The
World Book
Encyclopedia

N·O   Volume 14

World Book–Childcraft International, Inc.

A subsidiary of Field Enterprises, Inc.

Chicago Frankfurt London Paris Rome Sydney Tokyo Toronto

The World Book Encyclopedia

Copyright © 1978, U.S.A.
by
World Book—Childcraft International, Inc.

Nn

N is the 14th letter in our alphabet. It was also the 14th letter in the alphabet used by the Semitic peoples, who once lived in Syria and Palestine. They called the letter *nun*, their word for fish. But its symbol apparently came from the Egyptian hieroglyphic (or picture writing) for snake, which began with the same sound. The Greeks took over the letter from the Phoenicians and called it *nu*. See ALPHABET.

Uses. *N* or *n* is about the fifth most frequently used letter in books, newspapers, and other printed material in English. In mathematics, *n* represents an indefinite number. As an abbreviation, *n* may stand for *noun*, *neuter*, *noon*, *name*, or *not*. *N*, in chemical formulas, means *nitrogen;* in geographic descriptions, *north* or *northern*. As a printer's term, *en* means a medium blank space, half the width of the em (see MM [Uses]). In medieval Roman numerals, *N* represented 90 and *N̄*, 90,000.

Pronunciation. In English, a person pronounces *n* by placing the tip of his tongue against the gums behind his front teeth and making the sound through his nose. In such words as *hymn*, the final *n* is silent. But in such words as *gnostic* or *mnemonic*, the first *n* is pronounced, and the letter before it is silent. Double *n*, in words such as *manner*, is pronounced like *n*. In words like *pen-name*, each *n* is pronounced. The letter has much the same sound in classical Greek and Latin, and in French and German. In Spanish, when written with a tilde, *ñ*, it has a *ny* sound, as in the English word *canyon*. See PRONUNCIATION.　　　I. J. GELB and JAMES M. WELLS

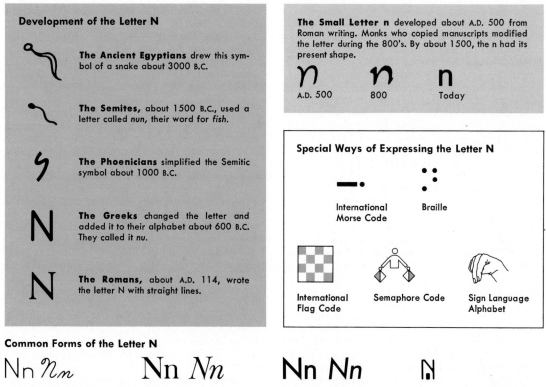

Development of the Letter N

The Ancient Egyptians drew this symbol of a snake about 3000 B.C.

The Semites, about 1500 B.C., used a letter called *nun,* their word for *fish.*

The Phoenicians simplified the Semitic symbol about 1000 B.C.

The Greeks changed the letter and added it to their alphabet about 600 B.C. They called it *nu.*

The Romans, about A.D. 114, wrote the letter N with straight lines.

The Small Letter n developed about A.D. 500 from Roman writing. Monks who copied manuscripts modified the letter during the 800's. By about 1500, the n had its present shape.

A.D. 500　　800　　Today

Special Ways of Expressing the Letter N

International Morse Code

Braille

International Flag Code

Semaphore Code

Sign Language Alphabet

Common Forms of the Letter N

Handwritten Letters vary from person to person. *Manuscript* (printed) letters, *left,* have simple curves and straight lines. Cursive letters, *right,* have flowing lines.

Roman Letters have small finishing strokes called *serifs* that extend from the main strokes. The type face shown above is Baskerville. The italic form appears at the right.

Sans-Serif Letters are also called *gothic letters.* They have no serifs. The type face shown above is called Futura. The italic form of Futura appears at the right.

Computer Letters have special shapes. Computers can "read" these letters either optically or by means of the magnetic ink with which the letters may be printed.

NAA. See NATIONAL AERONAUTIC ASSOCIATION OF THE U.S.A.

NAACP. See NATIONAL ASSOCIATION FOR THE ADVANCEMENT OF COLORED PEOPLE.

NABATAEANS. See JORDAN (Early Days); PETRA.

NABOKOV, *NAH boh kawf,* **VLADIMIR** (1899-1977), was a Russian-born author. His novels are noted for their complicated plots and the complex attitudes they express toward their subjects. Critics praised Nabokov's novels for their wit, intricate use of words, and rich language. His novels include *Invitation to a Beheading* (published in Russia, 1938; United States, 1959), *The Real Life of Sebastian Knight* (1941), *Lolita* (published in France, 1955; United States, 1958), *Pnin* (1957), *Pale Fire* (1962), and *Ada* (1969). Nabokov published collections of stories and poetry and translated several Russian literary classics into English. *Speak, Memory* (1951, expanded 1966) is his autobiography.

Nabokov was born in St. Petersburg (now Leningrad). His father was a wealthy landowner and a famous jurist and statesman. The family fled to Western Europe in 1919 because of the Bolshevik revolution. Nabokov attended Cambridge University in England from 1919 to 1922. From 1922 to 1940, he lived in Berlin and Paris among other Russians who had left their country because of the revolution. He wrote his novels in Russian, and most were later translated into English. In 1940, Nabokov settled in the United States and began to write in English. He became a U.S. citizen in 1945. Nabokov returned to Europe to live in 1959.   MARCUS KLEIN

NABONIDUS. See BELSHAZZAR; CYRUS THE GREAT.

NABOPOLASSAR, *NAB oh poh LAS ahr,* reigned as king of Babylonia from 625 to 605 B.C. About 612 B.C., he joined with the Medes to defeat the Assyrians who had ruled Babylonia for more than 100 years. He founded the New Babylonian Empire and started Babylonia on its last rise to greatness. The empire reached its peak under his son and successor, Nebuchadnezzar II. It is sometimes called the *Chaldean* Empire, because Nabopolassar belonged to one of the Chaldean tribes of southern Babylonia.   JACOB J. FINKELSTEIN

NABRIT, JAMES MADISON, JR. (1900-   ), won fame as a lawyer, university president, and diplomat. From 1960 to 1969, he was president of Howard University. He was the first black to become deputy U.S. representative to the United Nations (UN). He held the post in 1966 and 1967, while on leave from Howard.

Nabrit was born in Atlanta, Ga. He graduated from Morehouse College and Northwestern University Law School. In 1936, he joined the faculty of Howard University. At his suggestion, the university established—and he taught—the first civil rights course in an American law school. Nabrit was secretary of the university from 1939 to 1960, and dean of its law school from 1958 to 1960. As president of Howard, he encouraged greater student involvement in the operation of the university. As a lawyer, Nabrit specialized in civil rights cases, especially school desegregation cases.   EDGAR ALLAN TOPPIN

NACELLE. See AIRPLANE (The Wing).

NACRE. See MOTHER-OF-PEARL.

NADER, RALPH (1934-   ), an American lawyer, became famous for fighting business and government practices that he felt endangered public health and safety.

Newsweek

Ralph Nader

In his book *Unsafe at Any Speed* (1965), Nader argued that the U.S. automobile industry emphasized profits and style over safety. The National Traffic and Motor Vehicle Safety Act of 1966, which established safety standards for new cars, resulted largely from his work.

Nader's studies of the meat and poultry industries, coal mines, and natural gas pipelines also resulted in stricter health and safety laws. He publicized what he felt were the dangers of pesticides, various food additives, radiation from color television sets, and excessive use of X rays. He said the government was not strict enough in enforcing antipollution and consumer protection laws.

Nader's operating funds come mainly from his writings and speeches, from foundation grants, and from contributions. In the early 1970's, his organization included more than a dozen groups of lawyers, lobbyists, and researchers. Members of these groups assisted him in conducting investigations, preparing reports, bringing lawsuits, and lobbying for certain legislation. Nader and his staff conducted a major study of Congress in 1972. Their findings were published in a book, *Who Runs Congress?*, and in biographies of all U.S. senators and representatives.

Nader was born in Winsted, Conn., the son of Lebanese immigrants. He graduated from Princeton University and Harvard Law School.   LEONARD S. SILK

NADIR, *NAY duhr,* is the point in space directly below where one stands. To an observer on earth, the sky appears to be a half-dome whose edge forms a great circle resting on the flat surface of the earth. Imagine a plumb line suspended from the center of this dome, directly above your head, and passing through the center of the earth and into space as far as the central point of the invisible half-dome beneath the earth. The two points marking the ends of our imaginary plumb line are, respectively, the *zenith* and the *nadir*. They are the poles of the horizon, and each is 90° from the horizon. See also ZENITH.   OLIVER J. LEE

NADIR SHAH. See IRAN (Conquests of Nadir Shah).

NAGANA. See TSETSE FLY.

NAGASAKI, *NAH guh SAH kee* (pop. 421,114), is the Japanese city with which Westerners have had the longest contact. Its harbor was opened to foreign trade in 1568, and Portuguese ships occasionally called. After 1637, it was the only Japanese port where foreigners were allowed to trade. Dutch traders were permitted to set up a trading post on an island in the harbor, and one Dutch ship each year was allowed to call at the post. In 1857, it was one of the six Japanese ports opened to foreign trade.

Nagasaki is on the west coast of the island of Kyushu. It is important as the Japanese port city closest to the mainland of China. Nearby coal fields provide a source of soft coal for export. Nagasaki is on a land-locked bay, which is deep and large enough to hold many ships. For location, see JAPAN (political map).

Because Nagasaki has a large steel rolling mill, it is

an important shipbuilding center. Many of the factories in Nagasaki were destroyed on August 9, 1945, by the second atomic bomb used in warfare (see ATOMIC BOMB [pictures]). The blast destroyed 1.8 square miles (4.7 square kilometers) in the heart of the city. It injured 40,000 persons, and 40,000 were killed or missing. Since the war, most of Nagasaki has been rebuilt.　HUGH BORTON

NÄGELI, *neh JELL ee,* **KARL WILHELM** (1817-1891), a Swiss botanist and philosopher, studied the growth of roots, stems, and pollen grains. He discovered the nitrogenous nature of protoplasm, and described cell division in the formation of pollen and in simple algae. His philosophical views led him to scorn Gregor Mendel's proof of heredity (see MENDEL, GREGOR J.).

Nägeli was born in Kilchberg, Switzerland. He was professor of botany at the universities of Freiburg, Zurich, and Munich.　LORUS J. and MARGERY MILNE

NAGOYA, *nah GOH yah* (pop. 2,080,000), is a large city in Japan. It is the capital of Aichi prefecture on the island of Honshu. It stands on Nobi plain, facing Ise Bay (see JAPAN [political map]).

Nagoya was once the seat of the powerful *daimio* (baron) of Owari, a province of early Japan. In 1610, a great five-story castle was built in Nagoya. The castle was destroyed during World War II.

Nagoya is famous as a manufacturing center. It has an important textile industry. It also manufactures machines, pottery, porcelain, lacquerware, clocks, fans, and embroidery. Nagoya's industries and its population are crowded into a closely packed area.　HUGH BORTON

NAGPUR, *NAHG poor* (pop. 866,076; met. area pop. 930,459), India, is a city in the state of Maharashtra. For location, see INDIA (political map). Nagpur is a railroad center. Cotton from nearby farms is made into cloth in Nagpur, and shipped to other parts of India. The city also has oil mills and a large fruit-canning industry. Hislop College and Nagpur University are located in Nagpur.　ROBERT I. CRANE

NAGUIB, *nah GEEB,* **MUHAMMAD** (1901-　), was a leader in the Egyptian revolution of 1952 that forced King Faruk to abdicate. Naguib became prime minister in the new government. But in 1954, Gamal Abdel Nasser replaced Naguib as prime minister and forced him into retirement.

Naguib was born in Khartoum in the Sudan. He entered the army, and attended Fuad University and the Royal Military Academy in Cairo. He fought against Israel in 1948, and later became a major general. During the fighting, he realized how corruption in government had crippled the Egyptian army. He emerged from the war as a hero, and became a reformist. Naguib formed a secret group known as the Free Officers. This group led the revolution in 1952 that forced Faruk to leave Egypt.　T. WALTER WALLBANK

NAHUATL. See AZTEC (Life of the Aztec).

NAHUM, *NAY hum,* was one of the Hebrew "minor prophets" in the Bible. The Old Testament book bearing his name contains poems he wrote. The book opens with a poem believed to be the work of another author. The second and third chapters are Nahum's description of the fall of Nineveh, Assyria, in 612 B.C. Some scholars believe Nahum described the actual fall of the city. Others say the poems are his prophecy written before the capture of Nineveh.　WALTER A. WILLIAMS

NAIAD. See NYMPH (in mythology).

NAIL is the most widely used fastener for attaching one piece of wood to another. Nails can also be used to join wood and such materials as cloth, sheet metal, and wire. Special nails can hold wood and other materials to brick and concrete.

Most nails are made of steel, but some are made of aluminum, brass, copper, or stainless steel. Steel nails may be plated with cadmium, copper, or nickel to resist rust. Some nails have a coating of zinc or of an adhesive substance called *resin* that makes them hold more tightly.

Carpenters generally use a *claw hammer* to drive nails. This kind of hammer has a *claw* for pulling out nails. Many carpenters who build or remodel houses use a power tool called an *automatic nailer*. It can drive nails much more quickly than a regular hammer.

A nail should be hammered with quick, sharp blows. Tilting it at a slight angle to the wood surface makes it hold extra tightly. Driving a nail can be made easy by rubbing it with cake wax. Carpenters often lubricate nails by moistening them in their mouth.

The Parts of a Nail. A nail has three main parts: (1) the point; (2) the *shank*, or body; and (3) the head. The point acts as a wedge that separates the fibers of wood as the nail is driven. After the nail is in place, the fibers grip the shank and keep the nail from loosening. The head covers the hole made by the nail.

The most common type of nail point is the *diamond point*, a sharp point that works well in most kinds of wood. A *blunt point* works better in some hardwoods, such as maple and oak. This point breaks off some of the wood fibers and helps keep the wood from splitting.

Some Nail Sizes

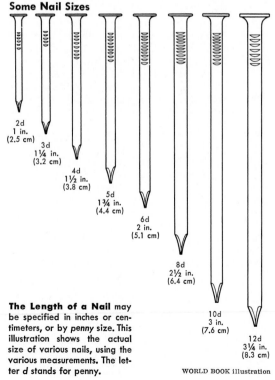

2d
1 in.
(2.5 cm)

3d
1¼ in.
(3.2 cm)

4d
1½ in.
(3.8 cm)

5d
1¾ in.
(4.4 cm)

6d
2 in.
(5.1 cm)

8d
2½ in.
(6.4 cm)

10d
3 in.
(7.6 cm)

12d
3¼ in.
(8.3 cm)

The Length of a Nail may be specified in inches or centimeters, or by *penny size*. This illustration shows the actual size of various nails, using the various measurements. The letter *d* stands for penny.

WORLD BOOK illustration

Some Types of Nails

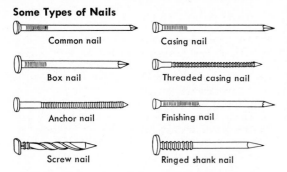

Common nail

Casing nail

Box nail

Threaded casing nail

Anchor nail

Finishing nail

Screw nail

Ringed shank nail

Nails Have Various Shapes, depending on the purposes for which they are used. The different types of nails can be distinguished by their head, *shank* (body), and point.

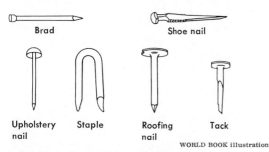

Brad

Shoe nail

Upholstery nail

Staple

Roofing nail

Tack

WORLD BOOK illustration

Specialty Nails and Other Metal Fasteners are made for specific jobs. For example, they may be used in making shoes, in upholstering furniture, or to hold roofing materials.

Most nails have a smooth, round shank. Nails with a twisted, threaded, or ringed shank hold better but cost more. A narrow shank helps prevent splitting of hardwoods or of thin boards. Nails with a square shank are used to attach wood flooring to concrete.

Most kinds of nails have a broad, flat head. A nail with a narrow head can be hidden in the wood by driving it completely below the surface with a punchlike tool called a *nailset*. The hole left by the nail can be filled with putty and then painted. Roofers use a nail with an extra wide head to install shingles. Upholsterers use tacks with decorative heads if the tacks can be seen in the finished work.

Sizes of Nails. Nails are usually measured in units called *pennies*, designated by the letter *d*. Nails measured in this way range in size from 2-penny nails that are 1 inch (2.5 centimeters) long to 60-penny nails 6 inches (15 centimeters) long. Nails that are shorter or longer than those are measured in inches or centimeters. The system of measuring nails in pennies probably began in England several hundred years ago. No one knows the source of the penny unit. Some people believe a penny once stood for the weight of 1,000 nails. For example, 1,000 4d nails weighed 4 pounds. Others think the unit represented the price of 100 nails, so that 100 4d nails would have cost 4 pennies.

How Nails Are Made. The earliest nails were made about 5,000 years ago in Mesopotamia. Artists used them to fasten sheets of copper to wooden frames to make statues. In the early 1700's, American colonists hammered nails by hand from a bar of hot iron. About 1775, Jeremiah Wilkinson, an inventor in Cumberland,

R.I., developed a process for cutting nails from a sheet of cold iron. About 1851, William Hassall (or Hersel), a machinist in New York City, invented the first machine for making nails from wire.

Today, almost all nails are made from wire by a machine that can produce more than 500 per minute. Wire is fed into the machine from a large coil. A set of cutters trims off a length of wire and forms the point of the nail at one end. At the same time, a hammer shapes the head at the other end. The nails are then polished, plated, or coated.

Nail manufacturers in the United States make nearly 300 kinds of nails. They sell nails in boxes of 1, 5, 10, 25, and 50 pounds. Special small nails, such as tacks and *brads*, may also be sold in 2- or 4-ounce boxes. ALVA H. JARED

NAIL. The horns, claws, talons, and hoofs of birds and animals are made up of the same materials as the nails on the fingers and toes of the human body. Deer antlers are another kind of growth. Horns, nails, claws, talons, and hoofs are special growths of the outer skin, or epidermis. These growths are made up of hardened skin cells.

The skin below the nail, from which it grows, is called the *matrix*. Near the root of the nail, the cells are smaller and carry less blood. The white, crescent-shaped spot indicating these cells is the *lunula* (from *luna*, meaning *moon*). If a nail is torn off, it will grow again, provided the matrix has not been severely injured. White spots on the nail are due to bruises or other injuries. They will grow out as the nail grows. The state of a person's health is often indicated by the nails. Illness often affects their growth. W. B. YOUMANS

Care of the Nails

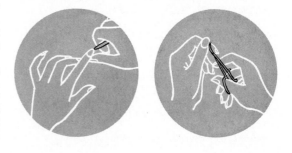

Shaping and Cleaning. Use a file to shape the nails to rounded points, *above*. Cleaning under the nails should be carefully done with an orangewood stick, *below*. Do not use a knife or other metal tool.

Removing the Cuticle. Soften the cuticle with a little Vaseline or oil. Then loosen it gently with an orangewood stick, *above*. Remove the loose cuticle carefully with manicure scissors, *below*.

NAINSOOK, *NAYN sook*, is a fine white cotton fabric often used for making women's blouses, baby dresses, and lingerie. It is like cambric, except that nainsook has a shiny finish. Nainsook is usually bleached white, but may be dyed. See also CAMBRIC.

NAIROBI, *ny ROH bee* (pop. 535,200), is the capital of Kenya, in East Africa. The city stands at the foot of Kikuyu Hills, about 330 miles (531 kilometers) northwest of Mombasa (see KENYA [map]). The Bantu, a black group, make up a large part of the population. More than a third of the Europeans and Indians of Kenya live in Nairobi. Most of the Europeans live in the hills above the city. Many big-game safaris start at Nairobi. See also BANTU; KENYA. HIBBERD V. B. KLINE, JR.

NAISMITH, JAMES A. (1861-1939), invented the game of basketball in 1891 (see BASKETBALL). He wanted to develop a game that could be played indoors during the winter months. He tacked up two peach baskets, and used a soccer ball for the first game. He invented the game when he was a physical-education teacher at the International YMCA Training School (now Springfield College), Springfield, Mass.

Naismith was graduated from McGill University in Montreal, Canada, in 1887. He was one of Canada's greatest rugby and lacrosse players. He studied for the ministry, but became a physical-education teacher. He became director of physical education at the University of Kansas in 1898. Naismith was born in Almonte, Ontario, Canada.   RICHARD G. HACKENBERG

NAM VIET. See VIETNAM (Early Years).

NAMATH, JOE (1943-   ), became one of the top quarterbacks in football history. He won fame for his accurate passing and skillful selection of plays.

Namath starred on the University of Alabama team that won the 1964 national championship. In 1965, he joined the New York Jets, who at that time were part of the American Football League (AFL). Namath was named AFL Rookie of the Year his first season. His skillful, dramatic play and colorful personality boosted the popularity of the AFL, which had been founded only five years earlier. The AFL's success helped lead to a 1966 agreement with the older National Football League (NFL) to merge in 1970.

United Press Int.
Joe Namath

In 1969, Namath led the Jets to a stunning upset of the Baltimore Colts of the NFL in the Super Bowl, football's world championship game. In 1977, he signed a contract to play with the Los Angeles Rams. Joseph William Namath was born in Beaver Falls, Pa. BOB WOLF

NAME, PERSONAL. Practically everyone since the beginning of history has had a name. Some explorers have reported discovering tribes whose people had no names. In those cases, the people probably did not want to reveal their names to a stranger. According to a superstition widespread among some peoples, anyone who knew another person's name could gain power over that person. At one time, some peoples kept their real names secret and were known only by nicknames.

Almost all names have meanings. Early peoples bestowed a name with a definite consciousness of its meaning. In the Bible, a widow exclaims, "Call me not Naomi (pleasant), call me Mara (bitter): for the Almighty hath dealt very bitterly with me" (Ruth 1:20). But today, people give little thought to the meanings. Most people have a given name and a family name. Many also have a middle name, and some have a nickname.

Given, or First, Names

Most of the common *given*, or *first*, names (often called *Christian* names) come from Hebrew, Greek, or Latin, or from Teutonic languages.

Hebrew Names taken from the Bible have provided the most important source of Christian names. The most common boy's name is *John*, which means *gracious gift of God*. The most common girl's name is *Mary*, which may mean *bitter*. Other common Hebrew names include *David* (beloved), *Elizabeth* (oath of God), *James* (may God protect, or one who takes the place of another), *Joseph* (the Lord shall add), *Hannah* (God has favored me), and *Samuel* (God has heard). These Biblical names occur in various forms among all Christian nations.

Greek and Latin Names often refer to abstract qualities. Common Greek names include *Alexander* (helper of mankind), *Barbara* (stranger), *George* (farmer), *Helen* (light), *Margaret* (pearl), *Philip* (lover of horses), and *Stephen* (crown or garland). Latin names include *Clarence* (famous), *Emily* (industrious), *Patricia* (of noble birth), *Victor* (conqueror), and *Virginia* (pertaining to spring).

Teutonic Names are widely used and are among the most popular Christian names, especially boys' names. They usually consist of two elements joined together without regard to their relationship. For example, *William* is composed of two name elements, *Wille* (will, or resolution), and *helm* (helmet). But the name *William* does not mean "helmet of will" or "resolute helmet." It means "will, helmet." Some of these name elements are found at the beginning, as *ead* (rich) in *Edwin* and *Edmund*. They may also occur at the end, as *weard* (guardian) in *Howard* and *Edward*.

Family Names. In Great Britain and the United States, family names may often be used as Christian names. Such names as Percy, Sydney, and Lincoln are now recognized Christian names. Some of the outstanding leaders in the United States, including Washington Irving, Hamilton Fish, Franklin Delano Roosevelt, and Jefferson Davis, had such names.

Saints' Names. The Roman Catholic Church, since the Council of Trent (1545-1563), has insisted that Catholic parents give a saint's name to each child. This is not difficult, because most common Christian names have now been borne by one or more saints.

Family, or Last, Names

Beginnings. The Chinese were the first known people to acquire more than one name. The Emperor Fushi is said to have decreed the use of family names, or *surnames*, about 2852 B.C. The Chinese customarily have three names. The family name, placed first, comes from one of the 438 words in the Chinese sacred poem *Po-Chia-Hsing*. It is followed by a *generation name*, taken from a poem of 20 or 30 characters adopted by each family; and a *milk name*, corresponding to a Christian name. In the United States, the Chinese often follow Western practice and put the family name last.

In early times, the Romans had only one name, but later they also used three names. The *praenomen* stood first as the person's given name. Next came the *nomen*, which indicated the *gens*, or clan. The last name, the *cognomen*, designated the family. For example, Caesar's full name was *Gaius Julius Caesar*. A person sometimes added a fourth name, the *agnomen*, to commemorate an illustrious action or remarkable event. Family names became confused by the fall of the Roman Empire, and single names once again became customary.

The Middle Ages. Family names came into use again in northern Italy about the late A.D. 900's, and became common about the 1200's. Nobles first adopted family names to set them apart from the common people. The nobles made these family names hereditary, and they descended from father to children. The nobility called attention to their ancestors in this way. A family name became the mark of a gentleman, so the common people began to adopt the practice too.

The Crusaders carried the custom of family names from Italy to the other countries of Western Europe. Throughout Europe, wealthy and noble families first adopted family names. At first, these were not hereditary, but merely described one person. For example, the son of Robert Johnson might be known as Henry Robertson, or Henry, son of Robert.

Origin of Family Names

It is difficult to work out a simple classification of family names, because of corruption and changes in spelling and pronunciation. Many old words are now obsolete or have obsolete meanings. For many years, spelling depended on the discretion of the writer. The same name might be spelled in different ways even in the same document. Some names appear to come from recognizable English words, but they are actually from another language. Foreign names are often altered into more familiar words. The Dutch *Roggenfelder* (dweller in or near a rye field) became the American *Rockefeller*.

Family names have come down to us in various ways. They may have grown out of a person's surroundings or job, or the name of an ancestor.

Place Names came from a person's place of residence. For example, if a man lived on or near a hill or mountain, he might be Mr. *Maki*, if from Finland; Mr. *Dumont* or Mr. *Depew* in France; Mr. *Zola* in Italy; Mr. *Jurek* in Poland; and Mr. *Hill* in England. In England, people might be known as *Wood*, *Lake*, *Brook*, *Stone*, or *Ford* because of their location. During the Middle Ages, few people could read. Signboards often exhibited the picture of an animal or object to designate a shop or inn. A person working or living at the place might be called *Bell*, *Star*, or *Swan*. A person might also be named after the town he came from, such as *Middleton* or *Kronenberg*. Many English place names may be recognized by the endings *-ham*, *-thorp*, *-ton*, *-wic*, and *-worth*, meaning a homestead or dwelling.

Occupation. Family names also come from a person's job. Names like *Baker*, *Carpenter*, *Clarke* (the British pronunciation of clerk), *Cook*, *Miller* and *Taylor* are quite common.

The most common surname in the English language is *Smith*. It is also common in many other countries. It takes the form of *Schmidt* in Germany, *Lefevre* in France, *Ferraro* in Italy, and *Kuznetzvo* in Russia.

Ancestor's Name. Many people took surnames from their father's given name. Practically every language has a suffix or prefix meaning "son of." Some names that include the term "son of" include Irish names beginning with *O'*, German names ending in *-sohn* or *-son*, and Scandinavian names ending in *-sen* or *-son*. Russian and Serbian names ending in *-ovitch* and Romanian names ending in *-escu* have the same meaning. Those describing the bearer of the name as the *son of John* include *Johnson* and *Jackson* in England; *Johns* and *Jones* in Wales; *Jensen*, *Jansen*, and *Hansen* in Denmark; *Jonsson* and *Johanson* in Sweden; *Janowicz* in Poland; *Ivanov* in Russia and Bulgaria; *Janosfi* in Hungary; and *MacEoin* in Ireland. Less common names indicating relationships include *Brothers*, *Eames* (uncle), and *Watmought* (Wat's brother-in-law).

Many surnames came from terms that described an ancestor. In the Middle Ages, most Europeans lived in small villages, and needed only a single name. When the village clerk had to note in his records that a villager had paid a tax, he often had to identify just which Robert was meant. The clerk would then add some descriptive word without consulting the man involved. For example, he might call a man *Robert, the small. Gross* and *Groth* come from the German, and indicate a fat, or large person. Names like *Reid*, *Reed*, and *Read* are early spellings of "red" and refer to a man with red hair. These red-haired men probably received the nickname of "Red" in the same way that boys of today with red hair acquire the name.

Other Family Names may have more than one origin. For example, the common English surname *Bell* may designate one who lived or worked at the sign of the bell, or it may refer to the bellmaker or bellringer. It may also indicate the descendant of *Bel*, a pet form of *Isabel*, or it may be a nickname for *the handsome one*, from the Old French word *bel*, or beautiful.

Jewish family names were the last to develop in most countries. In Europe, Jews usually lived apart from others in secluded communities. Many did not feel the need for family names. Laws passed in the early 1800's compelled them to adopt surnames. Many then chose pleasant combinations of various words like gold, silver, rose *(rosen)*, mountain *(berg)*, stone *(stein)*, and valley *(thal)*, to form such names as *Goldberg*, *Silverstein*, and *Rosenthal*. Others adopted place names of cities where they were born, such as *London* and *Modena*. Some took names with religious connotations. *Katz* is an abbreviation of *kohen tzedek*, Hebrew for *priest of righteousness*. Others took surnames from given names, such as *Benjamin* and *Levy*.

Other Names

Middle Names, or second Christian names, occur frequently today. Many people have as their middle name the *maiden name* of the mother, that is, the surname the mother had before her marriage. In France and Spain, double Christian names appeared in the Middle Ages. The Germans in Pennsylvania used several forenames in

This table shows the origin and probable meaning of a number of first names. Many names are so old that scholars can only guess at their meaning.

Name	Origin	Meaning	Name	Origin	Meaning
Alexander	Greek	helper of mankind	Jeffrey	Teutonic	God's peace
Amy	French	beloved	Jennifer	Celtic	white wave
Andrew	Greek	manly	Joan	Hebrew	gift of God
Ann, Anne	Hebrew	grace	John	Hebrew	God's gracious gift
Anthony	Latin	praiseworthy or priceless	Joseph	Hebrew	the Lord shall add
Barbara	Greek	stranger	Judith, Judy	Hebrew	Jewess or praised
Benjamin	Hebrew	son of the right hand	Julia, Julie	Latin	downy face
Brian	Celtic	strong	Karen	Greek	pure
Carl, Charles	Teutonic	man	Laura	Latin	laurel
Catherine	Greek	pure	Lois	Greek	desirable
Christopher	Greek	Christ bearer	Margaret	Greek	pearl
Daniel	Hebrew	God is my judge	Mark	Latin	of Mars, the Roman god of war
Darlene	Anglo-Saxon	darling			
Deborah	Hebrew	bee	Mary	Hebrew	bitter
Dennis	Greek	of Dionysus, the Greek god of wine	Matthew	Hebrew	gift of God
			Melanie	Greek	black
Dorothy	Greek	gift of God	Michael	Hebrew	godlike
Douglas	Celtic	dark water	Nancy	Hebrew	grace
Edward	Teutonic	rich guardian	Natalie	Latin	Christmas child
Elaine, Ellen	Greek	light	Patricia	Latin	of noble birth
Elizabeth	Hebrew	oath of God	Paul	Latin	little
Emily	Latin	industrious	Philip	Greek	lover of horses
Eric	Teutonic	kingly	Rachel	Hebrew	ewe
Francis, Frank	Teutonic	free	Richard	Teutonic	rule, hard
Frederick	Teutonic	peaceful ruler	Robert	Teutonic	bright fame
George	Greek	farmer	Ronald	Teutonic	advice, power
Gerald	Teutonic	strong with a spear	Samuel	Hebrew	God has heard
Gloria	Latin	glorious	Sara, Sarah	Hebrew	princess
Harold	Teutonic	warrior	Steven, Stephen	Greek	crown or garland
Helen	Greek	light	Susan, Susannah	Hebrew	lily
Henry	Teutonic	ruler of the home	Teresa, Theresa	Greek	harvester
James	Hebrew	may God protect, or one who takes the place of another	Theodore	Greek	gift of God
			Thomas	Aramaic	twin
			Virginia	Latin	pertaining to spring
Jane, Janet	Hebrew	gift of God	Walter	Teutonic	powerful ruler
Jean	Hebrew	gift of God	William	Teutonic	will, helmet

colonial times. But middle names did not become common in the United States until after the Revolutionary War (1775-1783).

Nicknames may be either descriptive terms or pet names. Descriptive terms, such as *Schnozzola* and *Gabby*, usually express a person's prominent characteristics. Physical characteristics account for the largest group of nicknames. Sometimes they go by contraries, as when a husky football player is called *Tiny*.

Sometimes a nickname results from a child's attempt to pronounce a word or name, as *Lilibet* for Elizabeth. In other instances, a nickname is a translation of the person's real name. Many persons called New York City's mayor, Fiorello H. La Guardia, *The Little Flower*, a literal translation of his Italian first name. In many other cases, a person's nickname may consist of the initials of his other names, such as *F.D.R.* for Franklin Delano Roosevelt.

Pet, or nursery, names often consist of abbreviations of Christian names, such as Bob, Jimmie, and Debbie. They may be terms of endearment, or represent surnames, such as *Smitty* for Smith.

Pseudonyms are fictitious names assumed for anonymity or for effect. A *nom de plume* (pen name) is the pseudonym of a writer. Many prominent authors have assumed pen names. For example, *Voltaire* was the pen name of François Marie Arouet. Eric Blair, an English writer, wrote under the name of *George Orwell*. See Pseudonym; Pen Name.

An *alias* usually refers to the name taken by a criminal to disguise his identity (see Alias). *Incognito* means the use of a fictitious name by a person, usually a celebrity, to avoid being recognized.

Stage Names are names that some entertainers assume in their professions. The French actress *Sarah Bernhardt*'s original name was Rosine Bernard. Most motion-picture actors have changed their names. Harry Lillis Crosby is better known as *Bing Crosby*.

The Legal Name of a person in the United States is the name by which he is known. Most legal names consist of a given name and a family name. Some states require that if a person does business under a name other than his or her own, the person must register it. A title such as *Mr.* or a suffix like *Jr.* is not part of one's legal name. In many countries, names can be changed only by governmental permission. In the United States, a person can change his or her name without any court order. But it is usually advisable to obtain a court order. See Signature, Legal. ELSDON C. SMITH

NAMIBIA. See South West Africa.

NAMUR, *nah MOOR* (pop. 32,574), is an industrial city in Belgium. It is located where the Sambre and Meuse rivers join. For location, see Belgium (color map). Its factories use the coal and iron mined nearby.

7

NANAIMO

Industries also include leather tanneries and machine factories.

In the 1600's and 1700's, the French captured the city three times, and the British seized it once. During both world wars, the Germans captured the forts that surrounded Namur. DANIEL H. THOMAS

NANAIMO, *nuh NY moh,* British Columbia (pop. 39,655), lies in the center of a forestry and farming district on Vancouver Island. It is on the southeast coast of the island and serves as a supply and transport center. Ferry service connects Nanaimo with Vancouver, 40 miles (64 kilometers) east. For location, see BRITISH COLUMBIA (political map).

Nanaimo ships lumber and pulp products to overseas markets, and is the center of a fishing industry. Its mild climate and good beaches make it a popular tourist resort. The Hudson's Bay Company founded Nanaimo in 1851, calling it Colvilletown until 1860. The city was incorporated in 1874. It has a mayor-council government. RODERICK HAIG-BROWN

NANAK, GURU. See SIKHISM.

NANCY, *NAN see,* or *NAHN SEE* (pop. 107,902; met. area pop. 280,569), lies 175 miles (282 kilometers) east of Paris. For location, see FRANCE (political map). Nancy is the commercial center of Lorraine because it is on the Eastern and Marne-Rhine canals and on the Meurthe River, 6 miles (10 kilometers) above its junction with the Moselle River. Factories there make furniture, glassware, and electrical equipment. The city has a university, founded in 1572, and a school of forestry and mining. EDWARD W. FOX

NANGA PARBAT. See HIMALAYA; KASHMIR.

NANKING (pop. 2,000,000) is an important center of industry, transportation, and government in east-central China. The city lies on the Yangtze River, about 200 miles (320 kilometers) from the East China Sea. For location, see CHINA (political map). Nanking is the capital of Kiangsu Province and was once the capital of all China.

The City. Government office buildings, two museums, and a stadium are in the center of Nanking. Commercial and residential areas lie outside the central area. Most of Nanking's people live in apartment buildings or in apartments above shops. The remains of an ancient defensive wall surround the built-up areas of Nanking. Areas of farmland outside the wall are included in the city limits.

Most of Nanking's people travel by bicycle or public bus. Trucks transport most products in the city, but some goods travel in carts pulled by animals.

Wharves that can handle ocean-going ships line the banks of the Yangtze River, which borders Nanking on the west. East of the city are Hsuan-wu Lake, a tourist attraction with several islands; and Purple Mountain, the site of an astronomical observatory. The tomb of Sun Yat-sen, who helped establish the Republic of China in 1911, lies on the mountain. Nanking's educational institutions include Nanking University, engineering colleges, and a medical school.

Economy. Nanking has hundreds of manufacturing plants. Leading products include cement, fertilizers, iron and steel, porcelain, textiles, and trucks. Nearby mines provide iron ore for the iron and steel plants. Several *communes* (farm communities) operate outside the city. The farmers raise cotton, rice, wheat, vegetables, and other crops.

Railroads link Nanking to Peking, the capital of China, in the north and to Shanghai in the east. Many ships dock at the city's wharves. A double-deck bridge that extends 3 miles (5 kilometers) across the Yangtze serves trains and motor vehicles.

History. People have lived in what is now the Nanking area since about the 400's B.C. Early settlers chose the site because of its location near a river and some roads. From A.D. 420 to 1421, the city served as the capital of various local Chinese *dynasties* (kingdoms). The Ming dynasty gained control of most of China in 1368. The first Ming ruler made Nanking—which means *southern capital*—the seat of the dynasty. In the early 1400's, the Mings moved the capital to Peking—which means *northern capital.*

In 1853, rebels called the Taipings seized Nanking from the Manchus, who ruled China at that time. The Taipings made the city the capital of their empire. The Manchus regained Nanking in 1864.

In 1911, Chinese revolutionaries overthrew the Manchus. The new rulers met in Nanking and founded the Republic of China. From 1928 to 1937, the city served as the capital of the republic. Japanese forces captured Nanking in 1937 and burned much of the city. Nanking again became China's capital in 1946, the year after Japan's surrender ended World War II.

The Chinese Communists took over China in 1949. They made Peking the capital, but Nanking remained a center of regional government. During the 1950's, 1960's, and 1970's, the Communists built hundreds of manufacturing plants in Nanking. The city quickly grew into a major industrial center. RICHARD H. SOLOMON

The Tomb of Sun Yat-sen lies on Purple Mountain, east of Nanking. Sun helped establish the Republic of China in 1911.

NANSEN, *NAN sun*, or *NAHN sen*, **FRIDTJOF,** *FRIT yawf* (1861-1930), was a famous Norwegian polar explorer. He was also a humanitarian, a statesman, a marine zoologist, and a pioneer oceanographer.

He made his first Arctic cruise in 1882 as a zoological collector aboard a whaler. In the summer of 1888, he and five other men crossed Greenland from east to west, a feat that experts had declared impossible.

Nansen hoped to obtain valuable scientific information by exploring the North Polar Basin. For this expedition, he had a ship specially built to withstand the grinding ice floes. This ship was named the *Fram* (Forward). Nansen left Norway in the *Fram* on June 24, 1893. After two years aboard ship, he and Hjalmar Johansen tried to reach the North Pole with kayaks and sleds. They came within 272 miles (438 kilometers) of the pole, nearer than anyone before them. After meeting many dangers, they reached Franz Josef Land. They boarded a British ship there in 1896, and sailed back to Norway.

U&U
Fridtjof Nansen

Nansen played a prominent part in the separation of Norway from Sweden in 1905. From 1906 to 1908, he served as Norwegian minister to Great Britain.

On his return to Norway, he became a professor of marine zoology (later oceanography) at the University of Christiania. He went on ocean voyages in 1910, 1912, 1913, and 1914, and published his results in many books. His writings include *Farthest North* (1897) and *In Northern Mists* (1911), a history of Arctic exploration.

After World War I, Nansen served as Norwegian delegate to the League of Nations. He aided Russian refugees in Asia Minor, and directed the return of German and Russian war prisoners to their homelands. He devised an identification certificate for refugees, called the *Nansen passport*. He received the 1922 Nobel peace prize for his services. Franz Josef Land in the Arctic Ocean is often called Fridtjof Nansen Land. Oceanographers use a metal container, called a *Nansen bottle* in honor of him, to trap seawater. Nansen was born in Christiania (now Oslo).   JOHN EDWARDS CASWELL

NANTAHALA GORGE. See NORTH CAROLINA (Places to Visit).

NANTES, *nants,* or *nahnt* (pop. 259,208; metropolitan area 393,737), a port near the mouth of the Loire River, lies 215 miles (346 kilometers) southwest of Paris (see FRANCE [political map]). A ship canal connects the city with the port of Saint Nazaire, nearer the mouth of the Loire, increasing the importance of Nantes as a trading center. The major industry in Nantes is shipbuilding. Other industries include the preparation of sardines for canning, and the manufacture of sugar, fishing nets, sailcloth, soap, and machinery.

Nantes has many fine buildings, including the ducal castle where Henry IV of France signed the Edict of Nantes.   EDWARD W. FOX

NANTES, *nants,* **EDICT OF.** The Edict of Nantes is one of the most famous royal decrees in history. It was the

first official recognition of religious toleration by a great European country. King Henry IV of France signed the edict in the city of Nantes, on April 13, 1598. By the decree, the French Protestants, or Huguenots, were allowed complete freedom of worship in about 75 towns. They were also given equal rights with the Catholics as citizens. The intolerant King Louis XIV abolished the edict in 1685, and thousands of Huguenots left France.   J. SALWYN SCHAPIRO

See also HENRY (IV) of France; HUGUENOTS; LOUIS (XIV); REFORMATION.

NANTUCKET, *nan TUK et,* Mass. (pop. 2,461), is a summer resort on Nantucket Island, off the coast of Massachusetts. The name was taken from the Indian word, *Nanticut,* meaning *The Far Away Land.* Nantucket is 18 miles (29 kilometers) south of Cape Cod and about 50 miles (80 kilometers) southeast of New Bedford. There are many summer homes there because of the scenery and mild climate. For location, see MASSACHUSETTS (political map).

During the late 1700's, Nantucket became one of the greatest whaling centers in the world. As many as 125 whaling ships had their home port there. James I of England granted Nantucket Island to the Plymouth Company in 1621. The island belonged to the province of New York from 1660 to 1692, when it became a part of Massachusetts.   WALTER F. DOWNEY

NAOMI. See RUTH.

NAPALM is a jellied gasoline used in war. A napalm bomb dropped from the air bursts, ignites, and splatters burning napalm over a wide area. The jellied gasoline clings to everything it touches, and burns violently. Napalm causes death from burns or suffocation. Napalm is also used in flame throwers that are carried by ground troops (see FLAME THROWER). Napalm was used in World War II, the Korean War, and the Vietnam War.

The word *napalm* comes from the two basic ingredients of the white, grainy powder used in the gasoline. *Na* stands for the naphthenic acids, and *palm* for the coconut fatty acids.   HAROLD C. KINNE, JR.

NAPHTHA, *NAP thuh,* or *NAF thuh,* is a liquid that is obtained when petroleum is evaporated during the refining process. Some types of naphtha are used to dissolve rubber and to thin paints and varnish. Others are used as a cleaning agent and as an ingredient in the manufacture of artificial gas.

Naphtha can also be made when coal tar, a sticky substance made from soft coal, is evaporated. Coal tar naphtha is used as a dissolving agent. It is also used in the manufacture of *synthetic* (artificial) resins. Pure naphtha is highly explosive when exposed to an open flame.   CLARENCE KARR, JR.

NAPHTHALENE. See HYDROCARBON (Aromatics).

NAPIER, *NAY pih er,* or *nah PEER,* **JOHN** (1550-1617), LAIRD OF MERCHISTON, a Scottish mathematician, became famous for his discovery of *logarithms* (see LOGARITHMS). He published his first statement of this system in his *Canonis Descriptio* (1614). He also invented "bones" or "rods" for multiplying and dividing, and for extracting square and cube roots. He originated formulas used in spherical trigonometry. He was born in Merchiston, near Edinburgh, Scotland.   PHILLIP S. JONES

Naples lies at the foot of low hills along the beautiful Bay of Naples. Volcanic Mount Vesuvius, rear, adds to the city's scenic beauty. Naples is a leading Italian port and manufacturing center.

NAPLES (pop. 1,223,659) is the third largest city of Italy. Only Rome and Milan are larger. Naples lies at the foot of a range of low hills on the west coast of southern Italy. For location, see ITALY (political map).

Naples ranks as a major manufacturing center, and the Bay of Naples makes it an important seaport. Tourists come from all parts of the world to see the many places of scenic and historical interest in the Naples area. The city's name in Italian is NAPOLI.

About 600 B.C., Greek colonists from Cumae, 14 miles (23 kilometers) to the west, founded a town near the site of present-day Naples. The Greeks called the town Parthenope. They later renamed it *Neapolis* (New City), and the people of Naples are still called Neapolitans. During much of the period from the 1100's until 1860, Naples was the capital of a kingdom. This kingdom included most of southern Italy and the island of Sicily. Since 1861, the city has been the capital of Campania, a political region of Italy.

The City. Naples is a city of extreme contrasts, with scenes of great beauty mixed with crowded slums. In the eastern section, church spires rise above old tenement buildings and factories. The Spacca-Napoli district, with its crowded, narrow streets, forms the heart of old Naples. The newer western part of the city lies along the Riviera di Chiaia, a broad drive that runs 3 miles (5 kilometers) along the Bay of Naples. A hilly, densely populated modern section called the Vomero lies inland from the bay.

The Cathedral of Saint Januarius, which was completed in 1323, honors Naples' patron saint. A number of castles in the city recall medieval times. The castles now house museum collections or government offices. The oldest of these structures, the *Castel dell'Ovo* (Castle of the Egg), takes its name from its shape. The Castel Sant'Elmo, built in the 1300's and enlarged in the 1500's, served as a prison for many years. Other interesting places in Naples are a botanical garden and a public park. The park includes one of Europe's finest aquariums.

Naples lies amid some of the most spectacular scenery in Europe. Artists from many countries go there to paint pictures of the landscape or the people. Mount Vesuvius, the only active volcano on the continent of Europe, rises from a plain 7 miles (11 kilometers) southeast of the city. The ruins of the ancient Roman cities of Herculaneum, Pompeii, and Stabiae are within 20 miles (32 kilometers) of Naples. The islands of Capri and Ischia, famous for their climate and scenic beauty, lie to the south across the Bay of Naples. Vineyards and citrus groves dot the hillsides on the bay's eastern shore. A few miles southwest of Naples, the town of Posillipo offers a beautiful view of the Bay of Naples. See CAPRI; HERCULANEUM; POMPEII; VESUVIUS.

The People of Naples impress many visitors as being livelier and more carefree than those of any other Italian city. Music plays an important part in Neapolitan life. Such songs as "O Sole Mio," "Funiculi, Funicula," and "Santa Lucia" have made the city's music familiar in many parts of the world. At the Piedigrotta, an annual music festival, the people hold an outdoor competition to choose the best of the new

Crowded, Narrow Streets run through the old sections of Naples. Naples is the third largest city in Italy, and its rapidly growing population has led to a severe housing shortage.

G. Barone from Madeline Grimoldi

popular songs. The Teatro San Carlo, one of the largest opera houses in Italy, has presented the first performance of many famous operas. It can seat an audience of 3,500.

Neapolitan food includes many varieties of dishes made with spaghetti, macaroni, or noodles. Naples is the birthplace of pizza, which a baker at the royal court may have invented in the 1700's. Neapolitans also eat much fish and other seafood.

Cultural Life. The National Museum in Naples displays one of the world's largest collections of ancient art objects. The collection includes glassware, mosaics, paintings, pottery, and statues from Herculaneum and Pompeii; and ancient Greek sculpture. The royal palace of Capodimonte, built in the 1700's as a residence for the kings of Naples, houses the National Gallery. The gallery owns a collection of paintings, porcelain, sculpture, and tapestries. The National Library, the largest of the city's several libraries, has more than a million volumes and thousands of rare manuscripts. The Carthusian monastery of St. Martin, which adjoins the Castel Sant'Elmo, features a museum collection devoted to the art and history of Naples. The University of Naples, the best known of the city's many schools and colleges, was founded in 1224 by Emperor Frederick II.

Economy. Products manufactured in Naples include automobiles, cement, chemical products, locomotives, office machinery, ships, and textiles. The highly industrialized area in and around the city has the greatest concentration of factories in southern Italy. Ships from

every part of the world use Naples' harbor, and the city ranks second only to Genoa among Italian ports. Naples still produces many traditional wares for which it became known through the years. They include kid gloves, wine, and articles, such as combs and jewelry, made of coral and tortoise shell.

History. After more than a century as a Greek colony, Naples came under Roman control about 326 B.C. The city's beauty and mild climate made it a favorite resort of wealthy Romans. The poet Virgil lived in Naples for more than 20 years and is buried on a nearby hill.

After the fall of the Roman Empire in A.D. 476, various peoples fought for control of Naples and the rest of southern Italy. The Byzantines, Franks, Lombards, Normans, and Germans held the city for periods during the Middle Ages. Naples came under Spanish rule in 1442, and Spain held the city for most of the next 250 years.

Austria ruled Naples during the early 1700's. In 1734, the city became the capital of an independent country called the Kingdom of the Two Sicilies. A Spanish branch of the royal Bourbon family governed this kingdom (see BOURBON). During the Napoleonic Wars (1799-1814), Naples had a series of French rulers, including Napoleon's brother, Joseph Bonaparte. The Bourbons regained power in 1815 and ruled until 1860. In 1861, the Kingdom of the Two Sicilies became part of the newly formed kingdom of Italy. See SICILIES, KINGDOM OF THE TWO.

During World War II (1939-1945), bombs destroyed many buildings in central Naples and the port area. The damaged areas have been rebuilt. In 1971, the government announced plans to relieve Naples' housing shortage by building two new cities less than 20 miles (32 kilometers) away.   EMILIANA P. NOETHER

See also CAMORRA.

NAPLES, BAY OF, is an inlet of the Tyrrhenian Sea, an arm of the Mediterranean Sea. It is famous for the beautiful scenery along its shores, and for the deep blue color of its waters. The bay cuts into the southwest coast of Italy. It is about 20 miles (32 kilometers) wide between Cape Miseno and Point Campanella, and cuts inland about 10 miles (16 kilometers). Two picturesque islands, Ischia and Capri, lie at the entrance to the Bay of Naples.   BENJAMIN WEBB WHEELER

Chase Manhattan Bank Money Museum
Face and Reverse Side of the French Napoleon

NAPOLEON was a French gold coin worth 20 francs. It was named for Emperor Napoleon I. The coin went out of general circulation during World War I.

NAPOLEON I (1769-1821) crowned himself Emperor of the French and created an empire that covered most of western and central Europe. He was the greatest military genius of his time. Napoleon's armies crushed one foe after another until he seemed invincible. For nearly 20 years, many European nations fought him.

Napoleon had an unimpressive appearance, but he carried himself well. He stood slightly below average height. His courage and short stature led to his early nickname of *le Petit Caporal*, or "the little corporal." He had heavy eyebrows and a weak mouth, but his powerful personality shone in his eyes.

His mother encouraged and helped him in his rise to the height of power. His soldiers adored him. He personally directed complicated military maneuvers and at the same time controlled France's press, its police system, its foreign policy, and its home government. He pioneered new strategy and tactics, and became one of the great military commanders in history. He proved himself a talented administrator. He supervised the work of preparing the system of laws called the *Code Napoléon*. He also founded the Bank of France, reorganized the French educational system, and established a strong centralized government. He created and juggled kingdoms at will. He placed his relatives and friends on the thrones of Europe. And, finally, he brought about his own downfall. His collapse came partly because his pride and stubbornness forced him to go ahead with doubtful plans, and partly because he betrayed the faith of many persons.

Early Years

Boyhood. Napoleon was born on Aug. 15, 1769, at Ajaccio, on the island of Corsica in the Mediterranean Sea. He was the fourth child and second son of Carlo Maria de Buonaparte (later given the French spelling *Bonaparte*) and Letizia Ramolino. His parents belonged to noble Italian families, and his father practiced law. Genoa had ceded Corsica to France in 1768, after a series of revolts on the island. During these troubled times, Napoleon's father skillfully followed a policy most likely to benefit himself and his family. He obtained for Napoleon an appointment to the military school at Brienne. The boy spent a few months learning French, then entered the school at the age of 10.

Napoleon soon transferred to the royal military school at Paris. He found the discipline here stern and the teaching more skillful. Napoleon did not have a brilliant scholastic career, but he showed a special aptitude for mathematics and history. He had great confidence in his own judgment and displayed persistence in carrying out decisions.

At 16, Napoleon received a commission as a second lieutenant of artillery in January, 1786. He had joined

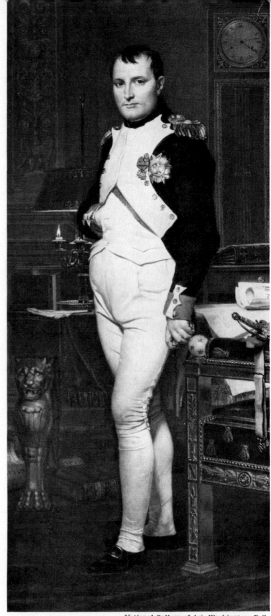

Napoleon I posed in his study for Jacques Louis David in 1810, *above.* David served as the court painter to the Emperor of the French. Napoleon's Great Seal, *upper left,* pictured him on his throne. The reverse side of the seal showed the imperial coat of arms.

an artillery regiment, and within three months had gone through the grades of private, corporal, and sergeant. Napoleon tried to master all the details of his new profession, and devoted much time to study. At first, his chief aim as a soldier seemed to be to free Corsica from French control. He spent many months of leave in Corsica, where the patriot Pasquale Paoli led an independence movement. Napoleon took part in the movement, but never got along with its leader.

The French Revolution broke out in 1789 (see FRENCH REVOLUTION). In 1792, when the mob attacked the royal palace called the Tuileries, Napoleon was again in Paris. He became an artillery captain that year. After Napoleon returned to Corsica, he quarreled with Paoli and abandoned his party. He joined the French revolutionaries on Corsica, and Paoli drove him from the island.

Napoleon rejoined the army and helped revolutionary forces occupy Marseille. His men also helped surround Toulon, which was strongly defended by English troops. The fall of Toulon was generally credited to Napoleon's strategy and organization. Now a major, he had handled his artillery command with such skill that he received a prompt promotion to brigadier general.

Napoleon's real military career began at this time. He developed a principle of war that formed the basis of his future campaigns. He learned to seek a weak point in the enemy's line and throw all his strength against it at the decisive hour of battle. With that point broken or weakened, the enemy collapsed.

In 1794, Robespierre fell from power in the new French government. The army suspended Napoleon and put him briefly under arrest, as a reaction to the violent reign of Robespierre (see ROBESPIERRE).

Fame at 26. A poorly-clad, ill-fed Napoleon waited in Paris for a change in his fortunes. The Convention that governed France grew steadily weaker, and many persons began to long for the monarchy again. In October, nearly 30,000 national guardsmen massed against the Convention, which was protected by 4,500 troops under Vicomte de Barras. Barras had seen Napoleon in action at Toulon, and now sent for him. The Convention appointed Napoleon as Barras' assistant. He showed superb resourcefulness by placing his artillery so that he cleared the streets of Paris "with a whiff of grapeshot."

Oct. 5, 1795, became a red-letter date in the history of Europe. Royalism had been crushed, and Napoleon had paved his own road to power. Barras appointed Napoleon his second in command in the army of the interior. The Directory succeeded the Convention as the government of France. But, in time, Napoleon would crush democracy and monarchy alike, concentrating supreme power in one person—himself.

Marriage. On March 9, 1796, Napoleon married Josephine de Beauharnais, a beautiful Creole from the West Indies (see JOSEPHINE). Her first husband had been guillotined two years earlier because he opposed Robespierre's revolutionary government. Napoleon first met Josephine at the home of Vicomte de Barras. She had become one of the society leaders of Paris. The young general fell violently in love with her. She was six years older than he, and Napoleon had no money. But he determined to marry her.

Two days after his wedding, Napoleon left Paris for Italy. He had prepared a plan to drive out the Austrians.

——————— IMPORTANT DATES IN NAPOLEON'S LIFE ———————

1769 (Aug. 15)	Born at Ajaccio, Corsica.
1796 (Mar. 9)	Married Josephine de Beauharnais.
1799 (Nov. 9)	Seized power in France.
1804 (Dec. 2)	Crowned himself Emperor of the French.
1805 (Dec. 2)	Crushed the allied armies at Austerlitz.
1806 (July 12)	Set up the Confederation of the Rhine.
1806 (Oct. 14)	Defeated the Prussians at Jena and Auerstädt.
1807 (June 14)	Overwhelmed the Russians at Friedland.
1810 (Apr. 2)	Married Marie Louise of Austria.
1812 (Sept. 14)	Occupied Moscow.
1814 (Apr. 11)	Abdicated his throne.
1814 (May 4)	Exiled and arrived on Elba.
1815 (Mar. 20)	Returned to power in France.
1815 (June 18)	Defeated in the Battle of Waterloo.
1815 (Oct. 16)	Exiled to Saint Helena.
1821 (May 5)	Died at Longwood in Saint Helena.

Culver

The Austrian Surrender at Austerlitz in 1805 Marked One of Napoleon's Greatest Military Triumphs.

NAPOLEON I

The Directory ordered Gen. Barthélemy Schérer, then in command in Italy, to carry out the plan. But Schérer thought the man who had prepared the plan should carry it out. The Directory agreed, and named Napoleon to command the French Army of Italy.

First Victories

Triumphs in Italy. Napoleon arrived in Nice, France, in March 1796. He found his army there poorly fed and clothed. He promised his men everything, and they believed him. After a few weeks in Italy, he had conquered Milan. Later he confessed that he had a vision of a great future for himself. "When I see an empty throne," he said, "I feel the urge to sit on it."

Napoleon began to hear rumors about his wife's infidelity. In his almost unreadable handwriting, he wrote passionate letters to her, filled with mingled love and hate. But Josephine continued to enjoy herself in Paris.

The Austrians had occupied large parts of northern Italy. After a series of battlefield triumphs, Napoleon forced Naples, Parma, and Modena to seek peace. His armies then crushed the Austrians. In 1797, Austria made peace in the Treaty of Campo Formio. Napoleon, now a national hero, returned in glory to Paris.

Egypt Invaded. Some men in the Directory feared, envied, and distrusted the young hero. Napoleon had great prestige in the army, and his men idolized him. Members of the Directory decided to get Napoleon out of the country. Great Britain had become France's greatest enemy, but Napoleon advised against an invasion of the British Isles. The Directory then ordered him to invade Egypt, a Turkish province, to avenge supposed insults to French merchants.

Napoleon's 35,000-man expedition reached Alexandria in July 1798. He defeated the Mamelukes within sight of the Egyptian pyramids (see MAMELUKE). But Lord Nelson's British fleet followed Napoleon to Egypt and defeated the French fleet in the Battle of Aboukir Bay. A tight blockade cut Napoleon's supply lines. The Turks declared war on France, and Great Britain and Russia formed an alliance with Turkey. Austria then reentered the war. The French forces marooned in Egypt advanced in 1799 into Palestine, and then into Syria. The Turks and British checked Napoleon in Syria. He retreated to Egypt and routed the Turkish army there. Napoleon learned that the Second Coalition, which included Austria, Britain, and Russia, had defeated the French in Italy. He also heard that Josephine had again been unfaithful to him.

First Consul of France. Napoleon gave the command of his army to Gen. Jean Kléber and sailed for Paris. He crossed the Mediterranean Sea in a small boat and avoided the British Blockade. In Paris, he and his followers seized power in a bold move called *the Coup d'État of Eighteenth Brumaire* on Nov. 9, 1799. Napoleon abolished the Directory and set up a new government of three members called *the Consulate*. He became First Consul. "The little corporal" now ruled as dictator of France.

The French people soon discovered that Napoleon had great gifts as a statesman. His government codified and revised the laws of France so well that today the *Code Napoléon* remains the basis of French law (see CODE NAPOLÉON). In 1800, Napoleon set up the Bank of France. He negotiated the Concordat of 1801 with Pope Pius VII, ending the confused church-state relations caused by the French Revolution. He also founded the Legion of Honor in 1802 to honor soldiers and civilians who had made contributions to France.

The Napoleonic Empire

Wars Against Austria. Napoleon ruled France with wisdom and vigor. But he found it difficult to settle down to peacetime government. His thoughts drifted to plans of conquests. Austria still controlled parts of northern Italy. Napoleon planned to strike a quick blow at his old enemy. In 1800, he led a famous march across the Alps, through the Saint Bernard Pass, into the Po Valley. His army clashed with the Austrians at Marengo in June. Napoleon's troops would have been cut to pieces if reinforcements had not arrived. A near defeat was turned into a victory. Austria agreed to sign a peace treaty on Feb. 9, 1801, at Lunéville.

Only Great Britain remained as France's major active enemy. The British and Turks drove the French from Egypt in 1801. This defeat shattered Napoleon's dreams of an empire in the Middle East and India. On March 27, 1802, after long negotiations, Great Britain kept Ceylon (now Sri Lanka) and Trinidad, but gave up its other colonial conquests to France and its allies in the Treaty of Amiens. France enjoyed its first real peace in 10 years. But the peace proved short-lived.

Napoleon felt that as long as Britain opposed him, his gains were not secure. But he needed more money to carry on any new wars. In 1803, he sold the Louisiana Territory to the United States (see LOUISIANA PURCHASE). On May 16, Britain declared war on France. Napoleon prepared to invade the British Isles.

Crowned Emperor. The French people in 1802 had voted Napoleon the title of First Consul for life. But the restless Napoleon was not satisfied. He began to whittle away all powers of the government that he did not control, and to strengthen his own authority. In May 1804, the French senate voted him the title of Emperor. The coronation ceremonies took place at Notre Dame Cathedral on December 2. As the pope prepared to crown him, Napoleon snatched the crown from the pontiff's hands and placed it on his own head, to show that he had personally won the right to wear it. Napoleon then crowned Josephine Empress.

Napoleon is probably most famous for his military achievements. But he guided the internal affairs of France as closely as he directed its armies. He set up a strong central government and appointed prefects to head the territorial areas, called *departments*. He reorganized the education system and founded the Imperial University. His measures later caused a break between the government and the Roman Catholic Church.

Dominates Europe. In 1805, Austria, Russia, and Sweden joined Britain in a new coalition against France and Spain. Emperor Napoleon I abandoned plans to invade Britain, and prepared to fight on the continent. On December 2, he smashed the Austrian and Russian armies at Austerlitz in one of his most brilliant victories. Later that month, Austria signed the Peace of Pressburg, and Russia stopped fighting. But off the southern coast of Spain, Lord Nelson had defeated the French and Spanish fleets at Trafalgar on October 21.

Napoleon now began to change the map of Europe.

He believed that "the object of war is victory. The object of victory is conquest. And the object of conquest is occupation." He made his brother Joseph king of Naples, and another brother, Louis, king of Holland. Even his sisters became sovereign rulers in Naples and Tuscany. He carved provinces of Germany and Italy into principalities and dukedoms, and awarded them to his favorite generals and marshals. Napoleon abolished the Holy Roman Empire. He set up a Confederation of the Rhine, made up of western German states under his protection. This action brought about a new war with Prussia. On Oct. 14, 1806, his armies overwhelmed the Prussians at Jena and Auerstädt. Napoleon made a conqueror's entry into Berlin. Here he issued the Berlin Decree that barred British goods from Europe.

Next, Napoleon turned to Russia. The Russian and French armies met at Eylau in February 1807, but fought to a draw. On June 14, 1807, Napoleon routed the Russian armies at Friedland, and forced Czar Alexander I to seek peace. Napoleon met the czar on a raft anchored in the Neman River near Tilsit, while Frederick William III of Prussia waited on the bank. Russia agreed to close its ports to all British trade. Prussia had to give up about half its territory to France. Napoleon's brother Jerome became king of Westphalia. Later that year, Napoleon issued the Milan Decree, stressing the ban on British goods in Europe.

Portugal had been friendly with Britain for hundreds of years, and had refused to obey Napoleon's Berlin Decree. In 1807, the French occupied Portugal. The following year, Marshal Joachim Murat's French forces invaded Spain. Napoleon removed Ferdinand VII from the throne, and appointed his brother Joseph as king of Spain. Murat took Joseph's place as king of Naples.

Great Britain finally felt strong enough to strike at Napoleon on land. The British invaded Spain and began the bloody Peninsular War, which lasted five years. Austria also declared war on France. At the end of the four-month campaign in 1809, the Austrians were completely defeated. The Peninsular War raged on.

Fall From Power

Divorce and Remarriage. Napoleon left the battlefield and returned to Paris. He had begun to develop a growing concern about the future of his vast empire after his death. Josephine had no children by Napoleon, and he had no heirs to his empire. He wanted a dynasty to rule France. Napoleon decided to divorce Josephine and marry a younger woman. On April 2, 1810, he married Archduchess Marie Louise, the daughter of Emperor Francis I of Austria (see MARIE LOUISE). She bore him a son in 1811. The son received the title of king of Rome (see NAPOLEON II). A revolt against French rule erupted in Spain in 1808. The French had to fight the British army and Spanish guerrillas. Finally, in 1813, the British forced Joseph Bonaparte to flee from Madrid.

Disaster in Russia. Napoleon had signed an alliance with Czar Alexander I of Russia in 1807. But the Russians did not fully carry out the Berlin Decree to close their ports to British trade. In 1812, Napoleon decided to teach the Russians a lesson. Long years of war had weakened France, but he raised an army of 600,000 men. His allies and subject nations furnished many of these conscripted soldiers. The Napoleonic

Empire now stretched from Spain to the fringes of Russia, and from Norway, an ally of France, to Italy.

Napoleon's army swept across the Neman River in the spring of 1812 and marched eastward. The Russians retreated slowly and destroyed everything of value. At Borodino, the French overwhelmed the czar's troops, but the main Russian force escaped eastward.

Napoleon pushed on to Moscow, where one of the greatest disappointments of his life awaited him. Most of the people had left the city. Those who remained set fire to it, and Napoleon soon found himself surrounded by ruins. The freezing Russian winter was approaching. The Russians rejected a French offer for a truce. Napoleon had no choice but to turn back and begin the long retreat from Moscow. His troops struggled homeward against snowstorms and terrible cold. They became weak because they had so little food. Swarms of Cossacks attacked the suffering French as they trudged through snow and tried to cross rivers. Hunger and the piercing cold accomplished what enemy armies had not been able to do—defeat the Grand Army. Of the 600,000 men in Napoleon's forces, over 500,000 were killed, were captured, deserted, or died of illness in the campaign and in the retreat from Russia.

The disaster proved to be the beginning of the end for Napoleon. He left Murat in command and hurried back to Paris to organize a new army before the news from Russia could reach his enemies. But the news swept across Europe like wildfire. Napoleon's reputation as a military genius suffered a fatal blow. New hope sprang up in countries that had long been under his heel.

The Enemy Alliance. Great Britain, Prussia, Russia, Spain, and Sweden allied themselves against Napoleon. With great effort, Napoleon raised another army. He battled with his old brilliance and defeated the allied armies at Lützen, Bautzen, and Dresden. But Napoleon could not match the strength of his enemies.

In October 1813, he fought them at Leipzig in the Battle of the Nations and met disaster. Returning again to France, he organized another army and held off the onrushing enemy forces. The Duke of Wellington's army headed for Paris from the south. Napoleon had nothing left but an army of old men and boys. Many trusted veterans of his great triumphs lay buried in the snows of Russia.

Rising nationalism had flared throughout Europe as a result of Napoleon's dictatorial rule. It now turned against Napoleon. He had aroused the anger of the German states, and, under Prussian leadership, the war became a conflict to liberate the Rhineland.

Exile to Elba. One by one, Napoleon's friends and allies began to desert him. By April 1814, he had decided that his cause was hopeless. The French senate called for a return of a Bourbon king to the French throne. Napoleon's commanders insisted that he give up the throne. On April 11, he abdicated at Fontainebleau. The French called upon Louis XVIII and crowned him king. Napoleon was made ruler of the tiny island of Elba off the coast of Italy, supposedly exiled from France forever.

Europe heaved a sigh of relief. Its diplomats met in the Congress of Vienna to undo many of Napoleon's many changes (see VIENNA, CONGRESS OF). But Napoleon's exile lasted less than a year. In February 1815, he

NAPOLEON'S EMPIRE

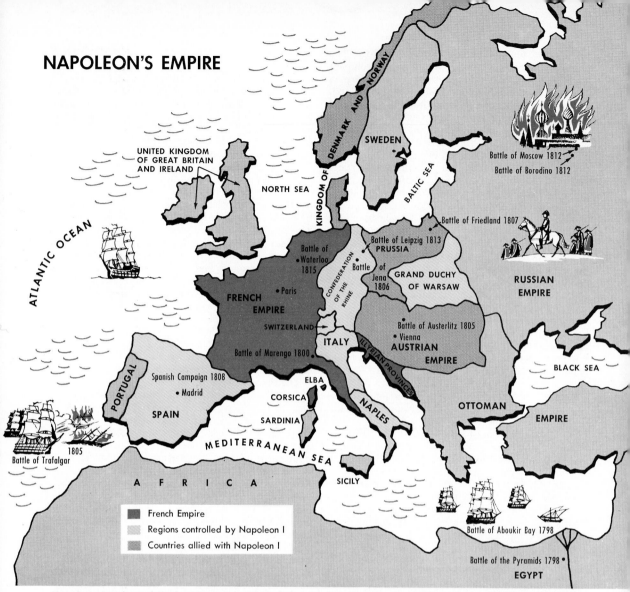

UNITED KINGDOM
OF GREAT BRITAIN
AND IRELAND

ATLANTIC OCEAN

NORTH SEA

DENMARK AND NORWAY

SWEDEN

KINGDOM OF

BALTIC SEA

Battle of Moscow 1812
Battle of Borodino 1812

Battle of Friedland 1807

Battle of Leipzig 1813
PRUSSIA

Battle of
Waterloo
1815

Battle of
Jena
1806

CONFEDERATION OF THE RHINE

GRAND DUCHY
OF WARSAW

RUSSIAN
EMPIRE

Paris

FRENCH
EMPIRE

SWITZERLAND

ITALY

Battle of Marengo 1800

ILLYRIAN PROVINCES

Battle of Austerlitz 1805
Vienna
AUSTRIAN
EMPIRE

BLACK SEA

PORTUGAL

Spanish Campaign 1808
Madrid

SPAIN

ELBA

CORSICA

SARDINIA

NAPLES

OTTOMAN

EMPIRE

Battle of Trafalgar
1805

MEDITERRANEAN SEA

SICILY

Battle of Aboukir Bay 1798

French Empire
Regions controlled by Napoleon I
Countries allied with Napoleon I

AFRICA

Battle of the Pyramids 1798

EGYPT

Napoleon Dominated Much of Europe in 1812, When He Attacked Russia. In Three Years, His Empire Collapsed.

escaped from Elba. He landed in France with a handful of followers on March 1, and began marching to Paris. Troops under Marshal Michel Ney sped from Paris to arrest him. But when they saw their old leader, the men joyfully joined him and hailed him as their emperor. Louis XVIII fled Paris as Napoleon approached. Once again, allied armies took the field against Napoleon.

The Hundred Days. The period from Napoleon's escape from Elba to his final defeat at Waterloo has been called *the Hundred Days.* Napoleon ruled once again. On June 12, he left Paris to take personal command of his troops. The Duke of Wellington and Marshal Gebhard von Blücher led separate armies against the French. Napoleon defeated Blücher at Ligny on June 16. Ney forced Wellington back to the Belgian village of Waterloo. On June 18, Napoleon attacked Wellington in one of history's most decisive battles. Wellington counted on the arrival of either nightfall or Blücher's reinforcements. At the decisive moment, Blücher's troops were seen approaching. The British and their allies fought

with renewed courage, and Napoleon suffered a crushing defeat (see WATERLOO, BATTLE OF).

Napoleon fled to Paris, abdicated, and tried to escape to the United States. But he failed, and surrendered to the captain of a British warship at Rochefort on July 15. The allied nations made him a prisoner of war. They took him to England, then exiled him to the barren island of Saint Helena, off the west coast of Africa.

Napoleon spent his last days under the care of a stern British governor. He died of cancer on May 5, 1821, and was buried on the island. In 1840, the French government took his body to Paris. There, beneath the dome of the *Église du Dôme* (Church of the Dome), the body of Napoleon Bonaparte was laid to rest.

Napoleon's Place in History

History would have given Napoleon Bonaparte a high place even if he had followed only one career. His military campaigns inspired many commanders, who sought the secret of his success. Napoleon's genius at making war lay in an ability to exploit an enemy's weakness.

Napoleon's achievements in government influenced both dictators and liberators of the 1800's and 1900's. His contributions to French law, embodied in the Code Napoléon, survive today. He also made major developments in education and banking. VERNON J. PURYEAR

Outline

I. Early Years
  A. Boyhood   B. Fame at 26   C. Marriage

II. First Victories
  A. Triumphs in Italy   C. First Consul of France
  B. Egypt Invaded

III. The Napoleonic Empire
  A. Wars Against Austria   C. Dominates Europe
  B. Crowned Emperor

IV. Fall From Power
  A. Divorce and Remarriage D. Exile to Elba
  B. Disaster in Russia   E. The Hundred Days
  C. The Enemy Alliance

V. Napoleon's Place in History

Questions

What military exploit started Napoleon on his great career?

What major civil reforms did Napoleon bring about?

What dealings did Napoleon promote with the United States?

Why did Napoleon's plans to invade Great Britain fail?

Why did Napoleon divorce Josephine and marry again?

When and why did Napoleon first abdicate?

In what battle was Napoleon decisively defeated? By whom?

What were *the Hundred Days?*

What was unusual about Napoleon's coronation as Emperor?

Why did Oct. 5, 1795, become a red-letter date in the history of Europe?

Books for Young Readers

FOSTER, JOHN T. *The Hundred Days: Napoleon Returns from Elba to Meet Defeat at Waterloo.* Watts, 1972.

KOMROFF, MANUEL. *Napoleon.* Messner, 1954.

ROBBINS, RUTH. *The Emperor and the Drummer Boy.* Parnassus, 1962. Fiction.

WHEELER, THOMAS G. *A Fanfare for the Stalwart.* Phillips, 1967. Fiction.

Ewing Galloway

Napoleon's Tomb stands in the *Église du Dôme* (Church of the Dome) in Paris. The remains of France's "Little Corporal" are in a block of red granite 14½ feet (4.4 meters) high.

Books for Older Readers

CASTELOT, ANDRÉ. *Napoleon.* Harper, 1971.

CRONIN, VINCENT. *Napoleon Bonaparte: An Intimate Biography.* Dell, 1972.

DURANT, WILL and ARIEL. *The Age of Napoleon: A History of European Civilization from 1789-1815.* Simon & Schuster, 1975.

HEROLD, J. CHRISTOPHER. *The Horizon Book of the Age of Napoleon.* Harper, 1963.

LUDWIG, EMIL. *Napoleon.* Liveright, 1926.

NAPOLEON II (1811-1832), DUKE OF REICHSTADT, *RYKE shtaht,* was the son of Napoleon I and Marie Louise of Austria. Napoleon I had long hoped for a son to inherit his empire, and greeted his son's birth with joy. He gave him the title of the King of Rome.

When Napoleon I was overthrown in 1814, he abdicated in favor of his young son. The senate did not recognize the title, and called Louis XVIII to the throne. Marie Louise took her son to live at the court of her father, Francis I of Austria. When Napoleon I was defeated at Waterloo in 1815, he proclaimed his son Napoleon II. But the French again ignored him and Napoleon II remained in Austria. His mother's family gave him the title of Duke of Reichstadt in 1818.

He was never strong, and grew into a tall, slender youth. He died of tuberculosis at the age of 21 and was buried in the Hapsburg family's church tomb in Vienna. The French government later requested that his body be returned to France, but the request was refused for many years. In 1940, Adolf Hitler had the body placed near that of Napoleon I in the *Église du Dôme* (Church of the Dome) in Paris. Napoleon II was born in Paris. Edmond Rostand based a play, *L'Aiglon* (The Eaglet), on his life. VERNON J. PURYEAR

NAPOLEON III (1808-1873) ruled as Emperor of France from 1852 to 1870, and was closely associated with major European political changes.

Early Life. He was born in Paris, the son of Louis Bonaparte, King of Holland and brother of Napoleon I. A French law of 1816 exiled the Bonapartes from

France, and Louis Napoleon spent his youth in Italy, Germany, and Switzerland. He became the head of his family in 1832. He was connected with such revolutionary groups as the *Carbonari* in Italy. He tried to overthrow the monarchy of Louis Philippe in 1836 at Strasbourg and again in 1840 at Boulogne (see LOUIS PHILIPPE). He was imprisoned in the fortress of Ham following the 1840 attempt. He escaped to England in 1846. During these years, he wrote his *Napoleonic Ideas* (1839), idealizing the career of his famous uncle, and *The Extinction of Poverty* (1844), proposing that the government act to end poverty and suffering.

Becomes Emperor. When the Revolution of 1848 led to the Second Republic in France, Louis Napoleon returned and was elected to the Assembly. In December, benefiting by the glamour of his name, he was elected president, winning $5\frac{1}{2}$ million votes out of $7\frac{1}{2}$ million cast. He swore an oath to the republic, but in December 1851, he managed to concentrate all power in his hands. He proclaimed himself emperor in 1852.

Napoleon's domestic policies were conflicting. He ruled as a dictator and was surrounded by dishonest adventurers. Although all men could vote, the legislature was powerless and the press could not publish legislative debates. When, after 1860, Napoleon moved in the direction of a liberal empire, it was too late. Léon Gambetta published *Belleville Manifesto* in 1869, demanding radical democracy. Yet Napoleon keenly realized the problems of the industrial age. He has been called a "socialist on horseback." He favored state help for industries, banks, railroads, and the poor.

Foreign Affairs. Napoleon was one of the first to propose general disarmament. He tried to settle disputes through international conferences, and he sympathized with claims of nationalism. He helped with independence for Romania, unification for Italy, and, unwittingly, unification for Germany.

He announced when he became emperor, "The Empire means peace," yet he led France into a long series of unfortunate adventures in other countries. In 1849, he helped overthrow the Roman Republic and restore the Pope. He joined England and Turkey in 1854 in the Crimean War against Russia. He secretly promised in 1859 to help the Count di Cavour drive the Austrians from Italy, in return for the promise of Nice and Savoy (see CAVOUR, COUNT DI). But he withdrew from the war when he saw that Italy, instead of forming a weak confederation, would be united. He tried unsuccessfully to help the Polish people in their 1863 revolt against Russia. He supported a scheme making Maximilian Emperor of Mexico in 1864 (see MAXIMILIAN). He hoped to increase French prestige, but American pressure in 1867 forced Napoleon to withdraw his troops and leave Maximilian to be shot.

His Defeat. Otto von Bismarck, the Prussian prime minister and secretary of foreign affairs, sought a common cause to unite the scattered German states. Napoleon gave Bismarck his chance by secret attempts to annex the Rhineland, Luxembourg, or Belgium. When these moves became known, they caused great indignation throughout Germany. Bismarck mobilized German opinion, maneuvered France into the Franco-Prussian War of 1870, and made the German Empire.

Napoleon surrendered at Sedan on Sept. 2, 1870, with 80,000 troops. Revolutionists overthrew the empire on Sept. 4, 1870. Napoleon III died in Chislehurst, England, only three years after the downfall of his empire. ERNEST JOHN KNAPTON

See also FRANCO-PRUSSIAN WAR; EUGÉNIE MARIE DE MONTIJO; BONAPARTE.

NAPOLEON OF THE STUMP. See POLK, JAMES KNOX (Lawyer and Legislator).

NAPOLEONIC CODE. See CODE NAPOLÉON.

NAPRAPATHY, *nuh PRAP uh thee*, is a system of drugless healing that attributes human ailments to a disorder in the ligaments, or bands of connective tissue. It attempts to correct these ailments by locating and treating the diseased ligaments. The word *naprapathy* comes from the Czech word *napravit*, meaning *to correct*, and the Greek word *pathos*, meaning *suffering*.

The naprapathic method is based upon the theory that strained or contracted ligaments in the spine, thorax, or pelvis cause irritation of the nerves which pass through ligamentous tissue. These irritated nerves then cause symptoms in the organs which they supply. Instead of treating the symptoms, the naprapath treats the diseased ligaments by special manipulation such as massage. Naprapathy is said to be different from both chiropractic and osteopathy. The system of naprapathy was originated in 1905 by Oakley Smith, a Chicago doctor.

NARCISSUS, *nahr SIS us*, is the name of a large group of early spring flowers with lovely blossoms. They grow from brown-coated bulbs. They were named for the legendary Greek youth Narcissus. Narcissuses are native to Europe and Asia, but many are cultivated in America. People like them because they have fragrant and delicately fashioned blossoms of yellow or white. The narcissus is a special flower of December. In Europe, in the springtime, fragrant masses of wild narcissuses cover the Alpine meadows. The bulbs of the narcissus plant are poisonous.

There are various types of narcissuses. All of them send up tall shoots from a group of sword-shaped leaves. They have six petals surrounding a trumpet-shaped tube which may be long or short. In one division, the trumpet in the center is the same length as the petals. *Daffodils* are long-trumpet narcissuses. *Jonquils* are short-trumpet narcissuses. Gardeners usually plant the bulbs in the fall. The flowers are perennial.

Another short-trumpet species is the *poet's narcissus*. It produces a single, wide-open blossom on each stalk. White petals surround a short, yellowish cup with a crinkled red edge.

The *paper white* and *polyanthus* narcissus, of the same group, can be grown indoors in winter from bulbs placed in water.

N.Y. Botanical Garden

The Poet's Narcissus has one blossom on each stalk.

They bear large clusters of pure white flowers that are very heavily scented. When cultivators cross these forms with the poet's narcissus, they get improved varieties. Florists value these beautiful hybrids. ·

Scientific Classification. Narcissuses belong to the amaryllis family, *Amaryllidaceae*. The daffodil is genus *Narcissus*, species *N. pseudo-narcissus*. The poet's narcissus is *N. poeticus;* the paper white is *N. tazetta*.   MARCUS MAXON

See also BULB; DAFFODIL; JONQUIL.

NARCISSUS was the son of the river god Cephisus in ancient Greek mythology. He was a handsome youth, and very proud of his own beauty. Many girls loved him, but he paid no attention to them. The nymph Echo, one of those who loved Narcissus, was so hurt by his coldness that all but her voice faded away.

The gods were angered at this, and they punished Narcissus by making him fall in love with his own reflection in a pool of clear water. He was so much in love with himself that he could not leave the pool. At last he died and was changed into the flower called *narcissus*. The Roman poet Ovid told the story of Narcissus in his *Metamorphoses*, a collection of mythological tales in verse.   VAN JOHNSON

NARCOLEPSY is a disease that causes excessive sleepiness. People with narcolepsy tend to fall asleep several times a day, even though they get enough sleep at night. The cause of the disease is not known. Doctors can help ease the problem with drugs, but narcolepsy cannot be cured.

Narcolepsy has several symptoms in addition to excessive sleepiness. For example, narcoleptics experience *episodes* (attacks) in which they remain fully awake but cannot move. This condition is called *cataplexy*. Most episodes are brought on by strong emotions, particularly anger or laughter, and last no longer than two minutes. Narcoleptics may also experience *sleep paralysis* and *hypnagogic hallucinations*. In sleep paralysis, the person suddenly becomes unable to move just as he or she is falling asleep. Hypnagogic hallucinations are vivid, realistic dreams that occur at the beginning of sleep.

Scientists believe the symptoms of narcolepsy are related to *REM (Rapid Eye Movement) sleep*, the phase of sleep during which people dream. The eyes move rapidly during this phase, and the body is paralyzed while dreaming occurs. Narcoleptics experience this same sort of paralysis—while awake—during a cataplectic episode. In addition, narcoleptics tend to have REM sleep at abnormal times, especially at the very beginning of sleep. In these cases, the REM dreams may be experienced as hypnagogic hallucinations.

Not all people who are abnormally sleepy have narcolepsy. But if they also experience cataplexy, they are almost certain to have narcolepsy.   WILLIAM C. DEMENT

See also CATAPLEXY; AMPHETAMINE (Medical Uses).

NARCOTIC, *nahr KAHT ik*, is a substance that has a strong *depressant effect* (lessens activity) upon the human nervous system. Narcotic substances cause insensibility to pain, stupor, sleep, or coma, according to the dose. The term *narcotic* comes from a Greek word meaning *to make numb*.

Opium is one of the most commonly used narcotics. Others include chloral hydrate, codeine, morphine, and heroin. When a narcotic is given in doses large enough to cause sleep or coma, the drug is called a *hypnotic*. The term *anodyne* is applied to a drug that relieves pain by numbing the nerves. Therefore, a narcotic may be both an anodyne and a hypnotic. In one sense, the general anesthetics ether and chloroform are narcotics.

Narcotic drugs are extremely useful in medicine, but they also have dangerous possibilities. Large doses of narcotics may cause death. The careless use of opium and substances made from it to relieve pain has often caused a drug habit. No one should use these drugs except under the direction of a physician.

The United States carefully regulates the importation of narcotics as well as the manufacture and distribution of narcotic by-products. Physicians must state certain facts on narcotic prescriptions, and druggists must keep records of them. The Drug Enforcement Administration in the U.S. Department of Justice oversees all narcotics laws.   A. KEITH REYNOLDS

Related Articles in WORLD BOOK include:

Analgesic	Drug Addiction
Anodyne	Hallucinogenic Drug
Barbiturate	Heroin
Belladonna	Morphine
Chloral Hydrate	Opium
Cocaine	

NARD. See SPIKENARD.

NARMADA RIVER, *nur MUD uh*, a large waterway in central India, has been sacred to Hindus for ages. Both banks of the 800-mile (1,300-kilometer) river are lined with shrines and temples. The Narmada rises in the state of Madhya Pradesh in central India. For location, see INDIA (physical map). It flows westward and empties into the Gulf of Cambay, about 200 miles (320 kilometers) from Bombay. Large boats can sail 80 miles (130 kilometers) up the river.   ROBERT I. CRANE

NARRAGANSET INDIANS, *NAR uh GAN set*, is the name of a tribe that lived in the Narragansett Bay region of Rhode Island in early colonial times. The Narraganset were of Algonkian stock. They were friendly to the colonists at first, but in 1675 they joined forces with Indian chief King Philip and made war on the whites. Only a few members of the tribe survive today.

NARRAGANSETT BAY is a narrow arm of the Atlantic Ocean. It extends 28 miles (45 kilometers) northward into the state of Rhode Island. The bay is about 20 miles (32 kilometers) across at its widest point. Harbors on its long, irregular coastline aid the trade and transportation of the state. Newport, a famous resort, lies on Aquidneck Island (officially named Rhode Island), the largest island in Narragansett Bay. Providence, the capital of the state of Rhode Island, lies on the western shore of Narragansett Bay.   BOSTWICK H. KETCHUM

NARRATION. See LITERATURE (Kinds of Discourse).

NARVÁEZ, *nahr VAH ayth*, **PÁNFILO DE** (1478?-1528), was a Spanish soldier, explorer, and Indian fighter. He helped conquer Cuba in 1511, and lost an eye trying to arrest Hernando Cortés in Mexico in 1521. Holy Roman Emperor Charles V granted him the unexplored land of Florida in 1526, and he led an expedition there in 1528.

He marched inland, and lost many of his men in storms and Indian attacks. While exploring, he was cut off from his ships, and they returned without him. Attacked by Indians, he and his men built five crude barges. They sailed along the coast to what is now

NARWHAL

south Texas. Narváez's boat was forced out into the Gulf of Mexico by winds and currents, and he was drowned. He was born in Valladolid.   FRANK GOODWYN

NARWHAL, *NAHR hwul,* is an unusual whale of the Arctic. The male has a spiral ivory tusk about 8 feet (2.4 meters) long jutting out of the left side of its head. The tusk is really the narwhal's only tooth. A few narwhals, mostly females, have two tusks. The female ordinarily has no tusk. Young narwhals use their tusks in play-fighting. So far as is known, the adult makes no use of its tusk. However, the tusks of most adult narwhals are worn at the tip. Perhaps the animal stirs up sand or mud with its tusk while feeding.

Narwhals grow about 18 feet (5.5 meters) long, not including the tusk, and weigh up to 2 short tons (1.8 metric tons). They are gray-white, and have dark-gray or black spots. The Eskimos of Greenland hunt narwhals. They eat the skin, which they call *muktuk,* and use the ivory to make tools.

Scientific Classification. The narwhal belongs to the whale order, *Cetacea.* It is genus *Monodon,* species *M. monoceros.*   RAYMOND M. GILMORE

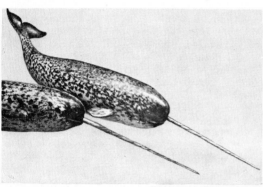

Field Museum of Natural History

Male Narwhals look like most other whales, but they have long, spiral tusks growing forward from the left sides of their heads.

NASA. See NATIONAL AERONAUTICS AND SPACE ADMINISTRATION.

NASBY, PETROLEUM V. See LOCKE, DAVID ROSS.

NASH, CHARLES WILLIAM (1864-1948), was a pioneer in the United States automobile industry. He became president of the Buick Motor Company in 1910, reorganized the company, and made it financially successful. He was elected president of General Motors Company (now Corporation) in 1912 when it was near bankruptcy. It also prospered under Nash's leadership.

Nash resigned from General Motors in 1916. He then bought an automobile firm from which he formed Nash Motors Company. He was president of the company until 1932, and board chairman until he died. The Nash firm merged with Hudson Motors in 1954, and became American Motors. Nash was born in De Kalb County, Illinois.   SMITH HEMPSTONE OLIVER

NASH, OGDEN (1902-1971), was a famous American writer of humorous and satirical poetry. He created a unique poetic style in his light-hearted verses.

Most of Nash's poems have lines of unequal length.

He often stretched sentences over several lines to produce surprising and comical rhymes. In "The Terrible People," for example, Nash wrote:

> People who have what they want are very
> fond of telling people who haven't what
> they want that they really don't want it,
> And I wish I could gather all
> such people into a gloomy castle on
> the Danube and hire half a dozen
> capable Draculas to haunt it.

Nash also used many puns and frequently made clever comparisons of apparently unrelated subjects. He sometimes invented words or misspelled real words to produce a carefully planned effect.

Although Nash wrote in a comic style, many of his poems make a serious point. He made satirical comments about American society and ridiculed what he considered foolish behavior, including his own. Nash described man as bewildered by all the complications of modern life. He regarded humor as the best means of surviving in a difficult world.

Kay Bell

Ogden Nash

The first collection of Nash's verses, *Hard Lines,* was published in 1931. His other collections include *Many Long Years Ago* (1945) and *You Can't Get There From Here* (1957). *The Old Dog Barks Backwards* (1972) appeared after his death. Nash was born in Rye, N.Y. Many of his poems were first published in *The New Yorker* magazine.   CLARK GRIFFITH

NASH, THOMAS (1567-1601?), was an English writer of the Elizabethan period whose works reflect his rowdy nature. He was involved in many disputes, and attacked his opponents in skillfully written pamphlets. Nash is probably best known today for *The Unfortunate Traveller* (1594), an example of Elizabethan prose fiction at its best. This book's narrative structure, realistic detail, and references to actual events and persons make it an important forerunner of the modern novel.

Nash was born in Lowestoft, Suffolk. He studied at Cambridge University, and belonged to a group of popular writers often called the *University Wits.* In 1589, Nash joined in the "Martin Marprelate" controversy between the Puritans and the Church of England. He wrote several pamphlets that attacked the Puritans. Nash and the poet Gabriel Harvey carried on a bitter feud through pamphlets. One of Nash's attacks is contained in *Pierce Penniless* (1592), which also satirizes Elizabethan society.   FRANK W. WADSWORTH

NASHUA, *NASH yoo uh,* N.H. (pop. 55,820; met. area 86,280), is the second largest city in the state. It lies on the west bank of the Merrimack River (see NEW HAMPSHIRE [political map]). Factories there make sheets, asbestos products, shoes, furniture, and blankets. The first permanent settlement was made there in 1656. A town charter was granted in 1673 under the name of Dunstable. Renamed for the Nashua Indians who once lived in the area, Nashua was incorporated in 1853. It has a mayor-council government.   J. DUANE SQUIRES

Downtown Nashville includes the Tennessee State Capitol, *center left*. Another landmark of the city is the 31-story National Life & Accident Insurance Company Building, *center right*.

NASHVILLE, Tenn. (pop. 447,877; met. area 699,-271), is the capital and second largest city of the state. Only Memphis is larger. Nashville is often called the *Athens of the South.* It received this nickname because of its many educational institutions and its buildings in the Greek classical style. Nashville is also called *Music City, U.S.A.* because it has become a recording and broadcasting center for country music. For location, see TENNESSEE (political map).

Nashville was founded in 1779, by settlers from North Carolina who were looking for fertile farmland. The settlers built a log stockade on a bluff overlooking the west bank of the Cumberland River. They called the settlement Fort Nashborough after Brigadier General Francis Nash, a Revolutionary War hero and a friend of one of the settlers. The settlement was renamed Nashville in 1784.

The City. Nashville covers all of Davidson County, an area of 533 square miles (1,380 square kilometers). It ranks as one of the nation's largest cities in area. The Nashville-Davidson metropolitan area covers 4,155 square miles (10,761 square kilometers) and consists of 8 counties.

The Cumberland River flows through downtown Nashville. The State Capitol overlooks Memorial Square. Nashville's tallest structure, the 31-story National Life & Accident Insurance Company Building, rises in the heart of the downtown area.

Almost all the people of Nashville were born in the United States. The city has small groups of Asian, British, Canadian, or German ancestry. Blacks form about a fifth of Nashville's population.

Baptists make up the largest religious group in Nashville. The Churches of Christ and the Episcopal, Methodist, Presbyterian, and Roman Catholic churches also have many members in the city.

Economy. Nashville has about 650 industrial plants. The manufacture of chemicals is the city's most important industry. Other manufactured products include aircraft parts, clothing, food products, heating and cooking equipment, phonograph records, tires, and trucks.

Nashville's economy received a big boost during the 1950's, when the city became a major music recording center. More than 180 recording companies, 23 recording studios, and about 450 song-publishing firms operate in the city.

Passenger and freight railroads serve Nashville, and about 10 airlines use its Metropolitan Airport. Barge lines connect the city with ports on the Cumberland River.

Nashville has two daily newspapers, the *Banner* and the *Tennessean.* Four television stations and 15 radio stations serve the city.

Large numbers of Nashville's people work for the state government. Many others have jobs with agencies of the federal or city government.

Education and Cultural Life. The metropolitan Nashville public school system consists of nearly 20 high schools and about 120 elementary schools. Their enrollment totals about 85,000 students. The city has about 40 private and parochial schools.

Vanderbilt University is the largest of Nashville's institutions of higher education. Other colleges and universities include Belmont College, Fisk University, George Peabody College for Teachers, Meharry Medical College, Scarritt College for Christian Workers, Tennessee State University, Trevecca Nazarene College, and the University of Tennessee at Nashville.

The Nashville Symphony Orchestra performs in the Municipal Auditorium. The state historical museum is also in Nashville. An exact replica of the Parthenon of Athens stands in Nashville's Centennial Park. The Tennessee Centennial of 1897 was held in the park. Nashville attractions include the Country Music Hall of Fame and Museum. Opryland, an outdoor entertainment park, is near the Nashville suburb of Donelson. It is the site of the Grand Ole Opry House, from which the "Grand Ole Opry" radio program is broadcast. This program, which began in Nashville in 1925, features country and western music. The Hermitage, the home of President Andrew Jackson, lies about 10 miles (16 kilometers) east of downtown Nashville. Jackson and his wife are buried on the grounds of the mansion.

Government. Nashville has a mayor-council form of government. The voters elect the mayor and the 40 council members to four-year terms. Property taxes provide most of the city's income.

History. The first white people who came to what is now the Nashville area found Shawnee Indians living along the Cumberland River. More settlers arrived after the establishment of Fort Nashborough in 1779. By 1780, the settlement consisted of seven forts with a total population of 300. Tennessee became a state in 1796, and Nashville was chartered as a city in 1806.

NASKAPI INDIANS

The first steamboat arrived in Nashville about 1818, and a brisk trade developed between Nashville and ports along the Ohio and Mississippi rivers. Various cities, including Kingston, Knoxville, and Murfreesboro, served as the capital of Tennessee. Nashville became the permanent capital in 1843. By 1850, the city's population had reached 10,165.

During the Civil War, Union troops held Nashville from 1862 until the fighting ended in 1865. Confederate General John B. Hood tried to recapture the city in 1864 but was defeated by Union forces under General George H. Thomas.

In 1900, Nashville had a population of 80,865. The busy river trade, plus income from the fertile farmlands surrounding the city, contributed to Nashville's prosperity. From 1920 to 1930, the city's population increased from 118,342 to 153,866.

In 1962, Nashville and Davidson County adopted a metropolitan form of government. This government combines city and county functions under one administration and provides services for the entire county.

An urban renewal project for downtown Nashville was scheduled for completion in 1978. This project included the widening and landscaping of city streets and the construction of office buildings.   ROBERT BATTLE

For the monthly weather in Nashville, see TENNESSEE (Climate). See also TENNESSEE (pictures).

NASKAPI INDIANS, *NAS kuh pee,* are a Far North tribe that lives in Schefferville, Que., and in Davis Inlet, a village near Hopedale, on the northeast coast of Labrador, Canada. Nearly 400 Naskapi live in Schefferville and hold a variety of jobs there. Most of the approximately 200 members of the tribe who live in Davis Inlet catch fish and hunt seals off the coast. The Naskapi speak an Algonkian dialect related to Macro-Algonkian, one of the 10 Indian language groups.

Before the 1900's, the Naskapi lived most of the year in the rugged forests and plains of the Labrador interior. They had moved there in the late 1700's and early 1800's to hunt *caribou* (wild reindeer), which lived on the plains. These animals supplied the Naskapi with food, clothing, hide for tents, and bone for needles and knives. During the fall, several bands of Naskapi united to hunt caribou. In winter, the Naskapi lived on meat that they had stored, and hunted caribou on the animals' winter feeding grounds. In spring and summer, fish and small game provided food for the tribe.

The Naskapi of Davis Inlet moved to the coast in the early 1900's because of a severe decline in the number of caribou. However, the tribe still has an annual caribou hunt in fall and winter.   JAMES A. TUCK

NASMYTH, JAMES (1808-1890), a Scottish engineer, invented the steam hammer. He also developed the *self-acting principle* in machine-tool design, by which a mechanical hand moving along a slide holds a tool. Using this principle, Nasmyth invented a planing mill and a nut-shaping machine.

Nasmyth was born in Edinburgh, the son of a noted artist. In 1829, he became assistant to Henry Maudslay, a tool designer and manufacturer. In 1834, Nasmyth started the Bridgewater Foundry at Manchester, which became famous for machine-tool and steam-engine construction. Nasmyth invented the steam hammer in 1839.

He retired in 1856 and devoted his time to studying astronomy.   ROBERT E. SCHOFIELD

NASSAU, *NAS aw* (pop. 100,000), is the capital of the Bahamas, an island nation in the West Indies, southeast of Florida. Nassau lies on the northeast coast of New Providence Island, the most important island in the group. For location, see BAHAMAS (map). It has a fine harbor and airport. The city is popular with winter vacationers. The British founded Nassau in the mid-1600's.   W. L. BURN

NASSER, *NAH sur,* **GAMAL ABDEL** (1918-1970), led the revolt that overthrew King Faruk in 1952 and established Egypt as a republic. He served as prime minister from 1954 until he was elected president of Egypt in 1956. Later that year, a world crisis occurred after Egypt seized the Suez Canal, then under international control. Nasser wanted to use the tolls collected from users of the canal to build the Aswan High Dam. When Syria and Egypt formed the United Arab Republic (U.A.R.) in 1958, Nasser became its president. Syria withdrew from the U.A.R. in 1961.

Nasser resigned after Egypt lost the six-day Arab-Israeli war of 1967. But the Egyptian National Assembly refused to accept his resignation, and massive demonstrations of public support led him to stay in office. He became both president and prime minister of Egypt. Fighting between Israel and the Arab nations continued into the 1970's. Nasser relied heavily on Russian military aid. In August 1970, he agreed to a 90-day cease-fire with Israel. His sudden death in September 1970 threatened the chances for a lasting peace.

Nasser's book, *Egypt's Liberation: The Philosophy of the Revolution* (1955), stated his aim to unite all Arabs under Egyptian leadership. Although his efforts toward this goal failed, he became one of the most influential men in the Arab world. Nasser claimed to follow a neutral foreign policy. His guiding principles were nationalism and economic reform. Nasser redistributed land to farmers and also advanced education.

Wide World

Gamal Abdel Nasser

Born in Alexandria, Nasser graduated from the Royal Military Academy in Cairo. He fought in the Arab war against Israel in 1948 and 1949.   T. WALTER WALLBANK

NASSON COLLEGE. See UNIVERSITIES AND COLLEGES (table).

NAST, THOMAS (1840-1902), was an American political cartoonist. He popularized the famous political symbols of the Democratic donkey, and originated the Republican elephant and the Tammany Tiger (see pictures with DEMOCRATIC PARTY; REPUBLICAN PARTY). His caricatures of the Tammany Tiger helped break up the notorious political organization headed by William "Boss" Tweed in New York City (see TWEED, WILLIAM MARCY).

Nast's cartoons began appearing in the popular magazine *Harper's Weekly* during the 1860's. He did his best work during the Civil War, when his political car-

Chicago Historical Society

Nast Drew the Tammany Tiger to symbolize the corrupt Tammany political machine in New York City. This cartoon appeared after the machine had defeated its Republican opponents in 1871.

toons influenced public opinion in favor of the North. In the presidential campaign of 1872, Nast's barbed cartoons helped bring about the defeat of Horace Greeley (see GREELEY, HORACE). Nast is also credited with starting the present-day idea of Santa Claus in sketches that appeared in *Harper's Weekly* in the 1860's.

Nast was an excellent draftsman and designer as well as cartoonist. His black-and-white drawings have been exhibited in many museums and galleries.

Nast was born in Landau, Bavaria, on Sept. 27, 1840, and came with his mother to the United States in 1846. He worked as a draftsman on *Frank Leslie's Illustrated Newspaper*, and sketched warfare in Italy for New York, London, and Paris newspapers. He published *Nast's Almanac* for many years. He was consul general in Ecuador when he died.   DICK SPENCER III

For other pictures by Thomas Nast, see the WORLD BOOK articles CARPETBAGGER; NEW YORK CITY; RECONSTRUCTION; and SANTA CLAUS.

NASTURTIUM, *nuhs TUR shum,* is the common name of a group of perennial plants native to tropical America. Nasturtium is a favorite garden flower of North America. There, it is a trailing or climbing annual that may reach about 10 feet (3 meters). Its blossoms are yellow, orange, or red. Dwarf nasturtiums are also grown.

The nasturtium flower has an interesting structure. There are five small *sepals* (outer "petals"). The three upper ones form a long spur that holds the nectar. There are also five petals. The three lower petals are a little apart from the upper two and have long, fringed claws. The long-stalked leaves are shaped like an umbrella. They have a spicy taste and are used in salads. The leaves also make an attractive light green background for the bright flowers.

Nasturtiums grow well from seeds sown outdoors

in spring. They can also be potted in the early spring and transplanted in May. The plants cannot stand frost, but may be grown indoors in winter. Nasturtiums are easy to grow. They thrive best in bright sunlight. Small insects, called black aphids, often attack the plants and live on the underside of the leaves. The insects will destroy the nasturtium unless they are controlled with insecticide. The name *nasturtium* is also given to the genus of the water cress (see CRESS).

W. Atlee Burpee

The Fragrant Nasturtium grows well in soil that is dry, sandy, or gravelly.

Scientific Classification. Nasturtiums belong to the tropaeolum family, *Tropaeolaceae*. The garden flower is genus *Tropaeolum*, species *T. majus*.   ROBERT W. SCHERY

NATAL, *nuh TAL,* is the smallest province in South Africa. Natal has an area of 33,578 square miles (86,967 square meters), and lies between the Indian Ocean on the east and the high Drakensberg (mountains) on the west on the southeastern coast of Africa (see SOUTH AFRICA [map]).

Warm, moist lowlands along the coast produce sugar cane and tropical fruits. Livestock and grain are raised farther inland. Coal is the chief mineral.

Natal has a population of 4,245,675. More than three-fourths of the people are black Africans. Pietermaritzburg is Natal's capital, and the seaport of Durban is the largest city. See DURBAN; PIETERMARITZBURG.

The Portuguese navigator Vasco da Gama sighted Natal on Christmas Day, 1497. Dutch settlers moved into Natal in the 1830's. The British annexed Natal in 1843. In 1844, Natal became a province of Britain's nearby Cape Colony. It was made a separate crown colony in 1856. Zululand was annexed to Natal in 1897. The British annexed part of Transvaal to Natal in 1902, after the Boer War had ended. Natal became a self-governing province in the new Union of South Africa (now South Africa) in 1910.   LEONARD M. THOMPSON

See also BANTU; ZULU.

NATCHEZ, Miss. (pop. 19,704), is the oldest city along the Mississippi River. It lies on the southwestern border of the state (see MISSISSIPPI [political map]). Products include automobile tires, lumber, oil, rayon pulp, and pecans.

Jean Baptiste le Moyne, Sieur de Bienville, a French governor of Louisiana, built Fort Rosalie on the site in 1716. In 1729, the Natchez Indians destroyed it. Settlers from the East re-established Natchez in 1771. The growth of the cotton industry made Natchez the center of wealth and culture in Mississippi before the Civil War. Natchez has a mayor-council government. It is the seat of Adams County.   CHARLOTTE CAPERS

See also NATCHEZ INDIANS.

NATCHEZ INDIANS were one of the few tribes in North America whose chiefs had complete power over their subjects' lives and property. The tribe once lived

23

near the city in Mississippi that was named after them.

They were farmers, and made excellent fabrics and pottery. Each member of the tribe inherited a place in a society of rigid class distinctions. There were three classes of nobility, as well as a large group of common people. The Natchez had a highly developed religious life based on sun worship. They believed that their chief was descended from the sun. Servants carried him about in a special litter, so that his feet would not touch the ground. When a chief died, his wives were strangled. Some other tribe members sacrificed their children.

The name of the Natchez first occurs in the reports of La Salle's descent of the Mississippi River in 1682. The Natchez, which probably included about 6,000 persons, were the largest and strongest tribe on the lower Mississippi at that time. They fought many wars with the French, but were so severely beaten in 1729 that they did not fight again. Only a few survivors remain today among the Cherokee and Creek Indians of Oklahoma.   WILLIAM H. GILBERT

NATCHEZ TRACE was an important commercial and military route between Nashville, Tenn., and Natchez, Miss. Pioneers who floated their goods on flatboats down the Mississippi River to New Orleans often returned on horseback along this route. Settlers moving into the Gulf States frequently traveled south on the trace. In 1800, Congress designated it as a post road, and the U.S. Army improved it. The trace was important in the early 1800's. In 1938, the Natchez Trace National Parkway was established. W. TURRENTINE JACKSON

See also NATIONAL PARK SYSTEM (table: Parkways).

NATCHITOCHES, *NAK uh tahsh,* La. (pop. 15,974), is the oldest town in Louisiana, and the trading center of a rich cotton-growing region (see LOUISIANA [political map]). It houses Northwestern State University of Louisiana.

Natchitoches was founded as Fort St. Jean Baptiste by Louis Juchereau de St. Denis in 1714. It served as a French military and trading post on the Red River. The town was later named after the Natchitoches Indians. It was the most important trading center of northwestern Louisiana until 1832, when the Red River moved its channel eastward. Natchitoches has a commission government. It is the seat of Natchitoches Parish.

NATHAN. See PARABLE.

NATHAN, ROBERT (1894-   ), is an American novelist and poet. He has written more than 25 successful novels, and many have been made into motion pictures. His first novel, *Peter Kindred,* was published in 1919. Others that became well known include *The Bishop's Wife* (1928) and *Portrait of Jennie* (1940). Nathan's war ballad, *Dunkirk* (1942), was widely hailed as effective propaganda. He is a skilled craftsman in poetry, and his sonnets are especially memorable. His books of poetry include *Youth Grows Old* (1922), and *The Green Leaf: Collected Poems* (1950). Nathan's work is touched with irony, and he has a gift for fantasy.

He was born in New York City, and graduated from Harvard University. He worked for two years in an advertising agency.   JOHN HOLMES

NATHANAEL. See BARTHOLOMEW, SAINT.

NATION is a large group of people that unite for mutual safety and welfare. A common language, origin,

history, and culture usually characterize a nation. *Nation* is a vague term, and nationhood exists largely because a group considers itself to be a nation. Nations that govern themselves independently may form states. The Serbians, Croatians, and Montenegrins form distinct ethnic groups in Yugoslavia, and consider themselves nations. But they are not states, because they are governed, with some other groups, by the Yugoslav government.   ROBERT G. NEUMANN

NATION, CARRY AMELIA MOORE (1846-1911), became well known for her violent efforts to stop the sale of alcoholic liquors. Although she was arrested often for disturbing the peace, she impressed many people with her sincerity and courage. Others considered her intolerant. She carried the temperance crusade from the level of education to that of action, and helped bring on national prohibition in 1919 (see PROHIBITION).

She was born on Nov. 25, 1846, in Garrard County, Kentucky. In 1867, she was married to Dr. Charles Gloyd, a drunkard who died soon after their marriage. She then taught school and rented rooms. In 1877, she married David Nation, a lawyer and minister. Her strong religious interests became more intense, and she began to see visions. Her belief that she was divinely protected increased in 1889, when a fire in her town left her hotel untouched. She thought, too, that her name (Carry A. Nation) had been preordained.

The Nations settled in Kansas in 1889. An 1880 state law banned liquor sales there. But it was not enforced. Mrs. Nation began in 1890 to pray outside saloons. Later she began to smash them. Nearly 6 feet (183 centimeters) tall and strong, she did much damage, first with stones and other implements, and later with hatchets. She closed the saloons of her own town, Medicine Lodge. She then conducted sensational campaigns, destroying saloons in the chief Kansas cities. When she entered states where liquor sales were legal, she was often arrested for disturbing the peace.

Carry Nation opposed tobacco, and immodesty in women's dress. She spoke eloquently, and inspired others to imitate her. Her husband divorced her for desertion in 1901.   LOUIS FILLER

NATIONAL. Many organizations are listed in THE WORLD BOOK ENCYCLOPEDIA under the key word in the

Brown Bros.

Carry Nation holds the weapons which she used in her crusade against alcoholic beverages in the early 1900's. The Bible was her text for many lectures. She used the hatchet often in her violent saloon-wrecking campaign.

name of the organization. Example: BUSINESS AND PROFESSIONAL WOMEN'S CLUBS, NATIONAL FEDERATION OF.

NATIONAL ACADEMY OF EDUCATION is a society devoted to furthering research in education. The academy consists of 50 scholars whose writings have contributed to educational history, practice, or theory. The academy is divided into four categories of membership: (1) history and philosophy; (2) anthropology, economics, politics, and sociology; (3) psychology; and (4) practices. Its purpose is to provide "a forum which will set the highest standards for educational inquiry and discussion." The academy is a private organization and has no connection with the U.S. government. It was founded by noted scholars in the United States in 1965. Critically reviewed by the NATIONAL ACADEMY OF EDUCATION

NATIONAL ACADEMY OF ENGINEERING. See NATIONAL ACADEMY OF SCIENCES.

NATIONAL ACADEMY OF SCIENCES is a nongovernmental organization that serves as a scientific adviser to the United States government. The academy also works to encourage research in the physical and biological sciences and promotes the use of these sciences for the general welfare. The National Research Council is an important part of the National Academy of Sciences. The National Academy of Engineering works with the National Academy of Sciences in advising the government on technological problems.

The National Academy of Sciences consists of about 800 scientists elected to the organization in recognition of their research accomplishments. Scientists from other countries may also be elected to the academy as foreign associates. A maximum of 50 Americans and 10 foreign associates may be elected each year.

The National Research Council enables other scientists to work with members of the academy. The council has about 300 members who are appointed by the president of the academy. They include representatives of major scientific and technological societies, and of the United States government.

The National Academy of Engineering consists of engineers who are elected because of their professional achievements. In 1964, the academy had 25 members. By the early 1970's, it had over 500 members. The academy is independent of the National Academy of Sciences, but cooperates closely with it.

More than 3,000 scientists and engineers take part in committees and other groups established by these three organizations. They devote their time without pay. Their work is financed by funds from both government and private sources.

The National Academy of Sciences was established in 1863 by an act of Congress signed by President Abraham Lincoln. Its charter requires it to advise the government on scientific matters as well as engaging in other scientific activities. The National Research Council was established by the academy in 1916 at the request of President Woodrow Wilson. The National Academy of Engineering was established in 1964 under the charter of the National Academy of Sciences. All three organizations have headquarters at 2101 Constitution Avenue NW, Washington, D.C. 20418.

Critically reviewed by the NATIONAL ACADEMY OF SCIENCES

NATIONAL AERONAUTIC ASSOCIATION OF THE U.S.A. (NAA) promotes the advancement of aviation and space flight in the United States. It is the U.S.

representative to the worldwide Fédération Aéronautique Internationale. The NAA documents and certifies flight records by U.S. aircraft and spacecraft. Groups associated with the NAA include the Academy of Model Aeronautics, the Balloon Federation of America, the Parachute Club of America, the National Pilots Association, and the Soaring Society of America. NAA annually presents four awards for achievements in flight. The NAA was chartered in 1922. Headquarters are at 806 15th Street NW, Washington, D.C. 20005.

Critically reviewed by the NATIONAL AERONAUTIC ASSOCIATION

NATIONAL AERONAUTICS AND SPACE ADMINISTRATION (NASA) conducts and coordinates United States nonmilitary research into problems of flight within and beyond the earth's atmosphere. NASA has about 12,000 scientists, engineers, and technicians. Its installations include the John F. Kennedy Space Center at Cape Canaveral, Fla.; the Lyndon B. Johnson Space Center, near Houston, Tex.; the Langley Research Center, Hampton, Va.; Wallops Station, Va.; Goddard Space Flight Center, Greenbelt, Md.; Lewis Research Center, Cleveland; George C. Marshall Space Flight Center, Huntsville, Ala.; Flight Research Center, Edwards, Calif.; Ames Research Center, Moffett Field, Calif.; and Jet Propulsion Laboratory, Pasadena, Calif.

NASA was established in 1958 as an independent agency, with headquarters in Washington, D.C. It absorbed the National Advisory Committee for Aeronautics (NACA). Critically reviewed by NASA

See also LYNDON B. JOHNSON SPACE CENTER.

NATIONAL AGRICULTURAL LIBRARY. See LIBRARY (United States Government Libraries).

NATIONAL AIR AND SPACE MUSEUM, in Washington, D.C., features exhibits of aviation and space materials. The museum is supported by the United States government and by private funds. Exhibits include the Wright brothers' first airplane; Charles A. Lindbergh's *Spirit of St. Louis;* Wiley Post's *Winnie Mae;* the X-1, the first supersonic airplane; the X-15 rocket-propelled airplane, which set a new altitude record in 1963; and the Mercury, Gemini, and Apollo spacecraft.

Congress created the National Air Museum in 1946 as a bureau of the Smithsonian Institution. The museum was renamed in 1966.

Critically reviewed by the NATIONAL AIR AND SPACE MUSEUM

NATIONAL ALLIANCE OF BUSINESSMEN (NAB) is an organization through which the United States government and industry cooperate to find jobs for the hard-core unemployed—people who have the most difficult time finding jobs. Through the NAB, the government's resources for locating the unemployed are linked with industry's resources for hiring and training them. Many hard-core jobless require special training and counseling because of poor education or lack of skills. Congress provides funds to pay back industry for the cost of hiring and training these persons.

The NAB was established in 1968. It started its program, called JOBS (*J*ob *O*pportunities in the *B*usiness *S*ector), in the nation's 50 largest metropolitan areas. In 1969, the program was expanded to 125 areas. The NAB has headquarters at 1730 K Street NW, Washington, D.C. 20006.

Critically reviewed by the NATIONAL ALLIANCE OF BUSINESSMEN

NATIONAL ANTHEMS are the official patriotic songs or hymns that are always played at ceremonious occasions or public gatherings. Sometimes they are songs inspired by a great crisis through which a nation has passed. Such a song is France's "La Marseillaise." National anthems, or national hymns, usually express the ideals that a country stands for. They also are used to stimulate patriotism and loyalty to one's country.

The national anthem of the United States is "The Star-Spangled Banner." Popular songs and hymns used upon patriotic occasions in the United States include "America," "Battle Hymn of the Republic," "Dixie," "God Bless America," "Semper Fidelis," and "Yankee Doodle."

In Great Britain and New Zealand, the national anthem is "God Save the Queen" (or "King"). This song is also used as the national anthem in Australia and Canada on royal occasions—events that involve the British monarch. Australia's anthem for nonroyal occasions is "Advance Australia Fair." Canada's anthem for such occasions is "O Canada."　　RAYMOND KENDALL

Related Articles: See Facts in Brief sections of country articles, such as NETHERLANDS (Facts in Brief). See also the following articles:

America	Hail Columbia
Battle Hymn of the Republic	Hail to the Chief
Deutschland über Alles	Horst Wessel
Dixie	Maple Leaf Forever
God Bless America	Marseillaise
God Save the Queen or King	Star-Spangled Banner
	Yankee Doodle

NATIONAL ARCHIVES. See ARCHIVES, NATIONAL.

NATIONAL ASSEMBLY. See FRENCH REVOLUTION.

NATIONAL ASSESSMENT OF EDUCATIONAL PROGRESS is a government program designed to evaluate the quality and progress of education in the United States. It tries to measure knowledge, skills, understanding, and attitudes.

The program's staff gives tests to four age groups—9-, 13-, and 17-year-olds, and adults from 26 to 35. The groups are tested in 10 subjects: (1) art, (2) career and occupational development, (3) citizenship, (4) literature, (5) mathematics, (6) music, (7) reading, (8) science, (9) social studies, and (10) writing. Two subjects are tested each year and are retested every five years. Over a period of time, the test results are intended to show whether education has improved.

The Education Commission of the States administers the program and reports the test results, which help educators plan courses of study. The commission consists of advisers from 41 states, Puerto Rico, and the Virgin Islands. The National Assessment of Educational Progress was established in 1964 and conducted its first tests in 1969.　　GEORGE B. BRAIN

NATIONAL ASSOCIATION FOR THE ADVANCEMENT OF COLORED PEOPLE (NAACP) is a civil rights organization in the United States. It works to end discrimination against blacks and other minority groups.

The NAACP achieves many of its goals through legal action. For example, it played an important part in the 1954 ruling of the Supreme Court of the United States that segregation of Negroes in public schools is unconstitutional. Thurgood Marshall, an NAACP lawyer, presented the argument in the case, known as *Brown v. Board of Education of Topeka*. Marshall later became a Supreme Court justice. See BLACK AMERICANS (The Legal Battle).

The organization also achieves its goals through legislative action. It played a leading role in obtaining passage of the Civil Rights Act of 1957, which protects the right to vote. This act established the Civil Rights Division of the Department of Justice and the Commission on Civil Rights. The NAACP worked for passage of the Civil Rights Act of 1964, which forbids discrimination in public places. This law established the Equal Employment Opportunity Commission. The association also helped bring into law the Voting Rights Act of 1965, which protects voter registration.

Activities. The NAACP has worked successfully to fight discrimination in housing and to strengthen the penalties against those who violate the civil rights of others. In 1970, the NAACP led a successful campaign to extend for five more years the Voting Rights Act of 1965, which banned literacy tests for voters. In 1975, it helped win a second extension of the act for seven more years. The NAACP also led successful efforts in 1972 to increase the power of the Equal Employment Opportunity Commission.

The organization strives to protect the rights of prison inmates. Its investigation of problems facing black military personnel led to changes in the system of military assignments and promotions. The NAACP sponsors a program of voter education and registration. It works for desegregation of public schools and fights dismissals and demotions of black teachers and administrators that it considers discriminatory. It urges publishers to produce textbooks that provide an accurate account of the achievements and activities of blacks.

The NAACP also acts to reduce poverty and hunger. In 1968, it established the Mississippi Emergency Relief Fund to feed poverty-stricken blacks in the Mississippi Delta area. In 1971, the NAACP Youth Council established a breakfast program for needy children in Nashville, Tenn.

History. The NAACP was founded in 1909 by 60 black and white citizens. In 1910, the organization began to publish *Crisis*, a magazine about blacks who have achieved success in the arts, business, and other fields.

During the NAACP's first 30 years, it worked to prevent violence against blacks, unjust legal penalties, and job discrimination. Much of its activity centered on passage and enforcement of antilynching laws. During World War II (1939-1945), the NAACP tried to obtain equal rights for black military personnel and more job opportunities for black civilians. After the war, the association stepped up its long struggle against the policy that treated blacks as "separate but equal." This policy had been established in 1896 by the Supreme Court's ruling in the case of *Plessy v. Ferguson*.

The NAACP has over 405,000 members and includes about 700 youth councils. It receives funds from membership fees and from donations by private groups and individuals. It has headquarters at 1790 Broadway, New York, N.Y. 10019. It has a legislative bureau in Washington, D.C.　　M. CARL HOLMAN

See also DUBOIS, W. E. B.; EVERS; MARSHALL, THURGOOD; WHITE, WALTER F.; WILKINS, ROY.

NATIONAL ASSOCIATION OF MANUFACTURERS (NAM) is an organization of American manufacturing companies. It serves as a policy-making body for the manufacturing industry on industrial and economic problems. It also interprets industry's policies to the federal government and the public. Many kinds of companies belong to the NAM. Most members are companies that employ 500 or fewer persons.

About 3,000 representatives of member companies form policy-making committees that make recommendations to the NAM's Board of Directors. The board and an Executive Committee meet several times a year to settle policies. The NAM was founded in 1895. It has headquarters at 1776 F Street, Washington, D.C. 20006. It also has several branch offices.

Critically reviewed by the NATIONAL ASSOCIATION OF MANUFACTURERS

NATIONAL ASSOCIATION OF SOCIAL WORKERS. See SOCIAL WORKERS, NATIONAL ASSOCIATION OF.

NATIONAL BANK. See BANKS AND BANKING (Commercial Banks).

NATIONAL BANK ACTS. See BANKS AND BANKING (Federal Regulations; The Wildcat Period).

NATIONAL BAPTIST CONVENTION OF AMERICA is an organization of black Baptists. It traces its history to the founding of the Foreign Mission Baptist Convention in 1880. The group merged in 1895 with the American National Baptist Educational Convention to form the National Baptist Convention of America. In 1915, this group split into the National Baptist Convention of America, commonly called the "unincorporated convention," and the National Baptist Convention, U.S.A.

The National Baptist Convention of America operates the National Baptist Publishing Board in Nashville, Tenn., and does missionary work in Jamaica, Panama, and Liberia. The convention also provides financial support for 10 colleges. The convention has about 2,650,000 members.

Critically reviewed by the NATIONAL BAPTIST CONVENTION OF AMERICA

NATIONAL BAPTIST CONVENTION, U.S.A., INC., is one of the largest religious organizations among American blacks. The convention has 30,000 churches and about 6,300,000 members. It is the second largest Baptist organization in the world, after the Southern Baptist Convention.

The convention was organized in 1880 to spread the gospel of Christ to other countries. Its founders stressed preaching the gospel to all people as an answer to what they considered the shortcomings of a segregating church. During 1967 and 1968, the convention reaffirmed its faith in civil rights through law and order by adopting the principles set forth in the book *Unholy Shadows and Freedom's Holy Light* by the convention's president, J. H. Jackson.

Critically reviewed by the NATIONAL BAPTIST CONVENTION, U.S.A., INC.

NATIONAL BASEBALL HALL OF FAME. See BASEBALL (table).

NATIONAL BASEBALL LEAGUE. See BASEBALL.

NATIONAL BASKETBALL ASSOCIATION. See BASKETBALL.

NATIONAL BATTLEFIELD. See NATIONAL PARK SYSTEM.

NATIONAL BLACK POLITICAL CONVENTION. See BLACK AMERICANS (Black Americans Today).

NATIONAL BOOK AWARDS are prizes given for distinguished books written by United States citizens. Awards in seven categories go each year to persons

whose books have been published in the United States during the previous calendar year. Panels of three judges choose the books. Each winner receives $1,000.

The National Book Awards were established in 1950. Until 1960, a volunteer committee from the book publishing industry conducted the program. From 1960 to 1975, the awards were administered by the National Book Committee, a nonprofit organization. In 1975, the National Institute of Arts and Letters took over sponsorship of the awards. In 1977, the Association of American Publishers became the sponsor. The awards are financed by the publishing industry.

For many years, awards were given in 10 categories. In 1976, the number of categories was reduced to six. In 1977, the number was increased to seven—fiction, poetry, biography and autobiography, history, contemporary thought, children's literature, and translation.

——————— NATIONAL BOOK AWARDS ———————

FICTION

1950*Nelson Algren, *The Man with the Golden Arm.*
1951*William Faulkner, *Collected Stories of William Faulkner.*
1952 James Jones, *From Here to Eternity.*
1953*Ralph Ellison, *Invisible Man.*
1954*Saul Bellow, *The Adventures of Augie March.*
1955*William Faulkner, *A Fable.*
1956*John O'Hara, *Ten North Frederick.*
1957 Wright Morris, *The Field of Vision.*
1958*John Cheever, *The Wapshot Chronicle.*
1959*Bernard Malamud, *The Magic Barrel.*
1960*Philip Roth, *Goodbye, Columbus.*
1961*Conrad Richter, *The Waters of Kronos.*
1962 Walker Percy, *The Moviegoer.*
1963 J. F. Powers, *Morte D'Urban.*
1964*John Updike, *The Centaur.*
1965*Saul Bellow, *Herzog.*
1966*Katherine Anne Porter, *The Collected Stories of Katherine Anne Porter.*
1967*Bernard Malamud, *The Fixer.*
1968*Thornton Wilder, *The Eighth Day.*
1969 Jerzy Kosinski, *Steps.*
1970 Joyce Carol Oates, *Them.*
1971*Saul Bellow, *Mr. Sammler's Planet.*
1972*Flannery O'Connor, *The Complete Stories.*
1973*John Barth, *Chimera;* John Williams, *Augustus.*
1974*Isaac Bashevis Singer, *A Crown of Feathers;* Thomas Pynchon, *Gravity's Rainbow.*
1975 Robert Stone, *Dog Soldiers;* Thomas Williams, *The Hair of Harold Roux.*
1976 William Gaddis, *JR.*
1977 Wallace Stegner, *The Spectator Bird.*

POETRY

1950*William Carlos Williams, *Paterson III and Selected Poems.*
1951*Wallace Stevens, *The Auroras of Autumn.*
1952*Marianne Moore, *Collected Poems.*
1953*Archibald MacLeish, *Collected Poems: 1917-1952.*
1954*Conrad Aiken, *Collected Poems.*
1955*Wallace Stevens, *The Collected Poems of Wallace Stevens.*
1956*W. H. Auden, *The Shield of Achilles.*
1957*Richard Wilbur, *Things of This World.*
1958*Robert Penn Warren, *Promises: Poems 1954-1956.*
1959*Theodore Roethke, *Words for the Wind.*
1960*Robert Lowell, *Life Studies.*
1961 Randall Jarrell, *The Woman at the Washington Zoo.*

*Has a separate biography in WORLD BOOK

NATIONAL BOOK AWARDS

1962 Alan Dugan, *Poems.*
1963 William Stafford, *Traveling Through the Dark.*
1964*John Crowe Ransom, *Selected Poems.*
1965*Theodore Roethke, *The Far Field.*
1966 James Dickey, *Buckdancer's Choice.*
1967 James Merrill, *Nights and Days.*
1968 Robert Bly, *The Light Around the Body.*
1969*John Berryman, *His Toy, His Dream, His Rest.*
1970 Elizabeth Bishop, *The Complete Poems.*
1971 Mona Van Duyn, *To See, To Take.*
1972 Howard Moss, *Selected Poems;* Frank O'Hara, *The Collected Poems.*
1973 A. R. Ammons, *Collected Poems: 1951-1971.*
1974*Allen Ginsberg, *The Fall of America: Poems of These States, 1965-1971;* Adrienne Rich, *Diving into the Wreck: Poems, 1971-1972.*
1975 Marilyn Hacker, *Presentation Piece.*
1976 John Ashbery, *Self-Portrait in a Convex Mirror.*
1977*Richard Eberhart, *Collected Poems, 1930-1976.*

NONFICTION

1950 Ralph L. Rusk, *Ralph Waldo Emerson.*
1951 Newton Arvin, *Herman Melville.*
1952*Rachel Carson, *The Sea Around Us.*
1953*Bernard De Voto, *The Course of Empire.*
1954*Bruce Catton, *A Stillness at Appomattox.*
1955 Joseph Wood Krutch, *The Measure of Man.*
1956 Herbert Kubly, *American in Italy.*
1957*George F. Kennan, *Russia Leaves the War.*
1958 Catherine Drinker Bowen, *The Lion and the Throne.*
1959 J. Christopher Herold, *Mistress to an Age.*
1960 Richard Ellmann, *James Joyce.*
1961 William L. Shirer, *The Rise and Fall of the Third Reich.*
1962*Lewis Mumford, *The City in History.*
1963 Leon Edel, *Henry James: The Conquest of London: 1870-1881* and *Henry James: The Middle Years: 1882-1895.*
1964 Award divided into three groups: Arts and Letters; History and Biography; and Science, Philosophy, and Religion.

ARTS AND LETTERS

1964 Aileen Ward, *John Keats: The Making of a Poet.*
1965 Eleanor Clark, *The Oysters of Locmariaquer.*
1966 Janet Flanner, *Paris Journal (1944-1965).*
1967 Justin Kaplan, *Mr. Clemens and Mark Twain.*
1968 William Troy, *Selected Essays.*
1969*Norman Mailer, *The Armies of the Night.*
1970*Lillian Hellman, *An Unfinished Woman.*
1971 Francis Steegmuller, *Cocteau.*
1972 Charles Rosen, *The Classical Style.*
1973 Arthur M. Wilson, *Diderot.*
1974 Pauline Kael, *Deeper into Movies.*
1975 Roger Shattuck, *Marcel Proust;* Lewis Thomas, *The Lives of a Cell: Notes of a Biology Watcher.*
1976 Paul Fussell, *The Great War and Modern Memory.*
1977 Award discontinued.

HISTORY AND BIOGRAPHY

1964 William H. McNeill, *The Rise of the West.*
1965 Louis Fischer, *The Life of Lenin.*
1966*Arthur M. Schlesinger, Jr., *A Thousand Days.*
1967 Peter Gay, *The Enlightenment: An Interpretation.*
1968*George F. Kennan, *Memoirs: 1925-1950.*
1969 Winthrop Jordan, *White Over Black.*
1970 T. Harry Williams, *Huey Long.*
1971 James MacGregor Burns, *Roosevelt: The Soldier of Freedom.*
1972-1975 Award divided into two groups: History and Biography.

*Has a separate biography in WORLD BOOK

1976 David Brion Davis, *The Problem of Slavery in the Age of Revolution: 1770-1823.*
1977 Award divided into two groups: History, and Biography and Autobiography.

HISTORY

1972*Allan Nevins, *The War for the Union: The Organized War, 1863-1864* and *The War for the Union: The Organized War to Victory, 1864-1865.*
1973 Robert M. Myers, *The Children of Pride: A True Story of Georgia and the Civil War;* Isaiah Trunk, *Judenrat: The Jewish Councils in Eastern Europe Under Nazi Occupation.*
1974 John Clive, *Macaulay: The Shaping of the Historian.*
1975 Bernard Bailyn, *The Ordeal of Thomas Hutchinson.*
1976 Award became History and Biography.
1977 Irving Howe, *World of Our Fathers.*

BIOGRAPHY

1972 Joseph P. Lash, *Eleanor and Franklin.*
1973 James Thomas Flexner, *George Washington: Anguish and Farewell (1793-1799).*
1974 Douglas Day, *Malcolm Lowry: A Biography.*
1975 Richard B. Sewall, *The Life of Emily Dickinson.*
1976 Award became History and Biography.

BIOGRAPHY AND AUTOBIOGRAPHY

1977 W. A. Swanberg, *Norman Thomas: The Last Idealist.*

SCIENCE, PHILOSOPHY, AND RELIGION

1964 Christopher Tunnard and Boris Pushkarev, *Man-Made America: Chaos or Control?*
1965*Norbert Wiener, *God and Golem, Inc.*
1966 No Award.
1967 Oscar Lewis, *La Vida.*
1968 Jonathan Kozol, *Death at an Early Age.*
1969 Award divided into two groups: The Sciences, and Philosophy and Religion.

THE SCIENCES

1969 Robert J. Lifton, *Death in Life: Survivors of Hiroshima.*
1970 No Award.
1971 Raymond Phineas Stearns, *Science in the British Colonies of America.*
1972 George L. Small, *The Blue Whale.*
1973 George B. Schaller, *The Serengeti Lion: A Study of Predator-Prey Relations.*
1974 S. E. Luria, *Life: The Unfinished Experiment.*
1975 Silvano Arieti, *Interpretation of Schizophrenia.*
1976 Award discontinued.

PHILOSOPHY AND RELIGION

1969 No Award.
1970 Erik H. Erikson, *Gandhi's Truth: On the Origins of Militant Nonviolence.*
1971 No Award.
1972 Martin E. Marty, *Righteous Empire: The Protestant Experience in America.*
1973 Sydney E. Ahlstrom, *A Religious History of the American People.*
1974 Maurice Nathanson, *Edmund Husserl: Philosopher of Infinite Tasks.*
1975 Robert Nozick, *Anarchy, State and Utopia.*
1976 Award discontinued.

CONTEMPORARY AFFAIRS

1972 Stewart Brand, *The Last Whole Earth Catalog.*
1973 Frances FitzGerald, *Fire in the Lake: The Vietnamese and the Americans in Vietnam.*
1974 Murray Kempton, *The Briar Patch: The People of New York v. Lumumba Shakur Et Al.*

1975 Theodore Rosengarten, *All God's Dangers: The Life of Nate Shaw.*

1976 Michael J. Arlen, *Passage to Ararat.*

1977 Award discontinued.

CONTEMPORARY THOUGHT

1977*Bruno Bettelheim, *The Uses of Enchantment: The Meaning and Importance of Fairy Tales.*

CHILDREN'S LITERATURE

1969*Meindert DeJong, *Journey from Peppermint Street.*

1970*Isaac Bashevis Singer, *A Day of Pleasure: Stories of a Boy Growing Up in Warsaw.*

1971*Lloyd Alexander, *The Marvelous Misadventures of Sebastian.*

1972 Donald Barthelme, *The Slightly Irregular Fire Engine or the Hithering Thithering Djinn.*

1973 Ursula Le Guin, *The Farthest Shore.*

1974 Eleanor Cameron, *The Court of the Stone Children.*

1975*Virginia Hamilton, *M. C. Higgins, the Great.*

1976*Walter D. Edmonds, *Bert Breen's Barn.*

1977 Katherine Paterson, *The Master Puppeteer.*

TRANSLATION

1967 Gregory Rabassa, for his translation of *Hopscotch* by Julio Cortazar; Willard Trask, for his translation of *History of My Life* by Giacomo Casanova.

1968 Howard and Edna Hong for their translation of *Søren Kierkegaard's Journals and Papers.*

1969 William Weaver for his translation of *Cosmicomics* by Italo Calvino.

1970 Ralph Manheim for his translation of *Castle to Castle* by Louis-Ferdinand Celine.

1971 Frank Jones for his translation of *Saint Joan of the Stockyards* by Bertolt Brecht; Edward G. Seidensticker for his translation of *The Sound of the Mountain* by Yasunari Kawabata.

1972 Austryn Wainhouse for his translation of *Chance and Necessity: An Essay on the Natural Philosophy of Modern Biology* by Jacques Monod.

1973 Allen Mandelbaum, *The Aeneid of Virgil.*

1974 Karen Brazell for her translation of *The Confessions of Lady Nijo;* Helen R. Lane for her translation of *Alternating Current* by Octavio Paz; Jackson Mathews for his translation of *Monsieur Teste* by Paul Valéry.

1975 Anthony Kerrigan for his translation of *The Agony of Christianity and Essays on Faith* by Miguel de Unamuno.

1976 No award.

1977 Li-li Ch'en for her translation of *Master Tung's Western Chamber Romance.*

*Has a separate biography in WORLD BOOK

NATIONAL BROADCASTING COMPANY (NBC) is

one of the largest broadcast organizations in the United States. NBC has more than 400 independently owned stations in its radio and television networks. It also owns and operates five television and five radio stations. NBC provides a national program service for its networks, including drama and comedy series, specials, news broadcasts, and sports coverage.

NBC organized the first radio network in the United States in 1926 with 25 radio stations. It also pioneered in television, introducing it as a regular service in 1939. In 1951, NBC inaugurated its coast-to-coast television network. It began televising programs in color soon after the federal government approved color television in 1953. By 1966, NBC was broadcasting all its programs in color. NBC is owned by the RCA Corporation

(formerly Radio Corporation of America) and has headquarters in New York City. It has color production facilities in New York City and Burbank, Calif.

Critically reviewed by the NATIONAL BROADCASTING COMPANY

See also RCA CORPORATION.

NATIONAL BUDGET is the financial plan for a nation's government. The budget forecasts the government's income and expenditures for one *fiscal year* (from October 1 to September 30 in the United States). It forecasts how much money the government will collect from taxes and other sources, and suggests how much money each government department should spend.

In the United States, the Office of Management and Budget prepares the proposed federal budget for the President. The office receives estimates of government income from the Department of the Treasury and spending estimates from all government departments. The Congressional Budget Office studies the President's proposal and may suggest changes. Using these recommendations, the budget committees of the Senate and House of Representatives prepare a revised budget and recommend general spending goals. These aims are debated and revised by both houses of Congress. Congress then passes spending bills based on the revised goals. If spending exceeds the goals, Congress must decide whether to borrow money, cut spending, or raise taxes.

The government gets most of its income from income and employment taxes paid by individuals and corporations. Most government expenditures are for national defense and for such domestic purposes as education, health, and social insurance benefits.

The national budget has grown in size and importance as the role of the federal government has grown. The U.S. budget is nearly 90 times larger today than in the early 1900's, after allowing for price changes. In the late 1970's, the national budget was more than $450 billion a year and amounted to more than 20 per cent of the country's gross national product. The Canadian budget has grown from about 5 per cent of the gross national product in 1900 to about 20 per cent today.

Economists once favored a *balanced budget,* in which income equaled spending. But many fiscal experts now favor a *budget deficit* (expenditures exceeding income) when the economy needs stimulating, and a *planned surplus* (income exceeding expenditures) in boom times to control inflation. K. PETER WAGNER

See also BUDGET (Government Budgets); MANAGEMENT AND BUDGET, OFFICE OF; TAXATION (illustration: The Federal Government Dollar).

NATIONAL BUREAU OF STANDARDS is a federal agency in the Department of Commerce that establishes accurate measurement standards for science, industry, and commerce in the United States. All measurements made in the United States depend on the primary standards maintained at the bureau. The bureau compares and coordinates its standards with those of other countries through international organizations.

The bureau works to maintain, improve, and apply fundamental systems of measurement, including length, time, and mass. It provides research and technical services to improve computer sciences and technology; materials technology; and such areas of applied technology as building construction and consumer product safety.

The bureau also provides measurement services and standards for other federal agencies and state and local governments. It helps private organizations promote the establishment of voluntary standards for commerce and industry. Published information on the bureau's work can be obtained from the Superintendent of Documents and the National Technical Information Service. The bureau was established in 1901 and became part of the Department of Commerce in 1903.

Critically reviewed by the NATIONAL BUREAU OF STANDARDS

NATIONAL CANCER INSTITUTE. See CANCER; NATIONAL INSTITUTES OF HEALTH.

NATIONAL CATHEDRAL. See WASHINGTON CATHEDRAL.

NATIONAL CATHOLIC EDUCATIONAL ASSOCIATION is an organization to encourage cooperation and mutual helpfulness among Catholic educators, and to promote, by study, conference, and discussion, Catholic educational work in the United States. The organization was founded as the Catholic Educational Association in 1904 in St. Louis, Mo., and, in 1927, became the National Catholic Educational Association. Its work is carried on by the departments of Major Seminary, Minor Seminary, College and University, Secondary School, School Superintendents, Elementary School, and Special Education. Headquarters are at 1 Dupont Circle, Washington, D.C. 20036. The organization has about 16,000 members. Critically reviewed by the

NATIONAL CATHOLIC EDUCATIONAL ASSOCIATION

NATIONAL CEMETERY is a burial place for men and women who served in the armed forces of the United States. Veterans are eligible to be buried in a national cemetery unless they received a dishonorable discharge. The spouses and dependent children of these veterans may also be buried there. The government maintains 122 national cemeteries throughout the United States and Puerto Rico. More than 50 of them have no space for additional graves. Over 1½ million persons are buried in national cemeteries.

Three government agencies operate the national cemeteries. The Veterans Administration (VA) maintains 106 of the cemeteries. The National Park Service, a bureau of the Department of the Interior, is responsible for 14 national cemeteries that are part of historic sites. The Department of the Army operates 2 cemeteries—Arlington National Cemetery in Arlington, Va., and Soldiers Home National Cemetery in Washington, D.C. The American Battle Monuments Commission maintains all U.S. military cemeteries outside the United States and its possessions.

The VA provides headstones and markers for all graves in national cemeteries and for all graves of veterans that do not have them. These unmarked graves include those of soldiers who served in the Union Army and the Confederate Army during the Civil War (1861-1865).

The national cemetery system was established in 1862, during the Civil War. That year, Congress granted President Abraham Lincoln permission to establish cemeteries for Union Army veterans.

One of the best-known national cemeteries operated by the National Park Service is in Gettysburg, Pa. A crucial Civil War battle was fought there in July 1863.

On November 19 that year, Lincoln delivered his Gettysburg Address at a ceremony dedicating part of the battlefield as a cemetery. The other historic cemeteries operated by the National Park Service are Andersonville in Georgia; Andrew Johnson, Fort Donelson, Shiloh, and Stones River in Tennessee; Antietam in Maryland; Battleground in Washington, D.C.; Chalmette in Louisiana; Custer Battlefield in Montana; Fredericksburg, Poplar Grove, and Yorktown in Virginia; and Vicksburg in Mississippi.

During the 1970's, the VA announced the sites for five more national cemeteries. They are in Bourne, Mass.; Calverton, N.Y., near Hampton Bays; Indiantown Gap, Pa., near Harrisburg; Quantico, Va.; and Riverside, Calif.

Critically reviewed by the NATIONAL CEMETERY SYSTEM
OF THE VETERANS ADMINISTRATION

See also ARLINGTON NATIONAL CEMETERY; BATTLEGROUND NATIONAL CEMETERY; CUSTER BATTLEFIELD NATIONAL MONUMENT.

NATIONAL COLLECTION OF FINE ARTS is a bureau of the Smithsonian Institution that preserves and displays certain works of art belonging to the United States government. The bureau also presents a continuing series of special exhibitions. The collection includes paintings, sculptures, prints, drawings, and decorative art works. Most items in the collection are by American artists. The bureau's Traveling Exhibition Service presents art exhibits throughout the United States and in other countries. The bureau lends works of art to federal agencies and provides facilities for art education and research. The collection is the oldest federal government art collection in the United States.

Critically reviewed by the SMITHSONIAN INSTITUTION

NATIONAL COLLEGIATE ATHLETIC ASSOCIATION (NCAA) establishes athletic standards and official playing rules for college sports. It conducts National Collegiate Championship events in 13 sports and keeps the official national statistics and records of college sports. It also conducts studies on athletic problems and maintains a large film library covering play in National Collegiate Championship events. The association sponsors an extensive postgraduate scholarship program. It also controls the televising of college football games.

The NCAA was founded in 1906. Its membership has grown from 13 schools to over 700, including colleges and universities, athletic conferences, and coaches' associations. Its headquarters are at U.S. Highway 50 and Nall Avenue, Shawnee Mission, Kans. 66222.

Critically reviewed by the NATIONAL COLLEGIATE ATHLETIC ASSOCIATION

NATIONAL CONFERENCE OF CHRISTIANS AND JEWS is a nonprofit human relations organization engaged in a nationwide program to eliminate prejudice and discrimination. The conference works to foster understanding among all ethnic, racial, and religious groups. Its educational program includes creative dialogues, institutes, seminars, and workshops. The conference works with teachers, parents, young people, police, clergy, business, labor, and community leaders. It sponsors Brotherhood Week (see BROTHERHOOD WEEK). The conference was founded in 1928. Its headquarters are at 43 W. 57th Street, New York, N.Y. 10019. Critically reviewed by the

NATIONAL CONFERENCE OF CHRISTIANS AND JEWS

NATIONAL CONGRESS OF AMERICAN INDIANS

is the oldest and largest American Indian organization in the United States. It evaluates government policies on Indian affairs and promotes programs to improve the economic opportunities, education, and health of Indians. It works to persuade members of the U.S. Congress to support legislation that benefits Indians.

The National Congress of American Indians was established in 1944 by Indian leaders representing more than 50 tribes. The goals of the organization included the development and protection of land, minerals, timber, and other resources owned by Indians. In 1946, the group supported the establishment of the Indian Claims Commission. This federal agency settles disputes between the government and Indian tribes over land claims. In 1953, the congress helped defeat a bill that would have placed under state control several Indian reservations that had been supervised by the federal government. The Indians declared that such a law would wipe out their property rights. The organization has helped Indians in the Southwest use their voting rights and has set up programs to provide scholarships and legal aid.

About 100 tribes belong to the congress, which represents approximately 350,000 Indians. The organization has headquarters at 1430 K Street NW, Washington, D.C. 20005. Leon F. Cook

NATIONAL CONGRESS OF PARENTS AND TEACHERS

is a volunteer organization that unites the forces of home, school, and community on behalf of children and youth. It is noncommercial, nonsectarian, and nonpartisan. Its educational program is developed through conferences, committees, and projects at national, state, and community levels. Local parent-teacher associations are known as PTA's. They encourage cooperation between home and school. The PTA's interpret the school to the community and the community to the school. They develop study-discussion groups in family life education and other areas of adult education. They also strive to improve the child's environment in home, school, and community. The National PTA works with other organizations in projects of common interest.

Objectives

Purposes are stated in the following *Objects:*

1. To promote the welfare of children and youth in home, school, church, and community.

2. To raise the standards of home life.

3. To secure adequate laws for the care and protection of children and youth.

4. To bring into closer relation the home and the school, that parents and teachers may cooperate intelligently in the education of children and youth.

5. To develop between educators and the general public such united efforts as will secure for all children and youth the highest advantages in physical, mental, social, and spiritual education.

Program. The National PTA conducts its program through national, state, and local activities. It works through five commissions that specialize in such fields as health and welfare, education, leadership development, individual development, and membership and organizational services.

The commissions work on various projects, such as providing children with wholesome material from com-

NAT'L. CONG. OF PARENTS AND TEACHERS

ics, motion pictures, radio, and television. The National PTA has set up standards for judging these media both as entertainment and as educational tools, and has encouraged state and local programs to improve them.

Nearly all of the state PTA's offer scholarships to encourage young people to become teachers, librarians, or guidance counselors. The National PTA has an ongoing program to support legislation aimed at improving the health, safety, and education of children. It urges adequate appropriations for such federal agencies as the Department of Health, Education, and Welfare.

The PTA publishes the monthly *National PTA Bulletin*, the annual *Proceedings*, and pamphlets used by local units.

Local PTA units throughout the nation have initiated such programs as drawing up teen-age conduct codes and providing clinics for reading assistance. Others have sponsored safety education programs and helped solve school traffic problems. Members' work has sometimes resulted in better streets around schools and improved traffic supervision. In some areas, PTA's have worked to keep schools open after hours as social centers. In others, they have helped local health authorities with polio vaccination programs and other health services.

The PTA encourages its members to become fully informed and to take an active interest in their school program. In 1973, the PTA changed its bylaws to enable its members to become more involved in school policymaking.

Organization

Government. Bylaws that govern the National PTA provide for a Board of Managers consisting of 95 members, 21 of whom serve on an Executive Committee. Annual conventions of the National PTA are open to all members, but voting is limited to the accredited state delegates and members of the National Board of Managers. Officers are elected for two-year terms.

National Congress of Parents and Teachers

The National PTA Board has both student and adult members. Board members frequently discuss such matters as proposed school legislation. Student members also serve on many state PTA boards of managers.

NATIONAL CONSERVATION COMMISSION

State Branches. Each state Congress of Parents and Teachers has a board of managers that handles the affairs within that state branch. Some state branches are divided into districts. Many states also have city and county councils. The state branches carry out the work of the National PTA within the state, and develop programs that meet particular state needs.

Local Units are formed in each school. A local parent-teacher association develops programs to fit the needs of its school and community. Local associations conduct monthly meetings, study groups, workshops, and programs of community service. A person who joins the local PTA automatically becomes a member of the state and national organizations.

Membership is open to "any person interested in the Objects of the National Congress who is willing to uphold its basic policies and subscribe to its Bylaws." The PTA has over 8 million members. Its headquarters are at 700 N. Rush St., Chicago, Ill. 60611.

Youth Involvement. During the late 1960's and early 1970's, the National PTA began to emphasize greater student involvement in PTA work. About 3,500 PTSA (Parent-Teacher-Student Association) units have been established throughout the United States. Many students are members of these units. Five students serve on the National PTA Board of Managers. One of these students is on the PTA Executive Committee.

History

The PTA organization was founded as the National Congress of Mothers. It first met in Washington, D.C., on Feb. 17, 1897. Alice McLellan Birney and Phoebe Apperson Hearst were the cofounders.

The first local units organized by the congress devoted themselves to child study. Very early in its history, the National Congress urged parents to study the curriculums of the schools their children attended. It also suggested reading courses to give both fathers and mothers information about children and schools.

One of the first large-scale projects the PTA undertook was to extend the kindergarten. In those days, kindergartens were still in the experimental stage. The congress has sponsored projects to meet recognized community needs, such as playgrounds and school lunches, until school or government authorities could take over their management. It initiated the Summer Round-Up of the Children, a health program for discovering and correcting physical defects of children about to enter school. In recent years, it has adopted a broader program for health supervision of children from birth through high school. It also has begun a long-range program to strengthen community resources for safeguarding the emotional health of children.

The first state congress was organized in New York in 1897. There is now a branch in every state and one in the District of Columbia.

Critically reviewed by NATIONAL CONGRESS OF PARENTS AND TEACHERS

See also EDUCATION; PARENT EDUCATION; PARENT-TEACHER ORGANIZATIONS; SCHOOL.

NATIONAL CONSERVATION COMMISSION. See CONSERVATION (National Policy).

NATIONAL CONSUMERS LEAGUE is an educational movement founded in 1899 to awaken interest in the conditions under which goods are made and distributed, and to show consumers their responsibility for these conditions. The league worked for child labor laws, the 8-hour day for women, minimum wage laws, social insurance, and national health insurance for the elderly under social security. It prepared legal briefs to defend these laws in court. The league also worked for the establishment of the Food and Drug Administration, meat inspection, and other consumer protection legislation. It now works to improve the conditions of migratory farmworkers, extend the Fair Labor Standards Act, and extend consumer protection. The National Consumers League has national headquarters at 1785 Massachusetts Avenue NW, Washington, D.C. 20036.

Critically reviewed by the NATIONAL CONSUMERS LEAGUE

NATIONAL COUNCIL OF CHURCHES is an agency through which churches work together to promote social justice and understanding among people in the United States and overseas. Its work includes community development, education, evangelism, medical aid, missions, relief, research, and social welfare programs. Each year, the council spends more than $20 million in overseas programs. It represents 30 Protestant and Orthodox denominations with about 40 million members.

A 240-member governing board directs the council's programs and policies. It meets twice a year. About half the board's members are lay people and half are clergy.

The council was formed in 1950 by the merger of 11 interdenominational agencies. Its full name is NATIONAL COUNCIL OF THE CHURCHES OF CHRIST IN THE UNITED STATES OF AMERICA. It publishes a quarterly newspaper called *NCCC Chronicles*. Headquarters are at 475 Riverside Drive, New York, N.Y. 10027.

Critically reviewed by the NATIONAL COUNCIL OF CHURCHES

NATIONAL COVENANT. See COVENANTERS.

NATIONAL CRIME INFORMATION CENTER. See FEDERAL BUREAU OF INVESTIGATION.

NATIONAL DEBT is the total amount that the federal government owes because of money it has borrowed by selling bonds or other securities. The national debt exists because the government's expenses often exceed its income from taxes. In such situations, the government sells bonds to get the extra money it needs. It must repay the bondholders the original amount of the bonds on a specified date, and it must also pay interest on this indebtedness.

Government debt differs from private debt because the government is not required to post any *collateral* (pledge of security) to guarantee payment. However, the U.S. government has always repaid its loans.

Causes of National Debt. The United States debt originated in the 1790's, when the newly established federal government assumed debts that the individual states had run up during the Revolutionary War. Wars have been by far the most common cause of increases in the U.S. national debt. For example, the federal debt was only $1 billion before World War I (1914-1918). The war raised it to about $25 billion. By the time World War II ended in 1945, the national debt had risen to about $259 billion. The Korean War in the early 1950's and the Vietnam War in the 1960's and early 1970's caused the debt to rise sharply again.

Wars have also been responsible for high national debts in other countries. In 1867, the newly formed

Dominion of Canada assumed the Canadian debt of $93 million. After increases caused chiefly by Canada's participation in two world wars, the debt totaled about $19 billion in the mid-1940's. By the mid-1970's, the Canadian national debt had risen to about $72 billion.

Public improvements also increase the national debt. These include such long-lasting improvements as canals, roads and highways, and dams for irrigation and elec-

trical power. Some of these yield enough income to pay the principal and interest on the bonds issued to finance them. Others, such as roads, benefit the nation, but generally do not yield money income.

In the United States, Congress has set both permanent and temporary limits or ceilings on how high the national debt may rise. In 1977, the permanent ceiling was $400 billion. However, the debt could exceed that

United States Gross National Debt and Gross National Product Since the Civil War

The gross national debt of the United States is about 236 times as large today as it was in 1865. But the U.S. population is only about 6 times as large. As a result, the debt per person is about 37 times as great as it was in 1865. In 1945, the national debt

exceeded the U.S. gross national product (GNP). The GNP is the total value of the goods and services produced during the year. Since the mid-1940's, the GNP has grown faster than the debt. Today the debt is only about two-fifths of the GNP.

Year	Gross National Debt	Debt per Person	Gross National Debt as Percentage of Gross National Product	Year	Gross National Debt	Debt per Person	Gross National Debt as Percentage of Gross National Product
1865	$2,677,929,000	$75	—	1930	$16,185,310,000	$132	18
1870	$2,436,453,000	$61	30	1940	$42,967,531,000	$325	43
1880	$2,090,909,000	$42	16	1950	$257,357,352,000	$1,697	90
1890	$1,122,397,000	$18	9	1960	$286,330,761,000	$1,585	57
1900	$1,263,417,000	$17	7	1970	$382,603,000,000	$1,867	39
1910	$1,146,940,000	$12	3	1975	$544,131,000,000	$2,548	36
1920	$24,299,321,000	$228	27	1976	$631,285,000,000	$2,935	37

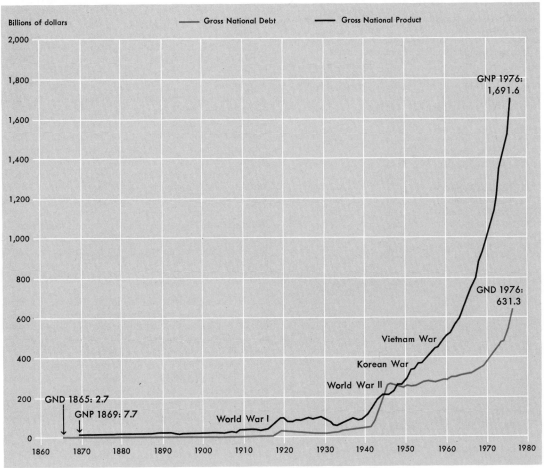

Sources: U.S. Department of Commerce; U.S. Department of the Treasury

limit by $300 billion on a temporary basis, if necessary.

Ownership of the Debt. About a fourth of the national debt is held by various government agencies. However, banks and private individuals are the largest owners of the debt. Banks and insurance companies buy government bonds as a safe investment and to earn interest on funds not used for other purposes. Individuals also buy bonds for family security and for patriotic reasons. During World War II, millions of Americans bought war bonds. Businesses also buy government bonds when they have extra cash which they wish to keep in a safe place while it earns interest. For those who wish to invest for a short time only, the government issues securities called *treasury bills* that mature after 13, 26, or 52 weeks. At the end of that time, these securities must be repaid out of income from taxes or from sales of newly issued bills to other investors. Banks and business firms buy most treasury bills.

Debt Policy. It is important to consider the national debt in relation to the nation's total economic strength. One way of doing this is to compare the national debt to the *gross national product* (GNP). The GNP is the value of a nation's entire production of goods and services in a given year. For example, the United States national debt rose from $259 billion in 1945 to $631 billion in 1976. But the 1945 debt amounted to 122 per cent of that year's GNP, while the 1976 debt was only about 37 per cent of the 1976 GNP. The 1976 national debt accounted for only about a sixth of all public (federal, state, and local) and private debts. In 1945, on the other hand, the U.S. national debt accounted for over three-fifths of all public and private debts.

Some persons argue that, just as in a family or business, federal government spending should be kept equal to or below its income. Others declare that this comparison is misleading. They point out that, except for the small portion of the debt held by persons in other countries, the size of the debt itself is not as important as the effects that increasing or reducing the debt might have on the economy. Both groups usually agree that taxes in prosperous times should be high enough to cover government spending and to reduce the debt.

Those who call for a balanced budget would not favor measures that would increase the national debt if a recession occurred or threatened to occur. But members of the second group would urge government borrowing to pay for public improvements as a sound way to prevent or end recession. They believe it is the government's responsibility to take such action to stimulate business activity, thereby creating more jobs to reduce unemployment.   K. PETER WAGNER

See also NATIONAL BUDGET; GROSS NATIONAL PRODUCT; KEYNES, JOHN MAYNARD; SAVINGS BOND.

NATIONAL DEFENSE. A nation must be able to defend itself if it is attacked. The problem of defense was easy when people lived in small tribes. There were only a few simple weapons, and everyone could use them in defending the tribe. As communities grew larger, and weapons more complicated, small armies of professional soldiers took over the job of defense. But today, when people have built weapons that can destroy entire cities, defense has become everyone's concern.

National defense affects almost every phase of a nation's life. It includes guns and butter, atomic bombs and cattle. The national defense policy of any nation is tied directly to its relationships with other countries. A nation must have the military strength to support its foreign policy. In time of peace, a nation must not spend so much on defense that it bankrupts the rest of its economy.

Planning for Defense

How strong must a nation be? It takes great leadership and planning to answer this question, not only for today, but for tomorrow. A nation, particularly a powerful country such as the United States, must study the other major political powers. It must estimate their strength now, two years from now, and even twenty years from now. Which nation is likely to be an aggressor, and provoke war? Which probably will be friendly? What about the natural resources, industry, and political and social make-up of other nations? All these questions must be considered.

The President of the United States is the head of all national defense activities. He is the commander in chief of the armed forces, and appoints civilian leaders

---

Canada National Debt and Gross National Product Since Confederation in 1867

Canada's national debt, like that of the United States, has increased because the government has borrowed huge sums to develop the country and to fight wars. Today, Canada's debt is rising more slowly than its gross national product.

Year	Gross National Debt	Debt per Person	Gross National Debt as Per Cent of Gross National Product
1867	$93,046,000	$27	—
1870	$115,994,000	$32	25
1880	$194,634,000	$46	33
1890	$286,112,000	$60	36
1900	$346,207,000	$65	33
1910	$470,663,000	$67	21
1920	$3,041,530,000	$355	55
1930	$2,544,586,000	$249	44
1940	$4,028,729,000	$354	60
1950	$16,750,756,000	$1,222	93
1960	$20,986,367,000	$1,174	58
1970	$38,150,097,000	$1,789	45
1975	$62,699,930,000	$2,749	39
1976	$71,773,759,000	$3,106	39

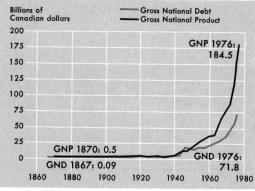

Billions of Canadian dollars
— Gross National Debt
— Gross National Product

GNP 1976: 184.5
GNP 1870: 0.5
GND 1867: 0.09
GND 1976: 71.8

Source: Statistics Canada

to supervise the federal government's defense activities.

The National Security Council is the highest defense planning group in the country. The President and the Vice-President meet with the Secretary of State and the Secretary of Defense to discuss all problems relating to the defense of the nation. These men bring together their knowledge of national and international problems, and decide on a unified policy designed to meet all the problems. They study the objectives and risks involved in any proposed policy.

The Council supervises the work of the Central Intelligence Agency, which has two jobs: (1) It must interpret information about foreign and domestic activities which could be a threat to national security; (2) it also provides facts and information to help the Council and other federal agencies in making plans and decisions.

Military Defense Forces

The Secretary of Defense is the President's appointed leader of the military defense activities. He is responsible for the entire military program of the United States, including problems of manpower, research, and supply.

The Joint Chiefs of Staff (JCS) forms the top strategic planning and military advisory group in the Department of Defense. The JCS is made up of a chairman; the Chief of Staff of the United States Army; the Chief of Naval Operations; and the Chief of Staff of the United States Air Force. On matters relating to the Marine Corps, the Commandant of the corps meets with the JCS as an equal member. The JCS is not a general staff group to exercise military command. It makes recommendations to the Secretary of Defense, the President, or the National Security Council.

Air Defense. Defense experts believe that the first blow in an atomic war probably would come by air. They have planned ways to detect, intercept, and destroy enemy planes and rockets in the air. Air defense of the United States and Canada is the job of the North American Air Defense Command (NORAD), with headquarters in Cheyenne Mountain near Colorado Springs, Colo. NORAD controls all Canadian and American air defense forces. Bands of radar stations in Canada and off the east and west coasts of the United States watch for attacking planes. Air Force planes equipped with radar patrol the skies over the Arctic and far out over the Atlantic and Pacific oceans. The Ballistic Missile Early Warning System (BMEWS) uses giant radar screens to watch for enemy rockets. All unidentified planes or missiles are reported to a direction center that operates every minute of every day in the year. The center can order interceptor planes or guided missiles into the air. See RADAR.

Sea Defense is designed to protect the United States from possible attack by submarines or surface vessels armed with atomic weapons. Navy patrol planes and ships at sea keep constant watch for potential enemy ships of any kind.

Land Defense is the third line of defense of the United States. Military experts believe that an invasion of the United States would not come until after bombardment from the air and attacks by sea. But the Army's job in defense also includes maintaining defense forces in Europe and in Asia. These forces are ready to repel aggression against Allied nations. Defense planners consider that the job of defending the United States is also a matter of defending its allies throughout the world.

Mobilizing for Defense

Making preparations to *mobilize*, or gather together, men and materials for war is one of the most important parts of the defense effort. This involves mobilization of all the natural resources, industries, and manpower.

Civil Defense is the responsiblility of the Defense Civil Preparedness Agency (DCPA) in the Department of Defense. The DCPA develops and directs an evacuation and fallout shelter program; a defense program against chemical, biological, and radiological warfare; and warning and communications systems. The agency also has programs to provide aid to state and local governments after an attack.

Natural Resources form the great strength of the country's defenses. The Federal Preparedness Agency in the General Services Administration (GSA) sees to it that critical and strategic materials are not wasted or used in nonessential industries. It also supervises the government's stockpiling of critical materials.

Industries which produce the country's civilian goods would, in case of war, have to be converted to making weapons and military supplies. The GSA must make plans for the government's part in shifting industry from a peacetime to a wartime economy.

Manpower programs are supervised by the GSA. Technicians and skilled workers in vital industries are often far more valuable in their jobs than they would be as soldiers. The government sees that such persons are not drafted into the armed forces.

The Selective Service System was set up before World War II, and again in 1948, for the purpose of supplying the armed forces with a "draft" of men. In the first six years of operation after World War II, more than 15 million men were registered under the system.

Research goes into the development of every new weapon and means of defense. Government researchers, working with industry and the armed forces, develop and test guided missiles, atomic weapons, atomic-powered ships and airplanes, and new types of jet aircraft.

History

In the early United States, the War Department was the only government department responsible for the defense of the country. Henry Knox served as its first secretary. The next addition was a Department of the Navy, with Benjamin Stoddert as its first secretary. These departments organized the nation's defense forces from the War of 1812 through World War I.

From 1789 to 1800, the government spent about $2,210,000 a year for defense. During the Civil War, this figure had risen to more than $613,000,000 a year. In the four-year period from 1916 to 1920, the average annual cost for defense was $4,095,000,000. During World War II, the government spent an average of $49,817,000,000 a year for the Army, Army Air Forces, and Navy alone. By 1970, the government was spending about $80,000,000,000 a year for defense.

The first major change in defense organization came in World War II, when the Joint Chiefs of Staff met to coordinate worldwide land, naval, and air operations.

NATIONAL DEFENSE EDUCATION ACT

Under the National Security Act of 1947, the War and Navy departments were united with a new Department of the Air Force in the National Military Establishment (NME). Only the head of NME, the Secretary of Defense, was a member of the President's Cabinet. James V. Forrestal was the first secretary. The National Security Council also was created.

In 1949, Congress changed the NME's name to the *Department of Defense*. The department was streamlined and the Secretary of Defense was given greater powers. The Army, the Navy, and the Air Force remained separately administered under the Secretary of Defense.

Two agencies were set up in 1953 to handle all problems of mobilization and foreign aid. The Office of Defense Mobilization (ODM) and the Foreign Operations Administration (FOA) were given centralized authority over problems that had been handled by separate agencies. The departments of State and Defense took over FOA functions in 1955. The ODM was reorganized as the Office of Civil and Defense Mobilization (OCDM) in 1958. In 1961, the Secretary of Defense established the Office of Civil Defense (OCD) to develop and direct civil defense programs. That same year, OCDM was renamed the Office of Emergency Planning. Its name was changed again in 1968, to Office of Emergency Preparedness. In 1972, the Secretary of Defense abolished OCD and established the Defense Civil Preparedness Agency (DCPA) to take over its civil defense programs. The Office of Emergency Preparedness was abolished in 1973.   John H. Thompson

Related Articles in World Book include:

Air Force, United States	Guided Missile
Antiaircraft Defense	Joint Chiefs of Staff
Army, United States	Marine Corps, U.S.
Atomic Bomb	National Security Council
Central Intelligence Agency	Navy, United States
Civil Defense	RAND Corporation
Defense, Department of	

NATIONAL DEFENSE EDUCATION ACT (NDEA) is a law enacted by the United States Congress in 1958. It was one of the most significant education bills in U.S. history. NDEA provides financial aid to states, educational institutions, and individuals to improve educational programs in the United States.

NDEA provides federal loans to superior students who can show financial need. A student in higher education may borrow a total of $5,000. He has 10 years to repay the loan, beginning one year after completing his course of study. He must repay only one-half the loan if he teaches in any nonprofit public or private institution for five years.

NDEA also provides funds for states, to buy teaching equipment in science, mathematics, language, English, reading, history, civics, and geography. Private schools also can borrow money for this purpose. Other NDEA programs include graduate fellowships, research into the use of communications media for educational purposes, the improvement of counseling and testing programs, expanded teacher-training programs in critical subjects, and the improvement of vocational education. States must match federal funds to get NDEA funds.

The NDEA is administered by the U.S. Department of Health, Education, and Welfare. Congress passed the NDEA on Sept. 2, 1958.   John D. Millett

NATIONAL EDUCATION ASSOCIATION OF THE UNITED STATES (NEA)

is the largest professional education organization in the world. The NEA has about $1\frac{2}{3}$ million members, most of whom are teachers. The organization's main goals include improving American education and increasing teacher benefits.

The NEA has branches in every state, Puerto Rico, and Washington, D.C. It also has overseas branches. Delegates from state and local associations meet annually in a Representative Assembly to plan the NEA's policies. Officers of the association, a board of directors, and an executive committee govern the NEA between the assembly's sessions.

The history of the NEA can be traced back to 1857, when 43 leaders from state teachers' associations organized the National Teachers Association. In 1870, this organization merged with the Association of School Superintendents and the American Normal School Association to form the National Educational Association. For many years, school administrators provided much of the NEA's leadership. But by the mid-1960's, classroom teachers held almost all offices in the NEA. The NEA requires that teachers make up at least 75 per cent of the members of each commission, committee, and council.

One of the NEA's main objectives is to unite the nation's nearly 3 million teachers. In 1973 and 1974, the association discussed a merger with the national teachers' union, the American Federation of Teachers (AFT). But the two groups did not agree to combine.

In 1957, the NEA established the Student NEA, an organization made up of college students enrolled in teacher education programs. The Student NEA promotes programs to improve the quality of teacher preparation.

The NEA publishes such periodicals as the *NEA Reporter* and *Today's Education*. It also publishes books, filmstrips, and leaflets, as well as materials for American Education Week. NEA headquarters are at 1201 16th Street NW, Washington, D.C. 20036.   Mario D. Fantini

See also Library (School Library Standards); Utah (The Mid-1900's); Education Week, American.

NATIONAL FARMERS ORGANIZATION (NFO)

helps United States farmers sell their products for prices it considers fair. Farmers who are members of the organization can sell their dairy products, grain, and livestock through the NFO. The organization believes that the prices of farm products should be set by the farmers, based on the cost of production.

Since 1974, the NFO has worked to control about 30 per cent of the production of any farm product of interest to its members. The NFO does this by bargaining with food processors for the prices and marketing conditions of the products. The farmers may hold their products from the market if the buyers do not purchase them at the prices set by the NFO. This refusal to sell is called a *holding action*. Some holding actions last until the buyers sign a contract with the NFO for the higher prices. Other such actions have ended when farmers could no longer afford to hold their products and resumed selling.

The NFO was founded in 1955. Its headquarters are in Corning, Iowa.   Ewell P. Roy

NATIONAL FARMERS UNION is a national organization made up of State Farmers Union organizations.

It is dedicated to obtaining parity prices for farm products. Parity prices are prices that give farmers the same purchasing power they had during a specific period in the past. The union promotes legislation that benefits farmers, and develops cooperative buying and selling methods and businesses. Founded in Texas in 1902, it represents more than 250,000 farm families. The union's national headquarters are at 1575 Sherman Street, Denver, Colo. 80201. Its official name is the FARMERS' EDUCATIONAL AND COOPERATIVE UNION OF AMERICA. Critically reviewed by the NATIONAL FARMERS UNION

NATIONAL FIRE PREVENTION WEEK is held to make the public more aware of fire prevention. It is held the calendar week of October 9, the commemoration date of the Great Chicago Fire of 1871. See also FIRE PREVENTION.

NATIONAL FLOWERS. See FLOWER (table).

NATIONAL FOOTBALL LEAGUE. See FOOTBALL (Professional Football).

NATIONAL FOREST is a forest area set aside by the Congress of the United States to be protected and managed by the federal government. The Forest Service, a part of the Department of Agriculture, manages 155 national forests in the United States and Puerto Rico. These forests cover a total area of about 183 million acres (74.1 million hectares), larger than California and Nevada combined. Most national forests are named for Indian tribes or famous people in American history. For location, size, and recreational facilities of these forests, see the *table* with this article.

Uses. National forests serve many purposes. Foresters mark individual trees or groups of trees, and the government sells them to the highest bidder for cutting into lumber, pulpwood, poles, and other wood products. But the Forest Service makes sure that forest growth exceeds the amount of timber cut or destroyed by disease, fire, or insects each year. Controlled grazing by

cattle and sheep is permitted on grass-covered sections of the forests. The government also allows private water-power development and mining operations in the forests. National forests safeguard *watersheds* (sources of creeks and rivers), provide a home for wildlife, and are valuable recreational areas.

Administration. A *forest supervisor* administers each national forest. The forests are divided into *ranger districts*, each headed by a *district ranger*. A ranger's first duty is to manage all forest uses and services. These include production of wood, water, forage, wildlife, and resources for outdoor recreation. One of his main duties is to prevent and fight forest fires.

U.S. national forests are grouped into nine regions. Regional foresters head each region. They direct the work of the forest supervisors in their regions. The regional foresters report to the chief of the Forest Service in Washington, D.C.

History. Early settlers in the United States adopted the first conservation laws. In spite of this encouraging start, destruction of forests became widespread during the settlement of the United States. In 1891, Congress established the first national forest-conservation policy. In that year, Congress authorized the President to set aside areas known as *forest reserves*. The first one was established in Wyoming. In 1907, the name was changed to national forests.

ROBERT T. HALL

National Forest Symbol

See also FOREST SERVICE.

NATIONAL FORESTS OF THE UNITED STATES

Forest	State	Area† In acres	In hectares	Chief Features
Allegheny*	Pennsylvania	506,102	204,812	Allegheny Mountains, Indian reservation, oil field, fishing, bear, turkey, and deer hunting, scenic drives, swimming, hiking
Angeles*	California	653,028	264,271	Old Baldy, riding, hiking, winter sports, fishing, hunting, wilderness area, Pacific Crest Trail
Angelina*	Texas	155,293	62,845	Shortleaf, loblolly pine, hardwoods, fishing, hunting, swimming
Apache*	Arizona and New Mexico	1,804,833	730,390	Spruce forests, prehistoric cliff dwellings, scenic drives, fishing, hunting, riding, primitive areas
Apalachicola*	Florida	557,729	225,705	Pine-hardwood forests, hardwood swamps, fishing, big-game hunting, boating, swimming
Arapaho*	Colorado	993,857	402,200	Mt. Evans, ghost towns, fishing, hunting, winter sports, scenic drives, dude ranches, primitive area, Moffat Tunnel, Continental Divide
Ashley*	Utah and Wyoming	1,383,904	560,046	Flaming Gorge National Recreation Area, fishing, hunting, riding, ancient geologic formations, primitive area
Beaverhead*	Montana	2,114,577	855,739	Historic sites, mountains, swimming, fishing, big-game hunting, hot springs, winter sports, wilderness area
Bienville*	Mississippi	177,077	71,661	Virgin loblolly pine, fishing, quail hunting
Bighorn*	Wyoming	1,107,342	448,125	Bighorn Mountains, glaciers, Indian Medicine Wheel, fishing, hunting, riding, scenic drives, winter sports, primitive areas
Bitterroot*	Idaho and Montana	1,575,895	637,742	Hot springs, fishing, hunting, Bitterroot Mountains, riding, dude ranches, winter sports, wilderness area
Black Hills*	South Dakota and Wyoming	1,233,404	499,141	Canyons, waterfalls, historic sites, Mt. Rushmore National Memorial, logging, mining, fishing, hunting, swimming, boating, hiking, riding, scenic drives, dude ranches
Boise*	Idaho	2,642,516	1,069,388	Ponderosa pine, abandoned mines, ghost towns, historic sites, fishing, hunting, scenic drives, winter sports, primitive areas

†National forest lands owned by the United States and administered by the Forest Service.   *Camping facilities available.

NATIONAL FORESTS OF THE UNITED STATES

Forest	State	Area† In acres	Area† In hectares	Chief Features
Bridger*	Wyoming	1,733,098	701,360	Glaciers, fishing, hunting, winter sports, wilderness area
Cache*	Idaho and Utah	679,953	275,167	Mountains, caves, canyons, winter sports, fishing, big-game hunting, scenic drives, riding, hiking
Calaveras Big-tree	California	380	154	Special group of big trees (giant sequoias)
Caribbean	Puerto Rico	27,846	11,269	Tropical trees, waterfalls, cliffs, swimming, hiking, scenic drives
Caribou*	Idaho, Utah, and Wyoming	987,534	399,641	Mountain ranges, historic trails, waterfalls, fishing, big-game hunting, scenic drives, riding, winter sports, soda springs
Carson*	New Mexico	1,391,369	563,067	Historic sites, Indian pueblo, hot springs, fishing, hunting, scenic drives, riding, winter sports, wilderness areas, Wheeler Peak
Challis*	Idaho	2,463,281	996,854	Mt. Borah, fishing, big-game hunting, scenic drives, riding, hiking, boating, primitive areas
Chattahoochee*	Georgia	739,493	299,262	Blue Ridge Mountains, waterfalls, small-game hunting, fishing, swimming, boating, hiking, archery hunting, Appalachian Trail
Chequamegon*	Wisconsin	839,565	339,760	Pine, spruce, and balsam, lakes, fishing, hunting, canoeing, skiing
Cherokee*	North Carolina and Tennessee	618,813	250,425	Mountains, river gorges, fishing, small- and big-game hunting, hiking, boating, swimming, Appalachian Trail
Chippewa*	Minnesota	655,623	265,321	Red pine, headwaters of the Mississippi, fishing, hunting, water sports, winter sports, scenic drives
Chugach*	Alaska	4,715,443	1,908,272	Glaciers, mountains, fiords, canneries, fishing, hunting, boating, hiking, mountain climbing, salmon-spawning runs
Cibola*	New Mexico	1,615,216	653,655	Mt. Taylor, antelope herds, Pueblo Indian villages, prehistoric ruins, hunting, scenic drives, winter sports, Sandia Crest
Clark*	Missouri	806,798	326,500	Ozark Mountains, oak and pine forests, redbud and dogwood, fishing, hunting, float trips, brilliant fall coloring
Clearwater*	Idaho	1,675,388	678,005	White pine, fishing, hunting, scenic drives, wilderness area, Lolo Trail, pack trips
Cleveland*	California	415,855	168,291	Palomar Observatory, fishing, hunting, scenic drives, primitive area, Pacific Crest Trail
Coconino*	Arizona	1,835,022	742,607	San Francisco Peaks, canyons, scenic drives, hunting, fishing, riding, boating, winter sports, primitive area
Coeur d'Alene*	Idaho	723,591	292,827	Mining, fishing, deer hunting, Cataldo Mission, winter sports
Colville*	Washington	943,793	381,939	Grand Coulee Dam, hunting, fishing, winter sports, Lake Roosevelt
Conecuh*	Alabama	83,957	33,976	Fishing, deer, turkey, and small-game hunting, swimming
Coronado*	Arizona and New Mexico	1,782,108	721,193	Mountains, desert, canyons, caves, hunting, scenic drives, dude ranches, winter sports, wilderness areas, Santa Catalina
Croatan*	North Carolina	156,589	63,369	Pine, swamp hardwoods, historic sites, hunting, fishing, boating
Custer*	Montana and South Dakota	1,187,381	480,516	Peaks and alpine plateaus, glaciers, ice caverns, fossil beds, fishing, big-game hunting, riding, winter sports, primitive area
Daniel Boone*	Kentucky	520,038	210,452	Cliffs, rock arches, caves, fishing, hiking, boating
Davy Crockett*	Texas	161,478	65,348	Shortleaf and loblolly pine, hardwoods, fishing, deer hunting, swimming, Red River Gorge
Deerlodge*	Montana	1,176,452	476,093	Fishing, big-game hunting, riding, winter sports, hiking, wilderness area, Tobacco Root Mountains
Delta	Mississippi	59,159	23,941	Flooded delta land, bayous, waterfowl preserve, hunting
Deschutes*	Oregon	1,600,670	647,768	Mountains, waterfalls, caves, fishing, winter sports, wilderness areas, Pacific Crest Trail, Lava Butte Geological Area
De Soto*	Mississippi	499,876	202,293	Quail hunting, fishing, boating, swimming
Dixie*	Utah	1,885,770	763,144	Canyons, peaks, colored cliffs, big-game hunting, fishing
Eldorado*	California and Nevada	667,043	269,943	Sierra Nevadas, Lake Tahoe, historic sites, fishing, hunting, scenic drives, riding, winter sports, dude ranches, wilderness and primitive areas, Gold Rush Country, Pacific Crest Trail
Fishlake*	Utah	1,423,900	576,232	Petrified forest, fishing, big-game hunting, scenic drives
Flathead*	Montana	2,363,415	956,440	Geological formations, glaciers, fishing, hunting, boating, riding, scenic drives, winter sports, wilderness and primitive areas
Francis Marion*	South Carolina	249,406	100,931	Oaks, yucca, dogwood, holly, historic sites, fishing, boating, bathing, alligator, deer, turkey, and quail hunting
Fremont*	Oregon	1,195,031	483,612	Indian paintings, antelope, deer hunting, wilderness area
Gallatin*	Montana	1,722,092	696,906	Mountains, waterfalls, winter sports, hiking, dude ranches, primitive areas, Madison River Canyon Earthquake Area
George Washington*	Virginia and West Virginia	1,038,447	420,245	Mountains, falls, caverns, fishing, hunting, scenic drives, swimming, hiking, Sherando Lake Recreation Area, Appalachian Trail
Gifford Pinchot*	Washington	1,251,051	506,282	Mt. Adams, fishing, scenic drives, riding, mountain climbing, winter sports, hunting, wilderness areas, Pacific Crest Trail
Gila*	New Mexico	2,705,239	1,094,771	Semidesert-to-alpine country, cliff dwellings, Indian reservation, fishing, hunting, scenic drives, hiking, dude ranches, wilderness and primitive areas
Grand Mesa*	Colorado	346,143	140,079	Grand Mesa and Uncompahgre plateau, cliffs, canyons, waterfalls, fishing, big-game hunting, scenic drives, riding, winter sports
Green Mountain*	Vermont	253,526	102,598	Historic battlegrounds, fishing, hunting, hiking, winter sports, Appalachian Trail

†National forest lands owned by the United States and administered by the Forest Service.   *Camping facilities available.

NATIONAL FORESTS OF THE UNITED STATES

Forest	State	Area† In acres	In hectares	Chief Features
Gunnison*	Colorado	1,662,938	672,967	Mountain peaks, ghost towns, trout fishing, big-game hunting, hiking, riding, winter sports, wilderness areas
Helena*	Montana	972,408	393,520	Continental Divide, ghost towns, fishing, elk and deer hunting, scenic drives, riding, winter sports, hiking, wilderness area
Hiawatha*	Michigan	863,885	349,602	Waterfalls, scenic drives, fishing, hunting, canoeing
Holly Springs*	Mississippi	145,141	58,736	Erosion gullies, quail and small-game hunting, swimming, fishing
Homochitto	Mississippi	189,039	76,501	Eroded loess country, excellent timber sites, fishing, swimming
Hoosier*	Indiana	177,501	71,832	Black walnut, dogwood, redbud, buffalo trail, hunting, fishing, scenic drives, swimming, Lost, White, and Ohio Rivers
Humboldt*	Nevada	2,528,076	1,023,076	Mountains, canyons, colorful cliffs, historic mining camps, elk herd, deer hunting, scenic trails, winter sports, wilderness area
Huron*	Michigan	417,108	168,798	Trout fishing, hunting, winter sports, swimming, Lake Huron
Inyo*	California and Nevada	1,843,837	746,506	Mt. Whitney, Palisade Glacier, fishing, deer hunting, winter sports, wilderness trips, Ancient Bristlecone Pine Forest Botanical Area
Jefferson*	Kentucky, Virginia, and West Virginia	674,105	272,801	Blue Ridge Mountains, rhododendron, hunting, swimming, Mount Rogers National Recreation Area, Appalachian Trail
Kaibab*	Arizona	1,556,964	630,081	Grand Canyon, game preserve, Kaibab squirrels, big-game hunting, scenic drives, fishing, riding, wild buffalo herd
Kaniksu*	Idaho, Montana, and Washington	1,622,333	656,535	Cedars, Chimney Rock, mountains, fishing, hunting, boating, swimming, scenic drives, winter sports, wilderness area
Kisatchie*	Louisiana	595,549	241,010	Longleaf, loblolly, and slash pine, bayous and lakes, fishing, hunting, boating, swimming, historic sites
Klamath*	California and Oregon	1,696,684	686,624	Mountain lakes and streams, salmon and steelhead trout fishing, deer hunting, riding, Pacific Crest Trail
Kootenai*	Idaho and Montana	1,827,375	739,512	Fishing, big-game hunting, scenic drives, winter sports, dude ranches, wilderness area
Lassen*	California	1,059,933	428,940	Volcanic lava flows, tubes, craters, ice caves, hot springs, mud pots, scenic drives, fishing, deer hunting, winter sports, wilderness areas, Pacific Crest Trail
Lewis and Clark*	Montana	1,835,264	742,705	Limestone canyons, mountains, fishing, big-game hunting, riding, Continental Divide, winter sports, wilderness area
Lincoln*	New Mexico	1,103,225	446,459	Ponderosa pine, firs, fishing, big-game hunting, winter sports, scenic drives, riding, wilderness area
Lolo*	Montana	2,089,810	845,716	Continental Divide, fishing, hunting, winter sports, wilderness area
Los Padres*	California	1,750,546	708,421	Coast redwood, California condor, peaks, hunting, trout fishing, winter sports, wilderness and primitive areas
Malheur*	Oregon	1,458,055	590,054	Ponderosa pine, mountains, fossil beds, fishing, elk and deer hunting, scenic drives, riding, wilderness area
Manistee*	Michigan	497,099	201,169	Fishing, deer and small-game hunting, skiing, swimming, canoeing
Manti-LaSal*	Colorado and Utah	1,265,256	512,031	Aspens, alpine meadows, cliff dwellings, unique geology, fishing, hunting, scenic drives, riding, hiking, winter sports
Mark Twain*	Missouri	631,471	255,547	Ozark Mountains, caves, scenic drives, fishing, quail hunting
Medicine Bow*	Wyoming	1,093,177	442,393	Beaver colonies, fishing, deer hunting, riding, winter sports
Mendocino*	California	875,925	354,474	Black-tailed deer, hunting, fishing, riding, wilderness trips
Modoc*	California	1,633,068	660,879	Lava flows, historic sites, deer herd, hunting, fishing, scenic drives, winter sports, wilderness area, bird refuge
Monongahela*	West Virginia	833,301	337,225	Cranberry glades, rhododendron, canyons, falls, historic sites, limestone caves, beaver colonies, fishing, swimming, Spruce Knob-Seneca Rocks National Recreation Area
Mount Baker*	Washington	1,282,921	519,180	Douglas fir, peaks, glaciers, fishing, hunting, winter sports, mountain climbing, wilderness areas, Pacific Crest Trail
Mount Hood*	Oregon	1,059,240	428,659	Alpine meadows, hot springs, glacier, scenic drives, fishing, swimming, winter sports, riding, mountain climbing, Mount Hood, wilderness areas, Pacific Crest Trail
Nantahala*	North Carolina	457,035	184,955	Azaleas, rhododendrons, falls, man-made lakes, fishing, hunting, swimming, boating, primeval forest, Appalachian Trail
Nebraska*	Nebraska	141,318	57,189	Planted forest on sand hills, fishing, swimming
Nezperce*	Idaho	2,205,742	892,632	Canyons, hot springs, big-game hunting, fishing, riding, scenic drives, winter sports, wilderness and primitive areas
Nicolet*	Wisconsin	652,001	263,855	Pine, spruce-balsam, hardwood, and cedar-spruce swamp forests, fishing, hunting, swimming, boating, hiking, snowshoeing, skiing
Ocala*	Florida	367,175	148,590	Palms, hardwoods, sand pine, springs, fishing, deer and bear hunting
Ochoco*	Oregon	843,644	341,411	Ponderosa pine, beaver colonies, historic sites, trout fishing, deer hunting, scenic drives, geologic formations
Oconee*	Georgia	104,045	42,106	Piedmont hills, archaeological remains, Rock Eagle Lake, 4-H center, wildlife refuge, deer and small-game hunting, fishing
Okanogan*	Washington	1,499,428	606,797	Alpine meadows, peaks, glaciers, Lake Chelan, fishing, boating, riding, winter sports, wilderness area, Pacific Crest Trail
Olympic*	Washington	651,635	263,707	Dense rain forests, peaks, fishing, hunting, scenic drives, riding
Osceola*	Florida	157,230	63,629	Cypress swamps, longleaf pine, fishing, hunting, swimming, boating
Ottawa*	Michigan	916,566	370,921	Victoria Dam, falls, fishing, deep-sea trolling, deer and bear hunting, scenic drives, winter sports, Lake Superior, canoeing

†National forest lands owned by the United States and administered by the Forest Service.   *Camping facilities available.

NATIONAL FORESTS OF THE UNITED STATES

Forest	State	Area† In acres	In hectares	Chief Features
Ouachita*	Arkansas and Oklahoma	1,574,939	637,355	Historic sites, caves, falls, medicinal springs, bass fishing, hunting, scenic drives, hiking, swimming
Ozark*	Arkansas	1,108,769	448,703	Oaks, fishing, hunting, swimming, scenic drives, rock cliffs and pools
Payette*	Idaho	2,307,897	933,973	Hells Canyon, fishing, big-game hunting, scenic drives, hiking, winter sports, dude ranches, primitive area, elk
Pike*	Colorado	1,104,911	447,142	Pikes Peak, historic sites, mountain sheep, hunting, fishing, riding, hiking, scenic drives, winter sports
Pisgah*	North Carolina	483,154	195,525	Rhododendron, fishing, hunting, hiking, riding, scenic drives, Linville Gorge, Mount Mitchell, wilderness areas, Appalachian Trail
Plumas*	California	1,158,374	468,777	Falls, historic sites, limestone caves, fishing, hunting, scenic drives, riding, hiking, winter sports, canyons, Pacific Crest Trail
Prescott*	Arizona	1,236,912	500,560	Hunting, riding, scenic drives, winter sports, dude ranches, primitive areas, ghost towns
Rio Grande*	Colorado	1,850,352	748,811	Rugged mountains, mining camps, trout fishing, hunting, hiking, scenic drives, winter sports, wilderness and primitive areas
Rogue River*	California and Oregon	636,725	257,673	Sugar pine, Douglas fir, Table Rock, waterfalls, trout fishing, hunting, riding, winter sports, Pacific Crest Trail
Roosevelt*	Colorado	781,626	316,313	Glaciers, Continental Divide, canyons, trout fishing, big-game hunting, hiking, scenic drives, winter sports, wilderness area
Routt*	Colorado	1,125,145	455,330	Continental Divide, trout fishing, hunting, scenic drives, riding, hiking, winter sports, wilderness area
Sabine*	Texas	186,691	75,551	Southern pine and hardwoods, swimming, fishing, fox hunting
St. Francis*	Arkansas	20,946	8,477	Indian burial mounds, wild game, fishing, swimming
St. Joe*	Idaho	862,992	349,240	White pine, canyons, big-game hunting, fishing, Bitterroot Range
Salmon*	Idaho	1,770,522	716,505	Fishing, big-game hunting, boating, scenic drives, winter sports, dude ranches, primitive area, Lewis and Clark Trail
Sam Houston*	Texas	158,648	64,203	Shortleaf and loblolly pine, hardwoods, fishing, swimming
Samuel R. McKelvie*	Nebraska	115,703	46,823	Planted forest on sand hills
San Bernardino*	California	628,246	254,242	Historic sites, fishing, hunting, riding, winter sports, wilderness areas, Pacific Crest Trail
San Isabel*	Colorado	1,107,830	448,323	Peaks, mines, alpine lakes, fishing, big-game and bird hunting, scenic drives, riding, winter sports
San Juan*	Colorado	1,867,089	755,584	Canyons, falls, cataracts, geologic formations, archaeological ruins, mines, fishing, hunting, scenic drives, riding, winter sports
Santa Fe*	New Mexico	1,579,462	639,186	Peaks, Indian villages, ancient pueblo and Spanish mission ruins, cliff dwellings, fishing, hunting, skiing, wilderness areas
Sawtooth*	Idaho and Utah	1,799,294	728,148	Wind- and water-worn rocks, hot springs, fishing, hunting, riding, Sun Valley, bathing, winter sports, primitive area
Sequoia*	California	1,123,908	454,829	Sequoias, canyons, caves, peaks, fishing, hunting, riding, hiking, swimming, boating, winter sports, wilderness and primitive areas, Pacific Crest Trail
Shasta*	California	1,118,136	452,494	Glaciers, lava beds, caves, chimneys, fishing, hunting, riding, winter sports, wilderness area, Whiskeytown-Shasta-Trinity National Recreation Area, Pacific Crest Trail
Shawnee*	Illinois	246,924	99,927	Prehistoric stone forts and Indian mounds, rock formations, fishing
Shoshone*	Wyoming	2,431,914	984,161	Glaciers, peaks, fishing, big-game and bird hunting, riding, scenic drives, winter sports, wilderness and primitive areas
Sierra*	California	1,285,909	520,389	Sequoias, falls, mountain climbing, fishing, hunting, boating, swimming, riding, winter sports, wilderness areas, John Muir Trail, Pacific Crest Trail
Siskiyou*	California and Oregon	1,091,295	441,631	Port Orford cedar, California laurel, wild lilac, rhododendron, azaleas, pitcher plants, Brewer weeping spruce, Saddler oak, fishing, hunting, boating, riding, wilderness area
Sitgreaves*	Arizona	814,974	329,808	Pueblo ruins, elk herd, hunting, riding, Mongollon Rim Drive
Siuslaw*	Oregon	623,453	252,302	Sitka spruce, western hemlock, cedar, Douglas fir, pitcher plants, dunes, fishing, hunting, swimming, boating, riding, scuba diving
Six Rivers*	California	968,660	392,003	Redwood, fir, fishing, riding, scenic drives, hunting, winter sports
Snoqualmie*	Washington	1,229,294	497,478	Douglas fir, peaks, falls, hunting, fishing, riding, winter sports, mountain climbing, wilderness area, Pacific Crest Trail
Stanislaus*	California	895,963	362,583	Canyons, historic sites, fishing, hunting, scenic drives, riding, winter sports, wilderness and primitive areas, Pacific Crest Trail
Sumter*	South Carolina	357,599	144,715	Rhododendron and other flowering shrubs, Piedmont Region and Blue Ridge Mountains, fishing, quail hunting, scenic drives
Superior*	Minnesota	2,061,470	834,247	Islands, sand beaches, 5,000 lakes, fishing, deer hunting, scenic drives, canoeing, Boundary Waters Canoe Area
Tahoe*	California	757,867	306,698	Lake Tahoe, historic sites, winter sports, fishing, hunting, riding, hiking, scenic drives, Squaw Valley, Pacific Crest Trail
Talladega*	Alabama	363,660	147,168	Hunting, fishing, swimming, scenic drives
Targhee*	Idaho and Wyoming	1,642,417	664,663	Grand Tetons, canyons, falls, big-game hunting, riding, hiking, scenic drives, winter sports, dude ranches, Snake River
Teton*	Wyoming	1,666,534	674,422	Tetons, Continental Divide, Jackson Hole, fishing, big-game hunting, scenic drives, swimming, winter sports, wilderness area

†National forest lands owned by the United States and administered by the Forest Service. •Camping facilities available.

NATIONAL FORESTS OF THE UNITED STATES

Forest	State	Area[†] In acres	In hectares	Chief Features
Toiyabe*	California and Nevada	3,156,117	1,277,235	Lake Tahoe, historic ghost towns, fishing, big-game hunting, riding, skiing, scenic drives, wilderness area, Pacific Crest Trail
Tombigbee*	Mississippi	65,412	26,471	Indian mounds, Davis and Choctaw lakes, Natchez Trace Parkway, deer and quail hunting, fishing
Tongass*	Alaska	16,000,046	6,474,988	Totems, Indian villages, glaciers, fiords, fishing, big-game hunting, boating, hiking, mountain climbing, Mendenhall Glacier
Tonto*	Arizona	2,874,843	1,163,408	Semidesert to pine-fir forest, prehistoric ruins, fishing, hunting, riding, scenic drives, wilderness areas, Superstition Mountains
Trinity*	California	1,040,204	420,956	Glaciers, lava beds, caves, chimneys, fishing, hunting, riding, scenic drives, winter sports, wilderness area, Whiskeytown-Shasta-Trinity National Recreation Area, Pacific Crest Trail
Tuskegee*	Alabama	10,778	4,362	Pine plantation, bream fishing
Uinta*	Utah	812,908	328,972	Maple, aspen, oak, canyons, waterfalls, geologic formations, big-game hunting, fishing, hiking, winter sports
Umatilla*	Oregon, Washington	1,390,283	562,628	Skyline drives, hot sulfur springs, hunting, riding, winter sports
Umpqua*	Oregon	988,309	399,954	Cataracts, falls, fishing, hunting, scenic drives, winter sports, Pacific Crest Trail
Uncompahgre*	Colorado	943,839	381,958	Wilson Mountains, wild flowers, cliffs, canyons, waterfalls, fishing, hunting, scenic drives, riding, winter sports, primitive areas
Uwharrie*	North Carolina	45,760	18,518	Uwharrie Mountain Range, deer hunting
Wallowa*	Oregon	982,040	397,417	Alpine meadows and rare flowers, peaks, glaciers, canyons, fishing, hunting, riding, scenic drives, dude ranches, wilderness area
Wasatch*	Utah and Wyoming	886,434	358,727	Mountains, canyons, skiing, fishing, hunting, boating, swimming, riding, skating, mountain climbing, primitive area
Wayne*	Ohio	163,345	66,103	Hardwoods, historic sites, hunting, fishing, hiking, riding, scenic drives
Wenatchee*	Washington	1,618,238	654,878	Alpine meadows, rare flowers, peaks, fishing, hunting, Lake Chelan, riding, winter sports, wilderness area, Pacific Crest Trail
White Mountain*	Maine and New Hampshire	720,045	291,392	Mount Washington, Presidential Range, falls, fishing, deer and bear hunting, scenic drives, skiing, mountain climbing, hiking, swimming, wilderness area, Appalachian Trail
White River*	Colorado	1,941,176	785,566	Canyons, falls, hot springs, caves, mines, fishing, hunting, hiking, riding, winter sports, wilderness and primitive areas
Whitman*	Oregon	1,264,731	511,818	Alpine meadows, rare flowers, fishing, hunting, wilderness area
Willamette*	Oregon	1,667,821	674,943	Peaks, waterfalls, hot springs, volcanic formations, fishing, hunting, riding, winter sports, wilderness areas, Pacific Crest Trail
William B. Bankhead*	Alabama	179,294	72,558	Limestone gorges, falls, natural bridges, hunting, fishing
Winema*	Oregon	1,042,803	422,007	Klamath Indian range lands, boating, winter sports area, ponderosa pine, Douglas fir, lodgepole pine, wilderness area, Oregon Cascades, Pacific Crest Trail

[†]National forest lands owned by the United States and administered by the Forest Service. *Camping facilities available.

NATIONAL FOUNDATION-MARCH OF DIMES is a health organization financed by funds gathered in the annual March of Dimes. It supports research, treatment, and professional and public education concerning birth defects. It also supports the Salk Institute for Biological Studies. The organization was founded by President Franklin D. Roosevelt in 1938 as the National Foundation for Infantile Paralysis. It financed the research that produced the Salk and Sabin vaccines, which help prevent poliomyelitis. The present name and goals were adopted in 1958. Headquarters are at 1275 Mamaroneck Avenue, White Plains, N.Y. 10605.

Critically reviewed by the NATIONAL FOUNDATION-MARCH OF DIMES

NATIONAL FOUNDATION ON THE ARTS AND THE HUMANITIES is an independent agency of the federal government. Its purpose is to develop and promote a broadly conceived national policy of support for the humanities and the arts in the United States.

The foundation is administered by a National Endowment for the Arts and a National Endowment for the Humanities. Each endowment is guided by a council composed of 26 private citizens distinguished for their knowledge and experience in the two allied cultural areas, the arts and the humanities. A Federal Council on the Arts and the Humanities coordinates the foundation's activities with related federal agencies.

The Arts Endowment is authorized to assist individuals and nonprofit organizations in a wide range of artistic endeavors. Additional funds are authorized to aid activities in the arts sponsored by the states.

The Humanities Endowment aids training and research in the humanities through fellowships and grants, and supports the publication of scholarly works.

Each endowment is headed by a chairman, who serves on the federal council, along with representatives of federal agencies whose programs are related to the arts and humanities. The foundation was established in 1965. It is located at 806 15th Street NW, Washington, D.C. 20506.

Critically reviewed by the NATIONAL FOUNDATION ON THE ARTS AND THE HUMANITIES

NATIONAL GALLERY OF ART in Washington, D.C., has nationally owned collections of paintings, sculptures, prints, drawings, and items of decorative art. Andrew W. Mellon, an American financier, made the original donation for the gallery in 1937. He gave the United States government his great art collection, and $15 million to build the gallery. The gallery opened in 1941.

The paintings and sculptures given by Mellon represent the works of many of the greatest European artists from the 1200's to the 1800's. Among the works are the *Alba Madonna* by Raphael, *The Annunciation* by Van Eyck, 23 paintings by Rembrandt, and 6 by

NATIONAL GEOGRAPHIC SOCIETY

Vermeer. The A. W. Mellon Educational and Charitable Trust also presented a collection of American paintings. Two of the most famous of these are Gilbert Stuart's portrait of Washington and Edward Savage's painting *The Washington Family.*

Samuel H. Kress, an American merchant, gave the gallery a collection of Italian art ranging from the 1200's through the 1700's. It includes works by such masters as Giotto, Raphael, and Bellini. The Samuel H. Kress Foundation has enlarged the gift of Italian art, and added to the collection in many other areas, including a gift of French paintings of the 1700's.

Joseph E. Widener, an American businessman, presented the National Gallery with a famous art collection that he and his father had gathered. The collection includes many works by Raphael, Bellini, Rembrandt, Vermeer, Van Dyck, and others. Lessing J. Rosenwald, another American businessman, gave a collection of over 17,000 prints and drawings. Many other donors have made important gifts to the National Gallery.

The National Gallery of Art is one of the largest marble structures in the world. It is 785 feet (239 meters) long, has more than 500,000 square feet (46,000 square meters) of floor space, and has about 238,000 square feet (22,111 square meters) for exhibits. The gallery has a resident composer-conductor who leads weekly concerts by the National Gallery Orchestra.

Critically reviewed by the NATIONAL GALLERY OF ART

NATIONAL GEOGRAPHIC SOCIETY is the world's largest scientific and educational organization. It was formed in 1888 to gather and spread geographic information throughout the world. It has more than 8 million members in approximately 185 countries. The society has sponsored and supported more than 2,000 expeditions and research projects that have expanded man's knowledge of the earth, sea, and sky.

The society distributes information through *National Geographic Magazine*, a monthly journal; *National Geographic World*, a magazine for children; authoritative books; and an information service for the press, radio, and television. It produces atlases, globes, maps, filmstrips, and television programs.

Among the projects the society has sponsored are the historic polar expeditions by Richard E. Byrd and Robert E. Peary. It also sponsored excavations in East Africa that uncovered fossils of a primitive being called *Homo habilis* that lived about 1,750,000 years ago. It helped back the first successful U.S. expedition to the top of Mount Everest and aided in the construction of livable quarters under the ocean. The society's headquarters are at 17th and M Sts. NW, Washington, D.C. 20036. Critically reviewed by the NATIONAL GEOGRAPHIC SOCIETY

NATIONAL GUARD is one of the organizations of the United States Army and Air Force. An outgrowth of the volunteer militia that was first authorized in 1792, the National Guard of the United States is a reserve group. Other types of civilian reserves, such as the Army, Air Force, and naval reserves, have no connection with the National Guard.

Each state, each territory, and the District of Columbia has its own National Guard. The National Guard Bureau of the Department of the Army directs Army units. The Department of the Air Force supervises Air

National Guard units. The two guards have an authorized strength of nearly 700,000, of which the Air National Guard's part is 60,000.

National Guard Emblem

Guardsmen enlist voluntarily, and are formed into distinctive units in the same manner as the active Army and Air Force. These two services supervise training. State funds provide armories and storage facilities. Federal funds provide clothing, weapons, and equipment.

During peacetime, National Guard men attend 48 weekly drill and training periods a year. They also receive two weeks of field training every year. The federal government pays members of the National Guard for the time that they spend training.

Guardsmen have a *dual status*, because they take an oath of allegiance to their state, as well as to the federal government. Until 1903, the state controlled the militia units entirely. The President had to call units into federal service through the governors of the states (see MILITIA). The National Defense Acts of 1920 and 1933 further extended federal authority. Since that time, the President may order units to active duty during any national emergency. State governors may order units to active duty during emergencies, such as strikes, riots, and disasters. CHARLES B. MacDONALD

See also AIR FORCE, UNITED STATES (Air Force Reserves); ARMY, UNITED STATES (Active Army, Reserves, and National Guard).

NATIONAL HISTORIC SITE. See NATIONAL PARK SYSTEM.

NATIONAL HOCKEY LEAGUE. See HOCKEY.

NATIONAL HOLIDAY. See HOLIDAY.

NATIONAL HONOR SOCIETY is an organization for high school boys and girls. Members are chosen on the basis of scholarship, leadership, citizenship, service, and character. College scholarships are awarded each year to top-ranking senior members. The society is sponsored by the National Association of Secondary-School Principals, which founded it in 1921. In 1929, the National Junior Honor Society was founded for students in junior high schools. The senior society has about 18,-000 local chapters; the junior society, 4,300. Both have headquarters at 1904 Association Drive, Reston, Va. 22091. Critically reviewed by NATIONAL HONOR SOCIETY

NATIONAL INCOME is the total of all income earned in a nation during a specific period, usually a year. This figure shows whether a nation's economy is growing or declining. Economists use national income figures to compare the economies of various nations.

Determining National Income. Economists calculate national income in either of two ways. One way is based on what individuals and businesses earn. The other is based on the production of goods and services. Each method provides the same national income figure because the amount that people earn equals the value of the goods and services produced.

National income based on earnings includes all the income earned in a nation during a certain period. This income consists of wages and salaries, interest, profits, and rents.

To find national income based on production, economists first determine a nation's *gross national product*. This figure represents the total value of the goods and services produced by a nation during a specific period. Economists find the national income by subtracting *depreciation* and *indirect business taxes* from the gross national product. Depreciation includes the normal decline in the value of buildings and machinery as a result of doing business. Indirect business taxes are paid by buyers of goods and include sales and excise taxes. Economists use the term *net national product* for the difference between gross national product and depreciation.

National income may be affected by both *inflation* (rising prices) and *deflation* (falling prices). For example, if the amount people earn increases 10 per cent in one year, the national income figure for that year will rise 10 per cent. But if prices also rise 10 per cent, people will not be able to buy any more goods or services than they did during the year before. Thus, the national income figure is 10 per cent higher because of inflation, not because of economic growth.

In order to compare national income figures for two or more years, economists adjust the national income to include inflation or deflation. The adjusted figure is called *real national income*.

Importance of National Income. National income figures show the rate at which a nation's economy changes. These figures also show the stability of the economy. For example, the economy may be unstable if national income varies greatly from year to year. National income figures also show how income is distributed in the forms of wages, interest, profits, and rents. In the United States, wages account for more than 75 per cent of the national income. Interest, prof-

its, and rents provide the rest of the national income.

Both government and industry must know the national income in order to form economic policy. They adjust their budgets in terms of the level, distribution, and rate of change in national income. If national income falls, for example, the government might cut taxes. A tax cut would give people more money to spend. If people spent this money on goods and services, business activity would rise. New jobs would be created, and the national income would increase.

National income figures include only payments and losses for which records are kept. As a result, these figures do not fully show the level of a nation's well-being. A housewife receives no salary for doing housework, and so her work does not raise the national income. On the other hand, environmental pollution causes great economic loss. But no one knows the total cost of this loss, and so economists cannot subtract it from the national income.

Changes in National Income. National income varies, depending on the efforts of workers, the level of employment, and the quality and quantity of *fixed capital*. Fixed capital includes the buildings and machinery used to provide goods and services. Improvements in fixed capital may create more jobs and raise the national income.

National income in the United States has generally risen from year to year. It has increased mainly because of additions to the nation's fixed capital, growth of the labor force, and improvements in the efficiency of both capital and labor.   THOMAS F. DERNBURG

See also CAPITAL; GROSS NATIONAL PRODUCT; INCOME; STANDARD OF LIVING.

UNITED STATES NATIONAL INCOME

National income has risen sharply since the depression years of the 1930's. This graph shows how it has risen and how much of it comes from the income of employees, the net income of businesses, and interest and rent.

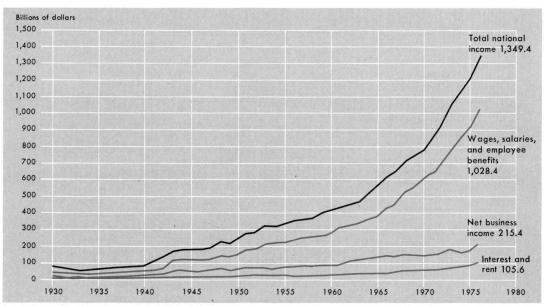

Source: Bureau of Economic Analysis, U.S. Department of Commerce.

NATIONAL INDUSTRIAL RECOVERY ACT. See NEW DEAL (Helping Industry and Labor).

NATIONAL INSTITUTES OF HEALTH (NIH) is an agency of the United States government. It is part of the Public Health Service, a division of the Department of Health, Education, and Welfare (HEW). NIH conducts and supports medical research. It provides funds for training medical researchers and building research facilities. It conducts programs for the prevention and treatment of mental illness. It also classifies and distributes biological and medical information. In the early 1970's, about a third of all the medical research in the United States was financed by the NIH.

NIH conducts research at its own laboratories and clinics in Bethesda, Md. There are 10 NIH institutes. They are: (1) allergy and infectious diseases, (2) arthritis and metabolic diseases, (3) cancer, (4) child health and human development, (5) dental research, (6) eye, (7) general medical sciences, (8) heart, (9) neurological diseases and stroke, and (10) environmental health sciences. A research hospital serves the institutes. The Bureau of Health Manpower and the National Library of Medicine are also part of NIH.

The National Institutes of Health adopted its present name in 1948. It traces its history to 1887, when the Hygienic Laboratory was set up at the U.S. Marine Hospital on Staten Island.

Critically reviewed by the NATIONAL INSTITUTES OF HEALTH

NATIONAL LABOR RELATIONS BOARD (NLRB) was created as an independent agency by Congress in 1935 to administer the National Labor Relations Act (Wagner Act). The NLRB has two major functions. It works to correct or prevent unfair labor practices committed by either employers or unions. When asked by a union, an employer, employees, or an individual, it conducts secret-ballot elections to determine whether employees wish to be represented in collective bargaining. The NLRB can ask the federal appeals courts to enforce board rulings.

The President of the United States appoints the five board members and the general counsel, with the consent of the Senate. Each board member serves a five-year term. The general counsel has a four-year term. The NLRB's main offices are at 1717 Pennsylvania Avenue NW, Washington, D.C. 20006. Petitions and charges are normally sent to regional offices.

Critically reviewed by the NATIONAL LABOR RELATIONS BOARD

See also INDUSTRIAL RELATIONS.

NATIONAL LEAGUE. See BASEBALL (Major Leagues; Professional Baseball).

NATIONAL LIBRARY OF MEDICINE. See LIBRARY (United States Government Libraries).

NATIONAL MEDIATION BOARD is an agency of the U.S. government that works to settle disputes between airline and railroad workers and their employers. The board also supervises elections that determine the proper representative of airline and railroad employees. The National Mediation Board was created in 1934. Its three members are appointed by the President with the consent of the Senate.

In a dispute, either party may apply for the board's services, or the board may act on its own if an emergency exists. Both sides are given solutions to consider.

This is called *mediation.* Neither party has to accept the solutions, however. If mediation fails, the board asks the parties to enter into *arbitration.* If the parties agree, the board may appoint a referee, whose decision is binding. Critically reviewed by the NATIONAL MEDIATION BOARD

NATIONAL MEDICAL ASSOCIATION (NMA) is a professional organization of American physicians. Almost all the members of the NMA are black. The organization works to raise the standards of medical practice and medical education. The NMA also strives to educate the public on matters concerning public health and to eliminate discrimination in medical institutions.

The NMA was founded by a group of black doctors in 1895 in Atlanta, Ga. Until 1960, it admitted dentists and pharmacists as well as physicians. About 6,600 physicians in the United States and its possessions and several other countries belong to the association.

The NMA publishes the monthly *Journal of the National Medical Association.* The organization has headquarters at 1720 Massachusetts Avenue NW, Washington, D.C. 20036.

NATIONAL MEMORIAL. See NATIONAL PARK SYSTEM.

NATIONAL MONUMENT. See NATIONAL PARK SYSTEM.

NATIONAL MOTTO, UNITED STATES, is *In God We Trust.* Congress made this phrase the official motto of the United States in 1956. It has appeared on coins since 1864, and probably originated from verse 4 of "The Star-Spangled Banner"—"And this be our motto: 'In God is our trust.'" See also E PLURIBUS UNUM.

NATIONAL MUSEUM OF HISTORY AND TECHNOLOGY features exhibits of the cultural and technological development of the United States. The museum, located in Washington, D.C., has more than 16 million items. The museum also conducts educational and research work. It is part of the Smithsonian Institution.

The history section of the museum includes displays of U.S. cultural, military, and political development. Visitors can see George Washington's sword, the desk at which Thomas Jefferson wrote the first version of the Declaration of Independence, and the original flag that inspired Francis Scott Key to write "The Star-Spangled Banner."

The technology section of the museum consists of exhibits of scientific and technological progress. These displays include Alexander Graham Bell's first telephone, Elias Howe's first sewing machine, and Samuel F. B. Morse's first telegraph.

The National Museum of History and Technology originally formed part of the U.S. National Museum. In 1967, the U.S. National Museum became two separate institutions, the Museum of History and Technology and the Museum of Natural History. The word "national" was added to both names in 1969. The National Museum of History and Technology is supported by annual grants from Congress. Critically reviewed by the NATIONAL MUSEUM OF HISTORY AND TECHNOLOGY

NATIONAL MUSEUM OF NATURAL HISTORY ranks as one of the world's major centers for the study of the natural sciences. The museum consists of the United States government's collections of items relating to human beings, the earth and its environment, and outer space. The museum also carries on educational and research work. The museum, which is located in Washington, D.C., forms part of the Smithsonian Institution.

The museum provides information for scientists in the fields of environmental pollution, medicine, development of food sources, and the evolution of the earth. It houses exhibits on such subjects as the archaeology of the Americas, cultures of Africa and Asia, ecology, and the evolution of human beings. The museum also has displays of animals and plants, dinosaurs and other fossils, and minerals and rocks.

The museum began as a branch of the U.S. National Museum, founded in 1848. The American naturalist Spencer F. Baird began to develop the natural history collections during the 1850's. The collections have grown to more than 50 million items.

In 1967, the U.S. National Museum became two separate institutions, the Museum of Natural History and the Museum of History and Technology. The term "national" was added to their names in 1969. The National Museum of Natural History is supported largely by annual grants from Congress. CRITICALLY REVIEWED BY THE NATIONAL MUSEUM OF NATURAL HISTORY

NATIONAL MUSEUMS OF CANADA is a government corporation established in 1968 to exhibit the artistic, historical, and scientific collections of the Canadian government. The corporation administers four national museums in Ottawa, Ont., plus 21 other museums and 30 exhibition centers throughout Canada. The national museums in Ottawa are the National Gallery of Canada, the National Museum of Man, the National Museum of Natural Sciences, and the National Museum of Science and Technology.

The National Gallery of Canada owns the world's largest collection of Canadian paintings and sculpture. It also displays many works by artists of other countries. The National Museum of Man features exhibits on the archaeology, folklore, and history of Canada. It includes the Canadian War Museum, which displays a wide range of military equipment and other mementos. The National Museum of Natural Sciences has five main halls with displays of dinosaurs, birds, mammals, other animal life, and minerals. The National Museum of Science and Technology offers exhibits dealing with Canadian contributions in such fields as agriculture, physics, and transportation. Displays include antique automobiles, scientific experiments, and early farm machinery. The National Aeronautical Collection, a

division of the museum, has a large collection of historic aircraft. CRITICALLY REVIEWED BY THE NATIONAL MUSEUMS OF CANADA

NATIONAL MUSIC CAMP is a summer school of music held every year in Interlochen, Mich. Its 1,100-acre (445-hectare) campus borders two lakes in northern Michigan. The school was founded in 1928 for students in all branches of music and allied arts. It is a nonprofit corporation affiliated with the University of Michigan and has a full-time faculty. The National High School Orchestra meets there in summer. JOSEPH E. MADDY

NATIONAL NAVAL MEDICAL CENTER, in Bethesda, Md., is the largest United States Navy facility for medical care, research, and training. It covers 242 acres (98 hectares) about 10 miles (16 kilometers) northwest of Washington, D.C. The center includes a hospital, medical and dental schools, a medical research institute, and a school of hospital administration. It opened in 1942. The first nuclear reactor installed in a hospital solely for medical use was dedicated at the center in 1957. JOHN A. OUDINE

NATIONAL OCEAN SURVEY is an agency of the United States government that gathers scientific data about the land, seas, and inland waters. It maps the nation's land areas, coastal waters, lakes, and rivers.

The survey prepares and distributes nautical and aeronautical charts to guide navigators on water and in the air. It publishes tables and charts of U.S. coastal tides and currents. The survey also records earthquake activity and issues warnings of *tsunamis* (huge sea waves caused by underwater earthquakes) in the Pacific Ocean area.

The National Ocean Survey was created in 1970 as part of the National Oceanic and Atmospheric Administration. The survey performs the functions of the former Coast and Geodetic Survey and the U.S. Lake Survey of the U.S. Army Corps of Engineers.

CRITICALLY REVIEWED BY THE NATIONAL OCEANIC AND ATMOSPHERIC ADMINISTRATION

NATIONAL OCEANIC AND ATMOSPHERIC ADMINISTRATION (NOAA) is a United States government agency that works to improve our understanding and use of the environment and of marine life. The NOAA combines the functions of several agencies that were formerly part of the Department of Commerce or

Eberhard E. Otto, Miller Services

The Canadian War Museum, a unit of the National Museum of Man in Ottawa, Ont., exhibits weapons and other equipment.

The National Gallery of Canada, Ottawa (Susan Campbell)

The National Gallery of Canada in Ottawa, Ont., a Canadian national museum, has metalwork, painting, and other art.

the Department of the Interior. It also administers several programs that were previously run by other government agencies or by the Army or the Navy.

The NOAA has nine major divisions: the National Ocean Survey, National Weather Service, National Marine Fisheries Service, National Environmental Satellite Service, Environmental Research Laboratories, Office of Sea Grant, National Oceanographic Instrumentation Center, Marine Minerals Technology Center, and National Data Buoy Project Office. The NOAA was created in 1970 as part of the Department of Commerce. Critically reviewed by the NATIONAL OCEANIC AND ATMOSPHERIC ADMINISTRATION

NATIONAL ORGANIZATION FOR WOMEN (NOW) is a civil rights group that fights sexual discrimination in all areas of society. NOW ranks as the largest organization in the women's liberation movement. It has about 64,000 members in the United States and other countries. Both men and women may join NOW.

One of the main goals of NOW is the passage of the Equal Rights Amendment to the United States Constitution. This amendment states that every person—regardless of sex—has equal rights under the law. NOW also works to obtain equal educational opportunities for women. It criticizes educational policies that it feels discourage women from entering such "male" professions as law and medicine.

In addition, NOW fights to end job discrimination against women. The group urges the Equal Employment Opportunity Commission to enforce the Civil Rights Act of 1964. This act prohibits job discrimination because of sex. NOW also calls for better child-care facilities that would free mothers for a career outside the home if they choose.

In 1971, NOW members helped form the National Women's Political Caucus, which encourages women to seek public office. NOW calls for more women delegates at political conventions and additional female appointments to high-level government positions.

NOW believes women can achieve equality only if basic changes occur in society. For example, the organization feels that men and women should be equal partners in society and share all responsibilities of citizenship and family life.

NOW was founded in 1966 by Betty Friedan, an American author, and 300 other leading American men and women. The group has headquarters at 425 13th Street NW, Washington, D.C. 20004.

Critically reviewed by the NATIONAL ORGANIZATION FOR WOMEN

See also WOMAN; FRIEDAN, BETTY.

NATIONAL PARK SERVICE is a bureau of the United States Department of the Interior. It manages about 300 areas of the National Park System. The National Park Service also preserves many historic and archaeological sites and structures. It was established in 1916, when the park system consisted of 37 areas. They included Yellowstone National Park, the world's first national park. The U.S. secretary of the interior appoints a director to head the bureau in its Washington, D.C., headquarters. It has eight regional offices, a National Capital Parks office, a planning and service center, and two training centers. See NATIONAL PARK SYSTEM; NATIONAL CEMETERY. GEORGE B. HARTZOG, JR.

Jack Zehrt, Shostal

Everglades National Park has a great variety of wildlife but is especially famous for its many species of birds.

NATIONAL PARK SYSTEM

NATIONAL PARK SYSTEM. The United States is rich in natural wonderlands, famous historic places, and sites for many kinds of outdoor recreation. The government has set aside nearly 300 such areas to preserve them for the benefit and enjoyment of the people. All these areas are called *parklands*, and all of them together make up the National Park System. They include parks, monuments, historic sites, memorials, cemeteries, seashores, lakeshores, and battlefields. Even the White House and the Statue of Liberty are part of the National Park System.

The first national park in the world, Yellowstone National Park, was established by the U.S. government in 1872. The National Park System developed with the creation of other parklands. Today, the system's parklands total about 48,600 square miles (125,900 square kilometers)—an area larger than that of Pennsylvania. Every state except Delaware has at least one national parkland. The District of Columbia, Puerto Rico, and the Virgin Islands also have national parklands.

The magnificent scenery of the national parks attracts more and more visitors every year. Yellowstone is world famous for hot geysers that erupt from the ground, thundering waterfalls that plunge into deep gorges, and sparkling lakes that lie high among snow-capped mountains. Bears, deer, elk, moose, and other wildlife roam Yellowstone's evergreen forests, free of danger from people. In Carlsbad Caverns, rock forma-

This article was critically reviewed by the National Park Service.

tions cover the floors and ceilings of great underground caves. The formations look like Oriental temples, strange beasts, and upside-down forests of icicles. The Olympic rain forests, almost as thick as tropical jungles, lie under rugged, towering peaks. On these mountains are mighty glaciers, and meadows blanketed by wild flowers. The breathtaking Grand Canyon has walls of black, brown, lavender, and red that are 1 mile (1.6 kilometers) deep. The weirdly beautiful Petrified Forest has rainbow-colored logs and tree trunks that are millions of years old and have turned into stone.

National monuments include the Statue of Liberty, ancient Indian pueblos, and forts dating from colonial or revolutionary times. Among the historical areas are the birthplaces of George Washington, Abraham Lincoln, Franklin D. Roosevelt, and John F. Kennedy.

The manager of the National Park System is the National Park Service, a bureau of the United States Department of the Interior. The director of the service names a superintendent to manage each individual area or a group of areas close together. Park rangers patrol the parklands to protect them from fire and other danger, and to perform various services for visitors. See the separate WORLD BOOK article on NATIONAL PARK SERVICE. See also the separate articles on the various parklands as listed in the tables with this article.

NATIONAL PARK SYSTEM / *Kinds of Areas*

The National Park System consists of three basic kinds of areas: (1) natural, (2) historical, and (3) recreational. Within these three groups, areas are identified by more than 20 types, such as national parks, national monuments, national historic sites, and so on. See the table of *Types of Areas*.

Congress must approve nearly all new areas for the National Park System, including any area planned as a national park. The President may establish a national monument if the government owns the land. The secretary of the interior may approve a national historic site.

The National Park Service acquires land for new areas through donations, exchanges, purchases, or reassignment of federal properties. Many parklands include some land that the government does not own. The government is gradually acquiring these sections as well. Sixteen areas are owned by state, local, or private agencies. Some of these areas are managed under cooperative agreements.

Natural Areas are preserved chiefly for the outstanding beauty or scientific importance of their natural features. These areas include all the national parks except Mesa Verde, which is preserved for its prehis-

John Arthur Polky, Tom Stack & Associates
Yellowstone National Park features famous Old Faithful geyser. Crowds watch Old Faithful erupt about every 65 minutes.

Werner Stoy, Camera Hawaii
City of Refuge National Historical Park preserves early Hawaiian culture and the history of the Polynesian people.

PARKLANDS OF THE NATIONAL PARK SYSTEM

This map shows the location of the parklands in the National Park System. Because of space limitations, the parklands within the East Coast area outlined in black are not named on the map. Their names can be found by matching their numbers with those in the tables on the right of the map.

WORLD BOOK map

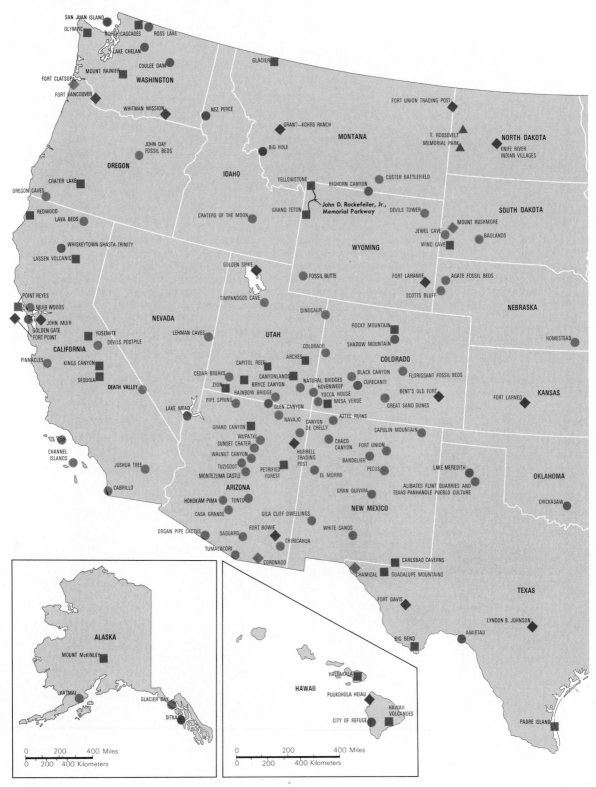

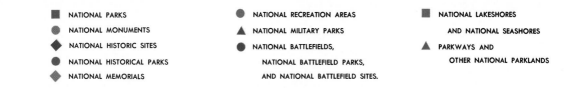

0   100   200   300   400 Miles
0   100   200   300   400 Kilometers

MAINE

MINNESOTA

VOYAGEURS

GRAND PORTAGE

ISLE ROYALE

APOSTLE ISLANDS

SAINT CROIX ISLAND

ACADIA

MICHIGAN

PICTURED ROCKS

ST. CROIX RIVERWAY

LOWER ST. CROIX RIVER

VERMONT

NEW HAMPSHIRE

SLEEPING BEAR DUNES

WISCONSIN

PIPESTONE

SAINT-GAUDENS

SARATOGA

FORT STANWIX

9, 10, 12, 13

MASSACHUSETTS

EFFIGY MOUNDS

MICHIGAN

NEW YORK

CONNECTICUT RHODE ISLAND

IOWA

HERBERT HOOVER

INDIANA DUNES

PERRY'S VICTORY

T. ROOSEVELT INAUGURAL

CUYAHOGA VALLEY

PENNSYLVANIA

NEW JERSEY

ILLINOIS

INDIANA

OHIO

ALLEGHENY PORTAGE RAILROAD

JOHNSTOWN FLOOD

MARYLAND

LINCOLN HOME

WILLIAM HOWARD TAFT

FORT NECESSITY

HARPERS FERRY

DELAWARE

WASHINGTON, D.C.

MOUND CITY GROUP

JEFFERSON NATIONAL EXPANSION MEMORIAL

GEORGE ROGERS CLARK

WEST VIRGINIA

WRIGHT BROTHERS

MISSOURI

LINCOLN BOYHOOD

ABRAHAM LINCOLN BIRTHPLACE

VIRGINIA

MAMMOTH CAVE

KENTUCKY

CUMBERLAND GAP

BOOKER T WASHINGTON

FORT RALEIGH

G. W. CARVER

WILSON'S CREEK

FORT DONELSON

A. JOHNSON

GUILFORD COURTHOUSE

CAPE HATTERAS

OZARK RIVERWAYS

GREAT SMOKY MOUNTAINS

NORTH CAROLINA

PEA RIDGE

STONES RIVER

CARL SANDBURG HOME

CAPE LOOKOUT

FORT SMITH

BUFFALO RIVER

SHILOH

KINGS MOUNTAIN

ARKANSAS

BRICES CROSS ROADS

RUSSELL CAVE

CHICKAMAUGA AND CHATTANOOGA

COWPENS

MOORES CREEK

HOT SPRINGS

TUPELO

TENNESSEE

KENNESAW MOUNTAIN

SOUTH CAROLINA

ARKANSAS POST

ALABAMA

FORT SUMTER

VICKSBURG

HORSESHOE BEND

OCMULGEE

FORT PULASKI

TUSKEGEE INSTITUTE

GEORGIA

MISSISSIPPI

ANDERSONVILLE

FORT FREDERICA

LOUISIANA

CUMBERLAND ISLAND

FORT CAROLINE

CASTILLO DE SAN MARCOS

BIG THICKET PRESERVE

FORT MATANZAS

GULF ISLANDS

CHALMETTE

CANAVERAL

SAN JUAN

VIRGIN ISLANDS

DE SOTO

PUERTO RICO

VIRGIN ISLANDS

FLORIDA

MAR-A-LAGO

BUCK ISLAND REEF

CHRISTIANSTED

BIG CYPRESS PRESERVE

BISCAYNE

0   50   100 Miles
0   50   100 Kilometers

EVERGLADES

FORT JEFFERSON

Appalachian Scenic Trail

Blue Ridge Parkway

Natchez Trace Parkway

Memorials ◆
1 FEDERAL HALL
2 GENERAL GRANT
3 HAMILTON GRANGE
4 JEFFERSON MEMORIAL
5 LYNDON B. JOHNSON GROVE
6 J. F. KENNEDY CENTER
7 T. KOSCIUSZKO
8 LINCOLN MEMORIAL
9 T. ROOSEVELT ISLAND
10 WASHINGTON MONUMENT
11 R. WILLIAMS

Parks ■
1 SHENANDOAH

Monuments ●
1 CASTLE CLINTON
2 FORT McHENRY
3 G. WASHINGTON BIRTHPLACE
4 STATUE OF LIBERTY

Historic Sites ◆
1 ADAMS
2 BARTON
3 EDISON
4 EISENHOWER
5 FORD'S THEATRE
6 HAMPTON
7 HOME OF F. D. ROOSEVELT
8 HOPEWELL VILLAGE
9 J. F. KENNEDY
10 LONGFELLOW
11 SAGAMORE HILL
12 SALEM MARITIME
13 SAUGUS IRON WORKS
14 SEWALL-BELMONT HOUSE
15 SPRINGFIELD ARMORY
16 T. ROOSEVELT BIRTHPLACE
17 VAN BUREN BIRTHPLACE
18 VANDERBILT MANSION

Historical Parks ●
1 APPOMATTOX COURT HOUSE
2 BOSTON
3 CHESAPEAKE AND OHIO CANAL
4 COLONIAL
5 INDEPENDENCE
6 MINUTE MAN
7 MORRISTOWN
8 VALLEY FORGE

Recreation Areas ●
1 DELAWARE WATER GAP
2 GATEWAY

Military Parks ▲
1 FREDERICKSBURG AND SPOTSYLVANIA
2 GETTYSBURG

**Battlefields,
Battlefield Parks,
and Battlefield Sites** ●
1 ANTIETAM
2 MANASSAS
3 PETERSBURG
4 RICHMOND

**Lakeshores
and Seashores** ■
1 ASSATEAGUE ISLAND
2 CAPE COD
3 FIRE ISLAND

**Parkways
and other Parklands** ▲
1 ARLINGTON HOUSE
2 CATOCTIN MOUNTAIN
3 F. DOUGLASS
4 FORT WASHINGTON PARK
5 GREENBELT PARK
6 NATIONAL CAPITAL PARKS
7 NATIONAL MALL
8 NATIONAL VISITOR CENTER
9 PISCATAWAY
10 PRINCE WILLIAM
11 ROCK CREEK PARK
12 WASHINGTON MEMORIAL PARKWAY
13 WHITE HOUSE
14 WOLF TRAP FARM

45

NATIONAL PARK SYSTEM

TYPES OF AREAS

Name	Number	Area In acres	In hectares
National Battlefield Parks	3	6,662	2,696
National Battlefield Sites	2	1,801	729
National Battlefields	7	5,990	2,424
National Capital Parks	1	6,452	2,611
National Cemeteries	*	218	88
National Historic Sites	51	13,556	5,486
National Historical Parks	16	78,171	31,635
National Lakeshores	4	192,269	77,808
National Mall	1	146	59
National Memorial Park	1	70,409	28,494
National Memorials	22	6,017	2,435
National Military Parks	11	34,597	14,001
National Monuments	81	9,849,441	3,985,927
National Parks	37	15,616,092	6,319,608
National Parkways	4	159,639	64,604
National Preserves	2	654,550	264,887
National Recreation Areas	16	3,506,513	1,419,035
National Scenic Riverways	4	244,306	98,867
National Scenic Trail	1	52,034	21,057
National Seashores	10	604,242	244,528
National Visitor Center	1	18	7
Parks (Other)	9	31,897	12,908
White House	1	18	7
TOTAL	**285**	**31,135,038**	**12,599,902**

*National cemeteries are administered with other historic areas and are not counted separately. However, their acreages are listed separately.

toric Indian cliff dwellings. They also include almost half the national monuments. Among these are the Agate Fossil Beds, world-famous deposits of ancient animal fossils; and Death Valley, a desert with strange and beautiful rock formations in the earth's crust. Death Valley has the lowest land surface in the Western Hemisphere—282 feet (86 meters) below sea level.

The largest natural area, Glacier Bay National Monument, is more than twice as large as the state of Delaware. It is also the largest area in the National Park System.

To keep the natural areas in their unspoiled condition, the *balance of nature* must be preserved. That is, the plant and animal life is left as undisturbed as possible (see BALANCE OF NATURE). Hunting and lumbering are prohibited, though fishing is allowed. Mining is permitted in only a few areas. Livestock grazing is limited and is steadily being eliminated. In most areas, water resources may not be used for such purposes as irrigation or the production of hydroelectric power.

The National Park Service encourages recreational activities in the natural areas if they do not disturb the surroundings. The service tries to enrich people's understanding of the natural processes that have made the land of each area what it is. Park rangers and other staff members are trained to explain natural and scientific features. The National Park Service also encourages research and educational activities in all the parklands.

Historical Areas are set aside to preserve their historical or archaeological features. Among these features are ancient Indian ruins, such as the remains of Mound Builders' towns at Ocmulgee National Monument. Others honor important persons or events in the history of the United States. These areas include battlefields, forts, national cemeteries and memorials, and his-

toric bridges, buildings, dams, canals, and farms. The most famous historical area is probably the White House.

The historical areas are made to look as much as possible as they did when they became important. For example, staff members sometimes restore buildings and natural features, raise animals on the farms, and wear clothing styles from the past.

Recreational Areas provide outstanding land and water resources for outdoor activities. Hunting is permitted in some of the areas.

In many recreational areas, including national seashores and lakeshores, visitors use the natural features for recreation. For example, 68 miles (109 kilometers) of white sand beaches and dunes line the Gulf of Mexico at Padre Island National Seashore. Its fishing, horseback riding, sailing, and swimming attract visitors from all parts of the country.

In other recreation areas, such features as roads, trails, and water reservoirs have been developed to provide recreational opportunities. For example, one of the world's largest artificially-created lakes, 254.69-square-mile (659.64-square-kilometer) Lake Mead, is a popular playground for water sports. Formed by Hoover Dam, the lake is part of the Lake Mead National Recreation Area. Recreational areas also include cultural areas that provide attractive settings for the enjoyment of fine arts performances. One such area is the Wolf Trap Farm Park for the Performing Arts. The park, in northeastern Virginia, presents concerts and other fine arts programs in its 3,500-seat auditorium. Lawns around the auditorium provide seating space for an additional 3,000 persons.

Jack Zehrt

Glen Canyon National Recreation Area includes Lake Powell, *above*. The lake was created by Glen Canyon Dam.

Each year, more and more people seek a relaxing change from city life or everyday routine. In the early 1970's, more than 200 million visits were made yearly to the national parklands, compared with about 80 million in 1960.

The Blue Ridge Parkway is one of the most popular national parklands in the National Park System. It has more than 12 million visits a year. This highway in the Blue Ridge Mountains winds from Virginia through North Carolina, and connects Shenandoah and Great Smoky Mountains national parks.

Visitors and park rangers share the responsibility of protecting the parklands. Carelessness can start a forest fire that could destroy lives and valuable resources. Visitors are not allowed to remove or damage any natural feature—not even a flower. The National Park Service repeatedly warns the public not to feed, tease, or touch any animals of the parklands.

Planning a Visit. Learning about a parkland beforehand will increase the enjoyment of a visit. Useful information includes the natural or historical features to look for, and why they are important. For an overnight stay, visitors should know whether the area has lodgings or campgrounds that will be open. Other useful information includes available services and recreational activities, traveling routes, and various fees.

The tables with this article show which parklands have overnight lodgings, permit camping, are closed part of the year, or are not yet open to the public. Area superintendents will mail other information upon request. For their addresses, write to Chief, Branch of General Inquiries, Office of Information, National Park Service, Department of the Interior, Washington, D.C. 20240.

Visitors should stop at a parkland's visitor center for pamphlets and maps that tell about the area's features and activities. At many parklands, staff members are available for campfire talks, guided trips, and amphitheater programs.

Visitors' Costs. About three-fourths of the parklands are free to the public. The others charge a daily entrance fee. Fees range from 50 cents to 75 cents for persons not entering by car and from $1 to $2 per carload. Persons under 16 and organized groups of high school age pay no entrance fee.

The park service sells Golden Eagle Passports for $10 a year. They may be used at all parklands that charge an entrance fee. Persons 62 or older may obtain a free Golden Age Passport. It offers the same privileges as the Golden Eagle Passport as well as a 50% discount on other fees.

Overnight lodgings vary in price, according to quality. They include cabins, cottages, lodges, motels, hotels, and trailer villages. These lodgings, available in nearly 40 areas, are operated privately under contract with the National Park Service. Visitors should make reservations early. The busiest periods, except in warm climates, are from late May to mid-October, and weekends and holidays the rest of the year.

Camping is permitted in about 95 national parklands—in the wilderness or on campgrounds. A wilderness site may be a great distance from such conveniences as drinking water and food supplies. Wilderness campers must notify the superintendent or a park ranger of their plans.

Inexperienced campers should camp on the campgrounds. Some of these sites have a few conveniences, and others have a wide variety, including play areas for children. Some campgrounds are designed for individuals or for families or other small groups. Other sites are intended for large, organized groups such as Boy Scout troops or school groups. Reservations can be made for group sites. For camping tips, see the CAMPING article.

Problems of Overcrowding. The growing numbers of visitors put more and more pressure on the national parklands. Problems include demands for such basic services as food, water, lodging, and transportation. Only through careful planning and management can these problems be handled without spoiling the parklands. Otherwise, overcrowding could result in too much automobile traffic, air pollution from automobile fumes and campfire smoke, dirty streams, and jammed campgrounds.

The National Park Service has taken many steps to correct early mistakes in parkland development. It has tightened controls on air and water pollution, food supplies, and health care. In Yosemite National Park, for example, public transportation was begun to reduce automobile traffic. The park's "firefall"—a huge bonfire pushed over a cliff every summer night—was eliminated to decrease smoke and traffic jams. The service also cut the number of campers permitted in overcrowded Yosemite Valley.

Redwood National Park, home of the world's tallest known tree, has many scenic sites that are ideal for picnicking.

David Muench, Van Cleve Photography

NATIONAL PARK SYSTEM

NATIONAL PARKS*

Name	Area In acres	Area In hectares	Location	Outstanding Features
Acadia†	37,722	15,266	Maine	Highest land on Atlantic Coast of the United States; rugged coastline
Arches†	73,379	29,695	Utah	Giant rock arches, windows, and towers formed by erosion
Big Bend†**	708,118	286,565	Texas	Chisos Mountains and Desert in big bend of Rio Grande
Bryce Canyon†**	37,277	15,085	Utah	Oddly shaped, beautifully colored rock formations in horse-shoe-shaped basins
Canyonlands†	337,570	136,610	Utah	Canyons, mesas, and sandstone spires; 1,000-year-old Indian rock carvings
Capitol Reef†	241,865	97,879	Utah	Colorful ridge 60 miles (97 kilometers) long with white dome-shaped rock
Carlsbad Caverns	46,755	18,921	New Mexico	Huge underground caves with strange rock formations
Crater Lake†**	160,290	64,867	Oregon	Lake in dead volcano; colorful lava walls almost 2,000 feet (610 meters) high
Everglades†**	1,400,533	566,776	Florida	Subtropical wilderness with plentiful wildlife
Glacier†**	1,013,598	410,189	Montana	Many glaciers and lakes among towering Rocky Mountain peaks
Grand Canyon†**	1,218,375	493,059	Arizona	Canyon 1 mile (1.6 kilometers) deep with brightly colored walls and rock shapes
Grand Teton†**	310,418	125,622	Wyoming	Rugged Teton peaks; winter feeding ground of large elk herd
Great Smoky Mountains†**	517,014	209,228	North Carolina, Tennessee	High mountains; large hardwood and evergreen forests
Guadalupe Mountains	76,398	30,917	Texas	Fossil limestone reef; evergreen forest overlooking desert
Haleakala†	27,824	11,260	Hawaii	Inactive volcano with large, colorful crater
Hawaii Volcanoes†**	229,177	92,745	Hawaii	Two active volcanoes; rare plants and animals
Hot Springs†	5,801	2,348	Arkansas	Mineral springs at base of Hot Springs Mountain
Isle Royale†**‡	539,280	218,239	Michigan	Island wilderness with large moose herd and wolves
Kings Canyon†**	460,136	186,210	California	Mountain wilderness of giant sequoia trees
Lassen Volcanic†**	106,372	43,047	California	Active volcano; steep domes of lava
Mammoth Cave†**	52,129	21,096	Kentucky	Huge cave with 150 miles (241 kilometers) of corridors; underground lakes, rivers, and waterfalls
Mesa Verde†**	52,036	21,058	Colorado	Prehistoric Indian cliff dwellings
Mount McKinley†**	1,939,493	784,885	Alaska	Highest mountain in North America; wildlife
Mount Rainier†**	235,404	95,265	Washington	Greatest single-peak glacier system in United States
North Cascades†	504,785	204,279	Washington	Mountain wilderness with glaciers, lakes, waterfalls, and jagged peaks
Olympic†**	897,909	363,371	Washington	Oceanside mountain wilderness with rain forest and elk
Petrified Forest	94,189	38,117	Arizona	Ancient, rock-hard wood; Indian ruins; Painted Desert
Redwood	62,147	25,150	California	World's tallest known tree in coastal redwood forest
Rocky Mountain†	263,793	106,753	Colorado	More than 100 peaks over 11,000 feet (3,350 meters) high
Sequoia†**	386,823	156,542	California	Giant sequoia trees; Mount Whitney
Shenandoah†**	190,532	77,106	Virginia	Blue Ridge Mountains; hardwood forest; Skyline Drive
Virgin Islands†**	14,470	5,856	Virgin Islands	White beaches; tropical plants and animals
Voyageurs	219,128	88,678	Minnesota	Beautiful northern forests of aspen, birch, pine, and spruce; more than 50 lakes
Wind Cave†	28,060	11,355	South Dakota	Limestone caverns; prairie wildlife
Yellowstone†**	2,219,823	898,330	Idaho, Montana, Wyoming	World's greatest geyser area; canyons and waterfalls; wide variety of wildlife
Yosemite†**	760,916	307,932	California	Mountain scenery with deep gorges and high waterfalls
Zion†**	146,553	59,308	Utah	Colorful canyons and mesas

*Each national park has a separate article in WORLD BOOK.
†Camping permitted.　　**Has overnight lodging.　　‡Closed part of the year.

NATIONAL RECREATION AREAS

Name	Area In acres	In hectares	Location	Outstanding Features
Amistad*	62,452	25,273	Texas	U.S. part of Amistad Reservoir on Rio Grande
Bighorn Canyon*	140,434	56,832	Montana, Wyoming	Reservoir created by Yellowtail Dam
Chickasaw*	9,294	3,761	Oklahoma	Cold mineral springs; Lake of the Arbuckles
Coulee Dam*	100,059	40,492	Washington	Franklin D. Roosevelt Lake, formed by Grand Coulee Dam
Curecanti*	41,572	16,823	Colorado	Blue Mesa and Morrow Point reservoirs
Cuyahoga Valley	29,112	11,781	Ohio	About 20 miles (30 kilometers) of Cuyahoga River from Akron, Ohio to Cleveland, Ohio
Delaware Water Gap	47,676	19,294	New Jersey, Pennsylvania	Scenery along Delaware River
Gateway	26,172	10,591	New Jersey, New York	Park in urban harbor area
Glen Canyon*†	1,235,080	499,819	Arizona, Utah	Lake Powell, formed by Glen Canyon Dam
Golden Gate	34,938	14,139	California	Urban recreational park
Lake Chelan*	61,890	25,046	Washington	Snow-fed Lake Chelan in forested valley
Lake Mead*†	1,492,795	604,113	Arizona, Nevada	Lake Mead, formed by Hoover Dam; Lake Mohave, formed by Davis Dam
Lake Meredith*	45,964	18,601	Texas	Lake Meredith on Canadian River
Ross Lake*	117,574	47,581	Washington	Lakes and forested valleys among snow-capped peaks
Shadow Mountain*	19,004	7,690	Colorado	Shadow Mountain and Granby lakes on Colorado River
Whiskeytown-Shasta-Trinity*	42,497	17,198	California	Whiskeytown Reservoir, formed by Whiskeytown Dam

*Camping permitted.   †Has overnight lodging.

Werner Stoy, Camera Hawaii

Yosemite National Park has many spectacular waterfalls, including Yosemite Falls, *above*, one of the world's highest falls.

Grand Canyon National Park offers a breathtaking view of the Inner Gorge of the Grand Canyon, *right*, from Toroweap Point.

Fred Bond, Publix

Vicksburg National Military Park includes relics of the famous Civil War battle. Many states whose soldiers fought in the battle have memorials in the park.

David Muench, Van Cleve Photography

E. Carle, Shostal

Fort Sumter National Monument is on the site where the Civil War began. Confederate guns attacked a Union force there.

Bernie Donahue, Publix

George Washington Carver National Monument marks the site where the famous scientist was born a slave.

NATIONAL MONUMENTS*

Name	Area In acres	In hectares	Location	Outstanding Features
Agate Fossil Beds	3,054	1,236	Nebraska	Deposits of animal fossils
Alibates Flint Quarries and Texas Panhandle Pueblo Culture†	93	37	Texas	Site of quarry used by prehistoric Indians in making tools and weapons
Aztec Ruins	27	11	New Mexico	Ruins of large Indian town of the 1100's
Badlands**‡	243,302	98,461	South Dakota	Rugged ravines, ridges, and cliffs; prehistoric animal fossils
Bandelier**‡	29,661	12,003	New Mexico	Ruins of prehistoric Indian pueblos and cliff dwellings; canyons
Biscayne	103,701	41,966	Florida	Living coral reef in Atlantic Ocean and Biscayne Bay
Black Canyon of the Gunnison**	13,672	5,533	Colorado	Narrow, steep-walled canyon with shadowed depths
Booker T. Washington	224	91	Virginia	Birthplace and childhood home of famous Negro leader and educator
Buck Island Reef	880	356	Virgin Islands	Marine garden in Caribbean Sea; underwater trail
Cabrillo	144	58	California	Memorial to Juan Rodríguez Cabrillo, who discovered West Coast
Canyon de Chelly**‡	83,840	33,929	Arizona	Prehistoric Indian ruins at base of cliffs and in caves
Capulin Mountain	775	314	New Mexico	Cinder cone of dead volcano, with trails around rim and into crater
Casa Grande	473	191	Arizona	Ruins of adobe tower built by Indians 600 years ago
Castillo de San Marcos	20	8	Florida	Fort begun by Spaniards in 1672 to defend St. Augustine
Castle Clinton	1	0.4	New York	Landing depot for 8¼ million immigrants from 1855 to 1890
Cedar Breaks**‡	6,155	2,491	Utah	Huge natural amphitheater in colorful Pink Cliffs
Chaco Canyon**	21,510	8,705	New Mexico	Ruins of large pueblos built by prehistoric Indians
Channel Islands**	18,388	7,441	California	Large sea lion breeding place; nesting sea birds; animal fossils

See footnotes at end of table.

Continued on next page

Ray Atkeson

Jack Zehrt, Shostal

Death Valley National Monument includes the lowest spot in the Western Hemisphere—282 feet (86 meters) below sea level.

Grand Portage National Monument in Minnesota marks the location of a famous fur-trading post of the 1700's.

NATIONAL MONUMENTS*

Name	Area In acres	Area In hectares	Location	Outstanding Features
Chiricahua**	10,648	4,309	Arizona	Strange, rocky landscape formed by nearly a billion years of erosion
Colorado**	17,669	7,150	Colorado	Canyons and unusual sandstone formations
Craters of the Moon**	53,545	21,669	Idaho	Lava fields with volcanic caves, cinder cones, craters, and tunnels
Custer Battlefield	765	310	Montana	Site of Battle of Little Bighorn in 1876
Death Valley**‡	2,067,832	836,822	California, Nevada	Great desert famous in Western history; lowest land surface in Western Hemisphere
Devils Postpile**§	798	323	California	Remains of lava flow forming rock columns up to 60 feet (18 meters) high
Devils Tower**	1,347	545	Wyoming	Volcanic rock tower 865 feet (264 meters) high
Dinosaur**	211,051	85,409	Colorado, Utah	Fossil deposits of dinosaurs and other prehistoric animals; canyons cut by rivers
Effigy Mounds	1,475	597	Iowa	Indian mounds in shapes of bears and birds
El Morro**	1,279	517	New Mexico	Soft sandstone with prehistoric rock carvings; inscriptions by early explorers and settlers
Florissant Fossil Beds	5,992	2,425	Colorado	Fossil insects, leaves, and seeds
Fort Frederica	215	87	Georgia	Built in the 1740's to protect British colonists from Spaniards
Fort Jefferson**	47,125	19,071	Florida	Built in 1846 to control Florida Straits
Fort Matanzas	299	121	Florida	Spanish fort built in the 1740's to protect St. Augustine from British
Fort McHenry	43	18	Maryland	Defended against British in War of 1812; battle inspired writing of "The Star-Spangled Banner"
Fort Pulaski	5,616	2,273	Georgia	Captured by Union forces during Civil War
Fort Stanwix	16	6	New York	Site of treaty with Iroquois Indians in 1768 and Revolutionary War siege in 1777
Fort Sumter	64	26	South Carolina	Site of beginning of Civil War
Fort Union	721	292	New Mexico	Ruins of fort built in 1851 to protect travelers on Santa Fe Trail
Fossil Butte	8,178	3,310	Wyoming	Fish fossils more than 40 million years old
George Washington Birthplace	456	185	Virginia	Plantation where Washington was born; memorial mansion and gardens

See footnotes at end of table.

Continued on next page

Ray Manley, Shostal

Wupatki National Monument in Arizona features pueblos built of red sandstone by prehistoric farming Indians. The Hopi tribe may have descended partially from these Indians.

NATIONAL MONUMENTS*

Name	Area In acres	In hectares	Location	Outstanding Features
George Washington Carver	210	85	Missouri	Birthplace and boyhood home of famous Negro scientist
Gila Cliff Dwellings	533	216	New Mexico	Prehistoric dwellings in overhanging cliff
Glacier Bay**‡	2,805,269	1,135,252	Alaska	Glaciers that move down mountainsides and break up into the sea; much wildlife
Gran Quivira	611	247	New Mexico	Ruins of Spanish mission buildings and Indian pueblos
Grand Portage	710	287	Minnesota	Fur-trading post on portage of canoe route to Northwest
Great Sand Dunes**	36,827	14,903	Colorado	Some of largest and highest dunes in United States
Hohokam Pima	1,555	629	Arizona	Remains of settlement of Hohokam Indians, ancestors of the Pima Indians
Homestead	195	79	Nebraska	One of first land claims under Homestead Act of 1862
Hovenweep**	785	318	Colorado, Utah	Prehistoric Indian cliff dwellings, pueblos, and towers
Jewel Cave	1,275	516	South Dakota	Underground limestone chambers connected by narrow corridors
John Day Fossil Beds	14,402	5,828	Oregon	Plant and animal fossils from five consecutive epochs in the earth's history
Joshua Tree**	559,960	226,608	California	Joshua trees; desert plants and animals
Katmai**	2,792,137	1,129,938	Alaska	Valley of Ten Thousand Smokes, scene of 1912 and 1913 volcanic eruptions
Lava Beds**	46,821	18,948	California	Unusual caves, cinder cones, and other results of volcanic action
Lehman Caves	640	259	Nevada	Limestone caverns with tunnels and corridors
Montezuma Castle	842	341	Arizona	Prehistoric Indian dwellings in limestone cliff
Mound City Group	68	27	Ohio	Burial mounds built by prehistoric Indians
Muir Woods	554	224	California	Grove of coast redwood trees
Natural Bridges**	7,779	3,148	Utah	Three gigantic natural bridges of sandstone
Navajo**	360	146	Arizona	Ruins of prehistoric Indian cliff dwellings
Ocmulgee	683	277	Georgia	Remains of Indian mounds and towns, some dating from 8000 B.C.

See footnotes at end of table.

Continued on next page

Bob and Ira Spring

Glacier Bay National Monument in Alaska lies in rugged country that can be reached only by airplane or boat. McBride Glacier, *left center,* is one of 16 glaciers in the monument.

NATIONAL MONUMENTS*

Name	Area In acres	In hectares	Location	Outstanding Features
Oregon Caves‡	466	189	Oregon	Limestone caverns with rock formations of beauty and variety
Organ Pipe Cactus**	330,690	133,825	Arizona	Organ-pipe cacti and other desert plants found nowhere else in United States
Pecos	341	138	New Mexico	Ruins of Spanish mission of 1600's and Indian pueblos of 1450's
Pinnacles**	14,498	5,867	California	Spirelike rock formations from 500 to 1,200 feet (150 to 366 meters) high; many caves
Pipe Spring	40	16	Arizona	Fort and other structures built by Mormon pioneers
Pipestone	282	114	Minnesota	Quarry where Indians took stone for making peace pipes
Rainbow Bridge	160	65	Utah	Largest known natural bridge—309 feet (94 meters) high and 278 feet (85 meters) long
Russell Cave	310	126	Alabama	Tools and other evidence of human life from 6500 B.C. to A.D. 1650
Saguaro	78,978	31,961	Arizona	Cactus forest, including giant saguaro cacti
Saint Croix Island	35	14	Maine	Site of 1604 French settlement
Scotts Bluff	2,988	1,209	Nebraska	Landmark on Oregon Trail
Statue of Liberty	58	24	New Jersey, New York	World's largest statue, gift of France
Sunset Crater	3,040	1,230	Arizona	Volcanic cinder cone and crater formed about A.D. 1100
Timpanogos Cave§	250	101	Utah	Limestone caverns known for coloring and twig-shaped wall formations
Tonto	1,120	453	Arizona	Indian cliff dwellings dating from 1300's
Tumacacori	10	4	Arizona	Spanish mission building built in 1700's
Tuzigoot	58	23	Arizona	Ruins of prehistoric Indian pueblos
Walnut Canyon	2,249	910	Arizona	Ancient cliff pueblos built in shallow caves under limestone ledges
White Sands	145,335	58,815	New Mexico	Glistening white dunes of gypsum sand
Wupatki	35,253	14,266	Arizona	Red sandstone pueblos built by prehistoric farming Indians
Yucca House†	10	4	Colorado	Ruins of large prehistoric Indian pueblo

*Each national monument has a separate article in WORLD BOOK.
†Not yet open to the public.   **Camping permitted.   ‡Has overnight lodging.   §Closed part of the year.

NATIONAL HISTORIC SITES

Name	Area In acres	In hectares	Location	Outstanding Features
Abraham Lincoln Birthplace	117	47	Kentucky	Log cabin inside memorial building on site of Lincoln's birthplace
Adams	8	3	Massachusetts	Home of Adams family, including Presidents John Adams and John Quincy Adams
Allegheny Portage Railroad	760	308	Pennsylvania	Honors Pennsylvania Canal and the railroad that carried canal boat passengers and cargoes over Allegheny Mountains
Andersonville	488	197	Georgia	Confederate prison camp during Civil War
Andrew Johnson	17	7	Tennessee	President Andrew Johnson's home, tailor shop, and grave
Bent's Old Fort	178	72	Colorado	Important fur-trading post of Old West
Carl Sandburg Home	247	100	North Carolina	The poet's home and farm
Christiansted	27	11	Virgin Islands	Honors Danish colonial development of Virgin Islands
Clara Barton	1	0.40	Maryland	Home of Clara Barton, founder of the American Red Cross
Edison	20	8	New Jersey	Laboratories and home of inventor Thomas A. Edison
Eisenhower*	493	199	Pennsylvania	Home and farm of Dwight D. Eisenhower during and after his presidency
Ford's Theatre	0.25	0.10	District of Columbia	Ford's Theatre, where President Lincoln was shot, and the nearby house where he died; Lincoln Museum
Fort Bowie	1,000	405	Arizona	Military headquarters for operations against Geronimo and his Apaches
Fort Davis	460	186	Texas	Major fort in west Texas defense system against Apaches and Comanches
Fort Laramie	571	231	Wyoming	Major post that guarded covered wagons going west
Fort Larned	718	291	Kansas	Protection of Santa Fe Trail
Fort Point	29	12	California	Brick and granite fort of mid-1800's
Fort Raleigh	159	64	North Carolina	Site of first attempted English settlement in what is now United States, in 1585
Fort Smith	19	8	Arkansas	One of first U.S. military posts in Louisiana Territory
Fort Union Trading Post	398	161	Montana, North Dakota	Major fur-trading post in upper Missouri River region
Fort Vancouver†	212	86	Washington	Western headquarters of Hudson's Bay Company
Golden Spike	2,203	892	Utah	Honors completion in 1869 of first coast-to-coast railroad in United States
Grant-Kohrs Ranch	1,528	618	Montana	One of the largest range ranches of 1800's
Hampton	45	18	Maryland	Great mansion built in late 1700's
Herbert Hoover	187	76	Iowa	Birthplace, boyhood home, and burial place of President Hoover
Home of Franklin D. Roosevelt	188	76	New York	Birthplace, home, "Summer White House," and burial place of President Franklin D. Roosevelt
Hopewell Village	848	343	Pennsylvania	Rural iron-making village of 1800's
Hubbell Trading Post	160	65	Arizona	Shows role of Indian reservation traders in settling West
Jefferson National Expansion Memorial	91	37	Missouri	Museum and Gateway Arch 630 feet (192 meters) high honor U.S. expansion west of Mississippi River
John Fitzgerald Kennedy	0.09	0.04	Massachusetts	Birthplace and early boyhood home of President John F. Kennedy
John Muir	9	4	California	Honors contributions to conservation and literature by explorer-naturalist
Knife River Indian Villages	1,304	528	North Dakota	Five Hidatsa Indian villages of 1845
Lincoln Home	12	5	Illinois	Only private home owned by Abraham Lincoln
Longfellow	2	0.80	Massachusetts	Home of American poet Henry Wadsworth Longfellow
Lyndon B. Johnson	241	97	Texas	President Lyndon B. Johnson's birthplace
Mar-A-Lago*	17	7	Florida	Private mansion of 1920's
Martin Van Buren*	42	17	New York	Home of President Martin Van Buren
Puukohola Heiau	77	31	Hawaii	Ruins of a temple built by King Kamehameha I, first ruler of the kingdom of Hawaii

See footnotes at end of table.

Continued on next page

NATIONAL HISTORIC SITES

Name	Area In acres	In hectares	Location	Outstanding Features
Sagamore Hill	85	34	New York	Last home of President Theodore Roosevelt
Saint-Gaudens**	86	35	New Hampshire	Home, studio, and gardens of sculptor Augustus Saint-Gaudens
Salem Maritime	9	4	Massachusetts	Derby Wharf and other important structures in New England history
San Juan	53	22	Puerto Rico	Spanish fort begun in 1539 to protect Bay of San Juan
Saugus Iron Works**	9	3	Massachusetts	One of first ironworks in North America, built in 1640's
Sewall-Belmont House	0.35	0.14	District of Columbia	Headquarters of National Women's Party
Springfield Armory	55	22	Massachusetts	Produced small arms, such as the Springfield rifle, for nearly 200 years
Theodore Roosevelt Birthplace	0.11	0.04	New York	Birthplace of 26th President
Theodore Roosevelt Inaugural	1	0.42	New York	House where Theodore Roosevelt was sworn in as President
Tuskegee Institute	70	28	Alabama	Student-made college buildings; home of Booker T. Washington; George Washington Carver Museum
Vanderbilt Mansion	212	86	New York	Magnificent country home built in 1890's
Whitman Mission†	98	40	Washington	Site where Indians killed missionaries Marcus Whitman and his wife
William Howard Taft	0.83	0.34	Ohio	President William H. Taft's birthplace

*Not yet open to the public.   †Has a separate article in WORLD BOOK.   **Closed part of the year.

Texas Highway Department

Fort Davis National Historic Site in western Texas reminds visitors of the frequent clashes between the U.S. Army and the Apache and Comanche Indians during the middle and late 1800's.

NATIONAL PARK SYSTEM

NATIONAL MEMORIALS

Name	Area In acres	In hectares	Location	Outstanding Features
Arkansas Post	385	156	Arkansas	First permanent white settlement in lower Mississippi Valley, founded in 1686
Chamizal	55	22	Texas	Honors peaceful settlement in 1963 of 99-year-old border dispute with Mexico
Coronado	2,834	1,147	Arizona	Honors Francisco Coronado's exploration of Southwest in 1540's
De Soto*	30	12	Florida	Near site of 1539 landing of explorer Hernando de Soto
Federal Hall	0.45	0.18	New York	Site of first U.S. Capitol, 1789-1790
Fort Caroline	129	52	Florida	Stockade overlooking attempted French settlement in 1560's
Fort Clatsop	125	51	Oregon	Winter campsite of Lewis and Clark expedition in 1805-1806
General Grant	0.76	0.31	New York	Tombs of President and Mrs. Ulysses S. Grant
Hamilton Grange	0.71	0.29	New York	Home of Alexander Hamilton, first U.S. secretary of the treasury
John F. Kennedy Center for the Performing Arts*	18	7	District of Columbia	National cultural center for the performing arts
Johnstown Flood	110	45	Pennsylvania	Memorial to more than 2,000 persons killed in Johnstown Flood of 1889
Lincoln Boyhood	200	81	Indiana	Farm site where Abraham Lincoln spent most of his boyhood
Lincoln Memorial*	164	66	District of Columbia	Marble building with a statue of Abraham Lincoln 19 feet (5.8 meters) high
Lyndon Baines Johnson Memorial Grove on the Potomac	12	5	District of Columbia	Grove of 500 white pines
Mount Rushmore*	1,278	517	South Dakota	Huge heads of four Presidents carved on face of granite cliff
Perry's Victory and International Peace Memorial	26	10	Ohio	Near site of U.S. naval victory in War of 1812; honors peace among United States, Canada, and Great Britain
Roger Williams†	5	2	Rhode Island	Honors founder of Rhode Island colony, a pioneer leader for religious freedom
Thaddeus Kosciuszko	0.02	0.008	Pennsylvania	Honors Polish patriot who built American fortifications during the Revolutionary War
Theodore Roosevelt Island	89	36	District of Columbia	Wooded island in Potomac River
Thomas Jefferson (Jefferson Memorial*)	18	7	District of Columbia	Circular marble building with a statue of Thomas Jefferson 19 feet (5.8 meters) high
Washington Monument*	106	43	District of Columbia	Four-sided pillar 555 feet (169 meters) high honoring George Washington
Wright Brothers	431	175	North Carolina	Site of Wright brothers' first airplane flight

*Has a separate article in WORLD BOOK.   †Not yet open to the public.

NATIONAL MILITARY PARKS

Name	Area In acres	In hectares	Location	Outstanding Features
Chickamauga and Chattanooga	8,093	3,275	Georgia, Tennessee	Civil War battles of 1863—Chickamauga, Lookout Mountain, Missionary Ridge, and Orchard Knob
Fort Donelson	545	221	Tennessee	First major Union victory of Civil War, 1862
Fredericksburg and Spotsylvania County Battlefields Memorial	6,019	2,436	Virginia	Civil War battles of Chancellorsville, Fredericksburg, Wilderness, and Spotsylvania Court House; 1862-1864
Gettysburg	3,864	1,564	Pennsylvania	Civil War battle that stopped Confederate invasion, 1863
Guilford Courthouse	220	89	North Carolina	Revolutionary War battle that led to British defeat at Yorktown, 1781
Horseshoe Bend	2,040	826	Alabama	Battle won by Andrew Jackson ending Creek Indian War, 1814
Kings Mountain	3,945	1,597	South Carolina	Revolutionary War victory of American frontiersmen, 1780
Moores Creek	77	31	North Carolina	Patriots' victory over Loyalists in Revolutionary War, 1776
Pea Ridge	4,300	1,740	Arkansas	Important Union victory of Civil War, 1862
Shiloh	3,753	1,519	Tennessee	Civil War battle of 1862 that led to fall of Vicksburg
Vicksburg	1,741	704	Mississippi	Battle that gave Union control of Mississippi River, 1863

NATIONAL BATTLEFIELDS, NATIONAL BATTLEFIELD PARKS, AND NATIONAL BATTLEFIELD SITES

Name	Area In acres	In hectares	Location	Outstanding Features
Antietam (NBS)	1,800	728	Maryland	Civil War battle that stopped first Confederate invasion of North, 1862
Big Hole (NB)	656	265	Montana	Battle between U.S. soldiers and Chief Joseph's forces in Nez Percé Indian War, 1877
Brices Cross Roads (NBS)	1	0.40	Mississippi	Large Union force defeated by outnumbered Confederate cavalrymen, 1864
Cowpens (NB)	826	334	South Carolina	American victory of Revolutionary War, 1781
Fort Necessity (NB)*	911	369	Pennsylvania	French defeat of colonial troops led by George Washington; first battle of French and Indian War, 1754
Kennesaw Mountain (NBP)	2,884	1,167	Georgia	Civil War battle during Gen. William T. Sherman's march to Atlanta, 1864
Manassas (NBP)	3,032	1,227	Virginia	Two battles of Manassas (Bull Run) in Civil War, 1861 and 1862
Petersburg (NB)	1,515	613	Virginia	Unsuccessful ten-month siege of Confederate railroad center, 1864-1865
Richmond (NBP)	746	302	Virginia	Several Union attempts to capture Richmond
Stones River (NB)	331	134	Tennessee	Beginning of Union drive to divide Confederacy into three parts, 1862-1863
Tupelo (NB)	1	0.40	Mississippi	Battle over Gen. William T. Sherman's supply line during march to Atlanta, 1864
Wilson's Creek (NB)	1,750	708	Missouri	Confederate forces defeated Union militia, 1861

*Camping permitted.

PARKWAYS AND OTHER NATIONAL PARKLANDS

Name	Area In acres	In hectares	Location	Outstanding Features
Appalachian National Scenic Trail* **	52,034	21,057	From Maine to Georgia	Wilderness trail through Appalachian Mountains; about 2,000 miles (3,200 kilometers)
Arlington House (Robert E. Lee Memorial)	28	11	Virginia	Home of Gen. Robert E. Lee, begun in 1802
Big Cypress National Preserve	570,000	230,671	Florida	Fresh water supply for Everglades National Park; home of Seminole and Miccosukee Indians
Big Thicket National Preserve	84,550	34,216	Texas	Alligator, red wolf, black bear, ocelot
Blue Ridge Parkway*†	81,784	33,097	Georgia, North Carolina, Virginia	Scenic mountain parkway; 469 miles (755 kilometers) long
Buffalo National River	94,146	38,100	Arkansas	High bluffs and deep valleys along river
Catoctin Mountain Park*	5,769	2,335	Maryland	Mountain scenery
Fort Washington Park	341	138	District of Columbia	Site of Fort Washington, built in 1814
Frederick Douglass Home	8	3	District of Columbia	Home of Negro leader from 1877 to 1895
George Washington Memorial Parkway	7,142	2,890	Maryland, Virginia	Potomac River sites associated with Washington's life; 49-mile (79-kilometer) road
Greenbelt Park*	1,078	436	Maryland	Woodland, 12 miles (19 kilometers) of marked trails
John D. Rockefeller, Jr., Memorial Parkway	23,777	9,622	Wyoming	82-mile (132-kilometer) parkway between Yellowstone and Grand Teton national parks
Lower Saint Croix National Scenic River	7,845	3,175	Minnesota, Wisconsin	About 26 miles (42 kilometers) of Saint Croix River
Natchez Trace Parkway*	46,936	18,994	Alabama, Mississippi Tennessee	Scenic 450-mile (724-kilometer) road along Indian and frontier trail
National Capital Parks	6,452	2,611	District of Columbia, Maryland, Virginia	A 346-unit park system in and near Washington, D.C.
National Mall	146	59	District of Columbia	Stretches from the Capitol to the Washington Monument
National Visitor Center	18	7	District of Columbia	Center for tourists in old Union Station building
Ozark National Scenic Riverways*	79,587	32,208	Missouri	Narrow river park along Current and Jacks Fork rivers; caves and springs
Piscataway Park	4,217	1,707	Maryland	View from Mount Vernon
Prince William Forest Park*	18,572	7,516	Virginia	Woodland with about 90 kinds of trees
Rock Creek Park	1,754	710	District of Columbia	Large urban park
Saint Croix National Scenic Riverway	62,728	25,385	Minnesota, Wisconsin	About 200 miles (320 kilometers) of Saint Croix and Namekagon rivers
Theodore Roosevelt National Memorial Park*	70,409	28,494	North Dakota	Badlands along Little Missouri River and part of President Theodore Roosevelt's ranch
White House**	18	7	District of Columbia	President's home and office
Wolf Trap Farm Park for the Performing Arts	130	53	Virginia	Concerts and dance performances in Filene Center auditorium

*Camping permitted.   †Has overnight lodging.   **Has a separate article in WORLD BOOK.

NATIONAL PARK SYSTEM

NATIONAL HISTORICAL PARKS

Name	Area In acres	In hectares	Location	Outstanding Features
Appomattox Court House	995	403	Virginia	Site of Gen. Robert E. Lee's surrender to Gen. Ulysses S. Grant, ending Civil War
Boston	35	14	Massachusetts	Includes Boston Naval Shipyard, Bunker Hill, Faneuil Hall, Old North Church, Old South Meeting House, Old State House, Paul Revere House
Chalmette	143	58	Louisiana	Scene of Battle of New Orleans in War of 1812
Chesapeake and Ohio Canal* †	20,239	8,190	District of Columbia, Maryland, West Virginia	One of the nation's oldest and least-changed lock canals for mule-drawn boats
City of Refuge	182	74	Hawaii	Prehistoric house sites and royal fish ponds
Colonial	9,834	3,980	Virginia	Major sites of colonial development—Jamestown, Williamsburg, and Yorktown; Yorktown battlefield
Cumberland Gap*	20,273	8,204	Kentucky, Tennessee, Virginia	Famous mountain pass explored by Daniel Boone and used by pioneers heading west
George Rogers Clark	24	10	Indiana	Honors Clark's Revolutionary War victories
Harpers Ferry	1,909	773	Maryland, West Virginia	Scene of 1859 raid by John Brown, foe of slavery, and his capture
Independence	21	8	Pennsylvania	Independence Hall and other buildings and sites related to founding of United States
Klondike Gold Rush	13,271	5,371	Alaska, Washington	Sites honoring the Alaska gold rush
Minute Man	745	301	Massachusetts	Landmarks of battles on first day of Revolutionary War
Morristown	1,544	625	New Jersey	Campsites in Revolutionary War; Washington's headquarters in 1777 and 1779-1780
Nez Perce	2,114	856	Idaho	Honors history and life of Nez Percé Indian region, and Lewis and Clark expedition
San Juan Island	1,752	709	Washington	Honors peaceful settlement of boundary dispute with Canada and Great Britain in 1872
Saratoga	2,432	984	New York	Scene of U.S. victory in Revolutionary War
Sitka	108	44	Alaska	Site of Tlingit Indians' last stand against Russian settlers in 1804
Valley Forge	2,550	1,032	Pennsylvania	Winter campsite of Washington's Continental Army in 1777-1778

*Camping permitted.   †Has a separate article in WORLD BOOK.

NATIONAL LAKESHORES AND NATIONAL SEASHORES

Name	Area In acres	In hectares	Location	Outstanding Features
Apostle Islands (NL)	42,012	17,002	Wisconsin	Cliffs and rock formations on 20 islands in Lake Superior; also on Bayfield Peninsula
Assateague Island (NS)*	39,631	16,038	Maryland, Virginia	Beaches and wild Chincoteague ponies
Canaveral (NS)	67,500	27,316	Florida	Beaches and birdlife
Cape Cod (NS)*†	44,600	18,049	Massachusetts	Beaches, birdlife, dunes, marshes, woodlands, and freshwater ponds
Cape Hatteras (NS)*	30,326	12,273	North Carolina	Beaches, dunes, and birdlife; "Graveyard of the Atlantic," scene of many shipwrecks
Cape Lookout (NS)	24,732	10,009	North Carolina	Beaches, dunes, salt marshes, and lighthouse
Cumberland Island (NS)	36,877	14,923	Georgia	Beaches, dunes, marshes, lakes, and forests
Fire Island (NS)*	19,357	7,833	New York	Beaches, dunes, marshes, and wildlife
Gulf Islands (NS)	142,009	57,469	Florida, Mississippi	Beaches, offshore islands, and historic forts
Indiana Dunes (NL)	8,330	3,371	Indiana	Dunes along Lake Michigan; woodlands
Padre Island (NS)*	133,919	54,195	Texas	Long beaches and bird and marine life
Pictured Rocks (NL)	70,822	28,661	Michigan	Beaches, dunes, woods, and cliffs
Point Reyes (NS)*	65,291	26,422	California	Beaches, cliffs, lagoons, and wildlife
Sleeping Bear Dunes (NL)*	71,105	28,775	Michigan	Beaches, dunes, woods, and lakes

*Camping permitted.   †Has overnight lodging.

NATIONAL PARK SYSTEM / History

During the 1800's, hunters and trappers returned from the Yellowstone region with reports of strange natural wonders. These stories—of hot springs, spurting geysers, and a mountain of black glass—seemed unbelievable. In 1870, an expedition led by General Henry D. Washburn, surveyor general of the Montana Territory, visited the region to check the reports.

After exploring by horseback, the men camped near the Madison River. They talked about the sights they had seen and discussed developing the land for resorts, or for lumbering and mining. Then, Cornelius Hedges, a Montana judge, proposed that the region be preserved as a national park to benefit all people for all time. The other men agreed enthusiastically.

Members of the expedition promoted the national park idea by writing articles in newspapers and magazines, giving lectures, and meeting with high government officials. Their efforts succeeded in 1872, when Congress established Yellowstone National Park. During the 1890's, four more national parks were established—Yosemite, Sequoia, General Grant (now Kings Canyon), and Mount Rainier.

In 1906, Congress passed the Antiquities Act to stop looting and destruction at prehistoric Indian sites in the Southwest. This law gave the President the power to establish national monuments on land owned or controlled by the government. Later in 1906, Devils Tower National Monument became the first such area. More than 30 national monuments were established during the next 10 years.

In 1916, Congress set up the National Park Service as a bureau of the Department of the Interior. Stephen T. Mather, a Chicago businessman, became its first director. Mather did much to promote and expand the National Park System. In 1916, there were 16 national parks and 21 national monuments, with a total area of 7,426 square miles (19,233 square kilometers). When Mather retired in 1929, the system consisted of 25 national parks, 32 national monuments, and a national memorial. It had a total area of more than 16,000 square miles (41,400 square kilometers).

In 1933, Congress transferred more than 70 areas from other government agencies to the Department of the Interior. These areas, most of them historical, were added to the National Park System. In 1935, the Historic Sites Act gave the secretary of the interior the power to approve national historic sites.

The Park, Parkway, and Recreation Area Study Act of 1936 led to establishment of recreational areas in the National Park System. The first such area, the Blue Ridge Parkway, was established later that year. An act of 1946 allowed the park service to manage recreational areas under cooperative agreements with other government agencies that controlled the areas.

By 1955, the National Park System had grown to almost 200 areas. About 50 million visits were recorded that year. During the 1960's, the National Park Service added 75 areas. Including boundary changes, over 7,300 square miles (18,900 square kilometers)—a total area almost as large as that of New Jersey—were added.

Grand Canyon of the Yellowstone was one of the paintings by Thomas Moran that helped persuade Congress to establish Yellowstone National Park in 1872. Easterners had found it hard to believe the reports of hunters and trappers of the region's magnificent beauty and natural wonders.

National Collection of Fine Arts, Smithsonian Institution

Since ancient times, rulers and members of the nobility have set aside parklands to preserve outstanding landscapes and wild animals. But these reserves were not open to the people. The idea of national parks for the public did not take shape until the United States established Yellowstone National Park in 1872. Since then, about 100 countries have established over 1,200 national parks and similar reserves. Many nations send people to the United States for training in park management by the National Park Service. The service also sends advisers to other countries.

Canada established its first national park in 1885. That year, the Canadian government set aside 10 square miles (26 square kilometers) in the Canadian Rockies. This land was the start of Banff National Park. Banff, Canada's best-known and most popular national park, has magnificent mountain scenery, glacier-fed lakes, and mineral hot springs. Wood Buffalo National Park, which covers 17,300 square miles (44,810 square kilometers), is the largest national park in the world. The largest buffalo herd in North America lives in this park. For information on these and other Canadian parks, see CANADA (National Park System).

In Africa, countless wild animals roam the vast plains, tropical rain forests, and thick bushlands of national parks and reserves. This wildlife includes buffaloes, elephants, giraffes, gorillas, lions, and zebras. Among the leading African national parks are Kafue in Zambia, Kruger in South Africa, Serengeti in Tanzania, and Virunga in Zaire.

In Asia, the Indian rhinoceros, largest of the Asian rhinoceroses, lives in the Kaziranga Reserve of India and the Chitawan Sanctuary of Nepal. The small number of lions still in Asia, outside zoos, make their home in the Gir Forest of India. Tigers and the rare Javan rhinoceroses live in Indonesia's Ujung Reserve.

The lakes, hills, and dales of Peak District National Park in England attract many tourists. Lüneburger Heath in West Germany has rolling sandy plains, and forests of birch, oak, and pine trees. Australia's Royal National Park is known for its rare, beautiful wild flowers. Japan's famous Mount Fuji is one of the magnificent natural features preserved in national parks. Another feature is Iguaçu Falls, over 2 miles (3.2

Norman Myers, Photo Researchers

Serengeti National Park in Tanzania has one of the world's largest animal reserves. Thomson's gazelles are common there.

Tom Myers

Waterton Lakes National Park is famous for its lakes, mountains, waterfalls, and trails. The park is the Canadian portion of Waterton-Glacier International Peace Park.

kilometers) wide, on the Argentine-Brazilian border.

The broadest worldwide park conservation effort is that of the International Union for Conservation of Nature and Natural Resources (IUCN). It was founded in 1948, and it has headquarters in Morges, Switzerland. Over 230 national governments and organizations, including the U.S. Department of the Interior, belong to the IUCN. The IUCN points out threats to resources and wildlife in individual countries and assists in park planning. It holds frequent international conferences and publishes books and reports on conservation.

Critically reviewed by the NATIONAL PARK SERVICE

NATIONAL PARK SYSTEM/*Study Aids*

Related Articles. See the WORLD BOOK articles on the national parklands as listed in the tables with this article. See also NATIONAL PARK SERVICE.

Outline

I. Kinds of Areas
  A. Natural Areas   C. Recreational Areas
  B. Historical Areas
II. Visiting the Parklands
  A. Planning a Visit C. Camping
  B. Visitors' Costs D. Problems of Overcrowding
III. History
IV. National Parks in Other Countries

Questions

How does the National Park Service acquire land?
What is the largest area in the National Park System?
What was the first national park in the world?
How are national parklands established?
Which national park has prehistoric cliff dwellings?
What is the world's largest national park?
Where is the lowest land surface in the Western Hemisphere?
What is the most popular parkland?
How many types of national parklands are there?
What is probably the most famous U.S. historical area?

NATIONAL PRIMITIVE BAPTIST CONVENTION IN THE U.S.A. is a religious organization that has more than 1,800 churches. Each church is independent, controlling its own membership. These Baptists follow three *ordinances* (established religious ceremonies)—baptism, holy communion, and feet-washing rites. They believe that a definite number of the human race were chosen for redemption before the world was created, and these persons will be saved before the final judgment. The convention was formed in 1907. It consists of state conventions and associations. It operates a publishing house, women's auxiliaries, training unions, and church schools. Headquarters are in Tallahassee, Fla. See also BAPTISTS.

Critically reviewed by the
NATIONAL PRIMITIVE BAPTIST CONVENTION IN THE U.S.A.

NATIONAL RADIO ASTRONOMY OBSERVATORY (NRAO) is an observatory used by scientists throughout the United States and from other countries. It is financed by the U.S. National Science Foundation. The NRAO has scientific offices in Charlottesville, Va., and it operates radio telescopes at Green Bank, W. Va., and Kitt Peak, Ariz.

Equipment at the main NRAO facility in Green Bank includes six radio telescopes. Each telescope has a large, dish-shaped metal mirror called a *reflector*,

which collects radio signals from space. The largest of these telescopes has a reflector 300 feet (91 meters) in diameter. The NRAO telescope at Kitt Peak has a 36-foot (11-meter) reflector designed to collect radio signals of extremely short wavelengths.

The NRAO is building the world's most powerful radio telescope near Socorro, N. Mex. This instrument, called the Very Large Array Telescope, consists of 27 reflectors, each 82 feet (25 meters) in diameter. It is to be completed by 1981.

The NRAO was founded in 1956 by the National Science Foundation to provide radio telescopes that are too expensive and complex to be built by individual universities. It is operated by Associated Universities, Inc., an association of nine U.S. universities.

Scientists using the NRAO facility at Green Bank were the first to detect radio signals from Uranus and Neptune. Scientists at the observatory also made key discoveries about the Milky Way and other galaxies, as well as about such phenomena as pulsars and quasars.

Critically reviewed by the NATIONAL RADIO ASTRONOMY OBSERVATORY

NATIONAL RAILROAD PASSENGER CORPORATION. See AMTRAK.

NATIONAL RECOVERY ADMINISTRATION (NRA), was a United States government agency in the early 1930's. The President set up the NRA in 1933 under the National Industrial Recovery Act as part of the New Deal program (see NEW DEAL). The NRA prepared and enforced codes of fair competition for businesses and industries. Hugh S. Johnson was the first head of the NRA. Donald R. Richberg succeeded him in 1934. The President abolished the NRA in 1935, after the Supreme Court ruled the recovery act unconstitutional. See also SCHECHTER V. UNITED STATES.

NATIONAL RECREATION AND PARK ASSOCIATION. See RECREATION AND PARK ASSOCIATION, NATIONAL.

NATIONAL RECREATION AREA. See NATIONAL PARK SYSTEM.

NATIONAL REPUBLICAN PARTY was a political party that arose when the Democratic-Republican party split during President John Quincy Adams' administration (1825-1829). Followers of Andrew Jackson opposed the party's conservative leaders, including Adams and Henry Clay. During Jackson's presidency (1829-1837), the National Republicans and other groups formed the Whig Party (see WHIG PARTY).   RAY ALLEN BILLINGTON

NATIONAL RESEARCH COUNCIL. See NATIONAL ACADEMY OF SCIENCES.

NATIONAL RIFLE ASSOCIATION OF AMERICA is an organization that encourages marksmanship and the use of firearms for hunting and other shooting sports. It opposes what it considers unnecessary restrictions on the right to own guns. The association, also known as the NRA, bases its opposition to gun control laws on the Second Amendment to the United States Constitution. This amendment establishes "the right of the people to keep and bear arms." However, the Supreme Court of the United States has ruled that the amendment was intended to ensure the arming of state militias.

Many law enforcement groups believe that stricter laws against owning and using guns would reduce the crime rate. The NRA feels that such laws would not help fight crime but would restrict the legal use of guns.

The NRA has been extremely effective at persuading Congress to block the passage of gun control bills. At the association's request, many of its more than 1 million members frequently send letters and telegrams to their legislators. The association was founded in 1871. Its headquarters are at 1600 Rhode Island Avenue NW, Washington, D.C. 20036.   ROBERT H. SALISBURY

See also GUN CONTROL.

NATIONAL ROAD. In the early 1800's, many settlers moved west of the Ohio River. They wanted their section to grow rapidly, and began demanding a better route from the East to the West. In 1811, work began on a road that, when completed, led from Cumberland, Md., to Vandalia, Ill. Over $7 million in federal funds was spent on the road. It was known at first as the Great National Pike, but later came to be called the National Road or the Cumberland Road.

For many years, the National Road was the chief road west. As railroads developed, the National Road became less important. Each of the states was finally given control of that part of the road which passed through it.

Now known as the National Old Trail Road, it is paved from Washington, D.C., to St. Louis, Mo. A monument to Henry Clay stands near Wheeling, W.Va. It honors Clay's great services in getting Congress to advance money for the road.   W. TURRENTINE JACKSON

NATIONAL SAFETY COUNCIL is a nonprofit educational organization that promotes accident prevention. It has about 10,600 members, including individuals, businesses, schools, government agencies, and trade, labor, and civic organizations. The council helps members solve their safety problems. It promotes public safety by carrying on publicity campaigns, cooperating with public officials, and helping to establish safety groups. It makes awards for outstanding safety achievements. The council's many publications include "Accident Facts," a yearly collection of accident statistics.

The council was founded in 1913, and was chartered by Congress in 1953. It has headquarters at 425 N. Michigan Avenue, Chicago, Ill. 60611.   HOWARD PYLE

NATIONAL SCIENCE FOUNDATION is an independent agency of the federal government. It supports research in the life, physical, engineering, and social sciences. The foundation also supports efforts to improve the quality of science education through grants to universities and colleges for activities aimed at upgrading science teaching. It also provides financial aid to outstanding students, and supports improvement in the spread of science information.

The foundation conducts studies that help the government formulate its science programs. It also supports such programs as Antarctic research, the use of computers for research and education, and studies of the oceans. It maintains, under contract, the National Radio Astronomy Observatory in Green Bank, W.Va., the Kitt Peak National Observatory in Arizona, and the National Center for Atmospheric Research in Boulder, Colo. It was established by the National Science Foundation Act of 1950. Headquarters are at 1800 G Street NW, Washington, D.C. 20550.

Critically reviewed by the NATIONAL SCIENCE FOUNDATION

See also KITT PEAK NATIONAL OBSERVATORY; NATIONAL RADIO ASTRONOMY OBSERVATORY.

NATIONAL SECURITY ACT OF 1947. See DEFENSE, DEPARTMENT OF (History); NATIONAL DEFENSE (History).

NATIONAL SECURITY AGENCY (NSA) develops security measures for the United States. This government agency also directs certain activities that provide *intelligence* (information) on other countries. NSA organizes research and operates facilities that obtain such information. President Harry S. Truman created NSA in 1952 as part of the Department of Defense.

NATIONAL SECURITY COUNCIL (NSC) serves as an interdepartmental defense cabinet of the United States government. It is a part of the Executive Office of the President. Members include the President, the Vice-President, and the secretaries of state and defense.

The NSC advises the President on a broad range of security problems. It brings together the departments and agencies most concerned with foreign policy and military matters. The council supervises the Central Intelligence Agency (see CENTRAL INTELLIGENCE AGENCY). Ordinarily, the NSC meets once a week. If a seri-

THE NATIONAL ROAD

One of the principal routes to the West used by the pioneers, the National Road was more than 500 miles (800 kilometers) long. It led from Cumberland, Md., to Vandalia, Ill.

▬▬ National Road
—— Other Road

WORLD BOOK map–FHa

ous world crisis develops, the President may summon the group into immediate session.

The NSC is assisted by a staff headed by the assistant to the President for national security affairs. The staff works with the member departments and agencies to prepare studies and policy papers for the council's action. Congress created the council in 1947.

Critically reviewed by the NATIONAL SECURITY COUNCIL

NATIONAL SECURITY MEDAL. See DECORATIONS AND MEDALS (table: U.S. Civilian Decorations).

NATIONAL SOCIALIST PARTY. See NAZISM.

NATIONAL SOCIETY FOR MEDICAL RESEARCH is an organization of more than 670 scientific and civic groups. The society is devoted to a cooperative program of informing the public on medical research. The groups include all medical schools, most veterinary and dental schools, health organizations such as the American Cancer Society, and all special medical societies in the United States. Among the groups are the American Medical Association, the Mayo Foundation, and the Rockefeller University. The society was founded in 1946. Headquarters are at 1330 Massachusetts Avenue NW, Washington, D.C. 20005.

Critically reviewed by NATIONAL SOCIETY FOR MEDICAL RESEARCH

NATIONAL TRAILWAYS BUS SYSTEM. See BUS.

NATIONAL TUBERCULOSIS AND RESPIRATORY DISEASE ASSOCIATION. See AMERICAN LUNG ASSOCIATION.

NATIONAL WAR COLLEGE, located in Washington, D.C., is a school for United States government career personnel. It was established in 1946 and placed under the direction of the Joint Chiefs of Staff.

The college prepares personnel to plan national strategy, and to exercise joint high-level policy, command, and staff functions. There are about 130 students in each class. Three-fourths are selected from the Army, Navy, and Air Force, and a fourth from government agencies, particularly the Department of State. A commandant from one of the military services heads the college. He is assisted by deputies, two from the military services and one from the Department of State. The faculty includes military and civilian members. The course lasts 10 months. RICHARD M. SKINNER

NATIONAL WILDLIFE FEDERATION is an organization founded to create interest and promote public education in the conservation, restoration, and protection of forests, lands, waters, and wildlife in the United States. The federation issues several free and inexpensive publications. It also publishes *National Wildlife* and *International Wildlife* magazines for adult members and *Ranger Rick's Nature Magazine* for younger members.

State wildlife federations and conservation leagues, made up of local clubs, are affiliated with the national organization. The federation has about 3 million members, counting members of affiliated organizations. The national group is financed by an annual direct-mail distribution of National Wildlife Conservation stamps and the sale of nature-related items. The federation began in 1936. It has headquarters at 1412 16th Street NW, Washington, D.C. 20036.

Critically reviewed by NATIONAL WILDLIFE FEDERATION

NATIONAL WOMAN SUFFRAGE ASSOCIATION. See WOMAN SUFFRAGE.

NATIONAL YOUTH ADMINISTRATION. See NEW DEAL (Leading New Deal Agencies).

NATIONAL ZOOLOGICAL PARK is a 175-acre (71-hectare) zoo maintained by the United States government in Rock Creek Valley in the District of Columbia. The Smithsonian Institution operates the park. The zoo has about 3,000 animals of all kinds. The park is used for public exhibitions, scientific research, and education. Biologists, artists, photographers, and writers do research there. The park provides information on buildings for housing animals, and cooperates with other governments in research work. JOHN C. BOLLENS

NATIONALISM is a people's sense of belonging together as a nation. It also includes such feelings as loyalty to the nation, pride in its culture and history, and— in many cases—a desire for national independence.

Since the mid-1700's, nationalism has become an important force in international relations. Nationalistic feelings, particularly the desire of each country to govern itself, have helped change the map of Europe several times since the 1800's. Since the late 1940's, nationalism has also transformed Africa and Asia.

Nationalism is widespread today, but it once did not even exist. People have not always had a sense of nationhood. Early people felt they belonged to cities or tribes. During the Middle Ages, people were loyal to a number of groups and rulers. For example, a French citizen might have owed loyalty to the duke of Burgundy, the king of France, the Holy Roman emperor, and the pope.

The Rise of Nationalism occurred along with the development of a political unit called the *nation-state*. A *nation* is a group of people who share a common culture, history, or language and have a feeling of national unity. A *state* is an area of land whose people have an independent government. A nation-state exists if a nation and a state have the same boundaries.

Nation-states began to develop during the late Middle Ages. Travel and communication improved at that time. As a result, people became increasingly aware of the part of their country that lay outside their own community. Loyalty to local and religious leaders began to weaken, and allegiance to kings grew stronger. By the 1700's, England, France, Spain, and several other countries had become nation-states.

Other peoples developed a sense of nationhood by the early 1800's. But most of them had not become nation-states. Many persons believed that a national group had the right to form its own state. This belief, known as the *doctrine of national self-determination*, caused many nationalistic revolutions in Europe. For example, Greece won independence from Turkey in 1829, and Belgium became independent of The Netherlands in 1830.

Different Forms of Nationalism later developed in various parts of the world. In the United States, for example, the spirit of nationalism expressed itself in rapid westward expansion during the 1800's. Many Americans became convinced that their nation had a *manifest destiny*—that is, a clear mission to take over all North America.

In Western Europe, new feelings of nationalism united the Italians and then the Germans, both of whom were still divided into many states. Each of these peoples combined to form one country out of the states.

NATIONALIST CHINA

The unification of Italy was completed in 1870, and Germany became a nation-state in 1871.

In Eastern Europe, on the other hand, national groups sought to create smaller states out of the huge Austro-Hungarian, Ottoman, and Russian empires. These demands for national self-determination helped cause World War I (1914-1918). They also broke up the empires after the war (see WORLD WAR I [Nationalism]).

During the 1930's, two dictators—Adolf Hitler of Germany and Benito Mussolini of Italy—used nationalism in demanding extreme loyalty from their people. They promoted *integral nationalism*, the belief that a certain nationality was superior to all others. This idea also placed strict limits on who could claim that nationality. In support of integral nationalism, the Nazis killed millions of Jews and other people whom they considered inferior human beings. Germany and Italy also set out to conquer the world. Their actions helped bring on World War II (1939-1945).

After World War II, nationalism led many African and Asian colonies to demand self-government. India and Pakistan won independence from Great Britain in 1947. The next year, a nationalistic movement called *Zionism* resulted in the establishment of Israel (see ZIONISM).

By the 1970's, more than 80 other nations had become newly independent. Many of them lacked the long history of shared experiences that had produced nationalism in Europe. But their leaders encouraged nationalism to help develop national unity.

Effects of Nationalism can be both good and bad. Nationalism gives people a sense of belonging and pride, and a willingness to make sacrifices for their country. They also take a greater interest in their nation's achievements in such fields as literature and music.

But nationalism also produces rivalry and tension between nations. Desires for national glory and military conquest may lead to war. Extreme nationalism may result in racial hatred and in persecution of minority groups.   JOSEPH S. NYE, JR.

See also FASCISM (Extreme Nationalism); NATION; PATRIOTISM. For a *Reading and Study Guide*, see *Nationalism* in the RESEARCH GUIDE/INDEX, Volume 22.

NATIONALIST CHINA. See TAIWAN.

NATIONALITY. In law, nationality is a person's status as a member of a particular country. Usually, a person's citizenship is the same as his nationality. But the terms do not mean exactly the same thing. For example, before the Philippine Islands became independent, their people were U.S. nationals. They owed allegiance to the United States, but were not U.S. citizens.

Nationality is acquired at birth according to either of two principles. The first is the *jus sanguinis*, or *right of blood*, which gives to a child the nationality of one of his parents, usually the father. The second, called *jus soli*, or *right of the place of one's birth*, makes a person a national of the country in which he is born. Most countries use both principles. Every country has the right to determine who its nationals shall be.

In the British Commonwealth, the difference between nationality and citizenship is extremely important. The people of the Commonwealth and of all British possessions are known as British subjects. This means that they have British nationality. But their citizenship comes from the particular country to which they belong. Thus, a British subject may be a citizen of Canada, of New Zealand, or of the United Kingdom itself.

Nationality Groups. A second meaning of nationality has nothing at all to do with law. It refers to the fact that many people continue the habits, the customs, and even the language of their native land when they go to live elsewhere. Many groups of people in U.S. cities try to keep alive the customs and traditions of other countries. Some of these people were born outside the United States. But in some cases, every member of the group was born in the United States.   HERBERT W. BRIGGS

See also CITIZENSHIP; NATURALIZATION.

NATIONALIZATION is the control and ownership of an industry on a national scale by the government of a country. Industries most commonly nationalized include airlines, electric and gas utilities, mines, postal services, telephone and telegraph companies, and railroads.

In some countries, nationalization plays a vital role in a set of economic, political, and social beliefs called *socialism*. These countries nationalize certain industries in an attempt to provide better products or services for their citizens. Socialists say that nationalization ensures democratic control of the industries concerned. France and Great Britain have nationalized many industries for these purposes.

Other countries, especially some underdeveloped nations, have nationalized certain industries to remove them from foreign ownership. In the 1960's and 1970's, for example, some countries in the Middle East and elsewhere began to take over oil companies that had been owned chiefly by Americans or Europeans. These countries gained higher profits for themselves by removing the oil industry from foreign ownership.

Forms of Nationalization. There are several forms of nationalization, based on how the nationalized industry is managed. In the most common form, a *public corporation* is set up as an independent body by law. The government appoints a board of directors that manages the industry much as the board of directors of a private corporation would manage it, but without private shareholders to serve. In another form of nationalization, a government department has control of the nationalized industry. Such action gives the government close control and management of the industry. In a third form, the government buys part of the stock in an ordinary corporation, and private investors own the rest of the stock. This action gives the government some control but does not require a new organization to manage the corporation.

Advantages and Disadvantages. Nationalized industries have some advantages over private industries. For example, a nationalized industry can provide vital products or services to the public that would not be profitable for private industry to provide. The government can encourage a nationalized industry to invest and expand during an economic *recession* (slowdown). Nationalized industries can also develop weak parts of the national economy and help hold down prices during periods of inflation.

Supporters of nationalization say that—in certain industries—a nationalized corporation can provide more efficient service than private industries. Such industries include electric and gas utilities and telephone and telegraph companies. Supporters also say that government is too weak unless it has some control over vital industries.

Nationalization has some disadvantages. Many nationalized industries do not make a profit. As a result, the government uses money from taxes to *subsidize* (help pay for) them. Critics of nationalization charge that a lack of competition causes nationalized industries to become inefficient. They say government subsidies keep unprofitable industries alive even though the industries are no longer useful. Opponents also fear that too much power is concentrated in a government if it controls vital industries.   LEONARD TIVEY

See also GREAT BRITAIN (Government Ownership; The Welfare State); SOCIALISM.

NATIVE SLOTH. See KOALA.

NATIVISM. See LATIN-AMERICAN LITERATURE (Romanticism; After World War I).

NATIVITY. See JESUS CHRIST (Nativity); CHRISTMAS.

NATO. See NORTH ATLANTIC TREATY ORGANIZATION.

NATTA, GIULIO. See NOBEL PRIZES (table: Nobel Prizes for Chemistry—1963).

NATURAL BRIDGE. Not only man, but also nature, builds bridges, some of which are hundreds or thousands of years in the making. A natural bridge is often the result of water working its way slowly through loose soil or soft rock. If there is a harder layer of rock on top of the soil or soft rock, the harder rock will stay firm and form a bridge. A stream or small valley may be beneath the bridge. See also OKLAHOMA (picture); RAINBOW BRIDGE NATIONAL MONUMENT; VIRGINIA (picture).

NATURAL BRIDGES NATIONAL MONUMENT is in southeastern Utah. It includes three natural sandstone bridges, among the largest examples of their kind. They are called by their Hopi Indian names: *Sipapu, Owachomo,* and *Kachina.* The largest bridge, Sipapu, is 220 feet (67 meters) high and 56 feet (17 meters) thick at the top of the arch. The arch is 37 feet (11 meters) wide and it spans 268 feet (82 meters). Second in size is Kachina bridge, with a span of 186 feet (57 meters) and a thickness of 107 feet (33 meters) at its smallest part. It arches 205 feet (62 meters) above water. Owachomo, the smallest and oldest bridge, is only 10 feet (3 meters) thick in the center, but is 108 feet (33 meters) high and 194 feet (59 meters) long. Many prehistoric drawings appear on Kachina. The monument was established in 1908. For its area, see NATIONAL PARK SYSTEM (table: National Monuments).   C. LANGDON WHITE

NATURAL COMMUNITY. See FISH (Fish in the Balance of Nature); PLANT (Where Plants Live).

NATURAL GAS. See GAS.

NATURAL HISTORY. See NATURE STUDY.

NATURAL KEY is the key of C major in music. It has no sharps or flats and is played on the white keys of a piano keyboard, usually starting with the note of C. See also MUSIC (The Elements of Music).

NATURAL RESOURCES are those products and features of the earth that permit it to support life and satisfy man's needs. Land and water are natural resources. So are biological resources on the land and in the water, such as flowers, trees, birds, wild animals, and fish. Mineral resources include oil, coal, metals, stone, and sand. Other natural resources are air, sunshine, and climate. Natural resources are used for

American Forest Institute

Conservation Practices, such as the replanting and selective cutting of trees, help to preserve valuable natural resources.

producing (1) food; (2) fuel; and (3) raw materials for the production of finished goods.

This article discusses natural resources in general. For information on the natural resources of specific areas, see the *Natural Resources* section in each state and province article, and in various country articles.

Uses and Importance. Biological resources are the most important natural resources. All the food we eat comes from plants or animals. Since early days, man has used wood from trees for fuel and shelter. Biological resources, in turn, are dependent on other natural resources. Most plants and animals could not live without air, sunshine, soil, and water.

Mineral resources are less important in supporting life, but they are extremely important to modern living. Mineral fuels—including coal, oil, and natural gas—provide heat, light, and power. Minerals serve as raw materials for the production of finished goods, such as automobiles, clocks, dishes, and refrigerators.

The wealth of a nation depends to an important degree on its natural resources. Most wealthy, or *developed,* countries—including Canada, Russia, and the United States—are rich in natural resources. But some well-to-do nations, such as Denmark and Ireland, have few resources. Poor, or *underdeveloped,* countries generally have fewer resources, though some—like Peru and Zaire—have many natural resources.

Conservation and Development. Since modern civilization—even life itself—is dependent on natural resources, many persons have been concerned about whether there will always be enough. They have asked, for example, what will happen if all the world's petroleum, iron, or coal gets used up.

Scientists and economists believe that man can never use up all the mineral raw materials like iron, aluminum, sand, and fertilizer. There are sufficient quantities in the earth and the sea, and most of the materials can be used over and over. For example, scrap iron can be melted down and used again in steelmaking. However, men may have to explore farther and dig deeper to get what they need. Or they may have to substitute one material for another that has become too scarce. For example, aluminum may be used in place of copper for many purposes. While copper is scarce, deposits of bauxite and clay contain more aluminum than the world can ever use.

Mineral fuels are different and can all be used up. The earth contains enough mineral fuels to last only one or two centuries. When these supplies run out, people may depend more on nuclear energy to power autos and factories and to heat homes. Even today, uranium and other nuclear fuels generate electricity. Such fuels will last for many centuries. Sunlight is already used to run the instruments in space satellites, and may someday be used to provide abundant energy. See NUCLEAR ENERGY; SOLAR ENERGY.

Preserving the delicate balance of nature in biological resources appears to be the most difficult and important part of saving our natural resources. People have often upset this balance. For example, poor farming methods have ruined much fertile farmland and left it barren. Each year, millions of tons of fertile topsoil that could produce good crops are washed away by rains. Chemicals sprayed on crops and washed off by rain sometimes end up in rivers and streams. Some of these chemicals kill the fish in the streams. Some entire species of birds and animals have been killed off by hunters.

Fumes from automobiles and trucks and smoke from factories poison the air. This *air pollution* in many cities kills trees and endangers human health. As more cars and factories are built, the problem gets worse. To correct these conditions, people will have to make big changes in ways of traveling and in ways of generating heat and power. See AIR POLLUTION.

Even if natural resources are conserved and developed, the earth will be unable to provide enough food if the population increases too much. With much effort, the amount of land under cultivation could be doubled, and farms in many developing countries could produce three or four times as much as they now do. Scientists also believe people can get much more food from the sea. All this might increase the food supply to 5 or even 10 times what it now is. But at the present rate of increase, the world's population would double in 35 years. If this rate of increase continued, the population would be 7 times as large in 100 years, and 53 times as large in 200 years.   NEAL POTTER

Related Articles in WORLD BOOK include:

Air	Industry (Natural Resources)
Conservation	Mineral
Developing Country	Soil
Forest	Water
Forestry	Wildlife Conservation
Game	World (The Wealth of Nations)

NATURAL SELECTION is a process of nature which was first explained by the English naturalist Charles Darwin. He believed it to be an important factor in the origin of new groups of plants and animals.

There is not nearly enough food, space, shelter, and other necessities for all the offspring that living things can produce. Living things, therefore, constantly compete with each other to live. Darwin's theory points out that even animals of the same kind are a little different from each other. In their struggle for existence, some will be a little better suited to live and have young. Others will be a little more likely to die or fail to produce offspring. This process is always going on, so the species lose unfavorable variations and keep the favorable ones. Variations can arise by *mutations*. Mutations are random changes in *genes* caused by radiation and certain chemicals found in the surroundings (see GENE). After thousands of years, the surviving members may be greatly different from their ancestors. The phrase "survival of the fittest" is applied to this process of change by natural selection. J. HERBERT TAYLOR

See also DARWIN (Charles Robert); EVOLUTION.

NATURALISM, in literature, is the attempt to apply scientific theory and methods to imaginative writing. Naturalists concentrate on the physical world to the exclusion of the supernatural. Naturalism thrived in the late 1800's and early 1900's, and has been most important in the novel and in drama.

Theory of Naturalism. Naturalists have been the most uncompromising realists. They believe that knowledge is acquired through the senses, and that the function of the writer is to report accurately what he or she observes. The naturalist tries to be as objective as a laboratory scientist. In their theory of life, naturalists are more pessimistic than realists. The realist believes people can make moral choices, but the naturalist believes they cannot. Naturalists believe that everything a person does is determined by heredity, or environment, or both. They try to show that people are trapped by one or both of these great forces over which they have no control.

In picturing people as trapped, the naturalist usually deals with the more sordid aspects of life. Characters in naturalistic literature are driven by their most basic urges. They are often brutal and usually failures. Their language is often coarse, their view of life hopeless, and their mood depressing. Yet in the best naturalistic works, there is a tone of compassion and even admiration for those who struggle against overwhelming odds.

Naturalism in Fiction. The principles of naturalistic fiction were first stated by the French author Émile Zola in *The Experimental Novel* (1880). Zola argued that novelists should treat their material as scientists treat theirs. Before 1880, psychological and physiological studies such as Zola recommended had appeared in works by Honoré de Balzac, Jules and Edmond de Goncourt, Gustave Flaubert, and other French writers. Zola's books shocked English and American readers, but his theories and novels established naturalism as an important literary movement.

Naturalism never became popular in England, but it has been a major influence in the United States since the 1890's. Stephen Crane, Hamlin Garland, and Frank Norris were the first Americans consciously to adopt the style. Most critics, however, consider Theodore Dreiser the best American naturalist. His novel *An American Tragedy* (1925) is a moving account of a young man trapped by circumstance. Later American naturalistic novelists include Nelson Algren, James T. Farrell, and Norman Mailer.

Naturalism in Drama has the same goals as naturalism in fiction. A highly realistic setting provides a sense of environment overwhelming the characters. The staging, acting, and plots are realistic and simple. Everything focuses upon the hopeless, but often admirable, struggle of the characters against fate.

Zola also led the movement in drama with his adaptation of his novel *Thérèse Raquin* into a play in 1873. August Strindberg of Sweden and Gerhart Hauptmann of Germany rank among the best European naturalistic playwrights. Strindberg's *The Father* (1887) and *Miss Julie* (1888) are two violent studies of sex. *The Weavers* (1892) by Hauptmann, a grim portrait of a workers' revolt, set the style for German naturalism. Naturalism also appears in plays by Henrik Ibsen of Norway and Leo Tolstoy and Maxim Gorky of Russia.

In the United States, naturalism became most popular and important in the plays of Eugene O'Neill. Many of O'Neill's plays, especially the trilogy *Mourning Becomes Electra* (1931), have pathetic characters and depressing atmosphere. Other American naturalistic playwrights include Sidney Kingsley, Arthur Miller, Clifford Odets, Elmer Rice, and Tennessee Williams.

Naturalism today has declined in influence, but its methods and its view of life are responsible for much of the imaginative power in today's fiction and drama. Excessive though naturalism may have been in its hopelessness and brutality, modern literature reveals life more honestly because of it. John C. Gerber

Each person mentioned in this article has a separate biography in World Book.

NATURALIST. See Nature Study with its list of *Related Articles.*

NATURALIZATION is the legal process by which a person changes his citizenship from one country to another. Not all countries have the same naturalization laws. The laws of most countries provide that a naturalized citizen has no further obligations to the land of his birth. He also loses any political rights there. He takes an oath of allegiance pledging loyalty to his adopted country.

In many countries, when a man is naturalized, his wife and minor children automatically become citizens. Unmarried women of legal age become naturalized in the same way that men do. Most countries that have compulsory military service do not allow men to become citizens of other countries until they have served their required time in the armed forces of the country of their birth. Occasionally a man leaves without performing this service. If he ever returns, he may still be forced to serve in the armed forces.

A naturalized citizen of the United States has the same rights as any other citizen, except that he cannot be elected President or Vice-President. He is entitled to full protection by the United States if he travels abroad. But, if he returns to the land of his birth, and if that country has not honored his withdrawal of allegiance, the United States might have difficulty in protecting him.

Naturalization in the United States

The procedure for naturalization in the United States involves three steps. These are: (1) a petition for naturalization, (2) an investigation and interview, and (3) final hearings in court. The law no longer requires a person to "take out first papers," or file a *declaration of intention* to become an American citizen. Some aliens still file such a declaration, however, because they need it to practice a profession under the laws of some states.

Petition for Naturalization. The Immigration and Nationality Act of 1952 requires an alien to apply for a petition for naturalization. This form may be obtained from any office of the Immigration and Naturalization Service, a division of the Department of Justice, or from any court authorized to naturalize aliens.

Before applying, an alien must be at least 18 years old and must have been lawfully admitted to live permanently in the United States. He must have lived in the United States for five years and for the last six months in the state where he seeks to be naturalized. In some cases, he need only have lived three years in the United States. He must be of good moral character and "attached to the principles of the Constitution." The law states that an alien is not of good moral character if he is a drunkard, has committed adultery, has more than one wife, makes his living by gambling, has lied to the Immigration and Naturalization Service, has been in jail more than 180 days for any reason during his five years in the United States, or is a convicted murderer.

Investigation and Interview. Officers of the Immigration and Naturalization Service investigate and interview the alien. He must appear with two citizen-witnesses who vouch for his qualifications. He must show that he can read, write, and speak simple English, if he is physically able to do so. Aliens who were more than 50 years old on Dec. 24, 1952, and had lived in the United States for at least 20 years, are exempted from this literacy test. The alien must also show that he knows something of the history and the form of government of the United States. The Service then makes its recommendation to the naturalization court.

Final Hearings are held in public sessions of the court after the petition has been filed. If the Immigration and Naturalization Service denies an alien's petition, he may request an examination by the judge. If the court denies his petition, he can appeal to the next higher court.

If the court approves the petition, the alien takes an oath renouncing all foreign titles and allegiance to any other country. He pledges to support and defend the Constitution, and to bear arms on behalf of the United States, unless he can prove that he is a conscientious objector whose beliefs forbid him to bear arms. The court clerk then gives him a certificate of naturalization, and the alien becomes a citizen.

Naturalization in Other Countries

Naturalization procedure differs in every country. In France, Germany, Great Britain, Italy, and Spain, a department in the executive branch of the government supervises naturalization. In Belgium, the legislature grants citizenship. Each Swiss canton (state) has the authority to naturalize an alien.

In Canada, the minister of manpower and immigration issues certificates of citizenship through county and district courts. The Citizenship Act of 1946 recognizes two types of citizens: *natural-born,* and *other than natural-born,* or naturalized. Naturalization of aliens consists of three steps: (1) the petition for citizenship, (2) the hearing in court, and (3) taking the oath of allegiance in a second court hearing.

NATURALIZATION

An alien generally must meet the following requirements for Canadian citizenship. He must be at least 21 years old, and have lived in Canada for a year before applying. He must have been lawfully admitted to live permanently in the country, and such residence must have been established for five years. He must be of good character, have an adequate knowledge of English or French, know the responsibilities of citizenship, and intend to live permanently in Canada.

The alien files his petition at the nearest court. The court posts the petition publicly for three months. At the court hearing, the alien must show evidence that he meets citizenship requirements. If the court approves, it sends the certified copy of the petition to the minister of manpower and immigration. The minister decides whether to issue a certificate of citizenship. If he does, the alien appears in court and takes the oath of allegiance. The court clerk endorses the certificate.

British Dominions and Colonies may naturalize aliens, but these persons do not then become citizens of other British dominions or colonies. All countries, however, recognize a person as a British subject if he is a naturalized citizen of the United Kingdom and its colonies under the British Nationality Act of 1948. This law provides that a citizen of any colony or of any member of the Commonwealth is a British subject, or a Commonwealth citizen.

Denaturalization

A naturalized citizen of the United States may be *denaturalized* or *expatriated*. The government may bring suit to *denaturalize* a person, or cancel his certificate of naturalization, based on his conduct and other circumstances *before* he was granted citizenship. The grounds for such action include the charges that he (1) concealed a fact bearing on his petition, (2) did not intend to live permanently in the United States, (3) took his oath with mental reservation, or (4) refused to testify before a congressional committee about his alleged subversive activities.

A naturalized citizen may also be *expatriated*, or be forced to give up his citizenship, because of acts he committed *after* he became a citizen. Such acts include becoming a citizen of another country, serving in the government or armed forces of another country, voting in another country's elections, formally renouncing United States citizenship, deserting the United States armed forces during time of war, avoiding military service, or committing treason. The Immigration and Nationality Act of 1952 provided that a naturalized citizen would lose his citizenship by living continuously in the country of his origin for more than three years. But the Supreme Court of the United States ruled in 1964 that this provision was unconstitutional.

The term *expatriation* also means voluntarily transferring allegiance from one country to another. See CITIZENSHIP (Expatriation).

History

Before the 1800's, a person always remained a citizen of his native land, no matter where he lived. According to an old saying in English common law, "Once an Englishman, always an Englishman." One of the causes of the War of 1812 was that the British arrested seamen who held American citizenship, but who had been born in Great Britain. In 1870, Britain finally recognized the right of an individual to *expatriate* himself, or leave the country and become the citizen of another country. Most governments have naturalization laws and recognize that their citizens can change citizenship.

United States naturalization laws caused other countries to liberalize their naturalization laws. The relaxed spirit of American laws spread first to the British dominions (in the late 1800's), then to South America, and later to Europe. Some European countries have even less strict laws regarding naturalized citizens than does the United States. In France, for example, a naturalized citizen can be elected president.

Nations usually make treaties concerning the rights of a naturalized citizen who returns to his native land. For example, a treaty between the United States and Italy provides that Italy may not claim naturalized Americans as citizens if they return to Italy during time of peace, but may do so in wartime.

In the United States. Congress passed its first naturalization law in 1790. This law gave certain courts the right to naturalize aliens. An alien could apply for citizenship after being in the country for two years. In 1795, the period of residence became five years, with one of these years spent in the state where the application was filed. An alien had to declare his intention to become a citizen at least three years before applying for citizenship. In 1906, Congress set up a Bureau of Immigration and Naturalization.

Originally, only "free white persons" could be naturalized. Negroes became eligible for naturalization in 1870. American Indians qualified in 1940. A law passed in 1943 allowed Chinese persons to be naturalized. Persons from India and the Philippines became eligible for U.S. citizenship in 1946. The Immigration and Nationality Act of 1952 removed all racial bars to naturalization in the United States. An average of 125,000 persons are naturalized yearly.

Status of Women. Before 1922, a woman's citizenship usually changed with that of her husband. A law passed that year provided that an alien woman does not automatically become a United States citizen through marriage to a citizen. She too must petition for naturalization. The alien wife or husband of a citizen may be naturalized after only three years' residence.

The Immigration and Nationality Act of 1952 combined in a single act all laws affecting naturalization and citizenship.   ROBERT RIENOW

Related Articles in WORLD BOOK include:

Alien	Immigration and	Immigration and
Citizenship	Emigration	Naturalization
Deportation		Service

NATURE STUDY means watching and learning about the things in nature. A student of nature does not merely learn the names of a few birds and flowers and rocks. He observes what is new every time he goes outdoors. Then he finds out why these things happen and when they may occur again.

The nature student learns about every new bird and flower he sees. He knows when certain trees will bud and burst into bloom. He finds out why the white butterflies hover over the cabbages in summer. The nature student watches long lines of ants and learns

Leo Choplin, Black Star

Nature Study includes identifying wild animals and learning their habits. These boys are studying the tracks of a marsh bird in a wildlife refuge.

plants, and grasses. But nature study really includes any of the things or doings of the natural world about us.

Studying Nature

Activities of Nature Students are followed all year long, both outdoors and in the home. Most students learn the names of unfamiliar plants and animals. But they usually go further than just learning names. They want to be sure that they will know a new bird the next time they see it. The student learns the size, shape, and color of the bird and some of its habits. Sometimes he learns its song or call. He finds out what family, or group of similar birds, it belongs to. Perhaps the observer will watch the new bird for a long time. He will want to know what it eats, where it can be found most often, where it nests, how it cares for its young, and whether it remains all winter or goes south in the fall.

Another common activity of the nature student is collecting. The collection may be an aquarium of fresh-water animals and plants gathered from nearby streams and ponds. It may be a collection of rocks, minerals, leaves, wild flowers, ferns, or shells, or a wild-flower garden. All collectors are careful not to destroy the forms of life from which they take their specimens.

Other common activities of nature students are field trips and excursions, nature hikes, gardening, and caring for pets. Many students make wildlife photographs or take part in wildlife-protection projects. These projects include such things as feeding birds in winter, providing field cover for birds and animals, winter protection, and setting up watering places for animals.

The Student's Notebook is an important part of his hobby. He has many questions to ask about the things in nature. To find answers to his questions, he makes careful observations of the plants and animals that interest him. He repeats the observations to find out if he always sees the same thing, or if the animal always behaves the same way under the same conditions.

People cannot always remember later exactly what they have seen. Thus, it is desirable for nature observers to make notes on what they see. The record is often

where they are going and why they are always so busy.

Almost always we associate nature study with the outdoors. Nature lovers like to be out in the fields, in the forest, on the mountains, or along the running streams. Nature lovers in the cities go to the parks or gardens if they cannot get into the open country.

Most persons think nature study is concerned only with living things—birds, wild animals, insects, fishes, frogs, snakes, trees, wild flowers, weeds, shrubs, water

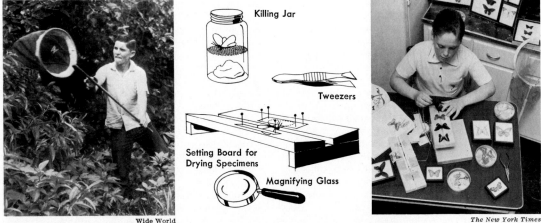

Killing Jar

Tweezers

Setting Board for Drying Specimens

Magnifying Glass

Wide World

The New York Times

A Butterfly Collector's Equipment includes a net and a killing jar containing poison-soaked cotton. He also needs tweezers, a magnifying glass, and rustproof pins for mounting the butterflies.

How to Display Insect and Plant Specimens

Insect and plant collecting are two popular hobbies of nature students. Insect specimens are often mounted on pins and displayed in special boxes. Plants are dried and mounted on paper.

WORLD BOOK diagrams by Marion Pahl

Dried Insects may be displayed in a cigar box with a glass top. A *fumigant box* is a small container that is filled with insect repellent and placed in the display box to protect the specimens. Each specimen should be properly labeled. Special insect pins, which are thinner and firmer than regular ones, are used for pinning. The top of the pin should stick up slightly from the insect's back. Tiny insects are glued onto the tips of small, stiff paper points.

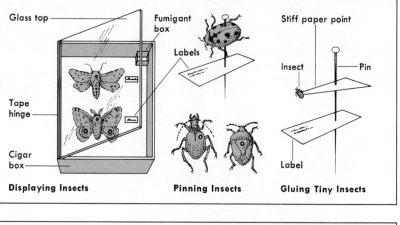

Displaying Insects   Pinning Insects   Gluing Tiny Insects

Dried Flowers are taped onto special mounting paper and labeled. Seeds of the plant are placed in an envelope. A drying press for flowers can be made with two plywood boards and leather straps. The plant specimens are placed between sheets of newspaper and blotting paper. A stack of specimens is then placed between the two boards, strapped together tightly, and left to dry.

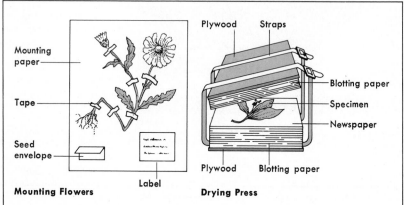

Mounting Flowers   Drying Press

more complete if it contains sketches made in the field.

Nature notebooks help in comparing observations of other seasons with those made at this season. For example, someone may say, "Robins are back early this year." A bird record kept for several years would show whether or not robins were early in their return.

Equipment for Nature Hobbies will grow as the student becomes more interested in nature. There are, of course, the nature books and pictures. In time the student will want field glasses for observing birds and animals, and a camera for photographs. He may want various magnifiers, and perhaps even a microscope for examining tiny objects. There are also collecting jars, nets, labels, and mounts of all kinds.

Perhaps the best way to start a new nature hobby is to find someone who has made a beginning. There are always other *naturalists* (nature students) with whom to exchange experiences and possibly specimens.

Information about Nature can be obtained from many different sources. The nature student can use them to compare his findings with those of others. He can talk with other workers, read nature books written by specialists, or visit the collections in the great natural-history museums. There are many useful articles about nature in THE WORLD BOOK ENCYCLOPEDIA. The student can use them to check his field observations against those of specialists in science and nature study.

Youth organizations such as the Boy Scouts, Camp Fire Girls, and Girl Scouts all have nature-study programs. The handbooks of these organizations are often useful. Many city parks have interesting trees and flowers, planted and labeled especially for nature students. The great state and national parks offer opportunities for study. Many of these parks have marked nature trails and nature directors who work with visitors.

Some cities have zoos and botanical gardens. Some have great natural-history museums with large collections of specimens. Often these specimens are arranged in natural groupings as they are found in nature. Examples of such museums are the National Museum of Natural History in Washington, D.C., the American Museum of Natural History in New York City, and the Field Museum of Natural History in Chicago.

Most states now have state conservation departments to help preserve and build up the wildlife of the state. These departments publish useful bulletins.

There are a great many books on nature-study subjects. Some are stories about animal life and are to be read for the story appeal. Others are stories and records of explorers who have found interesting plants and animals in out-of-the-way places. Besides these, there are books to help in learning animals, insects, trees, birds, wild flowers, rocks, and stars. Often these are beautifully illustrated in colors. Some are expensive sets for fine libraries. Others are inexpensive pocket and field guides that beginning students can buy for their own use. Every public library has many books about nature.

Nature Study Is a Science. At one time many schools and colleges had classes in nature study. But some science teachers objected. They said that people who are interested in nature study are carried away by their love of the beauties of nature. They said that much of the nature study was not good science. And they accused the nature students of careless work and inaccurate observations. For this reason, nature study is not so popular in schools as it once was. Schools now have classes in elementary science instead. But nature students can get much help from these science classes.

Much of our scientific knowledge has been gathered through careful and repeated observations of students of nature. Famous persons have been both naturalists and scientists. The nature student can read about Roy Chapman Andrews, Liberty Hyde Bailey, William Beebe, Frank M. Chapman, Anna Botsford Comstock, Charles Darwin, Raymond L. Ditmars, Henri Fabre, David Fairchild, William T. Hornaday, and John Muir.

For people who like to be outdoors and who are interested in animals, plants, rocks, or stars, nature study offers worthy and enjoyable hobbies. These can be carried on throughout life and will always provide something new. New material can be found everywhere.

Suggestions for Things to Do

1. Write to the Audubon Society nearest to you and ask for a price list of the pictures of birds. Buy a set of bird cards for the birds that are most often found in your region. Learn as many of these birds as you can in a season.

2. With a group of friends, find a path through a neighboring woods that has interesting natural features. If possible, find a path that reaches a stream, pond, or lake. Be sure to ask permission of the owner to use this path. Mark it as a nature trail with names of trees, shrubs, and wild flowers. Show spots where birds, squirrels, and other animals are usually seen. Perhaps you can get help with this project from your science teacher, a Scout leader, or a Camp Fire guardian.

3. If you have a camera, make a collection of photographs of 12 or 15 trees in winter and summer. Mount the photos and label each tree with its correct name.

4. Make three wren houses. Be sure to make the openings just one inch across so that wrens can get in and sparrows cannot. Put these houses up in suitable places about the lawn at home. If you can, also put up a bird bath where the birds can drink and splash about.

5. Set up a winter bird-feeding station outside a south or an east window. Insect-eating birds, such as woodpeckers, chickadees, or jays, will feed on bits of suet tied to the feeder or to the limb of a tree. Seed-eating birds, such as cardinals or juncos, feed on many kinds of small seeds, sunflower seeds, or cracked grain.

6. Make a tree-flowering calendar that shows the dates when trees in your area bloom in the spring. Mark the dates when fruit trees bloom. You may also record when these trees have seeds or fruit. RALPH K. WATKINS

Related Articles in WORLD BOOK include:

AMERICAN NATURALISTS

Agassiz (family)	Andrews, Roy C.	Audubon, John J.

Beard, Daniel C.	Burroughs, John	Seton, Ernest
Beebe, William	Muir, John	Thompson
Bessey, Charles E.	Osborn (Henry F.)	Vogt, William

BRITISH NATURALISTS

Bewick, Thomas	Murray, Sir John
Darwin (Charles R.)	Sloane, Sir Hans
Hudson, William H.	Wallace, Alfred R.

OTHER NATURALISTS

Asbjørnsen, Peter C.	Fabre, Jean H. C.
Cohn, Ferdinand J.	Lamarck, Chevalier de
Cuvier, Baron	Linnaeus, Carolus
De Vries, Hugo	

SOME NATURE STUDY SUBJECTS

Animal	Earth	Insect	Seed
Astronomy	Fish	Lake	Star
Balance of	Flower	Leaf	Tree
Nature	Forest	Mountain	Vegetable
Bird	Forestry	Ocean	Volcano
Botany	Fruit	Plant	Water
Butterfly	Game	River	Waterfall
Conservation	Gardening	Rock	Weather
Constellation	Geology	Season	Zoology
Desert	Hobby		

NATURE STUDY ORGANIZATIONS

Academy of Natural Sciences of Philadelphia	Camp Fire Girls
	Girl Scouts
Audubon Society, National	Izaak Walton League
Boy Scouts	of America

OTHER RELATED ARTICLES

Aquarium	National Forest	Planetarium
Arbor Day	National Park System	Telescope
Botanical Garden	Observatory	Terrarium
Museum	Park	Zoo

NATURE WORSHIP is a term used by some scholars for the religion of peoples who consider the objects and forces of nature sacred. In times past, people have regarded mountains, springs, rivers, fields, and even the earth itself as holy. Objects in nature were often seen as gods in the mythology of Greece and Rome. The sun, for instance, was a god who drove a flaming chariot across the sky. The moon was believed to be a goddess called Selene. Hindus worshiped the winds, and Persians the rainbow. The Maypole dance is possibly a survival of the worship of the oak tree by the ancient Britons, Vikings, and Slavs. WILSON D. WALLIS

See also ANIMISM; MAY DAY; MOTHER; PANTHEISM.

NAURU, *NAH roo*, is a small island country in the central Pacific Ocean. It has an area of 8 square miles (21 square kilometers) and a population of about 7,000. Nauru is the third smallest country in the world. Only Vatican City and Monaco are smaller. Nauru is rich in *phosphates*—valuable chemical compounds used in making fertilizers. Phosphate exports earn about $11 million a year for the government of Nauru. The government has used some of the income to build homes, schools, and hospitals. The government has also saved much of the income to help support the Nauruan people after all the phosphates have been mined.

Government. Nauru is a republic. An 18-member Parliament makes the country's laws. The members of Parliament are elected by the people to three-year terms. All Nauruans who are 20 years old or older may vote. The Parliament elects a president to a three-year term, and the president selects a Cabinet. The presi-

Nauru

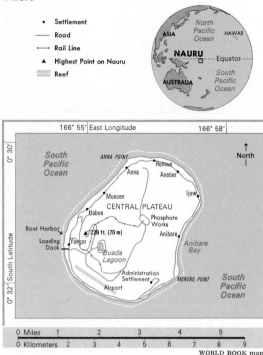

- • Settlement
- — Road
- ← Rail Line
- ▲ Highest Point on Nauru
- ▨ Reef

166° 55' East Longitude   166° 58'

0° 30'

South Pacific Ocean

ANNA POINT
Anna   Ronave
Anabar

Mueoen

CENTRAL PLATEAU
Uaboe
Phosphate Works
▲ 229 ft. (70 m)

Ijuw

Boat Harbor
Loading Dock   Yangor
Buada Lagoon

Anibare

Anibare Bay

Administration Settlement
Airport

MENENG POINT   South Pacific Ocean

South Latitude   0° 32'

0 Miles	1	2	3	4	5			
0 Kilometers	2	3	4	5	6	7	8	9

WORLD BOOK map

dent and the Cabinet carry out the operations of the government.

Land. Nauru, an oval-shaped coral island, lies 33 miles (53 kilometers) south of the equator. Most of the island is a plateau, 200 feet (61 meters) high, which contains deposits of phosphates. Near the center of the plateau is a lagoon surrounded by fertile land. Another belt of fertile land extends around the coast. Most of the people live along the coast. In the past, the people raised their own food. Now, they import most of their food and other products they need. Nauru has a tropical climate that is cooled by trade winds. Temperatures range from 76° F. (24° C) to 93° F. (34° C). About 80 inches (200 centimeters) of rain falls in Nauru yearly.

People. About half of Nauru's population are Nauruans—people of mixed Polynesian, Micronesian, and Melanesian ancestry. They are Christians. Most of them speak both the Nauruan language and English. Most Nauruan men work in the phosphate industry. The rest of Nauru's people are from the Gilbert Islands,

Tuvalu, Hong Kong, and Australia. They come for limited periods of time to help mine the phosphates.

The government provides Nauruans with modern homes at low rents, and 2 government hospitals and 11 clinics give them free medical care. The law requires Nauruan children between the ages of 6 and 17 to attend school. Nauru has two elementary schools, a high school, a Roman Catholic mission school, and a teacher training center. The government pays the expenses of students who go to college in other countries.

Economy. Phosphates are Nauru's only important resource and the country's only export. The government is trying to build a shipping industry. It also encourages such local industries as fishing and canoe building. Imported products include food, machinery, automobiles, furniture, shoes, and medicine.

History. John Fearn, an English explorer, was the first European to visit Nauru. He came in 1798. In 1888, Germany took over the island and administered it until 1914 when Australia took control. After World War I, Australia began to administer the island under a League of Nations mandate held also by Great Britain and New Zealand.

Japan seized Nauru during World War II. In 1945, Australian forces retook the island. In 1947, the United Nations provided for Australian control of the island under a trusteeship held also by Great Britain and New Zealand. In 1964, Nauru began to work for independence and control of the phosphate industry. The U.N. granted Nauru independence in 1968. In 1970, the Nauruan government gained control of the phosphate industry.   PETER PIRIE

NAUSEA, *NAW she uh,* or *NAW see uh,* is a disagreeable sensation best described by the familiar phrase "sick to my stomach." The word is strongly associated with seasickness. In fact, the word comes from Greek and Latin roots which mean *pertaining to the sea.* It is closely related in its origin to the words *nautical* and *navigate.*

In nausea the stomach muscle contracts gently in a direction that is the opposite of its normal contraction. A stronger contraction in this direction causes vomiting and the food is brought up into the mouth.

There are many causes of nausea, both physical and mental. Mental causes include revolting sights, disgusting odors, and sudden fright. Physical causes include severe pain arising anywhere in the body, blockage or obstruction of the digestive tract, and the stimulation of our balancing organs, the semicircular canals in the ears. Nausea often accompanies pregnancy, especially during the first three months.

The sensation of nausea may be produced by stimulating certain nerves which have their centers in the part of the brain called the *medulla.* It may come from the digestive tract or other parts of the body, from higher centers in the brain, or as a direct result of outside agents such as the drugs morphine and digitalis.

The tendency to nausea varies widely among different persons. Some can endure the tossing of a ship on the roughest sea without discomfort. Others are nauseated merely by the gentle swaying motion of a swing or hammock.

A tendency to nausea is sometimes a symptom of disease. Anyone who suffers from chronic attacks should consult a physician.   E. CLINTON TEXTER, JR.

See also CHLORPROMAZINE.

FACTS IN BRIEF

Capital: None.

Official Languages: English, Nauruan.

Area: 8 sq. mi. (21 km²). *Coastline*—12 mi. (19 km).

Population: *Estimated 1978 Population*—7,000; density, 862 persons per sq. mi. (333 persons per km²). *1966 Census*—6,057. *Estimated 1983 Population*—7,000.

Chief Product: Phosphates.

Flag: A horizontal gold stripe crosses a field of royal blue. Below the stripe is a white 12-pointed star. See FLAG (color picture: Flags of Asia and the Pacific).

Money: Australian dollar. See MONEY (table: Values).

58

NAUSICAA, *naw SIK ay uh,* is a character in the famous Greek epic the *Odyssey.* She was the daughter of Alcinous, king of the Phaeacians, and Arete. Nausicaa found Ulysses after he was shipwrecked on the shore of Scheria and conducted him to the court of her father.

NAUTICAL ALMANAC. See NAVIGATION (Celestial Navigation).

NAUTICAL MILE. See KNOT; MILE.

NAUTICAL TERMS. See SHIP.

NAUTILUS. See SUBMARINE (Early Submarines; Nuclear Submarines).

NAUTILUS, *NAW tuh lus,* is a sea animal whose soft body is partly covered with a coiled shell. The nautilus belongs to the same class of animals as the squid and octopus. A nautilus contains about 30 chambers which are lined with a rainbow-colored substance called *mother-of-pearl* or *nacre.* Because of this substance, the animal is often called a *pearly nautilus.* The nautilus lives at depths of 20 to 1,000 feet (6 to 300 meters) in the South Pacific and Indian oceans. It eats lobsters and crabs. Only 5 species of nautilus are living today. At least 2,000 fossil forms are known.

American Museum of Natural History

The Chambered Nautilus Has a Spiral-Shaped Shell. The animal adds a new, larger chamber to its shell each time it outgrows its old chamber. The shell shown above has been cut open lengthwise to show the many chambers of increasing size.

The body of a full-grown nautilus is about the size of a man's fist. Its cone-shaped head is surrounded by about 90 short *tentacles* (feelers). As the animal grows, its shell develops in the form of a spiral. The nautilus adds a new chamber to its shell each time it outgrows its old one. Each new chamber is closed at the rear, so the animal always lives in the outermost chamber of its shell. The closed chambers behind the animal are filled with a gas composed mainly of nitrogen. The *siphuncle,* a coiled, blood-filled tube that is enclosed in a limy covering, extends through all the animal's chambers.

Scientific Classification. The nautilus is in the phylum *Mollusca.* It belongs to the nautilus family, *Nautiliidae.* The pearly nautilus is genus *Nautilus,* species *N. pompilius.*   R. TUCKER ABBOTT

See also ARGONAUT; SHELL (Octopuses and Squids; pictures: Nautilus Shell).

NAUVOO. See ILLINOIS (Places to Visit); MORMONS (Mormons in the Middle West); SMITH, JOSEPH.

NAVAJO COMMUNITY COLLEGE. See ARIZONA (Schools).

NAVAJO INDIANS, *NAV uh hoh,* also spelled *Navaho,* are the largest Indian tribe in the United States. The Navajo reservation, which covers 14 million acres (6 million hectares), ranks as the nation's biggest reservation. It includes parts of Arizona, New Mexico, and Utah. The growth of industry on the reservation promises to make the Navajo one of the country's wealthiest tribes.

About 100,000 of the 140,000 Navajo in the United States live on the reservation. Some of the people live in traditional tribal houses called *hogans,* which are made of earth and logs (see HOGAN). Many Navajo practice the tribal religion. Large numbers of the tribe are farmers or sheep ranchers, but others are engineers, miners, teachers, or technicians. Skilled Navajo craftworkers weave wool blankets and make turquoise jewelry. Businesses owned by the Navajo, including coal mines, an electronics firm, and a lumber mill, earn millions of dollars yearly. Navajo Community College, the first college owned and operated by Indians, is in Tsaile, Ariz., near Lukachukai, on the reservation.

About A.D. 1000, the ancestors of the Navajo migrated to the southwestern United States from what is now Alaska and Canada. Their Pueblo neighbors taught them to raise crops. During religious rituals, Navajo medicine men created symbolic sand paintings to help heal the sick (see SAND PAINTING).

During the 1600's, the Navajo began to raise sheep. An increasing number of white settlers established ranches on the Navajo lands, and the Indians fought to drive the ranchers away. In 1864, U.S. Army troops led by Kit Carson destroyed the farms and homes of the Navajo. The soldiers forced about 8,000 Indians to march more than 300 miles (480 kilometers) to Fort Sumner, N. Mex. The Navajo call this march the "Long Walk." Thousands of Indians died during the march and their imprisonment at Fort Sumner. In 1868, the Navajo agreed to settle on the reservation. RUTH W. ROESSEL

See also INDIAN, AMERICAN (pictures); MANUELITO; ARMER, LAURA ADAMS.

NAVAJO NATIONAL MONUMENT is in northern Arizona. It contains three of the largest and most elaborate of known cliff dwellings. The Navajo Indian Reservation surrounds the monument. The monument was established in 1909. For its area, see NATIONAL PARK SYSTEM (table: National Monuments).

NAVAL ACADEMY, UNITED STATES. See UNITED STATES NAVAL ACADEMY.

NAVAL ARCHITECT. See SHIP (Designing and Constructing a Ship).

NAVAL ATTACHÉ. See ATTACHÉ.

NAVAL OBSERVATORY. Scientists at the Naval Observatory in Washington, D.C., study the stars, magnetism, and other facts and events in nature. They conduct studies to make time measurements more accurate throughout the world. The Naval Observatory also supplies official time signals to regulate clocks throughout the United States and its possessions. The Admiral's House, the official residence of the Vice-President of the

United States, stands on the observatory grounds. The Naval Observatory was established by the federal government in 1842. It is under the jurisdiction of the chief of naval operations. PAYSON S. WILD

See also NEWCOMB, SIMON.

NAVAL RESERVE. See NAVY, UNITED STATES (Regulars and Reserves).

NAVAL SHIPYARD is a waterside area where naval vessels are built or where logistic support is provided for the operating fleet. It is responsible for repairing damaged vessels and for overhauling ships after long periods at sea. It also alters or converts ships, and installs new types of gear and equipment. JOHN A. OUDINE

See also CHARLESTON NAVAL BASE; MARE ISLAND NAVAL SHIPYARD; NORFOLK NAVAL BASE; PHILADELPHIA NAVAL BASE; PORTSMOUTH NAVAL SHIPYARD.

NAVAL STORES. In the days of wooden sailing ships, the term *naval stores* referred to tar and pitch. These two materials were essential for shipbuilding. Today, the term includes the rosin, turpentine, pitch, and tar products from pine and other resinous trees.

NAVAL WAR COLLEGE, in Newport, R.I., is the highest educational institution of the United States Navy. The college prepares officers for higher command by teaching them the fundamentals of warfare, international relations, and interservice operations. The Navy Electronic Warfare Simulator, which imitates actual combat conditions, aids in the study of combat methods.

The staff and students of the Naval War College represent all the armed services. Since 1956, the college has offered a command course for officers from other countries. Commodore Stephen B. Luce, the college's first president, founded the Naval War College in 1884. The college is also the headquarters for the Institute of Naval Studies. The institute's functions include long-range studies on how to use changes in science and technology. JOHN A. OUDINE

NAVARINO, BATTLE OF. See GREECE (History).

NAVARRE, *nuh VAHR*, was once an independent kingdom which included a small part of southern France. It now forms the modern Spanish province of Navarre and the western part of the French department of Basses-Pyrénées. It covers 4,056 square miles (10,505 square kilometers). Its largest city is Pamplona.

Navarre is famous for its orchards and vineyards. Important products include flax, olive oil, hemp, livestock, lumber, fish, and small game. WALTER C. LANGSAM

NAVE. See BASILICA; CATHEDRAL; ARCHITECTURE (Architectural Terms; Early Christian and Byzantine).

NAVEL. See UMBILICAL CORD.

NAVEL ORANGE. See ORANGE.

NAVIGATION, *NAV ih GAY shun*, is the means of finding your way from one place to another and knowing where you are along the way. To find your way to a friend's house you follow such instructions as, "Go eight blocks north and six blocks east. The house is next to a grocery store. The address is 631 Stewart Street." *You are navigating* when you count the blocks you travel in each direction, look for the grocery store, and check the address of your friend's house. See DIRECTION.

Usually, however, when we speak of navigation we refer to guiding ships or aircraft from one place to

U.S. Coast Guard (WORLD BOOK photo)

A Navigator Plots a Course on a map before beginning a journey. The above photograph shows the navigator of a United States Coast Guard cutter marking a route to Greenland.

another. The word *navigate* comes from two Latin words, *navis*, meaning *ship*, and *agere*, meaning *to direct*.

Methods of Navigation

Principles of Navigation. Navigators on ships and aircraft must work mathematical problems to find where they are in relation to landmarks and stars. To solve these problems, the navigator uses navigational aids and instruments to get information about (1) *time*, (2) *direction*, (3) *distance*, (4) *speed*, and (5) *position*. With this information, the navigator figures out (1) what course to steer to arrive at the destination, and (2) what speed to use to arrive there at a certain time. The navigator uses algebra, geometry, and trigonometry in solving these problems.

There are four general methods of navigation. These are (1) *dead reckoning*, (2) *piloting*, (3) *celestial navigation*, and (4) *electronic navigation*. The four methods generally are used in combination with each other.

Dead Reckoning is a means of figuring, or *reckoning*, courses and distances from a known position by marking, or *plotting*, the ship's course and speed on a chart. The navigator figures out the distance traveled by multiplying the speed by the time traveled. Dead reckoning is the basis of all navigation and is used whether or not other methods are available or are used.

Piloting, called *contact flying* by pilots, is a means of navigating by watching for landmarks. Ship navigators use piloting, when close to land, by watching for lighthouses, buoys, and other landmarks. Air navigators check their position when contact flying by using such landmarks as rivers, bridges, and highways.

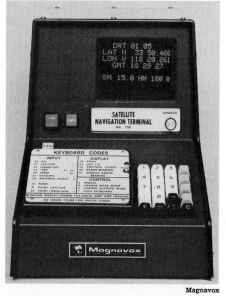

Magnavox

A Satellite Navigation System calculates the position of a ship in relation to the position of a satellite orbiting overhead. The navigator feeds such information as the ship's speed and destination into a computer by means of a keyboard on a terminal, *left*. The ship's latitude and longitude then appear on the display screen of the terminal, *above*.

Celestial Navigation is a means of checking a position by observing the sun, moon, planets, and stars. The ship navigator carries a book called the *Nautical Almanac*. This book gives the exact position of each heavenly body for exact times and dates. It tells the position of the heavenly body if it were to drop straight to earth at any instant. By observing the direction, or *bearing*, of a star, and by measuring its angle above the horizon, the navigator can figure out how far the ship is from the earthly position of the star. One observation gives a *circle of position*, but the circle is so large it is considered a straight line. This line is called a *line of position*. By observing several heavenly bodies, the navigator obtains several of these lines of position. The spot where the lines cross on the chart marks a *celestial fix*, or the position of the craft. The time used by a navigator for celestial navigation is *Greenwich Mean Time* (GMT), or the time it is in Greenwich, England. See GREENWICH OBSERVATORY, ROYAL.

Electronic Navigation makes use of such electronic devices as voice and code radio, radio direction finders, loran, shoran, radar, electronic depth finders, and communications satellites. In satellite navigation, a computer calculates the position of the craft in relation to the position of a satellite orbiting over the horizon.

A Trip with a Ship Navigator

Leaving Port. Before the ship gets under way for the voyage, the navigator makes sure that all the necessary navigation charts, books, and instruments are aboard. Then the navigator stands by on the bridge with the captain while a local pilot familiar with the harbor steers, or *cons*, the ship out into deep water. When the pilot turns the ship over to the captain and gets off to return to port, the navigator determines the ship's position and the exact time. This position, or *fix*, is known as the *point of departure*. It might be the time when the ship passes close to a buoy. The navigator marks a small circle on the chart and notes the time.

Near Land the navigator is a busy but unhurried person. The navigator draws on a large-scale Mercator chart the course the ship is to follow (see MAP [Cylindrical Projections]). The navigator observes lighthouses and other landmarks to get their bearing from the ship and plots each bearing on the chart. Each bearing line is a line of position. When the navigator obtains two lines of position, the spot where they cross gives the exact location of the ship. The navigator plots the position on the chart and notes its latitude and longitude in the *navigator's notebook*. The navigator also keeps a close check on the depth of the water by taking soundings with an instrument called a *fathometer*.

At Sea. As the ship steams away from land, the navigator does not need to check the ship's position so frequently. The ship's course and speed are plotted on the chart by dead reckoning. During the day the navigator regularly observes the sun and makes lines of position from these observations.

On clear nights, just after sunset and just before sunrise, the navigator figures out the ship's position by observing the stars. The navigator looks up at the sky and finds a familiar star, such as Betelgeuse in the constellation Orion. The navigator sights at the star through a *sextant* to measure its angle above the

How a Navigator Uses the Stars to Find the Position of a Ship

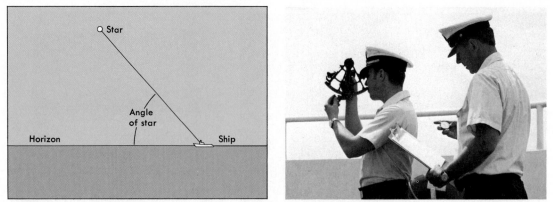

U.S. Coast Guard (WORLD BOOK photo)

The Angle of a Star above the horizon is measured by the navigator with an instrument called a *sextant*. An assistant records the angle and the time it was measured. This information is used to determine the star's *earthly position*, the point on the earth directly below the star.

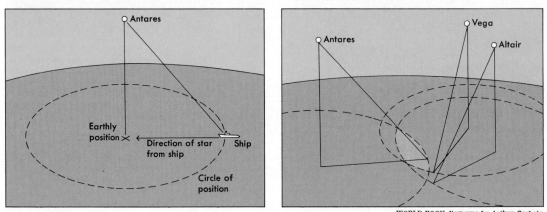

WORLD BOOK diagrams by Arthur Grebetz

The Earthly Position of a Star, such as Antares, *left,* is determined by means of special tables. The earthly position is the center of an imaginary circle called the *circle of position.* To find the ship's location, the navigator determines circles of position for two other stars, such as Vega and Altair, *right.* The ship is somewhere in the area where the three circles overlap.

U.S. Coast Guard (WORLD BOOK photo)

The Position of the Ship is marked on a navigational chart by drawing the overlapping portions of the three circles of position. The circles are so large that only a tiny part of each can be drawn. Therefore, the navigator draws three straight lines, each of which represents a portion of a circle. The three lines form a triangle. The ship's position is taken to be the center of the triangle.

horizon. Meanwhile, one of his assistants measures the direction of Betelgeuse from the ship. A second assistant stands by with a stop watch. When the navigator calls out "Mark!" the second assistant writes down the time, the angle of Betelgeuse above the horizon, and its bearing. The navigator makes such observations on several stars. Then he and his assistants go into the lighted charthouse and figure out the ship's position.

If the sky is cloudy or foggy, the navigator must depend on electronic devices to tell him his position. If he is within a few hundred miles or kilometers of land, he may use the radio direction finder to give him lines of position on radio beacons. If he is farther out to sea, he may use a loran receiving set to obtain lines of position on loran transmitting stations.

The good navigator also must be a weather forecaster. He must have training in meteorology and be able to read weather instruments.

Approaching Land. The first land sighted after a voyage is called a *landfall*. The navigator checks the landfall on his chart to make sure his navigation has been accurate. If the weather is stormy or foggy, the navigator depends on radar in approaching his destination. A *plan position indicator*, or *p.p.i.*, on the radar continuously provides the navigator with a circular map-picture of the sea and shoreline, with the ship at the center of the map. Ships and buoys also are shown on the radar screen, making it possible to pass safely through heavy traffic in a fog. From the radar operator, the navigator receives accurate distances and bearings on landmarks. The navigator also keeps a close check on the depth of the water by using a fathometer. At the entrance to the harbor, a local pilot usually comes aboard and takes charge of conning the ship into port.

Air Navigation

The air navigator's work is much the same as that of the ship navigator. However, he has less time in which to do it because aircraft travel much faster than ships. See AIRPLANE (Flight Navigation).

The air navigator is much more concerned with wind than the ship navigator is. This is because wind can change the course and speed of an aircraft more easily. In celestial navigation, the air navigator must use an artificial horizon in measuring the angles of heavenly bodies above the earth. He uses an *Air Almanac* to find the positions of heavenly bodies. The air navigator also has many special electronic instruments and aids to help him. Air navigation is sometimes called *avigation*.

Space Navigation

Scientists who are looking ahead to the building of spaceships for travel from the earth to other planets have worked out the problem of navigating in space, or *astrogation*. The navigator, or *astrogator*, of a space ship would have to have a special almanac with tables giving the positions of planets in relation to the sun at any time. The astrogator would measure the angle between the sun and each of at least two planets, then compute his distance from the sun by simple geometry. See SPACE TRAVEL (Aiming at the Moon).

Navigation Aids and Instruments

Aids. Most aids to navigation, such as buoys and lighthouses, are provided and maintained by the fed-

U.S. Air Force

An Airplane Navigator plots a course on charts that show such land features as airports, cities, and highways.

eral government. This is because safe sea and air commerce are vital to our way of life. The most important aid to navigation is an accurate *chart* which covers the area of the trip. Charts are marked in latitude and longitude and provide means of identifying any point on land or in coastal and inland waters. For details on many important aids to navigation, see separate articles listed in the *Related Articles* at the end of this article. Other navigation aids include:

Fog Signals, such as bells, whistles, and sirens, which can be identified easily in fog or darkness at a particular spot on the navigator's chart.

Light Lists, books which contain complete descriptions of each navigation aid maintained by the government, so that navigators can tell one lighthouse from another.

Nautical Almanac, a publication which contains tables of information about the position of stars.

Notices to Mariners, publications which regularly inform navigators of changes in aids to navigation.

Range Lights, two lights located some distance apart and one over the other, to mark the center line of a harbor channel.

Tide and Current Tables, publications which tell the navigator when to expect tides and currents in each locality.

Instruments. These are devices for determining the depth of water, the exact time of day, the direction the ship is traveling, the distance traveled, the ship's speed, and its position. The most important navigation instruments are the *compass*, which tells direction, and the *chronometer*, which tells time. A navigator also uses simple instruments to plot positions on a chart, such as a *geometry compass*, *dividers*, *parallel rules*, a *straightedge*, and a *protractor*. Other instruments used in navigation include:

Azimuth Circle, or *Bearing Circle*, a device like a gunsight mounted on a movable ring on a stand called a *pelorus* which contains a compass. By sighting through the azimuth circle, the navigator can determine the bearing of an object from his craft.

Computer, a device which the navigator uses to work out mathematical problems of time, speed, and distance. It may be a circular slide rule or a complicated electronic machine.

Plotter, a device combining a protractor with a ruler. It is used in plotting positions on a chart.

Plotting Board, or *Maneuvering Board*, a graph with concentric circles, used in solving triangle problems.

Star Finder, a map of the stars used by the navigator to identify stars used in celestial navigation.

History of Navigation

Early Navigators. For thousands of years man has sailed the seas. Early seafaring men such as the Phoeni-

Press Syndicate

Astrolabe was used by navigators before the invention of the sextant to determine the angle of stars above the horizon.

--------- IMPORTANT DATES IN NAVIGATION ---------

1100?-1200? Magnetic compass used by Chinese and Mediterranean sailors.

1519-1522 First circumnavigation of the earth by Ferdinand Magellan's fleet.

1569? Mercator chart invented by Gerhardus Mercator.

1730 Reflecting sextant invented, independently, by John Hadley in England and Thomas Godfrey in America.

1733 Bubble sextant, or artificial horizon sextant, invented by John Hadley. It made long-range air navigation possible 200 years later.

1735 First accurate chronometer made by John Harrison in England.

1767 First nautical almanac published in England by Nevil Maskelyne, an astronomer.

1767 Buoys first used in navigable waters of America, in the Delaware River.

1802 *American Practical Navigator* published by Nathaniel Bowditch.

1807 Coast Survey Bureau authorized by the United States Congress.

1837 Line of Position, or the Sumner Line, first discovered and used by Captain Thomas H. Sumner of Massachusetts.

1842 Ocean currents charted by Lieutenant Matthew F. Maury of the United States Navy. Maury helped found the U.S. Naval Observatory and the Hydrographic Office.

1881 First lighted buoy put in service outside New York Harbor. It burned oil gas.

1885 First bell buoy put in service in the United States.

1896 Ship-to-shore radio signals sent by Guglielmo Marconi.

1906 Gyroscopic compass invented by Hermann Anschütz-Kämpfe in Germany.

1910 Plane-to-ground radio messages sent over New York City by J. A. D. McCurdy.

1922 Radar effects first noted by A. Hoyt Taylor at Washington, D.C. This led to the development of radar in World War II.

1928 Second-setting watch for navigators invented by P. V. H. Weems in the United States.

1933 First air almanac prepared by P. V. H. Weems.

1940 Principle of loran discovered by Alfred L. Loomis. This led to the building of the first four loran transmitting stations by the U.S. government in 1942.

1953 Inertial guidance system developed. It navigates automatically without using outside signals, and can be used on ships, airplanes, and missiles.

1967 The U.S. Navy launched the first satellite navigation system for commercial use.

cians, the Carthaginians, and the Greeks moved chiefly from point to point along the coasts.

Scientific navigation began to develop in the 1100's. Crude magnetic compasses came into use. Prince Henry of Portugal (1394-1460) established an observatory and school in navigation at Sagres, Portugal, and was known as Henry the Navigator. He encouraged Portuguese sailors to sail to remote seas.

Early explorers were aided by the invention of the *astrolabe*. The astrolabe was a graduated circle with sights down which the navigator could roughly measure the angle between the horizon and heavenly bodies.

In the 1700's, the invention of the accurate chronometer and the sextant, which replaced the astrolabe, made it possible for navigators to know exactly where they were, even when far from land.

Modern Navigation. The invention of radio and its use on ships and aircraft at the beginning of the 1900's marked the start of electronic navigation (see RADIO [Navigation]). The development of electronic depth finders made it possible for ships to sail in shallow waters with less danger of going aground. The development of radar during World War II made navigation safer at night and in fog. *Loran* (**LO**ng **RA**nge **N**avigation) was invented in 1940. This system uses fixed radio station signals to determine the exact position of the navigator. After World War II, automatic navigation devices were developed for guided missiles (see GUIDED MISSILE). Other devices were developed that automatically computed celestial fixes and measured distances.

The U.S. Coast Guard maintains over 36,000 marine-navigation aids along more than 40,000 miles (64,000 kilometers) of seacoasts and navigable waters of the United States. The Federal Aviation Administration provides air-navigation aids, such as light beacons and markers on the tops of buildings, for over 70,000 miles (110,000 kilometers) of airways. P. V. H. WEEMS

Related Articles in WORLD BOOK include:

NAVIGATION INSTRUMENTS

Aircraft Instruments	Gyropilot	Protractor
Airplane	Gyroscope	Quadrant
(Flying an Airplane)	Gyrostabilizer	Radar
Astrolabe	Gyrosyn Compass	Radio
Chronometer	Inclinometer	Sextant
Compass	Lead, Sounding	Shoran
Direction Finder	Log	Sonar
Fathometer	Loran	Surveyor's
Gyrocompass	Plumb Line	Compass

FAMOUS NAVIGATORS

Bowditch, Nathaniel	Magellan, Ferdinand
Columbus, Christopher	Maury, Matthew Fontaine
Da Gama, Vasco	Mercator, Gerhardus
Dias, Bartolomeu	Phoenicia
Exploration and Discovery	Vikings
Henry the Navigator	

NAVIGATION AIDS

Airplane (Flight Navigation)	Coast Guard,
Airport (Air Traffic Control)	United States
Almanac	Inertial Guidance
Aviation (Aviation Agencies	Lighthouse
and Organizations)	Map
Beacon	Maritime Law
Buoy	National Ocean Survey
Chart	Ship

OTHER RELATED ARTICLES

Astronomy	Deneb
Dead Reckoning	Direction
Degree	Great-Circle Route

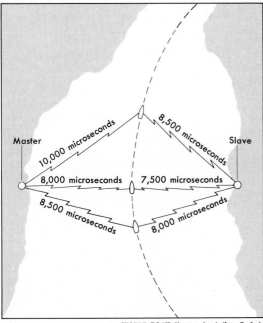

WORLD BOOK diagram by Arthur Grebetz

Loran, or long range navigation, uses two stations—a master and a slave—that continually send out radio signals. Receiver equipment on the ship or airplane measures the time intervals between signals to determine the position of the craft.

Greenwich Ob- servatory, Royal	Longitude	Tide
	Meridian	Time
Knot	North Star	Trade Wind
Latitude	Sailing	

Outline

I. Methods of Navigation
  A. Principles of Navigation
  B. Dead Reckoning
  C. Piloting
  D. Celestial Navigation
  E. Electronic Navigation

II. A Trip with a Ship Navigator
  A. Leaving Port   C. At Sea
  B. Near Land   D. Approaching Land

III. Air Navigation

IV. Space Navigation

V. Navigation Aids and Instruments
  A. Aids   B. Instruments

VI. History of Navigation

Questions

What information is provided by navigational instruments?
What is dead reckoning? Piloting?
How is celestial navigation done?
What is loran?
What is an astrolabe?
How does a sextant help the navigator?

NAVIGATION ACT. Several laws passed in the 1600's by the English Parliament were called the Navigation Acts. The purpose of the laws was to protect English trade. In 1645 a law forbade the importation of whale oil into England in vessels other than English, or in ships which were not manned by English sailors.

The act known officially as the First Navigation Act was passed by Parliament in 1651. This act was aimed against the English colonies and the Dutch, who were enjoying a greater part of the carrying trade between the West Indies and Europe. The act provided that no products from any foreign country might be shipped into England in any but English-built ships manned by English crews. The First Navigation Act was not strictly enforced. The Dutch continued to carry on their trade with the colonies. As a result the English Parliament passed other trade laws in 1660, 1663, and 1672. These acts repeated the former warnings. The act of 1660 required that all the tobacco from the colonies must be brought to England. The act of 1663 (Second Navigation Act) declared that almost all goods imported into the colonies must be landed in England first. In 1672, an act was passed requiring that goods had to be shipped to England before they could pass from one of the American colonies to another.

Before 1761, 29 acts had been passed in restraint of colonial trade. These included one law which prohibited the importation of molasses and sugar. America suffered little from these laws, because of the wholesale smuggling practiced by the colonists. Several provisions of the acts were favorable to American industry, especially shipbuilding, because they encouraged American shipping. But the restrictions on commerce were vigorously opposed by the Americans. This opposition was one of the principal causes of the Revolutionary War. The British Parliament, in 1849, repealed all the Navigation laws. BASIL D. HENNING

NAVIGATION SATELLITE. See SPACE TRAVEL (Artificial Satellites).

Naval Ships provide protection against enemy sea attacks. Ships of member nations of the North Atlantic Treaty Organization (NATO) conduct joint naval operations in the Atlantic Ocean, *left*.

NAVY

NAVY consists of a nation's combat fleet and supporting ships, their personnel, and land bases. All large navies also have an air force. Some navies, such as those of Great Britain, Russia, and the United States, have combat infantry units called *marines*.

Most maritime nations have a navy, but navies differ greatly in the size and fighting strength of their fleets. The smallest navies consist only of light warships, such as patrol boats and torpedo craft. These vessels are limited mainly to coastal operations. Larger navies also include such major warships as aircraft carriers, cruisers, destroyers, frigates, and submarines. These ships can operate far out at sea, and so they greatly extend a navy's range of operations. Support ships, which are called *auxiliary ships*, provide warships with fuel and supplies, and various other services.

Russia and the United States have the world's largest navies. Each includes hundreds of major warships and auxiliary ships. Each also has nuclear-powered submarines, nuclear weapons, and long-range guided missiles. Both navies operate on ocean waters throughout the world.

At one time, the most powerful nations were the ones with the strongest navies. The development of aircraft and missiles during the 1900's has changed the role of navies. Today, nations can rely on long-range bombers and guided missiles as well as on warships to extend their military influence overseas. Nevertheless, navies still have tremendous military and political value. International law allows ships—including warships—to sail to within 12 miles (19 kilometers) of a foreign coast. Thus, a group of warships can serve as a temporary military base. A large, well-equipped force can remain at sea up to a month without taking on fuel or supplies. More importantly, it can carry out its mission independently of foreign land bases.

The Missions of Navies

In wartime, nations use their navies chiefly to establish and maintain control of the sea and to attack or invade enemy coastal areas. Navies with nuclear weapons and long-range missiles would use them to provide a nuclear striking force in a nuclear war.

Control of the Sea. Nations seek control of the sea in wartime to ensure safe passage for their own ships and to deny passage to enemy ships. Most major warships perform this mission. For example, cruisers, destroyers, frigates, and submarines escort friendly merchant vessels, attack enemy ships, and defend offshore installations. Carrier-based aircraft may also carry out any of these assignments.

Coastal Attack and Invasion. Naval forces sometimes attack enemy coastal defenses. Cruisers and destroyers may sail within firing range of onshore targets and bombard them with heavy artillery. Carrier-based bombers can strike at targets farther inland. Navies use special *amphibious ships* to launch invasions from the sea. Most amphibious ships transport troops and supplies. These ships use helicopters, landing craft, and amphibious tractors to carry assault forces ashore. Cruisers, destroyers, and carrier-based aircraft provide support for amphibious landings.

Nuclear Attack and Defense. A submarine armed with long-range *ballistic missiles* provides a powerful striking force. The word *ballistic* refers to the long, arching path of the missiles in flight. A ballistic missile fired from a submarine can strike targets 4,000 miles (6,400 kilometers) or more away. Armed with a nuclear warhead, it could wipe out an entire city. A submarine that fires ballistic missiles is called a *ballistic missile submarine*. Some ballistic missile submarines are powered by diesel engines, but most are nuclear propelled. Nuclear submarines are the most useful type because they can remain on continuous patrol for long periods without coming to the surface.

Five nations—China, France, Great Britain, Russia, and the United States—each have one or more bal-

Norman Polmar, the contributor of this article, is the author of Ships and Aircraft of the U.S. Fleet *and the former editor of the U.S. sections of* Jane's Fighting Ships.

listic missile submarines. In 1977, Russia had by far the most—78. The United States had 41, and France and Great Britain each had 4. China had 1. The Chinese submarine and 22 of the Russian ones are diesel powered. All the rest are nuclear propelled.

Ballistic missile submarines have another important function. Military experts believe that these submarines could survive a surprise nuclear attack and launch a nuclear counterattack. Therefore, nations may avoid starting a nuclear war because of their fear of such a counterattack.

Other Missions. In peacetime, powerful nations sometimes send warships to guard their interests in politically troubled areas. Such shows of naval strength have helped prevent war in some cases. In 1958, for example, the presence of the U.S. Sixth Fleet in the Formosa Strait helped avoid a serious clash between Chinese Communist and Chinese Nationalist forces. A nation may also send warships to evacuate its citizens from areas of political or military conflict.

The World's Major Navies

The Five Largest Navies are, in order of size, those of Russia, the United States, Great Britain, France, and China. A navy's size may not reflect its fighting strength, however. For example, a large aircraft carrier can provide as much striking power as several cruisers, destroyers, or submarines. In addition, advanced weapons systems can give even a small navy superior striking power for a few days in a small geographical area.

The Russian Navy has about 335 submarines, 250 other major warships, and several hundred light combat vessels. The Russian naval air force, or *air arm*, has more than 1,200 aircraft and ranks second in size only to that of the United States. Unlike the U.S. naval air force, however, the Russian force operates almost entirely from land bases. It includes a large number of bombers armed with short-range missiles. The Russians have only one aircraft carrier. It carries helicopters and VTOL (*V*ertical *T*ake-*O*ff and *L*anding) planes. Missile-armed submarines and missile-firing bombers provide the navy's main striking power.

The United States Navy has about 120 submarines, 200 other major warships, and 45 light combat vessels. The Navy's air arm includes about 7,000 fixed-wing planes and helicopters. The U.S. Navy depends on ballistic missile submarines and naval aircraft for its main striking power. But the U.S. planes, unlike the Russian ones, operate from aircraft carriers as well as from land bases. The United States fleet has 13 large fixed-wing aircraft carriers, of which 3 are nuclear powered. Each aircraft carrier has from 85 to 95 aircraft and up to 6,000 personnel. The Navy's force of approximately

65 amphibious warships includes several helicopter carriers.

The British Navy, called the *Royal Navy*, has declined sharply in size since the 1950's. It has about 30 submarines, 75 other major warships, and a few light combat craft. The Royal Navy operates chiefly in the North Atlantic Ocean and depends on its four ballistic missile submarines for its strategic striking power. The navy's air arm has about 150 planes.

The French Navy has about 30 submarines, 55 other major warships, and a small number of light combat craft. Its air arm consists of over 300 planes. These ships and planes make up the navy's main striking force. The French fleet operates chiefly in the Atlantic Ocean and the Mediterranean Sea.

The Chinese Navy. Western naval experts know little about China's navy. It probably has about 45 submarines, 15 other major warships, and several hundred light combat vessels. Unlike other large navies, the Chinese Navy does not operate far from home. It has an air arm of about 450 aircraft, most of which are fighter planes assigned to coastal defense duties.

Other Major Navies include those of Canada, Greece, India, Italy, Japan, Turkey, and West Germany. These navies each have several major warships and a variety of light combat craft, such as minesweepers, missile boats, patrol boats, and torpedo craft. Each also has an air arm. The fleets chiefly patrol their own coastal waters, but they can operate in force some distance from home if necessary.

Members of the North Atlantic Treaty Organization (NATO) have treaty obligations that help determine their naval policies. For example, the Canadian Navy is pledged to help reinforce NATO forces in Western Europe in the event of war. Most of the fleet is therefore based on the Atlantic coast of Canada.

The History of Navies

Ancient Navies. The first warships were long, narrow wooden vessels called *galleys*. They were powered chiefly by oarsmen, but most galleys also had sails. In battle, a galley tried to ram an opponent or slice off the opponent's oars with its prow.

Most of the ancient Mediterranean civilizations used galleys to guard their seacoasts and trade routes. The Egyptians probably used them as early as 3000 B.C., but the Greeks and Romans made galleys highly effective weapons of war.

In 483 B.C., the Greek city-state of Athens began to build a large fleet of galleys to defend itself against invaders from Persia. The Athenians became the leading naval power in the Aegean Sea after defeating the Per-

STRENGTH OF MAJOR NAVIES
(Includes only warships in active service)

	Personnel	Carriers	Cruisers	Destroyers	Frigates	Submarines Conventional	Submarines Nuclear
China	172,000	0	0	8	10	45	1
France	68,315	2	1	21	30	24	4
Great Britain	76,200	2	2	11	60	19	13
Russia	500,000	1	32	100	110	195	140
United States	531,801	20	28	100	65	6	115

FAMOUS SEA BATTLES

480 B.C.—Salamis. Themistocles' 360 Greek ships routed a Persian fleet of 1,200 vessels under Xerxes. Persia lost naval command in the Aegean Sea and withdrew from Greece. See SALAMIS.

31 B.C.—Actium. Octavian (later Emperor Augustus) and Agrippa led a 400-ship Roman fleet that destroyed an Egyptian naval force of equal size under Mark Antony and Cleopatra off the coast of Greece. The victory ended a rivalry for the leadership of Rome and stopped Egyptian influence in Roman affairs.

1571—Lepanto. A fleet of 300 ships from Venice, Spain, and the Papal States, under Don John of Austria, defeated the 273-ship Turkish fleet under Ali Pasha. This was the last great battle of oar-driven ships. The battle, fought near Greece, marked a turning point of Muslim power in Europe.

1588—Spanish Armada. In a battle in the English Channel, Lord Howard's 197 warships smashed Spain's 130-ship "Invincible Armada" under the Duke of Medina Sidonia. The loss was a severe blow to the political prestige of Spain, the world's leading power at the time. See ARMADA.

1781—Chesapeake Bay. A French fleet of 24 warships under Comte de Grasse forced a British naval force of 19 ships led by Thomas Graves to withdraw from Chesapeake Bay. Neither side won the battle itself. But the fight prevented the British from reinforcing Lord Cornwallis and led to their surrender at Yorktown, ending the Revolutionary War in America.

1805—Trafalgar. Napoleon's dreams of invading England were shattered when Lord Nelson's 27-ship British fleet defeated a force of 33 French and Spanish warships under Pierre de Villeneuve off the coast of southern Spain. The battle ended a 100-year struggle for domination of the seas. See TRAFALGAR.

1862—Hampton Roads. During the Civil War in the United States, the North's *Monitor* fought the South's *Merrimack* (then called the *Virginia*) in the channel of Hampton Roads in Chesapeake Bay. This battle, though inconclusive, was the first between iron-armored ships and one of the first between ships powered solely by steam. See MONITOR AND MERRIMACK.

1905—Tsushima. Japan climaxed the Russo-Japanese War with its 106-ship fleet under Heihachiro Togo. The Japanese fleet, which included 57 torpedo boats, overwhelmed the Russian Baltic fleet of 29 vessels under Zinovy Rozhdestvensky in the Korean Straits. Japan thus began its rise as a great naval power.

1916—Jutland. The 151-ship British Grand Fleet under John Jellicoe repulsed the German High Sea Fleet of 103 ships under Reinhard Scheer in the North Sea. Although Britain lost more ships, the battle confirmed British command of the seas in World War I and forced Germany to adopt submarine warfare. See JUTLAND, BATTLE OF.

1942—Coral Sea. From May 4 to May 8, U.S. and Japanese carrier forces fought the first all-air naval battle. The opposing warships, which were almost evenly matched, did not fire a shot at each other. Each side lost one aircraft carrier, and the battle was inconclusive. But the Japanese assault on New Guinea was halted.

1942—Midway. From June 4 to June 6, U.S. carrier forces under Raymond A. Spruance and Frank J. Fletcher fought a much larger Japanese force under Isoroku Yamamoto. Four Japanese carriers and one U.S. carrier were sunk. The decisive U.S. victory marked the end of Japanese expansion in World War II. See MIDWAY ISLAND.

1944—Leyte Gulf. A U.S. force of 169 warships and a Japanese force of 64 ships fought a series of engagements off the Philippines. These clashes, known collectively as the Battle for Leyte Gulf, eliminated Japanese naval power and marked the end of the battleship as a major naval weapon.

1967—Port Said. Guided missiles fired by Egyptian missile boats sank the Israeli destroyer *Elath* off Port Said on the Egyptian coast. This battle was the first in which a warship was sunk by ship-to-ship missiles.

Famous Sea Battles

Actium (31 B.C.)—A 400-ship Roman fleet crushed an Egyptian force of equal size off the coast of Greece. The victory ended Egyptian influence on the Roman Empire.

Trafalgar (1805)—A 27-ship British fleet ended Napoleon's dreams of invading England by destroying a force of 33 French and Spanish warships off the coast of southern Spain.

Spanish Armada (1588)—Lord Howard's fleet defeated the "Invincible Armada" in the English Channel. Howard's victory ended Spain's plans to invade England.

sian fleet off the island of Salamis in 480 B.C. The Battle of Salamis was the first naval battle of which historians have a complete record. The Athenian navy included hundreds of *triremes* (galleys with three tiers of oars), each rowed by up to 200 oarsmen.

In 31 B.C., the fleets of two rival Roman leaders, Mark Antony and Octavian, fought a famous battle off Actium, a peninsula in western Greece. Antony was allied with Cleopatra, the queen of Egypt, who gave him command of the Egyptian fleet. Octavian's victory in the Battle of Actium enabled him to take control of Rome as Emperor Augustus. Rome then became the supreme power in the Mediterranean. For the next 400 years, Roman rulers considered the Mediterranean *mare nostrum* (our sea).

Navies in the Middle Ages. A new naval power—the Vikings—arose in Europe during the Middle Ages. The Vikings were bold Scandinavians who frequently went to sea in search of adventure and treasure. Viking galleys raided coastal and river settlements throughout western Europe from the A.D. 700's to the late 1000's. In the late 800's, the English king Alfred the Great built a great fleet of warships to defend his country against Viking raiders.

During the 1100's, European shipbuilders began to construct warships with deep hulls. Unlike the long, low galleys, deep-hulled ships could easily travel on the high seas. Sails became the chief means of propulsion. Oars in galleys were used when the wind failed, or to maneuver in battle. Most navies of the Middle Ages followed a set pattern in battle. Warships arranged themselves side by side. As they advanced toward the enemy, machines called *catapults* hurled rocks or flaming chemical mixtures. Ships then maneuvered to ram, and the crews tried to board the enemy vessels. Cannons were first used on warships during the 1300's but did not come into wide use until the 1500's.

Venice reigned as the major sea power in the Mediterranean during the late Middle Ages. By 1400, it had a fleet of more than 3,000 galleys. The Ottoman Turks were the chief naval rivals of the Venetians.

The Beginning of Modern Navies. Venice allied itself with the Papal States and Spain to prevent the Turks from overrunning the Mediterranean area. In 1571, the rivals fought a historic sea battle off the Turkish base of Lepanto in western Greece. Venice and its allies destroyed most of the Turkish fleet. The Battle of Lepanto was the last great naval fight between oar-driven galleys.

Spain also began to compete with England for control of the seas. During the mid-1500's, both nations had started to build large sailing vessels called *galleons* as the basic ships of their navies. A few Spanish galleons took part in the Battle of Lepanto.

In 1588, the English and Spanish fleets battled in the English Channel. The English galleons were easier to maneuver than the Spanish ones, and they also had better cannons. The Spanish fleet scattered, and many of its ships were lost in storms at sea. England's victory in this battle, known as the Battle of the Spanish Armada, marked the start of its rise as the world's leading sea power.

The Netherlands competed with England for control of the seas during the 1600's, and the two countries fought several naval wars. The first one, which lasted from 1652 to 1654, featured important changes in naval tactics. By the mid-1600's, combat fleets had become extremely large and difficult to manage. Naval commanders began to issue detailed instructions in order to coordinate the movements of their ships during a battle. They put the most powerful ships at the front of their fleets and kept the smaller warships near the rear. Bat-

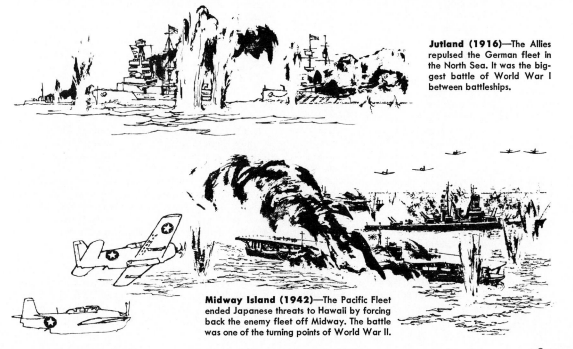

Jutland (1916)—The Allies repulsed the German fleet in the North Sea. It was the biggest battle of World War I between battleships.

Midway Island (1942)—The Pacific Fleet ended Japanese threats to Hawaii by forcing back the enemy fleet off Midway. The battle was one of the turning points of World War II.

tleships eventually became the backbone of the front-line formation.

During the 1700's, France became England's chief naval rival. In 1805, the British defeated the French off Cape Trafalgar, on Spain's Atlantic coast. After the Battle of Trafalgar, no nation could compete with Great Britain on the seas.

Engineering Advances. In 1814, the American inventor Robert Fulton built the first steam warship. Steamships could cruise faster than sailing ships, but steam warships faced a new problem. They needed fuel, and so they had to depend on land bases to supply coal and wood for refueling. Navies that ranged far from their home ports had to establish supply bases overseas.

Improvements in ship guns and armor had a tremendous effect on naval warfare. During the 1820's, inventors developed naval guns that fired explosive shells rather than solid cannon balls. In 1853, during the Crimean War, Russian warships fired the first explosive shells used in battle. The shells tore huge holes in the wooden vessels of the opposing Turkish fleet. Shipbuilders then began to construct warships with heavy iron armor over their wooden hulls. Soon, naval guns became so large and had so much recoil that even a large ship could carry only a few cannons. Rotating gun turrets were developed so that a large cannon could be aimed from either side of a ship.

The use of improved naval guns gave warships greater firing range and accuracy. Warships fought each other from a distance, with no more boarding and hand-to-hand combat in sea battles. As ship guns grew larger, heavier and heavier armor became necessary.

In 1862, during the Civil War in the United States, the North's *Monitor* battled the South's *Merrimack* (then called the *Virginia*). Neither ship was sunk in this battle in the channel of Hampton Roads in Chesapeake Bay. But the Battle of Hampton Roads became famous as the first duel between iron-armored ships. It also was one of the first battles between ships powered solely by steam. Most earlier steam warships were actually sailing ships that had auxiliary steam engines. See MONITOR AND MERRIMACK.

In 1906, the British Navy introduced the *Dreadnought* class of battleships. These ships mounted heavier guns than any previous warships and also traveled much faster than earlier battleships. The *Dreadnoughts* had a speed of 21 knots (nautical miles per hour). The next class of British battleships were even more heavily armed. These ships strengthened Britain's control of the seas. During the early 1900's, Germany ranked just behind Great Britain in naval power, followed closely by the United States. Heavily armored battleships, equipped with the largest guns ever made, formed the core of the fleets.

Navies in the Two World Wars. A new weapon, the submarine, brought sweeping changes to naval warfare during World War I. Soon after the war began in 1914, Germany started to use submarines to attack Allied shipping. In 1916, the British and German fleets fought the Battle of Jutland, the greatest naval battle of the war, off the coast of Denmark. The British suffered the heaviest losses but kept control of the sea (see WORLD WAR I [The Battle of Jutland]). World War I eliminated Germany as a major naval power, but the Germans rebuilt their fleet during the 1930's. The United States and Japan began to rival Britain in naval strength.

After World War II began in 1939, German submarines prowled the seas as they had during World War I. The Allies fought submarines with such new weapons as radar, sonar, fast-sinking depth charges, and rocket projectiles. The airplane, however, proved to be superior to all the other weapons that were used in the war.

On Dec. 7, 1941, Japanese bombers took off from six aircraft carriers and attacked the United States fleet anchored at Pearl Harbor in Hawaii. The surprise attack nearly wiped out the U.S. Pacific fleet. The United States quickly made adjustments, and aircraft carriers became the backbone of the Allied fleets. The U.S. Navy organized *carrier task forces*—that is, fleets assembled around carriers and assigned to specific tasks. Each carrier force had from 1 to 16 aircraft carriers surrounded by a defensive circle of cruisers and destroyers. Some carrier forces also included fast battleships.

The Battle of the Coral Sea in May 1942 was the first naval battle in which the opposing warships did not fire a single shot at each other. Carrier-based planes of the U.S. and Japanese task forces did all the actual fighting. The Battle for Leyte Gulf, in 1944, was the greatest naval battle of all time in terms of the tonnage involved. The opposing fleets weighed a total of more than 2 million long tons (2.03 million metric tons). This battle eliminated Japanese naval power from the war.

The Birth of Nuclear-Age Navies. In August 1945, U.S. warplanes dropped atomic bombs on the Japanese cities of Hiroshima and Nagasaki. Japan surrendered on September 2, and World War II ended.

World leaders realized that nuclear weapons had revolutionized warfare. Some believed navies were outdated and that future wars would be fought with air power alone.

The United States had the world's largest fleet at the end of the war. Great Britain no longer had the resources to compete for control of the sea. The French, German, Italian, and Japanese fleets had been wiped out, and the Russian Navy was still relatively small. The United States reduced its fleet immediately after the war and began to concentrate on building long-range, land-based bombers.

The Korean War (1950-1953) changed the thinking of many Western leaders about the importance of navies. Air power was not the deciding factor in ending the war, and neither side used nuclear weapons. During the fighting, the U.S. Navy launched carrier-based air attacks, staged amphibious landings, and bombarded enemy coastal defenses. Meanwhile, Russia had begun to enlarge and modernize its fleet. As a result of these developments, the United States again built up its naval strength.

In 1954, the United States Navy launched the submarine *Nautilus*, the world's first nuclear-powered ship. The first of a series of U.S. supercarriers, the *Forrestal*, was completed in 1955. By the mid-1960's, the United States and Russia both had a large force of nuclear submarines, many of which were armed with ballistic missiles.

Recent Developments. The U.S. Navy carried out extensive operations in the Vietnam War from 1965 through 1972. During this period, the U.S. fleet reached a peak strength of nearly 1,000 ships. After the United States withdrew from the war in 1973, it reduced the size of the fleet by more than half. However, the Navy has continually replaced outdated warships and weapons with improved ones, and it plans to continue such replacements. Russia has continued to enlarge and modernize its navy. Both nations armed their surface warships with guided missiles for defense against air attack and for attacking other ships. They also improved their submarine detection systems.

The cost of building and operating a navy has increased enormously since World War II. Such warships as aircraft carriers and nuclear-propelled submarines are extremely expensive, and only a few nations can afford them. Certain light warships, especially missile boats, provide superior striking power over a limited area, and they cost much less. Many small navies, such as those of Egypt and Israel, have added missile boats to their fleets.   NORMAN POLMAR

Related Articles in WORLD BOOK include:

BATTLES

Actium, Battle of	Pearl Harbor
Armada	Naval Base
Jutland, Battle of	Salamis
Midway Island	Trafalgar
Nile, Battle of the	

FAMOUS WARSHIPS

Alabama	Graf Spee
Bismarck	Maine
Constellation	Monitor and Merrimack
Constitution	

KINDS OF SHIPS

Aircraft Carrier	Dreadnought	Missile Boat
Amphibious Ship	Frigate	Privateer
Battleship	Galleon	Submarine
Corvette	Galley	Trireme
Cruiser	Minelayer	Warship
Destroyer	Minesweeper	

WEAPONS

Airship	Depth Charge	Torpedo
Blockade	Guided Missile	Turret
Bomb	Mine, Military	

OTHER RELATED ARTICLES

Admiralty	Naval Shipyard
Amphibious Warfare	Navy, United States
Canada, Armed Forces of	Prisoner of War
Convoy	Recruiting
Court-Martial	Salute
Decorations and Medals	Ship (History)
Desertion	Task Force
Dry Dock	Tromp, Martin H.
Insignia	Underwater
Logistics	Demolition Team
Marine	Uniform
Military School	Vikings
Military Training	War
Mutiny	

Outline

I. The Missions of Navies
   A. Control of the Sea
   B. Coastal Attack and Invasion
   C. Nuclear Attack and Defense
   D. Other Missions

II. The World's Major Navies
   A. The Five Largest Navies B. Other Major Navies
III. The History of Navies

Questions

What are the three main missions of navies?
What was the last great battle between ships propelled by oars?
What change in the construction of warships resulted from the use of shell-firing guns?
Which nation has the largest navy?
What are ballistic missile submarines? Which countries have them?
Why is a navy's size not necessarily an accurate indication of its fighting strength?
What was the first battle between two iron-armored ships?
Why did the opposing warships in the battle of the Coral Sea fire no shots at each other?
What great naval battle began England's rise as the world's leading sea power?
How do the U.S. and Russian navies differ in their use of aircraft carriers?

NAVY, DEPARTMENT OF THE, is one of the three military departments within the Department of Defense of the United States government. It serves as headquarters of the U.S. Navy, and is located in Washington, D.C. It includes the U.S. Marine Corps. In wartime, the President may assign the U.S. Coast Guard to the Department of the Navy. The department is responsible for having naval and marine forces ready to defend the nation's interests, guard its commerce, and improve international relations.

The *secretary of the Navy* heads the department, under the direction of the secretary of defense. The secretary of the Navy ranks equally with the secretaries of the Army and the Air Force. The position carries general responsibility for all naval affairs. The secretary's principal civilian aides include an undersecretary, a deputy undersecretary, four assistant secretaries, and a special assistant.

The *chief of naval operations,* an admiral, serves as the secretary's principal naval adviser, and commands such members and units of the Navy and Marine Corps as are determined by the secretary. Top assistants include the vice chief of naval operations and six deputy chiefs.

The commandant of the Marine Corps is responsible directly to both the secretary and the chief of naval operations.

Congress set up the Department of the Navy in 1798. The secretary of war had directed naval affairs for nine years before then. Congress reorganized the department in 1862, and created bureaus to manage such activities as construction, navigation, ordnance, medicine, steam engineering, and supplies. It created the office of chief of naval operations in 1915.

The secretary of the Navy has not served as a member of the President's Cabinet since 1947. In that year, the Department of the Navy was incorporated in the National Military Establishment. Then it became a military department within the Department of Defense in 1949. Critically reviewed by the DEPARTMENT OF DEFENSE

See also COAST GUARD, UNITED STATES (Supporting the Navy); DEFENSE, DEPARTMENT OF; MARINE CORPS, UNITED STATES; NAVY, UNITED STATES.

Aircraft Carriers provide the main striking power of the United States Navy's surface fleet. The carrier shown above, the U.S.S. *John F. Kennedy,* carries 95 planes and nearly 5,000 crew members.

NAVY, UNITED STATES, is the branch of the armed forces of the United States that acts to maintain command of the sea. In time of peace, the Navy often serves as an instrument of international relations. The very presence of naval vessels may be helpful in keeping a crisis from flaring into war. Navy ships also speed on errands of mercy, such as carrying food and medical supplies to disaster areas. Merchant vessels and passenger ships often call on the Navy for aid in emergencies.

In time of war, the Navy seeks out and destroys the enemy on, under, or above the sea. If attacked, it can return the blow almost anywhere on earth from its warships. Navy task forces can carry naval aircraft to any danger point. Powerful naval amphibious forces can support troop landings against heavy enemy resistance. Nuclear-powered submarines that carry missiles can travel around the world under water. Any enemy that might attack the United States must expect counterblows from these submarines, whose exact locations cannot be pinpointed in advance.

To perform its functions efficiently, the Navy has many types of ships, including aircraft carriers, battleships, cruisers, frigates, destroyers, submarines, and amphibious type ships. These fighting ships depend on the services of ammunition ships, minesweepers, oilers, repair ships, supply ships, and tugs. Both fighting ships and service ships rely on a shore organization, including naval bases, shipyards, docks, naval air stations, and

training stations, for supplies, repairs, training, and other services.

Many persons choose the Navy as a career because of their love of adventure and the sea. They may have an opportunity to visit many parts of the world.

The history of the United States Navy is a colorful story of daring deeds and famous ships at sea. It is the story of growth from a few sailing ships in Revolutionary War days to the greatest fleet ever to sail the seas. It recounts the changes from sails and cannon to nuclear power and guided missiles. It blazes with the achievements of such historic ships as the *Bonhomme Richard, Constitution, Monitor, Olympia, Enterprise,* and *Nautilus*.

Naval history tells of John Paul Jones, whose battle cry, "I have not yet begun to fight," established the Navy's fighting traditions. It includes the achievements of James Lawrence, who rallied his men with the historic words: "Don't give up the ship!" It reflects the deeds of David G. Farragut, the Navy's first admiral, who bellowed "Damn the torpedoes! Full steam ahead!" as his forces charged into Mobile Bay. It includes leaders such as Chester W. Nimitz, who directed the Pacific Fleet in its sweep from Pearl Harbor to Tokyo Bay. It shines with the names of famous ships, such as the *Nautilus*, the world's first nuclear-powered warship.

The Navy operates under the Department of the Navy. In the mid-1970's, it had a strength of about 485,000 men and about 42,000 women. The United States Naval Reserve numbered about 52,000. The department also maintains the 195,100-member United States Marine Corps, and employs 323,600 civilians in all parts of the world.

The Navy emblem was adopted in 1957. "Anchors Aweigh" is the Navy's famous marching song. Blue and gold are the official colors of the Navy.

Life in the Navy

Training a Sailor. The enlisted ranks of the Navy consist of three grades of seaman and six grades of petty officer, from seaman recruit to master chief petty officer.

Navy recruits first learn discipline and seamanship at a naval training center called a *boot camp*. They are called "boots" because, in early days, recruits wore leggings that looked like boots. Then they may attend a trade school, such as those for enginemen, cooks, and electricians. Or they may be assigned directly to a ship where they learn their duties and practice their trades. Sailors take competitive examinations for advancement through the *ratings* (ranks) to the highest enlisted grades. Some may be qualified to attend advanced schools.

Enlisted women receive basic training at the naval training center in Orlando, Fla. About half of them are assigned to advanced training schools, and the rest receive on-the-job training at naval bases. Qualified enlisted men and women can take examinations for admission to the U.S. Naval Academy at Annapolis, Md., or to other officer training programs.

Training an Officer. Navy officers train at the U.S. Naval Academy or in the following naval programs: (1) the Naval Reserve Officers Training Corps (NROTC) for high school graduates; (2) officer-candidate training for enlisted men and college graduates; (3) aviation-officer candidate programs for men and women with two or more years of college; and (4) programs to appoint warrant officers and limited-duty officers from the enlisted ranks. Doctors, dentists, and ministers may be commissioned without any military training. Officer candidates train at the Naval Officer Candidate School, Newport, R.I. The Navy admits women to NROTC programs at some universities and colleges.

Naval officers are assigned to one of three divisions: (1) line, (2) staff, or (3) warrant. *Line* officers usually command ships or aircraft and men. A *restricted line* officer specializes in such duty as engineering or public affairs. *Staff* officers include doctors, dentists, nurses, supply officers, lawyers, and chaplains. A *warrant* officer is usually appointed from the enlisted ranks as an administrative or technical specialist.

Newly appointed ensigns may apply for surface, submarine, or aviation duty. After about four years, they become eligible for many technical postgraduate programs. Senior-ranking officers may take command and strategy courses at the Naval War College in Newport, R.I., or at one of the joint service colleges, such as the National War College in Washington, D.C.

A Typical Day. Life at sea for a *bluejacket* (sailor) varies with the type of ship the person is on. Naval ships range from tugboats with a crew of five to giant aircraft carriers with a crew of thousands. Cargo ships spend long periods at sea. Repair ships usually stay in port. A sailor on a submarine gets to know every member of its crew. But on an aircraft carrier, each crew member does a specialized job and may never even see many areas of the ship.

In peacetime aboard a naval ship, a typical day begins about 6 A.M. Meals are generally served at 7 A.M., noon, and 5 P.M. These hours may be changed to meet operating requirements. The crew *musters* (assembles) at 8 A.M., after breakfast. Practically every crew member on a ship *stands watch*, or is at a post of duty, during four-hour periods. Each member has a battle station and a post for emergencies.

The Navy tries to make life aboard ship as comfortable and pleasant as possible for sailors who may have to live in limited space for weeks or months at a time without seeing land. Some ships have a library for the crew, and many have recreation rooms and hobby shops. Movies are shown every night when possible. Tailor and shoe-repair shops, laundries, and ship's stores provide for the crew's everyday needs. On large ships, doctors and dentists care for the sailors' health. When a ship is in port, crew members who are not on duty may be granted *liberty* (time off ashore).

Careers in the Navy. A sailor has a chance to see much of the world, and many learn to love the sea. A first enlistment may prepare a person for a civilian job or a naval career. Applicants must be between the ages of 17 and 31, and must meet the Navy's physical standards. A man or woman may enlist in the Navy for four to six years.

Qualified enlisted personnel may advance to chief petty officer in 12 to 14 years. They receive a pay increase with each promotion, and extra pay according to length of service. The Navy also pays money for *quarters* (housing) and *subsistence* (food). It gives additional pay for hazardous duty, such as submarine and aviation duty, and for sea duty and duty in some foreign countries. All Navy personnel are eligible for 30 days' *leave* (vacation) a year. They are entitled to free medical and dental care, and free hospital and medical care is available to their families. Men and women in the Navy may retire with pay after 20 years' service. For ranks and pay in the Navy, see RANK IN ARMED SERVICES.

Ships and Weapons of the Navy

Combat Ships of the U.S. Navy include warships, amphibious warfare ships, and mine warfare ships.

Smaller vessels, called *combatant craft*, patrol coastlines, land troops, and operate on rivers and other shallow waterways. This section discusses the U.S. Navy's warships. For information on amphibious warfare ships and mine warfare ships, see the WORLD BOOK articles on AMPHIBIOUS SHIP; MINE, MILITARY (Naval Mines); MINESWEEPER.

The U.S. Navy's *aircraft carriers* are its largest warships. Special carriers take part in helicopter amphibious assaults. *Guided missile cruisers* are used mainly to escort aircraft carriers. *Destroyers* defend amphibious ships and large warships from enemy attack. Some destroyers carry helicopters that can attack enemy submarines. *Frigates* escort other warships and amphibious ships and are also used for patrol duty. *Submarines* operate against surface ships, other submarines, and shore positions. *Command ships* carry elaborate communications equipment and serve as floating command headquarters.

Auxiliary Ships provide maintenance, fuel, supplies, towing, and other services to warships. There are four main kinds of auxiliary ships: (1) underway replenishment ships, (2) fleet support ships, (3) sealift ships, and (4) experimental, research, and surveying ships. *Service craft* generally are smaller vessels that provide services similar to those of auxiliary ships.

Underway replenishment (UNREP) ships provide fuel, ammunition, food, spare parts, and other materials to warships at sea. UNREP ships can transfer cargo to moving ships by means of lines rigged between the ships.

Fleet support ships provide maintenance and towing services to warships. Destroyer tenders, submarine tenders, and repair ships have machine shops that can repair the engines, weapons, and electrical systems of war-

ships. Ocean-going tugs provide the towing services.

Sealift ships carry cargo from port to port but cannot land their cargo on hostile beaches. Unlike UNREP ships, they cannot transfer cargo to moving ships.

Experimental, research, and surveying ships support warship development and operations. Experimental ships test hull designs, weapons, and other equipment. Research ships are used in studying the ocean and the ocean floor. Surveying ships map the ocean floor and coastlines.

Naval Aviation helps the Navy control the seas, takes part in amphibious attacks, and strikes at strategic shore targets. Navy pilots fly light and medium attack planes based on aircraft carriers. They also operate shore-based aircraft. The Navy's fighter planes are designed for low-speed landings and take-offs from carriers. Their wings can be folded, reducing the amount of storage space they need. Navy attack aircraft include the *A-6 Intruder* and the *A-7 Corsair II*. Fighters include the *F-14 Tomcat* and the *F-4 Phantom II*.

Navy planes can carry guided missiles and nuclear weapons. Planes such as the *P-3 Orion* and *S-3 Viking* have electronic devices to hunt enemy submarines. The Navy also operates helicopters for antisubmarine work and for carrying assault troops ashore.

Naval aircraft are classified by letters and numbers. For example, the F-4B is a fighter plane (F) of design number four (-4). It is the second model of that design (B). Other symbols that indicate the purpose of the aircraft are: *A*, attack; *C*, cargo/transport; *E*, special electronic installation; *H*, helicopter; *K*, tanker; *O*, observation; *P*, patrol; *S*, antisubmarine; *T*, trainer; *U*, Utility; *V*, vertical or short take-off and landing; *X*, research.

Ordnance Weapons include bombs, guns, mines, missiles, and torpedoes. Heavy cruisers, rather than battleships, now carry the Navy's largest guns, 8-inch

Inspection in the Ranks may be held ashore or aboard a ship. These men have just had an inspection during a commissioning ceremony and are beginning to march aboard the new ship.

guns that can hurl shells more than 17 miles (27 kilometers). Destroyers mount 5-inch guns in turrets that can shell targets more than 10 miles (16 kilometers) away. Surface warships also carry 3-inch rapid-fire guns for defense against enemy aircraft.

Naval mines may be fixed, moored, or mobile. Rockets such as *ASROC* and *SUBROC* combat submarines. The Navy has air-launched, surface-launched, and subsurface-launched torpedoes. They can be used against surface ships or submarines.

Missiles. Surface-to-air missiles include the *Stanard I, Talos, Tartar,* and *Terrier* missiles, with ranges from 10 to 65 miles (16 to 105 kilometers). Air-to-air missiles include the *Phoenix, Sidewinder,* and *Sparrow.* Such air-to-surface missiles as the *Bullpup* are used to support ground troops or hit targets at sea. The *Polaris* and the *Poseidon* can be launched under water to blast targets up to 2,500 miles (4,020 kilometers) away. *Trident* missiles, scheduled for completion in 1979, have a range of up to 4,500 miles (7,200 kilometers). Underwater-to-air-to-underwater missiles are launched from submarines. See GUIDED MISSILE.

Organization of the Navy

The U.S. Navy operates under the Department of the Navy in the Department of Defense. The Department of the Navy consists of (1) the Navy Department, (2) the Operating Forces, and (3) the Shore Establishment. The secretary of the Navy, a civilian, heads the entire naval establishment. He is responsible directly to the secretary of defense. The chief of naval operations is the Navy's highest-ranking officer. He serves as the secretary of the Navy's principal naval adviser and represents the Navy on the Joint Chiefs of Staff.

The Navy Department, located in Washington, D.C., is the central executive authority of the Navy. It includes the offices of the secretary of the Navy, the chief of naval operations, and the commandant of the Marine Corps, together with the assistants and staff organizations of these executives.

Operating Forces. The principal sea commands are the *Atlantic Fleet,* with headquarters at Norfolk Naval Base, Va., and the *Pacific Fleet,* with headquarters at Pearl Harbor Naval Base, Hawaii. The Navy divides these commands into smaller *fleets* for operations. These include the Third Fleet in the eastern and middle Pacific, the Second Fleet in the western Atlantic, the Sixth Fleet in the Mediterranean, and the Seventh Fleet in the western Pacific. These numbered fleets are divided into *task forces* that perform specific tasks and meet the changing needs of the Navy. Task forces are further divided into *task groups, task units,* and *task elements.*

Ships and forces of the same type in the major fleets are grouped for administration and training into *type commands.* For example, the commander of submarines for the Atlantic Fleet has administrative control over all submarines in that fleet. Other commands include fleet marine forces, mine forces, naval air forces, surface forces, and training commands.

The Military Sealift Command provides transportation of troops and cargo for the Department of Defense. It also operates ships that support scientific projects and other government programs. It is the only fleet command with civilian-staffed ships and its own supply and legal services.

The Shore Establishment trains men and women and provides and maintains supplies and equipment for the fleets and other operating forces. It includes bases, industrial plants, research centers, and other installations. Its commands provide facilities to repair and berth ships, and to perform other *logistic* (supply) operations.

U.S. Navy

Recreational Swimming is no problem for sailors at sea. The oceans provide the world's biggest swimming pools.

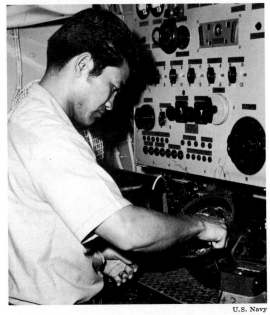

U.S. Navy

Navy Recruits Learn Trades and other useful skills. This electrician's mate is checking equipment aboard his ship.

WORLD BOOK photos with cooperation of U.S. Navy

U.S. Navy Uniforms are the same for officers and enlisted personnel. The service dress blue uniform, *left*, is the basic uniform. The women's uniform may be worn with a skirt or slacks. Summer uniforms include the tropical white long uniform, *center*, and the summer blue uniform, *right*.

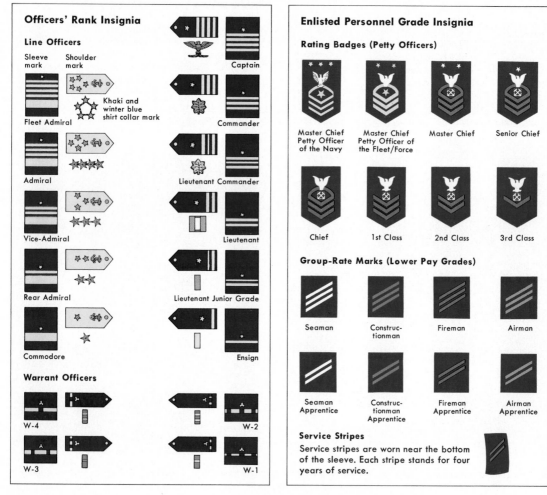

Officers' Rank Insignia

Line Officers

Sleeve mark	Shoulder mark		
Fleet Admiral			Captain
	Khaki and winter blue shirt collar mark		
Admiral			Commander
Vice-Admiral			Lieutenant Commander
Rear Admiral			Lieutenant
Commodore			Lieutenant Junior Grade
			Ensign

Warrant Officers

W-4   W-2
W-3   W-1

Enlisted Personnel Grade Insignia

Rating Badges (Petty Officers)

Master Chief Petty Officer of the Navy   Master Chief Petty Officer of the Fleet/Force   Master Chief   Senior Chief

Chief   1st Class   2nd Class   3rd Class

Group-Rate Marks (Lower Pay Grades)

Seaman   Construc-tionman   Fireman   Airman

Seaman Apprentice   Construc-tionman Apprentice   Fireman Apprentice   Airman Apprentice

Service Stripes

Service stripes are worn near the bottom of the sleeve. Each stripe stands for four years of service.

Some Officers' Devices

The emblems are embroidered on the sleeves of blue uniforms to indicate specialties. They also are worn on shoulder boards, and on the collars of khaki and winter blue shirts of staff officers.

Officer (Staff Corps)

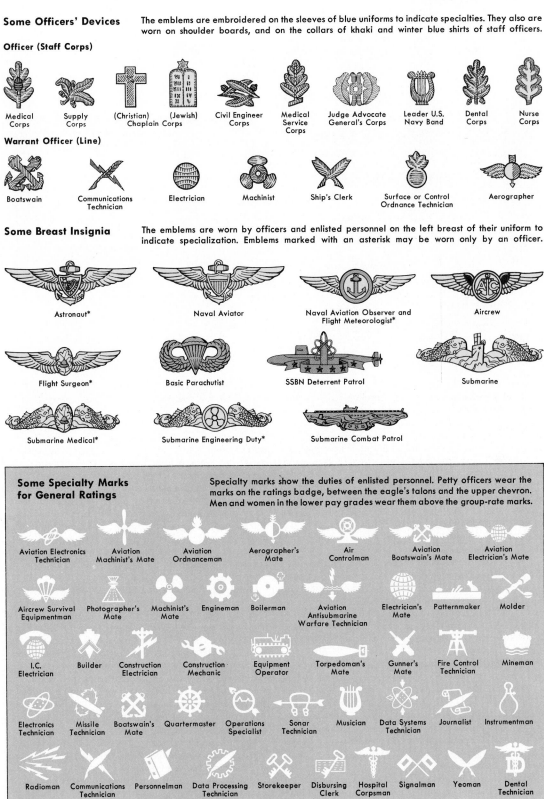

| Medical Corps | Supply Corps | (Christian) Chaplain Corps | (Jewish) | Civil Engineer Corps | Medical Service Corps | Judge Advocate General's Corps | Leader U.S. Navy Band | Dental Corps | Nurse Corps |

Warrant Officer (Line)

| Boatswain | Communications Technician | Electrician | Machinist | Ship's Clerk | Surface or Control Ordnance Technician | Aerographer |

Some Breast Insignia

The emblems are worn by officers and enlisted personnel on the left breast of their uniform to indicate specialization. Emblems marked with an asterisk may be worn only by an officer.

| Astronaut* | Naval Aviator | Naval Aviation Observer and Flight Meteorologist* | Aircrew |

| Flight Surgeon* | Basic Parachutist | SSBN Deterrent Patrol | Submarine |

| Submarine Medical* | Submarine Engineering Duty* | Submarine Combat Patrol |

Some Specialty Marks for General Ratings

Specialty marks show the duties of enlisted personnel. Petty officers wear the marks on the ratings badge, between the eagle's talons and the upper chevron. Men and women in the lower pay grades wear them above the group-rate marks.

Aviation Electronics Technician • Aviation Machinist's Mate • Aviation Ordnanceman • Aerographer's Mate • Air Controlman • Aviation Boatswain's Mate • Aviation Electrician's Mate

Aircrew Survival Equipmentman • Photographer's Mate • Machinist's Mate • Engineman • Boilerman • Aviation Antisubmarine Warfare Technician • Electrician's Mate • Patternmaker • Molder

I.C. Electrician • Builder • Construction Electrician • Construction Mechanic • Equipment Operator • Torpedoman's Mate • Gunner's Mate • Fire Control Technician • Mineman

Electronics Technician • Missile Technician • Boatswain's Mate • Quartermaster • Operations Specialist • Sonar Technician • Musician • Data Systems Technician • Journalist • Instrumentman

Radioman • Communications Technician • Personnelman • Data Processing Technician • Storekeeper • Disbursing Clerk • Hospital Corpsman • Signalman • Yeoman • Dental Technician

DEPARTMENT OF THE NAVY

The Department of the Navy is a military agency within the Department of Defense in Washington, D. C. The principal assistants of the secretary of the navy include an undersecretary, the chief of naval operations, and the Marine Corps commandant.

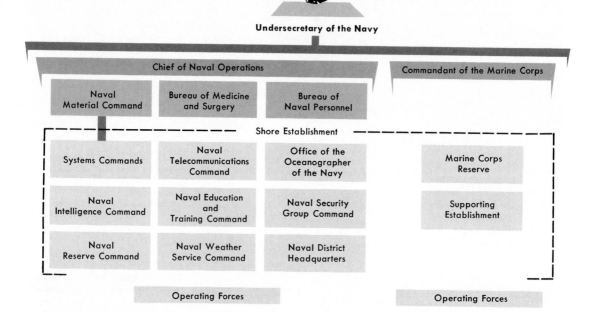

Secretary of the Navy

Undersecretary of the Navy

Chief of Naval Operations			Commandant of the Marine Corps
Naval Material Command	Bureau of Medicine and Surgery	Bureau of Naval Personnel	

Shore Establishment

Systems Commands	Naval Telecommunications Command	Office of the Oceanographer of the Navy	Marine Corps Reserve
Naval Intelligence Command	Naval Education and Training Command	Naval Security Group Command	Supporting Establishment
Naval Reserve Command	Naval Weather Service Command	Naval District Headquarters	

Operating Forces   **Operating Forces**

Other shore commands provide intelligence, oceanographic, and weather forecasts and analyses.

Naval Districts. The continental United States is divided into 11 naval districts. Two other districts lie outside the continental United States. The commandant of each naval district coordinates activities in the area. The naval districts and their headquarters are: 1st, Boston; 3rd, New York City; 4th, Philadelphia; 5th, Norfolk, Va.; 6th, Charleston, S.C.; 8th, New Orleans; 9th, Great Lakes, Ill.; 10th, San Juan, Puerto Rico; 11th, San Diego; 12th, San Francisco; 13th, Seattle; 14th, Pearl Harbor, Hawaii; and the Naval District, Washington, D.C.

Naval Bases are centers for the activities that support the fleet. Most bases include a naval shipyard, a naval air station, or a naval station. Naval stations perform administrative and housekeeping duties. Naval shipyards build and maintain Navy vessels (see NAVAL SHIPYARD). Vessels called *tenders* provide additional support in areas where the Navy may or may not have shore stations.

Other Naval Commands include such laboratories and test centers as the Naval Research Laboratory in Washington, D.C., and the Naval Air Test Facility in Lakehurst, N.J. Naval air stations serve as bases for fleet aircraft and aviation training. Naval reserve training facilities are in many cities. Shore commands also include hospitals, communications stations, and schools. The Navy assigns naval attachés and missions to many countries throughout the world.

Regulars and Reserves. The *Regular Navy* is the permanent professional naval force. It consists of men and women who join the Navy as a career.

The *Naval Reserve* provides additional forces in case of an emergency. The Naval Reserve has four divisions: (1) the Ready Reserve, (2) the Standby Reserve-Active, (3) the Standby Reserve-Inactive, and (4) the Retired Reserve. The Ready Reserve is made up of officers and enlisted men and women who take regular training and are alert for immediate mobilization in emergencies.

Reservists may apply for active duty in the Navy, and many active-duty naval officers are reservists. The Navy has continuing programs for three-, four-, five-, and six-year tours of active duty, and for extensions of active duty. Reservists on inactive duty, except members of the Retired Reserve, may earn points toward retirement by attending drills and by taking correspondence courses in various naval subjects.

Women in the Navy do not form a separate organization or unit, except for those in the Navy Nurse Corps. Women other than nurses serve as enlisted or commissioned personnel in the Regular Navy or Naval Reserve. Nurses serve as commissioned officers in the Naval Reserve and may transfer to the Regular Navy.

Navy women are trained, assigned, paid, and administered under essentially the same policies as are Navy men. They have the same service rights and benefits. Women are not assigned to combat units, but they may serve at overseas bases and on noncombatant ships. Navy nurses may serve in combat zones.

Women first served in the Navy during World War I. They performed *yeoman* (clerical and secretarial) duties to release enlisted men for active duty at sea. In 1942, during World War II, Congress authorized the establishment of the Women's Reserve of the United States Naval Reserve. Navy women became known as

WAVES, the abbreviation for the full name of this organization, *Women Accepted for Volunteer Emergency Service*. Mildred H. McAfee, a distinguished educator, served as the first director of the WAVES (see McAFEE, MILDRED H.). In 1948, women were authorized to become a permanent part of the Regular Navy and the Naval Reserve. Since then, they have not functioned as a separate organization within the Navy. The term *WAVES* is no longer an accurate or official title for Navy women.

The Marine Corps is a separate military service within the Department of the Navy. Its commandant is responsible directly to the secretary of the Navy. The corps assigns *fleet marine forces* (expeditionary troops) to the Atlantic and Pacific fleets. The Marines have the primary jobs of amphibious warfare and land operations performed in connection with naval campaigns. They also provide security forces that guard naval stations and ships and U.S. embassies in other countries. See MARINE CORPS, UNITED STATES.

The Coast Guard operates under the secretary of the Navy in wartime. It may then provide air-sea rescue services, carry out antisubmarine patrols, control and guard shipping in United States ports, and prevent waterfront disasters. In peacetime, the Coast Guard, operating under the Department of Transportation, helps enforce American laws and ensures safety at sea. See COAST GUARD, UNITED STATES.

History

The Colonial Navy was born in 1632, when the English colonists of Massachusetts built the first American warship, the 30-long-ton (30.5-metric-ton) *Blessing of the Bay*. They used it to fight pirates off the Atlantic Coast. By the late 1700's, the colonists had built hundreds of ships, including *privateers*, or privately owned war vessels (see PRIVATEER).

The Continental Congress established the Continental Navy in 1775. It set up a naval committee and later a marine committee to administer naval affairs and to build and equip warships. Several merchantmen were converted into combat vessels. In 1776, Esek Hopkins, the Navy's first commodore and its first commander in chief, raided Nassau in the Bahama Islands with a fleet of six ships. During the Revolutionary War, about 50 vessels served in the Continental Navy. Privateers usually operated on independent missions. Captain John Paul Jones's badly damaged *Bonhomme Richard* forced the British vessel *Serapis* to surrender in one of the war's most exciting battles. Jones uttered the Navy's famous watchword: "I have not yet begun to fight!" See REVOLUTIONARY WAR IN AMERICA.

In 1779, Congress organized a five-member Board of Admiralty to administer the Navy. It discontinued the board in 1781, and put Robert Morris, a financier, in charge of naval activities. The Navy ceased operations after the war. In 1785, the last warship was sold. But the need for a fleet soon arose again. Barbary pirates off North Africa preyed on American merchant ships, and killed or captured American sailors. In 1794, Congress voted to build six frigates to fight the pirates. This sea-going force operated under the secretary of war. The launching of the *United States* in 1797 marked the rebirth of the United States Navy.

Undeclared War with France. In the summer of 1796, relations between the United States and France had reached a state of undeclared war. France and Great Britain were at war with each other at this time. The French treated American merchant sailors like British subjects and, by 1798, the French had seized more than 300 American merchant ships. That year, Congress created a Navy Department under a secretary of the Navy. The 44-gun frigates *Constitution* and *United States* and the 36-gun *Constellation* formed the basis of a new fleet that had grown to 49 ships by 1801. Many battles raged between American and French ships. Napoleon Bonaparte ended the undeclared war with the United States after he seized power in France in 1799.

American relations with the Barbary states of Morocco, Algiers, Tunis, and Tripoli became worse. The Barbary rulers demanded more tribute money as the price for not attacking American ships in the Mediterranean. From 1812 until 1815, the United States fought chiefly with Algeria. Stephen Decatur commanded a powerful squadron that forced the Algerian forces to surrender and accept his terms in 1815.

The War of 1812. Great Britain declared a blockade of France when war broke out in 1803. It seized American ships that violated the blockade, and imprisoned

SOME SELECTED U.S. NAVY INSTALLATIONS

Name	Location
Adak Naval Station	Adak, Alaska
Alameda Naval Air Station	Alameda, Calif.
***Charleston Naval Base**	Charleston, S.C.
***Corpus Christi Naval Air Station**	Corpus Christi, Tex.
***Glenview Naval Air Station**	Glenview, Ill.
***Great Lakes Naval Training Center**	Great Lakes, Ill.
Jacksonville Naval Air Station	Jacksonville, Fla.
Little Creek Naval Amphibious Base	Little Creek, Va.
***Mare Island Naval Shipyard**	Vallejo, Calif.
***National Naval Medical Center**	Bethesda, Md.
Naval Air Development Center	Warminster, Pa.
Naval Air Engineering Center	Lakehurst, N.J.
***Naval Observatory**	Washington, D.C.
Naval Oceanographic Center	Bay St. Louis, Miss.
Naval Postgraduate School	Monterey, Calif.
***Naval War College**	Newport, R.I.
***New London Naval Submarine Base**	Groton, Conn.
***Norfolk Naval Base**	Norfolk, Va.
Oakland Naval Supply Center	Oakland, Calif.
***Pacific Missile Test Center**	Point Mugu, Calif.
Patuxent River Naval Air Test Center	Patuxent River, Md.
***Pearl Harbor Naval Base**	Pearl Harbor, Hawaii
***Pensacola Naval Air Station**	Pensacola, Fla.
***Philadelphia Naval Base**	Philadelphia, Pa.
***Portsmouth Naval Shipyard**	Portsmouth, N.H.
Puget Sound Naval Shipyard	Bremerton, Wash.
***San Diego Naval Base**	San Diego, Calif.
San Francisco Naval Support Activity	San Francisco, Calif.
***United States Naval Academy**	Annapolis, Md.
Whidbey Island Naval Air Station	Oak Harbor, Wash.

*Has a separate article in WORLD BOOK.

COMBAT SHIPS OF THE NAVY

Combat Ships include such warships as aircraft carriers, cruisers, destroyers, frigates, and submarines. Other naval combat vessels are amphibious warfare ships, mine warfare ships, and patrol craft. The Navy has about 40 types of combat ships. Major combat ships with their symbols are shown in the silhouettes below.

Aircraft Carrier (CV)

Dock Landing Ship (LSD)

Battleship (BB)

Command Ship (CC)

Guided Missile Frigate (FFG)

Ocean Minesweeper (MSO)

Guided Missile Destroyer (DDG)

Destroyer (DD)

Guided Missile Cruiser (CGN)

Fleet Ballistic Missile Submarine (SSBN)

their seamen. The U.S. Navy had only 16 warships when the War of 1812 began. In early victories, the *Constitution* captured the British ships *Guerrière* and *Java*, and the *United States* captured the *Macedonian*. The British *Shannon* destroyed the American *Chesapeake.* Captain James Lawrence of the *Chesapeake* issued as his dying command: "Don't give up the ship!"

The Royal Navy clamped a tight blockade on American ports, but American privateers continued to operate. They captured more than 1,300 enemy vessels and damaged British overseas trade. American ships won decisive victories on Lake Erie and Lake Champlain. By the end of the war in 1814, the Navy had established its place in national policy. See WAR OF 1812.

In the Mexican War, from 1846 to 1848, the Navy conducted amphibious operations and blockaded ports along Mexico's Gulf and Pacific coasts.

The Civil War found the Union Navy with only 42 ships. Within a month after the war began on Apr. 12, 1861, the Navy had blockaded the Southern States from Virginia to the Rio Grande to keep them from exporting cotton and importing supplies. The Confederacy countered with naval commerce raiders and blockade runners, which were operated independently. In March, 1862, the first battle between ironclad ships occurred at Hampton Roads, Va. The clash between the Confederate *Virginia* (*Merrimack*) and the Union *Monitor* ended in a draw. But the duel introduced a new kind of naval warfare (see MONITOR AND MERRIMACK).

In August, 1864, Rear Admiral David G. Farragut ran his fleet past defending forts at Mobile Bay, Ala., and forced a Confederate fleet in the harbor to surrender. As Farragut entered the bay, he shouted the famous command: "Damn the torpedoes! Full steam ahead!" He was the first U.S. naval officer to hold the rank of admiral.

The Navy played an important role during the Civil War. It was essential to the success of the land armies, and showed the powerful effect of control of the seas. The Union Navy came out of the war as the largest and most powerful naval force in the world. It had more than 670 ships and 57,000 men. See CIVIL WAR.

─────────── **NAMES OF NAVAL SHIPS** ───────────

The United States Navy names various types of ships after persons, places, or things, as follows:

Ammunition Ships—Volcanoes (*Mauna Kea*) or explosive terms (*Nitro*).

Amphibious Assault Ships—Famous battles (*Tarawa*).

Attack Aircraft Carriers—Famous ships (*Ranger*), battles (*Midway*), or men (*Forrestal*).

Battleships—States (*Missouri*).

Cargo Ships—Astronomical bodies (*Virgo*) or U.S. counties, especially those with college towns (*Muskingum*).

Cruisers—States (*California*) or naval heroes (*Halsey*).

Destroyers and Frigates—Naval heroes (*Forrest Sherman*), secretaries of the Navy (*Frank Knox*), or congressmen (*Norris*).

Destroyer Tenders—Geographic regions (*Cascade*).

Dock Landing Ships—Cities and places of historical interest or landmarks (*Monticello*).

Ocean Mine Sweepers—Abstract qualities (*Gallant*).

Ocean Tugs—Indian tribes (*Sioux*).

Repair Ships—Mythological characters (*Vulcan*).

Submarines—Fish or marine creatures (*Nautilus*) or, for ballistic missile submarines, famous heroes of American history (*George Washington*).

Submarine Tenders—Submarine pioneers (*Holland*).

The **Spanish-American War** started in 1898. The two major naval battles of the war took place half a world apart. On May 1, 1898, Commodore George Dewey's squadron steamed through the entrance to Manila Bay in the Philippines. As his flagship *Olympia* approached the Spanish fleet off Cavite, he gave the historic command: "You may fire when you are ready, Gridley." The battle ended with the 10-ship enemy fleet destroyed or burning. On July 3, Commodore Winfield S. Schley's warships crushed a Spanish fleet outside Santiago harbor in Cuba. After the war, the United States realized that it needed a Navy to guard its possessions. See MAINE (ship); SPANISH-AMERICAN WAR.

"The Great White Fleet." A force of 16 battleships and 4 destroyers of the Atlantic Fleet began a 14-month world cruise in 1907. It was called "the Great White Fleet," because the ships had been painted white. The 46,000-mile (74,000-kilometer) cruise proved that the Navy could easily shift from the Atlantic to the Pacific.

The Navy took two other major steps in the early 1900's. In 1915, it established the office of chief of naval operations. Admiral William S. Benson was the first to fill this position. Naval aviation was born during this same period. In 1911, the Navy purchased its first airplane. Shortly before, on Nov. 14, 1910, Eugene Ely had made the first shipboard take-off from a warship, the cruiser *Birmingham*. By 1914, the Navy had established its first naval air station at Pensacola, Fla., and in 1922, it built its first aircraft carrier, the *Langley*.

World War I began for U.S. combat forces on May 4, 1917, when a destroyer division docked in southern Ireland for duty with Great Britain's Royal Navy. In April, Rear Admiral William S. Sims had arrived in London to command U.S. Naval Forces in European waters. He found the British predicting an Allied defeat in six months unless the German submarine attacks could be stopped. The Allied navies began convoys, and assigned destroyers and submarine chasers to the Atlantic.

The Navy developed new types of mines, and laid a mine *barrage* (field) in the North Sea. It planted 56,000 mines in the largest mining operation in history. During the war, the Navy transported more than 2 million American soldiers across the Atlantic without a single loss of life. See WORLD WAR I.

After World War I, the Navy entered a period of decline. It scrapped, sank, or demilitarized about 2 million long or metric tons of ships, including 31 major warships, according to the 1921 Washington Conference that limited naval armament (see DISARMAMENT). By the 1930's, the United States had again started building ships. It planned a two-ocean Navy.

World War II. The Japanese attack against the Pacific Fleet at Pearl Harbor, Hawaii, on Dec. 7, 1941, brought the United States into World War II. Nearly four years later, the war ended with surrender ceremonies held aboard the battleship *Missouri* in Tokyo Bay, Japan.

The Navy had been involved in defense activities as early as September, 1939. On Oct. 31, 1941, a German submarine sank the destroyer *Reuben James*. This was the first casualty of the undeclared war in the Atlantic.

The Navy recovered quickly from its losses at Pearl Harbor. It salvaged and repaired many of the damaged or sunken ships. Admiral Ernest J. King became commander in chief of the United States Fleet, and later also served as chief of naval operations. Admiral

AUXILIARY SHIPS
OF THE NAVY

Auxiliary Ships support the combat vessels. The Navy has more than 40 types of auxiliary ships, ranging from large tankers to small tugs. Service craft include over 50 types of yard, harbor, and district craft, and floating dry docks. Some types of auxiliary ships with their symbols are shown in the silhouettes below.

Combat Store Ship (AFS)

Fast Combat Support Ship (AOE)

Fleet Ocean Tug (ATF)

Ammunition Ship (AE)

Cargo Ship (AK)

Hydrofoil Research Ship (AGEH)

Oiler (AO)

Destroyer Tender (AD)

Repair Ship (AR)

Salvage Ship (ARS)

Submarine Rescue Ship (ASR)

HISTORIC SHIPS OF THE UNITED STATES NAVY

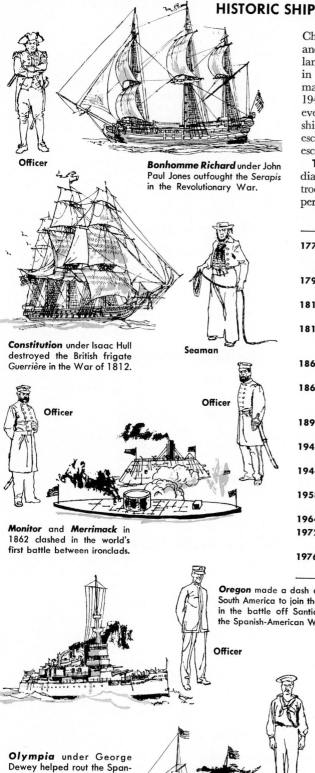

Chester W. Nimitz took command of the Pacific Fleet, and Admiral Royal E. Ingersoll commanded the Atlantic Fleet. By June, 1942, the Navy's decisive victory in the vital Battle of Midway Island had cut Japan's margin of superiority. When World War II ended in 1945, the Navy had become the most powerful fleet ever. It had 3,400,000 men and women, and 2,500 ships, including 24 battleships, 35 aircraft carriers, 77 escort carriers, 92 cruisers, 501 destroyers, 406 destroyer escorts, and 262 submarines. See WORLD WAR II.

The Korean War involved naval forces almost immediately after the conflict began. Aircraft carriers and troop transports played vital roles in holding the Pusan perimeter during the first three months of the war. On

Officer

Bonhomme Richard under John Paul Jones outfought the *Serapis* in the Revolutionary War.

Constitution under Isaac Hull destroyed the British frigate *Guerrière* in the War of 1812.

Seaman

Officer

Officer

Monitor and **Merrimack** in 1862 clashed in the world's first battle between ironclads.

IMPORTANT DATES IN NAVY HISTORY

1779 John Paul Jones' *Bonhomme Richard* outfought the *Serapis*, and gave the Navy its famous watchword: "I have not yet begun to fight."

1794 The United States Navy was formally established in a law providing for ship construction.

1812 The *Constitution* under Isaac Hull overwhelmed the British ship *Guerrière* in the War of 1812.

1813 James Lawrence and the *Chesapeake* fell before the cannons of British warship *Shannon*. The dying Lawrence commanded: "Don't give up the ship!"

1862 The first battle between ironclad warships was fought between the *Monitor* and the *Merrimack*.

1864 A Union fleet stormed into Mobile Bay as its commander, David Farragut, bellowed: "Damn the torpedoes! Full steam ahead!"

1898 The United States fleet under George Dewey crushed the Spanish fleet in Manila Bay.

1942 The Pacific Fleet repulsed a Japanese fleet that threatened Midway Island and Hawaii.

1944 In the biggest naval battle in history, the Pacific Fleet destroyed Japanese sea power off Leyte Gulf.

1958 The world's first nuclear warship, *Nautilus*, cruised beneath the North Pole, the first ship to reach it.

1964 A nuclear-powered task force cruised around the world.

1972 Alene B. Duerk became the first woman in the Navy to be promoted to the rank of admiral.

1976 Women were admitted to the U.S. Naval Academy for the first time.

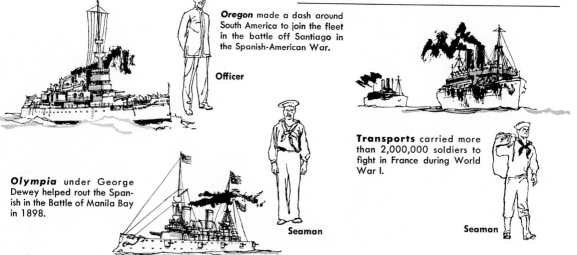

Oregon made a dash around South America to join the fleet in the battle off Santiago in the Spanish-American War.

Officer

Transports carried more than 2,000,000 soldiers to fight in France during World War I.

Olympia under George Dewey helped rout the Spanish in the Battle of Manila Bay in 1898.

Seaman

Seaman

Sept. 15, 1950, an amphibious landing at Inchon helped reverse the course of the war. A feature of the ground battles was the success of naval and marine close air support, with aircraft and infantry operations closely coordinated. Without command of the sea, the Korean War would have been lost. See KOREAN WAR.

The Nuclear Age Navy. In 1948, Captain Hyman G. Rickover was assigned the job of building a nuclear power plant for submarines. In 1954, the Navy commissioned the first nuclear-powered ship, the submarine *Nautilus*. By the early 1970's, the Navy fleet included more than 100 nuclear-powered submarines. These submarines can go over 60,000 miles (97,000 kilometers) before refueling, and can dive deeper and stay submerged longer than older types. Armed with Polaris and Poseidon missiles, they form a major part of the U.S. defense system. These submarines can cruise so deep, so fast, and so quietly that they are difficult for an enemy to detect. Each submarine keeps most of its missiles ready to fire in a short time if needed.

Such nuclear-powered surface ships as the cruiser *Long Beach* and the aircraft carriers *Enterprise* and *Nimitz* were also in service in the 1970's. In 1964, a nuclear-powered task force consisting of the *Enterprise*, *Long Beach*, and *Bainbridge* conducted Operation *Sea Orbit*, a cruise around the world. Construction of two more nuclear-powered carriers, the *Eisenhower* and the *Vinson*, was underway in the mid-1970's. The *Eisenhower* was scheduled for completion in 1978, and the *Vinson* was scheduled for completion by the early 1980's.

The Navy is strengthening its forces in other ways. It has added guided missile frigates and destroyers, and such large carriers as the *America* and the *John F. Kennedy*. In 1962, the Navy formed its first destroyer division and its first cruiser-destroyer flotilla of guided missile ships. Amphibious landing force ships, such as the amphibious assault ship *Tarawa*, are used for present-day naval operations. The Navy is also designing new combat support ships and guided missile frigates and destroyers. Critically reviewed by the UNITED STATES NAVY

Related Articles. See NAVY with its list of Related Articles, and articles on naval installations listed in the *Table* with this article. See also the following articles:

Outline

I. Life in the Navy
    A. Training a Sailor   C. A Typical Day
    B. Training an Officer   D. Careers in the Navy
II. Ships and Weapons of the Navy
    A. Combat Ships   D. Ordnance Weapons
    B. Auxiliary Ships   E. Missiles
    C. Naval Aviation
III. Organization of the Navy
    A. Navy Headquarters   D. Regulars and Reserves
    B. Operating Forces   E. Women in the Navy
    C. The Shore   F. The Marine Corps
       Establishment   G. The Coast Guard
IV. History

Questions

How does the Navy serve in peacetime emergencies?
What is a *fleet?* A *type command?* A *task force?*
What are the four divisions of the Naval Reserve?
Who was the first full admiral in the U.S. Navy?
When did the Navy reach its peak strength? How many ships and men did it have?
What is the role of naval aviation?
What are the naval operating forces? The shore establishment? Navy headquarters?
What was "the Great White Fleet"?
What was the world's first nuclear-powered warship?
How did the Union Navy rank as a naval force?

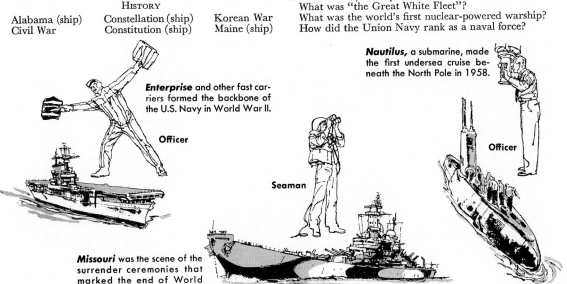

Enterprise and other fast carriers formed the backbone of the U.S. Navy in World War II.

Officer

Nautilus, a submarine, made the first undersea cruise beneath the North Pole in 1958.

Officer

Seaman

Missouri was the scene of the surrender ceremonies that marked the end of World War II.

NAVY AND MARINE CORPS MEDAL. See DECORA-TIONS AND MEDALS (Military Awards).

NAVY CROSS. See DECORATIONS AND MEDALS (Military Awards).

NAVY DAY. See ARMED FORCES DAY.

NAVY INTELLIGENCE SERVICE. See INTELLIGENCE SERVICE.

NAVY JACK is a flag of the United States Navy. It has 50 white stars on a blue background. It looks like the blue and white corner portion of the flag of the United States. The Navy Jack is flown from the bow of a ship from sunrise until sunset when the ship is in port. See also FLAG (color picture: The Shapes of Flags).   WHITNEY SMITH, JR.

NAVY LEAGUE OF THE UNITED STATES is a civilian organization that works for greater understanding of the importance of the seas to the nation's economy and security. It promotes a strong, progressive maritime policy for the United States. The league was founded in 1902, and has headquarters at 818 18th Street NW, Washington, D.C. 20006.

Critically reviewed by the NAVY LEAGUE OF THE UNITED STATES

NAVY ROTC. See RESERVE OFFICERS TRAINING CORPS (Navy ROTC); NAVY, UNITED STATES (Training an Officer).

NAVY YARD. See NAVAL SHIPYARD.

NAXOS. See CYCLADES.

NAY. See FLUTE.

NAYARIT, *nah yah REET*, is a state of Mexico. It lies along the Pacific Coast in west-central Mexico (see MEXICO [political map]). Nayarit has a population of 544,031. It covers 10,665 square miles (27,622 square kilometers) of narrow coastal lowlands and rugged mountains. Cattle, sheep, goats, and horses graze on plains in the northwest. Farmers grow sugar cane, tobacco, peanuts, vegetables, and cotton.

As a result of bad treatment by the Spanish colonists, the Indians of Nayarit fought a series of wars against the white people between the 1500's and 1800's. The territory became a Mexican state in 1917. Tepic is Nayarit's capital.   CHARLES C. CUMBERLAND

NAZARENE, *NAZ uh REEN*, refers to an inhabitant of Nazareth, an ancient town in Israel. The term is often applied to Jesus Christ, or to His followers (see JESUS CHRIST). A Nazarene was a member of an early Jewish-Christian sect that lived in Palestine until about the A.D. 300's. A group of German painters in the 1800's were also called Nazarenes. They moved to Rome and had the goal of restoring Christian art to its medieval purity. *Nazarene* also refers to a member of the Church of the Nazarene (see CHURCH OF THE NAZARENE).

NAZARETH (pop. 35,400), is a town in northern Israel. For location, see ISRAEL (color map). It was the home of Jesus Christ during His early youth. The town of Nazareth was in the Roman province of Galilee (see GALILEE).

The Old Testament does not mention Nazareth. Nathanael in the New Testament expressed the attitude of the times about the village when he said, "Can there any good thing come out of Nazareth?" (John 1: 46).

Nazareth remained insignificant for many years after the time of Christ. But pilgrims visited the town about A.D. 600, and a large basilica was built. The Arabs cap-

Russell Wright

Mary's Well in Nazareth, an ancient spring which flowed in Biblical times, still provides water for many people.

tured the city in the 600's. The Crusaders built several churches there, but the Ottoman Turks forced Christians to leave in 1517. A new town of Nazareth stands on the site of the old. Its population is far more than Nazareth had in Biblical times. The Latin Church of the Annunciation, completed in 1730, now rises where some persons think the home of Mary, the mother of Jesus, stood. Since the 1700's, several denominations have built churches and monasteries. An ancient well, called Mary's Well, still flows, and people still take water from it.   SYDNEY N. FISHER and BRUCE M. METZGER

See also ISRAEL (color picture).

NAZARETH COLLEGE AT KALAMAZOO. See UNIVERSITIES AND COLLEGES (table).

NAZARETH COLLEGE OF ROCHESTER. See UNIVERSITIES AND COLLEGES (table).

NAZARITE, *NAZ uh rite*, was a name given to certain holy men by the ancient Hebrews. A Nazarite was not allowed to drink wine, cut his hair, or touch a corpse. Nazarite was also a name once given to members of the Free Methodist Church.

See also NUMBERS.

NAZIMOVA, *nuh ZIM oh vuh*, **ALLA** (1879-1945), a Russian actress, became famous on the American stage and in motion pictures. She was one of the first in the United States to show the psychological approach in acting. She played leading parts in the stage plays *Ghosts, Hedda Gabler, The Master Builder, The Cherry Orchard, The Good Earth*, and *Mourning Becomes Electra*. She appeared in such motion pictures as *The Bridge of San Luis Rey, In Our Time*, and *Since You Went Away*.

Alla Nazimova was born in Yalta, in the Crimea. She performed at the famous Moscow Art Theatre before she came to the United States in 1906.   RICHARD MOODY

NAZISM, or NAZIISM, was the political and social doctrine of the German dictator Adolf Hitler and his followers. Hitler and the Nazis ruled Germany from 1933 to 1945. *Nazi* stands for the first word in the German name for the *National Socialist German Workers' Party* (*Nationalsozialistische Deutsche Arbeiterpartei*).

Nazism was part of the dictatorial political movement called *fascism*. The Nazis were extreme nationalists who believed in the superiority of the Germans and other members of the so-called "Aryan race." The Nazis worked to strengthen German military might in order to bring the world under German control. They believed in a totalitarian government, where all opposition is ruthlessly put down. See TOTALITARIANISM.

A small group started the Nazi Party in Munich, Germany, just after World War I. Hitler joined the group in 1919 and became its leader. Many discontented Germans turned to Nazism after the economic depression of 1930. The movement seemed to promise jobs for them and glory for their country. But the promises proved false. Hitler became chancellor of Germany on Jan. 30, 1933. He made the government a Nazi dictatorship. The Nazis set up concentration camps where they killed thousands of political opponents and members of religious minorities.

In 1939, the Nazi government started World War II by attacking Poland. It soon conquered most of Europe. Great Britain, Russia, and the United States fought against the Nazis and finally defeated them. Hitler committed suicide on April 30, 1945.

Millions of people died in the war the Nazis started. The Nazis murdered about 12 million civilians, including almost all the Jews who lived under German rule. After the war, the Allies prosecuted many Nazi leaders for taking part in these murders and abolished the Nazi Party in Germany.   WILLIAM EBENSTEIN

Related Articles in WORLD BOOK include:

Auschwitz	Goebbels, Paul Joseph
Belsen	Goering, Hermann Wilhelm
Bonhoeffer, Dietrich	Himmler, Heinrich
Buchenwald	Hitler, Adolf
Dachau	Horst Wessel
Eichmann, Adolf	Jews (Nazi Persecutions)
Fascism	Nuremberg
Flag (picture: Histor-	Nuremberg Trials
ical Flags of the World)	Swastika
Germany (History)	World War II (Causes of
Gestapo	Conflict)

NBC. See NATIONAL BROADCASTING COMPANY.

NCAA. See NATIONAL COLLEGIATE ATHLETIC ASSOCIATION.

N'DJAMENA, *na juh MEE nuh* (pop. 150,000), is the capital of Chad, an independent republic in Africa. For the location of N'Djamena, see CHAD (map). Founded in 1900, the city is a commercial center of Chad. Its industries include brick and tile manufacturing. The city was called Fort-Lamy until 1973.

NE PLUS ULTRA. See PILLARS OF HERCULES.

NE WIN, U (1911-   ), is the president of Burma. In 1962, he led a successful military revolt against the government and named himself Burma's leader. In 1974, he took the title of president under a new constitution created by the military.

After he gained power, U Ne Win set out to make Burma a socialist country. His government placed private businesses under government control. Despite such socialist goals and the fact that Burma borders China, U Ne Win maintained a generally neutral foreign policy. He also fought Communist rebels in Burma.

U Ne Win was born in Paungde, Burma. He became the head of the Burmese Army in 1950. In 1958, Prime Minister U Nu asked him to take over the government because of the threat of civil war. U Ne Win headed a

caretaker government from 1958 until elections were held in 1960 and U Nu returned to power. U Ne Win overthrew U Nu in 1962.   JOHN F. CADY

NEA. See NATIONAL EDUCATION ASSOCIATION OF THE UNITED STATES.

NEAGH, LOUGH. See LOUGH NEAGH.

NEANDERTHAL MAN, *nee AN duhr thawl*, was a type of prehistoric human being who lived in parts of Europe, Asia, and Africa from about 35,000 to 100,000 years ago. Many scientists classify Neanderthal man as an early subspecies of *Homo sapiens* (wise man). The word *Neanderthal* comes from the Neander Gorge near Düsseldorf, Germany. The first Neanderthal fossil, the top of a skull, was found there in 1856. Since then, similar fossils have been found in more than 40 other locations.

Scientists long thought of Neanderthal man as being stooped. But the fossils show that these people stood about 5 feet 2 inches (157 centimeters) tall and walked fully erect. They had heavy bones, slightly curved limbs, big brow ridges, and powerful teeth. Their brain was as large as that of modern people.

Stone tools and animal bones found with the human fossils show that the Neanderthal people were successful hunters in the subarctic environments of Europe. They lived in simple temporary shelters when following the animal herds and sometimes also in caves. The fossil remains show that at least some Neanderthal people buried their dead with great care.   KARL W. BUTZER

See also FAMILY (picture); PREHISTORIC PEOPLE.

NEAP TIDE. See TIDE (High Tides and Low Tides; diagram: Causes of Ocean Tides).

NEAR EAST is a name sometimes given to a region that includes non-Soviet Asia from the Mediterranean Sea to the eastern boundary of Iran, plus part of northeastern Africa. The British and French first called this region the Near East because it lay nearer to London and Paris than the Far East lay. Many people refer to the Near East region as the Middle East (see MIDDLE EAST).   SYDNEY N. FISHER

NEARSIGHTEDNESS is a defect of sight in which distant objects that should be clearly seen are blurred. Doctors call this condition *myopia*. A nearsighted person's eyeballs are too long. When the eye brings distant objects into focus, the image falls too far in front of the retina to produce a sharp picture. To correct this, nearsighted persons often wear contact lenses or glasses with lenses thin in the middle and thick at the edges.

Very few babies are born nearsighted. The defect usually develops in childhood and adolescence, and sometimes progresses rapidly until about the age of 21. Heredity is the most important cause of nearsightedness.

Nearsightedness cannot be cured. Vision should be kept as near to normal as possible by using properly fitted glasses.   JOHN R. McWILLIAMS

See also GLASSES; EYE (picture: Nearsightedness).

NEBO, *NAY boh*, the god of wisdom in Babylonian mythology, was said to have invented the art of writing. He was also a god of the sun, and some say he was a god of the water. Nebo was the son of Marduk, who controlled the fates of people. It was Nebo's duty to write down the judgments passed on to the dead souls.

NEBO, MOUNT. See MOUNT NEBO.

NEBRASKA

The Cornhusker State

NEBRASKA is one of the leading farming states in the United States. Yet it was once considered part of the "Great American Desert." The people of Nebraska, with their determined pioneer spirit, made the Nebraska "desert" a land of ranches and farms. They built irrigation systems and practiced scientific farming. Where crops could not be grown, Nebraskans grazed cattle.

Today, the sounds of busy tractors and other farm machinery are heard across Nebraska. In the west, waving fields of golden wheat stretch as far as the eye can see. In north-central Nebraska, huge herds of beef cattle graze on enormous ranches. On the fertile farms of the east, farmers grow corn, grain sorghums, and other crops. The farmers there also raise hogs and fatten cattle for market.

Nebraska's chief manufacturing activity is processing the food produced on its ranches and farms. Meat packing is the leading food-processing activity, and Omaha ranks as one of the world's largest meat-packing centers.

Much of the history of Nebraska is the story of the tough, strong-willed Nebraska farmer. Many of the first farm settlers built their homes out of the Nebraska sod because they found few trees on this grassy land. In the 1860's, the first great wave of homesteaders poured into Nebraska to claim free land granted by the federal government. Hard times, insect pests, and droughts discouraged many farmers, and they returned to the East. But most of them refused to give up.

The independent, pioneer spirit of the people of Nebraska also led them to adopt a *unicameral* (one-house) state legislature. Nebraska is the only state in the nation with a unicameral legislature. Lincoln is the capital of Nebraska, and Omaha is the largest city.

The name *Nebraska* comes from the Oto Indian word *nebrathka*. The word means *flat water*, and was the Indian name for Nebraska's chief river, the Platte. Nebraska's official nickname is the *Cornhusker State*. This nickname comes from corn, the state's leading crop, and from the cornhusking contests that were once held each fall in many rural communities.

Gerald R. Ford, the 38th President of the United States, was born in Omaha. Other famous Americans who have lived in Nebraska include the noted political leader William Jennings Bryan; novelist Willa Cather; and Edward J. Flanagan, the Roman Catholic priest who founded Boys Town.

For the relationship of Nebraska to other states in its region, see MIDWESTERN STATES.

The contributors of this article are William O. Dobler, Editor of the Lincoln Star; *Leslie Hewes, Emeritus Professor of Geography at the University of Nebraska; and James C. Olson, author of* History of Nebraska.

Dick Hufnagle, Publix
Stockyards in Omaha

FPG
Herding Cattle in Western Nebraska

Nebraska (blue) ranks 15th in size among all the states, and is the third largest of the Midwestern States (gray).

Autumn on a Nebraska Farm

Fred Ragsdale, Alpha

FACTS IN BRIEF

Capital: Lincoln.

Government: *Congress*—U.S. senators, 2; U.S. representatives, 3. *Electoral Votes*—5. *State Legislature*—members of the unicameral legislature, 49. *Counties*—93.

Area: 77,227 sq. mi. (200,017 km²), including 744 sq. mi. (1,927 km²) of inland water; 15th in size among the states. *Greatest Distances*—east-west, 415 mi. (668 km); north-south, 205 mi. (330 km).

Elevation: *Highest*—5,426 ft. (1,654 m) above sea level in southwestern Kimball County; *Lowest*—840 ft. (256 m) above sea level in Richardson County.

Population: *Estimated 1975 Population*—1,546,000. *1970 Census*—1,483,791; 35th among the states; distribution, 62 per cent urban, 38 per cent rural; density, 19 persons per sq. mi. (7 persons per km²).

Chief Products: *Agriculture*—beef cattle, corn, dairy products, grain sorghums, hogs, soybeans, wheat. *Manufacturing*—chemicals; electrical machinery; food products; instruments; metal products; nonelectrical machinery; printing and publishing. *Mining*—natural gas, natural gas liquids, petroleum, sand and gravel, stone.

Statehood: March 1, 1867, the 37th state.

State Motto: *Equality Before the Law*.

State Song: "Beautiful Nebraska." Words by Jim Fras and Guy G. Miller; music by Jim Fras.

Constitution of Nebraska was adopted in 1875. Nebraska had one earlier constitution, adopted in 1866. Amendments may be proposed in the legislature, by a constitutional convention, or by the people. An amendment proposed in the legislature becomes law after approval by three-fifths of the legislature and by a majority of voters casting ballots on the amendment.

A proposal to call a constitutional convention also must be approved by three-fifths of the legislature and by a majority of voters casting ballots on the proposal. Convention proposals become law after they have been approved by a majority of people voting on the proposals. The people of Nebraska may sign a *petition* (formal request) proposing a constitutional amendment. The number of signatures on a petition must equal 10 per cent of the total votes cast for governor in the last general election. The proposed amendment becomes law after a majority of the voters have approved it and the governor has proclaimed it a part of the constitution.

Executive. Nebraska voters elect the governor and lieutenant governor to four-year terms. The governor may serve any number of terms, but not more than two terms in succession. He receives a yearly salary of $25,000. For a list of all the governors of Nebraska, see the *History* section of this article.

In 1964, the voters approved a constitutional amendment, increasing the terms of other top state officials from two to four years. The new term went into effect in 1967 for the secretary of state, attorney general, treasurer, and auditor. All these officials except the treasurer may serve an unlimited number of successive terms. The treasurer may serve any number of terms, but not more than two in succession.

Legislature. Nebraska is the only state with a *unicameral* (one-house) legislature. The 49 members of the legislature are called *senators*. Voters in each of 49 legislative districts elect one senator. The people elect the senators on a *nonpartisan* ballot—the ballot has no political party labels. Nebraska is the only state in which the state legislators are chosen in nonpartisan elections. The people approved a constitutional amendment in 1962 increasing the legislators' terms from two years to four years. In the 1964 general election, 24 senators were elected to two-year terms and 25 senators were elected to four-year terms. Since the 1966 election, half the senators have been elected every two years to four-year terms.

The legislature meets every year. Regular sessions begin on the Wednesday after the first Monday in January. They are limited to 60 days in even-numbered years and 90 days in odd-numbered years. The governor may call special sessions. Between sessions, members of the legislature make up the legislative council. The council studies state problems and recommends new laws to the legislature.

Courts in Nebraska are headed by the state supreme court. It consists of a chief justice and six associate justices. Nebraska also has 21 district courts, with a total of 43 judges. A merit plan for selecting supreme court and district court judges went into effect in 1964. Under the plan, the governor appoints a judge to fill a vacancy in these courts from a list submitted by a nominating committee. Each judge appointed must be approved by the voters at the next general election after holding office for three years. If approved, he serves for six more years. Thereafter, the voters must approve him every six years.

Every Nebraska county has a county court presided over by a judge elected to a four-year term. Omaha and Lincoln each has a municipal court and a juvenile court. Judges of these courts are selected in the same way as are the judges of the supreme court and the district courts. No political party labels are allowed on the ballot for electing or approving any judge in Nebraska.

Local Government. Nebraska has 93 counties. About two-thirds of the counties have the commissioner-precinct form of government, and the rest have the supervisor-township form. Counties with the commissioner-precinct form are governed by a board of commissioners of three or five members. The commissioners are elected to four-year terms. Counties with the supervisor-township form are governed by a seven-man board of supervisors. The supervisors are also elected to four-year terms. Other officials in both kinds of Nebraska counties include the county clerk, treasurer, sheriff, and attorney.

Nebraska has about 540 cities and villages. Most cities have the mayor-council form of government. Nebraska City uses the commission form, and a few cities use the council-manager plan. Each village is governed by a five-man board of trustees. The Nebraska constitution gives *home rule* to all cities with more than 5,000 persons. Such cities may operate under their own charters. Only Lincoln and Omaha have chosen to adopt their own charters.

Taxation. Taxes and licenses bring in about two-thirds of the state government's income. Almost all of the other one-third comes from federal grants and other U.S. government programs. The state collects personal

Nebraska Game Commission

The Governor's Mansion, completed in 1958, stands south of the Capitol in Lincoln.

The State Seal

Symbols of Nebraska. On the state seal, adopted in 1867, the smith represents the mechanical arts. The settler's cabin, the growing corn, and the shocks of grain stand for agriculture. The steamboat and train symbolize transportation. The state flag, adopted in 1925, bears a silver and gold reproduction of the seal centered on a field of dark blue.

Seal, flag, bird, and flower illustrations, courtesy of Eli Lilly and Company

and corporation income taxes, a 2½ per cent sales and use tax, and taxes on alcoholic beverages, insurance payments, motor fuels, and tobacco. Nebraskans voted out the state property tax in 1966.

Politics. Nebraskans generally vote for Republicans when party labels are on the ballot. However, all members of the legislature, all judges and school officials, and many local officials are elected or approved on nonpartisan ballots. This system has weakened party politics in the state. In about two-thirds of the elections for President and governor, most Nebraskans have voted for Republicans. For Nebraska's electoral votes and voting record in presidential elections, see ELECTORAL COLLEGE (table).

Two of Nebraska's most famous citizens were national political leaders. William Jennings Bryan ran for President unsuccessfully three times. George W. Norris won fame as an independent statesman during his 40 years in the U.S. House of Representatives and Senate.

Nebraska's Capitol in Lincoln was completed in 1932. The central tower is 400 feet (120 meters) high. Lincoln was named the capital in 1867. Omaha was the capital from 1855 to 1867.
Nebraska Game Commission

The State Flag

The State Bird
Western Meadow Lark

The State Flower
Goldenrod

The State Tree
Cottonwood

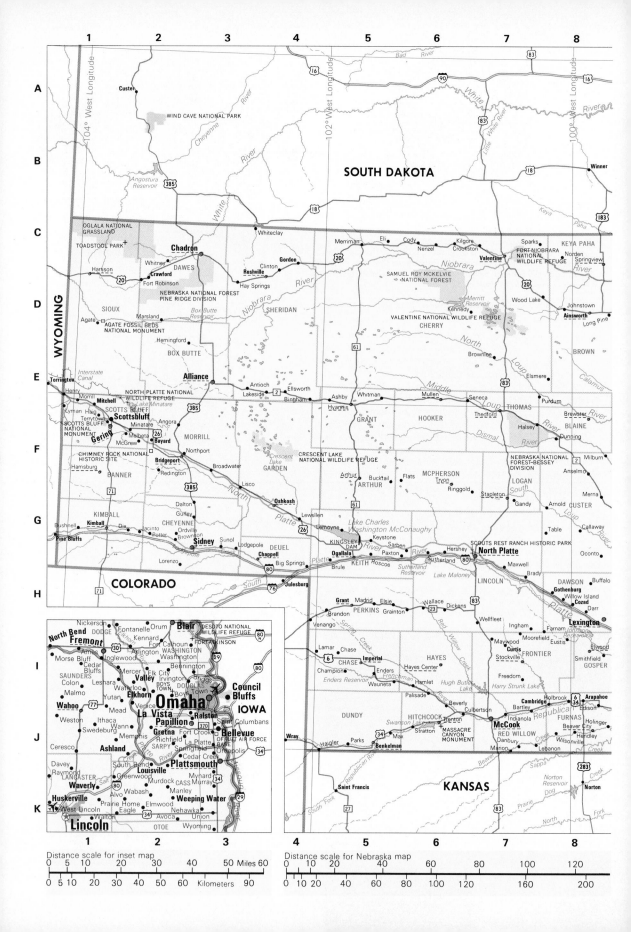

NEBRASKA Political Map

⊛ State capital	State boundary
Urban area in Nebraska	Park or other recreation area
Urban area outside Nebraska	Forest or other conservation area
• City or town	Water
◉ County seat	River
POLK County name / County boundary	Intermittent river
	Intermittent lake

Indian reservation
+ Point of interest
✈ Major airport
Military or other federal area

Highways:
Expressway
Other road
29 Interstate
20 U.S.
2 Other

Lambert conformal conic projection
WORLD BOOK map © Field Enterprises Educational Corporation

Population

1,546,000 Estimate..1975
1,483,791 ..Census..1970
1,411,330 ....“....1960
1,325,510 ....“....1950
1,315,834 ....“....1940
1,377,963 ....“....1930
1,296,372 ....“....1920
1,192,214 ....“....1910
1,066,300 ....“....1900
1,062,656 ....“....1890
452,402 ....“....1880
122,993 ....“....1870
28,841 ....“....1860

Metropolitan Areas

Lincoln 167,972
Omaha 542,646
(455,655 in Neb.; 86,991 in Ia.)
Sioux City (Ia.) .116,189
(103,052 in Ia.; 13,137 in Nebr.)

Counties

Adams ....30,553..I 11
Antelope ....9,047..E 11
Arthur ....606..G 5
Banner .....1,034..F 1
Blaine ....847..F 8
Boone ......8,190..F 11
Box Butte .10,094..E 2
Boyd ....3,752..C 10
Brown ......4,021..E 8
Buffalo ...31,222..H 9
Burt ....9,247..F 15
Butler ......9,461..G 13
Cass ......18,076..H 15
Cedar .....12,192..D 13
Chase ......4,129..I 5
Cherry ......6,846..D 6
Cheyenne ..10,778..G 2
Clay ....8,266..I 12
Colfax ......9,498..F 13
Cuming ....12,034..E 14
Custer ....14,092..G 8
Dakota ....13,137..D 14
Dawes ......9,761..C 2
Dawson ....19,771..H 8
Deuel ....2,717..G 4
Dixon ......7,453..D 13
Dodge .....34,782..F 14
Douglas ...389,455..G 15
Dundy ......2,926..J 5
Fillmore ....8,137..J 12
Franklin ....4,566..J 10
Frontier ....3,982..I 7
Furnas ......6,897..J 8
Gage ......25,731..I 14
Garden ......2,929..F 4
Garfield ....2,411..F 10
Gosper ......2,178..I 8
Grant ....1,019..F 5
Greeley .....4,000..F 11
Hall ....42,851..H 10
Hamilton ....8,867..H 12
Harlan ......4,357..J 9
Hayes ....1,530..I 6
Hitchcock ...4,051..J 6
Holt ....12,933..D 10
Hooker ....939..F 6
Howard ......6,807..G 11
Jefferson ...10,436..J 13
Johnson .....5,743..I 15
Kearney .....6,707..I 10
Keith ....8,487..H 5
Keya Paha ..1,340..C 8
Kimball .....6,009..G 1
Knox ......11,723..D 12
Lancaster .167,972..H 14
Lincoln ....29,538..H 7
Logan ....991..F 7
Loup ....854..F 9
Madison ...27,402..F 12
McPherson ....623..F 6
Merrick .....8,751..G 12
Morrill ......5,813..F 2
Nance ......5,142..G 12
Nemaha .....8,976..I 16
Nuckolls ....7,404..J 11
Otoe ....15,576..H 15
Pawnee .....4,473..J 15
Perkins .....3,423..H 5
Phelps ......9,553..I 9
Pierce ......8,493..E 12
Platte ......26,544..F 13
Polk ....6,468..G 12
Red Willow 12,191..J 7
Richardson 12,277..J 16
Rock ....2,231..E 9
Saline .....12,809..I 13
Sarpy ......73,479..G 15
Saunders ..17,018..G 14
Scotts Bluff 36,432..E 1
Seward .....14,460..H 13
Sheridan ....7,285..D 4
Sherman .....4,725..G 10
Sioux ....2,034..D 1
Stanton .....5,758..F 13
Thayer ......7,779..J 12
Thomas ......954..E 7
Thurston ....6,942..E 14
Valley ......5,783..F 10
Washington 13,310..G 15
Wayne .....10,400..E 13
Webster ....5,396..J 11
Wheeler ....1,051..F 10
York ......13,685..H 12

Cities and Villages

Abie ....78..G 13
Adams ....463..I 14
Agnew ....H 14
Ainsworth ..2,073.°D 8
Albion ......2,074.°F 12
Alda ....456..H 11
Alexandria ...225..J 13
Allen ....309..D 14
Alliance ....6,862.°E 3
Alma ....1,299.°J 9
Almeria ....F 9
Alvo ....151..K 1
Amelia ....E 10
Ames ....I 1
Amherst .....259..H 9
Angora ....F 2
Angus ....17..J 12
Anoka ....25..C 10
Anselmo ......180..F 8
Ansley ....631..G 9
Antioch ....E 3
Arapahoe ...1,147..J 8
Arcadia ......418..G 10
Archer ....G 11
Arlington .....910..I 2
Arnold ....752..G 8
Arthur ....175.°F 5
Ashby ....E 4
Ashland ....2,176..J 2
Ashton ....277..G 10
Assumption ....I 11
Atkinson ....1,406..D 10
Atlanta ......101..I 9
Auburn .....3,650.°I 16
Aurora .....3,180.°H 12
Avoca ....229..K 2
Axtell ....500..I 10
Ayr ....140..I 11
Bancroft ......545..E 14
Barada ....58..J 16
Barneston .....149..I 14
Bartlett ....140.°F 11
Bartley ....283..J 7
Bassett ....983.°D 9
Battle Creek ..771..E 12
Bayard .....1,338..F 2
Bazile Mills ....44..D 12
Beatrice ...12,389.°I 14
Beaver City ...802.°J 8
Beaver Crossing ....400..H 13
Bee ....156..H 13
Beemer ....699..F 14
Belden ....162..D 13
Belgrade ......210..G 11
Bellevue ...21,145..G 15
Bellwood ......361..G 13
Belvidere .....162..J 12
Benedict ......209..H 12
Benkelman ..1,349.°J 5
Bennet ....489..H 14
Bennington ....683..I 2
Bertrand ......662..I 9
Berwyn ....110..G 9
Big Springs ...472..H 4
Bingham ....E 4
Bladen ....293..I 11
Blair ....6,106.°F 15
Bloomfield ..1,287..D 12
Bloomington ...165..J 10
Blue Hill ......784..I 11
Blue Springs ..506..J 14
Boelus ....H 11
Boone ....F 12
Bostwick ....J 11
Bow Valley ....D 13
Boys Town ....989..I 2
Bradshaw .....347..H 12
Brady ....311..H 7
Brainard ......309..G 13
Brandon ....H 4
Brewster ....54.°F 8
Bridgeport ..1,490.°F 2
Bristow ......127..C 10
Broadwater ...141..F 3
Brock ....192..I 15
Broken Bow 3,734.°G 8
Brownlee ....E 7
Brownson ....G 2
Brownville ....174..I 16
Brule ....423..H 4
Bruning ....315..I 12
Bruno ....142..G 13
Brunswick .....229..E 12
Bucktail ....F 5
Burchard ......131..J 15
Burr ....108..I 15
Burton ....23..C 9
Burwell ....1,341.°F 9
Bushnell ......211..G 1
Butte ....575.°C 10
Byron ....171..J 12
Cairo ....686..H 10
Callaway ......523..G 8
Cambridge ..1,145..J 8
Campbell .....447..J 10
Carleton ......163..I 12
Carroll ....235..E 13
Cedar Bluffs ..616..I 1
Cedar Creek ..224..J 2
Cedar Rapids .449..F 11
Center ....111.°D 12
Central City .2,803.°H 12
Ceresco ......474..J 1
Chadron ....5,921.°C 3
Chambers ....321..E 10
Champion ....I 5
Chapman ....371..H 11
Chappell ....1,204.°H 3
Chester ....459..J 12
Clarks ....480..G 12
Clarkson ......805..F 13
Clatonia ....224..I 14
Clay Center ...952.°I 12
Clearwater ....398..E 11
Clinton ....55..D 4
Cody ....246..C 6
Coleridge .....608..D 13
Colon ....109..I 1
Columbus ..15,471.°G 13
Comstock ......144..F 9
Concord ....180..D 13
Cook ....328..I 15
Cordova ....141..H 13
Cornlea ....54..F 12
Cortland ......326..I 14
Cotesfield ......76..G 10
Cowles ....57..J 11
Cozad ......4,225..H 8
Crab Orchard ...96..I 15
Craig ....295..F 14
Crawford ...1,291..D 2
Creighton ...1,461..D 12
Creston ....171..F 13
Crete ....4,444..I 14
Crofton ....677..D 12
Crookston ......86..C 7
Culbertson ....801..J 6
Curtis ......1,166..I 7
Cushing ....43..G 11
Dakota City .1,057.°D 14
Dalton ....354..G 2
Danbury ....137..J 7
Dannebrog ....384..H 11
Darr ....15..H 8
Davenport .....427..I 12
Davey ....163..J 1
David City ..2,380.°G 13
Dawson ....251..J 16
Daykin ....192..I 13
Decatur ....679..E 15
Denton ....151..H 14
Deshler ....937..J 12
Deweese ....86..I 11
De Witt ....651..I 14
Dickens ....22..H 6
Diller ....287..J 14
Dix ....342..G 2
Dixon ....128..D 13
Dodge ....704..F 14
Doniphan ......542..H 11
Dorchester ....492..I 13
Douglas ....175..I 15
Dubois ....185..J 15
Dunbar ....252..H 15
Duncan ....298..G 12
Dunning ....162..F 8
Dwight ....224..H 13
Eagle ....585..K 1
Eddyville ....128..H 9
Edgar ....707..I 12
Edison ....199..J 8
Elba ....211..G 11
Eldorado ....I 12
Elgin ....917..E 11
Eli ....C 5
Elk City ....I 2
Elk Creek .....151..I 15
Elkhorn ....1,184..I 2
Ellis ....J 14
Ellsworth ....E 4
Elm Creek ....798..I 9
Elmwood ......548..K 2
Elsie ....125..H 5
Elsmere ....E 8
Elwood ....601.°I 8
Elyria ....55..F 10
Emerald ....H 14
Emerson ....850..E 14
Emmet ....70..D 10
Enders ....I 5
Endicott ....167..J 13
Enola ....F 12
Ericson ....122..F 10
Eustis ....400..I 8
Ewing ....552..E 11
Exeter ....759..I 13
Fairbury ....5,265.°J 13
Fairfield ....487..I 11
Fairmont ....761..I 12
Falls City ...5,444.°J 16
Farnam ....259..I 8
Farwell ....172..G 10
Filley ....138..I 14
Firth ....328..I 14
Flats ....F 5
Fordyce ....146..D 13
Fort Calhoun ....642..I 2
Fort Robinson .....D 2
Foster ....79..E 12
Franklin ....1,193.°J 10
Fremont ...22,962.°G 14
Friend ......1,126..I 13
Fullerton ...1,444.°G 12
Funk ....143..I 9
Gandy ....50..G 7
Garland ....244..H 13
Garrison ....60..G 13
Gates ....F 9
Geneva ......2,275.°I 12
Genoa ....1,174..G 12
Gering ......5,639.°F 1
Gibbon .....1,388..H 10
Gilead ....60..J 13
Giltner ....408..H 11
Gladstone ....J 13
Glenville ....332..I 11
Goehner ....113..H 13
Gordon .....2,106..C 4
Gothenburg .3,158..H 8
Grafton ....128..I 12
Grainton ....20..H 6
Grand Island ....31,269.°H 11
Grant ......1,099.°H 5
Greeley ....580.°G 11
Greenwood ....506..K 1
Gresham ....248..H 13
Gretna ......1,665..J 2
Gross ....8..C 10
Guide Rock ...318..J 11
Gurley ....233..G 2
Hadar ....172..E 13
Haigler ....237..J 4
Hallam ....280..I 14
Halsey ....131..F 7
Hamlet ....64..I 6
Hampton ....387..H 12
Hansen ....I 11
Harbine ....44..J 14
Hardy ....250..J 12
Harrisburg ....°F 1
Harrison ....377.°D 1
Hartington ..1,581.°D 13
Harvard .....1,230..I 11
Hastings ...23,580.°I 11
Hay Springs ..682..D 3
Hayes Center .237..I 6
Hazard ....72..H 10
Heartwell ....104..I 10
Hebron ......1,667.°J 12
Hemingford ...734..E 2
Henderson .....901..H 12
Hendley ....58..J 8
Henry ....147..E 1
Herman ....323..F 15
Hershey ....526..G 6
Hickman ....415..I 14
Hildreth ....352..I 10
Holbrook ....307..J 8
Holdrege ....5,635.°I 9
Holland ....I 14
Holmesville ....J 14
Holstein ....231..I 10
Homer ....457..E 14
Hooper ....895..F 14
Hordville ....147..H 12
Hoskins ....271..E 13
Howard City* .182..G 10
Howe ....I 16
Howells ....682..F 13
Hubbard ....151..D 14
Hubbell ....83..J 13
Humboldt ...1,194..J 15
Humphrey ......862..F 12
Huntley ....67..J 9
Hyannis ....345.°E 5
Imperial ....1,589.°I 5
Inavale ....J 10
Indianola ....672..J 7
Inglewood ......275..I 1
Inland ....I 11
Inman ....160..D 11
Irvington ....I 2
Ithaca ....121..J 1
Jackson ....232..D 14
Jamison ....C 9
Jansen ....191..J 13
Johnson ....350..I 15
Johnstown ....82..D 8
Julian ....80..I 16
Juniata ....480..I 11
Kearney ...19,181.°I 10
Keene ....I 10
Kenesaw ....728..I 10
Kennard ....336..I 2
Kennedy ....D 7
Keystone ....G 5
Kilgore ....110..C 6
Kimball .....3,680.°G 1
Kramer ....I 14
Kronborg ....H 12
Lakeside ....E 4
Lamar ....30..I 4
Lanham ....J 14
La Platte ....J 3
Laurel ....1,009..D 13
La Vista ....7,840..J 2
Lawrence ....343..J 11
Lebanon ....118..J 7
Leigh ....501..F 13
Lemoyne ....G 5
Leshara ....102..I 1
Lewellen ....376..G 4
Lewiston ....88..J 15
Lexington ....5,654.°H 8
Liberty ....118..J 14
Lincoln ...149,518.°H 14
Lindsay ....291..F 12
Lindy ....D 12
Linwood ....108..G 13
Lisco ....G 3
Litchfield ....248..G 9
Lodgepole ....407..G 3
Loma ....G 13
Long Pine ....363..D 8
Loomis ....323..I 9
Lorenzo ....H 2
Loretto ....F 11
Lorton ....47..I 15
Louisville ...1,036..H 15
Loup City ...1,456.°G 10
Lowell ....I 10
Lushton ....34..H 12
Lyman ....561..E 1
Lynch ....375..C 11
Lyons ....1,177..E 14
Macon ....J 10
Macy ....E 14
Madison ....1,595.°F 13
Madrid ....234..H 5
Magnet ....88..D 12
Malcolm ....300..H 14
Malmo ....131..I 1
Manley ....150..K 2
Marion ....J 7
Marquette ....239..H 12
Marsland ....17..D 2
Martell ....I 14
Martinsburg ...73..D 14
Mascot ....J 9
Maskell ....43..D 13
Mason City ...196..G 9
Max ....J 5
Maxwell ....282..H 7
Maywood ....309..I 7
McCook .....8,285.°J 7
McCool Junction ....289..H 12
McGrew ....79..F 2
McLean ....67..D 12
Mead ....488..J 1
Meadow Grove 372..E 12
Melbeta ....124..F 1
Memphis ....71..J 1
Menominee ....C 13
Merna ....322..G 8
Merriman ....172..C 5
Milburn ....F 8
Milford ......1,846..H 13
Miller ....130..H 9
Milligan ....319..I 13
Mills ....C 9
Minatare ....939..F 2
Minden ......2,669.°I 10
Mitchell .....1,842..E 1
Monowi ....16..C 11
Monroe ....295..G 12
Moorefield ....56..I 7
Morrill ....937..E 1
Morse Bluff ....162..I 1
Mullen ....667.°E 6
Murdock ....262..K 2
Murray ....286..K 3
Mynard ....K 3
Naper ....159..C 10
Naponee ....187..J 10
Nebraska City ......7,441.°H 16
Nehawka ....298..K 3
Neligh ......1,764.°E 11
Nelson ....746.°J 11
Nemaha ....207..I 16
Nenzel ....27..C 6
Newcastle ......347..D 14
Newman Grove ......863..F 12
Newport ....141..D 9
Nickerson ....214..H 1
Niobrara ....602..D 11
Nora ....43..J 12
Norfolk ....16,607..E 13
Norman ....52..I 10
North Bend .1,350..I 1
North Loup ...441..G 10
North Platte ...19,447.°G 7
Northport ....F 2
Oak ....100..J 12
Oakdale ....322..E 12
Oakland .....1,355..F 14
Obert ....36..D 13
Oconto ....155..G 8
Octavia ....97..G 13
Odell ....349..J 14
Odessa ....I 9
Offutt ....13,640..J 3
Ogallala .....4,976.°H 5
Ohiowa ....156..I 13
Omaha ...346,929.°G 15
O'Neill ......3,753.°D 10
Ong ....129..I 12
Orchard ....467..E 11
Ord ....2,439.°F 10
Orleans ....592..J 9
Osceola ....923.°G 12
Oshkosh ......1,067.°G 4
Osmond ....883..E 12
Otoe ....204..H 15
Overton ....538..H 9
Oxford ....1,116..J 9
Page ....177..D 11
Palisade ....372..I 6
Palmer ....391..G 11
Palmyra ....386..H 15
Panama ....153..I 14
Papillion ......6,493.°G 15
Parks ....J 5
Parkview* ...1,089..H 11
Paul ....I 15
Pauline ....I 11
Pawnee City ....1,267.°J 15
Paxton ....503..G 5
Pender ....1,229.°E 14
Peru ....1,380..I 16
Petersburg ......370..F 11
Phillips ....341..H 11
Pickrell ....182..I 14
Pierce ....1,360.°E 12
Pilger ....470..E 13
Plainview ....1,494..E 12
Platte Center .384..F 12

Plattsmouth .6,371.°H 15	Rose ....E 9	Snyder ....383..F 14	Taylor ....240.°F 9	Washington ....76..I 2
Pleasant Dale .258..H 14	Roseland .....212..J 11	South Bend ....86..J 2	Tecumseh ..2,058.°I 15	Waterbury ....81..D 14
Pleasanton ...261..H 10	Rosemont ....J 11	South	Tekamah ..1,848.°F 15	Waterloo .....455..I 2
Plymouth ....424..I 14	Royal ....86..E 11	Sioux City 7,920..D 14	Terrytown ....747..F 1	Wauneta .....738..I 8
Polk ....413..H 12	Ruby ....H 13	Spalding .....676..F 11	Thayer ....78..H 12	Wausa ....720..D 12
Ponca ....984.°D 14	Rulo ....299..J 16	Sparks ....C 7	Thedford .....303.°E 7	Waverly ...1,457..K 1
Poole ....19..H 10	Rushville ..1,137.°D 4	Spencer ......606..C 10	Thompson ....J 13	Wayne ....5,379.°E 13
Potter ....356..G 2	Ruskin ....229..J 12	Sprague ......119..I 14	Thurston .....117..E 14	Weeping
Powell ....J 13	St. Bernard ....F 12	Springfield ...795..J 2	Tilden ....947..E 12	Water .....1,143..H 15
Prague ....291..G 14	St. Columbans ...J 3	Springview ...260.°C 8	Tobias ....124..I 13	Weissert ....G 9
Prairie Home .....K 1	St. Edward ...853..F 12	Stamford .....207..J 9	Touhy ....G 14	Wellfleet .....51..H 7
Preston ....64..J 16	St. Helena ...102..C 13	Stanton ...1,363.°E 13	Trenton ......770.°J 8	West Lincoln .....K 1
Primrose ......88..F 11	St. James ....D 13	Staplehurst ..227..H 13	Trumbull .....220..I 11	West Point .3,385.°F 14
Princeton .....I 14	St. Libory ....H 11	Stapleton ....311.°G 7	Tryon ....°F 6	Western .....344..I 13
Prosser ....70..I 11	St. Mary ....I 15	Steele City ..176..J 13	Uehling ......249..F 14	Westerville ....G 9
Purdum ....E 7	St. Paul ...2,026.°G 11	Steinauer ....118..J 15	Ulysses ......312..H 13	Weston ....285..J 1
Raeville ....F 11	St. Stephens .....J 11	Stella ....282..J 16	Unadilla .....271..H 15	Whiteclay ....C 3
Ragan ....60..J 9	Salem ....214..J 16	Sterling ......476..I 15	Union ....275..K 3	Whitman ....E 5
Ralston ....4,731..J 2	Santee ....C 12	Stockham ......65..H 12	Upland ....205..I 10	Whitney ....82..C 2
Randolph ..1,130..D 13	Sarben ....G 6	Stockville ....61.°I 7	Utica ....602..H 13	Wilber ....1,483.°I 13
Ravenna ...1,356..H 10	Sargent ......789..F 9	Strang ....47..I 12	Valentine ..2,662.°C 7	Wilcox ....280..I 9
Raymond .....187..K 1	Saronville ....74..I 12	Stratton ......481..J 6	Valley ......1,595..I 2	Willow Island ....H 8
Red Cloud ..1,531.°J 11	Schuyler ..3,597.°G 13	Stromsburg .1,215..H 12	Valparaiso ...415..H 14	Wilsonville ...266..J 8
Republi-	Scotia ....354..G 10	Stuart ....561..D 9	Venango ......218..H 4	Winnebago ...675..E 14
can City ....179..J 9	Scottsbluff .14,507..F 1	Sumner ....222..H 9	Venice ....J 2	Winnetoon .....84..D 12
Reynolds .....115..J 13	Scribner ...1,031..F 14	Sunol ....G 3	Verdel ....74..C 11	Winside ......453..E 13
Richfield ....J 2	Sedan ....I 12	Superior ...2,779..J 11	Verdigre .....570..D 11	Winslow ....145..F 14
Richland .....123..G 13	Seneca ....III..E 6	Surprise ....77..H 13	Verdon ....265..J 16	Wisner ....1,315..E 13
Rising City ..344..G 13	Seward ....5,294.°H 13	Sutherland ...840..G 6	Virginia ....83..J 14	Wolbach .....366..G 11
Riverdale .....155..H 9	Shelby ....647..G 13	Sutton .....1,361..I 12	Wabash ....K 2	Wood Lake ..117..D 8
Riverton .....220..J 10	Shelton ....1,028..H 10	Swanton ......160..I 13	Waco ....214..H 13	Wood
Roca ....118..I 14	Shickley ......385..I 12	Swedeburg ....J 1	Wahoo ....3,835.°G 14	River .....1,147..H 10
Rockford ....J 14	Sholes ....22..E 13	Syracuse ...1,562..I 15	Wakefield ..1,160..E 14	Worms ....H 11
Rockville .....114..H 10	Shubert ....240..J 16	Table Rock ...429..J 15	Wallace ....241..H 6	Wymore ....1,790..J 14
Rogers ....95..G 14	Sidney .....6,403.°G 2	Talmage ......285..I 15	Walthill ......897..E 14	Wynot ....226..D 13
Rosalie ....204..E 14	Silver Creek ..483..G 12	Tamora ....93..H 13	Walton ....K 1	York ......6,778.°H 12
Roscoe ....G 5	Smithfield .....58..I 8	Tarnov ....63..F 12	Wann ....J 2	Yutan ....507..J 1

Sources: Latest census figures (1970 and special censuses). Places without population figures are unincorporated areas and are not listed in census reports.

NEBRASKA/People

The 1970 United States census reported that Nebraska had 1,483,791 persons. The population had increased 5 per cent over the 1960 figure, 1,411,330. The U.S. Bureau of the Census estimated that by 1975 the state's population had reached about 1,546,000.

About two-thirds of the people live in urban areas. Nebraska has two Standard Metropolitan Statistical Areas (see METROPOLITAN AREA). These are Omaha and Lincoln. The population of the Omaha metropolitan area is 542,646, and that of the Lincoln area is 167,972. The Sioux City, Iowa, metropolitan area also extends into Dakota County, Nebraska.

Omaha, the state's largest city, serves as the industrial and trade center of eastern Nebraska and western Iowa. Omaha is one of the nation's chief rail centers. Lincoln, the second largest city, became Nebraska's capital in 1867. The first Capitol stood on the open prairie.

Pioneers planted the trees that still shade many of Lincoln's streets. D Street is famous for its many huge pin oaks.

Lincoln is an educational, governmental, and retail-shopping center. Grand Island, Nebraska's third largest city, has a population of 31,269. It is an important shipping point for farm and manufactured products. Only nine other Nebraska cities have more than 10,000 persons. See the separate articles on the cities of Nebraska listed in the *Related Articles* at the end of this article.

About 98 out of 100 Nebraskans were born in the United States. Germans make up the largest group of Nebraskans born in other countries.

Roman Catholics make up the largest single religious group in Nebraska. The largest Protestant bodies in the state include Lutherans, Methodists, and Presbyterians.

POPULATION

This map shows the *population density* of Nebraska, and how it varies in different parts of the state. Population density means the average number of persons who live in a given area.

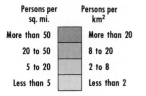

Persons per sq. mi.	Persons per km²
More than 50	More than 20
20 to 50	8 to 20
5 to 20	2 to 8
Less than 5	Less than 2

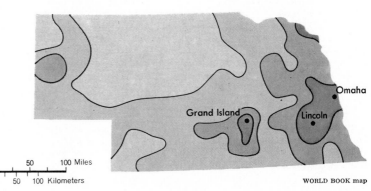

WORLD BOOK map

Schools. In the 1820's, the U.S. Army established Nebraska's first school, at Fort Atkinson (near present-day Fort Calhoun). During the 1830's and 1840's, missionaries of various religious faiths founded schools in many parts of the Nebraska region to teach the Indians. The first legislature of the Nebraska Territory adopted a free-school law in 1855, one year after the territory was opened for settlement. The state constitution, adopted in 1875, provides for the present system of public education. Children must attend school between their 7th and 16th birthdays.

The state department of education supervises the Nebraska school system. The department consists of a state board of education and a state commissioner of education. The people elect the eight members of the state board of education to four-year terms. The members of the board appoint the commissioner. For the number of students and teachers in Nebraska, see EDUCATION (table).

Libraries. Nebraska's first library was established in 1820 at the Fort Atkinson military post. The Kansas-Nebraska Act of 1854 provided for a territorial library in Nebraska. In 1871, Omaha established the state's first public library. The legislature passed a law in 1877 providing state funds to support public libraries. The Nebraska Library Commission was set up in 1901. It serves as a center for the development of libraries and the coordination of library services in the state.

Nebraska has more than 270 public libraries which are part of regional library networks. The state has 33 college and university libraries. The University of Nebraska library in Lincoln is the largest library in the state. It has more than 1 million books. The Nebraska State Historical Society in Lincoln owns the largest collection of historical documents concerning Nebraska. The Nebraska State Library is located in Lincoln. This library ranks among the best law libraries in the United States.

NEBRASKA/*A Visitor's Guide*

Every year, thousands of tourists drive along Nebraska highways that follow the historic Oregon and Mormon trails. Ruts left by the pioneers' covered wagons can still be seen along the roadsides. In western Nebraska, the forests and rugged rocks of the Pine Ridge are a camper's and hiker's paradise. Other scenic spots include the valleys of the Platte, Niobrara, Big Blue, Loup, and Republican rivers and the bluffs along the Missouri River. Fishermen delight in the lakes and streams of the Sand Hills area, which teem with bass, pike, and other game fish. On the broad prairies, hunters bag pheasants, quail, and other game birds.

--------- PLACES TO VISIT ---------

Following are brief descriptions of some of Nebraska's many interesting places to visit.

Bellevue is the oldest town in Nebraska. It was established about 1823 as a fur-trading center. Some of the town's buildings are more than a hundred years old.

Boys Town, near Omaha, is a home for neglected and homeless boys of all races and creeds.

Brownville was a leading river port of the 1850's. Many colorful reminders of pioneer days still stand.

Fort Atkinson, near Fort Calhoun, was the first U.S. military post west of the Missouri River. It stood from 1819 to 1827. A monument marks the site.

Massacre Canyon Monument, near Trenton, marks the site of the last battle between the Sioux and Pawnee Indians.

Scouts Rest Ranch, near North Platte, was the home of Buffalo Bill, the dashing frontiersman. His famous Wild West Show rehearsed there.

Toadstool Park, in the Badlands near Crawford, has huge, oddly shaped rock formations. Many of them resemble giant toadstools.

Union Stockyards, in Omaha, covers 90 acres (36 hectares). It is one of the world's largest livestock markets.

Buffalo Bill's Home at Scouts Rest Ranch near North Platte
Nebraska Information and Tourism Div.

National Forests and Parklands. Nebraska has two national forests, Nebraska in Blaine, Dawes, Sioux, and Thomas counties and McKelvie in Cherry County. These forests are the only national forests planted entirely by foresters. The Agate Fossil Beds National Monument contains famous deposits of animal fossils. The Homestead National Monument of America occupies the site of one of the first pieces of land claimed under the Homestead Act of 1862. The Scotts Bluff National Monument marks a landmark 766 feet (233 meters) above the North Platte River on the Oregon Trail. The spire at Chimney Rock National Historic Site rises about 500 feet (150 meters) above the North Platte.

State Parks. Nebraska has five state parks. For information on them, write to Director, Game and Parks Commission, Box 30370, Lincoln, Nebr. 68509.

Museums. The Nebraska State Historical Society museum features exhibits dealing with the history of Nebraska and the West. The Hastings Museum also has displays on Nebraska's history. The Harold Warp Pioneer Village in Minden features thousands of indoor and outdoor exhibits dealing with life in the West from 1830 on. The University of Nebraska State Museum in Lincoln has one of the nation's largest collections of fossils, including an exceptional display of prehistoric mammoth skeletons. The Joslyn Art Museum in Omaha owns many outstanding European and American paintings. The University of Nebraska Art Galleries in Lincoln display a large collection of paintings by modern American artists. These works are housed in the $3½ million Sheldon Memorial Art Gallery, which was completed in 1963. The National Park Service operates museums at Scotts Bluff National Monument near Scottsbluff, and at the Homestead National Monument of America near Beatrice.

─────── UNIVERSITIES AND COLLEGES ───────

Nebraska has 14 universities and colleges accredited by the North Central Association of Colleges and Schools. For enrollments and further information, see UNIVERSITIES AND COLLEGES (table).

Name	Location	Founded
Chadron State College	Chadron	1911
Concordia Teachers College	Seward	1894
Creighton University	Omaha	1878
Dana College	Blair	1884
Doane College	Crete	1858
Hastings College	Hastings	1882
Kearney State College	Kearney	1905
Midland Lutheran College	Fremont	1887
Nebraska, University of	*	*
Nebraska Wesleyan University	Lincoln	1887
Peru State College	Peru	1867
Saint Mary, College of	Omaha	1923
Union College	Lincoln	1891
Wayne State College	Wayne	1891

*For campuses and founding dates, see UNIVERSITIES AND COLLEGES (table).

Father Flanagan Memorial at Boys Town near Omaha
FPG

Chimney Rock National Historic Site near Bayard
Dick Hufnagle, Publix

─────── ANNUAL EVENTS ───────

The Nebraska State Fair and the Nebraskaland Days and Buffalo Bill Rodeo are the state's most important annual events. The fair is held in Lincoln in September. It features exhibits of crops, farm machinery, household equipment, and livestock. Nebraskaland Days, a week-long celebration, takes place in North Platte in June. It includes parades, old-time Wild West shows, and a rodeo. Almost every Nebraska county has a fair during the summer, and many communities hold annual fall festivals.

Other annual events held in Nebraska include the following.

April-May: Arbor Day, statewide (April); Fishing Derby in McCook (May); German Heritage Days in McCook (May); Women's College World Series in Omaha (May); Miss Nebraska Teen-age Pageant in North Platte (late May).

June-August: Sherman Cup Regatta and Laser National Championship at Sherman Dam near Ord (early June); Czech Festival in Clarkson (June); Danish Days in Minden (June); Rock and Mineral Show in Gering (June); Spring Festival in Schuyler (June); Swedish Festival in Stromsburg (June); Johnson Lake Regatta in Lexington (July); Old Mill Days in Neligh (July); Oregon Trail Days in Gering (July); Czech Festival in Wilber (August); Nebraska's Biggest Rodeo in Burwell (August).

September-December: Ak-Sar-Ben Livestock Show and Rodeo in Omaha (September); Applejack Festival in Nebraska City (September); Hay Days in Cozad (September); Fall Festival in Brownville (October); Light of the World Pageant in Minden (December).

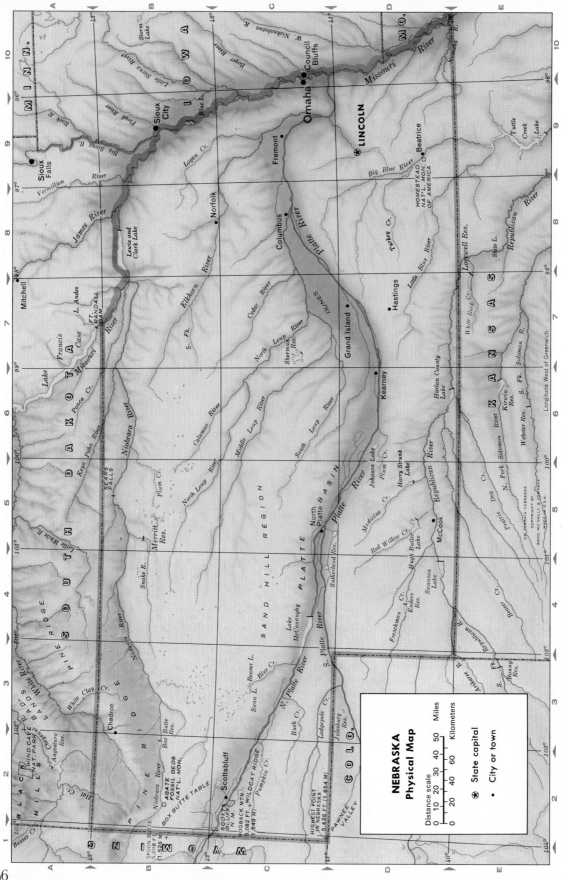

NEBRASKA
Physical Map

Distance scale
Miles
Kilometers

50
60
40
50
30
40
20
30
10
20
0
10
0

⊛ State capital
• City or town

96

Specially created for **World Book Encyclopedia** by Rand McNally and World Book editors

Land Regions of Nebraska

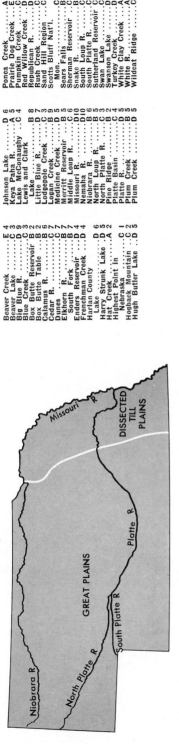

NEBRASKA/The Land

Land Regions. Nebraska rises in a series of rolling plateaus from the southeast to the extreme southwest. The land rises from about 800 feet (240 meters) above sea level to over 5,400 feet (1,650 meters). Nebraska has two major land regions. These are, from east to west: (1) the Dissected Till Plains and (2) the Great Plains.

The *Dissected Till Plains* cover about the eastern fifth of Nebraska and extend into South Dakota, Iowa, Missouri, and Kansas. Glaciers once covered the Till Plains. The last glacier melted several hundred thousand years ago. It left a thick cover of rich, soil-forming material called *till.* A deep deposit of wind-blown dust called *loess* then settled on the till. Streams have *dissected* (cut up) the region, giving it a rolling surface. In the southeastern section of Nebraska's Till Plains, the action of the streams has exposed glacial materials on the sides of the valleys. The *Loess Hills* of the Dissected Till Plains is known as the *Loess Hills.* Most of the Dissected Till Plains is well suited to farming with modern machinery.

The *Great Plains* region of Nebraska stretches westward from the Dissected Till Plains and extends into Wyoming and Colorado. A series of sand hills rises north of the Platte River in the central part of the region. The soil of the *Sand Hills* section consists of fine sand piled up by the wind. The sand was formed into low hills and ridges. The section covers about 20,000 square miles (51,800 square kilometers). Grasses that now cover the Sand Hills hold most of the sand in place. Sometimes, however, overgrazing by cattle kills the grass cover. The wind then cuts great holes called *blowouts* into the hillsides. Most ranchers take care not to overgraze the land. The Sand Hills make exceptionally fine cattle country because of the area's flowing streams, abundant well water, and excellent grasses. Some of the grass is cut as *wild hay.*

The soil of the Sand Hills acts like a giant sponge. It absorbs and holds most of the area's limited rainfall. The rainfall seeps down and creates vast underground reservoirs of *ground water.* Movements of the ground water make it possible to pump irrigation water to the surface in areas around the Sand Hills.

A deep deposit of loess covers the central and south-central parts of the Great Plains. Some of this loess country is rough and hilly. But in the southeast, a vast area of flat loess land covers about 7,000 square miles (18,000 square kilometers). This area, called the *Loess Plain,* is farmed even more intensively than the Till Plains.

North and west of the Sand Hills are the *High Plains,* which cover about 12,000 square miles (31,100 square kilometers). The High Plains in the west rise more than 1 mile (1.6 kilometers) above sea level along part of the Wyoming border. The High Plains receive little rainfall. Farmers there must use irrigation or practice *dry farming,* methods that make the most of the limited rainfall (see DRY FARMING). Rough parts of the High Plains are used mainly to graze cattle. Some of the rough areas, including the beautiful Wildcat Ridge and Pine Ridge, are covered with evergreen trees. The highest point in Nebraska is 5,426 feet (1,654 meters) above sea level in southwestern Kimball County.

A small area of *Badlands* is found in northwestern Nebraska. There, the forces of nature have carved weird formations in the sandstone and claylike rocks.

NEBRASKA

Rich Farmlands make up most of eastern Nebraska. Farmers use contour plowing on the rolling land. Rows of trees protect the flat areas from the weather.

The Badlands have little economic importance, but ranchers use some of the area to graze cattle.

Rivers and Lakes. The great Missouri River forms Nebraska's eastern and northeastern border. Nebraska's principal river, the Platte, flows into the Missouri at Plattsmouth. The North Platte and South Platte rivers join near the city of North Platte and form the Platte. The North Platte River flows into the state from Wyoming, and the South Platte enters from Colorado. The Platte River winds across central and southern Nebraska. In some places, it is as much as 1 mile (1.6 kilometers) wide. The Platte is too shallow for navigation. Nebraskans use the waters of the Platte River and its branches for irrigation and to generate hydroelectric power.

The Loup and Elkhorn rivers are the Platte's most important branches. Both rise in the Sand Hills. The abundant supplies of ground water in the Sand Hills keep these rivers flowing the year around. The Loup River is formed by the North, Middle, and South Loup rivers.

The Republican River enters southwestern Nebraska from Kansas. It flows near the southern edge of Nebraska for about 200 miles (320 kilometers), and then turns back into Kansas and empties into the Kansas River. Other branches of the Kansas River in Nebraska include the Big Blue and Little Blue rivers. These three branches of the Kansas River usually flow gently. But heavy rainstorms sometimes cause them to overflow and flood the countryside. This danger has been reduced by flood-control projects and by dams built for irrigation and generating electric power.

The Niobrara River flows into northwestern Nebraska from Wyoming. It winds across the northern part of the state. This narrow, swift river passes through many scenic spots. It joins the Missouri River in Knox County.

Nebraska has more than 2,000 lakes. None of the natural lakes is very large. Hundreds of small, shallow lakes dot the Sand Hills. Lake McConaughy, Nebraska's largest lake, is man-made. It covers about 55 square miles (142 square kilometers) and has a shoreline of 105 miles (169 kilometers). Lake McConaughy was formed on the North Platte River by Kingsley Dam. Other important man-made lakes on the Platte River irrigation and power system include Jeffrey and Sutherland reservoirs and Johnson Lake. Additional large man-made lakes in Nebraska are Swanson Lake and Harlan County Lake on the Republican River, and Enders Reservoir and Harry Strunk Lake on branches of the Republican River.

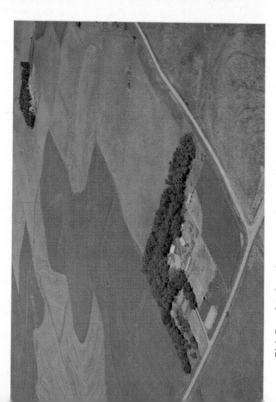

Photos by Dick Hufnagle, Publix

Mitchell Pass, at Scotts Bluff National Monument, was part of the Oregon Trail. The pass and bluffs are in the Great Plains Region of western Nebraska.

NEBRASKA / Climate

Nebraska's climate ranges from extremely hot in summer to extremely cold in winter. The weather changes suddenly—and sometimes violently. Hot, moist breezes from the Gulf of Mexico occasionally make summer nights uncomfortably warm in eastern areas. Nebraska sometimes has violent thunderstorms, tornadoes, blizzards, and hailstorms. The temperature varies only moderately from one section to another. Temperatures average about 77° F. (25° C) in July and about 25° F. (−4° C) in January. The state's record high temperature of 118° F. (48° C) was set at Geneva on July 15, 1934; at Hartington on July 17, 1936; and at Minden on July 24, 1936. Camp Clarke, near Northport, recorded the state's lowest temperature, −47° F. (−44° C), on Feb. 12, 1899.

Rainfall also decreases steadily from east to west. The east receives about 27 inches (69 centimeters) of rain yearly. Less than 18 inches (46 centimeters) fall in the west. The state has droughts in some years, floods in others. Most rain falls from April to September. The growing season ranges from about 165 days in the southeast to 120 days in the northwest. Snowfall averages almost 30 inches (76 centimeters) yearly in the east. The west generally has less snow.

SEASONAL TEMPERATURES

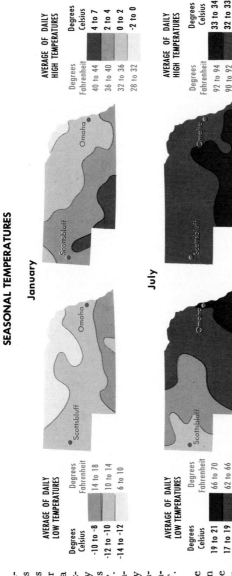

January

AVERAGE OF DAILY LOW TEMPERATURES

Degrees Fahrenheit	Degrees Celsius
14 to 18	−10 to −8
10 to 14	−12 to −10
6 to 10	−14 to −12

AVERAGE OF DAILY HIGH TEMPERATURES

Degrees Fahrenheit	Degrees Celsius
40 to 44	4 to 7
36 to 40	2 to 4
32 to 36	0 to 2
28 to 32	−2 to 0

July

AVERAGE OF DAILY LOW TEMPERATURES

Degrees Fahrenheit	Degrees Celsius
66 to 70	19 to 21
62 to 66	17 to 19
58 to 62	14 to 17
54 to 58	12 to 14

AVERAGE OF DAILY HIGH TEMPERATURES

Degrees Fahrenheit	Degrees Celsius
92 to 94	33 to 34
90 to 92	32 to 33

AVERAGE YEARLY PRECIPITATION
(Rain, Melted Snow, and Other Moisture)

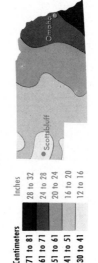

Centimeters	Inches
71 to 81	28 to 32
61 to 71	24 to 28
51 to 61	20 to 24
41 to 51	16 to 20
30 to 41	12 to 16

```
0        100        200 Miles
0   100   200   300  Kilometers
```

WORLD BOOK maps

AVERAGE MONTHLY WEATHER

	OMAHA				SCOTTSBLUFF			
	Temperatures		Days of Rain or Snow		Temperatures		Days of Rain or Snow	
	F°	C°			F°	C°		
	High Low	High Low			High Low	High Low		
JAN.	32 14	0 −10	6	JAN.	37 10	3 −12	5	
FEB.	37 18	3 −8	7	FEB.	42 15	6 −9	4	
MAR.	48 28	9 −2	8	MAR.	49 21	9 −6	6	
APR.	63 42	17 6	9	APR.	61 32	16 0	8	
MAY	73 52	23 11	11	MAY	70 42	21 6	12	
JUNE	83 62	28 17	11	JUNE	81 52	27 11	12	
JULY	89 68	32 20	9	JULY	90 59	32 15	7	
AUG.	86 65	30 18	10	AUG.	88 57	31 14	6	
SEPT.	78 56	26 13	7	SEPT.	78 46	19 8	6	
OCT.	67 44	19 7	6	OCT.	66 35	19 2	5	
NOV.	49 29	9 −2	5	NOV.	50 22	10 −6	4	
DEC.	36 19	2 −7	5	DEC.	40 14	4 −10	4	

A Sudden Snowstorm, typical of Nebraska's quick changes in weather, puts a frosty white blanket over this farm near Albion.

George W. Stewart

Natural Resources. Soil and water are Nebraska's most precious natural resources. They must be carefully conserved. Farmers rotate their crops and practice terracing and other soil-saving methods to keep the soil from wearing out or wearing away. Many dams have been built to provide water for livestock and irrigation. The dams are also used to help control the flow of rivers and to produce electric power.

Soil. A fertile silt loam covers eastern Nebraska, the state's best farming area. The soil of the Sand Hills consists of loose sand. It drifts badly if plowed. But if left untouched, it supports grasses on which cattle can graze. The High Plains in the west have a loamy soil. The Badlands have a clay soil.

Minerals. Nebraska has few minerals. Fields of petroleum and natural gas lie chiefly in western and south-central Nebraska. Sand and gravel can be found along the Platte and Republican rivers and their branches. Limestone quarries lie along the Missouri River in the southeast. Clay deposits are found throughout the state.

Forests. Trees covered only about 3 per cent of the land when white people first came to Nebraska. Most of the trees grew along the banks of rivers. There were not enough of them to be called forests. Many early settlers from wooded eastern states became active in programs to plant trees. A Nebraska City editor, J. Sterling Morton, originated the idea of Arbor Day, a special day set aside each year for planting trees. In 1872, Nebraska became the first state to celebrate Arbor Day. Charles E. Bessey, botanist of the University of Nebraska, did much to promote the planting of forests in the state. He was chiefly responsible for the establishment in 1902 of what are now the Nebraska National Forest and the Samuel R. McKelvie National Forest. These forests contain cone-bearing trees and were planted entirely by foresters. Common trees in eastern and central Nebraska include ashes, basswoods, box elders, cottonwoods, elms, hackberries, locusts, oaks, walnuts, and willows. Pines and cedars grow in the extreme western section of the state.

Other Plant Life. Pioneers in eastern Nebraska found tall prairie grasses, especially bluestem. These grasses still grow in uncultivated parts of the east. Short grasses, such as grama and buffalo grass, cover the land in drier western regions. Eastern shrubs include wild plums and chokecherries. Evening primroses, phloxes, and violets bloom in the east in spring. In summer, blue flags, columbines, larkspurs, poppies, spiderworts, and wild roses thrive throughout the state. Goldenrod and sunflowers brighten roadsides and fields in late summer.

Animal Life consists chiefly of mule deer and small animals such as badgers, coyotes, muskrats, opossums, prairie dogs, rabbits, raccoons, skunks, and squirrels. People hunt ducks, geese, pheasants, and quail, which are plentiful in the state. Common fish include bass, carp, catfish, crappies, perch, pike, and trout.

Agriculture accounts for about two-thirds of the value of all goods produced in Nebraska. The state, with a yearly total of about $4 billion, ranks as a leader in farm income. Nebraska has more than 70,000 farms. They average 634 acres (257 hectares) in size. Nebraska farms cover a total of about 46 million acres (19 mil-

lion hectares), of which almost 3 million acres (1.2 million hectares) are irrigated. Nebraska is a leading state in the amount of its irrigated land. Most of the irrigated farmlands lie in the south-central and far western areas.

Nebraska's largest farms are the cattle ranches of the Sand Hills area, some of which cover about 50,000 acres (20,200 hectares). The smallest farms are in the eastern and south-central sections. They produce livestock, and corn, small grains, and other field crops.

Livestock. Beef cattle provide the largest source of agricultural income—about $1¾ billion yearly. Only Texas and Iowa raise more beef cattle than Nebraska. The rich grasses that grow on the Sand Hills and in the west provide fine feed for range beef cattle. Ranchers ship calves and yearlings to farmers in the eastern corn-raising areas. These farmers, called *feeders,* fatten the young cattle on corn and other grains. Then they send the cattle to Omaha or other livestock markets. Nebraska is a leader in fattening cattle and lambs for market. Some farmers raise dairy cattle, and dairy products are a major source of income in the state.

Hogs rank next to cattle in value of livestock, and usually provide about $470 million in income yearly. Nebraska ranks high among the hog-producing states. Farmers throughout the state raise hogs, but most hogs come from corn-growing areas.

Field Crops. Farmers in the east and in irrigated areas raise most of Nebraska's corn, the state's chief crop. Corn

Production of Goods in Nebraska

Total value of goods produced in 1973—$6,203,275,000

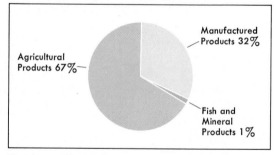

Agricultural Products 67%

Manufactured Products 32%

Fish and Mineral Products 1%

Percentages are based on farm income, value added by manufacture, and value of fish and mineral production. Fish products are less than 1 per cent.
Sources: U.S. government publications, 1975-1976.

Employment in Nebraska

Total number of persons employed in 1974—673,000

		Number of Employees
Wholesale & Retail Trade	𝌆	141,500
Agriculture	𝌆	120,000
Government	𝌆	114,800
Community, Social, & Personal Services	𝌆	98,400
Manufacturing	𝌆	92,300
Transportation & Public Utilities	𝌆	40,600
Finance, Insurance, & Real Estate	𝌆	33,600
Construction & Mining	𝌆	31,800

Sources: *Employment and Earnings,* May 1975, U.S. Bureau of Labor Statistics; *Farm Labor,* February 1975, U.S. Department of Agriculture.

provides a yearly income of about $755 million. Wheat, with an annual income of about $370 million, ranks second to corn. Most large wheat farms are in the west, though farmers in central and southeastern Nebraska also grow wheat. Many ranchers of the Sand Hills cut the grasses for hay. Nebraska leads the states in the production of this wild hay. Other important field crops include cultivated hay, grain sorghums, soybeans, and sugar beets. Farmers grow large crops of alfalfa, beans, corn, grain sorghums, potatoes, and sugar beets on the irrigated lands of the Platte River Valley.

Manufacturing accounts for about a third of the value of all goods produced in Nebraska. Goods manufactured in the state have a *value added by manufacture* of about $2 billion yearly. This figure represents the value created in products by Nebraska's industries, not counting such costs as materials, supplies, and fuel. Food processing is by far the leading manufacturing industry, with a yearly value added by manufacture of about $580 million.

Meat packing, the leading food-processing activity, is centered in Omaha. Omaha is one of the world's largest processors of meat products. Omaha and Lincoln make butter, ice cream, and other dairy products. Large flour mills are in Crete, Fremont, Grand Island, Humboldt, Lincoln, and Omaha. Nebraska City cans vegetables and other foods. Beet-sugar refineries are in Bayard, Gering, Mitchell, and Scottsbluff.

Nebraska mills produce large quantities of livestock feed. The biggest feed mills are in Crete, Fremont, Humboldt, Lexington, Lincoln, North Platte, and Omaha. Alfalfa-dehydrating plants operate along the Platte River and in a few other areas. Nebraska ranks first in the nation in the production of dehydrated alfalfa.

Other leading industries in Nebraska produce chemicals, electrical machinery, instruments, metal products, nonelectrical machinery, and printed materials. Omaha is the state's chief industrial center. Factories in Omaha make chemicals, farm implements, food products, machine tools, paper products, telephone equipment, and truck bodies. Plants in Lincoln produce bricks, candy, drugs, electrical equipment, golf carts, railroad cars, and rubber goods.

Mining accounts for only about 1 per cent of the value of goods produced in Nebraska, or about $80 million yearly. About a third of this sum comes from petroleum. Most of the state's crude oil and natural gas is produced in Banner, Cheyenne, Kimball, and Red Willow counties. Natural gasoline for fuel comes from the main gas fields. Construction companies use great quantities of sand and gravel from the Platte Valley. Manufacturers use clay from eastern Nebraska for bricks, tiles, and pottery. Limestone is used in construction, in making cement, and in treating soil.

Electric Power in Nebraska is produced and distributed by publicly owned plants and systems. Steam-generating plants provide most of the power. Hydroelectric plants supplement the steam plants in some

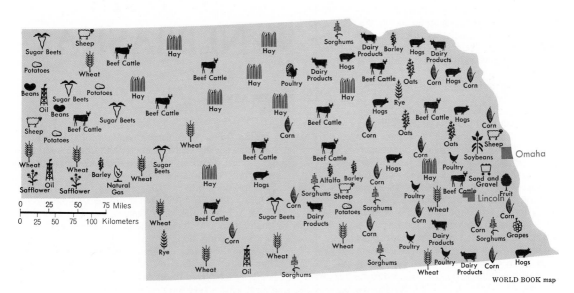

WORLD BOOK map

FARM AND MINERAL PRODUCTS

This map shows where the state's leading farm and mineral products are produced. The major urban areas (shown on the map in red) are the state's important manufacturing centers.

areas. The chief hydroelectric projects include the Central Nebraska Public Power and Irrigation District, the Loup River Public Power District, and the Platte Valley Public Power and Irrigation District. Over 30 rural power districts provide electricity for farm areas. Nuclear power plants generate electricity at Brownville and Fort Calhoun.

Transportation. Thousands of pioneers crossed the Nebraska region on their way to the West. The Oregon and Mormon trails followed Nebraska's Platte River.

Aviation. Seven commercial airlines serve Nebraska today. The state has about 275 airports, of which about 90 are public. Most of the other airports handle light aircraft only.

Railroads. In 1865, the Union Pacific began laying track westward from Omaha, and became part of the first transcontinental rail system in the United States. Today, railroads operate on about 5,500 miles (8,850 kilometers) of track in the state. Five rail lines provide freight service in Nebraska, and passenger trains serve five cities.

Roads and Highways. Nebraska has about 100,000 miles (160,000 kilometers) of roads and highways, of which about 75 per cent are surfaced. Interstate 80 crosses the state.

Waterways. Shippers use barges to transport huge quantities of grain, steel, and other bulky products on the Missouri River. Omaha, Nebraska City, and South Sioux City rank as the state's major river ports.

Communication. Thomas Morton began Nebraska's first newspaper, the *Nebraska Palladium and Platte Valley Advocate*, in Bellevue in 1854. Today, Nebraska publishers issue about 235 newspapers, of which 19 are dailies. Daily newspapers with the largest circulations include the *Lincoln Journal*, the *Lincoln Star*, and the *Omaha World-Herald*. Nebraska publishers also issue about 70 periodicals.

Nebraska has about 80 radio stations and about 25 television stations. Nebraska Wesleyan University established Nebraska's first radio station, WCAJ, in Lincoln in 1921. The first commercial station, WOAW (now WOW), began broadcasting from Omaha in 1923. Nebraska's first television stations, KMTV and WOW-TV, started operations in Omaha in 1949. The University of Nebraska established an educational television station, KUON-TV, in Lincoln in 1954. In 1963, the Nebraska legislature provided for a statewide educational television network.

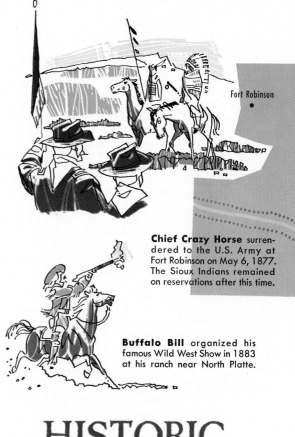

Fort Robinson

Chief Crazy Horse surrendered to the U.S. Army at Fort Robinson on May 6, 1877. The Sioux Indians remained on reservations after this time.

Buffalo Bill organized his famous Wild West Show in 1883 at his ranch near North Platte.

HISTORIC NEBRASKA

NEBRASKA/History

Indian Days. A prehistoric people probably lived in the Nebraska region between 10,000 and 25,000 years ago. Scientists base this belief on the discovery of tips of stone tools and weapons which were found buried in the Nebraska earth.

During the early 1700's, white explorers found several Indian tribes in the Nebraska region. The Missouri, Omaha, Oto, and Ponca Indians lived peacefully, farming and hunting along the rivers. The Pawnee hunted buffalo on the plains, and grew corn, beans, and squash. They fought fiercely with other tribes, especially with the Sioux who lived to the north. But the Pawnee were friendly with white settlers, and Pawnee scouts helped the U.S. Army in wars against the Sioux. The Arapaho, Cheyenne, Comanche, and Sioux hunted in western Nebraska. These wandering tribes built no villages and did not cultivate the soil. To keep their hunting grounds, the Arapaho, Cheyenne, and Sioux fought the white settlers.

Other Indian tribes moved into the Nebraska region

Largest Mammoth Fossil ever found was unearthed near North Platte in 1922. It stands 13 feet 4½ inches (4.08 meters) high.

Bellevue was the first permanent settlement in Nebraska. It was founded about 1823.

Gerald R. Ford, 38th President of the United States, was born in Omaha.

Pioneer Trails to the West followed the Platte and North Platte rivers. The Oregon Trail ran south of the rivers, the Mormon Trail north of them.

North Platte River

North Platte

MORMON TRAIL

Platte River

Omaha

LINCOLN

OREGON TRAIL

Beatrice

The First Arbor Day was celebrated in Nebraska in 1872. J. Sterling Morton of Arbor Lodge at Nebraska City was the one who first suggested the idea.

Unicameral Legislature. Nebraska's one-house legislature, adopted in 1934, is the only state government of its kind in the United States. The present state Capitol in Lincoln was completed in 1932.

One of the First U.S. Homesteads was granted to Daniel Freeman on Jan. 1, 1863. His 162-acre (66-hectare) farm near Beatrice became a national monument in 1939.

as whites drove them from their homes in the East. The Fox, Iowa, and Sauk tribes arrived in the late 1830's, and the Santee Sioux came in 1863. The last Indians to settle in Nebraska were the Winnebago, who originally lived in Wisconsin. White people drove the Winnebago first to Iowa and then to Minnesota and South Dakota. In 1863 and 1864, the Winnebago fled into what later became Thurston County. The Omaha and Winnebago now live on reservations in the state. See INDIAN, AMERICAN (Table of Tribes).

Exploration. In 1541, Francisco Vásquez de Coronado, a Spanish explorer, led an expedition across the American Southwest and into present-day Kansas. Spain claimed all this territory, including Nebraska, although the Spaniards made no settlements.

In 1682, the French explorer Robert Cavelier, Sieur de la Salle, traveled down the Mississippi River to its mouth. He claimed for France all the land drained by the Mississippi and its branches. La Salle named this vast territory, which included Nebraska, *Louisiana.*

Pony Express Station in Gothenburg stood on the trail to Oregon and California, which followed the Platte River through Nebraska. The station supplied fresh horses for the riders.

A. M. Wettach

NEBRASKA

French traders and trappers moved into the Louisiana region during the 1690's and early 1700's. In 1714, a French explorer and adventurer, Étienne Veniard de Bourgmont, traveled up the Missouri River to the mouth of the Platte River.

Spain objected to French explorers in regions that it claimed, and decided to remove the French. In 1720, a Spanish expedition under Pedro de Villasur marched from Santa Fe into the Nebraska region. But the expedition met a hostile group of Pawnee Indians along the Platte River and withdrew after being badly defeated.

Two French explorers, the brothers Pierre and Paul Mallet, traveled from French forts in Illinois to Santa Fe in 1739. They were probably the first whites to cross what is now the state of Nebraska.

The Louisiana Purchase. In 1762, France gave Louisiana to Spain. But French fur traders and trappers continued to operate in the Nebraska region, and the Spaniards never set up an effective government. In 1800, Napoleon Bonaparte, the ruler of France, forced Spain to return Louisiana to France. Three years later, Napoleon sold the Louisiana Territory to the United States. Nebraska, as part of the Louisiana Purchase, became part of the U.S. (see LOUISIANA PURCHASE).

American Exploration and Settlement. In 1804, President Thomas Jefferson sent an expedition under Meriwether Lewis and William Clark to explore the Louisiana Territory. Lewis and Clark traveled up the Missouri River and explored the eastern edge of Nebraska. Another American explorer, Zebulon M. Pike, visited the south-central part of Nebraska in 1806. Manuel Lisa, a Spanish-American trader, established fur-trading posts along the Missouri River between 1807 and 1820. One of these posts was Fort Lisa, about 10 miles (16 kilometers) from present-day Omaha.

In 1812, Robert Stuart, a fur agent, set out for New York City from the Astoria fur-trading post in Oregon. Stuart and his party spent the winter in Wyoming, and entered Nebraska early in 1813. They traveled along the North Platte and Platte rivers, and reached the Missouri River in April. Settlers moving to Oregon during the next 50 years followed the route explored by Stuart. This route became known as the Oregon Trail.

The U.S. Army established Fort Atkinson in 1819 on the Missouri River, about 16 miles (26 kilometers) north of present-day Omaha. The fort became the site of Nebraska's first school, library, sawmill, grist mill, and brickyard. The fort was abandoned in 1827.

In 1820, Major Stephen H. Long led an army expedition across Nebraska through the Platte and North Platte river valleys. Long described the region west of the Missouri River as "almost wholly unfit for farming." He called it the "Great American Desert."

During the 1820's, the American Fur Company and other fur companies set up trading posts at Bellevue and other points along the Missouri River. But until 1854, when Nebraska was made a territory, the federal government maintained Nebraska as Indian country. No white families were allowed to settle there. In 1843, thousands of pioneers began the "Great Migration" to the rich farmlands of Oregon and Washington. They followed the Oregon Trail through Nebraska to the West.

Territorial Days. In 1854, Congress passed the Kansas-Nebraska Act, which created the territories of Kansas and Nebraska. Earlier bills to create the territories had been defeated because Congress could not agree on the slavery question. Northerners wanted to forbid slavery in all new territories, but Southerners wanted to permit it. The Kansas-Nebraska Act provided that the people of the new territories could decide for themselves whether to permit slavery. Most Nebraskans opposed slavery. See KANSAS-NEBRASKA ACT.

The Nebraska Territory included what is now Nebraska and parts of Montana, North Dakota, South Dakota, Wyoming, and Colorado. President Franklin

---

IMPORTANT DATES IN NEBRASKA

1682 Robert Cavelier, Sieur de la Salle, claimed the region drained by the Mississippi, including present-day Nebraska, for France.

1714 Étienne Veniard de Bourgmont traveled up the Missouri River to the mouth of the Platte River.

1720 The Pawnee Indians defeated Spanish forces under Pedro de Villasur along the Platte River.

1739 Pierre and Paul Mallet were probably the first whites to cross Nebraska.

1762 France gave the Louisiana Territory to Spain.

1800 Spain returned Louisiana to France.

1803 The United States bought the Louisiana Territory, including Nebraska, from France.

1804 Meriwether Lewis and William Clark traveled up the Missouri River and explored eastern Nebraska.

1806 Zebulon M. Pike visited south-central Nebraska.

1813 Robert Stuart and his party followed the North Platte and Platte rivers across Nebraska.

1819 The U.S. Army established Fort Atkinson.

1843 The "Great Migration" began through Nebraska along the Oregon Trail to the West.

1854 Congress passed the Kansas-Nebraska Act, creating the Nebraska Territory.

1863 One of the first free homesteads was claimed by Daniel Freeman near Beatrice.

1865 The Union Pacific Railroad began building its line west from Omaha.

1867 Nebraska became the 37th state on March 1.

1874-1877 Vast swarms of grasshoppers invaded the Nebraska farmlands and damaged crops badly.

1890 Drought struck the state, and land prices collapsed.

1905 The North Platte River Project was begun to irrigate 165,000 acres (66,770 hectares) in western Nebraska.

1934 Nebraskans voted to adopt a unicameral state legislature.

1937 The unicameral legislature held its first session.

1939 Geologists discovered petroleum in southeastern Nebraska.

1944 Congress authorized the Missouri River Basin Project.

1954 Nebraska celebrated its territorial centennial.

1960-1964 Nebraskans approved a series of constitutional amendments that strengthened the state government by raising salaries and increasing terms of government officials.

1967 Nebraska adopted both a sales and an income tax. It also celebrated its statehood centennial.

Pierce appointed Francis Burt of South Carolina as the first territorial governor. Burt died shortly after he took office, and Secretary of State Thomas B. Cuming became acting governor. Cuming organized the territorial government and took a census so that elections could be held for the legislature. Nebraska had a population of 2,732 in 1854. By 1863, Congress had created several new territories from the region, and the Nebraska Territory was reduced to about the state's present area.

Many early settlers in the Nebraska Territory built their homes of sod, because so few trees grew on the prairies. These pioneers cut out blocks of sod with spades, and piled the blocks on top of each other to form walls. Most roofs consisted of sod blocks supported by a mat of branches, brush, and long grasses.

Statehood. By 1860, Nebraska's population had grown to 28,841. In 1862, Congress passed the first Homestead Act. This act granted 160 acres (65 hectares) of free land in the western frontier country to settlers. A great rush for land followed. One of the first homesteads was claimed by Daniel Freeman in 1863 near the present city of Beatrice. The 1862 Homestead Act and similar acts brought many thousands of homesteaders to Nebraska. See HOMESTEAD ACT (picture).

In 1865, the Union Pacific Railroad began building its line west from Omaha. The Union Pacific and the Burlington railroads also started campaigns to bring more settlers to Nebraska. They sent pamphlets describing the Nebraska farmland to people throughout the East, and even to Europe. These advertisements helped the population of Nebraska increase to 122,993 by 1870.

Early in 1867, Congress passed an act admitting Nebraska into the Union. In doing so, Congress overrode President Andrew Johnson's veto. Congress had required Nebraska to make certain changes in its constitution. Johnson believed this action violated the U.S. Constitution. Johnson also did not want Nebraska admitted into the Union because the territory had elected two Republicans to become Senators when statehood would be granted. The Republicans in Congress were trying to impeach Johnson, and the President believed the two new Senators might have been enough to convict him. Nebraska became the 37th state on March 1, 1867. The people elected David Butler, a Republican, as the first governor of the state.

Growth of Agriculture. The settlement of Nebraska slowed down between 1874 and 1877, when vast swarms of grasshoppers invaded the farmlands. The grasshoppers badly damaged oat, barley, wheat, and corn crops. Many settlers left their land and returned East. Farmers in the Midwest saw hundreds of wagons traveling east bearing such signs as "Eaten out by grasshoppers. Going back East to live with wife's folks." But another rush of farmers poured into the state during the 1880's. Prices for land soared higher and higher. In 1890, land prices collapsed because of drought, overuse of credit, and low prices for farm products. Farmers could not pay for land they had bought on credit at high prices.

The farmers blamed the railroads, banks, and other business organizations for their difficulties. Many farmers joined the Populist, or People's party, which sought reforms to help farmers. The party achieved its greatest strength in Nebraska during the 1890's. Many Populists supported William Jennings Bryan, a Democrat and the state's leading political figure of the period. See POPULIST PARTY.

In the 1890's, Nebraska farmers started to use irrigation and dry-farming methods. They also began to learn the value of cooperation in solving their marketing problems. They joined together to sell their products cooperatively and to fight the railroads over shipping rates. Cooperative marketing and purchasing organizations grew rapidly during the early 1900's.

Congress passed the Reclamation Act in 1902, authorizing federal aid for irrigation development. Three years later, construction started on the North Platte Project to irrigate 165,000 acres (66,770 hectares) in western Nebraska. The Kinkaid Act passed in 1904 and provided for 640-acre (259-hectare) homesteads in western Nebraska. But many settlers found much of the land unsuitable for farming. Cattle ranchers bought out most of the homesteaders and returned the land to grass.

Economic Depression. A boom in farm prices ended during the early 1920's. Then, in 1929, the stock market crashed and farm prices fell still further. In addition, drought again hit the state. Many farmers faced bankruptcy and the loss of their land. Banks and insurance

Homesteading Families, such as these posing on a farm near Ansley, were often called "sodbusters." They cut *sod* (soil with a thick growth of plants) into blocks and used it to build their houses. In spring, blossoming sod plants decorated the houses with flowers.

companies took over farmers' property because the farmers could not meet their mortgage payments. But so many families were affected that sheriffs often refused to carry out court orders for public sale of the land. During the Great Depression of the 1930's, the federal government provided long-term, low-interest loans and other aid for farmers.

In 1915, a committee of the Nebraska legislature had recommended a unicameral legislature. The committee believed that a one-house legislature would eliminate the delays and the shifting of responsibility that occurs in two-house legislatures. The unicameral legislature would be more economical, because there would be fewer members. The committee also felt that a one-house legislature would attract politicians of higher quality. The committee's recommendation formed the basis of discussions that lasted almost 20 years.

In 1934, U.S. Senator George W. Norris of Nebraska sponsored an amendment to the state constitution for the adoption of a unicameral legislature. The voters approved the amendment in the general elections of November 1934. The new unicameral legislature held its first meeting in 1937.

The Mid-1900's. Geologists discovered oil in southeastern Nebraska in 1939. Oil companies drilled many wells in the area during the early 1940's, and oil became the state's most important mineral.

During World War II (1939-1945), Nebraska farmers produced millions of tons of corn, oats, potatoes, and wheat to help meet wartime food shortages. The raising of beef cattle also expanded greatly. The state's enormous agricultural output was aided by plentiful rainfall and by the increased use of irrigation and scientific farming methods. By 1947, Nebraska's farm income reached a record of more than $1 billion yearly.

In 1944, Congress approved the Missouri River Basin Project. This huge project calls for construction of flood control dams, hydroelectric plants, and reservoirs in Nebraska and other states drained by the Missouri River. Nebraska has already benefited from the project, though it is far from completion. See MISSOURI RIVER BASIN PROJECT.

In 1948, the Strategic Air Command (SAC) established its headquarters at Offutt Air Force Base near Omaha. The base has been important to the economy of Omaha. In 1949, geologists discovered oil fields in western Nebraska. These fields were larger than those in the southeast.

During the 1950's, Nebraska farms became larger in size but fewer in number. The increased use of machinery lessened the need for farmworkers, and many moved to towns and cities in search of jobs. By 1970, over 60 per cent of Nebraska's people lived in urban areas.

The shift in population made Nebraska aware of the need to expand its industries and to attract new ones. In 1960, the voters approved an amendment to the state constitution allowing cities and counties to acquire and develop property for lease to private businesses. Many new firms moved into Nebraska during the 1960's, partly as a result of the state's campaigns to attract industry. Employment in manufacturing increased 44 per cent in the 1960's.

During the 1960's, the state legislature passed much important legislation. In 1963, it passed the Nebraska

U.S. Air Force

Underground Command Post of the Strategic Air Command is located near Omaha. The center would direct Air Force bombers and missiles against any enemy who might attack the United States.

THE GOVERNORS OF NEBRASKA

	Party	Term
1. David Butler	Republican	1867-1871
2. W. H. James	Republican	1871-1873
3. Robert W. Furnas	Republican	1873-1875
4. Silas Garber	Republican	1875-1879
5. Albinus Nance	Republican	1879-1883
6. James W. Dawes	Republican	1883-1887
7. John M. Thayer	Republican	1887-1892
8. James E. Boyd	Democratic	1892-1893
9. Lorenzo Crounse	Republican	1893-1895
10. Silas A. Holcomb	Fusion	1895-1899
11. William A. Poynter	Fusion	1899-1901
12. Charles H. Dietrich	Republican	1901
13. Ezra P. Savage	Republican	1901-1903
14. John H. Mickey	Republican	1903-1907
15. George L. Sheldon	Republican	1907-1909
16. Ashton C. Shallenberger	Democratic	1909-1911
17. Chester H. Aldrich	Republican	1911-1913
18. John H. Morehead	Democratic	1913-1917
19. Keith Neville	Democratic	1917-1919
20. Samuel R. McKelvie	Republican	1919-1923
21. Charles W. Bryan	Democratic	1923-1925
22. Adam McMullen	Republican	1925-1929
23. Arthur J. Weaver	Republican	1929-1931
24. Charles W. Bryan	Democratic	1931-1935
25. Robert Leroy Cochran	Democratic	1935-1941
26. Dwight Griswold	Republican	1941-1947
27. Val Peterson	Republican	1947-1953
28. Robert B. Crosby	Republican	1953-1955
29. Victor E. Anderson	Republican	1955-1959
30. Ralph G. Brooks	Democratic	1959-1960
31. Dwight W. Burney	Republican	1960-1961
32. Frank B. Morrison	Democratic	1961-1967
33. Norbert T. Tiemann	Republican	1967-1971
34. J. James Exon	Democratic	1971-

Education Television Act, and Nebraska became one of the first states to cover its entire area with educational television (ETV) broadcasts. In 1967, the legislature adopted sales and income taxes to make up for the revenue lost when the people voted out the state property tax in 1966. The 1969 legislature provided millions of dollars in aid to junior colleges.

Nebraska Today still depends heavily on agriculture, in spite of the rapid growth of manufacturing. In the 1970's, the trend toward fewer but larger farms is continuing. Agricultural production is also continuing to increase through the expanding use of machinery and modern farming methods.

The population shift from farms to cities remains one of Nebraska's chief problems. The rising urban population has created great demands on the cities to expand education, transportation, and other services.

In 1973, Gerald R. Ford, born in Omaha, became Vice-President of the United States under President Richard M. Nixon. Ford succeeded to the presidency in 1974 when Nixon resigned from the office because of his involvement in the Watergate scandal.

WILLIAM O. DOBLER, LESLIE HEWES, and JAMES C. OLSON

NEBRASKA/*Study Aids*

Related Articles in WORLD BOOK include:

BIOGRAPHIES

Bryan (family)	Ford, Gerald R.	Pound, Roscoe
Cather, Willa	Morton, Julius S.	Red Cloud
Cudahy, Michael	Norris, George W.	Sandoz, Mari S.
Flanagan, Edward J.		

CITIES

Boys Town	Lincoln	Omaha
Grand Island	North Platte	

HISTORY

Homestead Act	Railroad (The First Trans-
Kansas-Nebraska Act	continental Rail Lines)
Oregon Trail	Trails of Early Days
	Western Frontier Life

PHYSICAL FEATURES

Badlands	Kingsley Dam	Platte River
Great Plains	Missouri River	

PRODUCTS AND INDUSTRY

For Nebraska's rank among the states, see:

Agriculture	Bean	Corn
Alfalfa	Cattle	Hog

OTHER RELATED ARTICLES

Agate Fossil Beds	Midwestern States
National Monument	Offutt Air Force Base
Arbor Day	Scotts Bluff National
Homestead National Monument	Monument

Outline

I. **Government**
  A. Constitution D. Courts   F. Taxation
  B. Executive   E. Local   G. Politics
  C. Legislature   Government
II. **People**
III. **Education**
  A. Schools B. Libraries C. Museums
IV. **A Visitor's Guide**
  A. Places to Visit   B. Annual Events
V. **The Land**
  A. Land Regions   B. Rivers and Lakes
VI. **Climate**
VII. **Economy**
  A. Natural Resources   E. Electric Power
  B. Agriculture   F. Transportation
  C. Manufacturing   G. Communication
  D. Mining
VIII. **History**

Questions

What is unusual about Nebraska's state legislature?

Why did many early settlers in Nebraska build their houses of sod?

Why are the Sand Hills important to Nebraska?

How did the railroads help attract settlers to Nebraska?

Why did President Andrew Johnson oppose Nebraska's admission into the Union?

Nebraska became the first state to celebrate what widely observed day? Whose idea was it?

How does the Nebraska National Forest differ from all other national forests in the United States?

What famous Nebraskan ran unsuccessfully three times for the presidency of the United States?

Why is road building difficult in Nebraska? What famous pioneer trails crossed Nebraska?

Why did the settlement of Nebraska slow down between 1874 and 1877?

Books for Young Readers

BAILEY, BERNADINE. *Picture Book of Nebraska.* Rev. ed. Whitman, 1966.

BRUBAKER, ETHEL R., and others. *Our Nebraska.* Johnsen, 1963.

CARPENTER, ALLAN. *Nebraska.* Childrens Press, 1967.

FRANCHERE, RUTH. *Willa: The Story of Willa Cather's Growing Up.* Crowell, 1958.

SANDOZ, MARI. *The Horsecatcher.* Westminster Press, 1957.

Books for Older Readers

ADAMS, ANDY. *The Log of a Cowboy: A Narrative of the Old Trail Days.* Univ. of Nebraska Press, 1964. Originally published in 1903.

ALDRICH, BESS S. *A Lantern in Her Hand.* Scholastic Book Services, 1968. This novel was originally published in 1928.

BARNS, CASS G. *The Sod House.* Univ. of Nebraska Press, 1970. Originally published in 1930.

CATHER, WILLA. *O Pioneers!* Houghton, 1913. *My Ántonia.* 1918. *One of Ours.* Knopf, 1922. Three classic novels about Nebraska.

FAULKNER, VIRGINIA, ed. *Roundup: A Nebraska Reader.* Univ. of Nebraska Press, 1957.

MORRIS, WRIGHT. *The Home Place: Reminiscences of Nebraska.* Univ. of Nebraska Press, 1948.

NEIHARDT, JOHN G. *Black Elk Speaks: Being the Life Story of A Holy Man of the Oglala Sioux.* Pocket Books. Originally published by the Univ. of Nebraska Press in 1961.

NICOLL, BRUCE H., ed. *Nebraska: A Pictorial History.* Rev. ed. Univ. of Nebraska Press, 1975.

OLSON, JAMES C. *History of Nebraska.* 2nd ed. Univ. of Nebraska Press, 1967.

SANDOZ, MARI. *Love Song to the Plains.* Univ. of Nebraska Press, 1961.

WELSCH, ROGER L., ed. *A Treasury of Nebraska Pioneer Folklore.* Univ. of Nebraska Press, 1967.

The University of Nebraska is the largest university in Nebraska. It has campuses in Lincoln and Omaha. Oldfather Hall, *far left background*, stands on the City Campus in Lincoln. It houses faculty offices and some classrooms.

University of Nebraska

NEBRASKA, UNIVERSITY OF, is a state-supported coeducational university. It has two campuses in Lincoln, Nebr., and a campus and medical center in Omaha.

The Lincoln campuses have colleges of agriculture, architecture, arts and sciences, business administration, dentistry, engineering and technology, home economics, and law. These campuses also have a teacher's college and a graduate school.

The Omaha campus has colleges of arts and sciences, business administration, education, fine arts, engineering and technology, home economics, and public affairs and community services. This campus also has a graduate school.

The medical center has colleges of medicine, nursing, and pharmacy. Its facilities include a hospital, a rehabilitation institute, and a cancer research center.

The Lincoln campuses and the colleges of medicine, nursing, and pharmacy in Omaha grant bachelor's, master's, and doctor's degrees. The Omaha campus grants bachelor's and master's degrees.

The university carries on an extensive agricultural research program. It maintains six agricultural experiment stations in the state.

The University of Nebraska was chartered as a land-grant college in 1869. It held its first classes in 1871, in Lincoln. It merged with the Municipal University of Omaha in 1968. The municipal university became the University of Nebraska at Omaha. For enrollment, see UNIVERSITIES AND COLLEGES (table).

Critically reviewed by the UNIVERSITY OF NEBRASKA

NEBRASKA WESLEYAN UNIVERSITY is a coeducational, private liberal arts college in Lincoln, Nebr. It has a school of music and a department of teacher education, and it grants B.A., B.S., and B.F.A. degrees. It was founded in 1887. For enrollment, see UNIVERSITIES AND COLLEGES (table).   VANCE D. ROGERS

NEBUCHADNEZZAR, *NEB yoo kud NEZ er*, was the name of two kings of Babylon.

Nebuchadnezzar I (ruled 1124-1103 B.C.) was the greatest king of the second Isin dynasty, which followed the Kassite kings of Babylonia. He won fame by freeing Babylonia from Elamite control and by extending Babylonian rule over Elam, a country north of the Persian Gulf. Nebuchadnezzar's account of the Elamite battles is a fascinating document of ancient Babylonia.

Nebuchadnezzar II (ruled 605-562 B.C.) was the king of Babylonia about whom both the Old Testament and Babylonian sources have much to tell. He captured Jerusalem in 587 B.C., and destroyed the city. This battle ended the Judean kingdom. Nebuchadnezzar seized some Jews, and sent them to Babylon. The Old Testament tells of Nebuchadnezzar's spells of madness, when he would imagine himself an ox and would go out in the fields and eat grass.

Nebuchadnezzar was the son of Nabopolassar (see NABOPOLASSAR). He became king after his father's death in 605 B.C. Under Nebuchadnezzar's rule, Babylon became one of the most magnificent cities of the ancient world. In his own records, he rarely mentioned his military activities, but wrote of his building projects and his attention to the gods of Babylonia. He probably built the "Hanging Gardens," one of the Seven Wonders of the Ancient World (see SEVEN WONDERS OF THE WORLD [with picture]).   JACOB J. FINKELSTEIN

See also BABYLON; BABYLONIA; DANIEL.

NEBULA, *NEB yoo luh*, is a cloud of dust particles and gases in space. The term *nebula* comes from the Latin word for *cloud*. Early astronomers used the term for distant galaxies outside of the earth's galaxy, the Milky Way. Such galaxies, called *extragalactic nebulae*, looked like hazy patches of light among the stars. However, modern telescopes revealed that extragalactic nebulae are actually systems of stars similar to the Milky Way.

Today, most astronomers use the term *nebulae* only for the clouds of dust and gases in the Milky Way and other galaxies. They classify these masses into two general types: *diffuse nebulae* and *planetary nebulae*. Both types are also called *gaseous nebulae*.

Diffuse Nebulae are the larger of the two types. Some diffuse nebula contain enough dust and gases to form as many as 100,000 stars the size of the sun.

A diffuse nebula may occur near an extremely hot, bright star. The intense ultraviolet light from the star energizes the gas atoms of the nebula and enables the mass to emit light. A diffuse nebula of this kind is called an *emission nebula*.

Astronomers believe some emission nebulae are places where new stars are forming. Gravity causes a portion of a nebula's dust and gases to contract into a much smaller and denser mass. Pressure and temperature build up within the mass as contraction continues through millions of years. In time, the mass becomes hot enough to shine—and forms a new star.

A diffuse nebula also may occur near a cool star. In this case, the ultraviolet light from the star is too weak to energize the nebula's gas atoms and make them give off light. However, the dust particles in the nebula reflect the starlight. This kind of diffuse nebula is called a *reflection nebula*.

If a diffuse nebula occurs in an area that has no nearby stars, it neither emits nor reflects enough light to be visible. In fact, its dust particles blot out the light from the stars behind them. Astronomers call such a diffuse nebula a *dark nebula*.

Planetary Nebulae are ball-like clouds of dust and gases that surround certain stars. They form when a star begins to collapse and throw off a part of its outer gaseous envelope. When viewed through a small telescope, this type of nebula appears to have a flat, rounded surface like that of a planet. Because of this similarity, early astronomers called these nebulae *planetary nebulae*.　　　　　　　　　C. R. O'DELL

See also ASTRONOMY (pictures: Wonders of the Milky Way); GALAXY; MILKY WAY.

NEBULAR HYPOTHESIS, *NEB yoo ler*, is a theory advanced by the French astronomer Pierre Simon Laplace (1749-1827) to explain how our solar system was formed. He said the sun and planets were formed from a *nebula*, or cloud of intensely heated gas. Gravitation caused the nebula to condense and form globes. His theory has been changed and modified by new discoveries and different analyses of known facts.　　E. C. SLIPHER

See also NEBULA; EARTH; LAPLACE, MARQUIS DE.

NECK. See SKELETON; GIRAFFE (diagram); THROAT.

NECKER, *neh KAIR*, or *NECK er*, **JACQUES** (1732-1804), was a statesman in France under King Louis XVI. When he was appointed French finance minister in 1777, the nation had an unbalanced treasury. The situation grew worse after France joined the American Revolutionary War. Necker, a noted banker, borrowed heavily, and kept things going without increasing taxes. This only postponed trouble. He angered court circles by publishing, for the first time, a statement showing how taxes were spent and how much money went to court favorites. He resigned in 1781.

Necker was recalled in 1788, after less able successors had brought France close to bankruptcy. He proved too cautious and indecisive to provide the leadership that might have prevented the French Revolution. On July 11, 1789, the king suddenly dismissed Necker, but was forced to take him back, by public demand. Necker again resigned in 1790.

He was born in Geneva, Switzerland. His daughter, Madame de Staël, was a French writer (see STAËL, MADAME DE).　　　　　　　RAYMOND O. ROCKWOOD

NECKLACE. See JEWELRY; PEARL (Matching Pearls).

NECKTIE is a band of material or a bow that is worn around the neck. The *four-in-hand* and *bow* ties worn today have been about the same style since they were first worn in the 1870's.

Neckties originated in the neck cloths that men folded and wrapped around their necks, with ribbon tied over them to hold the ends in place. In the 1700's, men wore a whalebone *stock*. They fastened it in back with a strap or buckle, and tied it in front with a bow or knot. The *cravats* of the 1600's and 1700's were often frilly and lace-trimmed. By the mid-1800's, narrow string ties, knotted bow ties, and ascot ties had replaced the more elaborate cravat. Around 1870, the wider four-in-hand became popular for general wear, the white bow tie for evening wear, the black string tie for formal wear, and the soft windsor tie for sportswear. In the 1900's, formal black bow ties appeared, and more conservative men usually wore black string ties. Striped neckties also became popular.　　　　HAZEL B. STRAHAN

NECROLOGY, *neh KRAHL uh jee*, is a record of deaths, especially one kept by a church. Usually it shows the day, month, and year of the death. A necrology may be a list of persons who have died within a certain time. It also may be an obituary notice.

NECROMANCY, *NEHK ruh MAN see*, is a term taken from two Greek words meaning *corpse* and *divination*. It is the belief that the future can be discovered by communication with the spirits of the dead. Necromancy was a common belief in early times.

NECROPOLIS, *neh KRAHP uh lihs*, is a Greek word which means *city of the dead*, that is, a cemetery. Archaeologists and historians usually call the cemetery of an ancient city a *necropolis*.

Archaeologists have found large and well-known necropolises in Egypt, at such ancient cities as Memphis and Thebes, and also surrounding the pyramids at El Gîza. Another necropolis, dating from the Bronze

Lick Observatory

The Great Nebula in the Constellation Orion is a huge cloud of dust and gas. Its bright central area is shown above.

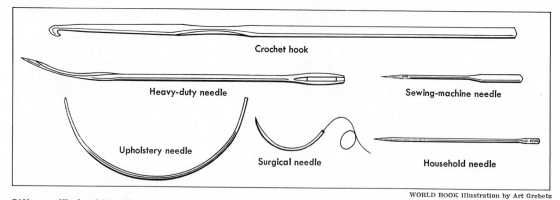

Different Kinds of Needles are made for special purposes. For example, a crochet hook has a hook to catch the thread. A heavy-duty needle is used to sew thick canvas or cloth for sails. Surgical needles are manufactured with thread attached to them for easy use in an operating room.

Age, is at Hallstatt, Austria. Many necropolises have also been found in America. A necropolis at Paracas, an archaeological site in Peru, dates back to the days before the Inca ruled there.

Ancient peoples often buried tools, weapons, and personal belongings with the dead. Sometimes they also carved or painted religious texts, information about the dead, and scenes from everyday life. Archaeologists and historians have learned much about ancient civilizations from necropolises. GEORGE R. HUGHES

See also TUTANKHAMON; VALLEY OF THE KINGS.

NECROSIS, *neh KROH sis*, is the death of a group of body cells and tissues due to some disease or external cause. *Phosphorus necrosis* is necrosis of the bone caused by exposure to phosphorus fumes (see MATCH [History]).

See also DEATH (Medical Aspects of Death).

NECTAR, *NECK ter*, is a sugary liquid produced by many flowers. Insects fly from flower to flower feeding on nectar. The nectar glands are usually at the bottom of the flower, and the insect has to brush past the pollen to reach them. It carries this pollen from one plant to another. Bees gather nectar, and change it to honey.

See also BEE (Making Honey).

NECTAR was the drink of the gods in Greek mythology. They drank out of cups brought to them by Hebe and Ganymede. Nectar was probably like sweet red wine. It was drunk with ambrosia, the food of the gods. Nectar and ambrosia gave youth and immortality to those who took them.

See also AMBROSIA; GANYMEDE; HEBE.

NECTARINE, *NECK ter EEN*, or *NECK ter in*, is a fruit much like the peach. The only important difference between the two is that nectarines have smooth skins and peaches are fuzzy. They come from identical trees. Nectarines often originate from peach seeds, and peaches may come from nectarine seeds. Botanists do not know which originated first, nectarine or peach.

Scientific Classification. The nectarine is a member of the rose family, *Rosaceae*. It is classified as genus *Prunus*, species *P. persica*. REID M. BROOKS

See also PEACH.

NEEDLE is a simple-looking tool, with a fine point at one end and a tiny eye at the other. But needles are not easy to make. Each needle passes through the hands of nearly 20 workers and undergoes at least 20 processes.

Sewing needles are made from coils of steel wire.

These coils are cut into pieces long enough for two needles. The pieces are then heated to a dull red and rolled on a flat steel plate to straighten them. The wires are pointed at each end on a grindstone. While they are being ground down to points, they are held in place by a device which makes them turn all the time they are touching the grindstone. This makes the points fine and even.

Only one end of the piece of wire is pointed at a time. After the ends are pointed, the center section of the wire pieces is stamped by a machine. This makes a flat place for the eyes. Next, the two eyes are punched in the middle of each piece of wire by another machine. Now each piece of wire has become a double needle. A piece of wire is now run through the eyes. The needles are then cut apart, leaving the needles hanging on the wire. Next, the heads, or eye ends, are rounded and smoothed. Finally, the needles are *tempered* (toughened), and polished, sorted, and packed.

Special needles are made for special uses. Sewing-machine needles are made with the eye near the point. They also have a groove on one side, which acts as a guide for the thread that goes through the eye.

A sewing needle for persons with poor vision has the eye split so that the needle can be threaded through the top. A crochet needle has a hook near the point. The

Nectarines Are Small Fruits Resembling Peaches. They have smooth skins much like those of plums.

thread is caught in the hook instead of going through an eye. Needles used for sewing shoes and upholstery are curved. Surgeons also use a curved needle for sewing up wounds and incisions. WALTER R. WILLIAMS, JR.

See also SEWING.

NEEDLE LEAVES. See LEAF.

NEEDLEFISH. See GAR.

NEEDLEPOINT is a type of embroidery made on a coarse background of open-mesh canvas. It is usually worked in woolen yarn, but silk, cotton, and some other materials may also be used.

The *continental* and the *half-cross* are the most common types of stitches used to make needlepoint. The continental stitch is more widely used, because it fills in the background evenly and fully on both the front and back of the canvas. It is also firmer and more durable than the half-cross stitch, which is used chiefly for products such as handbags, pictures, and pillows.

Needlepoint may be worked in *petit point* (fine, small stitches), or in *gros point* (larger stitches). Petit point is a single-yarn canvas. The yarns for it are split into two strands, and worked in the continental stitch. Gros point is a double-yarn mesh, and is usually used for upholstery. HAZEL B. STRAHAN

See also EMBROIDERY; LACE; PETIT POINT.

NEEDLEWORK. See CROCHETING; EMBROIDERY; KNITTING; LACE; NEEDLEPOINT; PETIT POINT; QUILT; SAMPLER; SEWING.

NÉEL, LOUIS E. F. See NOBEL PRIZES (table: Nobel Prizes for Physics—1970).

NEFERTITI, *neh fur TEE tee*, was an ancient Egyptian queen, the wife of Akhenaton, a *pharaoh* (king) who ruled from 1367 to 1350 B.C. Akhenaton was the first pharaoh to preach *monotheism* (belief in one god). Nefertiti was a firm supporter of Akhenaton's teachings and assisted him in the new religious ceremonies. The reign of Akhenaton and Nefertiti is called the *Amarna Revolution* because of the many changes in art, religion, and social practices they made.

Nefertiti is the subject of several sculptured portraits. A limestone head of Nefertiti in the Berlin Museum and an unfinished head kept in the Cairo Museum are among the best known. RICARDO A. CAMINOS

The Oriental Institute, University of Chicago

Nefertiti

See also EGYPT, ANCIENT (The Amarna Revolution).

NEGATIVE. See PHOTOGRAPHY (Developing Film).

NEGATIVE INCOME TAX. See POVERTY (Social Welfare Assistance); INCOME (Income Distribution).

NEGATIVE NUMBER. See ALGEBRA (Positive and Negative Numbers).

NEGEV, *NEHG uv*, or *nuh GEHV*, is the triangular southern half of Israel. It extends from Beersheba south to the port of Elat on the Gulf of Aqaba (see ISRAEL [map]). The Negev is a semidesert tableland from 1,000 to 2,000 feet (300 to 610 meters) above sea level. It is covered by a thick layer of fertile loam, which must have water to grow crops. The Israelis have farmed part of

Basket Weave Stitch

Cross Stitch

Stem Stitch

Checkerboard Stitch

WORLD BOOK photos

Needlepoint Embroidery is used to decorate many canvas products, such as handbags, pictures, and pillows. Most needlepoint is done with woolen yarn, and various kinds of stitches are used to create interesting patterns. The handbag on the left is decorated with squares of needlepoint. Close-up views of some of the stitches used to embroider the bag are shown on the right.

the Negev by irrigation. They have also mined phosphates and copper. Israel intends to draw water from the River Jordan to irrigate the Negev. But the surrounding Arab countries object to this water-diversion plan. See also WORLD (picture).   SYDNEY N. FISHER

NEGLIGENCE is the legal term for carelessness. The law uses negligence as a test to determine whether a person involved in an accident is responsible for any loss or injury that occurs in the accident.

The law considers negligence the failure to act the way a reasonable person would under the circumstances. But the law does not say what specific conduct is negligent. This decision is made by a judge or a jury after consideration of the circumstances in each case. The basic rule is that a person whose negligence harms another person must pay damages. If the person harmed also has been negligent, damages cannot normally be recovered. The law calls such action *contributory negligence*. For example, if a careless motorist hits a pedestrian who is reading a newspaper while crossing the street, the pedestrian's carelessness may be considered contributory negligence.

English and American law generally do not regard negligence as a crime. But in cases where someone is killed through negligence, the negligent person may be charged with a crime called *manslaughter* or *negligent homicide*. Most persons convicted of this type of manslaughter are punished seriously, but less severely than someone convicted of murder.

Some experts say the negligence test is no longer a good one for the law, especially in car accidents. Some suggest automobile cases should be handled as claims against some sort of insurance fund.   HARRY KALVEN, JR.

See also DAMAGES; TORT.

NEGOTIABLE INSTRUMENT, *nih GOH shuh buhl,* refers to a type of legal exchange or document that is either a promise or an order to pay money. Negotiable instruments can be used as evidence of indebtedness or as a substitute for money. A person holding a negotiable instrument is usually in a good legal position to collect from the person who signed it. The signer is called a *maker* or *drawer*. The use of negotiable instruments is regulated by the Uniform Commercial Code, which has been adopted by every state but Louisiana.

Negotiable instruments have six essential characteristics: (1) they must be in writing; (2) they must be signed by a maker or drawer, who promises to pay money; (3) they must contain an unconditional promise or order to pay; (4) payment must be in money; (5) instruments must be payable on demand or at a specific date in the future; (6) they must be payable to the bearer or to the order of a person.

Forms. Common forms of negotiable instruments include promissory notes, drafts, and checks. Promissory notes include bonds, certificates of deposits from banks, and real estate mortgage notes. Drafts include bills of exchange, bank drafts, cashier's checks, money orders, and traveler's checks.

Many instruments are not strictly negotiable but have some features of negotiable instruments. For example, instruments calling for the delivery of goods or property instead of money may possess many of the legal qualities of negotiability. Bills of lading and warehouse receipts

are examples. A bill of lading is given for goods in transit. A warehouse receipt is given for goods in storage. Each of these instruments can be written so that the promise to pay is negotiable.

Endorsement. Negotiable instruments are usually transferred or handed over to another person by endorsement. Any writing on the back is, in its broadest sense, an endorsement. The word comes from the Latin *in dorso*, meaning *on the back*. The term applies technically to the signature or other writing which indicates or proves that the instrument has been transferred.

An endorsement may be written in different ways. If the holder of the instrument simply signs it, the endorsement is called *in blank*. A *special endorsement* or an *endorsement in full* names the person to whom payment is to be made. A *restrictive endorsement* forbids further transfer. A check signed "Pay to First National Bank only" is a restrictive endorsement.

Every endorser of a negotiable instrument is usually liable for its face value, if the maker does not or cannot pay it. The endorser may add the words "without recourse" if he or she wishes to avoid liability. Such an endorsement does not affect the value of the instrument or prevent further endorsement.   JAMES B. LUDTKE

Related Articles in WORLD BOOK include:

Bill of Exchange	Bond	Draft	Note
Bill of Lading	Check	Money Order	

NEGRILLOS. See PYGMIES.

NEGRITOS are pygmies who live in southeast Asia, northern Australia, Indonesia, New Guinea, and the Philippines. They also include the Andamanese of the Andaman Islands and the Semang of the Malay Peninsula.

Negritos live in isolated mountainous interior areas. Almost all these people are less than 5 feet (150 centimeters) tall. Negritos fish, hunt, cultivate small fields, and gather fruits and plants to eat.   DONN V. HART

See also PYGMIES; PHILIPPINES (The People).

NEGRO. See BLACK AMERICANS.

NEGRO, RIO. See RIO NEGRO.

NEGRO HISTORY WEEK. See BLACK HISTORY WEEK.

NEGROES. See BLACK AMERICANS.

NEGROID. See RACES, HUMAN (How Races Are Classified; table).

NEGROS. See PHILIPPINES (The Islands).

NEHEMIAH, *NEE huh MY uh,* was a Jew who lived in the 400's B.C. His story is told in the book of Nehemiah in the Old Testament. He held the position of cupbearer to King Artaxerxes I in Persia. When he heard of bad conditions in Judah, Nehemiah asked the king to help. The king sent Nehemiah to Judah as Persian governor. There, he rebuilt the walls of Jerusalem and reformed the people.   WALTER G. WILLIAMS

NEHRU, *NEH roo,* is the family name of a father and his son, daughter, and granddaughter who became distinguished in Indian public affairs. The father and the son prefixed their names with their caste name, *pandit*. *Pandit* also means *scholar*. The daughter, the first woman president of the UN General Assembly, used Pandit as her last name (see PANDIT, VIJAYA L.). The granddaughter, Indira Gandhi, became the first woman prime minister of India (see GANDHI, INDIRA P.).

Motilal Nehru, *MO tih lahl* (1861-1931), came from a distinguished family in the province of Kashmir. He studied law at Muir College in Allahabad and built

Jawaharlal Nehru, *standing,* was the first prime minister of India. He served from 1947 until his death in 1964.

up a prosperous legal practice. He was at first a close friend of the English in India, a member of wealthy social groups, and a follower of Western ways. But in the 1920's he was converted to the cause of Indian independence, and became a follower of Mohandas Gandhi (see GANDHI, MOHANDAS K.). Nehru gave up his law practice and began to live in a simple manner.

He wrote the *Nehru Report* in 1928. It outlined a new constitution for India. In 1930, he became active in Gandhi's civil disobedience movement. His energetic efforts on behalf of freedom and several terms in prison weakened Nehru's strength, and he died the next year. Nehru was born in Agra.

Jawaharlal Nehru, *juh WAH hur lahl* (1889-1964), the son of Motilal Nehru, was India's first prime minister. He served as prime minister from 1947 until his death. He dominated Indian affairs. He worked to establish a democracy and to increase living standards. He favored a state-controlled economy.

Nehru gained international recognition for opposing alliances with the great powers and for promoting *neutralism* (nonalignment). He advocated nonaggression and ending atomic bomb tests. But he was criticized when Indian forces seized Goa and other Portuguese territories in India in 1961. Nehru acted as a spokesman for nonaligned nations in Asia and Africa. He favored admitting Communist China to the United Nations until Chinese forces attacked the Indian border in 1962.

Nehru and his father were fond and proud of each other, but occasionally disagreed. At one time, the father favored only dominion status for India, while the son demanded complete independence.

Nehru was born in Allahabad. He went to school in England and graduated from Harrow School and Cambridge University. He returned to India after his school-

ing and became active in politics. He supported Mohandas Gandhi's civil disobedience movement in 1920. Nehru served as general secretary of the All India Congress Committee in 1929. That same year, he was elected president of the Indian National Congress. He held that post again in 1936, 1937, and 1946. The British often imprisoned him for his nationalistic activities during this period. Nehru was a master of English, and his writings are widely read.   RICHARD L. PARK

See also INDIA (History).

NEIGHBORHOOD. See COMMUNITY.

NEKTON. See PLANKTON.

NELEUS. See NESTOR.

NELLIGAN, EMILE. See CANADIAN LITERATURE (Since 1900).

NELSON, British Columbia (pop. 8,919), is called the *Queen City of the Kootenays.* It lies along the west arm of Kootenay Lake (see BRITISH COLUMBIA [political map]). Nelson is a mining, lumbering, and transportation center. Water sports, skiing, and a Summer Curling Bonspiel attract tourists to Nelson. The city was named in 1888 for Hugh Nelson, then lieutenant governor of British Columbia. Nelson was incorporated in 1897. The city has a mayor-council form of government.   RODERICK HAIG-BROWN

NELSON, HORATIO (1758-1805), VISCOUNT NELSON, was Great Britain's greatest admiral and naval hero. He defeated the combined French and Spanish fleets at Trafalgar in the greatest naval victory in British history. His victory broke France's naval power, and established Britain's rule of the seas for the rest of the 1800's.

Early Life. Nelson was born at Burnham-Thorpe in Norfolk, on Sept. 29, 1758. His father was rector of the local church, and his mother was a member of the famous Walpole family. Nelson was a small, frail child. But he fell in love with the sea early in life, and made up his mind to be a sailor. He spent much time piloting small boats on the river near his home. When he was 12 years old, his uncle, Captain Maurice Suckling, planned a voyage to the Falkland Islands. Nelson begged his family for permission to go along, and was finally allowed to do so. He owed much of his early training to Captain Suckling, who had him transferred from time to time to ships engaged in different types of service. Suckling also encouraged him to study navigation and to practice boat sailing.

Joins the Navy. At the age of 15, Nelson went aboard the *Carcass* as a coxswain. He served on that vessel in an expedition to the Arctic seas. On his return, he was sent to the East Indies on the *Seahorse.* On the East Indies voyage he caught a fever that seriously damaged his health. But he became a lieutenant in the Royal Navy at 18.

In 1779, when not yet 21, he was given command of the frigate *Hinchinbrook.* He was known as a capable officer. His professional ability and his talent for

Horatio Nelson

getting along with his men helped him to rise rapidly in the service. A cruise to Central America brought on a second tropical illness and Nelson was sent home in feeble health.

He was given duty on the North Sea as soon as he recovered from the fever. He was then assigned to service in Canadian waters and developed a great fondness for Canada, where the climate strengthened his health. Nelson was given command of the frigate *Boreas*, stationed in the West Indies in 1784. He spent three years on this station.

Nelson married the widow of Josiah Nisbet, an English doctor, in the West Indies in 1787. Prince William, who later became King William IV of England, gave the bride away at the wedding. Nelson was recalled from active service soon afterward. He remained on the retired list until soon after the outbreak of war with France in 1793.

Wounded at Calvi. In 1793, he was placed in command of the *Agamemnon* and sailed to join the Mediterranean fleet. This voyage began seven years of almost continual warfare at sea. Nelson was one of the British commanders who blockaded Toulon and captured Corsica. He was wounded at Calvi, on the Corsican coast, and lost the sight of his right eye.

Nelson next distinguished himself at the Battle of Cape St. Vincent in 1797. He served under Admiral Sir John Jervis, who defeated the combined French and Spanish fleets. Nelson was made a Knight of the Bath for his part in this victory. He had become a rear admiral a week before the battle. A few months later, Nelson led a small landing party in an attack on the strongly fortified port of Santa Cruz de Tenerife in the Canary Islands. The attack was a bold gamble, but unlike others, it failed. The British were driven off with heavy losses and Nelson's right arm was badly mangled up to the elbow. The arm had to be cut off in a crude amputation in a pitching boat, and Nelson was invalided home to England in great pain. But he soon returned to duty.

Battle of the Nile. Napoleon, victorious in Europe, began to gather a French fleet for an expedition to conquer Egypt. Nelson was sent to watch the French ships at Toulon. A storm came up, and under its cover the French fleet escaped. Nelson followed it in a long and tiresome pursuit. He finally cornered the French fleet in the Bay of Aboukir, where he attacked and almost destroyed it on Aug. 1, 1798. This engagement is known to history as the Battle of the Nile. It cut off Napoleon's army in Egypt and ruined his Egyptian campaign. He was forced to desert his army in Egypt, and had to sneak across the Mediterranean in a tiny ship. This victory made Nelson world famous. He was made Baron of the Nile and given a large sum of money. See NILE, BATTLE OF THE.

Nelson was wounded again in this battle, and he went to Naples to recover. Lady Emma Hamilton, wife of Sir William Hamilton, the British Ambassador to Naples, fell in love with the battered, one-eyed, one-armed naval hero and became his mistress. Her influence over Nelson became so great that he disobeyed his orders to leave Naples and join a squadron in the Mediterranean. It was Nelson's good fortune that no British defeat resulted from his refusal to leave Naples. Nelson was condemned for his conduct, however, when he returned to England.

Battle of Copenhagen. Nelson became a vice-admiral in 1801, and sailed for Copenhagen in the squadron of Admiral Parker. Great Britain had claimed the right to search neutral ships for contraband of war. Denmark refused to allow its ships to be searched. A council of war chose Nelson to make the attack on the Danish

Nelson Falling (1825), an oil painting on canvas by
Denis Dighton; National Maritime Museum, London

Horatio Nelson led the British to victory over the French and Spanish fleets at Trafalgar in 1805.
Nelson, Britain's greatest naval hero, was fatally wounded in this battle, *above right*.

U.S. Navy

Nelson's Flagship, the *Victory*, led the British fleet at Trafalgar. It is kept in dry dock and is still in good condition.

fleet. Admiral Parker later became doubtful of the outcome. He signaled Nelson to retire. Nelson clapped his telescope to his blind eye and studied the signal. "I really do not see the signal," he said to an aide. He ignored the order and turned what might have been a defeat into a great victory.

Victory at Trafalgar. Nelson was made commander-in-chief of the fleet in May 1803. Sailing on the flagship *Victory*, he once more went in search of the French. He found the fleet at Toulon, but it slipped away from him. Nelson chased the French to the West Indies and back. It was more than two years before he was able to bring the French fleet to battle off Cape Trafalgar on the coast of Spain, on Oct. 21, 1805 (see TRAFALGAR). Nelson hoisted his famous signal, "England expects that every man will do his duty." With only 27 vessels, he attacked the combined French and Spanish fleets. One of the great naval battles of all time followed. Napoleon's fleet, with a total of 33 warships, was destroyed. Nelson was wounded at the height of the battle. He was carried below with a sharpshooter's bullet in his spine. He died during the battle, but he lived long enough to know that the British fleet had defeated the French and Spanish fleets. Nelson's last words were, "Thank God I have done my duty."

One of Nelson's great characteristics as a commander was his willingness to give full credit to his officers and men. After the Battle of Copenhagen, he refused an honor given him by the City of London because he alone was to be honored. Nelson replied, "Never till the City of London thinks justly of the merits of my brave companions of the second of April can I, their commander, receive any attention from the City of London." The poet Robert Southey wrote of Nelson, "England has had many heroes. But never one who so entirely possessed the love of his fellow countrymen. All men

knew that his heart was as humane as it was fearless . . . that with perfect and entire devotion he served his country with all his heart, and with all his soul, and with all his strength. And therefore they loved him as truly and fervently as he loved England."

Nelson is perhaps best remembered today by the members of the British Navy. He was a fighter. "I am of the opinion that the boldest measures are the safest," he once said. His frail body housed a great spirit. He had the power to inspire men with his own courage and confidence. Nelson is a symbol of Britain's navy.

Nelson Monument. A great monument to the memory of Nelson stands in Trafalgar Square, in the heart of London. It is one of the great landmarks of the world. It has been said that if you are looking for an English person whose address is unknown, that person will some day pass the Nelson monument in Trafalgar Square. See LONDON (picture). CHARLES F. MULLETT

NELSON, THOMAS, JR. (1738-1789), was an American patriot of the Revolutionary War period. He served as a delegate to the Continental Congress from 1775 to 1777 and again in 1779. He was one of the Virginia signers of the Declaration of Independence. During the Revolutionary War, he commanded the Virginia militia. He was born in Yorktown, Va. KENNETH R. ROSSMAN

NELSON, WILLIAM ROCKHILL (1841-1915), founded and built the *Kansas City* (Mo.) *Star*, a crusading newspaper, in 1880. The *Star* campaigned against municipal corruption, and for civic reform and a rehabilitation program. This program gave Kansas City parks, broad boulevards, and an art gallery. Nelson was born in Fort Wayne, Ind. KENNETH N. STEWART

NELSON RIVER is the longest river in Manitoba, Canada. From its outlet at the northern end of Lake Winnipeg, it flows about 400 miles (640 kilometers)

The Kansas City Star

William R. Nelson

northeastward to empty into Hudson Bay. It is the outlet of Lakes Winnipeg, Winnipegosis, and Manitoba, and the Winnipeg, Red, and Saskatchewan river systems. The watercourse to the head of the Saskatchewan's farthest tributary is 1,600 miles (2,570 kilometers) long. Once a transportation link for Hudson's Bay Company, the river is now a source of hydroelectric power. A power station at Kelsey Rapids supplies power to the nickel mines and refinery at Thompson, Man. Other stations are at Grand Rapids and Squaw Rapids on the Saskatchewan River. D. F. PUTNAM

NEMAN RIVER, sometimes known as the MEMEL or NEMUNAS RIVER, is a water route in Northern Europe. It rises in the Minsk region of Russia and flows northwest. The Neman River crosses Byelorussia and Lithuania before it empties into the Baltic Sea. The river is 580 miles (933 kilometers) long. The Viliya and Sheshupe streams are its chief branches. A canal connects the Neman, Bober, and Vistula rivers. Ships can sail 450 miles (724 kilometers) up the Neman. THEODORE SHABAD

NEMATHELMINTHES. See NEMATODA.

NEMATODA, or ROUNDWORMS, is a group of slender, round worms. Individuals in the group are called *nematodes*. Their bodies are usually pointed at the ends. Some are so small they can be seen only through a microscope, and others grow over 3 feet (91 centimeters) long. Males are usually smaller than females.

Some nematodes live in soil and water. Many, such as the eelworm, live as parasites in plants. Others, including hookworms, lungworms, pinworms, trichinella, and filariae, live as parasites in human beings, and such animals as dogs, sheep, and horses.

Scientific Classification. Nematoda is a class of the phylum *Aschelminthes* and is sometimes listed as a separate phylum *Nemathelminthes.*   JAMES A. MCLEOD

Related Articles in WORLD BOOK include:

Eelworm	Pinworm	Trichina
Hookworm	Roundworm	Vinegar Eel

NEMATOMORPHA. See HAIR SNAKE.

NEMEAN GAMES, *nuh MEE uhn*, were one of the four ancient Greek national festivals. The others were the Isthmian Games, the Olympic Games, and the Pythian Games (see the separate articles in WORLD BOOK for each festival). The Nemean Games occurred every other year, at the shrine of Zeus in Nemea, a valley in Argolis. They included athletic and musical contests. The first recorded Nemean Games took place in 573 B.C.   JOHN H. KENT

NEMERTINEA. See RIBBON WORM.

NEMESIS, *NEHM uh sihs*, was the goddess of vengeance in Greek mythology. She punished those human beings who angered the gods by becoming too proud of themselves. Nemesis stood for justice in all things.

The word *nemesis* today means a kind of punishing and relentless justice, which is deserved.   PADRAIC COLUM

NEMI, LAKE. See LAKE NEMI.

NENE, *nay nay*, known as *Hawaiian Goose*, is a rare bird of Hawaii. It is the official bird of Hawaii. Nenes are brown, and have long, buff-colored neck feathers. They live in open country and feed chiefly on grass.

Scientific Classification. The nene belongs to the water fowl family, *Anatidae*. It is classified as genus *Branta*, and is species *B. sandvicensis.*   GEORGE J. WALLACE

See also HAWAII (picture: The State Bird).

NEOCLASSICISM. See CLASSICISM; ENGLISH LITERATURE (The Classical Age); LITERATURE (The Age of Reason); PAINTING (The 1800's); SCULPTURE (1600-1900); SPANISH LITERATURE (Neoclassicism); DRAMA (French Neoclassical).

NEODYMIUM, *NEE uh DIHM ee uhm* (chemical symbol, Nd), is a metallic element belonging to the rare earth group. Its atomic number is 60, and it has an atomic weight of 144.24. C. F. Auer von Welsbach of Germany discovered the element in 1885. He separated the so-called element didymium into neodymium and praseodymium. Neodymium melts at 1010° C, and boils at 3127° C. The metal can be prepared by electrolysis of its halide salts, or by the reduction of these salts by alkaline earth metals in the presence of heat. The ceramic industry uses salts of neodymium to color glass and in glazes. The metal is present in *misch metal*, an alloy with many uses. See also RARE EARTH.   FRANK H. SPEDDING

NEOLITHIC PERIOD. See PREHISTORIC PEOPLE (How Prehistoric Farmers Lived); STONE AGE.

NEO-MALTHUSIANISM. See MALTHUS, THOMAS ROBERT.

NEON is a chemical element that makes up about 18 parts per million in the earth's atmosphere. The British chemists Sir William Ramsay and Morris W. Travers discovered it in the atmosphere while they were studying liquid air in 1898. Ramsay had predicted the existence of this gas one year earlier. Ramsay and Travers named the gas *neon*, for the Greek word meaning *new*.

Neon is used chiefly for filling lamps and luminous sign tubes. Its usual color in lamps is bright red. The addition of a few drops of mercury makes the light a brilliant blue. Many airplane beacons use neon light because it can penetrate fog. Pilots have reported that neon beacons were visible for 20 miles (32 kilometers) when it was impossible to see other lights.

Neon lamps are made by removing the air from glass tubes and then filling them with neon gas. When about 15,000 volts of electricity are applied to the tube, an electric discharge occurs and the tube glows fiery red. Instead of a filament, a neon tube has two electrodes sealed within it. The neon forms a luminous band between these electrodes.

Commercially, neon is obtained as a by-product of liquid air manufacture. It liquefies under normal pressure at −246° C. When air is liquefied at about −200° C, neon is left behind as a gas. It is sold in glass tubes that contain 1 quart (0.9 liter) of neon under pressure.

Robert H. Glaze, Artstreet

Neon Signs Brighten Shopping Areas throughout the world. These glowing signs in downtown Taipei, Taiwan, identify stores and advertise manufacturers and their products.

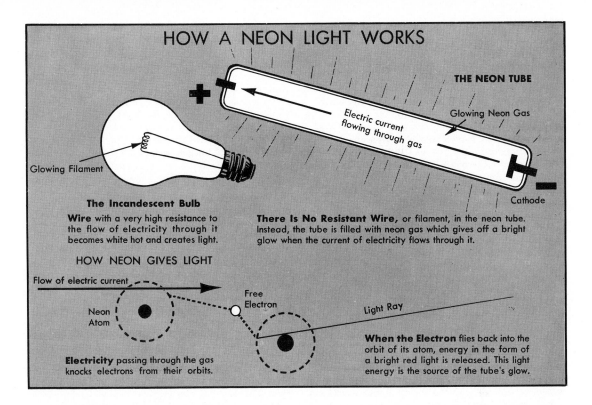

HOW A NEON LIGHT WORKS

THE NEON TUBE

+

Electric current flowing through gas

Glowing Neon Gas

Glowing Filament

Cathode

The Incandescent Bulb

Wire with a very high resistance to the flow of electricity through it becomes white hot and creates light.

There Is No Resistant Wire, or filament, in the neon tube. Instead, the tube is filled with neon gas which gives off a bright glow when the current of electricity flows through it.

HOW NEON GIVES LIGHT

Flow of electric current

Free Electron

Neon Atom

Light Ray

Electricity passing through the gas knocks electrons from their orbits.

When the Electron flies back into the orbit of its atom, energy in the form of a bright red light is released. This light energy is the source of the tube's glow.

Neon is expensive but very little is needed for lamps. Signs use 1 quart per 200 to 300 feet (1 liter per 64 to 97 meters) of tubing.

Neon is a colorless, odorless gas. It does not react readily with other substances. Neon is classed as a *noble gas*. Its symbol is Ne. It has the atomic number 10, and an atomic weight of 20.183.   FRANK C. ANDREWS

See also ELECTRIC LIGHT (Neon Lamps); NOBLE GAS.

NEON TETRA. See FISH (picture: Fish of Tropical Fresh Waters).

NEOPLASM. See TUMOR.

NEOPLATONISM was a dominant school of philosophy from the A.D. 200's to the 500's. Neoplatonism, which means *new Platonism*, developed from the philosophy of Plato. The leading philosophers of the school were Plotinus and Proclus.

The Neoplatonists developed their philosophy from Plato's theory of *forms*. According to this theory, all things owe their identities to unchanging forms in which they share. Our knowledge comes from recognizing the essential form of a thing, rather than from observing its many incidental qualities. The Neoplatonists carried the theory a step further. We are so wholly unreal, they believed, that only forms exist. The forms exist in a place, or divine mind, beyond the heavens, where our souls can "travel" when they leave our bodies.

In Neoplatonism, there is a single highest form, *The One*, which is completely self-sufficient and alone. It is a mistake even to say that The One *is*, because The One is beyond being. But, without changing, The One emanates or overflows, as light shines through darkness. The first and brightest level of emanation is *divine reason*, in which Plato's forms exist as ideas. The next level, dimmer and less real, is the world of souls. The

lowest order, the realm of bodies and matter, is almost total darkness. The two lower levels feel in themselves a desire, called an *anastrophe*, to turn upward and return. This is the feeling we sometimes have of homesickness or of being in an unreal world.

The Neoplatonists believed that the purpose of philosophy is to escape from the attachment we feel to our bodies and physical environment. In this way, we discover an impersonal immortality by finding our true identity in the world of form. As Plato tells in his myths, impure souls are destined to go from one human life to another. They seek permanent satisfaction, which attachment to their bodies prevents them from finding. Describing this cycle, Plotinus said: "The soul is a traveler, that sleeps every night in another inn."

Neoplatonism was an important philosophical movement. Plotinus influenced Saint Augustine in developing his principles of Christian theology. Proclus' views helped shape Christian *negative theology*, which points out the limits of human ability to comprehend a supreme being. The Neoplatonic emphasis on spiritual, as opposed to physical, beauty was important to the idea of *platonic love* in the Age of Chivalry during the Middle Ages. Neoplatonic commentaries appeared in the Near East as early as A.D. 529 and were generally accepted as the correct interpretation of both Plato and Aristotle.   ROBERT BRUMBAUGH

See also PLATO; PLOTINUS.

NEOPRENE. See RUBBER (Synthetic Rubber).

NEOPTOLEMUS, *NEE ahp TAHL uh muhs,* or PYRRHUS, was the son of Achilles in Greek legend. He killed Priam, the last king of Troy, when Troy was captured by the Greeks. See also HERMIONE.

NEP. See COMMUNISM (Communism Under Lenin).

NEPAL

NEPAL, *nih PAWL,* is a kingdom in south-central Asia. The world's highest mountain range, the Himalaya, covers more than nine-tenths of Nepal. Mount Everest, the tallest mountain in the world, rises 29,028 feet (8,848 meters) along Nepal's border with Tibet.

Nepal has a population of 13,545,000 and an area of 54,362 square miles (140,797 square kilometers). It is about as large as Illinois and has approximately the same number of people as that state. Patches of farmland lie among the mountains of Nepal. These cultivated areas account for only about 10 per cent of the country's total area, but more than 90 per cent of the people live there. Nepal is poor and undeveloped and has a high rate of disease and illiteracy.

Government. The king of Nepal serves as head of state and commander in chief of the armed forces. He appoints 22 of the 134 members of Nepal's legislative council, the *National Panchayat.* The king can veto any law passed by the Panchayat, and he can put into effect any law that it fails to pass. He selects all seven judges of the Supreme Court and can reverse any of the court's decisions. Many Nepalese believe the king is the descendant of the Hindu god Vishnu.

The Nepalese Constitution forbids political parties. Governmental processes are based on a system that the Constitution calls *Panchayat Democracy* (Guided Democracy). Under this system, Nepal has four levels of government: (1) village, (2) town, (3) district, and (4) national. The village, town, and district levels each consist of two legislative bodies—an assembly and a *panchayat* (council).

All villagers and townspeople who are 21 years old or older belong to their local assembly. They elect 11 representatives to the village or town panchayat. This panchayat then elects some of its members to the district assembly, which chooses its own 11 panchayat members. The district panchayat elects representatives to the national assembly. The national assembly, in turn, elects representatives to the National Panchayat. Thus, villagers and townspeople have a voice in local issues, and higher legislative bodies handle problems of broader national interest.

People of Nepal live chiefly in two regions. About two-thirds of the population make their homes in the central valleys and mountains that surround Kathmandu, Nepal's capital and largest city. About one-

---

FACTS IN BRIEF

Capital: Kathmandu.

Official Language: Nepali.

Form of Government: Constitutional Monarchy.

Area: 54,362 sq. mi. (140,797 km²). *Greatest Distances*— east-west, 500 mi. (805 km); north-south, 150 mi. (241 km).

Elevation: *Highest*—Mount Everest, 29,028 ft. (8,848 m). *Lowest*—150 ft. (46 m).

Population: *Estimated 1978 Population*—13,545,000; distribution, 94 per cent rural, 6 per cent urban; density, 249 persons per sq. mi. (96 per km²). *1971 Census*— 11,555,983. *Estimated 1983 Population*—15,117,000.

Chief Products: Cattle, corn, rice, oilseeds, wheat.

National Anthem: "Rashtriya Dhun" ("National Anthem").

Flag: The flag has two crimson triangles trimmed in blue, one above the other. The top triangle features the moon and the lower one the sun, symbols of the long life of Nepal. It is the only nonrectangular country flag. See FLAG (picture: Flags of Asia).

Money: *Basic Unit*—rupee. See MONEY (table: Values).

Nepal

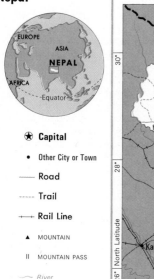

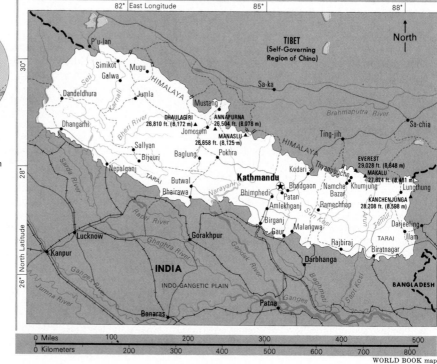

WORLD BOOK map

Hinduism is the official religion of Nepal. However, the Nepalese have combined the beliefs and practices of Hinduism with those of Buddhism. Buddha, the founder of Buddhism, was born in Nepal about 563 B.C. The Nepalese celebrate the festivals of both Buddhism and Hinduism, and Buddhist shrines and Hindu temples are considered equally sacred. Many of the people also worship primitive gods and spirits and consult *shamans* (witch doctors) in times of illness.

Nepal has few physicians, and such diseases as cholera, leprosy, malaria, and tuberculosis occur frequently. Since the early 1950's, the government has made an effort to control malaria. It also has launched campaigns to vaccinate as many people as possible against other diseases.

Some Hindus practice *polygamy*, a form of marriage in which a husband has more than one wife. *Polyandry*, the practice of a wife's having more than one husband, occurs among the Bhote tribe in northern Nepal. In most cases, a Bhote woman marries all the brothers of one family. The children born of such marriages regard all the husbands as fathers.

Illiteracy ranks as one of Nepal's chief problems. In the 1970's, only 15 per cent of the people over the age of 6 could read and write. Only about half of the population could speak Nepal's official language, Nepali. More than 30 other languages and dialects are spoken in the country. During the 1950's, the government began a program to build schools and train teachers throughout Nepal. Tribhuwan University in Kathmandu is Nepal's only university.

Land and Climate. Nepal has four principal regions: (1) the Himalaya, (2) the major valleys, (3) the Inner Terai, and (4) the Terai. Changes in altitude give each region a different climate. Each region also has its own kinds of plants and animals.

The Himalaya covers almost all of Nepal. The moun-

M. Philip Kahl, Jr., Bruce Coleman Inc.

Kathmandu, Nepal's capital and largest city, lies at the foot of the Himalaya. Towerlike buildings called *pagodas*, such as the ones shown above, line many of Kathmandu's streets.

third live in the *Terai*, a flat, fertile strip of land along Nepal's southern border. Nepal's population includes several ethnic groups, each of which lives in a certain area. Almost all the people live in small villages that consist of two-story houses made of stone or mud brick.

About 90 per cent of the people earn their living through farming. Most farms produce barely enough to support one family. Nepalese farmers trade any surplus crops they may raise for such important items as kerosene and salt. About 10 percent of the population consists of craftworkers, such as blacksmiths, goldsmiths, shoemakers, and tailors. A smaller number work as merchants and shepherds.

Two Nepalese ethnic groups—the Sherpas and the Gurung—are known for their special skills. The Sherpas, a Himalayan people, have won fame as guides and porters for mountain-climbing expeditions. Sherpa men and women carry heavy loads up to high altitudes. The Gurung group has contributed many men to Nepal's army. All Nepalese soldiers are called *Gurkhas*, after a province that is famous for its fighting men. Gurkhas became distinguished for their bravery while serving in the armies of Great Britain and India.

Malcolm Kirk from Peter Arnold

Porters on a Mountain-Climbing Expedition carry heavy loads up a steep trail in Nepal. The country's rugged mountains attract thousands of climbers and hikers yearly.

119

tains have long, harsh winters and short, cool summers. Steep river valleys cut through the glaciers and snow of the Himalaya. Forests cover the mountains up to about 12,000 feet (3,660 meters). Only grasses, lichens, and moss can grow in the cold, dry air above this altitude. Mountaineers in the Himalaya herd sheep and also long-haired oxen called *yaks*. Some people claim that a creature called the *abominable snowman*, or *yeti*, lives in the mountains (see ABOMINABLE SNOWMAN).

The Major Valleys lie to the south, in the foothills of the Himalaya. The valleys have a cool climate, and rain falls heavily in summer. Winters are chilly but dry. A wide variety of trees and bamboo grasses grow in thick forests in this region. Farmers in the valleys raise many crops, including corn, rice, millet, and wheat. They tend herds of cattle, sheep, and yaks.

The Inner Terai is south of the major valleys and the Mahabharat Mountains. This region has a tropical climate. Jungles and swamps in the Inner Terai have plentiful wild game, including crocodiles, elephants, deer, leopards, rhinoceroses, and tigers.

The Terai lies on Nepal's southern border. It has a warm, rainy climate. Farmers in the Terai grow corn, jute, millet, mustard, rice, sugar cane, tobacco, and other crops. Livestock raised in this region include cattle and water buffalo.

Economy of Nepal depends almost entirely on farming. Nepalese farmers attend small fairs and markets to trade their surplus crops for other items. Nepal has only about 60 miles (97 kilometers) of railroad track, and many parts of the country do not have paved roads. The lack of good transportation facilities makes large-scale trade difficult.

Roads link Nepal with India, and Nepal trades chiefly with that country. Nepal exports such produce as herbs, jute, rice, spices, and wheat. Principal imports include gasoline, kerosene, machinery, metals and metal products, and textiles.

Since the 1950's, large amounts of foreign aid have helped develop Nepal's economy. For example, China, Great Britain, India, Russia, Switzerland, and the United States have contributed money to Nepal. The funds have helped construct roads, maintain health centers, and start small industries throughout the country. The government spends about $50 million annually on development projects. Approximately 20 per cent of this money comes from foreign aid.

Gurkha soldiers employed in the British and Indian armies make a significant contribution to Nepal's economy. The salaries and pensions paid to these Nepalese soldiers total more than $240 million yearly. This sum is more than twice the amount that Nepal receives from foreign trade.

Money spent by visitors from other countries has helped improve economic conditions in Nepal. About 70,000 hunters, mountain climbers, and sightseers from other countries visit Nepal annually.

Nepal has deposits of such minerals as coal, copper, gold, iron, and mica. However, the country has few mines. Nepal's greatest natural resources are its forests and rivers. The swift mountain currents produce hydroelectric power, and Nepal has six hydroelectric plants.

History. Until the late 1700's, Nepal consisted of a number of small, independent kingdoms. The early history of the country centered in the Kathmandu valley, near what is now the Nepalese capital. About A.D. 400, that area came to be called Nepal. Through the centuries, bands of conquerors, nomads, and refugees from Central Asia, India, and Tibet came into the area. They became the ancestors of the Nepalese. For hundreds of years, India and Tibet controlled the area that is now Nepal.

In the mid-1700's, a Gurkha king named Prithwi Narayan Shah began a military campaign to unify the country. By the time of his death in 1775, he had conquered most of what is now Nepal. He took the title of king of Nepal, and his descendants have served as monarchs ever since.

In the early 1800's, Nepal fought a war against Great Britain. Nepal had attempted to expand its boundaries into northern India. A British trading corporation, the East India Company, controlled much of India at that time, and British soldiers guarded India's borders. Britain declared war on Nepal in 1814 after Gurkha troops attacked a British outpost.

The British expected an easy victory, but the Nepalese were accustomed to fighting in the mountains. The British Army suffered heavy losses but finally defeated the Nepalese in 1816. After the war, Britain and Nepal became allies. The Gurkha soldiers impressed the British, and Britain has recruited Gurkhas for its armies since that time.

In 1846, a political leader named Jang Bahudur Kunwar seized control of Nepal's government. He took the honorary title of *Rana* and declared that a member of his family would serve as prime minister from then on. Until 1951, members of the Rana family held complete control of the government. During this period, the king had no power. The Ranas dominated the army, imprisoned their opponents, and even killed rivals whom they considered dangerous.

During the 1930's and 1940's, opposition to Rana rule grew throughout Nepal. A revolution began in Nepal in 1950. It overthrew the government and restored the monarchy to power under King Tribhuwan Shah in 1951.

During the early 1950's, the government made various attempts to create a democracy in Nepal. King Tribhuwan died in 1955. He was succeeded by his son, Mahendra, who criticized Tribhuwan's efforts to form a democratic government. In 1960, Mahendra announced that these efforts had failed. He declared that Nepal needed a form of government that would suit the country's traditions. In 1962, Mahendra put into effect a constitution that set forth his royal powers and established the panchayat system.

Mahendra died in 1972, and his son, Birendra, succeeded him as king. Under Birendra's rule, the government has tried to modernize Nepal's educational system. Today, the schools stress scientific and technical training. The government has tried to improve transportation throughout the kingdom and to expand Nepal's industrial development.　　ROBERT I. CRANE

Related Articles in WORLD BOOK include:

Asia	Himalaya	Kathmandu
Buddha	Hinduism	Mount Everest
Colombo Plan		

NEPHITE. See Lehi.

NEPHRITE. See Jade.

NEPHRITIS, *nih FRY tihs,* or Bright's Disease, is a general term for several inflammatory diseases of the kidneys. *Glomerulonephritis* is the disease most often called nephritis. It results from swelling of the *glomeruli* (filtering units) of the kidneys. The inflammation reduces the production of urine by the kidneys. Urine carries waste materials out of the body.

Most cases of glomerulonephritis follow an infection of the throat or skin caused by certain types of the bacteria called *streptococci.* In some persons, such infections apparently cause the body to become allergic to the tissues of the glomeruli. The glomeruli may suffer serious damage as a result. If this damage occurs rapidly, the condition is called *acute glomerulonephritis.* If the damage occurs over a period of years, the condition is called *chronic glomerulonephritis.*

Acute glomerulonephritis occurs mostly in children. Symptoms include facial swelling, fever, headache, high blood pressure, vomiting, and blood and proteins in the urine. There is no specific treatment. Nearly all patients recover from their first attack of acute glomerulonephritis, but many have later attacks of the disease.

Chronic glomerulonephritis develops mostly in adults. Many cases involve only mild symptoms, and a person may not even know he has the disease. But in time, the chronic condition causes progressive, incurable kidney damage. Advanced stages may lead to kidney failure and a condition called *uremia.* Physicians use a *dialysis machine* or a kidney transplant to save victims of chronic glomerulonephritis.   Benjamin T. Burton

See also Kidney; Tissue Transplant; Uremia; Bright, Richard.

NEPHRON. See Kidney.

NEPHTHYS. See Mythology (Egyptian Mythology).

NEPOTISM, *NEP oh tiz'm,* is the practice of giving important political or business positions to members of one's family. The word *nepotism* comes from the Latin word for *nephew.*

NEPTUNE was the god of the sea in Roman mythology. He had power over the sea and seafaring. For example, he could cause—or prevent—storms at sea. Neptune resembled the Greek god Poseidon. Like Poseidon, he was also the god of earthquakes and horses.

The ancient Romans were a seafaring people and imported much of their food and other necessities by ship. As ruler of the sea, Neptune thus had an important role in their daily life. Sea travel was dangerous in ancient times, and Roman sailors prayed to Neptune for safe voyages. After their return, sailors often showed their gratitude by dedicating a valuable object to Neptune.

Neptune was the son of Saturn and Ops (called Cronus and Rhea by the Greeks). He married the sea nymph Amphitrite, and they had a son, Triton, who was half man and half fish. Triton played an important role in many ancient legends about the sea.

Neptune appears in a famous episode at the beginning of the *Aeneid,* an epic by the Roman poet Virgil. In this epic, Neptune calms a storm that had threatened to destroy the fleet of the Trojan hero Aeneas. Many ancient and modern seascapes feature Neptune, Amphitrite, and Triton. Artists portray Neptune as a man carrying a *trident* (three-pronged spear). Some show him riding in a chariot pulled by sea horses and accompanied by dolphins. Many fountains, notably the Trevi Fountain in Rome, include a statue of Neptune. One of the planets is named for him.   Paul Pascal

See also Poseidon; Triton; Nereid; Fountain (picture).

NEPTUNE is one of the two planets that cannot be seen without a telescope. It is much larger than the earth, but astronomers know little about it. Neptune is about 30 times as far from the sun as is the earth. Pluto is the only planet farther from the sun than Neptune. Before anyone had ever seen Neptune or Pluto, astronomers "discovered" them by using mathematics.

Neptune's diameter is about 30,760 miles (49,500 kilometers), or almost 4 times the earth's diameter. The

Roman copy (A.D. 100's) of a Greek statue of the 300's B.C.;
Museo Gregoriano Profano, The Vatican, Rome
(The Mansell Collection, London)

Neptune was the Roman god of the sea. The statue shown above portrays the god holding a three-pronged spear called a *trident.* The dolphin and ship at his feet symbolize his ocean kingdom.

planet is about 17 times as *massive* (heavy) as the earth, but is not so *dense* as the earth (see MASS; DENSITY).

Neptune travels around the sun in an *elliptical* (oval-shaped) orbit. Its mean distance from the sun is about 2,795,000,000 miles (4,498,100,000 kilometers). Neptune goes around the sun once about every 165 earth-years, compared to once a year for the earth. As Neptune orbits the sun, it spins on its *axis*, an imaginary line through its center. Neptune's axis is not *perpendicular* (at an angle of 90°) to the planet's path around the sun. The axis tilts about 30° from the perpendicular position. For an illustration of the tilt of Neptune's axis, see PLANET (The Axes of the Planets). Neptune spins around once in about 15 hours and 40 minutes.

Surface and Atmosphere. Neptune is so far from the earth that astronomers do not know much about its surface. They believe the portion of Neptune visible from the earth is the top of a thick layer of clouds. These clouds may consist of frozen ammonia, or combinations of crystals of ice, frozen methane, and frozen ammonia.

The atmosphere surrounding Neptune consists chiefly of hydrogen and methane gas, with some helium and ammonia. Astronomers believe this atmosphere is about 2,000 miles (3,200 kilometers) thick. The tilt of Neptune's axis causes the sun to heat the planet's northern and southern halves unequally, resulting in seasons and temperature changes. Temperatures are always much lower than on the earth. The plant and animal life of the earth could not live on Neptune because of the lack of oxygen and the low temperature. Astronomers do not know whether Neptune has any form of life.

Satellites. Two *satellites* (moons) travel around Neptune. One, named Triton, is about 3,000 miles (4,800 kilometers) in diameter and about 200,000 miles (320,-000 kilometers) from Neptune. It is the only large satellite in the solar system that travels in an east-to-west direction. Triton has a circular orbit, and travels around Neptune once every six days.

Neptune's other satellite, called Nereid, is only about 150 miles (241 kilometers) in diameter. It is about 3½ million miles (5.6 million kilometers) from the planet, and travels in an extremely elliptical orbit. Nereid goes around Neptune every 360 days.

Discovery. Neptune was discovered by means of mathematics before being seen through a telescope. Astronomers had noticed that Uranus, which they thought was the most distant planet, was not always in the position they predicted for it. The force of gravity of

---

NEPTUNE AT A GLANCE

Distance from Sun: *Shortest*—2,771,000,000 mi. (4,459,-500,000 km); *Greatest*—2,819,000,000 mi. (4,536,700,-000 km); *Mean*—2,795,000,000 mi. (4,498,100,000 km).

Distance from Earth: *Shortest*—2,678,000,000 mi. (4,309,-800,000 km); *Greatest*—2,750,000,000 mi. (4,426,000,-000 km).

Diameter: 30,760 mi. (49,500 km).

Length of Year: About 165 earth-years.

Rotation Period: 15 hours and 40 minutes.

Average Temperature: Unknown. Probably lower than −280° F. (−173° C).

Atmosphere: Hydrogen, methane, helium, and ammonia.

Number of Satellites: Two.

---

some unknown planet seemed to be influencing Uranus.

In 1843, John C. Adams, a young English astronomer and mathematician, began working to find the location of the unknown planet. Adams predicted the planet would be about 1 billion miles (1.6 billion kilometers) farther from the sun than Uranus. He completed his remarkably accurate work in September, 1845. Adams sent it to Sir George B. Airy, the Astronomer Royal of England. But Airy did not look for the planet with a telescope. Apparently, he lacked confidence in Adams.

Meanwhile, Urbain J. J. Leverrier, a young French mathematician unknown to Adams, began working on the same project. By the summer of 1846, Leverrier also had predicted the position of Neptune. He sent his predictions, which were similar to those of Adams, to the Urania Observatory in Berlin, Germany. Johann G. Galle, the director of the observatory, had just completed a chart of the fixed stars in the area of the sky where the unknown planet was believed to be. On Sept. 23, 1846, Galle and his assistant, Heinrich L. d' Arrest, searched with a telescope for an object that was not on the chart. They found Neptune near the position predicted by Leverrier. Today, both Adams and Leverrier are credited with the discovery. The planet was named for Neptune, the Roman sea god.   HYRON SPINRAD

See also PLANET; SOLAR SYSTEM.

NEPTUNIUM, *nehp TYOO nih um* (chemical symbol, Np), is a man-made element. Its atomic number is 93. Its most stable isotope has a mass number of 237. In the periodic system of the elements, neptunium follows uranium. Neptunium was discovered by Edwin M. McMillan and P. H. Abelson at the University of California in 1940. It was first produced by bombarding uranium with slow neutrons. Neptunium produced in this way has an atomic weight of 239. This isotope is unstable and decays to form an isotope of plutonium that can be used for nuclear fission. The longest-lived neptunium isotope, neptunium 237, has a half-life of 2,200,000 years (see RADIOACTIVITY [Half-Life]). See also PLUTONIUM; U-235.   EDWIN M. McMILLAN

NEREID, *NEER ee id.* The Nereids were the 50 daughters of Nereus and Doris. They were the lovely sea nymphs who attended the Greek sea god Poseidon and his Nereid wife, Amphitrite. They lived under the sea, and came to the surface to dance in the waves. Nereids are represented as beautiful maidens, sometimes part fish.   PADRAIC COLUM

See also ANDROMEDA; NYMPH.

NEREUS was a kindly sea god in Greek mythology. The Greeks believed that he lived at the bottom of the Aegean Sea and came to the surface only to help sailors and give them good advice. Nereus had the gift of prophecy and foretold the destruction of Troy at the end of the Trojan War. Nereus was born early in the earth's history and was sometimes called the Old Man of the Sea. His parents were Pontus, the oldest sea god, and Gaea, the ancient goddess of the earth. Nereus had 50 beautiful daughters called *Nereids* (see NEREID).

NERI, SAINT PHILIP (1515-1595), was the founder of the Oratorians, and a reformer of Rome during the Renaissance. Pope Gregory XIII recognized his group of priests as the Congregation of the Oratory in 1575. Neri, a popular leader, won over cardinals and popes to his unusual methods of reform. He was born in Florence, Italy.   JAMES A. CORBETT and FULTON J. SHEEN

NERNST, *nurnst,* **WALTHER HERMANN** (1864-1941), a German physical chemist, won the 1920 Nobel prize in chemistry for his formulation of the third law of thermodynamics (see Thermodynamics). His measurements of the specific heats of substances at low temperatures proved this law to be valid. Nernst also developed a theory of solutions that explains the voltage of electrochemical batteries (see Electrochemistry). He was born in Briessen, Germany.   Sidney Rosen

NERO, *NEER oh* (A.D. 37-68), was a Roman emperor and the last relative of the Caesars. He is remembered most for his mistreatment of Christians, and his neglect of government affairs while he pursued a musical career.

Nero was born Lucius Domitius in Antium at the court of his uncle, Emperor Caligula. Nero's father, Gnaeus Domitius Ahenobarbus, died when Nero was quite young. Caligula sent Nero's mother, Agrippina the Younger, away when the boy was three. Agrippina returned under Emperor Claudius after Caligula's death. Nero studied under Greek teachers, who encouraged his tastes in music, poetry, and sports. Agrippina married Claudius in A.D. 49. Claudius adopted the boy, changed his name to Nero Claudius Drusus Germanicus, and designated Nero as his eldest son. Agrippina chose Seneca, the philosopher, and Burrus, a military officer, to serve as Nero's teachers and advisers. Nero married Claudius' daughter Octavia in 53.

Nero became emperor when Claudius died in 54. Soon afterward, he had Claudius' son Britannicus poisoned, and buried him in haste and secrecy. Tired of his mother's interference, Nero had her murdered in 59. In 62, he had Octavia killed, and married Poppaea Sabina.

In some ways, Nero was a good administrator. Guided by Seneca and Burrus, he brought peace to the province of Britain after a revolt. He sent a fleet to protect Roman ships on the Black Sea, and chose excellent

Statue of Nero by an unknown Roman sculptor;
Uffizi Gallery, Florence, Italy (Alinari-SCALA)
Emperor Nero, who ruled Rome from A.D. 54 to 68, ordered the death of many Christians and several of his own relatives.

military commanders for wars in Armenia and Judea.

Nero has been accused of setting a fire that burned part of Rome in 64. This led to the popular saying, "Nero fiddled while Rome burned." Most historians, however, doubt Nero's guilt. Nero blamed the Christians for the fire, and had them put to death cruelly.

Late in his reign, Nero left Rome to sing in festivals in Greece. He returned to find the provinces in revolt and the Senate and his guards in Rome plotting against him. He committed suicide in 68.   Mary Francis Gyles

See also Agrippina the Younger; Seneca, Lucius.

NERUDA, *neh ROO thah,* **PABLO** (1904-1973), a Chilean poet, won the 1971 Nobel prize for literature. Many critics consider Neruda the finest Latin-American poet of his time. His use of surrealistic, violent, subconscious imagery and highly personal symbols makes his poetry sometimes difficult to understand. His works communicate a general sense of universal chaos.

Neruda was born in Parral, Chile. His real name was Neftalí Reyes. Several volumes of his poetry had been published before he was 20. His best volumes of poems include *Crepusculary* (1923), *Twenty Poems of Love and One Desperate Song* (1924), and *Residence on Earth* (1931, 1935). Attracted to Communism, Neruda sometimes allowed political views to detract from his art in his later works, including *Third Residence* (1947). His *A New Decade: Poems (1958-1967)* was published in 1969. Neruda served in the Chilean diplomatic service for many years as a consul and ambassador.   Marshall R. Nason

NERVAL, GÉRARD DE (1808-1855), was a French poet of the romantic period. His personal charm, odd behavior, periodic mental disorders, and mysterious suicide made him a hero typical of the romantic movement. Critics in the 1900's consider him a major visionary poet.

Nerval believed in *metempsychosis,* the passing of a soul at death from one body to another. In *Les Chimères* (1854), a collection of sonnets, this belief underlies many obscure references to the legendary past which contribute to the haunting beauty of the poems. His search for the eternal feminine ideal is reflected in the short stories of *Les Filles du Feu* (1854), notably in "Sylvie," a tale set in the Valois countryside. *Aurélia* (1855), a prose confession, begins with the phrase "Our dreams are a second life." It describes this "life," including the hallucinations Nerval suffered during his periods of insanity. He was born in Paris.   LeRoy C. Breunig

NERVE. See Nervous System.

NERVE GAS. See Chemical-Biological-Radiological Warfare.

NERVI, PIER L. See Architecture (Today; picture: Sports Arenas).

NERVOUS BREAKDOWN is a term often used to refer to anything from fatigue caused by overwork to a severe mental illness. It has no precise medical meaning. Psychiatrists and others who specialize in the study and care of patients with mental illness do not use the term. It is used by people who believe it is an accepted medical term, or by people who want to avoid using the term "mental illness." The original idea behind the term was that mental symptoms were caused by a failure of the nerves to function properly.   Charles Brenner

See also Mental Illness (Unhealthy Behavior).

NERVOUS SYSTEM

NERVOUS SYSTEM consists of the brain, the spinal cord, and the nerve cells and fibers that extend throughout the bodies of man and the higher animals. The nervous system keeps us in contact with the world outside our bodies by receiving messages from the sense organs, such as the eyes and ears. It interprets these messages and causes us to react. The nervous system enables all parts of our body, including the internal organs, to work together to keep us alive and well.

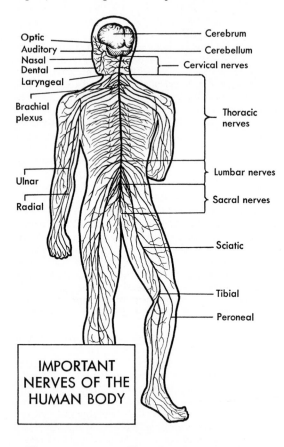

Optic
Auditory
Nasal
Dental
Laryngeal

Brachial plexus

Ulnar

Radial

Cerebrum
Cerebellum
Cervical nerves

Thoracic nerves

Lumbar nerves

Sacral nerves

Sciatic

Tibial

Peroneal

IMPORTANT NERVES OF THE HUMAN BODY

The nervous system, like other parts of the body, is made up of cells (see CELL). Nerve cells are called *neurons*. Like the other cells of the body, neurons have a nucleus surrounded by cytoplasm. The nucleus and the cytoplasm make up the *cell body*. The cytoplasm surrounding the nucleus of a neuron grows out into one or more fine threads or fibers. Most neurons have a single long fiber called an *axon* and several branched extensions of the cell body called *dendrites*. A *nerve* may be a single nerve fiber or a bundle of fibers. Neurons vary in shape and size depending on their function. Some neurons have short axons and dendrites, and others may have axons that are several feet or meters long.

The sense organs have specialized *nerve endings* (ends of nerve fibers) that respond to stimuli from the world around us. Such sense organs as the eyes and ears allow us to see and hear. Others, including some in the skin, tell us when we are hot or cold. Those in the nose and mouth enable us to smell and to taste. Still other sense

organs let us feel what is going on inside our bodies.

Neurons that carry messages from the sense organs to the spinal cord and brain are called *sensory neurons*. Neurons that control the muscles and glands of the body are called *motor neurons*.

The nerve endings in the sense organs respond to special stimuli, including light waves, sound waves, mechanical contacts, and chemicals. Neurons throughout the body—especially in the skin—respond to heat, cold, touch, and changes in posture. The nerve endings send messages to certain parts of the brain, and the brain interprets the messages as various sensations. Neurons respond to strong stimuli, such as extreme heat, with the sensation of pain.

Parts of the nervous system work automatically, without conscious commands from the brain. After a meal, for example, neurons cause the muscles of the intestine to contract and relax automatically, moving the food through the digestive system. Many other body functions are controlled by the *autonomic* (self-controlling) parts of the nervous system.

Nerve Impulses

The human nervous system has several billion neurons, all connected with one another. The dendrites of a neuron receive stimuli from other nerve fibers or from a *receptor organ*, such as a sense organ. The *impulse* (nerve signal) passes from the dendrite through the cell body to the axon. The axon carries impulses to the dendrite or cell body of another neuron, or to an *effector organ*, such as a gland or a muscle.

The place where an axon connects to a nerve cell or dendrite is called a *synapse*. The place where the ends of a motor axon and a muscle meet is called a *neuromuscular junction*. Structures called *end bulbs* and *end plates* are on the ends of axons at synapses or junctions. There, the impulse causes the release of a chemical substance. This substance transmits the message across the synapse, or neuromuscular junction. In some cases, both electrical and chemical transmission occur at synaptic junctions.

An axon and a dendrite are in close contact as a synapse, but they do not grow together. For an impulse to pass from a receptor organ to a neuron, from one neuron to another, or from a neuron to an effector organ, it must cross a synapse. For an impulse to pass from a receptor organ to the brain, or from the brain to an effector organ, it must travel over several neurons, crossing several synapses.

Kinds of Neurons

Neurons that receive impressions from the outside world are called *sensory neurons* or *afferent neurons*. They carry impulses from various sense organs to the brain. Neurons that carry impulses from the brain or other nerve centers to the muscles are called *motor neurons* or *efferent neurons*. *Association neurons* or *internuncial neurons* are in the brain and spinal cord. They carry impulses among the parts of the brain and among the parts of the spinal cord, and between the sensory and motor neurons.

Several nerves bound together by a tough sheet of tissue are called a *nerve trunk*. Some axons are covered by a fat-containing sheath called a *myelin sheath*. When the cell bodies of many neurons are bundled together

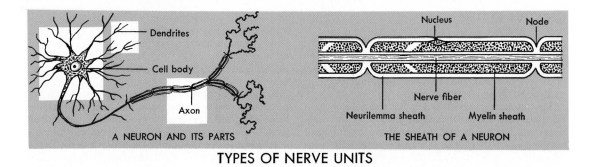

A NEURON AND ITS PARTS

THE SHEATH OF A NEURON

TYPES OF NERVE UNITS

outside the brain or spinal cord, they are called a *ganglion*.

Parts of the Nervous System

The nervous system can be separated into three divisions, the *central nervous system*, the *peripheral nervous system*, and the *autonomic nervous system*.

The Central Nervous System consists of the brain and the spinal cord. For a detailed description of the brain and its functions, see the article on BRAIN.

The spinal cord is a long, thick nerve trunk that runs from the base of the brain down through the spinal column, or backbone. The cord is composed of *white matter* (nerve fibers covered with a white myelin sheath), and *gray matter* (cell bodies and dendrites of neurons). A cross sectional view of the spinal cord shows the gray matter as an H-shaped area surrounded by white matter. Thirty-one pair of spinal nerves leave the spinal cord. Each of these nerve trunks is attached to the cord in two places. The root of the nerve that leaves the cord toward the front of the body is called the *ventral root* or *anterior root*. The root that leaves toward the rear of the body is called the *dorsal root* or *posterior root*.

Sensory nerves enter the spinal cord at the dorsal root. Motor nerves leave the spinal cord at the ventral root. If the ventral root of a nerve is cut, the part of the body to which the nerve goes cannot move, but it still has sensation. If the dorsal root of a nerve is cut, sensa-

tion disappears, but the body part can still move.

Some nerve impulses entering the spinal cord are directed to the brain. Others are routed to nerve centers, and then to the parts of the body that the nerves control. Responses from impulses that go almost directly to motor nerves are called *spinal reflexes*. See SPINE.

The Peripheral Nervous System consists of 12 pair of cranial nerves and the 31 pair of spinal nerves.

The Cranial Nerves come from the lower part of the brain. These nerves control many sensations and actions including sight, smell, chewing, and swallowing.

The Spinal Nerves come from the spinal cord and control the muscles of the body. There are 8 pair of *cervical nerves* that leave the spinal column from the first 7 vertebrae. Below them are 12 pair of *thoracic nerves*. The 5 pair of *lumbar nerves* leave the spinal cord at the small of the back. Each of the 5 pair of *sacral nerves* and the 1 pair of *coccygeal nerves* leave the spinal cord between the lowest vertebrae in the spinal cord.

The Autonomic Nervous System regulates the internal organs and blood vessels. This control is largely automatic and is strongly affected by an individual's emotional state. Some degree of voluntary control can be developed by a conditioning method called *biofeedback* (see BIOFEEDBACK).

Nerves of the autonomic nervous system are connected to the central nervous system and are normally regulated at a subconscious level. Each nerve consists

DIVISIONS OF THE NERVOUS SYSTEM

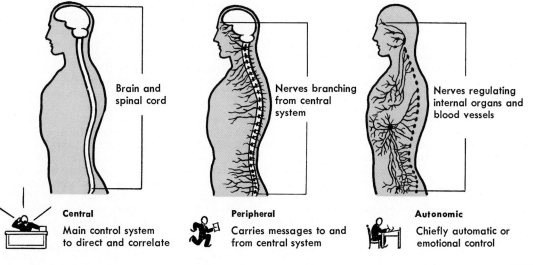

Brain and spinal cord

Nerves branching from central system

Nerves regulating internal organs and blood vessels

Central
Main control system to direct and correlate

Peripheral
Carries messages to and from central system

Autonomic
Chiefly automatic or emotional control

of a chain of two or more neurons leading from the spinal cord, through a ganglion, and to an organ. The nerve fibers have little or no myelin sheath. Most nerves in the autonomic system are *effectors* (motor nerves), but each trunk also has receptor fibers.

The autonomic nervous system has two main parts—the *sympathetic*, or *thoracolumbar, system*, and the *parasympathetic*, or *craniosacral, system*. Many organs have nerves coming from both the sympathetic and parasympathetic systems. Such nerves produce opposite reactions in the organs to which they go. For example, a nerve from one system speeds up the heart beat, and a nerve from the other system slows it down.

The nerves of the sympathetic system arise in the thoracic and lumbar portions of the spinal cord. They run from the cord to ganglia that lie along both sides of the spinal column. In the ganglia, the neurons from the cord, called *preganglionic* neurons, form a synapse with the neurons that continue to the various organs. The neurons that run from the ganglia to the organs are called *postganglionic* neurons.

The nerves of the parasympathetic system are divided into *cranial* and *sacral* sections. The cranial section begins with cells in the brain stem, the lowest part of the brain. The sacral section begins with cells in the lowest part, or sacral portion, of the spinal cord. The parasympathetic nerves run from the spinal cord to ganglia that are near, or even on, an organ.

How Nerves Work

Impulses in the largest human nerves travel at a speed of more than 300 feet (91 meters) per second. In the smaller fibers of the autonomic nervous system, impulses may travel as slowly as $1\frac{1}{2}$ to 6 feet (0.5 to 1.8 meters) per second.

The *membrane theory* is the most commonly accepted theory of how nerves work. The membrane that surrounds each nerve cell or fiber is *polarized*—that is, it has opposite electrical charges on either side. Positive *ions* (electrically charged particles) are located outside the membrane. Inside the membrane are negatively charged ions. At the point where the impulse begins, the membrane lets through only certain positively charged ions, such as sodium. These ions rush inside the membrane and cause a local *depolarization* (loss of polarization) of the nerve membrane. This produces a local negative electrical charge called the *action potential*. Depolarization lasts only from .001 to .005 of a second, and the nerve cannot conduct an impulse during this time, which is called the *refractory period*. Polarization is re-established by the movement of positively charged ions, such as potassium, from the inside to the outside of the membrane. This entire process passes down the nerve fiber to a synapse. As soon as the nerve is repolarized, it can conduct another impulse.

When an impulse reaches a synapse, it is passed on to another nerve fiber or to an organ. In most synapses, this occurs by release of a *chemical transmitter*. The chemical acts as a stimulus that starts an impulse along the next nerve fiber, or makes an organ or muscle react.

The strength and speed of the impulse or action potential in a nerve do not vary, regardless of the strength or nature of the stimulus. A nerve, however,

may send impulses more often when a strong stimulus is applied at the synapse or sense organ. In a nerve trunk, which contains many nerve fibers, a stronger stimulus may produce a stronger response because more fibers are being stimulated, and each may send impulses more rapidly.

After a sensory nerve has been stimulated, the impulses may pass up to the brain. The brain then decides how to respond. For example, you may see a pencil on a table and decide to pick it up. Impulses from the nerves in the eye pass along the sensory nerve to the brain. The brain sends impulses down the motor nerves to the muscles of the hand and arm.

Some impulses do not go to the brain. They are short-circuited more directly to make contact with motor nerves in the spinal cord. The path that the nerve impulse follows is called a *reflex arc*. For example, a pinprick on the skin stimulates a pain receptor. A sensory nerve carries the impulse to the spinal cord, where association nerves transfer it directly to motor nerves, by-passing the brain. The motor nerves send the message of pain to the muscles, which produce an involuntary jerk of the body.

Injuries to the Nervous System

If an axon or dendrite of a neuron is cut by an injury, the cut fiber will be absorbed by the body. If the injury occurs in the peripheral nervous system, the nerve cell may regenerate the fiber. However, if the cell body is damaged, or if the cut nerve fiber is in the central nervous system, the whole neuron will degenerate.   HERBERT H. JASPER

Related Articles in WORLD BOOK include:

Brain	Neuropathology	Plexus
Cerebrospinal Fluid	Palsy	Reflex Action
Epilepsy	Paralysis	Sciatica
Multiple Sclerosis	Parkinson's Disease	Senses
Neuritis	Physiological Psychology	Shingles
		Spine

See also *Nervous System* in the RESEARCH GUIDE/INDEX, Volume 22, for a *Reading and Study Guide*.

NESS, EVALINE (1911-   ), an illustrator of children's books, won the 1967 Caldecott medal for her illustrations for *Sam, Bangs, & Moonshine* (1966). She also wrote the novel. She previously had been a runner-up three times in the Caldecott competition.

Evaline Ness was born and grew up in Pontiac, Mich. She studied at the Art Institute in Chicago, the Art Students' League in New York City, and the Accademia di belle Arti in Rome.

NESS, LOCH. See LOCH NESS.

NESSUS. See HERCULES (Hercules' Death).

NEST is a place an animal prepares for raising its young. See ANIMAL (Animal Homes); ANT (Nests); BEE (The Nest); BIRD (Building the Nest; picture: Bird Nests); BIRD'S-NEST SOUP; HORNET; WASP.

NESTER. See WESTERN FRONTIER LIFE (The Cattle Boom).

NESTOR was the hero son of Neleus and Chloris, rulers of Pylos, Messenia, in Greek mythology. Late Greek legend said that Hercules killed Nestor's father and brothers. Nestor, a great warrior, fought in the battle between the Centaurs and the Lapiths (see CENTAUR). He helped kill the Calydonian boar, and he went on the voyage of the Argonauts (see ARGONAUTS).

He was over 60 when he took part in the Trojan War, and was outstanding in the Greek councils for his intelligent advice. He appears in Homer's *Iliad* and *Odyssey*. The word *Nestor* is used to describe a wise and clear-sighted person.   H. L. Stow

NESTORIAN CHRISTIANS are members of a religious sect that was prominent in the A.D. 400's. They follow the teachings of Nestorius, who was bishop of Constantinople. They believe that Jesus united in Himself two persons: the Word and the man. But these two persons were so closely united that they could almost be regarded as one. Nestorian doctrine does not recognize Mary as the mother of God. It teaches instead that Mary gave birth to a man who was the *instrument* of divinity, but was not divinity itself.

In A.D. 431, a Roman synod condemned Nestorius. He eventually died in exile. The sect continued to flourish in Arabia, Syria, and Palestine, and had missions in China, India, and Egypt. But it split in the 1500's. One group, now known as the Chaldean Christians, transferred its allegiance to the Roman Catholic Church. The other group maintained its old traditions.

NET is a fabric or cloth with an open mesh. It is made by interlacing threads and then knotting or twisting them at the points where they cross each other. The *bobbin threads* (fine cords) cross to the right and to the left. Net may be made of cotton, rayon, nylon,

or other fibers. A single twist net is most common, but a double twist is stronger. Narrow widths of net are called *footing*. Wider pieces, known as *yardage*, usually measure 72 inches (183 centimeters) across.

Crosswise bobbin net resembles Brussels handmade net, and is extremely fine. Its degrees of fineness are expressed in *points*—that is, the number of holes to $\frac{1}{2}$ inch (13 millimeters) crosswise. Its strength depends on the coarseness of the thread and the number of twists given to the pairs of threads that make up four of the mesh's six sides. Brussels net washes satisfactorily, but tends to thicken. It should be pulled or stretched into shape, usually on a frame, rather than ironed.

Handmade net has slight irregularities and costs more than machine-made net. *Filet net* has a square mesh that is made by knotting the threads to form corners.

Coarse mesh nets are often used for industrial purposes. They may be made into insect nets, tennis nets, heavy cable nets, and fish nets. Fish nets may be of several types, such as seine, drift, trawl, kettle, and trammel. A trammel net is a set of three nets. According to Norse mythology, Loki, the god of evil, invented fishing nets.   Hazel B. Strahan

See also FISHING INDUSTRY (How Fish Are Caught); LACE.

Nets have many uses. Volleyball, *above,* and other games require a net. Nets are also used by rescue crews to lift people from water, *above left,* and by dock workers to load ships, *below left.* In parts of the world, fishermen use nets, *below.*

Farrell Grehan, Photo Researchers

NETHERLANDS

Bicycle Riding is a popular way to travel in The Netherlands. About half the people own a bike, and many roads throughout the country have special bicycle lanes.

NETHERLANDS is a small kingdom on the North Sea in northwestern Europe. The Netherlands is often called *Holland*, though this name actually refers to only one part of the country. The people of The Netherlands call themselves *Hollanders* or *Nederlanders*, but in English-speaking countries they are known as the *Dutch*.

"God created the world, but the Dutch created Holland," according to an old Dutch saying. More than two-fifths of the country's land was once covered by the sea, or by lakes or swamps. The Dutch "created" this land by pumping out the water. In these drained areas, called *polders*, are the richest farmlands and largest cities of The Netherlands. Amsterdam, the capital and largest city, is on a polder.

To make a polder, the Dutch build a dike around the area to be drained of water. The water is pumped into a series of canals that flow into the North Sea. Windmills were once used to run the pumps, but electric motors have replaced most of them. The polders have no natural drainage because they are below sea level. As a result, the pumping must be continued after the polders are built.

Most of the Zuider Zee, once the largest bay in The Netherlands, is being drained. This project is creating about 860 square miles (2,227 square kilometers) of farmland. The rest of the Zuider Zee has been changed from salt water to fresh water, and is called IJsselmeer.

The Dutch have great pride in their long battle against the sea. They take extreme care to protect their hard-won land, and are famous for keeping their homes,

towns, and fields clean and neat. Land is especially valuable to the Dutch because The Netherlands is one of the most thickly populated countries in the world. It is about $1\frac{1}{2}$ times as large as Maryland, but it has about $3\frac{2}{5}$ times as many people as that state.

Most of The Netherlands is flat, with some uplands. Many canals cut through the country. They not only drain the land, but also serve as waterways and provide the farmers with extra water. Dairy farming is the most important form of agriculture in The Netherlands. The processing of dairy products is a major branch of Dutch manufacturing, the leading source of income.

The contributors of this article are Robert W. Adams, Professor of International Business at the University of Michigan; Lewis M. Alexander, Professor of Geography at the University of Rhode Island; and Herbert H. Rowen, Professor of History at Rutgers University.

--- **FACTS IN BRIEF** ---

Capital: Amsterdam.

Seat of Government: The Hague.

Official Language: Dutch.

Area: 15,892 sq. mi. (41,160 km²), including 1,175 sq. mi. (3,043 km²) of inland water. *Greatest Distances*—north-south, 196 mi. (315 km); east-west, 167 mi. (269 km). *Coastline*—228 mi. (367 km).

Elevation: *Highest*—Vaalser Berg, 1,057 ft. (322 m) above sea level. *Lowest*—Prins Alexander Polder, 22 ft. (6.7 m) below sea level.

Population: *Estimated 1978 Population*—14,091,000; distribution, 85 per cent urban, 15 per cent rural; density, 886 persons per sq. mi. (342 persons per km²). *1970 Census*—13,045,785. *Estimated 1983 Population*—14,810,000.

Chief Products: *Agriculture*—barley, dairy products, flower bulbs, oats, potatoes, sugar beets, wheat. *Manufacturing*—clothing, electronic equipment, iron and steel, machinery, petroleum products, processed foods, textiles, transportation equipment. *Mining*—natural gas, petroleum, salt.

National Anthem: "Wilhelmus van Nassouwe" ("William of Nassau").

Money: *Basic Unit*—guilder. For the value of the guilder in dollars, see MONEY (table). See also GUILDER.

NETHERLANDS / *Government*

The Netherlands has a democratic government based on the constitution of 1814. The constitution establishes a king or queen as head of state, but gives the ruler little real power. The ruler names all appointed government officials on the advice of various government bodies, and signs all laws passed by the parliament.

A queen has headed The Netherlands since 1890, when King William III died. Queen Juliana became ruler in 1948 in a ceremony called an *inauguration.* Dutch kings and queens, unlike those of other countries, are not crowned. Juliana's oldest daughter, Princess Beatrix, is first in line to inherit the throne. Beatrix' son, Prince William-Alexander, is second in the line of inheritance.

The national government meets in The Hague, though the capital is Amsterdam, 34 miles (55 kilometers) away. Invading French troops captured Amsterdam in 1795 and made it the capital. The Dutch restored their government in The Hague in 1814.

The Netherlands is part of the Kingdom of The Netherlands. The kingdom also includes the Netherlands Antilles—two groups of islands in the Caribbean Sea. These islands formed a Dutch colony until 1954, when they were made an equal partner in the kingdom. The Netherlands Antilles has an appointed governor, and a cabinet headed by a prime minister. The cabinet is responsible to a one-house legislature, whose members are elected by the people to four-year terms.

GOVERNMENT IN BRIEF

Form of Government: Constitutional monarchy.

Political Divisions: 11 provinces.

Head of State: King or queen.

Head of Government: Prime minister, appointed by the ruler. He heads a cabinet, also appointed, which runs the government departments. If the cabinet and the parliament cannot agree, either the cabinet resigns, or the parliament is dissolved and a new election is held.

Parliament (called the States-General): *First Chamber*—75 members, elected by the provincial legislatures to 6-year terms; *Second Chamber*—150 members, elected by the people to 4-year terms. Each house approves or rejects proposed laws, but only the Second Chamber can propose or amend bills. Legislation is also proposed by the ruler on the advice of the cabinet.

Provincial and Municipal Government: Councils elected by the people to 4-year terms. The number of members varies according to population. In the provinces, the chief executive is an appointed commissioner. In the cities and towns, he is an appointed burgomaster. Both are appointed by the ruler.

Courts: All judges are appointed by the ruler for life. They can be removed from office only by the highest court, the High Court of The Netherlands. The High Court has 17 judges and consists of three chambers— for civil, criminal, and tax cases.

Voting Age: 21.

Political Parties: *Largest*—Labor Party. Other major parties in The Netherlands include the Anti-Revolutionary Party, the Catholic People's Party, and the Liberal Party.

Armed Forces: Army, navy, and air force, with a total of almost 125,000 men. Men are required to serve from 16 to 21 months after reaching the age of 19.

WORLD BOOK photo by Bobbi Jones

Parliament Buildings in The Hague are the home of the two houses of the States-General, the Dutch parliament.

The Dutch Flag dates from about 1630. Until then, an orange stripe was at the top instead of a red one.

The Coat of Arms has old symbols of the Dutch royal family. The sword and arrows represent strength in unity.

Alan Band Associates

Queen Juliana, *second from left,* is the Dutch head of state. Her daughter Beatrix, *second from right,* is the heir to the throne.

The Netherlands is about one-half of 1 per cent as large as the United States, not counting Alaska and Hawaii.

WORLD BOOK map

The Netherlands is one of the most thickly populated countries in the world. It has 14¾ times as many people per square mile or kilometer as the United States. But few areas ever seem to be overcrowded. The Dutch keep their tidy homes, busy cities, and small farms as neatly arranged and sparkling clean as possible. Every Saturday, for example, many Dutch homemakers scrub the steps and sidewalks in front of their homes.

The Netherlanders are known for their good fellowship, called *gezelligheid*. This cozy friendliness, as well as Dutch orderliness, helps make life pleasant in the thickly populated country. Families welcome friends to drop in uninvited at almost any time. They enjoy making guests feel at home with generous servings of rich Dutch chocolates and pastries. Delicious Dutch cheeses such as Edam and Gouda are also popular. Dairy farmers sell the cheeses at weekly open-air markets.

The Dutch face their continuous battle against the sea—to "create" land and protect it from flooding—with great pride and courage. A famous story tells of a little Dutch boy who noticed water trickling through a dike one evening. There was no one nearby to tell. The boy plugged the hole with his finger, and held back the water until someone finally arrived the next day. A statue near Haarlem is inscribed in honor of this boy "who symbolizes the eternal struggle of Holland against the sea."

Population. In 1978, The Netherlands had about 14,-091,000 people. The following table shows some official census figures for The Netherlands through the years:

1970	13,045,785	1909	5,858,175
1960	11,461,964	1889	4,511,415
1947	9,625,499	1869	3,579,529
1930	7,935,565	1849	3,056,879
1920	6,865,314	1829	2,613,298

About 40 per cent of the people live in two coastal provinces—Noord-Holland (North Holland) and Zuid-Holland (South Holland). In these provinces are the two Dutch cities with populations of more than 500,-000—Amsterdam and Rotterdam. Fourteen other cities have populations between 100,000 and 500,000. See the separate articles on the Dutch cities listed in the *Related Articles* at the end of this article.

Religion. Protestants make up a little more than 40 per cent of the Dutch population, and another 40 per cent are Roman Catholics. Traditionally, the two groups have remained as separate as possible. This split in Dutch life has involved separate clubs, labor unions, neighborhoods, newspapers, schools, broadcasting companies, and political parties. Since the 1940's, the split has been slowly breaking down among young people and, because of a housing shortage, in many city neighborhoods.

Of the Protestants, about three-fourths belong to the Dutch Reformed Church. Members of the royal family traditionally belong to this church. Nearly 20 per cent of the Dutch are not church members.

Holidays and Recreation. The Dutch exchange gifts on St. Nicholas' Eve, December 5, instead of on Christmas. The children believe that Saint Nicholas visits their homes with presents for good boys and girls. A man dressed like a bishop represents Saint Nicholas and rides through the streets. In Amsterdam, he arrives by ship and is greeted by booming cannon, ringing bells, and cheering crowds.

During the 1600's, the Dutch brought the custom of Saint Nicholas' visit with them to America. There, the English settlers changed his Dutch nickname, *Sinterklaas*, to *Santa Claus* (see SANTA CLAUS).

On Palm Sunday, young people in Dutch villages sing Easter songs and carry lighted lanterns on their way to the market place for music and dancing. On Easter Sunday, children and adults play games with colored eggs. Many sports events are held on Easter Monday.

The Dutch are famous for raising tulips and other bulb flowers, and they hold many spectacular flower festivals each spring. Long parades of floats covered with blue, pink, red, and yellow blossoms wind through the towns near the bulb fields. Homes and lawns along the way are also decorated with beautiful floral designs.

The canals that carry water from the land are also used for ice skating, an extremely popular sport. But The Netherlands has mild winters, and the people do not have thick ice for skating so often as they would like. When the ice is hard enough, schools sometimes close to let the children skate. Even many business executives stop working and take "ice vacations."

Clothing. Most Netherlanders wear clothing similar to that worn in the United States and Canada. People in farm areas and fishing villages sometimes wear the famous wooden shoes called *klompen*. These shoes are noisy, but they protect the feet from damp earth better than leather shoes do. The Dutch rarely wear wooden shoes in their homes. They leave them outside and change to leather shoes.

Dutch national costumes also include full trousers for the men, and full skirts and lace caps for the women. They are still worn in a few regions, including the islands of Zeeland and the West Frisian Islands. See CLOTHING (picture: Traditional Costumes).

Language. The Netherlanders are a Germanic people, and the Dutch language is related to German. Many English words have been adapted from Dutch, including *brandy*, *skate*, *skipper*, and *yacht*. Most Netherlanders know English or German in addition to Dutch. The people of the northern province of Friesland also speak Frisian, another Germanic language.

Education. Dutch law requires children from the age of 6 through 14 to go to school. All schools, including religious schools, that meet national educational standards receive government funds. These standards, which are set by law, include courses of study and the hiring of teachers.

The Netherlands has no general high-school program like that of the United States. Instead, it has several kinds of high schools. Each kind trains students for a special purpose, such as university work, advanced study in various institutes, or jobs in business or industry.

All the universities are supported almost completely by the government. Tuitions are low, and many university students receive some form of government aid. The University of Amsterdam, with about 20,000 students, is the largest university. The State University of Leiden, founded in 1575, is the oldest.

Arts. The Netherlands has produced some of the world's greatest painters. During the 1600's, the country's Golden Age, masterpieces were painted by Pieter de Hooch, Frans Hals, Rembrandt, Jacob van Ruisdael, and Jan Vermeer. At that time, most European artists painted only for churches, nobles, or royalty. But Dutch artists painted ordinary persons and things, and many Dutch businessmen bought these works to beautify their homes. Later Dutch painters included Vincent van Gogh and Piet Mondrian. Paintings by most of these artists are shown in the PAINTING article.

Dutch literature is little known outside The Netherlands because few works have been translated. The most important Dutch writer was Joost van den Vondel. Others include Willem Bilderdijk, Herman Gorter, Constantijn Huygens, and "Multatuli" (Eduard Douwes Dekker).

The Netherlands has produced few noted composers. Among the better-known ones were Willem Pijper and Jan Pieterszoon Sweelinck. Several Dutch cities have fine symphony orchestras. The Concertgebouw Orchestra of Amsterdam is world famous, and frequently tours other countries.

Busy Amsterdam, the capital and largest city of The Netherlands, ranks among the chief European commercial centers.

Masterpieces of Dutch Art by such painters as Rembrandt and Jan Vermeer attract visitors to museums in The Netherlands.

Traditional Clothing of The Netherlands is worn by many of the Dutch people, especially in fishing and farming areas. It includes cap, baggy pants, and wooden shoes.

Land Regions. The Netherlands has four main land regions: (1) the Dunes, (2) the Polders, (3) the Sand Plains, and (4) the Southern Uplands.

The Dunes rise 15 to 25 feet (4.6 to 7.6 meters) above sea level. This region curves in a line along the entire North Sea coast of The Netherlands. In the north, the line consists of the West Frisian Islands. The line is unbroken in the center, but is broken in the south by wide river outlets. The sandy Dunes region cannot support farming, and few trees grow there.

The Polders lie below sea level, and are protected from the sea by the sand dunes or by dikes. The Prins Alexander Polder, the lowest point in The Netherlands, lies 22 feet (6.7 meters) below sea level. The Polders region makes up more than two-fifths of the country. It consists of flat, fertile areas of clay soils that were once covered by the sea, or by swamps or lakes. It has the country's most productive farmlands and largest cities.

The Sand Plains lie less than 100 feet (30 meters) above sea level in most places. In the southwest, the region rises higher. Low, sandy ridges cross the plains and create a rolling landscape. The soil is generally dry. Irrigation and fertilizers make farming possible. Pine forests cover much of the region. A broad valley of clay soils marks the courses of the Maas (or Meuse) River and of

LAND REGIONS OF THE NETHERLANDS

Polders

Dunes

Amsterdam

Sand Plains

Rotterdam

Polders

Southern Uplands

Distance Scale
0 Miles 25 50 75
0 Kilometres 50 75 100

WORLD BOOK map

Netherlands Map Index

Provinces

Cities and Towns

*Does not appear on map; key shows general location.
*Population of metropolitan area, including suburbs.
Sources: 1975 official estimates; 1971 census.

Netherlands
Political Map

International boundary
Expressway
Other road
Railroad
Canal
⊛ National capital
★ Provincial capital
• Other city

WORLD BOOK map

1 2 3 4 5 6 7

A

North Sea

East Frisian Islands

Norderney
Juist
Borkum
Norden
Borkum
Rottumeroog
Schiermonnikoog
Emden
West Frisian Islands
Ameland
Schiermonnikoog
Uithuizen
B
Terschelling
Hollum
Holwerd
Zoutkamp
Appingedam
Delfzijl
Westterschelling
Dokkum
Buitenpost
Dollard
Oostvlieland
GRONINGEN
Bay
Vlieland
Leeuwarden
Bergum
Groningen
Hoogezand-
Sappemeer
Winschoten
Harlingen
Franeker
Drachten
Roden
Veendam
Oude-Pekela
De Koog
Bolsward
Sneek
FRIESLAND
Stadskanaal
Aschendorf
Texel
Heerenveen
Makkinga
Assen
C
Den Helder
Den Oever
Workum
Musselkanaal
Ter Apel
Staveren
Wolvega
DRENTE
North Holland Canal
Lemmer
Steenwijk
Beilen
Ems
Emmen
Meppen
Wieringermeer
IJsselmeer
Northeast
Emmeloord
Hoogeveen
Coevorden
Polder
Schagen
Medemblik
Polder
Staphorst
Hardenberg
D
Bergen aan Zee
Enkhuizen
Urk
Meppel
Ommen
Den Ham
Nordhorn
Egmond aan Zee
Bergen
Hoorn
Kampen
OVERIJSSEL
Ootmarsum
Heemskerk
Alkmaar
Markerwaard
Zwolle
Vecht
Heerde
Den Ham
Polder
Lelystad
Elburg
Raalte
Almelo
Oldenzaal
Velsen
Edam
(under
Flevoland
Nunspeet
Olst
Hengelo
NORTH
construction)
Polder
Epe
Niverdal
HOLLAND
Zaandam
Harderwijk
Goor
Gronau
Haarlem
Amsterdam
NETHERLANDS
Deventer
Enschede
E
Zandvoort
Weesp
Nijkerk
Apeldoorn
Haaksbergen
Noordwijk
Bussum
Baarn
Zutphen
Lochem
Katwijk aan Zee
Hilversum
Amersfoort
Wassenaar
Leiden
Barneveld
Groenlo
The Hague
Woerden
Utrecht
Zeist
Ede
GELDERLAND
Winterswijk
SOUTH
UTRECHT
Arnhem
Doetinchem
Coesfeld
Hoek van Holland
HOLLAND
Delft
Gouda
Veenendaal
EUROPOORT
Naaldwijk
Lek
Rhenen
Wageningen
Aalten
Borken
Maassluis
Rotterdam
Schoonhoven
Kuilenburg
Oude IJssel
Vlaardingen
Waal
Nijmegen
Spijkenisse
Sliedrecht
Gorinchem
Tiel
Wesel
Ouddorp
Zwijndrecht
Zaltbommel
Oss
Rhine
F
Middelharnis
Dordrecht
Grave
Kleve
Lippe
Zierikzee
Waalwijk
Maas
Boxmeer
WEST GERMANY
Willemstad
Oosterhout
Uden
Domburg
Stavenisse
Steenbergen
Breda
NORTH BRABANT
Gelsenkirchen
Middelburg
Goes
Bergen op Zoom
Roosendaal
Tilburg
Gemert
Venraai
Oberhausen
Essen
Vlissingen
ZEELAND
Zundert
Dorschot
Helmond
Deurne
Maas
Duisburg
Westerschelde
Schelde-Rhine Canal
Eindhoven
Geldrop
Asten
Venlo
Ruhr
G
Oostburg
Terneuzen
Turnhout
Valkenswaard
Tegelen
Krefeld
Düsseldorf
Bruges
Sas van Gent
Hulst
Lommel
Weert
LIMBURG
Roermond
Mönchen-
Solingen
Antwerp
Brasschaat
Geel
Gladbach
Albert Canal
Ghent
Lier
Juliana Canal
Rur
Cologne
Sint-Niklaas
Schelde
Sittard
Erft
H
Dendermonde
Mechelen
Geleen
Jülich
Aalst
Demer
Diest
Genk
Heerlen
Kerkrade
BELGIUM
Louvain
Hasselt
Maastricht
Düren
Bonn
Brussels
Tienen
Vaals
Aachen
Rhine
Halle
Dender
Waremme
Liège
Soignies
Meuse
Verviers
Gembloux
Tournai
Kortrijk
Leie

0 25 50 75 100 125 150 Miles
0 25 50 75 100 125 150 175 200 225 Kilometers

THE LONG BATTLE AGAINST THE SEA

For hundreds of years, the Dutch have been "creating" areas of land called *polders* by pumping out the water that covered them. The map at the right shows the development of polders since 1300. The straight line between Den Helder and Zwolle indicates the area represented horizontally on the diagram below the map. The diagram shows how dikes keep water from polders.

Land Reclamation

- 1300 to 1600
- 1600 to 1900
- 1900 to present

AREA SHOWN IN CROSS-SECTION

Den Helder
Wieringermeer Polder
Northeast Polder
Zwolle
Markerwaard Polder (under construction)
Flevoland Polder
Amsterdam
Prins Alexander Polder 21.7 ft. (6.6 m) below sea level (Lowest point in The Netherlands)
Rotterdam

IJsselmeer
Waddenzee
North Sea
NETHERLANDS
Lek River
Waal River
Maas River
IJssel River
Rhine River

WEST GERMANY

Schelde-Rhine Canal
Antwerp
Schelde River

BELGIUM

50 Miles
100 Kilometers

WORLD BOOK map

Ralph Turner, Carl Östman

Dikes Pounded by Heavy Seas off The Netherlands must be strengthened from time to time.

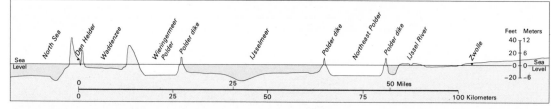

North Sea — Den Helder — Waddenzee — Wieringermeer Polder — Polder dike — IJsselmeer — Polder dike — Northeast Polder — Polder dike — IJssel River — Zwolle

Sea Level

Feet / Meters
40 / 12
20 / 6
0 / 0 Sea Level
-20 / -6

0 — 25 — 50 — 75 — 50 Miles
0 — 25 — 50 — 75 — 100 Kilometers

Russ Kinne, Photo Researchers

The Polders region has the richest farmland in The Netherlands. Canals that drain away water also irrigate the fertile soil of the region. Tulips and many other flowers grow there.

Fred Ward, Black Star

The Afsluitdijk, a dike 20 miles (32 kilometers) long, separates the North Sea, *left,* and the IJsselmeer.

branches of the Rhine River. These rivers are important waterways, and canals connect them with other rivers and canals to form a transportation network.

The Southern Uplands make up the highest land region of The Netherlands. The highest point, Vaalser Berg, rises 1,057 feet (322 meters) near Maastricht. The region has naturally fertile soils, and much fruit is grown in orchards there.

Deltas. Much of southwestern Netherlands consists of islands and peninsulas in the North Sea. These marshy areas are deltas of the Maas, Neder Rijn, and Wester-schelde rivers. In 1953, a storm broke through the dikes in this region. The sea flooded over 375,000 acres (151,-800 hectares), and over 1,800 persons drowned. In 1958, work began on the Delta Plan, a flood-control project, to prevent a similar disaster.

The Delta Plan includes a series of dams that will keep the sea from flooding into four wide outlets of the rivers. The first outlet was dammed in 1961, and a second was closed in 1968. Floodgates in the dams will allow ice in the rivers to flow to sea. Completion of the entire project was scheduled for 1978.

Ray Halin

The Sand Plains of The Netherlands are a low, mostly flat region with some ridges. Dairy cattle graze in pastures there.

NETHERLANDS / Climate

The Netherlands has a mild, damp climate, largely because the country is on the sea. In winter, the sea is not so cold as the land. In summer, it is not so warm. As a result, west winds from the sea warm The Netherlands in winter, and cool it in summer. In addition, winds carrying moisture from the sea make the skies over the country extremely cloudy. The clouds shield the land from the heat of the sun. Temperatures average from 60° to 65° F. (16° to 18° C) in summer, and a little above 30° F. (−1° C) in winter.

The country has no mountains to block the winds, so there are no great differences of climate from area to area. The extreme southeast, which is the highest part of The Netherlands, is also the wettest. It receives a yearly average of more than 34 inches (86 centimeters) of *precipitation* (rain, melted snow, and other forms of moisture). An average of 27 inches (69 centimeters) a year falls on the islands of Zeeland province and along the central Dutch-German border. Summer is the wettest season, but precipitation is fairly evenly distributed throughout the year. Brief showers may fall as often as every 30 minutes.

North Sea storms are heaviest in the coastal areas of The Netherlands. These storms have broken dikes and caused flooding, sometimes with great loss of life. The northern and western regions receive most of the mist from the sea. The mist is heaviest in winter.

Farrell Grehan, Photo Researchers

Strong Sea Winds require vacationers at the beach resort of Scheveningen to have chairs that also serve as shields.

The Netherlands has a thriving economy, even though the country's natural resources are limited. Dutch factories depend heavily on imported raw materials. Much of the total industrial production is exported, but the value of imports is greater than that of exports. The difference is made up by income from Dutch services—including shipping and banking—to other countries, and from tourism.

The great importance of foreign trade to The Netherlands makes the Dutch government and the people strong supporters of international economic cooperation. The Netherlands helped form the European Common Market—now called the European Community—in 1957. This economic union with Belgium, Britain, Denmark, France, Ireland, Italy, Luxembourg, and West Germany has done much to expand Dutch trade and improve the economy. See EUROPEAN COMMUNITY.

Natural Resources. The Netherlands has large deposits of salt and natural gas, and some coal and petroleum. The Polders region has extremely fertile soils.

THE NETHERLANDS' GROSS NATIONAL PRODUCT

Total gross national product in 1973—$59,978,000,000

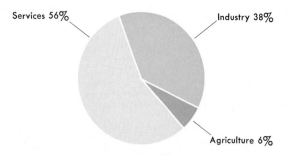

Services 56%

Industry 38%

Agriculture 6%

The gross national product (GNP) is the total value of goods and services produced by a country in a year. The GNP measures a nation's total annual economic performance. It can also be used to compare the economic output and growth of countries.

Production and Workers by Economic Activities

Economic Activities	Per Cent of GNP Produced	Employed Workers	
		Number of Persons*	Per Cent of Total
Manufacturing & Mining	28	1,132,000	24
Community, Social, & Personal Services	19	873,000	19
Government	15	607,000	13
Wholesale & Retail Trade	15	931,000	20
Construction	8	475,000	10
Transportation & Communication	7	302,000	6
Agriculture, Forestry, & Fishing	6	309,000	7
Utilities	2	44,000	1
Total	100	4,673,000	100

*Figures for persons are in man-years. A man-year is the amount of work performed by one person working one job full-time for one year.
Sources: Central Bureau of Statistics, The Netherlands; U.S. Department of State.

Forests—most of which are beech, oak, or pine—cover only about 8 per cent of the land.

Many rivers flow through The Netherlands. But the land is so flat that the rivers do not flow with enough force to generate hydroelectricity. As a result, the nation's electric power is produced entirely by fuel-burning power stations. The rivers, together with a connecting network of canals, provide cheap transportation. On these waterways, as well as the nearby sea, The Netherlands imports its industrial needs, exports its products, and carries on valuable shipping services. The coastal waters of the North Sea also have many kinds of fish.

Manufacturing is the most valuable economic activity of The Netherlands. By the mid-1960's, production had reached a level three times that of 1938. This expansion resulted largely from government industrialization programs to rebuild the shattered economy after World War II ended in 1945. The government and organizations of employers and workers have cooperated closely in establishing wages and other job policies. As a result, there have been almost no strikes.

Large iron and steel works operate near Velsen and Utrecht. They use imported ores. Amsterdam, Rotterdam, and other large cities have big shipyards. Eindhoven has one of the world's largest electronics factories. This factory produces household appliances, radios, and television sets. Machinery and transportation equipment also come from many Dutch factories.

Food processing is a major manufacturing industry. Dairy products—especially butter, cheese, and processed milk and eggs—are the chief foods. The Netherlands is one of the world's major cheese manufacturers. Other food products include beet sugar, chocolate, processed meats, and animal feed.

The fast-growing Dutch chemical industry produces drugs, fertilizers, paints, plastics, and synthetic rubber. There are several large oil refineries near Rotterdam. The Dutch textile industry produces goods of cotton, linen, wool, and synthetic fibers. Amsterdam has long been a famous center of diamond cutting and polishing. Other important Dutch products include bricks, cement, glassware, leather goods, paper, pottery, rubber products, and tobacco products.

Agriculture. The Dutch cannot afford to waste any land because their country is so thickly populated. The farmers fertilize their land heavily and use modern machinery to get the best results. Dutch farms cover an average of only 25 acres (10 hectares), compared with about 350 acres (142 hectares) in the United States. About two-thirds of the total land area is farmland. Almost 60 per cent of the farmland is used for grazing, and crops are grown on the rest.

Dairy farming is the most important branch of agriculture in The Netherlands. Most of the dairy farmers also grow crops, which are used mainly to feed the livestock. Almost 4 million cattle—mainly dairy cattle—graze on the grasslands. About 189,600 short tons (172,000 metric tons) of butter and 409,000 short tons (371,000 metric tons) of cheese are produced yearly. Farmers also raise beef cattle, hogs, and poultry.

Crops include barley, fruits, oats, potatoes, rye, sugar

beets, vegetables, and wheat. The Netherlands is a leading flax-producing country. Flower bulbs, especially tulips, are also important. Daffodils, hyacinths, narcissuses, and tulips carpet the countryside between Haarlem and Leiden every April and May. The bulbs of these flowers are shipped to all parts of the world.

Mining. The Dutch produce much natural gas. One of the world's largest reserves of this fuel—the Slochteren field—lies in Groningen province in the northeastern part of The Netherlands. It contains over 55 trillion cubic feet (1.6 trillion cubic meters) of natural gas.

Beds of salt lie near Hengelo. Miners dissolve the raw salt underground and pump the *brine* (salt water) to the surface, where it is evaporated to get the salt.

Oil wells operate in the northeastern province of Drente and near The Hague. They supply only a small part of the country's needs. The Netherlands has some coal mines in the southeastern province of Limburg. But mining conditions are poor, and almost all the mines are being closed.

Fishing. The Dutch have more than 1,500 commercial fishing boats, and catch about 415,000 short tons (376,500 metric tons) of fish and other seafood yearly. The catch comes mainly from the North Sea and the English Channel. The most important catch is mussels. Other important seafood products are flatfish, herring, and haddock. Fishermen also catch eels in IJsselmeer.

Transportation. Boats can travel on about 4,000 miles (6,400 kilometers) of rivers and canals in The Netherlands. Many of the canals are important waterways, and ocean-going ships use the larger ones. Motor barges on the inland waterways carry more than half the nation's total freight. The Netherlands has more than 28,500 miles (45,870 kilometers) of paved roads and highways. Over 2,000 miles (3,200 kilometers) of government-owned railroads also serve the country.

About half the people have a bicycle, and many roads have special lanes for bicycling. Sturdy motor-driven bicycles called *bromfietsen* (roar bikes) are becoming increasingly popular.

Rotterdam is the largest seaport in the world. It handles more cargo yearly than any other port. Rotterdam serves as a gateway to and from much of Europe by way of the Rhine River, Europe's busiest inland waterway. Amsterdam, the second largest Dutch port, is linked to the North Sea by the North Sea Canal, one of the world's deepest and widest canals. The canal is 49 feet (15 meters) deep and 525 feet (160 meters) wide.

Royal Dutch Airlines (KLM), established in 1919, is the oldest airline in the world still in operation. Its planes fly to about 65 countries.

Communication. The Netherlands has about 90 daily newspapers, with a total daily circulation of more than 3½ million copies. The largest newspaper is *De Telegraaf* of Amsterdam. It has a circulation of about 350,000 copies a day.

The government owns and regulates the nation's two radio networks and two television networks. Five large broadcasting companies prepare programs for them. These companies represent religious or political groups. The postal, telephone, and telegraph services are operated by the government.

I. Wimnell, Carl Östman

The Famous Alkmaar Cheese Market is held on Fridays from spring to fall. Porters in colorful hats carry the cheeses.

FARM, MINERAL, AND FOREST PRODUCTS

This map shows where the leading farm, mineral, and forest products of The Netherlands are produced. The map also points out the country's main industrial, pasture, forest, and crop areas. The manufacturing center of each industrial area is named on the map.

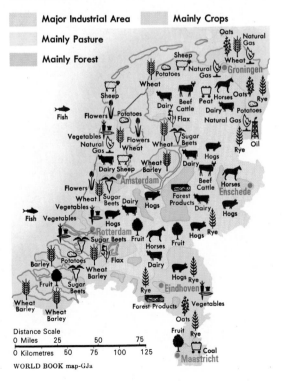

Major Industrial Area   Mainly Crops
Mainly Pasture
Mainly Forest

WORLD BOOK map-GJa

Early Days. In 58 B.C., Roman soldiers under Julius Caesar invaded what are now The Netherlands, Belgium, and Luxembourg. The Romans conquered much of the region, now called the Low Countries. The word *Netherlands* means *Low Countries*, but the Low Countries also include Belgium and Luxembourg.

During the A.D. 400's, Germanic tribesmen called Franks drove the Romans out of the Low Countries. The Frankish kingdom expanded, but broke apart during the 800's. In 870, the Low Countries were divided between the East and West Frankish kingdoms (later Germany and France). The northern part, including what is now The Netherlands, became part of the East Frankish kingdom.

The Rise of Commerce. At first, the French and German rulers of the Low Countries paid little attention to the region. Local dukes, counts, and bishops became increasingly powerful. But during the 1100's, trade and industry began to expand rapidly in the Low Countries. Fishing, shipbuilding, shipping, and textile manufacturing became especially important. The French and German kings became interested in the Low Countries after the thriving trade developed. The towns, which wanted to stay free, supported the local nobles in struggles against the foreign rulers.

Unification. Beginning in the 1300's, the French dukes of Burgundy won control of most of the Low Countries through inheritance, marriage, purchase, and war. They promoted central government there, and political and national unity began to develop.

In 1516, Duke Charles of Burgundy also became king of Spain. In this way, the Low Countries came under Spanish control. Charles became archduke of Austria and emperor of the Holy Roman Empire in 1519. Beginning in 1520, Charles further strengthened the central government of the Low Countries.

Freedom from Spain. During the early 1500's, the Protestant movement called the Reformation spread through the Low Countries. Charles tried to stop this threat to Roman Catholicism by persecuting Protestants. His son, Philip II of Spain, inherited the Low Countries in 1555. Philip stepped up the struggle against Protestants, and tried to take complete power over the Low Countries. In 1568, the nobles there revolted against his harsh rule. They were led by William I (called the Silent), prince of Orange.

The Spanish troops were generally successful in land battles, but the rebels' ships controlled the sea. The Spaniards attacked Leiden in 1573, but the city held out bravely. In 1574, the people opened dikes that held back the sea, and a Dutch fleet sailed over the floodwaters to rescue Leiden from the Spaniards.

By 1579, the revolt had started to break apart. Roman Catholic nobles in the southern provinces of the Low Countries (now Belgium) had become dissatisfied and returned to Spanish control. Protestantism was

William I, Prince of Orange, led nobles of the Low Countries in a revolt against Spain that began in 1568. The Dutch declared their independence in 1581, but fighting continued until 1648.

The Crossing over the River Maas, an etching (1569) by Mathis Zyndt, Rijksmuseum, Amsterdam, The Netherlands

Amsterdam, with Shipping in the River Y, an etching (1663) by Jacob van Meurs,
Nederlandsch Historisch Scheepvaart Museum, Amsterdam, The Netherlands

The Golden Age of The Netherlands was the 1600's. The nation was the leading sea power
and had a colonial empire. Ships bringing goods to Amsterdam made it the world trade center.

strongest in the northern provinces (now The Netherlands). In 1579, most of the provinces formed the Union of Utrecht and pledged to continue the revolt.

On July 26, 1581, the northern provinces declared their independence from Spain, beginning what later became known as the Dutch Republic or The Netherlands. The Dutch fought for their freedom until 1648, except for a temporary peace from 1609 to 1621. Spain finally recognized Dutch independence in 1648.

Prosperity and Power. The 1600's were the Golden Age of The Netherlands. The country became the leading sea power. Its merchant fleet tripled in size between 1600 and 1650, and Dutch ships supplied about half the world's shipping. Dutch explorers, including Dirck Hartog and Abel Janszoon Tasman, found new sea routes and fishing grounds. Expanding trade made Amsterdam the world's major commercial city, and gave the Dutch the highest standard of living. There were also outstanding cultural achievements, especially in painting.

During the Golden Age, the Dutch developed a great colonial empire in all parts of the world. In 1602, Dutch firms trading with the East Indies combined to form the Dutch East India Company. The company founded Batavia (now Jakarta, the capital of Indonesia) as its headquarters. The company's forces drove the British, French, Portuguese, and Spanish out of what later became the Netherlands Indies (now Indonesia). The company also colonized the southern tip of Africa.

The Dutch West India Company was founded in 1621 to trade in the New World and west Africa. In 1624, the company colonized New Netherland, which consisted of parts of present-day New York, New Jersey, Connecticut, and Delaware. In 1626, Dutch colonists bought Manhattan Island from the Indians for goods worth about $24. They had established New

IMPORTANT DATES IN THE NETHERLANDS

58 B.C. Julius Caesar conquered much of the Low Countries, including what is now The Netherlands.

A.D. 400's-800's The Franks controlled the region.

870 The Netherlands became part of the East Frankish kingdom (now Germany).

1300's-1400's The French dukes of Burgundy united most of the Low Countries.

1516 Duke Charles of Burgundy, ruler of the Low Countries, also became king of Spain.

1581 The Dutch Republic was begun.

1648 Spain recognized Dutch independence.

1600's The Netherlands became the world's major sea power, and developed a great colonial empire.

1652-1674 The Netherlands fought three naval wars with England, and kept leadership of the seas.

1702-1713 The Dutch lost control of the seas to England during a war against France.

1795-1813 France controlled The Netherlands.

1815 The Netherlands became an independent kingdom united with Belgium.

1830 Belgium revolted and became independent.

1914-1918 The Netherlands remained neutral during World War I.

1940-1945 Germany occupied The Netherlands during World War II. Queen Wilhelmina headed the Dutch government-in-exile in London.

1949 The Netherlands granted independence to the Netherlands Indies (now Indonesia).

1954 The colonies of Surinam and Netherlands Antilles became equal partners in the Dutch kingdom.

1957 The Netherlands helped form the European Common Market.

1962 The Netherlands gave up control of Netherlands New Guinea (now Irian Jaya) to the United Nations.

1967 Princess Beatrix gave birth to a son, the first male in line to inherit the throne since 1884.

1975 Surinam became a fully independent nation.

NETHERLANDS

Amsterdam (now New York City) there the year before. In 1634, the Dutch captured what is now the Netherlands Antilles from the Spaniards.

Wars with England and France. The Netherlands fought three naval wars with England between 1652 and 1674. The English hoped to seize the shipping and trading leadership from the Dutch, but failed. During this period, the Dutch won what is now Surinam from the English, and the English gained New Netherland.

France and England formed a secret alliance against the Dutch Republic in 1670, and attacked it in 1672. The Dutch fleet prevented the English from landing by sea, but French troops seized a number of Dutch towns. William III, prince of Orange, was then elected *stadholder* (governor). He stopped the French by opening some dikes and flooding the land. Spanish and German troops also helped the Dutch. The English suffered major defeats at sea, and made peace with the Dutch in 1674. The French were driven out, and signed a peace treaty in 1678.

William's wife, Mary, was a member of the English royal family. In 1689, he became King William III of England as well as the Dutch stadholder. The Netherlands, England, and other European countries defeated France in two more wars, fought from 1688 to 1697 and from 1702 to 1713.

The 1700's. The long wars against France exhausted The Netherlands. In the war that ended in 1713, The Netherlands lost leadership of the seas to England. Dutch industry and trade stopped expanding.

The Revolutionary War in America began in 1775, and the Dutch aided the Americans against the English. England started a naval war against the Dutch in 1780. The Dutch were severely defeated by 1784.

In 1795, the weakened Netherlands fell to invading French troops. The French renamed the country the Batavian Republic, and set up a new government. England seized most of the Dutch overseas possessions.

Independence. In 1806, Napoleon I of France forced the Dutch to accept his brother, Louis, as their king. The Batavian Republic became the Kingdom of Holland. Napoleon wanted tighter control over the country, and made it a part of France in 1810. The Dutch drove out the French in 1813.

After Napoleon's final defeat in 1815, Europe's political leaders remapped much of the continent at the Congress of Vienna. They united The Netherlands and Belgium into the Kingdom of The Netherlands to strengthen barriers against future French expansion. William VI, prince of Orange, became King William I of The Netherlands and grand duke of Luxembourg.

The customs, economies, languages, and religions of the Dutch and the Belgians differed greatly. Most of the Belgians were Roman Catholics, and the upper classes spoke French. In 1830, Belgium declared its independence. Luxembourg ended its political ties with the Dutch royal family in 1890. That year, 10-year-old Wilhelmina had become queen after the death of her father, William III. But Luxembourg's laws did not permit a female ruler.

The Netherlands remained neutral during World War I (1914-1918). British and German naval operations interfered with Dutch fishing, shipping, and trading.

World War II. On May 10, 1940, German troops invaded The Netherlands. Four days later, German bombers destroyed much of Rotterdam. The Dutch army surrendered. Most of the Dutch navy and merchant fleet escaped capture and supported the Allies.

The Dutch suffered greatly during the German occupation. The Germans killed about 75 per cent of the nation's Jews—about 104,000 persons—mostly in death camps. They also forced thousands of other Netherlanders to work in German factories. Secret Dutch groups fought the Germans, organized strikes, and aided escaped prisoners and Allied fliers who had been shot down. In March, 1942, the Netherlands Indies (Indonesia) fell to Japan, an ally of Germany. By the time Germany surrendered to the Allies in May, 1945, about 270,000 Netherlanders had been killed or starved to death. See WORLD WAR II.

Economic Recovery. World War II left much of The Netherlands in ruins. The destruction included almost half the nation's factories and shipping, and most of its railroads. The great harbors at Amsterdam and Rotterdam were crippled. About a seventh of the land was flooded as a result of war damage to the dikes.

The people dedicated themselves to rebuilding their country, and the government supported close international cooperation to achieve this goal. In 1945, The Netherlands became a charter member of the United Nations. In 1947, it joined the European nations working together for recovery under the Marshall Plan of the United States. The Netherlands received $1 billion in Marshall Plan aid. The Dutch also joined other programs to promote international unity, including Benelux, the Council of Europe, the European Coal and Steel Community, the European Common Market, and the North Atlantic Treaty Organization.

By 1955, Dutch industrial production had increased about 60 per cent over the pre-World War II level. Farm output was almost 20 per cent greater.

Political Changes. In 1948, the aging Wilhelmina gave up the throne to her daughter, Juliana. At that

Hit by German Bombers during World War II, the center of Rotterdam was destroyed. The city was rebuilt after the war.

Wide World

136

time, a revolt was underway in the Netherlands Indies. The fighting, which had started in 1945, continued until 1949, when The Netherlands recognized Indonesia's independence. See INDONESIA (History).

Surinam and the Netherlands Antilles were made self-governing and equal members of the Dutch kingdom in 1954. In 1962, the Dutch gave up Netherlands New Guinea (now Irian Jaya), their last colony, to United Nations control. Indonesia had claimed the region, and fighting had broken out earlier that year. The United Nations gave control of Irian Jaya to Indonesia in 1963.

The Netherlands Today has a high standard of living, largely because of its policy of economic cooperation. This cooperation has taken place not only with other countries, but also at home. After World War II, Dutch industry, labor unions, and the government worked together to keep wages and prices low. Their action encouraged the swift expansion of industries. The nation's political parties also cooperated to support the economic program. By the mid-1960's, Dutch prosperity had been re-established. Wage and price levels were then raised to those of other prosperous

European countries. During the 1970's, inflation became a serious problem in The Netherlands.

Thousands of people from the Netherlands Indies moved to The Netherlands after the Indies became independent under the name of Indonesia. Some of them, including people from the Molucca Islands, formed groups dedicated to freeing their homelands from Indonesian control. In the 1970's, Moluccans in The Netherlands began demanding that the Dutch government take steps to try to free their homeland. Some Moluccans staged terrorist acts to dramatize their demands. In 1975 and again in 1977, Moluccan terrorists seized a Dutch train and held passengers as hostages. Several people, including both passengers and terrorists, were killed during these incidents.

Surinam left the Dutch kingdom and became a fully independent nation in 1975. Many people from Surinam moved to The Netherlands shortly before independence.   ROBERT W. ADAMS,

LEWIS M. ALEXANDER, and HERBERT H. ROWEN

NETHERLANDS / Study Aids

Related Articles in WORLD BOOK include:

BIOGRAPHIES

Arminius, Jacobus	Mata Hari
Barents, Willem	Minuit, Peter
Bok, Edward W.	Mondrian, Piet
Bosch, Hieronymus	Rembrandt
De Hooch, Pieter	Ruisdael, Jacob van
DeJong, Meindert	Ruyter, Michel A. de
De Sitter, Willem	Spinoza, Baruch
De Vries, Hugo	Stuyvesant, Peter
Dubois, Eugene	Swammerdam, Jan
Einthoven, Willem	Tasman, Abel J.
Elzevir (Louis;	Thomas a Kempis
Bonaventure)	Tromp, Martin H.
Erasmus, Desiderius	Van der Waals,
Fokker, Anthony H. G.	Johannes D.
Frank, Anne	Van Gogh, Vincent
Goyen, Jan van	Van Leyden, Lucas
Grotius, Hugo	Van Rensselaer (Kiliaen)
Hals, Frans	Van't Hoff, Jacobus H.
Hobbema, Meindert	Vermeer, Jan
Huizinga, Johan	Wilhelmina
Huygens, Christian	William (III)
Juliana	William I
Lasso, Orlando di	William I, Prince
Leeuwenhoek, Anton van	of Orange
Lorentz, Hendrik A.	Zeeman, Pieter

CITIES

Amsterdam	Delft	Leiden
Arnhem	Haarlem	Rotterdam
Breda	Hague, The	Utrecht

HISTORY

Belgium (History)	New Guinea
Dutch East India Company	New Netherland
Dutch West India Company	United Nations
Indonesia (History)	(The Indonesian
Luxembourg (History)	Dispute)
Netherlands Indies	Vienna, Congress of

PHYSICAL FEATURES

Brabant	Meuse River	Rhine River
Frisian Islands	North Sea	Schelde River
Low Countries		

TREATIES AND AGREEMENTS

Benelux	North Atlantic Treaty
Europe, Council of	Organization
European Community	Ryswick, Treaty of
European Monetary	Western European Union
Agreement	

OTHER RELATED ARTICLES

Christmas (color picture)	Netherlands Antilles
Easter (In The	Nicholas, Saint
Netherlands)	Rubber (graph)
Europe (pictures)	Surinam
Gas (fuel)	Tulip
Hyacinth	Windmill

Outline

I. **Government**
II. **People**
   A. Population
   B. Religion
   C. Holidays and Recreation
   D. Clothing
   E. Language
   F. Education
   G. Arts
III. **The Land**
   A. Land Regions
   B. Deltas
IV. **Climate**
V. **Economy**
   A. Natural Resources
   B. Manufacturing
   C. Agriculture
   D. Mining
   E. Fishing
   F. Transportation
   G. Communication
VI. **History**

Questions

How do the Netherlanders "make" land?
What is the largest seaport in the world?
What is the leading branch of Dutch agriculture?
What part of the Kingdom of The Netherlands is in the Western Hemisphere?
What are "ice vacations"?
How did the Dutch lose leadership of the seas to the English? When?
When was the Golden Age of the Netherlands?
What does the word *Netherlands* mean?
How did the Dutch come under Spanish control? When did they officially win independence?
What is *gezelligheid?*

NETHERLANDS ANTILLES, also called the DUTCH WEST INDIES, consists of two groups of islands in the Caribbean Sea. One group lies about 50 miles (80 kilometers) from Venezuela. The smaller group is about 500 miles (800 kilometers) northeast of the main islands and about 160 miles (257 kilometers) east of Puerto Rico.

The islands have a total area of 383 square miles (993 square kilometers) and a population of 256,000. The combined coastline measures 140 miles (225 kilometers). The southern group, made up of Aruba, Bonaire, and Curaçao, covers 357 square miles (925 square kilometers) and has over nine-tenths of the population. Curaçao, which covers 171 square miles (443 square kilometers), is the largest island in either group. Willemstad, capital of the Netherlands Antilles, is on Curaçao. The northern group includes Saba and St. Eustatius islands, and the southern part of St. Martin Island. These islands cover only 26 square miles (67 square kilometers). See ARUBA; WILLEMSTAD.

Oil refining and tourism are the major industries in the Netherlands Antilles. Crude oil is shipped to refineries on Aruba and Curaçao from Venezuela. The other islands are of little economic importance. The land on Aruba and Curaçao is so rocky that little farming is possible. Most of the food must be imported. The people on Aruba and Curaçao speak Dutch, English, Spanish, and a mixture of the three called *Papiamento*.

The Spanish first occupied Curaçao in 1527. The Dutch captured the Antilles area in 1634, and soon settled on the other islands.

The Netherlands Antilles is an equal partner with The Netherlands in the Kingdom of The Netherlands. The islands are self-governing and have a governor who is appointed by the Dutch monarch. ISIDORE BLOCH

NETHERLANDS INDIES is the historic name for a group of volcanic islands in the Malay Archipelago, located between Asia and Australia. They were once known as the Dutch East Indies. In 1949, these islands were made into a federation of 16 states called the United States of Indonesia. In August 1950, these states became the Republic of Indonesia. Its capital is Jakarta. See also INDONESIA. JUSTUS M. VAN DER KROEF

NETHERLANDS NEW GUINEA. See NEW GUINEA.

NETHERLANDS WEST INDIES. See NETHERLANDS ANTILLES.

NETTLE, *NET'l*, is the common name of a group of plants with stinging bristles. They are coarse herbs, found in the north temperate regions. Nettles grow up to 4 feet (120 centimeters) tall. They have toothed leaves that grow in pairs opposite each other. The small, greenish flowers form in branching clusters.

The bristles of the nettle contain a watery juice that produces an intense itch when it enters a person's skin. This itch does not last long. In places where the skin is very thick, nettle bristles usually have no effect.

Young shoots of nettles can be cooked and eaten. The *great nettle* of Europe, now also found in the United States, has sometimes been cultivated for its fiber, from which a strong, coarse cloth can be made.

Scientific Classification. Nettles belong to the nettle family, *Urticaceae*. The great nettle is genus *Urtica*, species *U. dioica*. ARTHUR CRONQUIST

See also BOEHMERIA; RAMIE.

NETTLE TREE. See HACKBERRY.

NETWORK. See AMERICAN BROADCASTING COMPANIES, INC.; CBS INC.; MUTUAL BROADCASTING SYSTEM; NATIONAL BROADCASTING COMPANY.

NEUILLY, TREATY OF, ended hostilities between Bulgaria and the Allies after World War I. It was signed on Nov. 27, 1919, at Neuilly-sur-Seine, near Paris. The treaty forced Bulgaria to pay the Allies $450 million in reparations, to limit its army to 20,000 troops, and to give up territory to Greece, Romania, and Yugoslavia.

NEUMANN, SAINT JOHN NEPOMUCENE (1811-1860), was the first male United States citizen to be recognized as a saint by the Roman Catholic Church. He was *canonized* (declared a saint) in 1977.

Neumann was the bishop of Philadelphia from 1852 until his death. As bishop, he increased the number of Catholic elementary schools in the city from two to almost 100. He helped bring several sisterhoods from Europe to run the schools. He also founded a Philadelphia branch of the Sisters of St. Francis.

Neumann was born in Prachatitz, Bohemia. He came to the United States in 1836 and was ordained later that same year. In 1840, he joined the Redemptorist Fathers, a society of missionary priests. He traveled and preached among the German-speaking people of Pennsylvania and nearby states. Neumann became a U.S. citizen in 1848. FRANCIS L. FILAS

NEURALGIA, *nyoo RAL jah*, is a severe pain that occurs along a nerve. Its cause is not known. The pain may be limited to one part of the nerve, or it may extend along the nerve's branches. It may occur as repeated stabs of pain in the teeth, sinuses, eyes, face, tongue, or throat.

Neuralgia occurs in only two nerves. One nerve, the *trigeminal*, has three branches that enter the eyes, face, sinuses, and teeth. The other, the *glossopharyngeal*, leads to the back of the tongue and throat.

Neuralgia is sometimes confused with other conditions called *neuritis* and *radiculopathy*. But these occur in many different parts of the body. True neuritis is an inflammation that can permanently damage a nerve. Neuralgia does not harm the nerve.

Tic douloureux is a type of neuralgia that is common among older people. The name is French for *painful*

John H. Gerard

Wood Nettle Leaves are covered with fine, needle-shaped hairs that produce a stinging irritation on human skin.

twitching. Tic douloureux affects the trigeminal nerve and causes facial pain. The face muscles may contract each time a stab of pain occurs. The pain occurs very suddenly and then shoots along one side of the face. It usually begins at a specific part of the nerve called the *trigger zone.* It may then spread along various branches of the nerve, but it never involves other nerves. The pain may last only a few hours, or it may last several weeks. It may then disappear for a few months or years, but it usually returns.

Glossopharyngeal neuralgia is a very rare condition. It affects the throat and the back of the tongue.

Temporary relief for both types of neuralgia may be obtained by using drugs, or by numbing the nerve with an injection of alcohol. If the pain does not disappear, the only cure is a surgical operation to remove part of the nerve.   BENJAMIN BOSHES

See also NEURITIS.

NEURASTHENIA, *NYOO rus THEE nih uh,* is a term once used by doctors to describe a chronic mental and physical fatigue and lack of ambition. Such symptoms rarely occur without other physical or mental disturbances. In the past, neurasthenia was used to designate *anxiety reaction,* a form of neurosis (see NEUROSIS). In addition to fatigue and weakness, neurasthenia is characterized by dizziness, chest pain, heart palpitation, trembling, insomnia, and anxiety.   GEORGE A. ULETT

See also MENTAL HEALTH; NERVOUS BREAKDOWN.

NEURITIS, *nyoo RYE tis,* is an inflammation of a nerve caused by disease or injury. It is a painful condition that may affect one or many nerves. Neuritis is sometimes confused with a different disorder called neuralgia (see NEURALGIA).

Bacteria, viruses, and diet and vitamin deficiencies can cause neuritis. Infections such as tuberculosis, syphilis, and *herpes zoster* (shingles) can invade a nerve, resulting in neuritis. Neuritis can also develop when a disease, such as diabetes, changes the activities of the body's cells. Neuritis caused by physical injury to a nerve involves only the injured nerve.

If neuritis continues for a long period of time, a nerve may become so badly damaged that it can no longer function properly. As a result, a person may lose the ability to sense heat, pressure, and touch. The body also may lose control over such automatic activities as sweating. If a nerve no longer can stimulate a muscle, the muscle wastes away and eventually becomes paralyzed. Neuritis is a serious disorder that requires a doctor's care.   BENJAMIN BOSHES

NEUROLOGICAL SURGERY. See MEDICINE (table: Kinds of Medical Specialty Fields).

NEUROLOGY. See MEDICINE (table: Kinds of Medical Specialty Fields [Psychiatry and Neurology]).

NEURON. See NERVOUS SYSTEM.

NEUROPATHOLOGY, *NYOO roh puh THAL oh jih,* is the science that studies alterations in the tissues in diseases of the nervous system. It is concerned with the changes produced in the nerves, brain, and spinal cord. These may be changes in appearance studied with the unaided eye or with the microscope, or they may be changes that occur as a result of the normal chemical reactions of nerve cells.   BENJAMIN BOSHES

See also NERVOUS SYSTEM; PATHOLOGY.

NEUROPTERA, *nyoo RAHP ter uh,* is an order of insects that have thin, transparent wings netted with veins. The name *Neuroptera* means *nerve-winged.* Most members of this order are helpful because they feed on many destructive insects. The adults are delicate and fragile. Most of these insects are poor fliers, although their wings are well developed. See also ANT LION; LACEWING; INSECT (table).

NEUROSIS, *nu ROH sihs,* or PSYCHONEUROSIS, is a type of mild mental illness characterized by anxiety, unreasonable fears, insecurity, and depression. Most people have these feelings occasionally. But a *neurotic* person has them for a long time. Such feelings interfere with his life and relations with others, and he may seem hostile, selfish, or shy.

Neuroses rarely disable a person, and psychiatrists consider them mild mental disorders. Severe, disabling disorders are called *psychoses* (see PSYCHOSIS). Psychiatrists use *psychotherapy* to treat most neuroses. Through discussion, the physician and the patient work to overcome the patient's problems. See PSYCHOTHERAPY.

How Neuroses Develop. Psychiatrists believe that most neuroses begin in childhood, though symptoms may not appear until adulthood. A child's personality might be severely scarred by such conditions as parental conflict or divorce. A youngster could also be harmed by rejection, overprotection, or excessive strictness by his parents. Prolonged illness has helped bring about neurosis in many children. The emotional growth of a neurotic child may slow down, though his physical and intellectual growth continue normally.

An emotionally troubled child experiences guilt about his feelings, and so he pushes them into his unconscious mind. His mind forms barriers, called *defense mechanisms,* to keep the unwanted feelings from re-entering his awareness. One mechanism, known as *repression,* enables him to have no recollection of such feelings. Another defense mechanism, *reaction formation,* builds conscious attitudes opposite to the child's real feelings. Still another mechanism, *projection,* involves transferring unwanted feelings to someone else. A child might insist that a friend, not he, is angry.

As the disturbed child grows and his responsibilities increase, neurotic symptoms appear. His mind substitutes anxiety for his unwanted feelings. If he represses feelings of anger, for example, his mind will produce anxiety in situations in which anger would be normal.

Types of Neuroses. Psychiatrists classify neuroses by their major symptoms. One common classification includes (1) *anxiety neuroses,* (2) *conversion neuroses,* (3) *obsessive compulsive neuroses,* (4) *depressive neuroses,* (5) *phobic neuroses,* and (6) *traumatic neuroses.* Each group includes a variety of symptoms.

Anxiety Neuroses involve intense, baseless worry. Some neurotics worry about their health or job. Others feel constantly threatened by some undefined evil.

Conversion Neuroses cause a neurotic conflict to be expressed as a physical symptom. For example, a person may become temporarily blind to escape a desire to look at forbidden things.

Obsessive Compulsive Neuroses cause people to think about certain subjects or to feel forced to repeat certain acts. Some neurotics believe that repeating certain sayings in a special order keeps danger away.

Depressive Neuroses may result when a person overreacts to an unhappy event. Life seems to lose meaning, and he may blame himself for the event.

Phobic Neuroses involve one or more exaggerated, unrealistic fears called *phobias*. The patient may fear some animal, or he might panic in enclosed areas.

Traumatic Neuroses result from an overwhelming emotional experience. A soldier, for example, may collapse emotionally after repeatedly enduring the danger and fear of battle. STUART M. FINCH

See also ANXIETY; HYSTERIA; PHOBIA; MENTAL ILLNESS; PSYCHOANALYSIS.

NEUROSURGERY. See MEDICINE (table: Kinds of Medical Specialty Fields).

NEUTER GENDER. See GENDER.

NEUTRA, *NOY trah,* **RICHARD JOSEPH** (1892-1970), was an Austrian-born architect who worked in California. His best designs show his goal of creating buildings that meet man's biological and psychological needs, as well as artistic and technical considerations. In his book *Survival Through Design* (1954), he stated that man can survive only by controlling his environment through design, architecture, and city planning.

Neutra was born in Vienna. He moved to the United States in 1923 and settled in Los Angeles in 1925. His most famous work is the Lovell "Health" House (1929) in Los Angeles, one of the earliest examples of modern European architecture in the United States. This house is built of concrete and glass on a steel frame. Many of Neutra's later buildings, including the Tremaine House

Neutra's Lovell House in Los Angeles was one of the first homes in America to be constructed of concrete panels and glass.
Julius Shulman

(1948) in Santa Barbara, Calif., suggest a continuous flow of space by the use of vast sheets of glass and thin supports. STANFORD ANDERSON

NEUTRALITY is the official status of a government that does not take part in a war. The nations that do not take part, either directly or indirectly, are called *neutrals*. The warring countries are called *belligerents* (engaged in fighting). Belligerents want to defeat their enemies and prevent neutrals from trading with them.

Neutrals want to stay out of the war, and expect the belligerents to respect neutral territory, freedom of the seas, and the right to trade. *Neutralization* describes the position of a government that has been recognized as permanently neutral, such as Switzerland.

Since the late 1700's, the rights and duties of neutrals and belligerents have become part of international law. But warring nations have frequently ignored these rights and duties, and in most cases it has been difficult or impossible to enforce them. The rules of neutrality have been developed through both custom and treaty. In 1907, a group of nations at the second Hague Peace Conference set down in two treaties the traditional rules of neutrality on land and sea. These rules were an attempt to balance the differing, and often conflicting, interests of neutrals and belligerents. Individual governments also pass their own laws on neutrality.

Rights and Duties. Traditionally, a neutral must not help either of the belligerents. In return, belligerents must respect the rights of neutrals. They must not fight on neutral territory, or move troops across neutral countries. If belligerent troops enter neutral territory, the neutral has the right to disarm them and *intern* (hold) them until the war is over.

A neutral must not build or arm warships for a belligerent. During the U.S. Civil War, Great Britain failed to prevent the building and departure of the *Alabama* and other British warships for the Confederacy. These ships sank many Union ships. After the war, an international court ruled that Britain had violated its neutrality. Britain had to pay the United States $15½ million in damages (see ALABAMA [ship]).

Belligerent warships may enter a neutral port in an emergency. But if they stay more than 24 hours, they can be interned. Belligerents may not use neutral ports for naval operations.

Neutrals have the right to trade with other neutrals. But belligerents may search neutral ships. If these ships are carrying war materials to the enemy, the belligerent has the right to seize the goods. Belligerents often decide for themselves what to consider as war materials. They may blockade enemy ports and seize neutral vessels that try to *run* (slip through) the blockade.

World War I. In 1914, Germany violated the rules of neutrality by invading Belgium, whose permanent neutrality had been guaranteed by treaty in 1831.

The United States remained neutral in World War I from 1914 to 1917. During this time, the U.S. tried to defend its neutral rights at sea against violation by Great Britain, France, and Germany. Great Britain and France seized cargoes bound for neutral countries such as Denmark and Norway. They argued that such cargoes might eventually reach Germany. The United States insisted that Britain and France could not interfere with neutral rights or blockade neutral ports.

In 1917, the United States declared war against Germany, partly because Germany had violated U.S. neutrality. German submarines had sunk U.S. ships without warning. Under international law, Germany could capture ships carrying war materials to the enemy. But German submarines were unable to take captured ships into port, so they sank them. The loss of lives and property helped turn U.S. public opinion against Germany.

Between Wars. Conflicts over neutral rights had twice been major causes for the United States to go to war, once in 1917 and previously in 1812 (see WAR OF 1812 [Causes of the War]). In the 1930's Congress passed several neutrality acts hoping to keep the U.S. out of another war. These acts placed limits on U.S. neutral rights beyond those required by international law. They forbade the export of war materials and the extension of loans or credits to all belligerent nations. They also provided that other goods could be exported only on a *cash-and-carry* basis. This meant that the belligerent had to pay cash and use its own ships to carry the goods. If the ships were sunk, the United States would not suffer any losses.

World War II. Early in World War II, Germany violated the neutrality of Belgium, Denmark, The Netherlands, Norway, and Yugoslavia. The United States soon shifted from a policy of impartial neutrality to one of preparedness and aid to the Western allies. The laws of the mid-1930's were modified in November, 1939, to permit the export of all materials to belligerents on a cash-and-carry basis.

When German victories threatened Great Britain, the United States violated its neutral obligations by sending 50 destroyers and other war materials to the British. In March, 1941, Congress passed the Lend-Lease Act to aid countries fighting Nazi Germany. After Japan attacked Pearl Harbor in December, 1941, the United States declared war on both Germany and Japan.

Neutrality Today. Total warfare and the growth of world and regional organizations like the United Nations have changed the meaning of neutrality. Total warfare has erased most distinctions between civilian and military activities and materials. This destroys many of the arguments neutrals previously used to support their rights of neutral trade. Also, during a large-scale war, nations find it difficult to remain completely neutral. Most countries now belong to the United Nations. Collective action, such as use of the UN police force against an aggressor, is in many ways in disagreement with earlier practices of impartial neutrality.

Many countries, especially in Asia and Africa, have refused to support either the Communist or non-Communist blocs in the Cold War (see COLD WAR). These countries have sought security through policies of nonalignment and noninvolvement. They are called *neutralist*, *nonaligned*, or *uncommitted* nations. This group now has so many votes in the UN that neither Communist nor non-Communist powers can get resolutions adopted without support from at least some of the neutralist members. ELTON ATWATER

See also HIGH SEAS; INTERNATIONAL LAW.

NEUTRALIZATION, *NOO trull ih ZAY shun*, is a chemical reaction in which an acid and a base form a salt and water. If the reaction is complete, the final salt solution is usually *neutral* (neither acidic nor basic). Neutralization is one of the most important reactions in chemical analysis, and in many branches of industry. Important processes that go on in the human body include neutralization.

Acids and bases in water solution *ionize* (break down) into positive and negative ions as shown below for hydrochloric acid (HCl) and sodium hydroxide (NaOH).

$$HCl \rightarrow H^+ + Cl^- \quad \text{and} \quad NaOH \rightarrow Na^+ + {}^-OH$$

When the acid and base react together, the hydroxyl

($^-$OH) ion from the base combines with the hydrogen (H^+) ion from the acid to form water (H_2O).

$$H^+ + Cl^- + Na^+ + {}^-OH \rightarrow Na^+ + Cl^- + H_2O$$

The two remaining ions form a salt that usually stays in solution as ions. If the water is evaporated, the salt can be recovered in crystal form. Neutralization is more specifically defined as the reaction between hydroxyl and hydrogen ions to form water. Chemists can tell when a neutralization reaction is complete by using indicators, such as litmus. ESMARCH S. GILREATH

Related Articles in WORLD BOOK include:

Acid	Ion and	Litmus	Phenolphthalein
Base	Ionization	pH	Salt, Chemical
Hydrolysis			

NEUTRINO. See ATOM (Neutrinos); PAULI, WOLFGANG.

NEUTRON is one of the basic parts of all matter. It is a subatomic particle with a radius of about $\frac{1}{30,000,000,000,000}$ inch (0.000000000008 millimeter). Neutrons combine with protons to form the nucleus of an atom. Together, they make up 99.9 per cent of the atom's mass. A large cloud of electrons accounts for the rest of the mass. In the nucleus, neutrons and protons are held together by an extremely great force of attraction.

The nucleus of a stable atom contains as many neutrons as protons, or more. A *stable* atom is one that is not naturally radioactive. The number of neutrons in an atom of any element equals the difference between the element's mass number and atomic number. Neutrons have a mass slightly greater than that of protons.

Scientists use neutrons to make ordinary elements radioactive. They bombard such elements as iodine and cobalt with neutrons in a nuclear reactor. The nuclei of atoms become radioactive when they absorb neutrons. That is, they decay by giving off some kind of radiation. When the uranium isotope U^{235} absorbs a neutron, it splits into two large parts and several smaller parts. This process, called *fission*, releases a huge amount of energy. It also produces additional neutrons that cause more U^{235} atoms to split in a chain reaction. In this way, neutrons are responsible for nuclear energy and the atomic bomb.

The neutron was discovered in 1932 by Sir James Chadwick, an English physicist. But scientists are just beginning to understand its internal structure. It probably consists of at least two clouds of heavy mesons whose charges cancel each other. As a result, the neutron appears to have no electrical charge. The neutron spins and behaves in some ways like a bar magnet in a magnetic field. When a neutron is removed from a nucleus, it decays quickly into a proton, an electron, and a neutrino. The half-life of such a neutron is about 12.8 minutes. ROBERT HOFSTADTER

See also ATOM; NUCLEAR ENERGY; CHADWICK, SIR JAMES; RADIOACTIVITY; BARYON.

NEVA RIVER, *NE vuh.* This short stream, only 45 miles (72 kilometers) long, is an important link in three waterway systems in Russia. It rises at the southern end of Lake Ladoga and flows west into the Gulf of Finland at Leningrad. The Neva is part of the Ladoga-Volga system that connects the Baltic and Caspian seas. It is also a link in the canal system that connects the Baltic and White seas. THEODORE SHABAD

NEVADA

THE SILVER STATE

NEVADA, *nuh VAD uh,* or *nuh VAHD uh,* has one of the smallest populations of all the states. But every year Nevada has enough visitors to outnumber the population of most states. Nevada is the only state whose laws allow most kinds of gambling. Large, luxurious gambling casinos attract visitors from all parts of the world to Lake Tahoe, Las Vegas, and Reno. Las Vegas is Nevada's largest city and the chief tourist attraction.

Nevada is a land of rugged snow-capped mountains, grassy valleys, and sandy deserts. Pine forests cover many mountain slopes, and crystal-clear streams flow through steep, rocky canyons. Giant trout swim in sparkling valley lakes. In many places, geysers erupt and hot springs gush amid the rocks. In the south, big-horn sheep graze on jagged plateaus that glow red in the brilliant sunshine. Glistening white patches called alkali flats stretch across the deserts. The flowers of cactus, yucca, and sagebrush plants add splashes of color. The gray-green sagebrush gave Nevada one of its nicknames, the SAGEBRUSH STATE. The United States government maintains a testing center for nuclear weapons in the Nevada desert.

The state's most common nickname, the SILVER STATE, comes from the vast amounts of silver once taken from its many mines. Colorful ghost towns and historic mining towns, such as Virginia City, now attract thousands of tourists every year. But mining is still one of Nevada's chief industries. The most important minerals include barite, copper, diatomite, gold, gypsum, sand and gravel, silver, and stone. These resources support the state's growing manufacturing and processing industry.

Less rain falls in Nevada than in any other state. As a result, farming depends on irrigation. The Newlands Irrigation Project, near Reno, was the first system of its kind built by the federal government. Hoover Dam, on the Colorado River, created Lake Mead, one of the world's largest artificially created lakes. The dam supplies electricity for Arizona, California, and Nevada.

Nevada's main crops are alfalfa seed, hay, potatoes, and wheat. Cattle and sheep graze on vast ranches in the central and eastern areas of Nevada. Ranchers also feed their herds on public lands owned by the United States government. Public lands make up more than 85 per cent of the state.

Nevada lies mainly on a broad, rugged highland between the Rocky Mountains and the Sierra Nevada mountain range. In the 1820's and 1830's, the trappers Peter S. Ogden, Jedediah S. Smith, and Joseph Walker explored parts of the region in search of new fur sources. John C. Frémont began the first thorough exploration in 1843. By the 1860's, discoveries of gold and silver had brought thousands of miners to the area.

The name *Nevada* comes from a Spanish word meaning *snow-clad.* Miners and other settlers chose the name Nevada when the region became a territory in 1861. Nevada became a state in 1864 during the Civil War and was nicknamed the BATTLE BORN STATE.

For the relationship of Nevada to the other states in its region, see ROCKY MOUNTAIN STATES.

Desert Land near Las Vegas

Nevada (blue) ranks seventh in size among all the states, and second in size among the Rocky Mountain States (gray).

Downtown Las Vegas at Night

The contributors of this article are James W. Hulse, Professor of History at the University of Nevada; E. R. Larson, Professor of Geology at the University of Nevada; and Donald W. Reynolds, Publisher of the Nevada Appeal.

———————— FACTS IN BRIEF ————————

Capital: Carson City.

Government: Congress—U.S. senators, 2; U.S. representatives, 1. *Electoral Votes*—3. *State Legislature*—senators, 20; assemblymen, 40. *Counties*—16.

Area: 110,540 sq. mi. (286,297 km²), including 651 sq. mi. (1,686 km²) of inland water; 7th in size among the states. *Greatest Distances*—north-south, 483 mi. (777 km); east-west, 320 mi. (515 km).

Elevation: *Highest*—Boundary Peak, in Esmeralda County, 13,143 ft. (4,006 m) above sea level. *Lowest*—470 ft. (143 m) above sea level along the Colorado River in Clarke County.

Population: *Estimated 1975 Population*—592,000. *1970 Census*—488,738; 47th among the states; distribution, 81 per cent urban, 19 per cent rural; density, 4 persons per sq. mi. (2 persons per km²).

Chief Products: *Agriculture*—alfalfa seed, beef cattle, dairy products, hay, hogs, sheep, wheat, wool. *Manufacturing*—chemicals; electrical equipment; food products; metal products; printing and publishing; stone, clay, and glass products. *Mining*—barite, copper, diatomite, gold, gypsum, sand and gravel, silver, stone.

Statehood: Oct. 31, 1864, the 36th state.

State Motto: *All for Our Country.*

State Song: "Home Means Nevada." Words and music by Bertha Raffetto.

143

Constitution of Nevada was adopted in 1864, when the state entered the Union. Nevada's constitution may be *amended* (changed) only by a majority of the voters. An amendment proposed by the legislature must be approved by a majority of both houses in two successive regular sessions. Then the voters must approve it in the next general election. The people may amend the constitution directly by using the *initiative*. In this procedure, voters who support the amendment first sign a petition. The number of signatures must equal at least 10 per cent of the voters in the last general election in each of three-fourths of the counties, and at least 10 per cent of all the voters in the last general election. The petition states the proposed amendment and calls for a general election to vote on it. If the amendment is approved by a majority of the voters, it becomes part of the constitution.

The Nevada constitution may also be revised by a constitutional convention. To call such a convention, two-thirds of each legislative house must vote for it. Then a majority of voters must approve the convention in the next election.

Executive. The governor of Nevada is elected to a four-year term. He can serve no more than two terms. The governor receives a yearly salary of $40,000. For a list of all the governors of Nevada, see the *History* section of this article.

Key state officials also are elected to four-year terms. Elected officials include the lieutenant governor, secretary of state, treasurer, controller, and attorney general. The governor appoints the members of more than 150 bureaus, commissions, and administrative boards in the state.

Legislature consists of a 20-member senate and a 40-member assembly. Nevada has 10 senatorial districts and 40 assembly districts. Each senatorial district elects from one to seven senators, depending on population. Each assembly district elects one assemblyman. Senators serve four-year terms, and assemblymen serve two-year terms.

In 1965, a federal court ordered Nevada to redraw its legislative districts to provide equal representation. The legislature *reapportioned* (redivided) the legislative districts later that year, and the federal court approved the new districts in 1966. The legislature reapportioned the districts again in 1971.

The legislature meets on the third Monday of January in odd-numbered years. Legislators receive their salaries for 60 days, but legislative sessions have no time limit. Regular sessions last about 90 days. The governor can call special sessions.

Courts. The supreme court of Nevada has a chief justice and four associate justices, all elected to six-year terms. One or two justices are elected every two years. The justice who has served the longest acts as chief justice. Nevada has nine district courts, with 24 district judges who serve four-year terms. Court districts with large populations have divisions called departments. Each department is headed by a district judge. Municipal judges serve in city courts, and justices of the peace serve in townships.

Local Government. Three-man boards of county commissioners govern 14 of Nevada's 16 counties. Voters in Clark and Washoe counties elect five-man boards. A five-man board of supervisors governs the independent city of Carson City. County commissioners serve four-year terms. Other elected county officials include the assessor, auditor and recorder, clerk, district attorney, public administrator, and sheriff. Most cities have mayor-council governments.

Taxation provides about 50 per cent of Nevada's income. Almost all the rest comes from federal grants and other U.S. government programs. A 3 per cent sales tax supplies the chief state income, followed by taxes on gambling. Nevada allows many forms of gambling that are not legal in other states. However, Nevada collects less income from gambling taxes than some states that allow fewer kinds of gambling.

Other important sources of state revenue include taxes on alcoholic beverages, motor fuel, and tobacco; and license fees for automobiles, fishing, hunting, and the transportation of passengers and freight. State and local governments share income from a property tax.

To attract industry, Nevada enacted a "free port" tax law in 1949. This law applies to goods being held in Nevada for shipment outside the state. It allows manufacturers to process and store such goods in Nevada without paying property taxes on the goods. In most

Nevada Dept. of Economic Development

The Governor's Mansion in Carson City is ½ mile (0.8 kilometer) from the state Capitol. Stately white columns give a touch of formality to the mansion, which was built in 1908.

The State Seal

Symbols of Nevada. On the seal, the plow and the sheaf of wheat represent Nevada's agricultural resources. The quartz mill, mine tunnel, and carload of ore symbolize the mineral wealth of the state. The 36 stars around the outside show that Nevada was the 36th state to enter the Union. The seal was adopted in 1866. On the flag, the words *Battle Born* recall that Nevada gained statehood during the Civil War. The flag was adopted in 1929.

Flag, bird, and flower illustrations, courtesy of Eli Lilly and Company

states, manufacturers must pay taxes on such property. The free port law was written into the Nevada constitution in 1960.

Politics. Nevada has about twice as many registered Democrats as Republicans. The Democratic Party's strength lies mainly in Clark County, where about half of the voters live. Nevadans usually have elected a Democratic majority to the state assembly. But Republicans from rural counties generally have won a majority of seats in the state senate.

In national politics, Nevada Democrats have won more often than Republicans in elections for the United States Senate and House of Representatives. Since 1912, Nevada has voted for the winner in every presidential election except the 1976 race. For Nevada's electoral votes and voting record in presidential elections, see ELECTORAL COLLEGE (table).

The State Capitol in Carson City was built of Nevada stone. Gigantic wooden beams support the roof. The building was first used in 1871. A library annex was built in 1906, and north and south wings were added in 1914. Carson City has been the capital since the Nevada Territory was created in 1861.

Fred Bond, Publix

The State Flag

The State Bird
Mountain Bluebird

The State Flower
Sagebrush

The State Tree
Single-Leaf Piñon

145

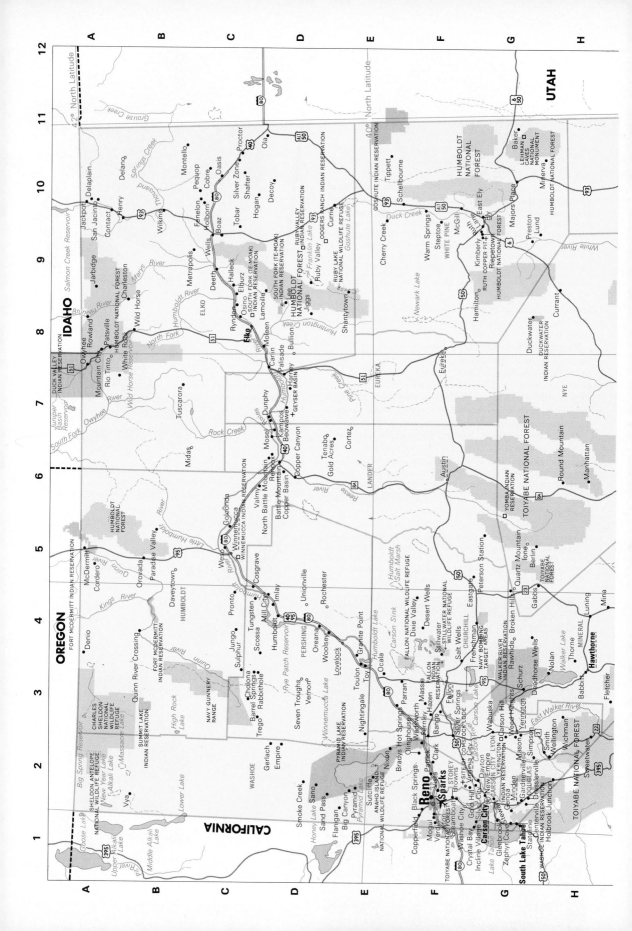

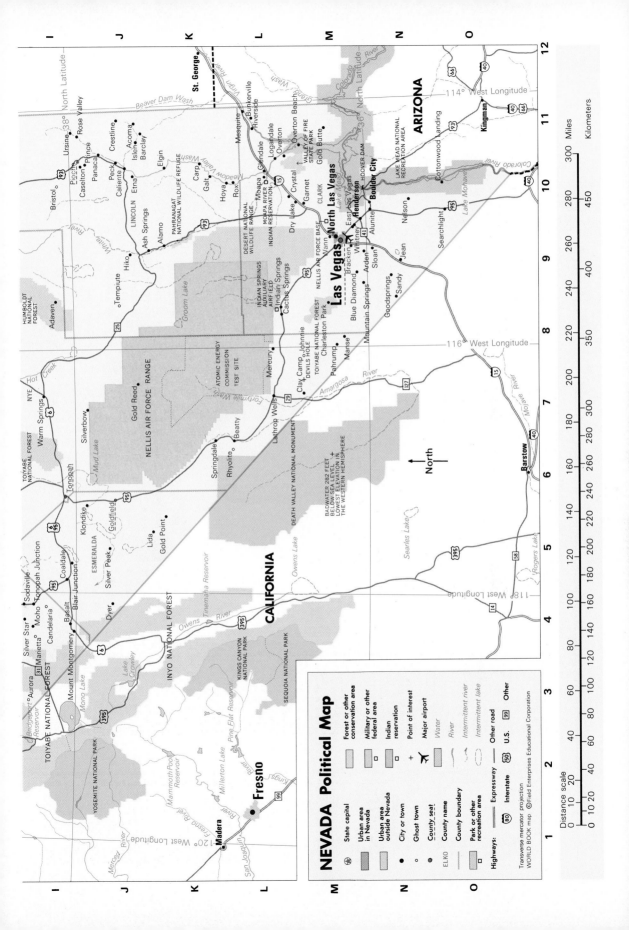

NEVADA Political Map

Highways:

Forest or other conservation area	
Military or other federal area	
Indian reservation	
+	Point of interest
✈	Major airport
	Water
	River
	Intermittent river
	Intermittent lake
Park or other recreation area	

⊛	State capital
	Urban area in Nevada
	Urban area outside Nevada
●	City or town
○	Ghost town
●	County seat
ELKO	County name
	County boundary

Highways: ══ Expressway · ══ Interstate · ⑤⑥ U.S. · ⑨⑨ Other

Transverse mercator projection
WORLD BOOK map ©Field Enterprises Educational Corporation

Distance scale

0 10 20 ... Miles
0 10 20 ... Kilometers

NEVADA MAP INDEX

Population

592,000 ..Estimate..1975
488,738 ...Census...1970
285,278 ......"......1960
160,083 ......"......1950
110,247 ......"......1940
91,058 ......"......1930
77,407 ......"......1920
81,875 ......"......1910
42,335 ......"......1900
47,355 ......"......1890
62,266 ......"......1880
42,491 ......"......1870
6,857 ......"......1860

Metropolitan Areas

Las Vegas 273,288
Reno 121,068

Counties

Churchill ...10,513..F 4
Clark .....273,288..M 10
Douglas .....6,882..G 2
Elko ....13,958..C 8
Esmeralda .....629..J 5
Eureka ....948..E 7
Humboldt ....6,375..B 4
Lander ......2,666..E 6
Lincoln .....2,557..J 10
Lyon ....8,221..G 2
Mineral .....7,051..H 4
Nye ....5,599..I 7
Pershing ....2,670..D 4
Storey ....695..F 2
Washoe ...121,068..C 2
White Pine .10,150..F 9

Cities and Towns

Acoma ....J 11
Adaven ....I 8
Alamo ....K 9
Alunite ....N 10
Arden ....N 9
Ash Springs ....J 9
Austin ....°F 6
Babbitt .....1,579..H 3
Baker ....G 11
Bango ....F 3
Barclay ....J 11
Barrel Springs .....C 3
Basalt ....I 4
Battle Mountain .1,856..D 6
Beatty ....L 7
Beowawe ....D 7
Berlin ....G 5
Big Canyon ....E 2
Black Springs ......F 2
Blair Junction .....I 5
Blue Diamond ......M 9
Boaz ....C 9
Boulder City 5,223..N 10
Bracken ....M 9
Bradys Hot Springs F 3
Broken Hills ....G 5
Browns ....F 2
Bunkerville ....L 11
Cactus Springs ......L 8
Caliente ......916..J 10
Carlin ....1,313..D 8
Carp ....K 10
Carson City 15,468†°G 2
Gold Acres ....E 7
Gold Butte ....M 11
Gold Hill ....G 2
Gold Point ....K 6
Gold Reed ....J 7
Goldfield ....°J 6
Goodsprings ....N 9
Granite Point ....E 4
Halleck ....C 9
Harney ....D 7
Hawthorne ..3,539.°H 3
Hazen ....F 3
Henderson ..16,395..M 10
Henry ....A 10
Hiko ....J 9
Hogan ....C 10
Holborn ....C 10
Holbrook Junction ..H 2
Hoya ....L 10
Humboldt ....D 4
Imlay ....D 4
Incline Village ......G 1
Indian Springs ......L 8
Islen ....J 11
Jackpot ....A 10
Jarbridge ....A 9
Jean ....N 9
Jiggs ....D 8
Jungo ....C 4
Kampos ....D 7
Kimberly ....G 9
Klondike ....J 6
Lamoille ....D 9
Lane ....G 10
Las Vegas 125,787.°M 9
Lathrop Wells ....L 7
Lawton ....F 1
Lee ....D 9
Lida ....J 5
Logandale ....L 11
Lovelock ....1,571.°E 4
Lund ....G 10
Luning ....H 4
Manhattan ....H 6
Manse ....M 8
Mason ....G 3
Massie ....F 3
McDermitt ....A 5
McGill ......2,164..F 10
Mercury ....L 8
Mesquite ....L 11
Metropolis ....C 9
Mill City ....D 4
Mina ....H 4
Minden°, see Gardnerville [-Minden]
Minerva ....H 11
Moapa ....L 10
Mogul ....F 1
Moho ....I 4
Moleen ....D 8
Montello ....B 11
Mosel ....D 7
Mount Montgomery .I 4
Mountain City ....A 8
Mountain Springs ..N 9
Nellis* ......6,449..K 7
Nelson ....N 10
New Empire ....G 2
Nixon ....E 2
Nolan ....H 3
North Battle Mountain ....D 6
North Las Vegas ....36,216..M 9
Oasis ....C 10
Ocala ....E 3
Ola ....D 11
Steamboat ....F 2
Steptoe ....F 10
Stewart ....G 2
Stillwater ....F 4
Sulphur ....C 3
Sun Valley* 2,414..M 9
Sunrise Manor* ..10,886..M 9
Sutcliffe ....E 2
Sweetwater ....H 3
Thorne ....H 4
Tippett ....E 11
Tobar ....C 10
Tonopah ....1,716.°I 6
Tonopah Junction ..I 4
Toulon ....E 3
Toy ....E 3
Trego ....D 3
Tungsten ....C 4
Tuscarora ....B 7
Ursine ....I 11
Valmy ....C 6
Vegas Creek* 8,970..M 9
Verdi ....F 1
Virginia City .....°F 2
Vista ....F 2
Vya ....B 2
Wabuska ....G 3
Wadsworth ....F 2
Wann ....M 9
Warm Springs ....I 7
Warm Springs ....F 10
Weed Heights ....G 3
Wellington ....H 2
Wells ....1,081..C 9
Weso ....C 5
White Rock ....A 8
Whitney ....M 10
Wichman ....H 3
Wild Horse ....B 8
Wilkins ....B 10
Winchester* 13,981..M 9
Winnemucca 3,587.°C 5
Woolsey ....D 4
Yerington ...2,010.°G 3
Zephyr Cove ....G 1

POPULATION

This map shows the *population density* of Nevada, and how it varies in different parts of the state. Population density means the average number of persons who live in a given area.

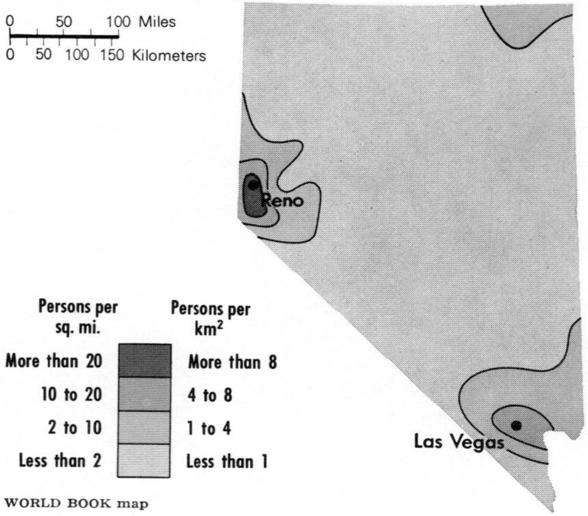

0 50 100 Miles
0 50 100 150 Kilometers
Reno
Las Vegas
Persons per sq. mi.
Persons per km²
More than 20
More than 8
10 to 20
4 to 8
2 to 10
1 to 4
Less than 2
Less than 1

WORLD BOOK map

NEVADA/*People*

The 1970 United States census reported that Nevada had 488,738 persons. The population had increased 71 per cent over the 1960 figure, 285,278. The U.S. Bureau of the Census estimated that by 1975 the state's population had reached about 592,000.

About 80 per cent of all Nevadans live in urban areas. But most of Nevada's cities and towns are small. Only 6 have populations greater than 10,000. More than half of the people live within 50 miles (80 kilometers) of Las Vegas, Nevada's largest city. About a fourth live within 30 miles (48 kilometers) of Reno, the second largest city. The only other cities with populations greater than 10,000 are North Las Vegas and Henderson, near Las Vegas; Sparks, near Reno; and Carson City, the state capital.

Las Vegas and Reno are population centers for Nevada's two Standard Metropolitan Statistical Areas (see METROPOLITAN AREA). The Las Vegas area includes all of Clark County, and the Reno area includes all of Washoe County.

People living in Las Vegas depend mainly on the tourist and gambling industries for their income. Las Vegas is famous for its gambling casinos and its night clubs. Reno, another tourist favorite, is the center of banking, commerce, and transportation in northern Nevada. See the separate articles on the cities of Nevada listed in the *Related Articles* at the end of this article.

About 96 per cent of the people of Nevada were born in the United States. More than a fifth of the people are Roman Catholics. Members of the Church of Jesus Christ of Latter-day Saints (Mormons) make up almost another fifth of the population. Eastern Nevada has several small Mormon communities. Other religious bodies include Baptists, Episcopalians, Jews, Lutherans, Methodists, and Presbyterians.

University of Nevada's Noble Getchell Library in Reno houses most of the school's library collections.

T. J. (Doc) Kaminski

Schools. Nevadans made plans for a tax-supported school system as early as 1861, when Nevada became a territory. In 1865, a year after statehood, the legislature established the first school districts.

Nevada had to overcome unusual problems in developing its public school system. Rural areas were thinly populated. In some places, taxpayers supported schools for as few as three or four school-age children living in a vast area. Some early schools were open only six months of the year because of a lack of funds. Until 1900, the state had only a few high schools. In some parts of Nevada, elementary school students still attend one-room schools.

In 1956, the state legislature made each county a school district. A nine-member board of education supervises Nevada's school system. The voters elect the board members to four-year terms. The board selects a superintendent of public instruction. Each school district also has its own elected board of education. Children must attend school between their 7th and 17th birthdays. For the number of students and teachers in Nevada, see EDUCATION (table).

The University of Nevada, with campuses in Reno and Las Vegas, is Nevada's only institution of higher learning accredited by the Northwest Association of Schools and Colleges (see NEVADA, UNIVERSITY OF). For the enrollment and further information, see UNIVERSITIES AND COLLEGES (table).

Libraries. The University of Nevada in Reno has the largest library in the state. The Nevada State Library in Carson City acts as the official library for the state government and as the reference and research center for other libraries throughout the state. Nevada has about 20 public libraries.

Museums. The museum of the Nevada Historical Society displays many items used by early Nevadans. Its collections include musical instruments, china, embroidery, and lace. The Nevada State Museum in Carson City displays examples of Nevada wildlife as well as historical relics. This museum also features life-sized mining exhibits built in tunnels beneath the build-

ing. The exhibits illustrate blasting, drilling, hoisting, and other mining operations. The Mackay School of Mines Museum in Reno specializes in displays on mining, metallurgy, and geology. The Lost City Museum in Overton has many items found at the Pueblo Grande de Nevada, an ancient Indian settlement. Lake Mead now covers part of the site of the ancient city. The Southern Nevada Museum in Henderson has exhibits that deal with the history of the southern part of the state.

Caselton	I 10	Olinghouse	F 2
Centerville	G 2	Oreana	D 4
Charleston Park	B 9	Orovada	B 5
Charleston Park	M 8	Osino	C 8
Cherry Creek	E 3	Owhon	L 11
Chiatana	F 2	Overton Beach	A 8
Clay Camp	M 7	Pahrump	M 8
Cobre	C 10	Palisade	D 8
Contact	A 10	Panaca	J 11
Copper Basin	D 6	Paradise* 24,477.	M 9
Copper Canyon	D 6	Paradise Valley	B 5
Copperfield	F 5	Parran	F 2
Cordero	A 5	Patrick	A 8
Cosgrave	C 5	Patsville	F 2
Cottonwood		Peck	C 10
Landing	O 10	Pequop Station	L 10
Crestline	L 11	Peterson Station	ol 10
Crystal	J 10	Pioche	G 10
Crystal Bay	H 9	Preston	F 9
Currant	E 10	Prince	J 10
Dayton	G 2	Proctor	C 11
Deadhorse Wells	D 10	Pronto	O E 2
Decoy	B 10	Pyramid	
Deeth	B 9	Quinn River	
Delaplain	A 6	Crossing	B 4
Denio	A 4	Rabbithole	D 3
Desert Wells	F 4	Rennox	D 8
Dixie Valley	F 4	Reno 72,863.	oF 9
Dresslerville	G 2	Riepetown	G 11
Dry Lake	M10	Riverside	D 1
Duckwater	G 7	Rixies Valley	D 7
Dunphy	D 8	Rose Valley	H 6
Dyer	J 4	Rowland Mountain	A 10
East Ely 1,992	G 10	Rox	L 10
East Las		Ruby Valley	D 9
Vegas 6,501	M10	Ruth	G 10
Eastgate	F 4	Ryndon	O C 8
Elburz	G 5	Salt Wells	F 4
Elgin	K 11	San Jacinto	A 10
Elko 7,621.	oC 8	Sand Pass	E 2
Ely 4,176.	oG 10	Sandy	N 9
Empire	D 2	Sano	F 10
Etna	J 10	Schellbourne	D 9
Eureka 2,959.	oF 8	Schurz	G 3
Fallon	F 3	Scossa	D 4
Fallon		Searchlight	O 10
Station* 1,045	F 3	Shafter	C 10
Fenelon	C 10	Shantytown	D 8
Fernley	F 3	Silver City	G 2
Franklin	I 6	Silver Peak	J 5
Fletcher	J 4	Silver Springs	F 3
Frenchman	G 4	Silver Star	I 6
Gabbs 874.	K 10	Silver Zone	C 10
Galt	G 5	Silverbow	H 7
Gardnerville		Simpson	G 3
[-Minden] 1,320.	G 2	Sloan	N 9
Garnet	M10	Smith	H 2
Genoa	G 2	Smoke Creek	D 2
Gerlach	D 2	Sodaville	J 4
Glenbrook	H 2	Sparks 24,187.	K 2
Glendale	G 2	Stateline	G 1
Goldonda	C 5	Stillsdale	C 10

*Does not appear on map; key shows general location.
†Independent city, not part of any county.
oCounty seat.
Source: Latest census figures (1970). Places without population figures are unincorporated areas and are not listed in census reports.

149

Ruth Copper Pit near Ely

NEVADA / A Visitor's Guide

Gambling and the colorful night life in Las Vegas and Reno draw millions of tourists every year. Virginia City and other towns remind travelers of the prospectors who came west seeking gold and silver. Sportsmen hunt mule deer and chukar partridge, and catch cutthroat, brown, and rainbow trout. Skiers race down the slopes of Mount Rose west of Reno, Mount Charleston near Las Vegas, and Ward Mountain near Ely. Vacationers also enjoy swimming and water skiing at Lake Mead, Lake Tahoe, and Pyramid Lake.

--------- PLACES TO VISIT ---------

Following are brief descriptions of some of Nevada's most interesting places to visit.

Atmospherium-Planetarium at the University of Nevada in Reno shows realistic motion pictures of hurricanes, tornadoes, and various weather conditions.

Bowers Mansion, a large Italian-style home near Carson City, was built by "Sandy" Bowers, a silver miner who made a fortune from the Comstock Lode.

Geyser Basin, near Beowawe, has active geysers, hot springs, and pools of bubbling mud. The geysers have created a terrace about $\frac{1}{2}$ mile (0.8 kilometer) long and 100 feet (30 meters) wide on the mountainside.

Hamilton, a ghost town between Eureka and Ely, once had nearly 15,000 people. It is now abandoned.

Hoover Dam, about 25 miles (40 kilometers) southeast of Las Vegas, is one of the world's largest dams. See HOOVER DAM.

Rhyolite, a ghost town near Beatty, has a museum of desert relics called the Bottle House. The house was built of bottles cemented with *adobe* (sun-dried brick).

Ruth Copper Pit, near Ely, is one of the largest open-pit copper mines in the world. It measures about 1 mile (1.6 kilometers) in diameter, and it is nearly 1,000 feet (300 meters) deep.

Lehman Caves National Monument near Baker

Bob and Ira Spring
Virginia City, a Famous Western Ghost Town

Fred Ragsdale, Shostal
Elephant Rock in Valley of Fire State Park

Art Marston, Shostal
Admission Day Parade in Carson City

National Forests and Monuments. Humboldt National Forest lies near Elko. Eldorado, Inyo, and Toiyabe national forests are partly in Nevada and partly in California. For the areas and chief features of these forests, see NATIONAL FOREST (table). In September, 1964, Congress set aside part of Nevada's national forests as a national wilderness. This area is to be preserved in its natural condition. Lehman Caves National Monument, near Baker, is on the eastern slope of Wheeler Peak. The northeast corner of Death Valley National Monument also is in Nevada. See LEHMAN CAVES NATIONAL MONUMENT; DEATH VALLEY NATIONAL MONUMENT. The National Park Service maintains Lake Mead as a national recreation area (see LAKE MEAD).

State Parks. Nevada has a total of 16 state parks, monuments, and recreational areas. The largest is the Valley of Fire, near Overton. The rocks in this park have been worn into odd shapes by the weather. For information on Nevada's state parks, write to Nevada State Parks Department, Nye Building, Carson City, Nev. 89701.

ANNUAL EVENTS

The Helldorado Rodeo in Las Vegas is one of Nevada's most exciting events. During this four-day celebration in May, men and women wear Old-West costumes for parades and street dances. Other annual events in Nevada include the following.

January-March: University of Nevada Winter Carnival at Mount Rose, near Lake Tahoe (February); Mint "400" Desert Rally in Las Vegas (March); Nevada Spring Square Dance Festival in Yerington (March).

April-June: Progress Days in North Las Vegas (mid-April); Spanish Fiesta in Overton (May); Carson Valley Days in Gardnerville (June); Reno Rodeo (June).

July-September: National Basque Festival in Elko (July); Jaycee State Fair in Las Vegas (August); Pony Express Days in Ely (August); National Air Races in Reno (September); National Camel Races in Virginia City (September); Wild Burro Races in Beatty (September).

October-December: Admission Day Celebration in Carson City (October); Colorado River Raft Race at Boulder City (October); Knights of Columbus Wine Tasting Festival in Winnemucca (December).

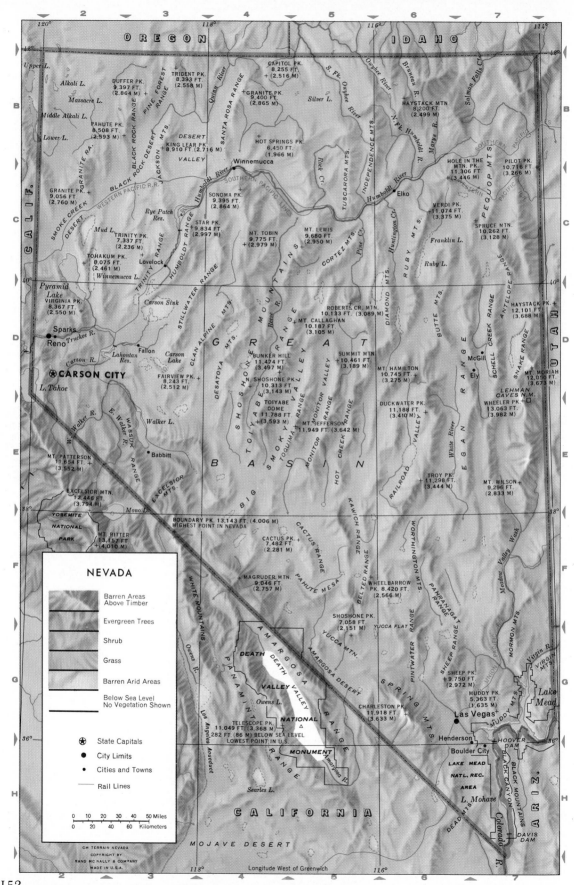

NEVADA

Barren Areas
Above Timber

Evergreen Trees

Shrub

Grass

Barren Arid Areas

Below Sea Level
No Vegetation Shown

⊛ State Capitals

● City Limits

• Cities and Towns

— Rail Lines

0 10 20 30 40 50 Miles

0 20 40 60 Kilometers

CM TERRAIN NEVADA
COPYRIGHT BY
RAND McNALLY & COMPANY
MADE IN U.S.A.

Specially created for **World Book Encyclopedia** by Rand McNally and World Book editors

OREGON   IDAHO

CALIF.

CARSON CITY

Reno
Sparks

Winnemucca

Elko

Las Vegas

Henderson
Boulder City

Lake
Mead

CALIFORNIA

ARIZ.

MOJAVE DESERT

Longitude West of Greenwich

Land Regions. Nevada lies almost entirely within the Great Basin, a huge desert area that extends into Oregon, Idaho, Wyoming, California, and Utah (see GREAT BASIN). The state has three main land regions: (1) the Columbia Plateau, (2) the Sierra Nevada, and (3) the Basin and Range Region.

The Columbia Plateau covers a small part of the northeastern corner of Nevada. Deep lava bedrock lies under the entire region. Streams and rivers have cut deep canyons, leaving steep ridges. The land flattens into open prairies near the Idaho border.

The Sierra Nevada, a rugged mountain range, cuts across a corner of the state west and south of Carson City. Lake Tahoe and other mountain lakes in this part of the state attract many vacationers. See SIERRA NEVADA.

The Basin and Range Region covers the remainder of the state. It consists mainly of an upland area broken by more than 30 north-south mountain ranges. The towering Sierra Nevada marks part of the western edge of the region. The Toiyabe and Toquima ranges rise in the center of the state. In the east are the Snake and Toana ranges. Between the mountains lie *buttes* (lone hills) and *mesas* (tablelike mountains), as well as flat valleys with lakes or alkali flats (see BUTTE; MESA).

The elevation of the Basin and Range Region varies from less than 500 feet (150 meters) above sea level near the Colorado River to more than 13,000 feet (3,960 meters) in the southwest. Boundary Peak, the highest point in Nevada, rises 13,143 feet (4,006 meters) in Esmeralda County near the California border. Hot springs and geysers in many places show that Nevada is an area of dying volcanoes.

The southeastern tip of the Basin and Range Region is not part of the Great Basin. But the land here closely resembles that of the Great Basin.

Map Index

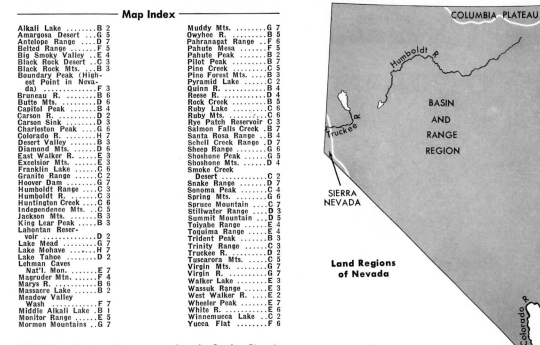

Land Regions of Nevada

COLUMBIA PLATEAU • Humboldt R • BASIN AND RANGE REGION • SIERRA NEVADA • Truckee R. • Colorado R.

Wild Horse Reservoir stores water from the Owyhee River, in the lava-covered Columbia Plateau region of northeast Nevada.

Nevada Highways & Parks Magazine

Mike Roberts Studios

Lake Tahoe, center of a famous resort area southwest of Carson City, lies in a valley in the Sierra Nevada Range. The lake is more than 6,000 feet (1,800 meters) above sea level.

Grazing Cattle, such as these on a range in the Ruby Mountains, are a common sight in the Basin and Range Region. This upland region covers most of Nevada.

Ray Atkeson

Rivers and Lakes. Most of Nevada's rivers are small and flow only during the wet season, from December to June. Only a few rivers have outlets to the sea. The Virgin and Muddy rivers join the Colorado in the southeastern tip of the state. The Owyhee (pronounced *oh WYE ee*), Bruneau, and Salmon flow northward across the Columbia Plateau to Idaho's Snake River.

All of Nevada's other rivers empty into the Great Basin. They flow into lakes without outlets or into wide, shallow *sinks* (low spots in the earth). In summer, the water evaporates from the sinks and leaves salty mud flats and dry lakes. The snow-fed Humboldt River is the longest river. It flows westward from the mountains of Elko County for about 300 miles (480 kilometers). Then it vanishes into the Humboldt Sink. The Carson River winds northeastward from California and empties into

Carson Sink. The Walker River also rises in California and empties into Walker Lake. The scenic Truckee River flows from Lake Tahoe into Pyramid Lake.

Lake Tahoe, on the Nevada-California border, is one of the nation's loveliest lakes. Lamoille, Liberty, and other beautiful lakes lie among the peaks of the Ruby Range in Elko County. Ruby and Franklin lakes are at the eastern foot of the Ruby Range. Pyramid Lake and Walker Lake are the remains of Lake Lahontan, an ancient lake that gradually dried up. Thousands of years ago, Lake Lahontan covered about a tenth of the present state of Nevada.

Lake Mead, a man-made lake, is the only Nevada lake with an outlet to the sea. Engineers formed this vast reservoir by building Hoover Dam across a canyon of the Colorado River.

154

NEVADA / Climate

Nevada has less rain than any other state. An average of only 7.4 inches (18.8 centimeters) of rain falls there annually. The driest regions include the state's southeastern tip and the land near Carson Sink. These areas have only about 4 inches (10 centimeters) of rain a year.

The rainiest parts of Nevada are in the Sierra Nevada and the eastern foothills of these mountains. As much as 25 inches (64 centimeters) of rain falls annually in the Lake Tahoe region of the Sierras. Most of the rain falls during winter. Clouds moving eastward from the Pacific Ocean bring the rain. But the clouds lose most of their moisture in California as they rise over the high Sierra Nevada. Snowfall varies from about 250 inches (635 centimeters) a year in the highest sections of the Sierras to about 1 inch (2.5 centimeters) in the southeast.

Nevada has a wide range of temperatures. The north and the mountains in all sections have cold, long winters and short, hot summers. The west has short, hot summers, but winters there are only mildly cold. In the south, summers are long and hot, and winters are mild.

July temperatures average about 70° F. (21° C) in the north and in the mountains, and 86° F. (30° C) in the extreme south. January temperatures average 24° F. (−4° C) in the north and 43° F. (6° C) in the south. The temperature often changes greatly during the day. In Reno, the temperature may change more than 45 degrees Fahrenheit (25 degrees Celsius) on a summer day. The highest temperature recorded in Nevada was 122° F. (50° C) at Leeland on August 12 and 18, 1914, and at Overton on June 23, 1954. The temperature reached a record low of −50° F. (−46° C) at San Jacinto on January 8, 1937.

SEASONAL TEMPERATURES

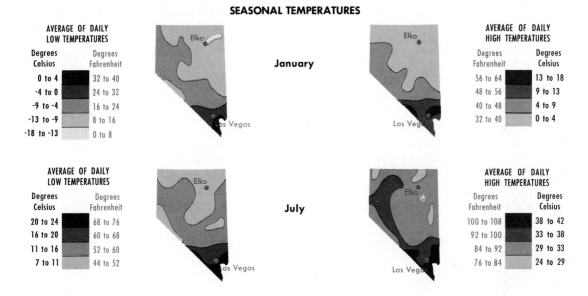

AVERAGE OF DAILY LOW TEMPERATURES — January

Degrees Celsius	Degrees Fahrenheit
0 to 4	32 to 40
-4 to 0	24 to 32
-9 to -4	16 to 24
-13 to -9	8 to 16
-18 to -13	0 to 8

AVERAGE OF DAILY HIGH TEMPERATURES — January

Degrees Fahrenheit	Degrees Celsius
56 to 64	13 to 18
48 to 56	9 to 13
40 to 48	4 to 9
32 to 40	0 to 4

AVERAGE OF DAILY LOW TEMPERATURES — July

Degrees Celsius	Degrees Fahrenheit
20 to 24	68 to 76
16 to 20	60 to 68
11 to 16	52 to 60
7 to 11	44 to 52

AVERAGE OF DAILY HIGH TEMPERATURES — July

Degrees Fahrenheit	Degrees Celsius
100 to 108	38 to 42
92 to 100	33 to 38
84 to 92	29 to 33
76 to 84	24 to 29

AVERAGE YEARLY PRECIPITATION
(Rain, Melted Snow and Other Moisture)

Centimeters	Inches
30 to 61	12 to 24
0 to 30	0 to 12

0   100   200   300 Miles
0   100 200 300 400 Kilometers

AVERAGE MONTHLY WEATHER

	LAS VEGAS					ELKO				
	Temperatures F°		Temperatures C°		Days of Rain or Snow	Temperatures F°		Temperatures C°		Days of Rain or Snow
	High	Low	High	Low		High	Low	High	Low	
JAN.	55	33	13	1	3	35	9	2	-13	9
FEB.	62	39	17	4	2	40	17	4	-8	9
MAR.	69	44	21	7	3	49	23	9	-5	8
APR.	79	53	26	12	2	60	29	16	-2	7
MAY	88	60	31	16	2	71	35	22	2	8
JUNE	99	68	37	20	0	79	42	26	6	5
JULY	105	76	41	24	3	91	49	33	9	3
AUG.	103	74	39	23	2	89	46	32	8	3
SEPT.	96	65	36	18	1	79	36	26	2	3
OCT.	82	53	28	12	2	66	29	19	-2	6
NOV.	67	41	19	5	2	49	20	9	-7	6
DEC.	58	36	14	2	3	39	15	4	-9	9

The tourist industry provides the greatest source of income in Nevada. The next highest sources of income are mining, manufacturing, and agriculture. Many of Nevada's mines and factories are controlled by individuals and corporations that have their headquarters in other states.

Natural Resources. Nevada's chief natural resources are its vast mineral deposits and beautiful scenery. In some areas, the poor soil and lack of water make it difficult or impossible to raise field crops. But thick grasses in the valleys provide grazing land for cattle.

Soil. Most of Nevada is covered with a gray soil containing large amounts of sodium carbonate. In most places, the soil has a heavy covering of underbrush. With irrigation, Nevada's soil can grow grain and other field crops. In some valleys, thick layers of sodium carbonate form gleaming white alkali flats, where nothing grows. These flats are sometimes called *dry lakes* because they may be covered with water after a rainstorm. Parts of western Nevada are covered by a reddish soil containing volcanic rocks washed down from the mountains. The northern section of the state has dark soil mixed with powdered lava.

Water. Nevada has a limited water supply because of its light rainfall. Water must be carefully conserved for personal needs and irrigation. Farmers and ranchers pump underground water for their crops and livestock in the Big Smoky, Diamond, Fish Lake, Las Vegas, Pahrump, Ruby, Smith, Spring, Truckee Meadows, and White River valleys. The largest irrigation systems operate along the rivers. The Newlands system includes the Lahontan Reservoir, which stores water from the Carson and Truckee rivers. It provides irrigation water for about 87,000 acres (35,000 hectares) in Churchill and Lyon counties. Other large irrigation projects include Rye Patch Dam on the Humboldt River, Hoover Dam at the southeastern tip of the state, and Wild Horse Dam in the Owyhee River Valley.

Minerals. Huge deposits of copper lie in Lander, Lyon, and White Pine counties. Pershing County leads the state in mercury production. Central and northwestern Nevada have large tungsten deposits. Gold and silver have been found in many parts of the state. Other mineral resources include antimony, barite, borates, clays, diatomite, fluorspar, iron ore, lead, magnesite, pumice, salt, and zinc. The state also has valuable deposits of gypsum, limestone, and sand and gravel. Petroleum has been found in some areas near the center of Nevada.

Forests in Nevada grow chiefly on the mountainsides. Commercially valuable trees include the Englemann spruce, lodgepole pine, mountain hemlock, ponderosa

Las Vegas News Bureau

Night Clubs in Las Vegas, Reno, and the Lake Tahoe area feature outstanding Broadway and Hollywood entertainers. These stars include such performers as Debbie Reynolds, *above*, shown during her act at a luxurious Las Vegas night spot. Nevada's night life helps attract about 12 million visitors to the state yearly.

Production of Goods in Nevada

Total value of goods produced in 1973—$574,868,000

- Mineral Products 35%
- Manufactured Products 39%
- Agricultural Products 26%

Percentages are based on farm income, value added by manufacture, and value of mineral production.
Sources: U.S. government publications, 1975-1976.

Employment in Nevada

Total number of persons employed in 1974—263,300

	Number of Employees
Community, Social, & Personal Services	104,500
Wholesale & Retail Trade	50,200
Government	43,000
Construction	16,900
Transportation & Public Utilities	16,800
Manufacturing	12,300
Finance, Insurance, & Real Estate	10,600
Agriculture	4,900
Mining	4,100

Sources: *Employment and Earnings*, May 1975, U.S. Bureau of Labor Statistics; *Farm Labor*, February 1975, U.S. Department of Agriculture.

pine, red fir, sugar pine, and white fir. Alder, aspen, cottonwood, and willow trees thrive on the banks of mountain streams. Many juniper trees and piñon pines grow on the mountain slopes and in some valleys. Most of the valleys receive too little rain for trees to grow. Nevada's forests support only a small local lumber industry. But they help conserve water, and they provide wildlife preserves and recreational areas for the state.

Plant Life. Nevada's deserts are dotted with cactus, yucca, and a variety of low brush plants. The most common desert plants include the bitter brush, mesquite, rabbit brush, sagebrush, and shadscale. Grasses grow in mountain and valley meadows. Nevada's meadows bloom in spring with Indian paintbrush, larkspur, shooting stars, and violets. In early spring, blood-red blossoms of the snow plant push through the snow in the pine forests. Wild peach blossoms and desert lilies brighten Nevada's foothills in spring and summer.

Animal Life. Nevada has few large animals, but hundreds of small animals live in the state. Mule deer roam the mountain forests. Pronghorns live mainly in the Charles Sheldon Antelope Refuge in Washoe County. Bighorn sheep climb the steep, rocky slopes of the Sheep Range in Clark County. Nevada's small animals include badgers, coyotes, foxes, minks, marmots, muskrats, porcupines, rabbits, and raccoons. A variety of lizards and snakes live in the desert. Game birds include chukar partridges, ducks, geese, pheasants, quail, and sage hens. Hundreds of white pelicans nest in the Anahoe Island Refuge in Pyramid Lake. Several kinds of trout make the state a favorite spot for fishermen. The *cui-ui* is a large sucker found only in Pyramid Lake. It was once an important food fish among the local Indians. Other fishes that swim in Nevada waters include bass, carp, catfish, and crappies.

Tourist Industry. Every year about 12 million visitors enjoy Nevada's night life, lovely scenery, and exciting sports. The tourist industry earns an annual income of about $2½ billion. Gambling is legal throughout the state. But about 90 per cent of the large casinos are in Las Vegas, Reno, and in the Lake Tahoe area. Forms of gambling include slot machines, blackjack, keno, poker, roulette, and dice games. Outstanding entertainers from Broadway, Hollywood, and Europe appear in floor shows at casinos and night clubs. Many restaurants and casinos never close. Signs announce "Breakfast Served All Day." Dude ranches, fishing resorts, and hunting lodges operate in many areas of the state.

Manufacturing. Nevada has few industrial areas. The most important industrial activity is food processing.

Manufacturing and Processing Plants make Henderson a major industrial center of southern Nevada. Plants in Henderson refine titanium and produce lime, weedkiller, and other chemicals. Nevada has few large industrial areas. Its main industrial activities include the processing of minerals from its mines.

Desert Farming. Farmers near Eureka in central Nevada use overhead sprinklers to turn vast areas of wasteland into fertile fields of potatoes, grains, and other crops. Irrigated farms operate chiefly in northern, western, and southeastern Nevada.
Photos, Nevada Dept. of Economic Development

FARM AND MINERAL PRODUCTS

This map shows where the leading farm and mineral products are produced. The major urban areas (shown in red) are the important manufacturing centers.

```
0    25   50   75   100 Miles
0    50   100   150 Kilometers
```

WORLD BOOK map

Gypsum · Mercury · Tungsten · Beef Cattle · Hay · Gold · Sheep · Sheep
Beef Cattle · Gold · Sheep · Silver · Lead
Tungsten · Iron Ore · Mercury · Gold · Silver · Beef Cattle
Wheat · Tungsten · Copper · Silver · Sheep · Beryllium
Beef Cattle · Poultry · Hogs · Barley · Silver · Silver · Tungsten · Copper
Reno · Dairy · Grapes · Diatomite · Beef Cattle
Gold · Silver · Mercury · Gold · Dairy Products · Barite · Gold
Copper · Poultry · Vegetables · Tungsten
Potatoes · Hay · Sheep
Sheep · Silver · Mercury · Oil · Silver
Barley · Gold · Tungsten · Gold · Antimony · Zinc
Silver · Manganese · Copper
Silver
Gold · Grapes · Zinc · Lead
Magnesium · Magnesium · Manganese · Silver
Tungsten · Poultry · Sand Gravel
Gold · Dairy Products · Gypsum · Las Vegas
Dairy Products
Fruit · Vegetables
Cotton · Limestone · Grapes

Hoover Dam, one of the highest concrete dams in the world, towers 726 feet (221 meters) from base to crest. The dam is located on the Colorado River, near the Arizona-Nevada border. The $120-million dam was completed in 1936.

Fred Bond, Publix

Nevada's industrial products have a value added by manufacture of about $225 million a year. This figure represents the value created in products by Nevada's industries, not counting such costs as materials, supplies, and fuels.

Meat packing, dairy, and bottling plants operate in the Las Vegas and Reno areas, the chief manufacturing centers in Nevada. Gypsum is crushed and graded in Empire. Copper mills and smelters operate near Yerington and in McGill. Henderson has chemical plants. A factory near Las Vegas manufactures plaster and wallboard. Plants in Reno make electronics and communications components and medical and surgical equipment. Las Vegas and Reno also have large printing and publishing companies.

Mining in Nevada accounts for an income of about $200 million a year. Copper is Nevada's most valuable industrial mineral. Mines near Ely and Yerington produce most of the state's copper. Most of the ore comes from open-pit mines. Nevada's next most valuable

mining product is gold. An open-pit gold mine began operating near Carlin in 1965. Within two years, this mine ranked as one of the top gold producers in the Western Hemisphere. An open-pit mine near Cortez also ranks among the most productive United States gold mines.

Sand and gravel are the third most valuable minerals produced in the state. Pershing County is the state's leading producer of mercury. Most of the mercury mines are in the western part of the state.

Gypsum, used for insulation materials, plaster, and wallboard, comes from pits in Clark, Lyon, and Pershing counties. Clark County also has a special sand that is used in making glass. Quarries in many sections produce building stone. Petroleum comes from Nye County. Other minerals include antimony, barite, clays, diatomite, fluorspar, lead, magnesite, pumice, salt, silver, tungsten, and zinc.

Agriculture provides an annual income of about $150 million in Nevada. Livestock ranching is the chief agricultural activity. Ranches average 5,070 acres (2,052 hectares) in size, but the largest ones cover as much as 275,000 acres (111,000 hectares). Farmers must depend on irrigation to raise field crops, but irrigation water reaches less than 2 per cent of the state. Most farms in the irrigated regions cover only about 260 acres (105.2 hectares).

Livestock and Poultry. Most of Nevada's large cattle and sheep ranches are in Elko, Humboldt, Washoe, and White Pine counties. Many ranchers graze their animals for part of the year on public lands that they rent from the federal government. Ranchers sell most of their cattle to farmers in California, Idaho, Nevada, and the Midwest for fattening. Stockmen also sell sheep, hogs, and lambs to meat packers, and wool to textile mills. Riding horses are raised in many parts of the state. Milk and butter come from Yerington and the Reno and Las Vegas areas.

Crops. Irrigated farms operate chiefly near the river valleys of northern, western, and southeastern Nevada. But irrigated farming projects are being developed throughout the state. Water for these projects comes from wells. Nevada's chief crops include alfalfa seed, barley, cotton, hay, oats, and wheat. Farmers use about 60 per cent of their hay and grain crops for livestock feed. Cotton, grapes, and melons come from farms in the southeast. Farmers also grow melons in Churchill County. Vegetables grown in Nevada include onions, potatoes, radishes, and tomatoes. Greenhouse and nursery products are also chief sources of farm income in Nevada.

Electric Power. Fuel-burning steam plants provide about 75 per cent of Nevada's electric power. Hydroelectric plants generate the rest. The Davis and Hoover dams on the Colorado River provide almost all the electricity for the southern and southeastern sections of the state. Small irrigation dams supply electric power in the north and west. Steam-powered plants operate near Las Vegas and Reno, and in east-central Nevada.

Transportation. Several transcontinental airlines serve Nevada and connect with routes of a local airline. Ranchers and farmers own most of the more than 50 private airfields in the state. Railroads operate on about 1,600 miles (2,570 kilometers) of track in Nevada. Four rail lines provide freight service in the state, and passenger trains serve Carlin, Elko, Sparks, and Reno. The state has about 50,000 miles (80,000 kilometers) of roads and highways, of which about a third are surfaced.

Communication. Nevada's first newspaper, the *Territorial Enterprise*, was established at Genoa in 1858. Mark Twain worked as a reporter on this daily paper from 1862 to 1864, after the paper was moved to Virginia City. The paper is now published weekly in Virginia City as the *Territorial Enterprise and Virginia City News*. More than 25 newspapers are published in Nevada, including about 15 weeklies. Daily newspapers with the largest circulations include the *Las Vegas Review-Journal*, the *Las Vegas Sun*, Reno's *Nevada State Journal*, and the *Reno Evening Gazette*.

Nevada has about 35 radio stations and 9 television stations. The state's first radio station, KOH, began broadcasting from Reno in 1928. The first television stations, KOLO-TV in Reno and KLAS-TV in Las Vegas, began operations in 1953.

Indian Days. Some of the earliest American Indians lived in the Nevada region. Bones, ashes, and other remains discovered near Las Vegas indicate that Indians may have lived there more than 20,000 years ago. Cave-dwelling Indians left picture writings on rocks in southern Nevada. Basket Makers once lived at Lovelock Cave, and Pueblo Indians lived around Las Vegas. Explorers of the early 1800's found Mohave, Paiute, Shoshoni, and Washoe Indians in parts of the region.

Exploration. Francisco Garcés, a Spanish missionary, possibly was the first white man to enter the Nevada region. He may have traveled through southern Nevada while journeying from New Mexico to California in 1776. Fur traders and trappers began to explore the region between 1825 and 1830. Peter S. Ogden explored the Humboldt River valley with a group of trappers of the Hudson's Bay Company (see HUDSON'S BAY COMPANY). Jedediah S. Smith led some trappers across the Las Vegas valley region into California and then back across the Great Basin.

In 1830, William Wolfskill blazed a route, called the Old Spanish Trail, from Santa Fe to Los Angeles. This trail opened Nevada to trade from the southeast. Trapper Joseph Walker blazed a trail along the Humboldt River on his way to California in 1833. Hundreds of wagons rolled westward over this same trail after gold was discovered in California in 1848. Between 1843 and 1845, Lieutenant John C. Frémont explored the Great Basin and Sierra Nevada. Frémont provided the first accurate knowledge of the Nevada region.

Early Settlement. At the end of the Mexican War in 1848, the United States acquired the Nevada region from Mexico. Nevada was then part of a territory that also included California, Utah, and parts of four other states (see MEXICAN WAR [The Peace Treaty]).

In 1849, the Mormon leader Brigham Young organized Utah, most of present-day Nevada, and parts of other present-day states as the State of Deseret. He asked Congress to admit his state to the Union. But in 1850, Congress established the Utah Territory, including Utah and most of present-day Nevada. President Millard Fillmore appointed Young governor of the territory.

In 1851, Mormons from the Great Salt Lake area in Utah built a trading post at Mormon Station (now Genoa) in the Carson Valley. The post supplied provisions for gold seekers heading for California. During the next few years, a few Mormon families came to farm and raise livestock in the Carson Valley and the surrounding region. This section of Utah Territory was organized into Carson County.

Many non-Mormons in Carson County did not want to be governed by Brigham Young. They pleaded unsuccessfully with Congress to make Carson County part of California. The Mormons themselves were troubled by a dispute with the federal government. In 1857, Young recalled the Mormon settlers to Great Salt Lake because he feared that federal troops would attack them. Two years later, the non-Mormons set up a provisional government in an attempt to establish Carson County as a separate territory. But Congress did not authorize the provisional government because only a few hundred persons lived in the Carson County area.

Gridley Sack of Flour. In 1864, R. C. Gridley of Austin collected $275,000 by auctioning a single sack of flour over and over again. He gave all the money to the U.S. Sanitary Commission, forerunner of the American Red Cross.

Trail Blazers. In 1776, Francisco Garcés may have become the first white man to enter the Nevada region. Jedediah Smith followed in 1826, and William Wolfskill arrived in 1830.

John C. Frémont mapped Nevada during trips across the region from 1843 to 1845. Kit Carson guided the expeditions.

● Virginia City

★
CARSON CITY

The Comstock Lode, a rich deposit of gold and silver, was discovered at the present site of Virginia City in 1859. Prospectors flocked to the area.

First Federal Irrigation Project, called *The Newlands Project*, was completed in 1907 along Nevada's Carson and Truckee rivers.

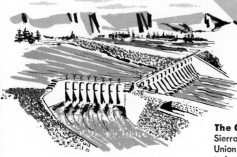

The Central Pacific cut 15 tunnels through the Sierras into Nevada in the 1860's. It met the Union Pacific tracks in Utah, forming the country's first transcontinental railroad system.

The Nevada Proving Ground of the Atomic Energy Commission began nuclear tests in 1951 at Yucca and Frenchman flats.

Hoover Dam was completed in 1936. Its reservoir, Lake Mead, is one of the world's largest man-made lakes. The reservoir is 115 miles (185 kilometers) long.

HISTORIC
NEVADA

The Comstock Lode, a rich deposit of silver ore, was discovered in 1859 at the present site of Virginia City. Henry Comstock, a prospector, took credit for the discovery, although other miners had found the ore. News of the Comstock Lode quickly spread to fortune hunters in California and the East. Hundreds of prospectors rushed to Carson County to "strike it rich." They settled in tents, rough stone huts, and hillside caves. Almost overnight, Virginia City became a thriving mining center.

The settlers led a difficult and dangerous life. They paid unbelievably high prices for provisions that had to be hauled from California over the Sierra Nevada. Some miners became millionaires. But many others found little or no wealth. Many mining camps were lawless, and many miners were rowdies or gunmen.

Nevada Becomes a Territory. By 1860, the booming mining camps of Carson County held more than 6,700 persons. In March, 1861, President James Buchanan signed an act creating the Nevada Territory. President Abraham Lincoln, who took office two days later, appointed James W. Nye, a New York City politician, governor of the territory.

The Civil War (1861-1865) began before Nevada's territorial government could be set up in Carson City. The war gave Nevada's rich mineral resources new importance. Both the North and the South needed silver and gold to pay the costs of the war. President Lincoln wanted Nevada's valuable minerals to help the Union. Also, most Nevadans favored the North. Lincoln needed another "northern" state to support his proposed antislavery amendments. At the time, the Nevada Territory had far less than the 127,381 residents required by law to become a state. But Nevadans held a convention anyway and drew up a state constitution.

Statehood. The convention met in November, 1863, but ended in failure. The voters rejected the proposed constitution because of its provisions for the taxing of mines. Congress then passed an act authorizing a second Nevada convention. In July, 1864, this convention met and completed its work. In September, the revised constitution won the approval of the voters. The people elected Republican Henry G. Blasdel, a mining engineer, their first governor. President Lincoln proclaimed Nevada a state on Oct. 31, 1864.

Mine Failure and Recovery. In the 1870's, mining companies dug the richest silver ore from Nevada's mines. Some of the state's mines produced only "low-grade" ores that contained small amounts of silver. Mine owners made a profit on these ores because silver had a high value.

During the early 1870's, the U.S. government limited the use of silver in its money system. As the government's demand for silver fell, the value of silver also dropped. Many mines closed because they could no longer produce low-grade ores at a profit. Unemployed persons began to leave Nevada by the thousands to find work elsewhere. The state's population dropped from 62,266 in 1880 to 47,355 in 1890. Several thriving communities became ghost towns.

As mining failed, ranching grew in importance. But the ranchers also faced difficult problems. They had to pay the railroad extremely high rates to ship their stock. In addition, severe winters in the late 1880's killed thousands of cattle. Many owners of small herds

became bankrupt and had to sell out to operators of large ranches.

Economic recovery began with new mineral discoveries in 1900. Prospectors found huge deposits of silver at Tonopah. They could be mined profitably, although silver still had a low value. Prospectors uncovered copper ores at Ely, Ruth, and Mountain City. In 1902, gold was discovered at Goldfield. Rich deposits discovered the next year brought thousands of miners rushing back to Nevada.

As the mining industry came to life again, the railroads built branch lines to the mining areas. Trains brought equipment to the mines and hauled ore away to processing plants. Cattlemen also used the new branch lines for speedy beef shipments.

Nevada's Newlands Irrigation Project, the country's first federal irrigation project, was completed in 1907. In this project, dams along the Carson and Truckee rivers create irrigation reservoirs and generate electricity. Water from this system supplies an agricultural region that developed near Fallon in west-central Nevada.

The richest of Nevada's gold and silver deposits were running out when the United States entered World War I in 1917. Industries then began to demand copper, tungsten, zinc, and other metals for weapons and wartime supplies. Many new mines opened in Nevada, and mine owners collected top prices for the metals. But prices fell after the war, and many mines closed.

In 1928, Congress authorized the construction of

IMPORTANT DATES IN NEVADA

1776 Francisco Garcés, a friar, may have become the first white man to enter the Nevada region.

1825-30 Peter S. Ogden discovered the Humboldt River. Jedediah S. Smith crossed southern Nevada.

1843-45 John C. Frémont and Kit Carson explored the Great Basin and Sierra Nevada.

1848 The United States received Nevada and other lands in the Southwest from Mexico under the Treaty of Guadalupe Hidalgo.

1859 The discovery of silver near Virginia City brought a rush of prospectors to western Nevada.

1861 Congress created the Nevada Territory.

1864 Nevada became the 36th state on October 31.

1877-81 The price of silver fell and caused many Nevada mines to close.

1880-90 Unemployed persons left Nevada and the population dropped by almost 15,000.

1909 The Nevada legislature passed laws making gambling illegal. The laws went into effect in 1910.

1931 The legislature reduced the divorce residence requirement to six weeks and also made gambling legal in the state.

1936 Boulder (now Hoover) Dam was completed.

1951 The Atomic Energy Commission began testing nuclear weapons in southern Nevada.

1963 The Supreme Court of the United States settled a 40-year dispute by specifying how much water the states of Arizona, California, and Nevada could draw from the Colorado River.

1967 The Nevada legislature changed state gambling laws to allow corporations that sell stock to the public to buy casinos and to hold gambling licenses.

1971 The Southern Nevada Water Project was completed.

NEVADA

Greater Reno Chamber of Commerce

Downtown Reno, which includes many of the city's large gambling casinos, lies on both sides of the Truckee River.

Boulder (now Hoover) Dam on the Colorado River. Work on the dam began in 1930. The huge project was completed in 1936. Hoover Dam provides power and stores up irrigation water for parts of Nevada, Arizona, and California.

Legal Gambling and Easy Divorce. As early as 1869, Nevada's legislature had permitted gamblers to operate games of chance in the state. By 1910, various groups of citizens had succeeded in having laws passed against gambling. But gamblers continued to operate illegally, and enforcement of the gambling laws required large amounts of money. Finally, the legislature decided it would be better to legalize gambling than to spend money trying to stop it. In 1931, Nevada made gambling legal. Many gambling casinos began to operate in the 1930's.

In the early 1900's, Nevada had passed laws that made it easy to get a divorce. A person had to live in Nevada for only six months to get a divorce there. In 1927, the Nevada legislature passed a law allowing persons to obtain a divorce if they lived in the state for only three months. In 1931, the period was reduced to six weeks. During the mid-1900's, thousands of persons went to Nevada each year to get divorces quickly and easily.

The Mid-1900's. World War II (1939-1945) created new business for Nevada's mining industry. Manufacturers of military supplies purchased large amounts of the state's copper, lead, magnesite, manganese, tungsten, and zinc. After the war, mining activities decreased. The industry gradually switched to the production of gypsum, lime, and other nonmetallic minerals.

In the late 1940's, Nevada began a widespread campaign to attract new industry. Although the campaign brought a number of factories into the state, Nevada's economy during the 1950's and 1960's depended chiefly on nuclear research and tourism.

In 1950, the Atomic Energy Commission (AEC) set up a testing center about 60 miles (97 kilometers) northwest of Las Vegas. The next year, the AEC began testing nuclear weapons. In 1962, it began a program to develop peaceful uses of nuclear energy.

Tourism remained Nevada's largest and fastest-growing industry during the 1950's and 1960's. By the late 1960's, the Las Vegas area alone attracted annually about 15 million tourists, who spent about $400 million. Tourists also flocked to the state's two other main resort centers, Reno and the Lake Tahoe area.

In the late 1950's, the Nevada legislature set up strict gambling regulations to prevent cheating and to stop criminals from entering or influencing the gambling industry. The regulations require every gambling house to have a state license, which is issued only after investigation by the Gaming Control Board and final approval by the Gaming Commission. In 1967, the legislature passed a law allowing corporations that sell stock to the public to hold gambling licenses. The new law was a further attempt to keep the underworld out of the gambling industry.

In 1963, the Supreme Court of the United States settled a 40-year dispute between Arizona, California, and Nevada over water supplies from the Colorado River. The court ruled on how much water each state could draw from the river every year.

In 1966, Howard Hughes, an American businessman and one of the world's richest men, moved to Las Vegas. He then bought airports, casinos and hotels, large tracts of land, and a television station in the area.

Nevada Today continues to depend heavily on the tourist industry. In addition, the state is looking forward to and planning for further growth of tourism in the 1970's. Nevada's tourist industry, however, depends on the prosperity of the nation.

With the expected increase in tourism, the Las Vegas and Reno-Lake Tahoe areas will continue their rapid growth. Already, more than four-fifths of the people of Nevada live in the Las Vegas and Reno metropolitan areas. Rural influence in the state legislature declined

THE GOVERNORS OF NEVADA		
	Party	**Term**
1. **Henry G. Blasdel**	Republican	1864-1871
2. **Lewis R. Bradley**	Democratic	1871-1879
3. **John H. Kinkead**	Republican	1879-1883
4. **Jewett W. Adams**	Democratic	1883-1887
5. **Charles C. Stevenson**	Republican	1887-1890
6. **Frank Bell**	Republican	1890-1891
7. **Roswell K. Colcord**	Republican	1891-1895
8. **John E. Jones**	Silver	1895-1896
9. **Reinhold Sadler**	Silver	1896-1903
10. **John Sparks**	Silver-Dem.*	1903-1908
11. **Denver S. Dickerson**	Silver-Dem.	1908-1911
12. **Tasker L. Oddie**	Republican	1911-1915
13. **Emmet D. Boyle**	Democratic	1915-1923
14. **James G. Scrugham**	Democratic	1923-1927
15. **Fred B. Balzar**	Republican	1927-1934
16. **Morley Griswold**	Republican	1934-1935
17. **Richard Kirman, Sr.**	Democratic	1935-1939
18. **Edward P. Carville**	Democratic	1939-1945
19. **Vail M. Pittman**	Democratic	1945-1951
20. **Charles H. Russell**	Republican	1951-1959
21. **Grant Sawyer**	Democratic	1959-1967
22. **Paul Laxalt**	Republican	1967-1971
23. **Mike O'Callaghan**	Democratic	1971-

*Silver-Democratic

during the 1970's as Nevada became basically a "two-city state."

Las Vegas and Reno are planning better airport and ground transportation facilities to accommodate the increased number of tourists expected to arrive in the 1970's on jumbo jets. In 1967, the Southern Nevada Water Project was created to provide increased water supplies for the expected growth in the Las Vegas area. The $80-million project, which brings water from Lake Mead, was completed in 1971.

Nevada cities face major problems as their populations continue to increase. Many of these problems will require help from the state government. City dwellers are demanding better police and fire protection, improvements in education, better recreational facilities, and other services. Blacks in Nevada feel that they do not have equal job opportunities. They also want a state open housing law. Air and water pollution has also become a serious problem in Nevada. In one program to control water pollution, Nevada has joined with California in the Tahoe Regional Planning Compact to fight pollution of Lake Tahoe.

JAMES W. HULSE, E. R. LARSON, and DONALD W. REYNOLDS

NEVADA/Study Aids

Related Articles in WORLD BOOK include:

BIOGRAPHIES

Beebe, Lucius M.	McCarran, Patrick A.
Carson, Kit	Pittman, Key
Frémont, John C.	Smith, Jedediah S.
Hughes, Howard R.	Wovoka
Mackay (John W.)	Young, Brigham

CITIES AND TOWNS

Carson City	Goldfield	Tonopah
Elko	Las Vegas	Virginia City
Ely	Reno	

HISTORY

Comstock Lode	Mexican War
Guadalupe Hidalgo,	Mormons
Treaty of	Western Frontier Life

PHYSICAL FEATURES

Colorado River	Lake Mead
Desert	Lake Tahoe
Great Basin	Sierra Nevada
Humboldt River	

OTHER RELATED ARTICLES

Copper (graph)	Lehman Caves National
Death Valley National	Monument
Monument	Nevada, University of
Gold (graph)	Ranching
Hoover Dam	Rocky Mountain States
Irrigation	

Outline

I. **Government**
    A. Constitution
    B. Executive
    C. Legislature
    D. Courts
    E. Local Government
    F. Taxation
    G. Politics
II. **People**
III. **Education**
    A. Schools
    B. Libraries
    C. Museums
IV. **A Visitor's Guide**
    A. Places to Visit
    B. Annual Events
V. **The Land**
    A. Land Regions
    B. Rivers and Lakes
VI. **Climate**
VII. **Economy**
    A. Natural Resources
    B. Tourist Industry
    C. Manufacturing
    D. Mining
    E. Agriculture
    F. Electric Power
    G. Transportation
    H. Communication
VIII. **History**

Questions

Where are about 90 per cent of Nevada's large gambling casinos?

Why did some Nevada mining communities become ghost towns during the 1880's?

How does Nevada's "free port" law attract new industries to the state?

From what country did the United States receive the land that includes the present state of Nevada?

What is the most valuable mining product produced in Nevada?

How many degrees may the temperature change in Reno on a summer day?

Why did President Abraham Lincoln support statehood for Nevada?

What is Nevada's most important industry?

What is the longest river in Nevada? Where does this river stop flowing and disappear?

Why does Nevada enforce strict regulations on gambling?

Books for Young Readers

BAILEY, BERNADINE. *Picture Book of Nevada*. Rev. ed. Whitman, 1965.

CARPENTER, ALLAN. *Nevada*. Childrens Press, 1964.

HENRY, MARGUERITE. *Mustang: Wild Spirit of the West*. Rand McNally, 1966. Fiction. Annie Bronn Johnston's fight to save the mustangs of Nevada.

LAXALT, ROBERT. *Nevada*. Coward, 1971.

MONTGOMERY, RUTHERFORD G. *Big Red: A Wild Stallion*. Caxton, 1971. Fiction.

Books for Older Readers

BEEBE, LUCIUS M., and CLEGG, C. M. *Legends of the Comstock Lode*. 5th ed. Stanford Univ. Press, 1956. *Steamcars to the Comstock*. 3rd ed. Howell-North, 1960.

BUSHNELL, ELEANORE. *The Nevada Constitution: Origin and Growth*. 3rd ed. Univ. of Nevada Press, 1972.

CARLSON, HELEN S. *Nevada Place Names: A Geographical Dictionary*. Univ. of Nevada Press, 1974.

ELLIOTT, RUSSELL R. *History of Nevada*. Univ. of Nebraska Press, 1973.

HULSE, JAMES W. *The Nevada Adventure: A History*. 3rd ed. Univ. of Nevada Press, 1972.

LAXALT, ROBERT. *Nevada: A Bicentennial History*. Norton, 1977.

PAHER, STANLEY W. *Nevada Ghost Towns and Mining Camps*. Howell-North, 1970.

TOLL, DAVID W. *The Compleat Nevada Traveler: A Guide to the State*. Univ. of Nevada Press, 1976.

NEVADA, UNIVERSITY OF, is a state-supported co-educational system of higher education. Its official name is the University of Nevada System. It operates campuses at Reno and Las Vegas, a Community College Division, and the Desert Research Institute.

The Reno campus offers programs leading to bachelor's, master's, and doctor's degrees. The Las Vegas campus grants bachelor's and master's degrees. The Community College Division operates two-year colleges at Elko, Carson City-Reno, and North Las Vegas. The Desert Research Institute studies water resources and other environmental concerns of desert areas. It has facilities in Boulder City, Las Vegas, and Reno.

The university was chartered in 1864 and began operation in Elko in 1874. It moved to Reno in 1886. For enrollment, see UNIVERSITIES AND COLLEGES (table).

Critically reviewed by the UNIVERSITY OF NEVADA SYSTEM

See also NEVADA (picture).

NEVADA FALLS is a waterfall in Yosemite National Park, California. This 594-foot (181-meter) drop of the Merced River represents a step in the "Giant's Stairway" as the river descends 2,000 feet (610 meters) in a distance of 1½ miles (2.4 kilometers) from Little Yosemite Valley to Yosemite Valley proper. Indians named it *twisted fall*, because a rock ledge spreads the fall's water spray to one side. JOHN W. REITH

NEVELSON, LOUISE (1900-   ), is an American sculptor. She is best known for her *assemblages*, often grouped within boxlike frames. Many of the large black walls of her compartments express a feeling of quiet and majesty. Most of her assemblages are made out of wood that is painted either black or gold or left in the natural color. She has also constructed "total environments" of everyday "found" objects and utensils, strips of molding, woodwork decorations, or Victorian debris that form powerful unified wholes.

Louise Nevelson was born in Kiev, Russia, and came

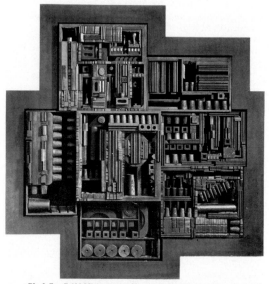

Black Zag B (1968) by Louise Nevelson, Pace Gallery, New York City
Louise Nevelson's Black Zag B is typical of the complex and mysterious large wooden constructions that have made her famous.

to the United States in 1905. She studied painting at the Art Students League in New York City. DOUGLAS GEORGE

NEVILLE, EMILY CHENEY (1919-   ), is an American author. She won the 1964 Newbery medal for her first book *It's Like This, Cat* (1963), a story about a boy and a cat in New York City. Emily Neville was born in Manchester, Conn.

NEVIN, *NEV in,* **ETHELBERT WOODBRIDGE** (1862-1901), an American composer, was known for his songs and piano pieces. His music is trivial, but charming. He wrote "The Rosary" (1898), one of the most successful songs ever written. He also wrote "Little Boy Blue" (1891), "Venetian Love Song" (1898), and "Mighty Lak' a Rose" (1901). His most popular piano piece is "Narcissus" (1891). He was born in Edgeworth, Pa., and studied music in Europe. GILBERT CHASE

NEVINS, *NEV inz,* **ALLAN** (1890-1971), an American historian and educator, twice was awarded the Pulitzer prize for biography. *Grover Cleveland: A Study in Courage* won the prize in 1933, and *Hamilton Fish: The Inner History of the Grant Administration* received the award in 1937. He won the Bancroft prize and the Scribner Centenary prize for *The Ordeal of the Union* (1947). Nevins' works are noted for being well balanced and thorough, with a distinctive literary style.

His *John D. Rockefeller*, a biography published in 1940, became very popular. It was revised and republished in 1953 as *Study in Power: John D. Rockefeller, Industrialist and Philanthropist*. Nevins and Frank Ernest Hill completed *Ford: the Times, the Man, the Company,* a study of Henry Ford, in 1954.

In addition to his histories and biographies, Nevins also edited collections of the letters of noted historical persons. He published his first book, *Life of Robert Rogers*, in 1914, and followed it with more than 50 other volumes. His other books include *The American States During and After the Revolution* (1924), *Frémont: The West's Greatest Adventurer* (1927), *A Brief History of the United States* (1942), *The Emergence of Lincoln* (1950), and *Herbert H. Lehman and His Era* (1963).

Born in Camp Point, Ill., Nevins was graduated from the University of Illinois. He wrote editorials for the *New York Evening Post* from 1913 to 1923. Nevins joined the staff of the *New York Sun* in 1924, and *The (New York) World* in 1925. He was a professor of history at Cornell University from 1927 to 1928, and at Columbia University from 1931 to 1958. In 1958, he became a senior fellow of research at the Henry E. Huntington Library in San Marino, Calif.

Nevins lectured on American history at several universities in other nations. He served as a special representative for the Office of War Information in Australia and New Zealand in 1943 and 1944, during World War II. MERLE CURTI

Columbia University
Allan Nevins

NEVIS, BEN. See BEN NEVIS.

NEVUS. See BIRTHMARK.

NEW AMSTERDAM. See NEW YORK CITY (History).

NEW BEDFORD, Mass. (pop. 101,777; met. area pop. 161,288), once the whaling capital of the world, is a textile center in southeastern Massachusetts. The city lies about 56 miles (90 kilometers) south of Boston, where the Acushnet River empties into Buzzards Bay. For location, see MASSACHUSETTS (political map).

The city's harbor and mild, damp climate provide favorable conditions for textile manufacturing, and New Bedford ranks high in cotton goods production. Other products include shoes and electrical equipment, glass and rayon fabrics, rubber, and copper products. Many fishing vessels use the port of New Bedford. It is also an important trade and distribution center for southeastern Massachusetts.

The first settlement on the site of New Bedford was made in 1652 on land purchased from Massasoit, chief of the Wampanoag Indians, by a company from Plymouth. It was named in honor of the Duke of Bedford's family. During the Revolutionary War, the New Bedford port harbored privateers that attacked British ships. British troops invaded the town in 1778, burning the homes, business places, and vessels of many American patriots. But the people soon rebuilt New Bedford, and it received its town charter in 1787.

New Bedford launched its whaling industry in the 1760's. Whaling prospered until 1859, when the discovery of petroleum in Pennsylvania ruined the whale oil industry. The Whaling Museum and the New Bedford Public Library exhibit mementos of whaling days. The Wamsutta Mills, the city's first major textile plant, started in 1846. A textile boom in the 1880's made the city a leading producer of cotton fabrics. New Bedford received its city charter in 1847. It has a mayor-council government.   WILLIAM J. REID

NEW BERN, N.C. (pop. 14,660), is the second oldest city in the state. It lies at the point where the Trent and Neuse rivers meet, about 35 miles (56 kilometers) from the Atlantic Ocean (see NORTH CAROLINA [political map]). Until 1776, New Bern was the capital of the North Carolina colony, and a major port. The coming of the railroads, the lack of a deep harbor, and the coastal dangers lessened New Bern's importance.

New Bern was founded in 1710 by Baron Cristoph von Graffenried of Switzerland and German Palatines, who had left their homes to escape religious persecution. Tryon's Palace, the colonial capital, has been restored. Thousands of servicemen were stationed at nearby Camp Lejeune and Cherry Point Marine Corps Air Station during World War II. New Bern, named for Bern, Switzerland, is the seat of Craven County. It has a council-manager government.   HUGH T. LEFLER

NEW BRITAIN is the largest island in the Bismarck Archipelago. It lies off the northeast coast of New Guinea and is part of the nation of Papua New Guinea. Rabaul is New Britain's largest city and chief port.

New Britain is about 300 miles (480 kilometers) long, but only about 50 miles (80 kilometers) wide. It covers an area of 14,100 square miles (36,519 square kilometers). A range of volcanic mountains runs the length of the island, rising to 7,546 feet (2,300 meters). There are many short rivers.

About 159,000 Melanesians live on the island. They are good fishermen and farmers, and have given up cannibalism. Most of the farming is done along the coasts.

In 1700, the English navigator William Dampier

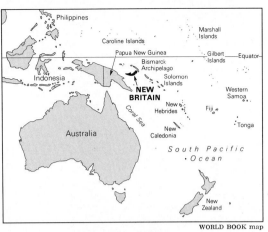

WORLD BOOK map

Location of New Britain

reached New Britain. In 1884, it became a part of the German Empire under the name of Neu Pommern. British forces took the island from Germany in 1914 during World War I. It was given to Australia as a mandate of the League of Nations in 1920. The Japanese captured Rabaul in 1942, during World War II, and held the area until 1945. During this time, Allied forces attacked the Japanese. Bombing raids destroyed most of Rabaul, but the city was rebuilt. New Britain became part of the new nation of Papua New Guinea in 1975.   EDWIN H. BRYAN, JR.

See also BISMARCK ARCHIPELAGO; SCULPTURE (Pacific Islands; picture: An Owl Mask).

NEW BRITAIN, Conn. (pop. 83,441; met. area pop. 145,269), often called the *Hardware City,* leads the nation in the production of builders' hardware and carpenters' tools. It lies in central Connecticut, about 10 miles (16 kilometers) southwest of Hartford (see CONNECTICUT [political map]). Factories produce ball bearings, automatic machinery, household appliances, electrical tools, and plumbing and heating supplies.

New Britain has more than 30 parks and public squares. The Art Museum of the New Britain Institute is known for its collection of American paintings. Central Connecticut State College is in New Britain. The town was settled in 1687, and became a city in 1870. It has a mayor-council government.   ALBERT E. VAN DUSEN

NEW BRUNSWICK, N.J. (pop. 41,885), is an educational and industrial center on the Raritan River about midway between Newark and Trenton (see NEW JERSEY [political map]). It produces medical supplies, pharmaceuticals, machinery, cigars and cigar boxes, and clothing. New Brunswick, Perth Amboy, and Sayreville form a metropolitan area with a population of 583,813. In World War II, nearby Camp Kilmer processed thousands of soldiers before they were sent to Europe.

In New Brunswick are Rutgers (the state university); Douglass College, which is part of Rutgers; the New Brunswick Theological Seminary; and the State Agricultural Experiment Station. The town became a transportation center early in its history. The Raritan River was part of the land-water route from New York City to Philadelphia. The city was chartered in 1730. It has a commission government. New Brunswick is the seat of Middlesex County.   RICHARD P. McCORMICK

Wild Flowers Brighten a Meadow at St. Andrews.

The contributors of this article are J. K. Chapman, Professor of History at the University of New Brunswick; Arnold L. McAllister, Professor of Geology at the University of New Brunswick; and Stuart Trueman, Contributing Editor to The Telegraph-Journal *and* The Evening Times-Globe *of Saint John.*

Fishermen on the Dock at Letite in Charlotte County

New Brunswick (blue) is eighth in size among Canada's provinces, and is second largest of the Atlantic, or Maritime, Provinces.

NEW BRUNSWICK

Hodgson, Miller Services
Falls of the Magaguadavic River at St. George

NEW BRUNSWICK is one of the four Atlantic Provinces of Canada. Clear, swift rivers rush down the many hills and sweep through the steep valleys of New Brunswick. Forests cover about 85 per cent of the land and add to its natural beauty. Saint John is New Brunswick's largest city and chief industrial and shipping center. Fredericton is the capital.

Every year, millions of logs from the thick forests are cut into lumber. Paper and pulp mills in New Brunswick use the wood to make *newsprint* (paper used in printing newspapers) and other paper products. The lumber and paper products industries rank among the leading manufacturing industries in the province.

New Brunswick is in an era of industrial expansion. Prospectors discovered huge deposits of copper, lead, silver, and zinc in northeastern New Brunswick during the 1950's. To develop these resources, a vast industrial program was begun. This program included the construction of new mines, processing plants, shipping facilities, and a steel mill. The provincial government built its greatest hydroelectric plant to generate power for these industries.

New Brunswick has rich farmland in the St. John River Valley and other regions. Farmers produce large crops of potatoes, and dairy farming is extensive. Lobsters are usually the most important catch in the waters off New Brunswick. Fishing fleets on the Bay of Fundy and the Gulf of St. Lawrence also make large hauls of crabs, herring, and redfish. The rivers and rolling woodlands of New Brunswick are among the best fishing and hunting grounds in North America.

In 1922, Andrew Bonar Law of New Brunswick became the only person born outside the British Isles to serve as prime minister of Great Britain. Richard B. Bennett, another New Brunswicker, became prime minister of Canada in 1930. Other well-known New Brunswickers include Bliss Carman, perhaps Canada's most famous poet; Sir Charles Roberts, an outstanding poet, novelist, and short-story writer; and Francis A. Anglin, chief justice of the supreme court of Canada. Lord Beaverbrook, who became a wealthy newspaper publisher and political power in Great Britain, spent most of his boyhood in New Brunswick.

New Brunswick was named for the British royal family of Brunswick-Lüneburg (the House of Hanover). Most of its early settlers were American colonists who had remained loyal to England during the American Revolutionary War. About 14,000 of these United Empire Loyalists, as they were called, began arriving in 1783. As a result, New Brunswick received the nickname of the *Loyalist Province*. It is also called the *Picture Province* because of its great natural beauty.

New Brunswick, along with Nova Scotia, Ontario, and Quebec, was one of the original provinces of Canada. For the relationship of New Brunswick to the other provinces, see ATLANTIC PROVINCES; CANADA; CANADA, GOVERNMENT OF; CANADA, HISTORY OF.

FACTS IN BRIEF

Capital: Fredericton.

Government: *Parliament*—members of the Senate, 10; members of the House of Commons, 10. *Provincial Legislature*—members of the Legislative Assembly, 58. *Counties*—15. *Voting Age*—18 years.

Area: 28,354 sq. mi. (73,437 km²), including 519 sq. mi. (1,344 km²) of inland water; eighth in size among the provinces. *Greatest Distances*—north-south, 230 mi. (370 km); east-west, 190 mi. (306 km). *Coastline*—1,410 mi. (2,269 km).

Elevation: *Highest*—Mount Carleton, 2,690 ft. (820 m) above sea level. *Lowest*—sea level, along the Atlantic Coast.

Population: *1976 Census*—677,250, eighth among the provinces; density, 24 persons per sq. mi. (9 per km²); distribution, 57 per cent urban, 43 per cent rural.

Chief Products: *Agriculture*—beef cattle, eggs, hay, hogs, milk, potatoes, poultry. *Fishing Industry*—cod, crabs, herring, lobster, redfish, tuna. *Forest Industry*—fuelwood, logs and bolts, pulpwood. *Manufacturing*—food and beverage products, lumber and wood products, paper and paper products. *Mining*—coal, copper, lead, peat moss, sand and gravel, silver, stone, zinc.

Entered the Dominion: July 1, 1867; one of the original four provinces.

Lieutenant Governor of New Brunswick represents Queen Elizabeth in the province. The lieutenant governor is appointed by the governor general in council of Canada. The position of the lieutenant governor is largely honorary, like that of the governor general.

Premier of New Brunswick is the actual head of the provincial government. The province, like the other provinces and Canada itself, has a *parliamentary* form of government. The premier is a member of the legislative assembly, where he or she is the leader of the majority party. The voters elect the premier as they do the other members of the assembly. The premier receives a salary of $25,000 a year, plus $16,000 if he or she heads a provincial department as a cabinet minister. For a list of all the premiers of New Brunswick, see the *History* section of this article.

The premier presides over the executive council, or cabinet. The council also includes ministers chosen by the premier from among members of his or her party in the legislative assembly. Each minister directs one or more departments of the provincial government. The executive council, like the premier, resigns if it loses the support of a majority of the assembly.

Legislative Assembly of New Brunswick is a one-house legislature that makes the provincial laws. It has 58 members elected from the province's counties and cities. Terms served by the members may last up to five years. However, the lieutenant governor, on the advice of the premier, may call for an election before the end of the five-year period. If the lieutenant governor does so, all members of the assembly, including the premier, must run again for office.

Courts. The highest court in New Brunswick is the supreme court. It is made up of three divisions: (1) ap-

peal, (2) chancery, and (3) queen's bench. The appeal and chancery divisions have the same judges—the chief justice of New Brunswick and three *puisne* (associate) judges. The queen's bench division, which hears criminal cases, has a chief justice and four puisne judges. Each county has a county court.

Judges of the supreme court and county courts are appointed by the governor general in council. They can serve until the age of 75. New Brunswick's minor courts include juvenile and magistrates' courts. Provincial authorities appoint officials of these courts.

Local Government changed throughout the province in 1967. The provincial government now assesses and collects local taxes, and administers all matters relating to education, health, welfare, and justice. City and town councils handle such things as streets, sewers, water service, and fire protection. All cities, towns, and villages have mayors and councils. The mayors and council members are elected to two-year terms. Some cities and towns also have managers.

Taxation provides about 40 per cent of the provincial government's income. A sales tax and a gasoline tax account for much of the tax money. New Brunswick also collects taxes on corporations and property. The province receives about 45 per cent of its income from federal-provincial tax-sharing arrangements and federal assistance. Most of New Brunswick's other income comes from the sale of liquor, which is under government control.

Politics. The major political parties of New Brunswick have always been the Liberal and the Progressive Conservative parties, or earlier forms of these groups. The Progressive Conservative party was formerly named the Conservative party, and today its members are

In the Assembly Chamber of New Brunswick's Legislative Building, a high throne symbolizes the British monarch. Sessions of the legislature are opened with a formal speech from the throne by the lieutenant governor. The paintings next to the throne show King George III and his wife, Queen Charlotte. They were painted by Joshua Reynolds.

The Provincial Coat of Arms

The Provincial Flag

Symbols of New Brunswick. On the coat of arms, the crown symbolizes New Brunswick's ties with Canada. The British lion represents the province's link with Great Britain. The galley stands for the early shipbuilding industry of the province. The coat of arms was adopted in 1868. The provincial flag, adopted in 1965, bears an adaptation of the coat of arms.

usually called simply Conservatives. The two parties have controlled the provincial government for about equal periods.

Newer political parties that have become popular in other provinces have received little support in New Brunswick. These groups include the New Democratic and Social Credit parties, which have tried to gain followers in New Brunswick.

The Floral Emblem
Purple Violet

The Legislative Building in Fredericton is built of limestone from nearby quarries. Landscaped grounds surround the stately three-story building. Fredericton has been the capital of New Brunswick since 1785. Some sessions of the legislature before 1788 were held in Saint John (then called Parrtown).

Hodgson, Miller Services

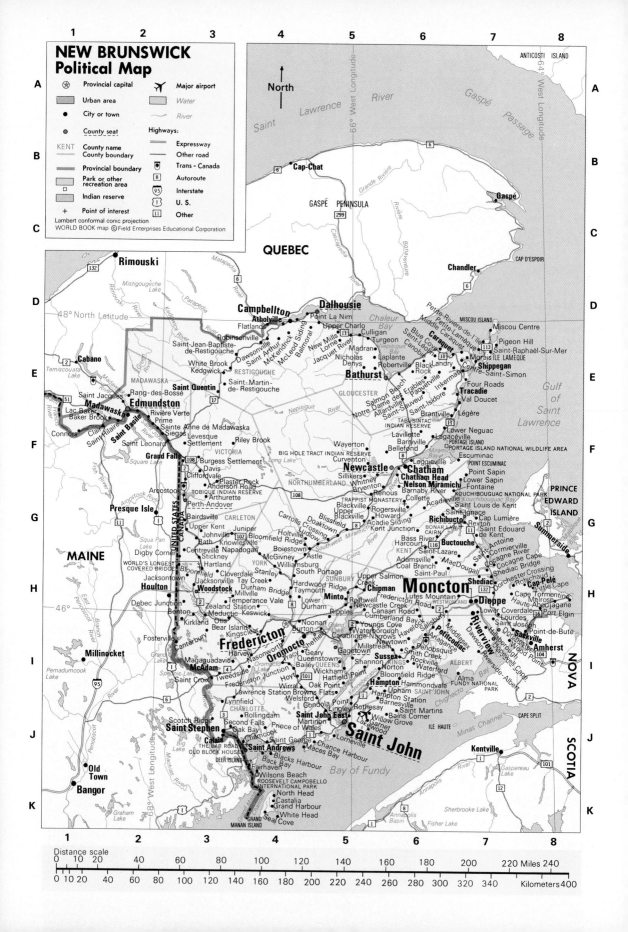

NEW BRUNSWICK Political Map

Provincial capital
Urban area
City or town
County seat
KENT   County name
County boundary
Provincial boundary
Park or other recreation area
Indian reserve
+   Point of interest

Major airport
Water
River

Highways:
Expressway
Other road
Trans – Canada
Autoroute
Interstate
U.S.
Other

Lambert conformal conic projection
WORLD BOOK map ©Field Enterprises Educational Corporation

North

ANTICOSTI ISLAND

Saint   Lawrence   River

Gaspé   Passage

Cap-Chat

GASPÉ PENINSULA

Gaspé

CAP D'ESPOIR

Chandler

QUEBEC

Rimouski

Mistigougèche Lake

Campbellton
Atholville
Flatlands
Point La Nim
Upper Charlo
Robinsonville
Saint-Jean-Baptiste-de-Restigouche
Dawsonville
White Brook
Kedgwick
Saint Arthur
McKendrick Siding
McLeod Siding
Balmoral
New Mills
Lorne
Jacquet River
Madran
Nicholas Denys
Laplante
Robertville
Black Rock
Landry

Dalhousie

MISCOU ISLAND
Miscou Centre
Pigeon Hill
Saint-Raphaël-Sur-Mer
Morais ILE LAMÈQUE
Shippegan

Chaleur   Bay

Petite-Rivière-de-l'île
Middle Caraquet
Blue Cove
Saint-Léolin
Canobie
Caraquet

Cabano
Temiscouata Lake

48° North Latitude

Culligan
Turgeon

MADAWASKA

Saint Quentin
Rang-des-Bossé
Edmundston
Madawaska
Lac Baker
Baker Brook
Connors
Saint Jacques
Rivière Verte
Prime
Sainte Anne de Madawaska
Siegas
Saint Basile
Saint Léonard
Levesque
Settlement
Riley Brook

RESTIGOUCHE

Saint-Martin-de-Restigouche

Centre-Saint-Simon

Bathurst

Tracadie
Val Doucet

Gulf
of
Saint
Lawrence

Four Roads

VICTORIA

Saint-Hilaire

Grand Falls
Burgess Settlement
Davis
Cliffordvale
Plaster Rock
Anderson Road
Arthurette
Perth-Andover
Aroostook

Wayerton
Curventon
BIG HOLE TRACT INDIAN RESERVE
Long Lake

GLOUCESTER

Salmon Beach
Notre Dame des Erables
Allardville
Saint-Sauveur
Saint-Isidore

Paquetville
Inkerman
Brantville
Légère

Lavillette
Barnyville
Belleford

TABUSINTAC INDIAN RESERVE

Lower Neguac
Lagacéville
PORTAGE ISLAND
PORTAGE ISLAND NATIONAL WILDLIFE AREA
Escuminac

Nepisiguit   River

Presque Isle

Square Lake

TOBIQUE INDIAN RESERVE

Bairdsville
Upper Kent
Johnville
Bath
Knowlesville
Centreville
Napadogan
Stickney

Newcastle
Silliker
Whitney
Bryenton

Chatham
Chatham Head
Nelson Miramichi

NORTHUMBERLAND

Renous
Barnaby River
Collette

Point Escuminac
Point Sapin
Lower Sapin
Fontaine

KOUCHIBOUGUAC NATIONAL PARK

PRINCE
EDWARD
ISLAND

MAINE

Squa Pan Lake

Aroostook River

UNITED STATES
CANADA

CARLETON

Juniper
Bloomfield Ridge

TRAPPIST MONASTERY
Blissfield
Doaktown
Blackville
Upper Blackville
Rogersville
Acadieville
Saint Louis de Kent

Kouchibouguac Bay

Carrolls Crossing
Holtville
Ludlow

Blackville
Howard
Acadie Siding
Kent Junction

Saint-Ignace
Cap Lumière
Rexton
Saint Edouard de Kent

Summerside

Digby Corner

WORLD'S LONGEST COVERED BRIDGE

Bloomfield
Cloverdale
Hartland
Williamsburg
South Portage

Astle

McGivney

Bass River
Harcourt
Saint-Lazare
Adamsville
Coal Branch
Saint-Paul

Richibucto
BONAR LAW CAIRN

Buctouche

Cormierville
Cocagne River
Cocagne Cape
Shediac Bridge

Jacksontown
Houlton

Debec Junction
Benton

Woodstock

YORK

Tay Creek
Durham Bridge
Millville
Zealand Station
Temperance Vale
Lower Durham
Ripples

Stanley
Taymouth
Hardwood Ridge
Upper Salmon Creek

SUNBURY

Minto
Chipman

Rothwell
Newcastle Creek
Canaan Road
Cumberland Bay

Moncton

KENT

MacDougall

Orchester Crossing
Cape Tormentine
Melrose
Shediac
Cap-Pelé
Little Cape

Dieppe

WESTMORLAND

Lutes Mountain
fredericton Road

Riverview

Haute-Aboujagane
Lower Coverdale
Lourdes
Saint Joseph
Dorchester
Point-de-Bute

Sackville
Amherst

Kirkland
Otis
Bear Island
Kingsclear

Fosterville

Millinocket

Pemadumcook Lake

46°

East Penobscot River

Canterbury
Magaguadavic

McAdam
Saint Croix

Tweedside
Fredericton Junction

Fredericton
Harvey
Nasonworth
Oromocto
Tracy
Sheffield
Geary
Queenstown
Bailey

Noonan
Burton
Gagetown

Cambridge-Narrows
Youngs Cove
Waterborough
Havelock
Newtown
Penobsquis
Anagance
Smith Creek
Millstream
Waterford

Salisbury
Middlesex
Petitcodiac

Dawson

Hampton
Hammondvale

Bains Corner

Alma
FUNDY NATIONAL PARK

NOVA

Haute-Aboujagane

Port Elgin

2
104

Graham Lake

Old Town

Bangor

Lynnfield

Scotch Ridge
Saint Stephen
Calais
THE BAR ROAD
OLD BLOCK HOUSE
Saint Andrews
DEER ISLAND

Rollingdam
Second Falls
Oak Bay
Prince of Wales
Chamcook
Saint George
Back Bay
Blacks Harbour
Chance Harbour
Maces Bay

Lorneville

Welsford
Lingley
Gondola Point
Rothesay
Marriton
Garnet

Saint John East

Saint John

Willow Grove
Barnesville
Saint Martins

ALBERT

SAINT JOHN

Upham

KINGS

Shannon
Norton
Hatfield Point
Bloomfield Ridge
Wickham
Oak Point
Browns Flats

Sussex

Fairhaven
Wilsons Beach
ROOSEVELT CAMPOBELLO INTERNATIONAL PARK
North Head
Castalia
Grand Harbour
White Head
Seal Cove

GRAND MANAN ISLAND

CHARLOTTE

Lawrence Station

Hoyt
Wirral

Bay of Fundy

ILE HAUTE

Minas Channel
CAPE SPLIT

Kentville

SCOTIA

Chignecto Bay

Sherbrooke Lake
Fisher Lake

Annapolis Basin

Gaspereau Lake

SEE Map scale
Distance scale
0 10 20   40   60   80   100   120   140   160   180   200   220 Miles 240
0 10 20   40   60   80   100   120   140   160   180   200   220   240   260   280   300   320   340   Kilometers 400

Population

677,250	...Census...	1976
634,557	...."....	1971
616,788	...."....	1966
597,936	...."....	1961
515,697	...."....	1951
457,401	...."....	1941
408,219	...."....	1931
387,876	...."....	1921
351,889	...."....	1911
331,120	...."....	1901
321,263	...."....	1891
321,233	...."....	1881
285,594	...."....	1871

Metropolitan Area

Saint John 112,974

Counties

Albert ....21,946..I 7
Carleton ..24,220..G 3
Charlotte .25,042..J 4
Gloucester .79,827..E 5
Kent .....28,727..G 6
Kings ....43,137..I 6
Madawaska 34,511..E 2
Northumberland ....53,134..G 4
Queens ...12,564..I 5
Restigouche 40,072..E 4
St. John ...87,039..I 6
Sunbury ..20,668..H 5
Victoria ..20,588..F 3
Westmorland 102,617..H 6
York ......70,433..H 4

Cities, Towns, and Villages

Acadie Siding .112..G 6
Acadieville ....144..G 6
Adamsville ....119..H 6
Allardville ....712..E 6
Alma ....327..I 7
Anagance ....109..I 6
Anderson Road .....149..G 3
Aroostook ....456..G 3
Arthurette ....299..G 3
Astle ....194..H 4
Atholville ..1,834..D 4
Back Bay .....567..J 4
Baie-Ste.-Anne* ...735..G 5
Bailey ....143..I 4
Bains Corner ..99..J 6
Bairdsville ....171..G 3
Baker Brook ..499..F 2
Balmoral ...1,663..D 4
Barnaby River ......87..G 6
Barnesville ....85..I 5
Barryville ....136..F 6
Bass River ...129..G 6
Bath ....864..G 3
Bathurst ..16,062.°E 6
Bear Island ...123..H 4
Belledune* ....738..D 5
Bellefond ....294..F 6
Benton ....149..H 3
Beresford* ..3,051..E 5
Bertrand* ..1,198..E 6
Blacks Harbour ..1,607..J 4
Blackville ....917..G 5
Blissfield ....130..G 5
Bloomfield Ridge .....162..I 5
Bloomfield Ridge .....218..G 4
Blue Cove ....519..E 6
Boiestown ....332..G 4
Boucher* .....800..E 2
Brantville ..1,072..F 6
Bristol* .....851..G 3
Browns Flats .262..I 5
Brynenton .....49..G 6
Buctouche ..2,546..G 7
Burton ....357.°I 4
Burtts Corner* 487..H 4
Cambridge-Narrows ...401..I 5
Campbellton 9,157..D 4
Canaan Road .130..H 6
Canobie .....149..E 6
Canterbury ...489..I 3
Cap-Bateau* .466..E 5
Cap-Lumière ..305..G 7
Cap-Pelé ...2,355..H 8
Cape Tormentine .261..H 8
Caraquet ..3,814..E 6
Carrolls Crossing ....188..G 4
Castalia .....199..K 4
Centre St. Simon ...517..E 7
Centreville ...603..G 3
Chance Harbour ....181..J 5

Charlo* ....1,268..D 4
Chatham ....7,517..F 6
Chatham Head .....1,440..F 6
Chipman ..1,962..H 5
Clair ....785..F 1
Cliffordvale ..110..F 3
Cloverdale ...133..H 3
Cocagne Cape .258..H 7
College Bridge* ...545..H 7
Collette .....178..G 6
Connors .....231..F 1
Cormierville ..194..H 7
Culligan .....55..D 5
Cumberland Bay ......246..H 6
Curventon ...144..F 5
Dalhousie ..5,593.°D 5
Darlington* ...585..E 4
Daulnay* ....539..E 6
Davis ....69..F 3
Dawson .....118..H 7
Dawsonville ..208..E 4
Debec Junction ....222..H 3
Dieppe ....7,424..H 7
Doaktown ..1,005..G 5
Dorchester ..1,120.°I 7
Dorchester Crossing ....574..H 7
Douglas* ....629..H 4
Douglastown* 1,028..F 6
Drummond* ..666..F 3
Dupuis Corner* ...218..H 8
Durham Bridge .....182..H 4
East Riverside-Kinghurst* 1,038..I 5
Edmundston 12,530.°F 2
Eel River Bridge* ...487..G 5
Eel River Crossing* .1,059..D 5
Escuminac ...134..F 7
Fairhaven ....118..J 4
Fairvale* ..3,201..I 5
Ferry Road* ..520..G 5
Flatlands ....280..D 4
Florenceville ..754..G 3
Fontaine .....318..G 7
Four Roads ...197..E 7
Fox Creek* ...488..H 7
Fredericton 44,572.°H 4
Fredericton Junction ...619..I 4
Gagetown ...647.°I 4
Garnet .....197..J 5
Geary ....1,023..I 4
Gondola Point .....1,831..I 5
Grand Bay* .2,930..I 5
Grand Falls .6,164.°F 3
Grand Falls Hill* ....559..E 2
Grand Harbour .....521..K 4
Grand Anse* .743..E 6
Hampton ..2,612.°I 5
Harcourt .....163..G 6
Hardwood Ridge .....222..H 5
Hartland ....936..H 3
Harvey .....366..I 4
Hatfield Point .....181..I 5
Haute-Aboujagane .308..H 7
Havelock ....513..H 6
Hillsborough 1,147..H 7
Holtville .....300..G 4
Hopewell Cape .....162.°I 7
Howard ....176..G 5
Hoyt ....97..I 4
Inkerman ....500..E 7
Jacksontown ..94..H 3
Jacksonville ..372..H 3
Jacquet River .718..D 5
Johnville ....115..G 3
Juniper .....585..G 3
Kedgwick ..1,257..E 3
Kent Junction ...105..G 4
Keswick .....308..H 4
Kingsclear ...132..I 4
Kirkland .....91..H 3
Knowlesville ..58..G 3
Lac Baker ....320..F 1
Lagacéville ...261..F 6
La Hêtrière* ..535..H 6
Lamèque* ....953..E 7
Landry .....268..E 6
Laplante .....240..E 5
Lavillette ....500..F 6
Lawrence Station .....221..I 3
Leech* .....515..E 6
Légère .....514..E 7
Le Goulet* ..1,155..E 7
Leighside* ...597..I 4
Lingley .....156..J 5
Little Cape ...454..H 8
Loggieville ...777..F 6
Lorne ....999..E 5
Lower Caraquet* .1,691..E 6

Lower Coverdale ......485..H 7
Lower Durham ...115..H 4
Lower Sapin ..186..F 7
Ludlow .....193..G 5
Lutes Mountain ..234..H 7
MacDougall ..148..H 7
Maces Bay ...133..J 4
Madran .....245..E 5
Magaguadavic .121..I 3
Maisonnette* ..620..E 6
Maltais* ....463..E 4
Manuels* ....546..F 6
Maugerville* ..346..I 5
McAdam ...1,960..I 3
McGivney ....232..H 4
McKendrick ..594..D 4
McLeod Siding ....307..D 4
Meductic ....165..H 3
Melrose .....144..H 8
Memramcook East* .....711..H 6
Middlesex ...246..H 6
Millstream ...100..I 6
Millville .....306..H 3
Minto .....3,654..H 5
Miscou Centre ....473..D 7
Moncton ..55,934..H 7
Nackawic* ..1,322..H 4
Napadogan ...123..G 4
Nasonworth ..158..I 4
Neguac* ...1,670..F 6
Nelson-Miramichi 1,527..F 6
New Maryland* .643..H 4
Newcastle ..6,296.°F 6
Newcastle Creek .....205..H 5
Nicholas Denys ....241..E 5
Nigadoo* ....796..E 5
North Head ..626..K 4
Norton ....1,277..I 5
Notre Dame des Érables* ...488..E 6
Oak Bay ....232..J 3
Oak Point ...100..I 5
Oromocto ..9,915..I 4
Paquetville ...690..E 6
Penobsquis ...79..I 6
Perth-Andover ...1,935.°G 3
Petit Rocher* .1,774..E 5
Petit Rocher Sud* ....538..E 6
Petitcodiac ..1,418..I 6
Petite-Lamèque ..352..E 7
Petite-Rivière-de-L'Île ....477..E 7
Pigeon Hill ..445..E 7

Plaster Rock 1,350..G 3
Point La Nim .383..D 4
Point Sapin ..349..F 7
Point-de-Bute .....199..I 8
Pointe-du-Chêne* ...484..H 7
Pointe Verte* .607..E 5
Pointe Verte* .833..E 6
Pont-Lafrance* ..856..E 6
Pont-Landry* ..562..E 6
Port Elgin ...417..H 8
Prime ....73..F 2
Prince of Wales ....131..J 5
Queenstown ..105..I 4
Quispamsis* .4,916..I 5
Rang St. George* ...485..E 6
Renforth* ..1,567..I 5
Renous .....211..G 5
Rexton .....865..G 7
Richardsville* ....892..D 4
Richibucto ..1,897.°G 7
Riley Brook ..166..F 3
Ripples .....230..H 5
Riverside-Albert ....447..I 7
Riverview ..14,069..H 7
Rivière-Verte .992..F 2
Robertville ...954..E 5
Robichaud ...350..H 7
Robinsonville ..202..E 4
Rockville ....43..I 6
Rogersville ..1,123..G 6
Rolling Dam ..124..J 4
Rothesay ...1,270..I 5
Sackville ...5,695..I 7
St. André ....309..F 3
St.-André-de-Madawaska* ..59..F 2
St. Andrews 1,684.°J 4
St.-Antoine* .1,049..H 7
St. Arthur ...521..E 4
St. Basile ..3,049..F 2
St.-François-de-Madawaska* 643..F 1
St. Edouard de Kent .....207..G 7
St. George ..1,134..J 4
St.-Hilaire ...167..F 2
St.-Ignace ...382..G 6
St.-Isidore ...477..E 6
St. Jacques .1,372..E 2
St.-Jean-Baptiste-de-Restigouche .293..E 3
St. John ..85,956.°J 5
St. Joseph ...719..H 7
St.-Lazare ...167..G 7
St.-Léolin ...694..E 6
St. Leonard 1,559..F 2
St.-Louis-de-Kent .....1,272..G 6
St.-Martin-de-Restigouche .145..E 3
St. Martins ..528..J 6
St.-Paul ....314..H 6

St. Quentin .2,225..E 3
St.-Raphaël-Sur-Mer ...588..E 7
St.-Sauveur ..626..E 6
St. Stephen .5,211..J 3
Ste. Anne de Madawaska ..1,326..F 2
Ste.-Rose-Gloucester* .479..E 6
Salisbury ..1,399..H 6
Salmon Beach 382..E 6
Saumarez* ...459..E 5
Seal Cove ...504..K 4
Second Falls .150..J 4
Shediac ...4,115..H 7
Shediac Bridge .....347..H 7
Sheffield ....112..I 5
Sheila* .....854..E 7
Shippegan ..2,317..E 7
Siegas .....393..F 2
Sillikers ....275..F 5
Smith Creek ..195..I 6
South Portage .169..H 4
Stanley .....431..H 4
Stickney .....266..H 3
Sunny Corner* 572..F 5
Sussex ....3,887..I 6
Sussex Corner* ...834..I 6
Tay Creek ...177..H 4
Taymouth ....280..H 4
Temperance Vale ......323..H 3
Tide Head* ...884..D 4
Tracadie ...2,525..E 6
Tracadie* ....869..E 6
Tracy ......650..I 4
Upham .....132..I 6
Upper Blackville ......224..G 5
Upper Gagetown* ...299..I 5
Upper Kent ..301..G 3
Upper Sheila* .748..E 7
Val-Comeau* ..495..E 6
Val d'Amour* .580..E 4
Val Doucet* ..486..E 7
Venoit* .....560..E 6
Verrett* .....900..E 2
Waterborough .126..I 5
Wayerton ....161..F 5
Welsford .....293..I 5
West End and Allison* ...1,279..I 7
Westfield* ..1,037..J 5
White Brook ..178..H 4
White Head ...97..K 4
Whitney .....282..F 5
Williamsburg .333..H 4
Willow Grove .336..J 5
Wilsons Beach .....911..K 4
Wirral .....115..I 4
Wood Point ...145..I 7
Woodstock ..4,803.°H 3
Youngs Cove ..118..H 5
Zealand Station .....442..H 4

°County seat.
*Does not appear on map; key shows general location.
Sources: Latest available census figures (1976 census, except 1971 census for unincorporated places).

Saint John, New Brunswick's Largest City, lies on the Bay of Fundy. The city's fine harbor is open all year, and ships from many parts of the world dock there. Saint John is the commercial and industrial center of the province.

New Brunswick Department of Tourism

New Brunswick Department of Tourism

Parade Watchers line a street in Shediac during the Lobster Festival. This annual event attracts visitors from many parts of New Brunswick. Lobstering is an important industry in the province.

NEW BRUNSWICK/*People*

The 1976 Canadian census reported that New Brunswick had 677,250 persons. The population had increased 7 per cent over the 1971 figure of 634,557.

More than half the people of New Brunswick live in cities and towns. About a sixth—112,974 persons—live in the metropolitan area of Saint John. Saint John has the province's only Census Metropolitan Area as defined by Statistics Canada.

Besides Saint John, New Brunswick has four cities and one town with populations of more than 10,000. They are, in order of size, Moncton, Fredericton, Bathurst, Riverview, and Edmundston. See the separate articles on the cities and towns of New Brunswick listed in the *Related Articles* section at the end of this article.

About 96 of every 100 New Brunswickers were born in Canada. Most of the others came from the United States or Great Britain. About 58 per cent of the people have English, Irish, Scottish, or Welsh ancestors. Many of them are descended from *United Empire Loyalists* (persons loyal to England who left the United States after the Revolutionary War). About 37 per cent of the people have French ancestors, and about 16 per cent speak only French. Many New Brunswickers are of Dutch or German descent. The province also has about 4,000 Indians. Most of them live on reservations along the St. John River and its branches.

More than half the people of New Brunswick, and nearly all the French-speaking population, belong to the Roman Catholic Church. Other large religious groups are Baptists and members of the United Church of Canada and the Anglican Church of Canada.

WORLD BOOK photo by Pridhams Studio of Photography Ltd.

The Main Shopping Area of Saint John, *above*, is on King Street near King Square. About a sixth of New Brunswick's people live in the metropolitan area of Saint John, the capital.

POPULATION

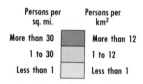

This map shows the *population density* of New Brunswick, and how it varies in different parts of the province. Population density is the average number of persons who live in a given area.

	Persons per sq. mi.	Persons per km²
More than 30		More than 12
1 to 30		1 to 12
Less than 1		Less than 1

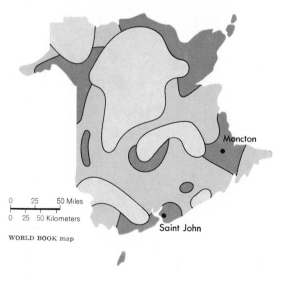

0   25   50 Miles
0   25   50 Kilometers

Moncton

Saint John

WORLD BOOK map

The University of New Brunswick's Old Arts Building was completed in 1828. It is Canada's oldest university building.

NEW BRUNSWICK / *Education*

Schools. During the 1700's, most schooling in the New Brunswick region took place in private homes. Traveling schoolteachers conducted the classes, and school was held only a few months of the year. The first schoolhouses were built of logs. New Brunswick's first *grammar* (high) school was established in Saint John in 1805. In 1816, the colonial legislature provided by law for grammar schools in every county.

During the early 1800's, schools were supported partly by the colonial government and partly by churches and other groups. In 1871, the provincial government established a free public school system and ended all church control. The schools were supported by provincial grants and by county and local taxation. In 1936, the cabinet office of minister of education was created to head the department of education.

New Brunswick law requires children between the ages of 7 and 16 to attend school. The province has about 500 public schools. About 200 of them, in French-speaking areas such as Edmundston, conduct classes in French. For information on the number of students and teachers in New Brunswick, see EDUCATION (table).

Libraries. New Brunswick has five regional public library systems, with about 35 libraries. The provincial legislative library is in Fredericton. Others include the Harriet Irving Library of the University of New Brunswick in Fredericton, the Ralph Pickard Bell Library of Mount Allison University in Sackville, and Pavillon Champlain of the University of Moncton.

Museums. The New Brunswick Museum in Saint John is Canada's oldest museum. It was founded in 1842. It has fine cultural, historical, and scientific exhibits. The Miramichi Natural History Museum in Chatham specializes in wildlife. The York Sunbury Historical Society operates a museum in Fredericton. The Beaverbrook Art Gallery in Fredericton owns works by British and Canadian artists.

UNIVERSITIES

New Brunswick has four degree-granting universities, listed below. For enrollments, see CANADA (table: Universities and Colleges).

Name	Location	Founded
Moncton, University of	Moncton	1963
Mount Allison University	Sackville	1858
New Brunswick, University of	*	1785
Saint Thomas University	Fredericton	1910

*For campuses, see CANADA (table: Universities and Colleges).

The New Brunswick Museum in Saint John is the oldest museum in Canada. It was founded in 1842. Visitors to the museum can see ship models in the Marine Section.

165

King's Landing, *left,* in Prince William, has been restored to its appearance of the early 1800's. This historic New Brunswick village includes a blacksmith shop, a sawmill, and several houses.

NEW BRUNSWICK/A Visitor's Guide

Thousands of visitors come to New Brunswick yearly. They enjoy boating and swimming off the beaches of the Bay of Fundy and the Gulf of St. Lawrence. The province's thick forests offer excellent camping facilities.

New Brunswick is one of the best fishing and hunting grounds in North America. Fishing enthusiasts cast for fighting Atlantic salmon—the prize catch—and bass, pike, and trout. In autumn, the hunting season, hunters shoot bear, deer, rabbits, and moose. They also hunt various game birds.

——— PLACES TO VISIT ———

Following are brief descriptions of some of New Brunswick's many interesting places to visit.

Barbour's General Store, in Saint John, is a restored country store that dates from the mid-1800's. Its shelves contain merchandise of this period.

Covered Bridge, over the St. John River in Hartland, is 1,282 feet (391 meters) long. It is believed to be the longest covered bridge in the world.

Huntsman Marine Laboratory and Aquarium is in St. Andrews. It features films and specimens of local marine life, including lobsters, salmon, and seals.

Islands in the Bay of Fundy. Campobello, Deer, and Grand Manan islands have excellent beaches. The islands also have fine harbors for yachting, and colorful fishing villages.

Keillor House, in Dorchester, is a large stone house built in 1813 by John Keillor, a wealthy county judge. The house, which has nine working fireplaces, is restored with furnishings and handicrafts that date from the early 1800's.

Kings Landing Historical Settlement, a restored village in Prince William, shows how the people in the region lived during the first half of the 1800's. The settlement includes a blacksmith shop, carpenter's shop, farm, sawmill, and school, as well as several houses. The village was established after the Revolutionary War in America (1775-1783) by the Kings American Dragoons. This group, a unit of the Royal Provincial Army, aided the British Army during the war.

Loyalist House, in Saint John, was built between 1810 and 1817 by David Merritt, a Loyalist from the United States. It was restored and opened in 1960.

Mactaquac is a 1,400-acre (570-hectare) park overlooking Mactaquac Dam near Fredericton. It has beaches, a marina, a camping area, and a golf course.

Magnetic Hill, near Moncton, offers a remarkable optical illusion. An automobile, left in neutral gear near what appears to be the bottom of the hill, will seemingly roll uphill to the top.

Rocks, at Hopewell Cape in Albert County, rise in fantastic forms. They are carved by tides from the Bay of Fundy.

Roosevelt Campobello International Park was the site of President Franklin D. Roosevelt's summer home. This park is on Campobello Island in the Bay of Fundy. See ROOSEVELT CAMPOBELLO INTERNATIONAL PARK.

Village Historique Acadien (Historic Acadian Village), near Caraquet, is a reconstructed settlement of Acadia from 1780 to 1880.

National Parks and Sites. New Brunswick has two national parks—Fundy and Kouchibouguac. National historic parks and sites include Carleton Martello Tower, Fort Beauséjour, and St. Andrews Blockhouse. For the areas and chief features of these parks and sites, see CANADA (National Park System).

Provincial Parks. New Brunswick has 59 provincial parks. For information on them, write to Tourism, New Brunswick, Box 12345, Fredericton, N.B., E3B 5C3.

Miller Services

Roosevelt Cottage on Campobello Island

Nick Karzes, Artstreet

Fundy National Park

ANNUAL EVENTS

New Brunswickers celebrate the landing of the American Loyalists in Saint John on May 18. A granite boulder at the harbor marks the site where the Loyalists landed in 1783. A similar stone marks their landing in Fredericton, up the St. John River.

Other annual events in New Brunswick include the following.

June-July: Miramichi Folk Song Festival in Newcastle (June); Salmon Festival in Campbellton (June); Codiac Hubbub Summer Festival in Moncton (June); Hospitality Days in Bathurst (July); Lobster Festival in Shediac (July); Fisheries Festival in Shippegan (July); Bon Ami Festival in Dalhousie (July).

August-September: International Festival in St. Stephen (August); Acadian Festival in Caraquet (August); International Hydroplane Regatta near St. Antoine (August); Mactaquac Handcraft Festival in Mactaquac Provincial Park, near Fredericton (September).

The City of Saint John

Celebration of the Loyalists' Landing in Saint John

Covered Bridge over the St. John River at Hartland
Hodgson, Miller Services

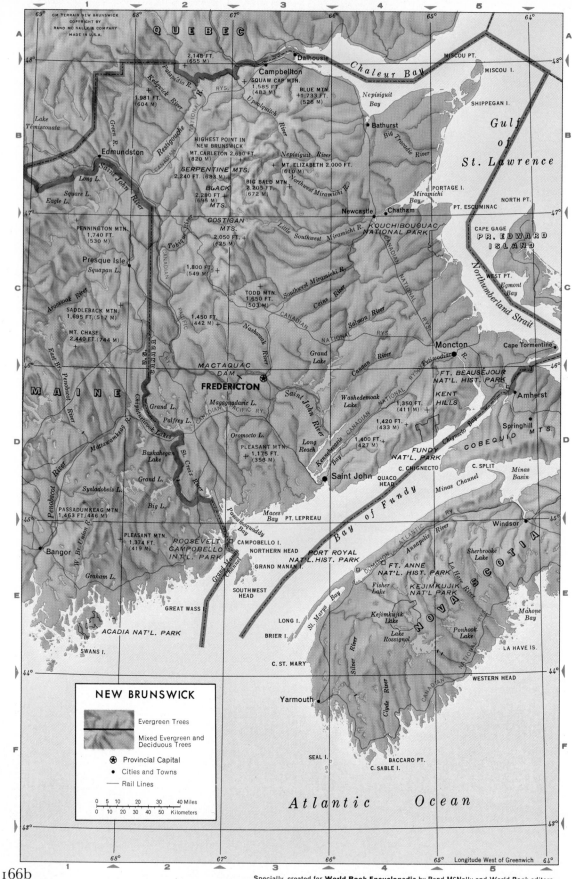

NEW BRUNSWICK

Evergreen Trees

Mixed Evergreen and Deciduous Trees

✱ Provincial Capital

• Cities and Towns

— Rail Lines

0 5 10   20   30   40 Miles
0 10 20 30 40 50 Kilometers

Specially created for **World Book Encyclopedia** by Rand McNally and World Book editors

New Brunswick Department of Tourism

New Brunswick's Most Important River, the St. John, flows through an area of rolling hills in the Appalachian Region.

NEW BRUNSWICK / *The Land*

Land Regions. New Brunswick is in the northeastern extension of the Appalachian mountain system of the eastern United States. This area is called the Appalachian Region. Most of it consists of wooded highlands with clear, swift rivers in steep valleys. The Coastal Lowlands, also part of the Appalachian Region, make up the rest of the province.

The highlands areas of the Appalachian Region consist of the Central Highlands, the Northern Upland, and the Southern Highlands. The Central Highlands are the highest section of New Brunswick. These rugged hills increase in height from the southwest to the northeast. Many rise over 2,000 feet (610 meters) above sea level. The hills include Mount Carleton, which stands 2,690 feet (820 meters) high. It is the highest point in New Brunswick. Northwest of the highlands is the flatter Northern Upland, with an elevation of about 1,000 feet (300 meters). The Southern Highlands, along

Villages Dot the Countryside in the Coastal Lowlands region of New Brunswick. These lowlands slope gently down to the east-

ern and southern coasts of the province. Trees, mostly evergreens, cover much of the land, and many rivers flow through the region.

New Brunswick Department of Tourism

NEW BRUNSWICK

the Bay of Fundy, have long ridges and valleys. Most of the hills are less than 1,000 feet (300 meters) high.

The Coastal Lowlands of the Appalachian Region are sometimes called the Eastern Plains. They slope gently down toward the east from the Central Highlands to the shores of the Gulf of St. Lawrence.

Coastline. New Brunswick has 1,410 miles (2,269 kilometers) of coastline. Deep bays and sharp inlets break the coastline in many places. The Bay of Fundy is the largest bay. Its tides are among the world's highest. The power of the tides generally keeps the bay's harbors free of ice in winter. But ice floes close ports on the Gulf of St. Lawrence. Other major bays include Chaleur, Chignecto, Miramichi, and Passamaquoddy.

Heavily wooded islands lie off the coast. Many of these coastal islands are summer resort areas. Numerous islands, many of which are only jagged rocks, lie in the Bay of Fundy. Grand Manan Island is the largest island in the bay. Miscou and Shippegan islands lie off the northeastern coast of the province.

Rivers, Waterfalls, and Lakes. No one in New Brunswick is ever far from a river. The St. John River, the longest in the province, flows 418 miles (673 kilometers). It rises in Maine, and drains the western half of New Brunswick and the lower part of the Coastal Lowlands. Its many branches include the Aroostook, Kennebecasis, and Tobique rivers. The St. Croix River forms part of New Brunswick's border with Maine. The Restigouche River forms part of the border between New Brunswick and Quebec. Other major rivers include the Miramichi, Nepisiguit, and Petitcodiac.

The great tides of the Bay of Fundy rush into the Petitcodiac River and other rivers in a high wall of water called a *bore*. This bore flows as far inland as Moncton, 20 miles (32 kilometers) away. The bore is one of the largest in the world, and sometimes rises to about 4 feet (1.2 meters). The Bay of Fundy's tides also produce the Reversing Falls at the mouth of the St. John River. At low tide, the water falls toward the sea. But high tide is so strong that it pushes the water backward over the falls. At the city of Grand Falls, the St. John River plunges 75 feet (23 meters) over a cliff.

Grand Lake, the largest lake in New Brunswick, forms an arm of the St. John River 20 miles (32 kilometers) long. Other large lakes include Magaguadavic, Oromocto, Washademoak, and the Chiputneticook chain of lakes.

Restigouche River, near Campbellton, forms part of New Brunswick's border with Quebec. New Brunswick has many large rivers.

Fish Ladder beside the falls in St. George helps fish swim upstream. New Brunswick has many waterfalls.

Hopewell Rocks, *left,* on the Bay of Fundy are worn away by strong tides.

NEW BRUNSWICK / *Climate*

New Brunswick's coastal regions have quick changes in temperature, but the seasonal differences are not so great as those inland. Saint John, on the coast, averages 20° F. (−7° C) in January and 62° F. (17° C) in July. Inland, Fredericton averages 14° F. (−10° C) in January and 67° F. (19° C) in July.

New Brunswick's record low, −53° F. (−47° C), was set at Sisson Dam on Feb. 1, 1955. The record high was 103° F. (39° C) in Nepisiguit Falls and Woodstock on Aug. 18, 1935, and in Rexton on Aug. 19, 1935.

Northern New Brunswick's *precipitation* (rain, melted snow, and other forms of moisture) averages 38 inches (97 centimeters) a year. The southern part of the province receives 44 inches (112 centimeters) a year. Snowfall averages about 96 inches (244 centimeters) a year.

Malak, Miller Services

Warm New Brunswick Summers Bring Colorful Flowers.

SEASONAL TEMPERATURES

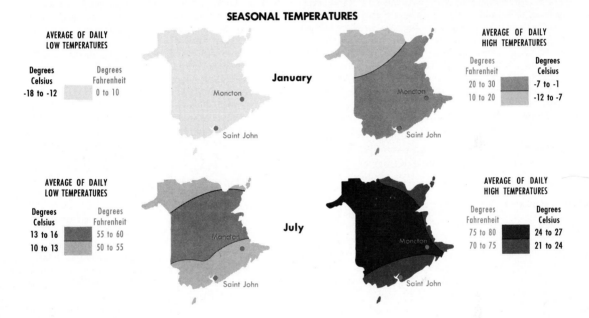

AVERAGE OF DAILY LOW TEMPERATURES

Degrees Celsius	Degrees Fahrenheit
-18 to -12	0 to 10

January

AVERAGE OF DAILY HIGH TEMPERATURES

Degrees Fahrenheit	Degrees Celsius
20 to 30	-7 to -1
10 to 20	-12 to -7

AVERAGE OF DAILY LOW TEMPERATURES

Degrees Celsius	Degrees Fahrenheit
13 to 16	55 to 60
10 to 13	50 to 55

July

AVERAGE OF DAILY HIGH TEMPERATURES

Degrees Fahrenheit	Degrees Celsius
75 to 80	24 to 27
70 to 75	21 to 24

AVERAGE YEARLY PRECIPITATION
(Rain, Melted Snow, and Other Moisture)

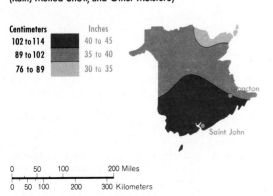

Centimeters	Inches
102 to 114	40 to 45
89 to 102	35 to 40
76 to 89	30 to 35

0   50   100   200 Miles

0   50 100   200   300 Kilometers

WORLD BOOK maps

AVERAGE MONTHLY WEATHER

	ST. JOHN					MONCTON			
	Temperatures F.°		C°		Days of Rain or Snow	Temperatures F.°		C°		Days of Rain or Snow
	High	Low	High	Low		High	Low	High	Low	
JAN.	28	12	-2	-11	14	25	7	-4	-14	11
FEB.	28	12	-2	-11	14	25	7	-4	-14	10
MAR.	37	22	3	-6	15	35	18	2	-8	11
APR.	46	32	8	0	14	46	29	8	-2	10
MAY	57	41	14	5	14	61	39	16	4	11
JUNE	65	48	18	9	14	69	47	21	8	12
JULY	70	54	21	12	14	77	55	25	13	10
AUG.	70	55	21	13	13	76	53	24	12	9
SEPT.	64	49	18	9	14	67	46	19	8	12
OCT.	55	41	13	5	13	56	36	13	2	11
NOV.	44	31	7	-1	16	42	27	6	-3	12
DEC.	32	17	0	-8	15	30	14	-1	-10	11

In the early days, the economy of the New Brunswick region was based chiefly on the fur trade and fishing. Agriculture, forestry, and shipbuilding became important during the 1800's. Today, manufacturing is New Brunswick's chief source of income.

All values given in this section are in Canadian dollars. For the value of Canadian dollars in U.S. money, see MONEY (table).

Natural Resources. Forests are New Brunswick's chief natural resource. Wilderness covers much of the land, and interferes with exploration for other purposes.

Forests cover about 85 per cent of the land area of New Brunswick—more than in any other province. Almost unbroken forest covers the central and northern parts of the province, except for a fringe of settlement along the coasts. More than two-thirds of the forest trees are evergreens. Balsam firs and spruces rank highest in commercial importance, followed by beeches, birches, cedars, maples, pines, and poplars.

Soil is not very fertile in most of New Brunswick. Farmers must use lime and fertilizers to make this soil productive. The flood plains of some rivers have a varying depth of extremely fertile black soil. Marshes and peat bogs cover parts of the east coast.

Minerals. Bituminous (soft) coal lies under the Minto-Chipman area near Grand Lake. The region south of Bathurst has about 250 million short tons (225 million metric tons) of ore that contains copper, lead, silver, and zinc. New Brunswick also has antimony, clay, coal, gypsum, manganese, natural gas, peat moss, petroleum, sand and gravel, and stone.

Plant Life. Purple violets and pink and white mayflowers carpet the forests late in spring. In summer, blackberries, blueberries, raspberries, and strawberries are plentiful. Fiddlehead ferns flourish along the muddy banks of the rivers. When one of these plants breaks through the earth, it looks like the head of a violin.

Animal Life. New Brunswick offers outstanding hunting. Forest animals include beavers, black bears, deer, martens, minks, moose, otters, rabbits, skunks, and squirrels. Game birds include ducks, geese, partridges, pheasants, and woodcocks. New Brunswick's many rivers offer excellent fishing. Anglers especially prize the Atlantic silver salmon, called the *king of game fish*. Other game fish include bass, landlocked salmon (salmon in fresh-water lakes), pike, and trout.

Manufacturing. Goods manufactured in New Brunswick have a *value added by manufacture* of about $600 million yearly. This figure represents the value created in products by New Brunswick's industries, not counting such costs as materials, supplies, and fuel.

New Brunswick's leading manufacturing activity is the production of paper and paper products, with an annual value added by manufacture of about $245 million. Huge paper and pulp mills operate in Bathurst, Campbellton, Dalhousie, Edmundston, Nackawic, Newcastle, and Saint John.

The food and beverage industry is New Brunswick's second-ranking manufacturing activity. This industry's products have an annual value added by manufacture of about $122 million. Factories produce soft drinks and process fish, dairy, and meat products and other foods. The main centers of production are in Florenceville, Moncton, and Saint John.

The manufacture of lumber and wood products is the third most important industry in New Brunswick. The province's sawmills cut about 293 million board feet (691,400 cubic meters) of lumber a year. Other important industries include the production of transportation equipment and fabricated metal products.

Mining in New Brunswick provides an annual income of about $210 million. Zinc is the greatest source of this income. Mining production increased rapidly in the province during the early 1960's. The greatest expansion took place in the region between Bathurst and Newcastle. Vast deposits of copper, lead, silver, and zinc were discovered there in 1952 and 1953. Although mining began in 1956, production did not boom until 1964.

The largest coal mines are in the Minto-Chipman field near Grand Lake. Natural gas and petroleum are produced near Moncton. Gypsum is taken in Albert County. Sand and gravel pits operate throughout the province. Other products include antimony, bismuth, cadmium, clay, gold, peat moss, stone, and sulfur.

Agriculture. New Brunswick's farm products provide an annual income of about $105 million. The province

Production of Goods in New Brunswick

Total value of goods produced in 1974—$1,011,473,000

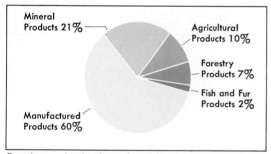

Mineral Products 21%
Agricultural Products 10%
Forestry Products 7%
Fish and Fur Products 2%
Manufactured Products 60%

Percentages are based on farm cash receipts, value added by forestry and manufacture, and value of fish, fur, and mineral production. Fur products are less than 1 per cent.
Sources: Canadian government publications, 1975 and 1976.

Employment in New Brunswick

Total number of persons employed in 1974—173,800

Economic Activities	Number of Employees
Community, Business, & Personal Services	48,400
Wholesale & Retail Trade	34,200
Manufacturing	34,000
Transportation, Communication, & Utilities	23,000
Government	15,000
Agriculture	6,000*
Finance, Insurance, & Real Estate	5,900
Fishing	4,900
Mining	2,400

*1975 figure.
Sources: *Estimates of Employees by Province and Industry, 1961-1974,* Statistics Canada; Fisheries and Marine Service, Environment Canada; Labor Force Survey Division, Statistics Canada.

FARM, MINERAL, AND FOREST PRODUCTS

This map shows where the leading farm, mineral, and forest products are produced. The major urban area (shown in red) is the province's important manufacturing center.

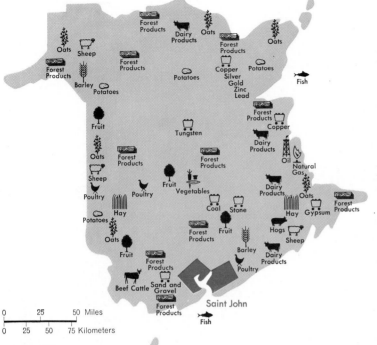

WORLD BOOK map

Wolfe Worldwide Films

Conveyors Stack Logs at a pulp mill near Saint John. Wood is the raw material for the production of paper and paper products, the leading manufacturing activity of New Brunswick.

has about 4,600 farms. They cover about 6 per cent of the land and average about 250 acres (101 hectares) in size. The best farmland lies in the valleys of the St. John River and its branches, and in the southeast.

Potatoes are the leading cash crop of New Brunswick. Most of the potatoes grow in the St. John River Valley. The province produces thousands of bushels of apples yearly. Milk and other dairy products also rank among the most important farm products of New Brunswick. Farmers raise dairy cattle throughout the province, but most dairying takes place in the better farming areas. Beef cattle and hogs are also raised in these areas. In addition, the province has poultry farms. Farmers in New Brunswick grow hay for livestock feed. They also raise oats and other grains such as barley, buckwheat, and wheat.

Forestry. Logging started in the New Brunswick region during the 1600's. The French and British navies cut tall white pine trees for masts and spars. *Masting*, as the cutting of such trees was called, employed many workers as late as the 1800's. Today, logs and pulpwood cut in New Brunswick have an annual value of about $75 million. Most of the trees cut down are balsam firs and spruces. The forests renew themselves every 20 years. This process provides continual forest growth.

Fishing Industry. New Brunswick has an annual fish catch valued at about $20 million. About half of this income comes from herring and lobster. Fishing crews also catch cod, crabs, redfish, and tuna.

Electric Power. More than half the electric power generated in New Brunswick is provided by steam

plants. Hydroelectric plants produce most of the rest. The largest hydroelectric plant, at Mactaquac Dam on the St. John River near Fredericton, began operating in December 1967.

Transportation. Charlo, Chatham, Fredericton, Moncton, and Saint John have airports. Two airlines, Air Canada and Eastern Provincial Airways, link these cities and towns with major cities in Canada and the United States.

The province has about 1,800 miles (2,900 kilometers) of main railway track. New Brunswick has about 12,500 miles (20,100 kilometers) of highways. About 6,000 miles (9,700 kilometers) of highway are paved.

Saint John is one of the few seaports of eastern Canada that are ice-free all year around. Transatlantic liners can dock at Saint John during the winter, even when ice shuts the ports on the Gulf of St. Lawrence.

Communication. The first newspaper in New Brunswick, the *Saint John Royal Gazette*, was founded in 1785. Today, the province has more than 20 newspapers, six of which are dailies. *The Telegraph-Journal* and *The Evening Times-Globe*, both of Saint John, have the largest daily circulations. *Le Progrès L'Evangeline* of Moncton is the chief French-language newspaper.

The first of New Brunswick's 12 radio stations, CFNB, began broadcasting in Fredericton in 1923. The Canadian Broadcasting Corporation sends programs overseas from its short-wave transmitter in Sackville. New Brunswick's first television station, CHSJ-TV, started in Saint John in 1954. The province now has three major television stations.

166g

Huge Ore Deposits, discovered near Bathurst in the early 1950's, boosted the economy of New Brunswick.

Fur Traders fought for control of the New Brunswick region during the 1600's. The British won complete control in 1763.

HISTORIC
NEW BRUNSWICK

Chaleur Bay

Bathurst

Jacques Cartier explored Chaleur Bay in 1534. He wrote in his journal that the land was ideal for farming.

The Aroostook War began when families from Maine and New Brunswick settled in the Aroostook Valley. A treaty signed in 1842 prevented any fighting.

Hartland

The Covered Bridge over the St. John River at Hartland probably ranks as the longest in the world. The bridge is 1,282 feet (391 meters) long.

★ FREDERICTON

A Great Forest Fire swept across about 6,000 square miles (16,000 square kilometers) of land in 1825. It burned the homes of about 15,000 settlers.

Saint John

Many American Loyalists moved to New Brunswick in 1783, after the United States separated from England.

Samuel de Champlain journeyed up the St. John River in 1604. His party arrived at the Reversing Falls.

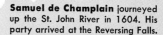

Indian Days. The first white settlers in what is now New Brunswick found Micmac and Maliseet, or Malecite, Indians living in the region. Both these tribes belonged to the Algonkian Indian family. The Micmac roamed the eastern part of the region, and the Maliseet lived in the St. John River Valley.

The Indians liked to camp downstream from waterfalls or near the farthest reaches of tidewater in rivers. These locations provided the best fishing for salmon and trout. On the coasts, the Indians caught porpoises and gathered clams and oysters. A few Indian groups also farmed, growing chiefly corn and pumpkins.

Exploration and Settlement. In 1534, the French explorer Jacques Cartier arrived in Chaleur Bay. He wrote of the New Brunswick region: "The land along the south side of it is as fine and as good land, as arable and as full of beautiful fields and meadows, as any we have ever seen...."

No further exploration took place until 1604. That year, the French explorers Samuel de Champlain and Pierre du Guast, Sieur de Monts, sailed into the Bay of Fundy. After exploring the coast, they established a settlement on St. Croix Island, near the mouth of the St. Croix River. In 1605, the settlement was moved across the Bay of Fundy to Port Royal, in what is now Nova Scotia. Throughout the 1600's, other Frenchmen arrived and established fur-trading and fishing stations. The French called the region Acadia (see ACADIA).

The Fight for Furs. The French fought among themselves for control of the valuable fur trade. The most famous struggle took place between Charles de la Tour and D'Aulnay de Charnisay. La Tour had a trading post and fort on the site of present-day Saint John. De Charnisay was a fur trader in Port Royal. In 1645, after many years of rivalry, De Charnisay attacked La Tour's fort while La Tour was absent. Marie de la Tour, the trader's wife, led the defense of the fort, but finally surrendered. De Charnisay ·forced her to watch him hang all members of the garrison except one, who served as executioner.

Competition among the French fur traders gradually gave way to rivalry between the French and the British. To the south, the British colonies were growing rapidly. Many British fishermen and fur traders were attracted to the New Brunswick region. The British conquered Acadia twice during the late 1600's. They returned it to France both times, in the Treaty of Breda (1667) and the Treaty of Ryswick (1697). After Queen Anne's War, France gave Acadia to England in the Peace of Utrecht (1713). The Acadians remained in the New Brunswick region, however. In 1755, during the last of the French and Indian Wars, the British captured the region. They drove out most of the Acadians. The Treaty of Paris (1763) confirmed British ownership of Acadia. See FRENCH AND INDIAN WARS.

English Settlement. Traders from New England arrived in Saint John in 1762. The next year, other New Englanders established the settlement of Maugerville, near what is now Fredericton. Also in 1763, the New Brunswick region became a part of the British province of Nova Scotia. Many Acadians whom the British had driven from the region were allowed to return. The Acadians received grants of lands in the north and east.

Beginning in 1783, after the American Revolutionary War, about 14,000 persons loyal to England arrived from the United States. These United Empire Loyalists, as they were called, landed in Saint John. Most of them settled in the lower St. John River Valley. They founded Fredericton. Others settled near Passamaquoddy Bay. In 1784, Great Britain established New Brunswick as a separate province. In 1785, Saint John became the first incorporated city in what is now Canada.

The timber trade and shipbuilding flourished during the early 1800's. After 1815, thousands of English, Irish, and Scottish settlers came to New Brunswick because they could not find jobs in Great Britain.

In 1825, a great forest fire blazed through about 6,000 square miles (16,000 square kilometers) in the Miramichi River region. The fire, fanned by a hurricane, destroyed the homes of about 15,000 New Brunswickers. The homeless settlers received clothing, money, and supplies from the other North American provinces, Great Britain, and the United States.

By the 1830's, about four-fifths of New Brunswick was still *crown lands* (lands owned by Great Britain). Timber traders had to pay high fees to operate in the forests. In 1833, the provincial legislature began a movement to acquire the crown lands. The British government gave the lands to New Brunswick in 1837.

The Aroostook War. Settlers from New Brunswick and Maine lived in the valley of the Aroostook River. Great Britain and the United States had never agreed on a boundary in this region, and disputes developed between the settlers. The climax came in 1839 when militiamen from New Brunswick and Maine assembled

───── **IMPORTANT DATES IN NEW BRUNSWICK** ─────

1534 The French explorer Jacques Cartier arrived in Chaleur Bay.

1604 Samuel de Champlain and Sieur de Monts of France established a settlement on St. Croix Island.

1713 France, in the Peace of Utrecht, gave the New Brunswick region to Great Britain.

1755 The British captured the New Brunswick region and expelled most of the French settlers.

1762 Traders from New England arrived in Saint John.

1763 France, in the Treaty of Paris, confirmed British ownership of the New Brunswick region.

1783 Thousands of Loyalists came from the United States to settle in New Brunswick.

1784 New Brunswick became a separate province.

1825 A great fire swept the Miramichi River region.

1842 The New Brunswick-Maine boundary dispute was settled.

1848 New Brunswick was granted self-government.

1867 New Brunswick became one of the original four provinces of the Dominion of Canada.

1890 Two national railway systems linked New Brunswick cities with Montreal.

1952 and 1953 Vast deposits of copper, lead, silver, and zinc were discovered in the Bathurst-Newcastle region.

1968 A $174-million industrial development program was completed in the Bathurst-Newcastle region and a hydroelectric plant opened at Mactaquac Dam on the St. John River near Fredericton.

New Brunswick Department of Tourism

Special Dock for Loading Ore towers over the port at Dalhousie. Huge ore discoveries near Bathurst spurred the construction of many mills and smelters in northern New Brunswick.

Ontario, and Quebec. Andrew R. Wetmore, of the Confederation party, became the first premier of New Brunswick after confederation of the provinces.

The province's fishing, lumbering, and mining industries expanded gradually. But the increasing use of iron steamships led to the end of New Brunswick's sailing-ship industry. During the 1870's and 1880's, many New Brunswickers moved to western Canada and the United States. These regions offered better job opportunities than New Brunswick did.

By 1890, two national railway systems linked cities in New Brunswick with Montreal. Saint John ranked with Halifax, N.S., as a chief winter port on Canada's east coast. But Ontario and Quebec controlled manufacturing and trade in Canada. New Brunswick's industries grew during the early 1900's. Public works programs improved communication and transportation.

The Mid-1900's. After World War II (1939-1945), the province's pulp and paper industries expanded greatly, and shipbuilding became important in the Saint John area. Huge deposits of copper, lead, silver, and zinc were discovered in the Bathurst-Newcastle region in 1952 and 1953. In 1953 and 1957, the province completed hydroelectric plants that provided additional power for mining and manufacturing.

A $174-million construction program related to the Bathurst-Newcastle metal discoveries began in 1962 and was completed by 1968. Projects in the program included chemical and fertilizer plants, docking and shipping facilities, milling and manufacturing firms, mines, and pipelines. Mining of the metal ores began to boom in 1964, when the region's largest mine started operations.

In 1968, a $120-million hydroelectric plant opened at Mactaquac Dam on the St. John River near Fredericton. More than half the power from this plant goes to industries in the Bathurst-Newcastle region.

to fight. No fighting took place, however. President Martin Van Buren sent General Winfield Scott to settle the dispute, which was called the Aroostook War. Scott arranged a truce with New Brunswick officials. In 1842, British and American authorities established the New Brunswick-Maine boundary.

As the population of New Brunswick grew, there were increasing demands for less political control by Great Britain. Political power shifted gradually from the British colonial office in London to the provincial legislature located in Fredericton. In 1848, Great Britain granted New Brunswick almost complete control over its own affairs.

Confederation and Progress. In 1864, delegates from New Brunswick, Nova Scotia, and Prince Edward Island met in Charlottetown, P.E.I., to discuss forming a united colony. Delegates from what are now Ontario and Quebec joined them and proposed a confederation of all the British provinces of eastern North America. The delegates met again later in 1864 in Quebec. They drew up a plan for Canadian confederation that led to the creation of the Dominion of Canada.

Many New Brunswickers feared they would lose their political powers in the proposed union. Samuel L. Tilley, a provincial political leader, played a major part in convincing the people that the larger provinces would not control them. On July 1, 1867, New Brunswick became one of the four original provinces of the Dominion of Canada. The others were Nova Scotia,

--- **THE PREMIERS OF NEW BRUNSWICK** ---

	Party	Term
1. **Andrew R. Wetmore**	Confederation	1867-1870
2. **George E. King**	Conservative	1870-1871
3. **George L. Hatheway**	Conservative	1871-1872
4. **George E. King**	Conservative	1872-1878
5. **John J. Fraser**	Conservative	1878-1882
6. **Daniel L. Hanington**	Conservative	1882-1883
7. **Andrew G. Blair**	Liberal	1883-1896
8. **James Mitchell**	Liberal	1896-1897
9. **Henry R. Emmerson**	Liberal	1897-1900
10. **Lemuel J. Tweedie**	Liberal	1900-1907
11. **William Pugsley**	Liberal	1907
12. **Clifford W. Robinson**	Liberal	1907-1908
13. **John D. Hazen**	Conservative	1908-1911
14. **James K. Flemming**	Conservative	1911-1914
15. **George J. Clarke**	Conservative	1914-1917
16. **James A. Murray**	Conservative	1917
17. **Walter E. Foster**	Liberal	1917-1923
18. **Peter J. Veniot**	Liberal	1923-1925
19. **John B. M. Baxter**	Conservative	1925-1931
20. **Charles D. Richards**	Conservative	1931-1933
21. **Leonard P. de W. Tilley**	Conservative	1933-1935
22. **A. Allison Dysart**	Liberal	1935-1940
23. **John B. McNair**	Liberal	1940-1952
24. **Hugh John Flemming**	Progressive Conservative	1952-1960
25. **Louis J. Robichaud**	Liberal	1960-1970
26. **Richard Hatfield**	Progressive Conservative	1970-

During the late 1960's, Premier Louis J. Robichaud, a Liberal, led the province in what he called a Program of Equal Opportunity. In this program, the provincial government took over the operation of all courts, schools, and health and welfare institutions. The action was taken to equalize the quality of services provided by such facilities throughout the province.

In 1969, the New Brunswick Legislative Assembly passed a law that made French an official language of equal status with English in the legislature itself and in courts, government offices, and schools. Later that year, the Canadian Parliament passed the Official Languages Act. This law requires federal facilities to provide service in both languages in districts where at least 10 per cent of the people speak French.

New Brunswick Today faces the problem of expanding its industry fast enough to provide jobs for its growing labor force. The province's shipping facilities were enlarged in 1970 when the first deepwater terminal

for oil tankers in North America opened near Saint John. In 1971, a terminal to handle ships that carry cargo in large metal containers opened at the port of Saint John. During the mid-1970's, the Saint John area experienced major industrial expansion. The chief projects included enlargement of the area's huge ship-building and oil refining complexes. Other plans for the area call for construction of two electric power plants, including the first nuclear power plant in the Atlantic Provinces.

Food-processing, mining, and pulp and paper industries are also expanding throughout New Brunswick. In addition, the federal government has announced plans to shift several federal departments from Ottawa to Bathurst and Moncton during the late 1970's.

J. K. Chapman, Arnold L. McAllister, and Stuart Trueman

NEW BRUNSWICK/Study Aids

Related Articles in World Book include:

BIOGRAPHIES

Anglin, Francis A.	Foster, Sir George E.
Beaverbrook, Lord	Law, Andrew Bonar
Bennett, Richard B.	Roberts, Sir Charles G. D.
Carman, Bliss	Tilley, Sir Samuel L.

CITIES AND TOWNS

Bathurst	Moncton	Saint Andrews	Sussex
Fredericton	Sackville	Saint John	

PHYSICAL FEATURES

Bay of Fundy	Passamaquoddy Bay
Campobello Island	Restigouche River
Gulf of St. Lawrence	Reversing Falls of Saint John
Miramichi River	Saint John River

OTHER RELATED ARTICLES

Acadia	Lead (graph)	United Empire Loyalist
Canada	Silver (graph)	

Outline

I. Government
   A. Lieutenant Governor
   B. Premier
   C. Legislative Assembly
   D. Courts
   E. Local Government
   F. Taxation
   G. Politics

II. People

III. Education
   A. Schools
   B. Libraries
   C. Museums

IV. A Visitor's Guide
   A. Places to Visit
   B. Annual Events

V. The Land
   A. Land Regions
   B. Coastline
   C. Rivers, Waterfalls, and Lakes

VI. Climate

VII. Economy
   A. Natural Resources
   B. Manufacturing
   C. Mining
   D. Agriculture
   E. Forestry
   F. Fishing Industry
   G. Electric Power
   H. Transportation
   I. Communication

VIII. History

Questions

Where is New Brunswick's greatest mining region? How did New Brunswick get its name?

What percentage of New Brunswickers have French ancestors? What percentage speak only French?

What is Canada's oldest museum? Where is it?

What causes the Reversing Falls?

Who was the only New Brunswicker to become prime minister of Great Britain?

Why do harbors on the Bay of Fundy remain free of ice in the winter?

Who established the first settlement in the New Brunswick region? Where? When?

What caused the Aroostook War? How was it settled?

What is New Brunswick's chief manufacturing activity?

Books to Read

Collie, Michael. *New Brunswick.* Macmillan (Toronto), 1974.

Cunningham, Robert J., and Prince, J. B. *Tamped Clay and Saltmarsh Hay: Artifacts of New Brunswick.* Brunswick Press (Fredericton), 1976.

Hayes, John F. *On Loyalist Trails.* Copp (Toronto), 1971. Fiction. For young readers.

MacNutt, W. Stewart. *New Brunswick: A History, 1784-1867.* Macmillan (Toronto), 1963.

Nowlan, Alden A. *Campobello: The Outer Island.* Clarke, Irwin (Toronto), 1975. For young readers.

Squires, W. Austin. *The Mammals of New Brunswick.* New Brunswick Museum (Saint John), 1968. *A Naturalist in New Brunswick.* 1972. *The Birds of New Brunswick.* 1976.

Sutherland, Neil. *New Brunswick: Story of Our Province.* Gage (Agincourt, Ontario), 1965.

Trueman, Stuart. *An Intimate History of New Brunswick.* McClelland (Toronto), 1970. *The Fascinating World of New Brunswick.* 1973.

NEW BRUNSWICK, UNIVERSITY OF, is a coeducational, provincially supported school with campuses in Fredericton and Saint John, N.B. The main campus, in Fredericton, offers courses in administration, arts, computer science, education, engineering, forestry, law, nursing, physical education and recreation, and science. The university grants bachelor's, master's, and doctor's degrees. It was established in 1785 as the Provincial Academy of Liberal Arts and Sciences. It assumed its present name in 1859. For enrollment, see Canada (table: Universities and Colleges).

Critically reviewed by the University of New Brunswick

NEW CALEDONIA

NEW CALEDONIA, *KAL uh DOHN yuh,* is an overseas territory of France. It consists of about 25 islands in the South Pacific Ocean (see PACIFIC ISLANDS [map]). The territory takes its name from New Caledonia, the largest and most important island. This island covers 6,530 square miles (16,913 square kilometers). The other islands cover a total of only 805 square miles (2,085 square kilometers). They include the Bélep Islands, the Chesterfield Islands, the Huon Islands, the Isle of Pines, the Loyalty Islands, and Walpole Island. The territory has a population of about 141,000.

Rugged mountains that are rich in mineral resources cover much of the island of New Caledonia. Farmers raise cattle and crops in fertile valleys and on plateaus in the interior. Nouméa—the capital, largest city, and chief port of the territory—is on the southwestern coast.

The original people of New Caledonia were Melanesians. Today, Melanesians make up about half the population. Most of the other people are Europeans of French descent or Polynesians.

Government. The French high commissioner in the Pacific serves as the governor of New Caledonia. A 35-member territorial assembly and a 5-member council assist the governor. The people elect the members of the assembly, and the assembly elects the council members.

New Caledonians are French citizens. They elect one representative to each house of the French parliament—the Senate and the National Assembly.

Economy. New Caledonia has great mineral wealth. Nickel mining and smelting are the leading industries. Other mineral resources of the territory include chromite, cobalt, iron, and manganese. Farmers raise coffee and copra for export and cattle and vegetables for local use. Mountain forests provide lumber.

Jobs are plentiful in New Caledonia, chiefly because

David Moore, Black Star

Nickel Mining provides New Caledonia with most of its income. Thousands of workers earn their living in the nickel industry.

of the nickel industry. Many workers from other South Pacific islands go to New Caledonia to find work.

History. James Cook, a British navigator, was the first European to visit New Caledonia. He arrived there in 1774. Other Europeans, including explorers, missionaries, and traders, followed. In 1853, France took control of the islands. France made New Caledonia a prison colony in 1864 and sent about 40,000 prisoners there during the next 33 years.

During the early years of French rule, the Melanesians fought to drive out the French. The last uprising took place in 1917. Since then, few New Caledonians have demanded independence. The United States had a military base on New Caledonia from 1941 to 1945 during World War II.   STUART INDER

See also CHESTERFIELD ISLANDS; LOYALTY ISLANDS; NICKEL (graph).

NEW CASTLE, Pa. (pop. 38,559), is an industrial center at the meeting point of the Shenango and Neshannock rivers, about 50 miles (80 kilometers) north of Pittsburgh. Its factories use much of the limestone, bituminous coal, sandstone, clay, and iron ore that are found in the region. Products of the city include chemicals, boxes, pottery, fireworks, and machinery.

About 1802, John Carlysle Stewart founded New Castle. It became a city in 1869. New Castle has a commission form of government.   S. K. STEVENS

NEW COMEDY. See DRAMA (Greek Drama).

NEW CONNECTICUT. See VERMONT (History).

NEW CROTON DAM is on the Croton River near New York City. It was built in 1905 to supply water to the city. The dam blocks the Croton River, and creates a lake from which water is piped to the city. The dam is 297 feet (91 meters) high and 2,168 feet (661 meters) long. See also DAM.

Jack Fields, Photo Researchers

Nouméa, the Capital of New Caledonia, is an important port and commercial center.

NEW DEAL was President Franklin D. Roosevelt's program to pull the United States out of the Great Depression in the 1930's. The New Deal did not end the depression. But it relieved much economic hardship and gave Americans faith in the democratic system at a time when other nations hit by the depression turned to dictators. Roosevelt first used the term *new deal* when he accepted the Democratic presidential nomination in 1932. "I pledge you, I pledge myself, to a new deal for the American people," he said.

When Roosevelt became President on March 4, 1933, business was at a standstill and a feeling of panic gripped the nation. The stock market crash in October, 1929, had shattered the prosperity most Americans enjoyed during the 1920's. The depression grew worse during the early 1930's. Banks, small businesses, and factories closed. Workers lost their homes and farmers lost their farms because they could not meet mortgage payments. An estimated 12 to 15 million Americans—1 out of 4 workers—had no jobs.

In his inaugural address, Roosevelt expressed confidence that the nation could solve its problems. "The only thing we have to fear is fear itself," he said.

The First Hundred Days

Roosevelt called Congress into special session on March 5, 1933. From March 9 to June 16, Congress passed a series of important laws aimed at speeding economic recovery, providing relief for victims of the depression, and making reforms in financial, business, agricultural, and industrial practices. Most of these passed swiftly and with little opposition. Never before had Congress approved so many important laws so quickly. The special session then became known as *The Hundred Days*.

The programs and policies that made up the New Deal did not come from one man. Some were Roosevelt's ideas. Others were proposed by members of the "Brain Trust," a group of unofficial presidential advisers. Congressional leaders suggested others. Some programs conflicted with each other. For example, the Economy Act cut the salaries of federal employees while the Public Works Administration increased government spending. But Roosevelt was willing to experiment and tried the ideas of one group and then another.

Helping Savers and Investors. Roosevelt's first goal was to end the banking crisis. A wave of bank failures in February had frightened the public. Depositors rushed to withdraw their money before their banks failed. Roosevelt declared a "bank holiday," closing all banks on March 6. On March 9, Congress passed the Emergency Banking Act. The new law allowed government inspectors to check each bank's records and to reopen only those banks that were in strong financial condition. Within a few days, half the nation's banks reopened. These banks held 90 per cent of the country's total deposits. This action did much to end the nation's panic.

The Glass-Steagall Banking Act of June 1933 provided further protection for investors. It gave the Federal Reserve Board more power to regulate loans made by banks and created the Federal Deposit Insurance Corporation (FDIC), which first insured bank deposits up to $2,500 and later, in July 1934, up to $5,000.

Congress passed the Truth-in-Securities Act in May, 1933. This law required firms issuing new stocks to give investors full and accurate financial information. Congress created the Securities and Exchange Com-

---

LEADING NEW DEAL AGENCIES

AAA —*Agricultural Adjustment Administration. Founded in 1933 to advise and assist farmers, and to regulate farm production.

CCC —*Civilian Conservation Corps. Founded in 1933 to provide jobs for the unemployed.

CCC —*Commodity Credit Corporation. Founded in 1933 to support the Department of Agriculture.

FCA —*Farm Credit Administration. Founded in 1933 to provide a credit system for farmers by making long-term and short-term credit available.

FCC —*Federal Communications Commission. Founded in 1934 to regulate radio, telephone, and telegraph systems.

FCIC —*Federal Crop Insurance Corporation. Founded in 1938 to provide insurance protection against unavoidable loss of certain crops.

FDIC —*Federal Deposit Insurance Corporation. Founded in 1933 to insure bank deposits.

FERA — Federal Emergency Relief Administration. Founded in 1933 to cooperate with the states in relieving hardships caused by unemployment and drought.

FHA —*Federal Housing Administration. Founded in 1934 to insure private lending companies against loss on home-mortgage loans and on loans for improving small properties.

FSA — Farm Security Administration. Founded in 1937 to help farmers buy needed equipment.

HOLC — Home Owners Loan Corporation. Founded in 1933 to grant long-term mortgage loans at low cost to homeowners in financial difficulties.

NLRB —*National Labor Relations Board. Founded in 1935 to administer the National Labor Relations Act.

NRA —*National Recovery Administration. Founded in 1933 to carry out the plans that were made by the National Industrial Recovery Act to fight depression.

NYA — National Youth Administration. Founded in 1935 to provide job training for unemployed youths and part-time work for needy students.

PWA — Public Works Administration. Founded in 1933 to increase employment and purchasing power through the construction of useful public works, such as bridges, in the various states.

REA —*Rural Electrification Administration. Founded in 1935 to aid farmers in the electrification of their homes.

SEC —*Securities and Exchange Commission. Founded in 1934 to protect the public from investing in unsafe securities and to regulate stock market practices.

SSB — Social Security Board. Founded in 1935 to secure a sound social security system.

TVA —*Tennessee Valley Authority. Founded in 1933 to help develop the resources of the Tennessee Valley.

USHA— United States Housing Authority. Founded in 1937 to aid in the development of adequate housing throughout the nation.

WPA — Works Progress Administration. Founded in 1935 to provide work for needy persons on public works projects.

*Has a separate article in WORLD BOOK.

mission (SEC) in 1934 to regulate the sale of securities and to curb unfair stock market practices.

Helping the Farmers. The Agricultural Adjustment Administration (AAA), created in May 1933, tried to raise farm prices by limiting production. The AAA used funds raised through a tax on processors of farm products to pay farmers not to produce as much as they had before. Farmers limited production by not planting crops on part of their land. The plan increased farm income, but critics said farmers should not cut food and cotton production at a time when people were hungry and needed clothing. The Supreme Court of the United States declared the AAA unconstitutional in 1936. The government then paid farmers to leave some land vacant as part of new soil conservation programs.

Helping Industry and Labor. The National Industrial Recovery Act of June 1933, was one of the most important of the new laws. This act created the National Recovery Administration (NRA) to enforce codes of fair practices for business and industry. Representatives of firms within each industry wrote the codes.

The industrial codes set minimum wages and maximum hours, and supported the right of workers to join unions. The codes primarily aided business. They allowed member firms to set standards of quality and establish the lowest prices that could be charged for goods. The Supreme Court declared the NRA unconstitutional in 1935 (see SCHECHTER V. UNITED STATES).

Helping the Needy. The Civilian Conservation Corps (CCC) launched the New Deal relief program. The CCC put young men from needy families to work at useful conservation projects, such as planting trees and building dams. The Federal Emergency Relief Administration provided the states with money for the needy. The Public Works Administration (PWA) created jobs for large numbers of people. Thousands of schools, courthouses, bridges, dams, and other useful public works projects were built through PWA projects. The Home Owners Loan Corporation (HOLC) provided money at low interest for persons struggling to pay mortgages. The Tennessee Valley Authority (TVA) built many dams to control floods and to provide electricity for residents of the Tennessee River Valley.

The Second Hundred Days

Congress approved several important relief and reform measures in 1935. These laws became the heart of the New Deal's lasting achievements. Most of the new laws were passed during the summer, and some historians call this period *The Second Hundred Days*. Some of the most important new measures were the Works Progress Administration (WPA), the National Labor Relations Act, and the Social Security Act.

Works Progress Administration provided jobs building highways, streets, bridges, parks, and other projects intended to have long-range value. It also created work for artists, writers, actors, and musicians. The WPA provided some work for about 8½ million persons.

The National Labor Relations Act guaranteed workers the right to organize unions. During the next few years, the American Federation of Labor (AFL) and the new Congress of Industrial Organizations (CIO) enrolled millions of workers in labor unions.

The Social Security Act provided pensions for the aged and insurance for the jobless. The law also provided payments for the blind and disabled and for needy children. See SOCIAL SECURITY.

The Final Measures

Roosevelt proposed a plan to add justices to the Supreme Court in 1937. Critics charged that he was trying to "pack" the court with judges who favored the New Deal. Roosevelt's plan divided the Democrats and cost him his solid support in Congress (see ROOSEVELT, FRANKLIN D. [The Supreme Court]). Congress passed only two other important reform measures after that. The first was the United States Housing Act of 1937, which provided money for more federal public housing projects. The second was the Fair Labor Standards Act of 1938, which set a minimum wage of 25 cents an hour and a maximum workweek of 44 hours, with extra pay for extra hours. It also banned children under 16 years of age from working in factories, and during school hours.

The economy faltered late in 1937. Farm prices dropped, and the number of jobless rose from about 5 million in September 1937 to almost 11 million in May 1938. The Democrats retained majorities in both houses of Congress in the 1938 elections, but Republicans gained back seats for the first time since 1928. Strong opposition in Congress forced Roosevelt to avoid further reforms, and he soon became occupied primarily with the growing threat of Nazi Germany.

Results of the New Deal

Most scholars agree the New Deal relieved much economic distress and brought about a large measure of recovery. But about 8 million Americans still had no jobs in 1940. Military spending for World War II, rather than the New Deal, brought back prosperity.

The New Deal tried to spend its way back to prosperity. It spent billions of dollars to create jobs for unemployed persons, so they could buy more and get business going normally. New Deal programs cost more money than the government received through taxes. The government borrowed much of the money it needed by selling bonds, and the federal debt grew from $22½ billion in 1933 to about $40½ billion in 1939.

The New Deal caused important political changes. The Democratic Party, generally a minority party since the Civil War, became the nation's largest political party. Its main source of strength shifted from the rural South to the urban North. Immigrants, union members, urban intellectuals, and reformers gained a stronger voice in party decisions.

Most scholars also agree that the New Deal preserved the essentials of the American free enterprise system. Profits and competition continued to play a leading part in the system. However, the program added new features. The federal government assumed responsibility for the economic security of the people and the economic growth of the nation. After the New Deal, the government's role in banking and public welfare grew steadily. Also, organized labor became an important force in national affairs.   DAVID A. SHANNON

See the separate articles listed in the table in this article; see also ROOSEVELT, FRANKLIN D.; TRUMAN, HARRY S. (The Fair Deal); LIBERTY LEAGUE.

NEW DELHI, *DEL ee* (pop. 301,801), is the capital of India. It lies close to the northern boundary of India, and is about 5 miles (8 kilometers) south and west of Delhi, the old capital. New Delhi stands on the west bank of the Jumna River, near the edge of the 74,000-square-mile (192,000-square-kilometer) Thar (or Indian) Desert. The Indian government began to irrigate the desert for farming in 1958. For the location of New Delhi, see INDIA (political map).

Description. New Delhi is an example of good city planning. Flowering trees line its flat, broad streets. The city is an administrative center. Important structures include Government House, the Parliament Building, the All-India War Memorial in Princes Park, and the great Raisina Court, which is 1,100 feet (335 meters) long and 400 feet (120 meters) wide. The Indian Supreme Court Building and the National Archives Building are also located in New Delhi.

An open-air observatory built by the astronomer-prince, Jai Singh of Jaipur, in the 1700's, still stands in New Delhi. The All-India Radio Station and the National Sports Stadium, holding 30,000 spectators, are located there.

The National Museum of India lies near the President's residence. Built in 1957, the National Museum houses art treasures of India. The city also contains many temples, historic monuments, and national institutes.

History. The seat of the Indian government was moved from Calcutta to Delhi in 1912 because: (1) Delhi had been the capital of the Mogul Empire and it seemed wise to take advantage of the traditional feeling Indians

had for Delhi; (2) Calcutta was the center of the Bengal terrorist movement, which was giving the Indian government much trouble.

Later, in 1912, government officials decided to erect the new public buildings away from the crowded conditions in the old city of Delhi. The city of New Delhi was founded for that purpose.

Work on the city continued until 1914, but was suspended during World War I (1914-1918). New Delhi was formally opened in 1931, at which time it became the capital of British India. New Delhi remained the capital after India gained its independence from Great Britain in 1947.

During World War II, New Delhi was headquarters of the Allied forces in southeastern Asia. The city is the center of celebration of India's Republic Day, held on January 26 every year since 1950.   ROBERT I. CRANE

See also DELHI; TEMPLE (picture); UNESCO (Education).

NEW DEMOCRATIC PARTY is a socialist political party in Canada. At various times during the 1960's and the 1970's, the New Democratic Party (NDP) controlled the provincial governments of British Columbia, Manitoba, and Saskatchewan. It also has had considerable influence in Ontario.

The NDP supports social-welfare policies. For example, it calls for the equal distribution of wealth among the Canadian people. The party opposes any increase in the number of foreign-owned corporations in Canada. It also opposes Canadian membership in such military alliances as the North Atlantic Treaty Organization (NATO) and the North American Air Defense Command (NORAD).

The NDP was founded in 1961. It resulted from a merger of the Co-operative Commonwealth Federation (CCF), a socialist political party, with several labor unions that belong to the Canadian Labour Congress. The congress is an association of labor unions.

During the 1960's and 1970's, the NDP achieved more in provincial elections than in national ones. It won control of the government of Manitoba in 1969 and of the government of Saskatchewan in 1971. It controlled British Columbia's government from 1972 to 1975. In the four national elections of the 1960's, the NDP ran far behind Canada's two major parties, the Liberal Party and the Progressive Conservative Party.

In the election of 1972, no party won a majority of the 264 seats in the House of Commons. The Liberals and the Progressive Conservatives each won about 110 seats, and the NDP won 31 seats. The NDP members influenced much legislation because, by allying themselves with one of the major parties, they could determine the fate of almost any bill. They used this *balance of power* to assure the passage of several social-reform bills. These bills included measures that increased government payments to unemployed people and provided greater benefits for the aged.

The NDP held the balance of power in the House until 1974. That year, the Liberals won a majority of the seats and the NDP won only 16. As a result of that election and tensions within the New Democratic Party, the party seemed to have become weak and divided.   J. L. GRANATSTEIN

Raghubir Singh, Woodfin Camp, Inc.
The Annual Republic Day Celebration in New Delhi marks the anniversary of India's establishment as a republic on Jan. 26, 1950. Many of the people at the Republic Day ceremony shown above wore special regional costumes for the occasion.

NEW ENGLAND

NEW ENGLAND forms the northeasternmost section of the United States. Captain John Smith, English explorer, gave the region its name when he explored its shores in 1614. New England includes six states: Maine, New Hampshire, Vermont, Massachusetts, Rhode Island, and Connecticut. These states have a combined area of 66,608 square miles (172,514 square kilometers). New England borders Canada on the north, the Atlantic Ocean on the east, Long Island Sound on the south, and New York on the west. All the states except Vermont lie along the Atlantic.

The Pilgrim settlers who came to New England in 1620 found a hilly, forested region with a long, jagged coast line. In general, New England is made up of a low coastal plain and two interior uplands. Several mountain ranges and river valleys separate the boulder-strewn uplands. Early-day farmers had to remove these rocks before they could till the soil. Many of the stone walls they built around their land still stand.

Of all the regions in the United States, New England is the most unified in its geography, history, and culture. Although the area consists of six states, it has developed as a unit. From its first settlement until about 1800, New England depended on agriculture, fishing, and shipping for its livelihood. During the early 1800's, the six states built up a profitable shipping trade with foreign countries. Great waves of European immigrants in the late 1800's worked in bustling factories that manufactured textiles, leather goods, and other products. Today, New England ranks as one of the nation's great manufacturing areas. It also is popular as a

Portland Chamber of Commerce

New England's Rocky Coast is dotted by many lighthouses. Portland Head Light, built in 1791, is the oldest lighthouse on the Maine coast. It rises 101 feet (31 meters) above high water.

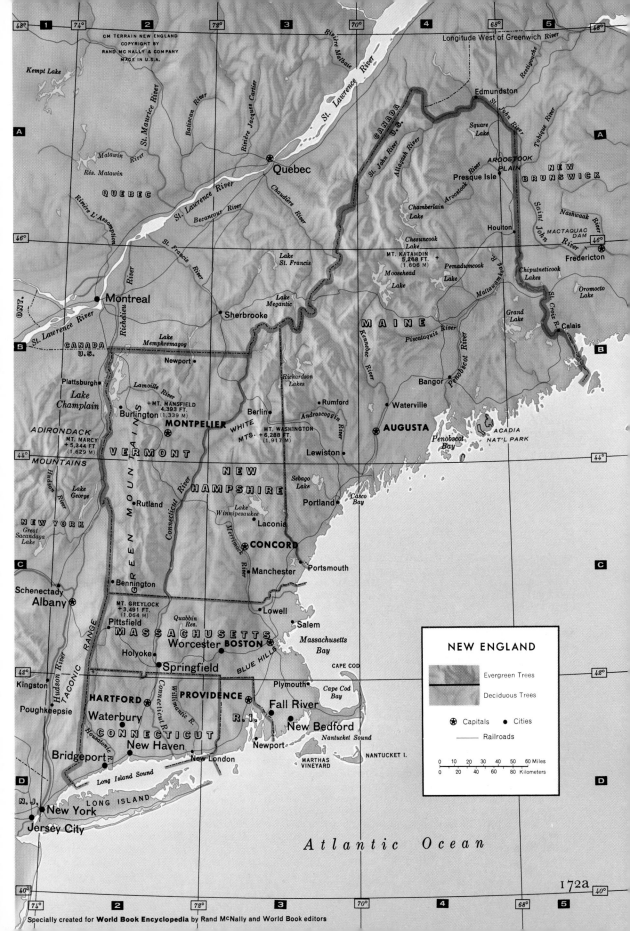

tourist and vacation center. Many interesting old villages add color to the rolling countryside.

The history of the region is rich with contributions to the American way of life. Early settlers in New England showed a strong desire for religious freedom, and for the liberty to speak, think, and write as they pleased. Their statesmen helped make these freedoms basic parts of the Constitution of the United States. New England became known as "the hotbed of the American Revolution." It played a chief part between 1765 and 1777 in defining the issues and hastening the actual hostilities of the Revolutionary War. Its people proudly recall the patriotic debates held in Boston's Faneuil Hall, the Boston Tea Party, and the famous ride of Paul Revere. The first shots of the Revolutionary War were fired at Lexington. General George Washington took command of the Continental Army in Cambridge. New England's statesmen include John Adams, John Quincy Adams, and Daniel Webster.

During the 1800's, New England became famous throughout the country for the products of its Yankee ingenuity. Peddlers sold the output of its many mills and factories, built at the fall line of rivers and streams. Famous Yankee inventions included the cotton gin, the six-shooter, the sewing machine, the telephone, and the Concord stagecoach, used in the opening of the West. The region is also rich in seafaring tradition. It produced the towering masts for the early sailing ships and the famous Yankee clippers. Whaling ships sailing from Nantucket and other ports brought back blubber to light oil lamps in American homes.

New Englanders also established the nation's first newspaper, printing press, and library, and the first college, public secondary school, and general high school. About 13 per cent of the nation's colleges and universities are in New England. These schools include such leading institutions as Amherst College, Bowdoin College, Brown University, Dartmouth College, Harvard University, Massachusetts Institute of Technology, Middlebury College, Wesleyan University, Williams College, and Yale University. New England also has about 16 per cent of the nation's scientific and research organizations.

New England has always been a center of artistic activity. It early became the home of many great libraries and museums. During the 1800's, the region produced such great writers as Emily Dickinson, Ralph Waldo Emerson, Nathaniel Hawthorne, Oliver Wendell Holmes, Henry James, Henry Wadsworth Longfellow, Henry David Thoreau, and John Greenleaf Whittier.

The Land and Its Resources

New England has no natural highway or inland waterway to the West. Its rivers run southward to the Gulf of Maine and Long Island Sound, or northward to Lake Champlain and Canada. A series of north-south mountain ranges rises between the waterways. These mountains discouraged the early settlers from developing commercial traffic with the growing Midwest and West. New England's location helped build a strong unity among its people.

Land Regions. New England has 10 natural land regions: (1) the Coastal Lowlands, (2) the Eastern New England Upland, (3) the Western New England Upland, (4) the White Mountains, (5) the Green Mountains, (6) the Taconic Mountains, (7) the Champlain Valley, (8) the Vermont Valley, (9) the Berkshire Valley, and (10) the Connecticut Valley Lowland.

The Coastal Lowlands stretch along the Atlantic Coast from easternmost Maine to westernmost Connecticut. They extend inland from 10 to 40 miles (16 to 64 kilometers) in Maine, and form the southeastern section of New Hampshire. This region covers the eastern third of Massachusetts, and includes Cape Cod, Nantucket Island, and Martha's Vineyard. The eastern two-thirds of Rhode Island and a narrow belt along the entire Connecticut coast make up the rest of the lowlands. This rolling land has many sandy beaches, rounded hills, glacial deposits, swamps, small lakes and ponds, and shallow rivers. Seaside resorts, state parks, and many cities and towns lie along the coastal plain. Excellent harbors, including those of Portland and Boston, are parts of the deeply indented coast. This area is New England's most populous and industrialized section.

The Eastern New England Upland lies west of the Coastal Lowlands. It extends southward from Maine's northern border in a wide sweep through Maine, the southern half of New Hampshire, central Massachusetts, western Rhode Island, and eastern Connecticut. This rough, hilly region is an extension of the White Mountains of New Hampshire. Its elevation varies from about 200 to 800 feet (61 to 240 meters). Small rivers cut through the land, separating its wooded hills. It is an area of many lakes, swift-flowing streams, small towns, and farm communities. The most fertile farming areas include the Aroostook Plateau of northern Maine and the New Hampshire section of the Connecticut River Valley. Many upland sections are tourist centers.

The Western New England Upland includes most of eastern Vermont, part of western Massachusetts, and almost all western Connecticut. Generally, this region is more rugged than the Eastern New England Upland. It includes the Granite Hills in Vermont, the Berkshire Hills in Massachusetts, and a section of forested hills and deep valleys in Connecticut. The region's best farmlands lie along the Connecticut River in eastern Vermont, and along the Housatonic River and its tributaries in western Vermont. The Berkshire Hills in Massachusetts are an important tourist area.

The White Mountains region includes western Maine, northern New Hampshire, and a small area of northeastern Vermont. The lofty ranges of the White Mountains include the Franconia and Presidential in New Hampshire. Their peaks usually remain snow-covered from late September to mid-May. The region has many lakes, and is a popular recreation area.

The Green Mountains region runs through the center of Vermont for the state's entire length. The peaks of this range rise more than 4,000 feet (1,200 meters) above sea level. Important deposits of asbestos, marble, and talc lie throughout the area.

The Taconic Mountains rise along half of Vermont's western border and run southward into Massachusetts. This region has many swift streams and beautiful lakes, and is noted for its scenery. Miners quarry slate and white marble in the Taconics in Vermont.

The Champlain Valley lies along the upper half of Vermont's western border. It is a region of rolling hills and low mountains that merge into fertile plains bordering Lake Champlain. Farmers raise corn, hay, potatoes, and other crops. Dolomite, slate, and red building stone come from the hills.

The Vermont Valley lies in southwestern Vermont between the Green Mountains and the Taconic Mountains. It is made up of the valleys of several small rivers, including the Batten Kill and Otter Creek. Large marble deposits may be found in the region.

The Berkshire Valley, less than 10 miles (16 kilometers) wide, extends north and south across Massachusetts in the far western part of the state. It also includes a small corner of northwestern Connecticut. The valley, drained by the Hoosic and Housatonic rivers, has many green meadows. Dairy farming is the main industry.

The Connecticut Valley Lowland is a fertile area of central Massachusetts and central Connecticut. Farmers raise onions, tobacco, and other crops on the flat, reddish land that borders the Connecticut River. This area also ranks as an important industrial region, and supplies traprock for roadbuilding.

Cities. New England has about 75 cities with populations of more than 20,000. Boston is by far New England's largest city. It serves as the manufacturing, shipping, financial, and cultural headquarters of the region. About 2,900,000 persons, or about a fourth of New England's entire population, live in Boston and the 77 other towns and cities that make up the Boston metropolitan district.

Providence ranks as New England's second largest city. It is the center of a busy manufacturing and ship-ping area. Other New England cities with populations of more than 100,000 include Cambridge, New Bedford, Springfield, and Worcester, all in Massachusetts; and Bridgeport, Hartford, New Haven, Stamford, and Waterbury, all in Connecticut.

The northern New England states of Maine, New Hampshire, and Vermont have no urban centers with 100,000 persons. Maine's largest city, Portland, has a population of 65,116. New Hampshire's largest city, Manchester, has 87,754. Burlington, with a population of 38,633, is Vermont's only city with more than 20,000 persons.

Climate. New England has long, cold winters. The average January temperature ranges from 18° F. (−8° C) in Vermont to 34° F. (1° C) in Massachusetts. In general, the northern interior regions, such as Maine's Aroostook Plateau and Vermont, have colder winter temperatures and receive more snowfall than the coastal and southern regions. Snowfall varies from about 150 inches (381 centimeters) annually in the White Mountains to about 50 inches (130 centimeters) along the coast. The brisk air, deep snows, and long winters in New Hampshire and Vermont help make these states popular winter playgrounds.

Summers are short and cool, with few hot days except in the valleys. The mountain regions generally have cooler summer days than the coastal plain. Average temperatures vary only slightly among the states, from 67° F. (19° C) in Maine, New Hampshire, and Vermont to 70° F. (21° C) in Rhode Island and Connecticut.

Maine Development Commission

White-Spired Churches, many of them built during colonial days, face the village green, or common, in many New England communities. The Congregational Church in the little fishing village and summer resort of East Boothbay, Me., was built in the early 1800's.

Eric M. Sanford

Harvard University stands beside the Charles River in Cambridge, Mass. It was founded in 1636.

Syd Greenberg, Alpha

Small Antique Shops attract many tourists. They feature articles once used by the American settlers.

Bullaty-Lomeo

A New England Potluck Dinner finds the table almost hidden under stacks of hearty, tasty food.

America's Seafaring History is displayed in the Stillman Museum at Mystic Seaport in Connecticut.

Eric M. Sanford, Alpha

Ralph Crowell Associates

A Vermont Farm is blanketed by winter's first snow. Parts of northern New England get about 10 feet (3 meters) of snow a year.

American Iron and Steel Institute

North America's First Successful Ironworks, at Saugus, Mass., was built in 1646. These restored buildings house the stone blast furnace, the forge, and the rolling mill.

Rain falls rather evenly throughout New England. Northern Maine and the Champlain Valley, with about 32 inches (81 centimeters) of rain annually, receive the least amount. The rest of New England has 32 to 45 inches (81 to 114 centimeters) of rainfall. Southern Connecticut and the higher mountain regions have the most rain.

New England's growing season ranges between 100 and 200 days. Northern Maine has between 100 and 125 frost-free days, central New England has about 150, and the coastal regions of Massachusetts, Rhode Island, and Connecticut have between 175 and 200.

Activities of the People

The People. Almost half of the people of New England live in Massachusetts, the nation's third most densely populated state. Connecticut, with the second largest share of New England's population, is the fourth most densely populated state.

The earliest settlers were Pilgrims and Puritans, who came to the region from England in the 1600's. Most of these people had a common cultural background. They were deeply religious individualists, and had a special resourcefulness and conservatism that became a strong New England tradition. The early people of New England received the nickname of *Yankees*. This name signifies their frugality, conservatism, and inventiveness. See YANKEE.

Because of New England's economic activities, personal income here exceeds the national average by 10 per cent. The people have 50 per cent more money in savings accounts, carry more life insurance, and own more home appliances than the average American. New England's savings institutions hold 20 per cent of the nation's resources kept in such banks. The region has become nationally famous for its insurance companies. New England's investment assets amount to more than 13 per cent of the country's total, making it the second most important financial center in the United States.

Manufacturing and Processing provides about a third of New England's personal income, and is the largest source of personal income. About 1,500,000 men and women work in the region's 24,000 plants and mills. Manufacturing ranks as the largest source of personal income in each of the six states. Massachusetts earns almost half of New England's personal income, and Connecticut accounts for about a third. This distribution of income-earning activities is one of New England's biggest economic problems. About four-fifths of the manufacturing activities center in the region's 26 metropolitan areas. These metropolitan areas have about three-fourths of New England's population, and have been

175

hard hit during economic recessions. This is especially true of cities whose economies depend on a single industry, such as textiles.

Raw materials for New England's plants and mills, and markets for its manufactures, lie at great distances. Long-distance hauling adds to the production costs. The region lost its top rank in the textile industry during the 1930's and 1940's, when the semiskilled labor required became available in the South and in other regions nearer the bulky raw materials. New England helped make up this economic loss by increasing its electronics and metal-fabricating industries. The value of the technical skills required in these industries more than offsets the increased transportation costs.

New England manufactures, in order of economic importance, include machinery, textiles, electrical machinery, transportation equipment; and metal, processed food, pulp and paper, and leather products. Factories in the six states make about 30 per cent of the nation's machine tools, 15 per cent of its electronics equipment, 38 per cent of its shoes, and 56 per cent of its newsprint. North America's largest single producer of newsprint operates at Millinocket and East Millinocket, Me. New England also manufactures 80 per cent of the country's sporting firearms, 80 per cent of its silverware, 50 per cent of its typewriters, 45 per cent of its cutlery, 37 per cent of its ball and roller bearings, 30 per cent of its abrasive products, and 30 per cent of its insulated wire and cable. Steel manufacturing in North America began in Hartford County, Connecticut, in 1728.

Massachusetts is a leader among the states in the production of clothing, leather, plastics, and textiles, and in printing and publishing. Rhode Island is a major glass maker and textile producer. Maine produces paper and leather.

Tourist Industry provides New England's second largest source of income. Over ten million tourists visit the region every year. Many come for the clean, crisp air, or to be lulled to sleep by the surf pounding against the craggy coast. Leading attractions include Cape Cod, the White and the Green mountains, hundreds of coastal beaches and mountain lakes, yachting harbors, and winter-sports areas. Many tourists visit Plymouth, Lexington, Concord, Salem, Boston, and other historic sites. Visitors enjoy displays of colonial and maritime life such as at Old Sturbridge Village, Mystic Seaport, the Shelburne Museum, the Old Dartmouth Whaling Museum, the Adams houses at Quincy, and the Wayside Inn. Along the way, they may visit the beautiful colonial homes that crowd the streets of Bath, Portsmouth, Newburyport, and other towns. The rural New England countryside has many charming old villages built around a common, or green, that faces a white-spired church. Luxurious resorts such as Bar Harbor, Bretton Woods, Chatham, Newport, Lenox, and Great Barrington also attract visitors.

Special New England events include the Berkshire Music Festival, several winter carnivals, maple-sugar making parties, clambakes, country fairs, fishing derbies, and autumn foliage tours.

Agriculture. Only about 1 per cent of the nation's farmland lies in New England. Most farms are small, because of the generally hilly terrain and rocky soil.

Poultry and eggs and dairy products account for almost two-thirds of the farm income. New England farms account for about 5 per cent of the value of the nation's poultry and dairy products. About 8 per cent of the United States potato crop comes from New England farms.

Several New England agricultural products are famous throughout the country. Cranberries grow in marshy bogs along the coast in Massachusetts and Maine. Massachusetts ranks as the leading cranberry-producing state. Vermont maple orchards make that state one of the country's leaders in the production of maple syrup and maple sugar. Potatoes from Maine's northern Aroostook Plateau are shipped throughout the country. Maine is a leader in potato production. Large crops of tobacco are grown under canvas shades in the fertile Connecticut Valley Lowland of Massachusetts and Connecticut.

Mining. Stone is New England's most valuable mineral product. All six states in the region produce granite. Maine and Vermont rank among the leading states in slate production. Vermont is also a major marble producer. Other important minerals include clay and sand and gravel.

Fishing Industry. New England totals about one-seventh of the nation's fish catch. Maine provides the country's largest supply of lobster. Massachusetts and New Hampshire are also leaders in lobster fishing. Important commercial fish include ocean perch, haddock, scallops, cod, flounder, whiting, pollack, and mackerel. New England plants process about four-fifths of the nation's packaged and frozen sea food.

Forest Products. New England has about 13 per cent of the country's commercial forests. Factories and mills throughout the region make boxes, wood pulp, furniture, and many other wood products.

Transportation. Shipping has been important in New England since early days. In 1786, Samuel Shaw, a New England businessman, established the first American mercantile house in China, at Canton. In 1787, the *Grand Turk* brought to Salem the first of many Oriental cargoes that, for a time, made Salem the third largest city in the nation. Between 1787 and 1790, Captain Robert Gray's *Columbia* carried the American flag around the world for the first time. His trip up the Columbia River laid the foundation for the country's claim to Oregon. It also began a very profitable trade with the northwest coast. New England ships exchanged furs from this region in China for teas and silks.

Today, Portland is New England's busiest port. About 28 million short tons (25 million metric tons) of cargo pass through the port each year. New England's next busiest ports, Boston and New Haven, together handle about 36 million short tons (33 million metric tons) of freight each year.

Early New England settlers built few roads. Boat service linked the towns along the coast and along rivers. Today, more than 95,000 miles (153,000 kilometers) of roads and highways serve the region. About 85,000 miles (137,000 kilometers) of these roadways are surfaced. Modern superhighways and toll roads link major centers. The Massachusetts Turnpike stretches from near Boston to the New York state line near Albany. The Northern Circumferential Highway swings around Boston and its suburbs from Gloucester to Cohasset. The New Hampshire Turnpike parallels the seacoast for 15 miles (24 kilometers), and the Spaulding Turnpike extends the seacoast road from Portsmouth to Rochester. The Everett Turnpike links Concord and the Massachusetts border. The Maine Turnpike extends from Kittery to Augusta. The Connecticut Turnpike runs from Greenwich to Killingly.

New England has about 6,230 miles (10,030 kilometers) of railroads. Boston is the region's main railroad center. Railroads in the area carry mostly freight and commuting passengers.

Logan International Airport, at Boston, is New England's major air center. The region has about 125 public airports, and all important cities have air service.

Regional Cooperation. New England has several regional organizations that study and seek solutions to the area's business and economic problems. The New England Council, established in 1925, is a region-wide association of manufacturers, bankers, business concerns, farmers, and representatives of labor, government, and other groups. Its programs are designed to make full use of New England's resources, and encourage development in industry, agriculture, recreation, and other fields. The New England World Trade Center promotes trade between the region's business firms and those in other countries.   HENRY F. HOWE

Related Articles. See the articles on the New England states with their lists of Related Articles. See also:

Berkshire Hills	Lake Winnipesaukee
Cape Cod	Long Island Sound
Colonial Life in America	Merrimack River
Connecticut River	Narragansett Bay
French and Indian Wars	Penobscot River
Green Mountains	Revolutionary
Housatonic River	War in America
Indian Wars	Saint John River
Lake Champlain	White Mountains

Outline

I. The Land and Its Resources
   A. Land Regions   B. Cities   C. Climate

II. Activities of the People
   A. The People   E. Mining
   B. Manufacturing and   F. Fishing Industry
      Processing   G. Forest Products
   C. Tourist Industry   H. Transportation
   D. Agriculture   I. Regional Cooperation

Questions

What states make up New England?
What is the largest source of income in New England?
Why are tourists important to New England?
What is New England's main air center?
What is one of New England's economic problems?
What is a popular nickname for New Englanders?
Who gave New England its name? When?
Why did New England's textile industry decline?
Which of the New England states has the most people?

NEW ENGLAND, DOMINION OF, was a group of English colonies in America united in 1686 by King James II of England. The colonies in the dominion were Connecticut, Massachusetts, New Hampshire, New Jersey, New York, Plymouth, and Rhode Island. King James believed the colonies could function best under a single government. But the colonists had no voice in the government, and most of them opposed the dominion. James was overthrown in England in 1688. The dominion broke up the next year, before it had begun to function completely as a government.   MARSHALL SMELSER

NEW ENGLAND COLLEGE. See UNIVERSITIES AND COLLEGES (table).

WORLD BOOK map

The New England Confederation was formed in 1643 by four New England colonies. The confederation hoped to discourage attacks by New Netherland, other nearby colonies, and Indians.

NEW ENGLAND CONFEDERATION was organized in 1643. Four colonies—Massachusetts, Plymouth, Connecticut, and New Haven—formed the UNITED COLONIES OF NEW ENGLAND, as it was called. They worked to solve boundary disputes and to meet the increased danger of attacks by the Dutch, French, and Indians. Maine, New Hampshire, and Rhode Island were excluded from membership for political and religious reasons.

The four colonies agreed to "enter into a firm and perpetual league of friendship and amity, for offence and defence, mutual advice and succor upon all just occasions, both for preserving and propagating the truth and liberties of the gospel, and for their own mutual safety and welfare."

Two commissioners from each member colony met each year to consider problems that were of mutual interest. The confederation had great power in theory, but, in practice, it could only advise. Under confederation regulations, three colonies comprised a decisive majority. A test of the confederation's power came in 1653, when Plymouth, Connecticut, and New Haven favored a war against the Dutch of New Netherland. The fourth colony, Massachusetts, did not agree and absolutely refused to yield. This action lessened the prestige of the organization. After 1664, the commissioners met only every three years, and in 1684 the confederation came to an end. Despite serious weaknesses, the confederation provided valuable experience in discussion and cooperation among the colonies. It also helped prevent the smaller colonies from being totally dominated by Massachusetts.   ALBERT E. VAN DUSEN

NEW ENGLAND CONSERVATORY OF MUSIC, in Boston, Mass., is the oldest music conservatory in the United States. It was founded in 1867. The conservatory grants the degrees of Mus.B. and Mus.M. It also grants the Undergraduate Diploma and Artist's Diploma. For enrollment, see UNIVERSITIES AND COLLEGES (table).   Critically reviewed by the
NEW ENGLAND CONSERVATORY OF MUSIC

NEW ENGLAND PRIMER. See LITERATURE FOR CHILDREN (The Puritans).

NEW FEDERALISM. See NIXON, RICHARD M.

NEW FRANCE. See CANADA, HISTORY OF.

NEW FRONTIER. See KENNEDY, JOHN F.

NEW GRANADA. See COLOMBIA (History).

NEW GUINEA

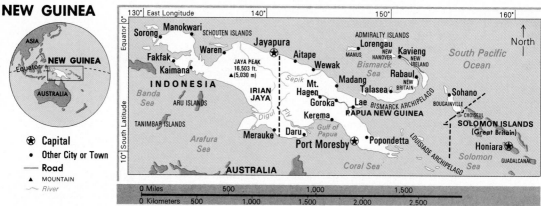

WORLD BOOK map

NEW GUINEA is a large tropical island in the Pacific Ocean, north of Australia. It ranks as the second largest island in the world. Only Greenland is larger.

New Guinea has an area of 311,796 square miles (807,548 square kilometers) and a population of about 3,389,000. Rugged, snow-capped mountains cover much of the interior of the island. In contrast, the lowlands along the northern and southern coasts are hot and humid.

Most New Guineans live in villages and supply all their own needs. Many of them lead simple lives. They build their houses of grass and sticks, wear little clothing, and fight with stone clubs and spears. Some of these people live in isolated mountain valleys and have never had contact with the outside world.

Political Units. Two political units—Irian Jaya and Papua New Guinea—occupy the island of New Guinea. Both of these units also include nearby islands.

Irian Jaya, formerly called West Irian, covers the western half of New Guinea. It is one of the provinces of Indonesia. Jayapura, a city on the northern coast, serves as the capital of the province. See INDONESIA (table: The Chief Islands; New Guinea).

Papua New Guinea occupies the eastern half of New Guinea. Formerly a territory of Australia, it became an independent nation in 1975. Port Moresby, a city on the southeast coast, serves as the nation's capital. See PAPUA NEW GUINEA.

People. Most New Guineans are Melanesians, a Pacific people who have dark skin and black, woolly hair. About 30,000 Asians, Australians, and Europeans also live on the island, most of them in coastal towns.

Most native New Guineans live in small, isolated villages in the central highlands. Other villages lie in the jungles, grasslands, and swamps of the coastal lowlands. In the highlands, most of the villagers live in round thatched huts and grow sweet potatoes as their main food. Pigs provide most of their meat. Many lowland villagers build their houses on stilts to keep them cool and dry. Their chief food crops are bananas, taro roots, and yams. People in the swamplands eat mostly sago, a starch that is taken from various kinds of palm trees.

The people of New Guinea speak more than 700 languages. Because of the number of languages, many people cannot communicate with neighbors who live only a short distance away. A growing number of eastern New Guineans speak pidgin English, a combination of English, German, and other languages. In the west, many of the people speak Malay as a second language.

Most New Guineans worship their ancestors and spirits, and many believe in magic. Some of the people are Christians or Muslims.

Missionaries operate most of the elementary schools in New Guinea. But many children, especially those in the interior, live far from schools and receive no formal education at all. The governments of Indonesia and Papua New Guinea are working to build public schools, train teachers, and provide higher education. The government of Australia also worked to upgrade education in Papua New Guinea when it controlled the territory.

The governments of both Australia and Indonesia have also taken steps to rid New Guinea of malaria, the island's most serious health problem. This campaign has sharply cut New Guinea's death rate.

Land and Climate. A great mountain system crosses New Guinea from east to west. It includes the Owen-Stanley Mountains in the east and 16,503-foot (5,030-meter) Jaya Peak, the highest point on the island, in the west. Mountain ridges, grassy plateaus, and deep, forested valleys cover much of the interior. Grasslands and jungles lie along the northern and southern edges of the island. Swamps with mangrove thickets border New Guinea in some areas.

Many streams and rivers flow down the mountain slopes and cross the lowlands. New Guinea's largest rivers, the Fly and Sepik, have large, swampy deltas near their mouths.

The coastal lowlands have a hot, humid climate. The temperature and humidity drop as the altitude increases toward the center of the island. The annual rainfall in parts of New Guinea averages more than 200 inches (510 centimeters).

Native animals of New Guinea include crocodiles, tree kangaroos, and such snakes as the death adder, the Papuan black, and the taipan. The island also has many bright-colored birds and butterflies.

The contributor of this article is Phillip Bacon, Professor and Chairman of the Department of Geography at the University of Houston.

Economy of New Guinea is one of the least developed of any area in the world. Most of the people farm the land, but they grow only enough food for their own needs. A few large plantations produce cacao, coconuts, and coffee for export. Australians and Europeans own most of the plantations.

A huge copper mine on the island of Bougainville in Papua New Guinea began production in 1972. This mine also yields enough gold to make Papua New Guinea one of the leading gold-producing areas of the world. Irian Jaya has some oil. Natural gas has been found, but it lies far from areas where it could be used to power industries.

Government leaders in New Guinea have encouraged economic development, but many New Guineans resist change. In addition, the rugged land makes the transportation of workers and materials difficult.

History. The earliest settlers in New Guinea probably migrated thousands of years ago from the Asian mainland by way of the Malay Peninsula and Indonesia. In 1526, Jorge de Meneses, the Portuguese governor of the Molucca Islands, became the first European to visit New Guinea. Dutch, English, French, and Spanish explorers stopped there during the next 300 years. The Netherlands claimed western New Guinea in 1828. In 1884, Germany gained the northeastern part of the island, and Great Britain took the southeastern part. Britain gave its territory to Australia in 1906. After Germany's defeat in World War I (1914-1918), the League of Nations made northeastern New Guinea a mandated territory under Australian rule (see MANDATED TERRITORY).

The Japanese seized northern New Guinea in 1942, during World War II, but by 1944 the Allies had reconquered the area. After the war, the northeastern part became the United Nations Trust Territory of New Guinea under Australian administration. Australia put the northeastern and southeastern units (now Papua New Guinea) under one government in 1949.

Indonesia gained independence from The Netherlands in 1949 and claimed western New Guinea. In 1962, The Netherlands agreed to turn over western New Guinea to the United Nations (UN). The UN placed the area under Indonesian administration in 1963, and Indonesia renamed it West Irian. In 1969, West Irian voted to remain part of Indonesia.

During the 1960's, some New Guineans in both West Irian and Papua New Guinea began demanding independence. In 1969, Indonesia put down an independence movement in West Irian. The province was renamed Irian Jaya in 1973. Australia granted Papua New Guinea total self-government over its internal affairs in 1973. In 1975, Papua New Guinea gained complete independence from Australia.   PHILLIP BACON

Related Articles in WORLD BOOK include:

Biak Island	New Britain
Bird of Paradise	Owen-Stanley Mountains
Bismarck Archipelago	Pacific Islands
Bougainville	Papua New Guinea
Clothing (picture:	Port Moresby
A Ceremonial Costume)	Races, Human (picture)
D'Entrecasteaux Islands	Schouten Islands
Echidna	Sculpture (Pacific Islands)
Idol (picture)	World War II (The South
Indonesia	Pacific)

APF; Department of Information and Extension Services, Port Moresby

Port Moresby, shown above, is the capital of Papua New Guinea. A deep, sheltered harbor helps make the town an important commercial center. In the picture at the right, a tribesman in a remote part of Papua New Guinea carries a ballot box to be used in a legislative election.

NEW HAMPSHIRE

THE GRANITE STATE

NEW HAMPSHIRE is a New England state noted for its natural beauty and year-round outdoor activities. In summer, vacationers flock to New Hampshire's rugged mountains, blue lakes, sandy beaches, and quiet villages. In the fall, visitors tour the countryside ablaze with brilliant red, orange, and yellow leaves. In winter, skiers race down snow-covered slopes and then warm themselves near crackling fires in friendly ski lodges. These and other attractions bring millions of tourists to tiny New Hampshire, and give the state a major source of income.

But New Hampshire is more than a vacation wonderland. New Hampshire is the home of freedom-loving, industrious people who built a prosperous state and helped form a nation.

New Hampshire was first settled in 1623, just three years after the Pilgrims landed in Massachusetts. Early New Hampshire settlers carved farms out of a wilderness and worked the land for food. Later, New Hampshirites turned their skills and their state's resources to industrial development. They cut down trees for the giant lumber and papermaking industries. They took minerals from the mountains and hills to start a mining industry. They used the rivers and lakes as sources of power for mills and factories. And they built ships along the state's small Atlantic coastline. In all, the people of New Hampshire changed a wilderness into a farming society, and then turned the farming society into a thriving industrial state.

New Hampshire and its people have played important roles in United States history. On Jan. 5, 1776, New Hampshire became the first of the 13 original colonies to adopt its own constitution. On June 21, 1788, it became the ninth state to ratify the U.S. Constitution. This act put the Constitution into effect. The U.S. Navy's first shipbuilding yard opened at Portsmouth in 1800. One of the country's first tax-supported public libraries was established at Peterborough in 1833. In 1853, Franklin Pierce of New Hampshire became the 14th President of the United States. Daniel Webster, a leading statesman and orator of the 1800's, was born in New Hampshire. So were Mary Baker Eddy, founder of the Christian Science religious movement, and Alan B. Shepard, the first American astronaut to travel in space.

New Hampshire's large granite deposits give it the nickname of the *Granite State*. Concord is the state capital and Manchester is the largest city. For the relationship of New Hampshire to other states in its region, see NEW ENGLAND.

A New Hampshire Village in Autumn

New Hampshire Harvest

New Hampshire (blue) ranks 44th in size among the states, and is the third largest of the New England States (gray).

The contributors of this article are Albert S. Carlson, former Professor of Geography at Dartmouth College; J. Duane Squires, author of The Story of New Hampshire; *and Paul H. Tracy, Managing Editor of the* Manchester Union Leader.

——————— FACTS IN BRIEF ———————

Capital: Concord.

Government: *Congress*—U.S. senators, 2; U.S. representatives, 2. *Electoral Votes*—4. *State Legislature*—senators, 24; representatives, 400. *Counties*—10.

Area: 9,304 sq. mi. (24,097 km²), including 277 sq. mi. (717 km²) of inland water; 44th in size among the states. *Greatest Distances*—north-south, 180 mi. (290 km); east-west, 93 mi. (150 km). *Coastline*—13 mi. (21 km).

Elevation: *Highest*—Mount Washington, 6,288 ft. (1,917 m) above sea level. *Lowest*—sea level, along the Atlantic Ocean.

Population: *Estimated 1975 Population*—818,000. *1970 Census*—737,681; 41st among the states; distribution, 56 per cent urban, 44 per cent rural; density, 79 persons per sq. mi. (31 persons per km²).

Chief Products: *Agriculture*—apples, beef cattle, dairy products, eggs, greenhouse and nursery products. *Fishing Industry*—cod, flounder, lobsters, shrimp. *Manufacturing*—electrical machinery, food products, instruments, leather and leather products, nonelectrical machinery, paper and paper products, printed materials, rubber and plastics products, textiles. *Mining*—clays, gemstones, sand and gravel, stone.

Statehood: June 21, 1788, the ninth state.

State Motto: *Live Free or Die.*

State Songs: "Old New Hampshire." Words by John F. Holmes; music by Maurice Hoffmann. "New Hampshire, My New Hampshire." Words by Julius Richelson; music by Walter P. Smith. "New Hampshire Hills." Words by Paul Scott Mowrer; music by Tom Powers.

181

Constitution of New Hampshire was adopted in 1784. It replaced a temporary constitution adopted in 1776. Constitutional amendments may be proposed by a three-fifths vote of each house of the state legislature, or by a constitutional convention. To become law, a proposed amendment needs the approval of two-thirds of the persons voting on the issue in an election.

A majority of the members of both houses of the legislature may propose a constitutional convention. The proposal must be approved by a majority of the citizens voting on it. In the absence of a proposal, the question of holding a convention must be voted on by the people every 10 years.

Executive. The governor of New Hampshire holds office for a two-year term. He may be re-elected any number of times. The governor receives a salary of $34,070 a year. For a list of all the governors of New Hampshire, see the *History* section of this article.

The executive branch of the New Hampshire government is somewhat unusual. The state has no lieutenant governor. But it does have a five-member executive council. Members of the executive council are elected by the people to two-year terms, and serve as advisers to the governor. The major executive officials appointed by the governor must be approved by the council. These officials include the adjutant general, attorney general, commissioner of agriculture, and comptroller. The New Hampshire legislature elects the secretary of state and state treasurer to two-year terms.

Legislature is called the *General Court*. By law, it consists of a 24-member Senate and a 400-member House of Representatives. The U.S. House of Representatives is the only legislative body in the country with more members than the New Hampshire house. New Hampshire's towns and *wards* (divisions of cities) send from one to 11 legislators to the House of Representatives, depending on their populations. Representatives serve two-year terms. Voters in each of the 24 senatorial districts elect one senator to a two-year term. Senatorial districts are also based on population. In 1965, the legislature *reapportioned* (redivided) all districts to give more equal representation based on population. The districts were redrawn again in the early 1970's.

The legislature meets on the first Wednesday of January in odd-numbered years. Legislators receive a fixed salary for regular sessions. Their allowance for travel expenses ends after July 1 or 90 business days, whichever comes first. Legislators are paid for 15 business days during special sessions of the General Court. The governor or the General Court can call special sessions of the legislature.

Courts. The Supreme Court of New Hampshire has a chief justice and four associate justices. The next lower court, the superior court, has a chief justice and 12 associates. A probate judge presides over each of the state's 10 probate courts, one in each county. In 1963, New Hampshire began replacing its 85 municipal courts with 37 district courts. The governor, with approval of the executive council, appoints all state and local judges. Judges may serve until they are 70 years old.

Local Government in New Hampshire operates as one of the purest forms of democracy in the world. The state's 222 towns are nicknamed "little republics." They are so named because they have almost complete self-government. Each year, the voters assemble for a town meeting at which they can participate directly in governmental decisions. Voters elect town officials, approve budgets, and decide on other local business. The chief town administrative officials are three *selectmen*. One selectman is chosen each year for a three-year term.

New Hampshire's 13 incorporated cities use either the mayor-council or city-manager form of government. The cities have *home rule*. That is, they are free to write and amend their own charters. Each of the state's 10 counties also has its own government. County officials include the sheriff, attorney, treasurer, register of deeds, register of probate, and county commissioners. These officials are elected to two-year terms.

Taxation provides about two-thirds of the state government's income. The other third comes from the federal government. Taxes on the sale of motor fuels, alcoholic beverages, tobacco products, restaurant meals,

State of New Hampshire

The Governor's Mansion stands in eastern Concord. The house was once owned by Styles Bridges, who served as governor of New Hampshire from 1935 to 1937. Bridges donated the mansion to New Hampshire in 1969. Previous governors had lived in homes rented by the state.

The State Seal

Symbols of New Hampshire. On the state seal, a reproduction of the Revolutionary War frigate *Raleigh* is surrounded by a laurel wreath to symbolize victory. The date 1776 is the year the state's first constitution was adopted. On the state flag, adopted in 1909, a copy of the state seal is surrounded by nine stars in a laurel wreath. This shows that New Hampshire was the ninth state to ratify the United States Constitution.

Seal, flag, and flower illustrations, courtesy of Eli Lilly and Company

The State Flag

and on motel and hotel room rates bring in a large share of the state's revenue. Other important sources of government revenue include license fees and taxes on business profits, and horse racing. New Hampshire also has a sweepstakes lottery to help pay public school costs.

Politics. New Hampshire became a Republican state shortly before the Civil War. Until 1850, the state usually voted Democratic. But most of New Hampshire's people opposed slavery and then became Republicans.

Republicans usually control the state legislature. Since 1856, most New Hampshire governors and U.S. Senators and Representatives have been Republicans. Republicans have won New Hampshire's electoral votes in all but six presidential elections since 1856. In 1964, the state voted Democratic in a presidential election for the first time in 20 years. For the state's electoral votes and voting record in presidential elections, see ELECTORAL COLLEGE (table).

State Capitol is in Concord, the capital since 1808. The building dates from 1819. Earlier capitals included Portsmouth (1679-1774), Exeter (1775-1781), and Concord (1782-1784).

New Hampshire Division of Economic Development

The State Bird
Purple Finch

The State Flower
Purple Lilac

The State Tree
White Birch

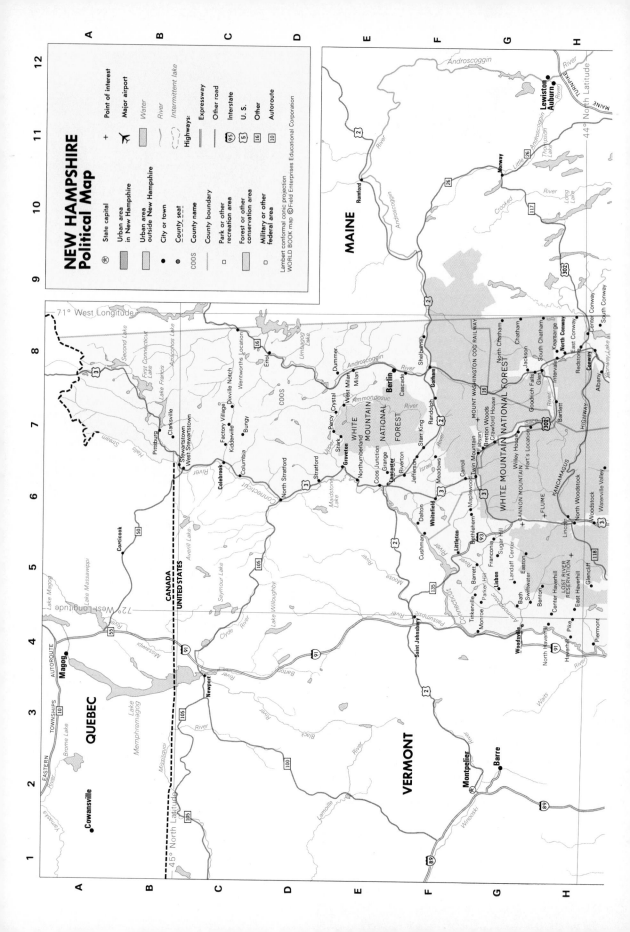

NEW HAMPSHIRE
Political Map

⊛	State capital
	Urban area in New Hampshire
	Urban area outside New Hampshire
●	City or town
●	County seat
COOS	County name
	County boundary
□	Park or other recreation area
	Forest or other conservation area
□	Military or other federal area

+	Point of interest
✈	Major airport
	Water
	River
	Intermittent lake

Highways:
	Expressway
	Other road
95	Interstate
5	U.S.
16	Other
10	Autoroute

Lambert conformal conic projection
WORLD BOOK map ©Field Enterprises Educational Corporation

QUEBEC

MAINE

VERMONT

CANADA
UNITED STATES

COOS

WHITE MOUNTAIN NATIONAL FOREST

MOUNT WASHINGTON COG RAILWAY

KANCAMAGUS HIGHWAY

LOST RIVER RESERVATION

Lewiston
Auburn
Norway
Rumford
Montpelier
Barre
Berlin
Gorham
Littleton
Whitefield
Lancaster
Groveton
Colebrook
Pittsburg
Clarksville
Lisbon
Woodsville
Conway
North Conway
Saint Johnsbury
Cowansville
Magog
Coaticook
Newport

44° North Latitude
45° North Latitude
71° West Longitude
72° West Longitude

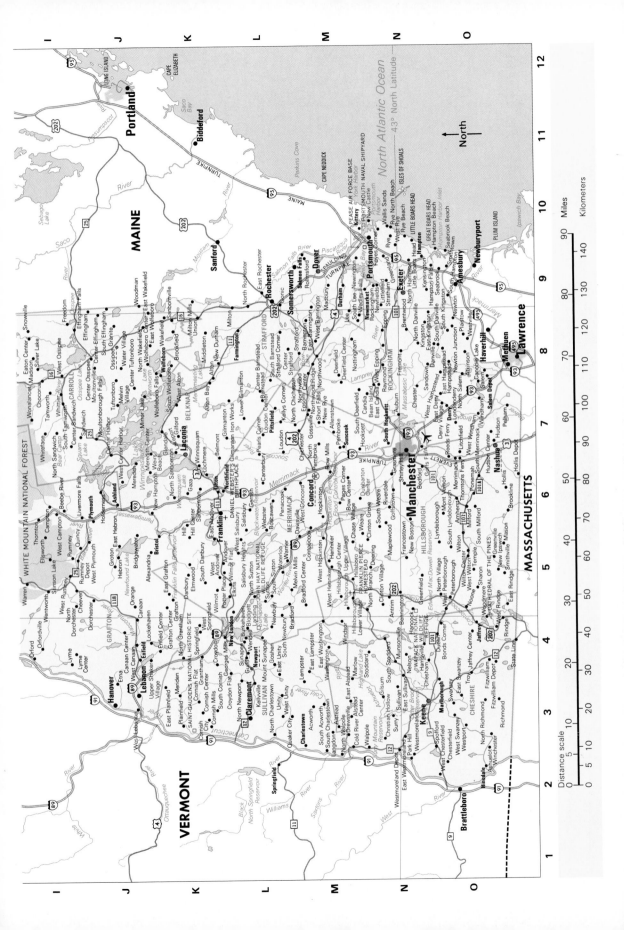

Population

818,000	Estimate	1975
737,681	Census	1970
606,921		1960
533,242		1950
491,524		1940
465,293		1930
443,083		1920
435,572		1910
411,588		1900
376,530		1890
346,991		1880
318,300		1870
326,073		1860
317,976		1850
284,574		1840
269,328		1830
244,161		1820
214,460		1810
183,858		1800
141,885		1790

Metropolitan Areas

Lawrence-Haverhill
(Mass.) ... 258,564
(221,208 in Mass.)
37,356 in N.H.)
Lowell (Mass.) ... 218,268
(212,860 in Mass.
5,408 in N.H.)

Counties

Belknap	32,367	K 7
Carroll	18,548	J 7
Cheshire	52,364	O 3
Coos	34,291	D 7
Grafton	54,914	J 4
Hillsborough	223,941	N 5
Merrimack	80,925	L 6
Rockingham	138,951	N 8
Strafford	70,431	L 4
Sullivan	30,949	L 3

Cities and Towns

Acworth .459▪ K 3
Albany .259▪ H 8
Alexandria .466▪ J 5
Allenstown 2,732▪ M 7
Alstead 1,185▪ M 3
Alton 1,647▪ K 8
Alton Bay K 8
Amherst 4,605▪ N 5
Andover 1,138▪ L 5
Antrim 2,122▪ N 5
Ashland 1,391 (1,599▪) J 6
Ashuelot O 2
Atkinson 2,291▪ O 8
Auburn 2,035▪ N 7
Barnstead 1,119▪ L 7
Barrington 1,865▪ M 8
Bath .607▪ H 4
Bedford 5,859▪ N 6
Beebe River J 6
Belmont 2,493▪ K 7
Bennington .639▪ N 4
Benton .194▪ H 4
Berlin 15,256▪ E 8
Bethlehem 1,142▪ G 6

Boscawen 3,162▪ L 6
Bow* 2,479▪ L 6
Bradford 1,362▪ L 5
Brentwood .679▪ L 8
Bretton Woods G 7
Bridgewater .398▪ J 6
Bristol 1,670▪ (1,080) J 5
Brookfield .184▪ K 8
Brookline 1,167▪ O 5
Campton 1,171▪ J 6
Canaan 1,923▪ J 4
Candia 1,997▪ N 7
Canobie Lake O 8
Canterbury .895▪ L 6
Carroll .310▪ F 7
Cascade E 8
Center Harbor 540▪ J 7
Center Ossipee J 8
Center Sandwich J 7
Charlestown 3,274▪ N 3

Chatham .134▪ G 8
Chesham N 4
Chester 1,382▪ N 7
Chesterfield 1,817▪ O 2
Chichester 1,083▪ M 7
Chocorua H 8
Christian Hollow N 3
Claremont 14,221▪ M 3
Clarksville .166▪ B 7
Colebrook 2,094▪ C 7
Columbia .467▪ C 7
Concord 30,022▪○ M 6
Contoocook L 6
Conway 1,489 (4,865▪) H 8
Coos Junction H 4
Cornish* 1,268▪ K 3
Crawford House G 7
Croydon .396▪ K 4
Dalton .425▪ F 5
Danbury .489▪ K 5
Danville 1,778▪ O 8
Deerfield 1,179▪ M 7
Deering .924▪ N 5
Derry 6,090 (11,712▪) N 7
Dorchester .144▪ J 4
Dover 20,850▪○ M 8
Dublin .895▪ O 4
Dummer .225▪ E 8
Dunbarton Center .825▪ M 6
Durham 7,221 (8,869▪) M 8

East Andover L 5
East Derry N 7
East Hampstead O 7
East Haverhill H 4
East Kingston 838▪ O 8
East Lempster L 3
East Swanzey O 3
East Wolfeboro K 8
Easton .92▪ G 5
Eaton .221▪ H 8
Effingham .360▪ J 8
Effingham Falls J 8
Elkins L 5
Ellsworth .13▪ I 5
Enfield 1,408 (2,345▪) K 4
Epping 1,097 (2,356▪) M 8
Epsom 1,469▪ M 7
Etna J 4
Exeter 6,439 (8,892▪)○ N 8
Fabyan G 7
Factory Village G 7

Farmington 2,884 (3,588▪) L 8
Fitzwilliam 1,362▪ O 4
Fitzwilliam Depot O 4
Francestown .525▪ N 5
Franconia .655▪ G 6
Franklin 7,292▪ L 6
Freedom .993▪ J 8
Freemont F 5
Georges Mills K 4
Gilford 3,160▪ K 7
Gilmanton 1,171▪ L 7
Gilmanton Iron Works L 7
Gilsum .570▪ N 3
Glen H 8
Glencliff H 5
Glendale K 7
Goffstown 9,284▪ N 6

Goodrich Falls H 8
Gonic L 8
Gorham 2,020 (2,998▪) F 8
Goshen .395▪ L 4
Gossville M 7
Grafton .370▪ K 5
Grantham .366▪ K 4
Grasmere N 6
Greenfield 1,058▪ N 5
Greenland 1,784▪ N 9
Greenville 1,332 (1,587▪) O 5
Groton .467▪ J 5
Groveton 1,597 E 7
Guild L 4
Hampstead 2,401▪ O 8
Hampton 5,407 (8,011▪) N 9
Hampton Beach N 9
Hampton Falls 1,254▪ N 9
Hancock .909▪ N 4
Hanover 6,147 (8,494▪) J 4

Harrisville .584▪ O 4
Haverhill 3,090▪○ H 4
Hebron .234▪ J 5
Henniker 2,348▪ M 5
Hillsborough 1,784 (2,234▪) M 5
Hinsdale 3,276▪ O 2
Holderness 1,059 J 6
Hollis 1,048▪ O 5
Hooksett 2,616▪ N 6
Hopkinton 1,303 (5,564▪) L 6
Hudson 3,007▪ O 6
Hudson Center 10,638▪ O 6
Intervale H 8
Jackson .404▪ G 8
Jaffrey 1,922 (3,353▪) O 4
Jefferson .714▪ F 7
Kearsarge H 8
Keene 20,467▪○ O 3
Kellys Corner M 8
Kellyville L 4
Kensington 1,044▪ N 8
Kingston 2,882▪ O 8
Laconia 14,888▪○ K 7
Lakeport K 7
Lancaster 3,166▪○ F 6
Landaff Center 292▪ G 5
Langdon .332▪ M 3
Lebanon 9,725▪ J 3

Lee 1,481▪ M 9
Lempster .360▪ M 3
Lincoln 1,341▪ H 6
Lisbon 1,247 G 6
Litchfield 1,480▪ O 7
Little Boars Head N 9
Littleton 1,420▪ (4,180) G 5
Livermore [5,290▪] land
Livermore Falls F 5
Lochmere K 7
Lochaven K 6
Londonderry 5,346▪ O 7
Loudon 1,707▪ L 7
Lower Gilmanton L 7
Lyme 1,112▪ J 4
Lyndeborough 789▪ N 5
Madbury .704▪ M 9
Madison .572▪ J 8
Manchester 87,754▪ N 7
Maplewood G 6
Marlborough 1,231 (1,670▪) O 3
Marlow .390▪ M 3
Mason .518▪ O 5
Meadows F 7
Melvin Mills L 7
Melvin Village J 7
Meredith 1,017 (2,904▪) J 7
Meredith Center J 7
Meriden K 3
Merrimack 8,595▪ O 6
Middleton .430▪ K 8
Milan .713▪ E 8
Milford 6,622▪ O 5
Milton 1,859▪ L 8
Milton Mills L 8
Mirror Lake K 8
Monroe .385▪ G 4
Mont Vernon .906▪ N 6
Moultonborough* 1,310▪ J 8
Moultonborough Falls J 7
Mount Sunapee L 4
Moultonville J 8
Munsonville N 4
Nashua 55,820▪○ O 6
Nelson .304▪ N 4
New Castle 1,975▪ N 10
New Durham 583▪ K 8
New Hampton 946▪ J 6
New Ipswich 1,803▪ O 5
New London 1,347 (2,236▪) L 5
New Rye L 4
Newbury .509▪ L 4
Newfields .843▪ N 8
Newington .798▪ N 9
Newmarket 2,645 (3,361▪) N 8
Newport 5,128▪ (5,899▪)○ L 4
Newton .136▪ (1,920▪) O 8
Newton Junction O 8
Noone O 4
North Branch M 5
North Chatham G 8
North Chichester M 7
North Conway 1,723 H 8
North Hampton 3,259▪ N 9
North Haverhill H 4
North Richmond O 3
North Rochester L 8
North Salem O 8
North Sanbornton J 6

North Sandwich J 7
North Stratford D 6
North Village M 5
North Walpole M 2
North Woodstock H 6
Northfield, see Tilton
Northfield* [-Northfield]
Northumberland 2,193▪ K 6
Northwood 2,493▪ E 6
Northwood Ridge M 8
Nottingham .952▪ M 8
Orange .376▪ J 5
Orford 1,384▪ J 4
Orfordville L 7
Ossipee 1,647▪○ J 8
Pages Corner M 6
Park Hill 213▪ G 2
Parker Hill L 7
Pearls Corner E 7
Pelham 5,408▪ O 7
Pembroke 4,261▪ M 7
Penacook L 6
Percy E 7
Peterborough 2,078 (3,807▪) N 4
Piermont .462▪ H 4
Pike H 4
Pittsburg .726▪ B 7
Pittsfield 1,662 (2,517▪) L 7
Plainfield 1,323▪ K 3
Plaistow 4,712▪ O 8
Plymouth 3,109 (4,225▪) J 6
Ponemah O 6
Portsmouth 25,717▪ N 10
Potter Place L 5
Quaker City J 4
Quincy O 6
Randolph .169▪ F 7
Raymond 3,003▪ N 8
Redstone H 8
Reeds Ferry O 6
Richmond .287▪ O 3
Rindge 2,175▪ O 4
Riverton E 8
Rochester 17,938▪ L 8
Rollinsford 2,273▪ M 9
Roxbury .161▪ N 3
Rumney .870▪ J 5
Rye Beach N 10
Rye 4,083▪ N 10
Salem 20,142▪ O 8
Salem Depot O 8
Salisbury .589▪ L 6
Salisbury Heights L 6
Salmon Falls M 9
Sanbornton 1,022▪ K 6
Sanbornville .741▪ K 8
Sandown .843▪ O 8
Sandwich .666▪ J 7
Seabrook 5,128▪ N 9
Sharon .136▪ O 4
Shelburne .199▪ F 8
Shirley Hill N 6
Short Falls M 7
Smithtown O 8
Snowville J 8
Somersworth 9,026▪ M 9
South Danbury K 5
South Danville O 8
South Hampton 558▪ O 9
South Hooksett N 6
South Lyndeboro N 5
South Merrimack O 6
South Newbury L 4
South Weare N 6

South Wolfeboro K 8
Spofford O 3
Springfield .310▪ K 4
Stark .343▪ E 7
Starr King F 7
State Line L 8
Stewartstown 1,008▪ B 7
Stoddard .242▪ N 4
Strafford .965▪ M 8
Stratford .980▪ C 8
Stratham 1,512▪ N 8
Sugar Hill .336▪ G 5
Sullivan .376▪ N 3
Sunapee 1,384▪ L 4
Surrook O 4
Sutton .642▪ L 5
Swanzey 4,254▪ O 3
Tamworth 1,054▪ J 8
Temple .441▪ O 4
Thornton .594▪ I 6
Thorntons Ferry O 6
Tilton [-Northfield] 2,579▪ K 6
Tilton K 6
Tinkerville H 8
Troy 1,123 (1,713▪) O 3
Tuftonboro 910▪ J 7
Twin Mountain G 7
Union L 8
Unity .709▪ L 3
Wadley Falls M 9
Wakefield 1,420▪ K 8
Wallis Sands N 10
Walpole 2,966▪ N 2
Warner 1,441▪ L 5
Warren .539▪ I 5
Washington .248▪ M 4

Waterloo L 5
Waterville H 7
Weare 1,854▪ N 6
Webster .680▪ L 6
Weirs Beach K 7
Wendell L 4
Wentworth 376▪ I 5
Wentworths Location .37▪ C 8
West Chesterfield O 2
West Epping M 8
West Lebanon J 3
West Milan E 7
West Ossipee J 8
West Peterborough N 4
West Rumney J 5
West Swanzey 998▪ O 3
Westmoreland N 2
Westport O 3
Westville O 8
Whitefield 1,538▪ F 6
Whitefield .441▪
Whittier J 8
Willey House G 7
Wilmot .516▪ K 5
Wilton 1,123 (2,420▪) O 5
Winchester 2,276▪ O 3
Windham 2,869▪ O 7
Windsor .43▪ M 4
Winnisquam K 7
Wolfeboro 1,718 (3,036▪) K 8
Wolfeboro Center K 8
Woodmere .897▪ H 4
Woodstock 1,336▪ G 4
Woodsville H 4

*Does not appear on the map; key shows general location.
▪Entire town (township), including rural area.
○County seat.
Sources: Latest census figures (1970 and special censuses).
Places without population figures are unincorporated areas
and are not listed in census reports.

UNIVERSITIES AND COLLEGES

New Hampshire has 13 universities and colleges
accredited by the New England Association of
Schools and Colleges. For enrollments, see UNI-
VERSITIES AND COLLEGES (table).

Name	Location	Founded
Colby-Sawyer College	New London	1943
Dartmouth College	Hanover	1769
Franconia College	Franconia	1965
Franklin Pierce College	Rindge	1962
Mount Saint Mary College	Hooksett	1934
Nathaniel Hawthorne College	Antrim	1962
New England Aeronautical Institute	Nashua	1965
New England College	Henniker	1946
New Hampshire, University of	*	*
New Hampshire College	Manchester	1966
Notre Dame College	Manchester	1950
Rivier College	Nashua	1933
St. Anselm's College	Manchester	1889

*For campuses and founding dates, see UNIVERSITIES AND
COLLEGES (table).

The 1970 United States census reported that New Hampshire had 737,681 persons. The population had increased about 21 per cent over the 1960 census figure, 606,921. The U.S. Bureau of the Census estimated that by 1975 the population had reached about 818,000.

About 56 of every 100 New Hampshirites live in urban areas. Almost half the people of New Hampshire live in the state's 13 incorporated cities. Manchester and Nashua form New Hampshire's two Standard Metropolitan Statistical Areas (see METROPOLITAN AREA). Manchester is the state's largest city. The Lawrence-Haverhill, Mass., metropolitan area extends into Rockingham County, New Hampshire. The Lowell, Mass., metropolitan area also extends into Hillsborough County, New Hampshire.

In addition to Manchester, New Hampshire's 12 other incorporated cities, in order of size, are: Nashua, Concord (the capital), Portsmouth, Dover, Keene, Rochester, Berlin, Laconia, Claremont, Lebanon, Somersworth, and Franklin. See the separate articles on New Hampshire cities that are listed in the *Related Articles* at the end of this article.

About 95 out of every 100 persons in New Hampshire were born in the United States. Many New Hampshirites are descendants of settlers who came from Canada and many European countries. The early settlers of New Hampshire came chiefly from the British Isles—England, Ireland, Scotland, and Wales. After the Civil War, thousands of French Canadians and European immigrants came to New Hampshire to work in the state's mills, shops, and factories.

Roman Catholics make up New Hampshire's largest single religious body. The largest Protestant groups include Baptists, Episcopalians, Methodists, and members of the United Church of Christ.

New Hampshirites, like other New Englanders, have long been called *Yankees*. This nickname calls to mind certain traits that are traditionally associated with the people of New England. These traits include business ability, thrift, conservatism, and inventiveness. See YANKEE.

POPULATION

This map shows the *population density of New Hampshire*, and how it varies in different parts of the state. Population density is the average number of persons who live in a given area.

Persons per sq. mi.	Persons per km²
More than 150	More than 58
70 to 150	27 to 58
30 to 70	12 to 27
Less than 30	Less than 12

Manchester
Nashua

0   25   50 Miles
0   25   50   75 Kilometers
WORLD BOOK map

Schools. The New Hampshire educational system dates from colonial days, when children of the settlers attended one-room schoolhouses. Some of these early schoolhouses still stand. Today's public schools operate under laws passed in 1789 and revised in 1919. A seven-member state board of education and a commissioner of education govern the public school districts.

The governor and the executive council appoint the board of education members. The board elects the commissioner of education. Members of school district boards are elected locally. Profits from the state sweepstakes lottery pay a small part of public school costs.

Children between the ages of 6 and 16 must attend school if they live in a district that has a high school. If their district has no high school, children must attend school until they are 14 years old. For the number of students and teachers in New Hampshire, see EDUCATION (table).

Dartmouth, New Hampshire's oldest college, ranks among the 10 oldest universities and colleges in the United States. It was chartered in 1769.

Libraries. In 1833, Peterborough founded a free, tax-supported, public library. Many historians believe that this was the first library of its kind in the United States. But others claim that a library founded in Salisbury, Conn., was the first. Today, almost every New Hampshire town has a library. The State Library Bookmobile Service is used by many small communities and rural areas. The largest New Hampshire libraries include the Baker Library at Dartmouth College in Hanover; the University of New Hampshire Library in Durham; the State Library in Concord; the Portsmouth Athenaeum; and the public library of Manchester.

Museums. The Morse Museum in Warren exhibits mounted animals from many parts of the world. The state's finest collection of paintings is in Manchester's Currier Gallery of Art. The Manchester Institute of Arts and Sciences has another noted collection of paintings. The New Hampshire Historical Society in Concord has four rooms with furnishings from colonial times.

NEW HAMPSHIRE / *A Visitor's Guide*

Visitors to New Hampshire enjoy a great variety of recreational activities in six major vacation areas: the White Mountains region, the Lakes area, the Seacoast region, the Merrimack Valley area, the Monadnock region, and the Dartmouth-Lake Sunapee area. The beautiful White Mountains, in the north, attract skiers, hikers, campers, and sightseers. The skiing season generally lasts from mid-December to mid-March. The Lakes area of central New Hampshire provides fun for water-sports enthusiasts. The Seacoast region of the southeast has several beaches along the Atlantic Coast. Also in the southeast is the Merrimack Valley area, where most of New Hampshire's chief cities are located. The Monadnock region, in the southwest, includes many natural beauty spots and some of the state's most interesting towns and villages. Many historic sites and educational institutions are in the Dartmouth-Lake Sunapee area, in the west.

Loran Percy
Profile Mountain at Franconia Notch

Winter Carnival, Dartmouth College

Sanford Photo Associates
Dick Smith
Mount Washington Cog Railway

PLACES TO VISIT

Following are brief descriptions of some of New Hampshire's most interesting places to visit.

Cathedral of the Pines is an interdenominational outdoor place of worship at Rindge. In 1957, Congress made this shrine to the nation's war dead a national memorial.

Daniel Webster's Birthplace, between Salisbury and Franklin, is a two-room cabin set in scenic surroundings. The cabin houses many mementos of the orator.

Flume is a *chasm* (deep, narrow valley) 800 feet (240 meters) long at Franconia Notch. Visitors can view scenic wilderness on a $\frac{1}{2}$-mile (0.8-kilometer) tour through the Flume.

Franklin Pierce Homestead, at Hillsboro, is a large two-story house where President Pierce spent his early years. Built in 1804, it has furniture, utensils, and imported wallpaper from the period.

Kancamagus Highway, a 34$\frac{1}{2}$-mile (55.5-kilometer) road between Lincoln and Conway, offers spectacular views of mountains, forests, and streams.

Mount Washington Cog Railway, near Fabyan House, runs to the top of Mount Washington. The railway, which is 2$\frac{3}{4}$ miles (4.43 kilometers) long, rises 3,625 feet (1,105 meters). Completed in 1869, it was the first cog railway in North America.

Profile Mountain, or CANNON MOUNTAIN, features a rock formation that looks like the side view of an old man's face. The formation, called the *Old Man of the Mountain*, stands about 48 feet (15 meters) high. It was made famous by Nathaniel Hawthorne's short story "The Great Stone Face."

Strawbery Banke, in Portsmouth, is a restored colonial seaport. It features homes built in the 1700's and 1800's, craft shops, and historical exhibits.

National Forest. The White Mountain National Forest, established in 1911, lies in north-central New Hampshire. Part of it extends into Maine. For the area and chief features of this forest, see NATIONAL FOREST (table).

State Parks and Forests. New Hampshire has 32 state parks and 6 state forests. Many of the parks have lakes and groves of stately trees, especially white birch. For information on the state parks and forests of New Hampshire, write to Director, Division of Parks, Department of Resources and Economic Development, P.O. Box 856, Concord, N.H. 03301.

Ski Lift Near Laconia

Daniel Webster's Birthplace Near Franklin

Flume at Franconia Notch

Eric Sanford

Sanford Photo Associates

Arthur Griffin

ANNUAL EVENTS

Many of New Hampshire's most popular annual events are sports contests. Summer months feature yacht regattas and races. Winter attractions include ski races, dog-sled races, and winter carnivals. The state's best-known annual events include the Winter Carnival held in early February at Dartmouth College in Hanover, and the League of New Hampshire Craftsmen's Fair held in early August in Newbury. Other annual events include:

January-March: Winter Carnivals in Berlin, Durham, Hanover, Manchester, Newport, and other communities (January and February); Annual World's Sled Dog Derby in Laconia (February).

April-June: Fast Day, statewide legal holiday honoring provincial governor John Cutt (fourth Monday of April); All-State Music Festival (no fixed date or place); Apple Blossom Festival in the Monadnock region (May).

July-October: Regatta races on lakes (July and August); Old Home Week, statewide (August); Annual summer fairs (at various places, August through October 12); Fall Foliage Tours, statewide (late September to mid-October).

The White Sand of Hampton Beach Chamber of Commerce

The White Sand of Hampton Beach attracts visitors who swim in the surf and enjoy the brisk, salt-tanged air of New Hampshire's Atlantic Coast.

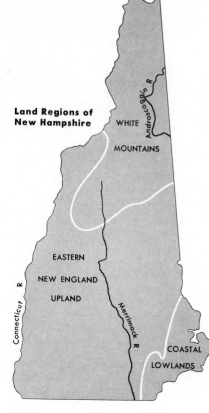

Land Regions of New Hampshire

WHITE

MOUNTAINS

Androscoggin R

Connecticut R

EASTERN

NEW ENGLAND

UPLAND

Merrimack R

COASTAL

LOWLANDS

Land Regions. New Hampshire has three main land regions: (1) the Coastal Lowlands, (2) the Eastern New England Upland, and (3) the White Mountains Region.

The Coastal Lowlands cover the extreme southeastern corner of the state. It is part of a larger land region of the same name that covers the entire New England coast. In New Hampshire, the region extends from 15 to 20 miles (24 to 32 kilometers) inland from the Atlantic Ocean. Along the coast, beaches provide popular recreational areas. Rivers winding through the Coastal Lowlands help supply hydroelectric power for the region's many industrial plants.

The Eastern New England Upland covers most of the southern, eastern, and western parts of New Hampshire. The entire Eastern New England Upland stretches from northern Maine to eastern Connecticut. In New Hampshire, the region consists of three areas: (1) the Merrimack Valley, (2) the Hills and Lakes area, and (3) the New Hampshire portion of the Connecticut River Valley.

The Merrimack Valley extends northward from the Massachusetts border to central New Hampshire. It is named for the swift Merrimack River, which winds through the hilly, uneven valley. Large crops of hay and fruits grow in the rich soil between the hills. Many of New Hampshire's chief mill and factory towns are in the Merrimack Valley.

The Hills and Lakes area surrounds the Merrimack Valley on the east, north, and west. It extends in a broad half-circle from Maine almost to the Vermont border. Here, most of New Hampshire's large lakes nestle among forested hills.

The Connecticut River Valley stretches in a long narrow strip down New Hampshire's western border. The Connecticut River flows through the area for 211 miles (340 kilometers). Rich farmland lies in the lowlands. Hardwood forests cover the hills. Hydroelectric plants supply power for public utilities. Their dams form long lakes in the valley.

The White Mountains Region lies north of the Eastern New England Upland. Here, rugged mountains rise sharply from wide flat areas

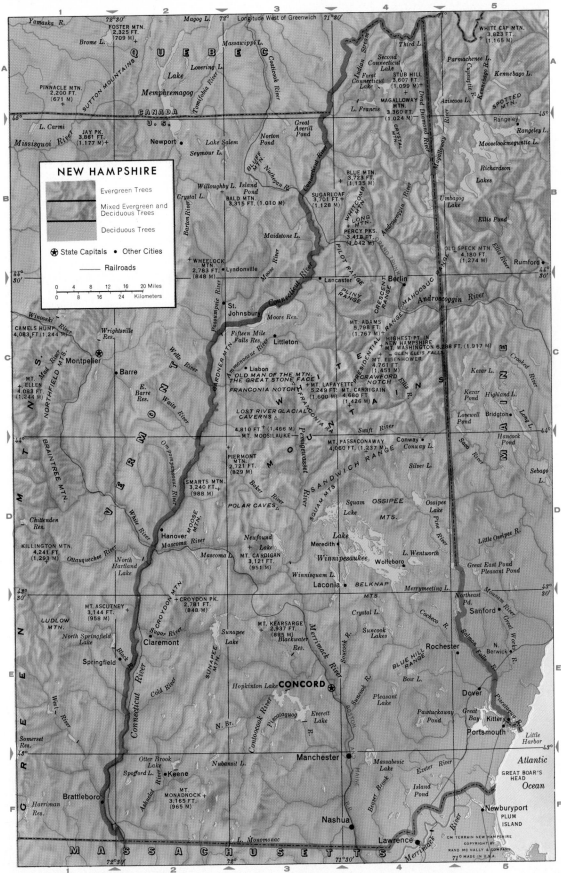

Dick Smith

Franconia Notch, a broad canyon in New Hampshire's White Mountains Region, separates the Kinsman and Franconia ranges. It has many attractions, such as Profile Mountain and the Flume.

Hampton, Rye, and other beaches lie along the shore. A group of islands called the Isles of Shoals lies 9 miles (14 kilometers) offshore. Four—Lunging, Seavey, Star, and White—belong to New Hampshire. The others are part of Maine.

Mountains. The Presidential Range of the White Mountains has the highest peaks in New England. Mount Washington (6,288 ft., or 1,917 m) is the highest mountain in this 86-peak range. Several other peaks in the Presidential Range are more than 1 mile (1.6 kilometers) high. These include Mount Adams (5,798 ft., or 1,767 m), Mount Jefferson (5,715 ft., or 1,742 m), Mount Clay (5,532 ft., or 1,686 m), Mount Monroe (5,385 ft., or 1,641 m), and Mount Madison (5,363 ft., or 1,635 m). The Franconia Range, also in the White Mountains, includes famous Profile, or Cannon, Mountain. Each year, thousands of sightseers view the remarkable profile of an old man's face caused by a rock formation near the mountaintop.

New Hampshire's mountains include five *monadnocks.* A monadnock is made up of rock that did not wear down when all the land around it was leveled by erosion. The monadnocks are Mount Moosilauke (4,810 ft., or 1,466 m), Mount Monadnock (3,165 ft., or 965 m), Mount Cardigan (3,121 ft., or 951 m), Mount Kearsarge (2,937 ft., or 895 m), and Sunapee Mountain (2,743 ft., or 836 m).

Rivers and Lakes. New Hampshire's chief rivers rise in the mountainous north. The Connecticut River begins near the Canadian border and flows generally southward. It separates New Hampshire and Vermont. After leaving New Hampshire, the 407-mile (655-kilometer) river cuts across Massachusetts and empties into Long Island Sound. The Pemigewasset River flows south from Franconia Notch. The swift Merrimack River is formed where the Pemigewasset meets the Winnipesaukee River at Franklin. The Merrimack flows south into Massachusetts. The Androscoggin and Saco rivers flow through northeastern New Hampshire, and then cross into Maine. The Piscataqua River, in the southeast, forms part of the New Hampshire-Maine border and empties into Piscataqua Bay.

About 1,300 lakes lie scattered throughout New Hampshire's hills and mountains. The largest, Lake Winnipesaukee, covers about 72 square miles (186 square kilometers) and has many islands. Other lakes include Ossipee, Squam, Sunapee, Umbagog (partly in Maine), and Winnisquam.

that were lakes thousands of years ago. Spruce, fir, and yellow birch provide wood for New Hampshire's paper mills. The towering White Mountains attract summer and winter tourists.

An area of forest-covered hills in Coos County forms the northernmost part of New Hampshire's White Mountains Region. Lumbering and paper manufacturing are this area's chief industries. Dairy and potato farms thrive in the west.

Coastline. New Hampshire has a general coast along the Atlantic of only 13 miles (21 kilometers). This is the shortest coastline of any state bordering an ocean.

Lake Winnipesaukee at Center Harbor nestles in a valley dotted with farms and surrounded by hills. The lake and valley are part of the Hills and Lakes region. The lake, largest in the state, covers about 72 square miles (186 square kilometers).

Dick Smith

NEW HAMPSHIRE /Climate

New Hampshire has cool summers with low humidity. In winter, heavy snow falls in much of the state. January temperatures average about 16° F. (−9° C) in the north and about 22° F. (−6° C) in the south. The state's lowest temperature, −46° F. (−43° C), was recorded at Pittsburg near First Connecticut Lake on Jan. 28, 1925. July temperatures average about 66° F. (19° C) in the north and 70° F. (21° C) in the south. The state's highest temperature, 106° F. (41° C), was recorded at Nashua on July 4, 1911. New Hampshire gets about 42 inches (107 centimeters) of *precipitation* (rain, melted snow, and other moisture) a year. Average yearly snowfall ranges from about 50 inches (130 centimeters) near the Atlantic Ocean to over 100 inches (250 centimeters) in the north and west.

Dick Smith

Mount Washington Has Sudden Storms. The strongest winds ever measured at the earth's surface—188 mph (303 kph)—struck here on April 12, 1934. One gust reached 231 mph (372 kph).

SEASONAL TEMPERATURES

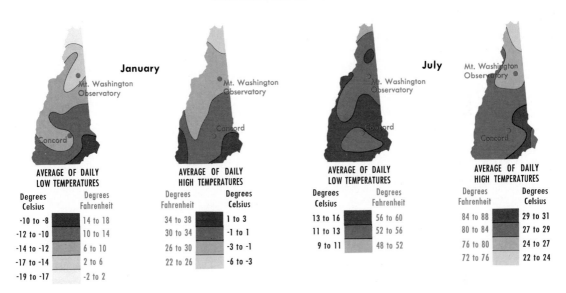

January

Mt. Washington Observatory

Concord

AVERAGE OF DAILY LOW TEMPERATURES

Degrees Celsius	Degrees Fahrenheit
-10 to -8	14 to 18
-12 to -10	10 to 14
-14 to -12	6 to 10
-17 to -14	2 to 6
-19 to -17	-2 to 2

AVERAGE OF DAILY HIGH TEMPERATURES

Degrees Fahrenheit	Degrees Celsius
34 to 38	1 to 3
30 to 34	-1 to 1
26 to 30	-3 to -1
22 to 26	-6 to -3

July

Mt. Washington Observatory

AVERAGE OF DAILY LOW TEMPERATURES

Degrees Celsius	Degrees Fahrenheit
13 to 16	56 to 60
11 to 13	52 to 56
9 to 11	48 to 52

AVERAGE OF DAILY HIGH TEMPERATURES

Degrees Fahrenheit	Degrees Celsius
84 to 88	29 to 31
80 to 84	27 to 29
76 to 80	24 to 27
72 to 76	22 to 24

AVERAGE YEARLY PRECIPITATION
(Rain, Melted Snow and Other Moisture)

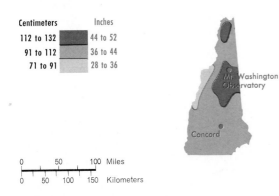

Centimeters	Inches
112 to 132	44 to 52
91 to 112	36 to 44
71 to 91	28 to 36

Mt. Washington Observatory

Concord

```
0        50       100 Miles
0    50    100    150 Kilometers
```

WORLD BOOK maps

AVERAGE MONTHLY WEATHER

	CONCORD					MT. WASHINGTON OBSERVATORY			
	High	Low	High	Low	Rain or Snow		High	Low	High	Low	Rain or Snow

	Temperatures F° High	Temperatures F° Low	Temperatures C° High	Temperatures C° Low	Days of Rain or Snow		Temperatures F° High	Temperatures F° Low	Temperatures C° High	Temperatures C° Low	Days of Rain or Snow
JAN.	32	9	0	-13	11	JAN.	14	-3	-10	-19	18
FEB.	33	10	1	-12	9	FEB.	14	-3	-10	-19	17
MAR.	43	21	6	-6	10	MAR.	20	4	-7	-16	19
APR.	56	30	13	-1	11	APR.	29	15	-2	-9	18
MAY	69	41	21	5	10	MAY	42	29	6	-2	17
JUNE	78	50	26	10	10	JUNE	51	38	11	3	16
JULY	83	55	28	13	10	JULY	55	43	13	6	17
AUG.	80	53	27	12	10	AUG.	53	42	12	6	15
SEPT.	72	45	22	7	10	SEPT.	47	35	8	2	15
OCT.	62	34	17	1	9	OCT.	38	25	3	-4	14
NOV.	48	26	9	-3	10	NOV.	26	13	-3	-11	18
DEC.	34	14	1	-10	10	DEC.	17	1	-8	-17	19

Manufacturing is New Hampshire's most important economic activity. The tourist industry ranks second, followed by agriculture. Manufacturing is centered in the cities of the south and southeast and in Connecticut River Valley communities. The millions of tourists who visit the state contribute about $400 million a year to the state's economy. Farms thrive in several areas.

Natural Resources. New Hampshire's climate and soils support dense forests and thick grasslands. Many kinds of animals live in the state. Minerals are found in many areas, but mining output is small.

Soil. A mixture of clay and rocks covers most of New Hampshire's hills and mountains. This soil was once farmland, and is now largely covered by trees. The soil in New Hampshire's valleys is chiefly clay and loam, and coarse gravel and sand. The clay and loam support farm crops. The gravel and sand supply low-cost road-building material.

Forests and Plant Life. Forests cover about 90 per cent of New Hampshire. Commercially valuable softwood trees include balsam fir, cedar, hemlock, spruce, tamarack, and white pine. Balsam fir, hemlock, pine, and spruce account for much of New Hampshire's lumber. Valuable hardwoods include ash, basswood, beech, birch, elm, maple, and oak.

Shrubs and flowering plants thrive in New Hampshire forests. The shrubs include American elders, chokeberries, red osiers, and sumacs. Wild flowers, which grow throughout the state, include black-eyed Susans, daisies, fireweed, gentians, goldenrod, purple trillium, violets, and wild asters.

Animal Life. Deer, rabbits, foxes, and raccoons are common in New Hampshire. Minks, beavers, pine martens, otters, squirrels, and chipmunks live in the central and northern mountains and forests. Game birds include ruffed grouse, pheasants, and ducks. Robins, bluebirds, purple finches, sparrows, and warblers nest throughout New Hampshire.

Among the state's fresh-water varieties of fish are brook, brown, lake, and rainbow trout; largemouth and smallmouth bass; and landlocked salmon, pickerel, perch, whitefish, and bullheads. Salt-water fish include cod, cunner, cusk, flounder, haddock, hake, mackerel, pollack, striped bass, and tuna. Coastal waters have lobster and shrimp.

Minerals. New Hampshire's chief mineral resources are its deposits of granite, gravel, sand, mica, feldspar, and quartz. The state's large beds of gray, red, and other kinds of granite give it the nickname of the *Granite State.*

Manufacturing accounts for 94 per cent of the value of goods produced in New Hampshire. Goods manufactured there have a *value added by manufacture* of about $1½ billion a year. This figure represents the value created in products by the state's industries, not counting such costs as materials, supplies, and fuel.

New Hampshire has about 1,500 factories, ranging from small plants to giant industrial works. The state's chief manufactured products, in order of value, are electrical machinery, nonelectrical machinery, paper and allied products, and leather and leather products. New Hampshire's main electrical machinery products

Production of Goods in New Hampshire

Total value of goods produced in 1973—$1,549,660,000

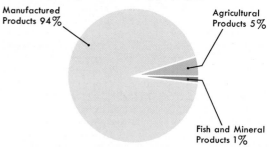

Manufactured Products 94%

Agricultural Products 5%

Fish and Mineral Products 1%

Percentages are based on farm income, value added by manufacture, and value of fish and mineral production.
Sources: U.S. government publications, 1975-1976.

Employment in New Hampshire

Total number of persons employed in 1974—307,300

		Number of Employees
Manufacturing	𝄃	95,000
Wholesale & Retail Trade	𝄃	63,900
Community, Social, & Personal Services	𝄃	53,300
Government	𝄃	45,100
Construction	𝄃	17,900
Finance, Insurance, & Real Estate	𝄃	14,000
Transportation & Public Utilities	𝄃	12,900
Agriculture & Mining	𝄃	5,200

Sources: *Employment and Earnings*, May 1975, U.S. Bureau of Labor Statistics; New Hampshire Department of Resources and Economic Development.

include electronic measuring instruments, lighting products, and radio and television equipment. Its chief non-electrical machinery products include machine tools and packaging and labeling machinery. New Hampshire ranks among the leading leather-manufacturing states. Shoes are its most important leather product.

Wood from New Hampshire's trees is the raw material for many manufactured products. Paper and pulp are the most important of these products. Many of New Hampshire's fir trees are cut down each year to be used as Christmas trees.

Other manufactured items include food and food products, instruments, printed materials, rubber and plastics products, and textiles.

Agriculture accounts for about 5 per cent of the value of goods produced in New Hampshire. New Hampshire farmers earn about $70 million a year. The state has about 2,900 farms, averaging 211 acres (85.39 hectares) in size.

Dairy farming is New Hampshire's most important agricultural activity. Milk and other dairy products have a value of about $25 million a year—about two-fifths of the state's total farm income. Dairy farms are especially numerous in the west and southeast. Poultry farming ranks next in importance. Eggs—the leading poultry product—and chickens and turkeys account for about a fourth of New Hampshire's farm income. Most poultry farms are in southern New Hampshire. Beef cattle are another important farm product in New Hampshire.

Apples rank as New Hampshire's leading fruit. New Hampshire farmers also grow peaches, blueberries, strawberries, and grapes. Potatoes and sweet corn are the state's most important vegetables. Greenhouse and nursery products also rank high among the state's chief agricultural goods.

Mining. Even though New Hampshire is famous as the *Granite State*, mining is of little importance to its economy. Mining accounts for about $15 million a year, or less than 1 per cent of the value of goods produced in New Hampshire. Granite, quartz, and sand and gravel are the state's chief minerals.

New Hampshire's largest granite quarries are in Hillsboro and Merrimack counties. The Concord quarries, in Merrimack County, are the biggest in the state. They have supplied granite for many famous buildings, including the Library of Congress in Washington, D.C. New Hampshire granite was also used as the cornerstone of the main United Nations building in New York City. All of New Hampshire's counties produce sand and gravel, and some produce clays and gemstones.

Fishing Industry is also a relatively minor economic activity in New Hampshire. Hampton, Portsmouth, and Rye are the chief salt-water fishing centers. Fishermen trap lobsters in the coastal waters. The lobster catch totals about 700,000 pounds (320,000 kilograms) a year. New Hampshire fishermen also catch cod, flounder, haddock, pollock, sandworms, shrimp, and smelt.

Electric Power. Over 70 per cent of New Hampshire's power needs are supplied by two large steam generating plants. One plant is near Manchester and the other is in Portsmouth. Large hydroelectric plants on the Connecticut River provide power during the peak periods to the New England Electric System. Chief plants on the river include Comerford Dam near Monroe, Wilder Dam near Hanover, and the Samuel C. Moore Dam near Littleton.

Transportation. New Hampshire's industrial growth during the 1800's encouraged the first great expansion of the state's transportation system.

New Hampshire has many small airfields. Larger airports link Concord, Keene, Lebanon, and Manchester with several major U.S. cities.

Railroads operate on about 900 miles (1,400 kilometers) of track in New Hampshire. Five rail lines provide freight service. Passenger trains serve the Lebanon-Hanover area. New Hampshire's first railroad began operating in 1838.

Roads and highways total about 15,000 miles (24,000 kilometers), and most of them are surfaced. The state's highway system includes modern toll roads. The New Hampshire Turnpike parallels the seacoast. The Spaulding Turnpike extends the seacoast turnpike from Portsmouth to Rochester. The Everett Turnpike links Concord and Massachusetts. New Hampshire highways include about 215 miles (346 kilometers) of the Federal Interstate Highway System.

Communication. About 45 daily and weekly newspapers are published in New Hampshire. The leading ones include *Foster's Democrat* of Dover; the *Manchester Union Leader;* the *Nashua Telegraph;* the *New Hampshire News* of Manchester; and the *Portsmouth Herald.*

New Hampshire's first newspaper began publication in 1756 at Portsmouth. It was called the *New Hampshire Gazette*, and is now the weekly supplement of the *Portsmouth Herald.* The state's first radio station, WLNH, was founded at Laconia in 1922. The first television station, WMUR-TV, began operation at Manchester in 1954. New Hampshire now has about 50 radio stations and 8 television stations.

Women Assemble Electrical Machinery at a factory in Manchester. This type of machinery ranks as New Hampshire's most valuable manufactured product.

Raytheon (Eric Sanford)

FARM, MINERAL, AND FOREST PRODUCTS

This map shows the areas where the state's leading farm, mineral, and forest products are produced. The major urban area (shown in red) is the state's important manufacturing center.

0   25   50 Miles

WORLD BOOK map

0   25   50   75 Kilometers

Indian Days. About 5,000 Indians probably lived in what is now New Hampshire before the white man came. Most of them belonged to two branches of the Algonkian Indian family—the Abnaki and the Pennacook. The Abnaki branch included the Ossipee and the Pequawket tribes. The Pennacook included the Amoskeag, Nashua, Piscataqua, Souhegan, and Squamscot tribes. New Hampshire Indians built wigwams of bark and skins. They hunted and fished, and farmed small fields of corn. The tribes lived together in peace, but often warred against their common enemy, the Iroquois.

Exploration. No one knows who was the first white man to reach New Hampshire. But wide-scale exploration of the area began in the early 1600's. In 1603, Martin Pring of England sailed a trading ship up the Piscataqua River. Pring and his men may have landed in Portsmouth. The French explorer Samuel de Champlain landed on the New Hampshire coast in 1605. In 1614, the English captain John Smith reached the Isles of Shoals. He named them *Smith's Islands*.

Settlement. In 1620, King James I of England founded the Council for New England to encourage people to settle in America. The council granted David Thomson land in present-day New Hampshire. In 1623, Thomson and his followers settled at Odiorne's Point (now a part of Rye). Edward Hilton settled Hilton's Point (now Dover) in the 1620's. Some historians believe this settlement began about the same time as Thomson's. Others believe it began a few years later. Other early settlements include Strawbery Banke (now Portsmouth), established in 1630; and Exeter and Hampton, founded in 1638.

In 1622, the Council for New England gave John Mason and Sir Ferdinando Gorges a large tract of land in present-day New Hampshire and Maine. In 1629, the land was divided between the two men. Mason received the part between the Merrimack and Piscataqua rivers. He named the land *New Hampshire*, after his native county—Hampshire, England. New Hampshire was made a part of Massachusetts in 1641. But in 1680, King Charles II again made New Hampshire a separate colony. The king appointed John Cutt as New Hampshire's first provincial governor (then called president).

French and Indian Wars were fought in New Hampshire and the rest of New England off and on from 1689 to 1763. The French and their Indian allies battled to gain control of the area from the British. Guided by Indians, French forces pushed down from Canada. Robert Rogers, the leader of a group of soldiers called Rogers' Rangers, and John Stark, both of New Hampshire, won fame as colonial military leaders during this period. See FRENCH AND INDIAN WARS.

Colonial New Hampshire was a rural society. Most of the people kept busy clearing the wilderness, building houses, and growing food. In 1767, when New Hampshire took its first census, the colony had 52,700 persons. The King of England appointed the governor and governor's council. But the people elected assemblymen to represent them in colonial affairs.

The Revolutionary War. During the 1760's, Great Britain passed a series of laws that caused unrest in New Hampshire and the other American colonies. Most of

──── **IMPORTANT DATES IN NEW HAMPSHIRE** ────

1603	Martin Pring of England explored the mouth of the Piscataqua River.
1614	Captain John Smith landed on the Isles of Shoals.
1620's	David Thomson and Edward Hilton made the first permanent settlements in New Hampshire.
1629	John Mason named the region *New Hampshire*.
1641	The Massachusetts Colony gained control of New Hampshire.
1680	New Hampshire became a separate royal colony.
1776	New Hampshire broke away from Great Britain and adopted a temporary constitution.
1784	New Hampshire adopted its present constitution.
1788	New Hampshire became the ninth state when it ratified the U.S. Constitution on June 21.
1838	The first railroad in New Hampshire was completed.
1853	Franklin Pierce of Hillsboro became the 14th President of the United States.
1944	The International Monetary Conference was held at Bretton Woods.
1961	Alan B. Shepard, Jr. of East Derry became the first American to travel in space.
1964	The New Hampshire sweepstakes lottery began. It was the first legal U.S. lottery since the 1890's.
1970	The legislature adopted a tax on business profits.

these laws either imposed severe taxes or restricted colonial trade. In December, 1774, Paul Revere rode to New Hampshire to warn the people of a British military build-up in Massachusetts. A band of New Hampshirites, led by John Sullivan, seized military supplies from a British fort in New Castle. This was one of the first armed actions by colonists against the British.

After the Revolutionary War broke out in Massachusetts in 1775, hundreds of New Hampshire "minutemen" hurried to Boston to fight the British. New Hampshire was the only one of the 13 original colonies in which no actual fighting occurred.

New Hampshire became the first colony to form a government wholly independent of Great Britain. It did so on Jan. 5, 1776, when it adopted a temporary constitution. On July 9, 1778, New Hampshire ratified the Articles of Confederation (the forerunner of the United States Constitution). On June 21, 1788, New Hampshire became the ninth state to ratify the U.S. Constitution. New Hampshire's ratification put the Constitution into effect.

The 1800's. New Hampshire remained an agricultural state from 1800 until the outbreak of the Civil War. But it began an industrial growth that has continued to the present day. Manchester, the largest industrial center, became the state's first incorporated city in 1846. Portsmouth developed as a leading clipper-ship port in the early 1800's, and the first railroad opened in 1838. During the 1850's, businessmen built hosiery plants, woolen mills, and factories that made boots and shoes, machine tools, and wood products.

New Hampshirites who gained national fame during this period included Franklin Pierce, the 14th President of the United States, and Daniel Webster, a leading orator and U.S. senator.

New Hampshire was a leading opponent of slavery. About 34,000 New Hampshirites served with the Union

HISTORIC NEW HAMPSHIRE

President Franklin Pierce
born at Hillsboro

Concord Wagons and Coaches, first made in 1813 by the Abbot and Downing Co. of Concord, were used during the 1800's to carry passengers and mail.

Bretton Woods Conference delegates in July, 1944, shaped financial and trade policies for the postwar world.

Bretton Woods

Dartmouth College at Hanover was chartered by King George III in 1769 "for the education and instruction of Youth of the Indian Tribes in this Land."

● Hanover

The Textile Industry grew rapidly in New Hampshire after the state's first cotton mill was founded at New Ipswich in 1804. The Amoskeag Mill, established at Manchester in 1809, became one of the world's largest cotton mills.

Daniel Webster's Birthplace stands near Franklin. The famous statesman was born in 1782.

● Franklin

Shoemaking developed into a major industry after Allen Sawyer established the state's first shoe factory at Weare in 1823.

Soldiers at Bunker Hill used gunpowder from 100 barrels captured from the British at Fort William and Mary in New Castle.

CONCORD ★

Hillsboro

Weare

The Library in Peterborough may be the nation's oldest tax-supported free public library. It was founded in 1833.

Peterborough ●

Manchester

New Castle ●

Independence from Great Britain was first achieved by New Hampshire of the 13 colonies. The state adopted a constitution on January 5, 1776, six months before the Declaration of Independence was signed.

New Ipswich

forces during the Civil War, and the Portsmouth Naval Shipyard built ships that blockaded Southern ports.

Industrial development increased greatly after the Civil War. The textile, woodworking, and leather industries were among those that grew at record rates. Thousands of French-Canadian and European immigrants came to New Hampshire to fill the labor needs caused by expansion of mills and factories. At the same time, many farmers left the state to claim free land in the West. Farming activity decreased as industry grew.

The Early 1900's. During World War I (1914-1918), the Portsmouth Naval Shipyard built warships. New Hampshire's cotton and woolen textile industries declined in the 1920's and 1930's. Leather and shoe manufacturing became the state's leading industry. New Hampshire greatly improved its highway system during the 1920's, and private utility companies built hydroelectric plants in the state. The Great Depression of the 1930's slowed the growth of New Hampshire's economy. Conditions improved after the depression eased in the late 1930's.

The Mid-1900's. During World War II (1939-1945), Portsmouth built submarines and repaired warships, and New Hampshire's textile mills supplied materials for military uniforms. In 1944, representatives of 44 nations held the historic International Monetary Conference at Bretton Woods in the White Mountains. They planned postwar world trade and simplified the transfer of money among nations. They also drew up plans for two United Nations agencies—the International Monetary Fund and the International Bank for Reconstruction and Development. See BRETTON WOODS.

New Hampshire became increasingly urban and industrial during the mid-1900's. In the 1950's, the state approved the formation of a Business Development Corporation and established an Industrial Park Authority. These agencies worked to aid new businesses and to attract industry to New Hampshire.

New Hampshire's once important shoe industry declined sharply because of competition from other states and from other countries, especially Italy. But the rapid growth of the state's electronics industry more than made up for shoe industry losses.

In 1961, Alan B. Shepard, Jr. of East Derry became

THE GOVERNORS OF NEW HAMPSHIRE

	Party	Term		Party	Term
Under Articles of Confederation			37. James A. Weston	Democratic	1871-1872
			38. Ezekiel A. Straw	Republican	1872-1874
1. Meshech Weare	None	1776-1785	39. James A. Weston	Democratic	1874-1875
2. John Langdon	None	1785-1786	40. Person C. Cheney	Republican	1875-1877
3. John Sullivan	Federalist	1786-1788	41. Benjamin F. Prescott	Republican	1877-1879
			42. Natt Head	Republican	1879-1881
Under United States Constitution			43. Charles H. Bell	Republican	1881-1883
1. John Langdon	*Dem.-Rep.	1788-1789	44. Samuel W. Hale	Republican	1883-1885
2. John Sullivan	Federalist	1789-1790	45. Moody Currier	Republican	1885-1887
3. Josiah Bartlett	*Dem.-Rep.	1790-1794	46. Charles H. Sawyer	Republican	1887-1889
4. John T. Gilman	Federalist	1794-1805	47. David H. Goodell	Republican	1889-1891
5. John Langdon	*Dem.-Rep.	1805-1809	48. Hiram A. Tuttle	Republican	1891-1893
6. Jeremiah Smith	Federalist	1809-1810	49. John B. Smith	Republican	1893-1895
7. John Langdon	*Dem.-Rep.	1810-1812	50. Charles A. Busiel	Republican	1895-1897
8. William Plumer	*Dem.-Rep.	1812-1813	51. George A. Ramsdell	Republican	1897-1899
9. John T. Gilman	Federalist	1813-1816	52. Frank W. Rollins	Republican	1899-1901
10. William Plumer	*Dem.-Rep.	1816-1819	53. Chester B. Jordan	Republican	1901-1903
11. Samuel Bell	*Dem.-Rep.	1819-1823	54. Nahum J. Batchelder	Republican	1903-1905
12. Levi Woodbury	*Dem.-Rep.	1823-1824	55. John McLane	Republican	1905-1907
13. David L. Morrill	*Dem.-Rep.	1824-1827	56. Charles M. Floyd	Republican	1907-1909
14. Benjamin Pierce	*Dem.-Rep.	1827-1828	57. Henry B. Quinby	Republican	1909-1911
15. John Bell	National		58. Robert P. Bass	Republican	1911-1913
	Republican	1828-1829	59. Samuel D. Felker	Democratic	1913-1915
16. Benjamin Pierce	Democratic	1829-1830	60. Rolland H. Spaulding	Republican	1915-1917
17. Matthew Harvey	Democratic	1830-1831	61. Henry W. Keyes	Republican	1917-1919
18. Samuel Dinsmoor	Democratic	1831-1834	62. John H. Bartlett	Republican	1919-1921
19. William Badger	Democratic	1834-1836	63. Albert O. Brown	Republican	1921-1923
20. Isaac Hill	Democratic	1836-1839	64. Fred H. Brown	Democratic	1923-1925
21. John Page	Democratic	1839-1842	65. John G. Winant	Republican	1925-1927
22. Henry Hubbard	Democratic	1842-1844	66. Huntley N. Spaulding	Republican	1927-1929
23. John H. Steele	Democratic	1844-1846	67. Charles W. Tobey	Republican	1929-1931
24. Anthony Colby	Whig	1846-1847	68. John G. Winant	Republican	1931-1935
25. Jared W. Williams	Democratic	1847-1849	69. Styles Bridges	Republican	1935-1937
26. Samuel Dinsmoor, Jr.	Democratic	1849-1852	70. Francis P. Murphy	Republican	1937-1941
27. Noah Martin	Democratic	1852-1854	71. Robert O. Blood	Republican	1941-1945
28. Nathaniel B. Baker	Democratic	1854-1855	72. Charles M. Dale	Republican	1945-1949
29. Ralph Metcalf	†American	1855-1857	73. Sherman Adams	Republican	1949-1953
30. William Haile	Republican	1857-1859	74. Hugh Gregg	Republican	1953-1955
31. Ichabod Goodwin	Republican	1859-1861	75. Lane Dwinell	Republican	1955-1959
32. Nathaniel S. Berry	Republican	1861-1863	76. Wesley Powell	Republican	1959-1963
33. Joseph A. Gilmore	Republican	1863-1865	77. John W. King	Democratic	1963-1969
34. Frederick Smyth	Republican	1865-1867	78. Walter R. Peterson, Jr.	Republican	1969-1973
35. Walter Harriman	Republican	1867-1869	79. Meldrim Thomson, Jr.	Republican	1973-
36. Onslow Stearns	Republican	1869-1871			

*Democratic-Republican   †Know-Nothing

the first American to travel in space. In 1962, New Hampshire voters elected a Democrat, John W. King, as governor. King was only the third Democrat since 1875 to serve as governor of New Hampshire. The Republicans regained control of the governorship in 1968, when Walter R. Peterson, Jr., was elected.

In 1963, New Hampshire adopted the first legal lottery in the United States since the 1890's. Lottery tickets are sold on horse races called *sweepstakes*. The state uses the profits from the lottery to help pay for public education. The first sweepstakes were held in September 1964.

New Hampshire Today. Manufacturing strengthened its position during the early 1970's as the leading economic producer in the state. Recreational and tourist activities rank second. Agriculture continues to

decline as an important economic force in the state. New Hampshire is one of the few states that does not collect a general sales tax. But many residents are demanding more state programs and services. In 1970, the New Hampshire legislature adopted a tax on business profits.

Pollution of New Hampshire's rivers and streams is becoming a major problem. The prevention of water pollution is particularly important because recreation has such an important part in the state's economy. Each year, the state's recreational facilities attract thousands of visitors for boating, camping, hiking, and skiing. ALBERT S. CARLSON, J. DUANE SQUIRES, and PAUL H. TRACY

NEW HAMPSHIRE/Study Aids

Related Articles in WORLD BOOK include:

BIOGRAPHIES

Adams, Sherman	Pierce, Franklin
Bartlett, Josiah	Porter, Fitz-John
Bridges, Styles	Shepard, Alan B., Jr.
Dearborn, Henry	Stark, John
Eddy, Mary Baker	Thornton, Matthew
French, Daniel C.	Webster, Daniel
Frost, Robert L.	Wentworth, Benning
Gilman, Nicholas	Whipple, William
Hale, John P.	Winant, John G.
Langdon, John	

CITIES AND TOWNS

Concord	Manchester
Exeter	Nashua
Hanover	Portsmouth

HISTORY

Colonial Life in America	Dartmouth College Case
French and Indian Wars	

PHYSICAL FEATURES

Connecticut River	Merrimack River
Lake Winnipesaukee	White Mountains

Outline

I. **Government**
  A. Constitution
  B. Executive
  C. Legislature
  D. Courts
  E. Local Government
  F. Taxation
  G. Politics
II. **People**
III. **Education**
  A. Schools
  B. Libraries
  C. Museums
IV. **A Visitor's Guide**
  A. Places to Visit
  B. Annual Events
V. **The Land**
  A. Land Regions
  B. Coastline
  C. Mountains
  D. Rivers and Lakes
VI. **Climate**
VII. **Economy**
  A. Natural Resources
  B. Manufacturing
  C. Agriculture
  D. Mining
  E. Fishing Industry
  F. Electric Power
  G. Transportation
  H. Communication
VIII. **History**

Questions

Why was New Hampshire's ratification of the U.S. Constitution especially important?

What record weather condition was recorded at Mount Washington?

What U.S. President was born in New Hampshire?

What is New Hampshire's main economic activity?

Why are New Hampshire's towns called "little republics"?

What important international conference was held in New Hampshire in 1944?

What religious movement was started by a New Hampshirite?

What are New Hampshire's three main land regions?

Why is New Hampshire's coastline unique?

What is New Hampshire's oldest college?

Books for Young Readers

BAILEY, BERNADINE. *Picture Book of New Hampshire.* Rev. ed. Whitman, 1971.

BAILEY, CAROLYN S. *Miss Hickory.* Viking, 1946. Fiction. Newbery medal winner.

CARPENTER, ALLAN. *New Hampshire.* Childrens Press, 1967.

GIFFEN, DANIEL H. *The New Hampshire Colony.* Macmillan, 1970.

LENGYEL, EMIL. *The Colony of New Hampshire.* Watts, 1975.

MEADER, STEPHEN W. *Red Horse Hill.* Harcourt, 1930. Fiction.

WOOD, JAMES PLAYSTED. *Colonial New Hampshire.* Nelson, 1973.

YATES, ELIZABETH. *Amos Fortune, Free Man.* Dutton, 1950. Fiction. Newbery medal winner. *New Hampshire.* Coward, 1969. *Sarah Whitcher's Story.* Dutton, 1971. Fiction. *We, the People.* Countryman, 1974. Fiction.

Books for Older Readers

CANNON, LeGRAND. *Look to the Mountain.* Holt, 1942. Fiction.

DIXON, PAIGE. *Promises to Keep.* Atheneum, 1974. Fiction.

HILL, RALPH N. *Yankee Kingdom: Vermont and New Hampshire.* Rev. ed. Harper, 1973.

HUNT, ELMER M. *New Hampshire Town Names and Whence They Came.* Bauhan, 1971.

LEAVITT, RICHARD F. *Yesterday's New Hampshire.* Seemann, 1974.

MORISON, ELIZABETH F. and E. E. *New Hampshire: A Bicentennial History.* Norton, 1976.

PRATSON, FREDERICK J. *New Hampshire.* Greene, 1974.

SPEARE, EVA A. C. *Stories of New Hampshire.* New Hampshire Publishing Co., 1975.

NEW HAMPSHIRE, UNIVERSITY OF

NEW HAMPSHIRE, UNIVERSITY OF, is a state-supported coeducational system of higher education. Its full name is the University System of New Hampshire. The system consists of the University of New Hampshire in Durham, state colleges in Keene and Plymouth, a two-year branch in Manchester, and a statewide school of continuing studies.

The Durham campus has colleges of engineering and physical sciences, liberal arts, and life sciences and agriculture. It also has a school of health studies, a school of business and economics, a graduate school, and a two-year school of applied science. It grants bachelor's, master's, and doctor's degrees. The Keene and Plymouth campuses grant bachelor's and master's degrees.

The University of New Hampshire was founded in 1866 as the New Hampshire College of Agriculture and Mechanic Arts. It took its present name in 1923. In 1963, Keene State College and Plymouth State College became part of the university. For enrollments, see UNIVERSITIES AND COLLEGES (table).

Critically reviewed by the UNIVERSITY SYSTEM OF NEW HAMPSHIRE

NEW HAMPSHIRE GRANTS. See VERMONT (Land Disputes); ALLEN, ETHAN.

NEW HARMONY, Ind. (pop. 971), became famous as an educational and cultural center during the 1820's. Today, this quiet town in Posey County is a trading center for a farming region in the lower Wabash River Valley (see INDIANA [map]).

George Rapp (1757-1847), the leader of a religious group called Harmonists, founded the village of Harmonie in 1814. Rapp brought the Harmonists from the kingdom of Würrtemberg in Germany to escape religious persecution. They spent 10 years in Butler County, Pennsylvania, then migrated to Indiana. The Harmonists practiced celibacy and members could not own property. In 1825, Rapp sold the town to Robert Owen, wealthy social reformer and industrialist from Scotland. The Harmonists returned to Pennsylvania and founded the village of Economy, now Ambridge, where the society died out toward the end of the 1800's.

Owen renamed his town New Harmony. He established a social order based on community ownership and equality of work and profit. His partner was William Maclure, a wealthy scientist from Philadelphia who is sometimes called the "Father of American Geology." In the 1820's, Maclure sent the first seed for the Chinese *golden-rain* trees to Thomas Say, another geologist who had come to New Harmony. These golden-rain, or *gate*, trees now line the streets of the town.

The experiment in community living made New Harmony famous. Scientists and scholars flocked to the town. But few of the 1,000 or more Owenites understood the principles of the experiment, and they split into several factions.

By 1827, it was apparent that Owen's plan had failed. New Harmony remained an educational, scientific, and cultural center until the Civil War. The Minerva Club, the first woman's club to have a constitution and by-laws, was organized at New Harmony in 1859. Some of the buildings erected by the Harmonists and Owenites have been restored.   PAUL E. MILLION, JR.

See also INDIANA (Education; Places to Visit; picture); OWEN (family).

NEW HAVEN, Conn. (pop. 137,707), is the home of Yale University. It is the third largest city in Connecticut and a commercial, cultural, and manufacturing center of New England. New Haven and West Haven form a metropolitan area with a population of 411,287.

New Haven is situated on an arm of Long Island Sound about 70 miles (110 kilometers) northeast of New York City (see CONNECTICUT [political map]). Three small rivers, the West, the Mill, and the Quinnipiac, meet to form the bay and harbor of New Haven.

New Haven is bordered on the east and west by hills 350 to 400 feet (107 to 120 meters) high. It is called the *City of Elms* because of its many elm-lined streets.

Industries. New Haven factories produce firearms, electrical appliances, automobile radiators, machine tools, rubber products, hardware, toys, and clothing. The city has a wide wholesale trade in oil, gasoline, coal, lumber, paints, and farm products.

Cultural Life. Yale University is one of the oldest schools in the United States (see YALE UNIVERSITY). Other schools located in New Haven include Albertus Magnus College and Southern Connecticut State College. The city's museums and galleries include the Peabody Museum of Natural History, the New Haven Colony Historical Society, the Yale University Art Gallery and Design Center, the Yale Center for British

Bettmann Archive; Ruohomaa, Black Star

New Harmony Settlers, *below,* lived in a communal society. The restored hedge labyrinth, *right,* was originally designed by George Rapp as entertainment for his followers.

Art, and the New Haven Art Gallery and Art Lending Library.

Recreation. New Haven has 15 city parks. Judges Cave in West Rock Park is a tourist attraction. In the 1660's, two English revolutionaries hid for several weeks in the cave to escape capture by forces of King Charles II. Yale Bowl seats 70,896 people. Yale's Payne-Whitney gymnasium, 16 stories high, is one of the world's largest sports buildings. Plays are often presented in New Haven before they open on Broadway in New York City. The city has one of the oldest symphony orchestras in the nation. It also has a city arena, golf courses, a baseball stadium, and a city-owned beach.

History. A company of Puritans, led by Theophilus Eaton and John Davenport, founded New Haven in 1638. The site was once occupied by an Indian village named *Quinnipiac*, which means *Long River Place*. The name was changed to New Haven, after the English city of Newhaven, in 1640. The town was part of New Haven Colony which also included the towns of Branford, Guilford, Milford, Stamford, and Southold. The New Haven Colony became part of the colony of Connecticut in 1665. New Haven was incorporated as a city in 1784. Roger Sherman, one of the committee of five who drafted the Declaration of Independence, was the first mayor. New Haven was one of Connecticut's two capitals from 1701 to 1875. The city is also the burial place of such famous men as Noah Webster and Lyman Beecher. Charles Goodyear, who discovered the process of vulcanizing rubber, was born in New Haven.

New Haven was a busy port during the 1700's and early 1800's. As steam-operated vessels replaced sailing ships, the harbor became less important, and the city turned to industry. Dredging of a deep channel to accommodate ocean-going ships began in 1927. By 1950, New Haven was again a major harbor. It has a mayor-council form of government.   ALBERT E. VAN DUSEN

NEW HEBRIDES ISLANDS, *HEB ruh deez*, form part of the Pacific region called *Melanesia*. The New Hebrides group lies in the southwest Pacific, about 1,000 miles (1,600 kilometers) northeast of the Queensland coast of Australia. Vila is the capital. The islands stretch across the sea routes between the United States and Australia. This position made them important during World War II. The United States set up a large air and naval base at Espiritu Santo during the war.

The New Hebrides are made up of 12 principal islands and many smaller ones. Their total area is 5,700

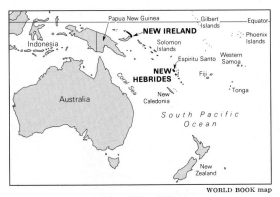

Location of New Hebrides

WORLD BOOK map

Ewing Galloway

A New Hebrides Tribesman, dressed in a warrior's costume, wears traditional head and nose ornaments. Most New Hebrides inhabitants are Melanesians, but some are Polynesians.

square miles (14,763 square kilometers). The islands' total coastline covers 1,300 miles (2,092 kilometers). The climate is damp, hot, and unhealthful. Some of the islands are fertile. The chief products include bananas, cocoa, coffee, copra, pineapples, and timber. The islands also have some cattle.

The New Hebrides have a population of about 104,-000. Fewer than 3,000 of these are white people. Most of the inhabitants are dark-skinned Melanesians. European governmental and religious influences have put a stop to their tribal wars and cannibalism. The islanders entertain visitors by diving from the tops of tall trees to the ground. The diver ties a vine to his legs. The other end of the vine is tied to a treetop. The vine breaks his fall just before he reaches the ground.

In 1606, Pedro de Queirós, a Portuguese explorer, became the first white person to see the New Hebrides. The British explorer James Cook reached other islands in the group in 1774, and mapped the entire region. Since 1906, the British and the French have jointly ruled the islands.   EDWIN H. BRYAN, JR.

See also ESPIRITU SANTO.

NEW HOLLAND. See AUSTRALIA (History).

NEW IRELAND is the second largest island of the Bismarck Archipelago. It covers 3,340 square miles (8,651 square kilometers) in the southwest Pacific (see NEW HEBRIDES ISLANDS [map]). It has a population of about 41,100. It is part of the nation of Papua New Guinea. New Ireland is a volcanic island about 230 miles (370 kilometers) long. In its center rise the Schleinitz Mountains, which are 2,000 to 4,000 feet (610 to 1,200 meters) high. The island has many coconut plantations. Kavieng is the largest town. NEAL M. BOWERS

195

Oil Refinery in Perth Amboy

NEW JERSEY

THE GARDEN STATE

FACTS IN BRIEF

Capital: Trenton.

Government: *Congress*—U.S. senators, 2; U.S. representatives, 15. *Electoral Votes*—17. *State Legislature*—senators, 40; assemblymen, 80. *Counties*—21.

Area: 7,836 sq. mi. (20,295 km²), including 315 sq. mi. (816 km²) of inland water but excluding 384 sq. mi. (995 km²) of Delaware Bay and New York Harbor; 46th in size among the states. *Greatest Distances*—north-south, 166 mi. (267 km); east-west, 57 mi. (92 km). *Coastline*—130 mi. (209 km).

Elevation: *Highest*—High Point, 1,803 ft. (550 m) above sea level. *Lowest*—sea level along the Atlantic Ocean.

Population: *Estimated 1975 Population*—7,316,000. *1970 Census*—7,168,164; 8th among the states; distribution, 89 per cent urban, 11 per cent rural; density, 915 persons per sq. mi. (353 per km²).

Chief Products: *Agriculture*—dairy products, eggs, greenhouse and nursery products, tomatoes. *Fishing Industry*—clams, flounder, lobsters, menhaden, oysters. *Manufacturing*—chemicals; electrical machinery; fabricated metal products; food and food products; nonelectrical machinery; printed materials; transportation equipment. *Mining*—sand and gravel, stone, zinc.

Statehood: Dec. 18, 1787, the 3rd state.

State Motto: *Liberty and Prosperity.*

NEW JERSEY is a state of industrial cities and towns, glistening beaches, and gay summer resorts. It is the fifth smallest state. Only Hawaii, Connecticut, Delaware, and Rhode Island have a smaller area. But New Jersey ranks eighth in population among the states, and few states manufacture more products or attract more vacationers.

About 89 per cent of New Jersey's people live in urban areas. Only California has a higher percentage. The state's cities include such busy manufacturing centers as Camden, Elizabeth, Jersey City, Newark, Paterson, and Trenton. But New Jersey also has many small, quiet towns. A large number of these are the homes of people who work in New York City and Philadelphia. Both of these giant cities are neighbors of New Jersey.

The thousands of New Jerseyans who work in New York City and Philadelphia commute daily by train, automobile, or bus. The Holland and Lincoln tunnels and the George Washington Bridge link the state with New York City. The Benjamin Franklin Bridge, the Tacony-Palmyra Bridge, and the Walt Whitman Bridge connect New Jersey with Philadelphia.

New Jersey's location gives it great economic importance. The state lies between the Hudson and Delaware rivers, and between New York City and Philadelphia. Miles of wharves stretch along the New Jersey side of the Hudson. Ocean liners, freighters, and other ships from all parts of the world dock there and along the Delaware. Products made in New Jersey are used throughout the United States and in many other countries. They find giant nearby markets in New York City and Philadelphia. New Jersey leads the states in chemical production. It ranks high among producers of machinery, metals, processed foods, and textiles.

The large city populations create a demand for New Jersey farm products. The state is an important supplier of poultry, vegetables, and fruits for many Eastern cities.

New Jersey's vacation areas along the Atlantic Coast contrast sharply with the state's industrial cities. More than 50 resort cities and towns, including Asbury Park and Atlantic City, line the New Jersey coast. They provide a wide variety of recreation activities.

New Jersey and its people have played important roles in United States history. The state earned the nickname *Cockpit of the Revolution* because of the many battles fought on its soil during the Revolutionary War. American patriots and British redcoats clashed nearly a hundred times in New Jersey. People compared these actions with cockfights. General George Washington turned the tide of the war at Trenton in 1776 when he led his tattered army across the Delaware River and surprised the enemy. Trenton and Princeton each served as the nation's capital during the 1780's.

In 1884, Grover Cleveland of New Jersey was elected the 22nd President of the United States. He was elected President again in 1892. Woodrow Wilson served as president of Princeton University and governor of New Jersey before he was elected the 28th President in 1912. Wilson was re-elected in 1916, and led the nation through World War I.

Three of the world's greatest scientists and inventors worked in New Jersey for many years. Thomas Edison invented the electric light and the phonograph in his laboratory in Menlo Park. Albert Einstein worked many years at the Institute for Advanced Study in Princeton. And Samuel F. B. Morse developed the first successful U.S. electric telegraph near Morristown.

New Jersey's many truck farms, orchards, and flower gardens give it the nickname of the *Garden State*. Trenton is the state capital, and Newark is the largest city. For the relationship of New Jersey to other states in its region, see MIDDLE ATLANTIC STATES.

The contributors of this article are Arthur Getis, Professor of Geography at Rutgers, The State University; Mort Pye, Editor of the Newark Star-Ledger; *and Richard P. McCormick, Professor of History and University Historian at Rutgers, The State University, and author of* New Jersey from Colony to State.

High Point, the Highest Peak in New Jersey
Scheller, Three Lions

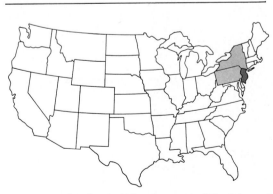

New Jersey (blue) ranks 46th in size among all the states, and is the smallest of the Middle Atlantic States (gray).

Constitution of New Jersey was adopted in 1947. New Jersey had two earlier constitutions, adopted in 1776 and 1844. Either house of the state legislature may propose constitutional amendments. Amendments must be approved by three-fifths of the members of both houses, or by a majority vote of both houses in two successive years. To become law, amendments must also be approved by a majority of the voters in a general election. The constitution makes no provision for a constitutional convention that can amend the constitution. But in 1966, the legislature set up a special convention to *reapportion* (redivide) the legislature.

Executive. The governor is the only New Jersey executive official elected by the people. The governor serves a four-year term and receives a yearly salary of $60,000. The governor may serve any number of terms, but may not serve more than two in succession. For a list of the governors of New Jersey, see the *History* section of this article.

The governor appoints most of the state's key executive officials. These officials include the attorney general; secretary of state; state treasurer; and the commissioners of conservation and economic development, education, health, and labor and industries. The state board of agriculture appoints the secretary of agriculture. The board members are recommended by an agricultural convention and appointed by the governor. All the governor's appointments are subject to approval by the state senate. Most executive officials serve four-year terms.

Legislature of New Jersey consists of a 40-member senate and an 80-member general assembly. Voters in each of the state's 40 legislative districts elect one senator and two members of the assembly. Senators serve four-year terms. Members of the assembly are elected to two-year terms. The New Jersey legislature meets annually, beginning on the second Tuesday of January. Legislative sessions have no time limit.

Courts. New Jersey's highest court, the state supreme court, hears cases involving constitutional problems,

capital punishment, and other major matters. The supreme court has a chief justice and six associate justices. The state superior court is New Jersey's chief trial court. It has three divisions—Appellate, Law, and Chancery. The superior court has 120 judges. The governor, with the senate's approval, appoints the members of both the supreme and superior courts to seven-year terms. If the governor reappoints them once, the judges may serve until they are 70 years old.

New Jersey's 21 county courts have from one to eight judges, depending on the population of the county. These judges serve five-year terms. Lower courts include county traffic courts, juvenile and domestic relations courts, single-municipal and multi-municipal courts, and surrogate courts.

The governor of New Jersey, with the senate's approval, appoints most lower court judges. Judges of single-municipal courts, called *magistrates*, are appointed by local governments. New Jersey voters elect surrogate judges.

Local Government. New Jersey is the only state in which county governments are called *boards of chosen freeholders*. This name comes from colonial days, when only *freeholders* (property owners) could hold public office. All 21 New Jersey counties have boards of from three to nine members. All freeholders in New Jersey's 21 counties are elected to three-year terms.

New Jersey's 567 municipalities include cities, towns, townships, boroughs, and villages. Most of them have the mayor-council, commission, or council-manager form of government. Most of New Jersey's large cities have the mayor-council form. New Jersey municipalities get their charters from the state. They can choose from among a variety of charters. But they cannot write or revise their own charters.

Taxation provides about 85 per cent of the state's income. Almost all the rest comes from federal programs and grants. The state's chief source of revenue is a general sales tax, adopted in 1966. Other sources include taxes on motor fuels, cigarettes, motor vehicles,

New Jersey Dept. of Conservation and Economic Development

The Governor's Mansion is a famous historic site in Princeton. The mansion, called *Morven*, was built in 1701 by Richard Stockton, on a plot purchased from William Penn. The buff brick structure consists of a central three-story unit and balancing wings at each end. It was given to the state in 1954 by Walter E. Edge, a former governor of New Jersey.

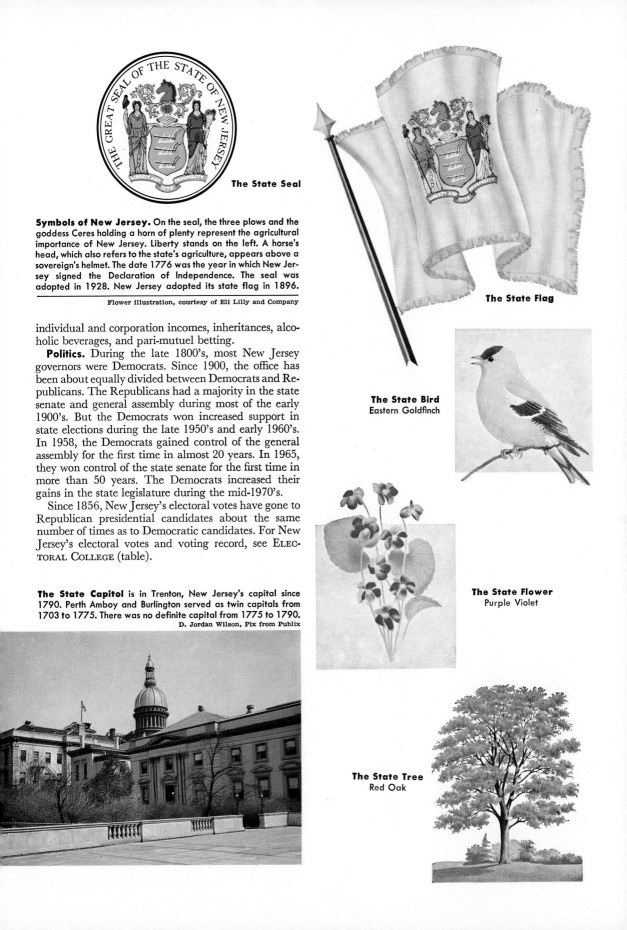

The State Seal

Symbols of New Jersey. On the seal, the three plows and the goddess Ceres holding a horn of plenty represent the agricultural importance of New Jersey. Liberty stands on the left. A horse's head, which also refers to the state's agriculture, appears above a sovereign's helmet. The date 1776 was the year in which New Jersey signed the Declaration of Independence. The seal was adopted in 1928. New Jersey adopted its state flag in 1896.

Flower illustration, courtesy of Eli Lilly and Company

The State Flag

individual and corporation incomes, inheritances, alcoholic beverages, and pari-mutuel betting.

Politics. During the late 1800's, most New Jersey governors were Democrats. Since 1900, the office has been about equally divided between Democrats and Republicans. The Republicans had a majority in the state senate and general assembly during most of the early 1900's. But the Democrats won increased support in state elections during the late 1950's and early 1960's. In 1958, the Democrats gained control of the general assembly for the first time in almost 20 years. In 1965, they won control of the state senate for the first time in more than 50 years. The Democrats increased their gains in the state legislature during the mid-1970's.

Since 1856, New Jersey's electoral votes have gone to Republican presidential candidates about the same number of times as to Democratic candidates. For New Jersey's electoral votes and voting record, see ELECTORAL COLLEGE (table).

The State Bird
Eastern Goldfinch

The State Capitol is in Trenton, New Jersey's capital since 1790. Perth Amboy and Burlington served as twin capitals from 1703 to 1775. There was no definite capital from 1775 to 1790.

D. Jordan Wilson, Pix from Publix

The State Flower
Purple Violet

The State Tree
Red Oak

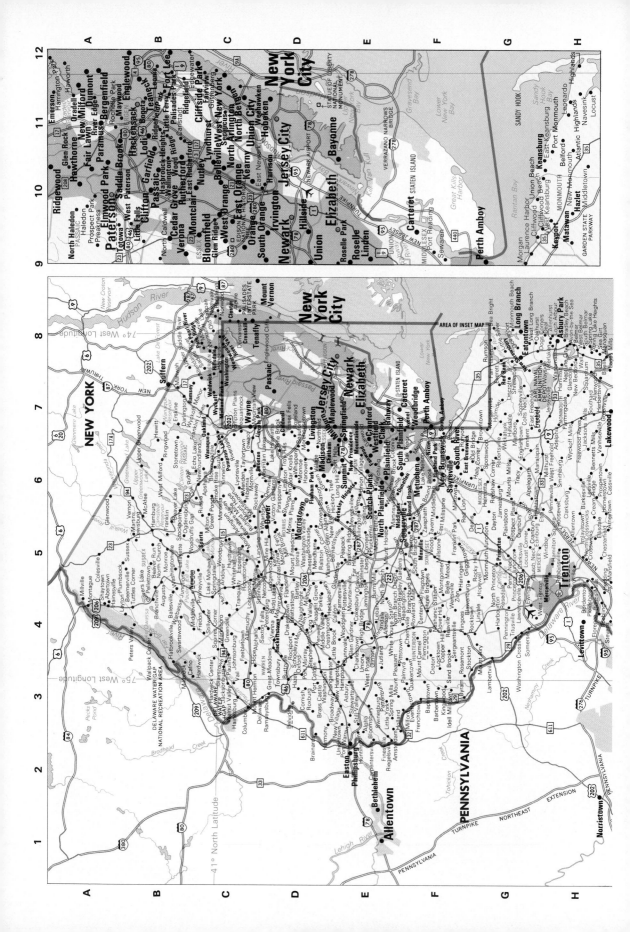

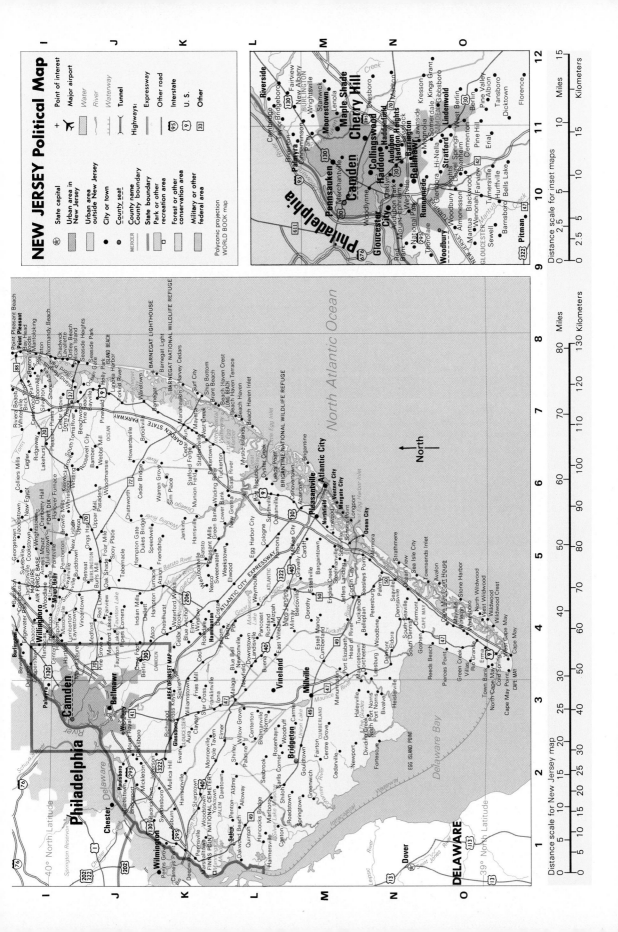

Population

7,168,164 ..Census..1970
6,066,782 ....“....1960
4,835,329 ....“....1950
4,160,165 ....“....1940
4,041,334 ....“....1930
3,155,900 ....“....1920
2,537,167 ....“....1910
1,883,669 ....“....1900
1,444,933 ....“....1890
1,131,116 ....“....1880
906,096 ....“....1870
672,035 ....“....1860
489,555 ....“....1850
373,306 ....“....1840
320,823 ....“....1830
277,575 ....“....1820
245,562 ....“....1810
211,149 ....“....1800
184,139 ....“....1790

Metropolitan Areas

Allentown-Bethlehem-Easton, Pa. ..594,382 (520,422 in Pa.; 73,960 in N.J.)
Atlantic City ...175,043
Jersey City 607,839
Long Branch-Asbury Park ..461,849
New Brunswick-Perth Amboy-Sayreville 583,813
New York City 9,943,800 (9,047,000 in N.Y.; 896,800 in N.J.)
Newark 2,057,468
Paterson-Clifton-Passaic 460,782
Philadelphia, Pa. ....4,824,110 (3,872,006 in Pa.; 952,104 in N.J.)
Trenton 304,116
Vineland-Millville-Bridgeton 121,374
Wilmington, Del. 499,493 (385,856 in Del.; 60,346 in N.J.; 53,291 in Md.)

Counties

Atlantic ..175,043..L 5
Bergen ...897,148..C 8
Burlington 323,132..J 5
Camden ...456,291..K 4
Cape May .59,554..O 4
Cumberland ....121,374..M 3
Essex .....932,526..D 7
Gloucester 172,681..K 3
Hudson ...607,839..D 8
Hunterdon .69,718..F 4
Mercer ....304,116..H 5
Middlesex 583,813..G 6
Monmouth 461,849..H 7
Morris ....383,454..D 5
Ocean .....208,470..J 7
Passaic ...460,782..B 6
Salem .....60,346..L 1
Somerset ..198,372..F 5
Sussex .....77,528..B 5
Union .....543,116..E 6
Warren ....73,960..D 3

Bloomsbury ...879..E 3
Blue Anchor ....K 4
Bogota ......8,960..B 11
Boonton* ...3,070▲.D 6
Boonton ....9,261..D 6
Bordentown* 7,303▲.H 5
Bordentown .4,490..H 5
Bound Brook ....10,450..F 6
Bradley Beach .....4,163..H 8
Bradley Gardens ...F 5
Brainards ....D 3
Branchburg* 5,742▲.F 5
Branchburg Park ...F 5
Branchville ...911..B 5
Brass Castle .....D 3
Breton Woods .....I 8
Brick* .....35,057▲.I 8
Brick Town ....I 7
Bridgeport ....J 2
Bridgeton ..20,435.°M 2
Bridgewater* ...30,235▲.E 5
Brielle ......3,594..H 8
Brigantine ..6,741..M 6
Broadway ....E 3
Brooklawn* ..2,870..N 10
Brookside ....D 5
Browns Mills 7,144..I 5
Budd Lake .3,168..D 5
Buena ......3,283..L 4
Buena Vista* 4,239▲.L 4
Bunnvale ....E 4
Burleigh ....O 4
Burlington* 10,640▲.I 4
Burlington .11,991..I 4
Butler .....7,051..C 6
Buttzville ....D 3
Byram* .....4,592▲.C 5
Caldwell ....8,677..D 7
Califon ......970..E 4
Camden ..102,551.°I 3
Candlewood* 5,629..H 7
Cape May ...4,392..O 4
Cape May Court House ....2,062.°O 4
Cape May Point ....204..O 3
Cardiff ....M 5
Carlstadt ...6,724..B 11
Carmel ....M 3
Carneys Point .....K 1
Carteret ....23,137..F 7
Cedar Brook ....K 4
Cedar Grove 15,582▲.B 9
Cedar Knolls ....D 6
Cedar Run ....K 7
Cedarville ....M 2
Cedarwood Park ...I 7
Changewater ......E 4
Chatham* ...8,093▲.E 6
Chatham ....9,566..E 6
Chatsworth ....J 6
Cherry Hill 64,395▲.N 11
Chesilhurst ...801..K 4
Chester* ....4,265▲.D 5
Chester .....1,299..D 5
Chesterfield .3,190▲.H 5
Cinnaminson ......16,962▲.M 11
Clark .....18,829▲.E 7
Clarksboro ....J 2
Clarksburg ....H 6
Clayton .....5,193..K 3
Clementon ..4,492..O 11
Clermont ....N 4
Cliffside Park .....18,891..C 12

Elizabeth .112,654.°E 7
Elk* ....2,707▲.K 3
Elmer ......1,592..L 3
Elsinboro* ..1,204▲.L 1
Elwood ....L 5
Emerson ....8,428..A 11
Englewood .24,985..B 12
Englewood Cliffs ....5,938..D 8
English Creek .....M 5
Englishtown .1,048..G 6
Erial ....O 11
Erma ....O 4
Espanong ....1,941..C 5
Essex Fells .2,541..D 7
Estell Manor ..539..M 4
Evesboro ....N 12
Evesham* ..13,477▲.J 4
Ewan ....K 2
Ewanville ....I 5
Ewing* .....32,831▲.G 4
Fair Haven .6,142..G 8
Fair Lawn .37,975..A 10
Fairfield* ...4,990▲.M 2
Fairfield* ...6,884..C 7
Fairton ....M 2
Fairview ...10,698..C 12
Fanwood ....8,920..E 6
Far Hills .....780..E 5
Farmingdale 1,148..H 7
Fieldsboro ....615..H 5
Finderne ....F 5
Finesville ....E 3
Flagtown ....F 5
Flanders ....D 5
Flemington ..3,917.°F 4
Florence* ...8,560▲.I 4
Florence ....O 12
Florence [-Roebling] 7,551..H 4
Florham Park ......8,094..D 6
Folsom ......1,767..L 4
Forked River 1,422..J 7
Fort Dix ...26,290..I 5
Fort Lee ...30,631..B 12
Frankford* ..2,777▲.B 5
Franklin* ...1,973▲.E 3
Franklin* ...2,154▲.F 3
Franklin* ..30,389▲.F 5
Franklin* ..8,990▲.K 3
Franklin ....4,236..B 5
Franklin Lakes .....7,550..C 7
Franklin Park ......F 6
Franklinville ....L 3
Fredon ......1,372▲.C 4
Freehold* ..13,185▲.H 7
Freehold ....10,545.°H 7
Freewood Acres ....H 7
Frelinghuysen* ...1,118▲.C 4
Frenchtown .1,459..F 3
Fries Mill ....K 3
Galloway* ..8,276▲.M 6
Garfield ....30,797..B 11
Garwood ....5,260..E 7
Gibbsboro ...2,634..O 11
Gibbstown ....J 2
Gilford Park 4,007..I 7
Gillette ....E 6
Gladstone, see Peapack [-Gladstone]
Glassboro ..12,938..K 3
Glen Gardner .874..E 4
Glen Ridge ..8,518..C 10
Glen Rock ..13,011..A 10
Glendola ....H 8
Glendora ....O 10
Glenwood ....A 6

Howell* ....21,756▲.H 7
Huntington ....E 3
Hurdtown ....C 5
Hurffville ....O 10
Imlaystown ....H 6
Independence* .....2,057▲.D 4
Interlaken ..1,182..H 8
Iona ....L 3
Ironia ....D 5
Irvington ...59,743..D 10
Island Heights ...1,397..J 7
Jackson* ...18,276▲.I 6
Jacobstown ....I 5
Jamesburg ..4,584..G 6
Jefferson* ..14,122▲.C 5
Jersey City 260,350.°E 8
Johnsonburg ....C 4
Juliustown ....I 5
Keansburg ..9,720..H 10
Kearny ....37,585..C 10
Kendall Park* ....7,412..G 5
Kenilworth* .9,165..E 7
Kenvil ....D 5
Keyport ......7,205..H 10
Kingwood ....2,294▲.F 3
Kinnelon ....7,600..C 6
Knowlton* ...1,738▲.C 3
Lacey* ......4,616▲.J 7
Lafayette ...1,202▲.B 5
Lake Hiawatha 11,389..D 6
Lake Mohawk ..6,262..C 5
Lake Telemark* .1,086..C 6
Lakehurst ...2,641..I 7
Lakewood ....17,874 (25,223▲)..H 7
Lambertville .4,359..G 4
Landing ....D 5
Lanoka Harbor .....J 7
Laurel Springs ...2,566..O 11
Laurence Harbor .....6,715..G 9
Lavallette ...1,509..I 8
Lawnside ...2,757..N 11
Lawrence* ..19,567▲.G 5
Lawrence* ...2,329▲.M 2
Lawrenceville ......G 5
Lebanon* ....4,235▲.E 4
Lebanon ......885..E 4
Ledgewood ....D 5
Leeds Point ....L 6
Leesburg ....N 3
Lenola, see Moorestown [-Lenola]
Leonardo ....H 11
Leonia ......8,847..B 12
Liberty* .....1,229▲.D 4
Lincoln Park 9,034..C 7
Lincroft ....G 8
Linden .....41,409..E 9
Lindenwold 16,265..O 11
Linwood ....6,159..M 5
Little Egg Harbor* ...2,972▲.K 6
Little Falls .....11,727▲.B 9
Little Ferry .9,064..B 11
Little Silver .6,010..G 8
Livingston ..30,127▲.D 7
Loch Arbour ..395..H 8
Locust ....H 11
Lodi ....25,163..B 11
Logan* ......1,840▲.J 2
Long Beach* 2,910▲.L 7

Millville ...21,366..M 3
Milmay ....M 4
Mine Hill ...3,557▲.D 5
Mizpah ....L 4
Monmouth Beach .....2,042..G 8
Monmouth Junction ....G 5
Monroe* .....9,138▲.G 6
Monroe* ....14,071▲.K 3
Monroe ....B 5
Monroeville ....K 3
Montague ...1,131▲.A 4
Montclair ..44,043..C 10
Montgomery .6,353▲.F 5
Montvale ....7,327..C 8
Montville ...11,846▲.C 6
Moonachie* .2,951..B 11
Moorestown 15,577▲.M 12
Moorestown [-Lenola] 14,179..M 12
Morganville ....G 7
Morris* ....19,414▲.D 6
Morris Plains 5,540..D 6
Morristown .17,662.°D 6
Mount Arlington .3,590..C 5
Mount Bethel ......E 6
Mount Ephraim ..5,625..N 10
Mount Fern ....D 5
Mount Freedom ..1,621..D 5
Mount Holly ....12,713▲°I 4
Mount Hope ....C 6
Mount Laurel ...11,221▲.J 4
Mount Olive 10,394▲.D 5
Mount Royal ....J 2
Mountain Lakes .....4,739..D 6
Mountainside 7,520..E 6
Mullica* ....3,391▲.L 5
Mullica Hill ....K 2
Mystic Islands .....L 6
National Park ......3,730..N 9
Navesink ....H 11
Neptune* ...27,863▲.H 8
Neptune City 5,502..H 8
Nesco ....K 5
Neshanic Station ...F 5
Netcong ......2,858..D 5
New Bedford ....H 8
New Brunswick .....41,885.°F 6
New Egypt ..1,769..I 6
New Gretna ....L 6
New Hanover* .27,410▲.I 5
New Lisbon ....I 5
New Milford 19,149..A 12
New Monmouth ....H 11
New Providence ....13,796..E 6
New Shrewsbury ......8,395..G 8
New Vernon ....E 6
New Village ....E 3
Newark ...381,930.°E 7
Newfield ....1,487..L 3
Newfoundland ......C 6
Newton ......7,297.°C 5
Newtonville ....L 4
Norma ....L 3
North Arlington 18,096..C 10
North Bergen ...47,751▲.C 12

Pine Hill ...5,132..O 11
Pine Valley ....23..O 11
Pinewald ....J 7
Piscataway* 36,418▲.F 6
Pitman ....10,257..O 10
Pittsgrove* ..4,618▲.L 3
Plainfield ..46,862..E 6
Plainsboro ...1,648▲.G 5
Pleasant Plains ....I 7
Pleasantville .....13,778..M 6
Pluckemin ....E 5
Plumsted* ...4,113▲.I 6
Pohatcong* ..3,924▲.E 3
Point Pleasant .15,968..I 8
Point Pleasant Beach ....4,882..I 8
Pomona ....L 5
Pompton Lakes ....11,397..C 7
Pompton Plains ....C 7
Port Colden ....D 4
Port Elizabeth .....M 3
Port Monmouth ....H 11
Port Morris ....D 5
Port Murray ....D 4
Port Norris .1,955..N 3
Port Reading ......F 9
Port Republic .586..L 6
Pottersville ....E 5
Princeton* ..13,651▲.G 5
Princeton ..12,311..G 5
Princeton Junction ....G 5
Prospect Park .....5,176..A 10
Quakertown ....F 4
Quinton ......2,567▲.L 1
Rahway ....29,114..E 7
Ramblewood* 5,556..J 4
Ramsey ....12,571..C 7
Rancocas ....I 4
Randolph* ..13,296▲.D 5
Raritan* ....6,934▲.F 4
Raritan .....6,691..F 5
Readington ..7,688▲.F 5
Reaville ....F 4
Red Bank ..12,847..G 8
Red Bank ....N 9
Richland ....L 4
Richwood ....K 3
Ridgefield ..11,308..B 12
Ridgefield Park .....13,990..B 11
Ridgeway ....I 7
Ridgewood .27,547..A 10
Riegelsville ....E 2
Ringoes ....F 4
Ringwood ..10,393..B 7
Rio Grande ..1,203..O 4
River Edge .12,850..A 11
River Vale ..8,883▲.C 8
Riverdale ...2,729..C 7
Riverside ....8,591▲.L 11
Riverton .....3,412..M 11
Riviera Beach ......I 7
Robbinsville ....H 5
Rochelle Park .....6,380▲.A 11
Rockaway* ..18,955▲.C 6
Rockaway ....6,383..D 6
Rockleigh .....308..C 8
Rocky Hill ....917..G 5
Roebling, see Florence [-Roebling]
Roosevelt .....814..H 6
Roseland .....4,453..D 7
Roselle ....22,585..E 9

Stillwater ...2,158▲.C 4
Stirling ....E 6
Stockholm ....B 6
Stockton ......619..G 3
Stone Harbor 1,089..O 4
Stow Creek* .1,050▲.M 1
Stratford ....9,801..O 11
Strathmore* 7,674..F 7
Succasunna ....D 5
Summit ....23,620..E 6
Surf City ....1,129..K 7
Sussex ....2,038..B 5
Swedesboro ..2,287..K 2
Tabernacle ..2,103▲.J 5
Tansboro ....O 12
Tavistock ....12..N 11
Taylortown ....C 6
Teaneck ...42,355▲.B 12
Tenafly ....14,827..C 8
Teterboro* .....19..D 8
Tewksbury* .2,959▲.E 4
Thorofare ....O 9
Three Bridges ......F 4
Titusville ....G 4
Toms River .7,303.°I 7
Totowa .....11,580..B 10
Towaco ....C 6
Town Bank ....O 4
Trenton ..104,786.°H 5
Troy Hills ....D 6
Tuckahoe ....N 4
Tuckerton ...1,926..L 6
Turnersville ....O 10
Union ....2,351▲.E 4
Union ......53,077▲.D 9
Union* .....1,539▲.K 7
Union Beach .....6,472..H 10
Union City .57,305..C 11
Uniontown ....E 3
Upper* ....3,413▲.N 5
Upper Deerfield* .6,648▲.L 2
Upper Freehold* .2,551▲.H 6
Upper Greenwood Lake* .....1,505..B 6
Upper Penns Neck* ....7,016▲.K 1
Upper Pittsgrove* ....2,884▲.L 2
Upper Saddle River .....7,949..C 8
Ventnor City .....10,385..M 6
Vernon ......6,059▲.B 6
Verona .....15,067..B 9
Victory Gardens ..1,027..D 6
Vienna ....D 4
Villas ....3,155..O 4
Vincentown ....J 5
Vineland ...47,399..L 3
Voorhees* ...6,214▲.J 3
Waldwick ..12,313..C 8
Wall ......16,498▲.H 8
Wallington .10,284..B 11
Walpack* .....384▲.B 4
Wanamassa ....H 8
Wanaque ...8,636..C 7
Wantage* ...4,329▲.B 5
Waretown ....K 7
Warren* ....8,592▲.E 6
Washington 10,577▲.C 8
Washington* 3,585▲.D 3
Washington* 6,962▲.D 4
Washington* 3,311▲.H 5
Washington* ....15,741▲.K 3
Washington* ..673▲.L 6

Cities, Towns, Townships, Boroughs, and Villages

Place	Pop.	Grid
Absecon	6,094	M 7
Adelphia		H 8
Albion		E 3
Alexandria*	2,127△	E 4
Allamuchy*	1,138△	C 4
Allendale	6,240	B 11
Allenhurst	1,012	L 8
Allentown	1,603	H 7
Allenwood		H 8
Alloway	2,550△	L 10
Almonesson		L 10
Alpha	2,826	C 3
Alpine	1,344	C 8
Andover	813	C 5
Annandale		E 4
Asbury		E 3
Asbury Park	16,533	K 8
Atco		M 6
Atlantic City	47,859	N 10
Audubon	5,102	H 11
Audubon Park	10,802	H 11
Avalon	815△	O 5
Avenel	1,283	K 7
Avon-by-the-Sea	2,163	K 8
Baptistown		F 3
Barnegat		K 7
Barnegat Light	554	K 8
Barrington	8,409	H 11
Basking Ridge		F 6
Bay Head	1,283	
Bayonne	72,743	J 7
Beach Haven	1,488	
Beachwood	4,390	
Bedminster	2,597△	F 5
Belle Mead		E 5
Belleville	37,629	
Bellmawr	15,618	H 11
Belmar	5,782	K 8
Belvidere	2,722	D 3
Bergenfield	29,000	B 11
Berkeley Heights	13,078△	E 4
Berlin	5,692	
Bernards*	13,355△	
Bernardsville	6,652	E 5
Beverly	3,105	
Blairstown	2,189△	C 4
Bloomfield	52,029	B 10
Bloomingdale	7,797	C 7

Place	Pop.	Grid
Cliffwood [-Cliffwood Beach]		
Clifton	82,056	G 10
Clinton	1,742	E 4
Closter	8,604	C 8
Collingswood	17,422	
Colonia	5,819△	
Colts Neck		G 7
Columbia		C 3
Columbus		H 7
Commercial*	3,667△	
Cookstown		H 7
Corbin City	258	
Cranbury	1,253	
Cranford	27,391△	G 7
Cresskill	8,298	C 8
Crosswicks		H 7
Culvers Lake		B 4
Dayton	2,401	H 6
Deal	554	K 8
Deerfield*	2,464△	
Delanco	4,157△	
Delaware*	3,249△	
Delran*	10,065△	
Demarest	5,133	C 8
Denville	14,045△	
Deptford*	24,232△	
Dover	15,039	
Downe*	1,177△	
Dumont	18,742	
Dunellen	7,072	
East Brunswick	34,166△	
Eagleswood*	823△	
East Amwell*	2,568△	
East Greenwich*	3,280△	
East Hanover	7,734△	
East Keansburg		H 8
East Millstone		
East Newark	1,922	
East Orange	75,471	
East Paterson	20,511	
East Rutherford	8,536	B 11
East Windsor	22,284△	
Eastampton*	1,385△	
Eatontown	14,619	
Edgewater	4,987	
Edgewater Park	7,412△	
Edison	67,120△	
Egg Harbor	9,882△	
Egg Harbor City	4,304	L 5

Place	Pop.	Grid
Gloucester*	26,511△	N 10
Gloucester City	14,707	
Goshen		O 4
Great Meadows		D 4
Green Bank	4,302△	
Green Village		G 7
Greenwich*	1,482△	E 3
Greenwich*	5,676△	
Greenwich*	3,667△	
Guttenberg	5,754	
Hackensack	36,008	B 11
Hackettstown	9,472	D 4
Haddon*	18,192△	
Haddon Heights	9,365	
Haddonfield	13,118	
Haledon	6,767	
Hamburg	1,820	B 7
Hamilton	79,609△	
Hamilton	7,299△	
Hamilton Square [-Hamilton Square]		
Hammonton	11,464	
Hampton	2,091△	
Hampton*	1,386	
Hanover*	10,700△	
Harding*	3,249△	
Hardwick	548△	
Hardyston*	3,499△	
Harmony	2,195△	E 3
Harrington Park	4,841	
Harrison	11,811	
Harvey Cedars	314	K 7
Hasbrouck Heights	13,651	B 11
Haworth	3,760	
Hawthorne	19,173	
Hazlet	22,239△	
Helmetta	955	
High Bridge	3,687△	
Highland Park	14,385	
Highlands	3,916	
Hightstown	3,431	
Hillsborough*	11,061△	
Hillsdale	11,768	
Hillside	21,636△	
Hi-Nella	1,195	
Hoboken	45,380	
Ho-Ho-Kus	4,348	
Holland*	3,587△	
Holmdel	6,417△	
Hopatcong	9,052	
Hope	1,030△	
Hopewell	3,970△	
Hopewell	1,395	
Hornerstown	6,470	

Place	Pop.	Grid
Long Branch	31,774	G 8
Long Valley	1,645	
Longport	1,225	N 6
Lopatcong*	3,144△	
Lower Alloways Creek*	1,400△	
Lumberton	3,945△	
Lyndhurst	22,729	
Madison	16,710	
Magnolia	5,893	
Mahwah	10,800	
Manahawkin	1,278	
Manalapan*	5,754	
Manasquan	4,971	
Manchester*	7,550△	
Mannington*	1,913△	
Mansfield*	2,597△	
Mansfield*	2,990△	
Mantoloking	319	
Mantua*	6,767	
Manville	10,643	
Maple Shade	16,464	
Maplewood	24,932	
Margate City	10,576	
Marlboro*	12,273△	
Marlton	10,180	
Matawan	9,136	
Maurice River*	3,743△	N 3
Mays Landing	1,272	M 4
Maywood	11,087	
Medford	17,680△	
Medford Lakes	4,792	
Mendham	3,697△	
Mendham*	3,729△	
Mercerville [-Hamilton Square]	24,465	H 5
Merchantville	4,425	
Metuchen	16,031	
Middle*	8,725△	
Middlesex	15,038	
Middletown*	54,623△	H 10
Midland Park	8,159	
Milford	1,344	
Millburn	21,089△	
Millstone	630	
Millstone*	2,535△	
Milltown	6,470	

Place	Pop.	Grid
North Branch		E 5
North Brunswick*	16,691△	F 6
North Caldwell	6,733	B 9
North Cape May	3,812	O 4
North Haledon	7,614	A 10
North Hanover*	9,858△	I 5
North Plainfield	21,796	E 6
North Princeton	5,488	G 5
North Wildwood	3,914	O 4
Northfield	8,875	N 6
Northvale	5,177	C 8
Norwood	4,398	C 10
Nutley	31,913	
Oakhurst	5,558	G 8
Oakland	14,420	C 7
Oaklyn	4,626	
Ocean*	18,643△	
Ocean City	10,575	N 7
Ocean Gate	1,081	
Oceanport	7,503	G 8
Ogdensburg	2,222	C 4
Old Bridge	25,176	F 7
Old Tappan	3,917	C 8
Oldmans*	2,088△	
Oradell	8,903	A 11
Orange	32,566	C 9
Oxford	1,411	D 3
Pahaquarry*	71△	C 3
Palisades Park	13,351	B 12
Palmyra	6,969	
Paramus	28,381	A 11
Park Ridge	8,709	
Parsippany-Troy Hills	55,112△	D 7
Passaic	55,124	
Paterson	144,824	O A 10
Paulsboro	8,084	J 2
Peapack [-Gladstone]	1,924	
Pemberton	1,344	
Pemberton*	19,754△	K 5
Pennington	2,151	G 4
Penns Grove	5,727	K 1
Pennsauken	36,394△	
Pennsville	13,296△	L 1
Pequannock*	14,350△	C 7
Perth Amboy	38,798	F 7
Phillipsburg	17,849	D 3
Pilesgrove*	2,706△	
Pine Beach	1,395	

Place	Pop.	Grid
Washington	5,943	D 3
Washington Crossing		G 4
Washington Valley		D 6
Watchung	4,750	
Waterford	4,073	K 4
Waterford Works		
Wayne	49,141△	B 11
Weehawken	13,383	C 12
Wenonah	2,364	O 10
West Amwell*	2,142△	G 4
West Belmar		H 8
West Caldwell	11,913	O 4
West Cape May	1,005	K 7
West Deptford*	13,928△	J 2
West Keansburg		H 10
West Long Branch	6,845	G 8
West Milford	17,304	B 6
West New York	40,627	C 12
West Orange	43,715	C 9
West Paterson	11,692	B 10
West Wildwood	235	O 4
West Windsor*	6,431△	G 5
Westampton*	2,680△	
Westfield	33,720	
Westville	5,170	
Westwood	11,105	
Weymouth*	998△	
Wharton	5,535	
Whippany		
White Horse [-White Horse]	2,326△	B 3
White House Station	1,019	E 4
White Meadow Lake	8,499	C 6
Whiting	14,058△	G 6
Wildwood	4,110	O 4
Wildwood Crest	3,483	
Williamstown	3,621	O 10
Willingboro	44,607△	
Winfield	2,184	
Winslow	11,202△	K 4
Wood Ridge	8,311	B 11
Woodbine	2,625	
Woodbridge	98,944△	J 7
Woodbury	12,408	O J 3
Woodbury Heights	3,621	
Woodcliff Lake	5,506	C 8
Woodland*	2,032△	
Woodlynne	3,101	N 10
Woodstown	3,137	
Woolwich*	1,147△	K 2
Wrightstown	2,719	
Wyckoff	16,039△	C 7
Yardville [-White Horse]	18,680	H 5

Source: Latest census figures (1970 and special censuses); 1972 U.S. Census Bureau estimate for New York Metropolitan Area. Places without population figures are unincorporated areas and are not listed in census reports.

*Does not appear on the map; key shows general location.
△Entire township, including rural area.
○County seat.

The 1970 U.S. census reported that New Jersey had 7,168,164 persons. The population had increased 18 per cent over the 1960 figure, 6,066,782. The U.S. Bureau of the Census estimated that by 1975, New Jersey's population had reached about 7,316,000.

About 89 out of 100 New Jerseyans live in urban areas. This percentage of urban dwellers is the second highest among the states. Only California has a higher percentage. Twelve Standard Metropolitan Statistical Areas lie either partly or entirely in New Jersey (see METROPOLITAN AREA). About 6¾ million New Jerseyans live in these areas. The metropolitan areas that lie entirely within New Jersey are Atlantic City, Jersey City, Long Branch-Asbury Park, New Brunswick-Perth Amboy-Sayreville, Newark, Paterson-Clifton-Passaic, Trenton, and Vineland-Millville-Bridgeton. Metropolitan areas that extend into New Jersey are Allentown-Bethlehem-Easton and Philadelphia, both in Pennsylvania; New York City in New York; and Wilmington, in Delaware and Maryland. For the populations of these metropolitan areas, see the *Index* with the political map in this article. Northeastern New Jersey and the New York City and Nassau-Suffolk Standard Metropolitan Statistical Areas form a Standard Consolidated Area with 16,293,700 persons.

Newark is New Jersey's largest city. Other cities with more than 100,000 persons, in order of population, include Jersey City, Paterson, Elizabeth, Trenton, and Camden. See the separate articles on New Jersey cities listed in the *Related Articles* at the end of this article.

About 90 per cent of all New Jerseyans were born in the U.S. Many of those born in other countries came from Italy. Roman Catholics make up the largest religious body. Other groups include Baptists, Episcopalians, Jews, Lutherans, Methodists, and Presbyterians.

Jersey Pictures Inc.

Factory Workers stream from a plant in Jersey City at the end of the day. Many of the city's industrial plants employ more than a thousand workers and operate two or even three shifts a day.

Farm Workers use special scooplike rakes to gather cranberries on a truck farm in southern New Jersey. The state's farmers find nearby markets for their products in several metropolitan centers.
Three Lions

POPULATION

This map shows the *population density* of New Jersey, and how it varies in different parts of the state. Population density means the average number of persons who live in a given area.

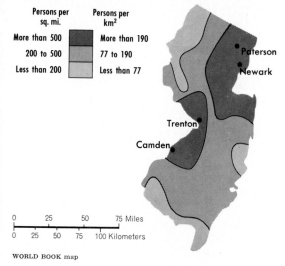

Persons per sq. mi.	Persons per km²
More than 500	More than 190
200 to 500	77 to 190
Less than 200	Less than 77

WORLD BOOK map

Schools. Colonial New Jersey had no public schools. Children attended school only if their parents could afford to pay tuition. New Jersey's public school system began in 1817, when the legislature established a permanent school fund. But taxes were not used to help support schools until 1829.

A state commissioner of education and a 12-member board of education direct New Jersey's public school system. The governor, with the senate's approval, appoints the commissioner to a five-year term and the board members to six-year terms. Local boards administer local school districts. The chancellor of higher education directs the state's public college system.

New Jersey law requires children between the ages of 6 and 16 to attend school. For the number of students and teachers in New Jersey, see EDUCATION (table).

Two of the oldest U.S. universities and colleges are in New Jersey. They are Princeton University (1746) and Rutgers, The State University (1766).

Libraries. Thomas Cadwalader founded New Jersey's first library at Trenton in 1750. Today, New Jersey has about 350 public libraries and more than 200 industrial and other special research libraries. The State Library in Trenton has large law and general reference collections that serve state government officials. The Interlibrary Reference and Loan Service loans books to libraries throughout the state. The Harvey S. Firestone Memorial Library of Princeton University is New Jersey's largest school library.

Museums. The New Jersey State Museum in Trenton features fine arts and natural history exhibits. It includes an auditorium, exhibition halls, and a planetarium. The Newark Museum includes a planetarium and art, science, and natural history exhibits. The New Jersey Historical Society in Newark has a museum featuring historic items. The Montclair Art Museum displays excellent collections of paintings and sculpture.

UNIVERSITIES AND COLLEGES

New Jersey has 29 universities and colleges accredited by the Middle States Association of Colleges and Secondary Schools. For enrollments and further information, see UNIVERSITIES AND COLLEGES (table).

Name	Location	Founded
Bloomfield College	Bloomfield	1868
Caldwell College	Caldwell	1939
Centenary College for Women	Hackettstown	1867
Don Bosco College	Newton	1938
Drew University	Madison	1867
Fairleigh Dickinson University	Rutherford	1941
Felician College	Lodi	1967
Georgian Court College	Lakewood	1908
Glassboro State College	Glassboro	1923
Jersey City State College	Jersey City	1921
Kean College of New Jersey	Union	1934
Monmouth College	West Long Branch	1933
Montclair State College	Montclair	1908
New Jersey Institute of Technology	Newark	1881
Northeastern Bible College	Essex Fells	1964
Princeton Theological Seminary	Princeton	1812
Princeton University	Princeton	1746
Ramapo College of New Jersey	Mahwah	1969
Rider College	Trenton	1865
Rutgers, The State University	New Brunswick	1766
St. Elizabeth, College of	Convent Station	1899
St. Peter's College	Jersey City	1872
Seton Hall University	South Orange	1856
Stevens Institute of Technology	Hoboken	1870
Stockton State College	Pomona	1969
Trenton State College	Trenton	1855
Upsala College	East Orange	1893
Westminster Choir College	Princeton	1926
William Paterson College of New Jersey	Wayne	1855

Holder Hall at Princeton University in Princeton

Joseph De Caro, Three Lions

NEW JERSEY / *A Visitor's Guide*

New Jersey is one of the great coastal playgrounds of the United States. Every year, millions of vacationers flock to the state's seaside resorts. They swim in the Atlantic Ocean, sunbathe on sandy beaches, and stroll along boardwalks lined with shops. Visitors also enjoy dozens of historic sites, chiefly in or near inland cities.

New Jersey attracts many sportsmen. Fishermen can catch game fish in the ocean. Inland, they can cast for trout in 1,400 miles (2,250 kilometers) of stocked streams. Hunters shoot ducks in coastal areas, and deer, pheasants, and rabbits on inland public shooting grounds. Sailing is popular in the coastal bays.

City of Atlantic City

Convention Hall in Atlantic City

Scheller, Three Lions

The Old Barracks in Trenton

Scheller, Three Lions

The Barn in the Colonial Village of Batsto

PLACES TO VISIT

Following are brief descriptions of some of New Jersey's many interesting places to visit.

Barnegat Lighthouse, near Barnegat Light, is a favorite subject of painters and photographers. The lighthouse is part of a state park that also includes a museum and a sandy beach.

Batsto is a partially restored colonial village in southeastern New Jersey. The community produced cannon balls for General George Washington's troops during the Revolutionary War. Attractions include an ironmaster's house, a blacksmith's shop, a general store, and a glassware exhibition.

Burlington features the birthplaces of novelist James Fenimore Cooper and James Lawrence, the naval officer whose famous dying command was "Don't give up the ship."

Camden includes *Walt Whitman House*, the great poet's home from 1884 until 1892. The house has many mementos of Whitman.

Delaware Water Gap is a deep narrow gorge formed where the Delaware River cuts through the Kittatinny Mountains. This scenic gap separates New Jersey and Pennsylvania north of Columbia, N.J.

Princeton is the home of Princeton University and Princeton Battlefield, the site of an important colonial victory in the Revolutionary War. The university's Nassau Hall served as the U.S. Capitol in 1783.

Seaside Resorts include Asbury Park, Atlantic City, Cape May, North Wildwood, Ocean City, Seaside Heights, Wildwood, and Wildwood Crest. Atlantic City, the most famous resort, has a 7-mile (11-kilometer) boardwalk and a convention hall that can seat 41,000 persons.

Trenton has many points of interest, including the New Jersey State Museum, the State Capitol, and the Old Barracks, used by British soldiers during the French and Indian Wars.

National Park and Historic Site. Morristown National Historical Park, established in 1933, lies in and near Morristown. It includes Ford Mansion, George Washington's headquarters during the winter of 1779-1780; Fort Nonsense, a restoration of a fort built in 1777; and several camps used by American soldiers during the Revolutionary War. See NATIONAL PARK SYSTEM (table: National Historical Parks). The Edison National Historic Site in West Orange includes the inventor's home, library, and models of some of his inventions.

State Parks and Forests. New Jersey has 25 state parks and 10 state forests. For information, write to New Jersey Office of Tourism and Promotion, Department of Labor and Industry, P.O. Box 400, Trenton, N.J. 08625.

New Jersey and New York together maintain Palisades Interstate Park. See PALISADES.

WORLD BOOK photo by Three Lions

Barnegat Lighthouse near Barnegat Light

The Miss America Pageant, held each September in Atlantic City, is New Jersey's best-known annual event. This nationally televised pageant features girls from every state. They compete for the title of Miss America on the basis of beauty, charm, and talent. Other annual events in New Jersey include the following.

January-March: Winter Sports Carnival near Mc-Affee (January-March); New Jersey Flower and Garden Show in Morristown (March).

April-June: Easter Sunday Promenades in Asbury Park, Atlantic City, and Seaside Heights (April); Cherry Blossom Display at Branch Brook Park in Newark (April); Dog Shows in Plainfield, Rumson, and Trenton (May); Art Show On-the-Rail in Atlantic City (May); Cavalcade of Sports Cars in Ocean City (June); National Marbles Tournament in Wildwood (June); Sussex County Outdoor Show (June).

July-September: Grand Prix Ocean Races at Point Pleasant Beach (July); Old Home Historical Tour in Cape May (July); "Night in Venice" Boat Parade in Ocean City (July); Miss New Jersey Beauty Pageant in Cherry Hill (July); National Shuffleboard Championships in Ocean City (July); Baby Parades in Avalon, Ocean City, Sea Isle City, and Wildwoods (August); Flemington Fair in Flemington (August); Striped Bass (Fishing) Derby in Atlantic City (September and October); State Fair in Trenton (September).

October-December: Striped Bass Derby at Long Beach Island (October); Memorial honoring Washington's crossing of the Delaware, at Washington Crossing (Dec. 25).

Beach at Ocean City on the Atlantic Coast
Scheller, Three Lions

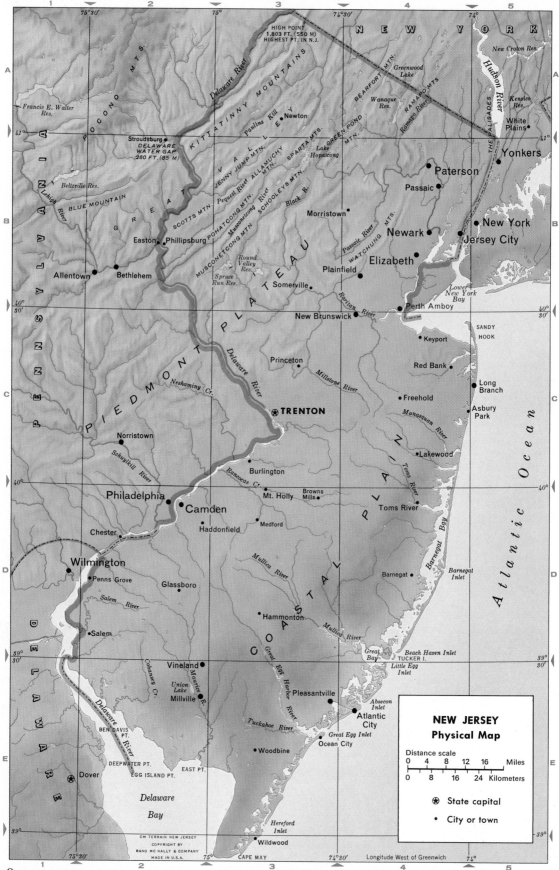

NEW JERSEY

Physical Map

Distance scale

0 4 8 12 16 Miles

0 8 16 24 Kilometers

✸ State capital

• City or town

CM TERRAIN NEW JERSEY
COPYRIGHT BY
RAND McNALLY & COMPANY
MADE IN U.S.A.

Longitude West of Greenwich

Specially created for **World Book Encyclopedia** by Rand McNally and World Book editors

Land Regions. New Jersey has four main land regions. They are, from northwest to southeast: (1) the Appalachian Ridge and Valley Region, (2) the New England Upland, (3) the Piedmont, and (4) the Atlantic Coastal Plain.

The Appalachian Ridge and Valley Region is a mountainous area in the northwestern corner of the state. It is part of a large region of the same name that runs from New York to Alabama. In New Jersey, it includes the Kittatinny Mountains and several valleys. The Kittatinny Mountains run parallel to New Jersey's northwestern border. The Delaware Water Gap, formed where the Delaware River cuts through the mountains, is one of the most scenic areas in the East. The Appalachian Valley lies southeast of the Kittatinny Mountains. This wide valley is part of the larger Great Valley. The Appalachian Valley is broken by ridges of shale and depressions of limestone. Herds of dairy cattle graze on grassy slopes in the valley, and farmers there raise apples and vegetables.

The New England Upland, usually called the *Highlands*, lies southeast of the Appalachian Ridge and Valley Region. The region extends into New York and Pennsylvania. Flat-topped ridges of hard rock, called *gneiss*, cover much of the New England Upland in New Jersey. Many lakes nestle among the ridges of the New England Upland in New Jersey. These lakes are among the state's most important tourist attractions.

The Piedmont crosses northern New Jersey in a belt 20 miles (32 kilometers) wide southeast of the New England Upland. The Piedmont covers an area from New York to Alabama. It covers only about a fifth of New Jersey, but about two-thirds of the state's people live there. The region includes such large industrial cities as Elizabeth, Jersey City, Newark, and Paterson. The cities of the Piedmont region owe much of their industrial importance to the many large rivers in the area. These rivers include the Hudson, the Musconetcong, the Passaic, the Ramapo, and the Raritan.

The Atlantic Coastal Plain is a gently-rolling lowland that covers the southern three-fifths of New Jersey. It is part of a plain with the same name that stretches from New York to Florida. In New Jersey, more than half the plain lies less than 100 feet (30 meters) above sea level. In the west and southwest, fertile soil supports many truck farms. Camden, Trenton, and other cities lie along the wide Delaware River in the western part of the plain. To the east, forests and salt marshes cover much of the Atlantic Coastal Plain. For this reason, large areas of the region are thinly populated. Salt marshes, shallow lagoons, and meadows lie near New Jersey's Atlantic coast. Over 50 resort cities and towns, including Asbury Park, Atlantic City, and Cape May,

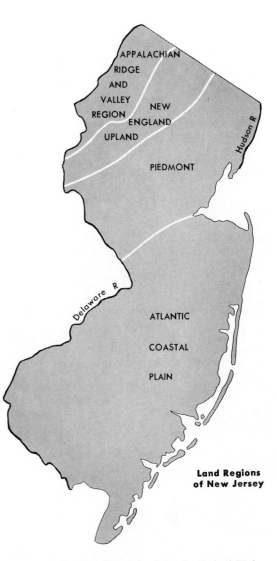

**Land Regions
of New Jersey**

lie on the eastern edge of the Atlantic Coastal Plain.

Coastline. A long, narrow sandbar makes up most of New Jersey's 130-mile (209-kilometer) coastline. Many inlets break the coast and lead to bays between the sandbar and the mainland. New Jersey's coastal bays include, from south to north, Great Egg Bay, Great Bay, Little Egg Harbor, Barnegat Bay, Sandy Hook Bay, Raritan Bay, and Newark Bay. The sandy beaches along New Jersey's coast make up one of the most popular vacation areas in the United States.

Map Index

NEW JERSEY

Mountains. New Jersey's only mountainous area is in the northwest. High Point, the state's highest peak, rises 1,803 feet (550 meters) in the northwestern corner of the state. It is in the Kittatinny Mountains, New Jersey's chief mountain range. Other ranges include the Sourland and Watchung mountains. They rise about 450 feet (137 meters) in the Piedmont region.

Rivers and Lakes. New Jersey's most important rivers are the Delaware and the Hudson. The Delaware forms the state's western border and empties into Delaware Bay. The Hudson separates New Jersey and New York in the northeast and flows into the Atlantic Ocean. The Raritan is the longest river entirely within New Jersey. It flows about 75 miles (121 kilometers) through the north. Other important rivers in the north include the Hackensack, Millstone, Musconetcong, and Passaic. Southern New Jersey rivers include Great Egg Harbor, Maurice, Mullica, and Toms.

Most of New Jersey's more than 800 lakes and ponds are in the north. Lake Hopatcong is the state's largest lake. Other large lakes include Budd, Culvers, Green Pond, Greenwood (partly in New York), Lake Mohawk, and Swartswood.

Lake Hopatcong, the state's largest lake, nestles among rocky, flat-topped hills in the New England Upland region of northern New Jersey.
Scheller, Three Lions

Grazing Horses feed in a rich green pasture in the gently rolling Piedmont region of north-central New Jersey.
Scheller, Three Lions

WORLD BOOK photo by Three Lions

Fertile Soil supports many truck farms in the Atlantic Coastal Plain region of southern New Jersey. The state is a chief producer of vegetables.

NEW JERSEY/Climate

New Jersey has a mild climate. Ocean breezes keep the eastern coast cool in summer and relatively warm in winter. Average July temperatures range from 76° F. (24° C) in the southwest to 70° F. (21° C) in the north. On July 10, 1936, Runyon had the state's highest temperature, 110° F. (43° C). Average January temperatures range from 34° F. (1° C) at Cape May to 26° F. (−3° C) in the Appalachian Ridge and Valley Region. On Jan. 5, 1904, River Vale had the state's lowest temperature, −34° F. (−37° C).

Snowfall averages about 13 inches (33 centimeters) a year in the south, and 50 inches (130 centimeters) in the north. New Jersey averages about 46 inches (117 centimeters) of *precipitation* (rain, melted snow, and other forms of moisture) a year. Precipitation is fairly evenly distributed throughout the state.

Scheller, Three Lions

Gentle Ocean Breezes keep Ship Bottom and other resort areas along the Atlantic Coast cool in summer and warm in winter.

SEASONAL TEMPERATURES

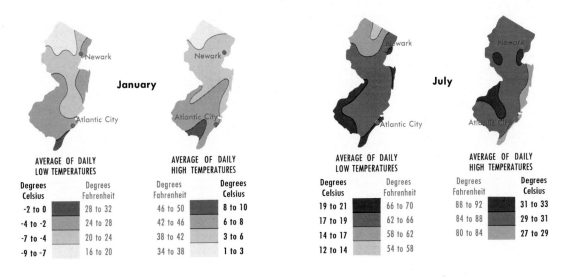

January

AVERAGE OF DAILY LOW TEMPERATURES

Degrees Celsius	Degrees Fahrenheit
-2 to 0	28 to 32
-4 to -2	24 to 28
-7 to -4	20 to 24
-9 to -7	16 to 20

AVERAGE OF DAILY HIGH TEMPERATURES

Degrees Fahrenheit	Degrees Celsius
46 to 50	8 to 10
42 to 46	6 to 8
38 to 42	3 to 6
34 to 38	1 to 3

July

AVERAGE OF DAILY LOW TEMPERATURES

Degrees Celsius	Degrees Fahrenheit
19 to 21	66 to 70
17 to 19	62 to 66
14 to 17	58 to 62
12 to 14	54 to 58

AVERAGE OF DAILY HIGH TEMPERATURES

Degrees Fahrenheit	Degrees Celsius
88 to 92	31 to 33
84 to 88	29 to 31
80 to 84	27 to 29

AVERAGE YEARLY PRECIPITATION
(Rain, Melted Snow, and Other Moisture)

Centimeters	Inches
112 to 122	44 to 48

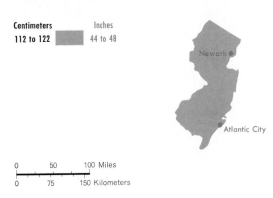

0	50	100 Miles
0	75	150 Kilometers

WORLD BOOK maps

AVERAGE MONTHLY WEATHER

	NEWARK					ATLANTIC CITY				
	Temperatures				Days of Rain or Snow		Temperatures			Days of Rain or Snow
	F.°		C°				F.°		C°	
	High	Low	High	Low			High	Low	High	Low	
JAN.	39	24	4	-4	12	JAN.	42	29	6	-2	12
FEB.	40	24	4	-4	10	FEB.	42	29	6	-2	10
MAR.	49	32	9	0	12	MAR.	48	35	9	2	12
APR.	60	40	16	4	12	APR.	56	43	13	6	11
MAY	71	51	22	11	12	MAY	65	53	18	12	11
JUNE	81	60	27	16	10	JUNE	75	62	24	17	10
JULY	85	66	29	19	10	JULY	79	68	26	20	10
AUG.	83	64	28	18	10	AUG.	79	67	26	19	10
SEPT.	77	57	25	14	8	SEPT.	74	62	23	17	8
OCT.	65	46	18	8	7	OCT.	65	51	18	11	9
NOV.	53	37	12	3	9	NOV.	55	41	13	5	9
DEC.	41	27	5	-3	11	DEC.	45	31	7	-1	10

Despite its small size, New Jersey ranks among the leading industrial states. Manufacturing, the state's most important economic activity, employs more than 800,000 workers in about 15,000 plants. These plants are mainly in the Elizabeth-Jersey City-Newark area in the northeast, and in the Trenton-Camden area in the west. New Jersey is sometimes called the *Workshop of the Nation* because of the great number of manufactured products its factories turn out.

The beach-lined Atlantic seaboard is the center of New Jersey's flourishing tourist trade. Tourism ranks as the state's second most important economic activity. The millions of tourists who visit the state each year contribute about $3½ billion to the economy.

New Jersey's location between New York City and Philadelphia helps the state's economy. Thousands of New Jerseyans work in these two cities.

Natural Resources of New Jersey include fertile soils, large forests, and small deposits of minerals. Unlike many other states, New Jersey does not rely on its own resources for the raw materials of its industries.

Soil. Three types of soil are most common in New Jersey. In the north, the soil has a high limestone and glacial mineral content. Farmers in this region raise field crops and operate dairy farms. A rich subsoil of greensand marl lies under rich loam in central New Jersey. This mixture yields good vegetable crops. When mixed with fertilizer, the sandy soil of the south supports fruit orchards and vegetable farms.

Minerals. Stone (especially basalt, granite, limestone, and sandstone) is New Jersey's most abundant mineral. The counties in northern New Jersey produce almost all the stone. Sand and gravel deposits are found throughout New Jersey. Bergen, Passaic, and other northern counties produce sand and gravel for construction. Cumberland, Camden, and other southern counties produce industrial sand for glassmaking and foundry work. Other minerals include clay, greensand marl, peat, and zinc.

Forests cover about half of New Jersey. Beech, birch, maple, oak, sweet gums, yellow poplar, and other hardwoods are the most valuable trees in the north. Important trees of southern New Jersey include cedar, pitch pine, and shortleaf pine.

Plant Life. The purple violet, the state flower, grows in wooded areas throughout the state. Honeysuckle, goldenrod, and Queen Anne's lace grow in many areas. Other flowers include azaleas, buttercups, mountain laurels, rhododendrons, and Virginia cowslips.

Animal Life. New Jersey animals include deer, foxes, minks, muskrats, opossums, otters, rabbits, raccoons, and skunks. Hunters shoot wild ducks and geese along the marshy shores of the Atlantic Ocean. Game birds of the meadows and woodlands include partridges, pheasants, quail, ruffed grouse, and wild turkeys.

Clams, crabs, lobsters, menhaden, and oysters live in New Jersey's coastal waters. The state's bays and streams abound with bass, bluefish, crappies, pickerel, pike, salmon, shad, sturgeon, trout, and weakfish.

Manufacturing accounts for about 97 per cent of the value of goods produced in New Jersey. Goods manufactured there have a *value added by manufacture* of about

Production of Goods in New Jersey

Total value of goods produced in 1973—$18,197,804,000

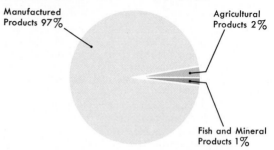

Manufactured Products 97%

Agricultural Products 2%

Fish and Mineral Products 1%

Percentages are based on farm income, value added by manufacture, and value of fish and mineral production.
Sources: U.S. government publications, 1975-1976.

Employment in New Jersey

Total number of persons employed in 1974—2,801,600

		Number of Employees
Manufacturing	🧍🧍🧍🧍🧍🧍🧍🧍🧍	822,000
Wholesale & Retail Trade	🧍🧍🧍🧍🧍🧍🧍	604,800
Community, Social, & Personal Services	🧍🧍🧍🧍🧍	474,900
Government	🧍🧍🧍🧍🧍	437,600
Transportation & Public Utilities	🧍🧍	184,400
Finance, Insurance, & Real Estate	🧍🧍	137,100
Construction	🧍🧍	117,700
Agriculture & Mining	🧍	23,100

Sources: *Employment and Earnings*, May 1975, U.S. Bureau of Labor Statistics; *Farm Labor*, February 1975, U.S. Department of Agriculture.

$18 billion a year. This figure represents the value created in products by New Jersey's industries, not counting such costs as materials, supplies, and fuels. New Jersey is a leader among the states in manufacturing and processing. New Jersey's chief manufacturing industries are, in order of importance, (1) the chemical industry, (2) electrical machinery manufacturing, and (3) food processing.

The Chemical Industry has a yearly value added of about $4½ billion. New Jersey leads the states in chemical production. Important products include basic chemicals, drugs and vitamins, cleaning solutions, explosives, paints and varnishes, plastics, and soaps. New Jersey has about 1,000 chemical plants. Most of these plants are near the Hudson River across from New York City, and in an area stretching from Newark to Camden.

Electrical Machinery Manufacturing in New Jersey has a value added of about $1¾ billion a year. New Jersey factories make lamps, phonographs, radios, stoves, television sets, washing machines, driers, and other electrical products for home use. They also turn out generators, motors, transformers, and other machines for industrial use. Homes and factories throughout the United States use telephones made by New Jersey manufacturers. The electrical machinery industry in New

Jersey is centered in three small northeastern counties. These counties are Essex, Hudson, and Union.

Food Processing accounts for about $1½ billion of New Jersey's value added by manufacture. Factories in northeastern New Jersey process a wide variety of foods, including meats, vegetables, and fruits. Plants in the southwest can and process fruits and vegetables from nearby truck gardens and orchards.

Other Industries, in order of importance, make nonelectrical machinery; fabricated metal products; transportation equipment (including automobiles); printed materials; and stone, clay, and glass products. Ranking next in importance are the manufacture of apparel, primary metals, and rubber products.

Industrial Research plants in New Jersey number more than 725. These plants spend about $3 billion a year to develop and improve products. This figure is about a tenth of all the money spent on industrial research in the United States. New Jersey researchers developed the transistor, and the electronic "brain" used for missiles. They also improved fuels, color television, and other products.

Agriculture accounts for about 2 per cent of the value of goods produced in New Jersey. New Jersey farmers earn about $310 million a year. The state's 8,493 farms average about 122 acres (49.4 hectares) in size.

Seabrook Farms, New Jersey's largest farm, covers nearly 5,000 acres (2,000 hectares) in Cumberland County. Seabrook Farms scientists carry on extensive studies of soil, weather, and growing methods to improve farm techniques.

Vegetables earn over a fourth of New Jersey's farm income. New Jersey is an important vegetable-growing state. It ranks high in the production of tomatoes, its chief vegetable crop. New Jersey farmers also raise asparagus, cabbage, lettuce, peppers, potatoes, and sweet corn. Vegetable farms thrive in many areas of New Jersey, but the largest ones are in the southwestern part of the state.

Dairy Products account for about 15 per cent of New Jersey's farm income. Milk, milkfat, and ice cream are the state's leading dairy products. Dairy farms flourish in the northwest, especially in Hunterdon, Sussex, and Warren counties.

Poultry and Poultry Products account for about 14 per cent of New Jersey's farm income. New Jersey chickens lay about 735 million eggs annually. Most of the eggs are sold as food, but many hatch into commercially valuable baby chicks. New Jersey farmers sell thousands of chickens and turkeys each year. Poultry farms are most numerous in Cumberland, Hunterdon, Monmouth, and Salem counties.

Greenhouse and Nursery Products are raised chiefly in northeastern New Jersey for sale in the New York City area. These products have an annual value of about $45 million. Millions of roses are grown in the state yearly. Nearly 1 million orchids a year come from Middlesex. New Jersey greenhouses also raise African violets, azaleas, chrysanthemums, geraniums, hydrangeas, lilies, and poinsettias. Leading nursery products in New Jersey include arborvitae, holly, junipers, yews, and a wide variety of other shrubs.

WORLD BOOK photo by Three Lions

A Research Chemist conducts an experiment on pigments and dyes in a laboratory in Toms River. New Jersey has about 1,000 chemical plants, and leads the states in chemical production.

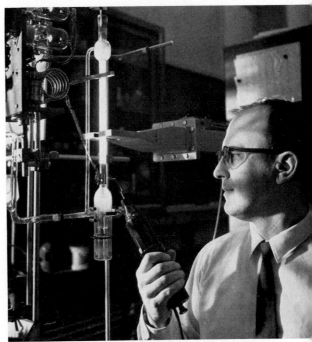

Bell Telephone Laboratories

An Electronics Researcher demonstrates a new electronic technique at Bell Telephone Laboratories near Berkeley Heights. Electrical machinery manufacturing is a chief New Jersey industry.

208e

Urwiller, Three Lions

FARM, MINERAL, AND FOREST PRODUCTS

This map shows where the state's leading farm, mineral, and forest products are produced. The major urban areas (shown on the map in red) are the state's important manufacturing centers.

0   10   20   30   40 Miles
0 10 20 30 40 50 60 Kilometers

WORLD BOOK map

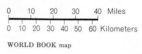

George Washington Bridge crosses the Hudson River, and links Fort Lee with New York City, background. The bridge is used daily by thousands of commuters who live in New Jersey and work in New York City.

Fruits. Large peach crops grow in southern New Jersey. Several varieties, including the Jerseyland and Sunhigh, were developed in the state. Apple orchards dot central and southern New Jersey. Other fruits include blueberries, cranberries, grapes, and strawberries.

Field Crops grown in the state are used chiefly to feed livestock. They include barley, corn, hay, and wheat.

Mining adds about $115 million a year to New Jersey's economy. Stone is the state's most important mineral. One of the most valuable types of stone in New Jersey is basalt, used to build roads. Miners take basalt from quarries in Essex, Hudson, Hunterdon, Mercer, Passaic, Somerset, and Union counties. Zinc also comes from Sussex County. Clay from Burlington, Cumberland, Middlesex, and Somerset counties is used in the state's brick and tile industries. Hunterdon, Morris, Passaic, and Sussex counties produce granite. Sussex and Warren counties are leading producers of crushed limestone. Most of the nation's greensand marl comes from Gloucester County. It is used chiefly as a water-softening agent. Other important minerals in New Jersey include sand and gravel and peat.

Fishing Industry. New Jersey's fish catch has an annual value of about $20 million. New Jersey fishermen take in about a fourth of the clams caught in the United States. Huge clam beds extend from Barnegat Bay to Cape May. New Jersey fishermen also catch crabs, flounder, lobsters, menhaden, oysters, porgy, scallops, tuna, and whiting.

Electric Power. Most of New Jersey's electric power comes from generating plants operated by the state's four investor-owned electric utilities. These plants burn oil and coal to produce electricity. Nuclear power plants also generate some electricity in New Jersey.

Transportation. New Jersey lies in the path between New York City and the western and southern states. This location makes New Jersey highways and railroads important links in the United States transportation system.

About 15 airlines serve New Jersey. The state has over 150 airports. Newark International Airport is one of the nation's chief air terminals. The first regular airplane passenger service in the United States began operating in 1919 between Atlantic City and New York City.

Railroads operate on about 1,850 miles (3,000 kilometers) of track in New Jersey. About 15 rail lines provide freight service. Passenger trains serve seven New Jersey cities. Swift commuter trains serve thousands of New Jerseyans who work in New York City and Philadelphia.

In 1891, New Jersey became the first state to help local communities build roads. New Jersey now has about 32,000 miles (51,500 kilometers) of roads and highways, most of which are surfaced. The 141-mile (227-kilometer) New Jersey Turnpike runs from Deepwater in the southwest to Ridgefield Park in the northeast. The turnpike was opened in 1952 and was extended in 1956. The 173-mile (278-kilometer) Garden

A Flower Grower waters plants in one of northeastern New Jersey's many greenhouses. Large numbers of roses, orchids, and geraniums are raised for sale in the New York City area. Many New Jersey nurseries grow ornamental landscaping shrubs.

State Parkway crosses New Jersey from the New York state line near Montvale to Cape May, at New Jersey's southern tip. The Garden State Parkway was completed in 1957. The Pulaski Skyway is a four-lane elevated road between Jersey City and Newark.

Bridges and tunnels link New Jersey and neighboring states. The George Washington Bridge, one of the world's longest suspension bridges, spans the Hudson River between Fort Lee and New York City. The Bayonne Bridge, the longest steel arch bridge in the world, crosses Kill Van Kull, a channel between Bayonne and Staten Island. Bridges across the Delaware River include the Benjamin Franklin Bridge between Camden and Philadelphia and the Delaware Memorial Bridge Twin Span between Deepwater and the New Castle, Del., area. The Holland and Lincoln tunnels and the Hudson tubes under the Hudson River link New Jersey and New York City.

New Jersey has important ports along the Hudson and Delaware rivers, in Newark and Raritan Bay, and along Kill Van Kull and Arthur Kill. New Jersey's part of the Atlantic Intracoastal Waterway extends for 117 miles (188 kilometers) from Manasquan Inlet to Cape May. The waterway is protected from the ocean by barrier beaches, and offers safe passage for small boats.

Communication. About 310 newspapers, including about 30 dailies, are published in New Jersey. The leading papers include the *Asbury Park Press*, the *Courier-Post* of Camden, the *Newark Star-Ledger*, and *The Record* of Hackensack. New York City and Philadelphia newspapers have wide circulation in New Jersey. The *New Jersey Gazette*, the state's first weekly newspaper, began publishing in Burlington in 1777. New Jersey's first daily newspaper, the *Newark Daily Advertiser*, was founded in 1832.

New Jersey has about 85 radio stations and 8 television stations. Many pioneer efforts in radio broadcasting took place in New Jersey. Joseph Henry transmitted the first radio impulse at Princeton in 1840. WJZ, the second licensed commercial broadcasting station in the United States, was established in Newark in 1921. This station now operates in New York City. The oldest radio station still broadcasting in New Jersey is WTNJ (formerly WAAT), which was established in 1923. The first New Jersey television station, WATV, began operating in Newark in 1948. It is now WNET of New York City. Today, only *UHF* (ultra high frequency) commercial stations broadcast in New Jersey. But stations broadcasting from New York and Pennsylvania also serve New Jersey.

New Jersey boasts many other "firsts" in communication. The first interstate long-distance telephone call was made from New Brunswick, N.J., to New York City in 1877. The first coast-to-coast direct dialing system was established in Englewood in 1951. *Telstar I*, the first communications satellite to transmit live television across the Atlantic, was designed at the Bell Laboratories in New Jersey. It was launched in 1962.

Alexander Hamilton was killed in 1804 in a duel with Aaron Burr at Weehawken.

Caldwell •

Weehawken •

• Hoboken

Inventions Developed in New Jersey include Samuel F. B. Morse's electric telegraph (1838), Thomas A. Edison's electric light bulb (1879), and John P. Holland's submarine (1898).

The First Game of Organized Baseball took place at Hoboken in 1846. The New York Nine defeated the New York Knickerbockers, 23 to 1.

Princeton •

Freehold *(formerly Monmouth)*

TRENTON
★

Princeton was the capital of the United States from June 30 to Nov. 4, 1783. Nassau Hall, built in 1756 as part of Princeton University, served for a time as the meeting place of Congress.

Washington Crossed the Delaware at the head of the American army on Christmas night, 1776. The next day, his forces defeated a Hessian army at Trenton.

• Indian Mills

Indian Mills in 1758 became the site of the first Indian reservation in what is now the United States.

Princeton University, founded in 1746, is the fourth oldest in the United States. Part of the Battle of Princeton was fought inside Nassau Hall in 1777.

Molly Pitcher took the place of her fallen husband on a cannon crew during the Battle of Monmouth in 1778.

The First Steam Locomotive in the United States was built by John Stevens in 1825 at Hoboken.

Grover Cleveland born in Caldwell

HISTORIC NEW JERSEY

Indian Days. About 8,000 Indians probably lived in what is now New Jersey before Europeans came. The Indians belonged to the Delaware tribe of the Algonkian Indian family. They called themselves *Leni-Lenape*, which means *original people*. The Indians spent most of their time hunting, but they also raised *maize* (corn), beans, squash, and other crops.

Exploration. Giovanni da Verrazano, an Italian navigator in the service of France, was probably the first white to explore the New Jersey coast. He reached the coast in 1524. Henry Hudson, an English sea captain employed by The Netherlands, explored the Sandy Hook Bay area in 1609. He also sailed up the river that now bears his name. The Dutch explorer Cornelius Mey sailed the Delaware River in 1614. Cape May was later named for him. Many Dutch trading ships visited the New Jersey area during the 1600's.

Settlement. The Dutch and the Swedes were the first white settlers in New Jersey. The Dutch founded an outpost in Pavonia (now part of Jersey City) about 1630. Indian uprisings prevented permanent settlement until 1660. That year, the Dutch built the fortified town of Bergen (now part of Jersey City). Bergen was New Jersey's first permanent white settlement.

Traders and settlers from Sweden arrived in southern New Jersey in 1638. The Dutch settlers feared Swedish competition in the fur trade. The Dutch forced the Swedes out of the New Jersey area in 1655.

English Control. English armies won control of New Jersey and other Dutch North American possessions in 1664. King Charles II of England gave the New Jersey area to his brother, James, Duke of York. James, in turn, gave it to two of his friends, Lord John Berkeley and Sir George Carteret. Berkeley and Carteret offered to sell the land to colonists at low prices. They also allowed settlers to have political and religious freedom. These policies attracted many settlers to New Jersey.

In 1674, a group of Quakers headed by Edward Byllynge bought Berkeley's share of New Jersey. Two years later, the colony was divided into two sections—West Jersey and East Jersey. Byllynge and his associates made West Jersey the first Quaker colony in America. Carteret owned East Jersey until his death in 1680. Another group of Quakers, called the *Twenty-Four Proprietors*, bought East Jersey in 1682.

During the late 1600's, the owners of East and West Jersey became unpopular with the colonists. Land grants made many years earlier caused disputes over property rights. The colonists also objected to paying rent to the owners. Many colonists rioted during the 1690's. The owners gave up East and West Jersey in 1702. England then united the two colonies as a single royal colony.

Colonial Days. New Jersey had twin capitals from 1703 to 1775. They were Perth Amboy, the former capital of East Jersey, and Burlington, the former capital of West Jersey. At first, the governor of New York also ruled New Jersey. But strong protests from the colonists forced England to give New Jersey its own governor in 1738. Lewis Morris, the first colonial governor, served from 1738 to 1746.

Colonial New Jersey was a rural society. Most of the

people kept busy growing their own food and building homes. By the 1760's, the colony had about 100,000 persons. The English king appointed the colonial governor and a 12-member council. The people elected a colonial assembly. But only freeholders who owned property valued at £50 (50 pounds) or more were allowed to vote. This sum equals about $140 today.

The Revolutionary War. During the 1760's, Great Britain passed a series of laws that caused unrest in New Jersey and the other American colonies. Most of these laws either set up severe taxes or restricted colonial trade. Some New Jerseyans urged the colonists to remain loyal to Britain in spite of the laws. But most of the colonists favored independence.

In 1774, a group of New Jerseyans dressed as Indians burned a supply of British tea stored in a ship at Greenwich, near Salem. This event, called the *Greenwich Tea Burning*, was similar to the more famous Boston Tea Party of 1773. Like the Boston Tea Party, the action symbolized colonial opposition to British taxation policies. See BOSTON TEA PARTY.

The Revolutionary War began in Massachusetts in 1775. Hundreds of New Jersey men joined the patriots in their fight for independence. New Jersey's location between New York City and Philadelphia made it a major battleground during the war. The Americans and British fought nearly a hundred engagements in New Jersey. The most important ones included the battles of Trenton in 1776, Princeton in 1777, and Monmouth in 1778. Before the Battle of Trenton, George Washington made his famous surprise crossing of the Delaware River on Christmas night. During the war, Washington's army camped two winters at Morristown and a third at Bound Brook. See REVOLUTIONARY WAR IN AMERICA (The Middle Years).

During the Revolutionary period, two New Jersey cities served as the temporary national capital. They were Princeton, from June 30 to Nov. 4, 1783, and Trenton, from Nov. 1 to Dec. 24, 1784.

New Jersey declared its independence from Great Britain and adopted its first constitution on July 2, 1776. On Nov. 26, 1778, New Jersey ratified the Articles of Confederation (the forerunner of the United States Constitution). New Jersey became a state on Dec. 18, 1787, when it ratified the U.S. Constitution. It was the third state to do so. William Livingston became New Jersey's first state governor.

The New Jersey delegates to the Constitutional Convention of 1787 proposed a plan to protect the interests of small states. This *New Jersey Plan* suggested that all states have equal representation in Congress. But the convention adopted the *Connecticut Compromise* instead. The compromise created the present two-house Congress. The states have equal representation in the Senate. Their representation in the House of Representatives is based on population.

The 1800's. During the early 1800's, New Jersey made many major improvements in its transportation system. These improvements included new turnpikes, canals, and railroads. Improved transportation in the state helped lead to industrial growth that has continued to the present day.

One of the most famous duels of all time was fought

New Jersey Dept. of Conservation and Economic Development
Urban-Renewal Project in Trenton calls for tearing down slums and building state office buildings and a cultural center.

at Weehawken in 1804. Aaron Burr, the Vice-President of the United States, shot and killed his political rival, Alexander Hamilton.

Public demand for a more democratic state government led to the adoption of a new state constitution in 1844. The new constitution provided for separation of powers among the legislative, judicial, and executive branches of the state government. It also provided for a bill of rights and for the election of the governor by the people. In 1845, Charles C. Stratton became the first New Jersey governor elected by the people.

About 88,000 New Jersey men served in the Union army during the Civil War (1861-1865). But there was much pro-Southern sympathy in the state during the Civil War period. In 1864, for example, New Jersey was one of only three states that voted against the re-election of President Abraham Lincoln.

During the late 1800's, New Jersey became the home of many of the nation's *trusts* (industrial monopolies). Trusts were illegal in many other states, but New Jersey law allowed them. New Jersey also attracted many *holding companies* during this period. A holding company is a company that controls the stock and policies of one or more other companies. By 1900, hundreds of large corporations obtained charters under New Jersey laws and set up headquarters in the state.

Industrial Development increased greatly after the Civil War. New Jersey factories turned out elevators, sewing machines, steam locomotives, and other new products. The great population growth of neighboring New York City helped New Jersey's food-processing industry expand by providing a larger market. The iron and steel industry and other businesses also expanded rapidly in the state.

As industry grew, thousands of Europeans came to New Jersey cities to work in factories. By 1910, more than half the state's people had been born outside the United States or had parents who were born in other countries. With the growth of industry, city populations increased and farm populations decreased. By 1900, more New Jerseyans were living in cities and towns than in rural areas.

The Early 1900's saw the rise of progressive government in New Jersey. In 1910, the people elected Woodrow Wilson governor. Under Wilson, the state passed laws providing for direct primary elections, workmen's compensation, and a public utilities commission. The legislature also passed laws restricting business monopolies. Wilson's achievements as governor helped lead to his election as President of the United States in 1912. He was re-elected in 1916.

Thomas A. Edison helped develop the motion picture while working in New Jersey. Fort Lee became the motion picture capital of the world in the early 1900's. There, "Fatty" Arbuckle, Mary Pickford, Pearl White, and other stars made movies that introduced a new era in entertainment.

After the United States entered World War I in 1917, Hoboken became a major port for shipping troops overseas. Thousands of American soldiers sailed for France from this Hudson River port. During the war, Camp Dix and Camp Merritt served as military training centers. New Jersey factories contributed chemicals, munitions, and ships to the war effort.

Between 1900 and 1930, New Jersey's population

more than doubled. During the same period, the state's annual value of manufacturing rose from about $500 million to almost $4 billion. New Jersey, like other states, suffered widespread unemployment during the Great Depression of the 1930's.

The Mid-1900's. New Jersey's electronics and chemical industries began large-scale operations about 1940. These industries grew during World War II (1939-1945), when the state produced communications equipment, ships, and weapons and ammunition.

In 1947, New Jersey voters approved a new state constitution. The constitution extended the governor's term from three to four years and increased the powers of the office. It also reorganized the state's court system.

During the mid-1900's, the state's population expanded steadily into many rural areas. The expansion included construction of homes and of commercial and industrial plants. Commercial and industrial growth occurred most rapidly among chemical, electronics, food-processing, pharmaceutical, and research firms.

The New Jersey Turnpike opened in 1952 and soon became one of the nation's busiest highways. The turnpike links the Philadelphia and New York City metropolitan areas. The Garden State Parkway, completed in 1955, runs along the New Jersey coast.

Although passenger railroad travel declined nationally during the mid-1900's, New Jersey kept its position as a major rail center. The freight yards in Hudson County remained among the largest in the world. Newark Airport started a major construction program in 1963 to expand passenger and cargo service.

During the 1960's, older New Jersey cities faced the problem of spreading slums, especially in black neighborhoods. In July 1967, riots broke out in black neighborhoods of several cities. The worst riot occurred in Newark, where 26 persons were killed and more than 1,000 were injured. Property damage totaled between $10 million and $15 million.

New Jersey Today, like many other states, has trouble providing enough money to run the state government. In the late 1960's, the state adopted a sales tax and several bond issues to help pay for major programs. One bond issue supplied money for new state colleges, highways, institutions, and commuter train facilities. Another paid for water conservation projects and for a program to fight water pollution. In 1969, voters approved a state lottery to raise money for the state government and for the schools.

The state continued to seek new sources of revenue in the 1970's. In 1976, the New Jersey Legislature adopted an individual income tax for the first time. That same year, New Jerseyans voted to allow gambling casinos in Atlantic City to help raise money for the disabled and the elderly.

THE GOVERNORS OF NEW JERSEY

	Party	Term		Party	Term
Under Articles of Confederation			Joel Parker	Democratic	1872-1875
			Joseph D. Bedle	Democratic	1875-1878
William Livingston	Federalist	1781-1789	George B. McClellan	Democratic	1878-1881
			George C. Ludlow	Democratic	1881-1884
Under United States Constitution			Leon Abbett	Democratic	1884-1887
William Livingston	Federalist	1789-1790	Robert S. Green	Democratic	1887-1890
Elisha Lawrence	Federalist	1790	Leon Abbett	Democratic	1890-1893
William Paterson	Federalist	1790-1793	George T. Werts	Democratic	1893-1896
Elisha Lawrence	Federalist	1793	John W. Griggs	Republican	1896-1898
Richard Howell	Federalist	1793-1801	Foster M. Voorhees	Republican	1898
Joseph Bloomfield	*Dem.-Rep.	1801-1802	David O. Watkins	Republican	1898-1899
John Lambert	Dem.-Rep.	1802-1803	Foster M. Voorhees	Republican	1899-1902
Joseph Bloomfield	Dem.-Rep.	1803-1812	Franklin Murphy	Republican	1902-1905
Charles Clark	Dem.-Rep.	1812	Edward C. Stokes	Republican	1905-1908
Aaron Ogden	Federalist	1812-1813	John Franklin Fort	Republican	1908-1911
William S. Pennington	Dem.-Rep.	1813-1815	Woodrow Wilson	Democratic	1911-1913
William Kennedy	Dem.-Rep.	1815	James E. Fielder	Democratic	1913
Mahlon Dickerson	Dem.-Rep.	1815-1817	Leon R. Taylor	Democratic	1913-1914
Jesse Upson	Dem.-Rep.	1817	James E. Fielder	Democratic	1914-1917
Isaac H. Williamson	Dem.-Rep.	1817-1829	Walter E. Edge	Republican	1917-1919
Garret D. Wall	Democratic	1829 (declined)	William N. Runyon	Republican	1919-1920
			Edward I. Edwards	Democratic	1920-1923
Peter D. Vroom	Democratic	1829-1832	George S. Silzer	Democratic	1923-1926
Samuel L. Southard	Whig	1832-1833	A. Harry Moore	Democratic	1926-1929
Elias P. Seeley	Whig	1833	Morgan F. Larson	Republican	1929-1932
Peter D. Vroom	Democratic	1833-1836	A. Harry Moore	Democratic	1932-1935
Philemon Dickerson	Democratic	1836-1837	Clifford R. Powell	Republican	1935
William Pennington	Whig	1837-1843	Horace G. Prall	Republican	1935
Daniel Haines	Democratic	1843-1845	Harold G. Hoffman	Republican	1935-1938
Charles C. Stratton	Whig	1845-1848	A. Harry Moore	Democratic	1938-1941
Daniel Haines	Democratic	1848-1851	Charles Edison	Democratic	1941-1944
George F. Fort	Democratic	1851-1854	Walter E. Edge	Republican	1944-1947
Rodman M. Price	Democratic	1854-1857	Alfred E. Driscoll	Republican	1947-1954
William A. Newell	Republican	1857-1860	Robert B. Meyner	Democratic	1954-1962
Charles S. Olden	Republican	1860-1863	Richard J. Hughes	Democratic	1962-1970
Joel Parker	Democratic	1863-1866	William T. Cahill	Republican	1970-1974
Marcus L. Ward	Republican	1866-1869	Brendan T. Byrne	Democratic	1974-
Theodore F. Randolph	Democratic	1869-1872			

*Democratic-Republican

NEW JERSEY

Also during the 1970's, large urban renewal projects were completed in several New Jersey cities. The program in Trenton included construction of a $35-million group of state government office buildings and a cultural center. In Newark, the state built or expanded several college and university facilities, including a new branch campus for Rutgers, The State University.

Another renewal plan involves the Meadowlands area of northeastern New Jersey. For years, nearby communities opposed development of the land, then covered by about 18,000 acres (7,280 hectares) of marshes. But plans that were begun in 1969 led to the construction of a sports complex there. A football stadium and race track opened at the complex in 1976.

ARTHUR GETIS, RICHARD P. McCORMICK, and MORT PYE

NEW JERSEY/Study Aids

Related Articles in WORLD BOOK include:

BIOGRAPHIES

Brearley, David	Lawrence, James
Burr, Aaron	Livingston, William
Case, Clifford P.	McClellan, George B.
Clark, Abraham	Paterson, William (1745-1806)
Cleveland, Grover	Pitcher, Molly
Crane, Stephen	Roth, Philip
Dayton, Jonathan	Saint Denis, Ruth
Dayton, William L.	Schirra, Walter M.
Edison, Thomas Alva	Stockton, Richard
Einstein, Albert	Van Fleet, James A.
Hague, Frank	Verrazano, Giovanni da
Halsey, William F., Jr.	Waksman, Selman A.
Hart, John	Williams, William Carlos
Hobart, Garret A.	Wilson, Woodrow
Hudson, Henry	Witherspoon, John
Kilmer, Joyce	

CITIES

Asbury Park	Morristown
Atlantic City	New Brunswick
Bayonne	Newark
Camden	North Bergen
Clifton	Paterson
East Orange	Perth Amboy
Elizabeth	Princeton
Hoboken	Trenton
Irvington	Union City
Jersey City	

MILITARY INSTALLATIONS

Cape May Training Center
Fort Dix
Fort Monmouth
Lakehurst Naval Air Station
McGuire Air Force Base

PHYSICAL FEATURES

Delaware Bay	Palisades
Delaware River	Piedmont Region
Delaware Water Gap	Raritan River
Hudson River	Sandy Hook

PRODUCTS AND INDUSTRIES

For New Jersey's rank among the states in production, see the following articles:

Automobile	Publishing
Chemical Industry	Textile
Clothing	Tomato
Peach	Wine

OTHER RELATED ARTICLES

Atlantic Intracoastal Waterway
Celluloid
George Washington Bridge
Hudson River Tunnels

Middle Atlantic States
New Netherland
Port Authority of New York and New Jersey

Outline

I. Government
  A. Constitution
  B. Executive
  C. Legislature
  D. Courts
  E. Local Government
  F. Taxation
  G. Politics

II. People

III. Education
  A. Schools
  B. Libraries
  C. Museums

IV. A Visitor's Guide
  A. Places to Visit
  B. Annual Events

V. The Land
  A. Land Regions
  B. Coastline
  C. Mountains
  D. Rivers and Lakes

VI. Climate

VII. Economy
  A. Natural Resources
  B. Manufacturing
  C. Agriculture
  D. Mining
  E. Fishing Industry
  F. Electric Power
  G. Transportation
  H. Communication

VIII. History

Questions

What unique name do New Jersey county governments have?

How did Lord John Berkeley and Sir George Carteret attract settlers to New Jersey?

What parts of New Jersey are included in a Standard Consolidated Metropolitan Area?

What is New Jersey's best-known annual event?

What New Jersey governor became President of the United States?

What is New Jersey's chief economic activity?

What percentage of New Jerseyans live in cities and towns?

What are New Jersey's six largest cities?

When and where was New Jersey's first library established?

What cities in New Jersey served as the national capital?

Books for Young Readers

BAILEY, BERNADINE F. *Picture Book of New Jersey*. Rev. ed. Whitman, 1965.
CARPENTER, ALLAN. *New Jersey*. Childrens Press, 1965.
COOK, FRED J. *The New Jersey Colony*. Macmillan, 1969.
CUNNINGHAM, JOHN T. *Colonial New Jersey*. Nelson, 1971.

DAHLSTEDT, MARDEN. *Shadow of the Lighthouse.* Coward, 1974. Fiction.
GAUCH, PATRICIA L. *This Time, Tempe Wick?* Coward, 1974. Fiction.
MCNEER, MAY Y. *Stranger in the Pines.* Houghton, 1971. Fiction.
NADEN, CORINNE J. *The Colony of New Jersey.* Watts, 1974.
RESNICK, ABRAHAM. *New Jersey: Its People and Culture.* Denison, 1974.
ROBERTSON, KEITH. *New Jersey.* Coward, 1969.
STOCKTON, FRANK R. *Stories of New Jersey.* Rutgers, 1961.
WOOLLEY, CATHERINE. *Cathy Uncovers a Secret.* Morrow, 1972. Fiction.

Books for Older Readers

BECK, HENRY C. *Roads of Home: Lanes and Legends of New Jersey.* Rutgers, 1956.
BILL, ALFRED H. *New Jersey and the Revolutionary War.* Rutgers, 1964.
CAWLEY, JAMES S. and MARGARET. *Exploring the Little Rivers of New Jersey.* 3rd ed. Rutgers, 1971.
CUNNINGHAM, JOHN T. *This Is New Jersey: From High Point to Cape May.* 2nd ed. Rutgers, 1968. *New Jersey: America's Main Road.* Rev. ed. Doubleday, 1976.
MCCORMICK, RICHARD P. *New Jersey from Colony to State, 1609-1789.* Rutgers, 1970. *Experiment in Independence: New Jersey in the Critical Period, 1781-1789.* 1972.
MCMAHON, WILLIAM H. *South Jersey Towns: History and Legend.* Rutgers, 1973.
MIERS, EARL S. *Crossroads of Freedom: The American Revolution and the Rise of a New Nation.* Rutgers, 1971. *Down in Jersey: An Affectionate Narrative.* 1973.
PEPPER, ADELINE. *Tours of Historic New Jersey.* Rev. ed. Rutgers, 1973.
PIERCE, ARTHUR D. *Iron in the Pines: The Story of New Jersey's Ghost Towns and Bog Iron.* Rutgers, 1957.
POMFRET, JOHN E. *Colonial New Jersey: A History.* Scribner, 1973.
SNYDER, JOHN P. *The Mapping of New Jersey: The Men and the Art.* Rutgers, 1973.
VECOLI, RUDOLPH J. *The People of New Jersey.* Rutgers, 1965.

NEW JERSEY PLAN. See CONSTITUTION OF THE UNITED STATES (The Compromises).

NEW JERSEY TURNPIKE. See NEW JERSEY (Transportation).

NEW LEFT is a radical political and social movement in the United States. The New Left movement began in the early 1960's and includes many college students and other young people. The New Left is "new" in relation to the "old left" of the 1930's. The "old left" generally was guided by Marxist ideas and supported Soviet policies.

Members of the New Left demand sweeping and fundamental changes in American society. They attack most major institutions for claiming to support democratic principles but failing to end such injustices as poverty, racial discrimination, and class distinctions. Many New Leftists oppose capitalism and believe the desire for profits leads to *imperialism*, a national policy that favors extending influence over another country.

People who identify themselves with the New Left are not all members of a single organization, and they frequently disagree among themselves. Members of the New Left range from pacifists to violent revolutionaries. Many New Leftists favor such tactics as nonviolent civil disobedience. But their actions have often led to bloody clashes with the police and other law-enforcement officials. The most important elements of the New Left include the militant wings of the peace

NEW MATHEMATICS

movement, the movement for racial equality, and the students' rights movement.

The peace and civil rights movements have appealed especially to young people. Their experiences in civil rights and peace demonstrations have convinced many of them that war and discrimination can be ended only by a general reformation of American society. Several radical student organizations appeared in the early 1960's, including the Students for a Democratic Society (SDS) and the Free Speech Movement. Radical students began to consider the university as an accomplice of war and racism. They used disruptive tactics in an effort to reform their universities or to use them as a base for revolutionary activities.

Most members of the New Left have shown little interest in conventional politics and have done little to get sympathetic candidates elected to public office. However, many people believe that the antiwar movement helped persuade President Lyndon B. Johnson not to run for re-election in 1968.

After 1968, the New Left split into several factions. For example, the revolutionaries split over tactics for defeating imperialism. Some urged an alliance with American workers, but others favored organizing the world's poor and nonwhite peoples.   CHRISTOPHER LASCH

See also RADICALISM (In the United States); BLACK PANTHER PARTY; STUDENTS FOR A DEMOCRATIC SOCIETY; RIOT (During the 1900's).

NEW LONDON, Conn. (pop. 31,630), is the home of the United States Coast Guard Academy. It is also the trading, banking, and distribution center for the southeastern region of Connecticut. The city's position at the mouth of the Thames River, near the eastern entrance of Long Island Sound, makes it an important seaport. For location, see CONNECTICUT (political map). New London and Norwich form a metropolitan area with 241,862 persons.

Military bases in the area include the U.S. Submarine Base and the U.S. Underwater Sound Laboratory. Factories make antibiotics, paper boxes, clothing, tooth paste, and burial vaults. The city is the home of Connecticut College. New London was founded in 1646 and incorporated in 1784. It has a council-manager form of government.   ALBERT E. VAN DUSEN

NEW LONDON NAVAL SUBMARINE BASE, Conn., is the chief training center of the United States Navy's submarine force. It also houses the Submarine School and headquarters of the Atlantic Fleet Submarine Force. The base covers 497 acres (201 hectares) on the Thames River, 1 mile (1.6 kilometers) northeast of New London. Connecticut gave the land to the federal government in 1868 for naval purposes. The Navy established a coaling station there in 1872. The Navy first used submarines at the New London base in 1900.

The New London Naval Submarine Base added a medical research laboratory after World War II. The laboratory conducts research on problems related to shipboard, submarine, and diving medicine. The New London base also houses a nuclear power school. The world's first atomic submarines were built in nearby Groton.   JOHN H. THOMPSON

NEW MATHEMATICS. See NUMERATION SYSTEMS; SET THEORY.

The Big Pasture by Peter Hurd for the Field Enterprises Educational Corporation Collection

Pastureland near the Sacramento Mountains

―――――――――― FACTS IN BRIEF ――――――――――

Capital: Santa Fe.

Government: *Congress*—U.S. senators, 2; U.S. representatives, 2. *Electoral Votes*—4. *State Legislature*—senators, 42; representatives, 70. *Counties*—32.

Area: 121,666 sq. mi. (315,113 km²), including 254 sq. mi. (658 km²) of inland water; 5th in size among the states. *Greatest Distances*—north-south, 391 mi. (629 km); east-west, 352 mi. (566 km).

Elevation: *Highest*—Wheeler Peak in Taos County, 13,161 ft. (4,011 m) above sea level; *Lowest*—2,817 ft. (859 m) above sea level at Red Bluff Reservoir in Eddy County.

Population: *Estimated 1975 Population*—1,147,000. *1970 Census*—1,016,000; 37th among the states; distribution, 69 per cent urban, 31 per cent rural; density, 8 persons per sq. mi. (3 persons per km²).

Chief Products: *Agriculture*—beef cattle, cotton, dairy products, eggs, grain sorghum, hay, lettuce, wheat. *Manufacturing*—electrical machinery; food and food products; lumber and wood products; printed materials; stone, clay, and glass products. *Mining*—coal, copper, natural gas, natural gas liquids, petroleum, potash, sand and gravel, uranium.

Statehood: Jan. 6, 1912, the 47th state.

State Motto: *Crescit eundo* (It grows as it goes).

State Song: "O, Fair New Mexico." Words and music by Elizabeth Garrett.

NEW MEXICO
THE LAND OF ENCHANTMENT

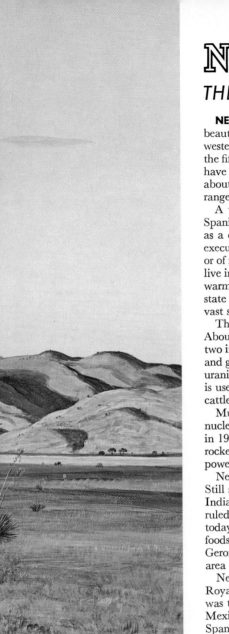

NEW MEXICO is called the *Land of Enchantment* because of its scenic beauty and rich history. Every year, thousands of tourists go to this southwestern state for hunting, fishing, skiing, or sightseeing. New Mexico is the fifth largest state in area. Only Alaska, Texas, California, and Montana have a greater area. But New Mexico is thinly populated. It averages only about 8 persons per square mile (3 persons per square kilometer). Mountain ranges, rugged canyons, and rocky deserts cover much of the state.

A vacationer might see New Mexico as a land of beautiful scenery, Spanish fiestas, and Indian ceremonies. But a scientist would think of it as a center of research into rockets and nuclear energy. An oil company executive might regard the state as a rich source of gasoline for automobiles, or of natural gas for cooking and heating. A retired couple might choose to live in southern New Mexico because its location and high altitude provide warm, sunny days and cool nights. A farmer might be disappointed in the state because of the lack of rain. But a rancher might be impressed by the vast stretches of grazing land.

The earth and its riches provide the basis of New Mexico's economy. About 85 per cent of the value of New Mexico's production comes from two industries that use the land, mining and agriculture. In addition to oil and gas, the mineral riches include two products important for the future—uranium and potash. Uranium is the raw material for nuclear power. Potash is used to make fertilizer that helps increase food production. Millions of cattle and sheep graze on the plains and in mountain valleys.

Much of New Mexico's growing industry springs from the science of the nuclear age. The first atomic bomb was built and exploded in New Mexico in 1945. Today, scientists in New Mexico search for a way to make space rockets travel on nuclear power. Others work on methods for using nuclear power to generate electricity, or to improve nuclear weapons for defense.

New Mexico's colorful past gives the state important tourist attractions. Still standing are the ruins of an 800-room apartment house built by the Indians hundreds of years before Columbus arrived in America. Spain ruled the land for more than 250 years. The Spanish influence may be seen today in the names of places, in the churches of early missionaries, in foods, and in customs and holidays. Colorful men such as Kit Carson, Geronimo, and Billy the Kid played major parts in the history of the area in territorial days.

New Mexico has the oldest road in the United States, *El Camino Real* (the Royal Road). It also has the oldest seat of government, Santa Fe. Santa Fe was the capital of a Spanish province in 1610, and is the capital of New Mexico today. The state's largest city is Albuquerque, founded by the Spaniards in 1706.

For the relationship of New Mexico to other states in its region, see the article on the SOUTHWESTERN STATES.

The contributors of this article are James B. Colegrove, former Editor of The Santa Fe New Mexican; B. LeRoy Gordon, Professor of Geography at San Francisco State University, and former Chairman of the Geography Department of the University of New Mexico; and Lynn I. Perrigo, Emeritus Professor of History at New Mexico Highlands University.

New Mexico (blue) ranks fifth in size among all the states, and second in size among the Southwestern States (gray).

Constitution. New Mexico is governed under its original state constitution. The constitution was adopted in 1911, a year before New Mexico became a state. It has been amended more than 60 times. Amendments may be proposed by either house of the state legislature. They must be approved by a majority of the voters in a regular or special election. Some sections of the constitution require special majority votes to be amended. These sections guarantee the voting rights and education of Spanish-speaking persons. Amendments to these sections must be approved by three-fourths of the voters in the state and by two-thirds of the voters in each county. A constitutional convention may be called by a two-thirds vote of the legislature, if a majority of the voters approve. The voters must approve any amendments proposed by a constitutional convention.

Executive. New Mexico's governor serves a four-year term. He receives a yearly salary of $35,000. Other executive officers elected to four-year terms are the lieutenant governor, secretary of state, auditor, treasurer, attorney general, and commissioner of public lands. None of the executive officers may hold any state office for two terms in a row except the lieutenant governor, who may seek the governorship. The 10 members of the state board of education are also elected by the people, for six-year terms.

Much of the governor's authority lies in his broad power of appointment. For example, he appoints three of the seven members of the powerful state board of finance, and is a member of the board himself. He also appoints most of the directors or board members who run state agencies and institutions. The governor may veto legislation passed by the state legislature. For a list of all the governors of New Mexico, see the *History* section of this article.

Legislature of New Mexico consists of a 42-member senate and a 70-member house of representatives. There are 42 senatorial districts and 70 representative districts. Voters in each senatorial district elect one senator.

Voters in each representative district elect one representative. Senators serve four-year terms. Members of the house of representatives serve two-year terms.

The legislature meets every year on the third Tuesday in January. The sessions are limited to 60 days in odd-numbered years, and to 30 days in even-numbered years. The governor may call the legislature into special session. The legislature may call itself into extraordinary session. The constitution provides for a referendum, but not for initiative (see INITIATIVE AND REFERENDUM).

Courts. The state supreme court, New Mexico's highest court, has five justices. They are elected to eight-year terms. Terms are staggered so an entirely new court is not elected in any one election. The justice with the shortest time to serve on the state supreme court acts as chief justice.

The court of appeals has five judges, who are elected to eight-year staggered terms. Panels made up of three judges hear appellate cases. Most cases which this court hears may be taken to the supreme court.

District courts are the state's principal trial courts. New Mexico has 29 district judges elected from 13 judicial districts. They hold district court sessions in each of the state's 32 counties. District judges are elected for terms of six years. They also serve as juvenile judges if the defendant is under 18 years old. Other courts include probate courts and magistrate courts.

Local Government. New Mexico has 32 counties. Each is administered by a board of three commissioners, who are elected to two-year terms. The state has about 90 *municipalities* (towns, villages, or cities).

State law gives municipalities a wide choice of form of government. Most common are the mayor-council, commission, and city manager-commission forms. Cities can adopt and amend their own charters. Albuquerque, Gallup, and Silver City have charters of their own. Towns and villages may elect trustees, one of whom serves as mayor. Municipal elections are held every two years in New Mexico.

New Mexico Dept. of Development

The Governor's Mansion stands on spacious landscaped grounds at the northeastern edge of Santa Fe. The simple lines of the building mark it as a fine example of the territorial style of architecture characteristic of New Mexico.

The State Seal

Symbols of New Mexico. On the state seal, adopted in 1913, the two eagles represent the annexation of New Mexico by the United States. The scroll beneath the birds bears the state's motto, *Crescit Eundo* (It grows as it goes). On the flag, adopted in 1925, the ancient sun symbol of the Zia pueblo of Indians appears in red on a yellow field. The colors represent the Spanish flag, a reminder that New Mexico was once Spanish territory.

Flag and flower illustrations, courtesy of Eli Lilly Company

Taxation. A sales tax is the largest single source of tax income for the state. New Mexico also has a state income tax on both individuals and corporations. In addition, the state collects taxes on cigarettes, alcoholic beverages, gasoline, and property. Almost all the rest of the state government's income, about 28 per cent, comes from federal grants and other U.S. government programs.

Politics. Since New Mexico became a state in 1912, it has voted for the winner in every presidential election except the 1976 race. In voter registration, Democrats usually outnumber Republicans by about 2 to 1. Democrats have won a majority of the state offices since the 1930's. But some Republicans have won election by large margins.

The eastern part of New Mexico was settled largely by southerners, who generally vote for Democrats. In the north-central counties, the Spanish-American population has been largely Democratic since the early 1930's. Centers of Republican strength lie in the northeast, northwest, and central portions of the state. For New Mexico's electoral votes and voting record in presidential elections, see ELECTORAL COLLEGE (table).

The State Capitol in Santa Fe was completed in 1967. Santa Fe was founded as the capital of the Spanish province of New Mexico in 1610. San Gabriel was the capital from 1599 to 1610.

New Mexico Department of Development

The State Flag

The State Bird
Road Runner

The State Flower
Yucca Flower

The State Tree
Piñon, or Nut Pine

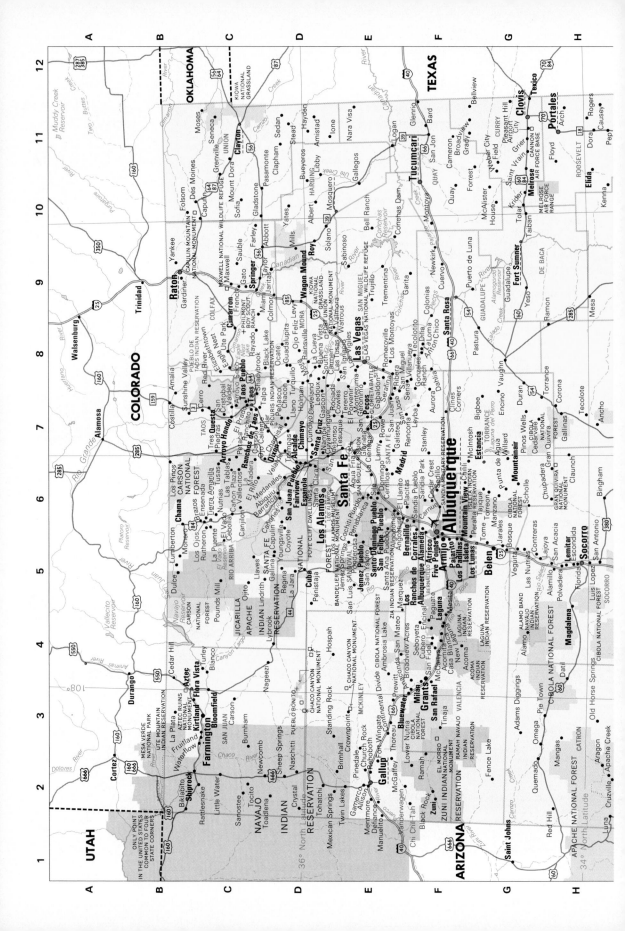

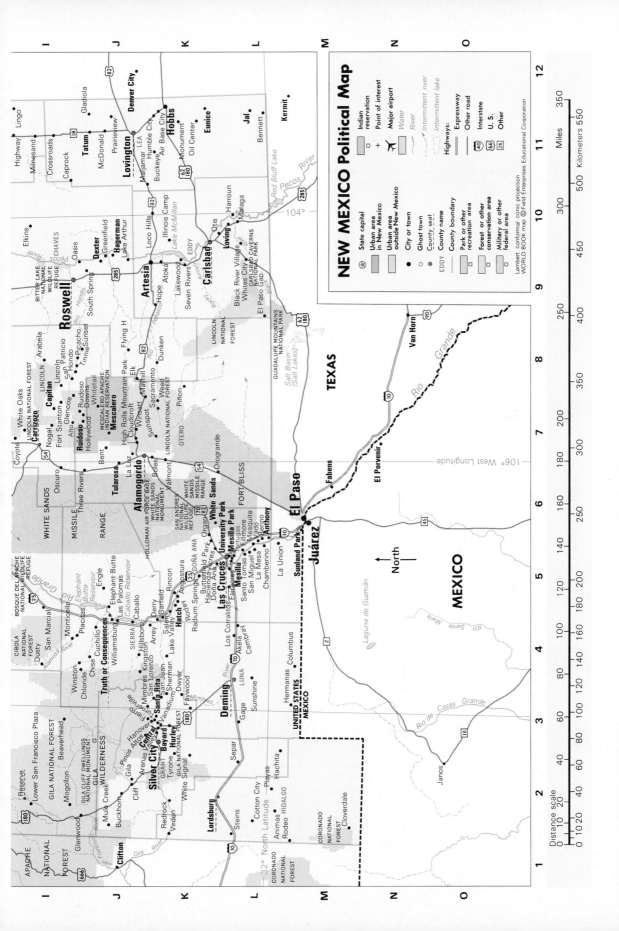

NEW MEXICO Political Map

	Indian reservation
+	Point of interest
✈	Major airport
	Water
	River
	Intermittent river
	Intermittent lake

Highways:

	Expressway
	Other road
⟨40⟩	Interstate
⟨66⟩	U.S.
⟨24⟩	Other

⊛	State capital
	Urban area in New Mexico
	Urban area outside New Mexico
●	City or town
○	Ghost town
●	County seat
EDDY	County name
	County boundary
	Park or other recreation area
	Forest or other conservation area
	Military or other federal area

Lambert conformal conic projection
WORLD BOOK map © Field Enterprises Educational Corporation

Distance scale

Miles 0 10 20 40 60 80 100 120 140 160 180 200 250 300 350

Kilometers 0 10 20 40 60 80 100 140 160 180 200 250 300 350 400 450 500 550

32° North Latitude

106° West Longitude

104°

North

MEXICO

TEXAS

Population

1,147,000	Estimate	1975
1,016,000	Census	1970
951,023	"	1960
681,187	"	1950
531,818	"	1940
423,317	"	1930
360,350	"	1920
327,301	"	1910
195,310	"	1900
160,282	"	1890
119,565	"	1880
91,874	"	1870
93,516	"	1860
61,547	"	1850

Metropolitan Area

Albuquerque ... 333,266

Counties

Cities, Towns, and Villages

*Does not appear on map; key shows general location.
°County seat.

Source: Latest census figures (1970). Places without population figures are unincorporated areas and are not listed in census reports.

NEW MEXICO / People

The 1970 United States census reported that New Mexico had 1,016,000 persons. The population had increased 7 per cent over the 1960 figure of 951,023. The U.S. Bureau of the Census estimated that by 1975 the state's population had reached about 1,147,000. New Mexico averages only about 9 persons per square mile (3 persons per square kilometer). Almost a third of the people live in the Albuquerque metropolitan area, the state's only Standard Metropolitan Statistical Area (see METROPOLITAN AREA).

Most New Mexicans are descended from one of the three major groups that settled the area—Indians, Spaniards, and English-speaking Americans. The modern Indian's way of life may be much like that of his ancestors. He might live in a *pueblo* (village) or on a large reservation.

Spanish Americans in New Mexico take part in most state activities, including politics. A Spanish American, Dennis Chavez, represented New Mexico in Congress for 31 years. The Spanish influence shows strongly in place names, foods, and holiday customs. Many New Mexicans speak both Spanish and English. About 98 out of 100 New Mexicans were born in the United States.

Albuquerque is the state's chief industrial, transportation, and trading center. Santa Fe, the capital and second largest city, has quaint, narrow streets, with buildings made of *adobe* (sun-dried bricks). See the separate articles on the cities of New Mexico listed in the *Related Articles* at the end of this article.

The majority of the people of New Mexico are Protestants, but Roman Catholics make up the largest single religious group. The largest Protestant groups are the Baptists, Episcopalians, Methodists, and Presbyterians.

POPULATION

This map shows the *population density* of New Mexico, and how it varies in different parts of the state. Population density means the average number of persons who live in a given area.

Persons per sq. mi.	Persons per km²
More than 90	More than 35
10 to 90	4 to 35
3 to 10	1 to 4
Less than 3	Less than 1

Albuquerque

0 50 100 150 Miles
0 50 100 150 200 Kilometers

WORLD BOOK map

NEW MEXICO / Education

Schools. Education in New Mexico began in the early 1600's, when Spanish priests started teaching the Indians. The state's first permanent school was established by the Roman Catholic Church at Santa Fe in 1853. The present system of free public education started in 1891.

The state board of education, an elected body, establishes school policies. The policies are carried out by a superintendent of public instruction hired by the board. The state constitution requires children between the ages of 6 and 18 to attend school. For the number of students and teachers in New Mexico, see EDUCATION (table).

Libraries and Museums. The New Mexico Territorial Library, now called the Supreme Court Law Library, was established in Santa Fe in 1851. The first public library in New Mexico was founded in Cimarron in 1881. New Mexico has about 40 public libraries.

The Museum of New Mexico in Santa Fe includes the Laboratory of Anthropology and the Museum of International Folk Art. The Los Alamos Bradbury Science Hall and Museum traces the development of nuclear energy. The Museum of Navajo Ceremonial Art is also in Santa Fe.

UNIVERSITIES AND COLLEGES

New Mexico has nine universities and colleges accredited by the North Central Association of Colleges and Schools. For enrollments and further information, see UNIVERSITIES AND COLLEGES (table).

Name	Location	Founded
Albuquerque, University of	Albuquerque	1940
Eastern New Mexico University	Portales	1934
New Mexico, University of	Albuquerque	1889
New Mexico Highlands University	Las Vegas	1893
New Mexico Institute of Mining and Technology	Socorro	1889
New Mexico State University	Las Cruces	1888
St. John's College	Santa Fe	1964
Santa Fe, College of	Santa Fe	1947
Western New Mexico University	Silver City	1893

An Indian Family buys food in a Gallup supermarket. The city is a shopping center for Indians of nearby reservations.

C. W. Herbert, Western Ways

NEW MEXICO / A Visitor's Guide

New Mexico's scenery and outdoor activities attract visitors throughout the year. The state offers skiing in winter, fishing in spring and summer, and hunting in the fall. Scenic beauty ranges from rose-colored deserts to snow-capped mountains. Lovers of history can visit Indian ruins, frontier forts, and Spanish missions.

Shostal

Fiesta in Santa Fe

Zimmerman, New Mexico Dept. of Development

Gila Wilderness near Silver City

FPG

Old Mission at the Isleta Pueblo

PLACES TO VISIT

Following are brief descriptions of some of New Mexico's most interesting places to visit.

Carlsbad Caverns National Park. This series of huge caves in southeastern New Mexico is one of the world's great natural wonders. Lighted trails offer an excellent opportunity for visitors to see fantastic rock formations. Tens of thousands of bats fly out at dusk and return at dawn. See CARLSBAD CAVERNS NATIONAL PARK.

Gila Wilderness, near Silver City, was the first area in the country to be set aside as a national wilderness. It is kept in its natural condition.

Glorieta Battle Site, west of Pecos, is the place where Union and Confederate troops fought for control of New Mexico during the Civil War.

Los Alamos Bradbury Science Hall and Museum shows the development of atomic energy.

Philmont Scout Ranch is a 137,000-acre (55,440-hectare) Boy Scout recreational area and a working ranch. Its headquarters, located near Cimarron, have a museum.

Puyé Cliff Dwellings are ancient Indian "apartment houses" west of Española.

San Miguel Mission, in Santa Fe, was built by the Spaniards in 1636 and was restored in 1710.

National Forests, Monuments, and Wilderness Areas. New Mexico has seven national forests, each with recreational areas. Gila Forest, north of Silver City, is the largest. The others are Apache, near Luna and Reserve; Carson, near Taos; Cibola, which consists of several separate forests; Coronado, near Rodeo; Lincoln, near Alamogordo; and Santa Fe, near Santa Fe. For the areas and features of these forests, see NATIONAL FOREST (table). In September, 1964, Congress designated five areas of the forests as national wilderness areas. These areas will be preserved in their natural form.

There are ten national monuments in New Mexico. They include some of the outstanding remains of ancient Indian civilization. These monuments are Aztec Ruins, an ancient pueblo; Bandelier, the ruins of four pueblos; Capulin Mountain, the cone of an extinct volcano; Chaco Canyon, the site of 18 pueblo ruins; El Morro, the site of Inscription Rock; Fort Union, an old military post; the Gila Cliff Dwellings, a onetime Indian settlement; Gran Quivira and Pecos, both with ruins of a pueblo and a Spanish mission; and White Sands, a large deposit of gypsum sand. Each monument is described in its own article in WORLD BOOK.

State Parks and Monuments cover large areas in New Mexico. There are 33 state parks and 9 state monuments. For detailed information, write Superintendent, State Park and Recreation Commission, P.O. Box 1147, Santa Fe, N.M. 87503.

Ceremonial Indian Dance at San Ildefonso Pueblo near Santa Fe

Rock Formations in Carlsbad Caverns near Carlsbad

ANNUAL EVENTS

Indian ceremonies and local rodeos are among the most interesting events for visitors. The dates of events may vary from year to year, and among the different tribes and pueblos. Numerous Indian ceremonies are held throughout the year.

Other annual events in New Mexico include the following.

January-March: King's Day Dances in most of the Indian pueblos (Epiphany, Jan. 6); Winter Ski Carnival in Red River (mid-February); Dances at most Indian pueblos (Easter).

April-June: State Science Fair in Socorro (mid-April); Ralph Edwards Festival in Truth or Consequences (late April or early May); Raft Races, Rio Grande River (mid-May); Mescalero Apache Indian Celebration in Ruidoso (late June); New Mexico Arts and Crafts Fair in Albuquerque (late June or early July).

July-September: Apache Indian Ceremonial in Mescalero (July 4th weekend); Rodeo de Santa Fe (mid-July); Puyé Cliff Ceremonial at Santa Clara Pueblo (last Saturday and Sunday in July); World Championship Steer Roping Contest in Clovis (August); "Billy the Kid" Pageant in Lincoln (early August); Annual Connie Mack Baseball World Series in Farmington (mid-August); Inter-Tribal Indian Ceremonial in Gallup (mid-August); Fiesta de Santa Fe (Labor Day weekend); Piñata Festival in Tucumcari (early September); New Mexico State Fair in Albuquerque (mid-September); Feast Day in Taos Pueblo (late September).

October-December: Eastern New Mexico State Fair in Roswell (early October); Navajo Fair in Shiprock (early October); Pecan Festival in Carlsbad (Thanksgiving weekend); Christmas Eve Dances in Mission Churches at many Indian pueblos (Dec. 24); Christmas Eve Luminaria Tours in Albuquerque (Dec. 24).

Land Regions. New Mexico has four main land regions: (1) the Great Plains, (2) the Rocky Mountains, (3) the Basin and Range region, and (4) the Colorado Plateau.

The Great Plains of New Mexico are part of the vast Interior Plain that sweeps across North America from Canada to Mexico. In New Mexico, the Great Plains cover roughly the eastern third of the state. They extend from a high plateau in the north to the Pecos River Valley in the south. Streams have cut deep canyons in the plateau as it slopes away from the Rocky Mountains. Cattle and sheep graze there. To the south are dry farming and irrigation. The eastern edge of the state, south of the Canadian River, is called the *High Plains* or *Llano Estacado* (Staked Plain). The Llano Estacado also covers much of northwestern Texas (see TEXAS [Land Regions]).

The Rocky Mountains extend into north-central New Mexico from Colorado south to a point near Santa Fe. In winter, deep snow piles up on the mountains. In spring, the snow melts and provides moisture for irrigated crops in the fertile Rio Grande Valley. The Rio Grande, which rises in Colorado, cuts between ranges of mountains. To the east are the Sangre de Cristo (Blood of Christ) Mountains. Wheeler Peak, 13,161 feet (4,011 meters) high, is the highest point in the state. The Nacimiento and Jemez ranges are west of the river.

The Basin and Range Region covers about a third of the state. It extends south and west from the Rockies to the borders with Arizona and Mexico. This region includes scattered ranges of rugged mountains—the Guadalupe, Mogollon, Organ, Sacramento, and San Andres ranges. Broad desert *basins* (low places where the streams have no outlet) lie between the mountains. The largest basins are the Jornada del Muerto (Journey of the Dead) and the Tularosa. The Rio Grande cuts through the Basin and Range region.

The Colorado Plateau, in northwestern New Mexico, is a broken country of wide valleys and plains, deep canyons, sharp cliffs, and rugged, lonely, flat-topped hills called *mesas*. The best-known mesa in the state is Acoma. The Indians built a city on top of Acoma. Ship Rock, a steep hill that resembles a ship under full sail, has been a famous landmark in San Juan County for hundreds of years. Ship Rock rises 1,678 feet

Dick Kent

Rugged Rock Formations are found in the Bottomless Lakes State Park near Roswell in the Great Plains region. Dry, treeless land makes up much of New Mexico's Great Plains. The soil of the region produces excellent crops when irrigated or dry farmed.

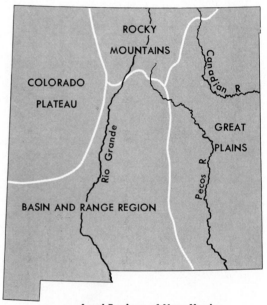

Land Regions of New Mexico

Map Index

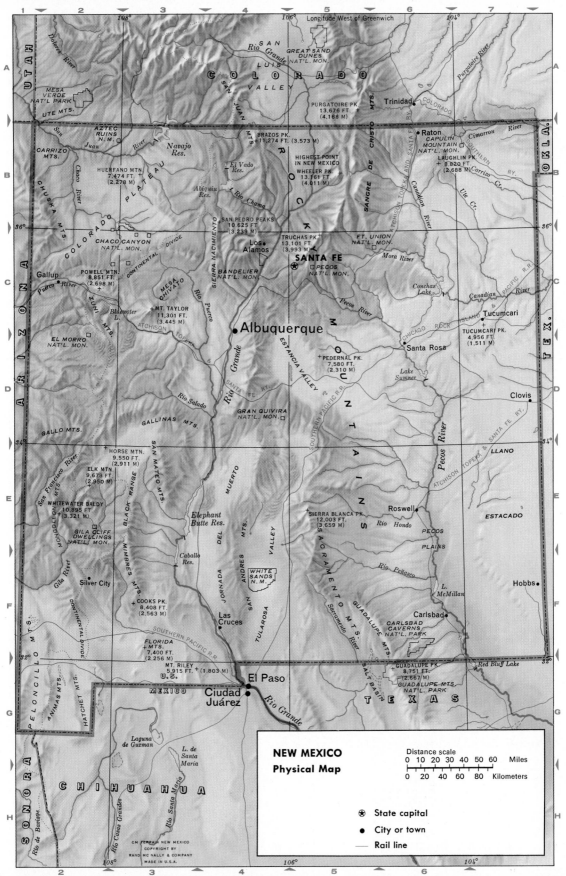

Longitude West of Greenwich

NEW MEXICO

Physical Map

Distance scale

0 10 20 30 40 50 60 Miles

0 20 40 60 80 Kilometers

✷ State capital

● City or town

— Rail line

CM TERRAIN NEW MEXICO
COPYRIGHT BY
RAND McNALLY & COMPANY
MADE IN U.S.A.

Huge Shifting Dunes of White Sands National Monument near Alamogordo form a magnificent scene of white gypsum sand.

This arid wilderness of southern New Mexico lies among the rugged mountain ranges and desert basins of the Basin and Range Region.

(511 meters) above the flat land around it. The San Juan Basin lies in the northwest section of the Colorado Plateau. To the south is a 40-mile (64-kilometer) strip of *malpais*, a badland of extinct volcanoes and lava plains. The *Continental Divide* winds through the plateau. Streams west of it run into the Pacific Ocean. Water east of the divide runs to the Gulf of Mexico.

Rivers and Lakes. The Rio Grande runs like a backbone down the length of New Mexico. At the state's southern boundary it turns east and forms the border between Texas and Mexico. A series of dams stores water for irrigation. Elephant Butte Dam, near Truth or Consequences, backs up the Rio Grande and forms Elephant Butte Reservoir, New Mexico's largest lake. Its water irrigates land in New Mexico, Texas, and Mexico. Another important river is the Pecos. It rises in the Sangre de Cristo Mountains, and then flows south. The Pecos provides irrigation water for the land around Carlsbad and Roswell. The San Juan River drains the northwest corner of the state. The Canadian River rises in the northeast part. Its waters are stored at the Conchas Dam, near Tucumcari, for irrigation. The Gila River, in the southwest, flows west into Arizona.

New Mexico has few natural lakes. Most famous are the deep Bottomless Lakes, a group of pools near Roswell. In addition to Elephant Butte, other man-made lakes are Abiquiu, Alamogordo, Avalon, Bluewater, Conchas, Eagle Nest, El Vado, McMillan, and Navajo.

Mesas and Desert Valleys form a landscape of rugged isolation. This stream and group of steep cliffs north of Gallup are part of the Colorado Plateau region of northwestern New Mexico.

Grazing Land in the Rocky Mountains region of northern New Mexico provides rich grass for cattle and sheep. These animals

find feed on much land that is too steep or too rocky to grow crops. Ranching is the chief agricultural activity in New Mexico.

NEW MEXICO / Climate

New Mexico has a dry, warm climate. A person may hang out clothes in the rain knowing the rain will stop soon, and the air will dry the clothes quickly. The state averages less than 20 inches (51 centimeters) of *precipitation* (rain, melted snow, and other forms of moisture) a year. It varies from over 20 inches in the northern mountains to less than 10 inches (25 centimeters) in the south and central areas. Snow falls throughout the state. The south receives only about 2 inches (5 centimeters) a year. The high mountains may get as much as 300 inches (760 centimeters).

The average July temperature is about 74° F. (23° C). January temperatures vary from about 55° F. (13° C) in the south to 35° F. (2° C) in the north. Day and night temperatures vary widely on the same day. The thin, dry air does not stay warm after sundown because of the high altitude. The lowest recorded temperature was −50° F. (−46° C) at Gavilan on Feb. 1, 1951. The highest temperature was 116° F. (47° C) at Artesia on June 29, 1918, and at Orogrande on July 14, 1934.

New Mexico Dept. of Development

New Mexico's Warm Climate helps produce rich crops if farmers irrigate the fertile land. This field is near Las Cruces. Not enough rain falls there to produce good crops without irrigation.

SEASONAL TEMPERATURES

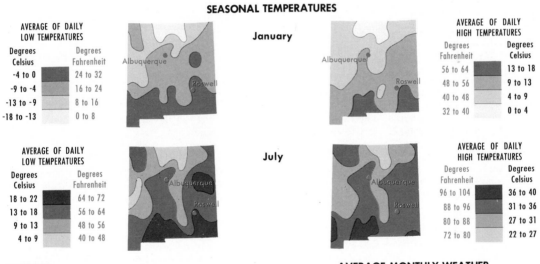

AVERAGE OF DAILY LOW TEMPERATURES

January

Degrees Celsius	Degrees Fahrenheit
-4 to 0	24 to 32
-9 to -4	16 to 24
-13 to -9	8 to 16
-18 to -13	0 to 8

AVERAGE OF DAILY HIGH TEMPERATURES

Degrees Fahrenheit	Degrees Celsius
56 to 64	13 to 18
48 to 56	9 to 13
40 to 48	4 to 9
32 to 40	0 to 4

AVERAGE OF DAILY LOW TEMPERATURES

July

Degrees Celsius	Degrees Fahrenheit
18 to 22	64 to 72
13 to 18	56 to 64
9 to 13	48 to 56
4 to 9	40 to 48

AVERAGE OF DAILY HIGH TEMPERATURES

Degrees Fahrenheit	Degrees Celsius
96 to 104	36 to 40
88 to 96	31 to 36
80 to 88	27 to 31
72 to 80	22 to 27

AVERAGE YEARLY PRECIPITATION
(Rain, Melted Snow, and Other Moisture)

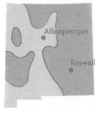

Centimeters	Inches
30 to 61	12 to 24
0 to 30	0 to 12

```
0    100    200    300 Miles
0  100 200 300  400 Kilometers
```

WORLD BOOK maps

AVERAGE MONTHLY WEATHER

	ALBUQUERQUE					ROSWELL			
	Temperatures				Days of	Temperatures			Days of
	F.°		C°		Rain or	F.°		C°	Rain or
	High	Low	High	Low	Snow	High	Low	High	Low	Snow
JAN.	46	22	8	-6	4	JAN.	54	25	12	-4	3
FEB.	52	27	11	-3	4	FEB.	60	30	16	-1	4
MAR.	60	32	16	0	4	MAR.	66	35	19	2	2
APR.	69	42	21	6	4	APR.	75	45	24	7	3
MAY	79	52	26	11	4	MAY	83	54	28	12	4
JUNE	89	61	32	16	4	JUNE	91	62	33	17	4
JULY	92	66	33	19	9	JULY	92	66	33	19	9
AUG.	89	65	32	18	10	AUG.	91	65	33	18	7
SEPT.	82	58	28	14	5	SEPT.	85	58	29	14	4
OCT.	71	45	22	7	5	OCT.	75	47	24	8	4
NOV.	57	31	14	-1	3	NOV.	64	33	18	1	2
DEC.	47	25	8	-4	4	DEC.	55	27	13	3	2

New Mexico's land is rich in many minerals, and at least part of the soil is fertile. But water is scarce. This lack of water has limited New Mexico's growth. The people are learning to make better use of their water resources. New industries that use little water are growing.

The federal government owns about a third of the land in New Mexico. National forests cover much of this land. The rest includes defense installations, grasslands, and Indian reservations. Many government agencies, among them the Energy Research and Development Administration, spend large sums of money in New Mexico. This makes the federal government vital to New Mexico's economy.

Natural Resources of New Mexico include large mineral deposits and rich, renewable resources based on the soil—forests, grasses, plants, and animals.

Minerals. New Mexico is rich in minerals that supply energy. The state has large reserves of coal, natural gas, petroleum, and uranium. Uranium is the main source of nuclear energy. New Mexico has about 150 million short tons (136 million metric tons) of uranium reserves. The largest U.S. reserves of potash, a vital fertilizer material, are in New Mexico. The state ranks as a leader in copper reserves. It also has important deposits of helium gas, natural gas liquids, perlite, salt, sand and gravel, stone, and zinc. Other minerals include clays, gemstones, gold, gypsum, iron, lead, manganese, mica, pumice, and silver.

Soil of New Mexico varies widely. More than half the soil is stony and shallow, and not good for farming. Some desert land has chemicals that prevent trees from growing. But it supports shrubs, flowers, and grasses. The eastern part of the state has brown and reddish-brown sandy soil.

Water is precious in New Mexico, and water resources are extremely important. New Mexico and other western states have joined with Mexico to share the use of water in various streams. Each area gets a share. For example, Colorado users must allow a certain amount of Rio Grande water to flow into New Mexico. New Mexico's resources include underground water. Some comes from *artesian wells* (see ARTESIAN WELL).

New Mexico has seven major storage projects that help make good use of water. These projects regulate the flow of the Canadian, Pecos, Rio Grande, and San Juan rivers, and some of their tributaries.

Forests cover about 18 million acres (7,280,000 hectares), or about a fourth of the state. There are commercially valuable timberlands in eight mountain areas. The most common trees include the aspen, cottonwood, Douglas fir, juniper, piñon (nut pine), ponderosa pine, scrub oak, spruce, and white fir.

Plant Life. The yucca, New Mexico's state flower, grows in most areas. Its dried stems provided the Indians with fire-making materials in the early days. Cattlemen must guard their livestock from the poisonous locoweed. Desert plants include cactus, creosote bush, grama grass, mesquite, white and purple sage, and soapweed. Wild mountain plants include forget-me-nots, saxifrages, sedges, alpine larkspur, and other flowers.

Animal Life is plentiful in New Mexico. Among the larger animals are black bears, coyotes, mountain lions, pronghorn antelope, and whitetail and mule deer. Others include badgers, beavers, bobcats, chipmunks, foxes, jack rabbits, minks, otters, and prairie dogs.

Among the game birds are ducks, grouse, pheasants, quail, and wild turkeys. Common fish include black bass, catfish, crappies, perch, suckers, and trout.

Two kinds of poisonous snakes, the rattlesnake and the coral snake, live in New Mexico. The southwestern desert is the home of such spiders as the tarantula and the poisonous black widow.

Mining is by far the biggest income-producing activity in New Mexico. Mineral products valued at more than $1⅓ billion a year account for half the value of all goods produced in the state and make New Mexico a leader in mining.

Petroleum makes up about a third of the value of New Mexico's mineral production, with a yearly output of about 100 million barrels. Natural gas is the second most valuable product, and the state is a leader in production of both oil and gas. The biggest producing fields are in San Juan County in the northwest, and in Lea and Eddy counties in the southeast.

New Mexico is the leading potash-mining state. Potash is mined near Carlsbad. The state is also a leader in copper production. Coal mines in Colfax, McKinley, and San Juan counties produce about 9 million short

Production of Goods in New Mexico

Total value of goods produced in 1973—$2,603,466,000

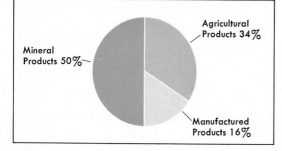

Agricultural Products 34%

Mineral Products 50%

Manufactured Products 16%

Percentages are based on farm income, value added by manufacture, and value of mineral production.
Sources: U.S. government publications, 1975-1976.

Employment in New Mexico

Total number of persons employed in 1974—380,700

	Number of Employees
Government	102,200
Wholesale & Retail Trade	79,600
Community, Social, & Personal Services	64,900
Manufacturing	29,100
Construction	24,700
Transportation & Public Utilities	23,200
Agriculture	21,700
Mining	19,000
Finance, Insurance, & Real Estate	16,300

Sources: *Employment and Earnings,* May 1975, U.S. Bureau of Labor Statistics; *Farm Labor,* February 1975, U.S. Department of Agriculture.

Harvey Caplin, Western Ways

Santa Rita Copper Mine is near Silver City. It has been a rich source of ore since the 1800's, when the Spaniards began to work the mine.

FARM, MINERAL, AND FOREST PRODUCTS

This map shows where the leading farm, mineral, and forest products are produced. The major urban area (shown in red) is the state's important manufacturing center.

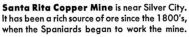

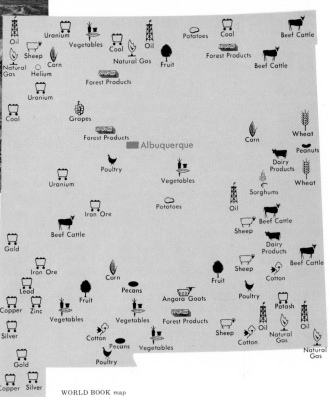

WORLD BOOK map

tons (8.2 million metric tons) of soft coal a year.

New Mexico ranks second only to Wyoming in uranium production, with about a third of the U.S. output. Large-scale production of New Mexico's uranium began after Paddy Martinez, a Navajo Indian, accidentally found uranium deposits in 1950 in the northwest region. Other important minerals are gypsum, molybdenum, natural gas liquids, perlite, salt, sand and gravel, silver, stone, and zinc.

Agriculture has a value of about $880 million a year, or about a third of the value of goods produced in the state. New Mexico has about 11,500 farms and ranches, covering about 46,792,000 acres (18,936,000 hectares). Farms average about 4,020 acres (1,627 hectares).

The most important agricultural activity is ranching. The state has more than twice as many cattle and sheep together as it has people. There are about $2\frac{1}{3}$ million cattle and sheep. They graze in areas where low rainfall or rough land prevents crop farming. About 45 million acres (18 million hectares) are used for grazing.

Dry farming is used on about half the state's cropland. This method is most successful in the eastern part of the state. But New Mexico's farmers are changing from dry farming to irrigation. New dams are providing more water, and many fields are being irrigated with water from deep wells. Nearly half the cropland is irrigated. The most important field crops are cotton, hay, and grain sorghum. Other important crops include let-

Huge Herds of Cattle, such as this one in the Animas Valley near Lordsburg, are rounded up by cowboys for shipment to mar-

ket. Cattle are one of New Mexico's most important products. The animals graze over vast areas of land unsuitable for crop farming.

Cletis Reaves, Alpha

tuce, onions, and wheat. Dairy products and eggs are also chief sources of agricultural income.

Fruits and vegetables grow well in the irrigated river valleys, particularly along the Rio Grande. Dona Ana county, near El Paso, Tex., has one of the nation's largest pecan groves. The nearly 200,000 trees in this grove bear about 7½ million pounds (3.4 million kilograms) of pecans a year.

Manufacturing has expanded since World War II, but it still provides only about a sixth of the value of all goods produced in New Mexico. Goods manufactured there have a *value added by manufacture* of about $415 million a year. This figure represents the value created in products by New Mexico's industries, not counting such costs as materials, supplies, and fuel. The state has a large atomic industry. The U.S. government finances the Los Alamos Scientific Laboratory, where the first atomic bomb was built. This laboratory and Sandia Laboratories, a private firm in Albuquerque, work on peaceful and military uses of nuclear energy.

Food processing is the chief manufacturing activity. Other manufactured goods include, in order of value, electrical equipment; stone, clay, and glass products; lumber and wood products; and printed materials.

New Mexico produces about 265 million board feet (625,300 cubic meters) of lumber a year. The major forest product is softwood lumber from ponderosa pines.

Electric Power is generated mostly by power plants that burn coal or natural gas. The only hydroelectric plant is a small one at Elephant Butte Dam. Privately owned power plants serve most urban areas. Municipally owned plants serve many medium-sized towns while electrical cooperatives serve most rural areas.

Transportation. New Mexico has about 70,000 miles (112,000 kilometers) of roads and highways, including about 20,000 miles (32,000 kilometers) of hard-surface roads. The oldest road in the United States—*El Camino Real* (the Royal Road)—runs from Santa Fe to Chihuahua, Mexico. Spaniards first traveled the road in 1581. The Santa Fe Trail was opened in 1821 between Missouri and New Mexico. Today, U.S. Highway 85 east of Santa Fe follows this old trail. See SANTA FE TRAIL.

Most commercial air traffic is centered around Albuquerque. Four major airlines serve the city. The state has about 130 airports. Railroads operate on about 2,200 miles (3,540 kilometers) of track in New Mexico. Five rail lines provide freight service, and passenger trains serve seven cities in the state. The Atchison, Topeka, & Santa Fe was New Mexico's first railroad. It began operating in the state in 1878.

Communication. The first Spanish-language newspaper in New Mexico, *El Crepúsculo de la Libertad* (The Dawn of Liberty), began publication in 1834 at Santa Fe. The *Santa Fe Republican*, the first English-language paper, was founded in 1847. Today, the state has about 60 newspapers, including about 20 dailies. The largest papers are the *Albuquerque Journal* and the *Albuquerque Tribune*. The state's first radio station, KOB, began broadcasting from Albuquerque in 1922. The first television station, KOB-TV, started regular programming from Albuquerque in 1948. New Mexico has about 90 radio stations and 11 television stations.

Indian Days. Indians probably have lived in what is now New Mexico for about 20,000 years. Stone spearheads found at Folsom and other places indicate that Indians hunted in northeastern New Mexico at least 10,000 years ago. The spearheads are known as *Folsom points*, and the people who made them are called *Folsom man*. See FOLSOM POINT.

From about 500 B.C. to A.D. 1200, the Mogollon Indians lived in the valleys in the area of the New Mexico-Arizona border. At first they lived in houses dug partly into the ground. Later, they built villages above the ground. See MOGOLLON.

Another group of ancient Indians lived in the region where the borders of New Mexico, Arizona, Utah, and Colorado meet. They were the Anasazi, some of the most civilized North American Indians. The Anasazi raised corn and cotton, and tamed wild turkeys. The big birds provided food and clothing. In winter, the Indians wore robes made of turkey feathers. Some Anasazi were cliff dwellers and built many-storied apartment houses of closely fitted stones. One such building, the *Pueblo Bonito* (pretty village), probably had about 800 rooms. Sometimes the Anasazi built towns on top of steep mesas. The Pueblo Indians are the descendants of these people. See CLIFF DWELLERS.

—— IMPORTANT DATES IN NEW MEXICO ——

1540-1542 Francisco Vásquez de Coronado explored New Mexico.

1598 Juan de Oñate founded the first permanent Spanish colony, at San Juan.

1610 Governor Pedro de Peralta established Santa Fe.

1680 The Pueblo Indians revolted and drove the Spaniards out of northern New Mexico.

1692 Diego de Vargas reconquered New Mexico for Spain.

1706 Francisco Cuervo y Valdes founded Albuquerque.

1821 New Mexico became a province of Mexico. William Becknell established the Santa Fe Trail.

1846 General Stephen W. Kearny took possession of New Mexico during the Mexican War.

1848 Mexico ceded New Mexico to the United States in the Treaty of Guadalupe Hidalgo.

1850 Congress created the Territory of New Mexico.

1853 New Mexico acquired part of the Gila Valley through the Gadsden Purchase.

1864 Colonel Kit Carson defeated the Mescalero Apache and Navajo Indians.

1876 Cattlemen began a 5-year series of fights called the Lincoln County War.

1886 The surrender of Geronimo ended the Apache Wars.

1912 New Mexico became the 47th state on January 6.

1916 Mexican bandits raided Columbus. Elephant Butte Dam was completed.

1922 Geologists discovered oil in the southeastern and northwestern regions of New Mexico.

1930 Carlsbad Caverns became a national park.

1945 The first atomic bomb was exploded at Trinity Site near Alamogordo.

1950 Paddy Martinez, a Navajo Indian, found uranium in the northwest region.

1964 Work started on the San Juan-Chama project to bring water through the Rocky Mountains to the Albuquerque area.

Coronado Explored New Mexico from 1540 to 1542, but could not find gold. The Spanish explorer proved that the fabled Seven Cities of Cibola were only poor pueblo villages.

The Santa Fe Trail opened a new trade route to New Mexico. Trader William Becknell established it in 1821, when he brought the first goods to Santa Fe from Missouri. Stagecoach service started from Independence, Mo., in 1849.

Taos

Santa Fe Trail

Los Alamos

SANTA FE

Americans Occupied Santa Fe in 1846. General Stephen W. Kearny led the troops into the city during the Mexican War. He met no opposition.

Oldest Government Building in the U.S. is the Palace of the Governors. The Spaniards used adobe to build it in 1610, when they founded Santa Fe. Now it houses an historical museum.

El Camino Real, the oldest road in the U.S., runs from Santa Fe to Chihuahua, Mexico. It first served travelers in 1581. It is now highway 85.

Alamogordo

Santa Rita

Copper Deposits were found by the Spaniards at Santa Rita in 1800. They used convicts to mine the metal, and mules to transport it to Mexico City.

World's First Atomic Bomb was exploded on July 16, 1945, near Alamogordo. It was produced at Los Alamos.

U.S. Army Signal Corps.

Carlsbad Caverns were first explored in 1901 by Jim White, a cowboy. He saw large numbers of bats come out of an opening in the ground.

HISTORIC NEW MEXICO

Pueblo Ruins in Coronado State Monument near Bernalillo symbolize the Indian and Spanish heritage of New Mexico. Indians lived in the pueblo before Columbus reached America. The Spanish explorer Coronado camped nearby in the 1540's.

The Navajo and Apache tribes came from the north about A.D. 1500. Utes and Comanches came into the region a few years later. See INDIAN, AMERICAN (Table of Tribes).

Exploration and Settlement. The first Spanish explorers reached the area almost by accident. Álvar Núñez Cabeza de Vaca was a member of a group seeking gold in Florida in 1528. The expedition was shipwrecked near the Texas coast. Most of the men were drowned. But Cabeza de Vaca and three companions —two white men and a Negro—landed on the Texas coast. In 1536, after wandering for eight years, they reached a settlement near the Pacific Coast of New Spain (now Mexico). They told stories of seven cities of great wealth, called the *Seven Cities of Cíbola*, to the north. See CÍBOLA, SEVEN CITIES OF.

The Spaniards were determined to find the seven rich cities. Guided by Cabeza de Vaca's Negro companion, Estevanico, also called Estéban, a priest named Marcos de Niza made a search in 1539. He claimed the area as a province of Spain. Marcos de Niza also reported that he had seen the cities from a distance.

Francisco Vásquez de Coronado, also in search of the seven cities, explored present-day New Mexico and Arizona from 1540 to 1542. But he found only the pueblos of the Indians. Fray Augustín Rodríguez and Captain Francisco Sánchez Chamuscado traveled up the Rio Grande from New Spain in 1581. The report of a later explorer, Antonio de Espejo, led to colonization.

The first Spanish colony in New Mexico was established in 1598 at the Pueblo of San Juan de Los Caballeros, near the Chama River. The colony was financed and established by Juan de Oñate. He became governor of the province of New Mexico. Oñate was succeeded as governor by Pedro de Peralta, who moved the capital to Santa Fe in 1610. Santa Fe is the oldest seat of government in the United States.

The colony had little wealth and grew very slowly. It was kept alive mainly by the efforts of missionaries. Roman Catholic priests from Spain established schools to teach Christianity to the Indians. But repeated quarrels occurred between the church and civil authorities, and between the Spaniards and the Indians.

The Spaniards set up a system of forced labor for the Indians that was almost like slavery. The Spaniards also kept the Indians from worshiping their ancient gods. Popé, an Indian from the San Juan Pueblo, led a revolt in 1680. The Indians killed more than 400 Spaniards, and drove the rest to El Paso del Norte (now El Paso, Tex.). The Indians destroyed almost every trace of the Roman Catholic Church. But they could not set up a permanent government.

In 1692, the Spanish governor Diego de Vargas took back the province with little trouble. Four years of scattered fighting broke the power of the Pueblo Indians. The colonists and priests returned to build homes and missions in and near Santa Fe. For the next 125 years, the Spaniards and Pueblo Indians lived fairly peacefully. The area remained a lonely outpost of the Spanish Empire.

Mexican Rule. Trappers and traders came to New Mexico from the United States during the early 1800's. Spanish officials feared the newcomers, and expelled them or put them in prison. But the Spanish officials were replaced in 1821, after Mexico won its freedom from Spain. New Mexico became a province of Mexico. That same year, William Becknell, an American trader, opened the Santa Fe Trail to bring goods to New Mexico from Missouri.

Mexico ruled the area for the next 25 years, a period filled with unrest. In 1837, Mexicans and Indians in New Mexico rebelled against the Mexican government. They executed the governor and seized the Palace of Governors in Santa Fe. A Taos Indian, José Gonzales, was installed as their chief executive. But a month later, Mexico's General Manuel Armijo crushed the rebellion and became governor.

In 1841, an expedition from Texas (then an independent country) invaded New Mexico. The Texans claimed the land east of the Rio Grande. However,

The Taos Rio Grande Gorge Bridge is a link in a highway that crosses northern New Mexico. The concrete and steel bridge spans a gorge 650 feet (198 meters) deep near Taos. It replaced a road that zigzagged down the sides of the gorge.

Mexican troops defeated the invaders and sent them as captives to Mexico City. They were later freed.

The Mexican War. As colonists from the United States pushed west, trouble developed between the United States and Mexico. In 1846, war broke out, and U.S. forces under General Stephen W. Kearny took control of New Mexico with little resistance. The Treaty of Guadalupe Hidalgo ended the war in 1848, and the U.S. took possession of the region. See MEXICAN WAR.

Territorial Days. In 1850, Congress organized New Mexico as a territory. James C. Calhoun was the first territorial governor. The territory also included what is now Arizona and parts of present-day Colorado, Nevada, and Utah. In 1853, the Gadsden Purchase enlarged the territory (see GADSDEN PURCHASE). Mexico sold the United States land south of the Gila River, between the Rio Grande and the Colorado River. New Mexico got its present boundaries in 1863, after Congress organized the territories of Colorado and Arizona.

Early in the Civil War (1861-1865), Confederate forces from Texas captured much of the region, including Albuquerque and Santa Fe. Union forces recaptured the territory in March, 1862, after two battles southeast of Santa Fe. The first clash was fought in Apache Canyon, and the second in Glorieta Pass. Between 1862 and 1864, Colonel Kit Carson, a famous frontier scout, led the New Mexicans in forcing both the Mescalero Apache and the Navajo Indian tribes to live on reservations.

During the late 1870's, cattlemen and other groups fought for political control of Lincoln County. The bitterness burst into open violence with the murder of rancher John G. Tunstall. Billy the Kid and other outlaws took a leading part in the fighting, which became known as the Lincoln County War. General Lew Wallace was appointed territorial governor in 1878. He declared martial law and used troops to end the bloodshed.

In the late 1800's, after the railroads linked the territory to the rest of the nation, New Mexico experienced a cattle and mining boom. Geronimo, one of the last hostile Apache chiefs, spread terror through the area until he surrendered on Sept. 4, 1886.

Early Statehood. New Mexico became the 47th state on Jan. 6, 1912. It had a population of about 330,000. The people elected William C. McDonald as the first state governor.

Mexican bandits, probably led by Pancho Villa, raided the town of Columbus in 1916, killing 16 Americans. The U.S. Army sent an expedition into Mexico to catch Villa, but it failed. During World War I, New Mexico sent over 17,000 men into the armed forces.

In the early 1920's, a long drought made life difficult for farmers and ranchers. Livestock prices dropped,

THE GOVERNORS OF NEW MEXICO

	Party	Term		Party	Term
1. William C. McDonald	Democratic	1912-1917	13. John J. Dempsey	Democratic	1943-1947
2. Ezequiel C. de Baca	Democratic	1917	14. Thomas J. Mabry	Democratic	1947-1951
3. Washington E. Lindsey	Republican	1917-1919	15. Edwin L. Mechem	Republican	1951-1955
4. Octaviano A. Larrazolo	Republican	1919-1921	16. John F. Simms	Democratic	1955-1957
5. Merritt C. Mechem	Republican	1921-1923	17. Edwin L. Mechem	Republican	1957-1959
6. James F. Hinkle	Democratic	1923-1925	18. John Burroughs	Democratic	1959-1961
7. Arthur T. Hannett	Democratic	1925-1927	19. Edwin L. Mechem	Republican	1961-1963
8. Richard C. Dillon	Republican	1927-1931	20. Jack M. Campbell	Democratic	1963-1967
9. Arthur Seligman	Democratic	1931-1933	21. David F. Cargo	Republican	1967-1971
10. A. W. Hockenhull	Republican	1933-1935	22. Bruce King	Democratic	1971-1975
11. Clyde Tingley	Democratic	1935-1939	23. Jerry Apodaca	Democratic	1975-
12. John E. Miles	Democratic	1939-1943			

and the stockmen's financial troubles spread. Banks closed and many persons lost their savings. But new businesses developed. Oil was discovered in the 1920's, and huge potash deposits at Carlsbad were opened. In 1930, the famous caverns near Carlsbad became a national park, and the tourist industry grew.

World War II. When the United States entered World War II in 1941, the 200th Coast Artillery, composed of New Mexico soldiers, was in the Philippine Islands. The Japanese overwhelmed the regiment, along with the rest of the U.S. forces on Bataan Peninsula. Many of the men were killed, and others spent more than three years in Japanese prison camps. The war ended after U.S. planes dropped two atom bombs on Japan in August, 1945. The bombs had been produced at Los Alamos, a town and laboratory built secretly in the New Mexico mountains. The world's first atomic bomb was exploded at Trinity Site, near Alamogordo, on July 16, 1945.

The Mid-1900's. After World War II ended in 1945, the government continued to spend large amounts of money in New Mexico for research. The state's economy and population both grew rapidly as the government provided funds for work on nuclear power development and experiments with rockets. The economy also was aided by the discovery of uranium in northwestern New Mexico in 1950.

During the 1960's, Albuquerque and Roswell went through a slowdown in their rate of growth. The government reduced the number of people it employed in Albuquerque and closed several military bases near Roswell. But by 1970, the cities had recovered from their losses by attracting nongovernment industries.

The state's coal industry grew in the mid-1960's. A large coal mine was opened near Raton, and coal-burning electric generating plants were built near Farmington. A molybdenum mine went into operation near Questa, a village in Taos County. But production of potash decreased in the Carlsbad area because of competition from Canadian potash mines.

New Mexico Today ranks as a leading center of space and nuclear research. The largest private employer in the state is the Sandia Laboratories of Albuquerque, which conducts research and does engineering work on the uses of nuclear energy. At Los Alamos, government scientists are working on many projects involving both military and nonmilitary uses of nuclear energy. New Mexico's vast mineral reserves assure the state a major role in solving problems created by an energy shortage that struck the nation in the 1970's.

The New Mexico tourist industry continues to grow. Income from tourists almost doubled from the mid-1960's to 1970. One reason for the increase was the construction and improvement of winter sports resorts.

Lack of water has always created problems in New Mexico. Many of these problems were expected to be solved with completion of the San Juan-Chama project in the late 1970's. This project, which was started in 1964, is already bringing water to the state through three tunnels from rivers in the Rocky Mountain area. The project included construction of reservoirs near Chama and Santa Fe. One of the reservoirs near Santa Fe will provide recreational facilities and water for irrigation.

JAMES B. COLEGROVE,
B. LeROY GORDON, and LYNN I. PERRIGO

NEW MEXICO/Study Aids

Related Articles in WORLD BOOK include:

BIOGRAPHIES

Anderson, Clinton P.
Billy the Kid
Carson, Kit
Chavez, Dennis
Condon, Edward U.
Coronado, Francisco
  Vásquez de

Garrett, Patrick F.
Geronimo
Hilton, Conrad N.
Oñate, Juan de
Ross, Edmund G.
Villa, Pancho
Wallace, Lew

CITIES

Albuquerque
Gallup

Las Cruces
Los Alamos

Santa Fe
Taos

HISTORY

Apache Indians
Cibola, Seven Cities of
Cliff Dwellers
Gadsden Purchase
Guadalupe Hidalgo,
  Treaty of
Indian, American
Indian Wars
Jefferson Territory

Mexican War
Mission Life
  in America
Mogollon
Navajo Indians
Pueblo Indians
Santa Fe Trail
Western Frontier Life
Zuñi Indians

PHYSICAL FEATURES

Canadian River
Carlsbad Caverns
  National Park
Dust Bowl
Elephant Butte
  Dam

Gila River
Mesa
Pecos River
Rio Grande
Rocky Mountains
Sangre de Cristo Mountains

PRODUCTS

For New Mexico's rank among the states in production, see the following articles:

Copper
Gas (fuel)
Lettuce

Mining
Petroleum

Sheep
Uranium

OTHER RELATED ARTICLES

Holloman Air Force Base
Kirtland Air Force Base
Rocky Mountain States

Southwestern States
White Sands Missile Range

Outline

I. Government
  A. Constitution
  B. Executive
  C. Legislature
  D. Courts
  E. Local Government
  F. Taxation
  G. Politics

II. People

III. Education
  A. Schools
  B. Libraries and Museums

IV. A Visitor's Guide
  A. Places to Visit
  B. Annual Events

V. The Land
  A. Land Regions
  B. Rivers and Lakes

VI. Climate

VII. Economy
  A. Natural Resources
  B. Mining
  C. Agriculture
  D. Manufacturing
  E. Electric Power
  F. Transportation
  G. Communication

VIII. History

What contribution did missionaries make to the development of New Mexico?

When and why did the Pueblos revolt in New Mexico?

How is Spanish influence evident in New Mexico?

Where is the oldest road in the United States? What is its name?

Why is New Mexico called the *Land of Enchantment?*

What states were formed from the New Mexico Territory?

Where is the oldest seat of government in the nation?

What historic weapons were built in New Mexico during World War II?

What are some of the chief minerals produced in New Mexico?

What is the main agricultural activity of New Mexico?

Books for Young Readers

BAILEY, BERNADINE. *Picture Book of New Mexico*. Rev. ed. Whitman, 1966.

CARPENTER, ALLAN. *New Mexico*. Childrens Press, 1967.

CLARK, ANN N. *Circle of Seasons*. Farrar, 1970. Describes ceremonies and festivals of the Pueblo Indians.

CONKLIN, PAUL. *Cimarron Kid*. Dodd, 1973. A boy's ranch life in New Mexico.

KRUMGOLD, JOSEPH. *... And Now Miguel*. Crowell, 1953. Fiction. This Newbery medal winner describes a boy and his family of New Mexico sheepherders.

MITCHELL, EMERSON B., and ALLEN, T. D. *Miracle Hill: The Story of a Navaho Boy*. Univ. of Oklahoma Press, 1967.

O'DELL, SCOTT. *Sing Down the Moon*. Houghton, 1970. Fiction. A story, set in the 1860's, of the conflict between the Navajos, Spanish slavers, and white soldiers.

REEVE, FRANK D., and CLEAVELAND, A. A. *New Mexico: Land of Many Cultures*. Pruett, 1969.

RYAN, J. CLYDE. *Revolt Along the Rio Grande*. Naylor, 1964.

Books for Older Readers

ARMSTRONG, RUTH W. *New Mexico: From Arrowhead to Atom*. 2nd ed. Barnes, 1976.

BECK, WARREN A. *New Mexico: A History of Four Centuries*. Univ. of Oklahoma Press, 1962.

BECK, WARREN A., and HAASE, Y. D. *Historical Atlas of New Mexico*. Univ. of Oklahoma Press, 1969.

BOLTON, HERBERT E. *Coronado: Knight of Pueblos and Plains*. Univ. of New Mexico Press, 1949.

BRADFORD, RICHARD. *Red Sky at Morning*. Lippincott, 1968. Fiction.

BUTCHER, RUSSELL D. *New Mexico: Gift of the Earth*. Viking, 1975.

CATHER, WILLA. *Death Comes for the Archbishop*. Knopf, 1927. Fiction.

FERGUSSON, ERNA. *New Mexico: A Pageant of Three Peoples*. 2nd ed. Univ. of New Mexico Press, 1973.

GILPIN, LAURA. *The Enduring Navaho*. Univ. of Texas Press, 1968.

HORGAN, PAUL. *The Centuries of Santa Fe*. Gannon, 1956. *Great River: The Rio Grande in North American History*. Holt, 1960.

JENKINS, MYRA E., and SCHROEDER, A. H. *A Brief History of New Mexico*. Univ. of New Mexico Press, 1975.

MINGE, WARD A. *Acoma: Pueblo in the Sky*. Univ. of New Mexico Press, 1976.

MOMADAY, N. SCOTT. *House Made of Dawn*. Harper, 1968. Fiction. Pulitzer prize winner.

ORTIZ, ALFONSO. *The Tewa World: Space, Time, Being, and Becoming in a Pueblo Society*. Univ. of Chicago Press, 1969.

RICHTER, CONRAD. *The Lady*. Knopf, 1957. Fiction.

SHERMAN, JAMES E. and B. H. *Ghost Towns and Mining Camps of New Mexico*. Univ. of Oklahoma Press, 1973.

SIMMONS, MARC. *New Mexico: A Bicentennial History*. Norton, 1977.

NEW MEXICO, UNIVERSITY OF, is a state-controlled coeducational school at Albuquerque, N.Mex. It has colleges of arts and sciences, business administration, education, engineering, fine arts, nursing, and pharmacy. It also has a graduate school, law school, medical school, government research division, bureau of engineering research, bureau of business research, extension division, summer session, and adult education program. A two-year branch campus is in Gallup, N. Mex.

The university's Institute of Meteoritics was the first of its kind in the world. The University of New Mexico also has anthropology, biology, and geology museums; art galleries; a 2,200-seat concert hall; and an audio-visual center. The University of New Mexico was founded in 1889. For enrollment, see UNIVERSITIES AND COLLEGES (table).   FERREL HEADY

NEW MEXICO HIGHLANDS UNIVERSITY. See UNIVERSITIES AND COLLEGES (table).

NEW MEXICO INSTITUTE OF MINING AND TECHNOLOGY. See UNIVERSITIES AND COLLEGES (table).

NEW MEXICO STATE UNIVERSITY is a coeducational institution on the outskirts of Las Cruces, N.Mex. It has colleges of agriculture and home economics, arts and science, business administration and economics, education, and engineering. The graduate school grants master's and doctor's degrees. Cooperative programs in education, engineering, mathematics, physics, and accounting provide for six months' study at the university and six months' employment in government agencies and in business. The university carries on scientific study and agricultural research. It was founded in 1888 as Las Cruces College, and in 1889 became New Mexico College of Agriculture and Mechanic Arts. It received its present name in 1960. For enrollment, see UNIVERSITIES AND COLLEGES (table).   GERALD W. THOMAS

NEW NETHERLAND was a region in America claimed by the Dutch in the early 1600's. It included parts of what are now Connecticut, Delaware, New Jersey, and New York. In 1621, merchants in The Netherlands formed the Dutch West India Company to compete with the Spanish Empire, colonize New Netherland, and develop the region's fur trade. Thirty families, sponsored by the company, began a Dutch colony at the mouth of the Hudson River in 1624. The company bought Manhattan Island from the Indians in 1626, and founded New Amsterdam (now New York City) there. The Dutch set up trading posts at what are now Albany, N.Y., Hartford, Conn., and Trenton, N.J.

The governors of New Netherland were harsh rulers. They allowed no religious freedom and quarreled with their own people and with neighboring colonies. They mistreated the Indians, and so the colony was often in danger of Indian attack. Many colonists became discontented. By the 1650's, a fierce trading rivalry had built up between the Dutch and the English. In 1664, the English sent a fleet of warships to capture New Netherland for the Duke of York. Many Dutch colonists refused to fight, and Governor Peter Stuyvesant was forced to surrender to the English. New Netherland became the English colony of New York.   MARSHALL SMELSER

See also NEW YORK (History); STUYVESANT, PETER.

NEW NOVEL. See FRENCH LITERATURE (The New Novel).

New Orleans' Famous Attractions include its historic French Quarter, *left*, and colorful Mardi Gras parades, *right*. The lacy iron grillwork that decorates many French Quarter buildings is a trademark of the city. The spectacular Mardi Gras festivities end the day before Lent begins.

NEW ORLEANS

NEW ORLEANS, *AWR lee uhnz*, is the largest city in Louisiana and one of the world's busiest ports. It is also a leading business, cultural, and industrial center of the Southern United States. New Orleans lies along the Mississippi River about 100 miles (160 kilometers) north of where the river flows into the Gulf of Mexico. This location has helped make the city a great shipping center.

Many people call New Orleans *America's Most Interesting City.* Each year, several million tourists visit New Orleans. The largest crowds come for the annual Mardi Gras celebration, with its spectacular parades and other merry festivities. Tourists are also attracted by the city's historic French Quarter, much of which has the charm of an old European town. Many other visitors come to New Orleans to hear top jazz musicians perform in the city that helped give birth to jazz in the early 1900's.

New Orleans is the oldest major city in the South. It was founded in 1718 by Jean Baptiste le Moyne, Sieur de Bienville. Bienville was the governor of the French colony of Louisiana. He named New Orleans after Philippe, Duke of Orléans, who ruled France for King Louis XV, then a youth. The flags of France, Spain, the Confederate States, and the United States have flown over the city.

Today, New Orleans is a colorful blend of old and new. Most of the city's historic sites have been preserved, while far-reaching urban renewal programs have replaced many decaying structures with striking new buildings. But like many other large cities in the United States, New Orleans faces such problems as crime, poverty, and slums.

The City

New Orleans covers 364 square miles (943 square kilometers), including 165 square miles (427 square kilometers) of inland water. The city occupies all of Orleans Parish and has the same boundaries as the parish. In Louisiana, counties are called *parishes*.

New Orleans is often called the *Crescent City*. It gained this nickname because the city's original section—the French Quarter—lay along a giant curve in the Mississippi River. Today, the main part of the city lies between the river on the south and Lake Pontchartrain on the north. Much of New Orleans is below sea level and lacks natural drainage. To prevent floods during heavy rainstorms, the city relies on one of the world's greatest systems of drainage pumps. The system's 112 pumps can draw off 25 billion gallons (95 billion liters) of water a day. New Orleans has also built about 130 miles (209 kilometers) of walls, called *levees*, to help prevent floods. The longest levees lie along the Mississippi and Lake Pontchartrain.

FACTS IN BRIEF

Population: *City Proper*—593,471. *Metropolitan Area*—1,046,470.

Area: *City Proper*—364 sq. mi. (943 km²). *Metropolitan Area*—2,958 sq. mi. (7,661 km²).

Climate: *Average Temperature*—January, 54° F. (12° C); July, 82° F. (28° C). *Average Annual Precipitation* (rainfall, melted snow, and other forms of moisture)—54 inches (137 cm). For the monthly weather in New Orleans, see LOUISIANA (Climate).

Government: Mayor-council. *Terms*—4 years for the mayor and the seven council members.

Founded: 1718. Incorporated as a city in 1805.

Ralph E. Thayer, the contributor of this article, is Director of the Urban Studies Institute of the University of New Orleans.

The Louisiana Superdome lies at the edge of downtown New Orleans. The 95,427-seat stadium, the world's largest indoor arena, is used for conventions, sports events, and trade shows.

Downtown New Orleans borders the east bank of the Mississippi. Most of the city's residential districts lie west, north, and east of the downtown area. The rest occupy a finger-shaped area on the river's west bank. This area, known as Algiers, is the only part of New Orleans on the west bank.

Downtown New Orleans includes the French Quarter and the main business district. The French Quarter was named after the French colonists who first settled the area. It is also called the *Vieux Carré* (pronounced *vee yoo cair RAY*), meaning *Old Square*. Most buildings in the French Quarter, however, look more Spanish than French. Terrible fires swept through the area in 1788 and 1794. At that time, Spain ruled Louisiana, and so the rebuilding favored the Spanish style of architecture. This style can be seen in many homes and other buildings with their lovely, landscaped patios and graceful balconies of lacy iron grillwork.

Several of New Orleans' most historic structures border Jackson Square in the heart of the French Quarter. One landmark, the magnificent St. Louis Cathedral, was completed in 1851. It stands between the Presbytère and the Cabildo. The Presbytère was built from 1794 to 1813 and used as a courthouse. The Cabildo, begun in 1795 and completed in 1799, was the seat of the Spanish government in the Louisiana Territory. The United States acquired the territory from France in the Louisiana Purchase of 1803, and the official transfer of the territory took place in the Cabildo. The Presbytère and the Cabildo are now museums.

The Pontalba Buildings, two block-long apartment buildings, face each other across Jackson Square. They were built as luxury town houses in 1849 and are among the city's most fashionable residences. The French Quarter is also known for its nightclubs on Bourbon Street and antique shops on Royal Street. It also has a number of restaurants famous for fine food.

New Orleans' main business district lies west of the French Quarter. Large department stores stand along Canal Street, the district's chief shopping area. This broad boulevard is 171 feet (52 meters) wide. The 33-story International Trade Mart rises at the south end of Canal Street. Many firms that deal in foreign trade have offices in the Trade Mart. A public observation deck at the top of the building offers a spectacular view of the city and the Mississippi River.

Many modern high-rise office buildings and hotels line Poydras Street between the riverfront and the gigantic Louisiana Superdome. The 95,427-seat Superdome, the world's largest indoor stadium, is used for conventions, sports events, and trade shows. City Hall stands in the nearby Civic Center.

Residential Districts. West of downtown New Orleans is a large residential area known as Uptown. It includes some of the city's oldest neighborhoods. The most famous one is the Garden District, with its majestic old mansions and beautiful gardens. Americans who came to New Orleans after the Louisiana Purchase in 1803 developed the Garden District. Also in Uptown are Tulane University of Louisiana, Loyola University, and 340-acre (138-hectare) Audubon Park.

City Park and a number of attractive communities along the Lake Pontchartrain shore cover much of northern New Orleans. City Park occupies 1,500 acres (607 hectares) and is one of the nation's largest city-owned parks. The New Orleans Museum of Art is in the park. Lake Vista, the oldest community on the lakefront, was laid out during the 1930's. This area remains one of the city's finest examples of urban planning with its ranch-style houses surrounded by a belt of parks. New Orleans Lakefront Airport and the University of New Orleans also lie on the lakefront.

Most of New Orleans' newest neighborhoods have been built in the northeastern part of the city, commonly called New Orleans East. Large-scale development began there during the 1960's.

The Metropolitan Area of New Orleans covers 2,958 square miles (7,661 square kilometers). It extends over

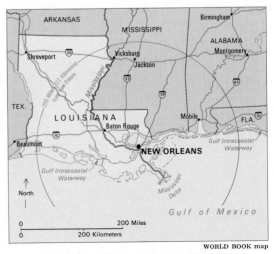

New Orleans Lies in Southeastern Louisiana

NEW ORLEANS

four parishes—Jefferson, Orleans, St. Bernard, and St. Tammany. About a million persons, approximately a third of Louisiana's people, live in this area.

New Orleans' largest suburb, Metairie, lies west of the city and has a population of 136,477. Fast-growing suburbs have sprung up along the Mississippi between New Orleans and Baton Rouge with the development of large industries. Suburbs north of Lake Pontchartrain are also growing rapidly.

People

About 55 per cent of New Orleans' people are white. Blacks and a small number of Orientals make up most of the rest of the population. Many white Orleanians are descendants of European immigrants who came to the city to find opportunity and freedom during the 1800's and early 1900's. Many other Orleanians arrived from Latin-American countries during the 1900's. Large numbers of blacks have lived in the city since the first slaves were brought in the early 1700's.

The New Orleans metropolitan area has experienced a shift in population common to other major urban centers in the United States. Since the 1950's, a large number of middle-class white families have moved from the city to the suburbs. As a result of this population

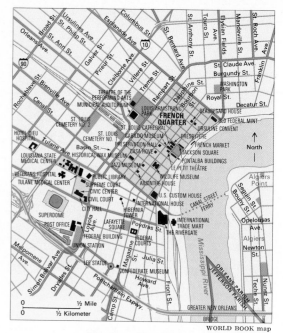

WORLD BOOK map

Downtown New Orleans

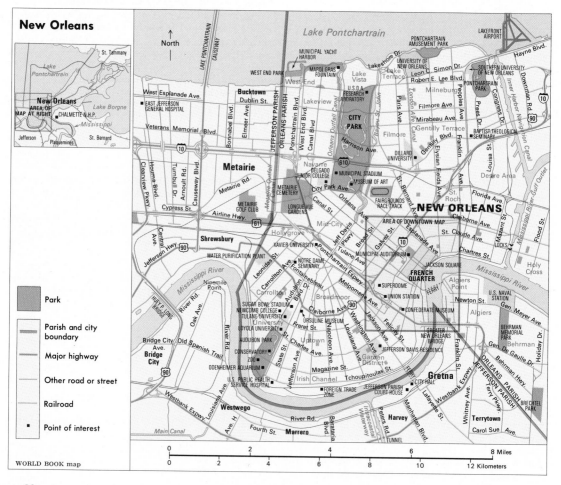

WORLD BOOK map

228b

Charming Old Homes line many streets in New Orleans' Garden District. Americans who came to the city after the Louisiana Purchase of 1803 developed this section.

Preservation Hall is one of the many places in New Orleans where fans can still thrill to the sounds of old New Orleans-style jazz. The city's musicians helped give birth to jazz during the early 1900's.

shift, wealthy whites and poor blacks now form the largest groups in New Orleans.

Roman Catholics make up New Orleans' largest religious group. Other major Christian groups in the city include Baptists, Episcopalians, Lutherans, Methodists, and Presbyterians.

Ethnic Groups. Nearly all the early black residents of New Orleans came from Africa as slaves. They worked on farms and plantations in and near the city. New Orleans also had many free blacks, who came from the West Indies. During the early 1900's, black musicians made New Orleans a world-famous center of jazz. Black jazz bands still follow a New Orleans custom and play in black funeral processions to and from the cemeteries. See JAZZ.

Today, about 240,000 blacks live in New Orleans and make up the city's largest ethnic group. Most of them are poor and live in mainly black communities near the downtown area.

Other groups of Orleanians include those of Chinese, Cuban, French, German, Guatemalan, Honduran, Irish, Italian, or Spanish ancestry. Many of the city's residents who came from Latin America live southeast of the downtown area.

The descendants of New Orleans' early French and Spanish residents are known as *Creoles*. The term *Creole* comes from the Spanish word *criollo*, which means *native to the place*. The Creole influence is still strong in New Orleans. For example, on All Saints' Day (November 1), a citywide holiday that honors the dead, many Orleanians follow the Creole tradition of going to the cemetery in family groups. Creole cooking, a spicy blend of French and Spanish dishes, remains popular in restaurants throughout New Orleans.

Housing. About 30 per cent of New Orleans' families own their homes. Most of the rest rent apartments. New high-rise apartment buildings have been erected in vari-

ous parts of New Orleans. But about half the city's housing was built before 1940. In fact, much of the housing dates from the 1800's. Many of the older homes, especially those in the French Quarter and the Garden District, have been beautifully restored. But much other housing, greatly in need of repair, is neglected because of high repair costs.

Education. New Orleans has about 135 public schools, with approximately 95,000 students. About 80 per cent of the students are black. New Orleans also has almost 60 Roman Catholic schools and a number of other church-supported and private schools. About 32,000 students attend the Catholic schools.

The University of New Orleans, the city's largest university, has an enrollment of over 12,000. It is part of the Louisiana State University system. Tulane University is New Orleans' oldest institution of higher learning. It was founded in 1834. Other universities and colleges in the city include Dillard University; Loyola University; New Orleans Baptist Theological Seminary; Notre Dame Seminary—Graduate School of Theology; Our Lady of Holy Cross College; Southern University of New Orleans; and Xavier University.

The Arts. New Orleans is a leading cultural center of the South. The New Orleans Theatre of the Performing Arts houses two of the city's finest musical organizations. They are the New Orleans Opera House Association and the New Orleans Philharmonic Symphony. Another popular organization, the New Orleans Summer Pops orchestra, performs in the Municipal Auditorium.

New Orleans has been known for its jazz ever since the city helped give birth to the music in the early 1900's. Black and a number of white musicians helped develop jazz in the bars and nightclubs on Basin, Rampart, and other streets in the French Quarter. Today, old New Orleans-style jazz can still be heard in many places in the city. One of the most famous places is Preservation Hall, a small building where fans sit on wooden benches or stand to hear jazz concerts.

Le Petit Théâtre du Vieux Carré is one of the city's best-known professional theater companies. The Dashiki Project Theatre is an outstanding black company.

Libraries and Museums. The New Orleans Public Library operates a main library and 12 branches. Tulane University has an outstanding collection of books on Louisiana history. Dillard University houses the Amistad Collection, a group of books on black life.

The New Orleans Museum of Art has a fine display of Spanish colonial paintings and decorative art. The Louisiana State Museum operates eight historic buildings in New Orleans, including the Cabildo and Madame John's Legacy, a beautifully restored house dating from the early 1700's. Other New Orleans museums include the Moss-Pitot House, a former plantation; the Confederate Memorial Museum; the Mardi Gras Museum; and the New Orleans Jazz Museum.

Chalmette National Historical Park in nearby Chalmette occupies the site of the Battle of New Orleans, the last clash of the War of 1812. A visitor center in the park features displays about the battle.

Recreation. New Orleans has more than 100 parks. The two largest parks, City Park and Audubon Park, were plantations during the 1800's. City Park includes a bandstand and the 27,000-seat Municipal Stadium. Audubon Park's attractions include an aquarium and a zoo. Lake Pontchartrain and other nearby lakes are popular for boating, fishing, and sailing.

New Orleans has two major professional sports teams. They are the New Orleans Jazz of the National Basketball Association and the New Orleans Saints of the National Football League. Both teams play in the Louisiana Superdome.

Annual Events. Every year, about a million visitors attend New Orleans' exciting Mardi Gras festival in February or March. The celebration climaxes the city's carnival season, which begins in January. Mardi Gras lasts about two weeks and ends on Shrove Tuesday, the day before the Christian observance of Lent starts. It features joyful parades and elaborate costume balls sponsored by private carnival organizations known as *krewes*. On Shrove Tuesday, also called Mardi Gras Day, the king of the Rex krewe leads a merry parade of several hundred floats. Brightly costumed riders on the floats toss beads, toys, and imitation gold coins to eager crowds.

Another popular annual event in New Orleans is the Spring Fiesta, held in April or May. This celebration includes guided tours through charming old houses in the French Quarter and the Garden District. Every New Year's Day, New Orleans hosts the famous Sugar Bowl football game. The game, held in the Superdome, features two of the nation's top college football teams.

Social Problems. The chief social problems in New Orleans, as in most other large U.S. cities, include poverty, slums, and crime. About a fourth of the city's families have a yearly income of $3,000 or less. Most of the needy have little education and work at low-paying jobs or are unemployed. Many of the unemployed have come to New Orleans from rural areas and lack the skills needed for jobs in the city. Most of the poor live in crowded, crime-ridden slums. The city has replaced many run-down structures with modern, low-cost public housing. But slums still cover large areas of New Orleans.

High unemployment and crime rates especially trouble the city's black neighborhoods and contribute to racial tension. But New Orleans also has many successful blacks in business, government, and other fields.

Economy

New Orleans' economy depends heavily on shipping and tourism. The Port of New Orleans is the second busiest port in the United States. Only New York City's port handles more cargo. The French Quarter

Karen A. Yops

A Lovely Terrace is the setting for this restaurant in New Orleans. Many of the city's restaurants are famous for fine food and feature Creole cooking, a blend of French and Spanish dishes.

Sara Dreyfuss

St. Louis Cathedral faces Jackson Square in the heart of the French Quarter. The towering spires of the church have made it a New Orleans landmark. The building dates from 1851.

Christopher R. Harris from Katherine Young

Shipbuilding is one of the leading industries in the New Orleans metropolitan area. The Avondale Shipyard of Jefferson Parish, above, is a major U.S. shipbuilding center.

helps attract more than 700 conventions to New Orleans yearly. The city is also one of the South's major centers of business, industry, and transportation.

Trade and Finance. The Port of New Orleans handles more than 125 million short tons (114 million metric tons) of cargo a year. About 5,000 ships from about 60 nations dock at the busy port annually. The chief exports are grain and other foods from the Midwestern United States and petroleum products. The leading imports include bananas, cocoa beans, and coffee. The port handles more trade with Latin America than does any other U.S. port.

New Orleans is also a busy port for barges. The barges use the nation's two main inland waterways, the Mississippi River and the Gulf Intracoastal Waterway, which meet at New Orleans (see GULF INTRACOASTAL WATERWAY). The port handles about 50,000 barges yearly.

The New Orleans metropolitan area is one of the South's chief centers of retail and wholesale trade. It has about 8,500 retail firms and over 2,000 wholesale firms. Their annual sales total about $7 billion.

The New Orleans area is also a financial center. More than 30 commercial banks and over 40 savings and loan associations operate in the area. Their loans help finance business expansion projects and other civic developments. The Sixth Federal Reserve District Bank operates a branch bank in New Orleans.

Industry. The New Orleans metropolitan area has about 1,000 manufacturing plants. They employ about 12 per cent of the area's workers and produce more than $1 billion worth of goods yearly.

The largest industrial complex in New Orleans is the Michoud Assembly Facility, where several companies produce equipment for the U.S. space program. Michoud made the Saturn V rocket that launched the Apollo 11 astronauts to the moon in 1969. The Avondale Shipyard, in Jefferson Parish, is one of the nation's largest shipbuilding centers. Other leading industries in the metropolitan area make food products, petrochemicals, petroleum products, and primary metals.

Transportation. Barges and oceangoing ships dock at wharves on the Mississippi River, the Inner Harbor Navigation Canal, and the Mississippi River-Gulf Outlet. The Navigation Canal links the Mississippi and Lake Pontchartrain. The 76-mile (122-kilometer) Gulf Outlet gives shippers a 44-mile (71-kilometer) short cut between New Orleans and the Gulf of Mexico.

New Orleans International Airport, in the nearby city of Kenner, serves about 15 commercial airlines. Private aircraft use New Orleans Lakefront Airport. About 60 trucking companies and several passenger and freight rail lines also serve the city. The Lake Pontchartrain Causeway, the world's longest bridge, extends about 29 miles (47 kilometers). It spans the lake and links New Orleans and its northern suburbs.

Communication. New Orleans has three daily newspapers—*The Daily Record*, the *States-Item*, and the *Times-Picayune*. The *Times-Picayune* has the largest circulation of Louisiana's daily newspapers. Five television stations and about 30 radio stations serve the city.

Government

New Orleans has a mayor-council form of government. The voters elect the mayor and the seven members of the City Council to four-year terms. The mayor may serve any number of terms but not more than two in a row.

The mayor appoints a chief administrative officer to help direct the city government. The mayor also plans civic improvements. The council makes the city's laws. The mayor may veto bills passed by the council. However, any bill the mayor vetoes may still become law if at least five council members vote to repass it.

A sales tax is the city government's largest source of local income. But New Orleans, like other big U.S. cities, does not raise enough money from local taxes to pay for the ever-increasing costs of services and improvements. As a result, the city depends on the state and federal governments for about half its income.

The Democratic Party has controlled the New Orleans city government since the late 1870's. Party members come from all classes and represent many views.

History

Chickasaw, Choctaw, and Natchez Indians lived in what is now the New Orleans area before Europeans arrived. In 1682, the French explorer Robert Cavelier,

New Orleans' Flag was adopted in 1918. The three stripes symbolize democracy. The fleurs-de-lis stand for the city's French heritage.

The City Seal dates from 1852. The two Indians honor the first inhabitants of the New Orleans area, and the alligator represents the city's swamps.

NEW ORLEANS

Sieur de la Salle, sailed down the Mississippi River from the Great Lakes region. He claimed the entire Mississippi Valley for France.

French and Spanish Rule. Sieur de Bienville founded New Orleans in 1718. In 1722, he made it the capital of the French colony of Louisiana, which covered the central third of the present-day United States.

In 1762, King Louis XV of France gave Louisiana to his cousin, King Charles III of Spain. The French Orleanians disliked the first Spanish governor of Louisiana, Antonio de Ulloa, and drove him from the city in 1768. But in 1769, soldiers arrived from Spain and restored Spanish rule in New Orleans.

The worst fire in what is now Louisiana broke out in New Orleans on March 21, 1788. It started in a house on Chartres Street and destroyed over 850 buildings. Rebuilding had just gotten well underway when a fire swept through 200 more structures in 1794.

In 1800, France secretly regained the Louisiana region from Spain but did not reveal the fact until March 1803. The next month, France sold Louisiana to the United States. On November 30, in preparation for the region's official transfer, the French took down the Spanish flag that still waved over New Orleans and raised the French flag. On December 20, the American flag became the third flag to fly over the city in less than a month.

The Early 1800's. In 1805, New Orleans was incorporated as a city. Louisiana joined the Union in 1812, and New Orleans became the state capital. Also in 1812, the steamboat *New Orleans* sailed from Pittsburgh down the Ohio and Mississippi rivers to New Orleans. It was the first steamer to navigate the Mississippi. River trade soon boomed at New Orleans.

During the War of 1812, British troops tried to capture New Orleans. The British sought the aid of Jean Laffite, leader of a pirate band based near the city. But Laffite joined the American forces that were defending New Orleans. General Andrew Jackson commanded the U.S. troops. Jackson's army and Laffite's pirates defeated the British in the Battle of New Orleans on Jan. 8, 1815. See WAR OF 1812 (The Needless Battle).

After the war, river trade brought increasing wealth to New Orleans. The city thrived as a cotton port and slave-trading center. The state capital was moved to Donaldsonville in 1830. But New Orleans again served as the capital from 1831 until 1849, when Baton Rouge became the capital. New Orleans held its first Mardi Gras celebration in 1838.

The *Paris of America.* By 1840, New Orleans had a population of 102,193 and was the nation's fourth largest city. In the mid-1800's, it attracted thousands of immigrants from Germany and Ireland. Professional opera and theater companies thrived in New Orleans during this period, and the lively and glamorous city became known as the *Paris of America.*

During the mid-1800's, New Orleans also gained a reputation as an unhealthy city. In 1832, a yellow fever epidemic swept through the city, taking about 7,700 lives. Doctors did not know that mosquitoes, which thrived in the swampy New Orleans area, were the chief carriers of the disease. The worst yellow fever epidemic in United States history hit New Orleans in 1853. It killed more than 11,000 persons.

The Civil War and Reconstruction. In 1861, Louisiana withdrew from the Union and joined the Confederate States against the North in the Civil War (1861-1865). New Orleans' importance as a port made it a chief target of the Union forces. In April 1862, a Union fleet commanded by Captain David Farragut sailed up the Mississippi from the Gulf of Mexico. After bombarding several forts, the fleet reached New Orleans and forced it to surrender on May 1. General Benjamin F. Butler took charge of the city and made it the Union capital of Louisiana.

Union troops remained in New Orleans during the Reconstruction period after the war. Blacks and Northerners then gained control of the city government. In 1866, a riot broke out between whites and blacks in New Orleans over a voting dispute. The riot resulted in

Lithograph (1851) by T. H. Muller; Mariner's Museum, Newport News, Va. (Katherine Young)

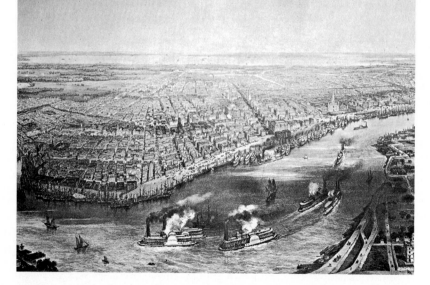

New Orleans' Riverfront served as a chief port for steamboats that traveled on the Mississippi River in the mid-1800's. The booming river trade of this period brought great wealth to New Orleans, which thrived as a cotton port.

the deaths of about 50 persons—most of them blacks—and increased racial tension in the city. Widespread corruption in government and rising city debts also troubled New Orleans during Reconstruction. In 1877, the United States government withdrew its troops from New Orleans.

During the Late 1800's, New Orleans struggled to rebuild its economy. Trade at the port had slumped sharply after the Civil War, when the coming of the railroads to the Mississippi Valley caused steamboat traffic to decline. In 1878, another yellow fever epidemic killed more than 3,800 Orleanians.

Port activity increased rapidly after 1879. That year, U.S. Army engineers directed by James B. Eads deepened the mouth of the Mississippi River. This project enabled oceangoing ships to reach New Orleans.

The 1900's. By 1900, New Orleans' population had reached about 287,000. It continued to climb steadily during the early 1900's, when thousands of Italian immigrants arrived. In 1905, New Orleans officials adopted a program to combat mosquitoes by destroying their breeding areas. This program ended the threat of yellow fever in the city. By 1920, black Orleanian musicians had helped New Orleans win fame as a jazz center. These musicians included Louis Armstrong, Jelly Roll Morton, and King Oliver. During the 1920's, the development of tugboats powerful enough to push long lines of barges on the Mississippi River greatly increased trade at New Orleans' port.

A major threat to New Orleans, floods from the Mississippi, was largely ended with the completion of the Bonnet Carré Spillway in 1932. This channel connects the river to Lake Pontchartrain west of the city. When floods threaten, water from the river is forced into the lake through the spillway.

In 1946, deLesseps S. Morrison, a Democratic reformer, was elected mayor of New Orleans. He served as mayor until 1961 and began a series of long overdue civic projects. In his first major accomplishment, Morrison combined five railroad stations into one, the Union Passenger Terminal. This station opened in 1954. Other projects included the opening of the Greater New Orleans Bridge in 1958 and completion of the Civic Center in 1959.

Recent Developments. During the 1960's, far-reaching social changes occurred in New Orleans. In 1960, black students entered all-white public elementary schools in New Orleans for the first time since the Reconstruction period. The city's libraries, restaurants, and other public facilities also became integrated during the decade.

Large residential developments began in New Orleans East during the 1960's. In the mid-1960's, the production of rockets at the Michoud industrial complex made New Orleans a space age industrial center.

The Louisiana Superdome opened in 1975. It led to the building of several hotels and motels in downtown New Orleans.   RALPH E. THAYER

Related Articles in WORLD BOOK include:

Outline

I. The City
A. Downtown New Orleans
B. Residential Districts
C. The Metropolitan Area

II. People
A. Ethnic Groups
B. Housing
C. Education
D. The Arts
E. Libraries and Museums
F. Recreation
G. Annual Events
H. Social Problems

III. Economy
A. Trade and Finance
B. Industry
C. Transportation
D. Communication

IV. Government

V. History

Questions

Why is New Orleans often called the *Crescent City?*

How has the Bonnet Carré Spillway largely ended the threat of floods to New Orleans?

When was New Orleans founded? By whom?

When does Mardi Gras take place?

Who led the Americans in the Battle of New Orleans?

What kind of music is New Orleans famous for?

Why do most buildings in the French Quarter look more Spanish than French?

How do many Orleanians celebrate All Saints' Day?

What historic event took place in the Cabildo?

What two main inland waterways of the United States meet at New Orleans?

NEW ORLEANS, BATTLE OF. See JACKSON, ANDREW (Glory at New Orleans); LAFFITE, JEAN; WAR OF 1812.

NEW ORLEANS BAPTIST THEOLOGICAL SEMINARY. See UNIVERSITIES AND COLLEGES (table).

NEW PROVIDENCE. See BAHAMAS.

NEW ROCHELLE, N.Y. (pop. 75,385), is a residential suburb of New York City. It was named for La Rochelle, France, the home of the early Huguenot settlers. New Rochelle lies on Long Island Sound, 15 miles (24 kilometers) northeast of the heart of Manhattan (see NEW YORK [political map]). It is noted for its bathing beaches, golf clubs, parks, and homes. New Rochelle has excellent transportation connections with New York City. It has the College of New Rochelle and Iona College. New Rochelle was founded in 1688, became a village in 1857, and a city in 1899. The city has a council-manager form of government.   WILLIAM E. YOUNG

NEW ROCHELLE, COLLEGE OF. See UNIVERSITIES AND COLLEGES (table).

NEW SALEM. See ILLINOIS (Places to Visit); LINCOLN, ABRAHAM (New Salem Years).

NEW SCHOOL FOR SOCIAL RESEARCH. See UNIVERSITIES AND COLLEGES (table).

NEW SOUTH WALES is the oldest and most heavily populated state in Australia. It lies in the east, facing the Pacific Ocean. New South Wales has high mountains and wide, rolling plains. Sydney is the capital and largest city (see AUSTRALIA [political map]).

The Land. New South Wales covers 309,433 square miles (801,428 square kilometers). Its coastline is 700 miles (1,127 kilometers) long. The coast rises sharply from the Pacific in rugged cliffs. These form rocky headlands that shelter several good harbors. Beyond the coast, a narrow strip of fertile land borders the mountains of the Great Dividing Range. The highest point in the range is 7,310-foot (2,228-meter) Mount Kosciusko. West of the mountains, the land broadens into a rolling plateau that slopes to grassy plains.

The state has a mild climate. Temperatures average about 50° F. (10° C) in July and 75° F. (24° C) in January. Average annual rainfall ranges from 100 inches (250 centimeters) in the eastern highlands to less than 10 inches (25 centimeters) on the western plains.

The People. Most of the 4,589,556 people of New South Wales are of British descent, and about three-fifths of them live in or near Sydney. The population includes about 28,000 Aborigines.

Economy. Most of the land suitable for agriculture lies along the coast and in the tablelands west of the mountains. Irrigation canals supply water for many areas. The chief industry in New South Wales centers around its grazing lands. About half of Australia's sheep graze on pastures there. Stock raising, dairy farming, and crop farming account for about a fourth of the state's total annual production of goods. Farmers grow wheat on over half of the farmland in New South Wales. Other products include bananas, citrus fruits, corn, hay, oats, potatoes, sugar, and tobacco.

More than half of Australia's mineral output comes from New South Wales. Coal production averages about 17 million short tons (15 million metric tons) a year. Australia's first gold discovery was made in New South Wales in 1851. Other minerals include copper, iron, lead, magnesite, opals, silver, tin, and zinc.

Most manufacturing is closely connected with stock raising and mining. The state has over 23,000 factories, including iron and steel foundries and woolen mills.

New South Wales has over 6,000 miles (9,700 kilometers) of railroads, all state owned. It has about 130,000 miles (209,000 kilometers) of roads. Chief exports include butter, coal, drugs, flour, fruits, hides and skins, iron and steel, lead, machinery, meats, textiles, wheat, and wool. The chief imports are manufactured goods.

Education and Religion. Children under 15 are required to attend school. About 590,000 students attend state public schools and 192,000 attend nongovernmental schools. The University of Sydney has over 16,000 students. The state also has the University of New South Wales, the University of New England, the University of Newcastle, and Macquarie University.

The Church of England has the largest number of members. There is no official state church.

Government. The chief executive of New South Wales is a governor appointed by the British monarch. The actual head is the premier, assisted by a Cabinet made up of the heads of the government departments. The state's Parliament consists of a 60-member Legislative Council, and a 94-member Legislative Assembly.

History. In 1770, the British explorer James Cook became the first European to reach the area (see COOK, JAMES). Captain Arthur Phillip landed with convict settlers at Port Jackson in New South Wales in 1788 to found the first settlement in Australia. At that time, New South Wales covered the eastern part of Australia and included land that now makes up the states of Queensland and Victoria and part of the state of South Australia. Free settlers began to arrive in the early 1800's, and convict immigration ended in 1852. The colonists drew up a constitution in 1853. The colony became self-governing in 1856.

In 1901, New South Wales became one of the six states of the Commonwealth of Australia. The state transferred 911 square miles (2,359 square kilometers) of territory to the federal government in 1911. This area became the Australian Capital Territory, surrounding Canberra. C. M. H. CLARK

See also CANBERRA; LORD HOWE ISLAND; MURRAY RIVER; MURRUMBIDGEE RIVER; SYDNEY.

NEW SWEDEN was the only Swedish colony in America. It extended along the Delaware River from the mouth of Delaware Bay to about what is now Trenton, N.J. Swedish settlers founded the colony in 1638, and built Fort Christina at what is now Wilmington, Del. The population of New Sweden never reached 200. The Dutch in New Netherland to the north tolerated Swedish competition in the fur trade as long as Sweden and The Netherlands were allies. In 1655, the Dutch took over New Sweden by a threat of force. See also DELAWARE (History). MARSHALL SMELSER

Australian News & Information Service

WORLD BOOK map

New South Wales lies in southeastern Australia. State agricultural societies stage annual shows where livestock are judged. The grand parade at Sydney's Royal Easter Show, *right*, displays some of the country's finest livestock.

NEW TESTAMENT is part of the Christian Bible. It is a record of the new *testament*, or promises made by God to man, as shown in the teachings and experiences of Christ and His followers.

Contents of the New Testament

Books. The New Testament consists of 27 books, and is about a third as long as the Old Testament. The first four books are the Gospels according to Matthew, Mark, Luke, and John. They represent a collection of the acts and words of Jesus. The authors wrote them for teaching purposes. The Acts of the Apostles, a continuation of the Gospel of Luke, is a volume of history. Twenty-one documents called *epistles*, or letters, follow. St. Paul is supposed to have written 13 of these; 7 books are the Epistles of Peter, James, John, and Jude; and the Epistle to the Hebrews is anonymous. The New Testament ends with the Book of Revelation, or Apocalypse.

The 27 books make up the *canon* of the New Testament, or all the books that Christians consider to be authoritative Scripture. During early Christian times, there were many books of religious writings, some of doubtful value and authority. These included fanciful gospels and acts designed to fill in details of the life of Jesus and His Apostles. By about the A.D. 300's, church scholars regarded the present books of the New Testament as authoritative Scripture. They considered other writings as *apocryphal*, or of doubtful authorship (see APOCRYPHA). Later, church councils ratified the decisions regarding the canon.

Writing the New Testament. The original language of the New Testament is the common vernacular Greek that was widely used at the time of Jesus. The Greek in the New Testament includes some Hebrew phrases and idioms, because all the New Testament writers except Luke were Jews. The authors of the original books of the New Testament wrote them on papyrus scrolls, none of which now exist. Scholars have used early Latin, Syriac, and Coptic translations of the Greek New Testament to help reconstruct the original text. They have also studied quotations of the New Testament. Several appear in the writings of the church fathers as early as about A.D. 150.

Dating the New Testament

It is impossible to give definite dates for all the events of the New Testament, just as it is impossible to give definite dates for many other incidents in ancient history. But scholars have been able to set approximate dates by connecting Bible narratives with facts known from history.

The Birth of Jesus. The Christian Era is represented by the Latin words *anno Domini*, which mean *in the year of our Lord*. The abbreviation A.D. is written before the year, as A.D. 1000. A mistake occurred when our calendar was set up. Early Christians dated the Christian Era about six years after the actual birth of Jesus.

Scholars have determined this in the following way: In Matthew 2 we learn that Jesus was born during the rule of Herod the Great. Herod died in 4 B.C. Some scholars believe that the birth of Jesus probably occurred two or three years before, or about 6 B.C.

Another attempt to find evidence for the date of Jesus' birth concerns the star of Bethlehem. Johannes Kepler, a great German astronomer, said that two planets seemed to come together in the skies over Bethlehem in 7 B.C. They must have looked like one bright star.

More evidence comes from Luke's mention of a decree of the Emperor Augustus (Luke 2: 1-3). The emperor, according to Luke, ordered that "all the world should be enrolled." Scholars have found documents that seem to show that a *census* (count of the people) took place in 8 B.C. Some persons believe it may have been shortly after this time that Joseph and Mary went to Bethlehem.

Nothing in the Bible tells us the day or month when Jesus was born. But the 25th of December comes at about the time of year called the winter *solstice* (see SOLSTICE). At this time, the days stop growing shorter as winter turns toward spring. The date serves as a symbol of the new life that came to the world when Jesus was born.

The Public Ministry of Jesus. The Gospel of Luke tells us that Jesus was about 30 years old when He began to preach (Luke 3: 23). The length of His public ministry is determined by the number of *Passovers* (annual Jewish Festivals) that He celebrated. The *Synoptic Gospels* (Matthew, Mark, and Luke) refer to only one Passover during Jesus' adult life, the one at the time of His Crucifixion. The Gospel of John mentions at least three Passovers, and the feast mentioned in John 5: 1 may have been a fourth Passover. The mention of these Passovers has led many scholars to believe Jesus' public ministry lasted for about two and a half or three and a half years.

The Crucifixion. All the Gospels imply that Jesus was crucified on a Friday. All except John tell us that this Friday was the day after Passover. In John, the Crucifixion occurs on the day of the Passover. Many scholars believe that the Crucifixion took place on either April

A Scene from the New Testament, *The Raising of Lazarus* by Peter Paul Rubens, shows Jesus calling Lazarus from his grave.
Staatliche Museen, Berlin, Germany

7, A.D. 30, or April 3, A.D. 33. The Jewish year differs in length from the calendar year now in general use. This difference makes it necessary to go through a complicated process of figuring to determine when Jesus died according to the calendar of the Christian Era.

The Conversion of Paul followed several incidents described in the opening chapters of Acts. These were the holiday of Pentecost, the organization of the church, and the martyrdom of Stephen. Paul was probably converted between A.D. 34 and 37.

Paul's Missionary Journeys. Paul and Barnabas brought food to the Christians at Jerusalem because of an expected famine, according to Acts 11: 27-30. Non-Biblical records show that a famine did occur in Judea about A.D. 46, during the rule of Claudius (41-54). Therefore, the visit of Paul and Barnabas must have taken place about A.D. 45 or 46. Paul made his first missionary journey soon afterward, and thus it must have occurred in A.D. 47 or 48. Two other missionary journeys followed. Then Paul was arrested in Jerusalem and put into prison by Felix, the Roman governor of Judea. Festus became governor two years later, and he allowed Paul to plead his cause before Herod Agrippa II. These references to names recorded in history make it possible for scholars to fix fairly precise dates for several events in Paul's life. An interesting inscription found at Delphi dates the governorship of Gallio (Acts 18: 12) in A.D. 50 or 51. Paul was probably in prison at Caesarea for two years, beginning about A.D. 58. From there, he was taken to Rome, where he remained in custody for two more years. Many scholars believe he wrote the Epistles to the Philippians, the Colossians, Philemon, and the Ephesians during this time.

Some scholars think that Paul may have made a missionary journey to Spain in about A.D. 64, and that he was again put in prison in Rome about the year 66. Tradition says that he died a martyr during the rule of Nero (54-68). We know that this emperor put a number of Christians to death after the burning of Rome in order to turn people's suspicions away from himself.

Critical Studies of the New Testament

The original manuscripts of the books of the New Testament, as they were written by the Apostles, have all been lost. Only copies remain, and none of them dates from the time when the Apostles were still living. Thousands of later copies exist. Many variations of wording occur in the old copies, although the variations in the Greek manuscripts rarely affect the meaning of the passage. But these differences have made it difficult to determine the original wording of some passages.

Efforts to determine original wordings through careful study and comparison of old manuscripts have sometimes met with opposition. But most church officials now accept such studies as necessary to determine the purpose and the original meaning of the Biblical writings. A study of this kind is called *criticism*. Biblical criticism is divided into two classes, lower criticism and higher criticism.

Lower, or Textual, Criticism is concerned with the recovery of the author's own wording, before copies were made. The process of making copies gave rise to errors, most of which were accidental. Lower criticism

requires a great deal of research and comparison, and scholars have spent years of work on it. They have put together all the variations of wording for the passages of the New Testament, and for the wording of the Old Testament as well.

Higher Criticism covers a broader field than textual criticism. Higher critics learn what they can of the Bible by comparing one passage with another. They also compare statements in the Bible with literary and historical works of the period. They study the literary form of the Biblical writings. By such means they can draw conclusions concerning the nature and authenticity of the sacred record. Higher critics have not always agreed in their findings. The more extreme higher critics have made such prejudiced interpretations that the general movement has at times met with hostile charges. Sometimes these charges are well-founded and sometimes not. Most persons believe that many good results have come from a wise and unprejudiced study of the Bible. The advanced schools of religious studies teach the New Testament in the light of all that modern learning and scholarship have achieved.   BRUCE M. METZGER

Related Articles. See BIBLE with its list of Related Articles. See also the following articles on Books of the New Testament:

Acts of the Apostles	Jude
Colossians, Epistle to the	Peter, Epistles of
Corinthians, Epistles to the	Philemon, Epistle to
Ephesians, Epistle to the	Philippians, Epistle to the
Galatians, Epistle to the	Revelation
Gospels (Matthew, Mark, Luke, John)	Romans, Epistle to the
Hebrews, Epistle to the	Thessalonians, Epistles to the
James, Saint (Epistles of)	Timothy
John, Epistles of	Titus

NEW THOUGHT is a philosophical idea that the mind is superior to all material conditions and circumstances. The idea was advanced in the 1800's by Ralph Waldo Emerson, American author and lecturer. It was somewhat revived in the early 1900's.

NEW WESTMINSTER, British Columbia (pop. 37,171), was the first Canadian city on the Pacific Coast. It became the first incorporated city in British Columbia in 1860. The second largest industrial center in the province, the city lies 12 miles (19 kilometers) southeast of Vancouver on the Fraser River. For location, see BRITISH COLUMBIA (political map).

New Westminster's lumber industry produces about 1 billion board feet (2.4 million cubic meters) of lumber a year. The city serves as headquarters of the International Salmon Fishing Commission and the Fraser River salmon fishing fleet. New Westminster is a distributing and canning center for Fraser Valley farm produce. Its port serves oceangoing ships.

Simon Fraser, a British fur trader and explorer, discovered the site in 1808. The city served as the capital of the colony of British Columbia from 1859 to 1868. British Royal Engineers named the city Queensborough in 1858. Queen Victoria changed the name to New Westminster in 1859, after the town of Westminster, England. Fire destroyed the main business district in 1898, but it was rebuilt. New Westminster has a mayor-council government.   RODERICK HAIG-BROWN

NEW WORLD is another name for the Western Hemisphere, which includes the continents of North America and South America. See OLD WORLD; HEMISPHERE.

Happy New Year

Εὐτυχές τό Νέον Ἔτος
(Greece)

Buon Capo d'Anno
(Italy)

Bonne Année
(France)

Szczęśliwego Nowego Roku
(Poland)

汽 **(Japan)**

Aith-bhliain fé mhaise dhuit
(Ireland)

Gott Nytt År
(Sweden)

ﮐﻮﯾﯽ ﻧﯽﺎﺳ
(Saudi Arabia)

Feliz Año Nuevo
(Spain)

Gelukkig Nieuwjaar
(Netherlands)

Gutes Neues Jahr
(Germany)

Hauoli Makahiki Hou
(Hawaii)

शुभ नव वर्ष
(India)

Leshana Tova
(Israel)

Maligayang Bagong Taon
(Philippines)

Godt Nytt År
(Norway)

С НОВЫМ ГОДОМ
(Russia)

Wide World

People Around the World Celebrate the New Year with special greetings, *above*. On New Year's Eve, a large crowd jams Times Square in New York City, *right*.

NEW YEAR'S DAY is the first day of the calendar year. It is celebrated as a holiday in almost every country. Generally, church services are held, with parties before or after them. New Year's Day is a time of gaiety in the Orient. Homes are decorated, and friends give one another gifts. In Europe, the day is celebrated by family parties, the giving of gifts, and visiting.

In the United States, people attend church, go to the theater, or to various places of entertainment. Parties are held on New Year's Eve to "watch the old year out." At one time, formal calls were made on New Year's Day, but this is no longer a general custom. Many persons hold "open house" on the afternoon or evening of New Year's Day. Their friends come to call, and refreshments are sometimes served.

Early Customs. The ancient civilizations all had customs that celebrated the new year. The Chinese, Egyptian, Jewish, Roman, and Islamic years all began at different times. But the first day of each year was marked with elaborate ceremonies. Thousands of years ago, the Egyptians celebrated the new year about the middle of June. This was the time when the Nile River usually overflowed its banks.

In ancient Rome, the first day of the year was given over to honoring Janus, the god of gates and doors and of beginnings and endings. The month of January was named after this god. Janus had two faces, and looked both ahead and backward. On the first day of the year the Roman people looked back to what had happened during the past year and thought of what the coming year might bring. Romans gave one another presents on New Year's Day. Many persons brought gifts to the Roman emperor and wished him good fortune. At first, the gifts were simply branches of bay and palm trees, but later more expensive presents were given. Roman senators received flowers and fruits and sometimes beautiful materials from persons who wanted favors. Roman merchants carried this custom of giving gifts as far east as Persia (now Iran). There the ancient Iranians, or Persians, followed the custom of giving eggs to their friends. Since an egg hatches into life, this custom meant much the same thing as "turning over a new leaf."

When the Romans invaded England, they found that the Druid priests celebrated New Year's Day on March 10. The priests cut off branches of mistletoe, which grew on their sacred oak trees, and gave them to the people

for charms. The early English took over many of the Roman New Year's Day customs. Later, English people followed the custom of cleaning the chimneys on New Year's Day. This was supposed to bring good luck to the household during the coming year. Today we say "cleaning the slate," instead of "cleaning the chimney." This means making resolutions to correct faults and bad habits, and resolving to make the new year better than the past year.

The Roman custom of giving gifts to the emperor was revived by the English in the 1200's. Jewelry, gloves, and other presents were brought to the English king or queen. Queen Elizabeth I (1533-1603) built up a collection of hundreds of pairs of richly embroidered and bejeweled gloves through this custom. By another English custom, English husbands gave their wives money on New Year's Day to buy enough pins for the whole year. This custom disappeared in the 1800's, when machines were developed to manufacture pins. But the term "pin money" still refers to small amounts of spending money.

The Date of New Year's. New Year's Day became a holy day in the Christian church in A.D. 487, when it was declared the Feast of the Circumcision. At first, parties were not allowed on this day because the pagans had followed that custom. This was gradually changed and celebrations could again be held. The opening of the new year has been celebrated on many different days in different countries. These days of celebration have included Christmas Day, Easter Day, March 1, and March 25, which is the time of the Feast of Annunciation.

January 1 became generally recognized as New Year's Day in the 1500's, when the Gregorian calendar was introduced. The Jewish New Year's Day, called Rosh Hashanah, is celebrated in late September or early October. The Chinese used the lunar calendar for about 4,000 years. This calendar is based on the waxing and waning of the moon. Today the Chinese New Year's Day falls between January 21 and February 19 each year.

The new year begins on March 21 in Iran. The date of the Hindu's new year depends upon his religion. The Hindus belong to many different religious groups, and each group considers a different date as the beginning of the year.   ELIZABETH HOUGH SECHRIST

See also JANUARY; JANUS.

NEW YORK

The Empire State

NEW YORK has richly earned its nickname—the *Empire State*. It is the leading center of banking, communication, finance, and transportation in the United States. New York far outranks all other states in foreign trade and in wholesale trade. It is second only to California in retail trade and manufacturing. New York ranked first among the states in population for more than a hundred years, until California gained first place during the 1960's.

Much of the state's greatness lies in huge, exciting New York City. New York City is the largest city in the United States and the fourth largest in the world. It is one of the nation's leading centers of business and industry. Its many theaters, museums, and musical organizations make it the cultural center of the Western Hemisphere. New York City is one of the world's biggest and busiest seaports. In its harbor stands the Statue of Liberty, long a symbol of freedom to people in all parts of the world. As the headquarters of the United Nations, New York City can be called the "capital of the world."

New York's factories turn out an incredible variety of products. They make more clothes than do factories in any other state. The New York City area does about a sixth of the nation's printing, and publishes about one-third of its books. New York also ranks as one of the leading U.S. producers of chemical products, food and food products, and machinery.

In addition to New York City, the state has five other cities with populations over 100,000. One of them is Albany, the state capital. These cities also are important manufacturing and trading centers.

But New York is not just a state of business and industry. It is also a land of fertile river valleys, forested hills, tall mountains, and sparkling lakes. New York's many scenic attractions draw countless vacationers. Niagara Falls, the state's most magnificent natural wonder, attracts millions of visitors every year.

New York was one of the original 13 states. Henry Hudson, an English explorer sailing under the Dutch flag, claimed the New York region for The Netherlands in 1609. The Dutch named the region *New Netherland*. On Manhattan Island, the Dutch established New Amsterdam, which later became New York City. The English took control of New Netherland in 1664. They renamed it New York in honor of the Duke of York (later King James II).

About a third of all the battles of the Revolutionary War were fought in New York. New York City became the first capital of the United States under the Constitution. George Washington took the oath of office there as the nation's first President. In the early 1800's, New York began its great era of canal and railroad building. By 1820, it had become the most populated state. By 1850, it was the leading manufacturing state.

Some historians believe New York's nickname—the *Empire State*—came from a remark made by George Washington. When Washington visited New York in 1783, he predicted that it might become the seat of a new empire. New York is also called the *Excelsior State*. *Excelsior*, a Latin word meaning *ever upward*, is the state motto. For the relationship of New York to other states in its region, see MIDDLE ATLANTIC STATES.

The contributors of this article are James A. Frost, coauthor of A History of New York State *and* New York, the Empire State; *John J. Leary, Executive Editor of the Albany* Times-Union; *and John H. Thompson, Professor of Geography at Syracuse University.*

The Lights of Manhattan

Three Lions

New York (blue) ranks 30th in size among all the states. It is the largest of the Middle Atlantic States (gray).

Bob Wyer

Delaware River Valley Between Delhi and Stamford

─── FACTS IN BRIEF ───

Capital: Albany.

Government: *Congress*—U.S. senators, 2; U.S. representatives, 39. *Electoral Votes*—41. *State Legislature*—senators, 60; assemblymen, 150. *Counties*—62.

Area: 49,576 sq. mi. (128,401 km²), including 1,745 sq. mi. (4,520 km²) of inland water but excluding 4,376 sq. mi. (11,334 km²) of Lakes Erie and Ontario, New York Harbor, and Long Island Sound; 30th in size among the states. *Greatest Distances*—east-west, 314 mi. (505 km); north-south, 307 mi. (494 km). *Coastline* (along the Atlantic Ocean) 127 mi. (204 km). *Shoreline*—775 mi. (1,247 km), including 371 mi. (597 km) along Lakes Ontario and Erie; 192 mi. (309 km) along the St. Lawrence and Niagara rivers, and 212 mi. (341 km) along islands.

Elevation: *Highest*—Mount Marcy in the Adirondack Mountains, 5,344 ft. (1,629 m) above sea level. *Lowest*—sea level along the Atlantic Ocean.

Population: *Estimated 1975 Population*—18,120,000. *1970 Census*—18,241,266; 2nd among the states; distribution, 86 per cent urban, 14 per cent rural; density, 368 persons per sq. mi. (142 per km²).

Chief Products: *Agriculture*—apples, beef cattle, dairy products, eggs, greenhouse and nursery products, potatoes. *Fishing Industry*—clams, flounder, lobsters, oysters, porgy. *Manufacturing and Processing*—chemicals; clothing; electrical machinery; fabricated metal products; food and related products; nonelectrical machinery; primary metals; printed materials; scientific instruments, and photographic equipment; transportation equipment. *Mining*—gypsum, salt, sand and gravel, stone, zinc.

Statehood: July 26, 1788, the 11th state.

State Motto: *Excelsior* (Ever Upward).

State Song: None official.

239

Constitution. New York adopted its first constitution in 1777. The present constitution was adopted in 1894, and has been *amended* (changed) more than 170 times. An amendment may be proposed in the state legislature. The proposal must be approved by a majority in both houses of two successive, separately elected legislatures. It must then be approved by a majority of the persons who vote on the proposal in an election. The constitution may also be amended by a constitutional convention. A proposal to call a convention must be approved by a majority of the legislature and by a majority of the voters. Amendments suggested by the convention become law after they have been approved by a majority of the citizens voting on them.

Executive. The governor of New York is elected to a four-year term. He may serve an unlimited number of terms. The governor receives a yearly salary of $85,000—the highest salary paid any governor in the United States. For a list of all the governors of New York, see the *History* section of this article.

The lieutenant governor, attorney general, and comptroller are also elected to four-year terms. The secretary of state is appointed by the governor with the approval of the state senate. The governor heads the executive department, one of the 20 departments that administer the state government. The governor, with senate approval, appoints most other department heads.

Legislature of New York consists of a senate of 60 members and an assembly of 150 members. Voters in senatorial and assembly districts elect the members of both houses to two-year terms. The legislature meets every year on the first Wednesday after the first Monday in January. There is no time limit on regular sessions. The governor may call special sessions of the legislature, which also have no time limit.

Courts. New York is divided into 11 judicial districts. The voters in each district elect a varying number of supreme court judges to 14-year terms. Altogether, New York has about 280 supreme court justices. They make up the state supreme court. New York is also divided into four judicial departments. Each department has an appellate division of the supreme court. The appellate divisions hear appeals from the supreme court. The governor selects the supreme court justices

of the appellate divisions. Two appellate divisions have seven justices each, and the other two have five each.

The highest court in New York is the court of appeals. It has a chief judge and six associate judges, all elected to 14-year terms. The court of appeals hears cases only from the appellate divisions of the supreme court.

Each New York county, except those that make up New York City, has a county court. County courts hear civil and criminal cases. A surrogate court in each county deals with wills and estates. Some counties have family courts that handle domestic matters. New York City has a civil court and a criminal court. There are also many justices of the peace, city courts, and village police courts in the state.

Local Government. New York has 62 counties, including the 5 that make up New York City. A board of supervisors or a county legislature governs each county except the New York City counties. The officials of these boards and legislatures are elected either from the towns and cities of the county, or from county legislative districts. The major responsibilities of the smallest counties include the administration of courts, highways, and welfare. The larger counties deal with community colleges, libraries, garbage disposal, and parks and recreation.

Within New York's counties are villages, towns, and cities. An elected mayor and board of trustees governs each village. Each town is governed by an elected supervisor and town board. Most New York cities have the mayor-council form of government. Some cities, including Niagara Falls, Rochester, and Yonkers, have the city manager form. A few small cities operate under the commission plan. The state legislature has the power to draw up city charters. Cities, in turn, may adopt and amend local laws and revise their charters, thus determining their own form of government. New York City, because of its large population and area, has a different government from that of the other cities (see NEW YORK CITY [Government]).

Taxation. Taxes bring in nearly four-fifths of the state government's income. Almost all the rest comes from federal grants and other U.S. government programs. A tax on personal income provides about a third of the state's income. It is the largest single source of income. New York has a sales tax, and taxes on alcoholic beverages, cigarettes, and motor fuels. It also taxes estates, race tracks, corporations and other businesses, stock transfers, and truck mileage.

Since 1967, the state has operated a lottery to raise educational funds from nontax sources.

Politics. Enrolled Democratic voters in New York City usually outnumber Republicans about 3 to 1. But there are about twice as many enrolled Republicans as Democrats in the rest of the state. Albany County is often the only upstate county to vote Democratic. Thus, the two parties are fairly evenly matched, because New York City has almost half the state's total population. Republicans, however, have generally controlled the legislature. From 1964 to 1966, the Democrats controlled the legislature for the first time in 30 years. In 1964 and 1965, Republicans and Democrats battled over *reapportionment* (redivision) of the

Governor's Mansion in Albany stands south of the Capitol. The building, begun in the mid-1850's, was originally a private home. The state bought it in 1877 for the governor's residence.
New York State Dept. of Commerce

The State Seal

Symbols of New York. On the seal, the figure on the left represents Liberty. The crown at her feet signifies that Liberty has rejected kings and monarchies. The figure on the right symbolizes Justice. A typical New York river scene is in the center of the seal, and an American eagle perches on the globe at the top. The seal was adopted in 1778. The state flag, adopted in 1909, has a reproduction of the seal.

legislative districts. But they did not agree on a reapportionment plan. In 1966, the court of appeals appointed a commission with representatives of both parties to draw up a plan. The court approved the commission's plan. The legislature redrew the districts in 1971. The new plan gave more representation to fast-growing suburban areas.

New York has 41 electoral votes—more than any other state except California. For this reason, New York plays a key role in presidential elections and its governors have always been considered possible presidential candidates. New York governors often have introduced national issues into state politics. Four men served as governor of New York before becoming President— Martin Van Buren, Grover Cleveland, Theodore Roosevelt, and Franklin D. Roosevelt. Five other governors— Horatio Seymour, Samuel J. Tilden, Charles Evans Hughes, Alfred E. Smith, and Thomas E. Dewey— were unsuccessful nominees for the presidency.

Since 1880, New Yorkers have voted for the winning presidential candidate in every election except those in 1916, 1948, and 1968. For New York's electoral votes and voting record, see ELECTORAL COLLEGE (table).

State Capitol in Albany was first occupied in 1879. Albany has been the capital since 1797. Kingston, Poughkeepsie, and New York City served as temporary capitals between 1777 and 1797.

The State Flag

The State Bird
Bluebird

The State Flower
Rose

The State Tree
Sugar Maple

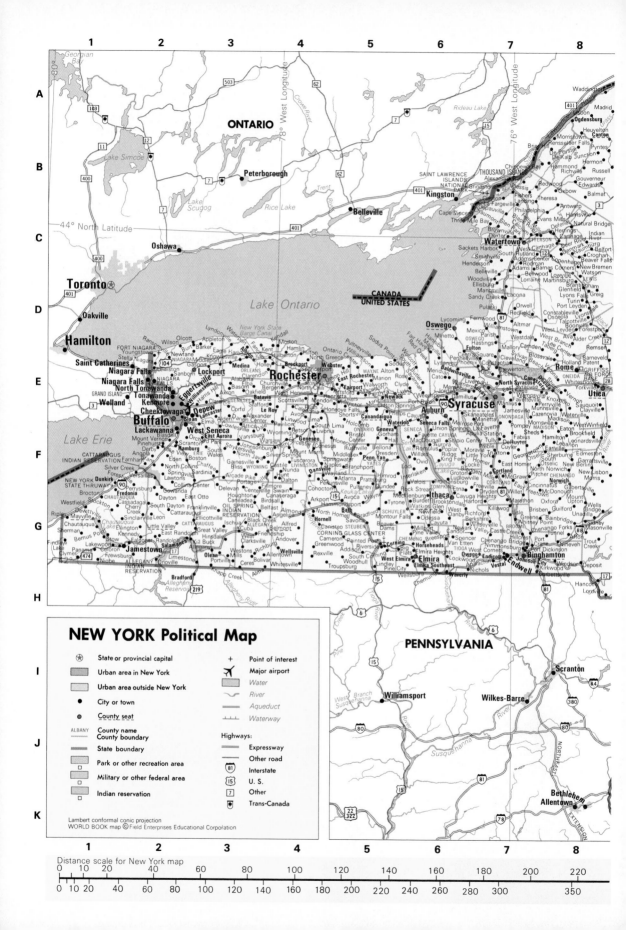

NEW YORK Political Map

⊛	State or provincial capital
	Urban area in New York
	Urban area outside New York
●	City or town
●	County seat
ALBANY	County name County boundary
	State boundary
	Park or other recreation area
	Military or other federal area
	Indian reservation
+	Point of interest
✈	Major airport
	Water
	River
	Aqueduct
	Waterway

Highways:
Expressway
Other road
81 Interstate
15 U.S.
7 Other
Trans-Canada

Lambert conformal conic projection
WORLD BOOK map © Field Enterprises Educational Corporation

Distance scale for New York map
0 10 20 40 60 80 100 120 140 160 180 200 220
0 10 20 40 60 80 100 120 140 160 180 200 220 240 260 280 300 350

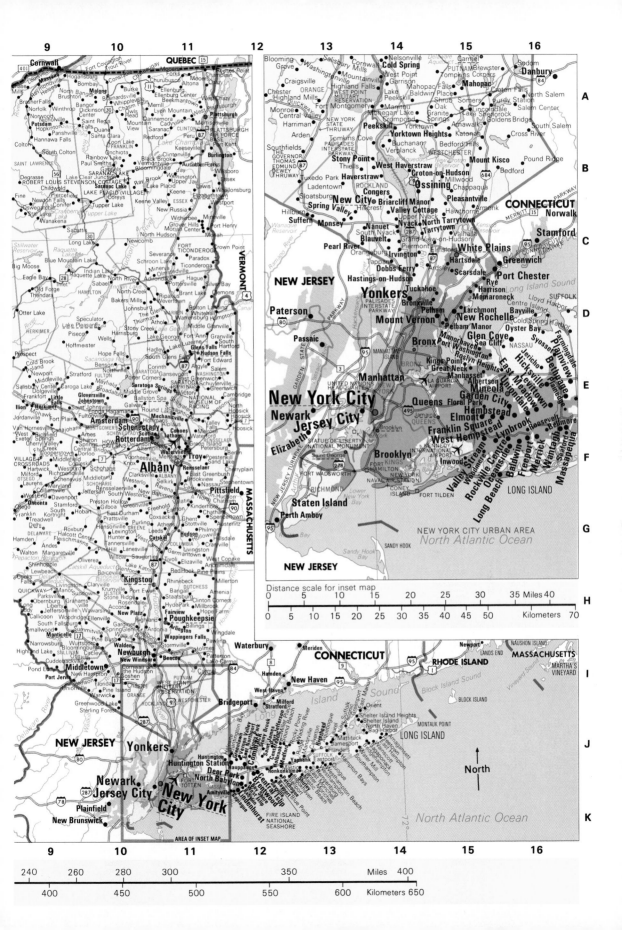

Population

18,241,266 .Census..1970
16,782,304 ....“....1960
14,830,192 ....“....1950
13,479,142 ....“....1940
12,588,066 ....“....1930
10,385,227 ....“....1920
9,113,614 ....“....1910
7,268,894 ....“....1900
6,003,174 ....“....1890
5,082,871 ....“....1880
4,382,759 ....“....1870
3,880,735 ....“....1860
3,097,394 ....“....1850
2,428,921 ....“....1840
1,918,608 ....“....1830
1,372,812 ....“....1820
959,049 ....“....1810
589,051 ....“....1800
340,120 ....“....1790

Metropolitan Areas

Albany-Schenectady-Troy 777,977
Binghamton .....302,672 (268,328 in N.Y.; 34,344 in Pa.)
Buffalo 1,349,211
Elmira 101,537
Nassau-Suffolk 2,555,868
New York City 9,943,800 (9,047,000 in N.Y.; 896,800 in N.J.)
Poughkeepsie 222,295
Rochester 961,516
Syracuse 636,596
Utica-Rome 340,670

Counties

Albany ...286,742..F 11
Allegany ..46,458..G 3
Bronx ...1,471,701..E 14
Broome ...221,815..G 7
Cattaraugus 81,666..G 2
Cayuga ....77,439..F 6
Chautauqua 147,305..G 1
Chemung ..101,537..G 6
Chenango ..46,368..F 8
Clinton ...72,934..A 11
Columbia ..51,519..G 11
Cortland ...45,894..F 7
Delaware ..44,718..G 9
Dutchess ..222,295..H 11
Erie ...1,113,491..F 3
Essex ......34,631..D 11
Franklin ...43,931..B 10
Fulton .....52,637..E 10
Genesee ....58,722..E 3
Greene .....33,136..G 10
Hamilton ...4,714..D 10
Herkimer ..67,633..D 9
Jefferson ...88,508..C 7
Kings ...2,602,012..F 14
Lewis ......23,644..D 8
Livingston ..54,041..F 4
Madison ....62,864..F 7
Monroe ...711,917..E 4
Montgomery 55,883..F 10
Nassau ..1,428,838..K 11
New York 1,539,233..E 14
Niagara ...235,720..E 2
Oneida ....273,037..E 8
Onondaga .472,835..E 7
Ontario ....78,849..F 5
Orange ...221,657..I 10
Orleans ....37,305..E 3
Oswego ...100,897..D 6
Otsego .....56,181..F 9
Putnam ....56,696..I 11
Queens ..1,987,174..F 14
Rensselaer 152,510..F 11
Richmond .295,443..F 13
Rockland .229,903..I 11
St. Lawrence ...111,991..B 9
Saratoga ..121,764..E 10
Schenectady ....161,078..F 10
Schoharie ..24,750..F 10
Schuyler ...16,737..G 5
Seneca .....35,083..F 6
Steuben ....99,546..G 5
Suffolk ..1,127,030..J 13
Sullivan ...52,580..I 9
Tioga ......46,513..G 6
Tompkins ..77,064..F 6
Ulster ....141,241..H 10
Warren ....49,402..D 11
Washington 52,725..E 11
Wayne .....79,404..E 5
Westchester ..894,406..I 11
Wyoming ...37,688..F 3
Yates ......19,831..F 5

Cities and Villages

Adams ......1,951..C 7
Addison ....2,104..G 5
Afton ......1,064..G 8
Akron ......2,863..E 3
Albany ....115,781.°F 11
Albertson ...6,825..E 16
Albion ......5,122.°E 3
Alden ......2,651..F 3
Alexandria Bay ......1,440..B 7
Alfred ......3,804..G 4
Allegany ....2,050..G 3
Almond ......658..G 4
Altamont ...1,561..F 10
Amenia ......1,157..H 11
Amityville ...9,794..K 12
Amsterdam 25,524..E 10
Andover ....1,214..G 4
Angelica .....948..G 4
Angola ......2,676..F 2
Angola on the Lake* ....1,573..F 2
Antwerp ......872..C 8
Apalachin ..1,233..G 7
Arcade ......1,972..F 3
Ardsley .....4,470..C 15
Arkport ....984..G 4
Arlington ..11,203..H 11
Asharoken* ...540..J 12
Athens .....1,718..G 11
Atlantic Beach* ...1,640..K 11
Attica ......2,911..F 3
Auburn ....34,599.°E 6
Aurora ......1,072..F 6
Averill Park* 1,471..F 11
Avoca ......1,153..G 5
Avon ....3,260..F 4
Babylon ....12,897..K 12
Bainbridge ..1,674..G 8
Baldwin ...34,525..F 16
Baldwinsville 6,298..E 7
Ballston Spa 4,968.°E 11
Balmville ...3,214..I 11
Barker ....567..E 3
Batavia ...17,338.°E 3
Bath ....6,053.°G 5
Baxter Estates* ...1,026..J 11
Bay Shore ..11,119..K 12
Bayport .....7,995..K 12
Bayville .....6,147..D 16
Beacon .....13,255..I 11
Belle Terre* ..678..J 12
Bellerose* ...1,136..J 11
Bellmore ...18,431..F 16
Bellport .....3,046..J 13
Belmont .....1,102.°G 4
Bergen ......1,018..E 4
Bethpage ..18,555..E 16
Big Flats ...2,509..G 5
Billington Heights* ..1,278..F 3
Binghamton 64,123.°G 7
Black River .1,307..C 7
Blasdell ....3,910..F 2
Blauvelt ....5,426..C 14
Bloomingdale .536..B 10
Bohemia* ...8,926..K 12
Bolivar .....1,379..G 3
Boonville ...2,488..D 8
Boysen Bay* 1,191..E 7
Brentwood .28,327..J 12
Brewerton ..1,985..E 7
Brewster ...1,638..A 16
Brewster Heights* ..1,265..I 11
Brewster Hills* .....1,745..I 11
Briarcliff Manor ....6,521..B 15
Bridgewater* ..601..F 8
Brightwaters* ...3,808..K 12
Brinckerhoff* .....2,094..I 11
Broadalbin ..1,452..E 10
Brockport ...7,878..E 4
Brocton ......1,370..G 1
Bronx ...1,471,701.°E 14
Bronxville ..6,674..D 15
Brookhaven ....J 13
Brooklyn 2,602,012.°F 14
Brookville* ..3,212..J 11
Brownville ..1,187..C 7
Brushton .....547..A 10
Buchanan ...2,110..B 14
Buffalo ...462,768.°F 2
Caledonia ...2,327..E 4
Cambridge ...1,769..E 12
Camden ......2,936..E 8
Camillus ....1,534..E 7
Canajoharie .2,686..E 10
Canandaigua ..10,753.°F 5
Canaseraga ...750..G 4
Canastota ...5,033..E 8
Candor ....939..G 7
Canisteo ...2,772..G 4
Canton .....6,398.°B 8
Cape Vincent .820..C 7
Carle Place* 6,326..K 11
Carmel .....3,395.°I 11
Carthage ....3,889..C 8
Cassadaga ....905..G 1
Castile ......1,330..F 4
Castleton-on-Hudson ...1,730..F 11
Cato ....601..E 6
Catskill .....5,317.°G 11
Cattaraugus .1,200..G 2
Cayuga ....693..F 6
Cayuga Heights ...3,130..G 6
Cazenovia ...3,031..E 7
Cedarhurst* .6,941..K 11
Celoron .....1,456..G 1
Center Moriches .3,802..J 13
Centereach ..9,427..J 12
Central Islip 36,369..J 12
Central Square ....1,298..E 7
Champlain ..1,426..A 11
Champlain Park* .....1,207..A 11
Chateaugay ...976..A 10
Chatham ....2,239..G 11
Chaumont .....567..C 7
Chenango Bridge, see Nimmonsburg [-Chenango Bridge]
Cherry Creek .658..G 2
Cherry Valley .661..F 9
Chester ......1,627..I 10
Chittenango* 3,605..E 8
Churchville .1,065..E 4
Clarence ....2,014..E 3
Clarence Center* ...1,332..E 3
Clark Mills* 1,206..E 8
Clayton ......1,970..B 7
Clayville ......535..E 8
Cleveland .....821..E 7
Clifton Knolls* ...5,771..F 11
Clifton Springs ...2,058..E 5
Clinton* ....2,271..E 8
Clyde ....2,828..E 6
Cobleskill ...4,368..F 10
Cohocton ......897..F 5
Cohoes ....18,653..F 11
Cold Spring .2,083..A 14
Cold Spring Harbor ...5,450..D 16
Colden Hill* 1,688..I 10
Colonie ......8,701..F 11
Commack ..24,138..J 12
Congers .....5,928..B 14
Cooperstown 2,403.°F 9
Copenhagen ...734..C 8
Copiague ...19,632..K 12
Corfu ....722..E 3
Corinth .....3,267..E 11
Corning ....15,792..G 5
Cornwall ....3,131..A 13
Cortland ..19,621.°F 7
Country Knolls* ...2,082..F 11
Coxsackie ...2,399..G 11
Croghan ......765..C 8
Croton-on-Hudson ..7,523..B 14
Cuba ....1,735..G 3
Dannemora ..3,735..A 11
Dansville ...5,436..F 4
Deer Park ..32,274..J 12
Delevan ......994..F 3
Delhi ....3,017.°G 9
Depew .....22,158..E 2
Deposit .....2,061..H 8
DeRuyter .....643..F 7
De Witt* ..10,032..E 7
Dexter ......1,061..C 7
Dix Hills* ..10,050..J 12
Dobbs Ferry ...10,353..C 14
Dolgeville ...2,872..E 9
Dryden ......1,490..G 7
Dundee ......1,539..F 5
Dunkirk ...16,855..F 1
Earlville ....1,050..F 8
East Aurora 7,033..F 3
East Bloomfield* ......643..F 5
East Cayuga Heights* ..2,611..F 6
East Glenville* .....5,898..E 10
East Half Hollow Hills* ...9,691..J 12
East Hampton .1,753..J 14
East Herkimer* 1,135..E 9
East Hills* ..8,624..J 11
East Islip* ..6,861..K 12
East Massapequa* ..15,926..K 11
East Meadow .46,252..E 16
East Middletown* ....2,640..I 10
East Moriches .1,702..J 13
East Neck* ..5,221..J 12
East Northport .....12,392..J 12
East Patchogue* 8,092..J 12
East Quogue* 1,143..J 12
East Randolph ......636..G 2
East Rochester .8,347..E 5
East Rockaway* ...11,795..K 11
East Syracuse ......4,333..E 7
East Vestal* ..10,472..G 7
East Williston* 2,808..J 11
Eastchester* 23,750..J 11
Eastport .....1,308..J 13
Eden ....2,962..F 2
Edwards .....576..B 8
Elba ....752..E 3
Elbridge* ...1,040..E 6
Elizabethtown ....607.°B 11
Ellenville ...4,482..H 10
Ellicottville ...955..G 3
Elma ....2,784..F 2
Elmira .....39,945.°G 6
Elmira Heights ...4,906..G 6
Elmira Heights North* ....2,906..G 6
Elmira Southeast .8,685..H 6
Elmont ....29,363..E 15
Elmsford ....3,911..C 15
Elwood* ....15,031..J 12
Endicott ...16,556..G 7
Endwell ...15,999..G 7
Evans Mills ..714..C 7
Fair Haven ...859..E 6
Fairmount* 15,317..E 6
Fairport ....6,474..E 5
Fairview ....8,517..H 11
Falconer ....2,983..G 2
Farmingdale ......9,297..E 16
Farnham .....546..F 2
Fayetteville .4,996..E 7
Fernwood ...3,659..D 7
Fillmore .....537..F 3
Firthcliffe* .4,025..I 10
Fishkill ......913..I 11
Flanders ....1,905..J 13
Floral Park 18,466..E 15
Florida .....1,674..I 10
Flower Hill* 4,486..J 11
Fonda ......1,120.°E 10
Forestville ....908..F 2
Fort Ann .....562..D 11
Fort Covington 983..A 10
Fort Edward 3,733..E 11
Fort Johnson* 711..E 10
Fort Plain ..2,809..F 9
Fort Salonga* ..1,604..J 12
Frankfort ...3,305..E 9
Franklin ......552..G 8
Franklin Square ...32,156..E 15
Franklinville 1,948..G 3
Fredonia ..10,326..G 1
Freeport ...40,374..F 16
Freetown ...1,543..J 14
Freeville ......664..F 7
Frewsburg ..1,772..G 2
Friendship ..1,285..G 3
Fulton .....14,003..E 6
Fultonville ....812..E 10
Gang Mills* 1,258..G 5
Garden City 25,373..E 16
Garden City Park* .....7,488..J 11
Gardnertown* .....4,614..I 10
Geneseo .....5,714.°F 4
Geneva ....16,793..F 5
Gilbertsville ..552..G 8
Glasco* ......1,169..G 11
Glen Cove .25,770..D 16
Glen Park .....587..C 7
Glenham* ...2,720..I 11
Glens Falls 17,222..E 11
Gloversville 19,677..E 10
Goldens Bridge .....1,101..A 15
Goshen .....4,342.°I 10
Gouverneur .4,574..B 8
Gowanda ....3,110..G 2
Granville ...2,784..D 12
Great Neck 10,798..E 15
Great Neck Estates* ..3,131..J 11
Great Neck Plaza* ....6,043..J 11
Green Island 3,297..F 11
Greene .....1,874..G 7
Greenlawn ...8,493..J 12
Greenport ...2,481..J 13
Greenwich ..2,092..E 11
Greenwood Lake ......2,262..I 10
Groton .....2,112..F 6
Hagaman ...1,410..E 10
Half Hollow Hills* ...12,081..J 12
Halfmoon Junction* .1,915..F 11
Hamburg ..10,215..F 2
Hamilton ...3,636..F 8
Hammondsport ......1,066..G 5
Hampton Bays ......1,862..J 13
Hancock ....1,688..H 8
Hannibal .....686..E 6
Harriman .....955..A 13
Harrisville ....836..C 8
Hartsdale ..12,226..C 15
Hastings-on-Hudson ...9,479..D 14
Hauppauge 13,957..J 12
Haverstraw ..8,198..B 14
Haviland* ..3,447..H 11
Head of the Harbor* ....943..J 12
Hempstead .39,411..E 16
Herkimer ...8,960.°E 9
Herricks* ...9,112..J 11
Heuvelton .....770..B 8
Hewlett* ....6,796..K 11
Hewlett Bay Park* ......586..K 11
Hewlett Harbor* ..1,512..K 11
Hewlett Neck* 529..K 11
Hicksville ..49,820..E 16
Highland ...2,184..H 11
Highland Falls .....4,638..A 14
Hillburn ....1,058..C 13
Hillcrest .....5,357..C 13
Hillis* ......2,750..H 11
Hilton ....2,440..E 4
Hobart ....531..G 9
Holbrook [-Holtsville] ....12,103..J 12
Holcomb .....778..F 5
Holland Patent .....556..E 8
Holley ......1,868..E 4
Holtsville, see Holbrook [-Holtsville]
Homer .....4,143..F 7
Honeoye Falls .....2,248..E 4
Hoosick Falls .....3,897..F 12
Hopewell Junction* .2,055..J 11
Hornell ....12,144..G 4
Horseheads .7,989..G 6
Houghton ...1,620..G 3
Hudson ....8,940 °G 11
Hudson Falls 7,917.°E 11
Huntington .12,601..J 12
Huntington Bay ......1,789..J 12
Huntington Station ..28,817..J 12
Hurley* .....4,081..G 11
Hyde Park ..2,805..H 11
Ilion ....9,808..E 9
Interlaken .....733..F 6
Inwood .....8,433..F 15
Irvington ...5,878..C 14
Island Park* 5,396..K 11
Islip* ....7,692..K 12
Ithaca .....26,226.°G 6
Jamaica ....°E 15
Jamestown .39,795..G 2
Jamestown West* ....2,491..G 1
Jefferson Valley, see Yorktown [-Jefferson Valley]
Jericho .....14,010..E 16
Johnson City .....18,025..G 7
Johnstown .10,045.°E 10
Jordan .....1,493..E 6
Keeseville ...2,122..B 11
Kenmore ...20,980..E 2
Kensington* 1,402..J 11
Kerhonkson* 1,243..G 11
Kinderhook .1,233..G 11
Kings Park .5,555..J 12
Kings Point .5,614..E 15
Kingston ...25,544.°H 11
Lackawanna 28,657..F 2
Lacona ....556..D 7
Lake* ....1,352..I 10
Lake Carmel 4,796..I 11
Lake Erie Beach* ....3,467..F 2
Lake George 1,046.°D 11
Lake Grove* 8,133..J 12
Lake Katrine 1,092..H 11
Lake Placid 2,731..B 10
Lake Pleasant ....°D 10
Lake Success* ..3,254..J 11
Lakeview* ..5,471..E 16
Lakewood ...3,864..G 1
Lancaster ..13,365..F 3
Larchmont ..7,203..D 15
Latham .....9,661..F 11
Lattingtown* 1,773..J 11
Laurel Hollow* ..1,401..J 11
Lawrence* ..6,566..K 11
Le Roy ......5,118..E 4
Levittown ..65,440..E 16
Lewiston ....3,292..E 2
Liberty .....4,293..H 9
Lima ....1,686..F 4
Limestone .....535..H 3
Lincoln Park* ....2,851..G 11
Lindenhurst 28,338..K 12
Little Falls .7,629..E 9
Little Valley 1,340.°G 2
Liverpool ....3,307..E 7
Livingston Manor .....1,522..H 9
Livonia .....1,278..F 4

Lloyd Har-
　bor ......3,371..D 16
Lockport ..25,399.°E 3
Locust
　Grove* ..11,626..J 11
Long Beach 33,127..F 16
Lorenz Park* .1,995..G 11
Loudonville* 9,299..F 11
Lowville ...3,671.°C 8
Lynbrook ..23,151..F 16
Lyndonville ...888..E 3
Lyons ......4,219.°E 5
Lyons Falls ..852..D 8
Macedon ...1,418..E 5
Mahopac ...5,265..A 15
Malone ....8,048.°A 10
Malverne* .10,036..K 11
Mamaro-
　neck .....18,909..D 15
Manchester .1,305..E 5
Manhasset .8,541..E 15
Man-
　hattan 1,539,233..E 14
Manlius ....4,295..E 7
Manorhaven .5,488..E 15
Marathon ..1,053..G 7
Marcellus* .2,017..E 7
Margaretville ..816..G 9
Marlboro ...1,580..I 11
Massapequa 26,821..F 16
Massapequa
　Park* ....22,112..K 11
Massena ..14,042..A 9
Mastic Beach 4,870..J 13
Matinecock* ..841..J 11
Mattituck ..1,995..J 13
Mattydale* .8,292..E 7
Maybrook* .1,536..I 10
Mayfield ....981..E 10
Mayville ...1,567.°G 1
McGraw ....1,319..F 7
Mechanic-
　ville .....6,247..F 11
Medina ....6,415..E 3
Melrose
　Park .....2,189..F 6
Melville* ...6,641..J 12
Menands ...3,449..F 11
Merrick ...25,904..F 16
Merriewold
　Lake* ....2,564..I 10
Mexico .....1,555..D 7
Middleburg .1,410..F 10
Middlehope* 2,327..I 10
Middleport .2,132..E 3
Middletown 22,607..I 10
Middleville ..725..E 9
Milford ......527..F 9
Mill Neck* ..982..J 11
Millbrook ..1,735..H 11
Millerton ..1,042..H 11
Milton* ....1,361..E 11
Mineola ...21,845.°E 16
Mineville [-Wither-
　bee] ......1,967..C 11
Minoa .....2,245..E 7
Mohawk ....3,301..E 9
Monroe ....4,439..A 13
Monsey ....8,797..C 13
Montgomery 1,533..I 10
Monticello ..5,991.°H 9
Montour
　Falls .....1,534..G 6
Mooers ......536..A 11
Moravia ...1,642..F 6
Morris ......675..F 8
Morrisonville 1,276..A 11
Morristown ..532..B 8
Morrisville .2,296..F 8
Mount
　Kisco ....8,172..B 15
Mount
　Morris ...3,417..F 4
Mount
　Vernon ..72,778..D 15
Munsey
　Park* ....2,980..J 11
Munsons
　Corners* .2,076..F 7
Muttontown* 2,081..J 11
Myers
　Corner* ..2,826..I 11
Nanuet ...10,447..C 14
Naples .....1,324..F 4
Nassau .....1,466..F 11
Nelliston* ...716..F 9
Nelsonville ..613..A 14
Nesconset* 10,048..J 12
New Berlin .1,369..F 8
New Cassel* 8,721..J 11
New City ..27,344.°B 14
New Hacken-
　sack* ....1,111..I 11
New
　Hamburg* .1,064..H 11
New Hart-
　ford* .....2,433..E 8
New Hyde
　Park* ...10,116..K 11
New Paltz .6,058..H 10
New Ro-
　chelle ..75,385..D 15
New Square* 1,156..J 10
New
　Windsor ..8,803..I 11
New York
　City ...7,895,563.°K 11

New York
　Mills* ....3,805..E 8
Newark ...10,717..E 5
Newark
　Valley ...1,286..G 7
Newburgh .26,219..I 11
Newfane ...2,588..E 2
Newport .....908..E 9
Niagara
　Falls ....85,615..E 2
Nichols ......638..H 6
Nimmonsburg
　[-Chenango
　Bridge] ..5,059..G 7
Niskayuna* .6,186..F 11
Nissequogue* 1,120..J 12
Norfolk ....1,379..A 9
North Amity-
　ville* ....11,905..K 12
North
　Babylon .39,526..K 12
North Ballston
　Spa* ....1,296..E 11
North
　Bellmore* 22,893..K 11
North
　Bellport* .5,903..J 13
North
　Boston* ..1,635..F 2
North Chili 3,163..E 4
North
　Collins ...1,675..F 2
North Great
　River* ..12,080..K 12
North
　Haven .....694..J 14
North
　Hornell ....919..G 4
North Linden-
　hurst* ...11,117..K 12
North Mas-
　sapequa* .23,123..K 11
North
　Merrick* .13,650..K 11
North New Hyde
　Park* ...18,154..J 11
North
　Patchoque 5,232..J 13
North
　Syracuse .8,687..E 7
North Tarry-
　town ....8,334..C 14
North Tona-
　wanda ...36,012..E 2
North Valley
　Stream* .14,881..F 15
North
　Wantagh* 15,053..K 11
Northport* .7,494..J 12
Northville ..1,192..E 10
Norwich ...8,843.°F 8
Norwood ...2,098..A 9
Nunda .....1,254..F 4
Nyack .....6,659..C 14
Oakdale* ...7,334..K 12
Oakfield ...1,964..E 3
Oceanside .35,372..F 16
Odessa ......606..G 6
Ogdensburg 14,554..A 8
Olcott .....1,592..D 2
Old Beth-
　page* ....7,084..K 11
Old Brook-
　ville* ....1,785..J 11
Old Field* ..824..J 12
Old West-
　bury* ....2,667..J 11
Olean ....19,169..G 3
Oneida ...11,658..E 8
Oneida
　Castle* ....788..E 8
Oneonta ..16,030..G 9
Oniad Lake* 1,587..I 11
Orange Lake* 4,348..I 10
Orchard
　Park .....3,732..F 2
Oriskany* ..1,627..E 8
Oriskany
　Falls* ......927..E 8
Ossining ..21,659..B 14
Oswego ...20,913.°D 6
Otego ......956..G 8
Otisville ....933..I 10
Ovid ....779..F 6
Owego .....4,686.°G 7
Oxford ....1,944..G 8
Oyster Bay
　Cove* ....1,320..J 11
Painted Post 2,496..G 5
Palatine
　Bridge] ....601..F 10
Palmyra ...3,672..E 5
Parish ......634..D 7
Patchogue .11,283..J 12
Pawling ...1,914..I 11
Pearl River 17,146..C 14
Peekskill ..19,283..A 14
Pelham ....7,260..I 11
Pelham
　Manor ...6,673..D 15
Penn Yan ..5,293.°F 5
Perry .....4,538..F 4
Peru ......1,261..B 11
Phelps .....1,989..E 5
Philadelphia ..858..C 8
Philmont ..1,674..G 11
Phoenix ...2,617..E 7

Piermont ...2,386..C 14
Pine Bush .1,183..I 10
Pine Neck-West
　Tiana* ...1,326..J 13
Pittsford ...1,755..E 5
Plainedge .10,759..E 16
Plainview .31,695..E 16
Plandome* .1,593..J 11
Plandome
　Heights* .1,032..J 11
Plandome
　Manor* .....835..J 11
Plattsburgh 18,715.°A 11
Plattsburgh
　Base* ....7,078..A 11
Pleasant
　Valley* ..1,372..H 11
Pleasantville 7,110..B 15
Poland ......629..E 9
Pomona* ..1,792..J 11
Ponquogue* 1,474..J 13
Port Byron .1,330..E 6
Port
　Chester .25,803..C 15
Port Dickin-
　son ......2,132..G 7
Port Ewen .2,882..H 11
Port Henry .1,532..C 11
Port Jeffer-
　son ......5,800..J 12
Port Jefferson
　Station* ..7,403..J 12
Port Jervis .8,852..I 9
Port Leyden ..862..D 8
Port Washing-
　ton .....15,923..E 15
Port Washington
　North* ...2,883..J 11
Portville ...1,304..H 3
Potsdam ..10,303..A 9
Pough-
　keepsie .32,029.°H 11
Prattsburg ..765..F 5
Pulaski ....2,480..D 7
Putnam
　Lake* ....1,425..I 11
Queens .1,987,174..F 14
Quogue ......865..J 13
Randolph ..1,498..G 2
Ransomville 1,034..E 2
Ravena ....2,797..G 11
Red Creek ..639..E 6
Red Hook ..1,680..H 11
Red Oaks
　Mill* .....3,919..H 11
Remsen ......602..E 8
Rensselaer .10,136..F 11
Rhinebeck .2,336..H 11
Richfield
　Springs ...1,540..F 9
Richmond-
　ville ......826..F 10
Ripley .....1,173..G 1
Riverhead .7,585.°J 13
Riverside ....911..G 5
Rochdale* .1,849..K 11
Rochester .296,233.°E 4
Rockville
　Centre ..27,444..F 16
Roesleville* 5,476..F 11
Rolling
　Acres* ...1,152..E 4
Rome ....50,148..E 8
Ronkonkoma 7,284..J 12
Roosevelt .15,008..F 16
Rosendale .1,220..H 10
Roslyn* ...2,607..J 11
Roslyn
　Estates* .1,420..J 11
Roslyn
　Harbor* ..1,125..J 11
Roslyn
　Heights* .7,242..E 16
Rotterdam .25,214..F 11
Round Lake ..886..E 11
Rouses Point 2,250..A 11
Rushville ....568..F 5
Russell
　Gardens* .1,207..J 11
Rye ......15,869..D 15
Sackets
　Harbor ...1,202..C 7
Saddle Rock* .895..J 11
Sag Harbor .2,363..J 14
St. George .....°F 13
St. James .10,500..J 12
St. Johns-
　ville ......2,089..E 9
Salamanca .7,877..G 2
Salem .....1,025..E 12
San Remo* .8,302..J 12
Sand Ridge* 1,109..E 7
Sandy
　Beach* ...1,691..E 2
Sands Point* 2,916..J 11
Sandy Creek ..731..D 7
Saranac
　Lake ....6,086..B 10
Saratoga
　Springs .18,845..E 11
Saugerties .4,190..G 11
Saugerties
　South* ...3,159..G 11
Savannah ...610..E 6
Savona .....933..G 5
Sayville ..11,680..K 12
Scarsdale .19,229..C 15

Schaghticoke ..860..F 11
Schenectady 77,958.°F 11
Schenevus ...540..F 9
Schoharie .1,125.°F 10
Schuylerville 1,402..E 11
Scotchtown* 2,119..I 10
Scotia .....7,370..F 11
Scottsville .1,967..E 4
Sea Cliff ..5,890..D 16
Seaford ...17,379..F 16
Selden* ...11,613..J 12
Seneca Falls 7,794..F 6
Setauket [-South
　Setauket]* 6,857..J 12
Sherburne .1,613..F 8
Sherman .....769..G 1
Sherrill ....2,986..E 8
Shirley ....6,280..J 13
Shoreham* ...556..J 13
Shortsville .1,516..E 5
Sidney .....4,789..G 8
Silver Creek 3,182..F 2
Silver Springs 823..F 4
Sinclairville ..772..G 1
Skaneateles 3,055..E 6
Slabtown* .2,753..G 5
Sloan .....5,216..F 2
Sloatsburg .3,134..B 13
Sodus .....1,733..E 5
Sodus Point 1,412..E 5
Solvay ....8,280..E 7
South
　Corning ..1,414..G 5
South Dayton ..688..G 2
South Falls-
　burg .....1,590..H 9
South Farm-
　ingdale* .20,464..J 11
South Floral
　Park* ....1,032..J 11
South Glens
　Falls ....4,013..E 11
South Hol-
　brook* ...6,700..K 12
South Hudson
　Falls* ...2,097..E 11
South Hunting-
　ton* .....9,115..J 12
South
　Lockport* .1,341..E 3
South Nyack 3,435..C 14
South Setauket, see
　Setauket [-South
　Setauket]
South Stony
　Brook* ..15,329..J 12
South Valley
　Stream* .6,595..K 11
South West-
　bury* ...10,978..J 11
Southampton 4,904..J 13
Southold* ..2,030..J 13
Spackenhill* 2,725..H 11
Spencer .....854..G 6
Spencerport 2,929..E 4
Spring
　Valley ..18,112..C 13
Springville .4,350..F 3
Sproutville* .1,871..I 11
Stamford ..1,286..G 9
Staten
　Island ..295,443..F 13
Stewart* ..1,230..I 10
Stewart
　Manor* ..2,183..J 11
Stillwater* 1,428..E 11
Stony Brook 6,391..J 12
Stony Point .8,270..B 14
Stottville ..1,106..G 11
Suffern ...8,273..C 13
Syosset ..10,084..E 16
Syracuse .197,297.°E 7
Tannersville ..650..G 10
Tappan ....7,424..C 14
Tarrytown .11,115..C 14
Theresa .....985..B 7
Thomaston* 2,811..J 11
Thornwood* .6,874..J 11
Ticonderoga 3,268..C 11
Tillson* ...1,256..H 10
Tivoli ......739..G 11
Tonawanda 21,898..E 2
Town Line* .2,434..E 3
Tribes Hill .1,184..F 10
Troy .....62,918.°F 11
Trumans-
　burg .....1,803..F 6
Tuckahoe .6,236..D 15
Tully ......899..F 7
Tupper Lake 4,854..B 10
Tuxedo Park .861..B 13
Twin Orchards, see
　Vestal [-Twin
　Orchards]
Unadilla ...1,489..G 8
Union
　Springs ..1,183..F 6
Uniondale .22,077..E 16
Unionville ...576..I 10
Upper Brook-
　ville* ....1,182..J 11
Upper
　Nyack ...2,096..C 14
Utica ....91,340.°E 8
Valatie ....1,288..G 11
Valley
　Cottage ..6,007..C 14

Valley Falls ..681..F 11
Valley
　Stream ..40,413..F 15
Van Etten ...522..G 6
Van
　Keurens* .3,292..H 11
Vernon ....1,108..E 8
Vernon
　Valley [-7,925..J 12
Vestal [-Twin
　Orchards] 8,303..G 7
Victor .....2,187..E 5
Victory .....718..E 11
Village of the
　Branch* .1,675..J 12
Viola* .....5,136..I 10
Voorhees-
　ville .....2,826..F 11
Waddington ..955..A 8
Walden ....5,277..I 10
Wallkill ...1,849..I 10
Walton ....3,744..G 9
Wampsville ..586.°E 8
Wantagh ..21,873..F 16
Wappingers
　Falls ....5,607..I 11
Wappingers Falls
　East* ....2,017..I 11
Wappingers
　Lake* ....1,958..H 11
Warrensburg 2,743..D 11
Warsaw ....3,619.°F 3
Warwick ...3,604..I 10
Washington
　Heights* .1,204..I 10
Washington-
　ville .....1,887..A 13
Waterford .2,879..F 11
Waterloo ...5,037..E 5
Watertown .30,787.°C 7
Waterville .1,808..E 8
Watervliet .12,404..F 11
Watkins
　Glen ....2,716.°G 6
Waverly ...5,261..H 6
Wayland ...2,022..F 4
Webster ...5,037..E 5
Weedsport .1,900..E 6
Wellsburg ...779..H 6
Wellsville .5,815..G 4
West Amity-
　ville* ....6,424..K 11
West
　Babylon* 12,893..K 12
West
　Carthage .2,047..C 8
West
　Elmira ...5,901..G 6
West End ..1,692..G 9
West Glens
　Falls* ....3,363..D 11
West Haver-
　straw ....8,558..B 14
West Hemp-
　stead ...20,375..E 16
West Islip 17,734..K 12
West Nyack 5,510..I 11
West Point .....A 14
West Sand
　Lake* ....1,875..F 11
West Say-
　ville* ....7,386..K 12
West Tiana, see
　Pine Neck-
　West Tiana
West
　Winfield ..1,018..F 8
Westbury* .15,362..J 11
Westfield ..3,651..G 1
Westhampton 1,156..J 13
Westhampton
　Beach ...1,926..J 13
Westmere* .6,364..F 11
Westport ....673..C 11
Westvale* .7,253..E 7
White
　Plains ..50,346.°C 15
Whitehall .3,764..D 11
Whitesboro .4,805..E 8
Whitney
　Point ....1,058..G 7
Williamson .1,991..E 5
Williams-
　ville .....6,835..E 2
Williston
　Park* ....9,154..J 11
Wilson ....1,284..E 2
Windsor ...1,098..G 8
Witherbee, see Mine-
　ville [-Witherbee]
Wolcott ....1,531..E 6
Woodbourne 1,155..I 9
Woodmere .19,831..F 15
Woodridge .1,071..H 10
Woodsburgh* ..817..K 11
Woodstock* 1,073..G 10
Wurtsboro ...732..I 10
Wyandanch* 15,716..K 12
Yaphank ...5,460..J 13
Yonkers .204,297..J 11
Yorktown
　Heights* .6,805..B 15
Yorktown
　[-Jefferson
　Valley] ..9,008..A 15
Yorkville ..3,425..E 8
Youngstown .2,169..E 2

*Does not appear on the map; key shows general location.
°County seat.

Sources: Latest census figures (1970 and special censuses); 1972
U.S. Census Bureau estimate for New York City metropolitan area.

245

NEW YORK/*People*

The 1970 United States census reported that New York had 18,241,266 persons. The population had increased 9 per cent over the 1960 figure of 16,782,304. The 1960 census had reported that New York ranked as the top state in population. But during the 1960's, California overtook New York. The U.S. Bureau of the Census estimated that by 1975 New York's population had dropped to about 18,120,000.

About 86 of every 100 of New York's people live in urban areas. That is, they live in or near cities and towns of 2,500 or more persons. The state has 10 Standard Metropolitan Statistical Areas (see METROPOLITAN AREA). For the populations of these areas, see the *Index* to the political map of New York.

New York City, with 7,895,563 persons, is the largest city in the United States. It ranks fourth in the world, after Shanghai, Tokyo, and Mexico City. The New York City metropolitan area, which includes eight counties in New York and one county in New Jersey, is also the fourth largest metropolitan area in the world. The state has five other cities with more than 100,000 persons. They are, in order of size, Buffalo, Rochester, Yonkers, Syracuse, and Albany. See the separate articles on the cities listed in the *Related Articles* at the end of this article.

New York, especially New York City, has long been known as a *melting pot*. Here, peoples of various races and many countries have settled and adopted a common culture. About 12 of every 100 persons in New York were born in another country. In addition, one or both parents of a fifth of the American-born New Yorkers were born in other countries. The largest groups born in other lands include, in order of size, Italians, Germans, Poles, Russians, English, Irish, Canadians, and Cubans. Many Puerto Ricans have come to New York since the end of World War II. More than 800,000 Puerto Ricans live in New York City. There are also more Negroes living in New York than in any other state—over 2 million.

Roman Catholics make up the largest single religious group in New York. Other large religious groups in the state include Episcopalians, Jews, Methodists, and Presbyterians. New York has more Roman Catholics and more Jews than any other state.

Ruth Sondak, FPG

Parade Watchers line the sidewalks in downtown Manhattan. New York City is the largest city in the United States. About 86 of every 100 persons in the state live in urban areas.

WORLD BOOK photo by Three Lions

Mohawk Indian works on a construction project in New York City. Indians come to the city from other parts of the state to find jobs. Many of them live in Brooklyn.

POPULATION

This map shows the *population density* of New York, and how it varies in different parts of the state. Population density means the average number of persons who live in a given area.

Persons per sq. mi.		Persons per km²
More than 1,000		More than 400
200 to 1,000		77 to 400
50 to 200		20 to 77
Less than 50		Less than 20

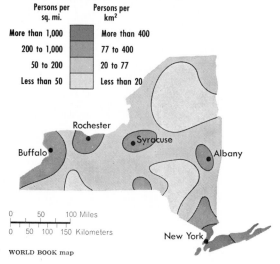

Rochester
Buffalo
Syracuse
Albany
New York

0   50   100 Miles
0   50   100   150 Kilometers

WORLD BOOK map

WORLD BOOK photo by Three Lions

A Puerto Rican Teacher discusses an art project with a student. Many Puerto Ricans live in New York City.

Schools. In 1784, the New York Legislature established an agency called the University of the State of New York. This agency controls and supervises the educational system in New York. The University of the State of New York is not a university in the usual sense of the word. A 15-member board of regents governs the University of the State of New York. The Legislature elects the regents, one each year, to seven-year terms. The regents receive no pay, but serve for the honor. The board has sweeping powers over all education in the state—elementary, secondary, and higher education—private and public. Its powers include setting educational standards, distributing public funds, awarding scholarships, and incorporating colleges and universities.

The powers and duties of the regents are administered by the state education department. The state commissioner of education heads the department. The regents appoint the commissioner for an indefinite term. In 1948, the Legislature established the State University of New York. This statewide university system has one of the largest enrollments of any U.S. university. Headquarters of the system are in Albany.

The state education department, responsible to the board of regents, supervises more than 750 local school districts. Each district has its own school board. Children between 6 and 16 must attend school. For the number of students and teachers in New York, see EDUCATION (table).

Libraries. The first libraries in New York were church libraries and private libraries established by Dutch colonists. The first libraries in the English colony of New York were set up about 1698 in New York City and Albany through the efforts of Thomas Bray, an Anglican missionary. The first public library in the New York region was founded in New York City about 1730. Today, the state has more than 1,000 public libraries. New York City has three independent library systems including more than 200 branches. One system, the New York Public Library, has the largest free circulating library in the nation.

Columbia University's libraries in New York City have about $4\frac{1}{2}$ million books. Other large college and university libraries include those at the City College of New York, Cornell University in Ithaca, the State University of New York in Buffalo, and Syracuse University. The Sibley Musical Library of the University of Rochester has the only library building in the nation devoted entirely to music.

New York's many special libraries include the Grosvenor Collection in the Buffalo and Erie County Public Library, which is an outstanding reference library; the Pierpont Morgan Library in New York City, which has a fine collection of rare manuscripts and early books; and the Frick Art Reference Library in New York City.

The New York State Library was founded in Albany in 1818. It is directed by the regents of the University of the State of New York. The library has a general reference collection of about $5\frac{1}{2}$ million books, pamphlets, manuscripts, and prints. It has an almost com-

Pickow, Three Lions

Baseball Hall of Fame and Museum in Cooperstown includes displays of equipment, trophies, and documents. The standing figure, above, shows the uniform worn by early baseball players.

State University of New York in Buffalo is part of the state's public system of higher education. The system includes university and medical centers, colleges of arts and science, and specialized, agricultural and technical, and community colleges.

State University of New York

plete collection of state and local histories on New York. The library's treasures include autographs of all of the signers of the Declaration of Independence, and the original copy of the first draft of the Emancipation Proclamation.

Museums. New York has over 300 museums. The New York State Museum, founded in Albany in 1836, is the nation's oldest state museum. The regents of the University of the State of New York supervise this museum. Its collections deal with natural history, science, and the art and history of the state. The Metropolitan Museum of Art in New York City is the largest art museum in the United States. Other outstanding museums include the Museum of Modern Art, the American Museum of Natural History, and the Guggenheim Museum, all in New York City; and the National Baseball Hall of Fame and Museum, in Cooperstown.

———— UNIVERSITIES AND COLLEGES ————

New York has 94 universities and colleges accredited by the Middle States Association of Colleges and Secondary Schools. For enrollments and further information, see UNIVERSITIES AND COLLEGES (table).

Name	Location	Founded	Name	Location	Founded
Adelphi University	Garden City	1896	Mercy College	Dobbs Ferry	1961
Alfred University	Alfred	1857	Molloy College	Rockville Centre	1955
Bank Street College			Mount Saint Alphonsus		
of Education	New York City	1916	Seminary	Esopus	1958
Bard College	Annandale-on-		Mount Saint Mary College	Newburgh	1954
	Hudson	1860	Mount Saint Vincent,		
Canisius College	Buffalo	1870	College of	New York City	1847
Cathedral College of the			Nazareth College of Rochester	Rochester	1924
Immaculate Conception	Douglaston	1948	New Rochelle, College of	New Rochelle	1904
Christ the King Seminary	East Aurora	1855	New School for		
Clarkson College of			Social Research	*	*
Technology	Potsdam	1896	New York, City University of	*	*
Colgate University	Hamilton	1819	New York, State University of	*	*
Columbia University	*	*	New York Institute of		
Concordia College	Bronxville	1972	Technology	Old Westbury	1958
Cooper Union	New York City	1859	New York University	New York City	1831
Cornell University	Ithaca	1865	Niagara University	Niagara University	1856
Dominican College of Blauvelt	Blauvelt	1972	Nyack College	Nyack	1882
Dowling College	Oakdale	1959	Pace University	*	*
D'Youville College	Buffalo	1908	Polytechnic Institute of		
Eisenhower College	Seneca Falls	1968	New York	New York City	1854
Elmira College	Elmira	1855	Pratt Institute	New York City	1887
Fashion Institute of Technology	New York City	1944	Rensselaer Polytechnic		
Fordham University	New York City	1841	Institute	Troy	1824
Hamilton College	Clinton	1793	Roberts Wesleyan College	North Chili	1866
Hartwick College	Oneonta	1928	Rochester, University of	Rochester	1850
Hebrew Union College—Jewish			Rochester Institute of		
Institute of Religion	New York City	1922	Technology	Rochester	1829
Hobart and William Smith			Rosary Hill College	Buffalo	1947
Colleges	Geneva	1822	Russell Sage College	Troy	1916
Hofstra University	Hempstead	1935	St. Bonaventure University	St. Bonaventure	1856
Houghton College	Houghton	1883	St. Francis College	New York City	1858
Immaculate Conception,			St. John Fisher College	Rochester	1951
Seminary of the	Huntington	1930	St. John's University	New York City	1870
Insurance, College of	New York City	1962	St. Joseph's College	New York City	1916
Iona College	New Rochelle	1940	St. Lawrence University	Canton	1856
Ithaca College	Ithaca	1892	St. Rose, College of	Albany	1920
Jewish Theological Seminary			St. Thomas Aquinas College	Sparkill	1972
of America	New York City	1887	Sarah Lawrence College	Yonkers	1928
Juilliard School	New York City	1887	Siena College	Loudonville	1937
Keuka College	Keuka Park	1892	Skidmore College	Saratoga Springs	1911
King's College	Briarcliff Manor	1938	Syracuse University	*	*
Kirkland College	Clinton	1965	Touro College	New York City	1970
Ladycliff College	Highland Falls	1933	Union College	Schenectady	1795
Le Moyne College	Syracuse	1946	Union Theological Seminary	New York City	1836
Long Island University	*	*	United States Merchant		
Manhattan College	New York City	1853	Marine Academy	Kings Point	1938
Manhattan School of Music	New York City	1920	United States Military Academy	West Point	1802
Manhattanville College	Purchase	1841	Vassar College	Poughkeepsie	1861
Mannes College of Music	New York City	1916	Wadhams Hall	Ogdensburg	1972
Marist College	Poughkeepsie	1946	Wagner College	New York City	1883
Maryknoll Seminary	Maryknoll	1911	Webb Institute of Naval		
Marymount College	Tarrytown	1907	Architecture	Glen Cove	1889
Marymount Manhattan College	New York City	1936	Wells College	Aurora	1868
Medaille College	Buffalo	1937	Yeshiva University	New York City	1886

*For campuses and founding dates, see UNIVERSITIES AND COLLEGES (table).

United States Military Academy in West Point, *right,* trains young men and women to be military officers. Another federal academy, the U.S. Merchant Marine Academy, is in Kings Point.

Guggenheim Museum in New York City, *below,* displays works of art in an unusual building designed by Frank Lloyd Wright.

New York State Museum in Albany, *below,* has displays of art, natural history, science, and state history.

Cornell University

Cornell University, *right,* is in Ithaca. Cornell also has schools of medicine and nursing in New York City.

NEW YORK / *A Visitor's Guide*

New York is one of the most popular vacationlands in the United States. Its forested mountains, shimmering lakes, sandy beaches, and vast areas of unspoiled wilderness attract millions of summer vacationers yearly. Winter sports fans enjoy New York's excellent facilities for skiing, snowmobiling, tobogganing, iceboating, and ice skating. Visitors also come to see New York's many historic forts and houses, and such magnificent wonders of nature as Niagara Falls. New York City's cultural and recreational attractions draw over 16 million visitors a year. See NEW YORK CITY.

Osborne, Three Lions
Niagara Falls at Night

PLACES TO VISIT

Following are brief descriptions of some of New York's many interesting places to visit.

Corning Glass Center, in Corning, includes the world's largest library devoted to glass, and a museum with exhibits of 3,500 years of glassmaking.

Farmers' Museum, near Cooperstown, has early agricultural tools and appliances. Nearby stands the **Village Crossroads.** It includes a country school, law office, village store, blacksmith shop, print shop, doctor's office, church, tavern, and farmhouse and barn. All were built in the late 1700's or early 1800's.

Fort Niagara, near Youngstown, was the scene of fighting during the French and Indian War and the War of 1812.

Fort Ticonderoga, on Lake Champlain, is a reconstruction of the colonial fort where Ethan Allen and his Green Mountain Boys defied the British and forced them to surrender in 1775.

Home of Franklin D. Roosevelt National Historic Site, in Hyde Park, includes the President's grave. Nearby, the Franklin D. Roosevelt Library and Museum has many of Roosevelt's books, ship models, and other personal belongings.

Howe Caverns, near Cobleskill, are colorfully lighted caves. Some are 200 feet (61 meters) underground.

Lake Placid, a village in the Adirondack Mountains, is a world-famous resort. It is noted for its glacial lake and its excellent facilities for winter and summer sports. John Brown, the abolitionist, is buried near there.

Literary Shrines may be seen throughout New York. They include John Burroughs' birthplace in Roxbury, Thomas Paine's home in New Rochelle, and Walt Whitman's birthplace near Huntington. Mark Twain's home and grave are in Elmira. The cottage in which Robert Louis Stevenson wrote several of his books is in Saranac Lake. The cottage in which Edgar Allan Poe wrote many poems is in New York City.

National Baseball Hall of Fame and Museum, in Cooperstown, honors great baseball players and displays historic equipment of the game.

Niagara Falls, in the city of Niagara Falls, is the most famous waterfall in the world. About 200,000 short tons (180,000 metric tons) of water plunge into a steep-walled gorge every minute.

Saranac Lake, in the Adirondacks, is a famous summer and winter sports center.

Saratoga Springs is noted for its health resort, owned and operated by the state, and for its race tracks. The National Museum of Racing has many exhibits of famous thoroughbred horses.

Vanderbilt Mansion, near Hyde Park, was the luxurious 50-room home of Frederick W. Vanderbilt. The

Watkins Glen State Park
Dean, Three Lions

Corning Glass Center in Corning
WORLD BOOK photo by Three Lions

WORLD BOOK photo
Fort Niagara near Youngstown

WORLD BOOK photo by Three Lions
Howe Caverns near Cobleskill

mansion was made a national historic site in 1940.

West Point, on the Hudson River north of New York City, is the home of the United States Military Academy.

National Parks and Monuments. Saratoga National Historical Park, near Stillwater, includes the battlefield on which the Americans defeated the British in the Battle of Saratoga in 1777. The park was established in 1938. Statue of Liberty National Monument, established in 1924, stands in New York Harbor. Castle Clinton National Monument, in New York City, was once a landing depot for immigrants. Here, more than 8 million persons entered the United States from 1855 to 1890. The monument was established in 1950. Fire Island National Seashore was established in 1964 on Fire Island, a reef off Long Island.

State Parks and Forests. New York has 128 state parks and about 50 forest areas. One of its most popular parks is Watkins Glen State Park, near Watkins Glen. This park is one of the scenic wonders of North America. It has 18 waterfalls, many caverns, Whites Hollow Lake, and a deep glen in which the water drops about 700 feet (213 meters) within 2 miles (3 kilometers). For information on the state parks of New York, write to the Office of Public Information, Parks and Recreation, Albany, N.Y. 12238.

Franklin D. Roosevelt Home in Hyde Park
WORLD BOOK photo by Three Lions

ANNUAL EVENTS

Many cultural festivals, historical celebrations, and sports competitions are held throughout New York every year. One of the most popular annual events is the New York State Fair, held in Syracuse in late August and early September. The opening of each theatrical and opera season in New York City is a glittering, exciting event. New York City also holds many gay and colorful holiday parades every year.

Other annual events in New York include the following.

January-March: Eastern States Speed Skating Championships in Saratoga Springs (January); Westminster Kennel Club Dog Show in New York City (February); Winter Carnival in Saranac Lake (February); St. Patrick's Day Parade in New York City (March).

April-June: Schoharie County Maple Festival in Jefferson (April); Hudson River White Water Derby in North Creek (May); Jaycee Canoe Race on the Ausable River in Lake Placid (May); National Lake Trout Derby on Seneca Lake near Geneva (May); Tulip Festival in Albany (May); Festival of Lilacs in Rochester (May); Intercollegiate Rowing Association Championship in Syracuse (late May); Belmont Stakes Horse Race in Long Island (early June); June Week Ceremonies at the United States Military Academy at West Point (June); Saratoga Fair in Saratoga Springs (late June or early July).

July-September: Annual Summer Ski Jump in Lake Placid (July); Newport Jazz Festival in New York City (July); Mormon Religious Pageant at Hill Cumorah near Palmyra (late July and early August); Central New York Scottish Games in Liverpool (August); Hall of Fame Baseball Exhibition Game in Cooperstown (August); United States Lawn Tennis Association Championships in Forest Hills, Long Island (August or September).

October-December: Columbus Day Parade in New York City (second Monday in October); U.S. Grand Prix (Formula 1 racing cars) in Watkins Glen (October); National Horse Show at Madison Square Garden in New York City (November); Thanksgiving Day Parade in New York City (November); Rockefeller Center Tree Lighting Ceremony in New York City (December).

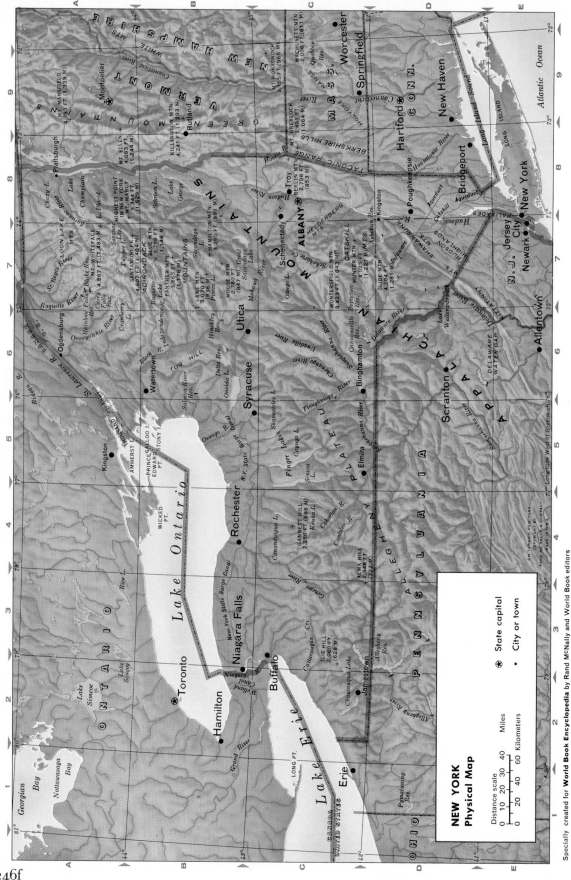

NEW YORK
Physical Map

Distance scale

Miles
0 10 20 30 40

Kilometers
0   20   40   60

⊛ State capital
• City or town

Specially created for **World Book Encyclopedia** by Rand McNally and World Book editors

NEW YORK / The Land

Land Regions. During the Ice Age, which ended about 10,000 years ago, glaciers spread across almost all the area now covered by New York. They formed many of New York's most striking natural features, and deposited stones, pebbles, and other materials. Most of New York's soils have been formed from materials deposited by the glaciers.

New York has seven major land regions: (1) the Atlantic Coastal Plain, (2) the New England Upland, (3) the Hudson-Mohawk Lowland, (4) the Adirondack Upland, (5) the St. Lawrence Lowland, (6) the Erie-Ontario Lowland, and (7) the Appalachian Plateau.

The Atlantic Coastal Plain covers Long Island and Staten Island. It forms part of the low, almost level coastal plain that stretches along the Atlantic Ocean from Massachusetts to the southern tip of Florida. Staten Island and the western end of Long Island lie within New York City. Both islands are important residential districts. Broad sandy beaches along the southern end of Long Island make it a popular summer resort area. Fishing is an important source of income on the Atlantic Coastal Plain. Farmers raise vegetables, fruits, flowers, and poultry.

The New England Upland, a region of hills and low mountains, extends along about half of New York's eastern border. The region includes the Taconic Mountains and the southern part of the Hudson River Valley. Manhattan Island, the heart of New York City, lies in the New England Upland. Lovely, forested Westchester County is also part of this region.

The Hudson-Mohawk Lowland covers most of the Hudson River Valley and the Mohawk River Valley. The Hudson Valley is part of the Appalachian Ridge and Valley Region of New Jersey and Pennsylvania. The Hudson-Mohawk Lowland is about 10 to 30 miles (16 to 48 kilometers) wide. It cuts through highlands over 1,000 feet (300 meters) high. The region is the only great break in the Appalachian Mountains. Since pioneer days, it has served as a highway into the interior. It is the only natural trade route within the United States between the Atlantic Ocean and the Great Lakes.

The fertile plains bordering the Hudson and Mohawk rivers are used for general farming, fruit growing, and dairying. Falls along the rivers provide abundant water power for generating electricity. Many of New York's great industrial and population centers are in the Hudson-Mohawk Lowland.

The Adirondack Upland is a roughly circular hill and mountain region in the northeastern part of New York. The region's mountains are formed of hard, ancient rocks, perhaps the oldest in North America. Many mountain peaks rise above 4,000 feet (1,200 meters). Mount Marcy rises 5,344 feet (1,629 meters) in the northeastern part of the region, and is the highest point in New York. The Adirondack Upland is famous for its wild and beautiful scenery, sparkling lakes, rushing streams, splashing waterfalls, and purple-tinted peaks. It ranks as one of the most popular recreation areas in the East. The Adirondack soils are poor for farming. But

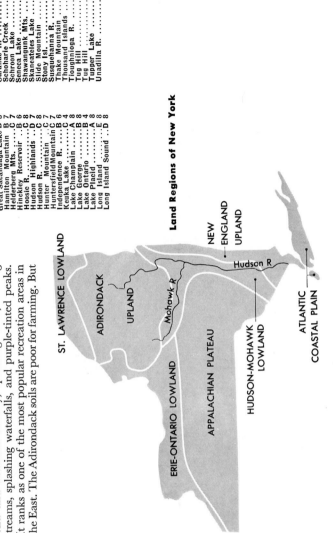

Land Regions of New York

Shostal

Higgs, FPG

Broad Sandy Beaches on the Atlantic Ocean, *left*, border Long Island's southern shores. The area is in the Atlantic Coastal Plain.

Mohawk River, *right*, serves as a major water link between the Atlantic Ocean and the Great Lakes. It is in the Hudson-Mohawk Lowland.

Southern Hudson River Valley, *below*, at Bear Mountain Bridge is in the New England Upland. This region extends along about half of New York's eastern border.

Pickow, Three Lions

NEW YORK

there is some lumbering in the region, as well as iron, lead, titanium, and zinc mining.

The Tug Hill Plateau lies in the western part of the Adirondack Upland region. This high, flat, rocky area has fewer lakes and smaller mountains than the rest of the region.

The St. Lawrence Lowland lies along the south bank of the St. Lawrence River. It borders the Adirondack Upland on the north. The region is less than 20 miles (32 kilometers) wide. The land is level to rolling, but seldom rises more than 500 feet (150 meters) above sea level. Some of the milk from the region's dairy farms is shipped all the way to New York City. Fruit growing is common near Lake Champlain on the New York-Ver-

Vineyards thrive near Seneca Lake, above, in the Finger Lakes area of the Appalachian Plateau. Fertile farmland lies in this area, which is also a famous resort center.

Eisenhower Lock, *right,* is part of the St. Lawrence Seaway. The lock is in the St. Lawrence Lowland region of northern New York.

mont boundary. Summer homes line the banks of the St. Lawrence River. Many resorts have been built on the river's beautiful Thousand Islands.

The Erie-Ontario Lowland is a low-lying region south of Lake Erie and Lake Ontario. Part of the region was once the flat bottom of ancient glacial lakes. Elsewhere, glacial deposits called *moraines* have produced a low, rolling surface. The glaciers also formed many *drumlins* in the area southeast of Rochester. Drumlins are oval-shaped hills about 50 to 300 feet (15 to 91 meters) high. The Erie-Ontario Lowland has unusually fertile soils. Fruit growing is a specialty. The region also has prosperous truck gardens, greenhouses, plant nurseries, and dairy farms. Excellent transportation and abundant

Tiny Village, *below,* nestles in the Keene Valley in the Adirondack Upland. The mountains in this region may be the oldest in North America. The region is famous for its beautiful scenery.

water power have spurred the growth of such industrial and commercial cities as Buffalo and Rochester.

The Appalachian Plateau, the state's largest land region, covers most of southern New York. It lies south and west of the Hudson-Mohawk Lowland, and south of the Erie-Ontario Lowland. The plateau stretches westward almost to Lake Erie. Glaciers and rivers have created a variety of surface features. These features range from rolling hills near the north end of Finger Lakes to the mountainous country of the Catskills in the east. The Catskill Mountains, with peaks rising from 2,000 to 4,000 feet (610 to 1,200 meters) or more high, are a favorite tourist area. Reservoirs in the Catskills help supply New York City with water (see WATER [map: How New York City Gets Its Water]).

Most farms of the Appalachian Plateau specialize in dairying. The best farming area lies in the Finger Lakes section in the north. Vineyards, nurseries, and truck gardens thrive here. The Finger Lakes received their name because they look like outstretched fingers of a hand. The beauty of the lakes and the wooded, rolling countryside provide a scenic attraction for vacationers. Many summer homes line their shores.

Coastline and Shoreline. New York's general coastline stretches 127 miles (204 kilometers) along the Atlantic Ocean. New York City has one of the world's best natural harbors. The harbor is almost completely protected by land. The state also has 371 miles (597 kilometers) of shoreline along Lakes Erie and Ontario, 174 miles (280 kilometers) along Lake Champlain, and 192 miles (309 kilometers) along the St. Lawrence and Niagara rivers. Buffalo is New York's chief lake port. Oceangoing ships reach it through the St. Lawrence Seaway.

Mountains. The Adirondacks, in northeastern New York, are the state's largest mountain range. In addition to 5,344-foot (1,629-meter) Mount Marcy, two other peaks in the Adirondacks rise over 5,000 feet (1,500 meters). They are Mount McIntyre and Algonquin Peak, both 5,112 feet (1,558 meters) high. The tallest peak in the Catskills is 4,204-foot (1,281-meter) Slide Mountain, west of the lower Hudson River. The Catskill's second highest peak, Hunter Mountain, rises 4,025 feet (1,227 meters). The low, narrow Shawangunk Mountains are south of the Catskills, and also form part of the Appalachian Plateau. The Shawangunks extend southward into New Jersey. The Taconic Mountains rise east of the Hudson River along the Massachusetts border. They are a western extension of Massachusett's Berkshire Hills. The Helderberg Mountains rise northeast of the Catskills.

Rivers. New York's most important rivers are the Hudson and the Mohawk. They make up one of the greatest trade waterways in the United States. The Hudson River rises in the wildest part of the Adirondacks, in a little lake called Tear-of-the-Clouds. The river flows almost straight south to New York Bay, where it becomes an arm of the Atlantic Ocean. The Hudson is 306 miles (492 kilometers) long—the largest river lying entirely within the state. Along its upper course, the Hudson is a narrow stream breaking into many falls and rapids, which are used to produce electric power. The Hudson widens and deepens as it flows to the sea. Some sections of the river are beautiful with their huge rock cliffs called *Palisades.* Oceangoing ships can sail up the Hudson as far as Albany, about 150 miles (241 kilometers) from the river's mouth.

The Mohawk River is the chief branch of the Hudson. It connects the Hudson with the Great Lakes lowland. The Mohawk drains central New York, and has been important in the development of the interior. The river rises in Oneida County and flows southeastward for about 145 miles (233 kilometers). It enters the Hudson River at Cohoes.

The Genesee River starts in Pennsylvania, flows northward through western New York, and empties into Lake Ontario north of Rochester. The Oswego River and its branch, the Seneca, also empty into Lake Ontario. The Delaware, Susquehanna, and Allegheny rivers drain the southern part of the state. The Delaware forms part of the boundary between New York and Pennsylvania. The Susquehanna rises in Otsego Lake in central New York and flows southward into Pennsylvania. The Allegheny begins in Pennsylvania, curves across the southwestern corner of New York, and swings back into Pennsylvania. The East River, which is actually a strait, separates Manhattan from Long Island. It is only about 16 miles (26 kilometers) long, but is an important New York City waterway. The St. Lawrence River, between New York and Canada, is one of the great water routes of North America.

Waterfalls. Many of New York's larger rivers flow through wide, fertile valleys for most of their courses. At certain points, some of the rivers pass through deep, rock-walled gorges and become waterfalls. The mountain streams have many small falls and rapids. Many of these falls provide water power for industries. Niagara Falls is the most famous of the state's waterfalls. Taughannock Falls, near Cayuga Lake in the Finger Lakes region, is one of the highest falls east of the Rocky Mountains. It drops 215 feet (66 meters). Near Portageville, the Genesee River breaks into three falls, the largest of which drops 110 feet (34 meters). Other falls in the Genesee at Rochester are used to generate power for the city's industries.

Lakes. New York has more than 8,000 lakes. Most of them were created by glaciers of the Ice Age. Lake Oneida, northeast of Syracuse, is the largest lake lying entirely within the state. It covers about 80 square miles (210 square kilometers), and empties into Lake Ontario. Lake George is a popular summer vacation area. It empties into Lake Champlain, which lies on the New York-Vermont border and extends into the Canadian province of Quebec. Lake Champlain covers about 500 square miles (1,300 square kilometers).

The glacial Finger Lakes consist of six bodies of water covering more than 10 square miles (26 square kilometers) each, and several smaller lakes. All are long and narrow, and lie nearly parallel in a north-south direction. The Adirondack Mountains have about 2,000 small lakes. Two of the most beautiful ones—Lake Placid and Saranac Lake—are popular summer and winter resorts. Chautauqua Lake, in southwestern New York, is a favorite summer vacation spot. It is also the birthplace of the Chautauqua Institution, famous for its summer adult education program.

NEW YORK / Climate

New York's climate varies greatly throughout the state because of differences in land forms and exposure to large bodies of water. The Adirondacks have the coldest winters, the heaviest snowfalls, and the coolest summers. The Atlantic Coastal Plain has the mildest winters, the lightest snowfalls, and the hottest summers.

The average January temperature in the Adirondacks is 17° F. (−8° C.), and on the coastal plain, 32° F. (0° C.). The average July temperature in the Adirondacks is 66° F. (19° C.), and on the coastal plain, 74° F. (23° C.). About 122 inches (310 centimeters) of snow falls yearly in the Adirondacks, and about 26 inches (66 centimeters) falls in the coastal plain. The climate of the other regions varies between the extremes of these two regions. Troy had New York's record high temperature, 108° F. (42° C.), on July 22, 1926. Stillwater Reservoir had the record low, −52° F. (−47° C.), on Feb. 9, 1934.

New York's annual *precipitation* (rain, melted snow, and other forms of moisture) ranges from 32 to 54 inches (81 to 137 centimeters). The southwestern slopes of the Adirondacks, Catskills, and other mountains, and the coastal plain receive the most precipitation.

SEASONAL TEMPERATURES

January

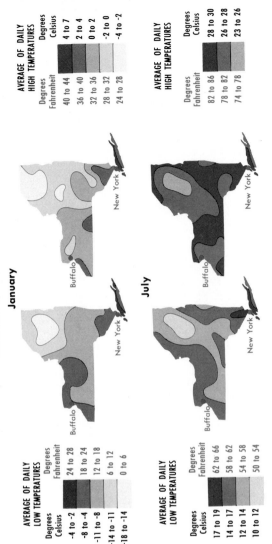

AVERAGE OF DAILY LOW TEMPERATURES

Degrees Celsius	Degrees Fahrenheit
−4 to −2	24 to 28
−8 to −4	18 to 24
−11 to −8	12 to 18
−14 to −11	6 to 12
−18 to −14	0 to 6

AVERAGE OF DAILY HIGH TEMPERATURES

Degrees Fahrenheit	Degrees Celsius
40 to 44	4 to 7
36 to 40	2 to 4
32 to 36	0 to 2
28 to 32	−2 to 0
24 to 28	−4 to −2

July

AVERAGE OF DAILY LOW TEMPERATURES

Degrees Celsius	Degrees Fahrenheit
17 to 19	62 to 66
14 to 17	58 to 62
12 to 14	54 to 58
10 to 12	50 to 54

AVERAGE OF DAILY HIGH TEMPERATURES

Degrees Fahrenheit	Degrees Celsius
82 to 86	28 to 30
78 to 82	26 to 28
74 to 78	23 to 26

AVERAGE YEARLY PRECIPITATION
(Rain, Melted Snow, and Other Moisture)

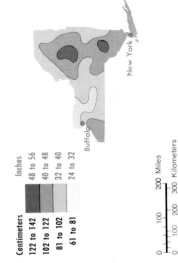

Centimeters	Inches
122 to 142	48 to 56
102 to 122	40 to 48
81 to 102	32 to 40
61 to 81	24 to 32

0   100   200 Miles
0   100   200   300 Kilometers

WORLD BOOK maps

AVERAGE MONTHLY WEATHER

	BUFFALO Temperatures F.° High	Low	C.° High	Low	Days of Rain or Snow		NEW YORK Temperatures F.° High	Low	C.° High	Low	Days of Rain or Snow
JAN.	32	19	0	−7	19	JAN.	40	26	4	−3	12
FEB.	32	17	0	−8	17	FEB.	40	25	4	−4	10
MAR.	41	25	5	−4	16	MAR.	49	33	9	1	12
APR.	53	34	12	1	14	APR.	58	42	14	6	11
MAY	66	45	19	7	13	MAY	69	53	21	12	11
JUNE	76	56	24	13	11	JUNE	78	62	26	17	10
JULY	81	60	27	16	10	JULY	82	67	28	19	11
AUG.	79	59	26	15	10	AUG.	80	66	27	19	10
SEPT.	73	52	23	11	11	SEPT.	75	60	24	16	9
OCT.	60	42	16	6	12	OCT.	65	50	18	10	9
NOV.	47	33	8	1	15	NOV.	53	40	12	4	9
DEC.	35	23	2	−5	18	DEC.	42	29	6	−2	10

Winter Snow covers Mount Whiteface. This area in the Adirondack Mountains attracts skiers from New York and other states.

Dean, Three Lions

New York is a great manufacturing and trading state. Its excellent location, huge population, and outstanding transportation facilities have helped make it a leader in business and industry. New York is also an important agricultural state. The state's farmers produce an enormous amount of food—especially dairy products and fresh vegetables—for the big cities of New York and other East Coast states.

Natural Resources of New York include fertile soils, mineral deposits, and abundant water supplies. The state has thick forests and other plant life, and a plentiful supply of fish and game.

Soil. In general, the soils of the Appalachian Plateau tend to be poor. Most of them are gray-brown, silty loam soils developed from glacial *drift*. Drift is material ranging in size from great boulders to fine rock dust laid down by melting glaciers. Soils of the New England Upland vary between stony and gravelly loams. Most of these soils also developed from glacial drift. The Adirondack Upland has rough, stony soils. The St. Lawrence Lowland, the Hudson-Mohawk Lowland, and the Erie-Ontario Lowland have fertile, loamy, well-drained soils. The Atlantic Coastal Plain has rich sandy and alluvial soils.

Minerals. Zinc is one of New York's chief metallic minerals. Most of the zinc is found in St. Lawrence County. This county also has deposits of lead and crude talc, which is used in ceramics, paints, and roofing. Deposits of iron ore lie throughout the Adirondacks. Clay deposits are found in the middle Hudson Valley and in Albany, Erie, and Onondaga counties. Many sections of the state have sand and gravel deposits. Reserves of petroleum and natural gas lie in the southwest. The Adirondacks supply a large part of the country's industrial garnets, used for watch jewels and in the manufacture of abrasives.

New York has large salt and gypsum deposits. The largest salt beds are in the Genesee Valley. Gypsum is also found in this area. The state has valuable deposits of granite, limestone, marble, and sandstone. Mines in Westchester County produce emery, used in grinding metals, gems, and lenses. This is the main emery-producing area in the United States. Slate deposits are found in Washington County.

Water is one of New York's most valuable resources, and the state has plentiful supplies. The water is used in homes and factories, for transportation, for recreation, and for powering electric generators.

Forests once covered all New York. In the 1800's and early 1900's, lumberjacks logged the forests heavily. Forested areas suitable for farms and cities also were cleared. Today, forests cover about half the state. Great tracts of trees grow throughout the Adirondacks. Smaller forests thrive throughout the Appalachian region. Trees of commercial importance in New York include the ash, birch, cherry, maple, spruce, walnut, and white pine.

Other Plant Life. Many wild flowers bloom in river valleys throughout the state. They include black-eyed Susans, devil's paintbrush, Queen Anne's lace, and white daisies. Buttercups, clover, goldenrod, strawberries, violets, and wild roses grow along the borders of wood lots. White and yellow water lilies thrive in many Adirondack lakes. Other common wild flowers include bunchberries, enchanter's nightshade, goldthreads, Indian pipes, starflowers, and trilliums.

Animal Life. Animals trapped for their furs in New York include foxes, gray squirrels, minks, muskrats, pine martens, raccoons, and skunks. Deer roam the forests, and rabbits range throughout the state.

More than 400 kinds of fresh- and salt-water fish live in New York waters. The most common include black crappies; brook, brown, and lake trout; northern and walleyed pike; pickerel; sunfish; white bass and smallmouth black bass; and yellow perch. New York's chief game birds include grouse, partridges, pheasants, quail, wild ducks, wild geese, and woodcocks.

Manufacturing accounts for about 95 per cent of the value of all goods produced in New York. Goods manufactured in the state have a *value added by manufacture* of about $35 billion yearly. This figure represents the value created in products by New York's industries, not counting such manufacturing costs as materials, supplies, and fuel.

New York ranks second only to California among the nation's leading manufacturing states. The value of its manufactured products accounts for about 8 per cent of the total U.S. output. New York has about 40,000 industrial plants. They employ about $1\frac{1}{2}$ million workers. New York's factories turn out an amazing variety of products—from huge machines to hairpins. New York is an industrial giant for many reasons. These include the state's favorable location, excellent air, rail, and water transportation facilities, and the markets provided by the large population of the East Coast. New York's chief manufacturing activities, in order of importance, are (1) printing and publishing, (2) the manufacture of instruments and related products, (3) the manufacture of nonelectrical machinery, and (4) the manufacture of clothing.

Printing and Publishing have a value added of about $4\frac{1}{2}$ billion yearly. New York is by far the leading state in this activity. New York City is the center of the publishing industry in the United States. It has more printing plants than any other U.S. city. The New York City area does about a sixth of the nation's printing and publishing. The city publishes about a third of all the books published in the United States.

Instruments and Related Products have a value added of about $4 billion annually. The Rochester area produces most of this total. Its chief products include photographic film and cameras.

New York City is also a leading manufacturer of instruments, especially medical instruments. The city also produces large quantities of mechanical measuring and control devices and engineering and scientific instruments. The Buffalo area produces medical and surgical instruments.

Nonelectrical Machinery produced in New York factories has a value added of about $3\frac{1}{2}$ billion yearly. The industry's leading products include electronic computing equipment, industrial equipment, metalworking machinery, and refrigeration equipment. The major centers of nonelectrical machinery production in the state include Buffalo, New York City, Rochester, and Syracuse.

Clothing manufactured in New York has a value added of about $3¼ billion yearly. New York leads all the states in the production of clothing and related products. The blouses, dresses, and women's coats made in the state have an annual value added of about $1½ billion. New York ranks as the leading producer of fur clothes in the United States. New York City is the nation's chief center for the manufacture of women's garments. New York City and Rochester are the leading men's clothing centers. New York City and the Triple Cities (Binghamton, Johnson City, and Endicott) produce shoes. Factories in Gloversville and Johnstown specialize in leather gloves and mittens. Shirtmaking centers include New York City and Troy.

Other Leading Industries produce chemicals and related products, electrical machinery, food and related products, metal products, and transportation equipment. The Hudson Valley is an important producer of cement. This region also makes bricks, porcelain for electrical appliances, tiles, and many similar products. Rome is a major center for the manufacture of copper products. Industries in Albany County manufacture products that include abrasives, paper goods, and steel. Buffalo is a major steel producer.

Agriculture. New York's farm income totals about $1½ billion yearly. But this enormous sum amounts to only about 4 per cent of the value of all goods produced in the state. New York has about 51,900 farms. They average 196 acres (79.3 hectares) in size. The state's farms cover a total of about 10,148,000 acres (4,106,700 hectares).

Dairy Products are New York's most valuable source of farm income. They bring in about $705 million yearly. New York's cool, moist climate and excellent pastureland have contributed to the development of the state's great dairy industry. But more important has been the huge demand for dairy products from New York City and other large cities on the East Coast. Dairying is carried on in almost every part of the state. Only Wisconsin and Minnesota have more milk cows than New York. New York is one of the leading milk-producing states. It also ranks high among the states in the production of butter and cheese.

Vegetables are the second most important farm products. They account for about $160 million annually. The demand for fresh vegetables from the big cities has encouraged the growth of New York's great truck farms (see TRUCK FARMING). New York ranks high among the states in the value of its vegetable crops. It is a leader in growing celery, lettuce, onions, potatoes, snap beans, and tomatoes.

Beef Cattle and Calves are also leading farm products in New York. They provide about $130 million annually. Cattle and calves are raised in most of the state.

Poultry and Eggs bring New York's farmers about $115 million annually. Long Island is one of the state's main poultry-raising areas. It supplies the nation with more than half of all the ducks marketed each year. People throughout the country enjoy Long Island ducklings. About 2 billion eggs and about 10 million chickens are produced on New York farms each year. Farmers also raise large numbers of geese, turkeys, and guinea fowl.

Other Farm Products. New York's most important fruit crops include apples, cherries, grapes, peaches, pears, and strawberries. Only California grows more grapes than New York. Most of New York's grapes come from vineyards along the Lake Erie shore in the far southwestern part of the state. Wine grapes are important in the Finger Lakes district and Chautauqua County. Only Washington raises more apples than New York. New York also ranks high among the states in growing pears and strawberries. Other fruits include currants, plums, and raspberries. There are many plant nurseries throughout the state, especially along the shores of Lakes Erie and Ontario, and on Long Island. These nurseries produce large quantities of flowers.

Other important New York farm products include hay and corn, grown for dairy and beef cattle, and maple syrup. New York ranks among the leading hay-producing states. New York and Vermont are leaders in the production of maple syrup.

Mining in New York has an annual value added of about $375 million. The state's most important mineral products include petroleum, salt, sand and gravel, stone, and zinc. Petroleum is produced in Allegany, Cattaraugus, Chautauqua, and Steuben counties. New

Production of Goods in New York

Total value of goods produced in 1973—$35,401,392,000

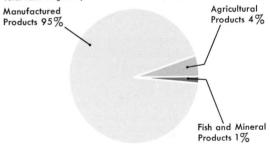

Manufactured Products 95%

Agricultural Products 4%

Fish and Mineral Products 1%

Percentages are based on farm income, value added by manufacture, and value of fish and mineral production. Fish products are less than 1 per cent.

Sources: U.S. government publications, 1975-1976.

Employment in New York

Total number of persons employed in 1974—7,189,900

		Number of Employees
Manufacturing	🧍🧍🧍🧍🧍🧍🧍🧍🧍🧍	1,581,200
Community, Social, & Personal Services	🧍🧍🧍🧍🧍🧍🧍🧍🧍	1,453,500
Wholesale & Retail Trade	🧍🧍🧍🧍🧍🧍🧍🧍🧍	1,443,000
Government	🧍🧍🧍🧍🧍🧍🧍🧍	1,292,000
Finance, Insurance, & Real Estate	🧍🧍🧍🧍	587,200
Transportation & Public Utilities	🧍🧍🧍	457,800
Construction	🧍🧍	262,700
Agriculture & Mining	🧍	112,500

Sources: *Employment and Earnings*, May 1975, U.S. Bureau of Labor Statistics; *Farm Labor*, February 1975, U.S. Department of Agriculture.

NEW YORK

York is also a leading salt-producing state. Most of the salt comes from the west-central counties. The nation's largest underground salt mine is in the Genesee Valley in Livingston County. Sand and gravel come from various parts of the state. The most valuable stones include basalt, limestone, sandstone, and slate. The state is the leading producer of emery, garnet, ilmenite, and wollastonite. New York mines also make the state a top producer of gypsum, talc, and zinc. Other minerals in the state include clay and natural gas.

Fishing Industry. New York has an annual fish catch valued at about $20 million. Fishermen take large catches from the rivers and inland lakes. But most of the commercial fishing takes place in Long Island waters and in Lakes Erie and Ontario. Butterfish, clams, flounder, lobsters, oysters, porgy, scallops, sea trout, striped bass, and whiting are taken from Long Island Sound. Fishermen catch bullheads, eels, perch, and pike in Lakes Erie and Ontario.

Electric Power. New York is a leader among the states in electric power production. Fuel-burning steam plants provide about 60 per cent of New York's electric power. Hydroelectric power plants supply about 25 per cent, and nuclear plants provide the rest. New York's two greatest hydroelectric power projects are the St. Lawrence Power Project and the Niagara Power Project. They were developed jointly by the Power Authority of the State of New York and the Hydro-Electric Power Commission of Ontario in Canada. In July, 1955, the General Electric Company plant in West Milton, near Schenectady, produced electricity through nuclear fission for commercial use. It was the first time this had been done anywhere.

Transportation. New York lies in the heart of the most thickly populated part of the United States. It is the chief gateway to the United States from other countries. It has one of the finest natural harbors in the world, and an excellent system of inland waterways. All these factors have helped New York become one of the nation's leaders in transportation.

Railroads operate on about 5,500 miles (8,850 kilo-

WORLD BOOK photo by Three Lions

Printer Checks Proofs in a New York City printing plant. New York City has more printing houses than any other U.S. city. It produces about one third of the books published in the country.

meters) of track in New York. About 20 rail lines provide freight service, and passenger trains serve nearly 15 New York cities. The state's first railroad, the Mohawk and Hudson, began running between Albany and Schenectady in 1831. New York City's subway, the world's busiest, covers about 232 miles (371 kilometers). More than 4 million passengers jam these trains every working day.

Aviation. New York has about 350 airports, 25 seaplane bases, and 40 heliports. All the principal cities have commercial airline service. About 40 domestic and international airlines serve New York. The John F. Kennedy International Airport in New York City handles more international flights than any other U.S. airport—about 275 every day. New York City is also served by La Guardia Airport and by two airports in New Jersey, Newark International Airport and Teterboro Airport.

Roads and Highways in New York cover about 105,000 miles (169,000 kilometers), most of which are surfaced. The Governor Thomas E. Dewey Thruway is the

WORLD BOOK photo by Three Lions

Racks of New Clothes are pushed through New York City's bustling garment district. New York leads all states in the production of clothing.

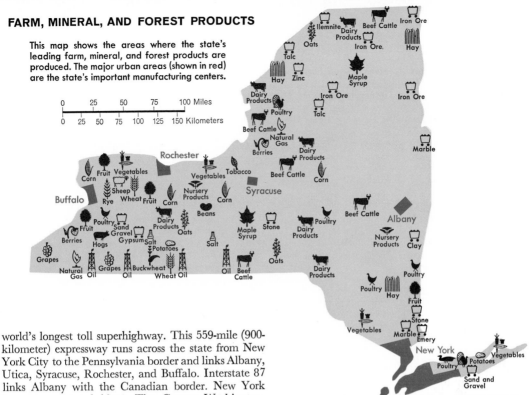

This map shows the areas where the state's leading farm, mineral, and forest products are produced. The major urban areas (shown in red) are the state's important manufacturing centers.

WORLD BOOK map

world's longest toll superhighway. This 559-mile (900-kilometer) expressway runs across the state from New York City to the Pennsylvania border and links Albany, Utica, Syracuse, Rochester, and Buffalo. Interstate 87 links Albany with the Canadian border. New York has many great bridges. The George Washington, Bear Mountain, Mid-Hudson, Newburgh-Beacon, and Rip Van Winkle bridges span the Hudson River. The Brooklyn and Triborough bridges cross the East River. The Peace Bridge links Buffalo with Fort Erie in Canada. The Verrazano-Narrows Bridge across the Narrows channel connects Brooklyn and Staten Island. Its 4,260-foot (1,298-meter) center span is one of the world's longest.

Waterways. New York has one of the nation's largest internal waterway systems—the New York State Barge Canal System. The system was completed in 1918, and includes parts of the old Erie Canal and several other waterways. The Erie Canal, which was opened in 1825, connected the Hudson River with Lake Erie. It played an important part in the economic growth of New York and the entire United States. The New York State Barge Canal System and its connecting waterways cover about 800 miles (1,300 kilometers). They extend from Lake Champlain and the Hudson River to Lake Erie and Lake Ontario. The St. Lawrence Seaway, which was opened in 1959, turned New York's Great Lakes ports into seaports.

Shipping. The Port of New York is the world's largest and busiest seaport. It handles more tonnage than any other U.S. port. It also handles more tonnage of foreign trade than any other American port. Huge ocean liners and freighters from all parts of the world dock at hundreds of piers in this great port. The port handles about 197 million short tons (179 million metric tons) of cargo each year. This cargo includes imports, exports, goods coming from other East Coast ports, and goods going to other coastal points.

Other major New York ports include Albany, Buffalo, Ogdensburg, Oswego, and Rochester. Buffalo, on Lake Erie, generally outranks all other Great Lakes ports in value of tonnage handled. Ogdensburg, on the St. Lawrence River, is an important shipping center for newsprint, petroleum products, pulpwood, and other products. Albany is a major shipping center although it lies almost 150 miles (241 kilometers) from the Atlantic Ocean. The Hudson River has been deepened so that ocean ships can reach Albany.

Communication. New York leads the nation in producing books, magazines, and newspapers. William Bradford established New York's first newspaper, the *New-York Gazette*, in New York City in 1725. Today, New York has about 90 daily newspapers and over 750 weeklies. One of the world's most influential newspapers, *The New York Times*, is published in New York City. Other well-known New York City newspapers are the *Daily News*, which has the largest circulation of any newspaper in the country, and the *New York Post* which is one of the nation's oldest papers. The Associated Press and United Press International have headquarters in New York City.

The General Electric Company set up New York's first radio station, WGY, in its Schenectady laboratories in 1922. The National Broadcasting Company established the first coast-to-coast radio network in 1926 in New York City. On Jan. 1, 1927, NBC made a 4,000-mile (6,400-kilometer) hookup with Pasadena, Calif., and carried the first broadcast of a Rose Bowl football game. The nation's first commercial TV station, WNBT, began operating in New York City in 1941. New York has about 325 radio stations and about 40 TV stations.

IMPORTANT DATES IN NEW YORK

1609 Henry Hudson explored the Hudson River. Samuel de Champlain visited the New York region.

1624 The Dutch established Fort Orange (Albany), the first permanent white settlement in the New York region.

1625 Dutch settlers began building New Amsterdam (New York City).

1664 The Dutch surrendered New Amsterdam to England.

1735 Editor John Peter Zenger was found innocent of libel, an important victory for freedom of the press.

1776 New York approved the Declaration of Independence.

1779 Military expeditions under Generals James Clinton and John Sullivan opened Iroquois land to white settlement.

1788 New York became the 11th state on July 26.

1789 George Washington was inaugurated in New York City as the first President of the United States.

1825 The Erie Canal was opened, linking the Hudson River and the Great Lakes.

1831 New York's first railroad, the Mohawk and Hudson, began running between Albany and Schenectady.

1863 Mobs rioted in New York City in opposition to drafting men into the Union Army.

1901 President William McKinley was assassinated at the Pan American Exposition in Buffalo.

1918 The New York State Barge Canal System was opened.

1939-1940 New York held a World's Fair.

1948 New York established its first state university—the State University of New York.

1952 United Nations Headquarters was completed in New York City.

1959 The St. Lawrence Seaway opening made "ocean" ports of New York's ports on Lake Erie and Lake Ontario.

1960 The New York State Thruway (now the Governor Thomas E. Dewey Thruway) was completed.

1964-1965 New York held another World's Fair.

1967 The state legislature established a lottery to help pay for education.

1972 A tropical storm caused 27 deaths and about $750 million in damages in New York.

Martin Van Buren
born in Kinderhook

Millard Fillmore
born in Locke

Theodore Roosevelt
born in New York City

Franklin Delano Roosevelt
born in Hyde Park

HISTORIC NEW YORK

First Woman Suffrage Convention in the United States was organized in Seneca Falls in 1848 by Lucretia Mott and Elizabeth Cady Stanton.

The Erie Canal, completed in 1825, helped to open the Midwest to settlers. It linked the Hudson River with the Great Lakes by way of the Mohawk Valley.

Indian Days. Two of the largest and most powerful Indian groups in North America lived in the New York region before white settlers came. One group consisted of the Delaware, Mohican, Montauk, Munsee, and Wappinger tribes of the Algonkian family of Indians. The other was the fierce and greatly feared Iroquois, or Five Nations. The Cayuga, Mohawk, Oneida, Onondaga, and Seneca tribes made up the Five Nations (see IROQUOIS INDIANS). Both Indian groups farmed, hunted, and fished. The Iroquois were especially advanced in political and social organization. See INDIAN, AMERICAN (Table of Tribes).

Exploration and Early Settlement. Giovanni da Verrazano, an Italian navigator and pirate, was probably the first white man to visit the New York region. Verrazano supposedly was hired by King Francis I of France to explore the northern part of America. Historians believe Verrazano may have sailed into New

George Washington took the oath of office as the nation's first President in New York City on April 30, 1789. New York City served as the capital of the United States from 1785 to 1790.

Turning Point of the Revolutionary War was General John Burgoyne's surrender to General Horatio Gates at Saratoga on Oct. 17, 1777.

Freedom of the Press won its first victory in the American Colonies when John Peter Zenger, editor of the *New York Weekly Journal*, was acquitted of criminal libel in 1735. He had criticized the British governor.

The National Baseball Hall of Fame and Museum at Cooperstown honors outstanding baseball players.

Henry Hudson, an English explorer, sailed up the Hudson River in 1609. He explored the New York region as far as the area near the present site of Albany.

The First Successful Steamboat, the *Clermont,* built by Robert Fulton, completed a trip from New York City to Albany in 32 hours on Aug. 19, 1807.

West Point, home of the United States Military Academy, lies on bluffs rising above the Hudson River. Congress established the school on March 16, 1802, after George Washington had twice recommended a national military academy be founded.

Manhattan Island Was Bought for $24. In 1626, Peter Minuit, director-general of New Netherland, paid the Manhattan Indians $24 in trinkets for Manhattan Island.

• Locke

Cooperstown •

Saratoga •

ALBANY ★

Kinderhook •

Hyde Park •

West Point •

• New York City

York Bay and reached the Hudson River about 1524.

In 1609, Henry Hudson, an Englishman employed by the Dutch, sailed up the river that now bears his name. He was looking for a Northwest Passage to the Orient. Hudson's voyage gave The Netherlands a claim to the territory covering much of present-day New York, New Jersey, Delaware, and part of Connecticut. The territory was named *New Netherland.*

Also in 1609, the French explorer Samuel de Champlain entered the northern part of New York from Quebec. His visit gave France a claim to the land.

The Dutch established several trading posts and prosperous settlements in the Hudson Valley soon after Hudson's visit. They built up a profitable fur trade with the Indians. In 1621, a group of Dutch merchants formed the Dutch West India Company. The government of The Netherlands gave the company all rights to trade in New Netherland for the next 24 years. In 1624, the company sent about 30 families to the region. Some of these families founded Fort Orange (now Albany), the first permanent white settlement in the colony. The rest established settlements in other parts of New Netherland. In 1625, a group of Dutch colonists began building a fort and laying out a town on Manhattan Island. They named their settlement *New Amsterdam.* In 1626, Peter Minuit, the Dutch governor (or director-general), bought Manhattan from the Indians for goods worth 60 Dutch guilders, or about $24. During the next few years, Wiltwyck (now Kingston), Rensselaerswyck (now Rensselaer), Breuckelen (now Brooklyn), Schenectady, and other settlements were established by Dutch colonists.

In 1629, the Dutch West India Company set up the *patroon* (landowner) system to speed the settlement of New Netherland. Members of the company were given huge tracts of land, which they could keep if they colonized the land with settlers. Only one patroonship was successful, that of Kiliaen Van Rensselaer, an Amsterdam diamond merchant. His land covered much of present-day Albany, Columbia, and Rensselaer counties. Van Rensselaer began the practice of leasing his land. He established the tenant system in New York, which lasted until the tenant farmers rebelled in the early 1800's. See PATROON SYSTEM.

Under English Rule. Many English colonists from Connecticut and Massachusetts settled on Long Island. For a long time, they cooperated with the Dutch. But gradually the English began to oppose the Dutch. In addition, King Charles II of England decided to take over New Netherland. He gave his brother James, the Duke of York, a charter for the territory. In 1664, the English sent a fleet to seize New Netherland. The warships dropped anchor in the harbor of New Amsterdam. Peter Stuyvesant, the Dutch governor, surrendered the settlement without a fight.

The English renamed the territory *New York*, after the Duke of York, who later became King James II of England. Under the Treaty of Breda, signed in 1667, the Dutch formally gave up all New Netherland to England.

At first, the colony prospered under English rule. Later, dishonest governors kept New York from developing rapidly. The farm tenant system further discouraged progress. Most of the land lay in large estates. Poor persons who wanted land of their own had to settle outside the colony.

Soon after the English won control of southern New York, the French began to take great interest in the northern part. In 1669, the French explorer Robert Cavelier, Sieur de la Salle, entered the Niagara region. In 1731, the French built a fortress at Crown Point on Lake Champlain. They prepared to take permanent possession of northern New York. Meanwhile, in 1689, war had broken out in Europe between England and France. New York soon became a battleground in the struggle between the two countries.

From 1689 until 1763, the region suffered severely through four wars, known in America as the French and Indian Wars. Battles were fought at Crown Point, Fort Niagara, Fort Ticonderoga, and many other places. The French received aid from the Algonkian Indians in the wars, but the Iroquois helped the English. The French and Indian Wars delayed settlement of the frontier regions and slowed the growth of sections that had already been settled. England and France signed a peace treaty—the Treaty of Paris—in 1763. But the wars cost France almost all its possessions in

Museum of the City of New York

Erie Canal opened in 1825 with a huge celebration. The canal provided an all-water route between the Hudson River and Buffalo. It greatly lowered the cost of transporting goods.

Immigrants of the 1880's wait for permission to enter the United States. The immigration station was on Ellis Island in New York Harbor. More than 16,000,000 persons passed through the station before it closed in 1954.

Pan American Exposition, held in Buffalo in 1901, sought to promote unity and understanding among the nations of North and South America. President William McKinley was shot on September 6 during a public reception at the exposition's Temple of Music.

North America. See FRENCH AND INDIAN WARS.

In 1735, John Peter Zenger, publisher of the *New York Weekly Journal*, won a great victory for freedom of the press. Zenger had criticized the English governor, and was charged with libel. In a historic trial, the jury found Zenger innocent.

The Revolutionary War. British policies angered many people of New York. They did not like the presence of British troops, the authority of royal judges, or the taxes passed by the British Parliament. Other New Yorkers, called Loyalists or Tories, did not oppose the British. Nobody knows how many persons were Loyalists. But after the Revolutionary War, more than 30,000 persons left the state. During the war, New York was the scene of many battles, on both land and water. The Loyalists helped the British and persuaded the Iroquois Indians to fight the patriots. American patriots won two important battles of the war in New York. These were the Battle of Oriskany and the Battle of Saratoga, both in 1777. See REVOLUTIONARY WAR IN AMERICA.

Statehood. On July 9, 1776, the provincial congress of New York met in White Plains. It approved the Declaration of Independence which the Continental Congress had adopted on July 4. The congress also organized an independent government. The next year, New York adopted its first constitution. George Clinton, who later became Vice-President of the United States, was elected governor.

On Feb. 6, 1778, New York approved the Articles of Confederation. On July 9, it ratified the Articles in the Continental Congress. It did not want a strong federal government. But it finally ratified the United States Constitution on July 26, 1788. New York was the 11th state to enter the Union. New York City served as the capital of the United States from Jan. 11, 1785, to March 2, 1789. In 1789, George Washington was inaugurated as the nation's first President. The inauguration took place in Federal Hall in New York City.

Settlement of the interior progressed rapidly. In 1779, General Washington sent an expedition to crush the mighty Iroquois. Troops commanded by General James Clinton raided Indian villages up through the Mohawk Valley. The soldiers then moved down the Susquehanna River to Tioga, Pa. There, they joined troops commanded by General John Sullivan. The combined force of about 3,500 men marched through the Finger Lakes region to the Genesee Valley. The soldiers wiped out Indian villages, killed the Indians' livestock, and burned their fields. The heart of the Iroquois territory was left in ruin. The military power of the Iroquois lay broken forever, leaving the area open to white settlement. After the Revolutionary War, soldiers who had fought in the area told of its level, fertile land. Many veterans settled on grants of land they received there.

War broke out between the United States and Great Britain in 1812 (see WAR OF 1812). Much of the fight-

255

ing took place in frontier regions near the New York-Canada border. After the war, pioneers began to settle in the northern and western sections of the state. Many came from other parts of New York, but many also came from New England, Canada, New Jersey, Delaware, and Pennsylvania. By 1820, about 500,000 persons lived in frontier settlements. New York had a population of over 1,370,000, more than any other state.

Growing Prosperity. As the frontier was opened, the people of New York realized that better transportation would be needed between the coast and the interior. Governor De Witt Clinton had long urged the construction of a canal to link the Atlantic Ocean and the Great Lakes. In 1825, the famous Erie Canal was completed. It crossed New York from Buffalo on Lake Erie to Troy and Albany on the Hudson River. The canal provided an important link in an all-water route between New York City and Buffalo. It greatly lowered the cost of transporting goods. Farmers in the West shipped their produce to the East by way of the Great Lakes and the Erie Canal. Products from New York's growing factories were, in turn, shipped on the canal to western markets (see ERIE CANAL).

The development of railroads across the state soon followed the opening of the Erie Canal. The canal and railroads greatly encouraged the state's growing prosperity. They also provided jobs for many of the thousands of European immigrants who were pouring into the state. By 1850, New York was firmly established as the *Empire State*. It led the nation in population, in manufacturing, and in commerce.

Wealthy merchants and great landowners had controlled New York since colonial days. During the early 1800's, the state adopted more and more democratic practices. In the 1820's, white men no longer had to own property to be able to vote. A new constitution adopted in 1846 required that all major state officials be elected by the voters. In 1839, the *antirent movement* began when tenant farmers refused to pay rent to wealthy landowners. The antirenters, disguised as Indians, ranged the countryside and terrorized the landlords. The antirent movement grew rapidly and became a powerful political force. During the 1840's, the great landlords began breaking up their estates into small independent farms. See ANTIRENTER.

Long before the Civil War began in 1861, many of New York's people strongly opposed slavery. But some did not. In July, 1863, mobs rioted for four days in New York City. They objected to drafting men into the Union Army. The mobs burned, robbed, and murdered recklessly. They killed or wounded about a thousand persons and destroyed more than $1½ million worth of property. Troops called from the battlefield finally ended the riots. Despite the draft riots, New York provided more soldiers, supplies, and money to the Union war effort than any other state.

After the Civil War ended in 1865, new manufacturing centers grew up in various parts of New York. More and more products of the Middle West flowed through Buffalo, the state's western gateway. Increased commerce between the United States and other countries passed through New York City, the state's eastern gate-

way. New York City, already the nation's industrial and financial capital, also became a leading cultural center. As manufacturing continued to increase, new waves of immigrants poured in, drawn by employment opportunities. They came from Italy, Poland, Russia, and other southern and eastern European countries. By 1900, the state had more than 7 million persons.

The Early 1900's. In 1901, a Pan American Exposition was held in Buffalo. The exhibition sought to promote unity and understanding between North and South America.

Theodore Roosevelt, a Republican, served as governor of New York in 1899 and 1900. He supported a number of reform bills, especially in the field of labor. In 1901, Roosevelt became Vice-President of the United States under President William McKinley. On Sept. 6, 1901, six months after the inauguration, an assassin shot McKinley at the opening ceremonies of the Pan American Exposition. McKinley died eight days later, and Roosevelt became President.

The United States entered World War I in 1917. New York City served as the great port from which thousands of American soldiers sailed for and returned from the battlefields of Europe.

The Great Depression of the late 1920's and the 1930's hit New York hard. Unemployment was severe. Men and women sold apples on street corners. Hungry persons lined up at soup kitchens, or stood in bread lines that stretched for blocks.

Alfred E. Smith, a Democrat, served as governor of New York from 1919 to 1921 and from 1923 to 1929. He lost to Republican Herbert Hoover in the 1928 presidential election. Franklin D. Roosevelt was governor from 1929 to 1932. He served as President from 1933 until his death in 1945. Herbert H. Lehman succeeded Roosevelt as governor and served until 1942. Much of the social legislation supported by Governors Roosevelt and Lehman attacked the depression. This legislation later served as a model for federal laws urged by President Roosevelt.

The Mid-1900's. New York became a center of the country's defense industry in the mid-1900's. Factories produced large amounts of war materials during World War II (1939-1945), the Korean War (1950-1953), and the Vietnam War. These materials came from the state's industrial centers—Buffalo, New York City, Rochester, Schenectady, and Syracuse—and hundreds of smaller communities. Growth occurred in several fields, including agriculture, banking, insurance, and manufacturing.

In 1946, the United Nations selected New York City as the site of its permanent home. Construction of UN headquarters was completed in 1952. Two world's fairs were held in New York City during the mid-1900's—in 1939 and 1940 and in 1964 and 1965.

In 1948, New York established its first state university—the State University of New York. The university has grown into a system of more than 60 campuses.

During the 1950's, New York and the Canadian province of Ontario developed a large hydroelectric project on the St. Lawrence River. In 1961, the first generator of a giant hydroelectric power plant began to produce electric power at Niagara Falls.

New York also greatly improved its transportation system. The St. Lawrence Seaway opened in 1959, allowing ocean-going ships to sail to ports on the Great

Lakes. In 1960, New York completed the world's longest toll superhighway, the New York State Thruway. This 559-mile (900-kilometer) expressway was renamed the Governor Thomas E. Dewey Thruway in 1964. Also in the 1960's, the state opened the 180-mile (290-kilometer) North-South Expressway and the 176-mile (283-kilometer) Adirondack Northway. The expressway runs through the middle of the state, connecting Pennsylvania with the province of Ontario. The scenic northway extends from Albany to Quebec. In 1964, the Verrazano-Narrows Bridge opened in New York City. It has one of the world's longest center spans.

During the 1960's, the Lincoln Center for the Performing Arts was built in New York City. The center serves as a home for some of the outstanding cultural institutions in the United States. These institutions include the Juilliard School of Music, the Metropolitan Opera, and the New York Philharmonic Orchestra.

New York Today needs more and better health facilities, schools, transportation, and welfare services. The state has pioneered in much social legislation—and its people continue to expect broad social programs. Welfare costs rank second only to education expenses in New York. Both state and local governments have raised taxes and borrowed more and more money to pay for their social programs. The people of New York pay more taxes per person than the residents of any other state.

The cost of education accounts for more than 40 per cent of New York's budget. The state uses profits from a lottery established in 1967 to help pay for education.

THE GOVERNORS OF NEW YORK

	Party	Term		Party	Term
1. George Clinton	None	1777-1795	29. Lucius Robinson	Democratic	1877-1879
2. John Jay	Federalist	1795-1801	30. Alonzo B. Cornell	Republican	1880-1882
3. George Clinton	*Dem.-Rep.	1801-1804	31. Grover Cleveland	Democratic	1883-1885
4. Morgan Lewis	*Dem.-Rep.	1804-1807	32. David Bennett Hill	Democratic	1885-1891
5. Daniel D. Tompkins	*Dem.-Rep.	1807-1817	33. Roswell Pettibone Flower	Democratic	1892-1894
6. John Tayler	*Dem.-Rep.	1817	34. Levi Parsons Morton	Republican	1895-1896
7. De Witt Clinton	*Dem.-Rep.	1817-1822	35. Frank Sweet Black	Republican	1897-1898
8. Joseph C. Yates	*Dem.-Rep.	1823-1824	36. Theodore Roosevelt	Republican	1899-1900
9. De Witt Clinton	*Dem.-Rep.	1825-1828	37. Benjamin B. Odell, Jr.	Republican	1901-1904
10. Nathaniel Pitcher	Independent	1828	38. Frank Wayland Higgins	Republican	1905-1906
11. Martin Van Buren	*Dem.-Rep.	1829	39. Charles Evans Hughes	Republican	1907-1910
12. Enos T. Throop	Democratic	1829-1832	40. Horace White	Republican	1910
13. William L. Marcy	Democratic	1833-1838	41. John Alden Dix	Democratic	1911-1912
14. William H. Seward	Whig	1839-1842	42. William Sulzer	Democratic	1913
15. William C. Bouck	Democratic	1843-1844	43. Martin Henry Glynn	Democratic	1913-1914
16. Silas Wright	Democratic	1845-1846	44. Charles S. Whitman	Republican	1915-1918
17. John Young	Whig	1847-1848	45. Alfred E. Smith	Democratic	1919-1920
18. Hamilton Fish	Whig	1849-1850	46. Nathan L. Miller	Republican	1921-1922
19. Washington Hunt	Whig	1851-1852	47. Alfred E. Smith	Democratic	1923-1928
20. Horatio Seymour	Democratic	1853-1854	48. Franklin D. Roosevelt	Democratic	1929-1932
21. Myron Holley Clark	Whig	1855-1856	49. Herbert H. Lehman	Democratic	1933-1942
22. John Alsop King	Republican	1857-1858	50. Charles Poletti	Democratic	1942
23. Edwin Denison Morgan	Republican	1859-1862	51. Thomas E. Dewey	Republican	1943-1954
24. Horatio Seymour	Democratic	1863-1864	52. W. Averell Harriman	Democratic	1955-1958
25. Reuben Eaton Fenton	Republican	1865-1868	53. Nelson A. Rockefeller	Republican	1959-1973
26. John Thompson Hoffman	Democratic	1869-1872	54. Malcolm Wilson	Republican	1973-1975
27. John Adams Dix	Republican	1873-1874	55. Hugh L. Carey	Democratic	1975-
28. Samuel Jones Tilden	Democratic	1875-1876			

*Democratic-Republican

Richard A. Peer

Robert Moses Power Dam is part of a large hydroelectric project on the St. Lawrence River. The project was developed jointly by the state of New York and the province of Ontario in the 1950's.

NEW YORK

Racial segregation is an urgent problem in New York's urban elementary and high schools, especially those in New York City. The population of certain areas of that city consists largely of blacks and Puerto Ricans. As a result, school enrollment in those areas is almost entirely black and Puerto Rican. The state has attempted to eliminate this *de facto* segregation by changing the boundaries of school districts and by busing children to schools outside their own districts. But both these efforts have created intense disagreement and sometimes violence.

New York is attacking the problem of water pollution with a $1-billion program. The state is also spending about $2½ billion to expand airport, highway, railway, and rapid transit systems.

Conflict between New York City and upstate New York remains a major problem. Government officials in each area have long tended to distrust each other. The city has claimed for years that it does not receive a fair share of state aid. The state legislature was reapportioned in 1966 to give New York City more representation. But the city lost three assembly seats in 1971, when the state's legislative districts were redivided to reflect population shifts to suburban areas.

In 1972, a tropical storm swept through the state, causing $750 million in damages and 27 deaths. Corning, Elmira, Painted Post, Waverly, and Wellsville suffered the most damage among New York cities.

JAMES A. FROST, JOHN J. LEARY, and JOHN H. THOMPSON

NEW YORK / Study Aids

Related Articles. See NEW YORK CITY with its list of Related Articles. See also the following articles:

BIOGRAPHIES

Abzug, Bella	La Guardia, Fiorello H.
Arthur, Chester A.	Leisler, Jacob
Astor (family)	Lewis, Francis
Baldwin, James	Lindsay, John Vliet
Bausch (family)	Livingston, Philip
Bryant, William Cullen	Livingston, Robert R.
Burr, Aaron	Miller, William E.
Cabrini, Saint Frances	Minuit, Peter
Champlain, Samuel de	Morris, Gouverneur
Chisholm, Shirley	Morris, Lewis
Clark, Mark W.	Moses, Grandma
Cleveland, Grover	Ochs, Adolph S.
Clinton, De Witt	Paine, Thomas
Clinton, George	Powell, Adam Clayton, Jr.
Cooper, James Fenimore	Pulitzer, Joseph
Cooper, Peter	Rockefeller (family)
Cornell, Ezra	Rockefeller, Nelson A.
Curtiss, Glenn H.	Rogers, William P.
Dewey, Thomas E.	Roosevelt, Eleanor
Eastman, George	Roosevelt, Franklin D.
Fargo, William G.	Roosevelt, Theodore
Farley, James A.	Roosevelt, Theodore, Jr.
Fillmore, Millard	Root, Elihu
Fish (family)	Runyon, Damon
Floyd, William	Schuyler, Philip J.
Forrestal, James V.	Seymour, Horatio
Fulton, Robert	Smith, Alfred E.
Gates, Horatio	Spellman, Francis Cardinal
Goodrich, Benjamin F.	Stuyvesant, Peter
Gould (family)	Sulzberger (family)
Greeley, Horace	Tilden, Samuel J.
Hale, Nathan	Tompkins, Daniel D.
Hamilton, Alexander	Van Buren, Martin
Harriman (family)	Vanderbilt (family)
Hayes, Patrick Cardinal	Van Rensselaer (family)
Hearst, William Randolph	Wagner, Robert F.
Hudson, Henry	Walker, James J.
Hughes, Charles Evans	Wharton, Edith N. J.
Irving, Washington	Wheeler, William A.
Javits, Jacob K.	Whitman, Walt
Jay, John	Zenger, John Peter
Johnson, Sir William	

CITIES AND OTHER COMMUNITIES

Albany	Ithaca	Niagara Falls
Buffalo	Kingston	Oswego
Cooperstown	Levittown	Plattsburgh
Corning	Mount Vernon	Poughkeepsie
Elmira	New Rochelle	Rochester

Rome	Schenectady	Troy	Yonkers
Saratoga Springs	Syracuse	Utica

HISTORY

Albany Congress	French and Indian Wars
Antirenters	Hunkers
Barnburners	Iroquois Indians
Bucktails	Loco-Foco
Colonial Life in America	New Netherland
Crown Point	Patroon System
Dutch West India Company	Revolutionary War
Federal Hall	in America
Fort Niagara	Tammany, Society of
Fort Ticonderoga	War of 1812
Free Soil Party	

PHYSICAL FEATURES

Adirondack Mountains	Long Island
Allegheny River	Mohawk River
Catskill Mountains	Montauk Peninsula
Delaware River	Niagara Falls and Niagara
Finger Lakes	River
Hudson River	Oneida Lake
Lake Champlain	Palisades
Lake Erie	Saint Lawrence River
Lake George	Saranac Lakes
Lake Ontario	Susquehanna River
Lake Placid	Thousand Islands

PRODUCTS AND INDUSTRY

For New York's rank among the states in production, see the following articles:

Apple	Cherry	Maple Syrup	Salt
Butter	Clothing	Milk	Textile
Cattle	Grape	Onion	Timothy
Cheese	Horse	Publishing	Wine
Chemical	Leather		
Industry	Manufacturing		

OTHER RELATED ARTICLES

Castle Clinton	New York State Barge
National Monument	Canal System
Chautauqua	Oneida Community
Erie Canal	Peace Bridge
Fort Stanwix	Sing Sing
Middle Atlantic States	United Nations

Outline

I. Government
  A. Constitution
  B. Executive
  C. Legislature
  D. Courts
  E. Local Government
  F. Taxation
  G. Politics

II. People

258

Questions

Why have New York's governors always been considered possible presidential candidates?

Why has New York earned its nickname the *Empire State?*

How many visitors does New York City usually have every year?

Why was the Erie Canal so important in New York's history?

Where did George Washington take the oath of office as the first President of the United States?

What are some of the reasons that New York is a great industrial state?

How does New York City rank in size with other cities in the United States? In the world?

Why has the Hudson-Mohawk Lowland been so important in the development of New York?

How was the power of the Iroquois Indians broken in New York in 1779?

Why is New York known as a *melting pot?*

Books for Young Readers

CARPENTER, ALLAN. *New York.* Childrens Press, 1967.

CHRISTENSEN, GARDELL D. *Colonial New York.* Nelson, 1969.

EDMONDS, WALTER D. *The Matchlock Gun.* Dodd, 1941. *Two Logs Crossing.* 1943. *Bert Breen's Barn.* Little, Brown, 1975. All are fiction.

ELLIS, DAVID M., and others. *New York: The Empire State.* 4th ed. Prentice-Hall, 1975.

FINK, WILLIAM B. *Getting to Know the Hudson River.* Coward-McCann, 1970. *Getting to Know New York State.* 1971.

GOODNOUGH, DAVID. *The Colony of New York.* Watts, 1973.

LORD, BEMAN. *On the Banks of the Hudson: A View of Its History and Folklore.* Walck, 1971.

NURENBERG, THELMA. *The New York Colony.* Macmillan, 1969.

ST. GEORGE, JUDITH A. *The Girl with Spunk.* Putnam, 1975. Fiction.

WILDER, LAURA I. *Farmer Boy.* Harper, 1953. Fiction. First published in 1933.

YATES, RAYMOND F. *Under Three Flags: Western New York State from the Ice Age to the Atomic Age.* Henry Stewart, Inc. (East Aurora, N.Y. 14052), 1958.

Books for Older Readers

DAVIDSON, MARSHALL B. *New York: A Pictorial History.* Scribner, 1977.

ELDRIDGE, PAUL. *Crown of Empire: The Story of the State of New York.* Barnes, 1957.

ELLIS, DAVID M., and others. *A History of New York State.* Rev. ed. Cornell, 1967.

IRVING, WASHINGTON. *Knickerbocker's History of New York.* Ed. by Anne Carroll Moore. Ungar, 1959.

KAMMEN, MICHAEL G. *Colonial New York: A History.* Scribner, 1975.

THOMPSON, JOHN H., ed. *Geography of New York State.* Syracuse Univ. Press, 1966.

NEW YORK, CITY UNIVERSITY OF, consists of 10 senior colleges, 7 community colleges, and a graduate school in New York City. The Mount Sinai School of Medicine is also affiliated with the university. The 10 senior colleges are Bernard M. Baruch College, City College, Hunter College, and John Jay College of Criminal Justice, all in Manhattan; Herbert H. Lehman College in the Bronx; Brooklyn College and Medgar Evers College in Brooklyn; Queens College and York College in Queens; and Staten Island-Richmond College on Staten Island. These colleges offer liberal arts and science programs leading to bachelor's degrees. Master's degrees are offered in business, education, engineering, liberal arts, library science, nursing, public administration, and social work. Doctor's degrees are offered in 27 fields.

The seven community colleges are Borough of Manhattan, Bronx, Hostos, Kingsborough, LaGuardia, New York City, and Queensborough. They offer associate degrees in arts and applied science.

The City University of New York is supported by the city, state, and federal governments, and by fees, gifts, and tuition. It gained university status in 1961. It is one of the largest systems of higher education in the United States. For the enrollment of the university, see UNIVERSITIES AND COLLEGES (table).

Critically reviewed by the CITY UNIVERSITY OF NEW YORK

NEW YORK, STATE UNIVERSITY OF, is the state-wide public system of higher education in the state of New York. It includes 4 university centers, 14 colleges of arts and science, 2 medical centers, 3 specialized colleges, 6 agricultural and technical colleges, 5 statutory colleges, and 30 community colleges.

The four university centers are in Albany, Binghamton, Buffalo, and Stony Brook. The 14 state colleges are in Brockport, Buffalo, Cortland, Fredonia, Geneseo, New Paltz, Old Westbury, Oneonta, Oswego, Plattsburgh, Potsdam, Purchase, Saratoga Springs, and Utica. The Downstate Medical Center is in Brooklyn, a borough of New York City; and the Upstate Medical Center is in Syracuse. Other professional colleges include the College of Environmental Science and Forestry adjoining Syracuse University, the State College of Optometry in New York City, and the Maritime College in the Bronx, a borough of New York City. The statutory colleges are the College of Ceramics at Alfred University and the state university colleges of agriculture and life sciences, human ecology, and veterinary medicine, and a school of industrial and labor relations at Cornell University.

The master's degree is offered at 25 campuses. The doctor of philosophy degree is granted at the four university centers and at nine other campuses.

Two-year courses are offered at the 30 community colleges and at the agricultural and technical colleges in Alfred, Canton, Cobleskill, Delhi, Farmingdale, and Morrisville. The community colleges and the agricultural and technical colleges offer associate degrees.

State University of New York was established in 1948. Headquarters are in Albany. For enrollment, see UNIVERSITIES AND COLLEGES (table).

Critically reviewed by the STATE UNIVERSITY OF NEW YORK

New York City is best known for the giant skyscrapers on Manhattan Island. The twin towers of the 110-story World Trade Center, *left*, rise above the city's financial district. New York City is the largest city in the United States in population and the fourth largest in the world.

NEW YORK CITY

NEW YORK CITY is the largest city in the United States and the fourth largest in the world. Only Shanghai, Tokyo, and Mexico City are larger. New York City is one of the world's most important centers of business, culture, and trade. It is also the home of the United Nations (UN). Much of what happens in New York City affects what happens throughout the United States and around the world.

New York City has a population of nearly 8 million. It is more than twice as large as Chicago, the nation's second largest city. In fact, only six states—not including New York State—have more people than New York City. Since its founding by Dutch settlers in 1624, New York has attracted immigrants from throughout the world. During the 1800's and early 1900's, millions of Europeans seeking a better life in a free land poured into the city. The Statue of Liberty, built in

This article was prepared by a committee of contributors headed by Robert H. Connery, President of the Academy of Political Science at Columbia University. The other contributors were William V. Farr of the Academy of Political Science, Columbia University; Roger Feinstein, Assistant Professor of Political Science at Boston State College; Floyd M. Shumway, Lecturer in American History, Columbia University; and Emanuel Tobier, Professor of Economics at the Graduate School of Public Administration, New York University.

New York Harbor in 1886, became the symbol of this new life. Since the mid-1900's, more immigrants—mainly blacks from the Southern States and Spanish-speaking Americans from Puerto Rico—have moved into the city. They have also looked to New York as a place to make a better life.

The business, financial, and trading organizations in New York City play a major role in the economy of the nation and of the world. The banks, stock exchanges, and other financial institutions in the city's famous Wall Street area help provide the money used by most large

---
————— FACTS IN BRIEF —————

Population: 7,895,563. *Metropolitan Area Population*—9,943,800. *Consolidated Metropolitan Area Population*—16,836,838 (11,632,436 in New York, 4,870,527 in New Jersey, and 333,875 in Connecticut.

Area: 365 sq. mi. (945 km²). *Metropolitan Area*—1,543 sq. mi. (3,996 km²). *Consolidated Metropolitan Area*—5,059 sq. mi. (13,103 km²), consisting of 2,807 sq. mi. (7,270 km²) in New York, 2,028 sq. mi. (5,252 km²) in New Jersey, and 224 sq. mi. (580 km²) in Connecticut.

Climate: *Average Temperature*—January, 33° F. (1° C); July, 74° F. (23° C). *Average Annual Precipitation* (rainfall, melted snow, and other forms of moisture)—44 in. (112 cm). For the monthly weather in New York City, see NEW YORK (Climate).

Government: Mayor-council. *Terms*—4 years for the mayor and the 43 council members.

Founded: 1624. Incorporated as a city in 1653.

Many New Yorkers Depend on Subways for transportation. During rush hours, subway trains are jammed with people traveling to and from their jobs in Manhattan's business districts.

Van Bucher, Photo Researchers

New York City lies in the southeastern corner of New York State at the mouth of the Hudson River. It covers about 365 square miles (945 square kilometers), including about 65 square miles (168 square kilometers) of inland water. New York City is divided into five areas called *boroughs*—Manhattan, the Bronx, Queens, Brooklyn, and Staten Island. Each borough is a county of New York State.

Manhattan, the smallest borough in area, covers 31 square miles (80 square kilometers). It occupies a long, narrow island bordered by the Hudson River on the west, the East River on the east, the Harlem River on the north and northeast, and Upper New York Bay (the mouth of the Hudson) on the south.

The Bronx lies across the Harlem River from Manhattan and covers 54 square miles (140 square kilometers). It extends north along the Hudson River and east along the East River. It is the only borough not separated from upstate New York by water.

Queens, the largest borough in area, occupies 127 square miles (329 square kilometers) on the northwest corner of Long Island. The East River separates Queens from the Bronx to the north and from Manhattan to the west.

Brooklyn covers 89 square miles (231 square kilometers) on the southwest tip of Long Island. It lies south and southwest of Queens and southeast of Manhattan across the East River.

Staten Island, formerly called the borough of Richmond, occupies a 64-square-mile (166-square-kilometer) island in Upper and Lower New York bays. It lies west of Brooklyn and southwest of Manhattan.

The state of New Jersey is directly west of New York City. It lies across two waterways, Arthur Kill and Kill Van Kull, from Staten Island; across Upper New York Bay from Brooklyn; and across the Hudson River from Manhattan and the Bronx.

Each of New York City's boroughs has a large population, important businesses and industries, and many fine educational and cultural institutions. Within the five boroughs are more than 100 neighborhoods, such as Manhattan's Chinatown, Greenwich Village, and

U.S. corporations. The skyscrapers that form the spectacular New York skyline house the home offices of many national and international business firms. The docks, warehouses, and shipping companies that line New York's huge natural harbor handle much of the nation's imports and exports.

As a cultural center, New York City has no equal in the United States. Most of the publishing houses that select and produce the nation's books have their headquarters in New York. The city's world-famous Broadway area is the center of professional theater in the United States. New York also has some of the nation's largest museums and art galleries. Outstanding orchestras and opera and dance companies perform at the Lincoln Center for the Performing Arts, one of the finest cultural centers in the world.

But along with all its greatness, New York City has many serious problems. Thousands of immigrants have not found the opportunities they had hoped for in New York. More than a million New Yorkers receive welfare aid, and thousands live in slums. Other problems include air pollution, traffic jams, crime, racial conflicts, and the ever-increasing cost of living in the city. All these problems are driving many families—especially white middle-class families—to the suburbs.

In spite of its problems, New York City remains one of the most interesting and exciting cities in the United States. In fact, many people consider it the most fascinating city in the world.

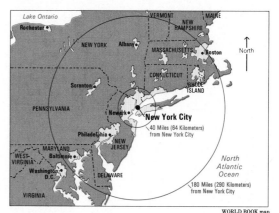

WORLD BOOK map

New York City lies at the center of a megalopolis, a group of metropolitan areas. These areas, shown in yellow on the map, extend from Boston to Washington, D.C.

NEW YORK CITY

New York City Metropolitan Area

The metropolitan area of New York City includes part of northern New Jersey. Hundreds of thousands of people who work in New York City do not live there. They commute daily from nearby areas, chiefly by train. The map shows the major commuter railroad lines.

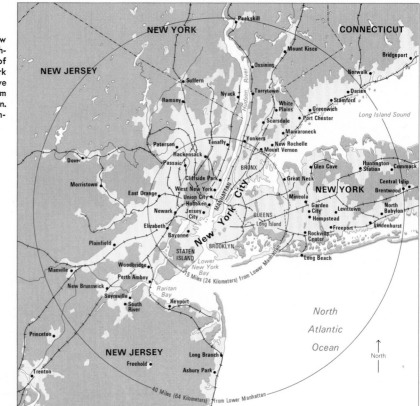

Built-up area

Non built-up area

Major commuter rail line

State boundary

Borough boundary

WORLD BOOK map

Allyn Baum, Rapho Guillumette

Outdoor Fruit Markets and other small shops serve customers in many New York City neighborhoods. The market above is in the Little Italy section of Manhattan.

Harlem. These neighborhoods are not official government units. They have similar types of housing or people with similar backgrounds or life styles.

New York City's metropolitan area spreads into northeastern New Jersey and southern New York State. Hundreds of thousands of people who work in New York live in suburban residential communities in the city's metropolitan area. Many industrial cities also lie in the area surrounding New York City.

Manhattan is the oldest and most important borough of New York City. It is about $13\frac{1}{2}$ miles (21.7 kilometers) long and $2\frac{1}{3}$ miles (3.8 kilometers) wide at its widest point. But over $1\frac{1}{2}$ million persons live there. The borough has the city's tallest buildings, some of the nation's largest schools and colleges, and the world's most famous financial and theatrical districts.

Manhattan is an area of many sharp contrasts. Some of the richest people in the United States live in its beautiful mansions and luxurious high-rise apartment buildings. But some of the nation's poorest people occupy its *tenements* (shabby apartment buildings) and low-rent public housing projects. Most of Manhattan is covered with concrete and asphalt, and skyscrapers make many of its streets look like deep canyons. But the borough's Central Park provides 840 acres (340 hectares) of grass, trees, and rolling hills. Manhattan has some of the world's most exclusive shops and largest department stores. They attract shoppers from all parts of the country. But the borough also has tiny neighborhood shops that sell to nearby residents.

New York City's Financial District lies at the southern tip of Manhattan and is centered on Wall and Broad streets. Many large banks, brokerage houses, and stock exchanges have their headquarters along the district's narrow streets. The giant World Trade Center rises in the Financial District along the Hudson River. The center includes twin 110-story towers.

Broadway, one of New York City's longest and best-known streets, begins in the Financial District and runs north and northwest across the length of Manhattan. On the east side of Broadway, a few blocks north of the Financial District, stands the Municipal

Civic Center. The center includes City Hall, handsome courthouses, and other government buildings.

Residential and commercial neighborhoods lie to the north and northeast of the Municipal Civic Center. These neighborhoods include Chinatown, Little Italy, and the Lower East Side. Both Chinatown and Little Italy have some of the city's oldest tenements. They also have many restaurants that specialize in Chinese or Italian food. For many years, most immigrants to New York City have first settled on the Lower East Side because of its many low-rent tenements. Jews once made up the largest group in the area, and they still own many stores there. Today, Puerto Ricans are the largest single group. But other groups, especially stu-

New York City

This map shows the five boroughs of New York City—the Bronx, Brooklyn, Manhattan, Queens, and Staten Island. These boroughs are also counties of the state of New York. County names appear in parentheses under each borough name.

Legend:
Bronx
Brooklyn
Manhattan
Queens
Staten Island
— Major road
■ Point of interest
Park area

WORLD BOOK map

263

Burt Glinn, Magnum

Abandoned, Decaying Buildings are a growing problem in New York City. Many property owners find it cheaper to abandon aging buildings than to repair them and pay taxes on them. Some people live in these buildings because better low-cost housing is not available.

dents and artists, have also been attracted to the Lower East Side by the low rents.

Greenwich Village lies north of the Lower East Side and west of Broadway. Traditionally, it has attracted artists, writers, musicians, actors, and other people in the arts. The Village has a variety of housing, many interesting shops and art galleries, and several small theaters.

North of Greenwich Village, Manhattan is laid out in a regular pattern of cross streets. Avenues run north and south, and numbered streets run east and west. Broadway cuts diagonally across this pattern.

Several of New York City's largest department stores are in the Herald Square and Greeley Square areas, where Broadway crosses the Avenue of the Americas (formerly Sixth Avenue). Just east of the department stores, on 34th Street, is the famous, 102-story Empire State Building, for many years the tallest building in the world. The busy Garment District, center of the city's large clothing industry, lies west of Herald and Greeley squares.

The intersection of Broadway and Seventh Avenue, between 42nd and 47th streets, forms world-famous Times Square, the heart of the New York Theater District. Much of the Times Square area is being redeveloped with large office buildings. But the area will remain the Theater District because many of the new buildings will have theaters.

United Nations headquarters occupy 18 acres (7.3 hectares) along the East River between 42nd and 48th streets. The UN's beautiful modern buildings have become New York City landmarks.

Rockefeller Center is another of the city's landmarks.

It lies on Fifth Avenue between 48th and 51st streets. The center consists of 21 buildings covering about 23 acres (9 hectares). It is the world's largest privately owned business and entertainment facility. The center's buildings include the RCA Building, which is 850 feet (259 meters) high, and the 6,200-seat Radio City Music Hall, the world's largest indoor theater. Many of New York City's finest stores line Fifth Avenue both north and south of Rockefeller Center.

Central Park, which runs from 59th to 110th streets between Fifth Avenue and Central Park West, separates Manhattan's Upper East Side and Upper West Side. The Upper East Side has long been the most fashionable neighborhood in Manhattan. At one time, the area had many mansions, which were owned by the city's richest residents. Today, cultural organizations and United Nations delegations occupy many of these mansions, and most of the people in the area live in luxurious apartment buildings. The Upper West Side is chiefly a middle-class neighborhood. It has many apartment houses, hotels, tenements, and long blocks of brick and brownstone row houses.

Harlem, the best-known Negro community in the United States, lies north of Central Park. It has been a center of black business and cultural activities for more than 60 years. A series of model housing projects extends along the Harlem River at the northern edge of Harlem. But much of the area consists of tenements.

Morningside Heights, the site of Columbia University and several other educational, cultural, and religious institutions, lies west of Harlem along the Hudson River. City College of the City University of New York is in Hamilton Heights, north of Morningside Heights.

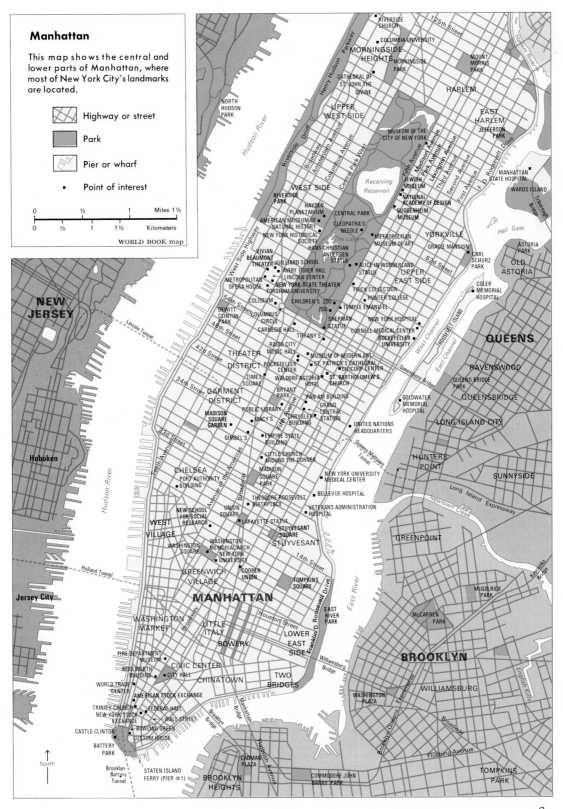

Russ Kinne, Photo Researchers

Brooklyn has hundreds of streets lined with long blocks of row houses. About 2½ million persons live in Brooklyn, more than in any other borough of New York City.

Van Bucher, Photo Researchers

The Bronx extends along the Hudson River north of Manhattan. Most people in the Bronx live in large apartment buildings. But the borough also has many old private homes.

Hamilton Heights was once the country estate of the American statesman Alexander Hamilton.

Washington Heights and Inwood are at the northern tip of Manhattan. Both have aging tenements, as well as modern housing projects. The Columbia-Presbyterian Medical Center; Yeshiva University; and the Cloisters, a museum featuring art of the Middle Ages, are in Washington Heights.

Brooklyn has more people than any other borough of New York City. If Brooklyn were an independent city, its population of more than 2½ million would make it the nation's fourth largest city.

Brooklyn is an important port and industrial center. Hundreds of ships carry freight to and from Brooklyn's docks each year. The borough's factories, most of which are along the waterfront, manufacture a wide variety of goods.

Housing in Brooklyn ranges from large mansions and towering apartment buildings to small cottages and run-down rooming houses. But most *Brooklynites* live in row houses and small apartment buildings that line the streets throughout the borough.

Downtown Brooklyn, the borough's main business and shopping district, lies near the approaches to the Brooklyn and Manhattan bridges. These two bridges are the main links between Brooklyn and Manhattan. A third bridge, Williamsburg Bridge, also connects the two boroughs. Brooklyn's downtown area has large department stores, tall office buildings, and several schools and colleges. Flatbush Avenue, one of the main downtown streets, begins at the Manhattan Bridge and runs through the heart of the borough.

Two of Brooklyn's oldest neighborhoods, Brooklyn Heights and Cobble Hill, lie along the East River west of the downtown area. These neighborhoods have more than 1,000 houses over 100 years old. Many of the houses stand on handsome, tree-lined streets and are carefully preserved.

The site of the former U.S. Naval Shipyard, which had been one of Brooklyn's chief industries, lies northeast of downtown. The Navy gave up the yard in 1968, and the area is now being made into an industrial park for factories and warehouses.

Bedford-Stuyvesant, east of the downtown area, is the largest black neighborhood in New York City. Blocks of well-kept row houses and many fine churches are found throughout the neighborhood. In contrast, Brownsville, a black and Puerto Rican neighborhood which lies southeast of Bedford-Stuyvesant, is the city's worst slum area. It has few well-maintained areas, and many of its buildings are abandoned and decaying.

Prospect Park, in the center of Brooklyn, is one of the finest landscaped parks in the nation. The park is designed so that its lakes, meadows, woods, and other features look larger than they are. Flatbush, once a fashionable suburb of Brooklyn, begins on the southeast edge of the park. Large homes built during the 1890's and early 1900's line many of its shaded streets.

Coney Island lies at the southern tip of Brooklyn. The area once was an island, but land has been filled in to make it a peninsula. In summer, many New Yorkers ride subways to Coney Island's beaches and to its famous Boardwalk, which has side shows, souvenir stands, and other attractions. At one time, Coney Island also had great amusement parks, but they have been replaced by housing developments.

The Bronx has a population of nearly 1½ million and is chiefly a residential borough. The western part of the Bronx consists of a series of hills and valleys crossed by boulevards. A major boulevard in the Bronx, the Grand Concourse, runs north and south through the area. It is lined with apartment houses, office buildings, and stores. The eastern section of the borough is a broad plain, with peninsulas extending into the East River and Long Island Sound.

Bronx Park lies in the center of the Bronx. It includes Bronx Zoo, one of the best-known zoos in the United States, and the New York Botanical Garden, an important scientific institution.

Fordham University and New York University (NYU) have handsome campuses to the west of Bronx Park. The NYU campus includes the Hall of Fame, which honors the memory of great Americans (see HALL OF FAME).

One of the most fashionable neighborhoods in the Bronx is Riverdale, in the northwest corner of the borough along the Hudson River. It has tall apartment buildings, estates and other large homes, and exclusive private schools. One of the poorest neighborhoods in the Bronx is Morrisania, which lies south of Bronx Park and east of Grand Concourse Boulevard. The area has many run-down and abandoned buildings.

Two huge housing developments lie in the eastern part of the Bronx. Parkchester, built between 1938 and 1942, is a rental development southwest of Bronx Park. Co-op City, built between 1968 and 1970, is in the northeast corner of the borough and is owned by its residents. Each development has more than 12,000 apartments, a large shopping area, and landscaped areas.

City Island lies east of the Bronx in Long Island Sound. It has several boat clubs and resembles a New England village. Edgewater Park and Silver Beach are at the southeastern tip of the Bronx. They were once summer resort communities. But the cottages in the areas have been winterized and are now used the year around.

Queens, with nearly 2 million residents, ranks second in population among New York City's boroughs. Queens grew rapidly between 1910 and 1930, when subways were built to connect it with Manhattan. A second period of fast growth began in the late 1940's, when the subways were extended, new highways were built, and two major airports were developed in the borough. Today, huge housing developments and busy expressways are the main features of Queens.

Much of the borough's industry is concentrated near the East River in an area called Long Island City. The area lies just south of the Queensboro Bridge, which connects Queens and Manhattan. It has giant rail yards of the Penn Central Railroad and many industrial plants and warehouses. Maspeth, southeast of Long Island City, also has large industrial plants, as well as pleasant residential areas.

Forest Hills lies near the center of Queens. Within

Larry Mulvehill, Photo Researchers

Queens is the largest borough in area. It has many busy expressways and large housing projects. Much of its development has occurred since the 1940's.

this neighborhood is Forest Hills Gardens, an attractive housing and shopping area built in 1913. Forest Hills Gardens was intended for families with low incomes. But it immediately became—and has remained—a community for the wealthy.

Northeast of Forest Hills is Flushing Meadows-Corona Park, site of the New York World's Fair of 1939 and 1964. The park has several features left from the fairs, including a botanical garden, an indoor ice-skating rink, and a science museum.

La Guardia Field, one of New York City's two main airports, is northwest of Flushing Meadows-Corona Park, across Flushing Bay. The neighborhood of Flushing, northeast of the park, has a busy shopping area and many large apartment houses.

Jamaica, in southeastern Queens, is one of the borough's chief commercial centers. It has large shopping and business areas and both rich and poor residential sections.

John F. Kennedy International Airport, the city's largest airport, lies immediately south of Jamaica. It has been expanding since 1942 and has become the borough's largest single source of employment.

Rockaway is a long peninsula that forms the southern

border of Jamaica Bay. It has a sandy beachfront, attractive private homes, and modern apartment buildings. It also has many summer cottages, some of which are occupied the year around.

Staten Island has about 295,000 persons, making it the smallest borough in population. It is the only borough not connected to Manhattan by a bridge or a tunnel. Until the completion of the Verrazano-Narrows Bridge in 1964, much of the island consisted of small farms and undeveloped areas. The bridge, which connects Staten Island with Brooklyn, has led to the construction of new housing and to industrial growth. But many of the borough's communities still look more like small towns than like sections of a major city.

St. George, on the northeast tip of Staten Island, serves as the downtown section of the borough and is the site of the Staten Island Ferry Terminal. The famous ferries carry automobiles and passengers between Staten Island and Manhattan and provide the only direct link between the two boroughs. A U.S. Coast Guard station, government and private office buildings, and a variety of stores are also in St. George.

The eastern shore of Staten Island is a decaying industrial area. But there are handsome homes and several colleges on the wooded hills just inland.

Parks and beaches line the southeastern and southern coasts of the island. Richmondtown, in the center of Staten Island, is being restored to show how it developed during the 1600's, 1700's, and 1800's. (See RICHMONDTOWN).

The industrial communities of Mariners Harbor and Port Richmond lie on the island's north coast. One of the three bridges that connect Staten Island and New Jersey is near Mariners Harbor. The others are on the northwest coast and near the southern tip of the island.

Small Islands. There are several small islands in the waters surrounding New York City. The most famous is Liberty Island, site of the city's greatest landmark—the Statue of Liberty. Ellis Island lies near Liberty Island. The U.S. Immigration Service used the island until 1954 as a detention and deportation center. Liberty and Ellis islands now form the Statue of Liberty National Monument. Governors Island, at the mouth of the East River, is the site of a military installation dating back to the late 1700's. Roosevelt, Wards, Randalls, and Rikers islands lie in the East River. Hospitals, prisons, and other institutions have been built on these islands. An aerial cable car system links Roosevelt Island and Manhattan. See ELLIS ISLAND; GOVERNORS ISLAND; LIBERTY ISLAND.

Metropolitan Area. The New York City metropolitan area, as defined by the federal government, consists of the five boroughs, Putnam, Rockland, and Westchester counties in southern New York, and Bergen County in New Jersey.

New York City's metropolitan area is the largest of nine metropolitan areas that make up the New York-Newark-Jersey City Standard Consolidated Statistical Area. This region includes the Nassau-Suffolk metropolitan area in New York, five metropolitan areas in northeastern New Jersey, and two metropolitan areas in southwestern Connecticut. The region has a population of more than 16 million.

Many communities in the New York area are commuter suburbs. Their residents work in New York City and commute by automobiles, buses, ferries, railroads, and subways. Some of these suburbs, such as White Plains in Westchester County, have become important centers of business and shopping outside the central city. Other communities in the New York area are industrial cities. They provide enough jobs so that most of their residents work in the communities themselves. Some of these industrial communities, such as Newark and Jersey City in New Jersey, are also experiencing the problems of pollution, poverty, and urban decay that affect New York City.

Kay Honkanen from Carl Östman

Staten Island has several sections that look more like small towns than like parts of a major city. Staten Island is the only borough not connected to Manhattan by a bridge or a tunnel. The famous Staten Island ferries link the two boroughs.

Don Morgan, Photo Researchers

Manhattan's Central Park attracts large crowds on warm summer days. The huge park has athletic fields, gardens, a lake, playgrounds, wooded areas, and a zoo.

The people of New York City represent nearly all races and nationalities. During the 1650's, only about 1,000 persons lived in the Dutch colony of New Amsterdam on Manhattan Island. But even then, 18 languages were spoken in the colony. Since that time, people from throughout the world have brought their skills, traditions, and ways of life to New York City.

People move to New York City for many reasons. Many are attracted by the city's job opportunities. Other people come to attend the city's schools and colleges or to enjoy its many cultural activities. Still others come simply because they want to be a part of a large, exciting city in which they can live almost any way they choose.

Ethnic Groups. Five ethnic groups—Irish, Italian, Jewish, Negro, and Puerto Rican—make up about 77 per cent of New York City's people. Neighborhoods consisting largely of people from these and many smaller groups are scattered throughout the city. Originally, most of the people in ethnic groups shared direct ties to a country, a language, or a common past with other members of their group. Today, this is less true. But the people still have some unity through such things as common religious beliefs and common economic interests.

Negroes are the largest ethnic group in New York City and make up about 21 per cent of the city's population. New York has about 1,667,000 Negroes, more than any other city in the world. Most of the blacks are immigrants—or the children of immigrants—from the rural South. But many have also come from the West Indies. A large number of New York City's blacks live in poor neighborhoods. Many of them have been prevented from leaving the ghetto areas by discrimination in jobs and housing and by a lack of education. But more and more black New Yorkers are becoming part of the city's middle class. Thousands of blacks live in racially integrated areas, and thousands more live in middle-class black neighborhoods.

Jews make up about 20 per cent of New York City's population. New York's Jews come from many countries. But they are considered an ethnic group because most of them live in Jewish neighborhoods and have similar religious and social beliefs. Many Jews own businesses. Many others work in garment factories, in offices, and in the legal, medical, and teaching professions.

About 15 per cent of New York City's people are of Italian ancestry. New York Italians are known for their well-kept homes and for their close neighborhood ties. They are the largest single group in the city's construction industry, and they play a key role in the restaurant and the wholesale and retail food-marketing industries. Many Italians have civil service jobs in the city's park, public works, sanitation, police, and fire departments. Most of New York City's Italians are Roman Catholics.

Puerto Ricans make up about 11 per cent of New

269

York City's population. They are the largest of several Spanish-speaking ethnic groups in the city. Large numbers of Puerto Ricans began to come to New York in the 1950's. Many of them found jobs as unskilled workers, especially in hospitals, hotels, and restaurants. At first, nearly all Puerto Ricans lived in East Harlem in Manhattan. But today, Puerto Rican neighborhoods are found in all the boroughs. Neighborhood associations, large church organizations, and the public school system have all developed programs to help newly arrived Puerto Rican people learn English and adjust to the city.

The Irish have traditionally been active in New York City's political life. During the late 1800's and early 1900's, they controlled the city government. But the percentage of Irish people in the city has dropped from 30 per cent in 1870 to about 10 per cent today. As a result, the Irish have lost much of their political power. But they are still the largest single group in New York City's police and fire departments. The Irish are also among the leaders of the Roman Catholic Church in the city.

New York City has many other ethnic groups besides the five major ones. Other large groups include Chinese, Cubans, Germans, Greeks, and Poles.

Housing in New York City differs in several ways from that in most other cities of the United States. About 60 per cent of New York's families live in apartment buildings or hotels. In other cities, most people live in one- or two-family houses. About 75 per cent of the families in New York rent their homes. In other U.S. cities, most families own their homes. About 70 per cent of the housing in New York City is more than 30 years old, and over 300,000 families live in buildings that are more than 70 years old. Most other cities have a far larger percentage of newer housing.

New York City has long been a leader in housing reform. In 1867, New York state, at the request of the city, passed the nation's first tenement house law. The law set minimum standards for room sizes and for ventilation and sanitation facilities. In 1943, the city passed a rent control law to protect tenants in privately owned buildings from unfair rent increases. Rent control laws passed in 1970 and 1971 were intended to help landlords make a reasonable profit. But many landlords complain that the higher rents they may charge do not cover rising costs. New York City has also built many public housing projects. Today, about 160,000 low-income families live in city-owned developments.

But housing remains one of New York City's most serious and difficult problems. Many old buildings are becoming unusable, and the demand for new housing, especially among poor people, is rapidly increasing. Yet steadily rising construction costs and a lack of large areas of open land make the development of new housing difficult.

Education. New York City has the largest public school system of any city in the world. The system includes more than 900 schools with over 1,100,000 students. An additional 400,000 students attend hundreds of privately operated schools in the city.

The public school system is governed by a central Board of Education and 32 elected local boards. Most of the boards were set up in 1969, after local communities—especially black and Puerto Rican communities—demanded more control over schools in their areas. A dispute over how local control should be organized led to a strike by teachers in 1968. The strike closed the city's schools for about 10 weeks.

New York City has neighborhood high schools like those found in most other cities. But it also has a wide variety of specialized high schools that prepare students

John Launois, Black Star

Crowded Tenements in Harlem house many of New York City's black residents. Blacks are the largest ethnic group in the city. They make up about 21 per cent of the population.

Allyn Baum, Rapho Guillumette

Kosher Food Shops are popular in New York's Jewish neighborhoods. Such shops sell foods prepared according to Jewish dietary laws. Jews make up about 20 per cent of the city's population.

for a specific occupation or for further training at the college level. These institutions include schools of automobile mechanics, aviation, the performing arts, printing, and science. Grade schools in poor neighborhoods have special programs to aid underprivileged children and children who do not speak English.

Many of New York City's colleges, universities, and other institutions of higher learning are world famous. One of the largest universities in the world, the City University of New York, is operated by the city with state and federal assistance. The university consists of 10 senior colleges, 7 community colleges, and a graduate school. The university has a total enrollment of about 240,000.

Columbia University, founded in 1754, is the oldest private university in New York City. The city's largest private university is New York University. Fordham and St. John's universities are important Roman Catholic schools.

New York City also has many smaller and more specialized institutions of higher education. The New School for Social Research deals mainly with adult education. Rockefeller University specializes in advanced research in biology and medicine. Pratt Institute and Cooper Union are largely devoted to architecture, engineering, and the fine arts. Other schools specialize in law, medicine, and social work.

Social Problems. New York City has many of the same problems other cities have. But New York is so much larger than other cities that the problems are greatly magnified. New York's major social problems include poverty, crime and drug addiction, and racial conflict.

Poverty is one of New York City's most expensive problems. The city spends more than $1 billion a year on welfare programs to feed, clothe, and house over a million people. Yet unskilled immigrants continue to move into the city while the demand for unskilled labor continues to decline. As a result, the problem of poverty is difficult to solve.

Because of its large population, New York City has more crime than any other U.S. city. But the crime rate—the number of crimes committed for every 100,-000 residents—is actually lower in New York than in many other cities. New York's crime and drug addiction problems are closely related. About half the drug addicts in the United States live in New York City. They commit many of the city's burglaries and attacks on individuals to get money for drugs.

Racial conflicts in New York City have had many causes. A major cause has been discrimination against blacks, Puerto Ricans, and other minority groups in jobs and housing. Many minority group members have had trouble obtaining well-paying jobs. Many also have had difficulty moving out of segregated neighborhoods and into neighborhoods where most of the people are white and of European ancestry. When members of a minority group have begun moving into such a neighborhood, the white residents often have begun moving out. In this way, segregated housing patterns have continued, and the chances for conflicts between the groups have increased.

Van Bucher, Photo Researchers

Fifth Avenue is one of New York City's most famous shopping areas. Its many fine stores are known throughout the world and attract both residents and tourists.

Arnold Hinton from Nancy Palmer

Traveling Storytellers visit parks and playgrounds to entertain, and help educate, New York youngsters. The Council on Interracial Books for Children sponsors the program.

New York City is one of the world's most important centers of industry, trade, and finance. Businesses, industries, and government agencies in the metropolitan area provide more than 7 million jobs. About 4 million of these jobs are within the city itself.

The economies of both New York City and its suburbs are growing. But since the 1940's, the economy of the suburban area has grown much faster than that of the city. The construction of new highways, a growing labor force, and the availability of land in the suburbs have led many businesses and industries to move from the crowded central city to the suburbs.

The types of jobs available in New York City have also been changing since the 1940's. The number of jobs for unskilled workers has decreased greatly because many industries have moved to the suburbs. This decrease has created a serious economic problem because most immigrants to the city are unskilled. At the same time, the number of jobs for skilled workers, especially office workers, has increased. But many of these jobs are being filled by people who live in the suburbs.

Industry. New York City ranks third after Chicago and Los Angeles-Long Beach among the leading manufacturing centers in the United States. The city has about 26,000 industrial plants. They employ about 775,000 workers. The city's two most important industries are (1) printing and publishing and (2) the production of clothing.

New York City is one of the nation's chief printing and publishing centers. It has more printing plants than any other U.S. city. New York does about a sixth of the nation's printing and publishing. It publishes about a third of the books published in the United States. The city's printing and publishing industry employs more than 160,000 persons.

New York City's clothing industry is centered in Manhattan's famous Garment District, southwest of Times Square. There, hundreds of factories employ about 217,000 persons and produce much of the nation's clothing. But the garment industry has been declining in New York. Many factories have left the Garment District because of the rising costs of doing business in the heart of crowded Manhattan.

Other leading manufacturing industries include those that produce chemicals, drugs, food products, furniture, paints, paper products, and textiles. The construction industry is also important. About 110,000 persons work in jobs related to the industry.

Trade. The Port of New York is one of the world's largest and busiest seaports. It employs about 60,000 persons and handles more cargo than any other U.S. port. This cargo includes foreign imports and exports, and goods going to or coming from other U.S. ports.

But New York City's port activity has been declining since the late 1940's. One reason for the decline has been the growth of other international U.S. seaports, especially along the Great Lakes. The opening of the St. Lawrence Seaway in 1959 allowed ships that previously docked in New York to reach Great Lakes ports. Another reason for the decline in New York's port activity has been the increased use of *container ships*—ships that carry cargo in huge prepackaged units called *containers*. Most of the docks in New York City are not equipped to load or unload container ships. As a result, nearly all these vessels in the New York area go through the New Jersey ports of Newark or Elizabeth, where special facilities have been built to handle them.

Large amounts of cargo are also handled at New York City's airports. Foreign air freight goes through Kennedy Airport. Domestic cargo is handled at both Kennedy and La Guardia airports.

The Port Authority of New York and New Jersey, a self-supporting agency of the states of New York and New Jersey, operates New York City's major airports and docking facilities, as well as several other transportation facilities. The port authority also owns and operates the World Trade Center, which serves as the headquarters of many firms involved in New York City's trading activities. See PORT AUTHORITY OF NEW YORK AND NEW JERSEY.

Wholesale trade plays an important part in New York City's economy. The city has more than 23,000 wholesale firms. They employ over 300,000 persons. The city's wholesale grocery and dry-goods businesses are the largest in the United States.

Retail business firms in New York City have more than 435,000 employees. The nation's largest retail center is in downtown Manhattan. Its department stores and specialty shops are known throughout the world.

Finance. More of the nation's largest and most important financial institutions have their headquarters in New York City than in any other city. Banks, brokerage houses, insurance companies, real estate firms, stock exchanges, and other financial organizations in New York employ about 465,000 persons. Unlike most industries in the city, the financial organizations offer a steadily increasing number of jobs.

Van Bucher, Photo Researchers

The Garment District is the center of New York City's important clothing industry. Its streets are nearly always crowded with trucks and with workers moving racks of clothing.

The most famous financial institution in New York City is the New York Stock Exchange, located at the corner of Broad and Wall streets in the heart of the Financial District. It is the largest stock exchange in the world. The American Stock Exchange, one of the nation's largest exchanges, is also in the Financial District. Many large brokerage houses have their headquarters near the exchanges.

New York City's banks are among the world's biggest. They help finance business ventures throughout the United States and in many parts of the world. The city's largest banks are in the Financial District.

Transportation. New York City has a huge, complicated transportation system. Much of the system is centered in the area of Manhattan south of Central Park. About 3½ million persons travel to and from that area each working day. Nearly all forms of air, land, and water transportation serve the city.

An extensive highway system has been developed to carry automobiles, buses, and trucks into, out of, and through New York City. The city's major expressways include the Major Deegan Expressway in the Bronx, the Shore and Gowanus parkways in Brooklyn, and Grand Central Parkway and the Long Island Expressway in Queens. Franklin D. Roosevelt Drive carries traffic along the eastern edge of Manhattan. The West Side Highway runs along the borough's western edge.

New York City includes 65 square miles (168 square

Land Use in New York City

The largest portion of land in New York City is used for houses and apartment buildings, shown in yellow. Many large industries, shown in dark brown, are located near the city's waterfront, and the commercial activities, shown in orange, are centered in Manhattan.

Industrial (factories, terminals, warehouses)

Commercial (banks, offices, stores, theaters)

Residential (houses, apartment buildings)

Recreational (beaches, parks, playgrounds)

Institutional (hospitals, schools)

Other land (cemeteries, vacant areas)

WORLD BOOK map

Adapted from *Land Use Policy New York City*, New York City Planning Commission

The New York Stock Exchange, *center,* is at the corner of Wall and Broad streets, the heart of New York's Financial District. The statue of George Washington, *foreground,* marks where he was inaugurated as the first U.S. President in 1789.

kilometers) of inland water, and so many bridges and tunnels are needed to link the city's boroughs. The famous Brooklyn Bridge crosses the East River and connects Brooklyn and the southern tip of Manhattan. It was completed in 1883 and declared a national historic landmark in 1964. Eight other bridges cross the East River. They are, from south to north, the Manhattan, Williamsburg, Queensboro, Roosevelt Island, Hell Gate, Triborough, Bronx-Whitestone, and Throgs Neck bridges. The Y-shaped Triborough Bridge links Manhattan, the Bronx, and Queens.

The Harlem River is spanned by High Bridge, Harlem Bridge, Henry Hudson Bridge, Alexander Hamilton Bridge, and several smaller bridges. High Bridge, which was opened in 1848, is one of the oldest bridges in the city.

One bridge, the George Washington Bridge, crosses the Hudson River and connects Manhattan and New Jersey. The Bayonne Bridge stretches 1,675 feet (511 meters) over Kill Van Kull channel between Staten Island and New Jersey. It has one of the longest arch spans in the world. Goethals Bridge and Outerbridge Crossing, which cross Arthur Kill channel, also connect Staten Island and New Jersey.

The Verrazano-Narrows Bridge, which links Staten Island and Brooklyn, opened in 1964. Its 4,260-foot (1,298-meter) suspension span is one of the longest in the world.

The Queens Midtown Tunnel runs under the East River and connects Manhattan and Queens. The 9,117-foot (2,779-meter) Brooklyn-Battery Tunnel links the southern tip of Manhattan with Brooklyn. The Lincoln and Holland tunnels run under the Hudson River between Manhattan and New Jersey.

New York City has three subway systems. They operate on about 235 miles (378 kilometers) of track. The Interborough Rapid Transit (IRT), the city's first subway, opened in 1904. The IRT operates in Manhattan and in a large part of the Bronx. It has branch lines into Brooklyn and Queens. The Independent Subway (IND) has lines in all the boroughs except Staten Island. The Brooklyn-Manhattan Transit Company (BMT) has lines in Brooklyn, Manhattan, and Queens. Buses operate throughout the city. The New York City Transit Authority, a state agency, controls all the subways and most bus lines in the city.

Two major railroad stations serve New York City— Grand Central Station at 42nd Street and Park Avenue and Pennsylvania Station on 31st Street at Seventh Avenue. In the mid-1960's, the upper level of Penn Station was torn down, but trains continue to operate beneath street level. Before the rapid growth of air travel in the 1950's, hundreds of thousands of railroad passengers from all parts of the country passed through Grand Central and Penn stations each day. Today, hundreds of thousands of persons still use the stations, but most are commuters.

La Guardia and Kennedy airports handle most of New York City's commercial air traffic. La Guardia serves domestic and Canadian airlines, and Kennedy serves domestic and international airlines. The city also has many smaller airports.

Communications. New York City is the nation's most important communications center. More publishing and broadcasting companies have their headquarters in New York than in any other city in the United States.

Three general newspapers—the *Daily News,* the *New York Post,* and *The New York Times*—are published daily in New York City. The *Daily News* has a circulation of over 2 million, the largest of any U.S. paper. The *Times* is one of the world's best-known papers and is often used as a reference source. The city has many community, foreign-language, and trade and union papers. The largest foreign-language papers are *El Diario-La Prensa* and *El Tiempo,* both published in Spanish. The major trade paper is *The Wall Street Journal.*

Most major national magazines and many specialized magazines have their editorial offices in New York City. New York also has more book publishers and advertising agencies than any other city.

New York City has about 45 radio and television stations and serves as the headquarters of the nation's four major broadcasting networks. Three networks— the American Broadcasting Company (ABC), the Columbia Broadcasting System (CBS), and the National Broadcasting Company (NBC)—provide both radio and television programming to stations throughout the United States. The fourth network—the Mutual Broadcasting System (MBS)—provides radio programming only.

New York City ranks as one of the world's greatest cultural centers. It has many art galleries, drama and dance groups, musical and literary societies, and other cultural organizations. It also has some of the world's finest concert halls, museums, and theaters. Many of the nation's greatest actors, artists, musicians, poets, and writers live in New York.

There are several reasons for New York City's leading position as a cultural center. Many of the city's wealthy residents have long given financial support to cultural activities. Traditionally, the city has also offered people in the arts an atmosphere that encourages freedom of expression. In addition, New York's many advertising agencies, broadcasting and film studios, recording companies, and publishing houses have provided jobs that attract creative people.

The Arts. Nearly all the arts thrive in New York City. Many new styles in American drama, literature, music, and painting have developed in New York and then spread to the rest of the country.

One of New York City's most famous and popular forms of art is the theater. Almost all important American plays and musical comedies have their premières in the city's famous Theater District. The theaters in this district are called *Broadway* theaters, though few are actually on that street. Most are on side streets near Times Square. Many plays and musicals by unknown authors and composers are presented in *off-Broadway* theaters, most of which are in Greenwich Village.

Musical organizations in New York City include the New York Philharmonic, one of the world's great symphony orchestras, and the Metropolitan Opera Associa-

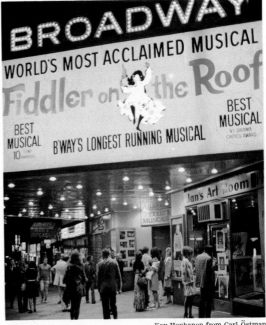

Kay Honkanen from Carl Östman

Broadway Theaters help make New York City one of the world's most important cultural centers. Nearly all major American musical comedies and dramas have their premières in New York.

Lincoln Center for the Performing Arts houses the New York Philharmonic, the Metropolitan Opera, the New York City Ballet, and several other cultural organizations.

Stephanie Dinkins, Photo Researchers

tion, an outstanding opera company. Both perform at the Lincoln Center for the Performing Arts. Lincoln Center also houses the New York City Ballet, the New York City Opera, and the Juilliard School of Music. The New York City Center of Music and Drama on W. 55th Street offers a variety of fine arts programs. Many concerts are held at Carnegie Hall, near Central Park. The Newport Jazz Festival sponsors jazz concerts in the city for several days each June and July.

Thousands of artists live and work in New York City. They display and sell their paintings, sculptures, and other works of art in the city's dozens of galleries. Many artists have made roomy studios in abandoned warehouses and factories in Manhattan. Most of the buildings were abandoned by industries that moved to suburban areas.

Architecture. New York's best-known style of architecture is the towering skyscraper. The giant buildings that form Manhattan's dramatic skyline are famous throughout the world.

One of the oldest and most famous skyscrapers in New York is the Flatiron Building, located on 23rd Street where Broadway crosses Fifth Avenue. The 21-story building was completed in 1903. It has a triangular shape like that of an old-fashioned flatiron.

During the 1930's, several famous skyscrapers were built in New York City. The most famous, the 102-story Empire State Building, was completed in 1931. It ranked as the world's tallest building for many years. The 77-story Chrysler Building at Lexington Avenue and 42nd Street and the 70-story RCA Building in Rockefeller Center were also completed in the 1930's.

Many glass-walled skyscrapers have been built in New York since the 1950's. These buildings include the United Nations Secretariat along the East River at 44th Street, Lever House on Park Avenue between 53rd and 54th streets, and the Seagram Building on Park Avenue between 52nd and 53rd streets. The twin towers of the giant World Trade Center on the Hudson River southwest of City Hall were completed in 1973.

Several New York City churches are famous for their Gothic style of architecture. They include the Episcopal Cathedral of St. John the Divine between 110th and 113th streets near Broadway, the Roman Catholic St. Patrick's Cathedral on Fifth Avenue between 50th and 51st streets, and the interdenominational Riverside Church on Riverside Drive and 122nd Street.

Other buildings of architectural interest in New York City include the many narrow brownstone houses that line side streets in Manhattan and Brooklyn. Most of these houses were built in the late 1800's as single-family homes. Today, many are divided into apartments.

Libraries. New York City has three public library systems. The New York Public Library serves Manhattan, the Bronx, and Staten Island. The Brooklyn Public Library serves Brooklyn, and the Queens Borough Public Library serves Queens. Altogether, the three systems have more than 200 branch libraries.

The New York Public Library is the largest public library in the United States. It has over 80 branches and about 9 million volumes. The library's Central Building on Fifth Avenue at 42nd Street is a Manhattan landmark.

In addition to the public library systems, New York

Hank Morgan, Black Star

The Metropolitan Museum of Art in New York City has more than 365,000 works of art. It occupies four city blocks and is the largest art museum in the United States.

City has more than 1,000 libraries operated by schools, colleges, and private organizations. Many of these libraries are highly specialized. For example, the Pierpont Morgan Library has rare books and manuscripts, and the Dag Hammarskjöld Library at the United Nations specializes in books dealing with international affairs and world peace.

Nearly all museums in New York have an associated library. The most important of these libraries include the Metropolitan Museum Art Reference Library, the Frick Art Reference Library, and the Museum of Natural History Library.

Museums. New York City has many kinds of museums. The largest museum is the Metropolitan Museum of Art on Fifth Avenue at 82nd Street. It has more than 365,000 works of art. These works represent nearly every culture of the last 5,000 years. The museum occupies four city blocks, yet it has space to display only about a third of its collection at one time. The Cloisters, a branch of the Metropolitan Museum, is devoted to art of the Middle Ages. The building is designed like a medieval monastery. It stands in Fort Tryon Park at the northern tip of Manhattan.

Several New York City museums specialize in modern art. They include the Museum of Modern Art on W. 53rd Street, the Whitney Museum of American Art on Madison Avenue and 75th Street, and the Guggenheim Museum on Fifth Avenue at 89th Street. The Guggenheim is in an unusual circular building designed by the famous American architect Frank Lloyd Wright. The Frick Collection on 70th Street at Fifth Avenue has a collection of art dating from the 1300's through the 1800's. The museum occupies one of Manhattan's few remaining mansions.

The American Museum of Natural History stands at 79th Street and Central Park West. It is the largest natural history museum in the world. Its exhibits include lifelike stuffed animals shown in reproductions of their natural surroundings. The Hayden Planetarium, which adjoins the American Museum, shows the changing patterns of the stars and planets on a 75-foot (23-meter) domed ceiling. Other scientific museums include that of the American Geographical Society at Broadway and 156th Street, the Museum of the American Indian at Broadway and 155th Street, and the Brooklyn Children's Museum in Brooklyn.

New York City also has several historical museums. They include that of the New-York Historical Society on Central Park West at 77th Street and the Museum of the City of New York on Fifth Avenue at 103rd Street.

Parks. New York has more parks, playgrounds, beaches, and other recreational areas than any other U.S. city. Yet many parts of the city are so crowded that children must still play in the streets.

Central Park, in the middle of Manhattan, is the best known of the city's more than 100 parks. It is 2½ miles (4 kilometers) long and ½ mile (0.8 kilometer) wide and has athletic fields, gardens, a lake, playgrounds, and wooded areas. Central Park includes the Mall, where outdoor concerts and other events are held, and the Ramble, an enclosed bird sanctuary. The Gateway National Recreation Area forms a 26,172-acre (10,591-

Katrina Thomas, Photo Researchers

Neighborhood Festivals allow New York City residents to enjoy cultural activities near their homes. The festivals are free and feature various types of entertainment.

hectare) park that lies along the Hudson River.

Other large parks in New York City include Bronx and Van Cortlandt parks in the Bronx, Prospect Park in Brooklyn, and Flushing Meadows-Corona Park in Queens. In many parts of the city, small parks and playgrounds have been developed on any open land that was available, including single empty lots.

New York City has several zoos and botanical gardens. Central Park Zoo features a special children's zoo. The Bronx Zoo in Bronx Park has the largest collection of animals of any zoo in the United States. Bronx Park also includes the New York Botanical Garden, which features plants from most parts of the world. Brooklyn and Queens also have outstanding botanical gardens.

Sports. The city has two major league baseball teams —the New York Yankees of the American League and the New York Mets of the National League. The Yankees play in Yankee Stadium in the Bronx. The Mets play in Shea Stadium in Queens. The city also has two National Football League teams. The New York Jets of the American Conference play in Shea Stadium. The New York Giants of the National Conference play their home games in Giants Stadium in nearby East Rutherford, N.J. New York City has a professional basketball team—the New York Knickerbockers of the National Basketball Association—and a professional hockey team—the New York Rangers of the National Hockey League. The basketball and hockey teams play in Madison Square Garden on Eighth Avenue between 31st and 33rd streets.

George Holton, Photo Researchers

United Nations Headquarters

Richard Lawrence Stack, Black Star

Museum of Modern Art Sculpture Garden

Lizabeth Corlett, DPI

Greenwich Village Theater

Each year, about 16 million tourists and delegates to conventions and trade shows visit New York City. To accommodate all these visitors, New York has hundreds of hotels, motels, and rooming houses and thousands of restaurants. Some of the city's hotels rank among the world's most luxurious. Many restaurants specialize in a certain type of cooking, such as French, German, or Italian. In fact, no other city in the world has so many kinds of restaurants as New York.

Following are descriptions of some of New York City's many interesting places to visit. Other places of interest are discussed and pictured earlier in this article.

Empire State Building on 34th Street between Fifth Avenue and the Avenue of the Americas is a 102-story New York City landmark. Public observation decks on the building's 86th and 102nd floors offer visitors spectacular views of the city.

Financial District is centered on Wall and Broad streets near the southern tip of Manhattan. Many banks, brokerage houses, and the world's largest stock exchanges are in the district. Tours are given of the New York Stock Exchange, located at the corner of Wall and Broad Streets.

Greenwich Village lies south of 14th Street and west of Broadway. Many actors, artists, musicians, and other people in the arts live in the area. The Village has several small theaters and many interesting shops and art galleries.

John Lewis Stage, Photo Researchers

Statue of Liberty

Kay Honkanen from Carl Östman

Saint Patrick's Cathedral

Richard Lawrence Stack, Black Star

Rockefeller Center Plaza

Museum of Modern Art on W. 53rd Street between Fifth Avenue and the Avenue of the Americas displays modern paintings, sculptures, films, photographs, and other works of art.

Rockefeller Center on Fifth Avenue between 48th and 51st streets includes the sunken Plaza, used for outdoor dining in summer and ice skating in winter; the 70-story RCA Building, which has a public observation roof; Radio City Music Hall, a 6,200-seat theater featuring films and stage shows; and the studios of the National Broadcasting Company (NBC). Tours are given of the NBC studios and of the entire center.

Saint Patrick's Cathedral at Fifth Avenue and 50th Street, across from Rockefeller Center, is the seat of the Roman Catholic Archdiocese of New York. It is one of the finest examples of Gothic architecture in the United States. See SAINT PATRICK'S CATHEDRAL.

Statue of Liberty on Liberty Island in New York Harbor is the world-famous symbol of American freedom. Boats carry visitors to the island from Battery Park at the southern tip of Manhattan. See LIBERTY, STATUE OF.

United Nations Headquarters lie along the East River between 42nd and 48th streets. Visitors may take tours of the Secretariat, General Assembly, and Conference buildings. A limited number of free tickets are available for meetings of the General Assembly and other UN organizations. See UNITED NATIONS.

274e

New York City's government is presently organized under a charter that was adopted in 1961 and that became effective in 1963. The government of New York is more centralized than that of most other U.S. cities. In New York, the central government is responsible for public education, correctional institutions, libraries, public safety, recreational facilities, sanitation, water supply, and welfare services. In most other cities, at least some of these services are provided by separate government units.

The mayor is the chief executive of New York City. He is elected to a four-year term and is responsible for the administration of city government. The mayor appoints the heads of about 50 city departments. He also may appoint two or more deputy mayors to assist him.

Each of New York City's five boroughs elects a borough president to a four-year term. The borough presidents serve on planning boards and advise the mayor on issues of interest to their boroughs.

New York City's legislature consists of the City Council and the Board of Estimate. The City Council has a president and 43 councilmen. The president is elected to a four-year term in a citywide election. He presides over council meetings but may vote only to break a tie. One councilman is elected from each of 33 districts in the city, and two are elected from throughout each of the five boroughs. The two elected from each of the boroughs cannot be members of the same political party. The Board of Estimate consists of the mayor, the city comptroller, the president of the City Council, and the borough presidents. Only the City Council may pass laws. But both the council and the Board of Estimate must approve the city budget, and the board may make recommendations to the council and the mayor.

New York has an annual budget of about $8\frac{1}{2}$ billion. The city gets part of its income from about 15 different taxes, including an income tax, real estate tax, and sales tax. The real estate tax provides the most tax income. But the total income from taxes is far from enough to meet the city's expenses. Additional money comes from the state and federal governments.

The Democratic Party has long been the most powerful political party in New York City. It has more than three times as many members as the Republican Party and usually controls between 75 and 85 per cent of the city's elective offices. Neither the Democratic nor the Republican party in New York City has a strong citywide organization. Both have separate organizations in each of the five boroughs. Two minor political parties, the Liberal and Conservative parties, also influence New York City politics. Both these parties have affected city elections chiefly by supporting candidates from one of the two major parties. But in 1969, Mayor John V. Lindsay was re-elected as the Liberal Party candidate after being defeated for renomination in the Republican primary election.

New York City's Flag was adopted in 1915. Its colors represent the Dutch flag that flew over the area between the 1620's and 1660's.

The City's Seal features an American eagle, an English sailor, and a Manhattan Indian. The date 1664 is the year England took the city from the Dutch.

Lizabeth Corlett, DPI

City Hall, completed in 1811, is one of New York City's architectural landmarks. It is part of the Municipal Civic Center and is surrounded by City Hall Park and by other city government buildings. The mayor and his staff have their offices in City Hall.

274f

Dutch Settlers Founded New York City at the southern tip of Manhattan in 1624. The settlement, which the Dutch called New Amsterdam, had about 1,000 persons by the 1650's, above.

The earliest people known to have lived in the New York City area were American Indians. Several tribes of the Algonkian family of Indians lived peacefully on the shores of New York Harbor and along the banks of the Hudson and East rivers. The Indians lived in small villages of bark huts. They fished, hunted, raised crops, and trapped animals. They traveled the area's waterways in sturdy canoes.

Exploration. The first European to enter New York Harbor was probably Giovanni da Verrazano, an Italian explorer employed by the king of France. Verrazano and his crew landed on Staten Island in 1524, while exploring the North American coast.

Other explorers visited the New York City region after Verrazano. But none of them reported seeing the island the Indians called *Man-a-hat-ta* (Island of the Hills). Finally, in 1609, Henry Hudson reached Manhattan and then sailed up the river that now bears his name. Hudson was an Englishman exploring for the Dutch, and so The Netherlands claimed the territory he had found.

Settlement. In 1613, the Dutch trader and explorer Adriaen Block and his crew became the first Europeans to live on Manhattan Island. They built several huts and spent the winter near the southern tip of the island after their ship was destroyed by fire. They built a new ship and left the island in the spring of 1614.

In 1624, the Dutch West India Company, a trading and colonizing firm, sent the first settlers to Manhattan. By 1626, the settlers had laid out a town and built a fort called Fort Amsterdam at the island's southern tip. That same year, the governor of the settlement, Peter Minuit, bought the island from the Indians for goods worth about $24.

Soon after Fort Amsterdam was built, the entire settlement was named New Amsterdam. The colony prospered slowly at first because the governors sent by the Dutch were poor administrators. But in 1647, Peter Stuyvesant became governor, and under his administration the town began to prosper rapidly.

About 1,000 persons lived in New Amsterdam during the 1650's. Their houses stood along narrow dirt lanes. In 1653, they built a wall along the northern edge of town because they feared attacks by Indians or by white enemies. But the wall fell down within a few years. Later, the colonists laid out a road in its place. The road became known as Wall Street.

While New Amsterdam was being established on Manhattan, colonists were also arriving in what is now the Bronx, Brooklyn, and Queens. Jonas Bronck of Denmark, after whom the Bronx is named, became the first settler in that area. He set up a 500-acre (200-hectare) farm in 1641 and was soon followed by other settlers. Dutch and English colonists established several small villages in Brooklyn and Queens. Staten Island developed more slowly than the other areas because settlers there often had trouble with Indians.

English Rule. The Netherlands and England fought three naval wars between 1652 and 1674. In 1664, English warships sailed into New York Harbor and forced Peter Stuyvesant to surrender New Amsterdam. The Dutch regained the colony a few years later but then gave it to England under the terms of a peace treaty. The English renamed the colony New York.

New York grew quickly under English rule. By 1700, its population reached about 7,000, and buildings filled lower Manhattan. The town's first newspaper, the *New-York Gazette*, appeared in 1725. King's College, now Columbia University, was founded in 1754.

New York played an important role in the American Colonies' fight for freedom from Great Britain. In 1765, the Stamp Act Congress met in New York to protest unfair taxes. In 1770, New Yorkers clashed with British soldiers, and one man was killed in the fighting. Soon after the Revolutionary War began in 1775, American forces took possession of the city. But the British regained New York after the Battle of Long Island in 1776 and held it until the war ended in 1783. In January 1785, New York became the temporary capital of the United States. Congress met there until March 1789, and George Washington was inaugurated in New York as the nation's first President in April 1789.

The Growing City. During the early years of the United States, Philadelphia and Boston were larger and more prosperous than New York. But New York's economy and population expanded rapidly. The city took advantage of its excellent natural harbor to increase its trade with other East Coast ports and with foreign countries. European immigrants began to pour into the city. By 1800, New York had about 60,000 persons, more than any other city in the country.

New York's growth continued during the early 1800's. In 1811, city officials, planning for further expansion, decided that all newly built Manhattan streets should run in straight lines. That decision resulted in the regular pattern of cross streets north of what is now Greenwich Village. The Erie Canal opened in upstate New York in 1825. The canal provided an important link in an all-water route between New York City and the rapidly developing Midwestern States (see ERIE CANAL). An increasing number of banks, insurance companies, and investment firms added to the city's economic growth.

New York's neighboring communities also grew quickly during the early 1800's. Brooklyn, the most important of these communities, was incorporated as a village in 1816 with 3,300 residents. By the time it became a city in 1834, Brooklyn had a population of about 24,000.

During the 1800's, thousands of European immigrants arrived in New York City every year. Until about 1890, most of them came from Germany, Ireland, and other countries of northern and western Europe. After about 1890, most immigrants came from southern and eastern European countries. Many immigrants had difficulty adjusting to the city. They lived in crowded slums and had trouble finding jobs.

Politicians, especially members of the Democratic Party machine in Manhattan called Tammany Hall, offered jobs, gifts, and advice to immigrants. In return, the immigrants voted to keep Tammany Hall in power. But the politicians actually did little to solve the immigrants' most important problems, such as the need for better housing, education, and medical care. In 1871, Tammany boss William M. Tweed and his followers were arrested and charged with cheating the city out of several million dollars. The Tweed Ring, as his group was called, was driven from public life. But the Tammany machine soon regained power. See TAMMANY, SOCIETY OF.

Formation of Greater New York. In 1883, engineers completed the Brooklyn Bridge, which provided the first direct link between Manhattan and Brooklyn. In 1898, Brooklyn and several communities in what became the Bronx, Queens, and Staten Island were united with Manhattan to form what was called Greater New York. The sprawling new city had over 3 million persons. Nearly 2 million of them lived in Manhattan. But during the early 1900's, subways and bridges were built to provide convenient transportation between Manhattan and the other boroughs. The city's people then spread out. As the populations of the other boroughs grew, Manhattan's population decreased.

But Manhattan remained the largest and most powerful borough of Greater New York, and so its Tammany Hall organization continued to control city politics. Occasionally, voters became angered enough by the illegal activities of Tammany leaders to elect mayors who promised reform. But none of these reform mayors lasted more than one term—until Fiorello La Guardia became mayor in 1934. La Guardia, an honest and outspoken reformer, served from 1934 to 1945. Since his administration, no political machine has been able to control New York politics.

Recent Developments. Since the 1940's, New York City has been troubled by many problems. These prob-

Harper's Weekly, The Newberry Library, Chicago

Tammany Hall, a powerful Manhattan political machine, was often attacked by cartoonist Thomas Nast. This cartoon appeared in 1871, after its leaders were caught cheating the city out of money.

Museum of the City of New York

Thousands of Immigrants arrived in New York City every year during the 1800's. Before entering the city, immigrants had to pass through the immigration station on Ellis Island, *above.* The island is now part of the Statue of Liberty National Monument.

Times Square in the 1930's was as much the heart of New York City's Theater District as it is today. Today, much of the area is being redeveloped but it will remain the Theater District.

A Financial Crisis hit New York City in 1975 and caused great concern for the city's future. A rally in Times Square, above, supported the use of federal aid to help the city.

lems have grown severe since the early 1960's. Air and water pollution have harmed the city's environment. Highways and mass transportation systems have become overcrowded and outdated. Housing shortages have increased. Racial conflicts have worsened.

New York City has also faced a series of damaging strikes by public employees. In 1966, transit workers struck for 12 days, halting all subway and bus service. In 1968, striking sanitation workers let garbage pile up on city streets for 9 days. In 1971, police officers refused to go on patrols for 6 days and fire fighters refused to perform nonemergency duties for a week. These strikes involved disputes over such matters as wages, various benefits, and working conditions.

Many citizen groups and government agencies have been set up to study and deal with New York City's problems. Some of these organizations have made progress toward solving some problems. But many groups have had little or no success.

New York City experienced a financial crisis in 1975, when the city's government lacked enough money to pay all its bills for the year. The state legislature helped ease the situation by establishing the Municipal Assistance Corporation, which lent the city some of the money it needed. The federal government also provided funds. To help pay its expenses during the late 1970's, the government of New York City increased city taxes, eliminated thousands of city government jobs, and reduced city services.   ROBERT H. CONNERY, WILLIAM V. FARR, ROGER FEINSTEIN, FLOYD M. SHUMWAY, and EMANUEL TOBIER

NEW YORK CITY / Study Aids

Questions

How does New York City rank in size with other cities in the United States? In the world?

What did Peter Minuit pay the Indians for Manhattan Island?

What are New York City's five boroughs? Which has the largest population? The largest area?

Which is the largest ethnic group in New York City?

Why is housing one of New York City's most serious and difficult problems?

What are New York City's two most important industries?

How do some high schools in New York City differ from those in most other cities?

When was New York City the nation's capital?

Which is the largest museum in New York City?

What provides the only direct link between Staten Island and Manhattan?

NEW YORK FOUNDATION is a fund for charitable purposes. The foundation was established in 1909 by Louis A. Heinsheimer, an American banker, by a grant of $1 million under his will. In 1926, the foundation received $2,200,000 from the estate of Lionel J. Salomon and, in 1929, $6 million from the estate of Alfred M. Heinsheimer.

The New York Foundation is nonsectarian and supports many organizations in the fields of public health, social welfare, and education, chiefly in New York City. It also helps support black organizations in the Southern United States. Headquarters are at 4 West 58th Street, New York, N.Y. 10019.

Critically reviewed by NEW YORK FOUNDATION

NEW YORK LIFE INSURANCE COMPANY. See INSURANCE (table: 15 Largest).

NEW YORK PUBLIC LIBRARY is the largest city public library in the United States in terms of its number of volumes and number of branch libraries. The library operates a group of research libraries supported mostly by its endowment funds. Public funds from the city support the system of branches that operate in the boroughs of Manhattan, the Bronx, and Staten Island. Two additional library systems that serve New York City are the Brooklyn Public Library and the Queens Borough Public Library.

The research libraries of the New York Public Library occupy a white marble structure at Fifth Avenue and 42nd Street. The main building contains over 5 million books. Its branch libraries and its bookmobiles have about 4 million additional books. The library also has about 10 million manuscripts, $3\frac{1}{2}$ million pictures, 307,000 maps, 120,000 reels of film and microfilm, and 80,000 books for the blind. The library also offers lectures, concerts, film showings, book discussions, and story hours for children. The New York Public Library was founded in 1895.

Critically reviewed by NEW YORK PUBLIC LIBRARY

NEW YORK STATE. See NEW YORK.

NEW YORK STATE BARGE CANAL SYSTEM connects the state's principal natural waterways. The toll-free canal system and its connecting waterways extend 800 miles (1,300 kilometers) from Lake Champlain and the Hudson River to Lakes Erie and Ontario. Nearly half the state of New York and 90 per cent of its population lie within 20 miles (32 kilometers) of some point on this huge waterways system. The canal system proper is 524 miles (843 kilometers) long.

The system consists of four canals—the Erie, the

The New York State Barge Canal System consists of the Erie Canal and three other canals. The system connects the principal natural waterways of New York.

WORLD BOOK map

Champlain, the Oswego, and the Cayuga and Seneca. The 338-mile (544-kilometer) Erie Canal connects Tonawanda on the Niagara River with Troy and Albany on the Hudson River. The Champlain Canal, between Whitehall on Lake Champlain and Waterford near Troy, is 60 miles (97 kilometers) long. The 24-mile (39-kilometer) Oswego Canal links Oswego on Lake Ontario and Three Rivers. The Cayuga and Seneca Canal extends 92 miles (148 kilometers) from Montezuma, on the Seneca River and the Erie Canal, to Ithaca and Watkins Glen. This waterway includes passages through Cayuga and Seneca lakes and to Montour Falls.

The New York state legislature authorized construction of the canal system in 1903. The system was opened in 1918. It has 57 locks, each 300 feet (91 meters) long and 43½ feet (13.3 meters) wide. It has a channel depth of 14 feet (4.3 meters) from Waterford to Oswego and 12 feet (3.7 meters) on all its other canals.

The system's locks can handle barges carrying more than 3,500 short tons (3,180 metric tons) of cargo. A vessel can pass through a lock in 20 minutes. About 2 million short tons (1.8 million metric tons) of goods and thousands of pleasure boats move through the system each year.   WILLIAM E. YOUNG

See also ERIE CANAL.

New York State Department of Transportation

A Series of Five Locks at Waterford, N.Y., above, lifts vessels 169 feet (52 meters) on New York's barge canal system. The system has a total of 57 locks.

NEW YORK UNIVERSITY, in New York City, is a privately endowed nonsectarian coeducational institution. It is one of the largest privately supported universities in the United States. The university offers more than 2,500 courses of study in many subject fields. It has more than 5,000 faculty members.

Nine major divisions of the university are located around Washington Square: two graduate schools (Arts and Science and Public Administration), the School of Continuing Education and Extension Services, Washington Square and University College of Arts and Science, and five professional schools (Law, Education, the Arts, Social Work, and Business and Public Administration).

The New York University Medical Center has a program of medical education, research, and patient care. The College of Dentistry offers instruction and conducts extensive clinics and research units. The Graduate School of Business Administration carries on an extensive educational program for business students and industrial executives. The Institute of Fine Arts specializes in scholarly studies of the history of art and in archaeological investigations. The Courant Institute of Mathematical Sciences is among the world's largest mathematics research and teaching centers. The university was founded in 1831. For enrollment, see UNIVERSITIES AND COLLEGES (table).   JAMES M. HESTER

See also HALL OF FAME.

NEW YORK WORLD'S FAIR has been held twice in New York City. The first fair opened in 1939. Its theme was *The World of Tomorrow,* and its symbols were the *Trylon* (a triangular obelisk 700 feet, or 210 meters, high) and the *Perisphere* (a ball-like structure 200 feet, or 61 meters, wide). The fair was held in Flushing Meadow Park in Queens. It promoted such inventions as television, nylon, and air conditioning. Scheduled to end in 1939, the fair was reopened in 1940 because of its popularity. It attracted almost 45 million persons.

The second New York World's Fair, held in 1964 and 1965, used the theme *Peace Through Understanding.* Its symbol was the *Unisphere* (a stainless steel globe 140 feet, or 43 meters, high). It was held on the same site as the first fair. The inventions displayed at the second fair included color television, picture telephones, computers, and communications satellites. Art treasures were also displayed. Vatican City sent Michelangelo's famous sculpture *Pietà.* The fair attracted about 51 million persons.

See also FAIRS AND EXPOSITIONS (picture: The Unisphere); TIME CAPSULE.

277

New Zealand's Beautiful Countryside provides excellent grazing land for millions of sheep. The nation ranks as one of the world's leading producers of lamb, mutton, and wool.

NEW ZEALAND

NEW ZEALAND is an island country in the Southwest Pacific Ocean. It lies about 1,200 miles (1,930 kilometers) southeast of Australia and about 6,500 miles (10,500 kilometers) southwest of California. New Zealand belongs to a large island group called *Polynesia.*

The country consists of two main islands—the North Island and the South Island—and several dozen much smaller islands. Most of the smaller islands are hundreds of miles or kilometers from the main ones. Altogether, the islands have an area about equal to that of Colorado. Wellington is the capital of New Zealand, and Auckland is the largest city. The country was once part of the British Empire. Today, it is an independent member of the Commonwealth of Nations, an association of countries that replaced the empire.

New Zealand is a beautiful country of snow-capped mountains, green lowlands, beaches, and many lakes and waterfalls. No place is more than 80 miles (130 kilometers) from the coast, and nowhere are mountains or hills out of view. Over three-fourths of the land lies at least 650 feet (198 meters) above sea level.

A brown-skinned people called *Maoris* were the first people to live in New Zealand. They came from Polynesian islands northeast of New Zealand. Europeans discovered the country in 1642, but they did not start to settle in the islands until the late 1700's. Today, most New Zealanders are descendants of early European settlers. About 8 per cent of the people are Maoris. A New Zealander of European descent is known as a

---

Gordon R. Lewthwaite, the contributor of this article, is Professor of Geography at California State University at Northridge.

---

pakeha (pronounced *PAH kay hah*). *Pakeha* is the Maori word for *white man.*

New Zealand's standard of living ranks among the highest in the world. The country has almost no extremely poor or extremely rich people. Most of New Zealand's income comes from the raising of sheep and cattle. The nation's economy depends on foreign trade. Butter, cheese, lamb, and wool are the chief exports.

New Zealand has a long tradition of equal rights and benefits for all its citizens. In 1893, it became the first nation to give women the vote. It was also among the first countries to provide social security benefits and old-age pensions for its people. Today, the nation has one of the world's finest public health programs.

--------------- FACTS IN BRIEF ---------------

Capital: Wellington.

Official Language: English.

Form of Government: Constitutional monarchy.

Area: 103,747 sq. mi. (268,704 km²). *North Island*—44,190 sq. mi. (114,453 km²); *South Island*—58,193 sq. mi. (150,718 km²); *Other Islands*—1,364 sq. mi. (3,533 km²). The North and the South islands extend in a curve more than 1,000 mi. (1,600 km) long. *Coastline*—about 3,200 mi. (5,150 km).

Elevation: *Highest*—Mount Cook, 12,349 ft. (3,764 m) above sea level. *Lowest*—sea level along the coast.

Population: *Estimated 1978 Population*—3,264,000; distribution, 82 per cent urban, 18 per cent rural; density, 31 persons per sq. mi. (12 per km²). *1971 Census*—2,862,631. *Estimated 1983 Population*—3,586,000.

Chief Products: *Agriculture*—butter, cheese, meat, wool. *Manufacturing*—chemicals, machinery, paper and wood pulp, petroleum products, plastics, processed foods, textiles, transportation equipment.

National Anthem: "God Save the Queen" (or "King").

National Song: "God Defend New Zealand."

Money: *Basic Unit*—New Zealand dollar. For its value in U.S. money, see MONEY (table: Values).

New Zealand is a constitutional monarchy. The nation recognizes Queen Elizabeth II of Great Britain as its monarch. The queen appoints a governor general to represent her in New Zealand, but the governor general has little real power. The New Zealand legislature and the prime minister and the Cabinet run the national government.

Great Britain gave New Zealand a constitution in 1852, when it was a British colony. But through the years, the New Zealand legislature has changed almost all its provisions. For all practical purposes, the nation today has no written constitution.

Legislature of New Zealand consists of only one house, the 87-member House of Representatives, also called Parliament. The people in each of 87 *electorates* (voting districts) elect one member of Parliament. Four electorates are reserved for Maori candidates and voters, but a Maori may vote in another electorate if he wishes. A parliamentary election must be held at least every three years, but one may be held sooner. All citizens 18 years old or older may vote.

Prime Minister and Cabinet. The leader of the political party that wins the most seats in a parliamentary election becomes prime minister. The prime minister appoints a Cabinet to run the various government departments. The Cabinet members, called *ministers*, are members of Parliament from the prime minister's party. The prime minister and the Cabinet are called the *Government*. The party that wins the second most seats in an election is called the *Opposition*. The Government proposes most new legislation to Parliament. If Parliament votes in favor of a bill, the bill becomes law. But if the Government loses the support of the majority in Parliament on an important issue, it resigns. Parliament is then dissolved, and a new election is held.

Political Parties. The main political parties in New Zealand are the Labour Party and the National Party. There is no clear division between the policies of the two parties. But in general, the Labour Party favors government control and public regulation of industry, and the National Party favors free enterprise.

Ombudsman is an official selected by Parliament to investigate complaints by New Zealand citizens against government departments. The ombudsman looks into the complaints and sends an opinion to the department involved. If the department does not take the action that the ombudsman believes is needed, the findings may be reported to Parliament. See OMBUDSMAN.

Courts. The Court of Appeal is New Zealand's highest court. It hears only cases that have been appealed from a lower court. The Supreme Court is the second highest court. It handles cases involving serious offenses and most appeals from magistrates' courts. Magistrates' courts, the lowest courts, hear most minor cases.

Local Government. New Zealand is divided into about 110 counties, 140 cities and small urban areas called *boroughs*, and 15 town districts. The voters in each of these units elect a governing council.

Armed Forces. New Zealand's regular army, navy, and air force have a total of about 13,000 men and women. All military service is voluntary.

Nerida F. Ellerton, Tom Stack & Associates

Parliament House in Wellington is the meeting place of the House of Representatives, New Zealand's one-house legislature.

New Zealand's Flag, officially adopted in 1902, features the British Union Flag and the constellation Southern Cross.

Coat of Arms. The symbols on the shield represent the importance of farming, mining, and trade to New Zealand.

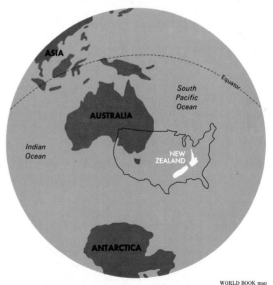

WORLD BOOK map

New Zealand lies about 1,200 miles (1,930 kilometers) southeast of Australia. It has an area about 3 per cent as large as that of the United States, not including Alaska and Hawaii.

Harrison Forman

Residential Sections of Auckland, like those of other New Zealand cities, consist mostly of single-family homes. Auckland is the country's largest city.

New Zealanders believe deeply in equal rights for all citizens. The Maoris and pakehas live in an atmosphere of common trust, and Maori political leaders and professional people play important roles in the life of the nation.

The New Zealand way of life combines an easy informality with a British sense of politeness. New Zealanders have kept close emotional ties to Britain and still follow many British customs. As a result, they have been slow to develop their own feeling of national identity.

Ancestry and Population. New Zealand has a population of over 3¼ million. About 85 per cent of the people were born in New Zealand. Many of them are descendants of British settlers who came to the country during the 1800's. Immigrants still come to New Zealand, chiefly from Britain, Australia, and other English-speaking countries. See IMMIGRATION AND EMIGRATION (Australia and New Zealand).

About 250,000 Maoris live in New Zealand. They make up the country's largest minority group. The Maoris are a Polynesian people whose ancestors came to New Zealand hundreds of years ago.

More than 70 per cent of all New Zealanders live on the North Island, and over 80 per cent live in urban areas. The country has five cities with more than 100,-000 persons. They are, in order of size, Auckland; Christchurch; Wellington, the nation's capital; Dunedin; and Manukau. See AUCKLAND; CHRISTCHURCH; WELLINGTON.

Language. English is the official language of New Zealand and is spoken throughout the country. Most of the people speak English with a New Zealand accent, which resembles a British accent with a slightly nasal sound.

Many Maoris speak their own language, Maori, in addition to English. The Maori language belongs to the Malayo-Polynesian group of languages (see LANGUAGE [Other Language Families]).

Way of Life. The people of New Zealand have a high standard of living. They have long been among the best-fed people in the world. They also receive excellent free health care under the government's medical program. The average annual income in New Zealand is higher than in any other country except the United States and Canada. About 70 per cent of New Zealand families own their homes, and almost every family has a car.

Most New Zealanders live in single-family houses with enough land for small flower or vegetable gardens. In the larger cities, some people live in high-rise apartment buildings. Almost all New Zealand homes have refrigerators, washing machines, and other modern electrical appliances. But few homes have air conditioning or central heating because New Zealand's weather rarely becomes extremely hot or extremely cold. In summer, open windows keep homes cool. In winter, fireplaces or electric heaters keep them warm.

Although about four-fifths of the people live in urban areas, New Zealand's cities are fairly uncrowded. Bad traffic jams seldom occur, even in the downtown areas. New Zealand's large cities have excellent restaurants as well as many *milk bars* (soda fountains) and *pubs* (taverns). These cities also have theaters, concert halls, and other places of entertainment. However, city life in New Zealand tends to be rather quiet. Most

New Zealanders prefer to dine and entertain at home.

About a fifth of New Zealand's people live in rural areas. In some rural areas, small settlements are linked by good roads, and so social contact is easy. But in rugged ranch country, a rancher's nearest neighbors may be many miles or kilometers away. As a result, many ranchers live almost in isolation. Most farms and ranches have electricity to provide light and to operate appliances and machinery. Many farm families run their farms with little or no hired help.

New Zealanders enjoy watching television in the evening, and more than three-fourths of New Zealand homes have TV sets. The nation has four television networks. None of them starts broadcasting before 2 P.M.

Food and Drink. New Zealanders eat more butter and meat per person than do the people of any other country. Lamb is a favorite meat. *Kumaras* (sweet potatoes) often accompany lamb and other meat dishes. A special treat is *toheroa* soup, made from a native green clam. Tea is the favorite drink of most New Zealanders. Beer is the most popular alcoholic beverage.

Recreation. New Zealanders love outdoor activities and sports. Many city families own small *baches* (cabins) in resort areas, where they go on weekends. The nation's mild climate the year around makes camping, hiking, hunting, and mountain climbing possible in any season. Skiing on New Zealand's snow-capped mountains is becoming increasingly popular. Many people also enjoy *cricket*, which somewhat resembles baseball; *Rugby*, a form of football; swimming; and tennis (see CRICKET; RUGBY FOOTBALL).

A Woodcarving School teaches young Maoris one of the chief skills of their ancestors. Maoris were New Zealand's first people.

Yachting along the coasts or on the lakes is a popular activity. Yachting in coastal waters offers the added attraction of fishing for marlin, shark, or swordfish. Such inland waters as Lake Taupo provide year-round trout fishing.

Education. New Zealand offers a free education to all students up to the age of 19. The law requires children from 6 through 14 to attend school, but most youngsters enter school at 5. Many children under 5 attend free kindergartens or play centers. About a tenth of the elementary school students go to private schools, most of which are operated by the Roman Catholic Church.

Some primary schools continue through what would be eighth grade in the United States. Other primary schools go only as far as fifth or sixth grade, and the students then continue in an *intermediate school*. Intermediate schools resemble junior high schools in the United States.

After completing elementary or intermediate school, most students go on to a *secondary school* or a *district high school*. Secondary schools resemble high schools in the United States. District high schools are the last four grades of schools that include all elementary and secondary classes. Secondary students may receive special training in agriculture, home economics, and technical subjects. About a seventh of all secondary students in New Zealand attend private schools. The Roman Catholic Church operates the majority of these schools.

New Zealand's government runs special buses to drive children who live in rural areas to and from school. Students who live too far from a bus route may receive instruction from the New Zealand Correspondence School in Wellington. This government-run school broadcasts daily lessons on the main radio stations. The school also mails lessons to the students, who send their homework back to the teachers.

Rugby Players fight for the ball during a match in Wellington. Rugby is a favorite game of the sports-loving New Zealanders.

280a

G. R. Roberts

New Zealand Children must attend school from age 6 through 14. The country offers a free education to all students to age 19.

G. R. Roberts from Carl E. Östman

Downtown Auckland, like the business areas of other large New Zealand cities, has many modern high-rise office buildings.

New Zealand has six universities—the Victoria University of Wellington and the universities of Auckland, Canterbury, Massey, Otago, and Waikato. Lincoln College is an agricultural college at the University of Canterbury. More than 30,000 students attend the universities. The universities are open to graduates of certain approved secondary schools and to any other student who passes an entrance examination. The government pays all or part of the expenses for about two-thirds of the university students. New Zealand also has nine teachers' colleges with about 6,000 students.

Religion. Many people who immigrated to New Zealand in the 1800's belonged to various church groups. These groups established their own religions in the areas where they settled. For example, members of the Anglican Canterbury Association helped found the city of Christchurch. There, they established the Church of England, which is Episcopal. Members of the Free Church of Scotland helped found Dunedin, where they established the Presbyterian faith. Today, the major religions in various parts of the country still reflect the settlement patterns and faiths of the early colonists and missionaries.

More than 900,000 New Zealanders belong to the Church of England. The country also has about 600,000 Presbyterians, 450,000 Roman Catholics, and 200,000 Methodists. Other religious groups include the Ratana and Ringatu churches of the Maoris. The beliefs of these groups combine Biblical teachings with the ideas of Maori prophets.

The Arts. Hundreds of years ago, the Maoris developed New Zealand's first and most individual arts. Their carefully detailed woodcarvings and poetic legends created a tradition that still continues among the Maoris of today.

When the first Europeans were settling in New Zealand, they had few chances to develop their artistic abilities. The hard work of building a new land left them little time for luxuries—and they looked on the arts as a luxury. The country's newness and its great distance from the old centers of Western culture also made New Zealanders feel apart from artistic developments in other countries. Perhaps for this reason, many New Zealanders tended to consider themselves inferior to the people of Europe and the United States in cultural matters. Most New Zealand artists who wished to develop their talents left their native land to live and work abroad. As late as the early 1900's, such gifted New Zealanders as the writer Katherine Mansfield, the painter Frances Hodgkins, and the political cartoonist Sir David Low moved to England.

Today, a new generation of New Zealand writers is becoming well known both at home and abroad. Such novelists as Sylvia Ashton-Warner and Ian Cross and such poets as James K. Baxter and Allen Curnow express the character of New Zealand and its people. Dame Ngaio Marsh's detective stories have become popular throughout the world.

All of New Zealand's major cities have art galleries and museums. The NZBC Orchestra, the country's national orchestra, is internationally known. Brass bands, choirs, and Scottish bagpipe bands have been popular since the days of the early settlers. Schools and universities teach fine arts, and many communities hold annual arts festivals. During the late 1960's, the pottery created by modern New Zealand potters began to attract the attention of art lovers in other countries.

New Zealand lies in the Southwest Pacific Ocean about 1,200 miles (1,930 kilometers) southeast of Australia. The Tasman Sea, a part of the Pacific, separates the nations. The North Island and the South Island are the largest islands of New Zealand. They cover over 98 per cent of the total area of 103,747 square miles (268,704 square kilometers). Cook Strait, 16 miles (26 kilometers) wide, separates the islands.

Stewart Island lies about 20 miles (32 kilometers) south of the South Island. Foveaux Strait separates the two islands. The Chatham Islands are also part of New Zealand. They lie about 500 miles (800 kilometers) east of the South Island. The nation has dozens of other islands in the South Pacific, but many are small and uninhabited. Inhabited islands include Campbell Island and one of the Kermadec Islands.

New Zealand administers several overseas territories, including Niue Island and the Tokelau Islands. The Cook Islands, once owned by New Zealand, became self-governing in 1965. But New Zealand is still responsible for their defense and foreign relations. For the location of New Zealand's island possessions, see PACIFIC ISLANDS (map). New Zealand also controls the Ross Dependency, a 160,000-square-mile (414,400-square-kilometer) region of Antarctica.

The North Island covers 44,190 square miles (114,453 square kilometers). It can be divided into three main land regions: (1) the Northern Peninsulas and Waikato Basin, (2) the Volcanic Region and Western Hill Country, and (3) the Eastern Hills.

The Northern Peninsulas and Waikato Basin occupy most of the northern part of the island. This region has forests, rich lowlands, citrus orchards, and undeveloped hill country. Long, sandy beaches line the west coast, and many inlets mark the east coast.

The Volcanic Region and Western Hill Country cover the western half of the island south of the Northern Peninsulas and Waikato Basin. Much of the region consists of volcanic rock. A large plateau covered with soft, gray *pumice*—the spongy stone thrown off by volcanoes—rises along the eastern part of the region in the center of the North Island. Active volcanoes in the region include Mount Ngauruhoe, Mount Tongariro, and the highest peak on the island, 9,175-foot (2,797-meter) Mount Ruapehu. This region also has many hot springs and geysers.

The Eastern Hills occupy the eastern part of the North Island. A mountain system runs through the region from East Cape to Cook Strait. The eastern slopes consist mainly of rugged hills, used for grazing sheep and beef cattle. The western slopes are greener and more fertile and are used for raising dairy cattle and lambs.

The South Island covers 58,193 square miles (150,718 square kilometers). It has three main regions: (1) the Southern Alps and High Country, (2) the Canterbury Plains, and (3) the Otago Plateaus and Basins.

The Southern Alps and High Country cover most of the island. The highest peak in New Zealand, 12,349-foot (3,764-meter) Mount Cook, rises in the Southern Alps. The Maoris named Mount Cook *Aorangi*, meaning the *cloud piercer*. The Mount Cook region has some of New Zealand's most beautiful and spectacular scenery. Gla-

Bill Noel Kleeman, Tom Stack & Associates

The Fertile Canterbury Plains make up New Zealand's chief grain-growing region. The plains lie along the east coast of the South Island. Farmland covers about two-thirds of the country. Most of this land is hilly or mountainous and is used to raise livestock, especially sheep.

NEW ZEALAND

ciers lie on mountain slopes high above thick, green forests. Sparkling lakes nestle in valleys throughout the Southern Alps and High Country region.

The western slopes of the Southern Alps and High Country region are rainy and rugged. The eastern slopes are lower and much less rainy than the western slopes. Rain forests cover most of the entire region. Along the southwest coast, long inlets of the sea, called *fiords*, cut into the land. They create a jagged coastline. Granite mountains border many of the fiords.

The Canterbury Plains lie along the east-central coast of the South Island. They form New Zealand's largest area of flat or nearly flat land and make up the chief grain-growing region. The plains are laid out in a patchwork of fields of barley, fodder crops, oats, and wheat.

The Otago Plateaus and Basins, in the island's southeast corner, is a region of plains and rolling hills.

Other Islands. Stewart Island occupies 670 square miles (1,735 square kilometers). Many trees once grew there. But most of them have been cut down for timber, and scrubby bushes now cover much of the land. Several hundred persons live on Stewart Island. Most earn their living by fishing and oyster gathering.

The Chatham Islands cover 372 square miles (963 square kilometers). About 700 persons, most of them Maoris, live on the islands. Fishing and sheep farming are their main occupations. For descriptions of other New Zealand islands, see KERMADEC ISLANDS; NIUE ISLAND; TOKELAU ISLANDS.

LAND REGIONS OF NEW ZEALAND

The map below shows the six land regions of New Zealand: the Northern Peninsulas and Waikato Basin, the Volcanic Region and Western Hill Country, the Eastern Hills, the Southern Alps and High Country, the Canterbury Plains, and the Otago Plateaus and Basins.

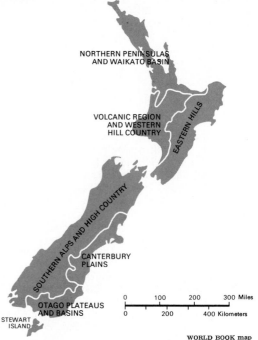

WORLD BOOK map

NEW ZEALAND MAP INDEX

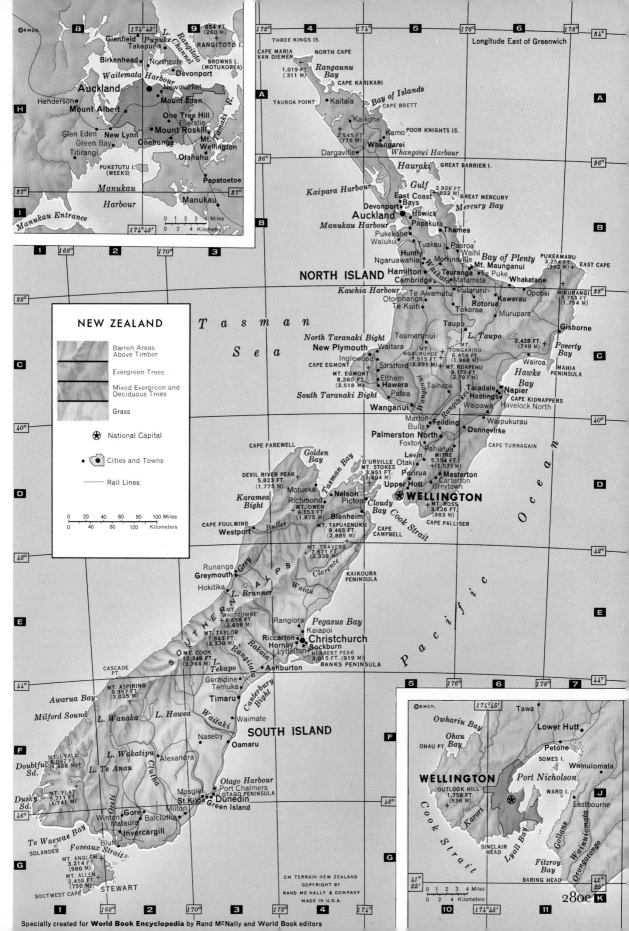

Coastline. New Zealand's coastline is about 3,200 miles (5,150 kilometers) long. Including the bays, fiords, and gulfs, the full length of the coast is about 4,300 miles (6,920 kilometers). Auckland and Wellington, the nation's chief seaports, overlook fine natural harbors on the North Island. The South Island has a few natural inlets in areas where seaports would be useful.

Lakes, Rivers, and Waterfalls are found throughout New Zealand. Most of the lakes lie in the volcanic plateau of the North Island and in glacial valleys near the Southern Alps of the South Island. The largest lake, Lake Taupo on the North Island, covers 234 square miles (606 square kilometers) and is a vacation spot.

On both islands, the rivers rise in the mountains and flow down to the sea. Most of the rivers flow very fast and are difficult to navigate. The Waikato River on the North Island is New Zealand's longest river, flowing 264 miles (425 kilometers). The Clutha River on the South Island carries the largest volume of water. The rapid flow of New Zealand's rivers makes them important sources of hydroelectric power.

New Zealand has hundreds of waterfalls. Sutherland Falls tumbles 1,904 feet (580 meters) down a mountain near Milford Sound on the South Island. It is the fifth highest waterfall in the world.

Animal Life. Most of New Zealand's animals have been introduced from other countries. Deer and rabbits —as well as cattle, pigs, and sheep—were all brought by the European settlers. Two species of bats are the only native land mammals. New Zealand has no snakes. But the tuatara, a native prehistoric reptile, still lives in New Zealand (see ANIMAL [picture: The Tuatara]).

Brian Carroll, Photographic Library of Australia

Natural Steam rises from a large volcanic plateau in the center of the North Island. Engineers harness the *geothermal steam* to generate electricity. The region also has geysers and hot springs.

New Zealand's lakes and rivers are well stocked with salmon and trout brought from other countries.

New Zealand has many native birds, including such flightless species as the kakapo parrot, kiwi, takahe, and weka. The kiwi may be the best known of all New Zealand birds, partly because *Kiwi* is a nickname for a New Zealander. The kiwi is the only known bird with nostrils in the tip of its bill. The kea, a parrot that can fly, is noted for its playfulness with human beings. New Zealand once had many ostrichlike moas, but they have become extinct. See KEA; KIWI; MOA.

Plant Life. The native forests of New Zealand consist mainly of evergreen trees and tree ferns. Volcanic eruptions in prehistoric times destroyed large areas of forest in the central plateau of the North Island. As a result, small shrubs, such as the manuka, now cover much of the region. Forests of pinelike kauri trees once thrived on the Northland Peninsula, but the early European settlers cut down so many of the trees that they almost destroyed the kauri forests. Yet many evergreen trees, including some kauris, still flourish in parts of both the North Island and the South Island. Beech forests grow on the cooler uplands of both islands.

Since 1900, many foreign trees have been introduced into New Zealand. The country's lumber industry depends mainly on the fast-growing radiata pine, originally imported from California.

J. Alex Langley, DPI

Majestic Mount Cook, New Zealand's highest mountain, soars 12,349 feet (3,764 meters) on the South Island. Mount Cook and hundreds of other peaks attract many mountain climbers.

New Zealand has a mild, moist climate like that of the Pacific Northwest Coast of the United States. But New Zealand lies south of the equator, and so its seasons are opposite those of the Northern Hemisphere. July is New Zealand's coldest month, and January and February are its warmest months. The country's mild climate results from ocean breezes that bring warmth to the land in winter and coolness in summer. Summer temperatures range from about 65° F. (18° C) to about 85° F. (29° C). Winter temperatures range from about 35° F. (2° C) to about 55° F. (13° C). Rain falls throughout the year. The amount varies little from month to month, but some regions regularly receive much more rain than others. Throughout New Zealand, the weather shifts suddenly from sunny to rainy and back to sunny again.

Climate Regions. Although New Zealand overall has a mild, rainy climate, the climate differs in various parts of the country. On the North Island, the Northland Peninsula is warm and humid the year around. But the island's central plateau has hot, sunny weather in summer and sharp frosts with occasional snow in winter. Wellington lies exposed to the frequent gales of Cook Strait. On the South Island, the rainy west contrasts with the drier east. The southern areas of the South Island average about 8° F. (4° C) cooler than the northern parts of the North Island. In mountain regions, temperatures are about 4° F. (2° C) cooler with each 1,000-foot (300-meter) increase in altitude. The interiors of both islands have cooler winters and warmer summers than the coastal regions.

Rainfall. The mountains chiefly control the distribution of rainfall in New Zealand. Winds from the west carry moisture from the ocean. This moisture falls as rain on the western slopes of the mountain ranges. Almost the entire west coast averages more than 100 inches (250 centimeters) of rain a year. Milford Sound, on the South Island, receives up to 300 inches (760 centimeters) a year. East of the mountains, the winds have lost most of their moisture. Some eastern regions average less than 20 inches (51 centimeters) of rain a year. Severe thunderstorms rarely occur in New Zealand. Snow seldom falls in lowland areas, though some mountain peaks remain snow-capped all year.

Earthquakes. New Zealand has about 400 earthquakes every year, but only about 100 of them are even strong enough to be felt. The country's most disastrous earthquake occurred in Hawke Bay in 1931. It killed 255 persons and badly damaged the cities of Hastings and Napier.

AVERAGE MONTHLY WEATHER

	AUCKLAND						CHRISTCHURCH				
	Temperatures				Days of Rain or Snow		Temperatures				Days of Rain or Snow
	F.° High	F.° Low	C° High	C° Low			F.° High	F.° Low	C° High	C° Low	
JAN.	79	53	26	12	10	JAN.	86	41	30	5	10
FEB.	79	53	26	12	10	FEB.	83	41	28	5	8
MAR.	77	51	25	11	11	MAR.	81	37	27	3	9
APR.	73	47	23	8	14	APR.	76	33	24	1	10
MAY	67	42	19	6	19	MAY	69	29	21	-2	12
JUNE	63	39	17	4	19	JUNE	62	26	17	-3	13
JULY	62	38	17	3	21	JULY	61	26	16	-3	13
AUG.	63	39	17	4	19	AUG.	65	26	18	-3	11
SEPT.	65	41	18	5	17	SEPT.	70	30	21	-1	10
OCT.	68	44	20	7	16	OCT.	76	32	24	0	10
NOV.	73	47	23	8	15	NOV.	79	36	26	2	10
DEC.	76	50	24	10	12	DEC.	84	39	29	4	10

Source: Meteorological Office, London.

The economy of New Zealand depends mainly on farming and foreign trade. The sale of butter, cheese, meat, and wool to other countries, particularly to Great Britain, provides most of the nation's income. But manufacturing has been increasing rapidly, and about twice as many New Zealanders work in factories as on farms.

Natural Resources. New Zealand's greatest natural resource is its land. About a third of the land consists of fertile cropland and rich pastureland. Another third is covered with forests that provide valuable timber and with grasses that offer fair grazing for farm animals. The remaining third consists of lakes, rivers, and unproductive mountain areas.

New Zealand has few minerals. The most important include coal, iron ore, and natural gas. The country also has a little copper, gold, silver, and tungsten.

Water power provides about 85 per cent of the nation's electricity. On the North Island, eight dams along the Waikato River are used to produce elec-

David Moore, Black Star

Special Airplane Flights take skiers to the top of Tasman Glacier, a popular ski area on the South Island. The country's many sports and scenic attractions have created a boom in tourism.

tricity. The Clutha and Waitaki rivers of the South Island have also been harnessed to provide hydroelectric power. A cable under Cook Strait carries electricity produced on the South Island to the more heavily populated North Island.

The underground steam in the volcanic area of the North Island is becoming an increasingly important source of power. Near Wairakei, engineers have drilled more than 60 deep holes to release *geothermal steam* for electric power plants.

Agriculture. New Zealand produces enough meat and dairy products to feed its own people as well as mil-lions of persons in other countries. The high farm production results from the country's mild climate the year around and the use of modern machinery and scientific farming methods.

New Zealand has more than 55 million sheep and almost 9 million cattle. It has about 25 times as many farm animals as people. No other country has so many farm animals in relation to its population. The size of farms varies with the type of farm and its location. A dairy farm in the lowlands may cover fewer than 100 acres (40 hectares), and a sheep ranch in the mountains up to 50,000 acres (20,000 hectares). But on the average, a dairy farm covers 147 acres (59 hectares) and a sheep ranch 1,141 acres (462 hectares).

Agriculture and Industry in New Zealand

This map shows how New Zealand uses its natural resources. Agriculture is the nation's chief economic activity and the source of most of its raw materials. Most of the land serves as pastures for sheep and cattle. Hydroelectric plants provide most of New Zealand's power supply. *Geothermal* power (underground steam) is becoming an increasingly important source of electricity.

- Mainly pasture
- Mainly pasture and cropland
- Mainly forest
- Mainly garden farming
- Mainly barren
- ● Manufacturing center

New Zealand's Gross National Product

Total gross national product in 1970—$5,327,800,000

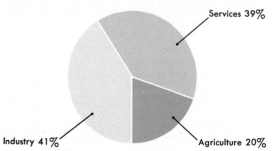

Services 39%
Industry 41%
Agriculture 20%

The gross national product (GNP) is the total value of goods and services produced by a country in a year. The GNP measures a nation's total annual economic performance. It can also be used to study economic trends and to compare the economic output and growth of countries.

Production and Workers by Economic Activities

Economic Activities	Per Cent of GDP Produced*	Employed Workers Number of Persons	Employed Workers Per Cent of Total
Other Services	39	202,400	19
Manufacturing	26	298,500	28
Agriculture	19	127,200	12
Construction	13	86,300	8
Forestry	1	7,400	1
Mining	1	6,900	1
Utilities	1	16,000	1
Fishing & Hunting	†	3,400	†
Finance, Insurance, & Real Estate	**	31,100	3
Government	**	40,800	4
Trade	**	158,000	14
Transportation & Communication	**	97,600	9
Total	100	1,075,600	100

*1968, latest information available. GDP is gross domestic product (gross national product plus net income from abroad).
†Less than 1 per cent.
**Included in Other Services.
Source: Department of Statistics, Wellington, N.Z.

0   100   200 Miles
0   100   200 Kilometres
WORLD BOOK map

Sheep are raised both for meat and for wool. Other products obtained from sheep include sausage *casings* (coverings), sheepskins, and *tallow* (animal fat). Cattle are almost as important as sheep. The country has almost 4 million dairy cattle and more than 5 million beef cattle. Dairy products account for a large share of the nation's income, but beef production is minor. Most of the beef cattle are kept on sheep ranches to help control weed growth.

Barley, corn, oats, and wheat are New Zealand's chief grain crops. Farmers also grow large quantities of apples and pears.

Manufacturing. New Zealand's chief manufactured products are agricultural, electrical, and woodworking machinery and transportation equipment. The country's factories also process dairy products and wool and freeze meat for export. Other manufactured items include chemicals, paper and petroleum products, plastics, and textiles. Auckland is the country's largest manufacturing center.

Forestry. New Zealand loggers cut down more than 700 million board feet (1.7 million cubic meters) of timber yearly. Most of this timber comes from the radiata pine, which grows mainly on the North Island's volcanic plateau. Native evergreen trees provide less than a third of the country's timber. The most important of these trees is the pinelike rimu.

Fishing Industry. Snapper and tarakihi are the chief fish caught in New Zealand waters. They are found off the coasts of the main islands. Fishermen sell most of their catch to local markets. But New Zealand also exports some of the fish, both fresh and frozen, to Australia. New Zealanders catch crayfish off the coasts of the main islands as well as off the coasts of the Chatham

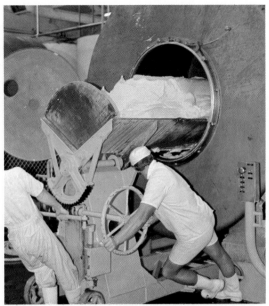

Bill Noel Kleeman, Tom Stack & Associates

Dairy Workers unload a huge batch of freshly churned butter at one of New Zealand's many creameries. Butter and other dairy products account for a large share of the country's exports.

Islands. Most of the crayfish are also sold to local markets, but the export of frozen crayfish tails to the United States is increasing steadily.

Trade. New Zealand's economy depends heavily on trade with other nations, especially its main trading partner, Great Britain. Other trading partners include Australia, Japan, and the United States. Butter, cheese, lamb, and wool make up about 85 per cent of the value of New Zealand's exports. Other exports include grass seed, logs, paper, and wood pulp. The country's chief imports include coffee, fruits, manufactured goods, tea, textile fibers, and vegetables.

Transportation and Communication. New Zealand has over 58,000 miles (93,300 kilometers) of roads, of which about 23,000 miles (37,000 kilometers) are paved. Nearly a million New Zealanders own a car.

The government owns New Zealand's two major airlines and its railroads. The National Airways Corporation handles domestic flights, and Air New Zealand operates international flights. The nation has more than 3,000 miles (4,800 kilometers) of railroad. Several ferries carry passengers, automobiles, and railroad cars between the North Island and the South Island. Auckland and Wellington are the nation's busiest seaports.

The New Zealand Post Office handles most communications. It operates the country's telephone and telegraph systems in addition to handling the mail. New Zealand has 8 major daily newspapers in the large metropolitan areas and more than 30 dailies in the smaller towns. The largest daily newspaper, Auckland's *New Zealand Herald*, has a circulation of about 210,000 copies. The government owns the nation's 2 TV networks and 45 of its 50 radio stations.

David Moore, Black Star

Sheep, New Zealand's Most Important Farm Animals, are raised for meat and wool. This rancher on the South Island is separating a flock into groups for fattening and shearing.

The first people to live in New Zealand were the Maoris. They probably came to the country by canoes from the Cook, Marquesas, or Society islands, which lie northeast of New Zealand. No one knows when or why the Maoris first came, but some of them may have arrived in New Zealand by A.D. 750. According to Maori legend, the hero Maui created the North Island by fishing it up from the sea.

The first Maoris lived mainly by fishing and hunting. They have been named the *moa hunters* because they chiefly hunted the giant, wingless birds called *moas*. Other groups of Maoris came to New Zealand after 750, but historians do not know exactly when. Some Maoris almost certainly arrived in the 1300's. By then, the moa hunters had killed most of the moas. The later Maoris developed a culture based on agriculture as well as on fishing and hunting. They were skilled woodcarvers and, working with stone tools, created highly elaborate carvings.

Discovery by Europeans. In 1642, the Dutch sea captain Abel Janszoon Tasman became the first European to sight New Zealand. He tried to send a group of men ashore, but Maoris attacked their two small landing craft and killed several of the men. Tasman made no further attempt to land. The Dutch named the islands *Nieuw Zeeland* after a province in The Netherlands. No other European came to New Zealand until 1769, when Captain James Cook of the British navy landed on the North Island. Cook made friends with the Maoris and explored and charted both the North Island and the South Island. The Maoris kept no written records, and so the written history of New Zealand dates back only to Cook's time.

Colonization. Explorers from France, Spain, and other countries visited New Zealand during the late 1700's. By 1790, the seals and whales in New Zealand's coastal waters had begun to attract American, Austral-

ian, and European hunters. Traders also came to buy flax and kauri timber from the Maoris. Some of the hunters and traders were convicts from the British penal colony at Sydney, Australia. These hunters and traders, almost all of them British, became the first colonists in New Zealand. In 1814, the first of many missionary groups to settle in the country arrived from Sydney. New Zealand had no legal government, and it remained a lawless frontier country until 1840.

The arrival of the foreigners brought great suffering to the Maoris. The pakehas introduced firearms, which increased the warfare among the Maori tribes. The newcomers also brought diseases against which the Maoris had no resistance. By 1840, warfare and disease had reduced the Maori population from about 200,000 to a little more than 100,000.

By the 1830's, British settlers and a number of Maoris had begun to ask Great Britain to provide law and order in New Zealand. But Britain hesitated to take action in a land it did not own. Finally, on Feb. 6, 1840, Captain William Hobson of the British navy and a group of Maori chiefs signed the Treaty of Waitangi. The treaty provided that the Maoris accept the British queen, Victoria, as their ruler in return for British protection of all Maori rights, including property rights. Under the treaty, the Maoris gave Britain *sovereignty* (control) over New Zealand, though some Maoris did not realize this at the time. Hobson became New Zealand's first governor. Soon after he signed the treaty, Hobson declared New Zealand to be a British colony.

Meanwhile, a British businessman, Edward Gibbon Wakefield, had formed the New Zealand Company in Great Britain to colonize the islands. Wakefield's company established colonies at Wellington and Wanganui in 1840 and at New Plymouth and Nelson in 1841. The company also joined with the Free Church of Scotland to establish Dunedin in 1848, and it joined with the

De Moordenaars Baay (The Murderers' Bay) (1726), an engraving by François Valentyn; Alexander Turnbull Library, Wellington, New Zealand

Discovery by Europeans. In 1642, Abel Janszoon Tasman, a Dutch sea captain, sailed his two ships along the New Zealand coast and became the first European to sight the country. He tried to send some men ashore, but Maoris in canoes killed several of them. Tasman made no further effort to land.

Anglican Canterbury Association to found Christchurch in 1850.

The South Island began to prosper soon after New Zealand became a colony. Few Maoris lived on the South Island, and so there was much available land that the settlers could buy or rent from the government. The island's rich grasslands provided good grazing for sheep imported from Australia, and soon the settlers could export wool. In 1861, gold was discovered in Otago. Immigrants poured into the country, hoping to strike it rich. Few miners found as much gold as they hoped for, but many stayed to become farmers. Farming developed rapidly on the South Island, and soon wheat was also being exported.

The Maori Wars. Settlers on the North Island had troubles almost at once. The thick forests made land clearance slow. Also, most of the Maoris lived on the North Island, and tension soon mounted between settlers who wanted to buy land and Maoris who did not want to sell. In 1845, Hone Heke, a Maori chief, headed an uprising on the North Island. The newly appointed governor, Sir George Grey, defeated Hone Heke in 1846. But racial tensions continued as many Maoris still refused to sell their land to pakehas. In 1858, to symbolize their unity, several Maori tribes joined to choose Chief Te Wherowhero as their king. War broke out again in 1860 and spread through much of the North Island. The fighting continued off and on until 1872, when the Maori leader Te Kooti was forced to

retreat. He withdrew to a remote area of the island, where the British troops decided not to pursue him.

During the Maori Wars, the government seized some areas of Maori land for public use. The Maoris' morale was shaken by their defeat and the seizure of their lands. Also, diseases continued to reduce their population.

Depression and Social Reform. For a short time after the Maori Wars, New Zealand prospered. But in the late 1870's, gold production declined and the prices of wheat and wool fell. By 1880, the country was in an economic depression that lasted until the 1890's.

In 1890, the Liberal Party won control of the New Zealand government. The party remained in power for 22 years. During this period, the Liberals carried out an extensive program of social reform. The Liberal reforms included old-age pensions, regulation of wages and working conditions, and the required settlement of disputes between workers and employers by an outside *arbitration court*. The Liberals also introduced taxes on income and land. In 1893, New Zealand became the first country to give women the vote.

Dominion Status. In the early 1900's, New Zealanders began to develop a sense of national identity. In 1907, Britain granted New Zealand's request to become a *dominion*, a self-governing country within the British Empire (see DOMINION).

Meanwhile, New Zealand had begun to prosper again. Agricultural production increased, and new refrigeration methods made it possible to ship large

---

——— IMPORTANT DATES IN NEW ZEALAND ———

A.D. 750 The first Maoris may have arrived in New Zealand.

1642 Abel Janszoon Tasman became the first European to sight New Zealand.

1769 Captain James Cook explored New Zealand's main islands.

1840 The Maoris signed the Treaty of Waitangi, which gave Great Britain sovereignty over New Zealand.

1845-1872 Settlers on the North Island fought the Maoris in the Maori Wars.

1852 Britain granted New Zealand a constitution.

1861 The New Zealand gold rush began.

1890 The New Zealand government started a program of social reform.

1907 New Zealand became a dominion within the British Empire.

1914-1918 New Zealand fought with the Allies against Germany in World War I.

1936-1938 The New Zealand government set up a social security program that included health care for all citizens.

1939-1945 New Zealand fought with the Allies against Germany, Italy, and Japan in World War II.

1945 New Zealand became a founding member of the United Nations (UN).

1951 New Zealand signed the ANZUS treaty.

1967 New Zealand changed its basic unit of money from the pound to the New Zealand dollar.

1973 New Zealand began increasing its trade with other countries after Great Britain—its chief trading partner—joined the European Economic Community.

The Treaty of Waitangi, a water color by Leonard C. Mitchell; Alexander Turnbull Library, Wellington, New Zealand

The Treaty of Waitangi was signed by Great Britain and the Maoris on Feb. 6, 1840. It gave Britain sovereignty over New Zealand in return for the protection of Maori rights.

quantities of butter, cheese, and meat to Britain. The Maoris were recovering in health and morale, and immigrants poured into the country. During World War I (1914-1918), New Zealand sent more than 100,000 troops overseas to fight with the Allies against Germany.

The Great Depression. The worldwide depression that started in 1929 hit New Zealand hard. By 1931, the value of the nation's exports had fallen 40 per cent. Many people lost their jobs. The National Party, then in power, took steps to help the country recover, but the depression dragged on. In 1935, the people voted the Labour Party into power. To help bring about relief and recovery, the Labour Party started a large public works program and guaranteed farmers minimum prices for their products. From 1936 to 1938, the government set up a social security program that included health care for all citizens and special benefits for the aged, children, and widows.

The Mid-1900's. During World War II (1939-1945), about 140,000 New Zealand troops fought with the Allies against Germany, Italy, and Japan. The war helped New Zealanders realize how close their country was to Japan and other Asian countries and how far it was from Britain. They became more aware that New Zealand's ties of friendship to Britain were not enough to guarantee them protection from an enemy nation.

In 1945, New Zealand became a founding member of the United Nations (UN). In 1951, New Zealand signed the ANZUS collective defense treaty with Australia and the United States. In 1954, the nation joined the Southeast Asia Treaty Organization (SEATO). New Zealand troops fought with the UN forces in the Korean War in the early 1950's, and a few combat units from New Zealand fought in the Vietnam War in the 1960's.

Until 1967, New Zealand's basic unit of currency was the New Zealand pound. The pound represented New Zealand's link to Britain and to the British *pound sterling* (see MONEY [Money Around the World]). In 1967, New Zealand adopted the New Zealand dollar as its basic unit of currency. In so doing, the nation took another step toward establishing its individuality.

New Zealand Today. New Zealand has avoided or reduced many of the problems that face other countries, such as environmental pollution, poverty, racial conflict, and urban overcrowding. The nation hopes to prevent such problems from becoming serious. New Zealand's top goals for the 1970's include conserving the environment, creating new job opportunities for its growing population, and helping more Maoris obtain positions of leadership in industry and the professions.

One of New Zealand's major concerns is finding new overseas markets for its dairy and meat products. In 1973, New Zealand's chief trading partner, Great Britain, joined the European Economic Community. This organization of European nations has no tariffs on trade among its members, but it does have a common tariff on goods imported from other countries (see EUROPEAN COMMUNITY). Thus, New Zealand can no longer rely heavily on British markets. New Zealand also hopes to increase the variety of its manufactured goods and to find overseas markets for such new products.

Sir Keith J. Holyoake, head of the National Party, served as prime minister from 1960 until he retired early

in 1972. John Ross Marshall, a Cabinet member, succeeded him. Later that year, the Labour Party won control of the government. Norman Eric Kirk, the party leader, became prime minister. Kirk died in 1974. Wallace E. Rowling, a member of the Cabinet, succeeded him. In 1975, the people voted the National Party into power. Robert D. Muldoon, the party's leader, became prime minister.   GORDON R. LEWTHWAITE

NEW ZEALAND / Study Aids

Related Articles in WORLD BOOK include:

BIOGRAPHIES

Hillary, Sir Edmund P.	Rutherford, Ernest
Holyoake, Sir Keith J.	Tasman, Abel J.
Mansfield, Katherine	Walpole, Sir Hugh S.
Muldoon, Robert D.	

CITIES

Auckland	Christchurch	Wellington

ISLANDS

Auckland Islands	Kermadec Islands	Tokelau Islands
Cook Islands	Niue Island	

OTHER RELATED ARTICLES

ANZUS	Moa	Southeast Asia Treaty
Colombo Plan	Mount Cook	Organization
Kea	Pacific Islands	Sutherland Falls
Kiwi	Ross Dependency	Tasman Sea
Maoris	Sheep	

Outline

I. Government
 A. Legislature
 B. Prime Minister and Cabinet
 C. Political Parties
 D. Ombudsman
 E. Courts
 F. Local Government
 G. Armed Forces

II. People
 A. Ancestry and Population
 B. Language
 C. Way of Life
 D. Food and Drink
 E. Recreation
 F. Education
 G. Religion
 H. The Arts

III. The Land
 A. The North Island
 B. The South Island
 C. Other Islands
 D. Coastline
 E. Lakes, Rivers, and Waterfalls
 F. Animal Life
 G. Plant Life

IV. Climate
 A. Climate Regions
 B. Rainfall
 C. Earthquakes

V. Economy
 A. Natural Resources
 B. Agriculture
 C. Manufacturing
 D. Forestry
 E. Fishing Industry
 F. Trade
 G. Transportation and Communication

VI. History

Questions

Who were the first people to live in New Zealand?

What is New Zealand's greatest natural resource?

What is an *ombudsman*?

Why do few New Zealand homes have central heating or air conditioning?

What flightless birds are native to New Zealand?

How do most persons on Stewart Island earn their living?

What were the terms of the Treaty of Waitangi?

What are New Zealand's most important farm animals?

What city is New Zealand's largest manufacturing center?

Who was the first European to sight New Zealand?

NEWARK, Del. (pop. 21,298), is one of the major fiber-making centers of the United States. It also manufactures fine book papers, and has an automobile-assembly plant. Newark lies in northern Delaware, about halfway between New York City and Washington, D.C. For location, see DELAWARE (political map). It is the home of the University of Delaware. Newark was chartered in 1758. It has a council-manager government.   JOHN A. MUNROE

NEWARK, N.J. (pop. 381,930; met. area pop. 2,057,-468), is the largest city in the state and one of the nation's leading centers of manufacturing and transportation. Newark lies on Newark Bay at the mouth of the Passaic River, about 10 miles (16 kilometers) west of New York City. For location, see NEW JERSEY (political map).

In 1666, 30 Puritan families from the Connecticut Colony settled in what is now eastern New Jersey. Developers of the area had offered them religious freedom and cheap farmland. The settlers founded a village on the Passaic because the site included a harbor and level, unforested land. They named the village Newark— probably for Newark-on-Trent, the English town where their pastor had entered the ministry.

The City. Newark, the county seat of Essex County, covers about 25 square miles (65 square kilometers). The Newark metropolitan area consists of all of Essex, Morris, Somerset, and Union counties and covers about 1,020 square miles (2,642 square kilometers).

Downtown Newark includes the city's tallest building, the 36-story Midatlantic National Bank. Nearby stands the First Presbyterian Church, Newark's oldest house of worship, completed in 1791. The Gateway, a group of office buildings and a hotel, rises in the eastern downtown area.

Blacks make up about 55 per cent of Newark's population. The city also has many people of Italian, Portuguese, or Puerto Rican descent. Large religious groups in Newark include Baptists and Roman Catholics.

Economy. The Newark metropolitan area has more than 4,000 manufacturing plants that employ about 25 per cent of the labor force. The production of drugs and chemicals ranks as the leading industrial activity. Newark also manufactures electric equipment, processed food, metal products, and nonelectric machinery.

Newark International Airport, a major air cargo center, lies at the south end of town. Port Newark, a leading New Jersey port, handles the ships of more than 100 ship companies. Passenger and freight railroads and about 240 trucking firms serve the city.

Newark ranks as the nation's third largest insurance center. Only companies in Hartford, Conn., and New York City sell more insurance. Newark is the home of Prudential Insurance Company of America, the largest of its kind in the world. The city also serves as New Jersey's leading center of finance and trade. Newark has five radio stations, two television stations, and one daily newspaper, the *Star-Ledger.*

Education and Cultural Life. Newark's public school system includes about 55 elementary schools and about 10 high schools. Blacks make up about 70 per cent of the public school enrollment. Spanish-speaking students account for another 15 per cent. The city has about 30 parochial and private schools. Institutions of higher learning include the College of Medicine and Dentistry

New Jersey Newsphotos

Newark, N.J., lies on the west bank of the Passaic River, *rear,* where the river flows into Newark Bay. The city forms the center of a large industrial area in northeastern New Jersey.

of New Jersey; the New Jersey Institute of Technology; the Newark campus of Rutgers, the State University; and the Seton Hall University School of Law.

The New Jersey Symphony Orchestra and the Opera Theater of New Jersey perform in Symphony Hall. The Newark Public Library has 8 branch libraries. The Newark Museum features art collections, exhibits of science and industry, and a planetarium. The New Jersey Historical Society has a museum of historic items.

Newark has about 50 parks. The largest one, Branch Brook Park, covers 486 acres (197 hectares) and includes about 3,500 cherry trees.

Government. Newark has a mayor-council form of government. The voters elect a mayor and nine council members, all to four-year terms. Property taxes are the city's leading source of income.

History. Delaware Indians lived in what is now the Newark area before white settlers first arrived in 1666. The city's industrial development began in the mid-1700's, when ironmakers began processing ore from nearby mines. During the late 1700's, a number of tanners settled in Newark. The area had many hemlock trees, which furnished the bark used in making leather. By the early 1800's, about a third of the labor force worked in shoemaking and other leather industries.

The work of Seth Boyden, a Newark inventor, helped the city grow industrially during the early 1800's. Boyden developed such products as patent leather and an improved kind of cast iron. Advances in transportation also contributed to Newark's industrial growth. For example, the Morris Canal, completed in 1831, linked Newark with coal-mining areas in the Lehigh Valley of Pennsylvania. By 1834, a railroad connected

285

NEWBERRY, WALTER LOOMIS

Newark and the Hudson River, which separates New Jersey and New York City. Newark had a population of 19,732 when it was incorporated in 1836.

From 1840 to 1860, many German and Irish immigrants settled in Newark to fill the growing number of industrial jobs. By 1860, the city had 71,941 people. A wave of immigration that began in the late 1880's brought thousands of Eastern and Southern Europeans to Newark. In 1910, the city had 347,469 persons.

Port Newark opened in 1915, during World War I. Newark's chemical industry, which began in the 1870's, expanded greatly during the war and the 1920's. In 1930, the population reached a record 442,337.

During the Great Depression of the 1930's, more than 600 Newark factories closed down and many neighborhoods became shabby. During World War II (1939-1945), jobs in defense plants attracted thousands of Southern Negroes to Newark. Blacks crowded into the city's run-down areas. Beginning in the 1950's, many middle-income families moved from Newark to the suburbs. The city's population fell to 405,220 by 1960.

By the mid-1960's, Newark had a large proportion of poor people. The city lacked money to provide adequate services. Almost half the voters were blacks, but they had little political power. As a result, racial tensions mounted. In July, 1967, five days of rioting shook the Negro section of Newark. The riots caused 26 deaths and from $10 to $15 million in property damage. Blacks had charged that widespread dishonesty existed in the city government. A series of investigations following the riots led to the conviction of Mayor Hugh Addonizio and other politicians for sharing illegal refunds on city contracts. In 1970, the voters elected Newark's first black mayor, Kenneth A. Gibson, who had been city engineer.

In 1971, a dispute over working conditions developed between white Newark teachers and the city's board of education. As a result of appointments made by Gibson, the board had a majority of black and Puerto Rican members. The dispute led to an 11-week strike by the teachers, the longest in the history of a major U.S. city. This strike increased racial tension in Newark. Gibson was re-elected mayor in 1974.

During the 1970's, Newark leaders worked to increase the city's job opportunities and improve its housing. The federal and state governments contributed large amounts of money to help with such problems. A series of urban renewal projects that began in the 1960's resulted in the construction of some factories and office buildings. Newark has a larger proportion of government-financed housing than any other major U.S. city. Several new university campuses and huge airport and seaport expansion projects were scheduled for completion in the 1970's.   HENRY A. STASIUK

For the monthly weather in Newark, see NEW JERSEY (Climate).

NEWBERRY, WALTER LOOMIS (1804-1868), was an American businessman and philanthropist. He left about half of his fortune to found the Newberry Library in Chicago (see NEWBERRY LIBRARY).

Newberry was born in East (now South) Windsor, Conn. His family moved to Sangerfield, N.Y., when he was a year old. He had little schooling, and went to work in his brother's store when he was 16. The two moved to Detroit, Mich., in 1826, where they built up a prosperous dry-goods business. Later, Newberry became interested in Chicago, which was then only a tiny trading community. He moved to Chicago in 1833, and made a fortune in real estate.   ROBERT H. BREMNER

NEWBERRY LIBRARY is a privately supported research library in Chicago. It specializes in books and manuscripts on literature, languages, history, genealogy, and music. The institution has about 850,000 volumes. Outstanding collections include the Edward E. Ayer collection on American Indians, the John M. Wing collection on printing, and the Louis H. Silver collection on European history and literature. The library, founded by Walter L. Newberry, opened in 1887. It is at 60 W. Walton Place, Chicago, Ill., 60610.

NEWBERY, JOHN (1713-1767), was an English publisher and bookseller. He is famous in the history of children's literature as the first person to print and sell books for children. He published *Mother Goose's Melody* and *Goody-Two-Shoes* (1765) and many other little volumes bound in "flowery gilt," a gay paper imported from The Netherlands. Many of Newbery's books were reprinted in America between 1749 and 1831.

Newbery's bookshop, The Bible and Sun, was in St. Paul's Churchyard, London. He was the friend and patron of Oliver Goldsmith, Samuel Johnson, and many other literary men of his day. Goldsmith portrayed him in his novel, *The Vicar of Wakefield* (1766). It is believed that Goldsmith wrote some of the quaint penny books published by Newbery. These little books are now highly prized. Thomas Babington Macaulay, a famous English essayist of the 1800's, called Newbery the "friend of children."

Newbery was born in Berkshire. The Newbery medal, which has been awarded each year since 1922 for the finest children's book written by an American, was named for him (see NEWBERY MEDAL).   JEAN THOMSON

See also LITERATURE FOR CHILDREN (The 1700's); MOTHER GOOSE.

NEWBERY MEDAL is an annual award given to the author of the most distinguished contribution to American children's literature published in the preceding year. The award was established and endowed in 1921 by Frederic G. Melcher, chairman of the board of R. R. Bowker Co., publishers of the *Library Journal* and *Publishers' Weekly*. He named it for John Newbery, an English publisher and bookseller. Melcher also founded the Caldecott medal. This award is presented annually to the illustrator of the outstanding children's picture book of the preceding year.

The Newbery Medal

Year	Author	Winning Book	Year	Author	Winning Book
1922	Hendrik Van Loon	*The Story of Mankind*	1952	Eleanor Estes	*Ginger Pye*
1923	Hugh Lofting	*The Voyages of Dr. Dolittle*	1953	Ann Nolan Clark	*Secret of the Andes*
1924	Charles Hawes	*The Dark Frigate*	1954	Joseph Krumgold	*. . . And Now Miguel*
1925	Charles Finger	*Tales from Silver Lands*	1955	Meindert DeJong	*The Wheel on the School*
1926	Arthur Chrisman	*Shen of the Sea*	1956	Jean Lee Latham	*Carry on, Mr. Bowditch*
1927	Will James	*Smoky*	1957	Virginia Sorensen	*Miracles on Maple Hill*
1928	Dhan Mukerji	*Gay-Neck*	1958	Harold V. Keith	*Rifles for Watie*
1929	Eric P. Kelly	*The Trumpeter of Krakow*	1959	Elizabeth G. Speare	*The Witch of Blackbird Pond*
1930	Rachel Field	*Hitty, Her First Hundred Years*	1960	Joseph Krumgold	*Onion John*
1931	Elizabeth Coatsworth	*The Cat Who Went to Heaven*	1961	Scott O'Dell	*Island of the Blue Dolphins*
1932	Laura Armer	*Waterless Mountain*	1962	Elizabeth G. Speare	*The Bronze Bow*
1933	Elizabeth Lewis	*Young Fu of the Upper Yangtze*	1963	Madeleine L'Engle	*A Wrinkle in Time*
1934	Cornelia Meigs	*Invincible Louisa*	1964	Emily C. Neville	*It's Like This, Cat*
1935	Monica Shannon	*Dobry*	1965	Maia Wojciechowska	*Shadow of a Bull*
1936	Carol Ryrie Brink	*Caddie Woodlawn*	1966	Elizabeth Borton de Treviño	*I, Juan de Pareja*
1937	Ruth Sawyer	*Roller Skates*	1967	Irene Hunt	*Up a Road Slowly*
1938	Kate Seredy	*The White Stag*	1968	Elaine Konigsburg	*From the Mixed-Up Files of Mrs. Basil E. Frankweiler*
1939	Elizabeth Enright	*Thimble Summer*			
1940	James Daugherty	*Daniel Boone*	1969	Lloyd Alexander	*The High King*
1941	Armstrong Sperry	*Call It Courage*	1970	William H. Armstrong	*Sounder*
1942	Walter D. Edmonds	*The Matchlock Gun*	1971	Betsy Byars	*The Summer of the Swans*
1943	Elizabeth Janet Gray	*Adam of the Road*	1972	Robert C. O'Brien	*Mrs. Frisby and the Rats of NIMH*
1944	Esther Forbes	*Johnny Tremain*			
1945	Robert Lawson	*Rabbit Hill*	1973	Jean C. George	*Julie of the Wolves*
1946	Lois Lenski	*Strawberry Girl*	1974	Paula Fox	*The Slave Dancer*
1947	Carolyn S. Bailey	*Miss Hickory*	1975	Virginia Hamilton	*M.C. Higgins, the Great*
1948	William Pène du Bois	*The Twenty-One Balloons*	1976	Susan Cooper	*The Grey King*
1949	Marguerite Henry	*King of the Wind*	1977	Mildred Taylor	*Roll of Thunder, Hear My Cry*
1950	Marguerite de Angeli	*The Door in the Wall*			
1951	Elizabeth Yates	*Amos Fortune, Free Man*			

Each author has a separate biography in WORLD BOOK.

René Chambellan designed the medal. It is awarded by the Children's Services Division of the American Library Association. ANNE J. RICHTER

See also NEWBERY, JOHN; MELCHER, FREDERIC GERSHOM; CALDECOTT MEDAL.

NEWCASTLE (pop. 249,962) is at the mouth of the Hunter River in New South Wales, Australia (see AUSTRALIA [political map]). It is the second largest city and the chief coal-mining town of the state of New South Wales. Newcastle exports chiefly coal, iron and steel, wool, timber, copper, and agricultural products.

NEWCASTLE UPON TYNE (pop. 217,220; met. area pop. 797,750) is one of the chief coal centers of England. It has given to the English language the expression "carrying coals to Newcastle," which means taking something to a place that already has more of it than is needed. Newcastle lies in northern England, near the North Sea (see GREAT BRITAIN [political map]).

The city received its name from a castle built by the son of William the Conqueror about 1080. Shipbuilding and the manufacture of locomotives are among the chief industries. FRANCIS H. HERRICK

NEWCOMB, *NOO kum,* **SIMON** (1835-1909), was an American astronomer. He became famous for his studies of the motions of the moon and other heavenly bodies.

In 1861, Newcomb was named professor of mathematics by the U.S. Navy, and assigned to the Naval Observatory in Washington, D.C. There, he supervised the construction of a 26-inch (66-centimeter) equatorial telescope. With George W. Hill, he used this telescope to determine the orbits of the moon, Venus, Mars, Uranus, Neptune, and Saturn.

From 1880 to 1882, Newcomb conducted experiments on the velocity of light. He used fixed and revolving mirrors on opposite banks of the Potomac River to gain his result of 186,328 miles (299,866 kilometers) per second.

Newcomb was born in Wallace, Nova Scotia, and came to the United States in 1853. He studied at Harvard University. From 1884 to 1894 and from 1898 to 1900, he served as a professor of mathematics at Johns Hopkins University. HELEN WRIGHT

NEWCOMEN, THOMAS (1663-1729), an English inventor, built one of the first practical steam engines in 1712. His atmospheric-pressure steam engine was used to pump water from British mines for almost 75 years. It was gradually replaced by James Watt's separate condenser engine (see WATT, JAMES).

Newcomen's was the first known engine to use a piston successfully. A water jet inside the piston cylinder condensed the steam, creating a vacuum. Air pressure then pushed the piston head into the vacuum. This engine was safer and more efficient than a similar machine designed by Thomas Savery and used at the time, because it avoided high steam pressures and wasted less fuel. Newcomen later worked with Savery in producing and building the new engine.

Newcomen was born in Dartmouth, England. He worked as a blacksmith until the problem of draining water from English tin mines caught his interest. According to tradition, Robert Hooke, the famous English scientist, directed Newcomen's attention to developing a steam engine that could drain the mines. Many Newcomen engines were used in Great Britain and on the continent of Europe. ROBERT E. SCHOFIELD

See also STEAM ENGINE; HOOKE, ROBERT.

Open Pit Mines Contain Labrador's Rich Iron Ore Deposits.

George Hunter, Shostal

N E W F O U N D L A N D

NEWFOUNDLAND, *new fun LAND*, is Canada's newest province. It includes the island of Newfoundland and the coast of Labrador, a part of the Canadian mainland. Newfoundland became a province of Canada in 1949. St. John's is the capital and largest city of Newfoundland. This bustling city ranks among the oldest communities in North America.

Fewer persons live in Newfoundland than in any other province except Prince Edward Island. Most of Newfoundland's land is rugged, especially along the rocky coast. Thick forests grow along tumbling rivers and around sparkling blue lakes. Barren, rocky ridges rise above the green valleys. The ridges surround many brown *peat bogs* (swamps of decayed plants). Arctic winds and ocean currents chill the land and keep the climate generally cool. Storms occur frequently, and fog often covers the coast.

Almost all Newfoundlanders live near the sea. Hundreds of villages and fishing settlements nestle in small, sheltered bays along the jagged coast. Some places, too small to appear on maps, have such unusual names as Blow-Me-Down, Little Heart's Ease, and Dragon Bay. One of the world's largest factories that produces paper for newspapers is in Corner Brook.

Most Newfoundlanders belong to families that originally came from the British Isles. The people of many lonely fishing settlements have kept much of the language and customs of their forefathers. Newfoundland fishermen are famed as a people made hardy by their struggle to earn a living from the sea.

Cod, salmon, and other fishes thrive along Newfoundland's shores. The fishing fleets of some nations sail halfway around the world to fish in an area called the Grand Banks, southeast of Newfoundland. Sportsmen come to the province to catch salmon in the streams or bluefin tuna in the offshore waters. Caribou and moose roam the wilderness areas. In winter, seals sun themselves on ice packs that drift down from the north.

Mining is Newfoundland's chief source of income. Miners dig iron ore and other minerals from deposits that rank among the world's largest. Manufacturing is also an important industry. Food processors prepare salted and frozen fish, and pack live lobsters for shipment to other countries. Manufacturers use the province's extensive timber resources to produce wood pulp and paper.

Newfoundland has a longer history than any other region of North America where the people speak English. Viking adventurers may have established settlements in Newfoundland as early as A.D. 1000. Sailors from the English port of Bristol probably reached the island of Newfoundland in 1481. In 1497, John Cabot, an Italian explorer in the service of England, sailed through the rich fishing grounds near Newfoundland. He brought news of the fishing grounds back to Europe. The fisheries attracted many fishermen, and some of them settled on the island. Newfoundland is sometimes called "Britain's oldest colony." But Great Britain considered Newfoundland only a fishing ground for English ships. It did not recognize Newfoundland as a colony until 1824.

For the relationship of Newfoundland to the other provinces, see CANADA; CANADA, GOVERNMENT OF; CANADA, HISTORY OF. See also LABRADOR.

The contributors of this article are Gordon Oliver Rothney, Professor of History at the University of Manitoba (formerly of the Memorial University of Newfoundland); Arch Sullivan, former writer for the Newfoundland Herald, *CJON radio and CJON-TV; and William F. Summers, Professor and Head of the Department of Geography at the Memorial University of Newfoundland.*

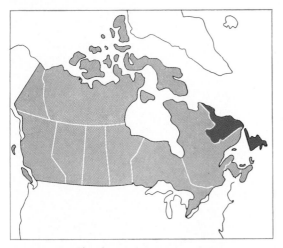

Newfoundland (blue) ranks seventh in size among the Canadian provinces, and is the largest of the Atlantic, or Maritime, Provinces.

FACTS IN BRIEF

Capital: St. John's.

Government: *Parliament*—senators, 6; members of the House of Commons, 7. *Provincial*—members of the House of Assembly, 51. *Voting Age*—19 years (provincial elections); 18 years (national elections).

Area: 156,185 sq. mi. (404,517 km²); the island of Newfoundland, 43,359 sq. mi. (112,299 km²); Labrador, 112,826 sq. mi. (292,218 km²); 7th in size among the provinces. *Greatest Distances*—north-south, the island of Newfoundland, 326 mi. (525 km); Labrador, 650 mi. (1,046 km); east-west, the island of Newfoundland, 320 mi. (515 km); Labrador, 450 mi. (724 km). *Coastline*—the island of Newfoundland, 8,495 mi. (13,676 km); Labrador, 9,498 mi. (15,286 km).

Elevation: *Highest*—5,232 ft. (1,595 m) above sea level in northern Labrador. *Lowest*—sea level.

Population: *1976 Census*—557,725, 9th among the provinces; density, 4 persons per sq. mi. (2 per km²); distribution, 57 per cent urban, 43 per cent rural.

Chief Products: *Manufacturing*—chemicals and chemical products; fabricated metal products; food and beverage products; paper and paper products; printed materials; stone, clay, and glass products; wood products. *Mining*—asbestos, copper, fluorspar, iron ore, lead, sand and gravel, zinc. *Fishing Industry*—cod, herring, lobster, redfish, salmon, turbot. *Agriculture*—blueberries, cranberries, eggs.

Entered the Dominion: March 31, 1949, the 10th province.

Provincial Motto: *Quaerite Prime Regnum Dei* (Seek Ye First the Kingdom of God).

Provincial Song: "The Ode to Newfoundland." Words by Sir Cavendish Boyle; music by Sir Hubert Parry.

Trinity, a Fishing Village on Trinity Bay

Malak, Miller Services

The Legislative Assembly Meets in the Confederation Building

NEWFOUNDLAND/Government

Lieutenant Governor of Newfoundland must approve all laws and executive orders. This position is largely honorary, like that of the governor general of Canada. The lieutenant governor always acts on the advice of the premier. The lieutenant governor is appointed by the governor general in council and serves as the representative of Queen Elizabeth in the province.

Premier of Newfoundland is the actual head of the government. The premier is a member of the Legislative Assembly, and is usually the leader of a political party. The premier must have the support of a majority of the Assembly. The premier receives $21,280 a year, in addition to allowances given to members of the Assembly.

The premier presides over the Executive Council, or Cabinet. The council includes ministers chosen by the premier, usually from among members of the premier's party in the Legislative Assembly. Most ministers direct one or more branches of the provincial government. The Executive Council, like the premier, must have the support of the majority of the Assembly. Otherwise, it must resign, or else its supporters must win a majority of seats in the Assembly in a new general election.

Legislative Assembly makes the provincial laws. This one-house legislature has 51 members. Voters in each of the province's 51 Assembly districts elect one member. Elections must be held at least once every five years. Usually, the lieutenant governor calls for the election after a shorter time, on the advice of the premier.

Courts of Newfoundland include the Supreme Court, district courts, and provincial courts. The Supreme Court consists of a chief justice and three other judges. Members of the Supreme Court and judges of the four district courts are appointed by the Canadian governor general in council. The lieutenant governor of Newfoundland appoints justices of the provincial courts.

Local Government. St. John's and Corner Brook, Newfoundland's only cities, operate under special city charters. Each of the province's towns and rural districts is governed by an elected council. Town councils have from 5 to 10 members who serve four-year terms. In some areas, the whole community meets once a year to elect a governing body called a community council. In other areas, trustees appointed by the lieutenant governor handle municipal duties.

Taxation. Federal grants, corporation taxes, and personal income taxes account for most of Newfoundland's income. The rest comes from service fees and from sales taxes on gasoline, tobacco products, alcoholic beverages, and other products. The province also collects license fees and royalties on the use of natural resources.

Politics. Newfoundland has two major political parties, the Liberals and the Progressive Conservatives. The Liberals gained power in 1949, when Newfoundland became a province, and held it throughout the 1950's and 1960's under the leadership of Premier Joseph R. Smallwood. The Conservatives won power in 1971 and formed their first government the next year.

290

The Provincial Coat of Arms

The Provincial Flag

Symbols of Newfoundland. On the coat of arms, *above*, the shield has two lions and two unicorns, which represent Newfoundland's ties to Great Britain. The Indians symbolize the province's first inhabitants. The coat of arms was granted by King Charles I of England in 1638. The British Union Jack, *above right*, was adopted as the provincial flag in 1952.

The Floral Emblem
Pitcher Plant

Confederation Building is in St. John's, Newfoundland's capital since 1729. The building serves as government headquarters, and the legislature meets there.

Newfoundland Tourist Development Office

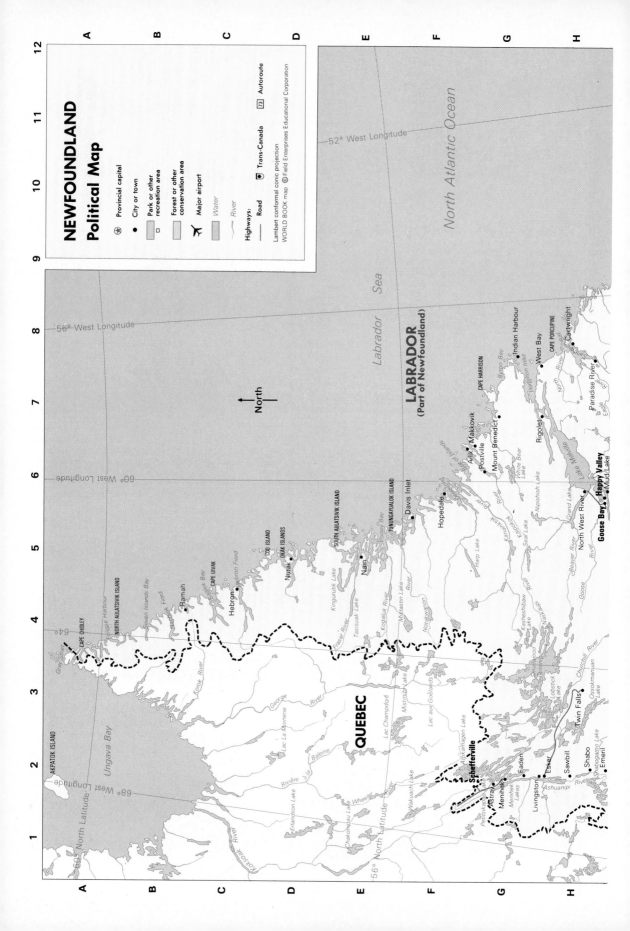

NEWFOUNDLAND
Political Map

⊕ Provincial capital

• City or town

▢ Park or other recreation area

▢ Forest or other conservation area

✈ Major airport

Water

River

Highways:

Road

◉ Trans-Canada

73 Autoroute

Lambert conformal conic projection
WORLD BOOK map © Field Enterprises Educational Corporation

North Atlantic Ocean

Labrador Sea

LABRADOR
(Part of Newfoundland)

QUEBEC

North

52° West Longitude

56° West Longitude

60° West Longitude

64° West Longitude

68° West Longitude

64° North Latitude

56° North Latitude

AKPATOK ISLAND

Ungava Bay

NORTH AULATSIVIK ISLAND

CAPE CHIDLEY

Gray Strait

Seven Islands Bay

Ramah

Saglek Bay

Hebron Fiord

Nachvak Fiord

CAPE UIVAK

COD ISLAND

OKAK ISLANDS

Nutak

SOUTH AULATSIVIK ISLAND

Nain

TUNUNGAYUALOK ISLAND

Davis Inlet

Okkak Bay

Voisey Bay

Hopedale

Hillsbury Bay

Kingurutik Lake

Kogaluk River

Fraser River

Tasisuak Lake

Mistastin Lake

Notakwanon River

Kokok River

George River

Rivière à la Baleine

Erlandson Lake

Lac La Monerie

Lac Champdoré

Lac aux Goélands

Mistinibi Lake

Chakonipau Lake

Wakuach Lake

Wheeler River

Koksoak River

Indian Harbour

West Bay

CAPE PORCUPINE

Cartwright

Paradise River

Eagle River

Hamilton Inlet

CAPE HARRISON

Makkovik

Aillik

Postville

Mount Benedict

Rigolet

Brop Bay

White Bear Lake

Lake Melville

North West River

Goose Bay · Happy Valley

Mud Lake

Grand Lake

Beaver River

Seal Lake

Naskaupi River

Nipishish Lake

Harp Lake

Kanairiktok River

Kenamu River

Grand Lake

Goose River

Churchill River

Lobstick Lake

Ossokmanuan Lake

Twin Falls

Chekogamio Lake

Emeril

Shabo

Sawbill

Esker

Livingston

Ashuanipi River

Faden

Menihek

Astray

Menihek Lakes

Attikamagen Lake

Petitsikapau Lake

Scheffervillle

North

A B C D E F G H

1 2 3 4 5 6 7 8 9 10 11 12

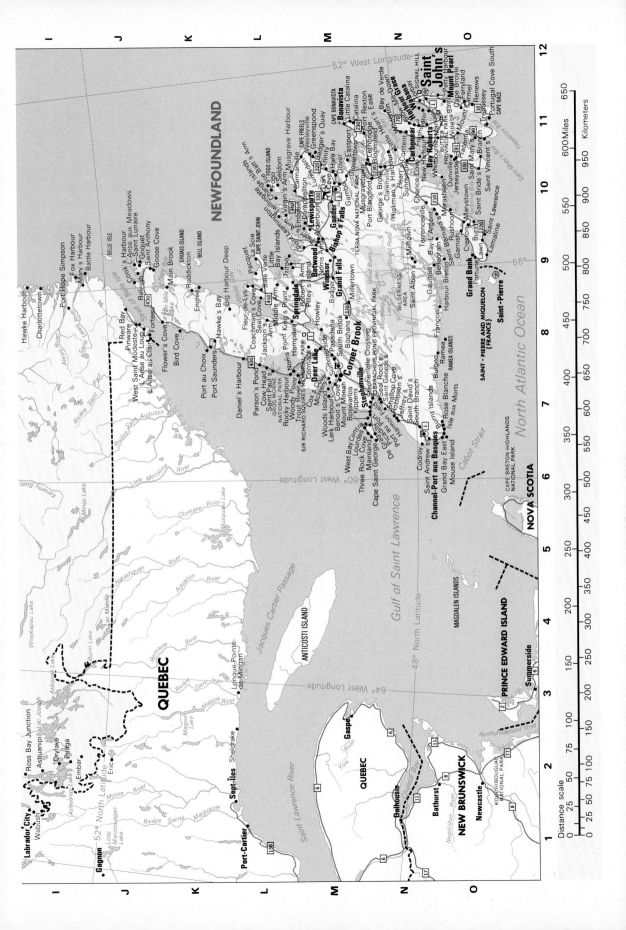

NEWFOUNDLAND/People

The 1976 Canadian census reported that Newfoundland had 557,725 persons. The population of the province had increased 7 per cent over the 1971 figure, 522,104. Most persons in Newfoundland are of English, Irish, Scottish, or French descent.

St. John's, on the Avalon Peninsula, is Newfoundland's capital and largest city. It is the center of the province's only Census Metropolitan Area as defined by Statistics Canada. For the population of this metropolitan area, see the *Index* to the political map of Newfoundland. About 40 of every 100 persons live on the Avalon Peninsula.

Corner Brook is Newfoundland's only other city. About three-fourths of Newfoundland's people live in communities with populations of more than 1,000 persons. Almost all these settlements lie near the coast. Only about 3 of every 100 Newfoundlanders live in communities on the coast of Labrador. See the articles on Newfoundland cities and towns listed in the *Related Articles* at the end of this article.

Less than 2 per cent of Newfoundland's population was born outside Canada. Most of these persons came to the province from England, Scotland, and the United States. The churches with the largest memberships in Newfoundland are, in order of size, the Roman Catholic Church, the Anglican Church of Canada, and the United Church of Canada. Many persons in Newfoundland also belong to the Salvation Army and to Pentecostal assemblies.

POPULATION

This map shows the *population density* of Newfoundland, and how it varies in different parts of the province. Population density is the average number of persons who live in a given area.

	Persons per sq. mi.	Persons per km²
▓	More than 30	More than 12
▒	1 to 30	1 to 12
░	Less than 1	Less than 1

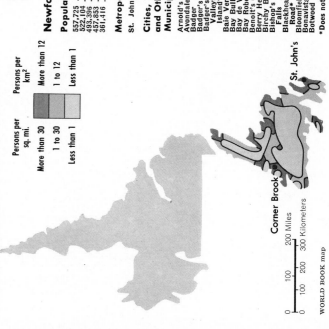

Corner Brook

St. John's

0   100   200 Miles
0   100   200   300 Kilometers

WORLD BOOK map

Newfoundland Map Index

Population

557,725	...Census	...1976
522,104	"	...1971
493,396	"	...1966
457,853	"	...1961
361,416	"	...1951

Metropolitan Area

St. John's 143,390

Cities, Towns, and Other Municipalities

Arnold's Cove 1,141..N10
Avondale* ......912..O11
Badger ....1,136..M9
Badger's Quay 904..M11
Valleyfield–Pool's
  Island* .....1,409..M11
Baie Verte ...2,462..L9
Bay Bulls* ...744..O11
Bay de Verde ...744..N11
Bay Roberts 3,997..O11
Benoit's Cove 1,187..M7
Birchy Head* ...907..N7
Bishop's Bay* ...624..M10
Bishop's
  Falls ....4,419..M9
Blackhead
  Road* ....1,672..N11
Bloomfield ....597..N10
Bonavista ...4,257..M11
Botwood .....4,484..M9

Brigus* ....859..O11
Buchans ......1,907..M8
Burgeo ....2,449..O8
Burin* ....2,779..O7
Burnt Islands 748..M10
Campbellton ...748..M9
Cape Broyle ...677..O11
Cape St. George–Pe-
  tit Jardin–Grand
  Jardin* ....1,697..N7
Carbonear ...4,920..N11
Carmanville ...903..M10
Cartwright ....663..H8
Catalina ....1,113..M11
Centreville* ...677..M11
Chamberlains* 988..O11
Channel–Port aux
  Basques ...6,080..O7
Chapel Arm* ...704..O11
Churchill* .....603..O11
Clarenville ...2,770..N10
Clarke's
  Beach* ......986..O11
Collier's* .....816..O11
Comfort Cove–
  Newstead* ...724..L9
Conception Bay
  South* .....9,559..O11
Conception
  Harbour* .....897..O11
Cormack* ......561..M8
Corner
  Brook ....24,798..M8
Cox's Cove .....633..L8
Cupids* ....741..O11
Daniel's
  Harbour .....570..L8

Dark Cove ...1,198..M10
Dark Cove–
  Middle Brook
Deer Lake* ..4,457..M8
De Grau* .....549..N7
Dildo* ....873..O11
Dover* ....947..M10
Dunville ....1,856..O11
Durrell* .....1,130..L10
Eastport ......560..M10
Embree ....848..M10
Englee ....970..K9
Ferryland* ....766..O11
Flat Rock* ....735..O11
Fleur-de-Lys* ...690..L9
Fogo ....1,083..L10
Fortune .....2,358..O7
Fox Cove–
  Mortier* ....488..O7
Fox Harbour* ...622..O11
Foxtrap* ....1,398..O11
Freshwater* ...631..M7
Freshwater–
  Long Cove* 1,312..M9
Gander ......9,117..M10
Garnish ....665..O9
Gaskiers–Point
  La Have* ....627..N10
Gaultois ....548..O9
Glenwood* ...1,105..M10
Glovertown ..2,247..M10
Goulds* .....3,211..O11
Grand Bank 3,745..O9
Grand Falls 8,786..M9
Green's
  Harbour* .....710..N11
Halfway Point–
  Benoit's Cove–John's
  Beach* .....1,005..M7
Hampden ....773..M8

Gambo* ......2,942..M10

*Does not appear on map; key shows general location.

Happy Valley–
  Goose Bay* 8,114..H6
Harbour
  Breton .....2,269..O9
Harbour
  Grace ......2,900..N11
Harbour
  Main* ......1,294..O11
Hare Bay ....1,588..M10
Harmon* .....1,525..N7
Heart's
  Content ......627..N11
Heart's Delight–
  Islington* ....823..N11
Hermitage* ....823..O9
Holyrood* ...1,598..O11
Horwood* ......878..M10
Irishtown* .....694..M7
Jersey aux
  Morts* .....1,243..O7
Jerseyside .....1,044..O11
Joe Batt's Arm 886..L10
Joe Batt's Arm–Barr'd
  Islands* ...1,010..L10
Kelligrews* ...2,046..O11
Kilbride* ....2,148..N11
Kippens* .....1,247..L7
King's Point ...762..L9
La Scie ......1,246..L9
Labrador
  City ....11,877..I2
Lark Harbour ...764..M7
Lawn ....1,003..O9
Leading Tickles
  West* ....589..M10
Lethbridge ....657..N11
Lewisporte ..3,746..M10
Little Catalina 728..M11
Long Harbour–
  Mount Arling-
  ton Heights* ...671..N11
Long Pond* ..1,758..O11
Lourdes* ......591..M7
Lumsden* .....591..M10
Manuels .....1,006..O11
Marystown ...5,823..O10
Marysvale* ....650..O11
Meadows* ......631..M7
Middle Arm ....850..L9
Middle Brook* ...875..M10
Milltown* ......560..O9
Milltown–Head of Bay
  d'Espoir* ..1,310..M9
Mount Carmel–
  Catherine's* ...662..O11
Mitchells Brook–St.
Mount Moriah 693..M7
Mount Pearl 10,053..N11
Musgrave
  Harbour ...1,517..M10
Musgravetown* 636..N10
Nain* ....804..E5
New Harbour ...704..N11
Norman's Cove–
  Long Cove* 1,136..O11
Norris Arm ...1,312..M9
Norris Point 1,047..M8
North West
  River* ......1,008..H6
Old Perlican* ...611..N11
Paradise* ...2,098..N11
Pasadena ...1,794..M8
Peterview* ...1,086..M9
Petty Harbour–
  Maddox
  Cove* ....910..O11
Piccadilly ......558..N7
Placentia ...2,064..O11
Point Leaming-
  ton ....875..M9

Port au Choix 1,077..K8
Port au Port West–
  Aquathuna–
  Felix Cove* ...986..N7
Port Blandford 799..N10
Port Hope
  Simpson ......545..I8
Port Saunders 680..K8
Port Union* ...666..M11
Portugal
  Cove* ......1,411..N11
Pouch Cove* 1,523..O11
Ramea ....1,217..O8
Robert's Arm 1,058..M9
Rocky
  Harbour ...1,244..L8
Roddickton ..1,205..K9
Rose Blanche .703..O7
Rose Blanche–Harbour
  Le Cou* ......957..O7
St. Alban's ..2,219..N9
St. Anthony 2,941..J9
St. Bernard's ...607..O10
St. Bride's ....573..O11
St. George's 1,953..N7
St. Jacques–Coomb's
  Cove* ......1,055..O9
St. John's ..86,576..N11
St. Lawrence 2,185..O9
St. Lunaire–
  Griquet* ......899..J9
St. Vincent's ...593..O11
Stephen–Peter's
  River* ....839..N11
Salmon Cove* ...728..N11
Seal Cove .....763..L9
Seldom–Little
  Seldom* ......518..L10
Shoal Har-
  bour* .....1,000..N10
Small Point–Bread
  Cove* ....672..N11
South Brook ...821..M8
Southern
  Harbour* .....752..N10
Spaniard's
  Bay* ......1,565..N11
Springdale ...3,454..M9
Stephenville 10,102..N7
Stephenville
  Crossing ...2,154..N7
Summerford* 1,085..L10
Summerside ...824..M8
Sunnyside .....717..N10
Terrenceville ...756..O10
Tilton* ....571..N11
Topsail* ......888..O11
Torbay ......2,839..N11
Trepassey ...1,403..O11
Trinity ....554..M11
Triton–Jim's Cove–Cards
  Harbour* ..1,079..L10
Trout River ..1,771..M7
Twillingate 1,385..L10
Upper Island* 728..O11
Victoria* ...1,746..N11
Virgin's Arm ...603..L10
Wabana .....4,745..N11
Wabush .....3,723..I2
Wedgewood
  Park* ......1,226..N11
Wesleyville ..1,149..M11
Whitbourne 1,251..O11
Windsor .....6,283..M9
Winterton .....768..N11
Witless Bay ...754..O11

Source: Latest available census figures (all 1976 census, except 1971 census for unincorporated places).

NEWFOUNDLAND /Education

Schools in Newfoundland are organized mainly on the basis of the province's religious denominations. Pentecostal, Roman Catholic, and Seventh Day Adventist denominations each operate one of Newfoundland's four consolidated school boards. The fourth board is operated jointly by Anglican, Presbyterian, Salvation Army, and United Church of Canada groups.

The provincial department of education supervises the four consolidated school boards. The minister of education, a member of the provincial Cabinet, directs the department. Newfoundland established the department of education in 1920.

Provincial law requires children to attend school from age 7 through 15. The provincial government pays almost all educational costs. Local taxes and assessments that are collected by some school districts pay for the rest. For the number of students and teachers in Newfoundland, see EDUCATION (table).

The province has one university—Memorial University of Newfoundland in St. John's. The university also maintains a two-year regional college in Corner Brook. See MEMORIAL UNIVERSITY OF NEWFOUNDLAND.

Libraries and Museums. In 1934, Newfoundland established its first public library, the Gosling Memorial Library in St. John's. Today, the province has about 100 libraries. The Arts and Culture Centre in St. John's has one of the finest libraries in Newfoundland. The Newfoundland Museum in St. John's features historical exhibits including relics of the Beothuk Indians. The Military and Naval Museum, also in St. John's, features weapons from early battles fought in the Newfoundland area. An aviation exhibit at Gander Airport has displays dealing with pioneer transatlantic flights. The Southern Newfoundland Seaman's Museum in Grand Bank has exhibits on the maritime history of Newfoundland's southern coast.

Houses of St. John's line the streets in areas familiar to such famous early explorers as Jacques Cartier and Sir Humphrey Gilbert. St. John's, inhabited in the 1500's, is one of the oldest continuously occupied North American cities. It serves as Newfoundland's capital, and is the commercial center of the province.

Fishermen Stop for Lunch in their open boat. Newfoundland's expert fishing crews do much of their fishing in the narrow strip of coastal waters near the shore. These waters provide enormous catches of such important fishes as cod, herring, and salmon.

The Memorial University of Newfoundland lies on a spacious campus in St. John's. It was founded as Memorial University College in 1925 and became a degree-granting university in 1949.

St. John's on the Atlantic Coast

NEWFOUNDLAND / A Visitor's Guide

Newfoundland's many bays and inlets offer camera fans a variety of colorful scenes. The blue waters of the bays may be rimmed by a sprawling city, wooded hills, or barren rocks. The resorts are all near the sea. Guides lead sportsmen inland to hunt bears, caribou, and moose, or to fish for salmon and trout.

PLACES TO VISIT

Following are brief descriptions of some of Newfoundland's most interesting places to visit.

Gander Airport, one of the finest terminals for air travel in Canada, includes a museum of transatlantic aviation.

L'Anse aux Meadows, near St. Lunaire in northern Newfoundland, was the site of a Viking village about A.D. 1000.

Placentia, on the west coast of the Avalon Peninsula, was established by the French in 1662. Prime Minister Winston Churchill and President Franklin D. Roosevelt drew up the Atlantic Charter on a warship near Placentia in 1941.

Port au Choix, on the Great Northern Peninsula, is the site of an Indian burial ground that is 4,000 years old.

Port de Grave Peninsula, in Conception Bay, is one of Newfoundland's most scenic areas. It attracts many artists and photographers.

Witless Bay, a small fishing village 20 miles (32 kilo-meters) south of St. John's, offers boat trips to sea bird nesting colonies on offshore islands.

National Parks and Sites. Newfoundland has two national parks—Gros Morne and Terra Nova. Gros Morne lies on the west coast, and Terra Nova is on the eastern shore. National historic parks and sites include Castle Hill near Placentia and Cape Spear and Signal Hill, both near St. John's. For the features of these parks and sites, see CANADA (National Park System).

Newfoundland has 44 provincial parks. The largest is Butter Pot Park, on the Avalon Peninsula. Barachois Pond Park lies near St. George's, in the middle of the towering Long Range Mountains. Sir Richard Squires Memorial Park, located on the Humber River, includes the famous Big Falls. Every spring, Atlantic salmon make spectacular jumps up the falls to reach their *spawning* (egg-laying) grounds upstream. For information on the provincial parks of Newfoundland, write to Chief Parks Officer, Department of Tourism, St. John's, Nfld.

Boats in a Harbor
on Conception Bay

Malak, Miller Services

Placentia Bay West of
the Avalon Peninsula
Horwood, Miller Services

Signal Hill Overlooking
the Harbor of St. John's

Jackson, Miller Services

ANNUAL EVENTS

Newfoundlanders observe Memorial Day on the Sunday nearest July 1. This day honors the Newfoundland regiment that was almost wiped out by German troops in the 1916 Battle of Beaumont-Hamel in France. Other annual events in Newfoundland include the following.

January-March: Kiwanis Music Festival in St. John's (February); St. Patrick's Day celebrations (March 17).

April-June: St. George's Day celebrations, throughout the province (April 23); Drama Festival in St. John's (May).

July-September: Regattas at Harbour Grace and Placentia (July); Summer Festival of the Arts in St. John's (July); Orangemen's Day celebrations, province-wide (July 12); Regatta Day boat races at Quidi Vidi Lake (August).

October-December: Various regional fairs and exhibitions.

NEWFOUNDLAND

Evergreen Trees

Mixed Evergreen and Deciduous Trees

Tundra

⊛ Provincial Capitals

• Cities and Towns

— Rail Lines

0 20 40 60 80 100 Miles
0 40 80 120 Kilometers

Longitude West of Greenwich

L a b r a d o r   S e a

Ungava Bay

AKPATOK ISLAND

C. CHIDLEY

NORTH AULATSIVIK I.

Abloviak Fd.

STONY PT.

Fort Chimo

TORNGAT MTS

FOUR PEAKS
4,415 FT. (1,346 M)

MT. ELIOT
4,553 FT. (1,388 M)

INNUIT MTN.
4,950 FT
(1,509 M)

HIGHEST POINT IN NEWFOUNDLAND
5,232 FT. (1,595 M)

Saglek Bay

C. UIVAK

Hebron Fjord

KAUMAJET MTS.
4,300 FT. (1,311 M)

L. LeMoyne

Rivière-la-Baleine

George River

Wheeler River

L A B R A D O R

SOUTH AULATSIVIK I.

Nain

Kogaluk River

TŪNUNGAYUALOK I.

A t l a n t i c

O c e a n

Q U E B E C

Lac Champdoré

Wakuach L.

2,873 FT. (876 M)

L. aux Goélands

Mistastin L.

Hopedale

C. HARRISON

Schefferville

Petitsikapau L.

Dyke L.

Attikamagen L.

Kanairiktok River

Kaipokok River

H I G H L A N D

Naskaupi River

Hamilton Inlet

Menihek Lakes

Sandgirt L.

Lobstick L.

Kasheshibaw L.

MOKAMI HILL
1,590 FT. (485 M)

MEALY MTS
4,300 FT. (1,311 M)

Sandwich Bay

Ashuanipi L.

Michikamau L.
1,860 FT. (567 M)

Grand L.

Lake Melville

Churchill Falls
245 FT. (75 M)

Ossokmanuan L.

Churchill River

Happy Valley
3,245 FT. (989 M)

Eagle River

Wabush L.

Shabogamo L.

Lac Joseph

Alexis River

St. Michaels Bay

Opocopa L.

Alikonak L.

Ashuanipi L.

3,440 FT. (1,049 M)

Little Mecatina River

St. Augustin River

St. Paul River

BRADORE HILLS

BELLE ISLE

52°

Q U E B E C

QUEBEC NORTH SHORE & LABRADOR RY.

Rivière Ste. Marguerite

Moisie River

R. St. Jean

Magpie River

Romaine River

Natashquan River

Aguanus River

Olomane River

Musquaro L.

Strait of Belle Isle

Hare Bay

GREY IS.

Sept Îles
(Seven Islands)

WEST PT.

Jacques Cartier Passage

ANTICOSTI ISLAND

HEATH PT.

C. WHITTLE

LONG RANGE MTS

White Bay

C. ST. JOHN

GROS MORNE
2,644 FT. (806 M)

GROS MORNE NAT'L PARK

Notre Dame Bay

FOGO I.

CANADIAN NATIONAL RY.

GASPESIAN PROV. PARK

MT. JACQUES CARTIER
4,160 FT. (1,268 M)

FORILLON NAT'L PARK

C. GASPÉ

Gulf

of

St. Lawrence

C. ST. GEORGE

Corner Brook

2,672 FT. (814 M)

LEWIS HILL

Grand L.

Humber R.

Gander R.

Bonavista Bay

C. BONAVISTA

TERRA NOVA NAT'L PARK

C. FREELS

GASPÉ PENINSULA

QUEBEC

Cascapédia R.

St. Georges Bay

Meelpaeg Lake

MT. SYLVESTER
1,234 FT. (376 M)

Trinity Bay

Campbellton
Chaleur Bay

MT. CARLETON
2,690 FT. (820 M)

SHIPPEGAN I.

MAGDALEN ISLANDS

C. RAY

LONG RANGE MTS.

Conception Bay
48°

ST. JOHN'S ⊛

Miramichi Bay

Cabot Strait

GREAT MIQUELON

ST. PIERRE AND MIQUELON
(FR.)

Fortune Bay

BURIN PEN.

Placentia Bay

C. RACE

N E W
B R U N S W I C K

KOUCHIBOUGUAC NAT'L PARK

Northumberland Strait

PRINCE EDWARD ISLAND

C. NORTH

CAPE BRETON HIGHLANDS NAT'L PARK

1,747 FT. (532 M)

CAPE BRETON ISLAND

LITTLE MIQUELON

St. Marys Bay

Charlottetown

N O V A   S C O T I A

Sydney

CM TERRAIN NEWFOUNDLAND
COPYRIGHT BY
RAND McNALLY & COMPANY
MADE IN U.S.A.

294b

Specially created for **World Book Encyclopedia** by Rand McNally and World Book editors

Land Regions. Newfoundland includes parts of two land regions: (1) the Canadian Shield, and (2) the Appalachian Region.

The Canadian Shield covers about half of Canada, including all Labrador. It is a rough plateau made up of ancient rocks. In Labrador, the edge of this plateau is cut by valleys and by swift rivers that drain into the Atlantic Ocean. Forests cover more than half of Labrador. Southwestern Labrador has many lakes. It also has rich deposits of iron ore. See CANADIAN SHIELD.

The Appalachian Region extends through the eastern part of North America from the island of Newfoundland to Alabama. Lowlands form the eastern edge of the island. To the west, the land gradually rises to a plateau with parts over 2,000 feet (610 meters) above sea level. In the central part of the island, rocky ridges rise from forested valleys. Lakes, ponds, and bogs dot the area. Three peninsulas—the Great Northern, the Avalon, and the Burin—stick out from the island. The mountainous Great Northern Peninsula points northeastward toward Labrador. Forests cover most of it. The Avalon Peninsula, in the southeast, is the most heavily populated part of Newfoundland. About 40 per cent of the people live there. To the west, across Placentia Bay, lies the hilly Burin Peninsula.

Coastline of Newfoundland is broken by *fiords* (long, narrow inlets) and many bays. Several of the bays rank among Canada's largest. The island of Newfoundland has 8,495 miles (13,676 kilometers) of coastline. Labrador's coastline is 9,498 miles (15,286 kilometers) long. Thousands of small islands dot the coastal waters.

Mountains. The highest point in Newfoundland is in the Torngat Mountains in northern Labrador. It rises 5,232 feet (1,595 meters) above sea level. The Mealy Mountains, in southern Labrador, are over 4,000 feet (1,200 meters) high. On the island of Newfoundland, the chief mountains are the Long Range Mountains, which rise along the Great Northern Peninsula. The Lewis Hills, southwest of Corner Brook, have the island's highest elevation—2,672 feet (814 meters) above sea level.

Rivers and Lakes. The Churchill River in Labrador is Newfoundland's longest river. It rises near the Quebec border and flows 600 miles (966 kilometers) to the Atlantic Ocean. On the island of Newfoundland, the Exploits River flows 153 miles (246 kilometers) northeast from Red Indian Lake into Notre Dame Bay.

Labrador's largest lake is Lake Melville, which covers 1,133 square miles (2,934 square kilometers). The next largest Labrador lakes are Michikamau, Lobstick, and Dyke lakes, and Lac Joseph. On the island of Newfoundland, Grand Lake is the largest, followed by Red Indian and Gander lakes. Grand Lake covers 205 square miles (531 square kilometers).

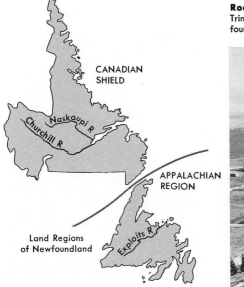

CANADIAN SHIELD

Naskaupi R

Churchill R

APPALACHIAN REGION

Exploits R

Land Regions of Newfoundland

Rocky Ridges rise near the village of Trinity on the shore of Trinity Bay. Trinity is in the Appalachian Region, which covers the entire island of Newfoundland. Many lakes, ponds, and bogs dot the area.

Miller Services

NEWFOUNDLAND / Climate

The cold Labrador Current and arctic winds keep Newfoundland cool (see LABRADOR CURRENT). But the climate varies greatly between Labrador and the island of Newfoundland. On the island, average January temperatures range from 24° F. (−4° C) in St. John's to 11° F. (−12° C) at the tip of the Great Northern Peninsula. Along the Labrador coast, average January temperatures range from 4° to −2° F. (−16° to −19° C). July temperatures average about 60° F. (16° C) in St. John's and about 50° F. (10° C) in coastal Labrador. The temperature may rise above 80° F. (27° C) in the summer in any part of the province. The highest and lowest temperatures in the province both were recorded in central Labrador. Goose Bay had the highest temperature, 100° F. (38° C), on July 4, 1944. The record

low, −55° F. (−48° C), occurred at Sandgirt Lake on Jan. 17, 1946, and at Ashuanipi on Feb. 7, 1950.

Frequent storms bring Newfoundland strong winds and regular *precipitation* (rain, melted snow, and other forms of moisture) throughout the year. Annual precipitation ranges from 50 to 60 inches (130 to 150 centimeters) around St. John's to less than 20 inches (51 centimeters) in northern Labrador.

Much of Newfoundland's precipitation falls as snow in the north. Snowfall is greatest in southern Labrador and in the central part of the island. These regions may receive up to 200 inches (510 centimeters) of snow annually. The southern part of the island averages 80 inches (200 centimeters) yearly. Some years, this region's snowfall is 5 inches (13 centimeters) or less.

SEASONAL TEMPERATURES

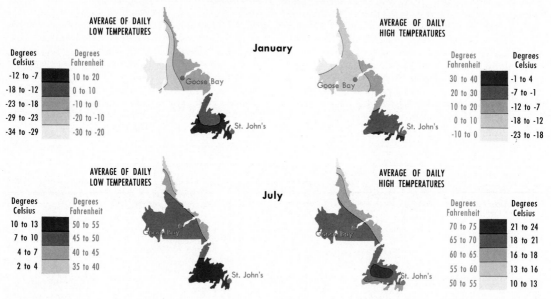

January

AVERAGE OF DAILY LOW TEMPERATURES

Degrees Celsius	Degrees Fahrenheit
-12 to -7	10 to 20
-18 to -12	0 to 10
-23 to -18	-10 to 0
-29 to -23	-20 to -10
-34 to -29	-30 to -20

AVERAGE OF DAILY HIGH TEMPERATURES

Degrees Fahrenheit	Degrees Celsius
30 to 40	-1 to 4
20 to 30	-7 to -1
10 to 20	-12 to -7
0 to 10	-18 to -12
-10 to 0	-23 to -18

July

AVERAGE OF DAILY LOW TEMPERATURES

Degrees Celsius	Degrees Fahrenheit
10 to 13	50 to 55
7 to 10	45 to 50
4 to 7	40 to 45
2 to 4	35 to 40

AVERAGE OF DAILY HIGH TEMPERATURES

Degrees Fahrenheit	Degrees Celsius
70 to 75	21 to 24
65 to 70	18 to 21
60 to 65	16 to 18
55 to 60	13 to 16
50 to 55	10 to 13

AVERAGE YEARLY PRECIPITATION
(Rain, Melted Snow and Other Moisture)

Centimeters	Inches
127 to 152	50 to 60
102 to 127	40 to 50
76 to 102	30 to 40
51 to 76	20 to 30
25 to 51	10 to 20

0   200   400 Miles
0   300   600 Kilometers

WORLD BOOK maps

AVERAGE MONTHLY WEATHER

	GOOSE BAY					ST. JOHN'S				
	Temperatures				Days of Rain or Snow	Temperatures				Days of Rain or Snow
	F° High	F° Low	C° High	C° Low		F° High	F° Low	C° High	C° Low	
JAN.	7	-9	-14	-23	21	30	18	-1	-8	15
FEB.	13	-6	-11	-21	19	28	16	-2	-9	15
MAR.	26	7	-3	-14	19	33	22	1	-6	14
APR.	36	19	2	-7	17	41	29	5	-2	12
MAY	49	32	9	0	16	51	35	11	2	13
JUNE	60	41	16	5	14	61	44	16	7	14
JULY	70	51	21	11	11	69	51	21	11	15
AUG.	67	49	19	9	13	68	54	20	12	14
SEPT.	57	41	14	5	14	61	47	16	8	12
OCT.	44	30	7	-1	18	53	40	12	4	13
NOV.	29	16	-2	-9	19	43	32	6	0	13
DEC.	16	1	-9	-17	21	35	24	2	-4	15

The leading source of income in Newfoundland is mining, followed by manufacturing and fishing. All production values given in this section are in Canadian dollars. For the value of the Canadian dollar in U.S. money, see MONEY (table).

Natural Resources. Newfoundland's most valuable resources are its large forests, extensive mineral deposits, and rich fishing grounds.

Soil of Newfoundland is coarse and rocky in most places. It contains granite, limestone, quartz rocks, sandstones, shales, slate, and other deposits left by ancient glaciers. The province's richest soil is in the valleys of the Codroy and Humber rivers.

Minerals. Newfoundland has some of the world's largest known iron-ore deposits. Other important minerals include asbestos, cadmium, copper, fluorite, gold, lead, limestone, pyrophyllite, sand and gravel, silver, stone, and zinc.

Plant Life. Forests cover about 49,000 square miles (127,000 square kilometers) of the province. Balsam firs and spruces, the most common trees, supply wood for Newfoundland's pulp and paper industry. Other trees include the aspen, birch, larch, pine, and white spruce. In areas over 1,200 feet (366 meters) above sea level, it is too cold for trees to grow. Only shrubs, lichens, and mosses grow at these elevations.

Animal Life. Newfoundland's fishing grounds became famous a few years after their discovery by John Cabot in 1497. Fisheries surround the island of Newfoundland and extend along the Labrador coast. Fishing crews from Europe and Japan fish on Newfoundland's Grand Banks, an underwater plateau. The Grand Banks extend 250 to 300 miles (402 to 483 kilometers) southeastward from the island. Fishing crews catch cod, flounder, herring, plaice, redfish, salmon, and lobsters.

About 30 kinds of animals live in the province. They include arctic hares, bears, beavers, caribou, foxes, lynxes, moose, otters, rabbits, seals, and weasels. Two famous breeds of dogs, the Labrador retriever and the Newfoundland, were developed in Newfoundland (see LABRADOR RETRIEVER; NEWFOUNDLAND DOG).

Few birds live in Newfoundland all year, but many kinds visit the province. Ptarmigans and ruffed grouse live on the island and in Labrador. Ducks, geese, and snipes visit the province every summer. Gulls, loons, murres, puffins, terns, and other sea birds feed in Newfoundland's coastal waters.

Mining in Newfoundland has an annual income of about $445 million. Iron-ore mining accounts for about four-fifths of all mining income. All of the iron ore comes from mines in Labrador. One of the world's largest iron-ore mines is in a border town known in Labrador as Knob Lake and in Quebec as Schefferville. Labrador City and Wabush, two thriving mining communities, grew up among valuable iron-ore fields in southwestern Labrador.

Mines at Buchans, near Red Indian Lake, produce most of Newfoundland's gold, lead, silver, and zinc. Buchans and Rambler Pond have copper mines, and Corner Brook has two limestone quarries. Other mining products include asbestos from Baie Verte, fluorspar from St. Lawrence, and gypsum from Flat Bay. Other

Production of Goods in Newfoundland

Total value of goods produced in 1974—$816,342,000

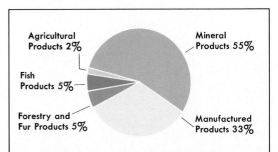

Agricultural Products 2%
Mineral Products 55%
Fish Products 5%
Forestry and Fur Products 5%
Manufactured Products 33%

Percentages are based on farm cash receipts, value added by forestry and manufacture, and value of fish, fur, and mineral production. Fur products are less than 1 per cent.

Sources: Canadian government publications, 1975 and 1976; Newfoundland Department of Agriculture and Forestry.

Employment in Newfoundland

Total number of persons employed in 1974—130,800

Economic Activities		Number of Employees
Community, Business, & Personal Services	𝕚𝕚𝕚𝕚𝕚𝕚𝕚𝕚𝕚𝕚	34,200
Wholesale & Retail Trade	𝕚𝕚𝕚𝕚𝕚𝕚𝕚	24,100
Transportation, Communication, & Utilities	𝕚𝕚𝕚𝕚𝕚𝕚	18,400
Manufacturing	𝕚𝕚𝕚𝕚𝕚	15,600
Fishing	𝕚𝕚𝕚𝕚𝕚	15,300
Government	𝕚𝕚𝕚𝕚	10,700
Mining	𝕚𝕚	6,000
Finance, Insurance, & Real Estate	𝕚	3,500
Agriculture	𝕚	3,000*

*1975 figure.

Sources: *Estimates of Employees by Province and Industry, 1961-1974,* Statistics Canada; Fisheries and Marine Service, Environment Canada; Labor Force Survey Division, Statistics Canada.

important mineral products include sand and gravel and stone.

Manufacturing. Newfoundland's industrial products have a *value added by manufacture* of about $270 million a year. This figure represents the value created in products by Newfoundland's industries, not counting such costs as materials, supplies, and fuels.

The manufacture of paper and paper products is Newfoundland's leading industrial activity, with an annual value added by manufacture of about $105 million. Corner Brook, in western Newfoundland, has one of the world's largest pulp and paper mills. Every day it produces more than 1,000 short tons (910 metric tons) of newsprint. The production of food and beverage products is the second-ranking industrial activity in the province. These products have a value added of about $70 million yearly. Dry salted cod and frozen *fillets* (boneless strips of fish) are major processed food products. Every year, Newfoundland ships over 115 million pounds (52 million kilograms) of frozen fillets to the United States and Europe.

Other important industries in Newfoundland include the production of chemicals and chemical products and of printed materials. The metal fabricating industry and the manufacture of stone, clay, and glass products are

Workers Prepare Codfish for Export in a port on Conception Bay. They spread the fish on wire racks to dry in the sun. Drying keeps the fish from spoiling. Newfoundland also exports large amounts of frozen fish.

Lyn; APF

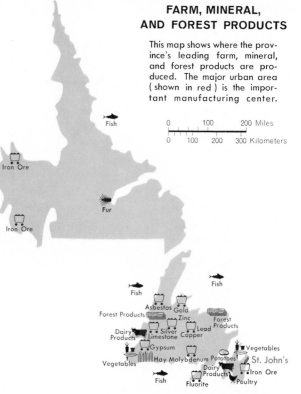

FARM, MINERAL, AND FOREST PRODUCTS

This map shows where the province's leading farm, mineral, and forest products are produced. The major urban area (shown in red) is the important manufacturing center.

WORLD BOOK map

also important manufacturing activities. Factories produce plywood, plasterboard and lath, wallboard, and cement. Industrial plants make clothing, leather goods, margarine, textiles, and wire.

Fishing Industry. Newfoundland ranks among the top fishing industry provinces, with an annual fish catch valued at about $45 million. Every year, the province's fisheries produce about 515 million pounds (234 million kilograms) of fish. Cod makes up the most valuable part of the catch, followed by redfish. Other fish caught in Newfoundland include herring, lobster, salmon, and turbot. Seals are also caught and processed for fur, leather, and oils.

Forestry in Newfoundland has an annual income of about $35 million. Every year, lumber workers produce about 113 million cubic feet (3,200,000 cubic meters) of timber, mainly pulpwood for Newfoundland's paper mills. The province has more than 1,100 sawmills.

Agriculture. Newfoundland's farm products provide an annual income of about $20 million. The province has about 880 farms. They average about 91 acres (37 hectares) in size. About half the farms are on the Avalon Peninsula. Newfoundland's chief farm products include blueberries, cranberries, and eggs.

Electric Power in Newfoundland comes almost entirely from hydroelectric plants. Steam or diesel-driven generators supply the rest of the electricity. Large hydroelectric plants supply power for the paper and pulp mills at Corner Brook and the mining operations in the Labrador City area. Construction of the largest single power project in the Western Hemisphere began in 1967 at Churchill Falls in Labrador. The power

plant, whose first generators began operating in 1971, can produce more than 5 million kilowatts of electricity.

Transportation. Newfoundland lies nearer Europe than any other part of North America except Greenland. This location makes the province an important stopping point for airplanes and ships traveling across the Atlantic Ocean.

Two major airlines serve Newfoundland. Many airplanes refuel at Gander Airport during transatlantic flights to and from Canada and the United States. Other important airports are at Torbay near St. John's, and at Goose Bay in Labrador. A 547-mile (880-kilometer) railway connects St. John's and Channel-Port aux Basques with Corner Brook and towns near the northern and eastern coasts. In Labrador, trains carry iron ore 357 miles (575 kilometers) from Knob Lake to Sept-Îles, Que.

Newfoundland has about 6,000 miles (9,700 kilometers) of roads. Most of the roads are not paved. Part of the Trans-Canada Highway runs from St. John's to Channel-Port aux Basques (see TRANS-CANADA HIGHWAY). Freighters sail to St. John's and Corner Brook from Toronto, Montreal, and Halifax. St. John's also serves a number of foreign fishing fleets.

Communication. Newfoundland has 3 daily newspapers and 10 weekly newspapers. *The Evening Telegram*, the oldest and largest daily, was established in St. John's in 1879. The province's first radio station, VOWR, began broadcasting from St. John's in 1924. In 1955, Newfoundland's first television station, CJON-TV, began operating in St. John's. About 20 radio stations and 4 television stations now serve the province.

Discovery. Viking explorers probably were the first white men to live in Newfoundland. In 1961, archaeologists discovered the ruins of a Viking settlement on the northern tip of the island. This settlement may have been built as early as A.D. 1000. English fishermen from Bristol probably reached Newfoundland in 1481. John Cabot, an Italian explorer in the service of England, may have landed on Newfoundland or Nova Scotia in 1497. Cabot thought he had reached Asia. He brought to Europe news of Newfoundland's rich fishing grounds.

Indian Days. After Cabot discovered the fishing grounds, hundreds of French, Portuguese, and Spanish fishermen visited Newfoundland. At that time, Beothuk Indians lived on the island. During the late 1700's, Micmac Indians invaded Newfoundland from what is now Nova Scotia. The Micmacs, like the white settlers, fought the Beothuks. This fighting, together with disease and starvation, wiped out the Beothuks by 1829.

The Micmacs settled around St. Georges Bay and along Newfoundland's southern coast. Naskapi and Montagnais Indians have lived in Labrador for as long as white men have known about the region.

Colonization. By the late 1500's, fishermen of several countries had established small settlements on Newfoundland. English fishermen worked and settled mainly along the southern part of the east coast. French fishing fleets controlled the north and south coasts. But English, French, Spanish, and Portuguese ships often anchored in the same harbor. Each harbor was ruled by a "fishing admiral." He was the master of the first ship to arrive at the beginning of the fishing season. He ruled until the end of the fishing season in early autumn. In 1634, King Charles I officially gave authority to the fishing admirals.

In 1583, the English explorer Sir Humphrey Gilbert landed at St. John's harbor. He claimed "200 leagues" (about 600 miles, or 970 kilometers) in every direction for England. John Guy, a merchant, arrived in 1610 with settlers sent by an English company. Guy formed a colony at Cupids, on Conception Bay. But English fishermen and pirates from the Mediterranean Sea attacked the colony, and it failed. In 1621, Sir George Calvert sent agents to set up a colony at Ferryland, in an area he named Avalon. French raiders and the harsh climate forced Calvert to abandon the project in 1629. In 1637, Charles I granted Newfoundland to Sir David Kirke and other nobles. Kirke set up headquarters at Ferryland, but he had no authority over the English fishermen who came to the island each summer. In 1651, the English government called Kirke back to England.

War with France. French settlers founded Placentia in 1662. Placentia quickly grew into a fortified colony that threatened the English in Newfoundland. But the English government considered Newfoundland only a fishery. English settlers were not allowed to own land within 6 miles (10 kilometers) of the sea. England and France did not quarrel openly until William III became king of England in 1689. William declared war on France, and Newfoundland became a battleground. The English and French attacked each other's ships and settlements until 1713, when they signed the Treaty of Utrecht. The treaty gave Britain the entire island.

France kept only the privilege of using part of the northern and western shore for drying fish. That area became known as the *French Shore*.

In 1729, the British government began to appoint naval officers as royal governors to rule Newfoundland. Captain Henry Osborne became the first such "naval governor." But Britain continued to favor the interests of the fishermen and to discourage the development of communities. Newfoundland's early governors lived on the island only during the fishing season, and returned to England for the winter.

During the Seven Years' War (1756-1763), English fishermen drove the French fishermen from the French Shore. In 1762, a French fleet seized St. John's and controlled the east coast for a few months. Britain finally obtained all of Canada by the Treaty of Paris in 1763. France received Saint Pierre and Miquelon islands from Britain, and also regained its right to use the French Shore. France gave up this right in 1904.

After the Treaty of Paris, the British government placed the Labrador coast under the authority of Newfoundland's royal governor. Newfoundland lost Labrador to Quebec in 1774, regained it in 1809, and then divided it with Quebec in 1825.

Representation and Independence. By the early 1800's, about 20,000 persons were living in Newfoundland. In 1817, Sir Francis Pickmore became the first governor to remain on the island after the close of the fishing season. Many Newfoundlanders wanted a strong local government. Led by William Carson, a Scottish surgeon, the people repeatedly asked Parliament for authority to make their own laws. In 1832, the British government established a legislature for Newfoundland. It consisted of a governor, his council, and a general assembly elected by the people.

Newfoundland's new government was a "representative government" because the legislature could make

The First Successful Atlantic Cable was completed in 1866 at the village of Heart's Content. Four previous attempts had failed. Cyrus W. Field, *second from right*, financed the project. He rented the British steamship *Great Eastern* to lay the cable, which stretched from Valentia, Ireland, to Heart's Content.

Confederation Life Collection

Newfoundland's Annual Seal Hunt takes place in spring. In the 1800's, schooners sailed out to the icefields.

The Labrador Boundary Decision of 1927 rejected Quebec claims, *dark area, left*, and defined Newfoundland's boundaries clearly, *right*.

Transatlantic Air Service made Goose Bay and Gander airports famous throughout the world.

Sir Humphrey Gilbert landed on Newfoundland in 1583 and claimed it in the name of Elizabeth I of England.

The First Transatlantic Flight, flown nonstop, left Lester's Field near St. John's on June 14, 1919.

Goose Bay •

HISTORIC NEWFOUNDLAND

John Cabot discovered the Newfoundland fisheries in 1497, and may have landed on the island of Newfoundland.

The First House of Assembly in Newfoundland was elected in the fall of 1832 and met on Jan. 1, 1833.

Corner Brook •   Gander •

1st Transatlantic Wireless Signal was received by Marconi in 1901 at Cabot Tower on Signal Hill, St. John's.

Torbay •
ST. JOHN'S ★

The Corner Brook Mill, one of the world's largest pulp and paper mills, turns out over 1,000 short tons (910 metric tons) of paper daily.

laws. But the British Parliament had to approve the laws, and a British governor enforced them. Soon, the assembly began to ask the British government for a "responsible government"—one in which the cabinet was controlled by the elected assembly and not by the governor. The British colonies in Canada had been granted this form of government in the 1840's. In 1855, Newfoundland was also allowed to set up a responsible government.

Economic Growth. In 1857, prospectors discovered copper at Tilt Cove. By 1888, copper mining had become an important industry. During the 1880's and 1890's, Sir William Whiteway served several terms as prime minister of Newfoundland. Whiteway encouraged the building of a Newfoundland Railway that later became part of Canadian National Railways. Newfoundland's first paper mill began operating in Grand Falls in 1909. The colony's fishing industry boomed during World War I (1914-1918) because of top prices paid for wartime food supplies.

In 1927, the government established the present boundary between the coast of Labrador and Quebec. This decision gave Newfoundland the vast mineral resources of the Knob Lake and Wabush Lake regions. See LABRADOR (History).

Ruin and Recovery. After World War I, Newfoundland's prosperity began to fade because there was no longer a demand for the province's products. During the 1920's, Newfoundland desperately tried to revive its lagging industries and to develop new ones. But by 1930, the Great Depression had struck most of the world. Newfoundland's fish, iron ore, and newsprint markets collapsed. Its government sank deeply into debt.

Under Prime Minister Frederick C. Alderdice, Newfoundland appealed to Great Britain for financial assistance under a new form of government. In 1934, Britain suspended Newfoundland's government and established a *Commission of Government*. This government consisted of a British governor and six other men, three of them Newfoundlanders. Newfoundland became a *dependency*, and Great Britain took over its debts.

Economic recovery came slowly. The Commission of Government reorganized the civil service, improved education and health facilities, and sponsored research to improve agriculture. Newfoundland's fishing and logging industries received much-needed financial aid.

World War II (1939-1945) gave new life to Newfoundland's economy. The fisheries, factories, and mines once again increased production to fill wartime demands. Canada and the United States built military bases in Newfoundland. Servicemen and employees at these bases created new demands for local products.

Confederation with Canada. In 1948, Newfoundland voters chose to unite with Canada rather than keep the Commission of Government or return to independent self-government. On March 31, 1949, Newfoundland became Canada's 10th province. Joseph R. Smallwood, a Liberal, took office as the province's first premier.

Newfoundland was in sound financial condition at the time of confederation. But a wide gap existed between the standard of living in Newfoundland and many of the other nine provinces. Through confederation, Newfoundland began to share in federal social security benefits. The province participated in federal programs, including development of trade schools and

the construction of over 500 miles (800 kilometers) of the Trans-Canada Highway. A federal-provincial project, begun in the 1950's, involved resettlement of a number of fishing outposts and villages. This program improved standards of living and educational opportunities for many fishermen and their families.

During the 1960's, Newfoundland expanded its industrial and educational facilities and its production and distribution of electricity. Following a boom in mineral production, mining began to rival manufacturing as the province's chief industry. New mines were opened, most of them in Labrador. Many new schools and trade schools were established to meet the demand for skilled workers.

By the late 1960's, Newfoundland's rural electrification program had brought electricity to more than 100 isolated communities in the province. The principal project in the program was a $950-million hydroelectric plant in Churchill Falls in Labrador. Construction started in 1967, and all of the plant's 11 generators were operating by 1974. This plant is the largest hydroelectric development in the Western Hemisphere.

Newfoundland Today has a major problem finding jobs to keep up with its rapidly increasing population. The province of Newfoundland has one of the highest birth rates and one of the lowest death rates among the provinces. A number of industrial complexes have been

--- IMPORTANT DATES IN NEWFOUNDLAND ---

1497 John Cabot raised the banner of King Henry VII on a "new found land" which may have been the island of Newfoundland or Nova Scotia.

1583 Sir Humphrey Gilbert landed in Newfoundland and claimed the region for England.

1637 Charles I granted Newfoundland to Sir David Kirke and his partners.

1662 The French established a garrison at Placentia.

1713 The Treaty of Utrecht gave Newfoundland to Britain.

1729 Captain Henry Osborne became Newfoundland's first royal governor.

1763 In the Treaty of Paris, France gave Labrador to Britain.

1832 Great Britain granted Newfoundland the right to elect a general assembly.

1855 Newfoundland gained a "responsible government" that was controlled by an elected assembly.

1904 France gave up its right to use Newfoundland's northern shore.

1909 Newfoundland's first paper mill began production in Grand Falls.

1934 Great Britain suspended Newfoundland's government, established a Commission of Government, and assumed Newfoundland's debts.

1949 Newfoundland became Canada's 10th province on March 31.

1958 Newfoundland introduced free hospitalization and programs for educational improvements.

1967 Construction began on a $950-million hydroelectric plant in Churchill Falls in Labrador. The plant's first two generators began operating in 1971.

1972 The Progressive Conservative Party won control of the Legislative Assembly, ending 23 years of Liberal Party control.

attracted to Newfoundland by the low-cost power generated at the Churchill Falls hydroelectric plant. Chief users include a linerboard mill in Stephenville and a phosphorous plant in Long Harbour.

Another big problem of Newfoundland is to find income to maintain the standards of public service reached since confederation. The cost of government programs has soared during that period.

As a result of the provincial elections in October 1971, the Liberals lost control of the legislature to the Progressive Conservative Party. Conservative leader Frank Moores became premier in January 1972, ending 23 years of Liberal Party rule under Joseph R. Smallwood.

GORDON OLIVER ROTHNEY, ARCH SULLIVAN, and WILLIAM F. SUMMERS

NEWFOUNDLAND/Study Aids

Related Articles in WORLD BOOK include:

BIOGRAPHIES

Bartlett, Robert A.	Grenfell, Sir Wilfred T.
Gilbert, Sir Humphrey	Prendergast, Maurice B.

CITIES AND TOWNS

Bonavista	Corner Brook	Saint John's
Carbonear	Placentia	

PHYSICAL FEATURES

Churchill River	Gulf of Saint	Gulf Stream
Grand Banks	Lawrence	Labrador Current

OTHER RELATED ARTICLES

Atlantic Provinces	Cod	Labrador
Beothuk	Goose Bay	Memorial University
Indians	Iron and Steel	of Newfoundland

Outline

I. **Government**
  A. Lieutenant Governor
  B. Premier
  C. Legislative Assembly
  D. Courts
  E. Local Government
  F. Taxation
  G. Politics
II. **People**
III. **Education**
  A. Schools
  B. Libraries and Museums
IV. **A Visitor's Guide**
  A. Places to Visit
  B. Annual Events
V. **The Land**
  A. Land Regions
  B. Coastline
  C. Mountains
  D. Rivers and Lakes
VI. **Climate**
VII. **Economy**
  A. Natural Resources
  B. Mining
  C. Manufacturing
  D. Fishing Industry
  E. Forestry
  F. Agriculture
  G. Electric Power
  H. Transportation
  I. Communication
VIII. **History**

Questions

What part of Newfoundland is most heavily populated?
What are Newfoundland's chief manufactured products? What are its two most important fish products?
How are Newfoundland's schools organized?
What part of Newfoundland produces most of the province's iron ore?
What are Newfoundland's only two cities?
When did Great Britain gain control of Labrador?
Why did Britain give Newfoundland a Commission of Government in 1934?
Why is Newfoundland an important stopping point for transatlantic airplanes and ships?

Books to Read

DeVOLPI, CHARLES P. *Newfoundland.* Longman (Don Mills, Ont.), 1972.
FEATHER, JEAN HAYES. *Sawtooth Harbour Boy.* Nelson (Don Mills, Ont.), 1973. Fiction. For young readers.

GOUDIE, ELIZABETH. *Woman of Labrador.* Peter Martin (Toronto), 1973.
HARRIS, LESLIE. *Newfoundland and Labrador: A Brief History.* Dent (Don Mills, Ont.), 1968. For young readers.
HORWOOD, HAROLD A. *Newfoundland.* Macmillan (Toronto); St. Martin's (New York), 1969. *The Foxes of Beachy Cove.* PaperJacks (Markham, Ont.), 1975. For young readers.
MAJOR, KEVIN, ed. *Doryloads.* Breakwater (Portugal Cove, Nfld.), 1974. Writings and art for young readers.
MOWAT, FARLEY. *This Rock Within the Sea: A Heritage Lost.* Rev. ed. McClelland (Toronto), 1976.
NEARY, PETER, and O'FLAHERTY, PATRICK, eds. *By Great Waters: A Newfoundland and Labrador Anthology.* Univ. of Toronto Press, 1974.
TAYLOR, STEPHEN, and HORWOOD, H. A. *Beyond the Road: Portraits & Visions of Newfoundlanders.* Van Nostrand (Scarborough, Ont. and New York), 1976.

NEWFOUNDLAND DOG, *noo FOWND luhnd,* is a breed developed by the earliest settlers of Newfoundland. It is famous for its work in saving people from drowning. One of the few truly American breeds, it is believed to have been the *forerunner* (ancestor) of the Labrador retriever.

The Newfoundland dog is a powerful, intelligent animal, which looks somewhat like the Saint Bernard or Great Pyrenees. It has a noble appearance, with a great head and shortened muzzle. The dog's color may vary, but the best-known type is black with a bronze tinge.

The Newfoundland has a dense oily coat which keeps water away from its body. The dog retrieves ducks, and can swim in the coldest water for hours. The males weigh from 140 to 150 pounds (64 to 68 kilograms). The dog is an excellent companion and guardian for children. It is fearless and has an even temper.

Few of the dogs live in Newfoundland today. Most of them have been taken to other countries. OLGA DAKAN
See also DOG (color picture: Working Dogs).

NEWGATE PRISON, a London jail, was England's main criminal prison for over 700 years. It was torn down in 1902, after years of protest about its shameful condition. The prison originally was part of London's West Gate, an entranceway to the city. West Gate was rebuilt and renamed Newgate in the 1100's. Prisoners were held in a room above the entranceway. Newgate was rebuilt again about 1423. But the Great Fire of London damaged it in 1666, and its condition grew steadily worse. Many prisoners died because of overcrowded rooms, poor food, and such contagious diseases as *jail fever* (typhus). Women, children, and debtors lived with hardened criminals. Few reforms were adopted until the 1800's. After 1815, debtors were held elsewhere. After 1847, only persons awaiting trial were kept at Newgate. VERNON F. SNOW

NEWMAN, JOHN HENRY CARDINAL (1801-1890), became a convert to the Roman Catholic Church in 1845, and was made a cardinal in 1879. Before his conversion, he had distinguished himself as a scholar and a preacher of the Church of England at Oxford University. In 1833, he joined the movement within that church to rid it of political domination and to ground it more firmly in traditional beliefs (see OXFORD MOVEMENT). The movement helped strengthen the established church, but Newman shocked his fellow reformers when he joined the Roman Catholic Church. In 1846, he became a Catholic priest.

Newman was born in London. For most of his life as a Catholic, he lived in Birmingham as rector of an *oratory*, a group of men devoted to prayer and studies. He was considered one of the great thinkers of the 1800's.

Cardinal Newman's autobiography, the *Apologia pro Vita Sua* (1864), was an answer to an attack upon him by Charles Kingsley, an Anglican minister and author. Among Cardinal Newman's many lectures is "The Idea of a University" (1852). *The Grammar of Assent* (1870) was his answer to religious skepticism. Newman also wrote the words of the hymn "Lead, Kindly Light". JOHN T. FARRELL and FULTON J. SHEEN

NEWMAN, PAUL (1925-   ), an American actor, won fame for his action roles and convincing character studies in motion pictures. He portrayed outsiders or rebels in many of his films.

Newman was born in Cleveland and studied acting at Kenyon College, Yale University, and the Actors Studio. He made his Broadway debut in *Picnic* (1953) after appearing in several television dramas. Newman's first movie was *The Silver Chalice* (1955). He gained stardom in *Somebody Up There Likes Me* (1957). Newman's other films include *The Long, Hot Summer* (1958), *The Hustler* (1961), *Hud* (1963), *Harper* (1966), *Hombre* (1967), *Cool Hand Luke* (1967), *Butch Cassidy and the Sundance Kid* (1969), *The Sting* (1973), and *Slap Shot* (1977). He also starred on Broadway in *Sweet Bird of Youth* (1959).

Paul Newman

Newman directed *Rachel, Rachel* (1968) and *The Effect of Gamma Rays on Man-in-the-Moon Marigolds* (1972). Both these films starred his wife, the Academy Award winning actress Joanne Woodward. ROGER EBERT

NEWMAN APOSTOLATE is a Roman Catholic organization in the United States. It serves students on campuses of universities and colleges not affiliated with the Roman Catholic Church. It has centers on about 1,250 campuses, serving more than 1½ million students.

Newman centers sponsor lectures, seminars, conferences, and study groups. They also conduct educational, leadership, religious, and social programs. A chaplain serves each center. The national office provides information, program aids, and publications for members. It sponsors chaplains' training schools, educational conferences, and a national student congress.

The first Newman group began in 1893. Headquarters are at 1312 Massachusetts Avenue NW, Washington, D.C. 20005.

Critically reviewed by the NATIONAL NEWMAN APOSTOLATE

NEWPORT, R.I. (pop. 34,562), is best known as a summer colony and resort. The city lies on Narragansett Bay (see RHODE ISLAND [political map]).

Newport was founded in 1639 by nine families from the Massachusetts Bay Colony who sought religious freedom. There are more than 300 colonial buildings in Newport, including the Old Colony House, which became a National Historic Landmark in 1962. Before the Revolutionary War, Newport rivaled Boston and New York City as a shipping center. It is the home of Salve Regina, The Newport College. The city has a council-manager government. CLARKSON A. COLLINS III

See also JEWS (picture: The Oldest Synagogue).

NEWPORT, CHRISTOPHER. See NEWPORT NEWS.

NEWPORT NEWS, Va. (pop. 138,177), is one of the largest Southern shipbuilding and coal-exporting centers. It stands on the northern shore of the harbor called Hampton Roads. See HAMPTON ROADS; VIRGINIA (political map). Newport News is a seafood center. It also produces auto parts; machinery; paints; ships and boats; and fish, foundry, paper, tobacco, and wood products.

The Mariners Museum in Newport News has more than 45,000 articles from ships of many countries. The city's War Memorial Museum of Virginia houses a large collection of relics from World Wars I and II. Newport News is the home of Christopher Newport College, a branch of the College of William and Mary.

The city is named after Captain Christopher Newport, who unloaded supplies there for the Jamestown colonists. He also brought news that more settlers were on the way. Permanent settlement began in 1621. Newport News grew rapidly during the 1800's. It merged with Warwick and took over Warwick County in 1958. The metropolitan area population of 338,581 persons includes Hampton. Newport News has a council-manager government. FRANCIS B. SIMKINS

NEWS COMMENTATOR. See COMMENTATOR.

NEWS SERVICE is an organization for the collection and distribution of news. News services make it possible for newspapers to give their readers news from all parts of the world. They furnish telegraphic news to radio and television stations and news magazines, as well as to newspapers. They also furnish photographs by messenger, mail, telegraph, radio, or facsimile.

The five principal news services in the world are the *Associated Press* and *United Press International* in the United States; *Agence France-Presse* in France; *Reuters* in Great Britain; and *Tass* in Russia. All except Tass are free from direct government control. Some 75 national news services distribute news daily.

During the Middle Ages, hand-written newsletters kept groups of nobles and business firms informed of recent events. Later, coffeehouses became the centers of news distribution. The first major news service in the United States, the Associated Press, was established in New York in 1848. EARL F. ENGLISH

Related Articles in WORLD BOOK include:

Associated Press	North American Newspaper Alliance	Tass United Press International
Kyodo	Reuters	

NEWSPAPER

The City Room of a daily newspaper is staffed by writers and editors. They quickly translate each day's important events into headlines, news stories, and pictures.

NEWSPAPER. In the United States, where about 97 out of 100 persons who are old enough have learned to read, almost everyone reads newspapers. Every day people in the United States buy about $62\frac{1}{2}$ million daily newspapers. They also purchase over 49 million Sunday newspapers and about 24 million weekly newspapers. These daily, Sunday, and weekly newspapers have become a part of the home life of most American families. They are so familiar to us all that we do not think of them as anything wonderful. But the newspaper is a daily miracle—a marvel of machinery, business organization, news coverage, and fast and clear writing.

In the United States there are about 1,800 daily, 8,800 weekly, and 460 semiweekly papers. These represent many differences in policy and great range in ethical standards and excellence. In discussing newspapers, we should keep in mind the fact that their great differences make many generalizations unsafe.

A large daily newspaper contains a variety of information. Up-to-the-minute news stories tell of foreign, national, state, and local affairs. Articles and columnists report developments in sports, society, finance, science, religion, education, and agriculture. Comment on the news appears in editorials and signed columns. Feature articles bring the readers information on such subjects as fashions, health, housekeeping, and child care.

Robert U. Brown, the contributor of this article, is editor and publisher of Editor & Publisher *magazine.*

Comic strips and crossword puzzles appear regularly.

A large newspaper would make a sizable volume if printed in book form. Like a book, it has a contents guide that tells where each feature may be found. In addition, most newspapers are divided into sections that make it easy for the reader to find various types of information. A large newspaper may have separate news, feature, entertainment, finance, and sports sections. Big Sunday and weekend editions may also include magazine sections, book review sections, and guides to the week's television viewing. Pictures and other illustrations appear throughout most newspapers.

Advertising usually fills about 50 to 70 per cent of a newspaper's space. The classified advertising section is filled with many small advertisements.

A newspaper that comes into any home with such a wide scope of reading matter can exert a great deal of influence. The modern newspaper, with its large circulation, usually tries to present both sides of a problem, instead of presenting only one viewpoint as newspapers usually did until the early 1900's. Nevertheless, it continually suggests ideas, beliefs, and ways of judging persons and events that help form our attitudes toward the important things of life.

What Is a Newspaper?

A newspaper is a publication devoted basically to presenting current news and commenting upon the news and related matters. The newspaper is usually printed on cheap paper known as *newsprint*. Neither the page size of a newspaper nor the number of pages has ever been standardized. But throughout the 1800's the folio page (about 16 by 23 inches, or 41 by 58 centimeters) was commonly considered the true newspaper form. Today, the folio (about 15 by 23 inches, or 38 by 58 centimeters) and the tabloid of about two-thirds that size are the common page sizes.

The *newsmagazine* is also devoted to news and comment, but it is issued with a cover and better paper. It is published weekly, but, unlike most weekly newspapers, it covers national and international news (see MAGAZINE). House organs, camp and army papers, and school papers are often newspapers in purpose and form.

Organization of a Newspaper

The number of men and women necessary to produce a newspaper varies greatly. There are some small one-man weekly papers, though the larger weeklies may have ten to thirty workers on their payrolls. The largest city papers have about 2,000 employees.

Such a staff, headed by the publisher, is divided into three departments: editorial, business, and mechanical.

The Editorial Department is headed by the editor in chief, who is nearly always called just the editor, or (by irreverent reporters) "the old man." Under the editor is the news staff, and a board of editorial writers who produce the editorial page. News is the paper's lifeblood, and the news staff is its heart. It is headed by the managing editor or by a news editor whom he appoints. Under the managing editor (or news editor) are the city editor, in charge of local news; the foreign (or cable) editor; the telegraph (or wire) editor; the state editor; and special editors for sports, society, the Sunday paper, the financial page, features, the book section, the woman's page, pictures, and similar special departments. The city editor has a staff of reporters, photographers, rewrite men, and copyreaders. Certain departmental editors, as those for sports and finance, have similar staffs. There is now a strong trend toward the "universal copydesk." Copy for all news departments passes over this desk for the inspection of the copyreaders, who edit the stories and write headlines.

The Business Department is headed by the business manager. The publisher also often gives this department a large part of his attention. The business manager has under him the circulation manager, with a large staff to handle distribution by carriers, street sales, mail, and trucks; the advertising manager, with assistants in charge of national, classified, department store, automotive, and other advertising fields; the promotion manager, with a staff whose job it is to advertise the newspaper itself in many ways; and the auditor, with his accounting staff.

The Mechanical Department is headed by a production manager or chief. It includes the composing room, where the type is set and made up into pages; the engraving room, where the photographers' prints

Chicago Daily News

A Breaking News Story is covered by a reporter and photographer. The reporter, *above left*, telephones the facts to a rewrite man in the newsroom. The photographer, *left*, receives a radio dispatch ordering him to the fire. He takes pictures, *above*, and rushes his film to the newspaper's photo lab.

Teletype Machines bring news service stories to newspapers from reporters stationed in all parts of the world.

are made into "cuts" for insertion into the pages for printing; the stereotyping room, where these pages go for casting before they are locked on the presses; the pressroom, where the papers are printed and folded; and the mailing room, where the papers are assembled, and turned over to the circulation department. Each of these divisions is headed by a foreman.

Each of the workers in these departments must do his job with the deadlines of each edition of the paper in mind. His own job must be finished at a certain time in order to fit in with the job that follows. For the newspaper must do its chief work not on a schedule of weeks or days or even hours, but minutes. It has to get its news on the street and in the home in the shortest possible time after an event occurs.

From News-Break to Fireside

Let us see how a typical news event is handled. A fire breaks out in an apartment house in the west end of a large city. A "beat" reporter from the *News*, who is at his daily job of visiting police and fire department news sources, telephones the city editor that this is a serious three-alarm fire.

Reporting the Story. The city editor calls to Stubbs, a general assignment man, "Get out to 18th and Oregon, Stubbs—three-alarm fire!" Stubbs crams some copy-paper into his pocket, seizes his hat, hurries to the street, and signals a taxi. There are only fifty minutes before

the home edition deadline, he notes by a glance at his wrist watch. When Stubbs arrives at the scene of the fire, he wastes no time observing picturesque effects. He may write a "color" story later, but now he wants the facts.

Stubbs finds out from the fire chief the probable cause of the fire, when it broke out, and any such features as rescues of residents or trouble with the water supply. He finds out who owns the property and locates him, getting his estimate of the damage and the amount of insurance. Most important of all, if there have been injuries or deaths, he must get the names and addresses of the injured and the dead, and the extent of their injuries or the causes of their deaths. Watching the time, Stubbs goes to a telephone 25 minutes before his deadline, calls his city editor. "Child dead from burns; fireman injured; $80,000 loss," he summarizes. "Give Wells half a column," says the city editor and switches Stubbs to a rewrite man. There will be a longer story, with pictures, in later editions, but now there is no time or space for more.

Writing the Story. Stubbs gives Wells the details—the location of the fire, the size of the building, the name of the owner, the probable loss, the insurance, and details of the traffic tie-up caused by the blaze. He gives the name, age, and parents of the dead child, and tells how it met its death. He gives the name and address of the fireman, tells the extent of his injuries and how they were received, and gives the name of the hospital to which he has been taken. He is very careful to spell names and to repeat figures. The form of the story takes shape in Wells' practiced mind as he takes down the facts at the telephone. As soon as Stubbs has finished, Wells writes his "lead," giving the chief facts, and then gives additional details in the paragraphs that follow.

Editing the Story. The city editor notifies the copy-desk that the story is coming. The news editor orders a headline. A copyreader takes the story in pages from a copy boy. He edits the story, checking accuracy and making it more readable. He then writes the headline for the story.

Setting the Story in Type. The news editor sends the copy down a pneumatic chute to the composing room just before the deadline. There it is divided into parts

At the Copy Desk, editors check stories for accuracy, grammar, and style. They also write a headline for each story.

Banner. The top headline on page 1.

Beat. A story obtained by a newspaper before rival papers publish it. A beat may not be exclusive, as a scoop. A beat may also mean any news source to which a reporter is regularly assigned, such as the city hall or a police district.

By-Line. The name of the writer of a news or feature story, or special column, usually carried between the headline and the item.

Copy. The manuscript of any kind of news matter prepared for the typesetter.

Date Line. The location and origin and date of a news story, such as, "New York, Sep. 4., (AP)—"

Deadline. The time limit for stages in preparing copy to get out a certain edition of a newspaper.

Edition. Any issue of the newspaper. Large newspapers issue several editions during the day or night.

Extra. An edition of a newspaper published at a time other than a scheduled regular edition.

Gazette. An ancient name for newspaper, often used today as part of newspaper titles. The term originated from a Venetian coin, *gazzetta*, which was the price of an early newspaper of Venice.

Lead. The opening paragraph of a news story. A *buried lead* consists of important facts which an inexpert writer has placed in the body of the story.

Line. See *Banner* (above).

Masthead. The title of the newspaper and statement of its ownership and policy, usually carried on the editorial page.

Morgue. The research library of a newspaper.

Obit. An obituary.

Scoop. A story obtained exclusively by a newspaper without the knowledge of its competitors.

Squib. A brief story, unimportant from a news standpoint and used primarily to fill space.

Subhead. Short headings used to break up the paragraphs of a long news story.

---

called "takes" so that several linotypers can set it in type. The lines of type, called slugs, are put together and proofs are printed, read, and corrected rapidly. The slugs, complete with head, are delivered to the editorial make-up man, who has left space for them in his front-page form. He shows a printer where to insert them, and gives the form to the stereotypers. During the 1960's, some newspapers began using computers to set type (see PRINTING [Electronic Computers]).

Printing and Distributing the Paper. In the stereotype room, a papier-mâché form, called a "mat," is made of the page. The mat is used as a mold for the plate. The printing plate is then cast from hot metal in the form of a half cylinder. This goes by roller conveyer to the press and is locked on a cylinder in printing position. The signal to start the presses is given, and the great press goes into action. The roll of paper is drawn through the length of the press, receiving the print of all the plates. At the farther end of the machine it is folded, trimmed, and counted.

The piles of paper are hurried to the mailing room, made into counted bundles, delivered methodically to a fleet of trucks, and rushed to newsstands, carriers, and post office. Two hours from the time Stubbs was assigned to cover the fire, the paper containing the fire story is delivered to your door. This kind of speed is common for a newspaper. A news bulletin often appears in an edition 15 minutes after it reaches a newspaper office in a large city.

News-Gathering Services

The chief U.S. services in covering world news are the Associated Press, which is owned by its member newspapers, and United Press International, owned by the Scripps-Howard chain of newspapers and serving many others as well. Each of these services has hundreds of correspondents at home and in most other countries. Each has regional bureaus and staffs of editors. Their dispatches and news photographs come into the newspaper offices over electrical Teletype and facsimile machines. They also serve radio and television stations.

Some large newspapers have their own staffs of foreign correspondents. These papers often *syndicate* (sell) their reports to other papers. Organizations with photographers and writers throughout the world syndicate

Chicago Sun-Times (WORLD BOOK photo)

Intertype Machines set stories that have been typed onto computer tape into lines of metal type called *slugs*.

Chicago Sun-Times (WORLD BOOK photo)

Type for Advertising Pages is set in segments by a computer and then pasted onto sheets and photographed.

Chicago Sun-Times

Printing Plates travel on a conveyer to the presses, where they are locked onto cylinders for printing.

pictures and features. Popular syndicated features include comic strips, public affairs columns, and puzzles.

All this material comes into the newspaper office in various ways. Feature stories, often called "time copy," usually come by mail. Most of these syndicated features can be prepared well in advance of their publication date. But most of the news from outside the local area comes in by Teletype. The stories are typed out on a Teletype recorder which receives electrical impulses over wires from a transmitter in a distant news bureau. Foreign dispatches come by cable or radio to New York or San Francisco and are then transmitted by Teletype. Radio was first used for reporting in 1899. Transmission of pictures by wire was begun by the Associated Press in 1935. A few years later, pictures were being sent by radio.

The Newspaper as a Business

Newspapers in the United States represent a $4\frac{1}{4}$-billion-a-year business. Newspapers receive about 70 per cent of their revenue from advertising and 30 per cent from newspaper sales. Newspapers get about one-third of all money spent for advertising in the U.S. In the mid-1960's, newspapers received over $3 billion a year from advertisers. Circulation (the sale of papers) brought about $1\frac{1}{4}$ billion.

Newspapers have billions of dollars invested in plants and equipment. Between 1954 and 1964, newspapers spent more than $100 million a year on plant modernization and expansion alone.

Daily newspapers employ about 250,000 persons. The weekly papers employ about 55,000. In addition, several hundred thousand carrier boys deliver daily, Sunday, and weekly newspapers to homes.

Newsprint is the largest expense item in operating all but the smallest newspapers. Each year, U.S. newspapers use about 9 million short tons (8.2 million metric tons) of newsprint costing over $1\frac{1}{3}$ billion. Newsprint costs rise with increases in circulation and volume of advertising and news. Newsprint accounts for about one-third of the expense in operating a large metropolitan newspaper. Among the smallest papers, it amounts to 15 per cent or less of total expenses.

Mechanical department costs range from 25 per cent for the smallest papers to about 15 per cent on the largest dailies. Editorial expenses account for about 14 per cent of total costs.

Newspapers in Other Countries

The circulation of newspapers for the entire world is about 350 million copies daily, or about one daily paper for every 10 persons. Luxembourg leads the world with about 560 copies sold daily for every 1,000 persons.

British newspapers greatly resemble American papers. This has been true ever since Lord Northcliffe (1865-1922), the most famous of modern British newspaper publishers, adapted many American techniques on his *London Daily Mail*. It is not true of the more conserva-

Chicago Sun-Times

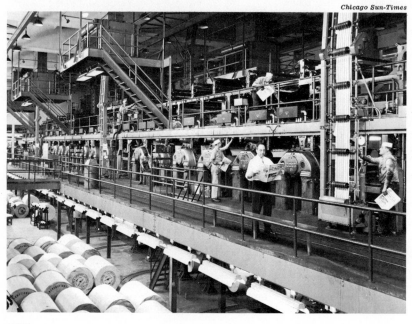

In the Pressroom, giant rolls of paper unwind through rows of presses that can print, cut, fold, and count as many as 1,000 newspapers a minute.

Ready for Delivery, newspapers are rushed to the mailing room, where they are bundled and sent to trucks.

tive *The Times* (London), which greatly influences English opinion. *The Times* carried classified advertising on its front page until early in 1966.

Many of the leading papers of France were founded during or after World War II. *France-Soir,* founded in Paris in 1941, has a circulation of over 800,000. Other papers include *Le Parisien Libéré, Le Figaro,* and *L'Aurore,* all published in Paris.

Leading independent papers published in West Germany include the *Frankfurter Allgemeine, Sueddeutsche Zeitung* of Munich, and *Die Welt* of Hamburg. The largest paper in East Berlin is the Communist-controlled *Neues Deutschland.* In Italy, outstanding papers are the independents, *Il Messaggero* and *Il Tempo,* and the Communist *L'Unità,* all in Rome; the Roman Catholic *L'Osservatore Romano,* in Vatican City; and *Corriere della Sera,* in Milan. Japanese papers include *Asahi Shimbun* and *Yomiuri Shimbun.*

In Russia, the Moscow *Izvestia* and *Pravda* are under strict Communist control. They claim to have daily circulations of several million. Among other Russian papers are the army *Red Star* and the navy *Red Fleet.* Russia claims a daily newspaper circulation of more than 33 million.

In China, mother of printing, papermaking, and the printed newspaper, newspapers have suffered from national disorders and wars. The Chinese tendency has been to develop many small dailies instead of a few papers with mass circulation. Once there were over a hundred dailies published at the same time in Peking.

In India, there are English-language papers in large cities, and many papers printed in other languages.

Australia and Canada have many prosperous and growing newspapers. The Melbourne *Sun News-Pictorial,* with more than 625,000 circulation, is the largest Australian daily paper. The *Toronto Daily Star,* with over 385,000, is the largest Canadian newspaper.

The Latin-American republics have many powerful and active newspapers. In a few of them the press is controlled in various degrees by the governments. *La Prensa* of Argentina, long outstanding for its full coverage of news, was taken over by Juan Perón's dictatorial government in 1951. After a revolution overthrew Perón, *La Prensa* was returned to its owners early in 1956. *La Nación* is another influential Argentine paper. *El Comercio* is the oldest paper of Peru. *El Mercurio* and *La Nación* of Santiago, Chile, have circulations of 100,000 or more. Mexico has about 100 dailies. The largest have circulations of over 100,000.

History

Beginnings. Probably the first newspaper was *Tsing Pao,* a court journal published in Peking. It is said to have started as early, as the 500's, and was continued until 1935. At first it was produced from carved blocks instead of from type. This method of printing was hundreds of years old in China when the paper began.

In Europe, the forerunners of printed newspapers were written newsletters. These were sent out regularly by Roman scribes to businessmen and politicians in distant cities to keep them informed of happenings in Rome. Newsletter service from European capitals continued to be used in the 1700's, even after printed papers had become common. Another Roman news publication was the posted bulletin. The leading bulletin was the *Acta Diurna* (Daily Events). This began to be posted in the Forum in 60 B.C., and was often copied by the scribes and dispatched abroad in newsletters.

After Gutenberg's invention of printing from movable type, there were occasional news pamphlets (news-

Newspapers Are Loaded onto Delivery Trucks that speed them to newsstands and carriers throughout the community.

A Newspaper Carrier delivers the latest news directly to a family's doorstep in the form of their daily newspaper.

books) issued in Europe, especially in Germany. But these pamphlets were not published frequently, since rulers generally frowned on news or comment on public affairs. In addition, only a few people were able to read. Apparently the first regularly published papers were issued in Germany in the early 1600's. The oldest on record is the *Strasbourg Relation* of 1609.

Early English Newspapers. The first paper to be published continuously in England was the *Courant*, or *Weekly Newes*, in 1622. This paper and those which followed were very small in page size. The first English newspaper of full size was the Oxford *Gazette*, which soon moved from Oxford to London. This was a court journal begun in 1665 and devoted to official notices of the royal court. It still continues with much the same function. The first daily paper in England was the *London Daily Courant*, begun in 1702 by a woman, Elizabeth Mallett. *The Times* (London) was founded in 1785 under the name of the *Daily Universal Register*.

First American Newspapers. The first newspaper published in the American colonies was *Publick Occurrences Both Forreign and Domestick*. It was issued in Boston in 1690 by Benjamin Harris, who had already been in trouble for bold publishing in England. His Boston paper was suppressed after the first issue. After that no paper was attempted until John Campbell began his *Boston News-Letter* in 1704. After that, other papers were attempted in Boston. One was the *New England Courant*, begun in 1721 by James Franklin, who employed his brother Benjamin in his shop.

The first paper outside Boston was Andrew Bradford's *American Weekly Mercury*, founded in Philadelphia in 1719. Andrew's father, William Bradford, started the first New York paper, the *Gazette*, in 1725. Benjamin Franklin published the *Pennsylvania Gazette* from 1729 to 1766. The first daily newspaper in America, the *Pennsylvania Evening Post and Daily Advertiser*, began in 1783 in Philadelphia. At the outbreak of the Revolutionary War, there were 35 newspapers being published in the colonies. The first published west of the Appalachian Mountains was the *Pittsburgh Gazette* in 1786. *The Alexandria* (Va.) *Gazette*, published daily since 1797, is one of the oldest continuously-published U.S. dailies.

The Penny Papers. In the early 1800's, the newspapers were chiefly political in both news and editorials.

They were often very large in page-size (blanket-sheets) and commonly sold for six cents. This put them out of reach of the poorer classes of people. When the penny papers were started in the 1830's, America had its first genuinely popular journalism. The first successful penny paper was the *New York Sun*, founded in 1833 by Benjamin H. Day. It was lively, gave more attention to news than politics, and was small in size. After the Civil War, the *Sun* came under the control of Charles A. Dana, a believer in independent journalism.

In 1835, James Gordon Bennett founded the *New York Herald*, which came to be considered by many people as the great representative American paper. In spite of his sensationalism, Bennett originated many new journalistic techniques, and is regarded as one of the greatest of American editors.

Another paper which started at one cent was the *New York Tribune*, founded in 1841 by Horace Greeley. Greeley was an outstanding humanitarian. He developed the modern editorial page and exerted a wide national influence. The Bennett and Greeley papers were merged in 1924 into the *Herald Tribune*. *The New York Times*, too, was a penny paper when it was started in 1851 by Henry J. Raymond and two associates. Adolph S. Ochs brought the *Times* to its present position in the top rank of journalism. Another penny paper was the *Baltimore Sun*, founded by A. S. Abell and two friends.

Other Great American Papers. Joseph Pulitzer, an immigrant boy, made both fortune and reputation in St. Louis, where he founded the *Post-Dispatch*. Later he bought *The* (New York) *World* (1883) and greatly influenced American journalism by his highly successful enterprise. The *World* was bought by the Scripps-Howard chain in 1931, and merged with the *New York Evening Telegram*. In 1950, the *World-Telegram* bought the *New York Sun* and became the *World-Telegram and The Sun*. The first Chicago paper was the *Chicago Democrat*, begun in 1833. The *Chicago Tribune* was founded in 1847. Joseph Medill and C. H. Ray made it an important paper in the 1850's.

A second penny-press movement developed in the 1870's and early 1880's. The *Chicago Daily News* was founded by Victor Lawson and Melville Stone in 1876. The *Kansas City Star* was founded by William Nelson in 1880. Certain Southern papers are historically important. These include the *New Orleans Picayune* (now *Times-Picayune*), founded in 1837 by George Kendall and his friend Francis Lumsden; and the *Atlanta Constitution*, edited in the 1880's by Henry Grady. Similarly important are two Western papers—the *San Francisco Chronicle*, started in 1865 by two teen-aged brothers named De Young, and the *Portland Oregonian*, edited from 1877 to 1910 by Harvey Scott.

Tabloids. During the 1920's, many tabloids adopted a policy of sensationalism coupled with large-scale use of illustrations. Most important of these newspapers was Joseph Patterson's *New York News*, founded in 1919. Many tabloids later gave up sensationalism and became respectable newspapers. Today there are a number of excellent tabloids published. Marshall Field III established *The Chicago Sun* in 1941. In 1948, he merged this paper with the *Daily Times* to form a tabloid, the *Chicago Sun and Times*, now called the *Chicago Sun-Times*. See FIELD (family).

Consolidation and Expansion. In the 1900's the number of newspapers in the United States was cut by consolidations, or combining of two or more papers. Advertisers found it cheaper to buy space in one paper with general circulation, even at increased rates, than in two with overlapping coverage. Combination papers often made special efforts to represent all points of view fairly, and they were able to avoid ruinous competition. Frank A. Munsey, millionaire magazine publisher, led a great movement of merging newspapers.

Newspapers expanded through modern chain ownership. E. W. Scripps established the first chain with his penny papers in 1878. William Randolph Hearst's chain began with the *San Francisco Examiner* in 1887. In 1895, he bought the *New York Journal* and made it the model of sensational papers. This sensationalism was called "yellow journalism," after the "Yellow Kid," a comic strip character (see OUTCAULT, RICHARD FELTON). In 1964, the Hearst chain had 10 daily papers and 8 Sunday papers. The Samuel Newhouse chain had 16 dailies and 10 Sunday papers, and a financial interest in 3 other dailies and 2 Sunday papers. The Scripps-Howard chain had 18 dailies and 8 Sunday papers.

In 1962, *The New York Times* began a West Coast edition in Los Angeles. This marked the first time a daily newspaper of general readership was published in two U.S. cities at the same time. But the western edition was suspended in 1964 after financial losses. For several years, *The Wall Street Journal* has been printed simultaneously in seven plants across the country.

Newspapers Today. Population shifts from large cities to suburban areas since the mid-1940's have changed the newspaper business. Large metropolitan papers must now compete with smaller suburban papers. These suburban papers give their readers more news of their local communities than the larger papers do. Metropolitan papers must appeal to readers over a wide area. They sometimes publish *zone* sections that feature local news and advertising for particular areas.

The number of U.S. dailies has changed little since the mid-1940's. Total circulation has increased about 14 million since then.

Major newspapers began to have financial problems during the early 1960's. Detroit, Houston, Los Angeles, New York City, and San Francisco lost newspapers during this period through mergers or closings. Because of costly strikes, New York City and Cleveland were without local newspapers during the winter of 1962-1963. The *New York Mirror* went out of business as an indirect result of the New York City strike.

In 1966, three New York City newspapers—the *Herald Tribune*, the *Journal-American*, and the *World-Telegram and the Sun*—merged to form the *World-Journal-Tribune*. But financial problems forced the paper to suspend publication in 1967. In 1972, two metropolitan dailies—the *Boston Herald-Traveler* and the Newark (N.J.) *Evening News*—ceased publication. That same year, the *Washington* (D.C.) *News* merged with the *Washington Star* to form the *Washington Star-News*. Today, Boston and New York City are the only U.S. cities with more than two separately owned newspapers having large circulations.   ROBERT U. BROWN

Related Articles. See the Communication section of the various state, province, and country articles. See also JOURNALISM with its list of Related Articles. Other related articles in WORLD BOOK include:

Advertising (Newspapers)	North American News-
Associated Press	paper Alliance
Audit Bureau of	Paper (Special Kinds)
Circulations	Photoengraving
Camera	and Photolithography
Cartoon	Printing
Comics	Proofreading
Editorial	Publishing
Facsimile	Reuters
Foreign Correspondent	Stars and Stripes
Fourth Estate	Stereotyping
Freedom of the Press	Tass
International News Service	Telephoto
Kyodo	Teletypesetter
Linotype	Teletypewriter
News Service	United Press International
Newspaper Guild	War Correspondent
Newspaper Syndicate	

Outline

Questions

About how many newspapers are distributed daily in the United States?

What is a large paper's greatest operating expense?

What was probably the first known newspaper?

What different kinds of material or information are usually found in a daily paper?

How did the term "yellow journalism" get started?

What country leads the world in the number of newspapers sold daily per 1,000 persons?

What are the three departments of a newspaper staff?

What is the work of the city editor?

What facts would a reporter covering a fire try to get?

What is (a) a beat reporter, (b) writing a lead, (c) a "mat," (d) a syndicated feature?

Reading and Study Guide

See *Newspaper* in the RESEARCH GUIDE/INDEX, Volume 22, for a *Reading and Study Guide*.

NEWSPAPER GUILD is a labor union whose members work in the news and commercial departments of newspapers, news magazines, news services, and related enterprises. The guild has local organizations in 100 cities in Canada, Puerto Rico, and the United States. For membership, see LABOR MOVEMENT (table).

The Newspaper Guild has advocated shorter hours, higher wages, severance pay, and greater job security for its members. It has contracts with newspapers whose combined circulation totals about one-half of the daily newspaper circulation in the United States.

The guild is affiliated with the AFL-CIO and the Canadian Labour Congress. It was founded in 1933 and was called the American Newspaper Guild until 1971. Its headquarters are at 1126 16th St. NW, Washington, D.C. 20036.   Critically reviewed by the NEWSPAPER GUILD

NEWSPAPER SYNDICATE. For a few cents a person can buy a newspaper that contains outstanding photographs and comics, and columns and features by famous writers, cartoonists, medical authorities, and other specialists. Newspaper syndicates make it possible for even small newspapers to carry features by highly paid contributors, because the syndicates sell the same material to many papers. They differ from *news services* because they do not deal in "spot news."

The amount of money a newspaper pays for a syndicated feature depends on the size of the newspaper's circulation. A paper with a circulation of 200,000 might pay $50 a week for a feature that would cost a smaller paper only $3.50 a week. Many syndicates are owned or controlled by newspapers which develop features for their own use and to sell to other newspapers.

There are several important newspaper syndicates in the United States. The best-known syndicates include Bell, Field Newspaper Syndicate (formerly called Publishers-Hall Syndicate), King Features, and United Features.   EARL F. ENGLISH

See also NORTH AMERICAN NEWSPAPER ALLIANCE; NEWS SERVICE.

NEWSPRINT. See NEWSPAPER (What Is a Newspaper?); PAPER (Special Kinds of Paper).

A **Red-Spotted Newt** is shown in the *eft* phase, during which it lives on land in wooded places.

Hugh Spencer

NEWT, *noot*, is a small animal with a slender body, thin skin, and four weak legs. It is a type of salamander, and is classified as an amphibian, along with frogs and caecilians (see AMPHIBIAN).

Newts and other salamanders are *tailed amphibians*. The tail of the adult newt is flatter than that of most other salamanders. Newts hatch from eggs which are laid singly in the spring on the leaves of plants under water. The young hatch after three to five weeks. They live in the water and breathe by means of gills. In time, they develop lungs and may take to the land. People then call them *efts*. The efts stay on land up to three years before they return to water to breed. They often shed their skins. If an eft loses a leg, it can grow it back. The kind of newt best known in the United States is the *red-spotted* newt. It is about 4 inches (10 centimeters) long. Newts eat insects, worms, and mollusks.

Scientific Classification. Newts are in the class *Amphibia*. They belong to the salamander family, *Salamandridae*. The American red-spotted newt is genus *Diemictylus*, species *D. viridescens*.   W. FRANK BLAIR

NEWTON, Mass. (pop. 91,263), is a suburban community 7 miles (11 kilometers) west of Boston. Often called the *Garden City*, Newton lies on the Charles River in a region of great natural beauty (see MASSACHUSETTS [political map]). Newton produces electrical equipment, knit goods, paper products, and plastics. Boston College is in the Chestnut Hill section of Newton. The city is also the home of the Andover-Newton Theological School.

Settlers first came to Newton in 1639. The settlement was then part of Cambridge. It consisted of 14 villages which still retain their separate identities within the city. John Eliot, called "The Apostle of the Indians," arrived in 1646, and later became pastor of Newton's first church. Other noted residents have included educator Horace Mann, and the authors Nathaniel Hawthorne and Ralph Waldo Emerson. Newton was known as New Cambridge until 1692, and received its city charter in 1873. It has a mayor-council type of government.   WILLIAM J. REID

NEWTON, SIR ISAAC (1642-1727), an English scientist, astronomer, and mathematician, invented a new kind of mathematics, discovered the secrets of light and color, and showed how the universe is held together. He is sometimes described as "one of the greatest names in the history of human thought," because of his great contributions to mathematics, physics, and astronomy.

Newton discovered how the universe is held together through his theory of gravitation. He discovered the secrets of light and color. He invented a branch of mathematics, *calculus* (see CALCULUS). He made these three discoveries within 18 months from 1665 to 1667.

The Theories of Motion and Gravitation. Newton said the concept of a universal force came to him while he was drinking tea in the garden and saw an apple fall. He suddenly realized that one and the same force pulls the apple to earth and keeps the moon in its orbit. He found that the force of universal gravitation makes every pair of bodies in the universe attract each other. The force depends on (1) the amount of matter in the bodies being attracted and (2) the distance between the bodies. The force by which the earth attracts or pulls a large rock is greater than the pull on a small pebble, because the rock contains more matter. The earth's pull is called *the weight* of the body. With this theory, Newton explained why a rock weighs more than a pebble.

He also proved that many types of motion are due to one kind of force. He showed that the gravitational force of the sun keeps the planets in their orbits, just as the gravitational force of the earth attracts the moon and an apple. The falling of an apple seems different from the motion of the moon, because the apple falls straight down to the earth, while the moon moves approximately in a circle around the earth. Newton showed that the moon falls just like the apple. If the moon did not fall constantly toward the earth, it would move in a straight line and fly off at a tangent to its orbit. Newton calculated how much the moon falls in each second and found the distance is $\frac{1}{3600}$ of the distance an apple falls in a second. The moon is 60 times as far from the earth's center as a falling apple. Consequently, the force of the earth on an object 60 times as far away as another object is $\frac{1}{3600}$.

The Principia. Newton concluded his first investigations on gravity and motion in 1665 and 1666. Nothing was heard of them for nearly 20 years. His original theory had been based on an inaccurate measurement of the earth's radius, and Newton realized differences between the theory and the facts. Although he later learned the true value of the earth's size, he was not led to complete his investigation or to produce a book for publication.

One day in 1684, Edmund Halley, an English astronomer, Robert Hooke, an English scientist, and Christopher Wren, the architect, were discussing what law of force produced the visible motion of the planets around the sun. They could not solve this problem. Halley went to Cambridge to ask Newton about it. He found Newton in possession of complete proof of the law of gravity. Halley persuaded Newton to publish his findings. Halley paid all the expenses, corrected the proofs, and laid aside his own work to publish Newton's discoveries. Newton's discoveries on the laws of motion and theories of gravitation were published in 1687 in *Philosophiae Naturalis Principia Mathematica* (Mathematical Principles of Natural Philosophy). This work, usually called *Principia* or *Principia Mathematica*, is considered one of the greatest single contributions in the history of science. It includes Newton's laws of motion and theory of gravitation. It was the first book to contain a unified system of scientific principles explaining what happens on earth and in the heavens.

Light and Color. Newton's discoveries in optics were equally spectacular. He published the results of his experiments and studies in *Opticks* (1704).

Newton's discoveries explained why bodies appear to be colored. They laid the foundation for the science of spectrum analysis. This science allows us to determine the chemical composition, temperature, and even the speed of such hot, glowing bodies as a distant star or an object heated in a laboratory.

Newton discovered that sunlight is a mixture of light of all colors. He passed a beam of sunlight through a glass prism and studied the colors that were produced. A green sweater illuminated by sunlight looks green, because it largely reflects the green light in the sun and absorbs most of the other colors. If the green sweater were lighted by a red light or any color light not containing green, it would not appear green.

Bausch & Lomb

By Passing a Beam of Sunlight through a prism, Newton showed that white light is made up of the rainbow's colors.

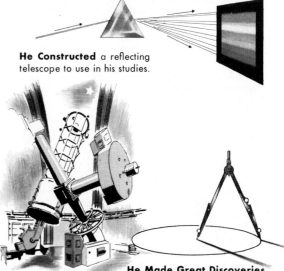

He Constructed a reflecting telescope to use in his studies.

He Made Great Discoveries in the field of mathematics. He is credited with inventing integral and differential calculus.

He Was the First to state the laws of gravitation.

The study of light led Newton to consider constructing a new type of telescope in which a reflecting mirror was used instead of a combination of lenses. Newton's first reflecting telescope was 6 inches (15 centimeters) long, and, through it, Newton saw Jupiter's satellites.

Early Life. Newton was born at Woolsthorpe, Lincolnshire, on Dec. 25, 1642. He attended Grantham grammar school. As a boy, he was more interested in making mechanical devices than in studying. He was considered a poor student. His youthful inventions included a small windmill that could grind wheat and corn, a water clock run by the force of dropping water, and a sundial. He left school when he was 14 to help his widowed mother manage her farm. But he spent so much time reading, he was sent back to school.

He entered Trinity College, Cambridge University, in 1661. He showed no exceptional ability during his college career, and was graduated in 1665 without any particular distinction. He returned to Cambridge as a fellow of Trinity College in 1667.

Newton became professor of mathematics at Cambridge in 1669. He lectured once a week on geometry, astronomy, optics, arithmetic, or other mathematical subjects. He was elected a fellow of the Royal Society in 1672.

Public Life. Newton became active in public life after the publication of *Principia*. He became the Cambridge University member of Parliament in 1689 and held his seat until Parliament dissolved the following year. He became warden of the mint in 1696. He was appointed master of the mint in 1699, a position he held until his death.

In 1699, he also became a member of the Royal Society council and an associate of the French Academy. He was elected to Parliament again from the university in 1701. He left Cambridge and settled permanently in London in 1701. He became president of the Royal Society in 1703 and was re-elected annually until his death. Queen Anne knighted Newton in 1705. He died in 1727 and was buried in Westminster Abbey.

Personal Characteristics. Newton did not enjoy the scientific arguments that arose from his discoveries. Many new scientific theories are opposed violently when they are first announced, and Newton's did not escape criticism. He was so sensitive to such criticism that his friends had to plead with him to publish his most valuable discoveries.

Newton was a bachelor who spent little of his time studying mathematics, physics, and astronomy. He was a student of alchemy, and made many alchemical experiments. He also spent a great deal of his time on questions of theology and Biblical chronology.

As a professor, he was very absent-minded. He showed great generosity to his nephews and nieces and to publishers and scientists who helped him in his work.

He was modest in his character. He said of himself shortly before his death, "I do not know what I may appear to the world, but to myself I seem to have been only like a boy playing on the seashore, and diverting myself in now and then finding a smoother pebble or a prettier shell than ordinary, whilst the great ocean of truth lay all undiscovered before me."

Albert Einstein, the German-American physicist, rejected Newton's explanation of universal gravitation but not the fact of its operation. He said that his own work would have been impossible without Newton's discoveries. He also said that the concepts Newton developed "are even today still guiding our thinking in physics."   I. BERNARD COHEN

Related Articles in WORLD BOOK include:

Aerodynamics (Pioneers)	Light
Color (History)	Motion
Force	Science (Galileo and
Gravitation	Newton)
Jet Propulsion	Tide

NEWTON'S LAWS OF MOTION. See MOTION.

NEWTON'S RINGS are a series of alternately bright and dark circles that can be seen when a slightly convex piece of glass is placed against a flat piece of glass. If the viewing light is a single color, the rings will have this color. If the light is white, the rings will have the colors of the spectrum from violet through red. Newton's rings are caused by interference between the light waves reflected from the top of the flat surface and those reflected from the bottom of the curved surface. The point of contact is dark. The rings were named for Sir Isaac Newton, who was the first to study them in detail.   ROBERT LINDSAY

NEXT OF KIN is a legal phrase for the closest blood relatives of a person who has died without making a will. These next of kin are entitled to share in whatever personal property the dead person owned. Laws of descent and distribution are complicated, and differ in the various states. The laws of each state determine how and to what extent the next of kin will share in the personal property left by a resident of that state who did not leave a will. In some instances such laws provide for the distribution of both real and personal property to the same people and to the same extent, thus treating next of kin the same as heirs. See HEIR.

People sometimes use the term *next of kin* to mean a person's nearest relative, without regard for the legal meaning of the phrase.   WILLIAM TUCKER DEAN

NEY, *nay,* **MICHEL** (1769-1815), was one of Napoleon Bonaparte's great soldiers. He served with great distinction in the campaign of 1792, when the French Army of the North defeated the Prussians and Austrians. His cool courage and military skill soon marked him as a most notable soldier. Napoleon made him a marshal of France in 1804. He received the title duke of Elchingen for defeating the Austrians at Elchingen in 1805. He fought at Jena and Eylau and commanded an army at Friedland, where the French defeated the Russians in the summer of 1807. His conduct at Friedland won him Napoleon's praise. He took charge of Napoleon's army for the march into Russia in 1812, and became Prince of Moscow. Napoleon and Joachim Murat left the army after its defeat and hastened back to France (see MURAT, JOACHIM). But Ney remained with the Grand Army during the terrible retreat.

When Napoleon was forced from power in 1814, Ney abandoned him, and became a supporter of King Louis XVIII, who succeeded Napoleon. But Napoleon escaped from Elba in 1815, and landed on the coast of France. Ney declared himself loyal to King Louis. He told the king that he would "bring Napoleon back in an iron cage," and started out with an army. He met Napoleon, who was marching toward Paris with a new army. But emotion swayed Ney. He embraced Napoleon, and joined him in the march on Paris. The king fled, and Ney and Napoleon entered the capital together.

The period of Napoleon's return to power, called the *Hundred Days*, ended in defeat. Ney led the last French charge at Waterloo in 1815. But the soldier who had fought so well for France was seized and tried for treason and rebellion. A court of his fellow officers refused to try him. But the House of Peers tried him, and condemned him to death. He was shot on Dec. 7, 1815. Ney was born in Saarelouis, in the Saar Basin.   VERNON J. PURYEAR

See also NAPOLEON I.

NEZ PERCÉ INDIANS, *nehz PURS,* are a tribe that lives in north-central Idaho. The rich farmlands and forests in the area form the basis for the tribe's chief industries, agriculture and lumber.

The name *Nez Percé* means *pierced nose,* but few of the Indians ever pierced their noses. In 1805, a French interpreter gave the name to the tribe after seeing some members wearing shells in their noses as decorations.

The Nez Percé originally lived in the region where the borders of Idaho, Oregon, and Washington meet. Prospectors overran the Nez Percé reservation after discovering gold there in the 1860's.

The Nez Percé resisted the efforts of the government to move them to a smaller reservation. In 1877, fighting broke out between the Nez Percé and U.S. troops. Joseph, a Nez Percé chief, tried to lead a band of the Indians into Canada. But he surrendered near the United States-Canadian border.   ALLEN P. SLICKPOO, SR.

See also JOSEPH, CHIEF; INDIAN WARS (The Nez Percé War).

NFO. See NATIONAL FARMERS ORGANIZATION.

NGO DINH DIEM, *noh din ZEE em* (1901-1963), was the first president of South Vietnam. He served from 1955 until a group of army officers seized control of the government and killed him in 1963.

Diem was born in central Vietnam, the son of a government official. During the 1940's, he worked for Vietnam's independence from France and opposed Communist control of Vietnam. In 1954, Communist-led rebels defeated the French. Vietnam was then divided into two parts, South Vietnam and North Vietnam. Bao Dai, emperor of South Vietnam, appointed Diem as his prime minister. Diem was elected president when South Vietnam became a republic in 1955.

At first, Diem restored some order to his war-torn country. But he soon began ruling like a dictator, and he became increasingly unpopular. Special police units brutally crushed his opponents. Also, Diem was unable to stop *Viet Cong* (Communist-led guerrilla) attacks on villages in South Vietnam. Many of his harsh actions were attributed to advice from his brother Ngo Dinh Nhu, and his sister-in-law, Madame Nhu. Nhu and Diem were killed together.   BERNARD B. FALL

See also VIETNAM (History); VIETNAM WAR.

NGUYEN VAN THIEU, *nwin vahn tyoo* (1923-   ), became president of South Vietnam in 1967, during the Vietnam War. In April 1975—under heavy pressure from his non-Communist political opponents—Thieu resigned in an attempt to encourage cease-fire talks between the Communists and the South Vietnam government. But the Vietnam War ended about a week later with a Communist take-over of South Vietnam.

Thieu was South Vietnam's deputy prime minister

and defense minister in 1965. From 1965 to 1967, he served as chief of state and chairman of the Directory, a 10-member executive committee in the military government that ruled South Vietnam.

Thieu was born in Phan Rang. As a military officer, he led a major attack during the military revolt that overthrew President Ngo Dinh Diem of South Vietnam in 1963. Born a Buddhist, Thieu became a Roman Catholic in 1958.   WESLEY R. FISHEL

See also VIETNAM (History); VIETNAM WAR.

NIACIN. See VITAMIN (Vitamin B Complex).

NIAGARA FALLS, N.Y. (pop. 85,615), is an industrial center on the Niagara River at Niagara Falls (see NEW YORK [political map]). The falls provide one of the greatest natural sources of water power in North America. The water power generated supplies homes and industries throughout New York and Pennsylvania, as well as the province of Ontario. The scenic beauty of the falls attracts thousands of tourists.

The city is a center for electrochemical and electrometallurgical industries. Factories there make paper products, carbons, graphite, abrasives, storage batteries, and aerospace equipment. Several charter air lines and a railroad freight line serve the city.

Father Louis Hennepin visited Niagara Falls in 1678 and sketched the falls. Robert Cavelier, Sieur de la Salle, later built Fort Conti, the first fort on the Niagara River, at this point. In 1759, this fort, later known as Fort Niagara, was captured by English forces. In 1819, Canada and the United States made the center line of the Niagara River their international boundary. Niagara Falls was incorporated as a village in 1848, and as a city in 1892. It has a city-manager government.

A footbridge over the Niagara River was completed in 1848. In 1855, John A. Roebling built the first railroad bridge. The twelfth bridge, a steel arch span known as the Rainbow Bridge, was completed in 1941. The development of Niagara power began in 1852. At that time, construction started on a hydraulic canal to lead the water from the upper river around the falls. The first electric power was delivered to the village of Niagara Falls in 1881. By 1895, electric power was available in quantity. In the early 1960's, the New York State Power Authority completed the $720 million Niagara Power Project, one of the largest hydroelectric facilities in the world.   WILLIAM E. YOUNG

See also NIAGARA FALLS AND NIAGARA RIVER.

NIAGARA FALLS, Ont. (pop. 69,423), is a gateway used by visitors to Canada from the United States. It lies on the Niagara River overlooking the Canadian side of the famous Niagara Falls (see ONTARIO [political map]). Driveways and parks stretch along the river.

Niagara Falls has become an industrial center of Ontario because of its location near the Queenston hydroelectric power development. The city's chief products include abrasives, chemicals, cereals, canned goods, industrial machinery, leather goods, iron and steel products, nitrogen fertilizers, paper, and silverware.

The city was incorporated in 1904. It has a mayor-council government. It became a gateway between Canada and the U.S. when a railroad bridge connected Canadian and U.S. railroads. Several bridges now cross the river at Niagara Falls.   D. M. L. FARR

Niagara Falls carries about 200,000 short tons (180,000 metric tons) of water a minute from one level of the Niagara River to the other. Horseshoe Falls, on the Canadian side of the river, is larger than American Falls. Four observation towers, from 282 to 500 feet (86 to 150 meters) high, give visitors a view of the falls. Rainbow Bridge links Niagara Falls, N.Y., *upper right*, and Niagara Falls, Ont.

NIAGARA FALLS AND NIAGARA RIVER. This waterway and its famous Falls make up one of the most beautiful natural regions in the world. Niagara Falls has become a favorite tourist center and is known throughout America as a *honeymooners' paradise*.

The River. The Niagara River connects Lake Erie and Lake Ontario. It forms part of the boundary line between New York and the Canadian province of Ontario. All the Great Lakes except Lake Ontario empty into this stream, which is only about 35 miles (56 kilometers) long.

The river flows quietly northward after leaving Lake Erie. Here, the stream is 326 feet (99 meters) higher than the surface of Lake Ontario, toward which it winds. Farther along in its course, the river divides and passes on either side of Grand Island, which is about 6 miles (10 kilometers) wide. Beyond the island, the river again forms a shallow stream. Goat Island then separates the river just before the Falls and a series of rapids occur. Then, the waters again flow quietly along the Ontario plain for the last 7 miles (11 kilometers). Ships can sail the length of the river except the 9 miles (14 kilometers) of waterfalls and rapids. The Welland Canal, which was built by the Canadian government, provides a shipping route around the Falls and rapids.

The Falls. Niagara Falls is located about midway in the river. At this point, the river plunges about 200,000 short tons (180,000 metric tons) of water a minute into a steep-walled gorge. The water drops in two streams.

The larger one falls over a rocky ledge of Niagara limestone on the Canadian side and forms the famous Horseshoe Falls. The smaller stream drops over the eastern shore and forms the American Falls. Horseshoe Falls is 158 feet (48 meters) high and 2,600 feet (792 meters) wide at the widest point (see ONTARIO [color picture]). This waterfall carries nearly the entire volume of the Niagara River. The American Falls is 167 feet (51 meters) high and about 1,000 feet (305 meters) wide. At night, wide beams of white and colored lights illuminate the Falls and present a beautiful picture of colored water. *The Maid of the Mist*, a steamer, takes visitors around the river at the base of the Falls.

The Whirlpool. The Whirlpool Rapids, near the northern end of the river, are almost as famous as the Falls. The current is so violent that it has carved a round basin out of the rock. Here, the rapids circle and twist about as fast as any other whirlpool in the world.

A cableway has been built in Ontario, high above the whirlpool. This cableway carries tourists from Colt's Point to Thompson's Point, on the opposite bank of the Niagara River. A passenger car provides seating space for 24 people, and standing room for 21 others. The car is hung from six cables, which are 1,800 feet (549 meters) long.

The Gorge. The steep-walled canyon through which the river flows downstream from Niagara Falls is 7 miles (11 kilometers) long. It stretches from the edge of Horseshoe Falls to Lewiston, N.Y. The gorge is made up

NIAGARA FALLS (N.Y.)

American Observation Tower

AMERICAN FALLS

HORSESHOE FALLS

James Studio, Niagara Falls

of layers of different kinds of stone. The top layer of hard limestone is about 80 feet (24 meters) thick. Beneath this layer are softer layers of limestone, shale, and sandstone. The ledge rests on a bed of soft shale. The top layer stretches out farther than the lower layers. The Cave of the Winds is under an extended shelf of hard rock. It is possible to see the falls from the inside by going down to the cave. Spray and water are wearing away at the base of the gorge. The gorge walls are steep but smooth at the southern and northern ends. But the rocks have been carved into strange shapes at the whirlpools and falls section.

The gorge is becoming longer, because the water pounds against it, wearing it down. The Falls were once at Lewiston, but they gradually moved back upstream toward Lake Erie. The ledge of Horseshoe Falls is being worn away at the rate of about 3 feet (91 centimeters) a year. The cutting away at the American Falls is much slower, since the action of the water is not so strong at this point. The rock bed of the American Falls moves back about 4 to 7 inches (10 to 18 centimeters) a year. In addition, slides have changed the appearance of the gorge. About 80,000 short tons (73,000 metric tons) of rock fell from the face of the American Falls in 1931. Several years later, 30,000 short tons (27,000 metric tons) of rock cracked off the upper edge of Horseshoe Falls. In 1934, 200 short tons (180 metric tons) of rock broke off from under Table Rock. On July 28, 1954, an estimated 185,000 short tons (167,800 metric tons) of rock

tumbled from the American Falls and nearby Prospect Point into the Niagara River. It was the biggest slide ever to occur at Niagara Falls. Engineers took steps to halt further erosion at the Falls. But on June 7, 1956, a series of giant rockfalls about $\frac{1}{2}$ mile (0.8 kilometer) below the Falls sent two-thirds of a huge power plant tumbling into the Niagara River gorge. A power-company employee was swept to his death in the disaster. Damage to the power station totaled several million dollars. Seepage of water into rock crevices between the lip of the gorge and the hydraulic canal feeding into the power station from above the Falls caused the collapse.

In 1969, U.S. Army engineers built a dam to temporarily stop the flow of water over the American Falls. They did this so they could study the rock ledge to find a way to prevent further erosion.

Origin of the Niagara Region. Niagara Falls was formed after the last great ice sheet withdrew from this region. The ice changed the surface of the land so much that waterways and streams were forced to seek new channels. The waters of Lake Erie overflowed and formed the Niagara River. This river had to pass a high cliff, known as the Niagara Escarpment, on its way northward. It is very difficult to tell when this occurred, because the water does not flow at an even rate, and it cuts away at both hard and soft rock. In some places, hard layers of rock cover softer layers, and the river cuts away the soft layers underneath to form caves. The Cave

HOW NIAGARA FALLS IS CHANGING

U.S. Army

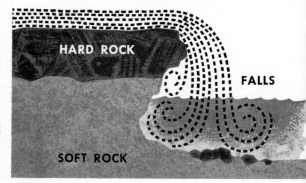

HARD ROCK

FALLS

SOFT ROCK

Swirling Currents, gaining force from plunging over the falls, eat away the soft under rock. The hard top rock then breaks off.

Erosion since Niagara Falls was first sketched in 1678 is shown by dotted lines, *below.* Horseshoe Falls, over which 95 per cent of the Niagara River flows, has eroded about ¼ mile (0.4 kilometer). The American Falls has receded only about 90 feet (27 meters) since 1842. In 1969, engineers temporarily stopped the flow over the American Falls, *left,* to study ways to prevent erosion.

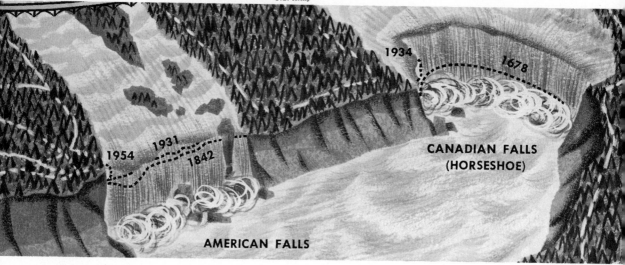

1934 · · · · · · · · 1678

1954 · 1931 · · · · 1842

CANADIAN FALLS (HORSESHOE)

AMERICAN FALLS

of the Winds was made in this way. Scientists believe that the Falls cannot be more than 20,000 years old.

Parks. In 1885, the New York state government took control of the land surrounding the falls on the American side and established Niagara Falls Park. The reservation covered about 430 acres (174 hectares). There are now about 1,700 acres (688 hectares) of parks on the U.S. side. In 1886, Canada set aside 196 acres (79 hectares) and established Queen Victoria Park. The entire Canadian side near the falls is now reserved as a park.

A drive follows the edge of the gorge in Canada. The drive is connected with Niagara Falls, N.Y., by the Niagara Rapids Boulevard and the Queenston-Lewiston Bridge. Niagara Rapids Boulevard links Devil's Hole State Park and Whirlpool State Park.

Bridges. The Cantilever Bridge, built in 1883 into solid rock, spanned the gorge above the whirlpool. It was the first bridge of its kind in America. A steel arch bridge replaced it in 1920. The famous Rainbow Bridge

was completed in 1941 between Niagara Falls, N.Y., and Niagara Falls, Ont. It replaced a bridge that collapsed under the weight of ice in 1938.

Water Power at the Falls was used as early as 1757 to run a sawmill built by a Frenchman, Chabert Joncaire, Jr. In 1881, the first hydroelectric power was generated at the Falls. But the first generators for the large-scale production of electric power were not installed on both sides of the Falls until the mid-1890's. Today, large power plants line both sides of the river. They have attracted to the Falls region electrochemical processing plants and other firms that require large amounts of electricity.

In 1950, the United States and Canada signed a treaty raising the amount of water that can be used to generate power. The authorized flow was increased from a total of 56,000 cubic feet (1,590 cubic meters) a second to 100,000 to 150,000 cubic feet (2,800 to 4,250 cubic meters) a second. The province of Ontario completed a power plant in 1958. This gave the Sir Adam Beck generating plants on the Canadian side of the Falls a total capacity of 1,811,000 kilowatts. That year, the United States began building a $720-million power plant with a capacity of 2,190,000 kilowatts. The plant, one of the world's largest hydroelectric facilities, was completed in 1962. GEORGE MACINKO

NIAGARA MOVEMENT was an organization founded by black Americans to fight racial discrimination in the United States. It existed from 1905 to 1910. At its height, the Niagara Movement had 30 branches in various U.S. cities. The movement failed to win the support of most blacks, but many of its ideas and programs were adopted in 1909 by a new interracial organization—the National Association for the Advancement of Colored People (NAACP).

The Niagara Movement was founded in Niagara Falls, Ont. W. E. B. Du Bois, a black professor at Atlanta University, led the organization (see DU BOIS, W. E. B.). The movement placed the responsibility for racial problems in the United States on whites. The movement thus opposed the view of the famous black educator Booker T. Washington, who urged blacks to stop demanding equal rights (see WASHINGTON, BOOKER T.). Various branches of the movement demanded voting rights for blacks, opposed school segregation, and worked to elect candidates who promised to fight race prejudice. ELLIOTT RUDWICK

See also BLACK AMERICANS (After Reconstruction).

NIAGARA UNIVERSITY is a coeducational school in Lewiston, N.Y. It is conducted by the Roman Catholic Vincentian Fathers. The university has colleges of arts and sciences, business administration, and nursing. It also has a graduate school, a school of education, the Soviet and East European Institute, and the Institute of Transportation, Travel, and Tourism. Courses lead to bachelor's and master's degrees. Niagara University was founded in 1856. For enrollment, see UNIVERSITIES AND COLLEGES (table). KENNETH F. SLATTERY

NIAMEY, *nyah MAY* (pop. 130,299), is the capital of the Republic of Niger in western Africa. An inland port on the Niger River, Niamey exports farm products of the region. For location, see NIGER (map).

NIBELUNG, *NEE buh loong,* was any one of a group of dwarfs in German mythology. They also were called *the children of the mist.* The Nibelungs owned a golden treasure that cursed all who seized it. The name Nibelung was later applied to anyone possessing the treasure. In the *Nibelungenlied,* a German epic of about A.D. 1200, the Burgundian kings are called Nibelungs.

See also OPERA (*Ring of the Nibelung, The*).

NIBELUNGENLIED, *NEE buh LOONG un LEET,* is a German epic poem written about A.D. 1200. The title means *Song of the Nibelungs.* The author is unknown but undoubtedly came from the Danube area of southeastern Germany or Austria.

The poem tells of Siegfried, king of the Nibelungs. Siegfried owns the fabulous Nibelung treasure and a cloak of invisibility. He has also killed a dragon and bathed in its blood. The blood hardened Siegfried's flesh, protecting it from wounds. But a linden leaf had fallen between his shoulders while he bathed, leaving an unprotected spot on his back.

Siegfried wants to marry Kriemhild, the sister of King Gunther of Burgundy. To gain Kriemhild, Siegfried helps Gunther win the maiden Brunhild, Queen of Iceland. Brunhild will marry only the man who can overcome her in combat. So Siegfried disguises himself as Gunther, and beats Brunhild, winning her for Gunther. Years later, Kriemhild tells Brunhild that Siegfried, not Gunther, had beaten her. In revenge, Brunhild orders Hagen, one of Gunther's *vassals* (servants), to murder Siegfried. Hagen kills Siegfried by shooting an arrow into the unprotected spot on Siegfried's back.

Several years later, Kriemhild marries Etzel, mighty king of the Huns. But she never forgets Siegfried. She invites the Burgundians to visit her and has them slaughtered. Only Hagen survives. Kriemhild asks him to reveal where he has hidden the Nibelung treasure. When he refuses, she kills him. Hildebrand, a warrior at the court of Etzel, horrified by Kriemhild's treachery, kills her.

The Background. Two actual events form the basis for parts of the *Nibelungenlied.* In A.D. 437, the Huns destroyed the Burgundians, an east Germanic tribe. The Burgundian king and members of his royal household died in the battle. The king of the Huns, Attila (called Etzel in the poem), was not connected with this event. Attila died suddenly on his wedding night in 453. Some historians said that he was murdered by his Germanic bride.

The Nibelungen-poet clearly was not the first to deal with this story material. The Icelandic *Edda,* composed before the *Nibelungenlied,* contains *lays* (short poems) on the same themes. The early Germanic peoples also composed lays to celebrate the great heroes and events of their past. The lays were revised, and in the course of centuries the original historical events were greatly altered. Unknown poets combined the events of 437 and 453 into a single historic lay. In this lay, a Burgundian bride kills Attila to gain revenge for the death of her relatives. Her relatives had been killed by Attila's Huns.

Many of the themes and much of the plot of the older Germanic lays can still be found in the *Nibelungenlied,* but the poet changed the material. Scholars have not been able to trace the *Nibelungenlied* story of Siegfried's death to particular historical personalities and events. In fact, Siegfried's supernatural powers give his story the quality of a fairy tale.

The Style. The *Nibelungenlied* is written in stanzas. Each stanza consists of four long lines of two pairs of rhymed couplets. The author shows a keen understanding of human psychology in developing the motives that cause the proud figures in the poem to act as they do. The great climaxes lie in the tense dialogues in which the rivals confront each other.

Scholars cannot say precisely what the Nibelungen-poet retained and what the poet added. The courtly aspects were probably added around 1200, however, when courtly culture flourished in Germany. The tender love between Siegfried and Kriemhild, the festivals of knights and ladies, and the many heroes of the epic reflect courtly virtues. These aspects provide the softer accents that contrast with and heighten the effect of the tragic ending. JAMES F. POAG

NICAEA, COUNCILS OF. See NICENE COUNCILS.

David Mangurian

The Nicaraguan Countryside includes sharply rising mountains, and grazing land for cattle and other livestock. The scene above is in western Nicaragua, near the city of León.

NICARAGUA

NICARAGUA, NIHK *uh* RAH *gwuh,* is the largest country of Central America. It is a little larger than New York, but has only about a tenth as many people as that state. Nicaragua extends from the Pacific Ocean to the Caribbean Sea. About three-fifths of the country's people live in a fertile region on the Pacific side. In this region is Managua, the capital and largest city of Nicaragua.

Most Nicaraguans have both Indian and Spanish ancestors. During the early 1500's, the Spaniards began arriving in what is now Nicaragua. They named the land for an Indian chief and his tribe—both called Nicarao—who lived there. The Nicarao way of life, like that of most other Indians of Nicaragua, has blended with Spanish customs and traditions. Today, Nicaragua has only a few Indian groups that still follow their old way of life.

Cotton is Nicaragua's leading source of income. It is grown on large farms in the Pacific Region. Few people live in the thickly forested Caribbean Region, on the other side of the country. In between, the people of the rugged Central Highlands raise beans, coffee, corn, and sugar cane on small farms.

Government

The Nicaraguan government has been controlled by the Somoza family directly or indirectly since 1937. That year, General Anastasio Somoza became president of Nicaragua. Partly by using terrorist methods, he achieved great political power and wealth. Each of

Richard N. Adams, the contributor of this article, is Professor of Anthropology at the University of Texas at Austin and the author of The Second Sowing: Power and Secondary Development in Latin America *and the coauthor of* Contemporary Cultures and Societies in Latin America.

Somoza's two sons later became president and tightened the family's control of the nation. Today, members of the Somoza family own all or part of almost every major economic operation in Nicaragua.

National elections are controlled to discourage voting against the Nationalist Liberal Party, which is run by the Somozas. Politicians opposed to the Somozas have never been a serious threat to their power. Opposition to the Somozas has been continuous, but it has been ineffective against their economic strength and government troops.

People

The great majority of Nicaraguans are *mestizos* (persons with white and Indian ancestors). Their general

---
FACTS IN BRIEF

Capital: Managua.

Official Language: Spanish.

Area: 50,193 sq. mi. (130,000 km²). *Greatest Distances*—north-south, 293 mi. (472 km); east-west, 297 mi. (478 km). *Coastlines*—Pacific, 215 mi. (346 km); Caribbean, 297 mi. (478 km).

Elevation: *Highest*—8,000 ft. (2,438 m) above sea level in the Cordillera Isabella. *Lowest*—sea level along the coasts.

Population: *Estimated 1978 Population*—2,373,000; distribution, 54 per cent rural, 46 per cent urban; density, 47 persons per sq. mi. (18 per km²). *1971 Census*—1,877,952. *Estimated 1983 Population*—2,791,000.

Chief Products: *Agriculture*—bananas, beans, beef cattle, coffee, corn, cotton, rice, sesame, sugar cane. *Manufacturing*—clothing and textiles, processed foods and beverages.

National Holiday: Independence Day, September 15.

National Anthem: "Himno Nacional de Nicaragua."

Money: *Basic Unit*—cordoba. See MONEY (table: Values). See also CORDOBA.

314

GOVERNMENT IN BRIEF

Form of Government: Republic.

Head of Government: President (elected to one six-year term).

Legislature: Senate (30 members elected to six-year terms); Chamber of Deputies (70 members elected to six-year terms).

Courts: The Supreme Court of Justice (7 justices elected by Congress until the age of 75) appoints judges of most lower courts to varying terms.

Political Divisions: 16 departments divided into 120 *municipios* (cities or townships). Administrators appointed by the president govern the departments. Mayors elected by the people head the municipios.

Voting Age: 21; 18 for persons who can read and write, are married, or have a high school degree.

Armed Forces: The National Guard of about 6,000 men is both an army and a police force. There are a small coast guard and air force within the National Guard. Military service may be required by law at any time.

---

way of life is somewhat similar to that of Spanish-Americans in other Central American countries. Most of the people of Nicaragua belong to the Roman Catholic Church and speak Spanish. The only Indian groups that still generally speak their own languages and follow their other old ways of life live in the thinly populated Caribbean Region. This region also has some black and mixed Indian-black communities that largely follow Indian customs and traditions.

Most of Nicaragua's people are poor farmers. Many of those in the Pacific Region are peasants who work on large estates owned by wealthy Nicaraguans. They live on or near the estates in shacks with palm-leaf roofs and walls of poles and branches. In the Central Highlands, many of the farmers have their own small farms. In the colder areas of that region, the farmers live in adobe homes with tile roofs. The Indians and blacks of the Caribbean Region live chiefly by farming small plots, or by fishing, lumbering, or mining.

Education. Nicaraguan law requires children to go to school from the age of 6 through 12. But only about half the children do so, and most of these live in cities or towns. Nicaragua does not have enough schools for all its youngsters, and many farm areas have no schools at all. There is also a shortage of teachers. About half the people cannot read and write.

Nicaragua has two universities. The National University of Nicaragua, in León and Managua, is the older and larger one. It was founded in 1812, and has more than 7,000 students. The Central American University is a Roman Catholic institution in Managua.

Population of Nicaragua increases about 3 per cent a year. To ease the pressure of this increase, the government encourages people of the Pacific Region, with loans and other help, to move to other regions. The Pacific Region still has about three-fifths of Nicaragua's population, although many people have moved to northern areas of the Central Highlands.

In 1978, Nicaragua had an estimated population of 2,373,000. The following table shows census figures of Nicaragua through the years:

1971	1,877,592	1940	835,686
1963	1,535,588	1920	638,119
1950	1,057,023	1906	505,377

Nicaragua has seven cities with populations over 20,-000. In order of size, they are Managua, León, Granada, Masaya, Chinandega, Matagalpa, and Estelí. See MANAGUA; LEÓN; and GRANADA.

The Land and Climate

Nicaragua has three main land regions: (1) the Pacific Region, (2) the Central Highlands, and (3) the Caribbean Region. The climate is chiefly tropical, with some differences among these regions.

The Pacific Region is largely a low area extending from Honduras to Costa Rica. Several volcanoes, some of them active, are in this low area. Lake Managua and Lake Nicaragua lie in the central and southern sections. Mountains up to 3,000 feet (910 meters) high rise along the Pacific coast. Nicaragua's largest cities and many large farms are in the Pacific Region.

The region receives about 60 inches (150 centimeters) of rain a year. The rainy season lasts from May to November. Temperatures average about 80° F. (27° C) throughout the year.

The Central Highlands make up Nicaragua's highest

Nicaragua's Flag was adopted in 1908 from that of the United Provinces of Central America. This union of the early 1800's consisted of Nicaragua and four other nations.

The Coat of Arms appears on the flag. The volcanoes stand for the Central American union, the triangle for equality, the rainbow for peace, and the cap for liberty.

Nicaragua, the largest Central American nation, is 1½ per cent as large as the United States, not counting Alaska and Hawaii.

WORLD BOOK map

Cotton, Nicaragua's Chief Product, makes up about 40 per cent of the country's exports. It grows in lowlands along the Pacific Ocean.

Leon Kofod

LAND REGIONS OF NICARAGUA

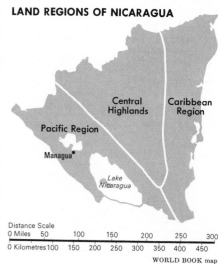

Central Highlands

Caribbean Region

Pacific Region

Managua*

Lake Nicaragua

Distance Scale

0 Miles	50	100	150	200	250	300

| 0 Kilometres | 100 | 150 | 200 | 250 | 300 | 350 | 400 | 450 |

WORLD BOOK map

and coolest region. They include the country's highest point, an unnamed peak that rises 8,000 feet (2,438 meters) above sea level in the Cordillera Isabella, a mountain range. Forests cover most of the region's slopes. Deep valleys lie between the mountains.

Some areas receive over 100 inches (250 centimeters) of rain a year. Most people live on farms in drier areas. Like the Pacific Region, the Central Highlands have a rainy season from May to November. Temperatures average 60° to 70° F. (16° to 21° C).

The Caribbean Region is mostly a flat plain, with some highlands sloping upward toward the west. Many rivers that rise in the Central Highlands flow through the plain. The region's only good farmland lies along the riverbanks. Rain forests cover most of the region. There are grasslands with palm and pine forests in the north. A number of small islands lie off the coast.

Easterly trade winds drench the Caribbean Region with an annual average of 165 inches (419 centimeters)

of rain, which falls throughout most of the year. Temperatures in the region average 80° F. (27° C).

Economy

Nicaragua's major natural resource is the rich soil of the Pacific Region. Ash from volcanoes makes this soil especially fertile. Farming is the country's leading industry, though farmland makes up less than 15 per cent of the land area.

Nicaragua has some deposits of copper, gold, and silver, but mining provides only a small part of the nation's income. United States and Canadian companies own most of the mines. Thick forests cover about half the land, and foreign firms also own much of the Nicaraguan lumber industry. Many mountain streams in the Central Highlands could furnish cheap hydroelectric power, but few of them have been used. The country is developing these power sources.

Agriculture. Exported farm products provide most of

Nicaragua Map Index

Departments

Boaco .....75,213..E 3		
Carazo .....86,139..F 2		
Chinandega 176,170..E 1		
Chontales ..78,532..E 3		
Esteli .....88,616..D 2		
Granada ....84,827..F 2		
Jinotega ..101,794..D 3		
León .....195,991..E 2		
Madriz ....59,077..D 2		
Managua ..499,568..E 2		
Masaya ...109,037..F 2		
Matagalpa 184,937..E 3		
Nueva Segovia ..75,777..D 2		
Río San Juan .....23,132..F 4		
Rivas .....86,015..F 3		
Zelaya ....161,866..D 4		

Cities and Towns

Acoyapa ....3,442..F 3		
Alta Gracia .1,739..F 3		
Belén .....3,487..F 3		
Bluefields .16,607..E 5		
Boaco .....7,870..E 3		
Camoapa ....5,252..E 3		
Catarina* ..2,273..E 2		
Chichigalpa 17,491..E 1		
Chinandega 34,902..E 1		

Ciudad Dario 6,716..E 2		
Condega ....3,835..D 2		
Corinto ...14,941..E 1		
Corn Island* 2,344..E 5		
Diriá* .....2,296..F 2		
Diriamba ..14,502..F 2		
Diriomo* ...4,706..F 2		
El Jícaro ...1,801..D 2		
El Sauce ...3,762..E 2		
El Viejo ..10,612..E 1		
Esquipulas ..2,556..E 3		
Esteli .....24,010..D 2		
Granada ...44,077..F 2		
Jalapa .....4,504..D 2		
Jinotega ..12,246..D 3		
Jinotepe ..15,434..F 2		
Juigalpa ..11,078..E 3		
La Concepción* ...3,387..F 2		
La Libertad .1,700..E 3		
La Paz Centro 7,933..E 2		
La Trinidad 4,019..E 2		
Larreynaga* .4,870..E 2		
León .....70,046..E 2		
Managua .364,337..E 2		
Masatepe ...8,267..F 2		
Masaya ...39,076..F 2		
Matagalpa .24,299..E 3		
Mateare ....1,678..E 2		
Matiguás ...2,620..E 3		
Moyogalpa ..1,791..F 3		
Muy Muy* ..2,001..E 3		
Nagarote ...8,817..E 2		

Nandaime ..7,098..F 2		
Nandasmo* .2,927..F 2		
Nindirí* ...2,699..F 2		
Niquinohomo* ...2,989..F 2		
Ocotal ...10,078..D 2		
Palacagüina* 1,689..D 2		
Posoltega* .1,538..E 1		
Prinzapolca* 5,794..D 5		
Pueblo Nuevo 1,799..D 2		
Puerto Cabezas ...6,376..C 5		
Puerto Morazán* .1,817..E 1		
Rama* .....2,256..E 4		
Rivas .....13,704..F 3		
San Carlos .3,104..F 4		
San Isidro ..2,818..E 2		
San Jorge .3,551..F 3		
San Juan de Limay ...2,376..D 2		
San Juan del Sur .....2,947..F 3		
San Lorenzo* 2,298..E 3		
San Marcos .4,447..F 2		
San Rafael del Norte .1,927..D 2		
San Rafael del Sur ...4,252..F 2		
Santa Teresa 3,602..F 2		
Santo Domingo ..1,895..E 4		
Santo Tomás 2,751..E 3		

Sébaco .....3,798..E 2		
Siuna .....4,126..D 4		
Somotillo ..2,305..E 1		
Somoto .....6,510..D 2		
Telica .....2,702..E 2		
Tipitapa ...8,904..E 2		
Tisma .....2,019..F 2		
Villa Somoza ...1,764..E 3		

Physical Features

Caribbean Sea ..F 5		
Coco (Wanks), Río C 4		
Concepción, Volcán (Volcano) ....F 3		
Darien, Cordillera de (Mountains) .....E 3		
Escondido, Río ...E 4		
Gorda, Punta (Point) ....C 5		
Grande, Río ......D 5		
Great Corn Island .E 5		
Huapi, Montañas de (Mountains) .....E 3		
Huaunta, Laguna (Lagoon) ......D 5		
Isabella, Cordillera (Mountains) .....D 3		
Lake Managua, see Managua, Lago de		
Lake Nicaragua, see Nicaragua, Lago de		

Managua, Lago de (Lake Managua) .E 2		
Marabios, Cordillera de los (Mountains) ....E 1		
Mico, Punta (Point) ......F 5		
Mosquito Coast ...F 4		
Negro, Río ......D 2		
Nicaragua, Lago de (Lake Nicaragua) F 3		
Ometepe, Isla de (Island) ......F 3		
Pacific Ocean ....F 2		
Pearl Cays (Islands) ......E 5		
Perlas, Laguna de (Lagoon) ......E 5		
Perlas, Punta de (Point) ......E 5		
Prinzapolca, Río ..D 4		
San Juan del Norte, Bahía de (Bay) .F 5		
San Juan, Río ....F 4		
Soletiname, Islas de (Islands) ......F 3		
Taberis, Laguna (Lagoon) ......C 5		
Tipitapa, Río* ....E 2		
Tuma, Río ......D 3		
Tyra Cays (Islands) E 5		
Venado, Isla (Island) ......F 5		

*Does not appear on the map; key shows general location.

Source: 1974 official estimates.

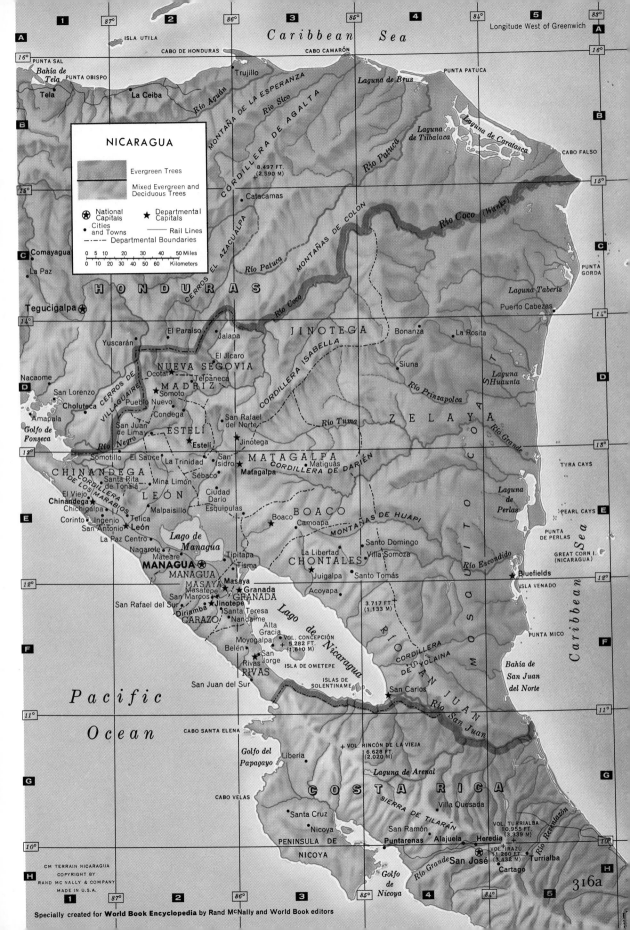

NICARAGUA

Legend:
- Evergreen Trees
- Mixed Evergreen and Deciduous Trees
- ⊛ National Capitals
- ★ Departmental Capitals
- • Cities and Towns
- ── Rail Lines
- ─ · ─ Departmental Boundaries

Scale:
0 5 10 20 30 40 50 Miles
0 10 20 30 40 50 60 Kilometers

Longitude West of Greenwich

Caribbean Sea

ISLA UTILA
CABO DE HONDURAS
CABO CAMARÓN
PUNTA PATUCA
PUNTA SAL
PUNTA OBISPO
Bahía de Tela
Tela
La Ceiba
Trujillo
Laguna de Brus
PUNTA PATUCA
Laguna de Tilbalaca
Laguna de Caratasca
CABO FALSO
Río Aguán
MONTAÑA DE LA ESPERANZA
Río Sico
CORDILLERA DE AGALTA
Río Patuca
8,497 FT. (2,590 M)
Catacamas
MONTAÑAS DE COLÓN
Río Coco (Wanks)
CABO FALSO
PUNTA GORDA
Comayagua
La Paz
CERROS EL AZACUALPA
Río Patuca
Río Coco
Laguna Taberis
Puerto Cabezas
H O N D U R A S
Tegucigalpa ⊛
El Paraíso
Jalapa
JINOTEGA
Bonanza
La Rosita
Yuscarán
El Jícaro
CORDILLERA ISABELLA
Siuna
Laguna Huaunta
NUEVA SEGOVIA
Ocotal ★
Telpaneca
MADRIZ
Somoto
Río Prinzapolca
Nacaome
San Lorenzo
CERROS DE VILLAGUAIRE
Pueblo Nuevo
Condega
San Rafael del Norte
Río Tuma
Z E L A Y A
Río Grande
Choluteca
ESTELÍ
San Juan de Limay
Esquipulas
Río Negro
Estelí
Jinotega
Río
Somotillo
El Sauce
La Trinidad
San Isidro
MATAGALPA
Matiguás
CORDILLERA DE DARIÉN
TYRA CAYS
Amapala
Golfo de Fonseca
CHINANDEGA
Santa Rita de Tonalá
Mina Limón
Ciudad Darío
Matagalpa
Laguna de Perlas
El Viejo
CORDILLERA DE LOS MARRABIOS
LEÓN
Malpaisillo
Esquipulas
B O A C O
MONTAÑAS DE HUAPI
PEARL CAYS
Chinandega
Chichigalpa
Boaco
Camoapa
PUNTA DE PERLAS
Corinto
Ingenio
Telica
Santo Domingo
GREAT CORN I. (NICARAGUA)
San Antonio
León
La Libertad
Villa Somoza
Río Escondido
La Paz Centro
Lago de Managua
CHONTALES
Bluefields
Nagarote
Mateare
Tipitapa
Juigalpa
Santo Tomás
ISLA VENADO
MANAGUA ⊛
MANAGUA
Tisma
3,717 FT. (1,133 M)
Masaya
MASAYA
Masatepe
Acoyapa
San Marcos
GRANADA
Granada
San Rafael del Sur
Santa Teresa
Jinotepe
PUNTA MICO
CARAZO
Nandaime
Diriamba
Alta Gracia
Lago de Nicaragua
CORDILLERA DE YOLAINA
Moyogalpa
VOL. CONCEPCIÓN 5,282 FT. (1,610 M)
Belén
San Jorge
Bahía de San Juan del Norte
RIVAS
Rivas
ISLA DE OMETEPE
ISLAS DE SOLENTINAME
Río San Juan
San Juan del Sur
San Carlos
Río San Juan
MOSQUITO COAST
Pacific Ocean
CABO SANTA ELENA
VOL. RINCÓN DE LA VIEJA 6,628 FT. (2,020 M)
Golfo del Papagayo
Liberia
Laguna de Arenal
Río Reventazón
C O S T A   R I C A
SIERRA DE TILARÁN
Villa Quesada
VOL. TURRIALBA 10,955 FT. (3,339 M)
CABO VELAS
Santa Cruz
Nicoya
San Ramón
Alajuela
Heredia
VOL. IRAZÚ 11,260 FT. (3,432 M)
Turrialba
PENÍNSULA DE NICOYA
Puntarenas
San José ⊛
Cartago
Golfo de Nicoya
316a

CM TERRAIN NICARAGUA
COPYRIGHT BY
RAND McNALLY & COMPANY
MADE IN U.S.A.

Specially created for **World Book Encyclopedia** by Rand McNally and World Book editors

NICARAGUA

Nicaragua's income. Cotton, the most valuable crop, is grown in the low Pacific areas. It accounts for about 40 per cent of the country's exports. Coffee and sugar cane are grown in the Central Highlands and the Pacific Region. Other farm exports include bananas, beef, rice, and sesame. Corn and beans are the main food crops raised for use in Nicaragua. They are grown in all regions, but chiefly in the Central Highlands.

Manufacturing. Nicaragua's industrial center is Managua, where most of the nation's electric power is generated. As in most Central American countries, the major products are processed foods and beverages, clothing, and textiles. Other products include cement, cigarettes, and goods made of leather, petroleum, and wood. Almost all the manufacturing companies are privately owned, about a third of them by foreign firms.

Foreign Trade. Nicaragua's main trading partner is the United States. Others include West Germany and Japan. Nicaragua belongs to the Central American Common Market, an economic union of five nations. This union is based on the General Treaty for Central American Economic Integration (see COMMON MARKET). Nicaragua's trade with the other four countries increased rapidly during the 1960's.

Transportation. Nicaragua has about 9,000 miles (14,000 kilometers) of roads, of which about 1,500 miles (2,410 kilometers) are paved. The Pan American Highway is the major highway (see PAN AMERICAN HIGHWAY). Many populated areas cannot be reached by automobile, and the people use mules or oxcarts to travel over crude trails. There are about 250 miles (402 kilometers) of railways, all in the Pacific Region. Managua has an international airport. The major seaport, Corinto, is on the Pacific Ocean.

Communication. Nicaragua has few newspapers. The largest is *La Prensa* of Managua. Government-operated postal, telegraph, and telephone systems serve only cities and towns. Most of the many radio stations and the two television channels are privately operated.

History

The Indian Period. Little is known of what is now Nicaragua before the Spaniards arrived in the early 1500's. A series of Indian states occupied the Pacific Region and the Central Highlands. They built fortified towns, and had highly developed markets and a system of social classes that included slaves. Less developed Indian societies lived in the Caribbean Region.

The Colonial Period. In 1502, Christopher Columbus arrived at what is now Nicaragua, and claimed the land for Spain. A Spanish expedition from Panama explored the Pacific Region in 1522. The Spaniards baptized many Nicarao Indians of the region into the Roman Catholic Church. Another expedition from Panama came to the region in 1524. The leader, Francisco Fernández de Córdoba, founded Granada and León near the main sources of Indian labor. The Indians worked on the Spaniards' farms and in their mines.

In 1570, Nicaragua came under the control of the Audiencia of Guatemala, a high court of Spanish judges and administrators that ruled most of Central America. Nicaragua was part of the colony of New Spain, but the court had great power because it was so far from Mexico City, the colonial capital.

The Spaniards explored the Caribbean coast of Nicaragua, but did not settle there. During the 1600's and 1700's, other Europeans—chiefly the English—occupied that region from time to time. English, Dutch, and French pirates had hideouts there, and attacked Spanish shipping in the Caribbean Sea. The pirates also raided Spanish towns to the west. During the 1700's, the English established control over the Miskito, or Mosquito, Indians of the Caribbean coast. Great Britain gave up its hold on the region to Nicaragua in the mid-1800's, under an agreement with the United States.

Independence. On Sept. 15, 1821, Nicaragua and other Central American states also declared their independence. They later became part of the Mexican empire, but broke away in 1823 and formed the United Provinces of Central America. This union generally followed liberal economic and political policies. For example, the member states established various civil rights, and ended the special rights of powerful nobles and the Roman Catholic Church.

Nicaragua's Gross National Product

Total gross national product in 1976—$1,526,000,000

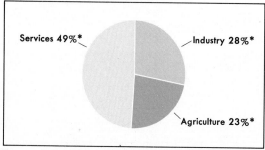

Services 49%*

Industry 28%*

Agriculture 23%*

The gross national product (GNP) is the total value of goods and services produced by a country in a year. The GNP measures a nation's total annual economic performance. It can also be used to compare the economic output and growth of countries.

Production and Workers by Economic Activities

Economic Activities	Per Cent of GDP* Produced	Labor Force	
		Number of Persons	Per Cent of Total
Agriculture, Forestry, & Fishing	23	315,127	46
Hotels, Restaurants, & Trade	22	83,622	12
Manufacturing	21	65,578	10
Community, Social, & Personal Services	7	137,458	20
Government	6	†	†
Transportation & Communication	6	28,960	4
Construction	5	29,637	4
Housing	5	—	—
Banking, Insurance, Real Estate, & Business Services	3	†	†
Mining	2	5,146	1
Utilities	**	5,216	1
Other economic activities	—	12,661	2
Total	100	683,405	100

*Based on gross domestic product (GDP). GDP is gross national product adjusted for net income sent or received from abroad.
†Included in Community, Social, & Personal Services.
**Included in Mining.
Source: Central Bank of Nicaragua.

The union began to fall apart under various pressures, including efforts by the conservative landowners and churchmen to regain their old privileges. In 1838, Nicaragua left the union. By that time, a great dispute had developed between León, the liberal center, and Granada, the conservative center. The cities struggled for control of Nicaragua, and fighting often broke out.

The liberals of León asked William Walker, an American military adventurer, to help them. In 1855, Walker arrived with a band of followers and captured Granada in a surprise attack. But instead of helping the liberals, he seized control of the government in 1856. The next year, the liberals and conservatives joined forces and drove Walker from the country.

The United States and Nicaragua. For many years, the United States had wanted to build a canal across Nicaragua to link the Atlantic and Pacific oceans. In 1901, President José Santos Zelaya of Nicaragua set certain limits on U.S. rights in the proposed canal zone. The United States did not accept these limits, and shifted its attention to Panama as the site of the canal. Zelaya then threatened to sell rights to the canal to some rival country of the United States. He also canceled contracts with a number of U.S. firms.

In 1909, a revolt broke out against Zelaya, a harsh ruler. He was driven from office after the United States sided with the rebels. In 1911, U.S. banks began to lend money to Nicaragua under agreements that gave them control over its finances until the debts were paid in 1925. At the request of the banks and President Adolfo Díaz, U.S. marines landed in Nicaragua in 1912 to put down forces that opposed American control. The marines remained there almost continuously until 1933 to protect U.S. interests and supervise elections.

Rebels led by General Augusto César Sandino made many raids on the U.S. marines from hideouts in the mountains. The Americans trained a new Nicaraguan army, called the National Guard, to help the marines. In 1934, after the marines had left, national guardsmen murdered Sandino under a flag of truce.

In 1916, the Bryan-Chamorro Treaty between the two nations gave the United States permanent, exclusive canal rights and 99-year leases on naval bases in Nicaraguan waters. Nicaragua received $3 million in return. United States plans for the canal were never developed, and, in 1970, the two nations signed an agreement to cancel the Bryan-Chamorro Treaty.

The Somoza Period. In 1936, General Anastasio Somoza, the head of the National Guard, forced President Juan Sacasa to resign. Somoza, who was Sacasa's nephew, became president the next year after an election in which he was the only candidate. He ruled as a dictator, and established great political and economic power for himself and his family.

Since 1937, a Somoza has ruled Nicaragua either as president or as the real power behind the government. Anastasio Somoza was assassinated in 1956, and his older son, Luis, replaced him as president. Luis held the presidency until 1963. His brother, Anastasio Somoza Debayle, became president in 1967. The Somozas have generally been eager to cooperate with the United States, and have always had U.S. government support.

Nicaragua's economy is expanding faster per person than that of any other Central American country. Political stability under the Somozas has attracted American

Wide World

The Somoza Family gained control of Nicaragua's government in 1937. Anastasio Somoza, *second from right,* shown with his wife, ruled from 1937 until 1956. His sons, Anastasio Somoza Debayle, *left,* and Luis Somoza, *right,* also became president.

investments. In 1968, the 160-mile (257-kilometer) Rama Road, built with U.S. aid, helped connect the Pacific and Caribbean coasts of Nicaragua.

In 1972, an earthquake in Nicaragua killed about 10,000 persons. It destroyed much of Managua, the capital and largest city. The city was rebuilt near the site of the earthquake. Also in 1972, President Somoza turned over power to a civilian junta. A presidential election was held in 1974, and Somoza was elected to a six-year term.   RICHARD N. ADAMS

Outline

I. **Government**
II. **People**
    A. Education   B. Population
III. **The Land and Climate**
    A. The Pacific Region
    B. The Central Highlands
    C. The Caribbean Region
IV. **Economy**
    A. Agriculture   D. Transportation
    B. Manufacturing   E. Communication
    C. Foreign Trade
V. **History**

Questions

How did Nicaragua get its name?
What is the main source of Nicaragua's income?
What family has controlled Nicaragua since 1937?
What is the most heavily populated part of Nicaragua?
What events led to the landing of U.S. marines in Nicaragua in 1912?
What are the main foods of the Nicaraguans?
Which two cities struggled for power in Nicaragua during the 1800's?
What are Nicaragua's chief manufactured products?
Why is the Pacific Region's soil especially fertile?
What country is Nicaragua's major trading partner?

NICARAGUA, LAKE. See LAKE NICARAGUA.

NICARAGUA CANAL was a proposed ship canal that was to extend across the Isthmus of Nicaragua and connect the Atlantic and Pacific oceans. The United States made several surveys of canal routes through Nicaragua during the 1800's and 1900's. The Nicaragua Canal was to extend across southern Nicaragua, through Lake Nicaragua (see NICARAGUA [map]). But plans for the canal were abandoned in 1970.

The Nicaragua Canal was first discussed in 1826 at the Panama Congress. Henry Clay instructed his commissioners to report whether the project was practical. Partial surveys were made in 1826 and 1837-1838. But nothing else was done until 1849, when Cornelius Vanderbilt formed and headed a company which was granted the right to build the canal. It never began construction, and the concession was annulled in 1856.

In 1849, Great Britain seized the land around the mouth of the San Juan River, which was to be the eastern end of the canal. Then the United States entered into the Clayton-Bulwer Treaty of 1850 with Great Britain. The treaty provided that, if the canal were built, Great Britain and the United States would control it (see CLAYTON-BULWER TREATY). The canal project was put off repeatedly. In 1887, a private company called the Nicaragua Canal Association was granted exclusive rights to build and operate the proposed canal. Two years later construction began, but cost of the canal was higher than had been expected, and within four years the company had spent $6 million. It then asked Congress for an additional $100 million. Congress denied the grant, and work was stopped.

The federal government appointed commissions to survey a route for a canal connecting the Pacific and Atlantic oceans in 1872, 1895, 1897, and 1899. Each time, the commissions favored a route across Nicaragua. But in 1909, Congress finally decided on a route through Panama. In 1914, the Panama Canal was completed. In 1916, the United States made a treaty with Nicaragua in which the Nicaraguan government granted the United States perpetual canal rights and other privileges for $3 million. In 1929, 1931, and 1938, Congress again authorized surveys. Some plans were also made after World War II (1939-1945). But in 1970, the United States and Nicaragua agreed to cancel the 1916 treaty.   ROLLIN S. ATWOOD

NICE, *nees* (pop. 322,442; met. area pop. 392,635), is a resort city on the French Riviera. It is also a Mediterranean port. Nice lies at the foot of the Alps near Italy (see FRANCE [political map]).

The beautiful city has wide avenues, luxurious hotels, and villas surrounded by gardens. The Paillon River divides it into the Old Town to the east and the modern, western part. The Alps protect Nice from cold northern winds and give it a mild winter climate. Most of the people depend for their living on the tourist trade. Most tourists come during the winter vacation season between January and April, or else from July to September. The Mardi Gras, which marks the height of the Riviera Carnival, is one of the city's many winter festivals (see MARDI GRAS). The industries of Nice produce olive oil, perfumes, processed fruit, soap, cement, and other products. Railroad lines to Marseille and to the Italian cities of Genoa and Turin pass through Nice. Greek settlers founded Nice about 400 B.C.   ROBERT E. DICKINSON

NICENE COUNCILS, *ny SEEN*, were two councils of the Christian Church held in Nicaea (Nice), in what is now northwest Turkey.

The first council was called in 325 by Emperor Constantine to settle the dispute caused by the Arian views of the Trinity. Arius was a priest of Alexandria who believed that Christ is not of the same essence as God, but of similar substance. The Council adopted the so-called *Nicene Creed*. This declared that God and Christ as God are of one substance. The Council also fixed the time for observing Easter. It was questioned whether the Christian Easter should be on the same day as the Jewish observance (Passover), or on a Sunday.

The *Nicene Creed* summarized the chief articles of the Christian faith of that time. It is next oldest to the Apostles' Creed. It was adopted originally in the following form, but has been amplified since:

> We believe in one God, the Father Almighty, maker of all things, both visible and invisible; and in one Lord, Jesus Christ, the Son of God, Only begotten of the Father, that is to say, of the substance of the Father, God of God and Light of Light, very God of very God, begotten, not made, being of one substance with the Father, by whom all things were made, both things in heaven and things on earth; who, for us men and for our salvation, came down and was made flesh, was made man, suffered, and rose again on the third day, went up into the heavens, and is to come again to judge both the quick and the dead; and in the Holy Ghost.

The second Council was called in 787 by the Empress Irene and her son Constantine. The Emperor Leo, Irene's deceased husband, had forbidden the use of images for any purpose. The Council was called because of opposition to the decree. The Empress revoked the decree after the Council had laid down principles governing the veneration of images.   FULTON J. SHEEN

See also ARIANISM; EASTER; ICONOCLAST; TRINITY.

NICHOLAS is the name of five popes of the Roman Catholic Church. Their terms were as follows:

Nicholas I, Saint	(858-867)
Nicholas II	(1059-1061)
Nicholas III	(1277-1280)
Nicholas IV	(1288-1292)
Nicholas V	(1447-1455)

Saint Nicholas I was a vigorous administrator. He asserted papal authority by excommunicating the archbishops of Cologne and Trier for approving King Lothair's second, adulterous marriage. He also excommunicated the archbishop of Ravenna for oppressing the poor.

Nicholas II called a council to set rules for electing future popes. He confined the election to a vote of the cardinals. This rule excluded the emperor and Roman nobility from papal elections.

The next two popes of this name were unimportant.

Nicholas V became famous as a scholar of the humanities. He founded the Vatican Library (see VATICAN LIBRARY). He started a vast building program that renovated Rome, and welcomed humanist scholars to Rome.   THOMAS P. NEILL and FULTON J. SHEEN

Nicholas II, the Last Czar of Russia, and His Family posed for this photograph shortly before the Russian Revolution of 1917. The Czar's family included his wife, Empress Alexandra; his son, Grand Duke Alexis; and his four daughters, the Grand Duchesses Maria, Tatiana, Olga, and Anastasia, *left to right.* Nicholas abdicated at the start of the revolution.

NICHOLAS was the name of two Russian czars.

Nicholas I (1796-1855) was noted for his harsh rule. He became emperor when his brother Alexander I died in 1825, and an older brother, Constantine, renounced his claim to the throne. Nicholas first put down a revolution staged by liberal-minded noblemen who desired reforms. This was called the *Decembrist* revolution because it occurred in December. Nicholas had five of the leaders executed, and exiled the rest to Siberia.

Nicholas fought all political reform after that. He created a powerful police, banned political organizations, introduced strict censorship, exiled liberal writers, and refused to abolish outdated institutions such as *serfdom* (see SERF). Corruption continued. He helped suppress revolutions abroad, and put an end to Polish independence when a revolution occurred there.

Despite these harsh measures, Nicholas eased and fixed the economic burdens of the farming class, and promoted the economic growth of the country through protective tariffs and a stable currency. He started railway construction. He introduced a new law code. Literature prospered despite persecution of liberal writers. Vocational schools were founded, but a free spirit in the universities was held in check.

Nicholas engaged in wars of expansion in Central and East Asia. He made war on Turkey in 1828, and almost achieved his aim of dominating the Bosporus and Dardanelles, exit to the Black Sea. Western Powers stemmed the Russian drive in the Crimean War (see CRIMEAN WAR). Nicholas died during the war. He was born at Tsarskoye Selo (now Pushkin).

Nicholas II (1868-1918), the last czar of Russia, ruled the country from 1894 to 1917. He was a charming and well-intentioned person, but he was politically weak and unreliable. Russia made economic progress, and became a major industrial power in oil, coal, iron, and textile production during his reign, with the help of loans from other countries. A trans-Siberian railway was completed. Science, music, and literature prospered. But Nicholas failed to re-establish good relations with his powerful neighbors, Germany and Austria. He allowed himself to become involved in a war with Japan in 1904, in an effort to control the Far East. Russia was defeated in 1905 (see RUSSO-JAPANESE WAR).

The lost war strengthened the disappointed Russian liberals, the discontented farmers and industrial workers, the oppressed Jews, and Polish, Finnish, and Baltic nationalists. Revolution broke out in 1905. Nicholas tried to crush it, but he was forced to compromise. He formed an elected assembly called the *Duma*, introducing a measure of representative government (see DUMA). He abolished flogging and canceled farm debts dating back to the time of emancipation. Farmers won the right to own their land. Although he introduced these reforms, broadened legislation, improved education, and increased industries, the lot of the common people seemed little improved. Nicholas disregarded demands for further reforms. This caused a renewal of revolutionary activities.

Russia entered World War I on the side of France and England. Soon terrible military defeats, coupled with an incapable, corrupt government, led to further suffering and unrest. Yet Nicholas, ill-advised by reactionaries, continued to neglect demands for reform. A new revolution broke out in 1917. Nicholas was forced to abdicate, and the rule of the czars ended. Nicholas and the members of his family were held as prisoners for a year. They were all reported shot on July 16, 1918, after Communists (Bolsheviks) seized the government. Nicholas was born at Tsarskoye Selo (now Pushkin), the son of Alexander III. W. KIRCHNER

See also RUSSIA (History); RASPUTIN, GRIGORI.

NICHOLAS, SAINT (A.D. 300's), one of the most popular saints of the Christian church, is the patron saint of sailors, travelers, bakers, merchants, and especially children. Little is known about his life except that he was Bishop of Myra in Lycia, on the coast of Asia Minor. It is believed that he was born in Patara in Lycia. Some stories say that he made a pilgrimage as a boy to Egypt and Palestine, that he was imprisoned during Diocletian's persecution, and released under Constantine. Some legends say he attended the Council of Nicaea in 325. Many miracles were credited to him.

Much of Europe still observes December 6, the date of Saint Nicholas' death, as a special holiday. In Germany, Switzerland, The Netherlands, and Belgium, men in bishops' robes pose as Saint Nicholas. They visit children, examine them on their prayers, urge them to be good, and give them gifts. This custom probably originated in the legend that Saint Nicholas gave gold to each of three girls who did not have dowries and so could not get married.

The Dutch brought "the visit of Saint Nicholas" to America. The visit of Santa Claus came from this custom. The name Santa Claus comes from *Sinterklaas*, Dutch for Saint Nicholas. WALTER J. BURGHARDT

See also BARI; CHRISTMAS (Saint Nicholas); NETHERLANDS (Holidays); SANTA CLAUS; SAINT NICHOLAS, FEAST OF.

NICHOLLS STATE UNIVERSITY. See UNIVERSITIES AND COLLEGES (table).

NICHOLS, MIKE (1931-   ), is a famous director known for his work both in motion pictures and on the stage. Nichols won an Academy Award for directing *The Graduate* (1967), his second movie. His other films include *Who's Afraid of Virginia Woolf?* (1965), *Catch-22* (1970), *Carnal Knowledge* (1971), and *The Day of the Dolphin* (1973).

Nichols began his directing career with *Barefoot in the Park* (1963), a Broadway comedy. He later directed such plays as *The Knack* (1964), *The Odd Couple* (1965), *Luv* (1966), and *Streamers* (1976).

Nichols was born in Berlin, Germany. His family came to the United States in 1939, and he became a U.S. citizen in 1944. Nichols joined a Chicago theater group in 1955. Later, he and another member of the group, Elaine May, formed a team that presented satirical comedy skits. ROGER EBERT

NICHOLSON, BEN (1894-   ), is an English artist noted for his abstract paintings, which feature geometric forms and pale colors. Nicholson also created *reliefs*, works of art which combine the techniques of painting and sculpture. In these reliefs, Nicholson created three-dimensional abstract pictures by cutting flat boards down to various levels and painting them.

Saint Nicholas was a kind-hearted Christian bishop who lived in the A.D. 300's. He became the patron saint of many European countries.

Bettmann Archive

Nicholson was born near Uxbridge, in England. His father was Sir William Nicholson (1872-1949), also an artist. Ben Nicholson's early works were realistic decorative paintings of great charm. He turned to abstract painting in the 1930's. He was especially influenced by the work of painters Piet Mondrian and Joan Miró. In 1956, he won the first $10,000 Guggenheim International Award for his painting, *August 1956—Val D'Orcia*. ALLEN S. WELLER

NICKEL (chemical symbol, Ni) is a white metallic chemical element often used in alloys. Its atomic number is 28 and its atomic weight is 58.71. Nickel is magnetic, takes a high polish, and does not tarnish easily or rust. It can be hammered into thin sheets or drawn into wires. One pound (0.4 kilogram) of pure nickel could be drawn into a wire 80 miles (130 kilometers) long. Axel Cronstedt, a Swedish scientist, discovered nickel in 1751.

Industrial Uses. Nickel is used in structural work and in electroplating chiefly because of its resistance to corrosion. Publishers often have printing plates electroplated with nickel to make them able to withstand hard use (see ELECTROPLATING). *Nickel peroxide*, a nickel compound, forms the active material of the positive electrode in the Edison storage battery. Nickel is also used in the nickel-cadmium storage battery (see BATTERY).

An important use for nickel is to promote certain chemical reactions by *catalysis* (see CATALYSIS). The

A Giant Nickel Ore Crusher, below, handles about 500 short tons (450 metric tons) of ore an hour, reducing it to 8-inch (20-centimeter) chunks. The machine operates in a mine in Ontario. Seven huge chains, foreground, regulate the flow of ore.

The International Nickel Co., Inc.

LEADING NICKEL-PRODUCING AREAS

Tons of nickel produced in 1972

Canada
256,500 short tons (232,700 metric tons)

Russia
*140,000 short tons (127,000 metric tons)

New Caledonia
110,400 short tons (100,200 metric tons)

Cuba
*40,000 short tons (36,300 metric tons)

Australia
39,400 short tons (35,700 metric tons)

*Estimate

Source: *Minerals Yearbook, 1972*, U.S. Bureau of Mines.

nickel itself is not changed in the process and can be used repeatedly. Nickel is used as a catalyst in a process called *hydrogenation*. In this process, the nickel causes some organic compounds to combine with hydrogen to form new compounds. Hydrogenation produces solid vegetable oils for cooking. See HYDROGENATION.

Nickel-Iron Alloys. Perhaps the largest use for nickel is as an additive to cast iron and steel. It improves the properties of these substances in many ways. It makes iron more *ductile* (easily formed) and increases its resistance to corrosion. Nickel also makes steel more resistant to impact. For this reason manufacturers frequently use steel alloyed with nickel to make armor plate and machine parts.

Invar, an alloy of nickel, iron, and other metals, is valued for meter scales and pendulum rods. It expands or contracts very little as its temperature changes.

Monel Metal is an alloy of copper and nickel used in sheet-metal work. See MONEL METAL.

Nickel Silver, also called *German silver*, is a nickel alloy used in tableware. See NICKEL SILVER.

Mining Nickel. The chief mineral ore of nickel is *pentlandite*, a mixture of sulfur, iron, and nickel. Other nickel ores include *millerite* and *niccolite*.

Sudbury District, in Ontario, supplies about a fourth of the world's nickel. Ores obtained there contain pentlandite and iron and copper sulfides. Other nickel-producing areas include Russia, New Caledonia, Cuba, and Australia. See SUDBURY.   ALBERT J. PHILLIPS

NICKEL is the common name for a U.S. copper-nickel coin. It is worth five cents, and its official name is the *five-cent piece*. The current Jefferson nickel has been minted since 1938. It has a profile of Thomas Jefferson on the *obverse* (front), and a picture of Monticello, Jefferson's home, on the *reverse* (back). A nickel with an Indian head on the obverse and a buffalo on the reverse was

Chase Manhattan Bank Money Museum

The U.S. Nickel Shows Thomas Jefferson and Monticello.

minted from 1913 through 1938. Nickels made from 1883 through 1912 had a head of Liberty on the obverse and a *V* (Roman numeral five) on the reverse. The earliest U.S. five-cent pieces had a shield on the obverse and a *5* on the reverse. They were minted between 1866 and 1883.   BURTON H. HOBSON

NICKEL SILVER is an alloy of copper, nickel, and zinc. A common composition is 60 parts copper, 25 parts zinc, and 15 parts nickel. The alloy is also called *German silver* because it was first made in the town of Hildburghausen, Germany. It is a yellowish metal that is harder than silver. Nickel silver tarnishes easily but takes a good polish.

Much of the silverware used today is made of nickel silver plated with real silver. It looks like solid silver when new, but the plate wears off with use.

The amounts of copper, zinc, and nickel are not always 60-25-15. Different proportions make the alloy better for some purposes. When it is used to make casts and candlesticks, a little lead is added. Iron or steel makes the alloy harder, whiter, and more brittle. Vinegar and strong salt solutions may combine with nickel silver to form substances that can make people ill. Silver-plated tableware should not be used with these liquids after the silver plate has worn away.   WILLIAM W. MULLINS

See also ALLOY.

NICKELODEON. See MOTION PICTURE (The History of Motion Pictures).

NICKLAUS, *NIK lus,* **JACK** (1940-   ), of the United States, is one of the world's leading golfers. He became the first golfer to win all four of the world's major golf titles at least twice. He won the U.S. Open in 1962, 1967, and 1972; the British Open in 1966 and 1970; the Professional Golfers' Association (PGA) tournament in 1963, 1971, 1973, and 1975; and the Masters tournament in 1963, 1965, 1966, 1972, and 1975. Before turning professional in 1961, Nicklaus won the U.S. Amateur title in 1959 and 1961. Jack William Nicklaus was born in Columbus, Ohio.   BOB WOLF

NICKNAME. See NAME, PERSONAL (Nicknames).

NICOBAR ISLANDS, *NICK oh bahr,* are a group of 19 islands in the Bay of Bengal. They have an area of 754 square miles (1,953 square kilometers), and about 22,000 persons. The islands, with the Andaman Islands, form a territory of India (see INDIA [physical map]).

People live on only 12 of the 19 islands. The thick forests and hot, wet climate make living conditions unpleasant. Most of the people on the islands trade in coconuts and copra.   ROBERT I. CRANE

NICODEMUS, *NICK oh DEE mus,* was a Pharisee and a member of the Sanhedrin, the Jewish court in Jerusalem. When Jesus Christ was tried before the Sanhedrin Nicodemus spoke in His behalf. He later helped care for and bury Christ's body. See PHARISEE; SANHEDRIN.

NICOLET, *nick oh LAY* or *nee kuh leh,* **JEAN** (1598-1642), was an early French explorer in America. Historians believe he was the first European to enter Lake Michigan and to travel in the territory that is now the state of Wisconsin. Little was known of his explorations until the middle 1800's when an account of his western journey was found in the *Jesuit Relations*.

It is now believed that Nicolet made a voyage up through Lake Huron in a large canoe in 1634. He passed through the Straits of Mackinac and entered Lake Michigan. Nicolet's party crossed the lake to Green Bay on the west side. There they met a tribe of Winnebago Indians, with whom Nicolet made a peace treaty. They honored him as a son of the gods. Nicolet is believed to have gone a short way inland and then to have returned to the French outposts.

Hank Lefebvre
Jean Nicolet

Nicolet was born in Cherbourg, France, and came to America when he was 20 with explorer Samuel de Champlain. Nicolet drowned when his boat overturned on the St. Lawrence River. FRANKLIN L. FORD

NICOMACHEAN ETHICS. See ETHICS (Greek and Roman).

NICOSIA, *NIHK uh SEE uh* (pop. 116,000), is the capital of Cyprus, an island in the Mediterranean Sea. It lies in the north-central part of the island, 150 miles (241 kilometers) northwest of Beirut, Lebanon. For location, see CYPRUS (map). The city serves as the business and administration center of the island. It is also a trade center in the Mesaoria Plain. Goods produced in this region include wheat, wine, olive oil, almonds, and citrus fruit. FREDERICK G. MARCHAM

NICOTIANA. See FLOWERING TOBACCO.

NICOTINE, *NIHK uh teen* (chemical formula $C_{10}H_{14}N_2$), is a colorless, oily, transparent vegetable chemical compound of the type called an *alkaloid*. It has a hot and bitter taste. It is found in small quantities in the leaves, roots, and seeds of the tobacco plant. It can also be made synthetically.

The quantity of nicotine in most tobaccos ranges from 2 to 7 per cent. Turkish tobacco has practically no nicotine. Good Havana tobacco contains little of it. Nicotine is most abundant in cheaper and domestic varieties. The amount of nicotine in the tobacco from which cigars, cigarettes, or pipe tobacco may be made is not the same as the amount in the finished product.

Nicotine is exceedingly poisonous. In a pure state, even a small quantity will cause vomiting, great weakness, rapid but weak pulse, and possibly collapse or even death. Nicotine varies in its effect. It harms some persons less than others. But physicians generally agree that use of tobacco in any form is not wise for young people. Overuse of tobacco may cause nausea, indigestion, and heart disturbances.

Nicotine is valuable as an insecticide. Physicians sometimes use nicotine compounds to treat tetanus and strychnine poisoning. A. KEITH REYNOLDS

See also TOBACCO (introduction).

NICOTINIC ACID. See VITAMIN (Vitamin B Complex).

NICTITATING MEMBRANE is a thin membrane under the eyelid that can be pulled over the eyeball. Birds and many reptiles have the membrane, but human beings do not have it.

NIDAROS, old name of Trondheim. See TRONDHEIM.

NIEBUHR, *NEE boor*, is the family name of two American brothers who became leading Protestant theologians.

Reinhold Niebuhr (1892-1971) won fame as a writer and teacher. He became dean of Union Theological Seminary in New York City in 1950 and served until 1960.

Niebuhr was ordained in 1915 and became pastor of an Evangelical church in Detroit, Mich. Detroit was growing into a vast, industrial city. Niebuhr defended labor and criticized such industrialists as Henry Ford. He became an active Socialist and a leader of the "social gospel" liberal Christians.

In 1928, he became an assistant professor of the philosophy of religion at Union Seminary. He was gradually disillusioned by Marxism, fascism, pacifism, and the "social gospel" theology. By 1939, he ranked as a leading anti-social gospel theologian. He worked on a theology that would retain Reformation values, especially those of Martin Luther, and that would apply to present-day social problems. He edited a small journal, *Christianity and Society*.

His writings include *Moral Man and Immoral Society* (1932), the two-volume *Nature and Destiny of Man* (1941 and 1943), *Christianity and Power Politics* (1940), and *Discerning the Signs of the Times* (1946). Niebuhr was born in Wright City, Mo. He was graduated from Yale Divinity School in 1915.

H. Richard Niebuhr (1894-1962) was an authority on Christian ethics and the history of Christian thought. He was a professor at Yale Divinity School from 1931 until his death. His writings include *The Kingdom of God in America* (1937), *The Purpose of the Church and Its Ministry* (1956), and *Radical Monotheism and Western Culture* (1960). Helmut Richard Niebuhr was born in Wright City, Mo. L. J. TRINTERUD

NIELLO. See ENAMEL (Decorative Enameling).

NIELSEN, *NEEL sun*, **CARL AUGUST** (1865-1931), was a Danish composer. He is best known for six symphonies and a comic opera, *Maskarade* (1906). He also composed chamber and choral music, and concertos. Nielsen was conductor of the Royal Opera from 1908 to 1914, and became director of the Royal Conservatory in Copenhagen in 1915. He was born on the island of Fyn, near Odense. HOMER ULRICH

NIEMEYER, OSCAR (1907-   ), is a Brazilian architect. He is best known as the designer of the principal buildings of Brasília, the Brazilian capital (see BRASÍLIA). Niemeyer often uses decorative shapes for entire buildings, and in repetitious architectural elements. He has said that his designs are inspired by Brazilian climatic and social conditions, and the nation's colonial baroque art heritage.

Niemeyer was born in Rio de Janeiro. His early work was influenced by brief contact with the architect Le Corbusier. An example of this work is the Ministry of Education (1937-1943) in Rio de Janeiro. It is shaped like a concrete slab, with windows set deeply into the building to provide sun shades. In the early 1940's, Niemeyer served as chief architect for Pampulha, a new residential suburb near Belo Horizonte. For pictures of his work, see ARCHITECTURE (Today) and LATIN AMERICA (Arts). STANFORD ANDERSON

NIÉPCE, *nyeps*, **JOSEPH NICÉPHORE** (1765-1833), a French scientist, invented the first photographic technique, *heliography*. Niépce began experimenting in 1816. He succeeded in making a crude photograph of a courtyard in 1826. He sensitized a metal plate with bitumen and exposed it eight hours. This plate, the world's first photograph, is in the Gernsheim Collection in London. Niépce also produced photogravure plates from engravings.

In 1829, Niépce became the partner of L. J. M. Daguerre, who based his researches for his daguerreotype process on Niépce's earlier technique of heliography (see DAGUERRE, LOUIS J. M.). Niépce was born in Chalon-sur-Saône.   BEAUMONT NEWHALL

See also PHOTOGRAPHY (History).

NIER, *near,* **ALFRED OTTO CARL** (1911-   ), an American physicist, won distinction for his development of a mass spectrograph and his use of it in nuclear research. He specialized in the study of *isotopes* (atoms of the same element with different atomic weights) and their accurate mass determination.

Nier separated a small amount of the two principal isotopes of uranium, U-235 and U-238, in 1940. This allowed physicist J. R. Dunning and his associates at Columbia University to prove that U-235 *fissions* (splits) when bombarded with slow neutrons. This discovery ranks as a milestone in the development of practical atomic energy. Nier also studied thermal diffusion, electronics, and the application of the mass spectrograph to chemistry, geology, and medicine.

Nier was born in St. Paul, Minn. He was graduated from the University of Minnesota. He became chairman of the physics department there in 1953.   RALPH E. LAPP

NIETZSCHE, *NEE chuh,* **FRIEDRICH** (1844-1900), was a German philosopher, poet, and classical scholar. Many philosophers, writers, and psychologists of the 1900's have been deeply influenced by him.

Nietzsche greatly admired classical Greek civilization. In his first book, *The Birth of Tragedy* (1872), he presented a revolutionary theory about the nature of Greek tragedy and civilization. He said they could best be understood as the results of a conflict between two basic human tendencies. The *Apollonian* tendency was a desire for clarity and order, represented by the Greek sun god, Apollo. The other, *Dionysian*, tendency was a wild, irrational drive toward disorder, represented by the god of wine, Dionysus.

The Palace of Justice was one of many buildings designed by Oscar Niemeyer in the 1950's for Brasília, the capital of Brazil.

Nietzsche criticized religion. In *Thus Spake Zarathustra* (1883-1885), he proclaimed, "God is dead." He meant that religion, in his time, had lost its meaningfulness and power over people. Thus, he argued, religion could no longer serve as the foundation for moral values. He believed that the time had come for man to critically examine his traditional values and their origins.

Nietzsche tried to begin this "re-evaluation of all values" in such works as *Beyond Good and Evil* (1886) and *Genealogy of Morals* (1887). He said that the warriors who originally dominated society had defined their own strength and nobility as "good," and the weakness of the common people as "bad." Later, when the priests and common people came to dominate society, they redefined their own weakness and humility as "good" and the strength and cruelty of the warriors whom they feared as "evil." Nietzsche criticized this second set of values because it was based on fear and resentment, and he associated these values with the Judeo-Christian tradition. He repeatedly criticized Christianity, particularly in *The Antichrist* (1895).

Nietzsche boasted that he was one of the few philosophers who was also a psychologist. Nietzsche's major psychological theory is that all human behavior is basically motivated by the "will to power." He did not mean that men wanted only to overpower each other physically. He thought that men also wanted to gain power and control over their own unruly passions. He thought that the self control exhibited by ascetics and artists was a higher form of power than the physical bullying of the weak by the strong. Nietzsche's ideal, the *overman* or *superman*, is the passionate man who learns to control his passions and use them in a creative manner.

Nietzsche said that one should accept and love one's own life so completely that he would choose to relive it, with its joys and sufferings, an infinite number of times.

Nietzsche was born in Saxony, the son and grandson of Protestant ministers. He studied at the universities of Bonn and Leipzig. When he was only 24, he became professor of classics at the University of Basel in Switzerland. There he became the close friend of the composer Richard Wagner, but the friendship ended in hostility. In 1870, Nietzsche became a Swiss citizen. After teaching at the university for only 10 years, he retired because of poor health. He then devoted all his time and energy to his writing. In 1889, Nietzsche suffered a mental breakdown from which he never recovered.

Nietzsche has unjustly suffered notoriety as a racist, anti-Semite, and forerunner of Nazism. This is largely due to the editing of his writings and misrepresentation of his ideas by Nazi propagandists and by his racist sister Elizabeth.   IVAN SOLL

NIFLHEIM, *NIHV'l haym,* in Norse mythology, was the land of mist and cold. Odin cast Hel, goddess of death, into Niflheim to rule over the "nine unlighted worlds" of the dead. All who died of sickness and old age went to Niflheim. It included the spring, Hvergelmin, from which ice streams flowed; the root of the world-tree that supported the universe; and Uller, god of winter. A bridge called Bifrost stretched from Niflheim to the world of men and gods.   CHARLOTTE E. GOODFELLOW

See also HEL; ODIN.

Niger

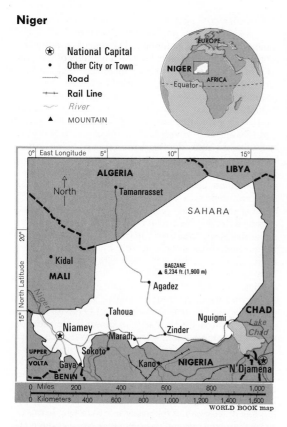

- ⊛ National Capital
- • Other City or Town
- —— Road
- +++ Rail Line
- 〜 *River*
- ▲ MOUNTAIN

WORLD BOOK map

NIGER, *NY juhr,* is a thinly populated country in western Africa. It sprawls over an area greater than the combined areas of Arkansas, Louisiana, Mississippi, Oklahoma, and Texas. But Niger has only slightly more people than the state of Louisiana.

Much of Niger is desert or semidesert. Most persons in the north are *nomads* (wanderers) who move from place to place in search of water and pasture for their livestock. The areas in the extreme southwest around the Niger River and along the southern border are the only places with enough water for farming. Farmers in the south raise millet, peanuts, and sorghum.

Niger is completely surrounded by other countries and has no outlet to the sea. Algeria and Libya border it on the north. Chad lies to the east and Nigeria and Benin to the south. Upper Volta borders Niger on the southwest, and Mali lies to the west.

Niger was once a territory in French West Africa. It became independent as the REPUBLIC OF NIGER in 1960. Its name in French, the official language, is RÉPUBLIQUE DU NIGER. Niamey (pop. 130,299) is the capital and most important town (see NIAMEY).

Government. Niger is a republic, with a president as head of state. He is also president of the *Supreme Military Council* (Cabinet), which has both military and civilian members.

The contributor of this article, R. J. Harrison Church, is Professor of Geography at the University of London and author of West Africa.

People of Niger belong to four main groups: (1) the Fulani, (2) the Tuareg, (3) the Djerma, and (4) the Hausa. These peoples live in widely separated areas, have little in common, and speak different languages. French is the official language of Niger, but few persons speak it. See FULANI; HAUSA.

There are about 414,000 Fulani in Niger. They live in the northern and central part of the country. About 250,000 Tuareg also live in the north. The Fulani and Tuareg are Muslims, but the Tuareg women do not wear veils, as most Muslim women do.

The Fulani and Tuareg are herders who travel from place to place with their livestock. The cattle are not raised as a source of income, but as the chief source of food. The Fulani and Tuareg live almost entirely on animal products. Their diet includes blood (which they draw regularly from healthy animals), meat, milk, and milk products. Men who own many animals have a high standing among their neighbors. Fulani and Tuareg sell animals only when they need money for taxes or special occasions such as a birth, death, or marriage.

About 545,000 Djerma, a branch of the Songhai peoples of western Africa, live in the southwestern part of Niger. Most Djerma raise such crops as rice, cotton, millet, and peanuts on small farms near the Niger River.

About 1,125,000 Hausa live in Niger. Most of them are farmers in the south. Their main food crops include beans, manioc, millet, peanuts, peas, and sorghum. Many other Hausa live in Nigeria.

About 8 of every 10 persons in Niger are Muslims. Most of the other people practice *fetish* religions, in which they worship objects such as stones or images (see FETISH). Many of the older people of Niger cannot read or write. The country has a shortage of schools and teachers, partly because Christian mission schools were not encouraged in this Muslim country. Only about 6 of every 10 school-age children go to school.

Land. Most parts of Niger lie less than 1,500 feet (457 meters) above sea level. The only extensive areas higher than 1,500 feet lie in the north-central part of Niger. The Sahara covers northeastern and east-central

--- **FACTS IN BRIEF** ---

Capital: Niamey.

Official Language: French.

Official Name: Republic of Niger.

Form of Government: Republic.

Head of State: President.

Area: 489,191 sq. mi. (1,267,000 km²). *Greatest Distances*— east-west, 1,100 mi. (1,770 km); north-south, 825 mi. (1,328 km).

Population: *Estimated 1978 Population*—4,979,000; distribution, 89 per cent rural, 11 per cent urban; density, 10 persons per sq. mi. (4 per km²). *1959-1960 Census*— 2,766,130. *Estimated 1983 Population*—5,689,000.

Chief Products: *Agriculture*—beans, chillies, cotton, henna, hides and skins, livestock (cattle, goats, sheep), manioc, millet, okra, onions, peanuts, peas, rice, sorghum. *Mining*—natron, salt, tin, uranium.

Flag: The flag has horizontal stripes of orange (for the Sahara), white (for purity), and green (for agriculture). An orange circle (for the sun) is in the center. See FLAG (color picture: Flags of Africa).

National Holidays: Independence Day, August 3, and Republic Day, December 18.

Money: *Basic Unit*—franc. See MONEY (table: Values).

Niger. The southern part of the country is a grassy plain. The Niger River flows through the southwestern corner of the country, and farmers plant crops there when the river floods. They also practice some irrigation near the river. Part of shallow Lake Chad lies in the southeast corner of Niger (see LAKE CHAD).

Niger has a hot, dry climate. The hottest season around Niamey in the southwest extends from March to late June when temperatures rise to about 110° F. (43° C). The rainy season, from late June to mid-September, is the coolest season. Temperatures average about 94° F. (34° C) during the day and about 73° F. (23° C) at night. They reach about 102° F. (39° C) in October and November, and range from 94° to 99° F. (34° to 37° C) from December to February.

At Agadez, in central Niger, May is generally the hottest month. Temperatures average up to 112° F. (44° C). Short rains occur in July and August, and January is the coolest month.

Average annual rainfall in Niger is 7 inches (18 centimeters). Only about a tenth of the country receives more than 21 inches (53 centimeters) of rainfall a year. About half of Niger receives less than 4 inches (10 centimeters), causing true desert conditions.

Economy. The economic development of Niger has been more difficult than that of many other African countries. Most of the people are herdsmen or farmers, but less than one-fourth of the country can be used for farming. Pasture for livestock is scarce. Niger's inland position makes transportation of exports difficult and expensive. Niger has few manufacturing industries.

Most farmers produce just enough food for their families. Some sell peanuts, cotton, and millet, however, and some animals and hides are exported to Nigeria. Mining companies produce a little tin in the north-central part of the country, and local residents dig salt and the mineral natron near Lake Chad. Rich deposits of uranium lie in west-central Niger. Niger's first plant for processing uranium ore began operating in 1971.

Niger has no railroads, but it has 3,500 miles (5,630 kilometers) of roads and trails. Niamey has an international airport, and there are smaller airports at Agadez, Maradi, Tahoua, and Zinder. A government radio station broadcasts from Niamey.

The most direct route for eastern Niger's overseas trade runs from Zinder or Maradi about 900 miles (1,400 kilometers) through Nigeria to the Nigerian port of Lagos. A 660-mile (1,060-kilometer) route from Niamey to the port of Cotonou in Dahomey is used for most of western Niger's trade. Niger is a member of the Council of the Entente, which promotes regional economic cooperation. Other members are Dahomey, Ivory Coast, Togo, and Upper Volta.

History. Areas of what is now Niger were part of the Kanem, Mali, and Songhai empires. These empires were powerful states that began during the Middle Ages. See KANEM; MALI EMPIRE; SONGHAI EMPIRE.

European explorers arrived in what is now Niger during the 1800's. The French began to occupy the area in 1897 and completed the occupation in 1900. They created the colony of Upper Senegal and Niger in French West Africa in 1904. In 1922, Niger became a separate colony in French West Africa.

Niger's first national assembly met in 1946. Also in 1946, representatives from Niger entered the French parliament in Paris, and the Grand Council of French West Africa in Dakar. In 1960, Niger became independent and Hamani Diori was elected president. He was re-elected in 1965 and 1970. In 1974, army officers, led by Lieutenant Colonel Seyni Kountche, overthrew Diori's government. Kountche then became president.

During the early 1970's, a severe drought caused widespread food shortages and other problems in Niger. The country's production of crops and livestock was sharply reduced.   R. J. HARRISON CHURCH

See also FRENCH WEST AFRICA; NIGER RIVER.

NIGER RIVER is the third largest river in Africa. The Nile and Congo rivers are larger.

The Niger rises in West Africa, only 150 miles (241 kilometers) from the Atlantic Ocean. But the river travels a winding course of about 2,600 miles (4,180 kilometers) before it reaches the Gulf of Guinea. The Niger River drains an area of 584,000 square miles (1,513,000 square kilometers). The middle Niger is navigable for about 1,000 miles (1,600 kilometers). But rapids interrupt its course for about 300 miles (480 kilometers) between the Republic of Mali and Nigeria. The lower Niger is navigable from Jebba to Onitsha, Nigeria. The delta begins at Onitsha, about 150 miles (241 kilometers) from the Atlantic. It is Africa's largest river delta.   KENNETH ROBINSON

See also AFRICA (physical map); RIVER (chart).

A Young Hausa Girl gathers wood for the family fire near the town of Tahoua in southwestern Niger. The Hausa tribe is one of the most important groups in Niger. Most Hausa tribesmen make their living by farming in southern Niger and the northern parts of Nigeria.

Jerry Frank, D.P.I.

Bruno Barbey, Magnum

Ways of Life in Nigeria present a sharp contrast between the new and the old. Many Nigerians live in modern, crowded cities, such as Lagos, the capital and largest city, *left*. But most people, such as the herdsmen at the right, live in rural areas and follow the traditions of their ancestors.

NIGERIA

NIGERIA, *ny JIHR ee ah,* a nation on the west coast of Africa, has more people than any other African country. More than 68 million people live in Nigeria, and the country ranks as the world's 10th largest nation in population.

Nigeria is a land of great variety. It has hot, rainy swamplands; dry, sandy areas; grassy plains; and tropical forests. High plateaus and rocky mountains rise up in parts of the country. The people of Nigeria belong to more than 250 different *ethnic* (cultural) groups. About three-fourths of the people live in rural areas. But Nigeria also has several large, crowded cities. Lagos, the nation's capital, ranks as the largest city.

Most Nigerians earn their livelihoods by farming, fishing, or herding. The country ranks as a leading producer of cacao, peanuts, and other crops. Nigeria also has a variety of mineral resources, including large deposits of petroleum. Since the late 1960's, profits from Nigeria's growing oil industry have brought new wealth to the nation. Nigeria has used this wealth to develop new industry and to improve its schools.

A number of ancient kingdoms developed in the area that is now Nigeria hundreds of years ago. Some of the kingdoms became important cultural and trade centers. Great Britain gained control of Nigeria during the late 1800's and early 1900's. Nigeria was a British

J. F. Ade Ajayi, the contributor of this article, is Vice-Chancellor of the University of Lagos in Nigeria, the author of Milestones in Nigerian History, *and joint editor of* A History of West Africa.

colony and protectorate until 1960, when it gained independence.

Government

Nigeria's 1963 Constitution established the country as a federal republic divided into four political regions. In 1966, military leaders took control of the government. They suspended parts of the Constitution and all elections, and banned all political parties. In 1976, the military leaders allowed elections for local government councils to be held.

National Government. The Federal Military Government holds all executive and legislative power. It consists of the Supreme Military Council, the National

───────── FACTS IN BRIEF ─────────

Capital: Lagos.

Official Language: English.

Official Name: Federal Republic of Nigeria.

Form of Government: Republic (Military Rule).

Area: 356,669 sq. mi. (923,768 km²). *Greatest Distances*—east-west, 800 mi. (1,287 km); north-south, 650 mi. (1,046 km). *Coastline*—478 mi. (769 km).

Elevation: *Highest*—Dimlang Peak, 6,699 ft. (2,042 m) above sea level. *Lowest*—sea level.

Population: *Estimated 1978 Population*—68,160,000; distribution, 73 per cent rural, 27 per cent urban; density, 192 persons per sq. mi. (74 per km²). *1963 Census*—55,670,055. *Estimated 1983 Population*—77,872,000.

Chief Products: *Agriculture*—beans, cacao beans, cassava, corn, cotton, livestock, millet, palm oil and palm kernels, peanuts, rice, rubber, yams. *Mining*—columbite, limestone, petroleum, tin. *Manufacturing*—cement, chemicals, clothing, food products, textiles.

National Anthem: "Nigeria, We Hail Thee."

Money: *Basic Unit*—Naira. For the value of the naira in U.S. dollars, see MONEY (table: Values).

326

Council of State, and the Federal Executive Council. The commander in chief of the armed forces is head of state and head of government, and presides over the three councils. The Supreme Military Council is the chief policy-making body of the government. It consists of the leaders of the army, navy, air force, and police force. The National Council of State is composed of the leaders of the federal government and each of the country's state governments. The Federal Executive Council is made up of military and civilian commissioners who head various government departments.

Local Government. Nigeria is divided into 19 states for purposes of local government. A military governor rules each state. Each state also has an executive council. The organization of local government below the state level varies from one part of the country to another. In general, the states are divided into provinces, which in turn are divided into divisions or districts. Towns and villages make up the smallest units of local government. Elected councils govern most of the local units.

Courts. The Federal Supreme Court is the highest court in Nigeria. It consists of a chief justice and six judges, all of whom are appointed by the federal government. The country's judicial system also includes state high courts of justice, magistrate courts, and district courts. Courts based on Islamic law operate in the northern part of the country, where many of the people are Muslims.

Armed Forces. About 200,000 persons serve in the Nigerian Army. The country also has a small navy and air force, and a federal police force. All military service is voluntary.

People

Population and Ancestry. Nigeria has a population of about 68,160,000. About three-fourths of all Nigerians live in rural areas. Since the mid-1900's, more and more Nigerians have moved to the cities. Lagos, the nation's capital and largest city, has more than a million people. Three other cities have populations of more than 400,000. They are, in order of size, Ibadan, Ogbomosho, and Kano. See IBADAN; LAGOS.

Almost all Nigerians are black Africans. The country has more than 250 different ethnic groups. These ethnic groups differ from one another in language and in some of their customs and traditions. The three largest ethnic groups are, in order of size, the Hausa, the Yoruba, and the Ibo (also spelled Igbo). These three groups account for about three-fifths of the total population.

The Hausa people live primarily in northern Nigeria and in the neighboring countries of Niger and Chad. Most of them are farmers, and many also work as craftworkers and traders. The Hausa have lived in the area for more than a thousand years. During the 1200's, the Fulani, a people who lived to the north and west, began to settle in the Hausa territory. The Fulani took control of the region during the early 1800's. Because of the intermixing of the two peoples, the group is sometimes called the Hausa-Fulani.

The Yoruba live mainly in southwestern Nigeria and in Benin and Togo, two nations that lie to the west. Many of the Yoruba live in cities and farm the land in the surrounding countryside. Several Yoruba cities, including Lagos, were founded hundreds of years ago.

The Ibo form a majority of the population in south-central Nigeria. Large numbers of Ibo also live in other areas of the country. During British rule in the 1900's, many Ibo accepted Western education and ways of life more quickly than the other ethnic groups and were more willing to travel away from home. As a result, the Ibo held many important positions in business and government during the period of colonial rule.

Nigeria's other leading ethnic groups include the Nupe and Tiv of central Nigeria; the Edo, Urhobo, and Itsekiri of the Bendel State; the Ijo of the Niger Delta area; the Efik and Ibibio of the Cross River State; and the Kanuri of northeastern Nigeria. The Kanuri trace their ancestry back to the ancient Kanem-Bornu empire (see KANEM).

Languages. English is the official language of Nigeria and is taught in schools throughout the country. But English is not the country's most commonly used language. Each of the more than 250 ethnic groups in Nigeria has its own distinct language. The three most widely used languages are those of the three largest ethnic groups—Hausa, Yoruba, and Ibo.

Many of the languages spoken in Nigeria have several different *dialects* (local forms). These dialects may make it difficult for two people of the same ethnic

Nigeria's Flag was adopted in 1960. The green represents agriculture, and the white symbolizes unity and peace.

Coat of Arms. The design on the shield stands for Nigeria's fertile soil and main rivers, the Niger and the Benue.

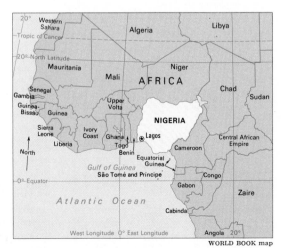

WORLD BOOK map

Nigeria, a large country in West Africa, lies on the Gulf of Guinea, just north of the equator.

NIGERIA

Nigeria
Political Map

International boundary
Road
Railroad
Oil pipeline
Oil field
National capital
State capital
Other city or town

WORLD BOOK map

*Does not appear on map; key shows general location.
*Population of metropolitan area, including suburbs.

Sources: 1978 official estimates for states; 1977 official estimates and 1963 census for cities and towns.

group to communicate with one another. Most Nigerians speak more than one language. They may use the language of their ethnic group on most occasions, and English or another language at other times. In addition, Nigerians who are Muslims use Arabic for various religious activities.

Way of Life. Most homes in rural Nigeria are made of grass, dried mud, or wood and have roofs of asbestos, corrugated metal, or thatch. A typical village consists of several *compounds* (clusters of houses). A group of related families lives in each compound. Well-to-do city dwellers in Nigeria live in modern houses or apartment buildings. The cities also have slums, where people live in mud huts that line unpaved streets. Overcrowding has become a serious problem in many Nigerian cities since the 1960's, when increasing numbers of people began moving from rural to urban areas in search of jobs.

In the cities, many Nigerians wear Western-style clothing. But other city dwellers and most people in rural areas wear traditional clothing. Traditional garments for men and women in Nigeria include long, loose robes made of white or brightly colored fabrics. The men may also wear short, full jackets with shorts or trousers. Small round caps are popular head coverings for men, and Nigerian women often wear scarves or turbans. Rural Nigerians in some parts of the country wear only a *loin cloth*, a small piece of fabric tied around the waist.

The chief foods of Nigeria include beans, corn, rice, and yams. The people also eat *plantains* (a kind of banana) and the roots of the *cassava* plant (see PLANTAIN; CASSAVA). Nigerian food is often cooked in palm oil or peanut oil, and it may be highly seasoned with red peppers. Some Nigerian meals feature beef, chicken, fish, or lamb. But in general, most Nigerians do not eat much meat. Popular beverages in Nigeria include beer and a wine that is made from the sap of palm trees. Some city dwellers also drink coffee and tea. Nigerian Muslims who obey the laws of Islam may not drink alcoholic beverages.

Religion. About half the people of Nigeria are Muslims. They make up the majority of the population in the north. About a third of the people are Christians. They live mainly in southern Nigeria. Many Nigerians, especially in the central part of the country and in rural areas, practice traditional religions based on the worship of many gods and spirits. People throughout the country may combine Christian or Muslim religious practices with traditional beliefs.

Education. About a fourth of the people of Nigeria can read and write. The country does not have enough schools or teachers to provide an education for all school-age children, and laws do not require school attendance. In the mid-1970's, about 5 million children attended elementary schools in Nigeria. About 500,000 students attended secondary schools. Nigeria has six universities. The largest is Ahmadu Bello University, in Zaria, with about 11,000 students.

In 1975, the Nigerian government announced a program to provide free elementary school education for all eligible children beginning in 1976. The government planned to build hundreds of elementary and secondary

Bruno Barbey, Magnum

Outdoor Markets bring farmers into Nigeria's cities to sell their fruits, grains, and vegetables. The market above is in Ibadan, one of the country's most important trade centers.

Bruno Barbey, Magnum

A Typical Village in rural Nigeria consists of clusters of homes much like those above. About three-fourths of all Nigerians live in rural areas and work as farmers, fishermen, or herders.

George Bookless, Terra Photos

Nigerian Muslims dressed in traditional costumes prepare to take part in a horsemanship event at the end of a religious festival. About half the people of Nigeria are Muslims.

326c

The Niger River flows southward through west-central Nigeria. It cuts through grassland, tropical forests, and swampy plains and then empties into the Atlantic Ocean. This picture shows a ferry crossing at the river's delta.

Bruno Barbey, Magnum

schools during the late 1970's. The plans also provided for a sharp increase in the number of teacher-training institutes and technical and vocational schools in Nigeria, and for the establishment of four new universities in the country.

Recreation. People in both urban and rural areas of Nigeria enjoy performances of traditional songs and dances. Motion pictures attract many people in the large cities, where radio and television are also popular. Soccer ranks as the favorite sport in Nigeria. Art festivals and special sports contests are held in many parts of the country.

The Arts. Nigeria is famous for the variety and quality of its art. The art of Nigeria and other African countries has also influenced art movements in many other parts of the world. For example, traditional African sculpture influenced Pablo Picasso and other modern Western artists.

The oldest known African sculptures are *terra-cotta* (clay) figures created by the Nok civilization in central Nigeria as early as 500 B.C. (see NOK). Other famous traditional sculptures include the bronze and brass figures of Benin and Ife, and the wood carvings of the Yoruba people (see BENIN; IFE). Various peoples who live in the forest areas of Nigeria are known for their elaborately carved wooden masks. Most of the traditional Nigerian painting is done on sculptures and textiles, or as body decoration.

Nigerian music often features drums, xylophones, and various string and wind instruments. Dance and dramatic performances are popular forms of entertainment in Nigeria. Many of these performances portray themes related to traditional beliefs or the everyday life of the people. Most of Nigeria's traditional literature is oral, rather than written. Popular forms of such literature include chants, folk stories, proverbs, and riddles. During

the mid-1900's, many Nigerian authors began to write novels, stories, and poetry. These works were written in English and in local languages.

The Land and Climate

Land Regions. Nigeria covers 356,669 square miles (923,768 square kilometers). The country can be divided into 10 land regions. They are: (1) the Sokoto Plains, (2) the Chad Basin, (3) the Northern High Plains, (4) the Jos Plateau, (5) the Niger-Benue River Valley, (6) the Western Uplands, (7) the Eastern Highlands, (8) the Southwestern Plains, (9) the Southeastern Lowlands, and (10) the Niger Delta.

The Sokoto Plains occupy the northwestern corner of Nigeria. Several rivers flow across the flat, low-lying plains and flood the area during the rainy season. The floodwaters deposit fertile soil that allows farmers to grow various crops in the area. But the floods also occasionally destroy homes and fields.

The Chad Basin extends across northeastern Nigeria, south and west of Lake Chad. Sandy ridges cut across parts of the low-lying basin. During the rainy season, parts of the region become swampy. But long dry spells occasionally cause serious droughts. Short grasses and thinly scattered trees grow in the Chad Basin.

The Northern High Plains cover almost a fifth of Nigeria's total area. They consist largely of flat grasslands, with a few hills and granite ridges. Most of the plains area has an elevation of about 2,500 feet (762 meters) above sea level.

Several branches of the Niger River have their source in the Northern High Plains. These branches include the Gongola, Sokoto, and Kaduna rivers. They flow gently across the plains and form beautiful waterfalls as they tumble into deep gorges in parts of the region.

The Jos Plateau lies near the center of Nigeria. It rises

up sharply from the surrounding plains. Parts of the region are more than 5,000 feet (1,500 meters) above sea level. Dairy cattle graze on the plateau's grasslands, and the area also has important tin mines.

The Niger-Benue River Valley forms an arc across central Nigeria, from east to west. The Niger River flows southeastward from Benin through west-central Nigeria. The Benue River cuts across east-central Nigeria. The two rivers meet near the center of the country and flow southward to the Niger Delta. Grasslands, palm forests, and swampy plains cover parts of the valley. Other areas are marked by rugged, rocky hills.

The Western Uplands, also known as the Plateau of Yorubaland, lie about 1,000 to 2,000 feet (300 to 610 meters) above sea level in the west-central part of Nigeria. Dome-shaped granite hills dot the grassy plains of the uplands.

The Eastern Highlands lie along the eastern border of Nigeria. They consist of plateaus and low, rocky mountains and hills. Much of the region is more than 4,000 feet (1,200 meters) above sea level. Dimlang Peak, the highest point in Nigeria, rises 6,699 feet (2,042 meters) above sea level in the Shebshi Mountains.

The Southwestern Plains consist of a heavily forested area that slopes gently northward from the Gulf of Guinea. Swamps and lagoons cover much of the coastal region. Lagos, the capital of Nigeria, occupies several islands in the Lagos Lagoon.

The Southeastern Lowlands resemble other parts of southern Nigeria, with swamps and forested plains covering much of the region. In the northwestern part of

this region, however, steep-sided plateaus rise up to about 1,000 feet (300 meters) above sea level.

The Niger Delta forms the southernmost region of Nigeria, along the Gulf of Guinea. It consists of deposits of clay, mud, and sand at the mouth of the Niger River. Lagoons and mangrove swamps cover much of the region. This area is also the site of Nigeria's important petroleum deposits.

Climate. Most of Nigeria has a tropical climate, with warm temperatures throughout the year. The north is generally hotter and drier than the south. The average annual temperature in the north is about 85° F. (29° C), but daily temperatures may rise above 100° F. (38° C). The average annual temperature in the south is about 80° F. (27° C).

Southern Nigeria receives far more rainfall than the northern part of the country. The coastal areas of Nigeria have an average annual rainfall of about 150 inches (381 centimeters). Parts of the north receive only about 25 inches (64 centimeters) of rainfall annually. The rainy season lasts from April to October in most parts of Nigeria, though it usually extends for a longer period of time in the south.

Economy

Nigeria has a developing economy based on agriculture and mining. Agriculture employs about three-fourths of all Nigerian workers, and it accounts for more than two-fifths of the total value of Nigeria's economic production. Since the late 1960's, however, the development of the oil industry has made mining the fastest

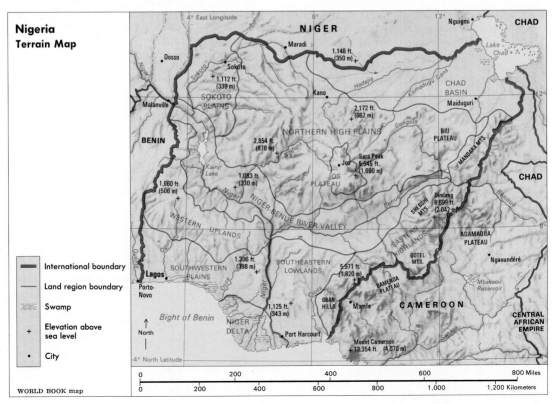

Nigeria
Terrain Map

International boundary
Land region boundary
Swamp
Elevation above sea level
City

WORLD BOOK map

growing part of the economy. In the early 1960's, mining accounted for less than 2 per cent of the value of economic production. By the mid-1970's, it accounted for nearly a fifth of the value of production, and revenue from oil exports provided the government with its chief source of income.

Nigeria does not have many large manufacturing plants. Manufacturing employs only about 10 per cent of the country's work force and accounts for less than 10 per cent of the value of economic production.

The federal and state governments of Nigeria control such areas as communication, transportation, and electric power production. Most businesses and industries are privately owned, but the federal government shares in the ownership of some. The government issues National Development Plans, which establish goals for economic growth. The plan for 1975 to 1980 called for increased agricultural output, the establishment of new industries, and improvement of transportation facilities.

Natural Resources. Nigeria has a variety of natural resources. More than half of Nigeria's land is suitable for farming and grazing. However, only about 10 per cent of the country's total area is actually used for growing crops. Forests cover about one-third of Nigeria. The country's lakes, rivers, and streams provide an abundance of fish.

Petroleum ranks as Nigeria's most valuable natural resource. Large oil fields lie in southwestern Nigeria and offshore in the Gulf of Guinea. The Jos Plateau of central Nigeria has important deposits of tin and columbite, a mineral used in the production of certain kinds of steel. Other important natural resources include coal, iron ore, lead, limestone, and zinc.

Agriculture. Nigeria ranks among the world's leading producers of cacao, palm oil and palm kernels, peanuts, and rubber. Other important crops include beans, cassava, corn, cotton, millet, rice, and yams. Farmers throughout Nigeria raise goats, poultry, and sheep. Cattle are raised primarily in the north. Nigerian fishermen catch shrimp and a variety of other seafoods.

Farms in Nigeria average only about $2\frac{1}{2}$ acres (1 hectare) in size. Most of the farmers use old-fashioned tools and methods, but the country usually produces enough food to feed its people. The government sponsors programs to distribute fertilizer, insecticides, and new varieties of seeds to farmers.

Mining. Nigeria ranks as one of the world's leading producers and exporters of petroleum. During the mid-1970's, Nigerian wells produced more than 2 million barrels of oil a day. Foreign oil companies operate most of the wells, but they pay the Nigerian government more than half their profits. In 1971, the government established a national oil corporation to explore for and produce oil. That same year, Nigeria joined the Organization of Petroleum Exporting Countries (OPEC).

In addition to petroleum, Nigeria produces coal, columbite, gold, iron ore, lead, limestone, natural gas, and zinc. The country also ranks as an important source of tin.

Manufacturing. Leading industries in Nigeria produce cement, chemicals, clothing, food products, lumber, metal products, and textiles. Nigeria also has a petroleum refinery and factories that process such agricultural products as rubber and oil palms.

Transportation and Communication. Nigeria has about 50,000 miles (80,000 kilometers) of roads, about 9,500 miles (15,300 kilometers) of which are paved. The Nigerian Railway Corporation operates about 2,180 miles (3,508 kilometers) of track. Rivers and streams form a network of more than 5,300 miles (8,500 kilometers) of inland waterways in Nigeria. The country's chief ports are Lagos and Port Harcourt. Lagos and Kano have international airports. Nigeria Airways provides domestic and international service.

More than 20 daily and weekly newspapers are published in Nigeria. The country also has more than 25 radio stations and 7 television stations.

Foreign Trade. During the mid-1970's, petroleum accounted for more than 90 per cent of the total value of Nigeria's exports. Because of the large income Nigeria receives from its oil exports, the country has a *favorable balance of trade*. This means that the value of its exports is greater than the value of its imports. In addition to oil, Nigeria exports cacao beans, palm products, pea-

Tomas D. W. Friedmann, D.P.I.

Sacks of Peanuts, ready for shipment to market, are piled in pyramid form by a continuous stream of Nigerian workers. Nigeria ranks as a leading peanut-growing country.

Bruno Barbey, Magnum

An Offshore Drilling Platform, *above,* sinks an oil well into the floor of the Niger Delta. Nigeria is a world leader in the production of petroleum, its most valuable natural resource.

nuts, rubber, timber, and tin. Chief imports include cement, chemical products, food products, machinery, manufactured goods, and textiles. Nigeria's most important trade partners are Great Britain, The Netherlands, West Germany, and the United States.

History

People lived in what is now Nigeria thousands of years ago. In parts of Nigeria, archaeologists have found stone tools that are 40,000 years old. Human skeletons, rock paintings, and other remains of prehistoric settlements have also been found.

The Nok civilization flourished in what is now central Nigeria from about 500 B.C. to A.D. 200. The clay figures produced by this civilization are among the oldest known examples of African sculpture. See NOK.

Early Kingdoms. The kingdom of Kanem developed in what is now Chad during the A.D. 700's. Beginning in the 1000's, Kanem adopted Islam as its religion and gradually expanded its territory. By the 1300's, Bornu, in what is now northeastern Nigeria, had become the political center of the kingdom. The Kanem-Bornu kingdom traded with countries in Africa, Asia, and Europe. See KANEM.

After about A.D. 1000, a number of Hausa states grew up in the region west of Bornu. Some of these states, such as Kano and Katsina, traded with other countries in North Africa and the Middle East. Kano, Kebbi, and some other Hausa states became part of the Songhai Empire, a west African state that flourished during the 1400's and 1500's (see SONGHAI EMPIRE). During the early 1800's, Uthman Dan Fodio, a Fulani who was a Muslim religious leader, declared war on the Hausa states. His forces gained control of almost all northern Nigeria except Bornu. He formed the area into a Muslim empire called the Sokoto Caliphate.

In the south, the Yoruba people had established an important cultural center at Ife as early as A.D. 1000. Yorubas from Ife later founded states in various parts of the surrounding territory. The most important of these was the kingdom of Oyo, which extended into what is now the country of Benin during the 1700's.

During the 1400's, the kingdom of Benin developed in the area between Lagos and the Niger Delta. Benin grew into a prosperous trade center. The kingdom also became famous for its sculptures of brass, bronze, and ivory. See BENIN (kingdom).

The Coming of the Europeans. The Portuguese were the first Europeans to reach Nigeria. They established a trade center near Benin in the late 1400's and developed a slave trade with the African chiefs. British, Dutch, and other European traders later competed for control of the trade. By the 1700's, the British were the leading slave traders on the Nigerian coast.

In 1808, the British government outlawed the slave trade. Britain signed treaties with other European countries and with local African rulers in an attempt to end the trade. British ships traveled along the Nigerian coast and captured ships that carried slaves. The British then set the slaves free at Freetown, in Sierra Leone. British missionaries converted many of the freed slaves to Christianity. Some of the freed slaves later returned to Nigeria and helped the British spread Christianity along the coastal areas and in the southwest.

British Rule. After 1808, British traders began to deal in palm oil and other agricultural products of the Nigerian coastal region. They explored the Niger River and other waterways in search of valuable natural resources. In 1851, Britain seized the port of Lagos in order to strengthen British influence over the area. Lagos served as a base from which the British continued their war against the slave trade. Lagos became a British colony in 1861.

During the late 1800's, Britain established protectorates in parts of southern Nigeria. A British trading firm called the Royal Niger Company controlled most of northern Nigeria until 1900. That year, the British government made the region the Protectorate of Northern Nigeria. In 1906, all of southern Nigeria, including Lagos, became the Colony and Protectorate of Southern Nigeria. Nigerians in some areas, especially in the north, fought against the establishment of British rule. But the British defeated them. In 1914, Britain joined the northern and southern regions into one unit called the Colony and Protectorate of Nigeria.

IMPORTANT DATES IN NIGERIA
---

c. 500 B.C.-A.D. 200—The Nok civilization thrived in what is now central Nigeria.

c. A.D. 1000-1400's—Various kingdoms, including Benin, Bornu, Ife, and the Hausa states, began to develop in different parts of Nigeria.

Late 1400's—The Portuguese became the first Europeans to reach Nigeria.

1851—Great Britain seized control of Lagos.

1914—The British formed the Colony and Protectorate of Nigeria.

1960—Nigeria became an independent federation.

January, 1966—Military leaders overthrew Nigeria's government.

July, 1966—A second revolt established a new military government in Nigeria.

1967—Nigeria's Eastern Region declared itself an independent republic called *Biafra.* Civil war broke out between Biafra and the rest of Nigeria.

1970—Biafra surrendered, and the civil war came to an end.

Wide World

An Independence Ceremony attended by representatives of Britain marked the opening of Nigeria's Federal Parliament in Lagos. Nigeria gained independence from Britain in 1960.

Independence. During the 1920's, Nigerians began to demand representation in the colonial government. At the same time, rivalries between the various peoples of Nigeria caused disunity in the country.

In 1946, Britain divided Nigeria into three regions—north, west, and east. Each region had an assembly composed of Nigerian and British members. The assemblies acted as advisory bodies to the central government in Lagos. A constitution adopted in 1954 gave the assemblies increased powers and established Nigeria as a federation. Sir Abubakar Tafawa Balewa, a northern leader, became the federation's first prime minister in 1957. On Oct. 1, 1960, Britain granted full independence to Nigeria. Balewa remained in office as prime minister.

In 1961, the United Nations (UN) organized a referendum in western Cameroon, a UN trust territory that bordered Nigeria on the east. As a result of the referendum, the northern part of the territory joined Nigeria, and the southern part joined the Republic of Cameroon. See CAMEROON.

During the early 1960's, various ethnic groups competed for political power within Nigeria's three regions. In 1963, a Mid-Western Region was created out of the Western Region. People in the Northern and Eastern regions also demanded separate political units.

At the same time, different groups competed for control of the central government. The people of southern Nigeria, especially the Ibo, resented the power of the Hausa people of the north. The northerners controlled the central government because the north had more people than the other regions. Censuses conducted in

1962 and 1963 showed that the north had an even larger population than had been expected. Many southerners protested against the census findings. Charges of dishonesty in a 1964 federal election and a 1965 regional election led to violent riots and added to the turmoil.

Civil War. In January 1966, a group of army officers, mainly Ibo, overthrew the central and regional governments. They killed Prime Minister Balewa and the prime ministers of the Northern and Western regions. General Johnson Aguiyi-Ironsi, commander of the army and an Ibo, took control of the government.

In May 1966, Aguiyi-Ironsi abolished the federal system of government. He set up a strong central government and appointed many Ibo as advisers. Many northerners feared that these actions would give the Ibo control over the entire country. Riots broke out in the north, and thousands of Ibo were killed.

In July 1966, a group of northern army officers revolted against the government and killed Aguiyi-Ironsi. Yakubu Gowon, the army chief of staff, became head of a new military government. But Colonel Odumegwu Ojukwu, the military governor of the Eastern Region, refused to accept Gowon as head of state.

In 1967, Gowon replaced the country's 4 political regions with 12 states, in order to give some of the smaller ethnic groups more political power. Ojukwu refused to accept the division of the Eastern Region into three states. On May 30, 1967, he declared the Eastern Region an independent republic called *Biafra.* Civil war between Biafra and the rest of Nigeria broke out in June 1967. Fighting continued until Biafra surrendered in January 1970.

Nigeria Today. The civil war caused widespread death and destruction in southeastern Nigeria. Beginning in 1970, the government sponsored reconstruction and relief programs to overcome the effects of the war. Many Ibo, including some who had fought with the rebel forces, were given government positions.

During the early 1970's, Nigeria's growing oil industry provided the country with an important source of wealth. Oil profits enabled the government to plan development programs to improve the standard of living of all Nigerians. Major goals included the establishment of manufacturing industries, new schools, and improved transportation facilities. But political problems continued in Nigeria. In 1975, military leaders overthrew General Gowon. General Murtala Ramat Mohammed became head of state and commander in chief of Nigeria's armed forces. In 1976, a group of military officers tried to overthrow the government. They failed, but they killed General Mohammed. Lieutenant General Olusegun Obasanjo succeeded him. Also in 1976, Nigeria increased its number of states from 12 to 19.   J. F. ADE AJAYI

Related Articles in WORLD BOOK include:

Africa (pictures)	Dancing (picture)	Ibadan
Chocolate (graph)	Gowon, Yakubu	Lagos
Clothing (pictures)		

Outline

I. Government

II. People

A. Population	C. Way of Life	F. Recreation
and Ancestry	D. Religion	G. The Arts
B. Languages	E. Education	

Questions

Where are Nigeria's oil fields located?
What are the three largest ethnic groups of Nigeria?
What was the Sokoto Caliphate?
What three organizations make up the Federal Military Government of Nigeria?
When did the Nok civilization exist? Why is it famous?
What are Nigeria's chief agricultural products?
What events led to the Nigerian civil war?
Where is Dimlang Peak located?
When did Nigeria gain independence from Britain?

NIGHT. See DAY.

NIGHT BLINDNESS. See BLINDNESS (introduction).

NIGHT HERON is a medium-sized heron which remains quiet during the day, and begins its activities at

G. Ronald Austing
The Nighthawk has black, white, and buff feathers, with a white bar on each wing. The bird feeds chiefly on insects.

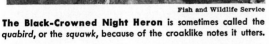
Fish and Wildlife Service
The Black-Crowned Night Heron is sometimes called the *quabird*, or the *squawk*, because of the croaklike notes it utters.

sundown. There are several species. They live in most parts of the world except the far northern regions. In America, the black-crowned night heron lives in colonies from Manitoba and New Brunswick, Canada, southward through South America. It is about 2 feet (61 centimeters) long, with a black head and back, grayish tail and wings, and white throat, breast, and forehead. In the spring, three white feathers hang from its crown. It usually nests in colonies and builds its bulky nest on the ground or in treetops, bushes, or reeds. The female lays from four to six pale-blue eggs.

Scientific Classification. The night heron is in the heron family, *Ardeidae*. The black-crowned night heron is genus *Nycticorax*, species *N. nycticorax*.   GEORGE J. WALLACE

NIGHT SCHOOL provides instruction after regular school hours. Most students who attend night school are people who work during the day. Many night school students want to complete the requirements for a high school diploma or a college degree. Others wish to increase their knowledge or skill in a certain field. The first night school in North America opened in Nieuw Amsterdam (New York City) in 1661. THOMAS J. McLERNON

See also VOCATIONAL EDUCATION (Night Schools).

NIGHTHAWK, also called *bullbat* and *mosquito hawk*, is a bird that looks much like the whippoorwill, to which it is related. It is not a hawk. The nighthawk is about 10 inches (25 centimeters) long, and has mixed black, white, and buff plumage, and a white throat patch. It has a white bar on each wing. Soon after sunset the nighthawk flies high to look for insects. It breeds throughout most of the United States and Canada. In winter, it is found in South America. The female lays two speckled eggs on the ground or on gravel rooftops.

Scientific Classification. The nighthawk belongs to the nightjar family, *Caprimulgidae*. The eastern nighthawk is genus *Chordeiles*, species *C. minor*.   HERBERT FRIEDMANN

See also BIRD (color picture: Color Protects Them).

NIGHTINGALE is a small bird of the thrush family. It lives in western and central Europe. The nightingale is famed for its beautiful voice, which has a sad quality.

The nightingale has a plain appearance, and shy habits. It is about 6 inches (15 centimeters) long, with russet-brown upper parts and a reddish rump and tail. The breast and underparts are mostly white. The bird is most at home deep in woods and hedges, especially along streams. It lives mainly on insects. It hops rapidly along the ground for a few moments and then stands motionless as if listening, as the robin does.

Nightingales have only one brood of young in a season. They build their nests near the ground in thickets or hedges. The female lays from four to six olive-brown eggs. The birds migrate to Africa for the winter.

Scientific Classification. The nightingale belongs to the thrush family, *Turdidae*. It is genus *Luscinia*, species *L. megarhynchos*.   GEORGE E. HUDSON

See also BIRD (color picture: Birds of Other Lands).

NIGHTINGALE, FLORENCE

NIGHTINGALE, FLORENCE (1820-1910), was the founder of the nursing profession as we know it today, and one of the greatest women of England's Victorian Age. British soldiers, wounded in the Crimean War, called her the *lady with the lamp* when she walked the halls of their hospital at night.

To all the world, the light that Florence Nightingale carried has come to mean care for the sick, concern for the welfare of the ordinary soldier, and freedom for women to choose their own work. She was called a "saintly woman." But her success was also due to her brilliant mind and her ability to organize and administer the details of hospital work.

Early Years. Florence Nightingale was named for Florence, Italy, where she was born on May 12, 1820, while her wealthy British parents were living abroad. Her childhood was spent at the two family estates in England, with her mother, father, and sister Parthenope. Her mother filled their home with guests. Mrs. Nightingale taught her daughters the social graces and how to manage a large household. William Nightingale was his daughters' teacher, and a strict one. He taught them Greek, Latin, mathematics, and philosophy.

Florence liked books better than parties. She was even more devoted to helping others. An example of her first handwriting is a copy of a medical prescription written in a book measuring only 1 inch (2.5 centimeters) square. She enjoyed caring for visiting babies and for sick farmers on her father's estates. She nursed her dolls in their imagined illnesses, and saved the life of an old shepherd's dog when its broken leg had condemned it to death. As Florence grew older, she took over the management of the large Nightingale households.

When she was 16, Florence Nightingale made a difficult personal decision. She decided that she must devote herself to service for others, but she did not yet know how she could do this. Both Florence and her sister were presented to Queen Victoria when they entered British society. Travels in Europe followed.

But Florence had not forgotten her purpose in life. Slowly, she began to realize what her work must be.

She turned down suitors, declined many parties, and spent much of her time studying health and reforms for the poor and suffering. This was unheard-of behavior for a wealthy girl. Mrs. Nightingale could not accept her daughter's wish to do hospital work.

Her family's opposition prevented Florence from working in a hospital, for at that time such places were dirty and disreputable. Nurses were often drunken women, unfit to care for the sick. Florence took her first step toward independence when she went to study in a hospital in Paris. She then entered nursing training at the Institute of Protestant Deaconesses in Kaiserswerth, Germany. At 33, she became superintendent of a women's hospital in London.

Service in Crimea. Great Britain and France went to war with Russia in the Crimea in 1854. The British people were angry when they heard that their troops had been sent to battle without enough supplies, to die under terrible conditions. The Secretary of War asked Florence Nightingale to take charge of nursing. She sailed for the Crimea with 38 nurses.

This little band, in ugly gray uniforms, stepped ashore in the mud of Scutari, across from Constantinople (now Istanbul), in late 1854. They faced a job which seemed impossible. Five hundred wounded troops had just arrived from the Battle of Balaclava, where the charge of the Light Brigade (made famous later in a poem by Alfred, Lord Tennyson) had taken place. Two-thirds of the British cavalrymen had been killed or wounded there in 25 minutes.

The hospital was an old Turkish barracks, huge, dirty, and unfurnished. The wounded lay on floors, bleeding and uncared-for. How much could 38 nurses do? Medical supplies, food, and bedding were not arriving. There were no cots, mattresses, or bandages. Nightingale found a few men well enough to clean the place, and she put them to work at once. She set up a nursing schedule for care, kitchen work, and diets. At night, her lamp burned as she walked the 4 miles (6 kilometers) of corridors and wrote countless letters demanding supplies from British military officials.

At first, doctors and officials resented the "dictatorship of a woman," as they regarded it, for Florence Nightin-

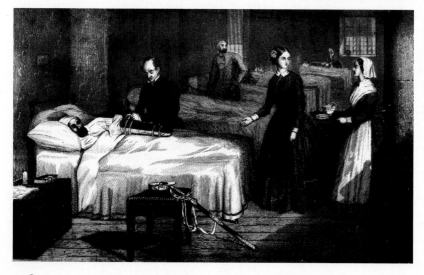

Florence Nightingale, *above,* introduced sanitary methods of nursing in wartime. She attended to the needs of British soldiers wounded in the Crimean War, *left.* It marked the first time that soldiers wounded away from home received good hospital care.

gale stood for no delays or slipshod ways. Then they came over to her side. Many people told her that the British soldiers were no better than animals and that she was "spoiling the brutes." But she believed that every human being's life was valuable. When the hospital was running better, she started classes to teach convalescent soldiers to read and write.

While on a visit to the front lines, Nightingale caught Crimean fever, and nearly died. By that time, she had become famous, and even Queen Victoria kept an anxious watch on her recovery.

After she returned to the Scutari hospital, Nightingale was urged to go to England to get her strength back. She replied firmly, "I can stand out the war with any man." Her success at Scutari became so widely recognized that she was given charge of all the army hospitals in the Crimea. By the end of the war, she had saved countless lives, and brought about worldwide reforms in hospital administration and nursing.

Return to England. England greeted her arrival in 1856 with big celebrations. Instead of attending them, Nightingale went quietly home to her family, and then moved to London. She used a gift of $150,000 from her grateful public to found the Nightingale Home for Nurses at Saint Thomas Hospital in London. She became a world authority on scientific care of the sick. The United States asked her advice for setting up military hospitals during the Civil War.

The strain of overwork and her Crimean illness had injured her health. Nightingale became a semi-invalid and seldom left her rooms. Instead, the world came to her. Ministers, heads of government, authors, reformers, and politicians came to ask her advice. By correspondence and by constant reading, she made studies of conditions in the British Army in India and in hospitals. Health conditions among the people of India especially concerned her. Her 800-page report to the War Department brought about the formation of the Royal Commission on the Health of the British Army in 1858. She received many public honors, and was the first woman to be given the British Order of Merit. MAY McNEER

NIGHTJAR. See GOATSUCKER.

NIGHTMARE is a frightening dream or dreamlike experience that awakens a sleeper. After awakening from most nightmares, the sleeper can recall the dream that caused the fright. But in another kind of nightmare, sometimes called an *incubus attack*, a deeply sleeping person feels a pressure as if a great weight were on the chest. The person wakes up in terror and does not remember much about any dream.

Nightmares may occur in times of severe tension. They have been experienced by many soldiers in combat and by persons withdrawing from alcohol or certain other drugs. All children between the ages of 2 and 6 probably have some nightmares. Some nightmares seem entirely real to a youngster after awakening. Most adults do not have nightmares. Frequent nightmares among older children or adults may indicate a physical or emotional problem. ERNEST HARTMANN

See also DREAM.

NIGHTSHADE is the common name of a family of plants that have the scientific name *Solanaceae*. The nightshade family includes herbs, shrubs, and tropical trees. The plants grow most abundantly in warm regions.

Some Members of the Nightshade Family

Nightshade

Jimson Weed

J. Horace McFarland Co.

Potato

Tomato

Among the more than 2,000 members of this family are such useful plants as the potato, tomato, ground cherry, capsicum (red pepper), and eggplant. The family also includes poisonous plants like belladonna (deadly nightshade), Jimson weed (stramonium), and bittersweet (woody nightshade). People in the United States once thought tomatoes were poisonous. The tobacco plant and the petunia also are members of the nightshade family. GEORGE H. M. LAWRENCE

Related Articles in WORLD BOOK include:

Apple of Sodom	Capsicum	Petunia	Tobacco
Belladonna	Eggplant	Potato	Tomato
Bittersweet	Jimson Weed	Solanum	

NIHILISM, *NI uh liz'm,* was a movement of ideas in Russia during the middle of the 1800's. The name comes from the Latin word *nihil*, which means *nothing*. It first appeared in Ivan Turgenev's novel *Fathers and Sons*. One character in the book says, "A nihilist is a man who does not bow down before any authority; who does not take any principle on faith, whatever reverence that principle may be enshrined in."

The idea of rejecting all authority greatly influenced the revolutionary movement in Russia. People in other countries believed that the nihilists were responsible for acts of terrorism against the Russian government. *Nihilism* and *revolution* came to have the same meaning when applied to Russia.

In Western Europe, nihilism meant a denial of objective truths and values. Friedrich Nietzsche called himself a nihilist because he attacked accepted ideas. Most Western nihilists find that they cannot remain wholly negative. They tend to replace old values with new ones. Pure nihilism seldom exists. JAMES COLLINS

See also NIETZSCHE, FRIEDRICH; TURGENEV, IVAN S.

NIIHAU. See HAWAII (The Islands).

NIJINSKY, *nih ZHIN ski,* **VASLAV** (1890-1950), was the most famous male dancer of his time. He was short, with thick thighs and sloping shoulders. Yet he acted out his roles so completely that his appearance seemed to change from one role to another.

Nijinsky had such amazing body control that his dancing looked spontaneous and effortless. One legend tells of a dramatic leap he made through an open window as his exit in *Le Spectre de la Rose*. He rose slowly, soared across the ledge, appeared to stop in midair, and was still at the height of his jump as he disappeared.

Nijinsky was born in Kiev, Russia. He first studied dancing at the St. Petersburg Imperial School of Ballet at the age of 10. He traveled with Sergei Diaghilev's ballet company to Paris in 1909, and enjoyed great international success until 1913. He married a dancer in the company in 1913, and Diaghilev dismissed him. Nijinsky rejoined the company in the United States in 1916, dancing as brilliantly as ever. But in 1917, mental illness ended his career.   P. W. Manchester

See also Ballet (Russian Ballet; picture).

Bettmann Archive

Vaslav Nijinsky created the choreography and also danced the part of the faun in *The Afternoon of a Faun* in 1912.

NIKE, TEMPLE OF. See Acropolis.

NIKE OF SAMOTHRACE. See Winged Victory.

NIKISCH, *NEE kish,* **ARTHUR** (1855-1922), was a Hungarian conductor, violinist, and pianist. He conducted the Leipzig Opera in Germany from 1879 to

1889, and then led the Boston Symphony Orchestra for four years. He conducted the Royal Hungarian Opera and the Philharmonic concerts in Budapest from 1893 to 1895. Nikisch became conductor of the Leipzig Gewandhaus Orchestra in 1895, and of the Berlin Philharmonic Orchestra in 1897. He held both positions until his death. He toured the United States in 1912.

Nikisch was born in Szent Miklós, Hungary. He performed as a pianist when only 8 years old.   David Ewen

NIKOLAYEV, ANDRIAN G. See Astronaut (table: Russian Cosmonauts).

NILE, BATTLE OF THE, took place between English and French fleets off the Egyptian coast on Aug. 1, 1798. Rear Admiral Horatio Nelson's British fleet defeated the French fleet, commanded by Admiral François-Paul Brueys. The battle re-established British supremacy in the Mediterranean Sea, and contributed to the failure of Napoleon's campaign in Egypt.

Napoleon's army had landed in Egypt early in July 1798. It captured Alexandria, routed the Mameluke army near the pyramids outside Cairo, and then took Cairo. Nelson, who had been searching in the eastern Mediterranean for the French fleet, sailed for Egypt after he learned of Napoleon's landing. He found the French fleet anchored by the island of Aboukir in the mouth of the Nile River. Nelson's fleet sank several of the 13 French ships, and damaged and captured most of the others. Brueys and several hundred French sailors were killed. Napoleon's army soon ran out of supplies, and he returned to France. Nelson was made Baron Nelson of the Nile and given a pension.   Vernon F. Snow

See also Mameluke; Napoleon I (Egypt Invaded); Nelson, Horatio (Battle of the Nile).

NILE RIVER is the longest river in the world. It flows for 4,160 miles (6,695 kilometers) through northeast Africa. The Nile rises near the equator and flows into the Mediterranean Sea. It irrigates about 7,600,000 acres (3,080,000 hectares) of land in Egypt and about 2,800,000 acres (1,130,000 hectares) in Sudan.

The Nile Valley and the Nile Delta rank among the world's most fertile farming areas. Until 1968, water from the Nile deposited fertile *silt* (particles of soil) in the valley and on the delta, where the Nile flows into the Mediterranean. The Nile also flooded certain areas every summer.

In 1968, the Aswan High Dam at Aswan, Egypt, began operating. This dam ended the annual floods and trapped the Nile's silt in Lake Nasser, behind the dam. Without the deposits of silt, Egyptian farmers had to use more artificial fertilizers on their soil. But the high dam and other dams built during the 1900's generate electricity and provide a steady flow of water for irrigation.

The Course of the Nile. The Nile flows generally northward throughout its course. Its southernmost source is the Ruvironza River in Burundi. Lake Victoria ranks as the largest source. The Nile flows through the Sudd, a vast swamp in southern Sudan, where high temperatures cause about half the water to evaporate.

The Nile is called the White Nile between the Sudd and Khartoum, Sudan. At Khartoum, the Blue Nile from Ethiopia joins the White Nile. North of Khartoum, the river is called simply the Nile. The Atbara River, another chief source of the Nile, drains into it in Sudan, about 175 miles (282 kilometers) north of Khartoum.

About 70 per cent of the Nile's water comes from the

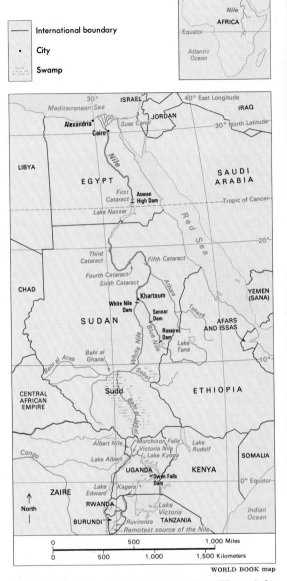

International boundary

• City

Swamp

WORLD BOOK map

Nancy Palmer Photo Agency Inc.

The Nile River irrigates large strips of farmland. The Egyptian farm village shown above lies north of the Aswan High Dam.

C. Pierre, De Wys, Inc.

The Blue Nile, one of the two main branches of the Nile, has carved out a deep valley in Ethiopia, *above.*

Blue Nile. The flow of water in the Blue Nile and the Atbara varies greatly. Flooding by these rivers caused the annual floods of the Nile in Egypt.

North of Cairo, Egypt, the Nile divides into separate channels in the Nile Delta. The delta has some swampy land and salty lakes, as well as highly fertile soil.

The Nile Valley and Nile Delta make up a total of about 3 per cent of Egypt's area. Almost all Egyptian farms lie in this densely populated region. Water from the Nile enables farmers in the valley and delta to raise various crops the year around. The chief winter crops, in order of area planted, include clover, wheat, and beans and other vegetables. The main summer crops are cotton, corn, rice, and millet. Cotton is Egypt's most important crop financially.   WILLIAM A. HANCE

See also ASWAN HIGH DAM; DELTA; EGYPT (The Land; picture); LAKE NASSER; RIVER (chart).

Marc & Evelyne Bernheim, Woodfin Camp, Inc.

Murchison Falls, *above,* is on the Victoria Nile in western Uganda, about 20 miles (32 kilometers) east of Lake Albert.

NILGAI. See ANTELOPE (Kinds of Antelope).

NILOTES. See AFRICA (People).

NILSSON, BIRGIT (1918-   ), is a Swedish dramatic soprano. She became noted for the power and clarity of her voice. Critics generally regard Nilsson as the finest singer of heroic roles in the operas of Richard Wagner. Kirsten Flagstad of Norway formerly held this distinction. Nilsson's performances as the Wagnerian heroines Isolde and Brünnhilde set the standard for her time. She also achieved fame as Aïda, Elektra, Lady Macbeth, Salome, and Tosca. But many critics rate her performance in the title role of Giacomo Puccini's opera *Turandot* as her outstanding achievement.

Birgit Nilsson was born in Västra Karup, near Malmö, Sweden. She began her career with the Stockholm Opera in 1947. She made a successful debut at the Metropolitan Opera in 1959 as Isolde. MAX DE SCHAUENSEE

NIMBA MOUNTAINS. See LIBERIA (The Land; map).

NIMBUS. See CLOUD.

NIMBUS is another name for *halo* in painting. It was developed in Christian art in the 400's. According to Greek myths, a radiant nimbus surrounded the heads of gods and goddesses when they came to earth.

NIMBUS WEATHER SATELLITE. See SPACE TRAVEL (Artificial Satellites).

NÎMES, *neem,* or NISMES (pop. 127,933; met. area pop. 131,638), is an industrial city of southern France. It is the center of a wine- and brandy-producing district. Its factories produce silks, cotton goods, and carpets. Nîmes was one of the most magnificent cities of the Roman Empire. For location, see FRANCE (political map). See also FRANCE (picture: The Amphitheater of Nîmes).

NIMITZ, CHESTER WILLIAM (1885-1966), served as commander in chief of the United States Pacific Fleet during World War II. He took command on Dec. 31, 1941, about three weeks after the fleet had been almost completely disabled in the Japanese attack on Pearl Harbor.

Admiral Nimitz painstakingly rebuilt U.S. strength in the Pacific. As commander of the Pacific Fleet and the Pacific Ocean Areas, Admiral Nimitz directed the Navy and the Marine Corps forces. The admiral's calm assurance of final victory did much to restore the U.S. Navy's faith in its own power and ability.

In the early months of the war, Admiral Nimitz refused to attack before U.S. forces were fully ready, in spite of angry questions from congress and newspapers. He waited until he had enough ships, supplies, and troops to assure victory. Nimitz developed much of the strategy of *island hopping* (seizing only key islands from which attacks on other key islands could be launched). This strategy saved lives and time. Nimitz led the fleet through many victories until it drove the Japanese back to Japan. He was promoted to fleet admiral in 1944. Nimitz signed for the United States at the Japanese surrender ceremonies in Tokyo Bay in 1945.

After the war, Nimitz became chief of naval operations. He left active duty in 1947, and then became special assistant to the secretary of the Navy. Nimitz headed the United Nations commission that mediated the dispute over Kashmir in 1949. Nimitz was born in Fredericksburg, Tex., and graduated from the U.S. Naval Academy in 1905. DONALD W. MITCHELL

See also WORLD WAR II (The War in Asia).

NIMROD is a Bible character mentioned in Genesis 10: 8-10 as a descendant of Noah. He lived some centuries after the Flood, when people were wandering over the earth. He is said to have been a grandson of Ham. He was a mighty ruler and builder of cities. His kingdom included Babylon, Erech, and Accad in Mesopotamia. He is supposed to have founded Nineveh in Assyria. He became famous as a hunter, and today we speak of a skillful hunter as a *Nimrod.* JOHN BRIGHT

NIÑA. See CARAVEL; COLUMBUS, CHRISTOPHER (First Voyage to America; picture: Columbus' Ships).

NINE-POWER TREATY. At the Washington Conference in 1921 and 1922, Belgium, China, France, Great Britain, Italy, Japan, The Netherlands, Portugal, and the United States signed a treaty to respect the independence and territorial integrity of China, and to maintain the Open Door there. But these powers failed to provide guarantees to keep the pledges. DWIGHT E. LEE

NINEPINS. See BOWLING (Other Kinds; History).

NINETEENTH AMENDMENT. See CONSTITUTION OF THE UNITED STATES (Amendment 19); WOMAN SUFFRAGE.

NINETY-FIVE THESES. See LUTHER, MARTIN.

NINEVEH was the last capital of the ancient Assyrian Empire. It stood on the east bank of the Tigris River, about 230 miles (370 kilometers) north of present-day Baghdad. The site of Nineveh was settled as early as 5000 B.C. In 612 B.C., a combined army of Babylonians and Medes captured and destroyed the city. In the 1800's, archaeologists unearthed the site and discovered the great royal library of King Ashurbanipal. This library included business documents, letters, and many examples of Babylonian and Sumerian literature. See also ASSYRIA; NIMROD. JACOB J. FINKELSTEIN

NINGPO (pop. 350,000), also called YIN-HSIEN, is an industrial center and port in the Chinese province of Chekiang. For location, see CHINA (political map). In 1842, Ningpo became one of five Chinese "treaty ports" in which Great Britain won special trading rights (see CHINA [The "Unequal Treaties"]). The city produces heavy industrial equipment. Its factories use iron from nearby mines. RICHARD H. SOLOMON

NIOBE, *NY oh bee,* was the daughter of King Tantalus in Greek mythology (see TANTALUS). She married Amphion, the king of Thebes, and had seven strong, talented sons and seven beautiful daughters. But her pride brought disaster. She boasted that she deserved more worship than the goddess Leto, mother of Apollo and Artemis, because she had so many children (see APOLLO; ARTEMIS). This angered Leto. She sent Apollo and Artemis to slay the children of Niobe with their arrows. Niobe's grief was so great that she could not stop weeping. The gods changed her into a stone cliff with a waterfall. PHILIP W. HARSH

NIOBIUM, or COLUMBIUM, one of the chemical elements, is a shiny-white, soft metal. It is used to toughen and harden steel. Niobium allows atomic particles called *neutrons* to pass through it without interference. For this reason, it may someday be used in nuclear reactors. Niobium occurs as niobium pentoxide (Nb_2O_5) in a mineral called columbite. It is always found with a similar element called tantalum.

Niobium (symbol Nb) has the atomic number 41 and the atomic weight 92.906. It melts at 2468° C (±10° C) and boils at 4927° C. It was discovered in 1801 by Charles Hatchett of England.   ALAN DAVISON

See also ELEMENT, CHEMICAL (tables).

NIOBRARA RIVER. See NEBRASKA (Rivers and Lakes).

NIPKOW, PAUL G. See TELEVISION (Early Development).

NIPPON. See JAPAN.

NIRENBERG, MARSHALL W. See NOBEL PRIZES (table: Nobel Prizes for Physiology or Medicine—1968).

NIRVANA. See BUDDHISM; TRANSMIGRATION OF THE SOUL; BUDDHA; RELIGION (Buddhism).

NISEI, *nee say*, is the Japanese name for the children of Japanese families who have migrated to other countries. The people who migrate are called *Issei*. Their children born in the new country are *Nisei*. The children of Nisei are called *Sansei*. The largest Japanese-American groups live in Hawaii and California. The Nisei and Sansei have rapidly adopted American ways of life. See also HAWAII (World War II); WORLD WAR II (Internment of Aliens).   FELIX M. KEESING

NIT. See LOUSE.

NITER. See SALTPETER.

NITRATE is any one of a number of chemical compounds. They always contain the nitrate radical (NO_3^-) and some other element, such as sodium or calcium. Some nitrates are salts of nitric acid. Others are formed by microorganisms that act on organic nitrogen compounds. They have many important uses in industry, medicine, and agriculture. Some heart remedies come from nitrates. Nitrates are also used in photographic films, fireworks, and explosives. The nitrates of sodium and calcium add nitrogen directly to the soil, and make valuable fertilizers. The large deposits of sodium nitrate found in Chile were long the chief source of nitrogen fertilizer. Synthetic nitrates are now being produced. See also CHILE (Mining); NITROGEN (Nitrogen in Agriculture).   K. L. KAUFMAN

NITRATE OF SILVER. See SILVER NITRATE.

NITRIC ACID is a strong inorganic acid that has many industrial uses. Its principal use is for the production of fertilizers, drugs, and explosives. Large quantities of nitric acid are produced during thunderstorms. It is also a by-product of nuclear explosions set off in the atmosphere. Nitric acid was one of the first acids known. Many alchemists of the Middle Ages used it in their experiments.

Nitric acid is such a powerful oxidizing agent that it dissolves many metals. But it does not attack two precious metals, gold and platinum. A drop of nitric acid on a piece of jewelry tells whether it is made of genuine gold or platinum. These two metals can be dissolved by *aqua regia*, a mixture of nitric acid and hydrochloric acid (see AQUA REGIA).

Nitric acid is used to manufacture ammonium nitrate, NH_4NO_3, an ingredient of many fertilizers, and to make explosives. The chemical industry uses nitric acid to prepare such organic compounds as dyes, drugs, and nitrate salts. Nitric acid reacts with toluene in the presence of sulfuric acid to form trinitrotoluene, better known as TNT. Cellulose is treated with nitric acid to make cellulose nitrate, which is used for guncotton and other explosives.

Commercially, most nitric acid is produced by oxidiz-

ing ammonia using a platinum catalyst. Ammonia and air are passed through heated platinum gauze. The gases react to form nitrogen oxide and water. Upon cooling, this gaseous mixture forms nitric acid. This method is called the *Ostwald process*, after Wilhelm Ostwald, the German chemist who developed it. Nitric acid is also produced by heating saltpeter with sulfuric acid. In this process, nitric acid is recovered by distillation.

Nitric acid is a colorless liquid with a suffocating odor. It develops a yellow color if kept in bottles that are not tightly stoppered. This is due to nitrogen dioxide gas, NO_2, that results from decomposition of the acid. Nitric acid is highly caustic and corrosive and can cause painful burns on the skin. Its chemical formula is HNO_3. The metal salts of nitric acid, called *nitrates*, are soluble in water.   S. YOUNG TYREE, JR.

See also ACID; OSTWALD, WILHELM; NITRATE.

NITRIFYING BACTERIA. See NITROGEN CYCLE.

NITRITE is a compound of the nitrite radical (NO_2^-) and some other element. Inorganic nitrites are stable and soluble. Organic nitrites are made from alcohol and aromatic substances, such as toluene. They are unstable when in the presence of acid, but they are preserved satisfactorily in neutral or mildly alkaline solutions. Nitrites are used in medicine for heart ailments. Sodium nitrite is important in making dyes. It is also added to cured meats, such as bacon, to prevent botulism and to give the meat a pinkish color. Under certain conditions, sodium nitrite may combine with other chemicals to form nitrosamines, which can cause cancer. The U.S. Department of Agriculture limits the amount of sodium nitrite allowed in cured meats. Nitrites are also used for explosives and to produce other chemicals.   K. L. KAUFMAN

NITROCELLULOSE, also called cellulose nitrate. See CELLULOID; GUNCOTTON.

NITROGEN is a chemical element that occurs in nature mainly as a gas. Nitrogen makes up about 78 per cent of the air by volume. Daniel Rutherford, a Scottish physician, discovered nitrogen in 1772.

Nitrogen belongs to the group of elements called *nonmetals*. Its symbol is N. Its atomic number is 7, and its atomic weight is 14.0067. Nitrogen gas is colorless, odorless, and tasteless. It is only slightly soluble in water, and it does not combine easily with most other elements. The boiling point of nitrogen is −195.8° C and its melting point is −209.9° C.

Nitrogen and Life

All organisms must have nitrogen to live. It makes up an important part of protein molecules, which are found in protoplasm. Protoplasm is the living material in all plant and animal tissues. Human beings and animals get protein by eating other animals and plants.

Most plants must manufacture their protein from simple nitrogen compounds dissolved in the soil. Some of this dissolved nitrogen comes from the atmosphere in the form of *nitric acid* (HNO_3). Lightning causes the nitrogen and oxygen in the air to form compounds called *nitrogen oxides*. These oxides react with water to form nitric acid, which is carried to the earth dissolved in rainwater.

Plants of the *legume* family produce protein from the

nitrogen of the air, with the help of certain types of bacteria. Legumes include such plants as alfalfa, peas, and soybeans. The roots of these plants have small swellings called *nodules*. The nodules contain *nitrogen-fixing bacteria*, which take nitrogen from the air and convert it into nitrogen compounds. The plants use these compounds to make protein. After the plants die and decay, the nitrogen compounds in the nodules become part of the soil.

As nitrogen is used and reused by living things, it goes through a continuous cycle of chemical changes. This cycle of changes is known as the *nitrogen cycle* (see NITROGEN CYCLE).

Uses of Nitrogen

Manufacturers make pure nitrogen by distilling liquid air (see LIQUID AIR). Air consists almost entirely of nitrogen and oxygen. During the distillation process, the nitrogen boils before the oxygen does, because nitrogen has a lower boiling point. As it vaporizes, the nitrogen is collected and stored under pressure in steel cylinders.

Production of Ammonia. The principal use of nitrogen is in the production of ammonia (NH_3), a gas that consists of nitrogen and hydrogen. Manufacturers produce ammonia chiefly by the *Haber-Bosch process*. In this process, nitrogen and hydrogen are combined at about 500° C and at about 500 times normal atmospheric pressure. The reaction takes place in the presence of a *catalyst*, a substance that increases the rate of a chemical reaction.

Ammonia is used as a fertilizer and in the production of explosives, nitric acid, and other chemicals. A common household cleaning agent consists of a dilute solution of ammonia in water.

Nitrogen in Agriculture. Almost all fertilizers used by farmers and gardeners contain nitrogen, which promotes the healthy growth of plants. Ammonia is the most common nitrogen fertilizer. Farmers inject ammonia gas directly into the soil, where it dissolves and helps plants grow. Liquefied ammonia and such compounds as ammonium sulfate and ammonium nitrate are also used as nitrogen fertilizers. Other sources of nitrogen include manure and *guano*, the waste material of sea birds. See FERTILIZER.

Farmers can also supply nitrogen to their fields by rotating certain crops. In crop rotation, a farmer plants a field one year with corn, wheat, or some other crop that removes nitrogen from the soil. The next year, the farmer plants the same field with a crop of legumes—such as alfalfa or soybeans—that restores nitrogen to the soil.

Uses of Liquid Nitrogen. The food industry uses liquid nitrogen to quick-freeze food (see FOOD, FROZEN [Nitrogen Freezing]). Liquid nitrogen also serves as a refrigerant for food during transport. Scientists use liquid nitrogen to produce the low temperatures necessary in some experiments.

Nitrogen and Pollution

Some nitrogen compounds contribute to the pollution of both water and air. Nitrogen fertilizer that is not used by plants can cause water pollution. Rainwater carries the unused fertilizer into streams or lakes, where the nitrogen compounds increase the rate of growth of algae and other water plants.

A compound called *nitric oxide* (NO) pollutes the air. Nitric oxide is formed as a by-product in the combustion of gasoline in automobile engines. Sunlight causes the nitric oxide in the lower atmosphere to react with oxygen to form *ozone*, one of the irritating substances in smog.

Supersonic airplanes produce nitric oxide in the stratosphere, where the chemical compound harms the environment in a different way. Nitric oxide acts as a catalyst for the decomposition of the ozone that is present in the stratosphere. In contrast to the ozone in the lower atmosphere, the stratospheric ozone layer benefits animals and plants by shielding them from harmful ultraviolet light.   WILLIAM L. JOLLY

Related Articles in WORLD BOOK include:

Borazon	Nitrite
Environmental Pollution	Nitroglycerin
Nitrate	Nitrous Oxide
Nitric Acid	Saltpeter

NITROGEN CYCLE is the circulation of nitrogen among the atmosphere, soil, water, and plants and animals of the earth. All living things require nitrogen, but most organisms cannot use the gaseous nitrogen (N_2) that makes up almost 80 per cent of the air. They must have nitrogen that has combined with other elements to form compounds. However, the supply of this *fixed nitrogen* is limited. Therefore, complex methods of recycling nitrogen have developed in nature.

After plants and animals die, they undergo decomposition by certain bacteria and fungi. These microorganisms produce ammonia (NH_3) from nitrogen compounds in dead organic matter and in body wastes excreted by animals. Plants absorb some of the ammonia and use it to make proteins and other substances essential to life.

Ammonia that is not absorbed by plants is changed into nitrates (NO_3^- compounds) by *nitrifying bacteria*. There are two types of nitrifying bacteria—*nitrite bacteria*, which convert ammonia into nitrites (NO_2^- compounds); and *nitrate bacteria*, which change nitrites into nitrates. Plants absorb most of the nitrates and use them in the same way as ammonia. Animals get nitrogen by eating plants or by feeding on animals that have eaten plants.

A process called *nitrogen fixation* constantly puts additional nitrogen into biological circulation. *Nitrogen-fixing* bacteria and algae take nitrogen from the air and convert it into ammonia. Much of this ammonia is absorbed by plants, but some of it is lost in the atmosphere.

Although nitrogen fixation removes nitrogen from the atmosphere, a reverse process called *denitrification* returns an approximately equal amount of nitrogen to the air. *Denitrifying bacteria* convert some of the nitrates in soil back into gaseous nitrogen or nitrous oxide (N_2O). However, fixed nitrogen may circulate many times between organisms and the soil before denitrification returns it to the atmosphere.

Some human activities interfere with the nitrogen cycle. For example, industry fixes vast quantities of nitrogen to produce fertilizer. The fertilizer provides great benefits, but excess amounts are washed off farmland and into waterways, polluting the water. In addi-

The Nitrogen Cycle Nitrogen makes up about 78 per cent of the earth's atmosphere, but most organisms cannot use nitrogen in its gaseous form. *Nitrogen-fixing bacteria* convert atmospheric nitrogen into a form that other living things can use. After nitrogen has been fixed by the bacteria, it circulates repeatedly between organisms and the soil. *Denitrifying bacteria* help regulate the amount of nitrogen in biological circulation by changing some fixed nitrogen back into a gas.

WORLD BOOK diagram

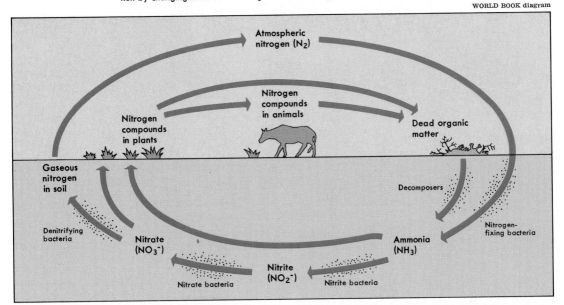

tion, the combustion of gasoline and some other fuels produces nitrogen compounds that contribute to air pollution.　　　　　　　　　　　WILLIAM A. REINERS

See also NITROGEN; LEGUME; NITRATE; NITRITE.

NITROGLYCERIN, NY troh GLISS ur in, or NITRO-GLYCEROL, is a powerful explosive. Its chemical formula is $C_3H_5(ONO_2)_3$. It is the principal explosive ingredient of dynamite. Pure nitroglycerin is a heavy, oily liquid that is as clear as water. But the commercial product is usually straw-colored. When nitroglycerin explodes, it expands to form gases that take up more than 3,000 times as much space as the liquid. The explosion of nitroglycerin is about three times as powerful as that of an equal amount of gunpowder, and the explosion speed is 25 times as fast as that of gunpowder.

Chemists make nitroglycerin by slowly adding glycerol, also known as glycerin, to concentrated nitric and sulfuric acids. The nitroglycerin forms a layer on top of the two acids. This layer is drawn off and washed, first with water, and then with a solution of sodium carbonate.

Ascanio Sobrero, an Italian chemist, discovered nitroglycerin in 1846. For many years, it was not used widely because it could not be depended on. In 1864, Alfred Nobel, a Swedish chemist, obtained a patent on a detonating cap made of mercury fulminate, which proved ideal for exploding nitroglycerin. In 1867, he invented dynamite, which provided a safe and convenient means for the transportation and use of nitroglycerin. Nitroglycerin quickly became the most widely used explosive.

Nitroglycerin is an ingredient of many smokeless powders, such as cordite and ballistite. It is seldom used alone as an explosive, except for blasting in oil wells.

Doctors use nitroglycerin to treat certain heart and blood-circulation diseases.　　　　　　　　JULIUS ROTH

See also DYNAMITE; EXPLOSIVE; GLYCEROL.

NITROUS OXIDE is a gas used as an *anesthetic* because it deadens pain. Nitrous oxide is commonly called "laughing gas," although people do not laugh when under its influence. When a person inhales nitrous oxide it causes loss of the sensation of pain. If a person inhales enough, it may cause loss of consciousness. But the effect does not last long. Nitrous oxide is used widely in dental and minor surgical procedures, because it acts quickly and because the patient recovers quickly.

Nitrous oxide is a relatively weak anesthetic, and must be used in high concentrations to be effective. The gas is usually mixed with pure oxygen. A mixture of air and nitrous oxide may not provide enough oxygen, because air is only 20 per cent oxygen. The body cannot use the oxygen found in the nitrous oxide compound itself.

Nitrous oxide is a colorless gas that has a sweetish odor and taste. Its chemical formula is N_2O. It does not burn, but wood will burn in an atmosphere of pure nitrous oxide. The gas was first prepared in the 1770's by English chemist Joseph Priestley.　　SOLOMON GARB

See also ANESTHESIA.

NIUE ISLAND, nee OOH ay, or SAVAGE ISLAND, is a coral island in the South Pacific. It belongs to New Zealand. The island covers about 100 square miles (259 square kilometers) and has a population of about 5,000. Niue exports copra and bananas. Alofi is the island's chief village. For the location of the island, see PACIFIC ISLANDS (map).

NIX was the name of a water sprite in German folklore. The nixes were little people with golden hair and green teeth, and they lived in lakes and rivers. Nixes were fond of music and dancing, and sometimes invited humans to their feasts. They were said to appear before anyone died of drowning.

See also FAIRY; NEREID.

RICHARD M. NIXON

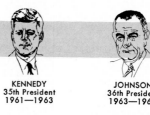

KENNEDY
35th President
1961—1963

JOHNSON
36th President
1963—1969

NIXON, RICHARD MILHOUS (1913-   ), was the only President of the United States ever to resign from office. He left the presidency on Aug. 9, 1974, while facing almost certain impeachment for his involvement in the Watergate scandal. This scandal included a burglary of Democratic national headquarters and other illegal activities by employees of Nixon's 1972 reelection committee. Nixon's attempts to cover up these crimes became a major part of the scandal. See WATERGATE.

Nixon was succeeded as President by Vice-President Gerald R. Ford. Ford had become Vice-President only eight months earlier when he replaced Spiro T. Agnew, who resigned from the vice-presidency while under criminal investigation for graft. Nixon chose Ford, then minority leader of the U.S. House of Representatives, to succeed Agnew. Shortly after Nixon resigned, Ford pardoned him for all federal crimes he may have committed during his presidency.

When Nixon was elected President in 1968, he climaxed one of the most extraordinary political comebacks in U.S. history. In 1960, while serving as Vice-President under President Dwight D. Eisenhower, Nixon ran for the presidency and lost to John F. Kennedy. In 1962, Nixon was defeated when he ran for governor of California, his home state. After this loss, one television network presented a program called "The Political Obituary of Richard Nixon."

But in 1968, Nixon showed that he was politically very much alive. He won several primary elections, and again became the Republican candidate for President. This time, Nixon defeated Vice-President Hubert H. Humphrey, his Democratic opponent, and former Governor George C. Wallace of Alabama, the candidate of the American Independent Party. In 1972, Nixon won a second term in a landslide victory over Democratic Senator George S. McGovern of South Dakota.

Nixon was the 12th former Vice-President who became President. He was the first of this group who did not succeed the President under whom he had served. Nixon became Vice-President at the age of 40, and was the second youngest man to hold that office. John C. Breckinridge was 36 when he became Vice-President under James Buchanan in 1857. Before Nixon was elected Vice-President, he was elected twice to the U.S. House of Representatives and once to the U.S. Senate.

After taking office as President, Nixon won respect for his conduct of foreign policy. He ended U.S. military participation in the Vietnam War and eased the tension that had existed for years between the United States and both China and Russia. Nixon became the first President to visit China while in office. He also visited Russia, and he won congressional approval of U.S.-Soviet agreements to limit the production of nuclear weapons.

At home, Nixon was challenged by sharply rising prices. He placed government controls on wages and prices to halt inflation, but the controls had little effect. Nixon ended the military draft and created an all-volunteer system for the U.S. armed services.

Friends knew Nixon as a painfully sensitive man. Nixon felt especially hurt by what he considered unfair criticism. But in politics, he won fame as a tough, forceful campaigner. He liked a good fight and had a fierce determination to succeed.

Early Life

Boyhood. Richard Milhous Nixon was born on Jan. 9, 1913, in Yorba Linda, Calif., a village 30 miles (48 kilometers) southeast of Los Angeles. He was the second of the five sons of Francis Anthony Nixon and Hannah Milhous Nixon. Nixon's father had moved from Ohio to southern California. There he met and married Hannah Milhous, who had come from Indiana with her parents and a group of other Quakers. Francis Nixon later gave up his Methodist faith and became a Quaker. At one time or another, he worked as a streetcar conductor, a carpenter, a laborer, and a farmer.

In 1922, the family moved to nearby Whittier. There the elder Nixon opened a combination grocery store and gasoline station. The President had four brothers, Harold (1909-1932), Arthur (1918-1925), Donald (1914-   ), and Edward (1930-   ).

At the age of about 10, Richard began working part time as a bean picker. During his teens, he worked as a handyman in a packing house, janitor at a swimming pool, and barker at an amusement park. While in college, Nixon served as bookkeeper and as manager of the vegetable department of his father's store.

Education. Nixon attended elementary schools in Yorba Linda, Whittier, and nearby Fullerton. At Whittier High School, history and civics were his favorite subjects. He played football and starred in debating. At the age of 17, Nixon entered Whittier College, a Quaker institution. He won several debating awards, and became president of the student body.

Nixon graduated from Whittier in 1934 and won a scholarship from the Duke University School of Law in Durham, N.C. Walter F. Dexter, then president of Whittier College, wrote in a letter of recommendation for Nixon: "I believe he will become one of America's

---

Earl Mazo, the contributor of this article, is former National Political Correspondent for Readers' Digest *and the author of* Richard Nixon: A Political and Personal Portrait.

FORD
38th President
1974—1977

CARTER
39th President
1977—

**37TH PRESIDENT
OF THE
UNITED STATES
1969-1974**

The United States flag had
50 stars when Richard M.
Nixon became President.

The White House

important, if not great, leaders." At Duke, Nixon was elected president of the student law association. He also won election to the Order of the Coif, the national law fraternity for honor students. Nixon ranked third in the 1937 graduating class of 44 students.

Lawyer. The Great Depression still gripped the United States when Nixon left Duke. There were few jobs. Nixon tried unsuccessfully to join the Federal Bureau of Investigation and then a law firm in New York City. He finally returned home and joined a Whittier law firm, in which he became a partner. Nixon and several investors later formed a company to make

––––––– **IMPORTANT DATES IN NIXON'S LIFE** –––––––

1913 (January 9) Born in Yorba Linda, Calif.
1934 Graduated from Whittier College.
1940 (June 21) Married Thelma Catharine (Pat) Ryan.
1942-1946 Served in the U.S. Navy during World War II.
1946 Elected to the U.S. House of Representatives.
1948 Re-elected to the House.
1950 Elected to the U.S. Senate.
1952 Elected Vice-President of the United States.
1956 Re-elected Vice-President.
1960 Defeated for President by John F. Kennedy.
1962 Defeated for governor of California by Governor Edmund G. (Pat) Brown.
1968 Elected President of the United States.
1972 Re-elected President.
1974 (August 9) Resigned as President.

and market frozen orange juice, but the company went bankrupt in 18 months.

At the age of 26, Nixon became the youngest member of the Whittier College Board of Trustees. He also taught a law course at Whittier.

Nixon's Family. Shortly after returning to Whittier, Nixon met Thelma Catharine Ryan (March 16, 1912-). She had been born in a mining camp at Ely, Nev. Her father nicknamed her Pat because she was born on the eve of St. Patrick's Day. When Pat was a baby, her parents moved to a farm in California. They died before Pat finished high school, but she put herself through the University of Southern California.

When Nixon met Pat, she was teaching commercial subjects at Whittier High School. Friends introduced them during tryouts for a community theater play. They were married on June 21, 1940. The Nixons had two daughters, Patricia (Tricia), born in 1946, and Julie, born in 1948. Julie married David Eisenhower, grandson of former President Eisenhower, in 1968. Tricia married Edward Cox in 1971.

Naval Officer. A movement among the Whittier faculty and alumni to choose Nixon as president of the school was halted by World War II. In January, 1942, while awaiting assignment by the Navy, he took a job in the tire rationing section of the Office of Price Administration in Washington, D.C. Eight months later, Nixon was called to active duty as a lieutenant junior grade. He served in a naval air transport unit in the

Wide World

Nixon's Birthplace was this small frame house in Yorba Linda, Calif. In the family picture, Nixon and two of his four brothers, Harold, *left*, and Donald, *center*, are shown with their parents. Richard went to work part time as a bean picker when he was about 10 years old.

Wide World

Pacific, and was promoted to lieutenant commander before the war ended in 1945.

Career in Congress

Nixon entered politics by invitation. Since 1936, the voters of his home congressional district had elected a Democrat, Jerry Voorhis, to the U.S. House of Representatives. Republican leaders searched for a "new face" to oppose Voorhis in the 1946 election. They turned to Walter F. Dexter, state superintendent of education and former president of Whittier College. Dexter declined, but suggested Nixon. Nixon, then awaiting discharge from the Navy, agreed to run.

Professional politicians gave Nixon little chance of defeating Voorhis, a veteran campaigner. At first, Voorhis ignored his relatively unknown opponent. Then he agreed to a series of public debates, and the campaign became a tough, hard-hitting race. Nixon's skill in debating helped him win the election.

U.S. Representative. In the House of Representatives, Nixon was proudest of his work on a committee that laid the groundwork for the Marshall Plan and other foreign aid programs (see FOREIGN AID). Nixon helped write the Taft-Hartley Act, which set up controls over labor unions. He also became a member of the House Committee on Un-American Activities.

In 1948, Nixon was re-elected to the House as the nominee of both the Republican and Democratic parties. At that time, California had a unique "cross-filing" system that allowed candidates to enter each party's primary election. Nixon won both of the primaries.

The Alger Hiss case, which began in 1948, brought Nixon into national prominence. Hiss, a former State Department official, was accused of having passed government information to a Russian spy ring during the 1930's. The matter rested with Hiss's word against that of his accusers. Many members of the Un-American Activities Committee wanted to drop the case, but Nixon insisted that the charges against Hiss be either proved or disproved. The question of Communists in government was a fierce political issue at the time. In 1950, a Federal District Court jury convicted Hiss of perjury in denying that he had ever given secret documents to Russian agents. See HISS, ALGER.

U.S. Senator. At the peak of his prominence in the Hiss case, Nixon ran for the U.S. Senate in 1950. He opposed Representative Helen Gahagan Douglas, a New Deal Democrat. Conservative Democrats regarded Mrs. Douglas as an extreme liberal. During the campaign, Nixon emphasized charges, made originally by Mrs. Douglas' foes in the Democratic primary election, that she did not realize the threat of Communism. In one of California's most savage political contests, Nixon defeated Mrs. Douglas by nearly 700,000 votes.

Nixon worked hard in the Senate, serving on the Labor and Public Welfare Committee. He also became a popular speaker at Republican Party affairs and at civic meetings in all parts of the United States.

The 1952 Campaign. In 1952, the Republican National Convention nominated Nixon for Vice-President to run with General Dwight D. Eisenhower. A highlight of the campaign was a dispute over an $18,000 fund set up by Nixon's supporters in California. They had organized the fund in 1950 to enable Nixon to campaign for Republican programs and candidates in both election and nonelection years. Nixon and his friends showed that they had used the money only for political expenses, but his Democratic opponents called it a "secret slush fund." Some Republicans, fearing that Nixon might hurt Eisenhower's chances of victory, demanded that Nixon withdraw from the campaign.

Nixon's cause seemed hopeless. Then, on Sept. 23, 1952, Nixon stated his case in an emotional address over television and radio. He discussed his personal finances in detail, showing that he had not profited personally from the fund. He said that "Pat doesn't have a mink coat. But she does have a respectable Republican cloth coat." And he vowed to keep Checkers, a cocker spaniel that had been a gift to his daughters. After the program, Republicans hailed Nixon as a hero. Eisenhower put his arm around Nixon when they next met and declared: "You're my boy." Eisenhower and Nixon went on to defeat their Democratic opponents, Governor Adlai E. Stevenson of Illinois and Senator John J. Sparkman of Alabama.

Vice-President (1953-1961)

Eisenhower succeeded Democratic President Harry S. Truman in 1953. He gave Nixon the job of working with members of Congress to smooth out possible quarrels with the new administration. Eisenhower also assigned Nixon to preside over Cabinet meetings and the National Security Council in the President's absence. Nixon took a greater role in the executive branch of the government than any previous Vice-President.

Eisenhower's Illnesses. Nixon's biggest test as Vice-President began Sept. 24, 1955, when Eisenhower suffered a heart attack. Nixon calmly went about his normal duties, presided at Cabinet meetings, and kept the wheels of government moving smoothly. He also stepped in when the President suffered another illness in June, 1956, and a stroke in November, 1957.

The 1956 Election. Many persons wondered whether Eisenhower would ask Nixon to run with him again in 1956. Angered by rumors that he planned to drop Nixon, the President declared: "Anyone who attempts to drive a wedge of any kind between Dick Nixon and me has just as much chance as if he tried to drive it between my brother and me." Eisenhower and Nixon defeated the Democratic nominees, Stevenson and Senator Estes Kefauver of Tennessee.

Overseas Missions. Nixon often acted as spokesman for the government on trips to other nations. As Vice-President, he toured nearly 60 countries, visiting every continent except Antarctica. During a tour of Latin America in the spring of 1958, Nixon faced violence and danger. In Peru, Communist agents led groups that booed and stoned him. In Venezuela, mobs smashed the windows of Nixon's car, but he was not hurt.

Nixon traveled to Russia in July, 1959, to open an American exhibit in Moscow. As he and Premier Nikita S. Khrushchev walked through a model home, they argued about Russian and U.S. plans for world peace. At one point in the "kitchen debate," Nixon startled the Russians by pointing his finger at Khrushchev and saying bluntly: "You don't know everything."

Defeat by Kennedy. Few persons doubted that Nixon would be the Republican presidential candidate in 1960. For a time, some party leaders thought that Governor Nelson Rockefeller of New York might make an

United Press Int.

Representative Nixon won national fame during the Alger Hiss case. Nixon worked with Whittaker Chambers, *left,* who accused Hiss of spying, and investigator Robert Stripling, *right.*

United Press Int.

Nomination in 1952 brought this joyful gesture from Nixon and Dwight D. Eisenhower. Their wives shared the excitement.

The "Kitchen Debate" between Nixon and Russian Premier Khrushchev occurred during a tour of a U.S. exhibit in Moscow.

Wide World

336c

John F. Kennedy and Nixon discussed the issues of the 1960 presidential campaign during four televised "great debates."

United Press Int.

all-out fight for the nomination. But Rockefeller withdrew, and the Republican National Convention nominated Nixon on the first ballot. The delegates chose Henry Cabot Lodge, Jr., American ambassador to the United Nations, as Nixon's vice-presidential running mate. The Democrats nominated Senator John F. Kennedy of Massachusetts for President and Senator Lyndon B. Johnson of Texas for Vice-President.

The campaign was close and hard-fought from start to finish. Kennedy argued that Republican methods had slowed U.S. economic growth, contributing to what he called a loss of American prestige on the international scene. Nixon cited figures to show that the economy was growing at a satisfactory rate. Nixon and Kennedy took part in a unique series of four televised debates. The television and radio audiences included most of the nation's voters. These "great debates" marked the first time in American history that presidential candidates argued campaign issues face-to-face.

Nixon lost to Kennedy in the closest presidential election since Grover Cleveland defeated James G. Blaine by 23,005 popular votes in 1884. Kennedy won by 119,-450 popular votes out of nearly 69 million. Nixon carried 26 states to 22 for Kennedy, but Kennedy received 303 electoral votes compared to Nixon's 219. Senator Harry F. Byrd of Virginia received 15 electoral votes.

Political Comeback

Defeat in California. In 1961, Nixon began to practice law in Los Angeles. In 1962, friends encouraged him to run for governor of California. Nixon won the Republican nomination for governor by defeating Joseph C. Shell in the state primary election. But the victory was costly. Conservative Republicans had supported Shell, and Nixon's triumph split the party. Democratic Governor Edmund G. (Pat) Brown beat Nixon by about 300,000 votes.

New York City Lawyer. Nixon moved to New York City in 1963 and began a new law practice. He became a partner in a Wall Street law firm, and his associates placed his name first in the list of partners.

Some of Nixon's supporters wanted him to run for President in 1964, but Nixon felt that most Republicans favored Senator Barry M. Goldwater of Arizona. Goldwater won the Republican presidential nomination, and Nixon campaigned for him and other party candidates. President Lyndon B. Johnson, seeking his first full term, defeated Goldwater by a huge margin.

Goldwater's overwhelming defeat put Nixon back into the political limelight. Liberal and conservative Republicans were quarreling bitterly, and he was the only nationally prominent man whom both groups could accept. In 1966, Nixon campaigned vigorously for Republican candidates in congressional elections. Republicans won 47 House seats and 3 Senate seats that had been held by Democrats. Nixon received much credit for the Republican victories.

In 1967, Nixon traveled around the world. His trip included visits to the Soviet Union and South Vietnam.

The 1968 Election. In February, 1968, Nixon announced that he would be a candidate for the Republican presidential nomination. Many Republicans wondered whether he could regain his voter appeal. They feared that his defeats by Kennedy and Brown had given him the image of a loser. But Nixon won primary elections by large margins in New Hampshire, Wisconsin, Indiana, Nebraska, Oregon, and South Dakota.

Nixon's chief opponents for the presidential nomination were Governors Nelson Rockefeller of New York and Ronald Reagan of California. But Nixon easily won nomination on the first ballot at the Republican National Convention in Miami Beach. The convention nominated Nixon's choice as running mate, Governor Spiro T. Agnew of Maryland.

The Democrats chose Vice-President Hubert H. Humphrey and Senator Edmund S. Muskie of Maine. Former Governor George C. Wallace of Alabama and retired General Curtis E. LeMay ran as the candidates of the American Independent Party.

Both Nixon and Humphrey promised to make peace in Vietnam their main goal as President. Nixon called for a program of what he termed "new internationalism." Under this program, other nations would take over from the United States more of the responsibility for preserving world peace and helping underdeveloped countries. Nixon also pledged to strengthen law enforcement in the United States.

In the election, Nixon defeated Humphrey by only about 812,000 popular votes, 31,710,470 to 30,898,055. Wallace received 9,446,167 popular votes. But Nixon

NIXON'S FIRST ELECTION	
Place of Nominating Convention	Miami Beach, Fla.
Ballot on Which Nominated	1st
Democratic Opponent	Hubert H. Humphrey
American Independent Opponent	George C. Wallace
Electoral Vote	301 (Nixon) to 191 (Humphrey) and 46 (Wallace)
Popular Vote	31,710,470 (Nixon) to 30,898,055 (Humphrey) and 9,446,167 (Wallace)
Age at Inauguration	56

won a clear majority of electoral votes, with 301. Humphrey received 191 electoral votes, and Wallace got 46. For the electoral vote, see ELECTORAL COLLEGE (table).

Nixon's First Administration (1969-1973)

Foreign Policy. Nixon's major goal was settlement of the Vietnam War. In his first inaugural address, Nixon said: "The greatest honor history can bestow is the title of peacemaker. This honor now beckons America."

The Vietnam War. The Vietnam peace talks, begun in 1968, continued in Paris. But the negotiators made little progress. In March, 1969, Nixon ordered a stepped-up training program for South Vietnamese forces so that they could gradually take over the major burden of fighting the war. In July, he began a gradual withdrawal of U.S. combat troops from Vietnam. This policy became known as *Vietnamization*. Many Americans favored the gradual withdrawal, but many others wanted the U.S. involvement to end immediately. Protests and demonstrations swept the nation.

In 1972, Nixon ordered a blockade of North Vietnam to cut off its war supplies from Russia and China. The blockade included the mining of North Vietnam's ports and the bombing of its rail and highway links to China.

The Nixon Doctrine. In 1969, during a visit to Southeast Asia, Nixon proposed a new policy. He declared that, in the future, Asian nations would have to bear the main responsibility for their defense. He pledged the aid of U.S. troops only if a non-Communist Asian nation were threatened by a major foreign power. This policy became known as the *Nixon Doctrine*.

Relations with China. In 1969, Nixon approved the removal of some restrictions on travel by Americans to China. He also encouraged the reopening of trade between China and the United States. The two nations had stopped trading with each other during the Korean War (1950-1953). In 1971, Nixon approved the export of certain goods to China. In February, 1972, the President visited China for seven days.

Relations with Russia. In May, 1972, Nixon visited the Soviet Union for nine days. During this visit, Nixon

President Nixon, in his inaugural address on Jan. 20, 1969, pledged that the United States would seek "the title of peacemaker." Vice-President Spiro T. Agnew sat to Nixon's left.

Wide World

----------- VICE-PRESIDENTS AND CABINET -----------

Vice-President............	*Spiro T. Agnew†
	*Gerald R. Ford (1973)
Secretary of State..........	*William P. Rogers
	*Henry A. Kissinger (1973)
Secretary of the Treasury.....	*David M. Kennedy
	*John B. Connally (1971)
	George P. Shultz (1972)
	*William E. Simon (1974)
Secretary of Defense........	*Melvin R. Laird
	*Elliot L. Richardson (1973)
	*James R. Schlesinger (1973)
Attorney General..........	*John N. Mitchell
	Richard G. Kleindienst (1972)
	*Elliot L. Richardson (1973)
	*William B. Saxbe (1974)
Postmaster General**........	Winton M. Blount
Secretary of the Interior......	Walter J. Hickel
	*Rogers C. B. Morton (1971)
Secretary of Agriculture......	Clifford M. Hardin
	*Earl L. Butz (1971)
Secretary of Commerce......	Maurice H. Stans
	Peter G. Peterson (1972)
	Frederick B. Dent (1973)
Secretary of Labor..........	*George P. Shultz
	James D. Hodgson (1970)
	Peter J. Brennan (1973)
Secretary of Health, Education, and Welfare........	*Robert H. Finch
	*Elliot L. Richardson (1970)
	*Caspar Weinberger (1973)
Secretary of Housing and Urban Development.......	*George W. Romney
	*James T. Lynn (1973)
Secretary of Transportation...	*John A. Volpe
	Claude S. Brinegar (1973)

*Has a biography in WORLD BOOK.   †Resigned on Oct. 10, 1973.
**Reduced to non-Cabinet rank, 1971.

and Leonid I. Brezhnev, leader of the Soviet Communist Party, signed agreements to limit the production of nuclear weapons. Later that year, Russia became a major buyer of U.S. wheat.

The National Scene. In August, 1969, Nixon proposed a series of major domestic reforms, which he termed the *New Federalism*. One of the reforms called for a minimum federal payment to every needy family with children. Nixon also suggested a *revenue sharing* plan in which the federal government would share its tax revenues with state and local governments. But action on the reforms was stalled as key Democrats in Congress asked for major changes.

Major Legislation. In spite of the legislative slowdown, Congress did enact several far-reaching laws. In 1969, it passed Nixon's proposal to establish a lottery system for the military draft. Also in 1969, Congress approved extensive reforms in federal tax laws. These reforms included increases in personal income tax deductions and cuts in tax benefits for foundations and oil companies. In 1970, Congress established independent agencies to replace the Post Office Department and to operate the passenger trains that linked the nation's major cities. Also in 1970, Congress lowered the minimum voting age in federal elections to 18. The 26th Amendment to the U.S. Constitution, ratified in 1971, set the voting age at 18 for all elections. In 1972, Congress approved Nixon's revenue sharing program. The legislation provided billions of dollars in federal tax money to state and local governments.

Inflation was one of Nixon's chief domestic concerns. Many Americans found that although they were earning more money than ever before, rising prices sharply cut their gains. In 1971, Nixon established a Pay Board to stop inflationary wage and salary increases and a Price Commission to regulate price and rent increases. Business increased during 1972. In addition, the rate of inflation slowed.

The ABM System. In March, 1969, Nixon proposed a plan to build an antiballistic missile (ABM) system called *Safeguard.* Nixon said the new missiles were needed to protect U.S. underground missiles and bomber bases from enemy missile attack. The plan became one of the most heavily debated issues of Nixon's Administration. Critics charged that the system would step up the arms race between the United States and Russia. They also claimed the new missiles would cost too much money and fail to destroy enemy missiles. In August, the Senate narrowly approved construction of the two ABM bases Nixon had requested.

School Desegregation was the subject of two major rulings by the Supreme Court of the United States during Nixon's first Administration. In 1969, the court ruled that all public school districts must end segregation "at once." This ruling replaced a 1955 Supreme Court decision calling for an end to segregation "with all deliberate speed." In 1971, the court ruled that children could be bused to integrate public schools in areas where state laws had required segregation. In March, 1972, Nixon proposed legislation to stop federal courts from issuing new busing orders.

Supreme Court Nominations. In 1969 and again in 1970, Nixon suffered a stinging defeat when he tried to appoint a conservative Southerner to the Supreme Court. In May, 1969, Associate Justice Abe Fortas resigned from the court under charges of personal misconduct (see FORTAS, ABE). Nixon nominated Judge Clement F. Haynsworth, Jr., of South Carolina to succeed Fortas. Some critics claimed that Haynsworth was anti-Negro. Others charged he was unethical for ruling in a case in which he had a financial interest. In November, the Senate rejected the nomination by a 55 to 45 vote.

In January, 1970, Nixon nominated Judge G. Harrold Carswell of Florida for the seat. Opposition to Carswell grew quickly after several judges and law school deans rated him unqualified for the Supreme Court. In April, the Senate defeated the nomination by a 51 to 45 vote. It was the first time that two Supreme Court nominees of a President had been rejected since 1894, when Grover Cleveland was chief executive.

After Carswell's defeat, Nixon charged that the Senate would not confirm a Southerner to the court. In May, the Senate unanimously approved Nixon's third choice, Judge Harry A. Blackmun of Minnesota.

The U.S. Space Program opened a new era of exploration and discovery in 1969. On July 20, Apollo 11 astronauts Neil A. Armstrong and Edwin E. Aldrin, Jr., became the first men to set foot on the moon. Nixon spoke to the men through a special telephone connection while they were on the moon. "Because of what you have done," he told them, "the heavens have become

WORLD EVENTS

1969 (July 20) Two U.S. astronauts, Neil A. Armstrong and Edwin E. Aldrin, Jr., became the first men to set foot on the moon.

1969 The United States began to withdraw its ground combat forces from South Vietnam.

1970 Charles de Gaulle, former president of France, died.

1971 China became a member of the United Nations.

1971 The Pakistan Civil War ended with the creation of the republic of Bangladesh.

1972 Nixon became the first President to visit China while in office.

1973 The United States completed its withdrawal of combat forces from South Vietnam.

UNITED STATES EVENTS

The United States flag had 50 stars when Nixon became President.

1969 Congress approved a lottery system for the military draft.

1970 The U.S. Postal Service, an independent government agency, replaced the Post Office Department.

1970 Congress authorized creation of the National Railroad Passenger Corporation (Amtrak) to operate passenger trains between cities.

*Amendment 26
1971*

1971 The 26th Amendment to the U.S. Constitution lowered the minimum voting age in all elections from 21 to 18.

1971 The Supreme Court approved busing as a way to integrate public schools in areas where state laws had required segregation.

1972 The State and Local Fiscal Assistance Act provided for sharing federal tax money with state and local governments.

1973 Vice-President Spiro T. Agnew resigned.

1974 Nixon became the first chief executive to resign from the presidency. He was succeeded by Vice-President Gerald R. Ford.

PRESIDENT NIXON

The First Men on the Moon were U.S. astronauts Neil A. Armstrong and Edwin E. Aldrin, Jr. The two men made their historic landing on July 20, 1969.

The U.S. Population in 1970 was 203,235,298, according to the federal census taken that year.

Average Monthly Living Expenses per Household

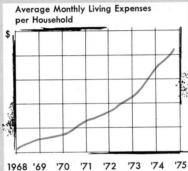

$

1968 '69 '70 '71 '72 '73 '74 '75

The Minimum Voting Age in all U.S. elections was lowered to 18 by the 26th Amendment to the Constitution, ratified in 1971.

Inflation was one of Nixon's major concerns. During 1973, prices rose at the fastest rate since 1947.

China Joined the United Nations in 1971. It became a permanent member of the UN Security Council.

EQUAL PAY FOR EQUAL WORK

United States Military Forces were gradually withdrawn from Vietnam in 1969 and the early 1970's.

UNSAFE FOR SWIMMING

Women's Liberation, a movement aimed at winning equal opportunities for women in all fields of life, gained fame in the early 1970's.

WATERGATE BREAK-IN

THE NEWS WATERGATE COVER-UP

TIMES PRESIDENT RESIGNS

Pollution of the air, land, and water became a growing problem in the United States during the late 1960's.

The Watergate Scandal shocked the nation and led to Nixon's resignation as President in 1974.

United Press Int.

Nixon and Chinese Premier Chou En-lai, *left,* toured Shanghai during the President's visit to China in 1972. With them were Mrs. Nixon and U.S. Secretary of State William P. Rogers.

part of man's world."

Environmental Problems attracted more and more attention during Nixon's Administration. Many Americans began to realize that pollution of the air, land, and water endangered not only the quality of life but also life itself. In 1970, Nixon set up the Environmental Protection Agency to deal with pollution problems.

The 1972 Election. Nixon and Agnew easily won renomination at the 1972 Republican National Convention in Miami Beach, Fla. The Democrats nominated Senator George S. McGovern of South Dakota for President. Sargent Shriver, former director of the Peace Corps, became McGovern's running mate.

In the election, Nixon won a landslide victory. He received over 17¾ million more popular votes than McGovern—the widest margin of any U.S. presidential election. Nixon got 520 electoral votes, and McGovern received 17. John Hospers of the Libertarian Party won 1 electoral vote. See ELECTORAL COLLEGE (table).

Life in the White House. The Nixons brought a calm and reserved way of life to the White House. The Johnsons and their two daughters had liked informal dress

---

NIXON'S SECOND ELECTION

Place of Nominating Convention.....Miami Beach, Fla.
Ballot on Which Nominated..........1st
Democratic Opponent...............George S. McGovern
Electoral Vote....................520 (Nixon) to 17 (McGovern) and 1 (Hospers)
Popular Vote.....................46,740,323 (Nixon) to 28,901,598 (McGovern)
Age at Inauguration...............60

---

and some jazz and rock music at their receptions. The Nixons preferred formal dress, including white ties and coats with tails for men and long gowns for women. They also favored fox trots and waltzes for dancing.

The Nixons' taste in art also was conservative. They replaced a number of the op art paintings that were on White House office walls with traditional landscapes and portraits.

Nixon was the first President to play the piano since Harry Truman. He occasionally played the White House piano for guests. The President followed sports closely, especially professional football. He impressed many White House visitors with his knowledge of baseball and football.

Pat Nixon worked hard to encourage Americans to volunteer for social work. She occasionally traveled across the country to support volunteer groups. "I want to make volunteerism the 'in' thing to do," she said.

Shortly after Nixon took office, he bought a large estate in San Clemente, Calif., a beach resort between San Diego and Los Angeles. The residence became known as the Western White House because Nixon spent working vacations there.

Nixon's Second Administration (1973-1974)

Foreign Affairs. On Jan. 27, 1973, the United States and the other participants in the Vietnam War signed agreements to stop fighting immediately and begin exchanging prisoners. The agreements climaxed several weeks of bargaining between North Vietnamese officials and Henry A. Kissinger, Nixon's chief foreign policy adviser. The United States completed its troop withdrawal from South Vietnam in March. Nixon privately assured South Vietnam that the United States would use "full force" to aid the South Vietnamese if the Communists violated the agreements. Fighting did continue in 1973, but no U.S. troops re-entered the war. Later that year, Kissinger succeeded William P. Rogers as secretary of state.

Nixon continued his efforts to improve relations between the United States and China. In 1973, the two nations opened diplomatic offices in each other's capital and exchanged visits by cultural groups.

Events at Home. Nixon carried out a key campaign pledge in January, 1973, when he ended the military draft. The military then became an all-volunteer force.

Disputes with Congress. Nixon's relations with the Democratic-controlled Congress grew increasingly strained during 1973. Nixon angered many congressmen by *impounding* (not spending) several billion dollars in federal aid on projects that Congress had approved. Nixon called the projects wasteful.

The President suffered a major defeat when Congress forced him to end U.S. bombing in Cambodia. Nixon had argued that the bombing was needed to prevent a Communist take-over of that nation. But Congress refused to provide money for bombing beyond August 15, 1973. This was the first time Congress had ever denied funds for U.S. combat operations in a war.

Nixon received another major setback in 1973 when Congress overrode his veto of a resolution that limited presidential war powers. The War Powers Resolution gives Congress the power to halt the use of any U.S. armed forces that the President has ordered into combat abroad. Passage of the resolution was the strongest

The Nixon Family. In the back row, *left to right*, are son-in-law David Eisenhower, the President, Mrs. Nixon, and son-in-law Edward Cox. Seated are the two Nixon daughters, Julie Nixon Eisenhower, *left*, and Patricia Nixon Cox.

The White House, Washington, D.C.

action ever taken by Congress to spell out the war-making powers of Congress and the President.

Economic Problems continued to challenge Nixon in 1973. In January, he ended most of the government-required limits that had been placed on wage and price increases in 1971. But prices soared, and another brief use of controls resulted in a shortage of beef and other foods. By the end of 1973, inflation had risen 8.8 per cent nationally—the largest increase in any year since 1947.

Also in 1973, a fuel shortage hit the nation. It led to reduced supplies of oil for home heating and industry, and to a form of gasoline rationing in a number of states. The shortage also caused a sharp drop in the demand for those automobiles that were relatively heavy users of gasoline. In 1974, Congress approved Nixon's proposal to establish a Federal Energy Administration to deal with the energy shortage.

The Watergate Scandal hit the Nixon Administration during 1973. It arose from a burglary of Democratic Party headquarters in the Watergate building complex in Washington, D.C., on June 17, 1972. Employees of Nixon's 1972 re-election committee were arrested in the break-in and convicted of burglary. Early in 1973, evidence was uncovered that linked several top White House aides with either the break-in or later attempts to hide information related to it.

Nixon insisted that he took no part in the break-in or the cover-up and promised a full investigation of the case. In May, Archibald Cox, a Harvard Law School professor, was named to head the investigation.

In July, a Senate investigating committee learned that Nixon had secretly made tape recordings of conversations in his White House offices since 1971. The President said that he taped the conversations to preserve an accurate record of his Administration. Cox and the Senate committee asked Nixon to give them certain tapes that they believed could aid their in-

vestigations. Nixon refused to give them the tapes. He argued that the Constitution gives a President the implied right to maintain the confidentiality of private presidential conversations. Nixon said the loss of that right would endanger the presidency.

In August, Cox and the committee filed petitions in court to obtain the tapes. U.S. District Court Judge John J. Sirica decided to review the tapes himself and ordered Nixon to give them to him. Nixon appealed the order, but a U.S. court of appeals supported Sirica.

On October 19, Nixon offered to supply summaries of the tapes to the Senate committee and to Cox. Cox refused, arguing that summaries would not be regarded as proper evidence in court. Nixon then had Cox fired. Leon Jaworski, a noted Texas attorney, later succeeded Cox. But Nixon's actions resulted in a move for his impeachment. See WATERGATE.

The Resignation of Agnew on Oct. 10, 1973, further stunned the nation. Federal officials had begun to investigate Agnew earlier that year in connection with charges of graft in Maryland. The investigation uncovered evidence that Agnew had accepted illegal payments while he had served as an officeholder in Maryland and as Vice-President.

Nixon became the first President to appoint a Vice-President under procedures established by the 25th Amendment to the Constitution. He named House Minority Leader Gerald R. Ford as Agnew's successor, and Ford became Vice-President on Dec. 6, 1973.

The Impeachment Hearings began before the House Judiciary Committee in October, 1973. The committee tried several times to obtain tapes of various White House conversations by issuing *subpoenas* (legal requests). But Nixon refused to give the committee any tapes.

In July, 1974, the committee finished reviewing evidence and voted to recommend three articles of impeachment against Nixon. The first article charged that the President obstructed justice by acting to delay the investigation of the Watergate burglary. It also accused Nixon of attempting to hide the identities of the people who ordered the burglary. The second impeachment article charged that Nixon abused presidential powers, and the third accused him of disobeying subpoenas.

Resignation and Pardon. On August 5, Nixon released records of taped White House conversations that severely damaged his struggle against impeachment. The conversations showed that he had approved a Watergate cover-up on June 23, 1972—six days after the burglary. As a result of the new evidence, Republican congressional leaders warned Nixon that he faced almost certain impeachment by the House of Representatives and removal from office by the Senate.

Nixon told his family on August 7 that he planned to resign as President, and he announced his decision to the American people during a nationwide television address the next day. On August 9, with about $2\frac{1}{2}$ years remaining in his second term, Nixon submitted his resignation as President. At noon that day, Vice-President Gerald R. Ford was sworn in as the 38th President of the United States.

Nixon's resignation ended the prospect of a struggle over impeachment. But many Americans continued to debate whether Nixon should be *prosecuted* (brought to trial) for his role in the Watergate cover-up. On September 8, President Ford granted Nixon a pardon for all federal crimes that Nixon may have committed while serving as President. Ford said he made the decision to "reconcile divisions in our country and heal the wounds that had festered too long."   EARL MAZO

Related Articles in WORLD BOOK include:

Outline

Questions

How did Nixon happen to enter politics?
What was the "kitchen debate"?
Why was Nixon's election as President in 1968 one of the greatest political comebacks in U.S. history?
How did Nixon first win national prominence?

Where did Nixon meet his future wife?
How was Nixon's career almost ruined in 1952?
Why was the 1960 presidential campaign unique?
What was the *Nixon Doctrine?*
What were some of the jobs Nixon held as a boy?
What kind of way of life did the Nixons bring to the White House?

NIZA, MARCOS DE. See ARIZONA (Exploration); NEW MEXICO (Exploration and Settlement).

NKRUMAH, *en KROO mah,* **KWAME,** *KWAH meh* (1909-1972), was president of Ghana from 1960 to 1966. Army leaders ousted him in 1966, and Nkrumah went into exile in nearby Guinea. Guinea's President Sékou Touré made Nkrumah honorary president of Guinea.

As president of Ghana, Nkrumah worked to develop the economy and improve the living conditions. He promoted industrialization, introduced health and welfare programs, and expanded the educational system. But Nkrumah made enemies with the methods he used to achieve these goals. He imprisoned his opponents. Taxes rose, the price of cacao (Ghana's chief export) fell, corruption became widespread, and government debt mounted. Army leaders took over the government while Nkrumah was visiting China.

Nkrumah was born in Nkroful, a village in Ghana. He led his country's drive for independence from Great Britain in the 1950's. He was prime minister of the Gold Coast, and kept that office when the colony became Ghana, an independent country, in 1957. His goal was to form a union of African nations.   IMMANUEL WALLERSTEIN

See also GHANA.

NLRB. See NATIONAL LABOR RELATIONS BOARD.

NO-FAULT DIVORCE. See DIVORCE.

NO-FAULT INSURANCE is a type of automobile accident insurance that was first proposed in the 1960's. It provides that if a driver, passenger, or pedestrian is injured, an insurance company—usually the driver's company—must pay, no matter who caused the accident. Injured people receive payment for medical costs and loss of income. However, many no-fault plans restrict a victim's right to sue for pain or other nonfinancial damage. Such restrictions forbid a damage suit unless the medical expenses exceed a certain amount or the victim was disfigured, disabled, or killed. Many other types of insurance, including fire, health, and life insurance, have always been no-fault.

Supporters of no-fault automobile insurance believe it corrects flaws in the older system, which requires that blame be determined before claims are settled. Many victims of automobile accidents go through costly legal battles and wait for years before receiving payment. Insurance companies fight large claims more vigorously than small ones. As a result, many seriously injured victims collect nothing, but many with minor injuries receive large settlements. People who favor no-fault insurance say it brings quicker settlements and fairer distribution of payments. They also believe that motorists pay less for insurance because there are fewer large damage suits and expensive court battles.

Opponents of no-fault insurance argue that it is unfair to release careless drivers from the responsibility for injuries they cause. They also say that no-fault plans do not reduce insurance costs.

In 1970, Massachusetts became the first state to adopt a no-fault insurance plan. By the late 1970's, 16 states had no-fault laws that included restrictions on damage suits. Eight other states had modified no-fault plans, without restricted suits. ROBERT E. KEETON

NO PLAY. See JAPANESE LITERATURE (Drama); DANCING (Oriental Dancing); DRAMA (Asian Drama).

NOAH, according to the Bible, was the only righteous, God-fearing man of his time. Genesis 6-9 tells that he was chosen by God to keep some people and animals alive during the Deluge, or great Flood. Noah warned people for 120 years that the Flood was coming. During that time, he built a ship, called the ark, which was 450 feet (137 meters) long. He took into the ark his family, and enough birds and animals to repopulate the earth. The rain poured for 40 days and 40 nights· (Gen. 7:12, 24). Even when the water rose above the highest mountaintops, all who were in the ark floated safely on the water.

The waters dropped enough 150 days after the Flood started that the ark was able to rest on top of Mount Ararat (see ARARAT). Noah let loose a raven which did not return. Then he sent out a dove, and it returned because it could find no place to perch. Later, he sent out the same dove two more times. On the second flight, it returned with an olive branch in its mouth. Noah and all the animals came out of the ark later to begin a new life. Noah offered sacrifice to God for deliverance, and God promised him that He would never send another flood to destroy the earth. He made the rainbow a sign of that promise. He commanded Noah and his descendants to respect human life and to punish murder with the death penalty.

Noah's sons were Shem, Ham, and Japheth. Shem became father of the *Semitic* peoples, including the Hebrews and the Arabs. Ham was father of the Hamitic peoples, and Japheth was father of peoples of Asia Minor and Europe. GLEASON L. ARCHER, JR.

NOBEL, *noh BEHL,* **ALFRED BERNHARD** (1833-1896), a Swedish chemist, invented dynamite and founded the Nobel prizes (see NOBEL PRIZES). As a young man, Nobel experimented with nitroglycerin in his father's factory. He hoped to make this dangerous substance into a safe and useful explosive. He prepared a nitroglycerin explosive, but so many accidents occurred when it was put on the market that for a number of years many persons considered Nobel almost a public enemy.

Finally, in 1867, Nobel combined nitroglycerin with an absorbent substance. This explosive could be handled and shipped safely. Nobel named it *dynamite* (see DYNAMITE). Within a few years, he became one of the world's richest men. He set up factories throughout the world, and bought the large Bofors armament plant in Sweden. He worked on synthetic rubber, artificial silk, and many other patented products. He also wrote several novels and plays, but with little success.

Nobel was never in good health. In later years, he became increasingly ill and nervous. He suffered from a feeling of guilt at having created a substance that

Amer. Swedish News Exch., Inc.
Alfred Nobel

caused so much death and injury. He hated the thought that dynamite could be used in war when he had invented it for peace. Nobel set up a fund of about $9 million. The interest from the fund was to be used to award annual prizes, one of which was for the most effective work in promoting international peace.

Nobel was born on Oct. 21, 1833, in Stockholm, the son of an inventor. He was educated in St. Petersburg (now Leningrad), Russia, and later studied engineering in the United States. K. L. KAUFMAN

NOBEL PRIZES are awarded each year in six different fields to persons, regardless of nationality, who have made valuable contributions to the "good of humanity." The awards are given for the most important discovery or invention in the fields of physics; chemistry; physiology or medicine; the most distinguished literary work of an idealistic nature; the most effective work in the interest of international peace; and the outstanding work in the field of economic science. Prizes in the first five fields were first presented in 1901. The economics award was offered for the first time in 1969. The original five prizes consist of equal shares from the income of the $9-million estate of the Swedish inventor Alfred Nobel. In his will, Nobel directed that his fortune be used in this way. The Swedish Central Bank established and provided money for the economics prize. In 1976, the value of each prize was $162,000.

The Royal Academy of Science in Stockholm chooses the physics, chemistry, and economics winners. The Caroline Institute, the faculty of medicine in Stockholm, awards the prize for medicine. The Swedish Academy of Literature in Stockholm awards the prize for literature. A committee of five elected by the Norwegian *Storting* (parliament) awards the prize for peace.

A candidate may not apply directly for a prize. A qualified person must submit each name in writing. For the literary prize, the Swedish Academy considers only works that have appeared in print and have been "proved by the test of experience or by the examination of experts." The academy usually selects an author for his complete work rather than an individual book.

The organizations that award the prizes appoint 15 deputies who elect a board of directors. The board holds office for two years and administers the fund. Winners receive their awards on December 10, the anniversary of the death of Alfred Nobel. The peace prize is awarded in Oslo, Norway. The other prizes are awarded in Stockholm, Sweden. Two or more persons may share a prize. Occasionally, prizes are not awarded or are awarded in a later year.

Through 1976, 136 persons who won a Nobel prize came from the United States, 68 from Great Britain, 62 from Germany, 41 from France, 21 from Sweden, 15 from Russia, 12 from Switzerland, 12 from The Netherlands, 11 from Italy, 11 from Austria, and 11 from Denmark. Eleven organizations have won prizes.

More Americans have won prizes in the fields of economics, physics, physiology or medicine, and peace than persons of any other country. The Germans lead in chemistry prizes and the French in literature.

There is a biography in WORLD BOOK of each prizewinner whose name is marked with an asterisk in the *tables* on the following pages.

NOBEL PRIZES

Alfred Nobel

Nobel Prizes consist of a medal and a cash award. Prizes are awarded for outstanding achievement in chemistry, physics, physiology or medicine, literature, world peace, and economics. The obverse side of each medal has a bust of Alfred Nobel, *left*, a Swedish chemist who established the prizes in the late 1800's. The chemistry and physics medals have identical reverse sides, *right*. The reverse side of each of the other four medals is different.

Physics and Chemistry

NOBEL PRIZES FOR PHYSICS

1901 *Wilhelm K. Roentgen (German) for discovering X rays.

1902 *Hendrik Antoon Lorentz and *Pieter Zeeman (Dutch) for discovering the Zeeman effect of magnetism on light.

1903 *Antoine Henri Becquerel and *Pierre and Marie Curie (French) for discovering radioactivity and studying uranium.

1904 Baron Rayleigh (British) for studying the density of gases and discovering argon.

1905 Philipp Lenard (German) for studying the properties of cathode rays.

1906 *Sir Joseph John Thomson (British) for studying electrical discharge through gases.

1907 *Albert A. Michelson (American) for inventing optical instruments and measuring the speed of light.

1908 Gabriel Lippmann (French) for his method of color photography.

1909 *Guglielmo Marconi (Italian) and Karl Ferdinand Braun (German) for developing the wireless telegraph.

1910 *Johannes D. van der Waals (Dutch) for studying the relationships of liquids and gases.

1911 Wilhelm Wien (German) for his discoveries on the heat radiated by black objects.

1912 Nils Dalén (Swedish) for inventing automatic gas regulators for lighthouses.

1913 Heike Kamerlingh Onnes (Dutch) for experimenting with low temperatures and liquefying helium.

1914 *Max T. F. von Laue (German) for using crystals to measure X rays.

1915 *Sir William Henry Bragg and Sir William L. Bragg (British) for using X rays to study crystal structure.

1916 No Award

1917 Charles Barkla (British) for studying the diffusion of light and the radiation of X rays from elements.

1918 *Max Planck (German) for stating the quantum theory of light.

1919 *Johannes Stark (German) for discovering the Stark effect of spectra in electric fields.

1920 Charles E. Guillaume (French) for discovering nickel-steel alloys with slight expansion, and the alloy invar.

1921 *Albert Einstein (German) for contributing to mathematical physics and stating the law of the photoelectric effect.

1922 *Niels Bohr (Danish) for studying the structure of atoms and their radiations.

1923 *Robert A. Millikan (American) for measuring the charge on electrons and working on the photoelectric effect.

1924 *Karl M. G. Siegbahn (Swedish) for working with the X-ray spectroscope.

1925 *James Franck and *Gustav Hertz (German) for stating laws on the collision of an electron with an atom.

1926 Jean Baptiste Perrin (French) for studying the discontinuous structure of matter and measuring the sizes of atoms.

1927 *Arthur H. Compton (American) for discovering the Compton effect on X rays reflected from atoms, and *Charles T. R. Wilson (British) for discovering a method for tracing the paths of ions.

1928 Owen W. Richardson (British) for studying thermionic effect and electrons sent off by hot metals.

1929 Louis Victor de Broglie (French) for discovering the wave character of electrons.

1930 *Sir Chandrasekhara Venkata Raman (Indian) for discovering a new effect in radiation from elements.

1931 No Award

1932 *Werner Heisenberg (German) for founding quantum mechanics, which led to discoveries in hydrogen.

1933 *Paul Dirac (British) and *Erwin Schrödinger (Austrian) for discovering new forms of atomic theory.

1934 No Award

1935 *Sir James Chadwick (British) for discovering the neutron.

1936 *Carl David Anderson (American) for discovering the positron, and Victor F. Hess (Austrian) for discovering cosmic rays.

1937 Clinton Davisson (American) and George Thomson (British) for discovering the diffraction of electrons by crystals.

1938 *Enrico Fermi (Italian) for discovering new radioactive elements beyond uranium.

1939 *Ernest O. Lawrence (American) for inventing the cyclotron and working on artificial radioactivity.

1940-1942 No Award

1943 Otto Stern (American) for discovering the molecular beam method of studying the atom.

1944 Isidor Isaac Rabi (American) for recording the magnetic properties of atomic nuclei.

1945 *Wolfgang Pauli (Austrian) for discovering the exclusion principle (Pauli principle) of electrons.

1946 *Percy Williams Bridgman (American) for his work in the field of very high pressures.

1947 *Sir Edward V. Appleton (British) for exploring the ionosphere.

1948 Patrick M. S. Blackett (British) for his discoveries in cosmic radiation.

1949 *Hideki Yukawa (Japanese) for discovering the meson.

1950 *Cecil Frank Powell (British) for his photographic method of studying atomic nuclei and his discoveries concerning mesons.

1951 *Sir John D. Cockcroft (British) and *Ernest T. S. Walton (Irish) for working on the transmutation of atomic nuclei by artificially accelerated atomic particles.

1952 *Felix Bloch and *Edward Mills Purcell (American) for developing magnetic measurement methods for atomic nuclei.

*Has a biography in THE WORLD BOOK ENCYCLOPEDIA

Physiology or Medicine

Literature

Peace

Economics

Nobel Foundation; Swedish Information Service

NOBEL PRIZES FOR PHYSICS (continued)

1953 Frits Zernike (Dutch) for inventing the phase contrast microscope for cancer research.

1954 *Max Born (German) for research in quantum mechanics, and Walther Bothe (German) for discoveries he made with his coincidence method.

1955 *Willis E. Lamb, Jr. (American), for discoveries on the structure of the hydrogen spectrum, and Polykarp Kusch (American) for determining the magnetic moment of the electron.

1956 *John Bardeen, *Walter H. Brattain, and *William Shockley (American) for inventing the transistor.

1957 *Tsung Dao Lee and *Chen Ning Yang (American) for disproving the law of conservation of parity.

1958 *Pavel A. Cherenkov, Ilya M. Frank, and *Igor Y. Tamm (Russian) for discovering and interpreting the Cherenkov effect in studying high-energy particles.

1959 Emilio Segrè and *Owen Chamberlain (American) for their work in demonstrating the existence of the antiproton.

1960 *Donald A. Glaser (American) for inventing the bubble chamber to study subatomic particles.

1961 Robert Hofstadter (American) for his studies of nucleons, and *Rudolf L. Mössbauer (German) for his research on gamma rays.

1962 *Lev Davidovich Landau (Russian) for his research on liquid helium gas.

1963 *Eugene Paul Wigner (American) for his contributions to the understanding of atomic nuclei and elementary particles, and *Maria Goeppert-Mayer (American) and *J. Hans Jensen (German) for their work on the structure of atomic nuclei.

1964 *Charles H. Townes (American) and *Nikolai G. Basov and *Alexander M. Prokhorov (Russian) for developing *masers* and *lasers*.

1965 *Sin-itiro Tomonaga (Japanese) and *Julian S. Schwinger and *Richard P. Feynman (American) for basic work in quantum electrodynamics.

1966 Alfred Kastler (French) for his work on the energy level of atoms.

1967 *Hans Albrecht Bethe (American) for his contributions to the theory of nuclear reactions, especially his discoveries on the energy production in stars.

1968 *Luis W. Alvarez (American) for his contributions to the knowledge of subatomic particles.

1969 *Murray Gell-Mann (American) for his discoveries concerning the classification of nuclear particles and their interactions.

1970 Hannes Olof Gosta Alfven (Swedish) for his work in *magnetohydrodynamics*, the study of electrical and magnetic effects in fluids that conduct electricity, and Louis Eugène Félix Néel (French) for his discoveries of magnetic properties that applied to computer memories.

*Has a biography in THE WORLD BOOK ENCYCLOPEDIA

Bettmann Archive

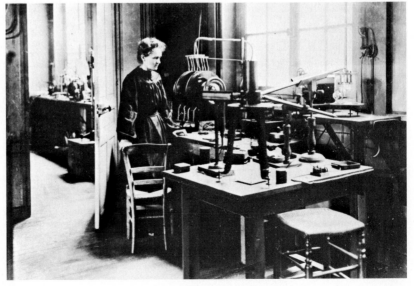

Marie Curie shared the 1903 physics prize with her husband, Pierre, and Antoine Becquerel for their discovery of radioactivity and studies of uranium. Mme. Curie also won the 1911 chemistry prize for her discovery of and work with the elements radium and polonium.

Black Star

Niels Bohr, *left,* a Danish physicist, received the Nobel prize for physics in 1922. Bohr conducted studies of the structure of atoms and the energy radiated by their electrons.

United Press Int.

Chen Yang and Tsung Lee, *right,* two American scientists, shared the Nobel prize for physics in 1957. They disproved the law of conservation of parity, which had been an accepted theory on the behavior of certain atomic particles.

NOBEL PRIZES FOR PHYSICS (continued)

1971 *Dennis Gabor (British) for his developmental work in *holography,* a method of making a three-dimensional photograph with coherent light produced by a laser.

1972 *John Bardeen, Leon N. Cooper, and John Robert Schrieffer (American) for their work on *superconductivity,* the disappearance of electrical resistance.

1973 Ivar Giaever (American), Leo Esaki (Japanese), and Brian Josephson (British) for their work on the phenomena of electron "tunneling" through semiconductor and superconductor materials.

1974 Antony Hewish (British) for the discovery of *pul-* sars, celestial objects that give off bursts of radio waves, and Sir Martin Ryle (British) for his use of small radio telescopes to "see" into space with great accuracy.

1975 L. James Rainwater (American) and Aage N. Bohr and Ben R. Mottelson (Danish) for their contributions to the theory of the structure of the atomic nucleus.

1976 Burton Richter and Samuel Chao Chung Ting (American) for their discovery of a new type of elementary nuclear particle called the *psi,* or *J, particle.*

NOBEL PRIZES FOR CHEMISTRY

1901 *Jacobus Henricus Van't Hoff (Dutch) for discovering laws of chemical dynamics and osmotic pressure.

1902 *Emil Fischer (German) for synthesizing sugars, purine derivatives, and peptides.

1903 *Svante August Arrhenius (Swedish) for his dissociation theory of ionization in electrolytes.

1904 *Sir William Ramsay (British) for discovering helium, neon, xenon, and krypton, and determining their place in the periodic system.

1905 Adolph von Baeyer (German) for his work on dyes and organic compounds, and for synthesizing indigo and arsenicals.

1906 Henri Moissan (French) for preparing pure fluorine and developing the electric furnace.

1907 Eduard Buchner (German) for his biochemical researches and for discovering cell-less fermentation.

1908 *Ernest Rutherford (British) for discovering that alpha rays break down atoms and studying radioactive substances.

1909 *Wilhelm Ostwald (German) for his work on catalysis, chemical equilibrium, and the rate of chemical reactions.

1910 *Otto Wallach (German) for his work in the field of alicyclic substances.

1911 *Marie Curie (French) for discovering radium and polonium, and for isolating radium and studying its compounds.

1912 *François Auguste Victor Grignard (French) for discovering the Grignard reagent to synthesize organic compounds, and Paul Sabatier (French) for his method of adding hydrogen to organic compounds, using metals as catalysts.

1913 Alfred Werner (Swiss) for his coordination theory on the arrangement of atoms.

1914 Theodore W. Richards (American) for determining the atomic weights of many elements.

1915 Richard Willstätter (German) for his research concerning chlorophyll and other coloring matter in plants.

1916-1917 No Award

1918 Fritz Haber (German) for the Haber-Bosch process of synthesizing ammonia from nitrogen and hydrogen.

1919 No Award

1920 *Walther Nernst (German) for his discoveries concerning heat changes in chemical reactions.

1921 *Frederick Soddy (British) for studying radioactive substances and isotopes.

1922 *Francis W. Aston (British) for discovering many isotopes by means of the mass spectrograph and

*Has a biography in THE WORLD BOOK ENCYCLOPEDIA

NOBEL PRIZES FOR CHEMISTRY (continued)

discovering the whole number rule on the structure and weight of atoms.

1923 Fritz Pregl (Austrian) for inventing a method of microanalyzing organic substances.

1924 No Award

1925 Richard Zsigmondy (German) for his method of studying colloids.

1926 *Theodor Svedberg (Swedish) for his work on dispersions and on colloid chemistry.

1927 *Heinrich O. Wieland (German) for studying gall acids and related substances.

1928 Adolf Windaus (German) for studying sterols and their connection with vitamins.

1929 Sir Arthur Harden (British) and Hans August Simon von Euler-Chelpin (German) for their research on sugar fermentation and enzymes.

1930 *Hans Fischer (German) for studying the coloring matter of blood and leaves and synthesizing hemin.

1931 *Carl Bosch and *Friedrich Bergius (German) for inventing high-pressure methods of manufacturing ammonia and liquefying coal.

1932 *Irving Langmuir (American) for his discoveries about molecular films absorbed on surfaces.

1933 No Award

1934 *Harold Clayton Urey (American) for discovering deuterium (heavy hydrogen).

1935 *Frédéric and Irène Joliot-Curie (French) for synthesizing new radioactive elements.

1936 Peter J. W. Debye (Dutch) for his studies on molecules, dipole moments, the diffraction of electrons, and X rays in gases.

1937 Sir Walter N. Haworth (British) for his research on carbohydrates and vitamin C, and Paul Karrer (Swiss) for studying carotenoids, flavins, and vitamins A and B_2.

1938 *Richard Kuhn (German) for his work on carotenoids and vitamins (declined).

1939 Adolph Butenandt (German) for studying the chemistry of sex hormones (declined), and Leopold Ružička (Swiss) for his work on polymethylenes.

1940-1942 No Award

1943 *Georg von Hevesy (Hungarian) for using isotopes as indicators in chemistry.

1944 *Otto Hahn (German) for his discoveries in atomic fission.

1945 *Artturi Virtanen (Finnish) for inventing new methods in agricultural biochemistry.

1946 *James B. Sumner (American) for discovering that enzymes can be crystallized, and *Wendell M. Stanley and *John H. Northrop (American) for preparing enzymes and virus proteins in pure form.

1947 *Sir Robert Robinson (British) for his research on biologically significant plant substances.

1948 Arne Tiselius (Swedish) for his discoveries on the nature of the serum proteins.

1949 William Francis Giauque (American) for studying reactions to extreme cold.

1950 *Otto Diels and Kurt Alder (German) for developing a method of synthesizing organic compounds of the diene group.

1951 Edwin M. McMillan and *Glenn T. Seaborg (American) for discovering plutonium and other elements.

1952 *Archer J. P. Martin and Richard Synge (British) for developing the partition chromatography process, a method of separating compounds.

1953 *Hermann Staudinger (German) for discovering a way to synthesize fiber.

1954 *Linus Pauling (American) for his work on the forces that hold matter together.

1955 Vincent Du Vigneaud (American) for discovering a process for making synthetic hormones.

*Has a biography in THE WORLD BOOK ENCYCLOPEDIA

Town and Country

Harold C. Urey of the United States won the Nobel prize for chemistry in 1934. Urey discovered deuterium, an isotope of hydrogen that is also known as heavy hydrogen.

United Press Int.

Glenn T. Seaborg shared the Nobel chemistry prize with Edwin M. McMillan, a fellow American, in 1951. Seaborg discovered several artificial elements that are heavier than uranium.

NOBEL PRIZES

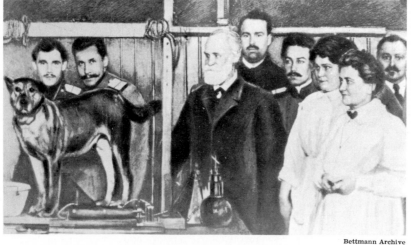

Ivan Petrovich Pavlov, a Russian physiologist, won the 1904 prize in physiology or medicine. Pavlov and his staff experimented with dogs to learn how nerves affect the process of digestion.

Bettmann Archive

NOBEL PRIZES FOR CHEMISTRY (continued)

1956 Sir Cyril Hinshelwood (British) and *Nikolai N. Semenov (Russian) for their work on chemical chain reactions.

1957 *Lord Todd (British) for his work on the protein composition of cells.

1958 *Frederick Sanger (British) for discovering the structure of the insulin molecule.

1959 *Jaroslav Heyrovský (Czech) for developing the polarographic method of analysis.

1960 *Willard F. Libby (American) for developing a method of radiocarbon dating.

1961 *Melvin Calvin (American) for his research on photosynthesis.

1962 *Sir John Cowdery Kendrew and *Max Ferdinand Perutz (British) for their studies on globular proteins.

1963 Giulio Natta (Italian) for his contributions to the understanding of *polymers,* and Karl Ziegler (German) for his production of *organometallic compounds.* The work of both men led to the production of improved plastics products.

1964 Dorothy C. Hodgkin (British) for X-ray studies of compounds such as vitamin B_{12} and penicillin.

1965 Robert Burns Woodward (American) for his contributions to organic synthesis.

1966 *Robert S. Mulliken (American) for developing the *molecular-orbital* theory of chemical structure.

1967 Manfred Eigen (German) and Ronald G. W. Norrish and George Porter (British) for developing techniques to measure rapid chemical reactions.

1968 Lars Onsager (American) for developing the theory of reciprocal relations of various kinds of thermodynamic activity.

1969 Derek H. R. Barton (British) and Odd Hassel (Norwegian) for their studies relating chemical reactions with the three-dimensional shape of molecules.

1970 Luis Federico Leloir (Argentine) for his discovery of chemical compounds that affect the storage of chemical energy in living things.

1971 Gerhard Herzberg (Canadian) for his research in the structure of molecules, particularly the fragments of some molecules called *free radicals.*

1972 Christian B. Anfinsen, Stanford Moore, and William H. Stein (American) for their fundamental contributions to the chemistry of *enzymes,* basic substances of living things.

1973 Geoffrey Wilkinson (British) and Ernst Fischer (German) for their work on *organometallic compounds,* substances which consist of organic compounds and metal atoms.

1974 Paul John Flory (American) for his work in polymer chemistry.

1975 John Warcup Cornforth (Australian-born) and Vladimir Prelog (Swiss) for their contributions to the chemical synthesis of medically important organic compounds.

1976 William N. Lipscomb, Jr. (American), for his studies on the structure and bonding mechanisms of *boranes,* complex compounds that consist of boron and hydrogen.

NOBEL PRIZES FOR PHYSIOLOGY OR MEDICINE

1901 *Emil von Behring (German) for discovering the diphtheria antitoxin.

1902 *Sir Ronald Ross (British) for working on malaria and discovering how malaria is transmitted.

1903 Niels Ryberg Finsen (Danish) for treating diseases, especially *lupus vulgaris,* with concentrated light rays.

1904 *Ivan Petrovich Pavlov (Russian) for his work on the physiology of digestion.

1905 *Robert Koch (German) for working on tuberculosis and discovering the tubercule bacillus and tuberculin.

1906 *Camillo Golgi (Italian) and Santiago Ramon y Cajal (Spanish) for their studies of nerve tissue.

1907 *Charles Louis Alphonse Laveran (French) for studying diseases caused by protozoa.

1908 *Paul Ehrlich (German) and *Élie Metchnikoff (Russian) for their work on immunity.

1909 *Emil Theodor Kocher (Swiss) for his work on the physiology, pathology, and surgery of the thyroid gland.

1910 Albrecht Kossel (German) for studying cell chemistry, proteins, and nucleic substances.

1911 *Allvar Gullstrand (Swedish) for his work on dioptrics, the refraction of light through the eye.

1912 *Alexis Carrel (French) for suturing blood vessels and grafting vessels and organs.

1913 Charles Robert Richet (French) for studying allergies caused by foreign substances, as in hay fever.

1914 Robert Bárány (Austrian) for work on function and diseases of equilibrium organs in the inner ear.

1915-1918 No Award

1919 Jules Bordet (Belgian) for discoveries on immunity.

1920 August Krogh (Danish) for discovering the system of action of blood capillaries.

1921 No Award

1922 Archibald V. Hill (British) for his discovery on heat production in the muscles, and Otto Meyerhof (German) for his theory on the production of lactic acid in the muscles.

1923 *Sir Frederick Grant Banting (Canadian) and *John J. R. Macleod (Scottish) for discovering insulin.

1924 *Willem Einthoven (Dutch) for inventing the electrocardiograph.

1925 No Award

1926 *Johannes Fibiger (Danish) for discovering a parasite that causes cancer.

1927 Julius Wagner von Jauregg (Austrian) for discovering the fever treatment for paralysis.

1928 Charles Nicolle (French) for his work on typhus.

1929 Christiaan Eijkman (Dutch) for discovering vitamins that prevent beriberi, and Sir Frederick G. Hopkins (British) for discovering vitamins that help growth.

1930 *Karl Landsteiner (American) for discovering the four main human blood types.

1931 Otto H. Warburg (German) for discovering that enzymes aid in respiration by tissues.

1932 Edgar D. Adrian and Sir Charles S. Sherrington (British) for discoveries on the function of neurons.

1933 *Thomas H. Morgan (American) for studying the function of chromosomes in heredity.

1934 *George Minot, William P. Murphy, and George H. Whipple (American) for their discoveries on liver treatment for anemia.

1935 *Hans Spemann (German) for discovering the organizer-effect in the growth of an embryo.

1936 Sir Henry H. Dale (British) and Otto Loewi (Austrian) for their discoveries on the chemical transmission of nerve impulses.

1937 Albert Szent-Györgyi (Hungarian) for his discoveries in connection with oxidation in tissues, vitamin C, and fumaric acid.

1938 Corneille Heymans (Belgian) for his discoveries concerning the regulation of respiration.

1939 *Gerhard Domagk (German) for discovering prontosil, the first sulfa drug (declined).

1940-1942 No Award

1943 Henrik Dam (Danish) for discovering vitamin K, and *Edward Doisy (American) for synthesizing it.

1944 Joseph Erlanger and Herbert Gasser (American) for their work on single nerve fibers.

1945 *Sir Alexander Fleming, *Howard W. Florey, and *Ernst B. Chain (British) for discovering penicillin.

1946 *Hermann Joseph Muller (American) for discovering that X rays can produce mutations.

1947 *Carl F. and Gerty Cori (American) for their work on insulin, and Bernardo Houssay (Argentine) for studying the pancreas and the pituitary gland.

1948 *Paul Mueller (Swiss) for discovering the insect-killing properties of DDT.

1949 Walter R. Hess (Swiss) for discovering how certain parts of the brain control organs of the body, and *Antônio E. Moniz (Portuguese) for originating prefrontal lobotomy.

1950 *Philip S. Hench, *Edward C. Kendall (American), and *Tadeus Reichstein (Swiss) for their discoveries on cortisone and ACTH.

1951 *Max Theiler (South African who worked in the United States) for developing the yellow fever vaccine known as 17-D.

1952 *Selman A. Waksman (American) for his work in the discovery of streptomycin.

1953 Fritz Albert Lipmann (American) and *Hans Adolf Krebs (British) for their discoveries in biosynthesis and metabolism.

1954 *John F. Enders, *Thomas H. Weller, and *Frederick C. Robbins (American) for discovering a simple method of growing polio virus in test tubes.

1955 Hugo Theorell (Swedish) for his discoveries on the nature and action of oxidation enzymes.

1956 André F. Cournand, Dickinson W. Richards, Jr. (American), and *Werner Forssmann (German) for using a catheter to chart the heart's interior.

1957 Daniel Bovet (Italian) for discovering antihistamines.

1958 *George Wells Beadle and *Edward Lawrie Tatum (American) for their work in biochemical genetics, and *Joshua Lederberg (American) for his studies of genetics in bacteria.

1959 *Severo Ochoa and *Arthur Kornberg (American) for producing nucleic acid by artificial means.

1960 *Sir Macfarlane Burnet (Australian) and *Peter B. Medawar (British) for research in transplanting human organs.

1961 Georg von Békésy (American) for demonstrating how the ear distinguishes between various sounds.

1962 *James D. Watson (American) and *Francis H. Crick and *Maurice H. F. Wilkins (British) for their work on nucleic acid.

1963 Sir John Carew Eccles (Australian) for his research on the transmission of nerve impulses, and Alan Lloyd Hodgkin (British) and *Andrew Fielding Huxley (British) for their description of the behavior of nerve impulses.

1964 *Konrad E. Bloch (American) and *Feodor Lynen (German) for their work on cholesterol and fatty acid metabolism.

1965 François Jacob, *André Lwoff, and *Jacques Monod (French) for their discoveries concerning genetic control of enzyme and virus synthesis.

1966 *Francis Peyton Rous (American) for discovering a cancer-producing virus, and Charles B. Huggins (American) for discovering uses of hormones in treating cancer.

1967 Ragnar Granit (Swedish) and H. Keffer Hartline and *George Wald (American) for their work on chemical and physiological processes in the eye.

1968 Robert W. Holley, H. Gobind Khorana, and Marshall W. Nirenberg (American) for explaining how genes determine the function of cells.

1969 Max Delbrück, Alfred Hershey, and Salvador Luria (American) for their work with *bacteriophages*.

1970 Julius Axelrod (American), Bernard Katz (British), and Ulf Svante von Euler (Swedish) for their discoveries of the role played by certain chemicals in the transmission of nerve impulses.

1971 Earl W. Sutherland, Jr. (American), for his discovery of the ways hormones act, including the discovery of cyclic AMP, a chemical that influences the actions of hormones on body processes.

1972 Gerald M. Edelman (American) and Rodney R. Porter (British) for their discovery of the chemical structure of antibodies.

*Has a biography in THE WORLD BOOK ENCYCLOPEDIA

NOBEL PRIZES FOR PHYSIOLOGY OR MEDICINE (continued)

1973 *Nikolaas Tinbergen (Dutch-born) and *Konrad Z. Lorenz and Karl von Frisch (Austrian) for their studies on animal behavior.

1974 Christian de Duve (Belgian) and Albert Claude and George E. Palade (American) for their pioneer work in cell biology.

1975 David Baltimore, Renato Dulbecco, and Howard M. Temin (American) for their research on how viruses affect the genes of cancer cells.

1976 Baruch S. Blumberg and D. Carleton Gajdusek (American) for their discoveries concerning the origin and spread of infectious diseases.

NOBEL PRIZES FOR LITERATURE

1901 *René Sully-Prudhomme (French) for his poems.

1902 *Theodor Mommsen (German) for his historical narratives, particularly his history of Rome.

1903 *Bjørnstjerne Bjørnson (Norwegian) for his novels, poems, and dramas.

1904 *Frédéric Mistral (French) for his poems, and José Echegaray y Eizaguirre (Spanish) for his dramas.

1905 *Henryk Sienkiewicz (Polish) for his novels.

1906 *Giosuè Carducci (Italian) for his poems.

1907 *Rudyard Kipling (British) for his stories, novels, and poems.

1908 Rudolf Eucken (German) for his philosophic writings.

1909 *Selma Lagerlöf (Swedish) for her novels and poems.

1910 Paul von Heyse (German) for his poems, novels, and dramas.

1911 *Maurice Maeterlinck (Belgian) for his dramas.

1912 *Gerhart Hauptmann (German) for his dramas.

1913 *Sir Rabindranath Tagore (Indian) for his poems.

1914 No Award

1915 *Romain Rolland (French) for his novels.

1916 Verner von Heidenstam (Swedish) for his poems.

1917 Karl Gjellerup (Danish) for his poems and novels, and Henrik Pontoppidan (Danish) for his novels and short stories.

1918 No Award

1919 *Carl Spitteler (Swiss) for his epics, short stories, and essays.

1920 *Knut Hamsun (Norwegian) for his novels.

1921 *Anatole France (French) for his novels, short stories, and essays.

1922 *Jacinto Benavente (Spanish) for his dramas.

1923 *William Butler Yeats (Irish) for his poems.

1924 Władysław S. Reymont (Polish) for his novels, particularly *The Peasants*.

*Has a biography in THE WORLD BOOK ENCYCLOPEDIA

1925 *George Bernard Shaw (British) for his plays and satires.

1926 Grazia Deledda (Italian) for her novels.

1927 *Henri Bergson (French) for his philosophic writings.

1928 Sigrid Undset (Norwegian) for her novels.

1929 *Thomas Mann (German) principally for his novel, *Buddenbrooks*.

1930 *Sinclair Lewis (American) for his novels.

1931 Erik Axel Karlfeldt (Swedish) for his lyric poetry.

1932 *John Galsworthy (British) for his novels, plays, and short stories.

1933 *Ivan Alexeyevich Bunin (Russian) for his novels, short stories, and poems.

1934 *Luigi Pirandello (Italian) for his dramas.

1935 No Award

1936 *Eugene O'Neill (American) for his dramas.

1937 *Roger Martin du Gard (French) for his novels.

1938 *Pearl S. Buck (American) for her novels.

1939 Frans Eemil Sillanpää (Finnish) for his novels.

1940-1943 No Award

1944 *Johannes V. Jensen (Danish) for his poems and novels.

1945 *Gabriela Mistral (Chilean) for her poems.

1946 *Hermann Hesse (German) for his novels, poems, and essays.

1947 *André Gide (French) for his novels.

1948 *T. S. Eliot (British) for his poems, essays, and verse plays.

1949 *William Faulkner (American) for his novels. (Award delayed until 1950.)

1950 *Bertrand Russell (British) for his philosophic writings.

1951 *Pär Fabian Lagerkvist (Swedish) for his novels, particularly *Barabbas*.

1952 *François Mauriac (French) for his novels, essays, and poems.

1953 *Sir Winston Churchill (British) for his essays, speeches, and historical writings.

1954 *Ernest Hemingway (American) for his novels and short stories.

1955 *Halldór K. Laxness (Icelandic) for his novels.

1956 *Juan Ramón Jiménez (Spanish) for his poems.

1957 *Albert Camus (French) for his novels.

1958 *Boris Pasternak (Russian) for his novels, especially *Dr. Zhivago* (declined).

1959 *Salvatore Quasimodo (Italian) for his lyric poems.

1960 *Saint-John Perse (French) for his poems.

1961 Ivo Andrić (Yugoslav) for his novels, especially *The Bridge on the Drina*.

1962 *John Steinbeck (American) for his novels, especially *The Winter of Our Discontent*.

1963 *George Seferis (Greek) for his lyric poetry.

1964 *Jean-Paul Sartre (French) for his philosophical works (declined).

1965 *Mikhail Sholokhov (Russian) for his novels.

1966 *Shmuel Yosef Agnon (Israeli) for his stories of Eastern European Jewish life, and *Nelly Sachs (German-born) for her poetry about the Jewish people.

1967 *Miguel Angel Asturias (Guatemalan) for his writings rooted in national individuality and Indian traditions.

Bettmann Archive

Rudyard Kipling, a British poet and storyteller, won the literature prize in 1907. Most of Kipling's writing is set in India, where he was born and lived for several years.

Sinclair Lewis became the first American to win the literature prize. He received the award in 1930 for his satirical novels.

André Gide of France won the 1947 literature prize for his novels. *The Counterfeiters* was one of his most famous books.

NOBEL PRIZES FOR LITERATURE (continued)

1968 Yasunari Kawabata (Japanese) for his novels about the Japanese people.

1969*Samuel B. Beckett (Irish-born) for his novels and plays.

1970*Alexander Solzhenitsyn (Russian) for his novels.

1971*Pablo Neruda (Chilean) for his poems.

1972 Heinrich Böll (German) for his novels, short stories, and plays.

1973*Patrick White (Australian) for his novels.

1974 Eyvind Johnson (Swedish) for his novels and short stories, and Harry Edmund Martinson (Swedish) for his essays, plays, novels, and poems.

1975 Eugenio Montale (Italian) for his poems.

1976*Saul Bellow (American) for his novels.

NOBEL PRIZES FOR PEACE

1901*Jean Henri Dunant (Swiss) for founding the Red Cross and originating the Geneva Convention, and Frédéric Passy (French) for founding a French peace society.

1902 Élie Ducommun (Swiss) for his work as honorary secretary of the International Peace Bureau, and Charles Albert Gobat (Swiss) for his work as administrator of the Inter-Parliamentary Union.

1903 Sir William R. Cremer (British) for his activities as founder and secretary of the International Arbitration League.

1904 The Institute of International Law for its studies on the laws of neutrality and other phases of international law.

1905 Baroness Bertha von Suttner (Austrian) for promoting pacifism and founding an Austrian peace society.

1906*Theodore Roosevelt (American) for negotiating peace in the Russo-Japanese War.

1907 Ernesto T. Moneta (Italian) for his work as president of the Lombard League for Peace, and Louis Renault (French) for organizing international conferences and representing France at two peace conferences.

1908 Klas Pontus Arnoldson (Swedish) for founding the Swedish Society for Arbitration and Peace, and Fredrik Bajer (Danish) for his work on the International Peace Bureau.

1909 Auguste M. F. Beernaert (Belgian) for his work on the Permanent Court of Arbitration, and *Paul d'Estournelles (French) for founding and directing the French Parliamentary Arbitration Committee and League of International Conciliation.

1910 The International Peace Bureau for promoting international arbitration and organizing many peace conferences.

1911 Tobias M. C. Asser (Dutch) for organizing conferences on international law, and Alfred H. Fried (Austrian) for his writings on peace as editor of *Die Friedenswarte*.

1912*Elihu Root (American) for peacefully settling the problem of Japanese immigration to California and organizing the Central American Peace Conference.

1913 Henri Lafontaine (Belgian) for his work as president of the International Peace Bureau.

1914-1916 No Award

1917 The International Red Cross for doing relief work during World War I.

1918 No Award

1919*Woodrow Wilson (American) for attempting a just settlement of World War I and advocating the League of Nations.

1920 Léon Bourgeois (French) for his contribution as president of the Council of the League of Nations.

1921 Karl Hjalmar Branting (Swedish) for promoting social reforms in Sweden and serving as the Swedish delegate to the League of Nations, and Christian Louis Lange (Norwegian) for his contribution as secretary-general of the Inter-Parliamentary Union.

1922*Fridtjof Nansen (Norwegian) for doing relief work among Russian prisoners of war and in famine areas in Russia.

1923-1924 No Award

*Has a biography in THE WORLD BOOK ENCYCLOPEDIA

Bettmann Archive

Elihu Root won the Nobel peace prize in 1912. As U.S. secretary of state, Root made important contributions to world peace.

Bettmann Archive

Woodrow Wilson in 1919 became the second U.S. President to win the peace prize. Theodore Roosevelt had received it in 1906.

Hull House Association

Jane Addams, an American social worker, shared the 1931 peace prize for her work with an international peace group.

United Press Int.

Albert Schweitzer of Germany won the 1952 Nobel peace prize. He devoted most of his life to humanitarian work in Africa.

NOBEL PRIZES FOR PEACE (continued)

1925 *Sir Austen Chamberlain (British) for helping to work out the Locarno Peace Pact, and *Charles G. Dawes (American) for originating a plan for payment of German reparations.

1926 *Aristide Briand (French) for his part in forming the Locarno Peace Pact, and *Gustav Stresemann (German) for persuading Germany to accept plans for reparations.

1927 Ferdinand Buisson (French) for his work as president of the League of Human Rights, and Ludwig Quidde (German) for writing on peace and participating in many international peace congresses.

1928 No Award

1929 *Frank Billings Kellogg (American) for negotiating the Kellogg-Briand Pact.

1930 Nathan Söderblom (Swedish) for writing on and working for peace.

1931 *Jane Addams (American) for her work with the Women's International League for Peace and Freedom, and *Nicholas M. Butler (American) for his work with the Carnegie Endowment for International Peace.

1932 No Award

1933 Sir Norman Angell (British) for his work with the Royal Institute of International Affairs, the League of Nations, and the National Peace Council.

1934 *Arthur Henderson (British) for his contribution as president of the World Disarmament Conference.

*Has a biography in THE WORLD BOOK ENCYCLOPEDIA

1935 *Carl von Ossietzky (German) for promoting world disarmament. (Award delayed until 1936.)

1936 Carlos Saavedra Lamas (Argentine) for negotiating a peace settlement between Bolivia and Paraguay in the Chaco War.

1937 Edgar Algernon Robert Gascoyne Cecil (British) for promoting the League of Nations and working with peace movements.

1938 The International Office for Refugees for directing relief work among refugees.

1939-1943 No Award

1944 The International Red Cross for doing relief work during World War II.

1945 *Cordell Hull (American) for his peace efforts as Secretary of State.

1946 *John R. Mott (American) for his YMCA work and for aiding displaced persons, and *Emily G. Balch (American) for her work with the Women's International League for Peace and Freedom.

1947 The Friends Service Council and the American Friends Service Committee for humanitarian work.

1948 No Award

1949 *John Boyd Orr (British) for directing the United Nations Food and Agriculture Organization.

1950 *Ralph J. Bunche (American) for his work as United Nations mediator in Palestine in 1948 and 1949.

1951 Léon Jouhaux (French) for his work helping to or-

Karsh, Ottawa, from Pix

Lester B. Pearson was the first Canadian to win the peace prize. He won the 1957 award for his work in the United Nations.

Wide World

Martin Luther King, Jr., won the 1964 peace prize for leading nonviolent civil rights demonstrations in the United States.

NOBEL PRIZES FOR PEACE (continued)

ganize national and international labor unions.

1952 *Albert Schweitzer (German) for his humanitarian work in Africa. (Award delayed until 1953.)

1953 *George C. Marshall (American) for his work in promoting peace through the European Recovery Program.

1954 Office of the United Nations High Commissioner for Refugees for providing international protection for millions of refugees and seeking permanent solutions to their problems. (Award delayed until 1955.)

1955-1956 No Award

1957 *Lester B. Pearson (Canadian) for organizing a United Nations force in Egypt.

1958 *Dominique Georges Pire (Belgian) for his work in resettling displaced persons.

1959 Philip Noel-Baker (British) for his work in promoting peace and disarmament.

1960 *Albert John Luthuli (African) for his peaceful campaign against racial restrictions in South Africa.

1961 *Dag Hammarskjöld (Swedish) for his efforts to bring peace to the Congo (awarded posthumously).

1962 *Linus Pauling (American) for trying to effect a ban on nuclear weapons.

1963 The International Committee of the Red Cross and The League of Red Cross Societies for humanitarian work.

1964 *Martin Luther King, Jr. (American), for leading

the black struggle for equality in the United States through nonviolent means.

1965 United Nations Children's Fund (UNICEF) for its aid to children.

1966-1967 No Award

1968 René Cassin (French) for furthering the cause of human rights.

1969 *International Labor Organization (ILO) for its efforts to improve working conditions.

1970 *Norman E. Borlaug (American) for his role in developing high-yield grains that increased food production in developing countries.

1971 *Willy Brandt (German) for his efforts to improve relations between Communist and non-Communist nations.

1972 No Award

1973 *Henry A. Kissinger (American) and Le Duc Tho (North Vietnamese) for negotiating the Vietnam War cease-fire agreement (Le Duc Tho declined).

1974 Sean MacBride (Irish) for working to guarantee human rights through international law, and *Eisaku Sato (Japanese) for his efforts to improve international relations and stop the spread of nuclear weapons.

1975 *Andrei D. Sakharov (Russian) for his efforts in support of peace and in opposition to violence and brutality.

1976 No Award

NOBEL PRIZES FOR ECONOMICS
The prize in economics was established in 1969.

1969 *Ragnar Frisch (Norwegian) and *Jan Tinbergen (Dutch) for their work in *econometrics*, the developing of mathematical models to analyze economic activity.

1970 *Paul A. Samuelson (American) for his efforts to raise the level of scientific analysis in economic theory.

1971 *Simon Kuznets (American) for his interpretation of economic growth.

1972 Kenneth J. Arrow (American) and Sir John Hicks (British) for their pioneering contribution to general equilibrium theory and to welfare theory.

1973 *Wassily Leontief (American) for his development

of the input-output method of economic analysis.

1974 *Friedrich von Hayek (Austrian) and *Gunnar Myrdal (Swedish) for their work in the theory of money and economic change and in the analysis of the relationship between economic and social factors.

1975 Leonid V. Kantorovich (Russian) and Tjalling C. Koopmans (American) for their work on how economic resources should be distributed and used.

1976 *Milton Friedman (American) for his work in the fields of economic consumption, monetary history and theory, and price stabilization policy.

*Has a biography in THE WORLD BOOK ENCYCLOPEDIA

349

NOBELIUM is an artificially created radioactive element. It has an atomic number of 102. Its isotopes range in mass number from 251 to 257. The most stable isotope has a mass number of 255 and a half-life of three minutes (see RADIOACTIVITY [Half-Life]). The chemical symbol for nobelium is No.

The discovery of element 102 was a subject of controversy. In 1957, scientists at the Nobel Institute for Physics in Stockholm, Sweden, bombarded curium with carbon 13. The result appeared to be an isotope of element 102, with a mass number of 254 and a half-life of 10 minutes. They named the element nobelium. However, later experiments in Russia and the United States did not confirm the discovery.

Element 102 was first identified with certainty in 1958 at the Lawrence Radiation Laboratory in Berkeley, Calif. The team of Albert Ghiorso, Glenn T. Seaborg, Torbjørn Sikkeland, and John R. Walton bombarded curium with carbon 12. They produced an element with a mass number of 254 and a half-life of 55 seconds. The Berkeley team had the right to name the element they had produced. In 1967, they decided to keep the name nobelium.   DANIEL J. KEVLES

NOBILITY. See TITLE OF HONOR.

NOBLE GAS is a term that refers to any of a group of six chemical elements. These elements are argon (Ar), helium (He), krypton (Kr), neon (Ne), radon (Rn), and xenon (Xe). They all occur naturally and can be found in the earth's atmosphere. The British scientists Lord Rayleigh and William Ramsay discovered the noble gases during the late 1890's.

Unlike most gaseous elements, the noble gases are *monatomic*—that is, they occur as single atoms. The atoms have stable *configurations* (arrangements) of electrons. Therefore, the atoms do not, under normal conditions, gain or lose electrons or share electrons with other elements. The six gases are called "noble" because they do not readily react with other elements. They are also sometimes called *inert gases* for this reason. However, krypton, radon, and xenon do combine with fluorine to form compounds.

The noble gases have various uses. Except for radon, which is highly radioactive, all of them are used as light sources in incandescent and gaseous-discharge lamps (see ELECTRIC LIGHT). Some also are used in devices called *gas lasers* (see LASER [Kinds of Lasers]).

Argon and helium are used in a welding process called *arc welding*. They provide a chemically inactive atmosphere in which certain metals, such as aluminum and magnesium, can be heated to their melting points without reacting chemically. Helium also is used in balloons that carry scientific instruments high into the earth's atmosphere, and in low-temperature research. Physicians sometimes use radon—because of its radioactivity—in treating cancer. Each noble gas has a separate article in WORLD BOOK.   NEIL BARTLETT

NOËL. See CHRISTMAS.

NOEL-BAKER, PHILIP. See NOBEL PRIZES (table: Nobel Prizes for Peace—1959).

NOGUCHI, ISAMU (1904-   ), is an American sculptor whose work represents a wide variety of styles. Noguchi has said that he is "suspicious of the whole business of style—again it is a form of inhibition."

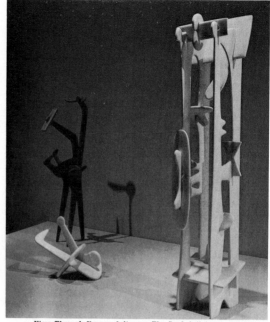

View Through Kouros, left rear; The Seed, left front; and *Strange Bird, right;* in polished marble and green slate. Kaz Inouye

Isamu Noguchi became famous for his abstract sculpture. He created these three works in the mid-1940's.

Noguchi works directly in nearly every sculptural material, avoiding such processes as casting, welding, or painting. Almost all his work has no recognizable subject matter. Noguchi seeks to preserve the nature of the sculptural material. He is intrigued by problems of weight, mass, and tension, and these elements are his constant themes.

Noguchi was born in Los Angeles of an American mother and a well-known Japanese poet and scholar. He lived in Japan from the age of 2 until he was 13. Noguchi gave up medical studies at Columbia University to return to sculpture, his earlier ambition. In the late 1920's, he studied in Paris with Constantin Brancusi, who had a strong influence on his work. Noguchi has designed furniture and settings for ballets. He also has collaborated with architects in planning gardens, playgrounds, and bridges.   DOUGLAS GEORGE

NOISE may be random sound or unwanted sound. It may also be unwanted signals, such as static that interferes with radio transmission. The sound we hear is caused by vibrations in air, water, steel, or other substances. A tuning fork produces an almost *pure tone*, with only one *frequency*, or rate of vibration (see TONE). Musical instruments produce *harmonic sound*. Such sound contains many frequencies, called *overtones*, that are harmonically related (see HARMONICS). *Random sound* has many overtones that are not harmonically related. Mechanical devices produce such sound.

Unwanted sound can be caused by any kind of sound—tones, harmonic sound, or random sound. Sound is unwanted if it is annoying or distracting, or if it damages the hearing mechanism. Persons exposed to a loud noise for a long time may suffer temporary or permanent loss of hearing. Workers continually exposed to loud noises may wear earplugs, earmuffs, or special helmets.

Noise can also be controlled by using heavy walls and tight doors to block its passage, or by using sound-absorptive materials to reduce its intensity. *Unwanted signals* can mean anything that interferes with any kind of communication. RICHARD H. BOLT

See also ACOUSTICS; DECIBEL; INSULATION (picture: Sound Insulation); MUFFLER; SOUND.

NOISE POLLUTION. See ENVIRONMENTAL POLLUTION. (Other Kinds of Pollution).

NOK was a West African civilization that flourished from about 500 B.C. until at least A.D. 200. It was centered in the valley where the Niger and Benue rivers meet. Today, Nok is the name of a village in Nigeria, about 100 miles (160 kilometers) northeast of Baro.

The people of ancient Nok produced the oldest sculptures found so far in black Africa. These sculptures of animal and human figures were identified by the British archaeologist Bernard Fagg, who named them after the village of Nok. Similar sculptures have been discovered at many other sites in the river valley.

The Nok sculptures are made of terra cotta, a kind of earthenware. They vary in size from 1 inch (2.5 centimeters) high to life size. All the human heads have pierced ears, and the eyes are hollowed out. Scholars do not know what function these sculptures had in the Nok society. Some believe that the sculpture of other West African peoples shows Nok influence.

The people of Nok probably farmed the land, but they also hunted and gathered food. They made tools and weapons of stone and at least started to learn to smelt and use iron. Scholars know from the decorations on Nok sculpture that the people probably wore beaded jewelry, including anklets, bracelets, and heavy collars. The Nok people apparently lived in clay huts in the lowlands and hills. Like some Nigerians today, they worshiped their ancestors and had many gods. Little is known about the end of the Nok culture. LEO SPITZER

NOLAN, PHILIP. See HALE, EDWARD EVERETT.

NOM DE PLUME. See NAME, PERSONAL (Pseudonym).

NOMAD, *NO mad,* is a person who wanders about and has no settled home. The word *nomad* is from a Greek word that means *one who wanders for pasture.* Most nomadic peoples wander through a general area in a cycle according to the seasons. The African Pygmies, the Negritos of Malaya, and the Australian Aborigines hunt animals and gather wild vegetables and fruits. Many of the American Indians lived as nomadic hunters and gatherers. There are few true nomads today.

Pastoral nomads live in the deserts of Arabia, Central Asia, and North Africa. These regions cannot be farmed, but have enough grass to feed grazing animals. Pastoral nomads raise camels, horses, sheep, and goats, and move seasonally to find new pastures. They generally live in portable tents, and have a simpler life than settled peoples. The Hebrews and other wandering tribes of Biblical times were pastoral nomads. This way of life still exists in the Middle East. FRED EGGAN

See also ARAB (Nomadic Life); ASIA (Way of Life in Southwest Asia; picture); BEDOUINS; GYPSY; MIGRATION (History); MONGOLIA (The People; picture).

NOME, Alaska (pop. 2,488), an ocean port and gold-mining center, lies on the northern shore of Norton Sound of the Bering Sea. It is about 2,400 miles (3,860 kilometers) by sea northwest of Seattle, Wash. For location, see ALASKA (political map).

Placer gold mining forms the backbone of Nome's economy. Three large dredges operate near the city. Ivory carving is the principal industry of the Eskimos in the area. Military construction and governmental offices also contribute to the income. The port of Nome is open from June to October. Two airlines serve the region. It also has a radio station.

Nome began as a boom town in 1899 when gold was discovered nearby. Within a short time, 40,000 miners, merchants, and adventurers had set up a tent city. Nome was incorporated in 1901. It has a mayor-council government. LYMAN E. ALLEN

NOMINATING CONVENTION. See POLITICAL CONVENTION.

NOMINATING ELECTION. See PRIMARY ELECTION.

NOMINATIVE CASE. See CASE.

NONAGGRESSION PACT is a treaty by which two or more nations agree to settle mutual disputes by peaceful means and not to attack each other. Between World War I and World War II, many nations signed nonaggression pacts because there was no international force strong enough to prevent aggression.

Nonaggression pacts sometimes were not effective because they lacked enforcement procedures, and also because participating nations violated their agreements. For example, during the 1920's and 1930's, Russia signed pacts with many of its neighbors. But Russia violated its agreements with Estonia, Finland, Latvia, and Lithuania when it occupied them in 1939 and 1940.

Since the end of World War II, there have been fewer attempts to establish nonaggression pacts. Many nations feel that the United Nations charter contains adequate pledges against aggression.

One of the major problems with nonaggression pacts is to determine an acceptable definition of *aggression.* The UN has debated this question, but has not been able to reach any agreement. Some nations believe that aggression includes only direct military attacks. Others feel that when one country aids revolution in another country through propaganda, subversion, or by taking over government posts, it constitutes indirect aggression. ELTON ATWATER

See also LEAGUE OF NATIONS; UNITED NATIONS.

NONCONDUCTOR. See ELECTRICITY (Current Electricity).

NONELECTROLYTE. See ELECTROLYTE.

NONES. See MONTH.

NONESUCH. See SHAMROCK.

NON-EUCLIDEAN GEOMETRY. See GEOMETRY.

NONGRADED SCHOOL. See EDUCATION (Elementary Education).

NONILLION, *noh NILL yun.* In the United States and France, nonillion is a thousand octillions, or a unit with 30 zeros. In England, it is a unit with 54 zeros.

NON-IMPORTATION ACT. See WAR OF 1812 (American Reaction).

NON-INTERCOURSE ACT. Congress passed the Non-Intercourse Act in 1809. The act prohibited American shippers from trading with Great Britain and France, which were then at war with each other. Both warring nations had interfered with American commerce by taking American ships. The British offense was aggravated by the policy of *impressing* (seizing) British, and sometimes American, sailors. President Jefferson felt that the Non-Intercourse Act would compel Britain and France to recognize American commercial rights.

In 1810, Congress passed the so-called Macon's Bill No. 2, which restored trade with both Great Britain and France. But Great Britain continued to interfere with American shipping until 1812, when open warfare broke out.   RAY ALLEN BILLINGTON

NONMETAL. See METAL.

NONPARTISAN LEAGUE, a political organization of farmers, was founded in North Dakota in 1915. Its aims were to restore government control to the farmers and to establish state-owned institutions for their benefit. From 1916 to 1921, the league controlled the government of North Dakota, and its influence spread to neighboring states. In Minnesota, it helped to create the powerful Farmer-Labor party.

After 1921, the power of the Nonpartisan League declined, except in North Dakota. For many years, most of the league candidates ran as Republicans, though they had little in common with Republicans elsewhere. In 1956, the league officially aligned itself with the Democratic party in North Dakota.   HAROLD W. BRADLEY

See also FARMER-LABOR PARTY.

NONSCHEDULED AIRLINE. See AIRLINE (Kinds of Airlines).

NONVIOLENT RESISTANCE. See KING, MARTIN LUTHER, JR.; BLACK AMERICANS (The Civil Rights Movement); GANDHI, MOHANDAS KARAMCHAND; CHAVEZ, CESAR ESTRADA.

NOODLE. See MACARONI.

NOON. See DAY; TIME.

NOOTKA INDIANS, *NOOT kuh*, were noted for the beauty and seaworthiness of their cedar canoes. No other hunting and fishing people in the world made such fine canoes. Some people say that this Nootka craft influenced the New England designers of the superb American clipper ships of the early 1800's.

Nootka villages dotted northwestern Washington state and the west side of Vancouver Island. Nootka craftworkers made remarkable wooden mechanical devices, such as puppets and masks with movable parts. The Nootka used Dentalium shells as a kind of money, and this custom spread to many other Indian groups in the Northwest region. In other respects, the Nootka way of life resembled that of other fishing groups in the Pacific Northwest (see INDIAN, AMERICAN [Indians of the Northwest Coast]). Little remains of the Nootka way of life. But many still speak the language and remember some of the old beliefs and customs.   MELVILLE JACOBS

NOPAL. See PRICKLY PEAR.

NORAD. See AIR FORCE, UNITED STATES (Defense); NATIONAL DEFENSE (Air Defense).

NORDENSKJÖLD, *NOOR dun SHOOLD,* **NILS ADOLF ERIK** (1832-1901), BARON NORDENSKJÖLD, was a Swedish polar explorer, mineralogist, and map authority. In 1878 and 1879, he became the first person to sail through the Northeast Passage between the Atlantic and Pacific oceans. He performed this feat by sailing along the northern coast of Europe and Asia. He tells of this journey in his book, *Voyage of the Vega* (1881).

Nordenskjöld was born in Helsinki, Finland. He moved to Sweden in 1857, and became a Swedish citi-

zen. He led two expeditions in an attempt to reach the North Pole. On the first one in 1868, he pushed to within about 400 nautical miles (740 kilometers) of the Pole. This was farther north (81°42′) than anyone had gone before. Nordenskjöld studied the geology of Greenland in 1870. He returned in 1883, and penetrated the ice barrier off the east coast. He traveled far enough over the inland ice to determine that it covered the interior of the island.   JOHN EDWARDS CASWELL

NORDHOFF AND HALL were a team of American novelists. Together they wrote a number of adventure stories of the South Seas. The best-known are *Mutiny on the Bounty* (1932), *Men Against the Sea* (1933), *Pitcairn's Island* (1934), and *The Hurricane* (1935). *Mutiny on the Bounty* and *The Hurricane* were made into movies.

Charles Bernard Nordhoff (1887-1947) wrote *The Fledgling* (1919), *The Pearl Lagoon* (1924), and *The Derelict* (1928). His first work with Hall was *Lafayette Flying Corps* (1920), a history of the famous World War I air group in which both served.

Nordhoff was born in London of American parents. During World War I, he served as a pilot, first in the French volunteer squadron the Lafayette Escadrille, and then in the United States Army Air Service. After the war, he and Hall lived in Tahiti.

James Norman Hall (1887-1951) wrote *Kitchener's Mob* (1916), *Dr. Dogbody's Leg* (1940), and his autobiography *My Island Home* (1952). He was born in Colfax, Iowa. In 1916, he joined the French Air Force, where he met Nordhoff.   JOHN O. EIDSON

NORFOLK. See ENGLAND (political map).

NORFOLK, Va. (pop. 307,951; met. area pop. 732,-600), is the largest city in Virginia and a leading seaport on the Atlantic Coast. Norfolk lies in southeastern Virginia, about 150 miles (241 kilometers) south of Washington, D.C. For location, see VIRGINIA (political map).

Hampton Roads, one of the world's finest natural deepwater harbors, forms Norfolk's northwestern boundary. The Norfolk Naval Base on Hampton Roads is one of the largest naval installations in the United States. It also serves as headquarters of the Atlantic Command of the North Atlantic Treaty Organization (NATO).

In 1682, the Virginia General Assembly founded a port in Norfolk County to serve ships sailing to and from England and the West Indies. The port was later named Norfolk for the county. It became an independent borough in 1736 and an independent city in 1845.

Description. Norfolk covers about 70 square miles (181 square kilometers), including 17 square miles (44 square kilometers) of inland water. The Elizabeth River borders the city on the south and west.

A feature of downtown Norfolk is a cultural and convention center called Scope. This $30-million building includes Chrysler Hall, where the Norfolk Symphony Orchestra performs. Norfolk's Chrysler Museum houses an art collection valued at up to $50 million. The city has several colleges and universities, including Norfolk State College, Old Dominion University, and Virginia Wesleyan College. Eastern Virginia Medical School also is in Norfolk.

Every spring, thousands of visitors come to the International Azalea Festival in Norfolk. Many tourists also visit St. Paul's Church, which dates from 1739. This church was one of only a few buildings that survived a

British bombardment during the Revolutionary War in America (1775-1783).

Economy of Norfolk depends heavily on Hampton Roads. The Norfolk Naval Base, the city's largest employer, lies on the shore of Hampton Roads. About 30,000 civilians work at the base. Hampton Roads—which includes Norfolk and other ports—handles more coal than any other port district in the world. It serves as the distribution center for the rich coal-mining regions of southwestern Virginia and West Virginia. The port of Norfolk handles about 50 million short tons (45 million metric tons) of cargo a year.

The Norfolk metropolitan area has about 500 manufacturing companies. Their chief products include automobiles, cork and rubber goods, and ships.

Government and History. Norfolk has a council-manager form of government. The voters elect seven councilmen to four-year terms. The councilmen choose one of their group as mayor and hire a city manager to carry out their policies.

Powhatan Indians lived in what is now the Norfolk area when white men first explored there in the early 1600's. Early Norfolk served as a colonial tobacco and naval supply port. In 1776, during the Revolutionary War, a British fleet bombarded and destroyed much of the town. Norfolk was incorporated as a city in 1845.

Norfolk grew slowly until the Navy began to build the naval base in 1917, shortly after the nation entered World War I. During World War II (1939-1945), thousands of civilians moved to the city to work in the navy yards and on the base. The population of Norfolk rose from 144,332 in 1940 to 213,513 in 1950.

In 1951, the city began an urban renewal program. This project included slum clearance and the construction of public housing. Civic plans for the 1970's included construction of several high-rise buildings and a waterfront hotel.   GARY J. DALTON

For the monthly weather in Norfolk, see VIRGINIA (Climate). See also NORFOLK NAVAL BASE.

NORFOLK ISLAND is an isolated island in the South Pacific Ocean. It lies 930 miles (1,500 kilometers) northeast of Sydney, Australia, and 630 miles (1,010 kilometers) northwest of New Zealand (see PACIFIC ISLANDS [map]). Many of the inhabitants are descendants of the crew of the sailing ship, *Bounty*. The sailors of the *Bounty* mutinied against their captain's treatment and settled on Pitcairn Island in 1790.

In 1774, the British explorer James Cook became the first European to reach Norfolk Island. For many years, the island was a part of the Australian state of New South Wales, which used it as a penal colony until 1856. In that year, settlers were moved to the island from Pitcairn Island, over 3,000 miles (4,800 kilometers) away. In 1914, Norfolk Island was separated from New South Wales and became a federal territory of the Australian Commonwealth.

Norfolk Island has a population of about 1,400, and covers an area of 14 square miles (36 square kilometers). It has fertile soil. The people grow citrus fruits, bananas, and vegetables.   EDWIN H. BRYAN, JR.

NORFOLK NAVAL BASE, Va., is the largest naval base in the United States. It includes the headquarters of the Atlantic Fleet, the Fifth Naval District, and the North Atlantic Treaty Organization (NATO) Allied Command Atlantic. Commissioned in 1917, the base

houses the Armed Forces Staff College and the navy's oldest supply center. Nearby are the Naval Amphibious Base at Little Creek, a weapons station at Yorktown, and a shipyard at Portsmouth.   JOHN A. OUDINE

NORFOLK SYSTEM. See INVENTION (The Industrial Revolution).

NORGAY, TENZING. See MOUNT EVEREST.

NORGE. See AIRSHIP (Italian Airships).

NORMAL CURVE. See STATISTICS (Frequency Distribution).

NORMAN. The Normans were a group of Vikings, or *Norsemen* (Scandinavians), who first settled in France, then spread into England, southern Italy, and Sicily. In the 800's, Norman warriors began their conquests by raiding French coasts and river valleys. By the early 900's, they had colonized the French territory near the mouth of the Seine River that is now known as Normandy. In 911, the Norman chief Hrolf, or Rollo (860?-931?), became a duke in the service of the Frankish king, Charles the Simple. The Normans became Christians and adopted French customs. Many became famous as administrators, church leaders, and crusaders.

In 1066, Norman warriors under the leadership of William, Duke of Normandy, conquered England, and Norman influence spread throughout the British Isles. During the same period, Norman groups won great victories in other lands. Robert Guiscard (1015?-1085), son of Tancred of Hauteville, conquered southern Italy. Roger, another of Tancred's sons, took the island of Sicily from the Muslims. These two territories were later united in the famous Kingdom of the Two Sicilies by Roger's son, Roger II.   WILLIAM C. BARK

See also NORMAN CONQUEST; NORMANDY; VIKINGS.

NORMAN ARCHITECTURE is a style of building which had its origin in Normandy, in northwestern France. It reached a high development in England after the Norman Conquest of 1066 and during the 1100's. Norman architecture is bold and massive, with short, heavy columns supporting semicircular arches. Geometric patterns of zigzags and similar forms were highly developed. Parts of some English Gothic cathedrals were done in the Norman style.   BERNARD LEMANN

NORMAN CONQUEST is the name given to the conquest of England in 1066 by William, Duke of Normandy. The duke, known as William the Conqueror, led a Norman army across the Channel into England.

William was a proud and ruthless ruler, and a vassal of the King of France. He hoped to follow his cousin, King Edward the Confessor, as King of England. William claimed that Edward had named him as his successor. The chief contender for the English throne was Harold, Earl of Wessex. But William also claimed that Harold, who had been shipwrecked on the Norman coast in 1064, had sworn a solemn oath to support William's claim to the throne. In 1066, King Edward died. The Anglo-Saxon Witan (Great Council) elected Harold king (see HAROLD [II]).

William at once declared his right to the throne. He secured the support of the pope and gathered an army of about 5,000 men. William landed in England without opposition at Pevensey, near Hastings.

The Normans were aided in their successful landing by a chance happening. While Harold was waiting for

Detail of the Bayeux Tapestry (1000's-1100's), embroidery on linen by unknown artists; Bayeux Museum, Bayeux, France (Giraudon)

The Norman Conquest of England Began in 1066 when William the Conqueror Sailed His Army Across the Channel.

the Normans to arrive, he received news that a Norwegian force had landed in the north of England. He hastened north and defeated the Norwegians. Meanwhile, William landed his force on the unprotected coast. Harold then marched back across England and attacked the Norman army near Hastings on October 14, 1066. This was the historic Battle of Hastings, which established the Norman rule of England. King Harold was defeated and slain. William marched on to London, where he was crowned King of England on Christmas Day, 1066. The Conqueror spent several years subduing the Saxons. At first he tried to win over the Saxon nobles, but they opposed him stubbornly.

William established the Norman rule in England on a strong foundation. He hesitated at no act which he thought would increase the power of the crown. He took the land of most of the English nobility, who had opposed him. However, William was generous in some cases and did not deprive the rebel of his lands or titles. The confiscated land was then divided among William's Norman followers. William forced all these landholders to swear direct loyalty to himself. In this way, he put all the lords of England under his direct control. In order to know conditions in England, the Conqueror directed the preparation of the famous Domesday Book. This was a survey of all the regions in his kingdom. Many English families trace their names to entries in the Domesday Book (see DOMESDAY BOOK).

The descendants of the Normans became the ruling class in England. For a time, they kept themselves aloof from the Anglo-Saxons and treated them as a conquered people. But as the years went by the Normans and the Anglo-Saxons intermarried. The two races, which even in the beginning were similar, blended into one.

The Normans were a race of conquerors, with a genius for law and government, and they ruled England with great ability. In addition, English language, literature, and architecture owe much to the Normans. At first the Normans spoke French. Later, the Norman French blended with the Germanic tongue of the Anglo-Saxons and became English. BASIL D. HENNING

See also ENGLAND (The Norman Conquest); HASTINGS, BATTLE OF; IRELAND (History); WILLIAM (I).

NORMANDY is a region in northwestern France. It was named after the Norsemen who conquered the area in the 800's. It lies along the English Channel coast between the regions of Picardy and Brittany. The famous towns of Normandy include Rouen, the capital of the old province; Le Havre, Harfleur, Caen, Bayeux, and Cherbourg. The inhabitants are well known as sailors and farmers. The farmers specialize in dairying and raising fruits, especially apples for cider and brandy. Iron ore is mined near Caen.

In A.D. 911, the Carolingian king, Charles the Simple, made Normandy a duchy under the Norman chieftain Hrolf, or Rollo. One of Rollo's most famous descendants was William the Conqueror, who won the English crown after the Battle of Hastings in 1066. Normandy was united with England during the reign of the English king, Henry I (1100-1135). England and France struggled for control of Normandy during the Hundred Years' War. The English recovered the region twice, but finally lost it in 1449 to Charles VII, king of France. Joan of Arc became famous as the leader of French troops in the fight for Normandy.

Normandy attracted worldwide attention on June 6, 1944, when Allied troops landed on its beaches. From Normandy, the Allies drove the Germans out of France. Visitors to the beaches may still see the wreckage of ships that took part in the historic invasion. Many Norman towns were damaged in the fighting, but have been repaired. ROBERT E. DICKINSON

See also FURNITURE (Norman); NORMAN; WORLD WAR II (D-Day).

NORMANDY, DUKE OF. See WILLIAM (I, the Conqueror).

NORNS were the three Fates of Scandinavian mythology. They were three sisters: Urd (Past), Verdandi (Present), and Skuld (Future). Urd was old and looked toward the past. Verdandi faced straight ahead into the present. Skuld represented the future, and looked in a direction opposite from that of Urd. The fate of men and gods was decided by the Norns.

The Norse people believed that there were many lesser Norns, and one for each person. PADRAIC COLUM

See also FATES.

(1922-   ), served as king, premier, and then chief of state of Cambodia between 1941 and 1970. Cambodia was a French colony when Sihanouk became king.

In the early 1950's, Sihanouk led his country's successful struggle for independence. He gave up the throne in 1955 to enter politics but took the title of prince. He became premier that same year and chief of state in 1960. Sihanouk established an up-to-date school system and many new industries in Cambodia. During the Vietnam War, he alternated between supporting South Vietnam and the United States and cooperating with North Vietnam. He claimed that his goal was an independent, peaceful Cambodia.

In March, 1970, while Sihanouk was out of the country, several members of his government overthrew him. These men favored a stronger anti-Communist policy. Sihanouk went to Peking, China, and formed a pro-Communist government-in-exile. By the end of 1970, war had erupted throughout Cambodia between government troops and Communist forces. The war ended with a Communist victory in 1975. The Communists gave Sihanouk the title of chief of state, but did not give him any important role in the government. He resigned from this office in 1976. Sihanouk was born in Phnom Penh.   DAVID P. CHANDLER

NORRIS, FRANK (1870-1902), was an American novelist and journalist and a leader of the naturalism movement in literature. Norris believed that a novel should serve a moral purpose. The novelist, he said, must "sacrifice money, fashion and popularity for the greater reward of realizing that he has told the truth." See NATURALISM.

Benjamin Franklin Norris was born in Chicago. He moved to San Francisco with his family in 1884 and attended the University of California from 1890 to 1894. At the university he came under the influence of the writings of the French naturalist writer Émile Zola and began to write *McTeague*, one of his finest novels. Norris then spent a year at Harvard University, where he wrote part of an unfinished novel, *Vandover and the Brute*.

In 1895 and 1896, Norris was a reporter in South Africa for *Collier's* magazine and the *San Francisco Chronicle*. In 1896, he returned to San Francisco where he became assistant editor of a magazine called *The Wave*. In 1899, he took a job as manuscript reader for a publisher in New York City. That same year Norris published *McTeague*, which tells how circumstances and a greedy wife force a man to become a murderer.

Norris planned a three-novel series called *Epic of the Wheat* to tell about the production, distribution, and consumption of wheat in the United States. *The Octopus* (1901) dramatizes how a railroad controlled a group of California wheat farmers by such means as charging excessive freight rates for hauling wheat. It ranks with *McTeague* as Norris' finest work. Both novels show the author's weakness for melodrama but illustrate his genius for revealing character and writing exciting action scenes. The second volume of the series, *The Pit*, was published in 1903, after Norris died following an operation for appendicitis. The final volume, *The Wolf*, was never written.   DOMINICK CONSOLO

NORRIS, GEORGE WILLIAM (1861-1944), was one of the great independent statesmen of American public life. During his 40 years in Congress, he ignored party politics to fight for whatever he believed to be right.

Norris was elected to the United States House of Representatives as a Republican from Nebraska in 1902. He served for 10 years. In 1910, he led the fight to free the House from the dictatorial power of Speaker Joseph Cannon.

Norris was elected a United States senator from Nebraska in 1912. He opposed American entry into World War I and into the League of Nations. But his main interest lay in the development of public ownership of public utilities. He wanted the U.S. government to develop the electric power of the Tennessee River Valley, despite the policies of his own Republican Party. In 1933, Congress finally passed his bill to create the Tennessee Valley Authority (TVA). A dam on the Tennessee was named in his honor.

Norris also helped pass the 20th (Lame Duck) Amendment to the United States Constitution. This amendment shortened the time gap between congressional elections and the first meeting of the new Congress. It reduced the influence of defeated congressmen.

Norris realized the danger to America resulting from the rise of Nazism and Fascism in Europe. He supported aid to Great Britain in the early years of World War II. Norris was defeated for re-election in 1942. He was born in Sandusky County, Ohio, and studied law at Valparaiso University. He moved to Beaver City, Nebr., in 1885.   JOHN A. GARRATY

NORRIS DAM. See TENNESSEE (color picture: Norris DAM); TENNESSEE VALLEY AUTHORITY (The Dams).

NORRIS-LA GUARDIA ACT OF 1932. See YELLOW-DOG CONTRACTS.

NORRISH, RONALD G. W. See NOBEL PRIZES (table: Nobel Prizes for Chemistry—1967).

NORSE MYTHOLOGY. See MYTHOLOGY (Teutonic Mythology).

NORSEMEN. See VIKINGS.

NORTH, LORD (1732-1792), FREDERICK, EARL OF GUILFORD, was a British prime minister whose shortsighted treatment of the American Colonies helped bring on the Revolutionary War.

North was closely associated with King George III, and managed the House of Commons in the king's interests (see GEORGE [III] of England). Even when he disagreed with his master's policy, he did not oppose it. He often asked to resign, but the king would not allow it. North supported the tea tax that became one of the causes of the Revolutionary War (see BOSTON TEA PARTY). As the Revolutionary War progressed, North's administration became increasingly disorganized and demoralized. He finally persuaded the king to accept his resignation in 1782. He became joint secretary of state with Charles Fox in 1783, but resigned after only nine months in office (see FOX, CHARLES J.).

He was born in London on April 13, 1732. He attended Eton College and Oxford University. His father had him elected to Parliament in 1754 from a "pocket borough" owned by the family. North later served in the Treasury and as a member of the Privy Council. He became chancellor of the exchequer and leader of the House of Commons in 1767. In 1770, North became prime minister.   W. B. WILLCOX

Alaskan Eskimo Girl

Yukon Territory, Canada

NORTH AMERICA

Clarence W. Olmstead, the contributor of this article, is Professor of Geography at the University of Wisconsin at Madison.

Niagara Falls

Guard at the Citadel, Quebec

New York City Harbor

Roundup in Wyoming

Panamanian Girl in Costume

Street in Mexico

─────── **FACTS IN BRIEF** ───────

Area: 9,417,000 sq. mi. (24,390,000 km²).
Greatest Distances (mainland)—north-south, 4,500 mi. (7,242 km); east-west, 4,000 mi. (6,437 km). *Coastline*—96,459 mi. (155,236 km).

Population: 358,000,000; density, 39 persons per sq. mi. (15 persons per km²).

Physical Features: *Chief Mountain Ranges*—Alaska, Appalachian, Cascade, Coast, Rocky, Sierra Madre, Sierra Nevada. *Highest Peaks*—McKinley (20,320 ft., or 6,194 m), Logan (19,520 ft., or 5,950 m), Orizaba (18,701 ft., or 5,700 m), Saint Elias (18,008 ft., or 5,489 m). *Lowest Point*—Death Valley (282 ft., or 86 m, below sea level). *Chief Rivers*—Arkansas, Colorado, Columbia, Fraser, Mackenzie, Mississippi, Missouri, Nelson, Ohio, Rio Grande, St. Lawrence, Yukon. *Chief Lakes*—Athabasca, Erie, Great Bear, Great Salt, Great Slave, Huron, Michigan, Nicaragua, Ontario, Superior, Winnipeg. *Chief Deserts*—Chihuahuan, Colorado, Great Basin, Mojave, Painted, Sonoran, Vizcaíno, Yuma. *Chief Waterfalls*—Niagara, Ribbon, Silver Strand, Takakkaw, Upper Yosemite. *Chief Islands*—Cuba, Greenland, Hispaniola, Jamaica, Newfoundland, Puerto Rico, Vancouver.

Chief Products: *Manufacturing and Processing*—airplanes, automobiles, cement, chemicals, clothing, electrical products, food products, furniture, leather products, locomotives, machinery, metals, paper, rubber products, textiles, tobacco products, wood products. *Agriculture*—beef cattle, coffee, corn, cotton, dairy products, fruits and vegetables, hay, hogs, oats, poultry and eggs, soybeans, sugar, tobacco, wheat. *Mining*—asbestos, bauxite, building stone, coal, copper, gold, gypsum, iron ore, lead, molybdenum, natural gas, nickel, petroleum, phosphate, potash, salt, silver, sulfur, uranium ore, zinc.

NORTH AMERICA, the third largest of the seven continents, extends from the cold Arctic Ocean in the north to the warm tropics in the south. Only Asia and Africa have greater areas. Canada and the United States occupy the northern four-fifths of North America. Mexico and Central America make up the southern part. North America also includes many widely separated islands, such as Greenland and the West Indies.

With about a tenth of the earth's people and about a sixth of its land area, North America produces more than a fourth of the world's manufactured goods and a large share of its mineral, forest, and farm products. Most of North America's vast wealth is centered in the United States and Canada. These countries, with great industries and vast natural resources, have the highest standards of living in the world. The Central American and Caribbean countries have fewer industries and resources, and lower living standards.

Nature gave North America many varieties of beautiful landscapes. The seacoasts of the Atlantic and Pacific oceans have great stretches of sandy beaches and rocky cliffs. In the interior, snow-capped mountains tower above gently rolling plains. The largest freshwater lakes in the world, the Great Lakes, are in North America. The continent also includes the world's most spectacular canyon, the Grand Canyon of the Colorado River. Fertile, green fields cover much of North America, but there also are immense, dry deserts.

When European explorers and colonists reached North America nearly 500 years ago, they found it largely a wilderness inhabited by primitive Indians. Only the Aztec and Maya Indians of Mexico and Central America had developed advanced civilizations that included written languages and large cities. The northern part of the continent was settled mostly by English-speaking (Anglo-Saxon) people. This region is sometimes called *Anglo-America*. The southern part of the continent was settled mostly by Spanish-speaking people. It is sometimes called *Middle America*, because it lies between Anglo-America and South America.

INDEPENDENT COUNTRIES OF NORTH AMERICA

Map Key	Name	Area In sq. mi.	In km²	Population	Capital	Official Language	Date of Independence
L9	Bahamas	5,380	13,935	230,000	Nassau	English	1973
M12	Barbados	166	431	251,000	Bridgetown	English	1966
G7	Canada	3,851,809	9,976,139	23,671,000	Ottawa	English; French	1931
N9	Costa Rica	19,575	50,700	2,137,000	San José	Spanish	1821
L9	Cuba	44,218	114,524	9,762,000	Havana	Spanish	1898
L10	Dominican Republic	18,816	48,734	5,115,000	Santo Domingo	Spanish	1821
N8	El Salvador	8,260	21,393	4,480,000	San Salvador	Spanish	1821
M12	Grenada	133	344	98,000	Saint George's	English	1974
M8	Guatemala	42,042	108,889	6,360,000	Guatemala City	Spanish	1821
M10	Haiti	10,714	27,750	4,810,000	Port-au-Prince	French	1804
M8	Honduras	43,277	112,088	3,431,000	Tegucigalpa	Spanish	1821
M9	Jamaica	4,244	10,991	2,137,000	Kingston	English	1962
L6	Mexico	761,605	1,972,547	66,692,000	Mexico City	Spanish	1821
N8	Nicaragua	50,193	130,000	2,373,000	Managua	Spanish	1821
N9	Panama	29,209	75,650	1,857,000	Panama City	Spanish	1903
M12	Trinidad and Tobago	1,980	5,128	1,113,000	Port-of-Spain	English	1962
J7	United States	3,615,122	9,363,123	219,103,000	Washington, D.C.	English	1776

OTHER POLITICAL UNITS IN NORTH AMERICA

Map Key	Name	Area In sq. mi.	In km²	Population	Status
L12	Antigua	171	442	74,000	State associated with Great Britain
M8	Belize*	8,867	22,965	154,000	British dependency; some self-government
J11	Bermuda*	21	53	59,000	British dependency; some self-government
M9	Cayman Islands*	100	259	11,000	British dependency
M12	Dominica	290	751	77,000	State associated with Great Britain
D9	Greenland*	840,004	2,175,600	52,000	Province of Denmark
L12	Guadeloupe*	687	1,779	373,000	Overseas department of France
M12	Martinique*	425	1,102	381,000	Overseas department of France
L11	Montserrat*†	38	98	12,000	British dependency
M11	Netherlands Antilles*	383	993	256,000	Self-governing part of The Netherlands
N9	Panama Canal Zone*	647	1,676	40,100	Territory under U.S. jurisdiction and control
L11	Puerto Rico*	3,435	8,897	3,385,000	United States commonwealth
L11	Saint Christopher (St. Kitts)-Nevis-Anguilla	138	357	66,000	State associated with Great Britain
M12	Saint Lucia	238	616	114,000	State associated with Great Britain
H11	Saint Pierre and Miquelon*	93	242	5,000	Overseas department of France
M12	Saint Vincent	150	388	121,000	State associated with Great Britain
L10	Turks and Caicos Islands*	166	430	7,000	British dependency
L11	Virgin Islands, British*	59	153	12,000	British dependency; some self-government
L11	Virgin Islands, U.S.*	133	344	120,000	U.S. organized unincorporated territory

Each independent country has a separate article in WORLD BOOK.
*Has a separate article in WORLD BOOK.
†Does not appear on map; map key shows general location.

Populations are 1978 estimates for independent countries and 1978 and earlier estimates for other political units based on the latest figures from official government and United Nations sources.

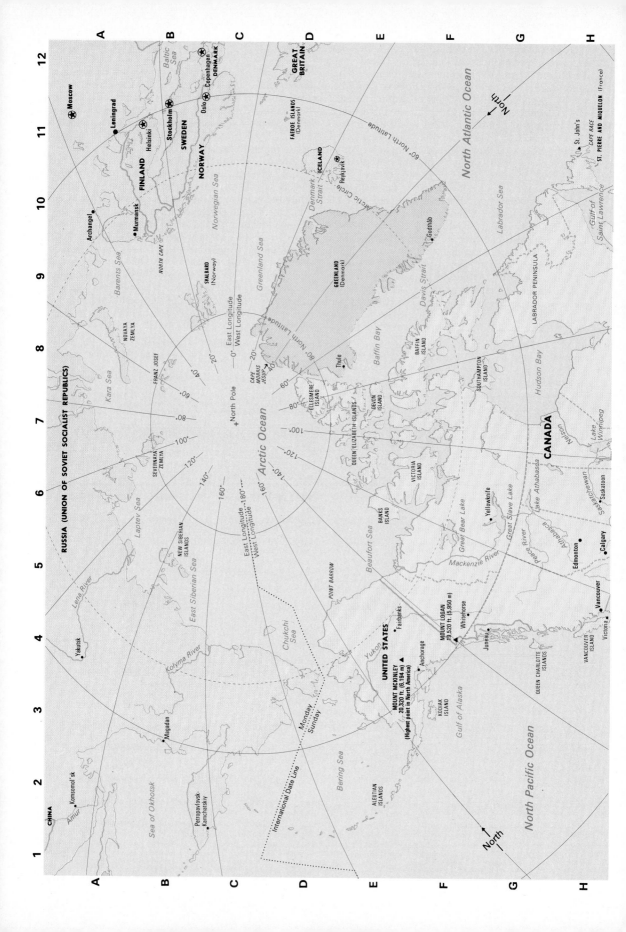

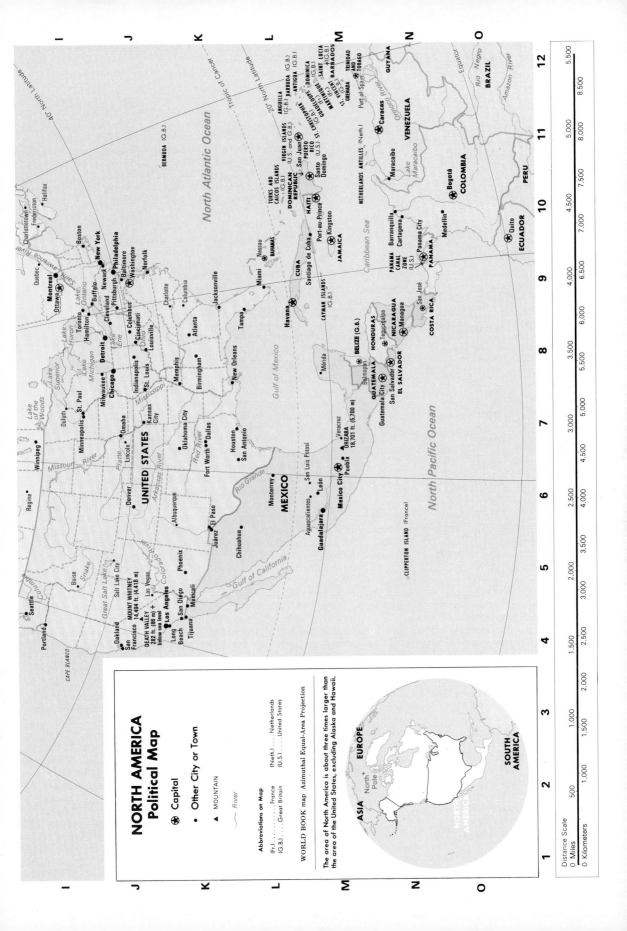

NORTH AMERICA
Political Map

⊕ Capital

• Other City or Town

▲ MOUNTAIN

〜 River

Abbreviations on Map

(Fr.) .... France   (Neth.) .... Netherlands
(G.B.) .... Great Britain   (U.S.) .... United States

WORLD BOOK map Azimuthal Equal-Area Projection

The area of North America is about three times larger than the area of the United States, excluding Alaska and Hawaii.

ASIA   EUROPE

North Pole

NORTH AMERICA

SOUTH AMERICA

Distance Scale

0 Miles   500   1,000   1,500   2,000   2,500   3,000   3,500   4,000   4,500   5,000   5,500

0 Kilometers   1,000   1,500   2,000   2,500   3,000   3,500   4,000   4,500   5,000   5,500   6,000   6,500   7,000   7,500   8,000   8,500

UNITED STATES

MEXICO

Mexico City

MOUNT WHITNEY 14,494 ft. (4,418 m)

DEATH VALLEY 282 ft. (86 m) + below sea level

ORIZABA 18,701 ft. (5,700 m) ▲

Seattle, Portland, Oakland, San Francisco, Los Angeles, Long Beach, San Diego, Salt Lake City, Las Vegas, Tijuana, Mexicali, Phoenix, Boise, Regina, Winnipeg, Denver, Lincoln, Albuquerque, El Paso, Juárez, Chihuahua, Duluth, Minneapolis, St. Paul, Omaha, Kansas City, Oklahoma City, Fort Worth, Dallas, San Antonio, Houston, Milwaukee, Chicago, Detroit, St. Louis, Indianapolis, Memphis, Birmingham, New Orleans, Toronto, Hamilton, Cleveland, Pittsburgh, Columbus, Cincinnati, Louisville, Atlanta, Tampa, Jacksonville, Columbia, Charlotte, Ottawa, Montreal, Quebec, Buffalo, Newark, New York, Philadelphia, Baltimore, Washington, Norfolk, Boston, Halifax, Fredericton, Charlottetown, Miami, Nassau, Monterrey, Aguascalientes, León, Guadalajara, San Luis Potosí, Veracruz, Puebla, Mérida

BAHAMAS, CUBA, Havana, Santiago de Cuba, CAYMAN ISLANDS (G.B.), JAMAICA, Kingston, HAITI, Port-au-Prince, DOMINICAN REPUBLIC, Santo Domingo, PUERTO RICO, San Juan, VIRGIN ISLANDS (U.S. and G.B.), TURKS AND CAICOS ISLANDS (G.B.), BERMUDA (G.B.)

ANGUILLA (G.B.), BARBUDA (G.B.), ANTIGUA (G.B.), ST. CHRISTOPHER (G.B.), GUADELOUPE (Fr.), DOMINICA, MARTINIQUE (Fr.), ST. LUCIA (G.B.), ST. VINCENT (G.B.), BARBADOS, GRENADA, TRINIDAD AND TOBAGO

BELIZE (G.B.), Belmopan, GUATEMALA, Guatemala City, HONDURAS, Tegucigalpa, EL SALVADOR, San Salvador, NICARAGUA, Managua, COSTA RICA, San José, PANAMA, Panama City, PANAMA CANAL ZONE (U.S.)

NETHERLANDS ANTILLES (Neth.), VENEZUELA, Caracas, Maracaibo, Lake Maracaibo, Barranquilla, Cartagena, Medellín, Bogotá, COLOMBIA, GUYANA, Port-of-Spain, Orinoco River, ECUADOR, Quito, PERU, BRAZIL, Rio Negro, Amazon River

North Atlantic Ocean

North Pacific Ocean

Gulf of Mexico

Gulf of California

Caribbean Sea

Great Salt Lake

Lake of the Woods

Lake Superior, Lake Michigan, Lake Huron, Lake Erie, Lake Ontario

Columbia River, Snake River, Colorado River, Rio Grande, Red River, Arkansas River, Missouri River, Platte River, Mississippi River, Saint Lawrence River

Tropic of Cancer, 20° North Latitude, 40° North Latitude, Equator

CAPE BLANCO, CLIPPERTON ISLAND (France)

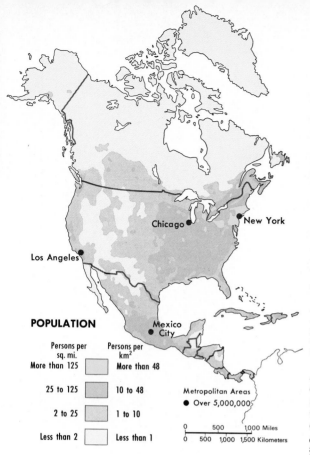

POPULATION

Persons per sq. mi.	Persons per km²
More than 125	More than 48
25 to 125	10 to 48
2 to 25	1 to 10
Less than 2	Less than 1

Metropolitan Areas
● Over 5,000,000

```
0        500      1,000 Miles
0    500   1,000  1,500 Kilometers
```

NORTH AMERICA / The People

The people of North America represent four vastly different backgrounds—European, African Negro, American Indian, and Eskimo.

The largest number of people of North America have European ancestors. About half of all Canadians trace their origin to Great Britain and Ireland, and about a third are the descendants of early French settlers. The United States became a melting pot of immigrants from many European countries. South of the United States, most of the European settlers came from Spain.

Negroes were originally brought to North America from Africa as slaves. In the United States, nearly 11 of every 100 persons is a Negro or has mixed Negro and white ancestry. The islands of the Caribbean also have large Negro populations. Nearly all the people of Haiti are Negroes or of mixed Negro and white descent.

Indians were the first North Americans. They have occupied the continent at least 20,000 years. Their ancestors probably came from Asia by way of a narrow crossing to Alaska. When Europeans first settled North America, the largest number of Indians lived in present-day Mexico and Central America. Today, many people in these regions have pure Indian ancestry, and even larger numbers are *mestizos* of mixed Indian and European descent. See INDIAN, AMERICAN; MESTIZO.

The Eskimos arrived after the Indians. They came from Asia by boat about 6,000 years ago and settled in Alaska, northern Canada, and Greenland. Today,

the descendants of these Arctic pioneers number about 90,000. See ESKIMO.

Language and Education. Most North Americans speak English, Spanish, or French. Generally, the early European colonists gave the language of their native countries to the regions that they settled. English is spoken throughout the United States and most of Canada. English and French both are spoken in Quebec and some other parts of Canada. Mexicans and most of the people of Central America and the Caribbean islands speak Spanish, although French, English, or Dutch is the language of some areas. Many Indians and Eskimos still use their native languages.

Most of the people of North America can read and write. Canada and the United States have extensive systems of public and private schools that provide the education needed to support a modern industrial democracy. The Latin-American countries south of the United States have been slower in providing mass education for all their young people.

The oldest university in North America is the University of Santo Domingo in the Dominican Republic. It was founded in 1538. For more about education in North America, see the *Education* section of the various country, state, and province articles.

Religion. Christianity is the major religion of North America. In the United States, the largest number of church members are Protestants. Roman Catholics account for about two-fifths of the church members of the United States, about half the church members of Canada, and nearly all of those in the Latin-American countries. Other chief religious groups in North America include Jews and Eastern Orthodox Christians.

Transportation and Communication. The most extensive transportation and communication systems in the world spread a network over a large part of the North American continent. On the Pan American Highway, automobiles can travel from Mexico in the north to Panama in the south and continue far into South America. In Canada and the United States, coast-to-coast highway systems connect most towns and cities. Airlines serve the cities of North America and provide jet travel across the continent in about five hours. They carry about 70 million passengers a year. The St. Lawrence Seaway, the Great Lakes, and the Mississippi River and its tributaries form the greatest inland waterway system in the world. In addition, intracoastal waterways run along the Atlantic and Gulf coasts of the United States and along the Pacific coast from Seattle to Alaska. The Panama Canal near the southern tip of the continent connects the Atlantic and Pacific oceans.

North Americans read more than 2,000 daily newspapers. Canada and the United States have an average of one telephone for about every three persons. More television sets are in North America than in all the rest of the world. In the United States alone, the Postal Service carries about 85 billion pieces of mail a year.

The continent's Latin-American and far-northern regions have fewer transportation and communication facilities than the United States and Canada. For example, Mexico has an average of only one telephone for about every 60 persons. Some areas of Central America cannot be reached by highway. In northern Canada and Alaska, airplanes provide much of the transportation in sparsely settled areas.

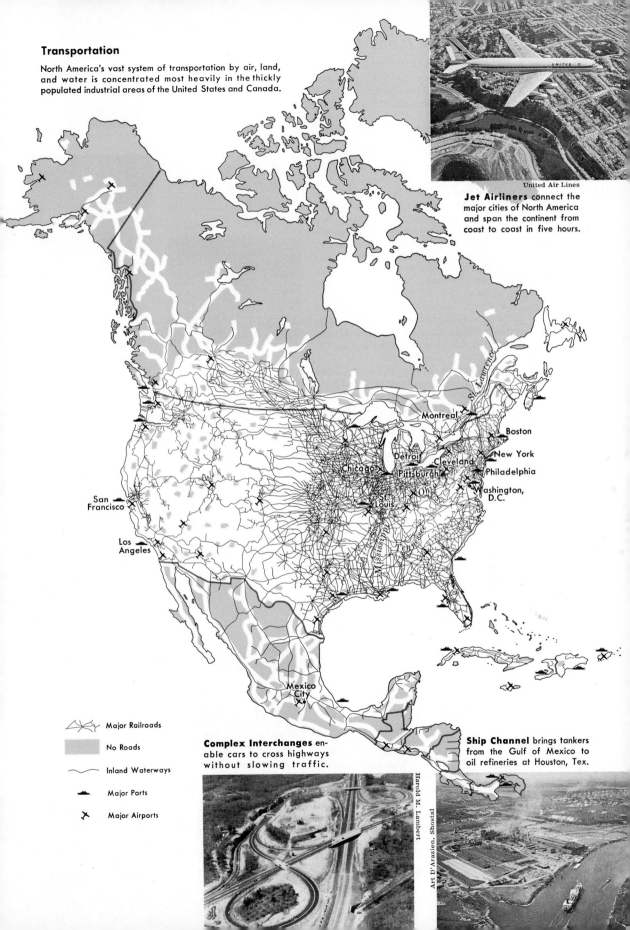

Transportation

North America's vast system of transportation by air, land, and water is concentrated most heavily in the thickly populated industrial areas of the United States and Canada.

United Air Lines

Jet Airliners connect the major cities of North America and span the continent from coast to coast in five hours.

Ship Channel brings tankers from the Gulf of Mexico to oil refineries at Houston, Tex.

Complex Interchanges enable cars to cross highways without slowing traffic.

Harold M. Lambert

Art D'Arazien, Shostal

Major Railroads

No Roads

Inland Waterways

Major Ports

Major Airports

Montreal

Boston

Detroit
Cleveland
New York

Chicago
Pittsburgh
Philadelphia

Ohio
Washington, D.C.

St. Louis

St. Lawrence

Mississippi
Tennessee

San Francisco

Los Angeles

Mexico City

NORTH AMERICA / *Land Regions*

North America is shaped roughly like a vast triangle. One point of the triangle connects with South America. The Atlantic, Pacific, and Arctic coasts form the three sides. Great mountain systems separated by wide plains run parallel to the Atlantic and Pacific coasts.

North America has seven major land regions: (1) the *Pacific Coastland*, (2) the *Intermountain Region*, (3) the *Rocky Mountains*, (4) the *Interior Plain*, (5) the *Canadian Shield*, (6) the *Appalachian Mountains*, and (7) the *Coastal Plain*.

The Pacific Coastland—Ray Atkeson, Publix

The Pacific Coastland extends from Alaska into Mexico. It consists of two roughly parallel mountain chains separated by valleys such as the Central Valley of California. The outer chain rises steeply from the Pacific Ocean. It includes the Olympic Mountains in Washington and the coastal mountains of Oregon and California. The inner chain includes the Alaska Range, the Coast Mountains of Canada, the Cascade Range in Washington and Oregon, and the Sierra Nevada in California. The Sierra Madre Occidental and the mountains of Lower California may be thought of as extensions of the Pacific Coastland mountains. Mount McKinley, North America's highest peak, rises 20,320 feet (6,194 meters) in the Alaska Range.

The Intermountain Region—Hal Rumel, Publix

The Intermountain Region divides the Pacific Coastland from the Rocky Mountains. Its basins and high plateaus include the Yukon River Basin in Alaska and Canada, the Interior Plateau of British Columbia, the Colorado Plateau, the Great Basin centered in Nevada, and the Mexican Plateau. The Intermountain Region includes such spectacular land features as the Grand Canyon. Death Valley, the lowest point in North America, lies 282 feet (86 meters) below sea level in the Great Basin.

The Rocky Mountains—John D. Freeman, Publix

The Rocky Mountains form the high inland spine of North America. They run from northern Alaska into New Mexico, and can be traced southward into Mexico as the Sierra Madre Oriental. The Colorado Rockies include 55 peaks that rise to 14,000 feet (4,270 meters) or more.

The Interior Plain is a lowland in the central part of the continent. It includes the Midwestern States of the United States and part of central Canada. The Rocky Mountains rise to the west, and the Appalachian Mountains to the east. The region has some hilly areas, such as the Ozark Mountains. The western part of the region is called the *Great Plains*.

The Interior Plain—Richard W. Hufnagle, Publix

The Canadian Shield stretches across half of Canada north and east of the Interior Plain. It also extends into northern Minnesota, Wisconsin, Michigan, and New York. The region is called a *shield* because of the old, hard rock that lies under the poor soil. Large forests cover much of the southern part of this region.

The Canadian Shield— George Hunter, Shostal

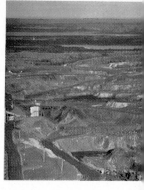

The Appalachian Mountains run parallel to the Atlantic coast. These low mountains extend about 1,500 miles (2,410 kilometers) from the Gulf of St. Lawrence into northern Alabama. The highest peak, Mount Mitchell in North Carolina, has an altitude of only 6,684 feet (2,037 meters).

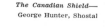

The Appalachian Mountains—Martin W. Swithinbank, P.I.P. Photos

The Coastal Plain is a lowland area along the Atlantic Ocean and the Gulf of Mexico. It extends from Cape Cod in Massachusetts, through the Yucatán Peninsula in Mexico, and into Central America.

The Coastal Plain—Joe E. Steinmetz, Publix

NORTH AMERICA
Physical Map

Distance scale

0   200   400   600   Miles

0   200 400 600 800   Kilometers

• City or town

---- National boundary

▬▬ Boundary of North America

ASIA

RUSSIA (U.S.S.R.)

East Siberian Sea

NORTH POLE

NORTHEAST FORELAND

Greenland Sea

JAN MAYEN I.

Norwegian Sea

ICELAND

Arctic Ocean

WRANGEL

C. MORRIS JESUP

POLAR ICE PACK

ELLESMERE ISLAND

GREENLAND

ICE CAP

Denmark Strait

Arctic Circle

Gulf of St. Anadyr

Chukchi Sea

SVERDRUP IS.

PARRY ISLANDS

NORTH MAGNETIC POLE

C. YORK

Baffin Bay

DISKO I.

Davis Strait

C. FAREWELL

Nome

ALASKA

BROOKS RANGE

Arctic Circle

MELVILLE I.

Viscount Melville Sound

BANKS I.

PRINCE OF WALES I.

BOOTHIA PEN.

Gulf of Boothia

BAFFIN ISLAND

Cumberland Sd.

C. CHIDLEY

Bering Sea

NUNIVAK I.

Yukon R.

Fairbanks

MT. McKINLEY 20,320 FT. (6,194 M) HIGHEST IN NORTH AMERICA

MT. KENNEDY 13,905 FT. (4,238 M)

MACKENZIE MTS.

Amundsen Gulf

VICTORIA ISLAND

Foxe Basin

Hudson Strait

Ungava Bay

Bristol Bay

KODIAK I.

Gulf of Alaska

ALEXANDER ARCHIPELAGO

Juneau

COAST

ROCKY

MOUNTAINS

Great Bear L.

Dubawnt L.

Great Slave L.

SOUTHAMPTON I.

Hudson Bay

QUEEN CHARLOTTE IS.

Hecate Str.

Peace River

Athabasca R.

L. Athabasca

Reindeer L.

Churchill R.

James Bay

L. Mistassini

Pacific

Ocean

VANCOUVER I.

Fraser R.

Calgary

Saskatchewan R.

Nelson R.

CANADA

Churchill R.

ANTICOSTI I.

Gulf of St. Lawrence

NEWFOUNDLAND

St. John's

PR. EDWARD

Vancouver

Seattle

Puget Sd.

MT. RAINIER 14,410 FT. (4,392 M)

CASCADE RANGE

Columbia R.

Regina

L. Winnipegosis

L. Manitoba

Winnipeg

Lake Winnipeg

Albany River

L. of the Woods

L. Superior

Quebec

Montreal

St. Lawrence River

Ottawa

Halifax

Portland

MT. SHASTA 14,162 FT. (4,317 M)

Great Salt L.

GREAT

Missouri River

Yellowstone River

Snake River

Minneapolis

Missouri R.

L. Huron

L. Michigan

Toronto

Detroit

L. Ontario

L. Erie

Boston

C. COD

New York

C. MENDOCINO

MT. WHITNEY 14,494 FT. (4,418 M)

SIERRA NEVADA

Salt Lake City

GREAT BASIN

BASIN

UNITED

MOUNTAINS

PLAINS

STATES

Denver

PIKES PK. 14,110 FT. (4,301 M)

Kansas City

Chicago

St. Louis

Pittsburgh

Ohio River

Washington D.C.

Philadelphia

Chesapeake Bay

C. HATTERAS

San Francisco

COAST RANGES

COLORADO PLATEAU

Colorado River

Red River

Arkansas River

OZARK PLATEAU

Mississippi River

APPALACHIAN MTS.

BERMUDA

Los Angeles

MOJAVE DESERT

Rio Grande

Dallas

Atlanta

Atlantic

Ocean

Gulf of California

SIERRA MADRE OCCIDENTAL

SIERRA MADRE ORIENTAL

Rio Grande

Houston

New Orleans

L. Okeechobee

Miami

BAHAMAS

Nassau

PTA. EUGENIA

PR.

MEXICO

Monterrey

Gulf of Mexico

Straits of Florida

Havana

CUBA

WEST INDIES

HAITI DOM. REP.

HISPANIOLA

C. SAN LUCAS

Tropic of Cancer

ISLE OF PINES

GREATER

ANTILLES

GREATER Windward Passage

JAMAICA

Guadalajara

Bay of Campeche

YUCATÁN PEN.

Caribbean Sea

IS. DE REVILLAGIGEDO

Mexico City

CITLALTÉPETL (ORIZABA) 18,701 FT. (5,700 M)

BELIZE

Gulf of Honduras

Maracaibo

VEN.

GUATEMALA

HONDURAS

NICARAGUA

Panama City

Magdalena R.

EL SALVADOR

L. Nicaragua

CANAL ZONE

PANAMA

Gulf of Panama

MTS.

COLOMBIA

CENTRAL AMERICA

COSTA RICA

ANDES

GALAPAGOS ISLANDS

COCOS

MALPELO

SOUTH AMERICA

Equator

Quito

ECUADOR

PERU

CM TERRAIN NORTH AMERICA COPYRIGHT BY RAND McNALLY & COMPANY MADE IN U.S.A.

363

Specially created for **World Book Encyclopedia** by Rand McNally and World Book editors

180°W   160°W   140°W   120°W   100°W   80°W   40°W

60°N   40°N   20°N   0°

NORTH AMERICA / *Natural Features*

Coastline. North America has a longer total coastline than any other continent. Including the many islands of North America, the total coastline is more than 96,000 miles (154,000 kilometers) long. The coastline of the mainland measures about 39,000 miles (62,800 kilometers). The Atlantic coastline is steep and rocky in the north, but south of Cape Cod it slopes gently to the sea. On the Pacific coast, high mountains rise abruptly from the sea. Great gulfs and bays jut into the mainland. The largest are the Gulf of Mexico in the south and Hudson Bay in the north.

Offshore Islands lie along North America's coasts. Greenland, the largest island in the world, is considered part of North America although it is a province of Denmark. Cuba, Hispaniola, and the other islands of the West Indies are part of North America. The Pacific coast islands, of which Vancouver is the largest, lie off southern Alaska and British Columbia. Other important North American islands include the Aleutians, Bermuda, Long Island, and Newfoundland.

Rivers. The crest of the Rocky Mountains divides North America into two great watersheds. West of this crest, called the *Great Divide*, water flows toward the Pacific Ocean. East of it, water flows toward the Arctic Ocean, the Atlantic Ocean, or the Gulf of Mexico. Together, the Mississippi and Missouri rivers form a river system of 3,710 miles (5,971 kilometers)—the longest on the continent. It drains much of the Interior Plain before emptying into the Gulf of Mexico. The Rio Grande separates Texas and Mexico.

The Mackenzie River, which forms part of the longest river system in Canada, flows from Great Slave Lake into the Arctic Ocean. The St. Lawrence River carries water from the Great Lakes to the Atlantic Ocean.

Great rushing streams that drain the western slopes of the Rocky Mountains include the Yukon, Fraser, and Columbia rivers. One of the western rivers, the Colorado, cuts through the Grand Canyon before it reaches the Gulf of California. Shorter, slower streams, such as the Hudson and Potomac rivers, drain the eastern slopes of the Appalachians.

Lakes. The Great Lakes are the most important group of lakes in the world. They make up part of North America's great inland waterway system. One of them, Lake Superior, is the world's largest body of fresh water. Four of the Great Lakes—Ontario, Erie, Huron, and Superior—lie between Canada and the United States. The fifth, Lake Michigan, lies entirely within the United States. Utah's Great Salt Lake, one of the natural wonders of North America, is from four to seven times saltier than the ocean. Great Bear Lake is the largest lake in Canada.

Waterfalls. North America's most famous waterfall is Niagara Falls, 167 feet (51 meters) high. It lies on the U.S.-Canadian border. More water passes over it than over any other falls in North America. Yosemite Falls in California, the highest waterfall in North America, drops 2,425 feet (739 meters).

Deserts. North America's major deserts are in the southwestern United States and northern Mexico. Like other west coast areas of similar latitude, this region receives scanty and irregular rainfall. The Chihuahuan, Sonoran, and Colorado deserts extend from Mexico into the United States. The largest North American desert region includes the area along the lower Colorado River, and the Mojave Desert and Death Valley of southeastern California. The land near the Arctic Ocean is a treeless area called the *tundra*.

NORTH AMERICA / *Climate*

North America is cold most of the year in the far north. The far south is always hot except in the highlands. The greater part of the continent, however, has a mixed climate, with warm summers and cold winters. In Chicago, for example, the average temperature in January is 26° F. (−3° C), and in July is 74° F. (23° C). The highest temperature ever recorded in North America was 134° F. (57° C) at Death Valley in 1913. The lowest temperature was −81° F. (−63° C) at Snag in the Yukon Territory in 1947.

Rainfall and snowfall vary from region to region. The western slopes of the Olympic Mountains in Washington get about 140 inches (356 centimeters) of rain a year. One of the driest areas lies between the Pacific coast ranges and the Rockies. Death Valley receives only about 1½ inches (3.8 centimeters) of rain a year.

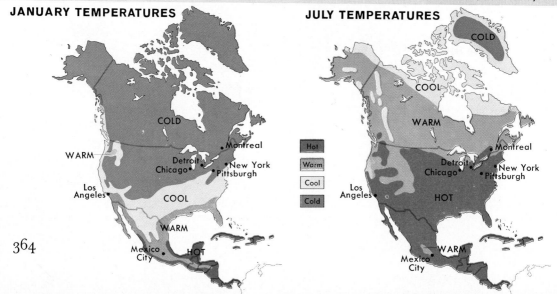

JANUARY TEMPERATURES

JULY TEMPERATURES

Hot
Warm
Cool
Cold

COLD

WARM

COLD

Montreal
Detroit · New York
Chicago · Pittsburgh

Los
Angeles ·

COOL

WARM

Mexico
City   HOT

COLD

COOL

WARM

Montreal
Detroit · New York
Chicago · Pittsburgh

Los
Angeles ·

HOT

Mexico
City

WARM

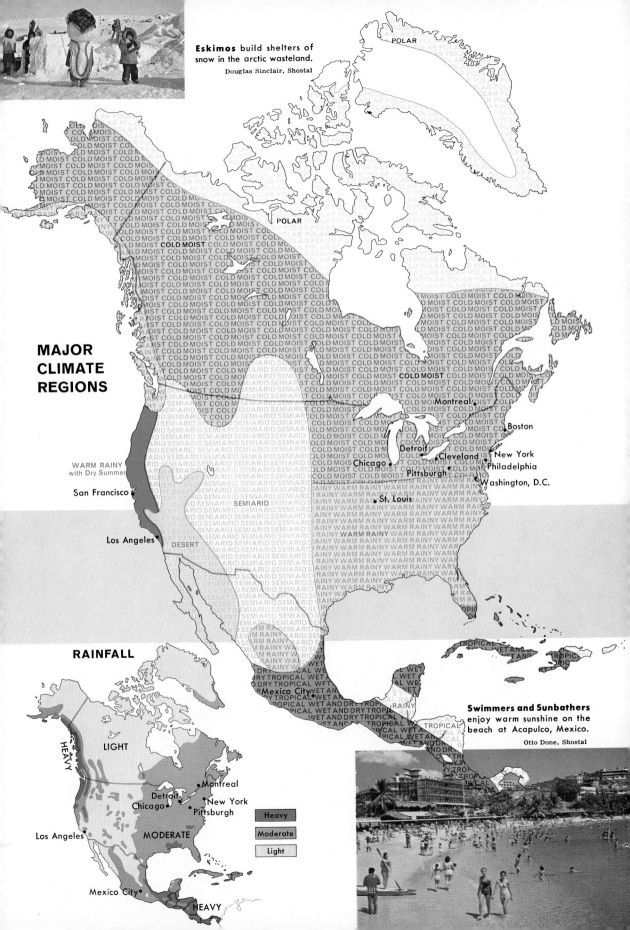

Eskimos build shelters of snow in the arctic wasteland.

Douglas Sinclair, Shostal

POLAR

MAJOR CLIMATE REGIONS

COLD MOIST

POLAR

COLD MOIST

WARM RAINY
with Dry Summer

San Francisco

SEMIARID

Los Angeles

DESERT

Montreal

Boston

Detroit

Cleveland

New York

Chicago

Philadelphia

Pittsburgh

Washington, D.C.

St. Louis

WARM RAINY

Mexico City

DRY TROPICAL

WET AND DRY TROPICAL

TROPICAL WET AND DRY

TROPICAL

RAINFALL

HEAVY

LIGHT

Montreal

Detroit

New York

Chicago

Pittsburgh

Los Angeles

MODERATE

| Heavy |
| Moderate |
| Light |

Mexico City

HEAVY

Swimmers and Sunbathers enjoy warm sunshine on the beach at Acapulco, Mexico.

Otto Done, Shostal

NORTH AMERICA /*Animals*

North America's wildlife varies from the polar north to the tropical south. Arctic foxes, caribou, fur seals, musk oxen, polar bears, and walruses live in the far north. Alligators, anteaters, armadillos, jaguars, monkeys, and colorful birds such as parrots are found in Central America. Eagles, elk, grizzly bears, and moose inhabit the forested western mountains. The wooded areas of the central and eastern regions have beavers, black bears, deer, muskrats, and porcupines. Smaller animals, such as pigeons, rabbits, and squirrels, live in and around populated regions and farm areas.

As more and more people settled the continent, many kinds of animals decreased in number or became extinct. Millions of buffalo once roamed the plains. Today, only a few scattered herds of buffalo live in game preserves. The passenger pigeon, native to North America, has disappeared entirely. Game laws and refuge areas protect wildlife today.

Polar Bears make their homes in the ice and snow of the arctic region of North America.

Musk Ox

Fur Seal

Bald Eagle

Kodiak Bear

Whooping Crane

Rocky Mountain Goat

Grizzly Bear

Timber Wolf

Canada Goose

Moose

Caribou

Salmon

Beaver

Black Bear

Porcupine

Mule Deer

Trumpeter Swan

Pronghorn

Skunk

Mountain Lion

Bighorn

Wood Duck

Snapping Turtle

Shad

Buffalo

Coyote

Prairie Chicken

White-Tailed Deer

California Sea Lion

Jack Rabbit   Sidewinder

Raccoon

Diamondback Rattlesnake

Prairie Dog

Gila Monster

Alligator

Horned Toad

Wild Turkey

Solenodon

White-Tailed Deer live in the forests of southern Canada and the United States.

Peccary

Quetzal

Illustrated by Margaret Estey
for WORLD BOOK

364b

NORTH AMERICA / *Plant Life*

The plant life of North America ranges from desert cactus to the largest trees in the world, the redwoods and sequoias of California. On the tundra, only moss, lichens, and some flowering plants can grow.

Trees and grass once covered most of North America. But as people settled the continent, they turned large areas of prairie and forest into farmland. Nevertheless, forests and grasslands are still two important natural resources. The grasslands of the Great Plains provide pasture for large herds of sheep and cattle. Evergreen forests of fir, spruce, and pine trees cover much of Canada and the western mountains of the United States. Large areas of hardwood and softwood trees grow in the forests that extend from Maine to Minnesota. The wooded regions of the eastern coastal plain produce several kinds of oak and pine. Forests near the Gulf of Mexico and the Caribbean Sea have palm, mahogany, cypress, mangrove, and other tropical trees.

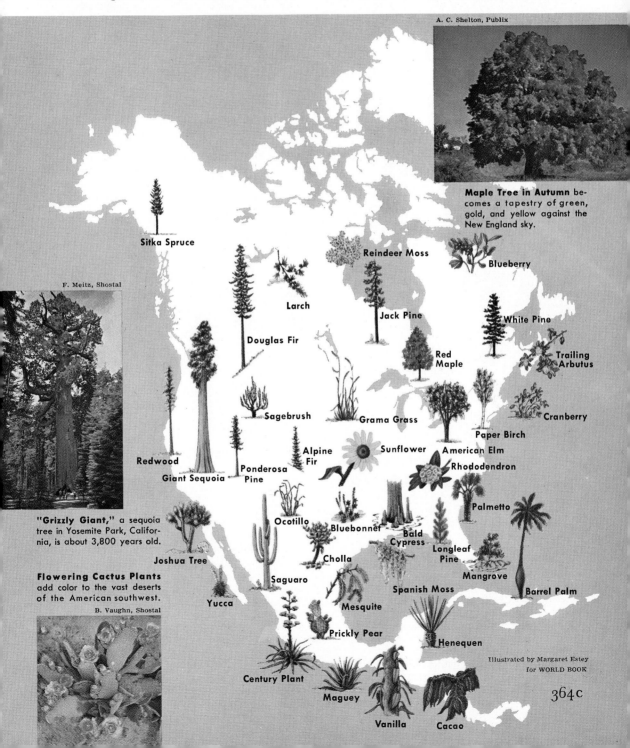

A. C. Shelton, Publix

Maple Tree in Autumn becomes a tapestry of green, gold, and yellow against the New England sky.

F. Meitz, Shostal

"Grizzly Giant," a sequoia tree in Yosemite Park, California, is about 3,800 years old.

Flowering Cactus Plants add color to the vast deserts of the American southwest.

B. Vaughn, Shostal

Sitka Spruce

Larch

Reindeer Moss

Blueberry

Jack Pine

White Pine

Douglas Fir

Red Maple

Trailing Arbutus

Sagebrush

Grama Grass

Cranberry

Paper Birch

Redwood

Alpine Fir

Sunflower

American Elm

Giant Sequoia

Ponderosa Pine

Rhododendron

Joshua Tree

Ocotillo

Bluebonnet

Bald Cypress

Palmetto

Cholla

Longleaf Pine

Mangrove

Saguaro

Spanish Moss

Barrel Palm

Yucca

Mesquite

Prickly Pear

Henequen

Century Plant

Illustrated by Margaret Estey for WORLD BOOK

Maguey

Vanilla

Cacao

364c

NORTH AMERICA / *Manufacturing and Mining*

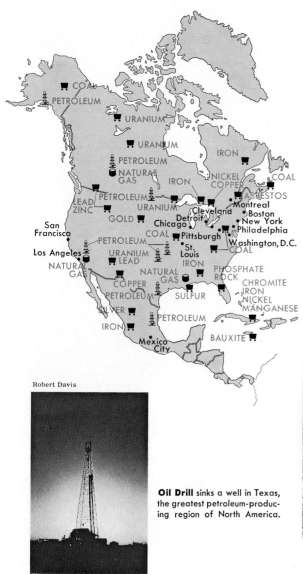

North America has large supplies of important minerals. The hills and plains contain some of the world's richest deposits of coal, gold, iron ore, nickel, petroleum, and other minerals. The United States produces about one-seventh of the world's petroleum and about a sixth of its coal. Canada is the leading producer of asbestos and nickel. Canada and the United States together mine about a third of the copper and about a sixth of the iron ore produced in the world. These two countries are also leading producers of gold and natural gas. Mexico is a major source of lead, silver, and zinc. Jamaica is one of the world's largest producers of bauxite, the ore used to make aluminum.

Many of the large cities of the United States and Canada are important industrial centers. As a result, both these countries rank among the leading manufacturing nations of the world. Their industrial greatness is based on their rich natural resources, their skilled workers, and their use of highly developed machinery, automation, and mass production.

The Latin-American countries of North America must import many of their manufactured goods. Most manufacturing is still done by hand, and cannot supply even all local needs. Modern factories are being established in some cities, especially in Mexico.

Robert Davis

Oil Drill sinks a well in Texas, the greatest petroleum-producing region of North America.

Yankee Atomic Power Plant, opened in 1960 at Rowe, Mass., produces 150,000 kilowatts of electricity for 10 privately owned power companies serving the New England area of the United States.

NORTH AMERICA / *Agriculture*

The United States and Canada have some of the largest and most fertile agricultural areas in the world. Their farms not only produce enough food for all their people, but also supply large quantities for export. Canada, for example, sends about three-fourths of its wheat to other parts of the world. Through the use of machinery and scientific methods of farming, the United States and Canada constantly increase the output of their land. Farmers in the United States grew about 26 bushels of corn per acre (64 bushels per hectare) in 1940. The yield had tripled by the late 1960's, and continues to increase.

The Latin-American countries of North America produce barely enough food for their own people. Large areas are either too dry or too wet for farming. Where farming is possible, primitive agricultural methods, such as the use of hand tools for tilling the soil, often prevent a large output. In some of these countries, one or two crops dominate the economy. Cuba, for example, depends largely on sugar for its foreign trade. Most Central American countries specialize in growing bananas in the lowlands and coffee in the highlands. In such regions, a poor growing season or low prices result in widespread hardship for the people.

Forests cover about a third of North America. This vast natural resource supplies more than a fourth of the world's lumber and half its pulpwood, from which paper is made. CLARENCE W. OLMSTEAD

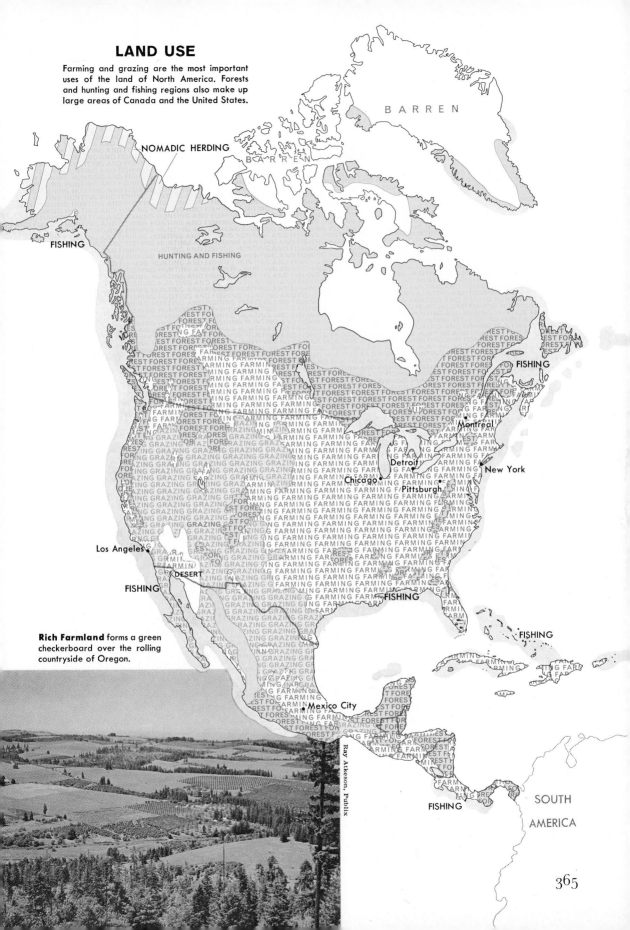

LAND USE

Farming and grazing are the most important uses of the land of North America. Forests and hunting and fishing regions also make up large areas of Canada and the United States.

BARREN

NOMADIC HERDING

BARREN

FISHING

HUNTING AND FISHING

FISHING

FOREST FOREST FOREST FOR
OREST FOREST FOREST FOREST FO
REST FOREST FOREST FOREST FOR
EST FOREST FARMING FARMING FAR
ST FOREST FARMING FARMING FA
OREST FARMING FARMING FARMING
FOREST FARMING FARMING FARMIN
FARMING FARMING FARMIN

Montreal

Detroit

FISHING

GRAZING GRAZING GRAZ
GRAZING GRAZING GRAZIN
GRAZING GRAZING GRAZING
GRAZING GRAZING GRAZING
GRAZING GRAZING GRAZING
GRAZING GRAZING GRAZING

Chicago

New York

Pittsburgh

Los Angeles

DESERT

FISHING

Rich Farmland forms a green checkerboard over the rolling countryside of Oregon.

FISHING

FISHING

FARMING FARMING FARMING FARMING FARMIN
FARMING FARMING FARMING FARMING FARMING
FARMING FARMING FARMING FARMING FARMIN
G FARMING FARMING FARMING FARMING FAR
G FARMING FARMING FARMING FARMING F
G FARMING FARMING FARMING FARMING FI

Mexico City

Ray Atkeson, Publix

FISHING

SOUTH
AMERICA

365

Related Articles in WORLD BOOK include:

COUNTRIES, COLONIES, AND TERRITORIES

Bahamas	Martinique
Belize	Mexico
Bermuda	Netherlands Antilles
Canada	Nicaragua
Costa Rica	Panama
Cuba	Panama Canal Zone
Dominican Republic	Puerto Rico
El Salvador	Saint Pierre and Miquelon
Greenland	Trinidad and Tobago
Guadeloupe	United States
Guatemala	Virgin Islands
Haiti	Virgin Islands, British
Honduras	West Indies (British)
Jamaica	

CITIES

See the following articles on the 15 largest cities of North America:

Baltimore	Havana	Milwaukee
Chicago	Houston	Montreal
Cleveland	Indianapolis	New York City
Dallas	Los Angeles	Philadelphia
Detroit	Mexico City	Washington, D.C.

NATURAL FEATURES

See the list of Related Articles with the articles on DESERT; INLAND WATERWAY; ISLAND; LAKE; MOUNTAIN; RIVER; WATERFALL; WATERWAY. See also the following articles on some of the most important physical features of North America:

Appalachian Mountains	Mississippi River
Arkansas River	Missouri River
Bridalveil Fall	Multnomah Falls
Canadian Shield	Nelson River
Coast Range	Newfoundland
Colorado River	Niagara Falls and
Columbia River	Niagara River
Death Valley	Orizaba
Fairy Falls	Parícutin
Grand Canyon National	Piedmont Region
Park	Popocatepetl
Great Basin	Ribbon Falls
Great Bear Lake	Rio Grande
Great Divide	Rocky Mountains
Great Lakes	Saint Lawrence River
Great Plains	Sierra Madre
Great Salt Lake	Sierra Nevada
Great Slave Lake	Takakkaw Falls
Greenland	West Indies
Ixtacihuatl	Yosemite Falls
Lake Nicaragua	Yosemite National Park
Lake Winnipeg	Yukon River
Mackenzie River	

COASTAL WATERS

Arctic Ocean	Gulf of California
Atlantic Ocean	Gulf of Mexico
Baffin Bay	Gulf of Saint Lawrence
Bay of Fundy	Hudson Bay
Bering Sea	James Bay
Caribbean Sea	Juan de Fuca, Strait of
Chesapeake Bay	Long Island Sound
Delaware Bay	Pacific Ocean
Florida, Straits of	Puget Sound

PEOPLE

Black Americans	Metropolitan Area
City	Mexican Americans
Clothing	Population
Eskimo	Shelter (Shelter
Food	Around the World)
Indian, American	World

HISTORY

See the History section of the articles on the countries, states, and provinces of North America. See also the following articles:

Canada, History of	Latin America (History)
Central America (History)	United States,
Exploration and Discovery	History of the

Outline

I. People
   A. Language and Education
   B. Religion
   C. Transportation and Communication

II. Land Regions
   A. The Pacific Coastland
   B. The Intermountain Region
   C. The Rocky Mountains
   D. The Interior Plain
   E. The Canadian Shield
   F. The Appalachian Mountains
   G. The Coastal Plain

III. Natural Features
   A. Coastline
   B. Offshore Islands
   C. Rivers
   D. Lakes
   E. Waterfalls
   F. Deserts

IV. Climate

V. Animals

VI. Plant Life

VII. Manufacturing and Mining

VIII. Agriculture

Questions

What mountain ranges rise to the east and west of the Interior Plain?

What is the largest island in the world?

What is North America's highest mountain?

What country is the world's leading producer of bauxite?

What is the largest body of fresh water in the world?

Which land region includes both the Grand Canyon and Death Valley?

What is the Great Divide?

What is North America's highest waterfall?

Which of the Great Lakes lies entirely within the United States?

Which countries form Anglo-America?

NORTH AMERICAN AIR DEFENSE COMMAND. See NATIONAL DEFENSE (Air Defense); AIR FORCE, UNITED STATES (Why We Have an Air Force).

NORTH AMERICAN NEWSPAPER ALLIANCE (NANA) is a worldwide independent news agency. It specializes in exclusive news coverage and in articles by famous persons. NANA provides its subscribing newspapers with important feature stories. The agency is noted for its memoirs of well-known political leaders. NANA was founded as a cooperative news alliance in 1922. Headquarters are at 229 West 43d Street, New York, N.Y. 10036.

NORTH ATLANTIC CURRENT is the continuation of the Gulf Stream that is carried northeastward by winds. It sweeps along the northwest coast of Europe, past the British Isles and Norway, and into the Arctic Ocean.

See also GULF STREAM (map); OCEAN (How the Ocean Moves).

NORTH ATLANTIC TREATY ORGANIZATION (NATO) provides unified military leadership for the common defense of 15 Western nations. NATO was established in 1950 by the nations allied by the North

United Press Int.

The North Atlantic Council, above, is the highest authority in NATO. It plans for the collective defense of North America and Western Europe. It consists of the representatives of the member countries. The NATO secretary general serves as council chairman. The presidency of the council rotates annually.

Atlantic Treaty, which provided for their collective defense against a possible attack by Russia or any other aggressor. Article 5 of the treaty provides that an armed attack against one or more member nations in Europe or North America shall be considered an attack against all members.

Twelve nations signed the North Atlantic Treaty on April 4, 1949, in Washington, D.C. They were Belgium, Canada, Denmark, France, Great Britain, Iceland, Italy, Luxembourg, The Netherlands, Norway, Portugal, and the United States. Greece and Turkey signed the treaty in October, 1951, and West Germany signed it in October, 1954.

Organization. NATO's military forces are organized into three main commands: the Atlantic Command, Channel Command, and Allied Command Europe. Most of NATO's forces are in Allied Command Europe, which is directed by the Supreme Allied Commander in Europe (SACEUR). The Military Committee of NATO, consisting of the chiefs of staff of the member nations, establishes military policy to be carried out by SACEUR. The committee is responsible to the North Atlantic Council, which consists of the heads of the member nations or their representatives. All decisions of the council must be unanimous.

NATO members have never been willing to maintain an army large enough to stand off the Russian Army. As a result, in order to prevent a Soviet attack, the United States has said it will use the nuclear weapons of its Strategic Air Command (SAC) against Russia if Russia starts a war in Europe. NATO's dependence on American nuclear weapons has made the United States the dominant member, and the supreme allied commander in Europe has always been an American general.

History. In 1949, the nations of Western Europe were weak and could not easily defend themselves against attack. The Communist seizure of power in Czechoslovakia in February, 1948, and the Russian blockade of Berlin in June, 1948, raised fears that Russia might use armed force to gain control of Western Europe.

By signing the treaty, the United States for the first time in its history joined a peacetime alliance that committed it to fight in Europe. United States leaders felt that the U.S. would have to fight against Russian seizure of Western Europe because this would add greatly to the power of Russia to attack the U.S. The United States hoped that Russia would not attack Western Europe if it knew it would have to fight the United States, too. At the same time, the United States also acted to help the nations of Western Europe to defend themselves by providing them with military weapons and economic aid as part of the Marshall Plan. The Communist attack on South Korea in June, 1950, increased fears of a Russian attack on Western Europe, and in September, 1950, the members of the alliance formed NATO.

Most alliances owe their unity to the fear of a common enemy. When this fear decreases, differences among the members can develop. In the 1960's, NATO members became less worried about the possibility of a Russian attack. At the same time, the European members began to wonder if the United States would really start a nuclear war in defense of Western Europe, in view of Russia's growing nuclear power. European members of NATO resented the fact that NATO had no control over SAC, the main instrument of European defense. They also disliked the fact that NATO could not influence U.S. foreign policy in other parts of the world, even though these policies might lead to a war in Europe. For their part, Americans resented the fact that Europeans did not furnish more ground forces, and Britain and France instead spent their money developing nuclear weapons.

These differences contributed to France's decision in 1966 to expel NATO forces and to withdraw French forces from NATO command. In 1967, the Supreme Headquarters Allied Powers Europe (SHAPE) moved from Paris to Casteau, near Brussels, Belgium.

NATO was further weakened in 1974. Greece withdrew its forces from NATO command because Britain and the United States did not prevent Turkey's invasion of Cyprus. But the West European nations and the United States remain interested in common defense. France and Greece are still members of the North Atlantic alliance. Greece permits U.S. forces to use Greek bases, and France still wants U.S. protection. As long as U.S. forces remain in West Germany as part of NATO, France has that protection.   WARNER R. SCHILLING

See also FLAG (color picture: Flags of World Organizations); WARSAW PACT.

NORTH BERGEN, N.J. (pop. 47,751), is one of the largest townships in the state. It lies in Hudson County, just north of Jersey City (see NEW JERSEY [political map]). Its factories make batteries, clothing, ink, machinery, paper boxes, and electric, electronic, and metal products. The township was founded in 1660, and was incorporated in 1843. North Bergen has a commission form of government.   RICHARD P. McCORMICK

NORTH BORNEO. See SABAH.

NORTH CAPE is a rocky point of land on the small island of Magerøy, which lies at the very northernmost tip of Norway on the shore of the Arctic Ocean. The cape has many cliffs and rocks which rise to 1,000 feet (300 meters) above the sea. Many tourists visit North Cape during the summer to see the *midnight sun.*

Cape Hatteras—Graveyard of the Atlantic

NORTH CAROLINA

THE TAR HEEL STATE

NORTH CAROLINA is the leading tobacco state of the United States. It leads the nation in tobacco farming and in the manufacture of tobacco products. North Carolinians grow tobacco, cure it, transport it, market it, and manufacture it. North Carolina also leads the nation in two other important areas. It manufactures more cloth and makes more wooden furniture than any other state. Most homes in the United States have wooden furniture that was made in North Carolina.

North Carolina is a southern state with a long coastline on the Atlantic Ocean. Islands, reefs, and sand bars make its shores some of the most treacherous in the world. Many ships have been wrecked at Cape Hatteras by the rough seas and difficult currents. Cape Hatteras is called the *Graveyard of the Atlantic*.

The state stretches westward from the coast across swamps and fertile farms. The land rises through lovely sand hills into industrial cities and towns. Tobacco farms, with neat rows of tobacco plants, are scattered throughout the state. The tobacco fields extend from the lowlands near the eastern coast high into the mountains at the western edge of the state. Mount Mitchell, more than $1\frac{1}{4}$ miles (2 kilometers) above sea level, is the highest peak in the eastern United States.

Manufacturing earns more money and provides more jobs than any other industry in North Carolina. But North Carolina's manufacturing depends on other industries and on the state's natural resources. Cotton and tobacco farms, on rich soils, provide the textile and tobacco industries with necessary raw materials. North Carolina's thick forests and its huge forest industry furnish wood for the furniture plants.

In 1585 and 1587, the first groups of English settlers in America built colonies on Roanoke Island off the

Thurston Hatcher, Shostal

North Carolina Burley Tobacco Field

Hallinan, FPG

The Blue Ridge Mountains near Waynesville

NORTH CAROLINA

———— **FACTS IN BRIEF** ————

Capital: Raleigh.

Government: *Congress*—U.S. senators, 2; U.S. representatives, 11. *Electoral Votes*—13. *State Legislature*—senators, 50; representatives, 120. *Counties*—100.

Area: 52,586 sq. mi. (136,197 km²), including 3,788 sq. mi. (9,811 km²) of inland water; 28th in size among the states. *Greatest Distances*—east-west, 503 mi. (810 km); north-south, 187 mi. (301 km). *Coastline*—301 mi. (484 km).

Elevation: *Highest*—Mount Mitchell in Yancey County, 6,684 ft. (2,037 m) above sea level. *Lowest*—sea level, along the Atlantic coast.

Population: *Estimated 1975 Population*—5,451,000. *1970 Census*—5,082,059; 12th among the states; distribution, 55 per cent rural, 45 per cent urban; density, 97 persons per sq. mi. (37 per km²).

Chief Products: *Agriculture*—beef cattle, broilers, corn, dairy products, eggs, hogs, soybeans, tobacco, turkeys. *Fishing Industry*—crabs, flounder, menhaden, shrimps. *Manufacturing*—chemicals; clothing; electrical machinery; fabricated metal products; food products; furniture and fixtures; nonelectrical machinery; textiles and related products; tobacco products. *Mining*—clays, feldspar, lithium, mica, phosphate, sand and gravel, stone.

Statehood: Nov. 21, 1789, the 12th state.

State Motto: *Esse quam videri* (To be, rather than to seem).

State Song: "The Old North State." Words by William Gaston; musical arrangement by Mrs. E. E. Randolph.

North Carolina coast. The first group returned to England. The later group vanished from the island, leaving behind only a mystery that has puzzled the ages. This group has been named the *Lost Colony*. Virginia Dare, the first child born to English parents in America, was a member of the Lost Colony. During colonial days, groups in North Carolina such as the *Sons of Liberty* defied English taxes and English rule. After the Revolutionary War began, North Carolina was the first colony to instruct its delegates at the Continental Congress to vote for independence.

Before the outbreak of the Civil War, North Carolina tried to preserve the Union. But after North Carolina left the Union, it did its best to help the Confederate cause. More than 10 battles were fought on North Carolina soil. During one fierce battle, some Confederate troops retreated, leaving North Carolina forces to fight alone. The North Carolinians supposedly threatened to put tar on the heels of the other troops so they would "stick better in the next fight." Since then, North Carolina has been called the *Tar Heel State*.

Raleigh is North Carolina's capital, and Charlotte is its largest city. For North Carolina's relationship to other states in its region, see SOUTHERN STATES.

North Carolina (blue) ranks 28th in size among all the states, and 4th in size among the Southern States (gray).

The contributors of this article are Robert Eli Cramer, Chairman and Professor in the Department of Geography at East Carolina University; Blackwell Pierce Robinson, Associate Professor of History and Political Science at the University of North Carolina at Greensboro; and Sam Ragan, Editor and Publisher of The Pilot *in Southern Pines.*

Constitution. North Carolina has had two Constitutions, the first adopted in 1776 and the present one approved in 1868. In 1970, the voters approved a major revision of the Constitution of 1868.

Amendments to the Constitution can be proposed in the state legislature or by a constitutional convention. An amendment proposed in the legislature must be approved by three-fifths of both houses. Then it must be approved by a majority of the voters in a general election. A constitutional convention must be approved by two-thirds of both houses, and by the voters, before it can meet to propose and adopt amendments.

Executive. North Carolina's governor and lieutenant governor serve four-year terms. They cannot serve two terms in a row. The governor receives a yearly salary of $38,500. For a list of North Carolina's governors, see the *History* section of this article.

The governor can appoint a number of important state officials, including the heads of nine executive departments. The voters elect eight other top administrative officers to four-year terms. They are the attorney general, auditor, secretary of state, superintendent of public instruction, treasurer, and commissioners of agriculture, labor, and insurance. These officials and the lieutenant governor make up the council of state, an advisory council to the governor. North Carolina is the only state in which the governor cannot veto a bill passed by the legislature.

Legislature, called the *general assembly*, consists of a 50-member senate and a 120-member house of representatives. Senators are elected from 27 senatorial districts. Representatives are elected from 45 representative districts. Members of both houses serve two-year terms from the day they are elected. The lieutenant governor is president of the senate. The house of representatives elects a speaker to preside over it. The legislature meets every year. Regular sessions of the legislature begin on the Wednesday after the second Monday in January.

In 1965, a federal court ordered North Carolina to redraw its legislative districts to provide equal representation. The general assembly reapportioned the districts in 1966. The legislative districts were reapportioned again in 1971.

Courts. North Carolina's court system consists of an appellate division, a superior court division, and a district court division.

The appellate division consists of the supreme court, the state's highest court; and the court of appeals, an intermediate appellate court. The appellate courts hear cases appealed from lower courts. The supreme court has a chief justice and six associate justices, and the court of appeals has nine judges.

The superior and district court divisions consist of 30 judicial districts. Each of these 30 districts is served by one or more superior court judges who hear civil and criminal trials. Each district also has two or more district court judges who handle minor civil and criminal cases.

Supreme court justices and superior court judges are elected to eight-year terms. Judges on the court of appeals are elected to six-year terms and district court judges to four-year terms. If any justice or judge leaves office, the governor appoints a successor.

Local Government. North Carolina has 100 counties. Each county is governed by a board of county commissioners. The boards consist of three to seven members, elected to two- or four-year terms, depending on the county. They meet monthly to supervise county affairs, and to perform such duties as appropriating funds and levying taxes. County officials include the sheriff, register of deeds, superior court clerk, treasurer, coroner, accountant, attorney, and tax officials.

State laws permit cities and towns to have *home rule* (self-government) to the extent that they can amend existing charters or adopt new ones. But control must remain in the hands of the general assembly. North Carolina has about 465 incorporated cities and towns.

The Legislative Building, *below,* is often called the *State House.* It was first used in 1963. The state senate and house of representatives meet there. It was the first building constructed by a state for the exclusive use of the legislature.

North Carolina Travel and Promotion Division

The Governor's Mansion, *right,* stands several blocks east of the Capitol. The red brick and sandstone building, completed in 1889, has many gables and porches. It is considered a classic example of the Victorian style of architecture.

North Carolina Travel and Promotion Division

The State Seal

Symbols of North Carolina. On the seal, the standing figure represents *Liberty* and holds a scroll inscribed "Constitution." The seated figure symbolizes *Plenty.* The date "May 20, 1775" is that of the supposed Mecklenburg Declaration of Independence. The seal was adopted in 1971. The state flag, adopted in 1885, bears the dates of the two North Carolina declarations of independence that were made before the national Declaration.

The State Flag

An area may incorporate by petitioning the general assembly. Most of the larger cities of North Carolina have the council-manager form of government. Other forms of municipal government are mayor-council and commission.

Taxation. Corporate and individual income taxes provide about 35 per cent of the state government's income. Sales and gross receipts taxes bring in about 25 per cent. Other sources of revenue include license fees and vehicle registrations. More than 20 per cent of the state government's income comes from federal grants and other U.S. government programs.

Politics. The Democratic Party dominates the state's politics. But the Republican Party is gaining strength. Since the Reconstruction period (1865-1877), Republican presidential candidates have won the state's electoral votes only three times—Herbert Hoover in 1928 and Richard M. Nixon in 1968 and 1972. For North Carolina's voting record in presidential elections, see ELECTORAL COLLEGE (table). In 1972, James E. Holshouser, Jr., became the first Republican to be elected governor of North Carolina since 1896. Also in 1972, Jesse A. Helms of Raleigh became the first Republican elected to the U.S. Senate from the state since 1896.

The Capitol Building is in Raleigh. The city became the capital in 1791, but was not used until 1794. New Bern was the capital from 1771 to 1776. There was no fixed capital, 1776 to 1794.

North Carolina Travel and Promotion Division

The State Flower
Flowering Dogwood

The State Bird
Cardinal

The State Tree
Pine

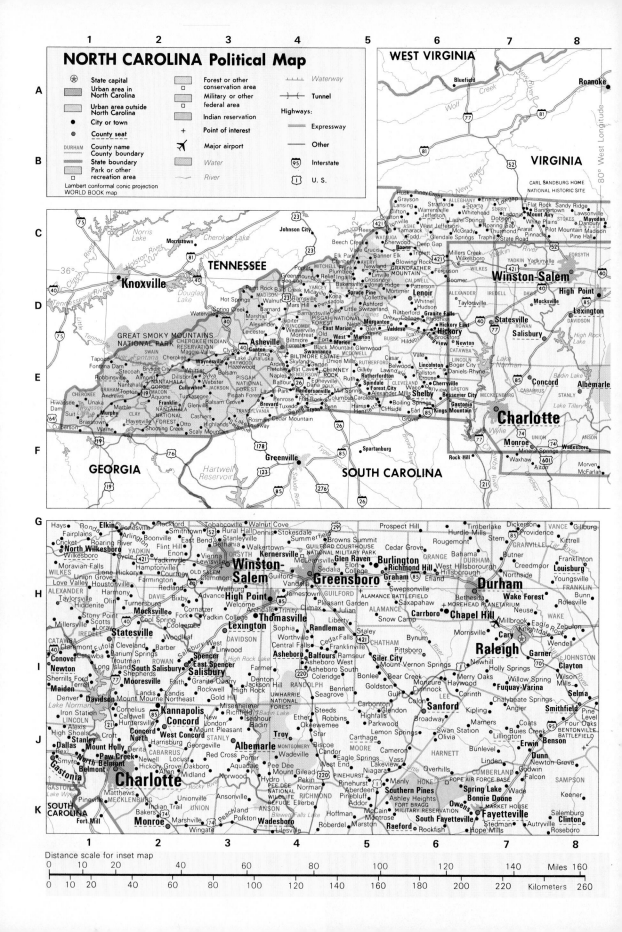

NORTH CAROLINA Political Map

Lambert conformal conic projection
WORLD BOOK map

Distance scale for inset map

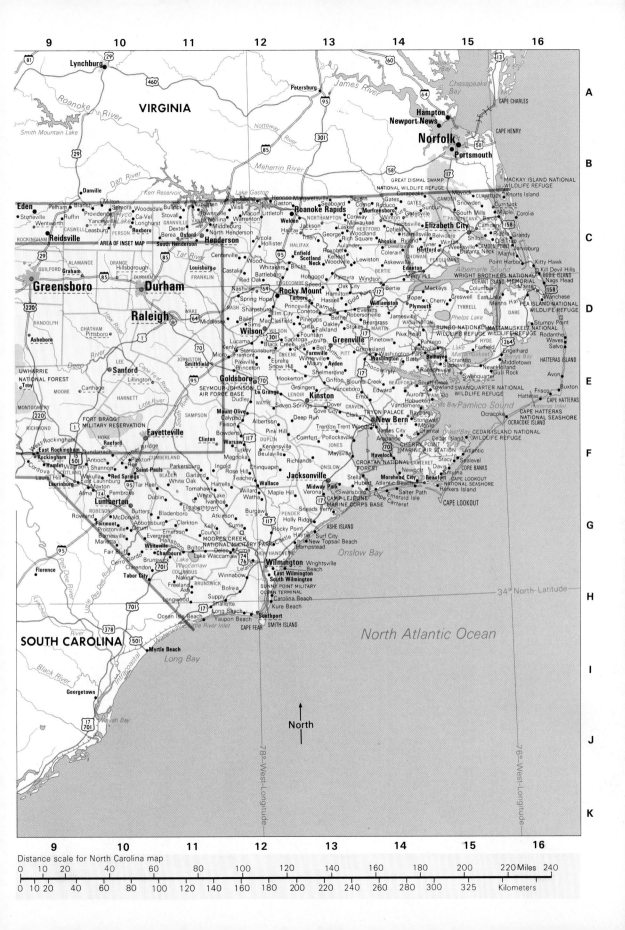

Population

5,451,000 Estimate..1975
5,082,059 ..Census..1970
4,556,155 ....“....1960
4,061,929 ....“....1950
3,571,623 ....“....1940
3,170,276 ....“....1930
2,559,123 ....“....1920
2,206,287 ....“....1910
1,893,810 ....“....1900
1,617,949 ....“....1890
1,399,750 ....“....1880
1,071,361 ....“....1870
992,622 ....“....1860
869,039 ....“....1850
753,419 ....“....1840
737,987 ....“....1830
638,829 ....“....1820
555,500 ....“....1810
478,103 ....“....1800
393,751 ....“....1790

Metropolitan Areas

Asheville 161,059
Burlington 96,362
Charlotte-Gastonia 557,785
Fayetteville 212,042
Greensboro-Winston-Salem-High Point 724,129
Norfolk-Virginia Beach-Portsmouth (Va.) ....732,600 (725,624 in Va.; 6,976 in N.C.)
Raleigh-Durham 419,394
Wilmington 107,219

Counties

Alamance ..96,362..C 9
Alexander .19,466..D 6
Alleghany ..8,134..B 6
Anson .....23,488..F 8
Ashe ......19,571..C 6
Avery .....12,655..C 5
Beaufort ...35,980..E 14
Bertie .....20,528..C 14
Bladen ....26,477..F 11
Brunswick .24,223..H 11
Buncombe 145,056..D 4
Burke ....60,364..D 5
Cabarrus ..74,629..E 7
Caldwell ...56,699..D 6
Camden ....5,453..B 15
Carteret ...31,603..F 14
Caswell ...19,055..C 9
Catawba ...90,873..E 6
Chatham ...29,554..D 9
Cherokee ..16,330..E 1
Chowan ....10,764..C 14
Clay ....5,180..E 2
Cleveland ..72,556..E 5
Columbus ..46,937..H 11
Craven ....62,554..E 13
Cumberland ....212,042..F 10
Currituck ...6,976..B 15
Dare ....6,995..D 16
Davidson ..95,627..D 8
Davie ......18,855..D 7
Duplin .....38,015..F 12
Durham ..132,681..D 10
Edgecombe 52,341..D 12
Forsyth ...215,118..C 8
Franklin ..26,820..D 11
Gaston ...148,415..E 6
Gates ....8,524..B 14
Graham .....6,562..E 1
Granville ..32,762..C 11
Greene .....14,967..E 12
Guilford ..288,645..C 9
Halifax ...53,884..C 12
Harnett ...49,667..E 10
Haywood ..41,710..E 3
Henderson .42,804..E 4
Hertford ...23,529..C 13
Hoke ......16,436..F 10
Hyde ....5,571..D 15
Iredell ....72,197..D 7
Jackson ....21,593..E 3
Johnston ...61,737..E 11
Jones ....9,779..F 13
Lee ....30,467..E 10
Lenoir .....55,204..E 12
Lincoln ....32,682..E 6
Macon .....15,788..E 2
Madison ...16,003..D 3
Martin ....24,730..D 14
McDowell ..30,648..E 5
Mecklenburg ....354,656..E 7
Mitchell ...13,447..C 4
Montgomery 19,267..E 9
Moore .....39,048..E 9
Nash ......59,122..D 12
New Hanover .82,996..G 12
Northampton ..24,009..C 13
Onslow ...103,126..F 13
Orange ....57,707..C 10
Pamlico ....9,467..E 14
Pasquotank 26,824..C 15
Pender ....18,149..G 12
Perquimans .8,351..C 15
Person .....25,914..C 10
Pitt ....73,900..D 13
Polk ....11,735..E 4
Randolph ..76,358..D 9
Richmond ..39,889..F 9
Robeson ...84,842..G 10
Rockingham 72,402..C 9
Rowan .....90,035..D 7
Rutherford 47,337..E 5
Sampson ..44,954..E 11
Scotland ...26,929..F 9
Stanly .....42,822..E 8
Stokes .....23,782..C 8
Surry .....51,415..C 7
Swain ......8,835..E 2
Transylvania 19,713..E 3
Tyrrell ......3,806..D 15
Union .....54,714..F 7
Vance .....32,691..C 11
Wake ....229,006..D 11
Warren ....15,810..B 11
Washington 14,038..D 14
Watauga ...23,404..C 5
Wayne .....85,408..E 12
Wilkes .....49,524..C 6
Wilson .....57,486..D 12
Yadkin .....24,599..C 7
Yancey ....12,629..D 4

Cities, Towns, and Villages

Abbottsburg ....G 11
Aberdeen ...1,592..K 5
Acme ....459..G 12
Addor ....K 5
Advance ......206..H 3
Ahoskie .....5,105..C 14
Albemarle .11,126.°E 8
Albertson ....F 12
Alexander ....D 4
Alexander Mills ....988..E 5
Alexis ....J 1
Allen ....J 2
Alliance* .....577..E 14
Alma ....G 10
Almond ....E 2
Andrews ....1,384..E 1
Angier ......1,431..J 7
Ansonville ....694..K 3
Antioch ....F 10
Apex* ......2,192..D 10
Aquadale ....J 3
Aquone ....E 2
Arapahoe .....212..F 14
Ararat ....C 7
Archdale ....4,844..H 4
Arcola ....C 12
Arden ....E 4
Arlington .....711..G 1
Asheboro ..10,797.°D 9
Asheboro South ....1,998..I 4
Asheboro West ......1,158..I 4
Asheville ...57,681.°E 4
Ashford ....D 5
Ashley Heights ....K 5
Askewville ....247..C 14
Atkinson ......325..G 12
Atlantic ....F 15
Atlantic Beach 300..F 14
Aulander .....947..C 13
Aurora ....620..E 14
Autryville ....213..K 7
Avon ....E 16
Avondale, see Henrietta [-Avondale]
Ayden ......3,450..E 13
Badin ......1,626..J 3
Bahama ....G 7
Bailey ....724..D 12
Bakers ....K 2
Bakersville ...409.°D 5
Bald Creek ....D 4
Balfour [-Druid Hills] .....2,014..E 4
Balfours ....4,836..I 4
Balsam ....E 3
Balsam Grove ....E 3
Banner Elk ...754..C 5
Bannertown .1,138..C 7
Barber ....I 2
Barco ....C 15
Barium Springs .....I 1
Barker Heights* ..2,933..E 4
Barnard ....D 3
Barnardsville ....D 4
Barnesville ....G 10
Bat Cave ....E 4
Bath ....231..E 14
Battleboro ....562..D 12
Bayboro ......665.°E 14
Bear Creek ....I 5
Beargrass ......99..D 13
Beaufort ....3,368.°F 14
Bee Log ....D 4
Belhaven ....2,259..E 14
Belmont ....5,054..J 1
Belmont South* ....2,125..C 8
Belmont-South Rosemary* 2,260..C 12
Belvidere ....C 14
Belwood ....E 6
Bennett ....I 5
Benson .....2,267..J 7
Berea ....C 11
Bessemer City ......4,991..E 6
Bethania ....G 3
Bethel ......1,514..D 13
Bethesda ....H 7
Beulaville ...1,156..F 12
Biltmore Forest ....1,298..E 4
Biscoe ......1,244..J 4
Bixby ....H 2
Black Creek ..449..D 12
Black Mountain .3,204..D 4
Bladenboro ....783..G 11
Bladenboro North* ....1,705..G 11
Blanch ....C 10
Blounts Creek ......E 14
Blowing Rock 801..C 5
Boger City ..2,203..E 6
Boiling Springs ...2,284..E 5
Boiling Spring Lakes* .....245..H 12
Bolivia ......185..H 12
Bolton ....534..G 11
Bonlee ....I 5
Bonnie Doone .....K 6
Boomer ....D 6
Boone ......8,754.°C 5
Boonville .....687..G 2
Bostic* ....289..E 5
Bowdens ....F 12
Brasstown ....F 1
Brevard ....5,243.°E 3
Bricks ....C 12
Bridgeton* ...520..E 14
Broadway ....694..J 6
Brookford ....590..D 6
Browns Summit ....G 4
Brunswick ....206..G 11
Bryson City .1,290.°E 2
Buies Creek .2,024..J 7
Bullock ....C 11
Bunlevel .....200..J 7
Bunn ....284..H 8
Burgaw ....1,744.°G 12
Burlington .35,930..H 5
Burnsville ..1,348.°D 4
Butner ......3,538..G 7
Butters ....G 10
Buxton ....E 16
Bynum ....I 6
Caldwell ....J 1
Calypso ......462..F 12
Camden ....°C 15
Cameron .....204..J 6
Camp Lejeune Central* .34,549..G 13
Candor ....561..J 4
Canton .....5,158..E 3
Cape Carteret .616..F 14
Carbonton ....I 5
Caroleen ....E 5
Carolina Beach ....1,663..H 12
Carrboro ....5,058..H 6
Carthage ....1,034.°E 9
Cary ....7,435..I 7
Casar ....E 5
Cashiers ......230..F 3
Castalia ....265..C 12
Castle Hayne ....G 12
Catawba .....565..I 1
Ca-Vel ....C 10
Cedar Falls ....I 4
Cedar Grove ....G 6
Cedar Island ....F 15
Cedar Mountain ...E 4
Celo ....D 4
Centerville ....123..C 12
Central Falls ......I 4
Cerro Gordo ..184..G 10
Chadbourn ..2,213..G 10
Chadwick Acres* ....12..G 13
Chalybeate ....J 7
Chapel Hill 25,537..H 6
Charlotte .305,500.°E 7
Cherokee ....E 2
Cherry ....D 15
Cherry Point* ...12,029..F 14
Cherryville ..5,258..E 6
China Grove* 1,788..E 7
Chinquapin ....F 12
Chocowinity ....566..E 14
Claremont ....788..I 1
Clarendon ....H 10
Clark ....E 13
Clarkton ......662..G 11
Clayton ....3,103..I 8
Clemmons ....H 3
Cleveland .....614..I 2
Cliffside ....E 5
Climax ....H 4
Clinchfield, see East Marion [-Clinchfield]
Clinton .....7,157.°F 11
Clyde ....900..E 3
Coats ....1,051..J 7
Cofield ....318..C 14
Colerain .....373..C 14
Coleridge ....I 5
Collettsville ....D 5
Colon ....I 6
Columbia .....902.°D 15
Columbus ....731.°E 4
Comfort ....F 13
Como ....211..C 14
Concord ...18,464.°E 7
Concord North .....2,350..J 2
Conetoe ......160..D 13
Conover ....3,355..I 1
Conway ......694..C 13
Cooleemee ..1,115..H 2
Corapeake ....B 14
Cordova ....F 9
Cornatzer ....H 2
Cornelius ...1,296..J 1
Corolla ....C 16
Council ....38..G 11
Courtney ....H 2
Cove City ......485..E 13
Cramerton* .2,142..E 6
Cranberry ....C 5
Creedmoor ..1,405..H 7
Creswell .....633..D 15
Cricket ....G 1
Crisp ....D 13
Croft ....J 1
Crossnore ....264..D 5
Crouse ....E 6
Culberson .....83..F 1
Cullowhee ....E 3
Cumnock ....I 6
Currie ....G 12
Currituck ....°C 15
Dallas ......4,059..J 1
Dana ....E 4
Danbury ......152.°C 8
Daniels-Rhyne ....2,273..E 6
Davidson ...2,931..J 1
Davis ....F 15
Deep Gap ....C 6
Deep Run ....F 12
Delco ....G 12
Dellview ....11..E 6
Denton .....1,017..I 3
Denver ....I 1
Derita ....J 1
Dickerson ....G 7
Dillsboro .....215..E 2
Dobson ....933.°C 7
Dover ....585..E 13
Drexel ......1,431..D 5
Druid Hills, see Balfour [-Druid Hills]
Dublin ....283..G 11
Dudley ....199..E 12
Dundarrach .....53..F 10
Dunn ....8,302..J 7
Durants Neck ......C 15
Durham ...95,438.°D 10
Eagle Rock ....I 8
Eagle Springs .....J 5
Earl ....E 6
East Bend ....485..G 2
East Flat Rock* ....2,627..E 4
East Gastonia* 2,370..F 6
East Lake ....D 16
East Laurinburg ....487..F 9
East Marion [-Clinchfield] ....3,015..D 5
East Rockingham ......2,858..F 9
East Spencer 2,217..I 2
Eden ......15,871..C 9
Edenton ....4,956.°C 14
Edneyville ....E 4
Edward ......115..E 14
Efland ....H 6
Elizabeth City .....14,381.°C 15
Elizabethtown .....1,418.°G 11
Elk Park .....503..C 5
Elkin ....2,899..G 1
Ellenboro* ....465..E 5
Ellerbe ....913..K 4
Elm City ...1,201..D 12
Elon College 2,150..H 5
Emerald Isle .122..G 14
Emerson ....G 11
Enfield .....3,272..C 12
Engelhard ....E 16
Enka ....E 4
Ennice ....B 7
Enon ....G 2
Ernul ....E 14
Erwin ......2,852..J 7
Ether ....J 4
Eure ....C 14
Eureka ....263..E 12
Everetts ......198..D 13
Evergreen ....G 10
Fair Bluff ..1,039..G 10
Fairfield ....E 15
Fairmont ...2,827..G 10
Fairplains ....G 1
Faison ....598..F 12
Faith ....506..I 2
Falcon ....357..K 7
Falkland ......130..D 13
Fallston ....E 6
Farmer ....I 4
Farmington ....H 2
Farmville ...4,424..E 13
Fayetteville 53,510.°F 10
Ferguson ....C 6
Flat Rock ...1,688..C 7
Flat Rock ....E 4
Fletcher ....1,164..E 4
Flint Hill ....G 2
Fontana Dam ......E 1
Forest City .7,179..E 5
Fork ....H 2
Fort Bragg* 46,995..F 10
Fountain ....434..D 13
Four Oaks ..1,057..J 8
Frank ....C 5
Franklin ...2,336.°E 2
Franklinton .1,459..H 8
Franklinville ..794..I 4
Freeland ....H 11
Fremont ....1,596..E 12
Frisco ....E 16
Fuquay-Varina ....3,576..I 7
Garland ......656..F 11
Garner ......4,923..I 7
Garysburg* ...231..C 13
Gaston .....1,105..C 12
Gastonia ...47,142.°J 1
Gastonia North* ...1,316..F 6
Gates ....B 14
Gatesville ....338.°C 14
George ....C 13
Gerton ....E 4
Gibson* ....502..F 9
Gibsonville* 2,019..D 9
Gieger, see New River-Gieger
Gilkey ....E 5
Glen Alpine ..797..D 5
Glen Raven .2,848..H 5
Glendale Springs ...C 6
Glendon ....J 5
Glenville ....E 3
Glenwood ....E 5
Godwin ......129..J 7
Gold Hill ....I 3
Gold Point ....108..D 13
Goldsboro .26,810.°E 12
Goldston .....364..I 5
Graham ....8,172.°D 9
Graingers ....E 13
Grandy ....C 16
Granite Falls 2,388..D 6
Granite Quarry ...1,344..I 2
Greenmountain .....D 4
Greensboro 144,076.°D 9
Greenville .29,063.°D 13
Grifton .....1,860..E 13
Grimesland ....394..E 13
Grover ....555..E 6
Guilford ....H 4
Guilford College* .....61..H 4
Gulf ....I 6
Gull Rock ....E 16
Halifax .....335.°C 13
Hallsboro ....G 11
Hamilton .....579..D 13
Hamlet .....4,627..F 9
Hampstead ....G 13
Hamptonville ....H 2
Harkers Island ....1,633..F 15
Harmony .....377..H 2
Harrells ......249..F 12
Harrellsville ..165..C 14
Harris ....E 5
Harrisburg ....J 2
Hassell ......160..D 13
Hatteras ....E 16
Havelock ....5,283..F 14
Haw River* 1,542..C 9
Hayesville ....428.°F 1
Hays ....G 1
Haywood ....I 6
Hazelwood ...2,057..E 3
Henderson .13,896.°C 11
Hendersonville ......6,443.°E 4
Hendersonville West* ....1,558..E 4
Henrietta [-Avondale] .....1,307..E 5
Hertford .....2,023.°C 15
Hickory ...20,569..D 6
Hickory East 4,181..D 6
Hickory Grove .....J 2
Hickory North* ...2,325..D 6
Hiddenite ....H 1
High Point 63,259..D 8
High Rock ....I 3
High Shoals ....J 1
Highfalls ....J 5
Highlands ....583..F 3
Hildebran ....481..D 6
Hillsborough ....1,444.°D 10
Hiwassee Dam .....E 1
Hobbsville ....C 14
Hobgood .....530..D 13
Hobucken ....E 14
Hoffman ......434..K 5
Holden Beach* 136..H 11
Hollister ....C 12

Holly Ridge ..415..G 13
Holly Springs .697..I 7
Hookerton ....441..E 13
Hope Mills .1,866..K 6
Hot Springs ..653..D 3
Hubert ....F 13
Hudson .....2,820..D 6
Huntersville 1,538..J 1
Hurdle Mills ......G 6
Husk ....B 6
Icard ....D 6
Indian Beach* 245..F 14
Indian Trail ..405..K 2
Ingalls ....D 5
Ingold ....F 11
Iron Station ......J 1
Ivanhoe ....G 12
Jackson ......762.°C 13
Jackson Hill ....I 3
Jacksonville 17,180.°F 13
James City ..2,577..F 14
Jamestown ..1,297..H 4
Jamesville ....533..D 14
Jarvisburg ....C 16
Jefferson .....943.°C 6
Jonas Ridge ......D 5
Jonesville ...1,659..G 1
Julian ....H 5
Jupiter ....208..D 4
Kannapolis 36,293..J 2
Kelford ......295..C 13
Kelly ....G 11
Kenansville ...762.°F 12
Kenly ......1,370..E 12
Kernersville .4,815..G 3
Kill Devil Hills ....357..C 16
King* ......1,033..C 8
Kings Mountain .....8,465..E 6
Kinston ...23,020.°E 13
Kipling ....J 7
Kittrell ......427..G 8
Kitty Hawk ....C 16
Knightdale ...815..I 8
Knotts Island .....B 16
Kona ....D 4
Kure Beach ...394..H 12
La Grange ..2,679..E 12
Lake Junaluska ....E 3
Lake Lure* ...456..E 5
Lake Toxaway .....F 3
Lake Waccamaw .924..G 11
Lakeview ....J 5
Landis .....2,297..I 2
Landis Northeast ......1,353..I 2
Lansing ......283..C 6
Lasker ....114..C 13
Lattimore* ....257..E 5
Laurel Hill .1,215..F 9
Laurel Park ..581..E 4
Laurinburg .8,859.°F 9
Laurinburg West* ....1,156..F 9
Lawndale ....544..E 6
Lawsonville ....C 8
Leasburg ....C 10
Leechville ....E 15
Leggett* ....120..D 12
Leicester ....D 4
Leland ....G 12
Lemon Springs .....J 6
Lenoir .....14,705.°D 6
Lewiston ......327..C 13
Lewisville ....H 2
Lexington ..17,205.°D 8
Liberty .....2,167..H 5
Lilesville .....641..K 4
Lillington ...1,155.°E 10
Lincolnton ..5,293.°E 6
Linden ....205..J 7
Linville ....D 5
Linwood ....I 3
Littleton .....903..C 12
Locust ......1,484..J 2
Lone Hickory ......H 2
Long Beach .1,656..H 12
Longhurst ..1,485..C 10
Longview ...3,360..D 6
Longwood ....H 11
Longwood Park* ....1,284..F 9
Loray ....H 1
Louisburg ..2,941.°C 11
Love Valley ...40..H 1
Lowell* ....3,307..E 6
Lowgap ....C 7
Lowland ....E 14
Lucama ....610..D 12
Lumber Bridge 117..F 10
Lumberton .16,961.°G 10
Lynn ....E 4
MacClesfield ..536..D 13
Mackeys ....D 14
Macon ....179..C 12
Madison ....2,018..C 8
Maggie Valley .....E 3
Magnolia .....614..F 12
Maiden ......2,416..I 1
Mamers ....J 6
Mamie ....C 16
Manly ....K 5
Manns Harbor .....D 16
Manteo ......547.°D 16
Maple ....C 15
Maple Hill ....G 13
Marble ....E 1
Margaretsville .95..B 13
Marietta ......70..G 10
Marion .....3,335.°D 5
Mars Hill ...1,623..D 4
Marshall .....982.°D 4
Marshville ..1,405..K 3
Marston ....K 5
Matthews ....783..K 2
Maury ....421..E 13
Maxton ......1,885..F 10
Mayodan ...2,875..C 8
Maysville .....912..F 13
McAdenville* .950..E 6
McCain ....K 5
McDonald ......80..G 10
McFarlan .....140..F 8
McGrady ....C 6
McLeansville ......H 5
Mebane* .....2,433..C 10
Merritt ....F 14
Merry Hill ....D 14
Merry Oaks ....I 6
Mesic* ....369..E 14
Micaville ....D 4
Micro ....300..E 12
Middleburg ...149..C 11
Middlesex .....729..D 12
Midland ....J 2
Midway Park .....F 13
Mill Spring ....E 4
Millbrook ....H 7
Millers Creek ......C 6
Millersville ....H 1
Milton ....235..C 10
Milwaukee .....376..C 13
Mineral Springs ...F 7
Minnesott Beach* ......41..E 14
Mint Hill* ..2,262..E 7
Misenheimer ....J 3
Mocksville ..2,529.°D 7
Moncure ....I 6
Monroe ....11,282.°F 7
Montreat .....581..D 4
Mooresville .8,808..I 1
Moravian Falls ....H 1
Morehead City ......5,233..F 14
Morganton .15,237.°D 5
Morgantown* 3,547..C 9
Morrisville ....209..H 7
Mortimer ....27..D 5
Morven ....562..F 8
Mount Airy .7,325..C 7
Mount Gilead 1,286..J 4
Mount Holly 5,107..J 1
Mount Mourne .....I 1
Mount Olive 4,914..E 12
Mount Pleasant ..1,174..J 2
Moyock ....B 15
Murfreesboro 3,508..C 13
Murphy .....2,082.°F 1
Nags Head ...414..D 16
Naples ....E 4
Nashville ...1,670.°D 12
Nebo ....D 5
Neuse ....H 7
New Bern .14,660.°F 14
New Holland ....E 15
New London ..285..J 3
New River-Gieger* ...8,699..G 13
New Topsail Beach ....41..G 13
Newell ....J 2
Newhill ....I 6
Newland ......524.°C 5
Newport .....1,735..F 14
Newton .....7,857.°D 6
Newton Grove .546..J 8
Niagara ....J 5
Norlina ....969..C 12
Norman ....157..K 4
North Belmont .10,672..J 1
North Henderson 1,997..C 11
North Wilkesboro 3,357..G 1
Northside ....H 7
Norwood ....1,896..J 3
Oak City .....559..D 13
Oakboro ......568..J 3
Ocean Isle Beach ....78..H 11
Ocracoke ....E 16
Okeewemee ....J 4
Old Fort .....676..D 4
Old Trap ....C 15
Olin ....H 1
Olivia ....J 6
Oriental ......445..F 14
Orrum ....162..G 10
Otto ....F 2
Owens ....K 6
Oxford ......7,178.°C 11
Paint Rock ....D 3
Palmyra ....27..C 13
Pantego ....218..D 14
Parkersburg ....56..F 11
Parkton ......550..F 10
Parkwood ...2,267..J 5
Parmele ......373..D 13
Patterson .....344..D 6
Patterson Springs* ....478..E 5
Paw Creek ....J 1
Peachland ....556..K 3
Pee Dee ....J 4
Pekin ....K 4
Pelham ....C 9
Pembroke ...1,982..G 10
Pensacola ....D 4
Phillipsville* 1,239..E 3
Pike Road ....D 14
Pikeville ......580..E 12
Pilot Mountain .1,309..C 8
Pine Hall ....C 8
Pine Knoll Shores* ......62..F 14
Pine Level .....983..J 8
Pinebluff .....570..K 5
Pinehurst ...1,056..K 5
Pinetops ....1,379..D 13
Pinetown ......278..D 14
Pineville ....1,948..K 1
Pink Hill .....522..F 12
Pinnacle ....C 8
Pisgah Forest ......E 3
Pittsboro ...1,447.°D 10
Pleasant Garden ...H 4
Plumtree ....D 5
Plymouth ...4,774.°D 14
Point Harbor ......C 16
Polkton ......845..K 3
Polkville* ....494..E 5
Pollocksville ...456..F 13
Poplar ....C 4
Porter ....J 3
Powellsville ...247..C 14
Princeton ...1,044..E 12
Princeville ....654..D 13
Proctorville ...157..G 10
Prospect Hill ......G 6
Providence ....C 9
Providence ....G 7
Raeford .....3,180.°F 10
Raleigh ...123,793.°D 11
Ramseur ....1,328..I 5
Randleman ..2,312..I 4
Ranlo* .....2,092..E 6
Ransomville ....E 14
Red Cross ....J 3
Red Oak ......359..D 12
Red Springs .3,383..F 10
Redland ....H 2
Reidsville ..13,636..C 9
Relief ....D 4
Rex ....F 10
Rex ....J 1
Rhodhiss ....784..D 6
Rhyne, see Daniels-Rhyne
Rich Square 1,254..C 13
Richfield .....306..J 3
Richlands .....935..F 13
Richmond Hill .....H 5
Riddle ....C 15
Roanoke Rapids ...13,508..C 12
Roaring Gap ....C 7
Roaring River .....G 1
Robbins .....1,059..J 5
Robbinsville ...777.°E 1
Roberdel ....K 4
Robersonville 1,910..D 13
Rockford ....G 2
Rockingham .6,255.°F 9
Rockwell .....999..I 3
Rocky Mount ...34,284..D 12
Rocky Point ....G 12
Rodanthe ....D 16
Roduco ....C 14
Rolesville .....533..H 8
Ronda ....465..G 1
Roper ....649..D 14
Rose Hill ...1,448..F 12
Roseboro ....1,235..K 8
Rosman ....407..E 3
Rougemont ....G 6
Rowan Mill* 1,184..D 7
Rowland ....1,358..G 10
Roxboro .....6,891.°C 10
Roxobel ....347..C 13
Royal Pines* 2,041..E 4
Ruffin ....C 9
Rural Hall ..2,338..G 3
Ruth ....360..E 5
Rutherfordton ...3,245.°E 5
St. Pauls ...2,011..F 10
Salemburg ....669..K 8
Salisbury ..22,515.°D 8
Salter Path ....F 14
Saluda ....546..E 4
Salvo ....D 16
Sandy Ridge ....C 8
Sanford ....11,716.°E 10
Sapphire ....F 3
Saratoga .....391..D 12
Saxapahaw ....H 5
Scaly Mountain ....F 2
Scotland Neck .....2,869..C 13
Scotts ....H 1
Scranton ....E 15
Seaboard ......611..C 13
Seagrove .....354..I 4
Sealevel ....F 15
Sedalia ....H 5
Selma ......4,356..I 8
Semora ....C 10
Seven Springs .188..E 12
Severn ....356..B 13
Seymour Johnson* ..8,172..E 12
Shallotte ......597..H 11
Shannon ....F 10
Sharpsburg ...789..D 12
Shelby .....16,328.°E 6
Shelmerdine ....E 13
Sherrills Ford ......I 1
Sherwood ....C 5
Shiloh ....C 15
Shooting Creek .....F 2
Siler City ...4,689..I 5
Sims ....205..D 12
Skyland ....2,177..E 4
Sladesville ....E 15
Smithfield ..7,025.°E 11
Smithtown ....196..G 2
Smyre ....J 1
Smyrna ....F 15
Sneads Ferry ......G 13
Snow Hill ..1,359.°E 13
Sophia ....H 4
South Creek ...73..E 14
South Fayetteville ..K 7
South Gastonia* .3,718..F 6
South Goldsboro* 2,094..E 12
South Henderson 1,843..C 11
South Mills ....C 15
South Rosemary, see Belmont-South Rosemary
South Salisbury .2,199..I 2
South Wadesboro* .109..F 8
South Weldon* ..1,630..C 13
South Wilmington ..H 12
Southern Pines .....5,937..K 5
Southport ..2,220.°H 12
Sparta ......1,304.°C 6
Speed ....142..D 13
Spencer .....3,075..I 2
Spencer Mountain* ..300..E 6
Spindale ....4,573..E 5
Spring Hope 1,334..D 12
Spring Lake 3,968..K 6
Spruce Pine 2,333..D 5
Stacy ....F 15
Staley ....239..I 5
Stanfield* .....458..E 8
Stanley .....2,336..J 1
Stanleyville .2,362..G 3
Stantonsburg ..869..E 12
Star ....892..J 4
State Road ....C 7
Statesville .20,007.°D 7
Stecoah ....E 2
Stedman ....505..K 7
Stem ....242..G 7
Stokes ....D 13
Stokesdale ....G 4
Stoneville ...1,030..C 9
Stonewall ....335..F 14
Stony Point .1,001..H 1
Stovall ....405..C 11
Stumpy Point ......D 16
Suit ....F 1
Summerfield ....G 4
Sunbury ....C 14
Sunset Beach* 108..H 12
Supply ....H 12
Surf City .....166..G 13
Swan Station .196..J 6
Swannanoa .1,966..E 4
Swanquarter ....°E 15
Swansboro ..1,207..F 14
Swepsonville ....H 5
Sylva ......1,561.°E 3
Tabor City ..2,400..H 10
Tapoco ....E 1
Tar Heel ....87..F 11
Tarboro .....9,425.°D 13
Taylorsville ..1,231.°D 6
Teachey ....219..F 12
Terrell ....I 1
Thomasville 15,230..H 3
Thurmond ....C 7
Tillery ....C 13
Timberlake ....G 6
Toast* ......2,635..C 7
Tobaccoville ....G 3
Todd ....98..C 6
Topton ....E 2
Townsville ....C 11
Traphill ....C 7
Trent Woods ..719..F 14
Trenton ....539.°F 13
Trinity ....H 4
Triplett ....C 6
Troutman ....797..I 1
Troy ....2,429.°E 9
Tryon ......1,951..E 4
Tungsten ....C 11
Turkey ....329..F 12
Turnersburg ....H 1
Tuxedo ....E 4
Tyner ....C 14
Unaka ....E 1
Union Grove ....H 1
Union Mills ....E 5
Unionville ....K 2
Valdese .....3,182..D 6
Valle Crucis ....C 5
Vanceboro ....758..E 13
Vandalia ....H 4
Vandemere ...379..E 14
Vass ....885..J 6
Verona ....G 13
Vienna ....G 3
Waco ....245..E 6
Wade ....315..K 7
Wadesboro ..3,977.°F 8
Wadeville ....J 4
Wagram ....718..F 9
Wake Forest 3,148..H 8
Wakulla ....F 10
Walkertown .1,652..G 3
Wallace ....2,905..F 12
Wallburg ....H 3
Walnut ....D 3
Walnut Cove 1,213..G 3
Walstonburg ..176..E 12
Wanchese ....D 16
Warrensville ..224..C 6
Warrenton ..1,035.°C 12
Warsaw ....2,701..F 12
Washington .8,961.°E 14
Washington Park ....517..E 14
Waterville ....D 3
Watha ....181..G 12
Waves ....D 16
Waxhaw ......1,248..F 7
Waynesville .6,488.°E 3
Weaverville .1,280..D 4
Webster ....181..E 3
Weeksville ....C 15
Welcome ....H 3
Weldon ......2,304..C 13
Wendell .....1,929..I 8
Wentworth ....°C 9
West Burlington* ......1,471..C 9
West Concord 5,347..J 2
West End ....J 5
West Hillsborough ...1,696..H 6
West Jefferson 889..C 6
West Marion 3,034..D 5
West Rockingham ..F 9
West Statesville* .....3,068..D 7
Whispering Pines* ......362..F 10
Whitakers ....926..C 12
White Lake ....232..G 11
White Oak ....F 11
White Plains ......C 7
Whitehead ....C 6
Whiteville ...4,195.°G 11
Whittier ....E 2
Wilkesboro ..1,974.°C 6
Willard ....G 12
Williamston .6,570.°D 14
Willow Spring .....I 7
Wilmington 46,169.°H 12
Wilson .....31,610.°D 12
Wilson Mills ...283..I 8
Windsor ....2,199.°D 14
Winfall ....581..C 15
Wingate .....2,569..K 2
Winnabow ....H 12
Winston-Salem ..133,683.°C 8
Winterville ..1,437..E 13
Winton ....917.°C 14
Wise ....C 12
Wood ....C 12
Woodfin* ...2,831..D 4
Woodland .....744..C 13
Woodleaf ....I 2
Woodsdale ....C 10
Woodville .....253..C 13
Worthville ....I 4
Wrightsville Beach .....2,525..H 12
Yadkin College ....H 3
Yadkinville ..2,232.°C 7
Yanceyville ..1,274.°C 10
Yaupon Beach 334..H 12
Youngsville .....555..H 8
Zebulon .....1,839..H 8
Zionville ....C 5

*Does not appear on the map; key shows general location.
°County seat.

Sources: Latest census figures (1970 and special censuses) and official estimate for Charlotte after annexations (1975). Places without population figures are unincorporated areas and are not listed in census reports.

NORTH CAROLINA /*People*

Tobacco Auctioneers and Buyers work rapidly. In these warehouses in Wilson, the world's largest bright-leaf tobacco market, more than 400 lots of tobacco can be sold in an hour.

The 1970 United States census reported that North Carolina had a population of 5,082,059 persons. The population had increased about 12 per cent over the 1960 figure of 4,556,155. The U.S. Bureau of the Census estimated that by 1975 the state's population had reached about 5,451,000.

About 45 per cent of North Carolina's people live in urban areas. That is, they live in or near cities and towns of 2,500 or more persons. About 55 per cent live in rural areas. But increasing numbers of people are moving from rural to urban parts of the state. About two-fifths of the people live in the state's seven Standard Metropolitan Statistical Areas (see METROPOLITAN AREA). These areas are Asheville, Burlington, Charlotte-Gastonia, Fayetteville, Greensboro-Winston-Salem-High Point, Raleigh-Durham, and Wilmington. For their populations, see the *Index* to the political map of North Carolina. Charlotte is the state's largest city. Other large cities, in order of population, are Greensboro, Winston-Salem, and Raleigh, the state capital. See the list of separate articles on the cities of North Carolina in the *Related Articles* at the end of this article.

More than 99 of every 100 North Carolinians were born in the United States. A majority of those from other countries came from Canada, Germany, Great Britain, Greece, and Japan. About 22 of every 100 North Carolinians are Negroes. Large numbers of Negroes have moved from the state to the industrialized areas of the North.

Baptists make up North Carolina's largest religious group. Other large church groups include Methodists, Presbyterians, and Roman Catholics.

POPULATION

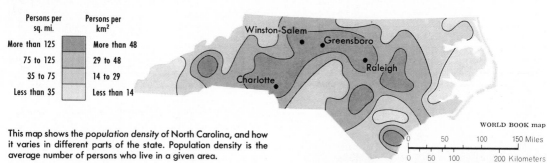

Persons per sq. mi.	Persons per km²
More than 125	More than 48
75 to 125	29 to 48
35 to 75	14 to 29
Less than 35	Less than 14

This map shows the *population density* of North Carolina, and how it varies in different parts of the state. Population density is the average number of persons who live in a given area.

WORLD BOOK map

WORLD BOOK photo

Handicraft Skills are part of the heritage of many persons who live in the mountain areas of western North Carolina. This potter makes graceful bowls and vases, using techniques that have been handed down through many generations.

Skills of the Past still form part of the daily life of Indians on the Qualla Reservation. This aged Cherokee woman pounds cornmeal with a mortar and pestle. Her full, pleated skirt and bandana are traditional garments for women.

Schools. Churches and religious leaders controlled most of the early education in North Carolina. In 1705, Charles Griffin, a schoolteacher and member of the Anglican Church, established what was probably North Carolina's first school. It was at Symons Creek near Elizabeth City. Early attempts at public education were opposed by church members, who believed that education belonged in the hands of the church. The constitution of 1776 provided for the establishment of a public school system and for chartering the University of North Carolina. In 1795, this university became the first state university in the United States to hold classes. But the state did not build its first public school until 1840. In 1901, Governor Charles B. Aycock began to improve North Carolina's system of public education.

The superintendent of public instruction administers the North Carolina public school system. He also serves as secretary of the state board of education, which consists of the lieutenant governor, state treasurer, and 11 members appointed by the governor to eight-year terms. Children between 6 and 16 must attend school. For the number of students and teachers in North Carolina, see EDUCATION (table).

Libraries. The state's first public library was founded about 1700 by Thomas Bray, an English missionary.

At this time, early groups of settlers were beginning to make their way into North Carolina. About five years later, Bray's library became part of Bath, the first town in North Carolina. In 1897, the state passed its first public-library law. That same year, the first tax-supported library in the state opened in Durham.

The Duke University library owns the largest collection of books in the state. The University of North Carolina at Chapel Hill also has an enormous collection of over a million volumes. Both universities have outstanding collections of documents relating to southern history and to the social sciences. The state library and the state department of archives and history, both in Raleigh, keep records of the history of North Carolina.

Museums. One of the outstanding art museums in the South, the North Carolina Museum of Art, opened in Raleigh in 1956. Among its exhibits are about 4,000 artistic treasures. The University of North Carolina's art museums include the William Hayes Ackland Memorial Art Center in Chapel Hill and the Weatherspoon Art Gallery in Greensboro. Other art galleries include the Mint Museum of Art in Charlotte and the Hickory Museum of Art in Hickory. The Greensboro Historical Museum and the North Carolina Museum of History at Raleigh portray the history of the state.

UNIVERSITIES AND COLLEGES

North Carolina has 30 universities and colleges accredited by the Southern Association of Colleges and Schools. For enrollments and further information, see UNIVERSITIES AND COLLEGES (table).

Name	Location	Founded	Name	Location	Founded
Atlantic Christian College	Wilson	1902	Livingstone College	Salisbury	1879
Barber-Scotia College	Concord	1867	Mars Hill College	Mars Hill	1964
Belmont Abbey College	Belmont	1876	Meredith College	Raleigh	1891
Bennett College	Greensboro	1873	Methodist College	Fayetteville	1964
Campbell College	Buies Creek	1887	North Carolina, University of	*	*
Catawba College	Salisbury	1851	North Carolina Wesleyan College	Rocky Mount	1964
Davidson College	Davidson	1836	Pfeiffer College	Misenheimer	1885
Duke University	Durham	1838	Queens College	Charlotte	1857
Elon College	Elon College	1889	Sacred Heart College	Belmont	1969
Gardner-Webb College	Boiling Springs	1969	St. Andrews Presbyterian		
Greensboro College	Greensboro	1838	College	Laurinburg	1858
Guilford College	Greensboro	1834	St. Augustine's College	Raleigh	1867
High Point College	High Point	1920	Salem College	Winston-Salem	1772
Johnson C. Smith			Shaw University	Raleigh	1865
University	Charlotte	1867	Wake Forest University	Winston-Salem	1834
Lenoir Rhyne College	Hickory	1891	Warren Wilson College	Swannanoa	1969

*For campuses and founding dates, see UNIVERSITIES AND COLLEGES (table).

North Carolina Museum of Art, in Raleigh, has a collection valued at more than $18 million. The museum has had strong state support. In 1947, the state gave $1 million to buy 200 paintings to start the first collection. In 1953, a state-owned building was remodeled to house the museum. The museum opened in 1956.

NORTH CAROLINA / *A Visitor's Guide*

Many Northerners come to North Carolina's sandhills area for relief from the cold winter weather. Blossoming mountain laurels, azaleas, and rhododendrons in spring and summer, and the beautiful colors of autumn, lure visitors to the mountains. Hunters track quail, deer, and black bears through the mountains. Fishermen, swimmers, and sunbathers enjoy North Carolina's lakes, rivers, and coastlines. Historic sites, battlefields, old mansions, and beautiful gardens throughout the state attract sightseers and students of American history.

All photos from North Carolina Travel and Promotion Division unless otherwise indicated.

Old Salem Restoration in Winston-Salem

Kabel, Publix

Wright Brothers National Memorial near Kitty Hawk

Chimney Rock in the Blue Ridge Mountains

Annual *Lost Colony* Drama in Manteo

--- PLACES TO VISIT ---

Following are brief descriptions of some of North Carolina's many interesting places to visit.

Alamance Battlefield, near Burlington, was the scene of a historic battle shortly before the Revolutionary War. About 2,000 frontiersmen, called the Regulators, rebelled against the eastern planters and suffered heroic defeat on May 16, 1771.

Bentonville Battlefield, near Smithfield, was the scene of one of the last important Civil War battles. There, on March 25, 1865, General William T. Sherman's Union forces defeated the Confederate troops of General Joseph E. Johnston.

Biltmore Estate covers about 12,000 acres (4,860 hectares) of forests and farmlands near Asheville. The Biltmore House, a masterpiece of early French Renaissance architecture, is the chief feature of the estate.

Cherokee Indian Reservation, at Cherokee, includes a replica of an Indian village as it looked in the 1700's. Visitors can see demonstrations of Cherokee handicraft.

Chimney Rock towers high above the mountains in Rutherford County. It offers an excellent view of the Blue Ridge Mountains.

Azaleas at Greenfield Park in Wilmington   Tryon Palace in New Bern

Grandfather Mountain, near Linville, looks like the huge sleeping face of an old man. Tourists may walk across a swinging bridge 1 mile (1.6 kilometers) high.

Market House, in Fayetteville, was once a slave market and now houses the local chamber of commerce. It stands on the site of the convention hall, where North Carolina ratified the U.S. Constitution in 1789.

Morehead Planetarium, at the University of North Carolina in Chapel Hill, is a widely known planetarium. Spectators can watch the movements of stars and planets across a 68-foot (21-meter) dome.

Nantahala Gorge, in Swain County, plunges deep into the mountains. Indians believed it was haunted.

Ocracoke Island, a hideout of Blackbeard, the pirate, and the site of many shipwrecks, lies about 20 miles (32 kilometers) offshore, southeast of Pamlico Sound.

Old Salem is a restored colonial village in Winston-Salem. Moravians founded the village of Salem in 1766.

Pinehurst, a popular and charming winter resort village in the sandhills region, is famous for its peaceful atmosphere and its golf facilities.

Tryon Palace, in New Bern, is the restored governor's mansion originally built by William Tryon, a royal governor. American patriots defied British authority by meeting in the palace in 1774.

U.S.S. *North Carolina* **Battleship Memorial** is located on the Cape Fear River at Wilmington. Visitors may tour the famous battleship, which took part in every major offensive in the Pacific during World War II.

National Parks, Forests, and Memorials. North Carolina has four national forests: Croatan, Nantahala, Pisgah, and Uwharrie. It shares another, the Cherokee National Forest, with Tennessee. For the area of each forest, see NATIONAL FOREST (table). In 1964, Congress set aside two areas of the national forests as national wilderness. North Carolina shares the Blue Ridge Parkway with Georgia and Virginia, and the Great Smoky Mountains National Park with Tennessee (see GREAT SMOKY MOUNTAINS NATIONAL PARK). The Wright Brothers National Memorial at Kill Devil Hills near Kitty Hawk honors the first powered airplane flight. For other areas, see NATIONAL PARK SYSTEM (tables: National Historic Sites, National Military Sites, and National Lakeshores and National Seashores.

State Parks. North Carolina has 18 state parks. For information about them, write to Director, Division of State Parks, Department of Natural and Economic Resources, Box 27687, Raleigh, N.C. 27611.

ANNUAL EVENTS

One of North Carolina's most popular annual events is the story of the *Lost Colony.* This historical drama is staged at Fort Raleigh in Manteo each night in July and August. It portrays some of the hardships faced by the early English colonists who disappeared mysteriously from Roanoke Island. Other annual events in North Carolina include the following.

January-March: Field Trials in Pinehurst (January); Old Christmas Celebration in Rodanthe (January); Camellia Show in Wilmington (February); Snow Carnival in Boone (February); Bird Dog Field Trials in Tryon (March); Moravian Easter Service in Old Salem (March or April).

April-June: Mountain Youth Jamboree in Asheville (April); Azalea Festival in Wilmington (April); Arts and Crafts Festival in Southeastern North Carolina in Lake Waccamaw (April); Stoneybrook Steeplechase in Southern Pines (April); Sports Car Hill Climb at Chimney Rock (April); Old Time Fiddlers Convention in Union Grove (April); Shad Festival in Grifton (April); Sedgefield Horse Show in Greensboro (May); Strawberry Festival in Chadbourn (May); National Hollerin' Contest in Spiney's Corner (June); Summer Festival of Music in Brevard (June-August); Singing on the Mountain at Grandfather Mountain (June); Rhododendron Festival on Roan Mountain and in nearby Bakersville (June).

July-September: Craftsman's Fair in Asheville (July); Highland Games and Gathering of Scottish Clans at Grandfather Mountain (July); Mountain Dance and Folk Festival in Asheville (August); Mineral and Gem Festival in Spruce Pine (August); International Cup Regatta in Elizabeth City (September); State Championship Horse Show in Raleigh (September); Mule Days Celebration in Benson (September).

October-December: State Fair in Raleigh (October); National 500 Auto Race in Charlotte (October); Surf Fishing Tournament in Nags Head (October); Carolinas Carousel in Charlotte (November); Formal Fox Hunt Meets, statewide (November); Anniversary of First Powered Airplane Flight in Kitty Hawk (December 17).

379

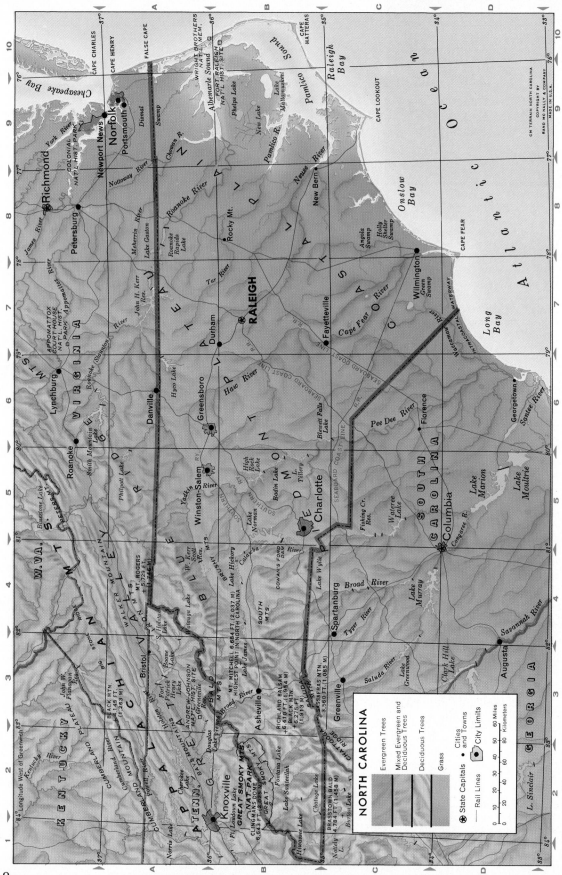

NORTH CAROLINA

Evergreen Trees

Mixed Evergreen and
Deciduous Trees

Deciduous Trees

Grass

⊛ State Capitals   • Cities
                      and Towns

— Rail Lines   ⊙ City Limits

0	20	30	40	50	60 Miles
0	20	40	60	80 Kilometers	

Specially created for **World Book Encyclopedia** by Rand McNally and World Book editors

**Land Regions
of North Carolina**

NORTH CAROLINA/The Land

Land Regions. North Carolina has three main land regions. These are, from east to west: (1) the Atlantic Coastal Plain, (2) the Piedmont, and (3) the Blue Ridge.

The Atlantic Coastal Plain extends from New Jersey to southern Florida. In North Carolina it looks somewhat like a giant foot, whose heel consists of a chain of slender land ridges that extend out to sea. The coastal plain has swamps, prairies, and rich farmland. It rises from sea level at the ocean to about 300 feet (91 meters) at the *Fall Line* of the rivers. The Fall Line is the zone in which the soft, low country ends and the rockier, hilly area begins.

The sand dunes, reefs, sand bars, and islands beyond North Carolina's shoreline are called the *outer banks*. Some of their individual names are far more colorful—Cape Fear, Cape Hatteras, Cape Lookout, and Nags Head. Like monsters of the deep, the outer banks have sent many ships to the bottom. Cape Hatteras has earned its nickname, the *Graveyard of the Atlantic*.

From the shore, the coastal plain extends inland through an area of low, level marshland, covered by trees and water. Many swamps, shallow lakes, and rivers reflect moss-hung cypress trees. The Dismal Swamp in the northeast is one of the country's largest swamps. Treeless, grassy prairies called *savannas* cover the eastern coastal plain. The western coastal plain has rich farmland. Sand hills rise along the southern part of the Fall Line. Popular winter resort areas such as Pine-hurst and Southern Pines are in the sandhills region.

The Piedmont extends from Delaware to Alabama. In North Carolina, its shape resembles the face of an elderly man, whose brow, nose, and jaw point westward. The region rises to about 1,500 feet (457 meters) at the mountains. Most of the state's manufacturing industries are in this region. The Piedmont has more people than the coastal and mountain regions together.

The Blue Ridge, or *Mountain,* region stretches from southern Pennsylvania to northern Georgia. It is named for the Blue Ridge Mountains, North Carolina's chief range. But in North Carolina the region also includes a number of other ranges. They include the Bald, Black, Brushy, Great Smoky, Iron, South, Stone, and Unaka ranges. All these mountains form part of the Appalachian Mountains. The Blue Ridge region rises from the Piedmont to heights of more than 1 mile (1.6 kilometers) above sea level. Mount Mitchell rises 6,684 feet (2,037 meters) and is the highest peak east of the Mississippi River. Forests cover much of the mountains, and the valley bottoms have good farmland. Great Smoky Mountains National Park and the Blue Ridge Parkway are in this region.

Rivers, Waterfalls, and Lakes. Most of North Carolina's rivers start in the Blue Ridge Mountains or in the Piedmont. They flow southeastward down the slopes of the mountains and hills until they reach the edge of the Piedmont region. There, they plunge down-ward in waterfalls and rapids to the Fall Line. The rivers race along narrow channels above the Fall Line. Then they become wider and flow slowly below the Fall Line, and end in wide *estuaries* (river mouths). Boats can sail inland from the coast as far west as the Fall Line. Some of the waterfalls and rapids at the Fall Line generate much of North Carolina's electric power.

One of the state's largest rivers, the Roanoke, flows into northeastern North Carolina, and empties into Albemarle Sound. The Neuse and Tar rivers drain the central part of North Carolina and flow into Pamlico Sound. The Cape Fear River crosses the southeastern portion of the Atlantic Coastal Plain. Several swift streams west of the Blue Ridge Mountains drain into Tennessee. North Carolina's largest dams are in this western area on the Hiwassee, Little Tennessee, and Nantahala rivers. Large dams also span the Catawba River, east of the Blue Ridge Mountains near Marion, and the Roanoke River near Roanoke Rapids.

Many lovely waterfalls add to the beauty of southwestern North Carolina. Some of the prettiest include Linville Falls and Bridal Veil Falls. Whitewater Falls, near Brevard, plunges 411 feet (125 meters) and is one of the highest falls in the eastern United States.

North Carolina's only natural lakes are on the Atlantic Coastal Plain. Lake Mattamuskeet, the largest, is about 15 miles (24 kilometers) long and 6 miles (10 kilometers) wide.

NORTH CAROLINA/*Climate*

Temperatures in the extreme southeast average 80° F. (27° C) in July and 48° F. (9° C) in January. The western mountains average 60° to 70° F. (16° to 21° C) in July, and as low as 28° F. (−2° C) in January. The state's highest recorded temperature was 109° F. (43° C) at Albemarle on July 28, 1940, and at Weldon on Sept. 7, 1954. The lowest temperature was −29° F. (−34° C) on Mount Mitchell on Jan. 30, 1966.

Rain makes up most of the state's *precipitation* (rain, melted snow, and other moisture). The Atlantic Coastal Plain averages about 50 inches (125 centimeters) a year, the Piedmont about 47 inches (120 centimeters), and the Blue Ridge region about 60 inches (150 centimeters). Snowfall ranges from 40 inches (100 centimeters) a year in some mountains to only a trace in some coastal areas. Since 1900, the state has averaged nearly one hurricane a year. In 1954, a hurricane killed 19 persons and caused over $100 million in damage.

Frank J. Miller

Mount Mitchell, the highest peak east of the Mississippi River, overlooks the scenic Blue Ridge Parkway. Rhododendrons and many other kinds of plants thrive in this region. The usually mild climate and heavy rainfall are ideal for plants.

SEASONAL TEMPERATURES

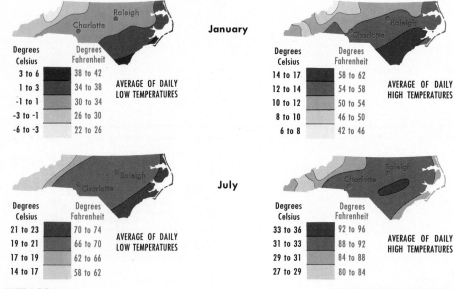

January

Degrees Celsius	Degrees Fahrenheit
3 to 6	38 to 42
1 to 3	34 to 38
-1 to 1	30 to 34
-3 to -1	26 to 30
-6 to -3	22 to 26

AVERAGE OF DAILY LOW TEMPERATURES

Degrees Celsius	Degrees Fahrenheit
14 to 17	58 to 62
12 to 14	54 to 58
10 to 12	50 to 54
8 to 10	46 to 50
6 to 8	42 to 46

AVERAGE OF DAILY HIGH TEMPERATURES

July

Degrees Celsius	Degrees Fahrenheit
21 to 23	70 to 74
19 to 21	66 to 70
17 to 19	62 to 66
14 to 17	58 to 62

AVERAGE OF DAILY LOW TEMPERATURES

Degrees Celsius	Degrees Fahrenheit
33 to 36	92 to 96
31 to 33	88 to 92
29 to 31	84 to 88
27 to 29	80 to 84

AVERAGE OF DAILY HIGH TEMPERATURES

AVERAGE YEARLY PRECIPITATION
(Rain, Melted Snow, and Other Moisture)

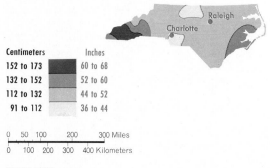

Centimeters	Inches
152 to 173	60 to 68
132 to 152	52 to 60
112 to 132	44 to 52
91 to 112	36 to 44

0 50 100   200   300 Miles

0   100 200 300   400 Kilometers

WORLD BOOK maps

AVERAGE MONTHLY WEATHER

	CHARLOTTE					RALEIGH			
	Temperatures F.°		C°		Days of Rain or Snow	Temperatures F.°		C°		Days of Rain or Snow
	High	Low	High	Low		High	Low	High	Low	
JAN.	52	32	11	0	11	51	32	11	0	10
FEB.	55	34	13	1	10	53	33	12	1	10
MAR.	62	40	17	4	12	62	39	17	4	11
APR.	71	48	22	9	10	71	46	22	8	10
MAY	80	57	27	14	10	79	55	26	13	11
JUNE	88	66	31	19	11	87	64	31	18	11
JULY	89	68	32	20	13	89	68	32	20	12
AUG.	87	67	31	19	11	88	67	31	19	11
SEPT.	83	62	28	17	8	84	62	29	17	8
OCT.	73	50	23	10	7	73	49	23	9	7
NOV.	61	39	16	4	7	62	39	17	4	7
DEC.	53	33	12	1	10	52	33	11	1	10

The line that separates the Atlantic Coastal Plain from the Piedmont also separates North Carolina's two major industrial areas. The state's richest farmland is in the Atlantic Coastal Plain. Most of the manufacturing takes place in the Piedmont. Mining industries operate in many parts of the state.

Natural Resources of North Carolina include rich soils and mineral deposits, thick forests, and plentiful plant and animal life.

Soil. Red and yellow soils cover most of North Carolina, except along the coast and in the mountains. Light and level sandy loam soils make the central and western coastal plain the richest farmland in the state. A strip of coastal land from 30 to 60 miles (48 to 97 kilometers) wide has marshy soils formed by dark peat or muck. These soils have poor drainage, but if drained properly, they provide good farmland. Deep sandy soils cover the sand hills along the Fall Line. The Piedmont has sandy, clay, and silt loams, mostly red in color. Strips of dark *alluvial* (water-deposited) soils lie along most of the streams. Grayish-brown loams cover most of the mountain section.

Minerals. Deposits of more than 300 kinds of minerals and rocks have been found in North Carolina. The mountains contain rich stores of feldspar and kaolin. The Blue Ridge and Piedmont regions have large deposits of gneiss. Sand and gravel are found in the coastal plain and in the Piedmont. The Piedmont region is also rich in clays, granite, and shale. Beaufort County, on the coastal plain, has one of the largest phosphate deposits in the world. Each of North Carolina's three main land regions has deposits of limestone.

Forests cover about 20 million acres (8,100,000 hectares), or about two-thirds of the state. Oaks and pines are the most common trees. Oaks grow along with such other hardwoods as hickories, maples, and tulip trees over the entire state. Tupelo and sweet gum forests spread along the coastal plain rivers and streams. Loblolly pine, the state's most common softwood, grows over the entire coastal plain. Pond pine, blackgum, cypress, and white cedar are found in the swamps.

Plant Life. Every January, camellias bloom along North Carolina's coastline. By April, redbud and dogwood blossoms have spread across the state. Each May and June, azaleas and rhododendrons color the mountainsides. Orchids, and insect eaters such as pitcher plants, sundews, and Venus's-flytraps flourish in the savannas.

Animal Life. Black bear and deer live in the western mountains and in the lowlands near the coast. North Carolina's fields, forests, and streams are filled with beavers, foxes, gray squirrels, opossums, otters, rabbits, raccoons, and skunks. Common songbirds include Carolina wrens and mockingbirds. Ducks, geese, and swans spend the winter near the coast. Mourning doves, partridge, and woodcocks inhabit much of the state. Dolphins, marlin, menhaden, sailfish, and sturgeon are found in the coastal waters. Fresh-water lakes and streams have bass, bluegills, crappies, sunfish, and trout.

Manufacturing accounts for 83 per cent of the value of goods produced in North Carolina. Manufactured goods have a *value added by manufacture* of about $15 billion a year. This figure represents the value created in products by North Carolina's industries, not counting such costs as materials, supplies, and fuels. The chief manufacturing industries, in order of importance, are (1) textiles and related products, (2) tobacco products, and (3) chemicals and chemical products.

Textiles and Related Products. North Carolina leads the United States and most nations of the world in textile production. The state's textile industries have a value added of about $3½ billion a year. This amount is about a fourth of North Carolina's total manufacturing income. The state has about 1,400 textile plants. Most of them are in the Piedmont region. Gaston County cotton mills spin more yarn than any other county in the United States. North Carolina produces nearly half the nation's hosiery. Greensboro has the world's largest mill for weaving denim. Kannapolis has the world's largest producer of household textiles, such as sheets and towels. Other leading textile products include nylon, polyester, and rayon fiber.

Tobacco Products. North Carolina leads all the states in the production of tobacco products. This industry has a value added of about $1½ billion a year. Cigarette factories at Durham, Greensboro, Reidsville, and Winston-Salem account for more than half the nation's cigarette production. North Carolina ranks among the leading states in the amount of taxes paid to the federal government. This is because a tax must be paid with the purchase of cigarettes or processed tobacco.

Production of Goods in North Carolina

Total value of goods produced in 1973—$15,196,683,000

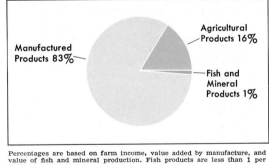

Manufactured Products 83%

Agricultural Products 16%

Fish and Mineral Products 1%

Percentages are based on farm income, value added by manufacture, and value of fish and mineral production. Fish products are less than 1 per cent.
Sources: U.S. government publications, 1975-1976.

Employment in North Carolina

Total number of persons employed in 1974—2,229,400

		Number of Employees
Manufacturing	𝍖	795,200
Wholesale & Retail Trade	𝍖	376,100
Government	𝍖	298,800
Community, Social, & Personal Services	𝍖	260,900
Agriculture	𝍖	182,000
Construction	𝍖	121,500
Transportation & Public Utilities	𝍖	104,100
Mining & Finance, Insurance, & Real Estate	𝍖	90,800

Sources: *Employment and Earnings*, May 1975, U.S. Bureau of Labor Statistics; *Farm Labor*, February 1975, U.S. Department of Agriculture.

FARM, MINERAL, AND FOREST PRODUCTS

This map shows where the state's leading farm, mineral, and forest products are produced. The major urban areas (shown on the map in red) are the state's important manufacturing centers.

WORLD BOOK map

Chemicals and Chemical Products have a value added of about $1¼ billion yearly. The chief chemical products of the state are plastic materials and such synthetic fibers as rayon. The leading centers of chemical production in North Carolina include Charlotte, Greensboro, Wilmington, and Winston-Salem.

Other Important Products. Furniture ranks fourth in North Carolina. It has a value added of about $890 million yearly. North Carolina leads the states in the production of household furniture, and High Point is often called the furniture capital of America. Factories at Hickory, Lenoir, Lexington, Statesville, Thomasville, and other towns produce wooden furniture. Electrical machinery ranks fifth. It has an annual value added of about $830 million. Other leading industries include the manufacture of clothing, fabricated metal products, food products, lumber and wood products, nonelectrical machinery, and paper and paper products.

North Carolina stands among the leading lumber-producing states. About two-thirds of the lumber comes from pines. Canton, New Bern, Plymouth, Riegelwood, and Roanoke Rapids have large pulp and paper mills. Other important wood products include cabinets, paneling, plywood, poles and piling, and veneer. North Carolina also ranks as the nation's leading producer of bricks.

Agriculture provides a yearly gross income of about $2½ billion, or about a sixth of the value of all goods produced. Farmland covers about 13 million acres (5,260,000 hectares), or nearly half the state.

Tobacco. North Carolina is the leading tobacco state, raising about 40 per cent of the nation's crop. Tobacco provides a yearly income of about $720 million—about a third of the state's total farm income.

The heart of the coastal plain is known as *Tobaccoland.* But farmers in most parts of the state raise tobacco. Most of the tobacco is the bright-leaf variety. But mountain farmers east of Jackson County raise golden-leaf Burley tobacco. Wilson sells more bright-leaf tobacco than any other city in the Western Hemisphere. North Carolina has about 50 tobacco markets.

Soybeans rank second among crops grown in North Carolina. They provide a yearly income of about $170 million and grow mostly in the eastern half of the state.

Corn is the third-ranking crop in North Carolina.

Farmers throughout the state raise corn, which they use both as feed for livestock and as a cash crop.

Other Field Crops. Peanuts rank fourth in North Carolina. They grow chiefly in the northern coastal plain. Sweet potatoes are raised in the warm, humid regions of the southern coastal plain. North Carolina leads the nation in sweet potato production. Coastal areas and the northern part of the mountain region supply Irish potatoes. Other crops raised in North Carolina include cotton, greenhouse and nursery products, hay, oats, and wheat.

Fruits and Truck Crops are raised mainly on the coastal plain and in the mountains. Some fruits, especially peaches, thrive in the sandhills region. Leading fruit crops include apples, grapes, melons, peaches, and strawberries. Burgaw is noted for its blueberries. Washington and other nearby coastal plain towns ship scuppernongs, a kind of grape. Cucumbers, snap beans, and tomatoes are among the most valuable *truck crops* (vegetables grown for market). Truck farmers also grow cabbages, peppers, and sweet corn.

Livestock Products provide a yearly income of about $975 million. North Carolina ranks among the leading raisers of *broilers* (chickens from 9 to 12 weeks old). Stanley, Surry, Wilkes, and Yadkin counties raise the most chickens. Eggs are a leading farm product in North Carolina. Duplin, Robeson, Scotland, Union, and Wayne counties raise the most turkeys. Most dairy farming takes place in the Piedmont and Blue Ridge regions. Hogs and beef cattle provide an important source of income.

Mining in North Carolina earns about $150 million a year. Stone provides the greatest income. Sand and gravel rank next in value, followed by phosphate, feldspar, and lithium. North Carolina is the leading producer of feldspar, lithium, and mica. It is also one of the leading states in crushed granite production. A huge quarry at Mount Airy supplies beautiful white granite. Granite quarries operate in about 50 counties. Avery County supplies all the state's kaolin, a type of clay used in making pottery, porcelain, and book paper. Other clays and shale are mined in about 20 counties.

Pottery made in Jugtown, in northern Moore County, has won national fame. Most counties supply sand and gravel. Other important minerals include asbestos, gemstones, iron ore, olivine, and talc. One of the largest supplies of phosphate in the United States and in the world was discovered in Beaufort County in eastern North Carolina in the 1950's.

Fishing Industry. North Carolina has an annual fish catch valued at about $15 million. Shellfish and menhaden provide much of the income. Leading fish products include crabs, flounder, and shrimp.

Electric Power. Fuel-burning steam plants produce about 85 per cent of the state's electric power. Nuclear generating plants supply about 10 per cent and hydro-electric power plants provide the rest.

Rural electric cooperatives and private companies furnish electricity to nearly all of the state's farms. North Carolina leads the nation in the percentage of farms with electrification. Fontana Dam, the largest in the state, spans the Little Tennessee River near the western tip of North Carolina. It belongs to the Tennessee Valley Authority, from which North Carolina buys some of its power. The state imports its coal, oil, and natural gas from other states.

Transportation. Rivers served as the first highways in North Carolina. Roads began to appear in the 1700's. But most of the roads remained poor until well into the 1900's. The first two major railroads—the Wilmington and Raleigh, and the Raleigh and Gaston—began service in 1840. At that time, the 161-mile (259-kilometer) Wilmington line was the longest in the world.

Today, about 77,000 miles (124,000 kilometers) of the

state's 85,000 miles (137,000 kilometers) of roads are surfaced. The Blue Ridge Parkway connects Great Smoky Mountains National Park with Shenandoah National Park in Virginia. Many bridges span rivers and inlets along the coast. Railroads operate on about 6,300 miles (10,080 kilometers) of track in North Carolina. About 25 rail lines provide freight service, and passenger trains serve about 10 cities in the state. Five commercial airlines serve North Carolina. Harbors at Morehead City, Southport, and Wilmington are part of the Atlantic Intracoastal Waterway (see ATLANTIC INTRACOASTAL WATERWAY).

Communication. James Davis, a printer and editor, established North Carolina's first newspaper, the *North Carolina Gazette*, at New Bern in 1751. The weekly *Raleigh Register* was founded in 1799. The state's largest daily newspapers today are the *Charlotte Observer* and the *Raleigh News and Observer*. North Carolina publishers print about 200 newspapers, of which about 50 are dailies. About 100 periodicals are produced in the state.

North Carolina's oldest radio station, WBT of Charlotte, began broadcasting in 1922. Television in the state started in 1949, with stations WBTV in Charlotte and WFMY in Greensboro. Today, North Carolina has about 300 radio stations, about 25 commercial television stations, and an educational television network.

NORTH CAROLINA / History

Indian Days. About 35,000 Indians, belonging to about 30 tribes, lived in the North Carolina region when white men first arrived. The most important tribes were the Cherokee in the western mountains; the Hatteras along the coast; and the Catawba, Chowanoc, and Tuscarora of the coastal plain and the Piedmont.

Exploration and Settlement. Giovanni da Verrazano, sailing in the service of France, was the first known white man to explore the North Carolina coast. He visited the Cape Fear area in 1524. Verrazano sent glowing reports of what he saw to King Francis I of France. But the king was not interested in colonizing the region. About two years later, Lucas Vásquez de Ayllón of Spain established a colony near Cape Fear. But disease and starvation killed so many of his followers that the survivors soon fled the area. In 1540, Hernando de Soto, also of Spain, led an expedition over the mountains at the southwestern tip of the North Carolina region. De Soto hoped to find gold. Instead, he became the first European to reach the Mississippi River. He arrived at the river in 1541. Other Spaniards also came to the region, but neither they nor the French established any permanent settlements. In 1585, Sir Walter Raleigh of England sent an expedition to settle on Roanoke Island. This group became the first English colony in America. But misfortunes forced the settlers to return to England in 1586. Raleigh sent a later expedition to Roanoke Island in 1587, with John White as governor. White established a colony, and sailed back to England for supplies that same year. When Queen Elizabeth allowed White to return to Roanoke Island

in 1590, his colony had disappeared. No one knows what happened to the more than a hundred men, women, and children of what has come to be called the *Lost Colony* (see LOST COLONY).

In 1629, King Charles I of England granted his attorney general, Sir Robert Heath, the southern part of the English claim in America. This included a strip of land containing what is now both North Carolina and South Carolina, and extending to the Pacific Ocean. The land was named the Province of *Carolana* (land of Charles). Heath made no attempts at settlement.

The first permanent white settlers in Carolina came from Virginia. They settled in the Albemarle Sound region around 1650. In 1663, Charles II of England regranted Carolina to eight of his favorite nobles. He made them *lords proprietors* (ruling landlords) of the colony. The proprietors divided Carolina into three counties: (1) Albemarle, in the northern part; (2) Clarendon, in the Cape Fear region; and (3) Craven, in what is now South Carolina. In 1664, William Drummond was appointed governor of Albemarle County, and government began in Carolina. Clarendon County lasted only until 1667. From then until 1689, Albemarle County had the only government in the North Carolina region.

Colonial Days. The colonists of Albemarle County believed that the proprietors and governors were more interested in making money than in governing wisely. In 1677, some Albemarle colonists revolted against their governor. They ran the county for over a year, with John Culpeper as governor. The revolt became known as *Culpeper's Rebellion*. Between 1664 and 1689, the colonists drove five of the Albemarle governors out of office.

After 1691, governors were appointed to govern the entire Carolina colony, with a deputy governor for the North Carolina region. The deputy governors ruled wisely and the colonists accepted them. The North Carolina region became a separate colony in 1712.

During the late 1600's and early 1700's, increasing

------ **IMPORTANT DATES IN NORTH CAROLINA** ------

1524 Giovanni da Verrazano, a Florentine explorer sailing in the service of France, visited the North Carolina coast.

1585 The English established at Roanoke Island their first colony in what is now the United States.

1629 King Charles I of England granted *Carolana* to Sir Robert Heath.

1650? The first permanent settlers came to the Albemarle region from Virginia.

1663 King Charles II granted the Carolina colony to eight lords proprietors.

1664 North Carolina's first government was established in Albemarle County.

1711 The Tuscarora Indians attacked settlements between the Neuse and Pamlico rivers. The colonists defeated the Indians in 1713.

1729 North Carolina came under direct royal rule.

1765 Colonists in North Carolina began to resist enforcement of the British Stamp Act and other tax laws.

1774 North Carolina sent delegates to the First Continental Congress in Philadelphia.

1776 The Whigs defeated the Tories at Moore's Creek Bridge. North Carolina adopted its first constitution.

1781 British forces withdrew from North Carolina and surrendered in Virginia.

1789 North Carolina became the 12th state on Nov. 21.

1835 Constitutional changes gave equal representation to most North Carolina taxpayers.

1861 North Carolina seceded from the Union.

1865 General Joseph E. Johnston surrendered to General William T. Sherman near Durham.

1868 North Carolina was readmitted to the Union.

1903 The Wright brothers made the first successful powered airplane flight at Kitty Hawk.

1915 The legislature established a highway commission.

1933 The state took over the support of public schools.

1945 Fontana Dam, the largest in the state, was completed.

1949 The people approved a large bond issue for road and public-school construction.

1950 Great industrial expansion began.

1958 Three North Carolina universities joined in the Research Triangle program for industry.

1962 The state's courts were reorganized under a general court of justice.

1963 The legislature adopted a single university plan for the University of North Carolina, beginning with campuses at Chapel Hill, Greensboro, and Raleigh. The plan made provisions for the addition of other campuses to the University of North Carolina system.

1969 The legislature adopted a state tax on cigarettes.

1971 A new state constitution went into effect.

1972 James E. Holshouser, Jr., became the first Republican to be elected governor since 1896.

numbers of settlers came to North Carolina. In 1705, North Carolina's first town, Bath, was incorporated near the mouth of the Pamlico River. By 1710, settlements had spread down the coast and along the riverbanks as far south as the Neuse River. In 1710, Swiss and Germans founded New Bern, a community several miles inland on the Neuse, in Tuscarora Indian territory. New Bern was one of the most peaceful and prosperous settlements in North Carolina. Then, at dawn on Sept. 22, 1711, disaster struck. Enraged Tuscarora tribesmen, whose land had been seized by white settlers, attacked New Bern and other settlements. Within two hours, most of the settlements between the Neuse and Pamlico rivers lay in ruins. The Indians had massacred hundreds of settlers, burned their homes, stolen their valuables, and destroyed their crops. The massacre marked the beginning of the Tuscarora War, the worst Indian war in North Carolina's history. The colonists defeated the Indians on March 25, 1713.

While settlers battled the wilderness and the Indians during the late 1600's and early 1700's, pirates ter-

President Andrew Johnson
born in Raleigh

President James K. Polk
born near Pineville

Lifeline of the Confederacy. North Carolina, "First at Bethel, farthest at Gettysburg, and last at Appomattox," furnished more than one sixth of the Confederate soldiers in the Civil War.

State of Franklin. In 1784, settlers in the western part of North Carolina (now east Tennessee) set up a state when cession of the territory to the United States left them without state or federal protection.

rorized North Carolina's coastline. Most piracy along the Atlantic Coast ended with the death of the famous pirate Blackbeard in a battle near Ocracoke Island in 1718.

In 1729, the lords proprietors sold their land back to England. North Carolina became a royal colony, ruled by royal governors appointed by the king. These royal governors ruled wisely and well, and helped the colony grow. In 1729, only about 36,000 persons lived in North Carolina, mostly along the coast. By 1775, the population had grown to nearly 350,000, and settlement had spread westward across the Piedmont and into the mountains.

Colonial Wars. North Carolina contributed money and troops to help England fight several colonial wars. The War of Jenkins' Ear (1739-1744) was fought against the Spaniards in what is now Georgia. The war was named for Robert Jenkins, an Englishman whose ear was believed to have been cut off by Spaniards. Other colonial wars included Queen Anne's War (1702-1713), King George's War (1744-1748), and the French and

Indian War (1754-1763). In 1760, Hugh Waddell of Wilmington led North Carolina troops to an important victory over the Cherokee Indians. This battle took place at Fort Dobbs, near present-day Statesville. In 1761, the Cherokee signed a peace treaty that opened a vast area of western Virginia and the Carolinas to settlement. See FRENCH AND INDIAN WARS.

Revolution and Independence. England had gone into debt as a result of the colonial wars. In an attempt to solve some of its financial problems, England imposed a series of taxes on the American colonies. But the colonists objected to these taxes. A group of North Carolinians called the *Sons of Liberty* led demonstrations and even armed rebellion against the taxes. Some western North Carolina farmers called the *Regulators* rebelled against taxes and against unjust treatment from eastern officials. William Tryon, the royal governor, needed more than a thousand troops to defeat the Regulators

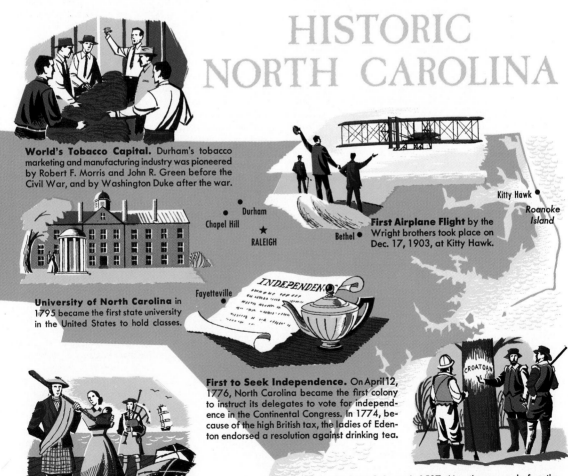

HISTORIC
NORTH CAROLINA

World's Tobacco Capital. Durham's tobacco marketing and manufacturing industry was pioneered by Robert F. Morris and John R. Green before the Civil War, and by Washington Duke after the war.

Kitty Hawk

Roanoke Island

Durham

Chapel Hill

★ RALEIGH

Bethel

First Airplane Flight by the Wright brothers took place on Dec. 17, 1903, at Kitty Hawk.

University of North Carolina in 1795 became the first state university in the United States to hold classes.

Fayetteville

INDEPENDEN

First to Seek Independence. On April 12, 1776, North Carolina became the first colony to instruct its delegates to vote for independence in the Continental Congress. In 1774, because of the high British tax, the ladies of Edenton endorsed a resolution against drinking tea.

CROATOAN

The Lost Colony. In 1587, thirty-three years before the Pilgrims landed at Plymouth Rock, an English colony was founded on Roanoke Island. Three years later, a supply ship found no trace of the colony except for the word "Croatoan" carved on a tree. Virginia Dare, first child born of English parents in America, was among the missing.

Scottish Highlanders settled around Fayetteville after Bonnie Prince Charlie was defeated in Scotland in 1746.

in the Battle of Alamance, fought on May 16, 1771.

North Carolina sent delegates to Philadelphia to attend the First Continental Congress in 1774. After the Revolutionary War began in April, 1775, North Carolinians quickly took sides. Those who opposed the British were called *Whigs*. Those who remained loyal to the king were called *Tories*. On Feb. 27, 1776, Whig forces, under Colonels Richard Caswell and Alexander Lillington, crushed the Tories in the Battle of Moore's Creek Bridge. This was the first battle of the Revolutionary War in North Carolina. The Whig victory prevented a planned British invasion of North Carolina. On April 12, 1776, North Carolina became the first colony to instruct its delegates to the Continental Congress to vote for independence. Later that year, North Carolina adopted its first constitution and chose Richard Caswell as governor. On July 21, 1778, North Carolina *ratified* (approved) the Articles of Confederation.

Much of the Revolutionary War was fought outside North Carolina's borders. But North Carolinians joined the fight against the British in Virginia, Georgia, and South Carolina. In 1780, British forces led by Lord Charles Cornwallis marched toward North Carolina from the south. Part of Cornwallis's army was slaughtered in the Battle of Kings Mountain, just south of North Carolina. But after a retreat, Cornwallis moved northward again, this time into North Carolina. On March 15, 1781, General Nathanael Greene's forces outlasted Cornwallis' troops in the Battle of Guilford Courthouse. The British abandoned North Carolina.

Statehood. North Carolinians delayed approving the United States Constitution because they opposed a strong federal government. At the Hillsboro Convention of 1788, they rejected the Constitution and suggested many amendments to it. The Bill of Rights to the Constitution, proposed by Congress in 1789, included some of these suggestions. North Carolina finally ratified the Constitution on Nov. 21, 1789.

North Carolina was called the *Rip Van Winkle State* from about 1800 to 1835. The state was so backward that it seemed to be asleep. It had little commerce or industry. It lacked seaports and transportation facilities. Most of its people worked on farms, using poor tools and wasteful methods. Many persons left North Carolina, including three men who later became President—Andrew Jackson, James K. Polk, and Andrew Johnson.

An age of progress began in 1835, when North Carolina revised its constitution, giving most taxpayers the right to vote. By granting equal representation, the constitution gave more power to the people of the western region and encouraged the development of that area. Public schools, railroads, and roads were built. Agriculture increased, and manufacturing started to grow. North Carolina led the nation in gold production until the California Gold Rush of 1849.

The Civil War and Reconstruction. North Carolina was part of the South, but it was also one of the original 13 states of the Union. It tried to preserve the Union even after most southern states had *seceded* (withdrawn). The Civil War began on April 12, 1861. When President Abraham Lincoln asked North Carolina for troops to fight the Confederate States, North Carolina refused.

The state seceded from the Union on May 20, 1861.

Union forces captured much of eastern North Carolina early in the war. But the port at Wilmington remained open to Confederate supply ships until January, 1865. More than 10 battles took place in North Carolina. The bloodiest of these was fought at Bentonville, on March 19-21, 1865. There, Union forces under General William T. Sherman defeated the Confederate troops of General Joseph E. Johnston. Johnston surrendered to Sherman near Durham on April 26. During the war, North Carolina supplied 125,000 men to the Confederate cause. About a fourth of all the Confederate soldiers killed came from North Carolina.

During the Reconstruction period, North Carolinians lived under federal military authority from 1867 until 1877. The Republican party, consisting mostly of Negroes, Union sympathizers, and Northerners called *carpetbaggers* gained control of the state government after the Civil War (see CARPETBAGGER). The Republicans drew up a new state constitution in 1868 which abolished slavery and gave Negroes the right to vote. The state rejoined the Union on June 25, 1868.

During the Reconstruction years, bitter struggles took place between Republicans and Democrats, and between Negroes and whites. The Ku-Klux Klan and other secret groups supported white supremacy and tried to keep Negroes from voting. Democrats gained control of the state legislature in 1870. They impeached Republican Governor William W. Holden in 1871, and removed him from office. Democratic influence spread to other state government departments. In 1875, the Democratic legislature added 30 amendments to the constitution. This action ensured white, Democratic control of North Carolina. See CIVIL WAR; RECONSTRUCTION.

Economic Progress. The Civil War had brought death, despair, and destruction to North Carolina. The abolition of slavery caused the loss of inexpensive farm labor. As a result, large plantations were divided into small farms. The number of farms in the state grew from about 75,000 in 1860 to about 150,000 in 1880.

The people of North Carolina rebuilt their state quickly. By the late 1800's, farm production equaled what it had been before the war. Tobacco and cotton crops led the growth. Industry also grew rapidly. Washington Duke opened a smoking-tobacco business at Durham in 1865. His son, James Buchanan Duke, founded the American Tobacco Company (now American Brands, Inc.), in 1890. Tobacco factories in the state numbered nearly 130 by 1880. Furniture making and cotton processing also became large-scale industries by 1900.

The Early 1900's. In 1901, Governor Charles B. Aycock started a vast, long-reaching program to improve North Carolina's public education system. Since then, the state's schools have continued to improve. In 1915, the legislature created the State Highway Commission. The commission began the largest road-building program in the state's history. This program earned for North Carolina the nickname of the *Good Roads State* during the 1920's.

The state's industries developed at a tremendous rate during the early 1900's. By the late 1920's, North Carolina led the nation in the production of cotton textiles, tobacco products, and wooden furniture.

The depression of the 1930's brought sudden drops in prices and wages. Businesses failed and banks closed. Workers lost their jobs and farmers lost their farms.

The federal and state governments tried to fight the effects of the depression. The North Carolina government reduced local taxes and took control of all highways and public schools. Federal control of agricultural production raised farm prices and income. The state passed welfare measures, raised teachers' salaries, and reduced working hours to help North Carolina out of the depression by the late 1930's.

The Mid-1900's. During World War II (1939-1945), North Carolina mills supplied the armed forces with more textile goods than any other state. It also mined over half the mica used in U.S. war production.

In the late 1940's, North Carolina built new hospitals and mental health facilities. The state also paved more than 13,000 miles (20,900 kilometers) of rural roads. Two dams increased the state's power output. Fontana Dam, at the edge of the Great Smoky Mountains, started operating in 1945, and Kerr Dam, near Henderson, went into operation in 1954.

In 1954, the Supreme Court of the United States ruled that compulsory school segregation was unconstitutional. North Carolina had separate schools for Negroes and whites. By 1970, almost all the state's school districts had been integrated.

During the 1950's, North Carolina continued to shift from a rural, agricultural economy to an urban, industrial economy. The state worked to attract new industries by providing businesses with technical and engineering assistance and by reducing taxes on corporations. In 1958, three universities—Duke University at Durham, North Carolina State University at Raleigh, and the University of North Carolina at Chapel Hill—combined their research resources. They formed the North Carolina Research Triangle, which provides research facilities for industry.

In 1962, the voters approved an amendment to the North Carolina Constitution that brought sweeping changes to the state's court system. All the courts became unified under a general court of justice.

In 1963, the legislature set up a system of community colleges and technical institutes. Also in 1963, the state adopted a single university plan for the University of North Carolina, beginning with campuses at Chapel Hill, Greensboro, and Raleigh. By 1969, campuses at Asheville, Charlotte, and Wilmington had become part of the university. In 1972, 10 other state-supported universities merged with the University of North Carolina, forming a 16-campus university system. These included the North Carolina School of the Arts, which had become the nation's first state-supported school for the arts when it opened in Winston-Salem in 1965. See NORTH CAROLINA, UNIVERSITY OF.

North Carolina Today faces growing demands for government services. These demands resulted largely from population movements. Almost half the state's people now live in urban, rather than rural, areas. In 1970, the voters approved a revised state Constitution, and a constitutional amendment that led to the merger of over 300 state agencies into 19 departments.

North Carolina also faces increased spending for community colleges, health programs and hospitals, highways, and prison improvement. In 1969, the

THE GOVERNORS OF NORTH CAROLINA

	Party	Term
Under Articles of Confederation		
1. Abner Nash	None	1780-1781
2. Thomas Burke	None	1781-1782
3. Alexander Martin	None	1782-1784
4. Richard Caswell	None	1784-1787
5. Samuel Johnston	Federalist	1787-1789
Under United States Constitution		
1. Alexander Martin	Unknown	1789-1792
2. R. D. Spaight, Sr.	*Dem.-Rep.	1792-1795
3. Samuel Ashe	*Dem.-Rep.	1795-1798
4. W. R. Davie	Federalist	1798-1799
5. Benjamin Williams	*Dem.-Rep.	1799-1802
6. James Turner	*Dem.-Rep.	1802-1805
7. Nathaniel Alexander	*Dem.-Rep.	1805-1807
8. Benjamin Williams	*Dem.-Rep.	1807-1808
9. David Stone	*Dem.-Rep.	1808-1810
10. Benjamin Smith	*Dem.-Rep.	1810-1811
11. William Hawkins	*Dem.-Rep.	1811-1814
12. William Miller	*Dem.-Rep.	1814-1817
13. John Branch	*Dem.-Rep.	1817-1820
14. Jesse Franklin	*Dem.-Rep.	1820-1821
15. Gabriel Holmes	Unknown	1821-1824
16. H. G. Burton	Federalist	1824-1827
17. James Iredell, Jr.	*Dem.-Rep.	1827-1828
18. John Owen	Unknown	1828-1830
19. Montfort Stokes	Democratic	1830-1832
20. D. L. Swain	Whig	1832-1835
21. R. D. Spaight, Jr.	Democratic	1835-1836
22. E. B. Dudley	Whig	1836-1841
23. J. M. Morehead	Whig	1841-1845
24. W. A. Graham	Whig	1845-1849
25. Charles Manly	Whig	1849-1851
26. D. S. Reid	Democratic	1851-1854
27. Warren Winslow	Democratic	1854-1855
28. Thomas Bragg	Democratic	1855-1859
29. John W. Ellis	Democratic	1859-1861
30. Henry T. Clark	Democratic	1861-1862
31. Z. B. Vance	Democratic	1862-1865
32. †W. W. Holden	Republican	1865
33. Jonathan Worth	Democratic	1865-1868
34. W. W. Holden	Republican	1868-1871
35. T. R. Caldwell	Republican	1871-1874
36. C. H. Brogden	Republican	1874-1877
37. Z. B. Vance	Democratic	1877-1879
38. T. J. Jarvis	Democratic	1879-1885
39. A. M. Scales	Democratic	1885-1889
40. D. G. Fowle	Democratic	1889-1891
41. Thomas M. Holt	Democratic	1891-1893
42. Elias Carr	Democratic	1893-1897
43. D. L. Russell	Republican	1897-1901
44. Charles B. Aycock	Democratic	1901-1905
45. R. B. Glenn	Democratic	1905-1909
46. W. W. Kitchin	Democratic	1909-1913
47. Locke Craig	Democratic	1913-1917
48. Thomas W. Bickett	Democratic	1917-1921
49. Cameron Morrison	Democratic	1921-1925
50. Angus Wilton McLean	Democratic	1925-1929
51. O. Max Gardner	Democratic	1929-1933
52. J. C. B. Ehringhaus	Democratic	1933-1937
53. Clyde R. Hoey	Democratic	1937-1941
54. J. Melville Broughton	Democratic	1941-1945
55. R. Gregg Cherry	Democratic	1945-1949
56. W. Kerr Scott	Democratic	1949-1953
57. William B. Umstead	Democratic	1953-1954
58. Luther H. Hodges	Democratic	1954-1961
59. Terry Sanford	Democratic	1961-1965
60. Daniel K. Moore	Democratic	1965-1969
61. Robert W. Scott	Democratic	1969-1973
62. James E. Holshouser, Jr.	Republican	1973-1977
63. James B. Hunt, Jr.	Democratic	1977-

*Democratic-Republican   †Provisional Governor

state legislature increased some taxes and passed North Carolina's first cigarette tax. The state is the nation's leading tobacco producer.

Other problems of North Carolina in the 1970's include conservation and pollution. In 1969, the state legislature passed laws to protect the coastal waters where fish and some game animals breed. The legislature also increased the powers of the state board of water and air resources. Cities and counties in North Carolina received permission to adopt air pollution laws. In 1974, the legislature adopted the Coastal Carolina Land Management Act. This law gave the state authority over the development of land on North Carolina's coast.

The Republican Party continued to increase its strength in the state during the 1970's. In 1972, James E. Holshouser, Jr., became the first Republican to be elected governor of North Carolina since 1896. Also in 1972, Jesse A. Helms was the first Republican to be elected to the U.S. Senate from North Carolina since 1896. In 1976, however, James B. Hunt, Jr., a Democrat, was elected governor. ROBERT ELI CRAMER, BLACKWELL PIERCE ROBINSON, and SAM RAGAN

NORTH CAROLINA/*Study Aids*

Related Articles in WORLD BOOK include:

BIOGRAPHIES

Aycock, Charles B.	Hooper, William
Blackbeard	Iredell, James
Blount, William	Johnson, Andrew
Bragg, Braxton	King, William R. D.
Daniels (family)	Penn, John
Dare, Virginia	Polk, James Knox
Duke, James B.	Spaight, Richard D.
Gaston, William	Vance, Zebulon B.
Hewes, Joseph	Williamson, Hugh

CITIES

Asheville	Fayetteville	New Bern	Wilson
Charlotte	Greensboro	Raleigh	Winston-Salem
Durham	High Point		

HISTORY

Civil War	Lost Colony	Reconstruction
Colonial Life in America	Mecklenburg Declaration of Independence	Revolutionary War in America
Franklin, State of		

PHYSICAL FEATURES

Black Mountains	Dismal Swamp	Mount Mitchell
Blue Ridge Mountains	Fall Line	Ocracoke Island
Cape Fear	Great Smoky Mountains	Pee Dee River
Cape Hatteras	Kill Devil Hill	Piedmont Region Roanoke River

PRODUCTS

For North Carolina's rank among the states, see:

Chicken	Nut	Sweet Potato	Tobacco
Clothing	Peanut	Textile	Turkey

OTHER RELATED ARTICLES

Camp Lejeune	Fort Bragg	Tennessee Valley
Cherry Point Marine Corps Air Station	Southern States	Authority

Outline

I. Government
  A. Constitution   D. Courts   F. Taxation
  B. Executive   E. Local   G. Politics
  C. Legislature   Government
II. People
III. Education
  A. Schools   B. Libraries   C. Museums
IV. A Visitor's Guide
  A. Places to Visit   B. Annual Events
V. The Land
  A. Land Regions
  B. Rivers, Waterfalls, and Lakes
VI. Climate
VII. Economy
  A. Natural Resources   B. Manufacturing

  C. Agriculture   F. Electric Power
  D. Mining   G. Transportation
  E. Fishing Industry   H. Communication
VIII. History

Questions

What was the *Lost Colony?*
Why is North Carolina one of the largest payers of federal taxes in the nation?
What North Carolina town produces famous pottery?
Why is North Carolina referred to as the *Tar Heel State?*
How did North Carolina attract industries in the 1950's?
What is the *Graveyard of the Atlantic?*
Why did North Carolina delay in approving the United States Constitution?
Who were the *Sons of Liberty?*
What is unique about the relationship between the governor of North Carolina and the state legislature?

Books for Young Readers

BELL, THELMA H. and CORYDON. *North Carolina.* Coward-McCann, 1971.
BURNEY, EUGENIA. *Colonial North Carolina.* Nelson, 1975.
CARPENTER, ALLAN. *North Carolina.* Childrens Press, 1965.
LACY, DAN M. *The Colony of North Carolina.* Watts, 1975.
ROBERTS, BRUCE and NANCY. *Where Time Stood Still: A Portrait of Appalachia.* Macmillan, 1970.
TAYLOR, THEODORE. *Teetoncey.* Doubleday, 1974. *Teetoncey and Ben O'Neal.* 1975. Both books are fiction.
TRAVELLER BIRD. *The Path to Snowbird Mountain: Cherokee Legends.* Farrar, 1972.
WALSER, RICHARD G., and STREET, J. M. *North Carolina Parade: Stories of History and People.* Univ. of North Carolina Press, 1966.

Books for Older Readers

CLAY, JAMES W., and others, eds. *North Carolina Atlas: Portrait of a Changing Southern State.* Univ. of North Carolina Press, 1975.
FLEER, JACK D. *North Carolina Politics: An Introduction.* Univ. of North Carolina Press, 1968.
GINNS, PATSY MOORE. *Rough Weather Makes Good Timber: Carolinians Recall.* Univ. of North Carolina Press, 1977. Oral history of North Carolina folkways.
LEFLER, HUGH T., and NEWSOME, A. R. *The History of a Southern State: North Carolina.* 3rd ed. Univ. of North Carolina Press, 1973.
LEFLER, HUGH T., and POWELL, W. S. *Colonial North Carolina.* Scribner, 1973.
ROBERTS, NANCY. *The Goodliest Land: North Carolina.* Doubleday, 1973.
WALSER, RICHARD G. *Literary North Carolina: A Brief Historical Survey.* North Carolina State Department of Archives and History (Raleigh), 1970.
WAUGH, ELIZABETH C. *North Carolina's Capital: Raleigh.* Univ. of North Carolina Press, 1967.
WETMORE, RUTH Y. *First on the Land: The North Carolina Indians.* Blair, 1975.

North Carolina State University at Raleigh is part of the University of North Carolina System. Harrelson Hall, *above*, a circular classroom building, can seat more than 3,500 students.

University of North Carolina campus at Chapel Hill includes the Louis Round Wilson Library, *right*. The library contains more than 1,200,000 volumes.

NORTH CAROLINA, UNIVERSITY OF, is a state-supported coeducational system of higher education. The system consists of 16 institutions that have a total of more than 90,000 students. Each of these institutions has its own chancellor, and a president heads the entire university.

Five institutions in the university system are called the University of North Carolina. They are in Asheville, Chapel Hill, Charlotte, Greensboro, and Wilmington. The other 11 institutions are Appalachian State University (in Boone), East Carolina University (in Greenville), Elizabeth City State University, Fayetteville State University, North Carolina Agricultural and Technical State University (in Greensboro), North Carolina Central University (in Durham), the North Carolina School of the Arts (in Winston-Salem), North Carolina State University at Raleigh, Pembroke State University, Western Carolina University (in Cullowhee), and Winston-Salem State University.

The multicampus university offers a wide variety of studies. For example, the North Carolina School of the Arts specializes in the performing arts. The University of North Carolina at Chapel Hill, the largest of the 16 institutions, offers programs in the arts and sciences, business administration, dentistry, education, journalism, law, library science, medicine, nursing, pharmacy, public health, and social work.

Each institution in the system grants bachelor's degrees. Appalachian State University, East Carolina University, North Carolina Central University, and Western Carolina University award master's degrees. North Carolina State University at Raleigh and the University of North Carolina at Chapel Hill and at Greensboro have programs leading to doctor's degrees.

The university was chartered in 1789. Its first campus opened in 1795 in Chapel Hill. From 1931 to 1969, five more institutions became part of the university. In 1972, the North Carolina General Assembly merged 10 other state-supported colleges and universities with the university to form the 16-campus system.

For the enrollment of each institution, see UNIVERSITIES AND COLLEGES (table). WILLIAM CLYDE FRIDAY

NORTH CAROLINA AGRICULTURAL AND TECHNICAL STATE UNIVERSITY. See UNIVERSITIES AND COLLEGES (table [North Carolina, University of]).

NORTH CAROLINA CENTRAL UNIVERSITY. See UNIVERSITIES AND COLLEGES (table [North Carolina, University of]).

NORTH CASCADES NATIONAL PARK is in northwestern Washington. The park's magnificent scenery includes mountain ridges, forested valleys, alpine lakes and meadows, waterfalls, and glaciers. Among the animals that live in the park are bears, cougars, deer, moose, mountain goats, and wolverines. The park also has valuable cedar and fir forests and mineral deposits. The park was established in 1968, along with the adjacent Lake Chelan National Recreation Area and Ross Lake National Recreation Area. For the area of the park, see NATIONAL PARK SYSTEM (table: National Parks). For its location, see WASHINGTON (political map). GEORGE B. HARTZOG, JR.

NORTH CENTRAL COLLEGE. See UNIVERSITIES AND COLLEGES (table).

NORTH CENTRAL STATES are the 12 states in the north-central part of the United States. They include Illinois, Indiana, Iowa, Kansas, Michigan, Minnesota, Missouri, Nebraska, North Dakota, Ohio, South Dakota, and Wisconsin. The western North Central States, sometimes called the Great Plains States, contain some of the richest farming land in the world. Corn and wheat fields cover the plains. The states on the eastern edge of the region are sometimes called the Lake States. They have great industrial centers, as well as farms. See also MIDWESTERN STATES.

NORTH DAKOTA

The Flickertail State

NORTH DAKOTA is a Midwestern state in the center of the North American continent. The geographic center of North America is near the town of Rugby. North Dakota is mainly a farm state. Its economy is based more heavily on farming than that of any other state except South Dakota. North Dakota has a larger percentage of workers in agriculture than any other state. About 56 of every 100 North Dakotans live on farms or in farming areas.

Farms and ranches cover nearly all North Dakota. They stretch from the flat Red River Valley in the east, across rolling plains, to the rugged Badlands in the west. The chief crop is wheat, which is grown in every county. Only Kansas raises more wheat. North Dakota harvests about half the nation's flaxseed. It is also the top producer of barley and a leader in rye production.

Soil is North Dakota's most precious resource. It is the base of the state's great agricultural wealth. But North Dakota also has enormous mineral resources. The nation's largest lignite coal reserves—about 16 billion short tons (14.5 billion metric tons)—are in North Dakota. The state also has large oil reserves. Petroleum was not discovered in North Dakota until 1951. But it quickly became the state's most valuable mineral.

Few settlers came to the North Dakota region before the 1870's. Transportation was poor, and newcomers feared attacks by Indians. During the 1870's, the Northern Pacific Railroad began to push across the Dakota Territory. Large-scale farming also began during the 1870's. Eastern corporations and some families established huge wheat farms covering thousands of acres or hectares in the Red River Valley. The farms made such enormous profits that they were called *bonanza* farms. Settlers flocked to North Dakota, attracted by the success of the bonanza farms. In 1870, North Dakota had 2,405 persons. By 1890, only 20 years later, its population had grown to 190,983. Farming became firmly established as North Dakota's major industry.

North Dakota was named for the Sioux Indians who once roamed the territory. The Sioux called themselves *Dakota* or *Lakota*, meaning *allies* or *friends*. One of North Dakota's nicknames is the *Sioux State*. But it is more often called the *Flickertail State*, because of the many flickertail ground squirrels that live in central North Dakota.

Bismarck is the capital of North Dakota, and Fargo is the largest city. For the relationship of North Dakota to other states in its region, see the article on MIDWESTERN STATES.

Cattle Ranch near Amidon

Harley Hettick, Alpha

Oil Well near Tioga

Harley Hettick, Alpha

Wendler, FPG

Rolling Hills in the Sheyenne River Valley

FACTS IN BRIEF

Capital: Bismarck.

Government: *Congress*—U.S. senators, 2; U.S. representatives, 1. *Electoral Votes*—3. *State Legislature*—senators, 50; representatives, 100. *Counties*—53.

Area: 70,665 sq. mi. (183,022 km²), including 1,392 sq. mi. (3,605 km²) of inland water; 17th in size among the states. *Greatest Distances*—east-west, 360 mi. (579 km); north-south, 210 mi. (338 km).

Elevation: *Highest*—White Butte, 3,506 ft. (1,069 m) above sea level in Slope County. *Lowest*—750 ft. (229 m) above sea level along the Red River in Pembina County.

Population: *Estimated 1975 Population*—635,000. *1970 Census*—617,761; 45th among the states; distribution, 56 per cent rural, 44 per cent urban; density, 9 persons per sq. mi. (3 per km²).

Chief Products: *Agriculture*—barley, beef cattle, dairy products, flaxseed, hogs, oats, potatoes, wheat. *Manufacturing*—nonelectrical machinery; printed materials; processed foods; stone, clay, and glass products. *Mining*—clay, coal, natural gas, natural gas liquids, petroleum, sand and gravel.

Statehood: Nov. 2, 1889, the 39th state.

State Motto: *Liberty and Union, Now and Forever, One and Inseparable.*

State Song: "North Dakota Hymn." Words by James W. Foley; music by C. S. Putnam.

North Dakota (blue) ranks 17th in size among all the states, and 5th in size among the Midwestern States (gray).

The contributors of this article are Jack U. Hagerty, Editor of the Grand Forks Herald; *Russell S. Reid, Former Historian of the State Historical Society of North Dakota; and Bernt Lloyd Wills, Professor of the Department of Geography at the University of North Dakota.*

Constitution. North Dakota is governed under its original constitution, adopted in 1889. An *amendment* (change) to the constitution may be proposed in the state legislature. The proposed amendment must be approved by a majority of each house of the legislature. Then a majority of citizens voting on the proposal must approve it. The people may also sign a *petition* (formal request) proposing an amendment. After 20,000 voters have signed the petition, the proposal is put on a state-wide ballot. The proposal becomes law if a majority of voters approve it.

Executive. The governor of North Dakota is elected to a four-year term, and may serve an unlimited number of terms. The governor receives a yearly salary of $18,000 and an expense allowance of $22,000 a year. For a list of all the state's governors, see the *History* section of this article.

The lieutenant governor, attorney general, secretary of state, treasurer, auditor, and superintendent of public instruction are also elected to four-year terms. All except the treasurer may serve an unlimited number of terms. The treasurer may serve only two terms in a row. The people also elect three public-service com-

missioners, and one commissioner each of agriculture, of labor, of insurance, and of taxation.

The governor, attorney general, and commissioner of agriculture make up the state industrial commission. This commission regulates the North Dakota oil industry. It also oversees the operation of the Bank of North Dakota in Bismarck and of the North Dakota Mill and Elevator in Grand Forks. Both these firms are state-owned and compete with private companies.

Legislature of North Dakota, called the *Legislative Assembly*, has a 50-member senate and a 100-member house of representatives. Voters in 48 of the state's 49 legislative districts elect one senator and two representatives. Voters in the other district, which includes two big U.S. Air Force bases, elect two senators and four representatives. Senators serve four-year terms, and representatives serve two-year terms. The Assembly begins its regular session on the first Tuesday after the first Monday in January in odd-numbered years. Regular sessions are limited to 60 legislative days. The governor may also call special sessions.

Courts of North Dakota are headed by the state supreme court. The supreme court has five judges, all elected to 10-year terms. The judge with the shortest remaining term serves as the chief justice. The people of the state's six judicial districts elect a total of 19 district court judges to six-year terms. Each county has a county court with one judge elected to a four-year term. All North Dakota judges are elected on a "no party" ballot—the ballot has no political party labels.

Local Government. North Dakota has 53 counties. Each is governed by a board of commissioners of three to five members elected to four-year terms. Other elected county officials include the auditor, sheriff, superintendent of schools, and treasurer. North Dakota has 358 cities. The 1967 legislature classed all cities and towns as cities. The cities have limited *home rule* (self-government). They are organized under either mayor-council or commission forms of government, with or without city managers.

Taxation. Taxes and license fees bring in nearly three-fourths of the state government's income. Almost all the rest comes from federal grants and programs. Retail sales taxes and motor vehicle license fees account for more than half the state's revenue. The state also collects taxes on alcoholic beverages, cigarettes, corporation and personal incomes, and other items.

Eva Luoma Photos

Memorial to Pioneer Families in North Dakota adds beauty to the Capitol grounds in Bismarck. The bronze statue shown above was completed in 1947.

North Dakota Travel Dept.

Governor's Mansion stands southwest of the state Capitol in Bismarck. The building was completed in 1960.

The State Seal

Symbols of North Dakota. On the seal, the elm tree and the setting sun represent the state's landscape. The plow, sheaves of wheat, and anvil symbolize agriculture. The bow and arrows and the Indian hunting a buffalo represent North Dakota's history. The seal was adopted in 1889. The regimental flag of the First North Dakota Infantry was adopted as the state flag in 1911. The design is a modified version of the coat of arms of the United States.

Bird and flower illustrations, courtesy of Eli Lilly and Company

The State Flag

Politics. Throughout most of its history, North Dakota has strongly favored the Republican Party. In 1889, the people elected a Republican as the first governor of their state. Since then, the state has had only six Democratic governors. North Dakotans have voted for Republican candidates in about three of every four presidential elections. For North Dakota's electoral votes and voting record in presidential elections, see ELECTORAL COLLEGE (table).

There are signs that North Dakota is becoming a two-party state. In 1915, the Nonpartisan League, a political organization of farmers, was founded in North Dakota. During its early years, the league often controlled the Republican Party. In 1956, the league joined with the state Democratic Party. In 1958, this new, strong political force elected the state's first Democrat to the U.S. House of Representatives. He was Quentin N. Burdick. Two years later, Burdick was elected to the U.S. Senate and William L. Guy, a Democrat, was elected governor. In 1964, Democrats won control of the state House of Representatives for the first time in the state's history. Also in 1964, Guy and Burdick won re-election. In 1966, the Republicans swept the election and regained control of the legislature. Guy served as governor until 1973, when he was succeeded by another Democrat, Arthur A. Link.

State Capitol in Bismarck is 18 stories tall. Bismarck has been the capital since 1889, when North Dakota became a state.

North Dakota Travel Dept.

The State Bird
Western Meadow Lark

The State Flower
Wild Prairie Rose

The State Tree
American Elm

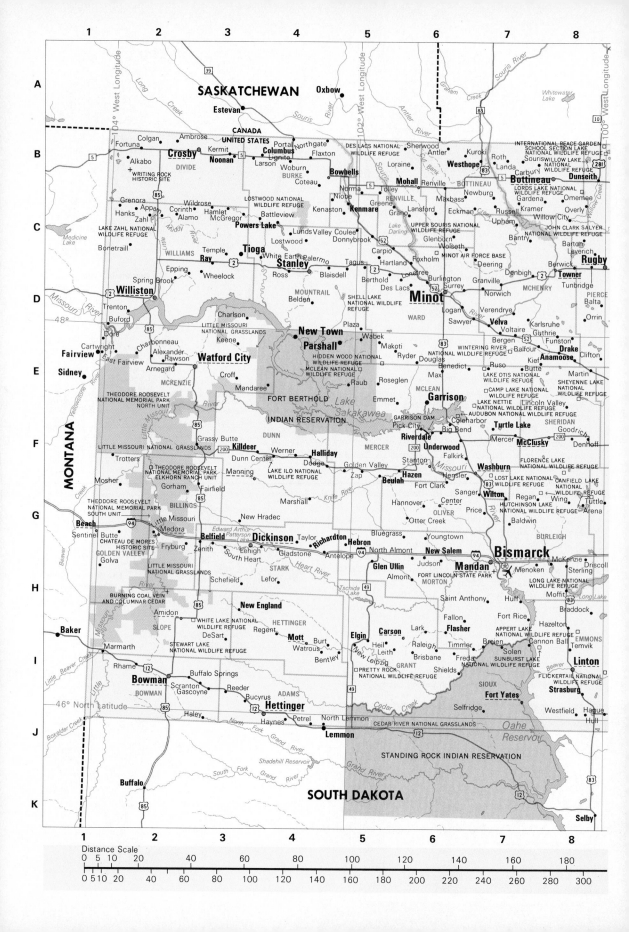

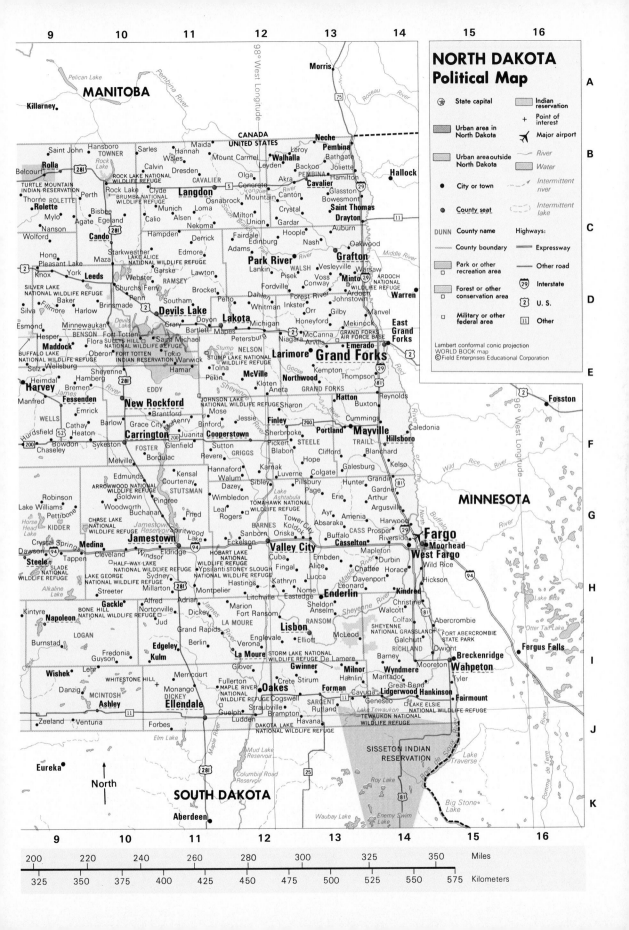

NORTH DAKOTA
Political Map

Legend:

- State capital
- Urban area in North Dakota
- Urban area outside North Dakota
- City or town
- County seat
- DUNN County name
- County boundary
- Park or other recreation area
- Forest or other conservation area
- Military or other federal area
- Indian reservation
- Point of interest
- Major airport
- River
- Water
- Intermittent river
- Intermittent lake

Highways:
- Expressway
- Other road
- 29 Interstate
- 2 U.S.
- 11 Other

Lambert conformal conic projection
WORLD BOOK map
©Field Enterprises Educational Corporation

MANITOBA

CANADA
UNITED STATES

MINNESOTA

SOUTH DAKOTA

North

SISSETON INDIAN RESERVATION

98° West Longitude

96° West Longitude

Miles							
200	220	240	260	280	300	325	350

Kilometers							
325	350	375	400	425	450	475	500	525	550	575

Population

635,000 ..Estimate..1975
617,761 ...Census...1970
632,446 ......"....1960
619,636 ......"....1950
641,935 ......"....1940
680,845 ......"....1930
646,872 ......"....1920
577,056 ......"....1910
319,146 ......"....1900
190,983 ......"....1890
36,909 ......"....1880
2,405 ......"....1870

Metropolitan Area

Fargo-Moorhead (Minn.) ......120,261 (73,653 in N. Dak.; 46,608 in Minn.)

Counties

Adams ......3,832..J 4
Barnes .....14,669..G 12
Benson .....8,245..D 9
Billings .....1,198..G 2
Bottineau ...9,496..B 6
Bowman ....3,901..J 2
Burke ....4,739..B 4
Burleigh ...46,079..G 8
Cass ......73,653..G 13
Cavalier ...10,977..B 11
Dickey ......6,976..J 11
Divide ......4,564..B 2
Dunn ....4,895..F 4
Eddy ....4,103..E 10
Emmons ....7,200..I 8
Foster ......4,832..F 10
Golden Valley ....2,611..H 1
Grand Forks ....61,102..E 13
Grant ....5,009..I 6
Griggs ......4,184..F 12
Hettinger ...5,075..I 4
Kidder ......4,362..G 9
La Moure ...7,117..I 12
Logan ......4,245..I 9
McHenry ....8,977..D 7
McIntosh ...5,545..I 10
McKenzie ...6,127..E 2
McLean ....11,251..E 6
Mercer ......6,175..F 5
Morton ....20,310..H 6
Mountrail ...8,437..D 4
Nelson ......5,807..D 12
Oliver ....2,322..G 6
Pembina ...10,728..B 13
Pierce ....6,323..D 8
Ramsey ....12,915..D 11
Ransom .....7,102..H 13
Renville ....3,828..C 5
Richland ...18,089..I 14
Rolette ....11,549..C 9
Sargent .....5,937..J 13
Sheridan ....3,232..F 8
Sioux ....3,632..I 7
Slope ....1,484..I 2
Stark ......19,613..H 4
Steele ....3,749..F 13
Stutsman ..23,550..G 11
Towner .....4,645..B 10
Traill ....9,571..F 13
Walsh ......16,251..D 13
Ward ......58,560..D 6
Wells ....7,847..F 9
Williams ...19,301..C 2

Cities

Abercrombie ..262..I 15
Adams ....284..C 12
Adrian ....H 11
Alamo ....124..C 2
Alexander ....208..E 2
Alfred ....H 10
Alice ....83..H 13
Alkabo ....B 2
Almont ....109..H 6
Alsen ....174..C 11
Ambrose ......109..B 2
Amenia ....80..G 14
Amidon ....54.°H 2
Anamoose ....401..E 8
Aneta ....376..E 12
Antler ....135..B 6
Ardoch ....70..D 13
Argusville ....118..G 14
Arnegard .....141..E 2
Arthur ....412..G 14
Arvilla ....E 13
Ashley ......1,236.°J 10
Ayr ....48..G 13
Baker ....D 9
Baldwin ....G 7
Balfour ....93..E 8
Balta ....133..D 8
Bantry ....40..C 7
Barlow ....F 10
Barney ....81..I 14
Bartlett ....32..D 11
Barton ....34..C 8
Bathgate .....133..B 13
Battleview ....C 4
Beach ......1,408.°G 1
Belcourt ....B 9
Belfield .....1,130..G 3
Benedict ......72..E 7
Bentley ....I 5
Bergen ....24..D 7
Berlin ....76..I 11
Berthold ....398..D 5
Berwick ....33..D 8
Beulah .....1,344..F 5
Big Bend ....F 6
Binford ......242..F 11
Bisbee ....305..C 10
Bismarck ..38,123.°H 7
Blaisdell ....D 5
Blanchard ....F 14
Bordulac ....F 10
Bottineau ...2,760.°B 8
Bowbells .....584.°B 4
Bowdon ......229..F 9
Bowesmont ....C 14
Bowman ....1,987.°I 2
Braddock .....106..H 8
Brampton ....J 13
Brantford ....F 10
Bremen ....E 10
Brinsmade .....36..D 10
Brocket ....95..D 11
Buchanan ....G 11
Bucyrus ....42..J 3
Buffalo ....241..G 13
Burlington .....495..D 6
Burnstad ....I 9
Burt ....I 4
Butte ....193..E 7
Buxton ....235..E 14
Caledonia ....F 14
Calio ....66..C 10
Calvin ....72..B 10
Cando ......1,512.°C 10
Cannon Ball ....I 7
Canton ....81..C 13
Carpio ....215..C 5
Carrington ..2,491.°F 10
Carson ....466.°I 6
Cartwright ....E 1
Casselton ...1,485..G 14
Cathay ....110..F 10
Cavalier ....2,433.°B 13
Cayuga ....116..J 13
Center ....619.°G 6
Chaffee ....H 13
Chaseley ....F 9
Christine ....H 14
Churchs Ferry 139..D 10
Cleveland .....128..G 10
Clifford ....84..F 13
Clyde ....B 10
Cogswell .....203..J 13
Coleharbor .....112..F 6
Colfax ....70..I 14
Colgate ....F 13
Columbus .....465..B 4
Conway ....57..D 13
Cooperstown .1,485.°F 12
Coteau ....B 4
Coulee ....C 5
Courtenay .....125..G 11
Crary ....150..D 11
Crosby ......1,545.°B 3
Crystal ....272..C 13
Cummings ....F 14
Dahlen ....D 12
Davenport .....147..H 14
Dawson ....131..H 9
Dazey ....128..G 12
Deering ....75..C 7
De Lamere ....I 13
Denhoff ....F 8
Des Lacs ......197..D 6
Devils Lake .7,354.°D 11
Dickey ....118..H 11
Dickinson ..12,405.°G 3
Dodge ....121..F 4
Donnybrook ...163..C 5
Douglas ....144..E 6
Drake ....636..E 8
Drayton .....1,095..C 14
Driscoll ....H 8
Dunn Center ..107..F 4
Dunseith ......811..B 8
Dwight ....93..I 15
East Fairview ....E 1
Eckleson ....G 12
Eckman ....9..C 7
Edgeley ....888..I 11
Edinburg ......315..C 12
Edmore ....398..C 11
Egeland ....96..C 10
Eldridge ....G 11
Elgin ....839..I 5
Ellendale ...1,792.°J 11
Elliott ....50..I 13
Emerado ......864..E 13
Enderlin .....1,343..H 13
Englevale ....I 12
Epping ....140..D 2
Erie ....G 13
Esmond ....416..D 9
Fairdale ......102..C 12
Fairmount ....412..J 15
Fargo .....55,815.°G 14
Fessenden .....815.°E 9
Fillmore ....D 9
Fingal ....166..H 13
Finley ....809.°F 12
Flasher ....467..I 6
Flaxton ....286..B 4
Forbes ....88..J 11
Fordville .....361..D 12
Forest River ...169..D 13
Forman ....596.°J 13
Fort Ransom ....H 12
Fort Totten ....E 10
Fort Yates ..1,153.°J 7
Fortuna ....216..B 2
Foxholm ....C 6
Fredonia ......100..I 10
Fullerton ......110..I 11
Gackle ....470..H 10
Galchutt ....I 14
Galesburg .....134..F 13
Gardar ....C 12
Gardena ....84..C 8
Gardner ....96..G 14
Garrison ....1,614..E 6
Gascoyne ....34..I 3
Gilby ....268..D 13
Gladstone ....222..G 4
Glasston ....C 13
Glen Ullin ..1,070..H 5
Glenburn ......381..C 6
Glenfield ......127..F 11
Golden Valley ......235..F 5
Golva ....104..H 1
Goodrich ......300..F 8
Grace City ....F 11
Grafton .....5,931.°C 13
Grand Forks ...40,060.°E 14
Grand Forks Base* ....10,474..E 13
Grandin ....187..F 14
Grano ....4..C 6
Granville .....282..D 7
Grassy Butte ....F 3
Great Bend .....86..I 14
Grenora ....401..C 1
Guelph ....J 12
Gwinner ....623..I 13
Hague ....146..J 8
Halliday ....413..F 4
Hamar ....E 11
Hamberg ....51..E 9
Hamilton ....110..B 13
Hampden ......114..C 11
Hankinson ..1,125..J 14
Hanks ....13..C 2
Hannaford ....244..F 12
Hannah ....123..B 11
Hansboro ....49..B 10
Harlow ....D 9
Harvey .....2,361..E 9
Hastings ....H 12
Hatton ....808..E 13
Havana ....156..J 13
Haynes ....53..J 4
Hazelton ......374..I 8
Hazen ....1,240..F 6
Heaton ....F 9
Hebron ......1,103..G 5
Heil ....I 5
Heimdal ....E 9
Hettinger ...1,655.°J 4
Hickson ....H 14
Hillsboro ...1,425.°F 14
Hoople ....330..C 13
Hope ....364..F 13
Horace ....276..H 14
Hovey Mobile Park* ....17..C 11
Huff ....H 7
Hunter ....362..G 14
Hurdsfield ....139..F 9
Inkster ....198..D 13
Jamestown .15,078.°G 11
Jessie ....F 12
Johnstown ....D 13
Jud ....110..H 11
Judson ....H 6
Karlsruhe .....172..D 7
Kathryn ....109..H 12
Keene ....E 3
Kempton ....E 13
Kenmare ...1,937..C 5
Kensal ....263..F 11
Kief ....46..E 8
Killdeer ....615..F 3
Kindred ....495..H 14
Kloten ....E 12
Knox ....104..D 9
Kramer ....125..C 7
Kulm ....625..I 10
Lakota .....1,144.°D 11
LaMoure ....951.°I 12
Landa ....61..B 7
Langdon ....3,957.°B 11
Lankin ....221..D 12
Lansford ....296..C 6
Larimore ....1,469..E 13
Larson ....35..B 3
Lawton ....123..D 11
Leal ....41..G 12
Leeds ....626..D 9
Lefor ....H 4
Lehr ....287..I 10
Leith ....92..I 5
Leonard ......221..H 14
Leroy ....B 12
Lidgerwood .1,000..J 14
Lignite ....354..B 4
Linton ......1,695.°I 8
Lisbon .....2,090.°I 13
Litchville .....294..H 12
Loma ....56..C 11
Loraine ....33..B 6
Ludden ....44..J 12
Luverne ....84..F 12
Maddock .....708..E 9
Makoti ....159..E 5
Mandan ...11,400.°H 7
Mandaree ....E 4
Manfred ....E 9
Manning ....°G 3
Mantador ....95..I 14
Manvel ....265..D 14
Mapes ....D 12
Mapleton ......219..G 14
Marion ....215..H 12
Marmarth ......247..I 1
Martin ....120..E 8
Max ....301..E 6
Maxbass ....174..C 6
Mayville ....2,554..F 13
Maza ....20..C 10
McCanna ....D 13
McClusky .....664.°F 8
McGregor ....C 3
McHenry ....152..F 11
McKenzie ....H 8
McLeod ....I 13
McVille ....583..E 12
Medina ....488..G 10
Medora ....129.°G 2
Mekinock ....D 13
Menoken ....H 7
Mercer ....132..F 7
Merricourt ....22..I 11
Michigan ......478..D 12
Milnor ....645..I 13
Milton ....293..C 12
Minnewaukan .496.°D 10
Minot .....32,290.°D 6
Minot Base* ...12,077..C 6
Minto ....636..D 13
Moffit ....H 8
Mohall ....950.°B 6
Monango ....112..I 11
Montpelier .....116..H 11
Mooreton ....158..I 14
Mott ....1,368.°I 4
Mountain ....146..C 12
Munich ....282..C 11
Mylo ....51..C 9
Napoleon ...1,036.°I 9
Nash ....G 13
Neche ....451..B 13
Nekoma ....138..C 11
New England ...906..H 3
New Hradec ....G 3
New Leipzig ..354..I 5
New Rockford. 1,969.°E 10
New Salem ....943..H 6
New Town ..1,428..E 4
Newburg ....125..C 7
Niagara ....115..D 12
Niobe ....C 5
Nome ....103..H 12
Noonan ....403..B 3
Norma ....C 5
North Lemmon ....J 4
Northgate ....B 4
Northwood ..1,189..E 13
Nortonville ....H 11
Norwich ....D 7
Oakes ......1,742..I 12
Oakwood ....C 13
Oberon ....151..E 10
Olga ....B 12
Omemee ....5..C 8
Oriska ....128..G 13
Orr ....D 13
Orrin ....D 8
Osnabrock ....335..C 12
Overly ....28..C 8
Page ....367..G 13
Palermo ....146..D 4
Park River ..2,056..C 13
Parshall ....1,246..E 5
Pekin ....120..E 12
Pembina ....741..B 13
Penn ....D 10
Perth ....44..B 9
Petersburg ....266..D 12
Pettibone ......173..G 9
Pick City ....119..F 6
Pillsbury ....50..G 12
Pingree ....76..G 10
Pisek ....154..D 13
Plaza ....291..D 5
Portal ....251..B 4
Portland ....534..F 13
Powers Lake .523..C 4
Raleigh ....I 6
Rawson ....10..E 2
Ray ....776..C 3
Reeder ....306..I 3
Regan ....82..G 8
Regent ....344..I 4
Reynolds .....236..E 14
Rhame ....206..I 2
Richardton ....799..G 4
Riverdale ....F 6
Riverside ......104..G 14
Robinson ......125..G 9
Rock Lake ....270..B 10
Rogers ....96..G 12
Rolette ....579..C 9
Rolla ....1,458.°B 9
Ross ....125..D 4
Rugby ......3,150.°D 8
Ruso ....15..E 7
Russell ....14..C 7
Rutland ....225..J 13
Ryder ....211..E 5
St. Anthony ....H 7
St. John ....367..B 9
St. Thomas ....508..C 13
Sanborn ....255..G 12
Sarles ....113..B 10
Sawyer ....373..D 7
Scranton ......360..I 3
Selfridge ......346..J 7
Selz ....E 9
Sentinel Butte ......125..G 1
Sharon ....201..F 12
Sheldon ....192..H 13
Sherwood .....369..B 6
Sheyenne ......362..E 10
Shields ....I 6
Sibley ....20..G 12
Solen ....180..I 7
Souris ....151..B 7
South Heart ..132..G 3
Spiritwood Lake ....G 11
Spring Brook ..27..D 2
Stanley .....1,581.°D 4
Stanton ....517.°F 6
Starkweather .193..C 10
Steele ....696.°H 9
Sterling ....H 8
Stirum ....I 13
Strasburg ......642..J 8
Streeter ....324..H 10
Surrey ....735..D 6
Sutton ....F 11
Sykeston ....232..F 10
Tagus ....14..D 5
Tappen ....294..H 9
Taylor ....162..G 4
Temvik ....I 8
Thompson ....291..E 14
Tioga ....1,667..C 3
Tokio ....E 11
Tolley ....163..C 5
Tolna ....247..E 11
Tower City ....289..G 13
Towner ....870.°D 8
Trenton ....D 2
Turtle Lake ..712..F 7
Tuttle ....216..G 8
Underwood .....781..F 6
Upham ....272..C 7
Valley City .7,843.°G 12
Velva ....1,241..D 7
Venturia ....77..J 9
Verona ....140..I 12
Veseleyville ....D 13
Voltaire ....54..D 7
Wabek ....E 5
Wahpeton ...7,076.°I 15
Walcott ....166..H 14
Wales ....113..B 11
Walhalla ....1,471..B 12
Walum ....F 12
Warsaw ....D 13
Warwick ....168..E 11
Washburn ....804.°F 7
Watford City .....1,768.°E 3
Webster ....D 10
Wellsburg ....E 9
Werner ....21..F 4
West Fargo .6,437..G 14
Westfield ....J 8
Westhope ....705..B 7
Wheelock ....21..D 3
White Earth ..128..C 4
Whitman ....D 12
Wild Rice ....H 14
Wildrose ....235..C 3
Williston ...11,280.°D 2
Willow City ...403..C 8
Wilton ....779..G 7
Wimbledon ...337..G 11
Wing ....230..G 8
Wishek .....1,275..I 9
Wolford ....81..C 9
Woodworth ...139..G 10
Wyndmere ....516..I 14
York ....102..D 9
Ypsilanti ....H 11
Zahl ....C 2
Zap ....271..F 5
Zeeland ....313..J 9

*Does not appear on map; key shows general location.
°County seat.

Sources: Latest census figures (1970 and special censuses). Places without population figures are unincorporated areas and are not listed in census reports.

The 1970 United States census reported that North Dakota had 617,761 persons. The state's population had decreased 2 per cent from the 1960 census figure, 632,446. But the U.S. Bureau of the Census estimated that by 1975 the state's population had increased to 635,000.

About 44 per cent of the people of North Dakota live in urban areas. Among the states, North Dakota has one of the lowest percentages of city dwellers. The Fargo-Moorhead (Minn.) metropolitan area is the state's only Standard Metropolitan Statistical Area (see METROPOLITAN AREA). For the population of this area, see the *Index* to the political map of North Dakota.

North Dakota has no large manufacturing industries to encourage the growth of big cities. Only 16 cities in the state have more than 2,500 persons. Only four have more than 25,000 persons. They are, in order of size, Fargo, Grand Forks, Bismarck, the state capital, and Minot. North Dakota's larger cities still serve their original function as centers of shipping, supply, and trade for the surrounding agricultural region. Most of the factories in North Dakota's cities are small. They manufacture, pack, and process food and food products. See the separate articles on the cities of North Dakota listed in the *Related Articles* at the end of this article.

Settlers began to pour into North Dakota by the thousands in the late 1800's. They were attracted by reports of the large profits that had been made in wheat farming. Most of the settlers came from states to the east and south. The largest number from other nations came from Norway. They settled throughout the region. Germans and Russians settled in the south-central area, and Canadians moved into the Red River Valley. Today, about 97 of every 100 North Dakotans were born in the United States. Most of the others came from Canada, Germany, Norway, and Russia.

The majority of immigrants who arrived in the late 1800's belonged to the Lutheran and Roman Catholic churches. Today, about three-fourths of the church members in North Dakota belong to these two churches. Other large religious groups in the state include Methodists and Presbyterians.

POPULATION

This map shows the *population density* of North Dakota, and how it varies in different parts of the state. Population density is the average number of persons who live in a given area.

Persons per sq. mi.		Persons per km²
More than 15		More than 6
5 to 15		2 to 6
Less than 5		Less than 2

```
0    25    50    75 Miles
0  25  50  75  100 Kilometers
```

WORLD BOOK map

Minot • Grand Forks • Fargo • Bismarck •

Indian Chief greets young paleface. Indians in North Dakota wear feathered headdresses at some ceremonies.
Alpha Photo Assoc.

Cowboys perform in exciting rodeos in Mandan and Dickinson every summer. These rodeos help preserve North Dakota's "wild west" heritage.
Greater North Dakota Assn.

Schools. In 1818, Roman Catholic missionaries established the first school in the North Dakota region, at Pembina in the extreme northeast. They taught the children of Scottish and Irish settlers who came from Canada. The school was discontinued in 1823, when the settlement was abandoned. In 1848, Father George Belcourt reopened the Pembina school as an Indian mission.

In the early days, teachers traveled from village to village, teaching groups of children in the settlers' homes. As the settlements grew, the colonists built new schools and hired teachers. Railroad companies, anxious to attract settlers to the region, helped by supplying building materials.

In 1862, the first legislature of the Dakota Territory passed "An Act for the Regulation and Support of Common (public) Schools." Between 1862 and statehood in 1889, the territory reorganized its educational system several times. The first state legislature created a fund for the support of all schools teaching the English language. State and local taxes now support the public schools.

The superintendent of public instruction administers the North Dakota public school system. The people elect him to a four-year term. The superintendent and his staff make up the state department of public instruction. Children must attend school between the ages of 7 and 16. For the number of students and teachers in North Dakota, see EDUCATION (table).

Libraries and Museums. Women's clubs did much to organize and improve North Dakota's early libraries. In 1897, a women's club opened the first public library in the state, at Grafton. Today, North Dakota has

NORTH DAKOTA /A Visitor's Guide

North Dakota's crisp autumn days attract thousands of hunters to streams and lakes where migrating waterfowl pause on their way south. Sportsmen also shoot grouse, Hungarian partridges, pheasants, and other game birds. Fishermen catch catfish, perch, pike, trout, and other fishes. Favorite summer-resort areas include the Badlands region; Devils Lake; and the Killdeer, Pembina, and Turtle mountains.

Rodeo in White Earth

Harley Hettick, Alpha

Relics of Fort Abercrombie in Abercrombie

Bernie Donahue, Publix

--------- PLACES TO VISIT ---------

Following are brief descriptions of some of North Dakota's many interesting places to visit.

Burning Lignite Beds, near Amidon, can be seen from a great distance at night. The lignite beds were probably set afire by lightning or by prairie or camp fires. The fire has advanced slowly, although it has been burning for many years.

Chateau De Mores, near Medora, was the home of a Frenchman, the Marquis de Mores, who founded Medora in 1883.

Fort Abercrombie, at Abercrombie, was the first U.S. military post in present-day North Dakota. The fort was established in 1857.

Lake Sakakawea, the reservoir for Garrison Dam, is about 60 miles (97 kilometers) north of Bismarck. The site is popular for swimming, boating, fishing, camping, and picnicking.

Whitestone Hill, near Ellendale, is the site of a battle in 1863 in which U.S. soldiers defeated the Sioux. The site has the graves of soldiers who died in the battle.

Writing Rock, near Grenora, is a large glacial boulder covered with Indian picture writing.

National Parklands. Theodore Roosevelt National Memorial Park lies in the scenic Badlands. It was established in 1947 in memory of President Roosevelt, who operated two ranches in the area in the 1880's. The park is a wildlife sanctuary. The Knife River Indian Villages National Historic Site, near Marshall, includes the remains of five Hidatsa Indian villages that were occupied until 1845.

State Parks. North Dakota has 12 state parks and campgrounds and many historic and military sites. Its most famous park is the beautiful International Peace Garden, which it shares with the Canadian province of Manitoba. The park lies in the Turtle Mountains. It symbolizes the long friendship between the United States and Canada. Fort Abraham Lincoln State Park, near Mandan, is one of the state's most important historic sites. In 1876, General George A. Custer set out from Fort Abraham Lincoln on the expedition that ended in the disastrous Battle of the Little Bighorn. For information on the state parks, write to Travel Division, State Highway Building, Bismarck, N. Dak. 58505.

about 70 public libraries. In 1898, the state department of public instruction set up a system of traveling libraries to serve the schools. In 1907, the legislature established the state library commission to administer the traveling libraries and provide other library services.

The University of North Dakota at Grand Forks has the largest library in the state. It owns about 370,000 books. The library's collection includes Scandinavian literature, manuscripts on North Dakota's history, and a complete set of the papers of the original Nuremberg trial (see NUREMBERG TRIALS).

The state historical society was organized in Bismarck in 1895. It operates a library with a large collection of books, manuscripts, maps, and papers relating to the state's history. The society also has a museum in Bismarck. The museum's collection includes exhibits dealing with the life of early North Dakota Indians, pioneer days, and natural history. The historical society has smaller collections in museums at Fort

Lincoln and Fort Abercrombie state parks, and at Camp Hancock, Fort Buford, Pembina, and White-stone Hill historic sites.

UNIVERSITIES AND COLLEGES

North Dakota has eight universities and colleges accredited by the North Central Association of Colleges and Schools. For enrollments and further information, see UNIVERSITIES AND COLLEGES (table).

Name	Location	Founded
Dickinson State College	Dickinson	1917
Jamestown College	Jamestown	1884
Mary College	Bismarck	1955
Mayville State College	Mayville	1889
Minot State College	Minot	1913
North Dakota, University of	Grand Forks	1883
North Dakota State University	Fargo	1889
Valley City State College	Valley City	1889

ANNUAL EVENTS

During the summer, musical comedies are offered at old Fort Totten, on an Indian reservation south of Devils Lake. Fort Totten has the nation's only restored "cavalry square." Variety shows are offered in the Burning Hills Amphitheater near Medora and in the Theodore Roosevelt National Memorial Park. Medora, a picturesque old cow town that has been restored, is a popular tourist attraction. Summer visitors to North Dakota also enjoy colorful Indian ceremonies conducted on reservations and exciting rodeos held in many communities. Other annual events in North Dakota are:

January-March: Snowmobile Races in Bismarck (January-March); North Dakota Winter Show in Valley City (March).

April-June: McLean County Fair in Underwood (June); Miss North Dakota Pageant in Bismarck (June);

White Earth Rodeo (June); International Peace Garden Music Camp (June and July).

July-September: Festival in the Park in Minot (July); Fort Seward Trail Ride in Jamestown (July); North Dakota State Fair in Minot (July); Rodeos in Dickinson, Fort Ransom, Fort Totten, Fort Yates, Mandan, New Town, and Raleigh (July); Indian Pow-Wows in Bismarck, Fort Totten, Fort Yates, Mandaree, and New Town (July and August); Medora Musical (July and August); Summer Theater in Dickinson, Fort Totten, Grand Rapids, and Minot (July and August); Bonanzaville Days in West Fargo (September); Oktoberfest in New Leipzig (September-October).

October-December: U.S. Durum Show in Langdon (October); Threshermen's Shows in Edgeley, Makoti, and Lansford (October); Indoor Rodeos in Bismarck and Minot (October-November).

Theodore Roosevelt National Memorial Park
Harley Hettick, Alpha

Indian Ceremonies near Mandan
Harley Hettick, Alpha

Land Regions. North Dakota has three major land regions: (1) the Red River Valley, (2) the Young Drift Plains, and (3) the Great Plains. These regions rise in three broad steps from east to west.

The Red River Valley lies along the Minnesota border. This region is extremely flat. The valley is part of the bed of an ancient glacial lake, Lake Agassiz (see LAKE AGASSIZ). The *silt* (soil particles) of the former lake bottom makes this valley one of the most fertile farming areas in the world. Dairy farms and fields of wheat and other crops cover most of the region. The valley is the most heavily populated part of North Dakota.

The Young Drift Plains rise on the western border of the Red River Valley. An *escarpment* (steep slope) separates the two regions. The escarpment is steepest in the north in the Pembina Mountains. The mountains tower several hundred feet or meters above the Red River Valley. Generally, the Drift Plains rise gradually toward the west and southwest. Near the region's western border, the land is from 300 to 2,000 feet (91 to 610 meters) above the Red River Valley. The glaciers that crossed the Drift Plains during the Ice Age left rich deposits of earth materials called *drift*. Most of the region has rolling hills, and is cut by stream valleys. In the north, the Turtle Mountains rise about 550 feet (168 meters) above the surrounding plains.

The Great Plains cover the southwestern half of North Dakota. This region is part of the immense highland that extends from northern Canada to southern Texas (see GREAT PLAINS). North Dakotans call the region the *Missouri Plateau.* The region begins at the Missouri Escarpment. The escarpment rises 300 to 400 feet (91 to 120 meters) above the Drift Plains just east of the Missouri River. It crosses the state from northwest to southeast. The area is hilly, and is used for grazing cattle. It is also rich in mineral deposits. The area has many small lakes where thousands of wild ducks nest every year.

A narrow band of lowlands called the *Missouri Breaks* follows the sweep of the Missouri River. The area south and west of the river is called the *Slope.* There, rough valleys and *buttes* (steep hills that stand alone) break up the flatness of the plains. Many small streams wind around the hills as they flow toward the larger rivers.

The Badlands of the Little Missouri River lie in the southwest. This strip of rough, beautiful land is 6 to 20 miles (10 to 32 kilometers) wide and about 190 miles (306 kilometers) long. The Badlands are a sandstone, shale, and clay valley in which wind and water have carved weird formations. Buttes, domes, pyramids, and cones—colored with bands of browns, reds, grays, and yellows—rise from the valley floor. One of the buttes, White Butte, is 3,506 feet (1,069 meters) above sea level, the highest point in North Dakota. In parts of the Badlands, the rocks contain lignite coal. Some coal beds have been burning for many years, turning the clay above them bright red and pink. This burned material, called *scoria*, is used for surfacing roads.

Rivers and Lakes. The Missouri and Red river systems drain most of North Dakota. The great Missouri winds through the western part of the state. Its branches include the Cannonball, Heart, Knife, and Little Missouri rivers. The James River begins in central North Dakota and flows southward into South Dakota. Gar-

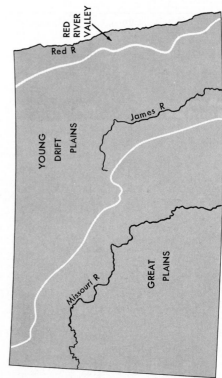

Land Regions of North Dakota

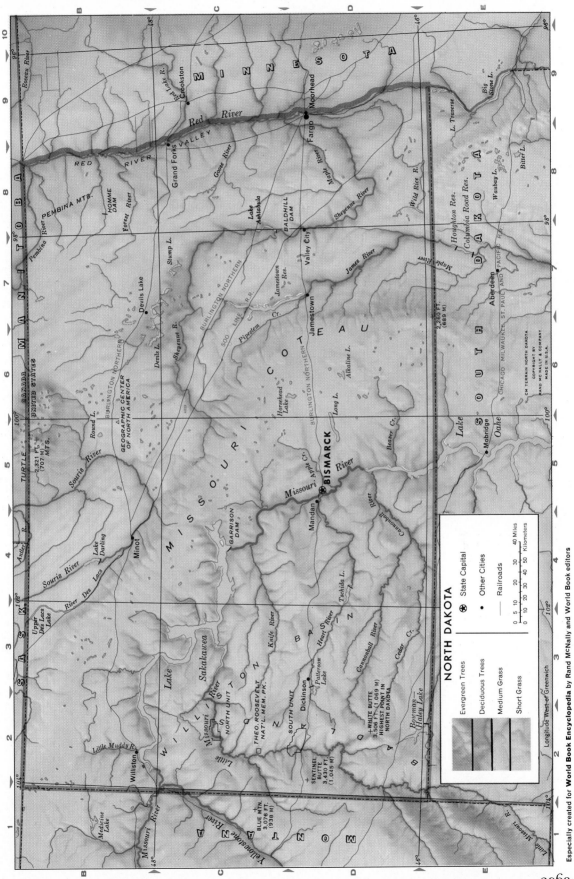

NORTH DAKOTA

Legend:
- ✳ State Capital
- • Other Cities
- — Railroads

Evergreen Trees

Deciduous Trees

Medium Grass

Short Grass

0 5 10 20 30 40 Miles
0 10 20 30 40 50 Kilometers

Especially created for **World Book Encyclopedia** by Rand McNally and World Book editors

Beds of Lignite smolder near Amidon in the Badlands of North Dakota. Some of these coal beds in the Great Plains have been burning for many years.

NORTH DAKOTA

rison Dam, 11,300 feet (3,444 meters) long, spans the Missouri near Riverdale. Its reservoir is 178 miles (286 kilometers) long and an average of $3\frac{1}{2}$ miles (5.6 kilometers) wide. The dam helps control floods, and provides water for irrigation and hydroelectric power.

The Red River and its branches flow northward through eastern North Dakota and empty into Hudson Bay in Canada. The largest branches include the Goose, Park, Pembina, and Sheyenne rivers. The Souris River drains a flat, fertile area in the north-central section. It flows southward from Saskatchewan, and then circles back north into Manitoba.

Numerous small lakes dot the Young Drift Plains. Many lie in beds scooped out by the glaciers. Devils Lake, in the north-central part of the region, is the largest natural lake in the state. It has no outlet, and its water is salty. The lake has been shrinking, and the state plans to raise the water level.

Fields of Soybeans ripen near Fargo in the Red River Valley. This region has some of the nation's most fertile farmland. Dairy farms and fields of crops cover most of the region.

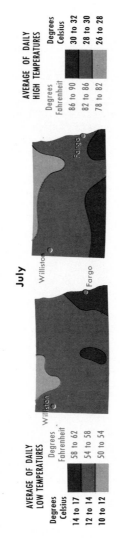

January

AVERAGE OF DAILY
LOW TEMPERATURES

Degrees Celsius	Degrees Fahrenheit
-16 to -13	4 to 8
-18 to -16	0 to 4
-20 to -18	-4 to 0
-22 to -20	-8 to -4
-24 to -22	-12 to -8

AVERAGE OF DAILY
HIGH TEMPERATURES

Degrees Celsius	Degrees Fahrenheit
-4 to -1	24 to 30
-8 to -4	18 to 24
-11 to -8	12 to 18
-14 to -11	6 to 12

July

AVERAGE OF DAILY
LOW TEMPERATURES

Degrees Celsius	Degrees Fahrenheit
14 to 17	58 to 62
12 to 14	54 to 58
10 to 12	50 to 54

AVERAGE OF DAILY
HIGH TEMPERATURES

Degrees Celsius	Degrees Fahrenheit
30 to 32	86 to 90
28 to 30	82 to 86
26 to 28	78 to 82

AVERAGE MONTHLY WEATHER

WILLISTON

	Temperatures F.°		C°		Days of Rain or Snow
	High	Low	High	Low	
JAN.	20	1	-7	-17	8
FEB.	23	4	-5	-16	6
MAR.	36	17	2	-8	7
APR.	54	32	12	0	7
MAY	66	43	19	6	9
JUNE	74	52	23	11	12
JULY	84	58	29	14	8
AUG.	81	55	27	13	8
SEPT.	70	45	21	7	7
OCT.	57	34	14	1	5
NOV.	37	19	3	-7	6
DEC.	25	7	-4	-14	7

FARGO

	Temperatures F.°		C°		Days of Rain or Snow
	High	Low	High	Low	
JAN.	17	-3	-8	-19	10
FEB.	21	1	-6	-17	8
MAR.	35	16	2	-9	9
APR.	53	31	12	-1	8
MAY	67	43	19	6	11
JUNE	77	53	25	12	11
JULY	84	58	29	14	10
AUG.	82	56	28	13	9
SEPT.	71	47	22	8	9
OCT.	57	35	14	2	6
NOV.	36	19	2	-7	7
DEC.	22	4	-6	-16	8

AVERAGE YEARLY PRECIPITATION
(Rain, Melted Snow, and Other Moisture)

Centimeters	Inches
41 to 51	16 to 20
30 to 41	12 to 16

```
0        100        200 Miles
|----|----|----|----|----|
0   100   200   300 Kilometers
```

WORLD BOOK maps

Harley Hettick, Alpha

North Dakota's Sunny Weather is ideal for growing wheat. This wheat crop in the Red River Valley is being harvested.

NORTH DAKOTA/Climate

Summers in North Dakota are generally clear and pleasant. The sun shines more than 15 hours on each clear day from mid-May through July. Even the hottest days are seldom uncomfortable because the humidity is low. Winters can be severe. Winds that sweep across the plains make the cold bitter.

July temperatures average 69° F. (21° C) in the north and 72° F. (22° C) in the south. The state's record high temperature was 121° F. (49° C), at Steele on July 6, 1936. January temperatures average 3° F. (−16° C) in the northeast part of the state and 14° F. (−10° C) in the extreme southwest. The state's lowest temperature, −60° F. (−51° C), was recorded at Parshall on Feb. 15, 1936.

The southeast has the most *precipitation* (rain, melted snow, and other forms of moisture)—about 18 inches (46 centimeters) a year. Some western areas receive only about 15 inches (38 centimeters). Most of the rain falls between April and September. Snowfall averages about 32 inches (81 centimeters) yearly.

Natural Resources. North Dakota's greatest natural resources are its outstandingly fertile soil and its enormous mineral deposits.

Soil is North Dakota's most valuable resource. It is the basis of the state's major industry—agriculture. North Dakota's richest soil lies in the Red River Valley. This fertile black soil is free of stones and contains much *organic matter* (decayed plant and animal remains). Loamy and sandy soils lie on the Drift Plains west of the Red River Valley. Shale and limestone make up most of the soil of the Great Plains region. The thin, brown soil in parts of the region produces well if irrigated.

Minerals. North Dakota has large deposits of petroleum in the west. These deposits lie in the great Williston Basin, which extends from North Dakota into northern South Dakota, eastern Montana, and southern Canada. In North Dakota, this enormous oil field has been developed in about 15 counties. McKenzie and Williams counties are the leading producers. Bowman County in southwestern North Dakota and other oil-producing counties in the northwest have natural-gas wells.

North Dakota has huge lignite coal deposits—about 16 billion short tons (14.5 billion metric tons). No other state has such enormous reserves of lignite coal. North Dakota's lignite deposits lie in the west. Sand and gravel are found throughout the state. The southwestern area of the state has great amounts of clay, ranging in quality from common brick to the finest pottery clay.

Plant Life. Forests cover only about 421,000 acres (170,400 hectares) of North Dakota, or about 1 per cent of the state's total area. Trees that grow in the east include the ash, aspen, basswood, box elder, elm, oak, and poplar. The largest stands of timber are in the Turtle and Pembina mountains and in the hills surrounding Devils Lake. Ash, cottonwood, elm, and willow trees grow along the Missouri and its branches.

In spring and summer, brilliantly colored flowers bloom throughout the countryside. They include beardtongues, black-eyed Susans, gaillardias, pasqueflowers, prairie mallows, red lilies, and wild prairie roses. The wild prairie rose is the state flower. Chokecherries, highbush cranberries, and wild plums grow in many parts of the state. Bluegrass thrives in the northeast, and buffalo and gama grasses in the southwest.

Animal Life. White-tailed deer graze throughout North Dakota. Mule deer and pronghorns range the western plains. In the Badlands, prairie dogs live in scattered colonies called *dog towns.* Fur-bearing animals include badgers, beavers, bobcats, coyotes, foxes, lynxes, minks, muskrats, rabbits, raccoons, skunks, and weasels. Flickertail ground squirrels are commonly seen.

Every summer, ducks migrate to North Dakota to breed in the lakes, marshes, and grainfields. More waterfowl hatch in North Dakota than in any other state. Hunters shoot grouse, Hungarian partridges, pheasants, and other game birds. Fishermen catch bass, carp, catfish, perch, pike, trout, and other fishes.

Agriculture is by far the leading industry in North Dakota. The state's farm income totals about $2¼ billion yearly. This is 84 per cent of the value of all goods produced in North Dakota. Crops are the largest source of the state's farm income. They bring in about $1⅔ billion yearly.

North Dakota has about 46,000 farms and ranches. They average about 930 acres (376.4 hectares) in size. North Dakota farms cover a total of about 43,100,000 acres (17,440,000 hectares). Of this total, about 63,000 acres (25,500 hectares) are irrigated.

Wheat is the most important crop in both value and production. It accounts for about $1⅓ billion of the state's annual farm income. Over 252 million bushels of wheat are harvested each year on about 9 million acres (3.6 million hectares) of land. Most of it is *spring wheat* (wheat planted in the spring). About 75 million bushels of *durum wheat* (a variety of hard spring wheat used for making spaghetti and macaroni) are usually grown in North Dakota each year. Durum wheat is harvested on about 2½ million acres (1 million hectares). North Dakota usually ranks second only to Kansas in total wheat production. But it leads the nation in durum wheat production. Wheat is grown throughout North Dakota, but the heaviest output is in the northern areas. The north-central areas lead in durum wheat production.

Other Field Crops. Farmers raise flaxseed on about 930,000 acres (376,000 hectares), chiefly in the eastern and central sections. They raise about 7 million bushels

Production of Goods in North Dakota

Total value of goods produced in 1973—$2,739,353,000

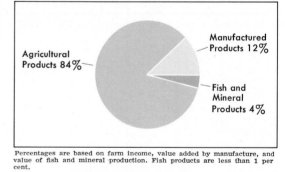

Agricultural Products 84%

Manufactured Products 12%

Fish and Mineral Products 4%

Percentages are based on farm income, value added by manufacture, and value of fish and mineral production. Fish products are less than 1 per cent.

Sources: U.S. government publications, 1975-1976.

Employment in North Dakota

Total number of persons employed in 1974—255,800

	Number of Employees
Agriculture	65,000
Wholesale & Retail Trade	52,800
Government	51,800
Community, Social, & Personal Services	37,100
Manufacturing	14,100
Transportation & Public Utilities	13,000
Construction	12,100
Finance, Insurance, & Real Estate	8,200
Mining	1,700

Sources: *Employment and Earnings*, May 1975, U.S. Bureau of Labor Statistics; *Farm Labor*, February 1975, U.S. Department of Agriculture.

Open-Pit Lignite Mine near Bismarck yields large amounts of soft coal. Much lignite is burned to produce electric power for North Dakota and nearby states.

Skyline of Towers rises from an oil refinery near Mandan. Petroleum is the most valuable mineral produced in North Dakota.

Greater North Dakota Assn.

of flaxseed annually, about half the nation's harvest. North Dakota also leads all states in barley production, with about 100 million bushels yearly. Farmers in the eastern counties raise most of the barley. North Dakota ranks second to South Dakota in rye production. It harvests about 6 million bushels annually. Most of the rye comes from the southeastern and southwestern areas. Other important North Dakota crops include oats, potatoes, soybeans, and sugar beets. Farmers also raise corn, dry beans, dry peas, hay, safflower, and sunflowers.

Meat Animals account for about $400 million in annual farm income. The central and western plains provide good pasturage and winter feed. Pastures cover about 13 million acres (5.3 million hectares), or about a third of the state's farmland. Farmers throughout the state raise beef cattle and sell them to eastern dealers who fatten them for market. Sheep are raised mainly in the southeastern counties. Farmers raise hogs in the southeast and south central areas, where corn is plentiful. Dairy cattle also graze in the southeastern part of the state, and in several central counties.

Manufacturing accounts for 12 per cent of the value of all goods produced in North Dakota. Goods manufactured in the state have a *value added by manufacture* of about $330 million yearly. This figure represents the value created in products by North Dakota's industries, not counting such costs as materials, supplies, and fuel. Among the states, only Alaska and Nevada rank lower than North Dakota in manufacturing. North Dakota has about 480 manufacturing plants. Most of them employ fewer than 20 persons.

Food processing is the chief manufacturing activity. Foods and related products processed in North Dakota have a value added of about $65 million yearly. North

Dakota creameries ship large amounts of butter and cheddar cheese. Creameries ship most of the butter, ice cream, and other dairy products to markets in other states. The state-owned flour mill in Grand Forks, established in 1922, is the largest west of Minnesota. Mills in Fargo produce wheat flour and cereals. A number of North Dakota mills prepare cattle feed. Sugar refineries operating in Drayton, Hillsboro, and Wahpeton process sugar beets that are grown in North Dakota and Minnesota.

North Dakota's second-ranking manufacturing activity is the production of nonelectrical machinery. This industry has an annual value added of about $40 million. Farm equipment is the chief product of the industry. North Dakota's third-ranking industry is the manufacture of stone, clay, and glass products. Printing and publishing and the manufacture of fabricated metal products are also important to North Dakota's economy.

Oil refineries are located in Dickinson, Mandan, and Williston. Plants in Alexandria, Lignite, McGregor, and Tioga recover gasoline, propane, butane, natural gas, and sulfur from the petroleum deposits of the Williston Basin.

Mining accounts for about $110 million, or about 4 per cent of the value of all goods produced in the state. Petroleum is the most valuable mineral. About 20 million barrels of oil are pumped annually from about 1,400 wells in western North Dakota. Pipelines carry most of the crude oil to North Dakota refineries. Trucks help transport the oil out of the state. North Dakota also produces about 28 billion cubic feet (793 million cubic meters) of natural gas annually.

About 7 million short tons (6.4 million metric tons) of lignite are mined yearly. Most of this coal comes

396e

from Mercer County. All the lignite is taken from *strip* (open) mines. The thin topsoil is removed, leaving the coal at the surface ready for mining by machinery. Coal production began to decline during the 1950's, when many coal users turned to natural gas and oil for fuel, and to the water power of Garrison Dam for electricity. However, construction of huge lignite-burning electric power plants near Stanton and Center has increased coal production. Almost all North Dakota counties produce sand and gravel. Other minerals produced in the state include clay, natural gas liquids, salt, and stone.

Electric Power. Steam plants that burn lignite coal generate about 65 per cent of North Dakota's electric power. The rest of the state's electric power comes from the hydroelectric project at Garrison Dam. Major coal-burning plants are located at Center, Mandan, and Stanton. Almost half of the power generated in North Dakota is exported by high voltage transmission lines to other midwestern states.

Transportation. North Dakota is a large state with a relatively small population. It also lies far from the nation's large population centers. These factors have hindered the growth of transportation in the state. The first railroad in North Dakota, the Northern Pacific, reached Fargo in 1872 and Bismarck in 1873. By 1881, the line ran to the Montana border. Until a bridge was built, trains crossed the Missouri River at Bismarck on a ferry in summer and on tracks over the ice in winter. By 1881, the Great Northern Railway established a route between Fargo and Grand Forks. It built a line

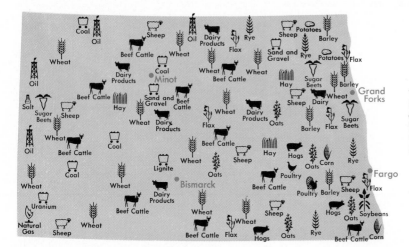
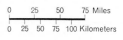

FARM AND MINERAL PRODUCTS

This map shows where the state's leading farm and mineral products are produced. The major urban areas (shown on the map in red) are the state's important manufacturing centers.

```
0    25    50    75  Miles
0   25  50  75  100  Kilometers
```

WORLD BOOK map

North Dakota Travel Division

North Dakota Cowboys round up cattle in the western part of the state. Many farmers throughout North Dakota raise beef cattle. They sell the animals to dealers who fatten them for market.

westward through Minot and Williston to the Montana border by 1887. Today, railroads operate on about 5,000 miles (8,000 kilometers) of track in the state. Four rail lines provide freight service, and passenger trains serve 10 North Dakota cities.

North Dakota has about 107,000 miles (172,200 kilometers) of roads and highways, of which about two-thirds are surfaced. Several scheduled airlines serve North Dakota, and the state has about 100 airports.

Communication. North Dakota's first newspaper, the *Frontier Scout*, was published in Fort Union in 1864. In 1873, Colonel Clement A. Lounsberry founded the *Bismarck Tribune*, the oldest newspaper still published in North Dakota. In 1876, Lounsberry wrote the first story of the Battle of the Little Bighorn. In this famous battle, Indians massacred General George A. Custer and all the troops under his immediate command.

In order to write the story, Lounsberry used notes found in the buckskin pouch of Mark Kellogg, a reporter who was killed in the battle.

The largest daily newspapers in North Dakota include the *Bismarck Tribune*, *The Fargo Forum*, the *Grand Forks Herald*, and the *Minot Daily News*. The state has approximately 100 newspapers, of which about 90 are weeklies. Publishers in North Dakota also issue about 20 magazines.

The first radio station in North Dakota, WDAY, started broadcasting in Fargo in 1922. The state's first television station, KCJB (now KXMC-TV), began operating in 1953 in Minot. North Dakota has about 40 radio stations and about 15 television stations.

NORTH DAKOTA / History

Indian Days. Several Indian tribes lived in the North Dakota region before white explorers first arrived. The Arikara, Cheyenne, Hidatsa, and Mandan peacefully farmed the land. Most of these Indians lived in the Missouri Valley. They lived in villages fortified against attacks by warring tribes. Hunter and warrior tribes included the Assiniboin, Chippewa, and Sioux. They mainly roamed the northeast. See INDIAN, AMERICAN (Table of Tribes).

Exploration and Early Settlement. In 1682, Robert Cavelier, Sieur de la Salle, claimed for France all the land drained by the Mississippi River system. This territory included the southwestern half of present-day North Dakota, because the Missouri River flows into the Mississippi. France also claimed the vast area south of Hudson Bay, which included the northeastern half of North Dakota. In 1713, France gave all this Hudson Bay territory to Great Britain.

North Dakota was first explored by a French Canadian, Pierre Gaultier de Varennes, Sieur de la Vérendrye. He set out from Canada in 1738, and reached the Mandan Indian villages near present-day Bismarck.

In 1762, France gave its land west of the Mississippi to Spain. Spain returned it to France in 1800. In 1803, the United States bought this region, called Louisiana, from France (see LOUISIANA PURCHASE).

In 1804, President Thomas Jefferson sent Meriwether Lewis and William Clark to explore the Louisiana Territory and to blaze a trail to the Pacific Ocean. Lewis and Clark reached central North Dakota in October, 1804. They built Fort Mandan on the east bank of the Missouri River, across from present-day Stanton. The explorers stayed at Fort Mandan until April, 1805. They passed through North Dakota again in 1806 on their return from the Pacific.

In 1812, Scottish and Irish families from Canada made the first attempt at a permanent settlement in North Dakota, in Pembina. In 1818, the United States obtained northeastern North Dakota by a treaty with Great Britain. All of present-day North Dakota then became U.S. territory. The 1818 treaty also set the United States-Canadian border at the 49th parallel. Some of the Pembina settlers moved north, to be sure they were on British territory. The rest left in 1823, when a survey

of the border confirmed that Pembina was actually located in the United States.

Territorial Days. Congress created the Dakota Territory in 1861. President Abraham Lincoln appointed William Jayne as governor. The territory included the present states of North and South Dakota and much of Montana and Wyoming. The first legislature met in Yankton (now in South Dakota) in 1862.

In 1863, the territory was opened for homesteading. Settlers were given free land if they lived on it and improved it. But the territory developed slowly. Transportation was poor, and the settlers feared Indian attacks. In 1862, Sioux Indians killed hundreds of settlers in an uprising in Minnesota. Some of the Indians then fled to the Dakota Territory. During the 1860's and 1870's, the U.S. government sent troops into the territory to punish the Indians who had taken part in the Minnesota massacre. Many battles were fought as the soldiers pursued the Indians across the territory.

The federal government signed several treaties with the Indians in the Dakota Territory, giving them land on reservations. But the whites often broke the treaties, causing more Indian uprisings. Peace came in 1881, when the great Sioux chief Sitting Bull voluntarily surrendered to U.S. troops. See INDIAN WARS (The Sioux Wars); SITTING BULL.

Large-scale farming began about 1875, when eastern corporations and some families established huge wheat farms. Most of the farms were in the Red River Valley, and ranged from 3,000 to 65,000 acres (1,200 to 26,300 hectares). The farms earned such tremendous profits they became known as *bonanza* farms. The farmers used machinery and orderly methods of planting, harvesting, and marketing. This was possible because only one crop —wheat—was raised. It was easy to cultivate the large, level fields with machinery, and the owners could afford equipment. In time, other crops were introduced on the bonanza farms. But difficulties arose as stockholders quarreled over how to operate the farms. Finally, most of the farms were divided into smaller lots and sold to newcomers.

Statehood. During the 1870's, the people began to ask Congress to divide the Dakota Territory into two parts. The population centers had developed in far cor-

NORTH DAKOTA

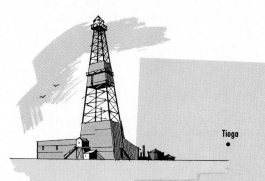

The Petroleum Industry in North Dakota began in 1951, when oil was discovered near Tioga. Oil quickly became the state's most valuable mineral.

Ranching Began in North Dakota in the late 1800's, when its western range lands became a fattening-up place for Texas cattle. Famous ranches included one owned by Theodore Roosevelt.

ners of the territory—in the northeast and the southeast. North-south travel between these two centers was difficult because the railroads had laid their tracks in an east-west direction. The two groups of settlers also had little in common, and wanted to develop their own governments.

In February, 1889, Congress established the present boundary between North Dakota and South Dakota. It also passed an enabling act, allowing the two regions to set up the machinery to become states (see ENABLING ACT). On Nov. 2, 1889, North Dakota became the 39th state, and South Dakota the 40th state. John Miller, a Republican, became North Dakota's first governor.

The Early 1900's. North Dakota's population increased rapidly following statehood. The state had 190,983 persons in 1890. In 1910, it had 577,056 persons. Farming also grew rapidly. But the farmers disliked having to deal with banks, grain companies, and railroad interests in Minnesota. They also disliked the power these out-of-state businesses held in North Dakota politics.

In 1915, the Nonpartisan League was founded in North Dakota. This organization supported the farmers. It called for state ownership of grain elevators, flour mills, packing houses, and cold-storage plants. It also wanted banks in farming areas that would grant loans at cost. Thousands of farmers joined the league.

In 1916, a league-supported candidate, Republican Lynn J. Frazier, was elected governor of North Dakota. During Frazier's administrations, from 1917 to 1921, the state legislature passed a number of progressive laws. Rural schools received more funds. Taxes on farm improvements were lowered. An industrial commission was set up to manage businesses begun by the state. In 1919, the Bank of North Dakota was established in Bismarck. In 1922, the North Dakota Mill and Elevator in Grand Forks began operating.

The Great Depression. North Dakota suffered a severe drought during the 1930's. In addition, the entire nation was hit by the Great Depression. North Dakota's farm production plunged sharply, and its population also began to decline. The population had reached a peak of 680,845 in 1930.

During the 1930's, the state and federal governments took many steps to help North Dakota farmers. In 1937, the state water conservation commission was created. Since that time, state, federal, and private agencies have set up projects to provide irrigation and prevent soil erosion. These agencies also encourage *dry farming*

HISTORIC NORTH DAKOTA

The First Explorer of the North Dakota region reached an Indian village at Mandan in 1738. He was Pierre de la Vérendrye, who was looking for a route west to the Pacific Ocean.

Scottish and Irish Families made the first attempts to settle at Pembina in 1812. Before that, only Indians and white fur traders lived in North Dakota.

The Huge Garrison Dam north of Bismarck is one of the largest dams in the world. It forms a lake 178 miles (286 kilometers) long. The dam was begun in 1946, and its generators started producing electricity in 1956.

The Northern Pacific Railroad built a line to Fargo by 1872, and reached westward to Bismarck in 1873. Railroad building brought a rush of settlers, and farming soon prospered in eastern North Dakota. The state now harvests about half the nation's flaxseed crop.

Lewis and Clark followed the Missouri into North Dakota in 1804. They wintered among Mandan Indians. On leaving, they took along the young Shoshoni, Sacagawea, who guided the expedition.

Wheat Raising on a Vast Scale boosted agriculture in the 1870's. The crop grew on rich "bonanza farms" that covered up to 65,000 acres (26,300 hectares). North Dakota leads the states in durum wheat production.

Dome-Shaped Lodges of the Mandan Indians have been restored. This community, near Mandan, is called Slant Village because the land it occupies slopes toward the Heart River.

Bernie Donahue, Publix

Garrison Dam Hydroelectric Project began operating in 1956. The project supplies much of North Dakota's electric power.

(farming methods that make the most of limited rain).

The Mid-1900's. North Dakota's economy recovered during World War II (1939-1945). Farmers broke all their production records in supplying much food for the armed forces. But in the late 1940's, farm prices sagged as a result of farm surpluses throughout the country. The increased use of machines on farms left large numbers of farmworkers unemployed. Many of these workers found jobs in towns and cities, and North Dakota's urban population increased. But thousands of farmworkers could not find other jobs in the state and left in search of opportunities elsewhere.

Construction of the great Garrison Dam near Riverdale began in 1946. This dam provides flood control, hydroelectric power, and water for irrigation. In 1956, the first generator at the dam went into operation. The dam was completed in 1960. Two lignite-burning power plants near Stanton have also helped the economy.

Oil was discovered near Tioga in 1951 and became the state's most valuable mineral. By 1970, oil wells were operating in 14 counties of western North Dakota.

In 1957, North Dakota established an economic development commission that works to attract industry to the state. More than 80 North Dakota communities now have their own development commissions. Largely as a result of these commissions, the state's rate of industrial growth ranked among the highest in the country from 1958 to 1969.

The U.S. Air Force gave a boost to the state's economy during the 1960's. It built Strategic Air Command (SAC) bases near Grand Forks and Minot. About 36,000 people live on the two bases.

North Dakota Today is working to broaden its economy, which still depends heavily upon agriculture. Farmers achieved record production again in the early 1970's. But state leaders, fearing a possible crop failure or a disastrous drop in farm prices, continue to seek new industry. The task of attracting new industry remains difficult because North Dakota lies so far from the nation's largest population centers.

The state's need for more industry is reflected in three related problems. These problems are (1) lack of job opportunities, (2) low *per capita* (per person) income, and (3) people moving out of the state. The number of nonagricultural jobs has been increasing, but not enough to keep up with the decline in farm jobs. North Dakota also hopes to expand the use of its mineral resources as a step toward broadening its economy.

The Garrison Diversion Project, started in 1967, was scheduled to begin operating in 1979. It includes a 2,000-mile (3,200-kilometer) canal system to bring water for irrigation from the Missouri River to 250,000 acres (101,000 hectares) of farmland. It will also supply water to 14 cities.

JACK U. HAGERTY, RUSSELL S. REID, and BERNT LLOYD WILLS

NORTH DAKOTA/*Study Aids*

Related Articles in WORLD BOOK include:

BIOGRAPHIES

Burke, John	Muench, Aloisius J.	Sacagawea
Maris, Roger	Cardinal	Sitting Bull

CITIES

Bismarck	Fargo	Grand Forks

HISTORY

Indian Wars	Lake Agassiz
(The Sioux Wars)	Lewis and Clark Expedition

Louisiana Purchase	Western Frontier
Nonpartisan League	Life

PHYSICAL FEATURES

Badlands	Missouri River
Great Plains	Red River of the North

PRODUCTS

For North Dakota's rank among the states in production, see the following articles:

Barley	Honey	Rye
Bean	Oats	Wheat
Flax	Potato	

Outline

I. Government
  A. Constitution   E. Local Government
  B. Executive   F. Taxation
  C. Legislature   G. Politics
  D. Courts
II. People
III. Education
  A. Schools
  B. Libraries and Museums
IV. A Visitor's Guide
  A. Places to Visit
  B. Annual Events
V. The Land
  A. Land Regions   B. Rivers and Lakes
VI. Climate
VII. Economy
  A. Natural Resources
  B. Agriculture
  C. Manufacturing
  D. Mining
  E. Electric Power
  F. Transportation
  G. Communication
VIII. History

Questions

What political organization was founded in North Dakota?

Why did few settlers come to the Dakota Territory in the early days even though they were given free land?

What mineral was discovered in North Dakota in 1951?

Why is soil the most precious resource of North Dakota?

How did trains cross the Missouri River at Bismarck before a bridge was built over the river?

North Dakota is the nation's leading producer of what crops?

What were the bonanza farms?

Why did the settlers of the Dakota Territory want the territory divided into two parts?

Where in the state have coal beds been burning for many years? How is the burned material used?

Why does North Dakota need more industry?

Books for Young Readers

BAILEY, BERNADINE. *Picture Book of North Dakota*. Whitman, 1971.

CARPENTER, ALLAN. *North Dakota*. Childrens Press, 1968.

SYPHER, LUCY J. *The Edge of Nowhere*. Atheneum, 1972. *Cousins and Circuses*. 1974. *The Spell of the Northern Lights*. 1975. *The Turnabout Year*. 1976. All are stories about family life in a North Dakota town in the early 1900's.

Books for Older Readers

DRACHE, HIRAM M. *The Day of the Bonanza: A History of Bonanza Farming in the Red River Valley of the North*. North Dakota Institute for Regional Studies, North Dakota State University, 1964.

OMDAHL, LLOYD B., and WRIGHT, B. L. *Governing North Dakota, 1975-77*. Bureau of Governmental Affairs, Univ. of North Dakota, 1975.

ROBINSON, ELWYN B. *History of North Dakota*. Univ. of Nebraska Press, 1966.

ROLFSRUD, ERLING N. *The Story of North Dakota*. Lantern Books, Alexandria, Minn., 1963.

TWETON, D. JEROME, and JELLIFF, THEODORE. *North Dakota: The Heritage of a People*. North Dakota Institute for Regional Studies, North Dakota State Univ., 1976.

NORTH DAKOTA, UNIVERSITY OF, is a state-supported coeducational institution in Grand Forks, N. Dak. It has colleges of arts and sciences, business and public administration, engineering, fine arts, human resources development, and nursing; a graduate school; and schools of law and medicine. The university also has a division of continuing education and a center for teaching and learning. It grants bachelor's, master's, and doctor's degrees. The University of North Dakota was founded in 1883. For enrollment, see UNIVERSITIES AND COLLEGES (table).   THOMAS J. CLIFFORD

NORTH DAKOTA STATE UNIVERSITY is a state-controlled coeducational school at Fargo, N. Dak. The university has undergraduate colleges of agriculture; education; engineering and architecture; home economics; humanities and social sciences; pharmacy; science and mathematics; and university studies. North Dakota State also has a graduate school. The university grants bachelor's, master's, and doctor's degrees.

The University includes the North Dakota Agricultural Experiment Station and the Cooperative Agricultural Extension. The school was founded in 1889 as the North Dakota Agricultural College. It took its present name in 1960. For the enrollment at North Dakota State University, see UNIVERSITIES AND COLLEGES (table).

Critically reviewed by NORTH DAKOTA STATE UNIVERSITY

NORTH EAST LAND. See SVALBARD.

NORTH EQUATORIAL CURRENT. See GULF STREAM (Cause; map).

NORTH GEORGIA COLLEGE is a coeducational liberal arts school at Dahlonega, Ga. It is a state-supported senior unit of the University System of Georgia. Courses at the college lead to B.A. and B.S. degrees. The college was founded in 1873. For the enrollment of North Georgia College, see UNIVERSITIES AND COLLEGES (table).

NORTH GERMAN CONFEDERATION. See GERMANY (The Unification of Germany).

NORTH ISLAND. See NEW ZEALAND (The North Island).

NORTH KOREA. See KOREA.

NORTH LITTLE ROCK, Ark. (pop. 60,040), an industrial and transportation center, lies in the center of the state on the north bank of the Arkansas River. For the location of North Little Rock, see ARKANSAS (political map). North Little Rock has large railroad repair shops. The city manufactures cottonseed products, fertilizer, furniture, concrete, iron products, railroad ties, barrels, and food products.

The city was laid out in 1839 as the town of De Cantillon and was incorporated under its present name in 1904. North Little Rock and Little Rock form a metropolitan area with a population of 323,296. North Little Rock has a mayor-council form of government.   WALTER L. BROWN

See also LITTLE ROCK.

NORTH MAGNETIC POLE. See NORTH POLE.

NORTH PARK COLLEGE. See UNIVERSITIES AND COLLEGES (table).

NORTH PLATTE, Nebr. (pop. 19,447), is the center of an important farming and cattle-raising region in western Nebraska. The people of this railroad and shipping city deal in livestock, grains, dairy products, meat packing, and pet food. Lake McConaughy, the reservoir of nearby Kingsley Dam, provides water for power and irrigation. The city lies at the fork of the North Platte and South Platte rivers (see NEBRASKA [political map]).

North Platte was first settled in 1866, as a construction camp for workers of the Union Pacific Railroad. William F. Cody, better known as "Buffalo Bill," operated a large cattle ranch nearby. The city has a mayor-council government.   JAMES C. OLSON

NORTH PLATTE RIVER. See PLATTE RIVER.

NORTH POLE is a term used for several invisible surface points located in the Arctic region. The best-known is the north geographic pole. But other important north poles include the instantaneous north pole, the north pole of balance, the north magnetic pole, and the geomagnetic north pole.

The North Geographic Pole lies near the center of the Arctic Ocean at the point where all the earth's lines of longitude meet. American explorer Robert E. Peary led the first expedition to reach the north geographic pole. The expedition included Matthew Henson, who was Peary's assistant, and four Eskimos. The party made the trip by dog team in 1909. In 1926, Admiral Richard E. Byrd and Floyd Bennett of the United States reached the pole by airplane. In 1958, the U.S.S. *Nautilus* became the first submarine to pass under the Arctic ice to the north geographic pole.

The Instantaneous North Pole lies at the point where the earth's *axis* (an imaginary line through the earth) meets the surface. The earth wobbles slowly as it turns around its axis, causing the instantaneous north pole to move. This pole takes about 14 months to move clockwise around an irregular path called the *Chandler Circle.* The diameter of this circle varies from less than 1 foot (30 centimeters) to about 70 feet (21 meters).

The North Pole of Balance lies at the center of the Chandler Circle. Its position locates the north geographic pole. Each year since 1900, the north pole of balance has moved about 6 inches (15 centimeters) toward North America. This motion has caused tiny changes in the latitude and longitude of points around the earth.

The North Magnetic Pole is the point toward which north-seeking compass needles point. This pole can move many miles or kilometers in a few years. In 1970, the north magnetic pole was located near Bathurst Island in northern Canada.

The Geomagnetic North Pole lies near Thule, Greenland. In the upper atmosphere, the earth's magnetic field points down toward this point.   PAUL A. SIPLE

Related Articles in WORLD BOOK include:

Arctic (Arctic Exploration)
Arctic Ocean (maps)
Bennett, Floyd
Byrd, Richard E.
Earth (The Earth's Magnetism)

Exploration and Discovery (Polar Exploration)
Henson, Matthew A.
Peary, Robert E.
Submarine (Nuclear Submarines)

NORTH SEA is a wide arm of the Atlantic Ocean that lies between Great Britain and the continent of Europe.

Location of the North Sea
WORLD BOOK map

In peacetime, heavily burdened ships, carrying food, manufactured products, and passengers, make the North Sea a busy trade highway. During wartime, the sea is closely guarded by the countries that lie on its shores.

The harbors of many of the greatest seafaring nations are on the shores of the North Sea. The most important ports of England, West Germany, Norway, The Netherlands, and Denmark border the sea. The entire eastern seaboard of England and Scotland is devoted to fishing. Water pollution and excessive fishing have been blamed for reduced catches since the mid-1900's.

The bottom of the North Sea has large deposits of petroleum and natural gas. The sea is an important European source of oil and gas.

The North Sea is nearly 600 miles (960 kilometers) long and about 360 miles (580 kilometers) wide. It has a shore line of about 4,000 miles (6,400 kilometers). The area of the North Sea is 221,000 square miles (572,000 square kilometers). About 2,500 square miles (6,500 square kilometers) of this area is taken up by islands.

The average depth of the North Sea varies from 100 feet (30 meters) in the south to 400 feet (120 meters) in the north. The deepest section is off the Norwegian coast. Here the water is more than 2,400 feet (730 meters) deep. Many rivers empty into the North Sea, including the Humber and Thames of Great Britain, and the Rhine, Elbe, Weser, Ems, and Schelde of the European continent.

Skagerrak, an arm of the North Sea, connects it with the Strait of Kattegat and the Baltic Sea. The Kiel Canal also connects the North and the Baltic seas. The English Channel and the Strait of Dover connect the North Sea with the Atlantic Ocean on the south.

Its location as a sea among seas causes strange tides in the North Sea. One tide wave comes through the English Channel and the Strait of Dover and sweeps northward. The other moves southward along Norway to the Danish coast. The two tides cancel near the southern tip of Norway, and they reinforce each other on the coast of West Germany, where the range of the highest tide is about 10 feet (3 meters). There is little rise and fall in the middle of the North Sea.

The position of the North Sea made it important during both world wars. During World War I, Great Britain controlled these waters and cut off the enemy from this route to the Atlantic. During World War II, both the German and British navies patrolled and mined the North Sea.   JOHN D. ISAACS

See also DOGGER BANK.

NORTH STAR, or POLESTAR. This star of the Northern Hemisphere has long guided mariners. Wherever one may be in northern latitudes, the direction north may be found by reference to it (see LATITUDE [picture]). The North Star is also called POLARIS. It is easily located, for two stars in the Big Dipper, part of Ursa Major, or Great Bear, always point to it.

The star is about one degree from the *north celestial pole*. It is the brightest star in the constellation Ursa Minor, or Little Bear. It is of the second magnitude in brightness. The Greeks called the polestar *Cynosura*, meaning *dog's tail*. In English, *cynosure* now means *center of attraction*.

The distance of the polestar from the north celestial pole is gradually becoming less, because of the motion of the pole of the heavens around the pole of the *ecliptic* (see ASTRONOMY [table: Astronomy Terms]). Within the next 100 years the distance will decrease to one-half degree, then begin to increase again. About 2,000 years from now, the star Alpha Cephei will be the polestar for people on earth. CHARLES A. FEDERER, JR.

See also ASTRONOMY (diagram: North Star); BIG AND LITTLE DIPPERS; STAR (How Man Uses Stars).

NORTH TEXAS STATE UNIVERSITY is a coeducational school in Denton, Tex. Courses offered include art, business administration, education, English, journalism, languages, music, political science, sciences, and speech and drama. The school grants bachelor's, master's, and doctor's degrees.

North Texas State University was established as Texas

Normal College in 1890. It became a state college in 1901, and received its present name in 1961. The graduate division was founded in 1935. The College of Arts and Sciences, and the schools of business administration, education, home economics, and music, were founded in 1946. For enrollment, see UNIVERSITIES AND COLLEGES (table). CALVIN CLEAVE NOLEN

NORTH VIETNAM. See VIETNAM.

NORTH WEST COMPANY was a famous fur-trading company organized in Canada during the late 1770's. It was set up to compete with the powerful Hudson's Bay Company. The North West Company sent its rugged traders across Canada to the Pacific Ocean and did much to open up the little-known regions of the Canadian Far West.

In the early 1800's, the North West Company began to build trading posts down the Pacific Coast toward the Columbia River. John Jacob Astor's Pacific Fur Company was also establishing posts in the Columbia region. Astor reached the entrance of the Columbia River first and, in 1811, founded Astoria. Later the North West Company bought out the Astor interests in this region. In 1821, the Hudson's Bay Company absorbed the North West Company. JOHN R. ALDEN

See also ASTOR (John Jacob Astor); HUDSON'S BAY COMPANY; FRASER, SIMON; McGILLIVRAY, WILLIAM.

NORTH-WEST MOUNTED POLICE. See ROYAL CANADIAN MOUNTED POLICE.

Yerkes Observatory

The North Star appears at the center of the time-exposure photograph shown at the right. Other stars seem to rotate around the North Star because of the earth's rotation on its axis. The North Star appears not to move because it lies on the axis. The North Star may be located by using the group of stars called the Big Dipper, shown above. Two of these stars, Dubhe and Merak, are almost in a direct line with the North Star.

North Star (Polaris)

Dubhe

Big Dipper

Merak

Smith College

Smith College in Northampton, Mass., was founded in 1871. The housing units, above, enclose a terraced quadrangle.

NORTHAMPTON, Mass. (pop. 29,664), is best known as the home of Smith College, one of the leading colleges for women in the United States.

Northampton lies on the Connecticut River in west-central Massachusetts, 17 miles (27 kilometers) north of Springfield (see MASSACHUSETTS [political map]). The city is noted for its wide, tree-lined streets and fine homes. Brushes, silverware, optical instruments, cutlery, and paper napkins are manufactured here.

Northampton was settled in 1654 and became a city in 1883. The seat of Hampshire County, it has a mayor-council government. Calvin Coolidge, 30th President of the United States, lived there.   WILLIAM J. REID

NORTHCLIFFE, VISCOUNT (1865-1922), ALFRED CHARLES WILLIAM HARMSWORTH, a famous English journalist and publisher, pioneered in the use of comics, special features, religious news, and tabloid newspapers. He had great political influence, and played an important part in the formation in 1916 of the Coalition Cabinet led by David Lloyd George. Northcliffe owned the Amalgamated Press, a large magazine publishing house, and the London *Evening News*, the *Daily Mail*, the *Daily Mirror*, and *The Times*. He was born in County Dublin, Ireland.   JOHN ELDRIDGE DREWRY

NORTHEAST LOUISIANA UNIVERSITY. See UNIVERSITIES AND COLLEGES (table).

NORTHEAST MISSOURI STATE UNIVERSITY. See UNIVERSITIES AND COLLEGES (table).

NORTHEAST PASSAGE. See ARCTIC OCEAN.

NORTHEASTERN ILLINOIS UNIVERSITY. See UNIVERSITIES AND COLLEGES (table).

NORTHEASTERN OKLAHOMA STATE UNIVERSITY. See UNIVERSITIES AND COLLEGES (table).

NORTHEASTERN UNIVERSITY is a private, coeducational school in Boston. It has colleges of business administration, criminal justice, education, engineering, liberal arts, nursing, and pharmacy and allied health professions. The university includes Boston-Bouvé College, which has courses in physical therapy and health, physical, and recreation education; Lincoln College, which offers training in engineering technology; and University College, which provides adult education programs. Northeastern also has schools of actuarial science, law, and professional accounting. It grants bachelor's, master's, and doctor's degrees.

The university has a cooperative plan of education in which undergraduates alternate periods of study with periods of work. Some graduate programs also use the cooperative plan. The university was founded in 1898. For enrollment, see UNIVERSITIES AND COLLEGES (table).

Critically reviewed by NORTHEASTERN UNIVERSITY

NORTHER is a cold winter wind that sweeps over the southern United States and the Gulf of Mexico, destroying crops and wrecking ships. The northers occur most frequently between September and March. Northers often cause the temperature to drop rapidly as much as 20 to 30 degrees Fahrenheit (11 to 17 degrees Celsius).

The wind usually blows over Texas and other regions that border the western part of the Gulf of Mexico. Sometimes the wind reaches as far south as Panama. Occasionally a norther starts as far north as Canada and extends over the entire Mississippi Valley. Scientists can predict the coming of a norther about 24 hours in advance. A similar cold wind, called *Friagem*, occurs in South America.   GEORGE F. TAYLOR

NORTHERN ARIZONA UNIVERSITY. See UNIVERSITIES AND COLLEGES (table).

NORTHERN CIRCLE. See TROPIC OF CANCER.

NORTHERN COLORADO, UNIVERSITY OF. See UNIVERSITIES AND COLLEGES (table).

NORTHERN HEMISPHERE. See HEMISPHERE.

NORTHERN ILLINOIS UNIVERSITY is a state-supported coeducational school in De Kalb, Ill. It has colleges of business, education, liberal arts and sciences, professional studies, visual and performing arts, and continuing education; and a graduate school. Courses lead to bachelor's, master's, and doctor's degrees. The school was founded in 1895. For enrollment, see UNIVERSITIES AND COLLEGES (table).

Critically reviewed by NORTHERN ILLINOIS UNIVERSITY

NORTHERN IOWA, UNIVERSITY OF, is a state-supported coeducational liberal arts and teacher education school in Cedar Falls, Iowa. It is controlled by the Iowa State Board of Regents. It offers courses that prepare students for preschool, elementary school, and high school teaching, supervisory, and administrative positions. It has a grade school and high school as a teaching laboratory. Founded in 1876, it grants B.A., M.A., and Ed.S. degrees. For enrollment, see UNIVERSITIES AND COLLEGES (table).   J. W. MAUCKER

Peter L. Gould

Belfast is Northern Ireland's capital and largest city. Shops and offices line Donegall Place, *above*, in the heart of Belfast.

Picturepoint from Publix

Green Valleys and Low Mountains lie along the coast of Northern Ireland. Rolling farmland covers most of the country.

NORTHERN IRELAND

NORTHERN IRELAND is the smallest of the four countries that make up the UNITED KINGDOM OF GREAT BRITAIN AND NORTHERN IRELAND. The other countries are England, Scotland, and Wales. Northern Ireland is slightly larger than the state of Connecticut, but it has only about half as many people as that state. Belfast is the capital and largest city.

Northern Ireland occupies the northeastern corner of the island of Ireland. It takes up about a sixth of the island. The independent Republic of Ireland occupies the rest of the island. Northern Ireland is often called *Ulster*. Ulster was the name of a large province of Ireland until 1920, when Northern Ireland was separated from the rest of Ireland.

Most of the people of Northern Ireland are of English or Scottish descent. The majority are Protestants, and they observe many English traditions and customs. Most of the rest of the people are Roman Catholics of Irish descent. The two groups have long been in conflict.

More than two-fifths of the people of Northern Ireland live in rural areas. The country's farmers produce large quantities of agricultural products for the rest of Great Britain. About a fourth of the people live in Belfast, the country's manufacturing and trading center.

This article tells about the people, geography, economy, and history of Northern Ireland. For a discussion

of Great Britain as a whole and of Northern Ireland's relation to the other British countries, see the WORLD BOOK article on GREAT BRITAIN. For information on the Republic of Ireland, see IRELAND.

Government

Northern Ireland is part of Great Britain, a constitutional monarchy. Queen Elizabeth II is the head of state, but a Cabinet of government officials called *ministers* actually rules Britain. The *prime minister*

The contributors of this article are John Magee, Senior Lecturer in History at St. Joseph's College of Education, Belfast, Northern Ireland; Norman Runnion, Editor of the Brattleboro (Vt.) Daily Reformer and former London Correspondent for United Press International; and J. Wreford Watson, Professor of Geography at Edinburgh University, Edinburgh, Scotland.

--------- FACTS IN BRIEF ---------

Capital: Belfast.

Official Language: English.

Form of Government: Constitutional monarchy; part of the United Kingdom of Great Britain and Northern Ireland (see GREAT BRITAIN [Government]).

Area: 5,452 sq. mi. (14,120 km²). *Greatest Distances—* east-west, 111 mi. (179 km); north-south, 85 mi. (137 km). *Coastline—*330 mi. (531 km).

Elevation: *Highest—*Slieve Donard, 2,796 ft. (852 m) above sea level. *Lowest—*The Marsh, near Downpatrick, 1.3 ft. (0.4 m) below sea level.

Population: *Estimated 1978 Population—*1,566,000; distribution, 55 per cent urban, 45 per cent rural; density, 287 persons per sq. mi. (111 per km²). *1971 Census—* 1,536,065. *Estimated 1983 Population—*1,589,000.

Chief Products: *Agriculture—*cattle, eggs, hogs, milk, potatoes. *Manufacturing—*aircraft, alcoholic beverages, animal feeds, canned foods, Irish linen and other textiles, ships, tobacco products.

Money: *Basic Unit—*pound. One hundred new pence equal one pound. For the value of the pound in dollars, see MONEY (table: Values [Great Britain]). See also POUND STERLING.

is the chief ruling official. *Parliament* makes the laws of Great Britain. Parliament is made up of the *House of Commons* and the *House of Lords*. Northern Ireland elects 12 of the 630 members of the House of Commons. Most members of the House of Lords are noblemen who inherit their seats. For more information on the British government, see GREAT BRITAIN (Government).

Central Government. Until 1972, Northern Ireland was the only British country with its own governor, parliament, prime minister, and cabinet. The governor served as the official head of state, but the prime minister and cabinet actually held most of the governing power. Northern Ireland's two-house Parliament handled such matters as maintaining law and order, administering the educational system, and regulating commerce and agriculture. Certain other powers, such as levying income taxes and maintaining armed forces, were reserved for the Parliament of Great Britain. Throughout the history of Northern Ireland, the Union-

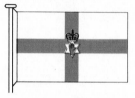 

Northern Ireland's Flag has the country's coat of arms over the St. George's cross of the English flag.

The Coat of Arms of Northern Ireland has a six-pointed star and the ancient Ulster symbol of a red hand.

Northern Ireland occupies about a sixth of the island of Ireland. The country is slightly larger than Connecticut.

WORLD BOOK map

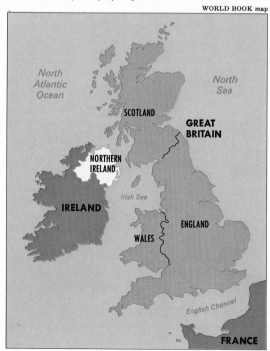

ist Party, a Protestant organization, controlled the government.

During the late 1960's and early 1970's, disagreements between Catholics and Protestants in Northern Ireland erupted in violent disorders and caused instability in the government. The Catholics demanded various reforms, including more political power. The continuing conflict led Britain to suspend Northern Ireland's government in March, 1972, and to establish direct rule over the country. Britain appointed a Secretary of State for Northern Ireland to take over executive and legislative powers.

In 1973, agreement was reached on a new government in which Catholics and Protestants shared power. The new government included a 78-member legislature, called the Northern Ireland Assembly, and a 15-member executive council made up of Catholic and Protestant assembly members. Legislative elections were held in June, 1973. The period of direct rule by Britain ended on Jan. 1, 1974, when the new executive council took office. Brian Faulkner, who had been prime minister of Northern Ireland before the British take-over, became head of the council.

But Catholic and Protestant extremist groups opposed the power-sharing government, and violence between the two sides continued. In May, 1974, Protestants led a general strike that severely disrupted the economy of Northern Ireland. The strike led to the resignation of the executive council. Britain then suspended the Northern Ireland Assembly and once again imposed direct rule over the country. In June, Britain announced that a constitutional convention would be held in Northern Ireland for the purpose of creating a new form of government that would unify the country. The delegates to the convention met early in 1976, but failed to reach agreement on a new government.

The Courts. The Supreme Court of Judicature is Northern Ireland's highest court. It consists of a chief justice and six associate justices. The British monarch appoints the justices on the advice of the British government. Other courts include the Court of Criminal Appeal and county and civil courts.

Local Government. Northern Ireland is divided into 26 districts for the purpose of local government. An elected council governs each district. District council members serve four-year terms. The district councils are responsible for such services as recreation, environmental protection, and garbage collection.

People

The way of life in Northern Ireland is closer to that in the rest of Great Britain than to that in the Republic of Ireland. This is because about two-thirds of the people of Northern Ireland are descended from English and Scottish Protestants. Most of the remaining third are of Irish Catholic descent.

Many Protestants of Northern Ireland belong to an organization called the *Orange Order* and are known as *Orangemen.* These terms date back to the late 1600's, when William of Orange, a Protestant, defeated James II, a Roman Catholic, in a struggle for the English throne. William became a hero to the Protestants of Ulster. On Orange Day, July 12, Orangemen still

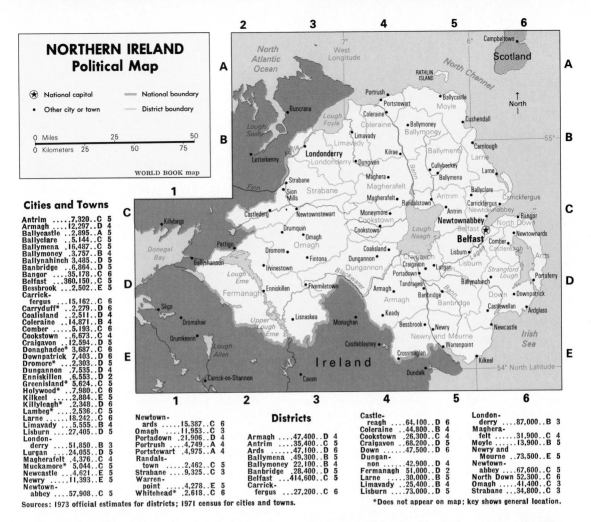

Cities and Towns

Antrim .....7,320..C 5
Armagh ...12,297..D 4
Ballycastle .2,895..A 5
Ballyclare ..5,144..C 5
Ballymena .16,487..C 5
Ballymoney .3,757..B 4
Ballynahinch 3,485..D 5
Banbridge ..6,864..D 5
Bangor ...35,178..C 6
Belfast ...360,150..C 5
Bessbrook ..2,502..E 5
Carrick-
  fergus ...15,162..C 6
Carryduff* ..2,279..D 6
Coalisland ..2,511..D 4
Coleraine ..14,871..B 4
Comber ....5,193..C 6
Cookstown ..6,673..C 4
Craigavon .12,594..D 5
Donaghadee* 3,687..C 6
Downpatrick 7,403..D 6
Dromore* ...2,303..D 5
Dungannon .7,535..D 4
Enniskillen .6,553..D 2
Greenisland* 5,624..C 5
Holywood* ..7,980..C 6
Kilkeel .....2,884..E 5
Killyleagh* .2,348..D 6
Lambeg* ....2,536..C 5
Larne .....18,242..C 6
Limavady ..5,555..B 4
Lisburn ...27,405..D 5
London-
  derry ...51,850..B 3
Lurgan ...24,055..D 5
Magherafelt .4,376..C 4
Muckamore* .5,044..C 5
Newcastle ..4,621..E 5
Newry .....11,393..E 5
Newtown-
abbey ....57,908..C 5

Newtown-
  ards .....15,387..C 6
Omagh ....11,953..C 3
Portadown .21,906..D 4
Portrush ...4,749..A 4
Portstewart .4,975..A 4
Randals-
  town .....2,462..C 5
Strabane ...9,325..C 3
Warren-
  point ....4,278..E 5
Whitehead* .2,618..C 6

Districts

Armagh ....47,400..D 4
Antrim ....35,400..C 5
Ards ......47,100..D 6
Ballymena .49,300..B 5
Ballymoney 22,100..B 4
Banbridge .28,400..D 5
Belfast ...414,600..C 5
Carrick-
fergus ....27,200..C 6

Castle-
  reagh ....64,100..D 6
Coleraine .44,800..B 4
Cookstown .26,300..C 4
Craigavon .68,200..D 5
Down ......47,500..D 6
Dungan-
  non ......42,900..D 4
Fermanagh 51,000..D 2
Larne .....30,000..B 5
Limavady ..25,400..B 4
Lisburn ...73,000..D 5

London-
  derry ....87,000..B 3
Maghera-
  felt ......31,900..C 4
Moyle .....13,900..B 5
Newry and
  Mourne ..73,500..E 5
Newtown-
  abbey ....67,600..C 5
North Down 52,300..C 6
Omagh ....41,400..C 3
Strabane ..34,800..C 3

Sources: 1973 official estimates for districts; 1971 census for cities and towns.   *Does not appear on map; key shows general location.

celebrate his victory in the Battle of the Boyne (see BOYNE, BATTLE OF THE).

Population. Northern Ireland has a population of about 1,566,000. More than half the people live in cities, towns, or villages. The country has three cities with over 50,000 persons. Belfast, the capital, has a population of 360,150. Londonderry has 51,850 persons, and Newtownabbey has 57,908.

Language. English is the official language throughout Great Britain, and nearly all the people of Northern Ireland speak it. A few persons in rural areas speak Gaelic, which was once used throughout Ireland (see GAELIC LANGUAGE).

Food and Drink. The people of Northern Ireland enjoy simple meals of meat, potatoes, vegetables, and bread. They also eat large amounts of poultry, eggs, dairy products, and fish.

Tea is the most popular drink in Northern Ireland. A favorite alcoholic beverage is beer. Many people enjoy drinking it in their local *pub* (public house). Pubs play an important role in social life throughout Great Britain.

Recreation. Northern Ireland's most popular organized sport is *football*, or soccer. The Irish Football Association regulates the country's nearly 600 amateur football teams. Professional and semiprofessional teams belong to the Irish League. Both amateur and professional teams compete in British and international football matches. See SOCCER.

Other popular sports include cricket, which is played with a bat and ball; Gaelic football, which resembles soccer; handball; hurling and camogie, which are somewhat similar to field hockey; and Rugby, a form of football. Many people enjoy boating, fishing, golf, hunting, and swimming. See CRICKET; FIELD HOCKEY; HANDBALL; RUGBY FOOTBALL.

Education in Northern Ireland is supervised by the Ministry of Education and five *area education boards*. All children in Northern Ireland between the ages of 5 and 16 are required to attend school. Nearly all of them go to schools supported by public funds.

Northern Ireland has three types of high schools—grammar schools, secondary schools, and technical schools. *Grammar schools* prepare students for college. *Secondary schools* provide general and vocational education. *Technical schools* offer specialized courses, with emphasis on mathematics and science. Education in secondary and technical schools is free. Grammar school students must pay fees, but about 90 per cent of them receive scholarships.

There are two universities in Northern Ireland—the Queen's University of Belfast and the New University of Ulster in Coleraine. The Queen's University has about 6,700 students, and the New University has about 1,700.

Religion. About two-thirds of the people of Northern Ireland are Protestants. The Church of Ireland, also called the Anglican Church, and the Presbyterian Church are the country's largest Protestant churches. Most of the remaining third of the people are Roman Catholics.

One of Northern Ireland's major problems is the serious split between Protestants and Catholics. Many Protestants fear that Catholics in both Northern Ireland and the Republic of Ireland want to unite the two countries and put Northern Ireland under Catholic control. On the other hand, Roman Catholics in Northern Ireland claim that the Protestants have violated their civil rights. For more information on the split between the Protestants and Catholics, see the *History* section of this article.

The Land

Northern Ireland occupies the northeastern corner of the island of Ireland. It covers 5,452 square miles (14,120 square kilometers). On the south and west, it is bordered by the Republic of Ireland, which occupies the rest of the island. The North Channel separates Northern Ireland from Scotland to the northeast, and the Irish Sea separates it from England to the southeast.

Surface Features. Northern Ireland is a land of rolling plains and low mountains. The plains, which cover the central part of the country, include fertile fields and pasturelands. The mountains, which are near the coast, have many deep, scenic valleys. In some areas, the plains reach to the coast.

The highest peak in Northern Ireland, 2,796-foot (852-meter) Slieve Donard, rises in the Mourne Mountains near the southeast coast. Other mountain ranges include the Sperrin Mountains in the northwest and the Mountains of Antrim in the northeast.

Lakes, Rivers, and Bays. Northern Ireland has many smooth, clear lakes called *loughs* (pronounced *lahks*). Lough Neagh, near the center of the country, covers 147 square miles (381 square kilometers) and is the largest lake in the British Isles (see LOUGH NEAGH).

The largest river in Northern Ireland is the River Bann. The Bann actually is two rivers. The Upper Bann, which is 47½ miles (76.4 kilometers) long, begins in the Mourne Mountains and flows northwestward into the southern end of Lough Neagh. The Lower Bann begins at the northern end of the lake and flows north 38 miles (61 kilometers) into the Atlantic Ocean. Many small, winding rivers empty into the Bann.

Several large bays, which are also called loughs, cut into Northern Ireland's coast. Lough Foyle and Belfast Lough provide excellent harbors for Londonderry and Belfast.

Economy

The economy of Northern Ireland depends mainly on manufacturing and agriculture. Manufacturing has been important since the Industrial Revolution began in Great Britain in the 1700's. Agriculture is important because more than 80 per cent of the land in Northern

Ireland is fertile enough for crop farming or grazing.

Natural Resources. Fertile fields and pasturelands are Northern Ireland's chief natural resources. The country also has large deposits of peat. The peat, which is cut from *bogs* (swamplands), is burned for heating and cooking (see PEAT). Other natural resources include chalk, granite, and sandstone. Excellent fishing grounds lie off the coast.

Manufacturing. Northern Ireland's chief manufactured product is Irish linen, which is world famous for its excellent quality. Most linen mills are near Belfast and Londonderry.

Other mills in Northern Ireland produce cord, twine, and rope; woolen and cotton textiles; and synthetic fibers. The production of synthetic fibers has grown rapidly with the construction of new factories near Belfast and Carrickfergus.

Heavy manufacturing in Northern Ireland is centered in the Belfast area. Shipyards there have built many warships and ocean liners, including the famous *Titanic*. Aircraft plants in the area make airliners and military planes. Aluminum produced in nearby Larne is used by the aircraft industry. Other products manufactured in Northern Ireland include alcoholic beverages, animal feeds, beet sugar, canned foods, chemicals, tobacco products, and vegetable oils.

Agriculture. Cattle, eggs, hogs, milk, and potatoes are Northern Ireland's most important agricultural products. Much barley, hay, and oats are grown for animal feed. Other farm products include butter,

PHYSICAL MAP OF NORTHERN IRELAND

A large plateau about 500 feet (150 meters) above sea level covers most of Northern Ireland. The surface is lowest near the center around Lough Neagh, the largest lake in the British Isles. The land rises gently in the mountains surrounding the plateau.

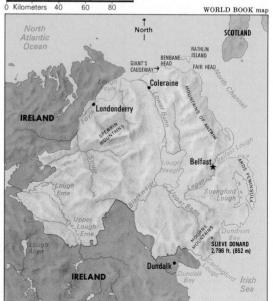

poultry, sheep, and turnips. Orchards in the south produce apples, pears, and plums.

Transportation and Trade. More than 14,000 miles (22,500 kilometers) of roads and highways and about 200 miles (320 kilometers) of railroad track crisscross Northern Ireland. Belfast is the country's main seaport. Ferry services run between ports in Northern Ireland and cities on the west coasts of England and Scotland. More than 150 miles (240 kilometers) of rivers and canals provide inland water routes. Aldergrove Airport, near Belfast, has flights to several countries.

Northern Ireland trades mainly with the Republic of Ireland and with the other countries of Great Britain. Its chief exports include clothing; finished cotton, linen, and rayon fabrics; and machines for weaving textiles. Northern Ireland also ships large quantities of eggs, livestock, meat, and poultry to the other British countries. Chief imports include cotton, flax, and rayon yarn; machinery; and unfinished cotton and woolen goods. Most of the flax fiber used in making Irish linen is imported from Belgium and France.

History

Protestant Settlement. Ireland came under English rule in 1541, when Henry VIII of England declared himself king of Ireland. Henry tried to introduce Protestantism into Ireland. But the Irish people, most of whom were Roman Catholics, objected and began a series of revolts against English rule. In 1603, Elizabeth I of England put down an uprising led by Catholics in Ulster, a large province in northeastern Ireland. James I, who followed Elizabeth as ruler of England, tried to prevent further revolts by seizing the Catholics' land in Ulster and giving it to English and Scottish Protestants. This action was partly responsible for the Prot-

estant majority that still exists in Northern Ireland.

Economic and Political Differences began to develop during the 1700's between Catholics in southern Ireland and Protestants in Ulster. In the south, an increasing population, unequal distribution of the land, and declines in industry led to low standards of living. In the north, textile manufacturing and shipbuilding flourished, and standards of living rose. The Protestants controlled Ireland's Parliament and, together with the British, restricted the rights of Catholics.

In 1800, the British and Irish parliaments each passed the Act of Union, which ended Ireland's Parliament and made the country part of Great Britain. But many Catholics still demanded freedom from Britain.

In 1886, the British Liberal Party supported a plan called *home rule*. Under this plan, all Ireland would have remained part of Great Britain, but the country would have had its own parliament for domestic affairs. Ulster Protestants, who feared a Catholic parliament, formed the Unionist Party to oppose the plan. The British Parliament passed a home rule bill over Ulster opposition in 1914. But the outbreak of World War I (1914-1918) prevented home rule from going into effect.

The Division of Ireland. In 1919, 73 Irish members of the British Parliament met in Dublin and declared all Ireland an independent republic. Violent fighting then broke out between the Irish rebels and British forces. In 1920, the British Parliament passed the Government of Ireland Act. This act divided Ireland into two separate countries and gave each some powers of self-government. Ulster Protestants accepted the act, and the state of Northern Ireland was formed from 6 counties in Ulster. But southern Catholics rejected the act and demanded complete independence. In 1921, southern leaders and Great Britain signed a treaty that

Textile Manufacturing is an important industry in Northern Ireland. These wool yarns will be woven into tweed, one of the many types of cloth made in Belfast and Londonderry mills.

Gordon Johnson, Photo Researchers

Pictorial Parade

British Troops built barricades in 1969 to separate the Protestant and Roman Catholic areas of Belfast. The troops were sent in following bloody fighting between the two religious groups.

created the Irish Free State from 23 southern counties and 3 counties of Ulster. In 1949, the Irish Free State cut all ties with Britain and became the independent Republic of Ireland.

Problems of Division. Many Roman Catholics in Northern Ireland refused to accept the 1920 division of Ireland, and the new government made little effort to win their loyalty. In some parts of the country where Catholics formed a majority, election districts were set up to make sure that Unionist minorities won control of local councils. The councils tried to establish separate living areas for Catholics and Protestants. As a result, the two groups, in time, became almost completely separated.

The division of Ireland was also opposed by the Irish Free State and, later, by the Republic of Ireland. Beginning in 1921, armed groups crossed into Northern Ireland and attacked British government installations. Between 1956 and 1962, frequent attacks were carried out by a group called the Irish Republican Army (IRA). The raiders hoped to force the British to give up control of the country. Because of these attacks, Northern Ireland's police force, the Royal Ulster Constabulary, was given heavy arms. In addition, an all-Protestant volunteer force called the Ulster Special Constabulary was formed to assist the police.

The Civil Rights Movement. Catholics in Northern Ireland have long claimed that Protestants have violated their civil rights and discriminated against them in jobs, housing, and other areas. In 1967, the Northern Ireland Civil Rights Association was established to work for equal rights for all citizens.

On Oct. 5, 1968, the association planned a march in Londonderry to demonstrate its strength and to demand reforms. The government tried to stop the march, and bloody riots broke out. Following the riots, the British government persuaded Northern Ireland's prime minister, Terence M. O'Neill, to establish a number of reforms. But conservative Unionists objected, and O'Neill resigned in 1969. James D. Chichester-Clark then became prime minister.

Serious riots occurred again in July and August, 1969, in Belfast and Londonderry. British troops were sent to Northern Ireland to maintain order, and the British government persuaded Chichester-Clark to accept far-reaching reforms, including an unarmed, nonpolitical police force and agencies to guard against discrimination. British troops remained in Northern Ireland, but they were unable to prevent rioting from occurring during the early 1970's. The Irish Republican Army and other militant groups carried out bombings and other terrorist activities. In 1971, Chichester-Clark resigned and was succeeded by Brian Faulkner. In 1972, the continuing violence led Britain to take over direct rule of Northern Ireland. For additional information on recent political events in Northern Ireland, see the *Government* section of this article.

Before 1920, the history of Northern Ireland was part of the history of Ireland. Since 1920, it has been part of the history of Great Britain. For further information, see IRELAND (History) and GREAT BRITAIN (History).

JOHN MAGEE, NORMAN RUNNION, and J. WREFORD WATSON

Related Articles in WORLD BOOK include:

Outline

Questions

What are Northern Ireland's most important natural resources?

Who was William of Orange?

What political party has controlled the government of Northern Ireland throughout most of the country's history? Why was this party formed?

What is Northern Ireland's chief manufactured product?

Why is there a split between Protestants and Roman Catholics in Northern Ireland?

What countries are Northern Ireland's chief trading partners?

Why was the Ulster Special Constabulary formed?

What is Northern Ireland's most popular organized sport?

What was the Government of Ireland Act?

Why is agriculture important in Northern Ireland?

NORTHERN LIGHTS. See AURORA BOREALIS.

NORTHERN MICHIGAN UNIVERSITY is a coeducational liberal arts school at Marquette. Its graduate school courses are conducted in cooperation with the University of Michigan. It grants A.B., B.S., and B.Mus. degrees. The university was opened in 1899. For enrollment, see UNIVERSITIES AND COLLEGES (table).

NORTHERN MONTANA COLLEGE. See UNIVERSITIES AND COLLEGES (table).

NORTHERN RHODESIA. See ZAMBIA.

NORTHERN STATE COLLEGE is a coeducational school at Aberdeen, S. Dak. The college offers bachelor's degrees in education and liberal arts, and master's degrees in education. Courses include fine arts, humanities, science, and mathematics. It was founded in 1901. For enrollment, see UNIVERSITIES AND COLLEGES (table).

NORTHERN TERRITORY is a tropical area in north-central Australia. It has large regions of only partly explored land. It covers 520,280 square miles (1,347,519 square kilometers). Its population of 85,519 includes many Aborigines whose ancestors lived in Australia before white people arrived (see AUSTRALIA [The Aborigines]). Tribal conditions still exist among some of the Aborigines. Darwin is the administrative center and largest city. For location, see AUSTRALIA (political map).

The territory's flat coastline of 1,040 miles (1,674 kilometers) has many bays. The interior is mostly flat. The northern area has excellent grazing regions. The south is sandy. Rivers include the Victoria, Daly, and Roper. Average January temperatures range between 80° F. (27° C) and 90° F. (32° C), and July temperatures average 70° F. (21° C). The annual rainfall varies. Darwin, on the northern coast, has an average of 58 inches (147 centimeters). In the dry interior, rainfall seldom exceeds 11 inches (28 centimeters) a year.

Cattle breeding is the chief industry in the Northern Territory. Large cattle *stations* (ranches) cover extensive areas in the territory. About 1,067,000 cattle, 36,000 horses, and 9,000 sheep graze in the Northern Territory. Other important industries include pearling and mining. Bauxite, copper, gold, mica, tantalite, tin, tungsten, and uranium are the chief minerals. Mining has developed slowly, because mineral deposits are located far from supply sources. The lack of good transportation and the distance from markets have delayed the full development of the Northern Territory.

Some of the people ride on horseback to hunt smooth-haired white buffaloes. These animals were imported from India about a hundred years ago, and now roam the Northern Territory plains in great numbers.

The federal government provides medical services for the Northern Territory. A "Flying Doctor" operation uses radio and aircraft service to help the sick and injured at isolated mines and cattle stations.

The government of South Australia operates the educational system in the Northern Territory for the federal government.

WORLD BOOK map

The Northern Territory

The Northern Territory was part of New South Wales until 1863 when it was annexed to the province of South Australia. The Australian Commonwealth government took over the administration in 1911. A commonwealth administrator now handles the territory's affairs. The territory has an 18-member council. The commonwealth appoints 10 of them. The people elect the other 8. The Legislative Council can adopt non-financial measures. The Northern Territory elects one member to the federal House of Representatives. This representative can vote only on matters that relate solely to the territory.

The explorer John McDouall Stuart entered the Northern Territory in 1860. His explorations opened up much of the Northern Territory. An overland telegraph line, completed in the 1870's, followed Stuart's trail from Adelaide to Darwin.   C. M. H. CLARK

See also DARWIN.

NORTHFIELD, Minn. (pop. 10,235), in the center of Minnesota's dairy country, is known for its Holstein-Friesian cattle and its large creameries. It lies about 40 miles (64 kilometers) south of St. Paul in southeastern Minnesota. For location, see MINNESOTA (political map).

Industries of Northfield include the manufacture of cereal, woodworking machines, sheet-metal products, and plastics goods. The city is named after John W. North, who founded it in 1856. It is the home of St. Olaf and Carleton colleges. Northfield has a mayor-council form of government.   HAROLD L. HAGG

NORTHLAND COLLEGE. See UNIVERSITIES AND COLLEGES (table).

NORTHMAN. See VIKINGS.

NORTHROP, JOHN HOWARD (1891-   ), an American biochemist, shared the 1946 Nobel prize in chemistry with James B. Sumner and W. M. Stanley. They prepared in crystalline form several pure enzymes and one of the viruses which destroy bacteria (see ENZYME). Northrop's writings on enzymes include *Crystalline Enzymes* (1939). He was born in Yonkers, N.Y. He received his doctoral degree from Columbia University in 1915 and became a member of the Rockefeller Institute (now Rockefeller University) in New York City in 1924.

NORTHROP UNIVERSITY is a privately controlled coeducational university in Inglewood, Calif. It has colleges of business and management, engineering, science and humanities, and technology. Courses lead to bachelor's and master's degrees. The school was founded in 1942 as Northrop Institute of Technology. It took its present name in 1975. For enrollment, see UNIVERSITIES AND COLLEGES (table).

NORTHWEST CHRISTIAN COLLEGE. See UNIVERSITIES AND COLLEGES (table).

NORTHWEST MISSOURI STATE UNIVERSITY is a state-controlled, coeducational teachers university at Maryville, Mo. It offers A.B. and B.S. degrees, and master's degrees in education. The school was founded in 1905, as the Fifth District Normal School. For the enrollment of Northwest Missouri State University, see UNIVERSITIES AND COLLEGES (table).

NORTHWEST NAZARENE COLLEGE. See UNIVERSITIES AND COLLEGES (table).

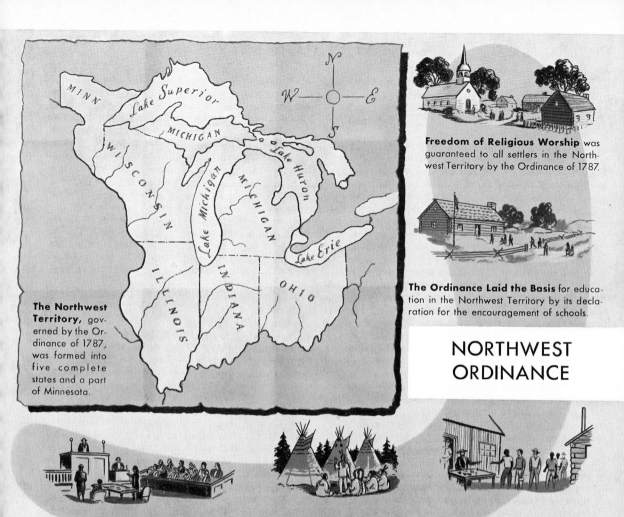

The Northwest Territory, governed by the Ordinance of 1787, was formed into five complete states and a part of Minnesota.

Freedom of Religious Worship was guaranteed to all settlers in the Northwest Territory by the Ordinance of 1787.

The Ordinance Laid the Basis for education in the Northwest Territory by its declaration for the encouragement of schools.

NORTHWEST ORDINANCE

Before State Governments were set up in the Northwest Territory, the laws of the thirteen original states were enforced there.

Just Dealing with Indians in the Northwest Territory was provided for in the Ordinance.

The Prohibition of Slavery strengthened the ranks of the antislavery states in the Union.

NORTHWEST ORDINANCE, passed by the United States Congress on July 13, 1787, was one of the most important laws ever adopted. The ordinance provided for the government of the region north of the Ohio River and west of Pennsylvania, then called the Northwest Territory. It became a model for all territories that later entered the Union as states. The ordinance was largely the work of General Nathan Dane, Rufus King, and Manasseh Cutler (see KING [Rufus]).

Under the terms of the ordinance, the territories could achieve equality with the older states by passing through three steps leading to full self-government. (1) Congress, which governed the territory, appointed a governor, a secretary, and three judges. (2) When the territory, or any division of it, attained an adult male population of 5,000, it could choose a legislature and send to Congress a delegate who could speak but not vote. (3) When the total population reached 60,000, the territory could apply for admission into the Union on terms of full equality with the older states. The ordi-

nance removed the danger of colonial rebellion, because it assured the territories of participation in the national government.

The Northwest Ordinance contained more than a plan of government. It laid the groundwork for social and political democracy in the West. It forbade slavery. All persons were guaranteed trial by jury and freedom of religious worship. The ordinance guaranteed fair treatment for the Indians, and declared that "means of education shall forever be encouraged."

The terms of the ordinance were so attractive that pioneers poured into the new territory. In 1788, one of the first groups of settlers founded the town of Marietta, Ohio. Thousands of families followed the first settlers in the westward movement. The territory eventually became five states—Ohio, Indiana, Illinois, Michigan, and Wisconsin. It included what is now the part of Minnesota east of the Mississippi River. RAY ALLEN BILLINGTON

See also NORTHWEST TERRITORY; OHIO COMPANY.

NORTHWEST ORIENT AIRLINES. See AIRLINE.

NORTHWEST PASSAGE. The explorers who followed Columbus soon found that North America was not a part of Asia, as they had believed at first. At this time, British, French, and Dutch adventurers were more interested in finding an easy route to Asia than they were in exploring and settling North America. So they began to look for a "Northwest Passage," or waterway, that would take them around or through the continent.

The search for the Northwest Passage is a tale of adventure and heroism. In 1524, Giovanni Verrazano, sailing under the French flag, tried to find the passage. He probably explored as far north as Maine.

Jacques Cartier, while exploring for France in 1535, found the St. Lawrence River. He was seeking a route to China. Henry Hudson was sent out many years later by the Dutch East India Company to find a shorter route to the South Seas. He thought he had found that route in 1609 when he sailed into New York Bay and some distance up the Hudson River. In 1610, Hudson explored the Hudson Strait and Hudson Bay while searching for the Northwest Passage.

No country tried harder than England to find the passage. Sir Martin Frobisher began a series of English expeditions in 1576. Other Englishmen continued these explorations for 300 years. These men sailed far to the north in their search. Frobisher made many important findings, including Frobisher Bay, an indentation in Baffin Island (later called Baffin Land). John Davis followed Frobisher, and sailed into the strait that now bears his name. In 1616, William Baffin and Robert Bylot sailed up Davis Strait and around the great channel ever since known as Baffin Bay. Russia, Holland, and Denmark took an interest in the search.

By the close of the 1700's, the territory that had been explored included Hudson Strait, Hudson Bay, Davis Strait, Baffin Bay, and the icy seas from Greenland to Spitsbergen and from Spitsbergen to Novaya Zemlya. For details of this important period of exploration, see EXPLORATION AND DISCOVERY.

Commander John Ross (1777-1856), a Scottish explorer, began the final series of expeditions in 1818. The most noted of the explorers to follow him was Sir John Franklin, a British explorer. Franklin died trying to find

a passage to Asia. Many people honor Franklin as the first discoverer of the passage, although he never completed the voyage through it. His ships reached a point not far from waters that lead directly to the Asiatic shore. In 1850 Sir Robert McClure (1807-1873) forced a passage northward to the northern shore of the island Banks Land. He anchored his ship in a bay which he named God's Mercy, and tried to continue his trip by foot. But his attempt did not succeed.

In 1906, Roald Amundsen's ship, the *Gjoa*, completed the first trip through the Northwest Passage. Amundsen traveled from east to west. The first west-to-east voyage was completed in 1942 by the Royal Canadian Mounted Police schooner, *St. Roch*. McClure Strait was conquered in 1954 by U.S. Navy and Coast Guard icebreakers. Three U.S. Coast Guard cutters, the *Spar*, the *Bramble*, and the *Storis*, aided by the Canadian Navy icebreaker, the *Labrador*, made the west-to-east trip in 1957. They traveled through *Bellot Strait*. This narrow channel is big enough for freighters. It permits cargo ships to unload supplies for the Distant Early Warning radar line in Northern Canada. The *Spar* was the first ship ever to sail completely around North America on a continuous voyage. It started from Bristol, R.I., and went south to the Panama Canal, then up the Pacific Coast, through the Northwest Passage, and back to Bristol.

In 1960, the U.S. atomic submarine *Seadragon* made the first underwater crossing of the Northwest Passage. It traveled 850 miles (1,368 kilometers) from Lancaster Sound, through the Canadian Arctic islands, and into McClure Strait. In 1969, the U.S. icebreaker-tanker *Manhattan* became the first commercial ship to complete the passage. The *Manhattan* sailed to Alaska by way of the Prince of Wales Strait.   RAY ALLEN BILLINGTON

Related Articles in WORLD BOOK include:

Amundsen, Roald	Franklin, Sir John
Arctic Ocean (Man and the Arctic Ocean)	Frobisher, Sir Martin
Baffin, William	Gilbert, Sir Humphrey
Cartier, Jacques	Hudson, Henry
	Parry, Sir William Edward

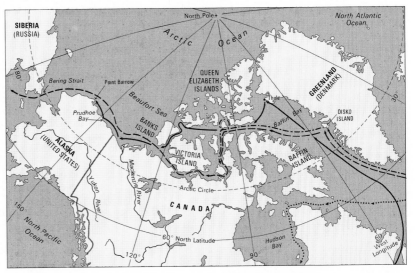

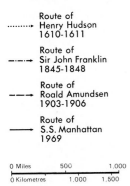

THE NORTHWEST PASSAGE

This map shows several routes traveled by explorers in search of a northern sea passage between Europe and Asia.

Route of
Henry Hudson
1610-1611

Route of
Sir John Franklin
1845-1848

Route of
Roald Amundsen
1903-1906

Route of
S.S. Manhattan
1969

0 Miles   500   1,000
0 Kilometres   1,000   1,500

WORLD BOOK map

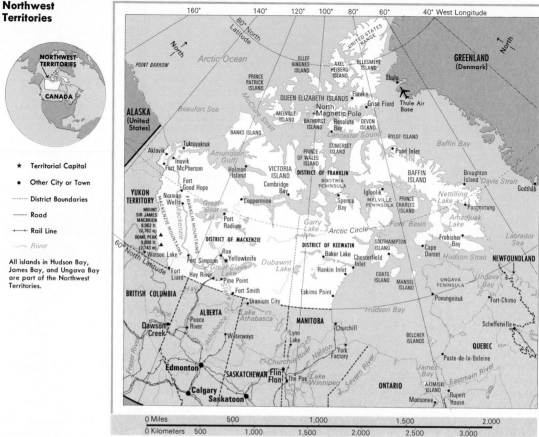

NORTHWEST
TERRITORIES

NORTHWEST
TERRITORIES

CANADA

★ Territorial Capital
• Other City or Town
----- District Boundaries
— Road
+—+— Rail Line
~ River

All islands in Hudson Bay,
James Bay, and Ungava Bay
are part of the Northwest
Territories.

WORLD BOOK map

NORTHWEST TERRITORIES is a vast region that covers about a third of Canada. It stretches from the northern boundaries of the Canadian provinces to within 500 miles (800 kilometers) of the North Pole. The region includes the Arctic homeland of about 11,400 Canadian Eskimos and about 7,200 northern Indians.

Until the 1950's, the Northwest Territories remained one of the world's last undeveloped frontiers. The region has one railroad and only one major highway. Pioneers are developing its great mineral wealth.

Yellowknife serves as the capital of the Northwest Territories. A commissioner and a 15-member council govern the Territories. The Canadian Department of Indian Affairs and Northern Development once handled the administration of the Northwest Territories. A territorial public service now handles these duties.

For the relationship of the Northwest Territories to the rest of Canada, see CANADA.

The Land and Its Resources

Location and Size. The Northwest Territories lies west of Greenland, and north and west of Quebec. The provinces of Manitoba, Saskatchewan, Alberta, and British Columbia border the Territories on the south. The Yukon Territory lies to the west. The Northwest Territories includes a group of Arctic islands north of the Canadian mainland, and all the islands in Hudson, James, and Ungava bays. The Territories covers

1,304,903 square miles (3,379,683 square kilometers). The *Map* shows that about half the Northwest Territories is located north of the Arctic Circle.

Districts. The Northwest Territories is divided into three geographic districts: Mackenzie, Keewatin, and Franklin.

The District of Mackenzie (527,490 square miles, or 1,366,193 square kilometers) lies east of the Yukon Territory. The district has a population of about 29,000. The rugged Mackenzie Mountains rise along the Yukon boundary. High peaks include Mount Sir James Mac-Brien (9,062 feet, or 2,762 meters) and Dome Peak (9,000 feet, or 2,743 meters).

East of the Mackenzie Mountains is the Mackenzie River Valley, a northward continuation of the Great Central Plain of North America (see PLAIN). The Mackenzie River is the longest waterway in Canada. From its most distant source to the point at which it empties into the Arctic Ocean, the river is 2,635 miles (4,241 kilometers) long. The Franklin Mountains rise to elevations of about 5,000 feet (1,500 meters), and lie along the east bank of the Mackenzie River.

More than half of Mackenzie District is east of the plains region in the rocky Canadian Shield area (see

S. M. Hodgson, the contributor of this article, is Commissioner of the Northwest Territories.

CANADIAN SHIELD). Lakes, swamps, and sand plains cover much of this area. Two of the largest lakes in Canada, Great Bear Lake and Great Slave Lake, lie east of the plain of the Mackenzie River.

The first main settlements of the Territories grew along the banks of the Mackenzie River during the late 1700's. In the 1930's, the center of population began to shift to mining areas around Great Slave Lake and Great Bear Lake, which supply most of the minerals mined in the Territories. Minerals include gold, lead, and zinc. The Mackenzie District is also the main source of forestry and fishery products. Nahanni National Park lies in the southwestern part of the district. Wood Buffalo National Park, which is largely in Alberta, extends into the district.

The District of Keewatin (228,160 square miles, or 590,932 square kilometers) lies east of Mackenzie District, within the Canadian Shield region. The district has a population of about 3,900. Keewatin extends eastward to Quebec and includes all the islands in Hudson, James, and Ungava bays. *Keewatin* means *north wind* in the language of the Cree Indians, who once hunted in the region. Most of Keewatin is a rocky plateau called the *Barrens*. It has little vegetation.

The District of Franklin (549,253 square miles, or 1,422,559 square kilometers) includes the Canadian Arctic islands and the Melville and Boothia peninsulas in the northeast. Large islands near the mainland in-

---

FACTS IN BRIEF

Capital: Yellowknife.

Government: *Parliament*—members of the Senate, 1; members of the House of Commons, 2. *Territorial*—members of the territorial legislative council, 15.

Area: 1,304,903 sq. mi. (3,379,683 km²), including 51,465 sq. mi. (133,294 km²) of inland water. *Greatest Distances*—east-west, 1,800 mi. (2,897 km); north-south, 1,660 mi. (2,672 km). *Coastline*—100,516 mi. (161,765 km), including mainland and islands.

Elevation: *Highest*—Mount Sir James MacBrien in the Mackenzie Mountains, 9,062 ft. (2,762 m) above sea level; *Lowest*—sea level along the coast.

Population: *1976 Census*—42,609; density, 3 persons per 100 sq. mi. (1 person per 100 km²); distribution, 52 per cent rural, 48 per cent urban.

Chief Products: *Mining*—gold, lead, silver, zinc. *Fishing Industry*—char, lake trout, whitefish. *Fur Industry*—bear, lynx, marten, muskrat, seal, white fox, wolf.

Territorial Coat of Arms: Two golden narwhals at the top guard the compass rose. The wavy line crossing the white chief (top of the shield) is blue. The field below has red and green sections. The bars of gold stand for mineral resources, and the fox for the fur industry.

Territorial Flag: The flag has three vertical panels. The panels on the left and right are blue for the skies and waters, and the wider center panel is white for the snows of the Territories. The shield from the territorial coat of arms appears in the center of the white panel. The flag was adopted in 1969. See FLAG (picture: Flags of Canada).

Territorial Flower: Mountain Avens.

Heavy Polar Ice dots the northern waters of the Northwest Territories the year around, often making navigation difficult.

The Territorial Coat of Arms

Yellowknife, the Capital of the Northwest Territories, lies on Yellowknife Bay, near Great Slave Lake. The main offices of the territorial government are in the building in the foreground.

clude Baffin, one of the largest islands in the world; Banks; and Victoria. The Arctic islands, north of Mc-Clure Strait and Lancaster Sound, are known as the Queen Elizabeth Islands. Ellesmere Island, the largest in the group, has a high mountain range, the United States Range. Its highest peak is 8,584 feet (2,616 meters) above sea level. Baffin and Ellesmere islands have rugged mountains and deep fiords. Auyuittuq National Park lies on the eastern side of Baffin Island.

Not one tree grows in the whole District of Franklin, because the average July temperature is below 50° F. (10° C). But colorful flowers bloom abundantly in some places in summer.

The District of Franklin has a population of about 9,200. The northern part of the district is almost completely uninhabited. There are some employees of government weather and radio stations, and of an airfield at Resolute Bay on Cornwallis Island. Some Eskimos live at Resolute Bay and at Grise Fiord. The Royal Canadian Mounted Police are also stationed in these two places.

Climate. Most of the District of Mackenzie has fairly warm summers and cold winters. Aklavik and Inuvik have average temperatures of 56° F. (13° C) in July, and −18° F. (−28° C) in January. Temperatures in Fort Smith, near the Alberta border, average 61° F. (16° C) in July, and −13° F. (−25° C) in January.

The District of Keewatin has an Arctic climate, with long, cold winters and short, cool summers. The average July temperature is about 42° F. (6° C), and January temperatures range around −25° F. (−32° C).

Temperatures on the Arctic islands vary little from the District of Keewatin, except in the Queen Elizabeth group. The far north averages 25° F. (−4° C) in July, and −40° F. (−40° C) in January.

Most of the Territories receives little moisture. Average annual precipitation ranges from 15 inches (38 cen-

timeters) in the southern Mackenzie District to about 2½ inches (6.4 centimeters) on Ellesmere Island. Most of it falls as snow. About 40 inches (100 centimeters) of snow falls every year on the mainland, and about 60 inches (150 centimeters) on some islands.

The highest temperature recorded in the Territories was 103° F. (39° C) at Fort Smith on July 18, 1941. The lowest, −71° F. (−57° C), also occurred at Fort Smith on Dec. 26, 1917.

Life of the People

The People. The Northwest Territories had a population of 42,609 in 1976. This was an increase of about 22 per cent over the 1971 figure. The Territories has an average of about 3 persons per 100 square miles (1 person per 100 square kilometers). The largest populated places, including Yellowknife, Hay River, Inuvik, Frobisher Bay, and Fort Smith, have a combined population of about 19,000. Most of the rest of the people live in small settlements that are scattered throughout the Northwest Territories. The population includes whites, Indians, Eskimos, and *métis* (persons who are of mixed white and Indian descent).

Most of the Eskimos live in the interior of Keewatin, around the shores of Hudson Bay, Baffin Island, and in the Arctic coast region. Most of the whites live in Mackenzie District.

All of the Indians live in the District of Mackenzie, and many of them make their living mainly by trapping and hunting. The Indians also work for government agencies, in industry and commerce, and as guides for tourists.

The income of the Eskimos comes chiefly from trapping, hunting, and handicrafts. Eskimos also work on government defense projects and in the public service. Many Eskimos in the west have gradually adopted the way of life of the white settlers. Most Eskimos now live in small, prefabricated houses. Igloos have almost disappeared.

The Roman Catholic, Anglican, and United churches are the largest churches in the Territories. Most Indians are Catholics. Most of the Eskimos belong to the Anglican Church. Most whites belong to one of those churches or to other denominations.

Municipalities. Yellowknife in 1970 became the first incorporated city in the Northwest Territories. Fort Smith, Hay River, Inuvik, and Pine Point are incorporated towns. Fort Simpson and Frobisher Bay are incorporated villages. Yellowknife is the capital and largest municipality. Aklavik, on the Mackenzie River Delta, long ranked second to Yellowknife in size. But frequent flooding of the area discouraged further growth. In 1955, the federal government began building Inuvik, about 30 miles (48 kilometers) away. Inuvik has replaced Aklavik as the administrative, educational, and medical-care center in the area. Many communities in the Northwest Territories were once fur-trading posts.

Work of the People

Mining is the most important activity in the Northwest Territories. It provides an annual income of about $225 million. Geologists believe that almost every known mineral can be found in the region. However, mining companies have developed only a small portion of the resources. Zinc and other base metals account for most of the mineral output. Gold mining centers in and around Yellowknife. Mines in this area yield about 177,000 troy ounces (5,505 kilograms) of gold a year. Petroleum comes from the Norman Wells area. A refinery in the town processes about 1 million barrels of crude oil annually. Pine Point, on the shore of Great Slave Lake, is the site of a lead and zinc mine that was completed in 1966. A railroad leading to the mine was built at the same time. Lead and zinc also come from northern Baffin Island. The Northwest Territories is a leading North American producer of lead

An Eskimo of the Northwest Territories cooks a meal on a camping stove. Nearly all the Eskimos and the Indians of the Territories use snowmobiles when hunting and trapping.

and zinc. One of the richest iron ore deposits in the world was found on northern Baffin Island near Milne Inlet in the early 1960's. But developers had difficulty transporting the ore out of the island's wilderness. Exploration for minerals continued into the 1970's.

Fur Trapping, which first attracted whites to the Territories in the late 1700's, remained the main source of income for more than a hundred years. It lost some of its importance as mining began to develop after 1920. It also suffered a great setback during the 1940's and 1950's, as fur prices fell and game became scarcer. Trapping provides an annual income of about $2 million. The principal furs include bear, lynx, marten, muskrat, seal, white fox, and wolf. Bear, muskrat, and seal ac-

A Roman Catholic Church in Inuvik is one of the largest churches in the Northwest Territories. The church, Our Lady of Victory, opened in 1961. Most Indians of the Territories are Catholics, and most of the Eskimos there belong to the Anglican Church.

count for a large part of the income from trapping.

Fishing Industry. The fish catch has an annual value of about $738,000. The total catch is about 3 million pounds (1.4 million kilograms). Almost all commercial fishing is on Great Slave Lake, which supplies whitefish and lake trout. *Char* (trout) fishing in the Arctic has attracted both sport and commercial interests.

Forest Industry and Agriculture. The forest industry of the Northwest Territories is located entirely in the District of Mackenzie. The most common trees include birch, pine, poplar, and spruce.

All the land that could be used for agriculture lies in the District of Mackenzie. The area has about 1 million acres (400,000 hectares) of possible farming land, including some grassland now used only for the grazing of buffaloes. The Northwest Territories has no full-time farmers. The government operates two experimental greenhouses in the eastern Arctic. Most food must be imported from the Canadian provinces.

Transportation. The great distances and the small number of passengers make transportation very expensive. The cheapest and oldest form of transportation is by water. But the Mackenzie River, the main water route, remains frozen for 8 to 9 months each year. A tug and barge service operates from the northern Canadian railroads in Hay River and Waterways, Alta. Waterways is the starting point of a historic route down the Athabasca and Slave rivers. The route then continues across Great Slave Lake to Yellowknife, or down the Mackenzie River to the Arctic Ocean.

Scheduled air services operate in each of the districts. Seaplanes that can land on lakes take supplies to mining and prospecting communities during the summer.

After the lakes freeze, airplanes use skis for landing. Jet aircraft serve Fort Smith, Frobisher Bay, Hay River, Inuvik, Resolute Bay, and Yellowknife. Motor vehicles use the highways south of Great Slave Lake. The Great Slave Lake Railroad provides freight service to Hay River and Pine Point. It runs parallel to Mackenzie Highway.

Communication. The Territories has seven weekly newspapers, including two each in Hay River and Yellowknife. The others circulate in Fort Smith, Frobisher Bay, and Inuvik. The Canadian Broadcasting Corporation has radio stations in Frobisher Bay, Inuvik, and Yellowknife. A telecommunications satellite provides a number of communications services, including television programs.

Education

Schools. The Northwest Territories has about 65 elementary and high schools. These include schools built and operated by the territorial government, and school districts financed by local taxation and grants from the territorial government. The federal government pays for the education of Indians and Eskimos. Students from isolated areas who attend high school in the larger communities live in dormitories during the school term. The Territories has no universities or colleges. But the Territories government provides grants and loans for students who wish to attend universities and colleges elsewhere in Canada.

Government

The people elect one representative to the Canadian House of Commons. The Territories also has one representative in the Canadian Senate. A commissioner and a legislative council of 15 members govern the Terri-

An Oil Refinery in Norman Wells is one of the largest industrial plants in the Northwest Territories. The refinery, which processes about a million barrels of oil annually, opened in 1921.

tories. The federal government appoints the commissioner. The voters elect one council member from each of 15 electoral districts. The council members serve four-year terms. The council meets at least twice a year. Its legislative powers are similar to those of provincial legislatures.

The territorial government maintains a departmentalized public service similar to those of provincial governments. The public service handles the administrative duties in the Territories. The federal government controls and administers all the Territories' natural resources except game, because their development requires substantial government investment in exploration, communications, and transportation.

The Northwest Territories Court has one judge appointed by the governor general of Canada. The judge holds court in Yellowknife and in other areas. There are also two magistrates appointed by the Territorial Government.

History

Exploration. The Vikings were probably the first Europeans to visit the Northwest Territories. They may have sighted the Arctic shores about A.D. 1000. The search for a Northwest Passage to the riches of China encouraged many explorers to look for a route around or through the North American continent to the West. Until 1770, all expeditions traveled by ship. Martin Frobisher, an English seaman, was the first known discoverer of any part of the Northwest Territories. He reached Baffin Island in 1576. See NORTHWEST PASSAGE.

The first white man to cross the Territories by land was Samuel Hearne, of the Hudson's Bay Company. He set out in 1770 from Churchill in present-day Manitoba. Traveling overland, he reached the mouth of the Coppermine River in 1771, and explored the Great Slave Lake region on the return journey. In 1789, Sir Alexander Mackenzie reached the Mackenzie River.

Northwest Territories. The eastern part of the Northwest Territories had belonged to the Hudson's Bay Company since 1670. In that year, King Charles II of England granted the company a vast area called Rupert's Land (see RUPERT'S LAND). In 1870, the Dominion of Canada acquired Rupert's Land. At the same time, it obtained from Great Britain a region called the North West Territory which lay north, west, and south of Rupert's Land. The Canadian government organized these two new possessions into the North West Territories, which later became known as the Northwest Territories. See SASKATCHEWAN (History).

The Territories lost part of the Manitoba area in 1870, when Manitoba became a province. The Yukon Territory was cut off in 1898, and the provinces of Alberta and Saskatchewan in 1905. In 1912, Manitoba, Ontario, and Quebec acquired certain areas.

1930's and 1940's. The discovery of radium ore on the shore of Great Bear Lake in the early 1930's brought the Northwest Territories into world prominence. During World War II, the importance of the radium mine increased because of the demand for uranium, which is found in the same ore as radium. Also, the requirements of the Allied armies brought about an intensified program for the building of airfields and weather stations in the Territories.

The Canadian government did little to develop the

Territories until after World War II. But then, it increased the number of the Royal Canadian Mounted Police detachments, and began to establish weather stations, post offices, schools, and medical services.

Recent Developments. The government expanded its programs for education and medical and social welfare during the 1950's. Interest in mineral and oil exploration also increased. Scheduled airplane flights to Mackenzie District and Baffin Island began in the 1950's. In the 1960's, the government carried on a major road building program. A railway was built from Peace River, Alta., to Great Slave Lake in the mid-1960's to serve mining operations in Pine Point. In 1967, Yellowknife became capital of the Territories. Ottawa had been the previous seat of government. In 1969, the federal government transferred its administrative responsibilities in the Northwest Territories to the territorial government in Yellowknife. Mineral production expanded on Baffin Island in 1976 when a $65-million center to mine and process lead and zinc opened there.   S. M. HODGSON

Related Articles in WORLD BOOK include:

Outline

Questions

What is the longest waterway in Canada?
What three groups of people make up the majority of the population of the Northwest Territories?
Why are there no trees in the District of Franklin?
What two large lakes are in Mackenzie District?
What firm once owned the land of the territories?
Why was the construction of a new town named Inuvik begun in the territories in 1955?
How do the people obtain most of their food?
What minerals account for much of the mining activity in the Northwest Territories?
What attracted explorers to the area of the Northwest Territories in the 1500's and 1600's?
How is public education provided in the territories?

NORTHWEST TERRITORY

NORTHWEST TERRITORY was a vast tract of land lying north of the Ohio River, west of Pennsylvania, and east of the Mississippi River. It extended to the northern limits of the United States. The states of Ohio, Indiana, Illinois, Michigan, Wisconsin, and part of Minnesota east of the Mississippi were carved out of the Northwest Territory.

Early History. The French, who first occupied the region, had established posts by the early 1700's. Competition between French traders operating from these posts and English trappers from Pennsylvania helped start the French and Indian War (1754-1763). The war ended with the cession of the area to victorious England. See FRENCH AND INDIAN WARS.

During the Revolutionary War (1775-1783), violent fighting took place in the Northwest between the settlers and the British and their Indian allies. The campaign of George Rogers Clark against British-held posts helped win the territory for the United States. The region was ceded after the war. Before the government could open the region to settlement, it had to deal with the claims of Massachusetts, Connecticut, Virginia, and New York. These states insisted that their colonial charters extended their boundaries into this area. The states ceded their claims to Congress between 1781 and 1785, because Maryland refused to approve the Articles of Confederation until it received assurance that the other states would yield their claims.

The land then became a territory of the United States. Congress, eager for revenue from the sale of lands there, adopted the Ordinance of 1785. This law provided for orderly rectangular surveys into mile-square units called *sections*. These were sold at auction at a minimum price of $1 an acre. Congress also struggled with the problem of a government for the territory. Thomas Jefferson in 1784 had drafted a plan that would have divided the territory into several units. These could become states when the population of any one unit equaled the population of the smallest state in the Union. The Eastern States rejected this pro-

Location of the Northwest Territory

posal, because they feared that the many Western States would dominate Congress. Instead, Congress adopted the Northwest Ordinance, or Ordinance of 1787. This provided for the division of the region into from three to five states, and the establishment of a governmental system that would allow them eventual membership in the Union. See NORTHWEST ORDINANCE.

Settlement began at once. The first arrivals were sent out by a New England speculating group called the Ohio Company (see OHIO COMPANY). They founded the town of Marietta at the mouth of the Muskingum River in Ohio. Other interests soon established rival settlements at such villages as Gallipolis and Cincinnati. To the north, colonists clustered about Cleveland in the "Western Reserve" area retained by Connecticut when it ceded its lands to Congress (see WESTERN RESERVE). Arthur St. Clair became the first governor of the Northwest Territory in 1787. He inaugurated the first territorial government on July 15, 1788.

The population grew slowly at first because of the continual Indian attacks. President George Washington sent three expeditions to fight the Indians, but the first two met with disaster. The territory became more peaceful after General Anthony Wayne defeated the Indians in the Battle of Fallen Timbers in 1794. In 1795, Wayne

The Garrison That Later Became the Site of Marietta, Ohio, Was Founded Soon After the Ordinance of 1787.

Northwestern University has an extensive library system that includes Deering Library, *front*, and University Library, *rear*.

Northwestern University

forced the Treaty of Greenville on the defeated Indians. In this treaty, they ceded most of the lands of southern Ohio and part of eastern Indiana to the United States. Other land cessions followed during the early 1800's. See INDIAN WARS (Along the Frontier).

As more settlers moved into the region, the Northwest Territory was divided. In 1800, the western part of the region became the Territory of Indiana, with William Henry Harrison as governor. The Michigan Territory was created in 1805, and the Illinois Territory in 1809. Ohio became a state in 1803, Indiana in 1816, Illinois in 1818, Michigan in 1837, and Wisconsin in 1848.   RAY ALLEN BILLINGTON

See also WESTWARD MOVEMENT (picture); CLARK, GEORGE ROGERS; HARRISON, WILLIAM HENRY; SAINT CLAIR, ARTHUR.

NORTHWESTERN COLLEGE. See UNIVERSITIES AND COLLEGES (table).

NORTHWESTERN STATE UNIVERSITY OF LOUISIANA. See UNIVERSITIES AND COLLEGES (table).

NORTHWESTERN UNIVERSITY is a private coeducational institution with campuses in Evanston and Chicago, Ill. The main campus, in Evanston, has a college of arts and sciences; schools of education, journalism, music, and speech; a graduate school; and a graduate school of management. The Technological Institute and the National High School Institute are also there. The university grants bachelor's, master's, and doctor's degrees.

The Chicago campus serves as a center for professional studies. Northwestern's McGaw Medical Center, one of the largest private medical centers in the world, is based there. It includes the university's dental and medical schools, and has seven member hospitals in the Chicago area—Children's Memorial Hospital, Evanston Hospital, the Institute of Psychiatry, Northwestern Memorial Hospital, the Rehabilitation Institute of Chicago, Veterans Administration Research

Hospital, and Women's Hospital and Maternity Center of Chicago. The university's law school and evening divisions are also on the Chicago campus.

Northwestern was the first university in the United States to establish a school of speech and to sponsor a children's theater. Its law school was the first to organize a scientific crime detection laboratory. The university also established the first program in African studies. Northwestern's Center for the Teaching Professions, Center for Urban Affairs, and Transportation Center are nationally known. The university's libraries have nearly $2\frac{1}{2}$ million volumes.

Northwestern University was founded in 1851. The Chicago campus opened in 1926. For the enrollment of Northwestern University, see UNIVERSITIES AND COLLEGES (table).   J. ROSCOE MILLER

NORWALK, Calif. (pop. 91,827), is a residential city 14 miles (23 kilometers) southeast of Los Angeles (see CALIFORNIA [political map]). The city's most important industry is oil refining. Norwalk was settled in 1868 and incorporated as a city in 1957. The city's greatest growth took place from 1940 to 1960, when its population grew from less than 4,000 to almost 90,000. It has a council-manager government.   GEORGE SHAFTEL

NORWALK, Conn. (pop. 79,113; met. area pop. 127,535), is an industrial city which takes its name from the Norwalk Indians who once lived in the area. It lies at the mouth of the Norwalk River, about 40 miles (64 kilometers) northeast of New York City (see CONNECTICUT [political map]). Norwalk's manufactured products include automobile accessories, clothing, compressors, computers, electrical and electronic equipment, laboratory apparatus, optical systems, and pumps.

Hartford colonists settled Norwalk in 1649. It was incorporated as a town in 1651. British Redcoats burned much of the town in 1779, during the Revolutionary War. Norwalk received a city charter in 1893. It has a mayor-council form of government. ALBERT E. VAN DUSEN

WORLD BOOK photo · George Holton, Photo Researchers

Norway's Rugged Coast is indented by many long inlets of the sea called fiords, *left*. Another famous symbol of Norway is the midnight sun. Every year, the sun shines day and night for 10 weeks at North Cape, *right*.

NORWAY

NORWAY is a long, narrow kingdom on the northwestern edge of the European continent. The northern third of Norway lies above the Arctic Circle and is called the *Land of the Midnight Sun*. Because this region is so far north, it has long periods every summer when the sun shines 24 hours a day. Oslo, Norway's capital and largest city, is in the southern part of the country.

Most of the Norwegian people live near or along the sea. Winds warmed by the sea give the coast much warmer winters than other regions so far north, and snow melts quickly there. Even north of the Arctic Circle, nearly all of Norway's harbors are free of ice the year around. Inland areas are colder, and snow covers the ground much of the year. For thousands of years, the people have used skis for travel over the snow. Today, skiing is Norway's national sport. Most Norwegians learn to ski before they even start school.

Norway, along with Denmark and Sweden, is one of the Scandinavian countries. Vikings lived in all three countries about a thousand years ago. Vikings from Norway sailed west and established colonies in Iceland and Greenland. About A.D. 1000, Leif Ericson sailed from Greenland and headed what was probably the first European expedition to the mainland of America.

Since the time of the Vikings, the Norwegians have been a seafaring people. Norway's coast is famous for its many long, narrow inlets of the sea called *fiords*, which provide fine harbors. Rich fisheries lie off the west coast, and dried fish were an important export as early as the 1200's. Norway began developing its great shipping fleet during the 1600's. Today, its fishing and shipping industries rank among the world's largest.

Norway is mostly a high, mountainous plateau covered chiefly by bare rock, and it has little farmland. But the rivers that rush down from the mountains provide much cheap electricity. Norway generates more hydroelectric power per person than any other country. Norwegian manufacturing is based on this cheap power. Important products include chemicals, metals, petroleum, processed foods, and wood pulp and paper.

The contributors of this article are H. Peter Krosby, Associate Professor of History and Scandinavian Studies at the University of Wisconsin; Mark W. Leiserson, member of the Development Policy Staff of the World Bank; and William C. Wonders, Professor of Geography at the University of Alberta.

──────── FACTS IN BRIEF ────────

Capital: Oslo.

Official Language: Norwegian (Bokmål and Nynorsk).

Official Name: *Kongeriket Norge* (Kingdom of Norway).

Form of Government: Constitutional monarchy. *Head of State*—King. *Head of Government*—Prime Minister. *Legislature*—Storting (150 members, 4-year terms).

Area: 125,182 sq. mi. (324,219 km²). *Greatest Distances*—northeast-southwest, 1,100 mi. (1,770 km); northwest-southeast, 280 mi. (451 km). *Coastline*—1,650 mi. (2,-655 km).

Elevation: *Highest*—Glittertinden, 8,104 ft. (2,470 m) above sea level. *Lowest*—sea level along the coast.

Population: *Estimated 1978 Population*—4,100,000; distribution, 55 per cent rural, 45 per cent urban; density, 34 persons per sq. mi. (13 persons per km²). *1970 Census*—3,874,133. *Estimated 1983 Population*—4,245,000.

Chief Products: *Agriculture*—barley, dairy products, hay, livestock, oats, potatoes. *Fishing*—capelin, cod, herring, mackerel. *Forestry*—timber. *Manufacturing*—aluminum, chemicals, processed foods, ships, wood pulp and paper. *Mining*—ilmenite, iron ore, lead, molybdenite, petroleum, pyrites, zinc.

National Anthem: "Ja vi elsker" ("Yes, We Love with Fond Devotion").

National Holiday: Constitution Day, May 17.

Money: *Basic Unit*—krone. For the value of the krone in dollars, see MONEY (table: Values). See also KRONE.

Norway is a constitutional monarchy with a king, a prime minister and cabinet, and a parliament. The government is based on the Norwegian constitution of 1814. This constitution, like that of the United States, divides the government into three branches—executive, legislative, and judicial. The prime minister is the actual head of the government. The king has little real power, and no queen can be the head of state.

The king usually appoints the leader of the strongest party in the parliament to be prime minister. Other high government officials, including judges and county governors, are appointed by the king on the advice of the cabinet. Most of them may serve until the age of 70, but the king can dismiss them earlier on the cabinet's advice. Like the other Scandinavian countries, Norway has a government official called an *ombudsman*. He investigates complaints by citizens against government actions or decisions. See OMBUDSMAN.

Cabinet of the Norwegian prime minister is also called the Council of State. It is formed by the prime minister to run the various government departments. There are 15 members, including the prime minister. The cabinet must resign if it receives a vote of no confidence from the parliament. Norway's cabinet system differs sharply from that of Canada and Great Britain. In those countries, cabinet members are generally also members of parliament. In Norway, a cabinet member cannot also be a member of the parliament.

Parliament of Norway is called the *Storting*. It has 150 members elected to four-year terms. Each of Norway's 20 counties elects from 4 to 13 members, depending upon its population. The Storting consists of one house, but its members form two sections to discuss and vote on proposed laws. They elect 38 of their number to the *Lagting*, and the other 112 make up the *Odelsting*.

To become law, most bills must first be approved by the Odelsting, and then by the Lagting. If the two sections do not agree on a bill, it can be approved by two-thirds of the parliament as a whole. Certain matters are voted on only by the entire parliament.

Courts. Norway's highest court is the Supreme Court of Justice. Five Courts of Appeal hear appeals of decisions made by the county and town courts. Each county and town also has a Conciliation Council, which tries to settle disputes before they go to court. This body consists of three persons elected to four-year terms.

Local Government. Norway has 20 counties, 2 of which are the cities of Oslo and Bergen. Each county, except Oslo and Bergen, has a governor. Cities, towns, and village districts elect councils of varying size to four-year terms. These councils select a chairman, or mayor, to serve two years.

Politics. Norway has seven political parties. The Labor party has been the largest since the 1920's. The others are the Center, Christian People's, Communist, Conservative, Liberal, and Socialist People's parties. Norwegians who are at least 20 years old can vote if they have lived in Norway five years or more.

Armed Forces. Norway's army, navy, and air force have a total of about 32,000 men. Norwegian men between the ages of 20 and 44 are required to serve from 12 to 15 months in the armed forces.

Sven Samelius from Carl Östman

Parliament Building in Oslo is the home of the *Storting*, Norway's one-house legislature. The Storting has 150 members.

Barto, Photo Researchers

King Olav V, *left,* came to Norway's throne in 1957. He heads the armed forces and the nation's Evangelical Lutheran Church.

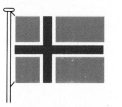

H. E. Harris & Co.

The Norwegian Flag was first approved for use by merchant ships in 1821. It became the national flag in 1898.

Norway's Coat of Arms dates from the 1280's, when the ax and crown of Saint Olav were added to the lion.

Norway is 4 per cent as large as the United States, not counting Alaska and Hawaii. The country lies just west of Sweden.

WORLD BOOK map

The Norwegians are a Scandinavian people, closely related to the Danes and the Swedes. The people of Norway have strong ties with Americans. During the late 1800's and early 1900's, more than 600,000 Norwegians migrated to the United States in search of better job opportunities. No other country except Ireland has provided the United States with so many immigrants in proportion to population.

About 20,000 Lapps live in far northern Norway (see LAPLAND). That region also has about 10,000 persons of Finnish ancestry.

Population. In 1978, Norway had a population of about 4,100,000. The following table shows some official census figures for Norway through the years:

1970	3,874,133	1920	2,649,775
1960	3,591,234	1900	2,240,032
1950	3,278,546	1855	1,490,047
1946	3,156,950	1801	883,487
1930	2,814,194	1769	723,618

More than 40 per cent of the people live in villages of fewer than 200 persons. Only six cities have populations over 50,000. They are Bergen, Drammen, Kristiansand, Oslo, Stavanger, and Trondheim. See the separate articles on Norwegian cities listed in the *Related Articles* at the end of this article.

Food. Norwegians usually eat four meals a day, but many farm families have five. Breakfast generally includes cereal and open-faced sandwiches with cheese, jam, or marmalade. Goat cheese is a favorite sandwich spread. Sandwiches are also eaten at lunch and at a late-evening supper. Dinner is usually the only hot meal of the day. It includes soup, meat or fish, potatoes, vegetables, and dessert. People in the cities and towns eat dinner in the evening, and those in farm areas have it at midday.

Language. The Norwegian language has two forms—Bokmål and Nynorsk. They are gradually being combined into a single form called Samnorsk. Bokmål and Nynorsk are similar enough for someone who speaks either form to understand a person who speaks the other. Both belong to the Scandinavian group of Germanic languages. Local school boards may select either as the chief form in a school, but all students learn to read both. The Lapps also use their own language, which is much like Finnish.

Bokmål, also called Riksmål, is the major form used in the cities and towns, and in most Norwegian schools. Bokmål is a Norwegian form of Danish. It has almost the same vocabulary and spelling as Danish, but is pronounced much differently. Bokmål developed during Norway's political union with Denmark, which lasted from 1380 to 1814. During that period, it replaced Old Norse, the early Norwegian language.

Nynorsk, originally called Landsmål, was created during the mid-1800's as a reaction against the Danish influence. Nynorsk was based on the many *dialects* (local forms of speech) that developed in the villages during Norway's union with Denmark.

Religion. The Norwegian Constitution establishes the Evangelical Lutheran Church as the nation's official church. About 96 per cent of the people are Evangelical Lutherans. Other religious groups have complete freedom of worship. They include members of the Baptist, Free Lutheran, Methodist, Pentecostal, and Roman Catholic churches.

The government largely controls the Evangelical Lutheran Church. It appoints the pastors and church officials, and pays their salaries. In 1956, the parliament passed a law permitting women to become pastors. The first woman pastor was named in 1961.

Education. Almost all the people of Norway can read and write. Norwegian law requires children from the age of 7 to either 14 or 16 to go to school. Until 1959, the elementary school program lasted seven years, until the age of 14. That year, the government provided for nine-year elementary schools. Each city, town, and village decided whether to adopt the new system, which required children to attend school until the age of 16. Today, about half the youngsters of Norway attend nine-year schools.

Norway's high schools offer three- or five-year programs. Norway also has many technical and specialized schools at the high school or college level. There are universities in Bergen, Oslo, Tromsø, and Trondheim.

The University of Oslo Library, which owns about 1,400,000 volumes, is the largest library in Norway. Oslo also has the country's largest city library, with about 720,000 volumes. All Norwegian cities and towns are required by law to have free public libraries. These libraries are partly supported by government grants.

Arts. Norwegians have contributed much to the development of the arts. Henrik Ibsen's realistic plays of the late 1800's brought him worldwide fame as the father of modern drama. Three Norwegian writers—Bjørnstjerne Bjørnson, Knut Hamsun, and Sigrid Undset—have won the Nobel prize for literature.

The painter Edvard Munch was a strong influence on the expressionist art style of the early 1900's. Statues by Gustav Vigeland, perhaps Norway's greatest sculptor, stand in Oslo's Frogner Park. Edvard Grieg, Norway's best-known composer, used many melodies from Norwegian folk songs and dances in his orchestral works. For more information on Norwegians in the various arts, see the biographies listed in the *Related Articles* at the end of this article.

Social Welfare. The government of Norway provides the people with many welfare services. All families with more than one child receive a yearly allowance for each youngster under the age of 16, beginning with the second one. These families also may receive financial aid in paying their rent. The government guarantees all employed persons an annual four-week vacation with full pay. Large families with medium or low incomes pay little or no national taxes, and their local taxes are reduced.

The National Insurance Act, which went into effect in 1967, combined many existing welfare programs. All Norwegians are required to take part in this combined plan. It includes old-age pensions, job retraining, and aid for mothers, orphans, widows, widowers, and handicapped persons. Another insurance plan provides free medical and hospital care, plus cash payments to employees during illness. The costs of these plans are shared by the insured persons, their employers, and the national and local governments.

Sports.

Outdoor sports are an important part of Norwegian life. Recreation areas lie within short distances of all homes. Skiing, Norway's national sport, may have started there thousands of years ago as a means of crossing the snow-covered land. Many Norwegians take cross-country ski trips to the country's mountains or wooded hills. Almost every town has a ski jump. The second most popular winter sport is ice skating. Norwegians also have long enjoyed *bandy*, a form of hockey played by 11-man teams on large rinks.

Soccer is the favorite summer sport. Sailing is popular along the coast. The lakes and rivers attract many fishermen, and a number of towns have rowing clubs. The people also enjoy hiking, hunting, and swimming.

Frogner Park in Oslo has about 150 works by Gustav Vigeland, one of Norway's greatest sculptors. The park, laid out by Vigeland, attracts visitors from many parts of the world.

John LaDue

Nordisk Pressefoto from Keystone Press

Lapp Children attend modern schools in the larger towns of far northern Norway. About 20,000 Lapps live here. They make their living largely by fishing or raising reindeer.

Oslo, the capital and largest city of Norway, has many colorful outdoor cafes. It is one of the most popular tourist centers of northern Europe, as well as a major industrial city.

Bob Serating, Birnback

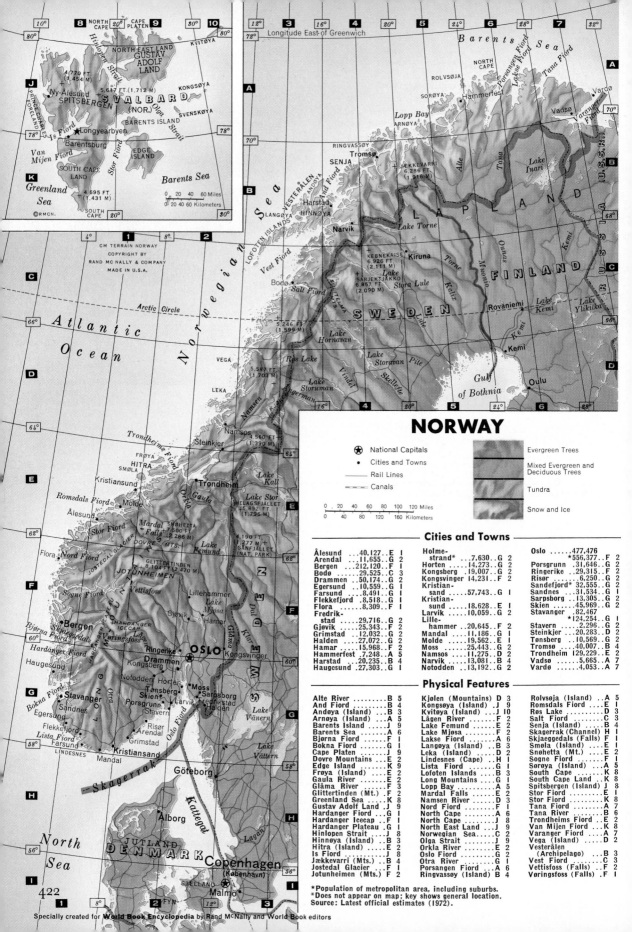

NORWAY

Longitude East of Greenwich

★ National Capitals
• Cities and Towns
— Rail Lines
— Canals

Evergreen Trees

Mixed Evergreen and Deciduous Trees

Tundra

Snow and Ice

0 20 40 60 80 100 120 Miles
0 40 80 120 160 Kilometers

Cities and Towns

Ålesund	40,127	E 1	Holme-		
Arendal	11,655	G 2	strand*	7,630	G 2
Bergen	212,120	F 1	Horten	14,273	G 2
Bodø	29,525	C 3	Kongsberg	19,007	G 2
Drammen	50,174	G 2	Kongsvinger	14,231	F 2
Egersund	10,559	G 1	Kristian-		
Farsund	8,491	G 1	sand	57,743	G 1
Flekkefjord	8,518	G 1	Kristian-		
Flora	8,309	F 1	sund	18,628	E 1
Fredrik-			Larvik	10,059	G 2
stad	29,716	G 2	Lille-		
Gjøvik	25,343	F 2	hammer	20,645	F 2
Grimstad	12,032	G 2	Mandal	11,186	G 1
Halden	27,072	G 2	Molde	19,562	E 1
Hamar	15,968	F 2	Moss	25,443	G 2
Hammerfest	7,248	A 5	Namsos	11,275	D 2
Harstad	20,235	B 4	Narvik	13,081	B 4
Haugesund	27,303	G 1	Notodden	13,192	G 2

Oslo	477,476	
*556,377	F 2	
Porsgrunn	31,646	G 2
Ringerike	29,315	F 2
Risør	6,250	G 2
Sandefjord*	32,555	G 2
Sandnes	31,534	G 1
Sarpsborg	13,305	G 2
Skien	45,969	G 2
Stavanger	82,467	
*124,254	G 1	
Stavern	2,296	G 2
Steinkjer	20,283	D 2
Tønsberg	10,569	G 2
Tromsø	40,007	B 4
Trondheim	129,229	E 2
Vadsø	5,665	A 7
Vardø	4,053	A 7

Physical Features

Alte River	B 5		Kjølen (Mountains)	D 3		Rolvsøya (Island)	A 5
And Fiord	B 4		Kongsøya (Island)	J 9		Romsdals Fiord	E 1
Andøya (Island)	B 3		Kvitøya (Island)	J 10		Røs Lake	D 3
Arnøya (Island)	A 5		Lågen River	F 2		Salt Fiord	C 3
Barents Island	J 9		Lake Femund	E 2		Senja (Island)	B 4
Barents Sea	A 6		Lake Mjøsa	F 2		Skagerrak (Channel)	H 1
Bjørna Fiord	F 1		Lakse Fiord	A 6		Skjaeggedals (Falls)	F 1
Bokna Fiord	G 1		Langøya (Island)	B 3		Smøla (Island)	E 1
Cape Platen	J 9		Leka (Island)	D 2		Snøhetta (Mt.)	E 2
Dovre Mountains	E 2		Lindesnes (Cape)	H 1		Sogne Fiord	F 1
Edge Island	K 9		Lista Fiord	G 1		Sørøya (Island)	A 5
Frøya (Island)	E 2		Lofoten Islands	B 3		South Cape	K 8
Gaula River	E 2		Long Mountains	G 1		South Cape Land	K 8
Glåma River	F 2		Lopp Bay	A 5		Spitsbergen (Island)	J 8
Glittertinden (Mt.)	F 2		Mardal Falls	E 2		Stor Fiord	E 1
Greenland Sea	K 7		Namsen River	D 2		Stor Fiord	K 8
Gustav Adolf Land	J 9		Nord Fiord	F 1		Tana Fiord	A 7
Hardanger Fiord	G 1		North Cape	A 6		Tana River	B 6
Hardanger Icecap	F 1		North Cape	J 8		Trondheims Fiord	E 2
Hardanger Plateau	F 1		North East Land	J 9		Van Mijen Fiord	K 8
Hinlopen Strait	J 8		Norwegian Sea	C 2		Varanger Fiord	A 7
Hinnøya (Island)	B 3		Olga Strait	J 9		Vega (Island)	D 2
Hitra (Island)	E 2		Orkla River	E 2		Vesterålen	
Is Fiord	J 8		Oslo Fiord	G 2		(Archipelago)	B 3
Jækkevarri (Mts.)	B 4		Otra River	G 1		Vest Fiord	C 3
Jostedal Glacier	F 1		Porsangen Fiord	A 6		Vettisfoss (Falls)	F 2
Jotunheimen (Mts.)	F 2		Ringvassøy (Island)	B 4		Vøringsfoss (Falls)	F 1

*Population of metropolitan area, including suburbs.
*Does not appear on map; key shows general location.
Source: Latest official estimates (1972).

422

Land Regions. Most of Norway is a high, mountainous plateau. Its average height is more than 1,500 feet (457 meters) above sea level. Only about a fifth of Norway, including two major lowlands, lies under 500 feet (150 meters). Norway has three main land regions: (1) the Mountainous Plateau, (2) the Southeastern Lowlands, and (3) the Trondheim Lowlands.

The Mountainous Plateau is covered largely by bare rock that was smoothed and rounded by ancient glaciers. Glaciers also formed many lakes and deep valleys, especially in the 4,500-square-mile (11,700-square-kilometer) Hardanger Plateau, Europe's largest highland plain. In Norway's uplands above 6,500 feet (1,980 meters), permanent snow and ice cover about 1,200 square miles (3,110 square kilometers). The 300-square-mile (780-square-kilometer) Jostedal Glacier is the largest ice field in Europe outside Iceland.

In the narrow northern half of Norway, the Kjølen mountain range extends along the border with Sweden. The jagged peaks form a ridge that looks like the keel on the bottom of an overturned boat. Norway's highest mountains rise in the wider southern half of the country. The Dovre Mountains extend in an east-west direction, and the Long Mountains rise to the south. The Jotunheimen range of the Long Mountains includes the highest point in Norway. It is 8,104-foot (2,470-meter) Glittertinden, northern Europe's tallest mountain.

The Southeastern Lowlands consist mostly of the middle and lower valleys of the Glåma River, which is 380 miles (612 kilometers) long, and several other rivers. The rivers are used to float timber to pulp mills and sawmills.

Their many waterfalls provide hydroelectric energy. The region also has narrow lakes, including Lake Mjøsa. Slopes are gentler than in most of the country, and the region is more suitable for farming and forestry. These lowlands are the most thickly settled part of Norway. They include Oslo, the capital and chief commercial, industrial, and shipping center.

The Trondheim Lowlands include the lower ends of several wide, flat valleys. In addition to providing good farmland, the valleys also serve as important railroad routes to other parts of Norway and to Sweden.

The lowlands have long been a major region of settlement. Trondheim, founded in A.D. 998, was once Norway's capital and leading city. Today, it is a leading center of industry and trade.

Coast and Islands. Many long, narrow inlets of the sea indent the rocky coast of Norway. These inlets, called *fiords*, make the coastline one of the most jagged in the world. The longest, Sogne Fiord, extends inland for more than 100 miles (160 kilometers). Norway has a coastline of about 1,650 miles (2,655 kilometers). Including all the fiords and peninsulas, the full length of the coast is about 12,500 miles (20,120 kilometers) —approximately half the distance around the world.

About 150,000 islands lie off the Norwegian coast. Some are only rocky reefs called *skerries*, which shield the coastal waters from stormy seas. The Lofoten Islands are the largest offshore island group. The waters around them have rich cod fisheries. The famous Maelstrom current sweeps between the two outermost Lofotens, and sometimes forms dangerous whirlpools.

Ernst A. Weber, Photo Researchers

The Trondheim Lowlands are among Norway's few farm regions. Crops include barley and potatoes. The region also has much dairy farming.

LAND REGIONS OF NORWAY

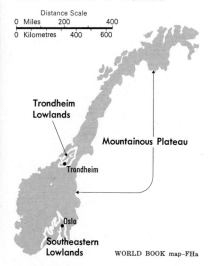

Distance Scale

0 Miles 200 400

0 Kilometres 400 600

Trondheim Lowlands

Mountainous Plateau

Trondheim

Oslo

Southeastern Lowlands

WORLD BOOK map–FHa

423

NORWAY/Climate

The climate of Norway is much milder than that of most other regions as far north, especially along the country's west coast. Near the Lofoten Islands, for example, January temperatures average 45 degrees Fahrenheit (25 degrees Celsius) higher than the world average for that latitude. Snow that falls along the coast melts almost immediately. The warm North Atlantic Current of the Gulf Stream keeps nearly all the seaports ice-free, even in the Arctic (see GULF STREAM).

Norway's inland regions are colder because mountains block the warm west winds that come from the sea. Snow covers the ground at least three months a year. In summer, when the sea is cooler than the land, the west winds cool the coast more than the inland. The warmest summers are in the inland valleys of the southeast. Less rain falls inland than along the coast.

The far north, known as the *Land of the Midnight Sun*, has continuous daylight from mid-May through July. The period of midnight sun decreases southward, and there is no 24-hour sunshine south of the Arctic Circle. In winter, northern Norway has similar periods of continuous darkness. See MIDNIGHT SUN.

Ingmar Holmasen from Carl Östman

Permanent Ice and Snow cover parts of Norway's uplands. The 190-square-mile (492-square-kilometer) Svartisen Glacier, near the Arctic Circle, is one of the largest glaciers in Norway.

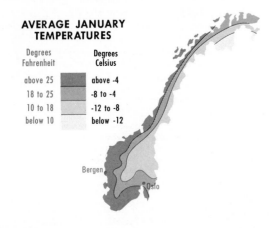

AVERAGE JANUARY TEMPERATURES

Degrees Fahrenheit		Degrees Celsius
above 25		above -4
18 to 25		-8 to -4
10 to 18		-12 to -8
below 10		below -12

Bergen
Oslo

AVERAGE JULY TEMPERATURES

Degrees Fahrenheit		Degrees Celsius
above 61		above 16
57 to 61		14 to 16
54 to 57		12 to 14
below 54		below 12

Bergen
Oslo

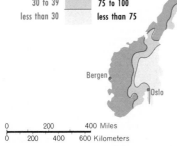

AVERAGE YEARLY PRECIPITATION
(Rain, Melted Snow, and Other Moisture)

Inches		Centimeters
more than 39		more than 100
30 to 39		75 to 100
less than 30		less than 75

Bergen
Oslo

```
0        200        400 Miles
0    200    400    600 Kilometers
```

WORLD BOOK maps
Sources: Meteorological Office, London; U.S. Navy

AVERAGE MONTHLY WEATHER

	OSLO					BERGEN			
	Temperatures				Days of	Temperatures				Days of
	F.°		C°		Rain or	F.°		C°		Rain or
	High	Low	High	Low	Snow	High	Low	High	Low	Snow
JAN.	30	20	-1	-7	8	43	27	6	-3	18
FEB.	32	20	0	-7	7	44	26	7	-3	14
MAR.	40	25	4	-4	7	47	28	8	-2	13
APR.	50	34	10	1	7	55	34	13	1	13
MAY	62	43	17	6	7	64	41	18	5	11
JUNE	69	51	21	11	8	70	46	21	8	13
JULY	73	56	23	13	10	72	51	22	11	13
AUG.	69	53	21	12	11	70	50	21	10	16
SEPT.	60	45	16	7	8	64	45	18	7	17
OCT.	49	37	9	3	10	57	38	14	3	18
NOV.	37	29	3	-2	9	49	33	9	1	16
DEC.	31	24	-1	-4	10	45	28	7	-2	18

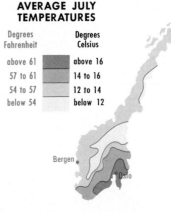

Norway has a thriving economy and nearly full employment. Since the late 1940's, the nation's total income from the production of goods and services has more than doubled. Unemployment has been kept below an average of 2 per cent of the labor force. During the 1920's and 1930's, a fourth to a third of the workers were usually jobless. The rapid economic expansion of the mid-1900's has resulted largely from (1) government programs to promote investment in industries, and (2) greater foreign demand for Norway's goods and services.

Natural Resources. Norway is not rich in natural resources. About three-fourths of the country consists of mountains and plateaus that are covered mostly by bare rock. Only 3 per cent of Norway is farmland. Forests, chiefly of pines and spruces, cover more than 20 per cent of the country. There are also many ash, beech, birch, and oak trees.

Norway's waters are its greatest natural resource. The many swift mountain rivers are used to produce hydroelectric power. The seas off the northern and western coasts are rich in cod and herring. The seas have also helped Norway carry on an extensive foreign trade and develop a great shipping industry.

Production of petroleum began in Norway's North Sea oil fields during the early 1970's. Iron ore and pyrites, from which copper and sulfur are taken, are mined in Norway. Other minerals include ilmenite, lead, molybdenite, and zinc. Coal is mined only in Svalbard, an island territory north of Norway.

Manufacturing developed much later in Norway than in the major industrial countries. Those countries had their own coal to provide power with which to run machines. In the 1800's, Norway had to import coal for its factories, which made manufacturing costly and held back its growth. By 1900, Norway had started to develop its sources of cheap hydroelectric power. Factories turned to hydroelectricity and expanded rapidly.

Today, manufacturing is Norway's most valuable industry. About half the factories are in the Oslo area. The most important products include chemicals and chemical products, such metals as aluminum and magnesium, processed foods, and wood pulp and paper. Norway is one of the world's leading producers of aluminum. This metal is processed from imported bauxite, which Norway lacks. The nation also produces clothing, electrical machinery, furniture, and small ships.

Agriculture. Norway's farms lie on narrow strips of land in inland valleys and along the coast. About 90 per cent of the farms cover 25 acres (10 hectares) or less, compared with an average of about 350 acres (142 hectares) in the United States. Many farmers have a second occupation so they can earn enough to support their families. Farmers own about two-thirds of Norway's commercial forests, and many are also loggers. Some farmers also work as commercial fishermen.

Dairy farming and livestock production account for over two-thirds of Norway's farm income. Most cropland is used to grow livestock feed. The major crops are barley, fruits and vegetables, hay, oats, and potatoes.

Forestry has been an important industry in Norway for hundreds of years. Lumber became a major export during the 1500's. Today, much timber is also used to produce pulp and paper. The chief commercial trees include birch, pine, and spruce. More than 12,000 miles (19,300 kilometers) of forest roads have been built to transport the logs. Much timber is also moved by way of rivers.

Norwegian loggers cut over 335 million cubic feet (9.5 million cubic meters) of timber a year. The forest growth rate is about 415 million cubic feet (11.8 million cubic meters) a year. Timber production could not be increased much without using up the forests, all of which are protected by government regulations.

Fishing. Norway has long been a great fishing country. Its total catch, chiefly capelin and cod, is about $3\frac{1}{2}$ million short tons (3.2 million metric tons) a year. Nor-

NORWAY'S GROSS NATIONAL PRODUCT

Total gross national product in 1970—$12,685,000,000

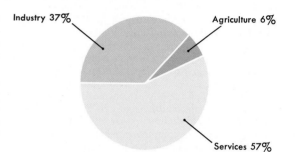

The Gross National Product (GNP) is the total value of goods and services produced by a country in a year. The GNP measures a nation's total annual economic performance. It can also be used to compare the economic output and growth of countries.

Production and Workers by Economic Activities

Economic Activities	Per Cent of GNP Produced	Employed Workers	
		Number of Persons	Per Cent of Total
Manufacturing	25	398,200*	27
Trade	17	208,500*	14
Water Transportation	11	57,300	4
Community, Business, & Personal Services	9	281,400	19
Construction	8	135,300*	9
Other Transportation & Communication	7	93,400	6
Housing	5	—	—
Government	4	75,200	5
Agriculture	4	117,100*	8
Utilities	3	14,800*	1
Banking, Insurance, & Real Estate	2	35,700*	2
Fishing, Sealing, & Whaling	1	36,500	3
Forestry	1	9,400*	1
Mining	1	8,400*	1
Other	2	—	—
Total	100	1,471,200	100

*Self-employed workers are included as follows: Banking, Insurance, & Real Estate in Trade; Forestry in Agriculture; Mining in Manufacturing; and Utilities in Construction.
Source: Norwegian Central Bureau of Statistics

wegian fishing crews also bring in large numbers of haddock, herring, and mackerel. Much of the catch is processed for export. Norway's once-great whaling industry declined sharply during the 1960's. Large catches by Norway and other major whaling nations made many kinds of whales increasingly scarce.

Electric Power. Norway produces more electric power in relation to its population than any other country. Industry uses most of it, but almost all Norwegian homes have electricity. Hydroelectric stations produce more than 99 per cent of the power. Since the late 1940's, hydroelectric production has increased 500 per cent. But Norway's still undeveloped sources of power could provide more than is now produced.

Foreign Trade. Norway depends heavily on foreign trade to help keep its standard of living high. The nation's trade is one of the largest in the world in relation to its population. Norway, with limited natural resources, imports a wide variety of foods and minerals as well as machinery and other manufactured goods. The imports have a value equal to about 40 per cent of all goods and services produced in Norway.

Norway's major exports include chemicals, fish, metals, and wood pulp and paper. The exported goods pay for only about half the imports. Income from Norway's merchant fleet, the fourth largest in the world, pays for more than a third of the imports. The fleet provides shipping services for countries in all parts of the world.

Transportation. During World War II (1939-1945), about half of Norway's merchant fleet was sunk while carrying cargo for the Allies. Since the war, the fleet has expanded over 600 per cent to a total of more than 26 million gross tons. About 450 vessels link the coastal cities and towns of Norway. Inland, ferries cross many fiords.

Norway has over 40,000 miles (64,000 kilometers) of roads and highways. Only the major routes are paved, but most of the others have well-kept gravel surfaces. About one-fifth of the people own automobiles.

The government owns and operates nearly all the railroads. There are about 2,700 miles (4,350 kilometers) of track. The government also owns part of Scandinavian Airlines, which flies throughout the world. Several airlines provide regular service to all parts of Norway.

Communication. Norway has about 85 daily newspapers with a total circulation of nearly 1½ million. The largest dailies include the *Aftenposten, Arbeiderbladet,* and *Dagbladet* of Oslo; the *Bergens Tidende* of Bergen; and the *Adresseavisen* of Trondheim.

The government-owned Norwegian Broadcasting Corporation operates the country's radio and television systems. No advertising is allowed on the programs. The corporation's income is provided by annual taxes on all radio and television sets. Most radio and television programs are cultural or educational, and less than a third of the broadcasting time is used for entertainment.

The government owns and operates the telegraph system and most telephone services. Telegraph and telephone lines connect all sections of Norway.

FARM, MINERAL, AND FOREST PRODUCTS

Crops and Livestock
Forest and Livestock
Mainly Livestock
Nonagricultural

● Major Manufacturing Center

Distance Scale
0 Miles 200
0 Kilometres 300

This map shows where the most important farm, mineral, and forest products of Norway are produced. Most Norwegian agriculture is in the Southeastern Lowlands. The map also shows the nation's major industrial centers.

Norway's Fishing Fleet brings in one of the world's largest catches every year. From January to April, huge amounts of cod are caught in waters off the Lofoten Islands.

Herbert Fristedt from Carl Östman

WORLD BOOK map-FHa

Early Days. Almost 11,000 years ago, people lived along the northern and western coasts of what is now Norway. Most of the region was covered by thick ice sheets, which took thousands of years to melt. By 2,000 B.C., a series of Germanic tribes had started to settle there permanently. They gradually spread throughout the region, and continued to arrive for hundreds of years after the time of Christ. The tribes formed local and regional communities ruled by chiefs and kings.

The Viking Period. Viking sea raiders from the Norwegian communities spread terror through much of western Europe for about 300 years. Beginning with the British Isles about A.D. 800, they attacked coastal towns and sailed away with slaves and treasure. The Vikings also sailed to the west and established colonies in the Faeroe Islands and other North Atlantic islands. About 870, they explored farther west and colonized Iceland. Eric the Red brought the first group of settlers to Greenland about 985. About 1000, his son, Leif Ericson, led what is believed to have been the first voyage of Europeans to the mainland of America. See ERIC THE RED; ERICSON, LEIF; VIKING (The Norwegian Vikings).

About 900, much of present-day Norway was united under Norway's first king, Harold I (called Fairhair), or Harald I. He defeated many local chieftains and kings, and others recognized his leadership. King Olav I introduced Christianity in Norway during the 990's. During the early 1000's, Olav II achieved full Norwegian unity and firmly established Christianity. He became Norway's patron saint in 1031.

The Viking period ended during the late 1000's. The church grew in power, foreign trade expanded, and religious and trading centers became important cities. Political confusion and bitter struggles for royal power also developed. Beginning in 1130, many regional leaders claimed the throne. They were defeated in a series of civil wars that lasted until 1240. Peace was restored under Haakon IV. By 1300, Norway's economy was largely controlled by north German merchants. Norway had become dependent on them for grain imports. The country was weakened further in 1349 and 1350, when about half the Norwegian people died in an epidemic of bubonic plague.

Union with Denmark. Margrete, the wife of King Haakon VI of Norway, was also the daughter of the king of Denmark. After her father died in 1375, she became the Danish ruler. Haakon died in 1380, and Margrete became ruler of Norway as well. In 1388, during political confusion in Sweden, Swedish noblemen elected her to rule that country, too. In 1397, in the Union of Kalmar, Margrete united Norway, Denmark, and Sweden, with power centered in Denmark. Sweden revolted against the Danish rule several times, and broke away from the union in 1523.

Under the Danish-controlled union, Norway grew weaker and Denmark became stronger. In 1536, Denmark declared Norway a Danish province and made Lutheranism the official Norwegian religion.

During the 1500's, Norway exported increasing amounts of lumber to the countries of western Europe. As a result, Norway began to develop a great shipping

National Museum, Copenhagen

King Olav II became Norway's patron saint in 1031. This wooden statue of Olav was carved by an unknown artist of the 1200's.

--- **IMPORTANT DATES IN NORWAY** ---

c. 870 Norwegian Vikings colonized Iceland.

c. 900 Harold I united Norway.

c. 985 Eric the Red colonized Greenland.

c. 1000 Leif Ericson sailed to North America.

1349-1350 An epidemic of bubonic plague killed about half the people of Norway.

1380 Norway was united with Denmark.

1536 Norway became a Danish province. Lutheranism was made Norway's official religion.

1814 Denmark gave up Norway to Sweden, but kept Norway's island colonies.

1884 The cabinet of Norway became responsible to the parliament instead of the king.

1905 Norway became independent.

1940-1945 German troops occupied Norway in World War II.

1945 Norway joined the United Nations.

1949 Norway became a member of the North Atlantic Treaty Organization.

1957 King Haakon VII died and was succeeded by Olav V.

1959 Norway and six other nations formed the European Free Trade Association.

1967 Norway began its greatest welfare program, which combined many established social security plans under the National Insurance Act.

424c

NORWAY

industry during the late 1600's. The industry expanded rapidly throughout the 1700's.

Union with Sweden. In 1807, during the Napoleonic Wars, Denmark sided with France against Great Britain. Britain had been Norway's chief trading partner, but now the British ended the trade. British warships blockaded Norway's trade with other countries, and many Norwegians starved. Norway was cut off from Denmark by the British blockade, and began to manage its own affairs. The Norwegians secretly began to trade with the British again.

Denmark was defeated in 1813 by Sweden, an ally of Britain against France. In 1814, in the Treaty of Kiel, Denmark gave Norway to Sweden. Denmark kept Norway's island colonies—Greenland, Iceland, and the Faeroe Islands.

The Norwegians did not recognize the Treaty of Kiel. Later in 1814, they elected an assembly to draw up a constitution for an independent Norway. The constitution was adopted on May 17, but Sweden refused to grant Norway independence. Swedish forces attacked Norwegian troops and quickly defeated them. In November, 1814, the Norwegian parliament accepted King Charles XIII of Sweden as Norway's ruler as well. Charles promised to respect the Norwegian constitution.

In 1884, after a long political struggle, the parliament won the right to force the cabinet to resign. Until then, the cabinet had been responsible only to the king.

Independence. During the 1890's, Norway's merchant fleet was one of the largest in the world. But the Swedish foreign service handled Norway's shipping affairs in overseas trading centers. Norway demanded its own foreign service, but Sweden refused. In May, 1905, the Norwegian parliament passed a law creating a foreign service, but the Swedish king vetoed it. On June 7, the parliament ended the union with Sweden.

Sweden nearly went to war against Norway. However, Sweden recognized Norway's independence in September, 1905, after all but 184 Norwegians voted for independence. In November, the people approved a Danish prince as their king. He became Haakon VII.

By the time of independence, Norway had started to develop its many mountain streams to produce hydroelectric power. Its industries expanded rapidly with this cheap power source. Norway's economy increased further during World War I (1914-1918). Norway remained neutral, but its merchant fleet carried much cargo for the Allies. About half its ships were sunk by German submarines and mines.

The Constitution of Norway was adopted in 1814 by an elected assembly at Eidsvoll, near Oslo. It has remained in effect since then with only minor changes. This painting of the assembly, presented to the parliament in 1885, hangs in the Storting's main chamber.

The National Assembly, Eidsvoll 1814 by Oscar Wergeland. Storting, Oslo (O. Vaering)

An economic depression hit Norway after the war. The nation's economy, dependent on trade and shipping, suffered further during the worldwide depression of the 1930's. Between a fourth and a third of Norway's workers were usually unemployed during this period.

World War II began in 1939, and Norway tried to remain neutral. But on April 9, 1940, Germany invaded Norway by attacking all its main seaports at once. The Norwegians fought bravely for two months, aided by some British, French, and Polish troops. On June 10, 1940, Norway surrendered. King Haakon VII and the cabinet fled to London and formed a government-in-exile. The Germans made Vidkun Quisling, a Norwegian who supported them, premier of Norway. His last name became an international word for *traitor*.

A secret Norwegian resistance army conducted sabotage against the German occupation force. These Norwegians were trained chiefly to join a hoped-for Allied invasion of Norway. Other Norwegians fled their country and trained in Sweden or Great Britain for the invasion. Some took part in British commando raids in Norway. After each raid, the Germans shot, tortured, or imprisoned many Norwegians.

Norwegian fighter pilots were trained in Canada, and operated from bases in Britain and Iceland. Norway's merchant fleet carried war supplies for the Allies. The Norwegian navy helped protect Allied shipping, and took part in the invasion of France in 1944.

On May 8, 1945, after Germany fell, the 350,000 German troops in Norway surrendered. Haakon VII returned in triumph on June 7, the 40th anniversary of Norwegian independence. About 10,000 Norwegians died during the war, and about half the merchant fleet was sunk. The far northern counties of Finnmark and Troms lay largely in ruins. See WORLD WAR II.

Postwar Developments. After the war, U.S. loans helped Norway rebuild its merchant fleet and industries. By the 1950's, the Norwegian economy was thriving.

Norway became a charter member of the United Nations in 1945. The next year, Trygve Lie of Norway became the first secretary-general of the UN. In 1949, Norway became a charter member of the North Atlantic Treaty Organization (NATO). But Norway refused to permit NATO bases or nuclear weapons on its territory for fear of angering Russia, its neighbor on the northeast. In 1959, Norway and six other countries formed the European Free Trade Association (EFTA), an economic union (see EUROPEAN FREE TRADE ASSOCIATION). Olav V became king of Norway in 1957.

Norway Today is more prosperous than ever. The nation has an extremely low unemployment rate. But the cost of living is rising. The government is promoting more foreign trade to help meet this problem.

In 1966, the parliament passed the National Insurance Act, probably the most important social reform in Norway's history. This program began on Jan. 1, 1967. It combines many social security plans, including old-age pensions, job retraining, and aid for mothers, orphans, widows, widowers, and handicapped persons.

In January, 1972, Norway signed a treaty to join the European Community, an economic union also known as the European Common Market. However, in September, 1972, Norwegian voters rejected entry into the Common Market and the treaty was not ratified.

H. PETER KROSBY, MARK W. LEISERSON, and WILLIAM C. WONDERS

NORWAY / Study Aids

Related Articles in WORLD BOOK include:

BIOGRAPHIES

Amundsen, Roald	Harold (kings of Norway)
Asbjørnsen, Peter C.	Ibsen, Henrik
Balchen, Bernt	Lie, Trygve
Bjørnson, Bjørnstjerne	Munch, Edvard
Eric the Red	Nansen, Fridtjof
Ericson, Leif	Olav V
Grieg, Edvard	Oscar (kings of Norway)
Haakon VII	Quisling, Vidkun A. L.
Hamsun, Knut	Undset, Sigrid

CITIES

Bergen	Oslo	Trondheim
Hammerfest	Stavanger	

HISTORY

Canute	European Monetary	Vikings
Europe, Council of	Agreement	World War II

PHYSICAL FEATURES

Arctic	Maelstrom	Skjaeggedals
Barents Sea	Mardal Falls	Skykje Falls
Fiord	Midnight Sun	Svalbard
Lapland	North Cape	Vettisfoss
Lofoten Islands	Skagerrak	

PRODUCTS AND INDUSTRY

For Norway's rank in production see:

Aluminum	Fishing Industry	Ship
Cod	Herring	

OTHER RELATED ARTICLES

Christmas (In Norway)	Krone
Clothing (picture: Traditional Costumes)	Scandinavia
Easter (In Scandinavian Countries)	Skiing
Europe (picture: Fiords)	

Outline

I. Government
II. People
    A. Population   D. Religion   G. Social Welfare
    B. Food   E. Education   H. Sports
    C. Language   F. Arts
III. The Land
    A. Land Regions   B. Coast and Islands
IV. Climate
V. Economy
    A. Natural Resources   F. Electric Power
    B. Manufacturing   G. Foreign Trade
    C. Agriculture   H. Transportation
    D. Forestry   I. Communication
    E. Fishing
VI. History

Questions

What families are covered by Norway's family allowance program?

Who led what was probably the first voyage of Europeans to the mainland of America?

How does Norway's cabinet system of government differ from that of Canada and Great Britain?

What is the northern third of Norway called? Why?

How did Norway, Denmark, and Sweden become united during the late 1300's?

How did Norway's two official languages develop?

Why is Norway's large merchant fleet essential to the country's economy?

Why does Norway's government regulate all logging?

What natural resource led to the rapid expansion of Norwegian manufacturing?

What led to Norway's independence from Sweden?

NORWAY HOUSE. See MANITOBA (Places to Visit).

NORWEGIAN ELKHOUND is a hunting dog that originated in Norway, probably between 5000 and 4000 B.C. Hunters claim the elkhound can scent an elk 3 miles (5 kilometers) away. The elkhound stalks its prey quietly and holds it at bay until the hunter arrives. It is also used in hunting bear and game birds. The elkhound's coat is thick and gray with black tips. The dog weighs about 50 pounds (23 kilograms). See also DOG (picture: Hounds). OLGA DAKAN

NORWICH TERRIER is an English dog, good at hunting rats and rabbits. It is named for Norwich, England. It has a head like a fox. Some Norwich terriers hold their ears straight up. Others let their ears droop. The Norwich has short legs and a wiry red coat. It weighs from 10 to 15 pounds (4.5 to 6.8 kilograms). The breed was developed in the 1880's by mating a small-sized Irish terrier with an English terrier. JOSEPHINE Z. RINE

The Norwich Terrier Originated in England.
WORLD BOOK photo by Walter Chandoha

NORWICH UNIVERSITY is a private coeducational school in Northfield, Vt. Norwich consists of a military college and the Vermont College Division. The University has courses in business, engineering, liberal arts and sciences, military science, and nursing. Courses lead to bachelor's, master's, and doctor's degrees. The school was founded in 1819. For enrollment, see UNIVERSITIES AND COLLEGES (table).

NOSE is the organ used for breathing and smelling. It forms part of the face, just above the mouth. Outwardly, it seems simple, but it is complicated inside.

When we breathe, air enters the nose through two openings called *nostrils*. The nostrils are separated by the *septum*, a thin wall of *cartilage* (tough tissue) and bones. Air passes from the nostrils into two tunnels called the *nasal passages*, which lead back to the upper part of the throat. From the nasal passages, air passes through the pharynx and windpipe into the lungs.

Both nasal passages have a lining of soft, moist mucous membrane covered with microscopic, hairlike projections called *cilia*. The cilia wave back and forth constantly, moving dust, bacteria, and fluids from the nose to the throat for swallowing.

Each nasal passage also has three large, shelflike bones that are called *turbinates*. The top two turbinate bones on each side are actually *processes* (extensions) of the *ethmoid* bone. The lowest one on each side is a separate bone. The turbinates warm the air before it enters the lungs. These turbinates also stir up the air so that dust in the air sticks to the mucous membrane of the turbinates and thus does not pass into the lungs.

The sense of smell is located in the highest part of the nasal cavity. The end fibers of the *olfactory nerve* lie in a small piece of mucous membrane about as big as a dime. These fibers carry sensations of smell along the olfactory nerve to the *olfactory lobe* of the brain, the part of the brain that is responsible for smell. The olfactory lobe is located on the lower surface of the brain's frontal lobe.

The sense of smell is closely related to the sense of taste. Some experts believe that much of our taste sensations are really sensations of odor that we have associated with certain tastes. For example, we really smell coffee, tobacco, wine, apples, and potatoes more

THE NOSE

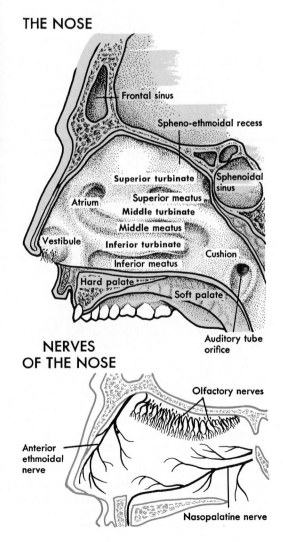

NERVES OF THE NOSE

than we taste them. If a person is blindfolded and his nose stopped up so he cannot smell, he has great difficulty telling apples from potatoes by taste. Red wine and plain coffee taste almost alike to such a person when they are at the same temperature and consistency.

We cannot smell when we have a cold, because the infection inflames the mucous membrane of the nasal passages and blocks the passage of air to the center of smell. It is important to keep nasal passages clean and to treat any inflammation of the mucous membrane at once. When neglected, colds can lead to more serious ailments, such as bronchitis and pneumonia. Sinuses, which empty into the nose, may also become infected. A. C. GUYTON

Related Articles in WORLD BOOK include:

Adenoids	Nosebleed
Catarrh	Respiration (with diagram)
Cilia	Rhinitis
Cold, Common (Symptoms)	Sinus
Cold Sore	Smell (with diagram)
Mucus	

HOW WE BREATHE

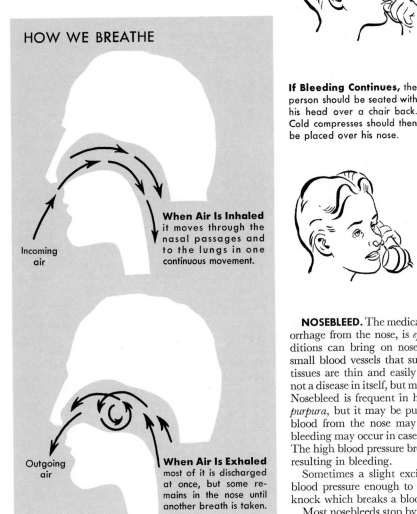

Incoming air

When Air Is Inhaled it moves through the nasal passages and to the lungs in one continuous movement.

Outgoing air

When Air Is Exhaled most of it is discharged at once, but some remains in the nose until another breath is taken.

HOW TO STOP NOSEBLEED

The Bleeding may often be stopped by pinching the nostrils together for four or five minutes, so that clots have time to form.

A Cold Compress made of a towel or other cloth wrung out of cold water can be placed at the back of the neck to stop bleeding.

A Small Pad or Roll of paper or cloth may be slid inside the upper lip above the teeth, and pressed from the outside with the finger.

If Bleeding Continues, the person should be seated with his head over a chair back. Cold compresses should then be placed over his nose.

A Doctor should be called to treat a severe nosebleed. Meanwhile, the nose should be plugged with gauze, with an end left hanging out.

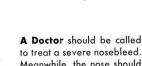

NOSEBLEED. The medical term for nosebleed, or hemorrhage from the nose, is *epistaxis*. Many different conditions can bring on nosebleed. There are numerous small blood vessels that supply the nasal tissues. These tissues are thin and easily broken. The hemorrhage is not a disease in itself, but may be a symptom of a disease. Nosebleed is frequent in hemorrhagic diseases such as *purpura*, but it may be purely local. Frequent flows of blood from the nose may even cause anemia. Severe bleeding may occur in cases of hardening of the arteries. The high blood pressure breaks small blood vessels, thus resulting in bleeding.

Sometimes a slight excitement can raise a person's blood pressure enough to start a nosebleed. Any hard knock which breaks a blood vessel may also cause it.

Most nosebleeds stop by themselves in about 10 minutes. It is helpful for the person to lie on his back, and to keep cool. The position helps lower the blood pressure. A cold pack against the nose may also be helpful. If the bleeding keeps up, it may be necessary to pack the nose with gauze. A physician may have to pinch off the blood vessel, or give drugs that cause it to close and help to clot the blood.

Nosebleeds that occur often or last a long time require medical care. In any case, a person with a nosebleed should not blow his nose once it has stopped bleeding. If he does, he may disturb the blood clots and start another nosebleed. WILLIAM DAMESHEK

NOSTRADAMUS, *NAHS truh DAY mus* (1503-1566) was the Latin name of MICHEL DE NOTREDAME, a French astrologer and physician. His fame rests on his book *Centuries* (1555), a series of prophecies in verse. Nostradamus won lasting fame in 1559 when King Henry II of France died in a manner predicted in the *Centuries*. Nostradamus' prophecies are vague and open to many interpretations. Some persons credit him with predicting various events in French and world history, including the rise of Adolf Hitler in the 1930's.

Nostradamus was born in St.-Rémy, in southern France. In 1525, while a medical student, he showed great courage and skill in caring for victims of a plague. He earned a doctor's degree in 1532, and became a professor at the University of Montpellier. The success of *Centuries* gained him an appointment as court physician to King Charles IX of France. ABRAHAM C. KELLER

NOSTRIL. See NOSE.

NOTARY PUBLIC is an officer who is authorized by state law to certify certain documents, and to take oaths. Many documents must be notarized before they become legally effective. The purpose of notarizing a document is to protect those who use it from forgeries. The notary, when he signs the document, certifies that the person who signed it appeared before him and was personally known to him. The signer of the document swears to the notary that the signature on the document is his own. The notary records that fact, then stamps his seal on the document.

The Notary Public Seal is pressed into paper with a small hand stamp.

In many states, any responsible person can get a commission as a notary public, on payment of a fee. A notary is usually allowed to charge for his services. In Great Britain and Canada, the Court of Faculties appoints notaries. ERWIN N. GRISWOLD

NOTATION, *noh TAY shun,* is any system of symbols and abbreviations that helps people work with a particular subject. Mathematics uses notation to simplify and consolidate ideas and problems. The Arabic numeral system is a notational device for writing numbers and making arithmetic operations easier. Chemistry, music, physics, and other subjects have also developed extensive notation systems. HOWARD W. EVES

See also ARABIC NUMERALS; NUMERATION SYSTEMS; MUSIC (The Language of Music); SYMBOL.

NOTE is an unconditional written promise to pay a specified sum of money on demand or at a given date to a designated person. The one who signs the note is called the *maker*. The one to whom it is made payable is called the *payee*. This written promise is called a *promissory note*. *Note of hand* is a name sometimes used for a promissory note.

Let us suppose that Arnold Shaw is a retail merchant who has a good business and a good financial standing. He needs $500 worth of merchandise, but does not have the cash on hand to pay for it. He knows that he has accounts coming due within 60 days. He will be able to pay the $500 when he is paid by those who owe him. He goes to Henry Brown, a wholesale merchant, who sells him the goods he needs and takes his note. The note is as follows:

$500   San Francisco, Calif.
                                      March 1, 1976
Sixty days after date I promise to pay to the order of Henry Brown $500, with interest at 8 per cent. Value received.

                              Arnold Shaw

Brown can endorse the note and cash it at the bank, if he needs the money before 60 days. Shaw will then pay the bank when his note becomes due.

Liability of the Maker. A note is *negotiable* when it is made payable to "bearer" or includes the word "order," like the one given above. When a note has been transferred by endorsement, the person in possession of the note is known as the *holder*. He can transfer it to another by adding his endorsement, and so on indefinitely, just as he can transfer a bank check. When the note falls due, the holder looks to the maker for payment. The law protects the holder under almost all conditions, including some kinds of fraud or cheating by the payee.

An endorser is liable in case the note fails to pay the note when it falls due. The endorser is served with a notice called a *protest*. It is signed by a notary public (see NOTARY PUBLIC), and one copy is sent to each endorser if there is more than one.

Caution. No one should sign a document unless he understands fully what he is signing. The maker should have a lawyer examine any document that he does not understand. The law holds the maker responsible for his signature, except when any part, or all, of the document is proved fraudulent in court, or is proved to have been altered, without the maker's knowledge, after he signed it in good faith. JAMES B. LUDTKE

See also DISCOUNT (Bank Discount); NEGOTIABLE INSTRUMENT.

NOTOCHORD. See AMPHIOXUS.

NOTRE DAME, CATHEDRAL OF, *NO t'r DAHM*, is a famous cathedral in the heart of Paris. It stands on the Île de la Cité, a small island in the Seine River. *Notre Dame* is the French expression for *Our Lady*, the Virgin Mary. The cathedral is one of the finest examples of early Gothic architecture. Its walls are supported by the first well-designed *flying buttresses* (stone beams built against the outside walls).

The cathedral was begun in 1163 and was completed about 150 years later. During the French Revolution in the late 1700's, a mob attacked the cathedral because they regarded it as a symbol of the monarchy. They smashed most of its statues and windows, and damaged the walls. Repairs were begun in 1845. The French ar-

Notre Dame Cathedral in Paris has many gracefully carved stone ornaments, figures, and gargoyles. But many of them are placed so high above the ground that it is said only an angel can admire their details.

Gendreau

chitect and writer Eugène Emmanuel Viollet-le-Duc (1814-1879) directed the restoration, and is largely responsible for the way Notre Dame looks today.

Many historic events have taken place in Notre Dame. Henry VI of England was crowned king of France there in 1431. Mary, Queen of Scots, married Francis II, the *dauphin* (crown prince) of France, there in 1558. Napoleon I was crowned ruler of France there in 1804.

Notre Dame is also the name of other famous cathedrals in France. One is located at Reims (see REIMS [picture]). Another is located at Amiens.   ALAN GOWANS

See also CATHEDRAL.

NOTRE DAME, COLLEGE OF. See UNIVERSITIES AND COLLEGES (table).

NOTRE DAME, UNIVERSITY OF, is a coeducational Roman Catholic school in Notre Dame, Ind. It is governed by a board of trustees consisting of 35 laymen, and 7 priests of the Congregation of Holy Cross—the Roman Catholic order that founded the university. Notre Dame admits students of all faiths.

The Campus. Notre Dame has a 1,000-acre (400-hectare) campus, with twin lakes and wooded areas that provide a beautiful setting for more than 70 buildings. Landmarks include the Log Chapel, which is a

replica of the first building erected at Notre Dame; and the Grotto of Our Lady of Lourdes, which is a replica of a shrine at Lourdes, France.

The 13-story Memorial Library, completed in 1963, has a capacity of about 2 million volumes. Nearly half of the university's undergraduates can study there at one time. The library's important collections include the Dante Library of books from the early 1500's; the Hiberniana collection of Irish history and literature; the Kirsch-Wenninger-Niewland Biology Library; and the Zahm South American Library.

Bordering the campus is Notre Dame Stadium where the "Fighting Irish" football team plays. Great football figures such as coach Knute Rockne, George Gipp, and the Four Horsemen of Notre Dame brought the university much fame (see ROCKNE, KNUTE).

Educational Program. Notre Dame's undergraduate school has colleges of arts and letters, business administration, engineering, and science. Courses in these colleges lead to bachelor's degrees. The College of Business Administration also grants the master's degree. Notre Dame's law school, the first law school at a Roman Catholic university in the United States, offers the Doctor of Laws degree. The graduate school at the

429

The Library at Notre Dame is the tallest building on campus and one of the largest university library buildings in the world. The 13-story building, built at a cost of $8 million, seats 2,900. The exterior features a mural, 132 feet (40 meters) high, made of 7,000 granite pieces. The mural depicts Christ, the Apostles, and various scholars.

The University of Notre Dame

University of Notre Dame offers advanced degrees in 24 departments.

The university has awarded the Laetare Medal each year since 1883. The award honors a leading Roman Catholic of the United States for his or her contributions to society.

Research Program. Notre Dame places a strong emphasis on research. It receives more than $8 million in grants annually for research. Researchers at the Lobund Institute for Germ-Free Life Studies use germ-free animals to study cancer and other diseases. *Lobund* stands for Laboratories of Bacteriology, University of Notre Dame.

The Medieval Institute conducts research and offers advanced courses in the culture, life, and thought of the Middle Ages. The Jacques Maritain Center conducts philosophical research. A $2,200,000 radiation laboratory, built by the U.S. Atomic Energy Commission, conducts research in radiation chemistry. Notre Dame was founded in 1842. For the enrollment of the University of Notre Dame, see UNIVERSITIES AND COLLEGES (table). THEODORE M. HESBURGH

See also HESBURGH, THEODORE MARTIN; INDIANA (picture: University of Notre Dame's Memorial Library).

NOTRE DAME COLLEGE. See UNIVERSITIES AND COLLEGES (table).

NOTRE DAME OF MARYLAND, COLLEGE OF. See UNIVERSITIES AND COLLEGES (table).

NOTRE DAME SEMINARY—GRADUATE SCHOOL OF THEOLOGY. See UNIVERSITIES AND COLLEGES (table).

NOTTINGHAM, *NAHT ing um,* England (pop. 294,-420) is a manufacturing city on the River Trent, 125 miles (201 kilometers) northwest of London. For location, see GREAT BRITAIN (political map). The city's industries include textiles and tobacco goods. Many of Robin Hood's legendary adventures took place in Nottingham and nearby Sherwood Forest. The city was founded in the 800's. In 1769, Richard Arkwright set up the first spinning frame for stockings in Nottingham. Another inventor, John Heathcoat (1783-1861), later produced a machine for making a kind of lace called *bobbinet.* JOHN W. WEBB

NOUAKCHOTT, *nwahk SHAWT* (pop. 50,000), is the capital of Mauritania, a West African republic. Nouakchott serves as a market center. The city is developing port facilities. For the location of Nouakchott, see MAURITANIA (map). CLEMENT H. MOORE

NOUN is a part of speech that identifies people, places, objects, actions, qualities, and ideas. The English language has a great variety of nouns. These nouns have been grouped into several classifications, some of which overlap.

Mass Nouns and Count Nouns. Mass nouns identify things that cannot be divided into separate units, such as *coal, fruit,* and *soil.* Count nouns identify things that can be divided into individual units, such as *apple, automobile,* and *rose.*

Mass nouns and count nouns do not differ completely because some words may belong to either group. In the sentence *I bought paper,* for example, *paper* is a mass noun. But in the sentence *I bought a paper,* the same word is a count noun. The category of a noun largely determines whether an article—*a, an,* or *the*—is used with the word. An article is generally used with a count noun but not with a mass noun.

Abstract and Concrete Nouns. Abstract nouns identify ideas and qualities that have no physical existence. *Bravery, effort,* and *knowledge* are abstract nouns. In contrast, concrete nouns identify objects that can be seen, heard, smelled, touched, or tasted. *Airplane, layer cake,* and *skyscraper* are concrete nouns. Some words can be used as either abstract or concrete nouns. For example, *red* as an abstract noun may specify the quality of redness. As a concrete noun, it may represent the particular color.

430

Abstract nouns usually function as mass nouns do. For example, an article may or may not be used with an abstract noun. It is correct to say either *He had courage* or *He had the courage*. However, an article must be used with a singular concrete noun—*He had an automobile*, not *He had automobile*.

Proper and Common Nouns. Proper nouns identify particular names or titles and are always capitalized. Examples include *Apollo II, Beacon Street, Cherokee Park, New Year's Eve,* and *President Lincoln.* Proper nouns generally are used without an article, though it is correct to say *the United States* or *the Mississippi River.*

All nouns that are not proper nouns are common nouns. They identify general categories of things. For example, *experiment, helper, holiday,* and *river* are all common nouns.

Collective Nouns identify groups of persons, animals, or things. Examples include *audience, class, crowd, family, flock, government,* and *team.* A collective noun may be considered singular if the word is used as a unit. In this instance, the noun takes a singular verb. For example, *The cast of the play* was *at its best.* A collective noun is considered plural if the word is used in terms of its parts. The noun then takes a plural verb—*The cast* were applauded *loudly for their performances.*

Nominals are words and phrases that function as nouns. Pronouns are the most common nominals, but other parts of speech may be used as nouns:

Adjective: *The* strongest *was not best.*
Gerund: *Clam* digging *is fun.*
Infinitive: To err *is human.*
Prepositions: *We knew the* ins *and* outs.
Pronoun: He *took a walk.*

Number and Case. English nouns may have endings that show *number* and *case.*

Number is the form which indicates that the noun refers to one (singular) or to more than one (plural). Singular nouns indicate one, such as *pear, apple, man,* and *mouse.* Plural forms for these nouns are *pears, apples, men,* and *mice.* Abstract nouns, mass nouns, and proper nouns do not ordinarily have distinct plural forms. But in special cases, these types of nouns may be used as concrete nouns, as in the sentence *There were three* Sams *in the room.*

Case is the form that helps show the relation of a noun to other words in a sentence. In some languages, words have many different endings to show relationships. In English, word order, rather than endings, shows relationships. Modern English nouns have only two cases, *common case* and *possessive case. Boy, man,* and *Sam* are common-case forms. *Boy's, man's,* and *Sam's* are possessive-case forms.

Gender. In English, nouns are sometimes said to have gender, but this feature is not regularly shown by endings. An English noun has gender only in the sense that it is referred to by one of three pronouns: *he* or *him, she* or *her,* and *it. I found Jim and brought* him *home, I found Sally and brought* her *home,* or *I found a book and brought* it *home.*

Nouns for which the corresponding pronoun is *he* or *him* are *masculine* nouns. Nouns for which the corresponding pronoun is *she* or *her* are *feminine* nouns. Nouns for which the corresponding pronoun is *it* are *neuter* nouns. Usually, masculine nouns name males, feminine nouns name females, and neuter nouns name inanimate or sexless things. However, there are some exceptions. Some people think of a ship as feminine and refer to it as *she,* though most authorities prefer the neuter pronoun *it.* We may use such expressions as *There she goes!* in connection with almost any object. Such nouns as *baby, mosquito,* and *mouse* do not name sexless things, but we usually use neuter pronouns in connection with them. In many languages, the connection between sex and gender in grammar is not so close as it is in the English language.   WILLIAM F. IRMSCHER

Related Articles in WORLD BOOK include:

Case	Person
Declension	Sentence (Subject and
Inflection	Predicate)
Number	

NOVA is a star that suddenly explodes and blasts part of its matter into space. An exploding nova quickly becomes much brighter than before. It remains bright for a time and then fades slowly. All novae observed so far have been distant stars too faint to be seen without a telescope before they exploded. Most became 10,000 to 100,000 times brighter when they flared up. One nova became several million times brighter. Astronomers do not know what causes novae. The word *nova* comes from the Latin word for *new.* People once believed that novae were newly created stars.

In a typical nova explosion, the star loses only about a hundred-thousandth part of its matter. The matter it throws off is a shell of glowing gases that expands outward into space at a tremendous speed.

Some novae develop so rapidly that they reach their greatest brightness in a few hours or a day. They start to fade gradually almost at once and return to their original brightness in several months or a year. Slower novae may take a month to reach maximum brightness. The fading process of these novae may last many years.

Several novae, called *recurrent novae,* have flared up more than once since they were first observed. Astronomers believe that all novae may be recurrent, but that most flare up so rarely that recurrence has not been noticed.

Astronomers observe about 2 novae a year in the Milky Way galaxy, but between 25 and 40 probably occur. Most novae go unnoticed because they are so far from the earth. Novae in one of the Milky Way's neighboring galaxies occur at about the same rate as novae in the Milky Way.

A *supernova* is a star that explodes much more violently and shines much more brightly than a nova. A supernova throws off as much as 10 per cent of its matter when it explodes. Supernovae and novae differ so much in the percentage of matter thrown off that scientists believe the two probably develop differently. A supernova may increase in brightness as much as a billion times in a few days. Astronomers believe that about 14 supernova explosions have taken place in the Milky Way during the past 2,000 years. The Crab Nebula, a huge cloud of dust and gas in the Milky Way, is the remains of a supernova seen in A.D. 1054. Supernovae are also rare in other galaxies.   ERIC D. CARLSON

NOVA EXPLOSION. See NOVA; SUN (How Long Will the Sun Shine?).

NOVA SCOTIA

NOVA SCOTIA, *SKO shuh,* is one of the four Atlantic Provinces of Canada. It includes a peninsula of the Canadian mainland and also Cape Breton Island. The province sticks out into the Atlantic Ocean from the Canadian mainland. Resorts along its coast have earned it the nickname *Canada's Ocean Playground*.

No part of Nova Scotia is more than 35 miles (56 kilometers) from the sea. The Atlantic Ocean, the Gulf of St. Lawrence, and the Bay of Fundy almost surround the province. Only a narrow strip of land—the Isthmus of Chignecto—joins the peninsula to the Canadian mainland. Ocean tides may rise higher in Nova Scotia than anywhere else in the world. Sometimes the tide rises more than 50 feet (15 meters) at the head of the Bay of Fundy. Sable Island, formed entirely of sand, lies about 100 miles (160 kilometers) off Nova Scotia's southern coast. Sailors call it the *Graveyard of the Atlantic* because it has caused many shipwrecks.

The sea keeps the climate of Nova Scotia from becoming either extremely hot or extremely cold. Thick forests cover much of the province. In the north, ranges of low hills stretch across parts of Nova Scotia. Seawater reaches far inland in many rivers that irrigate the rich soil of lowland farms. The Annapolis-Cornwallis Valley, famous for its apple orchards, glows with pink and white apple blossoms in spring.

White-tailed deer roam the wilderness areas. Many kinds of sea birds nest along the shore and on offshore islands. Cod, lobsters, scallops, and other seafoods caught off Nova Scotia help make the province a leader in the Canadian fishing industry.

Manufacturing is Nova Scotia's chief industry. The leading products include boats and ships, dairy products, paper, processed seafoods, and wood pulp. Nova Scotia leads the provinces in mining barite and ranks second in the production of gypsum and salt.

Nova Scotia is one of the four original Canadian provinces. In 1867, it joined with New Brunswick, Ontario, and Quebec to form the Dominion of Canada. The first British settlers in Nova Scotia had arrived from Scotland in 1629. The Latin words *Nova Scotia* mean *New Scotland*.

The American poet Henry Wadsworth Longfellow made Nova Scotia famous in his poem *Evangeline*. This partly fictional poem tells how French colonists, called *Acadians*, were driven from their homes in Nova Scotia by British colonial troops from New England. The Acadians had remained loyal to France after Great Britain won control of Nova Scotia in the early 1700's. The poem gave part of the province the nickname *Land of Evangeline*.

After the Revolutionary War in America, many

Halifax Harbor Is Canada's Busiest East Coast Port.
WORLD BOOK photo by Sherman Hines

November Sunset by Gerald Roach from the WORLD BOOK Collection

Countryside near Halifax

persons who remained loyal to Britain fled to Nova Scotia from the United States. These United Empire Loyalists, as they were called, nicknamed the Nova Scotians *bluenoses*. This nickname may have come from the "bluenose" potato, which the Nova Scotians grew and shipped to New England. Today, the people still call themselves bluenoses.

For the relationship of Nova Scotia to other provinces, see ATLANTIC PROVINCES; CANADA; CANADA, GOVERNMENT OF; CANADA, HISTORY OF.

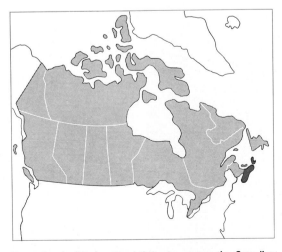

Nova Scotia (blue) ranks ninth in size among the Canadian provinces, and third among the Atlantic, or Maritime, Provinces.

FACTS IN BRIEF

Capital: Halifax.

Government: *Parliament*—members of the Senate, 10; members of the House of Commons, 11. *Provincial*—members of the House of Assembly, 46. *Voting Age*—19 years (provincial elections); 18 years (national elections).

Area: 21,425 sq. mi. (55,490 km²), including 1,023 sq. mi. (2,650 km²) of inland water; ninth in size among the provinces. *Greatest Distances*—southeast-northwest, 374 mi. (602 km); north-south, 100 mi. (161 km). *Coastline*—4,709 mi. (7,578 km).

Elevation: *Highest*—1,747 ft. (532 m) above sea level in Cape Breton Highlands National Park. *Lowest*—sea level.

Population: *1976 Census*—828,571, seventh among the provinces; density, 39 persons per sq. mi. (15 persons per km²); distribution, 57 per cent urban, 43 per cent rural.

Chief Products: *Manufacturing*—fabricated metal products; food and beverage products; paper and paper products; petroleum and coal products; printed materials; transportation equipment; wood products. *Mining*—barite, coal, gypsum, salt, sand and gravel, stone. *Fishing Industry*—cod, haddock, herring, lobster, redfish, scallops. *Agriculture*—apples, beef cattle, chickens, eggs, hay, hogs, milk.

Entered the Dominion: July 1, 1867; one of the four original provinces.

Provincial Motto: *Munit haec et altera vincit* (One labors, the other defends).

The contributors of this article are Basil W. Deakin, Arts Editor of the Halifax Herald, Ltd.; Charles Bruce Fergusson, Provincial Archivist of Nova Scotia and Associate Professor of History at Dalhousie University; and Bernard J. Keating, Professor of Geology at St. Francis Xavier University.

433

Lieutenant Governor of Nova Scotia represents Queen Elizabeth in the province. He is appointed by the governor general in council of Canada to a term of not less than five years. The lieutenant governor's position, like that of the Canadian governor general, is largely honorary.

Premier of Nova Scotia is the actual head of the provincial government. He is the leader of the majority party in the legislative assembly. The premier receives $39,400 a year, which includes his salary and the allowances he gets as a member of the assembly. For a list of all the premiers of Nova Scotia, see the *History* section of this article.

The premier presides over the executive council, or cabinet. The council is made up of the premier and other ministers. All the ministers are members of the majority party of the assembly. They are chosen by the premier. Each council member usually directs one or more departments of the government. The council resigns if it loses the support of a majority of the assembly.

Legislative Assembly makes the provincial laws. This one-house legislature has 46 members elected by the people. An election must be held at least every five years. But the lieutenant governor, on the advice of the premier, may call for an election at any time. If the premier loses the support of a majority of the assembly he resigns, or else a new election is held.

Courts. The supreme court has an appeal court division and a trial court division. The governor general in council of Canada appoints all supreme court members. The appeal division has a chief justice and three justices. The trial division has a chief justice and six justices. Justices serve until they are 75. The governor general in council also appoints seven county court judges. Nova Scotia's lieutenant governor in council appoints provincial magistrates, justices of the peace, and judges of probate and juvenile courts.

Local Government. Nova Scotia has 18 counties. They serve as the province's main judicial and administrative districts. The province has three cities, which operate under special charters, and 38 towns. Voters in each city and town elect a mayor and a council. All other communities in Nova Scotia are part of 24 districts called municipalities. Each of 12 counties is a single municipality, and each of the other 6 counties is divided into two municipalities. An elected council governs each rural municipality. Members of the council, called councilors, elect a *warden* (chief councilor) from their group.

Taxation. Nova Scotia's main source of income is a tax-sharing agreement with the Canadian government. Under this arrangement, the Canadian government collects income taxes and returns a special yearly grant to the province. The provincial government collects taxes on gasoline and alcoholic beverages. In 1959, Nova Scotia began collecting a sales tax to support a free-hospitalization plan.

Politics. Nova Scotia's leading political parties are the Liberal Party and the Progressive Conservative Party. An earlier Conservative Party changed its name to the Progressive Conservative Party in 1942. Since 1867, when Nova Scotia became a province, almost twice as many Liberals as Conservatives have been elected premier.

Government House in Halifax is the home of Nova Scotia's lieutenant governor. The mansion was first occupied in 1805. It is surrounded by parklike grounds.

The Provincial Coat of Arms

The Provincial Flag

Symbols of Nova Scotia. On the coat of arms, the center shield bears the blue cross of St. Andrew and a lion that represents Nova Scotia's ties with Scotland. An Indian, symbolizing the province's first inhabitants, and a unicorn, representing England, flank the shield. Charles I of England granted the coat of arms to Nova Scotia in 1626. The flag, granted by royal charter in 1621, bears the cross of St. Andrew and the lion of the Scottish kings.

The Floral Emblem
Trailing Arbutus

Province House in downtown Halifax is the meeting place of the Nova Scotia legislature. The three-story stone building was completed in 1818, and was first used by the legislature in 1819. Halifax, Nova Scotia's largest city, has been the provincial capital since 1749. Nova Scotia has had only one other capital—Annapolis Royal, from 1710 to 1749.

Nova Scotia Information Service

NOVA SCOTIA/*People*

The 1976 Canadian census reported that Nova Scotia had 828,571 persons. The population has increased 5 per cent over the 1971 figure, 788,960.

Most Nova Scotians belong to families that originally came from the British Isles or from France. Some persons in the province still speak the Gaelic language of their Scottish ancestors. During Scottish celebrations held each year in some communities, many persons wear colorful costumes and sing and dance to bagpipe music. Such gatherings are held in Antigonish and St. Ann's. Nova Scotia has about 4,500 Indians. Persons in the province who had French forefathers hold festivals in Chéticamp, Church Point, and Pubnico. These celebrations feature the dress and customs of old France.

Halifax is the capital of Nova Scotia and the largest of the province's three cities. It is one of Canada's most important ports and the chief railway and air terminal in Nova Scotia. Halifax is the population center of the province's only Census Metropolitan Area as defined by Statistics Canada. For the population of this metropolitan area, see the *Index* to the political map of Nova Scotia. Dartmouth, the second largest city in the province, lies across the harbor from Halifax. Sydney, the province's only other city, is on Cape Breton Island.

Nova Scotia's towns have populations of less than 25,000. See the separate articles on the cities and towns

POPULATION

This map shows the *population density* of Nova Scotia, and how it varies in different parts of the province. Population density means the average number of persons who live in a given area.

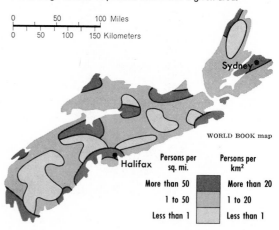

WORLD BOOK map

	Persons per sq. mi.	Persons per km²
More than 50		More than 20
1 to 50		1 to 20
Less than 1		Less than 1

listed in the *Related Articles* at the end of this article.

The churches with the largest memberships in Nova Scotia are, in order of size, the Roman Catholic Church, the United Church of Canada, and the Anglican Church of Canada. The Baptist Church and the Presbyterian Church also have many members.

NOVA SCOTIA MAP INDEX

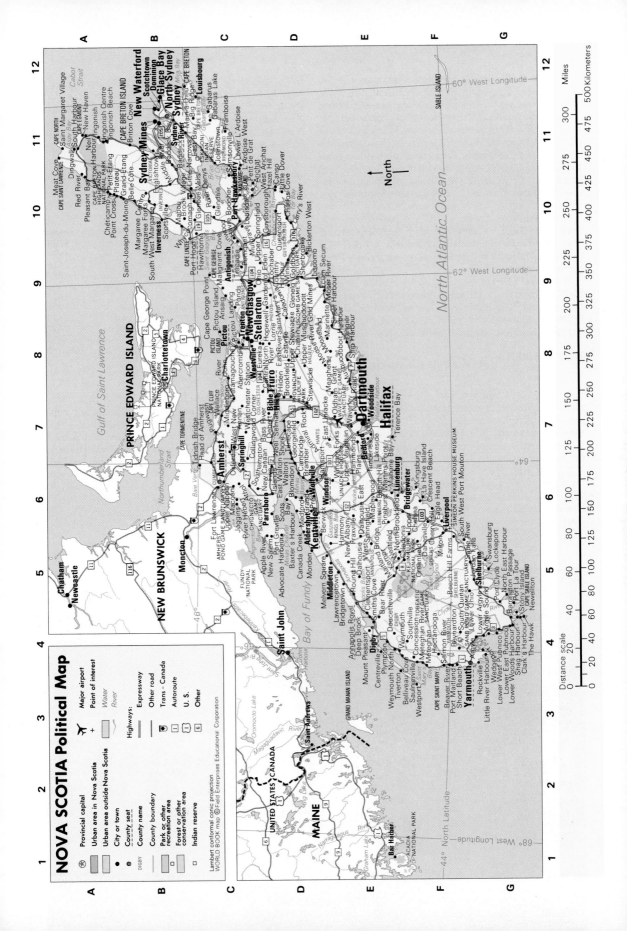

NOVA SCOTIA Political Map

✈	Major airport
+	Point of interest

Urban area in Nova Scotia
Urban area outside Nova Scotia

● City or town
Country seat
County name

DIGBY

County boundary
County boundary

Park or other recreation area
Forest or other conservation area
Indian reserve

Water
River

Highways:

Expressway
Other road

Ⓣ Trans - Canada
① Autoroute
① U.S.
⑥ Other

Lambert conformal conic projection
WORLD BOOK map ©Field Enterprises Educational Corporation

Distance scale

Miles

Kilometers

North

North Atlantic Ocean

Gulf of Saint Lawrence

Bay of Fundy

Northumberland Strait

PRINCE EDWARD ISLAND

NEW BRUNSWICK

MAINE

UNITED STATES
CANADA

Halifax

Dartmouth

Sydney

Sydney Mines

New Waterford

Glace Bay

North Sydney

Inverness

Antigonish

New Glasgow

Stellarton

Trenton

Westville

Truro

Amherst

Springhill

Parrsboro

Windsor

Kentville

Middleton

Bridgetown

Digby

Yarmouth

Shelburne

Liverpool

Bridgewater

Lunenburg

Charlottetown

Moncton

Saint John

Saint Andrews

Chatham

Newcastle

60° West Longitude

62° West Longitude

64°

66° West Longitude

68° West Longitude

44° North Latitude

Schools. Public schools in Nova Scotia operate under the provincial Education Act. Nova Scotia's first Education Act was passed in 1766. The provincial department of education supervises the school system. Schools are controlled by local school boards. Municipal councils and the lieutenant governor in council appoint the members of these boards. Local taxes and grants from the provincial government provide the chief sources of income for the Nova Scotia schools. Provincial law requires children to attend school from age 6 through age 16.

Libraries. Nova Scotia has 11 regional library systems, with about 50 branch libraries. Local taxes and grants from the provincial government support the regional libraries. The province also has about 20 college and university libraries.

Museums. The Citadel, a national historic park in Halifax, includes a military museum and a provincial museum. The Public Archives of Nova Scotia, at Dalhousie University in Halifax, contain public records and historic documents. The archives also have maps, ship models, and art collections. Other museums include the Alexander Graham Bell Museum in Baddeck, Fort Anne Historical Museum in Annapolis Royal, Fortress of Louisbourg Museum in Louisbourg, Nova Scotia Museum in Halifax, and Uniacke House in Mount Uniacke.

UNIVERSITIES AND COLLEGES

Nova Scotia has eight degree-granting universities and colleges. For enrollments, see CANADA (table: Universities and Colleges).

Name	Location	Founded
Acadia University	Wolfville	1838
Cape Breton, College of	Sydney	1974
Dalhousie University	Halifax	1818
Mount Saint Vincent University	Halifax	1873
Nova Scotia College of Art and Design	Halifax	1969
Nova Scotia Technical College	Halifax	1907
Saint Francis Xavier University	Antigonish	1853
Saint Mary's University	Halifax	1841

NOVA SCOTIA/*A Visitor's Guide*

Nova Scotia's beaches and shoreline resorts have given the province the nickname *Canada's Ocean Playground*. Fishing enthusiasts can catch striped bass and tuna along the coast, and salmon and trout in the inland streams. In the forests, people hunt deer, snowshoe rabbits, and grouse.

Tourists who spend three days or more in Nova Scotia may become members of the Order of the Good Time. This social organization was founded at Port Royal in 1606 by the French explorer Samuel de Champlain.

Many visitors come to the Gaelic festival in St. Ann's and the Highland Games in Antigonish. They enjoy watching the Scottish sport of tossing the caber. In this contest, men throw the *caber* (a heavy wooden pole) as far as they can. Hunting guides and lumbermen match skills during Sportsmen's Meets held at Beaver Dam near Shelburne and in Stillwater in Guysborough County. These contests include canoe racing and *log birling* (balancing on a spinning, floating log). Winter sports in Nova Scotia include curling, hockey, skating, and skiing.

A Queen and Her Court Reign at the Annapolis Valley Apple Blossom Festival.
Nova Scotia Communications and Information Centre

A Trout Fisherman Tries the
Rough Waters near Maitland.

John L. Stage, Photo Researchers

Bagpipers at Antigonish

Malak, Miller Services

Nova Scotia Communications and Information Centre
Tossing the Caber in a Highland Games Contest

PLACES TO VISIT

Following are brief descriptions of some of Nova Scotia's many interesting places to visit.

Alexander Graham Bell Museum, in Baddeck, displays inventions, models, notes, and photographs of Alexander Graham Bell, inventor of the telephone.

Bluenose II, based in Halifax Harbor, is a replica of *Bluenose,* a Canadian racing schooner that won the International Fisherman's Trophy in 1921, 1922, 1923, 1926, and 1938. Visitors may tour *Bluenose II* when the ship is in port.

Cabot Trail offers motorists a magnificent view of the sea. This highway winds through the wilderness areas of northern Cape Breton Island.

Cape Blomidon, near Wolfville, overlooks Minas Basin and nearby apple orchards.

The Lighthouse Route, between Yarmouth and Halifax, passes many small fishing villages with interesting traditions.

Sunrise Trail runs along the shore of the Northumberland Strait between Amherst and the Strait of Canso. The highway is 212 miles (341 kilometers) long.

National Parklands. Nova Scotia has two national parks—Cape Breton Highlands and Kejimkujik. Cape Breton Highlands National Park is on Cape Breton Island. Kejimkujik National Park lies in southwestern Nova Scotia. Canada's government also operates eight national historic parks and sites, including the Citadel and York Redoubt, in Halifax. For the area and features of each park and site, see CANADA (National Park System).

Other attractions include Wildlife Park in Shubenacadie, and four historic homes: Haliburton Memorial Museum in Windsor, Lawrence House in Maitland, Perkins House in Liverpool, and Uniacke House in Mount Uniacke. For information, write to Department of Tourism, P.O. Box 130, Halifax, N.S.

Nova Scotia Communications & Information Centre
Bluenose II, Based in Halifax Harbor

ANNUAL EVENTS

One of Nova Scotia's best-known annual events is the Annapolis Valley Apple Blossom Festival in Wolfville and nearby towns. The festival is held during late May or early June. Other annual events in Nova Scotia include the following.

July-September: Gathering of the Clans in Pugwash (Dominion Day, July 1); Lobster Carnival in Pictou (July); Highland Games in Antigonish (July); Theater Arts Festival International in Wolfville (July); Gaelic Mod in St. Ann's (August); Festival of the Tartans in New Glasgow (August); Nova Scotia Fisheries Exhibition in Lunenburg (September).

October: Joseph Howe Festival in Dartmouth and Halifax (late September and early October); Atlantic Winter Fair in Halifax (October).

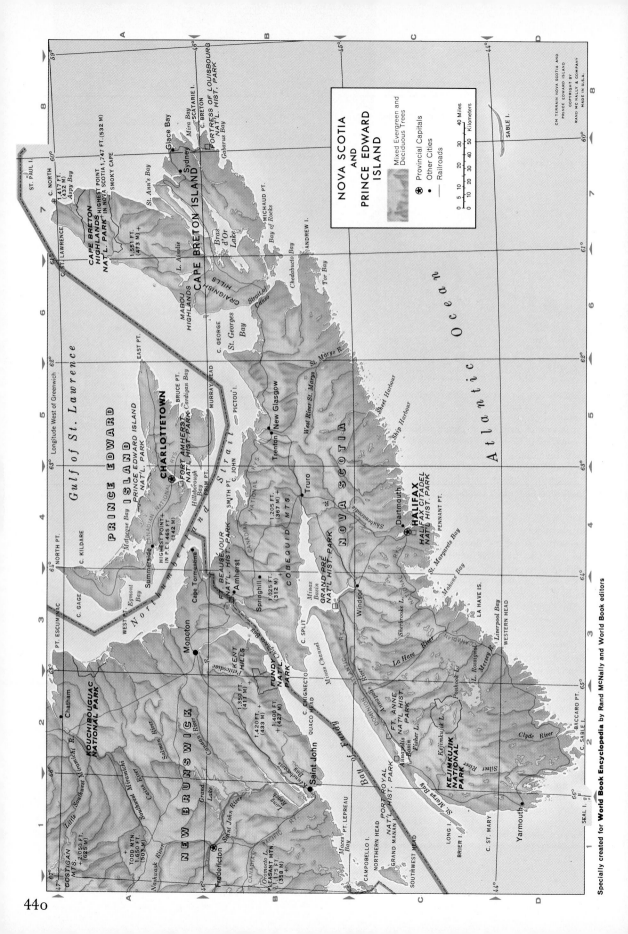

NOVA SCOTIA
AND
PRINCE EDWARD
ISLAND

Mixed Evergreen and
Deciduous Trees
⊛ Provincial Capitals
• Other Cities
— Railroads

0 5 10 20 30 40 Miles
0 10 20 30 40 50 Kilometers

CM TERRAIN NOVA SCOTIA AND
PRINCE EDWARD ISLAND
COPYRIGHT BY
RAND McNALLY & COMPANY
MADE IN U.S.A.

Specially created for World Book Encyclopedia by Rand McNally and World Book editors

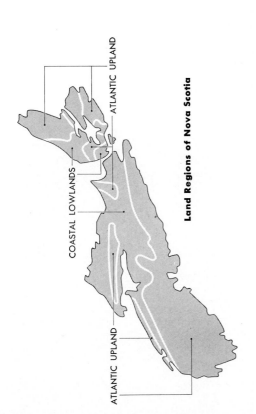

ATLANTIC UPLAND

COASTAL LOWLANDS

ATLANTIC UPLAND

ATLANTIC UPLAND

Land Regions of Nova Scotia

NOVA SCOTIA / The Land

Land Regions. Nova Scotia has two main land regions: (1) the Atlantic Upland and (2) the Coastal Lowlands.

The Atlantic Upland slopes upward from the Atlantic Ocean to hilly ranges near the northern shores of the province. The northern slopes of these hills drop steeply to the Bay of Fundy and to lowlands along the Gulf of St. Lawrence. North Mountain rises along the Bay of Fundy. The Cobequid Mountains extend along the northern shore of the Minas Basin.

The Atlantic Upland is part of a plain that once lay almost at sea level. Geologists believe this plain stretched northeast from Alabama to perhaps as far as the Arctic Ocean. About 70 million years ago, the plain tilted upward so that it sloped gently to the southeast. In Nova Scotia, this rocky slope is covered with forests. Rivers that flow down the slope are the source of most of the hydroelectric power generated in Nova Scotia. The Strait of Canso separates the Nova Scotia mainland from Cape Breton Island. At its narrowest point,

the strait is only ¾ mile (1.2 kilometers) wide. Steep hills rise in the northern part of Cape Breton Island. Thick forests grow close to the shores. The highest point in Nova Scotia rises 1,747 feet (532 meters) above sea level in Cape Breton Highlands National Park.

The Coastal Lowlands extend through central Nova Scotia and Cape Breton Island, and also surround the Cobequid Mountains. These lowlands were carved into the Atlantic Upland when rains and the weather wore away areas made up of soft rocks. In some places, the hard rocks of the upland region remained and formed flat-topped hills rising from the lowlands.

The lowlands have Nova Scotia's most valuable soils and mineral deposits. The rich farmland of the Annapolis-Cornwallis Valley is south of North Mountain. Fertile marshlands lie along the Bay of Fundy, Chignecto Bay, and the Minas Basin. These marshlands also extend far inland along many rivers. Beneath the lowlands are rich deposits of coal and gypsum. There are also deposits of limestone, rock salt, sandstone, and shale.

Coastline of Nova Scotia measures 4,709 miles (7,578 kilometers). This includes 2,517 miles (4,051 kilometers) of mainland, 1,170 miles (1,883 kilometers) of major islands and 1,022 miles (1,645 kilometers) of minor islands. The rocky southern shore has many inlets. Fishing fleets use the large inlets as harbors. Small islands lie off the southern coast.

Rivers and Lakes. Nova Scotia's rivers are all narrow, and few are over 50 miles (80 kilometers) long. The Mersey and the St. Marys rivers, both 72 miles (116 kilometers) long, are the longest in the province. The Mersey rises on South Mountain and flows through several lakes, including Lake Rossignol. Rich farmland lies along the Annapolis and Shubenacadie rivers, which flow into the Bay of Fundy. Other important rivers include the La Have and Musquodoboit, which flow into the Atlantic, and the Mira on Cape Breton Island. Ocean ships can sail 30 miles (48 kilometers) inland on the Mira River. Many of Nova Scotia's rivers rise and fall with the tides, and carry salt water inland. Dikes

Nova Scotia Communications and Information Center
Russ Kinne, Photo Researchers

NOVA SCOTIA

protect some lowlands from rivers that could overflow their banks at high tide.

Nova Scotia has more than 400 lakes. Most of them are small. Bras d'Or Lake, the largest, covers 360 square miles (932 square kilometers) on Cape Breton Island. This salt-water lake nearly divides the island in two. The largest fresh-water lakes are, in order of size, Lake Rossignol in Queens County, Lake Ainslie on Cape Breton Island, Kejimkujik Lake in Queens and Annapolis counties, and Grand Lake near Halifax.

Wild Daisies, below, brighten the rocky hillsides in the northern section of Cape Breton Island. These steep hills, part of the Atlantic Upland region, are among the highest in Nova Scotia.

Chas. R. Belinky, Photo Researchers

Cabot Trail, above, winds along steep bluffs overlooking the sea in northern Cape Breton Island. It is a favorite route for visitors.

Bay of Fundy Coast, right, in the Coastal Lowlands region, may have the world's highest tides. Low tide leaves boats on dry land.

SEASONAL TEMPERATURES

January

AVERAGE OF DAILY LOW TEMPERATURES

Degrees Fahrenheit	Degrees Celsius
10 to 20	-12 to -7
0 to 10	-18 to -12

AVERAGE OF DAILY HIGH TEMPERATURES

Degrees Fahrenheit	Degrees Celsius
30 to 40	-1 to 4
20 to 30	-7 to -1

July

AVERAGE OF DAILY LOW TEMPERATURES

Degrees Fahrenheit	Degrees Celsius
55 to 60	13 to 16
50 to 55	10 to 13

AVERAGE OF DAILY HIGH TEMPERATURES

Degrees Fahrenheit	Degrees Celsius
75 to 80	24 to 27
70 to 75	21 to 24
65 to 70	18 to 21

AVERAGE MONTHLY WEATHER

HALIFAX

	Temperatures F° High	Low	C° High	Low	Days of Rain or Snow
JAN.	32	17	0	-8	15
FEB.	31	16	-1	-9	14
MAR.	38	24	3	-4	14
APR.	47	32	8	0	13
MAY	58	41	14	5	14
JUNE	67	49	19	9	13
JULY	74	56	23	13	12
AUG.	73	57	23	14	10
SEPT.	67	51	19	11	12
OCT.	57	43	14	6	12
NOV.	47	34	8	1	15
DEC.	36	23	2	-5	15

SYDNEY

	Temperatures F° High	Low	C° High	Low	Days of Rain or Snow
JAN.	30	15	-1	-9	16
FEB.	28	11	-2	-12	15
MAR.	35	20	2	-7	15
APR.	44	29	7	-2	14
MAY	56	37	13	3	14
JUNE	67	46	19	8	12
JULY	75	55	24	13	11
AUG.	74	56	23	13	11
SEPT.	66	50	19	10	14
OCT.	56	41	13	5	14
NOV.	45	33	7	1	16
DEC.	35	23	2	-5	18

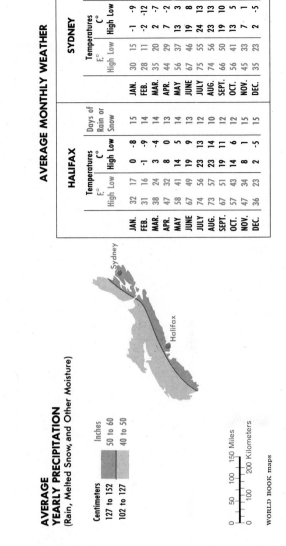

AVERAGE YEARLY PRECIPITATION
(Rain, Melted Snow, and Other Moisture)

Centimeters	Inches
127 to 152	50 to 60
102 to 127	40 to 50

WORLD BOOK maps

0 50 100 150 Miles
0 100 200 Kilometers

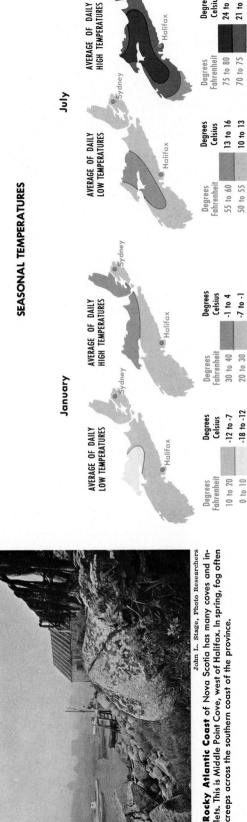

Rocky Atlantic Coast of Nova Scotia has many coves and inlets. This is Middle Point Cove, west of Halifax. In spring, fog often creeps across the southern coast of the province.

John L. Stage, Photo Researchers

NOVA SCOTIA/*Climate*

The sea nearly surrounds Nova Scotia and keeps the climate from becoming extremely hot or cold. The province has an average January temperature of about 25° F. (−4° C). The average July temperature is about 65° F. (18° C). Nova Scotia's northern Atlantic coast is the coldest part of the province. But even there, the winter temperature seldom falls below 5° F. (−15° C). In winter, Cape Breton Island and the eastern Nova Scotia mainland are chilled by winds crossing the ice-filled Gulf of St. Lawrence. In spring, occasional fogs cover the southwest coast of the province. Summer and autumn bring sunny skies over the coast, and pleasant southwesterly winds. The province's highest temperature, 101° F. (38° C), occurred at Collegeville on Aug. 19, 1935. Upper Stewiacke recorded Nova Scotia's lowest temperature, −42° F. (−41° C), on Jan. 31, 1920.

Nova Scotia's *precipitation* (rain, melted snow, and other forms of moisture) averages from 35 to 50 inches (89 to 130 centimeters) a year. Rainfall is heaviest along the Atlantic coast. Annual snowfall is about 90 inches (230 centimeters) on the uplands and from 60 to 80 inches (150 to 200 centimeters) on the lowlands.

The leading industry of Nova Scotia is manufacturing. Agriculture and fishing follow in importance. All production values given in this section are in Canadian dollars. For the value of the Canadian dollar in United States money, see MONEY (table).

Natural Resources. Nova Scotia's most valuable resources are its extensive mineral deposits, fertile lowlands, and rich fishing grounds.

Soil. The Annapolis-Cornwallis Valley has the best farmland. Other good farming areas include the marshlands along the Bay of Fundy and the plains between the Shubenacadie River and the Northumberland Strait. The Atlantic Upland has shallow, rocky soil.

Minerals in Nova Scotia include one of North America's largest deposits of gypsum, near Halifax. Valuable coal deposits lie underground from Chignecto on the Nova Scotia mainland to Glace Bay on Cape Breton Island. Other important minerals include barite, clay, lead, peat, salt, sand and gravel, silver, and stone.

Plant Life. Forests cover about 80 per cent of the province. Birch, firs, maples, pines, and spruces are the most common trees. Other plants found in Nova Scotia include the blueberry, bracken, mayflower, mountain laurel, raspberry, rhodora, sweet fern, and wintergreen.

Animal Life. The white-tailed deer is Nova Scotia's most common large animal. Some black bears, moose, and wildcats also are found in wilderness areas. Small animals of Nova Scotia include minks, muskrats, otters, porcupines, red foxes, skunks, and weasels. The province has several kinds of geese and ducks, as well as pheasants, ruffed grouse, and woodcocks. Salmon and trout swim in Nova Scotia's streams. The coastal waters contain cod, flounder, haddock, halibut, herring, lobsters, mackerel, pollack, redfish, scallops, and swordfish.

Manufacturing. Nova Scotia's industrial products have a *value added by manufacture* of about $600 million yearly. This figure represents the value created in products by Nova Scotia's industries, not counting such costs as materials, supplies, and fuels.

The production of paper and paper products is the chief manufacturing activity. The industry's products have an annual value added by manufacture of about $120 million. The chief products include cartons, newsprint, pulp, and stationery and envelopes. Major centers of production are Bridgewater, Centreville, Halifax, Port Hawkesbury, Stellarton, and Truro.

Food processing is the second-ranking manufacturing activity, with a value added of about $118 million yearly. Fish processing plants operate along the coast. The chief dairying regions lie around the Minas Basin and along the Bay of Fundy.

The production of transportation equipment is the third-ranking manufacturing activity. Ships are built in Dartmouth, Halifax, Lunenburg, and Shelburne. Factories in Trenton produce railway equipment, and aircraft parts are made in Amherst, Dartmouth, Halifax, and Yarmouth. Automobiles and automobile parts are manufactured at Halifax, Kentville, Lower Truro, and Sydney. Other important industries in Nova Scotia include the manufacture of fabricated metal products, lumber and wood products, petroleum and coal products, and printed materials.

Agriculture. Nova Scotia has about 5,400 farms. They average 224 acres (91 hectares) in size. Nova Scotia's farm products provide an annual income of about $105 million. Dairy farming is the province's most important agricultural activity. Milk is the most valuable source of farm income. Dairy cattle graze on the Truro plain and around the cities and large towns.

Hay is Nova Scotia's leading crop. Barley, hay, and wheat are grown along the Bay of Fundy. Apples are also an important product. Apple production totals about $2\frac{1}{4}$ million bushels yearly. Most of the apple orchards are in the Annapolis-Cornwallis Valley. The leading grain is oats. Other farm products include chickens, hogs, blueberries, eggs, and potatoes.

Fishing Industry. Nova Scotia ranks second only to British Columbia in commercial fishing among the provinces. Its annual catch is valued at about $80 million. Nova Scotia leads the provinces in lobster production. Other valuable seafoods include cod, haddock, herring, redfish, and scallops. Fish are sold to processing plants and then shipped to markets.

Mining in Nova Scotia has an annual income of about $75 million. The province's most valuable minerals, in order of importance, are coal, sand and gravel, and gypsum. The chief coal mines are on Cape Breton

Production of Goods in Nova Scotia

Total value of goods produced in 1974—$883,634,000

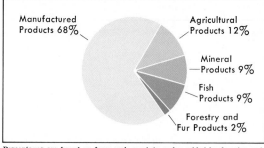

Manufactured Products 68%
Agricultural Products 12%
Mineral Products 9%
Fish Products 9%
Forestry and Fur Products 2%

Percentages are based on farm cash receipts, value added by forestry and manufacture, and value of fish, fur, and mineral production. Fur products are less than 1 per cent.

Sources: Canadian government publications, 1975 and 1976.

Employment in Nova Scotia

Total number of persons employed in 1974—233,700

Economic Activities		Number of Employees
Community, Business, & Personal Services	🧍🧍🧍🧍🧍🧍🧍🧍🧍🧍	69,400
Wholesale & Retail Trade	🧍🧍🧍🧍🧍🧍	41,900
Manufacturing	🧍🧍🧍🧍🧍🧍	40,400
Transportation, Communication, & Utilities	🧍🧍🧍🧍	25,600
Government	🧍🧍🧍🧍	24,500
Fishing	🧍🧍	10,500
Finance, Insurance, & Real Estate	🧍🧍	9,000
Agriculture	🧍🧍	8,000*
Mining	🧍	4,400

*1975 figure.
Sources: *Estimates of Employees by Province and Industry, 1961-1974,* Statistics Canada; Fisheries and Marine Service, Environment Canada; Labor Force Survey Division, Statistics Canada.

FARM, MINERAL, AND FOREST PRODUCTS

This map shows where the province's leading farm, mineral, and forest products are produced. The major urban area (shown in red) is the province's most important manufacturing center.

WORLD BOOK map

Grinning Fishermen proudly display a "big one" from their day's catch. Nova Scotia is a leader in Canada's fishing industry.

Malak, Miller Services

Island. Some coal is mined in Cumberland and Pictou counties. Much of the coal is used for fuel in steam-driven electric power plants. Gypsum comes from Halifax, Hants, Inverness, and Victoria counties. Salt is mined in Cumberland County. Nova Scotia leads the Canadian provinces in the production of barite and ranks second in gypsum and salt. The province also produces clay, limestone, peat, and quartz.

Forestry. Logs and pulpwood cut in Nova Scotia have an annual value of about $20 million. Nova Scotia's forests supply wood for its pulp and paper mills, boatyards, and furniture factories. Maple and yellow birch are the chief hardwoods of the province. The chief softwoods include balsam firs and spruces. Nova Scotia exports many Christmas trees to the United States.

Electric Power. Steam plants that burn coal and oil generate about 85 per cent of Nova Scotia's electric power. Steam plants operate in Dartmouth, Glace Bay, Halifax, Maccan, Point Tupper, Trenton, and Yarmouth. Hydroelectric dams produce the rest of the province's electric power.

Transportation. Nova Scotia has about 15,600 miles (25,110 kilometers) of roads. About a third of them are paved. Automobiles and trains travel about $1\frac{1}{2}$ miles (2.4 kilometers) from the Nova Scotia mainland to Cape Breton Island over a *causeway* (a road built on a high, man-made mound). Two airlines serve Nova Scotia. Halifax is a center for air traffic. Nova Scotia has about 1,200 miles (1,930 kilometers) of railroad track. Halifax is the largest seaport. Passenger ships connect Nova Scotia's coastal towns with Maine, New Brunswick, Newfoundland, and Prince Edward Island.

Communication. Nova Scotia has 30 newspapers, including 6 dailies. The *Halifax Gazette*, founded in 1752, was the first newspaper published in Canada. It is still published as the *Royal Gazette* by the provincial government. The province's main daily newspapers include *The Chronicle-Herald* and *The Mail-Star*, both of Halifax, and the *Cape Breton Post*, published in Sydney.

The province has 20 radio stations and 4 television stations. The first radio station, CHNS, began broadcasting from Halifax in 1920. The first television station, CJCB-TV, began operating in Sydney in 1954.

Trainloads of Coal from Cape Breton Island feed the steel mill furnaces of Sydney. Iron ore for Nova Scotia's mills comes from mines in nearby Newfoundland.

Malak, Shostal

Statue of Evangeline honors the French Acadians who were expelled from Grand Pré in 1755. Many of them were sent to what is now Louisiana.

First British Victory in Nova Scotia came when seamen captured and burned the French colony of Port Royal in 1613.

● **Port Royal**

Grand Pré ●

HISTORIC NOVA SCOTIA

Port Royal, one of the oldest cities in North America, was founded about 1605. It is now known as Annapolis Royal.

★ **HALIFAX**

Halifax Was Founded in 1749 by the English governor Edward Cornwallis. He made it the capital of Nova Scotia.

NOVA SCOTIA / *History*

Indian Days. When white explorers first came to the Nova Scotia region in the early 1500's, they found Micmac Indians living there. These Indians were the earliest known settlers in Nova Scotia. They fished along the coast in summer, and hunted moose and caribou in the forests in winter.

Exploration and Settlement. The English explorer John Cabot may have landed in Nova Scotia or in Newfoundland as early as 1497. Cabot believed he had landed in Asia. Between 1520 and 1524, several other explorers reached Nova Scotia while trying to find a westward sea route to Asia. These explorers included the Italian navigator Giovanni da Verrazano and two Portuguese sailors, João Alvarez Fagundes and Estevan Gomez. Verrazano explored in the service of France. Gomez sailed in the service of Spain. During the summers of the late 1500's, French fishermen used the Nova Scotia shore for drying codfish they had caught in the nearby fishing grounds. These fishermen returned to France every autumn.

In 1603, King Henry IV of France gave land including Nova Scotia to a French explorer, Pierre du Guast, Sieur de Monts. De Monts and another French explorer, Samuel de Champlain, sailed along the Nova Scotia coast in 1604. Champlain made the first accurate chart of the coast. The French called the Nova Scotia region and the land around it *Acadia* (see ACADIA). De Monts and Champlain established a colony in the New Bruns-

wick region near the mouth of the St. Croix River. In 1605, this colony was moved to Nova Scotia and became Port Royal.

The Struggle in Acadia. In 1613, the French colony at Port Royal was captured and burned by English raiders from Virginia. Samuel Argall, a sea captain, led the attack. For more than a hundred years the English and the French battled, off and on, for control of Acadia.

In 1621, King James I of England and Scotland granted Acadia to Sir William Alexander. The grant included what is now Nova Scotia and also New Brunswick, Prince Edward Island, part of Quebec, and part of Maine. Alexander named the region *Nova Scotia,* Latin for *New Scotland.* In 1629, Alexander's son, Sir William the younger, built a new fort at Port Royal. But the colony lasted only until 1632.

The English gave Port Royal to France in 1632, under the Treaty of St. Germain-en-Laye. Colonists sent by a French company took control of Port Royal and also settled at La Have. These settlers became known as Acadians. In 1636, the French built a new fort near Port Royal, on the present site of the town of Annapolis Royal.

English troops under Sir William Phips captured Port Royal in 1690. But England gave Port Royal back to France under the Treaty of Ryswick in 1697. A combined force of troops from England and New England

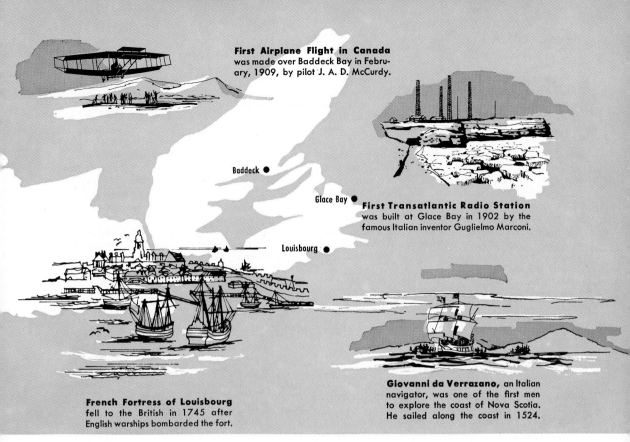

First Airplane Flight in Canada was made over Baddeck Bay in February, 1909, by pilot J. A. D. McCurdy.

First Transatlantic Radio Station was built at Glace Bay in 1902 by the famous Italian inventor Guglielmo Marconi.

Baddeck ●

Glace Bay ●

Louisbourg ●

French Fortress of Louisbourg fell to the British in 1745 after English warships bombarded the fort.

Giovanni da Verrazano, an Italian navigator, was one of the first men to explore the coast of Nova Scotia. He sailed along the coast in 1524.

took Port Royal again in 1710. That year, the British changed the name of the fort from Port Royal to Annapolis Royal.

The French finally gave up Nova Scotia under the Peace of Utrecht in 1713. This treaty made British subjects of the French Acadians who remained in Nova Scotia. It also gave Cape Breton Island and Prince Edward Island (then called *Ile Saint Jean*) to France. The French built a fortress at Louisbourg on Cape Breton Island to guard the entrance to the Gulf of St. Lawrence. British troops from New England captured the fortress in 1745 with the aid of the Royal Navy. France regained Louisbourg in 1748 under the Treaty of Aix-la-Chapelle, which settled a European war. But the French held the fortress for only 10 years. Louisbourg fell to the British during the Seven Years' War (1756-1763).

British settlers established Halifax in 1749, and it became the capital of Nova Scotia the same year. Many French, German, and Swiss Protestants came to Nova Scotia during the early 1750's to escape religious persecution in Europe.

In 1755, British colonial troops from New England began to drive out of Nova Scotia the Acadians who refused to swear allegiance to Britain. Several thousand Acadians fled to Prince Edward Island, Quebec, the French colony of Louisiana, and British colonies in America.

IMPORTANT DATES IN NOVA SCOTIA

1497-1524 European explorers reached Nova Scotia while seeking a sea route to Asia.

1603 King Henry IV of France commissioned Pierre du Guast, Sieur de Monts, to colonize Acadia.

1604 Samuel de Champlain charted the Nova Scotia coast.

1605 Champlain and De Monts founded Port Royal.

1710 The British captured Port Royal and changed its name to Annapolis Royal.

1713 Under the Peace of Utrecht, France gave Britain all Acadia except Cape Breton Island and Prince Edward Island.

1749 The British founded Halifax.

1755 British colonial troops from New England began to drive French Acadians from Nova Scotia.

1758 The British won Cape Breton Island from France. Nova Scotia's first provincial parliament met in Halifax.

1776-1785 United Empire Loyalists came to Nova Scotia from the United States.

1867 Nova Scotia joined with New Brunswick, Ontario, and Quebec in forming the Dominion of Canada.

1917 A French munitions ship exploded in Halifax harbor and killed about 2,000 persons.

1939-1945 Halifax became a base for warships sailing to and from Europe during World War II.

1955 The Canso Causeway was opened, linking the Nova Scotia mainland with Cape Breton Island.

1967 The Canadian Parliament established the Cape Breton Development Corporation to help attract new industry to the area.

Progress as a Province. In 1758, the British government allowed colonists in Nova Scotia to elect a representative assembly. The first assembly met in Halifax. It gave the people some voice in their government. But a governor and a council appointed by the king really ruled the province.

In 1760, more than 20 ships carrying New Englanders arrived in Nova Scotia. The New Englanders took over the land the Acadians had cleared, and established many new settlements. During and after the Revolutionary War in America (1775-1783), about 35,000 United Empire Loyalists came to Nova Scotia from the United States. The Loyalists were British colonists in America who refused to take up arms against Great Britain in the Revolutionary War. They established Shelburne and also settled in Aylesford, Digby, and other towns.

Settlers from Scotland began arriving in 1773. The greatest number of Scots arrived between 1815 and 1850. They settled in the eastern part of the Nova Scotia peninsula and in Cape Breton. Irish immigrants came to Nova Scotia after the 1845 potato famine in Ireland.

Nova Scotians gained complete control over their local affairs in 1848. That year, the British government granted Nova Scotia a governing council controlled by the elected assembly. Nova Scotia became the first completely self-governing colony within the British Empire. Joseph Howe, a forceful editor and statesman of Nova Scotia, had led the fight to win the new government for the colony.

During the 1800's, Nova Scotia thrived with growing industries and increasing world trade. Shipbuilders used timber from the province's forests to build merchant ships. By 1860, Nova Scotia had one of the largest merchant fleets in the world. For a short time, these ships and the profitable lumber industry made Nova Scotia the most prosperous Canadian province. But during the 1860's, steamships largely replaced sailing vessels. Nova Scotia then lost much of its shipping business. The lumber industry also suffered because of reckless tree cutting.

In 1867, Nova Scotia joined with New Brunswick, Ontario, and Quebec in forming the Canadian confederation (see BRITISH NORTH AMERICA ACT). During the next 30 years, economic difficulties slowed the growth of all the provinces. Nova Scotia began to recover during the late 1890's when farm production increased and the iron and steel industry developed.

The 1900's. During World War I (1914-1918), Halifax served as the headquarters of Allied fleets sailing between North America and Europe. In 1917, a French military supply ship exploded in Halifax Harbor. The blast killed about 2,000 persons and damaged much of the city.

In 1933, Angus L. Macdonald became premier of the province. Macdonald, a Liberal, served until 1940, when he resigned to take an administrative post in the Canadian government during World War II (1939-1945). He returned as premier in 1945 and served until his death in 1954. During Macdonald's administration, the Legislative Assembly passed new tax laws, a civil service act, and other laws dealing with economic, legislative, and social problems.

School expansion, highway construction, and industrial development marked the 1950's and 1960's in Nova Scotia. Several vocational and technical schools were built in the 1950's to meet the rising demand for skilled workers. The Nova Scotia Institute of Technology opened in Halifax in 1963. The Nova Scotia section of the Trans-Canada Highway—about 300 miles (480 kilometers) long—was built across the province. In 1955, the Canso Causeway was completed. It provided a highway and railway link between the mainland and Cape Breton Island. The causeway contributed to the province's economic growth and to expansion of the tourist industry. A suspension bridge across the northern part of Halifax harbor was also completed in 1955.

In 1957, the provincial government established Industrial Estates Limited, a corporation designed to attract new industry to Nova Scotia. This nonprofit corporation leases or sells manufacturing space and facilities to companies that wish to expand or to move into Nova Scotia. In 1967, the Canadian government set up the Cape Breton Development Corporation. This corporation was designed both to attract new industry and to close unprofitable coal mines. For almost 20 years, Nova Scotia's coal industry had suffered from rising production costs and a loss of markets.

Nova Scotia Today is developing industrially and its people have a higher standard of living than in past years. But a wide gap still exists in job opportunities, living standards, and wage levels between Nova Scotia and the heavily populated areas of Canada.

In 1970, the Port of Halifax opened a terminal that could handle the large containers of cargo widely used in shipping. This terminal increased business at the port. Industrial and mining expansion centered on Cape Breton Island during the early 1970's. A new coal mine and many new industries opened in the Sydney area. A $300-million industrial park was built on the shores of Canso Strait. The park included a deepwater port, a $60-million oil refinery, and a $65-million plant for making *heavy water*, used in nuclear reactors for producing electric power.   BASIL W. DEAKIN,

CHARLES BRUCE FERGUSSON, and BERNARD J. KEATING

——————— **THE PREMIERS OF NOVA SCOTIA** ———————

	Party	Term
1. Hiram Blanchard	Conservative	1867
2. William Annand	Liberal	1867-1875
3. Philip C. Hill	Liberal	1875-1878
4. Simon H. Holmes	Conservative	1878-1882
5. John S. D. Thompson	Conservative	1882
6. William T. Pipes	Liberal	1882-1884
7. William S. Fielding	Liberal	1884-1896
8. George H. Murray	Liberal	1896-1923
9. Ernest H. Armstrong	Liberal	1923-1925
10. Edgar N. Rhodes	Conservative	1925-1930
11. Gordon S. Harrington	Conservative	1930-1933
12. Angus L. Macdonald	Liberal	1933-1940
13. A. Stirling MacMillan	Liberal	1940-1945
14. Angus L. Macdonald	Liberal	1945-1954
15. Harold Connolly	Liberal	1954
16. Henry D. Hicks	Liberal	1954-1956
17. Robert L. Stanfield	*Progressive Cons.	1956-1967
18. George I. Smith	*Progressive Cons.	1967-1970
19. Gerald Regan	Liberal	1970-

*Progressive Conservative

Related Articles in WORLD BOOK include:

BIOGRAPHIES

CITIES AND TOWNS

PHYSICAL FEATURES

OTHER RELATED ARTICLES

Outline

I. **Government**
   A. Lieutenant Governor
   B. Premier
   C. Legislative Assembly
   D. Courts
   E. Local Government
   F. Taxation
   G. Politics
II. **People**
III. **Education**
   A. Schools
   B. Libraries
   C. Museums
IV. **A Visitor's Guide**
   A. Places to Visit
   B. Annual Events
V. **The Land**
   A. Land Regions
   B. Coastline
   C. Rivers and Lakes
VI. **Climate**

VII. **Economy**
   A. Natural Resources
   B. Manufacturing
   C. Mining
   D. Fishing Industry
   E. Agriculture
   F. Forestry
   G. Electric Power
   H. Transportation
   I. Communication
VIII. **History**

Questions

Where is Nova Scotia's best farmland?
How does Nova Scotia's provincial corporation attract new industries to the province?
What are Nova Scotia's three cities?
Who heads the provincial government?
What are Nova Scotia's chief manufactured products?
What bodies of water nearly surround Nova Scotia?
What are the leading mining products of Nova Scotia?
What is Nova Scotia's most valuable land region?
What was the first newspaper published in Canada?
Who were the United Empire Loyalists?

Books for Young Readers

BLAKELEY, PHYLLIS R., comp. *Nova Scotia: A Brief History.* Dent (Don Mills, Ontario), 1955.
COOPER, GORDON. *A Second Springtime.* Oxford (Don Mills, Ontario), 1973; Nelson (Nashville, Tenn.), 1975. Fiction.
KUMIN, MAXINE W. *When Great-Grandmother Was Young.* Putnam (New York City), 1971. Fiction.
SAUER, JULIA L. *Fog Magic.* Viking (New York City), 1943. Fiction.

Books for Older Readers

BRUCE, HARRY. *Nova Scotia.* Hounslow (Willowdale, Ontario), 1975.
BUCKLER, ERNEST. *Nova Scotia: Window on the Sea.* McClelland (Toronto); Crown (New York City), 1973.
Exploring Nova Scotia. Greey de Pencier (Toronto), 1976.
RADDALL, THOMAS H. *Halifax: Warden of the North.* McClelland (Toronto), 1950.

NOVA SCOTIA COLLEGE OF ART AND DESIGN is the only specialized school in Canada that offers degrees in fine arts and design. It is in Halifax, N.S., and gets most of its financial support from the provincial government. It offers four-year programs, some of which include preparation for careers in teaching, environmental design, and communication design. The college was founded in 1887. For enrollment, see CANADA (table: Universities and Colleges).   JAMES DAVIES

NOVA SCOTIA TECHNICAL COLLEGE is a coeducational university in Halifax, N.S. It is privately controlled, but receives federal and provincial grants. The university awards bachelor's, master's, and doctor's degrees. The undergraduate division offers the final two years of both a four-year and a five-year engineering course and the last four years of a six-year architecture course. The earlier years are offered by associated universities. Nova Scotia Technical College was founded in 1907. For enrollment, see CANADA (table: Universities and Colleges).

Critically reviewed by NOVA SCOTIA TECHNICAL COLLEGE

NOVALIS (1772-1801) was the pen name of Friedrich von Hardenberg, a German romantic poet. Five poems by Novalis, called *Hymns to the Night* (1800), express his religious, mystical nature, and a longing for death. In the essay *Christianity or Europe* (1799), Novalis tried to show that people lived more meaningful lives in the spiritual unity of the Catholic Middle Ages than in his own troubled time. This attitude became a major theme of German romanticism. Novalis died before finishing *Heinrich von Ofterdingen*, a novel about a legendary medieval poet.

Novalis was born in Saxony. The death of his 15-year-old fiancée in 1797 deepened his melancholy and religious temperament. Novalis' work as a mining engineer brought him close to the land and intensified his love of nature and its mysteries.   JEFFREY L. SAMMONS

NOVAYA ZEMLYA, *NAW vuh yuh zyim LYAH,* is the Russian name for two islands in the Arctic Ocean that belong to Russia. The name means *new land.* The northern island is about 20,000 square miles (52,000 square kilometers) in area. The southern island is about 15,000 square miles (38,800 square kilometers). The islands have a combined coastline of 1,700 miles (2,736 kilometers). Novaya Zemlya has an arctic climate. The islands have large deposits of coal, and some gold and copper. Russia has tested nuclear bombs there.

Russians first discovered Novaya Zemlya, probably in the A.D. 1000's, but the islands remained uninhabited until 1877. The Russian government has built villages for hunters, and a small colony of Russians and Samoyeds live on the southern island. Islanders raise reindeer, trap animals, and collect *eider down* (the feathers of eider ducks).   THEODORE SHABAD

NOVEL

NOVEL. A novel is a long prose story that is largely imaginary. Its chief purpose is usually to entertain, but its underlying aim is to help readers to understand life. Charles Dickens' *The Pickwick Papers* is mainly a funny story. Leo Tolstoy's great novel *War and Peace* not only gives pleasure but also offers much wisdom. While the reader is laughing at Mark Twain's humor in *Huckleberry Finn*, he learns about human nature and the history of part of the United States.

The novel is perhaps the broadest and least confined of all literary forms. It may be comparatively short. For example, Edith Wharton's *Ethan Frome* can be read in less than two hours. It may be long. Herman Melville's *Moby Dick* probably takes about twenty hours to read.

The novel is usually about people, but it is sometimes about animals or fabulous beings, such as those in *Gulliver's Travels* by Jonathan Swift. In George Stewart's *Storm*, the chief character is a wind. If the characters are people, they may be of high or low rank. They may be emperors or page boys. They may be saints or thieves.

Real people and imaginary people may appear in the same novel. In James Fenimore Cooper's *The Spy*, George Washington appears among "made-up" characters. Sir Walter Scott included King Richard I of England with many nonhistorical characters.

There is also much flexibility of action in the novel. The story can take place anywhere, and at any time. The action may occur in unexplored regions near the South Pole, as in Edgar Allan Poe's *The Narrative of A. Gordon Pym*. It can go under the sea. Its action can go through distant space, as in Jules Verne's *Hector Servadac*, the story of life on a comet.

The time of a novel may be in the past, the present, or the future. Sigrid Undset's *Kristin Lavransdatter* is a *trilogy* (series of three) of novels set in Norway in the 1300's. *Looking Backward* by Edward Bellamy is actually a forecast with events occurring in A.D. 2000.

Perhaps the great quality of the novel is the great variety of its subject matter. It may tell of practically unknown adventures. For example, few persons have had experiences like those of Robinson Crusoe. It may deal interestingly with familiar, everyday occurrences. For example, Sinclair Lewis' *Main Street* throws a new light on life in a small midwestern town. Reader interest is held by both types: *romantic* novels, which explore the new, and *realistic* novels, which recognize, analyze, and "check" the familiar.

The Power of the Novel

People read novels for fun, yet often they get much more than fun from them. The novel mirrors the history of mankind. W. M. Thackeray's *Henry Esmond* teaches us facts in English history; John Steinbeck's *The Grapes of Wrath* tells of the plight of United States dust-bowl farmers during the depression; George Santayana's *The Last Puritan* shows how a New England heritage shaped the character of a young man.

The novel may do more than mirror history: it may even influence it. Harriet Beecher Stowe's *Uncle Tom's Cabin* gave great impetus to the movement to free the slaves. Charles Dickens' *Nicholas Nickleby* told such a pathetic story of the treatment of children in an English school that it led to a movement to reform education.

The novel not only can teach people and help to shape society, but also it can make the reader a more understanding person, more tolerant and more sympathetic toward suffering. Reading a great novel like Fyodor Dostoevsky's *The Brothers Karamazov* or Victor Hugo's *Les Misérables* is an emotional experience that can serve to broaden the humanity of the reader. Like a great play such as William Shakespeare's *King Lear*, a great novel enriches the human spirit.

How the Novel Developed

The novel as it is now known in Western Europe and the Americas got its real start in the 1700's. Yet its beginnings are ancient. Many of the earliest narratives told for entertainment were about historical persons, but prose tales about imaginary persons are to be found even in ancient Greek writings.

Early Beginnings. The Italian stories called *novelle* are closely related to the novel of today in form. They are shorter than most novels of today. Giovanni Boccaccio's *Decameron* (1348-1353) is the most noted collection of novelle. The stories in the *Decameron* are supposedly told by a group of persons who left the city of Florence to escape the plague.

In Spain, two works of fiction became models for later writers. Garci Rodríguez de Montalvo published a romantic narrative, *Amadis of Gaul*, in 1508. This work was the most influential of the *romances of chivalry*. The first *picaresque novel*, *Lazarillo de Tormes*, appeared anonymously in 1554. It told of the adventures of a *pícaro*. A *pícaro* is a clever, witty, unscrupulous youngster who travels about in the service of various masters. He engages in cheating, practical jokes, and petty thievery. This type of story became very popular.

The most famous of all Spanish stories, *Don Quixote* by Miguel de Cervantes, was published early in the 1600's. Cervantes poked fun at the popular romances of chivalry through the idealistic knight Don Quixote. With his realistic squire Sancho Panza, Don Quixote, in a real world, tries to have the same kind of adventures that the knights did in the unreal, dreamy world of the old romances of chivalry. The effect is comic, but the tale is also sad. Don Quixote suffers much in body and in spirit.

In England, prose fiction began significantly during the Elizabethan period. The first notable work was John Lyly's *Euphues* (1578), remembered today for its

finished style, which set *euphuism* (artificial, elegant, alliterative style) as a standard for writers. There is very little incident, and the book is chiefly a running discussion of love, honor, and manners among fine ladies and gentlemen. Imitations of this popular piece included Thomas Lodge's *Rosalind* (1590). In the same year came Sir Philip Sidney's *Arcadia*, a long story using some materials of the romances of chivalry, but quieter in tone. It is partly pastoral; that is, it emphasizes the quiet charm of country living.

The Elizabethans wrote much picaresque material, especially after *Lazarillo de Tormes* was translated into English in 1576. Most notable was *The Unfortunate Traveller, or The Life of Jack Wilton* (1594) by Thomas Nash.

In the 1600's came many long, tedious romances, but no narratives of importance in the development of the novel until 1678. In that year, the first part of John Bunyan's *The Pilgrim's Progress* appeared. This is an allegory; that is, the characters and actions are represented by personifications, or symbols. It is the story of Christian, who left the City of Destruction as a pilgrim to the Celestial City. And yet it gives some realistic glimpses of English village life in the settings for its allegory. Bunyan's beautifully simple style reflects his familiarity with the Bible. Mrs. Aphra Behn's short *Oroonoko* (1688) was notable as one of the first stories to try to create sympathy for a slave.

The 1700's in England saw the novel well started. Defoe's *Robinson Crusoe* (1719) is the first novel of incident in which the author seems to try deliberately to create belief in the reality of his invented material. It has been said that Defoe "lied like truth." All his writings seem sincerely realistic. With Defoe, fiction seems more real than reality. The best known of his many other novels is *Moll Flanders* (1722).

Defoe's stories are not fully developed novels. Each is mainly a simple succession of adventures without a continued plot. Plot is a planned groundwork of action leading to a climax, which is the logical result. It creates suspense by the pattern of arrangement. This kind of planned action first appeared in *Pamela* (1740) by Samuel Richardson, the story of a servant girl's efforts to defend her honor. This was a long tale in the form of letters, but it had plot. Richardson's *Clarissa; or, The History of a Young Lady* (1747-1748) was a long novel in which the young woman was defeated instead of victorious like Pamela.

Henry Fielding also wrote novels in the modern sense of the word. His works were mainly humorous, as opposed to Richardson's seriousness. His novel, *Joseph Andrews* (1742), made fun of *Pamela* by showing, in highly exaggerated incidents, a young man trying to defend his honor against an older woman.

Some critics have said that Fielding's *Tom Jones* (1749) has the most perfect plot in all English fiction. It tells of the adventures of a lively young man who gets into many situations, both serious and humorous, before the mystery of his parentage is cleared up. Fielding used the picaresque method in much of his writing. Tobias Smollett, who wrote *Roderick Random* (1748), also used a picaresque framework for comic stories.

A very different kind of novel was produced by Laurence Sterne, who was interested in character more than incident. His *Tristram Shandy* (1760-1767) has been called a forerunner of the modern psychological novel. Oliver Goldsmith introduced the story of sentiment in his *The Vicar of Wakefield* (1766), one of the most loved English novels. In it, the gentle, humorous Dr. Primrose meets many family troubles with strength and courage before his story reaches a happy ending.

The Gothic novel appeared in the late 1700's. A Gothic novel belongs to what has been called the *goose-flesh* type of fiction. In it, the heroine in a lonely castle is exposed to such things as ghosts, strange lights, pictures that seem alive, mysterious voices, trapdoors, and statues that seem to drip blood. The first such English novel was Horace Walpole's short *The Castle of Otranto* (1764). The most famous was, perhaps, Ann Radcliffe's *The Mysteries of Udolpho* (1794). Many lesser and often more horrifying such novels were written.

The 1800's in England. The first novelist of importance was Jane Austen, who relied less on excitement than on careful use of detail. Her *Pride and Prejudice* (1813) is the story of a small-town family with several daughters to marry off. The chief interest lies in Mr. Darcy's courtship of Elizabeth Bennett, who is at first prejudiced against him because of his proud attitude toward village girls.

Sir Walter Scott had great success in colorful historical romance. His materials were often lovely ladies and gallant knights who were involved in tournaments, sieges, crusades, piracy, or border warfare. Scott did not forget the common people, however, and he was skilled in both tragic and comic action. His first novel, *Waverley*, appeared in 1814. Among his most famous were *The Bride of Lammermoor* (1819), *Ivanhoe* (1820), and *Kenilworth* (1821). Many persons think his best novel was *Old Mortality* (1816), about a religious problem among the Covenanters of Scotland at the end of the 1600's.

Charles Dickens' novels were compounded chiefly of humor, pathos, and interest in the welfare of the common people. His career began with the humorous *Pickwick Papers* in 1836-1837. In *Oliver Twist* (1837-1839), Dickens' talent for portraying pathos and tragedy was revealed, as well as his sympathy for the poor. His novels are especially informative on English schools, elections, poorhouses, prisons, and legal matters. Dickens also created memorable characters, such as Micawber in *David Copperfield* (1849-1850). *A Tale of Two Cities* (1859) is a vivid story of adventures, escapes, and heroism during the French Revolution.

William Makepeace Thackeray in *Vanity Fair*, published as a serial in 1847 and 1848, pictured the folly, insincerity, and emptiness of the London society of his time. His *Henry Esmond* (1852) is a historical novel of England in the early 1700's. Charlotte Brontë in 1847 brought out *Jane Eyre*, a story of the problems of a struggling young governess. Her sister, Emily Brontë, told in *Wuthering Heights* a tale of character conflict and violent incident in England's North Country.

The best of George Meredith's finely written, rather hard-to-read, psychological novels is probably *The Ordeal of Richard Feverel* (1859). About the same time, George Eliot (the pen name of Mary Ann Evans) was producing her stories of the English Midlands, notably *The Mill on the Floss* (1860) and *Silas Marner* (1861). Like Emily Brontë, George Eliot was deeply interested in the effects of environment on character.

Robert Louis Stevenson's novels *Treasure Island* (1883) and *Kidnapped* (1886) are exciting romantic stories of adventure, often involving young people.

On the Continent. François Rabelais's *Gargantua and Pantagruel* appeared in France in the 1500's. He specialized in exaggerated tales of gross humor. The psychological romance *La Princesse de Clèves* (*The Princess of Clèves*, 1678) by Madame de La Fayette was the only influential novel of the 1600's. As in England, the novel did not get underway until the 1700's.

In 1715, came the first part of Alain René Lesage's picaresque novel *Gil Blas*. L'Abbé Prévost produced a tragic love novel, *Manon Lescaut*, in 1731. Pierre Carlet de Marivaux published his *Marianne* in parts from 1731 through 1741. Perhaps the most famous early French novel was Jean Jacques Rousseau's *La Nouvelle Héloïse* (*The New Heloise*, 1761), a sentimental and tragic narrative about love problems.

The 1800's were rich in French novels. Stendhal's *The Red and the Black* (1831) showed an ambitious young man in complicated French society. Honoré de Balzac wrote many realistic novels. He intended an entire collection of novels (*La Comédie Humaine*) to give a picture of all life in France. The most famous single novel of the group is *Le Père Goriot* (1834).

Dumas produced many spectacular romances, *The Three Musketeers* (1844) being the most famous. Victor Hugo's *Les Misérables* (1862) is a complicated story springing from a poor man's theft of a loaf of bread. One of the most famous French novels of this time was *Madame Bovary* (1857), Gustave Flaubert's carefully finished study of a dissatisfied wife.

In the 1870's, Émile Zola's novels started the theory of naturalism. Naturalism treated character scientifically as the product of heredity and environment. Naturalism did not shrink from showing the most unpleasant or degrading aspects of life.

The novel as such developed late in Germany. Goethe's sentimental, tragic love story *The Sorrows of Young Werther* (1774) was read throughout Europe. His *Wilhelm Meister's Apprenticeship* (1795-1796) is a study of character development.

In Russia, Pushkin pioneered in 1836 with *The Captain's Daughter*. This novel treats of an unsuccessful Cossack revolt, led by peasants. Gogol's *Dead Souls* (1842) comically pictures a shrewd, scheming man, planning to gain money and land, but also gives realistic pictures of many aspects of Russian society.

Perhaps the most famous of all Russian novels is Tolstoy's *War and Peace* (1865-1869), a tremendous work portraying many aspects of society during the Napoleonic wars. His *Anna Karenina* (1875-1877) is a study of a tragic marriage.

Ivan Turgenev, also a powerful writer who used a finished style, brought out his most notable novel, *Fathers and Sons*, in 1862. During his life in Paris, he influenced and was influenced by French novelists.

Fyodor Dostoevsky, one of the most vivid Russian writers, wrote *Crime and Punishment* (1866). His novel *The Brothers Karamazov* (1880) has tremendous scope, including almost every human emotion from highest religious devotion to the most diabolical hatred. He was one of the most powerful shapers of the modern novel.

In the United States, sustained prose fiction became important with Charles Brockden Brown's *Wieland* (1798), a story of ventriloquism and religious mania. His *Edgar Huntly* (1799) has been called the first American detective novel.

James Fenimore Cooper, the "American Scott," wrote many historical novels, some of the best of which feature Indians. His *The Spy* (1821) was the first important novel to emphasize the American scene. Probably the most famous of his novels are *The Leatherstocking Tales*, with Natty Bumppo, master woodsman and brave fighter, as hero. *The Deerslayer* (1841) is perhaps his best. His pictures of frontier America and Indian life were excellently done. The heroines in his novels were usually weak and lovely.

Nathaniel Hawthorne wrote novels in which the "action" was often the destructive psychological effect of concealing sin, as in *The Scarlet Letter* (1850), picturing Puritan times, and in *The House of the Seven Gables* (1851), which mingles New England witchcraft and the inevitable punishment.

The greatest novel of the 1800's is probably Herman Melville's *Moby Dick* (1851). It is the story of a captain's pursuit of a huge white whale which symbolizes evil. Melville gave his readers both exciting incident and profound interpretation of man's problems.

William Dean Howells tried to make the novel realistic in *The Rise of Silas Lapham* (1885). Henry James used a rather difficult style for his *The American* (1877), in which the fine American characters face social and ethical problems in Europe.

Mark Twain's humorous stories of American boyhood, *The Adventures of Tom Sawyer* (1876) and *The Adventures of Huckleberry Finn* (1884), created patterns of natural speech and action that greatly influenced the novelists who came after him.

Stephen Crane treated war truthfully rather than romantically in *The Red Badge of Courage* (1895).

In the 1900's, most serious authors have been far more concerned with probing deep and even desperate problems than with entertainment. They show man as individual (in the psychological novel), and man's place in society (in the social novel). Joseph Conrad's *Lord Jim* (1900) shows what goes on in the mind of a chief mate after he deserts a sinking ship. Thomas Mann's *Buddenbrooks* (1901) is a study of the development and decay of a German merchant family. Mann's *The Magic Mountain* (1924) interprets the confusing world before World War I through the eyes of a sensitive young man in an Alpine tuberculosis sanitarium.

Sigmund Freud's studies of the unconscious mind influenced the writing of novels concerned with the fears, frustrations, and anxieties of modern people. Such a novel is James Joyce's *Ulysses* (1922), which gives a full account of one man's inner life during a period of 18¾ hours. D. H. Lawrence's *Sons and Lovers* (1913) studies the personality problems of a young Englishman torn between love of his mother and love of young women.

Thomas Wolfe's *Look Homeward, Angel* (1929) tells vividly of a young man who felt he did not "belong" to any social group in America. Marcel Proust's long and brilliant *À la Recherche du Temps Perdu* (*The Remembrance of Things Past*), published in several volumes from 1913 to 1927, deals in detail with the psychological states of several sensitive Frenchmen and women.

André Gide's *Les Faux-Monnayeurs* (1926; English title, *The Counterfeiters*) analyzes the lives and personalities of a group of characters, and the problems involved in writing a novel. In Ernest Hemingway's *The Sun Also Rises* (1926) and Aldous Huxley's *Point Counter Point* (1928), the chief characters suffer from lack of faith. Virginia Woolf made penetrating character studies in *Mrs. Dalloway* (1925) and *To the Lighthouse* (1927).

Problems of being black are presented in William Faulkner's *Light in August* (1932). The horrors of modern war is the theme of Hemingway's *A Farewell to Arms* (1929), Erich Maria Remarque's *All Quiet on the Western Front* (1929), and Faulkner's *A Fable* (1955).

Three novels of World War II are outstanding. Norman Mailer's *The Naked and the Dead* (1948) is long, but honestly and brilliantly written. It is noted for its stark realism. Irwin Shaw's *The Young Lions* (1948) is the dramatic, eloquent story of three young men in World War II, only one of whom survives. Herman Wouk's *The Caine Mutiny* (1951) traces the career of a Princeton graduate from midshipman to captain of the old minesweeper *Caine*.

Fear of mechanized control of human life is shown in Huxley's *Brave New World* (1932). Jakob Wassermann in *The World's Illusion* (1919) wrote of the need of faith, and kindness to fellow human beings.

Some novelists of the 1900's have dealt largely with economic problems. Erskine Caldwell's *Tobacco Road* (1932) pictures severe poverty in the South. In *My Ántonia* (1918), Willa Cather reported difficult pioneering conditions on the Nebraska prairie, as Ole Rölvaag did for Minnesota in *Giants in the Earth* (1927).

Sometimes novelists blame society when their characters violate moral codes, as Theodore Dreiser did in *Sister Carrie* (1900) and *An American Tragedy* (1925).

Other twentieth-century novelists deal with characters as groups. John Steinbeck did this in his realistic story of migrant workers, *The Grapes of Wrath* (1939). John Dos Passos in *Manhattan Transfer* (1925) presents the confused struggle for success, and the involved psychological and economic problems that are a part of city life today. In *The Emigrants* (1951), Vilhelm Moberg vividly recounts the extreme hardships of Swedish families voyaging to America.

Technique of the Novel

As the novel developed, its form changed almost as much as its content. At first, authors emphasized action, and it was generally easy to follow, as in the simple narrative *Tom Jones* (Fielding), or in the form of letters (Richardson's *Pamela*). Sometimes the authors used an autobiographical form, as Dickens did in *David Copperfield*.

The action was usually crystallized in a plot. Plot is organized action concerning a definite problem with foreshadowing (clues), climax, and dénouement (unfolding or untying). But even these rules were not always followed. Many novels have no recognizable plot.

The novel may be merely a description of a certain kind of life, as Dos Passos' *U. S. A.* (1937). Some novels have no central character wholly admirable. Often novelists may seem to be just observers of what they describe. In such cases, they are impartial, remote, as anonymous as newswriters. They offer no sympathy and no religious consolation. This is especially true of naturalistic writers.

Authors sometimes use special techniques to present setting and establish tone. Dos Passos uses the "camera-eye" and "newsreel" technique. Psychological novelists follow the "stream of consciousness" technique—giving the character's thoughts and feelings without any apparent selection, and without comment. Many modern novelists use symbolism, whereby an object represents an abstract quality, such as goodness or evil. In Franz Kafka's *The Castle* (1930), the castle symbolizes faith. Albert Camus' *The Plague* (1947) outwardly describes an epidemic of bubonic plague. At the same time, this novel symbolically relates humanity to the problem of evil in general.

The modern novelist probably does not offer as much clear explanation as the earlier novelist did. Sometimes the reader is lost in the complex presentation, which reflects the complexity of modern life.

The novel is not entirely different from all other forms of literature. It is most closely related to the short story, but it is longer and usually has more characters and more complicated events than the short story. It differs from drama because a play is more narrowly focused than a novel and the playwright seldom offers any explanation of the action.

The novel is not only the least confined and most experimental form of literature, but is also the longest lasting. If one form of the novel falls in popular favor, the novel can regain its vitality and its position in some new form. People write novels for self-expression, and read them to fill instinctive needs. Novels help people to endure and to enjoy life.   ALEXANDER COWIE

Related Articles. See LITERATURE and the articles on the various national literatures, such as AMERICAN LITERATURE and FRENCH LITERATURE. See also the following articles:

NOVELS

OTHER RELATED ARTICLES

NOVEMBER

NOVEMBER is the eleventh month of the year. *Novem* is the Latin word for *nine*. In the Roman calendar, November was the ninth month. Because July was named for Julius Caesar and August for Augustus Caesar, the Roman Senate offered to name the eleventh month for Tiberius Caesar. He refused modestly, saying, "What will you do if you have thirteen emperors?" Originally there were thirty days in November, then twenty-nine, then thirty-one. From the time of Augustus, it has had thirty days.

Nature in November. November comes between autumn and winter. In the North Temperate regions during November, the trees are bare, and the dead leaves on the earth have lost the brilliant color they had in October. Soft snow seldom hides the bareness of the fields, but the grays and browns of the landscapes are sometimes relieved by delightful days of hazy sunshine. The Anglo-Saxons referred to November as "the wind month" and sometimes "the blood month," probably because during this period they killed animals for their winter meat.

Many outdoor activities in the North come to a halt in November. Nature seems to be resting after the harvest. The crops have been stored or shipped to processing plants and mills, and farmers know whether or not they have had a successful year. Near the end of November, the people of the United States celebrate Thanksgiving Day. The Pilgrims celebrated the first New England Thanksgiving to express gratitude for their first harvests in the new land. In Canada, where the colder climate forces farmers to harvest their crops earlier, Thanksgiving is celebrated in October. Football

═══ IMPORTANT NOVEMBER EVENTS ═══

1 Benvenuto Cellini, Italian goldsmith, born 1500.
—Dr. Crawford W. Long, first to use ether as an anesthetic in surgery, born 1815.
—Sholem Asch, American novelist, born 1880.
2 Daniel Boone, American frontiersman, born 1734.
—Marie Antoinette, French queen, born 1755.
—Gaspar de Portolá reached San Francisco Bay, 1769.
—James K. Polk, 11th President of the United States, born near Pineville, N.C., 1795.

Warren G. Harding   **James K. Polk**

—Warren G. Harding, 29th President of the United States, born near Blooming Grove, Ohio, 1865.
—North Dakota became the 39th state, 1889.
—South Dakota became the 40th state, 1889.
—Arthur Balfour, British Foreign Secretary, proposed settlement of Jewish people in Palestine, 1917.
—First regular radio broadcasts began, over station KDKA in Pittsburgh, 1920.
3 Stephen Austin, colonizer of Texas, born 1793.
—William Cullen Bryant, American poet, born 1794.
—Canadian explorer Vilhjalmur Stefansson born 1879.
4 Erie Canal formally opened at New York, 1825.
—Will Rogers, American humorist, born 1879.
5 Gunpowder Plot to blow up Parliament failed, 1605. This day is celebrated as Guy Fawkes Day.
—Eugene V. Debs, American socialist and labor leader, born 1855.
—Will Durant, American historian, philosopher, and educator, born 1885.
—England and France declared war on Turkey, 1914.
—Reconstructed Vienna Opera House opened, 1955.
6 John Philip Sousa, American bandmaster, born 1854.
—Ignace Jan Paderewski, Polish pianist, composer, and statesman, born 1860.
—First intercollegiate football game in United States, Rutgers *vs.* Princeton, at Rutgers, 1869.
7 Gen. William Henry Harrison defeated Indians in Battle of Tippecanoe, 1811.

—Nobel physicist Marie Curie born 1867.
—Last spike driven in Canadian Pacific Railway (now CP Rail), 1885.
—French author Albert Camus born 1913.
—Bolsheviks ousted provisional Russian government, 1917. The date was Oct. 25 in the old Russian calendar.
—United States troops landed in North Africa, 1942.
8 Edmund Halley, British astronomer, born 1656.
—Mt. Holyoke Seminary for women opened, 1837.
—Montana became the 41st state, 1889.
9 Ivan Turgenev, Russian novelist, born 1818.
—Edward VII of England born 1841.
—Kaiser Wilhelm II abdicated German throne, 1918.
—The CIO established, 1935.
10 Martin Luther, German religious leader, born 1483.
—William Hogarth, English painter, born 1697.
—German poet Friedrich von Schiller born 1759.
—Sir John S. D. Thompson, Canadian prime minister, born 1844.
—Arctic explorer Donald MacMillan born 1874.
11 Russian novelist Fyodor M. Dostoevsky born 1821.
—Maude Adams, American actress, born 1872.
—Washington became the 42nd state, 1889.
—Armistice signed ending World War I, 1918.

—Veterans Day first celebrated in United States, 1954.
12 Joseph Hopkinson, American jurist and author of "Hail Columbia," born 1770.
—Reformer Elizabeth Cady Stanton born 1815.
—Auguste Rodin, French sculptor, born 1840.
13 James C. Maxwell, Scottish physicist, born 1831.
—Novelist Robert Louis Stevenson born 1850.
—John Drew, American actor, born 1853.
—Louis D. Brandeis, American jurist, born 1856.
—Holland Tunnel opened in New York City, 1927.
14 Robert Fulton, American inventor, born 1765.
—Claude Monet, French painter, born 1840.
—Leo H. Baekeland, American inventor, born 1863.
—Indian leader Jawaharlal Nehru born 1889.
—Canadian physician Frederick Grant Banting, famous for discovering insulin, born 1891.
—John Steuart Curry, American painter, born 1897.

is the outstanding sport in November. The weather is usually ideal for football, and thousands of spectators do not seem to mind sitting several hours in the frosty air to watch their favorite football teams play.

Special Days. Election Day in the United States falls on the first Tuesday after the first Monday in November. Veterans Day is celebrated on November 11 in the United States. Thanksgiving Day is celebrated on the fourth Thursday of the month. Children's Book Week is also observed in November.

November Symbols. The topaz is the November birthstone, and the special flower of the month is the chrysanthemum. GRACE HUMPHREY

Quotations

November's sky is chill and drear,
November's leaf is red and sear.
Sir Walter Scott

Autumn wins you best by this, its mute
Appeal to sympathy for its decay.
Robert Browning

The wild November comes at last
Beneath a veil of rain;
The night wind blows its folds aside,
Her face is full of pain.
Richard Henry Stoddard

November woods are bare and still;
November days are clear and bright;
Each noon burns up the morning's chill,
The morning's snow is gone by night.
Helen Hunt Jackson

See also CALENDAR; CHRYSANTHEMUM; THANKSGIVING DAY; TOPAZ.

IMPORTANT NOVEMBER EVENTS

14 Aaron Copland, American composer, born 1900.
—Prince Charles, heir to British throne, born 1948.
15 William Pitt, British statesman, born 1708.
—William Herschel, English astronomer, born 1738.
—Draft of Articles of Confederation approved by Congress, 1777.
—Zebulon Pike sighted Pikes Peak, 1806.
—American jurist Felix Frankfurter born 1882.
—First meeting of League of Nations Assembly, Geneva, 1920.
—Manuel Quezon inaugurated as first president of the Philippines, 1935.
16 Canadian poet Louis H. Fréchette born 1839.
—Composer Paul Hindemith born 1895.
—Oklahoma became the 46th state, 1907.

Franklin Pierce

—The United States recognized the Communist government of Russia, 1933.
17 Congress first met in Washington, D.C., 1800.
—Suez Canal opened, 1869.
—British General Bernard L. Montgomery, commander of the British 8th Army in World War II, born 1887.
18 Louis Jacques Daguerre, French painter and inventor of the daguerreotype, born 1787.
—Asa Gray, American botanist, born 1810.
—Standard time began in the United States, 1883.
—Sir William S. Gilbert, English dramatist who worked with composer Sir Arthur Sullivan, born 1836.
—Eugene Ormandy, American conductor, born 1899.
—United States and Panama signed treaty providing for Panama Canal, 1903.
19 Frontiersman George Rogers Clark born 1752.
—Danish sculptor Bertel Thorvaldsen born 1770.
—Ferdinand de Lesseps, French promoter of Suez Canal, born 1805.
—James A. Garfield, 20th President of the United States, born 1831.
—Abraham Lincoln delivered Gettysburg Address, 1863.
—Allen Tate, American poet and critic, born 1899.

James A. Garfield

—Indira Gandhi, first woman prime minister of India, born 1917.

20 Sir Wilfrid Laurier, Canadian statesman, born 1841.
—Selma Lagerlöf, Swedish novelist, born 1858.
—Kenesaw Mountain Landis, first commissioner of professional baseball, born 1866.
—United States forces landed on Tarawa, 1943.
21 Voltaire, French author and philosopher, born 1694.
—North Carolina ratified the Constitution, 1789.
22 French explorer La Salle born 1643.
—George Eliot, English novelist, born 1819.
—Charles de Gaulle, French statesman, born 1890.
—Benjamin Britten, British composer, born 1913.
—First transpacific air-mail flight began, 1935.
—U.S. President John F. Kennedy assassinated, 1963.
23 Franklin Pierce, 14th President of the United States, born in Hillsboro, N.H., 1804.
—Canadian novelist Sir Gilbert Parker born 1862.
24 Baruch Spinoza, Dutch philosopher, born 1632.
—Missionary Father Junípero Serra born 1713.
—Laurence Sterne, British novelist, born 1713.
—Zachary Taylor, 12th President of the United States, born near Barboursville, Va., 1784.
—French painter Henri de Toulouse-Lautrec born 1864.

Zachary Taylor

25 Lope de Vega, Spanish playwright, born 1562.
—Andrew Carnegie, American industrialist, born 1835.
—Pope John XXIII born 1881.
—Joe DiMaggio, American baseball star, born 1914.
26 First national Thanksgiving Day in United States proclaimed by President George Washington, 1789.
27 Charles A. Beard, American historian, born 1874.
28 William Blake, English poet and artist, born 1757.
—Stefan Zweig, Austrian biographer, born 1881.
29 Louisa M. Alcott, American author, born 1832.
—Commander Richard E. Byrd and crew of three were first to fly over South Pole, 1929.
30 Jonathan Swift, who wrote *Gulliver's Travels*, born 1667.
—Theodor Mommsen, German historian, born 1817.
—Mark Twain, American author, born 1835.
—British statesman Sir Winston Churchill born 1874.

NOVENA is a period of private or public devotion and prayer lasting nine days. It is used in the Roman Catholic Church as a period in which to obtain special graces. It is patterned after the action of the apostles. They gathered for prayer during the nine days between Ascension Thursday and Pentecost.   FULTON J. SHEEN

NOVERRE, JEAN GEORGES. See BALLET (History).

NOVI SAD, *NAW vee SAHD* (pop. 141,375), is a Yugoslav center of manufacturing and transportation. The city lies about 45 miles (72 kilometers) northwest of Belgrade. For location, see YUGOSLAVIA (map).

The Danube River and the Mali Bački Canal meet at Novi Sad. The canal forms part of a system of waterways that links the Danube and Tisa rivers. Novi Sad also lies on the main highway and railroad between Belgrade and Budapest, Hungary. The city produces electrochemical equipment and processed foods and is the home of the University of Novi Sad.

Novi Sad was founded in the early 1690's as the headquarters of the Serbian Orthodox Church. It grew as a trade center for the nearby farm area. A boom began in Novi Sad during the 1960's after petroleum and natural gas were found near the city.   ALVIN Z. RUBINSTEIN

NOVOBIOCIN. See ANTIBIOTIC (Kinds).

NOVOCAIN is a trade name for *procaine*, a drug used as a local anesthetic. When injected, Novocain paralyzes nearby nerves for a short time. The paralysis usually leaves no permanent or damaging effect. Novocain is not habit-forming and is rarely poisonous. Dentists often inject Novocain into the gums before pulling or filling teeth. An American physician, Albert Einhorn, discovered the drug in 1905. It is the most widely used local anesthetic.   SOLOMON GARB

NOVOSIBIRSK, *NAW vah sih BEERSK* (pop. 1,243,000), is the largest city of Siberia and an important Russian center of manufacturing. The city lies on the Ob River, about 1,700 miles (2,740 kilometers) east of Moscow. For location, see RUSSIA (political map).

Many factories in Novosibirsk manufacture heavy equipment, including farm and mining machinery and diesel trucks. The city also produces steel. Airlines, railroads, and riverboats serve Novosibirsk.

Novosibirsk was founded in 1893 as a settlement for workers building a railroad across Siberia. The city grew as a transportation center. Manufacturing boomed during World War II (1939-1945), when the government moved many factories from combat areas in western Russia to the safety of Novosibirsk. In 1958, the government built Akademgorodok, a suburb of Novosibirsk, as a Soviet center of research in chemistry, physics, and other sciences.   THEODORE SHABAD

NOW. See NATIONAL ORGANIZATION FOR WOMEN; WOMAN (In the United States and Canada); FRIEDAN, BETTY.

NOYES, *noyz*, **ALFRED** (1880-1958), was one of the most popular English poets of the early 1900's. He became famous for his ballads and lyric poems about English history. Many of Noyes's poems also show his love of the sea. Noyes's reputation has declined since the mid-1900's, but some of his poetry remains popular with children, especially the exciting ballad "The Highwayman" (1906).

Noyes was born in Wolverhampton. His first volume of poems, *The Loom of Years*, was published in 1902. Noyes established himself as a leading poet with *Drake*, an epic poem published as a serial from 1906 to 1908. This work deals with the famous English sea captain Sir Francis Drake. In *The Golden Hynde* (1908), Noyes filled his poems with colorful images of the sea and sea voyages. *Tales of the Mermaid Tavern* (1913) describes the adventures of noted Englishmen who lived during the reign of Queen Elizabeth I. The subjects include Sir Walter Raleigh and William Shakespeare.

Noyes's most ambitious work was perhaps *The Torchbearers*, a long three-part poem. It honors the contributions of the great scientists of history. The poem consists of *The Watchers of the Sky* (1922), *The Book of Earth* (1925), and *The Last Voyage* (1930).

In 1927, Noyes was converted to Roman Catholicism. His conversion influenced many of his later writings. In *The Unknown God* (1934), for example, he wrote a prose account of his change from an unbeliever to a devout Christian.

In addition to verse, Noyes wrote literary criticism, novels, plays, and short stories. Some of his literary essays were collected in *Pageant of Letters* (1940). Noyes also wrote an autobiography, *Two Worlds from Memory* (1953).   THOMAS A. ERHARD

See also POETRY (Image and Picture).

NOYES, JOHN HUMPHREY. See ONEIDA COMMUNITY.

NSA. See NATIONAL SECURITY AGENCY.

NSC. See NATIONAL SECURITY COUNCIL.

NU, U (1907-   ), is a Burmese politician and statesman. In the 1930's, he was a leader of a student strike that helped obtain independence for Burma. In 1948, he became the first prime minister of independent Burma. He left his post for eight months during 1956 and 1957 to reorganize the Anti-Fascist People's Freedom League, the country's most important political party. After a split in the ruling party, he resigned in 1958. He was named prime minister again in 1960, but was forced out of office in 1962 and placed under detention. He was released in 1966. U Nu was born in Wakema, in the Myaungmya District of Burma. *U* is an honorary title similar to *mister*. In March, 1960, U Nu became a Buddhist priest and took the name U Dhamma Dasa. See also BURMA (History).   GEORGE E. TAYLOR

NUBIA, *NOO bee uh*, was a region of ancient Africa. It covered part of what is now Sudan. Nubia extended along the Nile River from the southern boundary of ancient Egypt almost to present-day Khartoum, Sudan.

The earliest Nubians were probably Negroid peoples. They were controlled by Egyptian rulers at various times from about 2000 to 1000 B.C. The Egyptians regarded Nubia as a source of gold and as a trading center for cattle, ivory, and slaves from central Africa. Nubia's association with Egypt greatly influenced Nubian art and religion.

Kush, the most important civilization of Nubia, developed rapidly after 1000 B.C. This Nubian kingdom, which lasted until about A.D. 350, became a center of ironworking, learning, and trade. Kushites ruled Egypt from about 750 to 670 B.C. See KUSH.

During the A.D. 500's, the people of Nubia were converted to Christianity. A large part of Nubia remained Christian until the 1300's, when Arab invaders conquered the region. They firmly established Islam, the religion of the Muslims.   JOHN MIDDLETON

Idaho National Engineering Laboratory   Combustion Engineering, Inc.

The Tremendous Heat of Nuclear Energy is created deep within a *nuclear reactor, left,* a device that produces and controls nuclear energy. Water in the reactor keeps the device from melting. A nuclear power plant, *right,* uses the heat from a reactor to produce electricity.

NUCLEAR ENERGY

NUCLEAR ENERGY, or ATOMIC ENERGY, is the most powerful kind of energy known. It produces the tremendous heat and light of the sun and the shattering blast of atomic and hydrogen bombs. Nuclear energy results from changes in the *nucleus* (core) of atoms. Scientists and engineers have found many uses for this energy, especially in producing electricity. But they do not yet have the ability to make full use of nuclear power. If nuclear energy were fully developed, it could supply all the world's electricity for millions of years.

Scientists knew nothing about nuclear energy until the early 1900's. They then began to make important discoveries about matter and energy. They already knew that all matter consists of atoms. But scientists further learned that every atom consists mainly of its nucleus and that the nucleus is held together by an extremely powerful force. Their next challenge was to release the enormous energy bound in the nucleus.

Scientists first released nuclear energy on a large scale at the University of Chicago in 1942, three years after World War II began. This achievement led to the development of the atomic bomb. The first atomic bomb was exploded in the desert near Alamogordo, N. Mex., on July 16, 1945. As the bomb exploded in the predawn darkness, it produced a ball of fire that could be seen 180 miles (290 kilometers) away. Temperatures

Alvin M. Weinberg, the contributor of this article, is Director of the Institute for Energy Analysis of Oak Ridge Associated Universities. He is also the coauthor of The Physical Theory of Neutron Chain Reactors.

at the center of the blast about equaled those at the center of the sun. The next month, U.S. planes dropped atomic bombs on Hiroshima and Nagasaki, Japan. The bombs largely destroyed both cities and helped end World War II. Since 1945, scientists have learned how to control nuclear energy for peaceful uses.

Nuclear energy is useful chiefly because it creates great amounts of heat. The heat can be used to make steam, and the steam can be used to generate electricity. Engineers have invented devices called *nuclear reactors* to produce and control nuclear energy.

A nuclear reactor operates somewhat like a furnace. But instead of using such fuels as coal or oil, almost all reactors use uranium. And instead of burning the uranium, a reactor *fissions* it—that is, splits its nuclei in two. As a nucleus splits, it releases energy largely in the form of heat. The fissioning of 1 pound (0.45 kilogram) of pure uranium creates as much heat as the burning of 1,500 short tons (1,360 metric tons) of coal.

Electric power production is by far the most important use of nuclear energy. But nuclear energy also has great value because it produces high-energy particles and rays called *nuclear radiation*. Nuclear radiation has important uses in medicine, industry, and science. Nuclear energy also powers some submarines and other ships. Like nuclear power plants, these vessels have a reactor to create heat for making steam. The steam is used to turn the ship propellers.

This article deals mainly with nuclear energy as a source of electricity. To learn about other uses of nuclear energy, see the WORLD BOOK articles ATOMIC BOMB; HYDROGEN BOMB; RADIOACTIVITY (Uses of Radioisotopes); SHIP (Nuclear Power and Automation); SUBMARINE.

Almost all the world's electricity is produced by *thermal* and *hydroelectric* power plants. Thermal plants use the force of steam from boiling water to generate electricity. Hydroelectric plants use the force of rushing water from a dam or waterfall. The great majority of thermal plants burn *fossil fuels*, chiefly coal and oil, to produce the heat needed to boil water. Fossil fuels developed from the remains of plants and animals that died many millions of years ago. The remaining thermal plants fission uranium to create heat.

Hydroelectric plants cost much less to operate than do fossil-fuel plants. They are also cleaner than fossil-fuel plants, which produce much air pollution. But few countries have enough natural water power to generate large amounts of hydroelectricity. Most countries therefore depend mainly on fossil-fuel plants for their electric power.

The earth has only a limited supply of fossil fuels. Yet the worldwide demand for electricity increases every year. Nuclear plants may thus become more and more important. But today, they produce only about 4 per cent of the world's electricity.

Worldwide Distribution of Nuclear Energy. About 155 nuclear power plants operate in about 20 countries. Approximately 10 other countries plan to build at least one plant by the early 1980's. Most nations, however, cannot afford the expensive equipment that a nuclear power plant requires.

Growth of Nuclear Power Production

Nuclear power production has grown rapidly since the world's first full-scale nuclear plant began operations in England in 1956. The first U.S. plant opened the following year. Today, about 155 nuclear power plants are in operation in about 20 countries.

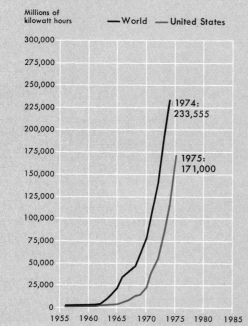

Sources: Federal Power Commission; *World Energy Supplies, 1950-1974*, UN, 1976.

The United States has about 55 nuclear plants and is by far the world's chief producer of nuclear power. The plants generate about 9 per cent of the country's electricity. Other leading producers include Canada, France, Great Britain, Japan, Russia, and West Germany. Canada has six nuclear plants. Five plants are in Ontario, and one is in Quebec. They produce about 5 per cent of the country's electricity. The United States, Canada, and some other leading producers have helped certain developing countries build nuclear plants. These countries include India and Pakistan.

The Advantages of Nuclear Energy. Nuclear power plants have two main advantages over fossil-fuel plants. (1) A nuclear plant uses much less fuel than does a fossil-fuel plant. The fissioning of 1 short ton (0.9 metric ton) of uranium fuel, for example, provides about as much heat energy as the burning of 3 million short tons (2.7 million metric tons) of coal or 12 million barrels of oil. (2) Uranium, unlike fossil fuels, does not release chemical or solid pollutants into the air during use. Nuclear power plants therefore cause much less air pollution than do fossil-fuel plants.

In spite of the advantages of nuclear energy, nuclear power development has been hindered by two chief difficulties. (1) Nuclear plants cost more to build than fossil-fuel plants. Many electric power companies decide against building a nuclear plant for this reason. (2) Nuclear plants are potentially hazardous and therefore must meet certain government requirements that most fossil-fuel plants do not have to meet. For example, a nuclear plant must satisfy government authorities that it can quickly and automatically deal with any kind of emergency. Failure to meet the various requirements often delays or prevents the building or licensing of nuclear power plants.

The Full Development of Nuclear Energy. Many experts believe that the benefits of nuclear power outweigh any problems involved in its production. These experts point out that the world's supply of oil may be nearly exhausted within the next 75 to 100 years. The United States, Canada, and some other countries have enough coal to meet their energy requirements for hundreds of years. But coal is an exceptionally dirty fuel that releases large amounts of sulfur and other pollutants into the air when it is burned (see ENVIRONMENTAL POLLUTION). If nuclear energy were fully developed, it could completely replace oil and coal as a source of electric power.

But a number of problems must be solved before nuclear energy can be fully developed. For example, almost all the power reactors used today require a type of uranium known as *U-235*. The world's supply of U-235, like its supply of fossil fuels, is limited. If U-235 continues to be used at the present rate, it will become increasingly scarce during the 1980's and 1990's and will eventually be used up. Therefore, nuclear power cannot permanently replace other power sources until scientists develop a method of producing nuclear energy that does not require U-235. But none of their experimental methods has yet been fully developed. The subsection *Nuclear Energy Today* discusses the main methods under development.

The process by which a nucleus releases energy is called a *nuclear reaction*. To understand the various types of nuclear reactions, a person must know something about the nature of matter.

The Composition of Matter

All matter is made up of *chemical elements*, which are in turn composed of atoms. A chemical element consists of a substance that cannot be broken down chemically into simpler substances. There are 106 known elements. Seventeen are artificially created, and the rest are found in nature. Scientists rank the elements according to *mass*, or weight. Hydrogen is the lightest natural element, and uranium the heaviest. Most of the artificially created elements are heavier than uranium.

Atoms and Nuclei. An atom consists of a positively charged nucleus and one or more negative electric charges called *electrons*. The nucleus makes up almost all of an atom's mass. The electrons, which are almost weightless, revolve about the nucleus. They determine the various chemical combinations that an atom enters into with other kinds of atoms (see CHEMISTRY [How Compounds Are Formed]). Electrons do not play an active part in nuclear reactions.

The nuclei of every element except hydrogen consist of particles called *protons* and *neutrons*. An ordinary nucleus of hydrogen, the lightest element, has one

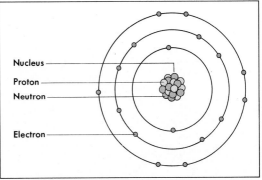

An Atom consists of a nucleus and one or more electrons. The nucleus, which makes up almost all of an atom's *mass*, or weight, consists of tiny particles called *protons* and *neutrons*. They are held together by an extremely powerful force.

proton and no neutrons. The heaviest elements, such as uranium and thorium, have the largest number of protons and neutrons in their nuclei.

Protons carry a positive charge. Neutrons carry no electric charge. Extremely strong forces, called *nuclear forces*, hold the protons and neutrons together in the nucleus. The nuclear forces of each type of nucleus determine the amount of energy that would be required to release its neutrons and protons. This energy is known as *binding energy*.

Isotopes. Most elements have more than one form. Different forms of the same element, called *isotopes*, have different weights. The atoms that make up each of the different forms also have different weights and are also called isotopes.

Scientists identify an isotope by its *mass number*—that is, the total number of protons and neutrons in each of its nuclei. All the isotopes of a given element have the same number of protons in every nucleus. Every hydrogen nucleus, for example, has just one proton. Every uranium nucleus has 92. But each isotope of an element has a different number of neutrons in its nuclei and so has a different mass number. For example, the most plentiful isotope of uranium has 146 neutrons. Its mass number is therefore 238 (the sum of 92 and 146). Scientists call this isotope *uranium 238 or U-238*. The uranium isotope that almost all nuclear reactors use as fuel has 143 neutrons, and so its mass number is 235. This isotope is called *uranium 235 or U-235*. The isotopes of other elements are identified in the same way.

No two elements have the same number of protons in their atoms. If an atom gains or loses one or more protons, it becomes an atom of a different element. If an atom gains or loses one or more neutrons, it becomes another isotope of the same element.

Nuclear Reactions

A nuclear reaction involves changes in the structure of a nucleus. As a result of such changes, the nucleus gains or loses one or more neutrons or protons. It thus changes into the nucleus of a different isotope or ele-

---

NUCLEAR ENERGY TERMS

Chain Reaction is a continuous, self-sustaining series of fission reactions in a mass of uranium or plutonium.

Fission is the only type of nuclear reaction that is controlled by people to produce energy. It occurs when a nucleus of uranium or another heavy element is split into two nearly equal parts.

Fusion is a type of nuclear reaction that occurs when two lightweight nuclei *fuse* (combine) and form a heavier nucleus. Fusion produces the sun's energy.

Half-Life is the time required for half the atoms of a radioactive substance to decay into another substance.

Isotopes are different forms of the same element. Their atoms, which are also called isotopes, have different mass numbers.

Mass Number is the total number of neutrons and protons in the nucleus of an atom.

Neutron is an electrically *neutral* (uncharged) particle in a nucleus.

Nuclear Radiation consists of high-energy particles and rays given off during a nuclear reaction.

Nuclear Reaction involves a change in the structure of a nucleus. Fission, fusion, and radioactive decay are the most important types of nuclear reactions.

Nuclear Reactor is a device for producing nuclear energy by means of controlled chain reactions.

Nucleus is the core of an atom and carries a positive charge. The nuclei of all elements except hydrogen consist of neutrons and protons. An ordinary hydrogen nucleus has one proton and no neutrons.

Proton is a positively charged particle in a nucleus.

Radioactive Decay, or radioactivity, is the process by which a nucleus *spontaneously* (naturally) changes into the nucleus of another isotope or element. The process releases energy mainly in the form of nuclear radiation.

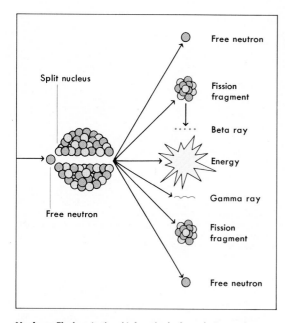

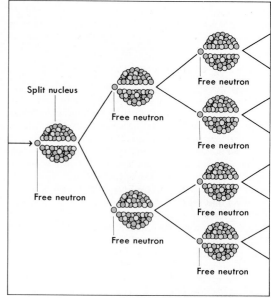

WORLD BOOK diagrams by Arthur Grebetz

Nuclear Fission is the chief method of producing nuclear energy. It involves using a free neutron to split a nucleus of a heavy element, such as uranium, into two *fission fragments*. Besides heat energy, fission releases neutrons and such nuclear radiation as gamma rays. The fragments give off beta rays.

A Chain Reaction results in the continuous fissioning of nuclei and so produces a steady supply of energy. To produce a chain reaction, each fissioned nucleus must give off enough free neutrons to fission at least two more nuclei, *above*. Uranium and plutonium are the materials used to produce a chain reaction.

ment. If the nucleus changes into the nucleus of a different element, the change is called a *transmutation* (see TRANSMUTATION OF ELEMENTS).

Three types of nuclear reactions release useful amounts of energy. These reactions are (1) radioactive decay, (2) nuclear fission, and (3) nuclear fusion. The matter involved in each reaction weighs less after the reaction than it did before. The lost matter has changed into energy.

Radioactive Decay, or radioactivity, is the process by which a nucleus *spontaneously* (naturally) changes into the nucleus of another isotope or element. The process releases energy chiefly in the form of particles and rays called *nuclear radiation*. Uranium, thorium, and several other natural elements decay spontaneously and so add to the natural, or *background*, radiation that is always present in the earth's atmosphere. Nuclear reactors produce radioactive decay artificially. Nuclear radiation accounts for about 10 per cent of the energy produced in a reactor.

Nuclear radiation consists largely of alpha and beta particles and gamma rays. An *alpha particle*, which is made up of two protons and two neutrons, is identical with a helium nucleus. A *beta particle* consists of a negative electrical charge and so is identical with an electron. It results from the breakdown of a neutron in a radioactive nucleus. The breakdown also produces a proton, which remains in the nucleus. The beta particle is released as energy. Alpha and beta particles are sometimes known as alpha and beta *rays*. *Gamma rays* are electromagnetic waves similar to X rays (see ELECTROMAGNETIC WAVES).

Scientists measure radioactive decay in units of time called *half-lives*. A half-life equals the time required for half the atoms of a particular radioactive element or isotope to decay into another element or isotope. Half-lives of radioactive substances range from a fraction of a second to billions of years. See ISOTOPE (Radioactive Isotopes); RADIOACTIVITY (Half-Life).

Nuclear Fission is the splitting of heavy nuclei to release their energy. All nuclear reactors produce energy in this way. To produce fission, a reactor requires a *bombarding particle*, such as a neutron, and a *target material*, such as U-235. Fission occurs when the bombarding particle splits a nucleus in the target material into two nearly equal parts, called *fission fragments*. Each fragment consists of a nucleus with about half the neutrons and protons of the original nucleus. A fission reaction releases only part of the energy of the nucleus. Most of the energy that is released takes the form of heat. The rest takes the form of radiation.

Scientists measure nuclear energy in units called *electron volts*. The burning of one atom of carbon in coal or oil produces about 3 electron volts of energy. The fissioning of one uranium nucleus produces about 200 million electron volts.

The Bombarding Particle must first be *captured* by a nucleus for fission to occur. Reactors use neutrons as bombarding particles because they are the only atomic particles that are both easily captured and able to cause fission. Neutrons can also pass through most kinds of matter, including uranium. Protons can cause fission. But protons and nuclei both have a positive charge, and so they normally *repel* (push away) one another. A nucleus easily captures neutrons because they have no electric charge.

The Target Material. Power reactors use uranium as their target material, or fuel. A uranium nucleus is the easiest of all natural nuclei to split because it has a large number of protons. Protons naturally repel one another, and so a nucleus with many protons has a tendency to "fly apart" and can easily be split.

Uranium also makes a good reactor fuel because it can create a continuous series of fission reactions. As a result, it can produce a steady supply of energy. To create a series of reactions, each fissioned nucleus must give off *free* neutrons in addition to the neutrons bound up in its two fission fragments. A free neutron can split still another uranium nucleus, thus releasing still more free neutrons. As this process is repeated over and over, it becomes a self-sustaining *chain reaction.* Only nuclei that have many more neutrons than protons, such as uranium nuclei, can produce a chain reaction.

U-238 would make an ideal reactor fuel because it is abundant in nature. But U-238 nuclei usually absorb free neutrons without fissioning. An absorbed neutron simply becomes part of the nucleus. The scarce uranium isotope U-235 is the only natural material that reactors can use to produce a chain reaction.

It is extremely difficult to separate the U-235 from the U-238 in uranium ore. For this reason, the fuel used by commercial power reactors contains many more U-238 atoms than U-235 atoms. To ensure capture by a U-235 nucleus rather than by a U-238 nucleus, a reactor must use *slow* neutrons as bombarding particles. Neutrons freed during fission normally travel about 12,000 miles (19,000 kilometers) or faster per second. These *fast* neutrons pass by the scarce U-235 nuclei in the fuel too rapidly to be captured. But a slow neutron travels about 1 mile (1.6 kilometers) per second and has a much better chance of capture by a U-235 nucleus. Reactors contain water or other substances, called *moderators,* to slow down fast neutrons.

Scientists are working to develop a commercial *breeder reactor* to replace reactors that depend only on U-235. A breeder reactor produces and fissions the man-made isotopes plutonium 239 or uranium 233. These fuels do not contain U-238 and so do not have to compete with U-238 nuclei for free neutrons. Most breeders can therefore use fast neutrons as bombarding particles. For this reason, such breeders are also called *fast breeder reactors.* The subsection *Nuclear Energy Today* discusses experimental breeders in more detail.

Nuclear Fusion occurs when two lightweight nuclei *fuse* (combine) and form a nucleus of a heavier element. The products of the fusion weigh less than the combined weights of the original nuclei. The lost matter has therefore been changed into energy.

Fusion reactions that produce large amounts of energy can be created only by means of extremely intense heat. Such reactions are called *thermonuclear reactions.* Thermonuclear reactions produce the energy of both the sun and the hydrogen bomb.

A thermonuclear reaction can occur only in a special form of matter called *plasma.* Plasma is a gas made up of free electrons and free nuclei. Normally, nuclei repel

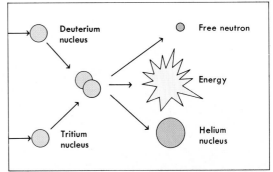

WORLD BOOK diagram by Arthur Grebetz

Nuclear Fusion occurs when two lightweight nuclei unite and form a heavier nucleus. In the example above, nuclei of deuterium and tritium unite and form a helium nucleus. This process releases energy and a neutron. Repeated many times, fusion creates the energy of both the sun and the hydrogen bomb. But scientists have yet to control fusion for use in energy production.

one another. But if a plasma containing lightweight nuclei is heated many millions of degrees, the nuclei begin moving so fast they break through one another's electrical barriers and fuse. See PLASMA (in physics).

Problems of Controlling Fusion. Scientists have not yet succeeded in harnessing the energy of fusion to produce power. In their fusion experiments, scientists generally work with plasmas that are made from one or two isotopes of hydrogen. One such isotope is *tritium,* a man-made radioactive isotope. Another isotope is *deuterium,* or *heavy hydrogen.* Deuterium is considered an ideal thermonuclear fuel because it can be obtained from ordinary water. A given weight of deuterium can supply about four times as much energy as the same weight of uranium.

To produce a controlled thermonuclear reaction, a plasma of deuterium or tritium or of both isotopes must be heated many millions of degrees. But scientists have yet to develop a container that can hold superhot plasma. Such extremely hot plasma has a strong tendency to expand and escape from its container. In addition, the walls of the container must be brought to extremely low temperatures to keep from melting. But if the plasma touches the walls, it becomes too cool to produce fusion. The plasma must therefore be kept away from the walls long enough for its nuclei to fuse and produce usable amounts of energy.

Fusion Devices. Most experimental fusion reactors are designed to contain superhot plasma in "magnetic bottles" twisted into various coillike shapes. The walls of the bottles are made of copper or some other metal. The walls are surrounded by a magnet. An electric current is passed through the magnet and creates a magnetic field on the inside of the walls. The magnetism pushes the plasma away from the walls and toward the center of each coil. All the fusion devices thus far developed, however, use much more energy than they create. The section *Nuclear Energy Today* discusses experimental fusion reactors in greater detail. For additional information on nuclear fusion, see HYDROGEN BOMB; SUN (How the Sun Produces Energy).

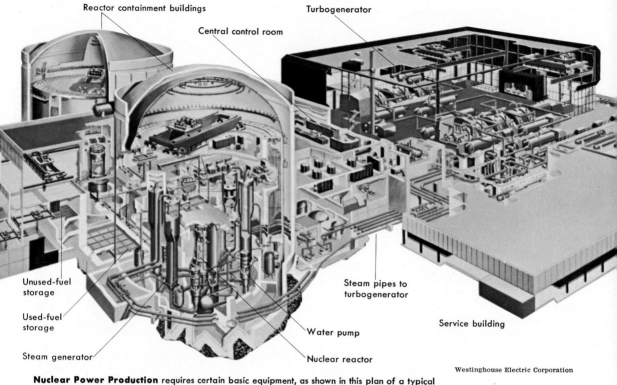

Reactor containment buildings

Central control room

Turbogenerator

Unused-fuel storage

Used-fuel storage

Steam generator

Steam pipes to turbogenerator

Water pump

Nuclear reactor

Service building

Westinghouse Electric Corporation

Nuclear Power Production requires certain basic equipment, as shown in this plan of a typical nuclear power plant. The equipment makes up two main systems. (1) The *nuclear steam supply system* includes the plant's reactor or reactors, any related steam-generating equipment, and pumps and pipes to move water and steam. Each reactor has its own *containment* building. (2) The *turbogenerator system* consists of a steam turbine and electric generator. Steam from the steam supply system spins the turbine, which drives the electric generator. The electric generator produces electricity. Other nuclear plant equipment includes special safety systems and storage for nuclear fuel.

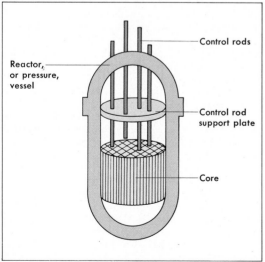

Control rods

Reactor, or pressure, vessel

Control rod support plate

Core

WORLD BOOK diagram by Arthur Grebetz

A Typical Nuclear Reactor consists mainly of a *core;* *control rods;* and a *reactor,* or *pressure, vessel.* The core holds the uranium that will be fissioned to create heat. The control rods regulate the chain reaction. The reactor vessel holds all other reactor parts and the water that will be heated to produce steam.

All large commercial nuclear power plants produce energy by fissioning U-235. But U-235 makes up less than 1 per cent of the uranium found in nature. More than 99 per cent of all natural uranium consists of U-238. The two types occur together in uranium ores, such as *carnotite* and *pitchblende*. Separating the U-235 from the U-238 in these ores is extremely difficult and costly. For this reason, the fuel used in reactors consists largely of U-238. But the fuel has enough U-235 to produce a chain reaction. Nuclear fuel requires special processing before and after it is used. The processing begins with the mining of uranium ore and ends with the disposal of fuel wastes. The entire process is known as the *nuclear fuel cycle*.

This section deals chiefly with the methods used in the U.S. nuclear power industry. But the methods described resemble those used in other countries.

Power Plant Design. Most nuclear power plants cover 200 to 300 acres (80 to 120 hectares). The majority are built near a large river or lake because nuclear plants require enormous quantities of water for cooling purposes.

A nuclear plant consists of several main buildings, one of which houses the reactor and its related parts. Another main building houses the plant's turbines and electric generators. Every plant also has facilities for storing unused and used fuel. Many plants are largely automated. Each of these plants has a central control room, which may be in a separate building or in one of the main buildings.

The reactor building, or *containment structure*, has a thick concrete floor and thick walls of steel or of concrete lined with steel. The concrete and steel guard against the escape of radiation from an accidental leak in the nuclear reactor.

Power Reactors used in U.S. nuclear plants consist of three main parts. They are (1) the reactor, or pressure, vessel; (2) the core; and (3) control rods.

The Reactor Vessel is a tanklike structure that holds the other reactor parts. It is installed near the base of the reactor building. The vessel has steel walls at least 6 inches (15 centimeters) thick. Steel pipes lead into and out of the vessel to carry water and steam.

The Core contains the nuclear fuel and so is the part of the reactor where fission occurs. The core is near the bottom of the reactor vessel. It consists mainly of the nuclear fuel held in place between an upper and a lower support plate.

Control Rods are long metal rods that contain such elements as boron or cadmium. These elements absorb free neutrons and thus help control a chain reaction. The control rods are attached to an elevatorlike mechanism just outside the reactor vessel. The mechanism inserts the rods into the core or withdraws them to slow down or speed up a chain reaction.

Reactor operations also depend on substances called *moderators* and *coolants*. A moderator is a substance, such as water or carbon, that slows down neutrons which pass through it. Reactors require a moderator because the neutrons released by fission are fast neutrons. But slow neutrons are needed to cause a chain reaction in the mixture of U-238 and U-235 that reactors use as fuel. A coolant is a substance, such as water or carbon dioxide, that conducts heat well but does not easily absorb free neutrons. The coolant carries heat from the chain reaction. It thus serves both to prevent the core from melting and to produce steam.

Almost all U.S. power reactors are *light water reactors*, which use *light* (ordinary) water as both the moderator and the coolant. The water is released into the core, where it serves as a moderator to start a chain reaction. Once the reaction has begun, the water also serves as a coolant. Many reactors in other countries use other substances as moderators and coolants. All Canadian power reactors, for example, are *heavy water reactors*. They use deuterium oxide, or heavy water, as both the moderator and the coolant.

Fuel Preparation. After uranium ore has been mined, it goes through a long milling and refining process to separate the uranium from other elements in the ore. Light water absorbs more free neutrons than do other types of moderators. The uranium used in light water reactors must therefore be *enriched*—that is, the percentage of U-235 must be increased. Free neutrons then have a better chance of striking a U-235 nucleus. In the United States, uranium that has been separated from the ore is sent to an *enrichment plant*.

Enrichment plants remove varying amounts of U-238

General Electric Company

A Reactor Vessel is carefully lowered into place at a power plant construction site. Reactor vessels are made of heavy steel. The largest weigh more than 800 short tons (720 metric tons).

General Electric Company

Refueling a Reactor. These workmen are loading a new *fuel assembly* into the core of a power plant reactor. The assembly consists of a bundle of long metal tubes filled with uranium pellets.

448g

A Nuclear Steam Supply System

The system shown in this diagram uses a *pressurized water reactor,* which heats water under high pressure. The pressure allows the water to heat past its normal boiling point without actually boiling. Heat from this water boils water in a *steam generator,* which produces steam. The water from the reactor is pumped back to the reactor for reuse. After the steam has operated the plant's turbine, it is sent to a *steam condenser,* which changes it back to water for reuse in the steam generator.

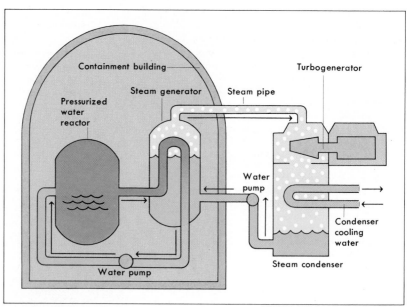

WORLD BOOK diagram by Arthur Grebetz

from the uranium, depending on the intended use of the uranium. Most light water reactors require fuel that contains no more than $97\frac{1}{2}$ per cent U-238 and $2\frac{1}{2}$ to 3 per cent U-235. Much higher amounts of U-235 are needed in nuclear weapons and in the fuel for nuclear ships. The enriched uranium used as reactor fuel is shipped to *fuel fabrication plants.*

A fuel fabrication plant changes enriched uranium into a black powder called *uranium dioxide.* The plant then shapes the uranium dioxide powder into pellets about $\frac{1}{3}$ inch (8 millimeters) in diameter and $\frac{1}{2}$ inch (13 millimeters) long. The pellets are inserted into tubes made of zirconium or stainless steel. Each tube measures about $\frac{1}{2}$ inch (13 millimeters) in diameter and 10 to 14 feet (3 to 5 meters) long. Free neutrons can pass through the walls of the tubes. But most other nuclear particles cannot.

After a tube has been filled with uranium dioxide pellets, its ends are welded shut. These *fuel rods* are then fastened together into bundles of 30 to 300 each. Each bundle weighs 300 to 1,500 pounds (140 to 680 kilograms) and forms a *fuel assembly,* or *fuel element,* for a reactor. Commercial power reactors require 50 to 150 short tons (45 to 136 metric tons) of uranium dioxide. The amount depends on the size of the reactor. A reactor therefore has a great many fuel assemblies in its core. The assemblies stand upright in the core between the two support plates.

Chain Reactions. A reactor requires exactly the right amount of fuel to keep up a chain reaction. This amount, called the *critical mass,* varies according to the design and size of the reactor. A chain reaction will die out if the amount of fuel in the reactor falls short of the critical mass. If the fuel supply exceeds the critical mass, the reactor will overheat. And if the heat becomes intense, the core may melt. Nevertheless, reactors are designed to hold more than a critical mass of fuel. But

the control rods slow down a chain reaction if it becomes too rapid.

To prepare a reactor for operation, the fuel assemblies are loaded into the core and the control rods are completely inserted. In a light water reactor, the water used as a moderator to slow down the neutrons fills the spaces between the fuel assemblies. The control rods are then slowly withdrawn, and a chain reaction begins. The farther the rods are withdrawn, the greater the intensity of the reaction because fewer neutrons are absorbed. More neutrons thus are free to cause fission. Meanwhile, the water in the core carries off the tremendous heat created by the chain reaction. To stop the reaction, the rods are again lowered all the way into the core to absorb most free neutrons.

Steam Production. The light water reactors used by almost all U.S. nuclear plants are divided into two main types. One type, the *pressurized water reactor,* produces steam outside the reactor vessel. The other type, the *boiling water reactor,* produces steam inside the vessel.

Most U.S. nuclear plants use pressurized water reactors. These reactors heat the moderator-water in the core under extremely high pressure. The pressure allows the water to heat past its normal boiling point of 212° F. (100° C) without actually boiling. The chain reaction heats the water to about 600° F. (316° C). Pipes carry this extremely hot, though not boiling, water to *heat exchangers* outside the reactor. These devices transfer heat from the pressurized water to water in a steam generator. This water then boils and so produces steam.

In a boiling water reactor, the chain reaction boils the moderator-water in the core. Steam is therefore produced inside the reactor vessel. Pipes carry the steam from the reactor to the plant's turbines.

Other Operations. In producing electricity, a nuclear plant's steam turbines and electric generators work like those in a fossil-fuel plant. The steam pro-

The Central Control Room of a large nuclear power plant contains hundreds of electronic devices. Some of the devices help regulate production operations. Others monitor the plant's many safety systems.

Westinghouse Electric Corporation

duced by a reactor spins the blades of the plant's turbines, which then drive the electric generators. Many plants have combination turbines and generators, which are called *turbogenerators*. For more information on how they work, see TURBINE; ELECTRIC GENERATOR.

After steam has passed through a plant's turbines, it is piped to a *condenser*. The condenser changes the steam back into water. A reactor can thus use the same water over and over. But a condenser requires a constant supply of fresh water to cool the steam. Most plants pump this water from a nearby river or lake. The water, which becomes warm as it passes through the condenser, is then pumped back into the river or lake. This warm waste water may cause a kind of water pollution called *thermal pollution*, which may endanger plant and animal life in some rivers and lakes where it occurs. Fossil-fuel plants also cause some thermal pollution.

To help solve the problem of thermal pollution, many nuclear plants have *cooling towers*. Hot water from the steam condensers is moved through the towers in such a way that the heat passes into the atmosphere as steam or water vapor. The cooled water is returned to the steam condenser for reuse.

Hazards and Safeguards. An ordinary power reactor cannot explode like an atomic bomb. Only a *supercritical* mass of plutonium 239 or of greatly enriched uranium 235 can cause such an explosion. A supercritical mass contains more than the amount of plutonium or uranium required to sustain a chain reaction. See ATOMIC BOMB (Chain Reactions).

The chief hazards of nuclear power production result from the great quantities of radioactive material that a reactor produces. These materials give off radiation in the form of alpha, beta, and gamma rays. The reactor vessel is surrounded by thick concrete blocks called a *shield*, which normally prevents almost all radiation from escaping.

Federal regulations limit the amount of radiation allowed from U.S. nuclear plants. Every plant has instruments that continually measure the radioactivity in and around the plant. They automatically set off an alarm if the radioactivity rises above a safe level. If necessary, the reactor is shut down. People who work with radioactive materials in nuclear plants must wear special clothing for protection.

A plant's routine safety measures greatly reduce the possibility of a serious accident. Nevertheless, every plant has emergency safety systems. Possible emergencies range from a break in a reactor water pipe to a leak of radiation from the reactor vessel. Any such emergency automatically activates a system that instantly shuts down the reactor, a process called *scramming*. Scramming is usually accomplished by the rapid insertion of the control rods into the core.

A leak or break in a reactor water pipe could have serious consequences if it results in a loss of coolant. Without sufficient coolant, a chain reaction can become so hot that it melts the reactor. A great amount of radiation might then be released into the atmosphere. This danger could occur even if scramming stopped the chain reaction. The radioactive materials in a reactor continue to give off much heat after a chain reaction stops. For this reason, all reactors have an *emergency core cooling system*, which automatically floods a reactor with water in case of a loss of coolant.

Wastes and Waste Disposal. The fissioning of U-235 produces more free neutrons than are needed to continue a chain reaction. Some of them combine with U-238 nuclei, which far outnumber U-235 nuclei in the reactor fuel. When U-238 absorbs neutrons, it quickly decays and forms U-239. The U-239 then decays into neptunium 239 (Np-239), which decays into plutonium 239 (Pu-239). This same process forms Pu-239 in a breeder reactor. Slow neutrons can fission Pu-239, as well as U-235. Some of the newly formed Pu-239 is thus fissioned during the fissioning of U-235. The rest of the Pu-239 remains in the fuel assemblies.

The fissioning of U-235 also produces many other radioactive isotopes, such as strontium 90, cesium 137, and barium 140. Like Pu-239, they remain in the fuel assemblies after fission. Some of these isotopes, especially Pu-239, are extremely poisonous and have long half-lives. Safe disposal of these wastes is one of the problems involved in nuclear power production.

Most nuclear plants need to replace their fuel assemblies only about once a year. The radioactive wastes generate heat, and so used fuel assemblies must be cooled after removal from a reactor. Nuclear plants cool the assemblies by storing them underwater in specially designed *storage pools*.

In the United States, the federal government has established guidelines for disposing of nuclear wastes. The guidelines propose that nuclear plants store their used fuel assemblies for only a few months or until the short-lived radioactivity has died away. The plants should then ship the assemblies to a commercial *reprocessing plant* for removal of unused U-235 and other useful elements. The reprocessing plant would also remove the radioactive wastes and store them temporarily in underground tanks. But Pu-239 and other long-lived wastes require safe, permanent storage for thousands of years. The federal guidelines therefore propose that reprocessing plants ship such *high-level* wastes to government facilities for permanent storage.

Scientists have proposed several methods for permanently storing high-level wastes. But the federal government has not yet decided which method to adopt. The government also has yet to decide whether to allow the *recycling* of plutonium from used fuel assemblies for use as reactor fuel. Uncertainty about the government's decision in these matters has delayed the building of commercial reprocessing plants. One such plant opened in West Valley, N.Y., in 1966, but it has been shut down for extensive remodeling since 1972. The plant is to reopen by the late 1970's, at which time several new plants are also scheduled to begin operations. Meanwhile, nuclear power plants store their used fuel assemblies in the storage pools on the plant grounds. The subsection *The Industry and the Environment* discusses the waste disposal problem in more detail.

NUCLEAR ENERGY / *The Nuclear Energy Industry*

In every country that has a nuclear energy industry, the government plays a role in the industry. But the nature and extent of the government's role vary greatly among countries. This section deals mainly with the U.S. and Canadian nuclear energy industries and with the role of government in these industries.

Organization of the Industry. Private utility companies own most U.S. nuclear power plants. The rest are publicly owned. Private companies also manufacture reactors, mine uranium, and handle most other aspects of nuclear power production in the United States. All uranium enrichment is done at three government-owned plants. But in the mid-1970's, the government began considering a plan to allow private industry to enter this field. No commercial reprocessing plants now operate in the United States. But several private plants are scheduled to open by the late 1970's.

Canada's nuclear power plants are all publicly owned. Atomic Energy of Canada Limited (AECL), a government corporation, has overall responsibility for the country's nuclear research and development program. AECL also designs the CANDU (*CAN*ada *Deu*terium oxide-*U*ranium) heavy water reactors used by all Canadian nuclear plants. Private companies make the various reactor parts and mine and process the country's uranium. Canada has no uranium enrichment plants because CANDU reactors operate with unenriched uranium fuel.

The Industry and the Economy. The main economic advantage of nuclear power plants is that they spend less money for fuel and so cost less to operate than fossil-fuel plants do. But nuclear plants cost considerably more to build than do fossil-fuel plants.

Under normal economic conditions, a nuclear plant's savings in fuel eventually make up for its higher construction expenses. At first, these expenses add to the cost of producing electricity. But after some years, a plant will have paid off its construction costs. It can then produce electricity more cheaply than a fossil-fuel plant can. But two main problems—sharply higher costs and equipment failures—have somewhat lessened this long-run economic advantage of nuclear plants.

The cost of building a nuclear plant has more than doubled since the late 1960's. The expense of building fossil-fuel plants, on the other hand, has not risen so sharply. Many nuclear plants in the United States have had to shut down for months at a time because of equipment failures. Such losses of operating time further add to the cost of producing electricity. But nuclear plants still cost less to operate than do fossil-fuel plants. To keep this economic advantage, nuclear plants are working to increase their operating efficiency.

The Industry and the Environment. A nuclear plant releases small amounts of radioactive gas into the air. In addition, the cooling water used in pressurized water plants picks up a small amount of *tritium* (radioactive hydrogen) in the steam condenser. The tritium remains in this water when it is returned to a river or lake. But these small amounts of radiation released into the environment are not believed to be harmful. Thermal pollution remains a problem at some nuclear plants. But cooling towers help correct this problem.

Unlike fossil-fuel plants, nuclear plants do not release solid or chemical pollutants into the atmosphere. However, many people believe that nuclear plants threaten the environment in various other ways. For example, these critics feel that as the number of nuclear plants grows, the possibility of a serious accident also increases. Such an accident could release much radioactivity and so endanger people in surrounding areas.

The subsection *Hazards and Safeguards* earlier in this article discusses the main methods of guarding against accidents.

Critics of nuclear power also fear another danger to the environment. As power production increases, the creation of high-level radioactive wastes also increases. These wastes remain extremely radioactive for about 600 years because of the presence of the isotopes strontium 90 and cesium 137. After about 600 years, the strontium and cesium will have decayed into stable isotopes and no longer present a danger. Yet the wastes will remain considerably radioactive and hazardous for thousands of years because they still contain plutonium and other artificially created heavy elements. Even in small amounts, plutonium can cause cancer or *genetic* (reproductive) damage in human beings. Larger amounts can cause radiation sickness and death (see RADIATION SICKNESS).

In the United States, most high-level wastes from nuclear plants are now stored temporarily on the plant grounds. The federal government plans to move these wastes eventually to a permanent storage place, but it has not yet decided what storage method to use. Most scientists recommend storing the wastes in underground salt deposits. However, any such storage place might have to be guarded for thousands of years to prevent future generations from digging into it and releasing the radioactivity.

Government Regulation. The Nuclear Regulatory Commission (NRC), an agency of the federal government, regulates nuclear power production in the United States. One of the NRC's main duties is to ensure that nuclear power plants operate safely. To carry out this responsibility, the NRC makes and enforces a variety of safety standards. In addition, every nuclear reactor and power plant must be inspected and licensed by the NRC before it may begin operations. The NRC also supervises the manufacture and distribution of nuclear fuels, and it controls the disposal of radioactive wastes.

The Atomic Energy Control Board, a Canadian government agency, regulates Canada's nuclear energy industry. The board's duties resemble those of the NRC.

Careers in Nuclear Energy cover a wide range of occupations and require widely varying amounts of training. A high percentage of the jobs require a college degree or extensive technical education. Many of these jobs are in large research laboratories, which work to improve nuclear processes and to lessen their hazards. Other careers that call for a high level of training are in such areas as uranium mining and processing, reactor manufacturing and inspection, power plant operation, and government regulation.

Many colleges and universities offer undergraduate and graduate degrees in such highly specialized fields as nuclear engineering, nuclear physics, and nuclear technology. People with degrees in these fields work throughout the industry. The industry also employs many workers with college degrees in various branches of engineering and in such fields as biology, chemistry, geology, and medicine. Many vocational and technical schools and some high schools prepare students for various specialized jobs in the industry.

Idaho National Engineering Laboratory

Samples of River Water taken near a nuclear plant are tested for radioactivity, as are samples of the soil and air. Nuclear plants release some radioactive gas into the environment. But the amounts are normally too small to be considered harmful.

Leading Nuclear Power Producing Countries

Kilowatt-hours of nuclear power produced in 1974

United States	171,000,000,000 kwh*
Great Britain	33,617,000,000 kwh
France	13,932,000,000 kwh
Canada	13,864,000,000 kwh
West Germany	12,136,000,000 kwh
Japan	10,000,000,000 kwh†
Russia	8,000,000,000 kwh†
Spain	6,700,000,000 kwh†
Switzerland	6,634,000,000 kwh
Italy	3,410,000,000 kwh

*1975 figure.
†Estimate.
Sources: Federal Power Commission; *World Energy Supplies, 1950-1974,* UN, 1976.

In 1972, scientists discovered that a natural chain reaction had occurred nearly 2 billion years ago in a uranium deposit in west-central Africa. Two billion years ago, radioactive decay had not progressed so far as it has today. The uranium ore therefore contained enough U-235 to start a chain reaction. An accumulation of ground water acted as a moderator to begin the reaction. As heat from the chain reaction changed the water into steam, less and less water was available to serve as a moderator and the reaction died out.

Except for such rare natural occurrences, nuclear energy was not released on a large scale on the earth until 1942. That year, scientists produced the first man-made nuclear chain reaction. Scientific discoveries within the last 100 years made the large-scale release of nuclear energy possible.

Early Developments

Before the late 1800's, scientists did not suspect that atoms contain energy. Then in 1896, the French physicist Antoine Henri Becquerel found that uranium constantly gives off energy in the form of invisible rays. He thus became the discoverer of natural radioactivity. Other scientists soon began experiments to learn more about this mysterious form of energy.

The Beginning of Nuclear Physics. Between 1899 and 1903, the great British physicist Ernest Rutherford found that some radioactive rays consist of high-energy particles. He discovered two kinds of radioactive particles, which he named *alpha* and *beta* particles. Experiments with these particles then led Rutherford to discover the atom's nucleus. This achievement, which Rutherford announced in 1911, marked the beginning of a new science—nuclear physics.

About 1914, scientists began trying to split light nuclei with alpha particles from naturally radioactive materials. Light nuclei do not repel positively charged particles, such as alpha particles, as strongly as heavy nuclei do. In 1919, Rutherford changed nitrogen into oxygen by this method. He thus achieved the first man-

made transmutation of one element into another. Oxygen weighs more than nitrogen. The reaction therefore consumed more energy, in the form of the alpha particle, than it produced. Although Rutherford did not succeed in producing fission, he showed that science can change the structure of a nucleus.

The First Man-Made Fission Reaction. To produce fission, scientists needed a particle that heavy nuclei would not repel. In 1932, the British physicist James Chadwick discovered such a particle—the neutron. In 1938, two German chemists, Otto Hahn and Fritz Strassmann, reported they had produced the element barium by bombarding uranium with neutrons.

At first, scientists could not explain how uranium had produced barium, which is much lighter than uranium. All previous transmutations had resulted in an element about as heavy as the original one. Then in 1939, the Austrian physicist Lise Meitner and her nephew Otto Frisch showed that Hahn and Strassmann had in fact produced the first known man-made fission reaction. The reaction had split a uranium nucleus into two nearly equal fragments, one of which consisted of a barium nucleus. Two neutrons were also emitted. The other fragment consisted of a nucleus of krypton, a somewhat lighter element than barium. These two nuclei, together with the emitted neutrons, weigh less than a uranium nucleus and a neutron. The reaction had therefore produced more energy than it consumed.

Scientists soon realized that if uranium produced a chain reaction, it would release tremendous energy. To find how much energy a chain reaction would release, scientists used a formula worked out by the great German-born scientist Albert Einstein in 1905. The formula, $E = mc^2$, illustrated Einstein's theory that matter and energy are equal. The formula states that the *energy* (E) in a substance equals the *mass* (m) of that substance multiplied by the *speed of light squared* (c^2). Light travels 186,282 miles (299,792 kilometers) per second. The speed of light *squared* is obtained by multiplying the speed of light by itself. Using this formula,

---

IMPORTANT DATES IN NUCLEAR ENERGY DEVELOPMENT

1896 Antoine Henri Becquerel, a French physicist, discovered natural radioactivity.

1905 The great German-born scientist Albert Einstein published his theory that matter and energy are equal.

1911 The British physicist Ernest Rutherford announced his discovery of the nucleus of the atom.

1932 James Chadwick, a British physicist, discovered the neutron.

1938 The German chemists Otto Hahn and Fritz Strassmann produced the elements barium and krypton by bombarding uranium with neutrons.

1939 The Austrian physicists Lise Meitner and Otto Frisch showed that Hahn and Strassmann had produced the first known man-made fission reaction.

1942 A group of scientists headed by the Italian-born physicist Enrico Fermi produced the world's first man-made chain reaction at the University of Chicago. The achievement made possible the development of the atomic bomb.

1945 The United States exploded the first atomic bomb near Alamogordo, N. Mex.

1946 Congress established the Atomic Energy Commission (AEC) to control U.S. nuclear energy development.

1952 The United States exploded the first hydrogen bomb at Eniwetok, a small island in the Pacific Ocean, and so produced the world's first large-scale fusion reaction.

1954 Congress allowed private industry to take over most aspects of U.S. nuclear power development.

1956 The first full-scale nuclear power plant began operations at Calder Hall in England.

1957 The United Nations (UN) established the International Atomic Energy Agency to promote the peaceful uses of nuclear energy. The first full-scale U.S. nuclear power plant opened in Shippingport, Pa.

1962 Canada's first full-scale nuclear power plant began to produce electricity in Rolphton, Ont.

1974 Congress divided the functions of the AEC between two newly formed agencies—the Energy Research and Development Administration (ERDA) and the Nuclear Regulatory Commission (NRC).

scientists determined that the fissioning of 1 pound (0.45 kilogram) of uranium would release as much energy as 8,000 short tons (7,300 metric tons) of TNT. Uranium could therefore be used to make an unbelievably powerful bomb.

The Beginning of the Nuclear Age

The Development of Nuclear Weapons. World War II broke out in Europe in September, 1939. The month before, Einstein had written to U.S. President Franklin D. Roosevelt urging him to commit the United States to developing an atomic bomb. Einstein had fled to the United States from Germany to escape Nazi persecution. He warned Roosevelt that German scientists might already be working on a nuclear bomb.

Roosevelt acted on Einstein's urging, and early in 1940 scientists received the first funds for uranium research in the United States. They sought to discover a method of preparing enough plutonium or greatly enriched uranium for a bomb. The United States entered World War II in 1941. The government then ordered an all-out effort to perfect an atomic bomb and established the top-secret Manhattan Project to achieve this goal (see MANHATTAN PROJECT).

A group of scientists at the University of Chicago had charge of producing plutonium for the Manhattan Project. The group included such noted physicists as Enrico Fermi, Leo Szilard, and Eugene Wigner, all of whom had been born in Europe and had settled in the United States. Fermi headed the group. Under the scientists' direction, workmen built an atomic *pile*, or reactor, beneath the stands of the university athletic field. The pile consisted of 50 short tons (45 metric tons) of natural uranium embedded in 500 short tons (450 metric tons) of graphite. The graphite served as a moderator. The pile was designed to start a chain reaction in the uranium, which would then produce plutonium by radioactive decay. Cadmium rods controlled the reaction. On Dec. 2, 1942, this primitive reactor produced the first man-made chain reaction.

The success of the University of Chicago project led the U.S. government to build a plutonium-producing plant in Hanford, Wash. The government also built a uranium enrichment plant in Oak Ridge, Tenn. Plutonium and greatly enriched uranium from these plants were used in the atomic bombs dropped on Japan in August, 1945. The bombs helped end the war quickly.

After World War II, scientists began work on developing a hydrogen bomb. The United States exploded the first hydrogen bomb in 1952 and so achieved the world's first large-scale thermonuclear reaction. Russia tested its first atomic bomb in 1949 and its first full-scale hydrogen bomb in 1953. China, France, Great Britain, and India have also exploded nuclear weapons. For more information on the development of nuclear weapons, see ATOMIC BOMB; HYDROGEN BOMB.

The First Peaceful Uses. While research on nuclear weapons continued, various countries also began experimenting with nuclear reactors. The United States and Russia had built uranium enrichment plants during the war. Both countries therefore started to develop light water reactors, which require enriched uranium

fuel. Canada, France, and Great Britain, on the other hand, began work on reactors moderated by graphite or heavy water. These reactors cost more to build than light water reactors, but they use unenriched uranium.

The U.S. Congress set up the Atomic Energy Commission (AEC) in 1946 to direct and control all aspects of nuclear energy development in the United States. In 1954, Congress allowed private industry to take over most aspects of commercial nuclear power development. But the AEC became responsible for regulating the nuclear energy industry. It also kept control in such areas as uranium enrichment and waste disposal.

The United States made the world's first full-scale use of controlled nuclear energy in 1954. That year, the U.S. Navy launched the first nuclear-powered vessel, the submarine *Nautilus*. The first full-scale nuclear power plant began operations in 1956 at Calder Hall in northwestern England. The next year, the first large-scale nuclear plant in the United States opened in Shippingport, Pa. It supplies electricity to the Pittsburgh area. Canada opened its first full-scale plant in 1962 in Rolphton, Ont.

The successful start of the nuclear power industry convinced world leaders of the need for international cooperation in the field. In 1957, the United Nations (UN) established the International Atomic Energy Agency to promote the peaceful uses of nuclear energy (see INTERNATIONAL ATOMIC ENERGY AGENCY; UNITED NATIONS [Peaceful Uses of Nuclear Energy]). Also in 1957, Belgium, France, Italy, Luxembourg, The Netherlands, and West Germany formed the European Atomic Energy Community (Euratom). The organization encourages nuclear power development among its member countries. Denmark, Great Britain, and Ireland joined Euratom in 1973.

Nuclear Energy Today

The Spread of Nuclear Capability. During the 1960's and early 1970's, a number of countries acquired reactors and used them to start nuclear power development. Progress was also made during this period toward limiting nuclear weapons tests and stopping the spread of nuclear weapons. In 1970, for example, a nuclear *nonproliferation treaty* went into effect. The treaty prohibits the United States, Russia, and the other nuclear powers that signed and ratified the document from giving nuclear weapons to nations that do not already have them. The treaty also prohibits nations without nuclear weapons from acquiring them.

But the nonproliferation treaty does not prohibit nations from selling or buying nuclear reactors. A reactor can be used not only for peaceful purposes but also to produce plutonium for nuclear weapons. India used a research reactor for this purpose and in 1974 exploded its first atomic bomb. Canada had supplied the reactor to India with the understanding it would be used for peaceful purposes only. Canada has signed the nonproliferation treaty, but India has not. Critics of India's action question the wisdom of supplying reactors to countries that do not already have them.

Meanwhile, the United States had been greatly increasing its nuclear power capacity. But opposition to

An Experimental Device called a *tokamak* holds promise for the development of fusion power. Ideally, a fusion reactor would use *heavy hydrogen* as its basic fuel. Heavy hydrogen is obtained from ordinary water, and so a successful fusion reactor could supply almost unlimited power.

Plasma Physics Laboratory, Princeton University

nuclear power development also increased in the United States during the late 1960's and early 1970's. Critics began to question nearly every aspect of nuclear power production, from the cost of uranium enrichment to the problems of waste disposal.

Many critics of the U.S. nuclear program charged that the government overlooked various safety risks at nuclear plants to promote nuclear power development. Partly as a result of such criticism, Congress disbanded the Atomic Energy Commission (AEC) in 1974 and divided its functions between two newly formed agencies. The Energy Research and Development Administration (ERDA) took over the AEC's development programs. The Nuclear Regulatory Commission (NRC) took over its regulatory duties. The NRC, it was believed, could better regulate the industry if it was not also responsible for the industry's growth and development. See Energy Research and Development Administration; Nuclear Regulatory Commission.

Present-Day Research. Increased nuclear power production has caused a variety of problems. One of the most serious is the growing shortage of U-235. In the mid-1970's, the U.S. government began to consider a plan to recycle waste plutonium for use as reactor fuel in place of U-235. But even if this plan is approved, it will relieve the nuclear fuel shortage only slightly. Large-scale relief calls for the development of a fusion reactor or commercial breeder reactor.

Experimental Fusion Devices. Ideally, a fusion reactor would use a superhot plasma of heavy hydrogen as its fuel. Heavy hydrogen could supply almost unlimited amounts of power because it is obtained from ordinary water. But few experts believe that a workable fusion reactor can be perfected in the 1900's, and some believe it may never be perfected.

The most successful fusion reactor, called a *tokamak,*

was originally designed by Russian scientists. Tokamak means *strong current* in Russian. Like other experimental fusion reactors, a tokamak uses a magnetic field to push superhot plasma away from its containing walls. But tokamaks also pass a strong current through the plasma. The current acts with the magnetic field to help confine the plasma.

Scientists in the United States and other countries have developed their own versions of the tokamak. But no tokamak has yet produced usable amounts of energy. Plasma must be heated to at least 180,000,000° F. (100,000,000° C) to produce a controlled thermonuclear reaction. But plasmas are extremely difficult to contain at such high temperatures.

Another experimental method to achieve fusion uses beams of *laser light* to compress and heat tiny pellets of frozen deuterium and tritium. This process creates miniature thermonuclear explosions that release energy before they reach the containing walls. But all experiments with this method have also failed to produce usable amounts of energy. See Laser.

Experimental Breeder Reactors. The most important type of experimental breeder uses the plentiful uranium isotope U-238 as its basic fuel. The reactor changes the U-238 into the man-made isotope plutonium 239 (Pu-239) by radioactive decay. Like U-235, Pu-239 can create a chain reaction and so can be used for energy production. Another type of experimental breeder uses the natural element thorium as its basic fuel. The reactor changes the thorium into the man-made isotope U-233, which can also produce a chain reaction.

France, Great Britain, Russia, and the United States have built successful experimental breeders. The French breeder, called the Phénix, is the most successful. It regularly produces 250,000 kilowatts of electricity. But no country yet has a breeder suitable for large-scale commercial use. Scientists expect the United States will have commercial breeders in operation in the 1990's. The breeder development program will cost more than $10\frac{1}{2}$ billion. The federal government will pay most of the cost. Utility companies will pay the rest.

The use of commercial breeders and the plan for recycling plutonium have drawn strong opposition in the United States. Critics point out that recycling plants and commercial breeders would create stockpiles of plutonium that could not easily be guarded against theft or sabotage. Political terrorists, for example, might steal enough plutonium to build an atomic bomb.

The Future of Nuclear Energy. Although the nuclear energy industry faces many problems, many experts believe that the problems will gradually be solved. Some countries have announced dramatic expansions of their nuclear power facilities. For example, Canada expects to obtain 25 per cent of its electricity from nuclear plants by 1990. In the United States, nuclear energy may supply nearly 30 per cent of the country's electricity by 1985. Meanwhile, the NRC is studying plans for the construction of floating nuclear plants in U.S. coastal waters. Another plan under consideration by the NRC calls for the building of large "nuclear parks" well away from built-up areas. Each park would have all the facilities needed to supply nuclear power for an entire region.   ALVIN M. WEINBERG

NUCLEAR ENERGY/Study Aids

Related Articles in WORLD BOOK include:

BIOGRAPHIES

OTHER RELATED ARTICLES

Outline

Questions

What two advantages do nuclear power plants have over fossil-fuel plants?

When did the first full-scale nuclear power plant begin operations? Where?

What is a chain reaction?

What is *U-235?* Why are scientists seeking a replacement for it?

How does a nuclear reactor produce fission?

What government agency regulates nuclear power production in the United States?

What part did Ernest Rutherford play in the development of nuclear energy?

How do U.S. nuclear power plants differ in their method of producing steam?

What is *radioactive decay? Nuclear radiation?*

What kinds of wastes are formed in power reactors? Why do they present a problem?

Reading and Study Guide

See *Nuclear Energy* in the RESEARCH GUIDE/INDEX, Volume 22, for a *Reading and Study Guide.*

NUCLEAR ENGINEERING. See ENGINEERING (table).

NUCLEAR FISSION. See FISSION; NUCLEAR ENERGY.

NUCLEAR NONPROLIFERATION TREATY. See UNITED NATIONS (Arms Control).

NUCLEAR PHYSICS is a branch of physics that deals with the nuclei of atoms. It involves a systematic study of the properties of the atomic nucleus. Such research has led to many important advances in science, medicine, and technology.

The atomic nucleus consists of protons and neutrons. These particles make up about 99.9 per cent of the mass of all matter. The neutrons and protons in a nucleus are packed together so tightly that the nucleus is extremely dense. The nucleus is held together chiefly by a powerful force called the *strong force.* This force causes the neutrons and protons in the nucleus to interact and bind together. However, it is effective only at extremely short distances—about 4 trillionths of an inch (10 trillionths of a centimeter). A less powerful force, called the *weak force,* also acts on the nuclear particles and helps bind them together.

The nuclei of most elements that occur in nature are stable, and so they do not break down easily. But the nuclei of some elements, such as radium and uranium, are unstable, as are many of those produced artificially in laboratories. Unstable nuclei are radioactive. They break apart spontaneously and release energy as radiations called *alpha, beta,* and *gamma rays.*

Nuclear physicists study the properties of the atomic nucleus to better understand its structure and the forces that hold it together. They also seek to learn more about the symmetries exhibited by nuclei and the rotations, vibrations, and other patterns of motion that occur within them.

Research in nuclear physics is based on high-precision experiments. Nuclear physicists use devices called *particle accelerators* to produce nuclear reactions, which involve changes in the structure of a nucleus. The development of increasingly more powerful accelerators and complex detection techniques has enabled researchers to conduct promising new studies. In the late 1970's, scientists began to explore reactions between nuclei and particles called *pi-mesons* and to investigate the interactions of fast heavy uranium nuclei.

The study of nuclear physics has become increasingly important. An understanding of the nuclear reactions called *fission* and *fusion* has enabled scientists to release the tremendous energy of the nucleus for practical use (see NUCLEAR ENERGY). The discovery of radioactive isotopes is another major contribution. The isotopes are used in industry, in medical research, and in diagnosing and treating diseases. Research into the nucleus has also led to the discovery of new physical phenomena and new laws of nature. Many scientific fields, particularly astrophysics, biochemistry, and solid-state physics, use such findings.   JOHN P. SCHIFFER

See also ATOM; PARTICLE PHYSICS.

NUCLEAR REACTOR is a device that produces a vast amount of energy from a small amount of fuel. It is sometimes called an *atomic reactor* or an *atomic pile*. A nuclear reactor generates energy mainly in the form of heat by means of a process known as *nuclear fission*. Nuclear fission is the splitting of the nuclei of atoms of uranium or plutonium.

An atomic bomb gets its destructive power from uncontrolled fission. A nuclear reactor, however, keeps fission under control. As a result, the energy it produces can be used for the generation of electricity and for other peaceful purposes. Reactors also are used to make various substances radioactive. These radioactive materials, called *radioisotopes*, have important uses in agriculture, industry, and medicine.

Growing concern about a possible future shortage of reactor fuel has encouraged the development of *breeder reactors*. These special reactors can produce more fuel than they use to produce energy. The surplus fuel can be utilized by other nuclear reactors.

Parts of a Nuclear Reactor

Nuclear reactors vary in design and size. But most of them have five basic parts: (1) the core, (2) the moderator, (3) the control rods, (4) the coolant, and (5) the pressure vessel. They also have a biological shield and a safety system to protect reactor operators and technicians.

The Core is the central part of a reactor and consists of the nuclear fuel. The fission process occurs in the core.

The nuclear fuel used by most reactors is a mixture of several *isotopes* (forms) of uranium. Only one of these isotopes, U-235, actually undergoes fission. But a breeder reactor can convert one of the other more abundant isotopes, U-238, to fissionable plutonium, Pu-239.

In a reactor that uses uranium fuel, fission occurs when the nucleus of a U-235 atom captures a neutron, a heavy uncharged atomic particle. The U-235 nucleus then splits into two smaller nuclei called *fission fragments*, releasing energy and several neutrons. These neutrons strike other atoms and cause them to break apart. These atoms, in turn, give off additional neutrons, which split still more atoms. This self-sustaining series of fissions in the nuclear fuel is called a *chain reaction*. Such a process can cause trillions of atoms to fission

within a fraction of a second—and produce an enormous amount of energy.

The Moderator is a material used in many reactors to increase the probability of fission and thus promote a chain reaction. Most moderators consist of graphite, water, or *heavy water*, a compound composed of oxygen and deuterium. Such a substance slows down the neutrons released by U-235 atoms during fission. By doing so, the moderator enables other U-235 atoms to capture the neutrons more readily and to split in turn. If a moderator did not reduce the speed of the neutrons, many of them would be absorbed by U-238 atoms, which do not fission.

The Control Rods regulate the rate of a chain reaction. They are made of boron, cadmium, or some other element that can absorb neutrons without being changed by them.

After loading the core with fuel, the operator of the reactor partially withdraws the control rods so that they absorb a relatively small number of neutrons. This ac-

Parts of a Nuclear Reactor

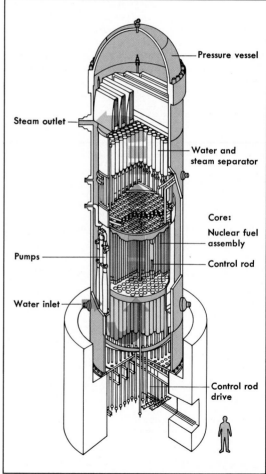

Pressure vessel

Steam outlet

Water and steam separator

Core:
Nuclear fuel assembly

Pumps

Control rod

Water inlet

Control rod drive

General Electric (WORLD BOOK diagram)

The Core is the heart of a nuclear reactor. Nuclear fuel in the core produces heat. Water or some other cooling material carries the heat to the machinery run by the reactor. A pressure vessel encloses the core and holds the cooling material.

tion allows a chain reaction to become self-sustaining. The operator then inserts the rods partway into the core to absorb enough neutrons to slow the reaction and prevent an explosion. If the operator wishes to increase the power level of the reactor, the control rods can be partly withdrawn to free more neutrons and speed up the reaction.

The Coolant carries the intense heat produced by fission out of a reactor. It makes the heat available to other systems of a nuclear power plant for the generation of electricity. At the same time, the coolant controls the temperature of the reactor core and prevents it from overheating. Various substances, including gases, liquids, and liquid metals, can be used as a coolant.

Reactors can be classified according to their coolant and the way they use it. For example, a *gas-cooled reactor* uses carbon dioxide or helium to transport heat to a steam generator outside the core. The generator makes steam for a turbine that drives an electric generator.

Two other types of reactors use water as the coolant. In a *boiling-water reactor*, the heat of the core causes the water to boil and turn to steam. The steam then flows from the reactor to a turbine connected to an electric generator. In a *pressurized-water reactor*, the water absorbs heat but does not boil because it is kept under high pressure. The hot water is transferred from the reactor to a separate boiler that produces steam for a turbine.

Some breeder reactors use liquid sodium as the coolant. In a *liquid-metal-cooled fast breeder*, for example, the sodium carries heat from the core to a system of *heat exchangers*. This system uses the heat to produce steam that drives a turbine.

The Pressure Vessel holds the core of most reactors. It also contains the circulation channels for the reactor's coolant. The walls of the vessel are designed to withstand the high pressure generated by a chain reaction. In most cases, the vessel walls are lined with thick steel slabs to reduce the flow of radiation from the core. Nuclear fission releases large amounts of penetrating neutrons and *gamma rays* (electromagnetic rays of extremely high energy). Both neutrons and gamma rays can harm people.

The Biological Shield consists of thick concrete blocks that surround the pressure vessel. The shield protects technicians from radiation exposure. Concrete absorbs the gamma rays and neutrons that escape from the vessel. Special instruments monitor the radiation level around the shield continuously to make sure no leaks occur.

The Safety System includes various devices designed to prevent serious reactor accidents. One such device is a set of *safety rods* that permits the rapid shutdown of a reactor. These rods, which function like control rods, are automatically inserted into the reactor core when neutron-counting instruments detect an abnormal increase in the rate of fission. A similar device, used for emergency shutdowns, consists of tiny balls of *samarium oxide*, a compound of samarium and oxygen. When these balls are dropped into the core, they quickly absorb enough neutrons to stop a chain reaction.

Most reactors also have an *emergency core-cooling system*. This emergency system keeps the core from overheating if its coolant is lost. For example, if a coolant pipe of a pressurized-water reactor ruptured, the emergency system would flood the core with water. The water would reduce the temperature of the core and prevent the nuclear fuel from melting.

If the fuel melted, large amounts of dangerous radioactive materials would be released from the reactor. To prevent the escape of radioactivity to the surrounding area, most power-reactor installations are enclosed in a leak-proof *containment structure*. Filters and similar devices trap and clear away most of the radioactive particles in this structure. Special airtight compartments called *air locks* enable technicians to flee from the structure without affecting the containment system.

How a Reactor Works

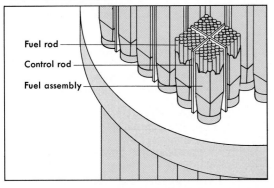

Fuel rod
Control rod
Fuel assembly

Fuel Assemblies in the reactor's core hold individual fuel rods that contain atoms of nuclear fuel. As the fuel atoms split, they produce energy and release neutrons. Other fuel atoms split when struck by the neutrons, and thus the nuclear reaction continues.

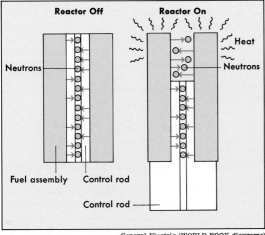

Reactor Off   Reactor On

Heat

Neutrons   Neutrons

Fuel assembly   Control rod

Control rod

General Electric (WORLD BOOK diagrams)

Control Rods limit the number of fuel atoms that can split. The rods are made of a material that absorbs neutrons. When the rods are deep in the core, they absorb so many neutrons that few atoms can split. To turn on the reactor, some rods are pulled out.

Reactors and the Environment

Nuclear reactors produce electric power without burning such fuels as coal or oil. They thus help conserve the world's supply of these fuels. Reactors also do not

give off smoke or gases that pollute the air. But they do create some new problems.

Nuclear power plants generate more excess heat than do power plants that burn coal or oil. Therefore, they need more water to cool their systems and, in turn, dump more hot waste water into lakes and streams. This addition of hot water, called *thermal pollution*, can harm animals and plants that live at lower temperatures. To help solve this problem, many nuclear power plants have installed *cooling towers* that use air to cool the hot water they produce.

Another problem involves the disposal of *fission products*, the radioactive wastes produced by reactors. These wastes remain highly radioactive for thousands of years and can cause serious radiation damage to all living things. Scientists have not found a permanent method of disposal. During the 1960's and 1970's, most radioactive waste from reactors in the United States was stored in shielded tanks buried in the earth.

Many people have become concerned about the possibility of a major reactor accident. Such a mishap could release large amounts of radioactive materials into the environment. This radioactive pollution would cause radiation sickness, a higher rate of cancer, and even death in nearby communities. But many experts point out that a disaster of this kind could occur only if a reactor's entire safety system failed. These experts declare that such a possibility is unlikely—especially because of continual efforts to improve the various kinds of safety features.

History

The first nuclear chain reaction was produced on Dec. 2, 1942, at the University of Chicago. The Italian physicist Enrico Fermi directed the work. His reactor consisted of a large pile of graphite blocks and chunks of uranium metal. After Fermi's success, other physicists in the United States developed larger and more complex reactors for various purposes.

The first experimental breeder reactor was built in 1951 by scientists at the National Reactor Testing Station, near Idaho Falls, Ida. In 1954, the U.S. Navy launched the submarine *Nautilus*, the first ship powered by energy from a nuclear reactor. In 1955, electricity for public use was first generated from a reactor at the National Reactor Testing Station. But it was done so only on a very limited basis.

A team of British engineers and scientists built the world's first large-scale nuclear power plant. This plant, at Calder Hall on the west coast of England, began to produce electricity in 1956. The first large nuclear power station in the United States was completed in 1957 in Shippingport, Pa., near Pittsburgh. By the mid-1970's, the United States had more than 50 huge plants that were using nuclear energy to generate electric power.

Scientists of several countries, including France, Russia, and the United States, are working to develop efficient breeder reactors for wide-scale commercial use. By the early 1990's, U.S. scientists expect to build power plants equipped with plutonium-breeding reactors.   FRANCIS T. COLE

See also ENERGY SUPPLY (picture: Sources of Energy); FERMI, ENRICO; ISOTOPE; NUCLEAR ENERGY; PLUTONIUM; URANIUM.

NUCLEAR REGULATORY COMMISSION is an independent agency of the United States government. The commission, also called the NRC, licenses and regulates the operation of civilian nuclear facilities, primarily nuclear power plants. The design and operation of all commercial nuclear reactors are subject to approval by the agency. The commission may fine or close down any operation that it believes could endanger public health and safety. The agency also supervises the handling, storage, and transportation of nuclear materials for civilian use.

The NRC and the Energy Research and Development Administration (ERDA) share responsibilities formerly handled by the Atomic Energy Commission (AEC). The Energy Reorganization Act of 1974 abolished the AEC and established the NRC and ERDA. The NRC began operations in 1975.

Critically reviewed by the NUCLEAR REGULATORY COMMISSION

NUCLEAR ROCKET. See ROCKET (Nuclear Rockets).

NUCLEAR SUBMARINE. See SUBMARINE (The Power Plant; Nuclear Submarines; pictures).

NUCLEAR WEAPON. See ATOMIC BOMB; HYDROGEN BOMB.

NUCLEIC ACID is a complex compound found in all living cells. Two types of nucleic acids are *deoxyribonucleic acid* (DNA) and *ribonucleic acid* (RNA). DNA is usually found only in the nucleus of a cell. But RNA may be found throughout the cell. Certain viruses, such as the plant viruses and poliomyelitis virus, contain only RNA. Other viruses contain only DNA.

DNA plays a vital part in heredity. It is the chief

material in *chromosomes*, the cell bodies that control the heredity of an animal or a plant. When a cell divides, the chromosomes in its nucleus must be duplicated exactly in the daughter cells. The DNA in the chromosomes furnishes the daughter cells with a complete set of "instructions" for the cells' own development and the development of their descendants for generations.

DNA contains *phosphate*, a sugar called *deoxyribose*, and compounds called *bases*. These are arranged in units of phosphate-sugar-base—phosphate-sugar-base, repeated thousands of times to form long, coiled chains. This fundamental chemical structure is common to all DNA. However, there are four different bases in DNA—*adenine*, *guanine*, *thymine*, and *cytosine*. The exact proportions of each of the bases, and the precise order in which they are arranged, are unique for each *species* (kind) of living thing. It is this exact order and composition that must be faithfully copied each time a cell divides. Each DNA molecule contains about 20,000 such phosphate-sugar-base units. A chromosome contains many thousands of DNA molecules. Scientists can *synthesize* (chemically reconstruct) some kinds of DNA molecules that are able to reproduce themselves.

RNA also consists of long chains of repeating phosphate-sugar-base units. However, the sugar in RNA is *ribose*. Its bases are *adenine, guanine, cytosine,* and *uracil* (rather than thymine as in DNA). Scientists believe that some RNA carries the materials used in making proteins. Other RNA carries the "instructions" for making different proteins.   ARTHUR and SYLVY KORNBERG

For a more complete discussion and diagrams, see CELL. See also HEREDITY; WATSON, JAMES D.; ENZYME.

NUCLEON. See ATOM (Inside the Atom).

NUCLEONICS is the study of nucleons, the central particles of atoms. See ATOM (Inside the Atom).

NUCLEUS. See AMEBA; ATOM; CELL; COMET.

NUEVA ISABELA. See SANTO DOMINGO.

NUEVO LEÓN, *NWAY voh lay AWN,* is a state in northeastern Mexico (see MEXICO [map]). It has an area of 24,925 square miles (64,555 square kilometers) and a population of 1,694,689. A dry plain covers northern Nuevo León. The Sierra Madre Oriental mountains are in the southern part of the state. Nuevo León grows grapes, cotton, wheat, corn, barley, and citrus fruits. It also produces cattle and lumber. Monterrey is the state capital.   CHARLES C. CUMBERLAND

NUFFIELD RADIO ASTRONOMY LABORATORIES, JODRELL BANK. See JODRELL BANK OBSERVATORY.

NUISANCE. When someone annoys you while you are working, you may call him a nuisance. In law, the term *nuisance* has much the same meaning.

A nuisance that annoys a large part of the community, such as an odorous slaughterhouse, is called a *public nuisance*. A slaughterhouse in open country that affects few people is a *private nuisance*. Most states have laws forbidding public nuisances.   FRED E. INBAU

NUKUALOFA, *NOO koo ah LOH fah* (pop. 18,200), is the capital of Tonga. The town lies on the northern coast of Tongatapu, one of the many islands of the South Pacific kingdom (see TONGA [map]). Nukualofa is Tonga's chief port and commercial center. Small shops and business offices line its wide streets. Most of the buildings are made of wood.

In 1643, Abel Tasman, a Dutch sea captain, became the first European to land at Nukualofa. Nukualofa was

named Tonga's capital during the reign of King George Tupou I, who ruled from 1845 to 1893.   STUART INDER

NULL SET. See SET THEORY (Empty Sets).

NULLIFICATION is the action of setting aside a law by declaring it *null and void*. The United States Constitution does not provide any way for a law of Congress to be declared unconstitutional after it has been signed by the President. Some delegates to the Constitutional Convention believed that the courts would naturally assume this authority. But only in 1803, with the case of *Marbury vs. Madison*, did the Supreme Court flatly assert the right of the courts to pass on the constitutionality of an act of Congress.

The theory that the states, rather than any branch of the federal government, should have the right to *nullify* (declare unconstitutional) a law of Congress, developed slowly. The Kentucky and Virginia Resolutions of 1798 protested the Alien and Sedition Acts passed by Congress. Many persons believed that these acts violated Amendment I. They wanted the states to join together to declare the acts unconstitutional. But no other state would join in the action. In 1799, the Kentucky legislature stated its belief in the legality of nullification, but merely entered a protest against the Alien and Sedition Acts.

Nullification was next seriously proposed in 1828, when John C. Calhoun prepared a document known as the South Carolina Exposition. Rising industrial interests of the Northeast had persuaded Congress to include in the tariff law of 1828 (the "tariff of abominations") protective duties that the cotton-growing South disliked. Sentiment against the tariff was strongest in South Carolina. There was even talk of secession.

Calhoun's motive in recommending nullification was to provide an alternative to secession. He argued that the federal government had no right to judge the constitutionality of its own acts. He also insisted that the states had given certain powers to Congress, and were alone competent to say whether or not Congress had exceeded its powers. Calhoun's reasoning was set forth by Senator Robert Y. Hayne in his famous debate with Webster in 1830. Webster said nullification would break up the Union, and closed with the words: "Liberty *and* Union, now and forever, one and inseparable!"

In 1832, Congress again passed a protective tariff act. South Carolina passed an ordinance which declared the tariff laws of 1828 and 1832 null and void in that state. It threatened to leave the Union if the federal government tried to enforce the tariff laws anywhere in South Carolina. President Andrew Jackson warned the people that the laws would be enforced. He also took measures to make sure that the tariff would be collected at the important port of Charleston. After Congress passed a Force Bill to uphold Jackson's position, it became clear that resistance was unwise. Besides, the Compromise Tariff of 1833, engineered through Congress by Henry Clay, greatly reduced the tariff duties.

Nullification was only one manifestation of the doctrine of states' rights which, insofar as it meant the supremacy of the states over the nation, was ended by the Civil War.   JOHN DONALD HICKS

See also CALHOUN, JOHN C.; FORCE BILL; HAYNE, ROBERT Y.; STATES' RIGHTS; WEBSTER, DANIEL.

NUMA POMPILIUS, the second of the seven legendary kings of Rome, reigned from 715 to 673 B.C. Many of his deeds are legendary. Supposedly, he became king a year after Romulus died. His chief contributions were in religion. He established the priesthoods, and created a calendar form which was used until the time of Julius Caesar. He also built a *shrine* (sacred place) to the god Janus (see JANUS). Numa, a Sabine, consulted the nymph Egeria who is said to have given Numa advice on religious matters (see EGERIA).   HERBERT M. HOWE

NUMBER, in grammar, is a feature of language that indicates how many persons or objects are referred to. In English, the form of a noun shows whether the reference is to one person, place, object, or idea, or to more than one. The form that indicates only one is called the *singular.* The form that indicates more than one is called the *plural.* Some other languages have a singular form, indicating one; a *dual* form, indicating two; and a plural form, indicating more than two. The plurals of English nouns are formed in *regular* and *irregular* ways.

Regular Plurals are formed by adding *-s* or *-es* to the singular forms of the noun, as in *cap, caps* and *church, churches.* Compound nouns form plurals with the addition of *-s* or *-es,* but the placement varies. For example, the plural of *brother-in-law* is *brothers-in-law.* But the plural of *grown-up* is *grown-ups.* And in *man-servant,* both parts take the plural form—*men-servants.*

Irregular Plurals are not formed according to any established rule, as are regular plurals. The plurals of some nouns of Old English origin are formed by a vowel change, as in *man, men* and *tooth, teeth.* A small number of nouns still have the Old English plural ending -en— for example, *ox, oxen* and *child, children.*

About a dozen nouns that end in *-f* or *-fe* are changed to *-ves* in the plural, among them *half, halves* and *wife, wives.* But not all nouns that end in *-f* or *-fe* follow this pattern. For example, *roof* and *chief* form regular plurals —*roofs* and *chiefs.*

Some nouns, such as *barracks, deer,* and *sheep,* have the same form in both the singular and the plural. A few expressions use a singular form even though a plural is actually called for. These include *two-inch nail, six-foot man,* and *two-gallon bucket.*

Some nouns, including *cowardice* and *brilliance,* have no plural. They differ from such nouns as *deer* and *sheep* because *two sheep* is correct, but *two cowardices* is not. The plural of *cowardice* would usually be expressed by saying something like *There are different kinds of cowardice.*

Foreign Plurals. Words coming into English from foreign languages sometimes keep their foreign plurals. Such foreign plurals are mostly from Greek and Latin words. Some of these are *phenomenon, phenomena; criterion, criteria; alumnus, alumni; alumna, alumnae; fungus, fungi;* and *thesis, theses.* There is a strong tendency for such words to go into the regular English plural group. For example, at an earlier period the plural of *stadium* was the foreign form *stadia.* Now, however, *stadiums* is the plural form commonly used.

The spelling of plurals in English has many irregularities that are not reflected in speech. Singular nouns that end in *-y,* following a consonant, are changed to *-ies* in the plural—for example, *lady, ladies; flurry, flurries;*

and *candy, candies.* For those ending in *-y,* preceded by a vowel, *-s* is added, as in *alley, alleys* and *day, days.* Some nouns that end in *-o* have *-s* added: *Eskimos* and *pianos.* Others, for no special reason, have *-es* added: *tomatoes* and *heroes.* Several even have optional forms, such as *zeroes* or *zeros* and *ghettoes* or *ghettos.*

English Pronouns also have plurals, but the relationship is not so consistent as in nouns. *We* can be called the plural of *I,* and *they* the plural of *he, she,* and *it. These* is the plural of *this,* and *those* the plural of *that.*

English Verbs reflect number by agreeing with the subject. For example, the verb *play* occurs with a plural subject in the sentence *The boys play baseball every day.* The verb appears with a singular subject in *The boy plays baseball every day.*   WILLIAM F. IRMSCHER

See also DECLENSION; INFLECTION; NOUN (Number and Case); PRONOUN; VERB.

NUMBER AND NUMERAL. Numbers are ideas. We think of a number when we consider how many objects are in a certain group. Numerals are names for number ideas. For example, we can use the word *five* or the symbol *5* to stand for the number of fingers on one hand. Both *five* and *5* are numerals.

Counting means arranging numerals in a certain order. In counting, each number is one more than the number that comes before it. Systems of counting or of naming numbers are called *numeration systems.* Today, most peoples use the *Hindu-Arabic* numeration system, also called the *decimal number system.* This system includes the familiar symbols 1, 2, 3, 4, 5, and so on.

Numbers used in counting are also called *natural numbers, positive numbers,* and *cardinal numbers. Ordinal numbers* such as "first," "second," "third," and so on, indicate an object's position in a series.

See also NUMERATION SYSTEMS; DECIMAL NUMERAL SYSTEM; ARABIC NUMERALS; INFINITY.

NUMBER LINE. See ADDITION (Regrouping).

NUMBERING MACHINE is a device for printing numbers on such papers as checks, invoices, and orders. The machine may print one number after another—1, 2, 3— or it may repeat the same number as many times as desired. The machines are either automatic or hand-operated.

A numbering machine consists of a set of little wheels, all mounted on the same shaft. Each of these wheels has numbers from 0 to 9 on its rim. The first wheel prints 0, 1, 2, 3, 4, 5, 6, 7, 8, 9. As it returns to 0, a tooth engages the second wheel and turns the wheel from 0 to 1, printing 10. After the number 99 has been printed, a tooth turns the third wheel from 0 to 1, printing 100. There are some numbering machines that can count as high as 99,999,999.   WILLIAM H. FISH

NUMBERS is the fourth book of the Bible. Its name comes from the *census,* or counting, of the Israelites in the desert after their escape from Egypt. The book includes experiences of the Hebrew tribes interwoven with important laws and poetic material. It contains the famous priestly blessing "The Lord bless thee, and keep thee" (6: 24), and the law of the Nazarites, who dedicated themselves to the service of God. It also tells about the prophet Balaam, who was hired to curse Israel. The book describes the grandeur and tragedy of Moses' career as leader of his people.   ROBERT GORDIS

See also NAZARITE; PENTATEUCH.

NUMERAL. See NUMBER AND NUMERAL.

NUMERATION SYSTEMS

NUMERATION SYSTEMS, or NUMERAL SYSTEMS, are ways of counting and of naming numbers. We cannot see or touch numbers, because they are ideas. But we can use symbols to stand for numbers. These symbols are called *numerals*. Here are four numerals that represent the number in a half dozen: 6, six, VI, and ⊦⊦⊦ I . Each of these numerals is a name for the number in a half dozen.

Our numeration system has only 10 basic numerals, called *digits:* 0, 1, 2, 3, 4, 5, 6, 7, 8, 9. With these 10 symbols we can represent any number, regardless of size. This system is called a *decimal* system because it is based on 10. The word decimal comes from the Latin word *decem,* which means *ten.* Ten is the *base* or the *scale* of the decimal system.

Kinds of Numeration Systems

It is possible to use any number as a base in building a numeration system. The number of digits used in the system is always equal to the base. For example, (1) the *decimal,* or *base 10,* system uses 10 digits; (2) the *quinary,* or *base 5,* system uses 5 digits; (3) the *binary,* or *base 2,* system uses 2 digits; and (4) the *duodecimal,* or *base 12,* system uses 12 digits.

The Decimal System represents numbers in terms of groups of ten. Suppose you wanted to count the pennies you have saved. Instead of counting them one by one, you could count them in groups of 10. You would put them in stacks of 10. Then you would arrange the stacks in groups, putting 10 in each group, as shown.

2 Groups of 10 Stacks of 10 Pennies   **4 Stacks of 10 Pennies**   **8 Pennies**

How many pennies are there? You could count them like this: 2 groups of 10 stacks of 10 = 2 × (10 × 10) = 200; 4 stacks of 10 = 4 × 10 = 40; plus 8 single pennies. In all, you have 200 + 40 + 8 = 248 pennies.

If you had counted the pennies one by one, you would have counted the same total. In decimal counting, you use one-digit numerals to count from 1 to 9. Then you use two-digit numerals to count from 10 to 99. In two-digit numerals, the digit on the left stands for the number of groups of ten. The digit on the right shows the number of ones. For example, the numeral 14 stands for 1 group of ten plus 4 ones. After 99, you use three-digit numerals. The first digit on the left of these numerals stands for the number of *hundreds* (groups of ten tens). Thus, the numeral 248 stands for 2 hundreds + 4 tens + 8, as shown in the illustration.

The value of each digit in a decimal numeral depends on its *place* (position) in the numeral. For example, the numeral 482 contains the same digits as the numeral 248. But 482 represents a different number because the digits are in different positions.

Charlotte W. Junge, the contributor of this article, is Professor of Education at Wayne State University, and Assistant Editor of The Arithmetic Teacher.

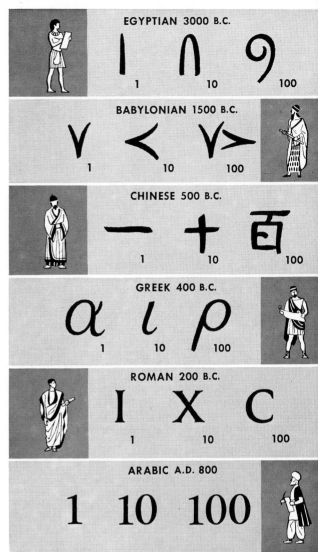

Numerals from Five Early Civilizations

Each position has a name that tells its value in terms of 10. In the numeral 248, the 8 is in the *ones* place; the 4 is in the *tens* place; and the 2 is in the *hundreds* place. In numerals with more than three digits, the additional positions are called the *thousands* place, the *ten thousands* place, and so on. Each position has a value 10 times greater than the position to its right.

Another way of expressing place value is to use *powers of 10* (10 multiplied by itself a certain number of times). The following table shows the meaning of several powers of 10.

Place Name	Power of 10	Meaning	Symbol
Ones		1	10^0
Tens	1st	1×10	10^1
Hundreds	2nd	10×10	10^2
Thousands	3rd	$10 \times 10 \times 10$	10^3
Ten Thousands	4th	$10 \times 10 \times 10 \times 10$	10^4

The 2 in 10^2, the 3 in 10^3, and the 4 in 10^4 are called *exponents.* The 10 is called the *base.* The exponent tells

NUMERATION SYSTEMS

the number of times the base is to be used as a *factor*. For example, 10^2 means 10 is used as a factor twice, or 10×10; and 10^4 means $10 \times 10 \times 10 \times 10$. We can write the numeral 248 as $200 + 40 + 8$, or we can write it as $(2 \times 10^2) + (4 \times 10^1) + 8$.

The value of any numeral is the sum of the values of the digits. The numeral 4,206 means "4 thousands plus 2 hundreds plus no tens plus 6 ones," or $(4 \times 10^3) + (2 \times 10^2) + (0 \times 10^1) + (6 \times 1)$. We could also write 4,206 as $(4 \times 10^3) + (2 \times 10^2) + (0 \times 10^1) + (6 \times 10^0)$. The exponent zero means ten is not used as a factor. 6×10^0 is another expression for 6×1.

The Quinary System groups numbers by fives and by powers of five. The word *quinary* comes from the Latin word *quinque*, meaning *five*. This system uses five digits: 0, 1, 2, 3, and 4. In the quinary system, the numeral 10 (one, zero) stands for *five*, the base of the system. It means "1 five plus no ones." To avoid confusion between quinary numerals and decimal numerals, you can write the word "five" next to a quinary numeral: 10_{five}. This numeral is read "one, zero, base 5."

Grouping by Fives. The groups of stars below show the meaning of several quinary numerals:

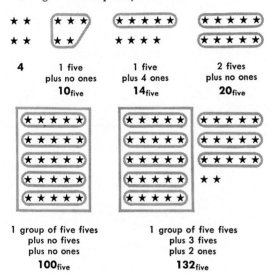

In quinary counting, the digits 1, 2, 3, and 4 are used to express numbers from 1 to 4. To show 5 in this system, we use the first two basic symbols. The number five is written 10_{five}. Two-digit numerals are used from 10_{five} to 44_{five} (4 fives plus 4 ones). The digit on the left represents the number of fives, and the righthand digit represents the number of ones. In the numeral 32_{five}, the 3 means 3 groups of 5, and the 2 means 2 ones. To show the counting numbers past 44_{five}, three basic symbols are used. The numeral 100_{five} means 1 twenty-five (5 fives) plus no tens and no ones. After 444_{five}, four-digit numerals are used, and so on.

Finding Place Value in Base 5. In a quinary numeral, the last digit on the right is in the ones place. Every other position has a value 5 times the value of the position to its right. In the quinary numeral 1402_{five}, the 2 means 2×1; the 0 means 0×5; the 4 means $4 \times 5 \times 5$; and the 1 means $1 \times 5 \times 5 \times 5$.

You can express the place value of each position in terms of powers of 5. The following table shows the meaning of several powers of 5 and their values in decimal numerals.

Base 5 Numeral		Meaning		Decimal Numerals		
1_{five}	$=$	1	$=$	1	$=$	5^0
10_{five}	$=$	5×1	$=$	5	$=$	5^1
100_{five}	$=$	5×5	$=$	25	$=$	5^2
$1,000_{\text{five}}$	$=$	$5 \times 5 \times 5$	$=$	125	$=$	5^3
$10,000_{\text{five}}$	$=$	$5 \times 5 \times 5 \times 5$	$=$	625	$=$	5^4

In the numeral 1402_{five}, 2 is in the ones place; 0 is in the 5^1 place; 4 is in the 5^2 place; and 1 is in the 5^3 place.

Quinary numerals may be changed to decimal numerals by adding the values of the digits in terms of decimal numerals. The following calculation shows how to change the quinary numeral 1402_{five} to the decimal numeral 227:

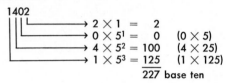

$$
\begin{array}{rll}
2 \times 1 = & 2 & \\
0 \times 5^1 = & 0 & (0 \times 5) \\
4 \times 5^2 = & 100 & (4 \times 25) \\
1 \times 5^3 = & 125 & (1 \times 125) \\
\hline
& 227 & \text{base ten}
\end{array}
$$

The Binary System groups numbers by twos and by powers of two. The word *binary* comes from the Latin word *bini*, meaning *two at a time*. This system uses only two digits: 0 and 1. The numeral 10_{two} (one, zero, base two) stands for *two*, the base of the system. It means "1 two plus no ones."

Grouping by Twos. The groups of squares below show the meaning of several binary numerals:

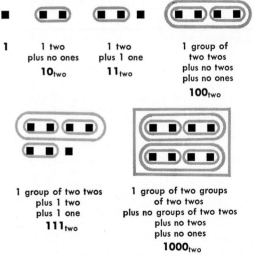

In binary counting, single digits are used for *none* and *one*. Two-digit numerals are used for 10_{two} and 11_{two} (2 and 3 in decimal numerals). For the next counting number, 100_{two} (4 in decimal numerals), three digits are necessary. After 111_{two} (7 in decimal numerals), four-digit numerals are used until 1111_{two} (15 in decimal numerals) is reached, and so on.

Finding Place Value in Base 2. In a binary numeral, every position has a value 2 times the value of the position to its right. For example, in the numeral 1010_{two}, the 0 on the right means 0×1; the 1 at the left of this 0 means 1×2; the next 0 means $0 \times 2 \times 2$; and the 1 at the far left of the numeral means $1 \times 2 \times 2 \times 2$.

The place value of each position can be expressed in terms of powers of 2. The following table shows the meaning of several powers of 2.

Base 2 Numeral		Meaning		Decimal Numerals		
1_{two}	=	1	=	1	=	2^0
10_{two}	=	2×1	=	2	=	2^1
100_{two}	=	2×2	=	4	=	2^2
$1,000_{two}$	=	$2 \times 2 \times 2$	=	8	=	2^3
$10,000_{two}$	=	$2 \times 2 \times 2 \times 2$	=	16	=	2^4

In the numeral 1010_{two}, the 0 at the right is in the ones place; the 1 next to it is in the 2^1 place; the next 0 to the left is in the 2^2 place; and the 1 at the far left is in the 2^3 place.

Binary numerals may be changed to decimal numerals by adding up the place values of the digits in terms of decimal numerals. The following calculation shows how to change the binary numeral 1010_{two} to the decimal numeral 10:

$$
\begin{array}{rclcl}
0 \times 1 &=& 0 & & \\
1 \times 2^1 &=& 2 & & (1 \times 2) \\
0 \times 2^2 &=& 0 & & (0 \times 4) \\
1 \times 2^3 &=& 8 & & (1 \times 8) \\
\hline
& & 10 & & \text{base ten}
\end{array}
$$

The Duodecimal System groups numbers by twelves and powers of twelve. The word *duodecimal* comes from the Latin word *duodecimus*, meaning *twelfth*. It is a combination of the Latin words *duo*, meaning *two*, and *decem*, meaning *ten*. Because the duodecimal system is based on 12, it uses 12 digits: 0, 1, 2, 3, 4, 5, 6, 7, 8, 9, T, and E. The symbols T and E stand for the number of objects called *ten* and *eleven* in the decimal system. The numeral 10_{twelve} (one, zero, base twelve) means "1 twelve plus no ones." The numeral 12_{twelve} (one, two, base twelve) stands for "1 twelve plus 2 ones." It represents the numeral 14 in the decimal system.

Grouping by Twelves. The groups of dots below show the meaning of various duodecimal numerals.

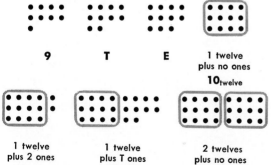

9	T	E	1 twelve plus no ones 10_{twelve}

1 twelve plus 2 ones 12_{twelve}	1 twelve plus T ones $1T_{twelve}$	2 twelves plus no ones 20_{twelve}

In duodecimal counting, you use single digits to count from 1 to E. Then you use two-digit numerals to count from 10_{twelve} to EE_{twelve}. The digit on the left stands for the number of twelves, and the digit on the right shows the number of ones. For example, in the numeral 45_{twelve}, the 4 stands for 4 twelves and the 5 for 5 ones. After EE_{twelve}, you use three-digit numerals. The first digit on the left then stands for the number of twelve twelves. For example, the number in one *gross* is twelve twelves (144 in decimal numerals). In the duodecimal system, one gross is written 100_{twelve}. This

numeral means "1 group of twelve twelves plus no twelves plus no ones." After EEE_{twelve}, you use four-digit numerals, and so on.

Finding Place Value in Base 12. In a duodecimal numeral, the last digit on the right is in the ones place. Every other position has a value 12 times the value of the position to its right. For example, in the numeral $E0T5_{twelve}$, 5 means 5×1; T means $T \times 12$; 0 means $0 \times 12 \times 12$; and E means $E \times 12 \times 12 \times 12$.

You can express the place value of each position in terms of powers of 12. The following table shows the meaning of several powers of 12 and their values in decimal numerals.

Base 12 Numeral		Meaning		Decimal Numerals		
1_{twelve}	=	1	=	1	=	12^0
10_{twelve}	=	12×1	=	12	=	12^1
100_{twelve}	=	12×12	=	144	=	12^2
$1,000_{twelve}$	=	$12 \times 12 \times 12$	=	1,728	=	12^3
$10,000_{twelve}$	=	$12 \times 12 \times 12 \times 12$	=	20,736	=	12^4

In the numeral $E0T5_{twelve}$, 5 is in the ones place; T is in the 12^1 place; 0 is in the 12^2 place; and E is in the 12^3 place.

Duodecimal numerals can be changed to decimal numerals by adding up the place values of the digits in terms of decimal numerals. The following calculation shows how to change the duodecimal numeral $E0T5_{twelve}$ to the decimal numeral 19,133:

$$
\begin{array}{rclcl}
\text{E0T5} & & & & \\
5 \times 1 &=& 5 & & \\
10 \times 12^1 &=& 120 & & (10 \times 12) \\
0 \times 12^2 &=& 0 & & (0 \times 144) \\
11 \times 12^3 &=& 19,008 & & (11 \times 1,728) \\
\hline
& & 19,133 & & \text{(base ten)}
\end{array}
$$

Working with Numeration Systems

Suppose you are asked to solve an addition problem: $4 + 4 + 4 = ?$. If you use the base 10 system, you know the answer is 12, as shown by these groups of dots:

4 ones	**4** ones	**4** ones	**12** 1 group of ten plus 2 ones

But if you use the base 5 system, the sum of 4 plus 4 plus 4 is 22_{five}, as shown below:

4 ones	**4** ones	**4** ones	22_{five} 2 groups of five plus 2 ones

On the other hand, if you use the base 12 system, $4 + 4 + 4 = 10_{twelve}$:

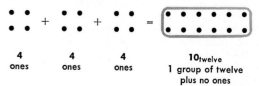

4 ones	**4** ones	**4** ones	10_{twelve} 1 group of twelve plus no ones

NUMERATION SYSTEMS

The numerals differ in each answer, but the number of dots is the same. The numerals are formed according to the principles of grouping and place value. Subtraction, multiplication, and division also follow these principles. You can study these principles by working problems in various numeration systems. In this way, you will get a better understanding of the use of numerals in arithmetic.

Decimal Arithmetic. Statements such as $4 + 5 = 9$, $9 - 4 = 5$, $9 \times 5 = 45$, and $45 \div 9 = 5$ are called *arithmetic facts*. We use many such facts in addition, subtraction, multiplication, and division.

Decimal Addition is a way of combining two or more groups into only one group. The principle of place value is used in adding ones to ones, tens to tens, and so on, as in the following example:

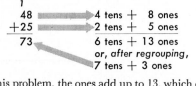

$$
\begin{array}{r}
24 \\
+12 \\
\hline
36
\end{array}
\quad
\begin{array}{l}
2 \text{ tens} + 4 \text{ ones} \\
1 \text{ ten} + 2 \text{ ones} \\
\hline
3 \text{ tens} + 6 \text{ ones}
\end{array}
$$

In this example, you use the addition fact $4 + 2 = 6$ and the fact $2 + 1 = 3$ (meaning 2 tens + 1 ten = 3 tens, or 30). Therefore, the sum is 3 tens plus 6, or 36. In some problems, the sum in one or more places is 10 or more. Then you must *regroup* the sum. Regrouping in addition is sometimes called *carrying*. The next problem shows how to regroup in decimal addition.

$$
\begin{array}{r}
^1 \\
48 \\
+25 \\
\hline
73
\end{array}
\quad
\begin{array}{l}
4 \text{ tens} + 8 \text{ ones} \\
2 \text{ tens} + 5 \text{ ones} \\
\hline
6 \text{ tens} + 13 \text{ ones} \\
or, after regrouping, \\
7 \text{ tens} + 3 \text{ ones}
\end{array}
$$

In this problem, the ones add up to 13, which can be regrouped into 1 ten plus 3 ones. So you write 3 in the ones place and a small 1 in the tens place above the 4. Then you add the tens: $1 + 4 + 2 = 7$ tens, or 70. Therefore, the sum is $70 + 3$, or 73.

Decimal Subtraction is a way of "undoing" addition. It follows the same principles as decimal addition:

$$
\begin{array}{r}
65 \\
-23 \\
\hline
42
\end{array}
\quad
\begin{array}{l}
6 \text{ tens} + 5 \text{ ones} \\
2 \text{ tens} + 3 \text{ ones} \\
\hline
4 \text{ tens} + 2 \text{ ones}
\end{array}
$$

In this example, you use the subtraction fact $5 - 3 = 2$, and the fact $6 - 2 = 4$ (meaning 6 tens − 2 tens = 4 tens). To subtract a large number from a smaller number in any place, you have to regroup. Regrouping in subtraction is sometimes called *borrowing*. The next example shows how to regroup in decimal subtraction.

$$
\begin{array}{r}
^6\!\!\not7\,3 \\
-25 \\
\hline
48
\end{array}
\quad
\begin{array}{l}
6 \text{ tens} + 13 \text{ ones} \\
2 \text{ tens} + 5 \text{ ones} \\
\hline
4 \text{ tens} + 8 \text{ ones}
\end{array}
$$

In the ones place, you must subtract 5 from 3, which is smaller. So you regroup 7 tens plus 3 ones to make 6 tens plus 13 ones. Show this by writing a small 1 in front of the 3, and by crossing out the 7 and writing a small 6 above it. Then use the subtraction fact $13 - 5 = 8$ to subtract the ones, and the fact $6 - 2 = 4$ to subtract the tens.

Decimal Multiplication is a way of putting together equal groups. The multiplication fact $4 \times 6 = 24$ means that 4 groups of 6 objects contain 24 objects. Here is the way you use place value to multiply 23 by 3:

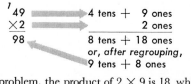

$$
\begin{array}{r}
23 \\
\times 3 \\
\hline
69
\end{array}
\quad
\begin{array}{l}
2 \text{ tens} + 3 \text{ ones} \\
3 \text{ ones} \\
\hline
6 \text{ tens} + 9 \text{ ones}
\end{array}
$$

First, think: "3×3 ones = 9 ones, and 3×2 tens = 6 tens, or 60." Then add $60 + 9 = 69$.

In multiplication, you regroup when the product in any place is 10 or more:

$$
\begin{array}{r}
^1 \\
49 \\
\times 2 \\
\hline
98
\end{array}
\quad
\begin{array}{l}
4 \text{ tens} + 9 \text{ ones} \\
2 \text{ ones} \\
\hline
8 \text{ tens} + 18 \text{ ones} \\
or, after regrouping, \\
9 \text{ tens} + 8 \text{ ones}
\end{array}
$$

In this problem, the product of 2×9 is 18, which can be regrouped into 1 ten plus 8 ones. So you write 8 in the ones place and a little 1 in the tens place above the 4. Next, multiply $2 \times 4 = 8$ in the tens place, and add the 1 to make 9.

When the multiplier has more than one digit, you repeat the operation for each digit and add the products:

$$
\begin{array}{r}
24 \\
\times 12 \\
\hline
48 \\
24 \\
\hline
288
\end{array}
\quad
\begin{array}{l}
2 \text{ tens} + 4 \text{ ones} \\
1 \text{ ten} + 2 \text{ ones} \\
\hline
4 \text{ tens} + 8 \text{ ones} \\
2 \text{ hundreds} + 4 \text{ tens} \\
\hline
2 \text{ hundreds} + 8 \text{ tens} + 8 \text{ ones}
\end{array}
$$

First, multiply 24 by 2, writing 8 in the ones place, and 4 in the tens place. Then multiply 24 by 1 ten, writing 4 in the tens place and 2 in the hundreds place. Then add the products to get 288.

Decimal Division is a way of "undoing" multiplication. It is a grouping apart of one group into several groups of equal size. Here is the way you divide 69 by 3:

$$
\begin{array}{r}
23 \\
3\overline{)69} \\
6 \\
\hline
9 \\
9
\end{array}
\quad
\begin{array}{l}
2 \text{ tens} + 3 \text{ ones} \\
3 \text{ ones }\,\overline{)6 \text{ tens} + 9 \text{ ones}} \\
6 \text{ tens} \\
\hline
9 \text{ ones} \\
9 \text{ ones}
\end{array}
$$

First, think: "6 tens ÷ 3 = 2 tens." Write 2 in the tens place above the 6. Then think: "9 ones ÷ 3 = 3 ones." Write 3 in the ones place above the 9. Therefore, $69 \div 3 = 2$ tens + 3 ones, or 23.

The principle of place value also makes it easy to divide larger numbers:

$$
\begin{array}{r}
82 \\
2\overline{)164} \\
16 \\
\hline
4 \\
4
\end{array}
$$

First, think: "16 tens ÷ 2 = 8 tens." Write 8 in the tens place above the 6. Then think: "4 ones ÷ 2 = 2 ones." Write 2 in the ones place above the 4. Therefore, $164 \div 2 = 8$ tens + 2 ones, or 82.

Quinary Arithmetic has fewer arithmetic facts than decimal arithmetic because it uses only 5 digits instead of 10. These digits are: 0, 1, 2, 3, 4.

Quinary Addition. You can use the following table to find the basic facts of quinary addition.

+	0	1	2	3	4
0	0	1	2	3	4
1	1	2	3	4	10
2	2	3	4	10	11
3	3	4	10	11	12
4	4	10	11	12	13

The numerals in the table run from left to right in *rows*, and from top to bottom in *columns*. Each row and each column begins with a digit from 0 through 4. You can use these digits to locate various sums in the chart. To find the sum of 3 + 3, for example, first find the row that begins with 3. Then run your finger to the right along this row until you come to the column that has 3 at the top. Your finger will be on 11 (1 five plus 1), the sum of 3 plus 3. You can use the table to solve the following problem:

Quinary Addition	Meaning	Decimal Addition
21	2 fives + 1 one	11
+13	1 five + 3 ones	+8
34	3 fives + 4 ones	19

When the sum in any place is greater than 4, you have to regroup, as shown in the next example.

Quinary Addition	Meaning	Decimal Addition
1		
24	2 fives + 4 ones	14
+14	1 five + 4 ones	+9
43	3 fives + 13 ones	23
	or, after regrouping,	
	4 fives + 3 ones	

First, use the fact 4 + 4 = 13 to add the ones. Regroup 13 ones into 1 five plus 3 ones. Write 3 in the ones place and a small 1 in the fives place above the 2. Next, add the fives: 1 + 2 + 1 = 4.

Quinary Subtraction. You can use the quinary addition facts table to find subtraction facts, too. For example, to subtract 3 from 11, first find the column that begins with 3. Next, run your finger down this column until you come to 11. Then run your finger to the left along this row to the beginning digit to find the answer, 3.

Use the table to solve the next problem:

Quinary Subtraction	Meaning	Decimal Subtraction
33	3 fives + 3 ones	18
−12	1 five + 2 ones	−7
21	2 fives + 1 one	11

The following problem shows how you regroup in quinary subtraction.

Quinary Subtraction	Meaning (after regrouping)	Decimal Subtraction
2 1		
3 1	2 fives + 11 ones	16
−14	1 five + 4 ones	−9
12	1 five + 2 ones	7

To subtract in the ones place, you must regroup 3 fives plus 1 one into 2 fives plus 11 ones. Then use the subtraction fact 11 − 4 = 2. Next, use the fact 2 − 1 = 1 to subtract the fives.

Quinary Multiplication also uses fewer facts than decimal multiplication. You can use the following table to find the basic quinary multiplication facts.

×	1	2	3	4
1	1	2	3	4
2	2	4	11	13
3	3	11	14	22
4	4	13	22	31

For example, to find the product of 3 × 4, first find the row that begins with 3. Then run your finger to the right until you come to the column that has 4 at the top. Your finger will be on the answer, 22 (2 fives plus 2 ones).

Here is a simple problem to solve with the table:

Quinary Multiplication	Meaning	Decimal Multiplication
21	2 fives + 1 one	11
×2	2 ones	×2
42	4 fives + 2 ones	22

When the product in any place is greater than 4, you have to regroup, as shown in the next example.

Quinary Multiplication	Meaning	Decimal Multiplication
1 14	1 five + 4 ones	9
×2	2 ones	×2
33	2 fives + 13 ones	18
	or, after regrouping,	
	3 fives + 3 ones	

First, you use the fact 2 × 4 = 13 to multiply in the ones place. Regroup 13 ones into 1 five plus 3 ones. Write 3 in the ones place and a small 1 in the fives place above the 1. Then use the fact 2 × 1 = 2 (meaning 2 × 1 five = 2 fives). Add the 1 five you got by regrouping in the ones place to make 3 fives, or 30 (three, zero) in quinary numerals. The sum is therefore 30 + 3, or 33 (three, three).

When the multiplier has more than one digit, repeat the operation for each digit and add the products:

Quinary Multiplication		Meaning	Decimal Multiplication
21		2 fives + 1 one	11
×12		1 five + 2 ones	×7
42		4 fives + 2 ones	77
21	2 twenty-fives +	1 five	
302	2 twenty-fives + 10 fives + 2 ones		
	or, after regrouping,		
	3 twenty-fives + 0 fives + 2 ones		

Quinary Division. You can also use the quinary multiplication table to find division facts. For example, to find the quotient 22 ÷ 4, first find the column that begins with 4. Next run your finger down this column until you come to 22. Then run your finger to the left along this row until you come to the beginning digit, 3. Use the table to work the following problem:

Quinary Division	Meaning	Decimal Division
12	1 five + 2 ones	7
2/24	2 ones/2 fives + 4 ones	2/14
2	2 fives	14
4	4 ones	
4	4 ones	

The next example shows how to divide with larger numerals.

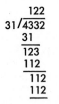

In this problem, think "3 will go into 4 once, so 31 will go into 43 once." Write 1 above the 3. Then finish the problem as you would a decimal division problem. But remember to use quinary arithmetic facts.

Binary Arithmetic has only a few facts because it uses only two digits—0 and 1.

Binary Addition is based on only these facts:

$$0 + 0 = 0 \quad 0 + 1 = 1 \quad 1 + 0 = 1 \quad 1 + 1 = 10$$

Here is the way you use these facts to add $11 + 11$:

Binary Addition	Meaning	Decimal Addition
1		
11	1 two + 1 one	3
+11	1 two + 1 one	+3
110	10 twos + 10 ones	6
	or, after regrouping,	
	1 four + 1 two + 0 ones	

First, you use the addition fact $1 + 1 = 10$ (meaning one 2) to add the ones. Regroup 10_{two} into 1 two plus no ones. Write 0 in the ones place, and a small 1 above the twos column. Then add the twos: $1 + 1 = 10$; $10 + 1 = 11$. Write 1 in the twos place, and 1 in the fours place. Thus, $11_{two} + 11_{two} = 110_{two}$.

Binary Subtraction is based on four facts:

$$0 - 0 = 0 \quad 1 - 0 = 1 \quad 1 - 1 = 0 \quad 10 - 1 = 1$$

Use these facts to subtract 11 from 110:

Binary Subtraction	Meaning *(after regrouping twice)*	Decimal Subtraction
110	0 fours + 10 twos + 10 ones	6
−11	1 two + 1 one	−3
11	1 two + 1 one	3

In the ones place, you have to subtract 1 from 0. So you regroup 1 four plus 1 two plus no ones into 1 four plus no twos plus 10 ones. Then use the fact $10 - 1 = 1$ to subtract the ones. To subtract the twos, you again have to take 1 from 0 because your first regrouping has left a 0 in the twos place. You regroup 1 four plus no twos

into no fours plus 10 twos, and use the fact $10 - 1 = 1$.

Binary Multiplication uses the following facts:

$$0 \times 0 = 0 \quad 0 \times 1 = 0 \quad 1 \times 0 = 0 \quad 1 \times 1 = 1$$

The product of two single digits is always either 0 or 1. However, you may have to regroup when adding products to complete a multiplication problem. For example, here is the way you multiply 11×11:

Binary Multiplication	Meaning	Decimal Multiplication
11	1 two + 1 one	3
×11	1 two + 1 one	×3
11	1 two + 1 one	9
11	1 four + 1 two	
1001	1 four + 10 twos + 1 one	
	or, after regrouping,	
1 eight + 0 fours + 0 twos + 1 one		

Multiply and write the products as you do in the decimal system. When you add the partial products, use binary addition facts. Bring down the 1 in the ones place. Add the twos: $1 + 1 = 10$. Regroup 10 twos to 1 four plus no twos. Write 0 in the twos place and add 1 to the 1 in the fours place: $1 + 1 = 10$. Write 0 in the fours place and 1 in the eights place to get 1001.

Binary Division "undoes" binary multiplication. The following example shows how to divide with a two-digit binary numeral:

$$\begin{array}{r} 11 \\ 11\overline{)1001} \\ \underline{11} \\ 11 \\ \underline{11} \end{array}$$

To divide 11 into 1001, think, "11 is larger than 10, but smaller than 100. So it must go into 100 once." Write 1 over the second zero. Then complete the problem by multiplying and subtracting as in a decimal numeral problem. But remember to use binary subtraction facts.

Duodecimal Arithmetic has more facts than decimal arithmetic because it uses more digits—0 through 9, plus T and E.

Duodecimal Addition. You can use the following table to find the basic facts of duodecimal addition.

+	0	1	2	3	4	5	6	7	8	9	T	E
0	0	1	2	3	4	5	6	7	8	9	T	E
1	1	2	3	4	5	6	7	8	9	T	E	10
2	2	3	4	5	6	7	8	9	T	E	10	11
3	3	4	5	6	7	8	9	T	E	10	11	12
4	4	5	6	7	8	9	T	E	10	11	12	13
5	5	6	7	8	9	T	E	10	11	12	13	14
6	6	7	8	9	T	E	10	11	12	13	14	15
7	7	8	9	T	E	10	11	12	13	14	15	16
8	8	9	T	E	10	11	12	13	14	15	16	17
9	9	T	E	10	11	12	13	14	15	16	17	18
T	T	E	10	11	12	13	14	15	16	17	18	19
E	E	10	11	12	13	14	15	16	17	18	19	1T

To find the sum of 6 + T, for example, first find the row that begins with 6. Then run your finger to the right along this row until you come to the column that has T at the top. Your finger will be on 14 (meaning 1 twelve plus 4), the sum of 6 plus T.

Use the table to solve the following problem:

Duodecimal Addition	Meaning	Decimal Addition
2T	2 twelves + T ones	34
+81	8 twelves + 1 one	+97
TE	T twelves + E ones	131

First, use the fact T + 1 = E to add the ones. Then use the fact 2 + 8 = T (meaning 2 twelves + 8 twelves = T twelves).

When the sum in any place is greater than E, you have to regroup in terms of the base, 12, as shown in the next example.

Duodecimal Addition	Meaning	Decimal Addition
$\overset{1}{6E}$	6 twelves + E ones	83
+34	3 twelves + 4 ones	+40
T3	9 twelves + 13 ones	123
	or, after regrouping,	
	T twelves + 3 ones	

In the ones place, E + 4 = 13, as shown in the table. Regroup 13 ones into 1 twelve plus 3 ones. Write 3 in the ones place and a small 1 in the twelves place over the 6. Then add the twelves: 6 + 3 = 9 twelves; 9 plus the 1 twelve you got by regrouping equals T twelves.

Duodecimal Subtraction. You can use the duodecimal addition facts table to find subtraction facts, too. For example, to subtract T from 14, first find the column that begins with T. Next, run your finger down this column until you come to 14. Then run your finger to the left along this row to the beginning digit to find the answer, 6.

Use the table to solve the next problem.

Duodecimal Subtraction	Meaning	Decimal Subtraction
E6	E twelves + 6 ones	138
−T4	T twelves + 4 ones	−124
12	1 twelve + 2 ones	14

First, use the fact 6 − 4 = 2 to subtract the ones. In the twelves place, use the fact E − T = 1 (meaning E twelves − T twelves = 1 twelve).

The next example shows how to regroup when the number you are subtracting in any place is larger than the one you are subtracting it from.

Duodecimal Subtraction	Meaning (after regrouping)	Decimal Subtraction
$\overset{6\,1}{\cancel{7}T}$	6 twelves + 1T ones	94
−3E	3 twelves + E ones	−47
3E	3 twelves + E ones	47

In the ones place, E is larger than T. So you regroup 7 twelves plus T ones into 6 twelves plus 1T ones. Cross out the 7 and write a small 6 above it, and write a small 1 in front of the T. Then use the subtraction fact 1T − E = E to subtract the ones. Use the fact 6 − 3 = 3 to subtract the twelves.

Duodecimal Multiplication also uses more facts than decimal multiplication. You can use the following table to find the basic duodecimal multiplication facts.

×	1	2	3	4	5	6	7	8	9	T	E
1	1	2	3	4	5	6	7	8	9	T	E
2	2	4	6	8	T	10	12	14	16	18	1T
3	3	6	9	10	13	16	19	20	23	26	29
4	4	8	10	14	18	20	24	28	30	34	38
5	5	T	13	18	21	26	2E	34	39	42	47
6	6	10	16	20	26	30	36	40	46	50	56
7	7	12	19	24	2E	36	41	48	53	5T	65
8	8	14	20	28	34	40	48	54	60	68	74
9	9	16	23	30	39	46	53	60	69	76	83
T	T	18	26	34	42	50	5T	68	76	84	92
E	E	1T	29	38	47	56	65	74	83	92	T1

For example, to find the product of 4 × 6, first find the row that begins with 4. Then run your finger to the right until you come to the column that has 6 at the top. Your finger will be on the answer, 20 (2 twelves plus no ones). Use the table to work the following problem:

Duodecimal Multiplication	Meaning	Decimal Multiplication
15	1 twelve + 5 ones	17
×2	2 ones	×2
2T	2 twelves + T ones	34

If the product in any place is greater than E, you have to regroup:

Duodecimal Multiplication	Meaning	Decimal Multiplication
$\overset{2}{3T}$	3 twelves + T ones	46
×3	3 ones	×3
E6	9 twelves + 26 ones	138
	or, after regrouping,	
	E twelves + 6 ones	

In the ones place, use the fact 3 × T = 26. Regroup 26 ones into 2 twelves plus 6 ones. Write 6 in the ones place and a small 2 in the twelves place above the 3. Then multiply 3 × 3 to get 9 and add the 2 to get E.

When the multiplier has more than one digit, repeat the operation for each digit and add the products. Can you find a mistake in the next duodecimal problem?

$$\begin{array}{r} \overset{1}{24} \\ \times 13 \\ \hline 70 \\ 24 \\ \hline 310 \end{array}$$

First multiply 24 × 3. In the ones place, use the fact 3 × 4 = 10. Regroup 10 ones into 1 twelve plus 0 ones. Write 0 in the ones place and a small 1 in the twelves place above the 2. Then use the fact 3 × 2 = 6 in the twelves place, and add the 1 to get 7. Next, multiply 24×1 twelve: $1 \times 4 = 4$ in the twelves place, and $1 \times 2 = 2$ in the one hundred forty-fours place. Finally, add the products. Bring down the 0. Add $7 + 4 = E$ (not $7 + 4 = 11$). Bring down the 2. The correct answer is 2E0 (not 310).

Duodecimal Division. You can also use the duodecimal multiplication table to find division facts. For example, to find the quotient $42 \div T$, first find the column that begins with T. Next, run your finger down this column until you come to 42. Then run your finger to the left along this row until you come to the beginning digit, 5.

Use the table to work the following problem:

Duodecimal Division	Meaning	Decimal Division
17	1 twelve + 7 ones	19
5/7E	5 ones/7 twelves + E ones	5/95
5	5 twelves	5
2E	2 twelves + E ones	45
2E	2 twelves + E ones	45

Think, "7 twelves divided by 5 is 1 twelve." Write 1 above the 7. Multiply 1×5 and write the product 5 below the 7. Complete the problem as you would in decimal division, but use duodecimal arithmetic facts.

History

How Numeration Systems Began. Primitive man had several ways of recording the few numbers he needed. A shepherd could collect pebbles to represent the number of sheep in his flock. Each pebble meant one sheep. A bag of pebbles stood for the whole flock. By matching the pebbles against his flock, he could see if he had all his sheep. Mathematicians call this kind of matching *one-to-one correspondence.*

Later, man developed other ways to record the number of his possessions. He tied knots in a leather thong, or he scratched tally marks (**JHt**) on the side of a rock. He matched the knots or marks against each item.

Then man began to use words to represent numbers. These words told him "how many." They helped him to match items mentally. For example, he used the word for "wings" to mean two objects. To refer to four things, he used the name of a fruit that grew in clusters of four. For five items, he used the word that meant "hand." Such number-names appeared in various primitive languages. They showed that man had begun to form ideas of numbers. Whether he had three fish, three pebbles, or three tally marks, he recognized a "threeness" about each of these groups.

Finally, man began to *count* by arranging his number-names in a certain order. To count, he spoke or wrote the word that meant "one," next the word for "two," then the word for "three," and so on. In time, people in many parts of the world developed various kinds of counting systems. Some were based on five, others on ten, and still others on twelve or sixty. We still use such measures as 12 inches in a foot and 60 minutes in an hour, taken from these ancient systems.

In most early systems, people formed numerals simply by repeating basic symbols and adding their values to get the number they wanted. The Egyptians, Greeks, and Romans used numeral systems of this kind.

The Hindus used a system superior to all others. It followed the principle of place value and used a symbol that meant *not any.* This system became the decimal numeral system, now used in most parts of the world.

The Egyptian Numeral System. About 3000 B.C., the ancient Egyptians used *hieroglyphics* (picture writing) to write numerals, as shown below.

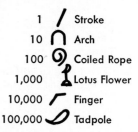

1	/	Stroke
10	∩	Arch
100	𝕯	Coiled Rope
1,000	⚘	Lotus Flower
10,000	∕	Finger
100,000	⟋	Tadpole

This system was based on 10. But it did not include a zero symbol, nor did it use the principle of place value. The Egyptians formed numerals by putting basic symbols together. For example, they wrote the numeral 1,326 like this:

$$ 𝚹 999 ∩∩ /// $$

With this system, Egyptians could put symbols in any order, because the value of a symbol did not depend on its position.

The Greek Numeral System. About 500 B.C., the Greeks developed a system based on ten. This system used a 27-letter Greek alphabet—the present-day 24-letter alphabet plus three letters no longer used. The first nine letters stood for numbers, from 1 through 9. The next nine letters stood for tens, from 10 through 90. The last nine letters were symbols for hundreds, from 100 through 900. The Greeks formed numerals by combining these symbols and adding their values.

The Roman Numeral System uses letters as symbols for numbers. But the early Roman system of about 500 B.C. differed from the system we use today. For example, the ancient Romans wrote 4 as IIII and 9 as VIIII. They used the symbol Ɫ for 50 and CIƆ for 1,000. Today, we use IV for 4, IX for 9, L for 50, and M for 1,000. The numerals VI, XV, and LX illustrate the *additive* principle. When the first of two symbols stands for a larger number than the second, you *add* the value of the first to the second to get the value of the combination. Thus, the Roman numeral VI represents 6, or $5 + 1$; XV represents 15 as $10 + 5$; and LX represents $50 + 10 = 60$.

The numerals IV and IX illustrate the *subtractive* principle. When the first of two symbols stands for a smaller number than the second, you subtract the value of the first from that of the second to get the value of the combination. Thus, in the Roman numeral IV, you subtract 1 from 5 to get 4.

The Babylonian Numeral System used *cuneiform* (wedge-shaped) symbols. An early system of about 3000 B.C. was based on 60. In this system, a numeral contained groups of symbols. One group stood for the number of ones, the next group stood for 60's, the next for (60×60)'s, and so on.

By 1500 B.C., the Babylonians had also developed

a system based on 10. In this system, the numeral for "one thousand" was a combination of the symbols for "ten" and "one hundred."

The Hindu-Arabic Numeral System. Hindu mathematicians of the 300's and 200's B.C. used a system based on 10. The Hindus had symbols for each number from one to nine. They had a name for each power of 10, and used these names when writing numerals. For example, a Hindu wrote "1 sata, 3 dasan, 5" to represent the number we write as 135. He wrote "1 sata, 5" for the number we write as 105.

Probably about A.D. 600, the Hindus found a way of eliminating place names. They invented the symbol *sunya* (meaning *empty*), which we call *zero*. With this symbol, they could write "105" instead of "1 sata, 5."

During the 700's, the Arabs learned Hindu arithmetic from scientific writings of the Hindus and the Greeks. Then, in the 800's, a Persian mathematician wrote a book that was translated into Latin about 300 years later. This translation brought the Hindu-Arabic numerals into Europe.

Several hundred years passed before the Hindu-Arabic system became widely used. Many persons liked Hindu-Arabic numerals because they could easily use them to write out calculations. Others preferred Roman numerals because they were accustomed to solving problems on a device called an *abacus* without writing out the calculations. After the development of printing from movable type in the 1400's, many mathematics textbooks were published. Most of them showed calculations using the Hindu-Arabic system. These books brought the system into widespread use.

Mathematicians regard the Hindu-Arabic system as one of the world's greatest inventions. Its greatness lies in the principle of place value and in the use of zero. These two ideas make it easy to represent numbers and to perform mathematical operations that would be difficult with any other kind of system.

Rediscovering Numeration Systems. During the late 1600's, the German mathematician and philosopher Gottfried Wilhelm Leibniz (1646-1716) developed the binary numeration system. However, mathematicians found no practical use for the system until the 1940's, when computers were developed. Today, many electronic computers use the binary system.

During the 1950's and 1960's, many educators recognized the value of teaching numeration systems. Students began studying various systems as a part of what was called the "new mathematics." By doing arithmetic with unfamiliar systems, students gained a better understanding of the familiar decimal system and of arithmetic in general. However, in the 1970's, educators recognized that students also needed practice in solving everyday arithmetic problems and learning basic computational skills. CHARLOTTE W. JUNGE

NUMERATION SYSTEMS PROBLEMS

1. The dots in the pattern below have been grouped by 10. Copy the dot pattern on a piece of paper. Then draw lines around the dots to group them by 5. Write the base 5 numeral for the number of dots.

2. How many stars are shown below? Give your answer in base 12 and in base 2.

★ ★ ★ ★ ★ ★ ★ ★
★ ★ ★ ★ ★ ★ ★ ★

3. What is the base of the system that uses the following numerals in counting?

1, 2, 3, 4, 5, 6, 7, 10, 11, 12, . . .

4. Fill in the digits for evaluating the binary numeral 101101. Write the decimal value of this numeral.

$1 \times 2^5 + \_ \times 2^4 + \_ \times 2^3 + 1 \times 2^2 + \_ \times 2^1 + 1$

5. Make groups of dots showing the numbers represented by the numeral 11 in (a) the duodecimal system, (b) the quinary system, (c) the binary system.

ANSWERS

1.

23_{five}

2. 16_{twelve}; 10010_{two}

3. Base 8

4. 0×2^4; 1×2^3; 0×2^1; decimal value = 45

5.

Base 12   Base 5   Base 2

Related Articles in WORLD BOOK include:

Abacus	Division
Addition	Duodecimal Numerals
Algebra (Positive and	Multiplication
Negative Numbers)	Notation
Arabic Numerals	Power
Arithmetic (Working with	Roman Numerals
Whole Numbers)	Set Theory
Binary Arithmetic	Subtraction
Decimal Numeral System	Zero

Outline

I. **Kinds of Numeration Systems**
  A. The Decimal System   C. The Binary System
  B. The Quinary System   D. The Duodecimal System
II. **Working with Numeration Systems**
  A. Decimal Arithmetic   C. Binary Arithmetic
  B. Quinary Arithmetic   D. Duodecimal Arithmetic
III. **History**

NUMERATOR. See ARITHMETIC (Common Fractions); FRACTION.

NUMEROLOGY, *NOO mer AHL oh jih,* is the practice of using a person's name and birth date in an attempt to tell his character and abilities, and see into his past and future. It is a *pseudo* (false) science. It has no scientific standing, and is not based on facts. Historians believe the ancient Chinese and Hebrews used it. The supposed basis for numerology is that all numbers vibrate. Each letter of the alphabet is supposed to have a numerical value. A person's name and birth date are said to give information about his vibrations. JOHN MULHOLLAND

NUMIDIA was an area in northern Africa during ancient times. It occupied part of what is now Algeria. Numidia was allied with nearby Carthage when the Second Punic War between Carthage and Rome began in 218 B.C. But Massinissa, a Numidian chieftain, sided with the Roman general Scipio. In return, Scipio made Massinissa king of all Numidia in 203 B.C. The next year, the Numidians helped Scipio defeat the Carthaginians; led by Hannibal, at Zama in North Africa.

Several times after the war, Massinissa seized land from Carthage. Finally, Carthage fought back, helping bring about the Third Punic War (149-146 B.C.). Rome destroyed Carthage in the war, but also halted Numidian expansion. By 112 B.C., Jugurtha, adopted grandson of Massinissa, had seized all of Numidia in defiance of Rome. He was defeated by the Roman general Marius in 106 B.C. In 46 B.C., Numidian King Juba fought Julius Caesar and was defeated. The Roman emperor Augustus made Numidia part of the Roman province of Africa in 25 B.C.   HENRY C. BOREN

NUMISMATIST. See COIN COLLECTING.

NUMITOR. See ROMULUS AND REMUS.

NUMMULITE, *NUHM yoo lite,* is the name for a large number of marine one-celled fossil animals. They can be recognized by their shells, which are shaped like flat disks. On the inside, each shell is coiled and divided into many little chambers. Some nummulites are smaller than a dime, others larger than a half dollar. The large-shelled nummulites are really giants among one-celled animals. During the Eocene and Oligocene periods of geologic time, nummulites lived in great numbers in the sea. Their shells made up thick layers of rock, especially in southern Asia and in the Mediterranean. The pyramids of ancient Egypt were built with blocks of such *nummulitic* limestone taken from large quarries.

Scientific Classification. Nummulites belong to the phylum *Protozoa* and the order *Foraminifera.* They are in the camerind family, *Camerinidae.*   SAMUEL PAUL WELLES

NUN is a woman who belongs to a religious community and dedicates her life to carrying out its goals. Various major religions, including Buddhism, Christianity, and Taoism, have orders of nuns. The Roman Catholic Church has more of these orders than any other Christian denomination.

WORLD BOOK photo

Many Roman Catholic Nuns, such as the one shown above, teach in parochial schools. Others devote their lives to nursing or to such services as caring for orphans and the aged.

Most Roman Catholic orders of nuns have different requirements for permanent membership, but they all require years of preparation. When a woman enters an order, she begins a period of spiritual training called a *novitiate.* During this period, which in many orders lasts from 5 to 10 years, she becomes thoroughly acquainted with the obligations of religious life (see RELIGIOUS LIFE). After her novitiate, the woman takes her final vows. She promises to give up possession of worldly goods, obey her superiors in the order, and remain unmarried. These promises may be either *simple vows* or *solemn vows.* Solemn vows are more binding.

A woman who has taken simple vows is known as a *sister.* One who has taken solemn vows is properly called a nun. But the term *sister* is commonly used as a form of address for a nun.

The first convents for women were founded in the Egyptian desert during the early 300's by Saint Pachomius. During the Middle Ages, nuns led strictly *cloistered* (secluded) lives in such convents. In 1633, Saint Vincent de Paul founded the Sisters of Charity, an order devoted to charity work outside the convent. The members of this order cared for orphans and the sick and taught children and adults.

The nun's way of life was modernized by Vatican Council II, a worldwide council of the Roman Catholic Church held from 1962 to 1965. Many orders now permit their members to live in small informal groups rather than in a convent. Many nuns no longer must wear the traditional robe and veil. Nuns continue to work in charitable and educational fields. They now also counsel youths in juvenile courts and perform other services as well.   RUTH McDONELL

Related Articles in WORLD BOOK include:

Carmelites	Sacred Heart of Jesus,
Convent	Society of the
Dominicans	Sisters of Charity
Franciscans	Sisters of Mercy
Little Sisters of the Poor	Ursulines

NUNCIO, *NUN shih oh,* or APOSTOLIC NUNCIO, is a Roman Catholic official somewhat like an ambassador. Nuncios represent the pope and are sent by the church to many countries that are largely Catholic. Nuncios are accredited, as are temporal ambassadors. They are concerned with the welfare of the church in countries to which they are accredited. *Internuncios* are officials with the same power as nuncios, but they are of a lesser rank.   FULTON J. SHEEN

See also LEGATE.

NUREMBERG, *NYOOR um berg* (pop. 477,100), is one of the oldest cities in Germany. Its German name is Nürnberg. The city is in West Germany and lies on the Pegnitz River, 92 miles (148 kilometers) northwest of Munich (see GERMANY [political map]). Nuremberg is noted for its historical landmarks and its toy industry. The city manufactures pencils, chemicals, and electrical supplies.

In the Middle Ages, the city was one of the most important cultural centers in Germany. The first German *gymnasium* (higher school) was established in Nuremberg. The first German paper mill stood in this city. About 1500, Peter Henlein invented in Nuremberg what may have been the first watch (see WATCH [History]).

The heart of Nuremberg was once its walled inner quarter. Many famous buildings, which were hundreds

German Tourist Information Office

An Old Wine-Storage House in Nuremberg, now a college dormitory, is one of Germany's finest medieval structures.

of years old, stood there. The Burg (royal palace), built between 1024 and 1158, stood on a hill overlooking the city. Allied bombs almost destroyed this section during World War II.

Nuremberg was known as a city as early as the 1000's. It became a Protestant center during the Reformation. Nuremberg was a free city at the time it became part of the kingdom of Bavaria in the early 1800's.

Nuremberg became an important political center after the National Socialists (Nazis) came to power in Germany in 1933. The Nazis held their nationwide assemblies and congresses in Nuremberg. In 1935, the Nazi-controlled national assembly (*Reichstag*) met at Nuremberg and approved the "Nuremberg Laws." These laws forbade Germans to marry Jews, deprived Jews of citizenship, and made the swastika Germany's flag.

American forces occupied Nuremberg in the last months of the war and continued to hold the city as part of the American zone. In 1945, various former officials of the German government, army, and navy were placed on trial in Nuremberg.   JAMES K. POLLOCK

See also NUREMBERG TRIALS.

NUREMBERG TRIALS were a series of 13 trials held in Nuremberg, Germany, from 1945 to 1949. In these trials, leaders of Nazi Germany were accused of crimes against international law. Some of the defendants were charged with causing World War II deliberately, and with waging aggressive wars of conquest. Nearly all were charged with murder, enslavement, looting, and other atrocities against soldiers and civilians of occupied countries. Some were also charged with responsibility for the persecution of Jews and other racial and national groups.

The Nuremberg trials were a new development in international law. Trials of war criminals have been carried on in one form or another for hundreds of years. But at Nuremberg, for the first time, the leaders of a government were brought to trial on the charge of starting an aggressive war.

The First Trial was held before the International Military Tribunal. This tribunal was set up under an agreement signed by representatives of the United States, Great Britain, France, and Russia at London in August, 1945. Judges and prosecutors from all four countries took part in the first trial. In it, 22 officials of

Nazi Germany were the defendants. Among these leaders were Hermann Goering, Rudolf Hess, Joachim von Ribbentrop, and Hjalmar Schacht. Martin Bormann was tried *in absentia* (while absent). On Oct. 1, 1946, the court convicted 19 defendants, and acquitted Schacht and two others. Seven, including Hess, were sentenced to prison. Bormann, Goering, von Ribbentrop, and nine others were condemned to death. Goering killed himself on October 15, and Bormann could not be found. The other condemned men were hanged at Nuremberg on October 16.

Further Trials. The four nations occupying Germany decided that additional war crimes trials should be held in each of the occupation zones. In the American zone, 12 trials were held in Nuremberg from 1946 to 1949. There were three trials of military leaders, three trials of principal officers in the SS (Hitler's private army), three trials of industrialists, one trial of government officials and diplomats, one trial of Nazi judges, and one trial of doctors who had conducted cruel and deadly medical experiments in concentration camps. About 200 leaders were brought to trial. Many were sentenced to prison, a few were sentenced to death and hanged, and some were acquitted.

Importance of the Trials. The nations responsible for conducting trials at Nuremberg hoped they would mark a great forward step in the development of international law, and in the preservation of peace and civilization. But some persons criticized the trials as acts of vengeance by the victorious nations. Others argued that there was no basis in international law for trying the German leaders on the charge of starting a war.   TELFORD TAYLOR

See also INTERNATIONAL LAW; WAR CRIME.

NUREYEV, *NUH reh yef,* **RUDOLF** (1938-   ), is a Russian dancer who *defected* (deserted) to the West in 1961. He joined England's Royal Ballet in 1962 as partner to Dame Margot Fonteyn, the company's prima ballerina. Nureyev and Dame Margot won praise for their performances in the classics of the 1900's and in *Marguerite and Armand*, created for the pair by Sir Frederick Ashton in 1963. See FONTEYN, DAME MARGOT (picture).

Critics have praised Nureyev for the apparently natural ease of his dancing. In addition to performing, he re-created several Russian works for the Royal Ballet. In 1966, he restaged Marius Petipa's four-act ballet *Don Quixote* for the Vienna State Opera. The next year, he composed a new version of *The Nutcracker*, which is based on Peter Tchaikovsky's music, for the Royal Swedish Ballet.   SELMA JEANNE COHEN

See also BALLET (picture: *Swan Lake*).

NURSE. See NURSING; HOSPITAL.

NURSERY raises trees, shrubs, and vines until they are ready for permanent planting elsewhere. Nurseries also scientifically develop such plants. People use these plants to beautify public and private property, to reforest vacant land, to control soil erosion, and in many other ways. The United States has over 100,000 acres (40,000 hectares) of nurseries. The federal and state governments operate many nurseries, but most are private enterprises. William Prince founded the first American nursery in New York about 1770.

From *Mother Goose*, illustrated by Pelagie Doane, and published by Random House. © 1940, by Random House, Inc. By permission of Artists and Writers Guild, Incorporated

"Pease Porridge Hot, Pease Porridge Cold."

NURSERY RHYME. Ever since the world was young, children have danced and played games. They have made up songs and rhymed words to go with their game-playing. This is as natural for children as their love of fairy tales and music. We do not know how most of these old rhymes began. The children probably made up many and passed them along to other children. Adults may have made up other rhymes.

The rhymes of childhood cover every subject and game a child is interested in. Some of these things are chasing games, counting games, guessing games, and games that are contests. Other rhymes are about familiar birds and beasts, the villages and cities that children know, the bridges they have crossed, and the activities and trades that go on around them. Almost everything has been made into rhyme. Children hear the rhymes and change them to fit their country and times.

Little girls have skipped rope in almost every country in the world, and counted the number of skips in rhymes such as this:

> Apple, peach, pumpkin pie,
> How many years before I die?
> One, two, three, - - - - - - - .

The following poem is usually recited to the clapping of hands.

> Pease porridge hot,
> Pease porridge cold,
> Pease porridge in the pot,
> Nine days old;
> Some like it hot,
> Some like it cold,
> Some like it in the pot,
> Nine days old.

Children of all time have been delighted with hunting games. They have used buttons, thimbles, handkerchiefs, and other small objects. A flower or nut was probably used the first time the game was played. All the players but the one who is *it* form a circle. The handkerchief, or other object, is hidden while the players sing:

> Drop the handkerchief Saturday night,
> Where do you think I found it?
> Up in the sky, ever so high,
> A thousand stars around it.
> Itiskit, Itaskit,
> Green and yellow basket,
> I sent a letter to my love
> And on the way I lost it.
> I lost it once; I lost it twice;
> I lost it three times over.

Riddles have always been among the best-loved rhymes. One that has a *river* for an answer is:

> Runs all day and never walks,
> Often murmurs, never talks;
> It has a bed and never sleeps;
> It has a mouth and never eats.

There have always been games to play with the baby's toes, or for children to play with their fingers. It is said that Oliver Goldsmith (1730?-1774), famous English writer, had one he taught to all the children he knew. He put two small pieces of black paper on the nails of his index, or pointing, fingers. He stretched out his hands, palms down, and then sang:

> Two bonnie blackbirds sitting on a hill;
> One named Jack and one named Jill.
> Fly away Jack; fly away Jill.
> Come back Jack; come back Jill.

Goldsmith would bend his fingers at the proper time in the rhyme and conceal the paper in his hand.

Children have had fun with tongue-twisters in rhyme in all languages. A famous tongue-twister in English is *Peter Piper*. Most of the fun from these rhymes comes in reciting them as fast as possible.

Peter Piper picked a peck of pickled peppers;
A peck of pickled peppers Peter Piper picked;
If Peter Piper picked a peck of pickled peppers,
Where's the peck of pickled peppers Peter Piper picked?

A counting rhyme that has delighted young and old for many generations is:

> One-ery, you-ery, e-kery, heaven,
> Hollow-bone, willow-bone, ten or eleven.
> Spin, spun—must be done—
> Hollow-bone, willow-bone, twenty-one.

Some rhymes are made up for their complete nonsense. One of these is:

> If all the world were paper,
> And all the sea were ink,
> And all the trees were bread and cheese,
> What would we have to drink?

The rhyme of *Little Jack Horner* has an interesting history. It is a tale of dishonest dealings in the days of King Henry VIII of England.

> Little Jack Horner,
> Sat in the corner,
> Eating his Christmas pie;
> He stuck in his thumb,
> And pulled out a plum,
> And cried, "What a bright boy am I."

But there is more to the story than appears in the nursery rhyme. It seems that a man by the name of John Horner, a steward of Glastonbury, England, was sent to London with a pie for the King. Title deeds for several estates in Somersetshire were baked in the pie. The greedy John Horner *stuck in his thumb* in the pie before he got to London. In other words, he stole the King's *plum*, which was the land deed for the Abbey of Mells. The estate formerly belonged to the Church of England. Another story is that Queen Jane's brother, Edward Seymour, received a pie in the 1500's from which some valuable papers had been stolen. Some scholars prefer this story to the first.

This legend seems more believable when we know that papers were often baked in pies at this time. It was a favorite trick in the 1500's to hide surprises of all kinds in pies. A rare old book of recipes tells a similar tale. It instructs a chef to make pies with live birds in them so that they may fly out when the pie is cut. This is probably the origin of the famous nursery rhyme:

Sing a song of sixpence,
Pocket full of rye,
Four and twenty blackbirds,
Baked in a pie;
When the pie was opened,
The birds began to sing,
Was not that a dainty dish,
To set before a king?

Several jingles were made up when the kings from the House of Hanover took over the English throne in 1714. A political party called *Jacobites* supported James III for the crown. They considered that George of Hanover, as a German, had no right to be King of England. They recited this rhyme when he became George I.

Hark, hark, the dogs do bark,
The beggars are coming to town;
Some are in rags, and some are in tags,
And some are in velvet gowns.

The Jacobites also used this rhyme:

Jim and George were two great lords,
They fought all in a churn;
And when that Jim got George by the nose,
Then George began to girn (whine).

This rhyme may shed some light on the same George's friendships with the women of the court.

Georgey Porgey, pudding and pie,
Kissed the girls and made them cry;
When the boys came out to play,
Georgey Porgey ran away.

A more recent rhyme tells of the adventures of Mary and her lamb. Here are the first three verses.

Mary had a little lamb,
Its fleece was white as snow,
And everywhere that Mary went,
The lamb was sure to go.

He followed her to school one day;
Which was against the rule;
It made the children laugh and play,
To see a lamb at school.

And so the teacher turned him out;
But still he lingered near,
And waited patiently about,
Till Mary did appear.

The *Mary* of the poem is generally said to be Mary Elizabeth Sawyer. Her lamb followed her to the Old Redstone Schoolhouse, near Sterling, Mass. Polly Kimball was the teacher who sent the lamb out. Sarah Josepha Hale wrote the verses, although they have been claimed by several others, including John Roulstone. The incident is a common one, and many have claimed to be the Mary of the poem.

The following rhyme is usually sung as a group of children dance in a circle. The first two verses are:

Here we go round the mulberry bush,
The mulberry bush, the mulberry bush,
Here we go round the mulberry bush,
So early in the morning.

This is the way we wash our clothes,
Wash our clothes, wash our clothes,
This is the way we wash our clothes,
On a cold and frosty morning.

Many of these nursery rhymes were written to tell a story with a lesson in it. This one suggests that little details are as important as big ones:

For want of a nail, the shoe was lost;
For want of the shoe, the horse was lost;
For want of the horse, the rider was lost;
For want of the rider, the battle was lost;
For want of the battle, the kingdom was lost;
And all for the want of a horseshoe nail!

For hundreds of years, babies have been lulled to sleep to the tune of *Bye, Baby Bunting*.

Bye, baby bunting,
Daddy's gone a-hunting,
To get a little rabbit skin,
To wrap the baby bunting in.

The Lord Mayor is another famous rhyme. Each line of the song represents a part of the face, which is touched as the line is recited:

Here sits the Lord Mayor, (forehead)
Here sit his two men, (eyes)
Here sits the cock, (right cheek)
Here sits the hen, (left cheek)
Here sit the little chickens, (tip of nose)
Here they all run in; (mouth)
Chinchopper, chinchopper,
Chinchopper chin! (chuck the chin)

There are many short verses that are probably as well known as many of the great classics of poetry. Some of them are:

Star light, star bright,
First star I see to-night;
I wish I may, I wish I might,
Have the wish I wish to-night.

A diller, a dollar,
A ten o'clock scholar,
What makes you come so soon?
You used to come at ten o'clock,
And now you come at noon.

Pussy-cat, pussy-cat, where have you been?
I've been to London to see the Queen.
Pussy-cat, pussy-cat, what did you there?
I frightened a little mouse under the chair.

Peter, Peter, pumpkin-eater,
Had a wife and couldn't keep her;
He put her in a pumpkin-shell,
And there he kept her very well.

The MOTHER GOOSE article in THE WORLD BOOK ENCYCLOPEDIA contains the nursery rhymes *Old King Cole*, *Little Jack Horner*, and *Hey Diddle Diddle*. The most popular nursery rhymes can be found illustrated in color in Volume I of CHILDCRAFT. This is published by World Book—Childcraft International, Inc., publishers of THE WORLD BOOK ENCYCLOPEDIA. For other books of nursery rhymes, see the Books to Read section (Beginning Books) following the WORLD BOOK article on LITERATURE FOR CHILDREN.   DOROTHY ELIZABETH SMITH

See also GAME (Games for Young Children).

NURSERY SCHOOL

NURSERY SCHOOL is a school for children from 3 to 4 years old. Children this age form important basic attitudes toward themselves, the people around them, and the world in which they live. These early attitudes strongly influence their behavior throughout later life. The nursery school aims at helping a child's physical, emotional, intellectual, and social growth during this critical period.

Nursery Schools in the United States

The United States has many nursery schools. But no reliable estimate of the number of nursery schools is available. Most of them are private. *Cooperative nursery schools*, owned and operated by parents, form the next largest group. Some churches have weekday nursery schools, and many colleges and universities operate them for educational research and practice-teaching.

A small but growing number of nursery schools care for handicapped children. For example, special nursery schools help crippled children and youngsters who suffer from defects in hearing, speech, and sight. Public-school systems seldom include nursery schools. But they often give funds to the special schools for handicapped children. *Day-care centers* are institutions that care for the children of working mothers.

Most private and cooperative nursery schools in the United States are half-day schools. Some schools, especially college-laboratory nursery schools, have full-day programs. They give the children luncheon at school and see that the children rest after the meal. Day-care centers are usually open from 6 A.M. to 6 P.M. Mothers who work can bring their children to the center at any time during the day.

Instruction in the Nursery School

Learning Through Play. Most nursery schools follow the principle that children from 3 to 4 can learn best through play. The youngsters spend a large part of their time playing with toys. A nursery school usually has many kinds of toys and equipment, including wagons, trucks, and boats; blocks, puzzles, and beads; clay, paints, and crayons; dolls, stuffed animals, and toys for make-believe housekeeping; sandboxes and sand toys; books; and a framework made of metal pipes on which the children can climb. There are also boards, planks, sawhorses, boxes, shovels, wheelbarrows, water, and pots and pans. Nursery schools also have some equipment found in schools for older children.

Selection of Play Materials. Nursery-school teachers select toys and other equipment with great care. The toys must promote a youngster's growth. They must also stimulate the child's development as a creative, self-reliant, and imaginative citizen in a democratic society. Nursery schools usually have few or no mechanical toys. A child only winds most mechanical toys and watches them work. Instead of these, nursery-school teachers choose toys and materials that can be used in many ways. These stimulate the imagination, and call for action on the child's part.

As children develop, they become more interested in other persons. Young children need practice in getting along with people, because a democratic society needs citizens who enjoy working with others. For this reason, nursery-school teachers prefer equipment that can best be used by children playing together.

At the same time, children are eager to explore the world in which they live. Nursery-school teachers also use play materials that help introduce children to this world. For example, nursery-school children often play with finger paints, water, mud, sand, clay, and wood. Each of these acquaints the child with a different feel and texture.

Nursery schools are concerned with the child's total development. Some kinds of equipment, such as a framework to climb on, promote a child's physical growth. Others, such as beads, teach a child to use the eyes and hands together. Still other kinds of play help social, intellectual, and emotional development.

Health forms an important part of most nursery-school programs. Nursery schools usually require a child to have a complete physical examination before entrance. Most nursery schools also require various immunizations and vaccinations. A doctor or nurse pays regular visits to the school, and a nursery-school teacher usually checks the children's health every day.

Most nursery-school programs recognize a child's need for adequate food and rest. They usually have a midmorning rest time and midmorning fruit or vegetable juice. Most full-day nursery schools give milk and crackers to the youngsters who stay through the afternoon. If the nursery school serves lunch, it either has an expert on child nutrition on its staff or follows the advice of an expert.

Other Training includes learning a number of important skills that the children can use in everyday life. The nursery-school teacher plans activities such as dressing and eating, so a child *learns independence*. Nursery schools have specially designed tables, chairs, plates, cups, and tableware that a child can learn to use easily. Almost all nursery-school furnishings, including those in the washrooms and coat closets, are of special design. For example, the designers place the hooks in a coat closet so that a child can reach them.

The Teacher

Children who go to nursery school leave their parents for the first time. This departure forms a critical step in

Wm. Franklin McMahon

Children in Nursery Schools take part in a variety of creative activities, including drawing and painting pictures.

their emotional and social development. Nursery-school teachers influence children's development in almost every way they act toward them. A nursery-school teacher must have a warm personality and the ability to be a friend to each child.

The Teacher's Role in a nursery school often seems different from that in a school for older children. For example, the teacher does not usually stand in the front of the room. Nor is the day divided into periods for studying particular subjects. A nursery-school teacher's biggest job is to plan indoor and outdoor activities so that the children learn chiefly from what they do, rather than from what they are told. Only rarely—during storytelling time or music time or when the group takes a trip—does the teacher take the center of the stage. Much time should be spent talking with individual children. Youngsters have many questions, and usually need help in solving their problems.

Training. Some nursery-school teachers take their professional training in home economics, because the nursery school in many ways serves as a supplement to the home. Others study in colleges of education or in child-study departments of liberal-arts colleges. They major in such fields as child development, child welfare, or *early childhood education*. Early childhood education is a field that includes educational programs for children from 3 to 8.

Associations. There are two national professional organizations that include nursery-school teachers: the Association for Childhood Education International and the National Association for the Education of Young Children, both with headquarters in Washington, D.C. The National Education Association also has a department that includes nursery-school instruction. Many nursery-school teachers have state and local associations. See CHILDHOOD EDUCATION INTERNATIONAL, ASSOCIATION FOR; NATIONAL EDUCATION ASSOCIATION OF THE UNITED STATES.

History

British factory owners began the first school groups for young children in the late 1700's. Hundreds of factories appeared in Great Britain at this time, and large numbers of women went to work in them. Many working mothers could not leave their younger children at home or keep the children with them at their jobs. The factory owners often provided special rooms for these youngsters, and hired untrained supervisors or older boys and girls to watch the children.

Robert Owen (1771-1858), a social reformer and mill owner, became the first to see the need for improving these schools. Owen set up the first regular teaching program for the children in his own factory in Great Britain. He hired persons with some teaching qualifications to supervise and teach the children. But schools such as Owen's remained rare until after World War I ended in 1918.

British law established the first public nursery schools in 1918. Other European countries, including France and Germany, followed Great Britain's example. In the United States, nursery schools developed on a private or cooperative basis. But the number of nursery schools grew rapidly. In 1918, the United States had only three nursery schools. In 1927-1928, it had 76. By 1930-1931, the number had risen to about 500. During the depres-

sion, the federal government maintained nursery schools as part of the Works Progress Administration (see NEW DEAL). The United States had 2,398 such nursery schools by 1933.

The federal government again supported nursery schools during World War II. It helped establish many nursery schools called *child-care centers*. At the peak of this program, these centers cared for 129,476 children. Nursery-school attendance dropped sharply when these centers closed after World War II, but the number of nursery schools, both public and private, continued to grow.   JAMES L. HYMES, JR.

Related Articles in WORLD BOOK include:

Day-Care Center	Education	Owen (Robert)
Early Childhood	Elementary School	School
Education	Kindergarten	Teaching

NURSE'S AIDE is a person who helps nurses in hospitals perform their work. A nurse's aide also may be called a *ward helper*, a *hospital attendant*, or a *nursing aide*. A man who performs this kind of work is usually called an *orderly*.

The nurse's aide does as much of a nurse's work as possible. By doing the jobs that require little or no training, the nurse's aide allows a regular nurse to concentrate on jobs that require special skills. Nurse's aides answer patients' calls; help feed, wash, and care for them; and keep their rooms in order. If patients have to go to some other part of the hospital, nurse's aides may go along. They may help support patients during treatment, or help move them onto or off of beds and stretchers. In larger hospitals, nurse's aides may act as diet assistants or as clerks.

There are two kinds of nurse's aides. The Red Cross trains volunteer workers who help out in community hospitals. Most of these are older women. But many nurse's aides are paid workers who have no nursing training. Many young girls work as nurse's aides in a hospital for a while in order to find out whether or not they want to become nurses.

See also NURSING.

NURSING. Most nurses work in hospitals taking care of sick persons and helping them get well. But nurses work in other places. Visiting nurses go to the homes of the sick. Some nurses assist in the offices of doctors and dentists. Others work in medical clinics, in schools, in stores and factories, in the armed forces, and on ships, trains, and airplanes. Nurses may be found wherever their skills are needed—in big cities, small towns, and farm areas in all parts of the world.

In addition to caring for the sick, nurses help healthy people stay well. They teach children and adults to protect themselves from disease. Nurses who have had advanced training may also teach in schools and colleges of nursing, where they help others to become professional nurses.

The two main groups of nurses are professional nurses and practical nurses. *Professional nurses*, generally called *registered nurses*, are graduates of two-year junior college programs, two- or three-year hospital programs, or four- or five-year college programs. *Practical nurses* complete a training program that usually lasts 12 months. These nurses perform many duties that relieve professional nurses for duties that require more preparation.

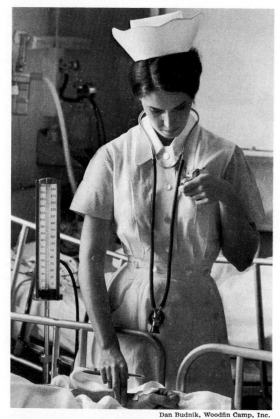

Dan Budnik, Woodfin Camp, Inc.

Most Nurses Work in Hospitals, where they help comfort and care for persons who are sick, injured, or recovering from surgery. The nurse shown above is taking a patient's pulse.

Most professional nurses are women. More women serve in the field of professional nursing than in any other profession except teaching. However, more and more men have been entering the nursing profession. Until the 1960's, men made up only 1 per cent of the total number of professional nurses. But by the early 1970's, nearly 6 per cent of the new students enrolled in professional nursing programs were men. Men also have found many career opportunities in the field of practical nursing, especially in caring for persons with chronic or mental illnesses.

Professional Nurses

Hospital Nurses. Most professional nurses serve as *general-duty* nurses in hospitals. They work with doctors to speed a patient's recovery. General-duty nurses may work in an operating room, where they play an important role as a member of the surgical team. Elsewhere in the hospital, nurses administer prescribed medicines and treatments to patients. In the nursery, nurses care for newborn babies. In other parts of the hospital, nurses assist with blood transfusions, give injections of drugs, or teach patients to care for themselves.

Nurses also take charge of the routine care of patients. They see that patients have a daily bath and that they

eat proper foods. They make sure that patients do exercises or treatments that will aid in recovery. Nurses keep a watchful eye on patients and report to the doctor any changes in physical condition, mental attitude, or reaction to drugs or other treatment.

The well-being of patients is of first importance to nurses. They take time to reassure worried patients and try to boost their morale. Nurses are trained to recognize and understand patients' needs and to provide emotional support as well as physical care. They take time to play with a lonely child, read to a person who cannot see, or write letters for a patient who has a broken arm.

A *head nurse* has charge of the nurses and patients in a ward or in some other unit of the hospital. With additional education, an experienced nurse may become a supervisor and direct several wards or may specialize in one kind of nursing. For example, a nurse who specializes in the care of newborn babies might become head of the hospital nursery. Specialization requires a master's degree, which prepares a nurse for teaching, supervision, or administration.

In other institutions, such as nursing homes and mental hospitals, nurses perform many of the same duties as do hospital nurses. Specialized knowledge or training usually is required because of the special needs of the patients. Many male nurses work in mental hospitals.

Private-Duty Nurses work in hospitals or in private homes. Unlike general-duty nurses, they are employed by the patient rather than by the hospital. Private-duty nurses may devote all their time to only one patient who needs constant care. Sometimes they may attend a small group of patients. Most hospitals keep a *registry*, or file, of nurses who are available for private duty.

Public, or Community, Health Nurses. Public health offers increasing opportunities for professional nurses. Those who wish to enter this field must take special

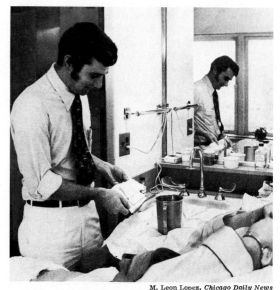

M. Leon Lopez, *Chicago Daily News*

A Male Nurse prepares to change a dressing for a patient. Since the early 1970's, more and more men have enrolled in nursing education programs.

college courses approved for community health work. Public health nurses usually help tend large groups of persons outside hospitals. Most of these nurses work for government or private agencies.

Visiting nurses are public health nurses. So are the nurses employed by city, county, or state health departments. Public health nurses may go into homes to care for patients who have just returned from hospitals. They often teach patients with chronic illnesses how to care for themselves. They also teach patients and their families about proper diet, personal cleanliness, and other ways of preventing illness. Public health nurses may take part in many community projects, such as polio-vaccination and immunization programs for communicable diseases. Some of them work in schools and summer camps.

Occupational, or Industrial, Health Nurses work in factories, stores, banks, and many business offices. They give first aid to the injured. They treat employees for colds, bruises, and other minor ailments. They also promote safety programs to prevent accidents on the job.

Nurse Practitioners, also called *nurse associates*, are professional nurses who have had additional training in a certain area of specialized practice. For example, some nurse practitioners specialize in *geriatrics* (caring for the aged) and others in *pediatrics* (caring for children). Nurse practitioners perform many tasks that were once done only by physicians. These nurses give physical examinations, diagnose and treat minor illnesses, and advise patients on health problems. By administering much of the routine health care, nurse practitioners free physicians to treat patients suffering more serious ailments. Most nurse practitioners work in private clinics or doctors' offices, or in a group practice with physicians or other nurse practitioners.

Other Nursing Careers. Many professional nurses combine the professions of teaching and nursing. To

Rush-Presbyterian-St. Luke's Medical Center, Chicago

Nurse Practitioners work closely with doctors. Special training enables these nurses to provide some kinds of direct patient care once given only by physicians. The nurse practitioner shown at the left above is discussing a patient with a physician.

teach in a school of nursing, a professional nurse must have advanced college preparation. A master's degree in nursing education is usually required for teaching.

Professional nurses may work in clinics or in doctors' and dentists' offices. Nurses also may work on research projects. Some nurses hold positions in nursing organizations. Others write books and articles about nursing. Companies that manufacture drugs and medical equipment often employ nurses as consultants on their products. Nurses serve in the army, navy, and air force. Other branches of the government, such as the Veterans Administration and Department of State, have nurses on their staffs.

Practical Nurses

Practical nurses are specially educated men and women who help professional nurses. They may work in hospitals, private homes, nursing homes, public health agencies, and doctors' offices. Practical nurses often attend mothers and babies, the aged, and chronically ill persons. Frequently they are responsible for such tasks as making beds, giving baths, feeding the helpless, and performing other selected nursing tasks.

Nursing as a Career

Nursing offers daily satisfaction to those who have a genuine desire to help others. It also provides such a wide range of job opportunities that a capable nurse can always be sure of a job.

Among the rewards of nursing are the challenges it offers. A badly injured person may need immediate and expert care. Medicines and equipment must be rushed to the patient's bedside. The family must be comforted, and the doctor must be given a detailed report on the patient's condition. A nurse's greatest reward often is the knowledge that his or her skill has helped to relieve suffering or to save a life.

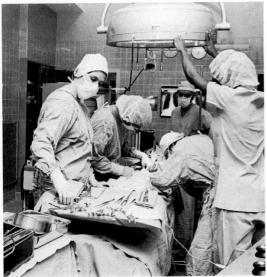

American Nurses' Association

Operating Room Nurses assist surgeons, *center,* during an operation. These nurses must react instantly and accurately to the surgeons' requests for operating instruments.

461

Persons planning a career in nursing should also consider a number of other factors. Advances are being made steadily in nurses' salaries. But beginning salaries may be below those for other professions that require comparable preparation. A person should also consider that some nurses must be active and on their feet a great deal, and may have to do some strenuous work, such as lifting patients. Special *body mechanics* courses taught in nursing schools help the nurse prepare for such tasks.

A nurse must like people and want to help them, and must also have self-reliance and good judgment. Patience, tact, honesty, responsibility, and ability to work easily with others are valuable traits. Good health is another "must."

Most professional nursing schools accept only candidates who rank in the upper half or upper third of their high-school graduating classes. Entrance requirements for practical nursing are less exacting. High-school graduates are preferred, but many practical nursing schools accept candidates with two years of high-school work or less.

Most professional schools admit nursing students between the ages of 17 or 18 and 35. But the upper age limit often is flexible, especially in colleges and universities. Schools of practical nursing admit candidates up to the ages of 45 or 50, but usually also have a flexible upper age limit.

Costs of a nursing education program vary widely. Most hospital schools require an entrance fee and charge tuition. In most college schools of nursing, the student pays tuition and also pays for all or part of her maintenance. Persons who want to enter nursing should inquire about costs at the schools being considered.

Professional Nursing Education. Three types of programs provide the necessary training for a career in professional nursing. They are (1) associate degree programs, (2) diploma programs, and (3) baccalaureate programs. The time needed to complete a program ranges from two to five years, depending on the type of program.

Associate degree programs consist of a two-year course of study in nursing care and related subjects. These programs lead to an associate degree in nursing. Many junior and community colleges offer such programs. Students also gain practical experience by working in local hospitals and other health agencies that cooperate in the programs.

Diploma programs are offered by hospital schools. Such programs require two or three years of study, after which the student receives a diploma. Students take nursing courses in classrooms and laboratories, and also work with patients in the hospital and at other health agencies.

Baccalaureate programs, which are offered by colleges and universities, lead to a bachelor of science degree. The course work requires four to five years. It includes experience with patients in hospitals and health agencies as well as courses in nursing and in the humanities.

All professional nursing education programs provide both classroom training and practical experience. They prepare the student for obtaining a license to practice as a Registered Nurse.

Classroom Work. Student nurses study such subjects as anatomy, chemistry, nutrition, pharmacology, physiology, psychology, and sociology, as well as the fundamentals of nursing care. They learn to care for the sick by working in the nursing laboratory. Frequently, the students practice on one another. For example, one student may take another's temperature, blood pressure, and pulse rate.

Clinical Experience. In all schools of nursing, classroom work or theory is interwoven with practice. Clinical experience, or practice, means the time the student spends in learning to care for different types of patients. As part of their clinical experience, students also learn something about hospital routine and the functions of various departments, and get the "feel" of hospital life.

Student nurses have experience with all types of patients. A teacher who is an expert nurse supervises all their early activities. As students gain experience and knowledge, they work more independently.

Licensing. After graduation from an approved school of nursing, professional nurses in the United States and Canada must pass examinations given by state or provincial boards of examiners. The nurse then receives a license to practice the profession. He or she is now an R.N., or Registered Nurse.

Nurses may advance their careers by additional study and experience. A master's degree is often the step to specialization, teaching, or administration. A nurse who wishes to advance her career even further may earn a doctoral degree.

Practical Nursing Courses usually last one year. Like professional nursing education, the course combines classroom study with actual experience.

There are two types of schools of practical nursing, public and private. Some public schools teach practical nursing as part of their vocational-training or adult-education programs. Private schools are operated by hospitals, health agencies, and by some junior colleges

Rush-Presbyterian-St. Luke's Medical Center, Chicago

A Nurse Keeps Watch over Patients by observing electronic equipment in a hospital's intensive care unit. These devices display information on the heart action, breathing rate, and other vital body functions of each of the patients in the unit.

and universities. Credits from practical nursing schools cannot be transferred to professional nursing schools. Practical nurses who want to become professional nurses may have to begin all over again.

In almost all the states, and some Canadian provinces, a practical nurse, like a professional nurse, must obtain a license to practice. He or she then becomes a Licensed Practical Nurse (L.P.N.), sometimes called a Licensed Vocational Nurse (L.V.N.).

Career Information. A high-school student who wants to learn about a nursing career should talk with a vocational guidance counselor, family doctor, school nurse, or other nurses. Many high schools have Future Nurses clubs whose members visit hospitals and schools of nursing and do volunteer work. Serving as a nurse's aide or as an orderly in a hospital is another way to learn more about nursing (see NURSE'S AIDE). Information on professional and practical nursing may be obtained from the ANA Committee on Nursing Careers, American Nurses' Association, 2420 Pershing Road, Kansas City, Mo. 64108; or from the Committee on Careers, National League for Nursing, 10 Columbus Circle, New York, N.Y. 10019.

The History of Nursing

Some form of nursing care has probably been practiced for thousands of years. For example, the early Hebrews and Egyptians hired women, later called *midwives*, who assisted at births.

Nurses first organized in groups during early Christian times. Noblewomen, including the wives of the emperors, helped care for the ill in ancient Rome. During the Crusades, military nursing orders of monks and knights tended the sick and wounded.

Many monasteries closed during the Reformation, and there were only a few places where religious orders could nurse the sick. The years from 1600 to 1850 were the darkest period in the history of nursing. Hospitals often were built as charity hospitals, and were usually staffed by untrained, sometimes disreputable, women. Wealthy persons never went to hospitals for treatment. The importance of sanitation and hygiene were unknown. People did not know how diseases spread. Often nurses who took care of patients with contagious diseases contracted these diseases themselves.

Nursing as we know it began in the 1850's with the work of the English nurse, Florence Nightingale, the founder of modern professional nursing. She established the first school of nursing, the Nightingale Home for Nurses, in London in 1860. Graduates of this school traveled to all parts of the world, including the United States, to teach nursing. The first nursing schools in the United States were established in 1873 at Massachusetts General Hospital in Boston, Bellevue Hospital in New York City, and the New Haven (Conn.) Hospital. The American Nurses' Association, Inc., an organization of professional registered nurses, was organized in 1896.

Many nurses have won world fame, including Clara Barton, Edith Cavell, Elizabeth Kenny, and Lillian D. Wald. EILEEN M. JACOBI

Related Articles in WORLD BOOK include:

NURSING HOME is a residential institution that provides medical or nonmedical care, chiefly for people who are 65 years old or older. The best nursing homes provide a comfortable, homelike environment for their residents.

The United States has about 22,000 nursing homes, and about 1,300,000 men and women live in them. The homes are privately owned; sponsored by various religious or civic groups; or operated by the federal, state, or local government. Each state has laws governing the operation of nursing homes and requires the institutions to have a license. The homes are inspected periodically to make sure they follow these laws.

There are three types of nursing homes: (1) skilled nursing care homes, (2) intermediate care facilities, and (3) supervised personal care homes. They differ according to the types of patients they care for and the kinds of services they offer.

Skilled Nursing Care Homes provide more extensive services than the other types of nursing homes. For example, they offer diagnostic, laboratory, and medication services; various therapy programs; and dental care. Registered nurses supervise the care of patients according to the instructions of the institution's medical director. Physicians visit skilled nursing care homes frequently.

Most of the patients in skilled nursing care homes require medical attention around the clock. Some have serious illnesses or disabilities. Others stay in these institutions after being hospitalized. They receive additional medical treatment there before returning to their homes.

Most skilled nursing care homes have transfer agreements with hospitals, intermediate care facilities, and other health-care institutions. Patients who become so ill that they need more medical care than a nursing home can provide are taken to a hospital. Those whose health improves, but who still require some nursing care, are transferred to an intermediate care facility or other health-care institution.

Patients in skilled nursing care homes pay about $16 a day. These institutions, which are run by a state-licensed administrator, are certified for participation in the Medicaid and Medicare programs (see MEDICAID; MEDICARE).

Intermediate Care Facilities, also called *basic nursing care homes*, provide basic nursing services. Registered nurses examine the residents periodically to determine what medical treatment is needed. Most men and women in intermediate care facilities suffer from a long-term illness. However, they require only minor medical care. Doctors visit nursing homes of this type at regular intervals.

Registered nurses direct the everyday nursing programs in intermediate care facilities, but an administrator runs these institutions. The patients in these homes are charged about $12 a day. Most intermediate care facilities are certified for participation in the Medicaid program.

Supervised Personal Care Homes provide nonmedical services. These services include preparing and serving the residents' meals and helping the men and women care for themselves. For example, members of the staff assist residents who have difficulty dressing themselves. The institutions also plan various social activities for the men and women.

Most of the residents of supervised personal care homes require only routine medical examinations, and so physicians visit these homes only when necessary. A supervisor of residential care directs the various services provided. Supervised personal care homes charge about $11 a day.   JAMES O. CARPENTER

NUT, Egyptian goddess. See MYTHOLOGY (Egyptian Mythology).

NUT is the popular name for a type of plant seed or fruit which grows in a shell of woody fiber. The term *nut* may mean the shell as well as the meat inside, or it may refer only to the seed of the fruit, as with the almond. The nut may be one of a large number of seeds lying inside a cone, like the pine nut or Indian nut. In the markets of the United States, whole nuts are called in-shell, or unshelled, nuts. Those with their shells removed are called shelled nuts, kernels, or nut meats.

The kernels of most edible nuts form highly concentrated foods, rich in protein. Most nuts are rich in fat, except the chestnut and a few others, which are fairly high in starch. Nuts are an important source of protein. In parts of Europe, nuts form a large part of the regular diet. Bread is sometimes baked from a flour made from chestnuts.

The Persian or English walnut, pecan, almond, cashew, pistachio, hickory, black walnut, Brazil nut, filbert or hazelnut, macadamia, and chestnut are the

most popular nuts in the United States and Canada. The Persian walnut is usually called the English walnut, although it probably was grown originally in Asia. Many walnuts and almonds are now grown in California. There are many pecan orchards in the southern and southwestern states.

The peanut is actually a relative of peas and beans. In the United States, peanuts are grown in many parts of the South (see PEANUT).

Several types of nuts come from the tropics. The coconut is a commercially important nut that grows in many parts of the tropics. The pili nut is a prized food in the Philippines and nearby islands. It is a hard-shelled triangular nut about 2 inches (5 centimeters) long. The sapuacia nut, which is sometimes called the paradise nut or cream nut, is related to the Brazil nut. It is triangular-shaped and about the same size as the Brazil nut. The sapuacia nut grows in the Amazon Basin. Its shell is much like soft cork, and its kernel has a pleasant taste. The ravensara nut and the breadnut are grown in the tropics. But botanists do not consider them to be true nuts. The ravensara nut supplies a spice called Madagascar clove nutmeg.

Several kinds of hickory trees bear nuts that are good to eat. Hickory nuts have hard shells. A hickory tree that grows in eastern United States and Canada bears a seed called a bitternut that is not good to eat. The outer hull is thin, and inside there is a thin inner shell purplish in color. The macadamia nut, sometimes called the Queensland nut or Australian nut, has a thin hard shell, but the kernel is good to eat. It is the fruit of an evergreen tree that comes from Australia, and it is now grown in Hawaii and parts of the American tropics. Some trees have been planted in California and Florida.

Several types of trees that bear pine nuts grow in western North America. The piñon, also called the pine nut, Indian nut, and pinyon, is the small, brown seed of the piñon pine. Its shell has yellow dots. The tree grows in areas from 5,000 to 9,000 feet (1,500 to 2,700 meters) above sea level. The stone pine, a close relative of the piñon pine, comes from southern Europe. Its kernels are known as pignolia.

The water chestnut, which is sometimes called the water caltrop or Jesuit nut, is the seed of a water plant that grows in Europe. A plant closely related to the water chestnut is called the Singhara nut, or horn nut. It comes from southern Asia.

Nut trees are pollinated by wind or insects. Varieties of *species* (kinds) of nut trees are often crossed. Parts of one variety are *grafted* (joined) to the rootstock of another variety (see GRAFTING).

Those nut trees which come from Europe grow better in the western part of the United States than in the East. Those transplanted from eastern Asia seem to do better in the eastern states.   REID M. BROOKS

Related Articles in WORLD BOOK include:

Acorn	Coconut Palm	Litchi
Almond	Copra	Macadamia
Beech	Fruit	Nut
Betel	Ginkgo	Nutmeg
Bitternut	Hazel	Pecan
Brazil Nut	Hickory	Piñon
Butternut	Horse Chestnut	Pistachio Nut
Cashew	Kola Nut	Walnut
Chestnut		

LEADING NUT-GROWING STATES
Tons of nuts grown in 1974

Georgia	861,000 short tons (781,100 metric tons)
California	344,000 short tons (312,100 metric tons)
Alabama	243,000 short tons (220,400 metric tons)
Texas	229,000 short tons (207,700 metric tons)
North Carolina	200,000 short tons (181,400 metric tons)
Virginia	145,000 short tons (131,500 metric tons)
Oklahoma	110,000 short tons (99,800 metric tons)
Florida	84,000 short tons (76,200 metric tons)
South Carolina	17,000 short tons (15,400 metric tons)
New Mexico	13,000 short tons (11,800 metric tons)

Source: U.S. Department of Agriculture.

NUTCRACKER is a bird of the crow family that lives in the mountainous evergreen forests of North America, Europe, and Asia. It received its name because of its supposed ability to crack nuts with its bill. It is somewhat smaller than a crow and has a strong, direct flight. Its feathers are a mixture of brown, white, and black, and its claws are heavy, curved, and very sharp.

The nutcracker feeds chiefly on the seeds of pine cones, and has the rather interesting habit of holding the cones in its claws while opening them. The American nutcracker is called *Clark's crow* and *Clark's nutcracker*. It is found in the western pine regions, usually at high altitudes, from Alaska to Mexico. This nutcracker hides its nest at the top of a tall pine tree. While there is still a deep blanket of snow on the ground, the female lays from three to five speckled, grayish-green eggs in the nest.

Scientific Classification. Nutcrackers belong to the crow family, *Corvidae*. The European nutcracker is genus *Nucifraga*, species *N. caryocatactes*. Clark's nutcracker is *N. columbiana*.   HERBERT FRIEDMANN

NUTHATCH is the name of a group of climbing birds. They are common throughout the temperate regions of are speckled with reddish-brown or lavender spots.

Other American nuthatches are the *red-breasted* nuthatch found in the northern states, the *brown-headed* nuthatch found in the southern states, and the *pygmy* nuthatch found in the West. The red-breasted and brown-headed nuthatches are smaller than the white-breasted nuthatch.

Scientific Classification. Nuthatches belong to the nuthatch family, *Sittidae*. The white-breasted is genus *Sitta*, species *S. carolinensis*. The red-breasted is classified as *S. canadensis*, the brown-headed as *S. pusilla*, and the pygmy as *S. pygmaea*.   GEORGE J. WALLACE

See also BIRD (pictures: Birds' Eggs, Birds That Help Us).

NUTMEG is the kernel of a tropical fruit, which is widely used as a spice. When the fruit is ripe it looks like a golden-yellow pear hanging among shiny, gray-green leaves. The tree grows to be as much as 70 feet (21 meters) high and is an evergreen. The trees originally grew in the Molucca (Spice) Islands, but they have been successfully raised in all of the East Indies, the West Indies,

John Sumner, Nat. Audubon Society
Clark's Nutcracker lives in western North America.

Allan Cruickshank
The Red-Breasted Nuthatch lives only in North America.

J. R. Watkins Co.
Kernels of Nutmeg provide the spice used in cooking. A membrane covering the kernel provides mace, another spice.

the world. Nuthatches get their name from their habit of wedging nuts into cracks in the bark of trees and then *hatching* (opening) them with repeated strokes of the bill.

The best-known American species is the *white-breasted* nuthatch. It lives the year-round in the United States and southern Canada. The bird is about 6 inches (15 centimeters) long. It is dark gray above. The top of its head and upper neck are black, and its under parts are white. These nuthatches are shy in summer, and live in wooded places. But in winter they can be seen around houses and orchards, where they are likely to find food. They particularly like to eat sunflower seeds and suet. They are fond of wild nuts, especially beechnuts, and of grain. They also eat many insects and insect larvae. In climbing trees, they zigzag in every direction, searching for insects under the bark. Nuthatches can even creep headfirst down trees. They have a peculiar wavering flight. The nuthatch builds its nest in holes in trees or stumps. The female bird lays from 5 to 10 eggs. The eggs are white or creamy in color and Brazil, India, and Sri Lanka. Nutmeg trees have long, pointed leaves with well-marked veins. The pale-yellow flowers droop in clusters, and look like lilies of the valley.

As the fruit ripens, the fleshy part becomes rather hard, somewhat like candied fruit. It finally splits open at the top, showing a bright-scarlet membrane, which partly covers the nut. The spice called *mace* comes from this membrane. The kernels are the familiar household nutmegs.

Nutmeg trees do not begin bearing until they are about nine years old. Each tree produces from 1,500 to 2,000 nuts yearly. The fleshy part of the fruit is often preserved and eaten like candy. A clear oil, called *oil of mace*, is made from the kernel.

Scientific Classification. Nutmeg trees belong to the nutmeg family, *Myristicaceae*. They are genus *Myristica*, species *M. fragrans*.   HAROLD NORMAN MOLDENKE

See also MACE.

NUTMEG STATE. See CONNECTICUT (Colonial Life).

NUTRIA. See COYPU.

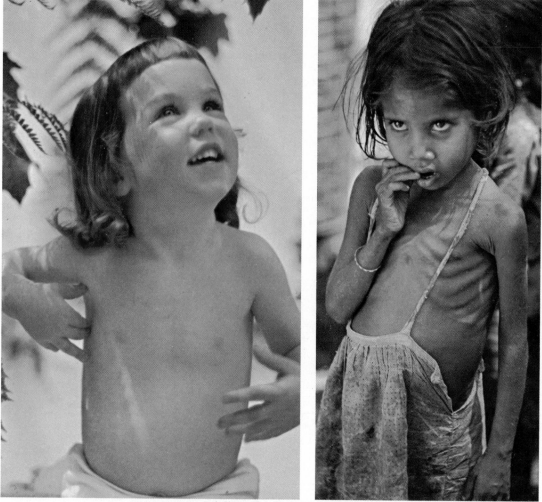

Doris Pinney, Photo Library   Wide World

Nutrition Plays an Important Part in Childhood Development. The child at the left has had a good diet. The child at the right suffers from malnutrition. Her deformed ribs and swollen abdomen are results of malnutrition, and she may also have rickets, a vitamin deficiency disease.

NUTRITION

NUTRITION is the science that deals with foods and the way the body uses them. Good food is essential for health as well as for survival. The word *nutrition* also refers to the process by which living things take in food and use it. Human beings depend for food on plants and on animals that eat plants.

The science of nutrition overlaps into several other fields of science. For example, nutrition is part of medicine because nutritionists study diseases caused by malnutrition. Nutritionists study digestion as part of physiology, the science that deals with how the body works. They also study biochemistry, the science of the various chemical reactions that take place in the body.

Many nutritionists work with community food programs. They may supervise the diets of patients in hospitals and the food served to children in schools. Nutritionists also develop and test new foods, such as the foods used in space exploration, foods made from *algae* (simple plants), and foods made from chemicals.

Experts in many professions try to solve problems concerning nutrition. Home economists study the management and preparation of food. Chemists make *synthetic* (artificial) foods from chemicals. Educators teach

Jean Mayer, the contributor of this article, is President of Tufts University. He was chairman of the First (1969) White House Conference on Food, Nutrition, and Health. He is a member of the President's Consumer Advisory Council and is the author of Overweight: Causes, Cost, and Control.

correct food habits. Agricultural researchers work to develop high-yield and high-quality crops.

Nutrients

The body uses certain parts of foods for energy and growth and for replacement of structures worn out by work or play. These food parts are called *nutrients*. Foods also provide vitamins, which are necessary to get energy out of food. The body needs energy to maintain all its functions. The energy in food is measured in units called *calories*. A food calorie is the amount of energy required to raise the temperature of 1,000 grams of water one degree Celsius.

The amount of energy needed varies from person to person. Children need more energy than adults because they are growing. Children also need more vitamins and nutrients. Pregnant women and nursing mothers require more nutrients than other women. Larger people need more food than smaller individuals. For some nutrients, such as vitamin A, the need is proportional to body size. For example, if one person is twice as large as another, his need for vitamin A is twice as great. The need for total calories also increases with size, though not proportionately. In cold weather, a person must have additional nutrients because his body uses more energy to stay at the same temperature. If a person does physical work or exercise, he also spends more energy than if he is resting.

Nutritionists classify nutrients into five main groups: (1) carbohydrates, (2) fats, (3) proteins, (4) minerals, and (5) vitamins.

Carbohydrates are the starches and sugars in foods. They serve as the main source of energy. Carbohydrates contribute about 45 per cent of the calories in a well-balanced diet. Starches are found in bread, breakfast cereals, flour, and potatoes. The main sugar in food is *sucrose*, ordinary white or brown sugar. Another important sugar, *lactose*, is found in milk.

Fats, another source of energy, furnish a little more than 40 per cent of the calories in the diet. Nutritionists classify fats as *visible* or *invisible*. Visible fats, such as butter, oil, and shortening, are added to foods. Invisible fats are already present in foods. They include the butterfat in milk and the fats in eggs, fish, meat, and nuts.

Fats are made up of substances called *fatty acids* and *glycerol*. Some fatty acids are *saturated*—that is, they contain as many hydrogen atoms as they can hold. Other fatty acids contain fewer hydrogen atoms than possible and are called *unsaturated*. If a fatty acid lacks four or more hydrogen atoms, it is called *polyunsaturated*. Too many saturated fatty acids in the body can raise the amount of *cholesterol*, a fatty substance in the blood and tissues. Too much cholesterol may cause heart attacks. See CHOLESTEROL.

Proteins are especially necessary for the growth and maintenance of body structures. The bones, muscles, skin, and other solid parts of the body are made up largely of proteins. Proteins also provide energy and make up from 12 to 15 per cent of the diet's calories. *Animal proteins* are found in cheese, eggs, fish, meat, and milk. *Vegetable proteins* are found in beans, grains, nuts, and vegetables.

Minerals are also needed for the growth and maintenance of body structures. Calcium, magnesium, and phosphorus are essential parts of the bones and teeth.

CHARACTERISTICS AFFECTING CALORIE REQUIREMENTS

Daily Calorie Requirements depend on many things. For example, a child needs more calories than an old man because the youngster is still growing. A man's body has a greater percentage of muscle tissue than a woman's, and he needs more calories than she does to keep this tissue healthy.

WORLD BOOK illustration

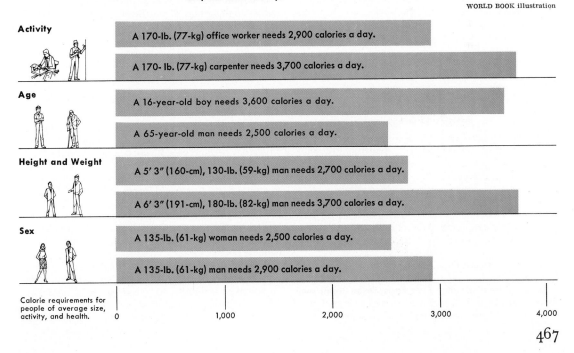

Activity
A 170-lb. (77-kg) office worker needs 2,900 calories a day.
A 170- lb. (77-kg) carpenter needs 3,700 calories a day.

Age
A 16-year-old boy needs 3,600 calories a day.
A 65-year-old man needs 2,500 calories a day.

Height and Weight
A 5' 3" (160-cm), 130-lb. (59-kg) man needs 2,700 calories a day.
A 6' 3" (191-cm), 180-lb. (82-kg) man needs 3,700 calories a day.

Sex
A 135-lb. (61-kg) woman needs 2,500 calories a day.
A 135-lb. (61-kg) man needs 2,900 calories a day.

Calorie requirements for people of average size, activity, and health.

0   1,000   2,000   3,000   4,000

467

In addition, calcium is necessary for blood clotting. Iron is an important part of hemoglobin, the red coloring matter in blood. Minerals are also needed to maintain the composition of the digestive juices and the fluids that are found in and around the body cells. Other vital minerals include iodine, potassium, sodium, and sulfur.

Vitamins are essential for good health. The body cannot manufacture vitamins and must depend on food to supply them. Vitamins are named by letters or by their chemical names. See VITAMIN (with table).

Vitamin A is found in green and yellow plants and in fish liver and fish-liver oils. It is necessary for healthy skin and development of the bones.

Vitamin B1, also called *thiamin*, is found in whole-grain cereals and in meat. It is necessary for the use of starches and sugars by the body.

Vitamin B2, or *riboflavin*, is essential for a number of complicated chemical reactions that take place during the body's use of food. It is found in liver, milk, and vegetables.

Vitamin B12 and *folic acid* are needed for the formation of red blood cells and the proper function of the nerves. Vitamin B12 is found in animal products, especially liver. Folic acid is present in leafy, green, and yellow vegetables.

Vitamin C, also called *ascorbic acid*, is found in fruit— especially oranges and lemons—and in potatoes. It is needed for the maintenance of the ligaments, tendons, and other supportive tissue.

Vitamin D is present in eggs, fish-liver oil, and liver. It is also formed when the skin is exposed to the sun. Vitamin D is necessary for the use of calcium by the body.

Vitamin K is manufactured by bacteria in the intestine. It is necessary for proper clotting of the blood.

Niacin is necessary for respiration of the cells. It is present in liver, yeast, lean meat, and some vegetables.

Pantothenic acid, pyridoxin, and *biotin* are other vitamins that play a role in chemical reactions in the body. Small amounts of these vitamins are found in many kinds of foods.

Water plays a vital role in the health of the body, but it is often considered separately from nutrients. Enough water is essential for a good, varied diet. See WATER (Water in Living Things).

Basic Food Groups

The key to good nutrition is a varied diet that includes every kind of nutrient. Nutritionists have grouped foods according to nutrient content to simplify the planning of a varied diet. The *Basic Seven* system of classification divides foods into seven groups.

Another system, called the *Basic Four*, puts foods of different nutritional values into the same groups. This system has (1) a milk group for all milk and milk products, (2) a meat group, (3) a bread and cereal group, and (4) a fruit and vegetable group.

Following are the Basic Seven groups, with the chief foods in each.

Group 1. Meat, Poultry, Fish, Eggs, Dried Beans and Peas, and Nuts. This group is a chief source of proteins and also provides vitamin B1, iron, niacin, phos-

phorus, and some starch. One or two daily servings are recommended.

Group 2. Leafy, Green, and Yellow Vegetables. This group includes greens of all kinds, such as asparagus, broccoli, green peas, and string beans. It also includes carrots, pumpkins, rutabagas, squash, sweet potatoes, and wax beans. All these vegetables supply large amounts of vitamin A, the B vitamins, vitamin C, calcium, and iron. They also provide fiber, which helps regulate the intestines. Nutritionists recommend one or more daily servings from this group.

Group 3. Citrus Fruits, Raw Cabbage, Salad Greens, and Tomatoes. This group includes all citrus fruits— such as grapefruit, lemons, and oranges—and their juices. These foods are good sources of vitamin C, and they also furnish vitamin A, calcium, and iron. One or more daily servings are recommended.

Group 4. Potatoes and Other Vegetables, and Non-citrus Fruits. This group includes all vegetables and fruits not in groups 2 and 3. At least one potato a day is recommended for active people, both children and adults. Potatoes are good sources of vitamin C if baked or boiled. A daily serving of another food from group 4 is also suggested. Group 4 foods supply carbohydrates, minerals, and small amounts of most vitamins.

Group 5. Bread, Breakfast Cereals, and Flour. This group includes biscuits and crackers. All these foods should consist of whole grains or enriched flour. Enriching is important because milling removes much of the grain's outer coat, which is rich in vitamins and minerals. At least four daily servings are recommended.

Group 6. Butter and Fortified Margarine. Margarine must be fortified with vitamin A to equal the amount of this vitamin found in butter. These foods are chiefly energy producers and sources of vitamin A. Butter or margarine should be included in the daily diet, but no specific amount is recommended.

Group 7. Milk and Milk Products. Milk in any form makes up this group. It may be fresh, dried, evaporated, or made into cheese or ice cream. A child needs 3 to 4 cups (0.7 to 0.9 liter) of milk daily, and an adult should have at least 2 cups (0.5 liter). Milk and cheese are valuable sources of vitamin A, vitamin B2, calcium, and proteins.

Selecting and Cooking Foods

Every day's meals should include foods from each group. A wise shopper buys foods that are as fresh as possible because many foods lose vitamins A and C when they become stale. Canned or frozen products add variety to meals because they make most foods available throughout the year. Modern food processing tries to ensure that canned and frozen foods retain their nutritional values. Some high-quality processed foods may be more nutritious than fresh foods. Fresh foods may lose some nutritional value if they are harvested before maturity or if they are kept for long periods before being eaten.

It is important not to add unnecessary calories, saturated fats, or sugar to food. Foods must be kept and cooked carefully to conserve their nutritional value. Many foods should be kept in the refrigerator. They should be cooked quickly and in as little cooking

BASIC FOOD GROUPS

The Basic Food Groups. Nutritionists recommend one daily serving from each of the Basic Seven groups. With the Basic Four system, they suggest four or more servings from both the vegetable-fruit and bread-cereals groups, and two or more servings from the meat group.

The Basic Seven

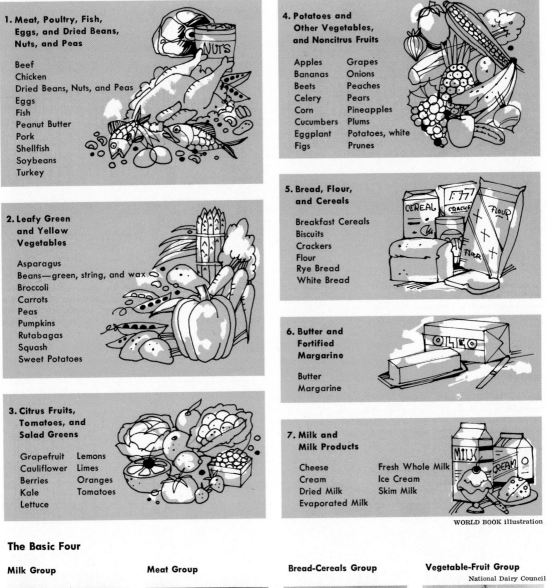

1. Meat, Poultry, Fish, Eggs, and Dried Beans, Nuts, and Peas

Beef
Chicken
Dried Beans, Nuts, and Peas
Eggs
Fish
Peanut Butter
Pork
Shellfish
Soybeans
Turkey

2. Leafy Green and Yellow Vegetables

Asparagus
Beans—green, string, and wax
Broccoli
Carrots
Peas
Pumpkins
Rutabagas
Squash
Sweet Potatoes

3. Citrus Fruits, Tomatoes, and Salad Greens

Grapefruit   Lemons
Cauliflower   Limes
Berries   Oranges
Kale   Tomatoes
Lettuce

4. Potatoes and Other Vegetables, and Noncitrus Fruits

Apples   Grapes
Bananas   Onions
Beets   Peaches
Celery   Pears
Corn   Pineapples
Cucumbers   Plums
Eggplant   Potatoes, white
Figs   Prunes

5. Bread, Flour, and Cereals

Breakfast Cereals
Biscuits
Crackers
Flour
Rye Bread
White Bread

6. Butter and Fortified Margarine

Butter
Margarine

7. Milk and Milk Products

Cheese   Fresh Whole Milk
Cream   Ice Cream
Dried Milk   Skim Milk
Evaporated Milk

WORLD BOOK illustration

The Basic Four

Milk Group

Meat Group

Bread-Cereals Group

Vegetable-Fruit Group

National Dairy Council

468a

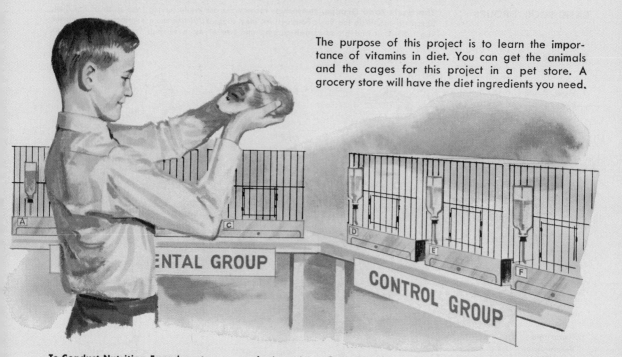

The purpose of this project is to learn the importance of vitamins in diet. You can get the animals and the cages for this project in a pet store. A grocery store will have the diet ingredients you need.

ENTAL GROUP

CONTROL GROUP

To Conduct Nutrition Experiments, a group of guinea pigs are divided into two groups—a control group and an experimental group. All animals get the same diet, which lacks one vital food element. This element is added to the food for the control group.

Comparison of the control group with the experimental group shows the effect of the deficiency of the food element in which you are interested. This project is concerned with vitamin deficiency. But you can conduct similar experiments with other food elements.

MATERIALS

Materials for this project include six young guinea pigs of about the same size and weight, six cages, a record book, graph paper, and adhesive tape. You will also need a gram scale for weighing the diet ingredients and each of the animals. Most drugstores sell such scales.

Illustrated by Bart Jerner for WORLD BOOK

Scale

Six cages

A

Six young
guinea pigs

Record book
and growth charts

B
D
C E
F
Adhesive tape labels

-380

-360

-340

-320

NUTRITION EXPERIMENT ON VITAMIN C DEFICIENCY

In this experiment, three guinea pigs make up the experimental group, and three make up the control group. Feed all the animals the same basic diet, which lacks vitamin C. But add foods with vitamin C to the daily ration for the guinea pigs in the control group. The formula for the basic diet and suggestions for foods with a high vitamin C content are given, *below.* Be sure to keep all the animals in comfortable and healthful surroundings. Give them fresh water at least once a day, and clean the cages daily.

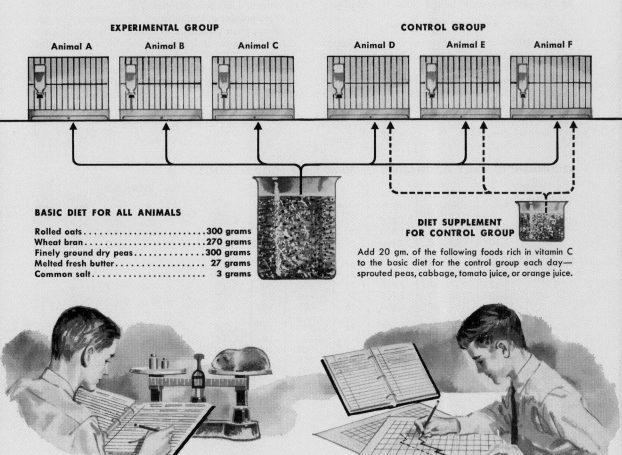

EXPERIMENTAL GROUP

Animal A   Animal B   Animal C

CONTROL GROUP

Animal D   Animal E   Animal F

BASIC DIET FOR ALL ANIMALS

Rolled oats . . . . .300 grams
Wheat bran . . . . .270 grams
Finely ground dry peas . . . . .300 grams
Melted fresh butter . . . . 27 grams
Common salt . . . . 3 grams

DIET SUPPLEMENT FOR CONTROL GROUP

Add 20 gm. of the following foods rich in vitamin C to the basic diet for the control group each day— sprouted peas, cabbage, tomato juice, or orange juice.

Keeping Records. In the log book, make daily entries for each animal, noting any changes in behavior or appearance. Make separate weight charts for the experimental group and for the control group. Weigh and record the weight of each animal daily. Use a different color lead or a different kind of line for each animal. Compare and analyze all your records at the end of the experiment.

ADDITIONAL EXPERIMENTS ON NUTRITION

You can show the effects of other vitamin deficiencies. For these projects, follow the same routine, but use mice instead of guinea pigs, and feed them a diet lacking the vitamin.

Vitamin A Deficiency. A special diet lacking this vitamin is given, *below.* The recipe makes about 300 grams, which is enough to feed six rats several days. Add 30 grams of fresh butter to this diet for feeding the control group. It may take from 5 to 7 weeks for the test animals to show any signs of vitamin A deficiency. As soon as they do, feed butter to them to restore them to normal health. Keep complete records during this period, too.

Vitamin B₁ Deficiency. A diet deficient in this vitamin is given, *below.* The recipe makes enough food for several days. To feed the control group, add 5 grams of bakers' yeast, 10 gm. of ground wheat, or 30 gm. of wheat bran to the basic diet. Any of these foods will supply vitamin B₁, so you need add only one of them. When the test animals begin to show signs of vitamin deficiency, add the yeast, wheat, or bran to their diet. Keep complete records.

BASIC DIET

Wheat . . . . .114 grams
Dried beef (or lean meat) . . . . 30 grams
Starch . . . . .150 grams
Common salt . . . . 3 grams
Slaked lime . . . . 3 grams

BASIC DIET

White flour . . . . .150 grams
Butter . . . . 30 grams
Dried beef . . . . 15 grams
Common salt . . . . 3 grams
Slaked lime . . . . 3 grams
Starch . . . . 99 grams

468c

liquid as possible. Because some vitamins and minerals dissolve in the liquid, it should be eaten with the food. Milk in glass containers should not be exposed to light for long periods because light destroys vitamin B_2.

Results of Malnutrition

Malnutrition is caused by poor intake, absorption, or use of nutrients by the body. If a person does not get enough food, *undernutrition* results. Starvation is extreme undernutrition. If a person does not eat enough food or if his diet lacks certain nutrients, the condition is called *primary malnutrition*. Sometimes, because of disease, the body cannot use nutrients even though they are present in the food eaten. The result is *secondary malnutrition*. A person's diet also may be faulty because it contains too many nutrients. Such a diet may be high in saturated fats or in calories.

Protein-Calorie Malnutrition occurs when the diet is low in both proteins and calories. The condition is called *kwashiorkor* if the diet is especially low in proteins. Symptoms of kwashiorkor include changes in the color and texture of the hair and skin, swelling of the body, and damage to the intestines, liver, and pancreas. The disease generally attacks children and is fatal unless the patient is given protein. If the diet is especially low in calories, the condition is called *marasmus*. Marasmus

RECOMMENDED DAILY ALLOWANCES OF SOME CHIEF FOOD ELEMENTS

	Age	Weight In lbs.	In kg	Calories	Protein (gm)	Calcium (mg)	Iron (mg)	A (I.U.)	C (mg)	D (I.U.)	Thiamine (mg)	Riboflavin (mg)	Niacin (mg)
Children	1-3	28	13	1,300	23	800	15	2,000	40	400	0.7	0.8	9
	4-6	44	20	1,800	30	800	10	2,500	40	400	0.9	1.1	12
	7-10	66	30	2,400	36	800	10	3,300	40	400	1.2	1.2	16
Males	11-14	97	44	2,800	44	1,200	18	5,000	45	400	1.4	1.5	18
	15-18	134	61	3,000	54	1,200	18	5,000	45	400	1.5	1.8	20
	19-22	147	67	3,000	54	800	10	5,000	45	400	1.5	1.8	20
	23-50	154	70	2,700	56	800	10	5,000	45		1.4	1.6	18
	51+	154	70	2,400	56	800	10	5,000	45		1.2	1.5	16
Females	11-14	97	44	2,400	44	1,200	18	4,000	45	400	1.2	1.3	16
	15-18	119	54	2,100	48	1,200	18	4,000	45	400	1.1	1.4	14
	19-22	128	58	2,100	46	800	18	4,000	45	400	1.1	1.4	14
	23-50	128	58	2,000	46	800	18	4,000	45		1.0	1.2	13
	51+	128	58	1,800	46	800	10	4,000	45		1.0	1.1	12

gm = grams; mg = milligrams; I.U. = International Units.
Above figures intended for normally active persons in a temperate climate.

Source: National Research Council.

NUTRITIONAL VALUES OF COMMON FOODS

Food	Portion	Calories	Protein (gm)	Calcium (mg)	Iron (mg)	A (I.U.)	C (mg)	D (I.U.)	Thiamine (mcg)	Riboflavin (mcg)	Niacin (mg)
Apple, raw	1 large	117	0.6	12	0.6	180	9	0	80	60	0.4
Banana, raw	1 large	176	2.4	16	1.2	860	20	0	80	100	1.4
Beans, green, cooked	1 cup	27	1.8	45	0.9	830	18	0	90	120	0.6
Beef, round, cooked	1 serving	214	24.7	10	3.1	0	0	0	74	202	5.1
Bread, white, enriched	1 slice	63	2.0	18	0.4	0	0	0	60	40	0.5
Broccoli, cooked	⅔ cup	29	3.3	130	1.3	3,400	74	0	70	150	0.8
Butter	1 tablespoon	100	0.1	33	0.0	460	0	5	tr.	tr.	tr.
Cabbage, cooked	½ cup	20	1.2	39	0.4	75	27	0	40	40	0.3
Carrots, raw	1 cup, shredded	42	1.2	39	0.8	12,000	6	0	60	60	0.5
Cheese, cheddar, American	1 slice	113	7.1	206	0.3	400	0	0	10	120	tr.
Chicken, fried	½ breast	232	26.8	19	1.3	460	0	0	67	101	10.2
Egg, boiled	1 medium	77	6.1	26	1.3	550	0	27	40	130	tr.
Liver, beef, fried	1 slice	86	8.8	4	2.9	18,658	10	19	90	1,283	5.1
Margarine, fortified	1 tablespoon	101	0.1	3	0.0	460	0	0	0	0	0.0
Milk, whole, cow's	1 glass	124	6.4	216	0.2	293	2	4	73	311	0.2
Oatmeal, cooked	1 cup	148	5.4	21	1.7	0	0	0	220	50	0.4
Orange, whole	1 medium	68	1.4	50	0.6	285	74	0	120	45	0.3
Pork, shoulder, roasted	2 slices	320	19.2	9	2.0	0	0	0	592	144	3.2
Tomatoes, raw	1 large	40	2.0	22	1.2	2,200	46	0	120	80	1.0
Potatoes, white, baked	1 medium	98	2.4	13	0.8	20	17	0	110	50	1.4
Rice, white, cooked	1 cup	201	4.2	13	0.5	0	0	0	20	10	0.7
Sugar, white, granulated	1 tablespoon	48	0.0	0	0.0	0	0	0	0	0	0.0

gm = grams; mg = milligrams; mcg = micrograms; I.U. = International Units; tr. = trace.

usually attacks infants, causing extreme underweight and weakness.

Protein-calorie malnutrition can stop or slow down the mental development of infants and children. Studies suggest that this can occur in three different ways, even without the development of physical disease. First, many poor children go to school so hungry that they cannot concentrate and are thus unable to keep up with their classwork. Second, many undernourished pregnant women have premature babies. Such babies have difficulty in both mental and physical growth. Third, a small number of children suffer severe malnutrition early in life. As a result, their brain cells fail to multiply as rapidly as they should. Brain cells of human beings multiply only until about eight months after birth. Additional brain cells are never developed later, even if the child obtains a better diet.

Vitamin Deficiencies are caused by a lack of vitamins. Symptoms vary according to the missing vitamin.

Vitamin A Deficiency causes *night blindness* (lack of vision in dim light) and momentary blinding by sudden exposure to light. It also causes dry, itchy skin. Extreme vitamin A deficiency leads to total blindness and death.

Vitamin B1 Deficiency, also called *beriberi*, causes swelling, damage to nerves, and a type of heart disease. Beriberi is widespread in many regions of the world. It is a major problem in areas of Asia where polished rice makes up a large part of the people's diet. When rice is polished, the outer shell of the grain is removed by milling. This shell contains most of the grain's vitamin B_1. In the United States, flour is enriched with vitamin B_1, vitamin B_2, iron, and niacin.

Vitamin B2 Deficiency causes cracking at the corners of the mouth, and itching.

Vitamin B12 Deficiency and lack of folic acid cause blood disorders. Abnormal red cells are formed, and the nervous system is affected.

From *Foundations of Nutrition* by Clara Mae Taylor and Orrea F. Pye

Vitamins are essential for important body processes. The two rats above were fed identical diets, except that the rat at the left did not receive vitamin B_2.

Minerals are also important for good health. The chickens below are both five weeks old and were fed identical diets, except that the chicken on the left did not receive zinc.

M. L. Sunde, University of Wisconsin

Vitamin C Deficiency, also called *scurvy*, causes sore and bleeding gums, slow repair of wounds, and painful joints. The walls of the *capillaries*, the smallest blood vessels, become so weak that slight pressure may cause them to break.

Vitamin D Deficiency, also called *rickets*, causes an abnormal development of the bones. Calcium is not properly deposited in the bones. Rickets may result in such conditions as knock-knees and chicken breast, in which the breastbone sticks out abnormally.

Mineral Deficiencies may also cause severe diseases. Lack of iron can cause *anemia*, an abnormal blood condition. A lack of iodine causes most cases of *goiter*, a disease in which the thyroid gland becomes enlarged.

Obesity results from eating more than the body needs for growth, energy, and maintenance. An obese person is simply too fat. More exercise and less food may be necessary to reduce body weight.

Heart and Circulatory Diseases can result from poor nutrition. An increase in the cholesterol in the blood may be caused by a diet with too many saturated fats. Increased cholesterol can increase the chances of heart attacks, strokes, and other diseases of the blood vessels.

History

Nutrition as a Science began in 1780. That year, the French chemist Antoine L. Lavoisier discovered that food and oxygen combine in the body to produce energy. But deficiency diseases had been studied earlier. In 1753, for example, James Lind, a Scottish physician, published a cure for scurvy. He studied the disease in sailors who lived for long periods on salted beef and *hard tack* (dry biscuits). Lind found that adding lemon juice to their diet cured and prevented the disease.

The deficiency diseases were conquered one by one. Christiaan Eijkman, a Dutch scientist, studied beriberi in military prison camps. About 1900, he found that people who depended largely on polished rice for food got beriberi. Those who ate whole rice did not get the disease. Eijkman concluded that something in the hulls was necessary for health.

In the early 1900's, scientists discovered vitamins and *amino acids*, organic acids that make up proteins. The British biochemists Frederick G. Hopkins and Edward Mellanby studied the composition of proteins and the role of vitamins. Mellanby also investigated the cause and cure of rickets. Two American biochemists, Elmer V. McCollum and Lafayette B. Mendel, demonstrated the body's need for amino acids and vitamins. Mendel identified vitamin A in 1913. Vitamin D was identified by McCollum in 1922. Joseph Goldberger, a physician of the U.S. Public Health Service, studied the disease *pellagra*. He found that it is caused by a lack of certain B vitamins.

Increased knowledge about nutrition was accompanied by improved techniques of food production. Intensive use of fertilizers, pesticides, and improved strains of plants greatly increased crop production in the developed countries. This abundance, with increased knowledge of nutrients, led to greater concern for the hungry and undernourished people of the world.

International Concern with nutrition began during the 1930's. In 1937, the League of Nations established a committee to study nutrition. During World War II (1939-1945), President Franklin D. Roosevelt of the United States proclaimed "Freedom from Want" as one of the goals of the war. The United Nations Relief and Rehabilitation Administration (UNRRA) distributed food to millions of persons, shipped livestock to war-torn areas, and helped revive agriculture.

Other United Nations (UN) agencies also were set up in the 1940's to deal with health and nutrition. The Food and Agriculture Organization of the United Nations (FAO) provides information on the production, consumption, and distribution of food throughout the world. The United Nations Children's Fund (UNICEF) provides food for needy mothers and children. The World Health Organization (WHO) deals with health problems.

Private agencies, such as the Ford and Rockefeller foundations, contributed to the development of high-yield strains of wheat and rice during the 1960's. In 1963, two American biochemists, Edwin T. Mertz and Oliver E. Nelson, developed corn containing *lysine*, an amino acid that is essential to good health.

Nutritional research has helped reduce hunger throughout the world. But millions of people still suffer from malnutrition and it remains one of the most important world problems. JEAN MAYER

Related Articles in WORLD BOOK include:

DIETARY DISEASES

Allergy	Beriberi	Malnutrition	Rickets
Anemia	Constipation	Pellagra	Scurvy

NUTRIENTS

Albumin	Fat	Lipid	Starch
Amino Acid	Gluten	Pectin	Sugar
Carbohydrate	Iron	Protein	Vitamin

OTHER RELATED ARTICLES

Baby (Feeding	Food	Starvation
Procedures)	Food Preservation	Trace Elements
Biochemistry	Food Stamp Program	Vegetarianism
Calorie	Health	Weight Control
Diet	Home Economics	Wheat (Wheat
Dietician	Meat	Flour)
Digestion	Metabolism	

Outline

I. Nutrients
  A. Carbohydrates   C. Proteins   E. Vitamins
  B. Fats   D. Minerals   F. Water
II. Basic Food Groups
III. Selecting and Cooking Foods
IV. Results of Malnutrition
  A. Protein-Calorie   D. Obesity
     Malnutrition   E. Heart and Circu-
  B. Vitamin Deficiencies   latory Diseases
  C. Mineral Deficiencies
V. History

Questions

What causes malnutrition?
What is a *nutrient?*
Why does the amount of energy needed vary from person to person?
Which group of the Basic Seven contains large amounts of vitamin A?
What is the danger of eating too many saturated fats?
How does careful cooking preserve nutritional values?
What is *kwashiorkor? Marasmus?*
What are the four groups in the Basic Four?
Who identified beriberi?
What was the first international agency to study nutrition?

NUTRITIONIST. See NUTRITION; FOOD (Research).

NUTTING, MARY ADELAIDE (1858-1948), was a Canadian-born leader in the development of professional nursing in the United States. She worked to establish professional standards in both the education of nurses and the practice of nursing. Nutting developed several training programs that supplemented practical experience in a hospital with classroom instruction in nursing principles.

Nutting was born in Waterloo, Que. She received a nursing certificate from Johns Hopkins Hospital Training School for Nurses in 1891. She then served as a head nurse at the school until 1894, when she became its principal. Nutting held this position until 1907. That year, when she joined the faculty of Teachers College at Columbia University, Nutting became the world's first professor of nursing. Nutting headed the Department of Nursing and Health at the college from 1910 until she retired in 1925.　　DONALD G. KEEN

NUX VOMICA, *nucks VAHM ih kuh,* is the name of a powerful drug containing two alkaloids, brucine and strychnine. It appeared in France during the 1400's or 1500's. Nux vomica is obtained from the dried, ripe seed of the nux vomica tree of India, Sri Lanka, northern Australia, and Vietnam. The seed is also called nux vomica. The drug is poisonous to both human beings and animals except in minute quantities. It is given in small doses as a stimulant in stomach and nervous disorders. In larger quantities, it causes convulsions and even death. Nux vomica is also the principal source of strychnine (see STRYCHNINE).　　AUSTIN SMITH

NYA. See NEW DEAL (table: Leading New Deal Agencies).

NYACK COLLEGE. See UNIVERSITIES AND COLLEGES (table).

NYASA, LAKE. See LAKE NYASA.

NYASALAND. See MALAWI.

NYE, BILL (1850-1896), an American humorist, wrote comic histories, such as *Bill Nye's History of the United States* (1894), and *Bill Nye's History of England* (1896). He did not use slang, dialect, or amusing misspellings, as did many other humorists of his time. He edited the *Laramie* (Wyo.) *Boomerang* for three years. He became famous as a staff member of *The* (New York) *World.* He made successful lecture tours, both alone and with the poet James Whitcomb Riley. He and Riley wrote *Nye and Riley's Railway Guide* (1888). Nye's other works include *Bill Nye and Boomerang* (1881), *Forty Liars and Other Lies* (1882), and *Baled Hay* (1884). He was admitted to the bar in 1876. Edgar Wilson Nye was born in Shirley, Me.　　EDWARD WAGENKNECHT

NYE, JAMES WARREN. See NEVADA (Nevada Becomes a Territory).

NYERERE, *ny RER ay,* **JULIUS KAMBARAGE** (1922-), became president of what is now Tanzania in 1964. He has been head of the Tanganyika African National Union party since 1954. A forceful African nationalist, he led Tanganyika to independence in 1961. In 1964, Nyerere united Tanganyika and Zanzibar to form what is now Tanzania. He introduced government controls to allow for more centralized economic planning. He has tried to set up a democratic society based on equality for all citizens.

Born near what is now Musoma, Tanzania, Nyerere was educated at Makerere University in Kampala, Uganda, and at the University of Edinburgh in Scotland. He became Tanganyika's first prime minister in 1961, and its first president in 1962.　　CARL GUSTAF ROSBERG

See also AFRICA (picture: Leaders of Africa); TANZANIA (History).

NYLON is the family name for a group of synthetic products. These products are made from chemicals derived from coal, water, air, petroleum, agricultural by-products, and natural gas. Nylon is one of the most important chemical discoveries. It ranks as one of the toughest, strongest, and most elastic substances. Nylon can be formed into fibers, bristles, sheets, rods, tubes, and coatings. It also can be made in powdered form for use in molding operations.

Nylon fabrics are not weakened by mildew. They are not harmed by most kinds of oil and grease or such chemicals as household cleaning fluids. Nylon absorbs little water.

Uses. Nylon was first made into hosiery in 1937. It was the first synthetic fabric thought to be superior to natural fabrics. Since then, many uses have been found for nylon. Dresses, underwear, bathing suits, lace, parachutes, tires, carpets, and upholstery are among the many products made of nylon. Industries use nylon to make bearings, gears, wire coatings, and machine parts. Single threads of coarse-fibered nylon are used for fishing line and for bristles in all types of brushes. Surgeons use nylon thread to sew up wounds.

How Nylon Is Made. Most nylon produced in the United States is made from two chemical compounds— *hexamethylenediamine* and *adipic acid.* Both these compounds contain carbon and hydrogen. Manufacturers combine the compounds to form *hexamethylene-diammonium-adipate,* commonly called *nylon salt.*

Most nylon factories make the substance by placing a solution of nylon salt in a machine called an *autoclave.* The autoclave heats the solution under pressure. The water is removed, and the molecules that make up each of the compounds combine and form very large molecules. This process of making large molecules from smaller ones is called *polymerization* (see POLYMERIZATION). In some factories, the newly formed nylon comes out of the machine as a plastic ribbon. The ribbon is cooled, hardened, and cut into chips that are used in making a variety of nylon products. See PLASTICS (How Plastics Are Made).

Nylon fibers are made by forcing molten nylon through tiny holes in a device called a *spinneret.* In some factories, the molten nylon travels to the spinneret as soon as the polymerization process is completed. Other

Fishing Line　　Furniture Casters

Du Pont

Nylon Is Used for Many Things. It is tough, strong, and elastic, and it cannot be damaged by oils, greases, and water.

factories melt nylon chips and pump the melted nylon through the spinneret. The streams of nylon harden into filaments when they strike the air. Then they are wound onto bobbins. From 1 to as many as 2,520 filaments are united into a textile nylon yarn.

Nylon fibers are *drawn* (stretched) after they cool. Some factories draw nylon after it has been spun into yarn. Others spin and draw the yarn in one operation. Drawing involves unwinding the yarn or filaments from one spool and winding them onto another. The winding rate is four or more times as fast as the unwinding rate. The pull between the spools stretches the fibers. Drawing makes the molecules in each filament fall into parallel lines. This process gives the fiber strength and elasticity. After being drawn, the yarn may be twisted a few turns per yard or per meter as it is wound onto spools. It may also be treated to give it a special texture or added bulk.

The size of nylon yarn is measured in *deniers*. A denier is the weight in grams of 9,000 meters (9,843 yards) of the yarn. For example, if 9,000 meters of a nylon yarn weigh 15 grams, the yarn is called *15-denier* yarn. See DENIER.

History. Wallace H. Carothers, a chemist of E. I. du Pont de Nemours & Company, was a leader in the development of nylon. In the late 1920's, he began to experiment with polymerization. He used a machine called the "molecular still," which made it possible to make longer molecules than had been made before. Carothers found that many of the fibers made from compounds which he polymerized could be pulled out to several times their original length after they were cooled. This pulling process made the fibers much stronger and more elastic.

But most of the compounds which Carothers had made so far melted at a temperature too low to make them practical for textiles which must be ironed. Then, in 1935, Carothers polymerized hexamethylenediamine and adipic acid. The product was called *polyhexamethylene adipamide*. This material had a melting point of 482° F. (250° C), which is satisfactory for textiles. The new fiber was named nylon and was hailed as a great discovery. Later, chemists referred to this original kind of nylon as *nylon 66*, because both chemicals used in making it had six carbon atoms.

Before nylon could be produced for the public market, scientists had to find a way to make large amounts of hexamethylenediamine and adipic acid. Researchers at Du Pont eventually developed a method for making these two chemicals from coal, air, and water. Nylon products first went on the market in 1938. Petroleum, natural gas, and agricultural by-products were developed later as raw materials.

Most manufacturers in the United States have continued to produce nylon 66. However, other types of nylon have also been developed. Nylon 6, made from a six-carbon chemical called *caprolactam*, is a major fiber produced in the United States and many other countries. A silklike nylon with the trademark *Qiana* is a popular fiber used for clothing.   ELIJA M. HICKS, JR.

NYMPH is a young or immature stage of insect larva of the type which has a gradual metamorphosis (see LARVA; METAMORPHOSIS). The larvae, or nymphs, of

these insects are small versions of their parents. They do not pass through four separate stages, taking on four separate appearances, like the insects which have complete metamorphosis. The nymphs look somewhat like the parents, but they have no complete wings, and have much smaller bodies, legs, and mouth parts. They grow gradually into adulthood, and do not pass through different stages. Grasshoppers, crickets, and earwigs have nymph stages.   WILLIAM C. BEAVER

NYMPH was a lovely maiden of mythology who guarded the different realms of nature. *Oreads* watched over the hills and mountains, and *nereids* over the Mediterranean Sea. The *naiads* were the nymphs of the rivers, brooks, and streams. The ocean was protected by the *Oceanids*. The *dryads* and *hamadryads* took care of the trees and forests. Many of the naiads watched over springs that were believed to inspire those who drank their waters. The naiads were thought to have powers to prophesy and to inspire people. The oreads were also known by names that came from the particular mountains where they lived.

Nymphs were friendly and kind to mortals. They were shy and fled from human beings, but sometimes they took revenge on people who hurt the things under their protection. Nymphs are represented with fauns and satyrs in the forest, or playing around the keels of ships. Only oreads and naiads were immortal.   PADRAIC COLUM

See also ARETHUSA; DRYAD; NEREID; NIX.

NYNORSK. See NORWAY (Language).

NYSTAGMUS, *nis TAG mus*, is an involuntary, rhythmical movement of the eyes. The eyes may move from side to side, up and down, in a circle, or in a combination of these movements. The motions may be rapid or slow, and jerky or smooth. Nystagmus occurs normally, as when a person watches scenery from a moving train. This condition may also be produced by diseases of the eye, the ear, or the brain. Some people are born with nystagmus.

A type of nystagmus known as *miner's nystagmus* is caused by darkness, and occurs among miners. *Positional nystagmus* occurs only when the patient's head is placed in an abnormal position or level. *Spontaneous ocular nystagmus* occurs as a result of complete blindness or from defective central vision. *Vertical nystagmus* is an up-and-down movement of the eyes. *Latent nystagmus* occurs when one eye is covered.   JOHN R. MCWILLIAMS

NYSWANDER, MARIE. See METHADONE.

NYX. See EREBUS.

NZINGA A NKUWA, *en ZING ah ah en KOO wah,* (? -1506), was the divine ruler of the Kongo kingdom in west-central Africa. His subjects believed he was God in human form.

After the first Portuguese trading ships came to Kongo in 1482, Nzinga a Nkuwa tried to increase his country's trade with Europe. At his request, Portugal sent a number of carpenters, farmers, traders, and other specialists to Kongo. But the Europeans became more interested in developing the slave trade than in aiding the Kongolese.

After Christian missionaries came to Mbanza, Kongo's capital, Nzinga a Nkuwa accepted Christianity as one of the country's religions. He was baptized in 1491 and took the name John I, or *João*, the name of the king of Portugal.   LEO SPITZER

See also KONGO.

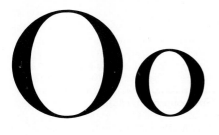

Oo

O is the 15th letter in our alphabet. It also appeared in the alphabet used by the Semites, who once lived in Syria and Palestine. They called the letter *'ayin*, their word for *eye*. For a symbol, they used a stylized picture of an eye. They probably borrowed it from an Egyptian *hieroglyphic*, or picture letter. The Phoenicians borrowed the letter from the Semites. Later, the Greeks borrowed it from the Phoenicians. They called it *omicron*. See ALPHABET.

Uses. *O* or *o* is about the fourth most frequently used letter in books, newspapers, and other printed material in English. In chemistry, *O* stands for the element *oxygen*. On maps, the letter is the abbreviation for *ocean*, as well as *Ohio*. In modern numbering, it represents the *cipher*, or zero. In medieval Roman numerals, *O* repre-

sented the number 11 or, when written $\bar{O}$, stood for 11,000. It may also be used as the abbreviation for *old*, *octavo* (a size of book or method of folding a printed sheet), or *ohm* (a unit used in measuring electrical resistance).

Pronunciation. The letter *o* is a vowel, and has several sounds in English. The main pronunciations are illustrated in the words *November* (long *o*), *not* (short *o*), and *home*, which scholars consider a *diphthong*, or combination of *o* and *u* sounds. Double *o* also has several sounds in English. When pronounced as a single vowel, it may have the sounds represented in the words *food* and *good*. There are some words in English in which each *o* is pronounced separately, as in *cooperate*. See PRONUNCIATION.

I. J. GELB and JAMES M. WELLS

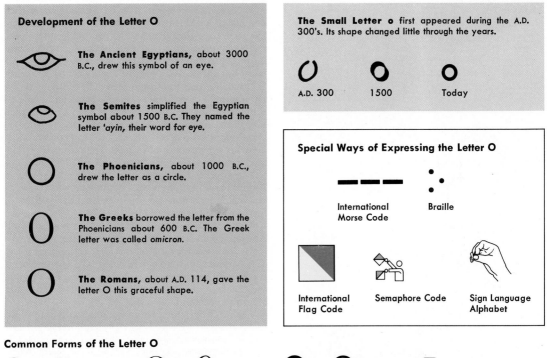

Development of the Letter O

The Ancient Egyptians, about 3000 B.C., drew this symbol of an eye.

The Semites simplified the Egyptian symbol about 1500 B.C. They named the letter *'ayin,* their word for eye.

The Phoenicians, about 1000 B.C., drew the letter as a circle.

The Greeks borrowed the letter from the Phoenicians about 600 B.C. The Greek letter was called *omicron.*

The Romans, about A.D. 114, gave the letter O this graceful shape.

The Small Letter o first appeared during the A.D. 300's. Its shape changed little through the years.

A.D. 300   1500   Today

Special Ways of Expressing the Letter O

International Morse Code

Braille

International Flag Code

Semaphore Code

Sign Language Alphabet

Common Forms of the Letter O

Handwritten Letters vary from person to person. *Manuscript* (printed) letters, *left,* have simple curves and straight lines. Cursive letters, *right,* have flowing lines.

Roman Letters have small finishing strokes called *serifs* that extend from the main strokes. The type face shown above is Baskerville. The italic form appears at the right.

Sans-Serif Letters are also called *gothic letters.* They have no serifs. The type face shown above is called Futura. The italic form of Futura appears at the right.

Computer Letters have special shapes. Computers can "read" these letters either optically or by means of the magnetic ink with which the letters may be printed.

OAK LEAVES
AND ACORNS

Bur Oak

Pin Oak

Live Oak

Red Oak

Black Oak

White Oak

O. HENRY. See HENRY, O.

OAHE DAM, near Pierre, S. Dak., ranks as one of the world's 10 largest earth-fill dams (see DAM [Embankment Dams]). It is 9,300 feet (2,830 meters) long and 245 feet (75 meters) high, and it has a volume of 92 million cubic yards (70 million cubic meters). The dam is part of the Missouri River Basin development program.

The dam's power plant includes seven generators, which can produce 595,000 kilowatts of electricity. The generators, 150 feet (46 meters) high, are among the world's tallest. The Oahe reservoir can store 23,600,000 acre-feet (29,110,000,000 cubic meters) of water. The United States Army Corps of Engineers completed the dam in 1963. T. W. MERMEL

OAHU. See HAWAII (The Islands).

OAK, *ohk.* For ages the oak tree has symbolized sturdiness and strength. Scientists know of about 275 different *species* (kinds) of oaks. These trees grow in many different lands. Oaks flourish from Malaya and China westward across the Himalaya and the Caucasus. They grow throughout most of Europe, from Sicily northward to the Arctic Circle. In North America, oaks can grow almost any place that other kinds of trees grow. But they do not live in regions of great cold. Oaks grow southward from North America into the Andes.

The acorn is the main feature that sets oaks apart from other trees. The acorn is the fruit of the oak tree. It is a rounded, smooth-shelled nut, pointed at the outer end. A scaly saucer or cup encloses the base of the nut. Most oak trees can also be recognized by their notched or lobed leaves. But a few kinds, including the live oak, have smooth-edged leaves, unlike the others.

Oaks grow slowly, and usually do not bear acorns until they are about 20 years old. But these trees live a long time. Most oak trees live about 200 or 300 years. In England, oak trees were sacred in the days of the Druids, more than 2,000 years ago. Some oak trees still thriving in England may have been seen by the Saxon kings, over 900 years ago. One oak tree growing in Gloucestershire is nearly 48 feet (15 meters) around. It is by far the largest known oak. The oak tree of England resembles the white oak of the United States.

The Charter Oak of Hartford, Conn., is famous in American history. The charter of the colony of Connecticut was hidden from the colony's English governor in this tree. See CHARTER OAK.

Kinds of Oaks. The *white oak* is the noblest of all American oaks. It sometimes grows 150 feet (46 meters) high. Its trunk may measure 8 feet (2.4 meters) thick. The bark of the white oak is pale gray. The tree bears leaves with round or finger-shaped lobes. In autumn, these leaves turn a deep red or golden brown. They add charm to autumn landscapes.

The white oak thrives from Canada south to the Gulf of Mexico and west to Texas. In dense forests it has a narrow *crown* (top). But when it grows in the open, it has wide-spreading branches. The wood of the white oak is hard and close-grained. It is valuable for its beauty, strength, and wearing qualities. Furniture makers value the white oak above all other kinds of oaks in the United States. The largest white oak in the United States is the Wye Oak, in Talbot County, Maryland. It is 95 feet (29 meters) high. The trunk is more than 27 feet (8 meters) around.

The *bur oak*, or *mossy-cup oak*, is a rugged tree that

The Red Oak is one of the most favored American ornamental trees.

The Magnificent Live Oak of the Southern States is famed for the great horizontal spread of its sturdy branches. It has leathery leaves.

The Oregon White Oak closely resembles its better-known relative, the stately white oak of the New England area.

The Rugged Bur Oak is sometimes called the mossy-cup oak. It has long, deep-cut leaves and yields valuable lumber.

The Pin Oak, often called the swamp oak, is the fine tree of low, marshy places. It is much used as a shade tree.

OAK

is attractive for parks. It has an irregular crown, deeply furrowed bark, and shaggy, spreading branches. It received its name because of its acorns, which are enclosed in a deep, fringed cup. The bur oak has large leaves with *sinuses* (deep notches). The two center sinuses are the deepest. This tree is grown both for shade and for lumber.

The *black oak* grows from Maine to Florida, and west to Minnesota, Kansas, and eastern Texas. Its leaves have broad, bristle-tipped lobes. The upper surface of the leaves is a glossy dark green in summer. In autumn, the leaves may turn a brilliant red. The tree itself does not usually grow more than 90 feet (27 meters) tall. It can be recognized by its dark gray bark. On old trees, the bark is almost black. It has orange-yellow inner layers rich in tannin.

The *red oak* is a handsome ornamental tree. It is common in the eastern parts of the United States. The red oak has grayish-brown bark. The inner layers of bark are red. The lobes of the leaves of this tree have irregular teeth, bristly points, and a triangular shape. They point forward more than outward. The red oak is the state tree of New Jersey.

The *live oak* ranks as a favorite avenue and park tree in the Southern States. It resembles somewhat an apple tree, because it has a thick, short trunk and long, spreading limbs. The live oak has thick, leathery leaves. They remain on the tree for a year, until new leaves appear. This oak has less showy foliage than some of the northern oaks. But its draperies of Spanish moss give the tree charm. The live oak has durable wood. See LIVE OAK.

The *holm oak*, sometimes called *holly oak*, or *ilex*, grows mainly in southern Europe. It reaches a height of about 80 feet (24 meters). Its leaves are dark green above, and light yellow underneath.

Uses. In some kinds of oaks, the acorn is sweet-tasting. But, in others, the acorn is very bitter. People in southern Europe often boil and eat acorns. The American Indians once used meal made from acorns. They first crushed the nuts, and then washed them in water to remove the bitter-tasting material. After the nuts dried, the Indians ground them into a meal. They pressed the meal into cakes which they cooked and ate. People chiefly eat the acorns of the white oak. Farmers feed all varieties of acorns to their hogs.

People have made use of timber cut from oak trees for many hundreds of years. The Shrine of Edward the Confessor, in Westminster Abbey, is built of oak. The wood seems as sound today as it was nearly 900 years ago. Oak wood rots very slowly, even if it is often exposed to dampness followed by drying. Oak ranked as the chief kind of lumber used for shipbuilding before the use of steel. The live oak was at one time the favorite kind of oak wood used for ships. Today, oak lumber is valued most of all for its beauty. Oak planks are especially attractive when they are *quartersawed* (cut from logs sawed lengthwise through the center).

Besides their valuable timber, oak trees yield tanbark, which is used in tanning leather. Cork oaks, which grow mainly in Spain and Portugal, produce cork. It comes from the thick, lightweight bark of these trees (see CORK).

An oak fungus that was isolated and identified about 1949 is killing a great many oak trees in the United States. The disease has spread eastward from the central Midwest.

Scientific Classification. Oaks belong to the beech family, *Fagaceae*. They make up the genus *Quercus*. The English oak is genus *Quercus*, species *Q. robur*. The white oak is *Q. alba*. The cork oak is *Q. suber*. The bur oak is *Q. macrocarpa*. The black oak is *Q. velutina*. The red oak is *Q. rubra*. The live oak is *Q. virginiana*. The holm oak is *Q. ilex*.   T. EWALD MAKI

See also ACORN; BIRD (Other Ways Birds Help Man); TREE (Familiar Broadleaf and Needleleaf Trees [picture]); BARK (picture).

OAK LEAF CLUSTER. See DECORATIONS AND MEDALS (Military Awards).

OAK RIDGE, Tenn. (pop. 28,319), the *Atomic Bomb City*, sprang up during World War II as a center for developing and producing materials for the atomic bomb. Oak Ridge now ranks as one of the largest cities in Tennessee. It lies about 18 miles (29 kilometers) northwest of Knoxville. For the location of Oak Ridge, see TENNESSEE (political map).

Federal authorities selected Oak Ridge as the site for atomic laboratories because of the abundance of water and electric power there. Also, its strategic location in hills and valleys helps isolate the various plants. About 1,000 families were removed to clear the area. By 1943, the town had a population of about 50,000. Its existence was not officially known until President Harry S. Truman announced production of the atomic bomb in August 1945. In 1949, the city was officially opened to the public. The Atomic Energy Communities Act of 1955 authorized self-government for Oak Ridge.

Energy Research and Development Administration

The Oak Ridge Gaseous Diffusion Plant was one of the installations that made World War II atomic-bomb materials.

Since 1948, the Oak Ridge National Laboratory has led in developing peaceful uses for nuclear energy. The Laboratory began nonatomic work in 1962 with basic research into the problems involved in changing salt water into fresh water. The Oak Ridge Associated Universities collaborates with the Laboratory. Oak Ridge is the home of the American Museum of Atomic Energy.   JEWELL A. PHELPS

Oakland, Calif., lies on the eastern shore of San Francisco Bay, 3 miles (4.8 kilometers) across the bay from San Francisco, *background*. Lake Merritt, *center*, is in the heart of downtown Oakland.

OAKLAND, Calif. (pop. 361,561), is one of the busiest shipping centers in the state. It forms part of the San Francisco-Oakland Metropolitan Area, which has a total population of 3,108,782. Oakland lies on the eastern shore of the San Francisco Bay, 3 miles (4.8 kilometers) across the bay from San Francisco. For location, see CALIFORNIA (political map).

Oakland was founded after the discovery of gold in California in 1848. The east bay area lay so near San Francisco, the center of the gold rush, that many prospectors extended their search there. Oakland was named for the oak trees that grew on its hills.

Description. Oakland, the county seat of Alameda County, covers about 80 square miles (210 square kilometers). This area includes about 25 square miles (65 square kilometers) of inland water. The San Francisco-Oakland Metropolitan Area covers 2,886 square miles (7,475 square kilometers). Lake Merritt lies in the heart of downtown Oakland. The Lake Merritt Wild Fowl Sanctuary, the oldest wildlife refuge in North America, opened in 1870. Jack London Square includes the bay waterfront that was visited frequently by the famous author for whom it was named.

Attractions in the city include the Oakland Museum, the Oakland Symphony Orchestra, and the Oakland Civic Ballet. The Oakland Zoo forms part of the Knowland State Arboretum and Park. Oakland has several colleges, among them the California College of Arts and Crafts, the College of the Holy Names, Mills College, and St. Albert's College. The city is the home of the Oakland Athletics baseball team of the American League, the Oakland Raiders of the National Football League, and the Golden State Warriors of the National Basketball Association.

Economy. Oakland is one of the world's busiest ports for container ships. These ships carry heavy cargo packed in metal containers of standard sizes to reduce shipping space. The western terminals of several freight railroad systems are located in Oakland. Passenger trains link Oakland with other U.S. cities. Air travelers use Oakland International Airport.

The city ranks as an important commercial center. About 25 per cent of Oakland's workers are employed in wholesale and retail trade, more than in any other economic activity. Oakland has about 750 manufacturing plants, and they employ about 20 per cent of the city's workers. The leading industries, in order of importance, produce processed foods, transportation equipment, fabricated metal products, chemicals, nonelectrical machinery, and electrical equipment.

Government and History. Oakland has a council-manager form of government. The voters elect a mayor and eight council members, all to four-year terms. The council appoints a city manager to carry out its policies.

Costanoan Indians lived in what is now the Oakland area before white settlers first arrived. During the 1770's, Spanish explorers became the first white people to reach the area. In 1820, Luis Maria Peralta, a Spanish soldier, received a land grant that included the entire east bay area. By 1849, gold seekers and other people had begun to settle in the area. Oakland received a city charter in 1854.

Oakland's population grew after trains reached the city from the East in 1869. About 65,000 persons settled in the city in 1906 after fleeing the San Francisco earthquake. Oakland's population had reached 150,174 in 1910. In 1936, the San Francisco-Oakland Bay Bridge linked the two cities. Oakland became an important port and shipbuilding center during World War II (1939-1945).

The Bay Area Rapid Transit system (BART), with headquarters in Oakland, began operating in 1972. A BART train route under San Francisco Bay between Oakland and San Francisco, opened in 1974. In 1973, Oakland completed a $1-million renewal project on the Paramount Theatre of the Performing Arts. A $150-million project called City Center, including office buildings, retail stores, and a hotel, was scheduled for completion in the early 1980's.   JAMES W. JOHNSON

OAKLAND UNIVERSITY. See UNIVERSITIES AND COLLEGES (table).

477

Annie Oakley became famous as one of the world's most accurate shots with pistol, rifle, and shotgun.

OAKLEY, ANNIE (1860-1926), an American markswoman, starred in Buffalo Bill's Wild West Show for 17 years. She was popular throughout the United States and Europe. She was an expert shot with a pistol, rifle, or shotgun. Once, with a .22 rifle, she shot 4,772 glass balls out of 5,000 tossed in the air on a single day. At 90 feet (27 meters), she could hit a playing card with the thin edge toward her, and puncture a card five or six times while it fell to the ground. Since then, free tickets with holes punched in them have been called "Annie Oakleys." She once shot a cigarette from the mouth of the German Crown Prince (later Wilhelm II) at his invitation.

Annie Oakley was born Phoebe Anne Oakley Mozee on Aug. 13, 1860, in a log cabin in Patterson Township, Ohio. She began shooting at the age of 9. After her father died, she supported the family by shooting small game. On a visit to Cincinnati she shot a match with Frank E. Butler, a vaudeville star. She won the match, and later married Butler. She joined his act, and became its star. Only 5 feet (152 centimeters) tall, she was called "Little Sure Shot." Annie Oakley joined Buffalo Bill's Wild West Show in 1885 (see BUFFALO BILL). The musical play *Annie Get Your Gun* portrayed her life.   HOWARD R. LAMAR

OAKUM, *O kum*, is loose fiber obtained by untwisting and picking at old, tarred hemp ropes. The fiber is used mainly to *calk*, or stuff, the seams of wooden ships to make them watertight. Plumbers use oakum for packing joints in waste pipes. *White oakum*, made from clean rope, was formerly used for medical purposes, such as dressings for wounds.   JOHN C. LE CLAIR

OAR. See ROWING.

OARFISH is a large fish that lives in the Atlantic and Pacific oceans. It sometimes reaches a length of 30 feet (9 meters). A long fin runs the length of its body. The oarfish swims with a snakelike, undulating motion.

Scientific Classification. The oarfish is in the family *Trachypteridae*. It is genus *Regalecus*, species *glesne*.

See also FISH (picture: Fish of the Deep Ocean).

OAS. See ORGANIZATION OF AMERICAN STATES; FRANCE (The Fifth Republic).

OASIS, *oh A sis*, is any watered spot in a desert region. In some cases, an oasis is only large enough to sustain the lives of a few persons. In other cases an oasis will be so extensive that 2,000,000 persons may live upon it.

Generally the soil in deserts is fertile but lacks the moisture to encourage plant growth. Oases develop in the places where springs, underground streams, or wells furnish water. The water from hills or mountains commonly percolates through rock debris down to the valleys, where much of it is held. The oases in the North American deserts are mainly formed in this way. Those in the Sahara result from springs, underground streams, or the nearness of mountains which are sufficiently high to cause moisture in the air to condense and rain to fall. People have reclaimed large tracts of land in these regions by drilling artesian wells and by irrigating the land from mountain streams.   ELDRED D. WILSON

See also DESERT; MERV; SAHARA (People).

OATES, JOYCE CAROL (1938-   ), is an American author. She gives most of her novels and short stories a nightmarish quality by emphasizing sex and violence. But her real subjects are society and insanity.

Oates dramatized the relationship between American society and its people in *A Garden of Earthly Delights* (1967). This novel shows how she believes society treats the poor. In *them* (1969), which won a National Book award in 1970, Oates portrayed the violent lives of a poor family in Detroit.

Many of Oates's characters are mentally ill. For example, in *Expensive People* (1968), a teen-ager who has difficulty distinguishing reality from fantasy confesses to the murder of his mother. However, he may not have committed the crime. The hero in *Wonderland* (1971) and the heroine in *Do With Me What You Will* (1973) have mentally ill fathers.

Collections of Oates's short stories include *By the North Gate* (1963) and *The Wheel of Love* (1970). She has also written essays, poems, and plays. Oates was born in Lockport, N.Y.   EUGENE K. GARBER

OATES, TITUS (1649-1705), was a conspirator who, in 1678, made up the story of a plot by Roman Catholics to assassinate the king of England and destroy Protestantism. He referred to the supposed plan as the *Popish Plot*. This was in 1678, when the English people were suspicious of Roman Catholics in general and of Jesuit priests in particular. Oates claimed knowledge of a Jesuit plot to suppress Protestantism through the assassination of King Charles II. He became a hero at first, and received a reward. But, in 1685, he was charged with perjury, fined, and imprisoned. William III released Oates in 1689, and he received a pension. Oates was born in Oakham, England.   F. A. NORWOOD

OATH is a pledge or promise. The *judicial* oath is probably the most common form of pledge. It is used in a court of law. A witness taking an oath in court swears

Irrigation Ditches that are filled with water from deep wells support the date palms and farm crops that are raised on El-Goléa, *above*, an oasis in Algeria.

An Artificially-Created Oasis in the Sahara has high sand walls built around it for protection against wind-swept sand.

that all of his or her statements are true. Frequently the person must lay one hand upon the Bible at the same time that the oath is being taken. This means that the person is making a declaration through God. A person swearing to the truth of an affidavit might be given the following oath:

"You do solemnly swear that the contents of this affidavit by you subscribed are true, so help you God."

A person who takes an oath in court and then makes a dishonest statement while under oath is guilty of perjury, which is a crime punishable by a fine or a jail sentence (see PERJURY).

All of us are familiar with oaths in everyday life. For example, a person who promises to give up a bad habit is said to "take an oath." This kind of oath is called *extrajudicial* because it has no force in a court of law. Oaths taken to show good faith in a private transaction are also extrajudicial.

Affirmation. Some religious groups, such as the Quakers, do not approve of swearing by an oath. They believe in the Bible's command "Swear not at all." When members of such groups testify in court they take an *affirmation* instead of an oath. The affirmation binds them to the truth just as strongly as an oath would.

Oath of Office. Many important officials take a pledge when they enter a public office. This *oath of office* is a promise to carry on the duties of the office honestly and faithfully. According to the Constitution, the President of the United States must take the following oath at his inauguration:

"I do solemnly swear (or affirm) that I will faithfully execute the Office of the President of the United States, and will to the best of my Ability, preserve, protect and defend the Constitution of the United States."

All United States officers lower in rank than the President take oaths much like the one above. An officer taking over a state public office promises to protect the state constitution as well as the U.S. Constitution.

In Canada many government officials take a pledge of faithfulness upon entering public office. But members elected to the federal Senate or House of Commons, and members of the legislative bodies of the provinces, must take the following oath of allegiance:

"I do swear that I will be faithful and bear true allegiance to His (or Her) Majesty . . ."

Military Oaths are taken by persons who enter the armed forces. Before a man or woman enters the service, he or she must take the following oath:

"I do solemnly swear (or affirm) that I will bear true faith and allegiance to the United States of America; that I will serve them honestly and faithfully against all their enemies whomsoever; and that I will obey the orders of the President of the United States and the orders of the officers appointed over me, according to the regulations and the Uniform Code of Military Justice."

Members of the armed forces of Canada, Great Britain, and other countries take a similar oath. In Germany, whole regiments were formerly sworn into the service together in a single ceremony. During conscription for World War II, the United States also followed the practice of swearing in large groups of men and women at the same time.   ERWIN N. GRISWOLD

See also CITIZENSHIP (The Oath of Allegiance); HIPPOCRATES (The Oath of Hippocrates).

479

OATMEAL

OATMEAL is a food product prepared from select cultivated oats. It is eaten chiefly as a cooked breakfast cereal. It is tasty and wholesome, and leads nearly all other grain products in food value. Oatmeal is made by removing the outer husk of the oat kernel. The *groat*, or inner portion of the kernel, is scoured to remove some of the outer skin. Then it is partially cooked by steaming, and rolled. The product is packaged in boxes or sacks.

The average portion of oatmeal contains about 67 parts carbohydrates, 16 parts protein, 7 parts fat, 2 parts mineral, and 7 parts water. Oatmeal is a good source of Vitamin B$_1$.　　　　W. B. DOHONEY

OATS are an important grain crop. Farmers grow them mainly to feed livestock, but oats also provide nourishing food for many people. The seeds of oat plants are processed and used in such foods as oatmeal, oatcakes, cookies, and ready-to-eat breakfast cereals.

Oats are a cereal grain and belong to the same family of plants as wheat, rice, corn, and barley. Oats have a higher food value than any other cereal grain. They are rich in starch and high-quality protein, and they provide a good source of Vitamin B$_1$, also called thiamine.

About 90 per cent of the oats grown in the United States are used as feed for livestock. Oats are the best grain to feed horses. Many farmers use the straw from oats as bedding for their livestock.

Russia produces more oats than any other country, followed by the United States, Canada, and the nations of northwestern Europe. More than 55 million short tons (50 million metric tons) of oats are grown annually.

The Oat Plant has a stalk that grows from 2 to 4 feet (61 to 120 centimeters) high. Many small branches spread out from the sides of the upper part of the stalk. Each branch ends in a single *spikelet* (flower cluster). The majority of oat plants have from 40 to 50 spikelets. Most spikelets contain two seeds, each enclosed by a husk. The husks must be removed before the seeds can be processed into oatmeal or other food products. The seeds of different varieties of oats are the same color as the husks and may be white, yellow, red, gray, or black.

The chief kinds of cultivated oats include *common*

Oat Plants have many flower clusters called *spikelets,* which contain the seeds. Each seed is enclosed by a husk.

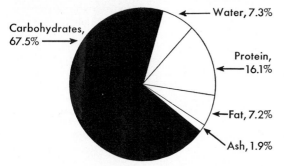

Carbohydrates, 67.5%

Water, 7.3%

Protein, 16.1%

Fat, 7.2%

Ash, 1.9%

The Food Value of Oatmeal makes it a nourishing breakfast cereal. One cup of oatmeal has about 130 calories.

Planting Oats. Many farmers plant oats with a machine called a *grain drill.* Planting takes place in early spring in most regions.

Harvesting Oats, a farmer may use a *combine.* This machine cuts down the stalks and separates the grain from them.

Leading Oat-Growing States and Provinces

Bushels of oats grown in 1975*

State/Province	Bushels
Minnesota	101,000,000 bu.
South Dakota	98,120,000 bu.
Alberta	95,625,000 bu.
Saskatchewan	90,313,000 bu.
Iowa	78,540,000 bu.
Wisconsin	74,250,000 bu.
North Dakota	56,170,000 bu.
Manitoba	54,188,000 bu.
Ohio	30,500,000 bu.
Ontario	29,219,000 bu.

*One bushel equals 32 pounds (15 kilograms).
Sources: U.S. Department of Agriculture; Statistics Canada.

Leading Oat-Growing Countries

Bushels of oats grown in 1975*

Country	Bushels
Russia	757,838,000 bu.†
United States	656,908,000 bu.
Canada	305,891,000 bu.
West Germany	237,341,000 bu.
Poland	222,529,000 bu.
China	206,683,000 bu.†
France	134,137,000 bu.
Finland	98,037,000 bu.
Sweden	93,696,000 bu.
Australia	82,673,000 bu.

*One bushel equals 32 pounds (15 kilograms).
†Estimate.
Source: FAO.

oats, red oats, side oats, and hull-less oats. Common oats are the type most widely grown in the United States. Red oats have reddish seeds. Side oats have all their branches on one side of the stalk. Hull-less oats, unlike the other types, have loose husks that separate from the seeds during harvesting.

Growing Oats. Oats can be grown in a variety of climates and soils. But they grow especially well in areas that have a cool, moist climate and fertile soil. Farmers may add fertilizer to poor soil to increase the yield.

Farmers grow two types of oats, *spring oats* and *winter oats.* Spring oats are planted in early spring and harvested in summer. The date of planting and harvesting depends on the climate of the area. Spring oats account for more than 85 per cent of the oat crop in the United States. Winter oats are planted in fall and harvested the next summer. They start growing before the weather turns cold. Growth stops during the winter and begins again in spring. Winter oats are not as hardy as other winter grains, and so they are grown chiefly in areas that have mild winters.

Oats grow best if the soil is prepared by plowing and *disking* before the seeds are planted. A *disk* is a type of farm machinery that has small blades. The blades break up clumps of earth into soil particles that absorb water better.

Some farmers plant oats by simply scattering the seeds over the field. But most farmers sow them with a *grain drill.* This machine drops the seeds into furrows and covers them with soil. The seeds are planted in rows about 8 inches (20 centimeters) apart and covered with about 2 inches (5 centimeters) of soil. Most farmers plant from 60 to 90 pounds of seeds per acre (67 to 100 kilograms per hectare) of land.

Harvesting Oats. Oats are harvested after the plants become dry and yellow and the seeds harden. The grain should not contain more than 12 to 14 per cent moisture when harvested. Farmers can take samples of the seed to a grain elevator for a moisture test.

Some oats are grown for hay or *silage.* Silage consists of chopped plant stalks, which are stored in a silo and used to feed livestock during the winter. Oats grown for hay or silage are harvested while the plants are still green and the seeds are soft.

Most farmers harvest oats with a machine called a *combine,* which cuts the stalks and separates the grain from the branches. The husks are later removed from the seeds at processing plants. The average yield of oats in the United States is about 48 bushels per acre (1,700 kilograms per hectare).

Diseases and Insect Pests. Various diseases sometimes attack oats and sharply reduce the yield. These diseases include smuts, rusts, septoria, and barley yellow dwarf. Oat crops can also be damaged by such insects as aphids, army worms, cutworms, cereal leaf beetles, and grasshoppers. Aphids are especially troublesome because they spread the barley yellow dwarf disease.

Some farmers use chemical sprays to control diseases and insects. But the best protection comes from planting resistant varieties of oats. Researchers continually develop new varieties that are more resistant to diseases and insects. The new varieties also produce higher yields and better grain. See SMUT; RUST; APHID; ARMY WORM; CUTWORM.

Scientific Classification. Oats belong to the grass family, Gramineae, and to the genus *Avena.* Common oats belong to the species *A. sativa.*   CHARLES M. BROWN

See also GRAIN; OATMEAL; FURFURAL.

OAXACA, *wah HAH kah,* officially OAXACA DE JUÁREZ (pop. 99,509), is the capital of Oaxaca, a state in southern Mexico. It stands in a rich mining, farming, and forest region (see MEXICO [political map]). Oaxaca has won fame for handicrafts. The ruins of two ancient Indian cities, Mitla and Monte Albán, lie near Oaxaca. Some historians believe the Aztec founded Oaxaca in

OAXACA

1486. But the Zapotec and the Mixtec Indians had lived in the area since the time of the early Christians. The people of colonial Oaxaca produced impressive architecture. JOHN A. CROW

OAXACA, *wah HAH kah,* is a mountainous state on Mexico's South Pacific Coast. It has a population of 2,171,733, and covers 36,820 square miles (95,363 square kilometers). For location, see MEXICO (political map). About half of the people are Indians. The chief tribes include the Zapotec and Mixtec. The ruins of their ancient cities show the splendor of these civilizations. Oaxaca's farmers grow wheat, bananas, tobacco, coffee, and other crops. The state also produces lumber, gold, silver, onyx, and marble. Oaxaca was one of the original states of Mexico. The capital is Oaxaca [de Juárez]. CHARLES C. CUMBERLAND

See also OAXACA (city); ZAPOTEC INDIANS.

OB RIVER, *ahb,* is one of the chief rivers of Russia in Asia. The Ob rises in the Altai Mountains of western Siberia and flows northwestward for 2,287 miles (3,681 kilometers) before it empties into the Arctic Ocean through the Gulf of Ob (Obskaya Guba). It drains 1,125,200 square miles (2,914,250 square kilometers), an area about four times the size of Texas.

The navigable waterways of the Ob and its tributaries total about 19,000 miles (30,600 kilometers). The lower part of the river is 2 to 4 miles (3 to 6 kilometers) wide, while the estuary averages 50 miles (80 kilometers) in width. It is blocked with ice from October to June. In summer, the Ob River is an important water route for shipping grain, dairy products, livestock, wool, and meat. Most of this moves to the railways for shipment to western Russia, but some is exported by way of the Arctic Ocean. See also RIVER (chart). THEODORE SHABAD

OBADIAH, *oh buh DIE uh,* the fourth book of the minor Hebrew prophets, is the shortest book in the Old Testament. It has only 21 verses. The book contains a prophecy that the kingdom of Edom will be destroyed, and that all nations except Judah will be punished. The name Obadiah (sometimes spelled *Abdias*) means *Servant of the Lord.* Nothing is known of the Obadiah who is supposed to have written this book. He probably lived after 540 B.C. WALTER G. WILLIAMS

OBBLIGATO. See MUSIC (Terms).

OBELISK, *AHB uh lisk,* is a great, upright, four-sided stone pillar. The sides slope slightly so that the top is smaller than the base. The top is shaped like a pyramid and ends in a point. The Washington Monument in Washington, D.C., is an obelisk.

The ancient Egyptians built huge obelisks. Most of them had inscriptions in *hieroglyphics* (picture writing). Two obelisks, now known as Cleopatra's Needles, were originally at Heliopolis, Egypt. In the 1800's, one was taken to New York City, and the other to London (see CLEOPATRA'S NEEDLES). An obelisk from the temple of Luxor, Egypt, is now in Paris' Place de la Concorde.

Obelisks were cut right at the quarry as single blocks of granite. The exact method the ancient Egyptians used is not known. It is believed they first made a horizontal, three-sided form by cutting deep trenches all around the form. Then they split away the fourth side either by inserting copper or wooden wedges, or by pounding through the underside with balls of diorite, a hard rock. Finally they polished the obelisk. Still unexplained is how they raised the huge stone pillar to an upright position at its final site. RICARDO A. CAMINOS

OBERAMMERGAU, *oh ber AHM er gow* (pop. 4,870), is a Bavarian village 45 miles (72 kilometers) southwest of Munich in Germany (see GERMANY [political map]). It is famous for its performances of the Passion Play, which normally take place every 10 years. This pageant portrays the suffering and death of Jesus. Residents perform all the parts. See PASSION PLAY.

Bible scenes cover the outside walls of many of the city's buildings. The Passion Play attracts thousands of tourists to Oberammergau. The people earn money from the tourist trade and by carving objects of wood and ivory. JAMES K. POLLOCK

OBERHAUSEN, *OH ber HOW zen* (pop. 249,000), is a coal-mining and industrial city in West Germany's Ruhr. The city was founded in 1862, and received its charter in 1874. Its industries include zinc refineries, furniture, chemicals, and glass. For location, see GERMANY (political map). JAMES K. POLLOCK

OBERLIN COLLEGE is a privately controlled, coeducational liberal arts school at Oberlin, Ohio. It was the first coeducational college in the United States. It has a college of arts and sciences and a conservatory of music. Courses lead to bachelor's and master's degrees. Oberlin was founded in 1833. The college has always had a policy

Oberammergau lies in the foothills of the Bavarian Alps in southern Germany. The town's Passion Play is usually presented every 10 years. It was first given in 1634.

of admitting all students regardless of their race, creed, or color. In 1841, Oberlin became the first U.S. school to award college degrees to women. For enrollment, see UNIVERSITIES AND COLLEGES (table). See also COEDUCATION; WOMAN (In Industrialized Societies).

Critically reviewed by OBERLIN COLLEGE

OBERLIN CONSERVATORY OF MUSIC is a coeducational school of music at Oberlin, Ohio. It is a division of Oberlin College. The school grants Mus.B. degrees. It was founded in 1865. Oberlin was the first music school in the United States to become an integral part of a collegiate institution.   J. ROBERT WILLIAMS

OBERON. See FAIRY; SHAKESPEARE, WILLIAM (*A Midsummer Night's Dream*).

OBERTH, HERMANN. See SPACE TRAVEL (Early Developments).

OBESITY. See WEIGHT CONTROL.

OBJECT, in grammar. See CASE.

OBJECTIVE CASE. See CASE (Pronouns).

OBJECTIVE LENS. See MICROSCOPE; TELESCOPE.

OBOE, *OH boh*, is the smallest and highest-pitched of the double-reed woodwind instruments. The name comes from two French words: *haut*, meaning *high*, and *bois*, meaning *wood*. The oboe is about 21 inches (53 centimeters) long. It was developed in France, probably in the mid-1600's.

The range of the instrument is almost three octaves, and the tone is made by means of a small double reed. The oboe is hard to play because so little air is needed to blow it. As a result, the player must breathe more slowly than normal. Early oboes gave off a loud, harsh tone, but today the oboe is known for its smooth and beautiful tone.

The oboe holds an important place in symphony orchestras, concert bands, and small ensembles. Sometimes it is used for solos. Among those who wrote important works for the instrument are Beethoven, Handel,

Mouthpiece ——→
(Double reed)

Keys

Tone holes

Bell ——→

WORLD BOOK photo, courtesy Chicago Symphony Orchestra

The Oboe is a high-pitched woodwind instrument. The musician plays it by blowing gently through the double-reed mouthpiece.

and Mozart. The English horn is an alto oboe, a fifth lower in pitch than the oboe.   CHARLES B. RIGHTER

See also ENGLISH HORN.

OBOLUS. See CHARON.

OBOTE, *oh BOH tee*, **APOLLO MILTON** (1926-   ), led Uganda, a British protectorate, to independence in 1962. He then served as the first prime minister of this east-central African nation. In 1966, Obote seized full control of the government and declared himself president. The people elected him president in 1967, but an army revolt deposed him in 1971.

Obote was born in the Lango district of Uganda. In 1958, he was elected to the Ugandan legislature. In 1960, Obote became leader of the Uganda People's Congress, a new political party he had helped create. As president of Uganda, Obote abolished the country's separate tribal kingdoms and ruled with absolute power. He put industry under government control and expanded trade with neighboring African nations. In 1969, an unidentified assassin failed in an attempt to shoot Obote.   ROBERT I. ROTBERG

See also UGANDA (History).

O'BOYLE, PATRICK ALOYSIUS CARDINAL (1896-   ), was named a cardinal of the Roman Catholic Church in 1967 by Pope Paul VI. Cardinal O'Boyle served as archbishop of Washington, D.C., from 1947 until he resigned in 1973. He also served as chancellor of the Catholic University of America in Washington. He won recognition for his welfare activities and his work in improving race relations.

From 1933 to 1936, he served as assistant director of the child care department of Catholic Charities of the New York archdiocese. He was executive director of the National Catholic Welfare Conference war relief activities from 1943 to 1947. Cardinal O'Boyle was born in Scranton, Pa. He was ordained a priest in New York City in 1921.   THOMAS P. NEILL

OBREGÓN, *oh bray GAWN*, **ÁLVARO** (1880-1928), a Mexican soldier, statesman, and rancher, was twice president of Mexico. Obregón succeeded Venustiano Carranza as president in 1920 (see CARRANZA, VENUSTIANO). The United States recognized his government in 1923. He was one of the most capable leaders of the Mexican Revolution. He was re-elected president in 1928, but was assassinated before he could take office.

In 1912, during a revolution against the government of President Francisco Madero, Obregón raised a force of Sonora Indians and went to Madero's aid. In 1913, Victoriano Huerta murdered Madero and seized the presidency. Obregón joined Venustiano Carranza against Huerta.

In 1914 and 1915, Obregón supported Carranza against Pancho Villa (see VILLA, PANCHO [with picture]). In his battles with Villa, Obregón used barbed-wire entanglements, machine-gun nests, and trench warfare for the first time in Mexico. Obregón was born in the Alamos district of Sonora.   DONALD J. WORCESTER

See also MEXICO (Economic and Social Changes).

O'BRIEN, LAWRENCE FRANCIS (1917-   ), served as postmaster general of the United States from 1965 to 1968. He had been a special assistant in charge of congressional relations to Presidents John F. Kennedy and Lyndon B. Johnson. He worked to get congressional approval of legislation that Presidents Kennedy and Johnson favored.

O'Brien helped direct John F. Kennedy's campaigns for the U.S. Senate in 1952 and 1958, and for the presidency in 1960. He helped direct Johnson's presidential campaign in 1964. He served as chairman of the Democratic National Committee from August, 1968, to January, 1969, and became chairman again in March, 1970. O'Brien resigned from the committee in July, 1972. He then became chairman of George S. McGovern's 1972 presidential campaign. In 1975, O'Brien became commissioner of the National Basketball Association (NBA). O'Brien was born in Springfield, Mass.   CARL T. ROWAN

O'BRIEN, ROBERT C. (1922-1973), an American author, won the 1972 Newbery medal for *Mrs. Frisby and the Rats of NIMH.* This children's story tells about a widowed mouse who willingly faces many dangers to care for her four youngsters.

Robert Carroll O'Brien was born in New York City. He worked as a free-lance author, magazine writer, and newspaper reporter. O'Brien began making up and telling stories while counseling at a boys' camp. His first children's book was *The Silver Crown* (1968).

OBSCENITY AND PORNOGRAPHY are terms used to designate written, recorded, or pictorial material—including motion pictures—that many people consider indecent and thus find offensive. The term *obscenity* can also refer to language or behavior believed to corrupt public morals. Some people consider violence and war obscene. *Pornography* refers chiefly to printed or pictorial material intended primarily to cause sexual stimulation. The terms obscenity and pornography are often used interchangeably.

Most states and cities in the United States have laws against publishing, distributing, or selling obscene materials. But these laws have been hard to enforce because judges, juries, lawyers, and the public all may interpret them differently. What some people regard as obscene may not seem so to others. For example, material acceptable for adults may be thought unsuitable for children. Also, what is considered obscene in one community may not be considered so in another.

The nature of obscenity and pornography and the laws governing them have been a continuing source of controversy. Some people are convinced that the distribution of pornographic material corrupts public morality. Others believe that anti-obscenity laws violate the rights of free speech and free press guaranteed by the First Amendment to the United States Constitution.

Congress passed the first federal law against obscenity as part of the Tariff Act of 1842. This law made it illegal to bring what it called "indecent and obscene" material into the country. In 1865, Congress passed legislation prohibiting the mailing of obscene material. By 1900, at least 30 states had passed laws to control distribution of such material.

In 1957, in the case of *Roth v. United States,* the Supreme Court ruled that freedom of the press—as guaranteed by the First Amendment—does not apply to obscenity. However, the court provided only loose guidelines for determining what can be considered obscene.

The public debate over obscenity intensified during the 1960's as many previous restraints on the content of books, magazines, and motion pictures were loosened.

In 1967, Congress created a national Commission on Obscenity and Pornography to study the matter. In 1970, the commission reported finding no reliable evidence that pornography caused crime among adults or delinquency among young people. The commission recommended repeal of all laws prohibiting the sale of pornography to consenting adults. But it also recommended that each state adopt laws against the sale of obscene pictorial material to young people. Not all members of the commission agreed with the majority viewpoint. One minority report declared that anti-obscenity laws should be strengthened and enforced; another recommended the repeal of all such laws.

The Supreme Court developed new guidelines for judging whether material is obscene in 1973, in the case of *Miller v. California.* According to the guidelines, material can be considered obscene (1) if the average person, applying contemporary community standards, finds that the material, taken as a whole, appeals to the *prurient* (sexually arousing) interest; (2) if the material shows, in a clearly offensive way, sexual conduct specifically defined as obscene by law; and (3) if the material lacks serious literary, artistic, political, or scientific value. States and cities were expected to use these guidelines in enforcing their anti-obscenity laws and in framing new legislation.

Many nations have anti-obscenity laws. In some, including Ireland and Italy, such laws are strictly enforced. In Canada and the United States, various anti-obscenity groups have fought for years for stronger legislation and strict enforcement of existing laws. Some Canadian provinces have obscenity boards that try to control the publication and distribution of obscene material. On the other hand, some nations have repealed their obscenity laws or are considering doing so. In the late 1960's, for example, Denmark dropped all legal barriers against pornography for adults. In England, Israel, and Sweden, various commissions have recommended similar action.   OTTO N. LARSEN

See also CENSORSHIP.

OBSERVATORY is a building or an institution where astronomers study the sun, planets, stars, and other objects in the universe. These scientists examine the various forms of *radiation* (energy) in space, including light, radio waves, and X rays. Astronomers also study how atoms behave in the vast spaces among the stars and in the high temperatures of the stars themselves.

There are two chief kinds of observatories. *Optical observatories* have optical telescopes for the study of light. *Radio observatories* have radio telescopes for the study of radio waves. Optical telescopes use such devices as lenses and mirrors to form magnified images of distant objects. Most radio telescopes use large antennas to capture radio waves from space. Observatories also have various instruments, including cameras, computers, and electronic sensors, to record the information gathered by optical and radio telescopes.

Astronomers build observatories in places that have good observing conditions, free of such difficulties as those caused by violent atmospheric disturbances, polluted air, and bright lights. Most optical observatories stand on high mountains, where the sky is almost always clear. Many radio observatories are in valleys, where the mountains protect them from radio interfer-

The Kitt Peak National Observatory, *above,* stands atop a high mountain near Tucson, Ariz. Its location, away from bright city lights and free of polluted air and violent atmospheric disturbances, provides astronomers with excellent observing conditions.

ence from cities and other highly populated areas. Astronomers also use balloons to send telescopes into the thin upper air to escape atmospheric distortion.

Some forms of radiation, including gamma rays, ultraviolet light, and X rays, are absorbed by the earth's atmosphere. To measure such radiation, instruments must be placed in an *orbiting astronomical observatory* or some other type of orbiting satellite. These satellites have special detectors to measure radiation in space.

Most observatories are operated by universities and are used by teachers and advanced students of astronomy. They are extremely expensive to build and operate, and so national governments or wealthy individuals support many of them. Most observatories have workshops that service the equipment used by astronomers. Optical observatories include photographic darkrooms to process pictures that astronomers take of the sky.

Optical Observatories. The telescope in an optical observatory stands under a large dome that has shutters. The dome and the shutters protect the telescope from the weather. Motors and precision gears keep the telescope pointed in the desired direction as the earth rotates. Observatories use two principal kinds of optical telescopes—*reflecting telescopes* and *refracting telescopes.* Reflecting telescopes use a curved mirror or a set of such mirrors to focus light, and refracting telescopes use a system of lenses.

Most optical observatories use reflecting telescopes, which can be made larger than refracting telescopes. The Hale telescope at the Palomar Observatory near San Diego ranks as one of the world's largest reflecting telescopes. Its mirror measures 200 inches (510 centimeters) in diameter.

Refracting telescopes need thick lenses for high magnification. Such lenses are difficult to make, and they absorb much of the light that they gather. The refract-

ing telescope at the Yerkes Observatory in Williams Bay, Wis., is the world's largest. Its lens measures 40 inches (100 centimeters) in diameter.

Many of the images produced by optical telescopes are too dim to be seen directly. As a result, astronomers rarely make their observations by looking through a telescope. They use cameras to make pictures of the dim images produced by the telescope. If the photographic film is exposed to dim light for a long time, a bright image results. Special television cameras can record even dimmer images.

Astronomers in optical observatories use an instrument called a *spectrograph* to separate the various colors that make up starlight. A spectrograph, which may be used with a telescope, spreads out starlight into a band of colors. Scientists can determine the composition of a star from these colors. A *photoelectric photometer* is used to measure the brightness of stars. It has filters that enable it to work with one color of light at a time.

Scientists at *solar observatories,* a type of optical observatory, specialize in studying the sun. Such observatories must make special provisions to reduce the effects of the sun's heat. This heat creates currents of hot air near the surface of the earth that blur photographs of the sun. Most solar observatories stand on high towers to escape the effects of the hot air.

Radio Observatories. The radio telescopes used by most radio observatories consist of a large bowl-shaped *reflector* that collects radio waves. A radio receiver picks up and amplifies the radio signals that enter the reflector. Scientists study these signals to determine the temperature and composition of various objects in space that give off radio waves.

The reflectors of radio telescopes are much larger than the lenses or mirrors of optical telescopes. As a result, radio telescopes can study objects too far away

485

SOME IMPORTANT OBSERVATORIES

Name	Location	Year Opened	Interesting Facts
Arecibo Ionospheric Observatory	Arecibo, Puerto Rico	1963	Has the world's largest radio telescope, with a reflector 1,000 feet (305 meters) in diameter
Cape of Good Hope Royal Observatory	Cape Town, South Africa	1820	One of the leading observatories in the Southern Hemisphere
Jodrell Bank Observatory	Jodrell Bank, England, near Manchester	1949	Includes the world's first radio telescope capable of being pointed in any direction
Mount Palomar Observatory	Mount Palomar, Calif., near San Diego	1948	Has the largest reflecting telescope in the United States, with a mirror 200 inches (508 centimeters) in diameter
National Radio Astronomy Observatory's Very Large Array Telescope Project	Socorro, N. Mex.	*	Will have the world's most powerful radio telescope, made up of 27 reflectors, each 82 feet (25 meters) in diameter
Naval Observatory	Washington, D.C.	1830	Establishes the official time for all places in the United States and its possessions
Paris Observatory	Meudon, France	1670	Observatory where the speed of light was first measured
Pulkovo Observatory	Leningrad, Russia	1839	Site of telescopic observations leading to major advances in understanding the earth's motion
Special Astrophysical Observatory	Zelenchukskaya, Russia, near Cherkessk	1974	Has the world's largest reflecting telescope, with a mirror 236 inches (600 centimeters) in diameter
Yerkes Observatory	Williams Bay, Wis.	1897	Has the world's largest refracting telescope, with a lens 40 inches (102 centimeters) in diameter

*Under construction; scheduled for completion in the early 1980's.

to be seen by optical telescopes. The Arecibo Observatory in Arecibo, Puerto Rico, has the world's largest radio telescope. This telescope has a reflector 1,000 feet (300 meters) in diameter.

Astronomers can connect two or more radio telescopes to form a *radio interferometer*. A radio interferometer can produce clearer images than a single radio telescope.

History. In ancient times, men built observatories to study the positions of the sun, the moon, and the stars. Stonehenge, a monument in Wiltshire, England, is the oldest known structure once used as an observatory. This arrangement of stone slabs was built about 1800 B.C. By about A.D. 300, Maya Indian astronomers in Central America had developed an accurate calendar based on observations of objects in the sky.

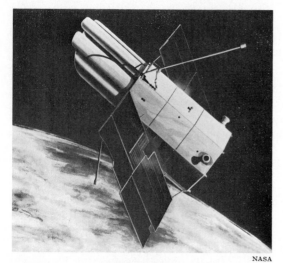

NASA

An Orbiting Astronomical Observatory can photograph objects far in space. Many such unmanned satellites can measure radiation that does not penetrate the atmosphere of the earth.

During the 1670's, observatories began to use refracting telescopes. These telescopes enabled astronomers to determine the positions of objects in the universe more accurately than ever before. In 1675, King Charles II of England founded the Royal Greenwich Observatory in Greenwich. This observatory provided charts that gave the exact locations of various stars for sailors to follow in navigation.

Many new scientific instruments came into use in observatories during the 1800's. With these instruments, astronomers could study the composition of the stars for the first time. For example, scientists at optical observatories started to use spectrographs in the mid-1800's. Cameras became one of the chief tools of observatories by the late 1800's.

During the 1900's, most large optical observatories began to use reflecting telescopes. Astronomers developed radio telescopes and orbiting astronomical observatories in the mid-1900's. Many observatories have taken part in the space exploration program by providing information needed to guide rockets and satellites.

Rising costs caused many governments to increase their support for observatories during the 1960's. The United States has four national observatories—the Cerro Tololo Inter-American Observatory near La Serena, Chile; the Kitt Peak National Observatory near Tucson, Ariz.; the National Astronomy and Ionosphere Center in Ithaca, N.Y. and Arecibo, Puerto Rico; and the National Radio Astronomy Observatory in Green Bank, W. Va.   FRANK D. DRAKE

Related Articles in WORLD BOOK include:

Astronomy
Cerro Tololo Inter-American Observatory
Greenwich Observatory, Royal
Hale Observatories
Jodrell Bank Observatory
Kitt Peak National Observatory
Lick Observatory

National Radio Astronomy Observatory
Radio Telescope
Space Travel (Scientific Satellites)
Spectroscope
Stonehenge
Telescope
Yerkes Observatory

OBSIDIAN, *ub SID ih un,* is a natural glass formed when hot lava from a volcano or an earth fissure cools quickly. Obsidian contains the same chemicals as granite, but the chemicals are melted together to make glass. Most obsidian is black, or black with red streaks. It is brittle and cannot be quarried in blocks. Indians used obsidian to make arrowheads. Obsidian Cliff, in Yellowstone National Park, is a huge mass of obsidian. See also IGNEOUS ROCK. RICHARD M. PEARL

OBSTETRICS. See MEDICINE (table: Specialty Fields).

OCARINA, AHK *uh RE nuh,* is a small toy wind instrument of the whistle type. It is made of molded clay or plastic, and shaped like a goose egg. Its name is a form of the Italian word for goose. The ocarina has a mouthpiece through which air is blown and 7 to 10 holes that sound a simple scale. Its tone is pleasing and soft. An Italian named Donati developed the ocarina in the 1860's, but forms of the

Jim Collins
The Ocarina

ocarina were known in ancient China. CHARLES B. RIGHTER

O'CASEY, SEAN (1880-1964), was perhaps the greatest Irish playwright of his time. Born in the Dublin slums and largely self-educated, he first gained fame when Dublin's Abbey Theatre staged three of his tragicomedies—*The Shadow of a Gunman* (1923), *Juno and the Paycock* (1924), and *The Plough and the Stars* (1926). Each deals with a phase of the violence Ireland experienced from 1916 to 1924, during and after its fight for independence from England. The plays show egotism, slogans, and abstract ideals such as patriotism as the enemies of life and happiness. The plays are full of colorful characters and speech, and are written in a vivid, realistic style.

O'Casey left Ireland for England in 1926, after *The Plough and the Stars* provoked rioting during its opening week. Some of the audience thought the play slandered Ireland's patriots and womanhood. O'Casey broke with the Abbey Theatre in 1928 after it refused to stage his play *The Silver Tassie.* Like his earlier work, this play was antiwar in tone, and shows war as the destroyer of individuality and heroism. The play also developed expressionistic tendencies found in O'Casey's earlier work. Symbolism and expressionism became more important in O'Casey's later plays.

Most of the plays O'Casey wrote during the 1930's and early 1940's have revolutionary heroes and call for a radical transformation of society. These works include *Purple Dust* (1940) and *Red Roses for Me* (1942).

O'Casey returned to Irish themes late in his career. He presented an Ireland that had exchanged British domination for domination by the Roman Catholic Church of Ireland and the new commercial class. Plays of this period include *Cock-a-doodle Dandy* (1949), *The Bishop's Bonfire* (1955), and *The Drums of Father Ned* (1958). O'Casey's most important nondramatic work is a six-volume autobiography in fictional form. MARTIN MEISEL

OCCIPITAL BONE. See HEAD.

OCCLUDED FRONT. See WEATHER (Fronts).

OCCULT, *uh KULT,* or *AHK ult,* is a term which refers to knowledge of a supernatural type, not bounded by the strict laws of modern science. People may be said to have knowledge of the occult if they claim to understand subjects which cannot be understood by others, and which are outside the field of recognized science. Occult means secret, or mysterious. Fortune-tellers claim to have knowledge of the occult when they tell a fortune, because they say that they can explain things which people in general cannot know.

During ancient times there was wide belief in occult sciences. The best-known of the old occult subjects included astrology, alchemy, necromancy, and magic. Many persons guided their lives by such false sciences. The physical sciences, with their exact answers, had not developed, and people were easily influenced by those who claimed to have unusual knowledge.

Several branches of the occult sciences are still alive today. Revivals of occultism occur from time to time in all parts of the world. WILSON D. WALLIS

Related Articles in WORLD BOOK include:

Alchemy	Fortunetelling	Spiritualists
Astrology	Magic	Superstition
Divination	Necromancy	Theosophist
Extrasensory	Psychical	
Perception	Research	

OCCUPANCY is a legal method by which a person or nation acquires title to a piece of property which does not have an owner. This manner of establishing title to unowned property was first recognized by Roman civil law. It was later taken into the English common law. Occupancy can be described as the act of taking possession of property which belongs to no one, with the intention of keeping it. Thus, a person who finds property that has been lost becomes its owner if the former owner makes no effort to reclaim it. If someone captures a wild animal and tames it, the animal becomes that person's property. British settlers landed in Bermuda in 1609, before there were any other inhabitants, and claimed the island as a British possession. This is an example of an effective occupancy. WILLIAM TUCKER DEAN

OCCUPATION. See CAREERS.

OCCUPATIONAL DISEASE. See DISEASE (Occupational Diseases).

OCCUPATIONAL SAFETY AND HEALTH ADMINISTRATION (OSHA) is an agency of the United States Department of Labor that promotes safe and healthful working conditions. OSHA's chief responsibility is the development and enforcement of job safety and health regulations. The agency also works to educate employers and employees about industrial hazards.

OSHA regulations deal with fire prevention, protective garments and railings, and many other safety matters. The rules also establish maximum levels of exposure to asbestos, lead, and other substances that could endanger the health of workers. OSHA inspectors check factories and other sites for violations, and employers who fail to make required changes are fined.

The agency encourages the states to develop their own health and safety programs to replace OSHA itself. By the late 1970's, about half the states had programs approved by OSHA. The federal government pays half the cost of such programs.

OSHA was established by the Williams-Steiger Oc-

OCCUPATIONAL THERAPY

cupational Safety and Health Act of 1970 and began operating in 1971. Many leaders of both business and labor criticized the agency's performance during its first few years. Executives complained that OSHA demanded too much paperwork and too many costly changes that did not increase safety. Labor leaders charged that the agency lagged in developing new regulations and failed to enforce existing ones. To improve the agency's performance, OSHA began additional training programs for inspectors and planned other changes.   JOHN V. GRIMALDI

OCCUPATIONAL THERAPY is a kind of treatment prescribed by doctors for persons who are physically or mentally disabled. It includes interesting occupations and pastimes that help patients overcome or reduce their handicaps. Patients with an artificial leg may be taught to dance. In this way, they gain confidence in their ability to live a normal life. Blind people who learn to travel, clothe, feed, and care for themselves are better prepared to live a useful life. Sometimes patients must relearn such basic skills of everyday living as dressing, writing, or eating. Occupational therapy is often described as "curing by doing," because the patients themselves must carry out the activities.

Activities used in occupational therapy are planned and supervised by professional experts called *occupational therapists*. These specialists work in hospitals, rehabilitation centers, and special schools. They also may provide treatment in the patient's home.

Occupational therapists determine what kind of therapy, or treatment, will best help patients. First, the therapist must become familiar with a patient's illness, interests, and background. Then, the therapist can plan a program that will help the patient overcome the disability. A woodworking project might provide the best exercise for a patient with an artificial arm. Or a mentally ill patient might be encouraged to learn to express his or her worries through painting.

The rehabilitation of the sick and injured often includes both occupational therapy and *physical* therapy. Therapists use both kinds of treatment to help the physically disabled. See PHYSICAL THERAPY.

The idea behind occupational therapy goes back to

A.D. 172 when Galen, the great Greek physician, said: "Employment is nature's best medicine and essential to human happiness." During the late 1700's, physicians in several countries used occupational therapy in treating mentally ill patients. These doctors included Philippe Pinel in France, Johann Christian Reil in Germany, and Benjamin Rush in the United States. By 1798, the Pennsylvania Hospital for the Insane in Philadelphia was teaching patients carpentry, shoe repairing, needlework, and music. The need to help disabled veterans of World Wars I and II stimulated the growth of occupational therapy.

Modern occupational therapy developed from a nursing course in "Invalid Occupations." This course was first offered to student nurses in 1906 by Susan E. Tracy, a Boston nurse. The term *occupational therapy* was first used in 1914 by George E. Barton, an architect from Clifton Springs, N.Y. He had been treated by this method.

What Occupational Therapy Does

Occupational therapy has two chief goals. These are (1) to help patients use their bodies more adequately after an injury or illness and (2) to help people overcome emotional problems.

Helping the Body is called *physical restoration* or *functional therapy*. Doctors prescribe physical restoration for patients with weak muscles or stiff joints. It is also used when muscles do not work together smoothly, when part of the body is permanently paralyzed, or when a patient must adjust to using an artificial limb.

Physical restoration provides exercise that helps restore muscle strength and usefulness. For example, a victim of poliomyelitis may lose the use of some muscles because the nerves that control those muscles have been damaged. The loss may be either partial or complete. The body itself can repair the nerve damage, but the muscles remain too weak to use. The occupational therapist suggests activities designed to strengthen the muscles. Such activities as throwing a ball or doing woodworking help build up a patient's arm muscles. A person can strengthen leg muscles by operating a potter's wheel, using a kicking motion on the pedal.

Sometimes a disease may cripple the body so that

Mitchell Payne, Jeroboam

Occupational Therapists teach skills to the handicapped. The blind girl shown at the left is working with a therapist in learning to write.

stricken muscles remain useless. Then the therapist must teach the patient new ways to perform familiar tasks by substituting one muscle or limb for another. Some patients might learn to dress and to eat with one hand instead of two. Others may have to develop strong arm and shoulder muscles to operate the crutches that do the work of their weakened leg muscles.

Physical restoration also helps patients learn how to use artificial limbs. The therapist might teach a person with an artificial hand to assemble an electric circuit. Handling the thin wires gives the patient skill in using the new hand, as well as a useful occupation.

Helping the Mind is called *psychological therapy*. Therapists use this technique to help physically or mentally ill patients solve emotional problems.

Patients often worry about the effect their illness will have on their own futures and on that of their families. Some persons are forced to limit their activities because of a disease such as tuberculosis or heart disease. Psychological therapy helps redirect their energies into activities and interests that are within their limitations. For example, people recovering from a heart attack might substitute chess or checkers for tennis. They may be encouraged to read about exploration instead of taking long hikes themselves.

Psychological therapy plays a vital part in helping patients with permanent disabilities such as blindness or the loss of a limb. Patients learn that they can do things in spite of their handicaps. An amputee might learn to drive a specially equipped car. A blind person might learn to travel alone. Each new thing a patient learns to do strengthens his or her self-confidence.

Doctors often prescribe psychological therapy for mentally ill patients who have trouble getting along with other people. The therapist plans activities that help the patient develop self-confidence and build satisfying relationships with others. Folk dancing and dramatics encourage social relationships. Patients may work in hospital kitchens or libraries as the first step toward returning to the responsibilities of home and community.

Careers in Occupational Therapy

A person must like people and enjoy serving them before considering occupational therapy as a career.

In addition, an occupational therapist must be emotionally stable.

Opportunities. Many positions are available for graduate therapists. They may work in the area of patient treatment, and in professional education, administration, and research. Salaries of therapists compare favorably with such professions as nursing and teaching.

Education. A therapist must be graduated from a college or university that offers a program approved by the American Medical Association. Professional subjects of the four-year course include the physical, biological, and social sciences; clinical medicine; rehabilitation; technical skills; and techniques for giving treatments. After their college work, students spend at least six months in clinical training. They divide this time between general and children's hospitals; and in institutions established for the mentally ill and for the rehabilitation of the handicapped. Upon completing these studies, the student receives a bachelor's degree in occupational therapy. A student can earn a master's degree in occupational therapy after an additional year of study.

After graduation, the therapist takes a national examination administered by the American Occupational Therapy Association. Therapists who pass the examination become Registered Occupational Therapists and use the letters "O.T.R." after their names. In Canada, certified occupational therapists use the letters "O.T.Reg."

To be effective in their work, therapists must continually add to their knowledge of medicine and psychology, as well as the arts, crafts, recreation, and homemaking skills. This broad range of interests and skills enables therapists to meet the needs of different patients.

Further information about occupational therapy may be obtained by writing to the American Occupational Therapy Association, 6000 Executive Boulevard, Rockville, Md. 20852; or to the Canadian Association of Occupational Therapy, 57 Bloor Street W., Toronto 5, Ont.   MARIE LOUISE FRANCISCUS

See also HANDICAPPED; HANDICRAFT; HOBBY.

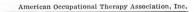

American Occupational Therapy Association, Inc.

Woodworking and similar activities can help patients overcome emotional problems. This picture shows an occupational therapist supervising a woodworking class.

OCEAN

OCEAN is the great body of water that covers more than 70 per cent of the earth's surface. The world is really one huge ocean, broken here and there by islands that we call continents. The ocean is so vast that you could sail across it for days without seeing land. It is also deep. In some areas, the ocean bottom lies more than 6 miles (10 kilometers) below the surface.

Seen from the top of a hill or from an airplane, the ocean seems calm and undisturbed. But the ocean is never still. There are always waves. They lap gently against the shore on calm days and pound heavily against the land on stormy days.

If you take a walk along the ocean shore, you see that the ocean constantly moves and constantly changes. You see what the waves have cast up on the shore—sea shells, starfish, bits of crabs, and stones and pebbles. You may find parts of wrecked ships or huge logs that

have been brought great distances by the current. Every day, changes take place in the shape of the waves and the slope of the beach.

The ocean is filled with life. Plants grow along the shore and on the ocean surface. They are the basis of all animal life in the sea. An amazing variety of animals lives in the ocean. Some of these animals can be seen only with a microscope, and others weigh many tons. Some animals float on the ocean surface, and others live on the ocean floor.

Scientists have only begun to learn many things about the sea, even after more than 90 years of study. There is still much they do not know about life in the sea and about the land beneath the sea. They have much to learn about the movements of the ocean waters. They can only guess how old the sea is and how it began.

Today, man is trying harder than ever to unlock the

Gendreau

INTERESTING FACTS ABOUT THE OCEAN

If the Greenland and Antarctic icecaps should suddenly melt, the world ocean would rise about 200 feet (61 meters). New York City would be submerged, with only the tops of the tallest buildings above the water.

The deepest spot in all the oceans, Challenger Deep, is 36,198 feet (11,033 meters) below the surface of the Pacific. If the highest mountain in the world, 29,028-foot (8,848-meter) Mount Everest, were put into this spot, more than 1 mile (1.6 kilometers) of water would cover the mountain.

The Composition of Seawater

All the natural elements can be found in seawater. Among the metallic elements dissolved in the ocean are millions of tons of gold and silver.

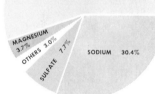

CHLORIDE 55.2%

SODIUM 30.4%

MAGNESIUM 3.7%

OTHERS 3.0%

SULFATE 7.7%

ocean's secrets. Scientists see many new ways to use the sea. The ocean has always been a major source of food. Someday, the sea may provide four or five times as much food as it does today. As the supply of minerals on land becomes smaller, people will turn more and more to the endless supply in the sea. People now get a small amount of fresh water from the sea by removing the salt. In the future, the ocean may be a major source of fresh water. After years of planning, the energy of the ocean's tides is being harnessed for power. The world's first tidal power plant, in France, uses the force of the tides to produce electricity.

This article was contributed by Joel W. Hedgpeth, an Environmental and Editorial Analyst, and former Resident Director and Professor of Oceanography at Yaquina Marine Laboratory, Marine Science Center, at Oregon State University.

Water pressure in the sea increases 14.7 pounds per square inch (1.03 kilograms per square centimeter) for every 33 feet (10 meters) of depth. At 30,000 feet (9,100 meters), the pressure could be compared to having the weight of an elephant pressed against every square inch of your body.

DEPTH		PRESSURE	
In feet	In meters	In pounds per square inch	In kilograms per square centimeter
Ocean Surface		14.7	1.03
600	183	269	18.9
1,200	366	536	37.7
3,000	914	1,338	94.1
7,200	2,195	3,208	225.5
18,000	5,486	8,019	563.8
30,000	9,144	13,363	939.5
36,198 (deepest spot)	11,033	16,124	1,133.6

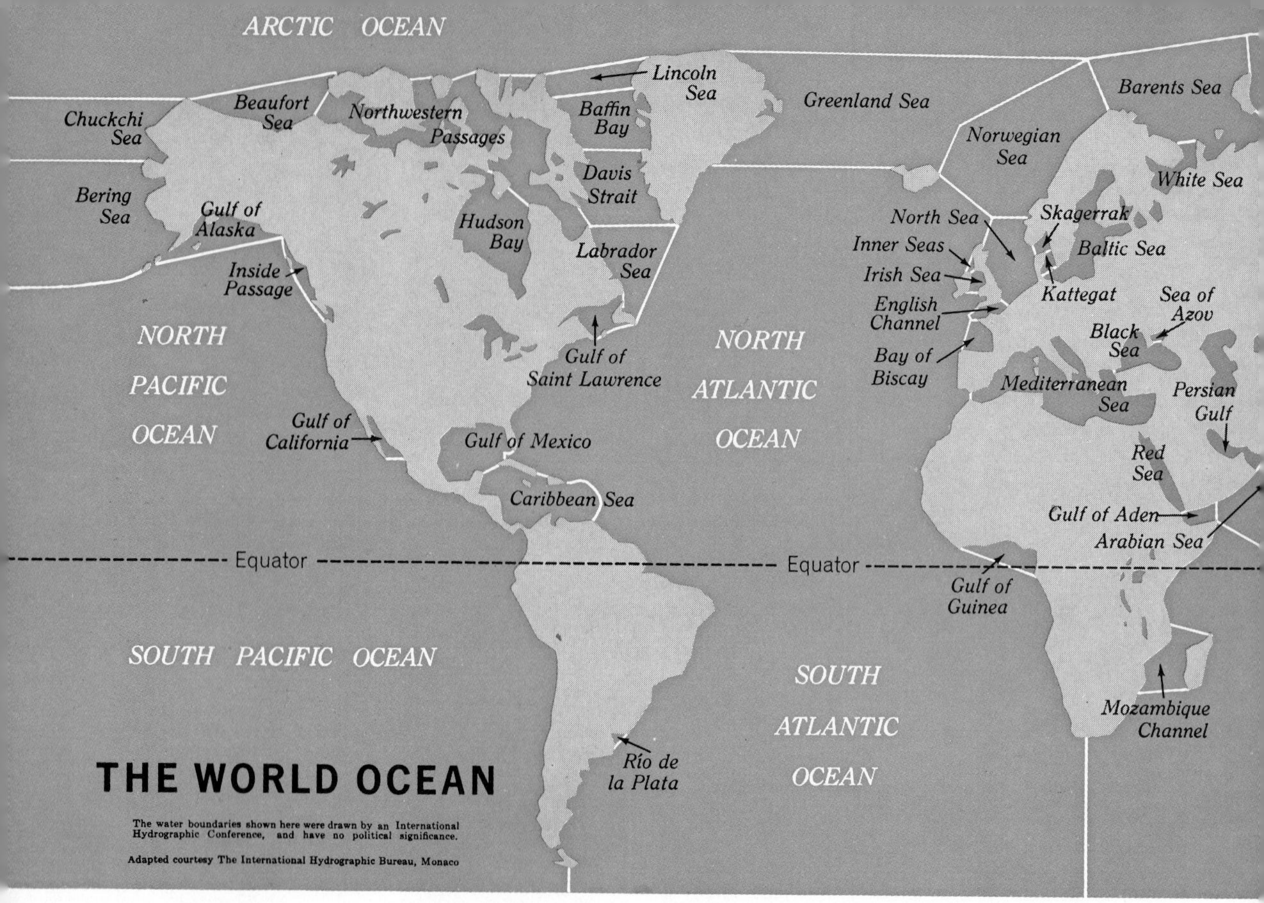

THE WORLD OCEAN

ARCTIC OCEAN

Chuckchi Sea · Beaufort Sea · Northwestern Passages · Lincoln Sea · Baffin Bay · Greenland Sea · Barents Sea · Norwegian Sea · White Sea · North Sea · Skagerrak · Inner Seas · Baltic Sea · Irish Sea · Kattegat · Sea of Azov · English Channel · Black Sea · Bay of Biscay · Mediterranean Sea · Persian Gulf

Bering Sea · Gulf of Alaska · Hudson Bay · Davis Strait · Labrador Sea · Red Sea

Inside Passage

NORTH PACIFIC OCEAN · Gulf of Saint Lawrence · NORTH ATLANTIC OCEAN · Gulf of Aden · Arabian Sea

Gulf of California · Gulf of Mexico

Caribbean Sea

Equator — — — Equator

Gulf of Guinea

SOUTH PACIFIC OCEAN · SOUTH ATLANTIC OCEAN · Mozambique Channel

Río de la Plata

The water boundaries shown here were drawn by an International Hydrographic Conference, and have no political significance.

Adapted courtesy The International Hydrographic Bureau, Monaco

OCEAN / *The World Ocean*

The three great oceans of the world, in order of size, are the Pacific, the Atlantic, and the Indian. Each includes smaller bodies of water called *seas, bays,* and *gulfs,* which are cut off by points of land or by islands. The word *sea* also means the ocean in general.

The three great oceans are really parts of one continuous body of water—the *world ocean.* You can see this if you turn a globe of the world upside down so that the South Pole is on top. The Pacific, Atlantic, and Indian oceans all come together around the continent of Antarctica in the Southern Hemisphere. There they form what is sometimes called the Antarctic Ocean. The Atlantic and Pacific meet again at the top of the globe, in the Arctic Ocean. The continents lie like islands in this vast world ocean.

The waters of the oceans mix together. For example, the waters around Antarctica are so cold that they are heavier than the surface waters of the surrounding oceans. Because they are heavier, they slide under the waters of the other oceans. *Oceanographers* (scientists who study the ocean) have found this cold Antarctic water far north of the equator. Storm waves on the Indian Ocean may travel across the Pacific to California. Some oceanographers estimate that one particle of water might move through all the oceans in 5,000 years.

The Pacific Ocean is the largest and deepest ocean. It covers about 63,800,000 square miles (165,200,000 square kilometers), more than a third of the earth's surface. The Pacific is so vast that it could hold all the continents. Near the equator, it stretches about 11,000 miles (17,700 kilometers), almost halfway around the earth. The average depth of the Pacific is about 14,000 feet (4,270 meters). The deepest known spot in the world ocean is Challenger Deep, southwest of Guam. It is 36,198 feet (11,033 meters) below the surface.

North America and South America lie to the east of the Pacific, and Asia and Australia are to the west. To the north, Bering Strait links the Pacific with the Arctic Ocean (see STRAIT).

The word *pacific* means *peaceful.* But some of the most disastrous storms on earth blow out of the Pacific. Thousands of volcanoes rise from the ocean floor, and earthquakes occur frequently. See PACIFIC OCEAN.

The Atlantic Ocean is the second largest body of water. Europe and Africa lie to the east, and North America and South America are on the west. The Atlantic meets the Arctic Ocean to the north. The Atlantic covers about 31,530,000 square miles (81,662,000 square kilometers). Its average depth is about 14,000 feet (4,270 meters). The ocean's greatest known depth is in the Puerto Rico Trench 28,374 feet (8,648 meters) below the ocean's surface.

Great storms rise in the North Atlantic, but there are also vast quiet areas. The chief industrial nations lie on the coasts of the Atlantic, making it the most important ocean for trade. See ATLANTIC OCEAN.

The Indian Ocean is smaller than the Atlantic. Africa borders it on the west, and Australia and the East Indies on the east. Asia lies to the north. The Indian Ocean covers about 28,356,000 square miles (73,441,700 square kilometers), and averages 13,000 feet (3,960 meters)

492

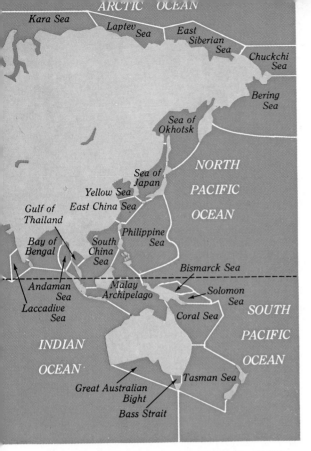

© Rand McNally

deep. The deepest known spot, 25,344 feet (7,725 meters) below the surface, is south of Java.

Gentle winds usually blow across the Indian Ocean, but it is sometimes swept by typhoons. North of the equator, the winds change with the seasons. The ocean currents change with the winds. See INDIAN OCEAN.

The Arctic and Antarctic Oceans are at opposite ends of the earth. The Arctic Ocean lies at the top of the world, north of Asia, Europe, and North America. On the west, Bering Strait links it with the Pacific. On the east, it merges with the Atlantic. Many geographers say it is a sea of the Atlantic, not a separate ocean.

The Arctic Ocean covers about 3,662,000 square miles (9,485,100 square kilometers). Its average depth is 4,362 feet (1,330 meters). Its greatest depth is 17,880 feet (5,450 meters). Ice covers much of the ocean during most of the year. In summer, the ice breaks up into drifting sections called *floes*. See ARCTIC OCEAN.

The Antarctic Ocean surrounds the continent of Antarctica. Many geographers say these waters are really the southern parts of the Pacific, Atlantic, and Indian oceans, not a separate ocean. See ANTARCTIC OCEAN; ANTARCTICA (The Antarctic Ocean).

The Ocean and Climate. The surface temperature of the ocean ranges from about 28° F. (−2° C) in the polar regions to about 86° F. (30° C) in the tropics. In the depths, temperatures vary throughout the ocean. But generally, the greater the depth, the lower the temperature. In the deepest parts, it is near freezing.

Water changes temperature more slowly than air and land do. Thus, it takes much longer for the sun to warm up the ocean than the land. The ocean controls the earth's climate because of the great area of the ocean, and the slowness of water to change temperature. The ocean has a steadying influence on land temperatures. It helps keep the air from becoming too hot or too cold.

The ocean also provides rainfall. As water evaporates from the ocean surface because of the sun's heat, it rises and forms clouds. Winds carry the clouds across the land. Clouds provide rain and snow that form rivers and lakes, and help plants grow. Without the ocean, the earth's climate would be like that on Mars—very cold at night and very hot during the day. Man could not live on a planet without an ocean. See CLIMATE (Differences in Land and Water Temperatures).

The Composition of Seawater. Swimming in the ocean is easier than in a lake. This is because seawater contains, on the average, about 3.5 per cent salts. These salts help a swimmer float. Seawater is not good to drink. It increases thirst and may make a person ill.

The salty material in the sea is mostly common table salt. Seawater also contains magnesium, sulfur, and calcium. In fact, seawater contains all the elements that make up the minerals in the earth's crust (see ELEMENT, CHEMICAL). The proportions of common salt and other elements in seawater are about the same throughout the world ocean. The mixing action of waves and currents causes this sameness.

Scientists have compared the composition of seawater with the composition of body fluids in man and animals. They have found that the proportions of the elements are much alike in seawater and body fluids. This seems to support the theory that life began in the sea. See LIFE (Later Theories).

493

Both plants and animals live in the ocean. Plants can be found wherever there is sunlight—on and near the surface, in shallow waters, and along the shores. Plants do not live in the deep, dark waters of the ocean. Animals, however, dwell everywhere in the sea—from the surface to the deepest parts of the ocean. The ocean is the home of the largest animals that have ever lived. Some of the smallest animals also live in the sea. Blue whales may grow 95 feet (29 meters) long. These animals are far larger than any dinosaur that walked the earth millions of years ago. The smallest animals in the sea measure only about 1/25,000 inch (0.001 millimeter) long.

All life in the ocean can be divided into three main groups: (1) the plankton, (2) the nekton, and (3) the benthos. The *plankton* consists of plants and animals that float about, drifting with the currents and tides. The *nekton* is made up of animals that swim freely in the water. The *benthos* consists of animals and plants that live on or in the ocean bottom, from the shore to the greatest depths of the sea.

Plankton

Plankton consists of small organisms—both plants and animals—that drift with the ocean currents and tides. The plants are called *phytoplankton*, and the animals are known as *zooplankton*.

WORLD BOOK illustrations by Alex Ebel

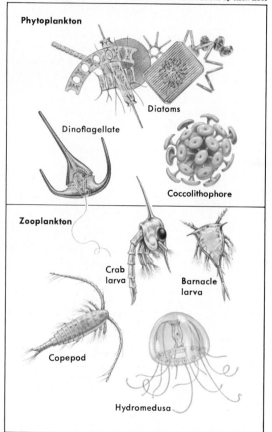

Phytoplankton

Diatoms

Dinoflagellate

Coccolithophore

Zooplankton

Crab larva

Barnacle larva

Copepod

Hydromedusa

The Plankton. Most of the floating, drifting plants and animals of the ocean are so small that they can be seen only under a microscope. The plankton plants make up the *phytoplankton*, and the plankton animals make up the *zooplankton*.

The Phytoplankton consists of several kinds of plants, including the diatoms, coccolithophores, and dinoflagellates. The most important and the most numerous are the diatoms (see DIATOM). The phytoplankton has been called the "pasture of the sea." It is the basic food supply of the ocean because all the animals feed on it, directly or indirectly.

Sea plants get their energy to grow from the minerals in seawater and from sunlight. But the sun's rays do not go deep into the water. In clear tropic seas, away from muddy rivers, light may reach several hundred feet or meters into the ocean. Near shores where rivers bring mud into the ocean, light does not go so deeply. Yet the rivers carry many substances that plants need to grow. For this reason, sea plants may grow thickly near shores.

The Zooplankton includes many kinds of animals, such as copepods, radiolarians, jellyfish, and arrowworms. Many of these animals have transparent bodies. Others are brightly colored. Some are light blue, some pink, some lavender. Some of the zooplankton float because they are mostly water themselves or because their bodies contain bubbles of gas. Other plankton animals have little fins or spines that help them float. See PLANKTON.

The Nekton. The animals of the nekton can swim about. The most important ones are the fishes. Over 20,000 kinds of fishes live in the sea. They range in size from sharks 50 feet (15 meters) long to gobies less than 1 inch (2.5 centimeters) long. The nekton also includes octopuses, squids, whales, and seals.

Although nektonic animals can swim about freely, they cannot all live anywhere in the world ocean. Some nektonic animals must live in certain parts of the ocean because of the temperature, the food supply, or the saltiness of the water. Most animals of the nekton are found only at certain depths. Sea animals can live under the pressure of the ocean because the pressure inside their bodies equals the water pressure outside. Many fishes have swimming bladders filled with gas that allow them to stay at certain depths. If they swim too high, they can be carried to the surface of the ocean. This happens because the pressure on the bladder inside no longer equals the water pressure outside. If a fish is carried too high in the water, it dies. A fish that strays too low is also in danger. The increased water pressure compresses the gas in the bladder so that the fish loses its ability to float. It then sinks to the bottom.

Most animals of the nekton, especially the fishes, have streamlined bodies. Their streamlined bodies help them swim easily and quickly in the pursuit of prey or to escape from enemies. Some of these animals can travel at remarkable speeds. The sailfish and the barracuda can swim 30 miles (48 kilometers) per hour. Many nektonic animals can also swim great distances. The eel and the salmon travel thousands of

Animals of the Ocean

The creatures shown below represent only a small part of the great variety of animal life found in the ocean.

WORLD BOOK illustrations by Tom Dolan and James Teason

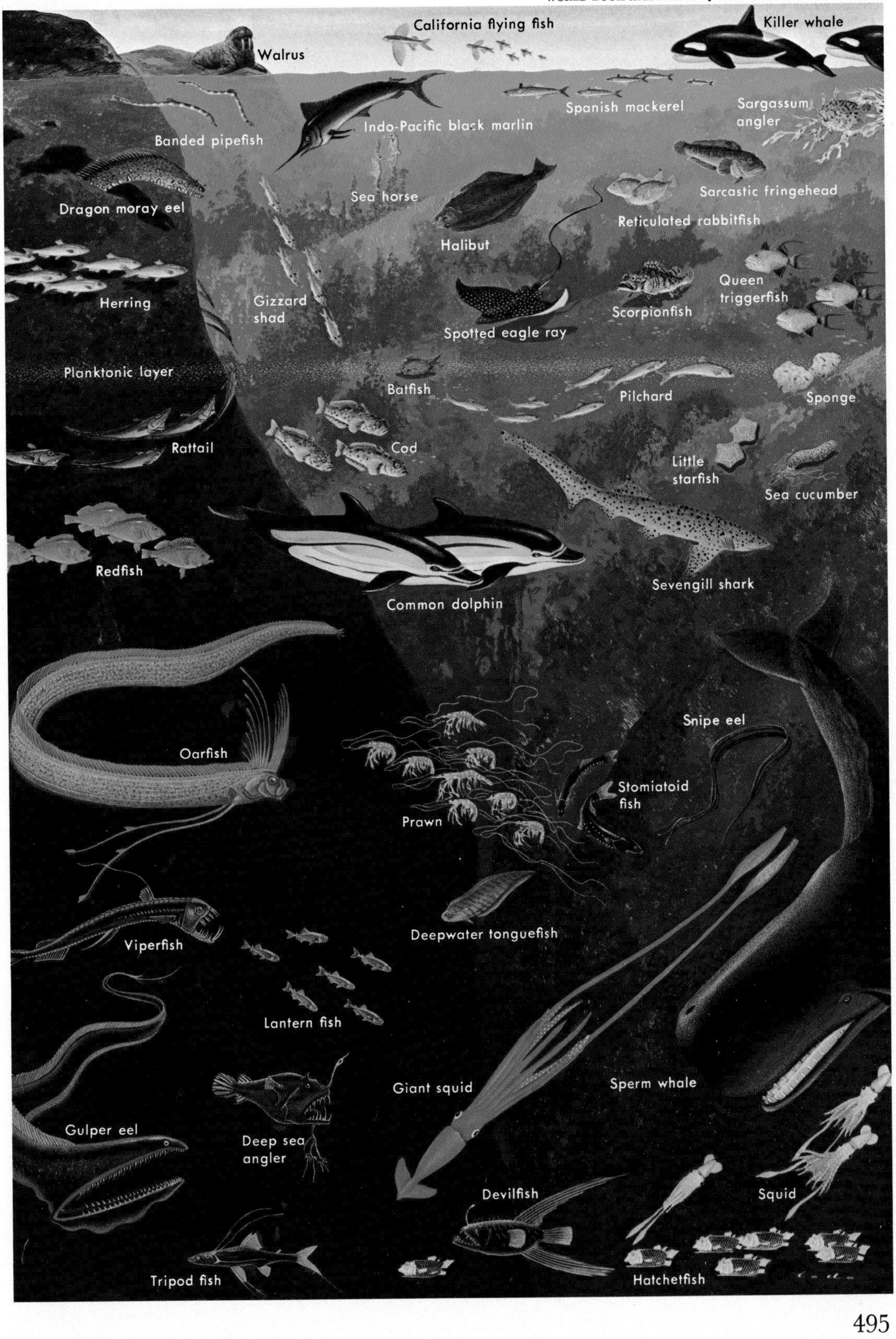

Killer whale

California flying fish

Walrus

Indo-Pacific black marlin

Spanish mackerel

Sargassum angler

Banded pipefish

Sea horse

Sarcastic fringehead

Dragon moray eel

Reticulated rabbitfish

Halibut

Herring

Gizzard shad

Scorpionfish

Queen triggerfish

Spotted eagle ray

Planktonic layer

Batfish

Pilchard

Sponge

Rattail

Cod

Little starfish

Sea cucumber

Redfish

Common dolphin

Sevengill shark

Snipe eel

Oarfish

Stomiatoid fish

Prawn

Deepwater tonguefish

Viperfish

Lantern fish

Giant squid

Sperm whale

Gulper eel

Deep sea angler

Devilfish

Squid

Tripod fish

Hatchetfish

495

miles or kilometers to and from their *breeding grounds*, where they lay their eggs.

The Benthos. Animals live everywhere on the sea bottom, from the shore to the deepest parts of the ocean. However, plants of the ocean bottom can be found only as deep as the rays from the sun go into the water.

Animals that dwell on the bottom include worms, snails, clams, sponges, sea lilies, and starfish. Some animals with heavy shells, such as crabs and lobsters, can carry this weight because the water buoys them up. Many of them are swimmers or walkers, and move about for food. Some animals are fixed to the bottom in one position throughout their lives. They include oysters, sea anemones, and corals. Ocean currents carry food to these animals, and some food drifts down to them from above.

Seaweeds grow along the shore or in shallow waters of the ocean. The largest kind of seaweed is the giant kelp. It usually grows about 70 feet (21 meters) long. Many kinds of small, bushy seaweeds grow over rocks that are covered by water at high tide. People have found many uses for seaweeds. But seaweeds are of little importance to the animals of the open sea. See SEAWEED.

The Food Cycle in the Sea. The phytoplankton is the food base for the animals in the world ocean. Certain animals of the zooplankton eat these plants. These animals, in turn, are eaten by other members of the zooplankton or by fish or other swimming animals. Generally, smaller sea animals are eaten by larger sea animals.

After an animal dies, it begins to sink. Before most dead animals sink very far, they are eaten by creatures that dwell at lower depths. When these animals die, they become a source of food for animals that live even deeper. Animals begin to *decompose* (decay) as soon as they die. This decomposition takes place at all depths. In addition, animals give off waste products. These waste products, and dead animals that are not eaten, are broken down into mineral salts by tiny living things called *bacteria* (see BACTERIA). Rising currents carry these minerals to the ocean surface, where plants of the plankton use them as food. Thus, the food cycle in the sea goes on and on.

Nekton

Nekton is made up of fish and other animals that have the ability to swim freely in water without the help of currents. Most nektonic creatures live in the upper layer of the ocean.

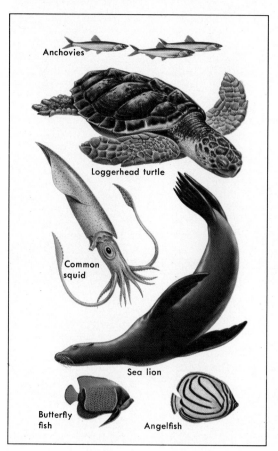

Anchovies

Loggerhead turtle

Common squid

Sea lion

Butterfly fish

Angelfish

Benthos

Benthos consists of plants and animals that live on the ocean bottom. All the plants and some of the animals of this group are attached to the bottom in one position throughout their lives.

WORLD BOOK illustrations by Alex Ebel

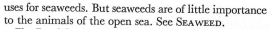

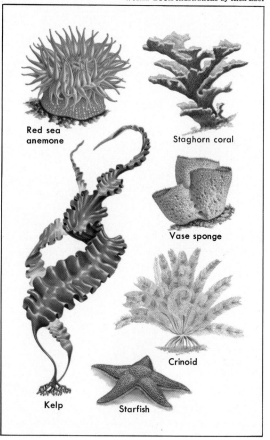

Red sea anemone

Staghorn coral

Vase sponge

Crinoid

Kelp

Starfish

People once believed that the floor of the sea was mostly a great level plain. Today, we know that the ocean bottom is just as irregular as the surface of the land. In fact, some of the earth's most spectacular scenery—towering mountains, deep trenches, vast canyons, and broad plains—is beneath the sea.

The Continental Shelf and Slope. In many places around the continents, the land gradually slopes under water to a depth of about 600 feet (180 meters). This submerged land is called the *continental shelf*. In some areas, the continental shelf extends hundreds of miles or kilometers. In other areas, it hardly exists, and the coastline drops nearly straight down into deep water. The shelf is covered by material called the *continental deposit*, which has been carried down from the land by rivers. In some ways, the continental shelf is the most important part of the land beneath the sea. The great fisheries of the world are there. The shelf also has rich oil fields.

The continental shelf slopes gently downward to the *continental edge*. There the *continental slope* begins. It is much steeper than the continental shelf. In many parts of the ocean, deep canyons gash the slope. Many of these canyons seem to have been cut by former rivers. Others may have been caused by the movement of sand and mud cutting down into the ocean bottom. The walls of some of the canyons are steeper and higher than the walls of the Grand Canyon. The continental slope plunges to the deep ocean bottom—the *abyss*.

Underwater Mountains and Valleys. Great mountains rise from the bottom of the ocean. Many are volcanoes. In some places, they stick out above the surface of the sea and form islands. The Hawaiian Islands were formed by volcanoes that rose from the sea floor.

Mountain ranges also rise from the bottom. An enormous range, 10,000 miles (16,000 kilometers) long, runs down the middle of the Atlantic Ocean. It is called the Mid-Atlantic Ridge. A deep valley cuts down through the middle of it. Some peaks of the ridge rise above the water's surface and form islands, such as the Azores.

Ridges also rise from the bottom of the Pacific Ocean, but they are smaller than the Mid-Atlantic Ridge. In addition, great cliffs thousands of miles or kilometers long are found on the Pacific floor. Some of the deepest parts of the world ocean may be found in the western Pacific. They are long, narrow valleys called *trenches*. Challenger Deep, in the Mariana Trench of the Pacific, is 36,198 feet (11,033 meters) below the surface. It is the deepest known spot in all the oceans.

Layers of muds cover the deep trenches and level parts of the ocean bottom. Some of these muds are full of the shells and skeletons of dead plants and animals from the plankton. Scientists call such muds *oozes*. The oozes have been formed over millions of years. They may be hundreds of feet or meters deep in places. Beneath them lies hard rock called *basalt*. See OOZE.

How the Oceans Began. How did the earth, the oceans, and the continents begin? No one really knows, but scientists have several theories. To understand the theories about how the oceans began, it is helpful to start with theories about how the earth itself began.

Some scientists believe the earth was torn from the sun and spun off into space. As it spun around, it became round and solid. Other scientists think the earth grew slowly, bit by bit. It increased in size by collecting particles floating in space.

Regardless of how the earth began, the rocks in its crust became separated. The heavier rocks sank deeper into the earth's crust, and lighter rocks rose to the surface. Today, the oceans lie in great basins of heavy basalt. Between them, floating on lighter rock called *granite*, are the continents.

According to one theory, the continents began as one great mass. The mass broke up into continents, which slowly drifted apart. This theory explains the similar shapes of the eastern coast of the Americas and the western coast of Africa. You can see this similarity on a globe. The margins of the continents seem to fit together like the pieces of a puzzle. According to another theory, the world is slowly growing larger, carrying North and South America farther away from Europe and Africa.

The great ocean basins became filled with water in two possible ways. Some scientists think the water came from the rocks inside the earth. As these rocks cooled and became solid, they released water. This water filled the depressions in the earth's crust. Other scientists believe that the water came from thick clouds that surrounded the earth. As the earth and clouds cooled, the clouds poured forth rain. The rain fell for hundreds of years, filling the ocean basins.

Many of the salts in the ocean come from the land. Scientists once thought they might learn the ocean's age by figuring out how long it took the ocean to get as salty as it is. But scientists now believe the ocean has been as salty as it is today for as long as there has been life in it. This period of time might be at least 500 million years.

Features of the Ocean Floor

This index lists the main features shown on the map on the following two pages.

OCEAN

The Land Beneath the Oceans has varied features. It consists of huge mountain ranges; broad basins and plains; and long, narrow valleys. The map below shows the major landforms of the world's ocean floor. The map index on the preceding page indicates their locations.

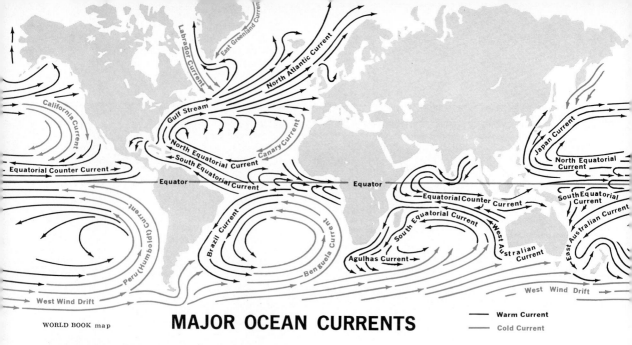

MAJOR OCEAN CURRENTS

WORLD BOOK map

— Warm Current
— Cold Current

OCEAN / *How the Ocean Moves*

Ocean Waves. The waters of the ocean never stop moving. The most familiar movements are the waves. Waves are set in motion by winds, earthquakes, and the gravitational pull of the moon and the sun. On shore, we see waves caused by the wind. Their size depends on whether they are driven by winds from storms nearby or from far across the ocean. In an ocean wave, water moves up and down. There is no forward motion of water as the wave goes through the water. This action is like the waves you can make in a rope tied to a tree. When you shake the free end of the rope, waves run along it. But the rope itself does not move forward. When an ocean wave reaches land, however, it starts to drag on the bottom. Then the water also moves.

As waves hit a sandy beach, they carry sand ashore and pile it up. They also move sand along the beach. Sometimes people build a *breakwater* (a wall to check the force of the waves) and stop the movement of sand along the shore. The sand may then be moved away below the breakwater, and rocks are exposed. This happened at Jones Beach on Long Island, N.Y. Now sand must be brought to this beach so people can use the area.

Storm waves are powerful. Out at sea, they may rise higher than 40 feet (12 meters). Waves can pick up huge boulders and throw them far up on the shore. They have carried large ships against rocks and smashed them. Waves also can cut holes in rocks, forming arches. Waves continually work against the land, breaking the rock into boulders, pebbles, and sand. See WAVES.

Earthquakes and shifts in the sea bottom often set in motion huge waves that move several hundred miles or kilometers an hour. This type of wave is often called a *tidal wave*, even though it is not caused by the tide. Scientists call these waves *tsunamis*. Most tsunamis start from Japan, Alaska, or Chile. Many earthquakes take place in these regions. Scientists can predict how fast tsunamis are moving, and warn people in their paths.

On the surface of the open ocean, a tsunami is hardly noticeable. But when it reaches a bay or harbor, it may pile up to a tremendous height in the narrow area. It then becomes very dangerous. Waves of this kind have destroyed large towns and drowned hundreds of persons. See TIDAL WAVE.

Ocean Currents. Waters move about in the ocean in streams called *currents*. The mighty Mississippi River is a

HOW OCEAN CURRENTS ARE FORMED

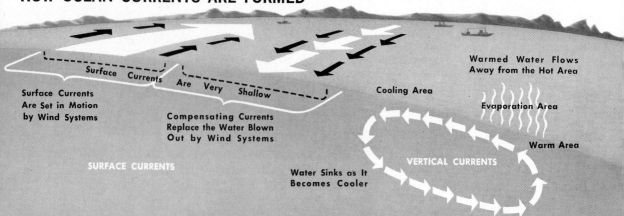

mere brook compared with the greatest of these streams. The wind systems set the ocean currents in motion (see WIND). Great circular currents move clockwise in the Northern Hemisphere and counterclockwise in the Southern Hemisphere. The earth's rotation makes the currents flow in this way. The strength of the ocean currents changes with the seasons. Often, deeper currents flow below the surface currents. These move in the opposite direction.

The currents move continuously, and they are never quite the same from year to year. The great surface currents of the ocean carry warm water away from the equator. This water gradually cools. When it gets even farther from the equator, it mixes with cold waters from high latitudes. Thus, when the current turns toward the equator again, it is a cold current.

In some years, a current may change its course. Or it may carry less water if the wind is not blowing so hard. Changes in currents may cause changes in the life of the sea. Fishes that depend on a current to bring them food may die if the current changes. A change in a current may change the temperature of the water so that fish eggs will not hatch as well. On the other hand, favorable changes in a current may mean many more fish—and a good year for people who catch fish for a living.

The Tides. If you stand on the ocean shore, you can see the water slowly rising higher and higher for about six hours. Then it slowly falls back for about six hours. The rise and fall of ocean waters are called *tides*. Tides are caused chiefly by the gravitational pull of the moon. When the moon is directly over any point in the ocean, it pulls the water toward it. The water on the opposite side of the earth also piles up. This action results from the spinning of the earth, which tends to make the water fly off the earth's surface. Tides are not high in mid-ocean, but near shore they may rise 6 to 8 feet (1.8 to 2.4 meters). In long, narrow bays, tides may rise 20 to 30 feet (6 to 9 meters). In the Bay of Fundy, between New Brunswick and Nova Scotia, the tide has risen 50 feet (15 meters).

When the moon is full or new, the earth, sun, and moon are in a straight line. At this time, the sun's gravitational pull, which is about half that of the moon's, combines with the moon's gravitational pull. The incoming tides then are at their highest, and the outgoing tides are at their lowest. These tides are called *spring* tides. At the quarters of the moon, the sun and moon are at right angles to one another. The *neap* tides that result are neither so high nor so low. See TIDE.

The Changing Shoreline. The movements of the ocean change the shoreline. Waves cut away sloping land and leave steep cliffs. They carve islands from the shore. Waves and currents build up sand bars along the shore. Sometimes waves and currents fill up harbors with sand and mud, making these waters useless for ships.

Shorelines also *emerge* (rise from the water) and *submerge* (sink). When shorelines emerge, all the caves and cliffs made by the waves are found far from the water. The new shore, once part of the ocean bottom, may have many sea shells on it. When shorelines submerge, hilltops become islands, and water flows into the valleys. Shores that have sunk, such as the coast of Maine, are very uneven. Shores that have risen, such as the east coast of Florida, are straighter.

HOW THE OCEAN CHANGES COASTLINES

Cutting Away the Land

As waves pound against the shore, they erode the land and leave a cliff. The earth that is worn away is deposited under water, where it piles up and forms a terrace. Further wave erosion steepens the cliff and cuts a notch in its base. In time, the unsupported earth above the notch falls and more land is carried out to sea.

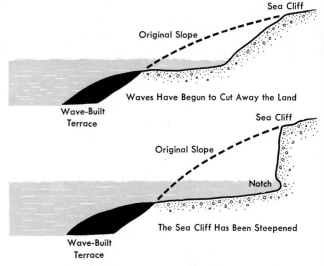

Building Up the Land

When large waves break some distance from shore, a sand bar forms as waves scoop up sediment from the ocean floor. Smaller waves build a lower bar near shore. A lagoon is formed after waves build the offshore bar above the water. Waves wash sand into the lagoon, and rivers and winds carry sediment into it. The lagoon becomes a marsh. Finally, the work of the waves, rivers, and winds turns the marsh into an area of sand dunes.

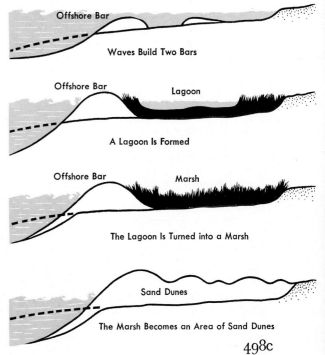

Seawater Becomes Fresh Water at this plant in Israel on the Red Sea. In dry regions near the ocean, man is turning more and more to the sea as a source of fresh water.

The Ocean's Energy is a source of power for man. Incoming and outgoing tides were first used to generate electricity in 1966, at this plant near St.-Malo, France.

State of Israel

OCEAN / *How Man Uses the Ocean*

Since early times, man has used the ocean and its products. He has captured its animals for food, pelts, and oil. He has taken out its valuable minerals. He has used the sea as a source of drinking water and as a highway of commerce. He soon will use its energy to light his homes and to run his factories. Man also uses the ocean as a dumping ground.

Fishing and Whaling. Every year, the world's fishing fleets bring in millions of tons of fish, shellfish, and whales. Some of the world's best fishing grounds are on the Continental shelves of the North Sea, the Atlantic Ocean near Newfoundland, and the Bering Sea. There, commercial fishermen catch haddock, herring, cod, and halibut. Clams, lobsters, oysters, and scallops also are taken in Atlantic waters off New England and Canada. Millions of tons of menhaden live in U.S. waters along the South Atlantic and Gulf coasts. Commercial fishermen of the United States catch more menhaden than any other kind of fish. Menhaden are ground up into meal for livestock. Oil pressed from the fish is used by chemical plants. The world's largest shrimp fisheries are in the same U.S. waters where menhaden are caught.

Other kinds of fishes are caught on the high seas, far from land. The most important is the tuna, which is eaten by the people of many countries. Fishermen catch tuna by hook and line and with nets in the Pacific and Atlantic oceans. See FISHING INDUSTRY.

Whales used to be hunted in the regions where tuna are now caught. Whaling now centers mostly in the waters of Antarctica and the North Pacific. Whales provide meat, oil, and other products. See WHALE.

The Ocean—A Liquid Mine. Seawater contains every mineral found on land. Man knows how to remove many of these minerals. But he must find cheaper ways to do it. For example, seawater holds tons of gold. This gold is so finely dissolved, however, that removing it would cost more than the gold is worth.

Salt was the first mineral that man took from the sea. He let seawater evaporate in shallow basins under sunlight, and used the salt that remained. In many parts of the world, people still gather salt in this way. Other minerals can be taken from the salt left after evaporation. These minerals include iodine, magnesium, and bromine. Evaporation is a cheap but inefficient way to mine the sea, so man uses other methods. Magnesium, for example, is taken by chemical and electrochemical processes (see MAGNESIUM).

On the bottom of the sea lies a fortune in rare minerals. These minerals include manganese, nickel, copper, and cobalt. They occur in lumps called *nodules*. Someday, man may be able to gather up the nodules in a device that works like a giant vacuum cleaner.

Other Products of the Sea include pearls, sponges, seaweeds, and fertilizer.

Pearls have been treasured since ancient times. Pearls are formed between the shell and body of an animal called the pearl oyster. The Japanese make cultured pearls by putting bits of shell in pearl oysters. See PEARL.

Sponges are gathered from the ocean bottom by divers. They also can be gathered by dragging a net along the bottom, but this method removes both young and mature sponges. Natural sponges have a higher quality than man-made ones. See SPONGE.

Seaweeds contain the minerals that are taken from seawater. These weeds are used for food, and as a source of iodine, soda, and potash. Seaweeds also are used in making medicines, ice cream, candy, jellies, salad dressing, and cosmetics. Some types are used as fertilizer. See SEAWEED.

Fertilizer. One of the best fertilizers for plants comes from huge deposits of bird droppings on Pacific islands near Peru. The sea birds of these islands feed on small fishes, which have eaten the rich plant life brought by the Peru Current. The birds fly out from the islands every day to eat the fish, and return at night. The bird droppings are called *guano*. The guano is shipped to many parts of the world. See GUANO.

A Source of Fresh Water. Many parts of the world have a shortage of fresh water. As the population of the world increases, this shortage will become greater. Man now makes a small amount of fresh water from seawater by removing the salt. In the future, he will have to use the sea more and more for water for farms, homes, and factories. He will have to find ways to change seawater into fresh water. Perhaps he will use nuclear energy to do this. See WATER.

498d

Transportation and Communication. The ocean has been a highway for trade ever since man first built sea-going ships. Today, ships are still the most important way to transport heavy machinery and such bulky products as grain and oil.

Telephone and telegraph cables crisscross the ocean bottom. These cables are thousands of miles or kilometers long. *Oceanographic ships* (ships equipped to explore the ocean) must be careful not to break the cables with instruments dragged along the sea floor. Special cable ships are used to find broken cables and bring them up to the surface for repair. See CABLE.

Harnessing the Sea's Energy. For years, men have tried to figure out ways to use the ocean's tremendous energy to provide electric power. The world's first tidal power plant began operating in June, 1966, on the Rance River, near St.-Malo, France. Twice a day, the incoming tide, up to 44 feet (13 meters) high, surges up the Rance. The tide reaches a volume of as much as 280 million gallons (1.06 billion liters) of water a minute. The plant was built to use this energy to produce 544,000,000 kilowatt-hours of electricity a year.

A Vast Dumping Ground. Man dumps all sorts of things into the sea. Barges carry garbage, tons of concrete, parts of wrecked automobiles, and other junk out to sea, where they are thrown overboard. Many cities dump sewage into the ocean. Radioactive wastes also are emptied into the sea in some places.

The ocean cannot hold all these things without endangering the life in the sea. Man will have to find other ways of getting rid of rubbish. As the world population increases, man will need more products from the sea. If he wants to harvest more fish, he will have to take better care of the ocean in which they live.

Peaceful Use of the Seabed. Many nations have come to realize the importance of exploring and using the ocean floor for peaceful purposes only. In 1969, the United Nations adopted a treaty that banned nuclear weapons from the seabed outside a 12-nautical-mile coastal zone. Great Britain, Russia, the United States, and several other countries signed this treaty, which went into effect in 1972. However, nations have been unable to resolve the problem of who owns resources that lie beneath the seabed, such as oil and gas.

Fernand Gigon, Pix from Publix

Seaweeds are used in making foods, drugs, and other products. In China, seaweeds help relieve the food shortage. These Chinese fishermen gather the weeds by age-old methods.

A Vast Supply of Minerals is dissolved in seawater. Magnesium is taken from the water at this plant in England.

WORLD BOOK illustrations by James Dunnington

A Great Highway of Commerce, the ocean has been used for trade ever since man first built ships to carry his goods.

The Port of New York Authority

Morin, Monkmeyer

Animals of the Sea are one of the ocean's greatest resources. Man catches them for food and for their oils and pelts.

OCEAN / *Discovering the Secrets of the Deep*

Early Exploration. People began to explore the ocean long before they started to record history. First they discovered the seashore. They found that they could use rocks as weapons and as tools for scraping and breaking things. They soon learned to eat clams, mussels, and seaweed. Then people developed rafts and small boats for fishing away from shore. Later, they built larger boats that could travel long distances for fishing. Now they could also exchange goods with other people in distant places.

Almost as soon as people discovered the sea and the shore, they became curious about them. Since the days of the ancient Greeks and Phoenicians, people have gone on voyages to find out what was beyond their own waters.

About 2,300 years ago, the Greek explorer Pytheas sailed out of the Mediterranean Sea and far north, perhaps closer to the Arctic Circle than any other explorer up to that time. About 100 years later, another Greek, Oppian, wrote the first known account of fish and fishing. In those days, people could not bring up fish from deep water. They could not dive far underwater nor take photographs. Most of the sea was unknown. No one had any idea of what was in the ocean depths. People believed that the sea held many secrets. Today, we still do not know all the secrets of the sea.

Scientific exploration of the ocean did not begin until accurate methods of finding the position of a ship at sea had been developed. The *sextant*, an instrument used for calculating latitude, was invented about 1730. Accurate clocks to help sailors determine longitude became available in the late 1700's. At this time, Captain James Cook, a British explorer, made accurate charts of the South Pacific Ocean. Naturalists accompanied Cook and later explorers who sought to find new lands or to make accurate maps of known regions. The scientists brought back plants and animals of the sea, as well as some knowledge of their behavior.

Nature studies by explorers of the early 1800's led to the first expedition to explore the ocean—its depths, waters, and living things. This expedition began in 1872, when the *Challenger*, the first ship equipped for ocean exploration, sailed from England. The *Challenger* expedition, supported by the Royal Society of London and by the British Admiralty, lasted $3\frac{1}{2}$ years. British scientists gathered information and specimens. Later, specialists from many parts of the world helped write the 50 volumes of the *Challenger Reports*. The expedition and the information it produced marked the beginning of *oceanography*, the scientific study of the sea.

Why Study the Sea? Today, people study the sea for many reasons. The oceans cover over 70 per cent

A Scuba Diver, *right,* carries his own air supply. He can move more freely than a diver in a diving suit, *left,* but cannot go down so deep.

Portholes in a chamber beneath the bow of *Atlantis II,* a research ship, permit direct undersea observation.

The **Deepstar,** a submersible, can carry a crew thousands of feet or meters beneath the surface.

The **FLIP (FLoating Instrument Platform),** *above,* glides through the water like any other ship. But when tanks in its long hull are filled with water, the stern of the vessel sinks. Its bow rises vertically and becomes a stationary oceanographic research laboratory, *right.*

of the earth, and they affect—directly or indirectly—all life on the earth. Scientists study the ways the ocean surface and the atmosphere act upon each other. They seek knowledge of the various kinds of plant and animal life in the sea. They also investigate the chemical composition of seawater and the structure of the ocean bottom. Scientists also study the behavior of currents, tides, and waves.

The actions of the oceans and the atmosphere on each other control the evaporation of water from the sea. The evaporated water forms *precipitation* (rain, snow, and other forms of moisture) that supplies water to the land. The interactions between the oceans and the atmosphere also affect the earth's climate. Water warms up or cools down much more slowly than do air or land. As a result, the mild temperatures of the air over the vast ocean surface help regulate the temperatures of the air over the land.

Knowledge about sea plants and animals may help man increase his food supply. Today, man gets only a small proportion of his food from the oceans. Yet, this amount is significant for nations that border the sea. Scientists are seeking ways to increase the yield of fish from the sea in order to meet the needs of an expanding world population. This goal involves the wise use of the food cycle in the sea. Scientists are also studying how pollutants dumped into the ocean affect the life cycles of living things of the sea.

Chemists want to know what seawater contains and how it behaves chemically. They seek to identify the materials in seawater that occur in extremely small quantities. Chemists hope to learn how these tiny amounts of material affect the plants and animals of the sea. This knowledge may also help man learn how certain pollutants could harm life in the ocean.

Studies of the sea bottom have revealed deposits of oil and natural gas near many land areas of the world. A number of these offshore sources of oil and natural gas have not yet been tapped by man. Someday they may become vital if man's need for fuel keeps on increasing at its present rate.

Scientists also seek additional knowledge of the currents, tides, and waves of the oceans. The navigation of atomic submarines that can stay underwater for weeks requires detailed understanding of the movements of ocean waters. The study of currents, tides, and waves includes gathering data on the sea's ability to mix and scatter the things that are put into it. Without such knowledge, man might pollute the oceans beyond tolerable limits.

How Man Studies the Depths. The scientists aboard the *Challenger* had only piano wire with which to measure ocean depths. They used heavy rope to tow nets along the ocean bottom to collect plants and animals. The men did have special thermometers to obtain the temperature of the sea at great depths. They also had a special kind of bottle to collect seawater far below the ocean surface. The Norwegian explorer Fridtjof Nansen later perfected this metal bottle. It is known as the *Nansen bottle*, and scientists still use it.

Lockheed Aircraft Corp.

Coring Devices bring up samples of the ocean floor. The corer shown above digs cores 8 feet (2.4 meters) deep and can cut through almost all sediment on the sea bottom.

Scripps Institution of Oceanography

A Wave-and-Current Channel reproduces the actions of ocean waves for scientific study in a laboratory. The glass-walled channel pictured here is 131 feet (40 meters) long.

UNDERSEA HABITAT

A habitat enables divers to remain underwater for several months. The two cylinders are 18 feet (5.5 meters) high and 12½ feet (3.8 meters) in diameter. Four compartments provide living and working quarters for five divers. A habitat carries equipment for scientific studies of the ocean.

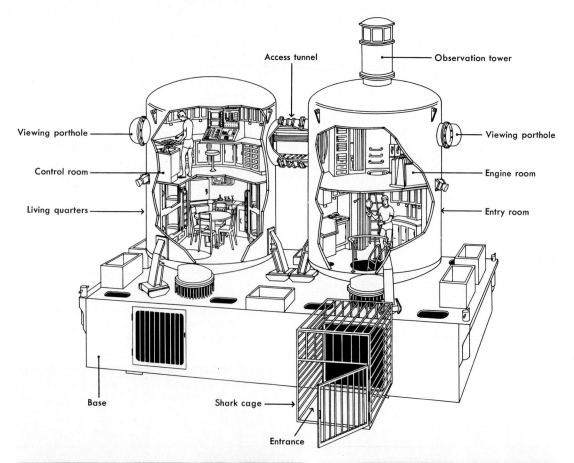

Access tunnel

Observation tower

Viewing porthole

Viewing porthole

Control room

Engine room

Living quarters

Entry room

Base

Shark cage

Entrance

Flip Schulke, Black Star

The Control Room of a Habitat has equipment to monitor activities in the vessel and to communicate with crews on the surface. It also holds instruments used by divers in their experiments.

Flip Schulke, Black Star

Outside a Habitat, a diver examines a marine specimen. The habitat allows divers to stay on the ocean floor far longer than they otherwise could.

Today, oceanographers have many modern instruments—though nets and dredges are still lowered to the bottom to collect specimens. Underwater cameras take photographs of the sea bottom. Devices called *corers* consist of long tubes that can bring up samples of bottom mud and sand. Scientists use such samples to study the history of both sea and land. Electronic instruments send back echoes from the bottom that provide information about the depth of the sea. The most powerful of these sounding instruments can send back echoes from layers of the earth deep below the water. Records of the echoes have provided information about the structure of these earth layers.

Other instruments help oceanographers analyze small amounts of various substances in the water. These devices detect the small amounts of the substances needed for life by the plants and animals of the sea. Such instruments also identify the substances that may harm the organisms. Large research vessels carry these delicate instruments and also have computers to help scientists analyze data quickly. The instruments require trained technicians to keep them working properly.

Oceanographic Diving. No oceanographic instrument, no matter how accurate, can take the place of direct inspection of the depths by man. Diving suits equipped with air hoses were developed during the 1800's, but they enabled men to go only about 200 feet (61 meters) down. These suits were so complicated and dangerous that only professional divers used them—and only for ship salvage or treasure hunting.

In the 1840's, the French biologist Henri Milne-Edwards became the first person to use diving gear for scientific studies. But scientists could not actually explore the depths until the invention of the aqualung in 1943. The aqualung, a free-diving device, was developed in France by Jacques-Yves Cousteau, an undersea explorer, and Émile Gagnan, an engineer. It gave a diver freedom by enabling him to carry his air supply.

Even with an aqualung, a diver is limited by the size of his air supply and by the pressure of the water. The pressure underwater increases with the depth of the water. A diver may be seriously injured if he descends or rises faster than his body can adjust to the change in pressure. See DIVING, UNDERWATER.

To eliminate the need for divers to keep adjusting to pressure changes, scientists developed underwater laboratories called *habitats*. Divers, called *aquanauts*, can live in a habitat for several months. The air pressure inside is kept equal to that of the surrounding water. The aquanauts can swim away from the habitat, returning only to eat, sleep, or refill their air tanks. Habitats enable divers to conduct various studies more carefully than was previously possible. These studies include the behavior of living things, the changes in the sea bottom, and the penetration of light into the sea.

Various types of diving spheres and small submarines enable man to descend much deeper than ever before. The first of these was the *bathysphere*, first used by William Beebe, an American naturalist, in 1930. In 1934, Beebe descended $\frac{1}{2}$ mile (0.8 kilometer) in a bathysphere that was connected to the surface by cables. A later craft, the *bathyscaph*, does not need cables.

The bathyscaph was invented in 1948 by Auguste Piccard, a Swiss physicist. It contains large tanks of *ballast* (weights). When the ballast is released into the water, the bathyscaph becomes light enough to rise to the surface. In the bathyscaph, man has descended more than 35,000 feet—or over 6 miles (10 kilometers)—into the ocean. See BATHYSCAPH.

A bathyscaph has little ability to move in any direction except down or up. But research submarines called *submersibles* can move about readily. One type has mechanical hands that can pick up objects from the sea bottom. It carries three men and has large windows for underwater study. It goes down about 4,000 feet (1,200 meters). Future submersibles will probably be able to dive 20,000 feet (6,100 meters). Submersibles can stay underwater for a day or two at the most.

Recent Discoveries. Oceanographers constantly discover new and interesting things about the sea. For example, they have found that water in deep pockets at the bottom of the Red Sea is extremely hot and salty. This water has somehow seeped from the underlying rock and does not mix with the water above it.

Oceanographers have collected evidence suggesting that man may be able to obtain four or five times as much food from the sea as he does today. But today's yield of food from the ocean is less than 4 per cent of the world's needs. The expected increase will not be enough to keep up with the increase in population. Much of the additional food might consist of *krill*, a small shrimp found in the Antarctic Ocean. Krill might be made into oil and livestock feed.

Another discovery was based on evidence provided by samples of bottom mud and sand and by *seismic refractions* (echoes from powerful sounding machines). This evidence showed that the sea bottom has large crumpled-up places somewhat like giant cracks. Scientists do not know the causes of these *mid-ocean ridges*. The ridges run down through the middle of the Atlantic Ocean and across the Pacific Ocean. Their existence suggests that the continents may be slowly drifting apart (see CONTINENTAL DRIFT).

Southwest Research Institute

A Naval Experimental Manned Observatory (NEMO) gives scientists a wide view of the underseas environment. The plastic sphere can descend as deep as 600 feet (180 meters).

Scientific Sailors. The ocean can be studied in many ways, and the science of oceanography has many different specialties. *Physical* oceanographers deal with waves, currents, and tides. *Chemical* oceanographers study the chemicals found in seawater. *Marine biologists* study the animals and plants of the sea. *Marine geologists* are concerned with the rocks beneath the sea, the sand and mud on the ocean floor, and how shores are formed.

An oceanographer, whatever his special interest may be, is really a scientific sailor. He must go to sea for his information. Therefore, he should enjoy life on the ocean. He should not mind being at sea in bad weather because he must understand the ocean on both stormy days and calm days. The oceanographer works on research ships that are equipped with special instruments to study the sea and everything in it.

Some oceanographers work with nets and dredges to capture animals. Others take samples of seawater in special bottles. Still other oceanographers work with echo sounding, or measure temperatures and magnetism in the sea.

Work at sea is often difficult, and research ships cost a great deal of money to operate. The oceanographer must plan trips carefully so he can do as much as possible in the time allowed. After the oceanographer obtains the information he wants, he must study and analyze it. Often he uses instruments that continuously measure and record the information he seeks, such as water temperature. The instruments record such information in the form of marks or numbers on rolls of paper. This data must be carefully analyzed. Animals and plants that have been taken from the sea must be identified. Usually an oceanographer can get enough information in a day at sea to keep him busy for 9 or 10 days on shore.

There are over 5,000 oceanographers in the United States. Many more will be needed in the future to work on new research vessels. Oceanographers work at institutions devoted to the study of the sea, and on ships maintained by these organizations. Some teach university courses. Oceanographers also work for various agencies of the U.S. government. These agencies include the Naval Oceanographic Office and the National Marine Fisheries Service of the National Oceanic and Atmospheric Administration.

Education and Training. The minimum educational requirement for a career in oceanography is a bachelor's degree. For research and teaching positions, a person must have graduate training in oceanography or one of the basic sciences. Many oceanographers have a doctor's degree in oceanography.

Oceanographers are expected to have had courses in physics, chemistry, biology, and geology. They also should have had enough mathematics—including calculus—to understand the complicated relationships of moving waters in the sea. A thorough knowledge of English is essential so the oceanographer can tell others what he has studied and discovered. An oceanographer must also be able to read about the studies being conducted in such countries as Russia, Germany, and France. His training should include the study of foreign languages, especially Russian and German.

Mechanical ability is valuable in some fields of oceanography. Equipment may break down on research ships and need immediate repair. Sometimes an oceanographer may have to design a special instrument for an unexpected task. Drawing ability is useful for marine biologists because so many of the animals and plants taken from the sea must be illustrated for reports. Most large oceanographic institutions have staffs of mechanics and artists. Electronics technicians are always in demand to care for the many electronic instruments used in oceanography.   JOEL W. HEDGPETH

Science Service, Inc.

Chemical Oceanographers study the composition of seawater. This scientist, on a perch on the side of his ship, lowers a *Nansen bottle* into deep water. It will bring up a sample of seawater.

Gar Lunney, National Film Board

Physical Oceanographers deal with waves, currents, and tides. These men, working with a model built to study the tides, adjust an instrument that measures the rise and fall of the tides.

OCEAN / *Study Aids*

Related Articles in WORLD BOOK include:

OCEANS

Antarctic Ocean	Atlantic Ocean	Pacific Ocean
Arctic Ocean	Indian Ocean	

SEAS

Adriatic Sea	Black Sea	Marmara, Sea of
Aegean Sea	Caribbean Sea	Mediterranean Sea
Andaman Sea	China Sea	North Sea
Arabian Sea	Coral Sea	Okhotsk, Sea of
Azov, Sea of	Ionian Sea	Red Sea
Baltic Sea	Irish Sea	Sulu Sea
Banda Sea	Japan, Sea of	Tasman Sea
Barents Sea	Java Sea	Tyrrhenian Sea
Bering Sea	Kara Sea	White Sea
Bismarck Sea	Ligurian Sea	Yellow Sea

CURRENTS

Gulf Stream	North Atlantic Current
Japan Current	Peru Current
Labrador Current	

OTHER RELATED ARTICLES

Animal (pictures:	Geology	Seiche
Animals	Grand Banks	Seven Seas
of the Oceans)	Guano	Ship
Bathyscaph	Life (Later	Skin Diving
Bore	Theories)	Sonar
Cable	Maelstrom	Sponge
Calms,	Magnesium	Tidal Wave
Regions of	Marine Biology	Tide
Climate	Mohole	Transportation
Continental Drift	Navigation	United Nations
Coral	Ooze	(Peaceful Uses
Crustacean	Pearl	of the Seabed)
Deep	Plankton	Water (Fresh
Diatom	Sargasso Sea	Water from
Diving,	Scripps	the Sea)
Underwater	Institution of	Waves
Dogger Bank	Oceanography	Whale
Fathometer	Sea Level	Woods Hole
Fish	Seashore	Oceanographic
Fishing Industry	Seaweed	Institution

Chris Lund, National Film Board

Marine Biologists study the animals and plants that live in all parts of the ocean. This scientist carefully examines some tiny animals of the plankton group that he has put into a bottle.

Outline

I. The World Ocean
  A. The Pacific Ocean
  B. The Atlantic Ocean
  C. The Indian Ocean
  D. The Arctic and Antarctic Oceans
  E. The Ocean and Climate
  F. The Composition of Seawater

II. Life in the Ocean
  A. The Plankton   C. The Benthos
  B. The Nekton   D. The Food Cycle in the Sea

III. The Land Beneath the Sea
  A. The Continental Shelf and Slope
  B. Underwater Mountains and Valleys
  C. How the Oceans Began

IV. How the Ocean Moves
  A. Ocean Waves
  B. Ocean Currents
  C. The Tides
  D. The Changing Shoreline

V. How Man Uses the Ocean
  A. Fishing and Whaling
  B. The Ocean—A Liquid Mine
  C. Other Products of the Sea
  D. A Source of Fresh Water
  E. Transportation and Communication
  F. Harnessing the Sea's Energy
  G. A Vast Dumping Ground
  H. Peaceful Use of the Seabed

VI. Discovering the Secrets of the Deep
  A. Early Exploration   D. Oceanographic Diving
  B. Why Study the Sea?   E. Recent Discoveries
  C. How Man Studies
     the Depths

VII. Careers in Oceanography
  A. Scientific Sailors   B. Education and Training

Questions

What would the climate on earth be like if there were no ocean? Why?

Why is it easier to swim in the ocean than in a lake?

What was the importance of the *Challenger* expedition?

What are some ways in which we use the ocean?

How long might it take for one particle of water to find its way through all the oceans on the earth?

How much of the earth's surface does the ocean cover?

What is meant by the food cycle in the sea?

Which is the largest and deepest ocean?

How do animals attached to the sea-bottom get food?

How can a change in an ocean current affect life in the ocean?

OCEAN CURRENTS. See OCEAN (How the Ocean Moves).

OCEAN ISLAND is a raised reef island near the equator in the west-central Pacific Ocean. It has an area of 2 square miles (5 square kilometers) and a population of about 2,300. It is part of the Gilbert Islands, a British dependency (see PACIFIC ISLANDS [map]).

The British discovered Ocean Island in 1804. They have mined its rich phosphate deposits for use in making fertilizer since 1890. This is the chief activity on the island.   EDWIN H. BRYAN, JR.

See also GILBERT ISLANDS.

OCEAN LINER. See SHIP (Ocean Liners); TRANSPORTATION (On Water); PROPELLER with picture.

OCEANARIUM. See AQUARIUM.

OCEANIA. See PACIFIC ISLANDS.

OCEANID. See NYMPH (myth).

OCEANOGRAPHY. See OCEAN (Careers in Oceanography).

The **Ocelot** prowls about the dense forest underbrush at night to hunt for food. It avoids bright sunlight by sleeping in dark caves or heavy thickets during the day.

Arizona-Sonora Desert Museum

OCELLI. See INSECT (Sight).

OCELOT, *O suh laht,* is a medium-sized animal of the cat family. It is known as the *leopard cat* or *tiger cat* of America. It is $3\frac{1}{2}$ to 4 feet (107 to 120 centimeters) long including the tail, which is 15 inches (38 centimeters) long. The ocelot stands 16 to 18 inches (41 to 46 centimeters) high at the shoulder. The ocelot lives in an area ranging from southeastern Arizona and southern Texas to Paraguay in South America. It spends most of its life on the ground, but often hunts in forest trees and is an agile climber. It eats mice, wood rats, rabbits, snakes, lizards, birds, young deer, and monkeys. In the tropics a favorite food is agoutis. If taken young, the ocelot can be tamed and makes an excellent pet.

The ground tint of ocelot fur varies greatly in different animals, from reddish-yellow to smoky-pearl. Black spots vary in size from dots on the legs and feet to large shell-shaped spots on other parts of the body. The ocelot has a pink nose and large, translucent eyes.

Scientific Classification. The ocelot belongs to the cat family, *Felidae*. It is classified as genus *Felis*, species *F. pardalis*. ERNEST S. BOOTH

See also ANIMAL (picture: Animals of the Tropical Forests).

OCHER, *O ker,* or **OCHRE,** is a kind of earth which is ground to a fine powder and used as a pigment with linseed oil or some other oil to form paint. Its color varies from pale yellow to brownish-red. Some yellow ochers turn red when heated. Ocher consists of iron oxide mixed with clay and sand. Georgia has large yellow ocher deposits.

OCHOA, *oh CHOH uh,* **SEVERO** (1905-   ), a Spanish-American biochemist, shared the 1959 Nobel prize for physiology or medicine. He and Arthur Kornberg won it for discovering ways to *synthesize* (put together) nucleic acids artificially. These acids play a basic role in life and reproduction. Born in Spain, Ochoa moved to the United States in 1940. He became professor of biochemistry at New York University in 1954, and made his discoveries there. IRWIN H. HERSKOWITZ

OCHS, *ahks,* **ADOLPH SIMON** (1858-1935), rose from a job as a newsboy to become the publisher and guiding influence of *The New York Times.* He separated editorial comment from news in the *Times,* and presented news truthfully and free from prejudice. In 38 years, the daily circulation of the *Times* rose from 9,000 to 460,000. Ochs also founded the magazine *Current History,* and gave $500,000 toward publication of the *Dictionary of American Biography.*

Ochs began his career at 14 as an errand boy at the *Knoxville* (Tenn.) *Chronicle.* Later, he bought a half-interest in the *Chattanooga Times,* and made it one of the region's strongest papers. He became manager of *The New York Times* in 1896, and gained controlling interest in 1900. He was born in Cincinnati, Ohio. I. W. COLE

OCKHAM, WILLIAM OF. See WILLIAM OF OCKHAM.

OCMULGEE NATIONAL MONUMENT is in central Georgia. It contains the most important prehistoric Indian mounds discovered in the Southeast, including a restored council chamber. Ruins dating from 8,000 B.C. were found there. The 683.48-acre (276.59-hectare) monument was established in 1934. C. LANGDON WHITE

O'CONNELL, DANIEL (1775-1847), an Irish statesman, was called the *Liberator.* He formed the Catholic Association in 1823 to help Irish Roman Catholics gain political rights. Pressure from the association and the fact that O'Connell, as a Catholic, could not take his seat in Parliament when he was elected in 1828, brought about the Catholic Emancipation Act of 1829. He was arrested in 1843 for conspiracy in advocating a free Ireland. He was convicted, but the House of Lords released him. He was born in County Kerry. JAMES L. GODFREY

See also DUBLIN (picture).

O'CONNOR, FEARGUS. See CHARTISM.

O'CONNOR, FLANNERY (1925-1964), was an American author whose novels and stories are filled with terror and violence. Many of her characters are physically deformed or emotionally or spiritually disturbed. Some are obsessed with religion and the possibility of their own damnation or salvation. But Miss O'Connor's books also contain humor, irony, and satire.

Mary Flannery O'Connor was born in Savannah, Ga. Her Southern heritage and her Roman Catholicism strongly influenced her writing. She suffered from poor health most of her life and could complete only a few works. They include two novels, *Wise Blood* (1952) and *The Violent Bear It Away* (1960). Her stories were collected in *A Good Man Is Hard to Find* (1955) and *Everything That Rises Must Converge*, which was published in 1965 after her death. The stories in these two collections are included in *Flannery O'Connor: The Complete Stories*, published in 1971. This collection won the 1972 National Book Award for fiction. *Mystery and Manners*, Miss O'Connor's essays and lectures on literature and writing, was published in 1969.   JOHN B. VICKERY

OCOTILLO, OH *koh* TEEL *yoh*, is a shrub that grows in the deserts of Mexico and southwestern United States. Other names for it are *candlewood, coachwhip,* and *vine cactus.* The plant stands 6 to 25 feet (1.8 to 7.6 meters) tall, and has many spiny stems growing out like switches from a base. After the wet season, the stems grow leaves and bunches of scarlet flowers. But in the dry season, they stand bare as dry thorny sticks. Ocotillos make good hedges that are hard to pass through.

Scientific Classification. Ocotillos belong to the fouquieria family, *Fouquieriaceae.* They are genus *Fouquieria,* species *F. splendens.*   EDMUND C. JAEGER

See also FLOWER (color picture: Flowers of the Desert).

Josef Muench

Ocotillo looks like a bunch of dry sticks thrust into the sand in dry periods. After a wet season, tiny green leaves cover the long spines, and brilliant red blossoms form at the tips.

OCRACOKE ISLAND is a coastal island in Hyde County, North Carolina. It is 16 miles (26 kilometers) long and 2 miles (3 kilometers) wide at its broadest part (see NORTH CAROLINA [political map]). Its chief industry is fishing and shrimping. According to tradition, the pirate Blackbeard hid there and was killed in a battle nearby in 1718. Before the Civil War, Ocracoke was an important port of entry.   HUGH T. LEFLER

OCTAGON, AHK *tuh gahn,* is a plane figure that has eight angles and eight sides. The word comes from the Greek terms for *eight* and *angle.*

OCTAHEDRON is a term used in geometry to mean a solid formed by eight planes. An example would be two solid pyramids with a mutual square base.

OCTANE, AHK *tayn,* is a petroleum hydrocarbon. Octane refers to *n-octane* (normal octane), a colorless, flammable liquid. Its chemical formula is written $CH_3(CH_2)_6CH_3$, and it boils at 125° C. There are 18 octane isomers in the *paraffin* series of hydrocarbons. *Isomers* are compounds that have the same molecular formula, but different chemical or physical properties.

Isooctane, the most important octane isomer, is used as a motor fuel and to determine anti-knock qualities of gasoline. It boils at 99° C and its chemical formula is written $(CH_3)_2CHCH_2C(CH_3)_3$.   LEWIS F. HATCH

See also HYDROCARBON; OCTANE NUMBER.

OCTANE NUMBER is a rating that tells how much a motor fuel "knocks." "Knocking" occurs when the last of the fuel in an engine cylinder burns. It causes some loss in engine power. Two test fuels, normal heptane and isooctane, are blended together for tests to determine octane number. Normal heptane has an octane number of zero, and isooctane a value of 100. Gasolines are then compared with these test fuel blends to find one that produces the same "knock" as the test fuel. If a test blend has 85 per cent isooctane and 15 per cent normal heptane, the gasoline is given an octane number of 85. Most gasolines today have octane numbers of from 90 to 100.   CLARENCE KARR, JR.

See also GASOLINE; TETRAETHYL LEAD.

OCTAVE, in music. See MUSIC (Terms).

OCTAVE, in poetry. See SONNET.

OCTAVIA (65?-9 B.C.) was the older sister of the Roman emperor Augustus. She was married to Mark Antony in 40 B.C. to seal a peace agreement that ended a civil war between Augustus and Antony. Octavia and Antony went to Athens and she bore him two daughters, Antonia the Elder and Antonia the Younger. Octavia also raised Antony's children by his former wife, Fulvia.

Antony treated Octavia badly. He had fallen in love with Cleopatra, queen of Egypt, before he married Octavia. About 36 B.C., Antony divorced Octavia and married Cleopatra. Octavia behaved with dignity throughout the civil wars which followed between Antony and Augustus, and won great respect as a virtuous Roman woman.   MARY FRANCIS GYLES

See also ANTONY, MARK; AUGUSTUS; CLEOPATRA.

OCTAVIAN, or OCTAVIANUS. See AUGUSTUS.

OCTAVO. See BOOK (Parts of a Book).

OCTILLION, *ahk* TILL *yun.* In France and the United States, an octillion is 1 followed by 27 zeros. In Great Britain, it is 1 with 48 zeros. See also DECIMAL NUMERAL SYSTEM (Larger Numbers).

OCTOBER

OCTOBER is the tenth month of the year. Its name comes from the Latin word for *eight*. October was the eighth month in the Roman calendar. The Roman Senate tried to name the month "Antoninus" after a Roman emperor, "Faustinus" after his wife, and "Tacitus" after a Roman historian. But the people continued to call it October. From the time of Julius Caesar, October has had 31 days.

In the North Temperate Zone, the first frost usually occurs in October. Farmers must finish harvesting most crops, but the cold weather does not come to stay. Days of warm, hazy sunshine come later, with a fresh autumn tang. They inspired poets to sing the praises of October and Indian summer. Leaves change to brilliant crimson, russet, and gold. Wild asters, goldenrod, and fringed gentians bloom at this time. The frost kills many insects, and most birds have left for the South, but sparrows are fond of October. They are seedeaters, and the fields and meadows are rich with seeds. Farmers should welcome sparrows at this time, because the birds eat millions of weed seeds that could otherwise damage the next crop.

Activities. Farmers bring in the fall crops and store them or ship them to market. A few fruits, such as apples and grapes, are still on trees and vines in some areas. Many apples are harvested at the end of October. The excitement of the football season dominates the sports scene, even though the World Series steals some of the spotlight early in the month. Hockey teams also begin their schedules in October.

Special Days. On the second Monday in October, schools and various organizations celebrate Columbus

---

IMPORTANT OCTOBER EVENTS

1 James Lawrence, the American naval officer who cried "Don't give up the ship!," born 1781.
— William E. Boeing, airplane manufacturer, born 1881.
— Free rural delivery of mail began, 1896.
— First "Model T" Ford put on the market, 1908.
— International Atomic Energy Agency's first general conference opened, Vienna, 1957.
2 Mohandas Gandhi, Indian political leader, born 1869.
— Cordell Hull, American statesman, born 1871.
— First Pan American conference, Washington, 1889.
3 George Bancroft, American historian, born 1800.
— William C. Gorgas, American physician, born 1854.
— Eleonora Duse, Italian actress, born 1859.
4 Rutherford B. Hayes, 19th President of the United States, born at Delaware, Ohio, 1822.

Rutherford B. Hayes

Chester A. Arthur

— Painter Jean François Millet born 1814.
— Michael Pupin, Serbian-American physicist and inventor, born 1858.
— Artist Frederic Remington born 1861.
— Russia launched first artificial satellite, 1957.
5 Gregorian calendar introduced, 1582.
— Denis Diderot, French author, born 1713.
— Chester A. Arthur, 21st President of the United States, born in Fairfield, Vt., 1829.
— Physician Edward L. Trudeau born 1848.
— Joshua Logan, American playwright, born 1908.
— President Harry S. Truman made the first presidential telecast address from the White House, 1947.
6 Jenny Lind, Swedish singer, born 1820.
— George Westinghouse, American inventor, born 1846.
— Le Corbusier, Swiss-born architect, born 1887.
— Austro-German forces invaded Serbia, 1915.
7 First double-decked steamboat, the *Washington*, arrived at New Orleans, 1816.
— James Whitcomb Riley, Hoosier poet, born 1849.
— Niels Bohr, Danish physicist, born 1885.
8 John M. Hay, American statesman, born 1838.
— Chicago fire began, and burned for about 30 hours, 1871.
— Eddie Rickenbacker, American air ace, born 1890.
9 Camille Saint-Saëns, French composer, born 1835.

9 Edward William Bok, noted American journalist, born 1863.
10 Henry Cavendish, English scientist, born 1731.
— Giuseppe Verdi, Italian opera composer, born 1813.
— United States Naval Academy opened at Annapolis, Md., 1845.
— Norwegian explorer and statesman Fridtjof Nansen born 1861.
— Helen Hayes, American actress, born 1900.
11 Eleanor Roosevelt born 1884.
— François Mauriac, French novelist, born 1885.
12 Columbus landed in America, 1492.
— George W. Cable, American author, born 1844.
— Ralph Vaughan Williams, British composer, born 1872.
13 White House cornerstone laid, 1792.
— Rudolf Virchow, German scientist, born 1821.
14 William the Conqueror won the Battle of Hastings, which assured the conquest of England, 1066.
— William Penn, founder of Pennsylvania, born 1644.
— Eamon de Valera, president of the Irish Republic, born 1882.
— Dwight D. Eisenhower, 34th President of the United States, born at Denison, Tex., 1890.
— E. E. Cummings, American poet, born 1894.
15 Virgil, Roman poet, born 70 B.C.
— J. F. Pilâtre de Rozier became first person to make an ascent in a captive balloon, 1783.
— Helen Hunt Jackson, American novelist, born 1830.
— Philosopher Friedrich Nietzsche born 1844.
— Clayton Antitrust Act became law, 1914.
16 Dictionary editor Noah Webster born 1758.
— Oscar Wilde, Irish dramatist, born 1854.
— John Brown and his men seized the United States arsenal at Harpers Ferry, Va., 1859.

Dwight D. Eisenhower

506

Day. This holiday honors Christopher Columbus' arrival in America on Oct. 12, 1492. In Canada, Thanksgiving Day is celebrated on the second Monday of the month. On the evening of Halloween, the last day of October, children disguise themselves with masks and costumes and go from door to door asking for a treat.

October Symbols. The calendula is the special flower for October. The birthstones for this month are the opal and the tourmaline. GRACE HUMPHREY

October gave a party;
The leaves by hundreds came;
The ashes, oaks, and maples,
And those of every name.
George Cooper

October turned my maple's leaves to gold;
The most are gone now; here and there one lingers;
Soon these will slip from out the twig's weak hold,
Like coins between a dying miser's fingers.
Thomas Bailey Aldrich

Quotations

There is something in October sets
  the gipsy blood astir;
We must rise and follow her,
When from every hill of flame
She calls and calls each vagabond
  by name.
Bliss Carman

Related Articles in WORLD BOOK include:

Autumn	Halloween
Calendar	Indian Summer
Calendula	Opal
Columbus Day	Tourmaline
Cosmos	

——— IMPORTANT OCTOBER EVENTS ———

16 David Ben-Gurion, Israeli prime minister and Zionist leader, born 1886.
—Eugene O'Neill, American playwright and Nobel prizewinner, born 1888.
17 British general John Burgoyne surrendered his army at Saratoga, 1777.
18 Henri Bergson, French philosopher and Nobel prizewinner, born 1859.
—The United States flag was formally raised over Alaska, 1867.
—James Truslow Adams, American historian, born 1878.

—Pierre Elliot Trudeau, prime minister of Canada, born 1919.
19 First general court in New England held, Boston, 1630.
—British troops under Cornwallis surrendered at Yorktown, 1781.
—Thomas Edison began first successful demonstration of his electric light, 1879.
20 Architect Sir Christopher Wren born 1632.
—John Dewey, American philosopher, born 1859.
21 Magellan entered strait that bears his name, 1520.
—Hokusai, Japanese artist, born 1760.
—Samuel Taylor Coleridge, English poet, born 1772.

—U.S.S. *Constitution,* or "Old Ironsides," launched, 1797.
—British Admiral Nelson was killed defeating the French and Spanish at Trafalgar, 1805.
—Alfred Nobel, Swedish philanthropist and founder of the Nobel Prize, born 1833.
22 Franz Liszt, Hungarian composer, born 1811.
—Sam Houston inaugurated as first president of the Republic of Texas, 1836.
23 British began offensive at El Alamein, 1942.
—Battle for Leyte Gulf began, 1944.
24 Anton van Leeuwenhoek, Dutch microscopist and naturalist, born 1632.
—First transcontinental telegram sent, 1861.
—United Nations formally established when necessary number of members ratified charter, 1945.
25 Henry V of England defeated French at Agincourt in Hundred Years' War, 1415.

25 Thomas B. Macaulay, English author, born 1800.
—"Waltz King" Johann Strauss, Jr., born 1825.
—Georges Bizet, French composer, born 1838.
—Painter Pablo Picasso born 1881.
—Richard E. Byrd, American explorer of the North and South poles, born 1888.
—Bolsheviks ousted provisional Russian government (this date based on the old Russian calendar), 1917.
26 Helmuth von Moltke, Prussian general, born 1800.
—Erie Canal opened to traffic, 1825.
27 Niccolò Paganini, Italian violinist, born 1782.
—The *Federalist* papers began appearing in New York *Independent Journal,* 1787.
—Theodore Roosevelt, 26th President of the United States, born in New York City, 1858.
—Captain James Cook, English explorer, born 1728.
28 Christopher Columbus landed in Cuba, 1492.
—Harvard College founded, 1636.
—Statue of Liberty dedicated, 1886.
—Jonas Salk, American developer of a polio vaccine, born 1914.
29 James Boswell, Scottish biographer of Samuel Johnson, born 1740.
—Cartoonist Bill Mauldin born 1921.
—Blackest day in stock market history, 1929.
30 John Adams, second President of the United States, born in Braintree (now Quincy), Mass., 1735.
—Benito Mussolini, founder of fascism, became premier of Italy, 1922.
31 Martin Luther nailed his 95 theses to the door of a church at Wittenberg, 1517.
—Jan Vermeer, Dutch painter, born 1632.
—King's College (now Columbia University) founded, 1754.
—Nevada became the 36th state, 1864.
—Sir Hubert Wilkins, Australian explorer, born 1888.

Theodore Roosevelt

John Adams

Many Octopuses Find Their Prey on the Ocean Bottom.

OCTOPUS is a sea animal with a soft body and eight arms called *tentacles*. The word *octopus* comes from two Greek words that mean *eight feet*.

Some people call octopuses *devilfish*, probably because of the animal's frightening appearance. An octopus has large, shiny eyes, and strong, hard jaws that come to a point like a parrot's bill. The octopus uses its arms to catch clams, crabs, lobsters, mussels, and other shellfish, and to break the shells apart. It cuts up food with its horny jaws. Some kinds of octopuses inject a poison that paralyzes their prey. Octopuses rarely attack people.

There are about 50 kinds of octopuses, and most are only about as big as a man's fist. The largest ones may measure 28 feet (8.5 meters) from the tip of one tentacle to the tip of another on the other side of the body.

Octopuses live chiefly in the China and Mediterranean seas, and along the coasts of Hawaii, North America, and the West Indies. Many people in these regions eat octopus meat. Octopuses belong to a group of shellfish called *mollusks*. This group includes clams, oysters, and snails. Like squid and cuttlefish, octopuses

are mollusks that have no outside shells. See MOLLUSK.

An octopus has no bones, and no inside shell as squid and cuttlefish do. A tough protective wrapper called a *mantle* covers the body and gives it shape. The tentacles are joined to the body and to one another by a web of tissue at their bases. Rows of round muscles

R. Tucker Abbott, the contributor of this article, holds the du Pont Chair of Malacology at the Delaware Museum of Natural History, and is the author of American Seashells *and* Sea Shells of the World.

BODY OF AN OCTOPUS

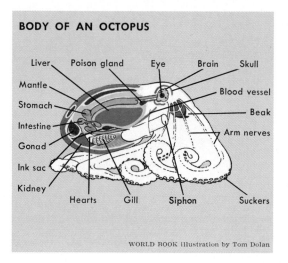

Liver · Poison gland · Eye · Brain · Skull · Mantle · Blood vessel · Stomach · Beak · Intestine · Arm nerves · Gonad · Ink sac · Kidney · Hearts · Gill · Siphon · Suckers

on the underside of each tentacle act much like suction cups. These suckers can fasten tightly to any object, and may hold on even if the tentacle is cut off. If an octopus loses a tentacle, a new one grows in its place.

An octopus has two eyes and sees well. It has the most highly developed brain of all the *invertebrates* (animals without backbones). It has three hearts that pump blood through its body. The animal breathes by means of gills, somewhat as fish do. An octopus swims by drawing water into its body. Then the animal squeezes the water out through its *siphon*, a funnel-shaped opening under the head. The force of the expelled water moves the animal backward. The octopus can also squirt a black fluid from the siphon. This fluid forms a dark cloud that hides the animal so it can escape from sharks, whales, men, and other enemies.

The skin of an octopus contains small bags of *pigments* (coloring matter). The pigment bags connect with the animal's nervous system. When an octopus becomes excited, it changes color—becoming blue, brown, gray, purple, red, white, or even striped. Many octopuses change color to blend with their surroundings.

A female octopus lays a cluster of as many as 180,000 nearly transparent eggs. The eggs are attached to rocks and hatch in about two months. The female tends the eggs and does not eat during this period. The young begin to find their own food as soon as they hatch.

Scientific Classification. Octopuses are members of the phylum *Mollusca*, and belong to the class *Cephalopoda*. They make up the genus *Octopus*.   R. TUCKER ABBOTT

See also CUTTLEFISH; MOLLUSK; NAUTILUS; SQUID.

OCULAR. See MICROSCOPE; TELESCOPE.

OCULIST is a physician who treats eye disorders and diseases. See OPHTHALMOLOGY.

ODD FELLOWS, INDEPENDENT ORDER OF, is one of the largest fraternal and benevolent orders in the United States. The order was founded in England. The date of its founding is not known, but Odd Fellows' groups probably existed in the early 1700's. The members founded a system of benefits and helped one another in time of misfortune. Branches called *lodges* grew up in the various English cities, but each branch refused to admit the superior rank of any other. Adjustments were finally made, and in 1814 the Manchester Unity of the Independent Order of Odd Fellows was organized. It has branches in various countries but has no present connection with the order in the United States.

The American Order. In 1819, the Washington Lodge of Odd Fellows was organized in Baltimore. The next year, Washington Lodge became a subordinate lodge in the Manchester Unity. Other American lodges were established later and assumed a like position.

But in 1843 the American lodges separated themselves from the parent order in England. The United States grand lodge became the head of the order in America and reserved for itself the right to found new lodges in Europe. The Canadian branch operated under a separate charter until 1852. In that year the society in Canada was merged with the grand lodge of the United States. The Order of Odd Fellows in the United States has a membership of 1,250,000.

Purpose and Organization. The chief purpose of the Order of Odd Fellows is to give aid, assistance, and com-

fort to its members and their families. It is a secret society and has its own system of rites and passwords. The three links in its symbol represent friendship, love, and truth. The skull and crossbones speak of mortality, and the single eye represents the all-knowingness of God.

A local lodge can confer three degrees of membership upon an Odd Fellow. When a member has reached the highest of these three grades he is ready for membership in an encampment. The encampment also has three degrees of membership, the Patriarchal, the Golden Rule, and the Royal Purple. The Patriarchal is an English degree. Since 1884, there has also been a military or uniformed degree called the Patriarch Militant.

The Rebekah lodges in Odd Fellows are chiefly for women, although some men belong. Rebekah assemblies were organized in 1851 and have more than 1 million members. Headquarters are at 16 W. Chase St., Baltimore, Md. 21201.

Critically reviewed by the INDEPENDENT ORDER OF ODD FELLOWS

ODE, *ohd,* a poem of moderate length, usually expresses exalted praise. Greek dramatists wrote *choral odes* that had three parts. Two parts, a *strophe* and an *antistrophe,* had identical meter. The third part, called an *epode,* had a contrasting meter. Pindar, of ancient Greece, wrote odes in praise of athletic heroes. He used the strophic form, which came to be called *Pindaric* (see PINDAR). Horace, of ancient Rome, wrote odes made up of uniform stanzas, called *stanzaic* form.

English poetry, from the time of Ben Jonson, included a variety of Pindaric odes, stanzaic odes, and *irregular* odes, or those with no particular stanza structure. John Dryden wrote two irregular odes in praise of St. Cecilia. "Ode to Evening," by William Collins, is a notable stanzaic ode. The great irregular and stanzaic odes of the 1800's include William Wordsworth's "Ode: Intimations of Immortality," Percy Bysshe Shelley's "Ode to the West Wind," John Keats' "Ode on a Grecian Urn," and Alfred, Lord Tennyson's "Ode on the Death of the Duke of Wellington." CHARLES W. COOPER

O'DELL, SCOTT (1903-), an American author, became known for his historical novels about southern California. He won the Newbery medal in 1961 for *Island of the Blue Dolphins,* his first novel for children. His other novels include *Woman of Spain* (1934) and *Hill of the Hawk* (1947). He was born in Los Angeles.

ODELSTING. See NORWAY (Parliament).

ODENSE, *OH thun suh* (pop. 165,520), is a seaport on Fyn island in Denmark. It is 3 miles (5 kilometers) from Odense fiord (see DENMARK [map]). A canal links the city and the fiord. Odense has important shipyards. Its factories produce machinery, glass, and textiles. During World War II, the city served as a center of Allied resistance against the Germans.   JENS NYHOLM

ODER. See FREYJA.

ODER RIVER is an important waterway of central Europe. It is 550 miles (885 kilometers) long and drains more than 43,000 square miles (111,000 square kilometers), which is about the area of Tennessee.

The Oder rises in the Carpathian Mountains of Czechoslovakia. It then flows northward across western Poland where it joins the Neisse River to form the boundary between Poland and East Germany. It empties into the Baltic Sea by way of the Oder Lagoon (see POLAND [terrain map]). Oceangoing vessels can sail into the port of Szczecin (Stettin), on the Polish side of the inlet. Other major cities on the Oder River include Frankfurt in East Germany, and Opole (Oppeln) and Wrocław (Breslau) in Poland.

The Oder's main tributary is the Warta (Warthe). It links the Oder with the Vistula River in Poland by means of the Notéc (Netze) River and a canal.

Because the Oder system provides many nations with an outlet to the sea, the navigable sections were put under international control by the Treaty of Versailles. After World War II, the lower part of the Oder, from about Frankfurt to Szczecin, became the boundary between East Germany and Poland. East Germany officially recognized this boundary, called the *Oder-Neisse Line*, in 1950. West Germany opposed the boundary until 1970 and then signed a treaty with Russia confirming the boundary.　　　M. KAMIL DZIEWANOWSKI

ODESSA, Tex. (pop. 78,380; met. area pop. 92,660), is an important petroleum refining center. It is also the world's largest oil-field service and supply center. It lies in western Texas (see TEXAS [political map]). The seat of Ector County, Odessa was founded in 1881 and incorporated as a city in 1927. It has a council-manager government.　　　H. BAILEY CARROLL

ODESSA, *oh DES uh* (pop. 913,000), is a seaport in Russia. It lies on the southwestern coast of the Ukraine, near the Romanian border. Odessa is on the Black Sea, 32 miles (51 kilometers) southwest of the mouth of the Dnepr River (see RUSSIA [political map]).

The harbor at Odessa is divided into five ports. One of these ports is for petroleum trade. Airplane service links Moscow, Kharkov, and Odessa. Odessa is one of the Ukraine's industrial centers. It is also an important transfer point for rail and ocean transportation. Its refineries produce large amounts of petroleum products, and its factories make machinery, automobiles, airplanes, and motion-picture equipment.

The Greeks first settled Odessa around 800 B.C. They named it *Odessos*, or *Ordyssos*. They were followed by the Tartars in the 1200's, the Lithuanians in the 1400's, and the Turks in the 1500's. Russia annexed the city in the 1700's. The Germans captured Odessa in 1941. Russian troops recaptured it later.　　　THEODORE SHABAD

ODETS, CLIFFORD (1906-1963), an American dramatist, is best known for his plays of social conflict written during the 1930's. His most successful works were presented by the famous Group Theatre.

Odets' one-act play *Waiting for Lefty* (1935) is about a taxi drivers' strike. It ranks among the most important of the many plays written in the 1930's that deal with the struggle of the working class. Odets' *Awake and Sing!* (1935) tells the story of a poor Jewish family in the Bronx during the Depression. It is less propagandistic than *Waiting for Lefty*, and its style has been compared to the style in Anton Chekhov's plays. Odets also wrote *Paradise Lost* (1935), *Golden Boy* (1937), *The Big Knife* (1948), and *The Country Girl* (1950).

Odets was born in Philadelphia. He helped form the Group Theatre in 1931. He worked as a film scriptwriter from 1936 until shortly before his death.　　　MARDI VALGEMAE

ODIN, *OH din*, was the king of the gods in Norse mythology. He held court in Asgard, in the hall named

Valhalla, where he gathered all the heroes who had died in battle. He was thought of as an old, one-eyed man, wisest of all the gods. On each shoulder he had a raven which he sent out daily to bring back news.

The worship of Odin came to Scandinavia from Germany, where he was known as *Wotan*. The ancient Anglo-Saxons called him *Woden*. From this name we get *Wednesday* (*Woden's Day*). Thor was the god of the common people. But Odin seems to have been worshiped by Viking chieftains. He was above all a god of war, and human sacrifices were made to him. He could be cunning and cruel, but in the final battle of Ragnarok he heroically led the gods against the evil giants that sought to destroy him.　　　EINAR HAUGEN

See also MYTHOLOGY; THOR; VALHALLA; BRUNHILD.

ODOACER, *oh doh AY ser* (A.D. 434?-493), was the Germanic leader who overthrew the last emperor of Rome in the West, ending the West Roman Empire.

Odoacer was probably born near the Danube River in what is now Germany. He joined the West Roman army and became a leader of barbarian troops serving the Romans. In 476, when the Roman government refused to give his troops land for settlement, Odoacer led them in a revolt. He deposed the West Roman emperor, Romulus Augustulus, and became the first barbarian king of Italy. Historians consider this event the end of the West Roman Empire. But for years, barbarian generals had been its real rulers. The emperors were symbolic rulers.

Odoacer ruled independently, although he pretended to serve Zeno, the East Roman emperor. Zeno never recognized Odoacer as ruler of Italy. In 489, Zeno sent the Ostrogoth king Theodoric to attack Odoacer. Odoacer retreated to Ravenna, where he surrendered in 493 and was executed (see THEODORIC).　　　WILLIAM G. SINNIGEN

ODOMETER. See SPEEDOMETER.

ODONATA is an order of insects made up of damsel flies and dragonflies. These insects are strong, graceful fliers. The adults spend little time on the ground. They cannot walk, but they use their legs to catch prey in the air. See also DRAGONFLY; INSECT (table).

ODONTOLITE. See TURQUOISE.

ODOR. See SMELL.

ODYSSEUS. See ULYSSES.

Odets' Awake and Sing! is a serious and realistic study of a poor Jewish family in New York City during the Depression.

New York Public Library

ODYSSEY, *AHD ih see,* an epic poem, is perhaps the most influential and most popular work in ancient Greek literature. The *Odyssey* ranks among the greatest adventure stories in literature. It became a model for many later adventure stories.

According to tradition, the *Odyssey* was composed by the Greek poet Homer, probably in the 700's B.C. The central character is Odysseus (Ulysses in Latin), the king of Ithaca. The poem describes Odysseus' adventures as he tries to return home after fighting for Greece against the city of Troy in the Trojan War. The author wrote about this war in the *Iliad*, another great epic poem. For information on the background and authorship of the *Odyssey* and the *Iliad*, see HOMER.

The *Odyssey* consists of 24 *books* (sections). The story takes place during a period of about 10 years in the 1100's B.C. The tale begins after much of the action has already occurred. This device of starting a story in the middle and returning to the start is called *in medias res.* Many later writers used it.

The *Odyssey* Begins on the island of Ogygia, where Odysseus has been the prisoner of the sea nymph Calypso for seven years. At a council of the gods on Mount Olympus, Zeus decides the time has come for Odysseus to return to his wife, Penelope, in Ithaca.

The scene then changes to Odysseus' palace in Ithaca, where a group of unruly young noblemen has settled. The noblemen want Penelope to assume that her husband is dead. They demand that she marry one of them and thus choose a new king of Ithaca. Odysseus' son, Telemachus, resents the noblemen. The goddess Athena suggests that he go on a journey to seek news of his father. Telemachus agrees and leaves Ithaca, and his travels become part of the story.

The tale next returns to Odysseus' adventures. The god Hermes makes Calypso release Odysseus. Odysseus sails away on a raft, but the sea god Poseidon causes a storm and he is shipwrecked on the island of the Phaeacians. Nausicaa, the beautiful daughter of the Phaeacian king, discovers him.

Odysseus Describes His Wanderings since the Trojan War while being entertained by the Phaeacians. He tells of his visit to the land of the lotus-eaters, whose magic food makes people forget their homeland. Some of Odysseus' men who ate the food want to stay with the lotus-eaters, but Odysseus forced them to leave with him. Odysseus and his men then sailed to an island where they were captured by Polyphemus, a one-eyed giant called a *Cyclops.* They escaped, but their ship was blown off course. The ship finally landed on the island of the enchantress Circe. Circe changed Odysseus' men into pigs and made Odysseus her lover. She told Odysseus that to get home, he must visit the underworld to consult the prophet Teiresias. In the underworld, Odysseus saw the ghosts of his mother and of Trojan War heroes. He also witnessed the punishment of sinners.

Teiresias told Odysseus the route home and Circe told him how to sail past the sea monsters Scylla and Charybdis. Circe also warned him about the Sirens, sea nymphs who use their beautiful singing to lure sailors to death on a magic island. Odysseus' ship sailed past these dangers and seemed ready to reach Ithaca without further trouble. But some of Odysseus' men stole and ate the sacred cattle of the sun on the island of Thrinacia. As punishment, the ship was de-

Painting (400's B.C.) on a Greek vase by an unknown artist; the British Museum, London

Odysseus Encountered the Sirens during his voyage home. The Sirens, part bird and part woman, lured seamen to their death with beautiful singing. Odysseus filled his sailors' ears with wax but had himself tied to the mast so he could safely enjoy the singing.

stroyed by a thunderbolt and Odysseus' men drowned. Odysseus made his way to Calypso's island—where the story began.

Odysseus Returns Home. After Odysseus finishes his story, the Phaeacians take him to a deserted shore in Ithaca. There, Athena tells him about the noblemen in his palace and advises him to return home in disguise for his own safety.

Odysseus goes to his palace disguised as a beggar. The noblemen are participating in an archery contest, with the winner to marry Penelope. Odysseus wins the contest, kills the noblemen, and is reunited with Penelope.

The *Odyssey* as Literature. The *Odyssey* is a skillfully written adventure story. It combines realistic accounts of life in ancient Greece and elements of historical events with fairy tales about imaginary lands.

The work also contains skillful characterization. Odysseus represents the model of a man of courage and determination. In spite of many setbacks, he never abandons his goal of returning home. But he has other human traits that keep him from being only a symbol. He enjoys life, even while struggling to get home. He is restless, clever, and even tricky and is able to invent lies easily. In fact, some later Greek dramatists made Odysseus a symbol of deceit. Penelope stands for the faithful, loving wife. Telemachus symbolizes the youth who matures by facing a difficult challenge. The travels of Odysseus and Telemachus may represent man's journey through life and his search for self-fulfillment and self-knowledge. GEORGE KENNEDY

Related Articles in WORLD BOOK include:

Aeneid	Circe	Iliad	Penelope	Siren
Calypso	Cyclops	Lotus-Eater	Polyphemus	Ulysses
Capri	Homer	Nausicaa	Scylla	

OECD. See ORGANIZATION FOR ECONOMIC COOPERATION AND DEVELOPMENT.

OEDEMA. See EDEMA.

OEDIPUS, *EHD uh puhs,* was an unfortunate king of Thebes in Greek mythology. He unknowingly killed his father and married his mother. His father, King Laius of Thebes, received an *oracle* (message) from Apollo which said that a son born to his wife Jocasta would kill him. When Jocasta gave birth to a son, Laius left the baby on a mountainside. But a shepherd found the child and carried him to King Polybus of Corinth. Polybus adopted the boy as his own and named him Oedipus *(swell foot)* because his feet were

From a painting by J. A. D. Ingres, courtesy of Bettmann Archive
Oedipus Solved the Riddle of the Terrible Sphinx.

swollen. Laius had pierced his feet with a spike.

Oedipus grew up in Corinth. One day a companion said that he was not really Polybus' son. Oedipus went to Delphi to find out the truth. Apollo told him not to go back to his own land because he would kill his father and marry his mother. Oedipus thought that Polybus was his father, and that Apollo meant that he should not return to Corinth. So he set out for Thebes.

Oedipus met a man who pushed him off the road. Not knowing that the man was Laius, his father, Oedipus killed him in anger. He found Thebes plagued by the Sphinx, a lioness with a woman's head (see SPHINX). She killed everyone who could not answer her riddle: "What has one voice and yet becomes four-footed and two-footed and three-footed?" Oedipus answered: "Man, who crawls on all fours as a baby, walks on two legs during his lifetime, and needs a cane in old age." The Sphinx killed herself after her riddle was solved.

Oedipus was made king because he had freed Thebes from the Sphinx. He married Jocasta, the widow of King Laius. Oedipus did not find out for many years that he had killed his father and married his mother. A plague came upon Thebes. An oracle said that it would not stop until the murderer of Laius had been driven from Thebes. Oedipus looked for the murderer,

and found that he was the man. Horrified, he blinded himself, and Jocasta hanged herself. Oedipus was banished from Thebes. He died at Colonus, near Athens. Sophocles' plays, *Oedipus Rex* and *Oedipus at Colonus,* tell part of the story. JOSEPH FONTENROSE

OEDIPUS COMPLEX, in psychiatry, is the strong attachment of a child to a parent of the opposite sex. The complex is usually accompanied by dislike for the other parent. The term comes from Oedipus, a hero in Greek mythology, who killed his father and married his mother. Sigmund Freud first used the term. See also OEDIPUS; FREUD, SIGMUND.

QERSTED is a unit used to measure the intensity, or strength, of a magnetic field in a vacuum. The number of oersteds of a magnetic field equals the number of magnetic lines of force per square centimeter in the field. The unit was named after Hans Christian Oersted, a Danish physicist who pioneered in the study of electromagnetism. The oersted is not as widely used today as another unit called the *weber* (see WEBER).

OERSTED, *UR steth,* **HANS CHRISTIAN** (1777-1851), a Danish physicist and chemist, laid the foundation for the science of electromagnetism (see ELECTROMAGNETISM). In 1820, he noticed that the needle of a compass wavered every time he put it near a wire carrying a current. He had discovered that every conductor carrying an electric current is surrounded by a magnetic field. Oersted is also credited with producing the first aluminum, in 1825 (see ALUMINUM [The First Aluminum]). He wrote *Spirit of Nature* (1850). Oersted was born at the town of Rudkøbing, on the island of Langeland, Denmark. R. T. ELLICKSON

OESOPHAGUS. See ESOPHAGUS.

OFF-BROADWAY THEATER. See THEATER (Theater in the United States).

OFFENBACH, *OHF un bahk,* **JACQUES** (1819-1880), a Franco-German composer, won fame as a manager, director, and composer of 90 French operettas, between 1855 and 1880. Few of the operettas have survived. He is remembered best for his opera, *The Tales of Hoffmann.* He worked on this opera for many years, but died before it was produced. Ernest Guiraud completed it for performance in 1881. His other works include *Orpheus in the Underworld* (1858), *La Belle Hélène* (1865), *La Vie Parisienne* (1866), and *La Grande Duchesse de Gérolstein* (1867).

Chicago Historical Society
Jacques Offenbach

He was born Jakob Offenbach, the son of a synagogue cantor, in Cologne, Germany. He began to study the violoncello at the Paris Conservatory when he was 14, and was shortly playing in the orchestra at the Opéra Comique. He became conductor at the Comédie-Française in 1850. He opened his own theater in 1855. Offenbach took his company to London in 1857, and to the United States in 1877. THEODORE M. FINNEY

OFFICE OF ————. Many offices are listed in WORLD BOOK under the key word in their names, as in EDUCATION, OFFICE OF.

OFFICE WORK is the process of recording, storing, and distributing the information needed to operate a business. The managers of the business use this information to make administrative decisions.

In the mid-1970's, about 15 million persons in the United States had a job as an office worker. They included bookkeepers and accounting technicians, file clerks, secretaries, and typists. Office workers do not include people involved in such activities as buying, selling, or management.

An office may receive information by telephone, by mail, or by computer. A company's reputation and success can depend on the way its office workers handle the information. A letter misplaced by a file clerk could result in the loss of an important customer. A slight error in arithmetic made by a bookkeeper might cause a loss of several thousand dollars.

An office worker must have skill in language and arithmetic to handle business information accurately. Almost all office jobs require at least a high school education. Many employers prefer people who have taken courses beyond the high school level. A person can get such advanced training at a community college, junior college, or business or vocational school. This training may include instruction in operating business machines and automated equipment.

A business office requires a skilled staff of managers to plan and direct work. As a business grows, so does the amount of paperwork that must be handled by its office workers. The management staff coordinates the activities of these employees so that accurate records can be kept concerning correspondence, inventory, payroll, sales, and taxes. Skillful management aids the process of recording, storing, and distributing business information efficiently.

Recording Information. Business information may be recorded by hand or by machine. The equipment that office workers use to record such data may be as simple as a pencil and paper or as complex as a computer.

Some handwritten information may be used in the form in which it is recorded. For example, a receptionist may keep a written record of visitors who come to the office on business. A secretary may take a telephone message for someone who is out of the office. Such information does not have to undergo further processing before it can be used.

Other types of information may be recorded by hand as the first step before processing it through a machine. For example, a stenographer takes notes in shorthand and then types letters or reports from the notes.

Information can also be recorded directly into a machine. A manager may dictate a letter into a dictating machine and have a secretary transcribe the message with a typewriter. Secretaries use manual, electric, and magnetic-tape and magnetic-card typewriters. Letters can be typed faster and more neatly with an electric typewriter than with a manual typewriter.

Magnetic-tape and magnetic-card typewriters are used to save time if the same letter is to be sent to many people. The secretary types the letter onto a magnetic tape or card, which is then fed into the typewriter. The typewriter prints perfect copies of the letter at over 140 words per minute, more than twice the speed of a good typist. Each copy of a letter typed by such a typewriter is actually an original copy.

Bookkeepers can also record information directly into a machine. Electronic calculators add, subtract, multiply, and divide with accuracy and lightning speed. Some calculators record figures with a special type that can be read by a computer. The computer tabulates and types financial reports automatically.

Storing Information. A business firm stores information to provide a record of all its transactions. Clerks keep correspondence and records of all kinds in systematic order in file cabinets so the information can be located quickly.

Many companies use key punch machines and computers, or microfilm, to reduce the size of the original records and thus save filing space. A key punch machine has a keyboard similar to that of a typewriter. The operator uses the keyboard to punch patterns of holes in cards inserted into the machine. A machine called a *card reader* "reads" information from these cards and puts it in the form of electric signals. The signals are sent to a computer, where a device called a *memory* records the information on magnetic tape or disks for storage. A computer can also receive information from an *optical scanner*, a machine that reads handwritten or printed material directly off a page.

Microfilm is used to photograph a reduced image of printed material. About 3,000 business letters can be photographed on a strip of microfilm 16 millimeters ($\frac{5}{8}$ inch) wide and 100 feet (30 meters) long. The strip can be wound up in a roll that occupies only about 16 cubic inches (262 cubic centimeters) of space. Microfilm strips are read on the viewing screen of a projection machine that enlarges the images on the film. Some projection machines can also make an enlarged paper copy of the images.

Distributing Information. Messenger service ranks as one of the oldest and most widely used methods of distributing information within an office. Messengers visit the various departments of a company at regular times every day to pick up and deliver communications.

Information to be distributed to many people in an office may be duplicated so that each person can have a copy. Duplicating machines make copies quickly and inexpensively. Some duplicators require the preparation of a *master*, a special form from which copies are made. Other machines can duplicate information that has been written or typed on ordinary paper. A computer can quickly find any information stored in its memory and then print copies.   FRANKLIN H. DYE

Related Articles in WORLD BOOK include:

OFFICE EQUIPMENT

Adding Machine	Computer	Duplicator
Addressograph	Dictating Machine	Typewriter
Calculator		

OTHER RELATED ARTICLES

Accounting (Industrial Accounting)	Information
Bookkeeping	Retrieval
Business	Microfilm
Business Education	Shorthand
Careers (Business and Office)	

OFFICER. See RANK IN ARMED SERVICES.
OFFICIAL LANGUAGES ACT. See CANADA, HISTORY OF (Trudeau Succeeds Pearson).

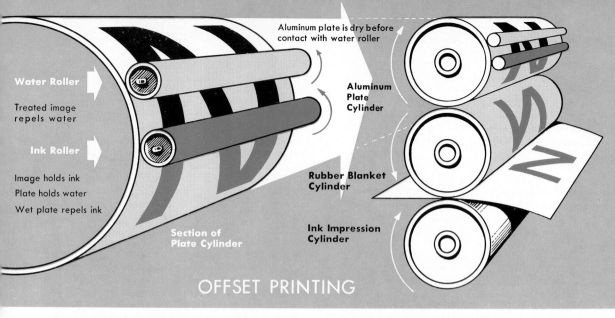

Aluminum plate is dry before contact with water roller

Water Roller

Treated image repels water

Ink Roller

Image holds ink
Plate holds water
Wet plate repels ink

Section of Plate Cylinder

Aluminum Plate Cylinder

Rubber Blanket Cylinder

Ink Impression Cylinder

OFFSET PRINTING

Offset Printing is not done directly from a printing plate or from type. Instead, the ink is transferred from the printing plate to a second roller, which in turn impresses it on the paper or other material to be printed.

OFFSET is a printing process in which the printing is done first on the rubber surface of a rotating cylinder. The impression is then transferred to paper by the pressure of other cylinders. The term *offset* describes the printing, or offsetting, of the ink from the rubber. In recent years, offset has grown more rapidly in popularity than any other printing process.

All ordinary offset printing is done from the metal surfaces of lithographic plates (see LITHOGRAPHY). The material to be printed is transferred onto the plates through a special photographic process. The plates are chemically treated so that only the traced design of the print will take up the ink. But the offset process is used for other methods also. Some printing is done from ordinary type and cuts, some from thin plastic relief or letterpress plates, some from gelatin surfaces, and some from *intaglio* plates, which are metal sheets that carry the ink in sunken lines.

Offset lithography is usually done on a press having three cylinders. A lithographic plate is wrapped around the first cylinder. This plate is a sheet of aluminum or zinc about as thick as heavy paper. The plate prints on a second cylinder which is covered by a rubber blanket. The impression on the rubber is then printed on the paper carried by the third cylinder. The third cylinder is equipped with steel fingers, called *grippers*, to hold the paper in position while it is squeezed against the rubber surface. Three-cylinder presses of this type can turn out 8,000 impressions an hour.

These cylinders are almost hidden while the press is in operation. They are covered by a great number of rollers which supply the lithographic plate with ink and water. The cylinders are also concealed by the mechanism for feeding and removing the sheets of paper.

The offset process has several advantages over other types of printing. The elastic rubber used transfers the impression to a rough surface as easily as to a smooth one. This makes it possible to print on rough paper, as well as on tin, celluloid, and other substances. Another advantage of offset is that the rubber on the cylinder fits itself easily to uneven surfaces. This greatly reduces the time pressmen must spend preparing the presses for printing. Offset is called a *planographic* technique.

Offset was developed in the early 1900's in America as a method of printing tin sheets for making cans and boxes. It has recently been applied to almost every class of printing, from the cheapest to the most expensive. Offset has replaced the older forms of lithography in which the impression was made directly on the paper from stone or metal plates. An offset press can turn out bank notes, stock certificates, letterheads, magazine covers, posters, and mail-order catalogues. The offset press is often used in printing weekly suburban newspapers. Offset is combined with rotogravure to make colored illustrations that are clear and delicate. It is also used for facsimile reproduction of old books.

The process is still being improved and applied to new purposes. The wearing qualities of the lithographic plates are being improved. Offset presses have been designed to print on a *web* (continuous sheet on a spool) of paper. The paper on this *web press* is passed between two rollers covered with rubber blankets, printing on both sides at the same time.   KENNETH G. SCHEID

See also PRINTING.

OFFUTT AIR FORCE BASE, Nebr., is headquarters of the U.S. Air Force Strategic Air Command. It covers about 1,900 acres (769 hectares), 10 miles (16 kilometers) south of Omaha. The base began as Fort Crook, an army post, in the early 1890's. In 1924, the airfield was named for Lt. Jarvis J. Offutt, Omaha's first air casualty in World War I. The Strategic Air Command established headquarters on the base in 1948. See also STRATEGIC AIR COMMAND.   RICHARD M. SKINNER

O'FLAHERTY, LIAM, *LEE uhm* (1897-), is an Irish writer of political and psychological novels and short stories. His *The Informer* (1926) and *The Puritan* (1932) made excellent motion pictures. He also wrote the novels *The Black Soul* (1925), *The Assassin* (1928), *Skerrett* (1932), and *Famine* (1937). He was born in the Aran Islands.   JOSEPH E. BAKER

OG, *ahg,* a Bible character, was an Amorite king whom the Israelites fought when they came to the edge of the Promised Land.' His kingdom was in Bashan, in what is today southern Syria and northern Jordan. Og was said to have been a giant (Deut. 3). The Israelites defeated and killed him, and took his land.   JOHN BRIGHT

OGASAWARA-GUNTO. See BONIN ISLANDS.

OGDEN, Utah (pop. 69,478), is the state's second largest city. It lies 35 miles (56 kilometers) north of Salt Lake City. See UTAH (political map). Ogden and Salt Lake City form a metropolitan area of 705,458. Ogden has the largest stockyards west of Denver. Its factories process agricultural products. Missiles are also produced in the area. Ogden is the home of Weber State College, the Utah State Industrial School, and the Utah School for the Deaf and Blind.

Mormons came to the Ogden region in 1847. Ogden was incorporated in 1861, and grew rapidly after becoming a link in the transcontinental railroad system in 1869. The Golden Spike, driven near Ogden in May, 1869, completed the railroad. Ogden was named for Peter Skene Ogden, an early fur trader. Ogden is the seat of Weber County. It has a council-manager government.   A. R. MORTENSEN

OGDEN, CHARLES K. See BASIC ENGLISH.

OGDEN, PETER SKENE. See OGDEN.

OGIER THE DANE, *OH jih er,* was a hero of several French romantic poems of the Middle Ages. The poems tell how he earned his knighthood in Charlemagne's war against the Saracens in Italy. Later, Charlemagne's son killed Ogier's son, and Ogier revolted against Charlemagne. He was imprisoned, but was set free when a Saracen army attacked France. Ogier killed the Saracen leader and saved France.   ARTHUR M. SELVI

OGLETHORPE, JAMES EDWARD (1696-1785), an Englishman, was the founder and first governor of the colony of Georgia.

He was born in London and attended Eton and Oxford. He joined the British Army at 14. He was elected to Parliament in 1722. Here, he became interested in persons who had been imprisoned for not paying their debts. Oglethorpe hoped to help them by establishing an American colony for debtors. In 1732, he and a group of associates received a charter from George II for the colony on territory between the Savannah and Altamaha rivers. Parliament also granted him $50,000.

Oglethorpe and 114 colonists arrived in America in January, 1733. He set up his first settlement where the city of Savannah now stands. He governed wisely for nine years and drove invading Spanish troops back into Florida. He defeated the Spaniards badly in the Battle of Bloody Marsh on St. Simons Island, in 1742.

Oglethorpe was so much in debt from his loans to colonists that he had to return to England in 1743. His enemies called him a coward for not capturing St. Augustine, Fla., when he attacked the Spaniards there in 1743. A court-martial dismissed the charges. He and the other trustees returned the Georgia charter to George II in 1752, and Georgia became a royal province.   JOSEPH CARLYLE SITTERSON

See also GEORGIA (Colonial Period).

OGLETHORPE UNIVERSITY. See UNIVERSITIES AND COLLEGES (table).

OGOTAI. See MONGOL EMPIRE (Invasions).

OGPU was the Soviet secret police. See MVD.

O'HARA, JOHN (1905-1970), was an American novelist and short-story writer. He is best known for his skillful use of dialogue spoken by middle-class Americans. Many of his novels and stories are set in the fictional town of Gibbsville, Pa.

O'Hara was born in Pottsville, Pa., and worked as a journalist before the success of his first novel, *Appointment in Samarra* (1934). The novel explores the social and psychological difficulties of the upper middle class in America. His novel *Butterfield 8* (1935) is a study of how sexual freedom affects both society and the individual. Of his later novels, *Ten North Frederick* (1955) has received the greatest praise from both critics and the public.

O'Hara published many collections of stories, including *The Doctor's Son* (1935) and *Sermons and Soda Water* (1960). His story sequence *Pal Joey* (1940) was adapted into a musical by Richard Rodgers and Lorenz Hart. This comic exposé expresses with an authentic American voice the frenzied life of a part of American society.   JOHN CROSSETT

O'HARA, JOHN CARDINAL (1888-1960), was the fifth archbishop of Philadelphia. He was named a cardinal of the Roman Catholic Church in November, 1958, by Pope John XXIII. He was ordained a priest of the Congregation of Holy Cross in 1916. He served as president of the University of Notre Dame from 1934 to 1939, and then became titular bishop of Mylassa. He became bishop of Buffalo in 1945, and archbishop of Philadelphia in 1951. Cardinal O'Hara was born in Ann Arbor, Mich.   JAMES A. CORBETT and FULTON J. SHEEN

O'HARA, MARY (1885-   ), is the pen name of Mary O'Hara Alsop Sture-Vasa, an American author. She wrote of people on the plains and their love for horses in her novels *My Friend Flicka* (1941) and *Thunderhead* (1943). She also wrote *The Son of Adam Wyngate* (1952), a novel of spiritual experiences. She was born in Cape May Point, N.J.

O'HARE INTERNATIONAL AIRPORT. See CHICAGO (Transportation); AIRPORT.

O. HENRY. See HENRY, O.

OHIA, *oh HE uh,* is a mountain apple tree that grows in Hawaii. The wood is used in furniture, flooring, and railroad ties. The ohia belongs to the family *Myrtaceae.*

O'HIGGINS, *oh HIG inz,* is the family name of two South American soldiers and statesmen, father and son.

Ambrosio O'Higgins (1720?-1801) was born in Ireland. He went to Spain, then to Peru to enter business. He became wealthy, and entered Spanish service in Chile. He was captain general of Chile from 1788 to 1796. O'Higgins became Marqués de Osorno in 1792. He served as viceroy of Peru from 1796 until his death.

Bernardo O'Higgins (1778-1842), the son of Ambrosio O'Higgins, was the liberator of Chile. After Spain defeated a Chilean army at Rancagua in 1814, O'Higgins joined the South American liberator José de San Martín, in Argentina. They crossed the Andes Mountains to Chile in 1817 and defeated the Spaniards at Chacabuco. O'Higgins won the final victory over the Spaniards at the Maipo River in 1818. He was ousted from power because of disputes over reform attempts. He was born in Chillán, Chile.   DONALD E. WORCESTER

See also CHILE (Independence; picture).

OHIO is one of the leading industrial states in the United States. It ranks third, behind California and New York, in the total value of manufactured products. Great numbers of people have moved to Ohio so they could work in the state's busy factories. Ohio stands 6th among the states in population, although it is 35th in area. Cleveland, the chief industrial center of Ohio, is the state's largest city. Columbus is the capital.

Ohio took its name from the Iroquois Indian word meaning *something great*. The Iroquois used the word for the Ohio River, which forms the state's southeastern and southern borders. Ohio is called the *Buckeye State*

OHIO *THE BUCKEYE STATE*

because of the buckeye trees that once grew plentifully on its hills and plains. Pioneers cut down many of the buckeyes, or horse chestnut trees, to build log cabins. In 1803, Ohio became the first state to be carved out of the Northwest Territory. Ohio later served as an important link to the West as canals, railways, and roads crossed the state. As a result, Ohio also came to be called the *Gateway State*.

Several natural advantages helped Ohio become a great manufacturing state. Ohio has an abundant supply of water and large deposits of coal, salt, and other important minerals. Its central location, near raw materials and major markets, has helped attract many

Covered Bridge in Southern Ohio Shostal

Sailing on Lake Erie James Busch, Foto/Find

Ohio (blue) ranks 35th in size among all the states, and 11th in size among the Midwestern States (gray).

large industries. Ohio ranks high among the states in the manufacture of machine tools and such transportation equipment as bus and truck bodies and truck trailers. Ohio's production of iron and steel ranks second only to that of Pennsylvania. No other state manufactures more rubber products than Ohio.

But Ohio is not entirely a manufacturing state. Fertile farmlands that make up part of the great midwestern Corn Belt stretch across much of Ohio. Farmers grow large crops of corn, soybeans, and wheat. Vineyards of grapes dot the shore of Lake Erie to the north. Ohio ranks among the leading hog-raising states.

Ohio claims the title of the *Mother of Presidents.* Seven Presidents of the United States were born in Ohio, more than in any other state except Virginia. In historical order, they were Ulysses S. Grant, Rutherford B. Hayes, James A. Garfield, Benjamin Harrison, William McKinley, William Howard Taft, and Warren G. Harding. William Henry Harrison was living in Ohio when he became President of the United States.

Two of the nation's most famous astronauts were born in Ohio. Neil A. Armstrong, the first man to set foot on the moon, was born in Wapakoneta. John H. Glenn, Jr., the first American spaceman to orbit the earth, was born in Cambridge and grew up in New Concord. He was elected to the U.S. Senate from Ohio in 1974. Many famous inventors also came from Ohio. Thomas A. Edison, the wizard of electricity, developed his scientific curiosity as a small boy in Milan. Orville Wright and Wilbur Wright made test flights in their first power-driven airplane from a field near Dayton. Charles F. Kettering of Dayton developed a self-starter for automobiles. The aluminum-refining process was discovered by Charles M. Hall of Oberlin.

For the relationship of Ohio to other states in its region, see the article on the MIDWESTERN STATES.

FACTS IN BRIEF

Capital: Columbus.

Government: *Congress*—U.S. senators, 2; U.S. representatives, 23. *Electoral Votes*—25. *State Legislature*—senators, 33; representatives, 99. *Counties*—88.

Area: 41,222 sq. mi. (106,764 km²), including 247 sq. mi. (640 km²) of inland water but excluding 3,457 sq. mi. (8,954 km²) of Lake Erie; 35th in size among the states. *Greatest Distances*—east-west, 230 mi. (370 km); north-south, 210 mi. (338 km). *Shoreline*—312 mi. (502 km) on Lake Erie, including 66 mi. (106 km) on islands.

Elevation: *Highest*—Campbell Hill in Logan County, 1,550 ft. (472 m) above sea level. *Lowest*—433 ft. (132 m) above sea level along the Ohio River in Hamilton County.

Population: *Estimated 1975 Population*—10,759,000. *1970 Census*—10,652,017; 6th among the states; distribution, 75 per cent urban, 25 per cent rural; density, 258 persons per sq. mi. (100 persons per km²).

Chief Products: *Agriculture*—beef cattle, corn, dairy products, eggs, greenhouse and nursery products, hogs, soybeans, wheat. *Fishing Industry*—carp, catfish, sheepshead, white bass, yellow perch, yellow pike. *Manufacturing*—chemicals; electrical machinery; food and related products; metal products; nonelectrical machinery; printed materials; rubber and plastic products; stone, clay, and glass products; transportation equipment. *Mining*—coal, petroleum, salt, sand and gravel, stone.

Statehood: March 1, 1803; the 17th state.

State Motto: *With God, all things are possible.*

State Song: "Beautiful Ohio." Words by Ballard MacDonald; music by Mary Earl.

The contributors of this article are Ralph W. Frank, Professor of Geography at Bowling Green State University; Ben Hayes, Columnist for the Columbus Citizen-Journal; *and James H. Rodabaugh, Professor of History at Miami University.*

Ohio Oil Refinery

G. Warstler, Foto/Find

Constitution of Ohio, the second in the state's history, was adopted in 1851. Ohioans adopted their first constitution in 1802. An amendment to the Constitution may be proposed by (1) the state legislature, (2) a petition signed by 10 per cent of the voters, or (3) a constitutional convention. A convention may be called if it is approved by two-thirds of each house of the legislature and by a majority of the voters. Ohioans also vote every 20 years as to whether they wish to call a convention. Constitutional amendments must be approved by a majority of the persons voting on them in an election.

Executive. The governor of Ohio is elected to a four-year term. He can serve an unlimited number of terms, but not more than two terms in succession. He receives a yearly salary of $40,000. For a list of all the governors of Ohio, see the *History* section of this article.

The governor has the power to appoint the heads of many of the state's administrative departments and agencies. These appointments must be approved by the state senate. The governor also appoints the adjutant general and the trustees of state-supported universities and institutions.

Legislature, called the *General Assembly*, consists of a 33-member Senate and a 99-member House of Representatives. Voters in each of Ohio's 33 senatorial districts elect one senator. Senators serve four-year terms. Voters in each of the state's 99 representative districts elect one representative. Representatives serve two-year terms. Regular legislative sessions begin on the first Monday of January in odd-numbered years and have no time limit.

A 1903 amendment to the state constitution required that each county have at least one representative, regardless of its population. In 1964, the Supreme Court of the United States ruled this amendment unconstitutional. In 1965, the governor, the state auditor, and the secretary of state drew up a *reapportionment* (redivision) plan for the Senate and House of Representatives. They set up single-member legislative districts that were as

equal in population as possible. A special three-judge federal district court approved the reapportionment plan for temporary use until a permanent plan could be drawn. The Supreme Court of the United States approved the federal district court's decision. In 1967, the Constitution was amended to provide for a permanent reapportionment plan.

Courts. The highest appeals court in Ohio is the Supreme Court. It has a chief justice and six other justices, elected to six-year terms. Ohio also has 11 courts of appeals. Each court has three judges, except the court of Cuyahoga County, which has six, and the court in Franklin County, which has five.

The highest trial courts are the courts of common pleas. Each of the 88 counties has one. These courts have varying numbers of judges, elected to six-year terms. Other courts in Ohio include county, juvenile, municipal, mayor, and probate courts.

Local Government. Each of Ohio's 88 counties is governed by a three-member board of commissioners, who are elected to four-year terms. By law, counties may have *home rule*. That is, a county may adopt its own charter. But no county in Ohio has done so.

Under Ohio law, cities are incorporated communities with at least 5,000 persons. Villages have populations under 5,000. Officially, Ohio has no towns. Ohio law allows cities and villages to adopt home rule, and about a fourth of the cities and villages have done so. The home-rule cities and villages have mayor-council, council-manager, or commission governments. Home rule in Ohio consists mainly of changing the form of local government, not its powers. In 1914, Dayton became the first large U.S. city to adopt council-manager government. About three-fourths of Ohio's cities and villages have a mayor-council government.

Taxation. A 4 per cent retail sales tax is the state government's largest single source of tax income. This tax provides about a fifth of the total income. Other state taxes include those on cigarettes, gasoline, inheritances, personal and corporation incomes,

The Governor's Mansion is in Bexley, a suburb of Columbus. The house, formerly a private residence, was given to the state in 1955. The brick and stone structure has 24 rooms. Three acres (1.2 hectares) of parklike grounds surround the mansion.

Ohio Dept. of Economic and Community Development

The State Seal

Symbols of Ohio. On the state seal, a sheaf of wheat represents the richness of Ohio's land. A bundle of arrows symbolizes Ohio's admission to the Union as the 17th state. The sun rising behind the mountains shows that Ohio was the first state west of the Allegheny Mountains. The seal was adopted in 1868 and revised in 1967. On the flag, adopted in 1902, the white circle stands for "O," the state's initial. The red circle represents the buckeye nut. Ohio is the only state with a pennant-shaped flag.

The State Flag

Flag, bird, and flower illustrations, courtesy of Eli Lilly and Company

property, and highway use by trucks. Federal grants and other U.S. government programs provide about a fourth of the state's income. The remainder comes from such sources as state-owned liquor stores and various state institutions such as hospitals.

Politics. Since the founding of the Republican party during the 1850's, Republicans have generally controlled Ohio politics. Almost twice as many Republicans as Democrats have been elected governor, and Republicans have usually controlled the state legislature. The rural areas and Cincinnati are centers of Republican strength. They usually combine forces to control the legislature. Cleveland is the major Democratic center.

Ohio is often called a *barometer state* in national politics. That is, Ohioans' political views frequently indicate those of most Americans. For example, the winning presidential candidates have won Ohio's electoral votes in a great majority of presidential elections since 1804. For Ohio's electoral votes and voting record in presidential elections, see ELECTORAL COLLEGE (table).

The State Capitol in Columbus was completed in 1861. The huge limestone building stands in a 10-acre (4-hectare) park. Columbus has been Ohio's capital since 1816. Other capitals were Chillicothe (1803-1810), Zanesville (1810-1812), and Chillicothe (1812-1816).

J. H. Hutton, FPG

The State Bird
Cardinal

The State Flower
Scarlet Carnation

The State Tree
Buckeye

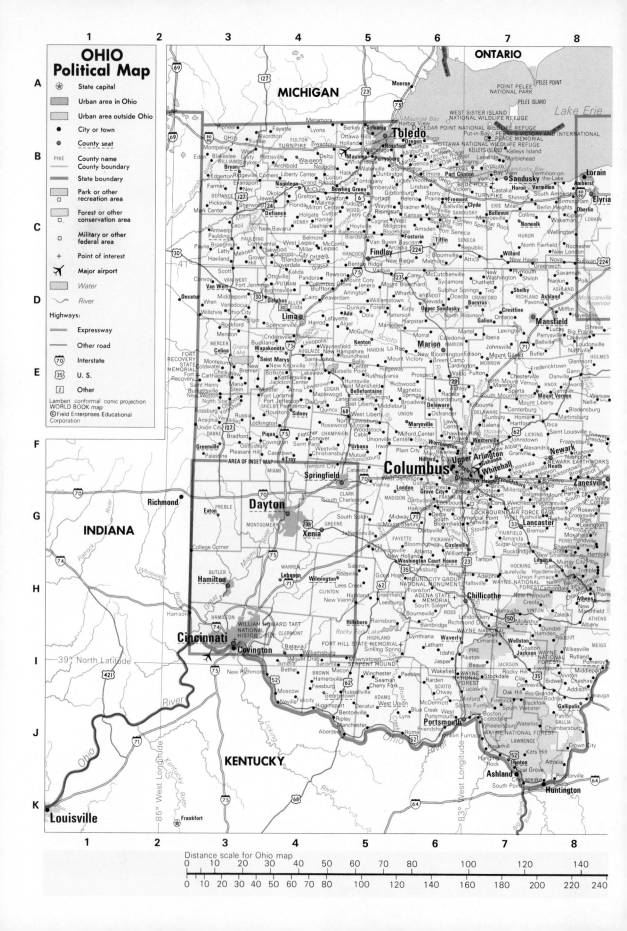

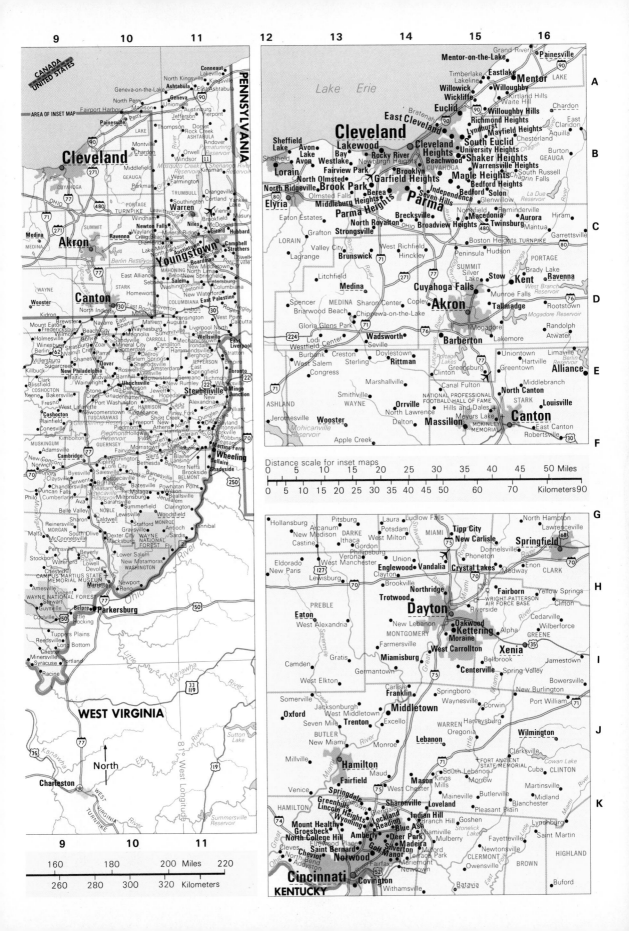

Population

10,759,000 Estimate.1975
10,652,017 .Census..1970
9,706,397 ....“....1960
7,946,627 ....“....1950
6,907,612 ....“....1940
6,646,697 ....“....1930
5,759,394 ....“....1920
4,767,121 ....“....1910
4,157,545 ....“....1900
3,672,329 ....“....1890
3,198,062 ....“....1880
2,665,260 ....“....1870
2,339,511 ....“....1860
1,980,329 ....“....1850
1,519,467 ....“....1840
937,903 ....“....1830
581,434 ....“....1820
230,760 ....“....1810
45,365 ....“....1800

Metropolitan Areas

Akron 679,239
Canton 393,789
Cincinnati 1,385,103
(1,104,717 in O.;
250,956 in Ky.;
29,430 in Ind.)
Cleveland 2,063,729
Columbus 1,017,847
Dayton 852,531
Hamilton-
Middletown ...226,207
Huntington
(W.Va.)-Ashland
(Ky.) 286,935
(144,499 in W.Va.;
85,568 in Ky.;
56,868 in O.)
Lima 210,074
Lorain-Elyria ...256,843
Mansfield 129,997
Marietta-Parkersburg
(W.Va.) 148,132
(90,972 in W.Va.;
57,160 in O.)
Springfield 187,606
Steubenville-Weirton
(W.Va.) 165,627
(96,193 in O.;
69,434 in W.Va.)
Toledo 762,658
(643,486 in O.;
119,172 in Mich.)
Wheeling (W.Va.) 182,712
(101,795 in W.Va.;
80,917 in O.)
Youngstown-
Warren 537,124

Counties

Adams ....18,957..I 5
Allen .....111,144..D 4
Ashland ...43,303..D 8
Ashtabula ..98,237..B 11
Athens .....55,747..H 8
Auglaize ...38,602..E 4
Belmont ...80,917..F 11
Brown .....26,635..I 4
Butler ....226,207..H 3
Carroll ....21,579..D 10
Champaign .30,491..F 5
Clark .....157,115..G 5
Clermont ...95,372..I 4
Clinton ....31,464..H 5
Colum-
biana ...108,310..D 11
Coshocton ..33,486..E 9
Crawford ..50,364..D 7
Cuyahoga 1,720,835..B 9
Darke .....49,141..F 3
Defiance ...36,949..B 3
Delaware ..42,908..E 7
Erie ....75,909..C 7
Fairfield ..73,301..G 7
Fayette ....25,461..G 6
Franklin ..833,249..G 6
Fulton .....33,071..B 4
Gallia .....25,239..J 8
Geauga ....62,977..B 10
Greene ....125,057..G 5
Guernsey ..37,665..F 10
Hamilton .923,840..H 3
Hancock ...61,217..C 5
Hardin .....30,813..E 5
Harrison ...17,013..E 10
Henry ......27,058..C 4
Highland ..28,996..I 5
Hocking ...20,322..H 7
Holmes ....23,024..E 8
Huron .....49,587..C 7
Jackson ....27,174..I 7
Jefferson ...96,193..E 11
Knox ......41,795..E 8
Lake ......197,200..B 10
Lawrence ...56,868..J 7
Licking ...107,799..F 7
Logan .....35,072..E 4
Lorain ....256,843..C 8
Lucas ....483,551..B 5
Madison ...28,318..G 5
Mahoning .304,545..D 11
Marion ....64,724..E 6
Medina .....82,717..C 9
Meigs ......19,799..I 8
Mercer .....35,558..E 3
Miami ......84,342..F 4
Monroe ....15,739..G 11
Montgom-
ery .....608,413..G 3
Morgan ....12,375..G 9
Morrow ....21,348..E 7
Muskingum 77,826..F 9
Noble ......10,428..G 10
Ottawa .....37,099..B 6
Paulding ...19,329..C 3
Perry ......27,434..G 8
Pickaway ..40,071..G 6
Pike ....19,114..I 7
Portage ...125,868..C 10
Preble .....34,719..G 3
Putnam ....31,134..D 4
Richland ..129,997..D 7
Ross ....61,211..H 6
Sandusky ...60,983..C 6
Scioto .....76,951..I 6
Seneca .....60,696..C 6
Shelby .....37,748..E 4
Stark ......372,210..D 10
Summit ...553,371..C 10
Trumbull .232,579..B 11
Tuscarawas 77,211..F 10
Union ......23,786..E 6
Van Wert ..29,194..D 3
Vinton ......9,420..H 7
Warren .....85,505..H 4
Washington 57,160..H 10
Wayne .....87,123..D 9
Williams ...33,669..B 3
Wood ......89,722..C 5
Wyandot ...21,826..D 6

Cities and Villages

Aberdeen ....1,165..J 5
Academia, see North
Mount Vernon
[-Academia]
Ada ....5,309..D 5
Addyston ....1,336..K 12
Adelphi ......455..H 7
Adena ....1,134..F 11
Akron ....275,425.°C 9
Albany ....899..H 8
Alexandria ....588..F 7
Alger ....1,071..D 5
Alliance ...26,547..E 16
Alvordton ......351..B 3
Amanda ....788..G 7
Amberly .....4,761..K 14
Amelia ....820..I 4
Amesville .....295..H 9
Amherst .....9,902..B 8
Amsterdam ....882..E 11
Andover .....1,179..B 11
Anna ....792..E 4
Ansonia .....1,044..F 3
Antwerp ....1,735..C 3
Apple Creek ..784..F 14
Aquilla ....389..B 16
Arcadia ....689..C 5
Arcanum ....1,993..G 13
Archbold ....3,047..B 4
Arlington ....1,066..D 5
Arlington
Heights* ..1,476..H 3
Ashland ....19,872.°D 8
Ashley ....1,034..E 6
Ashtabula ..24,313..A 11
Ashville ......1,772..G 6
Athalia ....287..J 8
Athens ......24,168.°H 8
Attica ....1,005..C 7
Aurora ....6,549..C 16
Austintown 29,393..C 11
Avon ....7,214..B 13
Avon Lake .12,261..B 13
Avondale* ...5,240..G 4
Bailey Lakes* .394..D 8
Bainbridge ..1,057..H 6
Ballville ....1,652..C 6
Baltic ....571..E 9
Baltimore ...2,418..G 7
Barberton ..33,052..D 15
Barnesville ..4,292..F 10
Barnhill ....339..E 10
Batavia ......1,894.°I 4
Bay ....18,163..B 13
Bay View ......798..B 7
Beach City ..1,133..D 9
Beachwood ..9,631..B 15
Beallsville .....452..G 11
Beaver ....317..I 7
Beaverdam .....525..D 4
Bedford .....17,552..B 15
Bedford
Heights ..13,063..B 15
Bellaire ....9,655..F 11
Bellbrook ....1,268..I 15
Belle Center ...985..E 5
Belle Valley ..393..G 9
Bellefon-
taine ....11,255.°E 5
Bellevue .....8,604..C 7
Bellville .....1,685..E 7
Belmont ....666..F 11
Belmore ....319..C 4
Beloit ....921..D 11
Belpre ......7,189..H 9
Bentleyville* ..338..B 10
Benton Ridge .329..C 5
Berea ....22,465..B 13
Bergholz ....914..E 11
Berkey ....294..A 5
Berlin Heights 828..C 7
Bethel ......2,214..I 4
Bethesda ....1,157..F 10
Bettsville ......833..C 6
Beverly .....1,396..G 9
Bexley ......14,888..F 6
Blacklick
Estates* ..8,351..F 7
Blanchester .3,080..K 16
Bloomdale ....727..C 5
Bloomingburg .895..G 6
Bloomingdale* 289..E 11
Bloomville ....884..C 6
Blue Ash ....8,324..K 14
Bluffton ....2,935..D 4
Boardman .30,852..C 11
Bolivar ......1,084..D 10
Boston Heights 846..C 15
Botkins ......1,057..E 4
Bowerston .....479..E 10
Bowersville ...358..I 16
Bowling
Green ...21,760.°B 5
Bradford .....2,163..F 3
Bradner ......1,140..C 5
Brady Lake ...450..D 16
Bratenahl ...1,613..A 14
Brecksville ..9,137..C 14
Bremen ......1,413..G 8
Brewster ....2,020..D 9
Briarwood
Beach ......508..D 13
Bridgeport* .3,001..F 11
Bridgetown* 13,352..I 3
Brilliant ....2,178..E 11
Broadview
Heights ..11,463..C 14
Brook Park 30,774..B 14
Brooklyn ...13,142..B 14
Brooklyn
Heights* ..1,527..B 9
Brookside .....939..F 11
Brookville ...4,403..H 14
Brunswick .15,852..C 14
Bryan ....7,008.°B 3
Buchtel ....592..H 8
Buckeye Lake 2,961..F 8
Bucyrus ...13,111.°D 6
Burbank ....354..E 13
Burkettsville ..279..E 3
Burton ....1,214..B 16
Butler ....1,052..E 8
Byesville ....2,097..F 9
Cadiz ....3,060.°E 11
Cairo ....587..D 4
Caldwell ....2,082.°G 10
Caledonia .....792..D 6
Cambridge .13,656.°F 9
Camden ......1,507..I 13
Campbell ..12,577..C 11
Canal Fulton 2,367..E 15
Canal
Winchester 2,412..G 7
Canfield ....4,997..C 11
Canton ...110,053.°D 10
Cardington ..1,730..E 7
Carey ....3,523..D 6
Carlisle .....3,821..I 14
Carroll ....614..G 7
Carrollton ..2,817.°E 10
Casstown ......380..F 4
Castalia .....1,045..B 7
Catawba ....323..F 5
Cecil ....295..C 3
Cedarville ...2,342..H 16
Celina ......8,072.°E 3
Centerburg ..1,038..E 7
Centerville .10,333..I 15
Chagrin Falls 4,848..B 15
Chardon ....3,991.°A 16
Chatfield ......291..D 7
Chauncey ....1,117..H 8
Chesapeake ..1,364..K 8
Cheshire ....315..I 8
Chesterhill .....361..H 9
Cheviot .....11,135..K 13
Chickasaw .....326..E 3
Chillicothe .24,842.°H 6
Chillicothe
West* ....1,122..H 6
Chippewa-on-
the-Lake ...341..D 13
Christiansburg 724..F 4
Churchill* ..7,457..C 11
Cincinnati 451,455.°I 3
Circleville .11,687.°G 6
Clarington ....338..G 11
Clarksburg ....457..H 6
Clarksville .....574..J 16
Clay Center ...370..B 6
Clayton ....773..H 14
Cleveland 750,879.°B 9
Cleveland
Heights ..60,767..B 15
Cleves ......2,044..K 12
Clinton ......1,335..E 14
Clyde ....5,503..C 6
Coal Grove .2,759..J 7
Coalton ....550..I 7
Coldwater ...3,533..E 3
College Corner 408..G 2
Columbiana .4,959..D 11
Columbus .540,025.°F 6
Columbus
Grove ....2,290..D 4
Commercial
Point ....320..G 6
Conesville .....448..F 9
Conneaut ..14,552..A 11
Continental .1,185..C 4
Convoy ....991..D 3
Coolville ......672..H 9
Corning ....838..G 8
Cortland ....2,525..B 11
Corwin ....346..J 15
Coshocton ..13,747.°E 9
Covedale ....6,639..I 3
Covington ...2,575..F 3
Craig Beach .1,451..C 11
Crestline ....5,947..D 7
Creston ......1,792..E 13
Cridersville .1,103..D 4
Crooksville ..2,828..G 8
Crown City ...371..J 8
Crystal Lakes 5,851..H 15
Cumberland ...463..G 9
Custar ....277..C 5
Cuyahoga
Falls ....49,678..D 15
Cuyahoga
Heights* ....866..B 9
Cygnet ....629..C 5
Dalton ......1,177..F 14
Danville .....1,025..E 8
Darbydale .....743..G 6
Dayton ...242,917.°G 4
Deer Park ..7,415..K 14
Defiance ...16,281.°C 4
De Graff ....1,117..E 4
Delaware ..15,008.°E 6
Dellroy ....363..E 10
Delphos .....7,608..D 4
Delta ....2,544..B 4
Dennison ....3,506..E 10
Deshler ......1,938..C 4
Devola ....1,989..H 10
Dillonvale ...1,095..F 11
Donnelsville ..278..G 16
Dover ....11,516..E 10
Doylestown ..2,373..E 14
Dresden .....1,516..F 8
Dublin ....681..F 6
Dunkirk .....1,036..D 5
Dupont ....302..C 4
East
Alliance ..1,175..D 10
East Canton 1,631..F 16
East
Cleveland 39,600..B 15
East Liver-
pool .....20,020..D 12
East Liverpool
North* ....6,223..D 11
East
Palestine .5,604..D 12
East Sparta ..959..D 10
Eastlake ....19,690..A 15
Eaton ......6,020.°G 3
Eaton
Estates ...2,076..C 13
Edgerton ....2,126..B 3
Edgewood* ..3,437..A 11
Edison ....569..E 7
Edon ....803..B 3
Eldorado ......483..H 13
Elida ....1,211..D 4
Elmore ......1,316..B 6
Elmwood
Place .....3,525..K 13
Elyria .....53,427.°B 8
Empire ....491..E 11
Englewood ..7,885..H 14
Enon ....1,929..H 16
Euclid ......71,552..A 15
Evendale* ..1,967..H 3
Fairborn ...32,267..H 15
Fairfax .....2,705..K 14
Fairfield ...14,680..K 13
Fairlawn* ...6,102..C 9
Fairport
Harbor ...3,665..A 10
Fairview
Park ....21,681..B 13
Farmersville ..865..I 14
Fayette .....1,175..B 4
Fayetteville ...415..K 16
Felicity ....786..I 4
Findlay ....35,800.°C 5
Fletcher ....539..F 4
Florida ....285..C 4
Flushing ....1,207..F 10
Forest ......1,535..D 5
Forest Park* 15,139..H 3
Fort Jennings 533..D 4
Fort Loramie .744..E 3
Fort McKin-
ley* .....11,536..G 3
Fort
Recovery ..1,348..E 3
Fort
Shawnee* .3,436..D 4
Fostoria ...16,037..C 6
Frankfort ......949..H 6
Franklin ...10,075..I 14
Frazeysburg ..941..F 8
Fredericksburg 601..D 9
Frederick-
town ......1,935..E 7
Freeport ......490..F 10
Fremont ...18,490.°C 6
Fulton ....377..E 7
Gahanna ...12,400..F 7
Galena ....361..F 7
Galion ......13,123..D 7
Gallipolis ...7,490.°J 8
Gambier ....1,571..E 8
Garfield
Heights ..41,417..B 15
Garrettsville 1,718..C 16
Gates Mills* 2,378..B 10
Geneva .....6,449..A 11
Geneva-on-the-
Lake ....877..A 11
Genoa ......2,139..B 6
Georgetown .3,087.°I 4
Germantown 4,088..I 14
Gettysburg ...526..F 3
Gibsonburg .2,585..B 6
Girard ......14,119..C 11
Glandorf ......732..C 4
Glendale ....2,690..K 14
Glenmont .....266..E 8
Glenwillow ...526..C 15
Gloria Glens
Park ....332..D 13
Glouster ....2,121..H 8
Gnaden-
hutten ....1,466..E 10
Golf Manor .5,170..K 14
Goshen .....1,174..K 15
Grafton .....1,771..C 13
Grand Rapids 976..B 5
Grand River ..613..A 16
Grandview
Heights ...8,460..F 6
Granville ....3,963..F 7
Gratis ....621..I 13
Green Camp ..537..E 6
Green
Springs ...1,279..C 6
Greenfield ..4,780..H 6
Greenhills ..6,092..K 13
Greenville ..12,380.°F 3
Greenwich ..1,473..C 7
Grove City .13,911..G 6
Groveport ...2,490..G 7
Grover Hill ...536..C 3
Hamden ....953..I 7
Hamersville ...567..I 4
Hamilton ...67,865.°H 3
Hamler ....681..C 4
Hanging Rock 278..J 7
Hanover ....626..F 8
Hanoverton ....483..D 11
Harpster ......291..D 6
Harrisburg ....556..G 6
Harrison ....4,408..H 2
Harrisville .....345..F 11
Harrod ....533..D 4
Hartford ......455..F 7
Hartville .....1,752..E 16
Harveysburg ..486..J 14
Haskins ....549..B 5
Hayesville ....506..D 8
Heath ....6,768..F 8
Hebron .....1,699..F 7
Helena ....298..C 6
Hicksville ...3,461..C 3
Higginsport ...383..J 4
Highland
Heights* ..5,926..B 10
Hilliard .....8,369..F 6
Hills and
Dales ......280..E 15
Hillsboro ...5,584.°H 5
Hiram ....1,484..C 16
Holgate .....1,541..C 4
Holland .....1,108..B 5
Hollansburg ..364..G 12
Holloway .....488..F 10
Holmesville ..412..D 9
Hopedale .....916..E 11
Hoytville ......403..C 5
Hubbard ....8,583..C 12
Huber
Heights* .18,943..G 4
Hudson .....3,933..C 15
Hunting
Valley* .....797..B 10
Huntsville ....475..E 5
Huron ......6,896..B 7
Inde-
pendence .7,034..B 14
Indian Hill .5,651..K 14
Irondale ......602..E 11
Ironton ....15,030.°J 7
Jackson .....6,843.°I 7
Jackson
Center ....1,119..E 4
Jacksonville ...545..H 8
Jamestown ..1,790..I 16
Jefferson ....2,472.°A 11
Jeffersonville 1,031..G 5
Jenera ....282..D 5
Jeromesville ...559..F 12
Jerry City .....470..C 5
Jewett ....901..E 11
Johnstown ...3,208..F 7
Junction City .732..G 8
Kalida ....900..D 4
Kent ......28,183..D 16
Kenton .....8,315.°D 5
Kenwood* .15,789..I 3
Kettering ..71,864..I 15
Killbuck .....893..E 9
Kingston ....1,157..H 7
Kingsville ...1,129..A 11
Kipton ....353..C 8

Kirkersville ...578..F 7
Kirtland* ...5,530..B 10
Kirtland Hills 452..A 16
Knollwood* .5,353..G 4
Lafayette .....486..D 4
Lagrange ...1,074..C 12
Lakemore ...2,708..D 15
Lakeview ...1,026..E 4
Lakewood ..70,173..B 14
Lancaster ..32,911.°G 7
La Rue ......867..E 6
Laura ....464..G 14
Laurelville ...624..H 7
Lawrenceville .687..G 16
Lebanon ....7,934.°H 4
Leesburg .....984..H 5
Leetonia ....2,342..D 11
Leipsic .....2,072..C 4
Lewisburg ..1,553..H 13
Lewisville ....294..G 10
Lexington ...2,972..D 7
Liberty Center ....1,007..B 4
Lima ......53,734.°D 4
Limaville .....303..E 16
Lincoln Heights ...6,099..K 13
Lincoln Village* .11,215..F 6
Lindsey ......652..B 6
Lisbon ......3,521.°D 11
Lithopolis ....705..G 7
Lockbourne ...420..G 6
Lockbourne Base* ....5,623..G 6
Lockland ...5,288..K 14
Lodi ....2,399..D 13
Logan ......6,269.°H 8
London .....6,481.°G 5
Lorain .....78,185..B 8
Lore City ....401..F 10
Loudonville .2,865..D 8
Louisville ...6,298..E 16
Loveland ...7,144..K 14
Lowell ....852..H 10
Lowellville ..1,836..C 12
Lucas ....771..D 8
Luckey ....996..B 5
Ludlow Falls .292..G 14
Lynchburg ..1,186..K 16
Lyndhurst .19,749..B 15
Lyons ....630..B 4
Macedonia ..6,375..C 15
Madeira ....6,713..K 14
Madison ....1,678..A 10
Madison North* ...6,882..A 10
Magnetic Springs .....349..E 6
Magnolia ...1,064..D 10
Maineville ....333..K 15
Malinta ......391..C 4
Malta ....1,017..G 9
Malvern ....1,256..D 10
Manchester .2,195..J 5
Mansfield .55,047.°D 7
Mantua ....1,199..C 16
Maple Heights ..34,093..B 15
Marble Cliff ..715..F 6
Marblehead ...726..B 7
Marengo ......330..E 7
Mariemont ..4,540..K 14
Marietta ..16,861.°H 10
Marion ....38,646.°E 6
Marion East* 1,079..E 6
Marshallville .693..E 14
Martins Ferry ....10,757..F 11
Martinsville ..500..K 16
Marysville ..5,744.°F 6
Mason ......5,677..K 14
Massillon ..32,539..F 15
Masury .....2,060..C 12
Maumee ...15,937..B 5
Mayfield* ...3,548..B 10
Mayfield Heights ..22,139..B 15
McArthur ...1,543.°H 7
McClure ......699..B 4
McComb ....1,329..C 5
McConnelsville ......2,107.°G 9
McDonald ..3,177..C 11
McGuffey ....704..D 5
Mechanicsburg ......1,686..F 5
Medina ....10,913.°C 9
Melrose ......302..C 3
Mendon ....672..D 3
Mentor ....36,912..A 16
Mentor-on-the-Lake .....6,517..A 16
Metamora .....594..A 4
Miamisburg 14,797..I 14
Middleburg Heights ..12,367..C 14
Middlefield ..1,726..B 10
Middlepoint ..543..D 3
Middleport ..2,784..I 8
Middletown 48,767..J 14
Midland ......388..K 16
Midvale .....636..E 10
Midway ......318..G 5
Milan ......1,862..C 7
Milford .....4,828..K 14
Milford Center 753..F 5
Millbury ......771..B 5
Millersburg .2,979.°E 9
Millersport ...777..G 7
Millville ......697..J 13
Mineral City ..860..E 10
Minerva ....4,359..D 10
Minerva Park ......1,402..F 7
Mingo Junction ......5,278..E 11
Minster .....2,405..E 3
Mogadore ...4,825..D 15
Monroe .....3,492..J 14
Monroeville 1,455..C 7
Montgomery* ..5,683..H 3
Montpelier ..4,184..B 3
Moraine ....4,898..I 15
Moreland Hills* ....2,952..B 10
Morral ....452..D 6
Morristown ...385..F 10
Morrow .....1,486..K 15
Moscow ......348..I 4
Mount Blanchard ..473..D 5
Mount Cory ..302..D 5
Mount Gilead 2,971.°E 7
Mount Healthy ...7,446..K 13
Mount Orab .1,306..I 4
Mount Pleasant ...635..F 11
Mount Sterling ...1,536..G 6
Mount Vernon ..13,373.°E 7
Mount Victory 633..E 5
Mowrystown ..465..I 5
Munroe Falls 3,794..D 15
Murray City ..562..H 8
Napoleon ...7,791.°B 4
Navarre .....1,607..D 10
Nelsonville ..4,812..H 8
Nevada ....917..D 6
New Albany ..513..F 7
New Alexandria .425..E 11
New Athens ..450..F 11
New Bloomington ......343..E 6
New Boston .3,325..J 7
New Bremen 2,185..E 3
New Carlisle 6,112..G 15
New Concord 2,318..F 9
New Holland .796..G 6
New Knoxville 852..E 4
New Lebanon 4,248..H 14
New Lexington ....4,921.°G 8
New London 2,336..C 8
New Madison .959..G 12
New Matamoras ......940..H 11
New Miami .3,273..J 13
New Middletown ......1,664..C 12
New Paris ..1,692..H 12
New Philadelphia ..15,184.°E 10
New Richmond .....2,650..I 4
New Riegel ...340..C 6
New Straitsville ....947..G 8
New Vienna ..849..H 5
New Washington .....1,251..D 7
New Waterford 735..D 11
Newark ...41,836.°F 8
Newburgh Heights ...3,396..B 14
Newcomerstown ......4,155..E 9
Newton Falls 5,378..C 11
Newtonsville ..385..K 15
Newtown ....2,038..K 14
Ney ....378..B 3
Niles ......21,581..C 11
North Baltimore 3,143..C 5
North Bend ...638..K 12
North Canton ..15,228..E 15
North College Hill .....12,363..K 13
North Fairfield ...540..C 7
North Hampton ...489..G 16
North Kingsville .2,458..A 11
North Lewisburg ..840..F 5
North Mount Vernon [-Academia] .....1,447..E 7
North Olmsted .34,861..B 13
North Perry ..851..A 10
North Randall* .1,212..B 9
North Ridgeville .....13,152..B 13
North Robinson ...277..D 7
North Royalton .12,807..C 14
North Star ...296..E 3
North Zanesville* .....3,399..F 8
Northfield ..4,283..C 15
Northridge .10,084..H 14
Northwood* .4,222..B 5
Norton* ...12,308..D 9
Norwalk ...13,386.°C 7
Norwood ...30,420..K 13
Oak Harbor .2,807..B 6
Oak Hill ....1,642..I 7
Oakwood* ...3,127..B 10
Oakwood ......804..C 3
Oakwood ....10,095..H 15
Oberlin .....8,761..C 8
Obetz ....2,248..G 6
Ohio City .....816..D 3
Olmsted Falls 2,504..B 13
Ontario .....4,345..D 7
Orange* ....2,112..B 10
Oregon ....16,563..B 6
Orient ....313..G 6
Orrville .....7,408..E 14
Orwell ....965..B 11
Osgood ....289..E 3
Ostrander .....399..F 6
Ottawa ......3,622.°C 4
Ottawa Hills 4,270..B 5
Ottoville ......914..D 4
Overlook-Page Manor* ..19,719..G 4
Owensville ....707..K 15
Oxford .....15,868..J 12
Page Manor, see Overlook-Page Manor
Painesville .16,536.°A 10
Painesville Southwest* 5,461..A 10
Pandora ......857..D 4
Parma ....100,216..B 14
Parma Heights ..27,192..B 14
Parral ....271..E 10
Pataskala ...1,831..F 7
Paulding ...2,983.°C 3
Payne ......1,351..C 3
Peebles .....1,629..I 6
Pemberville .1,301..B 5
Peninsula ....692..C 15
Pepper Pike* 5,382..B 10
Perry ....917..A 10
Perrysburg ..7,693..B 5
Perrysville ....752..D 8
Phillipsburg ..831..H 14
Philo ....846..G 9
Pickerington ..696..G 7
Piketon .....1,347..I 6
Pioneer ....968..B 3
Piqua .....20,741..F 4
Pitsburg ......462..G 13
Plain City ..2,254..F 6
Plains, The .1,568..H 8
Pleasant City .494..G 10
Pleasant Hill 1,025..F 3
Pleasantville .754..G 7
Plymouth ...1,993..D 7
Poland .....3,097..C 11
Polk ....435..D 8
Pomeroy ....2,672.°I 8
Port Clinton 7,202.°B 6
Port Jefferson 416..E 4
Port Washington ......550..E 10
Port William .323..J 16
Portage ......494..C 5
Portsmouth 27,633.°J 6
Potsdam ......311..G 14
Powell ....374..F 6
Powhatan Point .....2,167..G 11
Proctorville ...881..K 8
Prospect ....1,031..E 6
Put-in-Bay ...135..B 7
Quaker City ..510..F 10
Quincy ....686..E 4
Racine ....583..I 9
Ravenna ...11,780.°C 10
Rawson ....466..D 5
Rayland ....617..F 11
Reading ....14,617..K 14
Reno Beach* 1,049..B 6
Republic .....705..C 6
Reynoldsburg .....13,921..F 7
Richmond ......777..E 11
Richmond Heights ...9,220..A 15
Richwood ...2,072..E 6
Ridgeway .....379..E 5
Rio Grande ...814..I 8
Ripley ......2,745..J 5
Risingsun ....730..C 5
Rittman .....6,308..E 14
Riverlea ......558..F 6
Riverside ...1,107..H 15
Rock Creek ..731..B 11
Rockford ....1,207..D 3
Rocky Ridge ..385..B 6
Rocky River ....22,958..B 13
Rogers ....310..D 11
Rosemount* .1,786..J 7
Roseville ....1,767..G 8
Ross* ....1,661..H 3
Rossburg .....275..E 3
Rossford ....5,302..B 5
Roswell ......317..E 10
Rushsylvania .526..E 5
Rushville ....289..G 8
Russells Point .....1,104..E 4
Russellville ...399..I 5
Russia ....420..F 3
Rutland ......663..I 8
Sabina .....2,160..H 5
St. Bernard .6,080..K 13
St. Clairsville ......4,754.°F 11
St. Henry ...1,276..E 3
St. Louisville .385..F 8
St. Marys ...7,699..E 3
St. Paris ....1,646..F 4
Salem ......14,186..D 11
Salineville ..1,686..D 11
Sandusky ..32,674.°B 7
Sandusky South* ..8,501..B 7
Sardinia .....824..I 5
Savannah .....361..D 8
Scio ....1,002..E 10
Scott ....329..C 3
Seaman ......866..I 5
Sebring ....4,954..D 11
Senecaville ...497..F 10
Seven Hills 12,700..B 14
Seven Mile ...699..J 13
Seville ......1,402..E 13
Shadyside ..5,070..F 11
Shaker Heights ..36,306..B 15
Sharon West* ....3,120..B 11
Sharonville 11,393..K 14
Shawnee .....914..G 8
Shawnee Hills 428..F 6
Sheffield ...1,730..B 12
Sheffield Lake .....8,734..B 12
Shelby ......9,847..D 7
Sherrodsville .400..E 10
Sherwood .....784..C 3
Shiloh ....817..D 7
Shiloh* ....11,368..G 4
Shreve ......1,635..D 8
Sidney .....16,332.°E 4
Silver Lake .3,637..D 15
Silverton ...6,588..K 14
Smithfield ..1,245..E 11
Smithville ..1,278..E 13
Solon .....11,519..B 15
Somerset ...1,417..G 8
Somerville ....388..I 13
South Amherst ..2,913..B 8
South Bloomfield .610..G 6
South Charleston 1,500..G 5
South Euclid ...29,579..B 15
South Lebanon ..3,014..K 15
South Mount Vernon ...1,044..E 7
South Point .2,243..K 7
South Russell 2,673..B 16
South Solon ..415..G 5
South Webster 825..J 7
South Zanesville ......1,436..G 8
Spencer ....758..D 12
Spencerville 2,241..D 4
Spring Valley 667..I 15
Springboro ..2,799..I 14
Springdale ..8,127..K 13
Springfield 81,941.°F 5
Steubenville 30,771.°E 11
Stockport ......471..G 9
Stony Prairie 1,913..B 6
Stoutsville ....573..G 7
Stow ......19,847..D 15
Strasburg ...1,874..E 9
Stratton ....386..E 11
Streetsboro* 7,966..C 10
Strongsville 15,182..C 14
Struthers ..15,343..C 11
Stryker .....1,296..B 3
Sugar Grove ..469..G 7
Sugarcreek ..1,771..E 9
Summerfield ..306..G 10
Sunbury ....1,820..F 7
Swanton ....2,927..B 5
Sycamore ....1,096..D 6
Sylvania ...12,031..A 5
Syracuse ......684..I 9
Tallmadge .15,274..D 15
Tarlton ....412..H 7
Terrace Park 2,266..K 14
Thornville ....679..G 8
Thurston .....428..G 7
Tiffin .....21,596.°C 6
Tiltonsville .2,123..F 11
Timberlake ...964..A 15
Tipp City ...5,090..G 15
Tiro ....310..D 7
Toledo ...383,105.°B 5
Tontogany ....395..B 5
Toronto .....7,705..E 11
Tremont City .426..F 5
Trenton .....5,278..J 13
Trimble ....542..H 8
Trotwood ....6,997..H 14
Troy ......17,186.°F 4
Tuscarawas ..830..E 10
Twinsburg ..6,432..C 15
Uhrichsville 5,731..E 10
Union ......3,654..H 14
Union City .1,808..F 3
Uniopolis ....291..E 4
University Heights .17,055..B 15
Upper Arlington 38,727..F 6
Upper Sandusky .5,645.°D 6
Urbana ....11,237.°F 5
Urbancrest ...754..G 6
Utica ....1,977..F 8
Valley View* 1,422..B 9
Valley View* .909..F 6
Van Buren ...319..C 5
Van Wert .11,320.°D 3
Vandalia ..10,796..H 15
Vanlue ....539..D 5
Vermilion ...9,872..B 8
Verona ....593..H 13
Versailles ...2,441..F 3
Vienna ....545..F 5
Vinton ....352..I 8
Wadsworth 13,142..D 14
Waite Hill ....514..A 15
Wakeman .....822..C 8
Walbridge ..3,208..B 5
Waldo ....428..E 6
Walton Hills* 2,508..B 9
Wapakoneta 7,324.°E 4
Warren ....63,494.°C 11
Warrensville Heights ..18,925..B 15
Warsaw ......725..E 8
Washington ..346..F 10
Washington Court House ...12,495.°H 5
Washingtonville ....747..D 11
Waterville ..2,940..B 5
Wauseon ...4,932.°B 4
Waverly ....4,858.°I 6
Wayne ....921..C 5
Waynesburg 1,337..D 10
Waynesfield ..704..E 4
Waynesville .1,638..J 15
Wellington ..4,137..C 8
Wellston ...5,410..I 7
Wellsville ...5,891..D 11
West Alexandria 1,553..H 13
West Carrollton 10,748..I 14
West Elkton ..291..I 13
West Farmington 650..B 11
West Jefferson .3,664..F 6
West Lafayette .1,719..E 9
West Leipsic ..378..C 4
West Liberty 1,580..F 5
West Manchester .469..H 13
West Mansfield ..753..E 5
West Milton 3,696..G 14
West Portsmouth ....3,396..J 6
West Richfield .....3,228..C 14
West Salem .1,058..E 12
West Union .1,951.°J 5
West Unity .1,359..B 3
West View* .2,523..C 9
Westerville 12,530..F 7
Westfield Center .....715..D 13
Westlake ..15,689..B 13
Weston .....1,269..C 5
Wharton ......422..D 5
Wheelersburg 3,709..J 7
Whitehall ..25,263..F 7
Whitehouse .1,542..B 5
Wickliffe ..21,354..A 15
Willard .....5,510..C 7
Williamsburg 2,054..I 4
Williamsport .857..G 6
Willoughby 18,634..A 15
Willoughby Hills .....5,247..A 15
Willowick ..21,237..A 15
Willshire ......623..D 3
Wilmington 10,051.°H 5
Wilmot ....378..D 9
Winchester ...760..I 5
Windham ...3,360..C 10
Wintersville .4,921..E 11
Woodlawn ...3,251..K 13
Woodmere* ..1,041..B 10
Woodsfield .3,239.°G 10
Woodstock .....281..F 5
Woodville ...1,834..B 6
Woodworth* 1,054..D 11
Wooster ...18,703.°D 9
Worthington 15,326..F 6
Wren ....282..D 3
Wright-Patterson* ...10,151..H 15
Wyoming ...9,089..K 13
Xenia .....25,373.°G 4
Yellow Springs ...4,624..H 16
Yorkville ...1,656..F 11
Youngstown ....140,909.°C 11
Zaleski ....304..H 8
Zanesville .33,045.°F 8

°County seat.
*Does not appear on the map; key shows general location.

Source: Latest census figures (1970).

The 1970 United States census reported that Ohio had 10,652,017 persons, the sixth highest population among the states. Ohio's population had increased about 10 per cent over the 1960 figure of 9,706,397. The U.S. Bureau of the Census estimated that by 1975 the state's population had reached about 10,759,000.

About three-fourths of Ohio's people live in urban areas, and the rest make their homes in rural communities. Almost a third live in the metropolitan areas of Cincinnati and Cleveland. In all, Ohio has 15 Standard Metropolitan Statistical Areas that lie chiefly within the state. Ohio cities also help make up two metropolitan areas in bordering states (see METROPOLITAN AREA). For the names and populations of these metropolitan areas, see the *Index* to the political map of Ohio.

Cleveland, with a population of 750,879, is the largest city in Ohio. Ohio has five other cities with populations of more than 200,000. These cities are, in order of size, Columbus, Cincinnati, Toledo, Akron, and Dayton. See the separate articles on the cities of Ohio listed in the *Related Articles* at the end of this article.

About 97 of every 100 Ohioans were born in the United States. A majority of those born in other countries came from Germany, Great Britain, Hungary, Italy, Poland, and Yugoslavia.

Protestant churches have the largest membership in Ohio. Roman Catholics form the largest single religious group. Large Protestant groups in the state include Lutherans, Methodists, Presbyterians, and members of the United Church of Christ.

Ohio Dept. of Industrial and Economic Development

The Children's Zoo in Cleveland, Ohio's largest city, is a favorite attraction for children. In this part of the zoo, called "The Red Barn," a child can pet his favorite farm animals.

An Amish Family of Holmes County gathers for a quiet evening at home. These hardworking people lead simple lives and avoid modern ways. The women wear full-skirted dresses and sunbonnets. The men have beards. All the family's clothing is homemade. The Amish have lived in Ohio since the 1800's.

Cornell Capa, Magnum

POPULATION

This map shows the *population density* of Ohio, and how it varies in different parts of the state. Population density means the average number of persons who live in a given area.

Persons per sq. mi.	Persons per km²
More than 200	More than 77
90 to 200	35 to 77
Less than 90	Less than 35

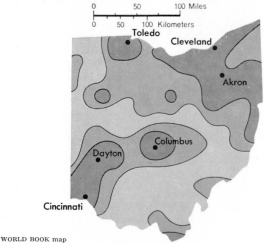

WORLD BOOK map

Schools. The first school in Ohio opened in 1773 at Schoenbrunn, near present-day New Philadelphia. It was set up for Indian children by David Zeisberger, a Moravian missionary. Ohio's public-school system began in 1825, and public high schools were authorized in 1853. During the 1800's, several Ohio educators wrote school textbooks that were used throughout the United States. The most famous of these educators was William H. McGuffey (see McGUFFEY, WILLIAM H.).

Many colleges were founded in Ohio during the 1800's, several of them by churches. Oberlin College, established in 1833, became the country's first college for both men and women.

All elementary and high schools in Ohio are under the supervision of the state board of education. This board heads the state department of education. It consists of 23 members elected to six-year terms. These members appoint the state superintendent of public instruction. Each of the state colleges and universities is supervised by a board of trustees appointed by the governor. Ohio law requires children between the ages of 6 and 18 to attend school. For the number of students and teachers in Ohio, see EDUCATION (table).

Libraries. A subscription library opened at Belpre in 1796. In 1804, the famous Coonskin Library was founded at Ames (now Amesville). Pioneers bought its first 51 books with skins of raccoons and other animals. Many of these books have been preserved by the Ohio Historical Society in Columbus. In 1817, Governor Thomas Worthington established the Ohio State Library in Columbus as a reference library for state officials. Ohio has about 250 tax-supported public libraries and library systems and about 385 branch libraries.

Cleveland is the largest library center in Ohio. The Cleveland Public Library is one of the biggest in the nation. Other large libraries include the Cincinnati Public Library, the University of Cincinnati Library, and the Ohio State University Library in Columbus.

The Rutherford B. Hayes Library in Fremont honors the 19th President of the United States. It opened in 1916 and was the nation's first presidential library. The Cincinnati Historical Society has a collection on early Ohio and metropolitan Cincinnati. The Martha Kinney Cooper Ohioana Library in Columbus collects the works of Ohio authors and books about Ohio.

Museums. The Cleveland Museum of Art owns the Severance collection of arms and armor, and several items from the famous Guelph Treasure from Germany. The Cincinnati Art Museum is well known for its Greek and Roman statues and other art objects. The Taft Museum in Cincinnati displays excellent collections of paintings and Chinese porcelain. The Toledo Museum of Art has a display of glass from all parts of the world.

Exhibits at the Ohio Historical Society in Columbus show the history of the state. The U.S. Air Force Museum, the only one of its kind, is at Wright-Patterson Air Force Base near Dayton. Its exhibits range from airplanes of World War I to jet aircraft.

UNIVERSITIES AND COLLEGES

Ohio has 59 universities and colleges accredited by the North Central Association of Colleges and Schools. For enrollments and further information, see UNIVERSITIES AND COLLEGES (table).

Name	Location	Founded	Name	Location	Founded
Air Force Institute of Technology	Wright-Patterson Air Force Base	1946	Lutheran Theological Seminary	Columbus	1830
Akron, University of	Akron	1870	Malone College	Canton	1957
Antioch College	Yellow Springs	1852	Marietta College	Marietta	1835
Ashland College	Ashland	1878	Miami University	Oxford	1809
Athenaeum of Ohio	Cincinnati	1829	Mount St. Joseph on the Ohio, College of	Mount St. Joseph	1852
Baldwin-Wallace College	Berea	1845	Mount Union College	Alliance	1846
Bluffton College	Bluffton	1900	Mount Vernon Nazarene College	Mount Vernon	1974
Borromeo College of Ohio	Wickliffe	1953	Muskingum College	New Concord	1837
Bowling Green State University	Bowling Green	1910	Notre Dame College	Cleveland	1922
Capital University	Columbus	1830	Oberlin College	Oberlin	1833
Case Western Reserve University	Cleveland	1826	Ohio Dominican College	Columbus	1911
Cedarville College	Cedarville	1887	Ohio Northern University	Ada	1871
Central State University	Wilberforce	1887	Ohio State University	*	*
Cincinnati, University of	Cincinnati	1819	Ohio University	Athens	1804
Cleveland Institute of Art	Cleveland	1946	Ohio Wesleyan University	Delaware	1842
Cleveland State University	Cleveland	1923	Otterbein College	Westerville	1847
Dayton, University of	Dayton	1850	Rio Grande College	Rio Grande	1883
Defiance College	Defiance	1850	Steubenville, College of	Steubenville	1946
Denison University	Granville	1831	Toledo, University of	Toledo	1872
Edgecliff College	Cincinnati	1935	United Theological Seminary	Dayton	1871
Findlay College	Findlay	1882	Urbana College	Urbana	1850
Franklin University	Columbus	1902	Ursuline College	Cleveland	1871
Hebrew Union College— Jewish Institute of Religion	Cincinnati	1875	Walsh College	Canton	1960
Heidelberg College	Tiffin	1850	Wilberforce University	Wilberforce	1856
Hiram College	Hiram	1850	Wilmington College	Wilmington	1870
John Carroll University	Cleveland	1886	Wittenberg University	Springfield	1845
Kent State University	Kent	1910	Wooster, College of	Wooster	1866
Kenyon College	Gambier	1824	Wright State University	Dayton	1967
Lake Erie College	Painesville	1856	Xavier University	Cincinnati	1831
			Youngstown State University	Youngstown	1908

*For campuses and founding dates, see UNIVERSITIES AND COLLEGES (table).

OHIO / A Visitor's Guide

Ohio has hundreds of historical, recreational, and scenic attractions. Historical points of interest include huge Indian burial mounds and forts that date back to prehistoric times.

Ohio's 2,500 lakes and 44,000 miles (70,800 kilometers) of rivers and streams offer boating, fishing, and swimming. Hunters shoot deer, ducks, and rabbits in the state's woods and on the rolling plains. Many vacationers enjoy hiking in Ohio's hilly eastern section, which has some of the state's most beautiful scenery.

Great Serpent Mound

PLACES TO VISIT

Following are brief descriptions of some of Ohio's most interesting places to visit.

Adena State Memorial, in Chillicothe, is a restored stone house built in 1807 by Thomas Worthington, who later became governor of Ohio. It is furnished with rare American antiques of the 1700's and early 1800's.

Blue Hole, a flowing spring near Castalia, pours forth 10 million gallons (38 million liters) of water daily. It has a constant temperature of 48° F. (9° C).

Campus Martius Museum, in Marietta, has been a state memorial since 1919. It stands on the site of the fortified stockade built by the first permanent white settlers in Ohio. The museum includes the home of Rufus Putnam, the founder of Marietta. Also on exhibit are models, pictures, and relics of riverboats.

Fort Recovery, in the village of Fort Recovery, is a reproduction of part of the fort built in 1793 by General Anthony Wayne. He used the fort during the Indian wars in Ohio.

Indian Mounds and Other Earthworks may be seen throughout the state. *Fort Ancient*, near Lebanon, is the largest hilltop earth structure in the United States. Its earthen walls, more than 20 feet (6 meters) high and 3 miles (5 kilometers) long, enclose over 100 acres (40 hectares). *Fort Hill*, near Bainbridge, is a 1,200-acre (486-hectare) area with a great walled enclosure on a high hill. Nature trails cross the area. *Great Serpent Mound*, near Hillsboro, is one of the best-known prehistoric structures in the world. The mound, shaped like a snake, has seven deep curves. It rises about 4 feet (1.2 meters) and extends over $\frac{1}{4}$ mile (0.4 kilometer). *Newark Earthworks*, at Newark, has circular walls 1,200 feet (366 meters) in diameter and 8 to 14 feet (2.4 to 4.3 meters) high. They enclose an earthen mound.

Kelleys Island, in Lake Erie near Sandusky, is a summer resort famous for its glacial markings and Inscription Rock. The markings—grooves cut into surface limestone by glaciers—are among the best examples of glacial action in the world. Inscription Rock is a large boulder with traces of prehistoric Indian carvings.

McKinley Memorial, in Canton, is the burial place of President and Mrs. William McKinley. It is a circular, domed structure that is 75 feet (23 meters) in diameter at the base and stands 97 feet (30 meters) high.

National Professional Football Hall of Fame, in Canton, honors outstanding professional football players. It includes a museum of equipment worn by famous players and used in famous games.

Rutherford B. Hayes Library and Museum, in Fremont, are at the former President's Spiegel Grove estate. The library has papers of Hayes and books on American life during the 1800's. The museum features exhibits on the life and times of Hayes and his family.

Schoenbrunn Village, near New Philadelphia, consists of reconstructed portions of the Moravian mission settlement founded there in 1772 for Indians. It includes a replica of the first schoolhouse in what is now Ohio.

Wright-Patterson Air Force Base, near Dayton, is the largest U.S. Air Force research field in the United States. The base includes the field on which the Wright brothers conducted their airplane experiments, and a national aeronautics museum. See WRIGHT-PATTERSON AIR FORCE BASE.

Zoar Village, near New Philadelphia, was founded in 1817 by a group of Germans seeking freedom from religious persecution. The home of their leader, Joseph Bimeler, and the old Zoar Garden can be seen.

National Forests and Parklands. Wayne National Forest, the only national forest in Ohio, lies in the southeastern part of the state. It was established as a national forest in 1934. For the forest's area and chief features, see NATIONAL FOREST (table). Perry's Victory and International Peace Memorial stands at Put-in-Bay on South Bass Island in Lake Erie. The memorial was completed in 1915. It honors the American victory in the Battle of Lake Erie during the War of 1812, and a hundred years of peace between the United States and Canada. The granite shaft, 352 feet (107 meters) high, is one of the nation's tallest memorials. It has an observation deck at the top. Mound City Group National Monument, near Chillicothe, has many prehistoric Indian mounds. The Cuyahoga Valley National Recreation Area stretches along the Cuyahoga River between Akron and Cleveland.

State Parks and Forests. Ohio has 62 state parks and 19 state forests. For information on the state parks of Ohio write to Chief, Division of Parks and Recreation, Fountain Square, Columbus, Ohio 43224.

Steve Bulkley, Foto/Find

Ohio Outdoor Historical Drama Association, Inc.

Outdoor Historical Play

Tom Root, Foto/Find

Schoenbrunn Village   **Geauga County Maple Festival**

Perry's Victory Memorial

Football Hall of Fame

Shostal

Frank Muth, Foto/Find

G. Warstler, Foto/Find

ANNUAL EVENTS

Two outdoor historical plays rank among Ohio's most popular annual events. "Tecumseh," a drama about the famous Shawnee Indian, is held near Chillicothe. "Trumpet in the Land," which concerns Ohio's first permanent white settlement, is performed near New Philadelphia. Both plays are presented from June to September. Other annual events include:

January-March: Butler Institute Art Show in Youngstown (January); American-Canadian Sports Show in Cleveland (March); Buzzard Sunday in Hinckley (first Sunday after March 15).

April-June: Geauga County Maple Festival in Chardon (April); International Festival in Toledo (early in May); May Music Festival in Cincinnati; Annual show of work by Cleveland artists (throughout May); Boy Scout Camporee in Greenville (second week in June);

National Clay Week Festival in Uhrichsville-Dennison (third week in June).

July-September: Steam Threshers Festival in London (July); Ohio Hills Folk Festival in Quaker City (July); Inter-Lake Yachting Association Regatta in Put-in-Bay (August); Portsmouth Regatta (August); Parade of the Hills in Nelsonville (August); Ohio State Fair in Columbus (late August-early September); Melon Festival in Milan (Labor Day Weekend); Jackson Apple Festival (September); Swiss Festival in Sugarcreek (September); Ohio State Farm Science Review at Ohio State University in Columbus (late in September).

October-December: Holmes County Antique Festival in Millersburg (early in October); Apple Butter Festival in Burton (October); Pumpkin Show in Circleville (October).

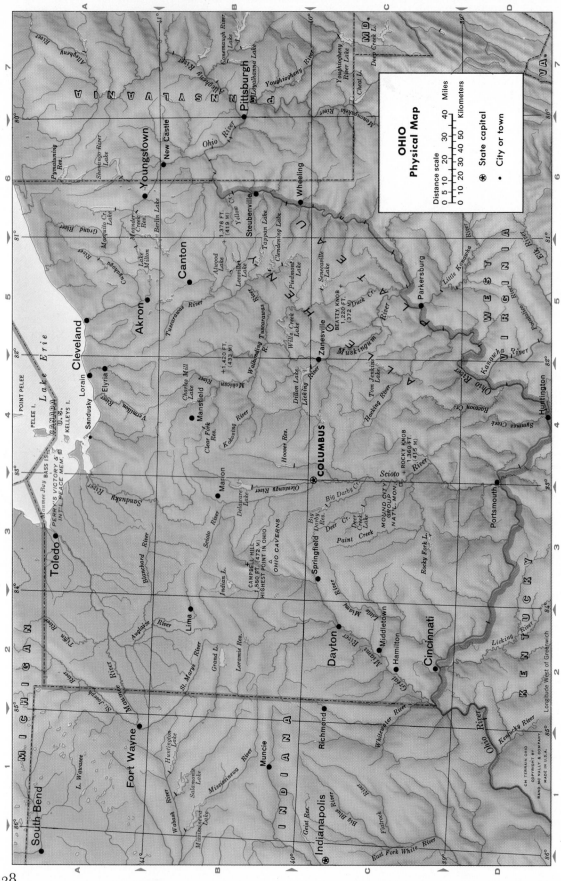

OHIO
Physical Map

Distance scale

| Miles |
| Kilometers |

⊕ State capital
• City or town

⊕ PERRY'S VICTORY & INTL PEACE MEM.

Specially created for **World Book Encyclopedia** by Rand McNally and World Book editors

528

Land Regions. Several glaciers moved down from the north thousands of years ago, during the Ice Age. They covered all of what is now Ohio except the southeastern part. These separate glacial movements helped create the state's four main land regions. These four regions are (1) the Great Lakes Plains, (2) the Till Plains, (3) the Appalachian Plateau, and (4) the Bluegrass Region.

The Great Lakes Plains of northern Ohio form part of the fertile lowland that lies along much of the Great Lakes. In Ohio, these plains make up a narrow strip of land that borders Lake Erie. The region is 5 to 10 miles (8 to 16 kilometers) wide in the east, and broadens to more than 50 miles (80 kilometers) in the Maumee Valley to the west. A few low, sandy ridges along the Lake Erie shore break the flatness of the plains. A wide variety of crops, especially fruits and vegetables, grows in the region's fertile soil. The region is one of the busiest manufacturing, shipping, and trading areas in the United States. It includes many lake ports and large industrial cities. The most heavily populated part of Ohio, the Cleveland metropolitan area, is in this region.

The Till Plains are the easternmost part of the rich midwestern Corn Belt, which stretches westward from Ohio. This region ranks among the most fertile farming areas in the country.

Some hills dot the gently rolling plains, which lie in most of western Ohio. One of them, Campbell Hill in Logan County, rises 1,550 feet (472 meters) and is the highest point in Ohio. From there, the land gradually slopes downward to the southwestern corner of the state in Hamilton County. This area, 433 feet (132 meters) above sea level, is Ohio's lowest point. Farmers of the Till Plains produce much grain and livestock. The area has many industrial cities where a wide variety of products is manufactured.

The Appalachian Plateau includes almost all the eastern half of Ohio. This highland extends eastward into Pennsylvania and West Virginia. The southern two-thirds of the region was not covered by glaciers. As a result, this section is the most rugged part of the state,

with steep hills and valleys. Most of the soil is thin and not fertile. The northern third of the Appalachian Plateau has rolling hills and valleys, and has less fertile soil than that of the Till Plains.

The rugged Appalachian Plateau has some of the most beautiful scenery in Ohio, including the state's largest forests and some waterfalls. It also has Ohio's richest mineral deposits—clay, coal, natural gas, oil, and salt. A few of its cities are important manufacturing centers.

The Bluegrass Region, Ohio's smallest land region, is an extension of the Bluegrass Region of Kentucky. This triangular area in southern Ohio has both hilly and gently rolling land. The hills of the Bluegrass Region have thin, less fertile soil.

Shoreline of Ohio stretches for 312 miles (502 kilometers) along Lake Erie, from Conneaut in the east to Toledo in the west. It includes 53 miles (85 kilometers) along Sandusky Bay, and 66 miles (106 kilometers) along offshore islands. The shoreline is mainly rocky,

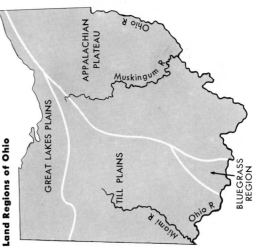

Meier's Wine Cellars, Inc.

Grape Packers stack wooden boxes of fruit for shipment to a winery in Sandusky. Fruits and vegetables grow well in the fertile soil of northern Ohio. This area is in the Great Lakes Plains region.

Land Regions of Ohio

Winter Snow covers a Marion County farm, *left.* This area of the Till Plains includes some of the country's most fertile farmland.

The Ohio River, *right,* forms Ohio's southern border. Gallipolis, settled in the 1790's, overlooks West Virginia across the river.

Gently Rolling Land of Highland County, *below,* has deep, fertile soil. The land forms part of the Bluegrass Region, a triangular section in southern Ohio.

with a few sandy beaches such as that at Cedar Point. Many fine harbors indent the shoreline. Two of the busy lake ports lie on large bays—Toledo on Maumee Bay, and Sandusky on Sandusky Bay. North and northwest of Sandusky in Lake Erie are some small islands. The largest ones are Kelleys and North, Middle, and South Bass islands. They are used chiefly as recreation areas.

Rivers and Lakes. Ohio has more than 44,000 miles (70,800 kilometers) of rivers and streams. They flow either south into the Ohio River or north into Lake Erie. A series of low hills separates the two groups of rivers. This *divide* forms an irregular line from the northeastern corner of Ohio to Mercer County, where it extends into Indiana. Except for the Maumee River, all the longer, wider rivers flow into the Ohio River. They drain about 70 per cent of the state.

The Ohio River, one of the chief rivers of North America, flows more than 450 miles (724 kilometers) along Ohio's southern and southeastern borders. The northern bank of the river forms the state boundary. Many bluffs from 200 to 500 feet (61 to 150 meters) high rise along the river, which winds through a valley less than 2 miles (3 kilometers) wide.

The Ohio River's longest tributary in Ohio is the Scioto River, which is 237 miles (381 kilometers) long. Other rivers flowing into the Ohio include the Hocking, Little Miami, Mahoning, Miami, and Muskingum. The largest rivers that flow into Lake Erie are the Cuya-

hoga, Grand, Huron, Maumee, Portage, Sandusky, and Vermilion. Some underground streams have formed caverns, such as Seven Caves near Bainbridge and Ohio Caverns near West Liberty. Many swift streams in the northeastern section of the state have rapids and waterfalls.

Ohio's lake waters include 3,457 square miles (8,954 square kilometers) of Lake Erie. The International Line between the United States and Canada runs through Lake Erie about 20 miles (32 kilometers) north of the Ohio shore. The state has more than 2,500 lakes larger than 2 acres (0.8 hectare). Over 20 of them are natural lakes with an area of 40 acres (16 hectares) or more. These lakes have beds formed by the ancient glaciers. Ohio also has more than 180 man-made lakes that cover at least 40 acres (16 hectares) each.

Several man-made lakes were built during the 1800's to feed water into two canals. These canals were the Ohio and Erie Canal, between Cleveland and Portsmouth, and the Miami and Erie Canal, between Toledo and Cincinnati. They were Ohio's chief means of transportation until the coming of the railroads. The largest lake in Ohio is 12,700-acre (5,140-hectare) Grand Lake near Indiana. It was created during the 1840's by damming two nearby creeks to provide water for the Miami and Erie Canal. Other large artificial lakes include Berlin, Indian, Mosquito Creek, and Seneca-ville lakes.

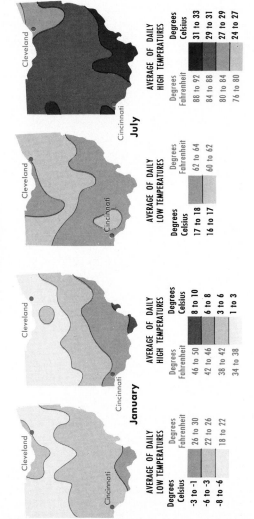

January

AVERAGE OF DAILY LOW TEMPERATURES

Degrees Fahrenheit	Degrees Celsius
26 to 30	-3 to -1
22 to 26	-6 to -3
18 to 22	-8 to -6

AVERAGE OF DAILY HIGH TEMPERATURES

Degrees Fahrenheit	Degrees Celsius
46 to 50	8 to 10
42 to 46	6 to 8
38 to 42	3 to 6
34 to 38	1 to 3

July

AVERAGE OF DAILY LOW TEMPERATURES

Degrees Celsius	Degrees Fahrenheit
17 to 18	62 to 64
16 to 17	60 to 62

AVERAGE OF DAILY HIGH TEMPERATURES

Degrees Fahrenheit	Degrees Celsius
88 to 92	31 to 33
84 to 88	29 to 31
80 to 84	27 to 29
76 to 80	24 to 27

Shostal

Autumn in Ohio is a season of colorful landscapes. Lake Hope, near Zaleski, is a man-made lake that attracts many tourists.

OHIO/Climate

Ohio has cold winters and warm, humid summers, with an average annual temperature of 52° F. (11° C). The average January temperature is 31° F. (−1° C), and the July temperature averages 74° F. (23° C). Ohio's lowest recorded temperature, −39° F. (−39° C), occurred at Milligan on Feb. 10, 1899. The highest temperature was 113° F. (45° C) at Thurman on July 4, 1897, and near Gallipolis on July 21, 1934.

Ohio's annual *precipitation* (rain, melted snow, and other moisture) averages 37 inches (94 centimeters) a year. The wettest area is in the southwest, where Wilmington's yearly precipitation is 44 inches (112 centimeters). The driest part of Ohio lies along Lake Erie between Sandusky and Toledo. It gets 32 inches (81 centimeters) of precipitation a year. Snowfall of Ohio averages 29 inches (74 centimeters) a year. It increases from west to east, and from south to north.

AVERAGE YEARLY PRECIPITATION
(Rain, Melted Snow, and Other Moisture)

Centimeters	Inches
102 to 112	40 to 44
91 to 102	36 to 40
81 to 91	32 to 36

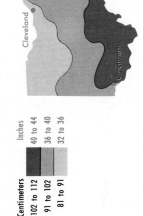

0	50	100	150 Miles
0	100	200 Kilometers	

WORLD BOOK maps

AVERAGE MONTHLY WEATHER

CLEVELAND

	Temperatures				Days of Rain or Snow
	F° High	Low	C° High	Low	
JAN.	36	21	2	-6	16
FEB.	36	21	2	-6	15
MAR.	45	28	7	-2	16
APR.	57	38	14	3	15
MAY	70	48	21	9	14
JUNE	80	58	27	14	11
JULY	85	63	29	17	10
AUG.	83	61	28	16	9
SEPT.	76	55	24	13	9
OCT.	64	45	18	7	10
NOV.	49	34	9	1	15
DEC.	38	25	3	-4	16

CINCINNATI

	Temperatures				Days of Rain or Snow
	F° High	Low	C° High	Low	
JAN.	41	25	5	-4	13
FEB.	43	27	6	-3	11
MAR.	53	34	12	1	13
APR.	64	43	18	6	12
MAY	74	53	23	12	12
JUNE	83	62	28	17	14
JULY	87	66	31	19	10
AUG.	85	64	29	18	10
SEPT.	80	58	27	14	9
OCT.	68	47	20	8	9
NOV.	53	36	12	2	10
DEC.	42	28	6	-2	11

The greatest source of income in Ohio is manufacturing. In fact, manufacturing provides all but a small share of the total value of all production in Ohio. Only California and New York rank above Ohio in industrial production. Several important natural advantages have helped develop Ohio's industries. They include large deposits of coal and other minerals, a plentiful water supply, and the state's central location near major markets and supplies of raw materials in other states.

Natural Resources. Fertile soils and valuable minerals are Ohio's most important natural resources. The state also has large forests and varied wildlife.

Soil. Fertile soils deposited by ancient glaciers are found in all parts of Ohio except the southeast. Many layers of these soils are several feet deep. Materials in the various kinds of soils include limestone, sandstone, and shale. Southeastern Ohio, which was not covered by glaciers during the Ice Age, has thin, infertile soil.

Minerals. Coal is Ohio's most important mineral. Deposits in eastern and southeastern Ohio have an estimated 21 billion short tons (19 billion metric tons) of coal. Oil and natural gas are found in several parts of Ohio. The state has about 125 million barrels of crude oil reserves. Ohio's minerals include huge reserves of rock salt and salt-water brine. The state could supply the United States with all the salt it needs for thousands of years. Most of the salt lies in deep rock-salt beds in northeastern Ohio. The state also has large deposits of clay, limestone, sand and gravel, and sandstone.

Forests cover about a fourth of Ohio. Most of the trees are hardwoods. They include beeches, black walnuts, hickories, maples, sycamores, red and white oaks, tulip trees, white ashes, and white elms. Nearly three-fourths of the state's lumber comes from farm wood lots. This wood consists of second-growth trees, which develop after the first growth of timber has been cut.

Animal Life. Ohio has few large wild animals, except white-tailed deer. Smaller wild animals include minks, muskrats, opossums, rabbits, raccoons, red foxes, squirrels, skunks, and woodchucks. Ohio has about 10 kinds of songbirds. Bald eagles and various shore birds live along Lake Erie. Game birds include ducks, geese, partridges, pheasants, quail, and ruffed grouse. Fish living in Ohio's waters include bass, bluegills, catfish, muskellunge, perch, and pike.

Manufacturing accounts for 92 per cent of the value of all goods produced in Ohio. Products manufactured in the state have a *value added by manufacture* of about $30 billion a year. This figure represents the value created in the products by Ohio's industries, not counting such costs as materials, supplies, and fuel.

Ohio's leading manufacturing activity is the production of nonelectrical machinery, with an annual value added by manufacture of about $4 billion. Ohio has long been a leader in the invention, improvement, and manufacture of farm machinery. Among the states, Ohio ranks third behind Michigan and Illinois in the manufacture of machine tools. Ohio factories also rank high in the manufacture of blast furnaces and rolling mills, heating and cooling equipment, office machinery, and refrigerating machinery. Dayton makes more cash registers than any other American city. Toledo has the

Production of Goods in Ohio

Total value of goods produced in 1973—$34,098,711,000

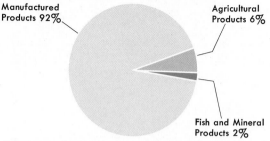

Manufactured Products 92%

Agricultural Products 6%

Fish and Mineral Products 2%

Percentages are based on farm income, value added by manufacture, and value of fish and mineral production. Fish products are less than 1 per cent.

Sources: U.S. government publications, 1975-1976.

Employment in Ohio

Total number of persons employed in 1974—4,340,100

		Number of Employees
Manufacturing	🧍🧍🧍🧍🧍🧍🧍🧍🧍🧍	1,415,400
Wholesale & Retail Trade	🧍🧍🧍🧍🧍🧍	876,100
Community, Business, & Personal Services	🧍🧍🧍🧍🧍	675,500
Government	🧍🧍🧍🧍	613,700
Transportation & Public Utilities	🧍🧍	229,900
Finance, Insurance, & Real Estate	🧍🧍	176,900
Construction	🧍🧍	169,200
Agriculture	🧍	159,000
Mining	🧍	24,400

Sources: *Employment and Earnings,* May 1975, U.S. Bureau of Labor Statistics; *Farm Labor,* February 1975, U.S. Department of Agriculture.

largest factory in the United States producing weighing scales.

The production of transportation equipment is Ohio's second-ranking manufacturing activity. This production has an annual value added of about $3¾ billion. Ohio ranks high among the states in the production of bus and truck bodies, motorcycles, and truck trailers. Cincinnati, Cleveland, Columbus, Hudson, Lorain, Toledo, and Twinsburg are major manufacturing centers for bodies and parts of automobiles and other motor vehicles. Elyria has the nation's largest factory producing automobile air brakes. Dayton is famous for the manufacture of airplane parts.

The third-ranking industry is the manufacture of primary metals, especially iron and steel. This industry's products have an annual value added by manufacture of about $3¼ billion. Among the states, only Pennsylvania's production is greater. Ohio's steel production totals about 20 million short tons (18.1 million metric tons) a year, about a sixth of the nation's total output. The chief steel mills in Ohio include those in the Cleveland-Lorain and Youngstown areas. Convenient transportation routes connect these areas with nearby supplies of coal and iron ore, used in steelmaking.

The manufacture of fabricated metal products is Ohio's fourth most important industry. This industry's products have an annual value added by manufacture

Libbey-Owens-Ford Glass Co.

Workers Examine Sheets of Plate Glass in a factory in Rossford. They use chalk to mark defects and cutting instructions on ground and polished glass. This eliminates waste when the sheets are cut. Ohio leads the states in the manufacture of glass products.

matches, musical instruments, paints and varnishes, and sporting goods. Many Ohio cities manufacture clothing and textiles. Papermaking, developed when the state was still heavily forested, is a profitable industry in Chillicothe, Hamilton, and Middletown. Publishing and printing are centered in Akron, Cincinnati, Cleveland, Columbus, and Dayton. Shipbuilding flourishes in Lorain. Several cities have oil refineries. Ohio ranks among the leading states in the production of coke. Important by-products of this steel-making fuel include chemicals, fertilizers, and tar.

Agriculture. Ohio has about 17,100,000 acres (6,920,-000 hectares) of farmland, and a farm population of about 371,000. The state's 111,000 farms average 154 acres (62.3 hectares) in size.

Agriculture in Ohio provides an annual income of about $2 billion. This amount is only 6 per cent of the state's total value of all production. The most valuable farm activity is the raising of meat animals. Ohio ranks among the leading hog-producing states. Farmers in the Miami River Valley developed the famous Poland China hog during the 1800's. But this breed is no longer produced in Ohio. A monument to the Poland China hog stands near Monroe.

Many farmers raise beef cattle or sheep. They raise both mutton and wool breeds of sheep, chiefly in the central part of the state. Ohio produces more wool than any other state east of the Mississippi River.

Dairy farming is Ohio's second-ranking livestock activity. About 95 per cent of the milk produced on the farms is sold in nearby cities. Cheese is a valuable by-product of the dairy industry. Tuscarawas County is called *America's Little Switzerland* because of its great Swiss cheese production. All Liederkranz cheese is produced in Van Wert.

Ohio cities provide a ready market for the state's large egg production. Poultry farmers also raise chickens and turkeys in hundreds of commercial hatcheries that produce about 30 million chickens a year.

Farmers in Ohio grow corn and wheat in nearly all parts of the state, especially in the Till Plains region. Ohio is a leading state in the production of corn. The state also ranks among the nation's leaders in the production of oats, popcorn, and soybeans. The state's farmers also grow crops of hay, mushrooms, red clover, and rye. They feed much of the grain crops to their livestock.

Ohio has been an important fruit-producing state since pioneer days, when Johnny Appleseed roamed the countryside planting apple seeds (see APPLESEED, JOHNNY). Ohio farms also produce large crops of grapes and peaches. The plains along Lake Erie and the offshore islands make up one of the leading grape-producing regions of the United States. The warm lake winds protect the grapes from frosts in late spring and early autumn. The state's 17 wineries produce about 625,000 gallons (2,360,000 liters) of wine annually.

Large crops of cucumbers, potatoes, sugar beets, sweet corn, tobacco, and tomatoes are grown in Ohio. The rich soils of the Great Lakes Plains and the warmer lowlands along the Ohio River are especially good for growing vegetables. These regions also have tree nurs-

of about $3 billion. The production of electrical machinery ranks next in importance, with a value added by manufacture of about $2¼ billion a year.

Ohio leads the states in the manufacture of rubber products. Its factories produce about a fourth of the rubber tires made in the United States. This industry is centered in Akron, where it was founded in 1870 by Benjamin F. Goodrich. The industry expanded rapidly because of the development of the automobile, and because of the industry's nearness to Michigan automobile factories. The nation's largest factory producing golf balls, a rubber product, is in Ashland.

The slaughtering and packing of meat animals is another leading Ohio industry. Important related industries include leather-tanning, shoe-manufacturing, and soapmaking. Ohio ranks second only to Illinois in soap production, and Cincinnati has the largest soap factory in the United States.

Ohio also leads the states in the manufacture of clay and glass products. Clay products include bricks and tile, roofing, and tableware. Much pottery is manufactured along the Ohio River, especially in East Liverpool. Toledo and various other cities are centers of the glassmaking industry. Two important natural advantages helped the establishment of this industry in Ohio. These were plentiful deposits of sand and natural gas, both used in glassmaking.

Other important Ohio products include aluminum, bicycles, butter and other dairy products, cement,

FARM AND MINERAL PRODUCTS

This map shows where the state's leading farm and mineral products are produced.
The major urban areas (shown in red) are the state's important manufacturing centers.

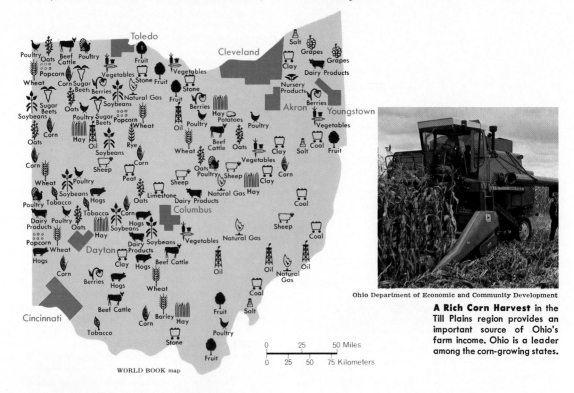

Ohio Department of Economic and Community Development

A Rich Corn Harvest in the Till Plains region provides an important source of Ohio's farm income. Ohio is a leader among the corn-growing states.

WORLD BOOK map

eries and flower greenhouses. Ohio leads the states in the production of hothouse vegetables. Ohio has about 1,000 acres (400 hectares) under glass, more than any other state.

Mining in Ohio provides an annual income of about $735 million. Coal is the greatest source of this income. Since coal mining began in Ohio during the early 1800's, about 4 billion short tons (3.6 billion metric tons) of coal have been mined. Ohio now produces about 46 million short tons (41.7 million metric tons) of coal a year, and is a leading coal-producing state. Ohio's great fields of *bituminous* (soft) coal lie mainly in the east and southeast. Nearly half the coal mined in Ohio comes from Belmont and Harrison counties. The fields there form part of the great Appalachian coal fields that include parts of Pennsylvania and West Virginia. About three-fifths of the coal is taken from strip mines (see COAL [Mining Methods]). Toledo is an important coal-shipping port.

Petroleum is taken from several parts of Ohio. At one time, most of it came from the Lima-Indiana field, which was opened in 1885. Ohio wells provide about 10 million barrels of oil yearly. The state has over 9,400 natural gas wells. They produce about 90 billion cubic feet (2.5 billion cubic meters) of gas annually.

Ohio ranks high among the states in the production of *nonmetallic minerals* (those that are neither metal ores nor fuels). The state leads in the production of building sandstone, supplying about a third of the country's supply. Ohio's best clays come from the eastern part of

the state, in or near the coal fields. These clays are used in the manufacture of such products as bricks and tile, cement, pottery, and stoneware. Sandstone is taken chiefly from quarries in eastern Ohio. The best-known variety of sandstone, Berea or *grit*, comes from Lorain County.

Ohio provides about a fifth of all the limestone used in the United States to make glass. The state also leads in the production of lime, made from limestone. Other uses of limestone include the manufacture of cement, chemicals, fertilizers, and steel. Limestone is quarried chiefly in north-central Ohio. The nation's deepest limestone quarry—about $\frac{1}{2}$ mile (0.8 kilometer) deep —is at Barberton.

Ohio's oldest mining industry is the production of salt, and the state is a leading salt producer. The deepest salt mine in the United States is near Fairport Harbor. The mine is about 2,000 feet (610 meters) deep. Sand and gravel are produced throughout the state. Other minerals include abrasive stones, gypsum, and peat.

Fishing Industry. Ohio has an annual fish catch valued at about $1 million. The state's annual commercial catch amounts to about 7 million pounds (3.2 million kilograms). Lake Erie used to be an extremely productive fishing area, but waste from cities and industries has killed off many fish. The cities of Port Clinton, Sandusky, and Vermilion are the only remaining fishing ports on Lake Erie today. Many fish caught in Lake Erie are shipped alive to commercial ponds in Kentucky, southern Ohio, and West Virginia. The most

532b

important fish caught in Ohio include carp, channel catfish, sheepshead, white bass, yellow perch, and yellow pike.

Electric Power. Almost all of Ohio's power comes from coal-burning steam plants. About 40 of these plants operate throughout the state. Ohio also has about 20 other fuel-burning plants and 1 hydroelectric plant.

Transportation. Ohio is a transportation link between the eastern and western United States. Cross-country railways and roads began going westward through the state during the 1800's.

About 10 airlines serve Ohio's cities. The state has more than 300 commercial airports and about 5 seaplane anchorages on Lake Erie and the Ohio River. Seaplane bases for private and training uses have also been established in fishing and hunting areas. Ohio has three federally owned airfields.

Railroads operate on about 8,000 miles (12,880 kilometers) of track in Ohio. About 15 rail lines provide freight service, and passenger trains serve about 10 cities in the state.

The first east-west roads in Ohio were the natural trails that followed the sandy ridges along Lake Erie. Later roads, paved with logs, followed Indian trails. The historic Zane's Trace, built for the federal government by Ebenezer Zane, opened in 1797. It ran from what is now Wheeling, W.Va., through the present-day Ohio cities of Zanesville, Lancaster, and Chillicothe to Maysville, Ky. Maysville was then the northern end of the road to New Orleans. During the early 1800's, the National (Cumberland) Road became an important link between the East and the West (see NATIONAL ROAD).

Today, Ohio has about 110,000 miles (177,000 kilometers) of roads, almost all of which have hard surfaces. Thirty federal highways and eight expressways cross the state. The 241-mile (388-kilometer) Ohio Turnpike runs from the Pennsylvania border across northern Ohio to Indiana.

The Great Lakes and the St. Lawrence Seaway connect Ohio with the Atlantic Ocean. The lakes also link Ohio with the north-central states and Canada. Another major waterway, the Ohio River, connects the state with the Mississippi River and the Gulf of Mexico. The entire length of this river is navigable all year.

Communication. The first newspaper published north and west of the Ohio River, the *Centinel of the North-Western Territory*, was founded in Cincinnati in 1793. The nation's first antislavery newspaper, the *Philanthropist*, began publication in Mount Pleasant in 1817. Today, Ohio has about 100 daily newspapers and about 300 weeklies. Newspapers with a circulation of over 150,000 are the *Akron Beacon Journal*, *Cincinnati Enquirer*, *The Cincinnati Post*, *Cleveland Press*, *The Columbus Dispatch*, *Dayton Daily News*, *Plain Dealer* of Cleveland, and *Toledo Blade*. About 320 magazines are published in Ohio.

Ohio's oldest radio station, WHK, began broadcasting in Cleveland in 1922. Also that year, Ohio State University in Columbus started WOSU, the first educational radio station in North America. The first Ohio television station, WEWS-TV, opened in Cleveland in 1947. Today, Ohio has about 295 radio stations and about 40 television stations.

Indian Days. Thousands of years ago, prehistoric Indians lived in what is now Ohio. These Indians were the ancestors of peoples called *Mound Builders*, some of whom had high forms of civilization. The Mound Builders left more than 6,000 burial mounds, forts, and other earthworks throughout the Ohio region. The Indians included the Adena and Hopewell peoples, who lived there from 1000 B.C. to A.D. 1300. See MOUND BUILDERS.

When the early white settlers arrived, several Indian tribes lived in the Ohio region. These tribes included the Delaware, Miami, Shawnee, and Wyandot, or Huron. See INDIAN, AMERICAN (Table of Tribes).

Exploration and Settlement. The French explorer Robert Cavelier, Sieur de la Salle, was probably the first white man to reach present-day Ohio. He is believed to have visited the region about 1670. The French based their claim to the entire Northwest on La Salle's explorations. But the British claimed all the territory extending inland from their Atlantic colonies. In 1750, the Ohio Company of Virginia sent Christopher Gist to explore the upper Ohio River Valley. This company, organized in 1747, was made up of Englishmen and Virginians who planned to colonize the Ohio region. See GIST, CHRISTOPHER; LA SALLE, SIEUR DE; OHIO COMPANY (The First).

The British-French dispute over territory in North America, including the Ohio region, led to the French and Indian War (1754-1763). In the peace treaty of 1763, France gave Great Britain most of its lands east of the Mississippi River. Pontiac, an Indian chief born in Ohio, started an Indian rebellion against the British in 1763 after the peace treaty was signed. See FRENCH AND INDIAN WARS; PONTIAC.

Fighting during the Revolutionary War forced a Moravian mission settlement named Schoenbrunn, near present-day New Philadelphia, to close down. The settlement, founded in 1772 by David Zeisberger, was abandoned in 1776. In 1780, George Rogers Clark defeated Shawnee Indian allies of the British in the Battle of Piqua, near present-day Springfield. Clark's campaigns in the Northwest helped win the region for the United States during the Revolutionary War.

The region, including Ohio, became the Northwest Territory in 1787. The Northwest Ordinance of 1787 provided for the eventual statehood of Ohio and other divisions of the territory. That year, the Ohio Company of Associates bought land northwest of the Ohio River in the Muskingum River Valley. Members of this company came from New England. On April 7, 1788, the company founded Marietta, the first permanent white settlement in Ohio. Rufus Putnam, a Revolutionary War general, was superintendent of the colony. Marietta became the first capital of the Northwest Territory in July, 1788. Within a short time, several other communities developed along the Ohio River. Many settlers were Revolutionary War veterans who received land in payment for their military service. See NORTHWEST TERRITORY; OHIO COMPANY (The Second); PUTNAM, RUFUS.

For several years, a series of Indian uprisings disturbed the settlers. Several raids were led by Little Tur-

HISTORIC OHIO
The Mother of Presidents

Rutherford B. Hayes
born at Delaware

Ulysses S. Grant
born at Point Pleasant

James A. Garfield
born at Orange

Control of Lake Erie was won for the United States by Commodore Perry's victory over the British near Put-in-Bay in 1813. In reporting the battle, Perry wrote: "We have met the enemy and they are ours."

Lake Erie

New Ideas in Education. Oberlin College, established in 1833, was the nation's first coeducational college. In 1870, Mount Union College, in Alliance, held one of the first summer schools. The University of Cincinnati began the cooperative plan (classwork combined with part-time employment) in 1906.

DOG
TOP
BEE
SUN

Famous Textbooks by Ohio authors were used in American public schools for many years. Best known were *Ray's Arithmetics* (1834), the *McGuffey Readers* (1836), the *Spencerian Writing System* (1848), and *Harvey's Grammar* (1868).

Rubber Manufacturing Center. B. F. Goodrich began to make fire hose and other products of rubber in 1870 in Akron. After the first pneumatic tire was used in 1895, Akron helped put the world on rubber tires.

• Orange
• Oberlin
Akron •
• Niles
• Alliance
Delaware •
COLUMBUS ★
• Yellow Springs
• Dayton
• Hillsboro
Marietta •

Air Pioneers. The Wright brothers built the first wind tunnel in North America at Dayton in 1901 to conduct experiments that led to the first successful airplane flight.

First Permanent White Settlement in Ohio was established in 1788 by General Rufus Putnam, who is sometimes called the Father of Ohio.

GROCERY

Home of Many Inventions. James Ritty invented the cash register in 1879 in Dayton. L. E. Custer invented the electric runabout there in 1899. Charles F. Kettering developed an automobile self-starter in Dayton in 1911.

Indian Mounds, near Hillsboro, were built by Indian tribes several thousand years ago. The Great Serpent Mound is about ¼ mile (0.4 kilometer) long. It looks like a serpent in the act of uncoiling. The snake has an egg in its jaws.

Benjamin Harrison
born near North Bend

William H. Taft
born at Cincinnati

William McKinley
born at Niles

Warren G. Harding
born near Blooming Grove

tle, a Miami chief. In 1794, General Anthony Wayne defeated the Indians near present-day Toledo in the Battle of Fallen Timbers. The next year, in the Treaty of Greenville, the Indians ceded the United States about two-thirds of what is now Ohio. The Indians accepted the treaty largely through the influence of Tarhe, or Crane, a Wyandot chief. With peace restored, more and more settlers poured into the region. Many settlements were founded in the valleys of rivers flowing into the Ohio. Some pioneers also settled in northeastern Ohio in the area called the Western Reserve (see WESTERN RESERVE).

In 1800, Congress passed the Division Act. This legislation created the Indiana Territory out of the western part of the Northwest Territory. Chillicothe became the capital of the eastern part, which continued to be called the Northwest Territory.

Statehood. Preparation for Ohio statehood began in November, 1802, when a convention in Chillicothe drew up the state's first constitution. Ohio became the 17th state on March 1, 1803, when the first state legislature met. Edward Tiffin, a Democratic-Republican, was the first governor. Ohio's population was about 70,000. Chillicothe was the capital from 1803 to 1810, when Zanesville became the capital. Chillicothe again became the capital in 1812, and Columbus in 1816.

The Louisiana Purchase in 1803 gave Ohio settlers a river outlet for their products. They could ship goods down the Mississippi River and through the port of New Orleans. A thriving river trade with New Orleans soon developed. The first steamboat to travel the Ohio River was the *New Orleans*, a wood-burning sidewheeler. It first went down the river in 1811.

Ohio took an active part in the War of 1812 (1812-1815). Commodore Oliver H. Perry sailed from Put-in-Bay at South Bass Island off the Ohio shore to battle a British fleet on Sept. 10, 1813. Perry won an important naval victory in this Battle of Lake Erie (see PERRY [Oliver H.]). After the war, thousands of persons moved to Ohio from the eastern states. Many came from New England, New York, and Pennsylvania. Immigrants arrived from Germany and Great Britain.

In 1818, the steamboat *Walk-in-the-Water* became the first steamboat on Lake Erie. It demonstrated the practical use of the Great Lakes as a waterway to the West. The Erie Canal across New York from Lake Erie opened in 1825. The Ohio and Erie Canal, joining Cleveland and Portsmouth, was completed in 1832. The Miami and Erie Canal, connecting Toledo and Cincinnati, was completed in 1845. These canals served as busy trade routes for more than 25 years. But the coming of the railroads reduced canal traffic. Ohio canals and railroads brought increased prosperity, and many mills and factories were built between 1830 and 1860.

An old border dispute between Ohio and the Territory of Michigan flared up in 1835 and led to the "Toledo War." Before any actual fighting broke out, President Andrew Jackson sent agents to Toledo to persuade the governors of Ohio and Michigan to accept a truce. In 1836, Congress awarded the disputed area, about 520 square miles (1,350 square kilometers) along Lake Erie, to Ohio. In 1841, William Henry Harrison of North Bend became the ninth President of the United States.

OHIO

The Civil War. During the years before the Civil War (1861-1865), many Ohioans had strong feelings on the question of slavery. Many *abolitionists* (persons opposed to slavery) lived throughout Ohio. They helped slaves who had escaped across the Ohio River on their flight to Canada (see UNDERGROUND RAILROAD). Most of Ohio's Southern sympathizers lived in the southern and north-central parts of the state. In 1862, Clement L. Vallandigham of Dayton became leader of the Peace Democrats party, which opposed President Abraham Lincoln's administration. Vallandigham and others who sympathized with the South were known as Copperheads.

Many famous Civil War commanders were born in Ohio, including Ulysses S. Grant and William T. Sherman. Ohio supplied about 345,000 men to the Union army. This was more than the total quotas requested by 10 presidential calls for soldiers from the state. In 1863, Confederate cavalrymen known as Morgan's Raiders crossed into Ohio and brought Civil War fighting to its northernmost point. Led by General John Hunt Morgan, they were captured in Columbiana County. Morgan later escaped and returned to the South. See MORGAN, JOHN HUNT.

Ohio's industrial centers grew rapidly after the Civil War. Many workers from other countries settled in the state. The shipping of coal, iron ore, and other bulk goods on Lake Erie increased. Farming continued to be a leading industry, but Ohio also developed into a top manufacturing state. In 1869, the Cincinnati Red Stockings (now Reds) became the first all-professional baseball team. Benjamin F. Goodrich began manufacturing rubber products in Akron in 1870.

Five Ohio-born Presidents, all Republicans, were elected during the 1800's. They were Ulysses S. Grant, Rutherford B. Hayes, James A. Garfield, Benjamin Harrison, and William McKinley. President William Henry Harrison of Ohio was born in Virginia.

The Early 1900's. Ohio's government was torn by political scandal and corruption during the late 1800's. Marcus A. "Mark" Hanna, political boss of Cleveland, and George B. Cox, boss of Cincinnati, both Republicans, controlled state politics. Reform movements began about 1900, and promoted honesty in both city and state governments. William Howard Taft of Cincinnati became the 27th President in 1909.

Ohio suffered the worst floods in its history during the spring of 1913. About 350 persons lost their lives after rivers overflowed their banks, and damage totaled about $100 million. Most of the destruction occurred in the Miami River Valley, especially at Dayton. In 1914, the state legislature passed the Conservancy Act, the first legislation of its kind in the United States. The chief purpose of the act was to permit the establishment of flood-control districts based on entire river systems. Many flood-control dams and reservoirs were built under this act, including those completed by 1922 in the Miami River Valley. The federal government also built about 20 flood-control dams in Ohio.

After the United States entered World War I in 1917, the state produced vast supplies of war materials. Newton D. Baker of Cleveland served as Secretary of War in President Woodrow Wilson's wartime Cabinet.

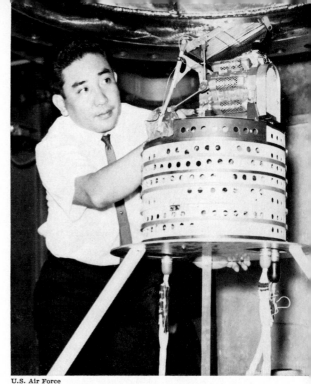

U.S. Air Force

Research in Space Technology contributes to Ohio's industrial expansion today. This scientist is examining the test model of an engine that may propel a spaceship. The engine was tested by the U.S. Air Force Systems Command at Wright-Patterson Air Force Base near Dayton.

Between World Wars. In 1921, Warren G. Harding of Marion became the 29th President. His Democratic opponent was Governor James M. Cox of Dayton. The 1920's were prosperous years in Ohio, because of continued industrial development. Cincinnati, Cleveland, Dayton, Toledo, and other industrial cities expanded rapidly. Many nearby farms disappeared as the cities grew. The Great Depression that began in 1929 hit these cities hardest in Ohio. Thousands of workers lost their jobs as factories closed. Many farmers lost their land when farm prices dropped sharply.

Government funds and federal agencies such as the Works Progress Administration (WPA) helped Ohio recover from the depression during the 1930's. In 1934, work began on the Muskingum River Valley flood-control project. This project came to national attention in the winter of 1937, when most of the dams withstood heavy floodwaters of the Ohio River. It was completed in 1938. Robert A. Taft, who became one of the most powerful men in the U.S. Senate, began his first term as Republican Senator from Ohio in 1939.

The Mid-1900's. During World War II (1939-1945), Ohio produced aircraft, ships, and weapons. It also contributed steel, tires, and materials to the war effort. The armed services established a number of training centers in the state.

During the 1950's, the Atomic Energy Commission (AEC) built several installations in Ohio. They included the Portsmouth Area Project in Pike County, which produces uranium-235 for use in nuclear reactors. In 1955, the 241-mile (388-kilometer) Ohio Turnpike across northern Ohio opened to traffic. Since 1958,

	Party	Term		Party	Term
1. Edward Tiffin	*Dem.-Rep.	1803-1807	33. Thomas L. Young	Republican	1877-1878
2. Thomas Kirker	Dem.-Rep.	1807-1808	34. Richard M. Bishop	Democratic	1878-1880
3. Samuel Huntington	Dem.-Rep.	1808-1810	35. Charles Foster	Republican	1880-1884
4. Return J. Meigs, Jr.	Dem.-Rep.	1810-1814	36. George Hoadly	Democratic	1884-1886
5. Othneil Looker	Dem.-Rep.	1814	37. Joseph B. Foraker	Republican	1886-1890
6. Thomas Worthington	Dem.-Rep.	1814-1818	38. James E. Campbell	Democratic	1890-1892
7. Ethan Allen Brown	Dem.-Rep.	1818-1822	39. William McKinley	Republican	1892-1896
8. Allen Trimble	Federalist	1822	40. Asa S. Bushnell	Republican	1896-1900
9. Jeremiah Morrow	Dem.-Rep.	1822-1826	41. George K. Nash	Republican	1900-1904
10. Allen Trimble	Federalist	1826-1830	42. Myron T. Herrick	Republican	1904-1906
11. Duncan McArthur	Federalist	1830-1832	43. John M. Pattison	Democratic	1906
12. Robert Lucas	Democratic	1832-1836	44. Andrew L. Harris	Republican	1906-1909
13. Joseph Vance	Whig	1836-1838	45. Judson Harmon	Democratic	1909-1913
14. Wilson Shannon	Democratic	1838-1840	46. James M. Cox	Democratic	1913-1915
15. Thomas Corwin	Whig	1840-1842	47. Frank B. Willis	Republican	1915-1917
16. Wilson Shannon	Democratic	1842-1844	48. James M. Cox	Democratic	1917-1921
17. Thomas W. Bartley	Democratic	1844	49. Harry L. Davis	Republican	1921-1923
18. Mordecai Bartley	Whig	1844-1846	50. A. Victor Donahey	Democratic	1923-1929
19. William Bebb	Whig	1846-1849	51. Myers Y. Cooper	Republican	1929-1931
20. Seabury Ford	Whig	1849-1850	52. George White	Democratic	1931-1935
21. Reuben Wood	Democratic	1850-1853	53. Martin L. Davey	Democratic	1935-1939
22. William Medill	Democratic	1853-1856	54. John W. Bricker	Republican	1939-1945
23. Salmon P. Chase	Republican	1856-1860	55. Frank J. Lausche	Democratic	1945-1947
24. William Dennison	Republican	1860-1862	56. Thomas J. Herbert	Republican	1947-1949
25. David Tod	Republican	1862-1864	57. Frank J. Lausche	Democratic	1949-1957
26. John Brough	Republican	1864-1865	58. John W. Brown	Republican	1957
27. Charles Anderson	Republican	1865-1866	59. C. William O'Neill	Republican	1957-1959
28. Jacob Dolson Cox	Republican	1866-1868	60. Michael V. DiSalle	Democratic	1959-1963
29. Rutherford B. Hayes	Republican	1868-1872	61. James A. Rhodes	Republican	1963-1971
30. Edward F. Noyes	Republican	1872-1874	62. John J. Gilligan	Democratic	1971-1975
31. William Allen	Democratic	1874-1876	63. James A. Rhodes	Republican	1975-
32. Rutherford B. Hayes	Republican	1876-1877			

*Democratic-Republican

the National Aeronautics and Space Administration (NASA) has operated Lewis Research Center in Cleveland. Scientists there conduct research on space propulsion systems. In 1959, Ohio voters approved an increase in the terms of the governor and other officials from two to four years.

Ohio's industrial growth moved forward rapidly during the 1960's. In 1963, the state launched a giant economic development program to attract more industry. Industrial expansion included new aluminum plants and chemical factories in cities along the Ohio River. Industries came to this area largely because it offered cheap, coal-generated power.

Ohio also entered international trade. Eight Ohio cities on Lake Erie—Ashtabula, Cleveland, Conneaut, Fairport, Huron, Lorain, Sandusky, and Toledo—became ports of the St. Lawrence Seaway, which opened in 1959. By 1970, Ohio ranked fourth among the states in the value of goods exported annually.

In 1963, Ohio voters approved a $250-million bond issue for improvements including expansion of state universities and public schools. In 1964, Ohioans approved a $500-million bond issue to step up expressway construction.

The Supreme Court of the United States ruled in 1964 that Ohio must *reapportion* (redivide) its House of Representatives to provide more equal representation based on population. A special session of the Ohio legislature drew up a reapportionment plan for the House, but the voters rejected it. In 1965, the governor, state auditor, and secretary of state proposed a reapportionment plan for both the House and the Senate. A federal district court approved the reapportionment plan for temporary use. The Ohio state legislature then drew up

a permanent plan, which the voters approved in 1967.

Also in 1964, the legislators drew up 24 congressional districts for Ohio. Previously, Ohio had 23 districts, each of which elected one representative. The 24th representative had been elected *at large* (by the entire state). Ohio's population declined in the 1960's. As a result, the state lost one seat in the U.S. House of Representatives. Ohio's congressional districts were redrawn in 1972 to reflect the change.

Ohio Today faces several problems. One of the state's most serious problems concerns its public school system. Between 1966 and 1970, several Ohio school districts closed their public schools because of lack of funds. Educators predicted more school closings in Ohio in the 1970's unless the voters approve tax increases to pay for higher teachers' salaries and better facilities.

Ohioans are also concerned with providing better police and fire protection for their communities. In 1969, the state established academies to improve the training of policemen and firemen. Another serious problem in Ohio is the pollution of Lake Erie and the state's rivers. In 1971, the Ohio state legislature enacted an income tax to help pay for the rapidly rising costs of state government.

Ohio is promoting tourism in the 1970's. New attractions include lakeside lodges and an Appalachia road through forest preserves in southern Ohio.

Electric power production has become vital to Ohio's economy. During the 1960's, 11 public utility electric power generators went into operation. Three electric companies are building a nuclear power station at Moscow on the Ohio River. The two-unit station was scheduled for completion in the late 1970's.

RALPH W. FRANK, BEN HAYES, and JAMES H. RODABAUGH

Related Articles in WORLD BOOK include:

BIOGRAPHIES

Allen, William	Krol, John Joseph Cardinal
Anderson, Sherwood	Logan
Appleseed, Johnny	McGuffey, William H.
Armstrong, Neil A.	McKinley, William
Brant, Joseph	Nicklaus, Jack
Bricker, John W.	Pendleton, George H.
Bromfield, Louis	Perry (Oliver H.)
Chase, Salmon P.	Pontiac
Cox, James M.	Putnam, Rufus
Dunbar, Paul Laurence	Rockefeller (John David;
Edison, Thomas A.	John David, Jr.)
Firestone, Harvey S.	Saxbe, William B.
Garfield, James A.	Shawnee Prophet
Glenn, John H., Jr.	Sherman (John; William T.)
Goodrich, Benjamin F.	Steinem, Gloria
Grant, Ulysses S.	Stokes, Carl B.
Green, William	Taft, Robert A.
Hanna, Mark	Taft, William H.
Harding, Warren G.	Tecumseh
Harrison, Benjamin	Thurman, Allen G.
Harrison, William Henry	Vallandigham, Clement L.
Hayes, Rutherford B.	Wayne, Anthony
Kettering, Charles F.	Wright Brothers

CITIES

Akron	East Cleveland	Marietta
Canton	East Liverpool	Mount Vernon
Chillicothe	Euclid	Parma
Cincinnati	Hamilton	Springfield
Cleveland	Lima	Toledo
Columbus	Lorain	Youngstown
Dayton		

HISTORY

French and Indian Wars	Pioneer Life in America
Indian Wars	Underground Railroad
Mound Builders	War of 1812
Northwest Ordinance	Western Reserve
Northwest Territory	Westward Movement
Ohio Company	

PHYSICAL FEATURES

Lake Erie	Ohio River
Miami River	Scioto River
Mound City Group	
National Monument	

PRODUCTS AND INDUSTRY

For Ohio's rank among the states in production, see the following articles:

Automobile	Corn	Salt
Building Stone	Horse	Soybean
Chemical	Iron and Steel	Tomato
Industry	Manufacturing	Vegetable
Coal	Publishing	

OTHER RELATED ARTICLES

Battelle Memorial Institute	National Road
Cleveland Institute of Art	Rookwood Pottery
Erie Canal	Wright-Patterson Air
Flood	Force Base
Midwestern States	

Outline

I. Government
   A. Constitution
   B. Executive
   C. Legislature
   D. Courts

II. People

   E. Local Government
   F. Taxation
   G. Politics

III. Education
   A. Schools
   B. Libraries

   C. Museums

IV. A Visitor's Guide
   A. Places to Visit

   B. Annual Events

V. The Land
   A. Land Regions
   B. Shoreline

   C. Rivers and Lakes

VI. Climate

VII. Economy
   A. Natural Resources
   B. Manufacturing
   C. Agriculture
   D. Mining
   E. Fishing Industry
   F. Electric Power
   G. Transportation
   H. Communication

VIII. History

Questions

How many U.S. Presidents came from Ohio? Which one of these men was not born in Ohio?

How did Ohio pioneer in flood-control legislation?

What is Ohio's most valuable farm activity?

Why is Ohio called a *barometer state* in politics?

What was the first U.S. college for both men and women?

What was the "Toledo War"? What was the result of this dispute?

What Ohio educator became famous as an author of reading books for schoolchildren?

What was the first educational radio station in North America? When and where was it established?

What is Ohio's rank among the states in manufacturing?

What city produces all Liederkranz cheese?

Books for Young Readers

BAILEY, BERNADINE. *Picture Book of Ohio.* Rev. ed. Whitman, 1967.

CAMERON, ELEANOR. *To the Green Mountains.* Dutton, 1975. Fiction.

CARPENTER, ALLAN. *Ohio.* Childrens Press, 1963.

HAMILTON, VIRGINIA. *The House of Dies Drear.* Macmillan, 1968. *M.C. Higgins, The Great.* 1974. Both books are fiction, and the second won the Newbery medal.

HUNT, IRENE. *Trail of Apple Blossoms.* Follett, 1968. Fiction.

RENICK, MARION L. *Ohio.* Coward, 1970.

SCHEELE, WILLIAM E. *The Mound Builders.* Collins-World, 1960.

Books for Older Readers

BARRY, JAMES P. *The Battle of Lake Erie, September, 1813.* Watts, 1970.

BASKIN, JOHN. *New Burlington: The Life and Death of an American Village.* Norton, 1976.

COLLINS, WILLIAM R. *Ohio: The Buckeye State.* 5th ed. Prentice-Hall, 1974.

HAVIGHURST, WALTER. *Ohio: A Bicentennial History.* Norton, 1976.

MOSER, DON. *A Heart to the Hawks.* Atheneum, 1975. Fiction.

ROSEBOOM, EUGENE H., and WEISENBURGER, F. P. *A History of Ohio.* 3rd ed. Ohio Historical Society, 1975.

SMITH, THOMAS H., ed. *An Ohio Reader.* 2 vols. Eerdmans, 1975.

WEISENBURGER, FRANCIS P. *Ohio: A Students' Guide to Localized History.* Teachers College Press, 1965.

WILCOX, FRANK N. *The Ohio Canals: A Pictorial Survey of the Ohio Canals.* Kent State Univ. Press, 1969. *Ohio Indian Trails: A Pictorial Survey of the Indian Trails of Ohio.* 1970.

Pioneers in Ohio settled in the Northwest Territory as a result of the forming of the second Ohio Company in 1786.

OHIO COMPANY. There were two Ohio Companies in American history. The purpose of each was to colonize the Ohio River Valley.

The First Ohio Company was formed in 1747. It is sometimes called the Ohio Company of Virginia. Its members included London merchants and wealthy Virginians. Among them were George Washington's brothers, Lawrence and Augustine Washington. In 1749, King George II granted the company 200,000 acres (81,000 hectares) west of the Allegheny Mountains in Maryland, Pennsylvania, and Virginia, and on both sides of the Ohio River. The company surveyed the Ohio River Valley. It traded with Indians, built storehouses and roads, and established the first fort at the forks of the Ohio. In 1753, a settlement called *Gist's Plantation* was founded near Mount Braddock, Pa. The French destroyed the company's strongholds in 1754. The French and Indian War blocked efforts to settle in the west. The company went out of business in 1792.

The Second Ohio Company was the more important. Its official name was the Ohio Company of Associates. It was organized at the Bunch of Grapes Tavern in Boston on March 1, 1786. Eleven delegates, elected by persons interested in the venture, set up the company. They planned to raise $1 million in $1,000 shares, which was payable in almost worthless Continental paper money. Within a year the company distributed 250 shares. The company appointed Manasseh Cutler, Rufus Putnam, and Samuel Parsons to petition the Continental Congress to sell it a tract beyond the Ohio River. Congress approved, and later passed the Northwest Ordinance of 1787 (see NORTHWEST ORDINANCE).

At first the Ohio Company contracted to buy 1½ million acres (610,000 hectares) at 66⅔ cents an acre. But because of financial difficulties, these terms were never fully carried out. Congress finally granted title to 750,000 acres (304,000 hectares) in what is now southeastern Ohio. The agreement provided that 214,285 acres (86,718 hectares) could be bought with army warrants, and that 100,000 acres (40,000 hectares) were to be offered free to settlers. One section of each township was reserved for schools, one for religion, and three sections for future disposal by Congress. This last term was designed to keep speculators from monopolizing the territory. Two townships of 46,080 acres (18,648 hectares) were set aside "for the support of an institution of higher learning." This institution was founded at Athens, Ohio, in 1804, and became Ohio University.

The Ohio Company appointed Rufus Putnam as its superintendent. He led an advance party of 47 surveyors, carpenters, boat-builders, blacksmiths, and laborers to lay out a town where the Muskingum and Ohio rivers joined. The group arrived at the mouth of the Muskingum on April 7, 1788. It founded there the first settlement under the Northwest Ordinance, and named it *Marietta* in honor of Queen Marie Antoinette of France. The settlers also built a fort called *Campus Martius* to protect their village. On July 15, Governor Arthur St. Clair established the first capital of the Northwest Territory at Marietta. By April, 1789, three new settlements had been established. The Ohio Company completed its land operations by 1797. It divided its assets among the shareholders, but did not go out of business until about 1832.   JAMES H. RODABAUGH

See also GIST, CHRISTOPHER; NORTHWEST ORDINANCE; NORTHWEST TERRITORY; PUTNAM, RUFUS.

OHIO DOMINICAN COLLEGE. See UNIVERSITIES AND COLLEGES (table).

OHIO NORTHERN UNIVERSITY. See UNIVERSITIES AND COLLEGES (table).

OHIO RIVER is a branch of the Mississippi River. It flows 981 miles (1,579 kilometers) through some of

OHIO RIVER

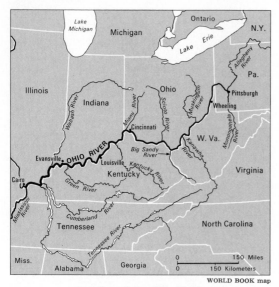

Location of the Ohio River

WORLD BOOK map

the richest farmlands and busiest industrial regions in the United States. Its entire length is navigable. Once early pioneers paddled their canoes down the Ohio on their way west. Today large towboats and barges carry more than 85 million short tons (77 million metric tons) of commerce on the Ohio every year.

Course and Branches. The Ohio River begins where the Allegheny and Monongahela rivers meet in Pittsburgh. The Ohio flows southwestward, and separates Ohio, Indiana, and Illinois from West Virginia and Kentucky. It empties into the Mississippi at Cairo, Ill. Its chief branches include the Muskingum, Scioto, Kanawha, Miami, Wabash, Big Sandy, Tennessee, Green, and Cumberland rivers. The entire Ohio system drains about 204,000 square miles (528,400 square kilometers), or more than twice the size of Wyoming. Among the large cities along the Ohio are Pittsburgh, Pa.; Wheeling, W. Va.; Cincinnati, Ohio; Louisville, Ky.; and Evansville, Ind.

Navigation. By 1929, a series of locks and dams were completed by the federal government to provide a minimum depth of 9 feet (2.7 meters) in the river. The improvement in navigation resulted in an increase of river traffic from about 10 million short tons (9 million metric tons) to over 20 million short tons (18 million metric tons) a year. Increased industry in the Ohio River Valley since World War II made a dam replacement and modernization program necessary. During the 1960's, army engineers built 19 modern highlift locks and dams to replace the 46 original structures. The old dams had locks 600 feet (180 meters) long. The new locks are 1,200 feet (366 meters) long.

Floods and Flood Control. The spring floods of the Ohio River often cause great damage. The region gets from 40 to 43 inches (101 to 109 centimeters) of rain a year. As a result of record floods in 1936 and 1937, Congress set up a program of flood control and protection. Dams and reservoirs in upland areas hold back runoff water until flood crests have passed. In addition, flood

walls, levees, and improved channels protect downstream communities.   PAUL B. MASON

Related Articles in WORLD BOOK include:

Allegheny River	Miami River	Scioto River
Cumberland River	Monongahela	Tennessee River
Flood	River	Wabash River
Kanawha River		

OHIO STATE UNIVERSITY is a coeducational state-supported institution with campuses in Columbus, Lima, Mansfield, Marion, and Newark, Ohio. The main campus is in Columbus. The university also operates a graduate center in Dayton.

The Columbus campus has colleges of administrative science, agriculture and home economics, the arts, arts and sciences, biological sciences, dentistry, education, engineering, humanities, law, mathematics and physical sciences, medicine, optometry, pharmacy, social and behavioral sciences, and veterinary medicine. It grants bachelor's, master's, and doctor's degrees. The campuses at Lima, Mansfield, Marion, and Newark offer liberal arts programs leading to a bachelor's degree.

The university operates its own radio and television stations. It has a 500-acre (200-hectare) airport near the Columbus campus. The university's Franz Theodore Stone Laboratory in Put-in-Bay, Ohio, studies the biology of the Great Lakes.

Ohio State University was founded in 1870 as a land-grant college. Originally called Ohio Agricultural and Mechanical College, the school opened in 1873. It took its present name in 1878. The Lima, Mansfield, Marion, and Newark campuses of the university were founded in 1972. For enrollment, see UNIVERSITIES AND COLLEGES (table).   NOVICE G. FAWCETT

Ohio State University

Ohio State University's ivy-covered Orton Hall, *above*, houses the geology department.

OHIO TURNPIKE. See OHIO (Transportation).

OHIO UNIVERSITY is a state-assisted coeducational school in Athens, Ohio. The university has eight colleges that grant undergraduate degrees—University College; the honors-tutorial college; and the colleges of arts and sciences, business administration, commu-

Harry Snavely, Ohio University

Ohio University is the home of Cutler Hall, *above,* one of the oldest college buildings in the Midwest. It was built in 1816.

nication, education, engineering and technology, and fine arts. University College offers associate of arts degrees and bachelor's degrees in general studies. The honors-tutorial college provides special programs for gifted students. The university also has a graduate college, which offers master's and doctor's degrees. In addition, the university maintains four regional campuses and an academic center in southeastern Ohio, and an extension division.

Founded in 1804, Ohio University was the first institution of higher learning in the vast Midwestern region called the Northwest Territory. For the enrollment of Ohio University, see UNIVERSITIES AND COLLEGES (table). Critically reviewed by OHIO UNIVERSITY

OHIO WESLEYAN UNIVERSITY. See UNIVERSITIES AND COLLEGES (table).

OHM is the unit used to measure resistance to the passage of an electric current. All materials resist the flow of electric current. But some materials offer more resistance than others. Materials that offer little resistance are called *conductors.* Materials that offer great resistance are called *insulators.* Electrical resistance, measured in ohms (R), is equal to the electromotive force producing a current, measured in *volts* (E), divided by the current, measured in *amperes* (I):

$$\text{ohms} = \frac{\text{volts}}{\text{amperes}} \quad \text{or} \quad R = \frac{E}{I}$$

The resistance of a conductor depends on its dimensions and its temperature as well as on the material from which it is made. For example, the resistance of a wire increases as its length increases or as its diameter decreases. Generally, a metal's resistance increases as its temperature rises.

The international standard for the ohm was adopted in 1893. It was defined as the amount of resistance to a uniform electric current offered by a thread of mercury with a cross-sectional area of one square millimeter and a length of 106.3 centimeters, at a temperature of 0° C. Engineers have worked out the resistance of standard-sized wires for the convenience of persons working with electrical circuits. Resistance in an electrical circuit can be measured with an *ohmmeter.* More accurate measurements of resistance can be obtained by using a device called a *Wheatstone bridge* (see WHEATSTONE BRIDGE). BENJAMIN J. DASHER

See also ELECTRIC CIRCUIT.

OHM, GEORG SIMON (1787-1854), a German physicist, in 1826 discovered the mathematical law of electric currents called Ohm's law (see OHM'S LAW). The *ohm,* a unit of electrical resistance, was named for him. His discovery was neglected until 1833, when he became a professor of physics at Nuremberg. He was appointed a physics professor at the University of Munich in 1849.

Ohm was born in Erlangen, Germany. He graduated from the University of Erlangen. SIDNEY ROSEN

OHM'S LAW expresses the relationship between electric current, electromotive force, and the resistance of electrical conductors. The law was discovered by a German physicist, Georg Simon Ohm. Ohm found that a current flowing through a conductor is directly proportional to the electrical force that produces it. In an equation that expresses Ohm's law, E represents electromotive force, measured in *volts;* I represents electric current, measured in *amperes;* and R represents electrical resistance, or *ohms.* The relationship is then expressed as:

$$E = IR.$$

For example, an electromotive force of eight volts is required to drive a four-ampere current through a circuit having a resistance of two ohms. The equation also states that if the resistance in a circuit remains constant, doubling the electromotive force doubles the current. See also OHM, GEORG SIMON. BENJAMIN J. DASHER

OIL. Any greasy substance that does not dissolve in water, but can be dissolved in ether, is classified as an oil. There are many different kinds of oil. Most are lighter than water and are liquid at room temperature. A few, such as lard and butterfat, are solid at room temperature.

Oils may be obtained from animal, mineral, or vegetable sources. This article chiefly discusses animal and vegetable oils. For more information on mineral oils, which include fuel oils, gasoline, and other petroleum products, see PETROLEUM.

Animal and vegetable oils consist chiefly of carbon, hydrogen, and oxygen. These oils are classified as (1) fixed or (2) volatile, depending on whether or not they evaporate under normal conditions.

Fixed Oils, which do not evaporate under ordinary conditions, are also called *fatty oils* or simply *fats.* They include all animal oils and many vegetable oils. Butterfat, lard, and tallow rank as the chief animal oils. Margarine and salad oil consist mainly of fixed vegetable oils. Other products made from fixed oils include candles, linoleum, lubricants, paint, and soap.

Butter makers churn cream to produce butter. People *render* (heat) fatty animal tissues to obtain other kinds

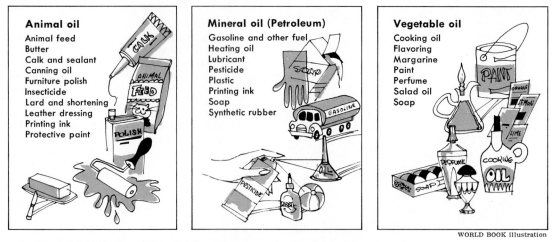

Animal oil

Animal feed
Butter
Calk and sealant
Canning oil
Furniture polish
Insecticide
Lard and shortening
Leather dressing
Printing ink
Protective paint

Mineral oil (Petroleum)

Gasoline and other fuel
Heating oil
Lubricant
Pesticide
Plastic
Printing ink
Soap
Synthetic rubber

Vegetable oil

Cooking oil
Flavoring
Margarine
Paint
Perfume
Salad oil
Soap

WORLD BOOK illustration

Oil Is Used in Making Many Products. The oil may come from animal, vegetable, or mineral sources. The above lists give examples of products containing oil from these three sources.

of animal oil. Lard is made from the fatty tissues of hogs, and tallow from cattle, goats, or sheep. Oils from such sea animals as fish and whales are called *marine oils.*

Most fixed vegetable oils are extracted from such seeds as corn, cottonseed, and soybeans. Processors obtain olive and palm oils from the fruit pulp surrounding the seed. For information on the processing of fixed vegetable oils, see VEGETABLE OIL.

Exposure to air causes fixed oils to thicken. The degree of thickening that occurs determines whether the oil is classified as (1) drying, (2) semidrying, or (3) nondrying.

Drying oils absorb oxygen from the air to form a tough film. They are widely used to make paints and varnishes. Important drying oils include linseed, perilla, tung or chinawood, soybean, oiticica, hemp, walnut, poppyseed, and sunflower. Linseed oil comes from flax seeds. It is one of the most important drying oils. It is used in paints and varnishes. Tung oil is a valuable oil used in waterproof varnishes and quick-drying enamels.

Semidrying oils absorb oxygen from the air to become very thick, but not hard. Cottonseed, corn, and sesame oils are of the semidrying type.

Nondrying oils absorb oxygen from the air with little increase in thickness. But they often develop unpleasant odors and flavors. Olive, peanut, and grape-seed oils, butterfat, and lard are examples of nondrying types.

Volatile Oils, also called *essential oils,* evaporate quickly, especially when heated. Some of these oils come from plants, and others are man-made. People use volatile oils chiefly for their flavor or odor. The taste of such food flavorings as lemon, mint, and vanilla extracts results from the volatile oils they include. Volatile oils also flavor chewing gum, tobacco, and toothpaste. Most fine perfumes include fragrant oils obtained from roses or other flowers. Manufacturers use such volatile oils as lemon oil to give a scent to soaps and other cleaning products.

Natural volatile oils are extracted from various parts of plants, including bark, flowers, leaves, roots, seeds, and twigs. Methods of obtaining plant oils used for their scent are described in the PERFUME article. Food

processors follow similar procedures in extracting natural volatile oils for flavoring.

Manufacturers use chemical processes to make artificial volatile oils from coal, petroleum, wood, and other substances. Some artificial oils duplicate natural oils. Others differ from any substance found in nature. Such products as artificial oil of rose and artificial vanilla extract cost much less than similar natural substances.   THEODORE J. WEISS

Related Articles in WORLD BOOK include:

Banana Oil	Hydrogenation	Palm Oil
Butter	Lard	Peanut
Castor Oil	Linseed Oil	Peppermint
Copra	Lubricant	Petitgrain Oil
Corn Oil	Margarine	Sesame
Cottonseed Oil	Oil Shale	Soybean
Fat	Olive Oil	Tung Oil

OIL FURNACE. See FURNACE; HEATING (Oil).

OIL OF VITRIOL. See SULFURIC ACID.

OIL PAINTING. See PAINTING.

OIL REFINERY. See PETROLEUM.

OIL SHALE is a sedimentary rock that may someday be an important source of oil. Some geologists believe oil shale is an undeveloped form of petroleum. It consists of *kerogen,* a waxy organic substance, mixed with sediment to form a hard rock ranging from tan to black. Refiners crush the rock and mix it with small, hot balls of aluminum oxide in a closed chamber. The heat drives crude oil vapors from the kerogen, and the vapors are later condensed into liquid oil in another chamber. The cost of producing crude oil from oil shale is greater than the cost of recovering liquid petroleum. For this reason, shale oil has not been widely used. But as liquid petroleum becomes scarce, refiners may begin using the vast deposits of oil shale. Colorado, Utah, and Wyoming have the richest deposits. See also BITUMINOUS SANDS; PETROLEUM (Oil Shale).   CLARENCE KARR, JR.

OIL WELL. See PETROLEUM.

OILCLOTH is a heavy, waterproof cloth used to cover tables and walls that must often be washed. It is made of coarse cloth coated with heavy paint. The cloth is stretched on a frame and stiffened with glue. The paint is put on in several coats. Each coat is smoothed with

538

pumice stone after it has dried. Patterns are then printed on, from blocks coated with paint. Oilcloth was first used in China between the 600's and 900's, and in England in the 1500's. The first American oilcloth was made in Philadelphia in 1809.   Effa Brown

OILSTONE is a rock found in Arkansas which can be used as a whetstone. See Whetstone.

OISE RIVER. See Aisne River.

OISTRAKH, *OY strahk,* **DAVID** (1908-1974), Russia's leading violinist, became known for his performances of works by Miaskovsky, Khatchaturian, and Prokofiev. He made his American debut in 1955.

Oistrakh began his concert career at 19. He won a Russian national contest in 1930, the international violinists' contest at Brussels in 1937, and the Stalin prize in 1942. He was born in Odessa.   Dorothy DeLay

OJEDA, ALONSO DE. See Colombia (History).

OJIBWA INDIANS. See Chippewa Indians.

OJOS DEL SALADO, *AW hohz thel sah LAH thoh,* is the second highest mountain in the Western Hemisphere. It rises 22,572 feet (6,880 meters). Only Aconcagua is higher. Part of the Andes range, it has four distinct peaks on the border between Argentina and Chile. Snow covers Ojos del Salado all year.   George I. Blanksten

O.K. See Slang (Types of Slang).

OKA RIVER, *uh KAH,* is a tributary of the Volga River in Russia. The Oka rises in central Russia, and flows north and northeast 915 miles (1,473 kilometers) to join the Volga at Gorki. Large vessels can sail up the Oka for about 550 miles (885 kilometers). But the river freezes over and halts ship traffic for 225 to 240 days each year. See also Volga River.

OKAPI, *oh KAH pih,* is a rare and strangely colored animal of the giraffe family. It is about 5 feet (1.5 meters) high at the shoulders, and has a long neck. Its sloping body makes the forelegs look longer than the

hind ones, as with the giraffe. Its body is reddish-brown, and its legs have creamy-white stripes and bands. Its face is creamy white, but its nose and pointed ears are deep brown or black. The male has a pair of short horns. The okapi has retiring habits and lives in remote jungles. It was discovered in 1900 in the dense forests of the Congo Valley in Africa. See also Giraffe.

Scientific Classification. The okapi belongs to the giraffe family, *Giraffidae.* It is genus *Okapia,* species *O. johnstoni.*   Theodore H. Eaton, Jr.

OKEECHOBEE, LAKE. See Lake Okeechobee.

O'KEEFFE, GEORGIA (1887-   ), an American artist, pioneered in modern movements in American painting. Her best-known paintings are those in which she enlarged flowers or the skulls of animals to fill the

Georgia O'Keeffe, *left,* won fame for her stark, simple paintings. She sought beauty by isolating and intensifying such things in nature as the skull and flowers in *Cow's Skull with Calico Roses.*

Candelario, U.S. Camera Annual

The Rare Okapi Resembles the Giraffe.
Underwood & Underwood

Courtesy of The Art Institute of Chicago, Gift of Georgia O'Keeffe

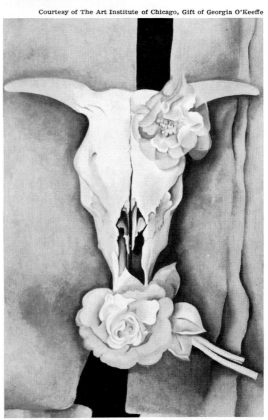

canvas, and transformed them into clear and precise designs. She painted early American buildings and city scenes, but began using subjects near Taos, N.Mex., after moving there in 1929. Her paintings include *A Cross by the Sea, Canada, Black Iris, Farmhouse Window and Door,* and *Lake George.*

Georgia O'Keeffe was born in Sun Prairie, Wis. Her work was first seen in 1916 at "291," the gallery started by Alfred Stieglitz to show work by artists trying new forms. Stieglitz, a famous photographer, encouraged her to seek her personal vision of the abstract design in nature. They were married in 1924 (see STIEGLITZ, ALFRED). Georgia O'Keeffe had exhibitions at the Art Institute of Chicago and the Museum of Modern Art. She also exhibited at the Intimate Gallery and at An American Place in New York City. During 1908 and 1909, she worked in advertising art in Chicago. In 1916 and 1917, she was supervisor of public schools at Amarillo, Tex., and in 1918 taught art in Texas. She studied at the Art Institute of Chicago, the Art Students' League in New York City, the University of Virginia, and Columbia University. She was elected to the American Academy of Arts and Letters in 1962.   GEORGE D. CULLER

OKEFENOKEE SWAMP, *O kuh fuh NO kee,* is a marshy, tropical wilderness in southeastern Georgia and northeastern Florida. Most of it was bought by the government in 1937, and 293,826 acres (118,907 hectares) in Georgia were set aside as a wildlife refuge.

The name *Okefenokee* comes from the Indian word *Owaquaphenoga,* which means *trembling earth.* It refers to the trembling of the small bushes and water weeds that float on the lakes of Okefenokee.

The swamp is about 40 miles (64 kilometers) long and 30 miles (48 kilometers) wide. It covers an area of 700 square miles (1,800 square kilometers). Fine timberlands and fresh-water lakes lie next to the marshy stretches. The region is drained by the St. Marys and the Suwannee rivers. Other bodies of water wind through the swamp. There are about 25 islands. For location, see color maps with FLORIDA; GEORGIA.

The swamp was once a favorite hunting ground of the Creek and Seminole Indians. Today as a government preserve it is the home of many animals, including deer, bears, wildcats, otters, raccoons, opossums, and alligators. The swamp is the winter refuge of many birds that spend the summer in the North. There are about 50 kinds of fish in its waters. Plants that grow there include white and golden lilies, Spanish moss, and cypress trees.   KATHRYN ABBEY HANNA

See also GEORGIA (color picture).

OKHOTSK, *oh KAHTSK,* **SEA OF,** is a large arm of the north Pacific Ocean on the eastern boundary of Russia. The sea is about 1,000 miles (1,600 kilometers) long and 600 miles (970 kilometers) wide, and covers 589,800 square miles (1,527,600 square kilometers). It is separated from the Bering Sea on the east by the Kamchatka Peninsula (see RUSSIA [map]). The Kuril Islands on the south separate the sea from the Pacific Ocean. Ice covers the Sea of Okhotsk from November to April, and heavy fogs and storms occur often. But the sea is used as a trade waterway for the ports of Magadan and Okhotsk in Russia. The Amur River and smaller streams empty into the sea.   BOSTWICK H. KETCHUM

OKINAWA

WORLD BOOK map

OKINAWA, OH *kah NAH wuh,* or in Japanese, *AW kee NAH wah,* is the largest and most important island of the Ryukyu Islands, a chain of islands in the western Pacific Ocean. Okinawa is a *prefecture* (district) of Japan. It covers 554 square miles (1,434 square kilometers) and has 945,111 persons. Naha, the capital and largest city of the Ryukyus, is on Okinawa.

Okinawa was a prefecture of Japan before World War II (1939-1945). The United States captured the island during the war and administered it until 1972, when it was returned to Japanese control.

Okinawa has had great military importance for the United States because it lies within easy flying distance of China, Hong Kong, Japan, the Philippines, Taiwan, and Vietnam. The United States built air bases and other installations on the island and continues to maintain them even after having given up control of Okinawa to Japan.

Richard Joseph Pearson, contributor of this article, is Professor of Anthropology at the University of British Columbia.

Government. Voters elect a governor to head the government of Okinawa. The island legislature, the *Prefectural Assembly*, consists of 44 members. Okinawans also elect seven representatives to the *Diet* (national parliament) in Tokyo.

People. The people of Okinawa look much like the Japanese, but Okinawans are shorter and have darker skin. Their language belongs to the Japanese language family, and most Okinawans also speak Japanese.

Many Okinawans live in small villages of red tile-roofed houses. Their main food is rice. Much pork is also eaten. Most village people are farmers or fishermen. Many wear traditional Japanese clothing—kimonos or cotton pants and jackets. Naha and other cities have modern buildings and traffic-choked streets. In the cities, many people wear Western-style clothing.

The University of the Ryukyus, in Naha, is Okinawa's major institution of higher education. About 265,000 students attend the island's elementary, junior high, and high schools. About 95 per cent of the people can read and write.

Land and Climate. Okinawa is 67 miles (108 kilometers) long and from 2 to 16 miles (3 to 26 kilometers) wide. Mountains and jungle cover the northern part of the island. The southern part has low, rocky hills. Most of the people live in the south.

Okinawa has a subtropical climate. The average daily temperature in Naha is 72° F. (22° C) the year around. Rainfall averages about 83 inches (211 centimeters) yearly, most of it falling in the typhoon season, from April to October.

Economy. Before World War II, Okinawa was a poor agricultural island. Today, it has one of the highest *per capita* (per person) incomes in the Far East. Its economy depends largely on U.S. military spending. The chief crops include pineapples, rice, sugar cane, and sweet potatoes. Tourism is growing in importance. Most of the tourists come from other parts of Japan.

Okinawan craftsmen make ceramics, lacquerware, and woven and dyed cloth. A pottery kiln in Naha has been operating since the 1600's. Okinawan arts and crafts are prized by art collectors, especially in Japan.

History. Okinawa became a prefecture of Japan in 1879. For the history of the island before that time, see the article on RYUKYU ISLANDS.

One of the bloodiest campaigns of World War II was fought on Okinawa between American and Japanese troops. The Americans landed on the island on April 1, 1945, and conquered it in late June. During the fighting, more than 90 per cent of the island's buildings were destroyed. See WORLD WAR II (Okinawa).

The peace treaty that ended the war gave the United States control of the Ryukyu Islands. In 1950, the United States began to grant some self-rule to the Ryukyuans. It returned the northern Ryukyus to Japan in 1953 but kept Okinawa and the southern islands. The United States built military bases on Okinawa after the Chinese Communists gained control of China in 1949 and the Korean War broke out in 1950.

During the 1950's and 1960's, many Okinawans demanded that the island be returned to Japanese rule. The United States returned the island to Japan in 1972. Under an agreement between the United States and Japan, U.S. military bases remain on Okinawa, but nuclear weapons may not be kept on the island without Japan's consent.   RICHARD JOSEPH PEARSON

A Farmworker in northern Okinawa cuts pineapples from their plants and drops them into a basket strapped to her back. Pineapples rank among the leading exports of Okinawa.

David Moore, Black Star

Naha, Okinawa's Capital and Biggest City, is a busy commercial center. The city was almost completely destroyed during World War II (1939-1945), but it was rebuilt after the war.

Kyodo News Service

An Oil Pump on the Prairie near Oklahoma City

OKLAHOMA

THE SOONER STATE

OKLAHOMA is a major fuel and food producing state in the Southwest. Thousands of oil and natural gas wells dot the Oklahoma landscape. Oil pumps operate even on the front lawn of the state Capitol. Millions of white-faced beef cattle graze on Oklahoma's flat plains and low hills. Fertile fields produce vast crops of wheat.

Oklahoma is also a manufacturing state. Manufacturing and processing rank with mining and farming as major sources of wealth for the people. Busy plants process petroleum and farm products. Factories making electrical equipment, metal products, and nonelectrical machinery produce a variety of manufactured goods.

The development of Oklahoma's vast resources began with the Indians. In the 1800's, the U.S. government made most of the region a huge Indian reservation. The Indians established separate nations, with their own governments and schools. The name *Oklahoma* is a combination of two Choctaw Indian words— *okla*, meaning *people*, and *homma*, meaning *red*.

The government first opened Oklahoma to white settlement during the late 1880's. Oklahoma became known as the *Sooner State* because some settlers were there "sooner" than the land was opened. It is also called the *Boomer State*, after the promoters who "boomed" white settlement. The land was settled rapidly, and whites soon far outnumbered the Indians.

During the early 1900's, the farms and ranches of Oklahoma were fertile and productive. In the 1930's, however, a long dry period and low farm prices brought disaster to the farmers. Many farmers and other workers left the state, and Oklahoma's population dropped.

Both these periods of Oklahoma history have become famous. The story of the state's farmers and cattlemen in territorial days is told in the musical play *Oklahoma!* The title song from the play became Oklahoma's state song. John Steinbeck's famous novel *The Grapes of Wrath* included a fictional, but widely accepted, description of the drought of the 1930's.

Today, Oklahoma's industries attract new residents. Farmers protect their land from drought with modern soil and water conservation methods. The state's oil and gas wells continue to yield their valuable products. Oklahoma City, the state capital and largest city in population, is one of the largest U.S. cities in area. It covers about 650 square miles (1,680 square kilometers).

For the relationship of Oklahoma to other states in its region, see the article on the SOUTHWESTERN STATES.

Bob Taylor
Combines Harvesting Wheat in Oklahoma

--- FACTS IN BRIEF ---

Capital: Oklahoma City.

Government: *Congress*—U.S. senators, 2; U.S. representatives, 6. *Electoral Votes*—8. *State Legislature*—senators,
48; representatives, 101. *Counties*—77.

Area: 69,919 sq. mi. (181,089 km²), including 1,137 sq.
mi. (2,945 km²) of inland water; 18th in size among the
states. *Greatest Distances*—east-west, 464 mi. (747 km);
north-south, 230 mi. (370 km).

Elevation: *Highest*—Black Mesa in Cimarron County,
4,973 ft. (1,516 m) above sea level. *Lowest*—along the
Little River in McCurtain County, 287 ft. (87 m)
above sea level.

Population: *Estimated 1975 Population*—2,712,000. *1970
Census*—2,559,253; 27th among the states; distribution,
68 per cent urban, 32 per cent rural; density, 37 persons per sq. mi. (14 persons per km²).

Chief Products: *Agriculture*—beef cattle, cotton, dairy
products, hogs, peanuts, wheat. *Manufacturing*—electrical equipment; food and food products; metal products; nonelectrical machinery; stone, clay, and glass
products. *Mining*—coal, helium, natural gas, natural
gas liquids, petroleum, sand and gravel, stone.

Statehood: Nov. 16, 1907, the 46th state.

State Motto: *Labor Omnia Vincit* (Labor Conquers All
Things).

State Song: "Oklahoma!" Words by Oscar Hammerstein
II; music by Richard Rodgers.

*The contributors of this article are W. Eugene Hollon,
former Professor of American History at the University of
Oklahoma; John W. Morris, Chairman of the Department of
Geography at the University of Oklahoma; and Charles L. Bennett, Executive Editor for* The Daily Oklahoman *of Oklahoma City and the* Oklahoma City Times.

Oklahoma (blue) ranks 18th in size among all of the states, and
is the smallest of the Southwestern States (gray).

Constitution. The Oklahoma Constitution was adopted in 1907, the year Oklahoma became a state. It may be amended by a majority vote of the people. Amendments may be proposed by the Legislature or by petitions from the voters. A constitutional convention may be called by the Legislature, subject to voter approval. The Constitution contains initiative and referendum clauses which allow the voters to propose and pass laws directly (see INITIATIVE AND REFERENDUM).

Executive. The governor is elected to a four-year term. The governor may serve any number of terms, but not more than two in a row. The governor receives a yearly salary of $35,000. For a list of all the state's governors, see the *History* section of this article.

The governor appoints the heads of the chief revenue and budget departments. Some department heads are chosen by a board or by a commission, not by the governor. But the top state officials—the lieutenant governor, secretary of state, attorney general, treasurer, auditor and inspector, and superintendent of public instruction—are elected to four-year terms.

Legislature of Oklahoma consists of a Senate with 48 members and a House of Representatives with 101 members. Each senator and representative is elected from a separate district. Senators are elected to four-year terms and representatives to two-year terms. The Legislature meets in annual sessions that begin on the Tuesday after the first Monday in January.

In 1964, a U.S. District Court changed many of the state's legislative districts to give fair representation to the larger cities. The Legislature had been *apportioned* (divided) to give rural areas more than their fair share of representatives. In 1971, the Legislature reapportioned both the Senate and the House of Representatives.

Courts. The Oklahoma Supreme Court has nine justices. They select a chief justice from their group. The governor appoints the justices with the aid of a judicial nominating commission. After serving at least one year,

Kurt Severin, Black Star

The Cowboy, a famous statue by Constance Whitney Warren, stands in front of the state Capitol in Oklahoma City.

a justice must win in the next general election for a six-year term. The Court of Appeals has six judges elected to six-year terms. The state also has a Court of Criminal Appeals with three judges. These judges are chosen in the same way that supreme court justices are selected. Oklahoma has 51 district court judges elected to four-year terms. Each county also has at least one associate district judge elected to a four-year term.

Oklahoma Industrial Development and Park Department

The Governor's Mansion stands a block east of the Capitol in Oklahoma City. The building, completed in 1928, has a white limestone facing and a red tile roof. Gardens surround the mansion.

The State Seal

Symbols of Oklahoma. On the state seal, the Indian and the white man shake hands before Justice to show the cooperation of all the people of Oklahoma. The large star has symbols of the Five Civilized Tribes, which first settled the region. The seal was adopted in 1907. The state flag, adopted in 1925, has two symbols of peace—a peace pipe and an olive branch. The shield behind these symbols stands for defensive warfare.

Local Government in Oklahoma operates in 77 counties and about 560 cities and towns. The counties have three commissioners, each elected from a separate district. Most cities and towns use the mayor-council or council-manager form of government. The state constitution allows cities of over 2,000 population to adopt and amend their own charters. This gives the cities some control over their own affairs.

Taxation. The state collects a sales tax and individual and corporate income taxes. State taxes, plus revenue from licenses, permits, and fees, provide about two-thirds of the money to run the state government. Almost all the rest of the state's income comes from federal grants and other United States government programs.

Politics. Oklahoma was once almost solidly Democratic. The state began to develop a two-party system in the 1960's. Oklahoma voters elected the state's first Republican governor in 1962, and the second in 1966. Oklahomans have favored Republican candidates in most presidential elections since 1948. For Oklahoma's electoral votes and for the state's voting record in presidential elections, see ELECTORAL COLLEGE (table).

The State Capitol was completed in 1917 in an area that later became a major oil field. Oklahoma City has been the capital since 1910. The only other capital was Guthrie (1890-1910).

Bob Taylor

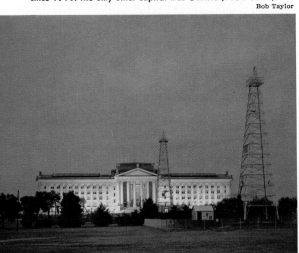

The State Flag

The State Flower
Mistletoe

The State Bird
Scissor-Tailed Flycatcher

The State Tree
Redbud

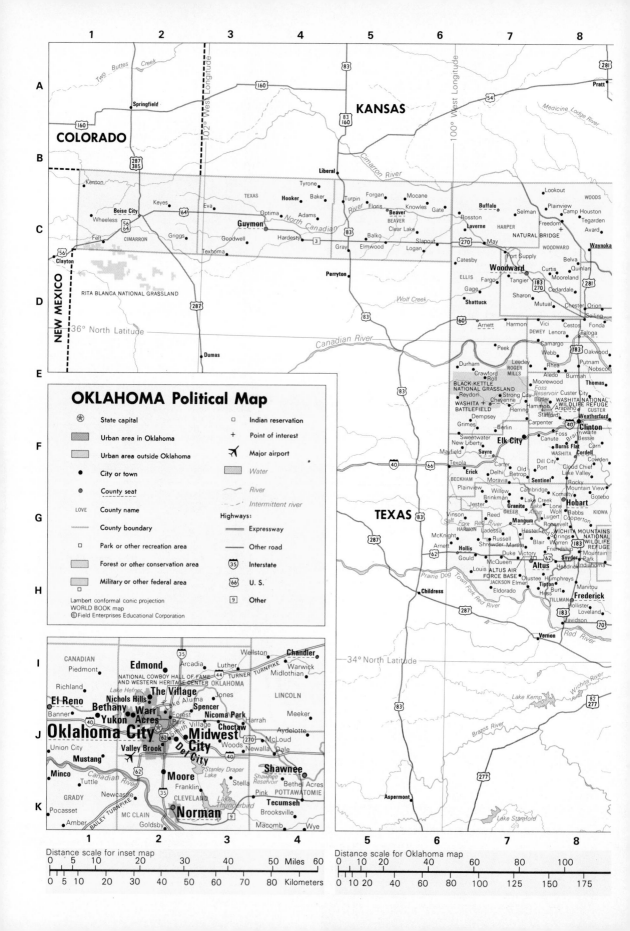

OKLAHOMA Political Map

⊛	State capital	⊡	Indian reservation
▨	Urban area in Oklahoma	+	Point of interest
▨	Urban area outside Oklahoma	✈	Major airport
●	City or town	▨	Water
●	County seat		River
LOVE	County name		Intermittent river
	County boundary	**Highways:**	
⊡	Park or other recreation area		Expressway
▨	Forest or other conservation area		Other road
⊡	Military or other federal area	35	Interstate
		66	U.S.
		9	Other

Lambert conformal conic projection
WORLD BOOK map
©Field Enterprises Educational Corporation

COLORADO

KANSAS

NEW MEXICO

TEXAS

102° West Longitude
100° West Longitude
36° North Latitude
34° North Latitude

Distance scale for inset map
0 5 10   20   30   40   50 Miles 60
0 5 10 20 30 40 50 60 70 80 Kilometers

Distance scale for Oklahoma map
0 10 20   40   60   80   100
0 10 20 40 60 80 100 125 150 175

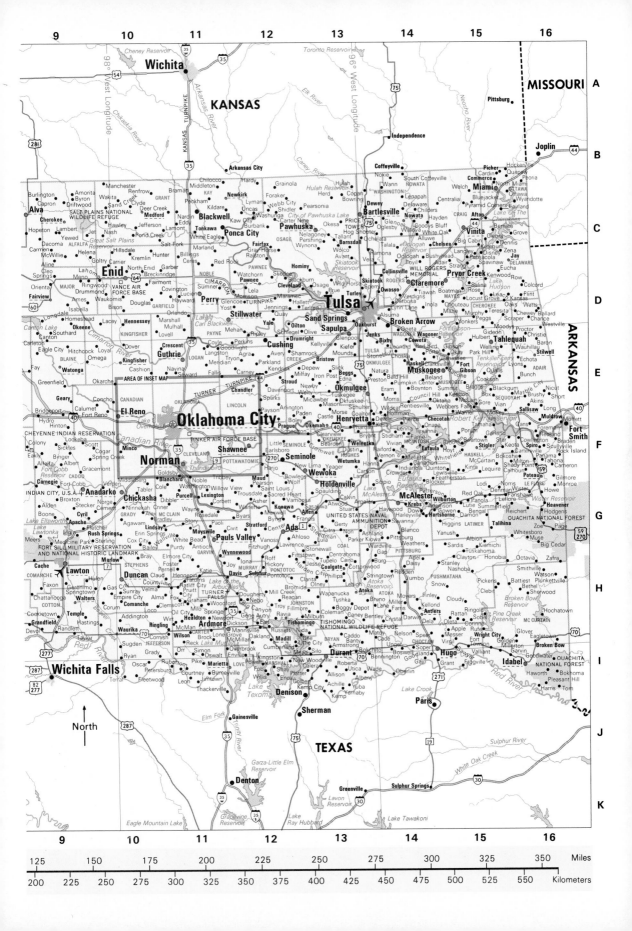

Population

2,712,000 Estimate..1975
2,559,253 ..Census..1970
2,328,284 ....“....1960
2,233,351 ....“....1950
2,336,434 ....“....1940
2,396,040 ....“....1930
2,028,283 ....“....1920
1,657,155 ....“....1910
790,391 ....“....1900
258,657 ....“....1890

Metropolitan Areas

Fort Smith (Ark.) 160,421
(104,914 in Ark.;
55,507 in Okla.)
Lawton 108,144
Oklahoma City ..699,092
Tulsa 549,154

Counties

Adair ......15,141..E 16
Alfalfa .....7,224..C 9
Atoka ......10,972..H 14
Beaver .....6,282..C 5
Beckham ...15,754..F 6
Blaine .....11,794..E 9
Bryan .....25,552..I 13
Caddo .....28,931..F 9
Canadian ..32,245..E 10
Carter .....37,349..I 11
Cherokee ...23,174..D 15
Choctaw ...15,141..I 14
Cimarron ...4,145..C 1
Cleveland ..81,839..F 11
Coal ....5,525..G 13
Comanche .108,144..H 8
Cotton .....6,832..H 9
Craig ......14,722..C 15
Creek .....45,532..E 12
Custer .....22,665..E 8
Delaware ..17,767..C 16
Dewey ......5,656..D 7
Ellis ....5,129..D 6
Garfield ...56,343..D 10
Garvin .....24,874..G 11
Grady .....29,354..G 10
Grant ....7,117..C 10
Greer ....7,979..G 7
Harmon ....5,136..G 6
Harper .....5,151..C 7
Haskell .....9,578..F 15
Hughes ....13,228..F 13
Jackson ....30,902..H 7
Jefferson ...7,125..I 10
Johnston ....7,870..H 12
Kay ....48,791..B 11
Kingfisher .12,857..D 10
Kiowa .....12,532..G 8
Latimer ....8,601..G 15
Le Flore ...32,137..G 16
Lincoln ....19,482..E 11
Logan .....19,645..E 11
Love ....5,637..I 12
Major ......7,529..D 9
Marshall ...7,682..I 12
Mayes .....23,302..D 15
McClain ...14,157..G 10
McCurtain .28,642..H 16
McIntosh ..12,472..F 14
Murray ....10,669..H 12
Muskogee ..59,542..E 15
Noble .....10,043..D 11
Nowata .....9,773..B 14
Okfuskee ...10,683..F 13
Oklahoma .527,717..F 11
Okmulgee ..35,358..E 13
Osage .....29,750..C 12
Ottawa ....29,800..B 16
Pawnee ....11,338..D 12
Payne .....50,654..D 11
Pittsburg ..37,521..G 14
Pontotoc ...27,867..H 12
Pottawat-
omie ....43,134..F 11
Pushmataha 9,385..H 14
Roger Mills .4,452..E 7
Rogers .....28,425..D 14
Seminole ...25,144..F 12
Sequoyah ..23,370..E 15
Stephens ...35,902..H 10
Texas ......16,352..C 3
Tillman ...12,901..H 8
Tulsa .....399,982..E 13
Wagoner ...22,163..D 14
Washington 42,302..B 14
Washita ...12,141..F 8
Woods .....11,920..C 8
Woodward .15,537..C 8

Cities and Towns

Achille ....382..I 13
Ada ....14,859.°G 12
Adair ....459..C 15
Adams ....C 4
Adamson ....G 14
Addington ....123..H 10
Afton ....1,022..C 15
Agawam ....G 10
Agra ....335..E 12
Ahloso ....G 12
Albany ....I 13
Albert ....F 9
Albion ....186..G 15
Alderson* ....215..G 14
Alex ....492..G 10
Alfalfa ....F 9
Aline ....260..C 9
Allen ....974..G 13
Alluwe ....116..C 14
Alma ....H 11
Altus ......23,302.°H 7
Alva ....7,440.°C 8
Amber ....K 1
Ames ....227..D 9
Amorita ....63..B 9
Anadarko ...6,682.°G 9
Antioch ....G 11
Antlers .....2,685.°H 14
Apache .....1,421..G 9
Arapaho ......531.°E 8
Arcadia ....I 3
Ardmore ...20,881.°I 11
Arkoma* ....2,098..F 16
Arlington ....E 12
Armstrong ....I 13
Arnett ....711.°D 7
Arnett ....G 6
Arpelar ....G 14
Asher ....437..G 12
Ashland ....73..G 13
Atoka ......3,346.°H 13
Atwood ....G 13
Avant ....439..C 13
Avard ....59..C 8
Avery ....E 12
Aydelotte ....J 4
Babbs ....G 8
Bacone ....E 15
Bailey ....G 10
Baker ....C 4
Bald Hill ....E 14
Balko ....C 5
Ballard ....D 16
Banner ....J 1
Banty ....I 13
Barnsdall ...1,579..C 13
Baron ....E 16
Bartlesville 29,683.°C 13
Battiest ....H 16
Bearden ....F 13
Beaver .....1,853.°C 5
Bee ....I 12
Beggs ......1,107..E 13
Beland ....E 14
Belva ....C 8
Bengal ....G 15
Bennington ...288..I 13
Bentley ....H 13
Berlin ....F 7
Bernice ....189..C 15
Bessie ....210..F 8
Bethany ...22,694..J 1
Bethel ....H 16
Bethel Acres 1,083..K 4
Big Cabin ....198..C 15
Big Cedar ....G 16
Billings ......618..C 11
Binger ....730..F 9
Bison ....D 10
Bixby ......3,973..E 14
Blackburn .....88..D 12
Blackgum ....E 15
Blackwell ...8,645..C 11
Blair ....1,114..G 7
Blanchard ..1,580..F 10
Blanco ....G 14
Blocker ....G 14
Bluejacket ....234..C 15
Boatman ....D 15
Boggy Depot ......H 13
Boise City ..1,993.°C 2
Bokchito .....607..I 13
Bokhoma ....I 16
Bokoshe ......588..F 16
Boley ....514..F 13
Boone ....G 9
Boswell ......755..I 14
Bowlegs ....F 12
Bowring ....C 13
Box ....E 15
Boynton ......522..E 14
Braden ....F 16
Bradley ......247..G 10
Braggs ....325..E 15
Braman ......295..B 11
Bray ....H 10
Breckinridge ...70..D 10
Briartown ....F 15
Bridgeport ....142..F 9
Brinkman ......7..G 7
Bristow .....4,653..E 13
Broken
Arrow ...11,787..D 14
Broken Bow 3,843..I 16
Bromide ......231..H 13
Brooken ....F 15
Brooksville ....K 4
Broxton ....G 9
Bruno ....H 13
Brushy ....E 16
Bryant ....86..F 13
Buffalo .....1,579.°C 7
Bunch ....E 16
Burbank ......188..C 12
Burg ....H 14
Burlington ....165..C 9
Burmah ....E 8
Burneyville ....I 11
Burns Flat ...988..F 8
Burt ....H 8
Bushyhead ....C 14
Butler ....315..E 8
Byars ....247..G 12
Byng ....G 12
Byron ....72..C 9
Cache ......1,106..H 9
Caddo ....886..I 13
Cade ....I 14
Cairo ....H 13
Calera ......1,063..I 13
Calhoun ....F 16
Calumet ......386..E 10
Calvin ....359..G 13
Camargo .....236..D 7
Cambridge ....G 8
Cameron .....311..F 16
Camp Houston .....C 8
Canadian .....304..F 14
Caney ....200..H 13
Canton ....844..D 9
Canute ....420..F 7
Capron ....80..C 9
Cardin ....B 15
Carleton ....E 9
Carmen ....519..C 9
Carnegie ....1,723..G 9
Carney ....396..E 12
Carpenter ....F 7
Carrier ....C 10
Carson ....F 13
Carter ....311..F 7
Carter Nine ....C 12
Cartersville ....F 16
Cashion ......329..E 10
Castle ....212..F 13
Catesby ....C 6
Catoosa ......970..D 14
Cement ....892..G 10
Center ....G 12
Centrahoma ...155..H 13
Centralia ......43..C 14
Ceres ....C 11
Cestos ....D 8
Chance ....D 16
Chandler ....2,529.°E 12
Chattanooga ..302..H 9
Checotah ...3,074..F 14
Chelsea .....1,622..C 14
Cherokee ....2,119.°C 9
Chester ....D 8
Chewey ....D 16
Cheyenne .....892.°E 7
Chickasha ..14,194.°G 10
Childers ....C 14
Chilocco ....B 11
Choctaw ....4,750..J 3
Choska ....E 14
Chouteau ...1,046..D 15
Christie ....D 16
Citra ....G 13
Civit ....G 11
Claremore ...9,084.°D 14
Clarita ....H 13
Clarksville ....E 14
Claud ....H 11
Clayton ......718..H 15
Clear Lake ....C 6
Clearview ....F 13
Clebit ....H 15
Clemscott ....H 11
Cleo Springs ..344..D 9
Cleora ....C 15
Cleveland ...2,573..D 13
Clinton .....8,513..F 8
Cloud Chief ....F 8
Cloudy ....H 15
Clyde ....C 10
Coalgate ....1,859.°H 13
Coalton ....F 14
Cogar ....F 10
Colbert ....814..I 13
Colcord ......438..D 16
Cold Springs ......G 8
Cole ....G 11
Coleman ....H 13
Collinsville ..3,009..D 14
Colony ....201..F 8
Comanche ...1,862..H 10
Commerce ...2,593..B 15
Concho ....E 10
Coodys Bluff ....C 14
Cookietown ....H 9
Cookson ....E 15
Cooperton .....55..G 8
Copan ....675..B 13
Corbett ....G 11
Cordell .....3,261.°F 8
Corinne ....H 15
Corn ....409..F 8
Cornish ....90..I 11
Corum ....H 10
Cottonwood ....H 13
Council Hill ...135..E 14
Countyline ....H 11
Courtney ....I 11
Covington ....605..D 10
Cowden ....F 8
Coweta .....2,457..E 14
Cowlington ...751..F 16
Cox City ....G 10
Coyle ....303..E 11
Crawford ....E 7
Crescent ....1,568..E 10
Criner ....G 11
Cromwell .....287..F 13
Crowder ......339..F 14
Crystal ....H 14
Cumberland ....I 12
Curtis ....D 8
Cushing ....7,529..E 12
Custer City ...486..E 8
Cyril ....1,302..G 9
Dacoma ......226..C 9
Daisy ....H 14
Dale ....J 4
Damon ....G 15
Darwin ....H 14
Davenport ....831..E 12
Davidson .....515..H 8
Davis ....2,223..H 11
Deer Creek ...203..C 11
Del City ...27,133..J 2
Dela ....H 14
Delaware .....534..C 14
Delhi ....F 7
Dempsey ....F 6
Denman ....G 15
Dennis ....C 15
Depew ....739..E 12
Devol ....129..I 9
Dewar ....933..F 14
Dewey ......3,958..C 13
Dibble ....184..G 10
Dickson ......798..I 12
Dill City .....578..F 8
Disney ....303..C 15
Dougherty ....211..H 12
Douglas ....79..D 10
Dover ....E 10
Dow ....G 14
Driftwood .....27..C 9
Drummond ...326..D 10
Drumright ..2,931..D 12
Duke ....486..H 7
Duncan ....19,718.°H 10
Durant ....11,118.°I 13
Durham ....E 6
Dustin ....502..F 13
Eagle City ....E 9
Eagletown ....I 16
Eakly ....228..F 9
Earl ....H 12
Earlsboro .....248..F 12
Echota ....E 16
Eddy ....C 11
Edmond ...16,633..I 2
Edna ....E 13
Eldorado .....737..H 7
Elgin ....840..G 9
Elk City ....7,323..F 7
Elmer ....138..H 7
Elmore City ...653..H 11
Elmwood ....C 5
El Reno ...14,510.°F 10
Empire City ...23..H 10
Enid ......44,986.°D 10
Enos ....I 12
Enville ....I 12
Eram ....E 14
Erick ....1,285..F 6
Erin Springs ....G 11
Eucha ....D 15
Eufaula ....2,355.°F 14
Eva ....C 3
Fair Oaks* ....23..D 14
Fairfax .....1,889..C 12
Fairland ......814..C 15
Fairmont .....154..D 10
Fairview ....2,894.°D 9
Fallis ....39..E 11
Fame ....F 14
Fanshawe ....199..G 15
Fargo ....262..D 7
Farris ....H 14
Faxon ....121..H 9
Fay ....E 8
Featherston ....F 14
Felt ....C 1
Fillmore ....H 13
Finley ....H 14
Fittstown ....H 12
Fitzhugh ....G 12
Fleetwood ....I 10
Fletcher ......950..G 9
Flint ....D 16
Floris ....C 5
Fob ....I 12
Foraker ....52..C 12
Forest Park ...835..J 2
Forgan ....496..C 5
Fort Cobb ....722..G 9
Fort Gibson .1,418..E 15
Fort Reno ....F 10
Fort Sill ..21,217..G 9
Fort Supply ..550..C 7
Fort Towson ..430..I 15
Foss ....150..F 8
Foster ....H 11
Fox ....H 11
Foyil ....164..C 14
Francis ......283..G 12
Franklin ....K 3
Frederick ...6,132.°H 8
Freedom .....292..C 8
Friendship ....G 8
Frogville ....I 15
Gage ....536..D 7
Gans ....238..F 16
Gap ....H 14
Garber .....1,011..D 10
Garland ....F 15
Garvin ....117..I 16
Gas City ....H 10
Gate ....151..C 6
Gay ....I 14
Geary ......1,380..E 9
Gene Autry ...120..H 12
Geronimo .....587..H 9
Gerty ....139..G 13
Gibson ....E 15
Gideon ....D 15
Gilmore ....F 16
Glencoe ......421..D 12
Glenoak ....C 14
Glenpool .....770..E 13
Glover ....I 16
Golden ....I 16
Goldsby ......298..F 11
Goltry ....282..C 9
Goodland ....I 14
Goodnight ....E 11
Goodwater ....I 16
Goodwell ...1,467..C 3
Gore ....478..E 15
Gotebo ....376..G 8
Gould ....368..G 7
Gowen ....G 14
Gracemont ....424..F 9
Grady ....I 10
Graham ....H 11
Grainola ......66..B 12
Grand Lake
Towne* ......23..D 15
Grandfield ..1,524..H 8
Granite .....1,808..G 7
Grant ....273..I 14
Gray ....C 5
Gray Horse ....C 12
Grayson* .....142..F 14
Greenfield ....143..E 9
Griggs ....C 2
Grimes ....F 7
Grove ......2,000..C 16
Guthrie .....9,575.°E 11
Guymon ....7,674.°C 3
Haileyville ....928..G 14
Hall Park* ...163..F 11
Hallett ....125..D 12
Hammon .....677..E 7
Hanna ....181..F 14
Harden City ....H 12
Hardesty .....223..C 4
Hardy ....5..B 12
Harjo ....F 12
Harmon ....D 7
Harrah .....1,931..J 3
Harris ....I 16
Hartshorne .2,121..G 14
Haskell .....2,063..E 14
Hastings .....184..H 10
Hawley ....C 10
Haworth .....293..I 16
Hayden ....C 14
Hayward ....D 11
Haywood ....G 14
Headrick .....139..H 8
Healdton ...2,324..H 11
Heavener ...2,566..G 16
Helena ....769..C 9
Hennepin ....H 11
Hennessey ..2,181..D 10
Henryetta ...6,430..F 13
Herd ....C 13
Herring ....E 7
Hess ....H 7
Hester ....G 7
Hickory ....62..H 12
Higgins ....G 15
Hillsdale ......77..C 10
Hinton ....889..F 9
Hitchcock ....160..E 9
Hitchita* .....160..E 14
Hobart .....4,638.°G 8
Hochatown ....H 16
Hockerville ....B 15
Hodgens ....G 16
Hoffman .....262..F 14
Hog Shooter ....C 14
Holdenville .5,181.°G 13
Hollis ......3,150.°G 6
Hollister .....105..H 8
Homestead ....D 9
Hominy .....2,274..D 13
Honobia ....H 15
Hooker .....1,615..C 4
Hopeton ....C 8
Howe ....403..G 16
Hoyt ....F 15
Hugo ....6,585.°I 14
Hulah ....B 13
Hulbert ......505..E 15
Hulen ....H 9
Humphreys ....H 8
Hunter ....274..C 10
Hydro ....805..F 9
Idabel ......5,946.°I 16
Indiahoma ....434..H 8
Indianola .....205..F 14
Ingersoll* .....17..C 9
Inola ....948..D 14
Iona ....H 12
Iron Post ....E 13
Isabella ....D 9
Jay ....1,594.°C 16
Jefferson .....128..C 10
Jenks ....1,997..D 13
Jennings .....338..D 12
Jesse ....H 13
Jester ....G 7
Jet ....317..C 9

Jimtown ....I 11
Jones ....1,666..J 3
Joy ....H 11
Jumbo ....D 14
Kansas ....317..D 16
Katie ....H 11
Kaw City ...283..C 12
Keefton ......E 15
Kellond ....H 14
Kellyville ...685..E 13
Kemp ......153..I 13
Kemp City ...117..I 13
Kendrick ...126..E 12
Kenefick* ...153..I 13
Kenton ....B 1
Kenwood ......D 15
Keota ......685..F 15
Ketchum ....238..C 15
Keyes .....569..C 2
Kiamichi ......G 15
Kiefer .....803..E 13
Kildare ....79..C 11
Kingfisher ..4,042..°E 10
Kingston ...710..I 12
Kinta ......247..F 15
Kiowa ......754..G 14
Knowles ....52..C 6
Komalty ....G 8
Konawa ...1,719..G 12
Krebs ....1,515..G 14
Kremlin ....200..C 10
Kusa ....F 14
Lacey ....G 7
Ladessa ....G 7
Lahoma ...299..D 10
Lake Aluma ..124..J 2
Lake Creek .....G 7
Lake Valley ....F 8
Lamar .....153..F 13
Lambert ....16..C 9
Lamont ....478..C 11
Lane ....H 14
Langley ....481..C 15
Langston ...486..E 11
Laverne ..1,373..C 6
Lawrence ......G 12
Lawton ..74,470..°H 9
Leach ....D 15
Leedey ....465..E 7
Leflore ....175..G 15
Lehigh ....296..H 13
Lela ....D 12
Lenapah ...325..C 14
Lenna ....F 14
Lenora .....D 8
Leon ......112..I 11
Leonard ......E 14
Lequire ......F 15
Lewisville ....F 15
Lexington .1,516..G 11
Lima* .....238..F 13
Lindsay ..3,705..G 11
Little ....F 12
Little City ..80..I 12
Loco ......193..H 10
Locust Grove 1,090..D 15
Lodi ....G 15
Logan ....C 6
Lone Grove .1,240..I 11
Lone Wolf ..584..G 8
Long ....E 16
Longdale ...331..D 9
Lookeba ...165..F 9
Lookout .....B 7
Lotsee* ....16..D 14
Louis ....H 6
Loveland ...36..H 8
Lovell .....28..D 10
Loyal .....107..E 10
Lucien ......D 11
Luport ......G 13
Lula ....G 13
Luther ....836..I 3
Lutie ......G 15
Lyman ......C 12
Lynn Lane ....D 14
Lyons ....E 15
Macomb ....41..K 4
Madill ...2,875..°I 12
Manchester ..165..B 10
Mangum ..4,066..°G 7
Manitou ...308..H 8
Mannford* ..892..D 13
Mannsville ..364..I 12
Maramec ...128..D 12
Marble City ..299..E 16
Marietta ..2,013..°I 11
Marland ....236..C 11
Marlow ...3,995..H 10
Marshall ...420..D 10
Martha .....268..G 7
Mason ......E 13
Matoy ....I 13
Maud .....1,143..F 12
Maxwell ......G 12
May ....91..C 7
Mayfield .....F 6
Maysville .1,380..G 11
Mazie ......D 15
McAlester .18,802..°G 14
McBride* ....44..I 12
McCurtain ..575..F 15
McKey ......F 15
McKnight .....G 6
McLain .....E 15
McLoud ..2,159..J 3
McMan ......H 11
McMillan ....I 12

McQueen ......H 7
McWillie .....C 9
Mead ....I 13
Medford ..1,304..°C 10
Medicine Park 483..G 9
Meeker ....683..J 4
Meers ....G 9
Mehan ......D 12
Mellette ....F 14
Meno ......119..D 9
Meridian ...104..E 11
Messer ......I 15
Miami ...13,880..°B 15
Micawber .....E 13
Middleberg ....G 10
Middleton .....B 11
Midlothian ...I 4
Midwest
City ....48,212..J 2
Milburn ....275..H 13
Milfay ......E 12
Mill Creek ..234..H 12
Miller ....H 14
Millerton ....I 15
Milo ....H 11
Milton .....F 16
Minco ....1,129..F 10
Mocane ......B 6
Moffett ....312..F 16
Monroe ......G 16
Moodys ......D 15
Moore ...18,761..K 2
Mooreland .1,196..D 8
Moorewood .....E 7
Moravia .....F 7
Morris ...1,119..E 14
Morrison ...421..D 12
Morse ....E 13
Mounds ....766..E 13
Mountain Park 458..G 8
Mountain
View ....1,110..G 8
Moyers ....H 14
Muldrow ..1,680..F 16
Mulhall ....250..D 11
Murphy ......D 15
Muse ....G 16
Muskogee .37,331..°E 15
Mustang ..2,637..J 1
Mutual .....94..D 8
Nardin ....135..C 11
Nash ......294..C 10
Nashoba ......H 15
Natura ......E 11
Navina ......E 11
Nebo ....H 12
Nelagoney ....C 13
Nelson ......D 11
New Liberty ...F 7
New Lima ....F 12
New Prue* ..202..D 13
New Tulsa* ..17..D 14
New
Woodville ..118..I 12
Newalla ......J 3
Newby ....E 13
Newcastle .1,271..K 2
Newkirk ..2,173..°C 11
Newport ......H 11
Nichols
Hills ....4,478..J 2
Nicoma Park 2,560..J 3
Nicut ....E 16
Nida ....I 13
Ninnekah ...910..G 10
Noble ....2,241..F 11
Nobscot .....E 8
Non ....G 13
Norge ....G 10
Norman ..52,117..°F 11
Norris ......G 15
North Enid ..730..D 10
North Miami ..503..B 15
Nowata ...3,679..°C 14
Noxie ......B 14
Oakhurst .....D 13
Oakland ...317..I 12
Oaks ....D 15
Oakwood ...129..E 8
Oberlin ......I 14
Ochelata ...330..C 13
Octavia ......H 16
Oglesby ......C 14
Oil City .....H 11
Oilton ...1,087..D 12
Okarche ...826..E 10
Okay ......419..E 15
Okeene ..1,421..D 9
Okemah ..2,913..°F 13
Okesa ....C 13
Okfuskee .....E 13
Oklahoma
City ..368,377..°F 11
Okmulgee .15,180..°E 13
Oktaha ....193..E 14
Old Retrop ...F 7
Oleta ....H 15
Olive ....D 13
Olney ....H 7
Olustee ....819..H 7
Omega ......E 9
Onapa ......F 14
Oneta ....D 14
Oologah ...458..C 14
Optima ....103..C 4
Orienta ......D 9
Orion ....D 8
Orlando ...202..D 11

Orr ....I 11
Osage .....170..D 13
Oscar ......I 10
Oswalt ......I 11
Ottawa ......B 15
Overbrook ....I 11
Owasso ..3,491..D 14
Paden .....442..F 12
Page ....G 16
Panama ..1,121..F 16
Panola ......G 15
Paoli .....480..G 11
Paradise Hill* .87..E 16
Park Hill .....E 15
Parker ......G 13
Parkland .....E 12
Patterson ....G 13
Pauls Valley 5,769..°G 11
Pawhuska ..4,238..°C 13
Pawnee ..2,443..°D 12
Payson ......E 12
Pearson .....G 12
Pearsonia ....C 13
Peckham .....C 11
Peek ....E 7
Peggs .....82..D 15
Pensacola ...56..C 15
Peoria .....179..B 16
Perkins ..1,029..E 12
Pernell ......H 11
Perry ....5,341..°D 11
Pershing .....C 13
Petersburg ...F 13
Pharoah .....F 13
Phillips ...106..H 13
Picher ...2,363..B 15
Pickens ......I 15
Piedmont ..269..I 1
Pierce ......F 14
Pike ....I 11
Pink ....K 3
Pittsburg ..282..G 14
Plainview ....C 8
Plainview ....G 7
Platter ......I 13
Pleasant Hill ..I 16
Plunkettville ..H 15
Pocasset .....K 1
Pocola* ..1,840..F 16
Ponca
City ...25,940..C 11
Pond Creek ..903..C 10
Pontotoc .....H 12
Port ....F 7
Porter ....624..E 14
Porum .....658..F 15
Poteau ...5,500..°F 16
Powell ......I 12
Prague ...1,802..F 12
Preston ......E 14
Proctor ......D 16
Prue ....D 13
Pruitt City ...H 11
Pryor Creek 7,057..°D 15
Pumpkin Center ..E 14
Purcell ..4,076..°G 11
Purdy ......G 11
Putnam .....84..E 8
Pyramid Corners ..C 15
Qualls ......E 15
Quapaw ....967..B 15
Quay ......41..D 12
Quinlan ....81..D 8
Quinton ..1,262..F 15
Raiford ......F 14
Ralston ....443..C 12
Ramona ....600..C 13
Randlett ...384..I 9
Ratliff City ..250..H 11
Rattan ......H 15
Ravia ......373..H 12
Reagan ......H 12
Reck ....I 11
Red Bird ...230..E 14
Red Oak ...609..G 15
Red Rock ...233..C 11
Redden ......H 14
Redland ......F 16
Reed ....G 7
Reichert .....G 16
Renfrow ....39..B 10
Rentiesville ..96..E 14
Reydon ....215..E 6
Rhea ....E 8
Richland .....I 1
Ringling ..1,206..I 11
Ringold ......H 15
Ringwood ...241..D 9
Ripley .....307..D 12
Roberta ......I 13
Rock Island ...F 16
Rocky .....260..F 8
Roff ......632..H 12
Roland* ....827..F 16
Roll ....E 7
Roosevelt ...353..G 8
Rose ....D 15
Rosedale ...98..G 11
Rosston ....56..C 6
Row ....D 16
Ruboutom .....I 11
Rufe ....I 15
Rush Springs 1,381..G 10
Russell ......G 7
Russett ......I 12
Ryan .....1,011..I 10
Sacred Heart ..G 12
St. Louis ..207..G 12

Salina ....1,024..D 15
Sallisaw ..4,888..°F 16
Salt Fork .....C 10
Sand Creek ...C 10
Sand
Springs .10,565..D 13
Sapulpa .15,159..°D 13
Sardis ......G 15
Sasakwa ...321..G 13
Savanna ...948..G 15
Sawyer .....I 15
Sayre ....2,712..°F 7
Schlegel .....D 12
Schoolton .....F 13
Schulter ......F 14
Scipio ......G 14
Scott ....F 9
Scraper .....D 15
Sculin* ....9..H 12
Scullyville ...F 16
Seiling ...1,033..D 8
Selman .....C 7
Seminole ..7,878..F 12
Sentinel ...984..F 8
Seward ......E 11
Shady Point ..F 16
Shamrock ...204..E 12
Sharon ....155..D 7
Shattuck ..1,546..D 6
Shawnee .25,075..°F 12
Shay ....I 12
Sherwood .....H 16
Shidler ....717..C 12
Short ......E 16
Shrewder .....F 9
Sickles ......F 9
Silo ....I 13
Simon ......I 11
Skedee ....117..D 12
Skiatook ..2,930..D 13
Slapout ......C 6
Slick ......171..E 13
Smith Village ..93..J 2
Smithville ..144..H 16
Snow ....H 14
Snyder ...1,671..H 8
Sobol ......H 15
Soper .....322..I 14
South Coffey-
ville .....646..B 14
Southard .....D 9
Sparks ....183..E 12
Spaulding .....G 13
Spavinaw ...470..C 15
Speer ....I 14
Spencer ..3,714..J 2
Sperry ...1,123..D 13
Spiro ....2,057..F 16
Spring Creek ..F 9
Springer ...256..H 11
Springlake
Park* ....14..F 11
Stafford .....F 8
Stanley .....H 14
Star ....F 15
Stecker .....G 9
Steedman .....G 13
Stella ......K 3
Sterling ...675..G 9
Stidham ....53..F 14
Stigler ...2,347..°F 15
Stillwater .31,126..°D 11
Stilwell ..2,134..°E 16
Stonebluff ...E 13
Stonewall ...653..G 13
Story ....G 11
Strang .....164..C 15
Stratford ..1,278..G 12
Stringtown ..397..H 13
Strong City ..40..E 7
Stroud ...2,502..E 12
Stuart .....294..G 13
Sugden ......I 10
Sulphur ..5,158..°H 12
Summerfield ..E 15
Summit ......E 14
Sumner .....16..D 11
Sunray ......H 10
Sweetwater ...F 6
Swink* ....88..I 15
Tabler ......G 10
Taft* .....525..E 14
Tahlequah .9,254..°E 15
Tahona ......F 16
Talala .....163..C 14
Talihina ..1,227..G 15
Tallant ......C 12
Taloga ....363..°D 8
Tamaha .....83..F 15
Tangier ......D 7
Tatums .....H 11
Taylor ......H 11
Tecumseh ..4,451..K 4
Tegarden .....C 8
Temple ...1,354..I 9
Teresita .....D 15
Terlton ....111..D 12
Terral .....636..I 10
Texanna ......F 14
Texhoma ...921..C 3
Texola .....144..F 6
Thackerville ..257..I 11
Thomas ..1,336..E 8
Tiawah ......D 14
Tipton ...1,206..H 8
Tishomingo .2,663..°H 12
Tom ....I 16
Tonkawa ..3,337..C 11

Tribbey .....F 12
Trousdale ....G 12
Troy ....H 12
Tryon .....301..E 12
Tullahassee ..183..E 14
Tulsa ..330,350..°D 13
Tupelo ....485..H 13
Turley ......D 13
Turpin .....C 5
Tushka .....230..H 13
Tuskahoma ....G 15
Tuskegee .....E 13
Tuttle ...1,640..K 1
Tyrone ....588..B 4
Uncas .....53..C 12
Unger ....J 4
Union City ..306..J 1
Utica ....I 13
Valley
Brook ..1,197..J 2
Valliant ...840..I 15
Vamoosa .....G 12
Vanoss ......G 12
Velma .....611..H 10
Vera ......215..C 14
Verden ....439..G 10
Verdigris .....D 14
Vernon ......F 14
Vian .....1,131..E 15
Vici ......694..D 7
Victory .....H 7
Village,
The ...13,695..J 2
Vinita ...5,847..°C 15
Vinson ......G 6
Virgil ......F 14
Vivian ......F 14
Wade ....I 13
Wagoner ..4,959..°D 15
Wainwright* ..135..E 14
Wakita .....545..C 10
Wallville .....G 11
Walters ..2,611..°H 9
Wanette ...303..G 12
Wann ......135..B 14
Wapanucka ..425..H 13
Wardville .....G 13
Warner ...1,217..F 15
Warr Acres 9,887..J 2
Warren ......G 8
Warwick ...146..I 4
Washington ..322..G 11
Washunga .....25..C 12
Watchorn .....G 15
Watonga ..3,696..°E 9
Watova ......C 14
Watson ......H 16
Watts .....326..D 16
Wauhillau .....E 16
Waukomis ...842..D 10
Waurika ..1,833..°I 10
Wayne .....618..G 11
Waynoka ..1,444..C 8
Weatherford 7,959..°F 8
Weathers .....G 14
Webb ....E 8
Webb City ...186..C 12
Webbers Falls .485..E 15
Welch .....651..B 15
Weleetka ..1,199..F 13
Welling ......E 15
Wellston ...789..I 4
Welty ....E 13
West Siloam
Springs ...210..D 16
Westport* .1,189..D 13
Westville ...934..D 16
Wetumka ..1,687..F 13
Wewoka ..5,284..°F 13
Wheeless .....C 1
White Bead ...G 11
White Eagle ..C 11
White Oak ....C 14
Whitefield ....F 15
Whitesboro ...G 15
Wilburton .2,504..°G 15
Wild Horse ...D 13
Wildcat .....F 14
Willis ......I 12
Willow .....188..G 7
Willow View ...G 11
Wilson ...1,569..I 11
Wirt ....H 11
Wister ....927..G 16
Wolco ......C 13
Wolf ....G 12
Woodford .....H 11
Woodlawn
Park* ....220..F 10
Woods ......J 3
Woodward .9,412..°D 7
Wright City .1,068..I 15
Wyandotte ...297..C 16
Wye ....K 4
Wynnewood .2,374..H 11
Wynona ....547..C 13
Yale .....1,239..D 12
Yanush ......G 15
Yarnaby ......I 13
Yeager ....107..F 13
Yewed ......C 9
Yonkers .....D 15
Yost ....D 12
Yuba ....I 13
Yukon ...12,980..J 1
Zafra ......H 16
Zena ....C 15
Zoe ....G 16

*Does not appear on the map; key shows general location.
°County seat.

Sources: Latest census figures (1970 and special censuses). Places without population figures are unincorporated areas and are not listed in census reports.

The 1970 United States census reported that Oklahoma had a population of 2,559,253 persons. The census showed that the state's population had increased 10 per cent over the 1960 figure of 2,328,284 persons. The U.S. Bureau of the Census estimated that by 1975 the population had reached about 2,712,000.

About two-thirds of the people of Oklahoma live in urban areas. Over half the people live in three metropolitan areas. These are, in order of size, Oklahoma City, Tulsa, and Lawton. These areas are the state's only Standard Metropolitan Statistical Areas (see METROPOLITAN AREA). The metropolitan area of Fort Smith, Ark., extends into Le Flore and Sequoyah counties in Oklahoma. For the populations of the metropolitan areas, see the *Index* to the political map of Oklahoma in this article.

Oklahoma has fewer than 30 cities with populations of over 10,000 persons. Most of these cities are near Oklahoma City and Tulsa. Oklahoma City is a rapidly expanding center of industry and trade. Tulsa started as a Creek Indian village in the early 1800's. The city boomed after oil was discovered nearby in the early 1900's. Lawton serves Fort Sill, a neighboring military center. See the separate articles on Oklahoma cities listed in the *Related Articles* at the end of this article.

More than 95 of every 100 Oklahomans were born in the United States. Indians make up about 4 per cent of the population.

Baptists make up the largest single religious group in Oklahoma. Other religious groups with large memberships include the Disciples of Christ, Methodists, Presbyterians, and Roman Catholics.

Bob Taylor

Harvesters Load Wheat into a trailer on a farm near Cordell. Many harvest workers own their own machinery. They work briefly on a farm, and then move to other areas as the wheat ripens.

Royce Craig, *Tulsa Tribune*

Busy Shoppers jam downtown Tulsa, Oklahoma's second largest city. Tulsa began as a Creek Indian village. The discovery of petroleum made the city a booming oil center in the early 1900's.

POPULATION

This map shows the *population density* of Oklahoma, and how it varies in different parts of the state. Population density means the average number of persons who live in a given area.

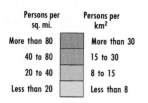

Persons per sq. mi.		Persons per km²	
More than 80		More than 30	
40 to 80		15 to 30	
20 to 40		8 to 15	
Less than 20		Less than 8	

```
0    25   50   75   100 Miles
0       50      100 Kilometers
```

WORLD BOOK map

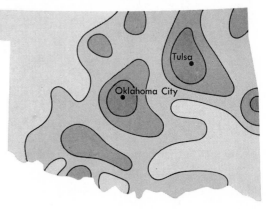

Schools. The first schools in Oklahoma were established for the Indians in the 1820's by missionaries. The Cherokee had the most advanced educational system, chiefly because of the work of one of their leaders, Sequoya. In 1821, Sequoya invented a system of writing. It was so simple that many Cherokee could learn to read and write in a few weeks. The territorial legislature first provided for schools for white children in 1890.

Oklahoma's present school system is headed by an elected superintendent of public instruction. He works with a board of education whose members are appointed by the governor. The U.S. government maintains nine boarding schools to assist in the education of Indian children. By law, children from age 6 through 17 must attend school. For the number of students and teachers in Oklahoma, see EDUCATION (table).

Libraries. Oklahoma has more than 100 public libraries and more than 30 college and university libraries. The first public library was founded in Guthrie in 1901. The Oklahoma Department of Libraries and the library division of the Oklahoma Historical Society are in Oklahoma City. The University of Oklahoma Library in Norman has the DeGolyer collection on the history of science and technology, the Bass Business History collection, and the Bizzell Bible collection.

Museums. Oklahoma's museums own many fine collections on Indian history and art. The Thomas Gilcrease Institute of American History and Art in Tulsa is devoted largely to these fields. The Woolaroc Museum near Bartlesville owns one of the world's finest collections of Indian blankets. Lawton has the Museum of the Great Plains, and the Southern Plains Indian Museum and Crafts Center is in Anadarko.

The Oklahoma Historical Society Museum is in Oklahoma City. The National Cowboy Hall of Fame and Western Heritage Center, also in Oklahoma City, features art of the American West and houses the National Rodeo and Great Western Performers Hall of Fame.

The Oklahoma Science and Arts Foundation operates a museum in Oklahoma City that features science exhibits and a collection of ivory. The Philbrook Art Center in Tulsa displays a number of paintings from the Italian Renaissance. The center also has collections of Chinese jade and art. Fort Sill, the United States Army Field Artillery and Missile Center near Lawton, displays unusual weapons in its artillery museum.

UNIVERSITIES AND COLLEGES

Oklahoma has 19 universities and colleges accredited by the North Central Association of Colleges and Schools. For enrollments and further information, see UNIVERSITIES AND COLLEGES (table).

Name	Location	Founded
Bethany Nazarene College	Bethany	1920
Cameron University	Lawton	1970
Central State University	Edmond	1890
East Central Oklahoma State University	Ada	1907
Langston University	Langston	1897
Northeastern Oklahoma State University	Tahlequah	1846
Northwestern Oklahoma State University	Alva	1897
Oklahoma, University of	Norman	1890
Oklahoma Baptist University	Shawnee	1910
Oklahoma Christian College	Oklahoma City	1962
Oklahoma City University	Oklahoma City	1904
Oklahoma Panhandle State University	Goodwell	1909
Oklahoma State University	Stillwater	1890
Oral Roberts University	Tulsa	1965
Phillips University	Enid	1906
Science and Arts of Oklahoma, University of	Chickasha	1908
Southeastern Oklahoma State University	Durant	1909
Southwestern Oklahoma State University	Weatherford	1901
Tulsa, University of	Tulsa	1894

University of Oklahoma in Norman operates this building, called Sooner House, as part of the Oklahoma Center for Continuing Education. Hundreds of adult groups use the building every year for special conferences and other educational programs.

Bob Taylor

OKLAHOMA / A Visitor's Guide

Will Rogers, the famous Oklahoma cowboy humorist, once said: "There ought to be a law against anybody going to Europe until they have seen the things we have in this country." Rogers may have been thinking of some of the scenic spots in his home state. Oklahoma's attractions include beautiful natural settings, Indian villages, and striking modern buildings.

Bob Taylor

Will Rogers Statue and Museum in Claremore

--- PLACES TO VISIT ---

Following are brief descriptions of some of Oklahoma's many interesting places to visit.

Church of Tomorrow, in Oklahoma City, has a 1,500-seat sanctuary, an educational building, and a theater-in-the-round.

Creek Capitol, in Okmulgee, is the building from which Creek Indians ruled their republic.

Fort Sill, a military center near Lawton, includes three historical sites—Stone Corral, Old Guardhouse, and an artillery museum. The fort was established in 1869.

National Cowboy Hall of Fame and Western Heritage Center was opened in Oklahoma City in 1965. Famous paintings and sculptures are on display.

Thomas Gilcrease Institute of American History and Art, in Tulsa, is an art gallery and library. It contains over 5,000 works of art, including many paintings on the history of the American West.

Tsa-La-Gi Indian Village, southeast of Tahlequah, re-creates an ancient Cherokee village. Cherokee Indians give tours of the village from May to early September.

Washita Battlefield, near Cheyenne, marks the site of an 1868 Indian fight. U.S. cavalry under General George A. Custer surprised the camp of Chief Black Kettle. General Custer's men killed or wounded more than 100 Cheyenne Indians, including women and children.

Will Rogers Memorial Building, in Claremore, honors the humorist. A stone ranch house, built as a museum, has exhibits about Rogers, Indians, and pioneers.

Woolaroc Museum, southwest of Bartlesville, displays over 55,000 historical exhibits. Much of its collection deals with the history of the Southwest, including paintings by artists Frederic Remington and Charles Russell.

National Recreation Area and Forest. The Chickasaw National Recreation Area lies in south-central Oklahoma. The area has six developed campgrounds, and facilities for swimming and boating at the Lake of the Arbuckles. Two sections of the Ouachita National Forest lie in southeastern Oklahoma. For the area and chief features, see NATIONAL FOREST (table).

State Parks. Oklahoma has 30 state parks and 22 recreation areas. For information, write: Director, Tourism Promotion Division, 500 Will Rogers Building, Oklahoma City, Okla. 73105.

National Cowboy Hall of Fame and Western Heritage Center, Oklahoma City

National Cowboy Hall of Fame in Oklahoma City

Bob Taylor

Natural Bridge in Alabaster Caverns State Park

552

Woolaroc Museum

Woolaroc Museum Near Bartlesville

Bob Taylor

Church of Tomorrow in Oklahoma City

ANNUAL EVENTS

Many Oklahoma towns and cities hold annual celebrations to honor pioneer days. One of the state's most popular annual events is the National Finals Rodeo (World Series of Rodeo), held in December in Oklahoma City. Another popular event is the "Trail of Tears" drama in a 1,800-seat amphitheater near Tahlequah. The play is held nightly, except Sunday, from late June through August. Other annual events in Oklahoma include the following.

January-March: International Rodeo Finals in Tulsa (February).

April-June: Azalea Festival in Muskogee (April); Cimarron Territory Celebration in Beaver (April); 89'ers Day Celebration in Guthrie (April); Pioneer Days in Guymon (April); Wichita Mountains Sunrise Easter Pageant near Lawton (Easter Sunday); Kolache (Czech) Festival in Prague (May); Rooster Day in Broken Arrow (May); Sequoyah Inter-Tribal Pow Wow in Elk City (May); Strawberry Festival in Stilwell (May); Walleye Rodeo in Canton Lake (May); Love County Frontier Days Celebration (June); National Sand Bass Festival in Madill (June).

July-September: International Brick and Rolling Pin Throwing Contest in Stroud (July); Tulsa Indian Pow Wow (July); World Championship Watermelon Seed Spittin' Contest in Pauls Valley (July); American Indian Exposition in Anadarko (August); Bluegrass Music Festival in Hugo (August); Italian Festival in McAlester (August); Peach Festival in Porter (August); Watermelon Festival in Rush Springs (August); State Fair of Oklahoma in Oklahoma City (September); Tulsa State Fair (late September).

October-December: Czech Festival in Yukon (October).

Oklahoma Industrial Development and Park Department

Tsa-La-Gi, a Cherokee Indian Village Southeast of Tahlequah

553

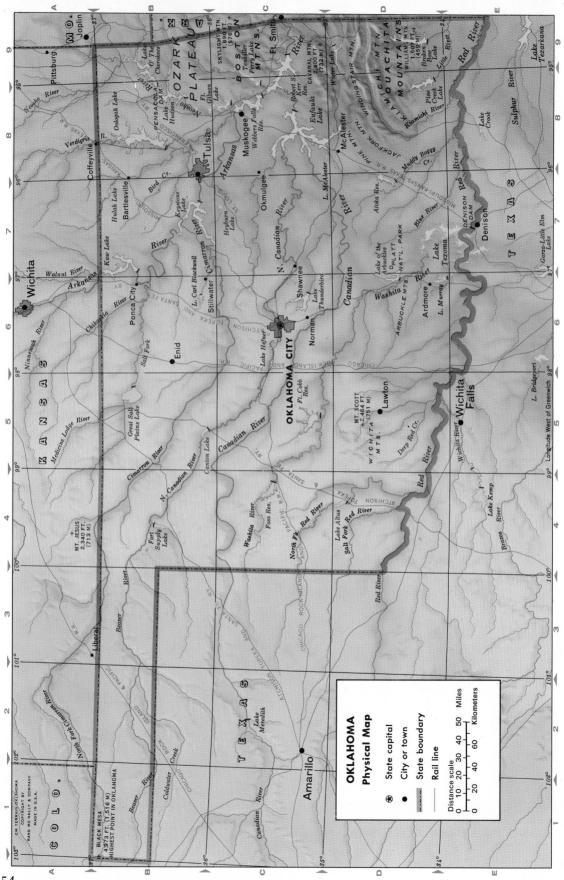

Specially created for **World Book Encyclopedia** by Rand McNally and World Book editors

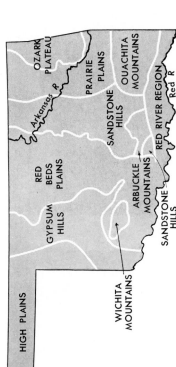

OKLAHOMA/The Land

Land Regions. Oklahoma has 10 main land regions: (1) the Ozark Plateau, (2) the Prairie Plains, (3) the Sandstone Hills, (4) the Ouachita Mountains, (5) the Arbuckle Mountains, (6) the Wichita Mountains, (7) the Red River Region, (8) the Red Beds Plains, (9) the Gypsum Hills, and (10) the High Plains.

The Ozark Plateau extends into northeastern Oklahoma from Missouri and Arkansas. This hilly region has swift streams and steep-sided river valleys. The areas between valleys are broad and flat. Steep bluffs have been formed where streams cut into the plateau.

The Prairie Plains include the land west and south of the Ozark Plateau. Farming and cattle ranching are the most important activities in this region. The Arkansas River Valley, east of Muskogee, produces such vegetable crops as spinach, snap beans, and carrots. Most of the state's coal and large amounts of petroleum come from this region.

The Ouachita Mountains rise in the southeastern part of the state on the border between Oklahoma and Arkansas. These mountains are a series of high sandstone ridges that form the roughest land surface in Oklahoma. The ridges run in a general east-west direction. They include Blue Bouncer, Buffalo, Jackfork, Kiamichi, Rich, and Winding Stair. The narrow valleys between the ridges have spring-fed streams. Lumbering is the region's most important industry.

The Sandstone Hills region extends south from the border with Kansas to near the Red River in southern Oklahoma. It is a region of hills 250 to 400 feet (76 to 120 meters) high. Many areas are covered with blackjack and post oak forests. Much of the early Oklahoma oil development took place in these hills. The region still has important oil fields. Farming is also important there.

The Arbuckle Mountains are wedged into an area of 1,000 square miles (2,600 square kilometers) in south-central Oklahoma. Millions of years ago these were tall mountains. Erosion has worn them down until they now rise only 600 to 700 feet (180 to 210 meters) above the surrounding plains. The erosion uncovered unusual rock formations that are often studied by geology students. The principal formations of this region include conglomerates, granite, limestone, sandstone, and shale. Ranchers use the land to raise cattle.

The Wichita Mountains are rough granite peaks in southwestern Oklahoma. The region has many small artificial lakes. These were created by damming the mountain streams to provide water for animals, and to control soil erosion. Most of the area lies within the Fort Sill Military Reservation and a federal wildlife refuge.

The Red River Region is a rolling prairie and forest area. Much of the soil is sandy and very fertile. Farmers in the region grow cotton, peanuts, and vegetables.

The Red Beds Plains extend from Kansas to Texas in a wide sweep through the middle of Oklahoma. Soft red sandstone and shale lie under the soil. This gently rolling plain, Oklahoma's largest land region, slopes downward from west to east. The eastern part has forested areas and the western part is mostly grassy. The Red Beds Plains have fairly fertile soil. Farmers grow cotton and wheat in the southwestern part of the region. Oil fields have been developed in some parts of the Red Beds Plains.

The Gypsum Hills, west of the Red Beds Plains, extend northward to the High Plains. These hills rise from 150 to 200 feet (46 to 61 meters), and are capped by layers of gypsum 15 to 20 feet (4.6 to 6.1 meters) thick. They are sometimes called the Glass, or Gloss, Mountains, because the gypsum sparkles like glass in the sun.

The High Plains, an area of level grassland, occupy the northwestern section. This region, which is part of

Bob Taylor

The Wichita Mountains in southwestern Oklahoma rise from a fertile plain. Fort Sill Military Reservation and a federal wildlife refuge occupy most of the land in the Wichita Mountains region. The mountains have many rough granite boulders.

Oklahoma Industrial Development and Park Department

High Sandstone Ridges in the Ouachita Mountains region of southeastern Oklahoma form the roughest land areas in the state.

Bob Taylor

The Highest Point in Oklahoma is Black Mesa, *background*, in the High Plains region. It is 4,973 feet (1,516 meters) high.

the vast Interior Plain of North America, includes Oklahoma's Panhandle. The Panhandle is the western portion of Oklahoma, a strip of land 166 miles (267 kilometers) long and 34 miles (55 kilometers) wide. The land of the High Plains rises from about 2,000 feet (610 meters) on the eastern edge of the region to 4,973 feet (1,516 meters) at Black Mesa, the highest point in Oklahoma. Black Mesa lies in Cimarron County in the northwestern corner of the state.

Rivers and Lakes. Oklahoma is drained by two great river systems—the Red and the Arkansas. These systems carry water from the state's rivers and streams eastward to the Gulf of Mexico. The winding Red River forms Oklahoma's southern boundary with Texas. Its main tributaries drain southern Oklahoma. These streams include the Blue, Kiamichi, Little, Mountain Fork, and Washita rivers, Cache Creek, and the North Fork of the Red River.

The Arkansas River flows through northeastern Oklahoma. Its principal tributaries flow in a broad, irregular semicircle across the entire width of the state. These include the Canadian and the Cimarron rivers. The Chikaskia, Illinois, Neosho (or Grand), Poteau, Salt Fork, and Verdigris rivers, which drain northern and eastern Oklahoma, are also important branches.

Oklahoma has more than 200 man-made lakes and about 100 small natural lakes. Lake Texoma, covering 91,200 acres (36,910 hectares), is the most popular resort center. Part of it lies in Texas. Lake O' The Cherokees is in northeastern Oklahoma. It backs up the waters of the Neosho River for 65 miles (105 kilometers). Lake Eufaula, in the east-central portion, covers over 100,000 acres (40,000 hectares). Fort Gibson Lake, Greenleaf Lake, Lower Spavinaw Lake, Upper Spavinaw Lake, Tenkiller Ferry Lake, and Lake Wister are in eastern Oklahoma. They have popular resorts for fishing and boating. Other large lakes and reservoirs in Oklahoma include Altus, Canton, Carl Blackwell, Ellsworth, Fort Supply, Foss, Great Salt Plains, Hefner, Heyburn, Hulah, Keystone, Lawtonka, Little River, McAlester, Murray, Oologah, Overholser, and Shawnee.

OKLAHOMA/*Climate*

Most of Oklahoma has a warm, dry climate. Northwestern Oklahoma is cooler and drier than the southeastern part. *Precipitation* (rain, melted snow, and other forms of moisture) varies greatly throughout the state. Average precipitation ranges from 50 inches (130 centimeters) a year in the southeast to 15 inches (38 centimeters) in the western Panhandle. Snowfall ranges from about 2 inches (5 centimeters) a year in the southeast to 25 inches (64 centimeters) in the northwest. The Panhandle gets the most snow.

The average July temperature in Oklahoma is 83° F. (28° C), and the average January temperature is 39° F. (4° C). The state's highest temperature, 120° F. (49° C), was recorded on four occasions during the summer of 1936—at Alva on July 18, at Altus on July 19 and August 12, and at Poteau on August 10. The same figure was reached at Tishomingo on July 26, 1943. The record low temperature, −27° F. (−33° C), was registered at two locations—at Vinita on Feb. 13, 1905, and at Watts on Jan. 18, 1930.

SEASONAL TEMPERATURES

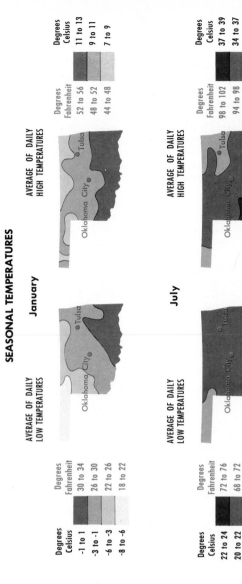

January

AVERAGE OF DAILY LOW TEMPERATURES

Degrees Fahrenheit	Degrees Celsius
30 to 34	-1 to 1
26 to 30	-3 to -1
22 to 26	-6 to -3
18 to 22	-8 to -6

AVERAGE OF DAILY HIGH TEMPERATURES

Degrees Fahrenheit	Degrees Celsius
52 to 56	11 to 13
48 to 52	9 to 11
44 to 48	7 to 9

July

AVERAGE OF DAILY LOW TEMPERATURES

Degrees Fahrenheit	Degrees Celsius
72 to 76	22 to 24
68 to 72	20 to 22
64 to 68	18 to 20

AVERAGE OF DAILY HIGH TEMPERATURES

Degrees Fahrenheit	Degrees Celsius
98 to 102	37 to 39
94 to 98	34 to 37
90 to 94	32 to 34

AVERAGE YEARLY PRECIPITATION
(Rain, Melted Snow, and Other Moisture)

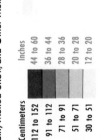

Centimeters	Inches
112 to 152	44 to 60
91 to 112	36 to 44
71 to 91	28 to 36
51 to 71	20 to 28
30 to 51	12 to 20

0   50 100   200 Miles
0   100 200 300 Kilometers

WORLD BOOK maps

AVERAGE MONTHLY WEATHER

OKLAHOMA CITY

	Temperatures				Days of Rain or Snow
	F° High	Low	C° High	Low	
JAN.	47	27	8	-3	6
FEB.	52	31	11	-1	7
MAR.	61	38	16	3	7
APR.	71	49	22	9	9
MAY	79	58	26	14	11
JUNE	88	67	31	19	9
JULY	93	71	34	22	6
AUG.	93	71	34	22	6
SEPT.	85	63	29	17	6
OCT.	74	52	23	11	6
NOV.	60	38	16	3	5
DEC.	50	30	10	-1	5

TULSA

	Temperatures				Days of Rain or Snow
	F° High	Low	C° High	Low	
JAN.	47	28	8	-2	6
FEB.	52	32	11	0	8
MAR.	61	39	16	4	8
APR.	71	50	22	10	9
MAY	78	58	26	14	11
JUNE	88	67	31	19	9
JULY	93	71	34	22	6
AUG.	93	71	34	22	7
SEPT.	85	63	29	17	6
OCT.	75	52	24	11	7
NOV.	60	39	16	4	6
DEC.	50	31	10	-1	6

Warm Summer Days bring many water skiers to the man-made lake in Great Salt Plains State Park near Cherokee.

Oklahoma Industrial Development and Park Department

Manufacturing is Oklahoma's most important economic activity. Agriculture ranks second, and mining ranks third.

Natural Resources. Oklahoma has vast reserves of minerals and large areas of fertile soils. Its mineral wealth includes petroleum and natural gas, important fuels of today's world. Large supplies of water and a favorable climate combine with rich soils to make Oklahoma a major producer of food.

Minerals. The state's oil reserves are among the largest in the United States. Large quantities of natural gas also are present in most of the oil fields. Deposits of petroleum and natural gas have been found in 70 of Oklahoma's 77 counties.

Rich beds of coal lie in the east-central and northeastern parts of the state. Experts estimate that about 1⅓ billion short tons (1.2 billion metric tons) of coal could be taken from these coal fields, which cover about 15,000 square miles (38,800 square kilometers).

The mountainous regions have deposits of stone and clays. High grade granite is found in the Wichita and Arbuckle mountains. Other minerals include copper, limestone of various kinds, glass sand, gravel, gypsum, and salt. Helium, one of the lightest gases, has been found in the natural gas of the Panhandle.

Soil varies from the fertile deposits in the river valleys to the unproductive shale and granite of the mountains. Much of the plains and grasslands area has a rich soil that produces abundant crops. Other areas have poor red clay soil.

Forests cover about 9,300,000 acres (3,760,000 hectares), or about a fifth of the state's land area. The most important commercial tree is the southern pine, used for softwood lumber. Hardwood trees of commercial value include the ash, elm, hickory, oak, red gum, and walnut. The main commercial forests are in the eastern and southeastern parts of the state.

Plant Life includes the prairie grasses that provide grazing for millions of cattle. Among these grasses are bluestem, sand grass, and the shorter buffalo grass, grama, and wire grass. Other common prairie plants are mesquite and sagebrush. Dogwood and redbud grow in the east, central, and southern areas. The anemone, goldenrod, wild indigo, petunia, phlox, primrose, spiderwort, sunflower, verbena, and violet grow in all regions of the state.

Animal Life. Coyotes, prairie dogs, and rabbits are common on the Oklahoma plains. Animals of the forest areas include deer, minks, opossums, otters, raccoons, and gray and fox squirrels. Common birds include blue jays, crows, doves, meadow larks, mockingbirds, robins, English sparrows, starlings, and swallows.

Manufacturing provides more than 40 per cent of the value of goods that Oklahoma produces annually. Goods produced in the state have a *value added by manufacture* of about $2½ billion a year. This figure represents the value created in products by Oklahoma's industries, not counting such manufacturing costs as materials, supplies, and fuels.

Oklahoma's leading industries, in order of value, produce nonelectrical machinery; food and food products; fabricated metal products; electrical equipment; stone, clay, and glass products; and transportation equipment.

The Tulsa and Oklahoma City areas lead in the manufacture of machinery. Blackwell, Duncan, Enid, Muskogee, Perry, Prior, and Shawnee also have machinery plants. Electronics and space equipment manufacturing has developed in Tulsa and Oklahoma City. These two cities also have important transportation equipment plants. Airplanes and trailers are produced in both places. Steel is a chief product of the Tulsa area.

Oklahoma City is the most important food-processing center. Canneries in Muskogee and Stilwell process many kinds of vegetables. El Reno, Shawnee, and Yukon are leading centers in grain milling. Plants in many cities handle meat processing and dairy products.

Oil-refining is concentrated in the north-central and south-central regions of the state. Bartlesville, Ponca City, and Tulsa are the leading refining centers. Duncan and Enid also have large oil refineries. About 70 plants in the state process natural gas.

Agriculture accounts for about 36 per cent of the value of goods produced in the state, or about $2¼ billion a year. The production of beef cattle is the state's leading source of agricultural income, and Okla-

Production of Goods in Oklahoma

Total value of goods produced in 1973—$6,155,165,000

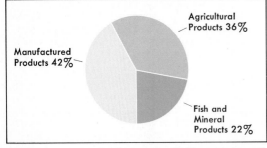

Manufactured Products 42%

Agricultural Products 36%

Fish and Mineral Products 22%

Percentages are based on farm income, value added by manufacture, and value of fish and mineral production. Fish products are less than 1 per cent.

Sources: U.S. government publications, 1975-1976.

Employment in Oklahoma

Total number of persons employed in 1974—989,900

	Number of Employees
Wholesale & Retail Trade	202,800
Government	197,200
Manufacturing	155,900
Community, Social, & Personal Services	135,500
Agriculture	111,000
Transportation & Public Utilities	56,700
Construction	46,800
Finance, Insurance, & Real Estate	45,500
Mining	38,500

Sources: *Employment and Earnings*, May 1975, U.S. Bureau of Labor Statistics; *Farm Labor*, February 1975, U.S. Department of Agriculture.

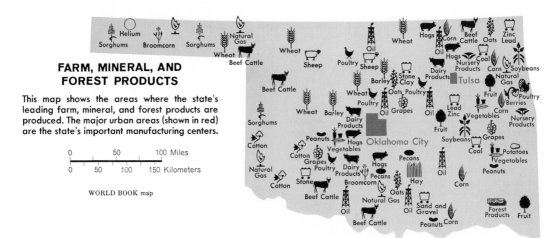

FARM, MINERAL, AND FOREST PRODUCTS

This map shows the areas where the state's leading farm, mineral, and forest products are produced. The major urban areas (shown in red) are the state's important manufacturing centers.

```
0        50        100 Miles
0    50      100     150 Kilometers
```

WORLD BOOK map

homa is one of the country's most important sources of beef. The state has about 5¾ million beef cattle.

Cowboys still ride the Oklahoma range as they did in earlier days, but ranching has become a modern business. Many ranchers graze their cattle on the range for a time, and then take them to *feed lots*. A feed lot is an enclosed area where cattle are fed special feed to fatten them for market. These animals do not need to search for feed, so they gain weight more rapidly than range cattle, and bring higher prices. Other important income from Oklahoma livestock comes from chickens, dairy products, eggs, hogs, sheep, and turkeys.

Winter wheat is the most valuable field crop for the state's farmers, and Oklahoma ranks as a leading wheat state. Vast fields of golden wheat are harvested early each summer by lines of combines. Peanuts rank second in value among Oklahoma's crops. Other crops, in order of value, are cotton, sorghum grain, hay, soybeans, greenhouse and nursery products, and pecans. Oklahoma often leads the states in the production of broomcorn, from which brooms are made. Orchards in eastern and central Oklahoma produce peaches and pecans. Other food products include corn, spinach, strawberries, and watermelons.

Mining in Oklahoma provides an annual income of about $1,323,626,000, or about 22 per cent of the value of goods produced in the state. Oil is the greatest source of this income. Oklahoma has about 75,000 oil wells. They produce about 190 million barrels of crude oil a

Beef Cattle feed on the rich grass of a ranch near Putnam. Beef cattle are the leading source of farm income in Oklahoma.

Bob Taylor

Mounds of Wheat cover the ground around a full grain elevator. This overflow wheat is quickly shipped to other storage areas or to flour mills. Oklahoma is a leading U.S. wheat-producing state.

Bob Taylor

Oil Derricks dot Lake Texoma, where wells pump oil from under the lake. Most parts of Oklahoma have oil wells. Pipelines carry the crude oil to refineries for processing.

Bob Taylor

year, putting Oklahoma among the leading states in oil production. Tulsa and Oklahoma City are the state's leading oil centers, but almost every section of Oklahoma has producing wells.

Natural gas is found in many places where there is oil, and Oklahoma ranks as a leader in gas production. Most of the gas is piped to other sections of the country for use as heating and cooking fuel. Natural gas liquids, such as natural gasoline and butane, are the state's third most important mineral product.

Stone ranks high in value among Oklahoma's minerals, as do sand and gravel. Coal is also an important income producer. In the early 1970's, miners took about 2 million short tons (1.8 million metric tons) a year from the coal beds in eastern Oklahoma. Other important mineral products include clays, copper, and gypsum.

Production of helium gas became important in the 1960's. Helium gained in value because of its use in rockets and for research. Natural gas in the Panhandle area contains a high percentage of helium. The U.S. Bureau of Mines built a large plant in Keyes to remove the helium from the natural gas. As a result, Oklahoma became one of the two leading states, with Texas, in the production of high-purity helium.

Electric Power. Oklahoma uses its gas, coal, or oil to generate almost all its electricity. Less than 10 per cent is produced by water power or nuclear energy. Most of the hydroelectric plants are in northeast Oklahoma. Privately owned plants generate over four-fifths of the state's power.

Transportation. Oklahoma has about 110,000 miles (177,000 kilometers) of roads and highways, about a third of which have hard surfaces. Toll highways link Tulsa, Oklahoma City, and Lawton.

Oklahoma has about 5,500 miles (8,850 kilometers) of railroad tracks. About 10 rail lines provide freight service. Passenger trains serve about 10 cities. Oklahoma's first railroad was the Missouri-Kansas-Texas Railroad, called "The Katy." It was built across Oklahoma to Denison, Tex., from 1870 to 1872.

Seven passenger airlines serve Oklahoma. Oklahoma City and Tulsa have the major commercial airports. There are about 240 public airports and about 145 private landing fields in the state. Tulsa and Muskogee, both on the Arkansas River, are Oklahoma's chief ports. Barges link them with Mississippi River ports.

About 50,000 miles (80,000 kilometers) of pipelines carry Oklahoma's oil, natural gas, and refined products to other states. Most of the pipelines run through central Oklahoma from southwest to northeast.

Communication. Oklahoma has more than 200 weekly and more than 50 daily newspapers. The first newspaper, the *Cherokee Advocate*, was published in Tahlequah in 1844. It was printed in both English and Cherokee. Today, the state's largest papers are *The Daily Oklahoman* of Oklahoma City, the *Oklahoma City Times*, the *Tulsa Daily World*, and the *Tulsa Tribune*.

Station WKY in Oklahoma City, the state's first commercial radio station, went on the air in 1921. The first television stations, WKY-TV in Oklahoma City and KOTV in Tulsa, began regular broadcasts in 1949. Oklahoma has 13 television and about 115 radio stations.

First White Man to explore Oklahoma was Francisco Coronado in 1541. He crossed western Oklahoma in search of the legendary Seven Cities of Cibola.

The Boomers, a group of homeseekers led by David L. Payne and C. C. Carpenter, promoted Oklahoma's opening to settlement in the 1870's and 1880's.

HISTORIC OKLAHOMA

OKLAHOMA /History

Early Days. Before the white men came, bands of Indians roamed the plains of the region that now includes Oklahoma. The Indians followed the huge herds of buffalo that grazed on the grasslands. The tribes included the Arapaho, Caddo, Cheyenne, Comanche, Kiowa, Osage, Pawnee, and Wichita. See INDIAN, AMERICAN (Table of Tribes).

Europeans first reached the Oklahoma region in 1541. That year, the Spanish explorer Francisco Vásquez de Coronado led an expedition from Tiguex, N.Mex. He reached what is now Oklahoma. Later the same year, Hernando de Soto, another Spaniard, probably entered the area. Both Coronado and De Soto were searching for gold, but they found none.

In 1682, the French explorer Robert Cavelier, Sieur de la Salle, traveled down the Mississippi River. He did not reach the Oklahoma area. However, he claimed for France all the land drained by the Mississippi, including

First White Settlements in Oklahoma were at Miller Court House, Salina, and Three Forks.

First Producing Oil Well in Oklahoma was drilled in 1889 by Edward Byrd, a Kansas prospector, near Chelsea. Over 100,000 commercial oil wells have been sunk in Oklahoma since then.

Chisholm Trail, running north from Texas through Oklahoma to Abilene, Kan., was used by millions of cattle in the 1870's.

Linking East and West, The Butterfield stage line, a mail and passenger route across Oklahoma from St. Louis to San Francisco, opened in 1858.

Greatest Oklahoma Land Run was the opening of the Cherokee Outlet on Sept. 16, 1893. More than 50,000 persons staked claims the first day.

The Five Civilized Tribes—Cherokee, Choctaw, Creek, Chickasaw, and Seminole—received their Oklahoma lands from the federal government in the 1820's for "as long as grass shall grow and rivers run," in return for their eastern lands.

the Oklahoma region. Soon afterward, other French explorers and traders entered the Oklahoma area.

American Ownership. France claimed the Oklahoma region as part of Louisiana until 1762, when France ceded Louisiana to Spain. Napoleon regained the province for France in 1800, but he needed money to fight wars in Europe. In 1803, he sold Louisiana to the United States (see LOUISIANA PURCHASE).

Congress reorganized the administration of Louisiana several times. The section that included present-day Oklahoma was first called the District of Louisiana. In 1805, it became the Louisiana Territory. Seven years later, in 1812, the Missouri Territory was organized from the Louisiana Territory.

In 1819, the United States settled several boundary disputes with Spain. As a result, the present Oklahoma Panhandle, one of the disputed areas, was given to Spain. The rest of Oklahoma became part of the Arkan-

sas Territory, which was created in 1819. Miller Court House (in present-day McCurtain County), Salina, and Three Forks were among the first white settlements established in Oklahoma.

The Indian Nations. After 1819, the federal government began prodding the Indian tribes in the southeastern United States to move to the Oklahoma area. The tribes—the Cherokee, Chickasaw, Choctaw, Creek, and Seminole—had lived in close contact with white men for more than a hundred years. They adopted many of the habits and customs of the whites, and became known as the Five Civilized Tribes.

At the time, Oklahoma was largely unoccupied. In 1824, to prepare the area for the Indian migration, the U.S. Army built Fort Towson and Fort Gibson. The government then forced the five tribes to give up most of their eastern lands and move west.

Between 1820 and 1842, sad processions of Indians

moved into the wooded hills and open grasslands of eastern Oklahoma. Many Indians died along the way. The Cherokee and Choctaw Indians speak of the trip as *The Trail of Tears.*

The immigrant Indians were given the right to all of present-day Oklahoma except the Panhandle. Each of the five tribes formed a nation. By treaties, the United States promised to protect the Indian nations. The government guaranteed that the Indians would own their lands "as long as grass shall grow and rivers run." Each Indian nation established its own legislature, courts, and written laws, and built its own capital. Most settlements were in the eastern part of the region, but the Indians made trips to the west to hunt buffalo.

After the first hard years, the Indians began to build schools and churches, clear land, and operate farms and ranches. They were protected from white settlement by their treaties, so the general westward movement of the pioneers passed them.

The Civil War (1861-1865) destroyed the prosperity and protection the Indians enjoyed. The Five Civilized Tribes had come from the South, and many of the Indians owned slaves. Delegations from Texas and Arkansas urged the Indians to join the Confederacy. In 1861, a Confederate military leader, Albert Pike, made treaties of alliance with some of the tribes. These tribes

Oklahoma Industrial Development and Park Department

Statue Honoring Pioneer Women stands in Ponca City. A nearby museum exhibits relics of pioneer days.

IMPORTANT DATES IN OKLAHOMA

1541 Francisco Vásquez de Coronado crossed western Oklahoma in a search for gold.

1682 Robert Cavelier, Sieur de la Salle, claimed Oklahoma as part of French Louisiana.

1762 France gave Louisiana, including the Oklahoma region, to Spain.

1800 France regained Louisiana.

1803 The United States bought the Oklahoma region, except the Panhandle, as part of the Louisiana Purchase.

1819 The Oklahoma region, except the Panhandle, became part of the Territory of Arkansas.

1824 The government established Fort Gibson and Fort Towson, the region's first military posts.

1820-1842 The Five Civilized Tribes moved to Oklahoma.

1870-1872 The Missouri-Kansas-Texas railroad was built across the region.

1872 Oklahoma's first commercial coal was mined near McAlester.

1889 The United States opened part of Oklahoma to white settlement. The region's first producing oil well was drilled near Chelsea.

1890 Congress established the Territory of Oklahoma and added the Panhandle region to it.

1893 Congress established the Dawes Commission to manage the affairs of the Five Civilized Tribes. The Cherokee Outlet was opened to white settlement.

1907 Oklahoma entered the Union on November 16 as the 46th state.

1910 The state capital was moved from Guthrie to Oklahoma City.

1920 The Osage County oil fields began to produce.

1928 The Oklahoma City oil field opened.

1963 Henry Bellmon became the first Republican governor of Oklahoma.

1970 The Arkansas River Development Program was completed.

---

included some Plains Indians who had moved into the area. At first the Cherokee leader, Chief John Ross, tried to avoid taking sides. But the Confederates won a battle near the Cherokee border, at Wilson's Creek in Missouri, and Ross pledged the Cherokee to the South. Pike then recruited and led a brigade of Indians to fight for the South. One Cherokee, Stand Watie, became a Confederate brigadier general. Other Indians, however, fought for the Union.

After the Civil War, Congress forced the Five Civilized Tribes to give up the western part of their land because they had supported the South. Some of this land was given or sold to other Indian tribes.

The land that bordered the Indian Territory filled rapidly with settlers. Soon there was no more free or cheap land available. The whites wanted to use the fertile Indian lands. During the late 1860's, many cattlemen drove their herds across Oklahoma on their way from Texas to the Kansas railroad centers. Some cattlemen paid the Indians for grazing rights, but others did not. From 1866 to 1885, more than 6 million longhorn cattle crossed the Indian lands. The East Shawnee, West Shawnee, Chisholm, and Great Western trails were the leading routes. In 1883, an association of cattlemen leased more than 6 million acres (2.4 million hectares) from the Indians for five years. But the United States government declared all the leases invalid. President Benjamin Harrison ordered the white men's cattle removed in 1890.

The Great Land Rushes. "Boomers" urged the government to open the land for white settlement. The boomer leaders included C. C. Carpenter, David L. Payne, and William L. Couch. Finally the government yielded. It bought over 3 million acres (1.2 million hectares) from the Creek and Seminole tribes. Authorities declared almost 1,900,000 acres (769,000 hectares) in central Oklahoma open for settlement at noon, April 22, 1889. Thousands of settlers moved to the border to await the opening. The army held them back until a pistol shot signaled the opening. Then a wild race began to claim the best farms and townsites. About 50,000 peo-

556f

Oklahoma's Greatest Land Rush was created by the opening of the rich Cherokee Outlet on Sept. 16, 1893. Thousands of settlers staked claims in this 6½ million-acre (2.6 million-hectare) area. Previously, the land had belonged to the Indians.

ple had moved into Oklahoma by that evening. In a single day, Guthrie and Oklahoma City became cities of 10,000 persons.

Some settlers, called Sooners, went into the area before the opening to claim the best land. To hide their early entry, many Sooners ran their horses hard on the day of the opening. Then the tired horses would be shown to the pioneers who had followed the rules, to "prove" that the owner had just arrived.

The Territory of Oklahoma was established by Congress in May, 1890, with Guthrie as the capital. The same act added the Panhandle to the territory. The Panhandle had become U.S. territory when Texas joined the Union in 1845. President Harrison appointed George W. Steele as the first territorial governor.

During the 1890's, more and more Indian tribes accepted individual *allotment* of their lands. This meant that the individual Indians, not the tribe as a whole, owned the land. The land not allotted to tribe members was opened for settlement. In some areas, settlers got their land by *run*, or land rush. Other land was distributed by a lottery.

The greatest opening occurred on Sept. 16, 1893. That day, the Cherokee Outlet, in north-central Oklahoma, and the Tonkawa and Pawnee reservations were opened. Over 50,000 persons claimed land in the 6½ million-acre (2.6 million-hectare) area the first day.

Progress Toward Statehood. After 1890, maps showed the Oklahoma area as the Twin Territories—Indian Territory and Oklahoma Territory. Indian Territory was the remaining land of the Five Civilized Tribes, plus a small area owned and settled by other tribes. The rest of the region was Oklahoma Territory.

White settlers now wanted the remaining Indian lands. In 1893, Congress created the Dawes Commission to bargain for the land, and to dissolve the Indian nations. Agents of the commission helped the tribes incorporate towns and prepare for citizenship. The commission divided the remaining land among members of the tribes. By 1905, commission leaders felt the Indian Territory was ready to become a state.

Leaders of the Five Civilized Tribes called a constitutional convention at Muskogee in 1905, and invited white citizens to take part. At the time, whites in the Indian Territory outnumbered the Indians five to one. The convention adopted a constitution for the proposed state of Sequoyah, and the people approved it in an election. But Congress refused to accept the area as a state. Congress wanted one state to be created from the Twin Territories. In 1906, delegates from both territories met in Guthrie to draw up a constitution.

Early Statehood. On Nov. 16, 1907, Oklahoma became the 46th state in the Union. Charles N. Haskell of Muskogee was elected the first governor. The new state had a population of 1,414,177. Guthrie was the first capital. In 1910, Oklahoma City became the capital.

Even before statehood, Oklahoma had become a center of oil production. A small well was drilled near Chelsea in 1889. The first important well was drilled at Bartlesville in 1897. Tulsa became an oil center after the Red Fork-Tulsa field was opened in 1901.

─── **THE GOVERNORS OF OKLAHOMA** ───

		Party	Term
1.	Charles N. Haskell	Democratic	1907-1911
2.	Lee Cruce	Democratic	1911-1915
3.	R. L. Williams	Democratic	1915-1919
4.	James B. A. Robertson	Democratic	1919-1923
5.	John C. Walton	Democratic	1923
6.	Martin E. Trapp	Democratic	1923-1927
7.	Henry S. Johnston	Democratic	1927-1929
8.	William J. Holloway	Democratic	1929-1931
9.	William H. Murray	Democratic	1931-1935
10.	Ernest W. Marland	Democratic	1935-1939
11.	Leon C. Phillips	Democratic	1939-1943
12.	Robert S. Kerr	Democratic	1943-1947
13.	Roy J. Turner	Democratic	1947-1951
14.	Johnston Murray	Democratic	1951-1955
15.	Raymond S. Gary	Democratic	1955-1959
16.	J. Howard Edmondson	Democratic	1959-1963
17.	George Nigh	Democratic	1963
18.	Henry Bellmon	Republican	1963-1967
19.	Dewey F. Bartlett	Republican	1967-1971
20.	David Hall	Democratic	1971-1975
21.	David L. Boren	Democratic	1975-

But there were problems, especially among farmers. The prices of farm products were low, and many settlers found they did not have enough land to farm profitably. After the United States entered World War I in 1917, these problems disappeared in the huge demand for Oklahoma's farm and fuel products.

The 1920's. During the 1920's, many of Oklahoma's problems returned. Farm prices dropped again, and economic distress led to unrest. Secret organizations, such as the Ku Klux Klan, stirred into action (see KU KLUX KLAN). The Klan won many members in all parts of the state, and controlled or elected many municipal and county officials. But Governor James B. A. Robertson, who served from 1919 to 1923, fought the Klan and refused to allow any state official to join it.

In 1923, John C. Walton became governor. He was impeached for abusing his powers. The state legislature removed him from office after only 9 months and 14 days. Among other things, Walton had used the National Guard to prevent a grand jury from meeting. Lieutenant Governor Martin E. Trapp became governor and served until 1927. Trapp was a "hard roads" governor who pushed the construction of all-weather highways. Trapp also backed a law that made it illegal to wear masks at public gatherings. This law helped control the Klan. Henry S. Johnston became governor in 1927, but he, too, was impeached. After two years in office, Johnston was found guilty of incompetence and removed by the legislature. In March, 1929, Lieutenant Governor William J. Holloway became governor.

Important discoveries of oil and gas helped Oklahoma during this period. The huge Oklahoma City field was opened in 1928. It had more than 1,500 producing wells within 10 years. The Greater Seminole area led the nation in production from 1925 to 1929.

The 1930's. The campaign of 1930 was highlighted by the election as governor of one of Oklahoma's most colorful politicians, William H. "Alfalfa Bill" Murray. A former congressman, Murray appealed to the "common folks" to vote for him. After his election, Murray shut down over 3,000 flowing oil wells. The price of oil had been dropping, and Murray wanted to keep some oil off the market to force up the price. After three months, he permitted production to start again.

Oklahoma suffered many hardships during the Great Depression of the 1930's. Business was bad and farm prices were extremely low. Many banks failed and people lost their savings. The entire Great Plains region suffered a severe water shortage. Crops failed for lack of rain, and there were unusually hot summers. High winds stripped away large areas of fertile topsoil, and whipped the dry dirt into massive dust storms that turned day into night. Much of the plains area became known as the *Dust Bowl* (see DUST BOWL). Many farmers left the land to try their luck elsewhere. Many miners and oil workers also left the state. Oklahoma suffered a large loss of population. See UNITED STATES, HISTORY OF (The Great Depression).

The Mid-1900's. During World War II (1939-1945), Oklahoma's major products—food and fuels—again came into great demand. Increased use of soil conservation practices helped restore many farms that had been damaged during the drought of the 1930's.

Tulsa's Port, the busiest in Oklahoma, lies on the Verdigris River at nearby Catoosa. The barge shown above is being loaded with a cargo of peanuts headed for The Netherlands.

From 1943 to 1947, Governor Robert S. Kerr brought about reforms in education, state finances, and pardon and parole procedures for convicts. After his term as governor, Kerr won election to the U.S. Senate.

During the 1950's, Oklahoma's economy began to shift from an agricultural to an industrial base. Both the size and number of farms declined. Johnston Murray, the son of Alfalfa Bill Murray, became governor in 1951 and started a campaign to develop new industry in the state. His successor, Raymond S. Gary, continued Oklahoma's industrial expansion.

New industries and construction projects highlighted the state's economic progress during the 1960's. Two large electronics plants were built in Oklahoma City, and Tulsa became the site of a space equipment factory. The Federal Aviation Administration built an aeronautics center in Oklahoma City. This center trains workers for civil aviation jobs, such as that of control tower operator, and conducts research into airplane crashes. In 1963, Henry Bellmon became the state's first Republican governor. Bellmon was elected to the U.S. Senate in 1967.

Construction of a number of dams and creation of several lakes began in the mid-1900's. Some of these projects were completed in the 1960's, and the others were to be finished in the 1970's. The man-made lakes were created to increase the state's hydroelectric power and water storage capacities.

The new dams and lakes assisted Oklahoma business and political leaders in their efforts to broaden the state's industrial activity. The state government advertised Oklahoma's abundant supplies of fuel, water, and electric power. In addition, the legislature revised the state's tax structure to attract manufacturers. As a result, Oklahoma gained new industries that do not depend on the products of the state's farms and mines.

Oklahoma Today is becoming increasingly industrialized. Carpet mills, plastics factories, and the manufacture of mobile homes have started to play an important role in the state's economy. The Arkansas River Navigation System was completed in 1970. This $1-billion federal project made it possible for barges on the Mississippi River to reach Oklahoma ports on the Arkansas River. Tulsa and Muskogee became important ports on the river system.

Like many other states, Oklahoma has had racial problems. During the 1960's, the state repealed laws

that had segregated schools and public accommodations and had prohibited racially mixed marriages. In the 1970's, Oklahoma continued to work toward eliminating racial segregation in the state's schools.

Economic growth continued in Oklahoma during the 1970's. The nationwide fuel shortage increased the demand for the state's oil and natural gas. Oklahoma also made efforts to attract tourist and convention business by providing new recreation and meeting facilities. The state government increased taxes in order to pay for better schools and other services.

W. EUGENE HOLLON, JOHN W. MORRIS, and CHARLES L. BENNETT

OKLAHOMA / Study Aids

Related Articles in WORLD BOOK include:

BIOGRAPHIES

Albert, Carl Bert	Rogers, Will
Chouteau (Jean P.)	Ross, John
Harris, Fred Roy	Sequoya
Harris, Roy	Tallchief, Maria
Hurley, Patrick J.	Thorpe, Jim
Roberts, Oral	Watie, Stand

CITIES

Enid	Muskogee	Tulsa
Lawton	Oklahoma City	

HISTORY

Caddo Indians	Indian Territory
Cheyenne Indians	Louisiana Purchase
Comanche Indians	Osage Indians
Five Civilized Tribes	Westward
Indian, American	Movement

PHYSICAL FEATURES

Arkansas River	Lake O' The	Ozark Mountains
Canadian River	Cherokees	Pensacola Dam
Dust Bowl	Lake Texoma	Red River
Fort Supply Dam		

PRODUCTS

For Oklahoma's rank among the states in production, see the following articles:

Cattle	Mining	Petroleum
Gas	Nut	Wheat
Horse		

OTHER RELATED ARTICLES

Fort Sill	Southwestern States

Outline

I. Government
A. Constitution   E. Local Government
B. Executive   F. Taxation
C. Legislature   G. Politics
D. Courts
II. People
III. Education
A. Schools   B. Libraries   C. Museums
IV. A Visitor's Guide
A. Places to Visit
B. Annual Events
V. The Land
A. Land Regions
B. Rivers and Lakes
VI. Climate

VII. Economy
A. Natural Resources   E. Electric Power
B. Manufacturing   F. Transportation
C. Agriculture   G. Communication
D. Mining
VIII. History

Questions

Why did Congress take land away from the Indians in the Oklahoma area after the Civil War?

What role did the Indian leader Sequoya play in the history of education in Oklahoma?

Why did a federal court order the reapportionment of the Oklahoma legislature?

What group of Indians was among Oklahoma's first permanent settlers?

What is the leading source of agricultural income in Oklahoma?

Why is Oklahoma called the *Sooner State?*

What part of Oklahoma is called the *Panhandle?*

How many of Oklahoma's 77 counties produce gas and oil?

Why is the phrase "as long as grass shall grow and rivers run" important in Oklahoma history?

Why did the population of Oklahoma drop in the 1930's?

Books for Young Readers

BAILEY, BERNADINE. *Picture Book of Oklahoma.* Rev. ed. Whitman, 1967.

CARPENTER, ALLAN. *Oklahoma.* Childrens Press, 1965.

HANCOCK, MARY A. *The Thundering Prairie.* Macrae Smith, 1969. Fiction.

KEITH, HAROLD. *Rifles for Watie.* Crowell, 1957. *Susy's Scoundrel.* 1974. Both books are fictional.

Books for Older Readers

FERBER, EDNA. *Cimarron.* Doubleday, 1930. Fiction.

HAMES, LIBBY W. *Under the Blackjack Trees.* Naylor, 1976. A collection of anecdotes about Oklahoma pioneers.

KIRKPATRICK, SAMUEL A., and others. *The Oklahoma Voter: Politics, Elections, and Political Parties in the Sooner State.* Univ. of Oklahoma Press, 1977.

McREYNOLDS, EDWIN C. *Oklahoma: A History of the Sooner State.* Rev. ed. Univ. of Oklahoma Press, 1964.

MORRIS, JOHN W., and others. *Historical Atlas of Oklahoma.* 2nd ed. Univ. of Oklahoma Press, 1976.

NYE, WILBUR S. *Carbine and Lance: The Story of Old Fort Sill.* 3rd ed. Univ. of Oklahoma Press, 1969.

WRIGHT, MURIEL H. *A Guide to the Indian Tribes of Oklahoma.* Univ. of Oklahoma Press, 1951.

WRIGHT, MURIEL H., and others. *Mark of Heritage.* 2nd ed. Oklahoma Historical Society, 1976. A guide to the state's historical sites.

OKLAHOMA, UNIVERSITY OF, is a state-supported coeducational institution in Norman, Okla. It has colleges of arts and sciences, business administration, education, engineering, environmental design, fine arts, law, liberal studies, and pharmacy, and a graduate college. Courses lead to bachelor's, master's, and doctor's degrees. The university also has a Medical Center in Oklahoma City. It has schools of dentistry, health, health related professions, medicine, and nursing. Research facilities on the Norman campus include Swearingen Research Park, the National Severe Storms Laboratory, and the Oil Information Center. The University of Oklahoma Press publishes *Books Abroad*, a quarterly review of international literature. The university was founded in 1890 by the Oklahoma territorial legislature. It opened in 1892. For enrollment, see UNIVERSITIES AND COLLEGES (table).   PAUL F. SHARP

OKLAHOMA CITY (pop. 368,377; met. area pop. 699,092) is the capital and largest city of Oklahoma. About a fourth of the state's people live in the Oklahoma City metropolitan area. The city ranks as one of the chief centers of oil production in the United States. It is a commercial and manufacturing center of Oklahoma and a distribution point for a large farming area.

Oklahoma City lies on the North Canadian River, near the geographic center of the state. For location, see OKLAHOMA (political map). White settlers first came to what is now the Oklahoma City area in 1889. The United States government had originally set this land aside for Indians. But the government later opened central Oklahoma for white settlement. On the first day, about 10,000 settlers flocked to a site near the Santa Fe Railroad tracks and pitched their tents. This settlement became Oklahoma City. The city's name came from two Choctaw Indian words—*okla*, meaning *people*, and *homma*, meaning *red*.

The City covers 649 square miles (1,681 square kilometers), including 15 square miles (39 square kilometers) of inland water. It is the nation's third largest city in land area. Only Juneau, Alaska, and Jacksonville, Fla., are larger. The Oklahoma City metropolitan area spreads over five entire counties—Canadian, Cleveland, McClain, Oklahoma, and Pottawatomie—and covers about 3,554 square miles (9,205 square kilometers).

The State Capitol stands in a major oil field on the northeast border of the city. Oil wells operate on the Capitol grounds and throughout the city—even on residential land. A statue called *The Cowboy* stands in front of the Capitol (see OKLAHOMA [pictures: The State Capitol; *The Cowboy*]).

The city's Myriad Convention Center is one of the nation's leading convention sites. It hosts many of the conventions held in Oklahoma City. The 35-story Liberty Bank Tower is the city's tallest building.

More than 98 per cent of the people of Oklahoma City were born in the United States. Persons of English, German, or Mexican ancestry form the largest groups. Blacks make up about 14 per cent of the city's population. Baptists make up the largest religious

Downtown Oklahoma City has many towering office buildings and hotels. Construction projects of the 1960's and early 1970's brought a number of new skyscrapers to the state capital.

Ray Jacoby

group, followed by Methodists and Roman Catholics.

Economy of Oklahoma City depends heavily on manufacturing. The leading industries of the city produce airplanes, food products, petroleum products, and space electronics equipment. About 600 manufacturing plants employ 15 per cent of the city's workers.

The federal and state governments employ another 27 per cent of Oklahoma City's work force. Tinker Air Force Base is the largest single employer. This base, an important supply station for the Air Force, employs about 21,000 civilians. The Federal Aviation Administration has about 4,000 civilian employees in the city.

Much of Oklahoma City's industrial importance results from its location in an area rich in natural resources for both oil production and farming. The more than 350 wells within the city produce about 5,000 barrels of oil daily. Over 1,800 wells pump oil in the Oklahoma City metropolitan area.

The city processes and distributes such farm products as feed, flour, and meat. It ranks as the nation's third largest cattle market, after Omaha, Nebr., and Sioux City, Iowa. Other Oklahoma City products include automobile bodies and parts, building materials, cottonseed oil, iron and steel products, paper products, telephone equipment, and transportation equipment.

Will Rogers World Airport lies at the southwest edge of the city, and passenger and freight trains also serve the community. Oklahoma City has three daily newspapers, *The Daily Oklahoman*, the *Oklahoma City Times*, and *The Oklahoma Journal*. Four television stations and about 20 radio stations broadcast from the city.

Education and Cultural Life. Oklahoma City's public school system includes about 85 elementary schools and 20 high schools. The city also has about 15 church-supported schools.

Colleges and universities in Oklahoma City include Oklahoma Christian College, Oklahoma City University, and the University of Oklahoma Health Sciences Center. The University of Oklahoma is in nearby Norman. The city's library system consists of a main library and five branches.

Oklahoma City is the home of the Lyric Theater of Oklahoma City University. The Oklahoma City Symphony performs at the Civic Center Music Hall. The National Cowboy Hall of Fame and Western Heritage Center displays paintings and sculptures of the American West.

The Oklahoma Historical Society Building and Museum has a collection of exhibits that trace the history of Oklahoma. The Oklahoma Science and Arts Foundation includes the Kirkpatrick Planetarium and exhibits of the nation's space program. Oklahoma City's famous Church of Tomorrow has a 1,550-seat sanctuary and a theater-in-the-round.

In December, Oklahoma City hosts the National Finals Rodeo, one of the state's most popular annual events. Oklahoma City's park system includes 128 parks, which cover about 3,500 acres (1,420 hectares). Lincoln Park, the largest, occupies 632 acres (256 hectares) and includes the Oklahoma City Zoo.

Government. Oklahoma City has a council-manager form of government. The voters elect a mayor and eight council members to four-year terms. The council appoints a city manager.

In 1971, the voters elected Patience S. Latting may-

or. She became the first woman mayor of a United States city of more than 200,000 persons. Sales taxes provide most of the city's income.

History. Creek and Seminole Indians lived in what is now the Oklahoma City area before white settlers first arrived. In 1889, the government bought the land there from the two tribes. On April 22, 1889, the government opened the area for white settlement, and a great land rush began. By the evening of that day, about 10,000 settlers had arrived there. Oklahoma City was incorporated in 1890. By 1910, it ranked as the state's largest city. Its population rose from 10,037 in 1900 to 64,205 in 1910. During that period, four railroads began to serve the city and two meat-packing plants opened. In 1910, Oklahoma City replaced Guthrie as the state capital.

The city's greatest problem during its early years was a lack of water sources. Shortly after 1900, Oklahoma City built its first municipal well. In 1919, it completed its first reservoir, Lake Overholser. Since then, the city has built several more reservoirs to assure a water supply.

By 1920, Oklahoma City had a population of 91,295. Oil was discovered in the city in 1928, and an oil boom began. Many oil companies built refineries there, and the area became a center of the nation's petroleum industry.

Tinker Air Force Base was built in Oklahoma City during World War II (1939-1945). By 1950, the population of the city had risen to 243,504.

Industrial expansion occurred during the 1950's and 1960's. Iron and steel plants were built, and the city also became a center of the electronics industry. Development took place in downtown Oklahoma City as well. During the 1960's, the city annexed many surrounding areas, and its area increased from about 310 square miles (803 square kilometers) in 1960 to about 635 square miles (1,645 square kilometers) in 1970.

Several problems resulted from Oklahoma City's rapid growth during the 1950's and 1960's. For example, the city faced the need for more hospitals and schools. In the late 1960's and early 1970's, Oklahoma City began several urban renewal projects to replace old buildings and slum areas.

Plans for the 1970's included construction of a cultural-recreational center called Myriad Gardens. This project, scheduled for completion by 1980, includes an arts and science center, a museum, and a sports hall of fame.

Oklahoma City's Medical Center Project, scheduled to be completed by 1980, includes a dental college, a hospital, a nursing school, and headquarters for the State Health Department. The city also started the John F. Kennedy Project, consisting of about 3,000 homes or apartment buildings, to replace 1,260 acres (510 hectares) of slum housing.   CHARLES L. BENNETT

For the monthly weather in Oklahoma City, see OKLAHOMA (Climate). See also OKLAHOMA (pictures).

OKLAHOMA STATE UNIVERSITY is a state-supported coeducational school in Stillwater, Okla. It has colleges of agriculture, arts and sciences, business administration, education, engineering, home economics, veterinary medicine, and a graduate college. It also offers a special program in fire protection and safety technology. The university grants bachelor's, master's, and doctor's degrees. It has a school of technical training in Okmulgee and a two-year technical institute in Oklahoma City. The university maintains an agricultural experiment station and a state extension service. It also has Army and Air Force ROTC units.

The university was established in 1890, and was opened to students in 1891. For enrollment, see UNIVERSITIES AND COLLEGES (table).

Critically reviewed by OKLAHOMA STATE UNIVERSITY

OKRA, *OH kruh*, is a plant cultivated for its immature pods, which are used in stews, to thicken and flavor soup, and as a vegetable, chiefly in the southern part of the United States. The plant is an annual. It grows 2 to 8 feet (0.6 to 2.4 meters) high. It bears rounded, fine-lobed leaves, and greenish-yellow flowers. The pods on the plant are from 4 to 6 inches (10 to 15 centimeters) long, but sometimes exceed 1 foot (30 centimeters) when fully grown. Okra pods are cooked and canned when young and tender.

U.S. Dept. of Agriculture
Pods of the Okra Plant

Okra is a kind of hibiscus, and it is closely related to cotton. It is a native of Africa. In the southern part of the United States, where okra is raised in large quantities, it is also known as *gumbo* or *okro*.

Scientific Classification. The okra belongs to the mallow family, *Malvaceae*. It is genus *Hibiscus*, species *H. esculentus*. JOHN H. MACGILLIVRAY

ÖLAND. See SWEDEN (The Land; map).

OLAV I. See NORWAY (The Viking Period); VIKINGS (The Danish Vikings).

OLAV II. See NORWAY (The Viking Period; picture).

OLAV V (1903-   ) became king of Norway in 1957 when his father, King Haakon VII, died (see HAAKON VII). Olav was born in England, and came to Norway when he was 2. He attended the Norwegian War College and Oxford University. He frequently served as regent during his father's illnesses. He was chief of Norwegian defense forces in World War II. His wife, Princess Märtha of Sweden, died in 1954. RAYMOND E. LINDGREN

Billedsentralen, Oslo
King Olav V

OLD AGE is a term that refers to the final period of life. For two main reasons, old age cannot be defined exactly. First, the aging process differs among individuals. A person of advanced age may have a healthier body and a more active mind than a much younger person has. Second,

an age considered old in some societies may be regarded as relatively young in other societies.

In some areas of the world where people have a short life expectancy, they may be considered old by the age of 40. On the other hand, a person in the United States, Canada, and other industrial countries lives an average of about 70 years. In those countries, people may not be considered old until 60 or 70.

Most nations define old age for legal purposes. For example, the U.S. and Canadian governments normally consider 65 as the legal beginning of old age. In both the United States and Canada, people in the 65-and-over age group are often called *senior citizens*.

About 10 per cent, or 20 million persons, of the U.S. population is 65 years old or over. This percentage has more than doubled since 1900, when old people made up only about 4 per cent, or 3 million persons, of the population. The 65-and-over age group includes about four women to every three men. It also includes a higher percentage of whites and of people born in other countries than does the population as a whole.

This article discusses the financial situation and ways of life of elderly people—those 65 years of age and over—in the United States. It also discusses public aid for the elderly. The WORLD BOOK article on SOCIAL SECURITY includes information on public aid for the elderly in Canada.

Financial Situation. The average income of the elderly is only about half that of younger people, mainly because most old people have retired. But even those who still work full time earn less than younger people. Younger workers may earn a higher salary because of more education or more recent training. Elderly women, many of them widows, are the worst off. Their income averages less than half that of elderly men.

Most elderly people receive federal social security payments. Many also receive funds from earnings, savings, private investments, or pension plans. Public health insurance pays about three-fourths of the total medical expenses of the elderly. Some elderly people who are extremely poor receive financial and medical assistance from state, county, or private welfare agencies.

Periodic increases in social security payments and improvements in private pension plans mean greater financial security for many old people. But a higher income from such sources disqualifies some of the elderly for certain welfare benefits provided by state and local governments.

Ways of Life Among the Elderly. In a modern industrial country, the elderly have difficulty finding a useful role in society. Most of them have retired, and so they lack the money and respect that an occupation provides. Many cannot afford to pursue interests or hobbies. Most younger people have gone to school longer and have had more up-to-date teaching than the elderly. As a result, the young may not regard the elderly as being wiser. Many Americans consider old age a period of decline and neglect. They have come to believe that the government should be responsible for the welfare of the elderly.

Most old people in the United States value their independence and want to be free to choose where and how they live. But many lack both the money and the opportunity to choose. Some elderly people live in extremely poor surroundings and have few of the conveniences and services that many other Americans take for granted.

A higher proportion of the elderly than of younger people live in rural areas, small towns, and the poorer sections of large cities. The government classifies about a fifth of the housing units occupied by the elderly as substandard. Much of this housing lacks such basic conveniences as private bathrooms and hot water. Some low-income apartment housing has been designed specially for senior citizens. But most elderly people do not want to move out of their old neighborhoods, even into less expensive or more convenient housing.

About 70 per cent of the elderly own their own homes. Almost 25 per cent live with their children, but the majority prefer not to. Another 25 per cent, mostly widowed, live entirely alone or with nonrelatives. Fewer than 5 per cent live in hospitals, nursing homes, or homes for the aged. More and more well-to-do elderly live in *retirement communities*.

Many of the aged have health problems, and some cannot afford adequate health care. About 80 per cent suffer from at least one disease. The Medicaid and Medicare programs have greatly lightened the financial burden of health care (see MEDICAID; MEDICARE). But the elderly must still pay about a fourth of their medical expenses. Other barriers to adequate health care include a severe shortage of hospitals and nursing homes, the low quality of many of these institutions, and the lack of preventive care and health education. However, most of the elderly, in spite of their problems, feel that their health does not prevent them from carrying out their major activities.

Only about 25 per cent of the elderly men and about 10 per cent of the aged women have jobs or are actively seeking them. Old people who do have jobs perform as well as younger workers. The working elderly seem to adjust better to old age than do those who have retired. Many retired people have difficulty finding useful or satisfying activities to occupy their free time.

Old people seem generally satisfied with their family relationships, and they consider these relationships important. Most old people visit with one or more of their children at least once a week. Many also spend much time visiting friends, watching television, reading, walking, or taking part in religious activities. A higher proportion of old people than young adults vote in elections and take an interest in public affairs. Some take an active part in clubs, lodges, or volunteer work. Golden Age and Senior Citizens' clubs have become increasingly popular.

Although the elderly sometimes seem less happy than younger people, this situation may be largely due to economic or social difficulties. Older people who have little money or education, no family ties, or poor health find less satisfaction in their lives than more fortunate individuals. For the more fortunate, old age can be an enjoyable time of life. They can lead active lives and, as a result, feel happier, more useful, and less lonely.

Public Aid. The federal social security program provides most public financial aid to the elderly through monthly pension payments. This program also helps finance state and local old-age assistance programs. In addition, the federal government provides special tax benefits and the Medicare program of financing health care for the elderly. Some state and local governments offer the elderly such special benefits as reduced property taxes, free legal service, or reduced fares for public transportation. For more information about public financial aid for the elderly, see the SOCIAL SECURITY article.

Many federal agencies work to help the elderly by financing special projects and by conducting research into the problems of aging. For example, the Administration on Aging, an agency of the Department of Health, Education, and Welfare, grants funds to state and local agencies. These agencies use the money to improve the health, living conditions, and educational and recreational opportunities of the elderly. The National Institute on Aging conducts and supports research on aging and on the diseases and other special problems of the aged.

The federal government also seeks to recruit elderly persons for various types of volunteer work. A White House Conference on Aging in 1961 and another in 1971 helped gain public recognition for the problems that old people face.   MARILYN JOHNSON

See also AGING; GERIATRICS; WELFARE; LIFE (Length of Life); LIBRARY (Services for Special Groups; picture: Music Lovers).

OLD-AGE AND SURVIVORS INSURANCE. See SOCIAL SECURITY.

OLD-AGE PENSION. See PENSION.

OLD BAILEY is the common name for the main criminal court in London. The Old Bailey has several courts, and each one holds sessions at least four times a year. The court is located on a street called Old Bailey. This street once formed part of a *bailey* (an area between the inner and outer city walls) in medieval London.

The London city government built the Sessions House in 1550. This building became known as the Old Bailey. Persons held at nearby Newgate Prison were tried in the Old Bailey. Famous cases held there included the treason trial of judges responsible for the execution of King Charles I; the treason trial of William Joyce, who broadcast for Nazi Germany during World

Camera Press from Publix
Old Bailey, London's main criminal court, dates from 1550. The present court building, *above*, opened in 1907.

War II as *Lord Haw Haw;* and the morals trial of the author and playwright Oscar Wilde.　VERNON F. SNOW

OLD BLOOD AND GUTS. See PATTON, GEORGE SMITH, JR.

OLD BULLION. See BENTON, THOMAS HART.

OLD CASCADE TUNNEL. See CASCADE TUNNEL.

OLD CATHOLIC CHURCHES are a group of Christian churches that split away from the Roman Catholic Church. The churches were formed by Roman Catholics who opposed the dogma of *papal infallibility* proclaimed at the first Vatican Council in 1870. This doctrine states that the pope is always right when he speaks as head of the church on matters of faith and morals.

The Catholics who withdrew from the Roman Catholic Church at that time established an independent church. Most of these Catholics lived in Germany, The Netherlands, Switzerland, and the Austro-Hungarian empire. The independent church formed a loose relationship with other dissenting Catholic churches under the terms of the Union of Utrecht in 1889.

Old Catholic churches generally follow Roman Catholic doctrine, although the clergy may marry. The churches encourage Bible study and conduct worship in the *vernacular* (local language).　FRANKLIN H. LITTELL

OLD COMEDY. See DRAMA (Greek Drama).

OLD DOMINION. See VIRGINIA.

OLD ENGLISH. See ENGLISH LANGUAGE; ENGLISH LITERATURE (The Anglo-Saxon Period).

OLD ENGLISH SHEEPDOG is best known for its long hair, "bobbed" tail, and odd, shuffling walk. Its hair hangs down over its eyes. Much brushing is required to keep the dog's long coat neat. The coat serves as excellent insulation. It is a grizzly gray or blue, often with white markings, or predominantly white, with markings. The dog stands about 22 inches (56 centimeters) high, and weighs from 50 to 65 pounds (23 to 29 kilograms).　OLGA DAKAN

See also DOG (picture: Working Dogs); SHEEPDOG.

OLD FAITHFUL. See WYOMING (color picture); YELLOWSTONE NATIONAL PARK.

OLD FUSS AND FEATHERS. See SCOTT, WINFIELD.

OLD GLORY. See DRIVER, WILLIAM.

OLD HICKORY. See JACKSON, ANDREW.

OLD IRONSIDES, locomotive. See BALDWIN, MATTHIAS WILLIAM.

OLD IRONSIDES, ship. See CONSTITUTION (ship).

OLD KING COLE. See MOTHER GOOSE.

OLD LINE STATE. See MARYLAND.

OLD MAN ELOQUENT. See ADAMS, JOHN QUINCY.

OLD MAN OF THE MOUNTAIN. See WHITE MOUNTAINS.

OLD MAN OF THE SEA. See NEREUS.

OLD NORTH CHURCH is the popular name for Christ Church, the oldest public building in Boston, Mass. The red-brick structure has a slender white steeple in the Christopher Wren style. Robert Newman hung the lanterns there as a signal from Paul Revere that the British were coming. The tower contains the first set of church bells in the American Colonies, cast in 1744. Storms in 1804 and 1954 toppled the spire. In 1955, it was rebuilt to its original 190 feet (58 meters). See also BOSTON; REVERE, PAUL.　WILLIAM J. REID

OLD ORCHARD BEACH. See MAINE (Land Regions).

OLD PRETENDER. See SCOTLAND (Union with England).

OLD ROUGH AND READY. See TAYLOR, ZACHARY.

OLD SOUTH MEETING HOUSE. See BOSTON (Downtown Boston; illustration: Boston's Freedom Trail).

OLD SPANISH TRAIL. See SANTA FE TRAIL.

OLD SQUAW. See DUCK (Diving Sea Ducks).

OLD STONE AGE. See PREHISTORIC PEOPLE (How Prehistoric Hunters Lived); STONE AGE.

OLD STONE MILL. See RHODE ISLAND (Places to Visit).

OLD TESTAMENT is the first part of the Bible. Together with the New Testament, it forms the Scriptures that are sacred to Christians. Jews accept only the Old Testament, which they call the *Hebrew Bible,* as sacred. The word *testament* is an old word for *covenant,* or agreement. The Old Testament emphasizes the idea of a covenant between God and His people, and contains a record of their history to show how faithfully they observed this covenant.

The Bible has been called "the Book of Books" because of the tremendous influence it has exerted on the human race. For over two thousand years, people have considered the Old Testament the word of God, and have turned to it for guidance on life's problems. Millions of persons have found in it great religious truths and inspired ethical teachings. As a cultural treasure, the Old Testament is one of the most important sources we have for knowledge of the past. In addition, the poetry and prose of the Old Testament include some of the greatest literary masterpieces of the world.

Contents. According to Jewish tradition, there are 24 books in the Hebrew Bible. Protestants accept the

Greater Boston Chamber of Commerce

The Graceful Steeple of Historic Old North Church pierces the skyline in the business district of Boston, Mass.

same books as the Old Testament, but arrange them differently. They divide several of them, making a total of 39. The Roman Catholic Old Testament consists of 46 books. It includes seven books that Protestants consider part of the Apocrypha (see APOCRYPHA). For a list of Old Testament books that are accepted by Jews, Protestants, and Roman Catholics, see the *table* with the WORLD BOOK article on the BIBLE.

Jews divide the Old Testament into three main sections called the Law, the Prophets, and the Writings.

The Law, or *Torah,* consists of the books of Genesis, Exodus, Leviticus, Numbers, and Deuteronomy. It is also called the *Pentateuch* or *Five Books* of Moses (see PENTATEUCH). The Hebrew word *Torah* is usually translated as *the Law,* but a more accurate translation would be *teaching* or *guidance.* The Law begins with an account of the creation of the world and the early traditions of humanity. It then concentrates on the careers of Abraham, Isaac, and Jacob, the *patriarchs* (fathers) of the Hebrew nation (see PATRIARCH). Other narratives include the story of Joseph, the history of the Israelites in Egypt, and the Exodus from Egypt under the leadership of Moses. The books of Numbers and Deuteronomy describe the experiences of the people in the desert and the death of Moses before they entered the Promised Land. Laws dealing with all phases of life are woven into the narratives. They include religious and moral teachings, ritual practices, and civil and criminal laws. Sections of the Old Testament also contain rules about health and even medical counsel.

The Prophets are divided into two parts, the Former Prophets and the Latter Prophets. The books of Joshua, Judges, Samuel, and Kings make up the Former Prophets. These books are often called the *historical books* because they trace the history of the Hebrew nation from the time it entered Palestine until the destruction of the kingdoms of Israel and Judah (see JEWS [History]). The books are included in the Prophets because they describe the lives and activities of many prophets, such as Nathan and Elijah. The Former Prophets also interpret the history of the Hebrews from the point of view of the prophets. The prophets taught that human destiny is determined by obedience or disobedience to God's laws. The Latter Prophets consist of four books— Isaiah, Jeremiah, Ezekiel, and the Twelve. The Twelve contains the teaching of 12 other prophets.

The Writings, or *Hagiographa,* are made up of a variety of books. Their authors include teachers, poets, and great thinkers. The Writings contain the books of Psalms, Proverbs, and Job, and the five *Megillot,* or Scrolls: Song of Solomon, Ruth, Lamentations, Ecclesiastes, and Esther. The book of Daniel and the later historical works of Ezra, Nehemiah, and Chronicles complete this section of the Old Testament.

For a fuller discussion of the Old Testament books, see the separate WORLD BOOK article on each book.

Christian and Jewish groups differ in the position of importance they assign to the books of the Apocrypha. Many of these books resemble those of the Old Testament in form. But they were written later, probably from about 200 B.C. to about A.D. 100.

Date. The Old Testament was written over a long period of time. The process was complicated because much of the material was recited or chanted out loud long before it was written down. Scholars disagree

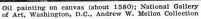
Oil painting on canvas (about 1580); National Gallery of Art, Washington, D.C., Andrew W. Mellon Collection

The Old Testament Story of Moses tells how Pharaoh's daughter found the infant Moses in the reeds along the Nile River. His mother hid him there after Pharaoh ordered all new-born Israelite boys killed. In his painting, *The Finding of Moses,* Paolo Veronese dressed his figures in the Venetian styles of his time.

about how and when the books were actually written. But most scholars today agree that the Old Testament does contain material from the days of Moses. One of the earliest poems is the "War Song of Deborah" (Judges 5), composed about 1100 B.C. Many parts of the historical and prophetic books were written during the time of the two kingdoms of Israel and Judah. Some of the most important prophets and poets lived during the Babylonian Exile, from 587 B.C. to 538 B.C. Many traditions, laws, and historical records that had accumulated were collected and put in order at that time. The books of Psalms and the Song of Solomon were assembled after 538 B.C., when many Jews returned to Palestine. Chronicles, Ecclesiastes, Esther, and Daniel were written later. The entire Old Testament existed by the time of the Maccabean Wars, from 168 B.C. to 165 B.C. The Biblical manuscripts of the Dead Sea Scrolls, written about 100 years later, show that the text of the Old Testament two thousand years ago was essentially the same as it is today (see DEAD SEA SCROLLS).

Translations. The entire Old Testament was written in Hebrew, except for some chapters in the books of Daniel and Ezra and a few words in Genesis and Jeremiah. These are in Aramaic, a language much like Hebrew (see ARAMAIC).

The Old Testament was probably the first work ever translated. The first translations were oral versions from Hebrew into Aramaic called *Targums* (see TARGUM). During the mid-200's B.C., Jewish scholars working in Alexandria, Egypt, translated the Law into Greek. This translation is called the *Septuagint* (see SEPTUAGINT). Translations of other Old Testament books followed. The best-known Latin translation was the *Vulgate*, completed by Saint Jerome in A.D. 405 (see VULGATE). Jerome's translation served as the official Old Testament text of the Roman Catholic Church for hundreds of years. For a historical discussion of other translations of the Old Testament, see BIBLE (Translations of the Bible). ROBERT GORDIS

See also BIBLE with its list of Related Articles.

OLD WATER TOWER. See CHICAGO (Downtown Chicago; map).

OLD WORLD is a general term applied to the Eastern Hemisphere. The Western Hemisphere is called the *New World*. The Old World includes the continents of Europe, Asia, Africa, and Australia. But the term *Old World* is often used to refer just to Europe or to European civilization. The terms Old World and New World are used in botany and zoology. For example, zoologists divide monkeys into two groups, Old World monkeys and New World monkeys. See also HEMISPHERE.

OLDENBURG, CLAES, *klows,* (1929-   ), is an American sculptor who became a leader of the pop art movement in the United States during the 1960's. He is best known for his exaggerated, oversized sculptures that represent such familiar objects as electric plugs, toothpaste tubes, and typewriters. Oldenburg makes many works from soft, floppy material, and these sculptures resemble caricatures of the original subjects. His *Giant Soft Fan, Ghost Version* appears in the WORLD BOOK article on SCULPTURE.

Oldenburg has used common objects in creating designs for large monuments. For example, he made a design of a giant pair of scissors to "replace" the Washington Monument in Washington, D.C. He designed a huge lipstick, called *Feasible Monument,* which was built at Yale University in 1969.

Claes Thure Oldenburg was born in Stockholm, Sweden, and became a United States citizen in 1953. He graduated from Yale in 1950 and studied at the Art Institute of Chicago from 1952 to 1954. GREGORY BATTCOCK

See also POP ART.

OLDFIELD, BARNEY (1877-1946), was the first person to drive an automobile at a speed of 1 mile (1.6 kilometers) per minute. His name became synonymous with speed after he did this in a much-publicized test at Indianapolis on June 15, 1903. His first racing car, the "999," was built by Henry Ford. In it, Oldfield won his first race at Detroit in 1902. In 1910, at Daytona Beach, Fla., he raced a mile at an average speed of 131 mph (211 kph), a record at that time. Berner Eli Oldfield was born in Wauseon, Ohio. See also AUTOMOBILE RACING (Early Automobile Races); AVIATION (picture: Airplanes Raced Against Automobiles). PAT HARMON

OLDS, RANSOM ELI (1864-1950), was a pioneer automobile inventor and manufacturer. Two automobiles,

the Oldsmobile and the Reo (from his initials), were named for him. In 1886, he began experimenting with steam-powered carriages in his father's machine shop in Lansing, Mich. He later made a four-wheeled steam car which he sold to a firm in India in 1893. It was the first U.S. car sold abroad.

Olds built his first gasoline-operated car in 1896. In 1899, he helped found the Olds Motor Works in Detroit, Mich. A lightweight, one-cylinder, low-cost model ($650) was in volume production by 1901. Many thousands of these cars were sold by 1906. In 1904, Olds left the Olds Motor Works, and organized a company to manufacture Reo automobiles and trucks. He was president of the Reo Motor Car Company from 1904 to 1924, and later became chairman of the board.

Olds was born in Geneva, Ohio. Many persons consider him the founder of the automobile industry. He built the first automobile factory, and was the first manufacturer to mass-produce cars. Furthermore, the success of the Oldsmobile attracted other manufacturers into the industry, and helped make the automobile popular with Americans. SMITH HEMPSTONE OLIVER

See also AUTOMOBILE (The Steam Car).

OLEANDER, *OH lee AN der,* is an ornamental flowering shrub which is valued as a house plant. The oleander sometimes grows 15 feet (4.6 meters) tall. It bears leathery lance-shaped leaves and showy roselike flowers. The two most common varieties have red and white blossoms. The oleander is native to the warm parts of Asia and to the Mediterranean region. Gardeners plant it outdoors in warm climates, but they grow it in pots and tubs in temperate regions. It is a favorite porch plant in summer.

Because all parts of the plant are poisonous to eat, children should be cautioned about eating the oleander. If the cuttings are placed in bottles of water, they will form roots in a few

J. Horace McFarland

The Oleander is a favorite indoor plant for gardeners.

weeks. Gardeners easily raise the oleander from cuttings. Then oleanders must be transplanted to moist, rich soil, where they grow well.

Scientific Classification. The oleander belongs to the dogbane family, *Apocynaceae.* It is genus *Nerium,* species *N. oleander.* J. J. LEVISON

OLEIC ACID. See FAT.

OLEIN. See LARD.

OLEOMARGARINE. See MARGARINE.

OLEORESIN. See RESIN.

OLERICULTURE. See HORTICULTURE.

OLFACTORY LOBE and **OLFACTORY NERVE.** See NOSE; SMELL.

OLIBANUM. See FRANKINCENSE.

OLIGARCHY, *AHL uh GAHR kee,* is a form of government in which a small group of persons holds the ruling power. These persons rule in dictatorial fashion, without the consent of the governed. A republic may be an oligarchy if only a few persons have the right to vote (see REPUBLIC).

Most persons today do not advocate oligarchical

forms of government. But many oligarchies existed in the past. Most ancient Greek city-states were classic examples of oligarchies. Another example is Venice during the Renaissance, when a small group of wealthy families controlled the city. In a broad sense, the word *oligarchy* can also be applied to some churches and to some business corporations. WILLIAM EBENSTEIN

OLIGOCENE EPOCH. See EARTH (table: Outline of Earth History).

OLIGOPOLY. See MONOPOLY AND COMPETITION.

Pat Oliphant; © 1969 *The Denver Post*, reprinted with permission Los Angeles Times Syndicate

A Cartoon by Patrick Oliphant deals with rising food prices. Punk the Penguin, *lower right*, a familiar character in Oliphant's cartoons, comments on the action in the drawing.

OLIPHANT, PATRICK BRUCE (1935-   ), is a well-known editorial cartoonist. The figures in his cartoons have very exaggerated features, and his work is more biting than that of most other editorial cartoonists. Most Oliphant cartoons include Punk the Penguin, a character that usually comments on the action in the drawings. Oliphant won the Pulitzer prize for cartooning in 1967.

Oliphant was born in Adelaide, Australia. In 1955, he became the editorial cartoonist of *The Advertiser*, the Adelaide newspaper. He came to the United States in 1964 to join the *Denver Post* as editorial cartoonist. In 1975, he joined *The Washington Star*. The Los Angeles Times Syndicate distributes Oliphant's cartoons to about 300 newspapers. Collections of his work have been published in *The Oliphant Book* (1969) and *Four More Years* (1973). ROY PAUL NELSON

OLIVE, *AHL iv*, is a fruit that grows in regions near the tropics. People have grown olives since prehistoric times. It is thought that this fruit first grew in the eastern Mediterranean basin. Hundreds of years ago it escaped from cultivation and began to grow wild all around the Mediterranean Sea. The Spaniards brought the olive to America, and it reached California in 1769.

Appearance of the Fruit and Tree. All its different parts give it an artistic appearance that people have admired for ages. Its bark and leaves are a soft gray-green, and its trunk is gnarled and uneven. Its shiny purple-black fruits are attractive.

Olive trees live longer than most other fruit trees. Some of the trees brought by the Spaniards to California are still alive. There are olive trees in Palestine which probably date back to the beginning of the Christian Era.

The olive tree has many small flowers. Most of the flowers are imperfect, and fruit cannot grow from them. They give off much pollen, and, as a rule, the wind

OLIVE

carries the pollen from flower to flower. In all the varieties of olive, a tree can fertilize its flowers with its own pollen. In occasional seasons there is evidence that the trees benefit if they receive pollen from other trees. Most varieties do not bear large crops one season after another. There is a slack season in between. This manner of growth is called *alternate bearing*.

The olive itself is a drupe, the type of fruit which has a pit. It is apple-shaped to plum-shaped, and the ripe fruit is purple to black. The most important material in it is the olive oil. Both seed and flesh contain much oil, which makes up 15 to 30 per cent of the weight of the fresh fruit. Fresh olives have a bitter substance which makes them unpleasant to eat. The substance is largely or entirely removed when they are prepared for market.

Cultivation. Parts cut off from an olive tree will readily take root and grow into new trees. The young trees will grow in many different types of soil, but need good drainage. To produce large fruit, the grower must irrigate and prune the trees, and thin the fruit. Early harvesting partially overcomes alternate bearing. Fertilizers that add nitrogen to the soil give a larger yield.

The olive tree has remarkable powers of growing where the climate is very hot and dry. But for bearing good fruit, it needs a moderate supply of water. The fruit matures from October to January, and is injured if the temperature falls below 26° F. (−3° C). The tree

J. Horace McFarland

Olives are a small, oval-shaped fruit. They are grown chiefly for their oil, which makes up about half the flesh of the fruit.

Arthur C. Smith

Olive Trees have small, gnarled trunks. The trees thrive in hot areas, such as those near the Mediterranean Sea.

Italy	●●●●●●●●●●●●●●●●●●●
	2,720,500 short tons (2,468,000 metric tons)
Spain	●●●●●●●●●●●●●●
	2,137,400 short tons (1,939,000 metric tons)
Greece	●●●●●●●(
	1,186,100 short tons (1,076,000 metric tons)
Turkey	●●●●●(
	741,900 short tons (673,000 metric tons)
Tunisia	●●●●
	573,000 short tons (520,000 metric tons)
Portugal	●●
	290,700 short tons (264,000 metric tons)
Morocco	●(
	267,000 short tons (242,000 metric tons)
Algeria	●(
	175,300 short tons (159,000 metric tons)
Syria	●
	156,800 short tons (142,000 metric tons)
Libya	(
	122,400 short tons (111,000 metric tons)

Based on a 4-year average, 1972-1975.
Source: FAO.

itself is not seriously injured until the temperature falls to 16° F. (−9° C). The fruit needs much heat to have a good quality when mature. The air must be dry when the flowers blossom, and when the fruit begins to grow.

Harvesting and Preparation for Market. Olives abroad are grown first of all for their oil. In the United States a large part of the industry is based on preparing the fruit for eating. Oil is a side line, but American olive oil is as good as the best imported oil.

Harvesting olives requires careful handling. Farmers pick the green fruit and haul it to the processing plant in small boxes. Over long distances it is shipped in barrels of light brine. At the plant, it is fermented a short time with lactic acid. The olives are then graded and put through a machine that separates the fruit of different sizes. Next comes a lye treatment, and washing to remove the bitter substance. Then the olives are treated with air to give them all the same dark color, and are canned in brine. After canning, they are sterilized at 240° F. (116° C). This treatment makes olives one of the safest of canned foods. Most of the American crop receives the California ripe-olive process, which gives a dark fruit, rich in flavor and food value. Other methods used include the Spanish green-olive process. The processed olives can be eaten whole, or they can be mixed with other foods to flavor them. California olives are becoming favorites.

Production. The countries bordering the Mediterranean Sea grow most of the world's olives. Italy and Spain together produce about three-fifths of the world output. There are about $13\frac{1}{2}$ million acres (5.5 million hectares) of cultivated olive trees in the world, which

produce about $8\frac{1}{2}$ million short tons (7.7 million metric tons) of olives a year.

Only a few places in the United States can support the olive industry. These places lie in central and southern California. There are 32,000 acres (12,900 hectares) of olive trees in California. These olive orchards produce over 60,000 short tons (55,000 metric tons) of olives a year. The olive tree grows in the states along the Gulf of Mexico, but it does not bear fruit there.

Scientific Classification. Olives belong to the olive family, *Oleaceae*. They are genus *Olea*, species *O. europaea*.   JULIAN C. CRANE

See also FORSYTHIA; FRINGE TREE; GREECE (picture: Olive Picking); GREECE, ANCIENT (picture: Greek Farmers); OLIVE OIL; SPAIN (picture: Olive Orchards).

OLIVE OIL is a fatty oil taken from olives. It is one of the most digestible of the edible fats. Like other fats, olive oil is a high energy food. Its chief ingredient is olein, a glycerin compound. Olive oil is used chiefly in salad dressings and as a frying fat. It is also used in soap, perfumes, and medicines.

In the manufacture of ordinary olive oil, the olives are crushed by corrugated metal rollers in brick trenches. The crushed pulp is placed in a coarsely woven fabric, and the fabric is folded over it to make a *cheese* (pulpy block) about 3 feet (91 centimeters) square and 3 inches (8 centimeters) thick. Ten or more of these cheeses are placed one above the other, with slats between them. Then pressure is applied.

The oil obtained by this method is filtered through woolen cloth, then allowed to settle for about 24 hours in funnel-shaped tanks. The sediment that settles to the bottom of the tank is drawn off. Then the oil is run into settling tanks lined with tin or glass. The oil stands in the tanks for a period of two to five months. The additional sediment that settles out is drawn off several times.

The flavor of olive oil depends upon the variety of olives used, their ripeness when picked, the way they are handled, and length of time they are stored before pressing. The best oil comes from olives which are picked just after they ripen and before they turn black. If the olives are picked too green, the oil is bitter. If they are picked too ripe, the oil is rancid. The flesh of ripe olives is about half oil. When the skin is broken, a great deal of the oil comes out of the pulp. Such oil is called "virgin," or "sublime," or "first expressed" oil. It is the highest grade of olive oil. A cheap grade of olive oil is made from the cheese pulp left over after the first pressing. The cheeses are broken up, mixed with hot water and then pressed again to produce the oil.

Most of the olive oil produced in the world comes from the Mediterranean countries. Italy and Spain combined usually produce about three-fifths of the world olive oil production of about $1\frac{3}{4}$ million short tons (1.6 metric tons) a year. In the United States, California produces about 1,100 short tons (998 metric tons) of the oil every year.   LEONE RUTLEDGE CARROLL

See also OLIVE.

OLIVES, MOUNT OF. See MOUNT OF OLIVES.

OLIVET NAZARENE COLLEGE. See UNIVERSITIES AND COLLEGES (table).

OLIVIER, *oh LIV ee ay,* **LAURENCE** (1907-   ), is one of the leading Shakespearean actors of his time. Many regard his motion pictures of the Shakespeare plays, *Henry V* (1946), *Hamlet* (1948), and *Richard III* (1955), as screen classics.

His first Shakespearean success was on the stage in *Hamlet* at the Old Vic Theater in London in 1937. He became a managing director of the Old Vic Company in 1944. He acted with it in New York City in 1945 and toured Australia and New Zealand in 1948.

United Press Int.

Laurence Olivier

Olivier became noted for his performances in the motion pictures *Wuthering Heights* (1938) and *Rebecca* (1940), and in the plays *Oedipus Rex* (1945) and *The School for Scandal* (1948). He was born in Dorking, England, and was knighted in 1947. In 1970, he became Lord Olivier, the first actor named a baron in English history.   RICHARD MOODY

See also MOTION PICTURE (picture: A Filmed Version of *Hamlet*).

OLMEC INDIANS developed one of the earliest high cultures in America. Their way of life flourished from about 1200 B.C. to about 100 B.C. They played an important role in the early stages of the ancient Mexican civilization. The word *Olmec*, meaning *rubber people*, comes from the Nahuatl language of the Aztec Indians. The Aztec gave the name to the people of the region along the eastern coast of Mexico, now part of the states of Veracruz and Tabasco, where they got their rubber. The name now applies to this ancient culture.

Much remains to be learned about the Olmec. But archaeologists have uncovered many remains of the culture. The Olmec carved in jade and stone, and sometimes buried the objects. Remains include stone altars and pillars; stone heads, some 9 feet (2.7 meters) tall and weighing 15 short tons (13.6 metric tons); and perfectly ground concave mirrors of polished hematite. The figure of a half-human, half-jaguar creature, thought to be a god, occurs often in their art. The Olmec had some knowledge of hieroglyphic writing. An Olmec slab, with a date corresponding to 31 B.C., is considered by some historians to be America's oldest known dated work. La Venta, the site of ruins in Tabasco, was a major Olmec settlement.   GORDON F. EKHOLM

See also SCULPTURE (American Indian).

OLMEDO, JOSÉ. See LATIN-AMERICAN LITERATURE (Literature After Independence).

OLMSTED, *AHM sted*, is the family name of two American landscape architects, father and son, who greatly influenced park planning in American cities.

Frederick Law Olmsted (1822-1903) and Calvert Vaux designed New York's Central Park, the first great American park, in 1858. When he signed these plans, Olmsted placed the words *landscape architect* under his name. He was the first man to use this term. Other large park systems he designed include the grounds for the United States Capitol in Washington, D.C. (1874), the World's Columbian Exposition in Chicago (1893), and parks in many of the larger American cities. Olmsted tried to preserve the natural scenery of the area as much as possible. He tried to create a rural atmosphere

in the hearts of great cities. Olmsted successfully combined beauty and function into his designs of parks.

In his early years, he traveled widely in Europe and the United States. His travels influenced him to write. His books include *Walks and Talks of an American Farmer in England* (1852), *A Journey in the Seaboard Slave States with Remarks on Their Economy* (1856), *A Journey Through Texas, with a Statistical Appendix* (1857), and *A Journey in the Back Country* (1860). Olmsted was born in Hartford, Conn., and studied at Yale University.

Frederick Law Olmsted, Jr. (1870-1957), studied landscape architecture with his father, and became a well-known landscape architect and a city planner. He served on the National Capital Park and Planning Commission in Washington, D.C., and as a professor of landscape architecture at Harvard University. He designed public parks in many American cities. Olmsted was born on Staten Island, N.Y., and was graduated from Harvard University.   ROBERT E. EVERLY

OLNEY, *AHL nih*, **RICHARD** (1835-1917), served under President Grover Cleveland as U.S. attorney general, and later as secretary of state. He was noted for breaking the Pullman strike of 1894. After the strike had tied up railroads running out of Chicago, Olney obtained an injunction against the strikers by claiming that they were interrupting the mails. Federal troops were sent in, the strike leaders were imprisoned, and the strike was broken.

In 1895, Olney vigorously upheld the Monroe Doctrine, which he believed was threatened by a boundary dispute between British Guiana (which has since been renamed Guyana) and Venezuela. He persuaded England to agree to arbitration of the matter. Olney was born in Oxford, Mass.   NELSON M. BLAKE

OLYMPIA is a valley about 11 miles (18 kilometers) from Pírgos, Greece. In ancient times, religion, politics, and athletics centered at Olympia. The Olympian games, held there every four years, were so important in Greek life that they were used as the basis for the calendar. All the buildings in Olympia were for worship or for games. The religious buildings were clustered in the *Altis* (sacred grove), which lies where the Cladeus River flows into the Alpheus River. They included the temples of Zeus and Hera, the Pelopion, the Philippeion, and the great altars.

The athletic buildings lay just outside the Altis. In the northwest corner was a gymnasium. Joining the gymnasium on the south lay the Palaestra, which was a wrestling and boxing school. On the east stood the great stadium. Southeast of the stadium was the Hippodrome, where chariot and horse races were held.

The Olympian games were prohibited in A.D. 394, and a fort was built inside the Altis. Later, earthquakes and floods covered Olympia with gravel and soil. Finally, it lay beneath 20 feet (6 meters) of earth.

In 1829, a French expedition began excavations at the temple of Zeus. The German government continued this work. Between 1875 and 1879 the entire Altis and many of the surrounding buildings were uncovered. Fragments of sculpture, coins, terra cottas, and bronzes have been found. The most important discoveries were two statues. These were the *Victory of Paeonius* (423 B.C.) and the *Hermes of Praxiteles*. Under an agreement between Germany and Greece, the originals of all discoveries remained in possession of Greece. The Germans reserved the right to take casts from sculptures, coins, or other discoveries. A museum with Olympian relics is at Olympia.   DONALD W. BRADEEN

See also OLYMPIC GAMES.

OLYMPIA, Wash. (pop. 23,296), is the state capital, and the gateway to southwestern Washington and the Olympic Peninsula. An important commercial port, the city lies on the southern point of Puget Sound. For location, see WASHINGTON (political map). Ocean-going ships use the harbor of Olympia to deliver petroleum products, lumber, and other goods. Beds of the delicious Olympia oyster lie in the shallow waters near Olympia. The city lists seafood processing among its major industries. Its other industries include brewing, food processing, and the manufacture of metal and lumber products. Many of the city's residents work at the state capitol. A 287-foot (87-meter) dome atop the Legislative Building towers over the area. See WASHINGTON (picture: State Capitol).

Fort Lewis, the largest United States Army post on the Pacific Coast, stands between Olympia and Tacoma. Evergreen State and St. Martin's colleges are located in Olympia.

Homesteaders began to settle there in the 1840's. Edmund Sylvester pioneered in the development of the Olympia townsite. Olympia was named the capital city when the Washington Territory was created in 1853. The city was incorporated in 1859. It is the seat of Thurston County, and has a mayor-commissioner type of government.   HOWARD J. CRITCHFIELD

OLYMPIAD, *oh LIM pih ad.* In the Greek system of telling time, an Olympiad was the period of four years that elapsed between two successive celebrations of the Olympian, or Olympic, Games. This method of figuring time became common about 300 B.C. All events were dated from 776 B.C., the beginning of the first known Olympiad.

The beginning of the year of the Olympiad was determined by the first full moon after the summer solstice, the longest day of the year. This full moon fell about the first of July. Therefore, only the last six months of the first year of the 195th Olympiad corresponded to the first year of Our Lord. This method of counting time ceased about A.D. 440, after the 304th Olympiad. The Olympiads were used as measures of time by later Greek historians and other writers to refer to preceding centuries, but they were never in everyday use, as were months and years.   JOHN H. KENT

OLYMPIAS (375?-316 B.C.) was the wife of Philip II of Macedonia, and the mother of Alexander the Great. A proud and emotional woman, she influenced Alexander greatly. She told Alexander that his real father was the god Zeus-Ammon, not Philip. Olympias feared that Philip might choose another heir. Many people believe that she had Philip killed in order to ensure that Alexander would become king. After Alexander's death in 323 B.C., Olympias tried to keep the empire for her grandson, Alexander IV. She failed, and in 316 B.C. was captured by Cassander, a Macedonian prince. Olympias was eventually killed.   THOMAS W. AFRICA

See also ALEXANDER THE GREAT; PHILIP II.

OLYMPIC GAMES

OLYMPIC GAMES bring together thousands of the world's finest amateur athletes to compete against one another. No other sports event attracts so much worldwide attention. Several million people attend the games, and hundreds of millions more watch the competition on television.

The Olympic Games take place every four years and consist of the Summer Games and the Winter Games. The Summer Games are held in a major city. The Winter Games are held in a city or town in a mountainous, snow-covered area.

Colorful ceremonies combine with thrilling athletic competition to create the special feeling of excitement that surrounds the Olympics. The opening ceremony of the games is particularly impressive. The Olympic athletes of Greece march into the stadium first, in honor of the original Olympics held in ancient Greece. The athletes of the other nations follow in alphabetical order by country. This order depends on the spelling of each nation's name in the language of the host country. The athletes of the host country enter last.

The chief of state of the host country declares the games open. The Olympic flag is raised, trumpets play, and cannons boom in salute. Hundreds of doves are released into the air as a symbol of peace.

The most dramatic moment of the opening ceremony is the lighting of the Olympic Flame. Runners in cross-country relays bring a lighted torch from the valley of Olympia, Greece, where the ancient Olympics were held. Thousands of runners take part in the journey, which starts four weeks before the opening of the games. They represent Greece and each country that lies between Greece and the host nation. Planes and ships

———— Sites of the Olympic Games ————

Year	Summer	Winter
1896	Athens, Greece	Not held
1900	Paris, France	Not held
1904	St. Louis, Mo.	Not held
1908	London, England	Not held
1912	Stockholm, Sweden	Not held
1916	Not held	Not held
1920	Antwerp, Belgium	Not held
1924	Paris, France	Chamonix, France
1928	Amsterdam, The Netherlands	St. Moritz, Switzerland
1932	Los Angeles, Calif.	Lake Placid, N.Y.
1936	Berlin, Germany	Garmisch-Partenkirchen, Germany
1940	Not held	Not held
1944	Not held	Not held
1948	London, England	St. Moritz, Switzerland
1952	Helsinki, Finland	Oslo, Norway
1956	Melbourne, Australia	Cortina, Italy
1960	Rome, Italy	Squaw Valley, Calif.
1964	Tokyo, Japan	Innsbruck, Austria
1968	Mexico City, Mexico	Grenoble, France
1972	Munich, West Germany	Sapporo, Japan
1976	Montreal, Canada	Innsbruck, Austria
1980	Moscow, Russia	Lake Placid, N.Y.

United Press Int.

The Opening Ceremony of the Olympic Games ranks among the most colorful spectacles in sports. The Olympic flag is raised, *left*, after all the athletes have marched into the stadium.

transport the torch across mountains and seas. The final runner carries the torch into the stadium, circles the track, and lights the Olympic Flame. The flame is kept burning until the end of the games.

The modern Olympics were organized to encourage world peace and friendship and to promote amateur athletics. The Olympic symbol consists of five interlocking rings that represent the continents of Africa, Asia, Australia, Europe, and North and South America. The rings are black, blue, green, red, and yellow. The flag of every nation competing in the games has at least one of these colors.

The Summer Games

The Summer Games are held in various months and draw as many as $4\frac{1}{2}$ million spectators during the 15 days of competition. The track and field, gymnastics, and swimming events usually attract the largest crowds and the widest coverage by the press.

A sport must be widely popular in at least 40 countries on three continents before it can be considered for the Summer Games. The approved list for the games consists of 21 sports. Sports with separate men's and women's events include archery, basketball, canoeing and kayaking, fencing, gymnastics, rowing, swimming and diving (including water polo for men only), team handball, track and field, and volleyball. Men and women may compete on the same team in *equestrian* (horseback riding) sports, shooting, and yachting. Only men compete in boxing, *cycling* (bicycle racing), field hockey, judo, soccer, weight lifting, wrestling, and the *modern pentathlon*, which consists of fencing, horseback riding, pistol shooting, running, and swimming. The program may include from 15 to all these sports.

The host city must provide a large stadium for the opening and closing ceremonies, the track and field

events, and soccer. Many host cities build special facilities for various Olympic events.

The Summer Games have grown tremendously since 1896, when about 285 male athletes, representing about 13 nations, competed in the first modern Olympics. More than 8,000 athletes, including more than 1,000 women, now take part. The athletes represent more than 100 nations.

The Winter Games

The Winter Games are held in January or February of the same year as the Summer Games. They last about 10 days. A sport must have great popularity in at least 25 countries on two continents to be considered for the Winter Games. There are seven approved sports for the Winter Games: the *biathlon* (a combination of cross-country skiing and shooting), bobsledding, figure skating, ice hockey, *luge* (a form of tobogganing), skiing, and speed skating. Only men compete in the biathlon, bobsledding, and ice hockey. The other sports have separate competition for men and women. More than 1,000 athletes, including about 250 women, take part in the Winter Games. They represent about 35 nations.

The host city of the Winter Games must provide an outdoor stadium. The opening ceremony and the speed skating races may be held in this stadium. The host city also must have at least one indoor stadium, for figure skating and ice hockey.

Skilled workers establish ski trails for the cross-country, downhill, and slalom races. The host city also must have two huge ski jumps. The ski-jumping competition may attract as many as 200,000 spectators.

The International Olympic Committee

The International Olympic Committee (IOC) is the governing body of the Olympic Games. The committee

1976 WINTER OLYMPIC GAMES

LEADING MEDAL-WINNING NATIONS

Nation	Gold	Silver	Bronze
Russia	13	6	8
East Germany	7	5	7
United States	3	3	4
Norway	3	3	1
West Germany	2	5	3
Finland	2	4	1
Austria	2	2	2
Switzerland	1	3	1
The Netherlands	1	2	3
Italy	1	2	1

BIATHLON

Event	Winner	Nation
Individual	Nikolai Kruglov	Russia
Relay	Elizarov, Biakov, Kruglov, Tihonov	Russia

BOBSLEDDING

Event	Winner	Nation
Two-man	Nehmar, Germeshausen	East Germany
Four-man	Nehmar, Babok, Germeshausen, Lehmann	East Germany

ICE HOCKEY

Winning nation
Russia

FIGURE SKATING

Event	Winner	Nation
Men	John Curry	Great Britain
Women	Dorothy Hamill	United States
Pairs	Irena Rodnina and Alexander Zaitsev	Russia
Ice Dancing	Ludmilla Pakhomova and Alexander Gorchkov	Russia

SPEED SKATING

Event	Winner	Nation	Time
Men			
500 meters	Evgeny Kulikov	Russia	39.17 s.*
1,000 meters	Peter Mueller	United States	1 m. 19.32 s.*
1,500 meters	Jan Egil Storholt	Norway	1 m. 59.38 s.*
5,000 meters	Sten Stensen	Norway	7 m. 24.48 s.
10,000 meters	Piet Klein	The Netherlands	14 m. 50.59 s.*
Women			
500 meters	Sheila Young	United States	42.76 s.*
1,000 meters	Tatiana Averina	Russia	1 m. 28.43 s.*
1,500 meters	Galina Stepanskaya	Russia	2 m. 16.58 s.*
3,000 meters	Tatiana Averina	Russia	4 m. 45.19 s.*

*Olympic record.

Wide World

Kathy Kreiner of Canada, above, won the giant slalom in the 1976 Winter Games. Rosi Mittermaier of West Germany, who finished second, won the downhill and slalom events.

SKIING

Event	Winner	Nation
Men		
Jump (70 meters)	Hans-Georg Aschenbach	East Germany
Jump (90 meters)	Karl Schnabl	Austria
Nordic combined	Ulrich Wehling	East Germany
Cross country		
15 kilometers	Nikolai Bayukov	Russia
30 kilometers	Sergei Saveliev	Russia
50 kilometers	Ivar Formo	Norway
40-kilometer relay	Pitkaenen, Mieto, Teaurajaervi, Koivistol	Finland
Downhill	Franz Klammer	Austria
Giant slalom	Heini Hemmi	Switzerland
Slalom	Piero Gros	Italy
Women		
Cross-country		
5 kilometers	Helena Takalo	Finland
10 kilometers	Raisa Smetanina	Russia
20-kilometer relay	Baldicheva, Amosova, Smetanina, Kulakova	Russia
Downhill	Rosi Mittermaier	West Germany
Giant slalom	Kathy Kreiner	Canada
Slalom	Rosi Mittermaier	West Germany

TOBOGGANING (LUGE)

Event	Winner	Nation
Single-seater (men)	Detlef Guenther	East Germany
Single-seater (women)	Margit Schumann	East Germany
Two-seater (men)	Rinn, Hahn	East Germany

1976 SUMMER OLYMPIC GAMES

Wide World

Sugar Ray Leonard of the United States, *right,* defeated Andres Aldama of Cuba for the light welterweight boxing title.

LEADING MEDAL-WINNING NATIONS

Nation	Gold	Silver	Bronze
Russia	47	42	35
East Germany	40	25	25
United States	34	35	25
West Germany	10	13	18
Japan	9	6	9
Poland	7	6	11
Bulgaria	6	8	9
Cuba	6	4	3
Romania	4	9	14
Hungary	4	5	12

WINNERS OF TEAM SPORTS

Sport	Nation
Basketball (men)	United States
Basketball (women)	Russia
Field Hockey (men)	New Zealand
Handball (men)	Russia
Handball (women)	Russia
Soccer (men)	East Germany
Volleyball (men)	Poland
Volleyball (women)	Japan
Water Polo (men)	Hungary

ARCHERY

Winner	Nation
Darrell Pace (men)	United States
Luann Ryon (women)	United States

BOXING

Class	Winner	Nation
Light flyweight	Jorge Hernandez	Cuba
Flyweight	Leo Randolph	United States
Bantamweight	Yong Jo Gu	North Korea
Featherweight	Angel Herrera	Cuba
Lightweight	Howard Davis	United States
Light welterweight	Ray Leonard	United States
Welterweight	Jochen Bachfeld	East Germany
Light middleweight	Jerzy Rybicki	Poland
Middleweight	Mike Spinks	United States
Light heavyweight	Leon Spinks	United States
Heavyweight	Teofilo Stevenson	Cuba

CANOEING AND KAYAKING

Event	Winner	Nation
Men		
500-meter kayak singles	Vasile Diba	Romania
500-meter kayak tandems	Mattern, Olbricht	East Germany
500-meter Canadian singles	Aleksandr Rogov	Russia
500-meter Canadian tandems	Petrenko, Vinogradov	Russia
1,000-meter kayak singles	Rudiger Helm	East Germany
1,000-meter kayak tandems	Nagorny, Romanovskiy	Russia
1,000-meter kayak fours	Chuhray, Degtiarev, Filatov, Morozov	Russia
1,000-meter Canadian singles	Matija Ljubek	Yugoslavia
1,000-meter Canadian tandems	Petrenko, Vinogradov	Russia
Women		
500-meter kayak singles	Carola Zirzow	East Germany
500-meter kayak tandems	Gopova, Kreft	Russia

CYCLING

Event	Winner	Nation
Individual road race	Bernt Johansson	Sweden
Sprint	Anton Tkac	Czechoslovakia
1,000-meter time trial	Klaus-Jurgen Grunke	East Germany
4,000-meter individual pursuit	Gregor Braun	West Germany
4,000-meter team pursuit	Braun, Lutz, Schumacher, Vonhof	West Germany
100-kilometer team time trial	Chukanov, Chaplygin, Kaminsky, Pikkuus	Russia

OLYMPIC GAMES

EQUESTRIAN

Event	Winner	Nation
Three-day, team	Coffin, Plumb, Tauskey, Davidson	United States
Three-day, individual	Tad Coffin	United States
Dressage, team	Boldt, Klimke, Grillo	West Germany
Dressage, individual	Christine Stueckelberger	Switzerland
Prix des nation, individual	Alwin Schockemoehle	West Germany
Prix des nation, team	Rogier, Parot, Roche, Roguet	France

FENCING

Individual Competition

Event	Winner	Nation
Foil (men)	Fabio Dal Zotto	Italy
Foil (women)	Ildiko Schwarczenberger	Hungary
Epee (men)	Alexander Pusch	West Germany
Sabre (men)	Victor Krovopouskov	Russia

Team Competition

Event	Winning Nation
Foil (men)	West Germany
Foil (women)	Russia
Epee (men)	Sweden
Sabre (men)	Russia

GYMNASTICS

Event	Winner	Nation
Men		
All-around	Nikolai Andrianov	Russia
Long horse vault	Nikolai Andrianov	Russia
Side horse	Zoltan Magyar	Hungary
Horizontal bar	Mitsuo Tsukahara	Japan
Parallel bars	Sawao Kato	Japan
Rings	Nikolai Andrianov	Russia
Floor exercise	Nikolai Andrianov	Russia
Team		Japan
Women		
All-around	Nadia Comaneci	Romania
Balance beam	Nadia Comaneci	Romania
Uneven parallel bars	Nadia Comaneci	Romania
Side horse vault	Nelli Kim	Russia
Floor exercise	Nelli Kim	Russia
Team		Russia

JUDO

Class	Winner	Nation
Lightweight	Hector Rodriguez	Cuba
Light middleweight	Vladimir Nevzorov	Russia
Middleweight	Isamu Sonoda	Japan
Light heavyweight	Kazuhiro Ninomiya	Japan
Heavyweight	Sergei Novikov	Russia
Open	Haruki Uemura	Japan

MODERN PENTATHLON

Individual Winner	Team Winner
Janusz Pyciak-Peciak, Poland	Great Britain

ROWING

Event	Winner	Nation
Men		
Single sculls	Pectti Karppinen	Finland
Double sculls	Hansen, Hansen	Norway
Pairs without coxswain	Landvoigt, Landvoigt	East Germany
Pairs with coxswain	Jahrling, Ulrich, Spohr	East Germany
Four sculls	Guldenpfennig, Reiche, Bussert, Wolfgramm	East Germany
Fours without coxswain	Brietzke, Decker, Semmler, Mager	East Germany
Fours with coxswain	Eshinov, Ivanov, Kuznetsov, Klepikov, Lukianov	Russia
Eights with coxswain	Baumgart, Dohn, Klatt, Luck, Wendisch, Kostulski, Karnatz, Prudohl, Danielowski	East Germany
Women		
Single sculls	Christine Scheiblich	East Germany
Double sculls	Otzetova, Yordanova	Bulgaria
Pairs without coxswain	Kelbetcheva, Grouitcheva	Bulgaria
Four sculls with coxswain	Borchmann, Lau, Poley, Zobelt, Weigelt	East Germany
Fours with coxswain	Metze, Schwede, Lohs, Kurth, Hess	East Germany
Eights with coxswain	Goretzki, Knetsch, Richter, Ahrenholz, Kallies, Ebert, Lehmann, Muller, Wilke	East Germany

Nadia Comaneci, a 14-year-old Romanian, won a gymnastics gold medal in the balance beam event, *above.* She also won the uneven parallel bars event and the all-around competition.

SHOOTING

Event	Winner	Nation
Skeet	Josef Panacek	Czechoslovakia
Trapshooting	Donald Haldeman	United States
Free pistol	Uwe Potteck	East Germany
Rapid-fire pistol	Norbert Klaar	East Germany
Small bore rifle— prone	Karlheinz Smieszek	West Germany
Small bore rifle— three positions	Lanny Bassham	United States
Running game target	Alexandr Gazov	Russia

Wide World

John Naber of the United States won gold medals in four swimming events. He finished first in the 100-meter and 200-meter backstroke races and swam on two championship relay teams.

SWIMMING AND DIVING

Event	Winner	Nation	Time
Men			
100-meter freestyle	Jim Montgomery	United States	49.99 s.*
200-meter freestyle	Bruce Furniss	United States	1 m. 50.29 s.*
400-meter freestyle	Brian Goodell	United States	3 m. 51.93 s.*
1,500-meter freestyle	Brian Goodell	United States	15 m. 02.40 s.*
100-meter backstroke	John Naber	United States	55.49 s.*
200-meter backstroke	John Naber	United States	1 m. 59.19 s.*
100-meter breaststroke	John Hencken	United States	1 m. 03.11 s.*
200-meter breaststroke	David Wilkie	Great Britain	2 m. 15.11 s.*
100-meter butterfly	Matt Vogel	United States	54.35 s.
200-meter butterfly	Mike Bruner	United States	1 m. 59.23 s.*
400-meter medley	Rod Strachan	United States	4 m. 23.68 s.*
400-meter medley relay	Naber, Hencken, Vogel, Montgomery	United States	3 m. 42.22 s.*
800-meter freestyle relay	Bruner, Furniss, Naber, Montgomery	United States	7 m. 23.22 s.*
Platform diving	Klaus Dibiasi	Italy	
Springboard diving	Phil Boggs	United States	
Women			
100-meter freestyle	Kornelia Ender	East Germany	55.65 s.*
200-meter freestyle	Kornelia Ender	East Germany	1 m. 59.26 s.*
400-meter freestyle	Petra Thumer	East Germany	4 m. 09.89 s.*
800-meter freestyle	Petra Thumer	East Germany	8 m. 37.14 s.*
100-meter backstroke	Ulrike Richter	East Germany	1 m. 01.83 s.*
200-meter backstroke	Ulrike Richter	East Germany	2 m. 13.43 s.*
100-meter breaststroke	Hannelore Anke	East Germany	1 m. 11.16 s.*
200-meter breaststroke	Marina Koshevaia	Russia	2 m. 33.35 s.*
100-meter butterfly	Kornelia Ender	East Germany	1 m. 00.13 s.*
200-meter butterfly	Andrea Pollack	East Germany	2 m. 11.41 s.*
400-meter medley	Ulrike Tauber	East Germany	4 m. 42.77 s.*
400-meter freestyle relay	Peyton, Boglioli, Sterkel, Babashoff	United States	3 m. 44.82 s.*
400-meter medley relay	Richter, Anke, Pollack, Ender	East Germany	4 m. 07.95 s.*
Platform diving	Elena Vaytsekhovskaia	Russia	
Springboard diving	Jennifer Chandler	United States	

*Olympic record.

Klaus Dibiasi, an Italian diver, won the gold medal in the platform competition.

Wide World

United Press Int.

Jennifer Chandler of the United States won the springboard diving championship.

Wide World

Alberto Juantorena of Cuba, *right*, set an Olympic record in the 800-meter race.

Wide World

Johanna Schaller of East Germany, *left*, won the women's 100-meter hurdles race.

Wide World

Vassili Alexeev, a Russian weight lifter, won the super heavyweight event.

TRACK AND FIELD

Event	Winner	Nation	Time or Distance
Men			
100 meters	Hasely Crawford	Trinidad and Tobago	10.06 s.
200 meters	Donald Quarrie	Jamaica	20.23 s.
400 meters	Alberto Juantorena	Cuba	44.26 s.
800 meters	Alberto Juantorena	Cuba	1 m. 43.50 s.*
1,500 meters	John Walker	New Zealand	3 m. 39.17 s.
5,000 meters	Lasse Viren	Finland	13 m. 24.76 s.
10,000 meters	Lasse Viren	Finland	27 m. 40.38 s.
110-meter hurdles	Guy Drut	France	13.30 s.
400-meter hurdles	Edwin Moses	United States	47.64 s.*
3,000-meter steeplechase	Anders Garderud	Sweden	8 m. 08.02 s.*
Marathon	Waldemar Cierpinski	East Germany	2 h. 9 m. 55.00 s.
400-meter relay	Glance, Jones, Hampton, Riddick	United States	38.33 s.
1,600-meter relay	Frazier, Brown, Newhouse, Parks	United States	2 m. 58.65 s.
20-kilometer walk	Daniel Bautista	Mexico	1 h. 24 m. 40.60 s.
High jump	Jacek Wszola	Poland	7 ft. 4 in. (2.25 m)
Long jump	Arnie Robinson	United States	27 ft. 4.7 in. (8.35 m)
Triple jump	Viktor Saneev	Russia	56 ft. 8.7 in. (17.29 m)
Pole vault	Tadeusz Slusarski	Poland	18 ft. 0.5 in. (5.50 m)*
Discus	Mac Wilkins	United States	221 ft. 5 in. (67.50 m)*
Javelin	Miklos Nemeth	Hungary	310 ft. 3 in. (94.58 m)*
Shot-put	Udo Beyer	East Germany	69 ft. 0.7 in. (21.05 m)
Hammer	Yuriy Sedyh	Russia	254 ft. 4 in. (77.52 m)*
Decathlon	Bruce Jenner	United States	8,618 pts.*
Women			
100 meters	Annegret Richter	West Germany	11.08 s.
200 meters	Baerbel Eckert	East Germany	22.37 s.*
400 meters	Irena Szewinska	Poland	49.29 s.*
800 meters	Tatiana Kazankina	Russia	1 m. 54.94 s.*
1,500 meters	Tatiana Kazankina	Russia	4 m. 05.48 s.
100-meter hurdles	Johanna Schaller	East Germany	12.77 s.
400-meter relay	Oelsner, Stecher, Bodendorf, Eckert	East Germany	42.55 s.*
1,600-meter relay	Maletzki, Rohde, Streidt, Brehmer	East Germany	3 m. 19.23 s.*
High jump	Rosemarie Ackermann	East Germany	6 ft. 4.0 in. (1.93 m)*
Long jump	Angela Voigt	East Germany	22 ft. 0.6 in. (6.72 m)
Discus	Evelin Schlaak	East Germany	226 ft. 4 in. (69.00 m)*
Javelin	Ruth Fuchs	East Germany	216 ft. 4 in. (65.94 m)*
Shot-put	Ivanka Christova	Bulgaria	69 ft. 5 in. (21.16 m)*
Pentathlon	Siegrun Siegl	East Germany	4,745 pts.

*Olympic record.

WEIGHT LIFTING

Class	Winner	Nation	Weight
Flyweight	Alexandr Voronin	Russia	535 lbs. (242.5 kg)*
Bantamweight	Norair Nurikyan	Bulgaria	579 lbs. (262.5 kg)*
Featherweight	Nikolai Kolesnikov	Russia	628 lbs. (285.0 kg)*
Lightweight	†		
Middleweight	Yordan Mitkov	Bulgaria	739 lbs. (335.0 kg)*
Light heavyweight	Valeri Shary	Russia	805 lbs. (365.0 kg)*
Middle heavyweight	David Rigert	Russia	843 lbs. (382.5 kg)*
Heavyweight	†		
Super heavyweight	Vassili Alexeev	Russia	970 lbs. (440.0 kg)*

*Olympic record. Weight is total of two lifts.
†Declared vacant; previously announced winner disqualified for using banned drugs.

WRESTLING

Class	Winner	Nation
Freestyle		
Paperweight	Khassan Issaev	Bulgaria
Flyweight	Yuji Takada	Japan
Bantamweight	Vladimir Umin	Russia
Featherweight	Jung-Mo Yang	South Korea
Lightweight	Pavel Pinigin	Russia
Welterweight	Date Jiichiro	Japan
Middleweight	John Peterson	United States
Light heavyweight	Levan Tediashvili	Russia
Heavyweight	Ivan Yarygin	Russia
Super heavyweight	Soslan Andiev	Russia

Class	Winner	Nation
Greco-Roman Style		
Paperweight	Alexey Shumakov	Russia
Flyweight	Vitaly Konstantinov	Russia
Bantamweight	Pertti Ukkola	Finland
Featherweight	Kazimier Lipien	Poland
Lightweight	Suren Nalbandyan	Russia
Welterweight	Anatolyi Bykov	Russia
Middleweight	Momir Petkovic	Yugoslavia
Light heavyweight	Valery Rezantsev	Russia
Heavyweight	Nikolai Bolboshin	Russia
Super heavyweight	Alexandr Kolchinski	Russia

YACHTING

Class	Winner	Nation
Finn monotype	Jochen Shumann	East Germany
Tornado	White, Osborn	Great Britain
470	Huebner, Bode	West Germany

Class	Winner	Nation
Soling	Jensen, Bandolowski, Hansen	Denmark
Flying Dutchman	Diesch, Diesch	West Germany
Tempest	Albrechtson, Hansson	Sweden

approves the sports to be included in the Olympics. The IOC also selects the host cities, one for the Summer Games and one for the Winter Games, six years in advance. The selection process includes a presentation by the mayor of each city that wishes to host the games.

The organizing committee of the host city and the international governing body for each Olympic sport work with the IOC in planning the games. These organizations decide the number of sports to be included in the games, the maximum number of athletes allowed to enter, and the schedule of events. The international sports organizations also conduct each event and appoint the judges and referees.

New members of the IOC are elected by the current members. A representative may be elected from any nation that has a national Olympic committee, but only nations that have hosted the Olympics may have two representatives. The IOC has no set rules regarding which eligible nations shall be represented. As a result, the size of the committee varies as members die or retire and new members are chosen. In 1976, the committee had 77 members. Originally, members were elected to the IOC for life. Today, any member elected after 1965 must retire at the age of 72. The members of the committee accept no instructions on voting from any government or other group or individual.

The IOC meets annually and during the Summer and Winter Games. Between meetings, its executive board handles the committee's business. This board consists of the president, three vice-presidents, and five members who serve four-year terms. The committee elects these officials from among its members. The president serves an eight-year term and then may be re-elected to any number of four-year terms.

Olympic Competition

Each national committee provides food, housing, and uniforms for its country's athletes while they prepare for and compete in the games. The committee also furnishes transportation for its team to the games and back.

Most countries use government funds to pay their Olympic expenses. The United States team is financed by contributions from corporations and individuals—a total of about $10 million every four years.

Selection of the Athletes. Every country represented in the Olympics has a national Olympic committee that selects the athletes who compete in the games. About 130 nations and territories have a committee, which is responsible for ensuring that the athletes meet the Olympic eligibility requirements.

An athlete who represents a country in the Olympics must be a citizen of that country. The athletes may be any age. Only amateur athletes may compete in the games. No Olympic athlete is permitted to have received money for coaching or competing in athletics. However, the IOC voted in 1974 to allow national Olympic committees to pay athletes during an unlimited training period before the games. Each athlete may receive expense money, plus the equivalent of the salary he or she would earn by working instead of training.

In the United States, Canada, and most other countries, athletes qualify by winning, or finishing high, in competitions called *selection trials*. Participation in most of these trials is by invitation only. The U.S. national committee invites athletes who have proved their outstanding ability in national championships or international competition.

Entries. In most Olympic sports, a nation may enter as many as three athletes in each individual event and one team in each team event. Two sports—swimming and track and field—require athletes to meet a minimum standard of performance if their country enters more than one competitor in an event.

Only 12 teams can compete in each men's team sport. No more than 18 teams can take part in each Olympic team sport that has competition for both men and women. At least six of these teams must be women's teams. If more than the maximum number of nations want to compete in a sport, a qualifying tournament is held before the Olympics. Such tournaments are the responsibility of the international governing body of the sport involved.

Judging. Several methods of judging are used in various Olympic events. For example, the eight fastest athletes qualify for the finals in most swimming and track and field events. The medals in diving, figure skating, and gymnastics are awarded on the basis of points given by judges. In bobsledding and luge, each contestant or team makes a certain number of timed runs down the course, and the lowest total time wins. Speed skaters are timed as they race, two at a time, over a course. The judging in archery and shooting is based only on accuracy. In wrestling, each man competes against at least two opponents before he can be eliminated. In boxing, each man remains in competition only until he loses one bout.

Medals. The top three athletes in each Olympic event receive a medal and a certificate. The next three receive only a certificate. The first- and second-place medals are made of silver, but the first-place medal has a gold coating. The third-place medal is made of bronze. All the members of a winning relay team get a medal. In team sports, only the members who played in their team's final game receive one. The design of the medals changes for each Winter Olympics, but it remains about the same for the Summer Games.

The winners receive their medals in an impressive ceremony held immediately after the event. The three medal winners stand at attention while the flags of their countries are raised. A band plays the national anthem of the homeland of the gold medal winner.

Olympic competition is intended to test the skill and strength of individuals, not nations. Therefore, the IOC does not keep an official score among the competing countries. No nation "wins" the Olympics. However, newspaper and television reporters from all parts of the world tell the public how many gold, silver, and bronze medals have been won by each country.

History

The Ancient Games. Athletics played an important part in the religious festivals of the ancient Greeks. The people believed such competition pleased the spirits of the dead. The religious festivals honored the gods, and many Greek tribes and cities held one every four years. These festivals probably began before 1400 B.C.

In time, four national festivals developed—the Isthmian, Nemean, Olympic, and Pythian games. The Olympic Games, which ranked as the most important, honored Zeus, the king of the gods.

The first known Olympic contest took place in the Stadium of Olympia in 776 B.C. This stadium stood in the valley of Olympia in western Greece. It had room for 40,000 spectators. For many years, the Olympics were for male contestants and male spectators only.

The Olympics were held every four years. The only event in the first 13 Olympiads was a footrace of about 200 yards (about 180 meters). Through the years, longer running races were added to the program. Other types

Wide World

Jesse Owens of the United States was the hero of the 1936 Summer Games. Owens won four gold medals in track and field.

of competition also became part of the Olympics. Wrestling and the pentathlon—which originally consisted of the discus throw, javelin throw, long jump, a sprint, and wrestling—were added in 708 B.C. Boxing became part of the games in 688 B.C., and the four-horse chariot race was added in 680 B.C. A savage and sometimes deadly sport called *pancratium*, which combined boxing and wrestling, was introduced in 648 B.C.

The Roman Empire conquered Greece during the 100's B.C., and the games soon lost their religious meaning. The contestants became interested only in winning money. In A.D. 394, Emperor Theodosius ordered the games ended because of their great decline in quality. No Olympics were held for more than 1,500 years.

The Modern Games. An earthquake destroyed the Stadium of Olympia in the A.D. 500's, and a landslide later buried the ruins of the structure. A group of German archaeologists discovered the ruins in 1875. The discovery gave Baron Pierre de Coubertin, a French educator, the idea of organizing a modern, international Olympics. De Coubertin believed that athletics played an important part in forming a person's character. He also thought that international sports competition would promote world peace. In 1894, de Coubertin presented his idea to an international meeting on amateur sports. The group voted to organize the games, and it formed the International Olympic Committee.

The first modern Olympic Games took place in 1896 in Athens, Greece. Women first competed in the modern games in 1900. The Winter Games began in 1924. No games were held in 1916, 1940, or 1944 because of World Wars I and II.

For many years, Finland and the Scandinavian nations—Denmark, Norway, and Sweden—had the best athletes at the Winter Games. From 1956 through 1976, Russians won more medals at the Winter Games than contestants of any other nation. From 1956 through

1972, Russia and the United States won most of the medals in the Summer Games. In the 1976 Summer Games, East Germany joined Russia and the United States as a major medal-winning nation.

The Olympics have been the scene of many exciting individual achievements. Paavo Nurmi, a long-distance runner from Finland, competed in 1920, 1924, and 1928 and won seven gold medals. Johnny Weissmuller of the United States won five gold medals in swimming in 1924 and 1928. Sonja Henie of Norway won the figure skating championship in 1928, 1932, and 1936. Jesse Owens of the United States won four gold medals in track and field in 1936. Emil Zatopek of Czechoslovakia won the 5,000- and 10,000-meter races and the marathon in 1952. Al Oerter of the United States won the gold medal for the discus throw in four straight Olympics, starting in 1956. Mark Spitz, a U.S. swimmer, set a record in 1972 by winning seven gold medals in a single Olympics. In the 1976 Summer Games, Alberto Juantorena of Cuba became the first runner to win the 400-meter and 800-meter races in the same Olympic Games.

Political disagreements threatened to disrupt the games in the 1970's. In 1972, political tension resulted in tragedy at the Summer Games in Munich, West Germany. Eight Arab terrorists attacked the quarters of the Israeli team. Two Israelis were killed resisting the attack, and nine others were taken hostage. All the hostages, five terrorists, and a West German policeman died in a gun battle with German police several hours later. In the 1976 Summer Games in Montreal, about 30 nations withdrew their teams just before competition began because of political disputes.

Some critics believe that rising costs place too great a financial burden on the host city. The 1976 Summer Games cost an estimated $1.5 billion. Some of the money pays for facilities that become permanent improvements in the host city. But some people believe the money should be spent on social programs they consider more worthwhile.   C. Robert Paul, Jr.

Related Articles. See Track and Field with its list of *Related Articles*. See also the following articles:

Basketball (International Competition)	Nemean Games
Flag (picture: Flags of World Organizations)	Olympiad
	Pythian Games
Hockey (Amateur Development)	Skiing (Skiing as a Sport)
Ice Skating (Figure Skating; Speed Skating)	Weight Lifting
Isthmian Games	World (picture: The Olympic Games)
Marathon	Wrestling

OLYMPIC MOUNTAINS are part of the Pacific Coast Range. The Olympics rise in northern Washington, south of Juan de Fuca Strait. They occupy an area of about 3,500 square miles (9,060 square kilometers), most of which lies in Olympic National Park. Mount Olympus (7,965 feet, or 2,428 meters) is the highest peak. There are over 100 small glaciers in the mountains. Forests of spruce, fir, cedar, and hemlock cover the lower slopes. The southwestern slopes receive over 140 inches (356 centimeters) of rain a year, one of the highest averages in the United States. See also Olympic National Park.   Howard J. Critchfield

OLYMPIC NATIONAL PARK lies in the Olympic Peninsula of Washington, not far from Seattle and Tacoma. The jagged peaks of the Olympic Range cover much of the park. For the area, see National Park System (table: National Parks). The National Park Service has set aside campgrounds and winter sports facilities for tourists. The park headquarters are at Port Angeles, Wash., a resort city on the Juan de Fuca Strait.

Of special interest are the rain forests consisting mainly of Douglas fir, Sitka spruce, western hemlock, and western red cedar. These rain forests, resulting from good soil and exceptionally heavy rainfall, are almost tropical in luxuriance, with an undergrowth of vine maple, big-leaf maple, ferns, and other junglelike growth. Mosses drape the branches and tree trunks. The park is the home of the world's largest herd of Roosevelt elk, estimated at 5,000 animals. Other wildlife species include black bear, cougar, and black-tailed deer.

This wilderness of glacier-clad peaks, flower-strewn alpine meadows, turbulent streams and jewel-like lakes, and deep valleys supporting a rich forest growth, is often described as America's "last frontier." Highways penetrate only its outer fringes, but several hundred miles of trails afford the horseback rider and hiker an opportunity to visit the wilderness. Nearly 1,000 varieties of flowers grow in the park's meadows and on its mountain slopes. Some varieties, such as the *Piper bellflower*, grow nowhere else.

Part of this region was set aside as Mount Olympus National Monument by President Theodore Roosevelt in 1909. In 1938, President Franklin D. Roosevelt signed the act establishing Olympic National Park. The park was formally dedicated in 1946. The Queets Corridor and Olympic Ocean Strip were added to the park by presidential proclamation in 1953.   James J. Cullinane

OLYMPICS. See Olympic Games.

OLYMPUS, *oh LIHM puhs*, is the highest mountain in Greece. It rises 9,570 feet (2,917 meters) at the eastern edge of the ridge which divides Thessaly from Macedonia. Its height and roughness made the early Greeks believe that it was the home of the gods. They believed the 12 major gods had palaces on the many peaks of the broad summit of the mountain.

Later the Greek people came to believe that Mount Olympus was not a fit home for the gods. It was usually covered with snow and hidden behind fog and clouds. Their voyages were also showing them that Olympus was not the exact center of the world as they had thought it was. They were beginning to be able to climb the mountain, and it was not good to have the gods living too close to their worshipers. For these reasons they began to believe in an imaginary Mount Olympus that was far away in the sky.

Greek poets did much to help this new idea. Homer holds to the first idea in the *Iliad*, but in the *Odyssey* he places the gods on a far-off mountain. No one knew where the new Olympus was.   Charlotte E. Goodfellow

See also Mountain (picture chart).

OMAGUA INDIANS, *oh MAH gwah*, were a South American tribe that held power at the time of the Spanish Conquest. The Omagua lived along the western part of the Amazon River, near the borders of present-day Peru and Brazil. Few of these Indians remain.

Milt & Joan Mann

Omaha is Nebraska's largest city and one of the world's leading cattle market and meat-packing centers. The 30-story Woodmen Tower building, *right,* is the tallest structure in Omaha.

OMAHA, *OH muh haw* or *OH muh hah* (pop. 346,929; met. area pop. 542,646), is the largest city in Nebraska. It ranks as one of the world's leading cattle market and meat-packing centers and as one of the nation's busiest railroad terminals. For the location of Omaha, see NE-BRASKA (political map).

Omaha took its name from the Omaha Indians. In 1854, this tribe gave most of its hunting grounds in the eastern Nebraska area to the United States government. That same year, the Council Bluffs and Nebraska Ferry Company, a land development firm, founded the town of Omaha. The company chose the site for settlement because of the rich farmland that surrounded it, plus the favorable location for trading. Today, Omaha serves as the trading center for eastern Nebraska and western Iowa.

The City covers 83 square miles (215 square kilometers) on the west bank of the Missouri River. The city of Council Bluffs, Iowa, lies across the river and makes up part of the Omaha metropolitan area. This area covers 1,558 square miles (4,035 square kilometers) and consists of Douglas and Sarpy counties in Nebraska and Pottawattamie County in Iowa.

Omaha's main business district lies near the Missouri River. The 30-story Woodmen Tower, a life insurance building in the heart of the downtown area, is the city's tallest structure.

More than 95 per cent of Omaha's people were born in the United States. The city also has large groups of Czech, German, Irish, Italian, Polish, Scandinavian, or Yugoslav ancestry. Blacks make up about a tenth of the population. Roman Catholics form Omaha's largest religious group, followed by Lutherans, Methodists, and Presbyterians.

Economy. Omaha has about 600 manufacturing plants. Food processing ranks as the city's most important industry, and meat packing is the leading indus-

trial activity. The city's 13 packing plants slaughter about 3 million head of livestock yearly. The Union Stockyards, one of the world's largest livestock markets, cover 90 acres (36 hectares) in southern Omaha. The city is one of the chief frozen food producers in the United States.

Other major Omaha industries include machinery manufacturing, metalworking, printing, publishing, and the manufacture of telephone and electric equipment. Omaha is one of the largest insurance centers in the United States. About 35 insurance firms have their home offices in the city, including Mutual of Omaha, the world's largest private health insurance company.

Eight railroads provide freight service to Omaha, and passenger trains also serve the city. Seven airlines use Eppley Airfield. Two bus lines and more than 140 trucking firms operate in Omaha. Five barge lines help make the city an important Missouri River port.

Omaha's one daily newspaper, the *World-Herald,* publishes both morning and evening editions. Three television stations and 12 radio stations serve the city.

Education and Cultural Life. Omaha's public school systems include about 10 high schools and more than 100 elementary schools. Their enrollment totals about 80,000 students. The city has more than 50 private and parochial schools with over 20,000 students. Omaha is also the home of the Nebraska School for the Deaf. Boys Town, a famous community for homeless and underprivileged boys, lies just west of Omaha (see BOYS TOWN). Colleges and universities in the city include the University of Nebraska at Omaha, Creighton University, and the College of St. Mary.

The Joslyn Art Museum owns works by many of the world's greatest artists. It also exhibits a fine collection of paintings and documents about American Indian life in the 1830's. The city has a symphony orchestra and a community playhouse.

Omaha has more than 120 parks that cover a total of about 5,000 acres (2,000 hectares). The Henry Doorly Zoo, in the southeastern part of the city, attracts many visitors. Fontenelle Forest, the largest unbroken tract of forestland in Nebraska, lies south of Omaha.

Every June, top college baseball teams come to Omaha to compete in the National Collegiate Athletic Association College World Series. The Knights of Ak-Sar-Ben, a civic organization with about 58,000 members, sponsors a rodeo and livestock show every September. This organization, whose name is *Nebraska* spelled backwards, was founded in 1895.

Government. Omaha has a mayor-council form of government. The voters elect the mayor and the seven council members to four-year terms. Omaha gets most of its income from a property tax and from a city sales tax.

History. Many Indian tribes, including the Missouri, the Omaha, and the Oto, once hunted buffalo in what is now the Omaha area. The famous expedition headed by Meriwether Lewis and William Clark passed through the area in 1804 on its way to the West.

In 1852, whites began to gather at Council Bluffs, Iowa. They were awaiting a chance to settle the land across the Missouri River. In 1854, a treaty between the United States government and the Omaha Indians opened the newly created Nebraska Territory for settlement. The Council Bluffs and Nebraska Ferry Company surveyed and laid out the site of Omaha. The firm sold land for $25 per lot.

Americans already were talking of a transcontinental railroad. Some Nebraskans wanted Omaha, though only a new settlement, to be the territorial capital. They thought the railroad companies would choose a territorial capital as a link in such a rail system. In 1855, the first territorial legislature selected Omaha as the capital. Omaha was incorporated as a city in 1857.

Many Nebraskans opposed Omaha as the capital. More than half the territory's people lived south of the Platte River. They felt that the capital should not be north of the Platte, as Omaha is. After Nebraska became a state in 1867, the capital was moved to Lincoln, 50 miles (80 kilometers) southwest of Omaha.

In the late 1850's, Omaha became an outfitting point for wagon trains headed for the newly discovered Colorado gold fields. The city had a population of 1,883 by 1860. In 1863, President Abraham Lincoln selected Council Bluffs as the starting point of the Union Pacific Railroad. But in 1865, the first tracks were laid westward from Omaha. The Union Pacific thus became part of the first U.S. transcontinental rail system.

During the 1880's, Omaha developed into an important meat-processing center. The city's location in a great cattle-raising area and at the heart of a rail network helped this growth. The opening of the Union Stockyards in 1884 further hastened the growth of Omaha. Thousands of immigrants, many of them from southern and central Europe, came to Omaha to work in its great meat-packing plants.

In 1898, the Knights of Ak-Sar-Ben organized the Trans-Mississippi and International Exposition, a fair that attracted more than 2½ million visitors to Omaha. By 1900, the city had 102,555 people. The population reached 191,601 in 1920, and 223,844 in 1940. The number of factories in Omaha grew from 150 in 1900 to 450 in 1950. In 1948, the Strategic Air Command, the long-range bomber and missile force of the U.S. Air Force, established its headquarters near Omaha.

In the 1970's, Omaha faced many problems shared by other large U.S. cities. These included a lack of money to finance city government. The growth of industry and population created problems of water and air pollution. Omaha completed a multimillion dollar sewage treatment plant on the Missouri River in 1969.

Extensive modernization of downtown Omaha began in 1968. This project included construction of a new hotel and large office buildings, with completion scheduled for the early 1980's. ALFRED L. FRISBIE

For the monthly weather in Omaha, see NEBRASKA (Climate). See also NEBRASKA (pictures).

OMAN, *oh MAN*, is a small country on the southeastern tip of the Arabian Peninsula. It is about as big as Kansas, but it has about one-third as many people.

Oman is one of the hottest countries in the world. Temperatures reach 130° F. (54° C). Only a few places get over 6 inches (15 centimeters) of rain a year. Much of inland Oman is desolate land where nothing grows. The border with Saudi Arabia, in the region of the *Rub Al Khali* (Empty Quarter) desert, never has been officially agreed upon.

The country has little manufacturing, no railroads, and few roads. But it has large deposits of petroleum

OMAN

and ranks as an important oil-producing nation. Muscat is the capital and leading port (see MUSCAT).

Government. A *sultan* (ruler) governs the country with the aid of a five-man council he appoints. But some people living in the mountains and other inland areas support the *imam*, their Islamic religious leader, rather than the sultan. *Walis* (governors) are in charge of local government units.

People. Most of the people are Arabs who belong to the Ibadite sect of Islam. Some are members of the Sunni Muslim sect. Many blacks, Indians, and *Baluchis* (people whose ancestors came from Baluchistan, Pakistan) live in the coastal towns. Members of the primitive Shuhuh tribe occupy the Musandam Peninsula at the northern tip of the country. They live in caves and exist mainly on fish from the Gulf of Oman.

Most of the people are poor and cannot read or write. They farm, or work in the petroleum industry or on the date and coconut plantations. A few fish for a living, or work for cattle and camel breeders. The people live in tents, or in houses that have mud and stone walls and flat roofs. The men wear flowing white robes and

――――――――――― FACTS IN BRIEF ―――――――――――

Capital: Muscat.

Official Language: Arabic.

Form of Government: Sultanate.

Area: 82,030 sq. mi. (212,457 km²). *Greatest Distances*—north-south, 500 mi. (805 km); east-west, 400 mi. (644 km). *Coastline*—about 1,200 mi. (1,930 km).

Population: *Estimated 1978 Population*—840,000; distribution, 94 per cent rural, 6 per cent urban; density, 10 persons per sq. mi. (4 persons per km²). *Estimated 1983 Population*—978,000.

Chief Products: Coconuts, dates, limes, petroleum.

Flag: A red vertical stripe appears at the left, with white, red, and green horizontal stripes at the right. The national coat of arms appears in white silhouette in the upper left corner. Adopted 1971. See FLAG (picture: Flags of Asia and the Pacific).

Money: Basic Unit—rial. See MONEY (table: Values).

Oman

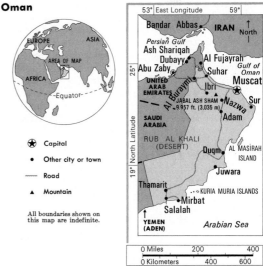

* Capital
• Other city or town
— Road
▲ Mountain

All boundaries shown on this map are indefinite.

WORLD BOOK map

headdresses to shield them from the sun and sand. Many of them carry knives or guns. Most of the women wear long, black dresses. They also wear masks that cover most of the face to keep them from being seen by strange men.

Land. The northernmost part of the country, the barren, rocky Musandam Peninsula, is separated from the rest of the country by the United Arab Emirates. Southeast of there, a low coastal plain stretches for about 1,000 miles (1,600 kilometers) along the Gulf of Oman and Arabian Sea. It rises to a plateau about 1,000 feet (300 meters) above sea level. Most farming is done in the Al Batinah area, which stretches about 200 miles (320 kilometers) along the Gulf of Oman.

The mountain range of Al Hajar stands south of Al Batinah. Jabal ash Sham (9,957 ft., or 3,035 m), part of Al Hajar, is Oman's highest point. The central Az Zahirah plateau is dry and mostly uncultivated. The fertile Dhofar region lies in southwestern Oman.

Economy. Oil fields yield large quantities of petroleum, which is the country's main product and export. Oases along the northern coast produce dates, limes, and pomegranates. Coconuts grow on the southern coast. Oman camels are bred throughout the country.

History. Portuguese forces captured what is now Oman in the early 1500's. But local Arabs expelled them in the mid-1600's and later took over other Portuguese possessions in East Africa. The present sultan's family came to power in 1743. In 1798, the British signed an agreement with the sultan and have maintained close relations ever since. In the 1800's, heirs to the sultanate formed Oman as it is known today.

In 1913, a newly elected imam acquired limited governing powers. The present imam headed resistance against Sultan Said bin Taimur in 1955 and 1957. When the sultan's forces defeated those of the imam in 1959, the imam fled into exile. In 1970, the sultan was overthrown by his son, Qabus bin Said. Qabus began reforms to modernize Oman.

During the mid-1960's, civil war erupted between rebels and government forces in the Dhofar region of Oman. In 1975, the government announced that it had defeated the rebels. GEORGE RENTZ

OMAR KHAYYAM, *O mahr ky YAHM* (1050?-1123?), was a Persian poet, astronomer, and mathematician. His one long poem, *The Rubaiyat*, has brought him lasting fame. *The Rubaiyat* (meaning a collection of quatrains, or four-line rhymes) first attracted attention in 1859 when Edward FitzGerald translated about 100 of the quatrains credited to Omar Khayyam. Omar wrote with gentle melancholy about nature, regret for the fleeting sweetness of life, and the pleasure of love.

Omar Khayyam was born and educated in Nishapur (now Neyshabur, Iran). As royal astronomer, he changed the Persian calendar. He devised one that may have been more accurate than the Gregorian calendar. Omar Khayyam also wrote an Arabic book on algebra that included a classification of equations. Khayyam is an epithet probably derived from his father's trade. It means *the tentmaker*. WALTER J. FISCHEL

See also FITZGERALD, EDWARD; RUBAIYAT.

OMAYYAD. See MUSLIMS (The Spread of Islam).

OMBU TREE. See TREE (table: Interesting Facts).

OMBUDSMAN, *AHM buhdz MUHN*, is a nonpartisan public official who investigates people's complaints about government officials or agencies. Most of his work involves complaints of unjust or harsh treatment of persons by police, prosecuting attorneys, or judges, and such matters as housing, taxation, voting, or welfare payments. After investigating a complaint, the ombudsman may dismiss it. Or he may seek correction of the problem—by persuasion, by publicity, or, occasionally, by recommending prosecution.

The ombudsman idea originated in Sweden in 1809. Since World War II, it has spread, in various forms, to Japan and to several European, Commonwealth, and newly independent countries. Hawaii has a comprehensive ombudsman plan, and other states and some cities of the United States have modified plans. The idea also has gained popularity in large organizations, including corporations and universities. Its growing popularity coincides with the increasing complexities of administration and with people's need for impartial and informal handling of complaints. HOLBERT N. CARROLL

See also COMMERCE, DEPARTMENT OF.

OMDURMAN, *AHM dur MAN* (pop. 185,000), the second largest city in the Sudan, lies across the Nile River from Khartoum. It was built in the 1880's as a model African city to replace Khartoum, which was destroyed during a war. See SUDAN (map).

OMEGA. See ALPHA AND OMEGA.

OMEN is supposedly a sign of future good or bad luck. A good omen foretells a desirable event, and a bad omen forecasts disaster. For example, a person may regard a dream about gold as an omen of success in business. Or he may believe that the death of a relative will follow a dream about losing a tooth. Sometimes omens come from a deliberate attempt to look into the future, such as a fortuneteller's "reading" cards.

Many ancient societies believed that lightning, thunder, or the behavior of animals foretold events. For example, the Mesopotamians thought fire would destroy the king's palace if a dog were seen lying on the throne. In Greece, the cry of a hawk warned of danger. Many leaders, when trying to decide on a particular course of action, asked the gods for a sign. In folklore, many heroes meet their death after disregarding such signs. ALAN DUNDES

See also AUGUR; DIVINATION; SUPERSTITION.

OMER. See LAG BA'OMER.

OMNIBUS BILL is a term sometimes used for a bill that includes several unrelated measures when it is put before a legislative assembly. It is used to pass several bills at once. The bill is named for an *omnibus* (bus), a vehicle that carries a number of people.

The term was first used in 1850. In that year there were a number of questions in dispute between the North and South in the Congress of the United States. Various bills had been offered dealing with slavery and the treatment of fugitive slaves. The Compromise of 1850 was proposed in an attempt to settle all these questions at once. It was denounced and jeered at as an omnibus bill. See COMPROMISE OF 1850.

Omnibus bills are considered bad practice. When a number of unrelated items are crowded into one bill, it is hard to give each the study it deserves. The constitutions of most states and provinces provide that a single bill shall relate to one topic only. THOMAS A. COWAN

OMNIVORE, *AHM nih vohr*, is an animal that eats both animals and plants. The bear, the brown rat, and the opossum are examples of omnivores. See also CARNIVORE; HERBIVORE.

OMSK, *awmsk* (pop. 850,000), is the second largest city in Siberia and an important Russian manufacturing center. Only Novosibirsk is larger. Omsk lies along the Irtysh River, about 1,360 miles (2,190 kilometers) east of Moscow (see RUSSIA [political map]).

Omsk manufactures farm machinery for the surrounding agricultural area. The city also has large food-processing, oil-refining, and petrochemical industries.

Omsk was founded in 1716, during the Russian expansion into Siberia. The Trans-Siberian Railroad reached the city in 1894, and Omsk became a commercial center of Western Siberia. During World War II (1939-1945), the government moved many factories from combat zones in western Russia to safe areas in Siberia. Omsk developed rapidly as a result, and its industries have continued to expand.   THEODORE SHABAD

ON-THE-JOB TRAINING. See CAREERS (The World of Work).

ON THE SUBLIME. See LONGINUS.

ONA INDIANS, *OH nah*, once lived on the island of Tierra del Fuego at the southernmost tip of South America. Their way of life was one of the simplest in all America. The two main divisions of Ona were the *Selknam* and *Haush*.

The Ona hunted the guanaco, a small wild relative of the llama. They used mainly the bow and arrow for hunting and fighting. The Ona wore little clothing. They had large capes and moccasins of guanaco skins, and sometimes used leggings. But Ona men often went without clothes, even in the snow. The people made simple windbreak shelters of guanaco hides.

Every few years, several bands of Ona would meet to initiate youths into manhood. This festival was the Ona's main religious ceremony and social celebration.

The Ona numbered about 2,000 around 1875. Then sheep ranchers and gold seekers invaded the island. They killed many Ona outright, and the new diseases they brought killed others. The tribe had disappeared entirely by 1930.   CHARLES WAGLEY

See also INDIAN, AMERICAN (illustration: Indian Ways of Life).

ONAGER, *AHN uh jer*, is the name of a fast-running animal which is a relative of the donkey. It is the *wild ass* mentioned in the Bible, where a good description of it may be found (Job 39: 5-8). The onager travels in herds on the hot, dry plains of west-central Asia. Its color varies from cinnamon-brown in summer to yellow-brown in winter. A yellow patch covers each thigh and a broad black stripe runs along its back. The onager also has a mane, and a tuft of hair at the end of its tail. It is about 4 feet (1.2 meters) high at the shoulders.

Scientific Classification. The onager is in the horse family, *Equidae*. It is genus *Equus*, species *E. hemionus*.

ONASSIS, ARISTOTLE SOCRATES (1906-1975), a Greek shipowner and business executive, became one of the world's wealthiest men. In 1968, he married Jacqueline Kennedy, the widow of President John F. Kennedy of the United States.

Onassis was born in Smyrna (now Izmir), Turkey, the son of a well-to-do tobacco importer. He emigrated to Argentina in 1923 after his father lost his fortune.

In Buenos Aires, he became a telephone switchboard operator and later a tobacco importer. He entered the shipping business during the Great Depression of the 1930's and bought several freighters at an extremely low price. He was a shrewd, daring investor and ignored the advice of many shipping experts after World War II, when he built several giant oil tankers. This venture was highly successful. Onassis owned Olympic Airways, the only Greek airline, from the mid-1950's until the government took it over in the mid-1970's.

Onassis was a citizen of both Greece and Argentina. He was a familiar figure in international high society and entertained world leaders and celebrities on his yacht *Christina*.   LEONARD S. SILK

OÑATE, *oh NYAH tay*, **JUAN DE** (1549?-1628?), was a Spanish frontiersman and explorer. He is remembered mainly for colonizing the territory now called New Mexico, in 1598. His explorations extended from the Colorado River to the plains of Kansas. He served for a time as governor of New Mexico, but later lost favor with the Spanish government, and resigned in 1607. He was brought to trial and found guilty of having disobeyed his king. It was largely because of Oñate's work that the city of Santa Fe was founded in 1610. Oñate was born in Guadalajara, Mexico.   RICHARD A. BARTLETT

ONE-CELLED ORGANISM. See PROTISTA; PROTOZOAN.

ONE-CROP FARM. See AGRICULTURE (Kinds).

O'NEALE, PEGGY (1796-1879), was a central figure in one of the greatest disputes in the history of Washington, D.C., society. The dispute caused President Andrew Jackson to reorganize his Cabinet.

Margaret O'Neale was born in Washington, D.C., the daughter of an innkeeper. Margaret, known by the nickname Peggy, married John B. Timberlake, a navy purser. She lived at the O'Neale tavern while Timberlake was at sea. Senator John H. Eaton of Tennessee lived there in 1818, and became fond of Peggy. Andrew Jackson, who became a U.S. senator from Tennessee in 1823, met Peggy at the inn. Peggy's husband died in 1828, and she married Senator Eaton on Jan. 1, 1829.

Eaton became secretary of war in 1829. Washington society refused to receive Peggy, because of her father's occupation and because of gossip about her conduct with Eaton. President Jackson stood by her, despite his family's protests. Several Cabinet members resigned, and Eaton resigned his post in 1831. He became governor of Florida in 1834, and then minister to Spain in 1836.   HELEN E. MARSHALL

See also JACKSON, ANDREW (Split with Calhoun).

ONEGA, LAKE. See LAKE ONEGA.

ONEIDA COMMUNITY, *oh NYE duh*, a cooperative settlement in Oneida, N.Y., was founded by John Humphrey Noyes in 1848. It was probably the most extreme form of communistic experiment ever established in the United States. Its members are often called "Bible communists."

The Oneida Community began in Putney, Vt. Its members believed that perfection in life is possible through personal communion with God, and that people must share all personal possessions and live as one family. They also believed in *complex marriage*, and everyone in the community was considered married to everyone else. Orthodox church leaders objected to this practice, and forced the community to leave Putney.

In Oneida, Noyes set up a system of "mutual criticism." Each individual was judged by the other members of the group for the sake of personal improvement. All work was considered dignified. Women had equal rights with men, and the community raised the children.

The community flourished financially. One of the members invented a steel game trap. Factories in the community manufactured these traps, and the people became wealthy by selling them. The community also manufactured several kinds of steel chains. It used much of the money it earned from these undertakings to build factories for making silk thread and for canning.

In 1879, because of outside opposition to complex marriage, Noyes advised the community to give it up. In 1881, the community was reorganized and incorporated as a joint-stock company that still exists. Only a few voluntary cooperative features, suggesting the original plan of the community, remain.   DONALD R. McCOY

ONEIDA INDIANS. See IROQUOIS INDIANS.

ONEIDA LAKE is one of the links in the New York State Barge Canal System. The lake was named for the Oneida Indians, who once had a village on its shores. Oneida Lake lies in central New York, about 10 miles (16 kilometers) northeast of Syracuse. Its area is 79.8 square miles (206.7 square kilometers). It is about 21 miles (34 kilometers) long, and 5 miles (8 kilometers) wide. It empties into Lake Ontario. For location, see NEW YORK (physical map).   WILLIAM E. YOUNG

O'NEILL, EUGENE GLADSTONE (1888-1953), is considered America's greatest playwright. He was the first American dramatist to write tragedy consistently. Before O'Neill, most successful American plays tended to be either melodramas or sentimental comedies.

O'Neill won the Nobel prize for literature in 1936. Four of his plays won Pulitzer prizes—*Beyond the Horizon* in 1920; *Anna Christie* in 1922; *Strange Interlude* in 1928; and *Long Day's Journey into Night* in 1957, after his death.

His Life. O'Neill was born on Oct. 16, 1888, in New York City. He was the son of James O'Neill, a well-known actor. He attended Princeton University briefly in 1906, and then left school and took a variety of jobs. As a seaman, he sailed to South Africa and South America

Random House
Eugene O'Neill

in 1910 and 1911. Many of O'Neill's plays reflect his experiences at sea. Others show his sympathy for the failures and outcasts of society he met during this time.

O'Neill was married three times, in 1909, 1918, and 1928. The first two marriages ended in divorce. O'Neill became ill with tuberculosis and entered a sanatorium in 1912. While recovering, he decided to become a playwright. In 1916, he became associated with the Provincetown Players, a theater group. It staged his first play, *Bound East for Cardiff* (1913-1914), in 1916.

O'Neill had written most of his plays by the mid-1930's. Later in life he suffered from Parkinson's disease, a form of palsy. The disease hampered his ability to write. O'Neill died on Nov. 27, 1953.

His Plays. O'Neill's 45 plays cover a wide range of dramatic styles and subjects. They vary in length from one act, to the nine-act *Strange Interlude* (written in 1926-1927) and the 11-act *Mourning Becomes Electra* (1929-1931). O'Neill wrote brutally realistic plays, including *Desire Under the Elms* (1924); expressionistic plays, including *The Hairy Ape* (1921); and satire, including *Marco Millions* (1923-1925).

O'Neill stated that his task as a playwright was to "dig at the roots of the sickness of today." He believed that science had robbed people of their faith in traditional beliefs and had not given them a new faith. People were left without any faith to satisfy their desire for meaning in life and to comfort them in their fear of death.

O'Neill's pessimistic view of life was influenced by the writings of German philosophers Friedrich Nietzsche and Arthur Schopenhauer and Swedish playwright August Strindberg. Modern psychology also influenced O'Neill. In *The Great God Brown* (1925), his characters wear masks to express their personalities. The characters in *Strange Interlude* speak their thoughts aloud, exposing their inner feelings. In *Days Without End* (1932-1933), two actors portray different parts of a character's personality. O'Neill used symbols in many plays. The drums in *The Emperor Jones* (1920) symbolize the primitive fears of the leading character.

Most of O'Neill's characters seek some meaning for their lives. In *Beyond the Horizon* (1918), *Anna Christie* (1920), and *Strange Interlude*, the characters turn to love to find meaning. In *Dynamo* (1928) and *Days Without End*, they turn to religion. All suffer disappointment. In *The Iceman Cometh* (1939), O'Neill's most pessimistic play, the characters in a waterfront saloon have ruined their lives. But they find meaning in their illusions about themselves. When these illusions are taken from them, they come close to despair. O'Neill says that all illusions are "pipe dreams." He seems to assert that humanity's only "hopeless hope" is in drink and death. But O'Neill also seems to say there is a certain admirable heroism in people who persist in living a life without hope.   HUBERT C. HEFFNER

See also AMERICAN LITERATURE (The Rise of American Drama); NATURALISM (Naturalism in Drama).

O'NEILL, THOMAS PHILIP (1912-   ), a Massachusetts Democrat, became speaker of the United States House of Representatives in 1977. He had served as majority leader since 1973. From 1971 to 1973, he had been majority *whip* (assistant leader) of the House of Representatives.

O'Neill was born in Cambridge, Mass. His boyhood friends nicknamed him Tip for James E. (Tip) O'Neill, a baseball player of the late 1800's. O'Neill graduated from Boston College in 1936 and was elected to the Massachusetts House of Representatives that same year. He became minority leader in 1947 and speaker of the Massachusetts House in 1948.

O'Neill won election to the U.S. House of Representatives in 1952. As a representative, he supported several changes in House rules. For example, he led a successful fight to record all votes in the House. Previously, representatives had voted on amendments to

Bermuda

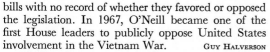

Red Globe

Southport Yellow Globe

J. Horace McFarland

Brown Spanish

Green

bills with no record of whether they favored or opposed the legislation. In 1967, O'Neill became one of the first House leaders to publicly oppose United States involvement in the Vietnam War.　　Guy Halverson

ONION, *UN yun,* is a plant that belongs to the amaryllis family. It is well known for its strong taste and odor. The odor is due to a mildly stimulating oil. This oil readily forms a vapor, which escapes into the air when onions are peeled or cut. It affects nerves in the nose connected with the eyes, and makes tears flow.

Onions first grew in Mongolia. They were raised in America as early as 1750. The leading onion-growing states include California, Idaho, Michigan, New York, Oregon, and Texas. But onions are grown in many other states and Canadian provinces. Mexico, Italy, and Spain are also noted for the size and quality of their onions.

The onion plant is a *biennial* (a plant that lives for two years). The upper part of the plant is a set of leaves growing inside each other. The lower parts of the leaves become very thick. The flowers are small and white, and grow in rounded clusters. The bulbs are enclosed in a thin papery covering made up of dried outer leaves. The onion plant has a few shallow roots.

The different kinds of onions have many different sizes, colors, and shapes. Men who trade in onions classify them as *American* (strong onions) and *foreign* (mild onions). The strong type includes the Yellow Globe types and the flatter Ebenezer type. The home gardener can grow these from *sets* (very small onions that have not completed their growth). These onions keep well, and they are usually eaten cooked. The foreign type are mostly Spanish and Bermuda onions. These large, mild onions are generally eaten uncooked.

Most onions that are sold in markets are raised from seeds. But home garden onions are usually raised from sets. Both sets and seeds are used to produce *scallions,* a popular name for young onions that are harvested before they have developed a bulb. Onions that have lost their ability to make seeds are raised from bulbs, and are known as *multiplier onions.* Some types produce tiny bulbs, called *aerial sets,* on their seed stalks. Seeds may be sown in the field or in greenhouses. Onions need a very moist soil for good growth.

The onion thrips is one of the worst insects that attacks onions. It can be checked by spraying seedlings with diazinon or malathion.

The onion is not particularly high in vitamins or in energy value. Cooking onions takes away some food value, but it makes them more digestible and tends to remove their odor. Onions are also pickled.

Scientific Classification. Onions belong to the amaryllis family, *Amaryllidaceae.* They are genus *Allium,* species *A. cepa.*　　Arthur J. Pratt

See also Bulb; Garlic; Ramp; Shallot; Chive.

ONOMATOPOEIA, *AHN oh MAT oh PE yuh,* is the formation of words to imitate natural sounds. The *buzz* of a bee, the *hoot* of an owl, and the *fizz* of soda water are examples of onomatopoeia. The term comes from two Greek words meaning *to make a name.*

ONONDAGA INDIANS. See Iroquois Indians.

ONSAGER, LARS. See Nobel Prizes (table: Nobel Prizes for Chemistry—1968).

LEADING ONION-GROWING STATES
Production of onions in 1974

California	1,085,400,000 lbs. (492,330,000 kg)
Texas	509,500,000 lbs. (231,110,000 kg)
New York	397,300,000 lbs. (180,210,000 kg)
Oregon	357,600,000 lbs. (162,200,000 kg)
Michigan	213,900,000 lbs. (97,020,000 kg)
Idaho	207,000,000 lbs. (93,890,000 kg)
Colorado	147,900,000 lbs. (67,090,000 kg)

Source: *Vegetables—Fresh Market, 1974 Annual Summary,* U.S. Department of Agriculture.

ONTARIO

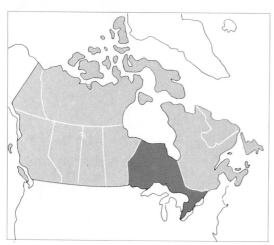

Ontario (Blue) Is Canada's Second Largest Province.

The contributors of this article are Norman L. Nicholson, Senior Professor of Geography at the University of Western Ontario; Val Sears, Washington correspondent and formerly Chief Editorial Writer of the Toronto Daily Star; *and John T. Saywell, Professor of History and Environmental Studies at York University.*

Steel Mill in Hamilton

ONTARIO, *ahn TAIR ee oh*, has more people than any other Canadian province. About a third of Canada's people live in Ontario. Ontario's manufacturing industries, its chief source of income, produce as much as those of the nine other provinces combined. Ontario ranks first among the Canadian provinces in farm income. It ranks second only to Alberta in mining. Toronto is the capital of the province, and the Toronto area is Canada's leading manufacturing center. Ottawa, the capital of Canada, lies on the Ottawa River in southeastern Ontario.

Ontario has a larger area than any other province except Quebec. It reaches down between New York and Michigan, and is Canada's southernmost province. In fact, Ontario extends a little farther south than the northern boundary of California. This province also extends so far north that some of the ground beneath the surface is *permafrost* (permanently frozen ground).

The busy factories, mills, and plants of Ontario have given it the nickname *Workshop of the Nation.* Most industries are in the warm southern region, south of Lake Nipissing. About 92 per cent of the people live there, on about 12 per cent of the land area. The richest manufacturing section, called the *Golden Horseshoe,* curves around the western shores of Lake Ontario.

Ontario's major industry is manufacturing automobiles. Most of the province's automobile plants are in the Golden Horseshoe. Almost all the automobiles made in Canada come from there. Hamilton, a city in the Golden Horseshoe, is Canada's greatest iron and steel center. Nearby is Toronto, one of the chief Canadian ports on the Great Lakes. The region's varied products travel from Toronto to many parts of the world by way of the St. Lawrence Seaway. Port Colborne, also part of the Golden Horseshoe, has one of the largest nickel-processing plants in North America.

The mines of Ontario provide about a fifth of all the minerals produced in Canada. Deposits near Sud-

Algoma by John Joy from the WORLD BOOK Collection

Wilderness near Lake Superior

bury yield about one-fourth of the world's supply of nickel and much of its copper and platinum. One of the largest known uranium deposits in the world lies near Elliot Lake. No other province or state produces more gold than Ontario.

But Ontario is not only an industrial province. It is Canada's leading producer of eggs and poultry, fruits, and vegetables. Ontario provides about a third of Canada's farm products. Herds of beef and dairy cattle graze in rich pastures between Lake Huron and Lake Ontario. Tobacco flourishes along Lake Erie, and colorful orchards thrive in the famous Niagara fruit belt. Northern Ontario has thick forests that provide wood for the pulp and paper industry. Trappers catch fur-bearing animals there, and campers hunt and fish.

The province's name came from the Iroquois Indians, who lived in the region when French explorers first arrived. The word *Ontario* may mean *beautiful lake*. Or it may mean *rocks standing high* or *near the water*—referring to Niagara Falls. These spectacular falls attract many visitors. The falls rank among the greatest natural sources of hydroelectric power in North America.

Ontario, together with New Brunswick, Nova Scotia, and Quebec, was one of the original provinces of Canada. For the relationship of Ontario to the other provinces, see CANADA; CANADA, GOVERNMENT OF; CANADA, HISTORY OF.

─────── **FACTS IN BRIEF** ───────

Capital: Toronto.

Government: *Parliament*—members of the Senate, 24; members of the House of Commons, 95. *Provincial Legislature*—members of the Legislative Assembly, 117. *Counties*—27. *Districts*—10. *Regional Municipalities*—10. *Metropolitan Municipalities*—1. *District Municipalities*—1. *Voting Age*—18 years.

Area: 412,582 sq. mi. (1,068,582 km²), including 68,490 sq. mi. (177,388 km²) of inland water; 2nd in size among the provinces. *Greatest Distances*—north-south, 1,075 mi. (1,730 km); east-west, 1,050 mi. (1,690 km). *Shoreline*—4,726 mi. (7,606 km) along the Great Lakes. *Coastline*—752 mi. (1,210 km) on Hudson and James bays.

Elevation: *Highest*—2,275 ft. (693 m) above sea level in Timiskaming District. *Lowest*—sea level.

Population: *1976 Census*—8,264,465; first among the provinces; density, 20 persons per sq. mi. (9 per km²); distribution, 82 per cent urban, 18 per cent rural.

Chief Products: *Agriculture*—beef cattle, hogs, milk, tobacco. *Fishing Industry*—perch, smelt, whitefish. *Forest Industry*—logs and bolts, pulpwood. *Fur Industry*—beaver, mink. *Manufacturing*—fabricated metal products, food products, primary metals, transportation equipment. *Mining*—copper, iron ore, nickel, zinc.

Provincial Motto: *Ut Incepit Fidelis Sic Permanet* (Loyal she began, loyal she remains).

Entered the Dominion: July 1, 1867; one of the original four provinces.

579

Lieutenant Governor of Ontario represents Queen Elizabeth in the province. The lieutenant governor is appointed by the governor general in council. The position of lieutenant governor, like that of the governor general, is largely honorary.

Premier of Ontario is the actual head of the provincial government. The province, like the other provinces and Canada itself, has a *parliamentary* form of government. The premier is a member of the Legislative Assembly, where he is the leader of the majority party. The voters elect him as they do the other members of the assembly. He receives a salary of $25,000 a year, in addition to allowances he gets as a member of the assembly. The head of Ontario's government was called the prime minister until 1972. That year, Prime Minister William Davis changed the title to premier. For a list of the prime ministers and premiers of Ontario, see the *History* section of this article.

The premier presides over the executive council, or cabinet. The council includes ministers chosen by the premier from his party's members in the Legislative Assembly. Each minister directs a government ministry, except for two who are designated *minister without portfolio*. The executive council, like the premier, resigns if it loses the support of a majority of the assembly.

Legislative Assembly is a one-house legislature that makes the provincial laws. It has 117 members who are elected from 117 electoral districts called *constituencies*. Their terms may last up to five years. However, the lieutenant governor, on the advice of the premier, may call for an election before the end of the five-year period. All members of the legislature then must run again for office.

Courts. The highest court in Ontario is the supreme court. It consists of the court of appeal and the high court of justice. The court of appeal is made up of a chief justice and 13 other justices. The high court of justice, which hears major civil and criminal cases, has a chief justice and 34 other justices. The governor general in council appoints all these justices, and they serve until the age of 75. He also appoints judges to county and district courts. These judges preside over small claims courts as well. Provincial authorities appoint judges of provincial criminal courts and family courts.

Local Government. The heavily populated southern tenth of Ontario is divided into 27 counties, 10 regional municipalities, and 1 metropolitan municipality. Three of these counties are called *united counties*. They each consist of two or three former single counties combined for purposes of government. Each of Ontario's county governments is headed by a council. This council consists of the reeves and deputy reeves of the county's towns, villages, and townships. The northern nine-tenths of Ontario is made up of 10 districts and 1 district municipality. The provincial government administers these areas.

Most of Ontario's cities and towns are governed by a mayor and a council, elected to two-year terms. Some of these municipalities have the council-manager form of government. The Municipality of Metropolitan Toronto, established in 1954, consists of the city of Toronto and five boroughs. It is governed by the metro council and metro executive chosen from the six municipal units. The council deals with such problems as highway construction, libraries, sewage disposal, traffic engineering, urban growth, water supply, and welfare.

Taxation. Taxes collected by the provincial government provide about two-thirds of its income. Most of this money comes from taxes on corporation income, gasoline, and retail sales. Ontario and Quebec are the only provinces that collect their own corporation income taxes. Other sources of Ontario's income include federal-provincial tax-sharing programs, license and permit fees, and the sale of liquor, which is under government control.

Politics. Ontario has three major political parties. They are, in order of strength, the Progressive Conservative, New Democratic, and Liberal parties. The Progressive Conservative party was formerly named the Conservative party, and today its members are usually called simply Conservatives. The New Democratic

Ontario Dept. of Travel & Publicity

The Legislative Chamber in the main Parliament Building in Toronto has hand-carved woodwork and mahogany paneling. The Legislative Assembly meets in this chamber.

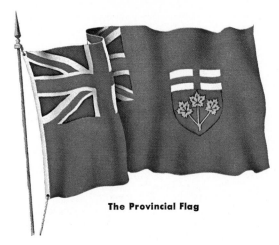

The Provincial Flag

Symbols of Ontario. On the coat of arms, the shield has the red and white cross of St. George, representing Ontario's ties with Great Britain. The three maple leaves are symbols of Canada. The bear above the shield stands for strength. The coat of arms was adopted in 1868. The provincial flag, adopted in 1965, has the shield of Ontario and the British Union flag.

The Provincial Coat of Arms

party is the youngest of Ontario's three major political parties. It developed partly from the old Co-operative Commonwealth Federation.

Ontario's first provincial government was a *coalition* (combination) of Liberals and Conservatives. The Liberals took full control of the government in 1871 and held it until 1905, when the Conservatives came to power. In 1919, during an economic depression, the United Farmers of Ontario took over the government. The Conservatives regained leadership in 1923 after the economy improved, but lost it to the Liberals in 1934. The Progressive Conservatives won control of the government in 1943, and have been in power ever since. An Ontario citizen must be at least 18 years of age to vote in federal or provincial elections.

The Floral Emblem
White Trillium

Miller Services

The Provincial Parliament Buildings are in Toronto, the capital of Ontario since 1867. Earlier capitals were Newark (now Niagara-on-the-Lake, 1792-1797); York (later renamed Toronto, 1797-1841); Kingston (the capital of combined Upper and Lower Canada, 1841-1844); Montreal, Que. (1844-1849); Quebec City, Que., and Toronto, alternately (1849-1865); and Ottawa (1866-1867).

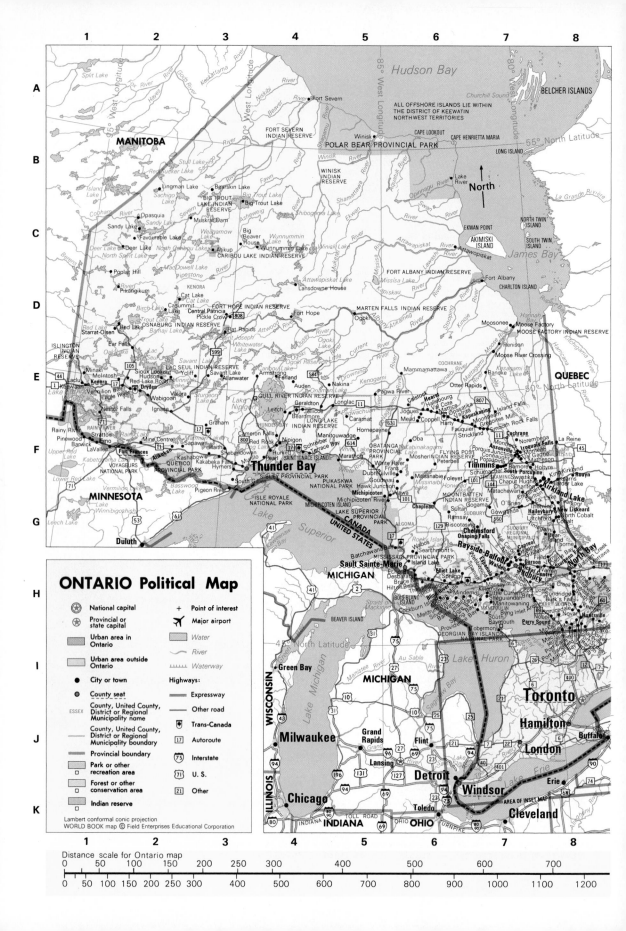

ONTARIO Political Map

Legend:

- National capital
- Provincial or state capital
- Urban area in Ontario
- Urban area outside Ontario
- City or town
- County seat
- ESSEX — County, United County, District or Regional Municipality name
- County, United County, District or Regional Municipality boundary
- Provincial boundary
- Park or other recreation area
- Forest or other conservation area
- Indian reserve
- + Point of interest
- ✈ Major airport
- Water
- River
- Waterway

Highways:
- Expressway
- Other road
- Trans-Canada
- 17 Autoroute
- 75 Interstate
- 71 U.S.
- 21 Other

Lambert conformal conic projection
WORLD BOOK map © Field Enterprises Educational Corporation

Distance scale for Ontario map
0 50 100 150 200 250 300 400 500 600 700
0 50 100 150 200 250 300 400 500 600 700 800 900 1000 1100 1200

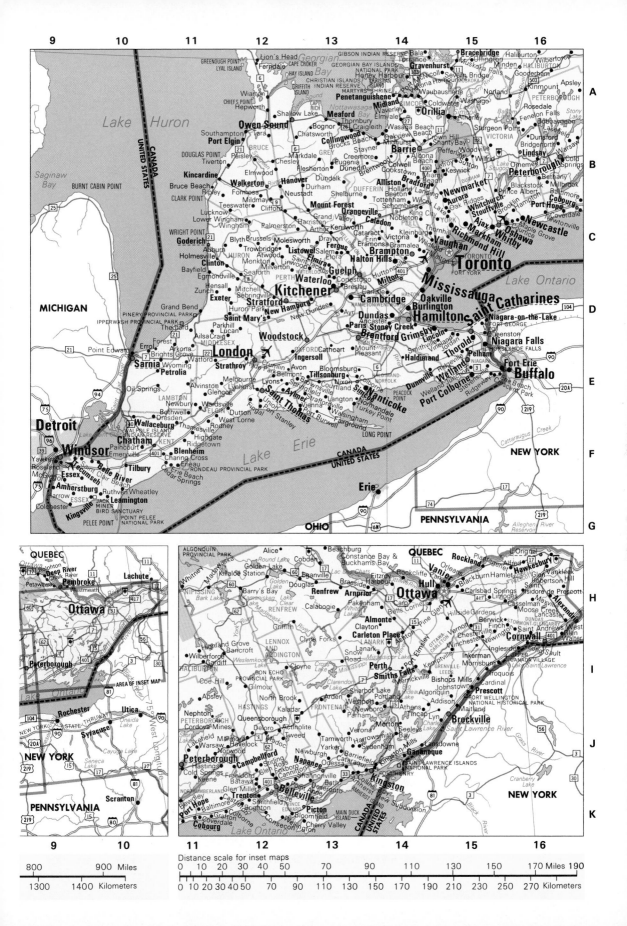

Population

8,264,465 ..Census..1976
7,703,106 ....."....1971
6,960,870 ....."....1966
6,236,092 ....."....1961
4,597,542 ....."....1951
3,787,655 ....."....1941
3,431,683 ....."....1931
2,933,662 ....."....1921
2,527,292 ....."....1911
2,182,947 ....."....1901
2,114,321 ....."....1891
1,926,922 ....."....1881
1,620,851 ....."....1871

Metropolitan Areas

Hamilton 529,371
Kitchener 272,158
London 270,383
Oshawa 135,196
Ottawa-Hull 693,288
(521,341 in Ontario; 171,947 in Quebec)
St. Catharines-Niagara 301,921
Sudbury 157,030
Thunder Bay 119,253
Toronto 2,803,101
Windsor 247,582

Counties

Brant ......98,089..E 14
Bruce ......56,557..B 12
Dufferin ...28,121..B 14
Elgin ......68,291..F 11
Essex .....305,585..G 10
Frontenac .106,166..J 13
Grey ....70,991..B 13
Haliburton .10,456..I 11
Hastings ..104,131..J 12
Huron .....54,876..C 12
Kent .....105,577..F 11
Lambton ..119,182..E 11
Lanark ....43,353..I 14
Leeds and Grenville† 77,371..I 14
Lennox and Addington 31,855..I 12
Middlesex .297,352..E 11
Northumberland .....63,752..K 11
Oxford .....83,729..E 13
Perth ......65,635..D 12
Peterborough .98,645..J 11
Prescott and Russell† .48,077..H 16
Prince Edward ..22,371..K 12
Renfrew ...87,757..H 12
Simcoe ...207,170..A 14
Stormont, Dundas, and Glengarry† ...97,612..I 15
Victoria ...42,773..A 16
Wellington 124,026..C 13

Districts

Algoma ..120,350..G 6
Cochrane ..95,668..E 6
Kenora ....57,298..D 3
Manitoulin .10,648..H 7
Nipissing ..80,790..H 11
Parry Sound ...32,157..H 8
Rainy River 24,562..F 1
Sudbury ...26,699..G 7
Thunder Bay ....148,972..F 4
Timiskaming ..43,148..F 7

Regional Municipalities

Durham ..245,131..C 16
Haldimand-Norfolk .88,301..E 14
Halton ....227,390..D 14
Hamilton-Wentworth ..405,579..D 14
Niagara ..360,974..D 15
Ottawa-Carleton 501,729..H 15
Peel ......371,719..C 14
Sudbury ..165,541..H 7
Waterloo ..286,545..D 13
York .....201,277..C 15

District Municipality

Muskoka ...36,119..I 8

Metropolitan Municipality

Toronto .2,081,521..C 15

Cities, Towns, and Villages

Aberfoyle* .....94..D 14
Actinolite .....100..J 12
Addison ....89..I 14
Adironto* .....595..I 14
Ailsa Craig ...696..D 11
Ajax ......20,669..C 15
Alban* ....420..G 7
Alberton* .....96..D 14
Alcona Beach* 659..I 8
Alexandria ..3,332..H 16
Aldercrest Survey* .....559..D 14
Alfred ......1,093..H 16
Algoma Mills ..89..H 6
Algonquin ....130..I 15
Alice ....95..H 12
Allanwater .....90..E 3
Alliston .....4,129..B 14
Almonte ....3,567..H 14
Alvinston .....610..E 11
Amherst Point* 392..G 10
Amherst View Subdivision ...3,121..K 13
Amherstburg 5,523..G 9
Ancaster ...14,151..D 14
Apsley ....250..I 11
Arden ....176..I 13
Arkona ....448..E 11
Armstrong ....574..E 3
Arnprior ....5,953..H 14
Arnstein* ......86..H 8
Arthur ......1,648..C 13
Ashton ....143..I 14
Astorville ....259..H 8
Athens ......1,025..J 14
Atherley ......392..A 15
Atikokan ....6,007..F 2
Attawapiskat* .532..D 3
Atwood ....690..C 12
Auburn ....209..C 12
Auden ....108..E 4
Aurora ....13,853..C 15
Avon ....87..E 12
Aylmer .....5,030..E 12
Ayr ....3,387..D 13
Baden* ....959..D 13
Bala ....462..A 14
Balmertown* ..977..D 2
Baltimore .....186..K 11
Bancroft ....2,285..I 12
Barrie .....33,524.°B 14
Barrie Island ......109..H 6
Barriefield ....247..J 14
Barry's Bay .1,231..H 12
Barwick ....40..F 1
Batawa ....667..K 12
Batchawana Bay* ....585..G 6
Bath ....746..K 13
Bayfield ......542..D 11
Bayside .....1,732..K 12
Baysville .....283..I 8
Beachburg ....645..G 13
Bear-Island ....85..H 7
Beardmore ....754..F 4
Beeton ......1,600..B 14
Belfountain* ..203..C 14
Bell Ewart* ..400..B 15
Belle River ..3,224..F 10
Belleville ..34,702.°K 12
Belmont ......735..E 12
Bent River* ...88..H 8
Berwick ....99..I 16
Bethany ......325..B 16
Binbrook* ....396..D 14
Biscotasing ....62..G 7
Bishops Mills ..83..I 15
Blackburn Hamlet* ..3,841..H 15
Blackstock ....251..B 16
Blenheim ...3,675..F 11
Blezard Valley* .....932..H 7
Blind River .3,104..H 6
Bloomfield ....744..K 13
Bloomsburg ....89..E 13
Blyth ....860..C 12
Bobcaygeon .1,561..B 16
Bognor ....88..B 13
Bondhead* ...683..A 14
Boninville* ....93..H 7
Bothwell ......886..E 11
Bracebridge .8,186.°A 15
Bradford ....5,031..B 15
Braeside ......523..H 14
Bramalea ..23,083..C 14
Brampton .103,459.°C 14
Brantford ..66,950.°D 13
Brentwood .....90..B 14
Breslau ....697..D 13
Bridgenorth .1,380..B 16
Brights Grove ......730..E 11
Brighton ....3,192..K 12
Britt ....500..H 7
Brockville ..19,566.°J 15
Brocks Beach .447..B 14
Brownsville ...295..E 13
Bruce Beach ...87..B 11
Bruce Mines ..513..H 6
Brussels .....1,029..C 12
Burk's Falls ..858..H 8
Burlington 104,314..D 14
Byng Inlet Area ....163..H 8
Cache Bay ....672..H 8
Caistorville* ...91..E 14
Calabogie .....299..H 13
Caledon ....22,210..C 14
Callander ...1,190..H 8
Calstock ....90..E 6
Cambridge .72,383..D 13
Cameron Falls 123..F 4
Campbellford 3,415..J 12
Cannifton* ....528..J 12
Capreol .....4,056..G 7
Caramat* .....520..F 4
Cardiff* ......525..I 11
Cardinal ....1,852..I 15
Carleton Place .....5,204..I 14
Carlisle* ......488..D 14
Carlsbad Springs .....226..H 15
Carol and Richard Park* ..703..H 7
Carp ....516..H 14
Cartier* ......740..G 7
Casselman ..1,411..H 15
Castleton .....289..K 11
Cataract ....90..D 14
Cathcart ....99..E 13
Cedar Springs .302..F 11
Central Patricia .....99..D 3
Centreton* .....94..K 11
Chalk River .1,080..H 9
Champlain Park* ......634..H 8
Chapleau ...3,365..G 6
Chaput Hughes ....873..G 8
Charing Cross .436..F 11
Charlton ......188..G 8
Chatham ..38,437.°F 10
Chatsworth ...392..B 13
Cherry Valley .238..K 13
Chesley .....1,825..B 12
Chesterville .1,319..I 15
Claremont* ...592..C 15
Clayton ....96..H 14
Clifford ....634..C 12
Clinton .....3,120..C 12
Cobalt ......2,033..G 8
Cobden ......1,020..H 13
Cobourg ...11,279.°K 11
Cochenour* ...610..D 2
Cochrane ....4,921.°F 7
Colborne .....374..E 13
Colborne ....1,708..K 12
Colchester ....752..G 9
Coldwater ....799..A 14
Collingwood 11,147..B 14
Collins Bay ..2,089..K 13
Colwell ....96..B 14
Conestogo* ....467..D 13
Connaught ....148..F 7
Consecon ......332..K 12
Constance Bay & Buckhams Bay* ....532..H 15
Cookstown ....861..B 14
Coppell ....38..F 6
Corbeil ....81..H 8
Cordova Mines 116..J 12
Cornwall .. 45,491.°I 16
Courtice ......519..C 16
Courtland ....574..E 13
Coverdale .....670..K 11
Craigleith ....131..B 13
Creemore ....1,040..B 14
Creighton* ..1,294..H 7
Crown Hill ....19..B 14
Crumlin ......240..E 12
Crystal Beach* .96..E 15
Cumberland Beach* .....477..A 14
Deep River ..5,527..H 9
Deloro ....238..J 12
Desbarats .....187..H 6
Deseronto ...1,877..K 13
Dobie* ....194..F 8
Dome Mines and Extension* ..453..E 6
Douglas ......307..H 13
Drayton ......795..C 13
Dresden ....2,435..F 11
Dryden .....6,682..E 2
Dubreuilville ..654..F 5
Dundalk ....1,143..B 13
Dundas ....19,115..D 14
Dunedin ....86..B 14
Dunnville ..11,556..E 15
Dunrobin* .....99..H 14
Dunsford ......96..A 16
Durham ....2,481..B 13
Dutton ....965..E 12
Eagle Lake ...187..H 8
Eagle River ....148..E 2
Ear Falls ...1,479..E 2
Earlton ....863..G 8
Echo Bay .....493..H 6
Eganville ...1,316..H 13
Egmondville ..492..D 12
Elk Lake .....627..G 7
Elliot Lake ..8,730..H 6
Elm View Subdivision* ....467..G 7
Elmira ......4,730..C 13
Elmvale .....1,166..A 14
Elmwood .....345..B 12
Elora ....2,422..C 13
Emeryville ..1,719..F 10
Emo ....768..F 1
Englehart ...1,739..G 8
Eramosa ....84..C 13
Erie Beach ...255..F 11
Erieau ....448..F 11
Erin ....1,982..C 14
Errol ....87..D 11
Espanola ...5,845..H 7
Essex ....5,549..F 10
Eugenia ......128..B 13
Exeter ......3,441..D 12
Fairground ....97..E 13
Fauquier .....643..F 7
Fenelon Falls .....1,618..A 16
Fergus ......5,980..C 13
Ferland ....87..E 3
Ferndale ......90..A 12
Field ....655..H 8
Finch ....402..H 16
Fingal ....322..E 12
Fitzroy Harbour ....317..H 14
Flesherton ....565..B 13
Foleyet ....637..F 6
Forest ......2,482..E 11
Formosa ......370..B 12
Fort Erie ..23,687..E 15
Fort Frances 9,198.°F 2
Foxboro ......590..K 12
Frankford ...1,811..K 12
Franz ....62..F 5
Gananoque ..5,056..J 14
Garson ......4,447..H 7
Geraldton ...3,033..E 4
Glen Cairn* .2,448..H 10
Glen Miller ...736..K 12
Glen Robertson 345..H 16
Glen Ross ......71..J 12
Glen Walter ..656..I 16
Glen Williams* .1,127..I 8
Glencoe .....1,806..E 11
Glenora* ....89..K 12
Goderich ....7,243.°C 11
Gogama ......578..G 7
Golden Lake ..229..H 12
Gooderham ...233..A 16
Gore Bay .....763.°H 7
Gowganda ....255..G 7
Grafton ......395..K 11
Grand Bend ..734..D 11
Grand Valley 1,072..C 13
Gravenhurst .7,908..A 15
Grimsby ...15,510..D 15
Grovesend* ....92..E 12
Guelph ....67,538.°D 13
Guilletville* .1,357..H 7
Haileybury ..4,657.°G 8
Haldimand .16,201..E 14
Haley Station* .97..H 9
Haliburton ...899..A 16
Hallebourg ....264..F 6
Halton Hills 34,232..C 14
Hamilton .312,003.°J 8
Hampton* ....597..I 8
Hanmer .....4,944..G 7
Hanover .....5,478..B 12
Harriston ...1,856..C 13
Harrow ....2,004..G 9
Harrowsmith ..550..J 13
Harty ....209..F 6
Hastings ......974..J 11
Havelock ....1,267..J 12
Hawk Junction 396..G 5
Hawkesbury .9,647..H 16
Hearst ......5,161..F 6
Hensall ....940..D 12
Hepworth .....374..A 12
Highgate .....411..F 11
Highland Grove ....82..I 11
Hillside* ......84..H 8
Hillside Gardens ....416..H 15
Hilton Beach .221..H 6
Holland Landing ....896..B 15
Holmesville ....97..C 11
Holtyre ....477..F 7
Honey Harbour ....239..A 14
Hornepayne .1,826..F 5
Hudson* ......543..E 2
Huntsville ..11,092..H 8
Hurkett ....54..F 4
Huron Park .1,217..C 12
Huttonsville ..448..C 14
Hyde Park ....208..E 12
Hymers ....83..F 3
Ignace ....334..F 2
Ingersoll ....8,034..E 13
Ingleside .....899..I 16
Inkerman ......86..I 15
Iona Station* ..88..E 11
Iron Bridge ...790..H 6
Iroquois ....1,263..I 15
Iroquois Falls .....6,807..F 7
Island Falls ...49..E 7
Island Lake ...89..H 6
Jellicoe ....160..F 4
Jersey* ....821..C 15
Jogues ....148..F 6
Johnstown* ...414..I 15
Kakabeka Falls ....325..F 3
Kaladar ......289..J 13
Kanata* ....4,635..H 10
Kapuskasing 12,542..F 6
Kashabowie ..110..F 3
Kearney ......279..H 8
Kearns ....451..F 8
Keene ....334..K 11
Keewatin* ..1,913..F 1
Kemptville ..2,483..I 15
Kenilworth ....89..C 13
Kenora ....10,361.°E 1
Keswick ....1,031..B 15
Killaloe Station .....693..H 12
Killarney .....475..H 7
Kincardine ..4,133..B 11
King City ...2,091..C 15
King Kirkland ...406..F 8
Kingston ...56,032.°K 14
Kingston Mills .40..J 14
Kingsville ...4,638..G 10
Kiosk ....332..H 8
Kirkland Lake .....13,486..G 8
Kitchener .131,870.°D 13
Kramer Subdivision* ....499..H 12
Laclu ....128..E 1
Lakefield ...2,218..J 11
Lakeside Beach* ......95..B 15
Lakeview* .....85..E 13
Lanark ....800..I 14
Lancaster .....533..H 16
Langton ......478..E 13
Lansdowne ...520..J 14
Larder Lake 1,427..G 8
Latchford .....451..G 8
La Vallee ......21..F 1
Leamington 11,036..G 10
Leaskdale ......90..B 15
Leckie Park Survey* .....443..D 14
Lefroy ....629..B 14
Limoges ......355..H 15
Lincoln ....14,235..D 15
Linden Beach* 508..G 10
Lindsay ...12,872.°B 16
Linwood* .....482..D 13
Lion's Head ..489..A 12
Listowel ....5,099..C 12
Little Current ...1,399..H 7
Lochiel* ....98..H 16
London ...240,392.°J 7
Long Sault ....965..I 16
Longlac .....1,400..E 5
L'Orignal ...1,366.°G 16
Louisville* .....91..F 11
Lower Wingham ...245..C 12
Lucan ......1,366..D 12
Lucknow ....1,127..C 12
Lukerville* ....94..G 10
Lynhurst ......463..E 12
Lyons ....88..E 12
MacTier ....794..I 8
Madawaska* ..371..H 11
Madoc ......1,357..J 12
Madsen* ......500..E 1
Magnetawan* .206..H 8
Maitland .....670..J 15
Manitouwadge ....3,258..F 5
Manitowaning .437..H 7
Mansfield and Dochart Area* ....1,128..H 10
Maple Grove ..550..C 16
Marathon ...2,409..F 5
Markdale ...1,357..B 13
Markham ..56,206..C 15
Markstay* ....491..G 7
Marmora ....1,313..J 12
Martintown* ..394..H 16
Massey ......1,330..H 7
Matachewan ..549..G 7
Matheson .....721..F 7
Mattagami Heights* ..1,670..F 7
Mattawa ....2,821..H 8
Mattice ....860..F 6
Maxville ......852..H 16
McGregor* ....665..G 10
McIntosh ......82..E 2
McKellar .....240..H 8
Mead ....31..F 6
Meaford ....4,253..A 13
Melbourne ....305..E 12
Meldrum Bay ..33..H 6
Merrickville ..871..I 14
Meyersburg* ...85..K 11
Miami Beach .504..B 14
Michipicoten ..202..G 5
Michipicoten River ....212..G 5
Middlemis* ....98..E 12
Middleville* ...85..I 14
Midhurst .....342..B 14
Midland ...11,444..A 14
Mildmay .....982..C 12
Milford Bay ..242..I 8
Millbrook .....885..B 16
Milton .....20,581.°D 14

Toronto, Canada's second largest city, is a busy Great Lakes port and industrial center. Downtown Toronto and the city's fine natural harbor are on the northwestern shore of Lake Ontario, *background.*

George Hunter, Miller Services

Milverton ...1,365..D 13	Pagwa River ...58..E 5	Rossmore* ....393..K 12	Stayner .....2,317..B 14	Vankleek
Minaki ......299..E 1	Paincourt ....324..F 10	Rummelhardt* .89..D 13	Stella* ....91..K 13	Hill ......1,591..H 16
Mindemoya ..458..H 7	Painswick* ...727..I 8	Ruthven .....461..G 10	Stirling .....1,527..J 12	Vaughan ...17,367..C 14
Minden .....697.°A 16	Paisley ....1,021..B 12	St. Agatha* ..542..D 13	Stockdale* ....89..K 12	Vermilion Bay 637..E 2
Mine Centre ..104..F 2	Pakenham ...371..H 14	St. Andrews	Stoney	Verner ....1,011..H 8
Mineral	Palmerston .1,943..C 13	West ......478..H 16	Creek ...29,944..D 14	Vernon .....237..H 15
Springs ......97..D 14	Paris ......6,487..D 13	St. Catha-	Straffordville .717..E 13	Verona .....689..J 13
Missanabie ...207..F 6	Parkhill ...1,295..D 11	rines ...123,351.°D 15	Stratford ..25,398.°D 12	Victoria .....91..C 14
Mississauga 250,017..D 15	Parry Sound 5,423.°H 8	St. Charles* ..468..G 7	Strathroy ..7,546..E 11	Victoria
Mitchell ....2,687..D 12	Pass Lake ....93..F 4	St. Clair	Stratton .....127..F 1	Harbour .1,291..A 14
Mitchell	Paynes	Beach ....1,948..F 10	Stroud* ......548..A 14	Vienna .....399..E 13
Corners* ....327..I 8	Mills* ....87..F 12	St. Clements* .843..J 8	Sturgeon Bay* .88..A 14	Vinemount* ...96..D 14
Molesworth ...91..C 12	Pearl* ....95..F 4	St. Isidore de	Sturgeon	Virginia-
Monkton* ....550..J 7	Pearson .....14..G 8	Prescott ....682..H 16	Falls ....6,352..H 8	town* ...1,279..G 8
Mono Centre* .89..B 14	Pefferlaw ...432..B 15	St. Jacobs ...787..D 13	Sturgeon	Wabigoon ....312..E 2
Moonbeam ...920..F 7	Pelham ....9,879..D 15	St. Mary's ..4,802..D 12	Point ......45..B 16	Wabos ....83..G 6
Moose	Pembroke ..14,722.°H 9	St. Pie X* ..1,067..E 7	Sudbury ...97,604.°H 7	Wahnapitae* 1,145..G 7
Factory ....849..D 7	Penetangui-	St. Thomas 26,721.°E 12	Sultan ......343..G 6	Walden ...10,366..H 7
Mooselanka	shene ....5,449.°A 14	Salem ....348..C 13	Sunbury* .....85..J 14	Walkerton ..4,591.°B 12
Beach* .....85..A 14	Perth ......5,639.°I 14	Sandford* ....86..B 15	Sundridge ...697..H 8	Wallaceburg 11,066..F 10
Moosonee ..1,793..D 7	Petawawa ..5,704..H 9	Sapawe ......91..F 2	Sunny Side* ..436..A 14	Walsingham ..233..E 13
Morrisburg .2,159..I 15	Peter-	Sarnia ...55,576.°E 10	Sutton ....2,500..B 15	Wardsville ...351..E 11
Morton ......91..J 14	borough .59,683.°I 9	Sault Ste.	Swastika .....627..F 7	Warren .....613..H 8
Mount Albert* 705..I 8	Petrolia ....4,338..E 11	Marie ...81,048.°H 6	Sydenham ....556..J 14	Warsaw .....242..J 11
Mount Forest 3,326..C 13	Pickering ..27,762..C 15	Savant Lake .202..E 3	Tamworth ....375..J 13	Wasaga
Mount Hope* .565..D 14	Pickering	Schomberg ...677..C 14	Tapleytown* ..85..D 14	Beach ...4,900..B 14
Mount	Beach* ....621..I 8	Schreiber ..2,072..F 4	Tara ....648..B 12	Washago ....423..A 15
Pleasant ...574..E 13	Picton ....4,612.°K 13	Schumacher .2,754..F 7	Taunton* .....89..B 15	Waterloo ..46,057..D 13
Murillo ......94..F 3	Pinecrest* ...485..G 7	Seaforth ...1,955..D 12	Tecumseh ..5,222..F 9	Watford ...1,349..E 11
Nairn ......461..H 7	Pinewood .....96..F 1	Searchmont ..375..G 6	Teeswater ...977..C 12	Waubaushene .718..A 14
Nakina .....673..E 5	Plantagenet ..900..H 16	Sebastopol* ...92..D 12	Terrace Bay 1,819..F 4	Waverley ....203..A 14
Nanticoke ..19,136..E 13	Pleasantview	Sebringville ..571..D 12	Thamesville ..960..F 11	Wawa ......4,375..G 5
Napanee ...4,765.°J 13	Survey* ....567..J 8	Seeleys Bay ..406..J 14	Thedford ....690..D 11	Webbwood ...456..H 7
Naughton ..1,076..H 7	Point	Shakespeare* .509..D 13	Thessalon ..1,803..H 6	Welland ...43,930.°E 15
Nephton .....83..J 11	Alexander* ...96..H 9	Shallow Lake .408..A 12	Thornbury ..1,276..B 13	Wellesley ....816..D 13
Nestor Falls ..296..E 1	Point	Shannonville ..325..K 13	Thorne ......441..G 8	Wellington .1,041..K 12
Neustadt ....536..B 12	Edward ...2,482..E 10	Shanty Bay ..316..B 14	Thornloe .....151..G 8	West Brook
New Dundee ..764..D 13	Pointe Anne ..373..K 12	Sharbot Lake .461..I 13	Thorold ...14,599..D 15	Heights* ....533..J 13
New	Porcupine ..1,303..F 7	Sharon* .....603..I 8	Thunder	West Lorne 1,145..F 11
Hamburg .3,008..D 13	Port Burwell .691..E 13	Shebandowan .235..F 3	Bay ....111,476.°F 3	Westmeath ...266..H 9
New	Port Carling .617..I 8	Sheguiandah ..126..H 7	Tilbury ....4,226..F 10	Westport ....638..I 14
Liskeard ..5,554..G 8	Port	Shelburne ..2,854..B 13	Tillsonburg .9,325..E 13	Westwood* ....86..J 11
Newboro ....255..J 14	Colborne .20,269..E 15	Silver Water ..126..H 6	Timagami ....693..G 8	Wharncliffe* ..98..G 6
Newburgh ....626..J 13	Port Elgin .4,909..B 12	Simcoe ...14,100.°E 13	Timmins ...44,010.°F 7	Wheatley ..1,613..G 10
Newbury ....387..E 11	Port Elmsley .86..I 14	Sioux	Tincap ....93..I 14	Whitby ...27,957.°C 15
Newcastle .31,582..C 16	Port Hope ..9,687..K 11	Lookout ..3,067..E 2	Tiverton ....815..B 12	Whitechurch-
Newington ...265..I 16	Port Loring ..331..H 8	Smiths Falls 9,149..I 14	Tobermory ...315..I 7	Stouffville 12,616..C 15
Newtonville ..272..C 16	Port	Smithfield ...319..K 12	Toronto ...633,318.°J 8	White River .945..F 5
Niagara	McNicoll .1,515..A 14	Smithville ..1,418..E 15	Torrance .....239..A 14	Whitefish* ...425..G 7
Falls ...69,423..D 15	Port Sandfield .56..I 8	Smooth Rock	Tottenham ..2,732..C 14	Whitney .....826..H 11
Niagara-on-the-	Port Stanley 1,706..E 12	Falls ....2,424..F 7	Trenton ...15,211..K 12	Wiarton ...2,087..A 12
Lake ...12,272..D 15	Portland .....253..J 14	Solina* ......93..C 13	Trout Creek .619..H 8	Wikwemi-
Nickel	Pottageville* .381..C 15	South	Trowbridge ...88..D 12	kong* ......895..H 7
Centre ..12,993..H 7	Powassan ..1,218..H 8	Baymouth ...73..H 7	Troy* ....84..D 14	Wilberforce ..229..I 11
Nipigon ....2,141..F 4	Prescott ...4,852..I 15	South Gillies ..15..G 3	Turkey Point .373..E 13	Wildfield ....373..C 14
Nixon ....86..E 13	Prince Albert .468..B 15	South	Tutela	Wilfrid ......87..B 15
Nobel ......484..H 8	Providence	Lancaster* ..264..H 16	Heights* ....457..E 14	Willisville* ...97..G 7
Nobleton ..1,356..C 14	Bay ......166..H 7	South	Tweed ....1,641..J 12	Winchester ..1,725..I 16
Noelville* ....856..H 8	Queensborough .99..J 12	Porcupine .4,843..F 7	Union ......235..E 12	Windsor ..196,526.°K 6
Norembega* ...88..F 7	Queensville* ..383..B 15	South River 1,084..H 8	Unionville ....781..F 7	Wingham ..2,851..C 12
Norland .....195..A 16	Queenswood* .757..H 15	Southampton 2,708..B 12	Val Caron ..4,036..H 7	Winona* ...1,411..J 8
Norman* .....224..H 7	Queenswood	Spanish ...1,257..H 7	Val Cote .....173..F 6	Woodstock .26,396.°D 13
Normandale ...86..E 13	Heights* ..1,980..H 15	Spragge .....240..H 6	Val Gagne ....292..F 7	Woodland
North Bay .51,639.°H 8	Rainy River 1,084..F 1	Spring Bay ..138..H 7	Val Therese* .903..H 7	Acres* .....389..J 11
North	Raith ....85..F 3	Springfield ...556..E 12	Valley	Woodville ....565..B 15
Brook ......221..J 13	Ramore .....125..F 7	Sprucedale ...209..H 8	East* ....19,427..H 7	Wyoming ..1,869..E 11
Northport* ....84..K 12	Ramsay ......111..G 6	Starratt-	Valrita* .....622..E 6	Yarker .....335..J 13
Norwood ..1,229..J 11	Rayside-	Olsen ......88..D 2	Vanier ...18,327..H 15	Zurich .....748..D 11
Nottawa* ....401..B 14	Balfour ..16,001..H 7			
Novar ....294..H 8	Red Lake ..2,155..D 2			
Oakville ..68,950..D 14	Red Lake			
Oba ....84..F 6	Road ......109..E 2			
Odessa ....1,020..J 13	Red Rock ..1,407..F 4			
Oil Springs ..619..E 11	Renfrew ...8,530..H 13			
Omemee ....763..B 16	Renton* ......99..E 13			
Onaping	Richmond			
Falls ....6,660..H 7	Hill ....34,504..C 15			
Opasatika ....537..F 6	Ridgetown ..3,078..F 11			
Orangeville 11,859.°C 14	Ripley .....571..C 12			
Orillia ...24,090..A 15	River Drive			
Orkney* ......86..D 14	Park* .....894..I 8			
Oshawa ..107,023..C 16	Roblin* ......92..J 13			
Osnabruck	Rockeliffe			
Centre* ....I 16	Park .....2,017..H 15			
Ottawa ..304,462.°H 16	Rockland ..3,881..H 15			
Owen	Rodney .....945..F 11			
Sound ...19,223.°A 13	Rolphton ....418..H 9			
Oxley* ....84..G 10	Rosedale .....91..A 16			
	Rosseau .....254..H 8			

Sources: Latest available census figures (1976 census, except 1971 census for unincorporated places).

585

The 1976 Canadian census reported that Ontario had 8,264,465 persons. The population had increased 7 per cent over the 1971 figure of 7,703,106.

The great majority of Ontarians—92 of every 100 persons—live in 12 per cent of the province's land area. This heavily populated region, the southernmost part of the province, lies south of Lake Nipissing. This area includes all of Ontario's metropolitan areas except those of Sudbury and Thunder Bay. Ontario has 10 Census Metropolitan Areas as defined by Statistics Canada. For the names and populations of these metropolitan areas, see the *Index* to the political map of Ontario.

About four-fifths of Ontario's people live in cities and towns. Ontario has 22 cities with populations of 50,000 or more. No other province has so many large cities. Toronto, the largest city of Ontario, is second in size only to Montreal among all Canadian cities. Other large cities of Ontario, in order of size, include Hamilton, Ottawa, Mississauga, London, Windsor, and Kitch-

ener. See the list of separate articles on the cities of Ontario listed in the *Related Articles* at the end of this article.

Almost 80 of every 100 Ontarians were born in Canada. The province also has large numbers of persons born in England, Germany, Italy, Scotland, and the United States. About 60 per cent of the people have English, Irish, Scottish, or Welsh ancestors, and 10 per cent are of French descent. About 95,000 of the French Canadians in Ontario speak only French.

Ontario has about 63,000 Indians, more than any other province. Most of the Indians live on 170 reservations, which cover a total of over 1½ million acres (610,-000 hectares) in the province.

Roman Catholics make up the largest single religious group in Ontario. Other large religious groups, in order of size, are members of the United Church of Canada and the Anglican Church of Canada. Ontario also has many Baptists, Lutherans, and Presbyterians.

POPULATION

This map shows the *population density* of Ontario, and how it varies in different parts of the province. Population density means the average number of persons who live in a given area.

	Persons per sq. mi.		Persons per km²
More than 30			More than 12
1 to 30			1 to 12
Less than 1			Less than 1

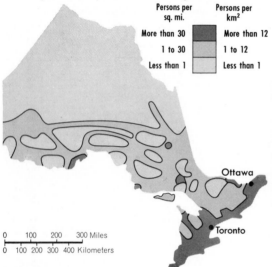

Ottawa

Toronto

0   100   200   300 Miles
0   100 200 300 400 Kilometers

WORLD BOOK map

George Hunter

Miners ride to the surface of a nickel mine in the Sudbury area. Ontario has rich deposits of nickel, gold, and uranium.

An Indian mends snowshoes in preparation for the Hudson Bay area's long, snowy winter. Most of the Indians in Ontario live on reservations.

Leavens, Photo Researchers

Farm Boys from Langton near Lake Erie tie tobacco leaves on a long stick. Then they hang the leaves in a barn to dry.

Don F. Smith, Miller Services

Carleton University's Maxwell MacOdrum Library symbolizes the modern design of the Rideau River campus. The university was established in Ottawa in 1942. A special feature is the school's Institute of Canadian Studies, founded in 1957.

ONTARIO /*Education*

Schools. The first *common* (elementary) schools in the Ontario region were established during the late 1780's. In 1807, the provincial government provided by law for a *grammar* (high) school in each of the province's eight districts. In 1816, the government provided for common schools throughout the province. A royal charter was granted in 1827 for a college in York (now Toronto). This college opened in 1843 as King's College, and became the University of Toronto in 1850.

Ontario's school system took its present basic form during the 1870's. All common and grammar schools became free elementary and high schools. Attendance between the ages of 6 and 16 was required by law, as it still is today. Ontario also set up provincial departments of education and university affairs headed by the minister of education, a cabinet member.

Today, Ontario has more than 4,600 public and *separate* schools. Separate schools are tax-supported schools operated mainly by Roman Catholics, but under control of the department of education. Catholics have a choice of supporting either the public schools or the separate schools with their taxes. Ontario has about 1,300 Roman Catholic separate schools. English is the language of instruction in most schools. The province has more than 300 French-language elementary schools and over 20 French-language secondary schools. Ontario offers a fifth year of high school education. It is usually required for entrance to universities. For information on the number of students and teachers in Ontario, see EDUCATION (table).

Libraries. By 1867, when Ontario became one of Canada's four original provinces, it had over 60 institutes that provided books. Today, Ontario has 320 public libraries, or about a third of all those in Canada. The province's libraries own over 8,400,000 volumes.

The Toronto Public Library is the largest library system in Canada. It has more than a million volumes, including a special collection of old children's books. Scholars of Italian literature visit the University of Toronto Library to study its famous collection of early Italian plays. The Legislative and Osgoode Hall law libraries in Toronto also own special collections. The National Library of Canada, and the libraries of the National Museum, National Research Council, Parliament, and Supreme Court of Canada are in Ottawa.

Museums. One of the world's outstanding collections of Chinese objects is owned by the Royal Ontario Museum in Toronto. The Ontario Science Centre, also in Toronto, features exhibits on lasers and space exploration. The National Museums of Canada in Ottawa have Indian and Eskimo displays, and exhibits on Canadian natural history.

Ottawa's Canadian War Museum displays objects from World Wars I and II. Articles of Canadian pioneers of the 1800's are featured in the Historical Museum of the Twenty, in Jordan. The Huronia Museum in Midland has exhibits on pioneer life of the region.

─── UNIVERSITIES AND COLLEGES ───

Ontario has 18 degree-granting universities and colleges, listed below. See the separate articles in WORLD BOOK on these institutions. For enrollments, see CANADA (table: Universities and Colleges).

Name	Location	Founded
Brock University	St. Catharines	1964
Carleton University	Ottawa	1942
Dominican College of Philosophy and Theology	Ottawa	1967
Guelph, University of	Guelph	1964
Lakehead University	Thunder Bay	1948
Laurentian University	Sudbury	1960
McMaster University	Hamilton	1887
Ottawa, University of	Ottawa	1848
Queen's University at Kingston	Kingston	1841
Royal Military College of Canada	Kingston	1874
Ryerson Polytechnical Institute	Toronto	1971
Toronto, University of	Toronto	1827
Trent University	Peterborough	1963
Waterloo, University of	Waterloo	1957
Western Ontario, University of	London	1878
Wilfrid Laurier University	Waterloo	1911
Windsor, University of	Windsor	1963
York University	Toronto	1959

Niagara Falls, with Horseshoe Falls and the Ontario Shore, *Background*, and the American Falls, *Foreground*

George Hunter, Publix

ONTARIO / *A Visitor's Guide*

About 18,000,000 tourists visit Ontario every year. The province's 250,000 lakes offer a variety of vacation attractions. Sparkling lakes and rushing rivers provide fine fishing and boating. Ontario's thick forests attract campers and hunters.

The sunny, southernmost resort region of the province, along Lakes Erie and Ontario, is known as *Canada's Sun Parlor.* Boat cruises take vacationers through the Thousand Islands and other islands in Ontario waters. The Kawartha and Muskoka lakes near Toronto are famous resort areas. Low, wooded hills line the shores of these lakes. The landscape becomes more rugged toward the northern and northwestern vacationlands of James Bay and Lake of the Woods. Many hunters fly in seaplanes to the far northern lakes. There they hunt bear, geese, moose, and other game.

───── PLACES TO VISIT ─────

Following are brief descriptions of some of Ontario's many interesting places to visit.

Bell Memorial is a huge stone sculpture of Alexander Graham Bell, inventor of the telephone. It stands near the Bell Homestead, now a telephone museum, in Brantford. There, in 1874, Bell worked on his invention.

Jack Miner's Waterfowl Sanctuary covers 300 acres (120 hectares) at Kingsville. It is dedicated to the memory of the famous Ontario naturalist.

Horseshoe Falls, near the Ontario-New York border, are the largest part of Niagara Falls. They are 2,600 feet (790 meters) wide and 158 feet (48 meters) high. See NIAGARA FALLS AND NIAGARA RIVER.

Manitoulin Island in Lake Huron is probably the world's largest fresh-water island. It is 90 miles (140 kilometers) long and 5 to 30 miles (8 to 48 kilometers) wide, and covers 1,068 square miles (2,766 square kilometers).

Martyrs' Shrine is 3 miles (5 kilometers) from Midland, near the site of old Fort Sainte Marie. The fort consists of the restored ruins of a Jesuit mission established in 1639. The Iroquois Indians destroyed this mission in 1649, during their war with the Huron Indians. Nearby stands a restored Huron village of the early 1600's.

Old Forts in Ontario that have been restored include Fort Erie in Fort Erie, Fort George in Niagara-on-the-Lake, Fort Henry in Kingston, Fort Wellington in Prescott, and Fort York in Toronto.

Ontario Place, in Toronto, is a cultural and recreational complex that features concerts, an ultramodern movie theater, and facilities for boating and picnics. It lies on artificially created islands in Lake Ontario.

Royal Botanical Gardens, in Hamilton, attracts visitors from many countries. It was established in 1941.

Upper Canada Village, near Morrisburg, shows life in the Ontario region from 1784 to 1867. Some buildings were moved to the village from the area now covered by Lake St. Lawrence.

National Parks. Ontario has four national parks— Georgian Bay Islands, in Georgian Bay; Point Pelee, on the Lake Erie peninsula; Pukaskwa, on the shore of Lake Superior; and St. Lawrence Islands, on the eastern Ontario mainland and on 17 of the Thousand Islands in the St. Lawrence River. Ontario also has seven national historic parks and sites. For the areas and main features of these parks, see CANADA (National Parks).

Provincial Parks. Ontario has more than 120 provincial parks. Most of them provide camping facilities and waterside ramps for small boats. For information on the provincial parks of Ontario, write to Ministry of Natural Resources, Division of Parks, Queen's Park, Toronto, Ontario M7A 1X5.

Ontario's best-known annual event is probably the Stratford Festival, held in Stratford from May to October. Famous actors appear in the dramas of William Shakespeare and other noted dramatists. Another popular event is the Royal Canadian Henley Regatta, the oldest rowing and sculling event in North America. This event is held in St. Catharines the last week of July. Other annual events in the province include the following.

January-March: International Boat Show in Toronto (January); Winter Carnivals throughout the province (January through March); Canadian National Sportsman's Show in Toronto (March).

April-June: Maple Festival in Elmira (April); Music Festival in Guelph (April); Blossom Festival on the Niagara Peninsula (May); Festival of Spring in Ottawa (May); Can-Am International Motor Racing at Mosport, near Oshawa (June); Queen's Plate Horse Race in Etobicoke (June); Annual Shaw Festival in Niagara-on-the-Lake (May-September).

July-September: Mariposa Folk Festival in Toronto (July); Annual Six Nations Indian Pageant in Brantford (August); Rockhound Gem-boree in Bancroft (early August); Central Canada Exhibition in Ottawa (late August); Canadian National Exhibition in Toronto (August-September).

October-December: Oktoberfest in Kitchener-Waterloo (October); Black Creek Pioneer Village Celebrations in Toronto (October-November); Royal Agricultural Winter Fair in Toronto (November).

Roger Jowett, Miller Services from FPG
Ontario Place in Toronto

Malak, Miller Services
Upper Canada Village near Morrisburg

Al Naidoff, Alpha
Fort Henry in Kingston

Thousand Islands in the St. Lawrence River near Lake Ontario
Photographic Survey Corp. from Photo Researchers

Land Regions. Ontario lies on a low plateau, crossed by two ranges of low hills. It has four main land regions. They are, from north to south: (1) the Hudson Bay Lowland, (2) the Canadian Shield, (3) the St. Lawrence Lowland, and (4) the Great Lakes Lowland.

The Hudson Bay Lowland curves around the southern part of Hudson Bay and extends as far south as Kesagami Lake. This flat region of northern Ontario is poorly drained, and has large *muskegs* (peat bogs). The lowland includes a narrow belt of *permafrost* (permanently frozen ground) near the Arctic.

The Canadian Shield is a vast, horseshoe-shaped region that covers almost half of Canada and part of the northern United States. This low, rocky region covers about half of Ontario. Small lakes and rivers surrounded by wooded hills attract many vacationers. The highest point in Ontario rises 2,275 feet (693 meters) in Timiskaming District.

The Canadian Shield is rich in game, minerals, and timber. Patches of clay are scattered throughout the region. These areas were formed by the soil of ancient glacial lakes. The largest clay area, known as the clay belt, extends from the Hearst area to the Quebec border. Farmers raise a variety of crops, including grains and vegetables, in the rich clay soil. Beef and dairy cattle graze on fenced grasslands. See CANADIAN SHIELD.

The St. Lawrence Lowland runs along the St. Lawrence River. In Ontario, it forms the tip of the wedge of land between the Ottawa and St. Lawrence rivers. Low hills rise above the fertile valleys. Farmers grow fruits, grains, and vegetables. Dairy farming is extensive there.

The Great Lakes Lowland lies along much of the Great Lakes in Canada and the United States. In Ontario, the region touches Lakes Erie, Huron, and Ontario. Great quantities of many crops are grown in the fertile gray-brown soil of the low, flat, southwestern section. These crops include corn, soybeans, tobacco, and tomatoes. The land rises gently in the northeast, where beef and dairy cattle are raised. The Niagara Escarpment, a high cliff or ridge, extends 250 miles (402 kilometers) from Manitoulin Island, through Bruce Peninsula, to Niagara Falls. The escarpment forms a natural shelter for Ontario's best fruit-growing belt. Many of Canada's largest cities and greatest industries are in the Great Lakes Lowland.

Shoreline and Coastline. Ontario's southern shores of bays, narrow inlets, and sandy beaches stretch 4,726 miles (7,606 kilometers). This shoreline, including 1,888 miles (3,038 kilometers) of offshore island shoreline, is on Lakes Erie, Huron, Ontario, and Superior. Ontario's Manitoulin Island is the world's largest inland island. It has an area of 1,068 square miles (2,766 square kilometers) in Lake Huron.

Oceangoing ships use the St. Lawrence Seaway to reach the Great Lakes ports of Ontario. These inland seaports include Hamilton, Port Colborne, Sarnia, Sault Ste. Marie, and Toronto. Thunder Bay on Lake Superior is the greatest wheat depot in North America. This city can store about 106,421,000 bushels of wheat for shipment. In northern Ontario, the province has a coastline of 752 miles (1,210 kilometers) on Hudson Bay and James Bay.

Rivers, Waterfalls, and Lakes cover a sixth of the province. A land rise separates the Ontario streams that flow into the Great Lakes from those that empty into the Ottawa River or Hudson Bay. Many lakes and rivers, some linked by canals, are important transportation routes.

Land Regions of Ontario

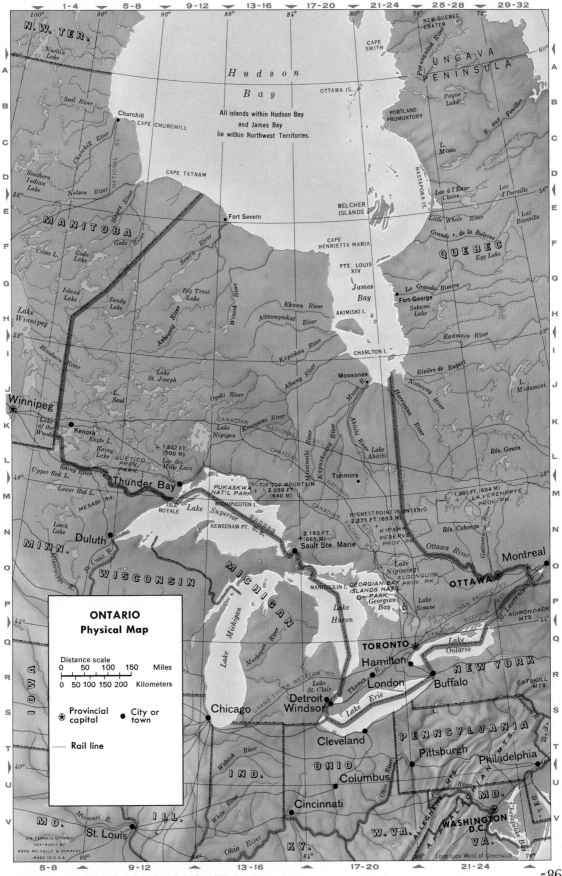

ONTARIO
Physical Map

Distance scale
0   50   100   150   Miles
0   50 100 150 200   Kilometers

⊛ Provincial capital   ● City or town

— Rail line

Specially created for World Book Encyclopedia by Rand McNally and World Book editors

Lowlands and Swamps surround the village of Moose Factory in the Hudson Bay Lowland. This poorly drained region in northern Ontario has large *muskegs*, which are marshes filled with peat.

Small Lakes, such as these in Quetico Provincial Park, are a familiar sight in the Canadian Shield region. The lakes and wooded hills of the region help attract many vacationers.

Rich, Fertile Soil makes farming an important industry around Bolton in the Great Lakes Lowland. Great quantities of many crops are grown in this region of Ontario.

The St. Lawrence River, a great natural highway for commerce, has contributed much to the growth of Ontario's economy. This waterway was enlarged during the 1950's to allow ocean vessels to reach the Great Lakes. Hydroelectric plants on the Niagara and other rivers provide Ontario with cheap power. The mighty Horseshoe Falls are formed by the Niagara River passing over the Niagara Escarpment.

The Ottawa River was part of the route of the early fur traders to Georgian Bay and the west. This river flows into the St. Lawrence River. The Ottawa drains the part of southern Ontario that does not lie in the Great Lakes basin. Other important southern rivers include the French, Grand, Thames, and Trent. The Detroit and St. Clair rivers are links between Lakes Erie and Huron. Lakes Huron and Superior are joined by the St. Marys River.

Ontario has about 250,000 lakes. Besides the Great Lakes, the largest are Lake of the Woods, Lake Abitibi, Lake Nipigon, Lake Nipissing, and Lake Seul.

Winds from the Great Lakes give southern Ontario a milder climate than the rest of the province. Northern Ontario gets bitter cold waves from the Arctic, or from the northwestern prairies. Frost-free periods range from six or seven months in the south to about three months in the north. The record high temperature in Ontario, 108° F. (42° C), occurred in Atikokan on July 11 and 12, 1936, and in Biscotasing on July 20, 1936. The lowest temperature, −73° F. (−58° C), occurred in Iroquois Falls on Jan. 23, 1935.

The Great Lakes and St. Lawrence lowlands have Ontario's longest summers and its highest temperatures. The average January temperature ranges from 12° F. (−11° C) in Ottawa to 24° F. (−4° C) in Windsor. The average July temperature is 69° F. (21° C) in Parry Sound and 73° F. (23° C) in Windsor.

The Hudson Bay Lowland and the Canadian Shield as far south as Lake Superior have long, cold winters. Summers are sunny, with hot days and cool nights. The temperature in January averages 12° F. (−11° C) in Trout Lake and −1° F. (−18° C) in Kapuskasing. The temperature in July averages 65° F (18° C) in Sioux Lookout and 61° F. (16° C) at Trout Lake.

Southern Ontario averages 38 inches (97 centimeters) of *precipitation* (rain, melted snow, and other moisture) a year. Rain falls fairly evenly all year, with no wet or dry seasons. In northern Ontario, precipitation averages 28 inches (71 centimeters) a year.

Heavy snow—over 10 feet (3 meters) a year—falls in a region extending from London to Owen Sound and Parry Sound. Annual snowfall in the rest of the province ranges from 5 to 9 feet (1.5 to 2.7 meters).

SEASONAL TEMPERATURES

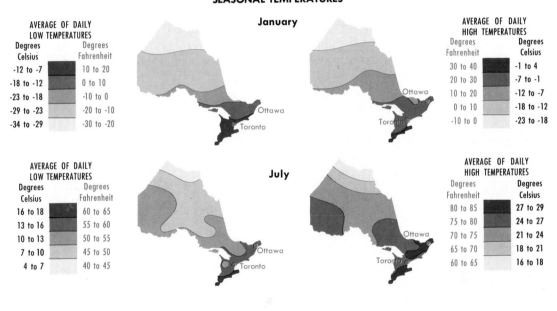

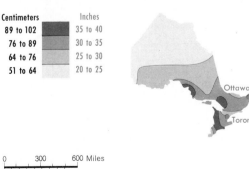

AVERAGE YEARLY PRECIPITATION
(Rain, Melted Snow, and Other Moisture)

Centimeters		Inches
89 to 102		35 to 40
76 to 89		30 to 35
64 to 76		25 to 30
51 to 64		20 to 25

WORLD BOOK maps

AVERAGE MONTHLY WEATHER

	TORONTO						OTTAWA				
	Temperatures				Days of		Temperatures				Days of
	F.°		C°		Rain or		F.°		C°		Rain or
	High	Low	High	Low	Snow		High	Low	High	Low	Snow
JAN.	31	18	-1	-8	16	JAN.	21	3	-6	-16	14
FEB.	31	17	-1	-8	12	FEB.	22	3	-6	-16	13
MAR.	39	25	4	-4	14	MAR.	34	17	1	-8	12
APR.	52	36	11	2	13	APR.	50	31	10	-1	12
MAY	65	46	18	8	12	MAY	65	43	18	6	12
JUNE	75	56	24	13	10	JUNE	75	53	24	12	10
JULY	81	61	27	16	10	JULY	80	58	27	14	11
AUG.	78	60	26	16	9	AUG.	78	55	26	13	10
SEPT.	71	53	22	12	11	SEPT.	69	48	21	9	11
OCT.	58	42	14	6	10	OCT.	55	37	13	3	12
NOV.	45	33	7	1	13	NOV.	40	26	4	-3	14
DEC.	34	23	1	-5	14	DEC.	25	10	-4	-12	15

The thriving industries of Ontario make it one of the richest economic regions of North America. Among the provinces and U.S. states, Ontario is a leading producer of numerous products. Ontario leads the provinces in manufacturing, its greatest source of income, and in farming and trapping. It ranks second only to Alberta in mining. Ontario is also a leader in the value of its forest products.

All values given in this section are in Canadian dollars. For the value of Canadian dollars in U.S. money, see MONEY (table).

Natural Resources. The valuable natural resources of Ontario have helped make the province rich. These resources include fertile soils, vast mineral deposits, great forests, wildlife, and plentiful supplies of water.

Soil in the northern Hudson Bay Lowland consists mostly of clay and muskeg. In the Canadian Shield, thin layers of clay and sand cover ancient rock. Near the Quebec border, glacial clays and silt cover the fertile clay belt. The St. Lawrence Lowland has black loams and well-drained sands over limestone and shale. The rich sandy soils in the Great Lakes Lowland help make it one of Ontario's chief farming regions.

Minerals. Sudbury District is famous for the variety and quantity of its minerals. It is the greatest single source of Ontario's mineral wealth. About one-fourth of the world's nickel supply and much platinum come from this region. The ores of the Sudbury District also contain large quantities of cobalt, copper, gold, and silver. In 1964, a huge field of copper, silver, and zinc ores was discovered near Timmins. Other major deposits lie in the Sturgeon Lake area of northwestern Ontario.

Rich iron ore deposits lie in Algoma District, in the Kirkland Lake and Timagami areas of northeastern Ontario, and near Marmora and Steep Rock Lake. In 1952, geologists discovered one of the Western world's largest single fields of uranium-bearing ore at Elliot Lake. A new area of copper and zinc ores was discovered in 1953 near Lake Manitouwadge.

Northern and central Ontario have large gold reserves, particularly around Kirkland Lake, Larder Lake, Red Lake, and Porcupine. Canada's first oil field, developed in Lambton County during the 1850's, still produces about 20,000 barrels of oil annually. Southern Ontario has pools of natural gas deep in the earth. This region also has deposits of gypsum, mica, and quartz.

Rich veins of silver and cobalt are near the town of Cobalt. The James Bay area has large reserves of clay and kaolin. Other minerals found in Ontario include asbestos, cadmium, calcium, lime, magnesium, salt, sand and gravel, and stone.

Forests. Ontario has about 167,000 square miles (432,500 square kilometers) of forest, of which about 137,000 square miles (354,800 square kilometers) are commercially valuable. Softwoods account for about 45 per cent of the commercial forests, and hardwoods for about 15 per cent. Mixed forests of both kinds of trees make up the remainder. The provincial government administers 90 per cent of the forest land, and individuals or firms must obtain cutting licenses.

Northern Ontario has huge forests of balsam, pine,

spruce, and other softwoods. It also has birch and poplar. Thick forests of hardwoods such as ash, beech, elm, maple, and walnut once covered the southern part of the province. Most of the timber in the south was cut during the 1800's, and the forests there now have second-growth trees.

Plant Life. Wild flowers are plentiful in Ontario. Trilliums and bloodroots blossom in spring. Autumn brings masses of asters and wild carrot blooms. Northern lakeside hills are thick with wild blueberry bushes in forest clearings. Shrubs and mosses grow in the far northern areas, where frost stays deep in the ground. Tamarack and spruce, which grow there, do not reach their usual height in this cold, poorly drained region.

Animal Life. Moose and caribou roam the wooded northlands of Ontario. Shy white-tailed deer pause to drink from streams in the Canadian Shield. People in this region often see the tracks of black bears. Fur-bearing animals such as beavers, minks, muskrats, foxes, and otters live throughout Ontario. Snowshoe hares are also plentiful in all parts of the province. Raccoons and rabbits are abundant in southern Ontario. Birds of Ontario include ducks, geese, and ruffed grouse. The haunting cries of loons pierce the air at dusk over Ontario's lakes. Brook trout, lake trout, northern pike,

Production of Goods in Ontario

Total value of goods produced in 1974—$23,091,743,000

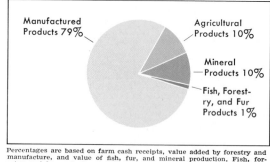

Manufactured Products 79%

Agricultural Products 10%

Mineral Products 10%

Fish, Forestry, and Fur Products 1%

Percentages are based on farm cash receipts, value added by forestry and manufacture, and value of fish, fur, and mineral production. Fish, forestry, and fur products are each less than 1 per cent.
Sources: Canadian government publications, 1975 and 1976.

Employment in Ontario

Total number of persons employed in 1974—3,016,100

Economic Activities		Number of Employees
Manufacturing	🧍🧍🧍🧍🧍🧍🧍🧍🧍	901,000
Community, Business, & Personal Services	🧍🧍🧍🧍🧍🧍🧍🧍	805,600
Wholesale & Retail Trade	🧍🧍🧍🧍🧍	517,700
Transportation, Communication, & Utilities	🧍🧍🧍	247,200
Government	🧍🧍🧍	226,200
Finance, Insurance, & Real Estate	🧍🧍	164,900
Agriculture	🧍🧍	118,000*
Fishing & Mining	🧍	35,500

*1975 figure.
Sources: *Estimates of Employees by Province and Industry, 1961-1974,* Statistics Canada, November 1975; *Fisheries Statistics of Canada, 1974,* Statistics Canada, July 1976; Labour Force Survey Division, Statistics Canada.

whitefish, and yellow pickerel are found in the lakes and rivers.

Manufacturing. Goods manufactured in Ontario have a *value added by manufacture* of about $18 billion yearly. This figure represents the value created in products by Ontario's industries, not counting such costs as materials, supplies, and fuels.

About half of Canada's industrial workers live in Ontario. They produce about half the country's manufactured products. The Toronto area ranks as Canada's leading industrial center. Since 1953, the provincial government's regional development program has established factory locations in many other parts of Ontario.

The production of transportation equipment is Ontario's chief industry, with an annual value added by manufacture of about $2⅔ billion. Automobile manufacturing is the chief activity. Most of Canada's motor-vehicle production takes place in Brampton, Oakville, Oshawa, and Windsor.

Food processing is Ontario's second-ranking industry. This industry's products have an annual value added of about $2 billion. More than half the province's slaughtering and meat packing takes place in Toronto. Fruit- and vegetable-canning plants and factories that make butter and cheese are scattered throughout the province.

The manufacture of fabricated metal products is the third most important industry, with an annual value added by manufacture of about $1,800,000,000. Primary metals industries in Ontario turn out products with an annual value added by manufacture of about $1,720,000,000. Hamilton is Canada's leading iron and steel producer. Sault Ste. Marie and Welland are also iron and steel centers. Other products manufactured in Hamilton include clothing, electrical equipment, and farm tools.

One of the Western world's largest papermaking machines is in Thunder Bay. Many pulp and paper mills operate in the Ottawa and Niagara Falls areas. Printing and publishing are also important industries, especially in Toronto.

Chemical plants in the Sarnia region produce gasoline, plastic resins, and other products. Canada's largest oil refinery and its only synthetic rubber factory are in Sarnia. Port Colborne has one of the largest nickel-processing plants in North America.

Agriculture. Ontario's farm products provide an annual income of about $2½ billion. The province has about 89,000 farms. They cover about 7 per cent of the province, and average 174 acres (70 hectares) in size.

Ontario farmers earn about 63 per cent of their income from livestock. The raising of beef cattle is the leading source of farm income. Milk ranks second among Ontario's farm products. Beef and dairy cattle graze on pastureland between the southeastern shores of Lake Huron and the lower western shores of Lake Ontario. Dairying is important eastward along Lake Ontario and the St. Lawrence River. Fine cattle, hogs, horses, and sheep come from Ontario stock farms.

Ontario farmers grow most of the feed crops they

FARM, MINERAL, AND FOREST PRODUCTS

This map shows where the leading farm, mineral, and forest products are produced. The major urban areas (shown in red) are the important manufacturing centers.

0   100   200 Miles
0   100   200   300 Kilometers
WORLD BOOK map

Grain Elevators dot the lakefront of Thunder Bay, *below.* This Lake Superior port forms the largest wheat depot in North America. From there, western grain moves east to Canadian and foreign markets.

Stage, Photo Researchers

587

A **Nickel Refinery** in Port Colborne, *left,* is one of the largest nickel-processing plants in North America. The production of primary metals is a leading industrial activity in Ontario.

George Hunter

need for their livestock. The major crops include barley, corn, hay, mixed grains, and oats. Ontario leads the provinces in the production of eggs and poultry. Its farmers also produce large quantities of butter and milk.

Ontario is also Canada's leading producer of fruits and vegetables. Orchards and vineyards of the famous Niagara fruit belt produce apples, cherries, grapes, peaches, pears, plums, and other small fruits. The chief vegetables include carrots, corn, cucumbers, onions, peas, and tomatoes. Tobacco, which flourishes along Lake Erie, provides about a tenth of Ontario's farm income.

Maple syrup and sugar are also produced in Ontario. Every spring, farmers in southern Ontario tap the gray-barked maples that grow in their *sugar bush* (groves of trees, mainly sugar maples).

Mining production in Ontario has an annual value of about $2 billion. Ontario accounts for about a fifth of Canada's total mineral production, and produces about two-fifths of its metallic minerals. Ontario leads all provinces and U.S. states in the production of gold, nickel, and silver. The province is also one of the leaders in uranium production.

Nickel is the most important mineral product of Ontario. Most of it comes from mines in Sudbury District. These mines also yield much of Canada's copper and platinum.

The principal gold-producing areas are near Kirkland Lake, Larder Lake, and Porcupine, all in northeastern Ontario. The Red Lake area in northwestern Ontario also produces gold. One of the Western world's largest uranium mines opened in 1955 at Elliot Lake, near Blind River.

Iron ore is mined at Capreol and Marmora, in Algoma District north of Sault Ste. Marie, at Kirkland Lake and Timagami in northeastern Ontario, and at Steep Rock Lake in southwestern Ontario. Natural gas and petroleum are obtained in southern Ontario and beneath the waters of Lake Erie. Other minerals produced in Ontario include cadmium, clay, cobalt, lime, magnesium, nepheline syenite, salt, sand and gravel, silver, stone, and zinc.

Forestry. Logs and pulpwood cut in Ontario have an annual value of about $188 million. Large stands of spruce trees in northern Ontario provide wood for much of the world's *newsprint* (paper used for newspapers).

Lumber camps in the northern forests cut logs of balsam, fir, jack pine, spruce, and white pine. Birch, maple, poplar, and other hardwoods are cut in southern Ontario.

Fur Industry accounts for about $13 million yearly. Pelts from mink raised on fur farms account for about $7 million of this total. Fur from animals caught by Ontario trappers accounts for the rest. Beaver are the most important animals trapped. The fur industry was important during the early days of the province. Today, about 12,500 trappers catch mostly beaver, fox, lynx, muskrat, otter, and raccoon.

Fishing Industry. Ontario's annual fish catch is valued at about $10 million. The province shares fishing rights with the United States in all the Great Lakes except Lake Michigan, the only one not bordering the province. Ontario also has important commercial fisheries in many other lakes and rivers. The most important fishes caught include bass, catfish, herring, perch, pickerel, pike, smelt, white bass, and whitefish. The province operates 14 fish hatcheries.

Ontario Editorial Bureau

Bunches of Ripe Grapes are picked by a mechanical harvester in a vineyard near St. Catharines, on the Niagara Peninsula of Ontario. Ontario is Canada's leading producer of grapes.

Factory Workers assemble a truck at Chatham. Automobile and truck manufacturing is Ontario's chief industry. Ontario does about half of Canada's manufacturing.

Electric Power. Hydroelectric power plants generate about half of Ontario's electricity. Plants operating on coal and other fuels supply the rest. Ontario Hydro, which operates the hydroelectric plants, is the largest publicly owned utility in Canada. Ontario and New York share the water of Niagara Falls under terms of a 1910 treaty between Canada and the United States. Ontario has about 70 hydroelectric plants, 5 fuel-electric stations, and 4 nuclear power plants.

Transportation. Waterways have played an important part in the history of Ontario. French explorers traveled up the Ottawa River in canoes. Early canals, particularly the Rideau and Trent systems, carried passengers and freight. The St. Lawrence Seaway, which was completed in 1959, brought oceangoing ships to the province's inland ports (see SAINT LAWRENCE SEAWAY).

During the navigation season, from mid-April to mid-December, many freighters travel between the ports of Ontario and those of the United States. Grain-carrying ships crowd the docks of Thunder Bay on Lake Superior. Ontario has 540 miles (869 kilometers) of canals, with over 100 locks. The largest is the Trent Canal, which extends 240 miles (386 kilometers) between Trenton and Georgian Bay. The Murray Canal, extending 7 miles (11 kilometers) through the Murray Isthmus, gives the Trent system an additional outlet to Lake Ontario.

More than 10 major airlines serve about 100 licensed airports in Ontario. A number of government, industrial, and private airlines carry passengers and supplies to distant mining and lumbering camps in the northern part of the province.

Ontario has about 10,000 miles (16,000 kilometers) of railways, about a fourth of Canada's total. About 4,000 miles (6,400 kilometers) of track stretch across northern Ontario. Southern Ontario, with about 6,000 miles (9,700 kilometers) of track, has Canada's finest railway network. Toronto is Ontario's chief rail center. CP Rail and the Canadian National Railways are the largest of the 12 railways operating in Ontario. The province owns the Ontario Northland Railway, whose main line runs through the clay belt and the silver-mining region to James Bay.

More than 75,000 miles (121,000 kilometers) of highways and roads crisscross the province. About a fourth of them are paved. Part of the east-west Trans-Canada Highway runs across Ontario. A 510-mile (821-kilometer) expressway from Windsor to the Quebec border was opened in 1963.

Communication. Louis Roy, a Frenchman from Quebec, published the first newspaper of the Ontario region. His paper, the *Upper Canada Gazette and American Oracle*, first appeared in 1793 in Newark (now Niagara-on-the-Lake). York (now Toronto) became the capital of Ontario in 1797, and the *Gazette* moved there in 1798. It was published until 1845. Today, about 300 newspapers are published in Ontario, including 50 dailies. The *Toronto Star* ranks first in circulation. Other leading dailies in Ontario, in order of size, include *The Globe and Mail* of Toronto, the *Hamilton Spectator*, the *Star* of Windsor, the *Ottawa Citizen*, and the *London Free Press*.

Station CKOC in Hamilton is Ontario's oldest radio station. It began broadcasting in 1922. The first television station, CBLT, was founded in Toronto in 1952. Today, Ontario has about 125 radio stations and approximately 25 television stations.

Indian Days. Three major Indian groups lived in what is now Ontario when white explorers first arrived. Chippewa Indians hunted beavers and small game in the forests north and east of Lake Superior. Huron Indians lived between Lake Huron and Lake Ontario. They depended mainly on cultivated crops for food. The Chippewa and Huron feared wandering bands of Iroquois Indians, who sometimes raided their camps.

Exploration. The first white man to explore the Ontario region was Étienne Brulé of France. He was sent in 1610 by Samuel de Champlain, the founder of Quebec. In 1613, Champlain paddled up the Ottawa River. He journeyed farther south in 1615, into the Lake Huron area. Champlain found this region rich in fur-bearing animals. Young Frenchmen followed his course into the wilderness to collect pelts. They traveled deep into the forests, and traded beads and knives to the Indians in exchange for furs. During the 1620's and 1630's, other French explorers, including Brulé and Jean Nicolet, traveled farther than Champlain. They explored the Lake Superior region and pushed on into Lake Michigan and beyond. See CHAMPLAIN, SAMUEL DE.

Early Settlement. French missionaries followed the fur traders into the Ontario region. In 1639, Jesuit priests built Fort Sainte Marie as the center of a group of missions. These missions, known as Huronia, were

Discovery of Nickel. In 1883, a curious railroad worker picked up some red mud, the first evidence of Ontario's rich deposits of nickel.

Life-Saving Insulin was discovered by Frederick G. Banting and Charles H. Best in Ontario in 1921.

IMPORTANT DATES IN ONTARIO

1610 Étienne Brulé of France became the first white man to explore the Ontario region.

1613 Samuel de Champlain of France explored the Ottawa River area.

1639 French missionaries founded Fort Sainte Marie.

1648-1649 Indians destroyed the French missions.

1763 The Ontario region became a British possession.

1784 Loyalists settled in the Ontario region.

1791 The region became the province of Upper Canada.

1812-1814 American forces invaded Upper Canada during the War of 1812.

1837 The Rebellion of 1837-1838 began.

1867 Ontario became one of the original four provinces of the Dominion of Canada on July 1.

1883 The world's largest copper-nickel reserves were discovered at Sudbury.

1904 Ontario's automobile industry began in Windsor.

1912 Ontario gained the territory north of the Albany River.

1945 Canada's first nuclear reactor started operating near Chalk River.

1952 The Western world's largest uranium deposit was discovered at Elliot Lake.

1959 The St. Lawrence Seaway opened.

1962 Canada's first nuclear power station began operating at Rolphton.

1964 Huge deposits of copper, silver, and zinc were discovered near Timmins.

1966 The first laboratory facilities of the Sheridan Park Research Community were opened near Toronto.

1967 The nuclear power station at Douglas Point began operating.

1972 Ontario began a program of free medical and hospital care for the elderly and the poor.

---

established among the Huron Indians. Later, the Iroquois made war on the Huron and their white allies. They destroyed the missions in 1648 and 1649.

During the 1650's and 1660's, French explorers entered the region north of Lake Superior. These men included Pierre Esprit Radisson and Médard Chouart, Sieur des Groseilliers. Their explorations led to the founding of the Hudson's Bay Company in London (see HUDSON'S BAY COMPANY).

In 1763, at the end of the French and Indian War, France gave the Ontario region to Great Britain. At that time, there were only a few scattered French settlements near what are now Kingston, Niagara Falls, and Windsor. Little further settlement took place until 1784. That year, after the American Revolutionary War, persons loyal to England began arriving from the United States. About 6,000 of these United Empire Loyalists, as they were called, had arrived by 1785. They settled west of the Ottawa River. The Loyalists had lost their homes and wealth. The British government gave them food, clothing, land, livestock, and seed. About 4,000 other settlers also arrived from the United States. See UNITED EMPIRE LOYALIST.

Upper Canada. In 1791, the Ontario region became the separate province of Upper Canada. Newark (now Niagara-on-the-Lake) was the capital. The British government appointed a lieutenant governor to govern the province. The lieutenant governor appointed a 7-member legislative council, and the people elected a 16-member legislative assembly. Colonel John Graves Simcoe, the first lieutenant governor, promoted road-building and expanded settlement. In 1793, Simcoe chose York (now Toronto) as the site for a new capital,

Thousands of Slaves fled from the U.S. to Ontario in the 1850's. Antislavery leader John Brown had many followers around Chatham.

Ontario's Northern Boundary was extended in 1912 from north of the Albany River to Hudson and James bays. The gray area of the map, *left*, shows Ontario from 1867 to 1912, and the light blue area shows the land added in 1912. The map on the *right* shows present-day Ontario.

The Famous Dionne Quintuplets were born at Callander in 1934.

American Forces Captured York (now Toronto), the capital of Upper Canada, during the War of 1812.

Alexander Graham Bell worked on the principle of the telephone in Brantford in 1874.

Callander

HISTORIC ONTARIO

TORONTO ★

Brantford

The Welland Canal, which opened in 1829, links the Great Lakes shipping lanes with the St. Lawrence River.

A Huge Power Plant on the Canadian side of Niagara Falls has produced electricity for Ontario since 1922.

and the government completed moving there in 1797.

Gradually, more settlers arrived, some in organized groups. Others were brought by land-development firms such as the Canada Company. These settlers were assigned farms on land owned by the companies. Many Americans who liked frontier life or wanted more land also came. Sometimes whole communities moved north. Such a group of Pennsylvania Dutch, for example, settled near what is now Kitchener. Men from the Hudson's Bay Company posts in the far north settled with their families in the southern towns. Most of these people were Scottish or English.

The War of 1812 between Great Britain and the United States began 21 years after Upper Canada was created. More than half the people of the colony were former Americans. But most of them were loyal to their new homeland. British and Canadian troops halted invading United States forces in several battles in Upper Canada. See WAR OF 1812 (Chief Battles of the War).

Early Industrial Growth. The population of Upper Canada grew rapidly during the 1820's. Towns such as Bytown (now Ottawa) became thriving centers of trade. Canals, mills and small factories, and roads were built. The Rideau, Trent, and first Welland canals date

591

from this period. In 1825, the Erie Canal linked Lakes Erie and Ontario with New York City. Large groups of immigrants, most of them from Ireland, came after these transportation improvements were made.

Political Unrest. During the 1830's, Upper Canadians became greatly dissatisfied with their government. They elected only the legislative assembly. The real power lay with the lieutenant governor, who was appointed by the British government. The lieutenant governor appointed the legislative council and his cabinet. The legislative council generally represented the wealthy and powerful persons of the province. The council often blocked legislation that the people wanted and the assembly had passed. This legislation included building new roads and schools, and providing free land to settlers.

Demands for political reform were ignored by both the provincial and British governments. In 1837, William Lyon Mackenzie, a member of the assembly, and a small group of followers rebelled. British troops put down the uprising easily and quickly. Several rebels were executed, some were imprisoned, and others, including Mackenzie, fled to the United States. See REBELLION OF 1837-1838.

After the rebellion, the British government sent the Earl of Durham to investigate the political situation in Upper Canada. Durham urged that Upper Canada and Lower Canada (part of present-day Quebec) be united under one government. He also recommended that the government be fully responsible to the voters. In 1840, the British government passed the Act of Union. The next year, Upper and Lower Canada formed the single province of Canada. By 1849, it had gained fully responsible government. See UNION, ACT OF.

Confederation. In 1864, delegates from the province of Canada proposed a federal union of all the British provinces in eastern North America. All except Prince Edward Island and Newfoundland agreed to join the confederation. On July 1, 1867, the British North America Act created the Dominion of Canada. New Brunswick, Nova Scotia, Ontario, and Quebec became provinces in the Dominion. Ottawa was made the federal capital, and Sir John A. Macdonald of Ontario became the first prime minister of Canada. John S. Macdonald, unrelated to him, was the first prime minister of Ontario. See BRITISH NORTH AMERICA ACT.

Progress as a Province. Ontario's economy grew slowly during the depression that followed confederation. Farming increased with the development of scientific methods and the use of machinery. Ontario's pulp and paper industry began, and woodcutting expanded in the Canadian Shield. During the 1880's, construction of the Canadian Pacific Railway and extension of canals helped attract settlers to western Ontario. Manufacturing increased, but many Ontarians moved to the United States for better job opportunities.

In 1883, the world's richest copper-nickel deposits were found near Sudbury. Major mining operations did not begin until after 1892, when a practical process for separating copper and nickel was developed.

The Early 1900's. The long depression ended in 1897, and manufacturing began to increase rapidly. Cobalt became a thriving mining center after a huge silver deposit was discovered near the city in 1903. Extensive mineral exploration took place throughout the Canadian Shield. Within a few years, many valuable new mineral deposits were discovered. The region soon became one of the world's richest mining areas.

In addition to mining, the pulp and paper industry and other manufacturing activities grew to major importance. Ontario's automobile industry began in 1904. Automobile parts were ferried across the Detroit River from Detroit, Mich., and cars were assembled in Windsor. In 1906, the provincial government established the Hydro-Electric Power Commission of Ontario. This agency developed and expanded Niagara Falls and other hydroelectric sources to provide more power for the growing industries.

In 1912, Ontario's northern boundary was extended from north of the Albany River to Hudson and James bays. This action gave the province its present area. The outbreak of World War I (1914-1918) hastened Ontario's economic growth. Ontario led the provinces in the production of weapons and other military supplies.

During the 1920's, after a short depression, old cities became larger and new ones grew in number. Bush pilots flew land surveyors and prospectors to the northern forest regions, and new mines were developed. Many Finns and Scandinavians, and French Canadians from Quebec, settled there. Industrial activity, especially automobile production, continued to grow. Other important activities included the manufacture of iron and steel, and of pulp and paper. The prosperity ended with the Great Depression of the 1930's. During the 1930's, many Jewish families escaped Nazi persecution in Germany and came to southern Ontario.

The Mid-1900's. During World War II (1939-1945), Ontario's factories, farms, and mines increased production to help arm and feed the Allied armies. Later, hundreds of thousands of Europeans left their war-torn countries and came to live in Ontario. More than half of the 3 million persons who settled in Canada between 1945 and 1970 made their homes in Ontario. Ontario's population rose from about 4 million to 7½ million.

--- **THE PRIME MINISTERS OF ONTARIO*** ---

	Party	Term
1. John S. Macdonald	Liberal	1867-1871
2. Edward Blake	Liberal	1871-1872
3. Oliver Mowat	Liberal	1872-1896
4. Arthur S. Hardy	Liberal	1896-1899
5. George W. Ross	Liberal	1899-1905
6. James P. Whitney	Conservative	1905-1914
7. William H. Hearst	Conservative	1914-1919
8. Ernest C. Drury	United Farmers of Ontario	1919-1923
9. George H. Ferguson	Conservative	1923-1930
10. George S. Henry	Conservative	1930-1934
11. Mitchell F. Hepburn	Liberal	1934-1942
12. Gordon D. Conant	Liberal	1942-1943
13. Harry C. Nixon	Liberal	1943
14. George A. Drew	Progressive Conservative	1943-1948
15. Thomas L. Kennedy	Progressive Conservative	1948-1949
16. Leslie M. Frost	Progressive Conservative	1949-1961
17. John P. Robarts	Progressive Conservative	1961-1971
18. William Davis	Progressive Conservative	1971-

*The title *prime minister* was changed to *premier* in 1972.

In 1945, Canada's first nuclear reactor went into operation near Chalk River. Laboratories there worked to find ways to develop cheap nuclear power for Ontario's expanding industries. By 1960, the station had five experimental reactors and other research facilities, including a particle accelerator.

Ontario experienced its greatest economic growth after World War II. By the early 1950's, manufacturing production in the province had doubled. Many mineral discoveries contributed to the economic boom. In 1952, one of the world's largest single uranium ore deposits was found at Elliot Lake. In 1953, prospectors discovered another huge uranium deposit near Bancroft and a rich zinc-copper field on the shore of Lake Manitouwadge.

Also during the 1950's, pipelines were laid to carry natural gas and oil to Ontario from western Canada. The oil, piped to Sarnia, led to the development of that city's great refining industry. Ontario's iron and steel industry grew rapidly. Ontario also expanded hydroelectric stations at Niagara Falls and other sites in the province.

In 1954, Toronto and its surrounding communities began to operate under a combined-government plan. Services for the entire area, including police protection and public transportation, are administered by the combined government. Such services as fire protection and health are handled by each community.

Ontario's economic growth continued during the 1960's. Factory production again doubled. The province's growing industries required great increases in electric power. Ontario began to make use of nuclear-power research conducted at the Chalk River reactor. Canada's first nuclear power station, at Rolphton, began operating in 1962. Its success led to the development of the nation's first full-scale nuclear station, which began operating at Douglas Point in 1967. A nuclear plant located at Pickering began operations in 1971.

Many other research programs were started to promote Ontario's industrial growth. In 1966, the Sheridan Park Research Community, consisting of several private industries, set up the first of its multi-million dollar facilities near Toronto.

In 1964, a huge field of copper, silver, and zinc ores was discovered near Timmins. An open-pit mine began operating there in 1966.

Automation caused unemployment in Ontario as machines replaced unskilled workers in factories and on farms. In 1965, the provincial and federal governments established a five-year program to fight poverty. The program included development of farmland through better land use and irrigation. Ontario also received federal aid for urban renewal in its rapidly growing cities.

Ontario Today accounts for about half of Canada's manufacturing, a third of the nation's farming, and a fifth of its mining. The province has one of the lowest unemployment rates in Canada. Manufacturing provides jobs for about a third of Ontario's workers. The chief industries manufacture automobiles, food products, and metal products. Large markets in the United States—plus access to European markets through the St. Lawrence Seaway—assure a continuing demand for Ontario's products in the 1970's.

Tourism is becoming vital to Ontario. The province's northern woods and lakes are attracting an increasing number of visitors. Private and government facilities, including a system of provincial parks and campsites, are being improved.

Ontario strongly supports progress in its schools and spends about 35 per cent of its budget on education. Since 1945, the province has combined most of its school boards, reducing the number from 5,649 to 194. In addition, 22 regional colleges of applied arts and technology have been established. They prepare students for technical and managerial jobs.

Ontario faces several problems in the 1970's. Along with rapid industrial growth have come overcrowded cities and polluted air and water. About 90 per cent of Ontario's people live in the southern 10 per cent of the province. In spite of the prosperity in Ontario, poverty exists among about 10 per cent of the province's families. In 1972, Ontario began to provide free medical and hospital care for persons aged 65 and older and for the poor.

NORMAN L. NICHOLSON, JOHN T. SAYWELL, and VAL SEARS

ONTARIO/Study Aids

Related Articles in WORLD BOOK include:

BIOGRAPHIES

Blake, Edward	King, W. L. Mackenzie
Bowell, Sir Mackenzie	Macdonald, Sir John A.
Brown, George	Mackenzie, Alexander
Cartwright, Sir Richard J.	Mackenzie, William Lyon
Dent, John C.	Macmillan, Sir Ernest C.
Diefenbaker, John G.	MacPhail, Agnes C.
Durham, Earl of	Massey, Vincent
Fleming, Sir Sandford	Mowat, Sir Oliver
Gordon, Charles W.	Mulock, Sir William
Gould, Glenn	Pearson, Lester Bowles
Hughes, Sir Samuel	Simcoe, John G.
Kerwin, Patrick	Thomson, Tom

CITIES

Brantford	Burlington	Cornwall
Hamilton	Oshawa	Sault Sainte Marie
Kingston	Ottawa	Sudbury
Kitchener	Peterborough	Thunder Bay
London	Saint Catharines	Toronto
Niagara Falls	Sarnia	Windsor

HISTORY

Canada, History of	Rebellion of 1837-1838
Fort Frontenac	United Empire Loyalist

PHYSICAL FEATURES

Canadian Shield	Lake Huron	Manitoulin Islands
Detroit River	Lake of the Woods	Moose River
Georgian Bay	Lake Ontario	Muskoka Lakes
Hudson Bay	Lake Saint Clair	Niagara Falls and
James Bay	Lake Superior	Niagara River
Lake Erie		

Ottawa River	Saint Lawrence	Saint Marys River
Rainy Lake	River	Thousand Islands

PRODUCTS

For Ontario's rank in production, see:

Automobile	Copper	Milk	Tobacco
Bean	Gold	Paper	Tomato
Butter	Grape	Salt	Turkey
Cattle	Iron and Steel	Silver	Uranium
Cherry	Maple Syrup	Textile	Wine

OTHER RELATED ARTICLES

Rideau Canal	Soo Canals
Saint Lawrence Seaway	Welland Ship Canal

Outline

I. Government
    A. Lieutenant Governor   E. Local Government
    B. Premier   F. Taxation
    C. Legislative Assembly   G. Politics
    D. Courts
II. People
III. Education
    A. Schools   C. Museums
    B. Libraries
IV. A Visitor's Guide
    A. Places to Visit   B. Annual Events
V. The Land
    A. Land Regions   C. Rivers, Waterfalls,
    B. Shoreline and Coastline   and Lakes
VI. Climate
VII. Economy
    A. Natural Resources   F. Fur Industry
    B. Manufacturing   G. Fishing Industry
    C. Agriculture   H. Electric Power
    D. Mining   I. Transportation
    E. Forestry   J. Communication
VIII. History

Questions

What is Ontario's chief manufacturing activity?
Where do the great majority of Ontarians live?
How did Ontario pioneer in Canada's development of cheap nuclear power?

What is Ontario's *Golden Horseshoe?* Where is it?
What is Ontario's most famous annual event?
What caused the Rebellion of 1837-1838?
What is the major mineral product of Ontario?
How do ocean vessels reach Ontario's inland ports?
How much of Canada's manufacturing, mining, and farming does Ontario account for?
When did Ontario's greatest period of economic growth begin?

Books for Young Readers

BURNFORD, SHEILA. *The Incredible Journey.* PaperJacks (Markham, Ont.); Little, Brown (Boston), 1961. Fiction.

FREEMAN, BILL. *Shantymen of Cache Lake.* James Lorimer (Toronto), 1975. Fiction.

HARRINGTON, LYN. *Ontario.* Scholars' Choice (Stratford, (Ont.); Childrens Press (Chicago), 1975.

HOUSTON, JAMES A., and KING, B. A. *Ojibwa Summer.* Longman (Don Mills, Ont.), 1973.

MINHINNICK, JEANNE. *At Home in Upper Canada.* Clarke, Irwin (Toronto), 1970.

REANEY, JAMES. *The Boy with an R in His Hand.* Macmillan (Toronto), 1965. Fiction.

REID, RAYMOND A. *Footprints in Time: Ontario.* Dent (Don Mills, Ont.), 1967.

STEVENS, JOHN, ed. *The Ontario Experience.* Macmillan (Toronto), 1976.

Books for Older Readers

DEAN, W. G., ed. *The Economic Atlas of Ontario.* Univ. of Toronto Press, 1969.

GREENHILL, RALPH A., and others. *Ontario Towns.* Oberon (Ottawa), 1974.

JOHNSON, J. KEITH, ed. *Historical Essays on Upper Canada.* McClelland (Toronto), 1975.

JUDD, WILLIAM W., and SPEIRS, J. M., eds. *A Naturalist's Guide to Ontario.* Univ. of Toronto Press, 1964.

KILBOURN, WILLIAM, ed. *The Toronto Book: An Anthology of Writings Past and Present.* Macmillan (Toronto), 1976.

MACDONALD, DONALD C., ed. *Government and Politics of Ontario.* Macmillan (Toronto), 1975.

WARKENTIN, GERMAINE, ed. *Stories from Ontario.* Macmillan (Toronto), 1974.

WISMER, CATHY. *Faces of the Old North.* McGraw (Scarborough, Ont., and New York City), 1974.

ONTARIO, LAKE. See LAKE ONTARIO.

ONTARIO PLACE. See ONTARIO (Places to Visit).

ONTOLOGY. See METAPHYSICS (Branches).

ONYX, *AHN icks,* is a term used loosely to apply to a banded marble and also to agate, a fine-grained variety of quartz (see AGATE).

Ordinary onyx of quartz or agate is dyed black and white, green and white, or red and white, and so on. *Sardonyx* is brown and white onyx. Onyx is strong and hard and takes a high polish. It is widely used in the carving of cameos and intaglios. Today, jewelers refer to dyed, single-color agate as *onyx.* When they speak simply of onyx, they mean the black stone. *Green onyx* is the same stone dyed green.

Onyx marble (Mexican onyx) is a variety of calcite marble which is found on the walls of caves. Mexican onyx shows a banding like that of agate, but it is much coarser. The colors of Mexican onyx range from white to green, red, and brown. Much of this soft onyx marble is cut into gem stones, colored with an aniline dye, then set in inexpensive native silver jewelry. The stones are brittle and are not durable. Mexican onyx is also used as a decorative stone.   FREDERICK H. POUGH

See also CAMEO; GEM (color picture); SARDONYX.

OOSTENDE. See OSTEND.

OOZE is a name for the mud found on the bottom of the ocean in deep waters. One variety of this mud consists of red clay and occurs extensively on the bottom of the Pacific Ocean. Another variety is made up mostly of shells and skeletons of tiny sea organisms called *foraminifera, radiolaria,* and *diatoms.* All three are termed *plankton,* which is the name for helpless forms of life which cannot swim, but can only float in the water and drift with currents. The foraminifera make their shells from calcium carbonate that is contained in solution in the sea water. A type of limestone called *nummulitic limestone* is made up mostly of the shells. The hard parts of the radiolaria and diatoms usually contain silicon.

The term ooze is also used for any mud, either on the surface of the earth, or in the beds of rivers, streams, ponds, or lakes.   ELDRED D. WILSON

OPA. See PRICE CONTROL.

OPAL is a gem stone that contains a rainbow of colors. But it is made mostly of the elements of common sand, or silica. An opal's background color may be black, brown, or white. But cut and polished opals reflect many colors when they are held to the light. The opal is the birthstone for the month of October.

The most prized opals are the deep-glowing black

gems from New South Wales, Australia. The finest of these stones are lightened by brilliant flashes of reds and yellows in addition to greens and blues.

The opal is unique among gem stones, because it is not found in nature in the form of crystals. Instead it is found in irregular patches, often filling cavities in rocks. Gemologists speak of an opal as a hydrated silica gel, because it contains water along with the silica. The water content makes some opals a risky buy. Many of them *check* (crack) after a long time in dry air. The checking occurs as the water in the gel dries out.

Most scientists believe the color flashes are caused by the water in the gems. Each layer of silica gel in an opal has a different *index of refraction*. That is, it bends light at a different angle. The angle varies according to the amount of water in the layer. Scientists believe that these different bendings break up the light that strikes the stone into its rainbow colors.

There are many different kinds of opals. They are classified according to the color of their background and the brilliance of the light rays that they reflect. Opals that give off brilliant flashes of color are *precious* opals. The black opals of New South Wales and the white opals of Europe, Queensland, and Mexico are examples of precious opals. The *girasol* is a precious opal. Its background is bluish-white with reddish reflections. The *common* opal is usually not a precious stone and shows no colors. The *fire* opal is a variety of common opal. It is red—often without color flashes. Other common opals may be transparent, and red, brown, green, or yellow. Some opals are almost colorless.

Since the beauty of the opal lies in its internal color flashes, it is never cut with facets, like a diamond. Instead, it is cut with a gently rounded convex surface.

Large opals of the world include a Hungarian opal that weighs 594 grams, now in the Museum of Natural History in Vienna. The *Roebling* opal, which was found in Nevada, is the most beautiful American opal. It is almost pitch black, with color flashes of great brilliancy. It weighs 530 grams and is on display at the National Museum of Natural History in Washington, D.C. The huge *Desert Flame of Andamooka* opal weighed over 6,800 grams when found in Australia in 1969. It was split in two and sold for over $1 million. FREDERICK H. POUGH

See also GEM (color picture).

OPAL GLASS. See GLASSWARE (Milk Glass).

OPARIN, ALEXANDER IVANOVICH (1894-   ), is a Russian biochemist. He developed a theory that explains how life on earth originated from chemical substances. His ideas became the basis of many modern scientific theories of the origin of life. Oparin has also done much research on the biochemistry of converting raw agricultural crops into such products as bread, sugar, tea, tobacco, and wine.

Oparin's theory of the origin of life rests on his belief that the earth's early atmosphere contained mostly ammonia, hydrogen, methane, and water vapor—not nitrogen and oxygen as it does today. He suggested that the chemical molecules necessary for life formed spontaneously in such an atmosphere. These molecules combined and formed more complex molecules. These complex molecules formed still larger combinations, and finally they developed into the first living cells through hundreds of millions of years.

Oparin was born near Moscow. He graduated from

Moscow State University in 1917. He first published his theory in 1923 and expanded it in a book called *The Origin of Life* (1936). In 1946, Oparin was appointed director of the Bakh Institute of Biochemistry in Moscow. HAROLD J. MOROWITZ

OPEC. See ORGANIZATION OF PETROLEUM EXPORTING COUNTRIES.

OPECHANCANOUGH. See INDIAN WARS (Jamestown).

OPEN CITY. See INTERNATIONAL LAW (The Laws of War).

OPEN-DOOR POLICY is a term used in international relations. It means that powerful countries have equal opportunities to trade with colonial, or so-called backward, countries. When countries agree to observe the Open-Door Policy in an area, they simply agree to permit their merchants and investors to trade freely there.

John Hay, United States secretary of state, started the idea of the Open Door in 1899. At that time, several Western powers had special interests in China. Each power was trying to get all the trading rights for itself. The U.S. secretary of state sent notes to the competing powers, asking them to maintain complete equality for all nations that wished to trade with China. The powers accepted Hay's proposal and signed treaties agreeing to observe the Open-Door Policy. Since then, the Open-Door Policy has been used in other areas. DWIGHT E. LEE

See also CHINA (Fall of the Manchus).

OPEN-END INVESTMENT COMPANY. See MUTUAL FUND.

OPEN-HEARTH FURNACE. See IRON AND STEEL (Methods of Making Steel).

OPEN HOUSING refers to the civil rights belief that a person may live wherever he chooses and can afford to live. The United States government and many local and state governments have passed laws and regulations to protect this right. The laws prohibit discrimination in the sale and rental of housing on the basis of race, religion, or nationality. Open housing laws are sometimes called *fair housing* laws or *open occupancy* laws.

The U.S. Civil Rights Act of 1968 contained the first national open housing law of the 1900's. The act prohibits discrimination in the sale or rental of about 80 per cent of all housing in the United States. It applies to all housing except (1) owner-occupied dwellings of four or fewer units, such as boarding houses; and (2) single-family houses sold or rented without the aid of a broker or realtor. In June, 1968, the Supreme Court of the United States went beyond the 1968 act. It ruled that a federal law passed in 1866 prohibits discrimination in the sale and rental of all property.

OPEN-PIT MINE. See IRON AND STEEL (How Iron Is Mined); MINING (Kinds of Mining; picture).

OPEN SEASON. See GAME (Game Laws).

OPEN SHOP is a business that employs both union and nonunion workers. It is the opposite of a *closed shop*, where only union members may be employed. A union may represent the workers in an open shop if a majority of them belong to the union. But no one must be required to belong to the union in order to be hired. See also CLOSED SHOP. GERALD G. SOMERS

OPENING OF THE WEST. See WESTERN FRONTIER LIFE; WESTWARD MOVEMENT.

Scene from a production by the Royal Opera, Covent Garden, London; Reg Wilson

Elaborate Scenery and Colorful Crowd Scenes add excitement to many operas. The spectacular "Triumphal March" shown above takes place in Act II of Giuseppe Verdi's tragic opera *Aida*.

OPERA

OPERA is a drama in which the characters sing, rather than speak, all or most of their lines. Opera is perhaps the most complex of all art forms. It combines acting, singing, orchestral music, costumes, scenery, and often ballet or some other form of dance.

In telling a story, opera uses the enormous power of music to communicate feeling. Music can often express emotions better than spoken words can. Singers, accompanied by an orchestra, may bring a dramatic situation to life more vividly than actors with spoken dialogue. Vocal and orchestral music can also tell an audience much about a character and his state of mind.

Because music expresses emotions so well, most opera composers base their works on highly emotional stories. An opera, more than a spoken play, is likely to emphasize passionate scenes of anger, cruelty, jealousy, joy, love, revenge, sadness, or triumph. Music can add excitement to scenes portraying spectacle. Some of the most stirring music in opera accompanies colorful crowd scenes, such as a coronation or a military parade.

Opera differs in several ways from other kinds of plays that have music. For example, William Shakespeare's comedy *A Midsummer Night's Dream* has scenes that call for music. Such music is called *incidental music* because the play is dramatically complete without it. Incidental music written by different composers may be used in different productions. The German composer Felix Mendelssohn wrote incidental music for *A Midsummer Night's Dream* that has become very popular.

Musical comedies and operettas resemble opera, but most of them have much more spoken dialogue than an opera has and their music is lighter. Compositions called *oratorios* also share certain features with opera. Like an opera, an oratorio has music for soloists, chorus, and orchestra. It may also tell a story. But unlike operas, almost all oratorios are intended to be performed in a concert hall and without acting, costumes, or scenery.

Organizations called opera companies produce most operas. Most companies are *repertory theaters*—that is, they present several operas alternately during a season. The operas a company presents are called its *repertoire*.

Most operas call for a large orchestra and a large cast of performers. As a result, operas are usually performed in specially designed theaters called *opera houses*. Most opera houses seat many more people than do theaters reserved for spoken drama. An opera house also has special facilities and equipment to provide the elaborate staging required by many operas. All modern opera houses have an orchestra pit between the stage and the seats of the auditorium. From the pit, the orchestra, led by the conductor, accompanies the singers onstage.

Most opera houses built in the 1700's and 1800's, and

Reinhard G. Pauly, the contributor of this article, is Director of the School of Music at Lewis and Clark College and the author of Music and the Theater: An Introduction to Opera.

some modern ones, have rows of boxes arranged in the auditorium. Originally, the boxes were reserved for the nobility who patronized the opera and for their families and guests. Because it is difficult to get a good view of the stage from many box seats, modern opera houses rarely feature this arrangement.

Opera, as we know it today, began in Italy in the late 1500's. Through the years, Italian composers, singers, and conductors have played a leading role in the history and development of opera. By the end of the 1600's, opera had spread from Italy to other European countries. Today, opera can be enjoyed in many parts of the world.

The best-known opera companies in Europe include those that perform at the Teatro alla Scala (La Scala) in Milan, Italy; the Paris Opéra; The Royal Opera House, Covent Garden, in London; the State Opera in Vienna; and the Festival Playhouse in Bayreuth, West Germany. The most famous company in the United States performs at the Metropolitan Opera House in New York City. Other cities in the United States that have important opera companies include Boston; Chicago; San Francisco; and Santa Fe, N. Mex.

Opening Night at the Opera ranks as one of the most glamorous social events of the year. The opening night crowd above mingles in the lobby of the Metropolitan Opera House.

TERMS USED IN OPERA

Aria, *AH ree uh,* is an elaborate vocal solo that usually expresses a character's feelings.

Bel Canto refers to a style of singing that emphasizes beautiful tone and technical skill.

Coloratura is a flowery, ornamental vocal style generally used by extremely high soprano voices.

Ensemble, *ahn SAHM buhl,* is a small group of singers, usually from two to five. The music the group sings is also called an *ensemble.*

Grand Opera refers to operas of the early 1800's that emphasized spectacular stage effects, big crowd scenes, and complicated, elaborate vocal and instrumental music. The term *grand opera* also means an opera with no spoken dialogue.

Leitmotif, *LYT moh TEEF,* is a short musical passage that identifies certain ideas, places, and characters each time they appear in the drama.

Libretto is the text of an opera.

Opera Buffa, *BOOF fah,* is an Italian comic opera concerned with humorous situations that occur in everyday life.

Opera Seria, *SEH ree ah,* was the leading opera form of the 1600's and early 1700's. It dealt primarily with historical and mythological themes and stressed spectacular stage effects and displays of brilliant singing.

Recitative, *REHS uh tuh TEEV,* is the part of the text that provides information about the action and moves the plot forward. It is sung in a simple, speechlike style, sometimes to orchestral accompaniment. In *secco recitative,* the accompaniment is provided by only a harpsichord or a harpsichord and cello or other bass instrument.

Score is the written or printed music for an opera, used by the conductor.

Singspiel, *ZIHNG shpeel,* is a form of German opera, usually comic, that has spoken dialogue instead of recitative. Most of the songs are simple and folklike.

Verismo, *vair EEHS moh,* is a style of realistic Italian opera that focuses on violent actions and emotions.

OPERA /*The Elements of Opera*

An opera has two basic elements: (1) the libretto and (2) the music. The libretto, which means *little book* in Italian, consists of the words, or text, of an opera. The music, which is also called the *score,* consists of both vocal and instrumental music. To translate the libretto and music into a performance, an opera must have singers, a conductor, and an orchestra.

The Libretto

To enjoy an opera fully, an operagoer should read the libretto or a summary of the action before attending a performance. It is especially important to read a translation of the libretto or a summary if an opera is sung in an unfamiliar language. Some public libraries have librettos. Most libraries have books that contain detailed summaries of the action in individual operas. Generally, an opera house provides its audiences with a program that has a summary of the plot.

The libretto of most operas is shorter than the text of a spoken play because it takes longer to sing a given number of words than to speak them. Librettos may also be shorter than the script of a spoken play because a few measures of music can often express emotions more vividly than many lines of spoken dialogue can. Because a libretto has to be relatively short, the story of an opera is likely to be simpler than that of a spoken play, with fewer characters and fewer secondary plots.

Many operas have been criticized for their poor librettos. Such operas give the impression that the composer used the text merely as a framework for the music. Yet flimsy plots and shallow characters do not bother many people. They attend the opera mainly to hear beautiful music sung by beautiful voices. Other people feel that a good opera must also be a good drama. And in fact, some librettos are outstanding works of literature. These librettos include those that the Austrian poet Hugo von Hofmannsthal wrote for the operas of Richard Strauss.

Many librettos seem dated today because the definition of good drama in opera has changed over the years. Numerous subjects that were popular in operas of the 1600's, 1700's, or 1800's are now out of fashion. Yet modern operagoers can still enjoy these older operas if they learn something about the customs in drama and music that influenced their composition.

Recitative and Arias. Certain parts of the libretto simply provide information for the audience. For example, one character may tell another about something that has happened. In some operas, the characters speak these portions of the text. But in many operas, the characters sing them in a simple, speechlike style called *recitative*. Most recitatives are written in everyday language—that is, they do not rhyme. Recitatives were especially popular in operas of the 1700's and early 1800's.

The most emotional parts of the libretto are solo numbers called *arias*. They usually express a character's feelings or thoughts. Most arias are written in rhythmical, rhymed verse. They are also set to far more elaborate music than are recitatives. In fact, arias provide the most beautiful and dramatic music in many operas.

Spoken dialogue or recitative carries the action forward. At intervals, the action stops and the characters sing arias to express their feelings. An example of the use of recitative and aria appears in the following passage from Wolfgang Amadeus Mozart's opera *Don Gio-*

vanni. In the passage, a character sings several lines of recitative, ending with:

> Every means must be sought to
> discover the truth . . . I shall avenge her!

He then sings an aria that begins with these lines:

> My peace depends on hers; that which
> pleases her gives life to me. . . .

The recitative above tells the audience about the character's future actions. The aria expresses his state of mind. The original Italian text for this aria was written in rhymed poetry.

Ensembles. In many operas, the libretto calls for two or more singers to engage in a musical dialogue, called an *ensemble*. The singers themselves are also called an *ensemble*. The most common ensembles are duets, trios, quartets, and quintets.

A special kind of ensemble requires several characters to sing at the same time and express their thoughts and feelings. They may sing the same words, showing agreement. Or they may sing different words and melodies, expressing conflicting feelings and thoughts.

The Music

The Singers. In an opera, each role calls for a singer with a specific voice range. Opera singers are therefore classified according to the range of their voices.

The basic vocal classifications for women, from highest to lowest range, are soprano; mezzo-soprano; and alto, or contralto. Each of these classifications can be divided into more specialized groups. For example, sopranos can be divided into coloratura sopranos, lyric sopranos, and dramatic sopranos. Coloratura sopranos have a very high range and can sing with great agility. Lyric sopranos have a light, graceful voice appropriate to youthful roles. Dramatic sopranos have a rich, strong voice suited to highly emotional parts.

The chief voice classifications for men, from highest to lowest range, are tenor, baritone, and bass. Each of these classifications can also be divided into more specialized groups. For example, tenors can be divided into lyric tenors and dramatic tenors. A lyric tenor has a light, high voice. A dramatic tenor, who is often called by the German word *Heldentenor*, has a rich, powerful voice with a lower range than a lyric tenor. Such voices are needed for the heroic roles in operas by Richard Wagner. Bass voices are classified as basso cantante, basso buffo, or basso profundo. A basso cantante has the highest bass voice, which has a range similar to that of a lyric tenor. A basso buffo has a deep, flexible voice and sings comic roles. A basso profundo has an especially low voice and usually sings majestic, serious roles.

Choral Singing. Most operas include choral singing as well as arias, recitatives, and ensembles. The function and importance of the chorus vary from opera to opera and even within an opera. A chorus may provide only visual background for a scene. For example, it might portray a crowd at a festival. Or a chorus may be required merely to shout an exclamation, such as "Hail to our great king!" But in some works, the chorus plays a leading part in the story and sings complicated music.

Acting in Opera. For a successful career in opera, a singer must have acting skill in addition to an outstand-

Scene from a production by the Lyric Opera of Chicago, with Regina Resnik, *left,* Joan Sutherland, *center,* and Spiro Malas (WORLD BOOK photo)

An Opera Ensemble consists of a small group of singers. The music they sing is also called an *ensemble.* A countess, her daughter, and a soldier sing a lively, comic ensemble in this scene from Act II of *The Daughter of the Regiment* by Gaetano Donizetti.

Scene from a production by the Lyric
Opera of Chicago (WORLD BOOK photo)

An Opera Chorus is a large group of singers who perform as a
unit. Members of the chorus must be able to act expressively while
they sing. The chorus above portrays an excited crowd outside a
bull ring in a scene from Act IV of *Carmen* by Georges Bizet.

ing voice. Most young singers who plan a career in opera
include several years of acting lessons in their training.

Opera acting presents special problems because it is
difficult to act and sing at the same time. Sudden movements, walking, running, and twisted body positions
may all interfere with the production of a beautiful,
clear, and steady tone. For this reason, opera acting
tends to be less lively and less realistic than acting in
other forms of drama.

The Conductor plays a key role in opera. Throughout
a performance, the conductor must keep the singers and
orchestra together. The beat must be clearly seen by
singers far from the conductor and by musicians sitting
in the dim light at the ends of the orchestra pit. Al-

Bruno Bartoletti conducting the orchestra of the
Lyric Opera of Chicago (WORLD BOOK photo)

The Conductor sets the tempo for both the musicians in the orchestra pit and the singers onstage. He or she must keep the
orchestra and vocalists together. The conductor must also adjust
the *balance* (loudness) between the singers and the orchestra.

though the conductor sets the tempo, he or she must be
able to react to unexpected circumstances. If a soloist
begins to sing too fast, for example, the conductor may
have to adjust the orchestra's tempo. Because of all
these special demands, opera conducting requires greater skills than does any other kind of conducting.

Some operas call for scenes in which musicians and
singers perform offstage. In such instances, an assistant
conductor directs the offstage music. In some modern
opera houses, the assistant conductor directs the offstage music while following the conductor's beat over
closed-circuit television.

The Orchestra. The number and kinds of instruments
in the orchestra depend on the particular opera being
performed. The instruments needed for Italian operas
composed in the late 1700's differ greatly from those
needed for operas written by Wagner in the late 1800's.

The particular opera being performed also determines
the orchestra's function. In most operas, the orchestra's
basic job is to accompany the singers. The accompaniment may be simple, providing only enough harmonic
and rhythmic background to keep the singers on pitch
and in time. But the orchestra may also serve a more
important role. For example, it might play music that
introduces the general emotional quality of an aria before a note has been sung. The orchestra may even emphasize a passage in the text. For example, a heavily
rhythmic beat might accompany the words "my heart
pounds faster."

In some scenes, one or more characters may be alone
on the stage a long time without singing or speaking.
During that period, the orchestral music expresses their
feelings. This kind of characterization through music is
one of the strengths of opera and is impossible in spoken
plays.

In many operas, the orchestra often repeats a melody
or short theme from an earlier scene. This melody or
theme, without singing or spoken words, is called a
leitmotif. Composers repeat the leitmotif to remind
listeners of some action, character, or idea previously
introduced in the opera. Composers of the 1800's,
notably Wagner, used the leitmotif most effectively.

Pieces of orchestral music called *interludes* are used to
connect scenes. Interludes provide time for scenery
changes or for new characters to enter. Interludes also
may indicate shifts in the emotional atmosphere in an
opera. Occasionally, orchestral music imitates the
sounds of nature. In Wagner's *Siegfried*, the orchestra
imitates the sounds in a forest.

Most operas begin with an orchestral overture. Some
overtures merely indicate that the performance is about
to begin. But other overtures have a much more important function. Some introduce the opera's principal
melodies. Other overtures set the mood for the opening
scene or for the opera in general. In some older operas,
the overture lasts less than a minute. A number of overtures of the 1800's are elaborate compositions that run
10 minutes or longer.

Musicians occasionally perform onstage in costume
and participate in the action of the opera. For example,
musicians may take part in such onstage activities as
a military parade or a religious procession.

An opera company produces several operas in a season. In selecting each work for production, the company must consider several factors. These factors include the estimated cost of presenting the opera and whether the work will attract a large audience. Most opera companies attempt to balance their season with both comic and tragic operas. They also try to select works by a variety of composers and from different historical periods.

The People Behind the Scenes

During an opera performance, the audience sees only the conductor, orchestra, and performers. But an opera production also requires the skills of many other people. These people include (1) the general manager, (2) the stage director, (3) costume and set designers, (4) the members of the technical staff, and (5) the stage manager. All these specialists perform about the same work for an opera as they would for a spoken play. But opera requires that they coordinate all parts of the production with the music.

The General Manager supervises the overall artistic and business policy of the opera company. This person plays a major part in choosing the repertoire and in hiring singers, conductors, and stage managers. The general manager follows each production through the planning and rehearsal stages to make sure it is progressing satisfactorily. Some companies have a music director to assist the general manager in such matters as the hiring of singers and conductors.

The Stage Director is responsible for the visual aspects of an opera production, just as the conductor is responsible for the music. The stage director must coordinate every action on the stage with the music. He helps singers interpret their roles, works with the designers on ideas for costumes and sets, and helps determine the lighting. See THEATER (The Director).

The stage director faces one of the greatest challenges in handling choral scenes. The chorus should not simply stand still and look at the conductor while singing. All dramatic illusion would be lost. The director must assign all members of the chorus some activity so they will appear natural on the stage. Some operas have scenes in which the chorus takes part in vigorous action while singing. One famous choral scene requiring vigorous action takes place near the end of Act II of Wagner's opera *The Mastersingers of Nuremberg*. A riot breaks out among a crowd of angry townspeople played by the chorus. In such scenes, the chorus must act convincingly while singing and following the conductor. The stage director has to plan choral scenes like these carefully and then rehearse the scenes frequently.

Sometimes, a stage director may create a new interpretation of an opera. Because the repertoire of opera companies consists chiefly of a few dozen works performed repeatedly, audiences may welcome a production that presents a familiar opera in a fresh way. But some directors have been criticized for taking too many liberties with an opera and thus distorting the composer's and librettist's intentions.

The Designers. The story of most operas in the standard repertoire takes place before the 1900's. Therefore, the costume and set designers must generally research the particular period of the story so their designs accurately reflect the time and place of the action. In Giuseppe Verdi's *Aida*, for example, the costumes and sets must realistically portray ancient Egypt.

The costumes and sets should be designed so that the performers can move about freely. In addition, the set designer always has to consider the requirements of the music. For example, the music may allow a singer a certain amount of time to move from a door to a table and begin an aria. The designer must arrange the set so the singer can move naturally and still arrive at the table at

Metropolitan Opera Association, New York City (WORLD BOOK photo)

The Set Designer makes a scale model of a set, *foreground*, to determine how the scenery will look on the full stage. The workers in the background are painting a large backdrop for a set.

Lyric Opera of Chicago (WORLD BOOK photo)

The Costume Designer creates costumes suitable to an opera's time and place. These designers fit a singer with a gown for Jules Massenet's *Manon*, which takes place in the 1720's in France.

Metropolitan Opera Association, New York City (WORLD BOOK photos)

Opera Rehearsals involve both technicians and performers. At a lighting rehearsal, *left,* an electrician in a lighting booth works with the director onstage to create desired lighting effects. The director also rehearses the singers, *right,* to develop stage movements and interpretations of roles.

the precise moment in the music when the aria begins. The set designer may also have to plan the sets to provide space for large choral or dance scenes. See THEATER (Scene Design; Costumes and Makeup).

The Technical Staff. Many technicians work with the stage director in planning and carrying out the visual aspects of the production. The electricians are especially important members of the technical staff. They operate

the complicated lighting equipment that is used to illuminate parts or all of the stage and to provide atmosphere. Some stage directors rely on lighting, rather than on realistic sets, to express an opera's mood. See THEATER (Lighting and Sound).

During an opera performance, the various crews of technicians and stagehands must work quickly and efficiently backstage. One crew changes the scenery be-

Lyric Opera of Chicago (WORLD BOOK photos)

The Stage Manager, *above,* has charge of backstage activity during an opera performance. He uses a score to follow the action onstage and watches the conductor over closed-circuit television. He communicates with backstage technicians over a headset.

A Crew of Stagehands changes the scenery between acts and scenes, *right.* Another stage crew puts such objects as chairs and weapons in their proper places onstage. A third crew arranges the lights. All three crews must work quickly and efficiently.

Lyric Opera of Chicago (WORLD BOOK photo)

The Prompter speaks the entire libretto during a performance in case a singer forgets a line. He works in a *prompter's box* below the stage where only the singers can see him. The prompter follows the conductor over closed-circuit television.

tween acts or scenes. Another crew adds the small objects, called *props*, that the performers use in the action. A third crew sets up and adjusts the lights. For changing scenery, some opera houses use revolving stages or stages that can be raised or lowered by elevator. Special technicians operate the machinery that moves these stages. See THEATER (Changing Scenery).

The Stage Manager has charge of all backstage activity during a performance. He sees that all the props needed for a scene are on the stage and in the correct place. He calls the performers from their dressing rooms at specific times so they can make their entrances on schedule. The stage manager also gives the electricians cues to change the lighting during the performance.

Preparing a Production

Planning a Production. After a company selects an opera, the general manager and the management staff establish the production's budget. They also choose the cast and assign a stage director and conductor to the production. Most companies employ a resident group of singers, conductors, and directors for an entire season. However, nearly all companies also hire guest singers to take the leading roles for a single production. In addition, companies frequently use guest conductors, stage directors, and designers.

In some cases, the most important consideration in selecting an opera is whether a company can hire a particular guest singer. Sometimes a company wants a certain singer so much it will let the artist choose the opera. In casting the leading parts, the opera company first of all seeks singers who have outstanding voices. But the performers should also act well and, preferably, have the physical appearance suited to the characters they are to portray.

During the early stages of a production, the key personnel hold many conferences. The stage director, for example, meets frequently with the costume and set designers. Sketches of the designs must be approved early

to allow enough time for the costumes and sets to be made. The costumes and sets may be manufactured in the opera house workshops or by outside firms. Sometimes, sets and costumes are borrowed or rented from another opera company.

Rehearsing a Production. After many months of planning the production, rehearsals begin. At first, the singers, chorus, and orchestra rehearse separately in rehearsal rooms. If the opera calls for dancing, the dancers also practice by themselves.

The stage director rehearses the principal singers to work out stage movements and establish interpretations of the roles. The chorus rehearses under the direction of a chorus master. A *choreographer* (dance composer) supervises dance rehearsals. The conductor and his assistants rehearse the orchestra.

A few weeks before the opera is to open, rehearsals move from separate facilities to the main stage. These rehearsals take place with piano accompaniment only.

Meanwhile, the stage director and the chief electrician hold lighting rehearsals. In most operas, directors use elaborate lighting that is changed frequently during the performance. Lighting rehearsals develop the best ways to achieve desired effects. The rehearsals also set the timing for the various lighting changes.

As the opening nears, the orchestra rehearses with the entire cast on the main stage. Because of the central function of the music, the conductor takes charge of these rehearsals.

A few days before opening night, the performers and orchestra stage a dress rehearsal. A dress rehearsal is presented like an actual performance, with costumes, makeup, and sets. By this time, the production should move with split-second timing. The music sets the pace for the action and should not be sped up or slowed down to adjust to what happens onstage.

Lyric Opera of Chicago (WORLD BOOK photo)

Offstage Music is required in some operas. An assistant conductor leads the musicians and singers hidden in the wings. He conducts from a score while following the beat of the conductor in the orchestra pit over closed-circuit television.

The first operas were composed and performed in the 1590's in Florence, Italy. There, a group of noblemen, musicians, and poets had become interested in the culture of ancient Greece, especially Greek drama. This group, called the *Camerata*, believed that the Greeks sang rather than spoke their tragedies. The Camerata attempted to re-create the style of ancient Greek tragedy in musical compositions. They took most of their subjects from Greek and Roman history and mythology. The Camerata called their compositions *dramma per musica* (drama for music) or *opera in musica* (musical work). The term *opera* comes from the shortened form of opera in musica. Jacopo Peri, a member of the Camerata, composed what is generally considered to be the first opera, *Dafne* (1597).

Baroque Opera

Opera emerged as an art form in western Europe during the *baroque* period in music history. This period began about 1600 and ended about 1750. Baroque music was elaborate and emotional. Italians composed the earliest baroque operas, and Italian-style opera dominated most of the period.

Early Baroque Opera. The first baroque operas consisted of recitatives, sung by soloists, and choral passages. A small orchestra accompanied the singers.

During the 1600's, the aria gradually emerged and developed as a separate function from that of the recitative. The recitative served to carry the plot of the opera forward. The arias became pauses in the action in which characters expressed their thoughts and feelings. Singers often used arias for showing off their vocal skills rather than for dramatic expression. A form of presentation called *secco recitative* developed in the 1600's. In secco recitative, the singers were accompanied by only a harpsichord—or by a harpsichord and cello or other bass instrument—rather than by the full orchestra.

Claudio Monteverdi, the first great composer of baroque opera, wrote the first opera masterpiece, *Orfeo* (1607). Monteverdi worked in Venice and made it the center of opera during the early 1600's. The world's first public opera house, the Teatro San Cassiano, opened in Venice in 1637.

By the late 1600's, operas were being written and performed in a number of European countries outside Italy, especially in England, France, and Germany. But Italian opera was the accepted style, and many non-Italian composers wrote operas in the Italian manner and to Italian librettos.

Opera Seria and Opera Buffa. Italian opera of the late baroque period developed into two basic types—(1) *opera seria* (serious opera) and (2) *opera buffa* (comic opera). Both types consisted of a succession of secco recitatives and arias.

Opera Seria. Composers of opera seria based their works on stories of ancient kings and queens and mythological gods and goddesses. These stories provided spectacular stage effects, such as earthquakes and floods and big coronation or battle scenes. The operas stressed much coloratura singing and long arias. Many singers were trained in a vocal style called *bel canto*, which emphasized technical skill and beauty of tone.

The *da capo* aria became a major feature of opera seria. It had three parts, the third being a repetition of the first. In the repeated part, the singer was expected to add difficult notes, passages, and other ornamentation not included in the score.

Opera Buffa began as comic skits, called *intermezzos*, performed in front of the curtain between the acts of an opera seria. The characters in opera buffa were common people, unlike the characters in opera seria. Characters in opera buffa represented the professions and social classes of the time, including doctors, farmers, merchants, servants, and soldiers. The typical opera

Engraving by Stefano della Bella of a scene from *The Wedding of the Gods* (1637) by Giovanni Carlo Coppola; The Newberry Library, Chicago

Opera Seria was a form of Italian opera popular in the 1600's and 1700's. It emphasized spectacular scenery and often dealt with ancient gods and goddesses. The Italian designer Alfonso Parigi created the elaborate set at the left for an opera seria. It shows the workshop of Vulcan, the blacksmith to the gods in Roman mythology. Parigi designed the workshop as a cave at the foot of several towering cliffs.

buffa dealt with humorous situations from everyday life. Many characters in opera buffa sang in *dialects* (local forms) of Italian rather than the formal Italian of opera seria. A very successful opera buffa was *La Serva Padrona* (1733) by Giovanni Pergolesi.

Italian opera seria and opera buffa were extremely popular. Hundreds of them were written, often in a short time. Most of these works were performed for one season and then forgotten. Because of the constant demand for new operas, composers used the same librettos over and over again. By today's standards, many librettos had unconvincing plots and unbelievable characters. Although some operagoers complained about the weak librettos of many Italian operas, most audiences of the 1600's and early 1700's enjoyed the works, chiefly for their music.

French Opera. A distinctly French style of opera appeared in the 1670's. Before that time, the French showed little interest in opera. The few operas performed in the country were written in the Italian style. Jean Baptiste Lully, though born in Italy, established a French form of opera. In the mid-1700's, Jean Philippe Rameau became the leading composer of French opera.

French opera composers avoided the secco recitatives and showy arias of Italian opera. Instead they preferred expressive melodies or simple songs. The recitatives were accompanied by a full orchestra and closely followed the rhythms of the French language. Ballet played an important part in French opera during the baroque period, as well as later.

In France, royalty became the chief patrons of opera. Lully acquired his fame at the court of King Louis XIV. Noblemen in France and other countries competed with one another in maintaining large opera companies. To impress audiences with their wealth, noblemen sponsored productions noted for expensive scenic effects, such as gods riding chariots in the sky.

Classical Opera

Dissatisfaction with Italian opera began to spread among operagoers during the early 1700's. Attacks centered on the far-fetched plots and lifeless characters in most operas. Many people particularly objected to the arias, which served only to glorify the singers. The reaction against Italian opera led to a new style, later known as *classical opera*. The classical period began about 1750 and lasted about 70 years. The first important classical composer was Christoph Willibald Gluck, a German. The greatest classical composer was Wolfgang Amadeus Mozart, an Austrian.

Gluck and Opera Reform. Gluck believed that the drama and music should be unified in opera. By integrating the music with the story in *Orpheus and Eurydice* (1762) and other works, Gluck put his beliefs into practice.

Gluck rejected improbable plots, elaborate scenic effects, and emphasis on showy arias. In his operas, the music served the story. Gluck simplified the action to make the stories and characters appear more natural. He also was one of the first composers to supervise all phases of a production, and he demanded many more rehearsals than had been customary.

Mozart, like Gluck, felt that the music in an opera should help make the story and characters believable. Mozart achieved this goal by carefully relating the instrumental and vocal music to the action. He showed particular skill in using music to create characterization—that is, to develop the personality of the characters. Mozart did this in ensemble scenes as well as in arias.

Mozart composed operas in both Italian and German. His best-known Italian operas are *The Marriage of Figaro* (1786), *Don Giovanni* (1787), and *Così Fan Tutte* (1790). His notable German operas include *The Abduction from the Seraglio* (1782) and *The Magic Flute* (1791). Both of these works contain elements of *Singspiel* (song play). Singspiel is a form of German opera that has spoken dialogue rather than recitative. Most stories are comic. The melodies often are simple and resemble the style of German folk and popular songs.

Opera in the 1800's

Romanticism was a movement from the late 1700's to the mid-1800's that emphasized emotionalism in the arts, including opera. The typical romantic opera had a setting in nature, a theme based on folklore or the supernatural, and colorful music. Carl Maria von Weber, a German, wrote one of the earliest and greatest romantic operas, *Der Freischütz* (1821). The story is set in a forest, and most of the chief characters are simple countrypeople. The orchestra has an important part in portraying many of the sounds of nature as well as supernatural forces.

Several Italians also wrote in the romantic style. The most typical of these composers were Vincenzo Bellini and Gaetano Donizetti. Many of their operas require voices trained in the bel canto style.

Grand Opera became popular in the early 1800's, especially in France. Composers of grand opera favored heroic episodes from history, in which they could use crowd scenes, spectacular stage effects, and complicated and elaborate vocal and instrumental music. Giacomo Meyerbeer, a German, became the leading composer of French grand opera with such works as *Les Huguenots* (1836) and *Le Prophète* (1849). Gioacchino Rossini, an Italian-born composer living in France, also wrote a famous grand opera, *William Tell* (1829).

Giuseppe Verdi dominated Italian opera during the mid- and late 1800's. He is still perhaps the most popular opera composer in history. Verdi's best-known works include *Rigoletto* (1851), *Il Trovatore* (1853), *La Traviata* (1853), and *Aida* (1871). All are noted for their emotional power, which is expressed through eloquent vocal music. *Aida* is also an example of grand opera.

Verdi wrote his last two operas—*Otello* (1887) and *Falstaff* (1893)—when he was in his 70's. Both works demonstrate that old age did not diminish his genius. The operas are masterpieces of characterization through music, and they show complete unity of vocal and instrumental writing.

Richard Wagner was the most important German opera composer of the 1800's. Wagner believed that all the parts of an opera production—acting, costumes, drama, orchestral music, singing, and staging—should have equal value. He wrote his own librettos and, whenever possible, supervised the staging and other aspects of a production. Wagner departed from tradition by making the orchestra as important as the singers. In many of Wagner's late works, instruments perform the main melodies.

As a young man, Wagner was greatly impressed by Weber's romantic opera *Der Freischütz*. *The Flying Dutchman* (1843), one of Wagner's early works, shows similar romantic qualities. These qualities include the supernatural aspects of the plot and the musical representation of the forces of nature, such as the wind and the sea. In *The Flying Dutchman*, Wagner first used musical themes to identify certain characters, places, or ideas each time they appear in the drama. Wagner expanded this *leitmotif* technique greatly in his later operas. *Tristan and Isolde* (1865) and the four works

called *The Ring of the Nibelung* (1876) represent Wagner's fully developed personal style.

Nationalism—the feeling of pride in one's country—influenced many composers throughout Europe during the 1800's. These composers based much of their work on the folk music of their nation or region. Czech nationalism, for example, dominates the operas of Antonín Dvořák and Bedřich Smetana. *The Bartered Bride* (1866) by Smetana and *Rusalka* (1901) by Dvořák are outstanding examples of nationalistic operas. Russian composers of nationalistic operas include Modest Mussorgsky with *Boris Godunov* (1874) and Alexander Borodin with *Prince Igor* (1890).

Verismo Opera. In the late 1800's, some Italian composers began to write grimly realistic operas dealing with everyday life. These *verismo* (meaning *true* or *realistic*) operas focused on violent emotions and actions. The earliest and best-known verismo operas are *Cavalleria Rusticana* (1890) by Pietro Mascagni and *I Pagliacci* (1892) by Ruggiero Leoncavallo.

The 1900's

Giacomo Puccini was the most popular Italian opera composer of the early 1900's. His operas are noted for their melodic and sometimes sentimental music and for their theatrically effective librettos. Puccini first gained widespread attention in the 1890's with *Manon Lescaut* (1893) and *La Bohème* (1896). He followed these works with *Tosca* (1900), a verismo opera. His other notable operas include *Madama Butterfly* (1904) and *Turandot* (produced in 1926, after his death).

Richard Strauss became the most important and successful German opera composer after Wagner. Strauss wrote operas that require singers with great vocal power. He is best known for three early operas—*Salome* (1905), *Elektra* (1909), and *Der Rosenkavalier* (1911). *Salome* and *Elektra* originally caused much controversy among operagoers because of their brutal action and harsh music. *Der Rosenkavalier*, however, is entirely different in mood and theme. In this opera, Strauss and the librettist, Hugo von Hofmannsthal, created an

Festspiele Bayreuth, Germany

New Techniques in Staging have given a fresh interpretation to many older operas. At its première in 1876, Richard Wagner's opera *Siegfried* was presented in a realistic setting, *above*. A modern staging of the work eliminates the detailed scenery and achieves mood largely through lighting effects, *below*.

Wilhelm Rauh, Festspiele Bayreuth, Germany

Scene from a production by the New York City Opera,
with Claramae Turner and Salvador Novoa; Fred Fehl

Bomarzo by Alberto Ginastera is one of the few modern operas
to gain international fame. The tragic opera concerns the tortured
mental state of Duke Bomarzo, a deformed Italian nobleman. In
Act I, *above*, Bomarzo and his grandmother sing an emotional duet.

affectionate portrait of aristocratic society in Vienna
in the 1700's.

The Search for New Forms. After World War I
(1914-1918), many composers began to search for new
forms of operatic expression. Some composers included
elements of American jazz in their operas. Ernst Křenek,
an Austrian, used jazz in his opera *Jonny spielt auf*
(1927). The German composer Kurt Weill wrote *The
Threepenny Opera* (1928) in the style of the music heard
in German *cabarets* (nightclubs).

Meanwhile, a movement called *expressionism* had developed in the arts. Expressionism aimed at exploring
man's subconscious and became especially important in
drama and painting. But expressionist qualities also
appeared in several operas. Such operas had a brooding,
nightmarish atmosphere, reinforced by unharmonious
music and symbolic and violent actions.

Strauss's *Salome* was an early example of the expressionist style. But Alban Berg and Arnold Schönberg, two Austrian composers, rank as the leading opera
composers in the movement. Berg wrote *Wozzeck*
(1925), the most successful expressionistic opera. Schönberg's major expressionistic work was *Erwartung* (completed 1909, first performed 1924). Other operas related
to expressionism include *Duke Bluebeard's Castle* (completed 1911, first performed 1918) by the Hungarian
composer Béla Bartók and *From the House of the Dead*
(1930) by the Czech composer Leoš Janáček.

American Opera. American composers wrote no
important operas until the 1900's. George Gershwin
wrote a highly original and popular American opera,
Porgy and Bess (1935). The work describes life among
Negroes in Charleston, S.C., in the 1920's. *Porgy and
Bess* has been acclaimed throughout the world as a
genuine American folk opera.

The most successful opera composer in the United
States is Gian Carlo Menotti. He composes in a tradi-

tional style that shows the influence of Puccini. Menotti wrote an opera for radio, *The Old Maid and the
Thief* (1939), and an opera for television, *Amahl and
the Night Visitors* (1951). His best-known stage operas
include two tense dramas, *The Medium* (1946) and *The
Consul* (1950).

In addition to Menotti, other Americans have composed notable operas. These works include *Trouble in
Tahiti* (1952) by Leonard Bernstein; *The Tender Land*
(1954) by Aaron Copland; *The Ballad of Baby Doe*
(1956) by Douglas Moore; *Vanessa* (1958) by Samuel
Barber; and *The Crucible* (1961) by Robert Ward.

Opera Today

The experimentation in opera that began after World
War I continues today. Some composers have explored
new dramatic and musical techniques, including the
use of electronic sounds, motion pictures, and color
slides. *Aniara* (1959), a science-fiction opera by the
Swedish composer Karl-Birger Blomdahl, takes place
in a space ship and uses taped and electronic sounds.
Bomarzo (1967) by the Argentine composer Alberto
Ginastera also features unconventional sound effects,
especially in fantastic, dreamlike scenes.

Operagoers today, however, still prefer older, traditional works. Only a few operas composed since the end
of World War I receive frequent productions. But many
changes have occurred in the way older operas are
staged. For example, stage directors often try to create
desired moods through lighting effects made possible
by modern lighting equipment. In many present-day
productions, Wagner's operas are simpler and less
realistic than they were in the 1800's.

Meanwhile, artistic and economic problems trouble
all major opera companies. Before the development of
fast, convenient air travel, leading singers remained
with one company an entire season. But jet travel enables singers to appear as guest artists in many opera
houses in a season. Artists earn more money as guests,
and audiences can see and hear many famous singers.
However, traveling artists often follow a tight, exhaust-
ing schedule that leaves too little time for rehearsal. As
a result, audiences often attend performances that
show a lack of adequate preparation.

The cost of producing opera has risen steadily during
the 1900's. Even if an opera house sells every ticket
for an entire season, it cannot meet expenses. In the
United States and Europe, ticket sales seldom provide
more than half the income needed to operate an opera
company. American companies rely on contributions
from individuals, corporations, and foundations to
make up losses. Many European countries, cities, and
states support opera with public funds. Numerous people in the United States believe the national government or local governments should help support opera
and the other arts, as governments do in Europe.

Most U.S. colleges and universities have opera
workshops. They provide training and experience for
young actors and singers and also present performances
for the general public. Some colleges and universities
have staged revivals of worthwhile but little-known
works.

Opera companies today present mainly works composed between the late 1700's and the early 1900's. Almost all the operas in this standard repertoire were written by Austrian, French, German, Italian, and Russian composers. This section describes some of the most popular operas in the standard repertoire. Some of the recommended books listed at the end of this article provide more detailed discussions of the repertoire.

Aida, a tragic opera in four acts by Giuseppe Verdi. Libretto in Italian by Verdi and Antonio Ghislanzoni. First performed in Cairo, Egypt, in 1871.

The *khedive* (ruler) of Egypt asked Verdi to write *Aida* to help celebrate the opening of the Suez Canal and the Cairo opera house. The story takes place in ancient Egypt and concerns the tragic love affair between Aida, an Ethiopian slave, and Radames, an Egyptian military officer. *Aida* is grand opera and so requires a large cast. The work has impressive crowd scenes, featuring choruses of soldiers, slaves, and priests, and an elaborate ballet. In Act I, Radames expresses his love for Aida in a beautiful aria, "Celeste Aida." Act II includes the stirring "Triumphal March," in which the Egyptian king reviews his victorious army.

Barber of Seville, The (*Il Barbiere di Siviglia*), a comic opera in two acts by Gioacchino Rossini. Libretto in Italian by Cesare Sterbini, based on the French play *The Barber of Seville* by Pierre Beaumarchais. First performed in Rome in 1816.

The story of *The Barber of Seville* takes place in Seville, Spain, in the 1600's. This work is a good example of Italian comic opera, or *opera buffa*. The libretto has many characters and situations typical of this style. The characters include an old man (Doctor Bartolo) who is interested in a beautiful and rich young woman (Rosina). He jealously watches over her but cannot prevent a dashing young nobleman (Count Almaviva) from meeting and finally marrying her. Other tradi-

tional characters include a drunken soldier, who is really the count in disguise, and an irritable housekeeper. Figaro, the barber in the opera's title, helps the count win Rosina.

Rossini developed the action primarily through secco recitative. In Act I, Rosina's aria "Una voce poco fa" provides opportunities for brilliant singing. Also in Act I, Figaro makes his first appearance singing a popular comic aria, "Largo al factotum," in which he boasts how clever he is. The opera also has a lively overture, which Rossini had used in two earlier operas, *Aureliano in Palmira* (1813) and *Elisabetta, Regina d'Inghilterra* (1815).

Bohème, La (*The Bohemians*), a tragic opera in four acts by Giacomo Puccini. Libretto in Italian by Giuseppe Giacosa and Luigi Illica, based on the French novel *Scenes from Bohemian Life* by Henri Murger. First performed in Turin, Italy, in 1896.

The bohemians in the opera's title are four poor but carefree young men who live together in an attic in Paris about 1830. They are Rodolfo, a poet; Marcello, a painter; Schaunard, a musician; and Colline, a philosopher. Mimi, a frail young girl in poor health, is their neighbor. She and Rodolfo meet and fall in love. But at the end of the opera, Mimi dies. The main secondary plot deals with a stormy love affair between Marcello and a young woman named Musetta.

Although *La Bohème* ends tragically, it has many humorous and sentimental moments. The opera also has a number of Puccini's most beloved melodies. One of these melodies is "O soave fanciulla," a love duet between Rodolfo and Mimi that ends Act I. Perhaps the opera's most familiar melody is the aria "Musetta's Waltz" in Act II.

Boris Godunov, a tragic opera in a prologue and four acts by Modest Mussorgsky. Libretto in Russian by the composer, based primarily on the Russian play *Boris Godunov* by Alexander Pushkin. First performed

The Barber of Seville by Gioacchino Rossini is one of the most popular comic operas. Act I ends in the wild argument shown here between Doctor Bartolo, *left center,* and Count Almaviva, *right center,* who is masquerading as a drunken soldier. Don Basilio, a music teacher, and Berta, a maid, try to hold back the doctor. Figaro, a barber, and Rosina, the count's sweetheart, attempt to restrain the nobleman.

Scene from a production by the Lyric Opera of Chicago, with
Luciano Pavarotti and Ileana Cotrubas (WORLD BOOK photo)

La Bohème by Giacomo Puccini deals with a love affair between
Rodolfo, a poet, and Mimi, a young seamstress in failing health.
Near the end of Act IV, *above*, Rodolfo and the dying Mimi sing a
beautiful love duet in the poet's attic lodging.

in St. Petersburg (now Leningrad), Russia, in 1874.

The opera takes place in Russia and Poland from 1598 to 1605 and concerns events in Russian history. Boris Godunov, an adviser to the czar, has the czar's young heir murdered. After the czar dies, Boris takes the throne. But in time, his feelings of guilt cause him to have visions of the murdered heir, and he finally collapses and dies. The "hero" of the opera is the Russian people, portrayed by the chorus. The chorus takes part in many scenes, including an impressive coronation.

Many musicians in Mussorgsky's time considered the music for *Boris Godunov* too harsh and crude. After Mussorgsky's death, his friend and fellow Russian composer Nicholas Rimsky-Korsakov wrote a completely new orchestration for the opera. Rimsky-Korsakov's version is often performed today.

Carmen, a tragic opera in four acts by Georges Bizet. Libretto in French by Ludovic Halévy and Henri Meilhac, based on the French story "Carmen" by Prosper Mérimée. First performed in Paris in 1875.

The action of *Carmen* is set in and near Seville, Spain, about 1820. Carmen is a beautiful Gypsy with no conscience or morals. While working in a cigarette factory in Seville, she meets Don José, a soldier, and has a love affair with him. Later, she leaves Don José for Escamillo, a bullfighter. At the end of the opera, Don José pleads with Carmen to return to him. After she scornfully refuses, Don José stabs the heartless girl to death in a jealous rage.

Scene from a production by the Bolshoi Theater Company, Moscow; Novosti Press Agency, Moscow

Boris Godunov by Modest Mussorgsky is a psychological tragedy based on events in Russian history.
In the prologue to the opera, *above*, Russian peasants in Moscow bow before Boris shortly after he
has been crowned czar. Members of the Russian nobility stand behind him.

The exciting plot, colorful Spanish setting, and stirring music have made *Carmen* one of the most popular works in the repertoire. Many of the opera's melodies have become almost as familiar as popular songs. They include Carmen's dancelike arias "Habanera" and "Seguidilla" in Act I and Don José's "Flower Song" and Escamillo's "Toreador Song" in Act II. The opera also has rousing choral and dance numbers.

Cavalleria Rusticana (*Rustic Chivalry*), a tragic opera in one act by Pietro Mascagni. Libretto in Italian by Guido Menasci and Giovanni Targioni-Tozzetti, based on the Italian story and play *Cavalleria Rusticana* by Giovanni Verga. First performed in Rome in 1890.

Traditionally, *Cavalleria Rusticana* is performed with Ruggiero Leoncavallo's one-act opera, *I Pagliacci*. The passion, realism, and violence of both works make them major examples of verismo opera.

The action in *Cavalleria Rusticana* takes place in a Sicilian village in the 1800's. There, Lola, a married woman, has a love affair with Turiddu, a young soldier. The title of the opera refers to the villagers' code of honor. According to this code, Alfio, Lola's husband, must seek revenge. He challenges Turiddu to a duel and kills him.

The composer and librettists used several effective dramatic devices. Halfway through the opera, the villagers are in church, and the stage is empty. During this interval, the orchestra plays the "Intermezzo." This gentle, melodic instrumental piece provides relief from the tense, highly emotional atmosphere of the opera. In another dramatic device, Turiddu's death takes place offstage. The opera audience learns of the outcome of the duel through the horrified reactions of the villagers onstage.

Don Giovanni, a partly comic and partly tragic opera in two acts by Wolfgang Amadeus Mozart. Libretto in Italian by Lorenzo da Ponte. First performed

Scene from a production by the Lyric Opera of Chicago, with Viorica Cortez and Lorenzo Saccomani (WORLD BOOK photo)

Carmen by Georges Bizet describes the love affairs of a beautiful Gypsy. In this scene from Act IV, Carmen sings a duet outside a bull ring with her latest lover, the bullfighter Escamillo.

in Prague, Bohemia (now part of Czechoslovakia), in 1787.

Mozart's opera *Don Giovanni* has become the best-known version of the legends about Don Juan, the Spanish lover. The action takes place in and near Seville, Spain, in the 1700's. In the opening scene, Don Giovanni (Don Juan) flees from the home of Donna Anna after seducing her, and then he kills her father in a duel. Several later episodes further show Giovanni's cruel nature. At the end of the opera, the marble statue of Donna Anna's slain father visits Giovanni and urges him to abandon his sinful ways. Giovanni refuses. The

Scene from a production by the New York City Opera; Beth Bergman

Don Giovanni by Wolfgang Amadeus Mozart has been praised as the greatest opera ever composed. It deals with the legendary Spanish lover Don Juan (Don Giovanni). Act I ends with this elaborate ball in Giovanni's castle.

scene is then enveloped in smoke and fire as he disappears into hell, accompanied by a chorus of demons.

The mixture of comic and tragic qualities in *Don Giovanni* has always fascinated audiences. Leporello, Giovanni's servant, provides most of the comedy. The most tragic figure is Donna Anna. In addition to many beautiful arias, *Don Giovanni* has highly dramatic recitatives and long, complicated ensembles. In one scene in Act I, three orchestras onstage perform three different dance numbers at the same time during a party given by Don Giovanni. While the three onstage orchestras play, the opera orchestra in the pit accompanies the singers.

Faust, a tragic opera in five acts by Charles Gounod. Libretto in French by Jules Barbier and Michel Carré, based on part I of the German play *Faust* by Johann Wolfgang von Goethe. First performed in Paris in 1859.

The story of *Faust* takes place in Germany in the 1500's. Faust is an old philosopher who yearns for his lost youth. Mephistopheles, the Devil, appears to Faust and grants him youth. Faust, in return, agrees that after he dies, he will serve the Devil in hell. The opera centers on the love story between the now young Faust and Marguerite, a beautiful village girl. At the end of the opera, Marguerite dies and a chorus of angels escorts her to heaven. The Devil then drags Faust down to hell.

In the 1800's, the German composers Louis Spohr and Heinrich Zöllner and the Italian composer Arrigo Boito also wrote operas based on the story of Faust and his agreement with the Devil. But Gounod's version has become the most popular. The 1859 version of the opera had spoken dialogue. Gounod substituted recitative in a production first given in 1869, and that version is performed today. In Act III, Marguerite sings the beautiful "Jewel Song." The lively "Soldiers' Chorus" in Act IV is one of the best-known choral numbers in the entire repertoire.

Lucia di Lammermoor, a tragic opera in three acts by Gaetano Donizetti. Libretto in Italian by Salvatore Cammarano, based on the Scottish novel *The Bride of Lammermoor* by Sir Walter Scott. First performed in Naples, Italy, in 1835.

Donizetti wrote *Lucia di Lammermoor* in the melodramatic style typical of Italian romantic opera of the early 1800's. The story takes place in Scotland in the late 1600's. It concerns a doomed love affair between Lucia Ashton and Edgardo di Ravenswood. Enrico Ashton, Lucia's brother, wrongfully holds Edgardo's estate. To prevent Lucia and Edgardo from marrying, Enrico tricks Lucia into wedding another man. Lucia goes insane, kills her husband, and then dies. Edgardo hears of Lucia's death and stabs himself to death.

The opera has one of the most dramatic ensembles in the repertoire, the sextet "Che mi frena." It is sung in Act II at Lucia's wedding. But the opera is probably best known for the "Mad Scene" in Act III, in which the insane Lucia sings of an imaginary wedding between herself and Edgardo. This scene, which is extremely difficult to sing, is considered one of the greatest challenges for a coloratura soprano in all opera.

Madama Butterfly, a tragic opera in three acts by Giacomo Puccini. Libretto in Italian by Giuseppe Giacosa and Luigi Illica, based on the American play *Madame Butterfly* by David Belasco, from a story by John Luther Long. First performed in Milan, Italy, in 1904.

The story of *Madame Butterfly* takes place in Nagasaki, Japan, about 1900. Cio-cio-san (Madame Butterfly) is a Japanese girl who falls in love with an American naval officer, B. F. Pinkerton. They marry in a Japanese ceremony. According to Japanese law, either the husband or the wife may cancel the marriage on a month's notice. Pinkerton must leave Japan with his ship. After he has left, the girl gives birth to his child. Three years later, Pinkerton sends a letter saying that

Madama Butterfly by Giacomo Puccini describes a tragic romance between Cio-cio-san, a Japanese girl, and B. F. Pinkerton, an American naval officer. In Act I, the girl and her friends arrive for the marriage ceremony. Standing on a bridge in the garden, Cio-cio-san sings of her love for Pinkerton.

The Magic Flute by Wolfgang Amadeus Mozart is a fairy-tale opera. Act II, the final act, ends with this scene in the sacred Temple of Wisdom, ruled by the high priest, Sarastro. Marc Chagall, the famous Russian-born modern artist, designed this set for a production at the Metropolitan Opera House.

he has married an American. Shortly after the letter arrives, Pinkerton appears with his American wife. The heartbroken Cio-cio-san agrees to give them the child. She then commits suicide.

Puccini tried to give *Madama Butterfly* an Oriental flavor by basing some of his score on Japanese music. He also included a passage from "The Star-Spangled Banner" in one of Pinkerton's numbers. The opera's best-known aria is the exquisite "Un bel dì" in Act II. In it, Cio-cio-san describes the happiness she will feel when Pinkerton returns.

Magic Flute, The (*Die Zauberflöte*), a fairy-tale opera in two acts by Wolfgang Amadeus Mozart. Libretto in German by Emanuel Schikaneder and perhaps Karl Ludwig Gieseke. First performed in Vienna, Austria, in 1791.

Mozart and Schikaneder were both members of a secret society called the Masons, and much of *The Magic Flute* deals symbolically with Masonic beliefs and rituals. However, the opera can be enjoyed simply as a fairy tale about two lovers, Tamino and Pamina. The opera takes its name from a magic flute that protects Tamino from danger.

The opera has spoken dialogue instead of recitative. Some of the music resembles simple folk songs, though several of the arias are dramatic and solemn. The Queen of the Night, Pamina's mother, sings two arias that are showpieces for a coloratura soprano. They have extremely difficult passages and high notes. The overture is often performed as a separate work in concerts.

Marriage of Figaro, The (*Le Nozze di Figaro*), a comic opera in four acts by Wolfgang Amadeus Mozart.

I Pagliacci by Ruggiero Leoncavallo is a tragedy about a company of traveling actors who stop in an Italian village to give a performance. In an aria in Act I, Canio, the leader of the company, describes the play the actors will present that night in the village.

Libretto in Italian by Lorenzo da Ponte, based on the French play *The Marriage of Figaro* by Pierre Beaumarchais. First performed in Vienna in 1786.

Beaumarchais wrote *The Barber of Seville* before *The Marriage of Figaro*. Mozart selected the second play for his opera. Thirty years later, Gioacchino Rossini composed an opera based on *The Barber of Seville*. The same principal characters appear in both works. The plot of *The Marriage of Figaro* follows the action begun in *The Barber of Seville*. Mozart's opera describes the problems that develop when Figaro, servant to Count Almaviva, tries to marry Susanna, Countess Almaviva's maid.

Operagoers have praised *The Marriage of Figaro* for its vivid, realistic characters. Unlike many opera composers of the time, Mozart relied far more on ensembles than on arias to develop his characters. The opera opens with a humorous overture. It is one of the most popular overtures ever composed.

Pagliacci, I (*The Players*), a tragic opera in a prologue and two acts by Ruggiero Leoncavallo. Libretto in Italian by the composer. First performed in Milan, Italy, in 1892.

A short verismo opera, *I Pagliacci* deals with life among members of a traveling company of actors in Italy in the 1860's. The story concerns the jealousy of Canio, the leader of the players. The opera opens with a prologue sung in front of the curtain by Tonio, who plays a clown. The prologue announces the theme of the drama.

Early in Act I, Canio learns that Nedda, his wife, is unfaithful. He discovers she is having a love affair, but he does not know the identity of the man. Canio sings one of the great tenor arias in all opera, "Vesti la giubba," which expresses his tragic fate of playing a clown while his heart is breaking. During a performance of a play, Canio learns that his wife's lover is

Silvio, a peasant who lives in the village where the actors are performing. Canio then stabs Nedda and Silvio as the opera ends.

Porgy and Bess, a folk opera in three acts by George Gershwin. Libretto in English by Gershwin's brother Ira and DuBose Heyward, based on Heyward's novel *Porgy*. First performed in Boston in 1935.

Gershwin's *Porgy and Bess* is one of the few American operas that has achieved worldwide fame. The opera portrays life among Negroes in Charleston, S.C., in the 1920's. It specifically deals with the love of the crippled Porgy for the beautiful Bess. The story is colorful and highly dramatic, and it has considerable humor. In his score, Gershwin captured the flavor of the songs sung by black people of the Southeastern United States.

The opera consists largely of individual songs and choral scenes, connected by spoken dialogue and some recitative. Some of the songs, including "Summertime," "I Got Plenty o' Nuttin'," and "It Ain't Necessarily So," have become popular hits.

Rigoletto, a tragic opera in three acts by Giuseppe Verdi. Libretto in Italian by Francesco Maria Piave, based on the French play *Le Rois' amuse* by Victor Hugo. First performed in Venice, Italy, in 1851.

The opera tells a story of treachery and revenge in the court of an Italian nobleman, the Duke of Mantua, in the 1500's. The chief characters include the duke; Rigoletto, a hunchback who is the duke's jester; and Gilda, Rigoletto's daughter. Through intrigue and deceit, Rigoletto's beloved daughter is murdered.

For *Rigoletto*, Verdi composed some of his most glorious melodies. In Act I, Gilda sings the beautiful aria "Caro nome," in which she expresses her love for the duke, who is disguised as a student. In Act III, the duke sings one of the most popular arias in the repertoire, "La donna è mobile." The aria is a humorous

Der Rosenkavalier by Richard Strauss portrays life among the aristocracy in Vienna in the 1700's. Part of the story concerns a romance between Octavian, a young nobleman, and Sophie, a wealthy young girl. They meet and fall in love in this scene from Act II. Octavian, *center*, brings Sophie, *left*, a silver rose sent by Baron Ochs. The baron, a coarse, middle-aged nobleman, plans to marry Sophie.

comment on how changeable women are in their affections. The emotional and melodic quartet "Bella figlia dell' amore" is sung later in Act III.

Ring of the Nibelung, The (*Der Ring des Nibelungen*), a cycle of four operas by Richard Wagner. Libretto in German by the composer. The three main parts are *Die Walküre* (*The Valkyrie*, 1870); *Siegfried* (1876); and *Die Götterdämmerung* (*The Twilight of the Gods*, 1876). Wagner called the fourth work, *Das Rheingold* (*The Rhine Gold*, 1869), the prologue to the other three. However, it is a complete opera. All four works were first performed as a cycle at the opening of the Festival Playhouse in Bayreuth, Germany, in 1876.

The four operas have a continuous plot based on ancient German legends. The Rhine-Maidens guard a treasure of gold on the bottom of the Rhine River. Alberich, one of a group of dwarfs called Nibelungs, steals the Rhine gold and makes a ring from it. The ring gives magic powers to whoever possesses it. After the ring is stolen from Alberich, he puts a curse on it. The ring changes owners several times during the four operas.

Many gods and goddesses take part in the action, including Wotan, their chief; and Fricka, his wife. Other important characters include Brunnhilde, one of several female warriors called Valkyries; Siegmund, a mortal son of Wotan; Siegfried, Siegmund's son; and Sieglinde, Siegmund's sister. The Ring cycle basically deals with the decline and downfall of the gods, brought about by their greed and lust for power as represented by the ring.

Rosenkavalier, Der (*The Bearer of the Rose*), a partly comic, partly serious opera in three acts by Richard Strauss. Libretto in German by Hugo von Hofmannsthal. First performed in Dresden, Germany, in 1911.

Unlike most opera texts, Hofmannsthal's libretto for *Der Rosenkavalier* is an outstanding work of literature. It glamorously portrays life among the aristocracy in Vienna in the 1700's. In most productions, the sets for the first two acts are spectacular, representing luxurious Viennese palaces. The work also calls for magnificent costumes.

The opera describes the love affairs of four chief characters: Princess von Werdenberg, called the Marschallin; Octavian, a young nobleman; Sophie, a beautiful girl; and Baron Ochs, a coarse and comic country nobleman. Strauss wrote the role of Octavian to be played by a female, and a mezzo-soprano sings the part.

Strauss composed many brilliant ensemble scenes for *Der Rosenkavalier*. One of the most impressive takes place in Act I when the Marschallin receives many visitors. The composer emphasized the light-hearted Viennese quality of the opera in a number of lilting waltzes. These waltzes are sometimes performed separately in concerts.

Salome, a tragic opera in one act by Richard Strauss. Libretto in German by Hedwig Lachmann; a translation of a play in French, *Salomé*, by the English author Oscar Wilde. First performed in Dresden, Germany, in 1905.

Wilde based his play on the story of Salome in the

Scene from a production by the Metropolitan Opera Association, with Birgit Nilsson; Frank Dunand, the Metropolitan Opera Guild

Salome by Richard Strauss is a passionate and violent opera that takes place in Palestine at the time of Christ. In the one-act opera's best-known scene, above, Salome performs the "Dance of the Seven Veils" before King Herod and his court.

New Testament, but he invented many details that shocked audiences of his time. In Wilde's play, Salome, a 15-year-old girl, is attracted to the religious prophet Jochanaan (John the Baptist). After Jochanaan rejects her advances, she decides to take revenge. Salome's stepfather, King Herod, asks her to dance for him and, in return, promises her anything she wishes. Salome performs the famous "Dance of the Seven Veils" and then asks Herod for Jochanaan's head on a silver dish. Herod, though horrified, keeps his promise and has Jochanaan beheaded. Salome kisses the head of the prophet, an act that audiences of the early 1900's considered especially objectionable.

Strauss's score captures perfectly the mood of Wilde's gruesome story. The music is often violent and harsh. At other times, it is vigorous and passionate. The orchestral music especially helps create the rich Oriental atmosphere of the opera. The role of Salome is one of the most difficult in the repertoire. The performer must not only sing extremely complicated music, but she must also act and dance well. In addition, she should look young and beautiful.

Tosca, a tragic opera in three acts by Giacomo Puccini. Libretto in Italian by Giuseppe Giacosa and Luigi Illica, based on the French play *La Tosca* by Victorien Sardou. First performed in Rome in 1900.

The story of *Tosca* takes place in Rome in 1800, when the city is torn by political intrigue. The chief characters are Floria Tosca, a famous singer; Mario, a painter and Tosca's lover; and Baron Scarpia, the villainous chief of police. In the story, Cesare Angelotti, an escaped political prisoner, has fled from Scarpia. Both Tosca and Mario know Angelotti's hiding place. Much of the action concerns Scarpia's attempts to force Tosca and Mario to reveal where Angelotti is hiding. Scarpia also wants to make Tosca his mistress.

La Traviata by Giuseppe Verdi describes a doomed love affair between Alfredo Germont, a young Frenchman, and Violetta Valery, his mistress. In this scene from Act I, the couple meet for the first time at a party given by Violetta at her home in Paris.

Scene from a production by the Santa Fe (N. Mex.) Opera, with George Shirley and Maralin Niska; Santa Fe Opera

Tosca kills Scarpia and then commits suicide after she watches a firing squad execute Mario.

Puccini's music powerfully expresses the passion and violence of the plot. The work also has several beautiful melodies, including Tosca's "Vissi d'arte" in Act II and Mario's "E lucevan le stelle" in Act III.

Traviata, La (*The Wayward One*), a tragic opera in three acts by Giuseppe Verdi. Libretto in Italian by Francesco Maria Piave, based on the French play *The Lady of the Camellias* by Alexandre Dumas the Younger. First performed in Venice, Italy, in 1853.

Although *La Traviata* failed dismally at its première, it has become one of the most frequently performed works in the repertoire. Verdi set the action in and near Paris in the mid-1800's. The opera shocked many people during the mid-1800's because Violetta, its heroine, leads an immoral life.

Unlike many earlier operas, *La Traviata* has realistic characters with complicated emotions. Their thoughts and feelings seem especially convincing because of Verdi's theatrically effective music. For example, in Act I, Violetta tries to decide whether to fall in love with Alfredo, who loves her. The music clearly reflects her indecision. In Act III, she sings one of the opera's most haunting arias, "Addio del passato," in which she bids farewell to the happy days of the past.

Trovatore, Il (*The Troubadour*), a tragic opera in four acts by Giuseppe Verdi. Libretto in Italian by Salvatore Cammarano, based on the Spanish play *El Trovador* by Antonio García Gutiérrez. First performed in Rome in 1853.

Like most of Verdi's operas, *Il Trovatore* tells a gloomy and violent story filled with passion. The action takes place in Spain in the 1400's. The principal characters include Manrico, a *troubadour* (poet-singer); Leonora, a noblewoman; Azucena, a Gypsy; and the

Count di Luna. Manrico and Leonora are lovers, but the count also loves Leonora. In addition, Di Luna and Manrico are brothers, though only Azucena knows it. Azucena seeks revenge against the count because his father had her mother burned at the stake. By the end of the opera, Leonora has committed suicide and the count has executed Manrico. After Manrico's death, Azucena tells the count he has killed his brother, and she thus has her revenge.

Despite a frequently confusing plot, *Il Trovatore* is brilliantly effective theater. The opera also has some of Verdi's most memorable music. In Act II, a band of Gypsies in their mountain camp sings what is perhaps the most familiar choral number in all opera, the stirring "Anvil Chorus."

Wozzeck, a tragic opera in three acts by Alban Berg. Libretto in German by the composer, based on the German play *Woyzeck* by Georg Büchner. First performed in Berlin in 1925.

Wozzeck is a private in the Austrian army about 1830. His superiors abuse and ridicule him. Even worse, Marie, the woman he loves, deceives him with another man. Driven almost insane by jealousy, Wozzeck stabs and kills Marie. Later, he throws the knife into a pond. Finally, he drowns in the pond while searching for the knife.

Much of the text for *Wozzeck* is set in an intensely emotional vocal style midway between spoken dialogue and singing. This style is known by the German term *Sprechstimme* (speaking voice). Most of the music is atonal—that is, it does not fall into the traditional keys.

Although *Wozzeck* is difficult to sing and play, it has been performed in many countries. Some people consider the music jarring and too hard to understand. But others feel that it effectively expresses a great variety of emotions.   REINHARD G. PAULY

OPERA / Study Aids

Related Articles in WORLD BOOK include:

AMERICAN COMPOSERS

Barber, Samuel
Bernstein, Leonard
Blitzstein, Marc
Bloch, Ernest
Copland, Aaron
Gershwin, George

Hanson, Howard Harold
Menotti, Gian Carlo
Moore, Douglas Stuart
Sessions, Roger
Thomson, Virgil

BRITISH COMPOSERS

Britten, Benjamin
Delius, Frederick
Purcell, Henry

Vaughan Williams, Ralph
Walton, Sir William

FRENCH COMPOSERS

Berlioz, Louis Hector
Bizet, Georges
Debussy, Claude
Delibes, Léo
Dukas, Paul
Fauré, Gabriel
Gounod, Charles
Honegger, Arthur
Lalo, Édouard

Lully, Jean Baptiste
Massenet, Jules
Milhaud, Darius
Offenbach, Jacques
Poulenc, Francis
Rameau, Jean Philippe
Ravel, Maurice
Saint-Saëns, Camille
Thomas, Ambroise

GERMAN-LANGUAGE COMPOSERS

Bach (Johann Christian Bach)
Beethoven, Ludwig van
Berg, Alban
Gluck, Christoph Willibald
Handel, George Frideric
Haydn, Joseph
Hindemith, Paul
Humperdinck, Engelbert
Meyerbeer, Giacomo

Mozart, Wolfgang Amadeus
Schönberg, Arnold
Schubert, Franz
Spohr, Louis
Strauss, Richard
Wagner, Richard
Weber, Carl Maria von
Weill, Kurt

ITALIAN COMPOSERS

Bellini, Vincenzo
Boito, Arrigo
Busoni, Ferruccio
Cherubini, Luigi
Dallapiccola, Luigi
Donizetti, Gaetano
Leoncavallo, Ruggiero

Mascagni, Pietro
Monteverdi, Claudio
Pergolesi, Giovanni
Puccini, Giacomo
Rossini, Gioacchino
Scarlatti (Alessandro)
Verdi, Giuseppe

RUSSIAN COMPOSERS

Borodin, Alexander
Glinka, Mikhail
Mussorgsky, Modest
Prokofiev, Sergei

Rimsky-Korsakov, Nicholas
Shostakovich, Dimitri
Stravinsky, Igor
Tchaikovsky, Peter Ilich

OTHER COMPOSERS

Bartók, Béla
Dvořák, Antonín
Falla, Manuel de
Ginastera, Alberto

Janáček, Leoš
Kodály, Zoltán
Smetana, Bedřich

AMERICAN OPERA SINGERS

Anderson, Marian
Callas, Maria
Farrar, Geraldine
Garden, Mary
Hayes, Roland
London, George
Maynor, Dorothy

Peerce, Jan
Ponselle, Rosa Melba
Price, Leontyne
Robeson, Paul
Sills, Beverly
Tucker, Richard

AUSTRALIAN OPERA SINGERS

Melba, Dame Nellie

Sutherland, Joan

EUROPEAN OPERA SINGERS

Bjoerling, Jussi
Caruso, Enrico
Chaliapin, Feodor

Fischer-Dieskau, Dietrich
Flagstad, Kirsten
Galli-Curci, Amelita

García (family)
Lehmann, Lilli
Lehmann, Lotte
Lind, Jenny
Malibran, Maria Felicita
Martinelli, Giovanni
McCormack, John
Melchior, Lauritz

Nilsson, Birgit
Patti, Adelina
Reszke (family)
Schumann-Heink, Ernestine
Schwarzkopf, Elisabeth
Tebaldi, Renata
Tetrazzini, Luisa

OTHER RELATED ARTICLES

Aria
Ballet
Chorus
Germany
 (Arts [picture])
Italy (The
 Arts [picture])

La Scala
Libretto
Metropolitan
 Opera Association
Music (History)
Musical Comedy
Operetta

Oratorio
Overture
Singing
United States
 (The Arts
 [pictures])

Outline

I. The Elements of Opera
   A. The Libretto   B. The Music
II. Producing an Opera
   A. The People Behind the Scenes
   B. Preparing a Production
III. The Development of Opera
IV. The Opera Repertoire

Questions

Why is the libretto of most operas shorter than the text of a spoken play?

What qualities make *The Barber of Seville* an example of opera buffa?

Why is the role of Salome one of the most difficult in the repertoire?

What is the difference between recitative and arias?

What dramatic function does the "Intermezzo" serve in *Cavalleria Rusticana*?

How does a coloratura soprano differ from a dramatic soprano?

What was the *Camerata*?

Why does opera acting tend to be less lively and less realistic than acting in other forms of drama?

Who was the most important German opera composer of the 1800's? Of the 1900's?

What is the function of a general manager in an opera company?

Books to Read

BULLA, CLYDE R. *Stories of Favorite Operas.* Crowell, 1959. *More Stories of Favorite Operas.* 1965. For younger readers.

EWEN, DAVID. *The New Encyclopedia of the Opera.* Farrar, 1971. *Opera: Its Story Told Through the Lives and Works of Its Foremost Composers.* Watts, 1972.

GISHFORD, ANTHONY, ed. *Grand Opera: The Story of the World's Leading Opera Houses and Personalities.* Viking, 1972.

GOLDOVSKY, BORIS. *Bringing Opera to Life: Operatic Acting and Stage Direction.* Prentice-Hall, 1968.

GROUT, DONALD J. *A Short History of Opera.* 2nd ed. Columbia, 1965.

KOBBÉ, GUSTAV. *The New Kobbé's Complete Opera Book.* Ed. & rev. by the Earl of Harewood. Putnam, 1976.

MARTIN, GEORGE. *The Opera Companion: A Guide for the Casual Operagoer.* Peter Smith, 1961.

PAULY, REINHARD G. *Music and the Theater: An Introduction to Opera.* Prentice-Hall, 1970.

ROSENTHAL, HAROLD D., and WARRACK, J. H., eds. *Concise Oxford Dictionary of Opera.* Rev. ed. Oxford, 1972.

STREATFEILD, NOEL. *The First Book of the Opera.* Watts, 1966. For younger readers.

The Victor Book of the Opera. 13th ed. rev. by Henry W. Simon. Simon & Schuster, 1968.

OPERA BUFFA. See OPERA (Opera Seria and Opera Buffa).

OPERA GLASS. See BINOCULARS.

OPERATION. See SURGERY.

OPERATION DEEP FREEZE. See ANTARCTICA (International Cooperation).

OPERATION HIGHJUMP. See ANTARCTICA (American Exploration).

OPERETTA is a light, short opera. It usually has gay, lilting music and an unpretentious plot. Much of the dialogue in an operetta is spoken. Operettas are sometimes called *light operas* because both forms are musical-dramatic works that are noted for their comedy. In England, the term *comic opera* is also used. A comic opera is sometimes longer than an operetta.

In American operettas, the dialogue may be both spoken and sung. The dialogue of most Italian operettas is carried in *recitativo secco* (dry, or unaccompanied, recitative), which means that the orchestra sounds only a few chords of music to enable the singer to hold to the key. In English, German, and French operettas, most of the dialogue of the recitative is spoken.

The operetta as known today began in the 1800's. An Austrian composer, Franz von Suppé, wrote more than 150 operettas, which were highly popular in Vienna. Two of his well-known works are *The Beautiful Galatea* and *Boccaccio*. Another Austrian, Johann Strauss the Younger, wrote such world-famous operettas as *Die Fledermaus* (The Bat) and *The Gypsy Baron*. Later, Franz Lehár's *The Merry Widow* became one of the most successful operettas ever written.

Jacques Offenbach made the operetta a popular form of entertainment in France in the 1800's. Many of his works, including *Bluebeard* and *Orpheus in the Underworld*, were performed with great success in both Europe and the United States. Two Englishmen, the composer Sir Arthur Sullivan and the dramatist Sir William S. Gilbert, together wrote some of the most delightful operettas of all time. Their most popular works include *H.M.S. Pinafore*, *The Mikado*, *Patience*, and *Iolanthe*.

Sigmund Romberg and Victor Herbert were well-known American composers of operettas. Romberg's works include *The Student Prince* and *Blossom Time*. Some of the songs from Herbert's operettas have become as famous as the operettas themselves. Among them are "Kiss Me Again" from *Mlle. Modiste*, "Italian Street Song" from *Naughty Marietta*, and "Toyland" from *Babes in Toyland*. The musical comedy developed from the operettas of the 1800's and early 1900's (see MUSICAL COMEDY). RAYMOND KENDALL

OPHIR, *O fer*, was an ancient region, perhaps in southern Arabia, which was famous for the abundance and fineness of its gold. The Bible says that Solomon built ships which brought him gold, silver, gems, ivory, apes, and peacocks from Ophir (I Kings 9-10).

OPHTHALMIA, *ahf THAL mee uh*, is a name for severe diseases affecting the eye membranes. These diseases may be caused by infections, poisons, or injuries. For example, *ophthalmia neonatorum* is an infection of the eyes of newborn babies, usually caused by the germ that causes gonorrhea. *Sympathetic ophthalmia* spreads to both eyes after an injury to one eye and often leads to blindness. See also BLINDNESS (Diseases). JOHN R. MCWILLIAMS

OPHTHALMOLOGY, *AHF thal MAHL uh jee*, is the field of medicine involving the diagnosis and treatment of eye diseases. An *ophthalmologist*, sometimes called an *oculist*, must have an M.D. degree and three to five years of specialized training in a hospital.

Ophthalmologists limit their medical practice to the eye. They examine the eye with special equipment and determine the degree of *refraction* in the lens of the eye. Refraction is a measurement of the eye's ability to see. If the examination shows that the patient needs glasses, the ophthalmologist gives the patient a prescription for them. Glasses are made by an *optician*. An ophthalmologist who discovers that an eye condition requires surgery performs the necessary operation to correct the condition.

By studying the retina, an ophthalmologist may discover signs of a disease of some other part of the body. For example, such diseases as diabetes, hypertension, and certain forms of anemia may involve changes in the appearance of the retina. SIDNEY LERMAN

See also SURGERY (Specialties).

OPHTHALMOSCOPE, *ahf THAL muh skohp*, is an optical instrument for examining the interior of the eye. Physicians trained to treat the eyes can make certain

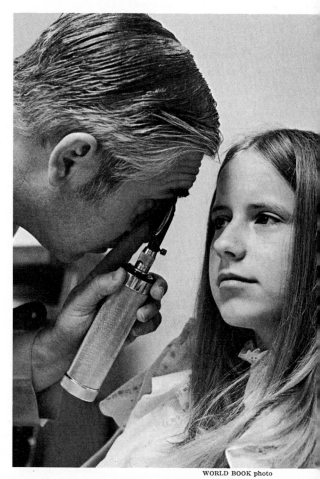

An Ophthalmoscope enables a physician to examine the interior of the eye. He peers through a tiny hole in the ophthalmoscope as he focuses light from the instrument into the patient's eye.

diagnoses by examining abnormalities of the eye's interior with the use of the ophthalmoscope. The ophthalmoscope contains an electric light and a prism to focus light on the interior of the eye. Lenses are mounted with the light and prism in the head of the instrument, which is attached to a handle containing a flashlight battery. The lenses make it possible for the physician to focus the light to provide a clear view of the interior of the eye.

The ophthalmoscope was invented by a German physicist, Hermann von Helmholtz, in 1851 (see HELMHOLTZ, HERMANN L.). Helmholtz' instrument consisted of a sandwich of three thin plates of glass mounted at a 45 degree angle on a handle. A light was placed to the side of the eye under examination. Some light passed through the glass plates, but some was reflected into the eye. The lighted inside of the eye was observed through the glass.　　WILLIAM L. BENEDICT

OPIATE, *O pih ayt,* is a type of drug made from or containing opium. *Codeine, heroin,* and *morphine* are opiates. Most opiates put a person to sleep, and partially or completely deaden the feeling of pain. Medicines of this kind are usually classed as *narcotics* (sleep inducers). Opiates are addicting, and should be taken only by prescription.　　SOLOMON GARB

OPINION. See THOUGHT AND JUDGMENT (Judgment); PUBLIC OPINION.

OPINION POLL. See PUBLIC OPINION POLL.

OPIUM is a drug that serves as the source of several medicines, including codeine and morphine. Heroin, an illegal drug, is also made from opium. Opium and most *opiates* (drugs made from or containing opium) can cause addiction. The United States and many other countries strictly regulate their manufacture, distribution, and use.

Opium is made from the juice of the opium poppy. Most opium used by U.S. drug manufacturers comes from poppies grown on farms in India. Processors near the poppy farms make dried poppy juice, called *raw opium,* into a brownish powder known as *refined opium.*

The Opium Poppy. At the left are (a) a ripe seed pod, and (b) a cross section of the pod showing the seeds inside.

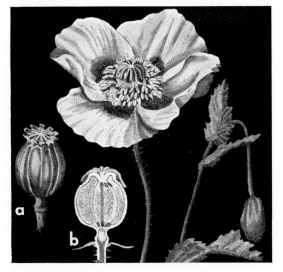

They also extract a yellowish powder called *morphine base* from the opium. Drug manufacturers use refined opium and morphine base to make codeine, morphine, and other medicines.

Heroin and most other illegal opiates are made from morphine base. Most illegal opiates are made in France, Latin America, the Middle East, and Southeast Asia.

Medical Uses. Opium ranked as the most effective pain-relieving drug until the development of morphine in the early 1800's. Opium was also used to stop coughing and diarrhea, to ease worry, and to cause drowsiness. Opiates serve many of the same purposes today. Physicians prescribe morphine to relieve severe pain. Codeine, probably the most widely used opiate, stops coughing. Paregoric, a drug that controls diarrhea, contains opium.

Opium Addiction. The misuse of opium or of drugs made from it can lead to addiction. Opium, when first used, can give a user a feeling of extreme calm and well-being. His troubles may seem unimportant, and he temporarily lives in an unreal world of isolated contentment. People smoke, sniff, or eat opium for these effects. But an opium addict may have vivid dreams and daydreams, which may be extremely unpleasant. Opium addicts tend to neglect their health and their families.

Addicts who want to stop taking opiates can obtain medical treatment and counseling. Some experimental programs use a drug called *methadone* to help patients overcome addiction to opiates (see METHADONE).

History. The use of opium began at least 6,000 years ago in the Middle East. Greek and Roman physicians prescribed the drug before the time of Christ. Arabian traders took opium to China and India, probably starting in the A.D. 600's. At first, the Chinese used the drug chiefly as a medicine. European traders introduced opium smoking into China in the early 1600's. The Chinese government outlawed opium in 1729, but traders continued to exchange it for silk, porcelain, and other Chinese products. In the late 1700's, opium addiction became widespread among the Chinese. The opium trade helped cause the so-called Opium War (1839-1842), in which England defeated China (see CHINA [The "Unequal Treaties"]).

During the 1800's, people in the United States and Europe could buy laudanum, morphine, and other opiates legally and without a prescription. By 1900, at least 200,000 Americans had become addicted to opiates. The Harrison Act, a group of laws passed in 1914, greatly reduced the problem in the United States. Addiction to opiates, particularly heroin, began to increase in the late 1940's and has continued to rise ever since. Today, a number of nations and international organizations cooperate in fighting the illegal manufacture and sale of opium and opiates.　　DONALD J. WOLK

Related Articles in WORLD BOOK include:

Codeine	Drug Abuse	Morphine
Drug (picture: The	Drug Addiction	Paregoric
Four Sources of Drugs)	Heroin	Poppy

OPIUM WAR. See CHINA (The "Unequal Treaties").

OPORTO. See PORTO.

OPOSSUM, *uh PAHS uhm,* is any member of a family of furry mammals that live in the Western Hemisphere. The female opossum carries its young in a pouch on its

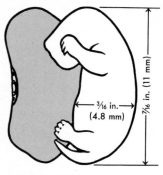

A Newborn Opossum is about the same size as a kidney bean.

Pix

A Mother Opossum carries its young on its back. Baby opossums stay in their mother's pouch for about two months after birth. They remain near the mother for several more weeks.

abdomen. Opossums, kangaroos, and other mammals that carry their young about in the mother's pouch after birth are called *marsupials*. Opossums are the only marsupials that are native to North America. They live from Ontario in Canada southward into South America.

There are many species of opossums, most of which live in Central and South America. Small, tree-dwelling *murine opossums* resemble mice. *Woolly opossums* have thick, soft fur. Another kind of opossum, the *yapok*, is the only marsupial that is adapted for living in water. Its webbed feet help make it a good swimmer.

The *common opossum* is the only kind of opossum found in the United States. This species grows about as big as a house cat. It has rough grayish-white hair, a long snout, dark eyes, and big hairless ears. This opossum has a long tail that does not have much hair on it. The animal can hang upside down by wrapping its tail around the branch of a tree. A common opossum has 50 teeth, more than any other North American mammal. Its teeth and claws are sharp. Opossum tracks are easy to recognize because the animal has long, widely separated toes.

Opossums are born in groups of from 5 to 20. At birth, an opossum is only about as big as a kidney bean. The female opossum carries its tiny babies in a pouch on the outer skin of its abdomen for about two months after birth. After leaving the pouch, the young stay near the mother for several more weeks. When they can take care of themselves, the young go off on their own.

Opossums hunt at night. They eat almost any kind of animal or vegetable food. When in danger, opossums lie motionless and appear to be dead. From this habit, we say a person is "playing possum" when he pretends to be injured.   FRANK B. GOLLEY

Scientific Classification: Opossums make up the opossum family, *Didelphidae*. The common opossum is genus *Didelphis*, species *D. marsupialis*.

See also ANIMAL (picture: Animals of the Temperate Forests); MARSUPIAL.

OPPENHEIMER, J. ROBERT (1904-1967), an American physicist, became known as the man who built the atomic bomb. From 1943 to 1945, Oppenheimer directed the Los Alamos laboratory near Santa Fe, N. Mex., where the design and building of the first atomic bomb took place.

After World War II, Oppenheimer served as a leading government adviser. He was consultant to the newly formed U.S. Atomic Energy Commission (AEC), and played a key role in drafting its policies. Oppenheimer also served as a policy adviser to the U.S. Department of Defense, and helped draft the first U.S. proposals for international control of nuclear energy.

In 1953, Oppenheimer's loyalty to the United States was questioned. His opposition to the development of the hydrogen bomb, together with his record of association with Communists, led to an investigation by an AEC security panel. The panel cleared Oppenheimer of all charges of disloyalty, but voted to deny him further access to official secrets. In 1963, however, the commission awarded Oppenheimer its highest honor, the Enrico Fermi award, for his work in the field of nuclear physics.

Oppenheimer was born in New York City. He studied theoretical physics at Harvard University, and graduated with honors in three years. From 1925 to 1929, he studied under some of Europe's leading physicists. He returned to the United States in 1929, and taught theoretical physics at the University of California and at the California Institute of Technology. Oppenheimer served as director of the Institute for Advanced

United Press Int.

J. Robert Oppenheimer

Study in Princeton, N.J., from 1947 until he retired in 1966.   RALPH E. LAPP

OPPER, FREDERICK BURR. See CARTOON (History).

OPPOSITION, in astronomy, is a term which refers to the point at which the sun, the earth, and one of the outer planets from the earth are in a direct line with one another. When Mars, for example, is in line with the earth and the sun, Mars is said to be *in opposition.*

OPTIC NERVE. See EYE (The Eyeball; diagram).

OPTICAL FIBER. See FIBER OPTICS.

OPTICAL GLASS. See GLASS (Specialty Glasses).

OPTICAL ILLUSION. As we look down a long, straight road, we see that it seems to grow narrower in the distance. Trees and telegraph poles along the road appear to grow smaller as they stretch away toward the horizon. We know that a white house looks larger than the same house painted a dark color, and that a person wearing a suit with up-and-down stripes looks thinner than he would if the stripes went crosswise. We call appearances of this kind *optical illusions* because we know that in such cases things are not the way they appear to be.

Optical illusions of the kind described above are called "normal" illusions, because every person with normal eyesight experiences them. But an optical illusion does not occur every time we are deceived by what

Some Common Optical Illusions

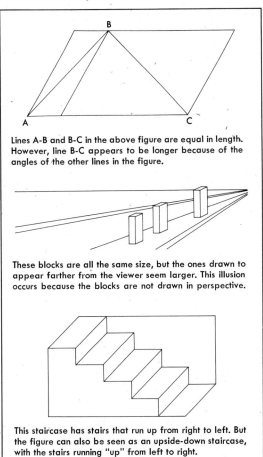

Lines A-B and B-C in the above figure are equal in length. However, line B-C appears to be longer because of the angles of the other lines in the figure.

These blocks are all the same size, but the ones drawn to appear farther from the viewer seem larger. This illusion occurs because the blocks are not drawn in perspective.

This staircase has stairs that run up from right to left. But the figure can also be seen as an upside-down staircase, with the stairs running "up" from left to right.

we see. Often we make mistakes in interpreting the impressions our eye receives. For example, many persons will read the sentence "he walked though the busy street," and never notice that the third word has no "r" in it. They *expect* to see "through" and therefore they *do* see "through." Such mistaken impressions are not optical illusions.   FRANK J. KOBLER

See also COLOR (How Color Fools the Eye); PSYCHOLOGY (picture: A Psychologist's Study of Perception); PERCEPTION (Factors Affecting Perception); MIRAGE.

OPTICAL MASER. See LASER (History).

OPTICAL SCANNER. See COMPUTER (Input Equipment).

OPTICIAN prepares, fits, and sells glasses prescribed for a patient by an ophthalmologist or an optometrist. See OPHTHALMOLOGY; OPTOMETRY.

OPTICS is the branch of physics that is concerned with the properties of light. It describes how light is produced, how it is transmitted, and how it can be detected and measured. Optics includes the study of visible light and of infrared and ultraviolet rays, both of which are invisible.

Many instruments, including binoculars, cameras, magnifiers, microscopes, projectors, and telescopes, operate according to the principles of optics. All these instruments have optical devices, such as lenses and mirrors, which transmit and control light. Light is detected and measured with instruments called *light meters* (see LIGHT METER).

Scientists have used the principles of optics to increase the number of ways to use light. For example, they can transmit light along a twisted or curved path by sending the light through a filament called an *optical fiber.* Scientists use a device called a *laser* as an important and powerful light source (see LASER).

There are two major branches of optics. *Physical optics* deals with the nature and behavior of light. *Geometrical optics* is concerned with optical instruments and what happens when light strikes them.

Basic Principles of Optics describe what light is and how it behaves. To study visible light, scientists use a *prism* (wedge of glass) that produces a band of colors called the *visible spectrum.* Scientists analyze this and other spectra with an instrument called a *spectroscope.* See LIGHT (The Visible Spectrum); SPECTROSCOPE.

Several reactions may occur when light strikes the surface of an object. Diffraction, interference, reflection, and refraction are basic principles that describe what may happen. Other principles include the chemical effects of light, dispersion, the photoelectric effect, and polarization. For a discussion of optical principles, see LIGHT (How Light Behaves).

History. The development of optics began chiefly during the 1600's. The Italian scientist Galileo built telescopes to observe the planets and the stars. Sir Isaac Newton, an English scientist, experimented with lenses and used a prism to break sunlight into its colors (see NEWTON, SIR ISAAC [Light and Color]). In Holland, the physicist Christian Huygens studied polarization and proposed a wave theory of light.

During the early 1800's, two physicists, Thomas Young of England and Augustin J. Fresnel of France, did much to confirm Huygens' theory. Young formulated the principle of the interference of light. Fresnel then developed a mathematical formula that supported this principle. Most scientists accepted the work of Young and Fresnel as proof of Huygens' theory.

During the mid-1800's, accurate measurements of the speed of light were made by the French scientists Armand H. L. Fizeau and Jean B. L. Foucault. At about the same time, two German scientists, Robert Bunsen and Gustav Kirchhoff, showed that atoms of chemical elements produced the color bands of the spectrum. In 1864, the English physicist James C. Maxwell introduced the electromagnetic theory of light.

Scientists made several important discoveries in optics during the late 1800's and the 1900's. Such scientists as Albert A. Michelson of the United States, Fritz Zernike of The Netherlands, and Dennis Gabor of England received the Nobel prize for physics for their work in optics.　　　　　　　　　　　　BRIAN J. THOMPSON

See also LIGHT with its list of *Related Articles*.

OPTIMIST INTERNATIONAL is an association of men's service clubs in the United States, Canada, and Mexico. Membership is by invitation only to business and professional men. Optimist clubs work to develop optimism as a philosophy of life. They also promote interest in good government and civic affairs, respect for law, patriotism, friendship among all people, and service to youth.

Optimist clubs sponsor a wide range of community service projects and programs. For example, the Respect for Law program urges citizens to help improve law enforcement by supporting local police departments and by becoming involved in fighting crime. Working with young people is another important Optimist activity. The clubs sponsor Bike Safety Week, Youth Appreciation Week, and an annual public speaking contest for young men and women of high-school age. Winners of the contest receive college scholarships.

Eleven Optimist clubs founded Optimist International in Louisville, Ky., in 1919. The organization now has about 120,000 members and more than 3,300 clubs. Headquarters are at 4494 Lindell Boulevard, St. Louis, Mo. 63108.　　　Critically reviewed by OPTIMIST INTERNATIONAL

OPTOMETRY, *ahp TAHM uh tree*, is a profession devoted to the care of vision. Optometrists prescribe about two-thirds of the glasses and contact lenses worn by people in the United States and Canada.

Optometrists give vision examinations that measure a person's ability to see nearby and distant objects and to judge distance. The tests also determine the ability of the eyes to work together and to perform such visual tasks as reading. Optometrists prescribe lenses to correct faulty vision. They also may recommend training methods to help a person overcome certain problems of vision. If an optometrist detects symptoms that indicate disease in the eye or any other part of a person's body, the person is referred to a physician.

To practice optometry in the United States or Canada, a person must pass an examination for a state or provincial license. Optometrists in the United States must have completed at least two years of pre-optometry college work and graduated from a four-year school or college of optometry. Since 1965, all schools and colleges of optometry have awarded Doctor of Optometry

(O.D.) degrees. Canada has similar educational requirements. Additional information on optometry may be obtained from the American Optometric Association, 7000 Chippewa Street, St. Louis, Mo. 63119.　　JAMES R. GREGG

OPUNTIA. See CACTUS (Kinds of Cactuses).

OPUS. See MUSIC (Names of Compositions).

ORACLES, *AWR uh kuhlz*, in ancient Greece and Rome, were the answers given by a god to some question. The word can also mean the priest or other means by which the answer was given, or the place where the answer was given. Two well-known Greek oracles were the oracles of Apollo at Delphi and Zeus at Dodona.

The ancient Greeks and Romans believed that their gods took a personal interest in human affairs. The people asked the gods for advice. The gods were supposed to answer them through the oracles. The meanings of the answers were often difficult to understand, so special priests or priestesses interpreted the god's meaning. The people rewarded the priests and priestesses with gifts.

At times, it was impossible even for the priests to know what the oracle meant. Croesus, king of Lydia, consulted the gods before he invaded Cappadocia. The oracle said that if he invaded this country he would bring ruin to an empire. Croesus thought this meant he would win, but the oracle had meant that the empire of Croesus would be ruined. And it was. Many dishonest people pretended to be oracles. They tricked worshipers and took their money.　　　　　　　　　　PADRAIC COLUM

See also CROESUS; DELPHI; DODONA.

ORAL CONTRACEPTIVE. See BIRTH CONTROL.

ORAL LAW is a body of Jewish laws, arising from interpretations and qualifications of the written law found in the Bible. These changes were made necessary by time, condition, and circumstances, and were handed down by word of mouth. They were finally put into writing in the Talmud, and helped Judaism to adjust itself to the changing science, philosophy, and sociology of new generations. After the Oral Law was codified and written, new interpretations of it in the form of commentaries arose to keep a dynamic tradition from becoming static. See also TALMUD.　　LOUIS L. MANN

ORAL MESSAGE. See FERLINGHETTI, LAWRENCE.

ORAL ROBERTS UNIVERSITY is a private coeducational liberal arts institution in Tulsa, Okla. It grants bachelor's degrees in about 25 fields. It offers courses in the fine arts, the humanities, mathematics, the natural sciences, the social sciences, and biblical studies. The evangelist Oral Roberts founded the university in 1965. For enrollment, see UNIVERSITIES AND COLLEGES (table). See also ROBERTS, ORAL.　　　　　　　ORAL ROBERTS

ORAL SURGERY. See DENTISTRY.

ORAN, *oh RAN*, or *oh RAHN* (pop. 485,139), is a Mediterranean Sea port in Algeria. It lies about 225 miles (362 kilometers) west of Algiers (see ALGERIA [color map]). Oran trades with cities of inland Africa and ports of southern Europe.

Oran was built by the Moors, and some of the old Moorish buildings are still standing. The city was captured by the Spaniards in 1509, by the Turks in 1708, and again by the Spaniards in 1732. Spain abandoned the city after it was destroyed in 1791 by an earthquake. In 1831, the French rebuilt Oran. American forces were stationed in the city during World War II, after they invaded North Africa.　　　　　　KEITH G. MATHER

ORANGE. See COLOR.

ORANGE. The orange is the most important of all citrus fruits. It is widely used as a source of vitamin C, and can be drunk as juice or peeled and eaten.

There are two kinds of oranges, both of them closely related. The *sweet orange* is the kind commonly grown and eaten in the United States. The other kind is called the bitter, sour, Seville, or bigarade orange. The tangerine is often considered an orange. Actually, it is a citrus fruit of the *mandarin* group.

The sweet orange is thought to have come from southern China. It seems not to have reached the Mediterranean until several hundred years after the bitter orange. The bitter orange came from India, and was grown in the countries surrounding the Mediterranean Sea a thousand years after the birth of Christ. Both kinds of oranges were brought to America by the Spanish and Portuguese in the 1500's. The early Spanish settlers in Florida planted orange trees. The mission fathers of southern California planted orange trees there in the latter part of the 1700's.

The Orange Tree. The orange tree has dark green leaves that are shed gradually in spring and other periods of *growth flush* (increased growth). The white, waxy flowers appear in abundance during spring, and in scattered blooms during growth flushes. For hundreds of years orange blossoms have been considered a symbol of marriage. Honey made from orange blossoms is very good. The orange tree has long been considered one of the most beautiful trees. To the people who lived in northern Europe it was a symbol of the beauty of the sunny lands of Italy and Spain.

The orange tree grows about 30 feet (9 meters) high. Its branches are very symmetrical and do not spread very much. The tree thrives in warm countries, and often requires irrigation. The bitter orange tree is somewhat hardier and resists cold somewhat better than the sweet orange. Both the bitter and the sweet orange resist cold better than limes or lemons.

U.S.D.A.

Washington Navel Orange Trees produce most of California's winter oranges. They were first imported from Brazil.

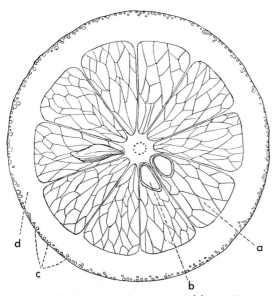

The Cross Section of an Orange shows (a) the edible part of the fruit; (b) location and cross section of the seed; (c) oil reservoirs just under the surface of the rind; and (d) the rind.

The Fruit of the orange is known to botanists as a *hesperidium*. It is really a special type of berry which grows only on citrus trees. The fruit has a soft central axis made of pith. Ten to fifteen segments surround the pith and contain the juice. The whole orange is enclosed in a soft rind. The *albedo* (inner part of the rind) is white and spongy. The *flavedo* (outer part) is orange-colored and is made up of small glands that contain an essential oil.

The juice of the orange contains sugars and citric acid. The spongy part of the rind contains a jelling substance called pectin. Orange juice is very high in vitamins A, B, and C, and it also contains mineral salts which are useful in the diet.

Oranges vary greatly in the number of seeds they contain. Most kinds of oranges contain many seeds. A few varieties have no seeds. Oranges are considered commercially seedless if they contain five seeds or less.

The Valencia orange is the most important late-season orange of California and Florida. Valencias account for almost half of the annual orange crop in the United States. They have a thin skin and a golden orange color, and are usually seedless.

The navel orange is really a double orange. A small second fruit that does not develop is embedded in one end of the main fruit to produce the so-called navel. All citrus fruits occasionally produce double fruits, but navel oranges do so regularly. The Washington navel

General Foods

Fruit Sizers separate oranges into groups. Some oranges go directly to market. Others are made into juice and marmalade.

It costs more to produce oranges in California than in Florida. The Florida rainfall is usually adequate, and irrigation is necessary only when the distribution of rainfall is irregular throughout a season. Irrigation is necessary in California and Texas. Also, labor costs are higher and crop yields are lower in California.

The orange tree is bud grafted onto the root systems of other citrus trees. The bitter orange is generally used because it is hardier and more resistant to disease than the root system of the sweet orange. But it is easily affected by a dreaded virus disease called *tristeza*. Other kinds of rootstocks used include those of the rough lemon, sweet orange, and grapefruit. The sweet lime tree is used in Israel. The orange tree can adapt itself to many different kinds of soil. But it requires soil that is well drained and not too acid or alkaline. It also suffers if too much irrigation is given. Orange trees yield best when they are very heavily fertilized. They respond mainly to applications of nitrogen and organic matter. They sometimes respond also to applications of magnesium. To make certain that the trees get enough of these necessary elements, salts containing zinc and copper are commonly sprayed on the trees. A complete nutritional program that includes manganese, molybdenum, and boron is needed in light, sandy soils.

To control insects and fungus diseases, the trees are sprayed with *pesticides* (pest-killers), the use of which is regulated by the federal government. In other cases, insects are controlled by introducing or aiding their enemies. Fungi which grow in the insects' bodies are sometimes sprayed on the trees. Sometimes insects which prey on harmful insects are especially raised for this purpose.

Oranges require a good deal of heat in order to ripen. Only in very hot places do oranges ripen during the fall and winter. In cooler climates, oranges ripen in the spring or summer a year after the trees have bloomed. Therefore, in late spring, a tree may carry ripe fruit, young green fruit, and flowers all at the same time.

Some kinds of oranges require more heat than others to ripen their fruit. Therefore, there are varieties which ripen early, others that ripen in midseason, and still others that are late in maturing. Oranges in California ripen throughout the year. Therefore, California oranges are the only ones that are commonly found in grocery stores during the summer months.

Harvesting and Marketing. Oranges are picked when the juice, sugar, and acid contents reach the levels established by state and federal laws. Most oranges are clipped off the trees in California. Workers prefer to pull Florida oranges. Oranges are usually sent to the packing house for immediate processing, unless it is necessary to color them with ethylene gas. The oranges are washed, dried, waxed, graded, and sized. They may also be color-added, stamped, and treated with a *fungicide* (fungus-killer). Most California oranges are shipped to serve as fresh fruit. As many as 80 per cent of the Florida oranges are sent to canneries that produce frozen orange concentrate.

Uses. Over three-fourths of the oranges processed in the United States are made into frozen orange juice concentrate. Other products include soft drinks, wine, and powdered instant orange juice.

Various by-products of the orange include the peel, which can be candied, dried, or made into marmalade.

orange, also called the California navel orange, is normally seedless. These oranges are harvested between November and April and account for most of California's winter oranges.

The *blood orange* is an interesting variation with juice that is colored by a red pigment called *anthocyanin*. It has a higher iron content than other oranges. It is more popular in Europe than in the United States.

Climatic factors cause Florida and California oranges to differ. Oranges become bright orange only in regions where the night temperatures are below 50° F. (10° C) during much of the ripening period. Florida oranges often require a red food-grade dye to obtain an orange color. The Florida orange is thinner-skinned, juicier, and has more sugar and less acid than California oranges. Florida oranges decay more easily and have a less attractive appearance. Green oranges from either state are often treated with ethylene gas to remove the green color and bring out the orange color.

Cultivation. Orange trees are sensitive to cold and sudden heat. If the temperature falls to 25° F. (−4° C), the fruit and the trees may be injured. If it falls to 20° F. (−7° C), injury may be severe. For this reason, the trees require a tropical or subtropical climate. In the latter, during occasional cold spells the trees are kept warm by means of orchard heaters.

While the orange tree itself grows very well in the tropics, the fruit is pale and flat in taste. For this reason its commercial culture is largely confined to the subtropics. In such areas, however, the trees are sometimes subject to sudden heat waves, which cause the young fruit to fall off. The tree is also sensitive to strong or prevailing winds. Living windbreaks are commonly used to provide wind protection.

The orange can be grown in a much wider range of climate than the lemon can, but it is not able to grow in as wide a range of climate as the grapefruit. In the United States, most oranges are grown in central and southern Florida, the lower Rio Grande Valley in Texas, and parts of Arizona and southern California.

LEADING ORANGE-GROWING STATES

Boxes of oranges and tangerines grown in 1973*

Florida
222,257,000 boxes

California
46,821,000 boxes

Texas
10,029,000 boxes

Arizona
5,989,000 boxes

*One box equals 70 pounds (32 kilograms).
Source: *Citrus Fruits, By States, 1972-73, 1973-74, and 1974-75,* U.S. Department of Agriculture.

Orange oil and pectin are other products made from the peel. It is also used in candymaking. Cannery wastes are used in the preparation of livestock feed. Orange oil is used for flavoring and perfumes.

The world production of oranges has increased greatly since World War II. It now averages over 1 billion 70-pound (32-kilogram) boxes a year. The United States is the largest producer in the world. More than a fourth of the oranges grown come from the United States. Brazil, Israel, Italy, Japan, Mexico, and Spain are other leading producers. Orange growing is also important in Algeria, Argentina, China, Egypt, India, Morocco, South Africa, and Turkey.

About 95 per cent of the oranges in the United States are produced in Florida and California. The states of Arizona, Texas, and Louisiana grow the remainder. About 250,000 acres (101,000 hectares) in California are planted in orange trees. The industry traditionally centered around Los Angeles, but the increased growth of cities in that area has forced the industry north and east. Nearly 300,000 acres (120,000 hectares) in Florida are used for growing oranges. The Florida industry centers chiefly in central Florida. Winter Haven and Orlando are important orange growing centers. But a series of severe freezes since 1957 caused growers to move south into newly reclaimed swamplands. About

LEADING ORANGE-GROWING COUNTRIES

Boxes of oranges and tangerines grown in 1973*

United States
285,096,000 boxes

Brazil
137,159,000 boxes

Japan
113,979,000 boxes

Spain
78,484,000 boxes

Italy
60,060,000 boxes

Mexico
59,840,000 boxes

Israel
36,219,000 boxes

*One box equals 70 pounds (32 kilograms).
Source: *Production Yearbook, 1973,* FAO.

35,000 acres (14,200 hectares) in Texas are used to grow oranges.

The Bitter Orange. The bitter orange is widely grown for use as *rootstock seedlings,* on which to bud-graft sweet oranges and other citrus fruits. It also is grown for other purposes in the Mediterranean region, particularly in Spain. Bitter orange marmalade is made from it. In southern France, the flowers of the bitter orange are distilled for their perfume. Eau de Cologne is made from it, and essential oils are made from the tender buds, shoots, and leaves of the trees.

Scientific Classification. The orange tree belongs to the rue family, *Rutaceae.* The common or sweet orange is genus *Citrus,* species *C. sinensis.* The bitter orange is *C. aurantium.*　　　　　　　　　　WILLIAM GRIERSON

See also LEAF (picture: Kinds of Tree Leaves); TANGOR; ISRAEL (picture); CALIFORNIA (picture); FLORIDA (Agriculture); SPAIN (picture).

ORANGE, HOUSE OF. See MARY (II); WILLIAM (III) of England; WILLIAM I, PRINCE OF ORANGE.

ORANGE BOWL. See FOOTBALL (table).

ORANGE FREE STATE is a province of South Africa. It is a land of rolling plains and light rainfall. The province covers 49,866 square miles (129,152 square kilometers). For location, see SOUTH AFRICA (map).

Most of the 1,715,589 people who live in the Orange Free State are black Africans. There are fewer than 300,000 white people, but they own nearly all the land. Most of the Africans work for white farmers or in gold and uranium mines in the northern part of the province. Farmers grow grain in the eastern districts. Bloemfontein is the capital of the province.

Europeans first entered the area in the 1700's. About 1836, Boers from Cape Colony settled the section. The British claimed the land in 1848 and called it the Orange River Sovereignty. In 1854 it was declared independent and renamed the Orange Free State.

In 1899, disagreements between the Boers and the British led to the Boer War (1899-1902). The Boers were defeated. In 1900, the Orange Free State again became a British possession, and was known as the Orange River Colony. Ten years later, as the Orange Free State, it became a part of the Union of South Africa (now Republic of South Africa).　　　　　LEONARD M. THOMPSON

See also BLOEMFONTEIN; BOER; BOER WAR; PRETORIUS.

ORANGE HAWKWEED. See DEVIL'S PAINTBRUSH.

ORANGE RIVER is the longest river in South Africa. It was named for the princes and noblemen of the Dutch House of Orange. The Orange rises in the high eastern mountains of Lesotho, less than 200 miles (320 kilometers) west of the Indian Ocean. The river follows a winding course westward for about 1,300 miles (2,090 kilometers) as it cuts across the continent to empty into the South Atlantic Ocean. The upper river forms the border between the Cape of Good Hope and Orange Free State provinces. The lower river separates the Cape Province and South West Africa. The Vaal River is the largest branch of the Orange River.

Steep banks border the Orange River. For the last 200 miles (320 kilometers) of its course the river flows through almost desert country. The stream has many rapids and falls. At King George's (Aughrabies) Falls, the waters drop nearly 400 feet (120 meters) into a deep canyon in solid rock. These rapids and a large sand bar at the mouth of the stream, which is 1 mile (1.6 kilometers) wide, make shipping impossible. But the waters above the Great Falls are useful for many irrigation projects. See SOUTH AFRICA (map).

In 1962, the South African government announced a 30-year development plan for the Orange River. The $630 million project includes 12 hydroelectric dams, and will irrigate 720,000 acres (291,000 hectares) of land.   KENNETH ROBINSON

See also VAAL RIVER.

ORANGEMEN. See WILLIAM (III).

ORANGEROOT. See GOLDENSEAL.

ORANGES, THE, are a group of cities in New Jersey. See EAST ORANGE.

ORANG-UTAN, *oh RANG oo tan,* is a large, rare ape that lives in Sumatra and Borneo. The name *orang-utan* comes from a Malay word meaning *man of the woods.* The orang-utan stands 3 to 5 feet (91 to 150 centimeters) tall, and has coarse reddish-brown hair. Male orang-utans may weigh from 150 to 200 pounds (68 to 91 kilograms). Some males have an arm spread of $7\frac{1}{2}$ feet (2.3 meters), one of the largest of all the apes. Females are about half as large as males. The orang-utan's arms reach to its ankles when the animal stands.

The orang-utan lives in trees, and rarely comes down to the ground. It moves carefully through the forest by climbing from branch to branch with its arms. It builds a nest in the trees to sleep in during the night. These nests are from 20 to 80 feet (6 to 24 meters) above the ground. Orang-utans eat fruits and leaves.

Orang-utans are silent, peaceful animals. Man is their main enemy. They live in groups of from two to five animals. These groups may not always stay together.

Arthur W. Ambler, National Audubon Society

Orang-Utans are powerful but peaceful apes. They use their long, strong arms to climb through branches in the forest.

Sometimes the animals travel through the forest alone.

Scientific Classification. Orang-utans belong to the anthropoid ape family, *Pongidae.* They are classified as genus *Pongo,* species *P. pygmaeus.*   GEORGE B. SCHALLER

See also ANIMAL (color picture: Animals of the Tropical Forests); APE.

ORATORIO, *AWR uh TOH rih oh,* is a musical composition using soloists, chorus, and orchestra. The subject is usually taken from the Bible, but may be a theme which is not strictly sacred. Scenery and action are not used in the performance. The oratorio is named from the Oratory, or mission hall, in Rome, where from 1571 to 1594 sacred musical performances were held. These were the basis of modern oratorios. The first and most popular subject was the Passion, or suffering of Christ. Johann Sebastian Bach's *Passion According to Saint Matthew* is the most famous. The next step was the epic oratorio, of which George Frideric Handel was the greatest writer. He composed 15 grand oratorios. The *Messiah* and *Judas Maccabaeus* are the best known of these. After these came Joseph Haydn's *The Creation* and *The Seasons,* and then Felix Mendelssohn's *Elijah* and *Saint Paul.*

Oratorios of today often have a dramatic element. Outstanding examples are Sir William Walton's *Belshazzar's Feast,* Ralph Vaughan Williams' *Sancta Civitas,* and Arthur Honegger's *King David.*   RAYMOND KENDALL

See also BACH (family); CHORUS; HANDEL, GEORGE FRIDERIC; OVERTURE.

ORATORS AND ORATORY. An orator is a skillful speaker who tries to influence his listeners by eloquent speeches. The art of an orator is called *oratory* or *rhetoric.* An orator follows rules of oratory. For some of the rules used today, see PUBLIC SPEAKING; DEBATE.

Beginnings. A mass of lawsuits arose when a democracy was established in Syracuse in Sicily in 466 B.C. They were brought by former exiles whose property had been seized by the tyrants. Many claims were several years old, and documentary evidence was often lacking. The claimants needed help in presenting their cases. Corax, a Sicilian Greek, was the first to supply this help, and is considered the founder of oratory. He established a system of rules for public speaking in the 460's B.C., with the aid of his pupil Tisias. He developed rules governing the organization of speech materials. He said that a speech usually should have five parts: (1) *proem* (introduction); (2) narrative; (3) arguments; (4) subsidiary remarks; and (5) summary.

Other early teachers of rhetoric include Protagoras, who developed the principles of debate; Gorgias, who emphasized style; Hippias, who was chiefly interested in the use of memory; and Lysias, who "showed how perfect elegance could be joined to plainness."

From Syracuse, the study of speechmaking spread to Athens, where the democratic form of government led to a general interest in the new art. During the 400's B.C., almost all male Athenian citizens attended the general assembly, where public policies were debated. They took part in the formulation of policies and the administration of justice. In the courts, they acted as jurors. The whole decision in each case rested with members of the jury, because there were no judges. Those who brought the charges and those who defended themselves pleaded their own cases. This led to a study of speechmaking.

Classical Orators. The first great Greek orator was Pericles. His speeches were reported by Thucydides in his famous *History of the Peloponnesian War*. Pericles' Funeral Oration is the best-known of all his speeches. The greatest Greek orator was Demosthenes. By patriotic speeches, he tried to inspire his countrymen to make Athens the leader of the Greek city-states.

The outstanding Greek writer on rhetoric was Aristotle. He defined rhetoric as "the faculty of discovering in every case the available means of persuasion." Aristotle emphasized three methods of proof: (1) *ethical* (the influence of the speaker's personality); (2) *pathetic* (the influence of the speaker's use of emotional appeal); and (3) *logical* (the influence of the use of formal principles of reasoning in proof).

Cicero holds first place among the important early Roman orators. Authorities believe that the *Rhetorica ad Herennium* was written by Cicero about 86 B.C. It states that an orator must divide the preparation of a speech into five steps. These steps are: (1) *invention* (analysis of speech situation and audience, investigation and study of subject matter, and selection of speech materials); (2) *disposition* (the arrangement of the speech materials under what we now call introduction, discussion, and conclusion); (3) *style* (the use and grouping of words to express ideas clearly, accurately, vividly, and appropriately); (4) *memory* (methods of memorizing material); and (5) *delivery* (the oral presentation).

Book I of Cicero's *De Oratore*, written about 55 B.C., develops the theme that a great orator must be a person of great learning and that the "proper concern of an orator . . . is language of power and elegance accommodated to the feelings and understandings of mankind." Book II emphasizes the importance of invention and disposition, with particular attention to court oratory. Book III deals with style and delivery. Here, Cicero shows that an orator should speak "correctly, perspicuously, elegantly, and to the purpose."

The Training of an Orator (A.D. 90) by Quintilian deals with the teaching of speechmaking and the education of orators. Even today, it is one of the most comprehensive works on training speakers.

Later Orators. With the coming of Christianity, the preacher replaced the political speaker. Famous early preachers include Paul, John Chrysostom, and Augustine. Outstanding speakers for religious reform were Savonarola in the late 1400's and Martin Luther and John Calvin during the Reformation in the 1500's.

Political oratory again became important in the 1700's. During the French Revolution, Comte de Mirabeau spoke for the common people fighting royal authority.

Great Britain has produced many distinguished speakers throughout its history of parliamentary government. They include Edmund Burke, Benjamin Disraeli, William Gladstone, and Winston Churchill.

American orators include Patrick Henry, John C. Calhoun, Daniel Webster, Stephen A. Douglas, and William Jennings Bryan. W. HAYES YEAGER

Related Articles in WORLD BOOK include:

FAMOUS AMERICAN ORATORS

Adams, John Q.	Henry, Patrick
Bryan (William J.)	Ingersoll, Robert G.
Clay, Henry	Lincoln, Abraham
Douglas, Stephen A.	Phillips, Wendell
Douglass, Frederick	Roosevelt, Franklin D.
Everett, Edward	Rutledge, John
Grady, Henry W.	Sumner, Charles
Hamilton, Alexander	Webster, Daniel

OTHER ORATORS

Aeschines	Isocrates
Burke, Edmund	Lysias
Chrysostom, Saint John	Mirabeau, Comte de
Churchill, Sir Winston	Pericles
Cicero	Pitt (family)
Demosthenes	Quintilian

ORBIT, in astronomy, is the path of any object in space whose motion is controlled by the gravitational pull of a heavier object. Astronomers call the heavier object the *primary* and the lighter object the *secondary*. The moon is a secondary that revolves in an orbit around the earth, a primary. The earth, in turn, is a secondary that travels in an orbit around the sun.

The term *orbit* is used for the path of either a natural object or a manufactured object, such as a spacecraft. Early spacecraft could travel only around the earth. Today, spacecraft can move out of earth orbit and become secondaries of the moon, sun, or another planet.

A certain speed is required before a secondary can orbit around its primary. If a secondary does not achieve *escape velocity*, the speed required to escape the gravita-

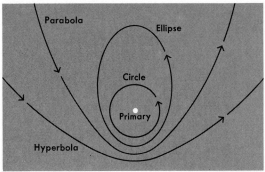

WORLD BOOK diagram

The Shape of the Orbit an object takes around a primary, such as the sun, depends on its speed in relation to the speed needed to escape from the primary. The shape may be a circle, ellipse, parabola, or hyperbola.

tional pull of its primary, its orbit is a closed curve called an *ellipse* (see ELLIPSE). The primary is not at the exact center of the ellipse, and so the secondary travels closer to the primary at some times than at others. The point in the orbit of any secondary of the earth where it is nearest the earth is called the *perigee*. The farthest point is called the *apogee*. An orbit could be a perfect circle, but truly circular orbits rarely occur.

If a secondary reaches escape velocity, its orbit becomes an open curve called a *parabola*. If a secondary moves faster than escape velocity, its orbit becomes a flatter open curve called a *hyperbola*. A spacecraft that leaves earth orbit on a trip to another planet must travel in a hyperbolic orbit. See PARABOLA; HYPERBOLA. ERIC D. CARLSON

See also MOON (How the Moon Moves); PLANET; SPACE TRAVEL.

ORBITING OBSERVATORY. See SPACE TRAVEL (Scientific Satellites); OBSERVATORY (picture).

ORCHARD. See FRUIT; HORTICULTURE.

ORCHESTRA

Robin Hood Dell

Outdoor Orchestra Concerts attract thousands of music lovers every summer. Such symphony orchestras as the Philadelphia Orchestra, *above*, perform in city parks and at summer music festivals.

ORCHESTRA is a group of musicians playing together. They may be playing on various stringed, wind, and percussion instruments. The term *orchestra* in ancient Greek theaters meant the space between the audience and stage, which was used by the chorus. Today the word still is used to mean the musicians' space before the stage, and sometimes the whole main floor. But it is more often used to mean the musicians themselves and their instruments.

Orchestras can be of almost any size. A string orches-

tra contains only stringed instruments. A symphony orchestra is large and has all the instruments needed to play symphonies. An orchestra may perform alone, it may accompany voices as in an opera or oratorio, or it may play with a solo instrument as in a concerto. It also may accompany dancers in a ballet, or provide "incidental" music between acts of a play.

Television and radio have special uses for the orchestra. It may introduce and identify a program by playing a "theme song," or add to the mood of a dramatic

The Conductor uses signals and gestures to tell the musicians how to play various parts of a composition. These photographs show how a conductor directs a performance. On the left, he asks the string section to play softly so a quiet passage by the brass section can be heard. On the lower left, he signals the orchestra to play vigorously. In the center picture, he gestures to the musicians to play with expression. On the lower right, he tells the orchestra to end the composition delicately.

Robert M. Lightfoot III,
Detroit Symphony Orchestra

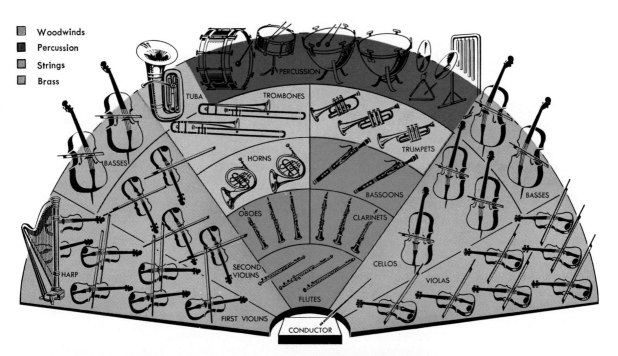

Woodwinds
Percussion
Strings
Brass

PERCUSSION

TUBA   TROMBONES

HORNS   TRUMPETS

BASSES   BASSES

OBOES   BASSOONS

CLARINETS

SECOND   CELLOS
VIOLINS

HARP   VIOLAS

FLUTES

FIRST VIOLINS

CONDUCTOR

Bernard Gotfryd, © *Newsweek*

Interlochen National Music Camp

Orchestra Seating is designed by the conductor to produce the desired blend of sounds from the different sections of an orchestra. The diagram above and the photograph on the left show two kinds of seating arrangements. In the diagram, the string section sits to the left and right of the conductor. In the photo, the strings form a semicircle around the conductor.

A Student Orchestra rehearses for a concert at a summer camp for teen-age musicians. At such camps, the young musicians study under skilled professional performers and teachers.

621

ORCHESTRA

Colin McPhee, courtesy *HiFi Review*

An Indonesian Orchestra includes gongs and instruments called *gambangs, above*. A gambang is played in somewhat the same way as a xylophone.

program by playing specially written "background" music. The motion picture uses orchestras more and more for this purpose. Sometimes music furnished by an orchestra tells part of the story, or furnishes clues as to what is happening. Producers have used orchestras in all kinds of productions. As a result, millions of people have come in contact with great orchestras.

A symphony orchestra is made up mainly of stringed instruments. It also has wind and percussion instruments, but fewer of them than of strings. A *band* usually has only wind and percussion instruments. A *dance orchestra* usually has wind and percussion instruments, a piano, and perhaps a few strings.

Orchestral Instruments can be grouped under four main types—strings, woodwind, brass, and percussion. The *string section* contains first violins, second violins, violas, violoncellos, and basses. The parts played by these instruments correspond roughly to the soprano, alto, tenor, baritone, and bass voices of a chorus. The symphony orchestra usually has about ten to fifteen first violins, ten to twelve second violins, and eight to ten violas, violoncellos, and basses.

The *woodwind section* chiefly provides different tone qualities. The flute, clarinet, and oboe are all high-pitched, but each has its own tone color. The flute tone is pure and velvety. The clarinet has a rich resonance in the low register and a trumpetlike tone in the high register. The oboe tone is thin, sweet, and rather shrill. The English horn is in a lower-pitch register and is more somber, or sad. Some other woodwinds are the bassoon, the piccolo, and the contra bassoon.

The *brass section* also has different pitch registers. The trumpets are the soprano brass, the French horns are the alto or tenor, the trombones are the tenor, baritone, or bass, and the tuba is the true bass.

The *percussion section* gives a rhythmic background and special tone-color effects. This group includes the timpani (or kettledrums), the snare drum, the bass drum, cymbals, gongs, bells, triangle, tambourine, and many other types of rhythm instruments.

The harp is sometimes used in the orchestra, especially in the symphony orchestra. The piano is not a regular orchestral instrument, but is often used in playing modern scores.

The Conductor is one of the most important members of the orchestra. He or she has two main duties. The conductor must first conduct the rehearsals, and then see that his or her directions are followed during the actual performance. First the conductor must see in rehearsal that all parts are played correctly and that the important melodies and harmonies are heard distinctly. The players must understand the conductor's style, interpretation, and choice of *tempo*, or speed. Stringed-instrument players must use their bows correctly and uniformly. Wind-instrument players must tongue and slur their parts carefully.

During the concert performance, the eyes of all players are on the conductor. Before the conductor is a "full score," which contains all players' parts. The conductor leads the musicians by means of the baton, hand gestures, facial expressions, and body movements. Each movement has a meaning which all players must know. Some conductors use no scores. They have memorized entire symphonies.

Learning About Orchestral Performance is simple for everyone. We can all hear the finest symphony orchestra music through radio or recordings. We can buy inexpensive miniature scores of most standard orchestral works. By following these scores, it is possible for us to *hear* the music and *see* it at the same time. With a little practice, we can easily identify the different instruments and their characteristics.

It is much more interesting to hear an actual performance by a symphony orchestra if one is familiar with the music and the score. Then, there is the added

Sam J. Lutz, Artists' Management

A Dance Orchestra plays popular music for both listening and dancing. A number of dance orchestras, such as the one led by Lawrence Welk, *above*, include a string section.

thrill of seeing the players at their work—the great body of violinists with arms and bows working in unison, the brasses and woodwinds making their entrances with precision and clarity, and the conductor producing seeming magic by the slightest movements of the baton or the hands.

History. Orchestras date back to the beginning of the human race. Even primitive peoples had crude musical instruments which they probably played in orchestral groups. The result probably would not have sounded like music to us, but it was probably rhythmic. Real orchestras did not appear until bowed string instruments became common, and wind instruments were developed so that the pitch could be controlled. It was also necessary to have a system of writing music before real orchestras could fully develop.

The modern orchestra began its slow growth about three hundred years ago. The small and poorly balanced groups of the 1600's were very different from the symphony orchestra of our day. The composer Jean Baptiste Lully (1632-1687) *scored* (arranged) much of his operatic music for stringed instruments, although he sometimes added flutes, oboes, trumpets, and drums. Lully also used bassoons. But these wind instruments did not have their own parts to play. They merely *doubled* (played along with) the string parts. Later composers, chiefly Alessandro Scarlatti (1659-1725) and Henry Purcell (1659?-1695), wrote special parts for wind instruments and included the French horn.

The orchestras of Johann Sebastian Bach (1685-1750) and George Frideric Handel (1685-1759) had two flutes, two oboes, one or two bassoons, two horns, two trumpets, drums, and strings. These orchestras were prominent in the early and middle 1700's. Christoph Willibald Gluck (1714-1787) added two clarinets and some special percussion instruments. Joseph Haydn (1732-1809) and Wolfgang Amadeus Mozart (1756-1791) enlarged the orchestra still further. During the period from about 1760 to 1800, the clarinet became a fixed part of the orchestra. At this time, a balance of stringed instruments was established in the orchestra, and improvements were made in wind instruments.

In the 1800's, the orchestra added the trombone and tuba, increased the number of horns, and enlarged the string section. Great progress was made in the manner and style of writing scores. By the end of the 1800's, the full symphony orchestra was established, with its 90 to 100 players.   CHARLES B. RIGHTER

Related Articles in WORLD BOOK include:

CONDUCTORS

Ansermet, Ernest	Klemperer, Otto
Barbirolli, Sir John	Koussevitzky, Serge
Barenboim, Daniel	Kubelik (Rafael)
Beecham, Sir Thomas	MacMillan, Sir Ernest C.
Bernstein, Leonard	Mahler, Gustav
Boulez, Pierre	Mehta, Zubin
Boult, Sir Adrian	Mitropoulos, Dimitri
Copland, Aaron	Monteux, Pierre
Damrosch (family)	Muck, Karl
Fiedler, Arthur	Nikisch, Arthur
Furtwängler, Wilhelm	Ormandy, Eugene
Ganz, Rudolph	Ozawa, Seiji
Goossens, Sir Eugene	Previn, Andre
Gould, Morton	Reiner, Fritz
Herbert, Victor	Richter, Hans
Iturbi, José	Sargent, Sir Malcolm
Karajan, Herbert von	Shaw, Robert

Solti, Sir Georg	Szell, George
Sousa, John Philip	Toscanini, Arturo
Spohr, Louis	Villa-Lobos, Heitor
Steinberg, William	Walter, Bruno
Stokowski, Leopold	Whiteman, Paul

OTHER RELATED ARTICLES

Band	Music
Chamber Music	Opera (The Orchestra)
Conducting	Symphony
Instrumental Music	Symphonic Poem

ORCHESTRA BELLS imitate the effect of real bells of cast bronze. The two types of orchestra bells are tubular chimes and metal bars. The chimes are usually from 1 to 2 inches (2.5 to 5.1 centimeters) in diameter and vary in length with the pitch. They are hung from a metal frame, and are struck with heavy leather-headed mallets. Their sound is deep and resonant. The metal bars are of varying size, usually not more than $\frac{1}{2}$ inch (13 millimeters) in thickness, and are arranged in rows much like the piano keyboard. They are struck with a hard mallet, and produce a ringing sound, more brilliant and higher-pitched than that of the tubular, hanging chimes.   CHARLES B. RIGHTER

See also MUSIC (picture: Percussion Instruments); XYLOPHONE.

ORCHID, *AWR kihd*, is one of the most beautiful flowers in the world. More than 6,000 *species* (kinds) of wild orchids grow throughout the world. Most of these are found in tropical and subtropical lands. But many kinds of orchids grow in cool, damp woods and in swamps.

Each orchid blossom has three sepals and three petals. The petals range in color from white to deep violet, and they may be speckled or streaked. One petal, called the *lip*, always has a special shape. It may be long and narrow, wide with a fringe, or shaped like a pouch. The lip of the *lady's-slipper orchid* is shaped like a pouch or slipper. This orchid grows in United States forests and swamps. Blossoms of the *butterfly orchid* of Britain look like white butterflies with red spots. Early Spaniards named the *Holy Ghost orchid*. They believed its blossoms were sacred because they looked like the holy dove that flew down at the baptism of Christ.

Each kind of orchid is fertilized by pollen carried by a particular kind of insect. The size and shape of an orchid's blossoms are suited to that insect. Special markings on the lip guide the insect toward the nectar inside the blossom. As the insect approaches this nectar, it brushes against pollen sacs in the blossom. Some of the pollen, and even the sacs themselves, may stick to the insect and be carried to another orchid of the same species. This process assures cross-fertilization within each kind of orchid (see FLOWER [How Flowers Reproduce; illustrations]).

In cool regions, orchids grow in the ground. But in tropical lands, many kinds of orchids grow high on the branches of trees. Their tiny seeds are carried there by the wind. When a seed sprouts, the young plant sends its roots out along the branch. These roots gather in a loose mass and some of them dangle in the air. Some of these orchids have a special corklike covering on their roots that enables the root to gather moisture directly from the air.

Raising orchids is a hobby that fascinates many people. They collect beautiful orchids from many lands

SOME KINDS OF ORCHIDS

More than 6,000 species of orchids grow throughout the world. These beautiful flowers have a wide variety of shapes and colors. Some of the orchids shown below grow in various countries and have no common name in English. The scientific name is given for such flowers.

Christmas orchid

Jim Annan

Loren McIntyre, Woodfin Camp, Inc.

Star orchid

E. S. Ross

Corcium nigrescens

Harold Hungerford

Boat orchid

Lynn M. Stone, NAS

Epidendrum oncidioides

M. P. L. Fogden, Bruce Coleman Inc.

Scorpion orchid

C. B. Sharp, Van Cleve Photography

Moth orchid

Bill Noel Kleeman, Tom Stack & Associates

Semi-terete hybrid orchid

624

and often build special greenhouses to raise them. Some of these orchids require six or seven years from the planting of the seed until they produce blossoms.

Some orchids produce useful items. For example, a climbing orchid called the *vanilla vine* has pods known as *vanilla beans* that produce the vanilla flavoring used in foods and beverages. Other orchids have potato-like swellings on their roots. These swellings are dried to make *salep*, a substance used in medicines.

Scientific Classification. Orchids make up the orchid family, *Orchidaceae*. Lady's-slippers make up the genus *Cypripedium*. Other genera in the Americas include *Arethusa*, *Calypso*, and *Habenaria*.   ROBERT W. SCHERY

See also FLOWER (color pictures: Cattleya Orchid, Flowers of the Woodland [Showy Orchis, Pink Lady's-Slipper], Mountain Flowers [Calypso]); LADY'S-SLIPPER; VANILLA.

ORCUS. See PLUTO.

ORCZY, BARONESS (1865-1947), was a Hungarian-born author known chiefly for her adventure-filled novels and detective stories. She also wrote several plays.

Orczy's most famous novel, *The Scarlet Pimpernel* (1905), is set during the French Revolution (1789-1799). The hero, an English aristocrat named Sir Percy Blakeney, appears to be an idle, useless person. But, as the mysterious Scarlet Pimpernel, he gallantly rescues aristocrats who have been sentenced to death. This character also appears in 12 other novels.

Orczy created several detectives in various short stories. For example, the Old Man in the Corner solves baffling crimes as he sits in the corner of a tea shop. He appears in *The Old Man in the Corner* (1909). Another detective, Lady Molly Robertson-Kirk, is featured in *Lady Molly of Scotland Yard* (1910).

Baroness Emmuska Orczy was born in Tarnaörs, Hungary, near Jászberény. Her family moved to London when she was 15. She learned English there and wrote her works in that language.   JAMES DOUGLAS MERRITT

ORD RIVER in Western Australia is the center of a development project that includes two dams and hydroelectric power plants. The project will supply water to irrigate about 200,000 acres (81,000 hectares) of land for cotton, rice, and other crops. Its power plants will supply power for the area.

The Ord River rises near Hall's Creek and flows northward for about 300 miles (480 kilometers) through the dry, sandy region in the northeast corner of Western Australia. It empties into Cambridge Gulf near Wyndham. With its tributaries, the Ord River drains about 17,000 square miles (44,000 square kilometers).

ORDER is a unit of scientific classification. Animals and plants are divided into seven major groups called kingdoms, phyla, classes, orders, families, genera, and species. Members of an order are more closely related than are members of a class. But members of orders are not so closely related as are members of families. See also CLASSIFICATION (table).   WILLIAM V. MAYER

ORDER, FRATERNAL. See FRATERNAL SOCIETY.

ORDER IN COUNCIL. Decrees issued by the British Crown when matters of great importance confront the nation are called Orders in Council. They get this name from the fact that they are proclaimed with the advice of the Privy Council. In 1807, Great Britain issued Orders in Council in answer to Napoleon's threat to blockade the island empire. By these orders, British ships blockaded the European coast and kept neutral trading vessels from entering ports of Napoleonic Europe. See also CONTINENTAL SYSTEM; PRIVY COUNCIL.   BASIL D. HENNING

ORDER OF ————. Many orders are listed in THE WORLD BOOK ENCYCLOPEDIA under the key word in the names of the order, for example: DE MOLAY, ORDER OF.

ORDERED PAIR. See ALGEBRA (Functions).

ORDINANCE is a public law or regulation made usually by the governing body of a city, town, or village. A *resolution* of a city council is another name for an ordinance. Ordinances are usually only local in nature.

The name *ordinance* has also been given to regulations that serve as laws, but are not actually constitutions. The Ordinance of 1787 was such a regulation (see NORTHWEST ORDINANCE). *Ordinance* may also refer to a church sacrament, such as Communion.

ORDINANCE OF SECESSION. See CIVIL WAR (Secession).

ORDINANCE OF 1785. See WESTWARD MOVEMENT (Solving Frontier Problems).

ORDINANCE OF 1787. See NORTHWEST ORDINANCE.

ORDINARY. See COLONIAL LIFE IN AMERICA (Recreation).

ORDNANCE, *AWRD nunce*, is a military term used for weapons and ammunition. Most armies, navies, and air forces have ordnance departments. It is the job of the departments to design, make, repair, and distribute weapons and ammunition. The term *ordnance* also includes the tools used in the manufacture of these items.

See also AMMUNITION; WEAPON.

ORDOVICIAN PERIOD. See EARTH (table: Outline of Earth History).

ORE, *ohr*, is a mineral or a rock that contains enough of a metal to make it worth mining. Often, two or more metals can be obtained from the same ore. Ores naturally occur in beds or veins, mixed in with valueless minerals called the *gangue*.

There are two types of ores—*native metals* and *compound ores*. In *native metals*, the valuable mineral occurs as a pure metal. It is not chemically combined with other substances. Gold, silver, platinum, and copper often occur as native metals. Smelting melts the bands or lumps of pure metal out of the gangue.

In *compound ores*, the valuable metal is joined to other substances such as oxygen, sulfur, carbon, or silicon to form various chemical compounds. The ores of iron, aluminum, and tin are usually found joined with oxygen and form compounds called *oxides*. Copper, lead, zinc, silver, nickel, and mercury are found joined with sulfur and form compounds called *sulfides*. Chemical changes free the metal from the compound. Some metals are freed by electric current in a process called *electrolysis*. Other metals are dissolved out of the ore by acids in a process called *leaching*. See METALLURGY (Extractive Metallurgy).   RICHARD M. PEARL

See also MINERAL; ROCK.

ÖRE, *UH ruh*, is a bronze coin used in Sweden. It is worth one-hundredth of a krona. See also KRONA.

ØRE, *UH ruh*, is a coin used in Denmark and Norway. It is worth one-hundredth of a krone. See also KRONE.

OREAD. See NYMPH.

OREGANO. See MARJORAM.

Sunset on the Oregon Coast at Cannon Beach

Ray Atkeson

Oregon (blue) ranks 10th in size among all the states, and 2nd in size among the Pacific Coast States (gray).

The contributors of this article are Jesse L. Gilmore, Professor of History at Portland State University; Richard M. Highsmith, Jr., Chairman of the Department of Geography at Oregon State University; and Robert C. Notson, Publisher of The Oregonian.

—————————— FACTS IN BRIEF ——————————

Capital: Salem.

Government: *Congress*—U.S. senators, 2; U.S. representatives, 4. *Electoral Votes*—6. *State Legislature* (Legislative Assembly)—senators, 30; representatives, 60. *Counties*—36.

Area: 96,981 sq. mi. (251,180 km²), including 797 sq. mi. (2,064 km²) of inland water but excluding 48 sq. mi. (124 km²) of Pacific coastal water; 10th in size among the states. *Greatest Distances*—east-west, 375 mi. (604 km); north-south, 295 mi. (475 km). *Coastline*—296 mi. (476 km).

Elevation: *Highest*—Mount Hood in Clackamas and Hood River counties, 11,235 ft. (3,424 m) above sea level. *Lowest*—sea level, along the Pacific Ocean.

Population: *Estimated 1975 Population*—2,288,000. *1970 Census*—2,091,385; 31st among the states; distribution, 67 per cent urban, 33 per cent rural; density, 22 persons per sq. mi. (8 persons per km²).

Chief Products: *Agriculture*—barley, beef cattle, dairy products, eggs, greenhouse and nursery products, hay, mint, onions, pears, potatoes, ryegrass seed, snap beans, wheat. *Fishing Industry*—Dungeness crabs, salmon, shrimp, tuna. *Manufacturing*—food and food products, lumber and wood products, nonelectrical machinery, paper and paper products. *Mining*—clay, diatomite, gemstones, gold, mercury, nickel, pumice, sand and gravel, silver, stone.

Statehood: Feb. 14, 1859, the 33rd state.

State Motto: The Union.

State Song: "Oregon, My Oregon." Words by J. A. Buchanan; music by Henry B. Murtagh.

OREGON

THE BEAVER STATE

OREGON, a Pacific Coast state, is known for its vast forests of evergreen trees. Forests cover almost half the state, and every large Oregon city has factories that make wood products. The state has about an eighth of the nation's timber, and it leads in lumber production.

The rugged beauty of Oregon's mountains, seacoast, and forest lands attracts more than 10 million tourists a year. Hunters shoot deer and elk and other game in Oregon's wooded regions. Sportsmen enjoy fishing in sparkling lakes and rivers, and in Pacific waters.

Oregon is often called the *Pacific Wonderland* because of its outstanding natural wonders. These include Crater Lake in the Cascade Mountains, the Columbia River Gorge, Hells Canyon on the Snake River, and Oregon Caves National Monument. Mount Hood, Mount Jefferson, and other snow-covered peaks rise majestically in the Cascade Range. The Wallowas, in northeastern Oregon, also offer spectacular mountain scenery. Steep cliffs rise along much of Oregon's wave-swept coast. But parts have sandy beaches and protected harbors.

The dry lands east of the Cascade Mountains have large livestock ranches. Potatoes, sugar beets, and other vegetables grow in irrigated areas of eastern Oregon. Wheat, Oregon's most valuable crop, comes chiefly from the north-central area. Orchard fruits from Oregon's Hood and Rogue river valleys are world famous.

The mighty Columbia River forms most of the boundary between Oregon and Washington. Huge dams on the Columbia supply electric power for homes and industries. The dams also improve the river for shipping, and provide water for irrigation. The Columbia was once called the Oregon, or *Ouragan*, which means *hurricane* in French. Some authorities think that Oregon's name came from this historic name. Oregon is known as the *Beaver State*, because the region supplied thousands of beaver skins during fur-trading days.

In the early days, Oregon meant the end of the trail for many pioneers. During the 1840's and 1850's, thousands of settlers traveled by covered wagon on the Oregon Trail to the fertile farmlands of the Willamette Valley. Today, the Willamette Valley is Oregon's greatest center for trade and industry. It is also important for dairy products, flower bulbs, fruits, and vegetables. Most of Oregon's large cities are in the Willamette Valley. They include Portland, the largest city, and Salem, the state capital. Portland extends along both banks of the Willamette River near the place where the Willamette flows into the Columbia. It is an industrial city and a major seaport.

For the relationship of Oregon to other states in its region, see the article on PACIFIC COAST STATES.

Artist's View of Eugene

Constitution. The present state Constitution was adopted in 1857, two years before Oregon joined the Union. Constitutional amendments may be proposed by either house of the state legislature. A majority of each house must approve the amendments. The voters must then approve the proposed amendments in the next regular general election, unless the legislature orders a special election.

Constitutional amendments may also be proposed and passed directly by the people, through their powers of *initiative and referendum* (see INITIATIVE AND REFERENDUM). In addition, the Constitution may be revised by a constitutional convention called after a majority of the legislators and the voters approve.

Executive. The governor of Oregon is elected to a four-year term. He cannot serve more than 8 years during any 12-year period. The governor receives a yearly salary of $38,500. He also receives an expense allowance of $1,000 a month. The governor appoints members of many state boards and commissions. The state has no official residence for its governor. For a list of all the governors of Oregon, see the *History* section of this article.

Other top state officials include the secretary of state, attorney general, treasurer, and labor commissioner. These officials are also elected to four-year terms. The secretary of state and the treasurer cannot serve more than 8 years during any 12-year period.

Legislature of Oregon is called the *Legislative Assembly*. It consists of a Senate of 30 members and a House of Representatives of 60 members. The state has 30 senatorial districts and 60 representative districts. Voters in each senatorial district elect one senator. Voters in each representative district elect one repre-

sentative. State senators serve four-year terms. Representatives hold office for two years. The assembly meets in regular session in odd-numbered years. Sessions usually begin on the second Monday in January. There is no limit to a session's length.

Courts. The highest court in Oregon is the state Supreme Court. It has seven justices elected to six-year terms. The court elects one of its members to serve a six-year term as chief justice. The next highest state court is the court of appeals. It has five judges who are elected to six-year terms.

Oregon is divided into 21 judicial districts. Each district has one or more circuit court judges. Circuit judges are elected to six-year terms by *nonpartisan* (no-party) ballot. A special tax court, created in 1961, ranks with the circuit courts. Lower courts include district courts, county courts, and justice courts.

Local Government. Oregon gives its cities and towns *home rule*. This means they have the right to choose their own form of government. Most cities with more than 5,000 persons have the council-manager form of government. Portland has a mayor and four commissioners. Most smaller cities have a mayor and a city council.

A 1958 amendment to the state Constitution extended home rule privileges to Oregon counties. However, only 4 of the state's 36 counties have taken action under this law.

A county judge and two commissioners rule on county business in most counties. A five-member board of commissioners exercises governmental power in most of the other counties. Most county judges and commissioners are elected to four-year terms.

Taxation. The state government receives most of its tax income from individual and corporation income

Entrance to Oregon's Capitol is flanked by massive marble monuments. One sculpture, *left*, honors the Lewis and Clark expedition through the Oregon region in 1805. The other sculpture, *right*, shows pioneers in a covered wagon on the Oregon Trail.

WESTWARD THE STAR OF EMPIRE TAKES ITS WAY

VALIANT MEN HAVE THRUST OUR FRONTIERS TO THE SETTING SUN

The State Seal

Symbols of Oregon. On the state seal, 33 stars represent Oregon's entry into the Union as the 33rd state. The departing British man-of-war and arriving American merchant ship symbolize the end of British influence and the rise of American power. The sheaf of grain, the pickax, and the plow represent Oregon's mining and agricultural resources. The seal was adopted in 1859. The flag, adopted in 1925, has a reproduction of the seal. The reverse side of the flag shows a beaver.

Bird and flower illustrations, courtesy of Eli Lilly and Company

The State Flag

taxes, gasoline taxes, and property taxes. The federal government provides about a fourth of the state's revenue, in the form of grants and other programs. Other sources of state revenue are inheritance taxes, gift taxes, and license taxes on motor vehicles, hunting, and fishing.

Politics. The Republican party has controlled Oregon politics during most of the state's history. Many industrial workers who settled in Oregon cities after World War II caused changes in the state's politics. In the mid-1950's, registered Democrats began to outnumber registered Republicans. The legislative districts were changed in the early 1960's and again in 1971. These actions gave more representation to urban areas, where the Democrats have their greatest strength. But the state continued to elect Republicans to the governorship and other high state offices. For Oregon's voting record in presidential elections since 1860, see ELECTORAL COLLEGE (table).

The State Bird
Western Meadow Lark

The State Capitol in Salem was completed in 1939. It has a cylinder-shaped dome topped by a golden statue called *Pioneer*. Salem has been Oregon's capital since 1855. Earlier territorial capitals were Oregon City (1849-1851), Salem (1851-1855), and Corvallis (1855).

Oregon State Highway Dept.

The State Flower
Oregon Grape

The State Tree
Douglas Fir

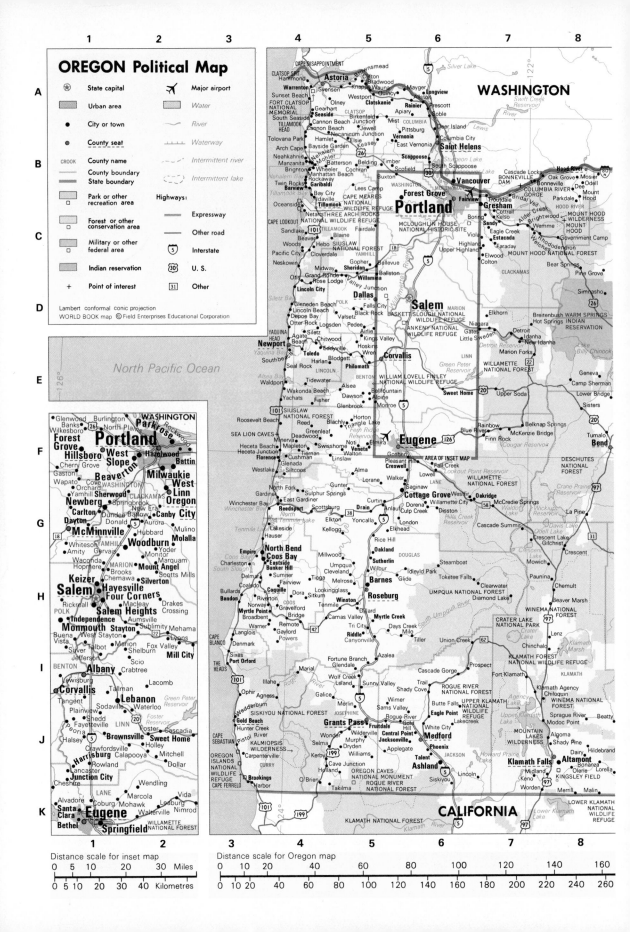

OREGON Political Map

⊛	State capital	✈	Major airport
	Urban area		Water
●	City or town		River
●	County seat		Waterway
CROOK	County name		Intermittent river
	County boundary		Intermittent lake
	State boundary		
	Park or other recreation area	**Highways:**	
	Forest or other conservation area		Expressway
	Military or other federal area		Other road
	Indian reservation	⑤	Interstate
+	Point of interest	㉚	U.S.
		㉛	Other

Lambert conformal conic projection
WORLD BOOK map ©Field Enterprises Educational Corporation

North Pacific Ocean

WASHINGTON

CALIFORNIA

Distance scale for inset map

0 5 10   20   30 Miles

0 5 10   20   30   40 Kilometres

Distance scale for Oregon map

0 10 20   40   60   80   100   120   140   160

0 10 20 40 60 80 100 120 140 160 180 200 220 240 260

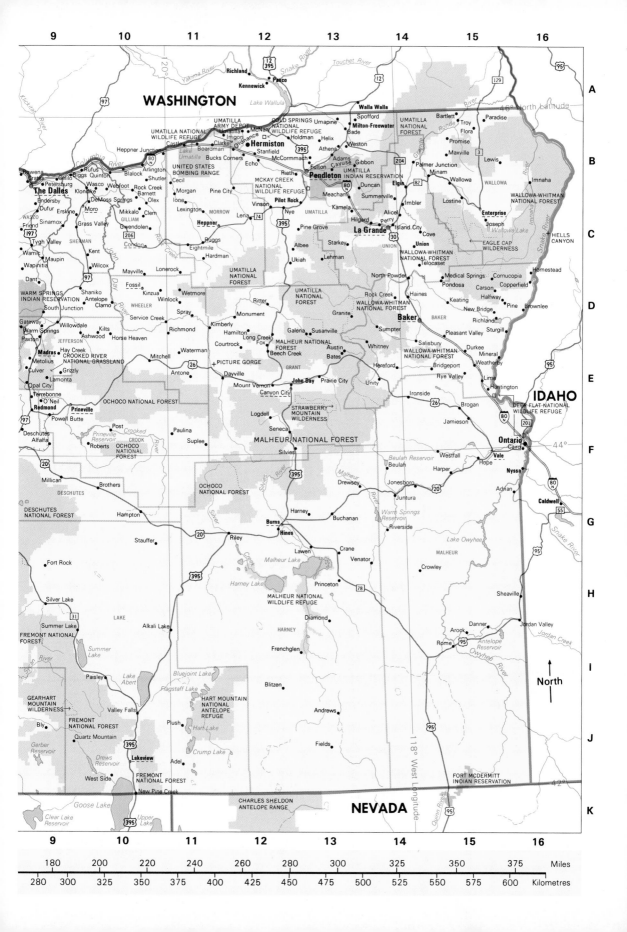

Oregon Map Index

North Bend .8,553..G 3	Powell Butte ......F 9	Scotts Mills ...208..H 2	Suver ....I 1	Walterville ....K 2

North Bend .8,553..G 3
North Fork ....G 4
North Plains ..690..F 1
North Powder .304..D 14
Norway ....H 4
Noti ....F 5
Nye ....C 12
Nyssa ...2,620..F 16
Oak Grove ....B 8
Oakland ..1,010..G 5
Oakridge ..3,422..G 7
O'Brien ....K 4
Oceanside ....C 4
Odell ....B 8
Olene ....J 8
Olex ....C 10
Olney ....A 4
O'Neil ....E 9
Ontario ...6,523..F 16
Opal City ....E 9
Ophir ....I 3
Ordnance ....B 12
Oregon City .9,176.°D 6
Otis ....D 4
Otter Rock ....D 4
Pacific City ....C 4
Paisley ......260..I 10
Palmer Junction ...B 14
Paradise ....A 15
Parkdale ....C 8
Parkrose ....F 2
Paulina ....F 11
Paunina ....H 8
Paxton ....D 9
Pedee ....D 5
Pendleton ..13,197.°B 13
Peoria ....I 1
Perry ....C 14
Petersburg ....B 9
Philomath ..1,688..E 5
Phoenix ...1,287..J 6
Pilot Rock ..1,612..C 13
Pine ....D 16
Pine City ....B 12
Pine Grove ....C 13
Pine Grove ....C 8
Pistol River ....J 3
Pittsburg ....B 5
Plainview ....J 1
Pleasant Hill ......F 6
Pleasant Valley ...D 15
Plush ....J 11
Pondosa ....D 15
Port Orford ..1,037..I 3
Portland ..379,967.°C 6
Post ....F 10

Powell Butte ......F 9
Powers ....842..I 4
Prairie City ..867..E 13
Pratum* ....H 1
Prescott .....105..A 6
Princeton ....H 13
Prineville ...4,101.°E 9
Promise ....B 15
Prospect ....I 6
Quartz Mountain ...J 9
Quincy ....A 5
Quinton ....B 10
Rainbow ....F 7
Rainier ....1,731..A 6
Redmond ...3,721..E 9
Reed ....F 4
Reedsport ..4,039..G 4
Remote ....H 4
Rhododendron ....C 7
Rice Hill ....G 5
Richland .....133..D 15
Richmond ....D 11
Rickreall ....H 1
Riddle .....1,042..I 5
Rieth ....B 12
Riley ....G 12
Ritter ....D 12
Riverside ....G 14
Riverton ....H 3
Roberts ....F 9
Rock Creek ....B 10
Rock Creek ....D 14
Rockaway ....665..B 4
Rockwood ....F 2
Rogue River ..841..J 5
Rome ....I 15
Roosevelt Beach ...F 4
Rose Lodge ....D 4
Roseburg ..14,461.°H 5
Rowena ....B 9
Rowland ....J 1
Rufus ....317..B 9
Ruggs ....C 11
Rye Valley ....E 15
Saginaw ....F 5
St. Helens ..6,212.°B 6
St. Paul* .....347..D 6
Salem ...68,480.°D 6
Salisbury ....D 14
Sams Valley ....J 6
Sandlake ....C 4
Sandy .....1,544..C 7
Santa Clara ....K 1
Scappoose ..1,859..B 6
Scio ....447..I 1
Scofield ....B 5

Scotts Mills ...208..H 2
Scottsburg ....G 4
Seal Rock ....E 4
Seaside ...4,402..A 4
Selma ....J 4
Seneca ....F 12
Service Creek .....D 11
Shady Cove ....I 6
Shady Pine ....I 8
Shaniko ....58..D 9
Sheaville ....H 16
Shedd ....J 1
Shelburn ....I 1
Sheridan ..1,881..C 5
Sherwood ..1,396..G 1
Shutler ....B 10
Siletz ....596..D 4
Siltcoos ....F 4
Silver Lake ....H 9
Silverton ..4,301..H 2
Silvies ....F 12
Simnasho ....D 8
Sinamox ....C 9
Siskiyou ....K 6
Sisters ......516..E 8
Sitkum ....H 4
Sixes ....I 3
Sodaville ....125..J 1
South Junction ....D 9
South
  Medford* .3,497..J 6
South Scappoose ...B 6
South Seaside ......A 4
Southbeach ....E 4
Spofford ....A 13
Sprague River ......I 8
Spray ....161..D 11
Springbrook ....G 1
Springfield .26,874..K 1
Stanfield ....891..B 12
Starkey ....C 13
Stauffer ....G 11
Stayton ...3,170..I 2
Steamboat ....H 6
Sturgill ....D 16
Sublimity ....634..H 2
Sulphur Springs ...G 4
Summer Lake ....H 9
Summerville ...76..B 14
Sumner ....H 4
Sumpter ......120..D 14
Sunny Valley ....I 5
Sunset Beach ....A 4
Suplee ....F 11
Susanville ....D 13
Sutherlin ..3,070..E 5

Suver ....I 1
Svensen ....A 5
Sweet Home 3,799..E 6
Swisshome ....F 4
Takilma ....K 4
Talbot ....I 1
Talent ....1,389..J 6
Tallman ....I 1
Tangent ....I 1
Telocaset ....C 14
Tenmile ....H 5
Terrebonne ....E 9
Tidewater ....E 4
Tiernan ....F 4
Tigard* ...5,302..C 6
Tillamook ..3,968.°C 4
Tiller ....I 6
Timber ....B 5
Tioga ....H 4
Toketee Falls ......H 6
Toledo ....2,818..E 4
Tolovana Park ......B 4
Trail ....I 6
Tri City ....H 5
Triangle Lake ......F 5
Troutdale ...1,661..B 7
Troy ....A 15
Tualatin* ....750..C 6
Tumalo ....E 9
Turner* ......846..D 6
Twin Rocks ....B 4
Tygh Valley ....C 9
Ukiah ....C 12
Umapine ....A 13
Umatilla .....679..B 12
Umpqua ....H 5
Union ....1,531..C 14
Union Creek ....I 6
Unity ....E 14
Upper Highland .....C 7
Upper Soda ....E 7
Vale ....1,448.°F 15
Valley Falls ....J 10
Valley Junction ...D 5
Valsetz ....D 5
Venator ....H 14
Veneta ....1,377..F 5
Vernonia ..1,643..B 5
Vida ....K 2
Vinson ....C 12
Viola ....C 7
Waconda ....H 1
Wakonda Beach ......E 4
Waldport .....700..E 4
Walker ....F 5
Wallowa .....811..B 15

Walterville ....K 2
Walton ....F 5
Wamic ....C 9
Wapato ....F 1
Wapinitia ....C 9
Warm Springs ....D 9
Warner ....H 4
Warrenton ..1,825..A 4
Wasco ....412..B 9
Waterloo .....186..I 2
Waterman ....E 11
Wauna ....A 5
Weatherby ....E 15
Webfoot ....B 10
Wedderburn ....J 3
Welches ....C 7
Wemme ....C 7
Wendling ....K 2
West Linn ..7,091..C 6
West Side ....K 10
West Slope ....F 2
West Stayton ....I 1
Westfall ....F 15
Westfir ....G 6
Westlake ....F 4
Weston ....660..B 13
Westport ....A 5
Wetmore ....D 11
Wheeler ......262..B 4
White City ....J 6
Whiteson ....G 1
Whitney ....D 14
Wilbur ....H 5
Wilcox ....C 10
Wilderville ....J 5
Wilkesboro ....F 1
Willamette City ....G 6
Willamina ..1,193..D 5
Williams ....J 5
Willowdale ....D 9
Wilsonville* .1,001..C 6
Wimer ....J 5
Winchester Bay .....G 4
Winlock ....D 11
Winston ...2,468..H 5
Wolf Creek ....I 5
Wonder ....J 5
Wood Village* 1,533..B 7
Woodburn ...7,495..G 1
Woods ....C 4
Worden ....K 7
Wren ....E 5
Yachats ......441..E 4
Yamhill ......516..G 1
Yoder ....G 2
Yoncalla .....675..G 5

*Does not appear on the map; key shows general location.
°County seat.

Source: Latest census figures (1970). Places without population figures are unincorporated areas and are not listed in census reports.

Portland is Oregon's largest city and the industrial, commercial, and cultural center of the state. Portland lies near the intersection of the Columbia and Willamette rivers, and is Oregon's leading port. Majestic Mount Hood rises east of the city.

Oregon State Highway Dept.

Branding Cattle, as these cowboys are doing near John Day, is a familiar sight on the ranches of eastern Oregon.

Surefooted Loggers guide logs to a sawmill. Oregon's forests provide about a fourth of the nation's lumber.

POPULATION

This map shows the *population density* of Oregon, and how it varies in different parts of the state. Population density means the average number of persons who live in a given area.

Persons per sq. mi.		Persons per km²
More than 50		More than 20
20 to 50		8 to 20
5 to 20		2 to 8
Less than 5		Less than 2

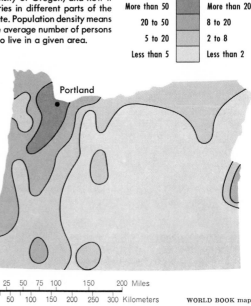

Portland

0	25	50	75	100	150	200 Miles
0	50	100	150	200	250	300 Kilometers

WORLD BOOK map

OREGON /People

The 1970 United States census reported that Oregon had 2,091,385 persons. The population had increased 18 per cent over the 1960 figure, 1,768,687. The U.S. Bureau of the Census estimated that by 1975 the population had reached 2,288,000.

About three-fifths of the people of Oregon live in the metropolitan areas of Portland, Eugene-Springfield, and Salem. These three areas are Standard Metropolitan Statistical Areas (see METROPOLITAN AREA). For the populations of these areas, see the *Index* to the political map of Oregon.

Most of Oregon's large cities lie in the rich Willamette Valley in the northwestern part of the state. Portland, the largest city, is the commercial, industrial, and cultural center of the state. Its lovely rose gardens give it the nickname *City of Roses.* Eugene, the second largest city, is a trading and processing center. The largest cities outside the valley are Klamath Falls in south-central Oregon, and Medford in the southwest. See the separate articles on the cities of Oregon listed in the *Related Articles* at the end of this article.

About 97 of every 100 Oregonians were born in the United States. Some trace their ancestry to settlers who came on the Oregon Trail. The largest groups of Oregonians born elsewhere came from Canada, Germany, Great Britain, and the Scandinavian countries. A majority of Oregon's people are Protestants. But Roman Catholics form the largest religious group. Other groups include Baptists, Disciples of Christ, Episcopalians, Lutherans, Methodists, Mormons, and Presbyterians.

Schools. Jason Lee, a Methodist missionary, established a school for Indian children in French Prairie as early as 1834. After the Oregon Territory was organized in 1848, an act provided that income from two sections (1,280 acres, or 518 hectares) of land in each township should be set aside for education. In 1849, the legislature passed laws providing for a free public school system. The first public school opened in 1851.

Today, a state board of education heads Oregon's public school system. The governor appoints the seven board members, subject to approval by the state Senate. The superintendent of public instruction is elected to a four-year term and administers the school system.

Children between the ages of 7 and 18 must attend school. For the number of students and teachers in Oregon, see EDUCATION (table).

Libraries. Oregon's first circulating library was organized in Oregon City in 1842. The Portland Library Association (now Multnomah County Library) was the first to serve the public on a large scale. It began in 1864 on a membership basis. This library became a free public library in 1902. Today, Oregon has over 180 public libraries and branches. The Oregon State Library in Salem serves chiefly as a reference and research center for state legislators and state agencies. The Astoria Public Library has a collection of Finnish language books.

Museums. The Portland Art Museum displays a large collection of paintings and sculpture. These works feature Indian art from the Northwest Coast and pre-Columbian Mexican art. The University of Oregon Museum of Art in Eugene owns the Warner Collection of Oriental Art, one of the finest in the country. The Oregon Museum of Science and Industry in Portland features demonstrations that show science at work in Oregon industries. The Oregon Historical Society in Portland has many items from pioneer days. The Favell Museum in Klamath Falls displays Indian artifacts and exhibits works of over 75 Western artists.

UNIVERSITIES AND COLLEGES

Oregon has 23 universities and colleges accredited by the Northwest Association of Schools and Colleges. For enrollments and further information, see UNIVERSITIES AND COLLEGES (table).

Name	Location	Founded
Columbia Christian College	Portland	1947
Eastern Oregon State College	La Grande	1929
George Fox College	Newberg	1892
Lewis and Clark College	Portland	1867
Linfield College	McMinnville	1849
Mount Angel Seminary	St. Benedict	1889
Museum Art School	Portland	1968
Northwest Christian College	Eugene	1895
Oregon, University of	Eugene	1872
Oregon College of Education	Monmouth	1856
Oregon Graduate Center	Beaverton	1966
Oregon Institute of Technology	Klamath Falls	1966
Oregon State University	Corvallis	1868
Pacific University	Forest Grove	1849
Portland, University of	Portland	1901
Portland State University	Portland	1946
Reed College	Portland	1910
Southern Oregon State College	Ashland	1926
Warner Pacific College	Portland	1937
Western Baptist Bible College	Salem	1955
Western Conservative Baptist Seminary	Portland	1927
Western Evangelical Seminary	Portland	1945
Willamette University	Salem	1842

Reed College

Reed College is a private coeducational college in Portland. Founded in 1910, it was one of the first colleges in the United States to install a nuclear reactor for use in undergraduate study.

WORLD BOOK photo by Alfred A. Monner

The Portland Art Museum, established in 1892, owns a fine collection of African pottery and sculpture, *above*. The museum also has a noted exhibit of American Indian art.

OREGON / A Visitor's Guide

Oregon is known for its beautiful mountain and coastal scenery. Majestic snow-covered Mount Hood towers above the Cascade Range about 50 miles (80 kilometers) east of Portland. U.S. Highway 26 skirts Mount Hood and offers close-up views of its glacier-clad slopes. U.S. Highway 101 follows the Oregon coastline for more than 300 miles (480 kilometers). Motorists driving along this route see views of white sand dunes, coastal lakes and bays, and cliffs rising above the shore.

Oregon is a sportsman's paradise. Deer, elk, and pronghorn roam the fields and forests. Fishermen battle steelhead trout and other major game fish. Grouse, pheasant, quail, and other game birds are plentiful.

Slopes in the Cascades, Wallowas, and other Oregon mountains offer excellent skiing. Timberline, on Mount Hood, is perhaps the most famous ski area in the state. The skiing season in most areas begins in December and lasts through April.

PLACES TO VISIT

Following are brief descriptions of some of Oregon's many interesting places to visit.

Bonneville Dam, the first major dam on the Columbia River, has a series of fish ladders. In season, salmon and other fish can be seen jumping up the ladders on their way upstream to spawn.

Columbia River Gorge. Here the Columbia River cuts through the Cascade Mountains on its way to the Pacific Ocean. Colorful basalt cliffs line the deep gorge for about 60 miles (97 kilometers) between The Dalles and Troutdale. Multnomah and other waterfalls tumble into the gorge.

Picture Gorge, by the John Day Highway (U.S. 26) near Dayville, is a canyon of basalt rock named for the Indian pictures on the walls. The John Day Fossil Beds have fossils of prehistoric animals and plants.

Sea Lion Caves, on the Pacific Coast near Florence, is the home of hundreds of sea lions. The best time for viewing the lions is from September through spring.

National Parks and Forests. Crater Lake National Park, the state's only national park, lies in the Cascade Mountains in south-central Oregon. Crater Lake, 1,932 feet (589 meters) deep, rests at the top of an ancient volcano. See CRATER LAKE NATIONAL PARK.

Eleven national forests lie entirely within Oregon. They are Deschutes, Fremont, Malheur, Mount Hood, Ochoco, Siuslaw, Umpqua, Wallowa-Whitman, Willamette, and Winema. Oregon shares Umatilla National Forest with Washington, and Klamath, Rogue River, and Siskiyou with California. Congress set aside 10 areas in Oregon's national forests as national wilderness areas, to be preserved in their natural condition. For the area and chief features of each national forest, see NATIONAL FOREST (table).

National Monuments, Memorials, and Historic Sites. Oregon Caves National Monument is in the Siskiyou Mountains of southwestern Oregon. Its limestone caverns contain beautiful stone formations. See OREGON CAVES NATIONAL MONUMENT.

Fort Clatsop National Memorial near Astoria was the site of the winter encampment of Meriwether Lewis and William Clark during their famous expedition to the region in 1805 and 1806. McLoughlin House National Historic Site in Oregon City was built by John McLoughlin, often called the *Father of Oregon.* He lived there from 1847 until his death in 1857.

State Parks. Oregon has 232 state parks. Many of them have overnight camping and recreational facilities. For further information, write to Superintendent, State Parks and Recreation Section, Oregon Highway Division, 301 Highway Building, Salem, Ore. 97310.

Shakespearean Festival in Ashland

Young Skiers Practice near Mount Hood

ANNUAL EVENTS

One of the most famous Oregon events is the Shakespearean Festival in Ashland, from mid-June through mid-September. Plays by Shakespeare are presented in an Elizabethan theater and in the Angus Bowmer indoor theater. "Dancing on the Green" before showtime features Shakespearean songs.

Other leading events are the Portland Rose Festival in early June and the Pendleton Round-Up and Happy Canyon Pageant in mid-September. The rose festival features a spectacular Grand Floral Parade. The four-day rodeo includes an Indian historical pageant.

Other annual events in Oregon include the following.

January-May: Ski Tournaments at Mount Ashland near Ashland, at Mount Bachelor near Bend, and at Government Camp near Mount Hood (January); Sled Dog Races in Bend and Union Creek (January-February); All Northwest Barber Shop Ballad Contest and Gay Nineties Festival in Forest Grove (late February); Pear Blossom Festival Parade in Medford (mid-April); All-Indian Rodeo in Tygh Valley (mid-May); Rhododendron Festival in Florence (mid-May); Fleet of Flowers Memorial Service in Depoe Bay (late May).

June-August: Strawberry Festival in Lebanon (early June); Rodeo in St. Paul (early July); World Championship Timber Carnival in Albany (early July); Buckeroo in Molalla (early July); Chief Joseph Days in Joseph (late July); Peter Britt Music and Arts Festival in Jacksonville (August); Regatta in Astoria (late August); State Fair in Salem (August-September).

September-December: Oktoberfest in Mount Angel (mid-September); Lord's Acre Auction and Barbecue in Powell Butte (early November); Pacific International Livestock Exposition in Portland (early November); Christmas Pageant in Rickreall (mid-December).

Fish Ladders at Bonneville Dam

Oregon Caves National Monument near Grants Pass

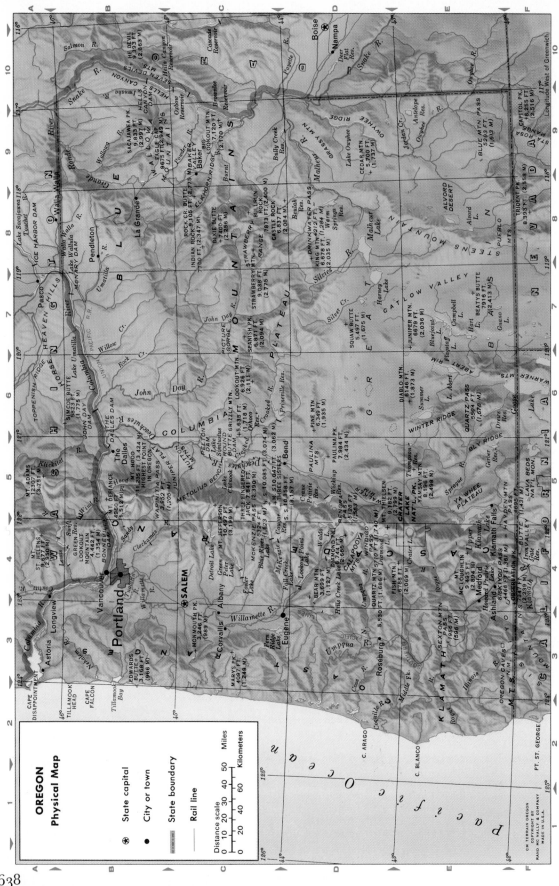

OREGON
Physical Map

⊛ State capital

● City or town

State boundary

Rail line

Distance scale

0   10   20   30   40   50 Miles

0   20   40   60 Kilometers

CM TERRAIN Oregon
COPYRIGHT BY
RAND MC NALLY & COMPANY
MADE IN U.S.A.

Specially created for **World Book Encyclopedia** by Rand McNally and World Book editors

638

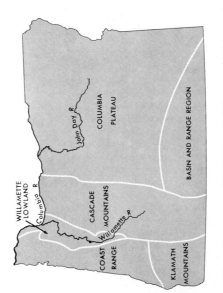

Land Regions of Oregon

OREGON | The Land

Land Regions. Oregon has six main land regions: (1) the Coast Range, (2) the Willamette Lowland, (3) the Cascade Mountains, (4) the Klamath Mountains, (5) the Columbia Plateau, and (6) the Basin and Range Region.

The Coast Range region borders the Pacific Ocean from Washington's Chehalis Valley on the north to the Klamath Mountains of Oregon on the south. The rolling Coast Ranges run parallel to the shoreline. They are the lowest of Oregon's main mountain ranges, with average elevations of less than 2,000 feet (610 meters). Marys Peak, southwest of Corvallis, rises 4,097 feet (1,249 meters) and is the highest point in the region. Forests of Douglas fir, hemlock, spruce, and other evergreen trees cover much of the area.

Several valleys in the region, such as Triangle Lake Valley, are beds of ancient lakes. Many small coastal lakes were formed when the mouths of streams sank and sand dunes dammed their waters. Along much of the coast, the land rises from the sea in sheer cliffs, some of them nearly 1,000 feet (300 meters) high. In some places, the coastal mountains rise in a series of terraces. Each terrace was once the coastline.

The Willamette Lowland is a narrow strip wedged between the Coast Ranges on the west and the Cascade Mountains on the east. The Willamette River and its branches flow north to the Columbia River. They drain the level and gently rolling farm and forest lands of the Willamette Valley. Over half the state's people live in the region. Rich soil, a favorable climate, and nearby water transportation make it the most important farming and industrial area in the state.

The Cascade Mountains region, a broad belt of rugged land crowned by volcanic peaks, includes some of the highest mountains in North America. Mount Hood, the highest peak in Oregon, rises 11,235 feet (3,424 meters) above sea level. Mount Jefferson is 10,497 feet (3,199 meters) high. Other beautiful Cascade peaks include the Three Sisters, over 10,000 feet (3,000 meters) high, and Mount McLoughlin, 9,495 feet (2,894 meters) high.

The Klamath Mountains cover the southwestern corner of Oregon. Thick forests grow on the mountainsides and provide shelter for game animals. This region also has the state's richest mineral deposits.

The Columbia Plateau covers most of eastern Oregon and extends northeastward into Washington and Idaho.

Mountains and Rocks line the Pacific Ocean at Cannon Beach near Ecola State Park in the Coast Range.

Crater Lake fills the hollow of a dead volcano in the Cascade Mountains in southwest Oregon.

Great Wheat Fields thrive in the Columbia Plateau of eastern Oregon. This field is located in Wasco County.

Thousands of years ago, lava flowed out of cracks in the earth's crust to form the plateau. Deep canyons of the Deschutes, John Day, and other rivers cut through the plateau in north-central Oregon. The state's great wheat ranches lie in this area. Much of the so-called "plateau" in Oregon is actually rugged and mountainous. The Blue and Wallowa mountains rise in northeastern Oregon. Rolling timberlands cover the Blue Mountain area. The Wallowa Mountains, cut by glaciers, provide spectacular scenery. The Snake River has carved the famous Hells Canyon on the Oregon-Idaho border. This great gorge lies between the Wallowa Mountains and Idaho's Seven Devils Mountains. Its depth is about 5,500 feet (1,680 meters).

The Basin and Range Region covers part of southeastern Oregon and extends into California and other nearby states. In Oregon, the region consists of a high basin broken by occasional low mountains. The Cascade Range to the west cuts off moisture-bearing winds from the Pacific Ocean and makes much of the area a semidesert.

Coastline. Oregon's coastline extends 296 miles (476 kilometers) along the Pacific Ocean. Much of the shore is rugged, with steep cliffs rising up from the sea. But many bays and harbors have been formed where rivers from the Coast Ranges and Klamath Mountains flow into the sea. These bays and harbors include Tillamook, Yaquina, Alsea, Winchester, and Coos.

Rivers, Waterfalls, and Lakes. The mighty Columbia River flows westward to the Pacific Ocean, forming most of the border between Oregon and Washington. The Columbia drains more than half of Oregon. The Columbia and its branch, the Willamette River, form the largest system of navigable waterways in the state. The Snake River forms much of the Oregon-Idaho border. It joins the Columbia in Washington. The Snake and its branches drain the easternmost part of Oregon. The Deschutes River travels northward through central Oregon and empties into the Columbia. The John Day River, rises in the Strawberry Mountains in eastern Oregon. It flows west and north to the Columbia and drains much of north-central Oregon.

Hundreds of streams in the Cascade Mountains rush down the slopes in rapids and waterfalls. Among the best known waterfalls are Benham, Pringle, Salt Creek, Steamboat, and the many falls along Silver Creek. About a dozen waterfalls, some of them over 200 feet (61 meters) high, tumble into the Columbia River Gorge. These waterfalls include Bridal Veil, Coopery, Elowah, Horsetail, Latourell, and Multnomah.

The Cascade Mountains region has many lakes. Crater Lake in the Cascades, 1,932 feet (589 meters) in depth, is the deepest lake in the United States. It lies in the *caldera* (crater) of an extinct volcano. Wallowa Lake in the Wallowa Mountains is famous for its sparkling clear water. Most of the lakes in southeastern Oregon are shallow and salty. Some evaporate during dry seasons and leave salt deposits in the lake beds. But a few, such as Harney and Malheur, are large year-round lakes. A number of small lakes near the Oregon coast were formed when deposits of soil and sand blocked the mouths of streams and kept the streams from emptying into the ocean.

OREGON / Climate

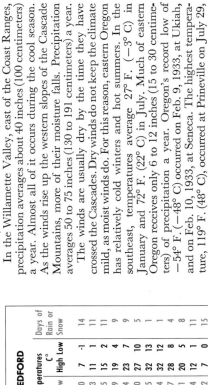

Ray Atkeson

Crops and Forests flourish in the moist, mild climate of the Willamette Valley in western Oregon.

Mild, moist winds from the Pacific Ocean give western Oregon an unusually mild climate for a state so far north. Coastal temperatures average 45° F. (7° C) in January and 60° F. (16° C) in July. The winds become cooler when they rise over the Coast Ranges. Much of their moisture condenses and falls as rain. In some coastal areas, yearly *precipitation* (rain, snow, and other moisture) exceeds 130 inches (330 centimeters).

In the Willamette Valley, east of the Coast Ranges, precipitation averages about 40 inches (100 centimeters) a year. Almost all of it occurs during the cool season. As the winds rise up the western slopes of the Cascade Mountains, more of their moisture falls. Precipitation averages 50 to 75 inches (130 to 191 centimeters) a year.

The winds are usually dry by the time they have crossed the Cascades. Dry winds do not keep the climate mild, as moist winds do. For this reason, eastern Oregon has relatively cold winters and hot summers. In the southeast, temperatures average 27° F. (−3° C) in January and 72° F. (22° C) in July. Much of eastern Oregon receives only 6 to 12 inches (15 to 30 centimeters) of precipitation a year. Oregon's record low of −54° F. (−48° C) occurred on Feb. 9, 1933, at Ukiah, and on Feb. 10, 1933, at Seneca. The highest temperature, 119° F. (48° C), occurred at Prineville on July 29, 1898, and at Pendleton on Aug. 10, 1898.

SEASONAL TEMPERATURES

January

AVERAGE OF DAILY LOW TEMPERATURES

Degrees Celsius	Degrees Fahrenheit
2 to 9	36 to 48
−4 to 2	24 to 36
−11 to −4	12 to 24
−18 to −11	0 to 12

AVERAGE OF DAILY HIGH TEMPERATURES

Degrees Fahrenheit	Degrees Celsius
48 to 56	9 to 13
40 to 48	4 to 9
32 to 40	0 to 4
24 to 32	−4 to 0

July

AVERAGE OF DAILY LOW TEMPERATURES

Degrees Celsius	Degrees Fahrenheit
13 to 18	56 to 64
9 to 13	48 to 56
4 to 9	40 to 48
0 to 4	32 to 40

AVERAGE OF DAILY HIGH TEMPERATURES

Degrees Fahrenheit	Degrees Celsius
92 to 100	33 to 38
84 to 92	29 to 33
76 to 84	24 to 29
68 to 76	20 to 24

AVERAGE MONTHLY WEATHER

PORTLAND

	Temperatures F° High	Low	C° High	Low	Days of Rain or Snow
JAN.	44	35	7	2	19
FEB.	50	38	10	3	16
MAR.	56	41	13	5	17
APR.	62	45	17	7	14
MAY	69	50	21	10	12
JUNE	73	54	23	12	9
JULY	79	58	26	14	3
AUG.	79	58	26	14	4
SEPT.	73	54	23	12	7
OCT.	64	49	18	9	12
NOV.	53	42	12	6	17
DEC.	47	38	8	3	19

MEDFORD

	Temperatures F° High	Low	C° High	Low	Days of Rain or Snow
JAN.	45	30	7	−1	14
FEB.	52	33	11	1	11
MAR.	59	35	15	2	11
APR.	66	39	19	4	9
MAY	73	44	23	7	9
JUNE	80	50	27	10	5
JULY	89	55	32	13	1
AUG.	89	54	32	12	1
SEPT.	82	47	28	8	4
OCT.	68	41	20	5	8
NOV.	54	34	12	1	11
DEC.	45	32	7	0	15

AVERAGE YEARLY PRECIPITATION
(Rain, Melted Snow and Other Moisture)

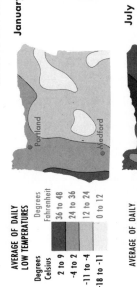
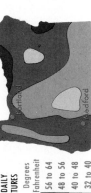

Centimeters	Inches
183 to 330	72 to 130
61 to 183	24 to 72
30 to 61	12 to 24
15 to 30	6 to 12

0   100   200 Miles
0   100   200   300 Kilometers

WORLD BOOK maps

The Cascade Mountains divide Oregon into two major economic regions. Manufacturing industries are concentrated in the Willamette Valley in western Oregon. This region also produces most of the state's dairy products, flower bulbs, fruits, and vegetables. The dry lands east of the Cascades are important for livestock and wheat production, and for vegetable production in irrigated areas.

The Hood River Valley in northern Oregon and the Rogue River Valley in southwestern Oregon are famous fruit-growing regions. Lumbering and wood processing are important industries in the forested parts of the state.

Natural Resources. Oregon's many natural resources include huge timber reserves, small deposits of many minerals, and a plentiful water supply.

Forests. Oregon has about an eighth of the nation's timber. Forests cover about 30½ million acres (12.3 million hectares), of which about 25,700,000 acres (10,400,000 hectares) are commercial forest land. Oregon has two forest regions: (1) the Douglas fir region west of the Cascade Mountains, and (2) the ponderosa (western yellow) pine region east of the mountains.

The Douglas fir, Oregon's state tree, provides the largest amount of timber. Ponderosa pine, western hemlock, western red cedar, Sitka spruce, and several kinds of true firs also grow in the Douglas fir region. Some Douglas fir trees grow in the ponderosa pine region, as do Engelmann spruce, Idaho white pine, lodgepole pine, sugar pine, and true firs. See FIR.

Oregonians conserve their timber reserves by protecting them from fire, harmful insects, and tree diseases. Forest owners plant seedlings in areas where large trees have been cut down. They also grow trees on tree farms. These farms cover more than 5 million acres (2 million hectares) in the state.

Minerals. Deposits of bauxite (aluminum ore) have been found in northwestern Oregon. Chromite occurs in several parts of the state. The Klamath Mountains region has important deposits of nickel ore. Veins of cinnabar, from which mercury is made, lie under many parts of the state. Other metallic minerals found in Oregon include copper, gold, iron ore, lead, silver, and uranium.

Deposits of coal, some of them 5 feet (1.5 meters) thick, occur near Coos Bay. Some parts of the state have deposits of high-grade limestone. Clay for bricks and tiles comes from the Willamette Valley and other areas. Oregon also has deposits of diatomite, peat, perlite, pumice, and semiprecious gems.

Water is one of Oregon's most important resources. Melted snow and winter rain from the mountains feed Oregon's rivers and provide unusually pure water for industry and home use. The Columbia River and its tributaries are important sources of water for power and irrigation.

Soils. Gray-brown soils cover the Coast Range and Klamath Mountains regions. The Willamette Lowland has deep, fertile soils. Shallow soils cover most of the eastern Cascade slopes, and the Basin and Range Region. The wheat belt of north-central Oregon has rich soils good for growing crops.

Production of Goods in Oregon

Total value of goods produced in 1973—$5,384,430,000

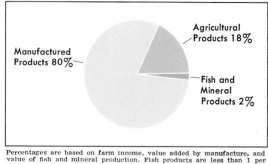

Agricultural Products 18%

Manufactured Products 80%

Fish and Mineral Products 2%

Percentages are based on farm income, value added by manufacture, and value of fish and mineral production. Fish products are less than 1 per cent.

Sources: U.S. government publications, 1975-1976.

Employment in Oregon

Total number of persons employed in 1974—891,600

	Number of Employees
Manufacturing	197,400
Wholesale & Retail Trade	194,700
Government	166,900
Community, Social, & Personal Services	140,900
Agriculture	54,000
Transportation & Public Utilities	52,400
Finance, Insurance, & Real Estate	44,500
Construction & Mining	40,800

Sources: *Employment and Earnings,* May 1975, U.S. Bureau of Labor Statistics; *Farm Labor,* February 1975, U.S. Department of Agriculture.

Plant Life. Many kinds of wild flowers grow in Oregon because the state has a variety of climates and elevations. Oregon is famous for its azaleas, laurels, rhododendrons, and other flowering shrubs. The state flower, the Oregon grape, grows in most parts of the state. Hardwood trees in Oregon include alder, ash, cottonwood, juniper, madroña, maple, and willow.

Animal Life. Columbian black-tailed deer and Roosevelt elk live in Oregon's mountain and coastal forests. Mule deer and Rocky Mountain elk are found east of the Cascades. Pronghorns thrive in the southeast. Small bands of mountain goats live in the Wallowa Mountains. Smaller animals found in Oregon include bobcats, beavers, coyotes, foxes, minks, muskrats, otters, and timber wolves. Seals and sea lions live along the coast in winter and early spring.

Oregon's most valuable commercial fish are tuna and salmon. They are also caught by sportsmen. Every year, thousands of salmon leave the ocean and swim up Oregon's rivers to lay their eggs. They leap up low waterfalls and climb fish ladders to get around dams. Cod, halibut, herring, ling cod, ocean perch, rockfish, sablefish, shad, and sole live in Oregon's coastal waters.

The steelhead trout is perhaps the most prized of Oregon's many game fishes. Other fishes in Oregon's rivers and lakes include perch, striped bass, and cutthroat and rainbow trout.

Rows of Daffodils carpet a valley near Portland. Farmers carefully tend these plants to provide flower bulbs, one of Oregon's profitable agricultural products. Similar farms throughout western Oregon grow gladiolus, iris, lily, and tulip bulbs.

Huge Logs from the thick forests of the Klamath Mountains region provide valuable timber for Oregon's lumber industry.

Manufacturing accounts for about four-fifths of the value of goods produced in Oregon each year. Products manufactured in the state have a *value added by manufacture* of about $4¼ billion a year. This figure represents the value added to products by Oregon's industries, not counting such costs as materials, supplies, and fuels.

Wood Processing is by far Oregon's most important manufacturing industry. Lumber and wood products have a value added by manufacture of about $1½ billion a year. Most cities have sawmills or plants that make wood products. Oregon leads the states in lumber production. It cuts about 8 billion board feet (19 million cubic meters) of lumber a year—about a fourth of the nation's supply. Oregon produces almost half the plywood manufactured in the nation. Oregon plants produce 2,919,000 short tons (2,648,000 metric tons) of pulp and about 3,151,000 short tons (2,859,000 metric tons) of paper a year.

Food Processing. Oregon plants process over 40 crops grown in the state. Portland, Salem, and other Willamette Valley cities have many canneries and freezing plants that pack fruits and vegetables. Several meat-processing plants also operate in the region. Canneries and freezing plants in Astoria pack a variety of fishes and shellfishes. Seafood is processed in Coos Bay, The Dalles, and other coastal and Columbia River cities.

Factories in Tillamook County produce world-famous Tillamook cheese. Large quantities of peas are processed in the Pendleton area. Sugar is made from sugar beets in Nyssa.

Other Leading Industries in Oregon produce electrical machinery, nonelectrical machinery, printed materials, and transportation equipment. Metal processing is also an important industry in Oregon. Aluminum-processing plants operate in The Dalles and Troutdale, near inexpensive hydroelectric power resources. They ship heavy materials on the Columbia River. Portland has a steel mill and metal-fabrication plants. Riddle has a

OREGON

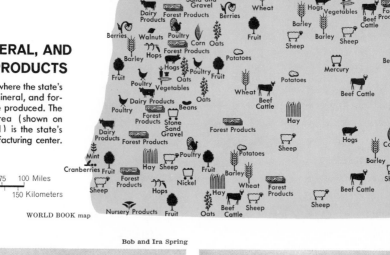

FARM, MINERAL, AND FOREST PRODUCTS

This map shows where the state's leading farm, mineral, and forest products are produced. The major urban area (shown on the map in red) is the state's important manufacturing center.

0   25   50   75   100 Miles

0   50   100   150 Kilometers

Yaquina Bay Harbor at Newport, *above,* exports many of Oregon's lumber products. The state has over 30½ million acres (12.3 million hectares) of trees. Oregon has two forest regions. One region, west of the Cascade Mountains, has Douglas fir forests. Ponderosa pine forests grow east of the Cascades.

Fruit Pickers Harvest Pears in the Rogue River Valley, *right.* Oregon is the country's leading producer of winter pears. Much of the state's best farmland lies in its river valleys. The Hood River Valley produces pears and apples. The Willamette River Valley is Oregon's most important vegetable-growing region.

640d

large ferronickel plant, and Albany has several plants that process such metals as titanium and zirconium.

Agriculture accounts for about $991 million a year, or about a fifth of the total value of goods produced in Oregon. The state has about 29,100 farms. They average 620 acres (250.9 hectares) in size.

Oregon has valuable herds of livestock, especially cattle and calves. Beef cattle are Oregon's most important farm product. They produce a yearly income of about $245 million. Most beef cattle are raised on ranges east of the Cascades. Western Oregon has large herds of dairy cattle. Dairy products are also an important source of farm income in the state.

Wheat is Oregon's most valuable crop. Much wheat grows in the plateau area of north-central Oregon. Hay is Oregon's second most important grain crop, followed by barley. Oregon usually produces more oats than any other state on the Pacific Coast.

Greenhouse and nursery products are another chief source of agricultural income in the state. Western Oregon is an important bulb-growing region. Farmers there grow daffodils, gladioli, irises, lilies, and tulips for bulbs. Such nursery products as shrubs and trees are also important.

Oregon leads the states in growing green snap beans. It also produces green peas, onions, and sweet corn. The Willamette Valley is the chief vegetable-growing region. Oregon farmers also grow large potato and sugar beet crops on irrigated land east of the Cascades. Oregon also produces hops, used in making beer. Marion County leads in hop production.

Oregon leads the states in the production of winter pears. The Hood and Rogue river valleys are famous pear-growing regions. Many Anjou, Bosc, and Comice pears from Oregon are used in gift packages. The Hood River Valley is also a center for apple production. Oregon fruit growers grow many cherries, especially in Wasco County. The western and northern counties produce peaches, plums, and prunes. Oregon ranks as a leading strawberry-producing state. Farmers in coastal areas grow cranberries. Other berries grown in Oregon include blackberries, blueberries, boysenberries, gooseberries, loganberries, and raspberries.

Oregon produces one of the nation's largest crops of nuts each year. About 96 per cent of the nation's filbert nuts come from the state.

Oregon farmers specialize in several crops that are not grown widely in many other states. For example, Oregon produces almost all the nation's seed for bent, fescue, and ryegrass, and most of the seed for common vetch, crimson clover, and merion bluegrass. These crops are grown mainly in northwestern counties. Oregon often leads the states in peppermint production.

Douglas County, in southwestern Oregon, leads in sheep raising. Sheep also graze on the eastern ranges and the Willamette Valley grasslands. Willamette Valley farmers raise most of the state's chickens. Umatilla County is the leading hog producer in Oregon. A number of fur farms operate in the state. Most of them specialize in raising mink.

Mining. Oregon mines about $80 million worth of minerals a year. Stone and sand and gravel account for about two-thirds of the value of Oregon's mineral output. These products are quarried in almost all counties. Basalt is the chief stone quarried. Oregon is the only state that produces nickel from raw ore. Other leading minerals include clay, diatomite, gemstones, gold, mercury, pumice, and silver.

Fishing Industry. Oregon has an annual fish catch valued at about $28 million. Tuna is Oregon's most valuable fishery product. The chief varieties landed are albacore and yellowfin tuna. Salmon ranks as the second leading fishery product of the state. Chinook and silver account for the major portion of the salmon produced. Other important seafoods from Oregon include Dungeness crabs, flounder, ling cod, oysters, rockfish, shad, shrimp, and steelhead trout.

Electric Power. Huge dams and power facilities stand on the Columbia River between Oregon and Washington. These dams include Bonneville, John Day, McNary, and The Dalles. They form part of a power pool that supplies electricity to the entire Pacific Northwest. Both private and public power generating sources contribute to the pool. The pool provides about 65 per cent of Oregon's electricity.

The rest of the electric power production is generated at dams that are entirely within Oregon. These dams include Detroit and Lookout Point on the Willamette River, and smaller dams on the Clackamas, Deschutes, Klamath, Rogue, and Umpqua rivers.

Transportation. From 1843 to the coming of the railroads in the 1860's, thousands of persons traveled the famous Oregon Trail to Oregon (see OREGON TRAIL). Today, Oregon has about 105,000 miles (165,000 kilometers) of roads. Railroads operate on about 3,000 miles (4,800 kilometers) of track. About 20 rail lines provide freight service. Passenger trains serve Eugene, Klamath Falls, Portland, and Salem.

Oregon has over 180 airports. The largest is Portland International Airport. Other major commercial airfields are located at Eugene, Klamath Falls, Medford, North Bend, Pendleton, and Salem. Portland is a major ocean port, although it is 100 miles (160 kilometers) inland. Portland ships more dry bulk cargo than any other West Coast port. Oceangoing ships follow a deepened channel up the Columbia and into the Willamette River to reach Portland's harbor.

A series of dams and locks allows barges to travel up the Columbia to Pasco, Wash. Oregon river ports near the Columbia include Hood River, The Dalles, and Umatilla. Coastal ports include Astoria, Bay City, Brookings, Coos Bay, Nehalem, Newport, Port Orford, and Tillamook.

Communication. Oregon's first newspaper, the *Oregon Spectator*, began publication at Oregon City in 1846. It is no longer published. *The Oregonian* was established in Portland in 1850 as the *Weekly Oregonian*. The *Oregon Statesman* appeared in Oregon City in 1851, and later moved to Salem. These two papers are still published today. Other leading newspapers include the *Mail-Tribune* of Medford, *Eugene Register-Guard*, and *Oregon Journal* of Portland. Oregon has about 135 newspapers, including about 20 dailies. Oregon publishers also issue about 75 periodicals.

Oregon's first commercial radio station, KGW, opened in Portland in 1922. The state's first television station, KPTV, began operating in Portland in 1953. Oregon has about 120 radio stations and 15 TV stations.

Fort Clatsop sheltered members of the Lewis and Clark expedition during the winter of 1805-1806 after their journey across the continent.

Captain Robert Gray visited the Oregon country in 1792. He sailed into the mouth of a great river which he named after his ship, the *Columbia*.

Salmon Runs take place on the Columbia River every year. For hundreds of years, Indians speared the salmon as they swam upstream to spawn.

Astoria

Astoria, founded by John Jacob Astor's fur company in 1811, marked the beginning of the settlement of Oregon.

The First U.S. Government in the Pacific Northwest was organized in 1843 at Champoeg by Oregon settlers in the Willamette Valley.

Willamette Valley Settlers, William Meek and Henderson Luelling, brought several hundred young fruit trees over the Oregon Trail from Iowa in 1847. Fruit from the valley is now world-famous.

Bonneville Dam and lock, completed in 1937, made the Columbia River navigable for seagoing vessels. It provides electricity for the Portland region.

HISTORIC OREGON

Indian Days. When the first white men entered the Oregon region, many Indian tribes lived there. The Chinook lived along the lower Columbia River, where they fished for salmon. The Clackama, Multnomah, and Tillamook tribes also made their homes in the northwest part of the region. The Bannock, Cayuse, Paiute, Umatilla, and a branch of the Nez Percé lived in the region east of the Cascade Mountains. The Klamath and the Modoc were in the south, near Oregon's present-day border with California.

Exploration and Settlement. Spanish sailors who went from Mexico to the Philippines during the 1500's and 1600's were the first white men to see the Oregon coast. Historians think that Sir Francis Drake of England touched Oregon's southern coast in 1579 while searching for an ocean route from the northern Pacific to the Atlantic. In 1778, the British explorer James Cook reached and named Cape Foulweather, north of Yaquina Bay. Robert Gray and other Americans landed on the Oregon coast in 1788. George Vancouver of Great Britain explored and mapped the coast in 1792. Also in 1792, Gray sailed into the river which he named for his ship, the *Columbia*. The explorers Meriwether Lewis and William Clark reached the mouth of the Columbia by land in 1805. Their expedition, together with Gray's trip on the river, gave the United States a strong claim to the Oregon region.

In the early 1800's, the Oregon region stretched from Alaska, which was claimed by Russia, to California, which was claimed by Spain. It extended eastward from the Pacific Ocean to the Rocky Mountains. Russia, Spain, Great Britain, and the United States claimed parts of the region. Russia based its claims on Russian explorations along the northern Pacific Coast. In treaties with Great Britain and the United States in 1824 and 1825, Russia gave up its interests south of latitude 54° 40'. In 1819, by treaty, Spain gave up its claim north of latitude 42°, Oregon's present southern boundary. Britain and the United States could not agree on a boundary line to separate their claims. They postponed a decision by signing a treaty in 1818 that permitted citizens of both countries to trade and settle in the region. The treaty was renewed in 1827.

John Jacob Astor, an American fur trader, began the white settlement of Oregon. He established a fur-trading post at Astoria in 1811. The Hudson's Bay Company, a powerful British trading firm, established Fort Vancouver (now Vancouver, Wash.) near the Columbia River in 1825. John McLoughlin directed the activities of the Hudson's Bay Company and ruled the region for about 20 years. He later became a U.S. citizen, and today he is known as the *Father of Oregon.*

In 1834, Methodist missionaries established the first permanent American settlement in the Willamette Valley. The first large overland migration into Oregon came in 1843. That year, about a thousand persons traveled the Oregon Trail and settled in the Willamette Valley. Hundreds of American settlers arrived each year from then on. The increasing number of settlers put pressure on the U.S. government to settle the boundary dispute with Great Britain. In 1844, James K. Polk based his campaign for the presidency partly on

IMPORTANT DATES IN OREGON

1579 Sir Francis Drake possibly touched the Oregon coast.

1792 Robert Gray sailed into the Columbia River.

1805 Meriwether Lewis and William Clark reached the mouth of the Columbia.

1811 John Jacob Astor founded Astoria.

1819 A treaty between the United States and Spain fixed the present southern border of Oregon.

1843 The Willamette settlers at Champoeg organized a provisional government.

1846 A treaty made the 49th parallel the chief boundary between British and U.S. territory in the Oregon region.

1848 Oregon became a territory.

1850 Congress passed the Oregon Donation Land Law.

1859 Oregon became the 33rd state on February 14.

1877 Chief Joseph helped lead the Nez Percé Indians in a war against the white men, but finally surrendered.

1902 Oregon adopted the initiative and referendum.

1912 The state adopted woman suffrage.

1937 Bonneville Dam was completed.

1950's McNary and The Dalles dams were built on the Columbia River.

1964 Heavy floods damaged western Oregon.

1974 Construction began on enlarging the powerhouse facilities of Bonneville Dam.

---

the claim that land south of latitude 54° 40' belonged to the United States (see FIFTY-FOUR FORTY OR FIGHT). In 1846, President Polk signed a treaty with Great Britain. This treaty fixed the 49th parallel as the chief dividing line between U.S. and British territory.

Indian Wars. In 1847, Indians massacred Marcus Whitman and 13 others, near present-day Walla Walla, Wash. (see WHITMAN, MARCUS). This massacre led to the Cayuse War of 1847, in which the Indian villages were destroyed. The Rogue River Wars of the 1850's resulted from the Indians' anger at being driven from their lands. Chief John, the Indian leader, surrendered in 1856 and was imprisoned.

One of the most spectacular Indian wars, the Modoc War, lasted from November, 1872, to June, 1873. White settlers tried to force the Modoc Indians onto the Klamath reservation. But the Indians hid near the California border among lava beds which provided natural defenses. A small band of warriors kept more than a thousand U.S. soldiers at bay until the Indians finally surrendered.

The Nez Percé War began in 1877. Chief Joseph and other Nez Percé leaders refused to let the government move their people from the beautiful Wallowa Valley to a reservation in Idaho. Joseph retreated slowly into Idaho and Montana. He hoped to wipe out the U.S. troops who pursued him. Joseph was finally captured near the Canadian border, where he surrendered. The Paiute and Bannock Indians rose against Oregon settlers in 1878, but were quickly defeated. See INDIAN WARS (In the Northwest).

Provisional and Territorial Governments. In 1843, settlers in the Willamette Valley met at Champoeg (near present-day Newberg) to organize a provisional government. A similar attempt had been made unsuccessfully two years before. In 1843, the settlers adopted a set of laws which were based on the laws of Iowa.

Oregon became a territory in 1848, with Oregon City as the capital. The capital was moved to Salem in 1850. Oregon's present boundaries were established in 1853, when Congress created the Washington Territory.

The Donation Land Law of 1850 spurred territorial growth and development. This law provided that any male American citizen over 18 who settled in Oregon before December, 1850, could receive 320 acres (129 hectares) of land. His wife could also receive 320 acres. To qualify for ownership, he had to cultivate his claim for four years. From December, 1850, to December, 1855, a settler had to be at least 21 to receive land, and he got only 160 acres (65 hectares).

Progress as a State. Oregon joined the Union as the 33rd state on Feb. 14, 1859. Salem became the state capital. John Whiteaker, a Democrat, served as the first state governor, from 1859 to 1862.

During the Civil War (1861-1865), state volunteers protected eastern Oregon against Indian attacks. The attacks continued for 15 years after the war. Oregon's population increased rapidly after the Civil War ended. Former soldiers from both sides sought new opportunities in the West. In 1860, about 52,000 persons lived in Oregon. By 1890, over 300,000 lived there.

During the 1890's, William S. U'Ren, a political leader, began a movement for governmental reform. U'Ren favored laws that would give the voters more direct control over the state government.

The Early 1900's. In 1902, Oregon adopted the *initiative and referendum*, procedures that permit voters to take a direct part in lawmaking (see INITIATIVE AND REFERENDUM). In 1908, it adopted the *recall*, a procedure for removing undesirable officials from office. The use of these direct-government procedures became known as the *Oregon System*. Many states have passed initiative, referendum, and recall laws based on this system.

In 1912, Oregon gave women the right to vote for the first time in the state's history. Passage of the law followed a long and difficult campaign for women's rights led by Abigail Jane Scott Duniway.

During the Great Depression of the 1930's, the federal government provided money to build Bonneville Dam on the Columbia River. The dam and nearby locks supplied electric power for industry and improved the river for navigation. Owyhee Dam, completed in 1932, provided irrigation water for vast areas of farmland in the Owyhee and Snake river valleys.

The Mid-1900's. By 1940, Oregon's population had grown to more than a million. During World War II (1939-1945), many of the state's factories produced military equipment. Portland became a major port for shipment of supplies to Russia and to U.S. armed forces in the Pacific. The city's shipyards produced cargo vessels and warships. Thousands of people from other states came to work in Oregon defense plants, and many of them settled in the state after the war.

During the 1950's, McNary and The Dalles dams were built on the Columbia River. These dams greatly increased Oregon's supply of low-cost electric power. In 1956, pipelines brought natural gas into the state

for the first time. Both developments contributed greatly to Oregon's industrial growth. Many people began to move from rural to urban areas to take manufacturing jobs.

Important changes took place in the Oregon timber industry during the 1960's. In the past, sawdust, bark, and other logging by-products had been wasted. Now, Oregon companies began to use many of these materials to make hardboard, pulp, and other wood products. Forestry specialists discovered new uses for forest products and studied ways to conserve the state's timber reserves. The industry replanted an increasing number of trees to replace those that had been cut down.

Changes also occurred in Oregon agriculture. The state's farms became larger and more closely linked with food processing. Farmers used more and more machinery. Irrigation projects allowed farmers to grow fruits and vegetables on land that once had been too dry for any crops except grasses.

Low-cost hydroelectric power from dams on the Columbia and Willamette rivers helped Oregon's economy grow during the 1960's. Gas pipelines were extended to many parts of the state. Industries, including the manufacture of metal products and electrical and electronic machinery, grew in importance.

The worst floods in Oregon's history hit the state in 1964. Storms and floods caused millions of dollars of damage, killed several persons, and forced thousands from their homes.

Oregon Today faces several problems. State leaders are searching for ways to pay for the high cost of schools and other public services in the 1970's. The legislature increased state income taxes in 1969 and again in 1973.

Air and water pollution have accompanied Oregon's

THE GOVERNORS OF OREGON

		Party	Term
1.	John Whiteaker	Democratic	1859-1862
2.	A. C. Gibbs	Republican	1862-1866
3.	George L. Woods	Republican	1866-1870
4.	La Fayette Grover	Democratic	1870-1877
5.	Stephen F. Chadwick	Democratic	1877-1878
6.	W. W. Thayer	Democratic	1878-1882
7.	Z. F. Moody	Republican	1882-1887
8.	Sylvester Pennoyer	Democratic-Populist	1887-1895
9.	William Paine Lord	Republican	1895-1899
10.	T. T. Geer	Republican	1899-1903
11.	George E. Chamberlain	Democratic	1903-1909
12.	Frank W. Benson	Republican	1909-1910
13.	Jay Bowerman	Republican	1910-1911
14.	Oswald West	Democratic	1911-1915
15.	James Withycombe	Republican	1915-1919
16.	Ben W. Olcott	Republican	1919-1923
17.	Walter M. Pierce	Democratic	1923-1927
18.	I. L. Patterson	Republican	1927-1929
19.	A. W. Norblad	Republican	1929-1931
20.	Julius L. Meier	Independent	1931-1935
21.	Charles H. Martin	Democratic	1935-1939
22.	Charles A. Sprague	Republican	1939-1943
23.	Earl Snell	Republican	1943-1947
24.	John H. Hall	Republican	1947-1949
25.	Douglas McKay	Republican	1949-1952
26.	Paul L. Patterson	Republican	1952-1956
27.	Elmo Smith	Republican	1956-1957
28.	Robert D. Holmes	Democratic	1957-1959
29.	Mark O. Hatfield	Republican	1959-1967
30.	Tom McCall	Republican	1967-1975
31.	Robert W. Straub	Democratic	1975-

industrial and urban growth. Oregon citizens have become concerned with such issues as the disposal of sewage and other wastes and the public's right to use recreational facilities including beaches and lakes.

Completion of a number of dams on the Columbia and Snake rivers in the early 1970's provided deepwater transportation across Oregon to Lewiston, Idaho. In 1974, construction began on enlarging the powerhouse facilities of Bonneville Dam, located on the Columbia River. The dams also increased the hydroelectric power

capacity in Oregon. However, demand for even more energy has caused both public and private utility systems to build power plants fueled by coal or nuclear energy. Oregon business and political leaders continue to seek industries that will not harm the state's natural resources.

JESSE L. GILMORE,
RICHARD M. HIGHSMITH, JR., and ROBERT C. NOTSON

OREGON/Study Aids

Related Articles in WORLD BOOK include:

BIOGRAPHIES

Astor (John Jacob)	Meeker, Ezra
Duniway, Abigail J. S.	Miller, Joaquin
Gray, Robert	Morse, Wayne L.
Lee, Jason	Palmer, Joel
McKay, Alexander	Parkman, Francis
McLoughlin, John	Pauling, Linus C.
McNary, Charles L.	Whitman, Marcus

CITIES

Astoria   Eugene   Portland   Salem

HISTORY

Fifty-Four Forty or Fight	Pioneer Life in America
Indian, American	Trails of Early Days
Lewis and Clark Expedition	Western Frontier Life
Oregon Trail	Westward Movement

NATIONAL PARKS AND MONUMENTS

Crater Lake National   Oregon Caves National
Park   Monument

PHYSICAL FEATURES

Bonneville Dam	Detroit Dam	Multnomah Falls
Cascade Range	Great Basin	Owyhee Dam
Coast Range	High Desert	Snake River
Columbia River	Mount Hood	Willamette River
Crater Lake		

PRODUCTS

For Oregon's rank in production, see:

Cherry	Onion	Pear
Forest Products	Paper	Plum
Lumber	Pea	Potato

OTHER RELATED ARTICLES

Columbia River Highway	Oregon Grape
Meteor (picture: The	Pacific Coast States
Willamette Meteorite)	Pacific Northwest

Outline

I. Government
  A. Constitution   D. Courts   F. Taxation
  B. Executive   E. Local Govern- G. Politics
  C. Legislature   ment
II. People
III. Education
  A. Schools   B. Libraries   C. Museums
IV. A Visitor's Guide
  A. Places to Visit   B. Annual Events
V. The Land
  A. Land Regions   C. Rivers, Waterfalls,
  B. Coastline   and Lakes
VI. Climate
VII. Economy
  A. Natural Resources   E. Fishing Industry
  B. Manufacturing   F. Electric Power
  C. Agriculture   G. Transportation
  D. Mining   H. Communication

VIII. History

Questions

What four nations once claimed parts of Oregon?
What is the deepest lake in the United States?
In what region are most of Oregon's large cities?
How did the United States obtain the Oregon region?
What are Oregon's two major forest regions?
Where does Oregon get most of its electric power?
How do oceangoing ships get to Portland?
Who was Chief Joseph?
What is Oregon's most valuable crop?
What changes have taken place in Oregon's lumber industry during the 1960's?

Books for Young Readers

BEATTY, PATRICIA. *Hail Columbia.* Morrow, 1970. Fiction.
BONHAM, FRANK. *The Friends of the Loony Lake Monster.* Dutton, 1972. Fiction.
CARPENTER, ALLAN. *Oregon.* Childrens Press, 1965.
HOLBROOK, STEWART H. *The Columbia River.* Holt, 1965.
LAMPMAN, EVELYN S. *Cayuse Courage.* Harcourt, 1970. Fiction.
McGRAW, ELOISE J. *Moccasin Trail.* Coward, 1952. Fiction.
NEUBERGER, RICHARD L. *The Lewis and Clark Expedition.* Random House, 1951.
NOBLE, IRIS. *Oregon.* Coward, 1966.
WARREN, MARY PHRANER. *Ghost Town for Sale.* Westminster, 1973. Fiction.

Books for Older Readers

ATKESON, RAY. *Oregon Coast.* Charles Belding (2000 N.W. Wilson, Portland, Ore. 97209), 1972. *Oregon II.* 1974.
BALDWIN, EWART M. *The Geology of Oregon.* Rev. ed. Kendall-Hunt, 1976.
CLARK, ELLA E. *Indian Legends of the Pacific Northwest.* Univ. of California Press, 1953.
FLORIN, LAMBERT. *Oregon Ghost Towns.* Superior, 1970.
McARTHUR, LEWIS A., ed. *Oregon Geographic Names.* 4th ed. Oregon Historical Society, 1974.
YOUNG, BOB and JAN. *54-40 or Fight! The Story of the Oregon Territory.* Simon & Schuster, 1967.

OREGON, UNIVERSITY OF, is a state-supported coeducational school in Eugene and Portland, Ore. On the main campus in Eugene are the college of liberal arts and the schools of architecture and allied arts, business administration, community services and public affairs, education, health, physical education and recreation, journalism, law, librarianship, and music, and the graduate school. The medical and dental schools are in Portland. Programs of study lead to bachelor's, master's, and doctor's degrees. The university offers special courses in radio and television production. It has museums of art and of natural history. The University of Oregon was chartered in 1872 and opened to students in 1876. For enrollment, see UNIVERSITIES AND COLLEGES (table).

ARTHUR S. FLEMMING

OREGON CAVES NATIONAL MONUMENT

OREGON CAVES NATIONAL MONUMENT is an area in Oregon containing the limestone caves in the Siskiyou Mountains, and a game preserve. The vast caves have unusual limestone formations created by the stream that runs through them. The national monument was established in 1909. For area, see NATIONAL PARK SYSTEM (table: National Monuments).

See also OREGON (color picture).

OREGON GRAPE. This wild plant, also called the Oregon hollygrape, is the state flower of Oregon. It grows from western Oregon through Washington into British Columbia. The Oregon grape is a low plant, and does not climb as the wild grape does. Its leaves look like those of the holly, and its wood is yellow. The clusters of dainty yellow flowers open in the early summer. The berries ripen late in the fall. They look like grapes or blueberries. The berries of this plant are often used for jelly. Despite its names, the Oregon grape is neither a grape nor a holly. See also BARBERRY; OREGON (color picture: The State Flower).

Scientific Classification. The Oregon grape belongs to the barberry family, *Berberidaceae*. It is genus *Mahonia*, species *M. nervosa*. EARL L. CORE

OREGON LAUREL. See LAUREL.

OREGON QUESTION. See POLK, JAMES KNOX ("Oregon Fever").

OREGON STATE UNIVERSITY is a state-supported, coeducational, land-grant school in Corvallis, Ore. The university includes colleges of liberal arts and sciences; and schools of agriculture, business, education, engineering, forestry, health and physical education, home economics, oceanography, and pharmacy. It grants bachelor's, master's, and doctor's degrees.

The university operates an extension service and agricultural experiment stations throughout the state. It also conducts a broad program of education and research in the marine sciences. The school was founded in 1868. For enrollment, see UNIVERSITIES AND COLLEGES (table). Critically reviewed by OREGON STATE UNIVERSITY

OREGON SYSTEM. See OREGON (The Early 1900's).

OREGON TERRITORY was created after the settlement in 1846 of a boundary dispute between the United States and Great Britain. It included the present states of Idaho, Oregon, and Washington and part of Montana and Wyoming. Before 1846, the Oregon Country, occupied jointly by the U.S. and Britain, included the area south of Alaska, north of California, and west of the Rocky Mountains. The 1846 settlement gave the United States the land south of the 49th parallel, except for Vancouver Island. The Oregon Country became a territory in 1848. Oregon was admitted to the Union on Feb. 14, 1859. OSCAR O. WINTHER

OREGON TRAIL was the longest of the great overland routes used in the westward expansion of the United States. It wound 2,000 miles (3,200 kilometers) through prairies and deserts and across mountains from Independence, Mo., to the Pacific Northwest. Even today, travelers can see the deeply rutted road cut by wagon wheels along sections of the trail.

Families traveling to the Oregon region usually gathered at Independence, near the Missouri River. They followed a trail which ran in a northwesterly course to Fort Kearny, Nebr. Then they traveled up the Platte River and its north branch to Fort Laramie, Wyo. From this point, they continued along the North Platte to its Sweetwater branch, and crossed through South Pass in the Rocky Mountains to the Green River Valley at Fort Bridger, Wyo. The route turned northwest to Fort Hall in the Snake River area, and on to Fort Boise, Ida. Settlers crossed the Grande Ronde Valley and the Blue Mountains to Marcus Whitman's mission at Walla Walla, Wash. Then they traveled down the Columbia River to Fort Vancouver and the Willamette Valley of Oregon.

Travel on the Oregon Trail was a severe test of strength and endurance. The journey in a covered wagon took six months. Settlers often had to cross flooded rivers. Indians attacked the wagon trains, and cholera and other diseases were common. Food, water, and wood were always scarce, and the travelers often encountered contaminated water holes.

Explorers and fur traders first traced the course of the Oregon Trail. In 1805, Meriwether Lewis and William Clark traveled on a western section of the route in the region of the Snake and Columbia rivers. Traders returning from Astoria also used the trail. Benjamin Bonneville is credited with taking the first wagons through South Pass in the 1830's. Nathaniel J. Wyeth also led companies over the trail. John C. Frémont surveyed a portion of the route in 1842 for the United States Army.

Settlers began following the trail to Oregon about 1841. By 1843, so many were there that a provisional government was organized. The Oregon country's northern boundary was set in 1846, and the Territory of Oregon was set up in 1848. W. TURRENTINE JACKSON

Related Articles in WORLD BOOK include:

Bridger, James	Pioneer Life in America
Meeker, Ezra	(Crossing the Plains)
Palmer, Joel	Westward Movement (Set-
Parkman, Francis	tling the Far West)

O'REILLY, LEONORA (1870-1927), was an American labor leader and reformer. She became well known as a lecturer and union organizer. O'Reilly strongly supported vocational training for girls.

O'Reilly was born in New York City and went to work in a shirt collar factory at the age of 11. In 1897, she helped organize a local garment workers' union. From 1902 until 1909, O'Reilly taught at the Manhattan Trade School for Girls, where she developed a strong belief in vocational education.

In 1903, O'Reilly helped establish the National Women's Trade Union League. This organization promoted laws to protect the rights of women factory workers. It also aided in the establishment of women's labor unions. In 1909, O'Reilly helped lead a strike in New York City by the International Ladies' Garment Workers' Union. Thousands of garment workers won wage increases after the five-month strike. O'Reilly also traveled and lectured throughout the United States and Canada.

O'Reilly helped found the National Association for the Advancement of Colored People (NAACP) in 1909. She also was active in the Woman Suffrage Party and the Socialist Party. CHARLES SHIVELY

ORELLANA, OH ray (L)YAH nah, **FRANCISCO DE** (1500?-1550?), was the first white man to explore the full course of the Amazon River, the longest river in South America (see AMAZON RIVER). He made the

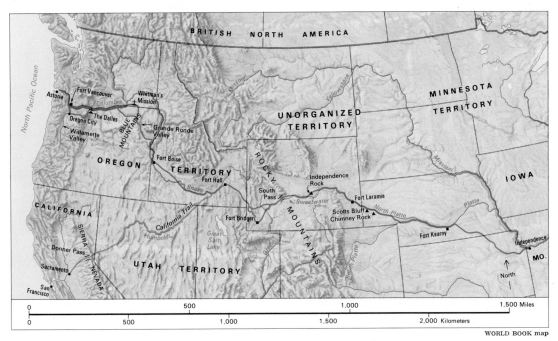

The Oregon Trail was the chief route to the Northwest in the mid-1800's. Thousands of pioneers traveled along the trail from Independence, Mo., to the Pacific Northwest. Other pioneers, attracted by gold in California, turned off near Fort Hall and followed the California Trail.

voyage in 1541 with about 50 Spaniards. On the journey, the Spaniards saw Indian warrior women. At this sight, some of the Spaniards were reminded of the Amazons, a race of female warriors in Greek mythology. Orellana called the country the *Land of the Amazons.* He was born in Trujillo, Spain.   CHARLES EDWARD NOWELL

ORESTES, *oh RES teez,* according to Greek legend, was the son of Agamemnon and Clytemnestra, rulers of Argos. When Clytemnestra killed Agamemnon on his return from Troy, Orestes was a young boy being educated away from home. He did not return to Argos until he was grown. Then, with the help of his vengeful sister Electra and a friend, Orestes killed his mother and her lover, Aegisthus. The Erinyes (Furies) punished Orestes by driving him insane. But he regained his sanity, and was acquitted of his sin.   H. L. STOW

See also ELECTRA; HERMIONE; IPHIGENIA.

ORGAN. See HUMAN BODY.

ORGAN is a keyboard musical instrument. There are two chief kinds of organs, *pipe organs* and *electronic organs.* Most pipe organs are found in churches, concert halls, and theaters. The history of the pipe organ can be traced back more than 2,000 years. Many masterpieces of music have been composed for it.

The electronic organ was invented in the mid-1900's. Most performers consider the pipe organ superior to the electronic organ. However, electronic organs are popular instruments in the home, and many churches also have them. The electronic organ ranks behind only the piano and the guitar as the most widely played instrument in the United States.

Both the pipe organ and the electronic organ have one or more keyboards that resemble a piano keyboard. However, a piano makes sounds by causing steel strings to vibrate. A pipe organ creates sounds by forcing air through metal or wooden tubes called *pipes.* An electronic organ produces sounds by means of electricity.

A pipe organ is the largest and most powerful of all musical instruments. Many pipe organs are so large that they must be built as part of the building where they are to be used. A large pipe organ can produce effects of grandeur that even a symphony orchestra cannot duplicate. It also can play delicate and refined music.

Pipe Organs. A small pipe organ has only a few hundred pipes, but a large organ has more than 5,000 pipes. Most pipes are made of lead or of lead mixed with tin. Some are made of other metals or wood.

An organist creates music by combining the sounds of different *ranks* (rows) of individual pipes. Each pipe in a rank is tuned to a single pitch and produces only one musical tone. Some ranks are pitched one or two octaves higher or lower than others.

Most organs have two types of pipes—*flue pipes* and *reed pipes.* A flue pipe works like a simple whistle. Air enters from a hole in the bottom of the pipe and causes a column of air inside the pipe to vibrate. The vibration creates the sound. A reed pipe contains a thin brass reed that vibrates as air passes around it.

About 80 per cent of the pipes in an organ are shaped like cylinders. But no two pipes of an organ look or sound exactly alike. The shape and size of the pipe determines the sound it makes. The longest pipes, which produce the lowest notes, may be more than 30 feet (9 meters) long and 1 foot (30 centimeters) in diameter. But most pipes measure less than 4 feet (1.2 meters) long. The smallest pipes, which produce the highest notes, are only 7 inches (18 centimeters) long and less than $\frac{1}{4}$ inch (6 millimeters) in diameter.

Most pipe organs have one, two, or three keyboards. A few have as many as six. The additional keyboards

643

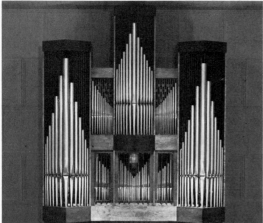

The Reuter Organ Company (Homer Frank)

Pipe Organs may have several thousand pipes. The pipe organ shown below has four manual keyboards and a pedalboard.

Jim Collins

Electronic Organs are popular in many homes. These organs occupy less space than pipe organs and they are easier to play.

The Reuter Organ Company (Homer Frank)

HOW A PIPE ORGAN WORKS

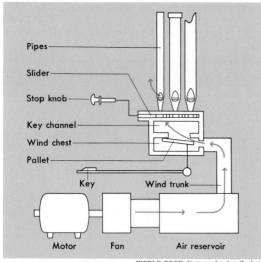

Pipes

Slider

Stop knob

Key channel

Wind chest

Pallet

Key

Wind trunk

Motor

Fan

Air reservoir

WORLD BOOK diagram by Art Grebetz

This diagram shows how wind flows through a pipe organ. An electric motor provides power for most modern organs. It operates a fan that forces wind into an air reservoir. The wind then moves through a wind trunk into a wind chest. When a key is pressed, a pallet opens and wind enters the key channel. From there a slider, controlled by a stop knob, allows wind to flow into the pipes. As the wind passes through a pipe, it produces a note.

enable the organist to create a wider variety of musical effects than would be possible with a single keyboard. The keyboards played with the hands are called *manuals*. Large organs may have up to five manuals called, in order of importance, the *great organ; swell organ; positive*, or *choir, organ; solo organ;* and *echo organ*. Most organs also have a *pedalboard*, a keyboard that the organist plays with his feet. Each keyboard—manuals and pedalboard—operates a number of ranks. Every key, in turn, controls several pipes. All the ranks operated by a keyboard are arranged on a box called a *wind chest*. Each wind chest receives an even flow of *wind* (air) from a reservoir. An electrically powered fan fills the reservoir with wind.

A thin strip of plastic or wood called a *slider* lies under each rank of pipes on a wind chest. A slider has holes in it that match the number and size of the holes in the rank of pipes above it. A slider regulates the passage of wind into the pipes. Sliders are controlled by *stop knobs*, commonly called *stops*, near the manuals. By pulling a stop, the organist moves the slider into position beneath the pipes so that wind can enter them.

To let wind into certain pipes, the organist presses the key that controls those pipes. This action opens a valve called a *pallet* in the wind chest and allows wind to flow into a compartment called the *key channel*. Wind enters the pipes from the key channel.

A cabinet called a *case* encloses all the pipes on a wind chest. The case blends the sounds of the various pipes. It projects this combination of sound out of the organ much as a megaphone projects the human voice.

Electronic Organs have no pipes. Devices called *oscillators* generate an electric current that produces the tones. The organ's sound is amplified electronically. An electronic organ cannot create the variety and richness of sound that a pipe organ can. But an electronic organ costs less and requires less space. The electronic organ has become a popular instrument in the home. It also is widely used in jazz and rock music.

History. In the 200's B.C., Ctesibius of Alexandria, a Greek engineer, built an organ called a *hydraulis*, or *hydraulus*, that used water power to force air into the pipes. Organs that used a bellows first appeared in Byzantium (now Istanbul, Turkey) during the A.D. 100's and 200's. The major features of the modern organ were developed from the 200's to the 1500's. For example, the keyboard was fully developed by the end of the 1400's.

From the 1500's to the mid-1700's, many composers wrote organ masterpieces. The greatest of these composers was Johann Sebastian Bach of Germany. Other leading composers of organ music included François Couperin of France and Girolamo Frescobaldi of Italy. During this period, organists accompanied singers in operas and oratorios. Large organs also provided music in churches, and small organs were popular in homes and at many public events.

By the late 1700's, small organs had lost their popularity. Many composers believed an orchestra or a piano could provide a wider range of musical effects. By 1900, interest in the organ had declined among composers and performers. The instrument was played regularly only in churches as part of religious services.

A revival of interest in the organ began in the early 1900's. The German humanitarian Albert Schweitzer, an accomplished organist, began this revival. Schweitzer gave organ concerts in many European cities and stimulated new interest in the instrument. In 1934, Laurens Hammond, a U.S. inventor, patented the first commercially practical electronic organ.   DALE C. CARR

Related Articles in WORLD BOOK include:

Bach (Johann Sebastian)	Music (picture: Keyboard
Hand Organ	Instruments)
Harmonica	Pipe (instrument)
Harmonium	Schweitzer, Albert

ORGAN OF CORTI. See EAR (How We Hear).

ORGAN PIPE CACTUS NATIONAL MONUMENT is an unspoiled desert in southern Arizona. It has organpipe cactus and other unusual plant and animal life found nowhere else in the United States. It was established as a national monument in 1937. For area, see NATIONAL PARK SYSTEM (table: National Monuments). See also CACTUS (picture).

ORGAN TRANSPLANT. See TISSUE TRANSPLANT.

ORGANIC ACID. See ACID.

ORGANIC CHEMISTRY. See CHEMISTRY.

ORGANISM is a living individual of any kind. Plants, animals, and microscopic living things called *protists* are organisms. All organisms are made up of living material called *protoplasm*, and almost all are composed of cells (see PROTOPLASM). Pieces of living tissue or a live organ, such as a heart, are not organisms. An organism is a complete living unit in itself. See also CELL; LIFE; MICROBIOLOGY; PROTISTA.   C. BROOKE WORTH

ORGANIZATION. See MANAGEMENT; PARLIAMENTARY PROCEDURE.

ORGANIZATION FOR ECONOMIC COOPERATION AND DEVELOPMENT is an association of 24 nations, most of which are in Western Europe. The organization, often called the OECD, works to promote the economic and social welfare of its members, and coordinates their efforts to aid developing countries.

The governing body of the OECD, called the Council, consists of one representative for each member nation. A 13-member Executive Committee assists the Council. The OECD has headquarters in Paris. It was established in 1961 to succeed the Organization for European Economic Cooperation (OEEC). Seventeen European nations formed the OEEC in 1948 as a re-

ORGANIZATION OF AFRICAN UNITY

MEMBERS OF THE OECD

Australia	France	Japan	Spain
Austria	Great Britain	Luxembourg	Sweden
Belgium	Greece	Netherlands	Switzerland
Canada	Iceland	New Zealand	Turkey
Denmark	Ireland	Norway	United States
Finland	Italy	Portugal	West Germany

sult of the Marshall Plan. Under the Marshall Plan, the United States helped Europe achieve economic recovery after World War II.   Critically reviewed by the ORGANIZATION FOR ECONOMIC COOPERATION AND DEVELOPMENT

ORGANIZATION OF AFRICAN UNITY (OAU) is an association of 49 African nations. It works to promote unity among the peoples of Africa and to strengthen their cultural, economic, military, scientific, and social ties.

The OAU opposes colonialism and believes all Africa should be independent of any non-African rule. The organization supports majority rule for Rhodesia and South Africa. Blacks make up a majority of the populations of these two countries, but whites control the governments. The OAU has also called for South Africa to end its system of rigid racial segregation, called apartheid (see APARTHEID). Although the OAU supports majority rule in other countries, its critics point out that most members of the OAU are themselves ruled by military or one-party dictatorships.

The OAU was founded in 1963 in Addis Ababa, Ethiopia, and originally had 30 members. Through the years, its influence has increased in both African and world affairs. The OAU has settled several boundary disputes between various member nations. It established a special fund to aid independence movements against colonial rule in Africa. Such movements helped end Portuguese colonial rule there (see PORTUGAL [History]). The OAU has forbidden its members to trade with Rhodesia and South Africa. The members have also tried to expel South Africa from the United Nations.

The organization does not have authority to force its members to follow its policies. For example, some members continue to trade with South Africa, though the OAU forbids such action. In addition, individual countries often pursue policies that differ from those of other members. For example, some OAU members want close relations with the Communist nations, but others prefer close ties with non-Communist countries.

The OAU has three administrative bodies: the As-

MEMBERS OF THE OAU

Algeria	Equatorial	Libya	Seychelles
Angola	Guinea	Madagascar	Sierra
Benin	Ethiopia	Malawi	Leone
Botswana	Gabon	Mali	Somalia
Burundi	Gambia	Mauritania	Sudan
Cameroon	Ghana	Mauritius	Swaziland
Cape Verde	Guinea	Morocco	Tanzania
Central African	Guinea-	Mozambique	Togo
Empire	Bissau	Niger	Tunisia
Chad	Ivory	Nigeria	Uganda
Comoros	Coast	Rwanda	Upper
Congo	Kenya	São Tomé and	Volta
Djibouti	Lesotho	Príncipe	Zaire
Egypt	Liberia	Senegal	Zambia

645

ORGANIZATION OF AMERICAN STATES

sembly of the Heads of States and Governments, the Council of Ministers, and the General Secretariat. The assembly holds an annual meeting attended by the leader of each member nation. The leaders vote on policies recommended by the council, which consists of foreign ministers or other officials appointed by the individual governments. The council meets at least twice a year. The General Secretariat, a permanent body located in Addis Ababa, works to make sure that the OAU's policies are carried out. LEWIS HENRY GANN

ORGANIZATION OF AMERICAN STATES (OAS) is an association of 25 Latin-American countries and the United States. The OAS is a regional organization within the framework of the United Nations. It seeks to provide for collective self-defense, regional cooperation, and the peaceful settlement of controversies. The OAS charter sets forth the group's guiding principles. They include a belief in the value of international law, social justice, economic cooperation, and the equality of all people. The charter also states that an act of aggression against one American nation is regarded as an act of aggression against all the nations.

The OAS functions through several bodies. Major policies are formed at annual sessions of the *General Assembly*. All member nations can attend, and each has one vote. Special *Meetings of Consultation of Ministers of Foreign Affairs* deal with urgent problems, especially those relating to defense or the maintenance of peace in the Americas. The *Permanent Council*, with headquarters in Washington, D.C., is the executive body of the OAS. Each member nation is represented. For convenience, diplomatic representatives in Washington serve as council members. The council supervises the *General Secretariat*, makes plans for General Assembly sessions, and oversees OAS administration. The secretary-general, the chief administrator of the OAS, is elected to a five-year term by the General Assembly. Specialized conferences promote inter-American cooperation.

The Organization of American States had its early beginning at the First International Conference of American States, which met in Washington, D.C., in 1889 and 1890. The delegates established the International Union of American Republics, with the Commercial Bureau of the American Republics as its central office. This bureau was renamed the Pan American Union in 1910. The Pan American Union became the permanent body of the OAS when it was organized in 1948 at the ninth Pan-American Conference, held in Bogotá, Colombia. The organization's original charter became effective in December 1951. An amended charter took effect in February 1970, and the Pan American Union was renamed the General Secretariat of the OAS.

Early in 1962, the OAS voted to exclude Cuba's Communist government from active membership. But Cuba itself remained an OAS member even though its government cannot participate in the organization's activities. In 1964, the OAS voted not to trade or have political relations with Cuba. They ended this policy, called an *embargo*, in 1975.

In 1965, a revolt in the Dominican Republic led the OAS to set up its first military force. Troops from six Latin-American countries and the United States took part. The troops and OAS committees worked to restore order in the Dominican Republic. In 1969, the OAS acted quickly to end a five-day invasion of Honduras by troops from El Salvador.

During the 1970's, economic development replaced peacekeeping as the major concern of the OAS. The

MEMBERS OF THE OAS			
Argentina	Cuba	Haiti	Peru
Barbados	Dominican	Honduras	Surinam
Bolivia	Republic	Jamaica	Trinidad and
Brazil	Ecuador	Mexico	Tobago
Chile	El Salvador	Nicaragua	United States
Colombia	Grenada	Panama	Uruguay
Costa Rica	Guatemala	Paraguay	Venezuela

organization promoted inter-American cooperation regarding such matters as investments, multinational corporations, energy shortages, and the exchange of technological information. The Special Committee for Consultation and Negotiation, created in 1970, dealt with trade and transportation. In 1973, the OAS established another special committee to recommend changes in the organization's charter and collective-security agreement. GEORGE W. GRAYSON

See also LATIN AMERICA (History; picture); PAN-AMERICAN CONFERENCES.

ORGANIZATION OF PETROLEUM EXPORTING COUNTRIES (OPEC), is an association of 13 nations that depend largely on oil exports for their income and foreign trade. The members of OPEC are Algeria, Ecuador, Gabon, Indonesia, Iran, Iraq, Kuwait, Libya, Nigeria, Qatar, Saudi Arabia, the United Arab Emirates, and Venezuela.

OPEC provides a common oil policy for its member nations. For example, it establishes taxes, royalties, and various trade rules on the oil exported by those countries. The members of OPEC produce more than half the oil used in the world. They also supply about 85 per cent of the oil imported by nonmember nations. As a result, OPEC has a major influence on the petroleum industry throughout the world (see PETROLEUM [In Other Countries; The Rising Cost of Oil]).

The Organization of Petroleum Exporting Countries was established in 1960 and has four main governing bodies. The OPEC Conference, the highest authority of the organization, meets twice a year to formulate general policies. The Economic Commission advises the conference on oil price matters. The Board of Governors, which consists of one representative from each member nation, meets at least twice annually. It supervises the affairs of the Secretariat, the administrative branch of OPEC. The Secretariat has permanent headquarters in Vienna, Austria. ZUHAYR MIKDASHI

ORGANIZED LABOR. See LABOR MOVEMENT.

ORGANUM. See MUSIC (The Middle Ages).

ORIENT, *O ree ent*, is another name for the Asiatic countries and islands, or the East. Sometimes the term is used to mean only the eastern part of Asia, which is also called the *Far East*. See also FAR EAST; ASIA.

ORIENTAL EXCLUSION ACTS, a series of acts passed by Congress in 1882, 1888, and 1892, prohibited Asians from entering the United States.

Chinese first came to the United States in large numbers after the discovery of gold in California in 1848. They were well received for a time, but met hostility when they moved to large cities. Between 1864 and 1869, Chinese coolies were brought to the United States to help build the Central Pacific Railroad. In 1868, China and the United States signed the Burlingame Treaty to protect this immigration.

However, Americans accused the Chinese of unfair competition in business, of lowering wages, and of immoral and unsanitary habits. During the economic depression of the 1870's, feeling against the Chinese increased. In some instances, they were victims of mob violence. Westerners demanded that Chinese immigration be halted. Despite the treaty of 1868, Congress passed the first Oriental Exclusion Act in 1882. These laws were first intended to be only temporary, but Congress made exclusion permanent in 1902.

Japanese began coming to the United States in increasing numbers during the late 1800's. Many of them settled on the West Coast and became farmers. Their farming methods and their low living standards made competition difficult for the white farmers. California adopted laws designed to drive the Japanese from agriculture in that state. A demand for the prohibition of the immigration of Japanese to the United States grew.

In 1907, the "gentleman's agreement" between the United States and Japan greatly reduced immigration, but it did not satisfy the people of the West (see GENTLE-MAN'S AGREEMENT). The Immigration Act of 1924 prohibited the entry of all Asiatic laborers.

During World War II, Congress repealed the laws against the Chinese. They may now enter the United States on a quota basis, and are eligible for citizenship. The Immigration and Nationality Act of 1952 extended the same privileges to other Asians, including the Japanese.   HAROLD W. BRADLEY

ORIENTAL INSTITUTE. See CHICAGO, UNIVERSITY OF.

ORIENTAL RUG. See RUGS AND CARPETS.

ORIFLAMME. See FLAG (picture: Historical Flags).

ORIGAMI, *AWR uh GAH me,* is the Japanese art of folding paper into decorative objects. The term is the Japanese word for *paper folding.* There are two types of origami—traditional and creative. Both types of origami are found in many parts of the world. Traditional origami, the simpler form, appeals mostly to children. Creative origami is more popular with adults.

Traditional origami dates back to at least 1682. Pieces of colored paper about 6 inches (15 centimeters) square are folded into simple figures without cutting or pasting. There are about 100 traditional figures, including a balloon, crane, frog, and helmet.

Creative origami has become popular since the mid-1940's. In this form of the art, people try to create original and more complicated figures. Sometimes figures are made by cutting, combining two folded pieces, or beginning with nonsquare pieces.   JAMES MINORU SAKODA

ORIGEN, *AHR ee jen,* (185?-254?) was an early Christian philosopher and writer. He believed that all knowledge comes from God, and finds its highest and most complete expression in Christianity. He had great influence in ancient times, and was said to have written 6,000 books on religious subjects. He was born and educated in Alexandria, Egypt. He died as a result of torture by the Roman Emperor Decius.   F. A. NORWOOD

ORIGIN OF SPECIES. See DARWIN (Charles Robert); EVOLUTION (History).

ORINOCO RIVER, *ohr uh NO koh,* is a South American river 1,281 miles (2,062 kilometers) long. It has two known sources, both in the Parima highlands in Venezuela, near the boundary of Brazil. It flows northwest to Colombia and forms the boundary between Colombia and Venezuela. Then it swings eastward. About 110 miles (177 kilometers) before it reaches the seacoast, it divides into many channels. For location, see VENEZUELA (color map).

Small oceangoing vessels can sail 260 miles (418 kilometers) upstream from the mouth of the Orinoco. Ships can use the river for about 500 miles (800 kilometers) above the Maipures and Atures rapids. Ciudad Bolívar is the center of the Orinoco river trade. Steamships run between Trinidad and Ciudad Bolívar most of the year. Major branches of the Orinoco are the Apure, Caroní, and Meta rivers. Including its branches, the Orinoco has a navigable length of 4,300 miles (6,920 kilometers).   MARGUERITE UTTLEY

ORIOLE, *O ree ohl.* In America, orioles form a subdivision of the blackbird family. In Europe, the name oriole is given to a family of orange and black birds

Origami is the Japanese art of folding paper into decorative objects. Most figures can be made without cutting or pasting.

An Orchard Oriole feeds its hungry young. These orioles breed in North America and spend the winter in the Caribbean Sea area.

647

related to the crows. Most of the American orioles live in or near the tropics. In Jamaica, they are known as *banana birds*. Two common species of orioles live in southern Canada and the United States—the *northern oriole* and the more southerly *orchard oriole*. The northern oriole is divided into two subspecies, the eastern *Baltimore oriole* and the western *Bullock's oriole*. Altogether there are eight species of native orioles.

Orioles have beautiful feathers and loud musical voices. They weave hanging nests, and help farmers by eating insects. But in some areas, these birds may eat ripening grapes. Some orioles are also called *troupials*.

Scientific Classification. The American oriole belongs to the icterid family, *Icteridae*. The northern oriole is genus *Icterus*, species *I. galbula;* the orchard oriole, *I. spurius*. GEORGE E. HUDSON

See also BALTIMORE ORIOLE; BIRD (Building the Nest; pictures: Favorite Songbirds, Bird Nests, Birds' Eggs).

ORION, *oh RYE un*, was a mighty hunter in Greek mythology. He was the son of the god Poseidon, who gave him the power to walk through the sea and on its surface (see POSEIDON).

The goddess Artemis fell in love with the handsome Orion. Her brother, Apollo, did not like this, and plotted to destroy Orion. One day while Orion was swimming, Apollo walked by with Artemis. Apollo challenged her to hit the target bobbing in the water. Artemis did not know that it was the head of her lover, and killed him with her arrow. Her sorrow was great. She placed Orion in the sky as a constellation.

Another story says that Artemis killed Orion because she was jealous of his attention to Aurora. VAN JOHNSON

ORION, the Great Hunter, is a brilliant constellation that straddles the celestial equator. The red star Betelgeuse marks the right shoulder of the hunter. The star Bellatrix marks the left shoulder. The blue-white star Rigel, at the southwest corner of the constellation, marks the giant's upraised left foot. Three bright stars mark the belt. A sword hilt, marked by faint stars, dangles from the belt. The Great Nebula of Orion, a mass of gases and dust, can be seen surrounding the center part of the sword. Orion faces the constellation of Taurus, the Bull, and seems to be warding off the bull's attack. He

Orion

holds a club in his right hand. In his left hand, he grasps a lion's skin, which he can use as a shield. I. M. LEVITT

See also ASTRONOMY (Skies of the Seasons); BETELGEUSE; RIGEL; STAR (picture: Possible New Stars).

ORISKANY, BATTLE OF. See SAINT LEGER, BARRY.

ORITHYIA. See BOREAS.

ORIZABA, *OHR uh ZAH buh* (pop. 92,517), is a resort and cotton-milling city in southern Mexico. It lies 65 miles (105 kilometers) southwest of Veracruz. For location, see MEXICO (political map). The city has cotton

and jute mills, cigar factories, railroad-repair shops, a brewery, and a paper mill. The Spaniards founded Orizaba in the 1550's. JOHN A. CROW

ORIZABA, or CITLALTÉPETL (*SEE tlahl TAY peht'l*), is the highest mountain in Mexico, and the third highest in North America. It rises 18,701 feet (5,700 meters) above sea level about 30 miles (48 kilometers) northwest of the city of Orizaba.

ORKNEY ISLANDS lie north of the British Isles. The Pentland Firth, 6 miles (10 kilometers) wide, separates them from Scotland (see GREAT BRITAIN [physical map]). The group has 67 islands and some rocky islets. They cover 377 square miles (976 square kilometers), and have a total coastline of about 100 miles (160 kilometers). People live on 25 of the islands.

The principal islands of the group are Mainland (Pomona), Hoy, North and South Ronaldsay, Flotta, Burray, Rousay, Shapinsay, Stronsay, Eday, Westray, and Sanday. Warm ocean currents give the islands a mild climate, and the soil is fertile.

About 17,000 persons live in the Orkneys. Most of them are of Scandinavian and Scottish descent. Agriculture and fishing are the chief occupations. The farmers grow barley, oats, turnips, and potatoes. Livestock, seafood, poultry, and eggs are exported. The Orkneys are so far north that they have scarcely any daylight in winter and scarcely any night in summer. Thousands of tourists visit the islands. Kirkwall (the capital) and Stromness are the only towns. Both are on Mainland.

In early times, a Celtic people lived on the islands, and Norse explorers often visited there. In the 900's, Norse earls settled and ruled the Orkneys. Scottish nobles replaced them in 1231, but the islands remained under the kings of Norway and Denmark. About 1468, the Orkneys were promised to Scotland as security for the dowry of Princess Margaret of Denmark, engaged to marry James III of Scotland. The dowry was never paid, and Scotland took the islands in 1472.

The islands are an important naval base. Scapa Flow, an enclosed anchorage that lies south of Mainland, served as the base of the British Grand Fleet during World War I. FREDERICK G. MARCHAM

ORLANDO. See ROLAND.

ORLANDO, Fla. (pop. 99,006; met. area pop. 453,-270), is a popular winter resort and tourist center. Orlando's warm climate has helped make it one of the fastest-growing cities in the United States. Walt Disney World opened about 15 miles (24 kilometers) southwest of the city in 1971. This famous entertainment center has contributed greatly to Orlando's rapid growth. Many people, including large numbers of retired citizens, have settled in Orlando because of the mild climate. Orlando's temperature averages 60° F. (16° C) in January and 83° F. (28° C) in July.

Orlando, the county seat of Orange County, covers 43 square miles (111 square kilometers) in central Florida (see FLORIDA [political map]). Museums in the city include the Central Florida Museum and Planetarium and the Orange County Historical Museum. Orlando is the home of Florida Technological University.

Walt Disney World is Orlando's chief employer. Other major employers include Martin Marietta, an aerospace firm; and the Orlando Naval Training Center. Orlando is the commercial center of a large fruit-growing area.

Seminole Indians lived in what is now Orlando before white settlers first arrived in 1837. In 1850, the settlement was named Jernigan for Aaron Jernigan, an Orange County trader. It became known as Orlando in 1857. This name probably honors Orlando Reeves, a soldier who died in a battle with the Indians. Orlando was incorporated in 1875.

Orlando's first major period of growth followed demands of early citrus fruit growers for better transportation for their crops. A railroad reached the city in 1881, and more planters started citrus groves during the 1890's. In the early 1900's, a real estate boom helped increase the population of Orlando and many other Florida communities. Orlando's population grew from 9,282 in 1920 to 52,367 in 1950.

The development of Walt Disney World led to many construction projects in Orlando. They included apartment buildings, banks, hotels, motels, restaurants, and shopping areas. In 1972, Orlando completed a new Municipal Justice Building. A $300,000 Civic Theater opened in 1973. Orlando has a mayor-council government. STAN ROBERTS

ORLANDO, *awr LAN doh,* **VITTORIO EMANUELE** (1860-1952), served as prime minister of Italy from 1917 to 1919. He took office just after the Italian Army suffered a terrible defeat in World War I. He helped raise civilian morale and spur the army on to victory.

Orlando began his political career in the Italian Chamber of Deputies in 1897. Between 1903 and 1917, he held various government jobs. He led the Italian delegation to the Versailles Peace Conference in 1919. He made strong demands there for increased territory for Italy. When the Allies failed to give Italy all that Orlando wanted, he was forced to resign as prime minister.

In 1922, Orlando supported the dictator, Benito Mussolini. But he denounced him in 1925, after Mussolini's henchmen murdered a Socialist leader. Orlando helped overthrow Mussolini in 1943. Orlando was born in Palermo, Sicily. R. JOHN RATH

See also WILSON, WOODROW (picture: Landing in France).

ORLANDO FURIOSO. See ARIOSTO, LUDOVICO.

ORLÉANS, *AWR LAY AHN* (pop. 106,246; met. area pop. 209,234), is an important commercial and transportation center in France. It is the capital of the department of Loiret. Orléans is in the heart of the Château Country, a region of many large estates and *châteaux* (country houses). It lies along the Loire River, southwest of Paris (see FRANCE [political map]).

Important industries in Orléans include textiles, food processing, tanning, distilling, and brewing. The city's factories produce clothing, candies, chocolates, liqueurs, vinegar, machinery, and pharmaceuticals.

Joan of Arc was called the *Maid of Orléans* after she led the French against the English, who besieged the city in 1429. A statue of Joan stands in the public square. Other places of historical interest in Orléans include the Cathedral of Sainte Croix, which was destroyed by the Huguenots in 1567 and rebuilt by Henry IV and his successors. Large sections of Orléans were damaged during World War II. EDWARD W. FOX

ORLÉANS, *AWR LAY AHN,* was the name of two branches of the royal French family, the houses of Valois-Orléans and Bourbon-Orléans (see BOURBON; VALOIS).

Louis (1372-1407) founded the house of Valois-Orléans. He was the second son of King Charles V, and the brother of Charles VI. Louis became duke of Orléans in 1392. He wanted to rule when Charles VI became mentally ill, but his uncle, Philip of Burgundy, ruled. Philip's son John plotted Louis' assassination.

Charles (1391-1465), the oldest son of Louis, was one of the greatest poets of France. His court at Blois attracted such noted poets as François Villon. Charles commanded French forces against the English in the Battle of Agincourt in 1415. He was captured and held in England until 1440. His son Louis XII was the first member of the Valois-Orléans branch to gain the throne (see LOUIS [XII]). The Duchy of Orléans was united with the crown after Louis became king.

Philippe (1640-1701), the son of Louis XIII and the only brother of Louis XIV, founded the house of Bourbon-Orléans. He became duke of Orléans in 1661.

Philippe (1674-1723), son of the founder of the Bourbon-Orléans branch, became duke of Orléans in 1701. He acted as regent of France until Louis XV came of age. He let John Law introduce a large amount of paper currency, which led to bankruptcy.

Louis Philippe Joseph (1747-1793), the grandson of Philippe, was known as Philippe Egalité (Equality). He took this name during the French Revolution to show the people that he sided with them against the nobles. He voted for the death of King Louis XVI. But Philippe and other members of the Bourbon family were arrested in 1793, and he was beheaded. He was the father of Louis Philippe (see LOUIS PHILIPPE). Ferdinand, the eldest son of King Louis Philippe, became the duke of Orléans when his father became king.

Louis Philippe Robert (1869-1926), the grandson of Ferdinand, was the last real claimant to the throne of France. He was a famous scientist, and led expeditions to the Arctic regions and to British East Africa. He was born in Twickenham, England, and was exiled from France in 1886. RICHARD M. BRACE

ORLÉANS, BATTLE OF. See ARMY (Famous Land Battles of History).

ORLON is a Du Pont Company trademark name for a widely used synthetic fiber. It can be woven or knit into fabrics. Orlon fabrics are comfortable to wear, dry quickly, and hold their shape. Orlon has a bulkiness that makes it suitable for garments such as sweaters.

Many different kinds of Orlon fibers are made to meet the needs of various materials. They vary in size, brightness, softness, and ability to absorb dyes. One fiber, Orlon Sayelle, has elasticity and a woollike feel.

Orlon production started in 1950 in Camden, S.C. Heavy yarns were produced there for industrial uses that required materials that resisted acids or exposure to sunlight. Manufacturers found that spun Orlon was excellent for wearing apparel, and fiber for knit and woven materials was produced. Manufacturers also developed Orlon fabrics for upholstery and carpets.

Orlon belongs to the *acrylic* class of plastics (see PLASTICS [table: Kinds of Plastics]). Orlon acrylic fiber was discovered when Du Pont chemists found that *polyacrylonitrile,* a synthetic chemical, dissolved in certain unusual solvents. The chemical produced a concentrated solution from which yarns could be spun.

Orlon is made from *acrylonitrile*, a chemical used as a *monomer* (basic building block). This substance is *polymerized*. In this process, the molecules of acrylonitrile join together to form long, chainlike molecules of polyacrylonitrile. Workers then dissolve the chemical in a solvent to produce a thick and sticky solution. The solution goes through machines which cast it into fibers by forcing the liquid through tiny openings called *spinnerets*. Machines also stretch the fibers to several times their original length to strengthen and toughen them. The Orlon is then dried and packaged in bales for shipment to textile mills.   ELIJAH M. HICKS, JR.

ORMANDY, *AWR muhn dee,* **EUGENE** (1899-   ), became one of the world's best-known conductors during his long career as director of the Philadelphia Orchestra. From 1936 to 1938, Ormandy shared the direction of the orchestra with Leopold Stokowski. Ormandy became the orchestra's sole music director in 1938. His performances stress romantic and neoromantic music and emphasize fine string playing and rich orchestral tones. Under Ormandy's leadership, the orchestra has toured many countries and made a great number of recordings.

Eugene Ormandy Blau was born in Budapest, Hungary. He studied the violin with Jenö Hubay, a noted Hungarian violinist. In 1921, Ormandy went to the United States to make a concert tour. Instead, he became a violinist in the orchestra of the Capitol Theater in New York City. Soon he had opportunities to conduct and in 1931 he became principal conductor of the Minneapolis Symphony Orchestra. He held this position until moving to Philadelphia. Ormandy became a U.S. citizen in 1927.   ROBERT C. MARSH

ORNAMENT. See ART AND THE ARTS, CLOTHING, GEM, and JEWELRY, with their lists of *Related Articles*.

ORNITHISCHIA. See DINOSAUR (Bird-Hipped).

ORNITHOLOGY, *AWR nuh THAHL uh jee,* is the bird-study branch of the science of zoology. It includes the description and classification of birds, their distribution, their activities, and their economic relations to people. The activities of birds which are studied include mating, nesting, rearing of young, feeding, and migrations. Photography has been used to record the activities of birds. Recordings have been made of bird songs.

The beauty of birds, their interesting habits, and their importance to people attract both professional and amateur scientists. Many persons belong to bird clubs. The American Ornithologists' Union was established in 1883. It has headquarters at the Museum of Natural History, Smithsonian Institution, Washington, D.C. 20560.   L. B. AREY

See also BIRD (Bird Study); AUDUBON, JOHN JAMES; AUDUBON SOCIETY, NATIONAL; BARTRAM (William).

ORNITHOPOD. See DINOSAUR (Bird-Hipped).

ORNITHOPTER, *AWR nih THAHP ter,* is a machine designed to fly by flapping its wings like a bird. No one has ever built a successful ornithopter, but people have dreamed of such a vehicle since ancient times. Some small-scale models have flown. But all attempts to build ornithopters that carry people have failed, because materials that are light enough and strong enough have not been developed.

Ornithopters are classified in two ways. The first type uses various forms of wings for support in the air, and fastens the wings to a person's body. The second type uses a cabin or cockpit to house the pilot. The wings are attached and operated from the cockpit. The English philosopher Roger Bacon suggested the idea of the ornithopter about 1250.   LESLIE A. BRYAN

See also AIRPLANE (Early Experiments and Ideas); BIRD (How Birds Fly); DA VINCI, LEONARDO (picture).

ORNITHOSIS. See PSITTACOSIS.

OROVILLE DAM. See CALIFORNIA (Natural Resources).

OROZCO, *oh ROHS koh,* **JOSÉ CLEMENTE** (1883-1949), was one of Mexico's best-known painters. His style was powerful, spiritual, and dramatic. His murals decorate the National Preparatory School in Mexico City and other public buildings in Mexico and the United States. A part of his mural in the Dartmouth College Library appears in the PAINTING article. Orozco was born in Zapotlán, Jalisco, and attended the Academy of Fine Arts in Mexico City.   ROBERT C. SMITH

See also FRESCO; MEXICO (picture: Palace of Justice).

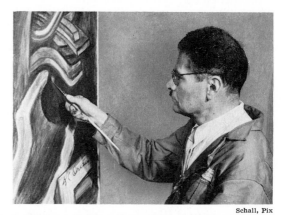

Schall, Pix

José Orozco Paints a Fresco on the southwest wall of the Museum of Modern Art in New York City.

ORPHANAGE is an institution that cares for homeless children. Some children may be left alone after both their parents die. Others may be abandoned by their parents because of poverty. Still other children may be homeless because their parents do not want the responsibility of rearing them. The oldest orphanage in the United States is Bethesda Home for Boys, near Savannah, Ga. It opened in 1740.

The number of orphanages in the United States has been declining steadily, largely due to the efforts of child psychologists, social workers, and other child welfare specialists. These authorities disapprove of the cold, impersonal atmosphere and the overcrowded conditions of most institutions. Instead, they believe that homeless children should live in a family environment.

Child welfare experts recommend placing homeless children in *foster homes* whenever possible. The parents in a foster home volunteer to care for a child in their own home, and they receive payment for the cost of the child's care. If a foster home is not available, specialists may recommend placing a child in a *group home*. In a group home, a professional staff cares for a small number of children, usually fewer than eight. Such organizations as religious groups and government agencies provide funds for group homes.   EDWARD ZIGLER

See also FOSTER PARENT.

ORPHEUS, *AWR fyoos,* or *AWR fee us,* was a musician in Greek mythology. He played such lovely music on his lyre that animals, trees, and stones followed him, and rivers stopped flowing to listen. He was the son of Apollo and the Muse Calliope. He married Eurydice, and loved her dearly (see EURYDICE). When she died, he went to the Lower World to bring her back. He played his lyre and charmed Hades and Persephone so much that they granted his request. They warned Orpheus that he must not look back at Eurydice on the way up to earth. But he glanced back too soon, and she disappeared. Because he wanted no woman but Eurydice, Orpheus angered some Thracian women, and they tore him to pieces. His head and lyre murmured sad music as they floated down the river Hebrus.   JOSEPH FONTENROSE

ORPHIC MYSTERIES. See MYSTERIES.

ORR, BOBBY (1948-   ), became famous as one of the greatest defensemen in the history of the National Hockey League (NHL). He was especially known for his skillful skating, high scoring, and team leadership.

Orr broke all major NHL scoring records for defensemen. He was the first defenseman to score more than 100 points in a season and the only one to lead the league in scoring. He won the scoring trophy twice. Orr also set the career record for most points scored by a defenseman. He was named the NHL's top defenseman eight times and was chosen the league's Most Valuable Player three times.

Robert Gordon Orr was born in Parry Sound, Ont. He played for the Boston Bruins from 1966 to 1976. His contract with Boston expired in 1976, and he signed with the Chicago Black Hawks.   BOB WOLF

United Press Int.

Bobby Orr

ORR, JOHN BOYD. See BOYD ORR, LORD.

ORREFORS, *awr uh FORSH,* Sweden (pop. 921), is famous for its crystal and glass works. It lies northwest of Kalmar, in southeastern Sweden. Orrefors glass is known for its design and its fused layers of colored and transparent glass.   JAMES J. ROBBINS

ORRERY. See PLANETARIUM.

ORRISROOT, *AWR is root,* is the dried, sweet-smelling *rhizome* (underground stem) of certain irises. It is used to give perfumes a scent of violets. The fragrant oil extracted from orrisroot is not so widely used as it once was, because of its high price and the availability of synthetic substitutes. But small amounts are still used in certain expensive perfumes. Orrisroot comes from three species—*Iris florentina, Iris germanica,* and *Iris pallida.* These irises are cultivated near Verona and Florence, Italy; and Grasse, France. The rhizomes are dug in the summer, and dried in the sun after the outer layer is peeled off. They yield a waxy material containing an oil that smells like violets and is used in perfumes. See also IRIS.   PAUL Z. BEDOUKIAN

ORT. See WOMEN'S AMERICAN ORT.

ORTEGA Y GASSET, *awr TAY guh ee gah SET,* JOSÉ (1883-1955), a Spanish philosopher, wrote *Meditations on Quixote* (1914). This book anticipated themes that existentialist philosophers made popular more than 10 years later (see EXISTENTIALISM). His later theory of truth and his best-known work, *The Revolt of the Masses* (1930), show the influence of Friedrich Nietzsche. In *The Dehumanization of Art* (1925), Ortega discussed the tendency of modern art to rid itself of human content.

Ortega was born in Madrid, and he also taught there. He lived in France, South America, and Portugal. He returned to Spain in 1949.   WALTER KAUFMANN

See also SPANISH LITERATURE (The 1900's).

ORTHOCLASE. See MINERAL (color picture).

ORTHODONTICS, *OR thoh DAHN ticks,* is the branch of dentistry that prevents or treats irregular positions of the teeth. These positions may be caused by heredity, or by early loss of the first teeth, dietary disorders, or thumb sucking and other undesirable habits. Teeth out of position prevent children from chewing their food properly, hurt their appearance, and may lead to cavities and gum diseases. Few children outgrow their irregularities, and most have to be treated. Dentists use a number of devices, commonly called *braces,* to correct these irregularities. Braces move the teeth by applying gentle pressure on them.   ROBERT G. KESEL

ORTHODOX, EASTERN. See EASTERN ORTHODOX CHURCHES.

ORTHOGRAPHIC PROJECTION. See MECHANICAL DRAWING.

ORTHOGRAPHY, *awr THAHG ruh fih,* is the art of spelling words correctly. See SPELLING.

ORTHOPEDICS is the correction of deformities of the skeletal system in persons of any age. See MEDICINE (table: Major Medical Specialty Fields).

ORTHOPTERA, *awr THAHP tur uh,* is a large order of destructive insects. The Orthoptera include the crickets, locusts, grasshoppers, katydids, cockroaches, walking sticks, and mantids. The name *Orthoptera* comes from two Greek words meaning *straight wings.* All members of the group have biting mouth parts, to bite off and chew food. Most of them feed on plants. The mantids, and a few other Orthoptera, eat other insects.

Related Articles in WORLD BOOK include:

Cockroach	Insect (table)	Locust	Mormon
Cricket	Katydid	Mantid	Cricket
Grasshopper	Leaf Insect	Mole Cricket	Walking Stick

ORTHORHOMBIC SYSTEM. See CRYSTAL AND CRYSTALLIZATION (Classification).

ORTOLAN, *AWR toh lun,* is a small bird that lives in the gardens of Europe and western Asia. It belongs to the finch family, and is about the size of an English sparrow. Its upper parts are brown, streaked with darker colors. Its ear region, throat, and rings around the eyes are lemon-yellow. Its upper breast is greenish-yellow, and the rest of the underparts are chestnut-brown. The well-known bobolink is sometimes called the *American ortolan,* as is the common sora, or sora rail.

In the spring, the ortolan breeds as far north as Lapland. When autumn draws near, it flies southward again to the Mediterranean countries. Hunters catch great numbers of ortolans, usually in nets. They feed and fatten the birds, and then kill them for eating.

Scientific Classification. The European ortolan is in the finch family, *Fringillidae*. It is genus *Emberiza*, species *E. hortulana*.   HERBERT FRIEDMANN

ORURO, *oh ROO roh* (pop. 110,490), is a mining center in Bolivia (see BOLIVIA [map]). It became a flourishing silver-mining town in the 1600's and 1700's. The city has been the center of a rich tin-mining area since the late 1800's. Railroads link Oruro with mining and farming areas in other parts of Bolivia. The Technical University of Oruro operates a mine on the outskirts of the city. The people of Oruro enjoy a colorful ceremony before Ash Wednesday each year. Masked dancers move through the streets of the city like the paraders in New Orleans' Mardi Gras. Oruro was founded in 1601.   HAROLD OSBORNE

ORWELL, GEORGE, was the pen name of Eric Arthur Blair (1903-1950), an English novelist and social critic. Orwell became famous with his novel *1984*, published in 1949. The book is a frightening portrait of a totalitarian society that punishes love, destroys privacy, and distorts truth. The grim tone of *1984* distinguishes it from Orwell's *Animal Farm* (1945), an animal fable satirizing Communism.

Orwell was a unique combination of middle-class intellectual and working-class reformer. A strong autobiographical element runs through most of Orwell's writing, giving both his novels and essays a sense of immediacy and conviction. For example, his experiences living in poverty color *A Clergyman's Daughter* (1935). The novel attacks social injustice and ranges from the miseries and hypocrisies of the poor of middle-class background to the near-starvation of

Paul Popper
George Orwell

the slumdweller. *Homage to Catalonia* (1938) is a nonfiction work based on Orwell's brief career as a soldier. He describes his disillusionment with the Loyalists during the Spanish Civil War.

Orwell was born in Bengal, India, the son of an English civil servant. He attended Eton from 1917 to 1921 and served with the Indian Imperial Police in Burma from 1922 to 1927. He lived in poverty in England and Europe until the mid-1930's.   FRANK W. WADSWORTH

ORYX. See ANTELOPE (Kinds of Antelope; picture).

OSAGE INDIANS, *oh SAYJ* or *OH sayj*, once roamed through Missouri, Arkansas, and Oklahoma. Oil discoveries on their lands in the early 1900's made them the richest tribe in the United States.

In early days, the round, mat-covered houses of the Osage lay in villages, with cornfields around them. The Osage camped on the plains, and hunted buffalo when they were not busy tending their crops. They had dignified ceremonies that they believed would make the corn grow and make their warriors brave. The Osage ceded most of their land to the United States by a series

of treaties between 1808 and 1870. After the tribe moved to a small reservation in Oklahoma, geologists found oil on their lands. The Bureau of Indian Affairs managed the oil leases for the tribe. Funds from the holdings were distributed among the Osage.   JOHN C. EWERS

OSAGE ORANGE is a small- to medium-sized tree planted across the United States for hedges, ornamental purposes, and shade. It originally was found in Texas, Oklahoma, and Arkansas. The name refers to the Osage Indians of that region, and to the greenish-yellow fruit that looks like an orange but is inedible. The tree is sometimes called *bodark*, *bois d'arc*, or *bowwood*.

The tree has a short trunk and crooked branches. Its long, pointed leaves are a shiny dark green. It has thorny twigs and a milky, bitter sap. Pioneers planted Osage orange trees as a "living fence" around their farms before barbed wire came into use.

The yellow wood of the Osage orange is hard, strong, and durable. The Indians preferred it for their bows and war clubs. It makes good fence posts and was used for wagon wheels. A yellow dye can be made by boiling chips of the wood in water.

New York Botanical Garden
Osage Orange Fruit

Scientific Classification. The Osage orange tree belongs to the mulberry family, *Moraceae*. It is genus *Maclura*, species *M. pomifera*.   ELBERT L. LITTLE, JR.

OSAKA, *oh SAH kah* (pop. 2,780,000), is the second largest city in Japan. Only Tokyo has more people. Osaka, an important industrial and commercial center, lies on Osaka Bay on the southern coast of Honshu Island. For location, see JAPAN (political map).

The City covers about 80 square miles (206 square kilometers). It is sometimes called the "Venice of Japan" because of its many canals and rivers. Since the 1960's, some of these waterways have been filled and highways built over them.

Downtown Osaka lies on the delta of the Yodo River. Office buildings, stores, hotels, restaurants, and entertainment centers fill this section of the city. Many shopping centers have been built underground because of a shortage of land.

Osaka has many museums, theaters, and religious shrines. Osaka Castle, built in 1584, houses a museum with historical exhibits. The Bunraku Theater presents puppet shows, and the Kabuki Theater offers regular stage performances. Osaka has 13 universities, including government-supported Osaka University. In 1970, Osaka was the site of Expo '70, the first world's fair held in Asia.

People. Most of Osaka's people are Japanese. The major foreign groups living in Osaka include Americans, Chinese, and Koreans. Like people throughout Japan, most Osakans practice both the Shinto and the Buddhist religion.

In the past, most Osakans lived in small wooden houses. Today, many Osaka residents live in large apartment buildings. The city's population increased by more than a million during the 1950's, and this

World Photo Service from Madeline Grimaldi

Osaka, Japan's second largest city, is an important commercial and cultural center. Numerous canals and rivers run through the city, which lies on the southwest coast of Honshu island.

rapid growth led to shortages of land and housing. Many of Osaka's people have moved to the suburbs to escape the city's crowded conditions, high prices, and pollution.

Osaka is famous for its good food, especially seafood. Local specialties include eel; shrimp; turtle; and *kaminabe,* a fish stew cooked in a paper pot.

Economy. Osaka produces about 25 per cent of all the products manufactured in Japan, including 40 per cent of the country's exports. Osaka exports clothing, electrical appliances, and fabrics. It imports raw materials, especially cotton. The city is also a financial and trade center.

Osaka has serious traffic problems in spite of efforts during the 1960's and 1970's to improve public transportation. Buses, a subway system, and commuter trains serve the city. The world's fastest trains travel between Osaka and Tokyo, a distance of about 250 miles (400 kilometers). These trains reach speeds of about 125 miles (201 kilometers) per hour.

History. Osaka was founded about A.D. 300. At that time, the city was called *Naniwa.* It later became Japan's major port and commercial center. Toyotomi Hideyoshi, the ruler of Japan from 1585 to 1598, encouraged merchants to move to Osaka from other areas. The government opened Osaka's port to foreign trade in 1868.

Allied bombing raids destroyed much of Osaka during World War II (1939-1945). The people rebuilt their city after the war. Osaka's population growth created a need for more housing, sewers, highways, and subways. Many of these improvements were completed during the city's preparations for Expo '70.   Lewis Austin

OSBORN is the family name of two American zoologists, father and son.

Henry Fairfield Osborn (1857-1935) was an authority on fossil vertebrate animals and evolution. He was best known for his studies of ancient reptiles and warm-blooded animals, or mammals. He wrote about rhinoceroses; elephants and their relatives; and *titanotheres* (creatures that once roamed the American West). His book, *From the Greeks to Darwin* (1894), treated evolution.

Osborn served as president of the American Museum of Natural History in New York City from 1908 to 1933. Under his administration, it became one of the world's largest museums. Osborn was born in Fairfield, Conn. He graduated from Princeton University.

Fairfield Osborn (1887-1969), was an outstanding conservation leader. He became president of the New York Zoological Society in 1940 and founded the society's conservation foundation in 1948. His conservation projects included the Save the Redwoods League, the International Commission for Bird Protection, the National Audubon Society, and the Boone and Crockett Club. He was instrumental in building the Marine Aquarium at Coney Island, N.Y., which opened in 1957.

Osborn was born in Princeton, N.J., and graduated from Princeton University.   A. M. Winchester

OSBORNE, JOHN JAMES (1929-   ), a British dramatist, won fame for his savage satirical attacks on British social institutions and values. Osborne's play *Look Back in Anger* (1956) was one of the most discussed plays of the 1950's. It shows the bitterness of certain young English adults over what they believe is mismanagement of most aspects of English life. The play earned Osborne the label of "angry young man." The phrase was soon applied to many English writers in the late 1950's.

Osborne also wrote *The Entertainer* (1957), *Luther* (1961), *Inadmissible Evidence* (1964), and *A Patriot for Me* (1965). Each has a central character who complains lengthily and loudly over the problems life has placed in his path. The strength of the plays lies in the complex characters, who are both sympathetic and outrageous. Osborne was born in London.   Malcolm Goldstein

OSBORNE, THOMAS MOTT (1859-1926), was an American prison reformer. In 1913, as chairman of the New York State Commission for Prison Reform, he spent a week in prison, secretly, so he could understand and help prisoners. He served as warden of Sing Sing (N.Y.) Prison (now the Ossining Correctional Facility) from 1914 to 1916 and of Portsmouth (N.H.) Naval Prison from 1917 to 1920. He organized the Mutual Welfare League to help prisoners rebuild their lives. He wrote *Within Prison Walls* (1914) and *Society and Prisons* (1916). He was born in Auburn, N.Y.   Louis Filler

OSCAN, *AHS kun,* was a language used by one of the earliest known races in Italy. It was part of the Indo-European family, and was distantly related to Latin.

OSCAR. See Motion Picture (Festivals and Awards).

OSCAR was the name of two kings of Sweden and Norway, father and son.

Oscar I (1799-1859) ruled as King of Norway and Sweden from 1844 until his death. He began a mild reform program for Sweden that made him popular with everyone except the upper classes. But he did not keep his early promises of major reforms, and they were not accomplished until the reign of his son, Charles XV. Oscar was born in Paris, the son of Jean Bernadotte, who became King Charles XIV John of Sweden and Norway (see BERNADOTTE, JEAN B. J.).

Oscar II (1829-1907), the third son of Oscar I, came to the throne in 1872 after the death of his brother, Charles XV. Oscar II became very popular with his people. He devoted himself to artistic interests, and supported museums and education. He wrote several books and poems. In 1905, he tried to prevent the separation of Norway and Sweden. But the Norwegian desire for independence was too strong, and Oscar had to give up the Norwegian throne in 1905. He continued as King of Sweden until his death two years later. He was born in Stockholm.   RAYMOND E. LINDGREN

OSCEOLA, AHS ee OH luh (1803?-1838), led the Seminole Indians in Florida in the Second Seminole War, which began in 1835. He resisted the attempts of the United States to force the Seminoles to move to the Indian Territory west of the Mississippi River. He hid his followers deep in the Florida Everglades, and inflicted a series of defeats on the American troops. In 1837, however, when invited by General Thomas Jesup to discuss peace under a flag of truce, Osceola was treacherously taken prisoner. He died soon afterward, in the Fort Moultrie prison near Charleston, S.C.

Osceola was one-quarter white. His grandfather was Scottish. After Osceola's father died, his Indian mother married a white man named Powell. Osceola was sometimes known by this name.

He took the name Osceola, or *Asi-Yaholo*, from *asi*, a black drink containing caffeine which was used in tribal ceremonies, and *Yaholo*, the long-drawn-out cry sung by the person who served this drink to the Indian braves. Osceola was born on the Tallapoosa River in Georgia, which was then a part of the Creek Indian territory.   E. ADAMSON HOEBEL

Detail of a painting (1838) by George Catlin; National Portrait Gallery, Smithsonian Institution.

Osceola

See also INDIAN WARS (In the South).

OSCILLATION. See ELECTRONICS (Oscillation).

OSCILLOGRAPH. See OSCILLOSCOPE.

OSCILLOSCOPE, uh SIHL uh skohp, is an electronic instrument that displays changing electrical signals. The signals appear as wavy lines on a fluorescent screen similar to that of a television set.

Oscilloscopes are used in such fields as industry, medicine, and scientific research. Electronics engineers use the instruments to test computers, radios, and other electronic equipment. Physicians use them to study electrical impulses from the brain or heart. Light, mechanical motion, and sound can also be studied with oscilloscopes. Devices called *transducers* change these forms of energy into electrical signals.

The screen of an oscilloscope is the front of a *cathode-ray tube*, a special type of vacuum tube. Inside the tube, a device called an *electron gun* projects a beam of

Tektronix, Inc.

An Oscilloscope shows electrical or sound waves or other vibrations as lines on a screen similar to a television screen.

electrons onto the fluorescent screen. Any movement of this beam leaves a glowing line on the screen. A circuit called the *time base* causes the beam to move repeatedly from left to right. At the same time, the signal to be studied is fed into the oscilloscope and causes the beam to move up and down. This movement corresponds to *oscillations* (vibrations) in the signal. The beam moves up and down while moving from left to right, and so it traces a wavy line on the screen. This line represents the oscillating signal.

An oscilloscope is a type of *oscillograph*, which is any instrument that displays or records electrical signals. Certain types of oscillographs change electrical signals into mechanical movements that are recorded on paper or photographic film. For example, some oscillographs use a lightweight pen called a *stylus* to draw a wavy line on a moving paper chart.   RICHARD W. HENRY

See also CATHODE RAYS; SOUND (picture: Seeing Sound).

OSCULUM. See SPONGE (The Body of the Sponge).

OSHAWA, Ont. (pop. 107,023; met. area pop. 135,-196), is an important Canadian industrial city that is sometimes called *Canada's Motor City*. It is the home of General Motors of Canada, the nation's largest manufacturer of motor vehicles. Oshawa lies on Lake Ontario in southeastern Ontario (see ONTARIO [political map]).

The Oshawa area was first settled in 1794, when Benjamin Wilson, a Pennsylvania farmer, and his family moved there. In 1842, the community was named *Oshawa*. The people of the village chose this name, an Indian word meaning *crossing between the waters*, because the community lay between Lake Ontario and Lake Scugog.

In 1908, R. S. McLaughlin established the McLaughlin Motor Car Company in Oshawa. This firm produced McLaughlin-Buick automobiles. The Chevrolet Motor Car Company of Canada was established in Oshawa in 1915. The two firms united in 1918 to form General Motors of Canada. Oshawa received a city charter in 1924.

General Motors of Canada is Oshawa's chief employer. Other companies in the city manufacture such products as fabricated metals, textiles, and woolens. Freight and passenger trains serve Oshawa. The city has a mayor-council form of government. JOHN L. McLEOD

654

OSHKOSH, Wis. (pop. 53,082), once had lumbering as its only industry. Today, its factories make sashes and doors, overalls, trucks, fiber and wool twine, coffins, matches, and metal products.

Oshkosh and Appleton form a metropolitan area with 276,948 persons. Oshkosh lies at the point where the Fox River empties into Lake Winnebago, about 85 miles (137 kilometers) northeast of Madison. For location, see WISCONSIN (political map). Oshkosh began as a fur-trading post. It was named for a Menominee Indian chief.

The city is the home of the University of Wisconsin-Oshkosh. It has a council-manager government. Oshkosh is the seat of Winnebago County.   JAMES I. CLARK

OSIER, *OH zhur*, is the name given to certain shrubs and small trees in the willow family. They grow best along streams. These willows have tough slender stems that can be used for making baskets and furniture. The coarse stems of the osier are not used for weaving, but the finer stems are peeled and bleached. The *common osier* and the *purple osier* are willows that have been brought to the United States from other parts of the world. They are cultivated for their flexible stems. One kind of dogwood is called *red-osier dogwood* because its bark resembles that of some willows.

Scientific Classification. Osiers belong to the willow family, *Salicaceae*. The common osier is genus *Salix*, species *S. viminalis*. The purple osier is *S. purpurea*. The red-osier dogwood is in the dogwood family, *Cornaceae*. It is genus *Cornus*, species *C. stolonifera*.   ROBERT W. HOSHAW

See also WILLOW.

OSIRIS, *oh SY rihs*, was the chief god of the underworld among the ancient Egyptians. He was worshiped in many great temples of Egypt. Osiris was the prince of the dead. He ruled the underworld of the tomb, which was populated by the souls of the dead. All good Egyptians believed that, when they died, they became Osiris.

Osiris was the husband of Isis and the father of Horus (see HORUS; ISIS). His brother was Set, who represented evil (see SET). According to a tradition, Set tricked Osiris into getting into a box, and then threw it into the Nile River. Isis found the box, but Set stole the body and cut it into 14 pieces. Isis found Osiris' body and brought it back to Egypt, where Horus was born. Horus avenged Osiris' death by defeating Set and his followers. Osiris was given new life. He then ceased to be a king of this world, and became king of the underworld. Thus, the idea of resurrection became the central theme in the worship of Osiris. Osiris is often represented in art as a mummy, wearing the crown of Upper Egypt on his head.   I. J. GELB

See also ANUBIS; APIS; MYTHOLOGY (Osiris Myth).

OSLER, *OHS ler*, **SIR WILLIAM** (1849-1919), was a Canadian physician and one of the greatest medical teachers. His brilliant teaching and informal and genial personality had a far-reaching influence on medical progress, and on many of his students.

One of Osler's most notable contributions to medicine was the organization of a clinic at the Johns Hopkins Hospital in Baltimore, Md., along systematic lines new to the United States. He strongly favored using "the patient for a text," and he perfected the method of teaching that encourages students to learn the practical art of medicine at the bedside. Osler once said that he would like his epitaph to read, "Here

Culver

Sir William Osler

lies the man who admitted students to the wards."

Osler discovered the presence in the blood stream of what later were called *disks*, or *blood platelets* (see BLOOD [Platelets]). He made studies of the heart and did research on typhoid fever, pneumonia, malaria, infant mortality, and various other public health menaces. Osler also helped found the National Tuberculosis Association (now the American Lung Association) in 1904.

His Writings. Osler published *Principles and Practice of Medicine* in 1891. It is still a standard textbook in the United States. In 1897, a member of John D. Rockefeller's philanthropic staff read the book and was amazed to learn how few infectious disease germs had been discovered. This incident led to the founding of the Rockefeller Institute for Medical Research in 1901 (see ROCKEFELLER UNIVERSITY). Osler also wrote *Aequanimitas* (1904), a collection of essays; *An Alabama Student* (1908); and *The Evolution of Modern Medicine* (1921).

His Life. Osler was born on July 12, 1849, in Bondhead, Ont., Canada. He graduated from McGill University in 1872. He served at McGill from 1875 to

Oriental Institute, University of Chicago

Osiris, One of the Principal Gods of Egypt, is shown on his throne in the lower world, where he ruled as king. The picture appears on an old papyrus made in Egypt about 330 B.C.

OSLO

1884 as a lecturer in physiology and as professor of medicine. He was pathologist at Montreal General Hospital at the same time. In 1884, he became clinical professor of medicine at the University of Pennsylvania. He was appointed professor of the principles and practice of medicine at Johns Hopkins University four years later. He was also made physician-in-chief to the new hospital there. Osler went to Oxford University in 1905 as regius professor of medicine, the highest medical position in Great Britain. He became a baronet in 1911. He organized the British medical profession during World War I to meet the war emergency. CAROLINE A. CHANDLER

OSLO, *AHZ loh* or *OHS loh* (pop. 477,476; met. area 556,377), is the capital and leading seaport of Norway. Until 1925, it was known as Christiania. Oslo is at the head of the great Oslo Fiord, located on the southeastern coast of Norway. It lies about 80 miles (130 kilometers) from the Skagerrak, an arm of the North Sea. For location, see NORWAY (map). Oslo extended its city limits in 1948, and now half the city is forested land. Christiania was founded by the Danes in 1624, on the site of a town called Oslo, founded in 1047. After 300 years, the Norwegian name of Oslo was used again.

The city is the seat of the Norwegian government. Oslo is largely a modern city. Brick and stone buildings have taken the place of older wooden ones. The Royal Palace stands severe and white in the center of the city. The Folk museum contains three famous ships which were used by the Norse Vikings of old. These ships were discovered and excavated in modern times. The museum has the *Fram*, the ship used by explorers Fridtjof Nansen and Roald Amundsen; and *Kon-Tiki*, Thor Heyerdahl's raft. A statue of Christian IV, the king who founded Christiania, stands in the market place.

The University of Oslo (The Royal Frederiks University until 1939) was founded in 1811 by a grant from King Frederik VI. The university has about 18,500 students. In Frogner Park, there is a bust of Abraham Lincoln, given by Norwegians in North Dakota.

Oslo is a favorite center of much northern European tourist traffic. Regular passenger steamers serve the port from Hull, Newcastle, and London, from Bergen and the Norwegian coast cities, and from numerous ports of northern Europe. Electric power is furnished by plants on the Glama River. Industry in Oslo centers in cotton and woolen mills, paper, match, and soap factories, food plants, shipyards, foundries, and machine shops. There is also a large granite paving-stone business and large ice storehouses. The chief products are timber, wood pulp, condensed milk, butter, and animal hides.

On the hills around Oslo there are sanatoriums and inns, and beautiful landscaped gardens. The Norwegians built three new theaters between World War I and World War II, and carried out various municipal improvements. Between 1912 and 1921 they spent large sums improving the harbor facilities. Vessels up to 10,000 long tons (10,200 metric tons) can be constructed in the shipbuilding yards.

Oslo was attacked and occupied by German forces on April 9, 1940, and held until the German surrender in 1945. The city was cut off from its import and export trade and suffered as a result. Rebuilding of world trade, because of its importance to the nation's economy, was given priority after the war. OSCAR SVARLIEN

For the monthly weather in Oslo, see NORWAY (Climate). See also NORWAY (pictures).

Dale Brown, DPI   Adeline Haaga, Tom Stack & Assoc.

Oslo is the capital and largest city of Norway. It also ranks as the country's leading seaport. Passenger ships, cargo vessels, and fishing boats dock at Oslo's busy harbor, *above left*. Many parks and gardens, such as the one shown above at the right, add to the scenic beauty of the city.

OSMIUM, *AHZ mee uhm* (chemical symbol Os), is a hard metallic element. It has the greatest density of all known elements. It is twice as heavy as lead, and has a specific gravity of 22.57. It has an atomic weight of 190.2 and its atomic number is 76. Smithson Tennant discovered it in England in 1804. Osmium is refined from the same ores in which platinum is found. Some osmium has been found in platinum mines in California and Tasmania.

The pure metal is a fine, black powder or a hard blue-gray mass. Its melting point is 3045° C ($\pm$30° C), but it can vaporize before a high temperature is reached. When heated above 93° C, osmium gives off a vapor which may cause total or partial blindness. The metal is used to tip gold pen points and to make standard weights and measures. Electric-light filaments are also made of osmium.   HARRISON ASHLEY SCHMITT

OSMOSIS is the movement of liquid from one solution into another through a membrane that separates them. The process is essential for the survival of living things. For example, a plant absorbs most of its water by means of osmosis. In animals, osmosis helps regulate the flow of water between body fluids and cells. Osmosis also has several industrial uses, such as water purification and food preservation.

How Osmosis Works. A mixture of substances that cannot be separated mechanically is called a *solution.* A liquid solution consists of a dissolved substance called a *solute* and a liquid called a *solvent.* During osmosis, some of the solvent from one solution moves through a membrane into another solution. The membrane is *semipermeable*—that is, it allows some substances, but not others, to pass through. The solvent moves between the solutions according to the number of the molecules of the solute and the temperature and pressure of each solution. In normal osmosis, the solvent moves into the solution that contains more solute molecules.

Osmosis can be demonstrated by performing the following experiment. First, fasten a piece of cellophane tightly over the bottom of a glass tube and put some sugar solution into the tube. Then, place the tube in a container of pure water so that the levels of the water and the sugar solution are equal. After several hours, the liquid inside the tube rises because water has moved into the sugar solution.

Water moves into the sugar solution because water molecules are smaller than sugar molecules. Thus, only water molecules pass through the cellophane, which is the semipermeable membrane. At the same time, the larger sugar molecules interfere with the water molecules in the tube and prevent some of them from moving through the membrane. As a result, more water moves into the tube than out of it.

As the water moves into the tube, the sugar solution rises and causes the pressure in the tube to increase. The solution continues to rise until the pressure in the tube equals the pressure of the water entering it. The pressure of the water is called *osmotic pressure.*

Osmosis and Life. In the human body, osmosis plays an important part in the function of the kidneys. It also results in the transfer of water and various nutrients between the blood and the fluid of the cells.

Plant roots take in water and some minerals as a result of the osmotic process. Osmosis helps to transport the water in a plant and to maintain a plant's shape and stiffness.

Uses of Osmosis. Chemists use a process called *reverse osmosis* to purify water. In normal osmosis, water flows from fresh water into seawater when the seawater and the fresh water are separated by a semipermeable membrane. But if pressure is applied to the seawater, the movement of water reverses direction, and fresh water is produced from seawater. Some shipwreck victims have used survival kits that filter drinking water out of seawater by osmosis.   KENNETH SCHUG

OSPREY, *AHS pree,* is a large bird of prey in the hawk family. Its name comes from a Latin word that means *bonebreaker.* It is also called *fish hawk* and *fishing eagle.*

How Osmosis Works

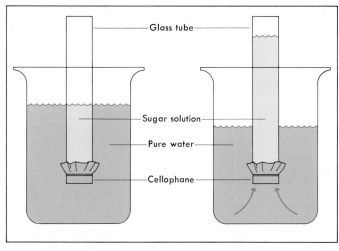

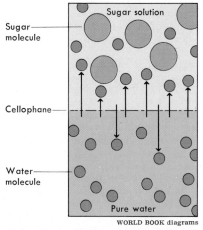

WORLD BOOK diagrams

The Process of Osmosis can be demonstrated in the experiment shown above. Water enters the glass tube through the cellophane, which serves as a semipermeable membrane. As the water mixes with the sugar solution, the solution rises.

Molecules of Water pass through the cellophane, as shown in the above diagram, but the larger sugar molecules do not. The level of the sugar solution rises because more water molecules move into the solution than out of it.

Allan Cruickshank

Ospreys live near large bodies of water. These birds plunge feet first into the water and grasp fish with the long, sharp talons on their feet. They are often called *fish hawks*.

The osprey lives near both fresh and salt water in almost every temperate and tropical country in the world. The American osprey breeds from northwestern Alaska to Newfoundland, and south to Lower California, western Mexico, and the Gulf States. It winters from the southern United States to northern Argentina and Paraguay.

The osprey is about 2 feet (61 centimeters) long, with a wingspread of nearly 6 feet (1.8 meters). It is dark brown above and has some white on its head. It is white below with a few streaks of dark brown.

Ospreys usually nest in the tops of tall trees near large bodies of water. Sometimes they nest in chimney tops, on telephone pole crossbars, on ledges, in dead stumps, and even on the ground. The birds usually lay three eggs, colored whitish and spotted with shades of brown.

Ospreys feed on fish that stay close to the surface and are of little value to man. The bird hovers over the water, then sets its wings and dives feet first, hitting the water with a great splash, and often going completely under. Its feathers are close, firm, and slightly oily, so it can plunge into water without becoming soaked.

Scientific Classification. The osprey belongs to the family *Accipitridae*. It is genus *Pandion*, species *P. haliaetus*, subspecies *carolinensis*.   OLIN SEWALL PETTINGILL, JR.

See also BIRD (picture: Hunters of the Sky).

OSSICLE. See EAR (The Middle Ear).

OSSIETZKY, *AWS ee ETS kee,* **CARL VON** (1889-1938), a German journalist, won the 1935 Nobel prize for peace. He was awarded the prize after he had been sent to a Nazi concentration camp for his antimilitaristic writings. Ossietzky fought for Germany in World War I, but he later wrote articles in his weekly publication de-

nouncing Nazi rearming. He was imprisoned as a "traitor" in 1933. He contracted tuberculosis in prison and was in a sanitarium when the Nobel award was announced. He was born in Hamburg.   ALVIN E. AUSTIN

OSSINING CORRECTIONAL FACILITY. See SING SING.

OSSOLI, MARCHIONESS. See FULLER, MARGARET.

OSTEND, *aws TAHND* (pop. 57,359), is a Belgian city on the North Sea, about 77 miles (124 kilometers) northwest of Brussels (see BELGIUM [color map]). Its name in Flemish is *Oostende*. Only Antwerp has a larger port in Belgium. Ostend conducts an export-import business with many countries. It is the harbor for cross-channel boats from Dover, England. Ostend fishermen catch cod and herring. Oysters are cultivated offshore. Ostend is a fashionable summer resort. Visitors enjoy its sea walk and listen to concerts in a building called the *Kursaal*, the center of social life.

Dutch, Spanish, and French troops have fought many battles for Ostend, because of its value as a port. In 1865, its fortifications were destroyed by the Belgian government, and Ostend became important for shipping. Ostend was damaged in World War I and again in World War II.   DANIEL H. THOMAS

OSTEND MANIFESTO. In 1854, the United States Secretary of State authorized three diplomats to negotiate for the purchase of Cuba by the United States. These men were James Buchanan, Minister to Great Britain, John Young Mason, Minister to France, and Pierre Soulé, Minister to Spain. They met at Ostend, Belgium, on October 18, 1854, and signed a dispatch later known as the Ostend Manifesto. It declared that if Spain would not sell Cuba, the United States would be justified in taking the island by force.

The three signers pretended to fear that a slave rebellion might turn Cuba into a disorderly Negro republic. But historians believe that they acted from the hope that Cuba might become a slave state of the United States. All United States political parties condemned the Manifesto.   JOHN DONALD HICKS

OSTEOLOGY, *AWS tee AHL oh jih,* is the study of the bones of man and animals. Osteologists can determine the sizes and living habits of prehistoric animals from bones. They can tell the age, sex, height, and weight of the person or animal from which the bones came. Osteology also includes the study of bone disorders and diseases. See also BONE.   IRVIN STEIN

OSTEOMYELITIS, *AHS tee oh MY uh LIE tihs,* is an inflammation of bone and *bone marrow*, the jelly-like material in the core of bones. Osteomyelitis can be caused by infection from any kind of germ, but the usual cause is a bacterium called *Staphylococcus aureus*. Infection of bone marrow may occur if a person has a compound fracture. In such a fracture, bone marrow may be exposed to the air. In some cases, the blood carries germs from a boil or from infected tonsils into the bone marrow. Symptoms of acute osteomyelitis include fever, chills, pain, and nausea. Doctors can check and cure the infection with penicillin.   MARSHALL R. URIST

OSTEOPATHY, *AHS tee AHP uh thee,* or OSTEO-PATHIC MEDICINE, is a system of medical practice that emphasizes the importance of the muscles and bones of the body and their connecting tendons and ligaments. These parts of the body make up the *musculoskeletal system*. Osteopathy maintains that the musculoskeletal system, which makes up 60 per cent of the body, has important interrelationships with all other body systems. Osteopathy involves all aspects of medicine and includes various medical specialties. Osteopathic physicians use all the medical, surgical, immunological, pharmacological, psychological, and hygienic procedures of modern medicine.

Osteopathic physicians believe that a disturbance in the musculoskeletal system can lead to three main conditions. It can produce symptoms that occur only in the musculoskeletal system itself. It can cause symptoms resembling those of diseases that affect other body systems. And it can affect the functioning of other body systems connected to the musculoskeletal system through nerves and the action of hormones. Osteopathic physicians are specially trained in the detection and treatment of musculoskeletal disturbances. They use massages and other types of *osteopathic manipulation* to treat these disturbances. This form of therapy is a distinctly osteopathic approach to the problems of health and disease.

History. The founder of osteopathy was Andrew Taylor Still, an American medical practitioner, who announced the basic principles of osteopathy in 1874. Still organized the first osteopathic college at Kirksville, Mo., in 1892.

The first law regulating osteopathy was passed in Vermont in 1896. There are now such laws in all the states, and in some of the provinces of Canada. In every state, graduates of recognized osteopathic schools are eligible to be licensed as physicians and surgeons.

Careers in Osteopathic Medicine. To become an osteopathic physician, a person must complete at least three years of preprofessional training in an accredited college or university and four years of professional education in an approved osteopathic college. The graduate receives a Doctor of Osteopathy (D.O.) degree. There are nine approved colleges of osteopathy in the United States. Some of these schools offer a year-round program in which the four-year curriculum can be completed in three years. After graduating, most osteopathic physicians gain additional training by spending a year

as an intern in an approved osteopathic hospital. About 70 of the more than 200 osteopathic hospitals in the United States offer intern training programs.

Osteopathic physicians may become certified specialists in any of a number of medical fields. Certification programs require two to five years of additional training after internship.

More than 15,000 osteopathic physicians practice in the United States. Most of them are members of the American Osteopathic Association, which has its headquarters in Chicago, Ill. The Association publishes three professional periodicals, *Journal of the American Osteopathic Association, D.O.,* and *Osteopathic Symposium.* It also publishes a magazine for laymen, *Health: An Osteopathic Publication.*

Critically reviewed by the AMERICAN OSTEOPATHIC ASSOCIATION

OSTEOSCLEROSIS, *AHS tee oh sklee ROH sihs,* means hardening, thickening, and increased density of bone. It may involve part of a bone, a whole bone, or the whole skeleton. The most common form occurs in children and is called *marble bones* or *osteopetrosis.* In this disease, the bones become chalky. Chalky tissue commonly replaces the bone marrow, the tissue that makes red blood cells. As a result, the child develops severe anemia. Osteosclerosis may develop in part of a bone from an infection or a tumor.   MARSHALL R. URIST

ÖSTERREICH. See AUSTRIA (table: Facts in Brief).

OSTRACISM. See TRIBE.

OSTRACODERM. See FISH (The First Fish).

OSTRAVA, *AW strahvah* (pop. 278,737), is the fourth largest city in Czechoslovakia. It is in northeastern Moravia, about 170 miles (274 kilometers) east of Prague. For location, see CZECHOSLOVAKIA (color map).

Ostrava is the center of the country's largest industrial area. The city is known for its great iron and steel works and for its manufacture of metal products. The region also has coal mines, petroleum refineries, and chemical plants. Other products of Ostrava include house-building materials, food products, wearing apparel, and furniture.   VOJTECH MASTNY

American Osteopathic Association

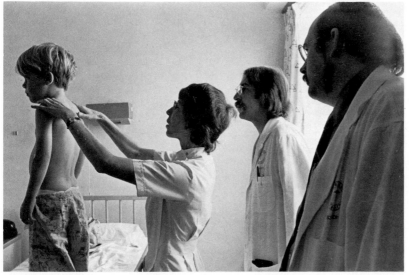

Most Osteopathic Physicians serve a year's internship at an approved osteopathic hospital. The intern shown at the left is examining a patient while experienced osteopathic physicians look on.

OSTRICH

Beth Bergman, N.A.S.

Richard Harrington, Three Lions

Ostrich Eggs are large, and usually weigh about 3 pounds (1.4 kilograms) each. Several ostrich hens usually lay their eggs in the same nest.

An Adult Ostrich, *left,* is the world's largest bird. It stands nearly 8 feet (2.4 meters) tall and may weigh over 300 pounds (140 kilograms) when fully grown.

A Week-Old Ostrich, *below,* has spotted down that blends with the ground, to protect the baby bird from its enemies.

Richard Harrington, Three Lions

OSTRICH, *AHS trich,* is the largest living bird. It may stand nearly 8 feet (2.4 meters) tall and weigh as much as 345 pounds (156 kilograms). Ostriches live on the plains and deserts of Africa. The extinct moas of New Zealand, which were 10 feet (3 meters) tall, were the only birds taller than ostriches. The extinct elephant birds of Madagascar, which weighed about 1,000 pounds (450 kilograms), were the only heavier birds. See ELEPHANT BIRD; MOA.

The ostrich is the only bird that has only two toes on each foot. The rhea, which is also called the *South American ostrich,* is three-toed, and it is not a true ostrich. See RHEA.

The male ostrich is a handsome bird. It has black feathers on its bulky body, with large white feathers, or plumes, on its small wings and tail. Its long, thin legs and upper neck and its small head have almost no feathers. The bare skin varies in color from pink to blue. Thick black eyelashes surround its eyes. The female's body, tail, and wings are dull brown.

The male ostrich has a strange voice. It gives a deep roar like that of a lion, but with a strange hissing sound. The ostrich cannot fly, but it is known for its speed. Its long legs can carry it in 15-foot (4.6-meter) steps at speeds up to 40 miles (64 kilometers) per hour. Its speed and its unusually good eyesight help the ostrich escape from its enemies, which are mainly lions and men. The

Ostrich Hide is valuable for making ladies shoes and handbags. The leather is durable, and it has an attractive quill design.

Fluffy Ostrich Feathers were popular in women's fashions before World War I. They were used to decorate hats and dresses.

ancient belief that the ostrich hides its head in the sand when frightened is not true. If the ostrich is exhausted and cannot run any farther, or if it must defend its nest, it kicks with its powerful legs. Its long toes, the largest of which is 7 inches (18 centimeters) long, have thick nails that become dangerous weapons when the bird is cornered.

How the Ostrich Lives. The ostrich usually eats plants, but it will eat lizards and turtles if it can find them. It also eats much sand and gravel to aid in grinding food for digestion. Ostriches drink water when they find it. But they can live for long periods without drinking if the plants they eat are green and moist.

Ostriches are *polygamous* (the male has more than one mate). Each *cock* (male) digs a shallow nest in sand, and from three to five *hens* (females) lay their eggs in the nest. Each hen lays as many as 10 eggs. Each egg is almost round, nearly 6 inches (15 centimeters) in diameter, and weighs about 3 pounds (1.4 kilograms). The eggs are a dull yellow, and have large pores and a thick shell.

The male sits on the eggs at night. But during the day the hens share the task of keeping them warm. The eggs hatch in five or six weeks. When an ostrich is a month old, it can run as fast as an adult. Ostriches live up to 70 years. Few other birds live so long.

Ostrich Farming. Hundreds of years ago, great flocks of ostriches roamed over Africa and western Asia. Arabs in western Asia hunted them for sport, and Africans took their eggs for food or killed them for feathers. But ostriches were seldom killed for food, because their flesh is tough and does not taste good.

Then in the late 1800's and the early 1900's, ostrich plumes came to be in great demand. They were used for decorating hats and clothing. Large numbers of birds were killed, and the ostrich disappeared from Asia and from much of Africa. The plumes were so expensive that it became profitable to raise ostriches in captivity. Plumes could be taken twice a year from live birds kept on ostrich farms.

Ostrich farms were established in North and South Africa, the United States, Australia, and southern Europe. Between 1914 and 1918, fashions changed

again, and the demand for ostrich plumes dropped sharply. Ostrich farming was no longer profitable. Today, about 25,000 birds are still raised in South Africa. But they are raised principally for their skins, which are made into fine quality leather.

Scientific Classification. The ostrich is in the ostrich family, *Struthionidae*. It is classified genus *Struthio*, species *S. camelus*.
R. A. PAYNTER, JR.

OSTROGOTH. See GOTH.

OSTROVSKY, ALEXANDER. See RUSSIAN LITERATURE (Early Realism).

OSTWALD, *OHST vahlt,* **WILHELM** (1853-1932), a German chemist, writer, and teacher, won the 1909 Nobel prize for chemistry. He received the award mainly for his studies in surface phenomena and speeds of chemical reactions. He wrote one of the early books on electrochemistry. His research on the oxidation of ammonia helped Germany make explosives during World War I. He was born in Riga, Latvia.
K. L. KAUFMAN

See also COLOR (Characteristics of Color).

OSTWALD PROCESS. See NITRIC ACID.

OSWALD, LEE HARVEY (1939-1963), was accused of assassinating President John F. Kennedy on Nov. 22, 1963, in Dallas, Tex. Two days later, while millions of television viewers looked on, Oswald was killed. He was shot to death by Dallas night-club owner Jack Ruby, while being transferred from the city jail to the county jail in Dallas. Ruby pushed through a ring of police officers to shoot Oswald down.

No one saw Oswald shoot the President. The high-powered Italian rifle said to have killed the President was traced to Oswald through a Chicago mail-order firm. Oswald worked in the Texas School Book Depository, the building from which the fatal shots were fired. A worker recalled seeing Oswald carry a long narrow package into the building the morning of the assassination. Police captured Oswald, who was armed with a revolver, in a Dallas motion picture theater about 90 minutes after the assassination.

Oswald was also charged with killing police officer J. D. Tippit. Tippit was shot to death in Dallas shortly after the President was killed. But Oswald denied killing either Tippit or the President. A presidential commission headed by Chief Justice Earl Warren investigated the case. After a 10-month investigation, the commission reported in September 1964, that Oswald, acting alone, had killed Kennedy and Tippit.

A Dallas jury convicted Ruby of Oswald's murder in 1964. The conviction was reversed in 1966 on the grounds that the trial judge had allowed illegal testimony. A new trial was ordered, but Ruby died in 1967 before the new trial started.

Oswald was born in New Orleans. Investigators said his school and military records showed emotional difficulty. Oswald dropped out of high school at 17 and joined the U.S. Marine Corps. He was discharged in September 1959, and went to Russia a month later. He tried to become a Russian citizen, but was turned down. He returned to the United States in 1962 with his Russian-born wife, Marina.   CAROL L. THOMPSON

See also KENNEDY, JOHN F.; WARREN REPORT.

OSWEGO, N.Y. (pop. 20,913), is the most eastern port on the Great Lakes. It lies at the point where the Oswego River empties into Lake Ontario (see NEW YORK [political map]). Coal and other products are shipped from Oswego to Canada. Wheat and lumber are brought into the port. Oswego produces aluminum, paper products, knitted underwear, engines and boilers, matches, oil-well supplies, silk, rayon, and cotton goods.

Oswego stands on the site of the earliest English trading post on the Great Lakes. The post was founded about 1722. During and after the Revolutionary War, the British held Oswego until 1796. In 1825, the Erie Canal was extended from Buffalo to the east, and Oswego lost importance as a port. Oswego became a village in 1828, and a city in 1848. It has a mayor-council form of government.   WILLIAM E. YOUNG

OSWEGO TEA is a horsemint plant that grows in eastern North America from Canada to Georgia. It is about 3 feet (91 centimeters) high and has small red flowers.

Scientific Classification. Oswego tea is in the mint family, *Labiatae*. It is genus *Monarda*, species *M. didyma*.

OTHELLO. See SHAKESPEARE, WILLIAM (Othello).

OTIS, ELISHA GRAVES (1811-1861), an American inventor, built the first elevator protected by safety devices against accidentally falling. While supervising the construction of a factory at Yonkers, N.Y., in 1852, he invented the improved elevator. Its safety device operated automatically in case the lifting rope or chain failed to hold the elevator. Otis demonstrated this safety device at the New York Fair in 1854 when he cut the lifting rope while standing on the elevator.

He also invented a steam plow in 1857, a bake oven in 1858, and a steam elevator in 1861. Otis was born on a farm near Halifax, Vt.   ROBERT P. MULTHAUF

OTIS, JAMES (1725-1783), was an American patriot and agitator against Great Britain. Otis was one of four representatives of Boston to the General Court, the provincial legislature, in 1761. There he proposed a meeting of representatives of all the colonies. His plan led to the Stamp Act Congress of 1765 (see STAMP ACT).

In 1768, Otis answered the British demand that the Massachusetts Assembly take back its plea to the colonies to fight the Townshend Acts by saying, "We are asked to rescind, are we? Let Great Britain rescind

Culver

James Otis became one of the most forceful leaders in the American colonies' struggle for independence from Great Britain.

her measures, or the colonies are lost to her forever."

The next year, as he entered the British Coffee House, Otis was attacked by British revenue officers, who resented his bitter criticism of their acts and methods. A head wound received during the attack eventually caused Otis to lose his mind. He was killed by lightning.

Otis was born in West Barnstable, Mass. He became king's advocate-general of the vice-admiralty court at Boston in 1756. Otis resigned four years later when the British revived the expiring writ of assistance (see WRIT OF ASSISTANCE). His sister Mercy Otis Warren was a writer who also became active in the American independence movement.   CLARENCE L. VER STEEG

OTOLARYNGOLOGY. See MEDICINE (table: Major Medical Specialty Fields).

OTOLOGIST. See EAR (Care of the Ear).

OTOSCLEROSIS. See DEAFNESS (Hearing Disorders).

OTOSCOPE is an instrument that doctors use to examine the eardrum. The otoscope consists of a magnifying lens and a light powered by a battery. The light illuminates the eardrum and the lens magnifies it about six times. The otoscope makes it possible for the doctor to see changes in the eardrum resulting from infections and diseases. NOAH D. FABRICANT

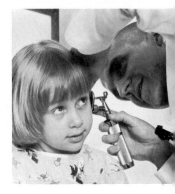

An Otoscope makes it possible for a physician to examine the eardrum of a patient.

WORLD BOOK photo by Henry Gill

Hans I. Blohm, Foto Blohm Associates Ltd.

Ottawa, the capital and eighth largest city of Canada, lies on the south bank of the Ottawa River. Canada's three Parliament buildings, *foreground,* are on Parliament Hill.

OTTAWA, *AHT uh wuh,* Ont., is the capital and eighth largest city of Canada. It lies on gently rolling hills along the south bank of the Ottawa River, about 120 miles (193 kilometers) west of Montreal. Parks, stately government buildings, and scenic drives add beauty to the city. Ottawa faces the city of Hull, Que., across the Ottawa River.

The Peace Tower, a memorial to Canada's war dead, rises 292 feet (89 meters). It is the first landmark seen by most travelers as they approach Ottawa. The memorial rises dramatically above the buildings of the Canadian Parliament on Parliament Hill, the highest point overlooking the river and the city.

In 1826, British troops founded the first settlement in the area that is now Ottawa. The soldiers had come to build the Rideau Canal, which links the Ottawa River and Lake Ontario. The town that sprang up around the construction site became known as Bytown. In 1855, the townspeople changed its name to *Ottawa,* an English version of the Algonkian Indian word *adawe,* meaning *to trade.* Other tribes used the name Adawe for an Algonquin tribe that traded in the area.

Ottawa was a small lumbering town when Queen Victoria chose it in 1857 to be the capital of the United Province of Canada. The Dominion of Canada was established in 1867, with Ottawa as its capital. The city's layout has been greatly changed through the years in keeping with Ottawa's standing as a national capital.

Metropolitan Ottawa

The City covers 48 square miles (124 square kilometers), including 5 square miles (13 square kilometers) of inland water. The Rideau River flows through Ottawa from the south. It plunges 37 feet (11 meters) over a cliff into the Ottawa River at the northeastern end of the city, forming the Rideau Falls. The Rideau Canal cuts through the city on its way from the Ottawa River to Lake Ontario (see RIDEAU CANAL).

Parliament Hill borders the Ottawa River just west

─────────── **FACTS IN BRIEF** ───────────

Population: 304,462. *Metropolitan Area Population—* 693,288.

Area: 48 sq. mi. (124 km²). *Metropolitan Area—*793 sq. mi. (2,054 km²).

Climate: *Average Temperature—*January, 12° F. (−11° C); July, 69° F. (21° C). *Average Annual Precipitation* (rainfall, melted snow, and other forms of moisture)— 34.24 in. (86.97 cm). For the monthly weather in Ottawa, see ONTARIO (Climate).

Government: Mayor-council. *Terms—*2 years for the mayor, 4 controllers, and 11 council members.

Founded: 1826. Incorporated as a city in 1855.

663

of the canal. The graceful spires and green roofs of the three Parliament buildings rise above a bluff near the river. The Peace Tower, topped by a lighted clock, stands out above the buildings. It houses a carillon of 53 bells that weigh a total of 60 short tons (54 metric tons). See CARILLON (pictures).

Upper Town, to the west of the Rideau Canal, and Lower Town, to the east, are the oldest parts of Ottawa. The city's chief shopping districts center around the Sparks Street Mall in Upper Town and Byward Market and Rideau Street in Lower Town. The municipalities of Rockcliffe Park and Vanier, each of which has its own government, lie entirely within Ottawa.

The Metropolitan Area of Ottawa includes Hull and covers about 793 square miles (2,054 square kilometers). It also includes the suburbs of Almonte, Bells Corners, Manotick, and Richmond in Ontario, and Aylmer and Pointe-Gatineau in Quebec.

South of Ottawa, flat farmland extends to the St. Lawrence River and Lake Ontario. North of the Ottawa River, the Gatineau Hills of Gatineau Park merge into the Laurentian Mountains. The Gatineau River, which drains these hills, empties into the Ottawa River opposite the Rideau Falls. The hills, lakes, and woods of the nearby Canadian Shield provide an excellent recreational area (see CANADIAN SHIELD).

A Visitor's Guide

About 3,550,000 tourists visit the Ottawa-Hull area yearly. They come to see Parliament in action and to view such attractions as the Peace Tower and the eight locks of the Rideau Canal. Ottawa's annual festivals and fairs also attract many visitors.

Following are brief descriptions of some interesting places and cultural attractions in Ottawa.

The Parliament Buildings rank as Ottawa's most popular tourist attraction. These three buildings—the Centre Block, the East Block, and the West Block—form three sides of a 35-acre (14-hectare) square.

The Prince of Wales, who later became King Edward VII of England, laid the first stone of the Centre Block in 1860. The three buildings were completed in 1865. Fire destroyed most of the Centre Block in 1916, and only the eight-sided Library of Parliament remained. After being rebuilt along the lines of the earlier structure, the Centre Block reopened in 1920.

The Centre Block includes the House of Commons, the Senate chamber, the Peace Tower, and offices of members of Parliament. Canada's prime minister has his office in the East Block. The West Block contains offices for some members of Parliament and other government officials. During July and August, the Governor General's Foot Guards and the Canadian Grenadier Guards perform a daily changing-the-guard ceremony in front of the Peace Tower.

Other Government Buildings include the Royal Canadian Mint, where visitors may watch coins being made. The National Library and Public Archives building exhibits historical documents. The Canadian Supreme Court building also attracts many visitors.

Rideau Hall, also called Government House, is the official residence of the Canadian governor general. It stands near the mouth of the Rideau River. Thomas McKay, a lumberman, built it in 1838. The Canadian government bought this gray limestone building in 1868 for Baron Monck, the first governor general. The home of the prime minister is nearby.

The National War Memorial, at Confederation Square, honors the Canadians who died in action during World Wars I and II. It consists of bronze figures of servicemen and servicewomen marching through a granite arch.

The Arts. The National Arts Centre, in the heart of Ottawa, opened in 1969. This $46,400,000 structure houses a 2,300-seat opera and concert hall, a theater with 800 seats, and a smaller theater with 300 seats. The National Arts Centre Orchestra performs in the concert hall. The nearby National Gallery of Canada has Canadian and European paintings and sculpture.

Museums. The National Museum of Natural Sciences features collections of animals, fossils, and minerals. The National Museum of Science and Technol-

The National Arts Centre stands in a landscaped area in the heart of downtown Ottawa. The center, which opened in 1969, houses a 2,300-seat opera and concert hall and two smaller theaters.

ogy has a section on Canadian aircraft. At the National Museum of Man, exhibits illustrate Indian and Eskimo cultures. Laurier House, the former residence of Canadian Prime Ministers Sir Wilfrid Laurier and W. L. Mackenzie King, has been preserved as a historical museum. The Canadian War Museum owns collections relating to World Wars I and II.

Parks and Recreation. Ottawa has more than 1,600 acres (647 hectares) of parks and playgrounds. Rockcliffe Park, the largest park, covers 240 acres (97 hectares). The Ottawa Rough Riders of the Canadian Football League play their home games at the Civic Centre in Lansdowne Park. The Central Experimental Farm includes attractive gardens.

Annual Events in Ottawa include the Canadian Tulip Festival during the last two weeks in May. More than 3 million bulbs bloom in parks, along roadways, and on the grounds of public buildings. Queen Juliana of The Netherlands sent the bulbs as a gift to Ottawa. During World War II, Juliana, then a princess, lived

in Ottawa while German troops occupied her country. After returning home, she sent Ottawa 100,000 tulip bulbs in gratitude for the city's hospitality and for Canada's role in freeing her country. Juliana has sent Ottawa 15,000 tulip bulbs for the festival annually ever since.

Ottawa holds a Winter Carnival from the last week of January through the first weekend of February. The carnival features such sports as broomball, car and motorcycle racing on ice, and dog-sled racing. The Summer Festival in Lakeside Gardens presents art exhibits, concerts, motion pictures, and plays. Every August, the Central Canada Exhibition at Lansdowne Park offers agricultural, industrial, and scientific exhibits. The Ottawa Winter Fair, held annually in October, also attracts many visitors.

People

About 85 per cent of Ottawa's people were born in Canada. About 55 per cent of the population have Brit-

City of Ottawa

Ottawa, the capital of Canada, lies on the Ottawa River in southeastern Ontario. It is the third largest city in Ontario and an important manufacturing center. The map at the right shows the major points of interest in and near Ottawa.

═══	City boundary
─ ─ ─	County boundary
─ ·· ─	Province boundary
═══	Main road
───	Other road
╫╫╫	Rail line
▪	Point of interest
▢	Built-up area
▨	Nonbuilt-up area
▨	Park
▨	Military area

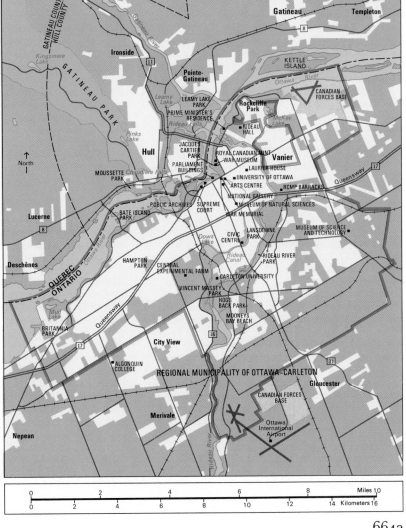

Sparks Street Mall, in the Upper Town section of Ottawa, is the heart of one of the city's chief shopping districts.

ish ancestry, and about 25 per cent are of French descent. Most of the rest of Ottawa's people trace their ancestry to other European countries. Most Ottawans speak only English, and a large number speak only French. An increasing number of Ottawans speak both English and French, especially those who work for the government. Roman Catholics make up Ottawa's largest religious group, followed by members of the United Church of Canada, the Anglican Church of Canada, and the Presbyterian Church.

Economy

Industry and Commerce. The Canadian government ranks as Ottawa's largest employer. More than 70,000 of the city's residents work for the Canadian government.

Ottawa has about 355 manufacturing and processing plants. They employ nearly 12,300 persons and produce almost $400 million worth of goods annually. Leading industries in Ottawa include the manufacture of communications equipment and the printing of business and financial forms. The city is also an important center of scientific research.

Transportation. Many major airlines use Ottawa International Airport, and passenger and freight trains also serve the city. Ottawa has a fine system of highways, including drives that run parallel to the Rideau Canal on both sides. The highway system extends across the Ottawa River into the Gatineau Hills. A city-owned bus company provides local service. Four automobile bridges and a railroad bridge connect Ottawa with Hull. The Ottawa River links the city with Montreal, and the Rideau Canal helps connect it with Kingston, Ont. But water transportation plays only a small part in Ottawa's economy.

Communication. Ottawa has three daily newspapers. The *Citizen* and the *Journal* are printed in English, and *Le Droit* is printed in French. Two local television stations broadcast in English and one broadcasts in French. Of the nine radio stations that serve the Ot-

tawa area, six broadcast in English and three in French.

Education

Schools. Ottawa has about 180 schools, almost evenly divided between public and Roman Catholic institutions. The schools have a total of about 77,000 students. More than 8,000 students attend each of the city's two universities, Carleton University and the University of Ottawa. The University of Ottawa, founded in 1849 as the College of Bytown, offers most of its courses in both English and French. Algonquin College of Applied Arts and Technology in Ottawa has an enrollment of more than 5,000.

Libraries. The Ottawa Public Library, which includes seven branches, has about 435,000 books and many films and other audio and visual aids. The Library of Parliament owns more than 350,000 books, and the National Library of Canada has about 450,000.

Government

Ottawa has a mayor-council form of government. The voters elect a mayor, 4 controllers, and 11 aldermen to two-year terms. The controllers supervise departments of the city government. Taxes on property, sales, and businesses provide most of the city's income. Ottawa also receives federal and provincial grants.

In 1968, Ontario established the Regional Municipality of Ottawa-Carleton, which combined Ottawa and Carleton County under a single government. The municipality covers about 1,100 square miles (2,850 square kilometers) and has a population of about 471,-931. It is governed by a council made up of elected officials from 2 cities, 1 village, and 8 townships. The regional government has taxing powers, and it controls health and welfare services, road and sewer construction, and water supply.

History

Early Days. Centuries ago, Algonquin and Iroquoian Indians traveled down the Ottawa River on hunting and trading trips. They went ashore at what is now Ottawa and carried their canoes around the Chaudière Falls. In 1613, the French explorer Samuel de Champlain passed through the area. French fur traders used the Ottawa River as a route to the west.

In 1800, Philemon Wright, a farmer from Massachusetts, took over a large tract of land on the north side of the Ottawa River. He built a sawmill and began a lumber business that grew into a thriving industry. Ira Honeywell, the first settler on the south bank, began to farm on the Ottawa side of the river in 1811.

Bytown. After the War of 1812, the British feared another war with the United States. As a result, they sought a way to send gunboats and supplies from Montreal to Lake Ontario without passing near U.S. territory. To carry out this project, the British sent the Royal Engineers under Lieutenant Colonel John By to build the Rideau Canal. A community known as Bytown grew up around By's headquarters.

Frequent conflicts between Irish canal workers and French-Canadian lumbermen made Bytown a stormy place during its early years. The lumber trade on the

Ottawa River had begun in 1806, when Wright took the first raft of processed timber down to the St. Lawrence River. Bytown became a center of this trade. Sawmills and other lumber industries sprang up, and by 1837, the population had reached 2,400. Bytown was incorporated as a town in 1850. It became a city in 1855, and the people changed its name to Ottawa. The community had a population of about 10,000 that year.

Capital of Canada. Upper and Lower Canada (present-day Ontario and Quebec) joined in 1840 and formed the United Province of Canada. For the next 17 years, the legislature debated the question of a permanent capital. Meanwhile, Kingston, Montreal, Quebec, and Toronto each served as capital. Canada referred the decision to Queen Victoria in 1857, and she chose Ottawa because of its beauty and location. Ottawa lay on the boundary of what had been Upper and Lower Canada. Yet the city was far enough from the United States to protect it from attack.

In 1867, Ottawa became the capital of the newly formed Dominion of Canada. Its population at that time had reached 18,000.

The city grew in a disorganized fashion, with numerous railroads crisscrossing through the center of town to accommodate the lumber trade. In 1896, Prime Minister Wilfrid Laurier called for a beautification program to make Ottawa the "Washington of the North." Three years later, the Ottawa Improvement Commission was formed to carry out this project.

The 1900's. In 1900, a great fire destroyed many houses, leaving a large number of Ottawa's 60,000 people homeless. But by 1912, the city had been rebuilt and its population had reached 90,000.

The Federal District Commission replaced the Ottawa Improvement Commission in 1927. Ten years later, Prime Minister W. L. Mackenzie King appointed Jacques Gréber, the Paris city planner, to replan Ottawa. But World War II broke out in 1939 and interrupted the project. Gréber returned to France and spent the war years there. Ottawa became the center of Canada's war effort. The population of the city rose from fewer than 155,000 in 1941 to over 202,000 in 1951.

After the war, Gréber went back to Canada. In 1951, Parliament accepted his plan to beautify Ottawa. The Gréber Plan brought about significant changes. Ottawa removed 32 miles (51 kilometers) of unattractive railroad tracks and relocated the railroad station at the edge of the city. It set aside land for a belt of parks around the capital. The commission also developed 88,000-acre (35,600-hectare) Gatineau Park just north of Ottawa. Instead of grouping all government offices in one area, the plan called for new government buildings on the outskirts of the city.

Recent Developments. The National Capital Commission replaced the Federal District Commission in 1959. The new commission has the responsibility of acquiring land for beautification purposes. It set up a national capital region of 1,800 square miles (4,660 square kilometers)—one 900-square-mile (2,330-square-kilometer) area in Ontario and another in Quebec. During the 1960's, developers created beaches, parks, and research laboratories within the capital region.

Ottawa established the Commercial and Industrial Development Corporation in 1962 to promote economic growth in the capital. This government corporation created 12 industrial parks in Ottawa during the late 1960's and early 1970's.

In 1973, the city repealed a law that had limited the height of buildings in the downtown area. As a result, larger buildings began to be constructed in Ottawa. City leaders predicted that the additional apartment dwellers and office workers in the new buildings—along with commuters from the growing suburbs—would strain Ottawa's transportation system. The provincial government announced a plan to avoid this problem by helping the city government build a rapid-transit railway system. This plan called for Ontario to pay 75 per cent of the estimated $195 million cost of the project. The system was scheduled to be in operation by 1982. D. M. L. FARR

OTTAWA, UNIVERSITY OF, is a coeducational school in Ottawa, Canada. It is supported by the province of Ontario. It was operated by the Roman Catholic Oblates of Mary Immaculate until 1965, when control was transferred to an independent board of governors. Classes are conducted in French and English. The university has *faculties* (colleges) of arts, civil and common law, education, management sciences, medicine, philosophy, psychology, science and engineering, and social sciences. There are also schools of graduate studies, library science, nursing, and physical education and recreation.

The University of Ottawa was founded as the College of Bytown in 1848. It received a civil charter in 1866 and a papal charter in 1889. In 1965, its civil and papal charters were transferred to the newly founded Saint Paul University. Saint Paul University students receive degrees from the University of Ottawa. For enrollment of the University of Ottawa, see CANADA (table: Universities and Colleges). ROGER GUINDON

OTTAWA RIVER is the chief branch of the Saint Lawrence River and one of the most important streams of Canada. Great quantities of lumber float down the Ottawa from forests in the north.

The river begins in Quebec, about 160 miles (257 kilometers) north of the city of Ottawa. For location, see QUEBEC (physical map). It flows west to the Quebec-Ontario border, and forms the border as it flows southeastward. It ends its 696-mile (1,120-kilometer) course near the island of Montreal, where it empties into the Saint Lawrence River. Canada's federal government buildings stand on the Ontario side of the river.

Rapids and falls along the river make it unnavigable for large ships. But the rapids and falls develop 1.5 million kilowatts of electric power a year. Chaudière Falls, north of the city of Ottawa, is the largest waterfall on the river. Dams and slides for large logs have been built on the Ottawa to aid the lumber industry. Canals built along the river once aided shipping. But they are now used only for pleasure boats. The Rideau Canal system connects the Ottawa River with Lake Ontario. The river was an early canoe route to the interior of Canada. French explorer Samuel de Champlain explored the river during the early 1600's. JOHN BRIAN BIRD

OTTAWA UNIVERSITY, Kans. See UNIVERSITIES AND COLLEGES (table).

OTTER is a member of the weasel family. Otters live close to water and spend much time in it. They are expert swimmers and divers and can stay under water for three or four minutes. An otter moves awkwardly on land.

Otters live on every continent except Australia. Most otters weigh from 10 to 30 pounds (4.5 to 14 kilograms) and grow from 3 to 4½ feet (0.9 to 1.4 meters) long, including the tail. The *giant otter* of South America may measure up to 7 feet (2 meters) long. Otters live along rivers, streams, lakes, and coastal waters, or in marshes. This article tells about otters that live in fresh waters. For information about the *sea otter*, which lives in the Pacific Ocean, see the article on SEA OTTER.

Body. An otter has a small flattened head; a long, thick neck; and a thick tail that narrows to a point. Special muscles enable the animal to close its ears and nostrils tightly to keep water out. Elastic webbing grows between the toes of all species of otters. In most species, the webbing is extensive enough to help the animals swim swiftly.

Otters, like beavers and muskrats, have long coarse *guard hairs* that cover and protect the short, thick underfur. This underfur traps air and keeps the otter's skin dry. In some species, a layer of fat under the skin insulates the otter from the cold. An otter's fur varies in color from brownish-gray to dark brown when dry, and appears darker when wet.

Otters often use their paws to handle objects. They hold and play skillfully with such things as stones and small shellfish. Some African and Asian species that have only a little webbing between their toes can use the toes like fingers. The ability of such *clawless* and *small-clawed otters* to handle food resembles that of raccoons. These otters feed on shellfish that live in shallow water. All otters have claws. Even the so-called clawless otter has short claws on the three middle toes of its hind feet.

The Life of an Otter. Otters eat crayfish, crabs, and fish. Although otters can sometimes catch such swift-swimming fish as trout, they generally capture slower fish. They also eat clams, frogs, insects, snails, snakes, and, occasionally, waterfowl. Otters are active the year around. Where man hunts them, they move about more

Paul Popper Ltd.

The African Clawless Otter eats mostly shellfish, but it also catches some fishes. This otter hunts in lakes and in slow-flowing streams. It handles its food skillfully with its forepaws.

at night than during the day. They hunt mostly alone, but sometimes they hunt in family groups.

Otters spend much time playing. They wrestle and romp and slide down steep muddy slopes in summer and down icy riverbanks in winter. Otters use a variety of sounds to communicate among themselves. All species have a warning growl. In addition, otters use various kinds of chirps, chuckles, screams, and squeals to express their feelings to other otters.

Most otters make their homes in burrows in riverbanks or under rocky ledges, or in abandoned dens of other animals. Most female otters give birth to two or three young at a time. The babies, called *cubs* or *pups*, are born blind. The young do not swim until they are several months old. Man hunts otters for their valuable and beautiful fur. Certain species, especially the giant otter, are in danger of becoming extinct.

Scientific Classification. Otters belong to the weasel family, *Mustelidae*. The North American otter is genus *Lutra*, species *L. canadensis*. The giant otter is genus *Pteronura*, species *P. brasiliensis*. The clawless and small-clawed otters form genus *Aonyx*. The clawless otter is classified *A. capensis*. The small-clawed otter is classified *A. cinerea*.   JOSEPH A. DAVIS

See also ANIMAL (picture: Animals of the Temperate Forests).

OTTER CREEK. See VERMONT (Rivers and Lakes).

OTTER HOUND was developed in Great Britain for the sport of hunting otter. It has a thick, rough coat, with an oily undercoat that enables it to stay in cold water for long periods. Its feet are slightly webbed, and this helps make the dog a good swimmer. The otter hound looks much like a bloodhound in size and build. But the otter hound has a longer coat and shorter ears than the bloodhound. The otter hound's color ranges from grizzled blue and white to sand, with black and tan markings. Some breeders believe the otter hound originally came from the bloodhound. Others believe its ancestors were bulldogs.   OLGA DAKAN

OTTERBEIN COLLEGE. See UNIVERSITIES AND COLLEGES (table).

OTTO. See ATTAR.

OTTO was the name of three German kings and emperors, father, son, and grandson. Their combined rule lasted from A.D. 936 to 1002.

Otto I, The Great (912-973), was the first king to become Holy Roman Emperor. He followed his father, Henry I, as king of Germany in 936. Otto's father had

Leonard Lee Rue, APF

The North American Otter is a swift, graceful swimmer. It lives in burrows along the banks of rivers. Crayfish and fish make up this otter's chief source of food.

actually ruled only his own duchy of Saxony, but Otto tried to rule all Germany. In 951, he crossed the Alps and declared himself the king of Italy. He was forced to return to Germany when the other German princes began a series of revolts. At the same time, the Slavs in Poland and Bohemia revolted, and the Magyars, or Hungarians, invaded Germany. Otto crushed the Magyars in the battle of the Lech River in 955. The Poles and Bohemians were forced to accept his rule. Otto was able to replace most of the rebellious German princes with members of his own family. The young king of Arles, or Burgundy, also had to accept German rule. Otto then turned his attention toward Italy. He married the widow of an earlier Italian king, and defeated a rival for the throne. In 961, Otto crossed the Alps to put down an uprising in Rome. For this service, Pope John XII crowned him emperor of what was later known as the Holy Roman Empire (see HOLY ROMAN EMPIRE).

Otto II (955-983) was Holy Roman Emperor from 973 to 983. He followed his father's example and tried to keep power over Lombardy, Burgundy, Germany, and the Slavic borderlands. Otto II tried to extend his power by claiming several provinces in southern Italy. But the Greek emperor opposed his claim, and called on the Saracens to help fight the Germans. Otto was defeated at Cotrone in 982 and left southern Italy. He died in Rome, where he was planning another campaign.

Otto III (980-1002), was 3 years old when his father died, but he was crowned king of the Germans. His mother and grandmother ruled for him as regents. He spent his life in Italy and took little interest in ruling Germany. He tried, instead, to bring back the glories of ancient Rome. His death ended the direct line of Saxon emperors. FRANKLIN D. SCOTT

OTTO I (1815-1867), a Bavarian prince, became the first king of Greece after it was liberated from Turkey in 1830 (see GREECE [Otto I]). Otto was an unpopular ruler. He was not Greek, and he failed to move toward the realization of the "Great Idea." This idea was to liberate all Greeks still under Turkish rule in such territories as Crete, Thessaly, and Macedonia.

Otto and the Greeks were prepared to join the Russians against the Turks during the Crimean War (1853 to 1856). Great Britain and France sent troops to

Joyce R. Wilson
The Otter Hound Is a Hardy Dog and a Good Swimmer.

Greece and prevented it. The Greeks blamed Otto and deposed him in 1862. Otto, however, worked hard for his people. He rebuilt Athens, established the first Greek university, and refounded Sparta. Otto was born in Salzburg, Austria, on June 1, 1815. R. V. BURKS

OTTO, NIKOLAUS AUGUST. See GASOLINE ENGINE (Development of the Gasoline Engine).

OTTO HAHN. See ATOMIC ENERGY (A Nuclear-Powered Ship, with pictures).

OTTO THE CHILD. See BRUNSWICK (family).

OTTOMAN EMPIRE. See TURKEY (History); ISTANBUL (History).

OUABAIN. See POISON.

OUACHITA BAPTIST UNIVERSITY. See UNIVERSITIES AND COLLEGES (table).

OUACHITA MOUNTAINS. See ARKANSAS (Land Regions; picture, Lake Hamilton); OKLAHOMA (Land Regions).

OUACHITA RIVER, *WASH ee taw*, begins in the Ouachita Mountains of western Arkansas and flows east and then south into Louisiana. Sometimes called the *Washita*, it is about 605 miles (974 kilometers) long. The Ouachita joins the Tensas River to form the Black River about 25 miles (40 kilometers) west of Natchez. Large ships can sail about 350 miles (563 kilometers) up the river to Camden, Ark. During high water seasons, ships can sail about 70 miles (110 kilometers) farther, to Arkadelphia. For location of the Ouachita River, see SOUTHERN STATES (color map). WALLACE E. AKIN

OUAGADOUGOU, *WAH guh DOO goo* (pop. 115,000), is the capital and commercial center of Upper Volta, a republic in western Africa. Factories there process the agricultural products grown in the surrounding region. See also UPPER VOLTA (map; History).

OUIDA, *WEE duh* (1839-1908), was the pen name of the English novelist Marie Louise De la Ramée. *Ouida* was the way she said *Louise*, as a child. Her romantic novels show a sharp sense of the dramatic. The best known is *Under Two Flags* (1867). She also wrote children's stories, including *A Dog of Flanders* (1872) and *Two Little Wooden Shoes* (1874). Her other works include *The Silver Christ* (1894) and *Street Dust* (1901). Ouida was born in Bury St. Edmunds, England, but she lived in Italy most of her life. The first of her nearly 20 novels, *Held in Bondage*, was published in 1863. She died in Viareggio, Italy. LIONEL STEVENSON

OUIJA BOARD, *WEE juh* or *WEE jee*, is a device used to supposedly ask questions of the spirits of the dead and receive answers from them. People who believe seriously in the Ouija board use it at gatherings called *séances*. Others use it for fun as a game.

A Ouija board is a small board with various symbols printed on its surface. These symbols include the letters of the alphabet, the numbers from 1 to 9 and 0, and the words *yes* and *no*. A smaller, three-legged board serves as a pointer.

Two or more persons hold a Ouija board on their laps and press their fingers lightly on the pointer. One of them asks the board a question. The pointer supposedly answers by indicating a word or a number or by spelling out words. According to people who believe in the Ouija board, spirits guide the pointer. Others think the fingers of the questioner influence the pointer. The

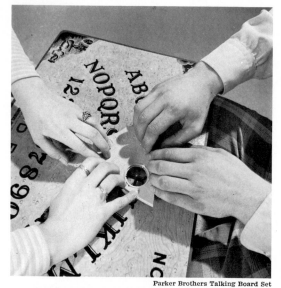

Parker Brothers Talking Board Set

A Ouija Board is used as a game or to supposedly exchange messages with the spirits of the dead.

Ouija board was invented about 1890 by William Fuld of Baltimore.   ALAN DUNDES

OUNCE. See SNOW LEOPARD.

OUNCE is a measure of weight and of volume. In *avoirdupois* weight, the ounce is equal to one-sixteenth of a pound, or $437\frac{1}{2}$ grains (28.3495 grams). In *troy* weight and *apothecaries'* weight, the ounce is equal to one-twelfth of a pound, or 480 grains (31.1035 grams). Grains are the same in all these systems. The avoirdupois ounce is a unit employed in weighing ordinary merchandise, such as foodstuffs. The troy ounce is used in weighing precious metals, and the apothecaries' ounce was once employed in compounding prescriptions. The name *ounce* comes from the Latin word *uncia*, meaning a *twelfth*.

In liquid measure, one fluid ounce equals 29.5735 milliliters. There are 16 fluid ounces in a liquid pint. The fluid ounce based on the Imperial gallon equals 28.4131 milliliters. Twenty ounces make a pint in the Imperial system.   E. G. STRAUS

See also WEIGHTS AND MEASURES.

OUR CHALET. See GIRL SCOUTS (In Other Countries).

OUR LADY OF ANGELS COLLEGE. See UNIVERSITIES AND COLLEGES (table).

OUR LADY OF FÁTIMA. See FÁTIMA.

OUR LADY OF THE ELMS, COLLEGE OF. See UNIVERSITIES AND COLLEGES (table).

OUR LADY OF THE LAKE UNIVERSITY OF SAN ANTONIO. See UNIVERSITIES AND COLLEGES (table).

OURAY. See UTE INDIANS; INDIAN WARS (The Southern Plains).

OURSLER, *OURZ ler*, **FULTON** (1893-1952), was an American writer and editor. He wrote *The Greatest Story Ever Told* (1949) and *The Greatest Book Ever Written* (1951). His daughter completed his *The Greatest Faith Ever Known* (1953) after his death. He was an editor of *Liberty* magazine from 1931 to 1942, and served as an editor of *Reader's Digest* from 1944 until 1952. Charles Fulton Oursler was born in Baltimore, Md. CARL NIEMEYER

OUTBOARD MOTOR is a gasoline or electric motor clamped to the stern of a small boat. It operates a vertical driving shaft to which a propeller is geared. The propeller spins under water to propel the boat.

Gasoline outboard motors are the most frequently used type. They may have either horizontal or "V-shaped" cylinders. There may be one, two, four, or six cylinders in a gasoline outboard motor.

Outboard motors operate at high speed and deliver their full power at 4,000 to 6,000 revolutions per minute. Some of the smaller types are also designed for low speeds and are used to troll for fish.

Electric outboard motors are less frequently used because their power comes from storage batteries that must be recharged frequently.

See also MOTORBOAT (Outboard Motorboats).

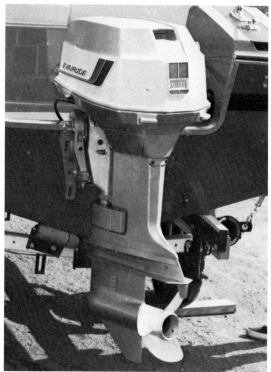

Evinrude Motors

An Outboard Motor is attached to the stern of a small boat. Such motors use electricity or gasoline for fuel.

OUTCAULT, *OWT kawlt*, **RICHARD FELTON** (1863-1928), was an American cartoonist. In about 1895, he created the comic strip "Hogan's Alley." The strip featured a young boy called the Yellow Kid. In 1896, the strip, renamed "The Yellow Kid," became the first comic strip to be printed in color.

Outcault introduced "The Yellow Kid" in *The* (New York) *World.* But he accepted an enormous salary from the *New York Journal* to draw the strip for that paper. The *World* hired another artist to draw "The Yellow Kid," and the papers began a sensational rivalry. Other newspapers called them the "Yellow Kid journals." The term *yellow journalism*, meaning a highly sensa-

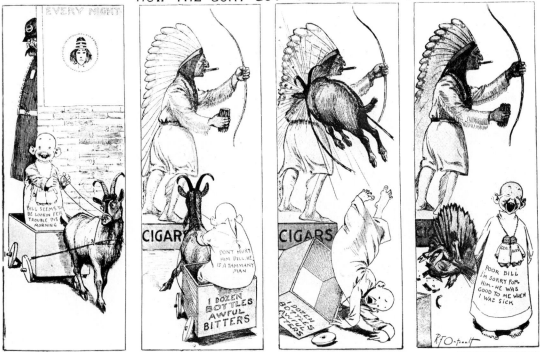

King Features Syndicate

Outcault's "The Yellow Kid" was the first comic strip printed in color. It featured a bald, grinning boy who became involved in humorous situations connected with New York City.

tional kind of newspaper writing, thus began with "The Yellow Kid" comic strip. Outcault was born in Lancaster, Ohio.   DICK SPENCER III

OUTDOOR RECREATION, BUREAU OF, is an agency of the United States government. It was established in 1962 as part of the Department of the Interior to coordinate federal recreation programs and handle long-range planning. It also provides assistance to states, encourages interstate and regional cooperation, and conducts outdoor recreation resource surveys.

OUTER MONGOLIA. See MONGOLIA.

OUTLAW. See BANDIT with its Related Articles.

OUTLINES AND OUTLINING. An outline gives the main topics, or principal ideas, of a subject. It is a writer's blueprint, or plan, for an article, a theme, or a book. It may also be used to summarize an article or a book for study, or to prepare a speech.

Formal outlines are of two kinds. The *topic outline* is a summary of topics and subtopics, or nouns and phrases, to indicate ideas. The *sentence outline* uses complete sentences for each division.

Organization. All topics of equal importance should be phrased in similar form and indented equally. The subject should be covered completely, but without too many main topics. Topic headings should be clear.

The topics and subtopics may be organized with Roman numerals (I), capital letters (A), Arabic numerals (1), and small letters (a), in that order. Use periods after the numbers and letters. If more subdivisions are needed, repeat the numbers and letters in parentheses. Do not use periods after parentheses. Always use at least two subheads. Capitalize the first letter of the

first word of each topic and subtopic. Use periods after complete sentences.

A Sample Topic Outline follows.

Outline on Floods

I. What Is a Flood?
  A. Its Extent
  B. Its Effects
    1. Bad effects
      a. Destroys property and homes
      b. Carries off topsoil
      c. Causes injuries and deaths
    2. Good effects
      a. Creates fertile regions
      b. Transports soil
        (1) Nile Valley
        (2) Mississippi delta

II. Kinds of Floods
  A. River Floods
    1. Rivers that commonly overflow
      a. Mississippi-Missouri system
      b. Hwang Ho, or Yellow River
    2. Causes
      a. Too heavy rains
      b. Too fast melting of snow and ice
    3. Great floods
      a. Ohio and Indiana, 1913
      b. Mississippi, 1927
  B. Seacoast Floods
    1. Causes
    2. Great Floods

III. Flood Control
  A. Reclaiming dry, barren highlands
  B. Planting trees
  C. Building reservoirs, levees, flood walls

Other Examples of outlines may be found in WORLD BOOK at the end of such articles as BIRD; FRANCE; OHIO; and in the article on PUBLIC SPEAKING.

An Outrigger in Java is a large framework that extends from each side of a canoe. The framework supports a pole that floats parallel to the boat and keeps it from capsizing in rough coastal waters. Javanese fishermen use double outriggers, *above*, to obtain maximum support.

Outriggers in the United States are used on small boats called *shells*, *above*. These outriggers are brackets that extend from each side of the shell and hold the oarlocks away from the boat. The extended oarlocks increase the shell's speed by giving the oarsman greater leverage.

OUTRIGGER BOAT is a rowing boat with the oarlocks mounted on *outriggers* (brackets) which run out from the sides of the boat. By moving the oarlocks farther from the oarsman, the leverage that the oarsman puts on the oars is increased. In the United States, outriggers are rarely used except in "shells," or very light boats such as are used in college or interclub boat racing. In the Indian and Pacific oceans, an "outrigger" is a canoe with a log attached to a framework extending from one side. The log is a counterbalance and keeps the canoe from capsizing. Some outriggers can hold 30 men. See also MARQUESAS ISLANDS (picture); INDONESIA (picture); CATAMARAN.   ROBERT H. BURGESS

OUZEL. See WATER OUZEL.

OVANDO, NICOLÁS DE. See COLUMBUS, CHRISTOPHER (Columbus in Disgrace; Fourth and Last Voyage).

OVARY. See FERTILIZATION; FLOWER (The Pistils); GLAND (The Sex Glands).

OVEN. See STOVE; BREAD (How Bread Is Baked; History); COOKING (History).

Hal Harrison, National Audubon Society
The Ovenbird Conceals Its Nest on the Forest Floor.

OVENBIRD is a common American bird that belongs to the family of warblers. The ovenbird looks like a small thrush. It is about 6 inches (15 centimeters) long, and has a brownish olive-green back, dull orange crown, and a white breast spotted with black. Its song sounds like the word *teacher*, repeated with increasing loudness. The ovenbird is often called the *teacher bird*.

The ovenbird nests from Oklahoma to Georgia, and north to Manitoba and Labrador. Its name comes from the shape of its nest, which looks somewhat like an old-fashioned rounded oven. The ovenbird hides its nest on the forest floor. It lays four to six white eggs, speckled with cinnamon brown. It eats mostly insects.

Scientific Classification. The ovenbird belongs to the wood warbler family, *Parulidae*. It is genus *Seiurus*, species *S. aurocapillus*.　　　　GEORGE J. WALLACE

See also WARBLER.

OVERDRIVE. See TRANSMISSION (Overdrive).

OVERLAND MAIL. See PONY EXPRESS.

OVERLAPPING SET. See SET THEORY.

OVERPOPULATION. See POPULATION; BIRTH CONTROL; EHRLICH, PAUL R.

OVERSEAS HIGHWAY. See FLORIDA (Transportation).

OVERTONE. See HARMONICS.

OVERTURE, *O ver tyoor*, is a musical composition written as an introduction to an opera, oratorio, or, in some cases, to a play or spoken drama. An overture may contain some of the principal themes of the main work, or it may be entirely independent. The overture may be in *sonata-allegro* (first movement) form (see SONATA). An overture to an opera compares with the first movement of a symphony. It is intended to put the listener into the proper frame of mind for what is to follow.

The musical introduction which leads to a drama is called a *dramatic overture*. Beethoven's overture to *Coriolanus* and Schubert's overture to *Rosamunde* are good examples. Other overtures are similar to symphonic poems and are written so that they may be played separately as concert pieces. These are known as *concert overtures*.

In the 1600's, the French-Italian composer Jean Baptiste Lully made the first important contribution to the development of the overture. Lully wrote short movements to be played as openings for his operas and ballets. These musical preludes became known as overtures.

In Italy, the first overture was probably written in 1607. The opera *Orfeo* by Claudio Monteverdi began with a musical overture of nine bars, played three times. Such an overture was known at that time as a *sinfonia*.

The first overture for an opera in which the music was directly related to the opera was written by Christoph Gluck, who wrote an overture to his opera *Iphigenia in Tauris*. The music of the overture prepared the listener for the opening act, which was a storm scene.

Mozart, an Austrian composer, made an important contribution to the development of the overture in 1787. He wrote an overture to his opera *Don Giovanni* that has become famous, and is played apart from the opera.

The next step in the development of the overture was made in the early 1800's by Beethoven. He wrote four overtures to his only opera, *Fidelio*. Three of them are called *Leonore* overtures, after the heroine of the story. All four contain themes from the music of the opera.

The overture reached its finest development in the preludes to the operas of Richard Wagner (1813-1883). The preludes to *Die Meistersinger*, *Lohengrin*, and *Tannhäuser* are really overtures.　　　RAYMOND KENDALL

OVERWEIGHT. See WEIGHT CONTROL.

OVID, *AHV ihd* (43 B.C.-A.D. 17 or 18), was a great Roman poet. He became best known for his witty, sophisticated love poems.

Perhaps Ovid's most famous work is the *Art of Love*, a kind of manual in verse on how to fall in love. He wrote this poem in a humorous, satirical style. Ovid considered the *Metamorphoses (Transformations)* his greatest work. It is a narrative poem that includes more than 200 tales taken from the favorite legends and myths of the ancient world. The stories tell of the adventures and love affairs of gods and heroes. Many of the stories involve a *metamorphosis* (change), such as the transformation of a woman into a bird. The *Metamorphoses* has become a vast and fascinating source of folklore and myth. For information about some of the stories, see the WORLD BOOK articles on ARETHUSA, NARCISSUS, PYGMALION, and PYRAMUS AND THISBE.

Ovid's other poems include the *Heroides* (*Letters of Heroic Women*). This work consists of 21 fictional letters written by famous women in mythology to their husbands or lovers.

Ovid was born in Sulmona, Italy. His full name was Publius Ovidius Naso. Ovid held some minor government positions in Rome, but he gave them up to write poetry. In A.D. 8, the emperor Augustus banished Ovid to an isolated city on the Black Sea for some reason that is not clear to scholars. Ovid's poetry apparently had offended Augustus. The poet's pleas to return to Rome were rejected, and he died in exile.　　HERBERT MUSURILLO

OVIPAROUS ANIMAL, *oh VIP uh rus*, is a type of animal that reproduces by laying eggs that hatch outside the parent's body. The young animals develop inside the egg. In *viviparous* animals, the young develop inside the parent until they are ready to be born. Viviparity is considered the higher method of birth, since it better protects and nourishes the young. Most vertebrates below mammals are oviparous, but there are exceptions. For example, certain sharks, lizards, and snakes bear live young. Among the mammals, the platypus is oviparous.　　　WILLIAM C. BEAVER

OVIPOSITOR. See GRASSHOPPER; ICHNEUMON FLY.

OVULE. See FLOWER (The Pistils).

OWEN

OWEN is the family name of two social theorists, father and son.

Robert Owen (1771-1858), a Welsh-born social reformer, pioneered in cooperative movements. He tried to prove as a businessman that it was good business to think of the employees' welfare. He set up the famous New Harmony community in Indiana in 1825.

Owen was part owner and the head of the New Lanark cotton mills in Scotland in 1799. It was during the Industrial Revolution, when machines were replacing home sewing and weaving. New factories were rarely built with the comfort of the workers in mind. Wages were low, and women and children were not treated with consideration.

He organized a model community. Instead of employing children, he built schools for them. He kept his mills in good repair, and tried to take care of his laborers' needs. The success of his mills impressed many visitors.

New Harmony. Owen wrote on the subject of proper social conditions, and tried to interest the British government in building "villages of cooperation." He thought these villages ought to be partly agricultural and partly industrial. He made up his mind to show they could succeed. He then set up New Harmony.

Owen believed in equal opportunity for all. His ideas in education were influenced by Johann Pestalozzi, a Swiss educator. Owen opposed mere book learning. He believed children also could be taught "correct ideas" by surrounding them with good examples.

He lost popularity by his antireligious views. Many of his associates at New Harmony refused to work. The community failed in 1827, and Owen returned to England in 1828.

Cooperatives. Owen retired from business to devote all his time to his social theories. He moved to London in 1828. There, trades unions became interested in his "villages of cooperation." In 1833, Owen organized the Grand National Consolidated Trades Union. It had more than 500,000 members. The movement tried to reorganize industry into cooperatives. The government and manufacturers opposed it, and by 1834, the union had collapsed. Owen continued to write and agitate for government aid. Although his plans were not accepted, his ideas influenced all later cooperative movements.

Owen was born in Newtown, Wales. He left school when he was 9 to work as a cotton spinner.

Robert Dale Owen (1801-1877) was a social theorist and an American legislator. He worked with his father, Robert Owen, in the New Lanark and New Harmony model communities. He edited the New Harmony *Gazette* with Frances Wright. When New Harmony collapsed in 1827, Owen moved to New York City. He and Frances Wright edited the *Free Enquirer* and tried to organize the Workingmen's party in 1829 in New York.

Owen was elected to the Indiana state legislature in

Brown Bros.
Robert Owen

Culver
Robert Dale Owen

Ruth Bryan Owen

1836 and served until 1838. He was a member of the U.S. House of Representatives from 1843 to 1847. He served as Minister to Naples from 1855 to 1858. Owen championed emancipation for black slaves, and influenced President Abraham Lincoln's views. He was a freethinker in religion, and a pioneer in advocating birth control and universal education. He was born in Glasgow, Scotland.   LOUIS FILLER

See also COOPERATIVE; NEW HARMONY; NURSERY SCHOOL; PESTALOZZI, JOHANN H.

OWEN, RUTH BRYAN (1885-1954), was the first American woman ever chosen to represent the United States in another country. She served as United States Minister to Denmark from 1933 to 1936.

Owen was born in Jacksonville, Ill., the oldest daughter of the well-known statesman, William Jennings Bryan. She served as a Democrat from Florida in the U.S. House of Representatives from 1929 to 1933. She served as alternate U.S. representative to the UN General Assembly in 1949.   GEORGE M. WALLER

OWEN-STANLEY MOUNTAINS lie in the eastern part of New Guinea. The highest mountain is Mount Victoria (13,240 feet, or 4,036 meters). Other peaks more than 10,000 feet (3,000 meters) high include Mounts Albert Edward, Suckling, Scratchley, Yule, and Obree. Streams from the southern slopes of the mountains flow into the Coral Sea. JUSTUS M. VAN DER KROEF

OWENS, JESSE (1913-   ), an American Negro athlete, held world track records in sprinting, hurdling, and jumping. On one day, May 25, 1935, he set three world records and tied another. The records were in the 220-yard dash, 220-yard low hurdles, and the running broad jump. He tied the 100-yard dash record. Owens won Olympic Games championships in 1936 at Berlin in the 100-meter dash, 200-meter dash, and running broad jump. He was born in Decatur, Ala., and attended Ohio State University.   PAT HARMON

OWENS, MICHAEL JOSEPH. See BOTTLE.

OWENS LAKE. See MOJAVE.

OWENSBORO, Ky. (pop. 50,329; met. area pop. 79,486), lies on the south bank of the Ohio River, 80 miles (130 kilometers) southwest of Louisville. Factories there make chemicals, liquor, road machinery, and steel. Owensboro was founded in 1797 as Yellow Banks, and later renamed in honor of Colonel Abraham Owens, who died in the Battle of Tippecanoe. Owensboro was incorporated in 1877, and has a council-manager government. Owensboro is the seat of Daviess County. For location, see KENTUCKY (political map).

OWL. The owl usually lives alone and hunts for food at night. It is known for its solemn appearance. The owl has been called the "night watchman of our gardens" because it eats harmful rodents at night. Although it is a bird of prey, or a bird which kills and eats other animals, the owl is a closer relative of the nighthawks, whippoorwills, and other goatsuckers than of the hawks.

Scientists have identified about 525 various kinds of owls. They live throughout the temperate, tropical, and subarctic regions of the world. Owls have been found on sea islands cut off from the mainland.

The smallest of owls is the tiny *elf owl* of the southwestern United States and western Mexico. It is hardly 6 inches (15 centimeters) long. The largest is the *great gray owl*, which lives in the deep woods of Canada and Alaska as far north as trees grow. It is 30 inches (76 centimeters) long, and has a wingspread of 54 to 60 inches (137 to 152 centimeters).

General Appearance. A person can recognize any owl at once by its large, broad head with a ruff of feathers around the eyes. This ruff is called the *facial disk*. It also covers enormous ear openings. The eyes are very large. These eyes point forward, unlike the eyes of most birds. For this reason owls can watch an object with both eyes at the same time. They have binocular vision like man. But unlike man, owls cannot move their eyes in their sockets, so they must move their heads to see a moving object. Their eyes have long lashes, and their upper eyelids close over them. Owls' eyes make them look as if they were wiser than other animals. The owl has long been a symbol of wisdom. The ancient Greeks thought it was sacred to Athena, their goddess of wisdom. Actually, geese, crows, and ravens are all smarter than owls.

Owls have short, thick bodies; strong, hooked beaks, and powerful feet with sharp claws. These are the only ways in which they resemble hawks. Some owls have tufts of feathers on their heads. The tufts are often called "ears" or "horns." Their feathers are soft and fluffy, and often make the birds seem larger than they are. The plumage is also dull, or colored so that the bird blends with its surroundings. Owls can fly fairly fast. Their fluffy feathers muffle the swishing sound that most birds make when they fly. An owl can swoop down on its prey unseen and unheard in the shadowy still night. All owls can see in the daytime, but usually not very well. A few can see well in the daytime, and hunt by day and night. Others hunt only at night. These birds usually have extremely sensitive eyes and see well in the dark.

Owls eat mostly mammals. The larger owls catch rabbits and squirrels, and the smaller ones catch many mice, rats, and shrews. Usually they capture their food alive, but now and then owls will pick up animals which have been recently killed along highways. Some owls will take a few birds and insects. Others have been known to fish in waters that are so shallow that the owls do not have to dive for their prey. Like the hawks, owls tear their prey into pieces when they eat it. Sometimes, if the prey is small enough, they swallow it whole. Later they throw up pellets of bones, fur, scales, and feathers which they cannot digest. These pellets can be found under their roosting places.

Owls are among the most useful birds to the farmer. They destroy harmful rodents, such as mice, rats, and

John Markham

The Barn Owl nests in old and abandoned buildings. It aids farmers by helping to keep farms free of rats and mice.

moles. But they seldom touch poultry, which are asleep and inside when owls come out to hunt.

Owls are not good nest builders. The nests are usually crude structures in hollow trees, caverns, underground burrows, barns, deserted houses, belfries, and old nests of hawks and crows. The eggs are nearly round, and are white tinged with buff or blue. There are usually three or four eggs, but some owls lay from two to twelve.

Both males and females help care for the nest. The larger owls bravely defend their nests against any intruder, including men. Sometimes they draw blood when they strike with their vicious talons. Young owls are attractive in their covering of thick white down. They are reared and fed in much the same way as young hawks. They stay in the nest longer than most birds.

Important Owls. There are two families of owls, which have certain body differences. They are the *barn owls* and the *typical owls*. There are ten species of barn owls. They live in most places except the colder regions. The *North American barn owl* ranges from the latitude of northern California and southern New England south to Central America. It is about 18 inches (46 centimeters) long. Sometimes it is called *monkey-faced owl* because its heart-shaped face, beady eyes, and amusing actions make it look like a monkey. It usually nests in a hollow tree, but sometimes selects a belfry or the dark places in a barn, which give it its name. Barn owls are very valuable birds. They eat many mice, rats, sparrows, blackbirds, and frogs.

Of the typical owls, the *great horned owl* lives in many places throughout North America. It is common in the heavy forests of the East and North, and among cliffs and canyons of the dry regions in the West. It grows 2 feet (61 centimeters) long, and is the only large owl with tufts of feathers on its head. Like other owls, it is heard more often than seen. It sounds like a barking dog in the distance—*whoo, hoo-hoo, whoo, whoo.*

The great horned owl is the only one which destroys poultry. It makes up for this destruction by keeping down the number of rabbits. This owl chooses old crow or hawk nests for its three eggs. Both males and females sit on the eggs at different times. The young cannot fly until they are 9 to 10 weeks old.

The *barred owl* lives only in the woodlands of eastern North America, from Canada south to Mexico. It is about the same size as the great horned owl, but has no ear tufts. Brownish-gray bars run across its breast and the length of its belly. This owl deserves the name hoot owl more than any other. It gives a series of eight or more loud hoots, the last one ending with an *ah: whoo, whoo, whoo, whoo—whoo, whoo, whoo, whoo-ah.*

The best known small owl is the *screech owl*. It is another woodland bird that lives in North America from the northern woodlands through Mexico. Most screech owls are about 10 inches (25 centimeters) long, and are the only small owls with ear tufts. Screech owls in the eastern United States may be reddish or grayish.

These owls like to spend the day in hollow trees and to nest there. They may live in a birdhouse if it has a single compartment and an opening 3 inches (8 centimeters) or more across. They often use the trees along the city streets and in parks. Screech owls may give no signs that they are around until night. Then they give their weird trembling calls and hollow whistles that run down the scale. Superstitious people think these sounds mean that death or disaster is near.

Screech owls eat mostly mice and other small rodents, insects, and sometimes birds. Most families have from four to six young, but sometimes there are as many as nine.

The adult male *snowy owl* is usually pure white, although it may have brown spots. It is about 20 inches (51 centimeters) long. It breeds in the Arctic and migrates in winter, sometimes as far as the Caribbean Sea.

The *long-eared owl* is another woodland bird. In summer it ranges from southern Canada to southern California and Virginia, and in winter it flies as far south as Florida. It is about two-thirds as large as the great horned owl, with ear tufts close together and lengthwise streaks on the breast.

The *saw-whet* also lives in the woods. Its name comes from its rasping call. In the course of the year this bird makes its home from Alaska and Nova Scotia south to Mexico. It is often tame and can be captured by hand.

Two kinds of owls live in open country and hunt by day as well as night. The *short-eared owl* is about the size of the long-eared owl. It is buff colored all over with many brown streaks. The ear tufts are so short that they are not noticeable. This owl nests from the Arctic south to California, Kansas, and New Jersey. It spends the winter in the United States and south to Central America. It lives mostly on prairies, meadows, and marshes, and nests on the ground. *Burrowing owls* live in the ground in burrows like snakes and prairie dogs. They have long legs which help them move on the ground, and they can

SOME KINDS OF OWLS

Owls are good hunters. They see and hear well and can fly almost noiselessly. Most owls build their nests in hollow trees. Others nest on ledges of cliffs or in burrows in the ground. Owls are helpful to man because they eat mice, rats, and other rodent pests.

Leonard Lee Rue III, Monkmeyer

Russ Kinne, Photo Researchers

Burrowing Owl
Speotyto cunicularia
Found on plains of Western Hemisphere
Body length: 9 inches (23 centimeters)

Snowy Owl
Nyctea scandiaca
Found in Arctic
Body length: 20 inches (51 centimeters)

Elf Owl
Micrathene whitneyi
Found in Southwestern United States and Mexico
Body length: 5½ inches (14 centimeters)

Walker, APF

see well in the daytime. They usually live near a colony of prairie dogs because these small animals are a favorite food of the burrowing owls.   OLIN SEWALL PETTINGILL, JR.

Scientific Classification. The owls in America north of Mexico belong to two families. The first is the barn owl family, *Tytonidae.* It includes the barn owl which is genus *Tyto,* species *T. alba.* The other family is the typical owl family, *Strigidae.* It includes the following:

Barred owl	*Strix varia*
Burrowing owl	*Speotyto cunicularia*
Elf owl	*Micrathene whitneyi*
Great gray owl	*Strix nebulosa*
Great horned owl	*Bubo virginianus*
Long-eared owl	*Asio otus*
Pygmy owl	*Glaucidium gnoma*
Saw-whet owl	*Aegolius acadicus*
Screech owl	*Otus asio*
Short-eared owl	*Asio flammeus*
Snowy owl	*Nyctea scandiaca*
Spotted owl	*Strix occidentalis*
Whiskered owl	*Otus trichopsis*

See also BIRD (color pictures: Hunters of the Sky, Bird Nests, Birds' Eggs); ANIMAL (pictures).

OWNERSHIP. See ABSTRACT; TITLE.

OWYHEE DAM, *oh WYE ee,* is one of the larger concrete arch gravity dams in the world. It lies on the Owyhee River in Oregon, about 11 miles (18 kilometers) southwest of the town of Adrian, Ore., near the Idaho state line. The dam is 417 feet (127 meters) high and 830 feet (253 meters) long. It can store 1,120,000 acre-feet (1,381,000,000 cubic meters) of water. It forms a reservoir 52 miles (84 kilometers) long which stores water for irrigating about 16,000 acres (6,470 hectares) of land. This dam was built by engineers of the United States Bureau of Reclamation. It was completed in 1932 at a cost of $6,671,000. See also DAM.

OX. Oxen include domestic cattle, water buffalo, bison, musk oxen, brahman, yak, banteng, and other members of the bovine family. Most oxen first came from Asia and Europe. The musk ox and bison are natives of North America. South America, Australia, and Madagascar have no native oxen.

Oxen have heavy bodies, long tails, and divided hoofs, and they chew their cud. Their smooth horns stand out from the side of the head, and are curved.

Domestic oxen give meat, milk, and leather. They are powerful work animals and serve as beasts of burden in some parts of the world.

Scientific Classification. The different kinds of oxen belong to the bovid family, *Bovidae.* Domestic cattle are genus *Bos,* species *B. taurus.*   DONALD F. HOFFMEISTER

Related Articles. For pictures of oxen see the articles IRAN; IRRIGATION; MAINE; URUGUAY. See also the following articles:

Bison	Cattle	Kouprey	Water Buffalo
Brahman	Gaur	Musk Ox	Yak

OXALIC ACID

OXALIC ACID, *ahks AL ik,* is a strong organic acid found in many vegetables and other plants. It occurs abundantly as its potassium salt in the sap of dock and other plants in the oxalis and rumex plant families. It is found in spinach, rhubarb, tomatoes, grapes, and sweet potatoes. Oxalic acid is also produced in the body. It has been known since early times.

Industry uses oxalic acid in processing textiles, bleaching straw hats, and removing paint and varnish. It is widely used in chemistry as an analytical reagent. Oxalic acid forms substances called *complexes* with various metals, especially iron. For this reason, it is also used as a rust and scale remover.

The acid is prepared commercially by heating sodium formate with sodium hydroxide. Oxalic acid can also be obtained by treating sugar with nitric acid, or by heating sawdust or other carbohydrates with sodium hydroxide.

Frank and John Craighead

Saw-Whet Owl
Aegolius acadicus
Found from Alaska to Mexico
Body length: 8 inches
(20 centimeters)

Great Gray Owl
Strix nebulosa
Found in northern North America and Western Eurasia
Body length: 30 inches
(76 centimeters)

Ron Austing, Photo Researchers

OXALIS

Oxalic acid occurs as clear, colorless crystals, soluble in water. It is highly poisonous if swallowed. Its chemical formula is $(COOH)_2 \cdot 2H_2O$, and it melts at 101.5° C (215° F.). This formula is the dihydrate form, as shown by the two water molecules. When heated to 212° F. (100° C), the crystals lose the water and have the formula $(COOH)_2$ (see HYDRATE). JOHN E. LEFFLER

See also ACID; OXALIS.

OXALIS, *AHK suh lis*, is the name of a group of plants, sometimes grown in hanging baskets, window gardens, or rock gardens. There are about 500 different kinds of oxalis. Most of the plants grow in Africa and the warm parts of America. Most kinds of oxalis grow from bulbs or tubers. They have showy flowers in various pastel colors. The leaves are shaped somewhat like clover leaves. Both leaves and flowers close up at night.

The leaves of these plants taste sour, because they contain *oxalic acid*. The acid is so named because it comes from the oxalis plant. The *wood sorrel* is a kind of oxalis that grows in the woods of North America. The leaves of some kinds of oxalis can be used in salads. Oxalis from South America have roots that can be eaten.

Scientific Classification. Oxalis belong to the wood sorrel family, *Oxalidaceae*. They form the genus *Oxalis*. The American wood sorrel is *O. montana*. DONALD WYMAN

OXBOW LAKE. The curves of winding rivers that have been cut off from the main stream are called oxbow lakes. Such a lake is usually formed when a river changes its course to a more direct path. The river leaves deposits of earth at either end of the curve and these deposits later separate it from the main stream. Oxbow lakes are often rather shallow and may disappear after a time, usually as a result of their being filled with sediment and decayed vegetation. Many of these lakes are found along the course of the Mississippi and Connecticut rivers. There are many oxbow lakes in Louisiana, Arkansas, and Mississippi along the slow-flowing tributaries of the Mississippi River. F. G. WALTON SMITH

OXEN. See OX.

OXENSTIERNA, *OOK sen sher nah*, **AXEL GUSTAFSSON** (1583-1654), a Swedish statesman, was friend and adviser to King Gustavus Adolphus. His brilliance as a statesman helped the king achieve great military victories. As chancellor, Oxenstierna directed Sweden's political affairs from 1612 to his death. This period marked Sweden's greatest influence in Europe.

Oxenstierna carried out important diplomatic missions for Gustavus Adolphus during the Thirty Years' War (1618-1648), a struggle between Roman Catholics and Protestants. After Gustavus died in battle in 1632, Oxenstierna directed Sweden's foreign affairs and provided vital leadership throughout the war. From 1636 to 1644, he headed the *regency* (temporary ruling group) that ruled Sweden during Queen Christina's childhood. He was born in Fåno, Sweden. THEODORE S. HAMEROW

OXFORD, England (pop. 111,680), is the seat of Oxford University. Oxford shares leadership in English education with Cambridge University. The inhabitants of Oxford are called Oxfordians or Oxonians. The city lies on the Thames River, about 50 miles (80 kilometers) northwest of London. For location, see GREAT BRITAIN (political map). Automobile factories are on the outskirts of Oxford. FRANCIS H. HERRICK

OXFORD GROUP. See MORAL RE-ARMAMENT.

OXFORD MOVEMENT is the name given to a revival in the Church of England which began in 1833 at Oxford. A powerful sermon was preached by John Keble (1792-1866), who tried to show the people the evils that were threatening the church because of their indifference and ignorance. Two leaders joined Keble in the Oxford Movement. One was the brilliant John Henry Newman, and the other was the learned Edward B. Pusey (1800-1882). They preached and wrote for a number of years, seeking to impress on the people that the church was "more than a merely human institution; that it had privileges, sacraments, a ministry ordained by Christ; that it was a matter of the highest obligation to remain united to the Church."

They wrote a series of essays called "Tracts for the Times." These were widely read and the movement grew. But in 1841 Newman wrote a tract which was so decidedly Catholic that the Anglican bishops condemned it. In 1845, Newman joined the Roman Catholic Church, and was eventually made a cardinal.

John Keble and Edward B. Pusey continued the work of the Oxford Movement, and new leaders took it up. A notable book, called *Lux Mundi* (*Light of the World*), edited by Charles Gore, afterwards Bishop of Oxford, was published in 1889. It created a great stir throughout the Anglican Communion.

The Oxford Movement had great influence upon the Anglican world, including the Episcopal Church in the United States. It revived faith in the church as the divine society, not to be controlled by the state. It made the pastor's office more important. It extended the church's work among the poor in larger cities. And in general it awakened church and laity to a broader view of their power and duty. WALTER H. STOWE

See also CHURCH OF ENGLAND; NEWMAN, JOHN HENRY CARDINAL; WILBERFORCE (Samuel).

OXFORD UNIVERSITY is the oldest university in Great Britain and one of the world's most famous institutions of higher learning. Oxford University started to develop during the 1100's. It is in Oxford, England, 58 miles (93 kilometers) northwest of London.

The university has more than 11,000 students. It consists of 34 colleges, plus 5 *private halls* established by various religious groups. Of the colleges, 19 are for men, 5 for women, and 10 for both men and women. The colleges include All Souls, Christ Church, Jesus, Lady Margaret Hall, Magdalen (pronounced *MAWD luhn*), Nuffield, St. John's, and Trinity.

At Oxford, each college is a corporate body distinct from the university and is governed by its own head and *fellows*. Most fellows are college instructors called *tutors*, and the rest are university professors, readers, and lecturers. Each college manages its own buildings and property, elects its own fellows, and selects and admits its own undergraduate students. The university provides some libraries, laboratories, and other facilities, but the colleges take primary responsibility for the teaching and well-being of their students.

Educational Program. Each student at Oxford is assigned to a tutor, who supervises the student's course of study. Much of the student's instruction comes through *tutorials*, which are weekly meetings of one or two students with their tutor. Students may see other tutors for specialized instruction. They may also attend lec-

Martha E. Bonham

The Tower of Magdalen College, Oxford University, Is Shown from Across the Cherwell River at Oxford, England.

tures by university teachers. Students choose which lectures to attend on the basis of their special interests and the advice of their tutor.

The university, not the individual colleges, grants degrees. The first degree in the arts or sciences is the Bachelor of Arts with honors. Oxford also grants graduate degrees and professional degrees in such fields as engineering, law, and medicine.

The Rhodes scholarship program enables students from the United States, Canada, and many other nations to study at Oxford for two years (see RHODES SCHOLARSHIP). The British government grants Marshall scholarships to citizens of the United States for study at Oxford and other universities in Great Britain.

History. During the 1100's, a university gradually developed from a number of schools in the city of Oxford. Its development was aided by a break in relations between England and France in 1167. Hostility between the two nations prevented English students from attending the University of Paris, and many of them went to Oxford instead. The university received its first official recognition in 1214.

The three oldest Oxford colleges—University, Balliol, and Merton—date from the 1200's. Twelve more colleges were founded between 1300 and 1555. The first colleges for women were established during the late 1800's. The university did not grant degrees to women until 1920.

See also ARCHITECTURE (Gothic [picture]); BODLEIAN LIBRARY; EUROPE (picture: Oxford University).

OXIDATION, *AHK suh DAY shun*, has two meanings in chemistry. The term originally referred to any chemical process in which a substance combines with oxygen. Today, the term also refers to the loss of electrons by a substance during a chemical reaction.

The rusting of iron is a common example of the original meaning of oxidation. In this process, iron (chemical symbol Fe) combines with oxygen to form iron oxide. Iron oxide then combines with water to form rust. Similar examples of oxidation include the decay of plant and animal matter and the formation of vinegar from cider. These oxidations take place slowly, and produce heat slowly as they proceed. Rapid oxidation, called *combustion*, produces heat fast enough to cause a flame. Methane (CH_4) is a gas that oxidizes rapidly.

Today, any process in which a substance loses electrons is also called oxidation. For example, iron atoms are oxidized in the presence of *ions* (electrically charged atoms) of copper (chemical symbol Cu). The chemical equation for this reaction is written:

$$Fe + Cu^{++} \rightarrow Fe^{++} + Cu.$$

In this reaction, each neutral iron atom loses two electrons and becomes an iron ion (Fe^{++}). This half of the complete reaction can be written:

$$Fe \rightarrow Fe^{++} + 2e^{-}.$$

Electrons released during oxidation must be captured by another substance. The process of gaining electrons is called *reduction*. In the reaction of iron and copper, electrons released by the iron atoms are captured by the copper ions. Each copper ion (Cu^{++}) captures two electrons and becomes a neutral copper atom. The re-

Oxidation With Oxygen occurs when oxygen combines with another substance. In a gas flame, *above*, oxygen combines rapidly with carbon and hydrogen atoms in methane molecules, producing carbon dioxide gas and water vapor. When metal rusts, *below*, iron combines slowly with oxygen and water, forming rust.

Electrochemical Oxidation occurs when a substance loses electrons. When an iron nail is dipped into a concentrated solution of copper sulfate, *above*, iron atoms in the nail are oxidized. Each iron atom loses two electrons and becomes an iron ion in the solution. Copper ions in the solution capture the released electrons, and become copper atoms which coat the nail.

duction half of the complete reaction can be written:

$$2e^- + Cu^{++} \rightarrow Cu.$$

One substance cannot be oxidized unless another substance is reduced. The combination of reduction and oxidation is called the *redox* process.   ESMARCH S. GILREATH

Related Articles in WORLD BOOK include:

Combustion	Food (Food as Fuel)	Reduction
Corrosion	Oxidation Potential	Rust
Fire	Oxide	

OXIDATION POTENTIAL is a measure, in volts, of an element's tendency to *oxidize* (lose electrons). The symbol for oxidation potential is E°. If a chemist knows an element's oxidation potential, he can predict how the element will react with another substance. He can also tell how much voltage would be produced if the element were used to make a battery.

Chemists measure the oxidation potential of a metal by means of an electrical cell that consists of two electrodes in a solution that conducts electricity. One electrode is the metal whose potential is to be measured. The other electrode is hydrogen. In this cell, a chemical reaction takes place that produces a voltage, E°, between the electrodes. This voltage produces a flow of electrons from the hydrogen electrode to the metal, if the metal's tendency to lose electrons is less than that of hydrogen. It produces a flow in the opposite direction if the metal's tendency to lose electrons is greater than that of hydrogen. Oxidation potentials are measured at the standard conditions of 25° C and one atmosphere of pressure (14.7 pounds per square inch, or 1.03 kilograms per square centimeter).

Chemists measure the voltages produced by the test cell with a voltmeter. In the United States, a metal is assigned a positive oxidation potential (+) if electrons go from the metal to hydrogen. A metal is assigned a negative potential (−) if electrons flow from hydrogen to the metal. Scientists in other countries use a system in which the plus and minus signs are opposite those in the U.S. system. For example, the E° of iron is +0.44 in the United States and −0.44 in other countries. In both systems, the oxidation potential of hydrogen is arbitrarily assigned as zero.

E° values are used extensively in chemistry and physics. Scientists can predict the total voltage of a battery cell by adding the E° values of the chemical elements that make up the reaction. Oxidation potentials can also be used to predict whether a chemical reaction will take place. Chemical reactions take place spontaneously if the total voltage of the reacting elements is positive.   F. BASOLO

See also ELECTROMOTIVE SERIES; ELECTRIC CURRENT; OXIDATION; ELECTRODE; BATTERY.

STANDARD OXIDATION POTENTIALS

Element	E° (volts)	Element	E° (volts)
Potassium	+2.92	Hydrogen	0
Magnesium	+2.37	Copper	−0.34
Aluminum	+1.66	Mercury	−0.79
Zinc	+0.76	Silver	−0.80
Iron	+0.44	Gold	−1.42

OXIDE, *AHK side*, is a chemical compound of oxygen with some other element. Oxides are commonly formed when the elements are oxidized. For example, burning the carbon present in coal or wood gives carbon dioxide (CO_2) and carbon monoxide (CO). Burning is rapid oxidation. Carbon dioxide is also formed by the slow oxidation of animal cells, and is exhaled from the lungs.

The rusting of iron is slow oxidation. Rust contains ferric oxide (Fe_2O_3).

Metallic oxides combine with water to form basic hydroxides, while nonmetallic oxides with water form oxygen acids. The oxides of sulfur and nitrogen are important because they can be used to form sulfuric and nitric acids. Nitrous oxide, a nitrogen-oxygen compound, is a common anesthetic. It is also called *laughing gas* because inhaling it makes some persons laugh.

Calcium oxide is *quicklime* (CaO). When mixed with water it forms the *slaked lime* used in whitewash and plaster. Sand, which is so important in glassmaking, is one form of *silicon dioxide*, called silica (SiO_2). Other forms are quartz, onyx, and opal.

See also MERCURIC OXIDE; NITROUS OXIDE; OXIDATION.

OXIDIZER. See ROCKET (Rocket Propellant).

OXNAM, G. BROMLEY (1891-1963), was a bishop of the Methodist Church. He was bishop of the Washington, D.C., area from 1952 to 1960, when he retired. His books and speeches emphasized his liberal social beliefs. They favor justice for laboring people and equal rights for all classes. Bishop Oxnam's books include *Russian Impressions* (1927), *Youth and the New America* (1928), *Facing the Future Unafraid* (1944), and *Labor in Tomorrow's World* (1945).

He was ordained a Methodist minister in 1916. He taught at the Boston University of Theology from 1927 to 1928. He was president of DePauw University in Greencastle, Ind., from 1928 to 1936. He was bishop of the Omaha area from 1936 to 1940, of the Boston area from 1940 to 1944, and of the New York area from 1944 to 1952.

Oxnam became president of the Federal Council of Churches of Christ in 1944, and later chairman of its Commission to Study the Bases of a Just and Durable Peace. He was president of the Methodist Church Council of World Service and Finance in 1956, and of the Council of Bishops of the Methodist Church in 1958. Garfield Bromley Oxnam was born in Sonora, Calif. He graduated from the University of Southern California and Boston University. He also studied in London and the Far East.

Brown Bros.

G. Bromley Oxnam

L. J. TRINTERUD

OXUS RIVER. See AMU DARYA.

OXYACETYLENE. See ACETYLENE.

OXYGEN, *AHK suh jun*, is a life-supporting gas and a chemical element. Nearly all living things need oxygen to stay alive. Oxygen combines with other chemicals in plant and animal cells to produce energy needed for life processes. Oxygen is also needed to make most fuels burn. During the burning process, oxygen combines with the fuel in a chemical reaction. Heat is released during this process.

Oxygen is one of the most plentiful chemical elements on the earth. It makes up about a fifth of the volume of air. Nitrogen makes up most of the other four-fifths. Oxygen is also found in the earth's crust and in water.

OXYGEN

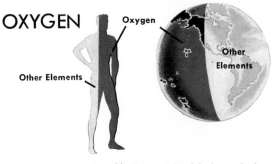

Oxygen

Other Elements

Other Elements

Oxygen makes up about ⅔ of the weight of the human body. The oxygen in the earth's crust weighs almost as much as all the other chemical elements put together.

This oxygen is not pure, but is combined with other elements. On the average, 100 pounds of the earth's crust contains $46\frac{1}{2}$ pounds of oxygen. Nearly half of the weight of most rocks and minerals is oxygen. Every 100 pounds of water contains about 89 pounds of oxygen. Hydrogen makes up the other 11 pounds.

How Oxygen Supports Life. Only a few kinds of living things, including certain germs, can live without *free* (chemically uncombined) oxygen. Human beings and the other land animals get oxygen from the air. Fish and most other water animals get dissolved oxygen from water. Free oxygen enters a person's blood stream through the lungs. It enters a fish's blood stream through the gills. The blood carries oxygen to the cells of the body. In the cells, oxygen combines with chemicals obtained from food. Energy produced during this process makes it possible for each cell to perform its function in the body. Carbon dioxide is produced in the cells as a waste product (see RESPIRATION).

People once believed that breathing pure oxygen would lead to an early death. They thought the body's cells would use oxygen too fast, and a person would die of exhaustion. But in certain situations, breathing pure oxygen may be necessary. For example, pilots who fly at high altitudes, where the air is too thin to supply enough oxygen, breathe from tanks of pure oxygen.

Plant cells use oxygen in much the same way that animal cells do. Plant cells also make oxygen in the process of *photosynthesis*. During this process, the cells use the energy of sunlight to make sugar from carbon dioxide and water. Oxygen is produced as a by-product, and is released into the atmosphere.

Other Uses of Oxygen. Oxygen has many uses in industry. Some steel is manufactured by the *basic oxygen process*. In this process, a stream of high-pressure oxygen blasts down on melted pig iron and burns out impurities. This process can change 100 short tons (91 metric tons) of pig iron to steel in about an hour. Welders mix oxygen with fuel in their torches to produce an extremely hot flame with a temperature of about 6000° F. (3300° C).

Liquid oxygen, called *LOX*, is used in rockets propelled by liquid fuels. LOX burns various fuels, including kerosene and liquid hydrogen, to produce the rocket's *thrust* (pushing force). LOX is also mixed with other fuels to make explosives for blasting.

Making Oxygen. Most commercial oxygen is distilled from liquid air. During the distillation process, the nitrogen boils before the oxygen does, because nitrogen has a lower boiling point. As the nitrogen boils away, the liquid air is left with a greater concentration of oxygen. Commercial oxygen is stored in steel tanks at a pressure of about 2,000 pounds per square inch (140 kilograms per square centimeter), more than a hundred times the pressure of the atmosphere.

Small amounts of oxygen can be made by heating potassium chlorate. A little manganese dioxide added to the potassium chlorate speeds up oxygen formation.

History. Oxygen was discovered by two chemists working independently. They were Carl Scheele of Sweden and Joseph Priestley of England. Scheele's laboratory notes show that he prepared oxygen between 1770 and 1773 by heating various compounds, including saltpeter and mercuric oxide. But Scheele's experiments were not published until 1775. Priestley also published his experiments in 1775. He described how he prepared oxygen in 1774 by heating mercuric oxide.

Scheele called oxygen *fire air*. Priestley called it *dephlogisticated air*. In 1777, the French chemist Antoine Lavoisier named the gas *oxygen*. The word means *acid producer*. Lavoisier and others had found that oxygen is a part of several acids. Lavoisier incorrectly reasoned that oxygen is needed to make all acids. He combined the Greek words *oxys* (meaning *sharp* or *acid*) and *gignomai* (meaning *produce*) to form the French word *oxygene*. This word is *oxygen* in English.

Chemical Properties. Oxygen is a colorless, odorless, and tasteless gas. Its chemical symbol is O. Its atomic number is 8 and its atomic weight is 15.9994. Ordinary oxygen molecules are made of two oxygen atoms. Molecules made of three oxygen atoms make up the gas *ozone*, O_3. Oxygen combines with many elements, forming a class of compounds called *oxides*. The process by which oxygen combines with other elements is called *oxidation*.

Oxygen changes to a pale blue liquid when cooled to its *boiling point*, $-183.0°$ C at atmospheric pressure. Oxygen liquefies at a higher temperature when the pressure is increased. At a pressure of 730 pounds per square inch (51 kilograms per square centimeter), oxygen liquefies at $-118.8°$ C. These values of temperature and pressure are oxygen's *critical temperature and pressure*. It is impossible to liquefy oxygen at a higher temperature at any pressure. Liquid oxygen is magnetic and can be held between the poles of a strong magnet. Oxygen freezes at $-218.4°$ C.   FRANK C. ANDREWS

Related Articles in WORLD BOOK include:

Anoxia	Liquid Air	Oxygen Tent
Element, Chemical	Oxidation	Ozone
Iron and Steel (The Basic Oxygen Process)	Oxide	Welding

OXYGEN TENT is a device used in medicine for patients who require more oxygen than is normally contained in the air. There are several types of tents. The simplest tent for emergency purposes is a dome-shaped hood made of material through which oxygen cannot pass. This tent is large enough to completely cover an infant. The oxygen enters through a hose at the top. Larger oxygen tents may cover the entire bed. Most tents are made of large sheets of transparent, fire-resistant material.

Oxygen tents are used mainly to treat infants and small children suffering from *anoxia* (a deficiency of oxygen supply to the body tissues). Anoxia may result from such conditions as pneumonia or heart ailments.

Physicians seldom use oxygen tents for adults. Other equally effective methods of administering oxygen have been developed that provide better access to the patient. For example, oxygen may be given through small tubes inserted into the patient's nostrils, or by a mask placed over his nose and mouth. Such methods require the patient to lie fairly still for long periods of time. Therefore, they cannot be used easily with infants or small children.

In some medical conditions, the patient must receive oxygen at pressures greater than atmospheric pressure. These patients are placed in a pressurized steel chamber and are given oxygen through a face mask. This treatment, called *hyperbaric oxygen therapy*, is especially useful in treating carbon monoxide poisoning, gas gangrene, and certain blood disorders. JOHN B. WEST

See also ANOXIA; OXYGEN.

OXYGENATED WATER. See HYDROGEN PEROXIDE.

OXYHEMOGLOBIN. See HEMOGLOBIN.

OXYTOCIN. See GLAND (The Pituitary Gland).

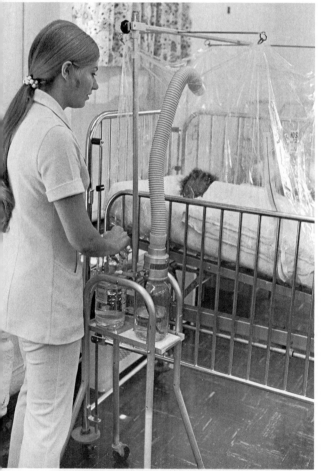

WORLD BOOK photo, courtesy Rush-Presbyterian-St. Luke's Medical Center

An Oxygen Tent provides a patient with air that contains more than the normal amount of oxygen. The air is pumped through a hose at the top of the tent, which may cover the entire bed.

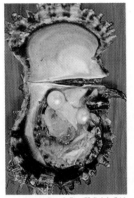

Sakata Pearl Co. (U.S.A.), Ltd.

The Pacific Pearl Oyster, *above,* has been cut to show the two gleaming jewels inside.

Young Oysters, *below,* are about as big as a needle point. They float and swim in the sea.
U.S. Dept. of Interior

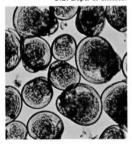

Joy Spurr, Bruce Coleman Ltd.

Oysters Fasten Their Shells to Rocks or other hard objects on the ocean bottom. Most species live in shallow coastal waters.

OYSTER is a sea animal with a soft body inside a hard, two-piece shell. Oysters live on the ocean bottom, mostly in inlets near shore where the water is usually quiet and not deep. They are found in many parts of the world that have a mild or warm climate.

Oysters are among man's most valuable shellfish. Oysters of the Persian Gulf and the Pacific Ocean make the pearls used as jewels. Man also uses oysters as food, and catches more oysters than any other shellfish. The United States produces about 800 million pounds (360 million kilograms) of oysters a year, more than any other country.

Man has eaten oysters for thousands of years. About A.D. 43, Roman pioneers in England caught oysters along the sea coasts. In winter, they packed the animals in snow and ice, put them in cloth bags, and sent them to Rome. Fishermen of ancient Rome raised oysters on "farms" in the waters off the Italian coasts. Today, about half the oysters in the United States come from undersea farms along the Atlantic Coast.

Oysters, like clams, scallops, and some other shell-

R. Tucker Abbott, the contributor of this article, holds the du Pont Chair of Malacology at the Delaware Museum of Natural History and is the author of American Seashells *and* Sea Shells of the World.

fish, are called *mollusks.* Mollusks make up a major division of the animal kingdom. For a description of other kinds of mollusks, see the article on MOLLUSK.

The Body of an Oyster

Shell. An oyster's shell is the animal's skeleton. It consists of two parts called *valves.* Oysters are often called *bivalves,* which means *two valves.* The valves are held together at one end by a hinge. One valve is deeper, larger, and thicker than the other, and the oyster's body rests in it. The second valve acts as a lid.

──────── **FACTS IN BRIEF** ────────

Names: *Male,* none; *female,* none; *young,* spat or seed oyster; *group,* bed.

Hatching Period: About 10 hours.

Number of Newborn: About 500 million a year for each oyster.

Length of Life: About 6 years.

Where Found: Mild or warm seas of the world.

Scientific Classification: Oysters used for food make up the oyster family *Ostreidae.* The oyster of the eastern North American coast is genus *Crassostrea,* species *C. virginica.* The European oyster is genus *Ostrea,* species *O. edulis.* The pearl oyster belongs to the pearl oyster family *Pteridae.* It is genus *Pinctada,* species *P. margaritifera.*

OYSTER

The oyster usually keeps the valves of its shell open just a bit. When an enemy comes near, the oyster snaps the valves shut by means of a strong muscle called an *adductor*. This muscle attaches the oyster's body to the inside of the shell. It holds the valves closed until danger has passed. An oyster can keep its shell closed for as long as several weeks.

The *mantle*, a fleshy organ, lines the inside of the shell and surrounds the body organs. It produces liquid substances that harden and form the shell. It also makes the colors that appear in the shell. The mantle adds material to the shell, so that the shell becomes larger as the oyster grows. Lines on the outside of the shell mark the additions of this material from the mantle. The inside of the shells of oysters used for food is dull white and purple. The inside of pearl oyster shells is covered with a smooth, shiny substance called *mother-of-pearl* or *nacre*. For information about how shells grow, see the WORLD BOOK article on SHELL (How Shells Are Formed).

Sometimes a grain of sand or some other object gets into the shell and rubs against the oyster's body. The mantle covers the object with thin layers of shell material, and in this way forms a pearl. Pearls used as gems come from pearl oysters, which live in tropical waters. Pearls produced by the oysters used as food have little value.

Body Organs. The oyster's soft body is a grayish mass of tissues that contain the body organs. The animal has no head. It has two pairs of W-shaped gills that look somewhat like the surface of a feather. The oyster uses its gills to breathe and also to capture food. Hair-like parts of the gills gather tiny plants and animals from

the water and push them toward the oyster's mouth. The mouth is a funnel-shaped opening at the narrowest part of the body. The oyster's digestive system includes a stomach, a digestive gland, and an intestine. The oyster's heart has two chambers that pump blood throughout the animal's body. The blood carries food and oxygen to all parts of the body, and removes waste materials.

An oyster has no eyes, ears, or nose, so it cannot see, hear, or smell. However, two rows of small feelers on the edges of the mantle respond to certain changes in the oyster's surroundings. The feelers hang over the edges of the open shell, and changes in light or in chemicals in the water cause them to contract. The contracting feelers signal the powerful adductor muscle to close the shell against possible danger.

The Life of an Oyster

An oyster spends all except the first few weeks of its life in one spot on the sea bottom. It uses the shell material produced by the mantle to fasten itself to a rock or to some other object in quiet waters. The shell substance hardens, and holds the larger valve firmly in place. Most oysters live about 6 years, but some live as long as 20 years.

Young. A female oyster may produce as many as 500 million eggs a year. The yellowish eggs are so tiny that a mass of them looks somewhat like thick cream. The female lays the eggs by spraying them into the water. The *spat* (young oysters) hatch about 10 hours later. Each spat is about as big as the point of a needle, and looks somewhat like a toy top. The young oysters swim by means of hairlike growths called *cilia*. The cilia beat the water like whips and push the oysters forward. When the oysters are about 24 hours old, their shells begin to grow.

An oyster spends about the first two weeks of its life floating and swimming. During this time, the animal has a muscular "foot" that extends from its body. The foot disappears after the oyster finds a place to settle. The oyster uses its foot as a feeler to test rocks, empty shells, and other hard objects. Then it fastens itself to one of the objects. Several oysters may use the same rock as a home. They may attach themselves not only to the rock, but also to each other. Large, crowded *beds* (groups) of oysters can be found in rocky inlets along the coasts.

Young oysters grow rapidly. A month-old oyster is about the size of a pea, and a year-old oyster is about 1 inch (2.5 centimeters) in diameter. Oysters grow about an inch a year for three or four years, and then grow even more slowly for the rest of their lives. Some oysters grow as long as 12 inches (30 centimeters).

Enemies. An oyster has many enemies, and no defense except its shell. Man is probably the oyster's greatest enemy. He catches and eats millions of oysters every year. Fish may swallow thousands of newly hatched oysters in one gulp. Crabs and other sea animals eat young oysters after crushing the soft new shells. Starfish pull the shells open with their tube feet and eat the oyster meat. Oyster-drill snails and whelks use their filelike teeth to bore holes in the shells and suck out the soft parts. A bird called the oyster catcher pries open the

THE BODY OF AN OYSTER

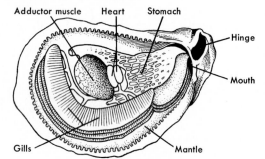

Adductor muscle Heart Stomach

Hinge

Mouth

Gills Mantle

THE PARTS OF AN OYSTER SHELL

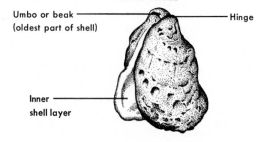

Umbo or beak
(oldest part of shell)

Hinge

Inner
shell layer

WORLD BOOK illustration by Tom Dolan

682

M. E. Warren, Photo Researchers

Harvesting Oysters with a dredge, oystermen watch the heavy net haul up their catch from the ocean bottom. The oysters are dumped in a pile on the ship's deck, and then are taken into port to be cleaned and packaged for market.

shells with its strong beak. Diseases caused by viruses that are harmless to man may kill millions of oysters in one year.

The Oyster Industry

Oyster Farming. Oysters are one of the most popular foods that man takes from the sea. Man's fondness for eating oysters—and his fear that they might die out—led him to raise the animals on undersea "farms."

An oyster farmer chooses an area of quiet water where the sea bottom is firm. Loose, shifting sand or deep, soft mud might cover and smother the oysters. Each farmer marks his plot with floats. He puts old shells or slabs of hardened clay called *tiles* on the sea floor. The shells and tiles provide places for the young oysters to attach them-

WHERE OYSTERS ARE FOUND

The black areas of the map show the parts of the world where edible oysters are found. The map includes oyster farm areas.

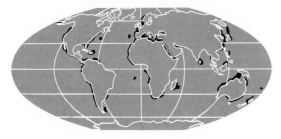

selves. The oyster farmer can buy *seed oysters* to "plant" in his farming area. The oysters grow there and are harvested when they are 2 to 4 years old and 2 to 4 inches (5 to 10 centimeters) in diameter.

Almost all the oysters that man raises for market come from oyster farms. One of the largest oyster-farming centers in the world is in the Bay of Arcachon, on the southwestern coast of France. More than 75 per cent of the oysters produced in the United States come from farms along the Atlantic Coast. The beds in American coastal waters, especially those of Chesapeake Bay, are also among the largest in the world. Oystermen fish in the waters along the Atlantic Coast from Maine to Florida, and along the Gulf Coast from Florida to Texas. They also fish along the Pacific Coast from California to Washington.

The leading oyster-producing states are Virginia, Louisiana, and Maryland. In Canada, the provinces of British Columbia and Prince Edward Island produce the most oysters. France, The Netherlands, and Italy are the largest oyster-producing countries of Europe. Japan, Australia, and New Zealand also produce many oysters.

Oyster Harvesting takes place during fall and winter in most regions. Groups of oysters in shallow waters are picked up with tongs that open and close somewhat as scissors do. Oysters in deeper waters are brought up by machines called *dredges*. The dredges are operated by hand or by steam power.

Some oysters are sold while still in their shells. Workers scrub the shells, pack the oysters in ice, and ship them to market. Most oysters are sold unshelled. Men called *shuckers* have great skill in removing the shells. A shucker places the edge of the shell on a chisel blade, which is fastened to a heavy block of wood. Then he hits the shell with a wooden hammer. The blow drives the tip of the chisel between the valves of the closed shell. The shucker then slips a knife blade into the shell and pulls it open so the valves lie flat. The adductor muscle, which attaches the body to the shell, is cut, and the soft flesh is removed, washed, and packed for shipment.

There is an old saying that oysters should be eaten only in months that have an "R" in their names. The saying once had some basis, because most oysters caught during the summer months are of poor quality. Today, with the use of modern preserving methods, oysters can be eaten safely the year round. They are caught when they are of top quality, and are canned or quick-frozen for later use. R. TUCKER ABBOTT

See also MOLLUSK; MOTHER-OF-PEARL; PEARL; SHELL; AQUACULTURE.

OYSTER CATCHER is the name of a family of wading birds which live on seacoasts in most sections of the world. The name comes from the sharp-edged, chisel-shaped bill with which an oyster catcher stabs open oysters, limpets, and clams upon which it feeds.

The common oyster catcher of the United States lives on both coasts of the Americas, but usually is not seen north of New Jersey in the east, and Lower California in the west. It has smoky-brown body feathers and a black head and neck. The under parts of its body are white. The black oyster catcher lives on the Pacific

Coast. The *sea pie* of Great Britain is the European kind of oyster catcher. Oyster catchers lay their three or four eggs among the bare pebbles.

Scientific Classification. Oyster catchers form the oyster catcher family, *Haematopodidae.* The east and west coast oyster catcher is genus *Haematopus,* species *H. palliatus;* the black is *H. bachmani;* and the European is *H. ostralegus.*   ALEXANDER WETMORE

E. R. Degginger
Oyster Catcher

OYSTER PLANT. See SALSIFY.

OZALID PROCESS is a method of producing copies of documents. The original paper is placed on a chemically treated sheet of Ozalid paper and fed into an Ozalid machine. Ultraviolet light shines through the translucent paper of the original copy and changes the chemicals on the Ozalid paper to a colorless compound. But it does not shine through the opaque lines or letters on the original copy. The Ozalid machine then develops the Ozalid paper, and the parts not struck by ultraviolet light appear, making an accurate copy.

OZARK MOUNTAINS. This range of hills extends from southern Illinois, across Missouri, and into Arkansas and Oklahoma. The Ozarks rise from 1,500 to 2,300 feet (457 to 701 meters) above sea level. The highest peaks of the Ozarks are the Boston Mountains of Arkansas.

The Ozark region covers about 40,000 square miles (100,000 square kilometers). The hills are covered with timber and have rich mineral deposits. Lead, coal, and iron are mined here, and marble is quarried. One of the low plateaus, known as Springfield Plain, covers about 10,000 square miles (26,000 square kilometers) in western Missouri, northwestern Arkansas, and northeastern Oklahoma. Corn, wheat, and fruits are grown on its good farmland. Other Ozark prairie regions have good grazing lands.   WALLACE E. AKIN

See also MISSOURI (Land); ARKANSAS (pictures).

OZARK NATIONAL SCENIC RIVERWAYS. See NATIONAL PARK SYSTEM (table: Parkways).

OZAWA, *oh ZAH wah,* **SEIJI,** *SAY jee* (1935-   ), is one of the outstanding symphony orchestra conductors of his time. He established his reputation with a broad range of music, including that of many modern Japanese composers.

Ozawa was born in Hoten, Manchuria. He went to Europe in 1959 and studied with the Austrian conductor Herbert von Karajan in West Berlin. There, Leonard Bernstein, conductor of the New York Philharmonic Orchestra, observed Ozawa and named him one of the or-

Chicago Daily News
Seiji Ozawa

chestra's three assistant conductors for the 1961-1962 season. Bernstein recalled Ozawa as sole assistant conductor for the 1964-1965 season. From 1965 to 1969, Ozawa served as conductor of the Toronto Symphony. He served as music director of the San Francisco Symphony from 1968 to 1976. In 1973, Ozawa also became artistic and music director of the Boston Symphony Orchestra.   KEITH POLK

OZONE, *O zone,* is a form of oxygen. Its sharp odor is often noticed near electric switches and machinery, and in the air after a thunderstorm. Ozone is a strong cleaning agent, because it reacts with dirt and soot. Ozone is also used to remove unpleasant odors from foods and from the air, to kill germs, and to bleach oils, fats, and textiles. It was discovered in 1840 by German chemist Christian Friedrich Schönbein.

Molecules of ordinary oxygen are made of two oxygen atoms joined tightly together. But ozone molecules have a third oxygen atom loosely attached to these two. The third atom can easily separate from the molecule and combine with other substances. As a result, ozone is a chemically active gas. Every flash of lightning converts some oxygen into ozone. The gas is also formed by electric sparks, such as those from motors. Commercial ozone is made in a machine called an *ozonizer.*

Very high energy radiation from the sun strikes oxygen in the earth's atmosphere and converts some of it to ozone. On the average, air at ground level contains less than 1 part of ozone per million parts of air. But 15 miles (24 kilometers) above the ground there is a more concentrated layer of ozone. This layer contains only about six parts of ozone per million parts of air. But it shields the earth from much of the sun's ultraviolet light. Ultraviolet rays harm living tissues. Without this protective ozone layer, plants and animals probably could not live on the earth.

Some scientists believe that the ozone layer can be destroyed by a group of chemical compounds called *fluorocarbons.* Fluorocarbons have been widely used as propellants in aerosol spray cans. After they are released from spray cans, fluorocarbons slowly rise into the earth's atmosphere. There, they are broken up by the sun's ultraviolet rays and release chlorine atoms. These chlorine atoms react with other chemical substances in the atmosphere and may gradually reduce the ozone concentration. If this happens, the earth would be exposed to increased amounts of harmful ultraviolet radiation. Because of this potential danger, the federal government has taken steps to ban fluorocarbon aerosols for most uses by 1979.

Ozone in the lower regions of the earth's atmosphere contributes to air pollution. In strong concentrations, ozone can kill plants and irritate a person's eyes and nose. Ozone may build up when sunlight acts on nitrogen oxides from automobile exhaust fumes. This excess ozone may contribute to additional pollution by reacting chemically with emissions of hydrocarbons from motor vehicles and some factories. Ozone changes these hydrocarbons into the pollutants found in smog. See SMOG.

The chemical symbol for ozone is O_3, and its molecular weight is 47.998. Concentrated ozone has a pale blue color. At atmospheric pressure, the gas liquefies at $-111.9°$ C ($-169.4°$ F.) and freezes at $-193°$ C ($-315.4°$ F.).   FRANK C. ANDREWS